DATE DUE

DEMCO 38-296

DICTIONARY

of

American
Foreign Affairs

DICTIONARY

of

American Foreign Affairs

Stephen A. Flanders
Carl N. Flanders

MACMILLAN PUBLISHING COMPANY
New York

MAXWELL MACMILLAN CANADA
Toronto

MAXWELL MACMILLAN INTERNATIONAL
New York   Oxford   Singapore   Sydney

Macmillan Publishing Company
A Division of Macmillan, Inc.
866 Third Avenue, New York, N.Y. 10022

Maxwell Macmillan Canada, Inc.
1200 Eglinton Avenue East, Suite 200
Don Mills, Ontario M3C 3N1

Macmillan Publishing Company is part of the
Maxwell Communication Group of Companies

Library of Congress Catalog Card Number: 92-46618

Printed in the United States of America

printing number
1   2   3   4   5   6   7   8   9   10

Library of Congress Cataloging-in-Publication Data

Flanders, Stephen A.
    Dictionary of American foreign affairs / Stephen A. Flanders, Carl N. Flanders.
       p.   cm.
    ISBN 0-02-897146-9
      1. United States—Foreign relations—Dictionaries. I. Flanders, Carl N.   II Title.
E183.7.F58 1993
327.73'003—dc20
                                                  92-46618
                                                           CIP

To
Stephen C. Flanders
who loved both America and foreign affairs

Contents

Acknowledgments

We are indebted to many for their help on this book. Our research was made possible largely through the assistance of numerous organizations and associations, many of which are cited in Appendix G. We would like to single out here the Office of the Historian, U.S. House of Representatives; House Foreign Affairs Committee; NASA History Office; U.S. Army Center of Military History; Council on Foreign Relations; and the Montclair, New Jersey, Public Library. We especially appreciate the support of the Sprague Library at Montclair State College and the use of its facilities. An unanticipated but very rewarding aspect of this project was the relationship we developed with the Sprague's responsive and professional staff, including Randal Cain, Barbara Fingerhut, Arthur Hudson, Hunter Jones, Kevin Prendergast, Patricia Sanders, and Thomas Trone.

We would particularly like to thank Eleanora von Dehsen and Mark Stafford for helping us get started; John M. Moore, our invaluable (and patient) computer expert; our cartographer, Thomas Nast; Peter Widulski, who generously reviewed the entries pertaining to the Constitution and international law; Norman A. Graebner, Lyman B. Kirkpatrick, Jr., and John Opie of our editorial advisory board; and our editorial staff at Macmillan: Alicia Cheng, Elizabeth Halleron, Michael Sander, Garrett Schure, Melissa Solomon, and Vicki Toyooka. Finally, there are four individuals who were the cornerstones of the book. Our editor, Philip Friedman, shepherded the project from concept to completion. Glenn Speer of our editorial board read the entire manuscript and immeasurably improved every facet of the book through his comments and corrections. Our indefatigable editorial assistant, Carol Flanders, somehow kept track of the project's myriad parts and unfailingly typed the complete manuscript through seemingly endless revisions. Eunhui Flanders retained an indispensable sense of proportion on what became at times an all-consuming undertaking and, for her husband, made the whole project worthwhile.

Introduction

The *Dictionary of American Foreign Affairs* is intended to meet the need for a single, multifaceted reference work devoted to U.S. foreign relations. There are many excellent books on the various aspects of U.S. foreign affairs. This dictionary is designed to provide a comprehensive, accessible source of information on the events, agreements, ideas, organizations, and people that have shaped America's involvement in the world from 1776 to the present. It is meant for a wide audience: informed lay readers and concerned citizens seeking better understanding of current issues; students, teachers, and researchers; and professionals in journalism, law, business, and government. The choice of material reflects a broad view of U.S. foreign relations as encompassing space, technology, and environmental matters as well as diplomacy, intelligence, and military and economic affairs. U.S immigration policy and relations with the Native American tribes similarly are covered. (The term Indian has been employed throughout for historical consistency and ease of reader access.) Particular emphasis has been placed on recent developments; the dictionary is current through the first half of 1992. All contents were researched and written by the authors and then reviewed by at least one member of the Editorial Advisory Board.

The heart of the book is the dictionary of approximately 1400 entries arranged in alphanumeric order. Entries share a standard structure. Each begins with a brief synopsis of the topic. Subject entries include applicable dates and participants, key background information, a description or summary of the item, and, as appropriate, an assessment of its outcome or significance. Where a subject entry has multiple aspects, such as an armed conflict, emphasis is on its relationship to foreign affairs. Biographical entries provide birth, death, and relevant active dates and focus on the person's role in foreign affairs. An entry is listed under its most familiar or accessible name. Cross-reference is made from other names or titles by which the entry is known. Two cross-referencing techniques are used within a given entry. The first time another dictionary entry is mentioned, it appears in SMALL CAPS. Other related entries or appendix items are identifed at the end of the entry following "See also."

The entries cover all the major accords to which the United States has been a signatory as well as all significant foreign affairs legislation passed by the Congress. Several relevant dates normally exist for each treaty or law (date of signing, ratification, enactment, and so on). Generally, the date most commonly identified with a given treaty or law has been provided. Biographical entries have been included on all the presidents and secretaries of state. Each presidential biography contains a broad overview of the foreign policy of that person's administration.

Several appendixes furnish a range of more specialized information. Appendix A is a graphic timeline presentation of American foreign affairs from 1776 to the present. It enables readers to place isolated individual facts within a historical context. Users can gain an overview of a given era, see the relationship of concurrent events, or simply and quickly identify a specific entry. Appendixes B and D profile the principal federal executive branch organizations and congressional committees involved in the formulation of U.S. foreign policy. Appendix C summarizes U.S. foreign relations with other key nations and international organizations. Appendixes B, C, and D also contain chronological listings of the people who have held the top U.S. foreign policy posts. Charts of the major conferences and summits participated in by the United States are provided in Appendix E. Appendix F is a glossary of the commonly used special terms in foreign affairs. Appendix H consists of maps illustrating the geographical issues and items addressed in the book. Readers desiring additional information can turn to the guide to further sources in Appendix G.

Abbreviations and Style Notes

As a general rule, acronyms are spelled out on first use in an entry or appendix. Exceptions are the following commonly used terms:

ABM	Antiballistic Missile
INF	Intermediate Nuclear Forces
MX	Missile Experimental
NATO	North Atlantic Treaty Organization
SALT	Strategic Arms Limitation Talks
START	Strategic Arms Reduction Talks
USSR	Union of Soviet Socialist Republics

Political party and state are always given for members of Congress, most often in parenthesis following the name, as in Senator Henry M. Jackson (D–WA). The two-letter abbreviation is used for states. Parties are abbreviated as follows:

D	Democrat
DR	Democratic–Republican
F	Federalist
R	Republican
I	Independent
W	Whig

The commonly accepted or known Chinese spelling is followed when possible. Otherwise, the Wade–Giles system is used through 1979, and the Pinyin system thereafter.

A

ABC MEDIATION See **VERACRUZ INCI-DENT**.

ABC-1 See **RAINBOW WAR PLANS**.

ABM TREATY See **ANTIBALLISTIC MIS-SILE TREATY**.

ABRAHAM LINCOLN BATTALION Unit of American volunteers that fought with the Republicans, or Loyalists, against the Nationalists in the Spanish Civil War (1936–1939). While foreign volunteers served on both sides of the conflict, the large majority of them enlisted in the Loyalist cause. Young, mainly working-class political leftists from the Western democracies actively sympathized with the Popular Front Republican government, which was opposed by the antileftist Nationalists under Spanish Army General Francisco Franco. The thousands of foreign volunteers who flocked to Spain to serve with the Republicans after Franco launched his uprising in July 1936 feared the spread of fascism in Europe and the rise of right-wing dictatorships across the continent. They were committed to defeating the Nationalist rebellion, which was supported by Adolf Hitler's Germany and Benito Mussolini's Italy, and preventing a Fascist victory in Spain.

The arriving volunteers were formed into separate International Brigades by the Spanish Republican command and deployed alongside native Loyalist forces. More than 35,000 men—and a scattering of women—from some 50 countries served in the brigades, which consisted of battalion-level units organized along lines of language or nationality. The first group of Americans to volunteer for the International Brigades left New York City in December 1936 and, so as to avoid violating U.S. NEUTRALITY ACTS, went initially to France before crossing into Spain in early 1937. Eventually about 3000 U.S. nationals fought with the Republicans. The Americans primarily filled the ranks of two units, the more celebrated Abraham Lincoln Battalion and the George Washington Battalion. The American units took part in several major military actions, sustaining heavy casualties. During the war roughly one-third of the American volunteers were killed. The Lincoln and Washington battalions absorbed such large losses at the battle of Brunete in July 1937 that afterward the Loyalist command merged what remained of the latter into the former.

The Lincoln Battalion was routed in March 1938 during a major Nationalist thrust that cut Republican Spain in two. With overseas enlistments virtually at an end, the battalion was rebuilt almost entirely with Spanish personnel. By midsummer the unit totaled 700 troops, only 150 of whom were Americans. Soon thereafter the Loyalist government decided to remove the remaining foreign volunteers from combat since they numbered so few and could no longer make a significant military contribution. In late September 1938 the Americans in the Lincoln Battalion were pulled from the battlefield for the last time. Thereupon a LEAGUE OF NATIONS commission arrived to help repatriate foreign volunteers, who began to leave Spain by year's end. Franco and the Nationalists overwhelmed the Loyalists and won a complete victory in April 1939.

ABRAMS, CREIGHTON WILLIAMS, JR.
(1914–1974) Army officer. Born in Spring-field, Massachusetts, Abrams graduated from West Point in 1936. He distinguished himself as a tank commander in WORLD WAR II. Promoted to general in 1956, he served in senior command and staff positions before assignment in 1967 as deputy commander of U.S. forces in the VIETNAM WAR. Abrams succeeded General WILLIAM C. WESTMORELAND the following year as commander of the half-million American troops in South Vietnam. He oversaw implementation of the Nixon administration's VIETNAMIZATION policy under which South Vietnam assumed increasing responsibility for fighting in its own defense. During the gradual winding down of the American military presence in Southeast Asia, he directed the CAMBODIAN INCURSION (1970) and LAOTIAN INCURSION (1971), attacks on Communist sanctuaries meant to disrupt North Vietnamese war-fighting abilities. In 1972 Abrams was named Army chief of staff, the service's top uniformed position. Stricken with cancer, he died in office. The M1 Abrams tank was named in his honor.

ACCIDENT MEASURES AGREEMENT See **NUCLEAR ACCIDENTS AGREEMENT**.

ACDA See **ARMS CONTROL AND DISARMAMENT AGENCY** in **APPENDIX B**.

ACHESON, DEAN GOODERHAM (1893–1971) Secretary of state. Born in Connecticut, Acheson graduated from Yale in 1915 and Harvard Law School in 1918. He served briefly as a junior officer in the Navy during WORLD WAR I. Private secretary to Supreme Court Associate Justice Louis D. Brandeis from 1919 to 1921, he then joined a Washington law firm. Over the next two years he specialized in corporate and international law. In 1933 newly inaugurated President FRANKLIN D. ROOSEVELT appointed him under secretary of the treasury. Acheson resigned the same year in sharp disagreement over Roosevelt's moves to lower the dollar's gold value. Following the outbreak of WORLD WAR II in Europe, he became in 1940 an active member of the COMMITTEE TO DEFEND AMERICA BY AIDING THE ALLIES. Acheson's assistance in the legal work for the DESTROYERS-FOR-BASES AGREEMENT (1940) with the British led Roosevelt

to bring him back into government in 1941 as an assistant secretary of state for economic affairs.

Acheson held the post throughout U.S. involvement in the world war. He helped coordinate LEND-LEASE aid to America's wartime allies, participated in the formation of the INTERNATIONAL MONETARY FUND and WORLD BANK at the BRETTON WOODS CONFERENCE (1944), and worked on planning for the UNITED NATIONS. In August 1945 he became under secretary of state. In 1946 he oversaw an expert committee that prepared the ACHESON-LILIENTHAL REPORT on the international control of atomic energy. The report was incorporated into the BARUCH PLAN for an international atomic development agency submitted to the United Nations and rejected by the Soviet Union. As U.S.-Soviet postwar relations deteriorated into COLD WAR, Acheson was a principal architect of the Truman administration's emerging strategy for the CONTAINMENT of Communist expansionism. He assisted in the formulation of the TRUMAN DOCTRINE (1947) committing the United States to the defense of European nations against Communist aggression and was an early advocate of the MARSHALL PLAN (1948) for massive U.S. economic aid to war-torn Europe.

Resigning in June 1947 to return to private law practice, Acheson remained active in public affairs, accepting appointment the same year to the Hoover Commission on the reorganization of the federal government and to the Permanent American-Canadian Defense Board. In January 1949 President HARRY S. TRUMAN named Acheson to succeed the retiring GEORGE C. MARSHALL as secretary of state. Acheson's attention turned first to Europe. In April 1949 the United States and its European allies finalized plans for the Western security alliance NATO. Convinced a restored Germany was key to the defense of Western Europe, he aligned U.S. policy behind the creation of an independent West German state and its inclusion in NATO.

Acheson's four-year tenure was dominated by events in Asia. In 1949 the Communist revolution under Mao Tse-tung gained power in China, driving the Nationalist government under Chiang Kai-shek to the island of Taiwan. In August 1949 Acheson released the CHINA WHITE PAPER defending the U.S. decision not to intervene in the

Chinese civil war on the side of the corrupt Chiang regime. The Truman administration, State Department, and Acheson all came under harsh attack by the pro-Chiang CHINA LOBBY for "losing" the giant Asian nation to communism. Beginning in 1950, Senator JOSEPH R. MCCARTHY (R-WI) raised charges, strongly denounced by Acheson, that alleged Communists in the State Department had subverted U.S. China policy.

In a January 1950 speech to the National Press Club in Washington outlining America's security commitments in Asia after the fall of China, Acheson failed to include Korea within the U.S. defense perimeter. When Communist North Korea invaded pro-Western South Korea in June 1950, Acheson's omission was criticized by Senator Robert A. Taft (R-OH) and other conservatives as having helped precipitate the KOREAN WAR. Acheson believed the Soviet Union ultimately responsible for the North Korean onslaught and strongly supported the commitment of U.S. ground forces to the conflict as essential to demonstrating American resolve to resist Communist aggression. The administration, worried that the invasion marked the first phase in a worldwide Communist offensive, also moved to bolster NATO defenses in Europe. Acheson endorsed Truman's decision, following Communist Chinese intervention in the fighting in November 1950, to pursue the more limited objective of restoring the 38TH PARALLEL boundary and thus avoid all-out war with China.

Acheson left office with the Truman administration in January 1953, having failed to secure a negotiated end to the Korean conflict. In the 1950s he was an outspoken critic of the Eisenhower administration's MASSIVE RETALIATION nuclear strategy for the DETERRENCE of communism. In 1958 he opposed GEORGE F. KENNAN's call for superpower DISENGAGEMENT in Central Europe, arguing such a policy eventually would drive West Germany into the Soviet fold and leave the continent vulnerable to Communist attack. Acheson served as an informal adviser to presidents JOHN F. KENNEDY and LYNDON B. JOHNSON. In 1968 he was one of the WISE MEN who, following the TET OFFENSIVE, counseled Johnson to deescalate U.S. involvement in the VIETNAM WAR. His memoirs, *Present at the Creation* (1969), won the Pulitzer Prize.

ACHESON-LILIENTHAL REPORT See **BARUCH PLAN**.

ACHILLE LAURO AFFAIR (1985) Hijacking of Italian cruise liner in the Mediterranean by Palestinian terrorists that became a sensitive international incident involving the United States, Italy, and Egypt. On October 7, 1985, the *Achille Lauro* was seized off Port Said, Egypt, by four Palestinian gunmen who threatened to kill passengers and blow up the ship unless their political demands were met. Leon Klinghoffer, an elderly passenger from New York City confined to a wheelchair, was shot and thrown overboard. After a tense standoff, the hijackers on October 9 surrendered to Egyptian authorities. The next day Egypt's president Hosni Mubarak approved the release of the Palestinian fugitives, who were put on a plane bound for Tunisia. The Egyptian aircraft, however, was intercepted by U.S. Navy jet fighters and forced to land in Sicily. President RONALD W. REAGAN's request for extradition of the four men to the United States was denied by the Italian government, which put the hijackers on trial. Defying U.S. government pleas, Italian officials allowed the alleged mastermind of the hijacking, renegade Palestinian leader Abu Abbas, who also had been on the intercepted Egyptian plane, to leave for Yugoslavia. The *Achille Lauro* affair briefly caused a rift in relations between the United States and both Italy and Egypt. Italian Prime Minister Benito Craxi resented the pressure America had exerted to gain extradition while Mubarak felt betrayed by the U.S. interception of a civilian Egyptian airliner. The Reagan administration for its part was upset with both Rome and Cairo for their failure to back its efforts against international terrorism.

ACT OF ... See **..., ACT OF**.

ACT TO ENCOURAGE IMMIGRATION (1864) Measure adopted by the federal government during the Civil War in response to a labor shortage. The act marked the first and ultimately only direct federal involvement in the promotion of immigration. Signed into law July 4, 1864, the bill endorsed the recruitment of foreign workers through contract labor agreements. The immigrant worker was bound to an employer for a set period in return for paid passage to the United States. The legislation was repealed in 1868 after wartime manpower requirements had abated. Contract labor arrangements continued in use until 1885 when Congress, under pressure from domestic labor, outlawed the practice in the FORAN ACT.

ADAMS, CHARLES FRANCIS (1807–1886) U.S. minister to Great Britain during the American Civil War, grandson of President JOHN ADAMS, son of President JOHN QUINCY ADAMS, and father of historian Henry Adams. Born in Boston, he graduated from Harvard in 1825, studied law under DANIEL WEBSTER, and was admitted to the bar in 1829. He practiced briefly in Boston before turning to journalism and politics. After serving from 1841 to 1845 as a Whig member of the Massachusetts House of Representatives, he emerged as a leader of the antislavery Conscience Whigs, who opposed the extension of slavery to U.S. territories. In 1848 Adams was the unsuccessful Free Soil candidate for vice-president on the ticket with MARTIN VAN BUREN. During the 1850s he compiled and edited a 10-volume edition of his grandfather's papers, the *Works of John Adams* (1850–1856). He returned to politics in 1858 with his election to the U.S. House of Representatives as a Republican. He resigned his congressional seat in 1861 to accept appointment by President ABRAHAM LINCOLN as minister to Great Britain, a post he held for seven years.

Arriving in London in the opening weeks of the Civil War, Adams served as an indispensable conduit between Secretary of State WILLIAM H. SEWARD and British Foreign Secretary Lord John Russell, with whom Adams developed a good relationship. His main task was to prevent British recognition of the Confederacy as an independent nation. He protested as unfriendly and premature Britain's recognition of Confederate belligerency, which Queen Victoria granted by way of a neutrality proclamation issued in May 1861. Under pressure from Adams, the British government refrained from receiving Confederate diplomatic agents as official envoys of an independent state. He played an instrumental part in defusing the Anglo-American diplomatic crisis precipitated by the TRENT AFFAIR (1861), the con-

troversial episode in which two Confederate commissioners en route to Europe were seized from the British vessel *Trent* by the commander of a U.S. Navy ship.

He pressured London to stop the British shipbuilders who were manufacturing and outfitting warships for the Confederacy in violation of British neutrality. The *Alabama* and other Confederate cruisers built in British ports were ravaging Union commercial shipping. Adams's protests eventually prompted British officialdom to take steps to prevent the delivery of British-built vessels to the Confederacy. A crisis developed in 1863 when the so-called Laird rams, a pair of ironclads made for the South and equipped to break the Union blockade of the Confederate coast, prepared to sail from British waters. Adams protested strenuously to Lord Russell, warning that the United States would deem it an act of war should the ships put to sea. As it was, the British government already had resolved not to let the vessels depart. Adams also presented the Lincoln administration's demand that the British government pay private American claims for damages inflicted on Northern merchant shipping by the *Alabama* and other British-built Confederate cruisers. London rejected Washington's repeated entreaties on this score, and the issue of the ALABAMA CLAIMS would remain deadlocked until 1871, when the two countries concluded the TREATY OF WASHINGTON, terms of which arranged for international arbitration of the American grievances.

After resigning his London post in 1868, Adams returned to the United States. He closed out his diplomatic career in 1872 as a U.S. commissioner on the tribunal at Geneva that arbitrated the Alabama Claims. He was an unsuccessful candidate for governor of Massachusetts in 1876. In the last years of his life he devoted himself to literary and historical pursuits, preparing for publication his father's monumental diary *Memoirs of John Quincy Adams* (12 vols., 1874–1877).

ADAMS, JOHN (1735–1826) Second president of the United States; father of sixth U.S. President JOHN QUINCY ADAMS. After graduating from Harvard College in 1755, John Adams studied law, was admitted to the Massachusetts bar in 1758, and opened a practice in his hometown at Braintree (now Quincy), Massachussetts. His early support for the cause of American independence vaulted him into colonial politics. He joined in the local revolutionary opposition to the Stamp Act (1765) and other British imperial taxes on the colonies. After moving to Boston in 1768, he solidified his reputation as an advocate of American liberties and foe of British tyranny. In 1770 he risked his rising political stature in successfully defending the British soldiers accused of murder in the Boston Massacre. Bad health forced Adams from the Massachusetts legislature after serving one term (1770–1771), but British retaliation for the Boston Tea Party (1773) drew him back into the radical politics of the coming AMERICAN REVOLUTION.

As a Massachusetts delegate to the Continental Congress (1774–1778), Adams helped draft the October 1774 petition of colonial rights and grievances to King George III, opposing reconciliation on any but American terms. He nominated GEORGE WASHINGTON as commander in chief of the Continental Army, successfully urged creation of a naval force to contend with British sea power, and forcefully defended the Declaration of Independence during the debate in Congress over its passage. He served on the COMMITTEE OF SECRET CORRESPONDENCE charged with developing foreign contacts for the new nation.

In 1778 Congress appointed Adams to replace SILAS DEANE as a member of the diplomatic mission in Paris seeking French recognition of American independence and expanded aid. Arriving after the FRANCO-AMERICAN ALLIANCE (1778) had been completed, he returned to Massachusetts and played a lead role in drafting that state's constitution. Named minister to the Netherlands in 1780, he obtained Dutch diplomatic recognition, a commerce treaty, and a substantial loan during his two-year stint at The Hague. Adams returned to Paris in October 1782 to take his place as a member of the American commission assigned to conclude a peace treaty with the British. With fellow members JOHN JAY and BENJAMIN FRANKLIN, he settled the preliminary articles of peace, which satisfied Adams's insistence upon American fishing rights off Canada and a U.S. western boundary of the Mississippi River. After signing the final TREATY OF PARIS (1783) formally ending the Revolution, Adams remained as a U.S. diplomat-at-large in Europe. He was appointed first U.S. minister to Great Britain in 1785. In three frustrating years in London, he was unable to secure British commercial concessions or move Anglo-American relations to friendlier terms.

Returning home at his own request in 1788, he won election the next year as the nation's first vice-president, an office he held for two terms (1789–1797). The Federalist Adams narrowly defeated Democratic-Republican THOMAS JEFFERSON in the 1796 presidential campaign to succeed President Washington. Adams took office in March 1797, inheriting a crisis in relations with France. Bitter French denunciation of the Anglo-American JAY'S TREATY (1794) and increasing French raids on American merchant ships were edging the two countries toward war. Convening a special session of Congress, Adams gained authorization for modest military preparations at the same time he won approval for a special diplomatic mission to Paris to try to reach a peaceful settlement of the conflict. The overture stalled when French Foreign Minister Charles Maurice de Talleyrand rebuffed U.S. envoys CHARLES COTESWORTH PINCKNEY, JOHN MARSHALL, and Elbridge Gerry in the XYZ AFFAIR (1797). Disclosure of Talleyrand's conduct quieted Democratic-Republican critics who had accused Adams of agitating for war with Paris.

The XYZ episode led the president to seek more extensive U.S. defensive preparations. At his direction, Congress created the DEPARTMENT OF THE NAVY, greatly bolstered the meager existing American fleet, empowered U.S. Navy ships and American privateers to raid armed French vessels, and authorized a large provisional army to defend against a possible French invasion. For two years the United States and France waged an undeclared QUASI-WAR (1798–1800). Federalists in Congress passed and Adams signed the controversial ALIEN AND SEDITION ACTS (1798), a series of measures aimed at controlling internal subversion and suppressing political opposition to Adams's French policy in the Democratic-Republican press. In 1799, in response to a French invitation to negotiation, the president dispatched a U.S. peace commission to Paris over ardent Federalist opposition in his cabinet and the Congress. The American commission finally concluded the CONVENTION OF 1800, which ended the Quasi-War and preserved U.S. neutrality by abrogating the Franco-American Alliance. Meanwhile Adams forced the resignation of Secretary of State TIMOTHY PICKERING and Secretary of War James McHenry who, hoping to widen the breach in U.S.-French relations, had schemed to thwart Adams's policies. The rancorous split between Adams and Federalist leader ALEXANDER HAMILTON divided their party. The politically weakened Adams lost the presidency to Thomas Jefferson in the 1800 election. He left office in 1801 and retired to Quincy.

ADAMS, JOHN QUINCY (1767–1848) Diplomat, secretary of state, sixth president of the United States, congressman; son of JOHN ADAMS, second U.S. president. John Quincy Adams was born in Braintree (now Quincy), Massachusetts. At age 10 he accompanied his father on diplomatic missions to Europe. He studied in France and the Netherlands, served as private secretary to the American commissioner to Russia, Francis Dana, in 1781, and was secretary to his father during the peace negotiations with Great Britain that produced the TREATY OF PARIS (1783) ending the AMERICAN REVOLUTION. Returning to the United States in 1785, he entered Harvard College, from which he graduated in 1787. He then read law, was admitted to the bar in 1790, and the same year entered practice in Boston. Under President GEORGE WASHINGTON, Adams served as U.S. minister to the Netherlands from 1794 to 1797 and, during his father's presidency, as minister to Prussia from 1797 to 1801. Returning to Boston and his law practice, he was elected as a Federalist in 1803 to the U.S. Senate.

His political independence in Congress put him at increasing odds with Federalist Party leaders in Massachusetts. After aligning with the Democratic-Republican Jefferson administration by voting for the EMBARGO ACT (1807), which was fiercely opposed by the Federalists, Adams was forced to resign his Senate seat in 1808. He was a professor of rhetoric and oratory at Harvard from 1806 to 1809. President JAMES MADISON named him the first American minister to Russia, where he served from 1809

to 1814. Nominated to the U.S. Supreme Court by Madison in 1810, he declined the appointment to remain in St. Petersburg. Adams headed the American commission that negotiated the TREATY OF GHENT (1814) with Great Britain, ending the WAR OF 1812. He concluded his long and remarkable career as a diplomat in Europe by serving as minister to Britain for two years.

President JAMES MONROE recalled Adams from London to become secretary of state in 1817. He held the post throughout Monroe's two terms. He directed negotiation of the CONVENTION OF 1818, a wide-ranging treaty that led to greatly improved ties with Britain by resolving several thorny issues in Anglo-American diplomacy. The convention extended the northwest boundary between the United States and Canada westward from the Lake of the Woods along the 49th parallel to the Rocky Mountains; deferred a final understanding on the OREGON QUESTION by leaving the Oregon country open to joint American and British occupation for 10 years, with neither side renouncing its claim to the territory; effected a compromise on the complex FISHERIES QUESTION by restoring American fishing privileges along limited coastal areas off Canada; and renewed the Anglo-American commercial convention of 1815 for a decade.

Relations with Spain preoccupied the Monroe administration, which sought a settlement of the long-standing differences between Washington and Madrid over Florida and the exact territorial limits of the LOUISIANA PURCHASE (1803). The secretary of state scored a major diplomatic triumph with his negotiation of the historic ADAMS-ONIS TREATY (1819), under which Spain ceded East and West Florida to America. Known also as the Transcontinental Treaty, it defined the frontier boundary between Spanish and U.S. possessions in North America from the Gulf of Mexico to the Pacific Ocean, with Spain accepting the 42nd parallel as the northern limit of its territory and the United States abandoning its claim to Texas. Monroe, following Adams's counsel, exercised great diplomatic caution by withholding U.S. recognition of the independence of Spain's former colonies in the Americas until the Adams-Onis agreement was safely ratified. The secretary of state sympathized with the Latin American revolutions but feared premature recognition might embroil the United States in a conflict with Spain and its fellow European monarchies. When an alliance of European powers appeared poised to invade Latin America to restore Spain's former colonies, Adams collaborated with the president in formulation of the MONROE DOCTRINE (1823), which established U.S. opposition to European intervention in the Western Hemisphere as a fundamental principle of American foreign policy. He resolved competing U.S. and Russian territorial claims along America's northwest coast through the RUSSO-AMERICAN TREATY OF 1824, in which Russia accepted 54° 40' as the southern boundary of Russian Alaska.

As one of four candidates for president in 1824, Adams finished second in the electoral vote to ANDREW JACKSON and ahead of William H. Crawford and HENRY CLAY. Because none of the candidates had commanded a majority, the election was forced into the House of Representatives. After private consultations between the two, Clay threw his support to Adams, who won the election in the House on the first ballot. With his victory, Adams named Clay secretary of state, whereupon Jackson's supporters made the charge that Clay and Adams had entered into a "corrupt bargain" to ensure the latter's election and the former's appointment to the cabinet. The general consensus among historians is that there was probably an implicit bargain but no corruption.

Adams entered office in March 1825. In foreign relations he was faced with the collapse of Spain's New World empire and its implications for American diplomacy. He welcomed the end of Spanish colonialism in Latin America, voicing the hope that the newly independent nations there would achieve stable, republican government and become partners in the economic expansion of the Americas. When the United States received an invitation to attend a pioneering conference of Latin American republics in Panama, Adams, with Clay's strong support, accepted. Political opposition in Congress to U.S. involvement in the scheduled Pan-American meeting significantly delayed the departure of the delegates whom Adams had appointed and ultimately prevented U.S. participation in the PANAMA CONGRESS (1826). Seeking to expand American overseas trade, the Adams administration completed general commercial treaties with Britain, France, the Netherlands, Mexico, and eight other countries. Efforts to win removal of the barriers to American trade with the British West Indies proved unsuccessful. On other fronts in Anglo-American relations, the administration concluded the CONVENTION OF 1827, which referred the U.S.-Canada northeast boundary dispute to international arbitration, and another agreement the same year that deferred the Oregon Question by renewing indefinitely the joint U.S.-British occupation of the Oregon Country.

The president embraced the American System, Clay's program for achieving national development under the direction of a strong federal government. He supported a protective tariff to foster American industry; however, Jacksonians in Congress manipulated the tariff issue to damage the president. In 1828 they orchestrated passage of the steep TARIFF OF ABOMINATIONS, which ignited fierce opposition from agricultural interests in the South and West. The Adams administration, which had pushed for higher tariffs, took the blame for the extremely unpopular legislation. Adams also endorsed federal protection of the Indian tribes against encroachment by the states. At the same time, eager to hasten westward expansion and settlement, he initiated what would develop under his successor into the INDIAN REMOVAL POLICY.

Defeated for reelection in 1828 by Andrew Jackson, Adams returned to Massachusetts, where voters elected him to the U.S. House of Representatives in 1830. He served 17 years in Congress, flourishing as a proponent of strong nationalism over states' rights. A champion of slavery's gradual abolition, he opposed its extension to newly acquired territories. His antislavery leadership in the House helped thwart the drive by proslavery Southern Democrats to annex Texas after it won its independence from Mexico in 1836 in the TEXAS REVOLUTION. In 1843 he helped defeat the UPSHUR-CALHOUN TREATY for annexation of the Lone Star Republic, only to see TEXAN ANNEXATION achieved by joint resolution of Congress in 1845. Beginning in 1836, he waged a yearly fight against adoption of the "gag rule," forbidding discussion or action in the House on antislavery petitions, until its defeat in 1844. In the AMISTAD AFFAIR (1841), involving a slave mutiny aboard a Spanish ship that was then captured by a U.S. warship, he appeared before the Supreme Court to argue successfully on behalf of the slaves' right to freedom. Adams died in office in 1848. His monumental 12-volume *Memoirs* (1874–1877) were edited by his son CHARLES FRANCIS ADAMS, the U.S. ambassador to Great Britain during the Civil War.

ADAMS-ONIS TREATY (1819) Treaty in which the United States acquired Florida from Spain and the two countries defined the western boundary between U.S. territory and remaining Spanish possessions in North America. The historic agreement, also known as the Transcontinental Treaty or the Florida Treaty, was signed February 22, 1819, by Secretary of State JOHN QUINCY ADAMS and Spanish Minister in Washington Don Luis de Onis. Florida and the boundaries of the LOUISIANA PURCHASE (1803) were long-standing disputes in Spanish-American diplomacy. The United States had coveted Florida virtually since Spain gained possession of it in 1783. American determination to prevent seizure of the Spanish colony by Great Britain or France prompted U.S. annexation of part of West Florida in 1810 and inspired President JAMES MADISON to assert the NO-TRANSFER PRINCIPLE in 1811. The imprecise Louisiana Purchase line had invited competing claims by Washington and Madrid for territory west of the Mississippi River.

Adams and Onis initiated their negotiations in December 1817. Spain suspended the talks after the FLORIDA INVASION by U.S. troops under General ANDREW JACKSON in March 1818. Negotiations resumed in October of the same year and culminated in the February 1819 treaty. Weakened by European war and by rebellion among its Latin American colonies, Spain acquiesced on most of the U.S. demands. By terms of the Adams-Onis accord, Spain ceded the Floridas, comprising Spanish colonial East and West Florida, to America. Instead of direct payment for the territory, the United States agreed to assume $5 million in outstanding claims by American citizens against Spain. Both countries settled on a new boundary between U.S. and Spanish domains reaching from the Mississippi River to the Pacific Coast. Spain surrendered its claims to the Oregon country and accepted the 42nd parallel as the northern limit to its posses-

sions. The United States abandoned its claims to Texas.

Following initial U.S. Senate approval, Spain delayed ratification while it sought a U.S. pledge neither to aid nor recognize revolting Spanish colonies in the Americas. The United States refused and the Spanish crown finally ratified the treaty in October 1820. The Senate approved it a second time in February 1821.

See also MAP 2.

ADDAMS, JANE (1860–1935) Social reformer. Addams was born in Illinois to a well-to-do family. She graduated from Rockford College in 1882. Addams spent several years traveling and studying in Europe, where she was exposed to the British social reform movement. In 1889 she bought an old mansion in a needy neighborhood in Chicago and formed Hull House, a settlement devoted to working-class education and recreation. She authored a number of well-received books that brought her work national attention. In the 1910s Addams became active in the international peace movement. A noted feminist, she presided over the International Congress of Women convened at The Hague in 1915 to seek an end to WORLD WAR I. She served as president of the WOMEN'S INTERNATIONAL LEAGUE FOR PEACE AND FREEDOM until her death in 1935. In 1931 she became the first American woman awarded the Nobel Peace Prize.

AFGHANISTAN WAR (1978–1992) Conflict in Afghanistan between the Soviet-backed Afghan regime and the U.S.-supported anti-Communist Afghan resistance. The leftist People's Democratic Party of Afghanistan overthrew the government of President Muhammad Daoud in a bloody coup in April 1978. The Democratic Republic of Afghanistan was established, with Noor Muhammad Taraki as president. The Soviet Union promptly established ties with the new regime and in December 1978 Moscow and Kabul concluded a treaty of friendship and cooperation. Taraki's revolutionary economic and social program led Islamic traditionalists and rural Afghan tribal groups to revolt against his regime, which relied increasingly on Soviet arms in its struggle against the growing insurgency.

Despite mounting efforts to suppress the guerrilla movement, the government's position continued to deteriorate. On December 25, 1979, Soviet military forces invaded neighboring Afghanistan and quickly gained control in Kabul. Babrak Karmal, leader of a pro-Soviet Afghan faction, was installed as president. His government remained dependent on Soviet military forces. The Soviet presence, which within a month grew to 85,000 troops, brought an intensification of the guerrilla rebellion, which was transformed into anti-Soviet resistance. The Soviet invasion of Afghanistan dealt a serious setback to superpower relations, bringing an end to the period of DE-TENTE and a resurgence of COLD WAR tensions. President JIMMY CARTER responded by withdrawing the SALT II arms control agreement from the Senate's consideration, imposing a grain embargo on the Soviet Union, and ordering the U.S. OLYMPIC BOY-COTT of the 1980 summer games scheduled to be held in Moscow. The Kremlin's intervention also was the impetus for the president's enunciation in January 1980 of the CARTER DOCTRINE declaring a U.S. commitment to protect the Persian Gulf against external attack.

The fighting in Afghanistan produced heavy casualties and caused severe population dislocations. About 3 million Afghan war refugees fled to Pakistan and roughly another 1.5 million found their way to Iran. The antigovernment Moslem guerrillas, or Mujahedeen, comprised dozens of factions united by the common goal of expelling the Soviet invaders. Operating from bases in Pakistan and Iran, the rebels were sustained by extensive military and economic assistance from abroad. The United States spearheaded international support for the Afghan insurgents. The Reagan administration, through the CENTRAL INTELLIGENCE AGENCY, furnished more than $2 billion in covert aid to the Mujahedeen between 1981 and 1988. President RONALD W. REAGAN made U.S. assistance to the Afghan rebels a hallmark of his policy, the so-called REAGAN DOCTRINE, of aiding anti-Communist insurgencies worldwide. The Reagan administration also sent substantial aid to U.S. ally Pakistan to help it with the Afghan refugee burden and to strengthen its position as a barrier state blocking further Soviet expansion.

By 1986, an estimated 115,000 Soviet troops and 50,000 Afghan government soldiers were pitted against approximately 130,000 guerrillas. Vast Soviet superiority in weapons and equipment was largely offset by Afghanistan's difficult mountainous terrain, where the Mujahedeen excelled as a fighting force and proved more effective than regular troops. Moreover, in 1986 the United States enhanced the rebels' military position when it began supplying them with Stinger antiaircraft missiles capable of downing Soviet helicopter gunships. The same year the Soviets orchestrated Karmal's replacement as president by Najibullah, former head of the Afghan secret police. Early in 1987 Najibullah proposed a cease-fire and national reconciliation policy, both of which were rejected by the guerrillas. By year's end, however, tedious negotiations pursued since 1982 within the UNITED NA-TIONS framework toward a political solution began to offer hints of a breakthrough. Since assuming power in 1985, Soviet leader Mikhail S. Gorbachev had made ending his country's intervention in Afghanistan a high priority. The intractable war there was increasingly unpopular with the Soviet public and a heavy drain on the beleaguered Soviet economy.

On April 14, 1988, the United States, Soviet Union, Afghanistan, and Pakistan concluded a set of U.N.-mediated agreements providing for Soviet withdrawal from Afghanistan and the voluntary repatriation of Afghan refugees. The accords, signed at Geneva, set out a scheme for ending the USSR's eight-year military occupation. They did not, however, end the ongoing Afghanistan War. The USSR pledged to pull out its 100,000-plus forces from Afghanistan within nine months after May 15, 1988. The Mujahedeen leaders, who were not a party to the Geneva accords, made clear that they did not feel bound by the agreements and vowed to continue their armed insurgency against the Soviet-backed regime in Kabul. The United States reserved the right to continue sending military aid to the resistance as long as the USSR continued to fortify its client Afghan government.

With the completion of the Soviet troop pullout on February 15, 1989, the focus of fighting shifted to the bitter struggle between the Mujahedeen and the Najibullah government. The United States placed an embargo on diplomatic contacts with Afghanistan and urged internationally monitored free elections, the possibility of which Najibullah endorsed in March 1990. U.S.-Soviet negotiations aimed at bringing about a settlement of the protracted conflict continued. Moscow dropped its demand Najibullah be guaranteed a place in any future Afghan government, while the United States backed off its insistence he be excluded from any role. Afghan guerrilla leaders, however, refused to participate in any peace talks with Najibullah or his ruling regime. Following the MOSCOW COUP, the newly reconstituted Soviet government and Bush administration in September 1991 reached an agreement halting all military aid to Afghanistan by the end of the year.

A Mujahedeen offensive against Kabul forced Najibullah's ouster on April 16, 1992, and presaged the Afghan government's imminent collapse. Moslem rebels met almost no resistance as they seized the Afghan capital on April 26, marking the end of their 14-year fight against the Communist regime. Rival guerrilla factions continued to battle one another for control of Kabul even as they formed an interim governing council.

AFRICAN DEVELOPMENT BANK (AfDB) Regional lending institution formed in 1963 by 33 independent African countries to accelerate economic and social developments of members by promoting investment. The agreement formally establishing the AfDB went into force in 1964 and the bank began operations at its headquarters in Abidjan, the capital of the Ivory Coast, in 1966. AfDB makes low-interest loans to finance both public and private development projects in agriculture, transportation, telecommunications, energy, water management, health, and sanitation. Membership in the bank was limited to African nations until 1982, when the AfDB, in search of badly needed additional capital, opened the institution to nonregional countries. By the end of 1983 more than 20 outside nations had joined the bank, including the United States. Under the agreement permitting entry of non-African states, African members still hold two-thirds of the capital stock, lending is restricted to African nations, and the AfDB's president is always an African national. The bank currently numbers 50 African and 25 non-African members.

In 1973 a group of non-African countries that included the United States joined with the AfDB to form the African Development Fund (ADF) as an affiliated, though legally distinct, lending institution. The fund provides interest-free loans with repayment over 50 years to the poorest African nations. All contributors to the ADF share in its management and exercise voting power over loan decisions in direct relation to the amount of ADF capital stock they hold. Together, the AfDB, the ADF, the Nigeria Trust Fund, and the International Financial Society for Investments and Development in Africa (known by its French acronym, SIFIDA) constitute the African Development Bank Group.

AFRICAN DEVELOPMENT FOUNDATION (ADF) U.S. government corporation created by Congress to support self-help development efforts of African groups and individuals at the grass-roots level. Authorized by lawmakers in 1980 as a complement to U.S. foreign aid programs, the foundation delivers economic assistance directly to local communities and organizations in African nations. The aid primarily funds farming, animal husbandry, manufacturing, and water management activities. The legislation creating the ADF mandated that its beneficiaries design and implement their own projects. The foundation's professed goal is to make local communities responsible for their own development through programs that meet their particular needs. The ADF encourages the use of traditional or local methods so as to avert the social and economic disruption that often follows the introduction of new equipment or production systems. Since the foundation became operational in 1984, it has subsidized programs and projects in some 20 countries. A seven-member board of directors appointed by the president with Senate confirmation governs the ADF. By law five members are drawn from the private sector and two from government.

AFRICAN DEVELOPMENT FUND See **AFRICAN DEVELOPMENT BANK**.

AFRICAN FAMINE RELIEF AND RECOVERY ACT (1985) Congressional legislation appropriating U.S. funds for emergency famine relief in Africa. With millions of people facing death from starvation on the continent, the United States in 1984 began sending an unprecedented amount of emergency aid to drought-stricken African countries as part of a larger international relief effort. America's response took two forms: emergency relief—food, seeds, and trucks to deliver them—and long-term aid targeted at helping countries develop their economies to avoid further food shortages. The majority of food aid was administered through the Agriculture Department's FOOD FOR PEACE program, an initiative launched in 1954 to help needy countries by supplying them with U.S. grain surpluses.

Congress furnished $90 million in emergency food aid to Africa in a special 1984 supplemental appropriations measure. The same bill also earmarked an additional $90 million from the Agriculture Department's Commodity Credit Corporation food stocks for distribution to African countries affected by the famine. Another emergency supplemental measure allocated $16 million for trucks, blankets, and seeds. The AGENCY FOR INTERNATIONAL DEVELOPMENT (AID), the U.S. government's principal agency for administering foreign assistance, reallocated an additional $172 million in emergency aid. When the famine spread during the year, AID approved another $200 million for the first weeks of fiscal year 1985. Ethiopia, the country most severely hit by the famine, received about $100 million. Kenya, the Sudan, Mauritania, and Mozambique were other major recipients. In late November 1984 the Reagan administration announced that it would, for the first time, release wheat from the U.S. emergency reserve for the benefit of needy African nations. President RONALD W. REAGAN agreed to furnish 300,000 tons, the maximum allowed under the 1980 law establishing the wheat reserve.

Continuing famine caused by drought and civil strife threatened some 20 countries in sub-Saharan Africa with large-scale starvation. In response to the unalleviated crisis, Congress on April 2, 1985, approved a bill appropriating $784 million for emergency relief. President Reagan signed the measure into law the same day. The money included $609 million for food aid and $175 million for nonfood assistance. The African Famine Relief and Recovery Act also authorized the Agriculture Department to give African countries 200,000 tons of Commodity Credit Corporation surplus food. Before sending any of the food, the agriculture secretary was required to certify to

Congress that none of it would end up directly in the hands of Ethiopia's Marxist government, which stood accused of obstructing emergency international aid. In the ensuing years the United States continued to furnish emergency assistance to ongoing international relief efforts in sub-Saharan Africa, which was plagued by a chronic cycle of civil war, drought, and famine.

AFRICAN SLAVE TRADE TREATY (1862) Anglo-American treaty for suppressing the African slave trade. The United States abolished the trade in 1808, a year after Great Britain had done so. In 1820 Congress declared it piracy under U.S. law, punishable by death. Despite the prohibitions the trade continued, driven by increasing manpower demands of plantation agriculture. Thus between 1808 and 1860 an estimated 250,000 African slaves were brought illegally into the United States. Animated by growing moral opposition to slavery, Britain spearheaded efforts in the early 19th century to halt the international slave traffic by policing the seas for violators. The United States, however, refused to grant the British the right to stop and search vessels flying the American flag and suspected of being slave ships. America withheld its cooperation because it objected to Britain's continued insistence on a right of IMPRESSMENT. The United States registered frequent complaints, moreover, that American ships engaged in legal commerce were intercepted and sometime unjustly seized by indiscriminate British patrols. U.S. grievances notwithstanding, the American flag was fraudulently flown by foreign traders seeking to evade capture while transporting African slaves across the Atlantic, especially to the profitable markets of Cuba and Brazil.

The United States took a step toward cooperation when it agreed under the WEBSTER-ASHBURTON TREATY (1842) to maintain an American naval squadron along the African coast to assist a similar British squadron interdict the illegal slave traffic. This joint cruising proved largely a failure since few American frigates were ever dispatched and successive Democratic administrations, generally sympathetic to Southern slave interests, did not vigorously carry out the 1842 treaty's provisions. The foreign slave trade emerged as an issue in the deepening sectional conflict in America over slavery. The Southern Commercial Convention at Vicksburg, Mississippi, in 1859 urged the repeal of all laws barring the international slave traffic. Some Southern leaders denounced all such legislation as unconstitutional.

The Civil War and the diplomatic challenges it presented the Union brought a change in U.S. policy. A captured slave trader, Nathaniel Gordon, was hanged in New York in February 1862 at President ABRAHAM LINCOLN's order, becoming the first person executed in the United States for the crime. Eager to curry the support of the European powers and forestall their diplomatic recognition of the Confederacy, Secretary of State WILLIAM H. SEWARD concluded a treaty with Britain on April 7, 1862, that provided for cooperative action to end the illegal commerce in African slaves. The agreement arranged for mutual right to stop and search off the coasts of Africa and Cuba, with joint courts in New York, Cape Town, and Sierra Leone to try alleged offenders. With the Southern states absent through secession, the Senate unanimously ratified the convention. Slavery's abolition in the United States and the end of the Civil War largely brought the African trade to a halt. Nonetheless, an illegal African slave traffic persisted through the second half of the 19th century. The United States was among the countries that met in Belgium and signed the 1890 General Act of Brussels, an international agreement for putting an end to the criminal activity.

AGEE, PHILIP (1935–) Former CENTRAL INTELLIGENCE AGENCY (CIA) officer, critic of U.S. intelligence activities. The Florida-born Agee graduated from Notre Dame in 1956 and joined the CIA. He was assigned to the agency's COVERT ACTION branch, serving as an agent in Ecuador, Uruguay, and Mexico. Disillusioned with U.S. policies in Latin America and strongly opposed to the VIETNAM WAR, Agee resigned from the CIA in 1968. He had come to believe the CIA's secret operations overseas were misguided and immoral and thus resolved to press for their discontinuation through public exposure. While living abroad in Cuba and Europe, he wrote a detailed account of CIA clandestine activities, listing the names of

hundreds of agency employees. His book, *Inside the Company: A CIA Diary*, was first published in England in 1975 to avoid possible U.S. censorship. Its release forced the CIA to cease or alter a number of its operations.

Agee continued his highly controversial campaign against U.S. intelligence activities, authoring articles, holding press conferences, and editing the magazine *Counterspy*, which identified and exposed U.S. intelligence officers. When CIA station chief Richard S. Welch was assassinated in Athens, Greece, in December 1975, senior agency officials bitterly condemned *Counterspy* for having previously published his name. In 1978 Agee released *Dirty Work*, an extensive compendium of anti-CIA articles. The same year he helped to launch the *Covert Action Information Bulletin*, which divulged names of CIA agents operating abroad. Expelled because of his activities from Great Britain, France, Belgium, and the Netherlands in the late 1970s, Agee settled in West Germany before moving finally to Spain.

Amid indications Agee might travel to Iran to participate in an anti-U.S. forum during the IRAN HOSTAGE CRISIS, Secretary of State CYRUS R. VANCE revoked his passport on national security grounds in December 1979. Agee challenged the constitutionality of Vance's decision. His counsel cited the 1958 U.S. Supreme Court decision in *Kent v. Dulles* that the State Department could not deny passports to individuals merely because of their beliefs or associations. On June 29, 1981, the Supreme Court ruled in *Haig* v. *Agee* that under the 1926 Passport Act, the State Department had the authority to revoke the passport of an American citizen deemed a threat to the nation's security. Agee remained an expatriate in Europe. Meanwhile, in 1980 the U.S. government had obtained a court order requiring that he submit all future writings on classified intelligence activities to a special CIA publications review board.

AGENCY FOR INTERNATIONAL DEVELOPMENT (AID) U.S. government agency that administers economic and humanitarian assistance to less-developed countries worldwide. Established within the State Department in 1961 by the FOREIGN ASSISTANCE ACT, AID represented the realization of the

Kennedy administration's proposal for a new federal organization under which U.S. foreign assistance programs would be consolidated. In 1979 it became a component of the newly founded INTERNATIONAL DEVELOPMENT COOPERATION ADMINISTRATION.

The purpose of AID is to help the world's poorer countries meet their basic human needs and improve their quality of life. Agency initiatives focus on increasing productivity, improving infrastructure and basic social services, and promoting equitable economic growth among developing nations. Development assistance programs address such areas as agriculture, nutrition, health, education, population planning, and environmental protection. The agency's efforts are geared toward pushing free-market-oriented growth and encouraging private U.S. investment in development projects. The agency also administers an Economic Support Fund whose primary aim is to shore up the economies of, and thereby promote political stability in, countries friendly to the United States. In addition, AID conducts U.S. international disaster relief efforts, providing emergency assistance to countries hit by natural calamities. It also shares responsibility with the Department of Agriculture for administering the FOOD FOR PEACE program.

AID See **AGENCY FOR INTERNATIONAL DEVELOPMENT**.

AIR AMERICA Airline owned and operated by the CENTRAL INTELLIGENCE AGENCY (CIA) in the Far East. In 1949 the CIA secretly purchased Civil Air Transport (CAT), a Taiwan-registered airline formed in 1946 by former U.S. General Claire L. Chennault, commander of the Flying Tigers in China during WORLD WAR II. Agency ownership was concealed through complex financial arrangements. CAT was used to support U.S. covert operations in Asia including OPERATION TROPIC and the INDONESIA REBELLION. In 1959 the airline's name was changed to Air America. It became a major enterprise with a large fleet of transport and combat aircraft and facilities throughout Southeast Asia. Air America became synonymous with covert air operations. It played a central role in clandestine activities in the LAOS SECRET WAR and the VIETNAM WAR. The CIA moved to liquidate the airline after the end of U.S. involvement in Indochina. By 1976 its various assets had been sold to private business.

AIR FORCE, DEPARTMENT OF THE See **DEPARTMENT OF THE AIR FORCE** in **APPENDIX B.**

AIRCRAFT SABOTAGE ACT See **HOSTAGE TAKING ACT**.

ALABAMA CLAIMS Demands for compensation made by the United States against Great Britain for damages to Union commercial shipping during the Civil War. The losses were inflicted by Confederate warships, notably the *Alabama, Florida,* and *Shenandoah,* built or armed in British ports. U.S. claims were based on Britain's alleged failure to uphold its obligations as a neutral nation to stop its citizens from assisting the Confederate war effort. The most notorious of the British-built vessels was the *Alabama,* which captured and destroyed scores of U.S. merchant ships before it was sunk in July 1864 outside Cherbourg, France, by the USS *Kearsarge.* Early in the war Secretary of State WILLIAM H. SEWARD had instructed U.S. Minister to Britain CHARLES F. ADAMS to demand redress from London for the depredations of the *Alabama* and other raiders on the North's maritime commerce. Repeated Lincoln administration protests gradually moved the British government to curb the building and outfitting of vessels for the South. U.S. claims for indemnity, ultimately totaling some $19 million, were resisted by Britain and remained a serious point of contention in Anglo-American diplomacy after the war.

A breakthrough appeared at hand in January 1869, when the Johnson-Clarendon Convention was signed. Negotiated under Seward's close supervision by U.S. Minister to Britain Reverdy Johnson and British Foreign Minister the Earl of Clarendon, the agreement arranged for the submission to international arbitration of all claims between citizens of the two nations since 1853. Political opposition in the Senate to President ANDREW JOHNSON, however, made the prospect for ratification of the agreement remote. Foreign Relations Committee Chairman Charles Sumner (R-MA) condemned the treaty in a celebrated anti-British speech. He argued that Great

Britain should pay not only for the value of Union ships and cargo destroyed by British-built Confederate cruisers but also for the indirect costs to northern shipping such as insurance rate increases and commercial traffic driven from the seas by British-built raiders. Moreover he contended that British moral and material support of the South had doubled the duration of the Civil War. He thus urged that London be assessed half the cost of the conflict to the Union treasury, a notion the British government dismissed as preposterous. Sumner's bill for Britain's indemnity amounted to more than $2 billion. He implied that as just compensation, the American claims might be settled by the cession of Canada to the United States. The Senate rejected the Johnson-Clarendon treaty in April 1869.

A renewed effort by Seward's successor as secretary of state, HAMILTON FISH, to resolve America's Civil War grievances culminated in the Anglo-American TREATY OF WASHINGTON (1871). Under its terms, the *Alabama* claims were referred to a five-member international arbitration board. The five arbitrators—one each from the United States, Great Britain, Italy, Switzerland, and Brazil—convened at Geneva in December 1871. On September 14, 1872, the board ruled that Great Britain had failed in its duties as a neutral country and awarded the United States $15.5 million for direct damages, all indirect claims having been dismissed. American opinion accepted the settlement as satisfactory and both nations emerged believing their honor intact. Great Britain paid the claims in 1873.

ALAMO, SIEGE OF THE (1836) Legendary stand by Texan forces against an overwhelmingly larger Mexican army during the Texan war for independence. Mexican forces sent in 1835 to quell the TEXAN REVOLUTION against Mexico's central authority were forced to abandon the Alamo, a group of fortified military buildings in San Antonio, to Texan colonists under arms. On February 23, 1836, a Mexican army of 3000 men led by General Antonio Lopez de Santa Anna appeared at San Antonio bent upon recapturing the fortifications. A force of about 150 Texan troops under Colonels William B. Travis and Jim Bowie took up defensive positions in the Alamo and defiantly rejected Santa Anna's demand for surrender. Besieged by the Mexicans, the grossly outnumbered Texans used cannon fire to repel repeated attacks. On the battle's eighth day some 30 Texas reinforcements breached Mexican lines and made it into the encircled Alamo.

Santa Anna launched his final assault in the fort early on March 6. Depite absorbing heavy losses, the Mexican forces routed the defenders, almost all of whom were killed in the intense fighting within the compound. Among the last to fall were Davy Crockett and his 12 fellow Tennessee volunteers. The combatants who surrendered were executed at Santa Anna's orders. News of the massacre stiffened resistance throughout the Lone Star Republic. Inspired by the rallying cry "Remember the Alamo," a Texan army commanded by SAMUEL HOUSTON defeated the Mexicans and captured Santa Anna at the decisive Battle of San Jacinto in April 1836, thereby gaining Texan independence.

ALASKA BOUNDARY DISPUTE (1898–1903) Controversy over the location of the boundary between Canada, at the time dependent on Great Britain for the conduct of its foreign relations, and Alaska. Resolution of the dispute in favor of the United States erased the last serious block to closer relations between America and Great Britain at the turn of the century. Following the discovery in 1896 of gold in Canada's Klondike region near Alaska, the Canadian government revived an old boundary dispute with the United States. The RUSSO-AMERICAN TREATY OF 1867, which transferred Alaska to the United States, had perpetuated the vague line between the Alaska panhandle and British North America. When Canada sought clarification and proposed that the boundary be drawn along the mouths of the numerous inlets from the Pacific Ocean, the United States vehemently objected. The dispute centered on the question of who controlled the headwaters of the Lynn Canal, the largest waterway into the prized Klondike region. Both sides understood that control of the canal was tantamount to control of the territory's emerging commercial possibilities. Great Britain initially backed Canada's claim by attempting to link the issue to concessions on the CLAYTON-BULWER TREATY, an 1850 pact that guaranteed equal British and American influence in Central America and thwarted independent U.S. development of an isthmian canal. London approached Washington about American relinquishment of Alaskan territory in exchange for enlarged rights in Central America. The United States rejected the overture and refused subsequent British offers to arbitrate the dispute. In 1902 Great Britain's Foreign Office, worried the boundary stalemate might derail its overall policy of Anglo-American rapprochement, and burdened by problems with the Boers in South Africa, pushed for a settlement. The Hay-Herbert Treaty, concluded in June 1903, established a U.S.-British-Canadian boundary commission to adjudicate the matter. In October 1903, the Alaska Arbitral Tribunal voted to grant the United States control of the Lynn Canal. Settlement of the dispute hastened improved relations between Great Britain and the United States in the decade after 1900.

See also MAP 5.

ALASKA PURCHASE (1867) Acquisition of Alaska in the Russo-American Treaty of 1867. When finalized, the purchase added to the United States an area nearly 600,000 miles square, or approximately twice the size of Texas. In December 1866, the czarist government directed its minister to the United States, Baron Edouard de Stoeckl, to offer to sell Russian America, or Alaska, to Secretary of State WILLIAM H. SEWARD, an ardent expansionist who as early as 1860 had revealed interest in the territory. Russia was willing to part with Alaska because it had become an economic liability and was vulnerable to British naval power projected from Canada. Secret negotiations between Seward and Stoeckl in Washington yielded a treaty, concluded March 30, 1867, in which the United States agreed to pay $7.2 million for Alaska. News of the purchase met with derision in Congress and among the public as critics questioned the value of the northern area to the United States.

Antiexpansionist newspapers mockingly dubbed the acquisition "Seward's Folly," "Walrussia," "Icebergia," and "Seward's Polar Bear Garden." The secretary of state campaigned to persuade Americans that Alaska's commercial and strategic importance in the Pacific region and its resources in fish, fur, and lumber justified the expense. By a vote of 37 to 2, the Senate approved the treaty on April 9, 1867. Although the House of Representatives delayed appropriating money for the purchase for more than a year, the American government took formal possession of Alaska in a ceremony at Sitka on October 18, 1867.

See also MAP 2.

ALBANIA OPERATION (1950–1952) Unsuccessful attempt by U.S. and British intelligence services to overthrow the Communist government of Albania. Albanian resistance to German occupation during WORLD WAR II was led by Enver Hoxha, founder of the Albanian Communist Party. After the war, Hoxha installed a Communist regime. In 1948 Albania's neighbor Yugoslavia broke with the Soviet Union over Moscow's direction of the international Communist movement. Yugoslavia's independent stance deprived the Soviet Union of direct land access to Albania. London and Washington sensed an opportunity for fomenting an anti-Communist uprising in Albania free from Soviet military intervention. Senior U.S. and British policymakers believed such a rebellion had the potential to undermine Soviet control in the Balkans and Eastern Europe.

In late 1949 the Truman administration approved a joint Anglo-American operation, code-named Valuable, to train and insert a force of Albanian emigre guerrillas back into their native country where they would mount a popular revolt. A special committee was established in Washington to coordinate the covert operation between the U.S. State Department and CENTRAL INTELLIGENCE AGENCY (CIA) and the British Foreign Office and Secret Intelligence Service (SIS). The two intelligence services recruited agents from Albanian exile groups in the eastern Mediterranean and established training camps on the British colonies of Malta and Cyprus.

The first agents were sent into Albania in April 1950. Over time it became apparent that the operation had been compromised. Alerted Albanian security forces captured most of the agents upon their arrival. The operation was stopped in 1952 after several hundred Albanian emigres had lost their lives. Later U.S. and British intelligence learned that Valuable had been betrayed by Kim Philby, the SIS representative to its joint oversight committee, who also had been a Soviet double agent.

ALGECIRAS CONFERENCE (1906) U.S.-brokered conference of major European powers on the status of Morocco. Held from January to April 1906 in Algeciras, Spain, it developed principally out of German-French rivalry over the North African sultanate. In 1904 France made agreements with Great Britain and Spain clearing the way for establishment of French dominion over Morocco. Germany, concerned about protecting its commercial interests in North Africa, sought to thwart the French plan. The Germans, endorsing Moroccan sovereignty and urging equal trade opportunity for all foreign powers in the sultanate, appealed for an international conference to deliberate the issue of Morocco's future. The French and British balked. Germany's declared determination to take part in any settlement on Morocco drew stiffened French opposition. This Franco-German diplomatic standoff on the Moroccan question threatened to escalate into a military conflict.

In June 1905 American President THEODORE ROOSEVELT, at the invitation of Germany, interceded in the crisis as a neutral conciliator seeking a peaceful solution. He persuaded France and Britain to accept a conference that would convene in the Spanish seaport town of Algeciras in January 1906. Roosevelt, defying domestic critics who attacked his intervention in the Morocco dispute as an unwarranted departure from the long-standing American tradition of avoiding entanglement in Europe's political controversies, sent diplomat Henry White as his personal representative to the negotiations in Spain. When the talks reached an impasse over German inflexibility, Roosevelt, through White, proposed a compromise that Berlin felt compelled to accept since the German government had promised the American president before the conference to support any settlement he deemed fair. The parley ended on April 7 with a treaty that, while affirming Moroccan independence and territorial integrity, left France in the most advantageous position in Morocco. When the U.S. Senate ratified this agreement in December, it attached a reservation formally stating that

American participation at Algeciras did not signify an abandonment of the U.S. policy of nonintervention toward Europe.

ALGERINE WAR (1815) Naval conflict between the United States and the North African Barbary state of Algiers. By its victory in the TRIPOLITAN WAR (1801–1805), the United States no longer had to make payments (so-called tribute) to Tripoli in order to keep Tripolitan pirates from plundering American commercial traffic in waters off the North African coast. Withdrawal of American naval forces from the Mediterranean Sea following the conflict left U.S. trade ships and their crews vulnerable to Barbary piracy, despite continued U.S. tribute payments to Morocco, Algiers, and Tunis. While the United States was preoccupied by the War of 1812 with Great Britain, Algiers captured American vessels and exacted ransom payments for their crews. The TREATY OF GHENT ended the Anglo-American conflict in December 1814 and freed President JAMES MADISON to respond to the Barbary troubles.

After Congress authorized hostilities against Algiers on March 2, 1815, Madison sent a naval squadron commanded by Commodore Stephen Decatur to the Mediterranean to redress Algerian assaults on U.S. shipping. After capturing the Algerian flagship *Mashuda*, Decatur sailed into Algiers harbor and on June 30 secured a peace treaty. By its terms, Algiers agreed to release all American captives, restore all U.S. property, and pay a $10,000 indemnity. The United States, moreover, would pay no future tribute money. Decatur proceeded with his squadron to Tunis and Tripoli, where he dictated similarly strict terms in order to halt violations of their previous treaties with the United States. America's decisive win in the Algerine War settled the long-standing conflict with the Barbary pirates, ensuring the safety of American commerce.

ALGIERS ACCORDS See **IRAN HOSTAGE CRISIS**.

ALIEN REGISTRATION ACT (1940) Federal statute to prevent foreign-sponsored subversion in the United States. The ANARCHIST ACT (1918) had excluded from America aliens who advocated the overthrow of the government. The rise of domestic radical activity during the Great Depression brought calls for more effective barriers to the admission of Communist immigrants. With fascism on the rise in Europe in the 1930s, measures were also proposed in Congress to block the entrance of its adherents. The Soviet-German non-aggression pact (1939) fueled anti-Communist sentiment while support for tighter controls over aliens grew after traitors, infiltrators, and other "fifth column" forces were involved in the initial German victories in WORLD WAR II. The Alien Registration Act was implemented June 28, 1940.

The act required the registration and fingerprinting of every alien over age 14 either living in the United States or seeking an entrance visa. Offenses for which an immigrant could be deported were expanded to include past membership in a subversive organization. Title I of the 1940 act, known as the Smith Act after its sponsor Representative Howard W. Smith (D-VA), pertained to citizens as well as aliens. The legislation, the first peacetime sedition law since the ALIEN AND SEDITION ACTS of 1798, made it a crime to espouse the violent overthrow of the government, to belong to any group advocating such action, or to attempt to undermine the loyalty and morale of the armed forces.

Concerns over an internal Communist threat abated as the United States and Soviet Union became allies during World War II. As COLD WAR tensions mounted after 1945, the Smith Act was used to fight alleged Communist subversion. In 1948 the federal government invoked the measure to indict Eugene Dennis and 10 other leading members of the American Communist Party. The Supreme Court upheld their convictions in *Dennis* v. *United States* (1951). The Court's ruling in *Yates* v. *United States* (1957), that the act applied only to direct efforts to overthrow the government and not to the advocacy of abstract doctrines substantially curtailed prosecution under its provisions. Supreme Court decisions in the mid-1960s that blocked enforcement of the INTERNAL SECURITY ACT against the Communist Party also effectively ended use of the Smith Act.

ALIEN AND SEDITION ACTS (1798) Series of four laws passed by Congress in June and July 1798 during a period of worsening relations with France. The controversial security measures were defended by the administration of President JOHN ADAMS as a necessary precaution in the event the two nations went to war over French harassment of U.S. shipping. Critics claimed the acts actually were an effort by the ruling Federalists to curtail opposition from the Democratic-Republican Party, many of whose leading members were foreign born.

Three of the acts reflected concerns over the possibility of divided loyalties and subversive activities among newly arriving European aliens who might be sympathetic to France. The Naturalization Act lengthened from 5 to 14 years the residency requirements for citizenship. The Aliens Act allowed the president to deport aliens regarded as dangerous to the nation's peace and safety. In times of war, the president was authorized by the Alien Enemies Act to seize and either imprison or expel the resident alien subjects of a hostile power. The final measure, the Sedition Act, made it a crime to slander maliciously or conspire against the federal government.

The CONVENTION OF 1800 provided a negotiated settlement to the undeclared maritime QUASI-WAR (1798–1800) with France. The increasingly unpopular Alien and Sedition Acts were repealed or allowed to lapse. Neither of the two alien acts had been enforced. Ten opposition editors and printers had been convicted under the Sedition Act before it expired in early 1801. All were pardoned during the presidency of THOMAS JEFFERSON.

"ALL OREGON" Slogan popularized between 1844 and 1846 that expressed an expansionist solution to the OREGON QUESTION. Anglo-American diplomacy since 1818 had failed to settle conflicting U.S. and British claims to the Oregon territory, leaving the two nations in joint occupation of the contested region, which stretched from the Rocky Mountains to the Pacific Coast between the 42nd parallel and 54° 40'. U.S. political discontent with the situation coalesced in the "All Oregon" movement, which made two related assertions: America had exclusive claim to Oregon, and the United States should acquire all of the Oregon territory to its northern limit of 54° 40'.

"All Oregon" became a popular Democratic slogan in the 1844 campaign in which pro-expansionist candidate JAMES K. POLK was elected president. In the following congressional session the Democratic-controlled House overwhelmingly passed a measure, later defeated by the Senate, that called for occupation and organization of "All Oregon" as an American territory. After 1845, the Democratic sentiment was revived in the western expansionists' slogan of "54° 40' OR FIGHT." Under the compromise ORE-GON TREATY of June 1846, the United States and Great Britain divided the Oregon territory along the 49th parallel.

ALLIANCE FOR PROGRESS (1961) U.S.-led program to promote the social and economic development of Latin America. Proposed by President JOHN F. KENNEDY in an address to a White House gathering of Latin American diplomats on March 13, 1961, the initiative had its roots in Operation Pan-America, a plan devised in 1958 by Brazilian President Juscelino Kubitschek for a large-scale hemispheric development program. The Act of Bogota, adopted by the ORGANIZATION OF AMERICA STATES (OAS) in 1960, had committed the United States and Latin American nations to work for economic growth and social reform in the region. In his White House speech, Kennedy called on the whole hemisphere "to join in a new alliance for progress . . . a vast cooperative effort . . . to satisfy the basic needs of the American people for home, work, and land, health and schools." The proposed alliance marked a shift toward a policy of expanded U.S. economic assistance to Latin America in the wake of Fidel Castro's successful Communist revolution in Cuba. U.S. policymakers were concerned to redress the poverty and social inequities that made Latin America ripe for violent leftist political upheaval and that might spawn other Cubas in the region. The Kennedy initiative, greeted positively by most Latin American leaders, immediately boosted U.S. relations throughout the hemisphere.

The charter formally creating the Alliance for Progress as an OAS program was signed by all the members of the organization except Cuba at a special meeting at Punta del Este, Uruguay, on August 17, 1961. The drafters of the charter stressed that the twin goals of economic develop-ment and social justice should be pursued simultaneously and that both should be paralleled by efforts to expand political freedom in the hemisphere. As a general proposition, the alliance called for the use of public funding to foster conditions in Latin American nations sufficiently attractive to invite investment of both domestic and foreign private capital. Among its objectives, as outlined in the Declaration to the Peoples of America that accompanied the founding charter, were comprehensive long-range social and economic planning; agrarian and tax reform; improvements in agriculture, industry and transportation; removal of intraregional trade barriers; strengthened health and education services; elimination of illiteracy; and construction of decent housing for the poor.

Self-help was made a central tenet of the alliance. The initiative adopted at Punta del Este foresaw a multibillion dollar investment, of which 80 percent was to be contributed by the Latin Americans themselves and the other 20 percent by external sources, including private and government funding. The United States pledged to provide a major part of the external assistance. At a special OAS meeting in Brazil in 1965, the original 10-year life span of the alliance was extended indefinitely. Between 1961 and 1969 external public economic aid to the Latin American states in the form of loans and grants was about $18 billion, of which roughly $10 billion came from official U.S. sources. While important political, social, and economic progress took place under the impetus of the alliance, a variety of forces within Latin America and a major shift of U.S. focus and energies to the VIET-NAM WAR sapped the program of its vitality. Although in 1967 President LYNDON B. JOHN-SON reaffirmed U.S. support for the alliance, by the early 1970s enthusiasm for it had waned in both the United States and Latin America. The decline resulted in large measure from the disappointing results of the opening decade and the growing belief that the alliance's goals were unrealistic. The program was formally terminated in 1980.

ALLIANCE, TREATY OF See **FRANCO-AMERICAN ALLIANCE**.

ALLIED CONTROL COUNCIL (1945–1948) Allied organization for governing Germany after WORLD WAR II. At the 1943 MOSCOW CONFERENCE, the United States, Great Britain, and Soviet Union created a European Advisory Commission to formulate Allied postwar policy for a defeated Nazi Germany. Commission planning for Allied administration of Germany in four separate occupation zones, with newly liberated France as the fourth occupying power, received final approval at the YALTA CONFERENCE (1945). The Allies also agreed to divide Berlin into four occupation zones. Following Germany's surrender in May 1945, the European Advisory Commission on June 5, 1945, officially established the occupation zones for Germany and Berlin. The administration of Berlin was placed under a four-power military panel known as the Berlin Kommandatura. An Allied Control Council was formed to coordinate and implement Allied policy in Germany and to serve, in effect, as a central government for the U.S., British, French, and Soviet zones. The council was composed of the commander of each occupation force. All its decisions required a unanimous vote. General DWIGHT D. EISENHOWER served as the first U.S. representative to the body. The POTSDAM CONFERENCE, ending August 2, 1945, dissolved the European Advisory Commission and established a four-power COUNCIL OF FOREIGN MINISTERS to negotiate a final peace settlement for Germany.

By the end of 1945, broad East-West differences over the future status of Germany had surfaced as the Soviet Union moved to tighten its hold on Eastern Europe. The Western powers favored eventual establishment of a democratic Germany while the Soviet Union pressed for formal recognition of the postwar rearrangement of Eastern European boundaries that gave it part of Poland and Poland part of Germany. Seeking to aid German reconstruction, the United States and Great Britain on December 2, 1946, against Soviet objections, joined their occupation zones into a single economic entity known as BIZONIA. France, apprehensive in the wake of World War II over the possible reemergence of a strong central German government, declined to include its zone in the merger. Mounting East-West COLD WAR tensions and the virtual partition of Germany into non-Communist and Communist areas, however, led the Western powers to consider

the formation of a separate democratic German government in their zones. The meetings of the Allied Control Council became the site of increasingly bitter East-West recriminations, with each side accusing the other of violating the principle of four-power control over Germany.

At the first session of the Western SIX-NATION CONFERENCE ON GERMANY (1948), representatives discussed the creation of a German federal government for the U.S., British, and French zones. Denouncing the move by the Western trio to unify their zones outside the four-power context, the Soviet delegate walked out of the March 20, 1948, session of the Allied Control Council. The council never met again and became defunct. The Soviet member withdrew from the Berlin Kommandatura on July 1, 1948, effectively marking the division of the city into East and West Berlin. The Cold War partition of Germany was formalized in 1949 with the creation of West Germany out of the Western zones and East Germany out of the Soviet zone. The Berlin Kommandatura continued to function in West Berlin until 1990, when it was dissolved as a consequence of German reunification under the FINAL SETTLEMENT WITH RESPECT TO GERMANY TREATY (1990).

"ALL-OF-MEXICO" MOVEMENT Campaign mounted during the MEXICAN WAR (1846–1848) by militant expansionist Democrats advocating U.S. annexation of Mexico. Frustrated by Mexico's refusal to make peace on terms proposed by Democratic President JAMES K. POLK, party extremists by late 1847 increasingly demanded the United States seize all of Mexico. The movement enlisted the ideas promoted in the notion of MANIFEST DESTINY to support its call for U.S. territorial expansion beyond America's continental boundaries. Proponents were motivated by a missionary zeal to "rescue" Mexicans from so-called political despotism by extending democratic principles and purportedly superior traditions of Anglo-Saxon civilization to America's southern neighbor. Polk disclaimed the movement's bold ambition and held to his own more limited, but still vast, demands of a Texas boundary settlement at the Rio Grande and U.S. acquisition of Mexico's California and New Mexico provinces. The "all-of-Mexico" drive receded after

Mexico accepted Polk's terms in the TREATY OF GUADALUPE HIDALGO (1848).

ALSOP, JOSEPH WRIGHT, JR. (1910–1989) Distinguished American journalist renowned as a political columnist. Born and raised in Connecticut, he graduated from Harvard University in 1932 and began working for the *New York Herald Tribune* as a staff reporter. The *Tribune* reassigned him in 1936 to Washington, where the following year he began writing a nationally syndicated column with fellow *Tribune* reporter Robert E. Kintner. Called "The Capital Parade," the column focused on domestic politics and established both men as topranking news commentators. The journalistic partnership ended in 1940 when Alsop joined the Navy as an officer. He resigned his naval commission in August 1941 to join the Flying Tigers, the famed volunteer air force in China led by American General Claire L. Chennault. Alsop spent most of WORLD WAR II in the Far East as a member of Chennault's staff. Returning to newspaper work at the war's conclusion, he teamed in 1946 with younger brother Stewart to start a Washington-based column on national and international affairs called "Matter of Fact." The Alsops were self-described New Deal liberals on domestic issues and foreign policy conservatives. Their column earned Overseas Press Club awards in 1950 and 1952 for best foreign news interpretation. After the brothers' collaboration ended amicably in 1958, Joseph Alsop continued to write "Matter of Fact" alone until his retirement from journalism in 1974.

A critic in the late 1930s of American ISOLATIONISM, he emerged after the war as a proponent of a vigorous U.S. policy against Soviet expansionism. He argued that if the United States were to prevail in the COLD WAR, it would have to build a strong national defense and resolutely oppose Communist aggression wherever in the world it might surface. In the early 1950s he defended the loyalty and integrity of several State Department officials accused of Communist affiliation. The Alsop brothers were among the first journalists to condemn the demagogic methods used by Senator JOSEPH R. MCCARTHY (R-WI) in his pursuit of alleged Communists in the U.S. government. Following the defeat of French forces by Vi-etminh insurgents at Dien Bien Phu in 1954, Alsop advocated an American military commitment in Vietnam to prevent a Communist takeover. Believing vital U.S. strategic interests to be at stake in Indochina, he became a hawkish supporter in the 1960s of American involvement in the VIETNAM WAR. Meanwhile in the late 1950s an alarmed Alsop grew certain that a dangerous MISSILE GAP between the United States and Soviet Union was widening. His good friend and kindred political spirit Senator JOHN F. KENNEDY (D-MA) seized the issue of a purported gap in INTERCONTINENTAL BALLISTIC MISSILES (ICBMs) to criticize the Eisenhower administration's defense policy. In retirement Alsop penned *FDR: A Centenary Remembrance* (1982), a popular biography of his cousin, President FRANKLIN D. ROOSEVELT. His memoirs, *I've Seen the Best of It* (1992), were published posthumously.

AMBRISTER AND ARBUTHNOT AFFAIR (1818) Anglo-American diplomatic dispute sparked by the execution of two British subjects during the FLORIDA INVASION. In March 1818 General ANDREW JACKSON invaded Spanish Florida with 3000 U.S. troops to suppress cross-border Indian raids into American territory. In April U.S. forces arrested private British traders Robert Ambrister and Alexander Arbuthnot in West Florida and charged them with conspiring to aid the Indians. Jackson accused Ambrister of plotting a Seminole uprising against the United States and Arbuthnot of incitement and espionage. Both were convicted in hastily conducted courts-martial. On April 29 at St. Mark's, Florida, Ambrister was shot by firing squad and Arbuthnot was hanged. Despite considerable public outrage in Great Britain over the punishment meted out by Jackson, the British government raised only cautious protest, since strong evidence of their complicity had been presented against Ambrister and Arbuthnot. Uproar over the affair faded and was supplanted by Spain's condemnation of Jackson's attack upon its territory and the American general's annexation of east Florida.

See also ADAMS-ONIS TREATY.

AMERASIA CASE Espionage case that raised concerns over Communist infiltration of the federal government. Founded in

New York City in 1936, *Amerasia* was a leftist journal on Asian affairs. In early 1945 an intelligence analyst at the OFFICE OF STRATEGIC SERVICES (OSS) connected an article in the magazine with a classified OSS report on Thailand. OSS agents broke into the periodical's offices and uncovered numerous classified government documents. An FBI investigation linked *Amerasia* editor Philip J. Jaffe to several federal employees who had access to classified information. In June 1945, Jaffe, coeditor Kate Mitchell, *Amerasia* writer Mark Gayn, Lieutenant Andrew Roth of Naval Intelligence, and State Department officials Emmanuel S. Larsen and JOHN S. SERVICE were arrested and charged with conspiracy to commit espionage. Although hundreds of classified documents were in *Amerasia* files, investigators found no indication that any secret materials had been passed to a foreign power. The defendants described the documents as background material provided for the journal's use by politically sympathetic government officials. The charges against all but Jaffe and Larsen were dropped for lack of evidence. Jaffe eventually pleaded guilty to a reduced charge of conspiracy to steal classified information. Larsen pleaded no contest and both paid small fines.

The case pointed out the need for improved safeguarding of classified materials. Jaffe's Communist ties and the role of U.S. government employees in the case helped bring about the HOUSE UN-AMERICAN ACTIVITIES COMMITTEE investigations into possible subversion in America. In 1950 Senator JOSEPH R. MCCARTHY (R-WI) cited the *Amerasia* case to support his controversial claim of Communist penetration of the State Department.

See also HISS CASE.

AMERICA FIRST COMMITTEE (1940–1941) Organization opposed to U.S. entry into WORLD WAR II. Following the outbreak of war in Europe in 1939, debate mounted in the United States over how the nation should respond. Interventionists, arguing that defeat of Nazi Germany and the Axis powers was essential to American security, favored greater U.S. aid to Great Britain to help obtain this end. Noninterventionists strongly opposed any U.S. involvement in the European conflict, believing it would lead inevitably to direct American participation in the war. The noninterventionist America First Committee was formed September 4, 1940, under national chairman General Robert E. Wood, head of Sears, Roebuck and Company, and national director R. Douglas Stuart, Jr., a Yale law student. The organization advocated concentrating America's full attention on domestic concerns and avoiding entanglement in an overseas war. At its peak the association had roughly 450 local chapters with a total membership of about 800,000. Prominent figures associated with the organization included famed aviator CHARLES A. LINDBERGH and Senator Gerald P. Nye (R-ND), who had chaired the NYE COMMITTEE hearings on the munitions industry in the mid-1930s. America First held rallies across the country and lobbied vigorously but unsuccessfully against such measures as the 1941 LEND-LEASE program to provide further aid to Great Britain. The organization was dissolved December 11, 1941, four days after the Japanese attack on PEARL HARBOR had brought America into World War II, with the national committee then pledging its support for the war effort.

See also ISOLATIONISM.

AMERICAN ACADEMY OF DIPLOMACY
Organization established in Washington, D.C., in January 1984 by a group of former U.S. foreign policy officials to evaluate the qualifications of nominees for American ambassadorships. Some 70 pillars of the U.S. diplomatic community, including six former secretaries of state, founded the academy to demonstrate their great concern about a decline in the quality of the diplomatic corps resulting from the rising percentage of amateur ambassadors—political appointees selected at the expense of career professional diplomats. From the academy's inception one of its main objectives was to advise presidents on the qualifications of ambassadorial nominees. In this capacity the organization hoped to serve in much the same way the American Bar Association functions as an advisory body in connection with federal judicial appointments. In March 1985 a bipartisan group of the SENATE FOREIGN RELATIONS COMMITTEE announced that it would seek information from the academy to aid the panel in its consideration of nominations to the ambassadorial corps. In June of the same year the

academy submitted its first-ever report to the committee regarding an ambassadorial appointment.

AMERICAN CENTURY Term coined by HENRY R. LUCE in a *Life* magazine article of February 17, 1941, expressing a vision of American world leadership as a decisive historical factor in the 20th century. "The American Century," authored almost 10 months before the Japanese bombing of PEARL HARBOR, predicted that the United States would enter and win WORLD WAR II and then undertake reconstruction of the postwar world. America had become, in Luce's view, the world's most vital and powerful nation. He contended at the same time that Americans, deeply isolationist by tradition, had not resolved themselves practically or intellectually to that fact or to the obligations this status conferred. Appealing for the rejection of American ISOLATIONISM and birth of a vigorous American INTERNATIONALISM, Luce asserted that the 20th century must be an American century if peace, prosperity, and freedom were to prevail around the world.

He described a vision of creative postwar American leadership in which the United States would champion economic free enterprise, make its technical skills available throughout the world, be the Good Samaritan to all, and disseminate American ideals and the great principles of Western civilization. Luce's ideas were rooted in his sense of America's moral mission, which in turn stemmed from his devout Christian beliefs.

AMERICAN ENTERPRISE INSTITUTE (AEI) Moderate conservative think tank based in Washington, D.C. Founded in 1943 as the American Enterprise Association and renamed the American Enterprise Institute in 1960, it aims to influence public policy through educational programs and research on both foreign affairs and domestic economic, political, and social issues. The independent AEI's staff of resident scholars and fellows includes prominent foreign policy experts who study national security, arms control, international law, and geopolitics. Results of their research appear in institute books, periodicals, and scholarly papers. The AEI's regular publications include the bimonthly journal *Public Opinion* and the monthly newsletter *AEI on the Issues*. In the 1980s the right-of-center think tank emerged as a consistent champion of President RONALD W. REAGAN's defense buildup and policy of U.S. support for anti-Communist resistance movements worldwide. The Reagan administration included dozens of individuals affiliated with AEI, most notably U.N. Ambassador JEANE D. KIRKPATRICK.

AMERICAN EXPEDITIONARY FORCE (AEF) U.S. troops that served in Europe during WORLD WAR I. When Congress declared war on Germany on April 6, 1917, the United States, with some 200,000 men in its Army, lacked a force capable of major combat operations in modern warfare. President WOODROW WILSON selected General JOHN J. PERSHING to organize and command the American Expeditionary Force, as U.S. overseas forces were designated. After arriving with his staff in Paris in June 1917, Pershing determined that Allied success would require vast American military assistance. He urged the War Department to send one million soldiers to France within a year and to plan for an ultimate force of three million. On the sensitive issue of U.S. military cooperation with Allied forces in combined operations against the Central Powers, Pershing would not allow American units to lose their distinct identity through consolidation with British and French armies. Wilson fully supported this position. When the Germans mounted a series of powerful offensives in spring and early summer 1918 that threatened to overwhelm the Allies, Pershing met the crisis by temporarily placing all the resources of the AEF at the disposal of the Allied high command. In July 1918 he oversaw formation of the American 1st Army under his independent command and won Allied consent to concentrate U.S. forces along their own sector of the battlefront in eastern France.

U.S. Navy forces abroad were commanded by Admiral William S. Sims. At the time the United States entered the war, German unrestricted submarine warfare was crippling Allied shipping. The American Navy immediately contributed a flotilla of destroyers to the antisubmarine effort. It later assisted the British fleet in keeping German U-boats out of the North Sea, cooperated in tightening the Allied maritime blockade on Germany, and escorted merchant vessels and troop transports across the Atlantic. The Navy reached a wartime strength of about 800,000 sailors. By the war's end, the U. S. Army had placed 4 million men under arms, approximately 2 million of whom reached France. American land and sea forces took a decisive part in the Allied victory. After the armistice was signed in November 1918 ending hostilities, the focus turned to bringing home the AEF. The last major U.S. units had departed for America by the end of August 1919.

AMERICAN FOREIGN SERVICE ASSOCIATION Private professional organization of the U.S. FOREIGN SERVICE. The group had its origin in the American Consular Association formed during WORLD WAR I. After the amalgamation of the diplomatic and consular services under the ROGERS ACT (1924), the association was reorganized in August 1924. With the addition to its ranks of members of the former diplomatic service, it became the American Foreign Service Association. The organization is composed of foreign service personnel of the DEPARTMENT OF STATE and career employees of other government agencies involved in service abroad. Dedicated to the welfare of the foreign service, it promotes the professional, economic, and personal interests of members. The association publishes the *Foreign Service Journal*, a monthly devoted mainly to the professional concerns of the foreign service community.

AMERICAN INSTITUTE See **TAIWAN MUTUAL DEFENSE TREATY.**

AMERICAN PROTECTIVE ASSOCIATION Secret society formed in Iowa in 1887 that was opposed to foreigners and Catholics. When the financial panic of 1893 raised concerns over the economic threat posed by new immigrants, the nativist group became an important force in midwestern Republican politics. At the peak of its influence in 1896, it had attained a million members. The same year the association divided over the free silver issue in the presidential campaign. Although the seriously weakened organization lasted until 1911, its membership and impact quickly waned.
See also KNOW-NOTHING MOVEMENT.

AMERICAN RELIEF ADMINISTRATION (ARA) Organization that provided emergency food to Europe after WORLD WAR I.

Following the armistice of November 1918, much of war-torn Europe faced critical food shortages. At President WOODROW WILSON's urging, Congress on January 24, 1919, voted $100 million in emergency aid credits to Europe. On March 2, 1919, Wilson issued an executive order forming the American Relief Administration to distribute the aid and appointed U.S. wartime food administrator HERBERT C. HOOVER its director general. In its four-month existence, the first U.S. foreign aid agency delivered some 23 million tons of food to 23 European countries. In July 1919, with the congressional appropriation almost fully used, Hoover transformed the ARA into a private organization that continued to oversee European food relief through 1923. From 1921 to 1923, the ARA provided assistance credited with saving millions of lives from famine in the Soviet Union.

AMERICAN REVOLUTION (1775–1783) War between Great Britain and its 13 American colonies that resulted in American independence and the establishment of the United States. Also known as the Revolutionary War and the American War of Independence, the conflict emerged from the confluence of economic, political, and ideological factors that fostered the idea of independence among the colonies.

Over the course of the 1700s, British imperial authority struggled to retain its control over the elected colonial assemblies. The royal governors, representatives of the British Crown, were vested with wide executive powers. In actuality, their authority was eroded by the ever more influential colonial assemblies, which gradually won the power to levy taxes and distribute funds. The contest for power reflected opposing conceptions of empire that took shape in the 18th century. In the British view, king and Parliament were vested with sovereign authority over the American colonies. Americans deemed their elective councils as the supreme legislative power in all internal affairs—each assembly, in effect, a miniature parliament. With imperial authority hampered by the physical distance between America and Great Britain, the British government through the 1750s was inclined to conciliate the American legislatures to avoid confrontation. This policy of accommodation, dubbed "salutory neglect" by the British statesman and political philosopher Edmund Burke, engendered a wide degree of political autonomy among the colonies.

The fuse of future royal-colonial confrontation in North America was ignited at the end of the French and Indian War (1754–1763), when British King George III and the leadership in Parliament resolved to end the long-standing policy of imperial administrative leniency and bring the colonies under tighter political and economic control. The French and Indian War, known also as the Great War for Empire, capped a long Franco-British struggle for North American supremacy. A victorious Great Britain emerged saddled with a burdensome national debt and facing the substantial challenges and increased costs of administering the newly acquired territories of Canada and the trans-Appalachian West. The British government decided that a standing army of 10,000 regulars had to be posted to the American colonies to defend the enlarged empire against possible French or Spanish aggression and keep peace on the American frontier between Indian tribes and white settlers eager to expand westward. Parliament concluded that, as a matter of fairness and financial necessity, the colonies must help pay for the new army and share in the costs of new imperial burdens. But the colonies, flush with aspirations for greater independence and feeling less reliant on Great Britain militarily following the explusion of France from Canada, desired less regulation from London and greater local autonomy.

Great Britain adopted a set of measures between 1763 and 1767 that precipitated a political crisis. A royal proclamation in 1763 forbade colonial settlement beyond the Allegheny Mountains; the Currency Act of 1764 barred colonial assembles from issuing paper money as legal tender; the Sugar Act passed the same year levied strictly enforced duties on molasses imported from the West Indies. The Quartering Act (1765) required the colonies to house and provide supplies to British troops stationed in America. Parliament's program mandated a range of new taxes and duties to raise money to help defray the expense of maintaining the British military in the colonies. The famous Stamp Act (1765) taxed newspapers, playing cards, and various legal documents. Its passage sparked vehement protest and open resistance in America. Secret organizations known as Sons of Liberty formed throughout the colonies to organize opposition to the measure. At the intercolonial Stamp Act Congress, convened at New York in October 1765, delegates proclaiming "no taxation without representation" organized an American boycott of British imports. Colonial economic coercion damaged British commerce and forced Parliament to repeal the Stamp Act in 1766. At the same time the British ministry held steadfastly to its right to tax the colonies. The Declaratory Act (1766), which accompanied the Stamp Act's repeal, asserted Parliament's power to make laws binding on the American colonies "in all cases whatsoever."

A lull in the crisis brought about by the revocation of the Stamp Act ended when Parliament in 1767 approved Chancellor of the Exchequer Charles Townshend's new program of taxes on lead, paint, paper, and tea imported by America. Townshend was careful to differentiate between "internal" taxes to raise revenue, which he knew the colonists would reject, and "external" taxes to regulate trade, which he mistakenly assumed the colonists would accept as a traditional Crown prerogative. The Townshend Acts elicited renewed colonial challenges to parliamentary authority and further persuaded Americans that their right to representative self-government was under serious threat. American resistance pressured the new British ministry of Lord North in March 1770 to repeal all Townshend duties except the one on tea, which was retained as a symbol of Parliament's power to tax.

A series of incidents in the colonies in the early 1770s heightened tensions and mutual suspicions: In the so-called Battle of Golden Hill in January 1770, citizens of New York City clashed with British troops who had destroyed a liberty pole, a symbol of local colonial resistance; British soldiers posted to Boston to enforce imperial trade laws opened fire on a mob on March 5, 1770, killing five Americans in what became known as the Boston Massacre; and Rhode Islanders angry with British policy destroyed the British customs schooner the *Gaspee* in June 1772. Beyond these episodes loomed the fundamental constitutional question of where political authority resided. Colonial thinking gravitated increasingly toward the idea of separation from the British empire. The nascent independence movement in the colonies looked to the work of English political philosopher John Locke, who had articulated the theory of government as a voluntary compact. Locke asserted that a free people, as a last resort, had a right to break this compact when their liberties were denied by an arbitrary government.

The British ministry revived the explosive taxation issue in 1773 by steering the Tea Act through Parliament. The measure was intended to save the government-chartered East India Company from financial ruin by exempting its tea from British duties and letting it sell its product directly in America. Such privileges threatened to undercut American tea importers. Colonial resistance leaders deplored the act as unjust and pledged to block the sale of East India Company tea. On December 16, 1773, townsmen dumped 90,000 pounds of tea into Boston Harbor in the most dramatic act of protest. The Boston Tea Party and rising tide of American opposition alarmed London. George III and the British ministry decided to punish the colonists and force their submission by a series of Coercive Acts (1774), or Intolerable Acts, that tightened royal control over the Massachusetts colony government and shut the port of Boston to all commerce. An intercolonial network of committees of correspondence reacted to the 1774 royal measures by mobilizing to exert unified opposition to British policy. All the colonies except Georgia were represented at the First Continental Congress, which convened at Philadelphia in September 1774 to petition the Crown for redress of American grievances. Reaffirming the sole power of the colonies to legislate their own affairs, the Congress demanded the repeal of objectionable royal laws and voted to impose a comprehensive economic boycott against Great Britain.

Early in 1775 King George and Parliament resolved to move militarily to uphold British sovereignty. By the time the Second Continental Congress gathered in May 1775, fighting had erupted. British troops clashed with Massachusetts militia on April 19, 1775, at Lexington and Concord, marking the opening battle of the War of Independence. In June the Continental Congress organized the patriot militias in New England as the nucleus of the American Continental Army and appointed GEORGE WASHINGTON as commander.

At the war's outset many Americans opposed a total rupture with Great Britain. Moderate colonists feared the social upheaval that might follow a complete break and questioned an independent America's ability to defend against European invasion. Conservatives deeply attached to the empire and British institutions favored reconciliation. Several conciliatory proposals from London early in the war failed to satisfy colonial demands. In August 1775 the king spurned the Continental Congress's so-called Olive Branch Petition, which reiterated colonial complaints while urging a peaceful settlement, and declared the American provinces in open revolt. Mounting sentiment for independence was articulated most potently in Thomas Paine's pamphlet *Common Sense* (1776), which attacked monarchial government and advocated America's separation from Great Britain. A resolution put before Congress on June 7, 1776, by Virginia delegate Richard Henry Lee declaring the colonies "free and independent states" passed on July 2. Congress on July 4 adopted the Declaration of Independence formally establishing the 13 colonies as the United States of America. The epochal document, drafted by THOMAS JEFFERSON, listed abuses by George III in asserting the right of the American colonies both to end their ties to Great Britain and to organize as an independent union. The minority of colonists who, opposing the rebellion, kept their allegiance to the British Crown were known as Loyalists or Tories. Thousands exiled themselves to Great Britain. Loyalists who remained in America during the war were maligned by patriots as traitors and faced harassment, physical attacks, and property confiscation. Between 15,000 and 30,000 served with the British military in the revolution.

The war became part of a larger European struggle in which major continental powers arrayed themselves against Great Britain. France, administered a humbling defeat in North America by the British in the French and Indian War, looked to capitalize on the American rebellion to avenge French losses and reduce British imperial power. Initially unwilling to risk war with London, the French monarchy adopted a careful policy of clandestine support to the colonies, which desperately needed military aid and money. In April 1776 the SECRET COMMITTEE and the COMMITTEE OF SECRET CORRESPONDENCE of the Continental Congress dispatched SILAS DEANE to France to procure war supplies and negotiate expanded French assistance. With the help of French Foreign Minister Charles Gravier Comte de Vergennes, the courtier and dramatist Pierre A. C. de Beaumarchais established the dummy trade firm HORTALEZ AND COMPANY to secretly funnel arms and munitions to the American rebels. French aid proved indispensable to the patriot military cause in the war's early stages.

By asserting American sovereignty, the Declaration of Independence in effect enabled the newly formed United States to establish formal diplomatic ties and make treaties. In September 1776 the Congress named Deane, BENJAMIN FRANKLIN, and Arthur Lee as special commissioners to Paris to secure recognition of American independence, solicit greater French military involvement, and negotiate a commercial treaty based on the PLAN OF 1776. France continued its cautious policy of secret assistance until the decisive American victory over the British at Saratoga, New York, in October 1777, news of which persuaded Vergennes of U.S. military strength and led him in December to assure the American envoys of impending French diplomatic recognition. Such recognition came when Vergennes and the American commissioners forged the historic FRANCO-AMERICAN ALLIANCE through the Treaty of Alliance and the TREATY OF AMITY AND COMMERCE, both signed on February 6, 1778.

The U.S.-French compact thwarted a British conciliation plan aimed at preventing a military union of the Americans and French. The Carlisle Commission, dispatched by Parliament to propose peace based on American home rule within the empire, arrived in Philadelphia after Congress had ratified the Franco-American treaties in May. The Earl of Carlisle and fellow commissioners were rebuffed by the patriot leadership, which would accept nothing less than independence. After entering the war in June 1778, France contributed troops and naval power to the fight against the British in North America. Meanwhile, faced with the mounting demands of American diplomacy, the Continental Congress had named the secret correspondence panel the Committee on Foreign Affairs in April 1777. Congress in January 1781 replaced the foreign affairs committee with an executive office of foreign affairs, the forerunner of the cabinet-level DEPARTMENT OF STATE.

In April 1779 Spain joined the war on the side of France. The Spanish monarchy refused to enter an alliance with the United States, fearing the influence of America's revolutionary example on Spain's own colonies in the Americas. American special envoy JOHN JAY gained neither Spanish recognition of U.S. independence nor a substantial war loan during his abortive diplomatic mission to Madrid from 1780 to 1782. British assaults on Dutch trade with the United States, France, and Spain brought the Netherlands into the war in late 1780. Russia, Sweden, and Denmark organized the ARMED NEUTRALITY OF 1780 to protest repeated British violations of the rights at sea of European neutrals. By 1781 London found itself diplomatically isolated from most of Europe and facing a deteriorating military position in America.

British General Charles Cornwallis's surrender at Yorktown, Virginia, in October 1781 effectively ended the fighting and presaged a final U.S. victory. Opposition in Parliament to prolonging the war forced King George to accede to peace negotiations. American commissioners Benjamin Franklin, JOHN ADAMS, John Jay, and Henry Laurens convened at Paris for talks with British representative Richard Oswald. Lengthy negotiations and diplomatic maneuvering yielded a preliminary Anglo-American treaty in November 1782 and the final TREATY OF PARIS on September 3, 1783. Under the Peace of Paris, Great Britain recognized American independence and ceded the territory between the Appalachian Mountains and the Mississippi River to the United States. From its inception as a sovereign nation, America was bounded by European neighbors. Great Britain still held Canada to the north while Spain retained the Floridas and Louisiana to the south and west. The Revolutionary War and the success of American democracy offered practical inspiration to the

French Revolution (1789–1799) and the Latin American independence movements of the early 19th century.

AMISTAD AFFAIR (1839)   Mutiny that involved the United States and Spain in a diplomatic dispute. In June 1839 the Spanish schooner *Amistad* set sail from Havana, Cuba, bound for the Caribbean with a cargo of some 50 black slaves who recently had been illegally abducted from Africa by renegade Portuguese slave hunters. At sea the slaves revolted, seizing the ship, killing part of the crew, and ordering their Spanish owners to sail to Africa. Intercepted that August by an American warship off Long Island Sound, the *Amistad* was taken to New London, Connecticut, where the Spaniards were freed and the Africans imprisoned on murder charges. Spain demanded the release of the *Amistad* and the extradition of the black mutineers to Cuba. In response to Spanish diplomatic protests, the State Department explained that the case had gone before the federal courts and that the U.S. government would not interfere in the legal proceedings.

Northern abolitionist groups funded the defense counsel for the accused, who were tried in U.S. district court in Hartford, Connecticut. The court ordered the defendents freed, ruling that they could not be held culpable for their mutinous actions since they had been enslaved illegally. Former President JOHN QUINCY ADAMS represented the blacks before the U.S. Supreme Court, which reviewed the case on appeal in March 1841. He insisted on the right of the accused to revolt to regain their freedom. Concurring with Adams, the Supreme Court upheld the lower court ruling, establishing as precedent under U.S. law that slaves escaping illegal bondage should be treated as free men and women. After the *Amistad* defendants were released, antislavery groups provided their transportation back to Africa. The outcome of the affair was a sore spot in U.S.-Spanish relations.

AMITY AND COMMERCE, TREATY OF (1778)   Historic agreement concluded with France on February 6, 1778, that provided the foundation for the FRANCO-AMERICAN ALLIANCE (1778). After the United States declared its independence from Great Britain

on July 4, 1776, a principal goal of American diplomacy became the establishment of formal relations with France, which remained unwilling to risk war with the British by open support of the U.S. rebellion. Clandestine French materiel aid to the American cause proved essential to the early U.S. effort in the AMERICAN REVOLUTION. The Continental Congress in September 1776 commissioned BENJAMIN FRANKLIN, SILAS DEANE, and Arthur Lee as special envoys to Paris with instructions to secure French war loans and recognition of American independence. Congress coveted French recognition for the boost it would provide to U.S. political legitimacy and stature in Europe. The decisive American victory over British forces at Saratoga, New York, in October 1777 assured France of U.S. military abilities and brought a shift in French policy. French Foreign Minister Charles Gravier Comte de Vergennes informed the American negotiators in December that France was prepared to forge official ties with the United States, but he insisted on a formal alliance between the two countries as the price of French recognition.

The visiting American commission consented to the demand and in early February 1778 the two sides completed the Treaty of Amity and Commerce, in which France recognized America as an independent nation, and the companion Treaty of Alliance. The latter agreement pledged the United States and France to join militarily against Great Britain in the event war broke out between Paris and London over French recognition of the United States (as it did in June 1778). Terms of the Treaty of Amity and Commerce closely conformed with the model articles drafted by Congress in the PLAN OF 1776, a treaty blueprint furnished to the American commissioners to guide their negotiations with France.

Beyond French diplomatic recognition, the two countries extended one another MOST-FAVORED-NATION privileges and agreed to all the principles of neutral rights and FREEDOM OF THE SEAS favored by the United States in its 1776 model plan. France also granted American commercial ships duty-free access to certain French Caribbean and home ports. The Continental Congress unanimously approved the treaty on May 4, 1778, and the following September appointed Franklin as the first U.S. minister to France. After the war relations between the countries became strained as American politics divided over whether to support the French Revolution (1789–1799) and the United States increasingly strove to avoid entanglement in European political and military conflicts. The United States and France terminated the Franco-American Alliance, and with it the Treaty of Amity and Commerce, through the CONVENTION OF 1800 ending the undeclared QUASI-WAR (1798–1800).

ANARCHIST ACT (1918)   Federal legislation that excluded aliens who were anarchists from the United States. As early as 1889, the FORD COMMITTEE's report on immigration had recommended denying admission to anarchists exiled from Europe. Following the assassination of President WILLIAM MCKINLEY by the foreign-born anarchist Leon Czolgosz in 1901, Congress banned anarchists in the Immigration Act of 1903. This legislation marked the first time aliens were barred on the basis of political beliefs.

The Russian Revolution (1917) and the rise of international workers' movements renewed concerns over the impact of radical doctrines on American society. Many leading American socialists and communists were immigrants and the ideologies they espoused were widely connected to foreigners in the public mind. Authorities worried that radical activities could hamper the nation's efforts in WORLD WAR I. Amid calls for more stringent controls on subversive aliens, the Anarchist Act was signed into law October 16, 1918.

The measure blocked the admission of anyone who either believed in or advocated the overthrow of the U.S. government in particular or government in general. It sanctioned the deportation of alien radicals already in the United States and made fraudulent entry of an anarchist a felony. The law was amended in June 1920 to apply also to those promoting assaults on public officials, sabotage, or property destruction, or who distributed subversive materials. The Anarchist Act served as the legal authority for the PALMER RAIDS, in which hundreds of allegedly radical immigrants were arrested and deported during the Red Scare of 1919 to 1920.

See also ALIEN REGISTRATION ACT.

ANGELL TREATY (1880)   Agreement between the United States and China that revised the open immigration provision of the BURLINGAME TREATY (1868). The steady volume of Chinese workers arriving in the western states throughout the 1870s raised anti-Chinese sentiments in the region. Congress, under increasing pressure to restrict Chinese immigration, was constrained by the nation's treaty obligations. At the urging of Congress, President RUTHERFORD B. HAYES dispatched a commission headed by University of Michigan president James B. Angell to China to negotiate changes in the Burlingame Treaty. In a pact concluded November 17, 1880, the Peking government consented to the regulation and limitation of Chinese immigration short of absolute prohibition. In return the United States promised to protect Chinese residents already in the country. The Angell Treaty paved the way for passage of the CHINESE EXCLUSION ACT in 1882.

ANGLETON, JAMES JESUS (1917–1987)   Intelligence officer. A native of Boise, Idaho, Angleton graduated from Yale and in 1943 joined the OFFICE OF STRATEGIC SERVICES (OSS), the nation's WORLD WAR II intelligence agency. With the dissolution of OSS after the war, he remained with the successor CENTRAL INTELLIGENCE GROUP and became part of the newly formed CENTRAL INTELLIGENCE AGENCY (CIA) in 1947. In the late 1940s he directed U.S. counterintelligence operations in Italy before returning to Washington, where he became head of the CIA's counterintelligence staff. He cemented his reputation as a skilled spymaster in 1956 when he obtained a copy of Soviet leader Nikita S. Khrushchev's secret speech denouncing Stalin before the Soviet Communist Party.

Responsible for countering the intelligence activities of foreign agents against the United States, Angleton handled CIA coordination with the FEDERAL BUREAU OF INVESTIGATION. In 1967 he was placed in charge of a covert investigation, requested by President LYNDON B. JOHNSON, into possible links between Communist governments or organizations and domestic dissent against the VIETNAM WAR. Over the next six years the special counterintelligence staff infiltrated radical political groups and compiled extensive computer files on antiwar individuals and activities. The effort, dubbed Operation Chaos, found no evidence of direct foreign involvement in the antiwar movement. In 1973 Angleton's new superior in the CIA's covert operations branch, WILLIAM E. COLBY, ended the Chaos program and a secret mail-opening operation run by Angleton since 1952. Colby grew increasingly troubled by Angleton's obsessive belief that a Soviet "mole" or double agent had penetrated the CIA. As the agency's new director, he forced Angleton's retirement in 1974. Angleton later testified on Chaos and the mail opening before both the ROCKEFELLER COMMISSION (1975) and congressional inquiries into CIA abuses. He served in retirement as chairman of the Security and Intelligence Fund, a private organization supporting American intelligence activities.

ANGOLAN CIVIL WAR (1975–1991) Long-standing armed conflict in Angola between the Soviet-supported government and U.S.-backed anti-Communist rebels. In January 1975 Portugal announced it would grant complete independence to its African colony Angola the coming November. The same month the Portuguese transferred power to a transitional coalition government comprising the three main rebel groups which had fought separately against colonial rule: the Popular Movement for the Liberation of Angola (MPLA), led by Antonio Agostino Neto; the National Front for the Liberation of Angola (FNLA), led by Holden Roberto; and the National Union for the Total Independence of Angola (UNITA), led by Jonas Savimbi. The battle over who would govern Angola was joined when the transitional government collapsed in August 1975 after fighting broke out between the Marxist MPLA and the two Western-leaning groups. Portugal withdrew from Angola on November 11, 1975, leaving the capital, Luanda, in the control of the MPLA, which received financial and military assistance from the Soviet Union and troop support from Fidel Castro's Communist Cuba.

The next day the FNLA and UNITA together established a rival administration backed by the United States and South Africa. Through a covert operation authorized by President GERALD R. FORD, the CENTRAL INTELLIGENCE AGENCY (CIA) furnished weapons and other support to the FNLA and UNITA. The U.S. decision to become involved had been driven by the escalation in 1975 of Soviet arms shipments to the MPLA and by Cuba's dispatch of military forces to Angola. The Ford administration feared the combined Soviet-Cuban aid would hasten an MPLA victory and thereby lead to establishment of a Communist regime in the African nation. U.S. COVERT ACTION in Angola ran into opposition in Congress, where many members were apprehensive, following the experience of the VIETNAM WAR, to commit the nation indirectly to a regional struggle that might lead to a direct U.S. military role. In early 1976 Congress approved the CLARK AMENDMENT to the annual U.S. foreign aid bill, effectively prohibiting U.S. support to rebel groups in the Angolan Civil War.

The MPLA, bolstered by Cuban troops, seized the initiative in 1976, eliminating the FNLA as a fighting force and pushing UNITA deeper into southern Angola. In the late 1970s, with the continued support of Moscow and Havana, the Marxist group consolidated its control over much of the country, establishing itself as the de facto Angolan government. UNITA, however, continued to mount an effective insurgency from its bases in southern Angola and neighboring Namibia. South Africa also was deeply involved in the Angolan conflict. Its military made raids into southern Angola beginning in earnest in the late 1970s to strike at forces of the South-West African People's Organization (SWAPO), who were using Angola as a haven from which to wage their armed struggle for NAMIBIAN INDEPENDENCE from South African control. By the early 1980s Pretoria's white minority government had stationed South African soldiers in southern Angola on a virtually permanent basis. South Africa, in addition to battling SWAPO, continued to provide aid to UNITA.

In 1980, in light of the State Department's estimate of a large Cuban troop presence in Angola, Congress revised the Clark Amendment to permit covert military support of UNITA if the president declared it to be in the national interest and Congress concurred. Seeking to reverse Soviet-sponsored Communist expansionism, the Reagan administration in the early 1980s advanced a policy of furnishing support to anti-Communist insurgencies worldwide. The Savimbi-led rebels became beneficiaries of the REAGAN DOCTRINE after Congress fully repealed the Clark measure in 1985. The next year, following a visit to Washington by Savimbi to appeal for U.S. assistance, the Reagan administration began supplying military aid to UNITA through the CIA. The aid was opposed by congressional liberals, who objected to supporting UNITA because of the rebel group's close ties to South Africa, whose system of racial separatism, known as apartheid, made it a pariah on Capitol Hill.

At U.S. insistence, regional peace efforts in the 1980s came to link the fates of Angola and neighboring Namibia. U.S. mediated talks between the Angolans and Cubans on one side and South Africans on the other yielded a breakthrough in late 1988, opening the way to resolution of the Angolan and Namibian conflicts. In December, at Brazzaville in the Congo, Angola, Cuba, and South Africa signed a U.S.-sponsored regional settlement tying Namibian independence from South Africa to the withdrawal of all Cuban forces from Angola. The pact called for Pretoria to give up control of Namibia in April 1989. A phased pullout of Cuba's 50,000 troops from Angola was scheduled to take place over a 27-month period. In connection with the agreement, Washington and Moscow urged their respective Angolan clients to enter into talks for a "national reconciliation."

In June 1989, the Marxist Angolan government and UNITA signed a truce, which fell apart after two months amid renewed fighting. Portugal organized a series of negotiations between the ruling MPLA and UNITA in 1990, the later rounds of which the United States and Soviet Union joined as advisers. These talks bore fruit when, on May 31, 1991, the Angolan government and rebel UNITA concluded a cease-fire agreement to end their 16-year-old civil war and hold the nation's first free elections. Meanwhile, in December 1990, in a move emblematic of the worldwide eclipse of communism, the MPLA had repudiated its Marxist ideology and promised a program of democratic reforms. Signing of the accord at Lisbon, Portugal, by Angolan President Jose Eduardo dos Santos and rebel leader Savimbi followed by a week the completion of the Cuban troop withdrawal from Angola. The peace accord arranged

for multiparty elections to take place by November 1992. Responsibility for monitoring the cease-fire fell to a UNITED NATIONS troop detachment. A joint political and military commission comprising the two Angolan sides and the U.S., Soviet, and Portuguese governments was established to prepare for elections and create a single Angolan army. Washington and Moscow had played an instrumental part in pushing the two factions to finalize a settlement and the Angolan cease-fire came about largely because of the newfound cooperation between the former adversaries following the end of the COLD WAR.

ANNECY ROUND   See **GENERAL AGREEMENT ON TARIFFS AND TRADE**.

ANTARCTIC TREATY (1959)   International agreement to cooperate on the scientific investigation of the Antarctic and to prevent the militarization of the continent. In May 1958 the United States proposed an international conference on the Antarctic to build on the scientific cooperation occurring in connection with the INTERNATIONAL GEOPHYSICAL YEAR (IGY) (1957–1958). The Eisenhower administration, concerned over the possible military use of the continent by the Soviet Union or other potentially hostile powers, also hoped to secure international agreement to reserve the Antarctic exclusively for peaceful purposes. The American initiative drew a favorable response. Representatives of 12 nations met in Washington from October 15 to December 1, 1959. Included were the seven countries with territorial claims in the Antarctic (Argentina, Australia, Chile, France, Great Britain, New Zealand, and Norway) and five countries both active in the IGY and interested in the continent's status (United States, Soviet Union, Belgium, Japan, and South Africa). The Antarctic Treaty was signed by all participants on the last day of the conference. The agreement prohibited any military activity on the continent, barred nuclear explosions or the dumping of nuclear wastes there, gave signatories the right to conduct aerial surveillance and to inspect each other's installations to safeguard against violations, and provided for international scientific cooperation in the Antarctic. The various, other overlapping territorial claims to the continent were placed on hold for the duration of the treaty. The first post–WORLD WAR II arms control agreement, the treaty effectively removed the Antarctic from East-West COLD WAR conflict. After ratification by all 12 signatories, the agreement came into force in June 1961. Other nations becoming full parties to the treaty, open to all UNITED NATIONS members, include Brazil, Communist China, India, and Germany. On October 4, 1991, members signed a protocol to the treaty intended to protect the Antarctic's environment. The measure banned mineral and oil exploration on the continent for at least 50 years and established new regulations governing wildlife protection, waste disposal, and marine pollution.

ANTIBALLISTIC MISSILE PROTOCOL See **ANTIBALLISTIC MISSILE TREATY**.

ANTIBALLISTIC MISSILE TREATY (ABM Treaty) (1972) U.S.-Soviet agreement to limit antiballistic missile (ABM) systems. In the 1960s the two superpowers grew concerned that ABM defenses, then under development by both sides, risked destabilizing the precarious U.S.-Soviet nuclear balance. If one side gained the ability to shoot down incoming nuclear missiles, the reasoning went, then the other side would be at a dangerous disadvantage and mutual nuclear DETERRENCE would be undermined. ABM systems were a central issue in the SALT I arms control negotiations begun in 1969. These talks produced the Treaty on the Limitation of Anti-Ballistic Missile Systems, signed on May 26, 1972, by President RICHARD M. NIXON and General Secretary Leonid I. Brezhnev at their historic first MOSCOW SUMMIT. The pact defined an ABM system as a combination of radars, launch sites, and interceptor missiles designed to "counter ballistic missiles or their elements in flight." The treaty prohibited either side from deploying a nationwide ABM system; limited each country to two ABM sites, one to defend its capital and the other to protect an INTERCONTINENTAL BALLISTIC MISSILE field, each with no more than 100 ABM launchers; and barred the further development or testing of ABM systems. Either party could withdraw from the agreement on six months' notice. The U.S. Senate ratified the treaty on August 3, 1972, and it entered into force October 3, 1972.

The ban on ABM systems effectively locked in place the strategic nuclear doctrine of MUTUAL ASSURED DESTRUCTION, under which neither superpower could risk a nuclear attack against the other for fear of certain devastating reprisal. At their second MOSCOW SUMMIT, Nixon and Brezhnev on July 3, 1974, signed a protocol to the ABM Treaty reducing from two to one the number of ABM sites allowed each side. The ABM Protocol was ratified by the U.S. Senate on November 10, 1975, and took effect May 24, 1976. In the 1980s the Reagan administration undertook the STRATEGIC DEFENSE INITIATIVE (SDI) to develop a space-based defensive shield against missile attack. The project, dubbed Star Wars, brought charges from both the Soviet Union and domestic American critics that it violated the ABM Treaty's ban on the continued development of ABM systems. The administration defended SDI as consistent with the treaty's provisions, citing language appended to the 1972 pact that left open to further discussion potential ABM systems based on "other physical principles."

ANTI-IMPERIALIST LEAGUE National political organization opposed to U.S. colonial expansion after the SPANISH-AMERICAN WAR (1898). Eastern anti-imperialists formed the league in Boston in November 1898 to protest the adoption by the Republican McKinley administration of an imperial expansionist policy fixed on acquiring Spanish colonies in the Caribbean and Pacific. Like-minded organizations sprang up around the country. In October 1899 they were joined as regional branches into a single American Anti-Imperialist League, which sought primarily to educate and shape public opinion. To promote its position, the league published articles and pamphlets, held conferences, circulated petitions, and sponsored speakers. Its members denounced U.S. acquisition of an island empire as an abandonment of America's commitment to self-government and a dangerous departure from the nation's historic ISOLATIONISM. The league suggested that IMPERIALISM would erode America's moral standing and undermine its democratic ideals. Members argued that it was inherently contradictory for a republic such as the United States to possess colonies. They also offered arguments against the constitutionality and strategic wisdom of an imperial policy. Colonial expansion, the league faithful asserted, would divert the nation's focus from pressing domestic problems, consume valuable resources, violate the spirit of the MONROE DOCTRINE, and entangle the United States in the rivalries of the European powers.

Intellectuals Carl Schurz, Charles W. Eliot, David Starr Jordan, and E. L. Godkin were among the prominent leaders of the league, which received much of its funding from the wealthy industrialist ANDREW CARNEGIE. Key figures dedicated to the anti-imperialist cause but working outside the league included WILLIAM JENNINGS BRYAN, labor leader Samuel Gompers, and the writer Mark Twain. The organization's members were mainly, though not entirely, Democrats. Despite its concerted campaign, the league proved unable to block U.S. acquisition, through the TREATY OF PARIS (1898), of the Philippines, GUAM, and Puerto Rico. It faded from the political scene following the decisive reelection in 1900 of President WILLIAM MCKINLEY in a race that had been billed by the Democrats as a referendum on the issue of imperialism.

ANTISATELLITE WEAPONS (ASAT) Various military technologies capable of tracking and destroying satellites in earth orbit. In the 1970s both the United States and Soviet Union pursued the development of ASAT systems. Negotiations begun in 1978 to limit ASAT weapons were derailed by worsening superpower relations following the 1979 Soviet invasion of Afghanistan. By the early 1980s the USSR had successfully tested a simple ASAT system that involved placing an explosive satellite in orbit, maneuvering it near a target satellite, and then detonating it. The Reagan administration pressed the development of the more sophisticated U.S. system, a homing missile fired by the highflying F-15 fighter plane.

In August 1983 the Soviet Union called for a resumption of ASAT negotiations and announced a moratorium on further tests of its ASAT system provided the United States did the same. President RONALD W. REAGAN rejected the Soviet overture as a ploy to prevent the testing of a U.S. ASAT weapon and thus leave the USSR with the only operational system. Spurred by liberal Democratic members who believed the development of ASAT systems represented a dangerous escalation in the arms race, Congress the same year attached to the defense appropriations act a requirement that the

Reagan administration report on its plans for ASAT arms control negotiations. Opponents of the U.S. ASAT program, such as the UNION OF CONCERNED SCIENTISTS, noted that both the United States and Soviet Union relied on satellites for early warning of a nuclear attack. By placing these satellites at risk, they argued the continued development of ASAT weapons would undermine superpower nuclear DETERRENCE.

In March 1984 the Reagan administration submitted the requested report to Congress, outlining its opposition to negotiations for a comprehensive ASAT ban. Such a ban, it contended, could never be verified and would lock the existing Soviet ASAT advantage in place. The administration also stressed that all existing and planned ASAT systems were for use in low earth orbit, not the high orbit where the early warning satellites were located. Over administration objections, Congress in October 1984 passed an amendment to the annual defense bill delaying until March 1, 1985, initial testing of the U.S. ASAT weapon against a target in space. After that date, tests could be conducted if the president certified that America actively was pursuing an ASAT arms control agreement.

With the improvement in superpower relations following the accession of Soviet leader Mikhail S. Gorbachev, broad U.S.-Soviet arms control negotiations resumed in March 1985 with ASAT weapons an important component. In September 1985 the United States successfully conducted the first space test of its ASAT missile. That December Congress, concerned that final development of the more advanced U.S. system might prompt a reciprocal Soviet effort and thereby undermine arms control negotiations, enacted a ban on further ASAT tests until September 30, 1986. The Reagan administration insisted the ban was undercutting the U.S. position in arms control discussions, but it was extended by Congress in 1986 and again in 1987. Although no ASAT agreement had been reached, U.S.-Soviet relations had improved dramatically by 1988. The same year the Defense Department, recognizing the congressional opposition to ASAT testing, requested no funds for this purpose, effectively terminating the existing U.S. ASAT program. In 1989 Congress approved funding for advanced ASAT research and development, while making clear its continued ban on testing. The Bush administration meanwhile continued U.S. participation in ASAT negotiations.

ANZUS TREATY (1951) Mutual security pact concluded by Australia, New Zealand, and the United States to safeguard the South Pacific. The name derived from the initials of the three countries. To allay Australia's and New Zealand's fears after WORLD WAR II of a revitalized and rearmed Japan and to win their consent to the JAPANESE PEACE TREATY (1951), the United States signed the tripartite defense treaty with them in San Francisco on September 1, 1951. The ANZUS pact provided that an armed attack on any of the signatories would be dangerous to all and that each should act to meet the common threat in accordance with its constitutional processes. It set up a council of foreign ministers that could meet at any time for consultation on defense issues. The treaty represented another link in the security system established by the United States in the early 1950s to prevent communism's expansion in the Pacific. The Senate approved the pact by a voice vote on March 20, 1952. In 1984, the New Zealand government declared its territory a nuclear-free zone. In February 1985 it refused permission for an American warship to dock in New Zealand waters when the United States, in keeping with long-standing policy, declined to reveal whether the vessel carried nuclear arms. In response, the United States officially suspended its defense arrangements with New Zealand under the ANZUS pact on August 11, 1986.

APACHE WARS Intermittent fighting from 1860 to 1886 between the United States and the southwest Apache Indians over efforts to confine the tribe to reservations. In the Apache and Navajo War of 1860–1865, the Apache and neighboring Navajo tribes in present-day Arizona and New Mexico joined together to oppose further encroachment on their land. Apache Chief Cochise wreaked early havoc after most regular federal forces in the southwest were withdrawn to fight in the Civil War. In 1865, following Colonel Christopher "Kit" Carson's successful campaign against the Indians, the Navajo surrendered while Cochise and the Apaches continued to stage raids from mountain hideouts.

The killing of more than 100 Apaches by white vigilantes at the Camp Grant Massacre in April 1871 ignited the Apache War of 1871–1873. Cochise made peace in 1872 while Chiefs Victorio and Geronimo fought on until 1873, when they and their forces surrendered and were settled on a reservation in southern Arizona. The Apache War of 1876–1886 erupted when U.S. troops sought to remove hundreds of Apaches to more remote areas. Indian bands under Victorio and Geronimo mounted attacks throughout the Arizona and New Mexico territories, evading the U.S. military by moving back and forth across the Mexican border. Victorio was killed in 1880. Geronimo was finally subdued by U.S. troops in September 1886. His surrender marked the end of the Apache resistance in the Southwest.
See also MAP 1.

APOLLO-SOYUZ (1975) U.S.-Soviet venture that was the first multinational manned spaceflight in history. On July 15, 1975, the American Apollo and Soviet Soyuz space ships rendezvoused in Earth orbit, whereupon the crew members of the COLD WAR rivals shook hands as a symbolic expression of the superpower DETENTE that made the mission possible. The U.S. astronauts were Thomas Stafford, Vance Brand, and Donald (Deke) Slayton. Their Soviet counterparts were cosmonauts Alexei Leonov and Valeri Kubasov. The extraordinary two-day linkup of the spacecraft, marking unparalleled U.S.-Soviet cooperation in space, was the centerpiece of the Apollo-Soyuz Test Project. The two crews also conducted a series of joint scientific experiments and demonstrated equipment and docking procedures for making space rescues, a capability needed for the manned orbital flights expected in the 1980s and beyond. Apollo-Soyuz received unprecedented publicity in the USSR where, for the first time, the public was allowed to view live television coverage of a space flight. Soyuz returned to Earth on July 21, three days in advance of Apollo. Continued U.S.-Soviet space cooperation stalled amid worsening superpower relations following the 1979 Soviet invasion of Afghanistan.

ARAB OIL EMBARGO (1973–1974) Oil embargo imposed by the Arab petroleum-producing countries to pressure the Western industrialized world to end its support for Israel. The October 1973 YOM KIPPUR WAR was the fourth in a succession of Arab-Israeli armed conflicts since Israel proclaimed its statehood in historic Palestine in 1948. Israel's Arab neighbors were pledged to the destruction of the Jewish state, whose right to exist they refused to recognize, and to the return of Palestine to Arab control. The Yom Kippur War began when Egypt and Syria staged a surprise attack against Israel on October 6 in a drive to recover territories lost to victorious Israeli forces in the 1967 Six-Day War. The United States, moving to counter heavy Soviet military aid to the invading Arab armies, undertook a massive airlift of weapons and supplies to the Israelis. In light of the U.S. intervention, the Arab oil-producing states resolved to use petroleum as a political and economic weapon on behalf of Egypt and Syria. The Arab strategy was to exploit the Western industrialized world's heavy dependence on Middle East oil. On October 17 the 11 members of the Organization of Arab Petroleum Exporting Countries (OAPEC) agreed on a coordinated program of cuts in oil exports aimed at forcing a change in pro-Israel U.S. policy and discouraging support of the Zionist state by Western Europe and Japan.

The heart of the embargo was a pledge by the participating Arab states to reduce oil production each month until Israel pulled out of the territories it occupied during the 1967 war and promised to respect the right of the Palestinians to self-determination. The Arab oil producers cut off all shipments to U.S. markets. The resulting shortages brought a rapid quadrupling of oil prices for all buyers and soaring inflation. Adoption by the UNITED NATIONS Security Council of an Egyptian-Israeli cease-fire agreement on October 25 marked the end of the Yom Kippur War. This development notwithstanding, the Arabs hewed to their oil strategy. The United States, which experienced a 12 percent decline in its total oil supply as a consequence of the embargo, moved diplomatically to contend with the oil crisis. U.S. Secretary of State HENRY A. KISSINGER met with Arab leaders in November and December to press for an end to the boycott, warning of possible U.S. retaliatory action if the Arab oil cutoff continued

indefinitely. He also called for a joint effort by the United States, Canada, Western Europe, and Japan to solve the world energy crisis and end their vulnerability to Arab oil cutoffs. In late December the major oil producers loosened the embargo by ordering modest increases in production. Despite the partial easing, the members maintained the total ban on exports to the United States. The Arab oil producers at the same time announced a doubling of the price of a barrel of oil. The price hike precipitated a chain reaction of similar increases by other, non-Arab oil-producing nations.

The conclusion of a U.S.-mediated Egyptian-Israeli troop disengagement agreement in mid-January 1974 led Egyptian president Anwar Sadat to urge fellow Arab leaders to lift the embargo. He contended Kissinger's SHUTTLE DIPLOMACY, which produced the agreement, reflected a change in America's Middle East policy that should be rewarded by a shift in Arab oil policy. Libya, Syria, and Iraq initially opposed Sadat's proposal. But support among the Arab oil producers for the Egyptian president's position gained momentum. In early March 1974 the Arab states, meeting in Libya, agreed to end the oil embargo and lift the boycott against the United States. Their decision was announced at a full meeting of the Organization of Petroleum Exporting Countries (OPEC) in Vienna on March 17. The Arab oil-producing states explained that recent movement in U.S. policy away from Israel had hastened the embargo's end. At Vienna the OPEC nations agreed not to roll back oil prices to pre-embargo levels.

ARABIC (1915) British passenger liner, sunk without warning in the Irish channel by a German submarine on August 19, 1915. Forty-four lives were lost, including two Americans. The *Arabic* was enroute from Liverpool, England, to New York when a German U-boat torpedoed it. The incident followed by less than four months the similar sinking of the LUSITANIA, which had resulted in 128 American deaths and was condemned by an indignant U.S. public as an unprecedented violation of neutral rights. The *Arabic* sinking exacerbated U.S.-German tensions and led Wilson to contemplate breaking off diplomatic relations.

German Ambassador to the United States Count Johann Heinrich von Bernstorff voiced regret for the *Arabic* incident and offered an indemnity. On September 1, 1915, acting on his own authority, he made the so-called *Arabic* Pledge, promising that German submarines would not attack unarmed passenger ships without warning and providing for the safety of passengers and crews. The German envoy's statement satisfied the Wilson administration. Within one week of Bernstorff's pledge, though, the German foreign office disclaimed responsibility for the *Arabic* attack. Wilson and Secretary of State ROBERT LANSING feared that the German government's announcement indicated Berlin would not abide by Bernstorff's promise of a suspension of unrestricted submarine warfare. They communicated to the German ambassador that his country's latest posture on the *Arabic* dispute was unacceptable and might bring a severing of U.S.-German relations.

Rather than risk a major diplomatic showdown, Germany on October 5, 1915, formally reaffirmed the *Arabic* Pledge, apologized for the torpedoing, and agreed to pay an indemnity for the two American lives lost. While the settlement was regarded as a significant diplomatic victory for the United States, the sinkings did not cease. The March 1916 U-boat torpedoing of the French passenger steamer SUSSEX, viewed by the Wilson administration as a deliberate breach of the *Arabic* Pledge, precipitated a serious crisis with Berlin. In April 1917 the United States entered WORLD WAR I on the Allied side, in large part over Germany's unrestricted submarine warfare.

ARIKARA "WAR" CAMPAIGN (1823) First large-scale U.S. punitive expedition against a Plains Indian tribe. The Arikara, reacting to encroachment on their lands along the upper Missouri River by white traders and fur hunters, launched a bloody attack on a party of trappers in 1823. Troops under Colonel Henry Leavenworth overran the Arikara villages in northern Nebraska, opening the area for continued white expansion. The Arikara, driven northward, eventually settled in present-day North Dakota.

See also MAP 1.

ARMED NEUTRALITY OF 1780 Code of maritime principles proclaimed in February 1780 by Catherine II, Empress of Russia, intended to protect neutral shipping from the interference of belligerents. Great Britain, at war both with the allied United States and France and with Spain, had antagonized neutral European nations by blockading their trade with the French and Spanish. Catherine invited other European maritime neutrals to join Russia in a League of Armed Neutrality committed to a set of principles already included in two key documents of early American diplomacy, the PLAN OF 1776 and the Franco-American TREATY OF AMITY AND COMMERCE (1778). Catherine's code asserted that FREE SHIPS MAKE FREE GOODS; stated that neutral ships had the right to enter belligerent ports; and limited the definition of contraband to cover only arms and munitions. The Netherlands, Sweden, the Holy Roman Empire, Prussia, Portugal and the Two Sicilies joined the league between 1781 and 1783. Great Britain rejected the Armed Neutrality since its principles threatened British naval dominance.

Although not invited to join the league, the United States on October 5, 1780, embraced its rules of neutrality and sought admittance as a step toward winning recognition of American independence from the member nations. The Continental Congress in the spring of 1781 dispatched Francis Dana as minister to Russia to secure its recognition of U.S. independence and to gain American entrance to the league. Dana's mission ended unsuccessfully in July 1783 after Russia declined to recognize the American rebellion. Catherine II steadfastly refused to receive the American envoy as long as Great Britain did not acknowledge American independence. By the summer of 1783, Congress had resolved that formal American participation in the League of Armed Neutrality would be unwise because it might entangle American interests with European politics.

ARMS CONTROL AND DISARMAMENT ACT See **ARMS CONTROL AND DISARMAMENT AGENCY** in **APPENDIX B.**

ARMS CONTROL AND DISARMAMENT AGENCY See same in **APPENDIX B.**

ARMS EXPORT CONTROL ACT (1968) Federal legislation governing U.S. foreign arms sales. In 1968 Congress moved to consolidate and revise the various provisions covering overseas arms transactions included in foreign aid legislation into a separate arms sales measure. Signed into law October 1968, the Arms Export Control Act stated that, while America supported the ultimate goal of arms control, it was U.S. policy to sell arms and military equipment to other countries for the purpose of common defense. The legislation stipulated that arms sales must conform to and serve U.S. foreign policy and national security objectives; limited such sales to friendly countries; prohibited sales to military dictators, unless certified by the president as vital to U.S. security; and required recipient nations to agree not to transfer the arms to a third party. The act also ended EXPORT-IM-PORT BANK involvement in the underwriting of overseas arms transactions and authorized funds to finance sales to nations in need of economic assistance. Renewed annually, the legislation has become the basic vehicle for controlling and funding foreign arms sales.

ARMSTRONG, JOHN (1758–1843) Soldier and diplomat. The Pennsylvania native left his studies at Princeton in 1775 to serve as a Continental Army officer during the AMERICAN REVOLUTION, achieving the rank of major. In May 1783 Armstrong anonymously penned the controversial "Newburgh Letters," which suggested that the soon-to-be disbanded army take action if the Continental Congress failed to satisfy the soldiers' demands for back pay. The so-called Newburgh Conspiracy ended without incident after General GEORGE WASHINGTON used his influence to dissuade the disgruntled army officers from moving against Congress. After the war he worked in Pennsylvania state government, was elected to the Confederation Congress in 1787, and two years later married into the influential Livingston family of New York. After a decade spent farming in his adopted state, Armstrong won election in 1800 to the U.S. Senate as a Democratic-Republican. He resigned his seat in 1804 to replace brother-in-law ROBERT R. LIVINGSTON as minister to France, a post Armstrong held until 1810.

In his tenure at Paris, he protested futilely against French confiscation of American shipping under decrees issued by Emperor Napoleon Bonaparte. Armstrong strongly advocated U.S. acquisition of the Floridas from Spain and, criticizing his administration's indecision and caution on the issue, advised President THOMAS JEFFERSON to take Spanish Florida by force. Before ending his frustrating mission at Paris, Armstrong received the so-called CADORE LETTER on August 5, 1810, from the French foreign minister. The controversial note, which attempted to persuade the U.S. government that Napoleon had rescinded his Milan and Berlin decrees against neutral American commerce, was intended to influence the United States to cut off its trade with Britain under terms of MACON'S BILL NO. 2.

By relaying the Cadore message to Washington without first probing the exact nature of his host country's intentions, Armstrong failed to uncover the fact that Napoleon had not committed unconditionally to a major shift in French policy. President JAMES MADISON'S decision to restrict commerce with Britain on the basis of the Cadore Letter widened the rift in Anglo-American relations that finally led to the War of 1812. Appointed secretary of war in 1813, Armstrong served a troubled year in the office, earning widespread blame for U.S. military setbacks in Canada and the British burning of Washington. He left the government in 1814, retiring to a life as a gentleman farmer in New York.

ARMY, DEPARTMENT OF THE See **DEPARTMENT OF THE ARMY** in **APPENDIX B**.

ARNOLD, BENEDICT (1741–1801) Revolutionary war general and infamous American traitor. Appointed a colonel in the Continental Army at the outbreak of the AMERICAN REVOLUTION, Arnold joined forces with Ethan Allen's Green Mountain Boys to capture British-held Fort Ticonderoga in upstate New York in May 1775. He subsequently conducted a brilliant although unsuccessful winter attack on Quebec and was promoted to general in January 1776. Arnold's battlefield leadership as second in command under General Horatio Gates was credited with securing the major American victory at Saratoga in October 1777. He was designated military commander of the Philadelphia area in June 1778. Bitter over the earlier promotion of less qualified peers, in need of money, and apparently opposed to the new FRANCO-AMERICAN ALLIANCE, Arnold began to disclose U.S. military information to the British. His plan to betray West Point was discovered when his contact, British Major John Andre, was captured and incriminating documents were found in his stocking. Arnold escaped to enemy lines, accepted a commission as a brigadier general in Great Britain's army, and led British raids on Virginia and his native Connecticut. After the war he went to England, where he died in 1801. His name became synonymous with treason for successive generations of Americans.

AROOSTOOK WAR (1838–1839) Undeclared, bloodless conflict between Maine and New Brunswick over the disputed U.S.-Canadian northeastern boundary. The episode raised tensions in Anglo-American relations and threatened to escalate into a violent clash. Location of the boundary dividing Maine from the Canadian province of New Brunswick had been a source of U.S.-British disagreement since 1783, when the TREATY OF PARIS ending the AMERICAN REVOLUTION failed to define clearly the northeastern border. After Maine achieved statehood in 1820, its legislature disregarded competing British territorial claims as it granted land to settlers along the Aroostook River. The United States and Britain, unable to resolve their differences through direct diplomacy, submitted the boundary dispute to arbitration by the king of the Netherlands in 1827. His compromise recommendation in 1831, while acceptable to the British, was rejected by the U.S. Senate on the grounds the king had exceeded his authority as an arbitrator and assumed the powers of a mediator.

The border issue came to a head in late 1838 after Canadian lumberjacks moved into the contested Aroostook region and began logging operations. In February 1839 land agent Rufus McIntire, an American appointed by and acting on the authority of the Maine legislature, entered the Aroostook area with a 200-man posse to expel the New Brunswick loggers. He and some of his men were captured by the

Canadians and put in jail. McIntire's arrest and the Canadian lumbermen's refusal to withdraw signaled the start of the so-called Aroostook War. Maine and New Brunswick mustered their respective militias and encamped them in the disputed territory. Congress, under pressure from its Maine members, authorized a federal force of 50,000 troops and $10 million for a possible military encounter. Determined to avert a confrontation, President MARTIN VAN BUREN sent U.S. Army General WINFIELD SCOTT to the trouble spot. Scott ended the tense standoff through his mediation of a March 1839 truce between the governor of Maine and the lieutenant governor of New Brunswick, at which point both sides withdrew their forces. Britain agreed to refer the long-standing dispute to a boundary commission. The northeastern boundary question was resolved in 1842 by the Anglo-American WEBSTER-ASHBURTON TREATY.

ARSENAL OF DEMOCRACY See **LEND-LEASE**.

ARTHUR, CHESTER ALAN (1829–1886) Twenty-first U.S. president. Born in Vermont, Arthur graduated from Union College in Schenectady, New York, in 1848. After studying law, he passed the New York bar in 1854, whereupon he became a successful New York City attorney, forming his own firm in 1856. An ardent abolitionist, he helped organize the newly founded Republican Party in the state. During the Civil War Arthur served as quartermaster general of New York, with responsibility for equipping and maintaining the state's volunteer militia. He remained prominent in the regular New York Republican organization after the war. His loyal support of President ULYSSES S. GRANT and his position as a leader of U.S. Senator Roscoe Conkling's state Republican machine won Arthur an appointment in 1871 as collector of the port of New York. In this key post, he supervised collection of three-fourths of the federal tariff revenues and administered one of the largest sources of federal political patronage. An investigation of the New York customs house launched in 1877 exposed lax management and led President RUTHERFORD B. HAYES to suspend Arthur. A bitter fight between the reformist Republican Hayes and the antireform Conkling machine ensued, culminating in Arthur's ouster in 1878.

Elected vice-president in 1880, Arthur assumed the presidency in September 1881 upon the death of JAMES A. GARFIELD, who had been cut down by an assassin's bullet in early July. To the surprise of political friends and foes alike, he ran an honest and independent administration, the main achievement of which was enactment of the landmark Pendleton Act (1883), which inaugurated civil service reform. In foreign affairs Arthur posted an unexceptional record. When Congress passed a bill to bar Chinese immigration to the United States, he vetoed the measure, contending it contradicted existing treaty arrangements with China. A revised version of the bill satisfied Arthur, who signed it into law as the CHINESE EXCLUSION ACT (1882). Secretary of State JAMES G. BLAINE, a Garfield appointee, resigned shortly after Arthur took over when he was unable to win the new president's endorsement for his ambitious proposal to develop a Pan-American political and economic union. Arthur's pick as the new secretary of state, FREDERICK T. FRELINGHUYSEN, shelved Blaine's Latin American plans. Arthur approved negotiation of the abortive FRELINGHUYSEN-ZELAYA TREATY, which granted the U.S. a canal route across Nicaragua. But Arthur's successor, Democrat GROVER CLEVELAND, withdrew the pact from the Senate on grounds it violated the CLAYTON-BULWER TREATY (1850). Arthur's proposal for a reduction in U.S. tariff rates was ignored by Congress, which passed a tariff in 1883 that maintained the highly protective existing duties. His administration launched a major construction program to increase the size and power of the U.S. Navy. Arthur was denied the renomination in 1884. He finished his term and retired in declining health to New York City, where he died in 1886.

ARTICLE X See **LEAGUE OF NATIONS**.

ARTICLES OF CONFEDERATION First governing document of the United States. In June 1776, at the same time it was drafting the Declaration of Independence, the Continental Congress appointed a committee to prepare a written instrument for governing the 13 former colonies in the newly formed nation. In July 1776 the committee reported a proposed set of articles of con-

federation. After more than a year of debate and revision, the articles were sent to the states for ratification in November 1777. The articles required unanimous approval and thus did not go into effect until March 1, 1781, when they were ratified by Maryland. The document established a federal government consisting of a congress made up of delegates from each of the states. There were no separate executive or judicial branches. Each state retained its sovereignty and independence but was forbidden to enter any treaty or alliance, conduct diplomatic relations, maintain military forces in peacetime other than militia, or make war unless suddenly invaded. Basic authority over foreign relations was entrusted to the Confederation Congress, which had the power to declare war and peace, negotiate treaties and alliances, send and receive ambassadors, determine maritime rules and conduct INDIAN AFFAIRS. These powers, however, could be exercised only with the consent of the congressional delegations from at least nine states.

The management of foreign relations was assigned to a congressionally appointed secretary of foreign affairs assisted by a small staff. Key international agreements concluded under the articles were the TREATY OF PARIS (1783) ending the AMERICAN REVOLUTION and the abortive U.S.-Spanish JAY-GARDOQUI TREATY. Because the federal government had no authority to raise revenues directly or regulate commerce and lacked the ability to enforce its measures on recalcitrant states, the articles proved ineffectual in governing the new nation. They were replaced by the U.S. CONSTITUTION on March 4, 1789. The new basic law incorporated many of the foreign affairs provisions of the earlier articles.

ASIAN DEVELOPMENT BANK (ADB) Regional lending institution whose purpose is to foster economic growth in Asia and help economic development of member countries in the region. Established formally in August 1966 under the auspices of the UNITED NATIONS Economic Commission for Asia and the Far East (ECAFE), now the Economic and Social Commission for Asia and the Pacific (ESCAP), the bank began operations in December of the same year at its Manila, Philippines, headquarters. The ADB's original membership of 31 gradually expanded and currently stands at 49, including 34 regional and 15 nonregional countries. The United States is a charter member. Communist China joined in 1986 after the ADB agreed to change Taiwan's membership title from "Republic of China" to "Taipei, China." The move prompted Taiwan to boycott bank meetings for a year before returning "under protest."

ADB offers financing for both public and private sector development projects in areas such as agriculture, industry, and energy. The bank's ordinary capital resources, which are used to make loans to more economically advanced nations in the region, comprise the financial contributions of member countries, money borrowed on world capital markets, and interest on the ADB's own undistributed assets. Individual country contributions account for the vast majority of these funds. The United States and Japan are the leading contributors, each providing 15 percent of the ADB's ordinary capital. The bank has other resources in the form of special funds. The Asian Development Fund (ADF), established in 1974, receives almost all its capital from voluntary contributions by major industrialized member nations. ADF makes very long-term interest-free loans to the poorest of ADB's developing member countries. The Technical Assistance Special Fund, likewise established in 1974 and also funded largely by members' voluntary contributions, furnishes grants for the bank's technical assistance operations.

See also COLOMBO PLAN.

ASIAN DEVELOPMENT FUND See **ASIAN DEVELOPMENT BANK**.

ASIA-PACIFIC TRIANGLE See **IMMIGRATION AND NATIONALITY ACT OF 1952**.

ASIATIC BARRED ZONE See **IMMIGRATION ACT OF 1917**.

ASIATIC EXCLUSION LEAGUE See **JAPANESE AND KOREAN EXCLUSION LEAGUE**.

ASSURED DESTRUCTION STRATEGY See **MUTUAL ASSURED DESTRUCTION**.

ASTRONAUT TREATY (1968) International agreement governing the rescue and repatriation of astronauts and objects returning from space. Formally titled the

Agreement on the Rescue of Astronauts, the Return of Astronauts, and the Return of Objects Launched into Outer Space, the treaty generally is referred to as the Rescue and Return of Astronauts Agreement. It was worked out by the United States and Soviet Union under the auspices of the Committee on the Peaceful Uses of Outer Space of the UNITED NATIONS General Assembly. Signed on April 22, 1968, by 74 countries, the agreement won U.S. ratification in October 1968 and went into effect on December 3, 1968. The treaty expanded on the provisions of the OUTER SPACE TREATY (1967) detailing the responsibilities of nations with regard to both the rescue and repatriation of foreign astronauts. Under its terms, signatory countries are obligated to take immediate steps to rescue and lend all necessary assistance to an astronaut in the event of an accident, emergency, or unintended landing in their territory. The agreement mandates that foreign astronauts, once rescued, will be promptly and safely repatriated. It also provides for the speedy return to the launching nation of objects (satellites, space vehicles) that land from space in foreign territory.

ATLANTIC CHARTER (1941) Joint declaration by President FRANKLIN D. ROOSEVELT and British Prime Minister Winston Churchill of the principles that would guide their two countries in the search for a more just and stable world. While maintaining official U.S. neutrality since the outbreak of WORLD WAR II in Europe in 1939, Roosevelt had progressively steered U.S. policy toward support of Great Britain in its struggle against Axis powers Germany and Italy. In August 1941 Roosevelt and Churchill met for the first time at the AT-LANTIC CONFERENCE to discuss what additional war materiel and other aid Washington might provide the beleaguered British government. The parley was kept secret for security reasons. At meetings from August 9 to 12 aboard the U.S. cruiser *Augusta* and British battleship *Prince of Wales* in Placentia Bay off Newfoundland, Roosevelt agreed to a larger U.S. Navy role in protecting British convoys in the North Atlantic. The two leaders, with the aid of assistants SUM-NER WELLES and Sir Alexander Cadogan, drew up a joint statement outlining their wartime and postwar policies and aims. The document contained eight broad principles: (1) neither nation sought territorial aggrandizement; (2) opposition to territorial changes without the free consent of the peoples concerned; (3) respect for the right of peoples to decide their own form of government; (4) support for free trade and equal access to raw materials; (5) support for international collaboration to achieve improved labor standards and economic advancement; (6) commitment to a world free from fear and want; (7) commitment to FREEDOM OF THE SEAS; and (8) peace based on abandonment of the use of force and disarmament of aggressor nations, to be guaranteed by the establishment of a permanent system of general security. The Atlantic Charter, released simultaneously in Washington and London on August 14, 1941, strengthened the nascent Anglo-American alliance and helped rally people worldwide to the Allied cause. By September 24, 15 anti-Axis nations, including the Soviet Union, had endorsed the document. The charter was incorporated into the UNITED NATIONS DECLARATION adopted by the United States and other Allied nations in January 1942.

ATLANTIC COMMUNITY Term used to describe the shared political, economic, and social interests, reinforced by a common Western cultural heritage, of the United States, Canada and the nations of Western Europe. The expression was coined by American columnist WALTER LIPPMANN during WORLD WAR II to refer to the ties forged between the United States and Europe as a result of the conflict. In the immediate postwar years, the idea that the nations bordering the North Atlantic formed a natural union was given additional impetus by the onset of East-West COLD WAR and the threat of Communist aggression against Western Europe. In 1949 the Western allies formed the NATO military alliance, providing an institutional framework to the Atlantic Community idea. Similarly, the MARSHALL PLAN (1948) for postwar European economic recovery evolved into the permanent transatlantic ORGANIZATION FOR ECONOMIC COOPERATION AND DEVELOPMENT. U.S. political leaders in the 1960s countered French President Charles De Gaulle's push to develop separate European institutions by emphasizing the importance of the larger Atlantic Community as the linchpin to Western security. In the 1980s the Reagan administration vigorously opposed what it perceived as Soviet attempts to split the Atlantic alliance by fomenting division between the United States and its West European partners. While no formal Atlantic Community organization exists, the United States and its European allies coordinate closely on political, economic, and security policy. With the end of the Cold War, discussion in the early 1990s about the future of the Atlantic Community centered on economic questions. At issue was whether the formation in 1992 of the European Community, with its scheduled economic integration of the continent, would cause the Atlantic Community to break apart into competing North Atlantic and European trading blocks.

ATLANTIC CONFERENCE See **WORLD WAR II CONFERENCES** in **APPENDIX E**.

ATOMIC ENERGY ACT (1946) Law that established civilian control over all aspects of atomic energy. On August 1, 1946, President HARRY S. TRUMAN signed the Atomic Energy Act, sponsored by Senator Brien McMahon (D-CT), creating the five-member civilian Atomic Energy Commission (AEC). Under the legislation, known also as the McMahon Act, full control over the use and development of atomic energy was transferred from the War Department to the presidentially appointed AEC. All production facilities and nuclear reactors were to be government owned and all technical information was to remain under the commission's sole authority. The military remained the custodian of the U.S. NUCLEAR WEAPONS arsenal. The AEC officially took control of the nation's atomic energy program in January 1947 under the chairmanship of David E. Lilienthal, noted lawyer and former chairman of the Tennessee Valley Authority. As revised in 1954, the Atomic Energy Act permitted private industry to own reactors and production facilities (but not fissionable material) and removed restrictions on disseminating technical information to other nations. A 1964 amendment to the 1954 statute permitted the AEC to sell fissionable material to private U.S. companies involved in the development of civilian uses of atomic energy.

ATOMS FOR PEACE (1953) Proposal by President DWIGHT D. EISENHOWER for cooperation among the nuclear powers and other nations in the peaceful development and application of atomic energy. In a speech before the UNITED NATIONS General Assembly on December 8, 1953, he outlined his Atoms for Peace scheme. The plan called for creation, under the U.N. aegis, of an international atomic energy agency to which the nuclear powers would contribute fissionable materials from their weapons stockpiles for peaceful uses. Eisenhower's proposal was offered as a dramatic new approach that might help restrain the nuclear arms race between the United States and Soviet Union and break the East-West disarmament deadlock. Before his U.N. appearance, the president had met at the BERMUDA CONFERENCE with British Prime Minister Winston Churchill and French Premier Joseph Laniel, who both endorsed Atoms for Peace. The USSR initially expressed guarded interest in Eisenhower's scheme. But in reply to a U.S. invitation to participate in discussions on the matter, the Soviet government insisted on prior U.S. agreement to a total global ban on atomic weapons. Rejecting Moscow's condition on account of Soviet unwillingness to accept an international verification regimen, Washington then undertook talks with its allies on the Atoms for Peace initiative. Part of Eisenhower's plan for the sharing of atomic energy for peaceful uses was realized with the creation in 1956 of the INTERNATIONAL ATOMIC ENERGY AGENCY.

AUSTRIAN STATE TREATY (1955) Peace treaty concluded with Austria by WORLD WAR II allies the United States, Great Britian, France, and Soviet Union. Nazi Germany annexed neighboring Austria in 1938. At the war's end in 1945, the Allies detached Austria from Germany and divided it into four occupation zones. Austrian capital Vienna similarly was separated into American, British, French, and Soviet sectors. A COUNCIL OF FOREIGN MINISTERS of the major Allied powers was established to begin preparing draft treaties with the defeated Axis nations. The ensuing deliberations underscored fundamental East-West differences over the future status of Germany

and Soviet-occupied Eastern Europe. Amid mounting COLD WAR confrontation, agreement finally was reached in 1949 on the basic outlines of an Austrian peace treaty. Negotiations on Germany, however, had reached a bitter impasse. Finalization of an Austrian agreement was blocked when the Soviet Union and Western Allies became deadlocked over Moscow's attempts to link further progress on Austria to a German settlement.

The emergence of new leadership in Moscow following the death of Soviet Premier Joseph Stalin in March 1953 enhanced the prospects for a British-proposed four-power summit to improve East-West relations. British, French, and Soviet interest in a meeting grew during 1954, but President DWIGHT D. EISENHOWER conditioned U.S. participation on the completion of an Austrian treaty. Eager both to resolve the Austrian question and to bring about a summit gathering where it might forestall West German rearmament within the Western NATO security alliance, the Kremlin invited the Austrian chancellor to Moscow for discussions on an accord in April 1955. The negotiations made considerable headway, leading the Western allies to accept a Soviet proposal for a conference of foreign ministers in Vienna to conclude a final agreement.

The United States, Great Britain, France, USSR, and Austria signed the Austrian State Treaty in Vienna on May 15, 1955. The pact reestablished Austria as a sovereign, independent, and democratic nation within its pre-1938 boundaries; prohibited political or economic union with Germany; and provided for the withdrawal of all occupation forces by the end of the year. It set no reparations but provided Moscow certain oil concessions; barred Austria from owning or making atomic weapons or guided missiles; and proclaimed Austria's perpetual neutrality. The U.S. Senate ratified the treaty on June 17. With the Austrian accord completed, Washington indicated its readiness to attend an East-West summit conference. The U.S., British, French, and Soviet heads of government subsequently met in July 1955 at the GENEVA SUMMIT.

B

BACON, ROBERT (1860–1919) Banker, diplomat, secretary of state. Bacon was born in Massachusetts. After graduating from Harvard University in 1880, he entered the banking business in Boston and in 1894 joined the New York firm of J. P. Morgan and Company. Long a student of foreign affairs, he became assistant secretary of state under ELIHU ROOT in 1905. Following Root's resignation in January 1909 to enter the U.S. Senate, Bacon was commissioned as secretary of state and served for the remaining weeks of President THEODORE ROOSEVELT's administration. In December 1909 President WILLIAM HOWARD TAFT named him ambassador to France. He remained in the post until January 1912. At the request of the CARNEGIE ENDOWMENT FOR INTERNATIONAL PEACE, Bacon traveled to South America in 1913 on a mission to promote better U.S. relations with Latin America. Following the outbreak of WORLD WAR I in Europe in August 1914, he went to France to help with the work of the volunteer "American Ambulance." With America's entry into the war in April 1917, he was commissioned a major in the Army and detailed to the staff of General JOHN J. PERSHING, commander of the AMERICAN EXPEDITIONARY FORCE. After his promotion to lieutenant colonel in 1918, Bacon served as chief of the American military mission at British General Headquarters. He returned from Europe in poor health and died in New York in May 1919.

BAGHDAD PACT See **CENTRAL TREATY ORGANIZATION**.

BAILEY, THOMAS ANDREW (1902–1983) Diplomatic historian who was an authority on both U.S. foreign policy and the presidency. He earned bachelor's, master's, and doctoral degrees from Stanford University, where he joined the history faculty in 1930. The California native spent most of his career at Stanford before retiring in 1968. His books examining America's experience in foreign relations included *A Diplomatic History of the American People* (1940), which went through 10 editions, *American Foreign Policies: Past and Present* (1943), *America Faces Russia: Russian-American Relations from Early Times to Our Day* (1950), and *The Art of Diplomacy: The American Experience* (1968). He explored America's decision at the end of WORLD WAR I not to join the LEAGUE OF NATIONS in *Woodrow Wilson and the Peacemakers* (1947). Among his works on the American presidency were *Presidential Greatness: The Image and the Man from George Washington to the Present* (1966) and *The Pugnacious Presidents: White House Warriors on Parade* (1980). Bailey also was widely known for *The American Pageant: A History of the Republic* (1956), which became a standard high school and college textbook.

BAKER, JAMES ADDISON, 3RD (1930–) White House chief of staff, secretary of the treasury, secretary of state. The scion of a prominent Houston, Texas, family, Baker graduated from Princeton in 1952, served two years in the Marine Corps, and earned a law degree from the University of Texas in 1957. He then joined a corporate law firm in Houston. In 1970 he entered politics as a county campaign manager for friend Representative GEORGE BUSH (R-TX), who ran unsuccessfully for the U.S. Senate. Baker became active in the Republican Party and in 1972 was named its state finance chairman. In 1975 he was appointed under secretary of commerce in the Ford administration. The following year he managed President GERALD R. FORD's reelection campaign. After Ford's defeat, he resumed his law practice. In 1978, in his only attempt at elective office, Baker lost a close contest for Texas state attorney general. He directed Bush's campaign for the 1980 Republican presidential nomination. With Bush's selection as vice-presidential candidate by eventual nominee RONALD W. REAGAN, Baker became a senior adviser to the Reagan campaign team.

In November 1980 President-elect Reagan named Baker White House chief of staff, a post he held throughout Reagan's first term. In February 1985, in a highly unusual move, Baker swapped positions with Secretary of the Treasury Donald T. Regan. At the Treasury Department, much of his attention was devoted to international economic issues. The INTERNATIONAL DEBT CRISIS was of particular concern to the Reagan administration. The inability of THIRD WORLD countries to repay their massive debts to Western commercial lenders threatened both to undermine the international financial system and to deny the developing nations desperately needed additional investment capital. In October 1985 Baker proposed initiatives to encourage free-market reforms in Third World nations to enable their economies to grow sufficiently to allow for debt repayment. The BAKER PLAN, with its emphasis on free-market-based growth, offered an incomplete solution to the Third World debt crisis and it was succeeded in 1989 by the BRADY PLAN, which incorporated both market reforms and debt relief. Also in 1985, Baker helped negotiate the PLAZA ACCORD, an agreement among the GROUP OF 5 Western industrialized nations designed to alleviate America's worsening trade deficit by lowering the value of the dollar.

He resigned his post in 1988 to manage Bush's successful presidential campaign. He took office as secretary of state in the new Bush administration on the eve of momentous worldwide change. The collapse of communism in Eastern Europe in 1989 hastened dramatically improved U.S.-Soviet relations and the end of the COLD WAR. Baker participated as Bush's principal adviser at the various summit meetings between the president and Soviet leader Mikhail S. Gorbachev. He worked closely with Soviet counterpart Foreign Minister Eduard A. Shevardnadze in the negotiation of the FINAL SETTLEMENT WITH RESPECT TO GERMANY TREATY (1990) ending the post-WORLD WAR II division of Germany and the CONVENTIONAL FORCES EUROPE TREATY (1990) providing for broad disarmament on the continent. Building on the momentum of U.S.-Soviet post–Cold War ties, he oversaw completion of the START Treaty (1991) reducing superpower long-range nuclear arsenals. Baker cautioned against massive Western assistance to the crumbling Soviet economy until Moscow committed fully to a free-market system. In the aftermath of the failed MOSCOW COUP (1991) and disintegration of the Soviet Communist Party, the Bush administration joined the other Western industrial powers in furnishing emergency humanitarian aid to the USSR.

Early in his tenure Baker moved to resolve the acrimony between the White House and Congress that had existed since the early 1980s over U.S. policy toward the leftist Sandinista government in Nicaragua. In March 1989, he negotiated a bipartisan accord on Central America with congressional leaders. The agreement represented a shift from the Reagan administration policy of providing military aid to the CONTRAS, Nicaraguan rebels waging a guerrilla campaign against the Managua regime. The Bush administration pledged to pursue a diplomatic solution in Nicaragua. Congress agreed in turn to continue the flow of nonlethal aid to the Contras, allowing them to remain in their bases in Honduras until the Sandinistas held promised national elections in February 1990. Sustaining the Contras as a viable insurgency in the interim, Bush and Baker maintained, was necessary to keep pressure on the Sandinistas to abide by their election pledge. The surprise victory of opposition candidate Violeta Chamorro in February 1990 presented U.S. policymakers with the departure of the Sandinista regime.

Following Iraq's August 1990 invasion of Kuwait, Baker helped construct the international political coalition that brought about a series of UNITED NATIONS Security Council resolutions condemning the action and demanding Iraq's withdrawal. The

U.S.-led coalition subsequently took military action under U.N. auspices in the PERSIAN GULF WAR to force Iraq's compliance with the resolutions. In 1991, moving to capitalize on enhanced U.S. credibility and influence in the region after the war, Baker spearheaded administration efforts to convene a Middle Eastern peace conference to resolve the long-standing Arab-Israeli conflict over Arab refusal to accept the Jewish state's right to exist and Palestinian Arab demands for a separate homeland in Israeli-occupied territories. After numerous trips to the region, entailing difficult negotiations with all concerned parties, his efforts culminated in the MIDDLE EAST PEACE CONFERENCE.

BAKER PLAN See **INTERNATIONAL DEBT CRISIS**.

BALANCE OF POWER Concept in international relations that describes how states safeguard their national security in a framework of shifting political and military alliances. A balance of power is a condition of equilibrium among rival countries. In theory, it secures the vital interests of nations while preserving peace by ensuring that no state or bloc of states attains dominance over another. Balance is achieved and maintained in two ways: by individual nations enhancing their own power, or by nations with shared interests forging a defensive alliance equal in power to that presented by a nation or alliance perceived as a threat. Diplomacy in this context is concerned with preventing the destabilizing accumulation of power by a single state or group.

A multiple power balance determined by shifting combinations of the leading European powers prevailed internationally from the mid-17th to early 20th century. Historically isolationist, the United States avoided involvement in the various balance-of-power arrangements. A breakdown of the European balance-of-power system, embodied in an intricate set of opposing alliances, was widely interpreted as having caused WORLD WAR I. Following the war, President WOODROW WILSON condemned a world order based on power calculations and spheres of influence. Wilson led efforts at the PARIS PEACE CONFERENCE (1919) to form an international peacekeeping body

that would serve instead as an instrument for global COLLECTIVE SECURITY. Reflecting the nation's traditional ISOLATIONISM, the U.S. Senate ultimately rejected American membership in the resulting LEAGUE OF NATIONS.

U.S. isolationism largely ended with the nation's entry into WORLD WAR II. America emerged from the conflict strongly committed to the international collective security arrangement embodied in the UNITED NATIONS. In the tense COLD WAR stalemate that developed shortly after the war, however, the United States found itself locked in ideological struggle with rival superpower the Soviet Union. This confrontation effectively evolved into a balance-of-power standoff between the FREE WORLD and the Communist bloc. The U.S.-led NATO Western security alliance was constructed to counter the massive Soviet armies in Eastern Europe and provide for the DETERRENCE of Communist aggression. The massive nuclear arsenals on each side gave rise to the expression "balance of terror" to convey the recognition by both superpowers that any nuclear conflict would result in their MUTUAL ASSURED DESTRUCTION and was thus unthinkable. A student of 19th-century European diplomacy, Secretary of State HENRY A. KISSINGER incorporated balance-of-power considerations into the formulation of the Nixon administration's policy of DETENTE with the Soviet Union in the early 1970s. Kissinger conceived of closer U.S.-Soviet ties based on a careful and pragmatic balancing of each nation's security concerns and geopolitical strengths and weaknesses rather than on a commitment to abstract ideals. The demise of Soviet communism and end of the Cold War at the outset of the 1990s removed the need for an East-West balance of power and steered the world back toward the U.N. collective security system. In the PERSIAN GULF WAR (1991), the United States and USSR supported the cooperative international effort to force Iraq's compliance with U.N. Security Council resolutions demanding it withdraw from Kuwait, which it had invaded in August 1990.

BALL, GEORGE WILDMAN (1909–   ) Lawyer, State Department official. An Iowa native, Ball graduated from Northwestern University in 1930 and went on to earn a law degree in 1933. He worked briefly for the Farm Credit Administration and Treasury Department in Washington before returning to Chicago in 1935 to practice law. He formed a lifelong friendship with fellow law firm member ADLAI E. STEVENSON. During WORLD WAR II Ball served as a counsel with the Office of LEND-LEASE Administration. In 1944 he was appointed director of the U.S. Strategic Bombing Survey, a civilian board established to assess the effects of the air campaign against Germany. After the war Ball was a founding partner in a law firm specializing in international trade. He assisted Jean Monnet, the architect of postwar European economic unification, on plans for the European Coal and Steel Community and later represented Common Market agencies in the United States. He played a major role in Stevenson's 1952 and 1956 unsuccessful presidential campaigns.

President-elect JOHN F. KENNEDY, impressed by a report Ball had authored on economic policy, named him under secretary of state for economic affairs in January 1961. In his new position Ball concentrated primarily on trade issues, helping to draft the TRADE EXPANSION ACT of 1962, which lowered tariffs on imported goods while giving the president broad authority to retaliate against foreign trade restrictions. Becoming under secretary of state in November 1961, the second-ranking post in the department, he played an important part in administration planning in the CONGO CRISIS (1960–1962) and CUBAN MISSILE CRISIS (1962). Under President LYNDON B. JOHNSON, Ball continued to oppose the mounting American military involvement in the VIETNAM WAR. He argued unsuccessfully against the bombing of North Vietnam before finally resigning in September 1966 over U.S. policy in Southeast Asia. He pursued a career in investment banking, which he interrupted briefly in 1968 to serve as U.S. ambassador to the UNITED NATIONS. In 1979 he conducted a special evaluation of the worsening situation in Iran for President JIMMY CARTER, recommending America withdraw its support from the shah. Ball published his memoirs, *The Past Has Another Pattern*, in 1982.

BALTIMORE AFFAIR (1891) Violent incident that pushed the United States and Chile to the verge of military conflict. Anti-American sentiment in the aftermath of the ITATA INCIDENT (1891) still ran deep when a party of 117 sailors from the U.S. cruiser *Baltimore* took shore leave in Valparaiso, Chile, on October 16, 1891. The lingering Chilean hostility, which stemmed from the feeling that the U.S. government had been antagonistic to the victorious rebel cause in Chile's 1891 civil war, erupted that evening as a Valparaiso mob attacked the American sailors, killing two and seriously wounding several others. News of the violence inspired calls in the United States for retaliation. President BENJAMIN HARRISON demanded an apology and swift reparations. The new Chilean government, denying responsibility for what it termed a drunken street brawl, rebuffed Washington, prompting Harrison to threaten strong U.S. action in his annual message to Congress on December 9.

Affronted by the threat, Chilean Foreign Minister M. A. Matte responded with a telegram denouncing the United States, further fanning U.S. indignation. Against the advice of Secretary of State JAMES G. BLAINE, who feared escalation of the crisis would imperil his nascent program for PAN-AMERICANISM and thus preferred a low-key diplomatic solution, Harrison on January 21, 1892, delivered an ultimatum to Chile in which he pledged to sever diplomatic relations unless apologies were tendered expeditiously. When no quick reply came, he sent a special message to Congress on January 25 virtually requesting a war declaration. Without allies and faced with superior U.S. military power, Chile decided to bow to U.S. demands, ending the crisis. The Chilean government submitted an official note of apology on January 26 and later paid a $75,000 indemnity to the injured sailors and the relatives of those who had died.

BAMBOO CURTAIN See **IRON CURTAIN.**

BARBARY TREATIES Succession of treaties from 1786 to 1797 between the United States and the four Barbary states of North Africa. Following the AMERICAN REVOLUTION, the United States faced assaults upon its commercial shipping in the Mediterranean Sea by the Barbary pirates of Morocco, Algiers, Tunis, and Tripoli. Before the Revolutionary War, Great Britain's payment of tribute money to the Barbary states had shielded American trade vessels and their crews in North African waters from capture and plunder by the corsairs. The newly independent United States after 1783 was left to negotiate its own arrangements with the Barbary rulers. Lacking the naval power to protect its commerce, America followed the late 18th century European practice of resorting to tribute. U.S. diplomacy also ventured to reach a formal Mediterranean settlement.

In treaties with Morocco (1786), Algiers (1795), Tripoli (1796), and Tunis (1797), the United States purchased pledges of unmolested passage for American ships traveling along the North African Barbary Coast. The U.S. government in each accord consented to a one-time payment of money and presents for Barbary assurances of "perpetual peace and friendship." Continuing Barbary piracy through the end of the 1790s flouted the ineffectual treaties, forcing further U.S. payments of tribute and ransom to safeguard American ships and win the release of captured American seamen. U.S.-Barbary maritime conflict at the outset of the 19th century erupted in the TRIPOLITAN WAR (1801–1805) and the later ALGERINE WAR (1815). American victories in these wars ended U.S. tribute payments to the Barbary states.

BARBOUR, JAMES (1775–1842) U.S. senator, secretary of war, and diplomat. Born in Virginia, he received no formal higher education but was admitted to the state bar. Barbour served in the Virginia House of Delegates from 1798 to 1805 and from 1807 to 1812, establishing himself as a vigorous advocate of states' rights. He supported the Virginia Resolutions (1798) drafted by JAMES MADISON that challenged the constitutionality of the ALIEN AND SEDITION ACTS (1798) and asserted the right of the states to nullify federal law. He was Virginia governor from 1812 until his election to the U.S. Senate in 1815. During his decade-long tenure in the upper house, Barbour served variously as chairman of the military affairs and foreign relations committees.

President JOHN QUINCY ADAMS appointed him secretary of war in 1825. He endorsed Adams administration policy in the Western Hemisphere that sought to limit British influence among the newly independent Latin American republics and likewise favored the president's decision to send a delegation to the PANAMA CONGRESS (1826) on Latin American unity. Barbour became involved in Indian policy through his difficult and ultimately unsuccessful negotiations with Georgia officials concerning the state's challenge to federal authority over INDIAN AFFAIRS. Georgia, determined to expel the Cherokee and Creek Indians, complained that Washington had reneged on its part of an 1802 settlement under which the state had agreed to cede immediately its western land claims to the federal government. In return the U.S. government had promised to act on the state's behalf to obtain title to Indian territory within Georgia as soon as feasible. The war secretary, who came to recommend Indian removal west of the Mississippi River, was unable to win Georgia's compliance with federal policy. The issue of sovereignty over Indian affairs was resolved in the federal government's favor through the landmark U.S. Supreme Court cases CHEROKEE NATION V. GEORGIA (1831) and WORCESTER V. GEORGIA (1832) while the fate of the Cherokee and Creek was sealed with the implementation of the federal INDIAN REMOVAL POLICY.

At his own request, Barbour was named U.S. minister to Great Britain in 1828. He served at London for less than a year before being recalled by Adams's successor, President ANDREW JACKSON. Following his uneventful diplomatic stint, Barbour returned briefly to the Virginia legislature (1830–1831) and later became involved in Whig politics until his death.

BARUCH, BERNARD MANNES (1870–1965) Financier, public official, and presidential adviser. Born in South Carolina, Baruch at age 10 moved with his family to New York City and graduated from the City College of New York in 1889. Beginning a Wall Street career in 1891, he made a large fortune by the time he was 30 and eventually purchased a seat on the New York Stock Exchange. His business acumen earned Baruch appointment by President WOODROW WILSON as a government adviser on wartime mobilization following the 1914 outbreak of WORLD WAR I in Europe. In 1916 Wilson named him to the advisory commission of the Council for National Defense, a cabinet committee responsible for national mobilization. After the United

States entered the war in 1917, Baruch became chairman of the War Industries Board, in which role he assumed virtual control over U.S. industrial production. He was selected as a member of the U.S. delegation to the PARIS PEACE CONFERENCE (1919), where he served Wilson as a key economic aide and worked on economics and reparations clauses of the TREATY OF VERSAILLES.

Although a Democrat, he was consulted often during the 1920s on agricultural matters and the economy by Republican presidents WARREN G. HARDING, CALVIN COOLIDGE, and HERBERT C. HOOVER. With the advent of the New Deal under President FRANKLIN D. ROOSEVELT in the 1930s, Baruch continued in his capacity as an unofficial adviser to the White House. Throughout the interwar years he waged a personal campaign for industrial preparedness in the event of war. In 1937 he submitted a plan to the Senate Military Affairs Committee on wartime mobilization. With America's entry into WORLD WAR II in 1941, Roosevelt enlisted Baruch's expertise in wartime use of industry. In 1942 the New York financier headed a special presidential committee charged with addressing the nation's acute rubber shortage. Appointed in 1943 as an unpaid assistant to JAMES F. BYRNES, then director of the Office of War Mobilization, Baruch prepared recommendations on wartime industrial adjustments and outlined a major postwar demobilization and reconversion program.

In March 1946 President HARRY S. TRUMAN named Baruch as first U.S. delegate to the newly created U.N. Atomic Energy Commission. At the commission's opening meeting that June, he presented the BARUCH PLAN for international control of atomic energy. Under the plan the United States would relinquish its nuclear monopoly; all atomic weapons would be outlawed; a proposed International Atomic Development Authority would control and inspect all atomic energy activities; and, to protect against violations of an international atomic energy covenant, the U.N. Security Council veto would be suspended in all atomic energy affairs. The USSR rejected the Baruch Plan and offered a counterproposal that outlawed atomic weapons but failed to provide for international control and inspection. The United States found the Soviet plan unacceptable and the issue ended in

stalemate. Baruch resigned his post in 1947, marking his last direct influence on government policy during the Truman years. In the 1950s he was an informal adviser to President DWIGHT D. EISENHOWER. A philanthropist, Baruch made gifts throughout his adulthood to universities and medical schools. He died at age 94 in New York City.

BARUCH PLAN (1946) U.S. plan for the international control of atomic energy submitted to the UNITED NATIONS. In January 1946 the U.N. General Assembly created the United Nations Atomic Energy Commission (UNAEC) to establish proper international controls over atomic energy and devise a scheme for nuclear disarmament. At the commission's opening meeting, on June 14, BERNARD M. BARUCH, American representative to UNAEC, presented the United States's official proposal for relinquishing its monopoly on atomic weapons under an international security system. The so-called Baruch Plan was based substantially on the Acheson-Lilienthal Report prepared by Under Secretary of State DEAN ACHESON and David Lilienthal, then head of the Tennessee Valley Authority, and issued by the State Department the previous February. It incorporated several major points. It proposed the creation of an International Atomic Energy Development Authority (IAEDA) that would control all phases of the development and use of atomic energy. The authority would have unprecedented powers of inspection within national territories to guard against forbidden atomic activity. Violators of atomic control agreements would face stiff penalities meted out by the IAEDA. Decisions of the authority and international control and inspection would not be subject to veto by the BIG FIVE powers (the United States, France, Great Britain, the Soviet Union, and China) in the U.N. Security Council. The Baruch Plan emphasized that the United States would stop manufacturing atomic weapons, dispose of its stockpiles, and disclose to the IAEDA its nuclear secrets after the proposed authority had established international control of atomic energy.

Unwilling to submit to an international regime in advance of U.S. nuclear disarmament and disclosure, the USSR promptly rejected the plan. A Soviet counterproposal to outlaw atomic weapons made no provision for international control and inspection and subjected questions of atomic energy to the veto in the Security Council. The United States dismissed the Soviet plan as completely unacceptable. Irreconcilable differences between Washington and Moscow produced a stalemate on the issue of international control of nuclear energy. The deadlock favored the Soviets, whose crash program to develop an atomic weapon culminated in the successful detonation of an atomic device in September 1949, thereby ending the American monopoly.

See also ATOMS FOR PEACE, INTERNATIONAL ATOMIC ENERGY AGENCY.

BASEL CONVENTION (1989)   Global treaty on the shipment and disposal of hazardous wastes across international borders. Appeals for an international agreement to control hazardous-waste exports followed increasing reports that dangerous toxic substances were being dumped in Africa and other areas of the developing world by unscrupulous companies in the industrialized countries. The measure was adopted March 22, 1989, by a UNITED NATIONS ENVIRONMENT PROGRAM conference in Basel, Switzerland, attended by more than 100 countries, including the United States. Officially called the Basel Convention on the Control of Transboundary Movements of Hazardous Wastes and Their Disposal, it was signed immediately by 34 nations. The United States has withheld signature pending further review of the convention's terms. The agreement will enter into force after ratification by the requisite 20 nations.

The Basel agreement aims to prevent international movement of hazardous waste to unsafe, inadequate sites by requiring waste exporters to notify and obtain formal written consent from receiving countries before shipping the refuse. It requires countries exporting waste and those receiving it to ensure that the hazardous material is disposed of in an environmentally safe manner. Treaty proponents have hailed it as an important step toward effective regulation of international hazardous-waste disposal. Critics contend the convention does not go far enough to control dangerous exports and lacks enforcement mechanisms.

BASKET I, II, III, IV   See **HELSINKI ACCORDS**.

BATTLE OF ...   See **..., BATTLE OF**.

BAY OF PIGS INVASION (1961)   Failed U.S.-sponsored invasion by Cuban exiles to overthrow the Castro regime on their former island homeland. The United States maintained close commercial ties with Cuba under strongman Fulgencio Batista, who had dominated Cuban politics since 1933. American firms owned much of the farmland and controlled Cuba's vital sugar crop. A guerrilla movement led by Cuban revolutionary Fidel Castro succeeded in driving Batista into exile and overthrowing his corrupt, authoritarian regime on January 1, 1959. The United States recognized the new Cuban government on January 7, but relations between the two nations soured as Castro executed hundreds of former Batista officials. As the Castro government began to take shape, thousands of Cubans opposed to its increasingly leftist character fled the island, many to the south of Florida.

U.S. concerns over possible imposition of a Communist government on Cuba escalated when Castro began to impose totalitarian control over the island. The Eisenhower administration viewed with alarm emerging diplomatic and security ties between Castro and America's COLD WAR adversary the Soviet Union. In response to Cuban expropriation of private American holdings on the islands, the U.S. government imposed a trade embargo on October 19, 1960. With the situation deteriorating, the Eisenhower administration severed diplomatic relations with Havana on January 3, 1961.

In early 1960 senior U.S. policymakers had begun to contemplate ways to remove Castro from power. President DWIGHT D. EISENHOWER in March 1960 approved a secret CENTRAL INTELLIGENCE AGENCY (CIA) plan for covert action against the Castro regime. The operation, code-named Pluto, arranged for establishment of an exile Cuban political organization, initiation of an anti-Castro propaganda campaign, development of an underground resistance in Cuba, and creation of an exile guerrilla force. The U.S. goal was the overthrow of Castro through a popular uprising led by the U.S.-backed guerrilla movement.

By the summer of 1960 Operation Pluto was well under way. The exile Cuban Democratic Revolutionary Front had been organized in Miami with CIA support. In May an agency radio transmitter on Swan Island off Honduras had begun anti-Castro broadcasts into Cuba. Young exiles were recruited in the United States and sent to Camp Trax, a secret guerrilla training base in Guatemala. The CIA also operated a clandestine airstrip in the Central American nation where it assembled a small rebel air force of aging transports and B-26 bombers. When a sufficient number of Cuban exile pilots could not be found, American volunteer pilots were drawn secretly from the Alabama Air National Guard.

As preparations continued for the guerrilla infiltration into Cuba, problems with the overall operation surfaced. Dissension plagued the exile political front. Intelligence showed that Castro was escalating efforts to crush remaining domestic opposition and receiving growing quantities of Communist-supplied arms. Underground activities on the island were proving ineffective and air drops of supplies to anti-Castro insurgents already in place were beset by troubles. Information on the operation was starting to leak. On October 30, 1960, the Guatemalan daily *La Hora* published an article on the training of Cuban guerrillas in the country.

U.S. planners increasingly doubted whether Castro could be overthrown by a guerrilla campaign. In November 1960 Eisenhower was briefed on a CIA proposal for an exile invasion of Cuba. The plan called for an amphibious landing and establishment of a beachhead that would become the seat of a provisional Cuban government. Eisenhower deferred any decision on the invasion to the incoming Kennedy administration. After President-elect JOHN F. KENNEDY gave tentative approval to the new plan, CIA preparations continued. In January 1961, after taking office, the Kennedy administration reviewed the entire Cuban project, weighing such concerns as the loss of suprise due to mounting news stories about the U.S.-backed exile force and the vital importance of keeping hidden the covert U.S. role in the operation. In March the president gave final approval to the scheduled April invasion. In giving the go-ahead, Kennedy stressed that no Americans were to be involved in the actual landing.

The invasion was staged out of Puerto Cabezas, Nicaragua, using a small fleet of CIA transport ships. On April 15, 1961, an initial rebel air attack on Cuba's three main airfields went as planned, but returning pilots reported that only one half of Castro's air force had been destroyed. One B-26 bomber flew to Miami to lend credibility to the cover story that the bombings were the work of defecting Cuban pilots. ADLAI E. STEVENSON, the U.S. ambassador to the UNITED NATIONS, had no knowledge of the Bay of Pigs venture and thus responded to Cuban accusations by denying any American involvement.

The operation from the outset encountered trouble. A planned diversionary landing had been canceled by its leaders the night before when Cuban troops were seen guarding the beach. On April 16 Kennedy, worried that the U.S. role was in danger of being exposed, called off a second rebel air strike against Cuban airfields. The main landing of some 1400 men at the Bay of Pigs on the island's southwestern coast went ahead as scheduled in the early morning of April 17, but quickly ran into problems. At dawn Castro's remaining air force sank two rebel transports bearing valuable ammunition supplies and the expedition's communication center. Alerted by the initial bombing raid on his airfields, Castro was able to rush a large force to the invasion site. By the morning of April 18 the small beachhead established by the invading force was under attack on all sides. Although exile commanders pleaded for assistance, Kennedy ruled out direct U.S. military intervention to save the invasion. On the third day the rebel force, almost out of ammunition and facing certain destruction, scattered into neighboring swamps. A few escaped to sea, but roughly 1200 were captured by Castro's soldiers. More than 100 exiles had been killed in the fighting, while Castro's losses were estimated at more than 3000 dead and wounded. In December 1962 Castro released 1179 prisoners in return for $50 million in U.S. medical supplies and other goods.

The Bay of Pigs invasion was a major embarrassment for the new Kennedy administration. Kennedy publicly acknowledged the U.S. role in the operation and took full responsibility for its failure. In the invasion's aftermath, he revived the PRESIDENT'S FOREIGN INTELLIGENCE ADVISORY BOARD, the civilian oversight panel on intelligence activities, and in September 1961 announced the retirement of CIA director ALLEN W. DULLES. Students of the Bay of Pigs episode continue to debate whether the loss of suprise and Kennedy's second-air-strike cancellation were decisive factors in the operation's ill-fated outcome.

The Bay of Pigs experience tempered the inclination of U.S. policymakers to resort to large-scale covert actions. The debacle damaged U.S. credibility and standing throughout Latin America while strengthening Castro's position at home and abroad. The Cuban dictator's ties with the Communist bloc grew tighter. Within 18 months, the United States and Soviet Union would face off in the CUBAN MISSILE CRISIS over the presence of Soviet nuclear missiles on the island.

BAYARD, THOMAS FRANCIS (1828–1898) U.S. senator, secretary of state, and diplomat. Born in Wilmington, Delaware, to one of the state's most prominent families, Bayard never attended college. He read law, was admitted to the Delaware bar in 1851, and went into practice. His first experience in public office was as U.S. attorney for his native state from 1853 to 1854. Elected as a Democrat to the U.S. Senate from Delaware in 1869, Bayard served until 1885. He was a member of the electoral commission of 1877 that decided the contested 1876 presidential election between Republican RUTHERFORD B. HAYES and Democrat Samuel J. Tilden in Hayes's favor. An unsuccessful candidate for the Democratic presidential nomination in 1880 and 1884, Bayard was named secretary of state in 1885 by President GROVER CLEVELAND.

Three major diplomatic issues confronted Bayard during his four-year term, none of which he was able to resolve. The troublesome North Atlantic FISHERIES QUESTION, a perennial source of Anglo-American conflict, surfaced anew with the expiration in 1885 of treaty clauses governing American fishermen's access to waters off Canada. The secretary of state's conciliatory approach resulted in the BAYARD-CHAMBERLAIN TREATY (1888), which a partisan Republican Senate rejected on grounds it surrendered U.S. rights and proposed lowering tariffs on Canadian fish products. The other issues emerged in the Pacific. Bayard was unable to secure a settlement either of the BERING SEA DISPUTE over pelagic sealing or

of conflicting U.S.-British-German interests in SAMOA.

With Cleveland's return to the White House in 1893, Bayard was appointed ambassador to Great Britain, becoming the first American ever to hold this higher diplomatic rank. (From its inception until the Cleveland administration decision to upgrade America's diplomatic missions, the United States had posted ministers rather than ambassadors overseas.) At London Bayard took a restrained stand during the VENEZUELA BOUNDARY DISPUTE. His speeches deriding tariff walls and advocating free trade led to his censure by the House of Representatives in 1896. He returned to the United States the following year and retired from public life to Massachusetts.

BAYARD-CHAMBERLAIN TREATY (1888) Abortive Anglo-American agreement negotiated as a resolution of the FISHERIES QUESTION. The long-standing dispute between Washington and London over the extent of American fishing liberties in Canadian territorial waters recurred in 1885 when for domestic political reasons the U.S. government terminated the fisheries clause of the TREATY OF WASHINGTON (1871). U.S. fishing privileges thus reverted to what they had been under the CONVENTION of 1818. American resentment was aroused when Canadian authorities, enforcing a narrow interpretation of the 1818 agreement, began seizing American fishing craft for technical violations of regulations governing the North Atlantic fisheries. Congress in 1887 passed a measure authorizing President GROVER CLEVELAND to retaliate by suspending Canada's trading privileges in America.

The threat to Anglo-American relations posed by the fisheries controversy induced the United States and Great Britain to negotiate a settlement of the issue by a joint commission. Secretary of State THOMAS F. BAYARD headed the U.S. commissioners and Colonial Secretary Joseph Chamberlain led the British representatives who convened in Washington, D.C., in November 1887. They concluded a compromise fisheries treaty on February 15, 1888. The Bayard-Chamberlain agreement arranged for an extension of Canadian fishing grounds eligible to American fishermen and promised further concessions if the United States lifted tariff duties on Canadian fish. In a vote driven by partisan political considerations, a Republican majority in the Senate rejected the new treaty on August 21, 1888, foiling the Democratic Cleveland administration's bid at a final resolution of the fisheries question. Nevertheless, Bayard and Chamberlain during their negotiations also had agreed on a two-year working arrangement that, pending ratification of the treaty, would allow Americans to continue fishing in Canadian waters by paying a licensing fee. In the absence of a treaty, this arrangement, renewed biennially, governed use of the Canadian fisheries until 1912, when a permanent settlement of the dispute was achieved by international arbitration.

BEAR FLAG REVOLT (1846) Rebellion against Mexican rule by American settlers in California's Sacramento Valley. In the decade leading up to the MEXICAN WAR (1846–1848), increasing numbers of Americans migrated to California, then a Mexican province. Unlike their counterparts to the south, who largely merged into the local society, American settlers in north central California formed a separate community. Mutual suspicions and tensions between the settlers and Mexican authorities came to a head in 1846 against a backdrop of worsening relations between the United States and Mexico. On June 14, 1846, settlers under William B. Ide seized the town of Sonoma and declared the Sacramento area the independent Republic of California. Their flag, a grizzly bear facing a red star, gave the revolt its familiar name. The rebellion was supported by American explorer JOHN C. FREMONT, whom the War Department had dispatched to California the year before as the leader of a 60-man armed exploring expedition. On July 5 Fremont was selected to head the new republic. Meanwhile, the May outbreak of hostilities between the United States and Mexico had brought U.S. Commodore John D. Sloat with his naval command to the coast off Monterey. Sloat put forces ashore on July 7 and proclaimed California a part of the United States. On July 9 the Americans at Sonoma replaced the Bear Flag with the Stars and Stripes. Shortly thereafter Sloat gave up command to Commodore Robert F. Stockton, who joined with Fremont to establish U. S. authority over the rest of the province by the end of 1846.

BEIJING SUMMIT (1984) Discussions between President RONALD W. REAGAN and the top Communist Chinese leadership held during Reagan's stay in the People's Republic of China April 26 to May 1. The China journey was the staunchly anti-Communist American president's first visit to a Communist country and reciprocated Premier Zhao Ziyang's January 1984 trip to the WASHINGTON SUMMIT. In talks with "Supreme Leader" Deng Xiaoping, Premier Zhao, and other high-level officials, Reagan maintained progress toward improved U.S. relations with China. On the summit's eve, the American president had called the establishment of diplomatic ties between the two countries in January 1979 one of the critical developments in U.S. foreign affairs since WORLD WAR II. Throughout the visit Reagan stressed vital U.S. strategic and commercial interests at stake in the Pacific that would be advanced by friendship with Beijing. He also restated American readiness to support Deng's program of economic modernization with capital investment and technology.

Chinese television twice censored remarks by the president praising capitalism and condemning adventurist Soviet foreign policy. Reagan reminded his hosts of the need for friendly Sino-American links to oppose the Moscow military threat. Premier Zhao responded with strong criticism of the Reagan administration foreign policy record, charging U.S. policies had fanned conflicts in Central America and left the Middle East deadlocked. Raising the sensitive issue of Taiwan, Chinese leaders indicated U.S. arms sales to the island nation and continuing contacts between Washington and Taipei remained the major obstacles to the strengthening of the U.S.-Chinese relationship. While reaffirming the long-standing U.S. friendship with the Taiwanese, Reagan described the issue of reunification of Taiwan and the mainland as an internal Chinese matter. During the summit, the leaders concluded three agreements: a pact renewing cultural and scientific exchanges; a tax treaty; and a long-awaited accord on the cooperative development of nuclear power.

BEMIS, SAMUEL FLAGG (1891–1973) Venerated American diplomatic historian and two-time recipient of the Pulitzer Prize.

Born in Worcester, Massachusetts, he attended Clark University, where he earned a bachelor's degree in 1912 and a master's in 1913. Bemis went on to Harvard University to complete a second master's in 1915 and his doctorate in 1916. He held several college teaching positions before joining the history faculty at Yale in 1935. Following his retirement in 1963, he continued his association with the school as professor emeritus until his death in 1973.

A leading authority on U.S. diplomatic history, he wrote prolifically in the field. His book *The Diplomacy of the American Revolution* (1935) remains the classic study of the period. He won the Pulitzer Prize for history in 1927 for the work *Pinckney's Treaty: A Study of America's Advantages from Europe's Distress* (1926). His second Pulitzer, for biography, was awarded in 1950 for *John Quincy Adams and the Foundations of American Foreign Policy* (1949). The historian's other books included *Jay's Treaty: A Study in Commerce and Diplomacy* (1923), *A Diplomatic History of the United States* (1936), *The Latin American Policy of the United States* (1942), and *American Foreign Policy and the Blessings of Liberty, and Other Essays* (1962).

BERING SEA DISPUTE International controversy beginning in the 1880s concerning pelagic sealing, or open-sea seal hunting, in the North Pacific. The sealing industry in the Bering Sea centered on the Pribilof Islands, where the fur seal herd gathered each year to breed. The United States had acquired the islands from Russia in the ALASKA PURCHASE (1867). In 1870 Congress granted the private Alaska Commercial Company exclusive right to hunt a regulated number of seals on the Pribilofs for 20 years. The prosperous North Pacific sealing attracted Canadian, European, and Japanese open-sea hunters, who after 1880 defied the monopoly and began preying on seals in the ocean beyond America's three-mile jurisdictional limit. The surge in commercial pelagic sealing threatened to wipe out the herd.

To protect the fur seals and uphold the American monopoly, U.S. Treasury Department vessels in August 1886 began to seize ships in the vicinity of the Pribilofs engaged in ocean hunting and to arrest their crews. The American action, defended officially on grounds the Bering Sea was *mare clausum*, or closed to foreign ships, touched off a long diplomatic dispute. Canada and Great Britain protested, insisting the United States had no right either to close the sea or to grab their ships beyond a three-mile limit in Alaskan waters. Continued sealing on the high seas led Congress in March 1889 to declare U.S. dominion over the Bering Sea and to empower the president to take steps necessary to stop foreign seal hunters. Secretary of State JAMES G. BLAINE contended the United States held a preeminent right over the seals, purportedly inherited from Russia through the Alaska acquisition. Great Britain denied Blaine's claim and warned America against violating established international principles of FREEDOM OF THE SEAS.

An Anglo-American treaty signed February 29, 1892, submitted the issue to an international arbitration tribunal. The commission on August 15, 1893, ruled against the United States on all major points, denying any American right of jurisdiction in the Bering Sea and affirming the freedom of the seas in peacetime. The U.S. government was ordered to pay damages to the British and Canadians for the shipping seizures. The tribunal decision at the same time banned pelagic sealing in a 60-mile zone around the Pribilof Islands and prohibited it for part of the year in waters north of the 35th parallel and east of the 180th meridian. Despite such regulations, large-scale slaughter continued and threatened the northern herd with extinction.

The United States, Great Britain, Russia, and Japan settled the long-festering dispute through the North Pacific Sealing Convention signed in July 1911 in Washington. The convention outlawed ocean seal hunting above the 30th parallel, established a U.S. monopoly of the Pribilof catch, and guaranteed Britain and Japan a percentage of the seal skins harvested in return for their withdrawal from pelagic sealing in the area. Japan, contending the seal herds were damaging important North Pacific fisheries, abrogated the convention in October 1940. The other signatories continued to abide by its terms. In 1957 the United States, Canada, the Soviet Union, and Japan concluded a new and revised convention prohibiting pelagic sealing in the North Pacific.

BERLE, ADOLF AUGUSTUS, JR. (1895–1971) American lawyer, teacher, diplomat, and public official. The Boston native attended Harvard University, earning a bachelor's degree in 1913 and a master's the following year. He graduated from Harvard Law School in 1916. After practicing law briefly in Boston, he joined the Army in 1917 as a private and subsequently became an intelligence officer. Berle was a member of the U.S. delegation to the PARIS PEACE CONFERENCE (1919) that negotiated the TREATY OF VERSAILLES (1919) ending WORLD WAR I. In 1919 he launched a successful career as a corporate lawyer in New York and, starting in 1927, also taught at Columbia Law School.

Berle plunged into public affairs in 1932 as an original member of Democratic presidential candidate FRANKLIN D. ROOSEVELT's so-called Brains Trust, the group of experts recruited to advise the nominee on means of attacking the economic crisis of the Great Depression. After Roosevelt's landslide victory, Berle became counsel for the Reconstruction Finance Corporation, the agency responsible for reforming the nation's banks, railroads, and insurance companies. He remained through the mid-1930s a regular consultant to the president on economic policy. Named assistant secretary of state for Latin American affairs by Roosevelt in 1938, Berle helped execute the administration's GOOD NEIGHBOR POLICY, attended several Pan-American conferences, and drafted the president's position paper on wartime relations with Latin America during WORLD WAR II. He was appointed ambassador to Brazil in 1945. During his year in the post, he represented the United States at the inter-American Mexico City Conference (1945) where he took part in drafting the ACT OF CHAPULTEPEC on Western Hemisphere security. Berle ended a 15-year hiatus from government service in 1960, when he accepted the invitation of President-elect JOHN F. KENNEDY to head a task force to advise the incoming administration on Latin American policy. In this role, Berle joined those recommending U.S. support of the disastrous BAY OF PIGS INVASION (1961) of Cuba to unseat Communist leader Fidel Castro. He was also an architect of the ALLIANCE FOR PROGRESS, Kennedy's social and economic development program for Latin America. From 1961 until his death, Berle wrote, taught, and practiced law in New York.

BERLIN AIRLIFT (1948–1949) Western air supply operation mounted to counter a Soviet blockade of Berlin. At the end of WORLD WAR II in 1945, major Allied powers the United States, Great Britain, France, and the Soviet Union each assumed responsibility for an occupation zone in defeated Germany. The German capital of Berlin, located in the Soviet zone, similarly was divided into four parts with each of the Allies receiving control over a sector. The Western nations had access to the city by both land and air. The occupying powers established an ALLIED CONTROL COUNCIL for the joint administration of their four zones and referred the question of Germany's future status to a COUNCIL OF FOREIGN MINISTERS. The Western allies were committed to a reunified democratic Germany, while the USSR moved to impose a Communist regime in its zone. The West opposed Moscow's efforts to formalize its hegemony over Eastern Europe. By 1947, the four-power discussions had broken down amid mounting COLD WAR confrontation between the Soviet Union and the Western nations. Protesting the separate Western SIX-NATION CONFERENCE ON GERMANY, the Soviet representative, in March 1948, withdrew from the Allied Control Council and the body ceased to function.

On June 7, 1948, the Western powers announced their intention, in the face of Soviet intransigence, to proceed with plans to integrate their three zones into a German state. The Soviet Union denounced the action as a violation of four-nation control over occupied Germany. On June 24, the Communist power imposed a blockade on all land traffic through its zone to Berlin, seeking to drive the Western allies from the city. While deciding against a direct challenge to the blockade, the Western powers began a massive airlift to resupply the isolated city. They also imposed economic countermeasures on the Soviet zone. Over the next 11 months hundreds of U.S. and British flights daily brought coal, food, and other supplies to western Berlin. The airlift became a symbol of Western resolve to stand firm against Communist aggression. Apparently concluding the blockade had been unsuccessful, the Soviets lifted it on May 12, 1949, in return for a resumption of four-power negotiations on Germany. These discussions again ended in stalemate and Berlin remained a key confrontation point throughout the Cold War. The airlift, which officially ended September 30, 1949, involved more than 275,000 flights carrying over 2.3 million tons of supplies. During the operation 31 Americans died in 12 accidental crashes.

See also BERLIN CRISIS.

BERLIN CONFERENCE (1954) Meeting of the foreign ministers of the United States, Great Britain, France, and Soviet Union in Berlin from January 25 to February 18, 1954. In April 1953 the Soviet Union proposed a five-nation conference of the three major Western powers, itself, and Communist China to address pressing international issues and reduce COLD WAR tensions. The U.S. policy of not recognizing the Chinese Communist government led the Eisenhower administration to reject the Soviet initiative. The U.S., British, and French governments instead suggested a four-power gathering on the still unresolved post–WORLD WAR II status of Germany and Austria. In November 1953 the USSR, desiring to halt Western moves to rearm West Germany and integrate it into NATO's military command, acceded to a four-power parley and called for a meeting of foreign ministers in Berlin. The Soviet government also made clear its intention to press for a subsequent five-power gathering. The three Western allies accepted the Soviet proposal for a four-power meeting during their December 1953 BERMUDA CONFERENCE.

The Berlin Conference marked the first official high-level East-West contacts since the sixth and final meeting of the COUNCIL OF FOREIGN MINISTERS in 1949. The discussions among U.S. Secretary of State JOHN FOSTER DULLES, British Foreign Secretary Anthony Eden, French Foreign Minister Georges Bidault, and Soviet Foreign Minister Vyacheslav Molotov made no progress on resolving fundamental East-West differences over Germany and Eastern Europe. Agreement was reached on holding a multilateral gathering to negotiate a final settlement of the KOREAN WAR, halted by an armistice in July 1953, and to address the Communist Vietnamese insurgency in French Indochina. The GENEVA CONFERENCE convened in April 1954.

BERLIN CRISIS (1958–1962) Protracted East-West confrontation over the German city. Following the Allied victory over Germany in WORLD WAR II, the United States, Great Britain, France, and the Soviet Union each assumed responsibility for an occupation zone in the defeated nation. Each also was given control over a sector in Berlin, the historic German capital located in the Soviet zone. By the late 1940s, negotiations among the former wartime allies over the future political disposition of Germany had broken down amid rising COLD WAR tensions. In 1948 the Western powers mounted the BERLIN AIRLIFT, overcoming a Soviet blockade of the city and making clear their intention to retain their sectors in West Berlin, which became a symbolic outpost of freedom behind the IRON CURTAIN. The effective division of Germany was realized the following year when the Western nations joined their occupation zones to form the democratic Federal Republic of Germany (West Germany) and the Soviet Union installed the Communist German Democratic Republic (East Germany) in its zone. Neither side recognized the other German state and the unresolved question of Germany's formal postwar status remained at the center of East-West struggle throughout the 1950s.

Sporadic negotiations over Germany remained stalemated. The Soviet Union adamantly opposed West Germany's integration into the Western security alliance NATO in 1955. The West refused to accept Soviet hegemony over Eastern Europe, including East Germany, and defended NATO as necessary to halt further Communist expansion. In November 1958 Soviet Premier Nikita S. Khrushchev, seeking to force Western recognition of the East German regime and its control over Berlin, precipitated an international crisis. The Soviet leader informed the Western powers that if a four-way agreement on Berlin were not reached within six months, the USSR would conclude its own separate treaty on the city with East Germany. The West rejected Khrushchev's ultimatum and stressed it would not acknowledge any East German authority over Berlin. A Western proposal for a four-power foreign ministers conference on Germany was accepted by the Soviets, in effect extending their earlier deadline for a settlement. When the conference, held at Geneva from May 11 to August 5, 1959, ended in deadlock, President DWIGHT D. EISENHOWER invited Khrushchev to the United States for direct talks on Germany and Berlin. At the September 1959 CAMP DAVID SUMMIT, Khrushchev agreed not to impose any time limits on negotiations concerning Germany and Eisenhower consented to a four-power summit in Paris the next year.

The May 1960 PARIS SUMMIT broke up after one session over the U-2 INCIDENT and the issue of Germany was never addressed. East-West tensions over Berlin again flared as growing numbers of refugees fled from East Germany into the western part of the city. At the June 1961 VIENNA SUMMIT, Khrushchev issued a new ultimatum, warning President JOHN F. KENNEDY that if a Berlin settlement was not achieved by the end of the year, then the USSR would sign a separate agreement with East Germany. Believing Khrushchev's ultimate intention was to force the Western allies from Berlin, Kennedy declared America's readiness to defend the city, increasing the U.S. garrison there and calling reserve military units to active duty. On August 13, 1961, the Soviets began construction of the BERLIN WALL between East and West Berlin to halt the steady exodus of East Germans into the Western sector. The West protested but did not physically challenge the barrier. Kennedy sent retired General LUCIUS D. CLAY, who had overseen the Berlin Airlift, to the city to communicate the U.S. commitment to West Berlin. In September 1961 the Soviets agreed to delay indefinitely their latest deadline in return for U.S. assurances of further negotiations on Berlin. While these discussions proved fruitless, the Soviets refrained from issuing further ultimatums and the Berlin Crisis abated by the end of 1962. East-West confrontation

over the city eased following the 1971 QUADRIPARTITE AGREEMENT ON BERLIN.

See also FINAL SETTLEMENT WITH RESPECT TO GERMANY TREATY, KENNEDY BERLIN SPEECH.

BERLIN KOMMANDATURA See **ALLIED CONTROL COUNCIL**.

BERLIN, TREATY OF (1889) Treaty completed June 14, 1889, among the United States, Germany, and Great Britain to settle their competition over SAMOA. Also called the General Act of Berlin, it established a three-nation protectorate over the Samoan islands, located in the south-central Pacific, about midway between Hawaii and Australia. The U.S.-sponsored WILKES EXPEDITION explored Samoa in 1839, returning with descriptions of the ideal harbor of Pago Pago on the island of Tutuila. American interest in the archipelago emerged after the Civil War and focused on Pago Pago, which was prized both as a coaling station for ships plying the growing South Pacific trade and as a possible naval base. By 1870 the United States was maneuvering for position in Samoa with Germany and Great Britain, both of which had established strong commercial footholds in the islands. To preempt expanding European influence, U.S. Navy Commander Richard W. Meade in 1872 made an unauthorized treaty with a Samoan chief on Tutuila that gave the United States exclusive control of Pago Pago. Opposition to U.S. overseas expansion prevailed in the Senate, which never approved the pact.

The United States signed a friendship treaty with leading Samoan chiefs in 1878 that granted America the right to establish a naval station at Pago Pago. The next year Germany and Great Britain countered by completing separate Samoan treaties securing similar naval privileges. A U.S.-German-British agreement struck in 1879 to exercise joint control of Samoa's government fell apart over German attempts to gain political advantage in the islands. In the summer of 1887, at the invitation of Secretary of State THOMAS F. BAYARD, Great Britain and Germany attended a three-power conference in Washington to deal with the Samoan controversy.

As the leading commercial force in the islands, Germany sought the dominant political role. Great Britain supported Germany's position in return for a promise of German concessions elsewhere in the South Pacific and Africa. When the United States refused Germany's demand, proposed equal three-way influence, and insisted on Samoan autonomy, the meeting ended without a settlement. Tensions mounted in 1888 after Germany declared war on Samoan King Malietoa, deported him from Upolu Island, and installed a pro-German native government. The United States and Great Britain responded by encouraging rebel chief Mataafa's uprising against the German-backed regime. By year's end, warships of the three countries were positioned at a standoff in Apia Harbor. Anti-German feelings swept the United States as congressional expansionists called for an aggressive U.S. stance, warning that Germany's policies threatened American strategic interests in the South Pacific.

Looming conflict led German Chancellor Otto von Bismarck to invite the United States and Great Britain to Berlin to renew the negotiations that had stalled at Washington in 1887. Delegates convened in late April 1889, a month after a deadly hurricane had devastated Apia and temporarily overshadowed the Samoa crisis. Six weeks later the three powers concluded the Berlin pact. It established tripartite control over the islands and arranged for restored native rule and nominal Samoan independence. The U.S. Senate approved the treaty over the objections of members who opposed a break in the long-standing American tradition of avoiding overseas political entanglements. The protectorate proved unworkable and was ended by the CONVENTION of 1899, which partitioned Samoa between the United States and Germany.

BERLIN, TREATY OF (1921) Agreement that formally ended hostilities between the United States and Germany after WORLD WAR I. Following the rejection of the TREATY OF VERSAILLES (1919) for a last time by the U.S. Senate in March 1920, America technically was still at war with Germany and Austria-Hungary, almost a year and one-half after the November 1918 armistice that had halted the fighting. Congress on May 20, 1920, passed a joint resolution declaring hostilities with the Central Powers at an end. The measure was vetoed by President

WOODROW WILSON, who remained bitter following his unsuccessful fight to gain ratification without reservations of the Versailles Treaty and accompanying LEAGUE OF NATIONS Covenant that constituted its first part. Wilson would not concede that the disapproval of his coveted league was final. He looked toward the coming presidential election as a national referendum on the issue of U.S. membership in the proposed multinational peacekeeping body. The landslide victory of Republican candidate WARREN G. HARDING in the 1920 election amounted to a final verdict against the league. After taking office Harding announced that the United States would not enter the international organization.

On June 2, 1921, Harding approved a joint congressional resolution proclaiming the war with the Central Powers ended. The measure reserved to the United States all rights and privileges secured by the victorious Allied nations under the Versailles and associated peace settlements. There was, however, no international agreement obliging the German government to respect the U.S. claim. On the basis of the congressional resolution, the Harding administration concluded a peace treaty with Germany at Berlin on August 25, 1921. The agreement specified that while the United States was not a party to the Versailles Treaty, it retained all rights and advantages accorded to it under the pact's terms. The Berlin settlement further made clear that the United States was not bound by the Versailles provisions pertaining to the League of Nations. Before the end of August, the United States also signed separate peace treaties with Austria and Hungary. The Senate gave prompt approval to all three pacts.

BERLIN WALL Barrier built by Communist East Germany beginning in August 1961 that cut off East Berlin from West Berlin and divided the city. At the VIENNA SUMMIT in June 1961, Soviet Premier Nikita S. Khrushchev fanned the BERLIN CRISIS by renewing a demand first made in 1958 that the United States, Great Britain, and France end their post–WORLD WAR II occupation of West Berlin. The Soviet leader contended long-standing unwillingness by the Western powers to recognize the East German regime continued to block a final peace settlement 16 years after the war. Khrushchev threatened to complete a separate peace treaty with East Germany by year's end that would abrogate the Western right of access to Berlin. President JOHN F. KENNEDY vowed the United States and its allies would uphold their postwar commitments in Germany. After the Vienna parley, he suggested the Soviets' real intention was to force the Western powers from Berlin. Kennedy called Khrushchev's threats a crucial test of the Western community's resolve and insisted the United States would not be driven from West Berlin.

An increasing stream of East German refugees into West Berlin coincided with the growing crisis atmosphere. More than 3 million East Germans had fled Communist rule and economic hardship since 1949. The rising refugee tide in the summer of 1961 embarrassed the Soviet Union and its East German client and represented a damaging drain of skilled workers that added to East Germany's worsening economic problems. On August 13, the East German regime, at the instigation of the Soviets, suddenly began to erect and militarily fortify a barbed-wire barricade between East and West Berlin. Within days construction started on the 28-mile-long concrete barrier that became known as the Berlin Wall. The barricade virtually halted the refugee exodus, although in years to come hundreds of East Germans seeking freedom would risk their lives attempting to scale over, tunnel under, or crash through the heavily guarded barrier. The Communists soon extended the wall by raising barbed-wire barriers along the entire East German–West German border. The United States and its European allies protested the sealing off of East Berlin but, caught off guard, made no attempt to tear down the wall. Warning the Soviets against any attempt to block Western access to the city, Kennedy bolstered the 5000-man U.S. garrison in West Berlin with 1500 more troops. At the same time he called for overall increases in American and NATO forces. The Soviets responded with a threat of military mobilization. The crisis mood eased gradually after Khrushchev backed off his Berlin ultimatum in October 1961.

The Berlin Wall became a symbol of the postwar division of Europe and of the long East-West COLD WAR struggle. The Western alliance for a generation proclaimed the barrier a monument to communism's social and economic failures and a stark reminder of Soviet-bloc tyranny. The collapse of the Berlin Wall began in late 1989 under the weight of sudden, remarkable political liberalization throughout Eastern Europe. On November 9 the East German government opened the wall, spurring dramatic changes that resulted in German reunification in October 1990.

BERMUDA CONFERENCE (1953) Meeting of U.S., British, and French heads of government at the British possession of Bermuda from December 4 to 7, 1953. The conference, sought by new U.S. President DWIGHT D. EISENHOWER as a vehicle for establishing a close working relationship with the leaders of principal U.S. allies Great Britain and France, originally had been scheduled for June 1953. It was postponed until December after a new French government came to power and British Prime Minister Winston Churchill became ill. Subjects discussed by Eisenhower, Churchill, and French Premier Joseph Laniel included the integration of West Germany into the Western NATO security alliance, the Communist Viet Minh insurgency in French Indochina, British control of the Suez Canal, and the recently ended KOREAN WAR. There was general agreement on the need to maintain Western defenses against the threat posed by COLD WAR adversary the Soviet Union. The three leaders decided to accept a Soviet invitation made November 26 for a four-power meeting of foreign ministers. The ensuing BERLIN CONFERENCE convened in January 1954. Eisenhower also briefed Churchill and Laniel on his ATOMS FOR PEACE proposal, which he presented to the UNITED NATIONS in New York City on December 8, 1953.

BERN CONFERENCE See **UNIVERSAL POSTAL UNION**.

BERN UNION See **WORLD INTELLECTUAL PROPERTY ORGANIZATION**.

BIDLACK'S TREATY See **CLAYTON-BULWER TREATY**.

BIG FIVE Informal name given to the United States, Great Britain, France, the Soviet Union, and China in the latter stages of WORLD WAR II. As the major international powers, the wartime BIG FOUR allies, joined by newly liberated France, took the lead in planning for the postwar world. The Big Five oversaw formation of the UNITED NATIONS in 1945 and became the five permanent members on the organization's pivotal Security Council. The catchphrase faded from use by the late 1940s as mounting COLD WAR tensions and the victorious Communist revolution in China brought an end to cooperation among the five nations.

BIG FOUR Catchphrase used in connection with both WORLD WAR I and WORLD WAR II to describe groups of Allied nations and their leaders. At the PARIS PEACE CONFERENCE (1919) following WORLD WAR I, the informal name "Big Four" was given to U.S. President WOODROW WILSON, British Prime Minister David Lloyd George, French Premier Georges Clemenceau, and Italian Premier Vittorio Orlando. As the heads of the four major powers at the gathering, they met as a separate body, known as the COUNCIL OF FOUR, to direct negotiations. During World War II, the term Big Four was applied to the United States, Great Britain, Soviet Union, and China as the principal Allied nations involved in the struggle against the Axis powers. The Big Three referred either to the United States, Great Britain, and Soviet Union or to their respective leaders President FRANKLIN D. ROOSEVELT, Prime Minister Winston Churchill, and Premier Joseph Stalin.

BIG STICK Catchphrase associated with THEODORE ROOSEVELT that denotes a policy of using the threat of force to help secure diplomatic goals. The expression was derived, according to Roosevelt, from a West African proverb that he first quoted in 1900 and thereafter used repeatedly in speeches during his presidency: "Speak softly and carry a big stick; you will go far." Anti-imperialist critics viewed the big stick image as a symbol of a bullying attitude on the part of the United States in its relations with Latin American neighbors. For his part, Roosevelt insisted that the Big Stick policy implied maintaining American military strength and overall resolve to safeguard national interests and honor wherever in the world they might come under challenge. His administration, he contended, affixed equal value

on the need for soft speech, by which he meant treating other nations respectfully and not committing offenses against them. The threat of U.S. intervention contained in the ROOSEVELT COROLLARY (1904) and the dispatch of the GREAT WHITE FLEET in 1907 marked more obvious instances of Big Stick diplomacy at work.

BIG THREE See **BIG FOUR**.

BILDERBERG CONFERENCE Three-day parley held annually, in great secrecy, among the power elite of Western Europe and North America to discuss major political and economic issues confronting the Western capitalist democracies. Conference members, traditionally numbering about 100 individuals in any given year, include heads of banks, industrialists, statesmen, ambassadors, government ministers, and scholars, all of whom attend the exclusive gathering by invitation. The meeting takes its name from the Bilderberg Hotel in Oosterbeek, Holland, site of the first conference in 1954. The idea for the gathering was conceived in the early 1950s by Polish political philosopher Dr. Joseph Retinger and American diplomat GEORGE W. BALL. They approached Prince Bernhard of Holland with a proposal that he chair a series of meetings of influential financial, political, and academic leaders that would help define the objectives of the ATLANTIC COMMUNITY. Participants were to come from Western Europe, America, and Canada only. Prince Bernhard agreed. Within months a small executive office had been set up at The Hague and steering committees established on both sides of the Atlantic. The committees were authorized to select conference participants and work out the discussion topics for each meeting. Since the inaugural parley in 1954, the Bilderberg group has met once a year in various out-of-the-way locations, except for 1976, when disclosure of Prince Bernhard's involvement in the LOCKHEED SCANDAL prompted embarrassed organizers to shelve the conference. The prince resigned his chairmanship. The conference's operating expenses are covered by the contributions of wealthy participants or their companies.

BIOLOGICAL WEAPONS CONVENTION (1972) International agreement barring biological weapons. The treaty, officially titled the Convention on the Prohibition of the Development, Production, and Stockpiling of Bacteriological (Biological) and Toxin Weapons and on their Destruction, was completed in 1971 by the CONFERENCE OF THE COMMITTEE ON DISARMAMENT meeting in Geneva, Switzerland, and approved by the UNITED NATIONS General Assembly the same year. Some 70 nations signed the convention in ceremonies in Washington, London, and Moscow on April 10, 1972. It was ratified by the U.S. Senate in December 1974 and signed by President GERALD R. FORD on January 22, 1975. The treaty, which supplemented the 1925 GENEVA PROTOCOL outlawing the use of chemical and biological weapons in war, prohibited any further development of biological weapons and committed each signatory nation, within nine months, to destroy or divert to peaceful purposes existing biological agents and related facilities and equipment. The convention represented the first international attempt to eliminate an entire class of weapons.

BITBURG INCIDENT (1985) Controversial visit by President RONALD W. REAGAN to a German military cemetery. The episode sparked a political uproar in the United States that focused attention on Nazi atrocities committed during WORLD WAR II. In January 1985 the president announced plans for a European trip in the spring both to commemorate the 40th anniversary of the Allied victory over Nazi Germany and to celebrate the success of the postwar Western alliance. On April 11 the White House revealed that on his state visit to West Germany Reagan planned to lay a wreath at the military cemetery in Bitburg for German soldiers.

The scheduled stop, intended to symbolize reconciliation since 1945 between former enemies and to emphasize West Germany's integral membership in the postwar alliance, quickly provoked a strong emotional reaction when it was learned that Bitburg cemetery contained the graves of some 50 soldiers of the Waffen SS, the fighting arm of Hitler's elite troops. Under Hitler, the SS had run the Nazi concentration camps where six million Jews were exterminated in the Holocaust. The SS also had massacred American prisoners of war. The revelation about the graves brought immediate protest from Holocaust sur-

vivors, Jewish organizations, and U.S. veterans' groups, all of whom implored Reagan to cancel the Bitburg ceremony. Congress joined the protest shortly before the president's trip was to begin. The Senate passed a resolution asking Reagan to change his plans, suggesting he visit a symbol of German democracy rather than Bitburg. A majority of the members of the House of Representatives sent a letter to West German Chancellor Helmut Kohl suggesting that the wreath laying threatened to engender enduring ill-will in America. They urged his government to find some alternative, appropriate site for Reagan to pay respect to the German people.

Despite the storm of domestic criticism, which had intensified rather than abated following Reagan's announcement that he also would visit a memorial to Holocaust victims at the Bergen-Belsen concentration camp enroute to Bitburg, the president refused to relent on the graveside ceremony. On May 5 the American president and West German chancellor visited Bergen-Belsen and Bitburg. Reagan and Kohl spent only a few minutes at the cemetery laying wreaths and saved their remarks for a nearby U.S. Air Force base. In the United States nationwide demonstrations were held in protest of the Bitburg visit, which was deplored, as well, by many senior Israeli political figures. The cemetery controversy overshadowed both the GROUP OF 7 economic summit at Bonn that Reagan had attended in the days before the Bitburg stop and the president's speech to the European Parliament at Strasbourg, France, on May 8, the anniversary date of Allied victory in Europe.

BIZONIA See **ALLIED CONTROL COUNCIL.**

BLACK HAWK WAR (1832) Brief war waged between the United States and the Sauk and Fox Indian tribes under the Sauk chief Black Hawk. The conflict stemmed from a forced cession of Sauk and Fox areas in Illinois to the United States under a disputed 1804 treaty. The Indians remained on the lands until forcibly driven west of the Mississippi in 1831. The following year Black Hawk led the tribes back to reclaim the Illinois territory and was confronted by a combined force of U.S. troops and volunteer militia. General Henry Atkinson pursued the Sauk and Fox into present-day Wisconsin and routed them in August 1832 at the Battle of Bad Axe River. The U.S. victory closed out the Indian possession of lands in the Illinois region.

See also MAP 1.

BLACK, JEREMIAH SULLIVAN (1810–1883) Jurist and U.S. secretary of state. Black was born in Somerset County in Pennsylvania, where he was admitted to the bar in 1830 and began a law practice. His legal abilities and political ties to Jacksonian Democrats brought him state judicial appointments. He was named deputy attorney general for the county in 1831. Black served as a common pleas court judge from 1842 until his election in 1851 to the Pennsylvania Supreme Court. After six years on the state's top bench, the last three as chief justice, Black stepped down in 1857 to accept appointment by Democratic President JAMES BUCHANAN, a fellow Pennsylvanian, as U.S. attorney general. Taking office amid the deepening sectional strife between North and South, he was confronted with difficult legal and constitutional problems stemming from the slavery issue. The greatest crisis was the prospect of imminent Southern secession following ABRAHAM LINCOLN's election as president in 1860. Black took the position that while the president could not coerce a seceding state to stay within the Union, he was constitutionally obligated to enforce federal laws and protect federal property. He urged Buchanan to bolster the garrisons in federal forts in the South as a precautionary measure. The president's failure to heed the attorney general's advice or to move decisively against secession brought the resignation of Secretary of State LEWIS CASS in December 1860.

Named immediately as Cass's replacement, Black entered the State Department just days before South Carolina seceded. His months in office were consumed by the secession crisis. On February 28, 1861, he instructed the principal U.S. diplomatic representatives in Europe to work to prevent recognition of the Confederacy by foreign powers. Black's tenure ended with the departure of the Buchanan administration on March 4, some five weeks before the start of the Civil War. Meanwhile, in early February, political adversaries of Black in the Senate had blocked confirmation of his nomination by Buchanan to the Supreme Court. He retired to Pennsylvania, where he resumed a law practice. He was appointed U.S. Supreme Court reporter in 1861. Black briefly reentered politics after the war as an adviser to President ANDREW JOHNSON on constitutional issues relating to Reconstruction. In 1877 he represented Democrat Samuel J. Tilden before the congressional Electoral Commission that decided the contested 1876 Hayes-Tilden presidential election in the Republican Hayes's favor.

BLACK WARRIOR AFFAIR (1854) Seizure of an American ship in Spanish colonial Cuba that caused a diplomatic uproar between the United States and Spain. The American merchant vessel *Black Warrior* had plied the coastal trade between New York City and Mobile, Alabama, since 1852. As it regularly stopped at Havana, Cuba, its owners had struck an informal agreement with Spanish port authorities that exempted the *Black Warrior* from the standard requirement of presenting a cargo manifest. When the American ship docked at Havana on February 28, 1854, Spanish officials broke from previous custom and demanded a manifest, which the vessel's captain was unable to produce. The *Black Warrior* was seized for violation of port regulations but restored to its owner by the end of March 1854 on payment of a $6000 fine.

Meanwhile in America the incident had drawn official U.S. government condemnation and excited a war clamor among southern Democratic expansionists in Congress who harbored ambitions of annexing Cuba from Spain and adding it to the Union as a slave state. President FRANKLIN PIERCE pledged to vindicate U.S. honor and win redress from Madrid for the conduct of the Havana authorities. Secretary of State WILLIAM L. MARCY directed U.S. Minister to Spain PIERRE SOULE to demand both an apology and an indemnity for the *Black Warrior* incident. The controversial Soule, an outspoken advocate of seizing Cuba as additional American slave soil, exceeded his instructions when, on April 8, he delivered the American demands to the Spanish foreign minister in the form of a 48-hour ultimatum. Spain ignored the ultimatum and

Marcy moved to rein in Soule. The affair was resolved in 1855 when the Pierce administration accepted a Spanish apology and reparation to the *Black Warrior*'s owners. The issue of America's expansionist designs on Cuba came to the fore with publication of the OSTEND MANIFESTO (1854), a report by three American diplomats, including Soule, urging the United States to take the island by force should Spain refuse to sell it.

BLAINE, JAMES GILLESPIE (1830–1893) National political figure, twice secretary of state. Born in Pennsylvania, Blaine graduated from Washington and Jefferson College in his native state in 1847. He taught school in Kentucky and Philadelphia until 1854. That year he settled near his wife's family in Augusta, Maine, purchasing an interest in the *Kennebec Journal* and joining the editorial staff of the *Portland Advertiser*. He entered politics as one of the founders of the Republican Party, serving as a delegate to the first national Republican convention in 1856. He won election to the Maine state legislature in 1859 and four years later entered the U.S. House of Representatives, where he was speaker from 1869 to 1875. Appointed in 1876 to fill a vacancy in the U.S. Senate, he held the seat until 1881. Opposition from the conservative "Stalwart" wing of the party, combined with Democratic accusations implicating him in a railroad graft scandal, deprived Blaine, leader of the "Half-Breed" faction, of the Republican presidential nomination in 1876. Four years later he again failed to capture the nomination, which instead went to fellow Half-Breed JAMES A. GARFIELD, who was elected president.

With Garfield's inauguration in 1881, Blaine became secretary of state. An apostle of PAN-AMERICANISM, he advocated closer U.S. trade and cultural ties with Latin America. To promote his goal he invited the Latin American republics to a proposed Pan-American Congress to be held in Washington, D.C. Blaine also sought to ensure U.S. control over any future transoceanic canal across Central America by attempting, without success, to gain British consent to modification of the CLAYTON-BULWER TREATY (1850). After Garfield was assassinated and Stalwart CHESTER A. ARTHUR became president in September 1881, Blaine resigned

from the cabinet, whereupon his successor, FREDERICK T. FRELINGHUYSEN, canceled plans for the Pan-American parley.

Nominated as the Republican presidential candidate in 1884, Blaine lost the election to Democrat GROVER CLEVELAND. The defeat notwithstanding, he remained party leader and was a chief influence behind the selection of BENJAMIN HARRISON as the Republican presidential candidate in 1888. When Harrison unseated Cleveland and took office in 1889, he appointed Blaine his secretary of state. In his second stint in the office, Blaine revived his Pan-American policy. He realized a long-delayed goal when he presided over the first PAN-AMERICAN CONFERENCE in Washington in late 1889. The gathering laid the groundwork for establishment of the BUREAU OF AMERICAN REPUBLICS. Looking to boost U.S. commerce in the Western Hemisphere, he promoted reciprocal tariff agreements with Latin American nations as authorized by the MCKINLEY TARIFF (1890). Concerned to protect the fur seal herds in Alaska's Pribilof Islands from poachers, he directed negotiation of an agreement with Great Britain that submitted the BERING SEA DISPUTE to international arbitration. U.S. interests in SAMOA were upheld when American, British, and German diplomats concluded the 1889 TREATY OF BERLIN establishing a three-way protectorate over the Pacific island group. Supporting America's rise as a nascent imperial power in the late 19th century, Blaine tried unsuccessfully to acquire naval stations in the Caribbean and Pacific and favored U.S. annexation of Hawaii. In declining health, he quit the cabinet in June 1892 and died in January 1893.

BOARD FOR INTERNATIONAL BROADCASTING See **RADIO FREE EUROPE**.

BOAT PEOPLE Term used to describe refugees who attempt to escape their native land by sea. The expression "boat people" was first applied to Vietnamese fleeing South Vietnam after the end of the VIETNAM WAR in 1975, when the victorious North united the country under a Communist government. Between 1976 and 1978, as the number of boat people slowly grew, the United States undertook several limited initiatives to admit refugees from its former ally.

In March 1978 the Vietnamese government began forcibly to expel the country's ethnic Chinese minority, expropriating their businesses as part of a drive to nationalize the economy. By the end of the year, tens of thousands of boat people were flooding refugee camps throughout Southeast Asia. The problem worsened after February 1979 when China initiated border hostilities with Vietnam over its invasion of Cambodia the previous December. Many local countries, overwhelmed by the volume, refused to allow additional boat people to land and the desperate plight of the refugees stranded at sea captured worldwide attention. Many thousands drowned, died of exposure, or were victimized by pirates. In June 1979, President JIMMY CARTER announced that America would double the number of Indochinese refugees it would accept by admitting 14,000 a month. The United States took an active role in the 65-nation Geneva Conference on Indochinese Refugees held the following month. Increasing international pressure on Vietnam succeeded in stemming the flow of boat people by the end of 1979.

The approximately 50,000 Haitians who made their way in makeshift ships to Florida's shores during the 1970s at times also were referred to as boat people. The federal government's position that the Haitians were fleeing economic poverty rather than political persecution disqualified them from admission as refugees under U.S. law. Many were detained pending deportation and most others became illegal aliens. An upsurge in Haitian boat people in the early 1980s led President RONALD W. REAGAN to issue an executive order on September 24, 1981, instructing the Coast Guard to interdict vessels carrying undocumented Haitians to the United States. Those Haitians already in America eventually were granted the right to stay under revised immigration statutes.

BOGOTA CONFERENCE See **ORGANIZATION OF AMERICAN STATES** in **APPENDIX C**.

BOHLEN, CHARLES EUSTIS (1904–1974) Career diplomat, Soviet expert. Bohlen graduated from Harvard in 1927. The New York native joined the FOREIGN SERVICE in 1929, specializing in Soviet affairs. Over the next four decades he played an important part in all major U.S.-Soviet developments. Following U.S. diplomatic recognition of the Soviet Union under the ROOSEVELT-LITVINOV AGREEMENT (1933), he was a member of the first U.S. mission to the Communist nation in 1934. After a tour in the State Department from 1935 to 1937 he returned to the U.S. embassy in Moscow. In 1940 he was posted to the American embassy in Tokyo. Following the Japanese attack on PEARL HARBOR in December 1941 he was interned for six months with the rest of the embassy staff before being returned to Washington. During WORLD WAR II Bohlen served as Russian interpreter for President FRANKLIN D. ROOSEVELT at the TEHERAN CONFERENCE (1943) and YALTA CONFERENCE (1945) and performed the same function for President HARRY S. TRUMAN at the POTSDAM CONFERENCE (1945). In 1947 he was made State Department counselor, essentially the senior assistant to the secretary of state.

In 1953 Bohlen was named ambassador to the Soviet Union. During his four-year tenure he reported extensively on developments there, cementing his reputation as the leading Kremlinologist in the U.S. diplomatic corps. In 1957 he was transferred to Manila as ambassador to the Philippines. He returned to Washington in 1959 to become Secretary of State CHRISTIAN A. HERTER's special adviser on Soviet matters. Bohlen was appointed ambassador to France in 1962. During his six years in Paris he strove to maintain good U.S.-French relations despite the strains brought by differences over NATO and the VIETNAM WAR. Bohlen's long career culminated with his service in 1968 as deputy under secretary of state for political affairs. He retired in 1969 and published his memoirs, *Witness to History, 1929–1969*, in 1973.

BOLAND AMENDMENTS Federal legislation in effect from 1982 to 1985 restricting U.S. aid to the CONTRAS, the guerrilla forces fighting the leftist Sandinista regime in Nicaragua. The various measures were named for their chief sponsor, Representative Edward P. Boland (D-MA), chairman of the House Intelligence Committee. In December 1981 President RONALD W. REAGAN authorized a program of covert U.S. assistance to emerging anti-Sandinista resistance groups. Liberals in Congress sharply criticized the policy, contending that the Contras were dominated by non-democratic elements and arguing that the United States should not support efforts to overthrow a foreign government. In December 1982 the first Boland amendment, or Boland I, was signed into law as part of an omnibus spending bill. Reagan strongly opposed the measure. As with all the Boland amendments, however, its attachment to key legislation sought by the president prevented Reagan from exercising his veto power. Boland I, in effect from December 1982 to December 1983, prohibited the PENTAGON and CENTRAL INTELLIGENCE AGENCY from furnishing the Contras military aid "for the purpose of overthrowing" the Nicaraguan government. The Reagan administration, denying it sought to topple the Sandinistas, justified continued covert support of the Contras as necessary to pressure Managua to stop supplying leftist rebels battling the U.S.-allied government in El Salvador. Boland II limited U.S. military assistance to the Contras from December 1983 to September 1984 to $24 million. Boland III, the most restrictive and comprehensive of the amendments, was in effect from October 1984 to December 1985. It barred any U.S. government agency involved in intelligence activities from providing any support to the Contras. Reagan administration efforts to circumvent the amendment resulted in the IRAN-CONTRA scandal. In August 1985 Congress approved $27 million in humanitarian aid to the Contras. With the expiration of Boland III in December 1985, Congress passed legislation that permitted only humanitarian assistance to the Contras through the end of September 1986. In June 1986 Reagan won congressional backing for a resumption of U.S. military aid to the Contras beginning in October 1986.

BONN CONVENTIONS See **PARIS AGREEMENTS**.

BOUNDARY WATERS TREATY (1909) Anglo-American agreement governing disputes over the waters along the Canadian-American border from Maine to Washington State. Signed in Washington, D.C., on January 11, 1909, by Secretary of State ELIHU ROOT and British Ambassador to the

United States James Bryce, the treaty established a permanent joint commission to settle disagreements that might arise concerning navigation or irrigation rights to the lakes and rivers traversing the U.S.-Canadian boundary. By removing a source of potential discord between Washington and London, the pact helped clear the way for a U.S.-British agreement in late January 1909 to submit the long-standing North Atlantic FISHERIES QUESTION to international arbitration. Both sides accepted the Hague Tribunal's 1910 compromise ruling on access to the Newfoundland fisheries in an Anglo-American convention in 1912.

BOWLES, CHESTER BLISS (1901–1986) Businessman, author, government official, and diplomat. Bowles was born in Massachusetts. After graduating from Yale in 1924, he co-founded the noted advertising firm Benton & Bowles. He entered government service during WORLD WAR II, holding positions in Connecticut's rationing program before becoming director of the federal Office of Price Administration in 1943. After the war he was active in the formation of the UNITED NATIONS EDUCATIONAL, SCIENTIFIC, AND CULTURAL ORGANIZATION (UNESCO). In 1948 Bowles, a Democrat, was elected governor of Connecticut. Defeated for reelection in 1950, he was named ambassador to India the following year. He resigned his post in 1953 with the arrival of the Republican Eisenhower administration. Bowles published an account of his experiences, *Ambassador's Report* (1954), and authored several books on foreign affairs before election to the House of Representatives as a Democrat from Connecticut in 1958.

Bowles served as chief foreign policy adviser to JOHN F. KENNEDY during his successful 1960 presidential campaign. Kennedy appointed him under secretary of state in January 1961. Advocating greater U.S. attention to the developing world, he quickly proved out of step with the East-West emphasis of Secretary of State DEAN RUSK and other senior department officials. He was removed from his post in November but remained in the administration as the president's special adviser on Asian, African, and Latin American affairs. Opposed to mounting U.S. military involvement in the VIETNAM WAR, Bowles submitted his resignation in December 1962 but was prevailed upon by Kennedy to return to his former post in India. During his second tour as ambassador from 1963 to 1969 he championed increased economic assistance to the giant nation, coordinating emergency U.S. wheat shipments in 1965 and 1966. Following the 1965 war between Pakistan and India, he pressed unsuccessfully for reducing U.S. military aid to Pakistan and increasing such assistance to India. Bowles retired in 1969 and wrote his memoir, *Promises to Keep: My Years in Public Life, 1941–1969* (1971).

BOXER REBELLION (1900) Violent uprising in China against foreigners and foreign influence. Following its defeat in the Sino-Japanese War (1894–1895), a weakened China was unable to resist foreign political and economic domination. In the late 1890s Japan and the European powers—Great Britain, France, Germany and Russia—undertook to carve China into spheres of influence and exacted commercial concessions and other privileges from the Chinese imperial dynasty. By decade's end the Chinese ruling class feared and anticipated that their country might be dismembered by the foreign powers. With its victory in the SPANISH-AMERICAN WAR (1898), the United States had acquired the Philippines and confirmed its standing as a major power in the Pacific. American business interests and expansionists envisioned enlarged U.S. trade with a potentially vast Chinese market. This trade would depend on preserving equal commercial opportunity for all nations in China, or what was called the OPEN DOOR policy. Thus the United States viewed with increasing alarm Japanese and European aggrandizement in China. Partitioning of the country into exclusive economic enclaves would spell the end of the Open Door and of America's ambitions for an enlarged stake in China's trade.

Foreign cultural penetration and infringement on Chinese sovereignty bred resentment and fostered strong nationalistic passions. In June 1900, members of a militant antiforeign secret society known as Boxers, supported by the imperial government under Dowager Empress Tzu Hsi, rose in rebellion to expel the "foreign devils" from China. The Boxers overran Peking, pillaging foreign buildings and churches and killing hundreds of Chinese Christians converted by foreign missionaries. Joined by Chinese imperialist troops, they laid siege to the foreign diplomatic legations in the city, where hundreds of foreign civilians had taken refuge. America joined with Britain, France, Germany, Russia, and Japan to form a rescue force of some 20,000 troops to lift the seige. President WILLIAM MCKINLEY decided to contribute U.S. forces to the rescue operation to discourage exploitation of the crisis by the other foreign powers, who he worried would use the Boxer rebellion as a pretext for abandoning the Open Door. In July, amid the crisis, Secretary of State JOHN M. HAY sent a circular note to the powers informing them that the United States was committed to a policy of preserving China's territorial integrity and independence and of safeguarding equal trade access to the great Asian nation.

On August 14 the international expedition raised the legation siege. The U.S. troops did not participate in the ensuing punitive expedition that brought the rebellion to an end. On September 7, 1901, after some seven months of negotiations toward a final settlement of the violent uprising, representatives of the foreign powers and the Chinese government signed the Boxer Protocol. Its harsh terms punished high Chinese officials involved in the rebellion and saddled China with a huge $333 million indemnity to be paid over 40 years. The U.S. share of the indemnity was originally set at $24.5 million. The American government later reduced this to $12 million and in 1924 set aside the unpaid balance.

BRACERO PROGRAM (1942–1964) Informal name, taken from the Spanish for "day laborer," for a program under which Mexican farm workers came to the United States. The manpower demands of WORLD WAR II created agricultural labor shortages in the Southwest. On August 4, 1942, the U.S. and Mexican governments completed an emergency wartime agreement, formally titled the Mexican Farm Labor Supply Program, to fill the shortfall with Mexican laborers. Mexican migrant workers subsequently played a major role in the production of southwestern crops.

Both governments favored continuing the Bracero Program after the war and it was extended periodically. American agricultural interests deemed the program essential, while in Mexico it was valued as a mechanism for relieving unemployment and providing an important source of national revenue. By the mid-1960s, enthusiasm for the program had waned as critics in both countries charged the migrant laborers were subject to intolerable working conditions and other abuses. The United States ended the program in December 1964. Approximately 5 million Mexican workers entered the United States during the 22 years it was in effect. Similar farm labor programs, with additional safeguards, have been proposed intermittently since 1964 as a way to alleviate the problem of illegal Mexican immigration.

BRADLEY PLAN See **INTERNATIONAL DEBT CRISIS**.

BRADY PLAN See **INTERNATIONAL DEBT CRISIS**.

BRANT, JOSEPH (1742–1807) Mohawk Indian chief and lifelong British loyalist, Brant aided Great Britain against the United States in the AMERICAN REVOLUTION. His success in enlisting the support of the Iroquois in New York State and Canada for the British cause earned Brant a colonel's commission in the British army. During the revolution, he was a leader at the Battle of Oriskany (1777) and took part in campaigns throughout New York's Mohawk Valley, notably the Cherry Valley Massacre (1778). Following the war, Brant blocked Iroquois efforts to strike a separate peace with the new American nation. His attempts during the 1780s to unite the six Iroquois tribes to oppose U.S. appropriation of their territories in New York, Pennsylvania, and Ohio failed. He subsequently settled in Canada.

BRETTON WOODS CONFERENCE (1944) Meeting of Allied nations during WORLD WAR II to plan for the postwar international economy. Officially titled the United Nations Monetary and Financial Conference, the gathering aimed to replace the chaotic economic conditions of the previous decade with a more cooperative international economic order. It was widely believed that the economic nationalism of the 1930s, in which the industrialized nations turned to trade barriers and other restrictive measures to aid their own economies, had exacerbated the worldwide Great Depression and contributed to the political frictions that finally brought world war. The conference, chaired by U.S. Treasury Secretary HENRY MORGENTHAU, JR., was held at Bretton Woods, New Hampshire, from July 1 to 22, 1944. Representatives from 44 nations, including the Soviet Union, attended. Building on the preliminary work of U.S. treasury official HARRY DEXTER WHITE and British economist John Maynard Keynes, the delegates concluded agreements forming two international financial institutions: the INTERNATIONAL MONETARY FUND (IMF) to regulate the world's money supply and the WORLD BANK to provide investment capital for economic development. Presaging its postwar opposition to Western market-based economic systems, the Soviet Union declined to participate in either organization. The IMF and World Bank, together with the 1947 GENERAL AGREEMENT ON TARIFFS AND TRADE, provided the institutional framework for postwar international economic cooperation.

BRICKER AMENDMENT Proposed constitutional amendment concerning the legal status of international agreements within the United States. America's greatly expanded international role after WORLD WAR II brought a proliferation of treaties and other international measures to which the nation was party. A combination of Southern Democratic and conservative Midwestern Republican members of Congress expressed concern over the degree to which these agreements were binding on U.S. domestic law. In MISSOURI V. HOLLAND (1920), the U.S. Supreme Court had ruled that under Article VI of the U.S. CONSTITUTION, ratified treaties were part of the supreme law of the land. The Court left unclear, though, whether treaties, like laws, had to conform to the Constitution or whether they actually could change the Constitution once adopted. Congressional skeptics worried that U.S. adherence to UNITED NATIONS agreements addressing HUMAN RIGHTS and other social and economic issues might bring state segregation laws in the American South into question or force the nation to adopt socialist principles. Also drawing congressional attention were EXECUTIVE AGREEMENTS, measures negotiated by the president with other nations. Unlike treaties, these agreements were not submitted for Senate approval. The mounting postwar use of the measures had invited criticism as a circumvention of the Senate's historic role in foreign affairs.

In January 1953 Senator John W. Bricker (R-OH) sponsored an amendment to the Constitution that would require any treaty or international agreement entered into by the United States to conform to the Constitution; restrict the impact of international agreements on powers reserved to the states; and subject all executive or other agreements to Senate approval. The measure sparked intense debate. Its supporters argued that national sovereignty and states' rights were at issue. Opponents contended that the amendment's provisions on state powers and executive agreements would undercut the president's authority as the principal architect of the nation's foreign policy. After attempting unsuccessfully to modify the measure, the Eisenhower administration came out against its passage. On February 26, 1954, the tally for the amendment was 60 to 31, one vote short of the two-thirds majority required to submit it for ratification by the states. In the mid-1950s, Bricker reintroduced several revised versions of the measure, none of which came before the full Senate for a vote. In its 1957 ruling in *Reid* v. *Covert*, the Supreme Court explicitly declared that treaties were subject to constitutional limits.

BRINKMANSHIP Catchword applied to a form of diplomacy first articulated by JOHN FOSTER DULLES, secretary of state under President DWIGHT D. EISENHOWER. As outlined in its NEW LOOK defense strategy, the Eisenhower administration relied on the threat of nuclear retaliation as the basic component in its DETERRENCE of Communist aggression. This reliance on nuclear weapons implied that senior administration figures were prepared to wage nuclear war to thwart Communist expansionism. Dulles saw the communication of an American readiness to go to war as a key diplomatic technique for prevailing in Cold War confrontations. In a famous 1956 interview with *Life* magazine, Dulles explained that the trick in convincing a possible adversary to back down lay in "the ability to get to the verge" without actually progressing to armed conflict. "If you cannot master it," Dulles asserted, "you inevitably get into a war. If you try to run away from it, if you are scared to go to the brink, you are lost." The term "brinkmanship" subsequently was coined to describe Dulles's approach. According to the secretary of state, the Eisenhower administration resorted to "brinkmanship," making known its willingness to use nuclear weapons to end the KOREAN WAR in 1953, to forestall a Chinese Communist move into Indochina in 1954, and to resolve the first of the QUEMOY-MATSU CRISES the same year. The ultimate instance of "brinkmanship" was the CUBAN MISSILE CRISIS (1962) between the United States and Soviet Union, after which there was broad recognition on both sides that the risks were too great to allow East-West confrontation to verge on nuclear war.

BRITISH BLACKLIST (1916) American firms and individuals singled out by Great Britain amid WORLD WAR I for suspected business dealings with the Central Powers. In July 1916 the British government published the names of 85 American firms and individuals suspected of trading with Britain's enemies. British subjects were barred from doing business with those blacklisted, who were to be denied access to British banking, shipping, and cable facilities. Britain's punitive step stirred public resentment in the United States and angered President WOODROW WILSON. When the British refused to revoke their blacklist following his protest, the president asked Congress for retaliatory powers. Prior to adjourning in September 1916, the Congress voted a pair of laws vesting Wilson with the authority he sought. The Shipping Board Act and Reserve Act empowered the president to withhold clearance papers or port facilities from British ships refusing to accept cargo from blacklisted firms. He never exercised these powers largely because the British government, under the pressure of the retaliatory U.S. legislation, eased its boycott of American firms. The United States entered World War I on the side of Britain and the Allies in April 1917.

BROOKINGS INSTITUTION Left-of-center think tank based in Washington, D.C.

Established in 1927, Brookings is an independent organization that seeks to influence public policy-making through research, education, and publications on issues in domestic and foreign affairs. Its staff includes scholars and former government authorities on foreign policy who conduct conferences, forums, and studies on U.S. national security, international trade, arms control, and relations with the Soviet Union, Latin America, the Middle East, Africa, and East Asia. The institution regularly publishes books on current issues in national defense and foreign affairs. Its flagship publication is the quarterly journal *The Brookings Review*. Although self-described as politically centrist, Brookings bears a long-standing reputation as a bastion of liberal Democratic thinking on American foreign policy.

BROWN, GEORGE SCRATCHLEY (1918–1978) U.S. Air Force officer, chairman of the JOINT CHIEFS OF STAFF (JCS). Born in New Jersey, Brown graduated from West Point in 1941. During WORLD WAR II he rose to the rank of colonel as a bomber pilot with the Eighth Air Force in Europe. In 1947 he became part of the newly independent U.S. Air Force and again saw action in the KOREAN WAR. In 1973 Brown was named Air Force chief of staff. During his Senate confirmation hearings he was questioned on his role in the secret bombing of Cambodia in 1969 and 1970, when he had commanded U.S. Air Force operations in the VIETNAM WAR. Brown acknowledged having concealed the bombing missions, explaining that he had done so on instructions from higher authority as a "special security precaution."

In 1974 Brown succeeded Admiral THOMAS H. MOORER as chairman of the JCS, the nation's highest military post. Shortly after taking office, he criticized an allegedly excessive Israeli influence on U.S. policy in a forum with students at Duke University. His remarks drew wide protest. President GERALD R. FORD reprimanded Brown, but retained him as chairman, strongly denying the general was anti-Semitic. Brown took part in the Ford administration's unsuccessful attempt to save South Vietnam from the final North Vietnamese offensive in the spring of 1975. The administration advocated sending military aid but was constrained by recent congressional legislation

limiting U.S. involvement in Southeast Asia. In subsequent years Brown cited a mounting military threat posed by the Soviet Union and pressed for production of both the B-1 bomber and CRUISE MISSILE. Stricken with cancer, he retired in 1978 and died the same year.

BROWN, HAROLD (1927–) Secretary of defense under President JIMMY CARTER. Brown was born in New York City. A brilliant student, he graduated from Columbia University in 1945 and completed a doctorate in physics there by age 21. In 1952 he joined the staff at the Lawrence Radiation Laboratory in California, which recently had been established as a center for NUCLEAR WEAPONS research. He became a protege of Dr. EDWARD TELLER, whom he succeeded as director of the laboratory in 1960. During the 1950s Brown served on several federal scientific bodies and was a scientific adviser to the U.S. delegation at the Geneva Conference for the Discontinuance of Nuclear Tests (1958–1959).

In 1961 Brown entered the Kennedy administration as director of research and engineering in the Defense Department. He was one of the "whiz kids," the term coined by senior military officers and defense officials for the group of young civilian intellectuals appointed to top leadership posts at the PENTAGON by Defense Secretary ROBERT S. MCNAMARA. Brown was named secretary of the air force in 1965. As American involvement in the VIETNAM WAR mounted, he supported selective U.S. bombing of North Vietnam. He left office with the Johnson administration in 1969, becoming president of the California Institute of Technology. He was a consultant to the U.S. negotiating team that concluded the SALT I arms control agreement with the Soviet Union in 1972 and was involved in the further talks for a SALT II accord.

Carter's choice for secretary of defense, Brown in 1977 became the first scientist to hold the post. Key concerns during his four-year tenure were improving U.S. strategic forces, strengthening NATO defenses, and advancing East-West arms control negotiations. Considering maintenance of a rough nuclear equivalence with the Soviet Union essential to U.S. DETERRENCE, he sought to upgrade the nation's NUCLEAR TRIAD of land- and sea-launched missiles and strategic bombers. He endorsed development of the MX missile and Trident nuclear submarine. While deciding to cancel the B-1 bomber, he approved development of stealth aircraft technology. In 1980 Carter issued PRESIDENTIAL DIRECTIVE 59 (PD-59) on U.S. nuclear warfare strategy. The directive called for America to be able to respond to any level of Soviet attack. Critics charged that the new strategic mandate validated the idea of a limited nuclear war. Brown replied that PD-59 was needed to ready the nation for any possible Soviet threat but emphasized that U.S. doctrine continued to regard nuclear war as unwinnable.

Brown assisted in the formulation of two major NATO initiatives to invigorate the regional security alliance. In May 1978 NATO countries endorsed a Long-Term Defense Program that called for sustained defense improvements. In response to Soviet deployment of new theater nuclear weapons, the alliance in December 1979 approved a DUAL-TRACK DECISION calling for deployment of U.S. intermediate-range PERSHING II and CRUISE MISSILES to Europe in the event of unsatisfactory progress in arms control negotiations. Brown helped gain Senate confirmation of the PANAMA CANAL TREATIES (1977). He strongly supported the June 1979 SALT II agreement, which was withdrawn from Senate consideration by Carter following the Soviet invasion of Afghanistan that December. He was involved deeply in the IRAN HOSTAGE CRISIS and took part in the planning of the ill-fated April 1980 hostage rescue mission. Brown left office at the end of Carter's term in 1981 and returned to academia. In 1983 he served on the SCOWCROFT COMMISSION on strategic nuclear forces.

BRUCE, DAVID KIRKPATRICK ESTE (1898–1977) Statesman and diplomat. Bruce was born in Baltimore. His father later would serve as a U.S. senator from Maryland. After attending Princeton for two years, he enlisted in the Army and served in France during WORLD WAR I. After the war he studied law at the University of Maryland and was admitted to the Maryland bar in 1921. He pursued a successful business career on Wall Street before establishing residence in Virginia, where he was elected to the state legislature in 1939. He married Alisa Mellon, daughter of American financier ANDREW W. MELLON in 1926. (They

were divorced in 1945.) During WORLD WAR II he helped organize the OFFICE OF STRATEGIC SERVICES and then headed the intelligence agency's operations in Europe.

In 1947 Bruce became assistant secretary under his former business associate, W. AVERELL HARRIMAN, at the DEPARTMENT OF COMMERCE. The following year he went to Paris to administer the MARSHALL PLAN in France. His skillful direction of the postwar economic recovery program led to his appointment as ambassador to France in 1949. He returned to Washington in 1952 to become under secretary of state, the second-ranking position in the department. Under the Eisenhower administration Bruce was U.S. representative to the European Defense Community, the precursor to the unified NATO military command, and the European Coal and Steel Community and ambassador to West Germany from 1957 to 1959. In 1961 President JOHN F. KENNEDY named Bruce ambassador to Great Britain, making him the first person to hold the top three U.S. diplomatic posts in Europe. He served in London until 1969.

In 1970 Bruce was selected by President RICHARD M. NIXON to replace HENRY CABOT LODGE, JR., a chief U.S. negotiator at the PARIS PEACE TALKS to end the VIETNAM WAR. During his 18-month tenure he was unable to bring about any real progress in the deadlocked negotiations. Following the initiation of relations between America and Communist China, Nixon in 1973 designated Bruce the first U.S. liaison officer in Peking. He returned in 1974 and the same year accepted assignment as U.S. ambassador to NATO, where he remained until his retirement in 1976.

BRUSSELS CONFERENCE (1937) International meeting on the growing war between China and Japan. During the MANCHURIAN CRISIS (1931–1933), the major Western powers, including the United States, protested to no avail the Japanese seizure of Manchuria, traditionally part of China, and the establishment of the puppet state of Manchukuo. Tensions mounted as the Nationalist Chinese government refused to recognize the Japanese-created state and Japanese military forces gradually pressed south into China. On July 7, 1937, Japanese and Chinese forces clashed at the Marco Polo Bridge north of Peking. Further hostilities quickly sparked a larger conflict.

By September it was clear Japan had launched a major invasion along the Chinese coast. China appealed to the LEAGUE OF NATIONS for assistance. Responding to the crisis, President FRANKLIN D. ROOSEVELT on October 5 delivered his QUARANTINE SPEECH, in which he called for an international "quarantine" of nations spreading the "epidemic of world lawlessness." When the League of Nations the following day denounced Japan's aggression and called for a conference of the signatories to the NINE-POWER TREATY (1922) guaranteeing Chinese sovereignty and territorial integrity and the principle of the OPEN DOOR, the United States readily agreed to participate.

The gathering, also known as the Nine-Power Conference, was held in Brussels from November 3 to 24, 1937. Present were representatives from all nine powers, including Japan and China, as well as other interested members of the League of Nations. Nazi Germany refused to attend. Japan defended its military actions as a matter of self-defense while the Western democracies, unwilling to commit themselves to possible war in Asia, agreed only on a verbal condemnation of Japan's violation of the 1922 pact. The conference ended with no concrete steps to halt the Sino-Japanese fighting. Japanese aggression in China effectively went unchecked until WORLD WAR II.

BRYAN "COOLING OFF" TREATIES (1913–1914) Series of bilateral agreements for maintaining peace concluded by Secretary of State WILLIAM JENNINGS BRYAN. On taking office in March 1913, Bryan made one of his immediate priorities the development of mechanisms that would promote the settlement of international disputes without resort to war. As early as 1905 he had advocated establishing a system for referring all international differences to a permanent court of arbitration. Shortly after becoming secretary of state, Bryan began negotiating with other countries a set of conciliation pacts collectively titled "Treaties for the Advancement of Peace" but popularly dubbed "cooling off" treaties. The agreements, which supplemented the ROOT ARBITRATION TREATIES (1908–1909), bound signatory nations to submit all diplomatically insoluble disputes, without exception, to a permanent international investigating commission. During the investi-

gation period, usually one year, the two disputants were barred from starting armed hostilities. Each nation could either accept or reject the commission's finding. The basic aim of the pacts was to provide a "cooling off" period during a time of worsening tensions. Bryan completed treaties with 30 nations during 1913 and 1914, including Great Britain, France, and Italy. Germany declined to negotiate a "cooling off" agreement. Since the recommendations of the international investigating commission would not be binding, the U.S. Senate concluded the treaties would pose no infringement of its foreign policy powers and approved most of the pacts without objection. The agreements effectively were rendered obsolete by the outbreak of WORLD WAR I in 1914.

BRYAN, WILLIAM JENNINGS (1860–1925) Political leader and secretary of state. Born in Illinois, Bryan graduated from Illinois College in 1881 and the Union College of Law in Chicago in 1883. He practiced law in his home state until 1887, when he moved to Lincoln, Nebraska, where he became active in Democratic politics. Elected to the U.S. House of Representatives in 1890 and reelected in 1892, he earned notice as a powerful and effective orator. He opposed high protective tariffs and voted against repeal of the Sherman Silver Purchase Act (1890). Defeated in a bid for the U.S. Senate in 1894, he then worked as editor-in-chief of the Omaha *World-Herald* and began what would become a 30-year vocation as a popular national Chautauqua lecturer. By the time the Democratic National Convention met in Chicago in 1896, he had become known nationally as a champion of the free coinage of silver. His famous "Cross of Gold" speech at the convention won him the party's presidential nomination. Campaigning on a platform supporting unlimited coinage of silver, he appealed to discontented farmers and workers, attacking the sound-money and high-tariff policies of the Republicans. Bryan narrowly lost the election to WILLIAM MCKINLEY. Though defeated, he emerged as the virtually undisputed leader of the Democratic Party and remained so until 1912.

Although opposed to the McKinley administration's imperialist policy of territorial acquisition at the end of the SPANISH-AMERICAN WAR (1898), Bryan wanted to see peace with Spain made official and thus used his influence with Democratic senators to help win approval of the controversial TREATY OF PARIS (1898). The Democratic presidential nominee again in 1900, he waged the campaign on the issue of IMPERIALISM and was defeated a second time by McKinley. In 1901 he established the weekly newspaper the *Commoner*, which he edited and published until 1913. Bryan headed the Democratic presidential ticket a third time in 1908 but lost to WILLIAM HOWARD TAFT. At the 1912 Democratic convention he helped nominate WOODROW WILSON. Bryan joined the incoming Wilson administration in 1913 as secretary of state.

In this post he negotiated the BRYAN "COOLING OFF" TREATIES (1913–1914), a series of some 30 bilateral agreements intended to prevent the outbreak of war during times of heightened international tensions. He supported the president's interventionist policy in Latin America as necessary to achieving political stability and protecting American interests in the hemisphere. The secretary of state joined Wilson in repudiating the Taft administration's DOLLAR DIPLOMACY in Central America. He concluded the BRYAN-CHAMORRO TREATY (1914) with the beleaguered Nicaraguan government. Under the agreement Nicaragua received $3 million to bolster its troubled finances. In return, it granted the United States both territorial concessions and exclusive rights to an interoceanic canal route. In the Far East, he firmly protested Japan's move in early 1915 to enhance its position in China by forcing a series of dictates, the so-called 21 Demands, on the Chinese government. When Bryan announced that the United States would refuse to recognize any agreement changing China's political or territorial status, Japan backed off its more extreme demands.

With the outbreak of WORLD WAR I in Europe in 1914, Bryan was staunchly committed to strict U.S. neutrality. He came to develop misgivings over what he viewed as the president's increasingly anti-German posture and orientation. He resigned from the cabinet in June 1915 in protest against Wilson's second note to Germany following the sinking of the LUSITANIA, a dispatch Bryan believed was unduly belligerent and provocative. He resumed his writing and lecturing. A Christian fundamentalist, he campaigned for state legislation prohibiting the teaching of evolution in public schools. When John T. Scopes, a Dayton, Tennessee, teacher, was tried in 1925 for violating such a law, Bryan joined the prosecution. The highlight of the celebrated case was the cross-examination of Bryan by renowned attorney Clarence Darrow, one of the defense counsels. Bryan died five days after the conclusion of the Scopes trial.

BRYAN-CHAMORRO TREATY (1914) Controversial agreement signed on August 5, 1914, by Secretary of State WILLIAM JENNINGS BRYAN and Nicaraguan Minister to Washington Emiliano Chamorro that gave the United States assorted rights and territorial concessions in Nicaragua. When a revolt against the pro-American regime of President Adolfo Diaz broke out in the Central American nation in July 1912, threatening American investments in the country, Diaz appealed for U.S. armed assistance. Contending that military intervention was needed to protect the lives and property of American nationals and other foreigners, President WILLIAM HOWARD TAFT sent U.S. marines into Nicaragua to crush the rebellion and save Diaz. A small guard from the Marines and Navy warship then were stationed in Nicaragua to deter further political unrest. Since 1911 American bankers, with the State Department's endorsement, had unofficially exercised a virtual protectorate over Nicaragua's chronically unstable finances. American fiscal stewardship was implemented by measures akin to those outlined in the abortive KNOX-CASTRILLO CONVENTION (1911). The Taft administration wanted to avert a level of economic disarray that might prompt Great Britain, France, or Germany, in violation of the ROOSEVELT COROLLARY to the MONROE DOCTRINE, to intervene in Nicaragua to reclaim the investments of European bankers.

The problem of Nicaragua's shaky treasury continued through the end of Taft's term. Soon after WOODROW WILSON became president in March 1913, Diaz approached the new American administration for aid to bolster his nation's economy. Negotiations between Bryan and Chamorro culminated in the August 1914 treaty, which granted the United States the exclusive right to build, control, and operate an interoceanic canal through Nicaragua in return for $3 million. In addition it gave the United States a 99-year renewable lease on the Great Corn and Little Corn islands and a right to establish a naval base in the Gulf of Fonseca. A clause patterned on the PLATT AMENDMENT (1901) that would have allowed American intervention in Nicaragua encountered strong anti-imperialist opposition in the U.S. Senate and was omitted from the final treaty text. The Senate ratified the Bryan-Chamorro pact in 1916.

When Costa Rica, El Salvador, and Honduras protested that the treaty infringed on their rights, Washington and Managua added a proviso disclaiming any intent to interfere with legitimate existing rights of other Central American countries. Unsatisfied, Costa Rica and El Salvador took their protest to the Central American Court of Justice, which ruled that Nicaragua had violated its neighbors' rights and should redress its action. The court did not declare the treaty invalid because it had no jurisdiction over the United States. Nicaragua ignored the decision and the Bryan-Chamorro agreement remained in force. The proposed naval base was never established and the Corn Islands remained under Nicaraguan jurisdiction except for a small area used by America for a lighthouse. The United States and Nicaragua agreed to abrogate the treaty in 1970.

BRZEZINSKI, ZBIGNIEW KAZIMIERZ (1928–   ) National security adviser under President JIMMY CARTER. Brzezinski was born in Poland. His family moved in 1938 to Canada where his father, a diplomat, had been posted. Following WORLD WAR II, when the Communists seized control of Poland's government, the family settled permanently in Canada. Brzezinski earned a B.A. degree in political science in 1949 and an M.A. the following year from McGill University in Montreal. He was awarded a Ph.D. from Harvard University in 1953 and joined the school's faculty the same year. In 1960 he became a professor at Columbia University, where he established himself as a leading authority on the Soviet Union and communism. He served as a consultant to the State Department during the Johnson administration and he was a foreign policy adviser in 1968 for Democratic presidential nominee Hubert H. Humphrey. Though staunchly anti-Communist, Brzezinski advocated a policy of "peaceful engagement" with the Soviet bloc. In 1973 he was named director of the TRILATERAL COMMISSION, a private organization encouraging greater cooperation among the United States, Western Europe, and Japan on common international concerns.

In 1976 he became a foreign affairs adviser to the presidential campaign of fellow commission member Jimmy Carter. Brzezinski held the post of national security adviser throughout Carter's presidency. He favored a continued policy of DETENTE toward the Soviet Union and supported the 1979 SALT II Treaty on nuclear arms. He was the principal American representative in negotiations leading to the initiation of full diplomatic relations between the United States and Communist China in January 1979. Brzezinski pressed for improved U.S. ties with the major developing nations in the THIRD WORLD, which he termed the "new influentials." Following the Soviet Union's invasion of Afghanistan in December 1979, he helped orchestrate the administration's hardening stance toward Moscow. Much of his attention during the Carter administration's final year was given to the protracted IRAN HOSTAGE CRISIS. In 1981 Brzezinski resumed his academic career and became a senior associate of the CENTER FOR STRATEGIC AND INTERNATIONAL STUDIES.

BUCARELI AGREEMENT (1923) U.S.-Mexican accord on subsoil mineral rights in Mexico. Amid the upheaval of the Mexican Revolution (1910–1920), U.S. military forces intervened at Veracruz to bring pressure for the ouster of dictator General Victoriano Huerta and again in northern Mexico in pursuit of revolutionary bandit Francisco "Pancho" Villa. The VERACRUZ INCIDENT (1914) and PUNITIVE EXPEDITION (1916–1917) antagonized Mexicans, seriously damaging America's relations with its southern neighbor. Tensions between the two countries mounted over a controversy stemming out of Article 27 of the Mexican Constitution of 1917, which vested ownership of subsoil mineral rights in the Mexican nation. Under the article, President Venustiano Carranza threatened to nationalize all of Mexico's oil holdings, many of which were owned by Americans and other foreigners. By a decree in February 1918 he declared oil an inalienable national resource and imposed a heavy tax on oil lands and the profits from their exploitation. American oil companies protested, deploring the Mexican government's actions as confiscatory and pressing President WOODROW WILSON to act to safeguard their property rights in Mexico. When Alvaro Obregon succeeded to the Mexican presidency in 1920, first Wilson, and then President WARREN G. HARDING, refused to recognize his government unless it formally agreed not to invoke Article 27 against American property owners.

Even as Obregon resisted the U.S. pressure, the two sides began negotiations in 1921 toward a settlement of differences. A final round of talks held at a location on Bucareli Avenue in Mexico City yielded an EXECUTIVE AGREEMENT in August 1923. Under the compromise accord, which became known as the Bucareli Agreement, the United States recognized Mexico's title to subsoil minerals, as spelled out in its 1917 constitution, while Mexico pledged to respect oil holdings acquired by American companies before 1917. After the Bucareli settlement was approved by Obregon and President CALVIN COOLIDGE, the United States extended diplomatic recognition to the Obregon government on August 31, 1923.

Trouble over subsoil rights reemerged with the election in 1924 of strongman Plutarco Calles as Mexican president. He did not feel bound to uphold the Bucareli Agreement since it was not a formal treaty. At his direction, the Mexican congress in December 1925 passed a pair of agrarian and petroleum laws that placed narrow restrictions on foreign ownership of Mexican land and oil holdings under terms of the 1917 constitution. The laws, which took effect in January 1927, violated the Bucareli settlement and provoked calls by American property owners in Mexico for U.S. intervention to protect their interests.

In a bid to ease rising tensions, Coolidge appointed Wall Street lawyer DWIGHT W. MORROW as U.S. ambassador to Mexico in September 1927. Morrow's conciliatory diplomacy was a great success, producing quick results and bringing a new cordiality between Washington and Mexico City. His efforts were aided in November of

the same year when the Mexican Supreme Court declared the limitations on foreign ownership imposed under the petroleum law unconstitutional. In December 1927 the Mexican congress reversed the effects of the land law by granting unlimited concession to those lands which American owners had begun to develop in some capacity before May 1, 1917.

See also MEXICAN OIL EXPROPRIATION CONTROVERSY.

BUCHANAN, JAMES (1791–1868) Secretary of state and 15th president of the United States. Born in eastern Pennsylvania, Buchanan graduated from Dickinson College in 1809. He studied law, was admitted to the bar in 1812, and established a successful practice at Lancaster, Pennsylvania. After brief service in the WAR OF 1812, he was elected in 1814 as a Federalist to the state assembly, where he served until 1816. Beginning in 1821, he spent five successive terms in the U.S. House of Representatives. With the demise of the Federalist Party in 1824, Buchanan aligned with the Jacksonian Democrats. He left the House in 1831 and the same year accepted appointment by President ANDREW JACKSON as U.S. minister to Russia. On his return to the United States in 1834 he was elected as a Democrat to the U.S. Senate from Pennsylvania. Buchanan held his seat until 1845, when he was appointed secretary of state by incoming President JAMES K. POLK.

He lent loyal support to the president's expansionist policies, which were anchored in the doctrine of America's MANIFEST DESTINY to extend its sovereignty over the continent. Buchanan's direction of U.S. diplomacy was limited by Polk's penchant for acting as his own secretary of state. Tensions in America's relations with Great Britain and Mexico dominated Buchanan's tenure. He managed a settlement with the British of the longstanding OREGON QUESTION through his successful negotiation of the OREGON TREATY (1846), which fixed the northern boundary of Oregon Country at 49°, thus ending a threat of war over competing Anglo-American territorial claims. To block suspected British ambitions in the Yucatan and Central America, he encouraged the president's formulation of the POLK COROLLARY to the MONROE DOCTRINE. The corollary elaborated on America's commitment to prevent further European territorial gains in the Western Hemisphere. He oversaw final arrangements for U.S. annexation of Texas. The crisis in U.S.-Mexican relations that followed in the wake of TEXAS ANNEXATION (1845) culminated in the MEXICAN WAR (1846–1848). While Polk orchestrated U.S. wartime diplomacy, Buchanan directed the negotiation of the TREATY OF GUADALUPE HIDALGO (1848), which ended the conflict and rewarded America for its victory with the vast MEXICAN CESSION. He sought unsuccessfully to purchase Cuba from Spain.

With the end of Polk's term in 1849, Buchanan retired to his Pennsylvania estate. In 1852 he was an unsuccessful candidate for the Democratic presidential nomination, which went to dark horse contender FRANKLIN PIERCE on the 49th ballot. Appointed U.S. minister to Great Britain by President Pierce in 1853, he spent three years in the London post. He joined with the American ministers to France and Spain, John Y. Mason and PIERRE SOULE, in drawing up the controversial OSTEND MANIFESTO (1854), which urged the United States to seize Cuba by force in the event Spain refused to sell its colony. Strong antislavery political opposition in the North forced the Pierce administration to repudiate the manifesto and abandon its goal of acquiring Cuba as slave territory.

When Buchanan returned from Britain he found the nation in the throes of a renewed and increasingly bitter sectional battle over slavery. The legislative Compromise of 1850 had effected an uneasy truce in the political struggle between North and South over the issue of slavery's extension into the territories. This was shattered when Pierce signed the controversial Kansas-Nebraska Act of 1854. By repealing the slavery restriction of the Missouri Compromise of 1820, the act invited vehement opposition from the Free-Soil North and reignited the sectional conflict. The Kansas-Nebraska measure provided that the residents of the territories should decide for themselves by a plebiscite whether or not to permit slavery, a principle that became known as popular sovereignty.

Against this backdrop, Buchanan won the Democratic nomination for president in 1856. Although personally opposed to slavery as a moral wrong, he held the "peculiar institution" to be constitutional, asserted that the federal government had no legal authority to interfere with it where it existed, and believed in each new state's right to choose for itself whether to be slave or free. Embracing the Compromise of 1850 as a final remedy, he ran on a platform that urged an end to northern agitation of the slavery question and endorsed concessions to the South to save the Union and avert civil war. In the election Buchanan defeated Republican JOHN C. FREMONT and American Party nominee MILLARD FILLMORE. Within days of his inauguration, the U.S. Supreme Court handed down its landmark *Dred Scott* (1857) decision declaring that Congress could not ban slavery from the newly formed territories. Buchanan accepted the *Dred Scott* ruling as the final word in the matter. His prediction that it would settle the controversy with respect to slavery in the territories proved wrong. Kansas became a bloody battleground, where antislavery and pro-slavery factions were engaged in a bitter struggle for control. Buchanan's recommendation in early 1858 that Congress approve a controversial state constitution, drafted at Lecompton, Kansas, calling for admission of the territory as a slave state divided the Democrats and brought his political undoing. The Lecompton Constitution was defeated in the House of Representatives and rejected in two subsequent referendums in Kansas. Slavery's opponents thereafter carried the initiative and Kansas was admitted as a free state in 1861.

Preoccupied with the deepening sectional crisis, Buchanan was unable to focus on foreign affairs. His diplomatic record was unexceptional. Congressional opposition blocked his scheme for expanding the national domain by acquiring Cuba. He managed to secure commercial treaties with China and Japan. His goal of checking European influence in Central America was advanced when Secretary of State LEWIS CASS persuaded Great Britain to accept the U.S. interpretation of the CLAYTON-BULWER TREATY (1850). Cass also won a victory for America's position on neutral maritime rights, persuading the British to relinquish their claim to a right to stop and search U.S. ships at sea.

Weakened by the Lecompton episode, Buchanan was not a candidate for reelection in 1860. The election in November of Republican candidate ABRAHAM LINCOLN as president triggered the secession crisis.

South Carolina left the Union on December 20, 1860, and other Southern states soon followed. In the remaining months of his term, Buchanan denied the legal right of states to secede, but held that the federal government lacked the constitutional authority to force them to remain in the Union. As Southern members of his cabinet resigned, he stiffened his stand against South Carolina, dispatching the vessel *Star of the West* in early January 1861 to reinforce the federal garrison at Fort Sumter in Charleston Harbor. The ship was fired on by Confederate artillery and driven away. Reverting to a policy of inaction, Buchanan mounted no further attempt to save Fort Sumter, which later fell to the South after Lincoln became president, marking the start of the Civil War. By the time he left office in March 1861, seven southern states had seceded and joined to form the Confederacy under President JEFFERSON DAVIS. After taking part in Lincoln's inauguration, Buchanan retired to his Pennsylvania estate. During the Civil War he supported the administration as a Union Democrat.

BUCHANAN-PAKENHAM TREATY See **OREGON TREATY**.

BUCKLEY, WILLIAM FRANK, JR. (1925–) Editor, columnist, television personality, and author who since the 1950s has endured as a champion of conservatism in the United States. Born in New York City, the son of a wealthy oilman, he grew up in France, Great Britain, and the United States. After serving in the U.S. Army from 1944 to 1946 as a second lieutenant, he entered Yale University, from which he graduated with honors in 1950. In 1955 he founded the influential magazine *National Review* as a forum for advancing the conservative viewpoint on leading social, political, and economic issues. His intellectual leadership and political activism helped transform conservatism into a viable political force in the 1960s and beyond. In 1964 he supported the unsuccessful presidential bid of Senator Barry M. Goldwater (R-AZ), whose candidacy marked the emergence of the contemporary American conservative movement. Buckley ran unsuccessfully for mayor of New York City in 1965 on the Conservative Party ticket. He served from 1969 to 1972 on an advisory committee of

the UNITED STATES INFORMATION AGENCY and in 1973 as a member of the U.S. delegation to the UNITED NATIONS General Assembly. Author of the nationally syndicated column "On the Right" since 1962, he also has hosted the award-winning television interview program "Firing Line" since 1966.

Ardently anti-Communist, Buckley viewed the long COLD WAR as a historic struggle of the U.S.-led Western capitalist democracies against the totalitarian, command-economy regimes of the Soviet bloc and China. He opposed the policy of DETENTE toward the Soviet Union initiated by the Nixon administration. He also protested American overtures to Communist China in the early 1970s and the 1979 establishment of full U.S. diplomatic relations with Peking as a sellout of longtime U.S. ally Taiwan. In 1978, he parted ways with many fellow conservatives when he supported the PANAMA CANAL TREATIES, which arranged for relinquishment of U.S. control over the waterway by the year 2000. Buckley celebrated former California Governor RONALD W. REAGAN's 1980 presidential election win as a triumph for the conservative movement. He promoted the massive Reagan defense buildup of the 1980s as necessary to counter the Soviet military threat. He has been a consistent enthusiast of the STRATEGIC DEFENSE INITIATIVE, the U.S. program to develop a space-based shield for protection against ballistic missiles. A proponent of the REAGAN DOCTRINE, the policy of American support for anti-Communist insurgency movements in the THIRD WORLD, he advocated U.S. aid for the anti-Sandinista Nicaraguan CONTRAS, the UNITA rebels fighting Angola's Marxist government in the ANGOLAN CIVIL WAR, and the Mujahedeen guerrillas resisting Soviet occupation in the AFGHANISTAN WAR. Buckley hailed the end of the Cold War and collapse of Soviet hegemony in Eastern Europe by 1990 as vindication of U.S. military and political resolve since 1945.

BUENOS AIRES CONFERENCE (1936) Special Pan-American peace conference held at Buenos Aires at the request of President FRANKLIN D. ROOSEVELT. The increasingly belligerent posture of Nazi Germany and Fascist Italy led Roosevelt to propose a special inter-American gathering on maintaining peace in the Western Hemisphere.

His main concern was Nazi infiltration in Latin America. Emphasizing the need for hemispheric unity to guard against external threats to peace, he sent personal letters in January 1936 to the leaders of the other American republics suggesting just such a parley. The Latin American nations accepted the proposal. Fresh from his election in November 1936 to a second term, Roosevelt traveled by battleship to Argentina and on December 1 delivered the opening address at the Pan-American Conference for the Maintenance of Peace. In his speech, he warned that aggression was on the rise in Europe, appealed for Pan-American solidarity, and urged the delegates to effect an arrangement for consulting among the American republics for "our mutual safety and our mutual good." Before adjourning on December 23, the conference adopted a pact, the Convention for the Maintenance, Preservation, and Reestablishment of Peace, that provided for Pan-American consultation in the event of any menace to peace in the Western Hemisphere. The delegates also adopted a separate protocol denouncing intervention by any American state, directly or indirectly, in the internal or external affairs of any other American state. This measure was stronger than the MONTEVIDEO PLEDGE adopted at the Seventh PAN-AMERICAN CONFERENCE in 1933. When the United States accepted the protocol without reservation, it committed itself fully to the principle of nonintervention. Amid the growing threat of war in Europe, the American republics took further steps to strengthen hemispheric cooperation under the 1938 DECLARATION OF LIMA.

BULLITT, WILLIAM CHRISTIAN (1891–1967) Diplomat. Bullitt was born to a wealthy family in Philadelphia, graduated from Yale in 1913, and briefly attended Harvard Law School. After a short stint as a newspaper reporter, he joined the State Department in 1917, following U.S. entry into WORLD WAR I, as head of the bureau of Central European Information. He accompanied the U.S. delegation to the PARIS PEACE CONFERENCE (1919). President WOODROW WILSON and British Prime Minister David Lloyd George sent him on a secret mission to Russia, then convulsed by civil war, to appraise the situation and report on the advisability of the Allies recog-

nizing the new Soviet regime. On his return to Paris, Bullitt, who had met Soviet revolutionary leader Nikolai Lenin in Moscow and favored Allied recognition of Lenin's government, mistakenly reported to Lloyd George first. This prompted Wilson to refuse to see Bullitt. Disillusioned by the rebuke and disenchanted with the harsh terms of the TREATY OF VERSAILLES (1919), which he characterized as cause for future wars, he resigned from the U.S. delegation and returned to America. He subsequently testified before the SENATE FOREIGN RELATIONS COMMITTEE on the secret deal making he had witnessed in Paris during the drafting of the Versailles pact, thereby helping to ensure the treaty's eventual failure to win Senate ratification.

Bullitt remained in private life for more than a decade, traveling widely and building on his knowledge of international affairs. In 1933 former Wilson administration colleague President FRANKLIN D. ROOSEVELT brought him back into government service as a special assistant to Secretary of State CORDELL HULL. Bullitt attended the WORLD ECONOMIC CONFERENCE in London and took part in the discussions leading to the ROOSEVELT-LITVINOV AGREEMENT (1933) extending U.S. diplomatic recognition to the Soviet Union. In November 1933 he went to Moscow as the first U.S. ambassador to the USSR.

Bullitt's tenure in the Communist nation was marked by increasingly tense contacts with the secretive, repressive regime under Joseph Stalin in the Kremlin. In 1936 he was named ambassador to France. In Paris Bullitt spoke out against the growing bellicosity of Adolf Hitler's Nazi Germany and carried on an extensive private correspondence with Roosevelt, serving in effect as the president's personal emissary in Europe. Following the fall of France to German invasion in June 1940, he returned to Washington, where he appealed for greater U.S. aid to Great Britain in its desperate struggle against the Axis powers. During WORLD WAR II he undertook a succession of special overseas assignments for Roosevelt. Denied enlistment in the U.S. Army because of his age, he joined Free French leader General Charles De Gaulle's wartime general staff in 1944. Bullitt returned to private pursuits after the war, but occasionally spoke out on foreign affairs issues.

A staunch anti-Communist, he was among the first to warn of the postwar threat posed by the Soviet Union and in the late 1940s supported Chiang Kai-shek and the Nationalist Chinese against the Communist revolution headed by Mao Tse-tung.

BUNCHE, RALPH JOHNSON (1904–1971) American educator, political scientist, UNITED NATIONS official, and 1950 winner of the Nobel Peace Prize. Born in Detroit, Michigan, he graduated Phi Beta Kappa from the University of California at Los Angeles in 1927. After earning a master's degree from Harvard University in 1928, he joined the faculty of Howard University in Washington, D.C., where he established and headed the political science department. In 1934 he completed his Ph.D. at Harvard and later did postdoctoral work in the United States, Great Britain, and South Africa. In the late 1930s he assisted Swedish sociologist Gunnar Myrdal with the pathbreaking research that became the basis of *The American Dilemma* (1944), Myrdal's classic study of blacks in the United States.

During WORLD WAR II Bunche served with the OFFICE OF STRATEGIC SERVICES as a specialist on Far Eastern and African affairs. Transferred to the State Department in 1944, he held a series of posts in which he worked on colonial problems. He became absorbed in planning for the United Nations, attending the DUMBARTON OAKS CONFERENCE (1944) that established the basic U.N. framework and the SAN FRANCISCO CONFERENCE (1945) that drafted the UNITED NATIONS CHARTER. In 1946 he was a delegate to the first General Assembly in London. Later that year, while on leave from the State Department, he joined the United Nations as director of the trusteeship division, which administered the world body's program for dependent colonies. He left the State Department in 1947 to become a permanent U.N. official.

Bunche was an accomplished diplomat and administrator at the United Nations for more than two decades. Named to its Palestine Commission in 1947, he became chief mediator in September 1948 of the Arab-Israeli peace talks following the assassination of original U.N. mediator Count Folke Bernadette of Sweden. Bunche successfully guided the arduous negotiations that resulted in the 1949 armistice between the new nation of Israel and the Arab states.

For his labors on the Palestine accord, he won the 1950 Nobel Peace Prize, becoming the award's first black recipient. In 1955 he was named a U.N. under secretary, in which position he supervised peacekeeping efforts in the SUEZ CRISIS in 1956, the CONGO CRISIS in 1960, and the Turko-Greek conflict in Cyprus in 1964. At the time of his retirement in 1971, Bunche held the office of under secretary for special political affairs and was a principal adviser to Secretary General U Thant.

BUNDY, McGEORGE (1919–) Educator, national security adviser, president of the Ford Foundation. Bundy was born in Boston, Massachusetts. His father, Harvey H. Bundy, served as assistant secretary of state under HENRY L. STIMSON during the Hoover administration and again as Stimson's special assistant at the War Department during WORLD WAR II. Bundy graduated from Yale in 1940 and was an Army intelligence officer in the European theater during the war years. Following his 1946 discharge, he helped Stimson research and write his autobiography, *On Active Service in Peace and War* (1948). After working briefly as an adviser in Washington on the MARSHALL PLAN for postwar European recovery and as a political analyst for the COUNCIL ON FOREIGN RELATIONS in New York, Bundy joined the faculty at Harvard University in 1949. He was appointed dean of arts and sciences in 1953 and became a full professor of government the following year.

Bundy impressed Harvard graduate Senator JOHN F. KENNEDY (D-MA), who was an overseer at his alma mater. In January 1961 newly elected President Kennedy made the Harvard dean his special assistant for national security affairs. His brother, WILLIAM P. BUNDY, also became part of the Kennedy administration as a senior official at the Defense Department. Responsible for directing the NATIONAL SECURITY COUNCIL staff and coordinating national security issues, McGeorge Bundy became a member of Kennedy's inner circle of advisers. He had a central role in the administration's handling of the CUBAN MISSILE CRISIS (1962). He supported American military involvement in South Vietnam and was a key architect of U.S. policies in Southeast Asia.

Following Kennedy's November 1963 assassination, Bundy continued as national security adviser to President LYNDON B.

JOHNSON. As attention focused in the mid-1960s on the situation in Indochina, he consistently maintained that a major U.S. commitment to the VIETNAM WAR was necessary to save South Vietnam and demonstrate American resolve to halt Communist aggression. After a trip to Saigon in February 1965, he recommended approval of a plan for full-scale U.S. bombing of North Vietnam. The bombing raids, known as Operation Rolling Thunder, began in March. In May 1965 he was sent by Johnson to the Dominican Republic to help resolve the DOMINICAN CRISIS. Bundy resigned in 1966 to become president of the Ford Foundation. He held the position until 1979, when he was named to the faculty at New York University.

BUNDY, WILLIAM PUTNAM (1917–) Senior national security officer, editor of *Foreign Affairs*. Bundy was born in Washington, D.C., to a prominent New England family. A brilliant student, he graduated from Yale in 1939 and earned a master's degree from Harvard the following year. During WORLD WAR II he served as an Army officer with the Signal Corps in the European theater. In 1943 he married Mary Eleanor Acheson, daughter of future Secretary of State DEAN ACHESON. Bundy obtained a law degree from Harvard in 1947 and went to work for the Washington firm of Covington and Burling. In 1951 he joined the CENTRAL INTELLIGENCE AGENCY (CIA), where he was involved in the preparation of top-level intelligence estimates.

In January 1961 Bundy entered the new Kennedy administration as deputy to Assistant Secretary of Defense for International Security Affairs PAUL H. NITZE. His brother, MCGEORGE BUNDY, was President JOHN F. KENNEDY's national security adviser. Responsible for coordinating military assistance programs, William Bundy was an early advocate of a strong U.S. stance against Communist aggression in Southeast Asia. In 1963 Nitze became Secretary of the Navy and Bundy moved up to fill the vacated position. He continued with the Johnson administration following Kennedy's assassination in November 1963. In February 1964 he was named assistant secretary of state for Far Eastern affairs.

Bundy's tenure coincided with the deepening American involvement in the VIETNAM WAR and he became a principal ar-chitect of U.S. policy in Southeast Asia. In the fall of 1964 President LYNDON B. JOHNSON directed a NATIONAL SECURITY COUNCIL panel headed by Bundy and Assistant Secretary of Defense John J. McNaughton to draw up recommendations on the future course of the war. The group's report, completed in November 1964, proposed an extensive air campaign against North Vietnam. Johnson consented to the plan in February 1965 and systematic bombing raids, code-named Operation Rolling Thunder, began the next month. Bundy believed the bombing could force North Vietnam to the negotiating table and in following years he helped orchestrate the air campaign. He left government service in 1969 and became a visiting professor of international studies at the Massachusetts Institute of Technology. From 1972 to 1984 he was the editor of the influential journal *Foreign Affairs* published by the COUNCIL ON FOREIGN RELATIONS.

BUNKER, ELLSWORTH (1894–1984) Businessman and diplomat. Bunker was born in Yonkers, New York. After graduating from Yale in 1916 he went into the family sugar business, eventually rising to president and then chairman of the National Sugar Refining Company. In 1951 he embarked on a distinguished diplomatic career with appointment as U.S. ambassador to Argentina. He served as ambassador to Italy from 1952 to 1953 and to India from 1956 to 1961. In the early 1960s Bunker earned a reputation as a skilled diplomatic troubleshooter. In 1962 he mediated a U.N.-sponsored settlement of the Dutch-Indonesian dispute over the western half of the island of New Guinea. Named U.S. ambassador to the ORGANIZATION OF AMERICAN STATES in 1964, he helped restore normal U.S.-Panamanian relations following the 1964 PANAMA RIOTS. Following the 1965 intervention of U.S. military forces in the Dominican Republic, he directed the negotiations resolving the DOMINICAN CRISIS.

In 1966 President LYNDON B. JOHNSON designated Bunker an ambassador-at-large. The following year Johnson posted him to Saigon as U.S. ambassador to South Vietnam. Bunker strongly supported the U.S. role in the VIETNAM WAR as necessary to halting Communist aggression in Southeast Asia. He forged close U.S. ties with the South Vietnamese government of President

Nguyen Van Thieu. Bunker agreed to stay on in Saigon under President RICHARD M. NIXON, backing the new administration's VIETNAMIZATION policy and endorsing the CAMBODIAN INCURSION (1970) and LAOTIAN INCURSION (1971), U.S.-directed military operations against Communist sanctuaries in neighboring Cambodia and Laos. He resumed his post as ambassador-at-large in 1973 following the PARIS PEACE ACCORDS that ended U.S. involvement in the war. The same year he took charge of deadlocked U.S.-Panamanian negotiations over the future of the PANAMA CANAL. Concluded after more than three years of talks, the PANAMA CANAL TREATIES (1977) represented Bunker's crowning achievement. The agreements, transferring eventual control of the canal to Panama, were ratified by the U.S. Senate in early 1978. Bunker retired the same year.

BUREAU OF AMERICAN REPUBLICS See **PAN-AMERICAN UNION**.

BUREAU OF INDIAN AFFAIRS (BIA) Federal agency primarily responsible for the Indian programs of the U.S. government since 1834. It has been variously and interchangeably referred to as the Office of Indian Affairs, the Department of Indian Affairs, the Indian Service, and the Indian Bureau. As it evolved in the 19th century, the bureau became the principal government agency for the management of Indian-white relations. It regulated the Indian trade, administered U.S.-Indian treaties, and assisted in the removal of tribes to reservations.

The bureau's forerunner was the Office of the Superintendent of Indian Trade, established in 1806 within the DEPARTMENT OF WAR to manage the system of U.S. government trading houses. The office evolved into a clearinghouse for all matters pertaining to federal relations with Indians. When Congress eliminated the FACTORY SYSTEM in 1822, the United States was left without a central agency for INDIAN AFFAIRS. Acting on his own authority, Secretary of War JOHN C. CALHOUN created a Bureau of Indian Affairs in March 1824 and named Thomas McKenney, a former superintendent of Indian trade, as its head. A department plan to reorganize the Indian office led to legislation in 1832 providing for a commissioner of Indian affairs authorized to direct and manage all relations with Indian tribes. The

commissioner fell under the war secretary and succeeded the head of the Indian bureau formed by Calhoun. In 1834 Congress passed the landmark law formally establishing the Bureau of Indian Affairs under the War Department. In 1849 the bureau was transferred to the newly created Department of the Interior.

BUREAU OF OCEANS AND INTERNATIONAL ENVIRONMENTAL AND SCIENTIFIC AFFAIRS Division within the DEPARTMENT OF STATE that has principal responsibility for planning and implementing U.S. government policy on international environmental matters. The bureau was established in 1974 in recognition of the growing impact of environmental and scientific concerns on America's international political and economic relationships. It assures that issues relating to oceans, fisheries, the atmosphere, population, and nuclear and space technology are taken into consideration when foreign policy decisions are made. The bureau advises the secretary of state on technical aspects of global environmental problems and represents the State Department at international gatherings relevant to its area of responsibility. The bureau since its inception has played a central role in the negotiation of international conventions in such areas as global climate change, tropical deforestation, wildlife conservation, and transport and disposal of hazardous wastes.

BURLINGAME TREATY (1868) Agreement negotiated between Secretary of State WILLIAM H. SEWARD and former American envoy to China Anson Burlingame, who at the time was representing the Chinese government. The pact, signed July 28, 1868, in Washington, added eight articles to the Sino-American agreement among the TREATIES OF TIENTSIN (1858). The articles reaffirmed Chinese territorial integrity, clarified the conduct of U.S. commercial activities in China, and established open immigration between the nations. The subsequent influx of Chinese workers raised tensions in the western United States and led to calls for measures to restrict their continued entrance. The ANGELL TREATY (1880) modified the provisions of the Burlingame Treaty to allow for limitations on immigration, laying the groundwork for passage of the CHINESE EXCLUSION ACT in 1882.

BURR CONSPIRACY (1804–1807) Ambiguous episode of political and military intrigue that ended in the treason trial of Aaron Burr, who was vice-president during President THOMAS JEFFERSON's first term (1801–1805). His political career in shambles after having killed ALEXANDER HAMILTON in a duel in July 1804, Burr soon embarked on an ultimately abortive scheme, the exact aims of which have never been conclusively established. Burr's reputed personal ambitions included annexation of Mexico and Spanish possessions in the present-day American Southwest, or secession of western territory from the United States—or perhaps both. While still vice-president, he approached British Minister at Washington Anthony Merry with a request for money to fund a proposed movement to detach Louisiana from the United States. The British government refused Burr. Upon leaving office in March 1805, he traveled down the Ohio River, stopping at towns in the trans-Appalachian West to make contacts with prominent people and enlist their support for his bold plans, the principal one of which apparently was a FILIBUSTERING expedition against Mexico. During a visit to New Orleans, Burr conferred with old friend General James Wilkinson, commander of the U.S. Army in the Mississippi Valley and governor of the Louisiana territory, purportedly about a secret two-pronged plot to wrest Mexico from Spain and to establish Louisiana as an independent republic.

In the summer of 1806 the former vice-president set up headquarters in Lexington, Kentucky, for organizing a military expedition to the Southwest. Burr's force of 60 to 80 men and 10 flatboats set out in August, descending first the Ohio and then the Mississippi River. At this point Wilkinson wrote to President Jefferson to warn him of Burr's machinations. Jefferson issued a proclamation cautioning American citizens against participation in illegal excursions against Spanish territory and at the same time ordered Burr's arrest. When Burr learned of Wilkinson's betrayal, he fled toward Spanish Florida, but was apprehended and brought to Richmond in March 1807 to stand trial before Chief Justice JOHN MARSHALL on the charge of treason against the United States. In the course of the trial, which ran from August 3 to September 1, Jefferson established the precedent of executive privilege by evading Marshall's subpoena to appear as a witness. The chief justice, in his instructions to the jury, insisted that the narrow constitutional definition of treason be strictly applied. Burr was acquitted and went into European exile.

BUSH, GEORGE HERBERT WALKER (1924–) Director of the CENTRAL INTELLIGENCE AGENCY (CIA), vice-president, 41st president of the United States. Bush was born in Massachusetts and raised in Connecticut. His father, Prescott Bush, represented Connecticut as a Republican in the U.S. Senate from 1952 to 1963. After graduating from prep school in 1942, he served as a Navy pilot in the Pacific during WORLD WAR II. He earned a B.A. from Yale in 1948 and moved to Texas, where he went into the oil business. Bush helped found Zapata Petroleum Corporation and became a millionaire in his own right. In 1964 he ran unsuccessfully as the Republican candidate for a U.S. Senate seat from Texas. In 1966 he won election to the House of Representatives from Houston. He was reelected in 1968. Two years later he was again defeated in a bid for the U.S. Senate.

In 1971 President RICHARD M. NIXON named Bush U.S. ambassador to the UNITED NATIONS. In 1973 he became national chairman of the Republican Party. President GERALD R. FORD in 1974 appointed Bush chief of the U.S. Liaison Office in Communist China. Ford brought him back from Peking to head the CIA in 1976. During his brief tenure in the post, Bush approved creation of TEAM A/TEAM B, a special study by outside experts of the Soviet military threat. He left office with the Ford administration in January 1977.

In 1980 Bush sought the Republican presidential nomination. When his own bid fell short, he accepted the vice-presidential nomination under Republican candidate RONALD W. REAGAN. The ticket swept to victory in 1980 and won a second term in 1984. As vice-president, Bush traveled extensively overseas and supported the administration's staunch anti-Communist policies. He coordinated with America's NATO allies on the 1983 deployment of U.S. PER-

SHING II and CRUISE MISSILES to Europe to counter similar Soviet intermediate NUCLEAR WEAPONS. He endorsed the steady improvement in U.S.-Soviet relations that followed reformist Soviet leader Mikhail S. Gorbachev's rise to power in 1985. Bush was linked to the IRAN-CONTRA scandal that shook the Reagan presidency in 1986 and 1987. He had participated in the decision to sell arms to Iran, but denied any knowledge of the diversion of the proceeds to the CONTRAS, the Nicaraguan rebels battling the leftist Sandinista regime in Managua. In 1988 he garnered the Republican presidential nomination and defeated Democratic candidate Massachusetts Governor Michael C. Dukakis in the general election.

Bush took office at a dramatic turning point in international affairs. In 1989 the political liberalization begun by Gorbachev in the USSR took hold across Communist Eastern Europe, resulting in the emergence of non-Communist governments in Poland and Hungary. When the Kremlin indicated it would not reimpose its will on its former East European satellites, the crumbling East German Communist regime in November 1989 opened the BERLIN WALL, long the symbol of Europe's COLD WAR division. The collapse of communism in Eastern Europe hastened the end of the East-West struggle that had dominated the postwar world. In December Bush and Gorbachev met at the MALTA SUMMIT to review the rapidly changing world situation and chart a course for post–Cold War U.S.-Soviet ties.

Developments in Latin America and Asia also drew Bush's attention in his first year. In March 1989 the administration reached a compromise with the Democratic leadership in Congress on a bipartisan U.S. policy toward Nicaragua. Under the plan, U.S. humanitarian aid would be furnished to the Contras until scheduled free elections were held in the Central American country in February 1990. The agreement emphasized diplomacy over military action but kept the Contras intact as a viable opposition force in the event the Sandinistas reneged on their electoral promises. The accord marked a sharp departure from the characteristically bitter White House-Capitol Hill debate over the Contras during the Reagan years. Bush came under criticism from Congress in June for his reaction to Communist China's brutal suppression of the TIANANMEN UPRISING. The president disputed charges his administration had not responded forcefully enough to Beijing's massacre of thousands of Chinese students demonstrating for democracy and contended that it was in America's interest to maintain effective ties with China. Simmering tensions between Washington and Panama City mounted after Panama's strongman General Manuel Antonio Noriega overturned the presidential election victory of opposition candidate Guillermo Endara in May 1989. In December 1989 Bush ordered the PANAMA INVASION to protect Americans in the CANAL ZONE and oust the Noriega regime. Noriega surrendered to U.S. forces in January 1990 and was flown to Florida to face drug-trafficking charges. In February 1990 opposition candidate Violeta Chamorro won an upset victory over Sandinista incumbent Daniel Ortega in the Nicaraguan presidential election, after which Bush initiated U.S. economic aid to the new Nicaraguan government.

In May 1990 Bush and Gorbachev conferred again at the WASHINGTON SUMMIT. The United States and USSR the same year spearheaded completion of the FINAL SETTLEMENT WITH RESPECT TO GERMANY TREATY ending that nation's postwar division and the CONVENTIONAL FORCES EUROPE TREATY reducing armaments on the continent. The new U.S.-Soviet cooperation first was tested when Iraq invaded Kuwait in August 1990. Joining the worldwide condemnation of the Iraqi aggression, Bush deployed U.S. forces to the defense of Saudi Arabia and took the lead in assembling an international coalition to reverse the invasion. The president and Gorbachev discussed their common strategy on the Persian Gulf crisis at the HELSINKI SUMMIT in September 1990. With Moscow's acquiescence, Bush was able to gain passage by the U.N. Security Council of a series of resolutions sanctioning the use of force to compel Iraq to withdraw from Kuwait.

In early 1991 a U.S.-led coalition force scored a quick victory over Iraq in the PERSIAN GULF WAR. In the war's aftermath Bush and Secretary of State JAMES A. BAKER 3RD built on enhanced U.S. influence in the region to press for a settlement of the longstanding Arab-Israeli conflict. The historic MIDDLE EAST PEACE CONFERENCE opened in

Madrid in October 1991 under joint U.S.-Soviet sponsorship. In May 1991 Washington and Moscow helped negotiate a cease-fire agreement ending the ANGOLAN CIVIL WAR. In July, at the MOSCOW SUMMIT, Bush and Gorbachev signed the START Treaty reducing superpower nuclear arsenals. The following month Bush aligned the United States behind Gorbachev and Russian leader Boris N. Yeltsin during the failed MOSCOW COUP by Communist hardliners. In September he announced the NUCLEAR REDUCTION INITIATIVE curtailing U.S. nuclear forces. Following the disintegration of the Soviet Union in December 1991, the Bush administration recognized as sovereign countries Russia and the other principal members of the newly formed Commonwealth of Independent States. The same month the administration helped conclude the U.N.-sponsored agreement ending the EL SALVADOR CIVIL WAR.

BUSH, VANNEVAR (1890–1974) Engineer and administrator who played a central role in mobilizing science and technology for the national war effort during WORLD WAR II. Bush was born in Massachusetts. He earned both bachelor's and master's degrees from Tufts College in 1913 and received his doctorate in engineering jointly from Harvard University and the Massachusetts Institute of Technology (MIT) in 1916. During WORLD WAR I he worked for the Navy on submarine-detection research. He joined MIT's faculty in 1919, becoming dean of its engineering school in 1932. He invented a number of advanced computational instruments, including the differential analyzer, forerunner of the modern computer. In 1939 Bush became president of the Carnegie Institution of Washington. He accepted appointment the next year as chairman of the National Defense Research Committee (NDRC), the federal panel formed to direct war-related scientific research. In 1941 he became chairman of the newly formed Office of Scientific Research and Development (OSRD), which absorbed the NDRC. As science administrator during World War II, he oversaw development of an array of new weapons and war-related technologies. Bush directed all scientific research related to the MANHATTAN PROJECT, the undertaking that produced the atomic bomb in 1945.

After the war he prepared a report, *Science: The Endless Frontier*, in which he urged continued massive government funding for basic scientific research in peacetime. His recommendations influenced creation of the National Science Foundation in 1950. Bush returned to the presidency of the Carnegie Institution in 1948. He gave up the post in 1955 to become director of the pharmaceutical firm Merck and Company and later served as the chairman of the MIT Corporation. Bush published his memoirs, *Pieces of the Action*, in 1970.

BUTLER, NICHOLAS MURRAY (1862–1947) American educator, political leader, and co-winner of the 1931 Nobel Peace Prize. The New Jersey native attended Columbia University, where he earned his bachelor's degree in 1882, his master's in 1883, and his doctorate in 1884. After study in France and Germany, he accepted a position teaching philosophy at his alma mater in 1885 and five years later became a full professor. In 1901 Butler was appointed university president, an office he held until his retirement in 1945. A lifelong conservative Republican, he was an influential party regular who served as a delegate to every Republican National Convention from 1904 to 1932 and advised Presidents THEODORE ROOSEVELT, WILLIAM HOWARD TAFT, WARREN G. HARDING, and CALVIN COOLIDGE on both domestic and foreign affairs. In 1912 he stepped in as Republican candidate for vice-president following the death during the campaign of regular nominee James S. Sherman.

Butler became closely acquainted with European leaders and political developments through frequent trips to Great Britain and the Continent after 1905. He was a charter member of the CARNEGIE ENDOWMENT FOR INTERNATIONAL PEACE and served as its president from 1925 to 1945. He urged U.S. entry into WORLD WAR I on the side of the Allies. In the postwar debate over the TREATY OF VERSAILLES and the issue of U.S. entry into the LEAGUE OF NATIONS, he sided with the so-called RESERVATIONISTS, the group of U.S. senators who generally favored American participation in the league but endorsed a set of reservations to the treaty clarifying U.S. interests. Involved in the formulation of the KELLOGG-BRIAND PACT (1928), which renounced war as a means for achieving national goals, Butler first suggested that the covenant be opened to all nations. He obtained the endorsement of Pope Pius XI for the pact and worked to win Senate ratification. For these efforts he shared the 1931 Nobel Peace Prize with peace activist and social reformer JANE ADDAMS.

BYRD AMENDMENT (1971) Federal legislation designed to bring about a resumption of U.S. chromium imports from Rhodesia. In 1965 white settlers had declared the British colony of Rhodesia (now Zimbabwe) in southern Africa an independent nation. The following year the UNITED NATIONS imposed trade sanctions against the white minority government in Salisbury (now Harare) to force it to accede to black majority rule. The United States implemented the sanctions, including a ban on the import of Rhodesian chromium, in 1968. In 1971 Senator Harry F. Byrd, Jr. (D-VA) sponsored an amendment to the Military Procurement Authorization Act that barred the president from blocking the import of strategic metals from non-Communist nations. With the strong support of the chromium-dependent U.S. speciality steel industry, the measure was signed into law November 17, 1971. As intended, it had the basic effect of restoring U.S. imports of Rhodesian chromium. At the urging of the Carter administration, which argued that full U.S. compliance with the U.N. sanctions against Rhodesia was essential to demonstrating America's commitment to majority rule in Africa, Congress overturned the Byrd Amendment on March 15, 1977, reimposing the ban on Rhodesian chromium imports. President JIMMY CARTER lifted U.S. economic sanctions on December 15, 1979, following agreement between the white minority government and Rhodesia's three major black political groups on a transition to majority rule.

See also CONSTRUCTIVE ENGAGEMENT.

BYRNES, JAMES FRANCIS (1879–1972) Congressman and senator, Supreme Court justice, secretary of state, governor of South Carolina. Byrnes was born in South Carolina. After attending public school until age 14, he studied law while a clerk in a law firm and was admitted to the bar in 1903. In 1910 he won election as a Democrat to the

U.S. House of Representatives, where he served seven terms. Defeated in a run for the U.S. Senate in 1924, he returned to private law practice. In 1930 he was elected to the Senate, where he emerged as an important backer of President FRANKLIN D. ROOSEVELT's New Deal legislative program. Reelected in 1936, he came to oppose the New Deal's more liberal facets but strongly supported Roosevelt's efforts, following the 1939 outbreak of WORLD WAR II in Europe, to aid Great Britain in its fight against Nazi Germany.

In June 1941 Roosevelt named Byrnes to the Supreme Court. He resigned his position as an associate justice in October 1942 to accept appointment as the head of the Office of Economic Stabilization during World War II. In 1943 he became director of the Office of War Mobilization. Known as the "assistant president on the home front," he supervised the nation's wartime economy. He accompanied Roosevelt in February 1945 to the YALTA CONFERENCE on postwar Europe. With Roosevelt's death in April 1945, Vice-President HARRY S. TRUMAN became president. The absence of a sitting vice-president placed the secretary of state next in line for the presidency, a fact that led Truman in June 1945 to name the experienced Byrnes to fill the cabinet post.

Byrne's 18-month tenure coincided with the end of World War II and the advent of COLD WAR confrontation with the Soviet Union. He attended the POTSDAM CONFERENCE with Truman, advocated dropping the atomic bomb on Japan, and initially favored continuing the U.S.-Soviet wartime alliance into the postwar administration of Europe. The September 1945 London Conference of the COUNCIL OF FOREIGN MINISTERS revealed deep U.S.-Soviet differences over the future of Soviet-occupied Eastern Europe and convinced Byrnes of the need for a firmer American policy toward the Communist nation. In March 1946 a visibly more assertive Truman administration successfully resolved the IRAN CRISIS, prevailing upon the USSR to withdraw its troops from their wartime positions in northern Iran. Byrnes headed the U.S. delegation to the 21-nation PARIS PEACE CONFERENCE, held from July to October 1946, that drafted peace treaties with the minor Axis powers. During the conference he delivered a major address at Stuttgart, Germany, on

September 6, in which he underscored the importance of a revived Germany to postwar European reconstruction and announced U.S. readiness to accept a divided Germany if agreement could not be reached with the Soviet Union on unification.

In January 1947 Byrnes, citing his health, resigned as secretary and became associated with a Washington law firm. In 1950 he won the governorship of South Carolina on a states' rights platform. During his four years in the office, Byrnes sought to preserve the state's system of legal racial segregation. Prohibited by state law from running again, he retired in 1955.

C

CADORE LETTER See **MACON'S BILL NO. 2**.

CAIRO CONFERENCES See **TEHERAN CONFERENCE**.

CAIRO DECLARATION See **TEHERAN CONFERENCE**.

CALHOUN, JOHN CALDWELL (1782–1850) Statesman and political philosopher who served in the Congress and as secretary of war, secretary of state, and vice-president. Graduating from Yale in 1804, he studied law in Connecticut and was admitted to the bar in 1807 in his native state of South Carolina. After a term in the South Carolina legislature (1808–1809), he was elected to the U.S. Congress as a Democratic-Republican, serving in the House of Representatives from 1811 to 1817. Calhoun quickly earned notice as one of the WAR HAWKS demanding war with Great Britain to uphold America's honor. As acting chairman of the House Committee on Foreign Relations, he introduced the June 1812 report recommending a war declaration against the British. Following the WAR OF 1812, he promoted a broad strengthening of the nation, supporting internal transportation improvements, a national bank, and the TARIFF OF 1816.

As secretary of war under President JAMES MONROE, he improved army organization and oversaw establishment of the BUREAU OF INDIAN AFFAIRS. Elected vice-president in 1824 and reelected in 1828, he served in succession under Presidents JOHN QUINCY ADAMS and ANDREW JACKSON. Calhoun emerged in the late 1820s as a major voice in the divisive national debate over the issue of commercial protectionism. Fearing that the steep TARIFF OF ABOMINATIONS (1828) threatened to drive the disgruntled South to rebellion, he prepared a report on his home state's behalf called the *South Carolina Exposition* (1828) that aired southern objections to a protectionist policy. In it he championed states' rights and first expounded the controversial doctrine of nullification, which asserted that a state had a right to not uphold federal legislation it judged unconstitutional. After Congress established systematic trade protection as the nation's fixed policy through the Tariff of 1832, parts of the South verged on revolt.

The brewing sectional political crisis was defused by the COMPROMISE TARIFF of 1833. Meanwhile disagreement with Jackson over nullification and growing personal friction between the two men had led to Calhoun's resignation as vice-president at the end of 1832.

Elected immediately by the South Carolina legislature to a vacated U.S. Senate seat, the states' rights advocate became absorbed with defending slavery against the challenges presented by abolitionist political activity in the North. In 1844, following the accidental death of ABEL P. UPSHUR, Calhoun was appointed secretary of state, serving in the post for the last year of JOHN TYLER's presidency. He completed negotiations begun by Upshur on a treaty for U.S. annexation of Texas.

Antislavery votes defeated the UPSHUR-CALHOUN TREATY in the Senate in 1844. Calhoun supported TEXAS ANNEXATION, finally accomplished by congressional joint resolution in March 1845, on the grounds it would increase the U.S. territory open to slavery and thereby help keep sectional balance in the Union. Favoring conciliation with Britain on the OREGON QUESTION, he initiated the talks with British Minister to the United States Richard Packenham that were pursued by Secretary of State JAMES BUCHANAN and finally culminated in the OREGON TREATY (1846) resolving the long-standing dispute in Anglo-American diplomacy.

The South Carolina legislature returned Calhoun to the Senate in 1846 on the eve of the MEXICAN WAR. A fervent opponent of the war, he directed the successful fight in the Senate against the WILMOT PROVISO, special legislation that would have mandated slavery's exclusion from any territory acquired from Mexico by the United States in the conflict. He continued to insist on an unqualified right of American citizens to carry slaves into any U.S. territory. Under the philosophy of government articulated by Calhoun, Congress could not legitimately restrict the spread of slaveholding. In his final speech to the Senate, on March 4, 1850, delivered by a colleague while the gravely ill Calhoun sat looking on, the South Carolinian denounced the Compromise of 1850, the legislative plan fashioned by HENRY CLAY to reconcile bitter sectional differences over the closely linked issues of U.S. territorial accession and slavery. Calhoun argued the act did not satisfactorily safeguard southern interests and presaged a sectional political imbalance that would favor the North. He died in Washington on March 31.

CAMBODIAN CIVIL WAR (1978–1991) Protracted armed struggle for control of Cambodia. The UNITED NATIONS mediated a settlement of the war at the end of 1991. The civil conflict in the Southeast Asian nation pitted a coalition of U.S.-supported resistance groups and Communist Khmer Rouge guerrillas against the Vietnamese-installed Communist government. Until his ouster by General Lon Nol in a coup in 1970, Cambodian ruler Prince Norodom Sihanouk had kept his country neutral in the VIETNAM WAR. Because Cambodia shared a long border with South Vietnam, it became a key staging area for North Vietnamese forces. Despite official Cambodian neutrality, Sihanouk had had little recourse but to tacitly acquiesce to the powerful Communist North Vietnamese military operating within Cambodia in its fight against U.S. ally South Vietnam. The United States responded by launching a secret bombing campaign of North Vietnamese bases in Cambodia in 1969. In 1970 President RICHARD M. NIXON ordered the CAMBODIAN INCURSION, an offensive mounted by U.S. and South Vietnamese forces against Communist sanctuaries along the border.

In the early 1970s Cambodia was drawn deeper into the Southeast Asian conflict. America supported the Lon Nol government in its struggle against an insurgency mounted by Cambodian Communist guerrillas known as the Khmer Rouge. In April 1975, at the same time North Vietnam was completing its conquest of South Vietnam, the Khmer Rouge drove Lon Nol from power. The triumph of Communist forces in both countries marked the collapse of U.S. post–WORLD WAR II policy in Indochina. Washington did not recognize the Communist governments in Cambodia (known as Kampuchea from 1976 to 1989) and Vietnam.

The Khmer Rouge under leader Pol Pot imposed a genocidal regime in Cambodia. More than a million Cambodians perished in a brutal reorganization of society based on radical Marxist agrarianism. Border clashes between historic enemies Cambodia and Vietnam prompted Hanoi to mount a full-scale invasion of its neighbor in November 1978. By January 1979 Vietnamese forces had overrun Cambodia and installed a friendly government in Phnom Penh under former Cambodian official Heng Samrin. The Khmer Rouge retreated to jungle camps along the Thailand border. A resistance group under non-Communist leader Son Sann and another faction loyal to Prince Sihanouk also waged a guerrilla campaign against the Heng Samrin government. In 1982 the three groups formed an alliance and established a government in exile. Under the anti-Communist REAGAN DOCTRINE, America funneled covert military supplies and aid to the two non-Communist groups.

The rebel coalition and Heng Samrin's Vietnamese-backed regime fought throughout the decade. Under international pressure, Vietnam withdrew its military forces from Cambodia in 1989. Meanwhile peace talks among the four Cambodian factions had begun in Indonesia in 1988. The end of the COLD WAR brought greater cooperation between the United States and Soviet Union in seeking a Cambodian settlement. In 1990 the five permanent members of the United Nations Security Council drafted a peace plan providing for a U.N. peacekeeping presence in the country pending national elections. Vietnam supported the peace process as part of its effort to improve relations with the West, particularly with the United States. After difficult negotiations, representatives of the Cambodian government, the three rebel factions, the five permanent U.N. security council members, and 13 other nations signed a final Cambodian peace settlement on October 23, 1991, at a conference in Paris. The treaty implemented a permanent cease-fire and provided for a Supreme National Council headed by Prince Sihanouk and including representatives from all four factions to govern the country pending U.N.-supervised free elections in 1993. To ensure Cambodia's peaceful transition to an elected government, the United Nations assumed responsibility for the basic functions of the Cambodian government, including foreign affairs, defense, and finance. A United Nations Transitional Authority, expected eventually to number some 25,000 civilian and military personnel, was established to administer the country.

Washington indicated it would open ties with the Supreme National Council but would wait to establish full diplomatic relations with a democratically elected Cambodian government. The Bush administration came under domestic criticism for accepting a coalition government that included the infamous Khmer Rouge. The White House contended that the Khmer Rouge was a well-armed and sizable faction that could not be ignored and maintained further that the peace treaty contained safeguards to preclude a Khmer return to power. In the wake of the Cambodian settlement the Bush administration announced plans to seek a gradual normalization of relations with Vietnam.

CAMBODIAN INCURSION (1970) U.S.-led military incursion into Cambodia during the VIETNAM WAR. Former French protectorate Cambodia emerged from the 1954 GENEVA CONFERENCE as an independent, neutral nation. Cambodian ruler Prince Norodom Sihanouk attempted to keep his country out of the growing conflict in neighboring Vietnam. By the mid-1960s, however, North Vietnamese units had established bases in eastern Cambodia to support their operations in South Vietnam. Because it was U.S. policy to respect Cambodian neutrality, the Communist bases in effect were sanctuaries free from American attack. In March 1969 the Nixon administration, seeking a way to hinder Communist operations without publicly violating Cambodian neutrality, began a secret bombing campaign against the sanctuaries. In the face of a mounting Communist Khmer Rouge insurgency, Prince Sihanouk was overthrown by anti-Communist General Lon Nol in March 1970.

The following month President RICHARD M. NIXON ordered an assault into Cambodia by U.S. and South Vietnamese forces to destroy Communist supply depots and staging areas. Nixon defended the operation as a necessary response to North Vietnamese violations of Cambodian neutrality. Its goals, he announced, were twofold: to assist the Lon Nol government in its battle against Communist forces; and to cripple North Vietnamese offensive capabilities, thus buying additional time for VIETNAMIZA-TION, the U.S. policy of transferring to the South Vietnamese army responsibility for fighting the war. Approximately 32,000 American and 48,000 South Vietnamese troops moved as far as 20 miles into Cambodia on April 29, 1970. The incursion sparked an upsurge in domestic antiwar dissent. On May 4, four college students were shot to death by Ohio National Guardsmen sent to keep order during a protest at Kent State University against U.S. policy in Southeast Asia.

In Congress, antiwar legislators introduced the COOPER-CHURCH AMENDMENT to halt U.S. operations in Cambodia and the broader McGOVERN-HATFIELD AMENDMENT to terminate American military involvement in Southeast Asia. Under pressure, Nixon on June 30, 1970, ended the incursion earlier than originally planned. The raid succeeded in capturing large quantities of enemy supplies and the administration claimed it set back North Vietnamese offensive operations by two years. The Cooper-Church measure, enacted in January 1971, blocked future U.S. combat operations in Cambodia. Antiwar critics on the political left have argued that the U.S. incursion into Cambodia brought full-scale war to the ancient kingdom and contributed to the eventual fall of Phnom Penh to the murderous Khmer Rouge in 1975.

CAMP DAVID ACCORDS (1978) Pair of U.S.-mediated agreements between Egypt and Israel providing the framework for both an Egyptian-Israeli peace pact and a comprehensive Middle East peace settlement. The accords culminated a process that began with the signing after the YOM KIPPUR WAR (1973) of two Egyptian-Israeli troop disengagement agreements, the first in 1974 and the second, the so-called Interim Agreement, in 1975. These measures, both reached through the SHUTTLE DIPLO-MACY of U.S. Secretary of State HENRY A. KISSINGER, had arranged for the separation of the Egyptian and Israeli armies along the Suez Canal and in the Sinai Peninsula. Israel had occupied the Sinai since capturing it from Egypt in the 1967 Six-Day War. When President JIMMY CARTER took office, he assumed from Kissinger the mantle of diplomatic broker in the volatile Middle East. Carter feared that a renewal of hostilities be-

tween the Jewish state and its Arab neighbors would imperil the supply of Mideast oil to the United States and might lead to a dangerous superpower confrontation in the region, where the Soviet Union wielded considerable influence. He hoped to achieve a settlement of the long-standing Arab-Israeli conflict, of which the historical enmity between Egypt and Israel was a major part.

Egyptian President Anwar Sadat's dramatic journey to Jerusalem in November 1977 brightened the outlook for a diplomatic breakthrough in the Middle East. Addressing the Israeli parliament, he set forth several principles which he contended must govern any peace settlement. Among them was Israel's consent to a homeland for the Palestinians residing in the Israeli-occupied Gaza Strip and West Bank. His visit led to the opening of Egyptian-Israeli peace talks in January 1978. Despite the boost Sadat's pilgrimage gave to the peace process, the negotiations reached an impasse by late summer 1978, whereupon Carter invited Sadat and Israeli Prime Minister Menachem Begin to meet with him for talks at the presidential retreat at Camp David, Maryland. On September 17, 1978, after 13 days of arduous negotiations mediated by the American president, Sadat and Begin signed two accords setting out guidelines for achieving a Middle East peace. Carter signed as a witness.

The first accord, a "Framework for Peace in the Middle East," dealt with the West Bank and Gaza Strip and the fate of their Palestinian inhabitants. It declared UNITED NATIONS Security Council Resolution 242 (1967) the basis for achieving a just and permanent settlement of the Arab-Israeli conflict. The resolution, adopted following the Six-Day War, called for Israeli withdrawal from occupied territories and for recognition by all states in the Middle East of one another's sovereignty and "right to live in peace within secure and recognized boundaries, free from threats or acts of force." The agreement provided for full Palestinian autonomy and self-government in the West Bank and Gaza Strip during a five-year transition period, in which time Israel, Egypt, Jordan, and elected Palestinian representatives would negotiate the permanent status of the two Israeli-occupied territories. Under the accord Israel would keep troops in designated areas of the West

Bank during the five-year period; withdraw at once its military government and allow the Palestinians to choose a form of local government in the West Bank and Gaza; and freeze new Israeli settlements on the West Bank during peace negotiations. The first Camp David document also provided for the normalization of relations between Israel and Egypt, Jordan, Syria, and Lebanon.

The second accord, a "Framework for the Conclusion of a Peace Treaty Between Egypt and Israel," called for completion within three months of an Egyptian-Israeli peace pact, based on total Israeli withdrawal from Egyptian territory in the Sinai within three years. The Camp David Accords made no mention of rival Arab and Israeli claims to East Jerusalem, which Israel had seized in 1967 and subsequently annexed. The second Camp David agreement finally led to the signing of a peace pact by Sadat, Begin, and Carter on March 26, 1979, in Washington. The Egyptian-Israeli Peace Treaty, the first peace settlement ever concluded between an Arab state and Israel, was brought to fruition through the perserverant personal diplomacy of Carter, who had visited Egypt and Israel earlier in the month to overcome last-minute obstacles and pressure Sadat and Begin to finalize the historic agreement. The treaty formally ended the state of war that had existed between the two countries since Israel's creation as a state in 1948. It arranged for a phased Israeli withdrawal of all military forces and civilian settlements from the Sinai over a three-year period. During the phased pullout U.N. buffer zones would be maintained in the peninsula, which would generally be demilitarized. To monitor the agreement, U.N. forces and observers were to be deployed in select Egyptian-Israeli border areas. Moreover, the United States agreed to conduct surveillance flights over the area to check on Israeli and Egyptian compliance.

Egypt and Israel pledged to establish normal diplomatic relations and exchange ambassadors following the first nine-month period of Israeli withdrawal. Egypt consented to end its economic boycott of Israel and grant Israeli ships and cargoes the right of passage through the Suez Canal. Also, Egypt and Israel agreed to begin negotiations, under U.S. supervision, on

Palestinian self-rule in the West Bank and Gaza Strip. These talks were scheduled to commence one month after the formal exchange of treaty ratification documents. The treaty did not mention the status of East Jerusalem. To help bring the accord to completion, Carter had promised some $4 billion in U.S. economic and military aid to Egypt and Israel over three years. As an adjunct to the treaty, the United States and Israel on March 26 also signed two separate memorandums of agreement. One memorandum provided U.S. assurances of military and political assistance to Israel in the event Cairo violated its pact with Jerusalem; the other contained a U.S. pledge to guarantee a satisfactory oil supply to the Jewish state. Egypt denounced the separate U.S.-Israeli agreements in a statement by Sadat on March 28. Egypt and Israel formally ratified their peace treaty in April 1979.

The Camp David agreements, for which Begin and Sadat were awarded the 1978 Nobel Peace Prize, met with swift and strong opposition within Sadat's own government and across the Arab world. Both the Egyptian foreign minister and ambassador to the United States promptly resigned, scoring the Camp David results as an abandonment of the other Arab states. Leaders of virtually all the Arab countries and the Palestine Liberation Organization (PLO) condemned the accords, charging that they failed to secure an Israeli pledge of total withdrawal from Arab territories and did not mention either a Palestinian right to statehood or a role for the PLO in the peace process. Sadat was accused of arranging a deal with Israel at the expense of the larger Arab cause. Hard-line Arab states severed diplomatic and economic relations with Cairo. After the signing of the Egyptian-Israeli Peace Treaty in 1979, Egypt was suspended from the Arab League and numbers of other Arab nations moved to cut diplomatic and economic ties with Sadat's government. Arab foes of the peace settlement cited it as evidence that the Carter administration was backing away from its commitment to seek a comprehensive settlement of the Arab-Israeli conflict. The Egyptian-Israeli talks on Palestinian autonomy began as scheduled but made no progress toward resolving that key question. The Camp David Accords and ensuing

Egyptian-Israeli peace pact failed to expand the Middle East peace process.

See also MIDDLE EAST PEACE CONFERENCE, REAGAN PLAN, SINAI PEACEKEEPING FORCE.

CAMP DAVID SUMMIT (1959) Talks between President DWIGHT D. EISENHOWER and Soviet Premier Nikita S. Khrushchev in September 1959 directed at easing long-standing COLD WAR tensions and resolving the BERLIN CRISIS. Throughout 1958 Khrushchev had sought a summit of the BIG FOUR (the United States, Great Britain, France, and Soviet Union) to address outstanding East-West conflicts over Germany's future, European security, and the international arms race. Failure of the Soviets and the Western powers to agree on a conference agenda precluded any top-level parley. Khrushchev raised international tensions in November 1958 when he declared that allied wartime agreements on Germany were no longer binding and demanded that the United States, France, and Great Britain terminate their post–WORLD WAR II occupation rights in West Berlin within six months. The Eisenhower administration responded by signaling its determination to hold Berlin by force if necessary. In March 1959, the Soviet government eased off the November ultimatum and agreed to a preliminary four-power conference of foreign ministers in preparation for a summit of leaders on Berlin and related issues.

The foreign ministers convened in Geneva, Switzerland, between May and July 1959 but their talks failed to produce a basis for a summit gathering. Unhappy at the lack of progress at Geneva, Eisenhower invited Khrushchev to visit the United States in the fall. In late August, the American president traveled to Bonn, London, and Paris to assure allied leaders that Khrushchev's pending trip represented neither a move toward unilateral U.S. negotiation with the Soviets nor a break in the continuity of American policy in Europe.

The Soviet premier arrived September 15, 1959, embarking on a high-profile and propaganda-filled nationwide tour from Washington to New York, the West Coast, Iowa, and Pennsylvania before returning for final face-to-face talks with Eisenhower at Camp David, Maryland, from September 25 to 27. At Camp David, Khrushchev accepted a postponement of his Berlin demands and Eisenhower agreed to a Big Four summit before the year's end. When France ruled out an imminent meeting, the summit was rescheduled for May 1960 in Paris.

The cordial "spirit of Camp David" proclaimed by Khrushchev appeared to clear the way for the long-discussed conference of Eisenhower, the Soviet premier, French President Charles de Gaulle, and British Prime Minister Harold MacMillan. But the U-2 INCIDENT, in which a U.S. spy plane was downed over the Soviet Union on the eve of the scheduled discussions, scuttled the 1960 PARIS SUMMIT at its outset, and ended the post–Camp David talk of an East-West thaw in relations.

CANADIAN RECIPROCITY AGREEMENT (1911) Abortive reciprocal trade pact between the United States and Canada. For more than 40 years after the abrogation of the MARCY-ELGIN TREATY (1854) in 1866, the United States had rejected proposals by Canada for trade reciprocity. Republicans, enjoying national political ascendency, had faithfully upheld high protective tariffs from the Civil War through the end of the 19th century. In 1909 they engineered passage of the PAYNE-ALDRICH TARIFF, a measure that struck at Canadian imports with severity and led Canada to threaten retaliation. To avert an anticipated tariff war, President WILLIAM HOWARD TAFT signed an agreement with Canadian Prime Minister Sir Wilfred Laurier on January 26, 1911, for commercial reciprocity.

The accord provided for reduction or elimination of duties on many of Canada's products, chiefly agricultural commodities, and for lowered rates on American manufactured items. Since the pact was not a treaty, it was subject to approval by both the House of Representatives and the Senate. The agreement won final approval in Congress in July 1911, despite opposition from domestic lumber, fish, and agricultural interests. But when Taft and several congressional supporters of the measure publicly remarked that free trade would lead to eventual U.S. annexation of Canada, feelings of nationalism in America's northern neighbor were aroused. In the Canadian general election of 1911, called as a virtual referendum on the trade issue, the Liberals, who favored the U.S.-Canadian agreement, were defeated by the antireciprocity Conservatives in the September vote. The outcome doomed the agreement and derailed trade reciprocity between the neighbors until 1935.

CANAL ZONE Ten-mile-wide strip of territory running through the Republic of Panama from the Atlantic to the Pacific Ocean. The zone, extending five miles on either side of the Panama Canal, was placed under American sovereignty by terms of the HAY-BUNAU-VARILLA TREATY (1903), which authorized U.S. construction of the isthmian canal. The 1903 treaty granted the United States use of the Canal Zone "in perpetuity" and authorized the American government to militarily fortify the zone and defend the waterway. A governor appointed by the U.S. president exercised authority over the Canal Zone and its civil administration. The governor, who reported to the secretary of the army, also served as ex-officio president of the Panama Canal Company, a federally owned corporation responsible for day-to-day operation of the canal.

Long-standing Panamanian resentments over sweeping American control of the canal flared in the decades after WORLD WAR II. Demand for U.S. withdrawal and a return of the Canal Zone to Panamanian authority intensified. Following the violent anti-American PANAMA RIOTS in January 1964, the Panamanian government insisted on complete revision of the Hay-Bunau-Varilla Treaty and briefly suspended relations with the United States. Intermittent U.S.-Panamanian negotiations brought no breakthrough until February 1974, when the two countries pledged that the Canal Zone would be restored to the sovereignty of Panama.

The two PANAMA CANAL TREATIES signed in September 1977 sealed final agreement on the future of the Canal Zone. The Panama Canal Treaty, which revoked the 1903 Hay-Bunau-Varilla accord, provided for the gradual transfer of the canal to complete Panamanian ownership and control by the year 2000. The pact also recognized Panama's territorial jurisdiction over the Canal Zone, which formally ceased to exist on October 1, 1979, the treaty's effective date. About 60 percent of the former Canal Zone came under direct Panamanian control at this time.

The United States retained provisional control of territory and installations in the zone needed to operate and defend the canal until the end of the century. In December 1989 the United States launched military operations against the government of Panamanian strongman General Manuel A. Noriega. The PANAMA INVASION, which removed Noriega from power, was justified as necessary to protect American lives and interests in the Canal Zone.

See also MAP 6.

CANCUN SUMMIT (1981) Meeting of the heads of government from 22 countries held in Cancun, Mexico, on October 22 and 23, 1981. The gathering, officially the International Meeting on Cooperation and Development, stemmed from a 1980 recommendation of the Brandt Commission, a private panel headed by former West German Chancellor Willy Brandt, for a summit conference of developed and developing nations to further the NORTH-SOUTH DIALOGUE on international economic issues. In March 1981, plans were drawn up for a North-South summit. A total of 22 nations—14 developing nations and 8 industrialized nations, including the United States—agreed to attend. The UNITED NATIONS secretary-general also was included. China accepted an invitation but the Soviet Union declined to participate, holding to its traditional position that North-South economic imbalances were the result of prior European colonialism and thus outside the responsibility of the Communist bloc. In August the foreign ministers of the 22 nations, conferring in Cancun, identified four subjects for discussion at the summit—food, energy, trade, and monetary and financial issues. The actual meeting made little progress in narrowing North-South differences. President RONALD W. REAGAN reiterated the U.S. commitment to free market economic activity as the key to stimulating THIRD WORLD development and growth. The leaders reached a provisional accord to pursue informal negotiations through the United Nations on global economic problems. The major industrial countries, led by the United States, opposed formal talks within the U.N. system, where they faced being outvoted by the more numerous developing countries, and proposed instead discussion under the auspices of the INTERNATIONAL MONETARY FUND and WORLD BANK. In the 1980s the INTERNATIONAL DEBT CRISIS came to dominate North-South relations while the UNITED NATIONS CONFERENCE ON TRADE AND DEVELOPMENT emerged as the principal forum for continuing North-South parleys on restructuring the world economy.

CARACAS EPISODE (1958) Violent anti-American demonstration targeted at Vice-President RICHARD M. NIXON during a visit to Venezuela. Economic difficulties in Latin America produced discontent and frustration that in the late 1950s took form in a rising tide of anti-Americanism. The region's economic woes were blamed on U.S. economic exploitation and on comparatively limited American foreign aid. Latin American critics also contended that the anti-Communist focus of U.S. foreign policy distracted attention from the economic and social ills that were the root cause of political instability in the Americas. Seeking to improve U.S. relations in the Western Hemisphere by promoting the Eisenhower administration's "Good Partner" policy (an offshoot of the GOOD NEIGHBOR POLICY), Nixon embarked on an eight-nation goodwill tour of South America in late April 1958.

His trip triggered anti-American outbursts. In Uruguay and Peru angry crowds, fueled by local Communist movements, greeted the vice-president by shouting him down, pelting him with eggs, and stoning him. Nixon arrived in Venezuela, his final stop, on May 13. In Caracas a large mob attacked his limousine, smashing in the window and nearly overturning the car before Nixon escaped. Shaken but unharmed, he departed the Venezuelan capital as scheduled on May 14 and, his tour completed, returned to Washington. Meanwhile an angered President DWIGHT D. EISENHOWER had mobilized U.S. military units for a possible mission to rescue the vice-president. Nixon's ordeal led the White House to rethink its Latin American policy. The Eisenhower administration promptly won congressional authorization for increased foreign aid and supported the creation in 1959 of the INTER-AMERICAN DEVELOPMENT BANK to furnish low-interest development loans to member Latin American nations.

CARIBBEAN BASIN INITIATIVE (CBI) U.S. sponsored inter-American program to develop stable, free-market democracies in the Caribbean and Central America. President RONALD W. REAGAN unveiled his initiative in an address to the ORGANIZATION OF AMERICAN STATES in Washington, D.C., on February 24, 1982. He outlined an economic and military aid package designed to safeguard the Caribbean basin against the threat of Communist insurgency. The centerpiece of Reagan's CBI was a free-trade provision to permit exports from participating Caribbean basin nations to enter the United States duty-free for 12 years. In a concession to pressures brought by domestic economic interests, Caribbean textiles, apparel items, and sugar exports were excluded under the initiative from duty-free treatment. The president's free-trade proposal represented no marked change in U.S. policy, since almost 90 percent of U.S. imports from Caribbean and Central American nations already were tariff-free. But Reagan contended that broadened duty-free access to U.S. markets would offer expanded opportunities for current Caribbean basin exports and furnish an incentive for Caribbean private investment in new products and services.

The CBI called for supplementary U.S. economic aid totaling $350 million to basin countries. Other parts of the initiative were directed toward the U.S. private sector, including the use of federal tax incentives to encourage investment by U.S. firms in the region and the formation of cooperative development programs among American businesses, U.S. government agencies, and international organizations such as the WORLD BANK. The Reagan proposal prohibited the extension of free-trade privileges and other CBI benefits to Communist nations; countries that had violated the HICKENLOOPER AMENDMENT ban on uncompensated expropriation of property belonging to U.S. citizens; and nations that gave preferential treatment to the exports of countries other than the United States, to the detriment of American commerce. The Reagan administration termed the various restrictions necessary to block CBI benefits from going to countries that were hostile to the United States or that discouraged free enterprise.

Reagan framed the initiative within the context of political unrest in the region, observing that U.S. economic and security interests were tied inextricably to the stability and welfare of basin countries. He described the threat posed by the Soviet Union and Cuba seeking to extend their "colonialist ambitions" in the region. Reagan denounced Soviet and Cuban sponsorship of armed leftist rebels in El Salvador and Guatemala and warned that without quick U.S. action, the violent conflicts in Central America would yield Communist dictatorships on the Cuban model.

Congress approved the basics of the proposal in the Caribbean Basin Recovery Act, signed into law August 5, 1983. But lawmakers, concerned that the CBI would add to U.S. unemployment, pared down the broad program of tax and trade benefits favored by the Reagan administration, leaving a modest package of incentives. The legislation specified that the initiative's provisions applied to the 27 nations in Central America and the Caribbean, as well as Guyana and Surinam, but not Cuba. It incorporated the eligibility criteria outlined by Reagan and added several others including cooperation with U.S. efforts to prevent illegal drug trafficking.

See also KISSINGER COMMISSION, LINOWITZ REPORT.

CARLUCCI COMMISSION (1983) Special panel appointed by Secretary of State GEORGE P. SHULTZ in February 1983 to examine ways to improve U.S. foreign assistance programs. Officially titled the Commission on Security and Foreign Assistance, the 24-member advisory board was headed by FRANK C. CARLUCCI 3RD, former deputy secretary of defense in the Reagan administration. Other members of the joint government-private sector panel included Nicholas F. Brady, future secretary of the treasury; U.S. Representative Dante B. Fascell (D-FL); retired Admiral THOMAS H. MOORER; David Rockefeller, former chairman of Chase Manhattan Bank; and U.S. Senator Paul S. Sarbanes (D-MD). The commission submitted its report November 21, 1983. Its key recommendation was the consolidation of all American foreign economic and military aid programs into a single new agency, tentatively called the Mutual Devel-

opment and Security Administration. While the proposal was never implemented, the panel was credited with focusing attention on U.S. foreign assistance, which had declined in real terms in recent years. Detractors contended the commission also served to advance the Reagan administration's goal of shifting U.S. aid emphasis away from economic development and toward security assistance.

CARLUCCI, FRANK CHARLES, 3RD (1930–) Diplomat, intelligence official, national security adviser, secretary of defense. Carlucci was born in Pennsylvania. He graduated from Princeton in 1952 and served two years in the Navy as a gunnery officer before briefly pursuing a business career. In 1956 he joined the U.S. FOREIGN SERVICE. Assigned to the American embassy in Leopoldville (now Kinshasa) in 1960, he was present during the CONGO CRISIS (1960–1962) over control of the African nation. He was posted to Tanzania in 1964 and from 1965 to 1969 held administrative positions at the U.S. embassy in Brazil. In June 1969 he joined the White House staff as the assistant director of the Office of Economic Opportunity and the following year moved up to director. In 1971 President RICHARD M. NIXON named Carlucci associate director of the Office of Management and Budget. He was elevated to deputy director under CASPAR W. WEINBERGER in 1972. When Weinberger became Secretary of the Department of Health, Education, and Welfare in 1973, he made Carlucci his under secretary.

In December 1974 President GERALD R. FORD appointed Carlucci ambassador to Portugal. In Lisbon, he helped with the implementation of democratic institutions following the April 1974 coup that deposed the nation's right-wing dictatorship. In January 1978 President JIMMY CARTER brought Carlucci back to Washington to become deputy director of the CENTRAL INTELLIGENCE AGENCY. He held the agency's second highest position until January 1981, when he again served under Weinberger as deputy secretary at the Defense Department in the new Reagan administration. In 1983 he left the administration to accept a senior executive position with the Sears World Trade Company. The same year he headed the CAR-

LUCCI COMMISSION, a special blue-ribbon panel that assessed U.S. foreign aid programs.

In January 1987 President RONALD W. REAGAN brought Carlucci back to government service as his national security adviser replacing Admiral JOHN M. POINDEXTER, who had resigned amid the IRAN-CONTRA scandal. Carlucci earned praise for restoring the credibility of the office. He was involved in final negotiations for the INTERMEDIATE NUCLEAR FORCES TREATY and backed the PERSIAN GULF INTERVENTION wherein the United States committed naval forces to protect neutral shipping during the Iran-Iraq War (1980–1988). In November 1987 Carlucci succeeded the retiring Weinberger as secretary of defense. Remaining in the post for the final year of the Reagan presidency, he supported the continuing improvement in U.S.-Soviet relations and worked to hold down defense spending amid a federal budget crisis. In 1989 he returned to private business.

CARNEGIE, ANDREW (1835–1919) Industrialist and philanthropist. Born in Scotland in humble circumstances, he came with his family in 1848 to Allegheny, Pennsylvania, where, at age 13, he found his first job in a cotton factory. Starting out as a telegraph operator with the Pennsylvania Railroad in 1853, he rose on the strength of his abilities to the position of superintendent of the Pittsburgh district. During the Civil War he worked for the War Department in Washington organizing the military telegraph agency and helping arrange for the transport of Union troops. After the war he turned to successful ventures in iron forging and railway bridge building. Beginning in 1873, Carnegie focused all his attention and capital on the nascent American steel industry. He spearheaded the remarkable expansion of U.S. steel manufacturing that, by 1890, enabled America to surpass Great Britain as the world's top steel producer. The hugely successful Carnegie Steel Company controlled most of the country's steel production at century's end. After selling his firm in 1901 to the newly formed U.S. Steel Corporation, he retired to a life of philanthropy. To distribute his vast wealth he set up a series of Carnegie trusts, or foundations.

Carnegie had taken an active interest in foreign affairs by the end of his business career. Prominent in the anti-imperialist movement of the 1890s, he was a major benefactor of the ANTI-IMPERIALIST LEAGUE, whose membership opposed U.S. acquisition of colonies in the Caribbean and Pacific as a result of the SPANISH-AMERICAN WAR (1898). Dedicated to the concept of PAN-AMERICANISM, Carnegie was a delegate to the pioneering inter-American Washington Conference (1889) convened by Secretary of State JAMES G. BLAINE and gave money to build the PAN-AMERICAN UNION building in Washington, D.C. He also funded construction in the Netherlands of the Hague Peace Palace, a center for arbitration of international conflicts. Having come to regard war as civilization's greatest tragedy, he established the CARNEGIE ENDOWMENT FOR INTERNATIONAL PEACE in 1910 with a $10-million fund.

CARNEGIE ENDOWMENT FOR INTERNATIONAL PEACE A trust founded in 1910 by philanthropist ANDREW CARNEGIE with $10 million to advance the cause of world peace. Carnegie intended the funds to be invested toward the abolition of war, which he termed the "foulest blot on our civilization." The endowment defined its basic goals as studying war's causes and prevention, championing the development of international law, and promoting friendly understanding among peoples and nations. Under first president ELIHU ROOT, a former U.S. secretary of state, and his successor, educator NICHOLAS MURRAY BUTLER, the peace trust established an extensive program of fellowships and grants to scholars and institutions worldwide. During WORLD WAR II the Carnegie Endowment joined with other organizations to support the creation of the UNITED NATIONS. In 1948 the trust stopped providing grants in order to focus on developing its own research and educational programs on international organizations, international law, diplomacy, and the role of military force in international affairs. The endowment over time has adjusted its emphasis as world events have changed. Throughout the 1980s it concentrated on East-West arms control, U.S.-Soviet relations, the Arab-Israeli political conflict in the Middle East, and the violence of apartheid in South Africa. Located in New York and Washington, with a European center in Geneva, Switzerland, the politically liberal endowment publishes the quarterly journal *Foreign Policy*.

CAROLINE AFFAIR (1837–1842) Episode along the Canadian-American border in New York that provoked a diplomatic dispute between the United States and Great Britain. In November 1837 William Lyon Mackenzie led a band of Canadian rebels in an uprising in Upper Canada, or present-day Ontario. The rebels sought Canadian independence from Great Britain. Thwarted by government forces, Mackenzie in December fled across the border and set up headquarters in Buffalo, New York, where he raised money and recruited volunteers to fight the British in Canada. He then relocated with his 1000-man rebel force to Navy Island on the Canadian side of the Niagara River and established a provisional government there. American sympathizers supplied the insurgents with food and arms transported from the New York shore on an American-owned steamboat, the *Caroline*. Determined to stop the supply effort, a party of some 50 Canadian troops on the night of December 29 crossed to the New York side of the Niagara River. Seizing and destroying the *Caroline*, the invading force killed American citizen Amos Durfee and wounded several others in the course of overpowering the crew.

The *Caroline* Affair sparked a patriotic uproar and raised anti-British sentiment in the United States. President MARTIN VAN BUREN lodged a strong protest with the British government over the raid and insisted on redress. Great Britain, ignoring complaints about violations of American territory and sovereignty, refused either to take responsibility for the assault or to meet demands for payment of an indemnity. Van Buren meanwhile took steps to quell border unrest in the aftermath of the *Caroline* conflict. In early January 1838 he issued a neutrality proclamation warning Americans against unlawful interference in British North America. Simultaneously, he posted U.S. forces under General WINFIELD SCOTT along the eastern Canadian frontier to prevent further border strife. The Canadian rebels abandoned Navy Island on January 13, surrendering their arms to the American military.

Threats of armed invasions into Canada and anti-British feelings continued through 1838. A group of Americans avenged the *Caroline* on May 29 by boarding and burning the Canadian vessel *Sir Robert Peel* on the U.S. side of the St. Lawrence River. Along the frontier of British North America, Canadian refugees and Americans formed secret societies committed to driving the British from Canada. Raids conducted by the societies fanned the border strife and invited Canadian retaliation. Anglo-American tensions subsided by the end of 1839 as the activities of the short-lived secret groups tailed off.

Interest in the *Caroline* Affair was rekindled by the so-called McLeod Case. Alexander McLeod, a Canadian deputy sheriff, was arrested in New York State in November 1840 and charged with the murder of Amos Durfee during the *Caroline* Affair. The British government demanded his immediate release. Secretary of State JOHN FORSYTH and his successor, DANIEL WEBSTER, replied that New York courts held exclusive jurisdiction over McLeod and that the federal government could not interfere with New York's legal authority in the case. New York Governor WILLIAM H. SEWARD informed Webster privately that he would pardon McLeod if found guilty so as to avoid international repercussions. McLeod was acquitted on October 12, 1841, and released. A final settlement of the *Caroline* incident was achieved during the negotiations on the WEBSTER-ASHBURTON TREATY (1842). Great Britain, insisting Canadian troops had invaded American territory in self-defense, expressed regret that no immediate explanation and apology were made after the raid. For its part the United States accepted the destruction of the *Caroline* as a self-defense measure and therefore abandoned the U.S. indemnity demand.

CARTER DOCTRINE (1980) Doctrine declaring American determination to protect the Persian Gulf region against external attack. President JIMMY CARTER extended the U.S. defense pledge to the Arab oil states and the region along the Soviet Union's border in the course of his State of the Union message on January 23. The doctrine, which defined the gulf area as a vital U.S. interest, was announced in the wake of the Soviet invasion of Afghanistan in late December 1979. Targeting his warning at the Soviets, Carter said the United States was prepared to use military force if necessary to safeguard the oil-supply routes of the Persian Gulf. The president, to demonstrate his resolve, revealed plans to reinstate the Selective Service System so national registration for a draft could begin. He also approved creation of the Rapid Deployment Force, which provided a quick-response military capability in the event of a gulf crisis. Both Carter and his successor, RONALD W. REAGAN, sought to strengthen the doctrine by fashioning a network of U.S. military facilities and assistance programs from Egypt to Pakistan.

CARTER, JAMES EARL, JR. (1924–   ) Governor, statesman, 39th president of the United States. Jimmy Carter was born and raised in rural Plains, Georgia. He graduated from Annapolis in 1946 and served in the Navy until 1953. On his father's death, he returned to Plains to run the family peanut business. From 1963 to 1967 he was a member of the Georgia state senate. Elected governor of Georgia in 1970, he emerged during his four-year tenure as one of a new generation of moderate Southern political figures who supported civil rights progress. In 1975, as part of a fledgling campaign for the presidency, he published an autobiography, *Why Not the Best?* Pledging to restore integrity and idealism to government after the experiences of the VIETNAM WAR and Watergate scandal, Carter gained the 1976 Democratic presidential nomination and went on to defeat President GERALD R. FORD in the general election.

On taking office in January 1977, Carter pardoned some 10,000 draft evaders from the Vietnam War era. He defended the controversial action, condemned by veterans groups, as an important step toward closing a divisive chapter in the nation's history. Carter's foremost foreign policy priority was to continue the process of DETENTE with the Soviet Union begun under President RICHARD M. NIXON and sustained by Ford. Conservatives attacked the administration's defense budgets as inadequate in light of a major military buildup underway in the Soviet Union. Carter's cancellation in 1978 of the controversial B-1 bomber prompted further criticism. In 1979 he approved initial deployment of the MX missile. The presence of a Soviet brigade in Cuba and Moscow's military assistance to leftist regimes in Angola and Ethiopia strained U.S.-Soviet relations. Nonetheless the superpowers made progress in arms control negotiations. In June 1979 Carter and Soviet General Secretary Leonid I. Brezhnev

met at the VIENNA SUMMIT, where they signed the SALT II arms control agreement. Carter also pursued closer ties with Communist China. In January 1979 he extended U.S. diplomatic recognition to Beijing and the same month Chinese leader Deng Xiaoping made the first official visit by a top Chinese Communist official to the United States and conferred with Carter at the WASHINGTON SUMMIT.

Other fundamental Carter foreign policy goals included placing a strong emphasis on HUMAN RIGHTS in international affairs, containing the further spread of NUCLEAR WEAPONS and materials, and curbing both U.S. foreign arms sales and the international arms traffic. In his first months in office Carter made a commitment to human rights a cornerstone of U.S. relations with other countries and sought to elevate the importance of human rights issues in world affairs. In February 1977 his administration announced that it was suspending U.S. foreign aid to Argentina, Uruguay, and Ethiopia because of human rights violations in those countries. Carter publicly denounced the Soviet Union's treatment of dissidents, spoke for the rights of persons behind the IRON CURTAIN, and scored the apartheid system in South Africa. The president defended his championing of human rights on practical as well as moral grounds, contending it strengthened American influence in the THIRD WORLD. He maintained it helped prevent the spread of Communist-sponsored revolutions by encouraging authoritarian regimes to end the repressive practices that fueled unrest and made societies susceptible to leftist appeals. The Carter human rights policy drew criticism from across the political spectrum. Liberals charged the administration ignored the human rights violations of key allies Iran, the Philippines, and South Korea. Conservatives, by contrast, worried that human rights concerns were being placed before vital American security considerations. The Carter administration throughout its tenure continued to link foreign aid to the human rights record of recipient nations.

In March 1977 the White House prevailed on Congress to repeal the BYRD AMENDMENT (1971), allowing the president to reimpose UNITED NATIONS-sanctioned economic sanctions on Rhodesia (now Zimbabwe) to force its white minority government to accede to black majority rule. Carter lifted the sanctions in December 1979 following agreement within Rhodesia on a transition to a black majority government. In March 1978 Carter signed the NU-CLEAR NON-PROLIFERATION ACT tightening controls on U.S. nuclear exports. In 1980 the administration endorsed the final draft of the multilateral NUCLEAR MATERIAL CONVENTION. Carter's efforts to limit international arms sales proved less successful. His administration, as part of its evolving Mideast policy, found it necessary to undercut its stance against the spread of sophisticated weapons, backing the transfer of advanced U.S. arms to allied countries in the region.

In 1978 Carter attained the two major foreign policy accomplishments of his presidency. In March and April, following months of debate, he narrowly won Senate ratification of the PANAMA CANAL TREATIES. U.S. and Panamanian representatives had concluded the two measures in 1977, culminating 13 years of negotiations. The treaties provided for the United States to turn over the CANAL ZONE to Panama at the end of 1999, with Washington retaining the right to use military force to safeguard the security and neutrality of the PANAMA CANAL. In the capacity of Mideast diplomatic mediator, Carter in September 1978 invited Egyptian President Anwar Sadat and Israeli Prime Minister Menachem Begin to the presidential retreat at Camp David, Maryland. After 13 days of negotiations the three leaders reached agreement on a framework for both a comprehensive Middle East peace settlement and an Egyptian-Israeli peace. The historic CAMP DAVID ACCORDS served as the basis for the March 1979 EGYPTIAN-ISRAELI PEACE TREATY ending 31 years of hostility between the two nations.

In November 1978 Carter won congressional enactment of a watered-down version of his national energy strategy. The legislation, intended to end U.S. dependence on foreign oil, pushed conservation measures and the conversion of industry from oil or gas to coal. In Africa he avoided U.S. involvement in the ANGOLAN CIVIL WAR. Carter twice ordered U.S. assistance to Zaire during the KATANGAN CRISIS (1977–1978) to help repel assaults by Kantangan rebels based in Angola. Hoping to build on the Panama Canal Treaties and continue to improve relations in Latin America, the Carter administration in 1979 extended U.S. recognition and aid to the new Sandinista government in Nicaragua.

Events in Southwest Asia dominated the last year of the Carter presidency. In November 1979 Iranian militants stormed the U.S. embassy in Teheran, seizing more than 60 American hostages. The ensuing IRAN HOSTAGE CRISIS consumed the Carter White House. Carter pursued a wide range of diplomatic initiatives and imposed economic sanctions in a futile effort to secure the release of the hostages from the Islamic fundamentalist and anti-Western Iranian government. In April 1980 he ordered a military rescue mission that ended in failure with eight Americans left dead in the Iranian desert. In December 1979 U.S.-Soviet detente was abruptly halted by Moscow's military intervention in the Afghanistan War. Carter led the worldwide response to the Soviet invasion of Afghanistan, withdrawing the SALT II Treaty from Senate consideration, suspending U.S. grain sales to the USSR, and organizing an OLYMPIC BOYCOTT of the 1980 games in Moscow. Concerned by potential Soviet inroads in the Persian Gulf region, in January 1980 he proclaimed the CARTER DOCTRINE, declaring U.S. readiness to repel "by the use of any means necessary including military force" any attempt by an outside force to gain control of the gulf region. U.S.-Soviet relations in 1980 reverted to COLD WAR confrontation.

Carter, seriously weakened politically by his seemingly ineffective handling of the Iran Hostage Crisis, was defeated by RONALD W. REAGAN in the 1980 presidential election. In its final weeks the Carter administration, working through intermediary Algeria, was able to negotiate the release of the Iranian hostages. Iran released the captives on January 20, 1981, just minutes after Carter left office. The former president returned to Georgia and remained active in public affairs. As a member of Habitat for Humanity, he worked as a carpenter helping build homes for families without shelter. He established the Carter Presidential Center in Atlanta and published his memoirs, *Keeping Faith*, in 1982. The Carter Center comprises a library, museum, and research center for international issues and conflict resolution. Among its various projects is GLOBAL 2000, a private aid program aimed at improving agriculture and health in the Third World. Carter has been most visible as the head of various international observer teams assembled to monitor elections in nations where the fairness of the voting was in doubt. In 1989 he observed the election in Panama and condemned the effort by Panamanian strongman General Manuel Antonio Noriega to alter the results. In 1990 he monitored elections in the Dominican Republic and Nicaragua, where he helped convince Sandinista leader Daniel Ortega to accept defeat by opposition candidate Violeta Chamorro. In 1991 Carter oversaw the election in Zambia that replaced longtime President Kenneth Kaunda.

CASABLANCA CONFERENCE See **WORLD WAR II CONFERENCES** in **APPENDIX E.**

CASE ACT (1972) Legislation requiring the executive branch to submit to Congress the text of all international agreements. Passage of the law stemmed from congressional concern over the growing use of EXECUTIVE AGREEMENTS in the conduct of U.S. foreign relations. Presidents since GEORGE WASHINGTON had relied on their foreign affairs authority as chief executive to conclude international agreements for handling routine matters such as postal conventions. Unlike treaties, these measures did not require Senate approval. During WORLD WAR II executive agreements replaced treaties as the most commonly used instruments in U.S. relations with other countries. By 1972, America was party to more than 4000 agreements in contrast to roughly 950 treaties. The proliferation in their use was a direct outgrowth of the nation's greatly expanded role in the postwar world.

While acknowledging that many agreements were administrative in nature, members of Congress worried that an increasing number contained important items, such as military commitments, that should have been addressed in treaties. The broad use of executive agreements, it was argued, threatened to bypass congressional involvement in foreign affairs. Disclosure by the SENATE FOREIGN RELATIONS COMMITTEE that the executive branch had withheld from Congress certain highly sensitive agreements so

as to preserve their secrecy drew strong criticism. In February 1972 the Senate approved by an 81 to 0 vote legislation sponsored by Clifford P. Case (R-NJ) that directed the secretary of state to transmit to Congress within 60 days of execution the text of any agreement made with another nation. If the president determined that public disclosure would harm national security, then the text was to be sent in secret to the Senate and House foreign affairs panels. The House subsequently endorsed the measure by voice vote and it was signed into law on August 22, 1972.

See also BRICKER AMENDMENT.

CASE-CHURCH AMENDMENT Congressional measure to end U.S. military involvement in the VIETNAM WAR. In the early 1970s antiwar members of Congress sought to terminate America's role in the conflict by cutting off funding for U.S. combat operations in Southeast Asia. Senators Clifford P. Case (R-NJ) and FRANK CHURCH (D-ID) in early 1972 sponsored an amendment to the 1973 State Department authorization bill that would prohibit funding for U.S. forces in or over North and South Vietnam, Laos, or Cambodia after December 31, 1972. The provision did not bar military assistance to America's Indochinese allies and was contingent on the release of American prisoners of war (POWs). Revised in early May to require the withdrawal of U.S. combat forces from Southeast Asia within four months after an agreement on the return of U.S. POWs, the amendment was defeated 47 to 43 on May 16, 1972.

In January 1973 the United States and North Vietnam signed the PARIS PEACE ACCORDS ending U.S. combat operations in Vietnam. U.S. bombing in neighboring Cambodia continued in the absence of a peace settlement between the pro-Western Cambodian government and the North Vietnamese-backed Communist Khmer Rouge insurgency. Congress debated the Nixon administration's constitutional authority to sustain the bombing without explicit congressional authorization. In May 1973 Case and Church sponsored another end-the-war amendment that would bar spending on U.S. military activities in Indochina without specific congressional approval. The Senate approved the measure by 67 to 15 on June 14, 1973. Meanwhile Congress attached to a supplemental appropriations bill a more specific provision mandating an immediate cutoff of funds for Cambodian operations. President RICHARD M. NIXON vetoed the legislation on June 27. He argued that the congressionally ordered bombing halt would undermine negotiations for a peace settlement in Cambodia. Under intense domestic political pressure, Nixon on June 30 signed a compromise measure that halted funding for U.S. combat activities in Southeast Asia after August 15, 1973. The version of the Case-Church Amendment requiring congressional consent before military operations could be resumed in Indochina was enacted as part of the 1974 State Department authorization measure on October 18, 1973.

See also COOPER-CHURCH AMENDMENT, MC-GOVERN-HATFIELD AMENDMENT, MANSFIELD AMENDMENT.

CASEY, WILLIAM JOSEPH (1913–1987) President of the EXPORT-IMPORT BANK, director of the CENTRAL INTELLIGENCE AGENCY (CIA). Born in New York, Casey graduated from Fordham University in 1934 and earned a law degree from St. John's University in 1937. He was admitted to the New York bar the following year. During WORLD WAR II Casey served in the OFFICE OF STRATEGIC SERVICES (OSS), the nation's wartime intelligence organization and precursor to the CIA. In 1944 he became chief of OSS intelligence operations in the European theater. Following the war he remained in government service as a special counsel to the U.S. Senate's Small Business Committee and as an associate general counsel to the MARSHALL PLAN for postwar European economic relief. In 1948 Casey returned to private law practice in New York. He also taught law at New York University and authored or edited more than 30 books on business and law subjects. His own investments and business ventures soon made him a millionaire.

In 1966 Casey was defeated in a Republican primary election for a New York seat in the U.S. House of Representatives. He actively supported RICHARD M. NIXON's successful 1968 presidential campaign. In 1971 Nixon named Casey chairman of the Securities and Exchange Commission. He became under secretary of state for economic affairs in 1973. In 1974 he headed the Export-Import Bank. He was a member under President GERALD R. FORD of the PRES-IDENT'S FOREIGN INTELLIGENCE ADVISORY BOARD in 1976.

Casey managed RONALD W. REAGAN's victorious 1980 presidential campaign. He was appointed director of the CIA and took office with the new Reagan administration in January 1981. Backed by Reagan, he moved to rebuild the agency's COVERT ACTION capabilities, curtailed by the Carter administration in the late 1970s in the wake of congressional investigations into INTELLIGENCE COMMUNITY abuses. Casey shared the president's staunch anti-communism and profound mistrust of U.S. COLD WAR adversary the Soviet Union. In 1981 he helped formulate the administration's policy of providing covert military aid to the CONTRAS, the Nicaraguan rebels battling the Soviet-backed Sandinista regime in Managua. The early Reagan years also saw a steady increase in U.S. covert assistance funneled to the Mujahedeen rebels fighting the leftist government in Kabul and Soviet military forces in the AFGHANISTAN WAR. Casey was an architect of the REAGAN DOCTRINE. Formally enunciated in 1985, it proclaimed U.S. support for anti-Communist insurgencies seeking to overthrow Marxist regimes in the THIRD WORLD.

During his tenure, clandestine U.S. aid was also furnished to Cambodian guerrillas opposing the Communist Vietnamese-installed government in Phnom Penh and to the Western-allied forces of Joseph Savimbi in the ANGOLAN CIVIL WAR. Casey came under criticism in 1984 for CIA involvement in the Contra mining of Nicaraguan harbors and the production of a Contra manual advocating the "neutralization" (a euphemism for assassination) of Sandinista officials. In 1986 he emerged as a key participant in the burgeoning IRAN-CONTRA scandal. Casey was hospitalized with a malignant brain tumor in December 1986, the day before he was to appear before a congressional panel probing his role in the affair. He never recuperated from surgery and died in May 1987. Later witnesses, most notably central Iran-Contra figure Lieutenant Colonel Oliver L. North, testified that Casey had approved of the secret U.S. arms sales to Iran and masterminded the diversion of the proceeds to the Contras to circumvent congressional restrictions on aiding the rebels. Casey's death, however, left unclear the full extent of his involvement. In 1991 allegations were raised by Gary Sick, a member of the NATIONAL SECURITY COUNCIL staff under President JIMMY CARTER, and others who contended that during the 1980 presidential campaign Casey had secretly arranged with Iranian government officials to postpone release of the U.S. hostages then being held during the IRAN HOSTAGE CRISIS. The charges, which remain unsubstantiated, relate to the so-called October Surprise. This rubric refers to the idea that Casey purportedly wanted to prevent a possible election-eve release of the hostages that might have boosted Carter to victory over Reagan.

CASH-AND-CARRY See **NEUTRALITY ACTS**.

CASS, LEWIS (1782–1866) Cabinet officer, diplomat, and U.S. senator. Born in New Hampshire, Cass was educated at Exeter Academy. In 1799 he went to Ohio, where he read law, was admitted to the bar in 1802 and began a practice in Zanesville. He won election to the Ohio legislature in 1806. After service in the WAR OF 1812, during which he attained the rank of brigadier general, Cass was appointed governor of the Michigan Territory in 1813. His vigorous pursuit of U.S. westward expansionist policy encouraged white settlement in the NORTHWEST TERRITORY and paved the way for eventual Michigan and Wisconsin statehood. In his capacity as governor he negotiated INDIAN TREATIES that secured extensive INDIAN LAND CESSIONS to the U.S. government.

Cass's achievements in Michigan led to his appointment as secretary of war in 1831 by President ANDREW JACKSON. He directed the Army in the BLACK HAWK WAR (1832) and at the outset of the second of the SEMINOLE WARS (1835–1842) and supervised implementation of the INDIAN REMOVAL POLICY that uprooted tribes and pushed them west of the Mississippi River. Appointed U.S. minister to France in 1836, his six-year tenure was marked by his antipathy toward Britain. Acting without State Department instructions, he persuaded the French government not to ratify a major British-sponsored treaty that both proposed legalizing London's interpretation of FREEDOM OF THE SEAS and called for a five-power European naval force to interdict the African slave trade. Cass contended the treaty threatened America's maritime rights. His unauthorized diplomacy, however, infuriated Secretary of State DANIEL WEBSTER, who forced Cass's resignation in 1842.

An ardent expansionist, he strongly urged the annexation of Texas during his unsuccessful bid for the Democratic presidential nomination in 1844. Elected to the U.S. Senate in 1845 from Michigan, he held his seat until 1857. In Congress, Cass opposed a territoral compromise with the British on the OREGON QUESTION; instead he endorsed the "ALL OREGON" movement's claim to the 54° 40' line. He also supported President JAMES K. POLK's policy on the MEXICAN WAR (1846–1848). Territories acquired by the United States as a result of the war forced the slavery issue to the fore. Cass expounded the so-called doctrine of popular sovereignty, which asserted the right of settlers in U.S. territories to determine for themselves whether to permit slavery. Democratic presidential standard-bearer in 1848, he lost the election to Whig candidate ZACHARY TAYLOR when dissident Democrats split from the party to help form the Free-Soil Party. In 1852 he was a losing candidate a final time for the Democratic presidential nomination.

Named secretary of state by President JAMES BUCHANAN in 1857, he won British acquiescence to the U.S. interpretation of the CLAYTON-BULWER TREATY (1850) and induced Britain to abandon its long-held claim to a right to stop and search American vessels at sea. He resigned his post in protest in 1860 over Buchanan's failure to take a strong stand against Southern secession. Cass retired to Detroit where he backed the Union cause in the Civil War and devoted himself to writing history.

CAYUSE WAR (1848–1855) Precipitated by the 1847 Whitman Massacre, the war between the United States and the Cayuse Indians stemmed from the Pacific Northwest tribe's resistance to increasing white immigration into Oregon in the 1840s. Blaming white missionaries for a deadly measles outbreak among the tribe, the Cayuse attacked one of their missions in November 1847, killing founder Marcus Whitman, his wife, and a dozen others. Fighting erupted between settlers in the Oregon Territory and the tribe. In 1848 U.S. troops joined the conflict as Cayuse raids on settlements escalated. Sporadic fighting continued until

1855, when the war-depleted tribe was subdued and forced onto reservation lands. The Cayuse uprising was a prelude to the ROGUE RIVER WAR and the YAKIMA WAR that raged in Oregon and Washington through the mid- and late 1850s.

See also MAP 1.

CENTER FOR STRATEGIC AND INTERNATIONAL STUDIES (CSIS) Influential right-of-center think tank that develops public policy recommendations on national security and foreign affairs. Founded in 1962, the center is an independent institution based in Washington, D.C. Its staff of scholars and fellows studies emerging world problems and the international issues they frame. Formerly called the Center for Strategic Studies, CSIS was affiliated with Georgetown University until 1987. It conducts education programs and research on arms control, science and technology, international economics, political-military affairs, regional studies, environmental studies, and international communications. The center also sponsors a series of prestigious conferences and forums that annually bring together senior statesmen and leaders from the corporate, academic, scientific, and media communities worldwide to examine current global issues. CSIS publications include *The Washington Quarterly* and the *Significant Issues Series*.

CENTO See **CENTRAL TREATY ORGANIZATION**.

CENTRAL AMERICAN TREATIES OF 1907 Set of agreements mediated by the United States and Mexico to bring peace to Central America. The search for stability in the politically turbulent region became an important facet of President THEODORE ROOSEVELT's Caribbean policy in his second term. He and Secretary of State ELIHU ROOT sought political tranquility among the five perpetually feuding Central American republics through establishment of a system of treaty law, whereby each would respect the governments and boundaries of its neighbors. Guatemala, Honduras, El Salvador, Nicaragua, and Costa Rica had a long-standing history of intervening in each others' affairs, aiding revolutions against one another, and turning internal conflicts into regional wars. Bitter rivalries exacer-

bated political struggles within and among the nations.

In June 1906 war broke out between Guatemala and allies El Salvador and Honduras. The United States and diplomatic partner Mexico persuaded the combatants to sign an armistice on July 20 aboard the U.S.S. *Marblehead*. At the same time an agreement was concluded arranging for a general Central American peace conference later in the year. The parley, sponsored jointly by Washington and Mexico City, met at San Jose, Costa Rica, in September and yielded a general peace treaty. Within months, though, new disturbances began, precipitated by Nicaraguan dictator Jose Santos Zelaya. He had boycotted the San Jose Conference as an expression of his adamant opposition to U.S. involvement in Central American affairs. Zelaya harbored ambitions of forging a Central American federation of republics, which he expected to dominate. Zelaya's interference in Honduran affairs through support of antigovernment rebels brought Nicaragua into conflict with both Honduras and its erstwhile ally El Salvador in early 1907. Nicaraguan troops invaded Honduras and captured its capital, Tegucigalpa, installing a government that would be friendly to Managua. Zelaya's scheme for regional dominance also placed him at bitter odds with Guatemala. With Central America on the verge of a general war, Secretary Root stepped forward in late August 1907 and, in conjunction with the Mexican government, proposed another regional peace conference. The leaders of all five Central American countries promptly agreed.

Representatives of the five republics met in Washington, D.C., from November 14 to December 20, 1907. The Washington Conference negotiations produced a series of eight treaties designed to settle regional problems. Key among them was an agreement under which the five countries obligated themselves to establish a Central American Court of Justice to resolve all future disputes among them. In other treaties the signatories pledged to forbid revolutionaries from using their territories as a base for striking against a neighboring state and agreed to withhold recognition from any government in Central America that seized power by force against the popular will. Another accord established the permanent neutrality of Honduras, whose succession of weak governments and central position in the isthmus often had made it a pawn in conflicts between its more powerful neighbors.

The conciliatory spirit that animated the Washington meeting did not last. Within the year renewed internal political unrest and sporadic fighting across borders jeopardized the treaties and threatened the tenuous Honduran neutrality. Zelaya had not abandoned his ambitious ideas and both Guatemala and El Salvador remained determined to resist him. In the face of these pressures the Central American treaty framework endorsed by the United States began unraveling. Political instability and violence brought U.S. intervention in both Honduras and Nicaragua in 1912.

See also HONDURAN INTERVENTIONS, NICARAGUAN INTERVENTIONS.

CENTRAL INTELLIGENCE AGENCY See same in **APPENDIX B**.

CENTRAL INTELLIGENCE GROUP (CIG) U.S. centralized intelligence service that was the predecessor to the CENTRAL INTELLIGENCE AGENCY (CIA). On January 22, 1946, President HARRY S. TRUMAN issued a presidential directive that established a NATIONAL INTELLIGENCE AUTHORITY (NIA). Consisting of the secretaries of state, war, and navy, and a personal representative appointed by the president, the NIA was charged with coordinating foreign intelligence activities throughout the government. The directive specified the formation of a Central Intelligence Group, a consolidated staff of experts drawn from the departments represented on the NIA, to accomplish the actual correlation, evaluation, and dissemination of intelligence information. The CIG was barred from law enforcement or involvement in domestic internal security or intelligence functions such as countering foreign subversion or espionage.

Truman designated the position of director of central intelligence to head the CIG. Admiral SIDNEY W. SOUERS served in the post until June 1946. His successor, General HOYT S. VANDENBERG, was able to expand CIG's size and scope, but the intelligence group was beset by interdepartmental rivalries and proved largely ineffe tive. It was replaced September 18, 194/,

by the newly created CIA under the NATIONAL SECURITY ACT of 1947.

CENTRAL TREATY ORGANIZATION (CENTO) Middle East regional security alliance. In 1955 Great Britain, Turkey, Iraq, Iran, and Pakistan formed the Middle East Treaty Organization, commonly called the Baghdad Pact, for their mutual defense and security. While it also fostered economic cooperation among its members, the organization was primarily a military alliance. The United States, concerned with preventing Communist inroads in the strategic region, strongly supported alignment of the northern tier of Middle Eastern states into a defensive barrier against possible Soviet aggression. Not wanting to inflame Egyptian and other Arab nationalist opposition to the alliance, America never formally joined the pact but associated closely with its defense committees and provided military and economic aid to its members. In 1958 a military coup overthrew the pro-Western Iraqi monarchy, whereupon the new government announced its withdrawal from the pact in March 1959. The same month the United States concluded bilateral defense agreements with Turkey, Iran, and Pakistan, underscoring its commitment to the area's security. The Baghdad Pact, minus Iraq, was reconstituted as the Central Treaty Organization on August 18, 1959. The alliance's name signified its position between NATO and SEATO in the band of COLLECTIVE SECURITY arrangements set up to block Soviet or Communist Chinese expansion. America again vigorously supported but did not enter the new pact. CENTO was disbanded in 1979 following the withdrawal of its Middle Eastern members.

CHAMBERS, DAVID WHITTAKER (1901– 1961) Journalist and Soviet spy who became an ardent anti-Communist. A native of Philadelphia, Whittaker Chambers left Columbia University short of graduation. He joined the Communist Party in New York in 1924 and was the editor of its paper, the *Daily Worker*. By his own admission he became a Soviet intelligence agent in 1932. Disillusioned with communism, Chambers quit the party in 1938 and obtained an editorial position with *Time* magazine. On several occasions over the next 10 years, he divulged his knowledge of

Communists in the federal government to the State Department and the FEDERAL BUREAU OF INVESTIGATION but no action was taken on his accusations.

In August 1948 Chambers was called to testify before a hearing of the HOUSE UN-AMERICAN ACTIVITIES COMMITTEE on Communist subversion in the United States. He acknowledged he had belonged to an underground Communist organization in the 1930s and named former Assistant Secretary of the Treasury HARRY DEXTER WHITE and former ranking State Department official ALGER HISS as other members. Appearing at a time of intensifying COLD WAR confrontation over Soviet expansionism in Europe, Chambers's allegations drew nationwide attention. The international dimensions of the HISS CASE were revealed when he produced evidence of Hiss's prior involvement in Soviet espionage. Hiss was convicted of perjury in January 1950. To many on the political right, Chambers became a symbol of the struggle of Western values against international communism. He published his renowned autobiography, *Witness*, in 1952. President RONALD W. REAGAN posthumously awarded the Medal of Freedom to Chambers in 1984.

CHAPULTEPEC, ACT OF (1945) Inter-American mutual-security agreement concluded near the end of WORLD WAR II. Plans for strengthening COLLECTIVE SECURITY arrangements in the Western Hemisphere were made at the special Inter-American Conference on Problems of War and Peace, which met from February 21 to March 8, 1945, at Chapultepec Castle near Mexico City. All the American republics except Argentina were represented at the gathering. The Argentine government, sympathetic to Nazi Germany, remained a diplomatic outcast in the Americas. For most of the war, Argentina had followed a policy of neutrality, refusing to break relations with the Axis powers. Under growing inter-American pressure, Buenos Aires finally severed relations with Berlin and Tokyo in January 1944. When, a month later, a group of nationalist and pro-Fascist Argentine army officers took control of the government and installed one of their own as acting president, the United States and several Latin American countries had refused to recognize the new regime. In August 1944 Ar-

gentina's gold assets in the United States were frozen in retaliation for its failure to cooperate against the Axis.

At the Mexico City Conference, delegates adopted the Act of Chapultepec on March 6, 1945. It provided for mutual defense by proclaiming that an attack on one American state would be regarded as aggression against all. The act also called for negotiation of a permanent hemispheric defense treaty at the end of the war. In a separate resolution, the American republics agreed to reorganize and strengthen the inter-American system under a formal written constitution. Delegates, moreover, invited Argentina to declare war against the Axis countries, and resolved that if it embraced the principles in the Act of Chapultepec, it would be eligible for membership in the UNITED NATIONS. Capitalizing on the opportunity to end their diplomatic isolation, the Argentinians declared war on Germany and Japan on March 27 and adhered to the Chapultepec agreement. The Argentine government thereupon won U.S. diplomatic recognition and support for admittance to the United Nations. The Act of Chapultepec was forerunner to the RIO TREATY of 1947, the formal inter-American mutual defense pact.

CHARTER OF PARIS FOR A NEW EUROPE See **CONFERENCE ON SECURITY AND COOPERATION IN EUROPE**.

CHENEY, RICHARD BRUCE (1941–) White House chief of staff, congressman, secretary of defense. Born in Nebraska, Cheney grew up in Wyoming, where he earned bachelor's and master's degrees in political science from the University of Wyoming in 1965 and 1966. After serving on the staff of Governor Warren Knowles and as an aide to Congressman William A. Steiger (R-WY), Cheney joined the White House staff of President RICHARD M. NIXON in 1969 as an assistant to DONALD RUMSFELD, director of the Office of Economic Opportunity and then presidential counselor. He left government service in 1973 to work in a Washington investment firm. In 1974 Rumsfeld, who had become chief of staff under President GERALD R. FORD, brought Cheney back to the White House as his deputy. In November 1975 Rumsfeld was named secretary of defense and Cheney was elevated to chief of staff, holding the position until the end of the Ford administration in January 1977.

He began a 10-year career in the House of Representatives in 1979. In 1987 he was a member of the joint select committee that investigated the IRAN-CONTRA scandal. The following year the Wyoming congressman was elected Republican Whip, the second-ranking party leadership post in the House. On March 9, 1989, President GEORGE BUSH's first choice for secretary of defense, JOHN G. TOWER, was rejected by the Senate. The next day Bush nominated Cheney for the position. He was swiftly confirmed and sworn in the same month. He took charge of the Defense Department just as communism was beginning to collapse in Eastern Europe. As American defense requirements in Europe and around the world began to change, he inherited responsibility for directing the reduction of U.S. armed forces in the post–COLD WAR era. Cheney supported the November 1990 CONVENTIONAL FORCES EUROPE TREATY with the Soviet Union and played a lead role in the U.S. response to the Iraqi invasion of Kuwait that culminated in the PERSIAN GULF WAR (1991).

CHEROKEE NATION v. GEORGIA (1831) Landmark case in which the U.S. Supreme Court held that Indian nations were not foreign states within the meaning of the CONSTITUTION. In 1829 Georgia extended its authority over Cherokee territories within its boundaries, seeking to uproot the Indians and open their lands for white settlement. The Cherokees, represented by former U.S. Attorney General William Wirt, asserted they were an independent nation and petitioned the Supreme Court to block Georgia from enforcing its laws in Indian areas. The justices dismissed the suit on procedural grounds, ruling four to two that the Cherokee tribe was not a foreign nation and therefore lacked standing to file its request. Chief Justice JOHN MARSHALL, writing for the majority, characterized the tribe's status as that of a "domestic dependent nation" under the sovereignty and protection of the United States. While maintaining the federal government's ultimate title to all Indian lands, Marshall recognized the Indians' internal political sovereignty, their ability to make treaties with the United States, and their right to the occupancy and use of their own territory. The decision did not address the issue of state authority over Indian areas. The Court would establish the federal government's exclusive jurisdiction over INDIAN AFFAIRS the following year in WORCESTER V. GEORGIA.

CHESAPEAKE AFFAIR (1807) Maritime confrontation between the United States and Great Britain over British IMPRESSMENT of American seamen. The controversial British practice, a bitter issue in Anglo-American diplomacy since the early 1790s, involved the seizure and forced enlistment of alleged British navy deserters serving on American ships. The impressed often included native-born Americans. On June 22, 1807, the U.S. Navy frigate *Chesapeake*, commanded by Commodore James Baron, was confronted by the British warship *Leopard* not far past the three-mile limit off Norfolk, Virginia. Claiming four men aboard the *Chesapeake* were British navy deserters, the British commander demanded their surrender and insisted the American ship submit to a search. When Baron refused the *Leopard* fired on the *Chesapeake*, killing 3 and wounding 18. A British search party boarded the damaged U.S. vessel and removed the four purported deserters, three of whom were Americans.

The bloody *Chesapeake* impressment, condemned in the United States as an assault on American sovereignty and national honor, provoked public outrage and raised a public clamor for war. President THOMAS JEFFERSON on July 2 ordered British warships to leave U.S. territorial waters and revoked their access under JAY'S TREATY (1794) to American ports. Jefferson then decided on economic pressure to try to bring an end to British impressment and to force European respect for American maritime rights. On December 14,1807, he allowed the NON-IMPORTATION ACT (1806) to take effect by lifting the suspension on the measure; and on December 22 he signed the EMBARGO ACT into law.

U.S. war sentiment faded during prolonged Anglo-American negotiations over the *Chesapeake* Affair. Although refusing to abandon impressment, Great Britain accepted blame for the incident and offered to make reparations for American losses. A final settlement came in November 1811, when the British formally renounced the

Leopard's action and returned two of the impressed Americans, the third having died in a British prison.

CHEYENNE AND ARAPAHO WAR (1864–1868) Conflict between U.S. forces and the allied Cheyenne and Arapaho Indians in Kansas intensified at the peak of westward expansion across the central Great Plains. Unhappy with lands reserved for them in the Colorado Territory under an 1861 treaty outlining Indian relocation, the tribes responded by raiding travel routes and white settlements. Settlers retaliated and full-fledged war erupted from Colorado to Texas after the Sand Creek Massacre in November 1864, in which an American military detachment killed 200 Cheyenne who believed they had been extended U.S. protection. Some Kiowa and Comanche Indians joined the fight against the U.S. Army.

A U.S. Army offensive in 1865 failed to subjugate the Cheyenne and Arapaho. Treaties concluded late that year briefly calmed the central Plains. Fighting resumed in 1867 when U.S. troops campaigned to end continuing warrior assaults on settlers and overland travel to the Southwest. The war wound down after a special INDIAN PEACE COMMISSION completed the October 1867 Medicine Lodge Creek Treaty, by which the Cheyenne and Arapaho agreed to leave Kansas and settle on reservations in Oklahoma and Texas.

See also MAP 1.

CHIEF JOSEPH See **JOSEPH, CHIEF**.

CHILE COUP (1973) Overthrow of Chilean President Salvador Allende Gossens by a military coup with at least tacit U.S. support. In 1970 the CENTRAL INTELLIGENCE AGENCY (CIA) funneled more than $1 million to the centrist Christian Democrats in an effort to prevent the Marxist Allende's victory in national elections. On September 4, 1970, Allende won a plurality of the vote, throwing the election into the Chilean Congress, where by custom he could expect to be selected as the next president. Concerned that an Allende government would establish a Communist foothold in South America, President RICHARD M. NIXON authorized a covert two-track strategy to prevent the Chilean leftist from coming to power.

Track I involved exerting U.S. political and economic pressure to influence the Chilean Congress to vote against Allende's election. Track II, which was entrusted to the CIA, involved the encouragement of a coup by members of the Chilean military. By early October 1970 the CIA had initiated secret contacts with anti-Allende police and military officials. U.S.-supported Chilean elements decided to abduct the head of the armed forces, General Rene Schneider, who opposed military intervention in politics, in preparation for a coup. On October 22, 1970, Schneider was killed in a gunfight with kidnappers who had intercepted his car. His assassination helped ensure Allende's victory in the congressional election held two days later.

U.S. efforts to remove Allende continued after his inauguration as president. The CIA covertly provided some $8 million to opposition groups in Chile between 1970 and 1973. The Nixon administration cut off U.S. economic assistance and discouraged private business investment. Allende stoked a worsening political and economic crisis in his country with his moves to socialize the economy, which triggered widespread middle-class opposition. Nationwide trucker strikes in 1972 and 1973 brought economic chaos. On June 19, 1973, loyal forces under Chilean General Carlos Prats put down a coup attempt. Within two months discontent in the armed forces had driven Prats from his post as chief of the Chilean military. He was replaced by General Augusto Pinochet, who headed the military junta that seized control of the Chilean government on September 11, 1973. Allende died at the presidential palace during the successful coup. The cause of death, whether assassination or suicide, is a matter of continuing dispute. According to the later congressional investigation conducted by the CHURCH COMMITTEE, the United States had no direct involvement in the actual coup.

CHINA CARD Expression describing a strategy of using improved U.S.-Communist Chinese ties to influence U.S.-Soviet relations. The term was coined in the 1970s when U.S. policymakers, capitalizing on the Sino-Soviet split of the early 1960s, were able to "play the China card" to induce greater cooperation from Soviet leaders worried over closer links between their American superpower rival and the hostile Communist Chinese state on their eastern border. The Nixon administration's historic 1971 opening with Communist China was widely seen as having hastened the emergence of U.S.-Soviet DETENTE. The Carter administration's decision in December 1978 to extend diplomatic recognition to Peking represented, in part, a China card policy to encourage U.S.-Soviet arms control negotiations. In the early 1980s, the Reagan administration looked to Communist China as an important counterbalance to strained U.S.-Soviet relations. Following Mikhail S. Gorbachev's rise to power in the USSR in 1985, the relevance of a China card strategy faded as internal Soviet reform brought rapidly improving U.S.-Soviet ties and then, in 1991, the collapse of the Soviet Communist state.

CHINA LOBBY Umbrella term encompassing the various organizations and individuals that emerged after WORLD WAR II as a powerful pressure group for U.S. support of the Nationalist Chinese government under Chiang Kai-shek in its struggle against Communist forces under Mao Tse-tung. After Mao's 1949 victory and Chiang's retreat to the island of Taiwan (then commonly known as Formosa), the China Lobby bitterly criticized the U.S. decision not to aid Chiang, accusing the Truman administration of "losing" the Chinese mainland to communism. In August 1949 Secretary of State DEAN ACHESON released the CHINA WHITE PAPER defending U.S. policy not to intervene in the Chinese civil war on behalf of Chiang's corrupt regime. In the early 1950s, the lobby actively backed Chiang's return to the mainland. As it became apparent this was infeasible, its emphasis shifted to the defense of Taiwan and the international isolation of the People's Republic of China. Former President HERBERT C. HOOVER in 1953 headed a national group that formed the Committee of One Million Against the Admission of Communist China into the UNITED NATIONS. Other prominent members of the China Lobby were publisher HENRY R. LUCE, former ambassador to China General Patrick J. Hurley, and U.S. Senator William F. Knowland (R-CA), known as "the senator from Formosa." The lobby's influence on U.S. policy faded in the 1960s and effectively ended with the

Nixon administration's historic 1971 opening to Communist China.

CHINA WHITE PAPER (1949) State Department study of U.S. policy in China. In December 1945 President HARRY S. TRUMAN sent recently retired Army General GEORGE C. MARSHALL as a special emissary to China to mediate the civil war between the Nationalist Chinese government headed by U.S. WORLD WAR II ally Chiang Kai-shek and Communist forces under Mao Tse-tung. Unable to attain a truce or promote a coalition government between the warring factions, Marshall ended his mission in January 1947. Under mounting pressure from the domestic CHINA LOBBY to aid Chiang, Truman dispached General Albert C. Wedemeyer in July 1947 to appraise the Nationalists' worsening situation. In his report Wedemeyer noted the need for Nationalist political and economic reform, but recommended a substantial increase in the limited U.S. assistance to Chiang. Truman, however, heeded the counsel of Marshall, who, having become secretary of state, advised against U.S. involvement in the conflict.

As the Communists neared victory in 1949, the Truman administration came under bitter attack for purportedly having abandoned Chiang. To head off the criticism, new Secretary of State DEAN ACHESON, on August 5, 1949, released a detailed report, known as a white paper, on U.S. policy toward China. The publication, officially titled *U.S. Relations with China with Special Reference to the Period 1944–1949*, consisted of some 1000 pages of documents and analysis. In an introduction Acheson defended the U.S. decision not to commit major U.S. aid to Chiang, arguing that nothing America could have done short of full-scale intervention would have prevented the corrupt Nationalist regime's ultimate defeat. Conservative Republican critics labeled the study a "whitewash" of the Democratic Truman administration's failed policy that had "lost" China to communism. The partisan debate continued throughout the 1950s while Senator JOSEPH R. MCCARTHY (R-WI) seized on events in China to buttress his demagogic accusations of Communist infiltration of the State Department.

CHINESE EXCLUSION ACT (1882) Legislation that blocked Chinese immigration to the United States. Starting with the gold rush of 1848, large numbers of Chinese had come to the West Coast to work in the mines and on the railroads. The BURLINGAME TREATY (1868) had endorsed the free immigration of Chinese laborers. Anti-Chinese feelings flared on the West Coast in the 1870s amid the perception that alien workers were to blame for the growing scarcity of jobs. Western legislators called for measures to halt the continuing influx of Chinese, arguing Asians were incapable of assimilation into American society. In 1879 Congress passed the Fifteen Passenger Act. Intended to restrict Chinese immigration by limiting their numbers on vessels bound to the United States, the bill was vetoed by President RUTHERFORD B. HAYES as a violation of U.S. treaty obligations.

The ANGELL TREATY, concluded with China the following year, revised the Burlingame Treaty to allow for limitations on immigration. The agreement cleared the way for Congress to enact legislation that suspended the entrance of Chinese laborers for 10 years. The Chinese Exclusion Act, signed into law May 6, 1882, was a major departure from America's traditional open immigration policy. It also represented the first instance of a group's being singled out for exclusion on the basis of race. In subsequent years Congress progressively tightened the restrictions on Chinese immigration. The 1892 GEARY ACT renewed the ban on Chinese immigration for another 10 years and the prohibition was extended indefinitely in 1902. In the GRESHAM-YANG TREATY (1894) the Chinese government consented to the existing limitations on immigration. Under pressure from a growing nationalist movement, the Chinese leadership refused to renew the treaty in 1904 and the anti-Asian aspects of American immigration policy remained a source of tension until WORLD WAR II. Congress repealed the various Chinese exclusion measures on December 17, 1943, reflecting the view that such discriminatory policies were inappropriate toward a wartime ally.

CHRISTMAS BOMBING See **OPERATION LINEBACKER**.

CHURCH COMMITTEE U.S. Senate investigation of the INTELLIGENCE COMMUNITY. In 1973 successive CENTRAL INTELLIGENCE AGENCY (CIA) directors JAMES R. SCHLESINGER and WILLIAM E. COLBY oversaw preparation

of a secret internal report, known as the FAMILY JEWELS, that identified previous agency improprieties. In December 1974 press reports of certain of these activities involving unlawful domestic surveillance operations set off a series of probes of U.S. intelligence agencies. President GERALD R. FORD in early January 1975 appointed the blue-ribbon ROCKEFELLER COMMISSION to determine whether the CIA had exceeded its charter. Ford hoped to prevent a congressional inquiry, but the Senate, increasingly inclined to assert its role in the oversight of intelligence matters, voted 82–4 on January 27 to create the Select Committee to Study Government Operations with Respect to Intelligence Activities. The bipartisan panel took its informal title from Senator FRANK CHURCH (D-ID), who was selected as chairman. Other members were Howard H. Baker (R-TN), Barry M. Goldwater (R-AZ), Gary W. Hart (D-CO), Philip A. Hart (D-MI), Walter Huddleston (D-KY), Charles McC. Mathias (R-MD), Walter F. Mondale (D-MN), Robert B. Morgan (D-NC), Richard Schweiker (R-PA), and JOHN G. TOWER (R-TX). In February the House followed with its own special probe conducted by the PIKE COMMITTEE.

The Senate panel undertook an extensive 11-month investigation. Former and incumbent senior intelligence officials were called to testify and large numbers of classified documents obtained from the CIA and other executive branch intelligence services were reviewed. The examination of previous CIA misdeeds was aided by the Family Jewels list provided by agency head Colby. The committee, disregarding a written request from Ford not to make the information public, released an interim report in November 1975 on prior U.S. involvement in the assassination of foreign leaders. The panel concluded U.S. government officials had ordered the assassination of Cuba's Fidel Castro and Patrice Lumumba of the Congo (now Zaire). Assassination plots against Dominican dictator Rafael Trujillo, Ngo Dinh Diem of South Vietnam, and Chilean General Rene Scheider had had at least tacit U.S support. In December another interim report found there had been no direct U.S. involvement in the 1973 CHILE COUP which overthrew Salvador Allende.

The committee issued its final report on April 26, 1976. Reflecting disagreements among members over its recommendations, Senators Goldwater and Tower did not sign the lengthy document. While signing the report, Senators Philip and Gary Hart and Mondale objected to the deletion of numerous passages from the public version for security reasons. The report found that the CIA had engaged in illegal, improper, and unethical activities. These included the maintenance of thousands of files on U.S. groups and individuals in violation of limits on domestic intelligence operations, a mail surveillance program that opened more than 200,000 envelopes over a 20-year period, and the testing of mind-altering drugs on unknowing subjects. It criticized what it described as an excessive reliance on COVERT ACTION by the United States. Many of these operations were said to be inconsistent with U.S. values and traditions and conducted without appropriate authorization. The committee recommended broad new legislation governing U.S. intelligence activities, better executive-branch control of covert operations, restrictions on intelligence activities such as assassination, and improved congressional oversight. Executive Order 11905 on U.S. intelligence issued by Ford the previous February had adopted many of the panel's proposals and Congress decided against enactment of an omnibus intelligence bill. On May 19, 1976, the Senate created a permanent Select Committee on Intelligence to monitor the intelligence community.

CHURCH, FRANK FORRESTER (1924–1984) U.S. senator. A native of Idaho, Church interrupted his studies at Stanford to serve as an Army officer during WORLD WAR II. He returned to earn an undergraduate degree in 1947 and a law degree in 1950. He practiced law in Boise before election to the U.S. Senate as a Democrat in 1956. Church became an influential member of the SENATE FOREIGN RELATIONS COMMITTEE. He emerged as an outspoken opponent of the mounting U.S. military role in the VIETNAM WAR. As early as 1963 he opposed American aid to any repressive regime in South Vietnam and in 1965 called for negotiations to end the conflict. After the CAMBODIAN INCURSION in April 1970, Church cosponsored the COOPER-CHURCH AMENDMENT that placed strict limits on U.S. military operations in Cambodia. In 1972 he coauthored the CASE-CHURCH AMENDMENT

that unsuccessfully sought to halt U.S. combat involvement in Southeast Asia. A modified version that barred future U.S. military activities in Indochina was adopted the following year. In 1975 and 1976 Church headed a special Senate inquiry into the U.S. INTELLIGENCE COMMUNITY. The CHURCH COMMITTEE's highly critical report of past abuses and illegalities helped prompt widespread reform. In 1976 he failed in a bid to win the Democratic presidential nomination. Church was defeated for reelection in 1980. He died of cancer in 1984.

CIA See **CENTRAL INTELLIGENCE AGENCY** in **APPENDIX B**.

CITES See **CONVENTION ON INTERNATIONAL TRADE IN ENDANGERED SPECIES**.

CITY OF NEW YORK v. MILN (1837) U.S. Supreme Court decision that upheld state laws regulating immigration. The justices declined to reverse a New York statute that required ships arriving from overseas to provide lists of their passengers. The Court ruled the measure was an appropriate exercise of a state's power to prevent an influx of indigent aliens. State governments retained broad control over immigration until the 1870s, although in the PASSENGER CASES (1849) the Court found that their authority did not extend to the right to impose taxes on arriving immigrants. In 1876 the Court concluded in HENDERSON v. MAYOR OF NEW YORK that state laws governing immigration were an unconstitutional usurpation of the power vested exclusively in Congress to regulate foreign commerce.

CIVIL AIR TRANSPORT See **AIR AMERICA**.

CIVIL OPERATIONS AND REVOLUTIONARY DEVELOPMENT SUPPORT U.S. PACIFICATION program during the VIETNAM WAR. In the early 1960s the United States sent military advisers to South Vietnam to help that nation defeat a Communist insurgency. By 1965 major U.S. combat units had been committed to the fight against North Vietnam's military campaign to unify the two Vietnams into a single Communist state. While U.S. military operations focused on the destruction of North Vietnamese forces, the Johnson administration continued to explore ways to combat the Viet Cong, the South Vietnamese Communist insurgents. In 1967 senior national security official ROBERT W. KOMER was named head of a new undertaking to improve U.S. pacification efforts in South Vietnam.

The Civil Operations and Revolutionary Development Support program, better known as CORDS, placed counterinsurgency resources from the military services, the State Department, the AGENCY FOR INTERNATIONAL DEVELOPMENT, the UNITED STATES INFORMATION AGENCY, and the CENTRAL INTELLIGENCE AGENCY under a single command. CORDS aimed to use a combination of civic action and local security to counteract Viet Cong influence in the countryside. Viet Cong use of assassination and other terrorist tactics for maintaining control had undermined previous U.S. initiatives. Komer, who enjoyed ambassador rank and reported directly to the senior U.S. leadership in Saigon, believed that for pacification to succeed it was necessary to root out the Viet Cong's covert infrastructure.

In 1968 he expanded CORDS to include the Intelligence Coordination and Exploitation (ICEX) program. ICEX pooled U.S. and South Vietnamese intelligence capabilities to identify and target Viet Cong cadres. Komer departed Vietnam at the end of 1968. His successor as CORDS director, veteran intelligence officer WILLIAM E. COLBY, redesignated ICEX as the Phoenix Program in 1969. The new name corresponded to the Vietnamese title for the operation, *Phung Hoang*, after a mythic bird similar to the phoenix.

The Phoenix Program evolved into a major operation. Centralized counterintelligence files were established and offices set up in each of South Vietnam's 235 local districts. Special strike teams were formed to arrest or otherwise "neutralize" individuals identified as Viet Cong agents. The program proved highly successful. In 1971 testimony before Congress Colby revealed that Phoenix had resulted in the defection of 17,000 Viet Cong, the capture of 28,000, and the death of another 20,000. According to Colby, almost all the dead had been killed in military actions or while resisting arrest. Critics of the increasingly controversial program charged that it involved widespread abuses including the use of torture in interrogation, the indefinite incarceration of suspects, and summary executions. Detractors denounced Phoenix as an assassination bureau. Colby defended the enterprise, contending that any abuses were infrequent and violated official policies.

CORDS significantly advanced U.S. anti-Communist pacification efforts. The Viet Cong, badly mauled in the 1968 TET OFFENSIVE, were largely eliminated as a threat by 1971. The Phoenix Program was terminated the same year amid the decreasing U.S. role in the war. American pacification initiatives continued through 1972, but the gains proved irrelevant as North Vietnam switched from guerrilla warfare to the conventional invasion that subdued South Vietnam in 1975.

CIVIL WAR DIPLOMACY Competing foreign policies pursued by the Union and Confederacy during the American Civil War. The complicated diplomacy bore significantly on the course of the conflict. Seceding Southern states formed the Confederate States of America as a separate, sovereign nation in February 1861. Taking office in March 1861, President ABRAHAM LINCOLN insisted the Union was indivisible and that the Confederacy could not and did not exist. The South, he contended, was in a state of insurrection. Following the outbreak of hostilities in April 1861, the Confederacy looked toward foreign diplomatic recognition, and the expected material advantages it would bring, as the key to its survival. The main diplomatic objective of the U.S. government, intent on preserving the Union, was to prevent foreign recognition of the Confederacy as an independent nation, particularly by leading European powers Great Britain and France. The Lincoln administration was determined to define and isolate the war as a domestic armed rebellion and thus preclude any foreign involvement.

Lincoln effectively contradicted his own position by his proclamation on April 19 of a naval blockade of southern ports. His administration pressed for international recognition of the maritime cordon. Under international law the Union blockade could have validity only if a state of war existed; and an acknowledged state of war would, by definition, confer belligerent status on the Confederacy. Starting with Great Britain on May 13, 1861, the European countries recognized the belligerency of the South, effectively granting the Confederacy the status of a nation within the context of its fighting a war. Secretary of State WILLIAM H. SEWARD and American Minister to Great Britain CHARLES FRANCIS ADAMS vigorously protested the neutrality proclamation by which London had conferred recognition on the South as a belligerent. Adams suspected that it prefigured British recognition of Confederate independence. Seward threatened the British government with a break in diplomatic relations should it receive Confederate diplomatic agents as official representatives of an independent state.

European recognition of the South's belligerency raised the issue of FREEDOM OF THE SEAS. In the unaccustomed role of major naval belligerent, the United States altered its traditional, staunch support for neutral rights at sea and instead sought British and French acquiescence in an expansive interpretation of maritime belligerent rights. The Lincoln administration championed broadened belligerent rights with a view to taking full advantage of the North's overwhelming naval superiority. The Confederacy insisted the North's blockade of the southern coast was never sufficiently effective to be binding under international law. The viability of the blockade depended on whether Great Britain, as the world's leading naval power, would respect it, since other nations would follow the British lead. Notwithstanding the fact that most of the trade ships seized by the U.S. Navy for intended breach of the blockade were British, London accepted the naval cordon as legally binding. The British government's acquiescence stemmed from its belief that, in the long run, British interests would be better served by having the United States committed to respecting a loose blockade as legal.

To halt blockade-running through neutral ports, the Union curtailed neutral rights through the so-called doctrine of continuous voyage, which Great Britain had developed during the Napoleonic Wars (1803–1815). In applying the doctrine, the Lincoln government went beyond traditional British practice. Throughout the Civil War, the South evaded the North's blockade with small, swift ships called blockade-runners, which ferried ammunition and supplies to the Confederates. By and large these ships had both British crews and financial backing. The blockade-running trade, which rewarded the Britons who plied it with handsome profits, was a recurring U.S. grievance against London. Ships loaded with goods typically sailed from Great Britain for neutral ports in the West Indies. From there blockade-runners would carry the supplies past the Union navy cordon to Confederate ports. To hinder the trade, the Union seized neutral ships in transit from Europe to the West Indies as blockade violators, on the grounds that the ultimate destination of their goods was blockaded Confederate ports. Though they sustained the most property losses through the Union confiscations, the British abided the expanded U.S. interpretation of the doctrine of continuous voyage, figuring that the U.S. shift on neutral rights over time would redound to their advantage.

The issue of neutral rights figured in the first major diplomatic crisis of the war. From the conflict's outset, Confederate President JEFFERSON DAVIS sent diplomatic agents to Europe to work for recognition, seek loans, and purchase supplies. Under pressure from the Lincoln administration, the European governments refused to meet officially with the South's representatives. On November 8, 1861, Captain Charles Wilkes, commanding the Union warship *San Jacinto*, stopped the British mail steamer *Trent*; he seized two passengers, Confederate diplomatic commissioners JOHN SLIDELL and James M. Mason who were bound for Paris and London, respectively, and took them to Boston where they were imprisoned. In the North, Wilkes was hailed as a hero. His deed outraged the British, who branded it a gross violation of maritime neutral rights under international law and an affront to their flag. With tensions in the controversial TRENT AFFAIR escalating dangerously, Seward acted to defuse the crisis. He acknowledged that Wilkes had erred and ordered the release of Slidell and Mason. His deft moves averted a possible war with Great Britain, sparing the Lincoln administration a confrontation it could ill afford.

The Confederate government expected to secure foreign assistance through its KING COTTON DIPLOMACY, based on the presumed economic strength of southern cotton. Southern leaders surmised that Great

Britain and France were so heavily dependent on the South's cotton crop for their textile industries that they would be forced to recognize Southern independence and break the Union blockade in order to maintain their access to the supply. Cotton diplomacy, however, proved a failure. At the war's onset, the British and French had two-year supplies of raw cotton on hand; and by 1863 European manufacturers had found ample substitute supplies from Egypt and India. Great Britain's need for Northern wheat owing to poor domestic harvests reinforced British reluctance to intervene on behalf of the Confederacy and risk a conflict with the Union. Moreover, whatever economic incentive existed for breaking the blockade was outweighed by the large war profits the British were making from the munitions industry, blockade-running for the Confederates, and the transfer of the American merchant marine to British registry to escape assault by Confederate raiders. Divided British popular opinion on the American conflict also dissuaded London from risking confrontation with Washington. Britain's upper classes, akin to France's, sympathized with the South. But the lower and middle classes, along with the liberals, opposed slavery and strongly sympathized with the Union. The French government of Emperor Napoleon III favored the Confederacy and was disposed to recognize it for self-interested economic and imperial reasons, but ultimately proved unwilling to take this step except in concert with the British.

The issue of intervention came to a head in Great Britain in September 1862. Following the Union defeat at the Second Battle of Bull Run on August 29 to 30, British Prime Minister Lord Henry Palmerston and his foreign secretary, Lord John Russell, agreed that the military situation in America warranted a joint proposal by Great Britain and France to mediate the Civil War on the basis of a permanently divided nation. Then news reached London of the key Union victory at the Battle of Antietam on September 17, prompting the British cabinet to delay on its mediation offer. The course of the war might have changed had the Confederacy prevailed at Antietam. The battle's outcome dealt a major blow to the South's chances of winning European recognition. Since prospects for British or French intervention hinged pri-

marily on Confederate military fortunes, Antietam represented a significant diplomatic turning point.

The French government also considered efforts at mediation. Napoleon III's suggestion to the British in the fall of 1861 of a joint intervention to open the Union blockade had been declined. After Lord Palmerston's mediation plan collapsed, the French emperor asked Great Britain and Russia whether they would join France in proposing both an armistice and suspension of the North's blockade. The British and Russians rejected the scheme, which would have validated Southern independence. Napoleon III's last attempt at mediation came in early 1863 when he proposed a meeting of Union and Confederate representatives at a neutral location to discuss peace terms. Secretary Seward, with Congress's firm support, flatly rejected the offer. Influenced by its desire to see the United States remain a strong and viable counterweight to the British Empire, Russia supported the Union cause throughout the Civil War. The czarist government was eager to stay on good terms with the Union to ensure Russian cruisers would have access to America's ice-free ports in the event of war with Great Britain.

The slavery question had a significant impact on wartime diplomacy with Great Britain, which in the 19th century spearheaded the international drive against the African slave trade. That Lincoln had not framed the war as a crusade to end human bondage had disappointed British and other European liberals. The Confederacy for its part discovered slavery to be a major diplomatic liability that hindered its ability to gain foreign support. With European opinion partly in mind, Lincoln issued his preliminary Emancipation Proclamation on September 22, 1862, intentionally timed to take advantage of the strengthened Union position following Antietam. The emancipation policy bolstered the North's moral and diplomatic standing in London and other European capitals. The final proclamation on January 1, 1863, strengthened sentiment abroad for the Union and greatly diminished Confederate chances of winning British or French recognition. With defeat closing inexorably in on the South, the Confederate leadership in December 1864 made a desperate offer to abolish slavery in return for British recognition of Southern independence. London rejected the last-ditch diplomatic effort.

A troublesome issue between Washington and London was the manufacture and outfitting in British shipyards of warships for the Confederacy. Since the South at the war's start possessed no navy nor the means to build one, it planned to acquire vessels in Great Britain and other European neutral countries. The Confederacy arranged with British firms for the construction of armed raiders such as the *Alabama* and *Florida*, which preyed with devastating effect on Union merchant shipping. Seward and Adams insisted that the British government's neutrality obligated it to prevent the delivery of ships built on British territory to the South. The Lincoln administration's repeated protests eventually moved British authorities to take concerted action to stop the supplying of British-made cruisers to the Confederacy.

Of particular alarm to the North were the so-called Laird rams, a pair of ironclads specially constructed for the South, each capable of smashing the Union's wooden warships and breaking the blockade. A crisis was touched off in 1863 as the ships became ready to sail from British waters. Adams warned the British foreign ministry that the United States would consider it an act of war if the ironclads were allowed to put to sea. The crisis was resolved when the British government took possession of the rams and tightened its neutrality policy. Throughout the war the Union demanded that the British government pay the claims of U.S. citizens for the depredations committed against Union merchant shipping by the *Alabama* and other British-built Confederate cruisers. Washington charged London with a failure to enforce its neutrality and held it accountable for the losses sustained by the North's maritime commerce. The ALABAMA CLAIMS would vex U.S.-British relations until they were disposed of through international arbitration in 1872.

France and Spain each took advantage of the Civil War to pursue imperial ventures in North America. In March 1861 Spain temporarily reannexed the Dominican Republic. Seward invoked the MONROE DOCTRINE in protesting the action and called upon Madrid to quit the island republic. Ignoring the secretary of state's appeal, the Spanish government declared its firm intention to hold onto its former colony. The burdens of the war kept Seward from forcefully confronting the Spanish. A Dominican revolt against Spanish rule broke out within two years and finally led Spain to end its costly enterprise. The last Spanish troops withdrew from the Dominican Republic in July 1865.

Napoleon III meanwhile undertook an imperial venture in Mexico. This scheme began in early 1862 when British, French, and Spanish troops mounted a joint military expedition against Mexico to force it to repay its debts to private European creditors. The British and Spanish pulled out within a matter of months but the French remained and extended their control over much of the country. In 1864 Napoleon III persuaded Austrian Archduke Maximilian to become emperor of Mexico, backed by French military forces. Seward condemned the French intervention and the Union refused to recognize the Maximilian puppet government. The demands of the Civil War prevented the Lincoln administration from taking decisive action against the French. Lincoln and Seward were concerned not to antagonize France and thereby give Napoleon III cause to recognize the Confederacy. As the Union moved closer to victory over the South, the Lincoln government became more assertive in protesting the French occupation. After the war's end in April 1865, Seward threatened American use of force if France did not withdraw from Mexico. Napoleon III capitulated and the last French troops departed in March 1867.

CLARK AMENDMENT (1976) Congressional legislation that prohibited U.S. involvement in the ANGOLAN CIVIL WAR. In April 1974 a leftist military coup overthrew the dictatorship in Portugal. The new government announced it would grant independence to Portuguese African colony Angola in November 1975. Three rebel groups that had fought separately against Portuguese colonial rule turned to battling one another over who would govern Angola. The Popular Movement for the Liberation of Angola (MPLA), an offshoot of the Angolan Communist Party, received support from the Soviet Union; the National Front for the Liberation of Angola (FNLA) relied mainly on aid from Communist China; and the National Union for the Total

Independence of Angola (UNITA) had ties with both China and South Africa.

In the spring of 1975 the Soviet Union escalated arms shipments to the MPLA while Communist Cuban leader Fidel Castro began to send military advisers. Concerned the Soviet and Cuban assistance would hasten an MPLA victory and thus lead to the installation of a Communist regime in Angola, the Ford administration in July 1975 approved a covert operation to provide weapons and other support to the FNLA and UNITA. By December CENTRAL INTELLIGENCE AGENCY (CIA) contingency funds had been exhausted and the administration requested additional monies from Congress. Senator Dick Clark (D-IA) led a concerted opposition to covert U.S. involvement in Angola. Following the bitter experience of the VIETNAM WAR, many members of Congress were reluctant to commit the United States to any regional conflict that might lead to a direct U.S. military role. Moreover, the recent congressional CHURCH COMMITTEE and PIKE COMMITTEE investigations of U.S. intelligence activities had invested COVERT ACTION with a generally negative connotation. In January 1976 Congress added to the annual foreign aid bill a measure, known as the Clark Amendment, that barred any American support to rebel groups in Angola. The legislation was signed into law by President GERALD R. FORD on February 9, 1976, marking the first time Congress had halted a covert operation.

With extensive Soviet and Cuban backing, the MPLA in the late 1970s consolidated its control over much of Angola. The increasingly pro-Western UNITA, however, under the leadership of Jonas Savimbi, mounted a successful guerrilla campaign in the south of the country. Following the December 1979 Soviet invasion of Afghanistan, the United States began providing secret assistance to the anti-Communist Afghan Mujahedeen guerrillas, signaling renewed U.S. willingness to resort to covert action. In 1980 Congress approved a revision of the Clark Amendment that permitted covert U.S. military aid to Angola provided the president determined it to be in the national interest and Congress then concurred. In the early 1980s President RONALD W. REAGAN steered U.S. policy toward furnishing support to anti-Communist insurgencies worldwide, an approach

that became known as the REAGAN DOCTRINE. In 1985 Congress repealed the Clark Amendment, opening the way for the Reagan administration to begin sending military arms to UNITA the following year. Conservative supporters hailed the vote as a statement of U.S. anti-Communist resolve while liberal opponents called it a return to unwarranted U.S. interventionism.

CLARK MEMORANDUM (1930) State Department study that repudiated the ROOSEVELT COROLLARY (1905) to the MONROE DOCTRINE (1823). Mounting Latin American resentment over U.S. interventionism in the Caribbean and Central America since the SPANISH-AMERICAN WAR (1898) contributed to a shift in U.S. policy in the late 1920s. Latin American nations at the Sixth PAN-AMERICAN CONFERENCE in Havana, Cuba, in early 1928 introduced a resolution, targeted at the United States, that disclaimed the right of any member state to intercede in the internal affairs of another state. Former Secretary of State CHARLES EVANS HUGHES, representing the Coolidge administration at the conference, persuaded fellow delegates to withdraw the measure and delivered what turned out to be the last high-level defense of an unequivocal U.S. right to intervene in the region.

Recognizing the need to review U.S. policy in Latin America, Secretary of State FRANK B. KELLOGG instructed Under Secretary J. Reuben Clark to study the use of the Monroe Doctrine to justify U.S. intervention in the region. Clark submitted his *Memorandum on the Monroe Doctrine* on December 17, 1928. The lengthy report concluded that the doctrine's principles could not properly serve as the basis for the Roosevelt Corollary, which had been invoked in support of U.S. interventions in Latin American nations. While effectively undercutting the Roosevelt Corollary, the memorandum was careful to retain the U.S. right to intercede in Latin American affairs under the principle of self-preservation.

Clark's analysis went unpublished until the State Department issued it in June 1930 at the direction of President HERBERT C. HOOVER. Determined to dispel charges of American IMPERIALISM, Hoover had entered office in March 1929 following a 10-week, 10-nation friendship tour of Latin America and embarked on a policy of good will and nonintervention. He endorsed the withdrawal of U.S. troops from Haiti and Nicaragua and revoked the moralistic diplomatic recognition policy that had angered much of Latin America since its introduction by President WOODROW WILSON in 1913. Hoover's decision to issue the Clark Memorandum confirmed the distinct new direction in U.S.-Latin American relations. President FRANKLIN D. ROOSEVELT continued the move toward greater mutual respect and cooperation in the GOOD NEIGHBOR POLICY.

CLAY, HENRY (1777–1852) Secretary of state under President JOHN QUINCY ADAMS. One of the most important congressional leaders of the pre-Civil War era, he was known as the Great Compromiser for his mediation of political conflict between the North and South, especially over the question of slavery. A Virginia native, Clay studied law and was admitted to the state bar in 1797. The same year he moved to Lexington, Kentucky, where he established himself as a top criminal lawyer. He first emerged politically in 1798 with a speech denouncing the ALIEN AND SEDITION ACTS, Federalist-sponsored measures intended to stifle dissent in the Democratic-Republican press during the undeclared QUASI-WAR (1798–1800) with France. He served in the Kentucky legislature from 1803 until 1806, when he was chosen to complete an unexpired term in the U.S. Senate. On his return to Kentucky in 1807, he was elected speaker of the state legislature, a post he held for two years. In 1810 he again was selected by the state legislature to finish another unexpired U.S. Senate term.

The same year Clay won election to the U.S. House of Representatives as a Democratic-Republican. Taking his seat in 1811, he promptly was elected House Speaker. He emerged as a leader of the WAR HAWKS, the aggressively nationalist congressmen from the South and West who successfully demanded that President JAMES MADISON go to war with Great Britain in June 1812. Clay was a member of the American peace commission in Belgium that negotiated the TREATY OF GHENT (1814) ending the WAR OF 1812. After returning from Europe in 1815, he reentered the House of Representatives and resumed the speakership. Harboring presidential ambitions, he began to develop in detail his famous "American System," a political program that called for

strong national defense, road and canal construction with federal aid, protection of American industries through high tariffs on foreign imports, and rechartering of the Bank of the United States.

In foreign affairs, Clay sympathized with the Latin American rebellions for independence from Spanish colonial rule, which he equated with America's own revolution against Britain. Beginning in 1817 the House speaker urged the U.S. government to recognize without further delay the independence of the Spanish-American republics. He attacked President JAMES MONROE and Secretary of State John Quincy Adams for following a hesitant, wait-and-see policy on the recognition issue. When Missouri's proposed statehood threatened the balance in Congress between free and slave states, Clay was instrumental in framing the so-called Missouri Compromise (1820). Under it, Missouri entered the Union as a slave state, Maine entered as a free state to preserve the balance in the Senate, and slavery was barred thereafter in any other new state north of 36° 30'. Resigning as speaker in 1820, he left Congress at the conclusion of his term the next year and returned to private interests in Kentucky. From 1823 to 1825 he again served in the House, once more filling the post of speaker.

As a candidate for president in 1824 he finished fourth in the electoral vote behind ANDREW JACKSON, Adams, and William H. Crawford. Since none of the candidates had tallied enough votes for outright victory, the election was thrown into the House of Representatives. Clay ignored the instructions of the Kentucky legislature to cast his vote for Jackson, his bitter political and personal adversary. Instead he voted for Adams, who won the election on the first ballot. After Adams named Clay secretary of state, Jacksonians persistently accused the Kentuckian of having struck a "corrupt bargain" to win the cabinet appointment, a charge Clay denied. In his tenure as secretary from 1825 to 1829, he was unable to realize his goal of forging a political and economic union of Pan-American nations. The American delegation appointed by Clay to attend the PANAMA CONGRESS (1826) was delayed from departing by congressional opposition and arrived too late to participate. In U.S.-British relations, he oversaw completion of the CONVENTION OF 1827, which submitted the long-standing Maine-Canada boundary dispute to international arbitration, and another treaty the same year that renewed indefinitely the Anglo-American diplomatic understanding on the OREGON QUESTION. During his term the United States completed 12 commercial treaties—more than any prior administration.

With the start of the Jackson presidency in March 1829, Clay withdrew from politics for two years. Reelected to the Senate from Kentucky in 1831, he held his seat until 1842. Following his unsuccessful run for president as the anti-Jackson, Whig candidate in 1832, Clay became absorbed in the Senate with the tariff controversy. The TARIFF OF ABOMINATIONS (1828) and other steep duties passed by Congress had been bitterly condemned in the South as unfair to southern economic interests. Clay's own vigorous defense of high tariffs as a cornerstone of his American System had drawn the ire of southern political leaders. The nation became embroiled in a sectional crisis when South Carolina in late 1832 moved to nullify federal tariffs and threatened secession if the Jackson administration took steps to enforce them. A showdown over nullification was averted when Clay secured passage of his COMPROMISE TARIFF of 1833.

He was defeated for the Whig presidential nomination in 1840 by WILLIAM HENRY HARRISON, who rode a wave of popularity to the White House. Harrison died soon after taking office. His successor, JOHN TYLER, resisted Clay's party leadership and rejected the Kentuckian's political program. A deeply disappointed Clay resigned from the Senate in 1842 and then persuaded Tyler's Whig cabinet to resign in protest. In 1844 he was the Whig nominee for president but lost the election to pro-expansion Democrat JAMES K. POLK. Clay's defeat in large part was due to his inconclusive stand on the issue of whether the United States should annex Texas and admit it to the Union. He supported the Polk administration's prosecution of the MEXICAN WAR (1846–1848), despite his earlier opposition to the U.S. war declaration. Troubled by the deepening sectional struggle over slavery, Clay returned to the Senate in 1849, where he hoped to modify the influence of Northern and Southern political extremists. He helped draft and supported the legislative Compromise of 1850, which was intended to satisfy both North and South by balancing their respective interests. Clay's last years were devoted to the cause of preserving the Union and preventing a civil war. He died in office in 1852.

CLAY, LUCIUS DUBIGNON (1897–1978) Army officer, military governor of Germany after WORLD WAR II. The son of U.S. Senator Alexander S. Clay (D-GA) and descendant of noted 19th century statesman HENRY CLAY, he graduated from West Point in 1918. The Georgia native served in a variety of command and staff positions as an Army engineer. In 1940, as an assistant to the administrator of civil aeronautics, he directed the organization and establishment of a national airport system. He was promoted to general in 1942. During World War II he held senior logistic positions and was a deputy to JAMES F. BYRNES at the Office of War Mobilization.

In April 1945 Clay was named the deputy military governor for the American zone in occupied Germany. He assisted in the formation of the ALLIED CONTROL COUNCIL by the United States, Great Britain, France, and Soviet Union for the joint administration of Germany after its wartime defeat. Responsible for civil affairs in the U.S. sector, Clay undertook to reconstruct the devastated country. He strove to eliminate Nazi influences from public life. Opposing harsh, punitive measures against the German people, he instead encouraged the development of democratic institutions. In January 1947 Clay became military governor of the American zone and commanding general of U.S. forces in Europe. His tenure was marked by mounting friction between the Western wartime allies and the Soviet Union. COLD WAR hostilities developed into open confrontation in June 1948 when the Soviet Union blocked Western access to Berlin. Clay directed the BERLIN AIRLIFT that supplied the beleaguered city for more than a year. He also helped draft the 1949 constitution for West Germany.

Clay relinquished his command and retired in May 1949. His 1950 book *Decision in Germany* described his postwar experiences. The same year he embarked on a business career as chairman and chief executive officer of the Continental Can Company. Amid renewed Soviet pressures on Berlin, President JOHN F. KENNEDY in August 1961 named Clay his personal representative to the city to underscore U.S. determination to resist Communist aggression. With an easing of the BERLIN CRISIS, Clay returned in May 1962 and retired from Continental Can the same year. From 1963 to 1973 he was a senior partner with the Lehman Brothers investment banking firm.

CLAYTON, JOHN MIDDLETON (1796–1856) Secretary of state under President ZACHARY TAYLOR. Clayton was born in Delaware. After graduating from Yale University in 1815, he read law and was admitted to the bar in 1819. Over the next decade he became a prominent Delaware courtroom lawyer. During this period he also entered politics, serving in the state legislature from 1824 to 1826 and as Delaware secretary of state from 1826 to 1828. Elected to the U.S. Senate in 1829, the staunch Whig Clayton held his seat seven years. He resigned in 1836 and the following year became chief justice of the Delaware Supreme Court. He stepped down from the bench in 1839 to devote himself to scientific farming. Returned to the U.S. Senate in 1845, he served there until 1849, when Taylor, whose candidacy Clayton had supported in the 1848 presidential election, rewarded Clayton with the State Department cabinet post.

As secretary of state, he is best remembered for negotiating the CLAYTON-BULWER TREATY (1850), the compromise settlement with Great Britain that provided for joint Anglo-American protection and control of any future transisthmian canal in Central America. Concerned that U.S. neutrality laws be enforced, Clayton worked to prevent the departure of FILIBUSTERING expeditions for Cuba. He stood firmly against violations of U.S. rights, as when he delivered an ultimatum to Portugal demanding an indemnity payment for the destruction of several U.S. vessels. Under a policy of promoting American commerce, he prepared a program for expanding U.S. trade relations with Asia that was followed by Commodore MATTHEW C. PERRY in his breakthrough expedition to Japan in 1853 and 1854. When Taylor died suddenly in office in July 1850, Clayton resigned his post and retired to his Delaware farm. In 1853 he again returned to the Senate, where he concentrated on defending the Clayton-Bulwer Treaty against increasing Democratic attack. He held his seat until his death in 1856.

CLAYTON-BULWER TREATY (1850) Compromise agreement reached between the United States and Great Britain on April 19, 1850, concerning their rival interests in Central America. Negotiated by Secretary of State JOHN M. CLAYTON and British Minister to the United States Sir Henry Lytton Bulwer, the treaty was intended to resolve the Anglo-American dispute over construction of a possible canal across the Central American isthmus. After the MEXICAN WAR (1846–1848), control of transit routes for a projected isthmian canal in Central America became an important issue in American diplomacy. The United States coveted a waterway to link its Atlantic coast with recently acquired California and Oregon.

The South American nation of New Granada (now Colombia) had watched with alarm in the mid-1840s as Britain enlarged its control over the eastern Mosquito Coast of Nicaragua and fixed its designs on Panama, at the time a New Granadan province. To preclude a British advance on the isthmus, New Granada's government completed a treaty with the American charge d'affaires in Bogota, Benjamin Bidlack, on December 12, 1846, that gave the United States transit rights across Panama. In return the United States pledged to uphold New Granada's sovereignty over Panama and to guarantee the isthmus's neutrality in time of war. The U.S. Senate approved the agreement in June 1848. Great Britain, then the dominant power in the Caribbean, was alarmed by Bidlack's Treaty because it reserved to the United States one of the two best routes for an interoceanic waterway. The British thus sought control of the other prized canal route, through Nicaragua. Nervous about British territorial ambitions, Nicaragua appealed for U.S. help. What followed was an Anglo-American struggle in which both countries maneuvered diplomatically and militarily to prevent each other from gaining exclusive control over the Central American canal routes. Mutually concerned that their rivalry might escalate into a serious conflict, Washington and London elected to seek a diplomatic settlement.

The British government in December 1849 dispatched a new minister to the United States, Bulwer, who undertook talks with Clayton to reconcile the differences on Central America. Their negotiations yielded a treaty the following April which stipulated that the two nations would jointly control and protect any canal or other transportation means built across the Central American isthmus. Both sides agreed not to erect fortifications along a canal route and guaranteed the neutrality of any future waterway. The signatories also pledged themselves against attempts at colonizing or exercising dominion over any part of Central America. This last provision became a lingering source of dispute between the two governments. The United States contended that the British had in effect consented to give up their protectorate over the Mosquito Indians and to withdraw from the islands they held in the Bay of Honduras. Rejecting the American view, Britain insisted that the treaty could not be applied retroactively to the existing British positions. Britain in the late 1850s finally acquiesced in the U.S. interpretation, withdrawing from Central America rather than risk a conflict that might threaten the prosperous Anglo-American cotton trade.

Domestic critics meanwhile charged that the agreement violated the MONROE DOCTRINE (1823) by bringing Britain into a protective partnership with America over a prospective interoceanic canal in the Western Hemisphere. As American interest in building a canal increased in the latter half of the 19th century, the U.S. government moved toward a policy that demanded exclusive American control of any Central American waterway. Presidents in succession from ULYSSES S. GRANT to CHESTER A. ARTHUR tried unsuccessfully to win revocation of the Clayton-Bulwer Treaty since it impeded U.S. canal ambitions. The agreement finally was abrogated in 1901 by the HAY-PAUNCEFOTE TREATY, which granted the United States exclusive rights to build and operate an isthmian canal.

CLEVELAND, STEPHEN GROVER (1837–1908)

Twenty-second and twenty-fourth president of the United States and the only one elected to two nonconsecutive terms. Born in New Jersey, son of a Presbyterian minister, Cleveland was raised in upstate New York. He studied law in Buffalo, was admitted to the bar in 1859, and went into practice. Entering local politics as a Democrat, he served as assistant district attorney and sheriff of Erie County. He was elected reform mayor of Buffalo in 1881 and governor of New York in 1882.

Integrity and political independence characterized his term in the statehouse and earned him the enmity of Tammany Hall, the powerful New York Democratic machine. The Democratic nominee for president in 1884, he won the election with the support of independent reform Republicans, known as Mugwumps, who disapproved of Republican candidate JAMES G. BLAINE. Cleveland's victory ended 24 years of unbroken Republican control of the presidency.

In his first term he strenuously sought to lower the nation's high tariffs, which he opposed as a federal subsidy to special business interests and as the main source of politically embarrassing and financially harmful treasury surpluses. In December 1887 he devoted his entire annual message to Congress to an appeal for reduction of the protective import duties. Cleveland, however, was unable to push legislation to curtail the tariff rates through the Republican-controlled Senate. His secretary of state, THOMAS F. BAYARD, attempted to resolve renewed Anglo-American difficulties over the Canadian FISHERIES QUESTION through the BAYARD-CHAMBERLAIN TREATY (1888). But the protectionist Republican majority in the Senate rejected the treaty in large part because it granted Canada tariff concessions. A separate diplomatic understanding negotiated by Bayard secured continued fishing privileges for Americans in Canadian waters. Rivalry among the United States, Germany, and Great Britain in the Samoan Islands prompted the Cleveland administration to convene a three-way conference on the South Pacific archipelago in Washington in 1885. The conference ended without a settlement on respective U.S., British, and German interests in SAMOA.

Renominated by the Democrats in 1888, he lost the ensuing election to Republican BENJAMIN HARRISON despite capturing a majority of the popular vote. On leaving office in 1889 Cleveland returned to private law practice in New York City. In 1892 he again received the Democratic nomination for president. Running on a platform that committed the party to tariff revision, Cleveland defeated Harrison handily in the November election. He took office just as the country was entering the worst economic depression it had yet experienced. Cleveland blamed the financial

Panic of 1893 on the Sherman Silver Purchase Act (1890) and the MCKINLEY TARIFF (1890), both of which he sought to have repealed. His struggle for tariff reform ended in frustration. The WILSON-GORMAN TARIFF (1894) that emerged from Congress was only marginally less protectionist than the McKinley Tariff. Cleveland denounced the measure but allowed it to become law without his signature.

The president took a more active hand in the conduct of foreign policy in his second term. He was an anti-imperialist. In 1893 he deplored American complicity in the overthrow of Queen Liliuokalani of Hawaii and withdrew from Senate consideration the treaty to annex the islands negotiated and submitted by the Harrison administration. Cleveland also sought to enforce strict U.S. neutrality in Cuba's rebellion against Spain in the mid-1890s. Cleveland supported Secretary of State RICHARD OLNEY's aggressive efforts to compel Great Britain to arbitrate the VENEZUELA BOUNDARY DISPUTE. With the president's wholehearted endorsement, the secretary of state enunciated the OLNEY COROLLARY to the MONROE DOCTRINE, which advised the British government of a U.S. claim to virtual sovereignty over the Americas. Under increasing pressure from the Cleveland administration, Britain agreed to submit the boundary issue to international arbitration. In 1896 the Democratic Party bypassed Cleveland to nominate WILLIAM JENNINGS BRYAN for president. On leaving office in 1897 Cleveland retired to private life in New Jersey, where he became a trustee of Princeton University. A movement to renominate him in 1904 failed.

CLIFFORD, CLARK McADAMS (1906–) Presidential adviser, secretary of defense. Born in Kansas, Clifford was raised in St. Louis, Missouri, where he earned a law degree from Washington University in 1928 and joined a local firm. He was commissioned a naval officer in 1944 during WORLD WAR II and was assigned to the logistics staff of the Pacific fleet in California. In 1945 he was transferred to Washington to serve as assistant to his friend and fellow Missourian James K. Vardaman, who was naval aide to President HARRY S. TRUMAN. Clifford succeeded Vardaman in January 1946. His naval service completed, he was named special counsel to the president the following June and soon became one of Truman's most trusted advisers.

At Truman's request, he undertook a study of U.S.-Soviet relations and prepared a highly secret memorandum in September 1946 that helped influence America's increasingly tough COLD WAR stance toward its wartime ally. Clifford helped draft the president's March 1947 message to Congress declaring U.S. readiness under the TRUMAN DOCTRINE to halt Soviet-sponsored Communist aggression. He assisted in the formulation of the MARSHALL PLAN (1948) to aid European postwar economic recovery and also in the formation of America's basic postwar national security institutions: the DEPARTMENT OF DEFENSE, CENTRAL INTELLIGENCE AGENCY, and NATIONAL SECURITY COUNCIL. He was the principal architect in 1948 of the Truman administration's decision to recognize the new Jewish state of Israel.

Clifford left the Truman White House in February 1950 and returned to private law practice, forming a prestigious Washington law firm. In 1960 President-elect JOHN F. KENNEDY turned to Clifford, who had served as an adviser during the campaign, to direct the transition team for his incoming administration. In May 1961 Kennedy appointed him to the PRESIDENT'S FOREIGN INTELLIGENCE ADVISORY BOARD. He was named chairman of the panel in April 1963. Clifford became one of President LYNDON B. JOHNSON's closest informal advisers, undertaking several unofficial fact-finding missions to Southeast Asia to assess the VIETNAM WAR. Although he had expressed private misgivings in 1965 over the pending escalation of U.S. military involvement in the conflict, Clifford publicly backed the Johnson administration's policies in Southeast Asia.

In January 1968 Johnson named Clifford to replace Secretary of Defense ROBERT S. MCNAMARA, who was resigning after seven years in the post. Clifford took office in the aftermath of the major Communist TET OFFENSIVE in South Vietnam. His brief tenure was dominated by the war. He chaired the administration's special Ad Hoc Task Force on Vietnam, convened to consider a request from U.S. commanders to increase American troop levels by 200,000. The committee's deliberations convinced Clifford that America could not prevail militarily in Vietnam and needed instead to disengage from the conflict and seek a negotiated settlement. Johnson initially resisted this assessment, but when it was echoed by a special advisory gathering of senior statesmen, known as the WISE MEN, the president decided to adopt Clifford's recommendation. On March 31, 1968, Johnson announced a halt to U.S. bombing of North Vietnam above the 20th parallel. In May 1968 the United States and North Vietnam agreed to begin formal peace talks in Paris.

Having played a central part in altering U.S. policy on Vietnam, Clifford then pressed for a complete halt to the bombing of North Vietnam as a means to spur the peace negotiations. In October 1968 Johnson ordered the cessation. Clifford left office with the Johnson administration in January 1969 and resumed his law practice. In July 1969 he authored an article in *Foreign Affairs* urging American withdrawal from Vietnam. He remained an influential figure in the Democratic Party and was an informal adviser to President JIMMY CARTER. He published his memoirs, *Counsel to the President*, in 1991. The following year he was indicted on charges of making millions in illegal profits in the financial scandal involving the Bank of Credit and Commerce International. Clifford denied any wrongdoing.

COFFIN, WILLIAM SLOANE, JR. (1924–) Christian clergyman active in the domestic antiwar movement. Born in New York City, he interrupted his studies at Yale to serve with the U.S. Army during WORLD WAR II as a liaison officer to the French and Soviet armies. Discharged from the military in 1947, he returned to Yale, graduating in 1949. From 1950 to 1953 he worked for the CENTRAL INTELLIGENCE AGENCY in Germany on top-secret operations against the Soviet Union. Returning to the United States, he studied at Yale Divinity School and was ordained a Presbyterian minister in 1956. In 1958 he became chaplain of Yale, a post he held for 18 years.

A political and social activist committed to the civil rights and antiwar movements in the 1960s, he was an early opponent of U.S. involvement in the VIETNAM WAR. Coffin served with the interdenominational peace group Clergy and Laity Concerned About Vietnam. Urging civil disobedience, he made his Yale chapel a sanctuary for draft-age men refusing to serve in the war. In 1968 he was convicted of conspiring to help draft resisters. His conviction was overturned on appeal in 1970 and the charges dropped. Named senior pastor of Riverside Church in New York in 1977, he was one of four clergymen invited by the Iranian government in 1979 to celebrate Christmas services for the American hostages at the U.S. embassy in Teheran during the IRAN HOSTAGE CRISIS. In 1987 he left Riverside to become president of the antinuclear arms group SANE/FREEZE.

COLBY, BAINBRIDGE (1869–1950) Lawyer and secretary of state. Born in Missouri, Colby graduated from Williams College in 1890 and the New York Law School in 1892. He was admitted to the bar and entered private practice in New York City. He won election as a Republican in 1901 to the New York State assembly, serving a single two-year term before resuming his law practice. He left the Republican fold in 1912 to help form the Progressive Party and support its presidential candidate, THEODORE ROOSEVELT. In 1914 he ran unsuccessfully for the U.S. Senate from New York as a Progressive. Two years later Colby supported the reelection of Democratic President WOODROW WILSON and soon afterward joined the Democratic Party. With American entry into WORLD WAR I in 1917, Colby accepted an appointment to the U.S. Shipping Board and was a member of the American mission to interallied meetings in France the same year. He resigned from the Shipping Board in 1919.

Named by Wilson in March 1920 to replace ROBERT LANSING as secretary of state, Colby spent just under a year in the post. He was a leader in the administration's ultimately unsuccessful fight for Senate approval of the TREATY OF VERSAILLES, forcefully defending Wilson's unyielding position on the LEAGUE OF NATIONS. The strongly anti-Communist Colby initiated the U.S. nonrecognition policy toward Soviet Russia in August 1920. His most significant accomplishments as secretary of state involved Latin America. Pursuing a program that presaged the GOOD NEIGHBOR POLICY of the 1930s, he avoided further armed intervention in the Caribbean, announced U.S. intention to begin withdrawing occupying forces from the Dominican Republic and Haiti, and made a goodwill tour of Latin America. He also opened talks with the Mexican government concerning its threats to expropriate foreign-held oil properties. These negotiations culminated in the BU-CARELI AGREEMENT in 1923 and normalization of U.S.-Mexican diplomatic relations. Colby left office with Wilson in 1921 and formed a law partnership with the former president. Following Wilson's death in 1924, he remained in private practice until his retirement in 1936. Revoking his early support for President FRANKLIN D. ROOSEVELT, he joined with other conservative Democrats in 1934 to form the anti-New Deal American Liberty League.

COLBY, WILLIAM EGAN (1920–) Intelligence officer and head of the CENTRAL INTELLIGENCE AGENCY (CIA). Colby was born in St. Paul, Minnesota, the son of a career Army officer. He graduated from Princeton in 1940. During WORLD WAR II he served as an Army officer with the OFFICE OF STRATEGIC SERVICES, the nation's wartime intelligence organization. He received a law degree from Columbia University in 1947. Colby left private practice in New York City in 1950 to join the recently formed CIA. He was assigned to the agency's covert operations branch.

In 1962 Colby was named chief of the clandestine department's Far East Division. He presided over expanded CIA involvement in the VIETNAM WAR, including agency direction of the LAOS SECRET WAR. In 1968 he took a leave of absence to serve as director of the CIVIL OPERATIONS AND REVOLUTIONARY DEVELOPMENT SUPPORT (CORDS) PACIFICATION program in Vietnam. The CORDS effort included the controversial Phoenix Program, which involved the identification and destruction of the Communist Viet Cong infrastructure in South Vietnam. Colby returned to the CIA in 1971 as its executive director-comptroller. In 1973 he became head of the covert operations department. Public disclosure the same year of prior agency involvement in illegal or questionable activities prompted CIA Director JAMES R. SCHLESINGER to instruct Colby to investigate and document previous transgressions. The report, known as the FAMILY JEWELS, initially remained within the CIA where it was used in the reform of internal procedures.

In May 1973 President RICHARD M. NIXON selected Colby to replace Schlesinger as director of central intelligence. The new CIA chief's tenure was dominated by presidential and congressional investigations. Allegations appearing in the *New York Times* in December 1974 of agency participation in an extensive illegal domestic intelligence operation brought probes by the ROCKEFELLER COMMISSION appointed by President GERALD R. FORD, the CHURCH COMMITTEE in the Senate, and the PIKE COMMITTEE in the House. In testimony before the various panels, Colby sought to balance the disclosure of agency misdeeds with the need to safeguard secret intelligence methods and sources. Many of the items in the Family Jewels list, including assassination of foreign leaders, the unsanctioned opening of domestic mail, and the testing of mind-altering drugs on unknowing subjects, were publicly revealed. Believing Colby's directorship had been undermined by the protracted investigations, Ford requested his resignation effective January 1976. In retirement Colby wrote his memoirs, *Honorable Men: My Life in the CIA* (1978), and began a law practice in Washington.

COLD WAR (1945–1990) Protracted struggle between the U.S.-led FREE WORLD and Soviet-dominated Commmunist bloc. The conflict evolved out of the post–WORLD WAR II contest for control of Central Europe and eventually became a worldwide ideological, political, and strategic competition. The East-West confrontation dominated and shaped international affairs for more than four decades. The term Cold War, coined by speech writer Herbert Bayard Swope, was first used by presidential adviser BERNARD M. BARUCH in a 1947 speech to characterize increasingly adversarial U.S.-Soviet relations. Popularized by columnist WALTER LIPPMANN, the phrase entered the international lexicon, describing a condition of East-West hostility intermediate between a state of peace and an actual shooting or "hot" war. The struggle between the West and the Communist world involved diplomatic maneuvering, psychological warfare and propaganda, COVERT ACTION, massive military buildups and the nuclear arms race, threats of force, and limited wars. The Cold War lasted from the end of World War II to the collapse of communism in 1990 and can be divided into five phases: confrontation from 1945 to 1955; coexistence and competition from 1955 to 1972; a period of DETENTE from 1972 to 1979; renewed confrontation from 1979 to 1985; and a final period of rapidly easing tension from 1985 to 1990.

The U.S.-Soviet alliance against Nazi Germany began to unravel almost as soon as World War II ended in August 1945. By 1946 the meetings of the COUNCIL OF FOREIGN MINISTERS revealed fundamental East-West differences over the future status of Germany and Eastern Europe. As Moscow moved to impose Communist regimes in the countries of Eastern Europe occupied by its armies during the war, British wartime leader Winston Churchill warned in 1946 of an IRON CURTAIN descending across Europe, partitioning East from West. Concern about possible Communist inroads in Western Europe, Greece, and Turkey led President HARRY S. TRUMAN in 1947 to enunciate the TRUMAN DOCTRINE committing U.S. policy to the CONTAINMENT of Soviet expansionism. By 1948 U.S.-Soviet relations had hardened into a tense standoff over Germany, which was divided after the war into Western and Soviet occupation zones. When the USSR blockaded Berlin, Washington mounted the BERLIN AIRLIFT (1948–1949), successfully resupplying the Western-administered sector of the city by air. In 1949 the United States spearheaded formation of NATO, the security alliance organized to defend Western Europe against Soviet-sponsored Communist aggression.

The same year a Communist revolution under Mao Tse-tung seized power in China. In 1950 a Truman administration study of U.S. security requirements yielded NSC-68, a top-level assessment identifying the Soviet-directed Communist drive for world domination as the principal threat to America and its allies. The Communist North Korean invasion of South Korea in June 1950 triggered the KOREAN WAR, raising Cold War tensions to a new high. Truman committed U.S. combat forces to the defense of South Korea, extending the American containment strategy to Asia. In the United States, Senator JOSEPH R. MCCARTHY (R-WI) exploited heightened domestic Cold War apprehensions by launching a demagogic campaign against alleged Communist subversion in the federal government.

The East-West confrontation began to ease in 1953 with the end of the Korean conflict and the emergence of a new leadership in the Kremlin following the death of Soviet Premier Joseph Stalin. The GENEVA SUMMIT (1955) of U.S., British, French, and Soviet leaders ushered in a brief thaw in Cold War hostilities. The positive "spirit of Geneva" was derailed by the brutal Soviet suppression of the HUNGARIAN REVOLT in 1956. Both sides, however, recognized that the advent of NUCLEAR WEAPONS and development of such means as the INTERCONTINENTAL BALLISTIC MISSILE for their long-range delivery made all-out war unthinkable. Soviet leader Nikita S. Khrushchev, abandoning classic Communist dogma positing the inevitability of a Communist-capitalist clash, spoke of "peaceful coexistence." At the same time Khrushchev also promoted leftist "wars of national liberation" in the THIRD WORLD, both underscoring and extending the continuing East-West Cold War competition. U.S.-Soviet hostilities flared during the BERLIN CRISIS (1958–1960) and the two superpowers went to the brink of war during the CUBAN MISSILE CRISIS (1962). This sobering brush with a possible nuclear conflict brought a new restraint in East-West relations. The LIMITED TEST BAN TREATY, the first major U.S.-Soviet arms control agreement, was concluded the following year. The U.S. commitment to preventing Communist gains in Southeast Asia brought a deepening and ultimately unsuccessful American involvement in the VIETNAM WAR in the mid-1960s.

President RICHARD M. NIXON shifted U.S. Cold War foreign policy toward a more pragmatic accommodation with the Communist bloc. Nixon aimed to achieve international peace and stability through a BALANCE OF POWER approach that recognized each side's vital national interests and security concerns. His dramatic 1972 journey to Peking initiated U.S.-Chinese ties, ending two decades of American isolation of the Communist nation. At the MOSCOW SUMMIT (1972), Nixon and Soviet leader Leonid I. Brezhnev formally inaugurated the burgeoning U.S.-Soviet detente. The 35-nation HELSINKI ACCORDS (1975) sought to codify the improving East-West relations. The new U.S.-Soviet relationship nonetheless did not spell the end of the Cold War. Washington and Moscow clashed during the 1973

Arab-Israeli YOM KIPPUR WAR and remained at odds over the Kremlin's support for Marxist regimes in Africa.

The USSR's intervention in the AFGHANISTAN WAR in 1979 ended the U.S.-Soviet detente. In response to the Soviet invasion, President JIMMY CARTER shelved the SALT II arms accord and organized the U.S.-led OLYMPIC BOYCOTT of the 1980 Moscow games. Renewed U.S.-Soviet hostilities intensified in the early 1980s under President RONALD W. REAGAN, who labeled the Soviet Union an "evil empire." The Reagan administration formulated a new U.S. Cold War strategy, involving U.S. support for anti-Communist insurgencies worldwide. Under this REAGAN DOCTRINE the administration funneled assistance to CONTRAS battling the leftist Sandinista government in Nicaragua, pro-Western UNITA forces in the ANGOLAN CIVIL WAR, and Mujahedeen guerrillas in Afghanistan.

In 1985 Mikhail S. Gorbachev became leader of the Soviet Union. Gorbachev's program of sweeping political and economic reform unleashed powerful movements for liberalization both in his country and across Eastern Europe. Gorbachev also achieved rapidly improved ties with the West. He and Reagan held a series of summit meetings and in 1987 concluded the landmark INF TREATY on nuclear arms. When it became apparent in 1989 that Moscow no longer would resort to force to maintain Communist regimes in its Eastern European satellites, the Communist governments of Eastern Europe collapsed under domestic pressure in a stunning sequence. In 1990 the FINAL SETTLEMENT WITH RESPECT TO GERMANY TREATY ended the postwar division of Germany, while the CONVENTIONAL FORCES EUROPE TREATY provided for the withdrawal of U.S. and Soviet military forces from Central Europe. The two agreements marked the end of the long East-West struggle over Europe and signaled the close of the Cold War. In 1991 Moscow cooperated with Washington in the PERSIAN GULF WAR to reverse Iraq's invasion of Kuwait. The Soviet Union itself was dismantled at the end of the year, whereupon the majority of the former Soviet republics joined, as sovereign nations, to form the non-Communist Commonwealth of Independent States.

COLLECTIVE SECURITY   Concept in international relations of an arrangement in which nations commit themselves to act in unison for their mutual security. The term is used to refer to either of two mutual security systems: an international body of all or most states, exemplified by the UNITED NATIONS, established to keep the peace among its members; or a regional security alliance, such as NATO, organized to provide for collective defense against outside aggression. From the final defeat of French Emperor Napoleon in 1815 to the onset of WORLD WAR I in 1914, the major European powers relied on a BALANCE OF POWER approach to preserve the peace and maintain international stability. The United States remained apart from the balance-of-power politics, observing its traditional aversion to involvement in overseas alliances first broadly articulated in WASHINGTON'S FAREWELL ADDRESS in 1796.

Following World War I, a wide consensus developed among Allied statesmen that the divisive European alliance system had contributed to the outbreak of conflict. Allied leaders called for a collective security arrangement to prevent a recurrence of the war's terrible carnage. President WOODROW WILSON led efforts at the PARIS PEACE CONFERENCE (1919) to devise an international peacekeeping organization to replace the earlier balance-of-power approach. The LEAGUE OF NATIONS was established through the TREATY OF VERSAILLES (1919) ending the world war. Deep-seated ISOLATIONISM and misgivings over the possible surrender of national sovereignty, however, led the U.S. Senate to reject American membership in the international body. Despite the participation of most nations, the league lacked effective means to curb the aggression of member states. Thus it proved incapable of preventing Japanese intervention in the MANCHURIAN CRISIS (1931–1933) and Fascist Italy's 1935 invasion of Ethiopia. The ineffectual body had lost all credibility by the time WORLD WAR II began in Europe in 1939.

During the war, U.S. President FRANKLIN D. ROOSEVELT championed the formation of a successor organization to the League of Nations. Roosevelt envisioned a global collective security arrangement with the major wartime allies—the United States, Great Britain, Soviet Union, and China—serving as the FOUR POLICEMEN for the postwar community of nations. America's political leadership was determined to avoid a return to prewar U.S. isolationism, which had come to be regarded as a cause of the global conflict. Senate ratification of the UNITED NATIONS CHARTER in 1945 signaled U.S. acceptance of the need for collective security. Roosevelt's policeman concept evolved into the U.N. Security Council, which was vested with the authority to enlist member nation armed forces for peacekeeping purposes. With the onset of the COLD WAR in the late 1940s, however, the United Nations became the site of East-West confrontation rather than of multinational mutual security cooperation.

The RIO TREATY (1947) for the joint defense of the Western Hemisphere marked the postwar emergence of the second, more limited form of collective security arrangement. The inability of the United Nations to fulfill its global collective security promise spurred the creation of regional security alliances. The Cold War-inspired fear of worldwide Communist aggression led the United States to join with its allies in Europe and Asia to form NATO in 1949 and the SOUTHEAST ASIA TREATY ORGANIZATION in 1954. NATO and its Communist counterpart, the Warsaw Pact, eventually produced what was in effect an East-West balance of power in Europe. The collapse of communism in Eastern Europe in 1989 and end of the Cold War raised the possibility the United Nations might finally develop, as intended, into the principal instrument for worldwide collective security. Following Iraq's August 1990 invasion of Kuwait, the U.N. Security Council voted a series of resolutions condemning the action and demanding Iraqi withdrawal. In an unprecedented instance of collective security at work, a U.S.-led U.N. coalition fought the PERSIAN GULF WAR (1991) to force Iraqi compliance with the Security Council resolutions.

COLOMBO PLAN International economic and social development program for Asia and the Pacific. Founded in 1950 by seven British Commonwealth nations at a meeting of Commonwealth foreign ministers in Colombo, Ceylon (now Sri Lanka), the plan was intended to promote the development of newly independent countries in Asia and the Pacific by providing capital and technical assistance. With the formal start of operations at its Colombo headquarters in 1951, the program began to expand its regional membership and opened itself to non-Commonwealth nations. By invitation, the United States and Japan joined the plan in 1951 and 1954, respectively. The Colombo Plan currently numbers 26 member nations, six of which are so-called major donors: Australia, Canada, Japan, New Zealand, Great Britain, and the United States.

The basic principles and policies governing assistance under the plan are determined by the Consultative Committee, the program's highest deliberative body, consisting of ministers representing all member governments. Negotiations for aid are made directly between a donor and a recipient country, within the framework of the policies adopted by the consultative panel. Assistance takes two principal forms: capital aid, which includes grants and loans from the major donors to recipient member countries for development projects; and technical cooperation, wherein experts and volunteers are provided, training fellowships awarded, and equipment for research and training supplied to assist in economic and social growth.

See also ASIAN DEVELOPMENT BANK.

COMMERCE, DEPARTMENT OF See **DEPARTMENT OF COMMERCE** in **APPENDIX B.**

COMMERCIAL BUREAU OF AMERICAN REPUBLICS See **PAN-AMERICAN UNION.**

COMMITTEE TO DEFEND AMERICA BY AIDING THE ALLIES (1940–1941) Organization that supported U.S. aid to Great Britain and other Allies fighting the Axis Powers in the years before American entrance into WORLD WAR II. The international advocacy group was formed in May 1940 under national chairman William Allen White, a distinguished newspaper editor from Kansas. The committee believed a victorious Nazi Germany would pose a dangerous threat to American security and thus pressed for U.S. assistance to the Allies, short of actual military intervention, to ensure its defeat. The private, bipartisan group quickly grew into a national organization with more than 300 local chapters and several hundred thousand members. Opposed to the traditional ISOLATIONISM espoused by such groups as the AMERICA FIRST COMMITTEE, the organization sought to mobilize public opinion behind greater U.S. involvement in overseas affairs and lobbied vigorously for measures to aid Britain, such as the DESTROYERS-FOR-BASES AGREEMENT (1940) and LEND-LEASE program (1941). The committee disbanded following the December 1941 Japanese attack on PEARL HARBOR, which brought U.S. entry into World War II.

See also FIGHT FOR FREEDOM COMMITTEE.

COMMITTEE ON DISARMAMENT See **CONFERENCE ON DISARMAMENT**.

COMMITTEE ON THE PRESENT DANGER Private advisory group founded in 1976 to counter what it believed was a growing threat to U.S. security posed by COLD WAR adversary the Soviet Union. Established by some 140 largely conservative former government officials, business and labor leaders, retired senior military officers, and academics, the committee warned that the U.S.-Soviet DETENTE since the early 1970s had not altered the Kremlin's drive for world domination based on a continuing massive military buildup. In advocating a large increase in U.S. defense budgets and a tougher stance toward the USSR, the group was at odds with the Carter administration's pursuit of continued detente with Moscow. The committee's influence grew amid deteriorating U.S.-Soviet relations following the Soviet invasion of Afghanistan in 1979. Its vantage point was embraced by President RONALD W. REAGAN in the 1980s. Members who figured prominently in the Reagan administration included CENTRAL INTELLIGENCE AGENCY Director WILLIAM J. CASEY; arms control negotiators PAUL H. NITZE and Max M. Kampelman; ARMS CONTROL AND DISARMAMENT AGENCY directors EUGENE V. ROSTOW and Kenneth L. Adelman; and UNITED NATIONS Ambassador JEANE D. KIRKPATRICK.

COMMITTEE OF SECRET CORRESPONDENCE Five-member committee formed by the Continental Congress at the outset of the AMERICAN REVOLUTION to develop contacts with friends and possible allies abroad. Initial members of the panel created November 29, 1775, included BENJAMIN FRANKLIN, THOMAS JEFFERSON, and JOHN JAY. Eager to find out how European powers regarded the American rebellion, the committee made Arthur Lee, a Virginia lawyer then in London, its first overseas correspondent. Following initial overtures by Lee to the French, the committee dispatched SILAS DEANE to Paris in April 1776 for further negotiations on French assistance to the colonies. The American envoy also represented the SECRET COMMITTEE, which was responsible for procuring war supplies.

In September 1776 the Congress appointed Deane, Lee, and Franklin as special commissioners to France. Undertaking the nation's first official diplomatic mission, the American representatives gained French recognition of American independence and completed the historic FRANCO-AMERICAN ALLIANCE (1778). The Committee of Secret Correspondence was redesignated the Committee on Foreign Affairs in April 1777 and assumed responsibility for the direction of American diplomacy. Thomas Paine, political philosopher and author of the influential revolutionary pamphlet *Common Sense* (1776), served as the new panel's secretary until January 1779. Organizational shortcomings drove Congress in January 1781 to replace the committee with an executive office of foreign affairs directed by a secretary of foreign affairs. ROBERT R. LIVINGSTON and Jay served in the post under the ARTICLES OF CONFEDERATION. The foreign affairs office evolved into the cabinet-level DEPARTMENT OF STATE, established in 1789 under the new CONSTITUTION.

COMMUNICATIONS SATELLITE CORPORATION See **INTERNATIONAL TELECOMMUNICATIONS SATELLITE ORGANIZATION**.

COMMUNIST CONTROL ACT See **INTERNAL SECURITY ACT**.

COMPACT OF FREE ASSOCIATION See **TRUST TERRITORY OF THE PACIFIC ISLANDS**.

COMPREHENSIVE TEST BAN TREATY Proposed agreement prohibiting all tests of NUCLEAR WEAPONS. A comprehensive ban on nuclear explosions has been a part of the international arms control agenda since the mid-1950s. The LIMITED TEST BAN TREATY (1963), THRESHOLD TEST BAN TREATY (1974), and PEACEFUL NUCLEAR EXPLOSIONS TREATY (1976) progressively limited nuclear testing to underground blasts below 150 kilotons (equivalent to 150,000 tons of TNT). The United States, Great Britain, and Soviet Union began discussions on a complete ban in 1977. Negotiations in Geneva over the next three years produced tentative accord on a pact that would halt all testing and rely on NATIONAL TECHNICAL MEANS to verify compliance. The talks stalled in 1980, however, amid worsening East-West relations following the December 1979 Soviet invasion of Afghanistan and were suspended by the Reagan administration in 1982. Discussions on a comprehensive test ban continued under the auspices of the CONFERENCE ON DISARMAMENT, but were unable to resolve U.S.-Soviet differences concerning American insistence on strict verification procedures. The development of highly sophisticated monitoring devices capable of recording any nuclear explosion raised the possibility in the early 1990s of a verifiable comprehensive ban. The Bush administration noted, however, that as long as the United States relied on nuclear DETERRENCE for its security, a minimum nuclear testing program was necessary.

COMPROMISE TARIFF (1833) Federal legislation that reduced U.S. tariffs and ended the Nullification Controversy. The TARIFF OF ABOMINATIONS (1828) had imposed record high duties on imported items, drawing harsh protests from both Southern agricultural and Northern manufacturing interests. The South Carolina legislature in December 1828 had declared the measure unconstitutional. Support for the right of a state to nullify objectionable federal laws mounted in South Carolina over the next several years. Passage of the Tariff of 1832, which eliminated many of the features of the 1828 tariff objectionable to Northern industries but left intact facets opposed by the South, brought South Carolina into open conflict with the administration of President ANDREW JACKSON. In November 1832 the South Carolina state legislature adopted an ordinance nullifying both the 1828 and 1832 tariffs. Jackson in turn is-

sued a proclamation denouncing nullification and asserted federal authority to use force if necessary to collect tariffs in South Carolina. The so-called Nullification Controversy was defused by new tariff legislation crafted by Senator HENRY CLAY (Whig-KY). Known as the Compromise Tariff, it was signed into law March 2, 1833. The measure provided for the general reduction of tariffs to 20 percent, satisfying Southern demands for fewer restraints on imports. To placate Northern desires for continued PROTECTIONISM, the rates were to be lowered gradually in two-year increments until 1842. South Carolina rescinded its nullification ordinance on March 15. Import duties were raised again briefly by the Tariff of 1842 and then returned to lower levels by the WALKER TARIFF (1846).

CONFERENCE OF THE COMMITTEE ON DISARMAMENT See **CONFERENCE ON DISARMAMENT**.

CONFERENCE ON DISARMAMENT Central international forum for multilateral arms control negotiations. Early post–WORLD WAR II multilateral arms control negotiations, conducted under the auspices of the UNITED NATIONS DISARMAMENT COMMISSION, ended in East-West COLD WAR stalemate in 1957. In 1959 a Ten-Nation Committee on Disarmament was formed apart from the United Nations but with U.N. backing. Composed of five NATO countries, including the United States, Great Britain, and France, and five Warsaw Pact countries, including the Soviet Union, its negotiations broke down in 1960. The following year the United States and Soviet Union took the lead in forming a successor Eighteen-Nation Committee on Disarmament. The committee, also separate from the U.N. system, was endorsed by a General Assembly resolution on December 20, 1961. In addition to five NATO and five Warsaw Pact countries, its membership included eight nonaligned nations. The committee began its meeting in Geneva, Switzerland, in 1962. Member France did not attend in protest against U.S.-Soviet domination of the deliberations. In 1969 the body's membership grew to 26 and its name was changed to the Conference of the Committee on Disarmament. The conference expanded to 31 nations in 1975. At the first

U.N. Special Session on Disarmament in 1978, agreement was reached to name the group the Committee on Disarmament, extend its membership to 40 nations, and rotate its chairmanship among all members on a monthly basis. With the participation of France in 1979 and China in 1980, all five major nuclear powers were represented at the meetings. In 1984 the committee redesignated itself the Conference on Disarmament, reflecting the ongoing nature of its negotiations. While still not an official U.N. body, the conference has developed increasingly close ties to the organization. A number of important multilateral arms control agreements have been reached under the disarmament forum's aegis: the Nuclear Non-Proliferation Treaty (1968), Seabed Arms Control Treaty (1971), Biological Weapons Convention (1972), and Environmental Modification Convention (1977).

CONFERENCE ON INTERNATIONAL ECO-NOMIC COOPERATION See **NORTH-SOUTH DIALOGUE.**

CONFERENCE ON THE LIMITATION OF ARMAMENT See **WASHINGTON NAVAL CONFERENCE.**

CONFERENCE FOR THE REDUCTION AND LIMITATION OF ARMAMENTS See **WORLD DISARMAMENT CONFERENCE.**

CONFERENCE ON SECURITY AND CO-OPERATION IN EUROPE (CSCE) Forum in which the European states, Canada, and the United States address European political and security issues. In 1969 the Soviet-dominated Warsaw Pact military alliance proposed an all-European conference to discuss common security matters. The basic Soviet goal in seeking such a gathering was to win international ratification of the post–World War II boundaries in Eastern Europe. At the wartime Yalta Conference (1945), the Soviet Union had gained possession of part of eastern Poland. As compensation for its loss, Poland provisionally received German territory east of the Oder-Neisse Line at the Potsdam Conference (1945). NATO, the U.S.-led Western security alliance, responded to the Communist overture by renewing its call for Mutual and Balanced Force Reduction Talks (MBFR)

among each side's conventional military forces in central Europe.

The Warsaw Pact pressed its conference proposal over the next few years. With U.S.-Soviet relations entering a period of detente, the Nixon administration in 1971 indicated the United States would support the Soviet-sponsored conference once a formal settlement of Berlin's postwar status had been reached. This was achieved with ratification of the Quadripartite Agreement on Berlin in June 1972. In October 1972, NATO endorsed preparatory East-West discussions to be held the next month in Helsinki on a European security conference. The alliance also accepted a U.S.-Soviet timetable for the NATO-sought MBFR talks in Vienna the following year.

Following the November 1972 preliminary discussions, representatives of 35 nations met in Helsinki on July 3, 1973, for the opening of the Conference on Security and Cooperation in Europe. In attendance were the 16 NATO countries, including the United States and Canada; the 7 Warsaw Pact countries; and 12 other European countries. All the European states except Albania were present. After two years of meetings in Helsinki and Geneva, the participants reached agreement on a CSCE Final Act providing a charter for East-West relations and codifying postwar European boundaries. The document, known as the Helsinki Accords, was signed by the leaders of the 35 CSCE nations at a final summit meeting in Helsinki from July 30 to August 1, 1975.

Follow-up conferences to review implementation of the accord were held in Belgrade (1977–1978), Madrid (1980–1983), and Vienna (1986–1989). The Madrid talks were the genesis of separate negotiations leading to the Stockholm Declaration on additional confidence-building measures to reduce NATO-Warsaw Pact tensions. The Vienna sessions produced the East-West Accord on Human Rights and an agreement to begin new talks on reducing conventional military forces in Europe. The collapse of communism in Eastern Europe in 1989 and ensuing dissolution of the Warsaw Pact altered the CSCE's basic role as a venue for East-West discussions. Both Moscow and its former Eastern European satellites envisioned the CSCE as providing the framework for a post–Cold War association of all European states. The Western European nations and United States endorsed an expanded CSCE, but stressed it would not supersede NATO or the European Community. At a November 1990 summit conference in Paris held in conjunction with the signing of the CONVENTIONAL FORCES EUROPE TREATY, CSCE nations concluded the Charter of Paris for a New Europe. The document, marking the end of the Cold War division of Europe, bound its signatories to a "steadfast commitment to democracy based on human rights and fundamental freedoms; prosperity through economic liberty and social justice; and equal security for all our countries." The charter transformed the CSCE into a permanent European institution. It established a CSCE secretariat in Prague and provided for annual meetings of foreign ministers and a summit gathering every two years of CSCE heads of governments. CSCE membership dropped to 34 with the reunification of Germany in October 1990 and returned to 35 with the inclusion of Albania in 1991. CSCE ranks swelled to more than 50 in early 1992 with the addition of newly sovereign states from both the former Soviet Union and civil war-torn Yugoslavia.

CONGO CRISIS (1960–1963) Violent political turmoil in the newly independent central African nation that became a major international crisis. Faced with mounting native opposition to its colonial rule, Belgium granted independence to the Congo (now Zaire) on June 30, 1960. National elections had been held that May and the new country was headed by a coalition government under President Joseph Kasavubu and Prime Minister Patrice Lumumba. From its inception the new government faced widespread upheaval. Reflecting their discontent with the fact independence had not brought the immediate elevation of Africans to command positions in the military, elements of the Congolese army mutineed on July 5, turning on their white officers and on European settlers. Amid an increasingly chaotic situation, Belgian military forces on July 10 reentered the country to restore order. The next day separatists led by Moise Tshombe declared the Congolese province of Katanga (now Shaba) an independent nation. Katanga contained most of the Congo's rich mineral resources and

Tshombe's separatist movement had the tacit backing of Western mining interests.

Fearing a plan by Belgium to reassume control of its former colony, Lumumba appealed to the UNITED NATIONS for assistance on July 12. The U.N. Security Council on July 14 called for the withdrawal of Belgian troops and authorized a U.N. peacekeeping force as their replacement. Within days several thousand soldiers from neighboring African countries and small nations elsewhere were serving under the U.N. banner in the Congo. The U.N. mandate was limited to keeping law and order and did not sanction intervention in internal Congolese affairs. In late July Lumumba visited the United States, seeking U.S. military aid for the suppression of the Katangan rebellion. The Eisenhower administration turned down the request, not wanting to involve America directly in the Congolese upheaval.

The Soviet Union was receptive to Lumumba's appeals for help. In August the Communist power began sending military supplies and technicians to the Congo. By threatening to intervene on the Lumumba government's behalf, Soviet Premier Nikita S. Khruschchev in effect extended the COLD WAR to sub-Saharan Africa. In response the United States asserted it would take whatever action was necessary to prevent the introduction of Soviet forces in the Congo. Alarmed by Lumumba's growing Soviet ties, the Eisenhower administration also undertook a covert operation to remove the prime minister from power. In late August 1960 Lumumba declared martial law and began arresting political opponents. On September 5 President Kasavubu dismissed him from office and ordered an end to the Soviet assistance. In the ensuing turmoil, General Joseph Mobutu assumed power. Lumumba remained under U.N. protection until November when, apparently with clandestine U.S. assistance, he was captured by Mobutu's forces. Lumumba was executed under dubious circumstances in January 1961.

Both the United States and Soviet Union favored ending the Katangan uprising. America wanted to see the Congo emerge as a stable, non-Communist nation, while the USSR opposed Western commercial control over Katanga's mineral resources and aimed to become the champion of African anticolonialism. In February 1961 the U.N. Security Council gave U.N. troops in the Congo greater leeway to use force to remove foreign mercenaries aiding the Katangan secession. In July 1961 Cyrille Adoula became the Congo's prime minister. With negotiations between Adoula and Tshombe showing no signs of progress, the U.N. command began limited military operations against foreign mercenaries in August. On September 18, 1961, U.N. Secretary-General Dag Hammarskjold died in a plane crash while en route to discussions with Tshombe on the fighting. Newly authorized to use whatever force necessary, U.N. soldiers in December mounted a larger operation against the foreign mercenaries, backbone of the Katangan rebellion. Amid the stepped-up U.N. campaign, Tshombe indicated willingness to negotiate. On December 21 he and Adoula concluded an agreement ending the Katangan secession.

Over the next year this agreement fell apart during protracted talks over its implementation. In late December 1962 U.N. forces, with U.S. airlift and logistical support, launched a major assault into Katanga and brought the rebellion to a close. Tshombe publicly announced the end of the secession on January 14, 1963, and subsequently went into exile. Resolution of the Congo Crisis was viewed as a victory for the United Nations.

See also KATANGAN CRISIS.

CONNALLY AMENDMENT (1946) Senate resolution declaring U.S. acceptance of the compulsory jurisdiction of the WORLD COURT. In ratifying the UNITED NATIONS CHARTER in 1945, the Senate endorsed U.S. participation in the U.N. tribunal. Under the World Court Statute, member nations that voluntarily commit themselves to abide by the tribunal's decisions do so with the understanding the judicial body will refrain from ruling in matters pertaining to any state's domestic affairs. In July 1946 the Senate considered a resolution, supported by President HARRY S. TRUMAN, stating U.S. adherence to the court's binding jurisdiction. Concerned that the court's statute vested the tribunal with exclusive authority to determine those items outside its purview, Senator Tom Connally (D-TX) sponsored a clarifying reservation. He proposed inserting the words "as determined by the United States" after the clause excluding U.S. domestic affairs from the court's jurisdiction. The so-called self-judging reservation was approved by a 51 to 12 vote on August 2, 1946, and the resolution, which became known as the Connally Amendment, took effect August 14. In years to follow critics contended that the Connally provision undermined U.S. leadership in the strengthening of international law. Detractors argued that the United States should not arbitrarily decide when it would or would not appear before the World Court. In 1985, however, the Reagan administration announced that it was withdrawing, as permitted under the court's statute, U.S. acceptance of the tribunal's compulsory authority in areas other than domestic affairs. The action stemmed from U.S. refusal to participate in the World Court case NICARAGUA V. UNITED STATES, concerning American efforts in the 1980s to overthrow the leftist Sandinista government in the Central American nation.

CONNALLY RESOLUTION (1943) Measure expressing U.S. Senate support for American involvement in an international peacekeeping organization. WORLD WAR II brought a dramatic alteration of America's traditionally isolationist foreign policy. During the conflict a broad political consensus emerged within the United States that the nation's ISOLATIONISM in the 1930s had accommodated the expansionist aggression of Germany and Japan that eventually resulted in global war. On September 21, 1943, the House of Representatives adopted the Fulbright Resolution, named for its sponsor J. WILLIAM FULBRIGHT (D-AR), favoring U.S. membership in a postwar international association "with power adequate to establish and maintain a just and lasting peace." A similar measure, introduced by Tom Connally (D-TX), passed the Senate by an 85 to 5 vote on November 5. The Connally Resolution endorsed creation of an international authority "to prevent aggression and to preserve the peace." The measures marked a growing American INTERNATIONALISM and signaled congressional backing for U.S. participation in the formation of the UNITED NATIONS.

CONSORTIUM LOAN TO CHINA (1911–1913) Collaborative lending arrangement established by European, U.S., and Japanese financiers for providing investment capital to China. Convinced that lagging U.S. influence in the Far East related directly to minimal private American investment in the region, President WILLIAM HOWARD TAFT and Secretary of State PHILANDER C. KNOX turned to DOLLAR DIPLOMACY, involving the promotion of an expanded U.S. overseas presence by active government support of private American enterprises abroad. The Taft administration concluded that by inducing American bankers to invest large sums in China, it could play a decisive role in preserving Chinese territorial integrity and upholding the OPEN DOOR policy of equal trade access in the Asian nation. A consortium of British, French, and German bankers received a concession in June 1909 to finance construction of the Hukuang Railways in southern and central China. At the State Department's suggestion, an American banking group was formed, and Knox asked that it be permitted to join the original consortium. When the Europeans resisted the U.S. bid for admission, Taft sent a personal appeal to the Chinese Prince Regent requesting a share of the loan for the American bankers. The Europeans and Chinese at last admitted the Americans under an agreement finalized in May 1911, whereupon the initial three-power consortium became a four-power consortium. In 1912, with the establishment of China as a republic following the overthrow of the Manchu dynasty, the United States, Great Britain, France, and Germany joined with Russia and Japan to form a six-power consortium. The bankers of the six nations maneuvered to make an enormous loan for the reorganization of China's government. As the six-power group sought to conclude its agreement with China, the American banking interests grew apprehensive about the fiscal soundness of the endeavor. After WOODROW WILSON became president in 1913 and repudiated the Taft administration's Dollar Diplomacy, the American financiers withdrew from both the four- and six-power consortiums.

CONSTITUTION Document establishing the U.S. government and setting forth its structure, purpose, and powers. American independence from Great Britain, declared in 1776, was recognized in the TREATY OF PARIS (1783) ending the AMERICAN REVOLUTION. Drafted in Philadelphia in 1787, the U.S. Constitution was ratified the following year and took effect in 1789. It replaced the ARTICLES OF CONFEDERATION, which had proved inadequate to the demands of governing the new nation. Both the original Constitution and its 26 amendments are concerned principally with the national government's organization, the separation of federal and state powers, and the safeguarding of citizens' individual liberties. The conduct of foreign affairs is addressed only sparingly. The Constitution generally is interpreted as taking for granted that foreign relations are a national concern and thus fall under federal rather than state control.

In keeping with the Constitution's emphasis on checks and balances, authority over foreign affairs is divided among the three branches of the federal government. The president is assigned four foreign affairs responsibilities. Article II, Section 2 designates the president the commander in chief of the armed forces and of the state militia when called into federal service. The same section confers on the president the authority to negotiate treaties and to appoint "ambassadors . . . [and] other public ministers and consuls." Article II, Section 3 similarly grants the president the responsibility to "receive ambassadors and other public ministers." Beyond these specific powers, presidents also have relied on the general "executive power" clause under Article II, Section 1 as the basis for their preeminent role in foreign policy.

Congress exercises a number of foreign affairs responsibilities. Article I, Section 8 confers on the legislative branch the authority to declare war, raise armed forces and "make rules for . . . [their] regulation," regulate foreign commerce, and legislate maritime law. Other powers granted in the same section with implications for foreign relations are the right to set rules for naturalization and immigration, establish a postal system, regulate patents and copyrights, and govern newly acquired territories. Article II, Section 2 calls for the "advice and consent" of the Senate in the president's negotiation of treaties and appointment of overseas envoys. Treaties must be ratified by a two-thirds vote while ambassadors and other foreign representatives require approval by a simple majority.

The general clause under Article I, Section 8 authorizing Congress to make all "necessary and proper" laws in the exercise of its responsibilities has served to justify the legislative branch's broad involvement in foreign relations. Finally, since most of the government's international activities require funding, Congress's power of the purse gives it considerable influence over the formulation and conduct of foreign affairs.

Article III, Section 2 places jurisdiction over legal controversies involving foreign states or parties in the federal court system. In its single specifically delineated foreign affairs power, the Supreme Court has original jurisdiction in "all cases affecting ambassadors . . . [and] other public ministers and consuls." Other provisions within the Constitution relating to foreign relations include the designation under Article VI of treaties as part of the "supreme law of the land"; a bar under Article I, Section 10 on individual states entering into "any agreement or compact . . . with a foreign power" without the consent of Congress; and a prohibition under Article I, Section 9 against public officials accepting foreign gifts or titles without congressional approval.

The president traditionally has enjoyed almost exclusive authority over the formulation and execution of foreign policy. Since the creation of the State and War departments in 1789, the nation's foreign affairs machinery has resided in the executive branch. During the GENET AFFAIR (1793), President GEORGE WASHINGTON drew on his power to receive foreign emissaries as the basis for his recognizing the new revolutionary government in France, thus setting the precedent of the president's authority to extend or withdraw U.S. diplomatic recognition of foreign governments. After an initial attempt to involve the Senate in the negotiation of several INDIAN TREATIES ended in failure, Washington also began the tradition of limiting its role in the treaty-making process to the ratification of completed agreements. Acknowledging the president's primary reponsibility for foreign relations, the Senate only rarely has declined to approve a treaty, most notably refusing to accept the TREATY OF VERSAILLES in 1920. When concerns have arisen over an agreement's scope or impact, the Senate usually has attached reservations, in effect amending the text, or adopted a resolution outlining its understanding of the treaty's meaning. Similarly, only a handful of presidential nominations for overseas posts have met with Senate rejection. Presidents ordinarily have not submitted for Senate confirmation the names of emissaries to peace negotiations or other international conferences or of personal envoys on special diplomatic missions. Presidents also can conclude EXECUTIVE AGREEMENTS with foreign governments. These international pacts are not submitted to the Senate for approval. In the 20th century they have come to vastly outnumber treaties. Amid concerns that growing use of these agreements threatened to circumvent congressional involvement in foreign policy, Congress in 1972 passed the CASE ACT requiring the president to make timely notification of such executive accords to the legislative branch.

The most serious and enduring struggle between the executive and legislative arms over foreign policy has concerned war powers. The Constitution assigns Congress the authority to declare war and the president the authority to conduct it. Since JOHN ADAMS and the undeclared maritime QUASI-WAR (1798–1800) with France, however, presidents regularly have directed the use of U.S. armed forces abroad without prior congressional assent. Only 5 of the nation's 12 major overseas conflicts were formally declared by Congress. Since WORLD WAR II, the trend has been away from official war declarations. The KOREAN WAR, VIETNAM WAR, and PERSIAN GULF WAR were waged under a combination of the president's authority as commander in chief and congressional resolutions. In 1973 Congress passed the WAR POWERS RESOLUTION requiring the president to obtain congressional approval when deploying U.S. forces into combat for an extended period.

The Supreme Court has avoided ruling on cases pertaining to foreign affairs. Under what is known as the "political question" doctrine, the Court maintains that matters touching on foreign relations involve policy rather than judicial questions and as such should be resolved by Congress and the president. In an important early application of the rule, the Court in 1829 in *Foster* v. *Neilson* refused to adjudicate a boundary dispute between the United States and Spain. The Court has limited its decisions in foreign affairs to instances where explicit constitutional issues have arisen out of cases involving domestic or internal legal matters.

As early as 1796, the Court held in WARE V. HYLTON that treaties, as the supreme law of the land, took precedence over state law. The same status was extended to executive agreements in UNITED STATES V. BELMONT (1937). In MISSOURI V. HOLLAND (1920) the Court gave an expansive definition to the federal treaty-making power, while later affirming in *Reid* v. *Covert* (1957) that a treaty, to be valid, had to conform to the Constitution. Beginning with the *Prize Cases* (1863) over the Union's blockade of the Confederacy during the Civil War, the Court in time of hostilities has afforded broad powers to the president as commander in chief. In UNITED STATES V. CURTISS-WRIGHT EXPORT CORPORATION (1936), the Court characterized the president as the "sole organ" of the nation's foreign relations with sweeping powers over foreign policy. This authority as commander in chief and chief executive was placed under clear constitutional limits in the STEEL SEIZURE CASE (1952). Following the SPANISH-AMERICAN WAR (1898), the Court faced the question of the Constitution's application in America's newly acquired overseas territories. In the INSULAR CASES (1902), the Court first developed the "incorporation theory," which held that the Constitution was fully in effect only in territories formally incorporated through treaty or act of Congress.

The emergence after World War II of international organizations such as the UNITED NATIONS and the creation of NATO and other regional security alliances raised new questions about the relationship of U.S. foreign relations to the nation's sovereignty and independence. U.S. membership in such associations occurs with the clear understanding that American participation remains subject to constitutional limits. Debate continues, though, over such issues as the extent to which either Congress or the president can commit the nation to a possible future conflict through its membership in a military alliance or the degree to which U.N. resolutions are binding on American policy or actions.

CONSTRUCTIVE ENGAGEMENT Term for the oft-criticized policy pursued by the Reagan administration to induce the government of South Africa to dismantle apartheid, that nation's legal system of racial separation and discrimination. Under the system, established by the white ruling party in 1948, all South Africans were classified by race. Institutional segregation divided the country's white, black, Asian, and mixed-race populations. The country's blacks, who outnumbered whites five to one, could not vote in national elections. Apartheid, and the police state apparatus used to uphold it, made South Africa an international pariah and the target of worldwide condemnation. The United States historically had expressed opposition to apartheid while preserving a strong relationship with a white majority South African government valued both as a pro-Western, anti-Communist ally and a supplier of strategic materials. American presidents since HARRY S. TRUMAN sought to encourage gradual change in South Africa in the interest of averting a civil war that could result in a takeover by a regime with ties to the Soviet Union. As part of its campaign for HUMAN RIGHTS, the Carter administration intensified U.S. criticism of apartheid and, in 1978, imposed an embargo on sales of U.S. computers and other items to South African armed forces.

After taking office in 1981, the Reagan administration embarked on a policy of so-called constructive engagement with South Africa. Devised by Assistant Secretary of State Chester A. Crocker and approved by President RONALD W. REAGAN, the policy advocated maintaining good relations with Pretoria while pressing discreetly, through friendly persuasion, for racial reform and for settlement of regional disputes involving South Africa and neighboring countries Angola, Mozambique, and Namibia. Under Crocker's leadership the approach brought a relaxation of the embargo restrictions implemented by the Carter administration, a deescalation of criticism of apartheid, and U.S. mediation of negotiations on regional issues. From the start critics contended that constructive engagement amounted to U.S. acquiesence in the institutionalized racism of South African society. At the end of Reagan's first term, highly publicized anti-apartheid demonstrations at the South

African embassy in Washington and a worsening cycle of racial unrest and government crackdowns in South Africa focused domestic political attention on his administration's policy.

Spurred by widening antiapartheid protests across the United States and escalating violence in South Africa, Congress in 1985 drafted legislation intended to signal firm U.S. condemnation of apartheid by leveling tough sanctions against Pretoria. In September of that year, yielding to bipartisan congressional pressure, Reagan signed an executive order imposing limited economic and political measures against South Africa. His step, milder than what the House and Senate had sought, temporarily deferred action on sanctions legislation. The executive order barred American banks from making new loans to most agencies of the South African government and urged U.S. companies doing business in South Africa to adhere to the SULLIVAN PRINCIPLES of fair and equal employment practices.

Pretoria's imposition of strict censorship and a state of emergency to counter the continuing racial turmoil fueled demands in the United States in 1986 for a tougher stance against the white minority government. On October 2, Congress overrode Reagan's veto of legislation imposing more severe economic sanctions against South Africa. The override, a major setback for the president, was the first on a foreign policy issue since Congress enacted the WAR POWERS RESOLUTION over President RICHARD M. NIXON's veto in 1973. The Comprehensive Anti-Apartheid Act barred importation of South African steel, coal, and agricultural products and suspended landing rights in the United States for the government-owned South African Airways. The 1986 law threatened further punitive steps if the South African government did not move to abolish apartheid. It also stipulated that the sanctions would be lifted if South Africa met a series of demands, including the release of jailed African National Congress (ANC) leader Nelson Mandela and other political prisoners, repeal of the state of emergency, legalization of democratic political parties, and incorporation of black South Africans into the political process. The sanctions repudiated constructive engagement and effectively established a new U.S. policy toward South Africa.

When GEORGE BUSH succeeded Reagan in 1989, he sought to work with Congress on fashioning a cooperative, bipartisan approach toward South Africa. Late in the year he persuaded the congressional leadership to hold off on additional sanctions until recently elected South African President F. W. de Klerk had ample opportunity to deliver on his promise to abolish apartheid and move the country toward multiracial democracy. The legalization of the ANC and dramatic release of Mandela by the South African government in February 1990 was praised in Washington but fell short of the changes needed to gain a suspension of U.S. sanctions. Bush and members of Congress met with Mandela in June 1990 and de Klerk the following September as the two leaders, on separate visits to the United States, vied for support from the American administration and lawmakers. Following further bold steps by de Klerk toward dismantling apartheid, Bush in July 1991 lifted economic sanctions, declaring that Pretoria had satisfied all the requirements of the 1986 sanctions law. Congress was divided over the repeal, with some members disputing the administration's claim that de Klerk's government had met the law's conditions.

CONTAINMENT U.S. strategic policy toward the Communist bloc for the duration of the COLD WAR. After WORLD WAR II, U.S. diplomatic relations with the Soviet Union deteriorated rapidly as its wartime ally moved to impose Communist governments on the nations of Eastern Europe. By 1947, the Truman administration had decided on a fundamental shift in America's approach to relations with the Soviet Union. The term containment, conceived by senior State Department official GEORGE F. KENNAN, described a strategic approach designed to counter further Soviet-directed Communist inroads in non-Communist nations. The logic of containment maintained that if Soviet expansionism were held in check, then contradictions internal to the Soviet system eventually would bring about a moderation of the Communist regime in Moscow, and thus a lessening of the Soviet threat to the West.

Implementation of the strategy evolved in the postwar era. Initially, containment applied primarily to Europe and was essentially nonmilitary in character, involving such measures as the MARSHALL PLAN. From the late 1940s, the policy's effectiveness hinged on the principle of DETERRENCE, or maintenance of sufficient military strength to dissuade a potential adversary from attack. As the Cold War intensified, the United States and its Western European allies formed the mutual security pact NATO as a bulwark against Soviet military power. After the Chinese Communists came to power in 1949, similar military alliances were established around the periphery of the Communist world. America's commitment to use military force if necessary to prevent the further spread of communism anywhere on the globe led to direct involvement in two major armed conflicts in Asia: the KOREAN WAR and the VIETNAM WAR.

In the early 1970s the Nixon administration sought to move beyond containment to a policy of DETENTE, or relaxation of East-West tensions. These efforts, derailed by the Soviet invasion of Afghanistan in 1979, resumed in the mid-1980s in response to political changes in the Soviet Union under General Secretary Mikhail S. Gorbachev. In 1989 Moscow accepted the collapse of its control over Eastern Europe. Scholars pointed to developments in the USSR, including political and economic reforms and tempering of military and foreign policies, as evidence of containment's long-term effectiveness. By 1990, with the reunification of Germany and an apparent end to superpower confrontation, leaders in both the East and West were declaring the Cold War over. The December 1991 demise of the Soviet Union was viewed widely as representing the final success of the West's containment strategy.

See also DISENGAGEMENT, LIBERATION.

CONTRAS U.S.-backed guerrilla forces opposed to the leftist Sandinista government in Nicaragua. The term is a shortened form of *contrarevolucianarios* (counterrevolutionaries), the Spanish word used by the Sandinistas to describe the groups. In 1978 the Sandinista National Liberation Front (FSLN) launched a major guerrilla offensive against Nicaraguan dictator General Anastasio Somoza. Named after Augosto Cesar Sandino, the celebrated rebel leader who fought U.S. intervention in Nicaragua in the late 1920s, the FSLN served as the umbrella organization for a broad range of opposition groups. As the popular insurgency grew, the Carter administration in January 1979 suspended U.S. aid to the Somoza government, long supported by Washington, and in June called upon the Nicaraguan strongman to step down. In July 1979 Somoza went into exile and a provisional Sandinista junta headed by Daniel Ortega took power. President JIMMY CARTER established relations with the new government and resumed U.S. aid to Nicaragua.

Carter's actions drew domestic criticism from conservatives who noted close ties between leftist elements within the FSLN and Soviet client Communist Cuba. Such conservatives voiced alarm over the possible establishment by the Soviet Union of a foothold in Central America. Concern in Washington mounted in 1980 as the moderate members of the Sandinista leadership withdrew and leftist hardliners led by Ortega consolidated their hold on power. Just before leaving office in January 1981, Carter suspended U.S. aid to Managua, citing Sandinista involvement in the training and supply of leftist rebels battling the Salvadoran government in the EL SALVADOR CIVIL WAR. President RONALD W. REAGAN adopted a tough stance toward the Sandinista regime, maintaining it posed a serious threat to the security of the region. In April 1981 the Reagan administration terminated U.S. aid to Nicaragua. The White House charged that the Sandinistas were part of a Soviet- and Cuban-directed operation to export Communist revolution throughout Central America, starting with El Salvador. Reagan in December 1981 authorized a program of covert U.S. assistance to the small groups of Nicaraguan anti-Sandinista rebels then forming across the border in Honduras. The Contras included former members of Somoza's National Guard, former Sandinistas, and Miskito Indians. With U.S. backing, the various Contra groups, collectively the Nicaraguan Democratic Front (FDN), comprised a force of 15,000 by the mid-1980s. The rebels mounted guerrilla attacks on Sandinista targets from bases in Honduras and Costa Rica. Support for the Contras became a mainstay of the REAGAN DOCTRINE of aiding anti-Communist insurgencies worldwide.

The White House denied that it was attempting to overthrow the Sandinista government. Reagan argued that U.S. assistance to the Contras was necessary to pressure Managua to cease aiding the leftist insurgency in El Salvador. The president championed the guerrillas as "freedom fighters" struggling against a repressive Marxist regime in Nicaragua. Liberal members of Congress, troubled by nondemocratic elements in the Contras and wary over U.S. covert involvement in Central America, grew disenchanted with the Reagan policy. In December 1982 Congress passed the first of the BOLAND AMENDMENTS, a series of measures curtailing U.S. aid to the Contras between 1982 and 1985. Press revelations in April 1984 of CENTRAL INTELLIGENCE AGENCY (CIA) involvement in the Contra mining of Nicaraguan ports sparked a congressional outcry and brought an end to the operation. Managua brought suit in the WORLD COURT in the case of NICARAGUA V. UNITED STATES but Washington refused to recognize the court's jurisdiction in the matter. Disclosure in October 1984 of CIA preparation of a Contra guerrilla warfare manual advocating the "neutralization" of Sandinista political targets prompted further congressional furor. White House efforts to circumvent the third and most restrictive Boland Amendment resulted in the IRAN-CONTRA scandal that shook the Reagan administration in 1987 and undercut support for its Central American policies. Amid evidence of a continuing Soviet-supplied military buildup in Nicaragua, Congress authorized a resumption of U.S. military aid to the Contras in October 1986.

Various proposals were advanced in the mid-1980s to halt the fighting. Little progress was made as Washington insisted that any settlement include the Contras and address El Salvador, while Managua refused to negotiate with the Contra leadership. In 1983 representatives of Colombia, Mexico, Panama, and Venezuela met on the Panamanian island of Contadora in search of a diplomatic solution for Central America. The Contadora Group, joined from 1985 by the Lima Group (Argentina, Brazil, Peru, and Uruguay), attempted to mediate the regional conflict. Building on the Contadora process, Costa Rican President Oscar Arias in 1986 proposed a comprehensive peace settlement among the five Central American countries. The presidents of Costa Rica, El Salvador, Guatemala, Honduras, and Nicaragua gathered in Guatemala City in August 1987 to conclude the Arias-sponsored regional peace accord. On August 5, on the eve of the Central American summit, Reagan announced a new bipartisan U.S. peace plan formulated between the Republican White House and House Speaker Jim Wright (D-TX). The so-called Wright-Reagan Plan called for a Nicaraguan cease-fire, democratic reforms within Nicaragua, and a halt to both U.S. military aid to the Contras and the flow of Soviet-bloc arms to the Sandinistas. The Arias Plan, signed at Guatemala City on August 7 by the five Central American presidents, rendered moot the Wright-Reagan proposal. The Arias initiative similarly provided for cease-fires in Nicaragua and El Salvador and the termination of outside aid to regional insurgencies. It required free elections be held in each country and guaranteed the participation of opposition parties. Unlike Wright-Reagan, the Arias Plan did not force Nicaragua to renounce Soviet bloc military aid. Arias won the 1987 Nobel Peace Prize for his efforts.

The peace process inaugurated by the Arias Plan led Congress in February 1988 to limit U.S. support to the Contras to humanitarian assistance. At a Central American summit in February 1989, Nicaragua agreed to hold presidential elections no later than February 25, 1990. In March 1989 the Republican Bush administration reached a bipartisan understanding on U.S. Nicaraguan policy with the congressional Democratic leadership, ending the generally adversarial White House-Capitol Hill relationship on the issue that characterized the Reagan years. The compromise agreement emphasized a diplomatic approach while providing enough nonlethal aid to keep the Contras intact pending the promised Nicaraguan elections. In a step that reflected the rapid thawing of the COLD WAR, Soviet leader Mikhail S. Gorbachev in May 1989 informed President GEORGE BUSH that the USSR had stopped supplying arms to Nicaragua. In August 1989 the Central American presidents agreed on a plan for disbanding the Contras and reassimilating them into Nicaraguan society. Former President JIMMY CARTER headed the international observer team that monitored the February

1990 Nicaraguan presidential election. During the campaign the Sandinistas permitted opposition parties and an independent press. Opposition leader Violeta Chamorro's upset victory over Ortega brought an end to Sandinista rule. Washington responded to Chamorro's election with an immediate program of U.S. economic aid.

See also KISSINGER COMMISSION.

CONVENTION OF 1800 Agreement signed by the United States and France at Morfontaine (outside Paris) on September 30, 1800, that ended the undeclared naval QUASI-WAR (1798–1800). The naval conflict between the two nations had developed out of bitter French resentment over the Anglo-American JAY'S TREATY (1794). U.S. efforts at rapprochement in 1797 were derailed by the XYZ AFFAIR, in which French Foreign Minister Charles Maurice de Talleyrand solicited a bribe from visiting American envoys as a precondition to his meeting with them. The episode provoked anti-French sentiment in the United States and prompted extremist Federalists, whose distaste for the French Revolution already was well established, to advocate full-scale war. Alarmed by the unexpectedly militant American response, France in late 1798 invited a resumption of negotiations.

Federalist President JOHN ADAMS overrode the opposition of his cabinet, which viewed skeptically the French peace overture, and sent a new diplomatic delegation to France. The American commission, composed of Oliver Ellsworth, William Vans Murray, and William R. Davie, arrived in March 1800 with two basic negotiating instructions: secure French reparations for raids, referred to at the time as spoliations, against American shipping since 1793; and gain French agreement to abrogate the FRANCO-AMERICAN ALLIANCE of 1778. The new French government of Napoleon Bonaparte, who had seized power in 1799, argued that the United States could not have both an indemnity and an annulment of the alliance. France would consider American claims only if the alliance treaties were still in force. When in September Talleyrand offered a compromise treaty that indefinitely deferred the alliance and indemnity questions, the American delegation accepted.

The Convention of 1800, or Treaty of Morfontaine, settled the Quasi-War, with both nations agreeing to mutual restoration of captured naval vessels and France pledging to grant American ships access to French ports. The U.S. Senate initially withheld approval of the accord, insisting upon termination of the 1778 alliance and settlement of the spoliation claims. Final ratification came in July 1801 after Napoleon consented to the alliance's abrogation in return for an American agreement to drop its indemnity demand. The 1800 treaty opened the way for Napoleon to pursue his imperial ambitions in North America. One day after the initial signing of the convention, France secretly acquired the Louisiana territory from Spain. The French later would cede the province to America through the LOUISIANA PURCHASE (1803). The Morfontaine agreement, in freeing the United States from its entangling alliance with France, manifested a growing American commitment to ISOLATIONISM at the start of the 19th century.

CONVENTION OF 1818 Wide-ranging diplomatic agreement between the United States and Great Britain. Completed in London on October 20, 1818, between British representatives and U.S. negotiators RICHARD RUSH, minister to Great Britain, and ALBERT GALLATIN, minister to France, the agreement settled several outstanding disputes in Anglo-American diplomacy not resolved by the TREATY OF GHENT (1814), which ended the WAR OF 1812. With the U.S.-British commercial convention of 1815 set to expire in 1819, President JAMES MONROE in 1818 named Rush and Gallatin as special commissioners to conclude a new trade pact and to reach settlement on the other predominant issues in relations with Great Britain: the disputed northwest boundary between the United States and Canada, or British North America; the FISHERIES QUESTION concerning U.S. right of access to the rich North Atlantic fishing grounds off Canada; confiscation of American slaves by British troops withdrawing from the United States after the War of 1812; the British practice of IMPRESSMENT, which often targeted neutral American ships; and competing Anglo-American claims to Oregon Country, an area extending from the Rocky Mountains west to the Pacific Ocean and north from the 42nd parallel to lattitude 54° 40'.

The TREATY OF PARIS (1783) ending the AMERICAN REVOLUTION defined the northwest boundary on the basis of a geographical misunderstanding of the frontier. The treaty described a boundary running from Lake of the Woods in present-day Minnesota due west to the Mississippi River. But the source of the Mississippi lay well south of such a line. This discrepancy left the Canadian-American border beyond Lake of the Woods open to interpretation and thereby invited a British claim to some territory below to the south. After its acquisition of the vast trans-Mississippi region in the LOUISIANA PURCHASE (1803), the United States was unable to gain British agreement to fix the boundary at the 49TH PARALLEL. America again suggested a settlement of 49° during the Treaty of Ghent negotiations but would not consent to Great Britain's demand for guaranteed access to the Mississippi headwaters. U.S. attempts at Ghent to win renewal of American fishing privileges along the east coast of British North America had also failed. U.S. fishing rights initially were insured by the Treaty of Paris. Great Britain contended the United States had lost whatever access rights the 1783 Peace of Paris had extended since mutual war declarations in 1812 had abrogated existing treaties between the two countries. Great Britain insisted the whole issue be renegotiated.

The October 1818 agreement renewed the 1815 commercial convention for 10 years and extended the Canadian-American boundary from the Lake of the Woods west along the 49th parallel to the Rocky Mountains. It crafted a compromise on the fisheries issue, granting the United States permanent fishing rights along limited coastal sections off Newfoundland, the Magdalen Islands, and Labrador, but excluding Americans altogether from the coasts of Nova Scotia, New Brunswick, and Prince Edward Island. U.S. fishermen were given the liberty to cure fish along the unsettled southern coast of Newfoundland but were barred from landing on the coast of any other British North American possession except to secure shelter, make repairs, or obtain water or wood. The U.S. indemnity request for slaves taken by British forces during the War of 1812 was referred to a friendly third country for mediation. Czarist Russia later was selected and awarded an indemnity to the United States which Great Britain paid in 1826.

Great Britain refused to surrender its right of impressment and the 1818 treaty made no mention of the issue. The United States and Great Britain agreed to keep the region west of the Rockies open to American and British settlement for 10 years, specifying that such "joint occupation" of Oregon territory would not compromise the long-standing territorial claims of either nation in the Pacific Northwest. The joint occupation arrangement in Oregon was renewed by an Anglo-American convention in 1827 and remained in effect until final settlement of the OREGON QUESTION in 1846.

See also MAP 2.

CONVENTION OF 1827 Anglo-American treaty signed September 29, 1827, that submitted the dispute over the U.S.-Canadian northeast boundary to arbitration. Since the end of the AMERICAN REVOLUTION, the United States and Great Britain had staked competing claims to a 12,000-square-mile stretch of land between Maine and Canada's New Brunswick province. The territorial dispute originated with the TREATY OF PARIS (1783), which had not defined clearly the location of the northeast boundary. Under the TREATY OF GHENT (1814) ending the WAR OF 1812, America and Great Britain agreed to seek a diplomatic settlement of the border disagreement. Intermittent talks brought no breakthrough until the 1827 convention, which resulted from negotiations between U.S. Minister at London ALBERT GALLATIN and British commissioners H. V. Addington and Charles Grant.

In the accord, the two countries agreed to put the boundary question to arbitration by a "friendly sovereign," to be chosen by mutual consent. The king of the Netherlands subsequently was selected. Unable to make a decisive determination based on the arguments presented by both sides, he proposed a territorial division that would have awarded the United States more than half of the contested land. The king's mediation offer satisfied the British since it gave them territory sufficient to build a much-desired military route from Quebec to the Canadian maritime provinces. Maine and Massachusetts, each with long-standing claims to the disputed border area, ardently objected to the king's proposal.

A U.S. Senate report opposed the compromise plan on principle. The report asserted that the United States was not obligated to accept the king's judgment because the Dutch sovereign had violated his charter by converting his role from an arbitrator to a mediator. The Senate on December 7, 1831, advised President ANDREW JACKSON to turn down the compromise settlement. The same day Jackson announced formal U.S. rejection of the king's ruling. The boundary problem finally was settled in 1842 by the WEBSTER-ASHBURTON TREATY.

CONVENTION OF 1899 Treaty signed by the United States, Germany, and Great Britain on December 2, 1899, that partitioned the Samoan Islands. Continuing rivalry among the three powers in the 1890s undermined the tripartite protectorate established over SAMOA by the TREATY OF BERLIN (1889). President GROVER CLEVELAND, an antiexpansionist Democrat elected a second time in 1893, objected to U.S. entanglement in the South Pacific islands. Joined by antiimperialist critics of American policy, he unsuccessfully urged Congress to withdraw the United States from the three-way condominium.

In the civil war that erupted in Samoa in early 1899, Germany backed one side while the United States and Great Britain supported the other. Following Anglo-American naval bombing of German positions at Apia, Germany proposed a division of the island chain to settle the conflict. The three powers met in Washington and, after Republican President WILLIAM MCKINLEY abandoned long-standing U.S. insistence on Samoan independence, agreed to partition the South Pacific archipelago. In the 1899 convention, the United States acquired all of Samoa east of the 171st meridian, including Tutuila Island and the prized harbor of Pago Pago. Thereafter the U.S. possessions were known as American Samoa. Germany received all islands west of 171 longitude, or what initially was called German Samoa and later became Western Samoa. Great Britain abandoned its Samoan claims in exchange for German concessions in the South Pacific Tonga Islands and in West Africa.

The Senate approved the treaty in January 1900 and McKinley placed American Samoa under the Navy Department the following month. Formal U.S. acceptance of the islands as American possessions came when Congress confirmed the Samoan ac-

quisition by joint resolution in 1929. American Samoa remains an unincorporated U.S. territory and one of the U.S. Pacific dependencies.

See also MAP 7.

CONVENTION ON INTERNATIONAL TRADE IN ENDANGERED SPECIES (CITES) (1973) Global treaty on regulating the international traffic in endangered plant and animal species. The convention was signed on March 3, 1973, at a conference held in Washington, D.C., under UNITED NATIONS auspices and attended by representatives of 80 countries. CITES, which entered into force on July 1, 1975, established an international system for controlling the trade in categories of endangered species designated by the participating nations. The system is carried out by the licensing of import and export operations and by various enforcement measures. The United States ratified the convention in August 1973.

Congress implemented CITES through the Endangered Species Act of 1973, which strengthened federal programs for protecting fish, wildlife, and plants. The legislation for the first time authorized federal officials to issue regulations to protect species "threatened" with extinction as well as "endangered" species at immediate risk of becoming extinct. It made violation of CITES restrictions on foreign trade a federal offense punishable by fines of up to $10,000. Amended in both 1978 and 1982, the Endangered Species Act directs the secretary of the interior, through the secretary of state, to encourage foreign countries to conserve fish and wildlife and to join in international covenants that provide for such conservation. The United States is the largest contributor to CITES.

CONVENTION FOR THE MAINTENANCE, PRESERVATION, AND REESTABLISHMENT OF PEACE See **BUENOS AIRES CONFERENCE.**

CONVENTION ON THE PREVENTION OF MARINE POLLUTION BY DUMPING See **LONDON DUMPING CONVENTION.**

CONVENTION FOR THE PREVENTION OF POLLUTION FROM SHIPS See **MARPOL CONVENTION.**

CONVENTION ON RIGHTS AND DUTIES OF STATES (1933) Agreement concluded at the Seventh PAN-AMERICAN CONFERENCE at Montevideo, Uruguay, that formally embraced the principle of nonintervention. By the late 1920s the United States faced growing hostility in Latin America toward its generation-long interventionism in the Caribbean and Central America. Resentful of the most recent of America's NICARAGUAN INTERVENTIONS, Latin American delegates arrived in Havana, Cuba, in 1928 for the Sixth PAN-AMERICAN CONFERENCE determined to win acceptance of nonintervention as a basic tenet of international conduct in the Americas. To parry the expected attack on U.S. policy, the Coolidge administration sent a strong delegation to Havana headed by former Secretary of State CHARLES EVANS HUGHES. President CALVIN COOLIDGE, at the urging of Secretary of State FRANK B. KELLOGG, went to the conference to deliver the opening address. By presenting a persuasive defense of America's right of intervention, Hughes managed to block the passage of a proposed resolution declaring that "no state has the right to interfere in the internal affairs of another."

U.S. policy in Latin America began to change under HERBERT C. HOOVER, who following his election as president in November 1928 embarked on a 10-nation goodwill tour of Central and South America. In office, he supported nonintervention, repudiated the ROOSEVELT COROLLARY to the MONROE DOCTRINE, and pioneered the idea of the "good neighbor" in inter-American relations. Hoover's successor, FRANKLIN D. ROOSEVELT, in his first inaugural address proclaimed the GOOD NEIGHBOR POLICY and expressed U.S. determination to respect the rights of other nations in the Western Hemisphere. In preparing for the Montevideo Conference scheduled for December 1933, the Roosevelt administration concentrated on promoting Pan-American cooperation. At the Uruguay gathering, delegates drafted the Convention on Rights and Duties of States, which included an article, the so-called Montevideo Pledge, asserting that "no state has the right to intervene in the internal or external affairs of another state." Secretary of State CORDELL HULL, head of the U.S. delegation at Montevideo, voted for the nonintervention clause and signed the convention, which was adopted unanimously on December 26. Two days later Roosevelt declared opposition to armed intervention to be the definite policy of the United States.

CONVENTION OF SHIMODA See **EDO, TREATY OF**.

CONVENTIONAL FORCES EUROPE TREATY (1990) Landmark arms control agreement limiting conventional military forces in Europe. At the end of WORLD WAR II, Soviet armies occupied Eastern Europe and the eastern part of Germany. With the onset of the East-West COLD WAR in the late 1940s, Western leaders grew concerned over the possible threat posed by the massive Soviet military force still in Eastern Europe. In 1949 the United States and its Western allies formed the NATO security alliance to provide for the defense of Western Europe. The Soviet Union in 1955 established the Warsaw Pact with its Communist satellites in Eastern Europe. The heavily armed sides faced each other along the border between East and West Germany, marking the Cold War division of Europe.

In 1968 NATO proposed discussions with the Warsaw Pact on mutual and balanced force reductions (MBFR) of the huge conventional military forces arrayed against each other in central Europe. NATO members argued that lower troop levels would eliminate the ability of either side to launch a surprise attack, lessening military tensions in Europe and reducing the possibility of a nuclear confrontation. In the climate of East-West DETENTE, the two sides agreed in 1972 to hold both a Soviet-proposed CONFERENCE ON SECURITY AND COOPERATION IN EUROPE (CSCE) and the NATO-suggested MBFR talks. The MBFR negotiations between representatives of the NATO and Warsaw Pact countries began in Vienna in 1973. The discussions specifically addressed conventional, or non-nuclear, military forces. The MBFR talks continued in Vienna throughout the 1970s and 1980s. Fundamental East-West differences soon emerged on several key issues. NATO maintained that Warsaw Pact forces were considerably larger, a claim rebutted by the Communist alliance, which contended there was rough parity between the two. NATO pressed for asymmetrical reductions to bring both sides to the same level. The Warsaw Pact in turn insisted on equal cuts among the two forces. Western demands for stringent verification provisions for any agreement were rejected by the Soviet-led Communist bloc.

Improving East-West relations in the mid-1980s brought a new momentum to the long-deadlocked conventional arms discussions. In 1987 the 16 NATO and 7 Warsaw Pact countries met in Vienna to explore new approaches to conventional disarmament in Europe. The "Group 23" sessions carried on into 1988. In January 1989 a review conference of the 35-nation CSCE, which counted all NATO and Warsaw Pact countries as members, called for a new set of conventional negotiations under a different aegis. The MBFR meetings formally ended in February 1989 and were followed by the opening of the Conventional Forces Europe (CFE) talks in Vienna in March.

Events in the Soviet bloc the same year soon outpaced the CFE negotiations. The collapse of the Communist regimes in Eastern Europe and emergence of non-Communist governments brought pressure on the Soviet Union to withdraw its forces from its former satellite countries. In February 1990 Moscow agreed to remove its troops from Hungary and Czechoslovakia by mid-1991. The rapid movement toward German reunification raised questions as to a united Germany's membership in NATO and the status of the hundreds of thousands of Soviet soldiers in East Germany. Throughout 1990 CFE negotiators struggled to keep up with developments and complete an agreement that would support and codify the dramatic changes taking place in Europe. In October 1990 U.S. Secretary of State JAMES A. BAKER 3RD and Soviet Foreign Minister Eduard A. Shevardnadze finalized a comprehensive CFE agreement that placed strict ceilings on the number of weapons that could be fielded by NATO and the rapidly disintegrating Warsaw Pact. The same month the FINAL SETTLEMENT WITH RESPECT TO GERMANY TREATY (1990) brought German reunification and the entry of a single Germany into NATO. The Soviet Union initially had opposed German participation in the Western alliance. The USSR changed its position amid a general European consensus that continued German membership in NATO was necessary to pre-

clude a reunified Germany's domination of central Europe.

The CFE treaty was signed in Paris on November 19, 1990, by the leaders of the 22 NATO and Warsaw Pact countries, including Presidents GEORGE BUSH and Mikhail S. Gorbachev. The agreement provided for broad conventional disarmament across the European continent. Under its terms, NATO and the Warsaw Pact were limited in the numbers of tanks, artillery pieces, armored troop carriers, armed helicopters, and combat aircraft they could deploy in an area stretching from the Atlantic Ocean to the Ural Mountains. To reach the designated levels, the treaty mandated the destruction of thousands of pieces of NATO military hardware and some 75,000 items in the larger Warsaw Pact arsenal. The Soviet Union was required to destroy many thousands of items and shift the bulk of its military equipment east of the Urals. The CFE Treaty did not address troop levels since the USSR had already pledged to withdraw all its forces from Eastern Europe by 1994. The United States indicated it would continue to maintain a small U.S. troop presence with NATO in Europe both as a guarantor of the American commitment to European security and to contribute to stability in central Europe.

The Bush administration initially expected to have the CFE pact ratified by the Senate in 1991. By January 1991, however, the treaty's future was clouded by two U.S.-Soviet disputes over the agreement's provisions. Washington alleged the USSR had maneuvered to avoid treaty limits by transferring units to its naval infantry and by moving equipment subject to destruction east of the Urals. In June 1991 Baker and new Soviet Foreign Minister Aleksandr A. Bessmertnykh struck a compromise formally resolving the disputes and paving the way for final CFE ratification. U.S. Senate approval of the pact again was temporarily thrown into question by the attempted MOSCOW COUP in August 1991. But with the failure of the Soviet reactionaries' bid to oust Gorbachev, the Senate ratified the treaty on November 25, 1991.

COOLIDGE, CALVIN (1872–1933) Thirtieth U. S. president. Coolidge was born and raised in rural Vermont. He graduated from Amherst College in 1895, studied law at a firm in Northampton, Massachusetts, and, after passing the bar, opened his own practice there in 1898. A Republican, he rose quickly in state politics after his election to the Massachusetts legislature in 1906, becoming lieutenant governor in 1915 and governor in 1918. He gained national attention after he mobilized the National Guard to restore order during the Boston police strike of 1919. Running mate of WARREN G. HARDING on the successful 1920 Republican presidential ticket, he served as vice-president from 1921 to 1923. Coolidge was sworn in as president following Harding's death on August 2, 1923.

He retained his predecessor's cabinet and continued the basic foreign policy of the Harding administration. Transatlantic ties increasingly were strained by the efforts of European nations to reduce their WORLD WAR I debts to the United States and to link repayment of the loans to their receipt of German war reparations. Coolidge reiterated U.S. opposition to any cancellation of the debts or any connection between them and reparations. With Germany facing financial chaos and European stability threatened, the Coolidge administration supported the DAWES PLAN (1924) easing German reparations payments. In his first term Coolidge also, with the support of influential Secretary of State CHARLES EVANS HUGHES, decided against extending diplomatic recognition to the Soviet Union and signed the highly restrictive IMMIGRATION ACT OF 1924.

Coolidge was reelected handily in 1924. In his second term FRANK B. KELLOGG replaced Hughes as secretary of state. Coolidge hoped to build on the progress toward naval disarmament achieved at the WASHINGTON NAVAL CONFERENCE (1921–1922) but the GENEVA NAVAL CONFERENCE (1927) made no headway. The major accomplishment in foreign affairs during his presidency was the KELLOGG-BRIAND PACT (1928) outlawing war as an instrument of national policy. The treaty, eventually subscribed to by 62 nations, brought Kellogg the Nobel Peace Prize. In Asia the Coolidge administration recognized the Nationalist Chinese regime under Chiang Kai-shek, which after a decade of internal strife had succeeded in bringing most of the giant Asian nation under a single government. In 1927 Coolidge sent American marines to Nicaragua to bolster the government against rebel attack. Special U.S. envoy HENRY L. STIMSON was able to negotiate the PEACE OF TIPITAPA (1927) between the various warring Nicaraguan factions, but civil war soon broke out again in the Central American nation. With U.S. intervention in Latin America under increasing attack in the region, Coolidge went to the Sixth PAN-AMERICAN CONFERENCE in Havana, Cuba, in 1928 to give the opening address. Relations, however, remained strained after the U.S. delegation blocked a proposed resolution supporting the principle of nonintervention. U.S. diplomacy was more successful in Mexico, where envoy DWIGHT W. MORROW was able temporarily to resolve a growing controversy over the Mexican government's threatened expropriation of American oil and land holdings. Coolidge chose not to run for reelection in 1928 and retired to Massachusetts.

COOPER-CHURCH AMENDMENT (1970) Congressional measure that limited further U.S. military operations in Cambodia during the VIETNAM WAR. In April 1970 President RICHARD M. NIXON ordered an attack by U.S. and South Vietnamese forces on Communist North Vietnamese sanctuaries in neutral Cambodia. The CAMBODIAN INCURSION sparked action in the U.S. Senate to reverse the apparently widening American role in the conflict in Southeast Asia. Antiwar Senators JOHN SHERMAN COOPER (R-KY) and FRANK CHURCH (D-ID) cosponsored an amendment to the foreign military sales bill that would prohibit the funding of U.S. military activities in Cambodia. After heated debate, the measure was adopted June 30, 1970, by a vote of 58 to 37. The same day Nixon reported that American ground forces had been withdrawn from Cambodia and would not return. The amendment, however, became bottled up in a joint House-Senate conference, delayed by opposition in the House of Representatives to its strict provisions. In December 1970 conferees agreed upon a compromise version barring U.S. troops or advisers in Cambodia, but allowing continued aerial bombing. Attached to a supplemental foreign aid authorization, the amendment became law January 12, 1971. It represented the first congressional restriction on U.S. involvement in Southeast Asia.

See also CASE-CHURCH AMENDMENT, MANS-
FIELD AMENDMENT, MCGOVERN-HATFIELD AMEND-
MENT.

COOPER, JOHN SHERMAN (1901–1991)
U.S. senator and diplomat. A Kentucky native, Cooper graduated from Yale in 1923
and attended Harvard Law School before
returning home following his father's
death. He was admitted to the Kentucky
bar in 1928, served in the state legislature,
and became a county judge. During WORLD
WAR II he saw action as an Army officer in
Europe. In 1946 Cooper won a special election to the U.S. Senate but was defeated in
the regular election in 1948. Adhering to a
bipartisan foreign policy, Democratic President HARRY S. TRUMAN the following year
named the Kentucky Republican a U.S. delegate to the UNITED NATIONS. Cooper was
elected to fill a vacant Senate seat in 1952
but again failed in a bid for a full term in
1954. From 1955 to 1956 he was ambassador to India. In 1957, following victory in
another special election, he began a final
16-year tenure in the Senate. In the mid-
1960s Cooper emerged as a leading opponent of the deepening American involvement in the VIETNAM WAR. In 1970 he
cosponsored the COOPER-CHURCH AMEND-
MENT that limited U.S. military operations in
Cambodia. Cooper retired from the Senate
in 1973. From 1974 to 1976 he served as
the first U.S. ambassador to East Germany.

**COORDINATING COMMITTEE FOR MUL-
TILATERAL EXPORT CONTROLS** See
TECHNOLOGY TRANSFER.

COUNCIL OF FOREIGN MINISTERS
Meetings of the foreign ministers of the major WORLD WAR II Allies to prepare peace
settlements following the conflict. At the
POTSDAM CONFERENCE (1945) the United
States, Great Britain, and Soviet Union
agreed to invite France and China to join in
forming a Council of Foreign Ministers. As
envisioned, the council would draw up
peace treaties for lesser Axis powers Italy,
Hungary, Bulgaria, Romania, and Finland;
propose settlements for postwar territorial
and boundary issues; and prepare a peace
settlement for Germany once a German
government capable of adhering to its
terms had been established. The council's
first session took place in London from

September 11 to October 2, 1945, to draft
peace treaties for the lesser Axis powers.
The London Conference ended in stalemate when the Soviet Union sought to exclude France and China from most of the
proceedings, insisting that only those council members that had signed the instruments of surrender with a given nation
should participate in the negotiations of its
peace terms. The United States disagreed,
maintaining that all five powers should take
part in all council deliberations.

At an interim council meeting in
Moscow in December 1945, U.S. Secretary
of State JAMES F. BYRNES, British Foreign Secretary Ernest Bevin, and Soviet Foreign
Minister Vyacheslav Molotov reached a
compromise on future council proceedings. The United States accepted the basic
Soviet position on limiting participation in
the initial formulation of the peace treaties.
In turn, the Soviet Union acceded to Western demands for an international conference of all council members and other concerned nations to finalize the peace
agreements. Since China had not signed
any European instruments of surrender,
the compromise effectively limited attendance at the council's working sessions to
the United States, Great Britain, France,
and Soviet Union. The second formal council meeting brought together the foreign
ministers of the four powers in Paris in
1946. Held in two separate sessions between April and July, the Paris Conference
prepared peace treaties for the minor Axis
powers and laid the groundwork for an international gathering to review and approve the draft measures. The 21-nation
PARIS PEACE CONFERENCE opened on July 29,
1946. Six weeks later it adjourned without
having reached final agreement on all
peace terms. The minor peace treaties were
completed at the third meeting of the
council from November 4 to December 12,
1946, in New York City.

The foreign ministers then turned to
the issues of Austria and Germany, both of
which had been divided since the war into
occupation zones administered by the four
powers. The fourth council meeting was
held in Moscow from March 10 to April 24,
1947. The Moscow Conference highlighted
growing East-West differences over the future of Eastern Europe and the emerging
de facto partition of Germany between the

zones administered by the Western democracies and the Soviet-controlled eastern Communist zone. Worsening COLD WAR tensions formed the backdrop to the fifth council meeting in London from November 25 to December 16, 1947, which was marked by acrimonious East-West debate over the continuing division of Germany and the extension of Soviet hegemony over Eastern Europe. U.S. Secretary of State GEORGE C. MARSHALL, reflecting Western frustration at the failure of the discussions to make any substantive headway, proposed the council's indefinite adjournment. The London Conference thus ended without the foreign ministers setting the date for a subsequent meeting.

The council did not convene for 18 months. It met for a sixth and final time in Paris from May 23 to June 20, 1949, to help resolve the international crisis involving the USSR's blockade of Berlin and the Anglo-American BERLIN AIRLIFT to relieve the German city's western sector. Fundamental East-West differences continued to block any agreement on either Austria or Germany. The unresolved status of central Europe dominated East-West relations throughout the Cold War. The AUSTRIAN STATE TREATY reestablishing Austria as an independent nation was completed in 1955. German reunification was achieved at the end of the Cold War through the FINAL SETTLEMENT WITH RESPECT TO GERMANY TREATY (1990).

See also COUNCIL OF FOREIGN MINISTERS CONFERENCES in APPENDIX E.

COUNCIL ON FOREIGN RELATIONS (CFR) Prestigious, bipartisan foreign policy research organization based in New York City. Founded in 1921, the council has a membership of some 2500 prominent individuals with specialized knowledge of international relations, including business executives, scholars, government officials, journalists, and lawyers. The CFR, through its analysis of international issues and study of political, economic, and military aspects of American foreign relations, seeks to help shape U.S. foreign policy. The center collaborates with the 38 affiliated branches of CFR around the country. A professional staff conducts research on long-range foreign-policy problems with guidance from selected statesmen, business leaders, and

academics. Through its library, lecture programs, and extensive publications the CFR serves as an information clearinghouse on international relations for both members and a wider audience. It publishes the journal *Foreign Affairs*, a compendium of articles contributed by established authorities in the field, and the annual *Political Handbook of the World*. The center regularly sponsors conferences and offers advanced academic and corporate study programs in foreign affairs.

COUNCIL OF FOUR Key working group, consisting of the heads of government of the United States, France, Great Britain, and Italy, which dealt with the major problems arising at the PARIS PEACE CONFERENCE (1919), the 32-nation parley at which the TREATY OF VERSAILLES ending WORLD WAR I was completed. Soon after the conference opened in January 1919, it became apparent that the hundreds of delegates in attendance constituted too unwieldy a body for effective deliberations. Thus a supreme executive council, the Council of Ten, was organized and given responsibility for making decisions on the most important questions. It comprised the heads of government and foreign ministers of the five leading powers—the United States, Great Britain, France, Italy, and Japan. In a move to hasten and streamline the conference's work, the Council of Ten was supplanted in March 1919 by the Council of Four. Known also as the BIG FOUR, it consisted of President WOODROW WILSON, British Prime Minister David Lloyd George, French Premier Georges Clemenceau, and Italian Premier Vittorio Orlando. A Council of Five, comprising the foreign ministers of the great five powers, also was established in March to discuss less important issues.

COUNCIL OF TEN See **COUNCIL OF FOUR**.

COVERT ACTION The use of secret means to advance foreign policy objectives or influence events abroad. The term is used interchangeably with covert operations, clandestine operations, special operations, and special activities. Covert action generally is understood to encompass propaganda and psychological warfare; political or economic activities designed to affect the political process or economy of another country; and paramilitary operations involving guerrilla or other unconventional forces. Most covert operations include a combination of measures.

The United States historically did not resort to covert action in peacetime. The global struggle of WORLD WAR II brought formation of the wartime OFFICE OF STRATEGIC SERVICES, the nation's first clandestine operations organization. America emerged from the conflict as a superpower with a vastly expanded international role. With the COLD WAR intensifying, the U.S. government by 1948 had turned to covert action as an alternative means between diplomacy and war for influencing foreign developments. In April 1948 an ad hoc CENTRAL INTELLIGENCE AGENCY (CIA) group secretly assisted in the defeat of the Italian Communist Party in the ITALIAN ELECTION OPERATION. From this initial success, U.S. use of covert operations expanded rapidly.

The Truman administration established the basic framework for U.S. covert activities, assigning responsibility for their control to the recently formed NATIONAL SECURITY COUNCIL (NSC). In June 1948 the NSC directed the formation of a permanent U.S. covert operations capability. The OFFICE OF POLICY COORDINATION (OPC) was formed as a semautonomous organization under the CIA. Early covert endeavors such as the ALBANIA OPERATION (1950–1952) were intended to undermine the Soviet Union's hold on Eastern Europe while thwarting further Communist advances. President HARRY S. TRUMAN initially placed the supervision of covert action under a special NSC panel composed of State and Defense department representatives. Committee membership was expanded in 1951 to include the head of U.S. psychological warfare programs. By 1952 the OPC had been fully integrated into the clandestine services branch of the CIA. The agency since has held primary responsibility for the execution of covert action.

The Eisenhower administration turned to covert action to overthrow leftist governments in the IRAN COUP (1953) and GUATEMALA COUP (1954). President DWIGHT D. EISENHOWER replaced the Truman administration's ad hoc approval procedures for covert operations with a more formal approach. In 1954 Eisenhower issued a top-

secret directive, NSC-5412, entrusting covert action to an NSC Operations Coordinating Board. Revisions to the directive in 1955 resulted in the formation of a senior NSC group, known as the 5412 Committee, to review and approve covert operations. The stated purpose of covert action was to counter the Soviet Union, Communist China, and the international Communist movement, and to strengthen the position of the United States and the FREE WORLD.

The Kennedy administration continued the emphasis on covert activities. Oversight functions were accomplished by an NSC "Special Group." Under the Johnson administration, the Special Group was renamed the 303 Committee after the 1964 NSC memorandum NSAM-303, updating its operation. In practice presidents JOHN F. KENNEDY and LYNDON B. JOHNSON relied on ad hoc advisory groups and more informal procedures. The United States suffered a serious setback with the failure of the CIA-sponsored BAY OF PIGS INVASION (1961) by Cuban exiles to overthrow Communist leader Fidel Castro. The debacle discouraged similar U.S. endeavors, although extensive covert operations were undertaken during the LAOS SECRET WAR and VIETNAM WAR.

In 1970 President RICHARD M. NIXON revived routine NSC supervision of covert activity in NSC memorandum NSDM-40. Under this directive, covert action planning came under a select panel, chaired by the NSC adviser, that became known as the 40 Committee. Nixon broadened the stated aim of U.S. covert action from its previously narrow anti-Communist focus to a general safeguarding of U.S. defense and security. Concern over establishment of a possible Communist foothold in South America prompted the Nixon administration's involvement in the CHILE COUP (1973).

Following revelations of past CIA abuses by the 1975 ROCKEFELLER COMMISSION, CHURCH COMMITTEE, and PIKE COMMITTEE investigations, President GERALD R. FORD in February 1976 issued Executive Order 11905, the first public regulation governing U.S. covert action. Ford replaced the 40 Committee with a cabinet-level Operations Advisory Group, stressing that covert operations would require approval at the highest levels of the executive branch. The tradition of limited congressional oversight of covert operations ended with the HUGHES-RYAN AMENDMENT (1974), which required that six separate congressional committees be briefed by the executive branch on covert activities. In a concession to security considerations, the number of committees was reduced to two under the 1980 Intelligence Oversight Act. In 1976 Congress for the first time blocked a U.S. covert action when it passed the CLARK AMENDMENT barring further U.S. involvement in the ANGOLAN CIVIL WAR.

President JIMMY CARTER continued the practice of public intelligence regulation in 1978 with Executive Order 12036. Ford's top-level NSC body became the Special Coordinating Committee. The Carter administration generally opposed the use of covert operations, reflecting the broad disfavor with which they were viewed following the 1975 investigations. When the Soviet Union invaded Afghanistan in December 1979, however, the United States provided clandestine support to the anti-Communist Mujahedeen guerrillas.

The Reagan administration placed a renewed emphasis on covert action. In December 1981 President RONALD W. REAGAN publicly outlined administration guidelines on intelligence activities in Executive Order 12333. Covert operations were assigned to a National Security Planning Group within the NSC. Military arms were funneled to the Mujahedeen rebels in the AFGHANISTAN WAR and, following the 1985 repeal of the Clark Amendment, to the UNITA guerrillas in Angola. In the mid-1980s members of the NSC staff mounted several secret operations that circumvented congressional oversight of covert actions. Disclosure of the secret arms sales to Iran and the unauthorized diversion of the proceeds to the CONTRAS in Nicaragua resulted in the IRAN-CONTRA scandal. The 1987 report of the TOWER COMMISSION underscored the need for covert activities to be properly approved, supervised, and executed.

CREEK WAR (1813–1814) Military conflict between the United States and the Red Sticks faction of the Creek Nation waged during the WAR OF 1812. U.S. victory over the British-allied Indians broke Creek fighting power and permanently weakened Indian resistance in the southeast to advancing white settlement across the Ap-palachians after 1815. The Creek defeat also spelled a wartime strategic setback for Great Britain, which had counted on Indian support in its planned invasion of the American Gulf Coast.

The Creeks were divided over who to support in the War of 1812. White Sticks remained U.S. loyalists. Red Sticks, hostile to federal efforts to forcibly civilize the southeast Indians, sided with Great Britain and in February 1813 launched an all-out attack in Mississippi and Alabama territories on American settlers. General ANDREW JACKSON mounted a retaliatory campaign against the Red Sticks and in March 1814 at the Battle of Horseshoe Bend in Alabama crushed their resistance. The Creek Nation was compelled to cede over half of its lands to the United States through the Treaty of Fort Jackson in August 1814.

See also MAP 1.

CREOLE AFFAIR (1841–1842) Anglo-American diplomatic dispute stemming from a slave-ship revolt. The *Creole*, an American ship transporting a cargo of 135 slaves, sailed from Virginia on October 27, 1841, headed for New Orleans. Early in November the slaves mutinied, killing a white crew member, taking possession of the vessel, and forcing the pilot to proceed to the free British port of Nassau in the Bahama Islands. British authorities held the instigators of the revolt on criminal charges but liberated all the other slaves. Secretary of State DANIEL WEBSTER demanded Great Britain return the slaves as mutineers and as the lawful property of U.S. citizens. He also insisted on an indemnity for the conduct of the Nassau officials. British rejection of the U.S. demands exacerbated tensions between Washington and London.

Great Britain had outlawed the African slave trade in 1807; the United States abolished it the next year, but continued to permit traders to ship domestic slaves between U.S. ports through American coastal waters. After slaves throughout the British empire were freed in 1833, Great Britain waged a strong international campaign against slavery. Treaties with other European nations authorized British cruisers to stop suspected slave ships. But the United States refused to let British vessels intercept and search ships sailing under the American flag. By 1840 America was the only major maritime nation not committed by formal agreement to helping Great Britain try to thwart the slave traffic out of Africa.

British cruisers after 1840 increasingly targeted slave ships that were not actually American but flew the American flag for the protection it provided. Sometimes legitimate American ships mistakenly were detained, leading to U.S. protest and charges of British interference with legal commerce and FREEDOM OF THE SEAS. Great Britain's drive against slave commerce on the seas and its criticism of slavery in the United States remained sensitive points in Anglo-American relations and were particularly galling to the American South. In the WEBSTER-ASHBURTON TREATY (1842), which settled several outstanding boundary disputes, the two countries agreed on an extradition arrangement that covered high crimes on the order of the *Creole* mutiny. At the same time the United States agreed to cooperate with Great Britain in suppressing the African slave trade. The *Creole* Affair finally was resolved in 1855 when a joint Anglo-American commission awarded the United States an indemnity of $110,330.

CRONKITE, WALTER LELAND (1916–) Celebrated American broadcast journalist. Born in Missouri, he dropped out of the University of Texas as a junior in 1935 and went to work as a reporter and newswriter for the Scripps-Howard newspaper syndicate. He joined United Press (UP) as a correspondent in 1939. From 1942 to 1945 Cronkite covered WORLD WAR II in Europe. Attached to American forces, he reported on such major military engagements as the Battle of the North Atlantic (1942), the Allied invasion of Normandy in June 1944, and the Battle of the Bulge in December 1944. He remained abroad after the war as chief UP correspondent at the NUREMBURG WAR CRIMES TRIAL in Germany and from 1946 to 1948 as Moscow bureau chief.

Hired by the Columbia Broadcasting System (CBS) in 1950, he was assigned to the network's new television station in Washington, D.C., as a news correspondent. From 1962 until his retirement in 1981, Cronkite served as anchorman and managing editor for the CBS Evening News, becoming perhaps the best-known and most credible figure in American journalism. His coverage of the VIETNAM WAR both reflected and influenced evolving American public opinion toward the conflict. On returning from South Vietnam after the TET OFFENSIVE in 1968, he offered his viewers a sober assessment that rejected the Johnson administration's optimistic war forecasts. He concluded: "It seems now more certain than ever that the bloody experience of Vietnam is to end in stalemate." Cronkite's report troubled President LYNDON B. JOHNSON, who interpreted it as evidence of a shift in public attitudes toward U.S. policy in Vietnam. Journalist DAVID HALBERSTAM later wrote how Johnson worried that "if he had lost Walter Cronkite he had lost Mr. Average Citizen." In addition to anchoring the network news, Cronkite hosted the program *Eyewitness to History* and the contemporary history series *Twentieth Century*. In charge of CBS coverage of America's space program, he became a great enthusiast of manned space flight. In retirement he remained a special CBS news correspondent and commentator.

CRUISE MISSILE Guided missile powered by a jet engine. With a sophisticated computer guidance system, the missile is able to fly very close to the ground, avoiding radar detection, and strike with pinpoint accuracy. Cruise missiles can be launched from the air, sea, or ground, and have a range up to several thousand miles. They can carry either nuclear or conventional warheads, with no difference in outward appearance, a fact which, together with their small size and easy concealment, makes them a difficult issue for arms control negotiations. In 1979 the Western security alliance NATO reached what became known as the DUAL-TRACK DECISION to station U.S. PERSHING II and ground-launched Tomahawk cruise missiles in Western Europe unless recently deployed corresponding Soviet medium-range nuclear weapons were withdrawn from Eastern Europe. Following Soviet rejection of this approach, the first U.S. missiles were fielded in 1983. In 1987 the United States and Soviet Union concluded the INTERMEDIATE NUCLEAR FORCES TREATY that eliminated medium-range nuclear missiles, including ground-launched cruise missiles.

CSCE See **CONFERENCE ON SECURITY AND COOPERATION IN EUROPE**.

CUBAN INTERVENTIONS U.S. armed interventions in the island nation during the opening decades of Cuban independence in the early 20th century. By the TREATY OF PARIS (1898) ending the SPANISH-AMERICAN WAR, Spain renounced its sovereignty over Cuba. Spanish authorities formally surrendered custody of the island to U.S. occupation forces on January 1, 1899. On the eve of the Spanish-American conflict, the United States, through the TELLER AMENDMENT (1898), had disclaimed any intent to annex Cuba or exercise sovereignty over it once peace was restored. In the war's aftermath, however, Washington feared that a rapid and total American military withdrawal might imperil Cuban political stability and thus jeopardize U.S. strategic and financial interests on the island. Control over Cuba fell to an American military government that was authorized to rule on a transitional basis until the Cubans established a viable self-government.

General LEONARD WOOD, U.S. military governor, assembled Cuban political leaders at a constitutional convention in November 1900. The following February the convention adopted a Cuban constitution providing for establishment of republican government. Secretary of War ELIHU ROOT, through Wood, informed the constitution's framers that the U.S. occupation of the island would not end until they accepted the PLATT AMENDMENT (1901) defining special future relations with the United States. Its main terms barred Cuba from entering any treaty with a foreign power that would compromise Cuban sovereignty, authorized the United States to intervene in Cuba to preserve its independence and maintain law and order, and enabled the United States to lease naval bases on the island. Under U.S. pressure the convention reluctantly added the Platt Amendment to the constitution in June 1901. With the inauguration of Conservative Tomas Estrada Palma as Cuba's first president in May 1902, President THEODORE ROOSEVELT withdrew American troops from the island, ending the U.S. occupation.

America's growing economic stake in Cuba at the turn of the century exerted a powerful influence on U.S. policy toward the island. In 1902 private American investment in Cuba, most of it in tobacco and sugar, was double what it had been in 1895. The CUBAN RECIPROCITY TREATY (1902) opened the way for even greater trade and investment. In its first years of ostensible independence, Cuba was troubled by bitter political rivalries. After Estrada Palma was reelected in 1906, his Liberal political adversaries revolted. When Estrada Palma resigned suddenly, Cuba was left without a functioning government and in general unrest. Amid increasingly chaotic conditions, Roosevelt invoked the intervention clause under the Platt Amendment and sent U.S. military forces into Havana on September 29, 1906. Secretary of War WILLIAM HOWARD TAFT formally declared American occupation and U.S. official Charles E. Magoon became governor of the island in mid-October. As the top civil authority in Cuba, Magoon enjoyed extensive powers, which he used to impose political and legal reforms, and to enforce peace and stability. In April 1909, following the inauguration of a newly elected Cuban president, Liberal Jose Miguel Gomez, the American Army of Cuban Pacification was withdrawn, and the island resumed an uneasy independence.

The United States next encountered crisis in Cuba after Conservative President Mario Garcia Menocal claimed to have won a second term in the November 1916 voting. The Liberals contended Menocal had stolen the election. In February 1917, after Cuban electoral authorities were unable to settle the dispute, the Liberals launched a revolt with the support of elements of the Cuban army. In the face of worsening political violence in eastern Cuba, where many of the largest American sugar holdings were situated, President WOODROW WILSON on March 8 landed U.S. marines at Santiago and Guantanamo to protect American lives and property and restore order. The U.S. presence shored up the Menocal government, which by late April was able to stamp out the Liberal rebellion as a viable political movement. Following U.S.-supervised elections on May 20, 1917, in which Menocal won another four-year term, American troops again were pulled out of Cuba.

Menocal protege Alfredo Zayas appeared to win a narrow victory in the 1920 presidential election. But Liberals, charging balloting fraud, refused to concede and appealed for U.S. supervision of new elections. The electoral dispute caused a political crisis that in turn was aggravated by a serious economic downturn precipitated by a sharp drop in world sugar prices. With the situation on the island deteriorating, the Wilson administration acted to uphold a stable Cuban government capable of protecting American lives and property. U.S. Army General Enoch H. Crowder, who previously had devised Cuba's legal code and helped draft its election laws, was sent to the island in an advisory capacity. Arriving in January 1921, he instructed Menocal on financial reorganization and pressed for a new presidential vote. Another election was held later in the year. Despite fresh Liberal accusations of fraud, Zayas was declared the winner and assumed office under Crowder's watchful scrutiny. Implementing fiscal and administrative reforms prepared by the American general, Zayas succeeded in bringing his country's worst financial problems under control. Crowder became U.S. ambassador to Cuba in 1923.

Zayas was succeeded in 1925 by Liberal General Gerardo Machado y Morales, who emerged as a tyrant. Machado's repressive regime aroused broad popular opposition. His resort to widespread terror tactics, which coincided with an economic depression produced by the collapse of the world sugar market in 1930, exacerbated civil unrest. In the face of the deepening Cuban crisis, President HERBERT C. HOOVER held throughout his term to a policy of nonintervention. After taking office in March 1933, President FRANKLIN D. ROOSEVELT sent SUMNER WELLES to Cuba as the new American ambassador with instructions to mediate an end to the political violence and seek to pave the way for free elections. Machado resisted Welles's diplomacy. On August 12, 1933, a cabal of Cuban army officers staged a bloodless coup that forced Machado to flee the country. He was succeeded by Dr. Carlos Manuel de Cespedes, who met with the U.S. ambassador's firm approval. Less than a month later, on September 4, Cuban noncommissioned officers led by Sergeant Fulgencio Batista (who in short order would become a colonel) overthrew Cespedes in the so-called Revolt of the Six Sergeants, which enjoyed the support of students and liberal intellectuals. The coup organizers established a civilian junta and installed prominent physician and university professor Dr. Ramon Grau San Martin as provisional president.

At the urging of Welles, who contended Grau San Martin's supporters were predominantly left-wing radicals, Roosevelt refused to recognize the new regime, claiming it lacked popular support. At the same time, amid continuing violence on the island, he sent U.S. warships to Cuban waters to protect American nationals but landed no troops. Colonel Batista, aware that Cuba had almost no hope of economic recovery absent U.S. diplomatic support, forced Grau San Martin's resignation in January 1934 and replaced him with the more conservative Colonel Carlos Mendieta, whom Roosevelt immediately recognized. In May 1934 the United States, in a demonstration of its GOOD NEIGHBOR POLICY toward Latin America, abrogated the Platt Amendment, thus giving Cuba its full political independence. America nevertheless retained its lease on the Guantanamo naval base. Mendieta was the first in a succession of presidents in the 1930s who served as fronts for Batista, who possessed the real power in Cuba.

See also BAY OF PIGS INVASION, MAP 6.

CUBAN MISSILE CRISIS (1962) U.S.-Soviet confrontation that went to the brink of war over the USSR's installation of offensive nuclear missiles in Cuba. Cuban leader Fidel Castro's imposition in 1959 of a leftist regime and subsequent development of close ties with the Communist world brought his island nation to the center of the U.S.-Soviet COLD WAR struggle. In April 1961 the U.S.-backed BAY OF PIGS INVASION by Cuban exiles to overthrow Castro ended in embarrassing failure. As Castro further aligned his nation with the Communist bloc, the United States led efforts to isolate its Caribbean neighbor. Washington welcomed Cuba's expulsion from the ORGANIZATION OF AMERICAN STATES (OAS) in January 1962. Cuba's alienation within the Western Hemisphere was offset, however, by increased military and economic aid from the Soviet Union.

By the summer of 1962, the Soviet Union had begun a major arms buildup in Cuba. American intelligence knew that such sophisticated conventional weapons as MiG-21 jet fighters and surface-to-air missiles (SAMs) were being stationed in

Cuba. Unbenownst to senior U.S. officials, the USSR also had decided to place nuclear-armed ballistic missiles on the island. The first missiles arrived in early September 1962 and were moved to secret launch sites then under construction. Assured by the Soviet government that its military assistance to Cuba was strictly defensive, President JOHN F. KENNEDY answered congressional criticism of his administration's inaction on Cuba by declaring that the Soviet arms shipments there posed no serious threat. He insisted that if the Communist buildup ever were to imperil either the United States or its allies, America then would do whatever was necessary to safeguard hemisphere security. Support in Congress for a clear statement of U.S. resolve resulted in passage of a joint resolution on September 26 backing the use of force, if needed, to respond to the Cuban situation.

Senior U.S. intelligence estimates continued to discount the possibility that the Soviet Union would risk a dangerous superpower confrontation by introducing offensive nuclear missiles into Cuba. CENTRAL INTELLIGENCE AGENCY (CIA) Director JOHN A. MCCONE thought otherwise. On his honeymoon in France that September he sent a series of messages back to Washington, dubbed "the honeymoon telegrams," urging greater consideration be given to a possible missile threat. McCone's suspicions were confirmed when an American U-2 reconnaissance aircraft on October 14 photographed a Soviet medium-range ballistic missile (MRBM) site in western Cuba near San Cristobal.

Kennedy was briefed on the discovery the morning of October 16. He immediately convened a meeting of his top advisers. The ad hoc group, later called the EXCOM for Executive Committee of the NATIONAL SECURITY COUNCIL (NSC), met almost continually as the Cuban Missile Crisis unfolded in the final weeks of October 1962. The group faced a dangerous situation. Aerial reconnaissance over Cuba revealed another MRBM site and two sites for more powerful intermediate-range ballistic missiles (IRBMs). The missiles represented a dramatic alteration of the U.S.-Soviet BALANCE OF POWER. Intelligence reports indicated the sites were close to completion. Once operational, the missiles could

launch a nuclear attack on targets throughout much of North and South America. The close proximity meant U.S. leaders would have almost no warning of an offensive strike. The presence of the missiles would undermine U.S. security guarantees to its fellow American states.

Kennedy from the start of the crisis set U.S. policy as the removal of the missiles from Cuba. Initial EXCOM support for a military strike against the missile sites was supplanted within several days by growing sentiment for a blockade of Cuba. By October 21 the president had decided on a naval quarantine, holding in reserve the option of direct military action. In a televised speech to the nation the following day, he disclosed that Soviet nuclear missiles had been found in Cuba, announced a blockade of further offensive military shipments to the island, and made clear U.S. determination to see the missiles removed. Kennedy placed the U.S. military on alert and ordered a possible invasion force readied.

Great Britain, France, and West Germany quickly signaled allied support of the U.S. stance, and the OAS voted to support the blockade on October 23. At the UNITED NATIONS, U.S. Ambassador ADLAI E. STEVENSON presented the case for the American actions. Questioning Soviet counterpart V. A. Zorin during a heated exchange over the presence of missiles in Cuba, Stevenson uttered his famous line about how he was "prepared to wait for my answer until hell freezes over." As people around the world grasped the gravity of the situation, there was widespread alarm over possible superpower hostilities and even nuclear war.

The quarantine was scheduled to go into effect on October 24. Soviet Premier Nikita S. Khrushchev vehemently denounced the U.S. measure, but at the last moment Soviet ships bound for Cuba stopped short of the U.S. blockade and turned away. The crisis, however, was not defused. Preparations on the missile sites continued at an accelerated pace. With tensions mounting, the U.S. Navy on October 26 for the first time stopped and boarded a ship, the Soviet-chartered Panamanian transport *Marcula*, to verify it was not carrying offensive weapons before allowing it to proceed to Cuba.

That evening Kennedy received a personal letter from Khrushchev indicating that the Soviet premier would be willing to withdraw the missiles from Cuba in return for an American commitment not to invade the island nation. A second letter from Khrushchev arrived the next morning. It demanded that the United States remove its nuclear missiles from Turkey in exchange for the withdrawal of Soviet missiles from Cuba. Following EXCOM deliberations on the two somewhat contradictory messages, Kennedy decided to answer only the first letter, accepting Khrushchev's original proposal. In addition, the president's brother, Attorney General Robert F. Kennedy, met privately with Soviet Ambassador to Washington Anatoly Dobrynin to convey U.S. desires for a peaceful solution based on Khrushchev's first letter. This diplomacy brought an end to the crisis as Khrushchev on October 28 confirmed that the Soviet Union would dismantle and ship home its missiles in return for a U.S. no-invasion pledge. The United States sought international verification of Soviet compliance, but Castro balked at U.N. or other outside inspection teams and America was forced to rely instead on aerial observation. On November 20 Kennedy stated that all known missile sites were dismantled and ended the quarantine. In notes to the United Nations in January 1962, the United States and Soviet Union announced a formal end to the crisis.

The episode, verging as it did on nuclear war, was the most serious U.S.-Soviet Cold War confrontation. The sobering experience pointed at the need for better communication links between Washington and Moscow and thus led to the first of the "HOT-LINE" AGREEMENTS. Why the Soviet Union risked a dangerous showdown with the United States by introducing nuclear missiles into Cuba remains a point of historical conjecture. It has been suggested Khrushchev left his 1961 VIENNA SUMMIT with Kennedy believing he could take advantage of the young, inexperienced American president. The Soviet leader ultimately was forced to retreat from his Cuban gambit by superior American military power. The Soviet agreement to remove the missiles was seen as a triumph for the Kennedy administration and hastened the weakened Khrushchev's replacement in Moscow. The crisis also precipitated a major arms buildup by a Kremlin

leadership determined never again to be forced to capitulate.

CUBAN RECIPROCITY TREATY (1902) Agreement concluded between the United States and Cuba that lowered tariffs on goods traded between the two nations. The former Spanish colony had gained its ostensible independence the previous May with the transition from American military rule to a newly elected sovereign Cuban government. As part of the agreement to end America's post–SPANISH-AMERICAN WAR (1898) occupation of the island, Cuba had consented to incorporate the PLATT AMENDMENT (1901) into its constitution. The measure, passed by the U.S. Congress, gave the United States a right to intervene in Cuba to maintain a stable and solvent government on the island. The U.S. government was determined to prevent a level of political turmoil or economic difficulty that might tempt European interference in Cuba or imperil American interests there.

The most pressing problem confronting newly independent Cuba, in Washington's judgment, was its depressed sugar industry, in which substantial private American capital was invested. Toward the end of the U.S. occupation of Cuba, the American military government had urged a reciprocal trade agreement that principally would help the island's sugar growers by cutting the duty on Cuban sugar exported to the United States. A pledge by President THEODORE ROOSEVELT and Secretary of War ELIHU ROOT to support trade reciprocity had helped to overcome Cuban resistance to the Platt Amendment. The Roosevelt administration believed a prosperous Cuban sugar economy was vital to Cuban political stability. Negotiations began following independence and the two nations signed a commercial pact in Havana on December 11, 1902. Under its terms, any U.S. and Cuban products already imported duty-free in either country would continue to enjoy tariff exemptions. The treaty stipulated that American duties on all other Cuban imports into the United States were to be 20 percent less than those on similar imports from any other country. Cuban duties on imports from the United States, with the exception of tobacco, were also to be 20 percent lower. The agreement was to remain in force for five years and from year to year thereafter until abrogated by either country. The treaty promptly benefited the Cuban economy and was responsible for much of the prosperity the country enjoyed in its first crucial years of independence. The value of sugar production soared between 1902 and 1912. Historians critical of the reciprocity agreement contend that in the long run it grossly distorted the Cuban economy by making the island nation excessively dependent on sugar. The treaty was suspended in 1934 in connection with the revocation of the Platt Amendment and advent of America's GOOD NEIGHBOR POLICY.

CUSHING, CALEB (1800–1879) Political leader and diplomat. Graduating from Harvard College in 1817, Cushing read law and was admitted to the bar in his native Massachusetts in 1821. He served in both chambers of the state legislature before his election as a Whig in 1834 to the U.S. House of Representatives, where he spent four successive terms and sat on the Committee of Foreign Affairs. On the death of President WILLIAM HENRY HARRISON in 1841, he broke with the Whigs and aligned with Harrison's vice-president and successor, JOHN TYLER, a states' rights Democrat. Appointed U.S. commissioner to China by Tyler in 1843, he negotiated the historic TREATY OF WANGHIA (1844), the first Sino-American treaty, which opened Chinese ports to U.S. trade and established the principle of EXTRATERRITORIALITY for U.S. citizens in China.

Back in the United States after his Asia mission, he won election once more in 1846 to the Massachusetts legislature, where he emerged as a proponent of U.S. expansionism. Cushing favored TEXAS ANNEXATION (1845) and the acquisition of "ALL OREGON." He supported President JAMES K. POLK on the MEXICAN WAR (1846–1848), during which he commanded a regiment of Massachusetts volunteers that he person-

ally had raised and organized. Cushing was made a brigadier general although he never saw field action. In 1853 President FRANKLIN PIERCE, whose candidacy Cushing had supported, named him attorney general. Influential in Pierce's cabinet, the expansionist Cushing championed the aims of YOUNG AMERICA and MANIFEST DESTINY. An advocate of U.S. acquisition of Cuba, he endorsed the controversial OSTEND MANIFESTO (1854), which urged America's annexation of Spain's island colony. In 1857 Cushing returned to the Massachusetts legislature.

As permanent chairman he presided over the Democratic National Convention in Charleston, South Carolina, in 1860 that nominated Illinois Senator Stephen A. Douglas for president. When defiant Southern extremist delegates withdrew and opened a rival convention in Baltimore, Maryland, Cushing also served as their chairman. The Baltimore seceders nominated John Breckinridge as their presidential standard-bearer. After the Civil War broke out, Cushing declared his loyalty to the Union and the federal cause. He became a Republican and served in the course of the war as a legal consultant to President ABRAHAM LINCOLN and Secretary of State WILLIAM H. SEWARD. He accepted appointment by President ULYSSES S. GRANT as senior American counsel to the arbitration at Geneva, Switzerland, in the early 1870s of the ALABAMA CLAIMS against Great Britain arising from the Civil War. Nominated by Grant in 1873 to be U.S. Supreme Court chief justice, Cushing was forced to withdraw his name after old political adversaries in the Senate mounted vigorous, partisan opposition to his selection. From 1874 to 1877 he served as U.S. minister to Spain, where his skillful diplomacy helped improve relations sullied by the VIRGINIUS AFFAIR (1873). Following his mission to Madrid, Cushing retired to Massachusetts.

D

DANIELS, JOSEPHUS (1862–1948) Newspaperman, secretary of the Navy, and diplomat. Daniels spent a summer studying law at the University of North Carolina, his only formal experience with higher education. He passed the state bar exam but never practiced law professionally. The North Carolina native embarked in earnest on a journalism career in 1885 when, with borrowed money, he bought the *Raleigh State Chronicle*. In 1887 he purchased the *Raleigh News and Observer* and merged it with the *Chronicle*, whose name he jettisoned. As editor and publisher of the *News and Observer* he emerged as a leading editorial voice in the South. A progressive Democrat, he was a close friend and loyal political ally of three-time unsuccessful presidential candidate WILLIAM JENNINGS BRYAN. In 1912 Daniels supported the winning presidential drive of WOODROW WILSON.

Appointed Wilson's Navy secretary, he served in the post from 1913 until 1921. Daniels, despite a lack of prior nautical experience, became an active Navy chief who implemented wide-ranging and sometimes controversial reforms. He banned liquor from officers' messes, provided compulsory schooling for illiterate sailors, and brought improvements to the U.S. Naval Academy and the Naval War College. Daniels insisted on competitive bidding by private companies on Navy contracts. Among his innovations was the establishment of the Navy Consulting Board, a panel headed by the famous inventor Thomas A. Edison and comprising distinguished scientists and engineers who advised the secretary on technical issues. During his tenure the Navy expanded greatly in size and performed effectively in WORLD WAR I.

Returning to his Raleigh newspaper in 1921, he continued to figure prominently in state and national Democratic politics. His former assistant at the Navy Department, FRANKLIN D. ROOSEVELT, on ascending to the presidency in 1933 named Daniels U.S. ambassador to Mexico. During his eight years at Mexico City, the North Carolinian served as an able and eloquent spokesman for Roosevelt's GOOD NEIGHBOR POLICY toward Latin America. Daniels' adroit diplomacy averted a serious rupture between the United States and Mexico after the Mexican government expropriated American oil holdings and implemented a land-reform program that nationalized American agricultural properties. His influence with Roosevelt set the stage for eventual settlement of the MEXICAN OIL EXPROPRIATION CONTROVERSY in November 1941. Daniels resigned his Mexican post late in 1941 because of his wife's declining health and returned to Raleigh. He maintained an active interest in the *News and Observer* until his death in 1948.

DANISH TREATY See **DANISH WEST INDIES ACQUISITION**.

DANISH WEST INDIES ACQUISITION (1916) Purchase of Denmark's Caribbean islands by the United States. Known today as the U.S. Virgin Islands, they comprise the main islands of Saint Croix, Saint Thomas, and Saint John and more than 60 other uninhabited small islands and cays. The Virgin Island chain is located 40 miles east of Puerto Rico in the Leeward Islands and totals 133 square miles. Acquisition of the islands became a principal aim of Secretary of State WILLIAM H. SEWARD's expansionist program after 1865. Seward coveted the Danish West Indies, especially Saint Thomas with its excellent harbor, as a prime location for a U.S. naval base in the Caribbean. Danish-American negotiations begun in January 1866 culminated in October 1867 with the Danish Treaty, in which the United States agreed to pay $7.5 million for Saint Thomas and Saint John. The sale was approved overwhelmingly by plebiscites in the islands themselves. But critics in Congress attacked the purchase as too costly and unnecessary and the U.S. Senate would not ratify the final treaty in 1870.

Interest in buying the Danish West Indies was revived at the outset of the 20th century. Concerned that Germany planned to acquire them in violation of the MONROE DOCTRINE restriction on European involvement in the Americas, President THEODORE ROOSEVELT offered to purchase the islands. In January 1902 the United States and Denmark completed an annexation treaty. The Senate quickly ratified the pact, but the Danish Parliament rejected it by a single vote. Afterward, the Roosevelt administration alleged, but was unable to substantiate, that German influence in Danish politics had blocked the sale.

Following the outbreak of WORLD WAR I in 1914, the United States feared Germany might take over the islands and thereby undermine America's strategic position in the Caribbean. Prospect of a German submarine base in the islands loomed as a threat to the security of the PANAMA CANAL. In a treaty signed August 4, 1916, Denmark agreed to relinquish its West Indies possessions to the United States for $25 million. The sale came after Secretary of State ROBERT LANSING had informed the Danish government the United States would seize the islands if German control of the chain seemed imminent. America accepted transfer of the islands on March 31, 1917. Formally an unincorporated U.S. territory, the islands since 1972 have sent one nonvoting delegate to the House of Representatives.

See also MAP 6.

DARTMOUTH CONFERENCES Ongoing series of informal parleys between promi-

nent private citizens from the United States and the Soviet Union to exchange views on predominant issues in Soviet-American relations. The unofficial conferences have been held periodically since 1960, when the first one was organized at Dartmouth College in Hanover, New Hampshire, by Norman Cousins, then editor of *The Saturday Review*. His aim was to establish a regular channel of communication between distinguished citizens of the rival superpowers as a vehicle for easing COLD WAR mistrust. While the conference takes its name from the inaugural site, subsequent ones have rotated among various other locations in America and the USSR. Participants are leading figures in business, academics, law, journalism, and politics and many have at one time held high office in their respective countries. The 1991 demise of the USSR left Dartmouth conferees to deliberate the course of post–Cold War U.S. relations with Russia and the former Soviet republics.

DAVIS, JEFFERSON (1808–1889) U.S. senator, secretary of war, and the only president of the Confederacy. Born in Kentucky, Davis was two years old when his family moved to Mississippi, where his father became a cotton planter. After graduating from West Point in 1828, he was assigned to frontier duty in the OLD NORTHWEST and served in the BLACK HAWK WAR (1832). He resigned his commission in 1835 to marry Sarah Taylor, daughter of his commander, Colonel ZACHARY TAYLOR, later president of the United States. The young couple settled on a cotton plantation in the Mississippi Delta. Within three months of the wedding, Sarah had died of malaria. The devastated Davis turned all his energies to developing the plantation. He remarried in 1845, the same year he was elected as a Democrat to the U.S. House of Representatives. He resigned his seat in 1846 to command a unit of Mississippi volunteers in the MEXICAN WAR. Severely wounded at the Battle of Buena Vista, he returned home and in 1847 was appointed to fill a vacancy in the U.S. Senate. The slaveholding Davis opposed the WILMOT PROVISO, the measure several times introduced in Congress to prohibit slavery in the territories acquired from Mexico as a result of the war. As a solution to the bitter sectional dispute at the end of the 1840s over the issue, he favored extending the Missouri Compromise line of 36° 30', above which slavery could not be introduced, all the way to the Pacific. Elected to a full Senate term in 1850, he resigned in 1851 to run unsuccessfully as the Democratic candidate for governor of Mississippi.

When FRANKLIN PIERCE became president in 1853, he made Davis secretary of war. His achievements in this post earned Davis national political stature. He strengthened coastal and frontier defenses, greatly enlarged the army, raised soldiers' pay, and introduced new weapons. With a view toward promoting the nation's continued westward expansion, he directed surveys for railway routes. He favored the southern route to the Pacific and played an instrumental part in securing the GADSDEN PURCHASE (1853) from Mexico. The purchase added territory in present-day New Mexico and Arizona, thereby completing the outline of the contiguous United States. Davis supported the Pierce administration's scheme to acquire Cuba from Spain as additional slave territory, but Northern antislavery opposition scuttled the plan. On the completion of his term as war secretary in 1857, he again was elected to the Senate. Now the South's recognized spokesman, he took his seat as the deepening sectional crisis over slavery edged the nation closer to disunion and impending civil war.

After Mississippi seceded on January 9, 1861, Davis resigned from the Senate and returned home where he was commissioned a general and placed in command of the state's defenses. Before he could assume his duties he was unanimously selected provisional president of the newly formed Confederate States of America by the provisional Confederate Congress. Inaugurated on February 18, 1861, at Montgomery, Alabama, the Confederacy's first capital, he pressed the South's military preparation. Steps ordered by President ABRAHAM LINCOLN to resupply the federal garrison at Fort Sumter in Charleston Harbor, South Carolina, led Davis to authorize the Confederate bombardment of Sumter on April 12 to 13, 1861, which marked the start of the Civil War.

At the conflict's outset, he sent diplomatic agents to European capitals seeking recognition for the Confederacy. Constrained by its well-established opposition to slavery, and under pressure from the Lincoln administration, the British government withheld recognition. The French government, while inclined to recognize the Confederacy, was afraid to act alone. Purchasing agents dispatched by Davis's government were able to procure ammunition, supplies, and ships. Confederate cruisers built and outfitted in British ports roamed the seas, exacting a heavy toll on Union commercial shipping. Davis pursued so-called KING COTTON DIPLOMACY, based on the coercive economic power of Southern cotton. Since British and French textile industries relied so heavily on cotton exported from the South, the Confederate leadership reasoned, London and Paris would be compelled to recognize the Confederacy and help it break the Northern blockade of the Southern ports in order to ensure continued access to the cotton supply. Economic circumstances and British and French unwillingness to risk war with the Union combined to doom the King Cotton policy. Following his election to a six-year term under the permanent Confederate constitution, Davis was inaugurated president on February 22, 1862, in Richmond, Virginia, which had become the new Confederate capital in June 1861. Two decisive events—Lincoln's Emancipation Proclamation, issued in September 1862, and the Confederate defeat at the Battle of Gettysburg in July 1863—dashed what remaining hope the Confederacy had of securing British or French diplomatic recognition.

With the Union army under General ULYSSES S. GRANT fast advancing on Richmond, Davis fled with his cabinet on April 3, 1865, and, following brief stays in Danville, Virginia, and Greensboro, North Carolina, set up a government for the last time in Charlotte, North Carolina. Conceding the end of the Confederacy, he was captured at Irwinville, Georgia, on May 10, 1865, and imprisoned at Fort Monroe, Virginia. Indicted for treason, he was never brought to trial. After two years in confinement he was released. He settled in Mississippi, where he spent the rest of his life and wrote *The Rise and Fall of the Confederate Government* (1881).

See also CIVIL WAR DIPLOMACY.

DAVIS, RICHARD HARDING (1864–1916) Newspaperman, war correspondent, and author. Born in Philadelphia, Pennsylvania, Davis attended Lehigh and Johns Hopkins universities, but never completed a degree. He began his career in journalism in 1886 as a reporter for the *Philadelphia Press*. In 1890 he joined the journal *Harper's Weekly* as managing editor, a position he held for three years. The best-known reporter of his generation, Davis enjoyed his greatest journalistic successes as a war correspondent for prominent New York and London papers. He covered the Cuban insurrection against Spain in 1895, the Greco-Turkish War (1897), the SPANISH-AMERICAN WAR (1898), the South African Boer War (1899–1902), the Russo-Japanese War (1904–1905), and, finally, WORLD WAR I. A friend and political admirer of President THEODORE ROOSEVELT, whom he had come to know while reporting on the Rough Riders during the Spanish-American War, Davis endorsed an expanded U.S. world role backed by a strong national defense and favored the BIG STICK diplomacy toward Latin America. He reported from the front lines in France and Serbia in the first year of World War I. After Germany's sinking of the LUSITANIA (1915), he became a strong advocate of U.S. intervention in the global conflict on the Allied side. Davis died suddenly of a heart attack at his Mount Kisco, New York, home in April 1916. A prolific writer of popular fiction throughout his career, he produced 7 novels, 25 plays, and 11 short story collections.

DAWES, CHARLES GATES (1865–1951) Financier and diplomat who served as U.S. vice-president under CALVIN COOLIDGE. Born in Ohio, Dawes graduated from Marietta College in 1884 and Cincinnati Law School in 1886. The following year he entered law practice in Lincoln, Nebraska, where he soon won acclaim for attacking the discriminatory freight rates of the railroads. Concurrently pursuing interests in banking and business, he became a Lincoln bank director and acquired control of utilities companies in the Midwest. He gave up his law practice and in 1895 moved to Chicago to oversee his profitable enterprises.

The Republican Dawes's first major involvement in politics came when he managed WILLIAM MCKINLEY's 1896 presidential campaign in Illinois. Following the election, the McKinley administration rewarded him with an appointment as comptroller of the currency. Dawes resigned the post to run for the U.S. Senate in 1902 from Illinois. He failed to gain the Republican nomination and thereafter devoted himself chiefly to business until 1917. He organized and became president of the Central Trust Company of Illinois. The new bank's great success assured his membership in the nation's leading financial circles.

Following America's entry into WORLD WAR I, Dawes was commissioned an Army major. In September 1917 General JOHN J. PERSHING assigned him to the headquarters staff of the AMERICAN EXPEDITIONARY FORCE and made him chairman of the general purchasing board and chief of supply procurement. Dawes conceived the idea of the Military Board of Allied Supply to coordinate purchases for all the Allied armies. He organized and ran the board and served formally as its American member. After the armistice he was on the United States Liquidation Commission established to dispose of surplus goods and war supplies. He resigned from the Army in August 1919 with the rank of brigadier general.

Dawes returned to public service in 1921 when he accepted appointment by President WARREN G. HARDING as first director of the Bureau of the Budget. In his one year in the post, Dawes reduced federal spending by more than one-third. In 1923 he was made chairman of the expert committee of the Allied Reparations Commission that met in Paris to seek a solution to the problem of chronic German delinquency on World War I reparations payments. He was principal architect of the so-called DAWES PLAN (1924), the program designed to enable Germany to restore and stabilize its shattered economy and at the same time pay reasonable reparations to its wartime adversaries. For the reparations plan, he shared the 1925 Nobel Peace Prize with British Foreign Secretary Sir Austen Chamberlain.

In 1924 Dawes was elected vice-president on the Republican ticket with Coolidge. After leaving office in 1929 he headed a commission to the Dominican Republic that advised its government on putting the island nation's finances in order. Later the same year he was appointed ambassador to Great Britain by president HERBERT C. HOOVER. During his mission he served as a delegate to the first of the LONDON NAVAL CONFERENCES (1930) and supported the HOOVER MORATORIUM (1931) on international debts and reparations. Dawes returned to the United States to become first director of the Reconstruction Finance Corporation (RFC), the federal agency created in February 1932 to provide emergency loans to the nation's banks and railroads threatened with insolvency amid the Great Depression. He resigned his post in June to head the board of the failing Central Republic Bank and Trust Company, the institution with which his bank earlier had merged. He guided the bank through reorganization as the City National Bank and Trust Company. Dawes remained active in business until his death and never again held public office.

DAWES PLAN (1924) Agreement governing the payment of German WORLD WAR I reparations. In April 1921 the Allied Reparations Commission, established under the TREATY OF VERSAILLES (1919), set at $33 billion the total amount defeated Germany had to pay to Great Britain, France, and other Allies as compensation for wartime damages. The United States, seeking no reparations, did not send a delegation to the commission. With its postwar economy in collapse, Germany was unable to meet the demanding payment schedule. Concerned that Franco-German differences over the reparations might bring renewed armed conflict, U.S. Secretary of State CHARLES EVANS HUGHES in December 1922 proposed creation of a panel of American financial experts to prepare a workable German payment plan.

The U.S. government adamantly rejected any connection between German reparations and Allied war debts to the United States. Nevertheless senior American officials also realized that the ability of the Allies to settle their U.S. debts hinged largely on their receipt of reparations. France initially ignored the Hughes offer, and, with Germany in default on the reparations, began a military occupation of the industrial Ruhr area in January 1923 to force a resumption of German payments. The following November, amid worsening Franco-German relations, the Allied Repara-

tions Commission revived Hughes's idea for a group of experts, forming a special committee to address the German fiscal crisis. Because it was not formally part of the commission, the United States did not participate officially in the committee's work. Hughes fully endorsed, however, the participation of American financiers CHARLES G. DAWES and Owen D. Young, in a private capacity, with British, Belgian, French, and Italian representatives on the expert panel. Dawes became the committee's chairman.

The group met from January 14 to April 9, 1924. Its report, known as the Dawes Plan, was approved by the Allied Reparations Commission and implemented effective September 1, 1924. The plan was based on the committee's determination of the amount Germany actually would be able to pay. It established an initial five-year schedule of reduced payments; provided for subsequent review and establishment of a permanent reparations schedule; and furnished Germany with funds for both reconstruction and reparations through $200 million in foreign loans and a bond issue secured by the German railroad system. The Dawes financial scheme remained in effect until replaced by the YOUNG PLAN in 1930.

DAWSON AGREEMENTS (1910) U.S.-sponsored measures for political and financial rehabilitation in Nicaragua following civil warfare. In October 1909 insurgents led by Juan J. Estrada rebelled against Nicaraguan dictator Jose Santos Zelaya. The revolt, in part encouraged and funded by American businesses in the country, was prompted by Zelaya's granting of lucrative monopolies to favored domestic and foreign parties to sell liquor, tobacco, and other goods. The anti-American Zelaya, who defiantly opposed foreign meddling in Central American affairs, already was viewed as a political adversary in Washington. The Taft administration considered the dictator the chief instigator of political upheaval in the isthmus and inhospitable to American business investments in his country. President WILLIAM HOWARD TAFT and Secretary of State PHILANDER C. KNOX saw Zelaya's chronic warring with neighbors, his violations of Honduran neutrality, and his iron-fisted rule at home as obstructions to their efforts at achieving peace and stability in the region within the framework of the CENTRAL AMERICAN TREATIES OF 1907.

When, in November 1909, Zelaya approved the execution of two American soldiers of fortune, Lee Roy Cannon and Leonard Groce, who had been captured in the service of the rebels, a furious Knox condemned Zelaya as a tyrant and his regime as a menace to Central American peace. At Taft's direction, the secretary of state broke off formal relations with the Nicaraguan government and threw U.S. moral support behind the revolution. A besieged Zelaya resigned in mid-December and, after naming Dr. Jose Madriz his successor, fled to Mexico. Madriz continued the struggle to suppress the rebellion. His request for U.S. diplomatic recognition was refused by Knox, who presumed the new leader was a Zelaya disciple. The Taft administration told both factions that the United States would not recognize any government until it controlled all of Nicaragua and promised to hold free elections for a new president. With the insurgency gaining strength and the rebels advancing on Managua, Madriz resigned in August 1910 and left the country. The revolutionaries captured the capital and Estrada was proclaimed provisional president.

The Taft administration welcomed the insurgents' victory as a positive development for its emerging DOLLAR DIPLOMACY in the Caribbean region. Knox believed Nicaragua's political salvation depended upon its financial rehabilitation, which he wanted to see achieved by means of loans to Managua from American bankers. Repayment of the loans, he ventured, would be guaranteed by a U.S.-administered customs collectorship in Nicaragua modeled on the one installed with success by President THEODORE ROOSEVELT in the debt-ridden Dominican Republic in 1905. Washington wanted such a scheme not only for Nicaragua but also for its financially troubled neighbors, particularly Honduras. In promoting Dollar Diplomacy, Taft and Knox surmised that Central American political order could be achieved by financial measures and without resort to U.S. armed intervention or military occupation.

Determined to meet the U.S. prescription for Nicaragua's financial reform, Estrada in September 1910 appealed for U.S. diplomatic recognition, promised to hold new elections, and requested help to procure a loan from American banks to be guaranteed by customs collections. Knox dispatched a special emissary to Managua, Thomas C. Dawson (who soon would become the first chief of the newly formed Latin American division at the State Department), to prepare Nicaraguans for elections and to ensure that the new government fulfilled the pledges made by Estrada. The Dawson agreements, completed in early November 1910, were signed by Estrada and fellow revolutionary leaders Adolfo Diaz and Generals Emiliano Chamorro and Luis Mena. The agreements abolished Zelaya's monopolies, established a claims commission to compensate foreign residents for property losses in the recent civil conflict, and assured that the murderers of Cannon and Groce would be punished. The measures also stipulated that the U.S. government would help the new Nicaraguan administration obtain a customs-guaranteed loan and provided for U.S. supervision of a customs receivership in Nicaragua. Finally, it was agreed that Estrada would assume the presidency of the republic and Diaz would become vice-president. In early January 1911 Estrada and Diaz were legally elected by a Nicaraguan constituent convention, whereupon the United States formally recognized the new Nicaraguan government.

Rivalries divided the revolutionary leadership and the signers of the agreement soon fell to infighting. Estrada came to suspect General Mena, his secretary of war, and General Chamorro, who had gone to Honduras, of plotting a rebellion. The president, believing himself surrounded by enemies, in March 1911 proposed creation of a full U.S. protectorate over Nicaragua, an appeal declined by Taft. Estrada then jailed Mena and tried to distribute weapons to his own political followers in Managua, but the army defied his orders. In May Estrada resigned and fled the country, whereupon Diaz became Nicaragua's new president. Cultivating American goodwill, Diaz promptly requested further U.S. help in stabilizing his country's precarious fiscal position. In June 1911 Washington and Managua completed the KNOX-CASTRILLO CONVENTION, which provided for American control over Nicaragua's finances.

See also BRYAN-CHAMORRO TREATY, NICARAGUAN INTERVENTIONS.

DAY, WILLIAM RUFUS (1849–1923) Secretary of state in the McKinley administration and U.S. Supreme Court justice. Born in Ohio, Day graduated from the University of Michigan in 1870, read law, and was admitted to the bar in 1872. He began practice in Canton, Ohio, where he became a friend of county prosecutor WILLIAM MCKINLEY. Day was elected judge of the county-level court of common pleas in 1886 as the nominee of both the Democratic and Republican parties. In 1889 he was named U.S. district judge for northern Ohio, but because of ill health never assumed office. Returning to private practice, Day also acted as an unofficial legal and political adviser to McKinley during his service as Ohio governor. Following his election as president, McKinley in 1897 appointed Day assistant secretary of state. When failing health forced the resignation of Secretary of State JOHN SHERMAN just as the SPANISH-AMERICAN WAR began in April 1898, Day accepted appointment as his replacement.

Although he lacked diplomatic training, Day performed very capably as State Department head. He succeeded at the war's onset in securing the neutrality of the Western European powers. The protocol that brought a summer cease-fire between Spain and the United States was prepared under Day's direction. Resigning his post in September 1898 to become chairman of the five-member U.S. commission appointed to make peace with Spain, he helped frame the TREATY OF PARIS (1898) that concluded the war. Opposed in principal to U.S. acquisition of territory by conquest, he paved the way for the treaty provision under which the United States paid Spain $20 million for the Philippines. After returning to the United States from Paris, he was appointed a judge of the U.S. Court of Appeals in 1899 and, four years later, an associate justice of the U.S. Supreme Court. He resigned from the high court in 1922 to serve on a multinational claims commission organized to hear the claims of American citizens against Germany stemming from WORLD WAR I.

DE LOME LETTER (1898) Controversial note written by Spanish Minister to the United States Enrique Dupuy de Lome that insulted President WILLIAM MCKINLEY. Published in the sensationalist American "yellow press," the intercepted private letter excited a diplomatic furor that presaged the start of the SPANISH-AMERICAN WAR (1898). The violent Cuban revolt in 1895 against Spain's rule was met by a brutal Spanish policy calculated to crush the insurrection. American sympathy favored the rebels. Joseph Pulitzer's *New York Tribune* and WILLIAM R. HEARST's *New York World* stoked pro-rebel sentiment in the United States through sensationalist coverage that depicted the insurrection as a struggle against Spanish barbarism. With the financial support of American benefactors, Cubans established U.S.-based revolutionary committees that organized and launched FILIBUSTERING expeditions. Madrid repeatedly protested the U.S. government's failure to enforce fully its neutrality laws to stop rebel smuggling and gunrunning from American soil to Cuba.

After 1895 a group of imperialist-minded politicians, naval strategists, and publishers emerged within the Republican Party to urge U.S. intervention in Cuba. Exponents of America's expansionist NEW MANIFEST DESTINY, they wanted to take advantage of the Cuban revolution to drive Spain from the Caribbean and establish U.S. dominion over the commercially and strategically vital island. The Republican McKinley distanced himself from the expansionists by disclaiming any aggressive territorial designs on the part of his administration toward Cuba. In September 1897 he offered to mediate the conflict between Spain and its rebellious colony, reiterating that the United States had no annexationist intent toward the island. A suspicious Spanish government refused McKinley's offer.

Spain's November 1897 offer of concessions to the insurgents, including a promise of eventual home rule for the island, brought a softening of U.S. government criticism of Spanish colonial policy toward Cuba. The short-lived easing of tensions between Madrid and Washington appeared to imperil the expansionist ambitions of American imperialists who favored a showdown with Spain over the island. Hearst's pro-war *Journal* on February 9, 1898, published a private communication of de Lome to a friend in Cuba. The letter had been filched from the Havana mails by a rebel spy and given to the Hearst press. In it the Spanish diplomat called McKinley "weak . . . a bidder for the admiration of the crowd . . . a would-be politician who strives to leave a door open behind himself while keeping on good terms with the jingoes of his party." The Spanish diplomat's digs at the president caused a public uproar that was fanned by the "yellow press." De Lome immediately cabled his resignation to the Spanish government. His pilfered letter nonetheless had already seriously harmed Spanish-American relations and contributed to the momentum carrying the two nations toward war.

DEANE, SILAS (1737–1789) Diplomatic agent and Continental congressman. Deane graduated from Yale in 1758. After passing the bar in his native Connecticut in 1761, he settled down to practice law. Active in colonial politics in the years preceding the AMERICAN REVOLUTION, Deane supported the patriot cause. He served in the Continental Congress and in March 1776 was appointed the diplomatic representative of the COMMITTEE OF SECRET CORRESPONDENCE to France. As the first envoy sent abroad by the colonies, Deane explored the prospects for French diplomatic recognition of American independence and an alliance. Working with Pierre A. C. de Beaumarchais, the noted dramatist and promoter of French aid to the American cause, Deane secured shipments of war supplies and recruited European military officers to serve with American forces against the British.

In September 1776, he, BENJAMIN FRANKLIN, and Arthur Lee were appointed special commissioners to France. Their negotiations with French Foreign Minister Charles Gravier Comte de Vergennes produced the TREATY OF AMITY AND COMMERCE (1778) and the FRANCO-AMERICAN ALLIANCE (1778). The Continental Congress recalled Deane in 1778 to answer accusations leveled by Lee and others that he had engaged in profiteering in his dealings with Beaumarchais. Deane denied the charges but Congress never fully exonerated him. Embittered, he journeyed to Europe and in 1781 began advocating peace without independence and a reconciliation with Great Britain. His views, expressed in letters to various influential American officials that came to be published in the New York newspaper the *Royal Gazette*, were regarded as traitorous in the United States.

Deane's contacts with reputed British spy Edward Bancroft, an American writer and inventor residing in Great Britain, brought further allegations of treason. The embattled Deane became an exile, living in Ghent, Belgium, and then London. In 1789 he died suspiciously aboard a ship en route from Great Britain to Canada. Some historians have suggested, but never clearly substantiated, that Bancroft poisoned Deane to prevent him from divulging information about Bancroft's involvement in British espionage.

DEBT-FOR-NATURE SWAP Practice of converting THIRD WORLD debts into funds for the conservation of tropical rain forests. The concept grew out of the INTERNATIONAL DEBT CRISIS of the 1980s, when developing nations increasingly were unable to meet the mounting interest payments on massive loans from Western banks and multilateral lending agencies such as the WORLD BANK. Much of the borrowing by Third World governments had financed environmentally destructive development projects. To raise the capital needed to service the interest due on outstanding loans, developing countries had indiscriminately exploited their natural resources, thereby adding to the environmental cost of the debt crisis. Recognition by the mid-1980s among lenders and their governments that many Third World loans could never be repaid spurred a drive to turn the debt problem to ecological benefit. This gave rise to debt-for-nature exchanges, whereby a country's unpaid foreign obligations are converted to funds for environmental protection. These schemes have targeted the problem of tropical deforestation, which has been most severe in Central and South America, India, and Southeast Asia. Two examples illustrate how such swaps are transacted. In 1987 the private U.S. environmental group Conservation International negotiated with Western banks to purchase some of Bolivia's debt at a substantial discount. In return, the group gained possession of part of Bolivia's rain forest and designated it a nature preserve. In 1989 American Express Bank, one of Costa Rica's major creditors, sold a portion of the Central American nation's debt at a discount to the Nature Conservancy, a Washington, D.C.-based environmental organization. The conservancy traded the notes back to the Costa Rican central bank for local currency bonds. The interest on the bonds is to be funneled into a series of local projects for forest conservation.

DECATUR, STEPHEN (1779–1820) U.S. Navy officer. Decatur was born in Maryland where his mother had gone to escape the British occupation of Philadelphia during the AMERICAN REVOLUTION. His father, also Stephen Decatur, was an early U.S. naval officer. Young Decatur began his naval career in 1798 as a midshipman during the maritime QUASI-WAR (1798–1800) with France. He rose to fame during the TRIPOLITAN WAR (1801–1805) when, on February 16, 1804, he sailed the *Intrepid* under cover of darkness into Tripoli harbor to set fire to the captured U.S. warship *Constitution* and deny its use to the enemy. His daring exploit brought promotion to captain. He served on the inquiries into the CHESAPEAKE AFFAIR (1807) and LITTLE BELT INCIDENT (1811), U.S.-British naval encounters. Following the outbreak of the WAR OF 1812 he scored an early victory over the British frigate *Macedonian*, but the American fleet on the Atlantic Coast soon found itself blockaded by superior British naval power. When Decatur ventured forth on the *President* in January 1815, he encountered a British squadron and was forced to surrender after a fight.

With the conflict's end, he was released by the British in February 1815. Almost immediately Decatur was given command of a nine-ship squadron and sent to the Mediterranean to prosecute the ALGERINE WAR (1815). By the end of June 1815, he had captured the Algerian flagship *Mashuda*, blocked the port of Algiers, and exacted favorable peace terms. Decatur sailed on to Tunis and Tripoli, securing indemnities for hostile acts during the War of 1812 and effectively ending Barbary piracy against U.S. shipping. On his return to America, Decatur was honored at a dinner at Norfolk, Virginia, where he made his famous toast, "Our Country! In her intercourse with foreign nations may she always be in the right; but our country, right or wrong." He was killed in a duel in 1820.

DECLARATION OF ... See ..., **DECLARATION OF**.

DECLARATION ON THE HUMAN ENVIRONMENT See **UNITED NATIONS ENVIRONMENT PROGRAM**.

DECLARATION ON LIBERATED EUROPE See **YALTA CONFERENCE**.

DECLARATION BY UNITED NATIONS See **UNITED NATIONS DECLARATION**.

DECONCINI RESERVATION See **PANAMA CANAL TREATIES**.

DEFENSE, DEPARTMENT OF See **DEPARTMENT OF DEFENSE** in **APPENDIX B**.

DEFENSE INTELLIGENCE AGENCY (DIA) Intelligence office in the DEPARTMENT OF DEFENSE. The agency was formed by Secretary of Defense ROBERT S. MCNAMARA in October 1961 to coordinate the efforts of the separate intelligence services of the Army, Navy, and Air Force; to function as the intelligence staff for the secretary of defense and the JOINT CHIEFS OF STAFF; and to strengthen the defense establishment's role in the preparation of national foreign intelligence estimates. In 1965 the director of the DIA replaced the representatives of the three military intelligence services on the United States Intelligence Board, now referred to as the NATIONAL FOREIGN INTELLIGENCE BOARD, the top interdepartmental panel of the INTELLIGENCE COMMUNITY. The director also heads the Defense Attache System, which supervises military attaches serving abroad at U.S. embassies.

DEFENSE REORGANIZATION ACT OF 1958 Legislation that reorganized the DEPARTMENT OF DEFENSE (DOD) and JOINT CHIEFS OF STAFF (JCS). Organizational shortcomings in the U.S. defense establishment revealed by the KOREAN WAR had elicited implementation of REORGANIZATION PLAN NO. 6 (1953), which continued the post–WORLD WAR II trend toward greater unification of the nation's armed forces under a centralized Defense Department. Rapid advances in military technology in following years, particularly long-range ballistic missiles, sparked continuing debate over how to make DOD's organization more responsive to the demands of modern warfare. In 1957 the secret report of the GAITHER COMMITTEE for the NATIONAL SECURITY COUNCIL concluded that U.S. strategic air forces, at the time the backbone of the nation's nuclear deterrent, were vulnerable to Soviet missile attack. American alarm over the Soviet Union's military capabilities was heightened by the launch of the Soviet satellite Sputnik in October 1957.

Influential studies early in 1958 by the Rockefeller Brothers Fund and the SENATE ARMED SERVICES COMMITTEE recommended reorganization of the Defense Department to improve decision making, speed the development of new weapons systems, and curtail waste and inefficiency resulting from rivalries among the Army, Navy, and Air Force. President DWIGHT D. EISENHOWER in his January 1958 State of the Union address identified defense reorganization as a top priority and that April forwarded to Congress a draft bill. In an accompanying message, Eisenhower stressed the need to integrate the nation's air, land, and sea forces into unified combat commands. His proposed legislation formed the basis of the Defense Reorganization Act of 1958, which he signed into law on August 6, 1958.

The 1958 law authorized the president to establish unified military commands composed of Army, Navy, and Air Force elements under a single headquarters. The control of forces in the unified commands was removed from the respective military services and placed directly under the secretary of defense, who also gained greater authority over defense procurement and the development of new weapons systems. While maintaining clear civilian control over the defense establishment, the act gave the JCS, the nation's ranking military officers, responsibility for helping to direct the unified commands. The 1958 legislation set the basic structure of DOD for almost three decades. The next major realignment of the Defense Department was the 1986 GOLDWATER-NICHOLS DEFENSE REORGANIZATION ACT.

DELAWARE INDIAN TREATY (1778) The first treaty between the United States and an Indian tribe, this historic agreement secured peace and friendship between the American colonies and the Delawares during the AMERICAN REVOLUTION. The treaty, concluded on September 17, 1778, fulfilled the key aims of federal Indian policy spelled out by the Continental Congress:

preserve friendly relations with tribes on the edges of colonial settlement and ensure Indian neutrality in the conflict with Great Britain.

Negotiation of the agreement followed a break in relations between the United States and the Iroquois Confederacy, which had sided with the British and was staging raids on colonial settlements in New York and Pennsylvania. In June 1778, Congress sent negotiators to seek a pact with the Delawares in the Ohio region. Already militarily stretched, the United States wanted peace on its western frontier, particularly since Great Britain held a strong military position along the Great Lakes. To allay Delaware fears of white encroachment on their lands, the American negotiators guaranteed the territorial rights of the tribe. Peace ended in 1782, when the Delawares joined with other hostile Ohio Indians to combat the continuing advance of white settlement in the area. The Indian resistance prefigured the warfare of the early 1790s between the United States and the Ohio tribes that concluded with the U.S. victory at the BATTLE OF FALLEN TIMBERS (1794).

See also MAP 1.

DEPARTMENT OF... See ..., DEPARTMENT OF.

DESTROYERS-FOR-BASES AGREEMENT (1940) Exchange of U.S. overage destroyers for British military bases in the Western Hemisphere. In May 1940 British wartime Prime Minister Winston Churchill asked Washington for a loan of 40 to 50 older U.S. destroyers to help the British navy defend itself against German submarine warfare. Because the United States was then officially neutral in WORLD WAR II, the request posed a dilemma for the Roosevelt administration. President FRANKLIN D. ROOSEVELT favored providing all aid possible to Great Britain short of war, but isolationist sentiment in America opposed any action that risked drawing the United States into the overseas conflict. To overcome potential domestic opposition to an arms transfer, Roosevelt fastened on the idea of a barter agreement whereby the United States would provide the destroyers in return for certain British military bases. On September 3, 1940, the two nations announced a destroyers-for-bases swap. Under the agreement, the United States transferred to Great Britain 50 overage destroyers. In exchange, the U.S. government acquired the right to 99-year leases on British naval and air bases in Newfoundland, Bermuda, the Bahamas, Jamaica, St. Lucia, Trinidad, Antigua, and British Guiana. The deal, Roosevelt observed, gave America control over important military facilities and improved U.S. defenses. It also served its basic purpose of furnishing much needed naval assets to Great Britain and signaled the deepening defense ties between the two nations.

DETENTE Name given to a period of improved U.S.-Soviet relations in the 1970s. Adopted from French diplomacy, the term refers generally to a relaxation of international tensions. On taking office in 1969, President RICHARD M. NIXON began to shift America's COLD WAR foreign policy away from its ideological orientation and toward a more pragmatic accommodation with the Communist world. While staunchly anti-Communist, Nixon subscribed to a realistic, power politics approach to foreign affairs. By the late 1960s the Soviet Union had achieved a rough parity in NUCLEAR WEAPONS with the United States. Nixon recognized that the dangerous nuclear stalemate that had developed was driving both superpowers toward negotiation rather than confrontation. The new president's most pressing concern was the VIETNAM WAR. Nixon believed Moscow and Peking, both of which supported U.S. adversary North Vietnam, held the key to resolving the protracted conflict in Southeast Asia. He saw in the rift between the Soviet Union and Communist China an opportunity for improved U.S. relations with both Communist powers. The United States had refused to recognize the government of Communist China since it came to power in 1949. Nixon conceived of a U.S. overture to Peking as both an inevitable acknowledgment of Communist China's existence and an incentive to Moscow to seek closer ties with Washington.

With national security adviser and key foreign policy aide HENRY A. KISSINGER, he undertook to establish U.S.-Communist Chinese contacts and pursue a policy of detente with the Soviet Union. The two Communist powers proved receptive to the U.S. initiatives. Communist China foresaw the end of its isolation from the West while the Soviet Union hoped to invigorate its troubled economy through greatly expanded East-West trade. In 1971 the Nixon administration announced an initial diplomatic opening between Peking and Washington and an unprecedented major American grain sale to the USSR. Nixon's meetings the following year with the Communist Chinese leadership at the PEKING SUMMIT and Soviet General Secretary Leonid I. Brezhnev at the MOSCOW SUMMIT underscored the thaw in Cold War tensions.

At Moscow, Nixon and Brezhnev signed the SALT I arms control agreement, a major trade pact, and measures for scientific and technical cooperation and cultural exchange. The Moscow parley ushered in an almost decade-long period of U.S.-Soviet detente and corresponding overall improvement in East-West relations. As developed by Nixon and Kissinger, detente involved constructing an interlocking set of agreements and understandings that took into account each side's vital national interests, reduced superpower tensions, and encouraged cooperation rather than competition. It was characterized by summit diplomacy, arms control negotiations, and closer economic, social, and cultural ties. Following Nixon's resignation in August 1974 over the Watergate scandal, President GERALD R. FORD continued his predecessor's detente policies. At the November 1974 VLADIVOSTOK SUMMIT, Ford and Brezhnev reaffirmed their commitment to deepening Soviet-American ties. U.S.-Soviet detente peaked in 1975 with the signing of the 35-nation HELSINKI ACCORDS on East-West relations.

Detente did not equal the end of the Cold War. U.S.-Soviet confrontation occurred during the 1973 Arab-Israeli YOM KIPPUR WAR, when Washington placed American forces on worldwide alert to dissuade Moscow from intervening on behalf of Egypt. The Soviet Union backed the 1973 PARIS PEACE ACCORDS ending U.S. involvement in Vietnam but continued to provide massive amounts of military aid to Communist North Vietnam, making possible the North's final victory over South Vietnam in 1975. The same year the Ford administration condemned Soviet assistance to the leftist faction in the ANGOLAN CIVIL WAR, which the Kremlin defended as support for an anticolonial national liberation struggle. Detente came under mounting U.S. domestic political criticism from conservatives who charged that the USSR had not modified its underlying expansionist behavior. These critics contended that America had lowered its guard while Moscow pursued a vigorous defense buildup. Under attack from rival candidate RONALD W. REAGAN and the conservative wing of his own party, Ford was compelled to drop use of the word "detente" during the campaign for the 1976 Republican presidential nomination. President JIMMY CARTER initially embraced the policy of continued U.S.-Soviet accommodation, meeting with Brezhnev at the VIENNA SUMMIT (1979), where the two concluded the SALT II arms control measure. The era of detente was abruptly halted by the Soviet invasion of Afghanistan in December 1979. To protest the Soviet aggression, Carter shelved the SALT II agreement and ordered the U.S. OLYMPIC BOYCOTT of the games scheduled for Moscow in 1980. By the early 1980s, the two superpowers had returned to Cold War confrontation.

DETERRENCE National security term referring to the discouragement of a possible enemy attack. Nations are said to achieve deterrence through possession of military strength sufficient to dissuade a would-be aggressor from starting hostilities. Such a potential aggressor is deterred from initiating conflict by a recognition that certain military retaliation would thwart its aims and defeat its interests. Deterrence of Communist aggression was at the heart of U.S. national security policy from the inception of the COLD WAR in the late 1940s. American thinking on the value of amassed military force to deter aggression had been profoundly influenced by the failure of the Western nations to stand up to German dictator Adolf Hitler in the late 1930s, which was interpreted as having led inevitably to WORLD WAR II. As the Soviet Union tightened its grip on Eastern Europe in the immediate postwar years, the Truman administration committed U.S. military power to the CONTAINMENT of further Soviet or other Communist expansionism.

The revelation in 1949 that the Soviet Union possessed atomic weapons and the emergence the same year of a Communist regime in China posed new tests for American deterrence of Communist aggression. Successive administrations sought to maintain a mix of nuclear and conventional military forces necessary to persuade the Soviet Union to avoid either nuclear war or a more limited conflict. Based on then overwhelming U.S. nuclear superiority, the Eisenhower administration's NEW LOOK defense strategy relied on a general threat of MASSIVE RETALIATION with nuclear weapons to block possible Communist advances. Continuing improvements in Soviet nuclear capabilities narrowed the U.S. advantage and thereby undermined America's unilateral nuclear deterrent. President JOHN F. KENNEDY adopted a FLEXIBLE RESPONSE strategy that called for the United States to counter the full range of potential Soviet military moves, from low-intensity conventional conflict to a full-scale nuclear war, with comparable forces. The Kennedy administration also emphasized the importance of conventional forces to the deterrence of Communist insurgencies and guerrilla campaigns around the world. The two instances when deterrence failed and America resorted to force were both limited conflicts in Asia: the KOREAN WAR and the VIETNAM WAR.

In the early 1970s President RICHARD M. NIXON began a process of DETENTE, or relaxation of tensions, with both the Soviet Union and Communist China. The goal was to eliminate the need for deterrence through improved East-West relations and the amelioration of Communist conduct. A series of U.S.-Soviet arms control agreements in the 1970s built on the shared recognition that each side's nuclear deterrent rested on the concept of MUTUAL ASSURED DESTRUCTION—the strategic reality that neither side would risk starting a nuclear war because it would result in its own destruction as well as that of its adversary.

The Soviet invasion of Afghanistan in 1979 derailed detente, but Mikhail S. Gorbachev's emergence as Soviet leader in 1985 led to a superpower thaw and dramatic improvement in U.S.-Soviet relations. With the virtual end of the Cold War by 1990, U.S. policymakers began to examine the question of what kinds of American forces would be needed in the future to deter which possible threats. These deliberations were interrupted by Iraq's

August 1990 invasion of Kuwait and subsequent U.S. involvement in the 1991 PERSIAN GULF WAR.

DEVELOPMENT LOAN FUND See **MUTUAL SECURITY ACT**.

DIEM COUP (1963) Overthrow of President Ngo Dinh Diem by South Vietnamese military officers with tacit U.S. approval. Following the partition of Vietnam by the 1954 GENEVA CONFERENCE, Diem served as prime minister in the French-installed Bao Dai regime in the South. He became president of the newly proclaimed Republic of Vietnam in 1955. The United States supported the Diem government with military and economic assistance. As South Vietnam came under mounting pressure in the early 1960s from a North Vietnamese-sponsored Communist insurgency, the Kennedy administration sent growing numbers of military advisers to the embattled nation.

Senior American officials believed that Diem's increasingly corrupt and authoritarian rule was undermining the South's struggle against the Viet Cong guerrillas. Many of his family members held key national or provincial positions. Of particular concern was the brutal conduct of his brother, Ngo Dinh Nhu, who headed the secret police. Diem resisted U.S. entreaties for reform. The political situation in South Vietnam worsened as Diem, a Roman Catholic, dealt violently with rising Buddhist opposition to his regime. In May 1963 police in Hue fired into a Buddhist protest against government persecution, killing or wounding more than 20 people. U.S. protests against repression of the Buddhists went unheeded and in late August Diem's security forces conducted bloody anti-Buddhist attacks throughout the country.

New U.S. Ambassador to Vietnam HENRY CABOT LODGE, JR. arrived in Saigon in the midst of the crisis. At the end of August 1963 he received a cable from State Department officials W. AVERELL HARRIMAN and ROGER HILSMAN instructing him to inform Diem that he risked losing U.S. backing unless he undertook immediate changes, including Nhu's removal. Lodge also was instructed to let the South Vietnamese military know that America would support a new government. The exact sequence of events that followed remains unclear. Diem

continued to disregard U.S. pressure for reform. Amid a flurry of varying messages from Washington regarding the proper extent of U.S. involvement in efforts to unseat Diem, Lodge informed South Vietnamese generals that the United States would not oppose a military coup. On November 1, 1963, Diem was overthrown by a group of senior South Vietnamese officers. He and Nhu were captured and shot the next day. Saigon subsequently underwent a series of military coups before the emergence of the Thieu government in 1965. While the Kennedy administration was not directly implicated in the Diem coup, tacit U.S. approval of his overthrow presaged the deepening American stake in the VIETNAM WAR.

DIES COMMITTEE See **HOUSE UN-AMERICAN ACTIVITIES COMMITTEE**.

DILLINGHAM COMMISSION Commonly referred to by the name of its chairman, Senator William P. Dillingham (R-VT), the Immigration Commission was established by Congress in 1907 to study U.S. immigration policy. The nine-member panel included three presidential appointees, three senators, and three members of the House of Representatives. It was formed amid mounting domestic concerns over the shift from northern to southern and eastern Europe as the major source of immigration to the United States. Groups such as the IMMIGRATION RESTRICTION LEAGUE worried that the nation's cultural and political institutions would be undermined by unassimilable aliens.

The Dillingham Commission issued its influential 41-volume report in 1911. Reflecting racial theories of the time, the report concluded that the "new" immigrants from southern and eastern Europe were inferior to the "old" immigrants from northern and western Europe. (Later critics pointed out that the report's evidence actually contradicted this conclusion.) The panel recommended that the numbers of new immigrants be limited through the use of a literacy test. Members also advocated a decrease in immigration as necessary to protect the U.S economy.

Senator Dillingham and another panel member, Senator HENRY CABOT LODGE, SR. (R-MA), played prominent roles in the subsequent passage of restrictive immigration measures. The commission's findings served as the basis for the IMMIGRATION ACT OF 1917, which introduced a literacy test for prospective immigrants, and the IMMIGRATION ACT OF 1921, which imposed ethnic quotas on U.S. immigration.

DILLON ROUND See **GENERAL AGREEMENT ON TARIFFS AND TRADE**.

DINGLEY TARIFF (1897) Act that set the highest tariffs up until that time in U.S. history. WILLIAM MCKINLEY, who as a member of Congress had sponsored the 1890 MCKINLEY TARIFF, campaigned for the presidency in 1896 on a Republican platform in favor of protective import duties and critical of the lower rates of the 1894 WILSON-GORMAN TARIFF. Following McKinley's victory, Representative Nelson W. Dingley (R-ME) introduced a tariff bill which, when enacted July 7, 1897, raised import duties to a record average level of 57 percent. The Dingley Tariff represented the height of the country's 19th century trade PROTECTIONISM. America's protectionist policy later entered a period of relative moderation with passage of the PAYNE-ALDRICH TARIFF (1909).

DIPLOMATIC SECURITY AND ANTITERRORISM ACT See **INMAN REPORT**.

DIRECTIVE ON DISPLACED PERSONS (1945) Executive action taken December 22, 1945, by President HARRY S. TRUMAN as an emergency response to the problem of displaced persons in war-torn Europe. The end of WORLD WAR II found millions of refugees in Germany and Austria. Many had been imprisoned in forced labor camps by the Nazis or had fled westward before the advancing Soviet army. Most eventually returned to their homelands, but many displaced persons from Eastern Europe refused repatriation for fear of political or religious persecution. Also housed in Allied refugee camps were thousands of Jewish survivors of the Holocaust. Truman directed that up to one-half of existing European immigration quotas be allocated to displaced persons. The order made available 40,000 visas a year, but efforts to bring refugees to America were hindered by the nation's restrictive immigration statutes. In his 1947 State of the Union address to Congress, Truman called for new legislation to assist in the resettlement of refugees. The

DISPLACED PERSONS ACT became law in June 1948. At the time, approximately 40,000 people had entered under the Truman directive.

DISENGAGEMENT Policy under discussion in the West in the late 1950s that called for the withdrawal of military forces from Central Europe and the neutralization of Germany. The idea had developed out of Soviet attempts earlier in the decade to forestall West German membership in NATO. Proposals by the Soviet Union for unification of its Communist satellite East Germany with democratic West Germany in a single neutral state were rejected by the West as a ploy to weaken NATO. West Germany joined the Western security alliance in 1955.

American diplomat and historian GEORGE F. KENNAN explored the concept of a demilitarized Central Europe in a series of lectures aired by the British Broadcasting Corporation in 1957 and published the next year as *Russia, the Atom and the West*. Kennan acknowledged that the removal of Soviet occupation forces from Eastern Europe was a basic goal of Western diplomacy, but noted that the Soviet Union had legitimate security concerns in Central Europe. He gave rise to the term *disengagement* when he advocated that NATO disengage from West Germany and accept its neutralization in return for a similar withdrawal of Soviet forces behind the USSR's borders. One of the principal architects in the late 1940s of the West's CONTAINMENT strategy, Kennan argued that, once withdrawn, Soviet armies were unlikely to return to Eastern Europe. At worst, he contended, the West's nuclear deterrent could ensure they remain in the USSR.

The proposed policy generated considerable interest among Western European liberals but otherwise met with general opposition. Former Secretary of State DEAN ACHESON provided an influential rebuttal in the journal *Foreign Affairs* in the spring of 1958. He pointed out that the creation of a neutral Germany eventually would lead to the withdrawal of all U.S. forces, the cornerstone of Western security, from Europe. American disengagement would leave a dangerous power vacuum in Central Europe which the Soviet Union could quickly fill. Even if they pulled their armies back,

Acheson reasoned, the Soviets would return to Eastern Europe rather than tolerate the demise of the Communist regimes there. Acheson's conclusion that the existing Western containment strategy, with its reliance on military force to block further Soviet advances, remained the best way to ensure European security and bring eventual change in the USSR was generally embraced among NATO allies. Discussion of disengagement had faded by 1959.

DISPLACED PERSONS ACT (1948) First major U.S. refugee legislation. WORLD WAR II and its aftermath left millions of people displaced in central Europe. Refugee camps operated by the Western allies in occupied Germany struggled to house the survivors of Nazi slave labor programs and concentration camps as well as growing numbers of Eastern Europeans fleeing the imposition of Communist regimes in their homelands. Adding to the burden were millions of ethnic Germans expelled from Eastern Europe by the Soviet Union under agreements reached at the POTSDAM CONFERENCE (1945).

The first formal American initiative to redress the refugee problem was the DIRECTIVE ON DISPLACED PERSONS issued by President HARRY S. TRUMAN in December 1945. The directive reallocated up to 40,000 immigration quotas per year to refugees. Resettlement was the only answer for the many displaced persons who faced political, racial, or religious persecution if they were repatriated. As the magnitude of the refugee situation became clear, the Truman administration called on Congress to allow greater numbers of the displaced to come to the United States. Lending assistance to the refugees was said to be consistent with the nation's humanitarian ideals. The administration also contended that America had a responsibility as a world leader to be at the forefront of efforts to resolve a crisis threatening to undermine European recovery.

President Truman signed the nation's first significant refugee measure on June 25, 1948. While accepting the bill's basic outline, Truman identified terms that effectively discriminated against Jewish and Catholic refugees and called for their quick revision. The Displaced Persons Act authorized the admission of 220,000 refugees over the next two years, giving priority to persons from territories annexed by the Soviet Union and agricultural workers. The law created no new immigration quotas; instead, refugee admissions were applied against a nation's future allocations.

As COLD WAR tensions mounted in the postwar period, refugee issues became an increasingly important element of America's anti-Communist foreign policy. Broad support for admitting "escapees" from Eastern Europe, who were pictured as living evidence of the bankruptcy of the Soviet system, led to extension of the Displaced Persons Act in June 1950. The ceiling for refugee admission was raised to 415,000, preferences were ended, and discriminatory restrictions on Jews and Catholics were eliminated. The amended legislation was followed in 1953 by the REFUGEE RELIEF ACT.

DOLLAR DIPLOMACY Policy during the Taft administration (1909–1913) aimed at enlarging U.S. diplomatic influence and advancing U.S. strategic objectives in Latin America and the Far East through the promotion of American commercial expansion. Devised by President WILLIAM HOWARD TAFT in collaboration with his secretary of state, PHILANDER C. KNOX, Dollar Diplomacy was based on two mutually reinforcing tenets: American foreign policy would mobilize to encourage and protect expanded American overseas trade and investment; and this very expansion would enhance U.S. power and influence and, presumably, act as a brake on rival European expansion. The focus of Dollar Diplomacy in the Far East was China, where the Taft administration wanted to boost American investment, strengthen the OPEN DOOR policy of equal foreign commercial access, and check widening Japanese and Russian influence in Manchuria. An American banking group was organized at Knox's urging to finance railroad concessions in China. Taft's personal interjections led European bankers to invite their American counterparts to take part in the CONSORTIUM LOAN TO CHINA for railroad construction. The consortium later fell apart and the administration's approach proved unsuccessful in the Far East.

Chronic political turmoil in the Caribbean region formed the underlying context for Dollar Diplomacy in Latin America. Taft and Knox surmised that such political unrest was a consequence of chronic fiscal instability compounded by heavy Latin American indebtedness to private European creditors. The administration feared that political disorder in countries such as the Dominican Republic, Haiti, Honduras, and Nicaragua imperiled U.S. interests in the region by raising the likelihood of European military intervention. Taft and Knox decided that financial rehabilitation achieved through the mobilization of American capital was the key to attaining stable governments in the Caribbean and Central America. They developed a general blueprint for fiscal reform in which troubled Caribbean republics would satisfy their obligations to European creditors with loans obtained from American banks. The U.S. government would guarantee the loans by establishing U.S.-administered customs collectorships in the borrowing countries, with a percentage of customs revenues specifically allocated for repayment of the American lenders.

Taft and Knox portrayed fiscal intercession as the constructive alternative to U.S. military intervention. The president characterized his administration's policy as "substituting dollars for bullets." He and Knox believed that the United States and Caribbean nations alike would benefit. America would gain increased trade and greater confidence for the security of the soon-to-be completed PANAMA CANAL; and the Latin Americans would reap peace, prosperity, and better social conditions. Dollar Diplomacy, however, did not amount to a renunciation of the use of American military power. The Taft administration asserted its readiness to intercede militarily in Latin America whenever necessary to restore stability or prevent foreign intervention. Dollar Diplomacy brought the establishment of U.S. financial protectorates in the Caribbean region and added to the legacy of American interventionism in Latin America from the SPANISH-AMERICAN WAR (1898) to the advent of the GOOD NEIGHBOR POLICY in the 1930s. The Taft policy led to charges of Yankee economic IMPERIALISM and engendered ill will and resentment in Latin America toward the "colossus of the North." Taft's successor, WOODROW WILSON, adopting a more idealistic stance in his foreign policy, publicly disassociated America from Dollar Diplomacy. In practice, however, the Wilson administration continued U.S. financial and military intercession in Latin America.

DOMINICAN CRISIS (1965–1966) Violent political upheaval in the Dominican Republic that brought U.S. military intervention to prevent the possible emergence of a Communist government. Dominican strongman Rafael Trujillo, who had ruled the Caribbean nation since 1930, was assassinated by local dissidents in May 1961. In ensuing months the Kennedy administration, which strongly supported the development of democratic institutions in the country, deployed U.S. naval forces off the Dominican coast to help block an attempt by the Trujillo family to return to power. Following a period of political flux, liberal Juan Bosch was elected president in December 1962 and inaugurated a month later. Amid continuing political unrest, he was deposed in September 1963 by a bloodless military coup, whose leaders installed a civilian junta headed by Donald Reid Cabral. On April 24, 1965, Bosch supporters, junior military officers, and other opponents of the government joined to mount a revolt against the Reid Cabral regime. Fighting between the rebel and loyalist forces quickly escalated into civil war.

The Johnson administration worried that the rebellion might result in the establishment of another Communist state, or "second Cuba," in Latin America. On April 28 President LYNDON B. JOHNSON sent 500 U.S. marines into Santo Domingo for the stated purpose of protecting Americans and other foreign nationals caught in the increasingly chaotic capital. With reports from the U.S. embassy in Santo Domingo indicating the presence of Communist elements in the revolt, Johnson ordered thousands of additional American troops to the island in what was the first U.S. armed intervention in Latin America in three decades. In a televised address on May 2, Johnson explained the deployment of U.S. forces as necessary to counter a Communist takeover of the Dominican Republic. In justifying the U.S. action, the president enunciated what became known as the JOHNSON DOCTRINE, making it U.S. policy not to permit the establishment of another Communist regime in the Western Hemisphere.

The U.S. presence reached a peak of nearly 24,000 troops on May 17. The American ground forces were able to separate the warring Dominican factions and effect a cease-fire in the capital. Eager to place its intervention within an inter-American framework, the Johnson administration sought to refer the Dominican crisis to the ORGANIZATION OF AMERICAN STATES (OAS). On May 6 a meeting of OAS ministers authorized an Inter-American Peace Force (IAPF) for the Dominican Republic. The IAPF, composed of troops from the United States and five Latin American nations, was deployed May 23, whereupon other U.S. forces were withdrawn. The OAS supervised the gradual restoration of order on the island and a provisional government was set up in September 1965. In national elections held in June 1966, conservative Joaquin Balaguer defeated Bosch for the presidency. The last U.S. units left the island with the departure of the IAPF in September 1966. U.S. casualties for the entire operation were 47 dead and 172 wounded.

The U.S. intervention met widespread criticism in Latin America as a violation of OAS agreements prohibiting the unilateral use of force. In a September 1965 speech to the U.S. Senate, J. WILLIAM FULBRIGHT (D-AR) voiced the major complaints of domestic opponents to the military action, charging the Johnson administration with an arrogant use of American power to interfere in the affairs of another nation. He contended the threat of a Communist takeover in the Dominican Republic had been greatly exaggerated and suggested the administration had been less than candid with the American public.

DOMINICAN INTERVENTIONS Military and political intervention of the United States in the Dominican Republic during the first half of the 20th century. The Caribbean nation at the outset of the 1900s was heavily burdened by debts to private foreign creditors. Repayment of the foreign lenders, the majority of whom were Europeans, was with income derived from the nation's customs houses. Torn by continuing civil strife, the republic by 1904 was nearly bankrupt and under increasing pressure from foreign governments to meet its financial obligations. After prodding from Washington, the Dominican government

arranged to pay its debt to a major American firm in monthly installments secured by customs revenue. When Santo Domingo failed to meet the first payment, the American concern, with Dominican consent, took control of the customs house at Puerto Plata in October 1904. The European nations protested the preferential treatment afforded the American firm and appeared ready to intervene militarily, as they had in the VENEZUELA CLAIMS controversy (1902–1903), to collect the debts owed their own nationals.

President THEODORE ROOSEVELT resolved to commit the United States to a policy of intercession in Latin America as necessary to preclude European armed intervention. He openly acknowledged the right of European creditors to seek protection from their governments for their investments abroad. But, in view of America's historic claim under the MONROE DOCTRINE to sovereign influence in its own backyard, he rejected the idea that chronic fiscal or political disorder in the Caribbean justified European armed intercession. The president reconciled these positions in his annual message to Congress in December 1904 when he announced the ROOSEVELT COROLLARY to the Monroe Doctrine. The corollary declared that the United States, to forestall European use of force in Latin America to collect debts, would assume responsibility for exercising an "international police power" in the Western Hemisphere; thus America, Roosevelt asserted, would intervene in delinquent, chronically unstable Latin American states to ensure that they fulfilled their international financial obligations.

Within weeks the debt-ridden Dominican Republic, fearing a possible German or British intercession, invited the United States to take charge of its customs collection. Under the banner of the Roosevelt Corollary, Washington and Santo Domingo in early 1905 concluded an agreement providing for U.S. collection and administration of Dominican customs duties and management of the nation's foreign debt payments. The accord authorized the United States to apply 45 percent of revenues to the Dominican national budget and 55 percent to foreign creditors. Opposition in the U.S. Senate to establishment of an American protectorate over the Dominican Republic blocked ratification of the protocol. Thereupon the Roosevelt administration bypassed the Senate by completing an EXECUTIVE AGREEMENT with the Dominicans in April 1905 that incorporated the terms of the protocol, placing the Caribbean nation under limited American control. U.S. custodianship brought financial stability to the Dominican Republic. The Senate finally endorsed Roosevelt's policy when, in February 1907, it approved a permanent treaty with Santo Domingo that authorized continuation of the American customs collectorship for 50 years.

The American financial protectorate temporarily relieved Dominican political unrest. But a renewal of revolution within five years threatened the U.S.-supervised customs scheme. In September 1912 insurrectionists seized several customs houses. Political conditions became so unruly by the summer of 1914 that President WOODROW WILSON interceded. In August he sent a diplomatic team headed by former New Jersey Governor John Franklin Fort to the Dominican Republic to seek an end to the civil turmoil. The U.S. delegation, on the first leg of the FORT MISSIONS, presented the so-called WILSON PLAN for restoring peace and establishing constitutional government, by force if necessary. Under threat of U.S. military intervention, Dominican factional leaders agreed to an immediate cease-fire. The United States oversaw prompt establishment of a provisional government and supervised elections in October 1914 in which Juan Isidro Jimenez won the Dominican presidency.

Jimenez came to be regarded as a U.S. puppet and before long faced a resurgent political opposition. In 1915 the Wilson administration resorted to GUNBOAT DIPLOMACY when it sent U.S. Navy forces to Dominican waters to thwart an anti-Jimenez uprising. By early the next year, though, revolution appeared imminent. In April 1916 Minister of War Desiderio Arias launched an attempt to overthrow Jimenez. In early May Wilson landed U.S. marines at several Dominican ports to surpress the rebellion. Bloodshed involving American forces was averted when Arias surrendered. Jimenez resigned and the Dominican Congress elected Dr. Francisco Henriquez Carvajal as provisional president. The United States then insisted on a new treaty granting it total control of

the Caribbean republic's finances and constabulary forces. Carvajal refused these conditions, contending they violated Dominican sovereignty.

On November 22, 1916, Secretary of State ROBERT LANSING recommended full American military occupation of the Dominican Republic as the only solution to establishing political and economic order. Wilson concurred and on November 29 declared martial law, whereupon the United States took complete control of the country and established a military government under the administration of the Navy Department. Captain Harry S. Knapp, in command of the American occupation forces, suspended the Dominican Congress and assumed broad powers. All revenues from the U.S. customs receivership henceforth were turned over to the American military governor, who exercised the major government functions. The Dominican occupation came just a year after the United States had taken control of Haiti and thus brought the entire island of Hispaniola under U.S. authority.

U.S. occupation on the whole brought stability to the country. Under the American military administration, sanitation was improved, roads and schools were built, and public finances were placed on a sounder basis. But Washington's resort to armed force and the strictness of U.S. military rule fostered a deep resentment among Dominicans toward the United States. Soon after WARREN G. HARDING became president in March 1921, his secretary of state, CHARLES EVANS HUGHES, began working on a plan to withdraw American marines from the Dominican Republic and end the military government. Hughes was sensitive to increasingly hostile criticism throughout Latin America regarding U.S. interventionism in the Caribbean and Central America. An agreement on withdrawal and restoration of Dominican independence was completed in June 1922 by American special envoy SUMNER WELLES and Dominican political leaders. Following U.S.-supervised elections, Horacio Vasquez was inaugurated in July 1924 as president under a newly adopted Dominican constitution. In September the U.S. forces were withdrawn from the country, marking the end of the occupation. The United States still exercised substantial control over Dominican finances through its customs collectorship, which continued in effect until 1940.

See also DOMINICAN CRISIS, DOMINICAN REPUBLIC ANNEXATION INITIATIVE.

DOMINICAN REPUBLIC ANNEXATION INITIATIVE Unsuccessful attempt by the Grant administration to annex the Dominican Republic, the eastern half of the Caribbean island of Hispaniola, to the United States. Early in his first term Republican President ULYSSES S. GRANT fixed his sights on acquiring the former Spanish colony, which he coveted as an American commercial foothold in the Caribbean and prime location for a U.S. naval base. In July 1869 he sent his private secretary, Colonel Orville E. Babcock, to the island to lay the diplomatic groundwork for annexation. The Dominican government, plagued by chronic financial troubles, was receptive to Grant's overture. Babcock signed an informal agreement in September committing the United States to annex the Dominican Republic and cover its national debt; however, should annexation fall through, America pledged to buy Samana Bay as a naval station site.

The Babcock agreement became the basis for two treaties submitted by Grant in January 1870 to the U.S. Senate for approval. The first provided for annexation of the island republic as a territory with the promise of ultimate statehood. The second, presented as a minimum alternative, gave the United States a 99-year lease on Samana Bay with the right of purchase at any time for $2 million. In the Senate, annexation encountered stiff antiexpansionist opposition spearheaded by Republican Charles Sumner of Massachusetts, chairman of the SENATE FOREIGN RELATIONS COMMITTEE. After long debate, and despite intensive lobbying by Grant, the Senate rejected the annexation treaty on June 30, 1870. The second treaty faced likely defeat and was not put to a vote. Sumner's dissent stung and embittered Grant who, as political retribution, used his influence to help strip Sumner of the chairmanship in March 1871.

DOMINO THEORY Geopolitical concept in currency in American foreign policy during the COLD WAR. It maintained that if one nation were to fall to communism, then surrounding countries would become susceptible to Communist expansionism and eventually would be toppled—as with a stack of dominoes—one after another. The theory first was spelled out by President DWIGHT D. EISENHOWER in April 1954. At a press conference on Indochina, Eisenhower referred to the "'falling domino' principle" to explain how the abandonment of Southeast Asia to the Communists ultimately would imperil all of the Far East. The Kennedy and Johnson administrations cited the domino theory and the threat posed by Soviet- and Communist Chinese-sponsored aggression in justifying the deepening U.S. military involvement in the VIETNAM WAR. What relevance the theory actually bore to the situation in Southeast Asia remains a matter of divided opinion. Detractors maintain that the Vietnam conflict essentially was a civil war over reunification of the country and not a case of Communist expansionism. Proponents note that neighboring "dominoes" Laos and Cambodia succumbed to Communist overthrow in 1975 along with South Vietnam. In the 1980s the Reagan administration invoked the domino theory in arguing for the need to furnish U.S. assistance to counter Communist inroads in Central America.

DONOVAN, WILLIAM JOSEPH (1883–1959) Army and intelligence officer; head of the OFFICE OF STRATEGIC SERVICES. After graduating from Columbia University in 1905 and Columbia Law School in 1907, William "Wild Bill" Donovan returned to practice law in his native Buffalo, New York. He organized a cavalry troop in the New York National Guard that served along the Mexican border during the PUNITIVE EXPEDITION (1916) against Mexican revolutionary Francisco "Pancho" Villa. In WORLD WAR I he saw extensive action with the Army in France. Wounded three times, he was awarded the Congressional Medal of Honor and attained the rank of colonel.

After the war, Donovan served as a U.S. attorney, became active in Republican politics in New York, and ran unsuccessfully for lieutenant governor in 1922 and governor in 1932. In 1929 he formed a prestigious Wall Street law firm. He also began an involvement in intelligence work that eventually would earn him the appellation "the father of American intelligence." In 1919 he undertook a confidential mission to Siberia for the State Department to evaluate the anti-Bolshevik movement of Admiral Alexander Kolchak and report on the Allied SIBERIAN INTERVENTION. Gaining a firsthand knowledge of Europe through frequent business travels, he went on an unofficial trip for the War Department in 1935 to observe Italy's military campaign against Ethiopia. Over the next few years he made similar excursions to gather intelligence on the Spanish Civil War (1936–1939) and military developments in the Balkans and eastern Europe.

Following the outbreak of WORLD WAR II in Europe, President FRANKLIN D. ROOSEVELT sent Donovan overseas in 1940 to assess Great Britain's desperate fight against Nazi Germany. Donovan returned believing Britain could prevail with U.S. aid and advocated American assistance. Impressed by British intelligence operations, he proposed to Roosevelt in 1941 the formation of a similar centralized agency to direct U.S. foreign intelligence. In July 1941, five months before America's entrance into World War II, Roosevelt established the position of coordinator of information and named Donovan to the post. While the president's directive stopped short of creating an intelligence service, Donovan in practice quickly built the OFFICE OF THE CO-ORDINATOR OF INFORMATION into his proposed intelligence agency.

In June 1942 Donovan's intelligence staff was established formally as the Office of Strategic Services (OSS). Donovan headed the OSS, which was responsible for clandestine and paramilitary operations as well as intelligence activities, throughout World War II. He urged that the intelligence service be retained after the war, but the OSS was disbanded in September 1945. His recommendation for a permanent foreign intelligence agency prevailed with the formation of the CENTRAL INTELLIGENCE AGENCY in 1947. Donovan retired from active duty following the war with the rank of major general and renewed his law practice. He served briefly as U.S. ambassador to Thailand in 1953 and 1954.

DOOLITTLE COMMITTEE (1954) Special panel appointed by President DWIGHT D. EISENHOWER to examine the covert activities of the CENTRAL INTELLIGENCE AGENCY. The four-man board was headed by retired Air Force General James H. Doolittle. Other members were William B. Franke, former assistant secretary of the Navy; New York lawyer Morris Hadley; and William D. Pawley, former ambassador to Brazil. The committee submitted its report with a classified set of recommendations in October 1954. In an often-cited passage reflecting the COLD WAR mood of the time, the Doolittle Report noted the threat posed by the nation's Communist adversaries and endorsed the use of COVERT ACTION. It concluded the United States "must develop effective espionage and counterespionage services and must learn to subvert, sabotage and destroy our enemies by more clever, more sophisticated and more effective methods than those used against us."

DRIFTNET IMPACT MONITORING, ASSESSMENT, AND CONTROL ACT (1987) U.S. law concerned with the threat to marine life posed by driftnet fishing. Driftnets, used in commercial fishing, are panels of fine plastic or nylon webbing strung together, placed in the water, and allowed to drift. In the 1980s Japanese, Taiwanese, and South Korean fishing enterprises in particular made increasing use of a driftnet technique characterized by some conservationists as "biological stripmining." Hundreds of fishing vessels working in conjuction lay nets spanning an extensive ocean area to trap squid. These nets ensnare and kill other maritime creatures, such as fur seals, dolphins, porpoises, and sea birds. As the decade wore on concern grew that the substantial secondary loss of marine animals to driftnet fishing imperiled some species and might affect the aquatic ecosystem. The initial U.S. response to the problem was the Driftnet Impact Monitoring, Assessment, and Control Act, which became law on December 29, 1987.

The legislation, noting a need for more information on the various species affected, recommended increased efforts at monitoring, assessing, and regulating driftnet fishing. The measure directed the secretary of commerce, acting through the secretary of state, to undertake negotiations immediately with foreign governments whose citizens engage in the practice in the North Pacific. The negotiations were to be geared toward reaching agreements to gather information on the types and amounts of U.S.

marine life depleted by fishing fleets using driftnets. Under the law, the commerce secretary also was required to report to Congress on the impact of driftnet fishing on the marine environment.

DRUG SUMMIT (1990) Four-nation parley held in Colombia on strategy for their collective war on drugs. U.S. President GEORGE BUSH and presidents Virgilio Barco Vargas of Colombia, Alan Garcia of Peru, and Jaime Paz Zamora of Bolivia met on February 15, 1990, in Cartagena, where they signed a joint declaration pledging cooperation in the fight against illegal narcotics trafficking. The accord emphasized that reducing the international demand for drugs was as important as halting their production. The presidents observed that a successful war on drugs would hurt the economies of the South American drug-producing countries, which had grown dependent on the illegal trade. They agreed that an antidrug strategy, to be effective, had to involve increased economic cooperation and encourage trade and investment in the three Andean drug-producing nations. Bush pledged to seek funding from the U.S. Congress to help Colombia, Peru, and Bolivia "counteract the severe socioeconomic impact of an effective fight against illicit drugs." The four leaders concluded few specific agreements on law enforcement or military measures and sidestepped such sensitive issues as the extradition of drug suspects to America and the use of U.S. troops to interdict cocaine shipments out of South America. The conference took place under heavy security following unsubstantiated reports that drug traffickers might try to assassinate Bush.

DUAL-TRACK DECISION See **INTERMEDIATE NUCLEAR FORCES TREATY**.

DULLES, ALLEN WELSH (1893–1969) Director of central intelligence and head of the CENTRAL INTELLIGENCE AGENCY (CIA) from 1953 to 1961. The grandson of Secretary of State JOHN W. FOSTER, Dulles graduated from Princeton in 1914. After travel in the Far East and a stint teaching English in India, he returned to Princeton, earning his master's degree in 1916. The same year he entered the FOREIGN SERVICE, then under the direction of his uncle, Secretary of State ROBERT LANSING. Assigned to the American embassy in Vienna, he was transferred to Bern, Switzerland, after the United States declared war on Germany and Austria in 1917. Dulles was part of the U.S. delegation to the PARIS PEACE CONFERENCE (1919) that negotiated the TREATY OF VERSAILLES ending WORLD WAR I. He served briefly in Berlin and Istanbul before returning to Washington in 1922 to head the State Department's Near Eastern Affairs Division.

After earning his law degree from George Washington University in 1926, Dulles left the Foreign Service and joined the New York international law firm of Sullivan and Cromwell, where his older brother JOHN FOSTER DULLES was senior partner. He maintained an official involvement in foreign affairs, serving as legal adviser to American delegations at several international disarmament conferences. With the outbreak of WORLD WAR II, Dulles joined the OFFICE OF STRATEGIC SERVICES (OSS), the nation's wartime intelligence service. In November 1942 he established an OSS station in Switzerland. Among his accomplishments there were early reports on the German V-1 and V-2 missile programs and secret negotiations leading to the surrender of enemy forces in northern Italy.

Dulles resumed his legal career after the war. In 1946 he became president of the influential COUNCIL ON FOREIGN RELATIONS, a private organization of individuals interested in U.S. foreign policy. He helped draft the section of the NATIONAL SECURITY ACT of 1947 that established the CIA and the following year headed a three-member panel that studied the effectiveness of American intelligence activities for the NATIONAL SECURITY COUNCIL. In 1950 WALTER BEDELL SMITH, the new director of central intelligence (DCI), invited Dulles to implement his recommended reforms at the CIA. Dulles oversaw the agency's newly formed covert operations branch before becoming deputy director in August 1951.

In February 1953 President DWIGHT D. EISENHOWER elevated Dulles to the position of DCI. He assumed a central role in the formulation and conduct of U.S. foreign affairs alongside John Foster Dulles, whom Eisenhower had appointed secretary of state. The Dulles brothers initially supported U.S. commitment to the LIBERATION of Eastern Europe from Soviet domination. Eventual recognition that the West could not force the Soviet Union to withdraw led the Eisenhower administration to continue supporting the policy of CONTAINMENT of further Soviet expansionism.

The first civilian head of the CIA, Dulles promoted the use of clandestine operations in the COLD WAR struggle against communism. Early in his tenure the United States covertly instigated the overthrow of leftist governments in the IRAN COUP (1953) and GUATEMALA COUP (1954). He also presided over the development of the advanced U-2 and SR-71 spy planes and SATELLITE RECONNAISSANCE over Communist bloc countries. Dulles continued as DCI under President JOHN F. KENNEDY. Following the failure of the CIA-sponsored BAY OF PIGS INVASION of Cuba in April 1961, he was replaced by JOHN A. MCCONE. He returned to his law practice and later served on the Warren Commission that investigated Kennedy's assassination.

DULLES, JOHN FOSTER (1888–1959) Lawyer, diplomat, secretary of state. Dulles was born in Washington, D.C., to a family with a tradition of diplomatic and missionary service. He was named for his maternal grandfather, JOHN W. FOSTER, who was secretary of state under President BENJAMIN HARRISON. In 1907 he was secretary to his grandfather, who was representing the Chinese government at the second of the HAGUE PEACE CONFERENCES. Dulles graduated from Princeton in 1908, spent a year at the Sorbonne in Paris, and studied law at George Washington University. He passed the bar in 1911 and began a long and highly successful career with the distinguished New York firm of Sullivan and Cromwell, becoming an expert in international law. During WORLD WAR I he was commissioned an Army officer and, because of poor eyesight, assigned to an administrative position with the Trade Board in Washington. In 1919 he accompanied his uncle ROBERT LANSING, secretary of state to President WOODROW WILSON, to the PARIS PEACE CONFERENCE, where he was a legal adviser to the American delegation. Dulles returned to private law practice, but remained active in foreign affairs. He helped draft the DAWES PLAN (1924) for stabilizing postwar German finances and was involved

in the early 1930s in efforts to resolve German war debt repayment problems.

Following the outbreak of WORLD WAR II in 1939, he became chairman of the National Council of Churches' Commission on a Just and Durable Peace. The commission concluded that Christian faith and unity could provide a solution to the global hostilities. With American entry into the war in 1941, Dulles became associated with the internationalist wing of the Republican Party. His influential 1943 pamphlet, *Six Pillars of Peace*, called for creation of a postwar international organization to keep the peace. Committed to a bipartisan foreign policy during the war years and their COLD WAR aftermath, he underook several assignments for the Democratic Roosevelt and Truman administrations. He was a U.S. delegate to the SAN FRANCISCO CONFERENCE (1945) and to the UNITED NATIONS General Assembly from 1946 to 1950. He endorsed the anti-Communist TRUMAN DOCTRINE, the MARSHALL PLAN for postwar European recovery, and U.S. membership in NATO. He was an adviser to New York Governor Thomas E. Dewey during his unsuccessful 1944 and 1948 presidential campaigns and emerged as a leading Republican spokesman on foreign affairs. In 1949 Dewey appointed him to fill a vacant U.S. Senate seat. Dulles was defeated in his bid for a full term that November. In 1950 he became a special consultant to the State Department, serving as the principal negotiator of the JAPANESE PEACE TREATY (1951).

By the early 1950s Dulles had come to view the Truman administration's policy of CONTAINMENT of communism as both ineffective and immoral. Asked to draft the foreign policy plank of the 1952 Republican platform, he condemned containment as the abandonment of "countless human beings to a despotism and godless terrorism" and proposed instead the LIBERATION of Communist-controlled Eastern Europe. Made secretary of state by President DWIGHT D. EISENHOWER in 1953, Dulles brought to the formulation of U.S. foreign policy his moralistic view of the West's struggle against the evil of communism. His brother ALLEN W. DULLES served during the Eisenhower years as head of the CENTRAL INTELLIGENCE AGENCY.

While remaining committed rhetorically to rolling back Communist advances in Eastern Europe, the new administration was not prepared to risk war with the Soviet Union to do so, as became apparent with the U.S. decision not to intervene in the 1953 East German bread riots or the 1956 HUNGARIAN REVOLT. In practice, the administration continued Truman's basic Cold War containment policy. Dulles helped shape Eisenhower's NEW LOOK defense strategy that emphasized NUCLEAR WEAPONS as the most modern, cost-effective means of safeguarding the nation's security. In a January 1954 speech he explained the policy's reliance on the threat of MASSIVE RETALIATION to deter Communist aggression around the world. In 1956 Dulles coined the term BRINKMANSHIP to describe the administration's readiness to go to the brink of nuclear conflict as necessary in its handling of Cold War crises.

Events in Asia figured prominently in Dulles's first years in office. In 1953 the administration negotiated an armistice ending the KOREAN WAR, after Eisenhower reportedly threatened North Korea with nuclear attack. Dulles briefly headed the American delegation at the 1954 GENEVA CONFERENCE on Indochina before turning it over to his deputy, WALTER BEDELL SMITH. He distanced the United States from the conference's final settlement, not wanting to endorse Communist control over the northern part of Vietnam. The United States subsequently began to provide military and economic aid to the pro-Western government of Ngo Dinh Diem in South Vietnam. In September 1954 Dulles concluded a treaty in Manila forming the SOUTHEAST ASIA TREATY ORGANIZATION as a bulwark against further Communist expansion in the area. The same month Communist Chinese artillery began shelling Nationalist Chinese islands, precipitating the first of the QUEMOY-MATSU CRISES. In December 1954 Dulles affirmed the U.S. commitment to Nationalist China's security by signing the TAIWAN MUTUAL DEFENSE TREATY. A month later Congress passed the FORMOSA RESOLUTION authorizing the president to use force as necessary to protect Taiwan. The crisis slowly abated as the Communist bombardment tapered off by the end of April. When the shelling began again in 1958, Dulles defused the second Quemoy-Matsu Crisis by prevailing upon Taiwan to reduce its military garrisons on the offshore islands. The United States also

communicated to Communist China that it would not back a Nationalist Chinese invasion of the mainland.

In Europe Dulles pressed for strengthening the Western alliance against possible Communist bloc aggression. When France balked in 1954 at the formation of an inter-European army that would include West German forces, Dulles threatened an "agonizing reappraisal" of American commitments in Europe. The same year the Western allies agreed on the integration of West Germany into the unified NATO command. Dulles opposed any attempt at conciliation with the USSR, believing it would lend credence to Soviet claims on Eastern Europe. He counseled unsuccessfully against Eisenhower attending the 1955 GENEVA SUMMIT, which he saw as achieving nothing of significance. He supported a firm U.S. response when Soviet leader Nikita S. Khrushchev triggered the BERLIN CRISIS in 1958 by demanding withdrawal of Western forces from the divided German city.

Dulles was also confronted by crisis in the Middle East. His efforts to form a regional security alliance to forestall Communist expansion in the region were frustrated by the growing nationalism of Arab countries, which declined membership in any organization including former colonial powers Great Britain and France. Determined to avoid direct association with prior European colonialism, he limited American participation in the 1955 BAGHDAD PACT military alliance to observer rather than member status. During the 1956 SUEZ CRISIS, Dulles strongly opposed the British, French, and Israeli invasion of Egypt. Under U.S. pressure the invading forces were compelled to withdraw. Faced with mounting Soviet influence in the region following the Suez episode, Dulles helped craft the 1957 EISENHOWER DOCTRINE committing the United States to the defense of the Middle East against Communist subversion. Under the doctrine, Eisenhower ordered the LEBANON INTERVENTION in 1958 to aid the pro-Western government there against possible Communist revolt. Gravely ill with cancer, Dulles resigned on April 15, 1959, and died five weeks later.

DUMBARTON OAKS CONFERENCE (1944) Meeting of the major Allied powers during WORLD WAR II at which the basic plan for the UNITED NATIONS organization was drafted. Held at a large estate known as Dumbarton Oaks in Washington, D.C., the parley was conducted in two separate phases. The first phase, from August 21 to September 28, 1944, was attended by representatives of the United States, Great Britain, and the Soviet Union. The second phase, from September 29 to October 7, brought together representatives of the United States, Great Britain, and China. This arrangement accommodated the fact that the Soviet Union was not yet involved in the war in the Far East against Japan. Delegates of the four powers adopted a set of proposals for establishing a permanent postwar international organization for maintaining world peace and security. The Dumbarton Oaks proposals, which served as the basis for the UNITED NATIONS CHARTER, were concerned with the purposes and principles of the proposed organization, its membership and main organs, and its jurisdiction in economic and social as well as security matters. The key body in the organization was to be the Security Council, on which the BIG FIVE—the United States, Great Britain, France, the USSR, and China—were to be permanently represented. A number of issues remained unresolved and became the subject of negotiations at the subsequent YALTA CONFERENCE (1945) and SAN FRANCISCO CONFERENCE (1945).

E

EASTERTIDE OFFENSIVE (1972) Major North Vietnamese invasion of U.S.-supported South Vietnam during the VIETNAM WAR. Under its policy of VIETNAMIZATION, the Nixon administration by 1972 had transferred primary responsibility for the defense of South Vietnam to the South Vietnamese military. U.S. troop strength in Vietnam had declined from a high of 540,000 in 1969 to approximately 70,000. On March 30, 1972, North Vietnam launched a massive cross-border attack against the South. Named the Eastertide Offensive after the time of year, it was the largest Communist military thrust since the 1968 TET OFFENSIVE. President RICHARD M. NIXON responded by ordering a resumption of U.S. bombing around Hanoi in North Vietnam, given the name OPERATION LINEBACKER, and directed the mining of Haiphong and other North Vietnamese ports to interdict war supplies. Nixon's actions rekindled domestic antiwar protests. After initial successes, the Communist offensive was halted by a combination of South Vietnamese ground forces and U.S. air power. The Nixon administration hailed the North Vietnamese setback as proof of Vietnamization's effectiveness. The U.S. bombing and mining ended with the conclusion of the PARIS PEACE ACCORDS in January 1973.

EAST-WEST ACCORD ON HUMAN RIGHTS (1989) Statement of principles adopted on January 15, 1989, at the end of a meeting in Vienna of the CONFERENCE ON SECURITY AND COOPERATION IN EUROPE (CSCE). The enunciation of a common stand on HUMAN RIGHTS among the 35 CSCE members, including the Soviet Union and the other Communist states of the Warsaw Pact, testified to the political liberalization taking place in Eastern Europe in the late 1980s and the rapid easing of East-West COLD WAR tensions. In previous decades the West had condemned the Soviet bloc's human rights record. The CSCE agreement committed its signatories to respect political, economic, social, and cultural rights; religious freedom; freedom of movement and travel, including the right to emigrate; the equality of men and women; and the inherent dignity of each individual. Soviet endorsement of the accord foreshadowed the Kremlin's readiness later the same year to relinquish its hegemony over Eastern Europe and permit the overthrow by democratic movements of the Soviet-installed Communist regimes behind the crumbling IRON CURTAIN.

EC-121 INCIDENT (1969) Downing of an American reconnaissance aircraft by North Korea. On April 14, 1969, a U.S. military EC-121 four-engine turboprop departed Atsugi Naval Air Station in Japan for a routine intelligence flight intercepting North Korean communications in international airspace off the Communist nation's eastern coast. Some seven hours into its mission the EC-121 was shot down over the Sea of Japan by North Korean jet fighters and its crew of 31 lost. The U.S. government protested the incident but could do little more than provide fighter escorts to future flights.

See also PUEBLO INCIDENT.

ECONOMIC SUMMITS Annual meetings of the leaders of the major industrialized nations. The initial gathering evolved out of a 1975 proposal by French President Valery Giscard d'Estaing for a conference of the GROUP OF 5 (G-5) and other industrialized countries to coordinate economic policy in the wake of massive increases in world oil prices. The suggested meeting, held in France in November 1975, was attended by the heads of government of the G-5 nations (the United States, Great Britain, France, West Germany, and Japan) and Italy. It be-

came the first in an annual series of summit conferences hosted on a rotating basis among its participants. Canada joined the second summit in 1976, forming the GROUP OF 7. The European Community has been represented in the deliberations since 1977. The agenda of the summits has expanded to include international political developments as well as economic issues. Although not included in the summit itself, Soviet President Mikhail S. Gorbachev was invited to the July 1991 meeting in London. Gorbachev, seeking to reverse long-standing Soviet Communist opposition to the Western market-based economic system, met informally with the G-7 leaders to discuss the integration of the Soviet Union into the INTERNATIONAL MONETARY FUND, the WORLD BANK, and the international financial community.

See also ECONOMIC SUMMITS in APPENDIX E.

EDGE ACT See **WEBB-POMERENE ACT**.

EDO, TREATY OF (1858) Major commercial treaty concluded between the United States and Japan. Formally named the Treaty of Commerce and Navigation, it was negotiated by U.S. representative TOWNSEND HARRIS and represented Japan's first such agreement with a Western nation. Commodore MATTHEW C. PERRY's breakthrough expedition to Japan yielded the U.S.-Japanese TREATY OF KANAGAWA (1854), which opened the long-isolated island empire to limited trade and diplomatic contacts and whetted American determination for expanded ties. Harris arrived in Shimoda, Japan, in August 1856 as U.S. consul general with full diplomatic powers to negotiate a comprehensive commercial treaty. His initial negotiations with Japanese authorities resulted in the June 1857 Convention of Shimoda. This agreement affirmed that the United States, by dint of the MOST-FAVORED-NATION clause in the Treaty of Kanagawa, possessed the same trade and EXTRATERRITORIALITY rights in Japan as had been granted to European countries in treaties struck with the Japanese within months of Perry's opening.

Harris, aware that the 1857 convention failed to fulfill American diplomatic aims, then initiated talks on the comprehensive treaty coveted by Washington. During year-long negotiations, he fanned Japanese suspicions that Britain, France, and Russia had territorial designs on Japan and would use military force to exact further trade concessions. Unlike the Europeans, Harris assured his hosts, the United States did not seek territory and supported Japan's independence. He persuaded Japanese authorities that, by accepting a U.S. treaty offer, they would thwart the ambitions of the Europeans, who Harris suggested would then settle for treaties identical to the proposed American one.

On July 29, 1858, at an official ceremony aboard the American warship *Powhatan* in Edo (now Tokyo) Bay, the U.S. consul general and Japanese government representatives signed a full commercial treaty. The historic agreement arranged for the exchange of diplomatic representatives between Washington and Edo. Japan agreed to open six more ports to American trade and residence and accepted a fixed tariff on Japanese goods purchased by American vessels. Americans in Japan were granted permission to practice their religion freely. Three Japanese ports were made available to U.S. Navy ships as supply depots. Japan gained permission to buy ships and munitions in the United States. A special provision, inserted at Japan's urging, designated the U.S. president to act as a mediator in possible Japanese-European conflicts. The treaty served as a model for similar agreements completed between Japan and other Western nations before the end of 1858. Its terms guided Japanese foreign relations until the end of the 19th century. Following an exchange of ratifications in Washington in February 1860, Harris was appointed first U.S. minister to Japan. The Edo and related European treaties exacerbated political unrest in Japan among opponents of the government's decision to open the country to foreign influences. A strong wave of antiforeignism swept Japan from 1858 until 1868, when the imperial government under the Meiji Restoration embraced a policy of inviting increased relations with the West.

See also JAPANESE-AMERICAN TREATY OF *1894.*

EGYPTIAN-ISRAELI PEACE TREATY See **CAMP DAVID ACCORDS**.

EIGHTEEN-NATION COMMITTEE ON DISARMAMENT See **CONFERENCE ON DISARMAMENT**.

EISENHOWER DOCTRINE (1957) Declaration by President DWIGHT D. EISENHOWER on January 5, 1957, expressing U.S. determination to use military force to defend Middle East nations against Communist aggression. Following the SUEZ CRISIS (1956), the Soviet Union pressed the advantage it had earned by its support of Arab nationalism to extend its influence in the Middle East. Moscow, exploiting Arab hostility to Anglo-French colonialism and to Israel, developed close links with Egypt and Syria and became a major arms supplier to Cairo and Damascus. Eisenhower and Secretary of State JOHN FOSTER DULLES believed the Soviet Union sought regional domination and would move militarily to achieve its expansionist aims. The Eisenhower administration decided a clear statement of American resolve was imperative to deter Kremlin aggression and restore the BALANCE OF POWER in the wake of the British and French reversal. The BAGHDAD PACT, the regional defense alliance comprising Great Britain, Turkey, Iraq, Iran, and Pakistan, was deemed no longer able to serve as a northern barrier against Soviet expansion into Arab areas because of waning British influence in the region.

Eisenhower appeared before a joint session of Congress in early January 1957 to announce that the United States would defend the Middle East against Soviet inroads. He then asked legislators to support the Eisenhower Doctrine through a joint resolution. After extended debate, during which critics scored the administration for overstating the threat of an overt Soviet attack, Congress approved the Eisenhower dictum March 5 and the president signed it March 9. The resolution defined the preservation of the territorial integrity and political independence of Middle East countries as vital to U.S. national security; it authorized the president to use armed force to support any Middle East nation requesting assistance against attack "from any country controlled by international communism"; and it gave the president the power to allocate $200 million in economic and military aid among Middle East states to help keep them out of the Soviet orbit. The doctrine effectively extended to the Middle East the post–WORLD WAR II U.S. policy of CONTAINMENT. Eisenhower's pledge also placed primary responsibility for the defense of Western strategic interests in the region on the United States.

U.S. actions in 1957 in the JORDANIAN CRISIS and the SYRIAN CRISIS underscored the American intention to stem Communist gains in the region. Eisenhower's decision to deploy 15,000 troops in the LEBANON INTERVENTION in July 1958, the most forceful demonstration of his doctrine, was condemned in the Arab world as further evidence that the United States ignored Arab nationalism and viewed the problems of the Middle East exclusively in COLD WAR terms. Opposition to Soviet involvement in the area became a fundamental aspect of American foreign policy.

See also CARTER DOCTRINE.

EISENHOWER, DWIGHT DAVID (1890–1969) Army officer, 34th president of the United States. Born in Texas, Eisenhower was raised in Abilene, Kansas and graduated from West Point in 1915. His military career flourished after he finished at the top of his class at the Army's Command and General Staff School in 1926. He served under Chief of Staff DOUGLAS MACARTHUR in Washington and from 1935 to 1939 was MacArthur's aide in the Philippines. Eisenhower was promoted to general in 1941. With U.S. entry into WORLD WAR II, he was named head of the War Department's plans division. In 1942 he was given command of the U.S. invasion of North Africa. He commanded the Allied invasions of Sicily and Italy in 1943 and the invasion of France on D-Day, June 6, 1944. Promoted to five-star general in December 1944, he directed the final Anglo-American assault on Nazi Germany that culminated in Berlin's surrender on May 8, 1945.

Eisenhower emerged from the war a national hero and renowned international figure. In November 1945 he became Army chief of staff. Following his retirement in 1948, he assumed the presidency of Columbia University. The same year he declined overtures from both major political parties for a possible presidential bid. President HARRY S. TRUMAN called Eisenhower

back to active duty in 1950 to assume command of the military forces of NATO, the newly formed Western security alliance in Europe. Persuaded to run for president in 1952 by the moderate wing of the Republican Party, he resigned his NATO post, garnered the Republican presidential nomination, and went on to defeat Democratic standard-bearer ADLAI E. STEVENSON. During the campaign he pledged to go to Korea if elected to assess firsthand the KOREAN WAR, then in its third year.

President-elect Eisenhower visited South Korea in December 1952, whereupon he concluded that the conflict was an unwinnable stalemate. He made ending the war an immediate priority on taking office in January 1953. Eisenhower secretly warned Communist China that if a negotiated settlement was not forthcoming, the United States was prepared to extend the conflict beyond Korea and use atomic weapons. The degree to which the atomic threat influenced Commmunist China and North Korea to enter serious negotiations remains unclear. Revived peace talks led to an armistice agreement on July 27, 1953. Eisenhower committed the United States to the defense of the South against future North Korean aggression in the SOUTH KOREA MUTUAL DEFENSE TREATY (1953).

Asia continued to command the administration's attention. The 1954 GENEVA CONFERENCE on Korea and Indochina failed to reach a final Korean peace settlement. Not wanting to ally America with European colonialism, Eisenhower ruled out direct U.S. military intervention in French Indochina to help France avert defeat by the Communist Viet Minh insurgency fighting for Vietnamese independence. The final accords of the Geneva Conference divided newly independent Vietnam into a Communist North and non-Communist South. Aligning U.S. policy behind the security of the South Vietnamese state that emerged under President Ngo Dinh Diem, the Eisenhower administration began a program of U.S. military and economic aid to Saigon. Eisenhower's strategic outlook on Southeast Asia was informed by the DOMINO THEORY, the idea that if one country fell to communism then other neighboring countries were liable to be toppled in a chain reaction. In September 1954 Washington spearheaded formation of the SOUTHEAST ASIA TREATY ORGANIZATION for the defense of the region against Communist aggression. That same month, Communist China's shelling of offshore islands under the control of the Nationalist Chinese regime on Taiwan precipitated the first of the QUEMOY-MATSU CRISES. The Eisenhower administration in December 1954 concluded the TAIWAN MUTUAL DEFENSE TREATY with the Nationalist government. In January 1955 the president gained congressional passage of the FORMOSA RESOLUTION, authorizing him to use force as necessary to defend Taiwan. The crisis eased by the end of April 1955, but flared again briefly in 1958, prompting Eisenhower to reiterate U.S. readiness to stand with the Nationalist Chinese.

The 1952 Republican Party platform castigated the Truman administration's policy of CONTAINMENT toward the Communist bloc and called instead for the LIBERATION of Eastern Europe from Soviet domination. Eisenhower had prevailed over the isolationist wing of the Republican Party to gain the presidential nomination. Espousing an internationalist foreign policy, he had pledged during the campaign to lead a great crusade for "freedom in the world." The new administration's liberation policy was exposed as largely rhetorical when, in June 1953, Eisenhower took no steps to aid an uprising among workers in Communist East Germany that was crushed by the Soviet Union. In practice, the Eisenhower White House continued the basic containment policy fashioned by Truman. Eisenhower did alter U.S. military strategy for holding Communist expansionism in check. Concerned about the impact of rising defense costs on the federal budget, he adopted the NEW LOOK defense policy that trimmed conventional forces and emphasized comparatively less expensive NUCLEAR WEAPONS. Under the New Look, U.S. DETERRENCE of Communist aggression rested on the threat of MASSIVE RETALIATION with nuclear arms. This approach came under mounting criticism in the late 1950s from congressional Democrats and allied defense analysts, who contended that an excessive reliance on nuclear weapons left America unable to respond to a wide spectrum of limited conflicts and crises.

Eisenhower took office amid a continuing national scare over alleged Communist infiltration of the federal government. He shared the widely held view that Soviet espionage posed a very real danger to the nation's security. Despite international pleas for clemency, he declined to commute the death sentences of Americans Julius and Ethel Rosenberg, convicted in the ROSENBERG CASE of passing atomic secrets to the Soviets. They were executed in June 1953. During the 1952 election, Eisenhower tacitly abided the charges leveled by demogogic Senator JOSEPH R. MCCARTHY (R-WI) of Communist subversion in the executive branch. As president he grew increasingly outraged by McCarthy's unsupported accusations. But Eisenhower largely refrained from speaking out against the senator, preferring instead, he explained, to let McCarthy's outlandish behavior bring his own downfall, as it did in 1954.

The COLD WAR formed the overarching context for foreign policy throughout Eisenhower's presidency. The PARIS AGREEMENTS (1954) achieved the long-standing U.S. goal of integrating West Germany into NATO and strengthening the alliance against possible Soviet attack. Moscow's cooperation in completing the AUSTRIAN STATE TREATY the following year convinced Eisenhower to attend an East-West summit conference with the leaders of Great Britain, France, and the Soviet Union. The July 1955 GENEVA SUMMIT ushered in a brief thaw in U.S.-Soviet relations. The improved East-West atmosphere, or so-called spirit of Geneva, ended with the brutal Soviet suppression of the HUNGARIAN REVOLT in 1956.

Eisenhower again defeated Stevenson in the 1956 presidential race to win a second term. In 1957 the Soviet Union startled the world when it put into orbit the first artificial satellite, Sputnik, inaugurating the Space Age. Americans were stunned by the Soviet feat, which underscored the ability of Soviet INTERCONTINENTAL BALLISTIC MISSILES to strike the United States and seemed to confirm a Soviet lead in advanced technology. The Eisenhower administration responded by establishing an American space program under the newly formed NATIONAL AERONAUTICS AND SPACE ADMINISTRATION (1958) and securing passage of the NATIONAL DEFENSE EDUCATION ACT (1958) to spur U.S. science education. Democratic critics raised charges, which Eisenhower strongly denied, that his administration had permitted a dangerous MISSILE GAP to develop between the United States and the Soviet Union.

In 1959 Soviet Premier Nikita S. Khrushchev accepted Eisenhower's invitation to visit the United States for discussions on the BERLIN CRISIS (1958–1962) and other issues. Their CAMP DAVID SUMMIT marked another brief respite from Cold War confrontation. The 1960 PARIS SUMMIT among Eisenhower, British Prime Minister Harold MacMillan, French President Charles de Gaulle, and Khrushchev fell apart, however, over the U-2 INCIDENT, involving the Soviet downing of an American spy plane. The episode left U.S.-Soviet relations strained in Eisenhower's last months as president.

The THIRD WORLD emerged during the Eisenhower years as European colonies in Africa and Asia gained their independence. In the Middle East Eisenhower sought to balance America's goal of blocking any Communist inroads in the strategic region with its determination to avoid any identification with European colonialism. In 1953 the U.S.-orchestrated IRAN COUP overthrew the leftist government of Mohammed Mossadegh and restored Shah Mohammed Reza Pahlavi to power. In 1955 the Eisenhower administration backed the formation of the British-led BAGHDAD PACT to provide for the security of the Middle East's northern tier. The following year, however, Eisenhower opposed the British and French intervention in Egypt during the SUEZ CRISIS. With Soviet influence in the region on the rise in the wake of the crisis, the president in January 1957 formulated the EISENHOWER DOCTRINE asserting U.S. readiness to defend any Middle Eastern country threatened by Communist aggression. The same year Eisenhower deployed U.S. naval forces to the eastern Mediterranean to support King Hussein during the JORDANIAN CRISIS and to discourage suspected Communist-inspired plots emanating from Syria against its pro-Western neighbors during the SYRIAN CRISIS. In 1958 he dispatched U.S. troops to Beirut in the LEBANON INTERVENTION to prevent a possible Communist takeover there.

Eisenhower also took action to prevent the emergence of a Communist state in Latin America. In 1954 the administration orchestrated the GUATEMALA COUP that re-placed the Central American nation's leftist government with a U.S.-allied regime. Interest in Latin America mounted in Eisenhower's second term. The CARACAS EPISODE (1958), in which Vice-President RICHARD M. NIXON was attacked by a violent mob in the Venezuelan capital, highlighted growing anti-Americanism in the region and galvanized the administration to increase U.S. involvement and economic aid there. Fidel Castro's successful revolution and installation of a leftist government in Cuba in 1959 led to a break in U.S.-Cuban relations and prompted Eisenhower to authorize planning for a covert operation to topple the Cuban leader.

Eisenhower left office in January 1961 and retired to his farm in Gettysburg, Pennsylvania. In his renowned farewell address he warned against the danger of a U.S. MILITARY-INDUSTRIAL COMPLEX. He authored his memoirs, *Mandate for Change* (1963) and *Waging Peace* (1964), remained active in Republican politics, and served as an informal adviser to succeeding presidents.

EL SALVADOR CIVIL WAR (1979–1992) Violent struggle between leftist rebels and the U.S.-supported El Salvadoran government. In October 1979 the military government of General Carlos Humberto Romero was ousted in a coup led by younger, more politically progressive officers. The new military-civilian junta proved unable to quell mounting violence between left- and right-wing groups. Charging that the ruling junta had swung to the right, a coalition of leftist organizations and dissident political groups in April 1980 formed the Democratic Revolutionary Front (FDR). The Farabundo Marti National Liberation Front (FMLN) was organized as the coalition's military arm. Named for the leader of a Salvadoran peasant uprising in 1932, the FMLN waged the growing guerrilla campaign to install a leftist government in El Salvador. In December 1980 three American nuns and a lay worker were found murdered near San Salvador. The apparent involvement of government security forces in the slayings prompted President JIMMY CARTER to suspend U.S. military and economic aid to El Salvador. The ruling junta was reorganized the same month, with centrist leader Jose Napoleon Duarte being named the country's first civilian president in a half-century. In January 1981 the FMLN launched a major offensive. Responding to both the Duarte government's emergence and evidence that Communist Cuba and the leftist Sandinista regime in Nicaragua were supplying the FMLN, Carter resumed U.S. aid to San Salvador.

President RONALD W. REAGAN believed the guerrilla war in El Salvador was part of a concerted Communist offensive in Central America. In February 1981 the Reagan administration, as part of its effort to gain congressional backing for increased U.S. assistance to El Salvador, issued the EL SALVADOR WHITE PAPER. The report charged the Soviet Union and Cuba were sponsoring the FMLN , which was said to be receiving arms and training from several Communist countries. Managua's alleged role in funneling assistance to the FMLN contributed to worsening U.S.-Nicaraguan relations. The Reagan White House began a program of covert U.S. aid to the CONTRAS, Nicaraguan guerrillas opposed to the Sandinista government. Reagan won reluctant congressional support in 1981 for greater U.S. military aid to San Salvador, including the training of Salvadoran army units.

As the fighting continued and reports of atrocities committed by both sides mounted, debate intensified in Washington over U.S. Salvadoran policy. In Salvadoran elections in March 1982 the conservative Arena Party defeated Duarte's Christian Democrats. Arena leader Roberto d'Aubuisson, a former army major widely identified with right-wing death squads, became head of the national assembly. Duarte was replaced as president by the independent Dr. Alvaro Magaña. Reagan prevailed on Congress in 1982 and 1983 to provide several hundred million dollars in military and economic aid to El Salvador. Liberal members made the assistance conditional on the Salvadoran government moving to end right-wing HUMAN RIGHTS abuses and making progress on political and economic reform. In April 1983 the LINOWITZ REPORT, the work of an influential private inter-American forum, held that political unrest in Latin America stemmed ultimately from social and economic inequalities rather than from East-West COLD WAR competition. In July 1983 Reagan appointed the KISSINGER COMMISSION on Central America. Its report, submitted in January 1984, concluded that the

Soviet Union and Cuba had exploited the region's social and economic conditions to promote Communist revolutions that threatened the security of the entire Western Hemisphere. The commission endorsed the Reagan administration's anti-Communist policies.

Under U.S. pressure, the Salvadoran government had moved to curtail the death squads by 1984. In May 1984 Duarte won a national presidential election over d'Aubuisson. The same month five members of the Salvadoran national guard were convicted of killing the American nuns in 1980. The election of the much-respected Duarte moderated the divisive debate in Congress over El Salvador and ensured a steady flow of U.S. aid. The civil war in El Salvador reached a bitter stalemate. Various peace proposals advanced by both sides and other Latin American countries met with no success. Washington's attention in the mid-1980s focused increasingly on Nicaragua and the controversial U.S. backing of the Contras.

Arena Party candidate Alfredo Cristiani's election to succeed the retiring Duarte as president in March 1989 raised concerns in the United States about the possible reemergence of a repressive Salvadoran government. Cristiani assured Washington that he represented the more moderate elements in Arena and U.S. assistance to San Salvador continued. In November 1989 the FMLN unleashed a major urban offensive. The same month six Salvadoran Jesuit priests, their housekeeper, and her daughter were slain by army troops in San Salvador. Amid an international outcry over the killings, the Cristiani government in January 1990 charged nine members of the military with the murders. Suspecting a cover-up, Congress conditioned future U.S. aid on a thorough investigation of the affair.

In February 1990 an opposition movement led by Violeta Chamorro emerged victorious in national elections in Nicaragua. The Sandinista defeat, coinciding as it did with the end of the Cold War and collapse of communism in the Soviet bloc, left the FMLN increasingly isolated. With its support evaporating and its November 1989 offensive stalled, the rebel leadership welcomed negotiations. The Cristiani government, facing a possible cutoff in U.S. aid and eager to end the costly conflict, also indicated a readiness to compromise. UNITED NATIONS-sponsored peace talks began in May 1990. In September 1991 the two sides signed an agreement meant to pave the way to a cease-fire. On December 31, 1991, a comprehensive peace agreement was concluded under U.N. auspices in New York City. The pact called for the civil war to end February 1, 1992, followed by the reassimilation of the FMLN into Salvadoran society.

EL SALVADOR WHITE PAPER (1981) Disputed State Department report issued February 23, 1981, on the arms buildup by left-wing insurgents in El Salvador. Entitled "Communist Interference in El Salvador," the study claimed to furnish definitive evidence that the Soviet Union and Cuba, with the active support of other Communist states, secretly shipped arms through Nicaragua to Marxist-Leninist rebels in El Salvador fighting to overthrow the government of President Jose Napoleon Duarte. Based on documents purportedly captured from areas controlled by leftist rebels in El Salvador, the report outlined the growth of Soviet- and Cuban-sponsored Communist involvement in the EL SALVADOR CIVIL WAR.

Before releasing the white paper, Reagan administration Secretary of State ALEXANDER M. HAIG, JR. had used it to brief members of Congress, whom he was lobbying for increased military aid for the Duarte government. Such aid had been cut off by President JIMMY CARTER after the December 1980 murder of three American Catholic nuns and one lay worker in El Salvador. Carter's move was intended to pressure the Salvadoran authorities to investigate the slayings and crack down on political violence by the military. It was initially suspected—and later established—that members of the Salvadoran national guard had killed the women. In the closing days of his administration Carter had decided to restore some of the suspended American military assistance in response to a concerted Salvadoran rebel offensive against the governing civilian-military regime.

Despite congressional testimony by former American Ambassador to El Salvador Robert E. White and others that right-wing groups with close ties to the Salvadoran armed forces were primarily responsible for violent political repression in the Central American country, Haig was able to persuade the House and Senate to approve a Reagan administration request for $5 million in additional military loans to El Salvador. In June 1981 the *Wall Street Journal* and the *Washington Post* challenged the authenticity of the captured documents that formed the basis of the white paper and questioned the accuracy of the conclusions drawn by the State Department concerning Soviet-bloc covert interference in the Salvadoran conflict. The department defended the report in a point-by-point rebuttal issued on June 17. The Reagan administration and Congress battled through the 1980s over the extent of U.S. aid to El Salvador.

EMBARGO ACT (1807) Legislation urged by President THOMAS JEFFERSON that sanctioned a policy of economic coercion to force British and French respect for the neutral rights of American shipping. Signed into law December 22, 1807, the act embargoed all American commerce abroad by halting U.S. exports and prohibiting American merchant vessels from sailing for foreign ports. The embargo was Jefferson's response to escalating abuses on American seaborne commerce committed by Great Britain and France during the Napoleonic Wars (1803–1815). Seeking to deny to one another sources of resupply, and thereby diminish each other's capacity to wage war, the European belligerents schemed to restrict neutral commerce. The American merchant marine had undergone remarkable growth in the course of the French Revolutionary Wars (1792–1802), profiting from the expanded opportunities for neutral shipping created by prolonged Anglo-French conflict. American commercial prosperity continued with the outbreak of renewed warfare in 1803, by which point the United States was the world's leading neutral trader.

British policy after 1804 turned hostile toward American shipping. Parliament resolved to crack down on the lucrative U.S. trade between the French West Indies and France. In London's judgment, neutral American commerce principally benefited the French, whose own overmatched fleets had been forced from the Atlantic by superior British sea power and who thus relied heavily on the American merchant marine to ferry goods between French Caribbean colonies and continental Europe. Britain's highest admiralty court, ruling in the 1805 case of the captured American merchant ship *Essex*, insisted this Franco-American commerce was an attempt to circumvent the Rule of 1756, a maritime principle unilaterally proclaimed by the British. The Rule of 1756 in essence said that a belligerent nation could not initiate trade with a neutral nation during war when the same trade had been denied the neutral nation in peacetime. By British thinking, American ships were forbidden from transporting cargoes from the French West Indies to France since such traffic had been closed to the United States prior to the Anglo-French war.

Following the *Essex* decision, the British navy took aim at American vessels in the Caribbean and outside U.S. harbors along the Atlantic Coast, seizing ships, confiscating cargoes bound for France, and subjecting American sailors to IMPRESSMENT, or forced naval recruitment. British depredations drew U.S. outrage and dealt a damaging blow to Anglo-American relations. Congress retaliated with the NON-IMPORTATION ACT (1806), which authorized a ban on assorted British products to the United States. Jefferson delayed enforcement of the measure pending outcome of negotiations held in 1806 aimed at resolving U.S.-British differences concerning neutral rights. These talks yielded the MONROE-PINKNEY TREATY (1806), the terms of which were so unsatisfactory to Jefferson that he never submitted it to the Senate.

Neutral American trade meanwhile had become the main casualty of a stepped-up campaign of Anglo-French economic warfare. Britain provoked the back-and-forth commercial battle in May 1806 by imposing a blockade on French-controlled European ports. French Emperor Napoleon Bonaparte responded by issuing the Berlin Decree in November, inaugurating his so-called Continental system for interdicting British commerce with the rest of Europe. Britain struck back with a series of Orders in Council, or edicts, that tightened its blockade on the French. Napoleon retaliated in kind with more restrictive decrees against British trade. U.S. merchant ships were squeezed from both ends in the esca-lating Franco-British battle of blockades. American vessels attempting to trade in Europe or the British Isles faced harassment and assorted penalties whenever they failed to comply with arbitrary dictates of one or the other of the warring powers.

Apart from maritime trade difficulties, the United States endured the humiliation of the CHESAPEAKE AFFAIR (1807), in which a British navy search party forced its way onto the U.S. frigate *Chesapeake* and impressed four sailors, three of whom ultimately proved to be American citizens. The incident entailed the loss of American lives and aroused bitter U.S. indignation. The Chesapeake Affair, coupled with the British and French assaults on U.S. merchant shipping, prompted Jefferson and Secretary of State JAMES MADISON in December 1807 to resort to economic pressure to gain European recognition of America's neutral rights. The president lifted the suspension on the Non-Importation Act against Britain and a special session of Congress called by Jefferson passed the remarkable Embargo Act, which closed off virtually all of America's foreign trade. The Jefferson administration estimated wrongly that dependence on U.S. manufactured and agricultural products would drive the British and French to acknowledge America's neutral maritime rights in order to win repeal of the embargo. Despite additional legislation tailored to improve the trade ban's effectiveness, the 1807 act proved difficult to enforce against smuggling and other means of noncompliance. The embargo caused far greater harm to the United States than to Britain or France, both of which were only marginally affected. A congressional report in October 1808 concluded that Jefferson's sweeping trade prescription had severely damaged the U.S. economy while failing to coerce its intended targets, the two European belligerents.

Popular domestic opposition to the embargo grew steadily, especially in New England, which had suffered most under the policy of economic reprisal. State legislatures questioned the embargo's constitutionality and governors turned down federal requests for militia to help enforce the commercial ban. In Congress, the intensifying opposition of Federalists and a dissident faction within Jefferson's own Democratic-Republican Party forced the repeal of the Embargo Act on March 1, 1809, three days before Jefferson left office. The departing president, who had strived to preserve the embargo, signed the replacement NON-INTERCOURSE ACT, reopening trade with all nations except France and Great Britain. The new law authorized Jefferson's successor Madison to resume commerce with whichever of the two warring countries first ceased violating America's neutral rights.

EMERGENCY DETENTION ACT See **INTERNAL SECURITY ACT**.

EMERGENCY TARIFF (1921) Federal act that marked the return to full PROTECTIONISM in U.S. trade policy. The 1913 UNDERWOOD TARIFF, meant to spur America's foreign commerce, had reduced import duties to roughly 30 percent, their lowest level since the mid-19th century. Following WORLD WAR I, mounting economic troubles brought renewed calls for higher tariff rates to protect domestic markets from overseas competition. The sharp downturn in U.S. agriculture in 1921 resulted in passage of the Emergency Tariff Act. Adopted May 27, 1921, the legislation imposed increased customs fees on imported farm products. It was succeeded the following year by the broadly protectionist FORDNEY-MCCUMBER TARIFF.

"THE END OF HISTORY?" Provocative article in the summer 1989 issue of the *National Interest*, a neoconservative journal published in Washington, D.C., proclaiming the final triumph of Western liberal democracy over communism. In his widely publicized essay, author Francis Fukuyama, a little known U.S. State Department official, sought to explain the course of world events at the end of the 1980s—communism's demise in Eastern Europe and the Soviet Union, the virtual end of the East-West COLD WAR, economic liberalization in mainland China, and the emergence of nascent democracies worldwide—as the fulfillment of a great historical scheme. Fukuyama, borrowing heavily from the thinking of the German philosopher Georg Hegel, argued that history has represented a long struggle to achieve a political state that realizes the idea of freedom inherent in human consciousness. In the 20th century, he contended, the forces of Commu-

nist—and Fascist—totalitarianism had been decisively defeated by the United States and its allies. The West's victory, Fukuyama asserted, confirmed liberal, pluralist, capitalist democracy as the realization of the Hegelian ideal and thus marked the end point of mankind's ideological evolution. The article became an international cause celebre, eliciting widespread debate over its premises and conclusions. Critics complained that Fukuyama failed to address nationalism and religious fundamentalism as ideological forces, ignored the possibility of reactionary crackdown and totalitarian resurgence in the Soviet Union, and altogether overlooked the THIRD WORLD.

ENVIRONMENTAL MODIFICATION CONVENTION (1977) Agreement to prohibit environmental modification as a means of warfare. The measure was signed in Geneva, Switzerland, on May 18, 1977, following four years of negotiations by the CONFERENCE OF THE COMMITTEE ON DISARMAMENT. Officially titled the Convention on the Prohibition of Military or Any Other Hostile Use of Environmental Modification Techniques, it entered into force October 5, 1978. The convention, which grew out of concerns about the development of weather-modification technologies with potential military applications, banned the "deliberate manipulation of natural processes" meant to cause a change in the Earth's ecosphere for hostile purposes. Examples of prohibited activities included the alteration of climate patterns, the triggering of an earthquake or tidal wave, or the upset of a region's ecological balance. The United States formally ratified the measure on December 13, 1979, after approval by a 98 to 0 vote in the Senate.

ERSKINE AGREEMENT (1809) Abortive understanding struck between British Minister at Washington David M. Erskine and Secretary of State ROBERT SMITH outlining a settlement of Anglo-American differences over commerce and neutral rights. America's neutral trade was a recurring casualty of the war between Great Britain and France in the early 19th century. In retaliation for British and French interference with U.S. merchant shipping, Congress in March 1809 passed the NON-INTERCOURSE ACT prohibiting all American trade with the two European belligerents. In April British Foreign Secretary George Canning directed Erskine to seek a negotiated end to the crisis in U.S.-British relations. Through diplomatic notes exchanged on April 18 and 19, Erskine and Smith entered into an agreement that obligated Britain to revoke its 1807 Orders in Council, or edicts, against American shipping and committed the United States to restore commercial relations with the British.

On the basis of the Erskine Agreement, President JAMES MADISON immediately proclaimed the Non-Intercourse Act no longer in effect against Britain and thus renewed Anglo-American trade. Madison's move, however, proved premature. In his determination to reach a settlement with Smith, Erskine had exceeded his negotiating instructions. In late May 1809, after learning of Erskine's diplomatic improvisation, Canning repudiated the Erskine Agreement and recalled the British minister to London. Canning's action forced a chagrined Madison to reverse himself and reimpose the Non-Intercourse Act against Britain in August. The deterioration in Anglo-American relations that followed the collapse of the Erskine Agreement culminated in the WAR OF 1812.

ESPIONAGE ACT (1917) Federal legislation enacted following America's entrance into WORLD WAR I that imposed severe penalties for treasonable or disloyal activities. The United States declared war on Germany in April 1917. A German campaign of subversion in America that included explosions and fires, propaganda, and political agitation brought passage of the nation's first espionage statute, the Espionage Act of June 15, 1917. The law sanctioned up to 20 years imprisonment for anyone divulging information concerning national defense, obstructing recruitment or promoting insubordination in the armed forces, refusing military duty, or otherwise aiding the enemy. The law authorized the postmaster general to prevent the mailing of treasonous or seditious material. In April 1918 Congress passed related legislation that identified specific acts of sabotage as crimes. The SEDITION ACT of May 1918 extended the provisions of the Espionage Act to subversive speech or writing. The Supreme Court upheld the constitutional-

ity of the Espionage Act in *Schenck* v. *United States* (1919).

See also ESPIONAGE AND SABOTAGE ACT.

ESPIONAGE AND SABOTAGE ACT (1954) Federal legislation that updated and broadened U.S. laws against enemy intelligence activities. Amid COLD WAR concerns over Communist subversion, fueled in part by congressional investigations into Communist infiltration of America, the Eisenhower administration in 1954 called for the strengthening of the nation's internal security laws. The basic U.S. sanctions against espionage had originated during WORLD WAR I with the ESPIONAGE ACT of 1917. Statutes criminalizing sabotage had been enacted in 1918 and 1940. The Espionage and Sabotage Act became law on September 3, 1954. The measure increased the allowable punishment for peacetime espionage to death or life imprisonment and removed existing statutes of limitations for espionage offenses. The act made sabotage laws effective during national emergencies as well as wartime and extended the definition of sabotage to include the use of radioactive materials or biological and chemical agents.

EUROPEAN ADVISORY COMMISSION See **ALLIED CONTROL COUNCIL**.

EUROPEAN BANK FOR RECONSTRUCTION AND DEVELOPMENT (EBRD) London-based international lending agency created in 1990 to boost the state-controlled economies of Eastern Europe and facilitate their conversion to free market activity. The idea for the bank, based on a proposal by French President Francois Mitterand, gained the endorsement of the European Community (EC) in December 1989 amid the accelerating collapse of communism in Eastern Europe. After months of planning, during which most other leading Western nations were brought into the project, a treaty to establish the EBRD with initial capitalization of $12 billion was signed by 40 countries on May 29, 1990, in Paris. Its organizers characterized the bank as one of the most important international aid projects since WORLD WAR II.

The EBRD's purpose is to promote private and entrepreneurial initiative in Eastern European countries demonstrably committed to multiparty democracy and market economies. The United States and Great Britain pressed unsuccessfully for lending to Eastern Europe to be limited entirely to the region's nascent private sector. The bank's charter permits up to 40 percent of EBRD's money to be allocated for public sector projects, such as roads and telecommunications. All of the Eastern European countries except Albania signed the EBRD treaty and became eligible for bank membership. Despite strong initial U.S. opposition to its participation, the Soviet Union was allowed to become a member—but on the condition that it not borrow more from the bank than it contributed in capital for at least the first three years. This restriction was imposed out of Western concerns that the Soviets, themselves wracked by economic problems and in dire need of capital, would draw most of the EBRD's resources. Washington argued further that Moscow had not yet met the democracy and market orientation criteria. The United States became the largest shareholding member of the bank with 10 percent of the capital. It was followed by Germany, France, Japan, Italy and Great Britain, each with 8.5 percent, and the Soviet Union with 6 percent. The remaining eight EC nations, the EC itself, and the European Investment Bank held roughly 20 percent of the capital while the seven Eastern European members held approximately 7.5 percent.

EUROPEAN RECOVERY PROGRAM See **MARSHALL PLAN**.

EVARTS, WILLIAM MAXWELL (1818–1901) Lawyer, statesman, and secretary of state. The Boston native graduated from Yale College in 1837, attended Harvard Law School, and was admitted to the New York bar in 1841. Evarts practiced in New York City and became one of the most renowned American trial lawyers of his time. From 1849 to 1853 he was assistant U.S. district attorney for the southern district of New York. An active Republican, he twice was sent during the Civil War on diplomatic missions (1863 and 1864) to Great Britain by Secretary of State WILLIAM H. SEWARD to seek an end to British building of Confederate ships. In 1867 he took part in the abortive prosecution of former Confederate president JEFFERSON DAVIS for

treason. The following year, as chief counsel, he successfully defended President ANDREW JOHNSON at his impeachment trial. Evarts then served in the Johnson administration as attorney general until 1869.

In 1871 and 1872 he was the chief U.S. counsel before the tribunal at Geneva, Switzerland, that arbitrated the ALABAMA CLAIMS, which stemmed from damages to Union shipping inflicted during the Civil War by Confederate ships built or outfitted in Britain. He represented the Republican Party before the congressionally created electoral commission that awarded the disputed 1876 presidential election to Republican candidate RUTHERFORD B. HAYES over Democrat Samuel J. Tilden. Appointed secretary of state by Hayes in 1877, he served in the post until 1881. During his tenure he defined America's independent construction and operation of an interoceanic canal across Central America as a fundamental objective of U.S. foreign policy. To protest raids across the U.S. border by Mexican bandits, he withheld diplomatic recognition of the Mexican government that came to power in 1877. While Mexico would not agree to permit, as Evarts wanted, U.S. troops to pursue the bandits back into Mexican territory, it pledged greater cooperation in halting the raids. The climate between the neighbors improved and Evarts extended recognition. He directed negotiation of the ANGELL TREATY (1880) with China, the terms of which laid the groundwork for the restrictive immigration provisions of the CHINESE EXCLUSION ACT (1882). After leaving the State Department he was a delegate to the International Monetary Conference at Paris in 1881. Elected to the U.S. Senate in 1885 as a Republican from New Jersey, he served only one term before retiring because of increasing blindness.

EVERETT, EDWARD (1794–1865) Educator, diplomat, legislator, statesman, and noted orator. Born in Massachusetts, Everett was educated at Harvard University, where he completed a bachelor's degree in 1812 and a master's in theology in 1814. After a year as a Unitarian pastor, he received his doctorate in philosophy from the University of Gottingen in Germany and joined the Harvard faculty in 1819. Entering politics, he served in the U.S. House of Representatives from 1825 to 1835 and was Whig governor of Massachusetts from 1836 to 1839. In 1841, through the efforts of close personal friend Secretary of State DANIEL WEBSTER, he was appointed U.S. minister to Great Britain, where he served until 1845. Taking leave from politics on his return from London, he became president of Harvard in 1846, remaining in the post three years. In 1850, at Webster's request, he drafted for the State Department the so-called HULSEMANN LETTER to the Austrian charge d'affaires in Washington, asserting the right of the United States to extend sympathy to the participants in the Hungarian revolt (1848–1849) against Austria.

Named secretary of state following Webster's death in 1852, Everett served during the last four months of President MILLARD FILLMORE's term. Highlight of his brief tenure was his rejection of a proposal by France and Great Britain that the United States join with them to guarantee Spanish colonial control of Cuba and to make a three-way pledge against trying to acquire the island. Invoking the spirit of the MONROE DOCTRINE in his reply, he warned Paris and London against undue meddling in Cuba and expressed the intention of the United States to be the dominant influence in the Caribbean. In 1853 he won election to the U.S. Senate from Massachusetts. He was morally opposed to slavery, but avoided criticizing it because he feared that agitation of the abolition issue would deepen sectional strife and divide the Union. Under fire in the North for his moderate public posture on slavery, Everett resigned his seat in May 1854 and devoted himself to professional oratory. In 1860 he was the vice-presidential nominee on the unsuccessful Constitutional Union ticket. During the Civil War he wholeheartedly backed the Union cause. Everett delivered the oration at the dedication of the national cemetery at Gettysburg, Pennsylvania, on November 19, 1863, that preceded President ABRAHAM LINCOLN's famous Gettysburg Address.

EVIAN CONFERENCE (1938) International meeting on refugees held at the French town of Evian in the summer of 1938. By the mid-1930s, Nazi persecution of Jews and others in Germany had created a burgeoning refugee problem. German dictator Adolf Hitler's annexation of Austria into the Third Reich in March 1938 placed additional hundreds of thousands of Jews and political opponents of fascism in danger of persecution. The same month President FRANKLIN D. ROOSEVELT announced he was inviting European and American nations to join the United States at a proposed conference on German and Austrian refugees. The invitation drew a positive response and representatives from 31 countries met at Evian in July 1938. The American emissary, Myron Taylor, served as conference chairman.

The United States and several other nations indicated they would accept more refugees but little was accomplished before the outbreak of WORLD WAR II. America and most other participants were reluctant to alter significantly their existing immigration policies. The sole tangible achievement at the conference was the formation of the Intergovernmental Committee on Refugees. Although limited in its ability to assist refugees during the war, the organization took a lead role in aiding displaced persons after the conflict. The Evian parley later came under much criticism for its failure to help save Jews from extermination in the Holocaust.

EXECUTIVE AGREEMENT International agreement made by the president or his designated representatives. Unlike treaties, executive agreements are not submitted to the Senate for ratification. Their authority derives solely from the president's constitutional power as chief executive and commander in chief to conduct the nation's foreign affairs. Presidents since GEORGE WASHINGTON have relied on executive agreements to handle routine diplomatic and commercial matters where a full-fledged treaty was unwarranted. Although the agreements are not specifically mentioned in the CONSTITUTION, the Supreme Court has upheld their legal standing, most notably in UNITED STATES V. BELMONT (1937) and *United States* v. *Pink* (1942). WORLD WAR II and the expansion of America's role in international affairs brought a dramatic increase in the use of executive agreements. Between 1789 and 1940, roughly 1200 executive agreements and 800 treaties were concluded. Between 1946 and 1971, however, the United States completed more than 5550 agreements as compared to some 360 treaties, a shift that attested to the nation's extensive new overseas diplomatic, security, and commercial interests. Concerned that the proliferation of executive measures threatened to bypass its involvement in foreign affairs, Congress in 1972 adopted the CASE ACT requiring the president to inform it of all agreements made with other countries.

See also BRICKER AMENDMENT.

EXIMBANK See **EXPORT-IMPORT BANK**.

EXPORT ADMINISTRATION ACT (1969) Legislation that extended and revised the federal government's authority to restrict U.S. exports to other nations for national security, foreign policy, or domestic economic reasons. Federal controls on the shipment of American goods overseas traced back to the Export Control Act of 1949, a measure adopted amid worsening COLD WAR tensions between the United States and Soviet Union. The law authorized the president to limit or ban exports to Communist bloc nations whenever such sales conflicted with U.S. national security or foreign policy interests. It also sanctioned export controls to prevent domestic shortages of scarce materials. The 1949 law designated the Commerce Department to administer controls through an export licensing system. Under the system the department, with the input of other agencies, compiled a so-called commodity control list of goods, the export of which required a license authorizing shipment. Generally, U.S. policy under the Export Control Act prohibited all exports to Communist China, North Korea, North Vietnam, and Cuba; barred the export of arms and strategic materials to the USSR and most of its East European satellites; and placed almost no limits on exports to non-Communist nations.

Renewed periodically, the law was replaced by the less restrictive Export Administration Act of 1969. Signed into law December 30, the new legislation permitted the American sale of items to Communist countries if they already were available from such areas as Western Europe or Japan. This shift reflected U.S. acknowledgment that all but 200 of the 1200 items subject to controls at the end of 1968 were obtainable by the Communist nations from

allies of the United States. Congress further revised export control guidelines in 1977. The updated legislation provided that U.S. policy for controlling exports should be predicated on a nation's current and potential relations with the United States rather than on whether it was a Communist state. The 1977 measure also barred U.S. companies from participating in an attempted Arab economic boycott of Israel. The antiboycott provisions prohibited American firms from refusing to trade with Israel as a precondition for trading with an Arab nation.

The House and Senate undertook few significant changes when, as required, the legislation was renewed in 1979. As signed into law September 29, the act extended and amended export control programs authorized under the 1969 legislation. The new measure outlined criteria for the president to consider before imposing export restrictions for foreign policy reasons. It streamlined export licensing procedures and directed the Commerce Department to scale back the number of items subject to limitations. The legislation also continued restrictions designed to curb American complicity in an Arab trade boycott against Israel. After the law expired in 1984, the White House controlled exports under emergency powers while the House and Senate engaged in protracted negotiations on renewal legislation. Congress in 1985 approved a measure to extend export administration. The act strengthened the president's power to block highly sensitive military exports and authorized new curbs on trade to protest other nations' foreign policies.

EXPORT CONTROL ACT See **EXPORT ADMINISTRATION ACT**.

EXPORT TRADING COMPANY ACT (1982) Federal law designed to increase U.S. exports. Congress on October 1, 1982, passed legislation to encourage formation of export trading companies to help U.S. firms sell their goods and services abroad. As signed into law October 8, the measure eased antitrust restrictions that had inhibited joint export activities in the United States. It set up a mechanism for federal officials to grant American export trading companies limited exemption from U.S. antitrust laws. The act also, for the first time, allowed bank holding companies and certain banking institutions, commercial banks excluded, to invest in combined export ventures. The law defined trading companies as organizations primarily engaged in exporting U.S. goods or services or providing export trade services, such as marketing, transportation, or processing foreign orders. The development of such companies had lagged in the United States largely because of the uncertainties presented by U.S. antimonopoly statutes and banking regulations. Historically, banking and commerce had been kept separate to ensure the soundness of banking institutions.

EXPORT-IMPORT BANK (Eximbank) Federal lending institution formed to stimulate the nation's overseas trade by helping finance U.S. exports. Founded in 1934 as a federal corporation to spur the sale of American goods overseas during the Great Depression, the bank was made an independent U.S. government agency in 1945. Situated in Washington, D.C., Eximbank is headed by a board of directors comprising five full-time members appointed to four-year terms by the president with Senate confirmation. In addition, the secretary of commerce and U.S. trade representative are *ex officio* members. All Eximbank lending is directed toward helping American exporters meet government-subsidized competition from other countries. Concerned primarily with promoting the sale of U.S. products abroad, Eximbank under various programs provides direct loans and export credits to foreign governments, corporations, and citizens to help finance their purchase of American goods and services. In a related capacity, it makes loans to foreign banks which in turn lend to foreign buyers of U.S. exports. In addition, the bank extends loans and credit guarantees to U.S. exporters to protect them against

undue risks of doing business abroad. Eximbank is authorized to insure American exports against nonpayment by foreign purchasers. Reasons for nonpayment include war and expropriation by a foreign government. Bank funds are derived from stock subscribed by the U.S. Treasury in 1945, loans from the federal treasury and private banks, and interest earnings. Eximbank is not supposed to compete with private capital but to supplement it when monies available in the private sector are inadequate.

EXTERRITORIALITY See **EXTRATERRITORIALITY**.

EXTRATERRITORIALITY Principle by which nationals of one country are exempted from the legal jurisdiction and law courts of another country in which they are residing. Based either on specific treaty terms or international custom, the privilege was conceded under pressure in the 19th century by African and Asian states to the Western nations. The Western powers regarded African and Asian institutions as inferior and insisted upon immunity from local laws for European and American subjects or citizens. As a result, extraterritoriality courts were established to administer Western law. After securing limited extraterritoriality provisions in agreements with the Barbary states, the United States concluded an 1830 treaty with Turkey that exempted American citizens from Islamic law. This immunity was repealed in 1923. The United States gained extraterritoriality privileges in China under the TREATY OF WANGHIA (1844) and in Japan under the TREATY OF EDO (1858). By the end of WORLD WAR II the European nations and United States had abandoned extraterritoriality. The international practice of exempting diplomats and their families from local jurisdictions is called exterritoriality and remains in effect.

F

FACTORY SYSTEM System of trade with the Indian tribes enacted by Congress on March 3, 1795, and in operation until 1822. At the urging of the Washington administration, lawmakers established the factory system to shield the Indians against exploitation by private traders, promote peace on the American frontier, and counteract British and Spanish influence among the tribes. The system comprised a network of federally operated trading posts where Indians could obtain goods at cost. Factory referred to the factors, or agents, in charge of the government stores.

The United States, hoping for improved Indian-white relations, sought an end to the abuses committed upon the Indians by traders eager to capitalize on the lucrative frontier commerce of the late 18th century. The Trading House Act of 1806 extended the system beyond the Mississippi River and established a superintendent of Indian trade to operate the program. From its inception, the factory system struggled to compete with more efficient British traders from Canada and private U.S. trading interests. Frontier merchants, fur companies, and Indian agents opposed its continuation and Senator Thomas H. Benton (D-MO) led a successful campaign in Congress for the system's abolition. Legislation passed May 6, 1822, repealed the factory system and a companion law established a curtailed federal program for regulating and licensing the Indian trade.

FAIR SHARE REFUGEE ACT (1960) Refugee assistance measure passed as a consequence of U.S. participation in the UNITED NATIONS-sponsored World Refugee Year. In December 1958 the U.N. General Assembly approved a concentrated campaign to resolve worldwide refugee issues. A major goal was the final resettlement of remaining post–WORLD WAR II refugees in Europe. American involvement in the Refugee Year, designated from July 1, 1959, to June 30, 1960, was announced at a May 1959 White House Conference on Refugees. As part of the U.S. initiative, the Eisenhower administration urged a loosening of strict U.S. immigration quotas and adoption of a liberalized refugee admissions policy.

The Fair Share Refugee Act, the nation's broadest refugee legislation to that point, was enacted July 14, 1960. Unlike previous measures, which had provided access to a specific nationality or responded to a particular emergency, the law established general procedures for refugee admissions. "Fair share" derived from the act's formulation of an appropriate percentage of refugees to be absorbed by the United States. Also referred to as the World Refugee Year Law, the act authorized the Justice Department to admit refugees from Europe and the Middle East at a maximum rate of 25 percent of the total refugee admissions of other nations. The law's admission provisions were extended by the MIGRATION AND REFUGEE ASSISTANCE ACT in 1962.

FAIRBANK, JOHN KING (1904–1991) Historian long considered among the world's leading authorities on modern China and Asia's relations with the West. The South Dakota native graduated from Harvard University in 1929. He spent two years on a Rhodes Scholarship to Oxford

University in England and in the early 1930s went to China to study and teach. After receiving his Ph.D. degree from Oxford in 1936, he joined the faculty at Harvard as a history instructor. During WORLD WAR II he held a succession of U.S. government posts, serving with the OFFICE OF STRATEGIC SERVICES and the OFFICE OF WAR INFORMATION, and spending time in China as an assistant to the American ambassador and as director of the United States Information Service there. He returned to Harvard in 1946, becoming a full professor in 1948.

In the postwar years Fairbank added his voice to the growing debate on U.S. policy toward China. He urged that the United States come to terms with the 1949 Communist victory over Chiang Kai-shek's Nationalist regime and adopt a more pragmatic approach toward Peking. Fairbank became a target of congressional investigations in the early 1950s into alleged Communist subversion in government and academia. Senator JOSEPH R. MCCARTHY (R-WI), who spearheaded the congressional probes, claimed that Fairbank and other prominent "China hands" had, through their influence on U.S. policy, essentially "lost" China to the Communists. In 1951 ex-Communist Louis F. Budenz fingered Fairbank as a former Communist, a charge the Harvard professor denied. In testimony before the Senate internal security subcommittee in 1952, he repeated under oath his earlier assertions that he had never been a Communist. Ultimately he was cleared of the charges. Fairbank continued to call for the establishment of diplomatic relations with Communist China and admission of the Peking regime to the UNITED NATIONS. He suggested that Communist China should be contained but not isolated and advocated that some manner of political accommodation be struck between the mainland and Taiwan. In the mid-1960s he urged a negotiated end to the VIETNAM WAR and by 1970 had joined in the domestic opposition to American policy in Southeast Asia. Among the many books he authored or co-authored were his classic The *United States and China* (1948); *East Asia: The Great Tradition* (1960), done in collaboration with EDWIN O. REISCHAUER; *East Asia: The Modern Transformation* (1965), written with Reischauer and Albert Craig; and his memoirs *Chinabound* (1982).

FALL, BERNARD B. (1926–1967) Historian of the VIETNAM WAR and war correspondent. Born in Vienna, Austria, he grew up in France as a French citizen. Fall fought with the French resistance against German occupation during WORLD WAR II. After working briefly as a researcher at the NUREMBURG WAR CRIMES TRIALS, he studied in Paris and Munich. He came to the United States in 1951, eventually earning his Ph.D. in political science from Syracuse University. In 1956 he became a professor of international relations at Howard University in Washington, D.C., a position he retained until his death.

Fall ventured to Indochina in 1953 to research his doctoral dissertation on the Viet Minh insurgency against French colonial occupation. Based in Hanoi, he accompanied French forces on combat operations. He captured his observations on these excursions in *Street Without Joy* (1961). First of his seven books on Vietnam, it established his reputation as an authority on the country. He honed his expertise through numerous return trips to Southeast Asia. After U.S. forces became significantly involved in Vietnam in the early 1960s, Fall wrote more than 250 magazine and newspaper articles examining the war and relating the experiences of the soldiers fighting it. His best known work, *Hell in a Very Small Place* (1966), recounted the siege of Dien Bien Phu in 1954 and the decimation of the trapped French forces in that critical battle.

Fall was a leading voice in the American debate in the 1960s on the Vietnam War. Detractors branded him a French apologist with a defeatist outlook toward U.S. involvement in Indochina. He was, in fact, a strong critic of French colonialism in the early 1950s. His concern about Soviet- or Chinese-sponsored communism in Indochina tempered his opposition to the U.S. military presence there. Neither hawk nor dove, he opposed escalating U.S. military involvement even as he rejected a complete withdrawal of American forces. He felt President LYNDON B. JOHNSON had not satisfactorily defined American war goals. Fall regarded the Johnson administration's assessment of the military situation as unwarrantably optimistic and was among the first to warn about the capacity of the regular North Vietnamese forces and the Viet

Cong to take punishing losses. A seasoned combat correspondent, he expressed contempt for commentators who wrote on war from the safety of the United States. Fall, who kept his French citizenship, was killed on February 21, 1967, by a Viet Cong land mine while on patrol with American marines.

FALLEN TIMBERS, BATTLE OF (1794) Climactic engagement in the frontier war between the United States and Ohio Indian tribes confederated under the Miami Chief LITTLE TURTLE. Between 1784 and 1786, the United States appropriated vast lands in the Ohio Valley through treaties dictated to the northern Indian tribes at Fort Stanwix and Fort McIntosh. By the late 1780s the Ohio Indians had resorted to hostilities to stem the steady advance of white settlement on tribal areas. American forces under General "Mad Anthony" Wayne defeated the Indians on August 20, 1794, at Fallen Timbers in northwest Ohio. The victory capped the U.S. campaign to quell Indian opposition to white expansion north and west of the Ohio River.

By terms of the Treaty of Greenville, signed on August 3, 1795, the Ohio Indians ceded most of present-day Ohio to the United States; the federal government pledged to protect the Indians from further white encroachment; and boundaries were drawn clearly distinguishing Indian lands from areas open to settlement. The outcome at Fallen Timbers also cleared the way for American enforcement of JAY'S TREATY (1794) between the United States and Great Britain. This agreement arranged for the British to abandon the frontier military posts they had maintained in the OLD NORTHWEST and along the U.S.-Canadian border since the AMERICAN REVOLUTION.

See also MAP 1.

FAMILY JEWELS Name given to an internally prepared account of transgressions at the CENTRAL INTELLIGENCE AGENCY (CIA). In May 1973 press reports disclosed a CIA link to an illegal search of the office of the psychiatrist for ex-government official Daniel Ellsberg, pivotal figure in the PENTAGON PAPERS. CIA director JAMES R. SCHLESINGER instructed senior aide WILLIAM E. COLBY to undertake an internal probe of past agency involvement in unlawful or questionable activities. Colby oversaw the preparation of a lengthy report detailing some 700 possible abuses or improprieties since the agency's inception in 1947. The secret list was dubbed the "Family Jewels." It included CIA participation, outside its charter, in the surveillance of domestic groups and individuals; an illegal mail-opening operation; the testing of mind-altering drugs on unsuspecting subjects; and agency involvement in assassination attempts or plots against foreign leaders.

Colby, who became head of the CIA in September 1973, used the Family Jewels to guide internal reforms of agency procedures. In December 1974 the *New York Times* published an article on items leaked from the list. Amid mounting public pressure for an investigation, the Ford administration in January 1975 appointed the ROCKEFELLER COMMISSION to look into CIA activities. Congress formed the CHURCH COMMITTEE in the Senate and the PIKE COMMITTEE in the House. Colby furnished each of the inquiries with the Family Jewels document. Its information subsequently was released to the public in official reports or through leaks. In February 1976 President GERALD R. FORD issued Executive Order 11905 on intelligence activities to prevent future violations.

FAR EAST WAR CRIMES TRIALS Post–WORLD WAR II proceedings against Japanese officials accused of committing war crimes during the conflict. As the supreme commander of Allied forces in occupied Japan, U.S. GENERAL DOUGLAS MACARTHUR in September 1945 was given the authority to arrest, prosecute, and punish Japanese war criminals. On January 19, 1946, MacArthur established the International Military Tribunal for the Far East and issued guidelines, similar to those adopted for the NUREMBURG WAR CRIMES TRIALS of German Nazis, to be followed in war crimes proceedings. The trial of the major Japanese war criminals, those with a direct connection to the Japanese government's wartime policies, was held from June 3, 1946, to November 12, 1948. Twenty-five high-ranking officials were charged variously with "conventional war crimes," such as mistreatment of prisoners; "crimes against peace," including the illegal instigation of war; and the commission of atrocities and other "crimes against humanity." All were found guilty by a panel of justices from 11 nations. Seven were sentenced to death and the others received extended prison terms. On December 20, 1948, the U.S. Supreme Court declined to hear an appeal of the verdict, stating it lacked jurisdiction over an international tribunal, and the seven, including wartime premier Hideki Tojo, were hanged in Tokyo three days later. Trials of other accused Japanese war criminals, primarily military officers, were conducted before special tribunals throughout the Far East; more than 4000 were convicted and in excess of 700 executed.

FBI See **FEDERAL BUREAU OF INVESTIGATION**.

FEDERAL BUREAU OF INVESTIGATION (FBI) The principal federal law enforcement agency, the FBI conducts counterintelligence activities within the United States. The bureau was established in 1908 to provide the Justice Department with its own detective force. It was formally named the Bureau of Investigation the following year. With the onset of WORLD WAR I in 1914, German operatives began a campaign of sabotage and espionage within the United States to hinder neutral America's trade with German foes France and Great Britain. The Secret Service, the agency in the Treasury Department responsible for protecting the president, assumed the role it had filled during the SPANISH-AMERICAN WAR (1898) of counteracting the activities of foreign agents within the United States. The bureau was brought into the counterintelligence efforts in 1916. Its participation grew rapidly after America's entry into the war in April 1917, to include the monitoring of foreign nationals and the enforcement of new espionage statutes.

In 1919 Attorney General A. Mitchell Palmer, in response to an upsurge in bombings and other radical activities in America, established a separate General Intelligence Division (GID) in the Justice Department to investigate foreign-sponsored or -inspired subversion. Palmer named 24-year-old Justice Department agent J. Edgar Hoover to head the new unit. The GID and bureau together orchestrated the mass arrests of suspected radicals in 1919 and 1920 known as the PALMER RAIDS. In 1924 Assistant Director

Hoover was appointed chief of the bureau, beginning his nearly half-century tenure in the top position. Elimination of the GID ended the Justice Department's role in countering domestic subversion, but the bureau continued its involvement in counterintelligence through enforcement of the espionage laws.

The agency was renamed the Federal Bureau of Investigation in 1935. The following year President FRANKLIN D. ROOSEVELT instructed the FBI to investigate suspected subversive activities of Communists, Fascists, and foreign agents. With the start of WORLD WAR II in Europe, Roosevelt in 1939 directed the creation of an Intelligence Coordinating Committee to merge the efforts of the FBI and the intelligence services of the Navy and War departments. The FBI was given broad authority for counterintelligence within the United States. In 1940 the agency gained responsibility for countering enemy espionage throughout the Western Hemisphere and Hoover formed a Special Intelligence Service (SIS) within the FBI for foreign operations.

Active throughout Latin America and the Caribbean during World War II, the SIS was responsible for the arrest of more than 400 enemy agents and detection of a plan by pro-Nazi Bolivians to overthrow their government. Hoover's aspirations for a larger overseas role were thwarted with the formation in 1942 of the OFFICE OF STRATEGIC SERVICES, the separate wartime U.S. foreign intelligence service. Hoover pressed for a worldwide mission for the SIS after the war, but the office was closed and its operations in Latin America transferred to the newly formed CENTRAL INTELLIGENCE GROUP in 1947. The Truman administration and Congress agreed that domestic law enforcement and foreign intelligence activities should not be consolidated in the same agency. The CENTRAL INTELLIGENCE AGENCY, established in 1947, was barred from conducting intelligence operations within the United States. The FBI retained its domestic counterintelligence responsibilities, playing a key part in such early COLD WAR espionage epiosodes as the ROSENBERG CASE. The agency's image was tarnished by revelations in the 1970s of previous excesses in its investigations into domestic dissent in the 1960s. These abuses included mail openings and break-ins. Since reformed and placed under tighter restraints, the FBI remains an active member of the INTELLIGENCE COMMUNITY.

FENIAN RAIDS Incursions across the U.S. border into Canada by Irish-Americans committed to the Irish republican revolutionary movement. The raids became a thorny issue in Anglo-American relations as London pressured Washington to crack down on Fenian violations of U.S. neutrality laws. The Fenians were a secret Irish brotherhood organized in the late 1850s in America, predominantly in New York City, to suport the fight for Irish independence from Great Britain. Growing divisions within the parent society in the mid-1860s led a Fenian faction to abandon the approach of sending arms and men to Ireland for one of striking at British interests in North America. These Fenians plotted moves on Canada, then a British dominion. Soldiers from the recently disbanded armies of the Civil War were recruited and plans of attack were devised. Their opening gambit, an attempt in April 1866 to seize Campobello Island, a part of New Brunswick, Canada, was derailed when U.S. troops and vessels intercepted a shipment of Fenian arms.

On June 1, 1866, a Fenian force of several hundred crossed the Niagara River at Fort Erie, engaged and defeated a column of volunteer Canadian troops, and then withdrew back to Buffalo, New York. No other Fenian action matched even the transient success of the Niagara invasion. Similar follow-up raids along the St. Lawrence River and in Nova Scotia and New Brunswick were easily repulsed by regular Canadian militia. The U.S. military thwarted Fenian invasions staged from St. Albans, Vermont, and Monroe, New York, in May 1870 and arrested the raiders, although political pressures forced their swift release. By 1871 redoubled Canadian defenses and U.S. vigilance had brought an end to the Irish-American raids.

"54° 40' OR FIGHT" Slogan adopted in 1846 by expansionists in the Democratic Party during the national debate on the OREGON QUESTION. Unable to settle conflicting claims to the Oregon country, the United States and Great Britain since 1818 had jointly occupied the territory, which spanned from the 42nd parallel to 54° 40' along the Pacific Coast and inland to the Rocky Mountains. By 1844, western expansionists demanding U.S. acquisition of the whole of Oregon had gathered under the banner of "ALL OREGON" and that year helped elect JAMES K. POLK as president. Polk in 1845 asserted exclusive U.S. title to Oregon in both his inaugural address and annual message to Congress. "54° 40' or fight," first used by Senator William Allen (D-OH) in a speech before the Senate in 1844, emerged in early 1846 during congressional deliberations on Oregon and became the signature phrase of expansion-minded Democrats. Those who voiced the slogan, referred to as "fifty-four forties," insisted on sole American occupation and control of Oregon territory to 54° 40' even at the cost of war with Great Britain. The imminent MEXICAN WAR inclined the Polk administration toward an Oregon compromise. In the OREGON TREATY of June 1846, the United States and Great Britain agreed to divide the region at the 49th parallel.

5412 COMMITTEE See **COVERT ACTION**.

FIGHT FOR FREEDOM COMMITTEE (1941) Private, bipartisan advocacy group formed in April 1941 to press for U.S. entry into WORLD WAR II. Following the outbreak of war in Europe in 1939, growing numbers of Americans viewed with alarm the possibility of a victory by Nazi Germany over Great Britain and the other European allies. Such an outcome, they believed, would imperil the United States. Formed in 1940, the COMMITTEE TO DEFEND AMERICA BY AIDING THE ALLIES lobbied for U.S. assistance to Great Britain short of war to prevent the besieged nation's defeat. In April 1941 American interventionists, convinced that aid short of war would not be enough to prevail over Germany, organized the Fight for Freedom Committee to push for U.S. participation as a full belligerent in the fight against the Axis powers. Its national chairman was Henry W. Hobson, Episcopal bishop of southern Ohio. Senator Carter Glass (D-VA) was honorary chairman. In the months before the Japanese attack on PEARL HARBOR the influential group squared off against the proponents of ISOLATIONISM, who argued for American detachment from the overseas conflict. Its objective realized, the committee disbanded following the U.S. declaration of war in December 1941.

See also AMERICA FIRST COMMITTEE.

FILIBUSTERING Private armed expeditions mounted against nations targeted for political overthrow or economic exploitation. The expression was derived from the Spanish *filibustero*, meaning "freebooter" or pirate. Conspicuous instances of filibustering in early U.S. history were the abortive BURR CONSPIRACY (1804–1807) and the seizure by American settlers in 1810 of Spanish West Florida during the WEST FLORIDA CONTROVERSY. The term came into currency in America in the mid-1800s when it was applied to the exploits of adventurers who, with the financial and material backing of sympathetic private sponsors, undertook armed forays against Latin American nations or colonies with which the United States was at peace. Active between the MEXICAN WAR (1846–1848) and the Civil War, the filibusters, as they became known, staged invasions of Cuba, Mexico, and Central America, with the general intent of capturing territory and establishing local governments that would apply to the United States for annexation.

Conditions in America in the mid-19th century bode favorably for filibustering. A strong expansionist spirit emerged in the "spread eagle" nationalism of the YOUNG AMERICA movement and in the ideology of MANIFEST DESTINY, which at its boldest foresaw an extension of U.S. sovereignty over the whole of North and South America. In the domestic sectional political battle over slavery, Southern expansionists wanted the accession of new slave territory to the Union as a way to solidify the South's power and safeguard its "peculiar institution" of human bondage. Political leaders in the lower South contended that territorial acquisitions in Latin America were needed to preserve the balance in Congress between slave and free states.

Among the filibusters who sailed from U.S. soil, several were noteworthy. From 1849 to 1851 Narciso Lopez, a former Spanish general and self-styled political revolutionary, supported by a number of prominent Southern expansionists, launched three unsuccessful expeditions

out of New Orleans against Cuba with the intent of freeing the island from Spanish rule. On the last foray, he and a number of his American and Cuban exile volunteers were captured and executed by the Spaniards. The most remarkable filibuster leader was the American adventurer WILLIAM WALKER, who in 1853 led an armed expedition into Mexico that was foiled by U.S. government authorities and in 1855 mounted an operation against Nicaragua, where he briefly established a regime with himself as president. Walker's Central American exploits ended with his execution before a Honduran firing squad in 1860.

The American filibustering of the 1850s occurred despite federal neutrality laws forbidding such operations. Most of the filibusters at some point were in trouble with the U.S. courts. However, they enjoyed public sympathy in the South and Far West—where their trials were invariably held—and juries would not convict them. The armed expeditions came to be a nettlesome problem in American foreign relations and an increasingly divisive issue in domestic politics. Pressure from antislavery political forces in the North led President FRANKLIN PIERCE to pledge a crackdown on adventurers violating the neutrality laws. Faced with the impossibility of patrolling the whole U.S. southern coastline, President JAMES BUCHANAN in 1857 posted American naval vessels outside Central American ports to prevent the landing of any filibusters who might have evaded the detection of federal officials. Filibustering virtually ended with the coming of the Civil War, which brought the abolition of slavery and an ebb in the Manifest Destiny tide.

FILLMORE, MILLARD (1800–1874) Thirteenth president of the United States. Fillmore was born and raised on the frontier in western New York. He read law, was admitted to the bar in 1823, and went into practice in East Aurora. He became a political protege of Thurlow Weed, an influential state leader of the Anti-Masonic movement. Fillmore was elected in 1828 to the New York legislature and went on to complete three terms. Meanwhile he moved in 1830 to Buffalo, where he built a thriving law practice. In 1832 he won a seat in the U.S. House of Representatives. After a single term he left Congress and, following

Weed's lead, joined the new Whig Party in 1834. Again elected to the House in 1836, he held office for three successive terms, joining the Whig faction under HENRY CLAY. Fillmore ran unsuccessfully in 1844 for governor of New York. In 1848 he was elected vice-president, having been nominated on the Whig ticket with standard-bearer ZACHARY TAYLOR to placate the Clay wing of the party, which had opposed Taylor's nomination for president. As vice-president, Fillmore presided over the great Senate debate on slavery and its extension into the new territories acquired in the MEXICAN WAR (1846–1848). Unlike Taylor, who opposed any concession to the South on the "peculiar institution," Fillmore favored the Compromise of 1850, Henry Clay's legislative plan for resolving the slavery question and averting a civil war.

On Taylor's sudden death in July 1850, Fillmore became president and subsequently signed the five separate acts that constituted Clay's compromise initiative. His strict enforcement of one of the measures in particular, the stringent Fugitive Slave Act, alienated abolitionists and cost him the support of the northern Whigs. Fillmore's one major foreign affairs initiative was his effort to expand U.S. trade with the Far East. The president in 1852 authorized the historic expedition under Commodore MATTHEW C. PERRY to Japan. Perry's mission culminated in the TREATY OF KANAGAWA (1854), which opened Japanese ports to American commerce and established initial diplomatic contacts between the United States and the long-isolated Pacific empire. Fillmore was defeated for renomination in 1852 by General WINFIELD SCOTT. Nominated for president four years later by the antiimmigration, nativist American Party of the KNOW-NOTHING MOVEMENT, he ran a distant third in the election to Democrat JAMES BUCHANAN and Republican JOHN C. FREMONT. The defeat ended his political career. Thereafter Fillmore was active in Buffalo civic affairs.

FINAL SETTLEMENT WITH RESPECT TO GERMANY TREATY (1990) Historic agreement providing for the reunification of Germany and final settlement of WORLD WAR II in Europe. At the war's end in 1945, victorious Allied powers the United States, Great Britain, France, and the Soviet Union di-

vided defeated Nazi Germany into four occupation zones. Negotiations among the Allies on a German peace treaty soon reached an impasse amid mounting COLD WAR tensions over Soviet establishment of hegemony in Eastern Europe. The de facto postwar partition of Germany was formalized in 1949, when the Western allies formed democratic West Germany in their zones and the USSR established Communist East Germany in its sector. Germany remained divided over the next four decades, reflecting the continuing geopolitical contest between the FREE WORLD and the Communist bloc.

The process of political and economic liberalization launched in the Soviet Union in the late 1980s by reformist leader Mikhail S. Gorbachev unleashed powerful movements against Communist rule in the Soviet satellites in Eastern Europe. Following the emergence in the first half of 1989 of non-Communist governments in Poland and Hungary, Gorbachev publicly declared that Moscow would not oppose the political changes sweeping Eastern Europe. In October Soviet foreign ministry spokesman Gennadi I. Gerasimov joked that the Brezhnev Doctrine, the policy named for former Soviet leader Leonid I. Brezhnev that proclaimed a Soviet right to intervene militarily in Eastern Europe to protect Communist regimes, had been replaced by the Sinatra Doctrine. The reference to the famous American singer Frank Sinatra and his song "My Way" conveyed the Kremlin's acknowledgment of the right of its East European satellites to govern as they saw fit. The same month hardline East German leader Erich Honecker was ousted as pro-democracy rallies swept the nation and tens of thousands of East Germans fled to the West through recently liberalized Poland and Hungary. On November 9 the BERLIN WALL, the tangible symbol of Germany's partition, collapsed as the new more moderate East German leadership ended most travel restrictions. In the following days millions of East Germans visited the West. As the East German Communist regime crumbled, huge demonstrations urged reunification with West Germany.

The stunning developments, occurring at a time of rapidly improving U.S.-Soviet relations, raised anew the question of Germany's status. On November 28 West German Chancellor Helmut Kohl seized the initiative, unveiling a plan for a confederation of the German states leading ultimately to a united nation. Momentum for reunification built as East Germany in December scheduled the country's first free elections for 1990. At an East-West conference of foreign ministers held in Ottawa, Canada, in February 1990, the United States, Great Britain, France, Soviet Union, and the two Germanys agreed to a so-called two-plus-four formula for formal talks on German reunification. Under the formula the two Germanys would negotiate all domestic or internal reunification issues. Joining them in resolving all external aspects of German unity would be the four powers still responsible for achieving a postwar German settlement. The two-plus-four talks opened in Bonn in March 1990. The delegations decided to include Poland in future discussions, particularly regarding a united Germany's eastern border. At the 1945 POTSDAM CONFERENCE at the close of World War II, Poland had received part of eastern Germany as recompense for the part of eastern Poland transferred to the Soviet Union. The Polish government, fearing that a reunited Germany might try to reclaim its former territory, sought guarantees of Poland's western border in any reunification agreement.

All the parties involved initially speculated that German reunification would take a long time. But events quickly outpaced the negotiating process. The first East German elections, held in March 1990, brought to power a broad coalition government favoring rapid unification with the West. In May the two Germanys concluded a treaty for their monetary and economic union effective that July. The movement toward reunification was slowed, however, by disagreement between the Western allies and the Soviet Union over European security arrangements following Germany's reunion. The Western powers, as well as the two Germanys, pressed for a united Germany to be a member of the Western security alliance NATO. Moscow supported German membership in both NATO and its Soviet-led counterpart, the Warsaw Pact. President GEORGE BUSH and Gorbachev were unable to resolve the issue at the May 1990 WASHINGTON SUMMIT. The debate on European security also involved ongoing U.S.-Soviet negotiations on the reduction of conventional military forces on the continent.

In July 1990, after face-to-face talks with Kohl, Gorbachev consented to German membership in NATO. Kohl agreed to limit German weaponry and military manpower and to allow Soviet troops to remain on East German territory for several years. Soviet acquiescence reflected consensus European thinking that NATO membership would serve as a brake on any resurgence of historic German expansionism. The same month the two-plus-four discussions produced an agreement guaranteeing Poland's existing western border along the ODER-NEISSE LINE. With the major hurdles to reunification surmounted, the two Germanys signed a unity treaty in August providing for their full political and legal merger.

The two-plus-four talks culminated in the signing on September 12, 1990, in Moscow of an agreement paving the way to German reunification. The measure ended the responsibility of the four Allied powers for Germany and granted full sovereignty to the newly united nation. Formally the Treaty on the Final Settlement with Respect to Germany, it provided for German membership in NATO, set limits on future German troop levels, and banned German possession of nuclear, biological, and chemical weapons. The Allied powers suspended their jurisdiction pending the treaty's ratification so German reunification could take effect on October 3, 1990. The U.S. Senate ratified the treaty on October 10 by a 98 to 0 vote.

See also BERLIN CRISIS, CONVENTIONAL FORCES EUROPE TREATY, COUNCIL OF FOREIGN MINISTERS, PARIS AGREEMENTS, QUADRIPARTITE AGREEMENT ON BERLIN, SIX-NATION CONFERENCE ON GERMANY.

FISH, HAMILTON (1808–1893) Secretary of state under President ULYSSES S. GRANT. Fish was born in New York City. After graduating from Columbia College in 1827, he studied law, was admitted to the bar in 1830, and practiced in New York City. Entering politics as a Whig, he was elected to the U.S. House of Representatives in 1842, serving one term. He was New York's lieutenant governor from 1847 to 1848 and its governor from 1849 to 1850. While a U.S. senator from 1851 to 1857, he joined the newly formed Republican Party. During the Civil War he served in New York's Union

Defense Committee and as a federal commissioner for the relief and exchange of prisoners. Appointed secretary of state in 1869, he held the post for the length of Grant's two terms. The most notable achievement of Fish's busy tenure was settlement of the ALABAMA CLAIMS against Great Britain for damages caused to Union commercial shipping during the Civil War by British-built Confederate raiding craft. Under the Anglo-American TREATY OF WASHINGTON (1871), the claims were submitted to an international arbitration tribunal in Geneva which ultimately decided in favor of the United States. The Washington agreement also cleared the way for resolution of the SAN JUAN ISLANDS CONTROVERSY and updated U.S.-British understanding on the long-controversial FISHERIES QUESTION.

In the Caribbean, Fish pressed Grant's abortive DOMINICAN REPUBLIC ANNEXATION INITIATIVE. Cuba presented the secretary of state with problems throughout his term. A Cuban rebellion against Spanish colonial rule, the Ten Years' War (1868–1878), resulted in injuries to Americans on the island, causing Fish to seek redress from Spain. Washington and Madrid reached an agreement in 1871 to form a joint commission to adjudicate the American claims. Meanwhile Fish successfully resisted domestic pressure to formally recognize the Cuban rebels as belligerents and provide them with support. He persuaded Grant to remain neutral in the Cuban independence struggle. The VIRGINIUS AFFAIR (1873), in which Spanish colonial authorities in Cuba executed crew members and passengers of a vessel under American registry but owned by the Cuban insurrectionists, was resolved peacefully by Fish, who secured an indemnity from the Spanish government. In the role of mediator, he presided over a peace conference in Washington in 1871 that ended an intermittent war pitting Spain against allies Peru, Chile, Ecuador, and Bolivia. He also concluded the HAWAIIAN RECIPROCITY TREATY in 1875. His efforts to obtain rights to build an interoceanic canal in Panama or Nicaragua failed. After leaving office in 1877, Fish declined an appointment to the U.S. Supreme Court and retired to private life.

FISHERIES QUESTION Recurring dispute between the United States and Great Britain over the fisheries off continental Canada's northern Atlantic coast and its adjacent maritime provinces. The controversy vexed Anglo-American relations for more than a century after American independence. The TREATY OF PARIS (1783) ending the AMERICAN REVOLUTION granted American citizens the liberty to fish within the territorial waters of Canada and to cure fish on the unsettled coasts of all the maritime provinces except Newfoundland. When the WAR OF 1812 broke out, Great Britain declared the 1783 treaty terminated and directed Canadian officials to deny American fishermen access to the fishing grounds. The United States insisted the fishery provisions of the Paris agreement could not unilaterally be voided. The TREATY OF GHENT (1814) ending the war made no mention of the fisheries, leaving the troublesome issue unsettled. A compromise was achieved in the CONVENTION OF 1818, under which Great Britain recognized the right of Americans to fish along certain designated Canadian coasts. In turn the United States renounced other fishing liberties it had previously enjoyed or claimed in British North America.

In the ensuing 30 years, competition between Canadian and American fishermen precipitated various disputes over the limits of U.S. treaty privileges. The MARCY-ELGIN TREATY in 1854 appeared to offer a solution to the enduring controversy. America agreed to commercial reciprocity with Canada in return for greatly extended U.S. fishing access in the maritime provinces. When the United States terminated the commercial agreement in 1866, however, the provisions governing the fisheries reverted to those contained in the 1818 convention. The TREATY OF WASHINGTON (1871), a comprehensive settlement of outstanding issues in Anglo-American relations, restored the expanded fishing privileges. Dissatisfaction with facets of the treaty concerning Canadian-American commercial relations led the United States to abrogate the fisheries provisions in 1885. Thus American fishing rights again returned to what they had been under the 1818 convention.

The BAYARD-CHAMBERLAIN TREATY of 1888 proposed a final settlement of the dispute but it was rejected by the U.S. Senate for domestic political reasons. Nonetheless, during the Bayard-Chamberlain negotiations, Washington and London had reached a temporary understanding on the fisheries that gave American fishermen access to Canadian territorial waters under a licensing system that involved payment of modest annual fees. In the absence of a formal treaty, this makeshift arrangement was renewed every other year until 1907, when it was replaced by a similar temporary agreement. Finally, in 1909, the United States and Great Britain concluded a treaty that submitted the whole North Atlantic fisheries matter to the PERMANENT COURT OF ARBITRATION at The Hague in the Netherlands. This tribunal issued its award on September 7, 1910. The British claim of a right to regulate the fisheries at question was in principle upheld, but with the proviso that such regulation must be reasonable and in good faith, and not aimed at unfairly hampering U.S. fishermen. America and Britain formally accepted the Hague award in 1912, bringing the long-standing fisheries controversy to an end.

FIVE-POWER TREATY (1922) Agreement concluded between the United States, Great Britain, France, Italy, and Japan at the WASHINGTON NAVAL CONFERENCE (1921–1922) on the limitation of naval armaments. At the gathering's first session on November 12, 1921, U.S. delegate Secretary of State CHARLES EVANS HUGHES proposed that the world's five major sea powers not only restrict future naval construction but also scrap many of their warships already afloat. Hughes's disarmament plan served as the basis for the Five-Power Treaty signed February 6, 1922. Also known as the Washington Naval Treaty, the measure provided for a 10-year "holiday" in the construction of capital ships (vessels of more than 10,000 tons or having 8-inch or larger guns) and aircraft carriers; set limits on the size and armaments of major warships; and fixed each nation's tonnage in capital ships and aircraft carriers at a ratio of 5 to 5 to 3 to 1.67 to 1.67 for the United States, Great Britain, Japan, France, and Italy, respectively. To gain Japan's acceptance of the smaller ratio, the other four powers consented to a ban on fortifications on island possessions in the western Pacific, thus assuring Tokyo's continued naval superiority in its home waters. Under the treaty, the first ever international agreement on naval limitations, the United States, Great Britain, and Japan each was required to scrap more

than 15 capital ships. The pact did not address smaller warships such as cruisers, destroyers, and submarines, which subsequently were covered in 1930 under the first of the LONDON NAVAL TREATIES. Japanese withdrawal terminated the Five-Power Treaty at the end of 1936.

FLEXIBLE RESPONSE Defense policy adopted by the Kennedy administration. In the 1950s the United States had relied extensively on NUCLEAR WEAPONS for the DETERRENCE of Communist aggression. The successful Soviet launch of the unmanned satellite Sputnik in 1957 brought the Eisenhower administration's NEW LOOK defense strategy, which hinged on the threat of nuclear retaliation, under greater scrutiny. Policymakers and defense planners noted that the same rocket that had propelled Sputnik into orbit could also be used to attack the United States. Critics such as Senator JOHN F. KENNEDY (D-MA) argued that improvements in the Soviet Union's nuclear capability undercut existing U.S. strategy because any American use of nuclear weapons would risk a Soviet nuclear response. Thus, the U.S. nuclear threat had little credibility other than in the defense of vital national interests in a general war. By this reasoning, then, the United States needed a greater range of conventional, or non-nuclear forces, to respond to limited conflicts. Military strategists such as General MAXWELL D. TAYLOR in the late 1950s called for strengthened American conventional forces to meet such challenges as Communist insurgencies and the wars of national liberation promoted by Soviet leader Nikita S. Khrushchev.

On taking office in 1961, President Kennedy announced a U.S. defense strategy of "Flexible Response." The new policy took its name from the strategy outlined by General Taylor in his book *The Uncertain Trumpet* (1959). As elaborated by the Kennedy administration, it was designed to provide U.S. policymakers with a range of options, from covert and paramilitary operations to conventional and nuclear war, for responding to a possible adversary. Implementation of the Flexible Response strategy had three parts: retention of an effective nuclear deterrent; increased conventional and counterinsurgency capabilities such as the Army's Green Berets; and improved command and control procedures to allow senior officials to take full advantage of the various options available.

The Kennedy administration viewed the CUBAN MISSILE CRISIS (1962) as a textbook example of its Flexible Response strategy at work. The president was able variously to order a naval quarantine of Cuba, prepare a conventional invasion force, and place U.S. strategic nuclear forces on alert. The strategy's emphasis on counterinsurgency operations led to escalating American involvement in the VIETNAM WAR. The need to retain a flexible mix of military means to respond as necessary to foreign developments remains a basic principal of U.S. strategic thinking.

FLORIDA INVASION (1818) Foray into Spanish Florida by U.S. forces under General ANDREW JACKSON. After 1815, American settlers in the southeast increasingly were targets of deadly raids staged from Spanish territory by Creek and Seminole Indians. When Seminoles massacred an American encampment on the Apalachicola River near Georgia's southern border in late 1817, President JAMES MONROE ordered Jackson to pursue the Indians into Spanish Florida if necessary and to punish them. The general's instructions, however, did not sanction attacks on Spanish military posts. The Monroe administration defended its decision on the grounds Spain had failed to meet its obligations under PINCKNEY'S TREATY (1795) to restrain the Indians within Spanish possessions from mounting assaults on American territory.

Jackson in early January 1818 wrote to Monroe seeking permission to annex East Florida. In March, the general invaded the Floridas with 3000 troops in the first of the SEMINOLE WARS. He seized most major Spanish military forts, including St. Marks; executed British subjects Robert Ambrister and Alexander Arbuthnot for allegedly inciting America's Indian enemies; and captured Pensacola. The AMBRISTER AND ARBUTHNOT AFFAIR provoked a public uproar in Great Britain and nearly touched off an Anglo-American diplomatic crisis. Jackson's campaign ended in May 1818. He had defeated Seminole resistance, occupied West Florida between the Perdido and Apalachicola rivers, and virtually conquered East Florida. Critics in Congress and within Monroe's

cabinet accused the general of having exceeded his orders. Jackson contended he had interpreted the president's lack of response to his January letter as consent to the conquest plans. Monroe denied he had authorized Jackson to take East Florida but decided against disciplining the general. Four congressional resolutions to censure Jackson were voted down by substantial majorities.

Spain condemned the invasion, demanding an indemnity and restoration of East Florida. Secretary of State JOHN QUINCY ADAMS, in answer to Madrid, justified the American incursion as self-defense and insisted Spain either take control of Florida or cede it to the United States. Jackson's expedition had disrupted talks between Adams and Spanish Minister to Washington Don Luis de Onis on the issues of Florida and the disputed boundaries of the LOUISIANA PURCHASE (1803). Negotiations resumed when Monroe placated Spain by agreeing to return its East Florida posts. The United States acquired all of Florida from Spain in the historic February 1819 ADAMS-ONIS TREATY.

See also MAP 4.

FLORIDA TREATY   See **ADAMS-ONIS TREATY**.

FOOD AND AGRICULTURE ORGANIZATION OF THE UNITED NATIONS (FAO) Principal international body that deals with issues of food and agriculture. The Conference on Food and Agriculture held by the United States and other WORLD WAR II allies in May 1943 at Hot Springs, Virginia, formed an interim commission to draft plans for the organization. FAO came into being on October 16, 1945, when Allied nations meeting in Quebec, Canada, signed its constitution. The organization became a UNITED NATIONS specialized agency in December 1946. Its membership now stands at more than 160 nations, including the United States. FAO's stated aims are to raise nutrition levels and living standards worldwide and to improve the production and distribution of food and agriculture products from farms, forests, and fisheries. It promotes investment in agriculture, improved soil and water management, and higher crop and livestock yields. The organization encourages conservation of natural resources and environmentally sound use of pesticides and fertilizers. It provides technical assistance to member governments, especially in the developing world, in such areas as soil-erosion control, reforestation, irrigation, and control of infestation. The organization administers special programs to provide emergency relief to countries hit by famines. FAO sponsors the World Food Program (WFP) within the United Nations. The WFP, set up in 1963 at the suggestion of the United States, uses food commodities, money, and services contributed by member states to support social and economic development initiatives as well as to provide emergency relief services. Drought-induced famine in Africa in the early 1980s became a predominant focus of FAO, which got involved in the search for long-term solutions to the continent's cyclical food shortages. Its Global Information and Early Warning System provides current information on the world food situation and identifies countries threatened by shortages.

FOOD FOR PEACE Federal foreign aid program that disburses U.S. agricultural products abroad. In the early 1950s mounting U.S. government stocks of surplus farm commodities acquired under federal price-support programs brought calls to finance the disposal of the extra agricultural goods with foreign aid funds. Congress dealt with the surplus issue by establishing the Food for Peace program under the 1954 Agricultural Trade Development and Assistance Act, better known as Public Law 480 (PL 480). Enacted July 10, 1954, the legislation arranged for the liquidation of surpluses abroad under the program by two principal means: sales to needy capital-poor countries (subsidized by U.S loans and grants to the purchasing nations); and outright donations of commodities to friendly countries for famine or related emergency-relief purposes. In its first 10 years Food for Peace disposed of approximately $12-billion worth of surplus American agricultural staples, or roughly 27 percent of the total value of all U.S. farm exports during the decade.

By the mid-1960s the U.S. had largely succeeded in controlling its farm surpluses. At the same time demands for assistance from underdeveloped nations were rising.

Congress in 1966 passed legislation extending and amending PL 480. The revised law changed the program's basic emphasis from surplus disposal to foreign aid aimed at combating world hunger. It also, for the first time, mandated that recipient nations begin implementing self-help measures to increase local food production. Under Title I of the revamped PL 480, the United States lends money at below-market terms to foreign nations to purchase American farm products. Since the mid-1970s food sales under the program have been allocated by fixed percentages. Seventy-five percent go to the poorest countries as defined by the WORLD BANK; the remaining 25 percent go to relatively well-off nations. Under Title II, farm commodities are donated to governments friendly to the United States and, in certain emergency situations brought on by natural disaster, directly to needy populations without regard to the status of U.S. relations with their government. Much of the donated food is channeled through voluntary international relief organizations that have distribution networks in place in recipient countries. Under Title III, a portion of the funds raised through Title I food sales is applied toward agricultural development initiatives to improve indigenous food production. Food for Peace, also called Food for Freedom, is administered jointly by the AGENCY FOR INTERNATIONAL DEVELOPMENT and the Department of Agriculture.

FORAKER ACT (1900) Federal legislation approved April 12, 1900, that provided for the establishment on May 1 of civil government in Puerto Rico. After its defeat in the SPANISH-AMERICAN WAR (1898), Spain ceded Puerto Rico to the United States under the TREATY OF PARIS (1898). The American military took control of the island in October 1898 following the departure of the Spanish governor-general and remained in authority pending congressional action to establish civil rule.

The Foraker Act, named for sponsor Senator Joseph B. Foraker (R-OH), defined the former Spanish colony as an unorganized U.S. territory and granted it limited self-government. Control over Puerto Rico's affairs effectively remained with the federal government. The law created an executive department composed of an American governor and an 11-member council (5 of whom were to be native Puerto Ricans), all appointed by the president with the Senate's consent. The council also served as the upper house of a national bicameral legislature. The lower chamber was a popularly elected house of delegates. All laws were made subject both to the governor's veto and to congressional annulment. Under the 1900 act, reduced federal tariffs were to be levied on Puerto Rican goods and the island was exempted from federal taxes.

Puerto Rican aspirations in the early 20th century for greater self-rule were manifested in competing political movements for full U.S. territorial status, U.S. statehood, and independence. The Wilson administration's support for greater Puerto Rican autonomy brought passage of the Jones Act on March 2, 1917. In the legislation, which was sponsored by Representative William A. Jones (D-VA), Congress made Puerto Rico an organized but unincorporated U.S. territory and granted its inhabitants American citizenship. The act separated the upper house of the legislature from the executive branch and made it elective. In 1947 the Jones measure was amended to allow Puerto Ricans to elect their own governor.

To further the island's internal autonomy, Congress in 1950 passed legislation that allowed Puerto Rico to draft its own constitution and form a government of its own choosing. A constitution drawn up by a popularly chosen convention was approved by plebiscite on March 3, 1952, and accepted by Congress. Effective July 25, Puerto Rico became a free commonwealth voluntarily associated with the United States. Their relations since have been governed by the United States-Puerto Rico Federal Relations Act (1952). Under this law, the Commonwealth of Puerto Rico has virtual autonomy in internal affairs while the island's international trade and foreign policy remain under U.S. control. As provided for in the Foraker Act, Puerto Ricans elect a nonvoting resident commissioner to the U.S. House of Representatives.

The island's political disposition has endured as the central issue in Puerto Rican politics since 1900. A 1967 popular referendum upheld Puerto Rico's commonwealth status as voters rejected the alternatives of statehood or independence. In the plebiscite, approximately 60 percent of the electorate chose commonwealth; approximately 39 percent chose statehood; and less than 1 percent opted for independence. Momentum appeared to be building in Congress in the early 1990s for legislation that would submit the question of Puerto Rico's political future to another popular vote on the island.

See also MAP 6.

FORAN ACT (1885) Legislation passed by Congress to prohibit immigrant contract labor. Officially entitled the Alien Contract Labor Law of February 26, 1885, the measure became known by the name of its sponsor, Representative Martin A. Foran (D-OH). The economic recession of the mid-1880s prompted calls from domestic labor organizations for tighter curbs on foreign contract workers. Congress in 1864 had sanctioned contract labor in its ACT TO ENCOURAGE IMMIGRATION. This bill was repealed in 1868, but the use of contract labor agreements remained widespread. The Foran Act made it unlawful to subsidize in any way the transportation or passage of an alien to the United States in exchange for that person's labor for a designated period upon arrival. Exceptions were provided for skilled workers and domestic servants. The Knights of Labor, and later the American Federation of Labor, successfully campaigned for more restrictive amendments in the following decades.

FORD COMMITTEE (1888–1889) Select five-member committee of the House of Representatives appointed in the summer of 1888 to review initial federal attempts to regulate immigration to the United States. Under the direction of its chairman, Representative Melbourne H. Ford (D-MI), the Select Committee on Investigation of Foreign Immigration conducted the first major federal study of American immigration. Submitted in January 1889, the panel's report concluded that the nation's immigration facilities and controls were inadequate and that the enforcement of existing provisions was ineffective. The commission's findings served as the basis for the Immigration Act of 1891, which greatly expanded the federal immigration service. The panel broke new ground when it recommended barring a specific group for political reasons, advocating the exclusion of anarchists being driven from Germany and Great Britain.

See also ANARCHIST ACT.

FORD DOCTRINE (1975) New doctrine for the Pacific announced by President GERALD R. FORD on December 7 during a stopover in Honolulu, Hawaii, on his way back from the 1975 PEKING SUMMIT. Ford, providing a framework for his Pacific Doctrine, described the United States as a nation of the Pacific Basin with vital strategic and economic stakes in Asia. His pronouncement came amid concerns in the region over a growing Soviet military presence and wide uncertainty over U.S. commitments following the fall of Saigon and the end of the VIETNAM WAR earlier in the year. The doctrine set forth a series of premises, foremost of which defined American strength as basic to a stable BALANCE OF POWER in the Pacific. The president called the U.S. partnership with Japan a pillar of American strategy in the region and said normalization of relations with Communist China remained a paramount aim of U.S. diplomacy. Other tenets of the doctrine included a pledge of continued U.S. commitment to the stability and security of Southeast Asia, particularly the Philippines and Indonesia; and an assertion that peace in Asia depended on settlement of political conflicts in Korea and Indochina. Developing upon the NIXON DOCTRINE (1969), Ford's dictum concluded by stressing that U.S. national interests were served by strengthening the self-reliance and regional security of America's friends and allies in Asia.

FORD, GERALD RUDOLPH, JR. (1913–) U.S. representative, vice-president, 38th president. Born in Nebraska, Ford was raised in Grand Rapids, Michigan. He graduated from the University of Michigan in 1935 and Yale Law School in 1941. During WORLD WAR II he saw extensive combat as a Navy officer aboard an aircraft carrier in the Pacific theater. After the war Ford practiced law in Grand Rapids until his election as a Republican to the U.S. House of Representatives in 1948. He served in Congress until 1973, rising in the Republican Party hierarchy to become House minority leader in 1965. He first gained national attention as a member of the Warren Commission that investigated the assassination of President JOHN F. KENNEDY. An internationalist in foreign affairs, Ford supported the U.S. COLD WAR commitment to the CONTAINMENT of Communist aggression. In the mid-1960s he advocated more decisive U.S. military action in the VIETNAM WAR.

He endorsed Republican President RICHARD M. NIXON's handling of the conflict in Southeast Asia as well as his 1971 overture to Communist China and policy of DETENTE with the Soviet Union. In October 1973 Nixon nominated Ford to succeed Vice-President Spiro T. Agnew, who had resigned over involvement in a bribery scandal. He was confirmed by Congress and took office in December 1973. On August 9, 1974, Ford became president following Nixon's resignation under the threat of impeachment for his role in the Watergate scandal. The traditional "honeymoon" from criticism enjoyed by a new president ended abruptly on September 8 when Ford granted Nixon a "full, free, and absolute pardon" for any offenses committed during his tenure in the White House. The action brought charges that Nixon had received unwarranted special treatment. Ford denied allegations he had made a deal with the former president, defending the pardon as necessary to allow the nation to put Watergate behind it.

He continued the broad outlines of the Nixon administration's foreign policy, retaining influential Secretary of State HENRY A. KISSINGER. In November 1974 Ford met with Soviet General Secretary Leonid I. Brezhnev at the VLADIVOSTOK SUMMIT. The two leaders reaffirmed their commitment to U.S.-Soviet detente and signed the VLADIVOSTOK ACCORD providing a framework for a SALT II arms control agreement. In July 1975 Ford journeyed to Finland for a summit meeting of the 35-nation CONFERENCE ON SECURITY AND COOPERATION IN EUROPE, at which delegates signed the HELSINKI ACCORDS on improved East-West relations. He continued to build on Nixon's opening to the People's Republic of China, holding four days of talks with the senior Communist Chinese leadership at the December 1975 PEKING SUMMIT. At a stopover in Honolulu on his return trip to Washington, he declared the FORD DOCTRINE reasserting U.S. commitment to the security and stability of the Pacific region.

Ford had been unable to prevent the final collapse of U.S. policy in Southeast Asia in 1975. The last American combat forces had departed South Vietnam in 1973 and Congress the same year had passed the CASE-CHURCH AMENDMENT barring further U.S. military involvement in Indochina. Beginning in January 1975, amid growing indications of a major North Vietnamese offensive against South Vietnam, Ford pleaded unsuccessfully with Congress to provide emergency military aid to Saigon. When it became apparent the Communist offensive would prevail, he directed all American personnel be evacuated. U.S. allies Cambodia and South Vietnam both fell to the Communist forces in April 1975. The following month he ordered a military operation that rescued an American merchant vessel seized by Cambodian Communists. Ford's use of force in the MAYAGUEZ INCIDENT was seen widely as conveying America's readiness to defend its interests in the wake of its Vietnam debacle.

Following press disclosures of widespread abuses by the CENTRAL INTELLIGENCE AGENCY (CIA), Ford in January 1975 named a panel headed by Vice-President NELSON A. ROCKEFELLER to examine the charges. ROCKEFELLER COMMISSION findings of unlawful and improper CIA activities, along with the investigations of the congressional CHURCH COMMITTEE and PIKE COMMITTEE, prompted Ford in February 1976 to issue an executive order governing the activities of the U.S. INTELLIGENCE COMMUNITY. Disregarding his warnings of a Communist threat to southern Africa, Congress the previous month had passed the CLARK AMENDMENT ending covert U.S. aid to the pro-Western factions in the ANGOLAN CIVIL WAR. In the Middle East he supported Kissinger's SHUTTLE DIPLOMACY, undertaken in the aftermath of the 1973 YOM KIPPUR WAR. The secretary of state's labors yielded Egyptian-Israeli and Syrian-Israeli troop disengagement agreements. Ford was defeated for reelection in 1976 by Democratic candidate JIMMY CARTER. In retirement he remained active in national politics and served on a number of corporate boards. He published his memoirs, *A Time to Heal*, in 1979.

FORDNEY-McCUMBER TARIFF (1922) Legislation that completed America's return to a protectionist trade policy. The UNDERWOOD TARIFF (1913) had lowered U.S. import duties, shifting U.S. trade policy from PROTECTIONISM to the encouragement of international commerce. Following WORLD WAR I, worsening domestic economic conditions in 1921 brought passage of the EMERGENCY TARIFF, which imposed steeper customs fees on imported agricultural items. In 1922 Representative Joseph W. Fordney (R-MI) and Senator Porter J. McCumber (R-ND) sponsored a tariff bill that restored high protectionist rates on manufactured goods as well as farm products. Enacted September 21, 1922, the measure included a reciprocity provision that authorized the president to raise or lower a tariff by 50 percent in response to changes in foreign rates. Negotiations with Great Britain and France in the 1920s for mutual tariff reductions proved unsuccessful. The Fordney-McCumber Tariff was replaced in 1930 by the even steeper SMOOT-HAWLEY TARIFF.

FOREIGN AFFAIRS See **COUNCIL ON FOREIGN RELATIONS**.

FOREIGN AGENTS REGISTRATION ACT (1938) Legislation governing the activities of foreign agents operating in the United States. Adopted as the aggressive actions of Nazi Germany and Fascist Italy raised the threat of war in Europe, the act was devised to protect the U.S. government against subversion from abroad. It stemmed out of a congressional probe into Nazi and other subversive propaganda circulated in the United States. The measure, which became law on June 8, 1938, required firms and individuals (excepting diplomats) who represented a foreign government to register with the Justice Department. Registrants were required to detail what work they planned to do, list their offices and employees, and disclose all funds received and spent in the United States and propaganda disseminated. Under the law, violaters faced penalties of up to five years imprisonment and a $10,000 fine. Exclusively commercial groups were exempted from the registration requirements.

In 1966 Congress passed legislation updating and broadening the 1938 act. By the mid-1960s, lawmakers' concern had shifted from foreign subversion to the need to place tighter controls over the proliferating number of lobbyists, often U.S. citizens, who sought to influence or otherwise affect the U.S. government and its policies on be-half of foreign interests. Signed into law July 4, 1966, the revised measure imposed stricter disclosure requirements for foreign lobbyists and expanded the scope of activities for which foreign agents must register. It required agents representing foreign interests to make known their status when contacting government officials and members of Congress. The legislation also prohibited contingent fee contracts between agents and their foreign principals based on the success of political activities undertaken by the agents, outlawed campaign contributions on behalf of foreign interests, and broadened registration exemptions for commercial activities.

FOREIGN ASSISTANCE ACT (1961) Federal law that initiated a new phase in post–WORLD WAR II foreign aid, following the MARSHALL PLAN (1948) and MUTUAL SECURITY ACT (1951). It was first in a series of annual pieces of legislation authorizing U.S. foreign assistance programs. When JOHN F. KENNEDY became president in 1961, he sought to reorient America's foreign aid program from military to economic assistance. Kennedy believed the prevailing emphasis on military aid, meant to assist the CONTAINMENT of Communist expansion, was unsuited to an emerging shift in the East-West COLD WAR struggle from direct confrontation to ideological competition in the THIRD WORLD. In his first message to Congress on overseas aid, he declared that the United States and other free industrialized nations should mount a major economic assistance effort aimed at helping underdeveloped countries achieve self-sustained economic growth.

At Kennedy's urging Congress passed the Foreign Assistance Act of 1961, which replaced the decade-old Mutual Security Act as the fundamental law on American economic and military aid. The new measure scrapped the consolidated approach to foreign aid in effect since 1951 by separating military from nonmilitary assistance. The Mutual Security Assistance program—the military aid component—was placed under the administration of the Defense Department. The 1961 act established the new AGENCY FOR INTERNATIONAL DEVELOPMENT (AID) within the State Department. AID absorbed the functions of the INTERNATIONAL

COOPERATION ADMINISTRATION and the DEVELOPMENT LOAN FUND, both of which were abolished, and administered virtually all U.S. economic and technical assistance programs. Two other Kennedy administration foreign aid initiatives also were launched in 1961: the ALLIANCE FOR PROGRESS, a multibillion dollar plan for economic development in Latin America, and the PEACE CORPS, a program for sending young American volunteers to less-developed nations to furnish technical skills. In the 1950s military assistance had been roughly double the level of development aid. During the first half of the 1960s the ratio was reversed. The Foreign Assistance Act remains the basic yearly legislative vehicle for authorizing America's overseas aid program.

FOREIGN CORRUPT PRACTICES ACT (1977) Federal law that prohibits American corporations from bribing foreign officials. The measure grew indirectly out of the domestic Watergate scandal that brought the resignation of President RICHARD M. NIXON in 1974. While probing illegal corporate contributions to the 1972 Nixon presidential campaign, the Watergate special prosecutor uncovered a series of corporate political slush funds that had been hidden from regular accounting controls. The Securities and Exchange Commission (SEC), insisting such practices undermined corporate accountability to stockholders, launched an independent investigation of the concealed funds in 1974. After the SEC probe exposed large-scale overseas bribery involving corporate slush funds, the Senate moved to curb the corruption.

By the time Congress cleared legislation in early December 1977 criminalizing foreign bribes, more than 400 U.S. companies had admitted making highly questionable payments to officials in other countries. As signed into law on December 19, 1977, the Foreign Corrupt Practices Act barred American firms from bribing foreign officials either to win business contracts from their governments or to influence their nations' laws or regulations. The measure set criminal penalities of fines and/or imprisonment for violations of the bribery ban by corporations or their individual officers, employees, or shareholders. The act also required corporations to publicly divulge purchasers of more than 5 percent of their stock. This provision was included as a device for gauging the stake that foreign investors had acquired in U.S. companies.

See also KOREAGATE, LOCKHEED SCANDAL.

FOREIGN INFORMATION SERVICE See **OFFICE OF WAR INFORMATION**.

FOREIGN OPERATIONS ADMINISTRATION See **MUTUAL SECURITY ACT**.

FOREIGN POLICY ASSOCIATION Organization dedicated to stimulating interest in international relations and educating the public on current issues in U.S. foreign policy. Founded in New York City in 1918 by a group of liberal intellectuals as the League of Free Nations Association, it embraced internationalist ideas and endorsed U.S. participation in the LEAGUE OF NATIONS formed following WORLD WAR I. In 1921, after the Senate's failure to ratify the TREATY OF VERSAILLES (1919) prevented U.S. membership in the league, the organization changed its name to the Foreign Policy Association. During WORLD WAR II its publications and meetings focused on informing Americans about the creation of the UNITED NATIONS. The association sponsors the "Great Decisions" discussion series on national public radio and television networks, arranges special conferences on world affairs, and holds open forums in New York featuring prominent speakers on contemporary international issues. Association publications include the periodical *A Citizen's Guide to U.S. Foreign Policy* (issued prior to national elections) and the monthly *Foreign Policy Preview*, a newsletter that addresses pending elections, legislation, and diplomatic negotiations.

FOREIGN RELATIONS OF THE UNITED STATES State Department publication. These volumes are digests of the diplomatic correspondence of the United States. Compiled and edited by the State Department's Office of the Historian, the Foreign Relations series includes one or more volumes for each year beginning in 1861, except for 1869, when no volume was issued. Orginally entitled *Papers Relating to Foreign Affairs Accompanying the Annual Message of the President*, the name of the series was changed in 1870 to *Papers Relating to the Foreign Relations of the United States*, and in 1947 to the present title. In addition to the annual volumes, the department occasionally has published special supplements on major diplomatic issues or events, for example, a 13-volume series on the PARIS PEACE CONFERENCE (1919) and volumes on the major Allied WORLD WAR II conferences. The overwhelming quantity of relevant documentary material of American foreign affairs since World War II has resulted in a 30-year publication backlog. The series provides, subject to restrictions dictated by federal security regulations, a comprehensive documentary record of major U.S. foreign policy decisions.

FOREIGN SERVICE U.S. diplomatic and consular establishment. The ROGERS ACT of 1924 created the Foreign Service of the United States by merging the formerly separate American diplomatic and consular services into a single entity under the DEPARTMENT OF STATE. The service conducts day-to-day relations between the United States and other countries. Its functions include execution of U.S. foreign policy, protection of American citizens and interests abroad, reporting on events and conditions in foreign countries, negotiation of agreements, and ceremonial representation. Entry to the service is governed by a nationwide competitive examination system and promotion within is based on merit. There are three key categories of personnel: chief of mission, a senior career officer or political appointee, who serves either as an ambassador to a foreign country or as head of a permanent U.S. delegation to an international organization; Foreign Service officer (FSO), the designation for the various grades of career diplomatic and consular officers who form the backbone of the service; and Foreign Service reserve officer (FSRO), a technical specialist or expert known generally as an attache, who serves on a temporary basis at the discretion of the secretary of state. Diplomatic officers are concerned primarily with political affairs. Consular duties pertain mainly to business and commercial relations. A consular officer's functions include promoting and protecting America's foreign trade and furnishing legal and administrative support to American nationals overseas.

The establishment of the modern Foreign Service was the culmination of developments dating to the AMERICAN REVOLUTION. The secret diplomatic agents appointed by the Continental Congress to enlist European support for America's struggle against Great Britain were forerunners of the diplomatic service. These agents evolved into the foreign representatives of the newly independent United States. During the revolution, the Continental Congress also appointed commercial agents who carried out fiscal and consular functions and in effect were the nation's first consuls. Following ratification of a consular treaty with France in 1790, Congress passed legislation in 1792 providing for a formal consular service. Several factors discouraged the development of a professional foreign service during the 19th century. The low salaries and allowances allotted to diplomats forced most to spend their own money to fulfill their diplomatic duties and extensive social obligations. Thus independent wealth became a virtual necessity to represent the nation abroad. Moreover, with the spoils system taking a hold on the distribution of federal offices in the 1830s, diplomatic and consular appointments were determined increasingly by partisan, domestic political considerations. The United States did not move to establish a career foreign service until the 20th century, a delay attributable to a number of key factors, among them popular attitudes. Americans for the most part viewed diplomatic service as an extravagance, disdained its pomp and ceremony, and believed it to be inherently antirepublican. The antipathy for traditional diplomacy was reflected in the fact that the United States refrained from appointing ambassadors until 1893. In its first century the nation was represented abroad by envoys of the lower rank of minister.

The emergence of the United States as an international power after the SPANISH-AMERICAN WAR (1898) generated pressure for improving the quality of America's overseas services. A 1915 federal "act for the improvement of the foreign service" removed overseas appointments and promotions below the rank of minister from politics and placed them on a merit basis. The proliferation of American economic interests abroad and expansion of the United States' world role following WORLD WAR I highlighted flaws in the U.S. diplomatic and consular machinery. Congress answered the need

for fundamental reorganization with the Rogers Act, which forged the modern Foreign Service and anchored it on a secure professional basis.

Between 1927 and 1935 the departments of Commerce and Agriculture and the Bureau of Mines of the Department of the Interior created three additional overseas services. In so doing, the departments contended that the Foreign Service could not satisfactorily handle all the specialized functions abroad that each required. The presence abroad of representatives from numbers of government agencies led to frequent jurisdictional disputes, duplication of effort, and confusion. The situation was remedied in 1939 when Congress approved President FRANKLIN D. ROOSEVELT'S proposal to fold the foreign operations of the Commerce and Agriculture departments into the Foreign Service. The few foreign specialists in the Bureau of Mines were absorbed in 1943.

WORLD WAR II created vast new requirements for American representatives abroad. During the conflict the career Foreign Service was augmented by a temporary Foreign Service Auxiliary and other emergency agencies were formed to assist in handling the various war-related foreign duties. The 1946 Foreign Service Act prepared the Foreign Service to meet greatly enlarged responsibilities stemming from America's leading role in the postwar world. The legislation, which superseded the Rogers Act, strengthened the service's administration, significantly improved salaries and allowances, and reclassified employees into the structure that, with minor changes, remains in effect. The act also granted career personnel more flexibility to assume a temporary assignment elsewhere—another federal agency or international organization—and established the Foreign Service Institute for the training of FSOs.

In 1949 the Hoover Commission on the reorganization of the federal executive branch recommended combining State Department civil service personnel and Foreign Service personnel into a single foreign affairs branch. Its report noted that FSOs, because of prolonged duty abroad, lost touch with their own country while departmental officers in Washington had too little contact with or understanding of other nations. Strong institutional resistance prevented action on this integration proposal until 1954, when Secretary of State JOHN FOSTER DULLES appointed a committee, headed by Brown University president Henry M. Wriston, to reprise the questions of department organization and U.S. overseas representation. The concluding Wriston Report, echoing the Hoover Commission, urged rapid integration. This recommendation was promptly approved and within several years, through a process that became known as "Wristonization," other department personnel were absorbed into the Foreign Service, tripling its size. Other influential studies that brought additional refinements in Foreign Service organization were the HERTER REPORT (1962) and the MURPHY COMMISSION (1975).

FOREIGN SERVICE ACT See **FOREIGN SERVICE**.

FOREIGN TRADE ZONES (FTZs) Designated areas in the United States, usually located near ports of entry, that are considered legally outside U.S. customs territory. They are the U.S. version of what internationally are known as free trade zones. Authority for the FTZs derives from the Foreign Trade Zones Act of 1934. They were created to encourage port activity during the Great Depression. Foreign and domestic merchandise may be moved into these areas for warehousing, manufacture, and assembly without incurring federal duties. Products destined for sale in the United States are not subject to U.S. duty payments until they exit the FTZ and pass through customs. No U.S. duty is paid on products exported overseas from the FTZs. The federal agencies responsible for FTZ operations are the Foreign Trade Zones Board and the Customs Service. The board, located administratively under the DEPARTMENT OF COMMERCE, is responsible for reviewing applications, licensing, and regulating zones. Customs is responsible for zone security and control and for collection of duties.

FORMOSA RESOLUTION See **QUEMOY-MATSU CRISES**.

FORRESTAL, JAMES VINCENT (1892–1949) Secretary of the navy and first secretary of defense. Forrestal was born in

Beacon, New York. He studied at Dartmouth for a year before transferring to Princeton, which he left in 1915 short of graduation. In 1916 he joined the investment banking firm William A. Read and Company (later Dillon, Read and Company) in New York, where he remained, except for a period of naval service during WORLD WAR I, until 1940. He became president of the company in 1938. Forrestal entered government service as a special administrative assistant to President FRANKLIN D. ROOSEVELT in June 1940 and two months later was named under secretary of the navy. During the first years of WORLD WAR II he supervised the Navy's industrial mobilization, gaining a reputation as a highly capable administrator. In May 1944 he succeeded Secretary of the Navy Frank Knox, who had died of a heart attack.

Reflecting his deep distrust of the Soviet Union, Forrestal warned against the threat of postwar Communist inroads in Europe and argued unsuccessfully against the rapid demobilization of the American military following the Allied victory. With the onset of the COLD WAR, he supported the TRUMAN DOCTRINE (1947), the MARSHALL PLAN (1948), and the emerging U.S. policy of CONTAINMENT of Soviet expansionism. He figured prominently in the formulation of the NATIONAL SECURITY ACT of 1947. The Navy, fearing a reduction in its traditional power and influence, opposed the postwar movement toward unification of the armed services, and Forrestal lobbied effectively against the creation of a centralized defense department. The resulting 1947 legislation brought the Army, Navy, and newly formed Air Force together in a loosely organized NATIONAL MILITARY ESTABLISHMENT under the direction of a secretary of defense.

President HARRY S. TRUMAN selected Forrestal to become the first secretary of defense in September 1947. During his brief tenure, he argued for larger defense budgets to deter Soviet aggression, took an active part in the formation of the Western security alliance NATO, and worked to improve coordination among the three armed services. In March 1948 he met with the JOINT CHIEFS OF STAFF, the uniformed heads of each of the military services, at Key West, Florida, to iron out differences over the missions and roles of the various branches under what became known as the

KEY WEST AGREEMENT. Convinced the secretary of defense required greater authority over the service secretaries, he endorsed the NATIONAL SECURITY ACT AMENDMENTS OF 1949. Suffering from exhaustion, Forrestal resigned at the end of March 1949. He underwent a nervous breakdown and was admitted to the Bethesda Naval Hospital in Maryland where he committed suicide by leaping from a window on May 22, 1949.

FORSYTH, JOHN (1780–1841) Member of Congress, diplomat, and secretary of state. The Virginia native graduated from the College of New Jersey (now Princeton) in 1799. Forsyth was admitted to the Georgia bar in 1802 and opened a practice in Augusta. His political career began with his appointment in 1808 as Georgia attorney general. Elected as a Democratic-Republican, he served in the U.S. House of Representatives from 1813 until 1818, when he won a seat in the U.S. Senate. The following year he resigned to become President JAMES MONROE's minister to Spain, where he secured the Spanish king's ratification of the ADAMS-ONIS TREATY (1819) ceding Florida to the United States. Returning from his four-year mission to Madrid, Forsyth in 1823 reentered the House of Representatives. He held the seat until his election in 1827 as governor of Georgia. After one term he again was elected to the U.S. Senate, where he served from 1829 to 1834.

A strong unionist and staunch supporter of President ANDREW JACKSON, he vigorously led the opposition to Senator JOHN C. CALHOUN (D-SC) and the nullification movement in the fight over protective tariffs. Forsyth attacked the doctrine of nullification, which asserted a state's right to suspend enforcement, within its own territory, of any federal law it deemed unconstitutional. He condemned on political and legal grounds South Carolina's annulment of the TARIFF OF ABOMINATIONS (1828) and Tariff of 1832. His forceful antinullification stand dissuaded Georgia from following South Carolina's lead.

Named secretary of state by Jackson in 1834, he continued in the post under President MARTIN VAN BUREN and served until 1841. Forsyth's tenure coincided with a fallow period in American foreign relations. He oversaw successful settlement of the long-standing controversy with France concerning payment of FRENCH SPOLIATION CLAIMS for American commercial shipping losses during the Napoleonic Wars (1803–1815). On the issue of Texas, which had declared its independence from Mexico in 1836, Forsyth opposed either U.S. diplomatic recognition or annexation of the Lone Star Republic. There was no decisive development on the Texas question during his tenure. He died shortly after leaving office in 1841.

FORT GIBSON, TREATY OF See **OSCEOLA**.

FORT HARMAR, TREATIES OF (1789) A pair of treaties between the United States and the northern Indians, the terms of which signaled an important shift in federal Indian policy. Completed on January 9, 1789, the two Fort Harmar accords, one with the Iroquois and the other with the Delaware, Wyandot, Ottawa, and Chippewa tribes, marked an end to the federal practice since the AMERICAN REVOLUTION of acquiring lands from the Indians by right of conquest, and a return to the colonial-era principle of purchase. The agreements confirmed the boundary lines and land cessions made in the TREATY OF FORT STANWIX (1784) and TREATY OF FORT MCINTOSH (1785). The United States agreed to pay the Indian nations for the territory ceded in those earlier accords. The treaties failed to halt settlers and land speculators from encroaching on Indian areas and frontier hostilities mounted. Indian resistance to white expansion northwest of the Ohio River was crushed at the BATTLE OF FALLEN TIMBERS (1794).

See also MAP 1.

FORT JACKSON, TREATY OF See **CREEK WAR**.

FORT LARAMIE, TREATY OF See **SIOUX WARS**.

FORT McINTOSH, TREATY OF See **FORT STANWIX, TREATY OF**.

FORT MISSIONS (1914–1915) Pair of diplomatic missions sent to Hispaniola (the Caribbean island that comprises the Dominican Republic and Haiti) to seek restoration of peace and order. Following formal establishment of an American financial protectorate over the Dominican Republic in 1907, the Caribbean nation was able to meet its loan payments to foreign creditors and experienced a five-year reprieve from serious internal political disorders. The mechanism for U.S. control of Dominican finances was a customs collectorship, whereby U.S. officials collected the country's customs and settled its foreign debts by earmarking part of the revenue for this purpose.

Renewed political unrest in 1912 presaged the revolution that broke out against the U.S.-supported Dominican government in 1913. Worsening political violence finally led President WOODROW WILSON to intercede in the interests of preserving the customs collectorship and protecting American lives and property. In July 1914 he prepared a plan for ending the Dominican turmoil. The proposal, which became known as the Wilson Plan, declared U.S. determination to see peace restored and stable, constitutional government established. It called upon contending Dominican political factions to lay down their arms and select a provisional president, after which elections for a president and congress would be held under U.S. supervision to ensure they were "fair and free." The United States would recognize the new government while insisting there be no further revolutions. Wilson then appointed a three-man commission headed by former New Jersey Governor John Franklin Fort to present the plan to the Dominicans and insist on immediate compliance with its terms. The American commissioners were instructed to convey that the United States was prepared to use military force if necessary to effect Wilson's scheme for the republic. The Fort panel arrived in Santo Domingo in August and arranged an armistice in the civil warfare. All the principal factional leaders quickly accepted the Wilson Plan. Before the month was out, a provisional executive had been chosen and an interim government established. Juan Isidro Jimenez was elected president in October and took office in December.

In January 1915 Wilson decided to dispatch another commission under Fort to Haiti, where political violence and public financial delinquency threatened American investments and strategic interests. Fort and his fellow commissioners arrived in Port-au-Prince in March with orders to seek Haiti's consent to a treaty granting the United States a customs collectorship and lease to a naval base. The commission also was expected to gather information on the popularity and qualifications of General Vilbrun Guillaume Sam, a Haitian revolutionary leader who recently had assumed the presidency. The U.S. delegation stayed only a few days, failed to negotiate a treaty, and accomplished little else. The mixed results of the Fort missions were overshadowed by subsequent developments. Continued political disorder brought U.S. military intervention in Haiti in July 1915 and the Dominican Republic in May 1916.

See also DOMINICAN INTERVENTIONS, HAITIAN INTERVENTION.

FORT STANWIX, TREATY OF (1784)   The Iroquois made the first Indian land cession to the United States when they surrendered their claims to the Ohio Valley in the Treaty of Fort Stanwix. Signed October 22, 1784, this was the first of several treaties concluded after the AMERICAN REVOLUTION between the new nation and northern Indian tribes that had been allied with the British in the war. The agreements laid down peace terms, established Indian lands to be ceded north of the Ohio River, and defined the boundaries designating territories reserved to the various tribes. Following the Iroquois action at Fort Stanwix, the Delaware, Wyandot, Chippewa, and Ottawa yielded lands in present-day eastern and southern Ohio in the Treaty of Fort McIntosh in 1785.

The 1783 TREATY OF PARIS ending the war with Britain did not address the Indians. The United States was left to conclude its own settlements with the Indian nations. By 1784 Congress had adopted the position that tribes which had sided with the British during the war had forfeited their land rights. The Fort Stanwix and Fort McIntosh agreements incorporated American territorial claims based on a right of conquest over Great Britain and its Indian allies. Responding to increased warfare on the frontier waged by Indians hostile to the forced land cessions, Congress after 1787 abandoned its practice of dictating treaties and reverted to colonial-period methods of negotiating with the tribes and obtaining land through purchase. The United States signed the TREATIES OF FORT HARMAR in January 1789 confirming the land cessions made at forts Stanwix and McIntosh and arranging for U.S. compensation for the ceded areas.

See also MAP 1.

FORTRESS AMERICA Expression denoting a policy of America concentrating on its own defense and avoiding involvement in overseas military alliances. Its use evolved in the years after WORLD WAR II. Until the war the United States, reflecting a historic ISOLATIONISM reinforced by its geographic separation from Europe and Asia, eschewed any participation in COLLECTIVE SECURITY arrangements or other foreign alliances. At the war's end in 1945, America found itself the world's dominant power with a greatly expanded international role. The Soviet Union's postwar subjugation of Eastern Europe, the onset of the COLD WAR, and the threat of Communist aggression forced Washington to confront the question of whether and how to safeguard Western Europe's security. The Truman administration committed the United States to the defense of the FREE WORLD and the CONTAINMENT of Soviet expansionism. In 1949 the United States joined in the formation of the NATO security alliance for Western Europe and in 1950 President HARRY S. TRUMAN sent American combat units to help repulse Communist North Korea's invasion of South Korea.

U.S. entry into the KOREAN WAR was followed by the decision to deploy American ground forces to NATO in Europe, occasioning the GREAT DEBATE over U.S. defense policy. Conservative Republican critics of Truman's internationalist foreign policy, most notably former President HERBERT C. HOOVER and Senator Robert A. Taft (R-OH), contended that American military commitments on the European continent and Asian mainland dangerously overextended U.S. defenses and risked drawing the nation into draining, unwinnable conflicts, as in Korea. Instead, they advocated a strategy where America would rely on its sea and air power to guarantee its own security and avoid direct involvement in the defense of Europe or Asia. In a nationwide radio address in December 1950, Hoover evoked the image of a Fortress America, calling for defense policies to preserve the United States as a "Western Hemisphere Gibraltar." The idea of a Fortress America was generally rejected as an unworkable return to the nation's isolationist past. The expression came to be invoked disparagingly by critics of the notion that America could retreat from its world role and provide for its own security in isolation from its allies.

40 COMMITTEE See **COVERT ACTION**.

49TH PARALLEL Latitude that forms the Canadian-American boundary west of the Great Lakes. The TREATY OF PARIS (1783) ending the AMERICAN REVOLUTION drew a sinuous line from Maine to Lake of the Woods in present-day Minnesota as the border between the United States and Canada, or British North America. With the LOUISIANA PURCHASE (1803), the United States acquired from France the vast region between the Mississippi River and the Rocky Mountains. Great Britain disputed American interpretations that favored fixing the Louisiana territory's indeterminate northern limit at the 49th parallel. The British continued to claim areas south of 49° latitude in Minnesota and the Dakotas. By the Anglo-American CONVENTION OF 1818, Great Britain surrendered its claim and agreed with the United States to extend the U.S.-Canadian boundary west along the 49th parallel from the Lake of the Woods to the Rocky Mountains.

See also OREGON QUESTION.

FOSTER, JOHN WATSON (1836–1917) Lawyer, diplomat, and secretary of state. Foster graduated from Indiana University in his native state in 1855. He attended Harvard Law School briefly, was admitted to the Indiana bar in 1857, and began practicing in Evansville. Fervently antislavery, he served in the Union army during the Civil War, rising to the rank of brigadier general. Foster was editor of the *Evansville Daily Journal* from 1865 to 1869 and then spent four years as Evansville postmaster. Meanwhile in 1872 he was Republican state committee chairman, in which capacity he worked for the reelection of President ULYSSES S. GRANT. Named minister to Mexico by Grant in 1873, Foster served there seven years, achieving good relations with the

Mexican government during the turbulent transition from the Sebastian Lerdo de Terjeda regime to the Porfirio Diaz regime.

In 1880 President RUTHERFORD B. HAYES transferred him to Russia, where he spent a year as minister engaged in little more than ceremonial functions. On his return to the United States, Foster established an international law practice in Washington, D.C. In 1883 he was appointed minister to Spain by President CHESTER A. ARTHUR. During his two-year tenure in Madrid, he negotiated a reciprocity treaty affecting American trade with Cuba that subsequently was rejected by the U.S. Senate. President BENJAMIN HARRISON sent him as a special envoy to Spain in 1890 to negotiate another reciprocity agreement. The treaty Foster concluded won Senate approval and encouraged American trade with Spanish colonies Cuba and Puerto Rico in the early 1890s.

From 1892 to 1893 he was the U.S. agent in the arbitration stemming out of the BERING SEA DISPUTE over the hunting of fur seals. The United States, standing for the protection of fur seals, lost the case on all major points. For eight months during 1892 and 1893 Foster served as Harrison's secretary of state. In his short term he completed an annexation treaty with the Republic of Hawaii. This negotiation occurred so soon after the republic's establishment under the domination of American economic interests in the islands, and under such suspect circumstances, that when GROVER CLEVELAND became president a second time he withdrew the treaty from the Senate prior to a vote. Foster also presided over the final diplomatic resolution of the BALTIMORE AFFAIR (1891), the deadly run-in between U.S. Navy sailors and a Valparaiso mob that had precipitated a serious crisis in America's relations with Chile.

After leaving the State Department he lived in Washington. At the invitation of the Chinese government, Foster served in a private capacity as one of its commissioners in the negotiation of the peace treaty that ended the Sino-Japanese War (1894–1895). He returned to U.S. government service as its official representative before the arbitration tribunal that in 1903 decided the ALASKA BOUNDARY DISPUTE largely in America's favor. He again represented China in 1907 at the second of the HAGUE PEACE CONFERENCES. In later years Foster taught

courses on international relations at George Washington University. He also wrote extensively on American diplomatic history. His works included *A Century of American Diplomacy, 1776–1876* (1900), *American Diplomacy in the Orient* (1903), and a two-volume autobiography, *Diplomatic Memories* (1909). He was the grandfather of JOHN FOSTER DULLES and ALLEN W. DULLES.

FOUR FREEDOMS Basic human freedoms enunciated by President FRANKLIN D. ROOSEVELT in his 1941 State of the Union message. Roosevelt delivered the annual address to Congress on January 6, 1941, against the backdrop of WORLD WAR II in Europe and 11 months before the United States entered the conflict. Describing the struggle against the Axis powers as a common cause among democratic nations, he called for a LEND-LEASE program to provide war materials and supplies to Great Britain in its fight against Nazi Germany. The president drew attention to the Fascist menace to basic liberties by articulating the goal of a postwar world "founded upon four essential human freedoms": freedom of speech, freedom of worship, freedom from want, and freedom from fear.

FOUR NATIONS ON GENERAL SECURITY, DECLARATION OF . See **MOSCOW CONFERENCE** (1943).

FOUR POLICEMEN Catchphrase coined by President FRANKLIN D. ROOSEVELT during WORLD WAR II to express his idea for postwar COLLECTIVE SECURITY. Roosevelt envisioned the four major Allied wartime powers—the United States, Great Britain, Soviet Union, and China—serving in effect as the world's policemen, working together to prevent or halt armed aggression and conflict. The basic concept of the great powers collectively maintaining the peace was incorporated in 1945 into the Security Council of the newly formed UNITED NATIONS, with the council's key permanent membership made up of Roosevelt's four policemen and France.

FOUR-POWER TREATY (1921) Agreement concluded December 13, 1921, at the WASHINGTON NAVAL CONFERENCE by the United States, Great Britain, France, and

Japan. The treaty bound the four powers to respect one another's island possessions in the Pacific, to settle any Pacific disputes through negotiation, and to consult on the measures to be taken in the event of an "aggressive action of any other Power." The pact effectively ended an Anglo-Japanese alliance that America had construed as a threat to its interests in the western Pacific. Dating to 1902, the alliance had pledged Great Britain and Japan to come to each other's defense in the event of war in the Far East. By resolving the Pacific security concerns of its signatories, the four-power agreement paved the way for completion of the FIVE-POWER TREATY on naval arms limitations at the Washington conference in February 1922. The Senate ratified the four-power measure in March 1922 after adding the reservation that it entailed no alliance, defense obligation, or commitment to use armed force. Japan terminated the treaty in 1936.

FOURTEEN POINTS U.S. aims in WORLD WAR I as defined by President WOODROW WILSON in an address delivered before Congress on January 8, 1918. Political pressure in Europe for a statement of Allied war aims intensified following the November 1917 Russian Revolution. The Bolsheviks, having seized power, immediately appealed for an armistice based on principles of no annexations and no indemnities. To expose Allied ulterior designs, Soviet Commissar for Foreign Affairs Leon Trotsky published the texts of the so-called SECRET TREATIES concluded earlier in the conflict between czarist Russia and other Allies that apportioned the anticipated territorial spoils of war. Condemning these pacts as imperialistic, the Bolsheviks began negotiations on December 3 with the Central Powers for an armistice. The Allies spurned Trotsky's invitation to join these negotiations and did not respond to his request to declare their war objectives. On December 15 the Bolsheviks and Germans completed a separate armistice. (Germany and Russia subsequently completed a separate peace, the Treaty of Brest-Litovsk, in March 1918.) The Allies meanwhile were unable to agree on a joint statement of aims. Bolshevik propaganda began to have a significant impact on liberal opinion on Allied home fronts, bringing mounting demands for an answer

to Soviet and German peace overtures. Wilson decided to formulate an independent American reply.

The Fourteen Points address drafted by Wilson was based on consultations with his personal adviser Colonel EDWARD M. HOUSE and the recommendations of The Inquiry, a group of outside experts assembled by House to study the war aims of all the belligerents and advise the president on specific terms of an American peace program. Addressing Congress on January 8, Wilson presented his Fourteen Points as the expression of America's own war aims. The first five dealt with sweeping general principles. They called for (1) the end of secret diplomacy; (2) FREEDOM OF THE SEAS in peace and in war; (3) removal of barriers to free trade among nations; (4) worldwide reductions in armaments consistent with domestic security; and (5) impartial adjustment of colonial claims.

The next eight dealt with specific territorial adjustments in Europe and the Near East. They proposed (6) German evacuation of Russian territory and self-determination for Russia; (7) German evacuation of Belgium and restoration of Belgian sovereignty; (8) return of Alsace-Lorraine (taken by Prussia in 1871) to France; (9) readjustment of Italy's boundaries along lines of nationality; (10) autonomy for the peoples of Austria-Hungary; (11) reorganization of the Balkan states along lines of nationality, with an outlet to the sea for Serbia; (12) full sovereignty for the Turkish portions of the Ottoman Empire, autonomous development for other portions, and free passage through the Dardanelles for ships of all nations; and (13) an independent Poland with free access to the sea.

The final point proffered the idea of COLLECTIVE SECURITY to ensure future peace. Prefiguring the LEAGUE OF NATIONS, it proposed (14) creation of a general association of nations to provide mutual guarantees of political independence and territorial integrity for all nations. Wilson later added other points calling for a just peace and for the right of national self-determination. Ultimately, 27 points and principles were included under the general rubric of the Fourteen Points. Wilson's program represented an appeal for a new international order and a rejection of the old diplomacy. Captivated by Wilsonian idealism, labor groups and liberals throughout the Western world rallied behind the Fourteen Points. The Wilson administration did not seek Allied acceptance of the U.S. war aims until Germany in October 1918 appealed for peace on the basis of the Fourteen Points. The November 1918 armistice agreement, at Wilson's insistence, recognized his program as the blueprint for peacemaking, subject to reservations on freedom of the seas, reparations, and some territorial particulars. The president lobbied determinedly for the points during the 1919 PARIS PEACE CONFERENCE that hammered out the TREATY OF VERSAILLES ending the war.

FRANCO-AMERICAN ALLIANCE (1778) Alliance struck during the AMERICAN REVOLUTION between the United States and France that secured French recognition of American independence. Since May 1776 France had provided secret aid to the rebel colonies in the form of munitions. Clandestine French support, channeled through a dummy firm set up by the influential and ardently pro-American French courtier Pierre A. C. de Beaumarchais, was indispensable to the early American war effort against French nemesis Great Britain. France's hostility toward the British in part stemmed from Great Britain's decisive victory in the Seven Years' War (1756–1763), the consequence of which was destruction of French power in North America.

Adoption of the Declaration of Independence by the Second Continental Congress on July 4, 1776, changed the diplomatic situation by enabling the United States to establish formal diplomatic relations and negotiate treaties. The declaration also was intended to communicate to France and other possible allies that America's break with Great Britain was complete and irreversible. In September the Congress named BENJAMIN FRANKLIN, SILAS DEANE, and Arthur Lee as official diplomatic envoys to Paris, where they sought French loans and recognition of U.S. independence. French Foreign Minister Charles Gravier Comte de Vergennes promised the American commissioners more secret aid. But the French crown would not risk war with Great Britain by either openly supporting or recognizing the United States until the Americans showed themselves capable of

military success against the British. The British surrender to victorious U.S. forces at Saratoga, New York, in October 1777 persuaded France of American battlefield abilities and led Vergennes in December to assure American negotiators of French readiness to recognize the United States. After Spain refused a French invitation to join in a three-way pact against the British, the United States and France forged their alliance through two historic treaties completed in Paris on February 6, 1778.

In the TREATY OF AMITY AND COMMERCE, France recognized the United States as an independent nation and the two countries granted one another MOST-FAVORED-NATION status. The second accord, the Treaty of Alliance, was to take effect in the event French recognition provoked war between France and Great Britain. Under terms of the alliance, both pledged not to make a separate peace without the other's consent and agreed to fight together until absolute U.S. independence was achieved. France vowed to guarantee American sovereignty and territory; the United States obligated itself to defend French possessions in the West Indies. France disclaimed any intention of trying to regain territory on the North American mainland it had held prior to 1763.

The Continental Congress, spurning British reconciliation offers aimed at forestalling the Franco-American union, ratified the alliance May 4, 1778. France joined the conflict in June and ultimately contributed 12,000 troops in addition to naval power. After the war, its independence secured, the United States came to view the perpetual alliance as a burden that threatened to draw the young nation into endless European warfare on the side of France. Worsening U.S.-French relations in the 1790s culminated in the undeclared maritime QUASI-WAR (1798–1800). The CONVENTION OF 1800 restored peace and formally abrogated the 1778 alliance.

FRANKLIN, BENJAMIN (1706–1790) Printer, statesman, and diplomat; prominent figure in American politics in the era of the Revolutionary War. Born in Boston, Franklin attended school briefly and apprenticed in the print shop of his brother James. He moved to Philadelphia in 1723 and by 1730 had acquired sole ownership of the newspaper the *Pennsylvania Gazette*, which he edited until 1748. From 1732 to 1757 he published the immensely popular *Poor Richard's Almanack*. A patron of local cultural affairs, he organized a prestigious debating club called the Junto; established a circulating library; formed the American Philosophical Society; and helped found what became the University of Pennsylvania. A series of inventions, starting with the Franklin stove (1742), and his experiments on electricity and lightning earned Franklin international renown as an inventor and scientist.

Franklin's remarkable political career began in earnest with his election in 1751 to the Pennsylvania colonial legislature. The British Crown in 1753 appointed him postmaster general for the colonies, an office he held until 1774. A delegate to the Albany Conference (1754) convened at the start of the French and Indian War (1754–1763), his proposed plan for an intercolonial union to defend against the French was rejected by both the colonies and Great Britain.

Twice Franklin was sent to London by the Pennsylvania assembly to act as its agent to the British government. During his second mission from 1764 to 1775 he in effect became a liaison of the colonies to Parliament and plunged into the politics of the coming AMERICAN REVOLUTION. In London, Franklin increasingly spoke out against British tax and commerce policies that he believed foreclosed any possibility of reconciliation between the colonies and the mother country. Following his participation in last-ditch and unsuccessful secret negotiations to settle the mounting crisis, he returned to Philadelphia in 1775.

Elected the same year to the Second Continental Congress, he served simultaneously as the first postmaster general and sat on several key congressional committees, including the SECRET COMMITTEE, which was responsible for procuring war supplies; the COMMITTEE OF SECRET CORRESPONDENCE, which conducted foreign relations; and the special committee that drew up the PLAN OF 1776. Franklin also served on the panel that oversaw drafting of the Declaration of Independence, which he signed. He was part of an American commission that tried in vain to win Canadian cooperation against the British. Named by the Continental Congress in September 1776 as one of three special American envoys to France, he arrived in Paris in December. He was received enthusiastically by the French people, who welcomed his wit, courtesy, and simple manners and who heralded him as an embodiment of Enlightenment ideas. Together with fellow commissioners Arthur Lee and SILAS DEANE, Franklin secured French war loans and completed the historic treaties of the FRANCO-AMERICAN ALLIANCE (1778). Following his appointment in September 1778 as first U.S. minister to France, he continued to borrow money and acquire supplies for the American war effort. In June 1781 he, JOHN ADAMS, and JOHN JAY were chosen to negotiate peace with Great Britain. Franklin was instrumental in the often complicated diplomacy that finally resulted in the TREATY OF PARIS (1783) ending the war.

Returning from Europe to Philadelphia in 1785, he became involved in Pennsylvania politics. In 1787, at age 81, Franklin attended the Constitutional Convention, where he gained distinction as an effective voice of compromise and conciliation. In his last public act, he signed a petition to Congress advocating slavery's abolition. He died in Philadelphia in 1790, leaving his famous *Autobiography* unfinished.

FREE SHIPS MAKE FREE GOODS Doctrine of neutral maritime rights developed by the small-navy European powers in the 17th and 18th centuries and championed by the United States in its early national history. This maxim, distinctly advantageous to neutral shipping, was the centerpiece of an expansive interpretation of FREEDOM OF THE SEAS. "Free ships make free goods" asserted that neutral vessels in wartime could carry, without threat of interference or seizure, all enemy cargoes except for contraband, which covered goods that might be legally confiscated and which generally included weapons of war. The doctrine did not apply in instances where a port was sealed off completely by an effective blockade. Its adherents conceded that neutral property on enemy ships should be subject to confiscation—in other words, "unfree ships make unfree goods." The United States incorporated the free ships make free goods principle in both its PLAN OF 1776, which outlined a model treaty to be negotiated with European nations, and its TREATY OF AMITY AND COMMERCE (1778) with France. Great Britain, reigning naval power in the late 18th and 19th centuries, opposed the doctrine because it undercut the rewards of British maritime supremacy. Instead London embraced the narrower interpretation of neutral rights known as the *consolato del mare*, which essentially proclaimed any enemy property transported on neutral ships subject to capture.

Determined to win British diplomatic concessions and to avert an Anglo-American war, the United States abandoned the free ships make free goods maxim and accepted the more restrictive British concept of neutral rights in JAY'S TREATY (1794). American capitulation on freedom of the seas drew French condemnation and contributed to a deterioration in Franco-American relations that culminated in the undeclared QUASI-WAR (1798–1800).

FREE WORLD   Term used throughout the COLD WAR to describe those parts of the world not under Communist domination. The phrase referred generally to every non-Communist country. U.S. policymakers often stressed the importance of not allowing another part of the Free World to fall to Communist aggression. The term also was used to refer more specifically to the Western alliance led by the United States that stood in opposition to the Communist bloc headed by the the Soviet Union.

See also THIRD WORLD.

FREEDOM FLIGHT PROGRAM   Airlift of Cuban refugees to the United States. In a September 1965 speech in Havana, Cuban leader Fidel Castro invited his domestic critics to leave the country. During signing ceremonies for the IMMIGRATION ACT OF 1965 held at the Statute of Liberty on October 3, President LYNDON B. JOHNSON announced the United States was prepared to accept any Cubans able to depart the Communist island nation. Castro almost immediately opened the port of Camarioca and some 5000 dissident Cubans sailed to America in small boats the same month. The chaotic nature of the boatlift prompted Washington to enter into negotiations with the Cuban government to establish an orderly migration. A "Memorandum of Understanding" between the United States and Cuba,

concluded November 6, 1965, arranged for daily refugee flights from Havana to Miami.

Dubbed the Freedom Flight Program, the airlift brought more than 250,000 Cubans to the United States. Top American foreign policymakers defended the program both on humanitarian grounds and as a way to draw attention to the political and economic failures of Castro's communism. The Cuban government unilaterally ended the airlift in April 1973. The flow of Cuban refugees to the United States resumed with the MARIEL BOATLIFT in 1980.

FREEDOM OF THE SEAS   Principle that no nation has sovereignty over ocean areas outside of its territorial waters. Under international law, the high seas are regarded as the common property of humankind; thus, all states have the right to exercise certain freedoms of commerce and travel on them with due consideration for the interests of other parties. This concept had become a universally recognized rule under international law by the first half of the 19th century. The question of restrictions on maritime freedoms in wartime, however, remained a source of dispute in international relations until WORLD WAR II. The debate centered on the issue of neutral versus belligerent rights.

From its inception the United States championed an interpretation of freedom of the seas that was rooted in the principle FREE SHIPS MAKE FREE GOODS and thus strongly protective of the rights of neutral countries in wartime. During the AMERICAN REVOLUTION, the Continental Congress drafted the PLAN OF 1776, outlining maritime freedoms supported by the United States. The issue of maritime rights dominated early U.S. foreign relations. America's neutral merchant shipping became a casualty of nearly uninterrupted Anglo-French war between the early 1790s and 1815. French assaults on American vessels precipitated the undeclared QUASI-WAR (1798–1800) and plagued Franco-American relations during the Napoleonic Wars (1803–1815). IMPRESSMENT of American sailors and other British violations of U.S. neutral rights at sea were among the causes of the WAR OF 1812. After its indecisive victory, the United States sought in vain to include in the war-ending TREATY OF GHENT (1814) terms affirming the U.S. position on freedom of the seas.

In the mid-1850s the main European powers set out to write a definition of freedom of the seas into international law. Meeting in France, they agreed on articles that generally embraced the principles the United States had endorsed since its founding as a nation. America refused an invitation to adhere formally to the articles of the Declaration of Paris (1856) because the great maritime powers had not explicitly prohibited the capture on the high seas of all private property other than contraband of war.

The United States protested British and German violations during WORLD WAR I of neutral maritime rights of trade and travel. Britain's expanded definition of contraband squeezed neutral commerce with much of Europe and thus threatened to cause a serious breach in Anglo-American relations over freedom of the seas. Germany's policy of unrestricted submarine warfare against neutral shipping eventually drew America into the war in April 1917 on the Allied side. U.S.-British differences over contraband resurfaced at the onset of WORLD WAR II, but again were resolved by America's entry into that conflict in 1941. Since the war, the recurring UNITED NATIONS CONFERENCE ON THE LAW OF THE SEA has served as the international forum for addressing legal issues pertaining to the sea.

FRELINGHUYSEN, FREDERICK THEODORE (1817–1885) U.S. senator and secretary of state. He was born in Millstone, New Jersey, grandson of Continental congressman and U.S. senator Frederick Frelinghuysen. Following his father's death he was adopted at age three by his uncle, Theodore Frelinghuysen, also a U.S. senator (and president of Rutgers College). Frederick Frelinghuysen graduated from Rutgers in 1836, read law, passed the New Jersey bar in 1839, and inherited the family practice. Gradually turning to politics, he helped establish the Republican Party in New Jersey. He was state attorney general from 1861 until his appointment to the U.S. Senate in 1866. Frelinghuysen lost his seat in the 1869 election. He declined President ULYSSES S. GRANT's offer the following year to become minister to Great Britain. In 1871 he returned to the Senate, where he served until 1877. He was a member of the electoral commission that ruled Republican RUTHERFORD B. HAYES the winner in the disputed 1876 Hayes-Tilden presidential election.

Named by President CHESTER A. ARTHUR in 1881 to replace JAMES G. BLAINE as secretary of state, Frelinghuysen held the post until 1885. On taking the State Department reins, he canceled his predecessor's plan for a Pan-American Congress and recalled the commission sent to South America by Blaine to mediate an end to the Chilean-Bolivian War of the Pacific (1879–1881). He fostered closer U.S.-Latin American commercial bonds through his negotiation of reciprocal trade treaties with Mexico, the Dominican Republic, and Spain. Committed to independent U.S. construction and operation of an interoceanic canal in Central America, Frelinghuysen pressed unsuccessfully for abrogation of the CLAYTON-BULWER TREATY, the 1850 agreement that mandated joint Anglo-American control over rights to such a waterway. His proposed Frelinghuysen-Zavala Treaty (1884) with Nicaragua gave the United States an exclusive right to build a canal across that Central American country. But Arthur's successor, Democrat GROVER CLEVELAND, withdrew the treaty from the Senate prior to a ratification vote because it conflicted with the Clayton-Bulwer pact. Frelinghuysen initiated diplomatic relations with Korea under the KOREAN-AMERICAN TREATY OF 1882, concluded negotiations in 1884 for a U.S. Navy base at PEARL HARBOR in Hawaii, and successfully mediated a boundary dispute between Mexico and Guatemala that threatened peace in the region. He also authorized U.S. participation in the Berlin Conference of 1884 that regulated the affairs of the Congo. In failing health, he died shortly after leaving office.

FRELINGHUYSEN-ZAVALA TREATY See **FRELINGHUYSEN, FREDERICK THEODORE**.

FREMONT, JOHN CHARLES (1813–1890) Soldier, explorer, and politician. Born in Savannah, Georgia, Fremont attended Charleston College and joined the U.S. Topographical Corps, receiving a commission as a second lieutenant in 1838. He became a noted explorer, earning the sobriquet "the Pathfinder" for his three major expeditions: an investigation of the Oregon

Trail in 1842, an exploration of the Great Basin between the Rocky and Sierra mountains in 1843 and 1844, and an 1845 journey to the Sierra Nevada in California, at the time a Mexican province. Early 1846 found Fremont and his expedition of 60 men at Monterey on the Pacific Coast. Informed by a messenger from Washington of imminent war between the United States and Mexico, Fremont in May 1846 committed his armed band to the conquest of California. In June he joined the BEAR FLAG REVOLT of American settlers in the Sacramento Valley and briefly headed a newly proclaimed Republic of California. Learning of the MEXICAN WAR in July, he formed a California Battalion of settlers and expedition members that assisted forces under Commodore Robert F. Stockton and Colonel Stephen W. Kearny to establish American control over the southern part of the province.

Fremont sided with Stockton in his dispute with Kearny over who would administer the newly seized California territory. Kearny accused Fremont of disobedience to a superior officer and later pressed charges. In a famous court-martial in Washington, concluded in January 1848, he was found guilty of mutiny and insubordination. President JAMES K. POLK remitted the sentence, but Fremont resigned his Army commission. He returned to California and in 1850 was elected to the U.S. Senate. In 1856 he was the unsuccessful first presidential candidate of the newly formed Republican Party. During the Civil War he served as a major general, briefly commanding Union forces in the Department of the West in 1861 and the western Virginia mountains in 1862 before resigning over disagreements with the Lincoln administration. After several failed railroad ventures Fremont was saved from poverty by his appointment as territorial governor of Arizona from 1878 to 1883. In retirement he returned to California.

FRENCH SPOLIATION CLAIMS American claims for losses resulting from French attacks on neutral U.S. commercial shipping during the Napoleonic Wars (1803–1815). In the Anglo-French conflict that spanned the end of the 18th and beginning of the 19th centuries, adversaries Great Britain and France regularly seized American trade ships in the Atlantic Ocean and Caribbean Sea and confiscated their cargoes. Such raids on neutral vessels were called spoliations. The French and British by these attacks aimed to prevent one another from carrying on wartime commerce with the United States.

U.S. damage claims against France accrued during the French Revolutionary Wars (1792–1802) had been resolved in part through the CONVENTION OF 1800. In this accord the United States assumed responsibility for paying the indemnity demands of its citizens up to the amount of $20 million in return for French agreement to abrogate the FRANCO-AMERICAN ALLIANCE (1778). Another adjustment of French spoliation claims occurred in the LOUISIANA PURCHASE (1803) treaty, when as part of the purchase price the United States agreed to compensate further American shipping losses up to 20 million francs.

Mounting American grievances after 1803 stemmed primarily from French assaults on U.S. seaborne commerce under a series of Napoleonic decrees issued between 1806 and 1810. Presidents JAMES MADISON, JAMES MONROE, and JOHN QUINCY ADAMS each failed in efforts to win an indemnity settlement. President ANDREW JACKSON dispatched William C. Rives as minister to France in 1829 with instructions to press for payment of the outstanding spoliation claims. Following negotiations that were interrupted by the Revolution of July 1830 in France, Rives and new French King Louis Philippe concluded a spoliation treaty on July 4, 1831. The agreement provided for French payment of 25 million francs in six annual installments as recompense for American claims. But the French legislature objected to the size of the indemnity and balked at appropriating the claims money. The prolonged delay in making payment opened a rift in Franco-American relations. President Jackson, in his annual message to Congress in 1834, deplored French conduct and sought permission to force France's compliance with the 1831 spoliations treaty in the event of further delinquency. Jackson's remarks drew angry French protest and demands for an apology. With tensions mounting, Washington and Paris severed diplomatic ties in late 1835. Following British mediation in early 1836, the French consented to pay the overdue installments and the United States and France resumed normal relations.

FULBRIGHT ACT See **FULBRIGHT SCHOLARSHIPS**.

FULBRIGHT, JAMES WILLIAM (1905–) U.S. senator, chairman of the SENATE FOREIGN RELATIONS COMMITTEE. Born in Missouri, Fulbright grew up in Arkansas and graduated from the University of Arkansas in 1925. After earning a master's degree at Oxford University on a Rhodes Scholarship, he completed a law degree at George Washington University in 1934. He served briefly as an attorney for the Justice Department and taught law at George Washington before joining the faculty at the University of Arkansas. From 1939 to 1941 he was president of the school. The following year he won election as a Democrat from Arkansas to the U.S. House of Representatives, where he quickly evinced an interest in foreign affairs and emerged as a leading internationalist. In 1943 he sponsored the FULBRIGHT RESOLUTION, which expressed House support for an international peacekeeping organization after WORLD WAR II, helping pave the way for U.S. participation in the UNITED NATIONS. In 1944 Fulbright was elected to the first of five terms in the U.S. Senate. In 1946 he crafted legislation that established an educational exchange program between the United States and foreign nations. The education grants under the program became known as FULBRIGHT SCHOLARSHIPS. Fulbright became chairman of the Senate foreign relations panel in 1959. In the early 1960s he backed the foreign policy of the Democratic Kennedy and Johnson administrations. At President LYNDON B. JOHNSON's request he introduced the August 1964 TONKIN GULF RESOLUTION authorizing the president to take military action in Vietnam. Within 18 months, however, Fulbright had become an outspoken opponent of the American role in Southeast Asia as U.S. involvement in the VIETNAM WAR continued to escalate.

In February 1966 he conducted televised hearings before the Foreign Relations Committee on the conduct of the war. The influential hearings served as a forum for early criticism of U.S. policy in Indochina. Fulbright, who had also dissented against the 1965 U.S. intervention in the DOMINICAN CRISIS, explained his opposition to the use of American military force in local conflicts in his 1967 book *The Arrogance of Power*, which became a national best-seller. After chairing Senate hearings in 1968 on the TONKIN GULF INCIDENT (1964), he charged the Johnson administration with having misrepresented the event so as to gain congressional backing for the Tonkin Gulf Resolution. Fulbright continued his attacks on U.S. Vietnam policy during the Nixon years, endorsing the various legislative measures introduced to halt U.S. combat activities in Indochina. He was a key supporter of the 1973 WAR POWERS RESOLUTION meant to limit the president's ability to commit U.S. troops to hostilities abroad. Defeated for reelection in 1974, Fulbright went into law practice in Washington.

FULBRIGHT RESOLUTION See **CONNALLY RESOLUTION**.

FULBRIGHT SCHOLARSHIPS Grants made by the U.S. government to teachers, researchers, and students participating in educational programs abroad. The scholarships are named for Senator J. WILLIAM FULBRIGHT (D-AK), who sponsored the legislation under which they were originally awarded. The 1946 Fulbright Act, an amendment to the Surplus Property Act of 1944, set aside monies accruing to the United States from the sale of its property left overseas at the end of WORLD WAR II for the funding of educational travel grants. Subsequent legislation, notably the 1961 Mutual Education and Cultural Exchange Act, or Fulbright-Hays Act, broadened the program and provided additional sources of revenue. Under the supervision of a presidentially appointed national Board of Foreign Scholarships, fellowships are awarded to U.S. citizens for graduate study, postdoctoral research, and teaching assignments abroad. In addition, educational exchange programs have been established with most nations of the world, providing opportunities for foreign students and instructors to come to the United States.

G

GADSDEN, JAMES (1788–1858) Railroad promoter and U.S. minister to Mexico. A Charleston, South Carolina, native and 1806 graduate of Yale College, Gadsden served in the U.S. Army from 1811 to 1821, participating in the WAR OF 1812 and the FLORIDA INVASION (1818) against the Seminole Indians. During General ANDREW JACKSON'S incursion into Spanish Florida, he won distinction when he intercepted the incriminating correspondence that led to the execution of two British subjects for collaborating with the Indians against the United States in what became known as the AMBRISTER AND ARBUTHNOT AFFAIR. Gadsden settled in Florida and was chosen by President JAMES MONROE in 1823 to arrange for the forced removal of the Seminoles to reservations in the south of the territory. That year he negotiated terms for the Indian relocation in the Treaty of Fort Moultrie. He returned to Charleston in 1839 and the following year became president of the Louisville, Cincinnati, and Charleston Railroad. He held the post for a decade, in which time he became a strong Southern nationalist and advocate of a transcontinental railroad along the southern route from New Orleans to California.

Through the influence of his friend, Secretary of War JEFFERSON DAVIS, Gadsden was appointed minister to Mexico by President FRANKLIN PIERCE in 1853. His chief mission was to acquire territory to accommodate the construction of a southern railway to the Gulf of California. Gadsden's negotiations with Mexican President Santa Anna resulted in the GADSDEN PURCHASE (1853), in which the United States obtained territory in southern Arizona and New Mexico sufficient for the railroad route in exchange for $10 million. Replaced as minister in 1856, Gadsden returned to Charleston, where he died in 1858.

GADSDEN PURCHASE (1853) U.S. territorial acquisition from Mexico that completed the continental expansion of the contiguous United States. President FRANKLIN PIERCE fixed American designs on land in northern Mexico for an eagerly sought railroad route from New Orleans to the Pacific Ocean. In May 1853 he appointed South Carolina railroad promoter JAMES GADSDEN minister to Mexico to negotiate with President Santa Anna about U.S. purchase of territory for the proposed southern transcontinental railroad. Santa Anna spurned the American envoy's initial offer of $50 million for nearly 250,000 square miles in the north of Mexico, or about one-third of the country.

On December 30, 1853, they signed the Gadsden Treaty, whereby Mexico sold to the United States the southern parts of present-day Arizona and New Mexico, including a disputed region near El Paso called Mesilla Valley, for $15 million. The treaty encountered opposition in the U.S. Senate from antislavery members who feared further acquisition of territory that might become a region for slavery's expansion. The Senate made amendments that reduced the size of the Gadsden Purchase from 55,000 to the approximately 45,000 square miles judged essential for the railroad route and cut the U.S. payment to $10 million. Santa Anna accepted the treaty changes and the two nations exchanged ratifications on June 30, 1854.

See also MEXICAN CESSION, MAP 2.

GAITHER COMMITTEE (1957) Panel that prepared an influential secret report on U.S. defense policy. In April 1957 President DWIGHT D. EISENHOWER appointed an 11-member committee of private citizens to examine the adequacy of the nation's civil defense in the event of nuclear attack. The panel's director was H. Rowan Gaither, Jr., chairman of the board of the Ford Foundation. Other members included former Secretary of Defense ROBERT A. LOVETT; William C. Foster, later director of the ARMS CONTROL AND DISARMAMENT AGENCY in the 1960s; scientist Jerome B. Wiesner; and Robert C. Sprague, chairman of Sprague Electric Company, who headed the committee when Gaither became ill. In the course of its study, the panel also was instructed to assess the deterrent value of U.S. strategic nuclear forces.

The committee submitted its findings to the NATIONAL SECURITY COUNCIL in the fall of 1957. Although extracts of the Gaither Report were leaked to the press in November 1957, Eisenhower refused to make the document public, invoking the historic principle of safeguarding confidential advice to the president. The report was never released. As later revealed by Eisenhower in his memoir *Waging Peace* (1965), the committee had projected that by 1959 the Soviet Union would be able to launch a major nuclear attack by INTERCONTINENTAL BALLISTIC MISSILE against the United States. Such a Soviet capability threatened the suddenly vulnerable bombers of the Strategic Air Command, the centerpiece of the American nuclear deterrent. Acting on the panel's prediction, the Eisenhower administration took steps to place more strategic bombers on alert status. Committee recommendations for improving Defense Department management and decision making were incorporated into the DEFENSE REORGANIZATION ACT OF 1958. Proposals for a massive fallout-shelter program and enhanced limited warfare forces did not fit Eisenhower's economy-minded NEW LOOK defense policy and received less attention. Cited in press accounts shortly after the surprise Soviet launch in October 1957 of the first artificial satellite, Sputnik, the Gaither Report fanned domestic debate over a MISSILE GAP between the United States and the Soviet Union.

GALLATIN, ALBERT (1761–1849) Statesman and diplomat. Born in Geneva, Switzerland, Gallatin graduated from Geneva Academy in 1779 and the following year emigrated to America. He went from Maine to Massachusetts and in 1784 settled in the western Pennsylvania back country, where he engaged unsuccessfully in land speculation. Serving in the Pennsylvania legislature from 1790 to 1792, Gallatin was an early leader of the state's emerging Democratic-Republican Party. Elected to the U.S. Senate in 1793, he was denied his seat by a Federalist majority because he had not been an American citizen the mandatory nine years under the CONSTITUTION. Gallatin served in the U.S. House of Representatives from 1795 to 1801, where he became the leader of the Democratic-Republican minority and distinguished himself by his expertise on public finance. Appointed treasury secretary by President THOMAS JEFFERSON in 1801, Gallatin held the post until 1814. His program for reforming the national economy and paying off the public debt was derailed by the impact of the Napoleonic Wars (1803–1815) on neutral U.S. trade and by the Anglo-American WAR OF 1812.

Gallatin served as a member of the peace commission that negotiated the TREATY OF GHENT (1814) ending the 1812 conflict. In 1816 he became U.S. minister to France. During his uneventful eight-year tenure in Paris, Gallatin was unable to win settlement of the FRENCH SPOLIATION CLAIMS for damages inflicted on American commercial ships under a series of Napoleonic decrees issued between 1806 and 1810. He did join with American Minister to Great Britain RICHARD RUSH in negotiating the CONVENTION OF 1818, which settled a number of outstanding conflicts in U.S.-British diplomacy. In 1826 Gallatin took the post of minister to Great Britain. Serving one year in London, he negotiated both the CONVENTION OF 1827, which referred the Canadian-American northeast boundary dispute to the arbitration of the king of the Netherlands, and a second 1827 treaty that renewed indefinitely the joint Anglo-American occupation of Oregon. After returning from Europe, Gallatin served as president of the National Bank in New York City. The so-called father of American ethnology, he published works in the field and in 1842 founded the American Ethnological Society.

GARFIELD, JAMES ABRAM (1831–1881) Twentieth U.S. president. Garfield attended Western Reserve Eclectic Institute (now Hiram College) in his native Ohio before enrolling at Williams College, from which he graduated in 1856. He was a teacher and administrator at the Eclectic Institute before his 1859 election as a Republican to the Ohio senate, where he denounced slavery and advocated force to prevent Southern secession from the Union. Meanwhile he studied law and was admitted to the bar. When the Civil War began in 1861, Garfield was commissioned a lieutenant colonel in the Union army and given command of an Ohio volunteer regiment he had helped raise. He held a series of field commands and was promoted to general before resigning from the military in the fall of 1863 to enter the U.S. House of Representatives, to which he had been elected the year before by his Ohio district. He held his seat until 1881. He served on the military affairs committee and from 1871 to 1875 was chairman of the appropriations committee. In 1876 Garfield became House minority leader.

Implicated in the Credit Mobilier and DeGolyer paving contract scandals in the 1870s, he weathered these political tribulations and went on to win election to the Senate in 1880. But Garfield never took his seat. Emerging as the Republican presidential nominee in 1880, he won the general election and entered the White House in March 1881. His brief presidency largely was consumed by patronage fights and struggles over political appointments. His secretary of state, JAMES G. BLAINE, had barely begun laying the foundations for improved U.S. relations with Latin America when, on July 2, 1881, nearly four months after his inauguration, Garfield was gunned down at a Washington railway station by assassin Charles J. Guiteau, a mentally unstable and disgruntled lawyer who had unsuccessfully sought a federal appointment. After lingering for almost three months in a critical condition,the president died on September 19, 1881.

GATES, THOMAS SOVEREIGN, JR. (1906–1983) Secretary of the navy and then secretary of defense during the Eisenhower administration. After graduating from the University of Pennsylvania in 1928, Gates went to work at the investment firm Drexel and Company in Philadelphia. The Pennsylvania native became a partner in 1940 before interrupting his business career to serve in the Navy during WORLD WAR II. Appointed under secretary of the navy by President DWIGHT D. EISENHOWER in October 1953, Gates promoted the development of naval nuclear forces as part of the administration's NEW LOOK defense strategy. He became secretary of the navy in April 1957 and deputy secretary of defense in June 1959 before succeeding NEIL H. MCELROY as head of the Defense Department in December 1959. Defense secretary during the final year of the Eisenhower presidency, Gates rebutted continuing Democratic charges of a MISSILE GAP between the United States and the Soviet Union. Following the Soviet downing of an American spy plane in the U-2 INCIDENT (1960), he defended U.S. reconnaissance flights over the Communist adversary as a national security necessity.

Gates joined Morgan Guaranty Trust Company in New York, becoming chairman in 1965. President RICHARD M. NIXON selected him in 1969 to head the influential Advisory Commission on an All-Volunteer Force, which submitted a report advocating an end to the military draft. He served from 1976 to 1977, with the rank of ambassador, as chief of the U.S. Liaison Office in the Communist People's Republic of China.

GATT See **GENERAL AGREEMENT ON TARIFFS AND TRADE**.

GEARY ACT (1892) Law that extended the 1882 CHINESE EXCLUSION ACT for another 10 years. Named for its sponsor, Representative Thomas J. Geary (D-CA), the May 5, 1892, measure reflected the strong anti-Chinese sentiment of the time. In addition to renewing the bar on the immigration of Chinese workers, the act required Chinese aliens already in America to obtain a certificate of residence and provided for the deportation of those ruled to be in the country illegally. In order for a Chinese immigrant to prove lawful residency, the supporting testimony of "at least one credible white witness" was required.

The Chinese government protested the discriminatory legislation and threatened to impose similar measures against Americans in China. Relations were improved by the GRESHAM-YANG TREATY of 1894. China consented to the provisions of the Geary Act and the United States agreed to relax the travel restrictions on Chinese residents implemented previously in the SCOTT ACT (1888).

GENERAL ACT OF BERLIN See **BERLIN, TREATY OF** (1899).

GENERAL ACT OF BRUSSELS See **AFRICAN SLAVE TRADE TREATY**.

GENERAL AGREEMENT TO BORROW See **INTERNATIONAL MONETARY FUND**.

GENERAL AGREEEMENT ON TARIFFS AND TRADE (GATT) International organization that promotes and regulates trade among member countries. In 1946 the newly formed UNITED NATIONS undertook to establish an International Trade Orgnization (ITO) to provide for the orderly development of world commerce after WORLD WAR II. The United States, Great Britain, and other major trading nations were determined not to return to the high tariffs and other protectionist measures of the 1930s that, in their estimation, had prolonged and worsened the Great Depression and thus helped trigger the outbreak of world war. Western leaders also believed that the postwar reconstruction of Europe hinged on the growth of international trade.

As a first step toward the formation of the ITO, 23 nations, including the United States, met in Geneva, Switzerland, in 1947 under the auspices of the U.N. Conference on Trade and Employment to negotiate an agreement for the mutual and reciprocal reduction of tariffs and other trade barriers. The General Agreement on Tariffs and Trade was concluded October 30, 1947, and came into effect January 1, 1948, under a provisional arrangement that also established an administrative office to implement its terms. Both the GATT agreement and office were scheduled to be incorpo-

rated into the proposed ITO. The ITO charter was completed at the 1948 Conference on Trade and Employment in Havana, Cuba. The so-called Havana Charter failed to gain U.S. Senate ratification, however, and the ITO never came into being. The GATT measure, implemented as an EXECUTIVE AGREEMENT by the Truman administration under the authority of the TRADE AGREEMENTS ACT (1934), had not required Senate approval. GATT by default became the central international trade agreement and its administrative office evolved into a permanent secretariat with headquarters in Geneva. The term *GATT* came to refer primarily to the organization, which is closely associated with but not actually part of the U.N. system.

The 1947 General Agreement set forth detailed rules for governing world commerce founded on four basic principles: trade between GATT members should be on a MOST-FAVORED-NATION basis; tariffs should be the only means of protecting domestic industries, with all non-tariff barriers, such as import quotas, prohibited; members should consult on trade issues; and GATT should provide the framework for tariff-reduction and other trade negotiations. The agreement bound participating states to curtail restrictive trade practices, but a so-called escape clause was included that allowed nations to impose temporary trade restrictions if domestic industries were threatened with serious economic harm. The pact also outlined specific tariff reductions for each nation.

Seven additional sessions, or "rounds," of multilateral trade negotiations have been held under GATT auspices. The first four rounds—conducted at Annecy, France, in 1949; Torquay, England, from 1950 to 1951; and Geneva from 1955 to 1956 and again from 1960 to 1962—reduced tariffs on more than 70,000 items representing over one-half of total world trade. The trade talks from 1960 to 1962, known as the Dillon Round after U.S. Secretary of the Treasury C. Douglas Dillon, cut tariffs on industrial goods by more than 20 percent. The Kennedy Round, held from 1964 to 1967 and named after key early sponsor President JOHN F. KENNEDY, lowered import duties an additional 35 percent and for the first time addressed tariff reductions by broad categories of products rather than by single items.

By the late 1960s, GATT faced mounting charges from developing nations that the international trade system worked against them. For many THIRD WORLD countries, export earnings represented the only means of funding their economic development. Since most developing countries were unable to compete with the more advanced industries of the developed world, their access to international markets was for all intents foreclosed. Recognizing the need to redress the trade difficulties of developing nations, GATT in 1971 adopted a Generalized System of Preferences (GSP), which authorized developed nations to grant special trade advantages to Third World countries. The United States in 1976 became the last major industrialized nation to subscribe to the GSP.

The sixth set of GATT trade talks, the Toyko Round, opened in the Japanese capital in 1973 and subsequently moved to Geneva. The sessions concentrated on nontariff barriers to trade such as import quotas, special product standards, and licensing procedures. Negotiations on a comprehensive set of trade agreements were completed in Geneva in 1979. The measures removed or restricted a wide range of structural barriers to trade and broadly reformed and updated GATT rules and procedures. The Uruguay Round, the latest series of trade negotiations, began in the South American country in 1986. Concerned with unfair trading practices, such as government subsidies to aid export industries, the talks continued past their originally scheduled 1990 completion. The United States and the European Community remain divided over American calls for an end to special subsidies and protections for European agriculture. The United States, Europe, and Japan have all stressed the importance of a successful conclusion of the Uruguay Round to future international economic relations.

By the early 1990s, more than 100 nations were members of GATT. The Communist world historically did not participate in the international trade system, but in 1990 the Soviet Union, following the example of its former Eastern European satellites, gained observer status in preparation for eventual full membership. Following the December 1991 demise of the USSR, Russia and other newly sovereign former Soviet republics moved to join GATT.

See also NORTH-SOUTH DIALOGUE, *GENERAL AGREEMENT ON TARIFFS AND TRADE ROUNDS in APPENDIX E.*

GENERALIZED SYSTEM OF PREFERENCES See **GENERAL AGREEMENT ON TARIFFS AND TRADE.**

GENET AFFAIR (1793–1794) Controversial diplomatic mission of the French Republic's first minister to the United States, Citizen Edmond C. Genet. Relations with France became a major issue in U.S. domestic politics after the revolutionary French government declared war on Great Britain, Spain, and Holland in February 1793. This development spawned concern in America that the French would seek to involve the United States in the conflict under terms of the FRANCO-AMERICAN ALLIANCE (1778).

France decided not to invoke the alliance, since America offered far greater benefit to the French as a neutral merchant trader than as a military partner. Genet, who had adopted the revolutionary title "citizen," landed at Charleston, South Carolina, on April 8, 1793, with instructions to curry pro-French sentiment and to secure an interpretation of the TREATY OF AMITY AND COMMERCE (1778) that would benefit France's war effort. The bold French emissary immediately took steps that threatened to compromise American neutrality. He hired and outfitted privateers in South Carolina ports and dispatched them to plunder British commercial shipping. Genet also offered military commissions to Americans willing to fight with the French and attempted to organize expeditions in the United States against Canada and the Spanish possessions of the Floridas and Louisiana.

The French minister's freewheeling actions troubled President GEORGE WASHINGTON, who on April 22, 1793, issued his NEUTRALITY PROCLAMATION declaring the United States at peace with Great Britain and France and warning American citizens against involvement in the Anglo-French hostilities. Genet meanwhile traveled overland to the U.S. capital at Philadelphia, where he was received coolly by Washington on May 18. The French envoy clashed with Treasury Secretary ALEXANDER HAMILTON over the meaning of the 1778 commerce treaty. Genet insisted the pact authorized French use of U.S. ports to equip privateers. Hamilton contended the treaty only obligated the United States to keep American ports closed to the outfitting of British privateers. The treasury secretary denied Genet's request for advance payment of America's Revolutionary War debt to France. In early June Secretary of State THOMAS JEFFERSON informed the French minister his military recruiting on American soil violated U.S. sovereignty and neutrality. Washington then insisted that Genet order all French privateers to leave American ports. Genet defied the president when he armed the *Little Sarah*, a captured British ship, and dispatched it from Philadelphia as a French privateer. The brash French diplomat reportedly also threatened to bypass President Washington in order to appeal directly to the American public for support.

On August 2 the Washington administration demanded Genet's recall. A new revolutionary government in France consented. The replacement French minister, Joseph Fauchet, arrived in 1794 under orders to arrest Genet and return him for trial. Afraid Genet might face the guillotine, Washington would not permit the extradition of the discredited French envoy. Genet later married the daughter of New York Governor Henry Clinton, became an American citizen, and spent the rest of his life in the United States. British objections to Genet's conduct prompted the United States to define its neutral obligations in the Neutrality Act of June 1794. The Genet Affair marked the start of a steady decline in U.S.-French relations that culminated in the undeclared QUASI-WAR (1798–1800).

GENETRIX PROJECT Program of unmanned high-altitude balloon reconnaissance of the Soviet Union. In the late 1940s and early 1950s, the United States relied on secret intelligence agents for its knowledge of Soviet military capabilities. Concerned about Soviet NUCLEAR WEAPONS programs, U.S. intelligence agencies turned to aerial reconnaissance as a means of obtaining much more timely and extensive informa-

tion. In 1950 the Air Force began development of a camera-equipped balloon capable of taking detailed photographs as it floated at high altitude across the Soviet Union. After several delays, the system was successfully tested in 1955.

In January 1956 Air Force crews in Europe launched the first of several hundred reconnaissance balloons eventually sent over the Soviet Union. The secret project, code-named Genetrix, was concealed by an actual meteorological program involving weather balloons called Moby Dick. In February 1956 the Soviet Union protested the overflights and held a press conference at which captured balloons and cameras were displayed. The United States responded publicly that the balloons were part of a meteorological study; privately the Eisenhower administration decided to halt the reconnaissance project. Approximately 40 balloons reached the Pacific recovery area with useable photographs. Experts disagreed as to the intelligence value of the photographs, but the project itself generally was considered a failure.

GENEVA ACCORDS See **GENEVA CONFERENCE** (1954).

GENEVA CONFERENCE (1954) International diplomatic conference on Korea and Indochina. In the early 1950s military conflicts in Asia captured worldwide attention. In July 1953 an armistice halted the fighting in the KOREAN WAR (1950–1953); continuing negotiations between North Korea and Communist China on one side and South Korea and the U.S.-led UNITED NATIONS coalition on the other, however, showed no signs of achieving a final settlement. In Southeast Asia, meanwhile, Communist Viet Minh forces were nearing victory in their struggle to end French colonial rule in Vietnam. Communist insurgencies also were active in Laos and Cambodia, then semiautonomous states in the French Union. Meeting in Berlin in January and February 1954, the foreign ministers of the United States, Great Britain, France, and Soviet Union agreed to hold a conference of all concerned parties in Geneva on the Far Eastern conflicts. America reluctantly consented to Communist China's presence at the gathering but emphasized that this did not constitute U.S. diplomatic recognition of the Peking government. Later, at Geneva, American representative Secretary of State JOHN FOSTER DULLES would refuse to shake hands with Chinese envoy Chou En-lai, a gesture that came to symbolize U.S. COLD WAR policy toward the mainland.

The conference opened in the Swiss city on April 26, 1954, with 19 nations in attendance for the first phase of talks on Korea. In addition to the 4 convening powers and Communist China, participants included the 2 Koreas and 12 other countries that had contributed to U.N. forces in the Korean conflict. Uneasy about negotiating the future of the Far East with the Communists, Dulles departed Geneva early, leaving his deputy, WALTER BEDELL SMITH, to head the American delegation. The discussions on Korea ended in stalemate on June 15 when the 16 non-Communist nations released a statement announcing there was no reason to continue. They blamed the deadlock on Communist rejection of both U.N. involvement in the Korean question and the principle of Korean unification through free elections.

The first session on Indochina was held on May 8, one day after the French had suffered a devastating defeat in Vietnam at Dien Bien Phu. French will to continue fighting had collapsed and France came to Geneva ready to end the French Indochina War (1946–1954) and grant Vietnam its full independence. Attending the Indochina talks were the convening powers, Communist China, the Viet Minh Democratic Republic of Vietnam, and the French Union states of Vietnam, Laos, and Cambodia. The discussions culminated in three agreements signed on July 20, 1954, and a final declaration issued at the conference's end the following day.

Known collectively as the Geneva Accords, the four measures provided for the end of hostilities in Indochina; recognition of Cambodia and Laos as independent nations; and the temporary partition of Vietnam along the 17TH PARALLEL into two zones, with the north controlled by the Viet Minh and the south under the French-installed regime of the Emperor Bao Dai. Vietnamese civilians were to be free to move to either zone. Nationwide elections were scheduled for 1956 in Vietnam to decide its future government and bring about unification. The agreement prohibited the Indochinese states from entering into military alliances or accepting foreign military assistance beyond that needed for self-defense. Foreign forces were to be withdrawn from Cambodia and Laos and no additional foreign military personnel introduced into the Vietnamese zones. To implement the accords, the conference established an International Control Commission of Canadian, Indian, and Polish representatives.

All of the participants except the United States and the French-backed Vietnamese government in Saigon endorsed the accords. America was unwilling publicly to accept the installation of a Communist regime in the northern Vietnamese zone. The Eisenhower administration nonetheless acknowledged the conference results and pledged not to use force to disturb their implementation. The Saigon government for its part announced it would adhere to the cease-fire but refused to be bound by the accords. With U.S. backing, a newly independent South Vietnam declined to hold the scheduled national elections in 1956, arguing that a fair vote was impossible in the Communist zone. By the end of the decade the Communist North had moved to unify Vietnam by force. America became increasing involved in the ensuing VIETNAM WAR. Resumption of fighting between the North Vietnamese-backed Communist Pathet Lao, neutralist factions, and the pro-Western government in Laos precipitated the LAOTIAN CRISIS and another international conference in Geneva in 1961 and 1962.

See also SOUTHEAST ASIA TREATY ORGANIZATION.

GENEVA CONFERENCE (1961–1962) International diplomatic meeting that settled the LAOTIAN CRISIS. Laos emerged from the 1954 GENEVA CONFERENCE on Indochina with full independence from French colonial rule. Conference agreements on the withdrawal of foreign troops from the Southeast Asian nation and a ban on its membership in military alliances were intended to establish Laotian neutrality. Later the same year, however, the treaty forming the U.S.-led SOUTHEAST ASIA TREATY ORGANIZATION (SEATO) extended the pact's COLLECTIVE SECURITY guarantees to Laos under a special protocol. A constitutional monarchy, Laos was ruled initially by a coalition government. By the late 1950s civil war had erupted among rightist, neutralist, and Communist factions struggling for control of the country. In early 1961 the Kennedy administration looked with growing concern on a joint offensive by neutralist and Communist Pathet Lao forces that threatened to overthrow the U.S.-backed rightist regime then in power.

Communicating U.S. readiness to intervene militarily if needed to prevent a Communist North Vietnamese-supported Pathet Lao takeover in Laos, the United States prevailed upon Great Britain and the Soviet Union, co-chairs of the 1954 conference, to convene another international gathering in Geneva on the Laotian situation. The second Geneva Conference opened on May 16, 1961. In attendance were delegates from 14 countries: the world powers—the United States, Great Britain, France, Soviet Union, and Communist China; the member nations of the International Control Commission created in 1954 to supervise agreements on Indochina—Canada, India, and Poland; and the nations of Southeast Asia—Burma, Thailand, Laos, Cambodia, and the two Vietnams. The U.S. representative was veteran diplomat W. AVERELL HARRIMAN. Each of the three rival Laotian factions was included in the negotiations.

Prospects for resolving the Laotian Crisis increased substantially when President JOHN F. KENNEDY and Soviet Premier Nikita S. Khrushchev, meeting at the June 1961 VIENNA SUMMIT, expressed a common interest in a fully neutral Laos with a coalition government. By early October, the warring Laotian groups had agreed in principle to joint participation in a neutralist, national unity government. This tentative settlement fell apart amid renewed fighting among the factions. In May 1962 Kennedy responded to new Communist military advances in Laos by ordering 5000 U.S. soldiers to neighboring Thailand. At the same time the United States increased its pressure on the rightist regime in Laos to accede to a political solution. On June 11 the three factions finally consented to joint rule under neutralist Prince Souvanna Phouma.

After almost 15 months, the 14 conference nations signed agreements on July 23, 1962, that guaranteed Laotian neutrality, recognized the new coalition government, and specified the withdrawal of all foreign forces within 75 days. The Laos Accords

also made clear that an expressly neutral Laos no longer considered itself under the protection of SEATO. The Geneva settlement only temporarily halted the civil war in Laos. America continued to aid the Laotian anti-Communist elements fighting the Pathet Lao. In practice, Laotian neutrality was violated by North Vietnam, which used its Ho Chi Minh Trail through the Laotian panhandle to move men and equipment south during the VIETNAM WAR. The United States in turn disregarded the 1962 agreements by waging a massive bombing campaign against the North Vietnamese operations. In 1975 the Pathet Lao seized power and proclaimed Laos a Communist state.

See also LAOS SECRET WAR.

GENEVA CONFERENCE ON THE MIDDLE EAST (1973) Historic peace conference convened by the United States and Soviet Union to begin negotiations toward a permanent settlement of the Arab-Israeli conflict. The mandate for the parley was UNITED NATIONS Security Council Resolution 338, adopted on October 22, 1973, as Israel moved toward a decisive victory over Egypt and Syria in the YOM KIPPUR WAR. The three-part resolution, drafted during talks in Moscow between U.S. Secretary of State HENRY A. KISSINGER and Soviet General Secretary Leonid I. Brezhnev, called for an immediate cease-fire in place; implementation of Security Council Resolution 242 in all its parts; and the start of negotiations between the "parties concerned under appropriate auspices aimed at establishing a just and durable peace in the Middle East." Resolution 242 had been adopted unanimously in November 1967 in the aftermath of the June 1967 Arab-Israeli Six-Day War. In the conflict Israeli forces had captured the Gaza Strip and Sinai Peninsula from Egypt, the West Bank and East Jerusalem from Jordan, and the Golan Heights from Syria. Resolution 242 called for a comprehensive Mideast peace based on the withdrawal of Israeli armed forces from territories occupied during the war; the recognition of the sovereignty and independence of all states in the region and "their right to live in peace within secure and recognized boundaries, free from threats or acts of force"; and a just settlement of the refugee problem, referring to the more than one million Palestinian Arabs living in the Israeli-occupied territories as well as those who had been displaced from their homes in historic Palestine by the formation of the Jewish state in 1948.

During and after the Yom Kippur War, Kissinger assumed the role of diplomatic mediator in the Mideast. Proceeding within the framework of Resolution 338, he proposed, with Moscow's endorsement, a conference on the Arab-Israeli conflict as a first major step in the peace process. Egypt and Jordan agreed to participate provided they did not have to meet directly with Israel but could negotiate through intermediaries. Israel also consented to take part, but announced it would not sit with the Syrians unless they provided lists of Israeli prisoners taken in the Yom Kippur War and allowed the International Red Cross to visit the captives. Syria, however, refused to attend, citing Israel's unwillingness to pledge beforehand to withdraw its forces to the truce line drawn in Resolution 338. The Palestine Liberation Organization (PLO), the erstwhile representative of the Palestinian people and their quest for an independent homeland, was not invited to attend. Israel was inalterably opposed to negotiations involving the PLO, which the Israeli government condemned as a terrorist organization pledged to the Jewish state's destruction, so long as it refused to recognize Israel's right to exist and failed to accept Resolutions 242 and 338.

Scheduled to begin in Geneva on December 18, 1973, the conference was delayed several days because of differences over the role of the U.N. Security Council. Mideast peace negotiations "under appropriate auspices" had been understood at the time Resolution 338 was adopted to mean under the sponsorship of the United States and USSR. Israel insisted that the conference be held under joint U.S.-Soviet aegis, opposing Arab wishes that the United Nations play an important part in the meeting. Israel's aversion to significant U.N. involvement stemmed from a belief that the international body was generally pro-Arab and hostile to the Jewish state. Washington and Moscow advised U.N. Secretary-General Kurt Waldheim on December 18 that they intended to conduct the parley but welcomed him to preside at its opening session.

The first-ever Arab-Israeli peace conference convened in the Swiss city on December 21, 1973, under formal U.N. auspices, with the U.S., Soviet, Egyptian, Jordanian, and Israeli foreign ministers in attendance. Kissinger and Soviet counterpart Andrei A. Gromyko were co-chairmen of the parley. After officially opening the conference, Secretary-General Waldheim remained as an observer. Policy speeches by the assembled foreign ministers dominated the historic two-day gathering, which brought no breakthrough in the substantive disagreements at the root of the Arab-Israeli conflict. Kissinger appealed to all Mideast parties to put aside their long-standing antagonisms and work for a realistic peace based on full implementation of Resolution 242. He pledged U.S. determination to help achieve a Mideast solution on the basis of strict adherence to the October ceasefire; separation of Egyptian and Israeli armies along the Suez and in the Sinai; withdrawal of Israeli forces from Arab lands occupied in the Yom Kippur War; internationally recognized borders and satisfactory security arrangements for all states in the region; and settlement of the Palestinian problem. Gromyko invoked the possibility of Moscow re-establishing diplomatic ties with Israel, severed after the 1967 Six-Day War. But he reiterated the Soviet government's firm support for the fundamental Arab demand that Israel withdraw from all territories occupied in 1967. In concurrence with Kissinger, he stressed that the most urgent priority was to secure an Israeli-Egyptian troop disengagement agreement as the base for continued regional peace negotiations.

The Egyptian and Jordanian foreign ministers, Ismail Fahmy and Said al-Rifai, linked any peace settlement to Israel's return to its 1967 boundaries, and resolution of the Palestinian issue on the basis of self-determination. Israeli Foreign Minister Abba Eban insisted that his country's security requirements made a return to 1967 borders unacceptable. He called for a negotiated peace under which all parties would renounce the use of force and unequivocally recognize one another's political sovereignty and independence. He indicated Israel was prepared to make a territorial compromise that would preserve its security, but sidestepped the Palestinian question.

The Geneva parley adjourned following a closed session on December 22, after agreement had been reached to resume troop disengagement negotiations between Israeli and Egyptian military officials on December 26. To monitor these talks and the work of various committees that were expected to be established to deal with other Mideast issues, the decision was made to continue contacts in Geneva at the ambassadorial level, with the understanding the conference would resume at the foreign minister level when and if developments warranted. Kissinger's SHUTTLE DIPLOMACY hastened the completion of an Egyptian-Israeli troop disengagement accord in January 1974 and a similar Syrian-Israeli agreement in May 1974. The Geneva Conference on the Middle East never reconvened. Egypt and Israel pursued the peace process through other channels, concluding the U.S.-mediated CAMP DAVID ACCORDS in 1978.

See also MIDDLE EAST PEACE CONFERENCE.

GENEVA CONVENTIONS (1949) Four international agreements governing the care of wounded and sick combatants, prisoners, and civilians during war. Because the conventions were developed under the auspices of the International Red Cross, they also have been referred to as the Red Cross Conventions. The first Geneva convention, which provided for the care of wounded and sick combatants regardless of nationality, was signed by delegates from 16 European nations at Geneva, Switzerland, in 1864. The measure provided for the protection of medical personnel and facilities, identified by the distinctive emblem of the Red Cross (later the Red Crescent for Moslem countries). The United States became a party to the convention in 1882.

The convention was amended and extended at Geneva in 1906. Its terms were applied to maritime warfare by the HAGUE CONVENTIONS formulated at the HAGUE PEACE CONFERENCES of 1899 and 1907. A second Geneva convention, regarding the treatment of prisoners of war, was adopted in 1929. The new measure, an outgrowth of the experiences of WORLD WAR I, expanded on the earlier Hague Conventions and established additional safeguards to protect the welfare of prisoners. The Nazi genocide of Jews in the Holocaust, the Axis mistreatment of prisoners, and other major humanitarian abuses during WORLD WAR II were the impetus for further modifications. The conventions were approved in their pres-

ent form by delegates of 58 countries, including the United States, in Geneva on August 12, 1949. To the two existing agreements, both of which underwent revisions, was added a third convention covering the wounded, sick, and shipwrecked at sea; and a fourth convention addressing the protection of civilians in wartime. The four measures have been signed by the vast preponderance of nations, including all the major powers.

An international Diplomatic Conference on Humanitarian Law Applicable in Armed Conflicts, convened at the invitation of the Swiss government, met in Geneva from 1974 to 1977. On June 10, 1977, delegates from 109 nations, including the United States, adopted two protocols to the 1949 conventions. Protocol I recognized so-called wars of national liberation as international conflicts and extended prisoner of war status to captured armed guerrillas. Protocol II set forth humanitarian provisions to be followed in civil wars. The measures prohibited indiscriminate attacks on civilians or the starvation of noncombatants. The United States has not ratified the protocols.

GENEVA DISARMAMENT CONFERENCE See **WORLD DISARMAMENT CONFERENCE**.

GENEVA NAVAL CONFERENCE (1927) International gathering that sought unsuccessfully to curb naval armaments. The FIVE-POWER TREATY concluded between the United States, Great Britain, France, Italy, and Japan at the WASHINGTON NAVAL CONFERENCE (1921--1922) had set limits on the number of large, or capital, ships in each country's navy. The accord, however, had not addressed smaller vessels such as cruisers, destroyers, and submarines. Concerned by British and Japanese naval expansion, President CALVIN COOLIDGE in February 1927 called for a five-power conference to reach an agreement restricting those classes of vessels not covered by the earlier five-power pact. Great Britain and Japan agreed to the meeting but France and Italy declined, contending that naval armaments should be discussed within a broader context of general security concerns. The conference was held in Geneva, Switzerland, from June 20 to August 4,

1927. The parley ended without an agreement after the United States and Great Britain were unable to concur on a formula for the number of cruisers permitted each nation. The deadlock at Geneva helped ensure congressional passage in 1929 of a naval bill authorizing the construction of 15 large cruisers. The five powers in the 1930s returned to the issue of naval arms limitations at the LONDON NAVAL CONFERENCES.

GENEVA PROTOCOL (1925) International agreement prohibiting the use of chemical and biological weapons in war. The horrifying experience of poisonous gas in WORLD WAR I brought a concerted international movement to eliminate chemical warfare. At the 1925 Geneva Conference for the Supervision of the International Traffic in Arms, the United States suggested barring the export of gases used in war. The proposal served as the basis for a broader conference agreement on chemical weapons. Signed June 17, 1925, the Geneva Protocol banned the use in war of lethal gases as well as deadly bacteriological, or biological, agents. The pact was ratified before WORLD WAR II by all the major powers except the United States and Japan. Strong opposition in the U.S. Senate to American involvement in international arrangements kept the measure from coming up for a vote. In 1969 President RICHARD M. NIXON restated the long-standing U.S. commitment not to initiate use of chemical weapons and resubmitted the 1925 protocol to the Senate. Approval was delayed by debate over the Nixon administration's contention that the pact did not apply to herbicides, or defoliants, and tear gas, then in use by U.S. forces in the VIETNAM WAR. Following the Ford administration's renunciation of first use of herbicides and tear gas in war as a matter of U.S. policy, the Senate approved the protocol by a 90 to 0 vote on December 16, 1974, and it was signed by President GERALD R. FORD on January 22, 1975. The U.S. ratification included the common reservation that adherence to the protocol was no longer binding in the event of enemy use of chemical warfare.

See also BIOLOGICAL WEAPONS CONVENTION.

GENEVA ROUND See **GENERAL AGREEMENT ON TARIFFS AND TRADE**.

GENEVA SUMMIT (1955) Conference among the leaders of the United States, Great Britain, France, and the Soviet Union. The historic meeting was the first in the succession of East-West summits in the post–WORLD WAR II era. It also marked the first direct contact between the Soviet and major Western heads of government since the POTSDAM CONFERENCE in 1945. The onset of the COLD WAR in the late 1940s had foreclosed further top-level meetings between the Kremlin and the Western allies. British Prime Minister Winston Churchill first proposed a summit conference to break the diplomatic deadlock in May 1953. Soviet Premier Joseph Stalin's death in March of that year had left a government in charge that appeared more receptive to negotiations with the West. Churchill believed face-to-face contacts among leaders could serve to improve East-West relations.

The United States balked at the summit idea. A wary Secretary of State JOHN FOSTER DULLES feared a lessening of tensions might promote a dangerous complacency among the United States and its allies. He was concerned that negotiations might weaken NATO and disrupt allied plans to integrate West Germany into the West European defense structure. The Eisenhower administration faced vocal opposition to a top-level meeting with the Soviets from within party ranks. The staunchly anti-Communist Republican "Old Guard" continued to invoke the YALTA CONFERENCE (1945) as a symbol of appeasement and warned against a possible return to U.S. concessions through conference diplomacy. Throughout 1954 the United States resisted mounting international pressure for a summit. President DWIGHT D. EISENHOWER would not agree to talks until the Western allies completed ratification of West German independence and membership in NATO; and the Soviet Union consented to an Austrian peace treaty. With these conditions met by May 1955, the situation in Europe had evolved enough to make a summit possible.

Meeting in Geneva, Switzerland, from July 18 to 23, 1955, President Eisenhower, British Prime Minister Anthony Eden (who had succeeded Churchill), French Premier Edgar Faure, Soviet Premier Nikolai A. Bulganin, and Soviet Communist Party head Nikita S. Khrushchev discussed four major items: the reunification of Germany, European security, disarmament, and increased East-West contacts. Eisenhower captured attention with his vow that the United States would never wage aggressive war and with his OPEN SKIES proposal, which called for mutual aerial surveillance of Soviet and American military installations as a guard against surprise attack. The Soviets rejected the "open skies" plan and the summit ended with no clear breakthrough aside from the so-called spirit of Geneva, a purported thaw in the Cold War that indicated a wish on both sides for a relaxation in tensions. At the close of the conference, the leaders turned over the agenda to their foreign ministers who then met in Geneva in October and November 1955 but likewise reached no agreement. The 1955 Geneva Summit signaled a move toward increased East-West contacts and a measure of improvement in relations between Cold War adversaries. U.S. and Soviet leaders next met at the CAMP DAVID SUMMIT (1959) following Khrushchev's instigation of the BERLIN CRISIS in November 1958.

GENEVA SUMMIT (1985) Meeting between President RONALD W. REAGAN and Soviet leader Mikhail S. Gorbachev from November 19 to 21, 1985, in Geneva, Switzerland. First of the Reagan-Gorbachev summits, it marked the resumption of top-level contacts suspended since the Soviet Union's invasion of Afghanistan in 1979. In early 1985 the superpowers agreed to reinitiate arms limitation talks that had been stalled since Moscow suspended negotiations in late 1983 following the U.S. deployment of medium-range PERSHING II and CRUISE MISSILES in Europe. U.S. Secretary of State GEORGE P. SHULTZ and Soviet Foreign Minister Andrei A. Gromyko announced the two countries would begin separate but parallel negotiations in Geneva the coming spring on three kinds of weapons: strategic nuclear forces, intermediate-range nuclear forces (INF), and space weapons.

The start of the three-layered arms talks in March coincided with a change in Kremlin leadership that brought Gorbachev to power as general secretary of the Soviet Communist Party. Reagan, more inclined in his second term to negotiations with Moscow, offered to meet with the new Soviet head. Gorbachev in early April signaled his willingness for a superpower parley. He

seized the initiative by declaring a Soviet moratorium on INF deployment in Europe and calling on the United States to reciprocate. The Reagan administration dismissed the proposal as Kremlin propaganda aimed at splitting the NATO allies. In July the two sides formally agreed to a summit in Geneva in late autumn. Reagan then ordered continued U.S. adherence to the unratified 1979 SALT II agreement to demonstrate Washington's determination to curb the arms race.

As the summit neared, Reagan vowed to confront Gorbachev at Geneva about Soviet HUMAN RIGHTS violations and bars on Jewish emigration, the Soviet occupation of Afghanistan, and Kremlin interference in regional conflicts in Central America, Africa, and Southeast Asia. For its part Moscow looked to steer the pre-summit focus to arms control. On September 30 Gorbachev made a dramatic new negotiating offer: a bilateral 50 percent cut in strategic nuclear arms, contingent on U.S. agreement to strictly limit research on space-based antimissile defense, known as the STRATEGIC DEFENSE INITIATIVE (SDI). The Reagan administration rejected Soviet efforts to link overall arms control progress to a ban on SDI. Harsh rhetoric accompanied the renewed U.S.-Soviet dialogue on arms issues. Mutual accusations of violations of existing arms control agreements were a source of superpower tensions.

The Geneva parley, held under a press blackout, brought no breakthroughs on arms control, human rights, or regional conflicts between the superpowers. In a final joint communique, Reagan and Gorbachev declared mutual support for the principle of a 50 percent cut in strategic NUCLEAR WEAPONS but left unresolved what arms should be counted in the 50 percent. Both sides called for accelerated progress toward an interim agreement on medium-range missiles in Europe. The leaders also pledged to continue efforts to reduce conventional forces in Europe and to ban biological and chemical weapons. The communique made no mention of the deep Soviet-American division over SDI. But in post-summit remarks, Gorbachev reasserted the Kremlin's insistence on strict SDI curbs as a precondition to any major arms-reduction accord. The conference yielded a series of minor pacts on cultural exchanges, air safety, environmental protection, and resumption of civil aviation ties. Gorbachev and Reagan made tentative plans for follow-up talks in the United States in 1986 and the USSR in 1987. They next met at the impromptu REYKJAVIK SUMMIT (1986).

GENOCIDE TREATY (1948) International agreement that defined genocide as the intentional destruction of a national, ethnic, racial, or religious group and declared it a crime punishable under international law. The pact was drafted in response to Nazi Germany's systematic murder of 6 million Jews in the Holocaust during WORLD WAR II. Officially the Convention on the Prevention and Punishment of the Crime of Genocide, it was approved by the UNITED NATIONS on December 9, 1948, and entered into force on January 12, 1951. The United States was among the original signers and in 1949 President HARRY S. TRUMAN submitted the treaty to the Senate for ratification. Conservative opponents, however, viewing the agreement as a potential infringement on American sovereignty, blocked its approval for more than three decades. The senate finally ratified the treaty on February 19, 1986, under prodding by the Reagan administration, which argued that adoption of the measure was important to U.S. international standing. To assuage conservatives' concerns, the Senate attached reservations to its ratification, affirming that the U.S. CONSTITUTION takes precedence over any treaty provisions and withholding the United States from the compulsory jurisdiction of the WORLD COURT.

GENTLEMEN'S AGREEMENT (1907–1908) Diplomatic understanding that resolved a dispute over Japanese immigration to the United States. The JAPANESE-AMERICAN TREATY OF 1894 permitted free entry between the two countries, although each government retained the right to limit the immigration of laborers. The large influx of Japanese workers to the West Coast sparked a backlash against the new arrivals, who were widely viewed as a threat to local employment. In August 1900, at American urging, the Japanese government stopped issuing passports to emigrant laborers bound for the U.S. mainland under an arrangement sometimes referred to as the first Gentlemen's Agreement.

Many Japanese circumvented this development by traveling first to Hawaii, then an American territory, and subsequently to the U.S Pacific Coast. Tensions on the West Coast mounted over the continuing influx. Formed in 1905, the JAPANESE AND KOREAN EXCLUSION LEAGUE was representative of the anti-Asian sentiments. In October 1906 the San Francisco school board ordered the segregation of Japanese and other Asian students. The Japanese government protested the discriminatory action as a violation of the 1894 treaty and anti-American demonstrations erupted in Japan. The Roosevelt administration sought to defuse the international incident. At a Washington meeting in February 1907, President THEODORE ROOSEVELT persuaded the San Francisco school board to reverse its decision. At the same time Roosevelt exercised authority granted to him by the just-completed Immigration Act of 1907, signing an executive order that halted the entry of foreign workers who had journeyed either to another country or an American possession en route to the United States. This effectively blocked the movement of Japanese immigrants from Hawaii to the mainland.

Roosevelt's intervention with the San Francisco school board paved the way for negotiations between Secretary of State ELIHU ROOT and Japanese Foreign Minister Tadasu Hayashi over the status of Japanese immigration to the United States. In an exchange of diplomatic notes culminating in February 1908, they reached an understanding, known as the Gentlemen's Agreement, that the United States would not single out the Japanese as undesirable or inferior by barring their entry by law. Japan in turn would accept the further restriction on the immigration of its laborers to America. The Gentlemen's Agreement averted a crisis that threatened to damage Japanese-American relations. The agreement governed Japanese immigration to the United States until passage of the IMMIGRATION ACT OF 1924, which totally excluded Japanese immigrants. Viewing the U.S. legislation as a violation of previous understandings, Japan abrogated the Gentlemen's Agreement the same year.

GHENT, TREATY OF (1814) Treaty between the United States and Great Britain that ended the WAR OF 1812. Almost as soon as hostilities began in June 1812, both sides made peace overtures. These first efforts at arranging an armistice failed because the British would not, as America demanded, yield on the question of IMPRESSMENT, claiming it as an indispensable national right. A Russian offer extended in September 1812 to mediate the Anglo-American conflict was accepted by the Madison administration but rejected by the British government. In November 1813 British Foreign Secretary Lord Castlereagh offered to negotiate without intermediaries. President JAMES MADISON, faced with intensifying Federalist opposition to the unpopular war, a bleak military outlook, and an economy withering under the British naval blockade of the American seaboard, eagerly accepted. The five-member American peace commission appointed by the president comprised JOHN QUINCY ADAMS, ALBERT GALLATIN, John Russell, James A. Bayard, and HENRY CLAY. The U.S. commissioners and their British counterparts James Gambier, Henry Goulburn, and William Adams convened in Ghent, Belgium, where negotiations began on August 8, 1814.

The U.S. commission was directed to win recognition of American neutral rights, abolition of impressment, an end to "illegal blockades," and adjustment of other maritime grievances. Instructions forwarded by Secretary of State JAMES MONROE at the end of July had afforded the American representatives greater negotiating flexibility by authorizing them to drop the once-indispensable impressment issue if necessary. Emboldened by its superior military situation, Britain made sweeping initial demands. These included establishment of an Indian buffer state in the OLD NORTHWEST between the United States and Canada, U.S. territorial concessions along a line from Maine west to the headwaters of the Mississippi River (amounting to about one-third of U.S.-held territory), and exclusive military control over the Great Lakes. The U.S. delegation flatly rejected these terms, whereupon the British fell back on a proposal for restoration to their Indian allies of the lands they held before the war—an arrangement in principle accepted by the Americans. When, on September 27, 1814, the British received news of the burning of Washington, D.C., by their troops, they held out for peace on the basis of *uti possidetis* (the principle that each nation would keep the territories it held in actual possession). After learning on October 21 of U.S. Commodore Thomas Macdonough's critical victory on Lake Champlain, the U.S. commissioners rejected *uti possidetis* and instead proposed the principle of *status quo ante bellum* (restoration of territories held prior to the war). A temporary deadlock ensued.

Great Britain grew eager to break the stalemate and bring an end to the war. The conflict in North America was a heavy strain on the depleted British treasury and a detriment to British foreign policy in Europe, where statesmen were absorbed with negotiations at the Congress of Vienna on the settlement of the Napoleonic Wars (1803–1815). The Duke of Wellington, offered command of British forces in America, warned his government that a clear victory was unattainable absent British supremacy on the Great Lakes and suggested that Britain, based on the prevailing military situation, was in no position to demand a cession of territory. His counsel was a decisive factor in persuading the British government in November to yield to the American view.

On December 24, 1814, the U.S. and British delegates signed the Treaty of Ghent restoring peace on the basis of *status quo ante bellum*. The agreement was silent on the major issues over which the two nations had gone to war. No mention was made of impressment, neutral rights, or indemnity for losses incurred by American merchant shipping during the nearly uninterrupted war between Great Britian and France since 1793. Indians who had fought with the British were assured amnesty. The treaty provided for the appointment of several joint commissions to settle U.S.-Canadian boundary problems. By mutual agreement, the military status of the Great Lakes and the FISHERIES QUESTION were deferred to future negotiations. Both sides also pledged to exert themselves to abolish the African slave trade. The treaty was widely popular in America. It was approved by the Senate on February 15, 1815, and proclaimed by Madison two days later.

GLASSBORO SUMMIT (1967) Impromptu meeting between President LYNDON B. JOHN-

SON and Soviet Premier Aleksei N. Kosygin in which the two leaders discussed a range of outstanding international issues. Held on June 23 and 25, 1967, at Glassboro, New Jersey, the conference marked the fifth postwar summit of U.S. and Soviet heads of government and the first since President JOHN F. KENNEDY and Soviet Premier Nikita S. Khrushchev met at the VIENNA SUMMIT in June 1961. Kosygin had come to the United States June 17 to present his country's views on the 1967 Arab-Israeli war before a special session of the UNITED NATIONS. Shortly after Kosygin's arrival, Johnson proposed that he and the Soviet premier meet for wide-ranging talks. After several days of diplomatic back-and-forth sparring the two leaders settled on an appropriate summit agenda and agreed to hold their meeting at Hollybush, home of the president of Glassboro State College, roughly halfway between the United Nations and the White House.

In two separate sessions on the state of U.S.-Soviet relations, Johnson and Kosygin discussed their differences on the Middle East crisis and the VIETNAM WAR and reviewed efforts to stop the proliferation of NUCLEAR WEAPONS. Neither claimed substantive gains as a result of the talks. Both stressed the importance of reaching an international agreement to halt the spread of nuclear arms. The two heads of state characterized the summit as useful, made a preliminary agreement to meet again, and directed their top foreign affairs advisers to continue the discussions. Despite claims of a new mood of optimism, dubbed the "spirit of Hollybush," Glassboro failed to clear up any major differences between the two nations. Conference diplomacy resumed in 1972 with the historic trip of President RICHARD M. NIXON to the MOSCOW SUMMIT.

GLOBAL CHANGE RESEARCH PROGRAM See **UNITED STATES GLOBAL CHANGE RESEARCH PROGRAM**.

GLOBAL 2000 (1980) Report outlining the findings of a three-year U.S. government study on the projected state of the world environment in the year 2000. In May 1977 President JIMMY CARTER commissioned a study of global environmental trends to be conducted by the State Department and the executive-branch Council on Environmental Quality. The product of their labors was published in July 1980 under the title *Global 2000 Report to the President: Entering the Twenty-First Century*. Prepared with the input of 13 federal agencies, it represented the first full-scale demographic and ecological projection ever done by a government. (Earlier models had been prepared by various UNITED NATIONS commissions and by the WORLD BANK.) The report forecast a troubled future for planet Earth. It concluded that "if present trends continue, the world in 2000 will be more crowded, more polluted, less stable ecologically, and more vulnerable to disruption than the world we live in now. Serious stresses involving population, resources and environment are clearly visible ahead." The study's authors suggested that only international cooperation could halt the destruction of the environment, exhaustion of natural resources, and overpopulation. The report called on the United States to spearhead efforts to counteract these global problems. The considerable short-term interest generated by *Global 2000* faded with the departure of the Carter administration in 1981. The former president subsequently organized and became chairman of Global 2000, Inc., a private organization dedicated to helping improve health and agriculture in developing countries.

GOLDWATER v. CARTER See **TAIWAN MUTUAL DEFENSE TREATY**.

GOLDWATER-NICHOLS DEFENSE REORGANIZATION ACT (1986) Major reorganization of the U.S. military establishment. Following WORLD WAR II, both the changing nature of modern warfare and the desire for greater economy in defense spending led the United States to unify its air, land, and sea forces in a single DEPARTMENT OF DEFENSE (1949). The DEFENSE REORGANIZATION ACT OF 1958, which provided the Defense Department's basic structure for almost three decades, balanced the traditional prerogatives of the Army, Navy, and Air Force with the need for greater coordination among the armed services in order to meet the nation's global defense commitments. The secretary of defense, assisted by the JOINT CHIEFS OF STAFF (JCS) comprising the nation's top uniformed officers, was granted broad authority over the defense establishment and the joint military commands, made up of forces from each of the armed services. At the same time the Army, Navy, and Air Force were not merged into a single military service but retained their basic autonomy and continued to exercise control over their respective armed services.

In the reexamination of U.S. defense policy in the late 1970s following the Vietnam War, attention began to focus on ways to improve the joint functioning of the military services. The drive for reform of the Pentagon gathered momentum following the failed rescue mission during the Iran Hostage Crisis (1980) and the serious difficulties in interservice coordination evident in the Grenada Invasion (1983). Widely publicized "horror stories" of Defense Department waste and mismanagement, such as the $640 toilet seat, also spurred congressional support for further centralization of authority over the defense establishment. In 1985 President Ronald W. Reagan appointed the blue-ribbon Packard Commission to examine defense reorganization. The commission's February 1986 report endorsed basic changes similar to ones under consideration in the Congress.

On October 1, 1986, Reagan signed legislation that shifted additional authority from the separate military services to the Defense Department as a whole. The measure's two key sponsors were Senator Barry M. Goldwater (R-AZ) and Congressman William Nichols (D-AL), both of whom had been long involved in defense issues. To encourage a multiservice outlook on defense issues and limit parochialism, the act made the chairman of the JCS the principal military adviser to the president. Prior to 1986 the entire panel had held this responsibility, but it was widely thought that the uniformed chiefs too often concentrated on the interests of their own services at the expense of overall U.S. defense planning. The 1986 law created the position of vice chairman, to be filled by an officer from a different branch than the chairman, to further reinforce a multiservice emphasis. The legislation also strengthened the authority of the commanders of the nation's seven joint or unified commands. The commands, each responsible for military actions in a specified geographic region such as Europe, gained full control over all units assigned them. The new command arrangement received generally high marks for its performance in the Panama Invasion (1989) and the Persian Gulf War (1991).

GONDRA TREATY See **INTER-AMERICAN CONFERENCES** in **APPENDIX E.**

GOOD NEIGHBOR POLICY U.S. policy toward Latin America formally inaugurated by President Franklin D. Roosevelt based on the principles of equality and partnership among the American republics. American economic and military intervention dating from the beginning of the 20th century had engendered deep resentment in Latin American, where U.S. policy was branded "Yankee imperialism." Republican administrations during the 1920s took steps to allay hostility and suspicion throughout the region toward the United States, which was pejoratively dubbed the "colossus of the north." President Herbert C. Hoover, eager to diminish anti-American sentiment among the Latin American countries, first gave shape to the good neighbor idea. Expressing his disapproval of intervention, in 1930 he issued the Clark Memorandum, which repudiated the Roosevelt Corollary to the Monroe Doctrine. The corollary, formulated in 1904 by President Theodore Roosevelt, had provided the principal justification for U.S. interventions in the Western hemisphere.

Hoover's successor, Franklin D. Roosevelt, expanded the good neighbor idea and transformed it into policy. Together with Secretary of State Cordell Hull and career diplomat Sumner Welles, he made it the center of his administration's approach toward Latin America. In his first inaugural address in March 1933, Roosevelt stated that "in the field of world policy I would dedicate this nation to the policy of the good neighbor—the neighbor who resolutely respects himself, and because he does so, respects the rights of others—the neighbor who respects his obligations and respects the sanctity of his agreements in and with a world of neighbors." The president subsequently made clear that the Good Neighbor Policy applied specifically to the Western Hemisphere.

The Roosevelt administration's acceptance of the principle of nonintervention marked the first major step toward implementing the policy. At the Montevideo Conference in 1933, Secretary Hull, head of the U.S. delegation, signed the CONVENTION ON RIGHTS AND DUTIES OF STATES, which asserted that no American state had the right to intervene in the internal affairs of another. After Montevideo Roosevelt abandoned all right of armed intervention. In 1934 he withdrew the last U.S. marines from Haiti, ending a 19-year occupation and completing the pullout of all U.S. armed forces from Latin American countries. With the abrogation of the PLATT AMENDMENT the same year, the United States relinquished its right to intervene in Cuba, as it also did with respect to Panama under a treaty concluded with the Panamanian government in 1936. At the BUENOS AIRES CONFERENCE the same year, the United States concurred in a nonintervention protocol even stronger than the 1933 pledge at Montevideo. Successive U.S. presidents abided by the nonintervention vow until 1965, when President LYNDON B. JOHNSON sent U.S. forces into the Dominican Republic during the DOMINICAN CRISIS.

As part of its Good Neighbor Policy, the Roosevelt administration sought successfully to increase U.S. trade with Latin America through tariff cuts negotiated under authority of the TRADE AGREEMENTS ACT (1934). Alarmed by the increasingly belligerent posture of Nazi Germany and Fascist Italy, Roosevelt began to emphasize the need for hemispheric unity to protect against possible European threats to peace. At the 1936 Buenos Aires Conference, the American states concluded a pact providing for Pan-American consultation in the face of any menace to Western Hemisphere security. With the specter of war growing in Europe, the American republics took further steps in 1938 under the DECLARATION OF LIMA to strengthen hemispheric solidarity and consultation in case of external threat to their peace or territorial integrity. With the outbreak of WORLD WAR II in Europe in 1939, the American foreign ministers met in Panama at the behest of the United States, where they adopted the DECLARATION OF PANAMA announcing the neutrality of the Western Hemisphere.

Following U.S. entry into the war in December 1941, the American foreign ministers gathered for the RIO DE JANEIRO CONFERENCE (1942), recommending that their governments break relations with the Axis powers. The broadening of the Good Neighbor Policy helped the United States to secure the strong support of nearly all Latin American nations during World War II. Plans for strengthening hemisphere COLLECTIVE SECURITY were made at a special inter-American conference in Mexico in 1945, where delegates adopted the ACT OF CHAPULTEPEC, which provided for mutual defense among the American states. The Chapultepec measure was forerunner to the RIO TREATY of 1947, the formal inter-American mutual defense pact. The cooperative spirit underpinning the drive for a system of collective security culminated in the creation in 1948 of the ORGANIZATION OF AMERICAN STATES, an umbrella inter-American organization and the first regional security arrangement under the UNITED NATIONS.

See also ALLIANCE FOR PROGRESS.

GOODPASTER, ANDREW JACKSON (1915–   ) Army officer, commander of NATO forces in Europe. A native of Illinois, Goodpaster graduated from West Point in 1939 and saw action in Europe during WORLD WAR II as commanding officer of an engineer battalion. After the war he attended Princeton University, where he completed a master's in engineering in 1948 and a doctorate in international relations in 1950. The same year he became an aide to General DWIGHT D. EISENHOWER, in which capacity he assisted in the organization of NATO's military command. In 1954 President Eisenhower made him a special assistant at the White House. As staff secretary, he served in effect as the president's aide. He gave special attention to national security issues and briefed Eisenhower on developments daily. He was promoted to general in 1957.

Departing the White House in 1961 following completion of the transition to the Kennedy administration, Goodpaster took command of a division in Germany. He returned to Washington in 1962 as an assistant to General MAXWELL D. TAYLOR, chairman of the JOINT CHIEFS OF STAFF (JCS). In 1968 he became deputy to General CREIGHTON W. ABRAMS, JR., the commander of U.S. forces in the VIETNAM WAR. The following year he was selected by President RICHARD M. NIXON for the position of NATO supreme allied commander. Goodpaster assumed his duties at a time when America's attention was diverted from Europe by the conflict in Southeast Asia. He worked to improve communications between Washington and its European allies and began an extensive modernization of NATO forces. He was succeeded at NATO by General ALEXANDER M. HAIG, JR. in 1974 and retired from the Army, becoming a senior fellow at the Woodrow Wilson International Center for Scholars. In 1977 he was recalled to active duty by President JIMMY CARTER to serve as commandant of West Point. He retired again in 1981.

GORE-McLEMORE RESOLUTIONS (1916) Tandem congressional measures intended to limit Americans from traveling on belligerent merchant ships subject to torpedoing by German submarines in WORLD WAR I. At the time the United States had not yet entered the war. The abortive resolutions challenged President WOODROW WILSON's insistence on upholding the neutral right of Americans under international law to take passage on Allied ships without restriction. German submarine warfare, however, had been responsible for the sinking in 1915 of the British passenger liners LUSITANIA and ARABIC, which resulted in American deaths and precipitated a crisis in relations between Washington and Berlin. Germany's declaration on February 8, 1916, that after March 1 its U-boats would sink armed Allied merchant ships without warning stoked fears among a group of congressional Democrats who worried that further loss of American lives would draw the United States into the conflict. This sentiment in Congress coalesced around a pair of initiatives intended to preempt such a possibility.

Representative Jefferson A. McLemore (D-TX) introduced a resolution February 17 requesting the president to warn Americans not to travel on armed vessels. On February 25, Senator Thomas P. Gore (D-OK) introduced a resolution to deny passports to Americans who planned to travel on armed belligerent vessels. Wilson responded to the measures by reiterating his adamant opposition to any U.S. retreat on the issue of neutral rights. He construed the resolutions as a threat from within his own Democratic Party to his control over foreign policy. In an open letter to the SENATE FOREIGN RELATIONS COMMITTEE drafted amid the imbroglio over Gore-McLemore, the president emphasized that he "could not consent to any abridgement of the rights of Americans in any respect." The Wilson administration successfully pressured the congressional leadership to defeat the measures. The Senate tabled the Gore resolution on March 3 by a 68–14 vote while the House shelved the McLemore resolution on March 7 by a 276–142 vote.

GRANT, ULYSSES SIMPSON (1822–1885) Army general and 18th president of the United States. Grant was born in Ohio and baptized Hiram Ulysses. Upon entering the U.S. Military Academy in 1839, he learned that he was enrolled as Ulysses Simpson through an error of the congressman who had arranged for his appointment. Choosing to accept the change, Grant dropped Hiram from his name. He graduated from West Point in 1843. In the MEXICAN WAR (1846–1848) he served with distinction under General ZACHARY TAYLOR, earning promotion to captain for his bravery at the Battle of Chapultepec. He resigned from the Army in 1854 and settled with his wife and children in Missouri, where over the next six years he struggled unsuccessfully at farming and selling real estate. In worsening financial straits, he moved to Galena, Illinois, in 1860, becoming a clerk in his father's leather goods store.

Following the outbreak of the Civil War, he was appointed a colonel in command of an Illinois volunteer infantry regiment in June 1861 and promoted to brigadier general two months later. His capture in February 1862 of Forts Henry and Donelson in Tennessee brought him to the attention of President ABRAHAM LINCOLN and won him promotion to major general. When the Confederate commander at Donelson asked for terms of capitulation, Grant replied "No terms except an unconditional and immediate surrender can be accepted," earning him the nickname "Unconditional Surrender Grant." He was promoted to lieutenant general and put in command of all Union armies in March 1864. Waging a successful campaign of attrition, he finally forced the surrender of General Robert E. Lee and his army at Appomattox, Virginia, on April 9, 1865.

He was promoted to general of the army in July 1866, the first to hold the rank since GEORGE WASHINGTON. When President ANDREW JOHNSON dismissed Secretary of War Edwin M. Stanton in August 1867, Grant agreed to act as secretary ad interim, spending five months in the cabinet. But when the Senate acted to restore Stanton, Grant surrendered the position without protest, earning a bitter rebuke from Johnson, who publicly accused the general of bad faith. The favored candidate of the Radical Republicans, who opposed Johnson's lenient postwar policy toward the South and endorsed a harsh program of Reconstruction, Grant captured the Republican presidential nomination in 1868. He was elected and won reelection in 1872. Grant allowed Radical Reconstruction to run its course, continuing the occupation of the South by federal troops. Under authority of the so-called Force Acts (1870–1871), his administration threatened use of armed force against states denying the vote to blacks.

On foreign policy Grant generally followed the counsel of Secretary of State HAMILTON FISH. The one notable exception was the president's ill-fated scheme to annex the Dominican Republic. Strong opposition in the Senate defeated the DOMINICAN REPUBLIC ANNEXATION INITIATIVE. Fish averted a serious crisis in Spanish-American relations by persuading Grant to withhold recognition of the belligerent status of Cuban rebels and to maintain U.S. neutrality in the Ten Years' War (1868–1878), Cuba's failed struggle for independence from Spanish rule. The secretary of state also secured a peaceful adjustment with Spain of the VIRGINIUS AFFAIR (1873). Negotiations undertaken by the Grant administration with Great Britain produced the TREATY OF WASHINGTON (1871). This watershed agreement submitted to international arbitration outstanding Anglo-American diplomatic disputes, most notably the ALABAMA CLAIMS, the U.S. financial grievances against Britain for damage inflicted on Union shipping during the Civil War by Confederate vessels built and armed in British ports.

Though Grant himself was never involved in corruption, his administration was wracked by a series of scandals that spanned his two terms, including the Credit Mobilier railroad bribery scheme and the implication of Grant's private secretary, Orville E. Babcock, in the Whiskey Ring liquor-tax-diversion scam. He was willing to run for a third time in 1876, but opposition to him within Republican ranks prevailed and RUTHERFORD B. HAYES captured the nomination. Upon leaving office in March 1877, Grant made a two-year world tour with his family. A bid to nominate him for a third term failed at the Republican National Convention in 1880. He moved the following year to New York City, where he was left bankrupt when the brokerage firm he had co-founded failed in 1884. To provide for his family, Grant wrote his hugely successful *Personal Memoirs* (1885) while battling cancer in the last year of his life. His remains eventually were buried in Grant's Tomb, the monument dedicated in New York City in 1897.

GREAT DEBATE (1951) Debate in the U.S. Congress over the deployment of American ground forces to defend Europe. The months-long confrontation revolved around two main issues: the relationship of the legislative and executive branches in the formulation of national security policy and the role the United States would adopt in world affairs in the post–WORLD WAR II period. In April 1949 America broke with its historic tradition of avoiding peacetime military alliances when it joined NATO, the newly formed security alliance for Western Europe. In June 1950 President HARRY S. TRUMAN committed U.S. troops to rolling back Communist North Korea's invasion of South Korea. Worried that the KOREAN WAR presaged a Soviet Communist offensive in Europe, the Truman administration decided on a major expansion of the U.S. military and a buildup of NATO forces. When Truman announced plans in September to augment the two U.S. divisions already in Europe, the nation's attention was focused on mounting U.S. military involvement in Korea.

The sudden Chinese Communist attack in Korea in late November 1950 rekindled U.S. concerns about possible moves in Europe by the Soviet Union. On December 19, 1950, Truman named General DWIGHT D. EISENHOWER as supreme commander of NATO forces and announced that additional American troops would be sent to Europe as quickly as possible. The next day former President HERBERT C. HOOVER criticized Truman's actions in a nationwide radio address. Hoover opposed any further U.S. involvement in possible land wars either in Europe or Asia. He argued that America should rely on its air and sea power to defend the British Isles, Japan, Formosa, and the Philippines. By initiating such a strategy, Hoover contended, the United States could safeguard the Atlantic and Pacific oceans and thereby preserve itself as a "Gibraltar of Western civilization."

In a Senate speech on January 5, 1951, Senator Robert A. Taft (R-OH) endorsed Hoover's isolationist views. Taft also accused Truman of exceeding his constitutional powers by ordering American combat forces overseas without congressional approval. His remarks launched what was called at the time the "Great Debate" over U.S. foreign and military policy. On January 8 Senator Kenneth S. Wherry (R-NE) introduced a resolution to express the sense of the Senate that American troops not be deployed abroad without the consent of the Congress. The same day Truman in his State of the Union message reasserted his authority as president to dispatch American soldiers overseas.

The ensuing debate pitted conservative Republicans led by Taft and Wherry against moderate Republicans, such as former Minnesota Governor Harold E. Stassen and State Department adviser JOHN FOSTER DULLES, and majority party Democrats. Together the moderate Republicans and Democrats opposed the idea of FORTRESS AMERICA and endorsed greater American involvement in world affairs. General Eisenhower curried support for the deployment of U.S. ground forces when he returned from an initial inspection of his NATO command. In an address to an informal joint session of Congress at the Library of Congress on February 1, 1951, the venerated former World War II commander described U.S. military assistance to Europe as essential.

Over the next month the debate was dominated by joint hearings of the Senate Armed Forces and Foreign Relations committees. Secretary of Defense GEORGE C. MARSHALL testified that the Truman administration intended to send four additional Army divisions to Europe and maintained that no plans existed to deploy more Americans later. On March 14 the committees recommended passage of a Senate resolution approving the appointment of Eisenhower as NATO commander, endorsing a

"fair share" contribution of U.S. forces to the alliance, and calling on the president to consult with Congress before dispatching more troops abroad. Following heated debate on the Senate floor, the resolution was amended to state that no more than four divisions should be sent to NATO without further Senate approval. The measure passed on April 4. Truman praised the resolution as a clear affirmation of U.S. commitment to the defense of Europe. The Great Debate effectively determined that America would not revert to its prewar ISOLATIONISM and confirmed the president's authority to deploy U.S. forces without prior congressional backing.

GREAT WHITE FLEET (1907–1909) Name given to the U.S. fleet sent on a voyage around the world by President THEODORE ROOSEVELT to demonstrate America's naval might and stature as an ascendent global power. The United States emerged from the SPANISH-AMERICAN WAR (1898) with new Pacific and Caribbean possessions and a belief in the importance of sea power as an instrument of foreign policy. In the conflict's aftermath, the American Navy grew to be the world's second largest.

Dispatch of the fleet stemmed out of increasingly strained Japanese-American relations in the opening years of the 20th century over Japanese immigration to the United States. Mounting anti-Japanese sentiment on the West Coast brought discrimination against Japanese residents there and a movement to exclude them altogether from the United States. The mistreatment excited strong anti-American feelings in Japan. The segregation of Japanese children by the San Francisco school board in October 1906, deplored by the Japanese government, pushed Washington and Tokyo to the brink of a major diplomatic crisis. The two sides averted a showdown through negotiation the following year of the so-called GENTLEMEN'S AGREEMENT limiting Japanese immigration to America. The continuing anti-Japanese agitation on the Pacific coast, however, prompted belligerent intimations from Japan and rumors of war circulated. Eager to dispel the lingering crisis, Roosevelt decided to send the bulk of the Navy on a world cruise to impress upon the Japanese leadership that armed conflict with the United States would be ill-advised and futile. The president also wanted to communicate that the United States would not brook Japanese challenges to American hegemony in the Philippines.

The armada of 16 battleships and 4 destroyers, all painted white for the voyage, departed in December 1907, by which time the Japanese government was anxious to avoid war. At the invitation of the Japanese emperor, the fleet visited the Pacific island nation, where it was greeted with great fanfare and left a vivid impression of American naval strength. The cruise ended in February 1909 having fulfilled its diplomatic objectives and provided the Navy with practical information helpful to the further development of the modern U.S. fleet.

GREENVILLE, TREATY OF See **FALLEN TIMBERS, BATTLE OF**.

GREER INCIDENT (1941) Armed hostilities between the U.S. Navy destroyer *Greer* and a German submarine. Despite offical U.S. neutrality in the opening years of WORLD WAR II, President FRANKLIN D. ROOSEVELT gradually steered U.S. policy toward full support, short of war, to Great Britain in its fight against Nazi Germany. British convoys carried increasing amounts of critical U.S.-supplied war materiel across the North Atlantic. German submarines, however, exacted a mounting toll on Allied shipping. At the August 1941 ATLANTIC CONFERENCE, Roosevelt promised the beleaguered British that U.S. naval forces would escort their convoys as far east as Iceland. Convoy operations were underway by early September, but the president, wary of domestic isolationist opposition to further U.S. involvement in the world war, held off on announcing the action to the American people. On September 4 the *Greer* and a German submarine exchanged fire in waters off Iceland, with neither ship sustaining any damage. On September 11 Roosevelt used the incident to reveal the new U.S. escort policy, declaring it imperative that Nazi raiders not gain control of the North Atlantic. U.S. ships would patrol as far east as Iceland and the Azores with authority to "shoot-on-sight" intruding German and Italian vessels.

U.S. military involvement in the Atlantic, often referred to as the "undeclared war," drew widespread domestic support since it seemingly satisfied the desire of Americans both to stay out of World War II and to see Hitler defeated. On October 17, 1941, the U.S. destroyer *Kearny*, on escort duty in Icelandic waters, went to the aid of a convoy of merchant ships under German attack. In the ensuing action, a German submarine fired a torpedo that struck the *Kearny*, killing 11 U.S. sailors. Undeclared hostilities continued to escalate. On October 30, a German submarine sank the U.S. destroyer *Reuben James* with the loss of 115 lives. This incident helped bring repeal of the U.S. NEUTRALITY ACTS on November 17, 1941. The Japanese surprise attack on PEARL HARBOR on December 7, 1941, brought war between the United States and Japan. On December 11, Japanese ally Germany declared war on the United States and the U.S. Congress reciprocated the same day.

GRENADA INVASION (1983) U.S. armed intervention in the Caribbean island of Grenada. On October 25, 1983, U.S. ground, air, and sea forces invaded the tiny island, where a hardline Marxist military faction had recently staged a successful coup, seizing power after murdering Prime Minister Maurice Bishop. During 1983, the Reagan administration had insisted that a Soviet- and Cuban-sponsored buildup was underway in Grenada for the export of revolution in the Caribbean basin and warned that the country represented a security risk to the United States. President RONALD W. REAGAN undertook the military action, he explained, after member nations of the Organization of Eastern Caribbean States (OECS) had urgently requested U.S. help in restoring order and democracy in Grenada and curbing Communist Cuba's growing influence in the island. He contended that the invasion, codenamed Operation Urgent Fury, was necessary to ensure the safety of some 1000 Americans on the island, mostly medical students, who were considered to be in imminent danger. The Marxist regime's small army, joined by about 700 Cubans who had been on the island to construct an airstrip, put up a fierce resistance for several days but were overwhelmed by the invasion force, which at its peak numbered more than 7000 troops. Within several weeks the leaders of the military government were arrested by U.S. forces and turned over to Grenada's governor general. By mid-December 1983 all U.S. combat forces had been withdrawn from the island. An advisory council was appointed to govern Grenada until promised elections could be held. The reported invasion death toll was 18 Americans, 25 Cubans, and 116 Grenadans.

GRESHAM, WALTER QUINTIN (1832–1895) Jurist and secretary of state. Gresham was born in Indiana. After attending Indiana University for one year, he studied law and was admitted to the bar in his native state in 1854. A local organizer of the Republican Party, he was elected to the state legislature in 1860. He served in the Union army during the Civil War, attaining the rank of major general of volunteers before a serious wound forced his retirement. After the war he returned to private law practice in Indiana and in 1866 ran unsuccessfully as a Republican for Congress. In 1869 President ULYSSES S. GRANT named Gresham a federal district judge in Indiana. He left the bench in 1883 to become postmaster general under President CHESTER A. ARTHUR. In September 1884 Arthur made him treasury secretary following the incumbent's death. A month later Gresham resigned to accept a federal circuit judgeship. He was an unsuccessful candidate for the Republican presidential nomination in 1888. His growing hostility to protective tariffs led him to bolt the Republican Party and become a Democrat in 1892.

President GROVER CLEVELAND appointed him secretary of state in 1893. The antiimperialist Gresham firmly opposed HAWAII ANNEXATION. Believing Hawaii's provisional government, which was dominated by American sugar growers, to be illegitimate, he influenced Cleveland to withdraw from Senate consideration the treaty of annexation negotiated under his predecessor as president, Republican BENJAMIN HARRISON. Gresham's quiet diplomacy brought about settlement in 1895 of a dispute between Great Britain and Nicaragua, helped facilitate an end to the Sino-Japanese War (1894–1895), and defused tensions with Italy following the lynching of Italian nationals in Colorado. He also negotiated the Sino-American GRESHAM-YANG TREATY (1894) on Chinese immigration to the United States. In failing health, Gresham died on May 28, 1895, while still in office. He was replaced by RICHARD OLNEY.

GRESHAM-YANG TREATY (1894) Treaty concluded in Washington March 17, 1894, between Secretary of State WALTER Q. GRESHAM and Chinese envoy Yang Yu. The agreement amended the ANGELL TREATY of 1880. In the earlier measure, the Chinese government had consented to limits on the immigration of Chinese laborers to the United States. Congress subsequently passed the CHINESE EXCLUSION ACT (1882), which suspended the admission of Chinese workers for 10 years.

Demands for more effective enforcement mounted amid charges that Chinese laborers were fraudulently entering America. Under the 1882 act, Chinese workers already in the United States were allowed to visit their homeland. Many workers going back to China for a supposed visit were alleged to be remaining there while other laborers returned in their place. In 1888 U.S. and Chinese negotiators reached agreement on a pact to place tighter controls on the departure and reentry of Chinese workers. When China hesitated over ratification, Congress passed the SCOTT ACT (1888) barring the return of all Chinese laborers. The GEARY ACT (1892) extended the ban on Chinese immigration another 10 years.

Concerned over its deteriorating ties with China, the United States negotiated a new immigration accord. The 1894 treaty improved relations strained by the recent U.S. legislation and the continuing mistreatment of Chinese immigrants on the American West Coast. The Chinese government accepted the Geary Act constraints on the immigration of its laborers. In return, the United States pledged to reinstate freedom of travel to and from their homeland for Chinese immigrants either with family or property worth $1000 in America and to provide greater protection for Chinese residents. An increasingly nationalistic Chinese leadership later refused to renew what it had come to consider an unequal agreement and the Gresham-Yang Treaty expired in 1904.

GREW, JOSEPH CLARK (1880–1965) Prominent career diplomat best remembered as U.S. ambassador to Japan. Born into a wealthy Boston family, Grew attended the Groton School and graduated from Harvard University in 1902. After traveling in Europe and the Far East, he started his diplomatic career with an appointment in 1904 as a clerk to the U.S. consulate in Cairo, Egypt. From 1906 to 1916 he held junior posts in Mexico City, St. Petersburg, Berlin, and Vienna. When the United States entered WORLD WAR I in 1917, Grew returned to Washington to serve as acting chief of the State Department's division of western affairs. After the war he was a secretary to the U.S delegation to the PARIS PEACE CONFERENCE (1919). Named American minister to Denmark in 1920, he was transferred the following year to Switzerland, where he attended the Lausanne Conference (1922–1923) on the Near East as a U.S. delegate. From 1924 to 1927 he was in Washington as under secretary of state, in which capacity he supervised the restructuring of the FOREIGN SERVICE authorized under the ROGERS ACT (1924). For his efforts he became known as the father of the career diplomatic service. Made ambassador to Turkey in 1927, he spent five uneventful years at Ankara before accepting assignment as ambassador to Japan, where he served from 1932 to 1941.

Grew arrived in Tokyo shortly after Japan's seizure of Manchuria. Throughout his tenure he sought in vain to avert a serious deterioration in Japanese-American relations and to steer Japan away from its scheme for conquest in Asia. He tried to persuade President FRANKLIN D. ROOSEVELT and Secretary of State CORDELL HULL that attempts by the United States to thwart Japan's policy toward China through expressions of legal or moral disapproval would prove counterproductive. By 1940, though, he accepted U.S. economic sanctions against Japan as necessary to confront its expansionist militarism. Almost 11 months before the Japanese strike on PEARL HARBOR (1941), Grew alerted Washington in a cable to Hull about a possible Japanese surprise attack on the Hawaiian naval base. His warning apparently went unheeded. After the attack he was interned at Tokyo. Repatriated in 1942 through a U.S.-Japanese exchange of diplomats, he became special assistant to Secretary Hull. In 1944 he was made director of the State Department's Office of Far Eastern Affairs. He

served as under secretary of state again for eight months before retiring in August 1945. Toward the war's end he had urged Americans to look past victory to a healing peace with Japan. In retirement, Grew was board chairman of the Free Europe Committee, the organization responsible for operation of RADIO FREE EUROPE, and wrote his autobiography, *Turbulent Era* (1952).

GROUP OF 5 (G-5) Name given to the five principal non-Communist economic powers. In 1967 finance ministers from the United States, Great Britain, France, West Germany, and Japan met outside London for informal discussions on international monetary issues. In subsequent years the finance officials of what quickly became known as the Group of 5 convened on numerous occasions, often in conjuction with the meetings of the INTERNATIONAL MONETARY FUND, to coordinate economic policy. In 1975 it was decided to hold a more formal annual gathering of the G-5 heads of government to confer on the global economic picture. In years since, the ECONOMIC SUMMITS also have become important forums for the leaders of the major industrial democracies to consider international political developments. Italy joined the meetings in 1976 and Canada the following year, thus making the Group of 7 (G-7). From 1977 to 1986 the G-5 finance ministers continued to meet as a separate body. At the G-7 summit in Tokyo in 1986, agreement was reached to include finance ministers from Italy and Canada in the original quintet's deliberations. Since then the Western economic powers essentially have worked together under the G-7 aegis. In 1990 newly unified Germany assumed West Germany's place in the group.
See also GROUP OF 10.

GROUP OF 7 See **GROUP OF 5.**

GROUP OF 10 (G-10) Informal title given to the major industrial nations that established the General Agreements to Borrow (GAB) within the INTERNATIONAL MONETARY FUND (IMF) in 1962. Under the GAB, the 10 wealthier members of the IMF stood ready to make loans to the fund when it needed extra resources to cope with a disruption in the international monetary system. G-10 originally was composed of the GROUP OF 7 countries and Belgium, the Netherlands, and Sweden. Switzerland became a participant in 1984, but the group continues to be referred to as G-10. The finance ministers of group members meet regularly to coordinate economic policies and are known as the Paris Club.

GUADALUPE HIDALGO, TREATY OF (1848) Peace treaty concluded between the United States and Mexico that formally ended the MEXICAN WAR. In April 1847, after Veracruz had fallen to American forces under General WINFIELD SCOTT, President JAMES K. POLK decided to send Nicholas P. Trist, chief clerk of the State Department, secretly to Mexico to accompany Scott's army as a peace commissioner. Trist was authorized to arrange a suspension of hostilities and to receive any possible Mexican peace proposals that satisfied American demands for Mexican territory. His instructions, drafted by Polk and Secretary of State JAMES BUCHANAN, were substantially those that envoy JOHN SLIDELL had carried in his earlier abortive diplomatic sojourn to Mexico, the so-called SLIDELL MISSION. Trist was told to secure peace on the basis of the Rio Grande as the boundary between Texas and Mexico and the cession of Mexican provinces California and New Mexico to the United States. He also was expected to negotiate for acquisition of Lower California and the right of transit across the isthmus of Tehuantepec. Trist's instructions were kept strictly confidential since the Democrat Polk had not yet publicly disclosed his territorial aims for fear of stoking opposition to the war among Northern Whigs, who since its outset had suggested the conflict was part of a Southern scheme to wrest land from Mexico to accommodate the extension of slavery.

Trist reached Veracruz in May 1847, where he fell to quarreling bitterly with Scott, who challenged the extent of the envoy's authority. The two men patched up their dispute and in August Scott arranged an armistice with Mexico. Ensuing negotiations between Trist and a Mexican commission headed by former President Herrera foundered and hostilities resumed in early September. After learning at the end of September of the armistice and preliminary peace talks, Polk became concerned that Trist was perhaps straying from his instruc-

tions and giving the Mexicans the false impression that the United States was so anxious for peace it would ultimately accede to Mexican terms. The president ordered Trist's recall. In mid-November the emissary received the letter ordering him home. Delaying his departure, he eventually decided to disregard the president's instruction and to assume responsibility for negotiating a peace treaty. Polk toward the end of the year announced for the first time his full territorial aims, which predictably aroused powerful Whig objections. At the same time he faced pressure from ardent expansionists within his own party, who spearheaded the "ALL-OF-MEXICO" MOVEMENT, demanding U.S. annexation of the whole of Mexico.

Trist entered unauthorized negotiations with the Mexican commissioners on January 2, 1848. These talks produced a treaty, signed on February 2, 1848, at the village of Guadalupe Hidalgo near Mexico City. Under its terms the Rio Grande was established as the U.S.-Mexican boundary. Mexico, in addition to relinquishing all claims to Texas above the Rio Grande, ceded New Mexico and California to the United States. The territory embraced all or part of the present-day states of Arizona, California, Colorado, Nevada, New Mexico, Utah, and Wyoming. Including Texas, which had been annexed in 1845, the area amounted to more than one million square miles, representing a loss to Mexico of half of its national territory. In return for the vast MEXICAN CESSION, the United States agreed to pay $15 million and to assume the unpaid indemnity claims of U.S. citizens against the Mexican government up to $3.25 million. When the treaty reached Washington, Polk at first was inclined to reject it on account of Trist's insubordination. But after discovering it met his territorial objectives, he accepted the agreement and submitted it to the Senate, where Democrats clamoring for all of Mexico and Whigs who opposed any acquisition of Mexican soil sought, unsuccessfully, to block it. The Senate, after defeating a motion to add the antislavery WILMOT PROVISO, approved the measure on March 10, 1848, by a vote of 38 to 14. After ratification by the Mexican Congress, Polk proclaimed the treaty in effect July 4, 1848.

See also GADSDEN PURCHASE, MAP 2.

GUAM U.S. territorial dependency located in the western Pacific Ocean between Hawaii and the Philippines. Largest and most populous of the Mariana Islands, Guam is about 30 miles long and 4 to 7 miles wide. Spain ceded the island to the United States in 1898 under the TREATY OF PARIS that ended the Spanish-American War. Guam was placed under the jurisdiction of the DEPARTMENT OF THE NAVY and became the site for an American naval station. Japanese occupation of Guam during WORLD WAR II lasted from December 1941 until July 1944, when U.S. forces recaptured the island.

Under the 1950 Organic Act of Guam, passed by the U.S. Congress, the island was established as an unincorporated territory of the United States. The legislation also shifted responsibility for Guam's civil administration from the Navy to the Interior Department, gave Guamanians U.S. citizenship, and introduced internal self-rule. The island sends a nonvoting member to the U.S. House of Representatives. The governor of Guam, until 1970 appointed by the U.S. president, has since been popularly elected. Islanders also vote for a unicameral legislature, which acts as local lawmaking authority. The U.S. Congress can annul any measure passed by the island legislature. In a September 1982 island referendum, 72 percent of voters favored U.S. commonwealth status similar to that of the neighboring Northern Marianas Islands. Since the plebiscite, no change in Guam's political status has taken place. U.S. military installations on the island, including a major air force base and a naval air station and submarine base, form an important cog in America's Pacific defenses and have become a mainstay of Guam's economy.

See also MAP 7.

GUAM DOCTRINE See **NIXON DOCTRINE**.

GUATEMALA COUP (1954) U.S.-directed overthrow of Guatemalan President Jacobo Arbenz Guzman. In 1944 Guatemalan dictator Jorge Ubico was forced from office and leftist educator Dr. Juan Jose Arevalo was elected president. In 1951 Army officer Arbenz succeeded Arevalo, continuing his predecessor's land reform program. He signed an agrarian reform law in 1952 that expropriated much of the large land holdings of the American-owned United Fruit Company. Arbenz's actions, enthusiastically endorsed by the Guatemalan Communist Party, were viewed with alarm in Washington as possible indication of an emerging Communist state in Latin America.

The Truman administration approved, then canceled, covert assistance to Nicaraguan leader Anastasio Somoza Garcia, who had offered to remove Arbenz. In March 1953 an uprising of anti-Communist army officers was put down by the Guatemalan government. In August the Eisenhower administration directed the State Department and CENTRAL INTELLIGENCE AGENCY (CIA) to plan a coup d'etat in the Central American nation. The operation, code-named Success, had three components: diplomatic pressure on the Arbenz administration; a campaign to undermine support for Arbenz in the Guatemalan military; and paramilitary assistance to former army officer Carlos Castillo Armas, a leading opposition figure and U.S. choice to replace Arbenz. The CIA established training bases for Castillo Armas's small exile army in Honduras and Nicaragua, installed clandestine radio stations, and assembled a private air force of aging fighters and light bombers.

The U.S. government stepped up its political and economic pressure on Guatemala in early 1954. At a conference of the ORGANIZATION OF AMERICAN STATES in March, Secretary of State JOHN FOSTER DULLES secured passage of a declaration that condemned communism and called for "appropriate action" to prevent its introduction in the Western Hemisphere. In April U.S. intelligence learned that the Swedish freighter *Alfhem* was bound for Guatemala with a shipment of Czechoslovakian arms provided by the Soviet Union. On May 17, two days after the freighter docked at the Guatemalan port of Puerto Barrios, Dulles decried the arrival of the Communist arms, characterizing it as a violation of the MONROE DOCTRINE. The same day an emergency secret session of the NATIONAL SECURITY COUNCIL chaired by President DWIGHT D. EISENHOWER gave the final go-ahead to Operation Success.

Eisenhower announced a U.S. naval blockade of Guatemala. On June 18, 1954, Castillo Armas's "Army of Liberation" crossed the border from Honduras and advanced to the town of Esquipulas, a short distance inside Guatemala. It remained there over the next several days as the CIA's air force conducted air strikes throughout the country. Meanwhile, broadcasts by CIA-operated "Voice of Liberation" radio transmitters reported that Castillo Armas was marching on the capital with thousands of rebel troops and encouraged Guatemalans to rally to the liberation movement. On June 27 Arbenz succumbed to the combination of military and psychological pressure, turning over the government to a military junta and going into exile overseas. Castillo Armas became president on September 1. The Guatemala Coup was viewed in Washington as a critical reversal of a possible Communist takeover in Central America, but it engendered lasting hostility across Latin America to the United States and its interventionist policies.

GULF OF SIDRA INCIDENTS (1981, 1989) Encounters, occurring eight years apart, between U.S. and Libyan warplanes in the Gulf of Sidra. In 1981, U.S.-Libyan relations deteriorated in the face of evidence that Libyan leader Colonel Muammar Qaddafi was a major source of support for international terrorism, much of it directed against American interests. In May the State Department expelled all Libyan diplomats from the United States because of Tripoli's alleged terrorist actions worldwide. In August, U.S. and Libyan aircraft battled over the Gulf of Sidra. According to the U.S. account of events, two Libyan planes were shot down after they made an unprovoked attack on American aircraft involved in a naval exercise in what the Reagan administration maintained were international waters. Qaddafi, though, claimed the Gulf as Libyan territorial waters and condemned the U.S. naval presence as a violation of Libyan sovereignty. Later in the year President RONALD W. REAGAN said the United States possessed evidence that Qaddafi's regime had sent an assassination squad to America to kill him and other U.S. leaders. He barred U.S. travel to Libya and called on the 1500 Americans living in the country, mostly oil workers, to leave.

In January 1989, two U.S. carrier-based F-14 jet fighters shot down two Libyan MiG-23 fighters over the Gulf of Sidra. The Reagan administration justified the action as self-defense, explaining that the Libyan aircraft had approached the U.S. planes in a "hostile manner" while the latter were engaged in training. The confrontation occurred in the wake of U.S. government allegations that Libya was building a chemical weapons plant at Rabat and after the terrorist destruction of PAN AM FLIGHT 103 over Lockerbie, Scotland. A draft resolution put before the UNITED NATIONS Security Council condemning the American action was vetoed by the United States, Great Britain, and France.

GULF OF TONKIN...   See **TONKIN GULF....**

GUNBOAT DIPLOMACY Catchphrase for a policy of using the threat of naval power to uphold national interests abroad or serve diplomatic aims. Between 1890 and WORLD WAR II, the United States variously exercised such an approach in China and Latin America. U.S. Navy gunboats were stationed on Chinese rivers and harbors to protect America's position in the Asian nation and discourage European or Japanese violations of the OPEN DOOR. From the SPANISH-AMERICAN WAR (1898) until the advent of the GOOD NEIGHBOR POLICY in the early 1930s, the Navy patrolled the seas off Caribbean and Central American countries experiencing internal political instability. The naval presence was intended to bolster pro-U.S. governments or pressure competing political factions in the nations to restore order. The goal, in either event, was to quell threats to U.S. economic or strategic interests in Latin America through a show of force short of direct military intervention. The Navy vessels were the agents of American armed interventions, through the early 20th century, in the Dominican Republic, Cuba, Haiti, Honduras, Nicaragua, and Mexico.

GUNTHER, JOHN JOSEPH (1901–1970) Journalist and author. The Illinois native graduated from the University of Chicago in 1922 and by 1924 was covering events in Europe as a correspondent for the *Chicago Daily News*. Until his resignation from the newspaper in 1936, he reported from most of the major nations of west and central Europe, the Balkans, and the Middle East. From 1937 to 1939 Gunther toured the

Near East and Asia as a special correspondent for the North American Newspaper Alliance, a news syndicate. Meanwhile he had completed the first of the "Inside" books of personal reportage destined to win him worldwide fame. *Inside Europe* (1936), a country-by-country survey of the continent, examined existing political crises and provided personality profiles of such major political leaders as Nazi Germany's Adolf Hitler, Fascist Italy's Benito Mussolini, and the Communist Soviet Union's Joseph Stalin.

He followed the enormously successful *Inside Europe* with *Inside Asia* (1939). In 1940 and 1941 he visited 20 Latin American countries, interviewing 18 heads of state, in advance of writing *Inside Latin America* (1941). During WORLD WAR II, he worked for the NBC radio network as a commentator on international affairs and as a correspondent covering Allied campaigns in Europe. From 1942 to 1944 he served as special consultant to the U.S. War Department. After the war the prolific Gunther wrote numerous books, including *Inside Africa* (1955) and *Inside Russia Today* (1958), volumes on FRANKLIN D. ROOSEVELT and DOUGLAS MACARTHUR, and *Death Be Not Proud* (1949).

H

HAGUE CONVENTIONS   See **HAGUE PEACE CONFERENCES**.

HAGUE PEACE CONFERENCES (1899, 1907) International meetings held at The Hague, Netherlands. The first conference was convened at the suggestion of Russian Czar Nicholas II to discuss disarmament, the development of rules and laws governing warfare, and the formation of an international mechanism for the peaceful settlement of disputes. Support for a multinational gathering to foster peace reflected the widespread belief emerging in the late 19th century that nations could resolve their differences through reason rather than force. Delegations from 26 countries, including the United States, assembled from May 18 to July 29, 1899. America's attendance was an early instance of the nation's growing involvement in world affairs following its victory in the SPANISH-AMERICAN WAR (1898). While failing to make any progress on the central goal of disarmament, delegates reached agreement on four conventions. Referred to collectively as the Hague Conventions, they established the PERMANENT COURT OF ARBITRATION for resolving international disagreements; set forth laws for land warfare; applied the 1864 Geneva Convention to maritime warfare; and prohibited aerial bombardment from balloons. The provisions of the convention on the rules of war became known as the Hague Regulations. The United States ratified all four conventions, with the reservation that its acceptance of an international court of arbitration did not entail any involvement in foreign alliances or amount to a renunciation of the MONROE DOCTRINE.

A second conference was held from June 15 to October 15, 1907, with 46 nations in attendance, including the United States. A total of 14 conventions were adopted. These included revisions of the four 1899 conventions as well as new measures addressing the formal start of hostilities between nations; the rights and duties of neutral countries and persons in wartime; the wartime status of merchant ships; naval bombardment and mine-laying; and an international prize court for ruling on the status of captured ships. While again not reaching agreement on disarmament, delegates approved a ban on armed intervention to collect foreign debts. The United States became a party to all the conventions except those pertaining to merchant ships and the prize court, which were viewed as conflicting with the traditional American position on FREEDOM OF THE SEAS. A third gathering scheduled for 1915 never convened because of WORLD WAR I. The Hague Conferences represented an emerging commitment to international meetings and institutions and presaged the development of the LEAGUE OF NATIONS, WORLD COURT, and UNITED NATIONS.

See also GENEVA CONVENTIONS.

HAIG, ALEXANDER MEIGS, JR. (1924–)
Army officer, NATO supreme allied commander, secretary of state. Haig was born in Pennsylvania. He attended Notre Dame for two years before gaining an appointment to West Point, from which he graduated in 1947. He saw action in the KOREAN WAR, served in Europe, and earned a master's in international relations from Georgetown University in 1961. In 1964 he was named military assistant to Secretary of the Army CYRUS R. VANCE. After a combat tour during the VIETNAM WAR, Haig became deputy commandant of cadets at West Point. In 1969 HENRY A. KISSINGER, national security adviser in the new Nixon administration, selected him as his military assistant. He was promoted to general the same year. In 1970 he was named deputy national security adviser. While on the NATIONAL SECURITY COUNCIL, he made numerous fact-finding trips to Southeast Asia to help formulate the administration's Vietnam policy and headed the White House advance team that went to Communist China to prepare for the 1972 PEKING SUM-

MIT. In 1972, in what was described as part of a move to bring younger officers into senior leadership posts, Haig was promoted from two-star to four-star rank and appointed Army vice-chief of staff. In May 1973 President RICHARD M. NIXON brought Haig back to the White House to replace H. R. Haldeman, who had been forced to resign as chief of staff over the worsening Watergate scandal. Haig remained in the post until Nixon's resignation in August 1974. Recalled to active military service by President GERALD R. FORD, in December 1974 he assumed his new duties as supreme allied commander of NATO forces in Europe. Haig held the NATO command for five years, overseeing the initial upgrade and modernization of the Western security alliance's forces in response to a major Soviet military buildup. He retired in 1979 and became president of United Technologies.

In 1981 Haig became President RONALD W. REAGAN's first secretary of state. He supported the administration's hard-line stance toward the Soviet Union, concurring in Reagan's assessment of the Communist superpower as a dangerous, expansionist threat. In Latin America he pressed for aid to El Salvador to help that country defend itself against a Marxist-Leninist guerrilla insurgency, and was an architect of the Reagan administration's policy of opposition to the leftist Sandinista regime in Nicaragua. His suggestion that America might have to deal with the flow of arms from Cuba to the Sandinistas and El Salvador guerrillas "at the source" raised concerns over U.S. intervention in Latin America and prompted Reagan to state publicly that the United States was not contemplating an assault on the Communist island nation. After Argentine military forces seized the Falklands from Great Britain in April 1982, Haig attempted to mediate the long-standing dispute over the South Atlantic islands. When full-scale fighting broke out in May, he shifted U.S. policy in support of Great Britain's successful campaign to recapture the Falklands. From the outset, Haig's tenure had been marked by conflict within the administration over his efforts to centralize all foreign policy authority in the State Department. With the secretary of state increasingly at odds with other senior aides, Reagan accepted his resignation in June 1982. Haig returned to his business career and published his memoirs, *Caveat: Realism, Reagan, and Foreign Policy* (1984). He served in 1983 on the SCOW-CROFT COMMISSION on U.S. strategic nuclear forces. In 1988 he was an unsuccessful candidate for the Republican presidential nomination.

HAITIAN INTERVENTION   U.S. military intervention that resulted in American occupation of the Caribbean nation from 1915 to 1934. Financial instability stemming from chronic political turmoil, corruption, and economic underdevelopment rendered Haiti increasingly unable in the early 1900s to pay its debts to foreign creditors, mainly American and European bankers. Political violence in this period often placed foreign lives and property in Haiti at risk. On several occasions the French and German governments landed small numbers of troops to protect their nationals. In July 1914 the United States, looking to stabilize Haitian finances and forestall further European interventions, tried without success to complete a treaty with Port-au-Prince giving Washington control over the collection of Haitian customs revenue. The Wilson administration sought to uphold historic American claims under the MONROE DOCTRINE (1823) and its ROOSEVELT COROLLARY (1904) to sovereign influence and international police power in the Caribbean.

When revolution broke out in Haiti in January 1915, threatening American lives and private investments, President WOODROW WILSON sent a diplomatic commission to the country on the second of the FORT MISSIONS with instructions to negotiate a treaty granting the United States a naval base and a customs receivership. By the time the commission arrived, a new Haitian government had come to power under General Vilbrun Guillaume Sam, who assumed the presidency. The mission foundered when Sam declined to negotiate.

The Wilson administration meanwhile rejected a Franco-German proposal for a three-way customs collectorship in Haiti as a method for guaranteeing repayment of the Caribbean country's outstanding foreign obligations. Secretary of State William JENNINGS BRYAN announced that the United States would not permit European nations to take formal part in political or financial control of Haiti. Another revolution erupted in the summer of 1915 after President Sam brutally executed 167 Haitian political prisoners. On July 28 Sam's regime was toppled and he was assassinated by a Port-au-Prince mob. This new round of violence and political disorder prompted U.S. intervention. On July 29, at Wilson's order, U.S. troops landed in Haiti to protect American lives and property and restore order. American forces imposed a military occupation over the entire country.

In mid-August 1915 Sudre Dartiguenave, a figure acceptable to Washington, was chosen president by the Haitian national assembly in an election supervised by American authorities. Under pressure from the Wilson administration, Dartiguenave signed a treaty on September 16, 1915, that effectively made his country a U.S. protectorate. The agreement, renewable after 10 years, rendered Haiti's government a puppet regime by investing the United States with control over Haitian finances, police forces, public works, and sanitation. Under its terms, American marines remained stationed in the country to keep order. The U.S. Senate unanimously approved the agreement in February 1916.

U.S. State Department officials drafted a new constitution that was approved by Haitians in 1918 in a national plebiscite conducted by American military forces. The same year a guerrilla revolt broke out against U.S. occupation. American troops suppressed the two-year insurgency, during which more than 2000 resisting Haitians and a dozen or so marines were killed. High-handed U.S. policies and exercise of strict control by American authorities bred deep resentment among the Haitian people. Nevertheless, U.S. civilian and military officials under General John H. Russell, American high commissioner of Haiti from 1922 to 1930, achieved widespread financial reforms and improvements in public works, education, sanitation, and public health. In 1922 Dartiguenave was replaced as president by Louis Borno, whose unpopular administration followed Russell's dictates.

Labor strife and mounting opposition to the U.S. occupation led to a Haitian uprising in 1929 that brought renewed clashes with U.S. forces. Before the year was out, President HERBERT C. HOOVER, apostle of a less-imperialistic policy toward Latin America, appointed a special commission to survey the situation in Haiti and devise recommendations for ending the American occupation. Hoover began to implement the commission's plan in the remaining two years of his term. Borno resigned in May 1930 and was replaced by Eugene Roy, who served as interim executive until November 1930, when the national assembly selected Stenio Vincent as the new president. With the gradual withdrawal of American officials, many governing powers were restored to Haitian authorities. The U.S. occupation ended in 1934 with the withdrawal of the U.S. Marines by President FRANKLIN D. ROOSEVELT. A Haitian national guard, trained by U.S. officers, took over the policing of the country. Washington relinquished control over Port-au-Prince's finances in 1947, upon full redemption of a loan made by an American bank to the Haitian government in 1922.

HALBERSTAM, DAVID (1934–) Journalist and author. After graduating from Harvard University in 1955, the New York City native worked as a reporter for daily newspapers in Mississippi and Tennessee. He joined the Washington bureau of the *New York Times* as a staff writer in 1960 and the following year was posted to the Congo (now Zaire) as a foreign correspondent. Reassigned to South Vietnam in 1962, Halberstam became embroiled in controversy over his coverage of the VIETNAM WAR. His dispatches describing South Vietnamese military shortcomings, the growing strength of the Communist Vietcong forces, and a deteriorating political situation in Saigon contradicted official versions of events in Indochina and called into question U.S. government optimism about the war.

The American embassy in Saigon, the PENTAGON, and the White House all attacked his coverage as inaccurate, biased, and sensationalized. American officials and the South Vietnamese government exerted pressure on him by monitoring his sources and tracking his whereabouts. In October 1963 President JOHN F. KENNEDY suggested to *Times* publisher Arthur Ochs Sulzberger that Halberstam was "too close to the story" in Indochina and should be reassigned. Sulzberger declined, although Halberstam did leave Vietnam in 1964, the

same year he garnered the Pulitzer Prize for international reporting. His book *The Making of a Quagmire* (1965) recounted his experiences covering the war and indicted U.S. policy in Vietnam.

Sent to the *Times* Warsaw bureau in January 1965, he was expelled before year's end by Poland's Communist regime, which disapproved of his forthright coverage. After working in Paris and New York, Halberstam resigned from the *Times* in 1967 to become a contributing editor at *Harper's* magazine, where he remained until 1971. He is the author of the best-sellers *The Best and the Brightest* (1972), an examination of America's entry into the Vietnam War, and *The Powers That Be* (1979), a study of major media in the United States.

HAMILTON, ALEXANDER (1757–1804) Statesman, first secretary of the treasury, and a leader of the Federalist Party. Born out of wedlock in the British West Indies, Hamilton journeyed to New York City in 1772, entering King's College (now Columbia University) in 1774. He plunged into the politics of the AMERICAN REVOLUTION as a pamphleteer who supported the patriot cause and attacked British imperial policies. Commissioned an artillery captain early in 1776, he became secretary and aide-de-camp to General GEORGE WASHINGTON in March 1777, with lieutenant colonel's rank. Miffed by his failure to win a field assignment, he quit the general's staff in February 1781. Washington soon after gave Hamilton command of an infantry regiment, which he led in the decisive campaign at Yorktown.

With the fighting over, he went to Albany, New York, to study law and in July 1782 was admitted to the state bar. After serving in the Continental Congress from 1782 to 1783, Hamilton opened a law practice in New York City, where in 1784 he helped found the Bank of New York. An ardent nationalist and leader of the movement for a strengthened federal government, he became a forceful critic of the ARTICLES OF CONFEDERATION, which Hamilton deemed too weak to govern the Union or place its public finances on a solid footing. At the Annapolis Convention (1786) he drafted the influential report that led to the convening of the Constitutional Convention at Philadelphia in May 1787. A New York delegate to the convention, Hamilton advocated a powerful national government under a strong executive, clashing with proponents of states' rights who favored strict curbs on federal powers. He fought wholeheartedly for adoption by the states of the CONSTITUTION, collaborating with JAMES MADISON and JOHN JAY on *The Federalist*, a renowned series of interpretive articles that urged ratification, and successfully leading the battle for ratification in New York. Hamilton was a member of the Confederation Congress from 1788 to 1789, when the new government under the Constitution was formed.

Appointed first secretary of the treasury by President Washington in September 1789, he was architect of an ambitious fiscal program that restored the credit of the United States to a sound basis and created a national financial machinery. An economic nationalist, Hamilton instituted policies that bound the states closer to the new central government and emphasized the federal government's authority. His watershed *Report on Public Credit* (1790) established a national debt by committing the federal government to pay off in full both its domestic and foreign loans. He implemented as well a plan by which the federal government assumed the unpaid portion of debts incurred by the states during the revolution. Legislation chartering the Bank of the United States in 1791 was based on ideas developed by Hamilton in his *Report on a National Bank* (1790). The treasury secretary established a U.S. mint in 1792 and created a standard currency. His famous *Report on Manufactures* (1791), which advocated modest import duties to protect nascent American industries, prompted Congress in 1792 to raise the rates under the TARIFF OF 1789. Congress also enacted Hamilton's proposed excise tax on distilled liquor, which he recommended as a revenue source supplementary to the tariff. Opposition to the resented liquor excise coalesced in the so-called Whiskey Rebellion in western Pennsylvania. Hamilton in 1794 personally led 15,000 federal troops to the scene of the insurrection to enforce the whiskey tax.

Philosophical differences made Hamilton and Secretary of State THOMAS JEFFERSON political arch-enemies. The split between the top two members of Washington's cabinet was emblematic of the division in American political life between Hamilto-

nian Federalists and Jeffersonian Democratic-Republicans. Hamilton's substantial influence over the conduct of foreign policy contributed to Jefferson's decision to leave the State Department in December 1793.

Antipathy for the French Revolution and its bloody excesses shaped the conservative Hamilton's outlook on the conflicts embroiling Europe in the 1790s. After France declared war on Great Britain in 1793, and the revolutionary French government maneuvered for U.S. support, Hamilton advocated strict American neutrality, which Washington made official policy through his NEUTRALITY PROCLAMATION. The treasury secretary argued for a narrow interpretation of U.S. treaty obligations under the FRANCO-AMERICAN ALLIANCE (1778) and assailed French meddling in domestic American politics during the notorious GENET AFFAIR. He also aimed to limit anti-British sentiment in Congress stemming from deliberate British interference with America's neutral shipping in the Atlantic and French West Indies. Washington considered sending Hamilton to London as a special envoy to negotiate outstanding Anglo-American differences, but ardent Democratic-Republican opposition in Congress blocked the treasury secretary's appointment. At Hamilton's urging, fellow Federalist and Chief Justice JOHN JAY was sent in his place. Despite misgivings about the resulting JAY'S TREATY (1794), notably its silence on neutral rights, Hamilton supported the controversial agreement because his national economic program depended heavily upon revenues from stable Anglo-American trade.

Under relentless personal attack from the Jeffersonian opposition, which called him captive to British influence and accused him of improper involvement in financial speculation, he resigned from the cabinet in January 1795. Resuming a law practice in New York, Hamilton remained a trusted adviser of the president and helped draft WASHINGTON'S FAREWELL ADDRESS (1796). Staying active in Federalist Party politics, he exercised influence with cabinet members such as Secretary of State TIMOTHY PICKERING to interject himself in the succeeding Adams administration's affairs. President JOHN ADAMS deeply resented the former treasury secretary's interference. When the undeclared QUASI-WAR (1798–1800) with France flared, threatening to become a full-scale war, Adams was forced by Federalist political pressures to appoint Hamilton in July 1798 inspector-general of the Army, second in command to Washington. Hamilton's embryonic plans for mobilizing U.S. forces to conquer Spanish Florida and Louisiana were deflated when Adams opted for a peaceful settlement of the naval conflict with France. In the presidential campaign of 1800, he contributed to the splitting of the Federalist Party by his support for CHARLES COTESWORTH PINCKNEY over Adams. In the ensuing election, after an electoral college tie forced a final vote in the House of Representatives, Hamilton thwarted the presidential aspirations of his bitter New York political rival, Aaron Burr, by throwing his support behind old antagonist Thomas Jefferson as the lesser of two evils. Hamilton also helped defeat Burr's run for governor of New York in 1804 and impugned his adversary's character. Challenged to a duel by the insulted and embittered two-time loser, Hamilton was mortally shot by Burr at Weehawken, New Jersey, on July 11, 1804, and died the next day.

HAMMER, ARMAND (1898–1990) Wealthy industrialist who maintained lifelong business interests in the Soviet Union and was an acquaintance of Soviet leaders from Lenin to Gorbachev. After graduating from Columbia University Medical School in his native New York City in 1921, he went to the Soviet Union to treat victims of the typhus epidemic ravaging that country in the aftermath of the Russian Revolution. Finding the graver problem to be famine, Hammer considered emergency steps that might be taken to ward off widespread starvation. Turning from doctor to business entrepreneur, he proposed to Soviet officials the idea of bartering American grain for furs and other Soviet goods. Soviet leader Nikolai Lenin, in need of foreign investment, soon awarded Hammer trade, mining, and manufacturing concessions that marked the start of the American's hugely profitable commercial dealings with the Soviet Union.

With the rise of Lenin's successor, Joseph Stalin, Hammer left the Soviet Union in 1930 for New York. In the following decade, he prospered in part through the sale of art acquired in the USSR. In the mid-1950s he invested in the Occidental Petroleum Company, soon becoming its chairman and chief executive officer. He built Occidental into one of the nation's largest and most lucrative energy enterprises. In the early 1970s, amid a thaw in U.S.-Soviet relations, he signed a multi-million dollar 20-year deal in Moscow arranging for Occidental to build a chemical fertilizer plant in the USSR. Over the last two decades of the COLD WAR, he promoted peace between the United States and Soviet Union. In the role of self-appointed, unofficial envoy, he sought to use his influence with political leaders of both nations to bring about expanded Soviet-American economic and cultural ties. Often praised, Hammer also was attacked by critics who termed him a self-serving tycoon and apologist for Soviet domestic political repression and foreign policy adventurism.

HARDING, WARREN GAMALIEL (1865–1923) U.S. senator, 29th president. Born in Ohio, Harding graduated from Ohio Central College in 1882 and two years later was one of three partners who bought the troubled *Marion Daily Star*. Harding soon gained full ownership and built the newspaper into a successful enterprise. In 1899 he entered the state legislature as a Republican. From 1903 to 1905 he was Ohio's lieutenant governor. Defeated in a run for the governorship in 1910, he won election to the U.S. Senate in 1914. He first came to national attention as the keynote speaker at the 1916 Republican National Convention. While in the Senate, Harding favored higher tariffs and immigration restrictions and was among the RESERVATIONISTS opposed to the proposed LEAGUE OF NATIONS under the TREATY OF VERSAILLES (1919). He emerged as the compromise presidential nominee at the deadlocked 1920 Republican convention and went on to claim an easy victory over Democratic candidate James M. Cox, the governor of Ohio, in the general election.

Though Harding was never personally implicated, his administration was tarnished by corruption, including the famed Teapot Dome Scandal, in which federal oil reserves were illegally diverted from the government facility at Teapot Dome, Wyoming. With Senate rejection of the Versailles Treaty, the White House in 1921 concluded the TREATY OF BERLIN formally ending WORLD WAR I with Germany. The

Harding presidency's principal foreign affairs accomplishment, the Washington Naval Conference (1921–1922), which produced several major agreements on naval disarmament and the Far East, was largely the work of Secretary of State Charles Evans Hughes. Harding signed into law the restrictive Immigration Act of 1921 and the protectionist Fordney-McCumber Tariff (1922). He had been president for little more than two years when he was felled by a stroke and died in San Francisco on August 2, 1923. He was succeeded by Vice-President Calvin Coolidge.

HARKIN AMENDMENT (1975)   human rights rider attached by Congress to the 1975 bill authorizing U.S. financial contributions to the Inter-American Development Bank and the African Development Fund. Sponsored by Representative Thomas R. Harkin (D-IA), the amendment required that U.S. representatives to both of the international lending institutions vote against loans to nations that consistently violated human rights unless it could be shown that the loans would directly benefit impoverished people in those countries. Congress approved the final version of the bank bill and its Harkin rider on December 9. The measures were incorporated into the two-year foreign economic aid legislation passed by Congress the same day. The Harkin Amendment anticipated the emphasis placed by President Jimmy Carter on human rights as an integral foreign policy issue. Since 1975 similar human rights provisions have regularly been affixed to congressional bills governing U.S. participation in international financial institutions. In 1978 Harkin successfully added a rider to legislation authorizing a U.S. role in a new International Monetary Fund (IMF) lending program for low-income nations with chronic balance-of-payments deficits caused by rising oil prices. The amendment required the U.S. executive director of the new IMF program to ensure that loans not be used in any way that might contribute to human rights violations.

HARRIMAN, WILLIAM AVERELL (1891– 1986)   Industrialist, government official, statesman, and prominent diplomat. Born in New York City, Harriman was the son of a wealthy financier. He graduated from Yale in 1913 and joined the family railroad

business. He founded the Merchant Shipping Corporation and W. A. Harriman and Company, an investment banking firm, and in 1932 became chairman of Union Pacific Railroad. He first entered public life as an administrator with the National Recovery Administration in the mid-1930s. In 1940, on the eve of U.S. entry into World War II, he returned to the federal executive branch to help direct the nation's growing armaments production. From 1941 to 1943 he coordinated Lend-Lease assistance to Great Britain and the Soviet Union. As ambassador to the Soviet Union from 1943 to 1946, he worked to continue aid to America's wartime ally and attended the major Allied wartime conferences. With the conflict drawing to a close in 1945, he became an early advocate of a firm stance toward the Soviet Union, warning of Moscow's expansionist designs on Eastern Europe. His thinking influenced President Harry S. Truman to adopt a more confrontational policy toward the Communist nation.

Truman named Harriman ambassador to Great Britain in March 1946. Seven months later he was called back to Washington to become secretary of commerce. In 1948 he returned to Europe as chief administrator of the Marshall Plan, the postwar program of massive U.S. economic assistance to war-torn Western Europe. During the final two years of the Truman administration he headed the Mutual Security Agency, responsible for the distribution of foreign aid. From 1955 to 1959 Harriman, a Democrat, was governor of New York. In 1961 he joined the new Kennedy administration as a roving ambassador and the same year became assistant secretary of state for Far Eastern affairs. He was the American representative to the Geneva Conference (1961–1962) that produced a negotiated settlement of the Laotian Crisis. As under secretary of state for political affairs from 1963 to 1965, he negotiated the historic Limited Test Ban Treaty (1963).

In 1965 President Lyndon B. Johnson appointed Harriman an ambassador-at-large. He made several worldwide trips seeking support for U.S. policy in the Vietnam War. In 1968 he was named chief U.S. negotiator in the peace talks beginning in Paris to end the conflict in Southeast Asia. The discussions had made little headway when he left government service in 1969 with the arrival of the Republican Nixon administration. Harriman remained active in foreign affairs, coming to oppose further American military involvement in Southeast Asia, and served as an elder statesman to the Democratic Party.

HARRIS, TOWNSEND (1804–1878) First U.S. minister to Japan. Born in Sandy Hill, New York, he received little formal education and at age 13 began working in a dry goods store in New York City. With his father and brother he later went into the importing business. Harris read widely and acquired a knowledge of several European languages. Active in local civic and political affairs, he was elected in 1846 to the New York Board of Education, serving as president for two years. His leadership was integral to the founding of what is now the College of the City of New York. After his mother's death in 1847, the bachelor Harris quit the family business and purchased a merchant ship, embarking on trading voyages to the Far East. He applied in 1853 with the U.S. Consular Service for a position in East Asia and was appointed America's consul to Ningpo, China, the following year. In August 1855 he was named first U.S. consul general to Japan, a post established through the pathbreaking TREATY OF KANAGAWA (1854) negotiated by Commodore MATTHEW C. PERRY. Harris was elevated to the rank of minister to Japan in 1859 when the United States upgraded its diplomatic mission at Edo (now Tokyo). The American diplomat is best remembered for negotiating the TREATY OF EDO (1858), a major U.S.-Japanese commercial agreement that remained in force until the end of the 19th century and became a model of its kind. Achieving substantial influence with the Japanese government, he often advised it on its conduct of relations with other Western nations. While careful not to turn to U.S. advantage the domestic turmoil in Japan fostered by its sudden opening to the West, he insisted upon strict Japanese observance of American treaty rights. He was instrumental in keeping Japanese doors open to the outside world in the mid-1800s. Harris resigned his post in 1861 and returned to New York, where he lived out his life in retirement.

HARRISON, BENJAMIN (1833–1901) Twenty-third president of the United States; grandson of WILLIAM HENRY HARRISON, ninth U.S. president. Benjamin Harrison was born in Ohio. After graduating from Miami University in Ohio in 1852, he studied law and in 1854 settled in Indianapolis, Indiana, where he went into practice. He entered politics as a Republican. Elected reporter of the Indiana Supreme Court, he held the post from 1860 to 1862 and, following service in the Civil War, again from 1864 to 1868. During the war he commanded an Indiana infantry regiment, attaining the rank of brigadier general. Defeated as the Republican candidate for governor in 1876, he was chairman of the Indiana delegation to the 1880 Republican National Convention, playing a prominent part in the nomination of JAMES A. GARFIELD for president. Declining a position in Garfield's cabinet, he was elected to the U.S. Senate, where he served from 1881 to 1887. He captured the Republican nomination for president in 1888 and went on to defeat incumbent Democratic President GROVER CLEVELAND in the general election.

In foreign affairs Harrison abetted the rise in the late 19th century of a nascent American IMPERIALISM. He expanded the merchant marine, advocated creation of a two-ocean navy, and explored possible opportunities for acquiring naval bases in the Caribbean and Pacific. His Navy secretary, Benjamin F. Tracy, supervised a program to build armor-clad ships of the most modern design. The Harrison administration concluded an agreement with Great Britain to arbitrate the BERING SEA DISPUTE over pelagic sealing, established a three-way protectorate, with Britain and Germany, over SAMOA, and made an abortive attempt at annexing Hawaii. Controversies with Italy and Chile produced tense diplomatic crises. The MAFIA INCIDENT (1891–1892) was defused when Harrison condemned the lynching of Italian nationals by a New Orleans mob and arranged for indemnification of the Italian government. The United States narrowly missed going to war over the BALTIMORE AFFAIR (1891), which stemmed out of lingering Chilean resentment over the ITATA INCIDENT earlier the same year. Hostilities were averted when the Chilean government met Harrison's demands of a formal apology and indemnity for the deadly attack on U.S. sailors on leave in the Chilean port city of Valparaiso.

The administration's Latin American policy was the brainchild of Secretary of State JAMES G. BLAINE, who in 1889 convened the First PAN-AMERICAN CONFERENCE in Washington to promote political and economic cooperation among Western Hemisphere nations. Passage of the McKINLEY TARIFF (1890) maintained very high protectionist duties on goods imported into the United States. The McKinley measure included a reciprocity provision that allowed the president to lower tariffs in response to reductions by other countries. Harrison and Blaine utilized this provision to begin negotiating limited reciprocal trade agreements with Latin American nations. Renominated in 1892, Harrison was defeated by Cleveland and left office in 1893. Resuming his law practice, he served as senior counsel for Venezuela in the arbitration of the VENEZUELA BOUNDARY DISPUTE with Great Britain. In his last years, he spoke and wrote on leading economic and political issues.

HARRISON, WILLIAM HENRY (1773–1841)   Territorial governor of Indiana, Army general, and ninth president of the United States. Harrison was the first president to die in office. Born in Virginia, he attended Hampden-Sydney College from 1787 to 1790, studied medicine briefly in Philadelphia, and in 1791 accepted a commission in the U.S. Army. Serving in the campaign in the early 1790s against the Ohio Indian tribes in the OLD NORTHWEST, Harrison became an aide-de-camp to General "Mad Anthony" Wayne and fought in the decisive U.S. victory at the BATTLE OF FALLEN TIMBERS (1794). After resigning from the Army with the rank of captain in 1798, he accepted appointment as secretary of the NORTHWEST TERRITORY. In 1799 the territorial legislature elected him its first delegate to Congress. With the division in 1800 of the Northwest Territory into the Ohio and Indiana territories, President JOHN ADAMS appointed Harrison governor of the Indiana Territory, a position he held for the next 12 years. Instructed to win the trust of the territory's Indians and protect them from abuses by white settlers, he also was urged to acquire for the government as much land as possible from the tribes. Through a series of INDIAN TREATIES negotiated during his governorship, he secured enormous land cessions in present-day Indiana and Illinois, opening a large new area to westward expansion.

Continued settlement invited increasing Indian hostility after 1805. Shawnee warriors TECUMSEH and his brother, the Prophet, organized an Indian confederation to fight further white encroachment on Indian lands. With authorization from Washington, Harrison led a force of 1000 men to northwestern Indiana, where he defeated the tribal confederation at the BATTLE OF TIPPECANOE (1811) and razed the nearby Indian settlement called Prophetstown. His successful campaign presaged the end of organized Indian resistance to white advances in the region. After the outbreak of the WAR OF 1812 with Great Britain, Harrison was commissioned a brigadier general and given supreme command of the Army of the Northwest. Promoted to major general, he decisively defeated the British and their Indian allies at the Battle of the Thames in Canada in October 1813. Harrison's victory broke the power of the British and Indians in the Northwest, paving the way for greatly expanded American settlement after 1815. His War of 1812 exploits and earlier Indian fighting made him a national hero.

In May 1814 he resigned from the Army and returned to his farm in North Bend, Ohio. Elected to the House of Representatives, he served from 1816 to 1819. Harrison was an Ohio state senator from 1819 to 1821. In 1825 he won election to the U.S. Senate, where he was chairman of the committee on military affairs and the militia and supported the Adams administration's program for protective tariffs. He resigned his Senate seat in 1828 to accept appointment by President JOHN QUINCY ADAMS as U.S. minister to Colombia. Reaching Bogota in February 1829, he was soon thereafter recalled by Adams's successor, ANDREW JACKSON, for largely political reasons. Harrison retired to his Ohio farm, where he weathered a series of personal financial setbacks and developed presidential aspirations. Nominated by the emerging Whig Party as its candidate for president in 1836, he lost the general election to Democrat MARTIN VAN BUREN. In 1840 Harrison again was selected by the Whigs as their presidential nominee. Running with vice-presidential candidate JOHN

TYLER on the slogan "Tippecanoe and Tyler Too," he won a landslide victory over the incumbent Van Buren. At his inauguration on March 4, 1841, he contracted pneumonia and died one month later. He was the grandfather of President Benjamin Harrison.

HART-CELLER ACT See **IMMIGRATION ACT OF 1965**.

HAVANA, ACT OF (1940) Declaration adopted early during WORLD WAR II at the Second Meeting of American Foreign Ministers held in Havana, Cuba. The act was designed to prevent German acquisition of existing European colonies in the Western Hemisphere. In May and June 1940, Germany overran and occupied the Netherlands and France, raising fears in the United States that the Nazis might gain control of French and Dutch possessions in the Americas and use them as military bases. The U.S. Congress evidenced its great concern when on June 18 it overwhelmingly approved a joint resolution sponsored by Senator Key Pittman (D-NV) and Representative Solomon Bloom (D-NY). The Pittman-Bloom Resolution, reaffirming the historic NO-TRANSFER PRINCIPLE (1811), notified Germany and Italy that the United States would refuse to recognize any transfer of territory in the Western Hemisphere from one non-American power to another non-American power. Secretary of State CORDELL HULL at the same time invited the Pan-American states to a special consultative meeting on the issue.

The American foreign ministers convened in Havana on July 21, 1940. Inspired by the Pittman-Bloom measure, the delegates of the 21 American republics unanimously approved the Act of Havana on July 30, the gathering's closing day. It stipulated that if a non-American nation should attempt to gain control of European colonies in the New World, one or more of the American republics could, in the interest of hemispheric security, take over and administer such possession on a provisional basis. The machinery established at Havana was never set in motion since Germany did not attempt to extend its control over the French and Dutch holdings. The ministers also agreed on a declaration stating that any outside attack on an American state would be regarded as an act of aggression against the other republics of the Western Hemisphere. This statement of general security exceeded the DECLARATION OF LIMA (1938) and served as the basis for later wartime cooperation in the Americas.

HAWAII ANNEXATION (1898) U.S. acquisition of the Hawaiian islands. By the mid-19th century, America was the preeminent trade and shipping power in the small kingdom of Hawaii. The emerging commercial and strategic advantages of the islands led Secretary of State DANIEL WEBSTER in 1842 to declare U.S. opposition to their annexation by a foreign power. Webster's statement, directed at growing British influence, extended the MONROE DOCTRINE to Hawaii and was repeated by successive U.S. administrations. America's acquisition of Oregon in 1846 and California in 1848 brought greater contacts between the West Coast and the islands and kindled domestic interest in annexation of Hawaii. An 1854 U.S.-sponsored treaty arranging for immediate admission of the island kingdom as a state was defeated in the Senate.

After 1860, sugar growing became the pillar of Hawaii's economy. American planters who dominated the islands' sugar industry sought favorable trade terms in the United States through reciprocal commercial agreements. Twenty years in the making, the HAWAIIAN RECIPROCITY TREATY was signed in 1875 despite the bitter opposition of U.S. sugar growers. By its terms, Hawaii was allowed to ship its sugar to the United States duty free. In return, Hawaii pledged to make no territorial concessions to other foreign countries. The Hawaiian sugar economy boomed and the islands developed ever closer ties to the American mainland.

In 1890, Congress passed the MCKINLEY TARIFF, provisions of which boosted sugar grown in the United States and hurt Hawaii planters by wiping out their reciprocity advantages. American growers in the islands began to favor U.S. annexation as the solution to regaining privileged treatment of their sugar. In 1891 Queen Liliuokalani came to the Hawaiian throne determined to reverse American influence in her kingdom. She revoked the 1887 liberal constitution imposed by white elites and granted herself autocratic powers by royal decree.

American planters under the leadership of Sanford B. Dole already had organized to overthrow the native monarchy, with the apparent support of pro-annexationist U.S. minister to Hawaii John L. Stevens. During the group's January 26, 1891, uprising, Stevens ordered 150 marines ashore from a U.S. cruiser, ostensibly to safeguard American lives and property. With the Marines' backing, the rebels deposed the queen and seized political control of the islands. Acting without authorization, Stevens recognized the regime the next day and on February 1 raised the American flag, proclaiming Hawaii an American protectorate. Dole became president of the new government.

An annexation treaty prepared by the Hawaiian provisional leadership was submitted to the U.S. Senate on February 15. Expansionists, mostly Republicans, supported it and warned that U.S. failure to act might result in British or Japanese annexation of the island chain. Democrats disclaiming American IMPERIALISM in the Pacific led opposition to the pact. The treaty had not been acted on by the time Republican President BENJAMIN HARRISON left office in March 1893. Incoming Democratic President GROVER CLEVELAND withdrew the treaty from the Senate and dispatched fellow Democrat and former Georgia Congressman James H. Blount as a special commissioner to Hawaii to investigate the uprising.

After a four-month inquiry, Blount concluded that Stevens had acted improperly, that most native Hawaiians opposed annexation, and that the American sugar planters had directed the revolt. The provisional government rejected Cleveland's plea that it relinquish power and restore the queen to the throne. The revolt's leaders established the Republic of Hawaii on July 4, 1894. While the Cleveland administration formally recognized the new government on August 7, the president blocked all attempts at U.S. annexation to the end of his term. His successor, Republican WILLIAM MCKINLEY, favored acquisition and concluded a new Hawaii annexation treaty on June 16, 1897. Opposition by Democrats and anti-imperialist Republicans prevented its ratification.

Hawaii's role as a key naval installation for U.S. operations in the Philippines during the SPANISH-AMERICAN WAR (1898) under-scored the archipelago's strategic value, thus raising annexationist pressures. By the joint Hawaiian Islands Resolution, Congress annexed Hawaii on July 6, 1898. McKinley signed the measure the next day and the United States formally gained the islands on August 12. Japan muted its vigorous objection to the action following U.S. assurances that the rights of Japanese living in Hawaii, the islands' most numerous ethnic group, would be protected. From 1900 a succession of territorial governors, appointed by the U.S. president, exercised local rule. On August 21, 1959, Hawaii joined the Union as the 50th state.

See also MAP 2.

HAWAIIAN RECIPROCITY TREATY (1875) Commercial agreement between the United States and the Kingdom of Hawaii allowing both to trade freely in most goods. Hawaii's sugar industry, foundation of the island's economy, was dominated by American growers, who sought a reciprocal trade accord that would give them free access to U.S. markets. The United States recognized Hawaii's growing commercial and strategic value. Washington was eager to increase American ties with the islands and at the same time secure a guarantee against establishment of European political or economic hegemony in the archipelago. Hawaiian King Kalakua's visit to the U.S. capital in November and December 1874 facilitated negotiations for a trade pact. Henry A. P. Carter, the commissioner appointed by the Hawaiian kingdom as its representative, and Secretary of State HAMILTON FISH concluded the reciprocity treaty on January 30, 1875. By its terms, Hawaii was allowed to export unrefined sugar, rice, fruits, nuts, vegetables, and other goods to the United States duty free and American goods such as wool, iron, steel, and textiles were granted duty-free entry into Hawaii. The kingdom also pledged not to lease or dispose of any of its territory to a foreign country other than the United States. The U.S. Senate ratified the treaty, which was to remain in effect seven years and which either side could terminate after one year's notice, on March 18, 1875, by a 50 to 12 vote.

In December 1884 the Senate refused to approve a renewal of the reciprocity agreement because it did not guarantee the

United States use of PEARL HARBOR as a coaling and naval station. Secretary of State THOMAS F. BAYARD proceeded to win Hawaiian consent to an amendment to the treaty that granted America an exclusive right to establish a fortified naval base at Pearl Harbor. With the addition of the naval base article, which itself became known as the Pearl Harbor Treaty, the Senate ratified the extension of the Hawaiian Reciprocity Treaty on January 20, 1887.

See also HAWAII ANNEXATION.

HAWES-CUTTING ACT See **TYDINGS-MCDUFFIE ACT**.

HAY, JOHN MILTON (1838–1905) Writer, diplomat, and secretary of state under Republican presidents WILLIAM MCKINLEY and THEODORE ROOSEVELT. He was born in Salem, Indiana. After graduating from Brown University in 1858, he studied law in his uncle's office in Springfield, Illinois, where he became acquainted with ABRAHAM LINCOLN, whose office was next door. When Lincoln became President in 1861, he brought Hay to Washington as an assistant private secretary. Hay served Lincoln until the president's death in 1865. For the next five years he held a succession of junior diplomatic posts in Paris, Vienna, and Madrid. Returning from Europe with literary ambitions, he joined the *New York Tribune* in 1870 as an editorial writer. After marrying into wealth, Hay left the paper in 1875 and moved to Cleveland, where he devoted himself mainly to writing and dabbled in Republican politics.

Except for a stint as assistant secretary of state from 1879 to 1881, he pursued his literary career exclusively for the next 20 years and made frequent trips to Europe. A poet and novelist, as well as historian, he wrote, with John G. Nicolay, the monumental 10-volume *Abraham Lincoln: A History* (1890) and edited, with Nicolay, *Abraham Lincoln: Complete Works* (2 vols., 1894). Hay worked on behalf of longtime friend William McKinley in the 1896 presidential campaign, becoming a valued adviser. In 1897 McKinley named Hay ambassador to Great Britain, in which position he secured British neutrality toward the United States in the SPANISH-AMERICAN WAR (1898). McKinley recalled Hay in September 1898 to replace WILLIAM R. DAY as secretary of state. Hay remained in the post until his death in 1905.

Notable among his accomplishments were the two sets of notes elaborating the OPEN DOOR policy, which guaranteed freedom of commerce in China and Chinese territorial integrity. Advocate of an Anglo-American entente, Hay settled several outstanding problems in U.S.-British relations. Under the terms of the HAY-HERBERT TREATY (1903), the two nations agreed to resolve the ALASKA BOUNDARY DISPUTE through arbitration. The HAY-PAUNCEFOTE TREATY (1901), which abrogated the CLAYTON-BULWER TREATY (1850), removed remaining British resistance to American construction and fortification of an interoceanic canal in Central America. The PANAMA CANAL became a reality after the signing of the HAY-BUNAU-VARILLA TREATY (1903). By its provisions, newly independent Panama granted the United States the right to a 10-mile-wide CANAL ZONE in which to build the waterway.

HAY-BUNAU-VARILLA TREATY (1903) Agreement between the United States and Panama that cleared the way for America's construction of a canal across the Panamanian isthmus. Toward the end of the 1890s a canal in Central America had become a leading American policy aim. To proponents, new island possessions in the Caribbean and Pacific made an interoceanic waterway appear more vital than ever to U.S. national security and economic expansion. American battleships forced to voyage around Cape Horn during the SPANISH-AMERICAN WAR (1898) had underscored the need for a canal that would dramatically cut sailing time between the Atlantic and Pacific oceans. President WILLIAM MCKINLEY in December 1898 called on the U.S. government to build, fortify, and operate such a canal. The long-standing obstacle to this goal, the CLAYTON-BULWER TREATY (1850), which mandated joint Anglo-American action on a waterway, was removed in 1901 by the HAY-PAUNCEFOTE TREATY. By its terms the British relinquished their claim in Central America in exchange for an American pledge that any future canal would be open to the ships of all nations on equal terms.

McKinley named a special isthmian canal commission to evaluate possible canal routes in Panama, then a province of

Colombia, and Nicaragua. The panel was known as the Walker Commission after its chairman, Admiral John G. Walker. In November 1901 the commission recommended the Nicaraguan option, citing cost as the decisive factor. The New Panama Canal Company, a French-chartered firm that held Colombia's canal concessions in Panama, wanted $109 million from the United States. The Walker panel judged the asking price on Panama as too steep. Acting on the commission's findings, the U.S. House of Representatives passed the Hepburn Bill on January 8, 1902, authorizing a Nicaraguan canal. When the New Panama Canal Company, fearing similar Senate action and the loss of its investments, dropped its price to $40 million, the Walker panel reversed itself and endorsed the Panamanian option. Congress followed suit by adopting an amended version of the Hepburn Bill known as the Spooner Act. This measure, enacted June 28, 1902, authorized a Panama route provided the United States could come to satisfactory terms with Colombia. If not, the president was free to proceed with a Nicaraguan canal.

The State Department began discussions with Colombian officials on an agreement to allow U.S. construction of a Panamanian waterway. In January 1903, negotiators signed the HAY-HERRAN TREATY, which gave the United States a 10-mile-wide strip of land in Panama in exchange for $10 million and annual payments of $250,000 after nine years. The U.S. Senate approved the Hay-Herran agreement in March 1903. After failing in its attempts to exact higher payments from the United States, the Colombian senate rejected the treaty that August, confounding President THEODORE ROOSEVELT and Secretary of State JOHN M. HAY.

In early October 1903, Philippe Bunau-Varilla, an affiliate of the governing junta in Panama, met with Roosevelt in Washington, D.C. He expressed his support for an American canal and predicted an imminent uprising in Colombia's Central American protectorate. Roosevelt then sent American naval forces to the Caribbean with orders to prevent any Colombian military interference in a possible Panamanian revolt. Panama declared its independence on November 4, 1903, following a swift, blood-less uprising. Two days later Hay officially recognized the Republic of Panama. On November 18 Hay and Bunau-Varilla, the new Panamanian government's ambassador to Washington, concluded an agreement resolving the canal question. The treaty granted the United States perpetual lease over a CANAL ZONE in which to build the waterway. In return, the United States agreed to guarantee Panama's independence and to pay $10 million immediately and $250,000 annually from canal revenues. The U.S. Senate ratified the treaty on February 23, 1904. American relations with an embittered Colombia deteriorated after the canal episode. Under the THOMSON-URRUTIA TREATY of April 1921, the U.S. government agreed to pay a $25 million indemnity to Colombia in an effort to mend fences.

See also PANAMA CANAL TREATIES.

HAYES, RUTHERFORD BIRCHARD
(1822–1893) Nineteenth U.S. president. Hayes was born in Ohio. After graduating from Kenyon College in 1842 and Harvard Law School in 1845, he was admitted to the Ohio bar and went into practice in present-day Fremont, moving to Cincinnati in 1849. Entering politics as a Whig, Hayes joined the new Republican Party in the mid-1850s. When the Civil War began he was commissioned a major of Ohio volunteers and during the conflict rose to the rank of brigadier general. His Union war service helped launch his political career. Without leaving his military command to campaign, he won election to the House of Representatives from Ohio in 1864 and took his seat the next year. He was reelected in 1866 but resigned the following year to run for governor of Ohio. He captured the election and served two successive terms from 1868 to 1872. Elected governor a third time in 1875 in a campaign that made him a national political figure, Hayes gained the Republican presidential nomination in 1876. His election day contest with Democratic nominee Samuel J. Tilden ended in bitter dispute, with each claiming victory in the extremely close vote. The impasse led Congress to form a special bipartisan electoral commission to determine the winner. On March 2, 1877, Hayes was awarded the presidency by a single electoral vote.

Foreign relations were relatively uneventful under Hayes. His administration was dominated by domestic concerns, namely the post–Civil War sectional tensions engendered by military occupation of the defeated South, labor and monetary issues, and the need for civil service reform. In 1877 he ended Reconstruction by withdrawing the last federal troops from the South. The major problem in foreign affairs involved Mexico, where Porfirio Diaz had overthrown the established government in 1876. Early in his term Hayes withheld diplomatic recognition from the Diaz regime because it was unable to curb raids by Mexicans and Indians into U.S. territory. In June 1877 Hayes authorized army units in Texas to pursue the raiders back across the border into Mexico. His administration finally extended recognition in April 1878, although the "hot pursuit" policy remained in effect until Diaz satisfactorily suppressed the raids in 1880. The question of Chinese immigration also loomed important. The accelerated influx of Chinese workers to the western states in the 1870s had aroused violent anti-Chinese feelings in the region, placing pressure on Congress to restrict further immigration. A commission sent to China by Hayes concluded the ANGELL TREATY (1880), which revised terms of the BURLINGAME TREATY (1868) to allow for the regulation of Chinese immigration to America. Upon taking office Hayes had said he would not consider a second term. He retired to his Ohio home in 1881 and devoted the remaining years of his life to various philanthropic causes and public speaking engagements.

HAY-HERBERT TREATY See **ALASKA BOUNDARY DISPUTE**.

HAY-HERRAN TREATY (1903) Proposed treaty between the United States and Colombia concerning canal rights in Panama. Signed January 22, 1903, by Secretary of State JOHN M. HAY and the Colombian charge d'affaires in Washington, Tomas Herran, the agreement arranged for U.S. construction of an isthmian canal across Colombia's province of Panama. The Colombian government agreed to lease a 10-mile-wide strip of Panamanian territory to the United States for 100 years in return for $10 million immediately and annual payments of $250,000 beginning in nine

years. The U.S. Senate approved the treaty on March 17. Colombian legislators, dissatisfied with financial terms of the settlement, sought unsuccessfully to exact higher U.S payments. A defiant Colombian senate unanimously rejected the Hay-Herran Treaty on August 12.

This failure of ratification frustrated Hay and President THEODORE ROOSEVELT, who began weighing other options for achieving American aims in Central America. In November 1903 Panama declared its independence from Colombia following a successful revolt that enjoyed tacit U.S. support. The Roosevelt administration and new Panamanian government swiftly negotiated the HAY-BUNAU-VARILLA TREATY giving the United States an exclusive right to build a transisthmian canal. U.S. complicity in the Panamanian uprising led to worsening relations with a resentful Colombia through the early 1900s. By terms of the THOMSON-URRUTIA TREATY (1921), Washington paid Bogota $25 million as belated compensation for American involvement in Panama's 1903 revolt.

HAY-PAUNCEFOTE TREATY (1901) Agreement between the United States and Great Britain abrogating the CLAYTON-BULWER TREATY (1850). Concluded on November 18, 1901, by Secretary of State JOHN M. HAY and British Ambassador at Washington Lord Julian Pauncefote, it granted the United States exclusive rights to build and operate an interoceanic canal on the Central American isthmus, provided the waterway would be open to the commerce of all nations on equal terms. The British had rejected as unacceptable an earlier Hay-Pauncefote Treaty (1900) after the U.S. Senate amended it to allow American fortification of a prospective canal. Great Britain, increasingly committed to its policy of improved Anglo-American relations, finally surrendered to this U.S. demand. The treaty signaled London's acceptance of American preeminence in the Caribbean. It moved the United States closer to its objective of an interoceanic waterway in Central America. This goal was essentially realized two years later when the HAY-BUNAU-VARILLA TREATY, concluded with Panama, gave the United States the land and permission it required to build an isthmian canal.

HEARST, WILLIAM RANDOLPH (1863–1951) American newspaper and magazine publisher. The San Francisco native was the only child of George Hearst, a wealthy mine owner, U.S. senator, and publisher of the *San Francisco Daily Examiner*. Following his expulsion from Harvard College in 1885 for a prank, William Randolph Hearst took charge of his father's faltering publication. Through a mix of sensationalism and social reform-minded coverage borrowed from Joseph Pulitzer's *New York World*, he made the paper hugely profitable. With his purchase of the *New York Journal* in 1895, Hearst challenged Pulitzer on his own turf. The ensuing circulation war between the publishing giants ushered in an era of "yellow journalism" characterized by coverage that was alternately sensational, lurid, exaggerated, and untruthful.

In the fierce competition for readers, Hearst and Pulitzer seized on the Cuban revolt against Spain in 1895. The *Journal* and *World* offered inflated accounts of purported Spanish "atrocities," exciting public indignation and a mood of jingoism in the United States. Hearst advocated an imperialist policy of U.S. military intervention to drive Spain from Cuba. When noted artist Frederic Remington, sent by the *Journal* to draw scenes of the Cuban insurrection, requested to return because there was no war, Hearst cabled back: "Please remain. You furnish the pictures and I'll furnish the war." The *Journal* published the intercepted DE LOME LETTER, in which the Spanish minister to the United States made insulting remarks about President WILLIAM MCKINLEY. Disclosure of the letter's contents evoked anger among Americans and further damaged U.S.-Spanish relations. Inflammatory coverage and deliberate misrepresentations by the *Journal* and *World* alike hastened the outbreak of the SPANISH-AMERICAN WAR (1898). Calling it the "*Journal*'s war," Hearst sailed with a group of his correspondents on a chartered steamship to Cuba in June 1898 to take part in the paper's reporting of the conflict.

After the turn of the century he began to expand his holdings, launching the Hearst newspaper chain, creating news and feature wire services, and acquiring a host of profitable magazines. Meanwhile he remained keenly interested in politics and public office, his prize personal ambition being the presidency. A Democrat, he represented his Manhattan district in Congress from 1903 to 1907. In 1904 he mounted a strong campaign but finally lost the Democratic presidential nomination to Alton B. Parker. He was defeated in runs for mayor of New York in 1905 and 1909. In 1906 he lost a close race for New York governor to CHARLES EVANS HUGHES.

From atop his print empire, Hearst voiced his strong views on key issues in American foreign affairs. His ardent opposition to U.S. entry into WORLD WAR I exposed him to charges of being pro-German. At war's end the isolationist Hearst fought U.S. membership in the LEAGUE OF NATIONS and later helped block U.S. participation in the WORLD COURT. After visiting Germany in 1934 and meeting at length with Adolf Hitler, he came under attack for allegedly cozying to Nazism. In the mid-1930s he campaigned against communism abroad and purported "radicalism" among college faculties in the United States. Economic losses brought on by the Great Depression forced Hearst in 1937 to surrender control of his business interests to a legal trustee, who then consolidated, sold, or closed some of his properties. The return of domestic prosperity during WORLD WAR II stabilized his enterprises and salvaged Hearst. After suffering a heart seizure in 1947 he became an invalid. He died in 1951.

HELMS, RICHARD McGARRAH (1913–) Intelligence officer who headed the CENTRAL INTELLIGENCE AGENCY (CIA) from 1966 to 1973. Helms graduated from Williams College in 1935 and began a career in journalism. The Pennsylvania native joined the Navy in 1942 and the following year transferred to the OFFICE OF STRATEGIC SERVICES, the U.S. WORLD WAR II intelligence service. He remained in intelligence after the war, serving in the CENTRAL INTELLIGENCE GROUP and then helping to organize the CIA in 1947. A careerist in covert operations, he was named chief of the clandestine branch in 1962. In 1965 he became the deputy director of central intelligence, the number two position in the agency.

Appointed director of the CIA by President LYNDON B. JOHNSON in 1966, Helms held the post during the period of greatest

U.S. involvement in the VIETNAM WAR. In Vietnam the agency conducted special counterinsurgency operations such as the PHOENIX PROGRAM while also directing the LAOS SECRET WAR against Communist forces in the neighboring Southeast Asian country. Helms received high marks for the CIA's intelligence estimates on the 1967 Arab-Israeli Six-Day War. In 1970 the agency unsuccessfully attempted to prevent Marxist Salvador Allende from coming to power in Chile.

Helms ended his CIA career in January 1973 and was named U.S. ambassador to Iran. During Senate confirmation hearings he denied any agency involvement in efforts to overthrow Chilean President Allende. While ambassador, Helms was called back to answer questions from the ROCKE-FELLER COMMISSION, CHURCH COMMITTEE, and other inquiries into past CIA abuses such as illegal domestic surveillance. He retired as ambassador in January 1977 and became a private consultant. That fall he pleaded guilty to two misdemeanor counts of misleading the Senate rather than face perjury charges on his previous testimony regarding the CIA's role in Chile. He received a $2000 fine and a two-year suspended sentence. In 1983 he served as a member of the SCOWCROFT COMMISSION on U.S. strategic nuclear forces.

HELSINKI ACCORDS (1975) Multilateral agreement adopted at the conclusion of the CONFERENCE ON SECURITY AND COOPERATION IN EUROPE (CSCE). In 1973 representatives of the United States, Canada, the Soviet Union, and 32 European states convened in Helsinki for a Soviet-proposed conference on European security issues. The Soviet Union hoped to win international recognition of Eastern Europe's post–WORLD WAR II boundaries. At the wartime YALTA CONFERENCE (1945), the United States and Great Britain had acquiesced in Soviet acquisition of a slice of Eastern Poland. At the POTSDAM CONFERENCE (1945), Poland had provisionally received as compensation for its loss the German territory east of the ODER-NEISSE LINE. When the USSR moved after 1945 to impose Communist regimes on the nations of Eastern Europe, the wartime alliance among the United States, Great Britain, and Soviet Union degenerated into East-West COLD WAR; thus the redrawn Ger-

man, Polish, and Soviet frontiers never gained final Western approval. The United States and its Western allies agreed to the CSCE as a means of building on the burgeoning East-West DETENTE of the early 1970s.

After two years of meetings in Helsinki and Geneva, the CSCE, comprising the 16 members of the NATO Western security alliance, the 7 Communist Warsaw Pact nations, and 12 other European states, concluded an agreement outlining measures to promote and strengthen improved East-West relations. Titled the Final Act of the CSCE, it was signed August 1, 1975, at a final CSCE summit meeting in Finland. Most nations were represented at the Helsinki Conference, held July 30 to August 1, 1975, by their heads of state or government. Among those in attendance were U.S. President GERALD R. FORD and Soviet General Secretary Leonid I. Brezhnev. During the conference the two leaders met for private talks on strategic arms control issues.

Known as the Helsinki Accords, the Final Act had four sections, referred to as "baskets." Basket I contained a set of 10 principles to guide East-West relations and a series of so-called confidence-building measures meant to reduce military tensions in central Europe. The principles, beyond ratifying the postwar European boundaries, committed the signatories to settle disputes by peaceful means and refrain from the use of force; respect each other's sovereignty and territorial integrity; adhere to the rights of each nation to self-determination and nonintervention in its internal affairs; abide by the rule of international law; and respect HUMAN RIGHTS and the fundamental freedoms of thought, conscience, religion, and belief. Basket II addressed economic, scientific, technical, and environmental cooperation. Basket III called for cooperation in humanitarian efforts and educational and cultural exchanges. Basket IV provided for follow-up conferences to review and expand on the accords.

Conservatives in the United States scored the Helsinki Accords as a capitulation to Soviet hegemony over Eastern Europe. The Ford administration defended the agreement as an important milestone that both cemented the progress already made under detente and opened the way for further improvements in East-West ties.

The period of detente represented by the agreement ended with the Soviet invasion of Afghanistan in 1979. The accords' human rights provisions came to serve as a standard by which the internal policies of the Soviet and other Communist governments were judged, both by groups emerging within their societies and by the international community. As provided for under Basket IV, review conferences were conducted in Belgrade (1977–1978), Madrid (1980–1983), and Vienna (1986–1989). The 1990 FINAL SETTLEMENT WITH RESPECT TO GERMANY TREATY retained the boundaries agreed to under the Helsinki Accords.

HELSINKI SUMMIT (1990)   Parley held September 9, 1990, in Helsinki, Finland, between President GEORGE BUSH and Soviet President Mikhail S. Gorbachev to consult on the Persian Gulf crisis. Bush requested the meeting to show united U.S.-Soviet opposition to Iraq's August 1990 invasion and occupation of Kuwait and to facilitate cooperation between the superpowers in responding to the gulf situation. In the invasion's immediate aftermath Bush had assumed leadership of the condemnatory international reaction against Iraq's aggression. He had deployed U.S. military forces to Saudi Arabia to protect its oil fields against the threat of Iraqi seizure and had persuaded America's Arab allies to commit troops to the anti-Iraq effort. At the same time the United States had spearheaded passage by the UNITED NATIONS Security Council of a set of resolutions that mandated unconditional Iraqi withdrawal from Kuwait and imposed economic sanctions on Iraq. On the eve of the summit, Iraqi President Saddam Hussein issued a defiant open message to the two leaders reiterating his country's intention of holding onto Kuwait, and insisting that the crisis was for the Arabs, not the United States and Soviet Union, to resolve.

At the end of the day-long talks, Bush and Gorbachev issued a joint statement pledging to force Iraq's withdrawal from Kuwait. They asserted that the Iraqi aggression, if allowed to stand, would destabilize the Middle East and foil the establishment of a post–COLD WAR peaceful international order. While declaring their preference for resolving the crisis without resorting to hostilities, the U.S. and Soviet leaders stressed that, in the event political and economic sanctions failed to bring an Iraqi retreat, they were prepared to consider military action under the U.N. aegis to drive Iraq from Kuwait. Bush assured the Soviet leader that U.S. armed forces in the gulf would be withdrawn as soon as Iraq pulled out of Kuwait and the security requirements of the region were met. Preoccupied with his country's internal political and economic problems, Gorbachev for the time being ruled out adding Soviet military forces to the anti-Iraq U.N. coalition. Western analysts attributed his reluctance to make a military commitment to lingering weariness among the Soviet people from the AFGHANISTAN WAR and concern that a deployment to the gulf might spark unrest among the USSR's Moslem population.

The summit also yielded a significant development regarding the Middle East peace process. In a departure from the long-standing American policy of striving to curb Soviet political influence in the Arab world, Bush invited Moscow to exercise a greater diplomatic role in the region and suggested U.S.-Soviet cooperation in seeking a settlement of the Arab-Israeli conflict and other problems. The president voiced American willingness to consider an international conference on the Mideast, a proposal long advocated by the USSR, provided such a gathering did not link the resolution of the Palestinian issue with the gulf crisis.

The two leaders next met in November 1990 at the CONFERENCE ON SECURITY AND COOPERATION IN EUROPE summit in Paris, where the heads of the NATO and Warsaw Pact nations signed the historic CONVENTIONAL FORCES EUROPE TREATY. In a private discussion concerning the gulf, Bush was unable to gain Gorbachev's public endorsement for a U.N. Security Council resolution, sought by Washington, authorizing the use of force to expel Iraq from Kuwait. Through further diplomatic maneuvering, the Bush administration obtained Soviet approval of the November 29 U.N. Security Council resolution that sanctioned military action if the Iraqis did not withdraw from Kuwait by January 15, 1991. On December 12, at the same time he approved $1 billion in federal loans to the USSR to enable it to buy U.S. food, Bush disclosed that he and Gorbachev would confer in mid-February

1991 in Moscow, where they hoped to sign a final START arms control agreement. The MOSCOW SUMMIT, postponed due to the PERSIAN GULF WAR (1991), subsequently was held in July 1991.

HENDERSON v. MAYOR OF NEW YORK
(1876) Major U.S. Supreme Court ruling in three companion cases that declared state laws governing immigration unconstitutional because they impinged on the exclusive power of Congress to regulate foreign commerce. In a decision handed down March 20, 1876, the justices overturned measures in California, Louisiana, and New York that imposed various fees on shipowners for their alien passengers. Historically the states had exercised broad control over immigration. This authority had been endorsed by the Court in CITY OF NEW YORK v. MILN (1836). State regulation of immigration was first limited by the Court in the PASSENGER CASES (1849). In proceeding to strike down state measures, the *Henderson* opinion called for the enactment of federal immigration legislation. State officials, no longer able to handle the growing influx of new arrivals, petitioned the Congress for action. The result was the IMMIGRATION ACT OF 1882, the nation's first general federal immigration law.

HEPBURN BILL   See **HAY-BUNAU-VARILLA TREATY**.

HERITAGE FOUNDATION   Influential Washington-based conservative think tank. Founded in 1973, the research institute examines current issues in domestic and foreign policy. Its stated aim is to provide the national news media, members of Congress, and White House policymakers with information, analysis, and ideas on leading political, economic, and social developments from the vantage point of the "New Right." Foundation scholarship on foreign and national security affairs includes ongoing studies on East-West relations, UNITED NATIONS agencies and programs, strategic defense, and international economic development. The Asian Studies Center, a special research division of the institute, focuses on U.S. policy toward China, Korea, Japan, and the Philippines, and Western security concerns in the Pacific. The foundation also sponsors a slate of annual conferences, roundtables, and seminars with

government and private-sector decision makers. Publications that regularly address foreign affairs include the quarterly journal *Policy Review* and the monthly *National Security Record*. During the 1980s Heritage emerged as a bastion of conservative thought, maintaining a special relationship with the Reagan administration, whose ardent anticommunism and program for a strong national defense it strongly endorsed.

HERSEY, JOHN (1914–   ) Journalist and author. Hersey was born in Tientsin, China, the son of American missionaries. At age 10 he moved with his parents to the United States. After graduating from Yale University in 1936, he went to Cambridge University in England for postgraduate study. He worked briefly in 1937 as secretary to the American novelist Sinclair Lewis before joining *Time* magazine as a writer later that year. Dispatched to the Far East in 1939 as a *Time* foreign correspondent, he developed strong first hand knowledge of political developments in China and Japan. Hersey covered WORLD WAR II for *Time* and *Life*, reporting from both the Pacific and Europe. His wartime experiences and observations became the basis for three books: *Men on Bataan* (1942), about the Pacific battle in the Philippines; *Into the Valley* (1943), about the fighting on Guadalcanal; and his first novel, the Pulitzer Prize-winning *A Bell for Adano* (1944), about life in a war-torn Italian town. The *New Yorker* devoted an entire issue to Hersey's *Hiroshima* (1946), a moving journalistic account of the atomic bombing of the Japanese city on August 6, 1945. Since the end of the war he has been a successful writer of fiction and nonfiction. Among his more notable works are the novels *The Wall* (1950), the story of the Jewish resistance in the Warsaw ghetto during World War II, and *The Call* (1985), about the missionary experience in China.

HERTER, CHRISTIAN ARCHIBALD
(1895–1966) Congressman, governor, secretary of state, U.S. trade representative. Herter was born in France to expatriate American artists. He grew up in Paris and New York. In 1915 he graduated from Harvard and the following year entered the FOREIGN SERVICE. The multilingual Herter served briefly at U.S. embassies in Germany

and Belgium and was assigned to the State Department in Washington during WORLD WAR I. He accompanied the American delegation to the 1919 PARIS PEACE CONFERENCE as a secretary and strongly supported the TREATY OF VERSAILLES (1919) and the LEAGUE OF NATIONS. He left the diplomatic service in 1919 to become an assistant to HERBERT C. HOOVER, then director of the AMERICAN RELIEF ADMINISTRATION providing aid to war-torn Europe. When Hoover became secretary of commerce in 1921, Herter joined him as his special assistant.

Herter departed government service in 1924 to pursue a career in publishing and was an owner and editor of the *Independent* and *Sportsman* magazines. He also lectured on international relations at Harvard. In 1931 he began a 12-year tenure in the Massachusetts state legislature. Elected as a Republican to the U.S. House of Representatives in 1942, he served there during WORLD WAR II, gaining a reputation as an internationalist and staunch backer of a postwar UNITED NATIONS. In 1947 he headed a special House Select Committee on Foreign Aid. Known as the HERTER COMMITTEE, the panel undertook an 18-nation visit to Europe. Its report on the need for massive American assistance to the war-devastated continent helped ensure passage of the MARSHALL PLAN for European economic recovery.

In 1952 Herter took part in DWIGHT D. EISENHOWER's successful presidential campaign. The same year he was elected governor of Massachusetts. After two terms in the state house, he joined the Eisenhower administration in 1957 as under secretary of state, the second-ranking post in the State Department. In April 1959 he succeeded the terminally ill JOHN FOSTER DULLES as secretary of state. During his brief tenure Herter continued the basic U.S. COLD WAR policy of CONTAINMENT of Soviet and other Communist expansionism. His 1960 plan for U.S.-Soviet disarmament talks was derailed by the U-2 INCIDENT, during which Herter publicly admitted that American spy planes had been flying over the Soviet Union. He faced recurring difficulties in the BERLIN CRISIS (1958–1962), CONGO CRISIS (1906–1962), and LAOTIAN CRISIS (1960–1962), and worsening relations with Cuba and Fidel Castro.

Herter left office with the end of the Eisenhower presidency in January 1961. In 1962 he headed a special private panel of experts that prepared for the State Department the so-called Herter Report on the organization and manning of the Foreign Service. The same year President JOHN F. KENNEDY appointed him U.S. trade representative. He participated in various trade negotiations, most notably the KENNEDY ROUND on tariff reductions. Herter remained in the trade representative post until his death in December 1966.

HERTER COMMITTEE   See **MARSHALL PLAN**.

HERTER REPORT   See **HERTER, CHRISTIAN ARCHIBALD**.

HICKENLOOPER AMENDMENT (1962) Rider to the federal FOREIGN ASSISTANCE ACT of 1962 mandating a suspension of U.S. aid to nations that expropriate American-owned property without just compensation. Sponsored by Senator Bourke B. Hickenlooper (R-IA), the amendment required the president to halt economic aid to any country that nationalized, expropriated, or otherwise seized control of U.S. property unless the offending country made provision for adquately compensating the owner within six months of the takeover. The measure also applied to discriminatory taxes or restrictive operating conditions on U.S. firms, which had the net effect of expropriation. Hickenlooper's provision applied to confiscations that took place after January 1, 1962, and was prompted by the Brazilian province of Rio Grande do Sol's February 1962 expropriation of International Telephone and Telegraph property. A similar but less stringent amendment that had been approved as part of the 1954 MUTUAL SECURITY ACT had expired in 1961. The earlier provision had suspended aid to expropriating countries but gave the president discretionary authority to waive the suspension if U.S. interests so warranted. The Hickenlooper Amendment was signed into law with the foreign assistance legislation on August 1, 1962.

HIGGINS, MARGUERITE (1920–1966) War correspondent. Born in Hong Kong, she graduated from the University of California at Berkeley in 1941 and earned her master's degree the following year from

Columbia University's Graduate School of Journalism. She became a newspaper reporter with the *New York Herald Tribune*. In 1944 the *Tribune* sent her to its London bureau and then to Paris where she used her fluency in French to advantage in reporting on WORLD WAR II. Higgins accompanied Allied forces on their victorious march across Europe to Berlin. Named the *Tribune*'s Berlin bureau chief in 1945, she covered the liberation of the Dachau and Buchenwald concentration camps, the NUREMBURG WAR CRIMES TRIALS, and the BERLIN AIRLIFT (1948–1949).

Her coverage of the KOREAN WAR brought her national prominence. Rushed to Korea by the *Tribune* at the war's outset in 1950, she was ordered to leave by U.S. field commander Lieutenant General Walton H. Walker, who objected to a woman's presence on the front line. On appeal, General DOUGLAS MACARTHUR reversed Walker's order, allowing Higgins to stay. Her dispatches from Korea earned her a Pulitzer Prize for international reporting in 1951. Higgins left the *Tribune* in 1963 to write a syndicated column for the Long Island daily *Newsday*. Venturing several times to Southeast Asia to report on the VIETNAM WAR, she became a fierce critic of U.S. policy in Southeast Asia. Higgins died at age 45 from a rare tropical ailment contracted on her last tour of the Far East.

HILLENKOETTER, ROSCOE HENRY (1897–1982) Career naval officer and first director of the CENTRAL INTELLIGENCE AGENCY (CIA). A native of Missouri and 1920 graduate of the Naval Academy, Hillenkoetter served in a variety of sea and shore assignments. He began the first of several tours as a naval attache in France in 1933. During WORLD WAR II he served as the intelligence officer on the staff of Pacific commander Admiral Chester W. Nimitz. Promoted to admiral in 1946, Hillenkoetter was named director of central intelligence by President HARRY S. TRUMAN in May 1947 and assumed responsibility for heading the CENTRAL INTELLIGENCE GROUP (CIG). When the CIG was reconstituted as the CIA under the NATIONAL SECURITY ACT of July 1947, he continued as the first director of the new agency.

The CIA faced criticism in April 1948 for its alleged failure to predict the bloody riots in Bogota, Colombia, that disrupted the Ninth PAN-AMERICAN CONFERENCE, which Secretary of State GEORGE C. MARSHALL attended as the head of a U.S. delegation. Hillenkoetter testified before a House subcommittee that a CIA warning of possible Communist-sponsored agitation in Colombia had not been forwarded to Marshall by State Department officials. Two years later he defended the agency against charges it had not provided advance warning of the North Korean invasion in June 1950 that launched the KOREAN WAR, noting that the CIA had reported a North Korean military buildup for more than a year. Hillenkoetter was succeeded by WALTER BEDELL SMITH in October 1950. He returned to naval duty, commanding the 7th Task Force in the waters off Taiwan and then the 3rd Naval District before his retirement in 1957.

HILSMAN, ROGER (1919–   ) State Department official, educator. Hilsman graduated from West Point in 1943. During WORLD WAR II, the Texas native served in the China-Burma-India theater with the famed Merrill's Marauders and the OFFICE OF STRATEGIC SERVICES, the wartime intelligence agency. In 1945 he led a parachute rescue mission that liberated U.S. prisoners at a Japanese camp in Manchuria. Among those freed was his father, an Army officer captured three years earlier in the Philippines. Earning a Ph.D. in international relations from Yale University in 1951, he worked on the initial military planning for NATO, taught international politics at Princeton University from 1953 to 1956, and was deputy director of the legislative reference service at the Library of Congress.

In 1961 Hilsman joined the new Kennedy administration as director of the State Department's Bureau of Intelligence and Research. Emerging as one of the architects of the administration's nascent VIETNAM WAR policy, he prepared a plan in January 1962 that defined the struggle against Communist insurgency in the Southeast Asian nation as primarily political rather than military. He endorsed relocation of the rural population into fortified, secure villages or "strategic hamlets" as a key PACIFICATION measure. South Vietnamese President Ngo Dinh Diem in March 1962 implemented a largely ineffective strategic hamlet program. Promoted to assistant secretary of state for Far Eastern affairs in May

1963, Hilsman assumed his new post amid mounting Kennedy administration unease over the Diem regime's domestic political repression. Hilsman helped draft an August 1963 cable to the American embassy in Saigon stating that Washington would not oppose Diem's overthrow. In the aftermath of the DIEM COUP (1963), the U.S. government was seen widely to have given tacit support to the South Vietnamese leader's ouster. Opposed to the Johnson administration's escalation of the U.S. role in Vietnam, Hilsman left government service in February 1964 and joined the Columbia University faculty. In 1967 he published *To Move A Nation* on the foreign policy of the Kennedy years.

HISS, ALGER (1904–   ) State Department official who was the central figure in a major and still controversial espionage case. A 1929 graduate of Harvard Law School, Hiss was legal secretary for Supreme Court Justice Oliver Wendell Holmes, Jr., before taking a position in 1933 in the New Deal Agricultural Adjustment Administration. He subsequently served as a legal assistant to the NYE COMMITTEE's investigation of the WORLD WAR I armaments industry and then joined the Justice Department in 1935. The following year he began a decade-long career at the State Department. Hiss worked on foreign trade problems and Far Eastern political relations until 1944, when he moved to the new Office of Special Political Affairs. He participated in planning for the UNITED NATIONS, attending the DUMBARTON OAKS CONFERENCE (1944) and the YALTA CONFERENCE (1945). He was elected temporary secretary general at the SAN FRANCISCO CONFERENCE (1945) and served as an adviser to the U.S. delegation at the first session of the U.N. General Assembly in London in 1946.

Hiss left the State Department at the end of the year and became president of the CARNEGIE ENDOWMENT FOR INTERNATIONAL PEACE. In August 1948 former Communist WHITTAKER CHAMBERS testified before the HOUSE UN-AMERICAN ACTIVITIES COMMITTEE (HUAC) that he and Hiss had belonged to an underground Communist cell in the 1930s. The HISS CASE drew worldwide attention and brought HUAC member RICHARD M. NIXON (R-CA) to national prominence. Hiss maintained his innocence in

appearances before the committee. In December 1948 Chambers produced documents and microfilm to support his claim that Hiss had engaged in espionage for the Soviet Union.

The controversial evidence contributed to Hiss's eventual conviction for perjury in January 1950. He served 44 months in federal prison. After his release he continued to assert his innocence and was reinstated to the Massachusetts bar in 1975. His supporters considered Hiss the victim of a COLD WAR witch-hunt. Many on the political right saw him as part of alleged Communist-sponsored subversion behind the U.S. "sell-out" of Eastern Europe at Yalta. In February 1950 demagogic Senator JOSEPH R. MCCARTHY (R-WI) launched his accusations about Communist agents in the State Department.

HISS CASE Major post–WORLD WAR II espionage case that came to symbolize the debate over the extent of Communist subversion in the United States and its impact on the nation's foreign policy. In August 1948 WHITTAKER CHAMBERS, then a senior editor with *Time* magazine, testified before the HOUSE UN-AMERICAN ACTIVITIES COMMITTEE (HUAC) that in the 1930s he had been part of a secret Communist underground organization that included former Assistant Secretary of the Treasury HARRY DEXTER WHITE and former State Department official ALGER HISS. White, who died of a heart attack three days after his testimony, and Hiss both appeared before the committee to deny Chambers's accusations. Hiss challenged Chambers to repeat his allegations outside the legal protection of a committee hearing. When he did so, Hiss sued for slander.

The committee's further investigation of Hiss pitted conservative Representative RICHARD M. NIXON (R-CA), who spearheaded the inquiry, against the Harvard-educated New Dealer and leading member of the foreign policy establishment. During pretrial discovery hearings for the slander suit, Chambers produced classified 1938 State Department documents he claimed to have received from Hiss for relay to the Soviet Union. Chambers also then handed over to HUAC five rolls of microfilm, two of which contained secret State Department documents initialed by Hiss. Because the highly publicized film had been hidden in a hollowed-out pumpkin, the materials became known as the "Pumpkin Papers."

In December 1948 Hiss was indicted on two counts of perjury for lying about his involvement with former Communist Chambers. No espionage charges were brought because the statute of limitations had expired. A first trial ended in a hung jury. Hiss was convicted after a second trial on January 21, 1950, and served 44 months in prison. Still insisting on his innocence, he published his account of the case, *In the Court of Public Opinion*, in 1957.

The controversial Hiss case made Nixon a national figure. With COLD WAR concerns over Soviet subversion and international communism mounting, Hiss's conviction was seen widely as confirmation of Communist infiltration of the nation's foreign policy apparatus. Hiss's detractors linked him to American acquiescence at the YALTA CONFERENCE (1945) to Soviet control over Eastern Europe. He had attended the Crimean parley as part of the U.S. delegation. His defenders argued he had been singled out as a scapegoat for the loss of Eastern Europe and was wrongly convicted in the midst of an anti-Communist hysteria.

HONDURAN INTERVENTIONS U.S. military and political interventions in Honduras in the first quarter of the 20th century. Under the U.S.- and Mexican-mediated CENTRAL AMERICAN TREATIES OF 1907, the five Central American republics (Guatemala, El Salvador, Honduras, Nicaragua, and Costa Rica) agreed to neutralize Honduras. The step was undertaken to end chronic violations of the country's sovereignty and territory by its stronger neighbors. Poorest of the isthmian nations, Honduras struggled under a legacy of weak governments that left it vulnerable to outside interference. U.S. interest in Honduras had grown after American fruit companies began banana production along the Honduran north coast in the early 1900s. These firms, led by the United Fruit Company, soon became a powerful force in the country's political and economic life. By 1910 U.S. enterprises controlled 80 percent of Honduran banana lands and bananas had become a mainstay of the economy.

Continuing political turmoil in Central America frustrated the successive efforts of presidents THEODORE ROOSEVELT and WILLIAM HOWARD TAFT to promote regional stability within the framework of the 1907 treaties. The Taft administration eventually sought a remedy to the upheaval in a policy of DOLLAR DIPLOMACY. Secretary of State PHILANDER C. KNOX, architect of the approach, believed that financial rehabilitation was the key to achieving political tranquility in Central America. By 1909 several isthmian countries had begun defaulting on their foreign debts, the overwhelming share of which had been contracted with European creditors. Taft and Knox were fearful of possible European military intervention to exact repayment—a move that would mark a direct challenge to the ROOSEVELT COROLLARY (1904).

Knox devised a plan whereby the financially troubled Central American states would meet their foreign obligations with loans obtained from American bankers. Washington would guarantee the loans by establishing U.S.-controlled customs collectorships in the borrowing countries. A percentage of customs revenues would be earmarked for repayment of the American banks. The plan was modeled on the successful arrangement implemented by Roosevelt in 1905 in the Dominican Republic. During 1910 the secretary of state developed a specific plan to take control of Honduras's public finances. On January 10, 1911, Washington signed a treaty with Tegucigalpa providing for a customs-secured loan to Honduras, an American customs collectorship, and a plan for refunding the Honduran national debt. The agreement was virtually identical to the KNOX-CASTRILLO CONVENTION that the United States was to conclude with Nicaragua several months later.

Meanwhile in the final stages of the treaty negotiations Honduras plunged into civil war, with General Miguel Davila and his regime facing a revolt plotted and launched from New Orleans, Louisiana, by archenemy Manuel Bonilla. Davila's position had grown precarious following the overthrow in December 1909 of his ally and patron, Nicaraguan dictator Jose Santos Zelaya. Bonilla and his followers landed on Honduras's north coast the same day the U.S.-Honduran customs collectorship accord was signed. With the outbreak of fighting Taft sent American warships to

Honduras's Caribbean coast to protect American lives and property. U.S. marines were landed in late January 1911 to establish a so-called neutral zone for American nationals in the town of La Ceiba, which Bonilla was about to attack. Davila then suffered a damaging political setback when his effort to win domestic approval of the loan treaty failed. A defiant Honduran congress overwhelmingly rejected the agreement on January 31.

The United States urged an armistice and offered its mediation to end the war. When both sides accepted, State Department official Thomas C. Dawson was dispatched to oversee a peace conference that convened on February 21. Just before the parley a New Orleans jury indicted Bonilla for violation of U.S. neutrality laws. This development notwithstanding, the rebel leader enjoyed predominant influence in Honduras. In early March Dawson crafted a mutually acceptable compromise. Davila would step down and a Bonilla follower would become provisional president, pending general elections. When the new Honduran government took form following elections in October 1911, Bonilla became president. In the meantime the U.S. Justice Department, for diplomatic reasons, had decided not to pursue the indictment against him. Despite several earlier promises to support the proposed loan treaty with the United States, Bonilla grew increasingly unreceptive to the idea of an American customs collectorship in his country. In mid-April 1912 he declared Honduran rejection of the treaty final. The failure of the U.S. Senate to approve the agreement the following month killed any hope of sustaining the initiative and marked the defeat of the Taft administration's Dollar Diplomacy in Honduras.

More than a decade later, the United States intervened following the outbreak of civil war in Honduras in 1924. The conflict, a struggle between rival Liberals and Conservatives, grew out of the contest for the Honduran presidency. Conservative candidate Tiburcio Carias Andiro, chief challenger to incumbent Liberal President Rafael Lopez Gutierrez, claimed victory in the disputed election, which was thrown into the national congress for a decision. Thereupon, Gutierrez declared martial law, cracked down on Carias's supporters, and

resolved to hold office past the end of his official term. His move to establish a dictatorship touched off a revolt led by Carias. A large battle erupted between Honduran government and rebel forces at La Ceiba in late February 1924. The adjacent waters were patrolled by an American Navy squadron created after WORLD WAR I to cruise the Caribbean and Pacific coastlines of Central America, serving as the instrument of America's GUNBOAT DIPLOMACY. When the fighting intensified, Secretary of State CHARLES EVANS HUGHES sent a U.S. military detachment into the Honduran port city in mid-March to protect American lives and property.

In April 1924 U.S. diplomat SUMNER WELLES was sent as a special envoy to Honduras with instructions to settle the conflict. Welles convened the leaders from various competing Honduran factions aboard the U.S.S. *Milwaukee* and negotiated a peace agreement. The settlement arranged for a provisional presidency to be followed by free elections—from which the major revolutionary leaders would be barred as candidates. In 1925 Welles supervised the Honduran presidential balloting, which was won by Conservative Miguel Paz Barahona. U.S. diplomacy failed to bring lasting stability as Honduras was beset by continuing political turbulence.

HOOVER, HERBERT CLARK (1874–1964) Secretary of commerce, 31st president. Hoover was born in Iowa. Orphaned on the death of his mother in 1884, he was raised by relatives in Oregon, graduated from Stanford University in 1895, and became a mining engineer. His work often took him overseas. In China during the BOXER REBELLION (1900), he directed the construction of barricades to protect the foreign community at Tientsin. By 1908, Hoover was pursuing independent mining ventures that brought him wealth and international recognition. In London at the outset of WORLD WAR I in August 1914, he agreed to serve as head of the private American Relief Committee, which provided for the repatriation of some 120,000 Americans stranded in Europe by the hostilities. In October 1914 he formed the Committee for the Relief of Belgium, overseeing, until America entered the war in April 1917, the flow of food, clothing, and other humanitarian aid to German-occupied Belgium. In August 1917 President WOODROW WILSON named him U.S. wartime food administrator. In 1919 he became director general of the AMERICA RELIEF ADMINISTRATION that furnished emergency food aid to war-ravaged Europe.

President WARREN G. HARDING appointed fellow Republican Hoover secretary of commerce in 1921. He continued in the post under the succeeding Coolidge administration. Hoover gained the 1928 Republican presidential nomination and won a commanding victory over Democrat Alfred E. Smith. He took office at a time of peace and prosperity, but his presidency soon was consumed by the stock market crash of October 1929 and the ensuing Great Depression. Before his inauguration, Hoover made a goodwill tour of Latin America. His administration began the shift in the region from GUNBOAT DIPLOMACY toward the GOOD NEIGHBOR POLICY developed in full by his successor, President FRANKLIN D. ROOSEVELT. In 1930 he instructed the State Department to issue the CLARK MEMORANDUM repudiating the ROOSEVELT COROLLARY (1904) that had justified U.S. intervention in Latin America. In Asia, Hoover faced the MANCHURIAN CRISIS (1931–1933). When it became apparent that Western condemnation would not force Japan to abandon its conquest of Chinese Manchuria, the administration in January 1932 announced the STIMSON DOCTRINE. Framed by Hoover and Secretary of State HENRY L. STIMSON, it declared U.S. refusal to recognize any change in China's status brought about by force.

Hoover hoped to build on the naval disarmament achievements of the WASHINGTON NAVAL CONFERENCE (1921–1922). In 1930 the United States, Great Britain, and Japan reached agreement on further naval arms limitation at the first of the LONDON NAVAL CONFERENCES. The WORLD DISARMAMENT CONFERENCE (1932–1934), strongly supported by Hoover, proved unsuccessful. As the worldwide economic depression worsened, the increasingly beleaguered Hoover administration found itself hamstrung by events. The highly protectionist SMOOT-HAWLEY TARIFF (1930) brought a sharp drop in U.S. overseas trade. The economic collapse in Europe led the president to devise the HOOVER MORATORIUM (1931) on the re-

payment of Allied World War I debts and German reparations. Hoover won renomination but was defeated by Franklin D. Roosevelt in the 1932 presidential election. He remained active in Republican Party politics, oversaw the development of the HOOVER INSTITUTION ON WAR, REVOLUTION, AND PEACE at Stanford, and served in the late 1940s and mid-1950s as chairman of special committees, each known as the Hoover Commission, on the reorganization of the federal governmment.

HOOVER INSTITUTION ON WAR, REVOLUTION, AND PEACE Conservative think tank affiliated with Stanford University in California. Founded by future President HERBERT C. HOOVER in 1919, the institution is a prestigious research and educational organization whose resident scholars study worldwide political, economic, and social change in the 20th century. Its two-fold purpose is to develop and impart knowledge, and by extension, to serve as a fund of ideas for public policymakers and the private sector. Research is organized into three main areas: domestic studies, including U.S. government spending and taxation, welfare, and income distribution; international studies, including American foreign policy, foreign area studies, and international economics; and national security affairs, including defense and arms control. As a supplement to its program of scholarship, the Hoover Institution regularly conducts conferences and seminars that bring together government, academic, business, and media leaders from around the world.

HOOVER MORATORIUM (1931) Temporary freeze on the payment of German reparations to the European Allies and of Allied war debts to the United States. Great Britain, France, and other European Allied nations had borrowed more than $11 billion from the United States during and immediately after WORLD WAR I. When approached by the financially strapped European countries for relief, American presidents beginning with WOODROW WILSON refused either to cancel the debts or to link their repayment to the monies the Allies were scheduled to receive in German reparations. In 1922 the U.S. Congress voted to create the World War Foreign

Debt Commission to negotiate debt-settlement agreements. Between 1922 and 1926 the eight-member commission completed low-interest, long-term repayment pacts with 13 Allied debtor nations. The problem of German delinquency on reparations was temporarily resolved by the DAWES PLAN of 1924 and payment on both the reparations and the Allied war debts was made until the end of the decade.

The onset of the worldwide Great Depression in 1929 undermined both the ability of the European nations to repay their war debts and of Germany to continue to meet its reparations obligations. By June 1931 the German economy was in collapse, threatening the financial stability of both Europe and America. As foreign capital fled Germany and the crisis worsened, President HERBERT C. HOOVER on June 20 proposed a one-year moratorium on Allied war debts to the United States, with the proviso that the Europeans similarly would allow Germany to delay payment on its reparations. By July 6 the European Allies had agreed to the moratorium. To stop the flow of foreign investments out of Germany, delegates from the United States, Great Britain, Belgium, France, Italy, Germany, and Japan convened in London the same month and agreed to implement a "standstill" on financial withdrawals. A committee of international bankers subsequently concluded what became known as the "Standstill" Agreement, imposing a six-month suspension on withdrawals effective September 1, 1931. The standstill measure was renewed periodically by U.S. banks until 1940.

On December 23, 1931, Congress passed a resolution formally approving the debt moratorium. The legislation set the next scheduled debt payment for December 1932. With no end in sight to the worldwide depression, it became apparent that the Hoover Moratorium would need to be extended. The European Allies moved to revise the 1929 YOUNG PLAN governing the payment of German reparations. In July 1932 the European nations agreed to cancel 90 percent of the remaining German reparations on the condition that the United States in turn write off the Allied war debts it was owed. The Hoover administration rejected the arrangement. In December 1932 all of the European debtor nations except Finland defaulted on their U.S. obligations, straining transatlantic relations for the balance of the decade. Following Adolf Hitler's rise to power in 1933, Germany renounced its World War I reparations. In 1934 America enacted the JOHNSON DEBT DEFAULT ACT barring further loans to countries that defaulted on their U.S. war debts.

HOOVER-STIMSON DOCTRINE   See **STIMSON DOCTRINE**.

HOPEWELL, TREATY OF (1785)   First of the peace treaties made after the AMERICAN REVOLUTION between the United States and southern Indian nations. America completed the agreement with the Cherokees on November 28, 1785, at Hopewell, South Carolina. The Cherokees ceded lands in North Carolina and Tennessee and acknowledged the right of Congress to regulate trade with the Indian nation. The treaty established boundaries recognizing the remaining Cherokee territories.

U.S. negotiators, looking to limit the appropriation of Indian lands by the states, repudiated earlier accords dictated by Georgia and North Carolina that had confiscated Cherokee areas. Congress exercised exclusive authority under the ARTICLES OF CONFEDERATION to manage INDIAN AFFAIRS and therefore rejected independent treaty-making by the states as an intrusion on federal powers. After the treaty with the Cherokees, the United States completed similar agreements at Hopewell in January 1786 with the Choctaws and Chickasaws. By the end of the year, the Hopewell treaties proved unenforceable. Defiant southern states and settlers ignored the boundary lines and the Indian tribes resorted to fighting to preserve their lands against further encroachment.

See also MAP 1.

HORTALEZ AND COMPANY   Fictitious French trading company formed during the AMERICAN REVOLUTION to channel covert aid to the American colonies. In September 1775 the dramatist Pierre A. C. de Beaumarchais, an agent of the French government who was sympathetic to the American cause, urged French Foreign Minister Charles Gravier Comte de Vergennes to secretly assist the colonists in their struggle for independence from Great Britain. Vergennes was unwilling to risk war with the British by openly supporting the Americans. To preserve official French neutrality and allay the foreign minister's apprehensions, Beaumarchais proposed establishing a dummy firm through which war supplies could be funneled to America.

On May 2, 1776, King Louis XVI sanctioned secret aid when he authorized an initial one million livres (about $200,000) for arms and munitions; in July the Spanish monarchy contributed an equal sum. In August Beaumarchais organized the firm Roderique Hortalez and Company, which in its first year was responsible for shipping more than six million livres worth of French and Spanish guns, gunpowder, and other supplies to America. France had committed itself to clandestine backing of the rebellion before America declared its independence and even before the Continental Congress's envoy Silas Deane arrived in Paris to solicit aid. Hortalez and Company's generous disbursements between 1776 and 1778 were indispensable to American fighting fortunes. The Franco-American Alliance (1778) brought France into the war against Great Britain and thereby removed the need for covert assistance. Some controversy surrounded the firm during its operation when Beaumarchais and Deane faced accusations, never substantiated, of enriching themselves with funds siphoned from Hortalez.

HOSTAGE TAKING ACT (1984) Federal law to prevent and punish the crime of abducting American hostages. The measure was part of the Comprehensive Crime Control Act of 1984, a sweeping anticrime package signed into law October 12 by President Ronald W. Reagan that culminated a decade-long effort to overhaul the federal criminal code. The Hostage Taking Act represented a new weapon in the Reagan administration's professed war against international terrorism. It sought to deter abductions committed for political purposes by mandating severe criminal penalties. The legislation required life imprisonment for anyone found guilty of taking American nationals hostage either inside the United States or outside the country in order to compel the U.S. government or a third person to act or abstain from acting as a condition for releasing the hostages. The Aircraft Sabotage Act, also part of the comprehensive 1984 crime package, established steep fines and lengthy prison terms for anyone who damaged civil aircraft or aircraft facilities in the United States or committed acts of violence against passengers or crews on such aircraft.

"HOT-LINE" AGREEMENTS Measures providing for direct communications links between U.S. and Soviet leaders for use in an emergency. The 1962 Cuban Missile Crisis revealed the need for an official, immediately available communications link between Washington and Moscow to ensure that a misunderstanding, miscommunication, or accident did not trigger a nuclear war. The United States and Soviet Union completed the "Hot-Line" Agreement in Geneva on June 20, 1963, establishing a teletype communications link, or "hot-line," between the two governments. The "Hot-Line" Modernization Agreement, concluded in Washington on September 30, 1971, replaced the teletype link with satellite communications. In July 17, 1984, the two sides initialed an agreement adding a facsimile capability to the system.

HOUSE ARMED SERVICES COMMITTEE See same in **APPENDIX D**.

HOUSE, EDWARD MANDELL (1858–1938) Public figure, known as Colonel House, who was President Woodrow Wilson's closest adviser. He was born in Houston, Texas, son of a prosperous cotton planter. After briefly attending Cornell University, he returned home, where he managed family business and agricultural enterprises and became involved in Democratic politics. Eschewing elective or appointive office, he served as campaign manager and intimate counselor to successive governors of Texas from 1892 to 1904. Governor James S. Hogg insisted on naming him to his staff with the title of colonel, an appellation that clung to House throughout his life.

House met Wilson in 1911, quickly winning his friendship and trust. After Wilson's election in 1912, House declined an official appointment to the administration and instead became the president's closest confidante and right-hand man, especially in foreign affairs. Following the outbreak of WORLD WAR I in 1914, he endorsed Wilson's neutrality policy. He served in ensuing years as the president's personal agent in negotiations for possible U.S. mediation of the conflict. Wilson twice sent House to Europe, in 1915 and 1916, to attempt to broker a peace. On his second mission, the colonel concluded an agreement with the British foreign secretary, known as the HOUSE-GREY MEMORANDUM (1916), which called for a U.S.-sponsored peace conference and revealed the Wilson administration's growing partiality toward the Allies. Nothing, however, came of the memorandum. After the United States entered the war in April 1917 House emerged as Wilson's key intermediary in dealings with the Allied governments. He assembled and supervised THE INQUIRY, a group of experts that prepared for peace negotiations and also helped formulate Wilson's FOURTEEN POINTS and the president's LEAGUE OF NATIONS proposal. He represented the United States at the Allied meetings in France in October 1918 that drafted the pre-armistice agreement ending the fighting. House scored a diplomatic triumph when he won the consent of the Allied leaders to establishing the Fourteen Points as the basis for a final peace settlement.

At the PARIS PEACE CONFERENCE (1919), House served as Wilson's chief deputy. Differences developed between the two men over the degree to which the United States should yield to British and French demands, with House favoring conciliation and acquiescence. Wilson, though forced by necessity to accept compromise, began to lose faith in his long-standing aide. When House urged the president to compromise with the Senate on the League of Nations Covenant in order to secure ratification of the TREATY OF VERSAILLES, Wilson refused. After returning from Paris, the president broke off his relationship with House. The two never saw each other again. In later years House traveled frequently in Europe and kept up his contacts with European leaders.

HOUSE FOREIGN AFFAIRS COMMITTEE See same in **APPENDIX D.**

HOUSE UN-AMERICAN ACTIVITIES COMMITTEE (HUAC)   Controversial congres-

sional panel that investigated alleged subversion in American society. In 1938 the House of Representatives established a Special Committee on Un-American Activities under the chairmanship of Martin Dies, Jr. (D-TX). The panel, known as the Dies Committee, was empowered to inquire into Fascist, Communist, and other "un-American" activities in the United States. It was renewed five times by members of Congress worried over the domestic influence of foreign agents from Nazi Germany and the Soviet Union. The committee's heavy-handed investigation into the possible subversive infiltration of labor and civic organizations such as the National Labor Relations Board drew widespread criticism. During WORLD WAR II Dies directed several inconclusive inquiries into the purported security threat posed by Japanese-Americans and the suggested lax management of their internment by the War Relocation Authority.

On January 3, 1945, the Dies special committee was replaced by the permanent House Un-American Activities Committee, often referred to by its acronym, HUAC. The committee enjoyed its greatest influence over the next five years. Against a backdrop of mounting COLD WAR tensions and concerns over the potential threat of Soviet-sponsored subversion, the committee in 1947 launched a controversial investigation into Communist infiltration of Hollywood and the film industry. Other hearings probed alleged subversion in government, labor unions, and the press. His central role in the committee's handling of the highly publicized HISS CASE brought member RICHARD M. NIXON (R-CA) to national prominence. Critics condemned committee tactics, such as the use of contempt citations against unfriendly witnesses, as an infringement of basic civil liberties.

HUAC's major legislative effort was the INTERNAL SECURITY ACT (1950). In the early 1950s, the panel was overshadowed by Senator JOSEPH R. MCCARTHY (R-WI) and his demagogic charges of Communist penetration of the federal government. The panel maintained its lower profile following McCarthy's political downfall in 1954. HUAC's diminished activity in the late 1950s reflected a gradual decrease in concerns over Communist subversion. In the 1960s, amid violent civil rights protest and mounting domestic opposition to American involvement in the VIETNAM WAR, the panel turned its attention to possible foreign subversion in radical youth organizations, black militant groups, and the antiwar movement. Under attack by liberals and civil libertarians as a vestige from the McCarthy era, HUAC was renamed the Internal Security Committee in 1969. The panel's mandate was limited to investigations of groups seeking the violent overthrow of the government. The House abolished the committee in January 1975.

HOUSE-GREY MEMORANDUM (1916) Anglo-American proposal for securing a negotiated peace in WORLD WAR I. With the onset of war in Europe in August 1914, President WOODROW WILSON had declared U.S. neutrality. His administration, reflecting overwhelming American sentiment, was determined to keep the United States out of the conflict. Developments through the first year of the war persuaded Wilson that the only certain way to avoid U.S. military involvement was to bring the struggle to a negotiated end. His initial try at brokering a peace had come in December 1914 when he sent his personal adviser, Colonel EDWARD M. HOUSE, as an unofficial emissary to London, Paris, and Berlin to propose American mediation. House's months of discussions with the major belligerents ended inconclusively. To Washington, in frustration, he cabled, "Everbody seems to want peace but nobody is willing to concede enough to get it."

In January 1916 Wilson dispatched House on a second European peace mission. The president by that time had concluded that American entry in the war would be preferable to a German victory. That judgment notwithstanding, he considered the military situation in Europe a stalemate and believed the United States had an opportunity to push a settlement in which neither side would emerge an overwhelming loser. House conferred with British, French, and German leaders. His discussions at London with British Foreign Secretary Sir Edward Grey produced what became known as the House-Grey Memorandum. Signed on February 22, 1916, the draft agreement stipulated that Wilson would summon a peace conference whenever Great Britain and France deemed the

moment "opportune." By terms of the memorandum, if the Allies accepted the invitation and Germany rejected it, the United States "would probably enter the war against Germany." Should the Germans accept, Wilson would help the Allies gain a favorable peace. The president relayed his approval of the memorandum to House on March 8. The House-Grey scheme, though, fell flat. Neither the Allies nor the Central Powers desired a peace conference since both remained confident in the spring of 1916 that they could achieve a military victory. While nothing further came of the House-Grey understanding, it revealed that the Wilson administration, despite its avowed neutrality, was partial toward the Allies and presaged American entry into the war in April 1917.

HOUSTON, SAMUEL (1793–1863) American soldier and statesman who led Texas's drive for independence from Mexico and twice served as president of the Republic of Texas. Born in Virginia, he grew up in Tennessee near Cherokee Indian country. He left home in his teens and lived three years among the Cherokees, who called him "the Raven." Through his experience he gained a lasting affection and sympathetic understanding for Indian life. In the WAR OF 1812 he served under General ANDREW JACKSON against the Creek Indians and was wounded at the decisive Battle of Horseshoe Bend (1814). Resigning from the army in 1818 with the rank of lieutenant, he studied law in Nashville, Tennessee, passed the bar, and entered private practice.

Turning to politics, Houston spent two terms in the U.S House of Representatives (1823–1827) before his election in 1827 as governor of Tennessee. In 1829, after his newlywed wife Eliza Allen left him for reasons never divulged, he abruptly resigned the office and became an Indian trader and adopted son of the Cherokees, settling near Fort Gibson in present-day Oklahoma. During visits to Washington in the early 1830s, he represented Cherokee grievances about the U.S. government's failure either to fulfill its obligations to the tribe under the INDIAN REMOVAL POLICY or to protect the Indians from abuses by white settlers and land speculators. President Jackson sent him to Texas in December 1832 to broker a peace between the Cherokees and the Comanches. Attracted by the opportunities for land, Houston decided to settle in the territory and soon joined the leadership of the burgeoning Texas revolt against Mexico.

With the outbreak of the Texan War of Independence in 1835, he was appointed commander in chief of the Texan army by the provisional government. In March 1836, after Texas formally declared itself an independent republic, his overall military command was reaffirmed. Forces under Houston surprised and routed the Mexican army at San Jacinto on April 21, 1836, capturing Mexican General Antonio Lopez de Santa Anna. The victory guaranteed Texan independence. Elected president of the Republic of Texas, he served from 1836 to 1838 and again from 1841 to 1844. He secured formal U.S. diplomatic recognition of the republic in 1837. Houston in his first term advocated annexation of Texas by the United States. But political opposition in the North to the admission of Texas to the Union as a slave state led President MARTIN VAN BUREN to reject annexation proposals.

After Congress finally annexed Texas in 1845, Houston became one of the state's first two U.S. senators, serving in Washington from 1846 to 1859. An ardent Union Democrat, he grew politically alienated from his Southern colleagues in the Senate following his vote for the Compromise of 1850 and against the Kansas-Nebraska Act (1854), legislation formulated to resolve the sectional crisis over the extension of slavery into new territories. Elected Texas governor in 1859, he opposed Southern secession from the Union, denouncing it as treason. His refusal to swear allegiance to the Confederacy led to his removal from office on March 18, 1861. He died two years later at Huntsville, Texas. The city of Houston was named after him.

HUGHES, CHARLES EVANS (1862–1948) Secretary of state, Supreme Court justice. Born in New York, Hughes graduated from Brown University in 1881 and Columbia Law School in 1884. He practiced law in New York City, was a faculty member at Cornell Law School, and served as counsel for several investigatory committees of the New York state legislature. A Republican, he won the governorship of New York in 1906 over Democratic candidate and renowned publisher WILLIAM RANDOLPH HEARST. Reelected for a second two-year term, Hughes resigned in 1910 to accept appointment by President WILLIAM HOWARD TAFT as an associate justice on the U.S. Supreme Court. He stepped down from the Court in 1916 to garner the Republican presidential nomination. Narrowly defeated by President WOODROW WILSON in the general election, Hughes resumed his private law practice.

In 1921 he was named secretary of state in the new Harding administration. Following the death of President WARREN G. HARDING in 1923, he continued in the post under CALVIN COOLIDGE. In contrast to the abstract INTERNATIONALISM of the Wilson years, Hughes brought a more pragmatic, legalistic approach to U.S. foreign relations. The highlight of his tenure was the WASHINGTON NAVAL CONFERENCE (1921–1922), at which he presided. The international meeting on naval disarmament and the Far East produced the FOUR-POWER TREATY on the security of the western Pacific, the FIVE-POWER TREATY limiting naval armaments, and the NINE-POWER TREATY on China and the OPEN DOOR. Before taking office, Hughes had favored U.S. participation in an amended LEAGUE OF NATIONS. Realizing the Senate would not ratify the TREATY OF VERSAILLES that ended WORLD WAR I and established the league, he negotiated a separate peace agreement, the 1921 TREATY OF BERLIN, with Germany. He played a central role in the formation of the committee that prepared the DAWES PLAN (1924) for shoring up the collapsing German economy and restructuring the defeated nation's war reparations. Hughes shifted U.S. policy away from Wilson's legacy of armed intervention in the Caribbean and was credited with improving relations with Latin America. He oversaw negotiation of the BUCARELI AGREEMENT (1923) extending U.S. diplomatic recognition to the post-revolutionary Mexican government and guaranteeing private American land and oil holdings in Mexico. He continued the Wilson administration's policy of nonrecognition of the Soviet Union.

Hughes left office in 1925 to rebuild his personal finances, returning to his Wall Street law practice. He remained active in public affairs, serving as a member of the international PERMANENT COURT OF ARBITRATION from 1926 to 1930 and as head of the

U.S. delegation at the sixth PAN-AMERICAN CONFERENCE in Havana in 1928. In 1930 President HERBERT C. HOOVER appointed Hughes to a second term on the Supreme Court, where he replaced WILLIAM HOWARD TAFT as chief justice. Hughes presided over the Court during a period of dramatic political and social change brought by the Great Depression and President FRANKLIN D. ROOSEVELT's New Deal programs for restoring the American economy and society. He generally helped form a majority favoring the constitutionality of New Deal legislation vesting broad new powers in the federal government. But he sucessfully opposed Roosevelt's 1937 court-packing scheme, in which the president attempted to appoint additional justices to the Court in order to influence its decisions. Hughes retired from the bench and public life in 1941.

HUGHES-RYAN AMENDMENT (1974) Legislation that first established formal congressional oversight of U.S. COVERT ACTION. With the emergence of the various U.S. foreign intelligence agencies following WORLD WAR II, Congress deferred to the executive branch in the management of U.S. intelligence in general and the direction of covert operations in particular, reflecting a traditional respect for the president's foreign policy prerogatives. Congress assumed an increasingly assertive role in the formulation of foreign policy in the late 1960s as opposition to the VIETNAM WAR mounted among House and Senate members. Revelations of CENTRAL INTELLIGENCE AGENCY (CIA) involvement in the CHILE COUP (1973) prompted calls for greater congressional control over U.S. covert activities. In 1974 Congress added an amendment on intelligence oversight to that year's foreign assistance act. The measure, sponsored by Senator Harold E. Hughes (D-IA) and Representative Leo J. Ryan (D-CA), stipulated that covert action could be carried out only when the president had determined specifically that it was important to the national security. The president also was required to notify promptly relevant congressional committees of this finding. The amendment, which became law when President GERALD R. FORD signed the foreign aid bill on December 30, 1974, represented a major expansion of congressional involvement in intelligence. The 1980 Intelligence Oversight Act for security reasons reduced from six to two the number of committees required to be kept informed of covert operations.

HULL, CORDELL (1871–1955) U.S. representative, senator, secretary of state. Born in Tennessee, Hull entered National Normal University in Lebanon, Ohio, in 1889. The following year he studied law at Cumberland University in Tennessee and in 1891 was admitted to the state bar. From 1893 to 1897 he was a member of the state legislature. During the SPANISH-AMERICAN WAR (1898) he served as a captain in a Tennessee infantry regiment. His unit arrived in Cuba after the fighting had ended. After the war he returned to the practice of law and in 1902 was appointed a state circuit judge. A Democrat, Hull was elected in 1906 to the U.S. House of Representatives. He held the seat, except for the two years between 1921 and 1923, until 1930, when he won election to the U.S. Senate.

In March 1933 Hull became secretary of state in the new Roosevelt administration. He remained in the position almost 12 years, the longest tenure in U.S. history. His influence and accomplishments were limited, though, by FRANKLIN D. ROOSEVELT's domination of foreign affairs throughout his presidency. Hull was most active in trade policy and Latin American relations. He was an ardent free trade advocate, believing high tariffs and trade barriers stifled international commerce and led to war. He headed the U.S. delegation to the 1933 WORLD ECONOMIC CONFERENCE, where he hoped to help effect a reversal of the worldwide Great Depression through greater international economic cooperation. The gathering broke down, however, after Roosevelt rejected European calls for currency stabilization. The following year he led administration efforts to gain passage of the TRADE AGREEMENTS ACT authorizing the negotiation of reciprocal tariff-reducing measures with other nations. Hull eventually concluded some 20 bilateral agreements under the law. The idea of international commerce based on open access and reciprocity subsequently would provide the basic framework for the 1947 GENERAL AGREEMENT ON TARIFFS AND TRADE.

Hull championed Roosevelt's GOOD NEIGHBOR POLICY toward Latin America. In 1933 he chaired the U.S. delegation at the

PAN-AMERICAN CONFERENCE at Montevideo, Uruguay, where he voted for the CONVENTION ON RIGHTS AND DUTIES OF STATES, committing America to the principle of non-intervention in the Western Hemisphere. The vote, as well as Hull's cordial and respectful manner, did much to improve U.S. relations with Latin American nations long resentful of American intervention in the region. In subsequent years, against the backdrop of impending war in Europe, he worked for the establishment of hemispheric security arrangements. Hull directed U.S. involvement in the formulation of the DECLARATION OF LIMA (1938) calling for inter-American consultation in the event of an outside threat to the hemisphere, the DECLARATION OF PANAMA (1939) affirming Pan-American neutrality in WORLD WAR II and creating a hemispheric security zone, and the ACT OF HAVANA (1940) providing for Pan-American trusteeship of any European possession in the hemisphere in danger of falling under Nazi Germany's control.

From 1939 to 1941 Roosevelt's attention largely focused on events in Europe. Hull in turn handled negotiations begun with the Japanese in 1941 over the status of the Far East. The United States opposed Japanese aggression in China and sought to prevent Japan from taking advantage of the war in Europe to advance its interests in the Western Pacific. Insisting it held a special, paramount position in the Far East, Japan continued its military campaign against China and moved to occupy French Indochina. As U.S.-Japanese relations deteriorated, Hull in late November 1941 warned of the possibility of war. On December 7, 1941, he received Japanese envoys informing him of a state of war between the two nations after Japanese planes had already struck at PEARL HARBOR. During World War II Hull's efforts centered largely on planning for the postwar UNITED NATIONS. Roosevelt chose not to have Hull accompany him to the wartime conferences with the other Allied leaders, reserving to himself the formulation and conduct of American diplomacy. Hull aided in the drafting of the UNITED NATIONS DECLARATION (1942) and oversaw U.S. involvement in the initial preparation of the UNITED NATIONS CHARTER. He attended the 1943 MOSCOW CONFERENCE of Allied foreign ministers. He resigned his post in 1944 for health reasons. Roosevelt called him the

"father of the United Nations"; in 1945 he won the Nobel Peace Prize for his work on the international organization. Hull published his two-volume *Memoirs* in 1948.

HULSEMANN LETTER See **WEBSTER, DANIEL**.

HUMAN RIGHTS Concept of fundamental political and civil rights possessed by all individuals. The modern idea of inalienable human rights derived from the American and French revolutions of the late 18th century and the doctrine of natural rights that was their legacy. The precedent established by the United States and France of enacting constitutional guarantees against arbitrary government abridgement of individual rights and liberties gained growing acceptence among nations worldwide in the ensuing 200 years. Twentieth-century Socialist and Communist systems first asserted the inalienability of certain basic economic and social rights, elevating them to a level of importance equal to political and civil rights. Notwithstanding initial development of a humanitarian law of war and achievement of a ban on the international slave trade in the 19th century, human rights did not emerge as a major international issue until after WORLD WAR I. The Covenant of the LEAGUE OF NATIONS, the charter for the postwar international organization created to provide COLLECTIVE SECURITY, did not formally recognize fundamental rights of mankind. Certain of its provisions did, however, suggest a nascent concern for the basic rights and welfare of human beings. League members, for example, accepted an obligation to secure fair and humane working conditions and pledged to treat justly the native inhabitants of their colonies. The INTERNATIONAL LABOR ORGANIZATION (ILO), formed in 1919 as an autonomous part of the league, advanced human rights by its promotion of worker health, safety, and welfare.

The Nazi atrocities of WORLD WAR II, most notoriously the extermination of 6 million Jews in the Holocaust, as well as Germany's persecution of other religious and ethnic minorities and use of slave labor, raised international consciousness regarding human rights and led the victorious Allied powers to formulate international standards of humane conduct and fundamental rights to be enjoyed by all people. In the ATLANTIC CHARTER (1941) and UNITED NATIONS DECLARATION (1942), the United States and other Allied nations had made preservation of human rights a basic peace aim. At war's end, the Allies formed an international military tribunal at Nuremburg, Germany, to try alleged Nazi war criminals. The tribunal was given jurisdiction to prosecute not only war crimes but also "crimes against humanity," which encompassed Nazi abominations against civilians. It was at the NUREMBURG WAR CRIMES TRIALS (1945–1946) that a country's treatment of its own people was for the first time made subject to criminal proceedings in an international forum. In response to the Nazi atrocities, the international community adopted the GENOCIDE TREATY (1948), which made genocide a crime punishable under international law, and revised the GENEVA CONVENTIONS in 1949 to provide for the protection and humane treatment of civilians in wartime.

Since World War II, international activity with respect to human rights has been conducted mainly within the framework of the UNITED NATIONS. In December 1948, the General Assembly adopted the landmark UNIVERSAL DECLARATION OF HUMAN RIGHTS, comprising a catalog of basic rights and freedoms to serve as a "common standard of achievement for all peoples and all nations." A pair of U.N. covenants drafted between 1948 and 1954 expanded on and put into binding legal form the rights contained in the declaration. The two covenants finally entered into force in 1976 after ratification by the necessary number of member nations.

Emphasis on human rights in America's post–World War II foreign policy reached its apogee under President JIMMY CARTER. Throughout the COLD WAR, the United States drew attention to fundamental East-West differences on human rights, contrasting the FREE WORLD's commitment to political and civil rights with the Soviet bloc's totalitarian repression of basic human freedoms. To protest the Kremlin's policy of restricting Soviet Jewish emigration, Congress passed the JACKSON-VANIK AMENDMENT (1974) denying MOST-FAVORED-NATION trade status to the Soviet Union. At the CONFERENCE ON SECURITY AND COOPERATION IN EUROPE (CSCE) in 1975, the United States and USSR were among the 35 nations that concluded the HELSINKI ACCORDS, the terms of which committed the signatories to uphold human rights and the basic freedoms of thought, conscience, and religion. The Helsinki provisions became the standard by which the West criticized the Soviet Union's human rights record and pressed for improvement. The 1989 EAST-WEST ACCORD ON HUMAN RIGHTS, concluded under CSCE auspices, underscored the process of liberalization underway in the Soviet bloc and presaged the collapse of communism in Eastern Europe and the USSR.

HUNGARIAN REVOLT   Anti-Communist uprising in Hungary that was brutally suppressed by the Soviet Union. In 1956 Soviet leaders Nikolai A. Bulganin and Nikita S. Khrushchev, successors to the tyrannical Joseph Stalin, advanced a softened policy toward Eastern Europe, which had fallen under the control of Soviet-installed Communist regimes after WORLD WAR II. In 1955, the Soviets had reached an accord with Marshal Tito's Yugoslavia that recognized the Balkan nation's right to choose its own path to socialism, free of Moscow's dictation. Yugoslavia's experience, combined with disclosure of Khrushchev's dramatic secret speech in February 1956 to the 20th Communist Party Congress denouncing Stalinism and the "cult of personality" associated with it, kindled the aspirations of the satellite nations of Eastern Europe to break free from Soviet domination. On October 20, 1956, Hungarian students began demonstrations in Budapest demanding freedom from communism. Full-fledged rebellion broke out on October 23. With much of the world's attention riveted on the SUEZ CRISIS in the Middle East, and with America entering the final days of a presidential election campaign, the Kremlin on November 4 sent Soviet tanks and artillery into Budapest and other Hungarian cities to ruthlessly crush the revolt. The organized Hungarian resistance quickly collapsed and Moscow installed a loyal Communist regime in the country.

The United States condemned the Soviet action before the UNITED NATIONS and in other forums. President DWIGHT D. EISENHOWER took no tangible steps to aid the Hungarian "freedom fighters," however, out of concern that U.S. intervention might precipitate a world war. Domestic and foreign detractors accused the Eisenhower administration of having incited the Hungarian people to rebellion through its enunciation of a policy of LIBERATION, and then failed to support them in the face of overwhelming Soviet armed might.

I

ICBM See **INTERCONTINENTAL BALLISTIC MISSILE**.

IMF See **INTERNATIONAL MONETARY FUND**.

IMMIGRATION ACT OF 1875 Federal law that excluded convicts and prostitutes from admission to the United States. The measure also reinforced prohibitions against American involvement in the coolie labor trade, in which workers were involuntarily transported overseas from their native China. Signed into law March 3, 1875, the legislation represented the first direct regulation of immigration by Congress. Broad federal control over immigration was established in the IMMIGRATION ACT OF 1882.

IMMIGRATION ACT OF 1882 First comprehensive federal immigration law. Control over immigration traditionally had been left to the states. This situation began to change in the decades after the Civil War. The rising volume of immigrants, the need for uniform national rules governing their arrival, and the increasing impact of immigration issues on foreign relations caused the federal government to assume a more active role.

Congress took an initial step toward federal regulation of immigration in the IMMIGRATION ACT OF 1875. The following year the Supreme Court made further federal involvement inevitable when it ruled in HENDERSON V. MAYOR OF NEW YORK that state immigration statutes were unconstitutional. Congress accepted broad responsibility for immigration in the Immigration Act of 1882. Enacted August 3, the measure assigned the supervision of immigration to the Treasury Department; imposed a head tax on aliens to fund immigration programs; and added idiots, lunatics, and paupers to the roster of those excluded from the United States. The Immigration Act of 1891 completed the transition from state to federal regulation, establishing a permanent national immigration administration.

IMMIGRATION ACT OF 1917 Federal law imposing a literacy test and other restrictive provisions on immigration to the United States. The legislation signaled the end of the traditional American commitment to open immigration. The massive wave of transatlantic immigration beginning in the 1890s brought increasing pressure for federal limits on newly arriving aliens. Nativist groups such as the IMMIGRATION RESTRICTION LEAGUE argued that the large influx of allegedly inferior immigrants from southern and eastern Europe exerted an adverse influence on American society. Labor organizations advocated lower immigration levels to protect the economy and safeguard jobs.

Opponents of free immigration waged a quarter-century campaign to establish a literacy requirement for prospective immigrants. The literacy test, while defended as a means of selecting qualified entrants, was generally understood to be primarily directed at halting the flow of less-educated southern and eastern Europeans. In 1897 President GROVER CLEVELAND vetoed an initial attempt by Congress to enact a literacy measure. A similar bill, passed after the influential DILLINGHAM COMMISSION endorsed a literacy exam, received a presidential veto from WILLIAM HOWARD TAFT in 1913. When President WOODROW WILSON rejected another literacy measure in 1915, he remarked that excluding immigrants because they lacked an education contradicted American ideals. He refused to sign a similar measure two years later, but the Immigration Act of 1917 became law when Congress overrode Wilson's veto on February 5.

The legislation barred immigrants over age 16 unable to pass a basic reading test in their native language. Exceptions were provided for close family members and religious refugees. The act also established an Asiatic Barred Zone encompassing Afghanistan, Arabia, India, Indochina, and the East Indies. The law blocked laborers from the zone from coming to the United States. The literacy test did not curtail immigration as expected and the influx in 1921 was only slightly below previous levels. Congress moved the same year to enact more stringent measures, imposing ethnic quotas on the number of new arrivals in the IMMIGRATION ACT OF 1921.

IMMIGRATION ACT OF 1921 Second of three measures enacted between 1917 and 1924 that marked the adoption of a restrictive U.S. immigration policy. The act placed the first quotas on immigration to America. Congress had imposed a literacy requirement on newly arriving aliens in the IMMIGRATION ACT OF 1917, but the test proved ineffective in limiting the heavy volume of transatlantic immigration. By 1921, several factors had contributed to a growing national alarm over immigration. Congress worried that WORLD WAR I had produced a flood of European refugees bound for the United States. The postwar downturn in

the nation's economy led the American Federation of Labor to renew its calls for a halt to immigration. The American Legion and other nationalistic groups favoring the Americanization, or complete cultural assimilation, of immigrants urged a suspension of immigration until the large backlog of recently arrived foreigners could be absorbed.

Responding to the perceived immigration crisis, Congress passed a quota bill that became law on May 19, 1921. Known variously as the Quota Act, the Per Centum Limit Act, and the Johnson Act, after its sponsor Albert Johnson (R-WA), chairman of the House Immigration Committee, the Immigration Act of 1921 was enacted as an emergency measure until Congress could formulate a permanent U.S. immigration policy. The legislation limited the annual immigration for each national group to three percent of the foreign born of that nationality in the 1910 U.S. census. The quotas were the first direct limits on European immigration. Reflecting ethnic biases of the time, the law's use of the 1910 census sharply curbed allegedly less desirable immigration from southern and eastern Europe. Western Hemisphere countries were exempted from quotas, both to preserve good relations and to ensure a continuing flow of Mexican agricultural workers.

The 1921 act reduced overall immigration to the United States by two-thirds. The numbers of immigrants from southern and eastern Europe fell to one-quarter of their levels before World War I. The legislation, extended for two years in 1922, served as the foundation for the national origins system established by the IMMIGRATION ACT OF 1924.

IMMIGRATION ACT OF 1924 Major legislation that established the framework of U.S. immigration policy for nearly a half-century. The law marked the end of a prolonged debate over how to respond to a massive influx of European immigrants to the United States since the 1890s. America had departed from its basic policy of open borders in the IMMIGRATION ACT OF 1917, which instituted a literacy test for would-be immigrants and created an ASIATIC BARRED ZONE from which immigration was not accepted. The temporary IMMIGRATION ACT OF 1921 continued the movement toward restriction. It imposed the first annual quotas on immigration. During this period sentiment for stringent limits on immigration, already supported by labor and nationalistic organizations, mounted as nativist groups such as the IMMIGRATION RESTRICTION LEAGUE and the KU KLUX KLAN convinced large numbers of Americans that immigrants from southern and eastern Europe were racially inferior and posed a threat to the nation's future.

President CALVIN COOLIDGE signed a permanent immigration bill on May 26, 1924. The Immigration Act of 1924, also known as the National Origins Act and the Johnson-Reed Act, after its sponsors Representative Albert Johnson (R-WA) and Senator David A. Reed (R-PA), was substantially more restrictive than the 1921 measure it replaced. The law established a national origins system as the basis for determining immigration quotas. Beginning July 1, 1927, the total number of immigrants allowed annually into the United States would be 150,000. Each nationality received a quota equal to the percentage of people in the 1920 census of that ancestry or national origin. The U.S. population in 1920 was largely of northern European descent and the national origins formula had the intended result of severely curtailing immigration from southern and eastern Europe. During a transition period from 1924 to 1927, the quotas in the 1921 act were reduced to two percent of the 1890 census. As with the 1921 law, the 1924 legislation placed no limits on immigration from Western Hemisphere countries.

Because it ended Japanese immigration, the Immigration Act of 1924 has also been referred to as the Japanese Exclusion Act. Immigration from most of Asia had been blocked by the CHINESE EXCLUSION ACT (1882) and the 1917 immigration law. In the GENTLEMEN'S AGREEMENT (1907–1908), the Japanese government had consented to limit the emigration of its workers to the United States. The 1924 act included a provision that barred immigrants who were ineligible for U.S. citizenship. The measure, which relied on the Supreme Court's decision in OZAWA V. UNITED STATES (1922) that the naturalization law did not apply to Asians, aimed principally at halting all Japanese immigration. During Senate debate over the provision, the Japanese am-

bassador to the United States sent Secretary of State CHARLES EVANS HUGHES a formal note warning of "grave consequences" if a ban on Japanese immigration were enacted. Hughes forwarded the letter to Congress where Senator HENRY CABOT LODGE, SR. (R-MA), expressing the mood of the chamber, called the note an unacceptable "veiled threat" and the provision barring Japanese immigration was overwhelmingly approved.

The Japanese government considered the measure a violation of previous understandings and abrogated the Gentlemen's Agreement. The effective date of the ban, July 1, 1924, was declared a day of national mourning by the Tokyo press. The exclusion policy contributed to the gradual worsening of Japanese-American relations in the period before WORLD WAR II. Racial barriers to immigration and naturalization were eliminated by the IMMIGRATION AND NATIONALITY ACT OF 1952. The national origins system of quotas was halted by the IMMIGRATION ACT OF 1965.

IMMIGRATION ACT OF 1965 Broad revision of the IMMIGRATION AND NATIONALITY ACT OF 1952 that represented an important shift in U.S. immigration policy. The legislation replaced the restrictive measures that had framed American policy over the previous half-century with more liberal immigration provisions. Following passage of the 1952 act, which retained the national origins system of ethnic quotas, four successive presidential administrations sought to eliminate the racial bias built into the nation's basic immigration law. Critics of the immigration code contended its discrimination against southern and eastern Europeans, Africans, and Asians contradicted U.S. ideals; undermined America's leadership of the FREE WORLD; and blocked the development of good relations with the new nations of Africa and Asia.

In July 1963 President JOHN F. KENNEDY called for the liberalization of U.S. immigration policy. President LYNDON B. JOHNSON continued the reform drive. After extensive congressional hearings, he signed the Immigration Act of 1965 at a ceremony October 3 at the Statue of Liberty. The Hart-Celler Act, named after sponsors Senator Phillip A. Hart (D-MI) and Representative Emanuel Celler (D-NY), abolished all immigration quotas based on race or ethnic type. It eliminated the designation in the 1952 act of an ASIA-PACIFIC TRIANGLE and provided for equal immigration access regardless of nationality.

The annual limit on immigration visas was raised to 290,000. Of this total, 170,000 were allocated to the Eastern Hemisphere. No more than 20,000 immigrants could come from the same country in a given year. The 1952 act had given preference to immigrants with needed professional skills. The new law shifted the emphasis to family reunification and the granting of visas to immediate relatives of citizens and resident aliens. Departing from the tradition of providing open access to other Western Hemisphere countries, the 1965 measure placed an overall quota of 120,000 on immigration from these nations. The yearly total of 20,000 visas per country and the preference system were extended to the Western Hemisphere in the WESTERN HEMISPHERE ACT (1976). The 1965 statute also provided for the acceptance of refugees. U.S. refugee policy was revised in the REFUGEE ACT OF 1980 while immigration law was next updated in the IMMIGRATION REFORM AND CONTROL ACT (1986).

IMMIGRATION ACT OF 1990 Federal legislation revising and updating U.S. immigration law. The IMMIGRATION REFORM AND CONTROL ACT (1986) had capped a half-decade of congressional debate over transforming the nation's statutes on illegal immigration. The act granted amnesty to millions of illegal aliens and imposed penalties on employers hiring undocumented workers. Congress then set out to overhaul the country's legal-immigration laws, last comprehensively revised under the IMMIGRATION ACT of 1965. The 1965 legislation had made family reunification the priority consideration in granting immigrant visas to the United States. This had resulted, by the 1980s, in almost 90 percent of all new immigrants coming from Latin America and Asia. The situation generated calls for greater "diversity" and a more flexible system that would allocate more immigrant visas to other nations. The Immigration Act of 1990, signed into law by President GEORGE BUSH on November 29, increased annual legal immigration from roughly 500,000 to about 700,000 people. While family reunification remained the priority, a

new category of "diversity" visas was created for nationals from countries, mostly European, that had sent few immigrants under the 1965 law. The act also expanded the number and types of work visas; stipulated that aliens not be barred because of their political beliefs; and established a national commmission on immigration reform to report by September 30, 1994.

IMMIGRATION AND NATIONALITY ACT OF 1952 Comprehensive revision of U.S. immigration and naturalization laws. In 1947 the Senate Judiciary Committee undertook a major investigation of U.S. immigration policy. Following its three-year study the committee, under the leadership of Senator Patrick A. McCarran (D-NV), drafted a broad overhaul of U.S. immigration law. After extensive debate, the Immigration and Nationality Act of 1952 was enacted on June 27 over President HARRY S. TRUMAN's veto.

Known as the McCarran-Walter Act, after sponsors McCarran and Representative Francis E. Walter (D-PA), the legislation consolidated all previous immigration and naturalization measures into a single statute. The law retained the national origins system of quotas established by the IMMIGRATION ACT OF 1924. The method of calculating the quotas intentionally favored immigration from northwestern Europe; under the 1952 act these countries continued to account for more than four-fifths of the roughly 150,000 immigration visas allocated annually. The statute, by establishing quota preferences for those with professional skills needed in America, facilitated the "brain drain" of talented newcomers to the United States in the postwar years. The act removed any gender-based distinctions and granted the husbands of American citizens the same immigration rights as alien wives.

By 1952 there was broad consensus among U.S. policymakers that existing bans on Asian immigration were undermining efforts to counteract Communist anti-American propaganda in the region. The country's exclusionary immigration code exposed the United States to charges that it viewed its Asian allies as inferior. While the new law eliminated racial bars on immigration and naturalization, Asians still did not receive equal consideration. An Asia-Pacific Triangle replaced the ASIATIC BARRED ZONE created by the IMMIGRATION ACT OF 1917.

The triangle included the area bounded by Pakistan, Japan, and the Pacific islands north of New Zealand. Most countries in the region received a minimum annual immigration quota of 100. Japan's allocation was 185 and China retained its quota of 105.

Debate on the 1952 act occurred against a backdrop of widespread concern over Communist infiltration of the United States. The 1950 INTERNAL SECURITY ACT had blocked the immigration of members of totalitarian organizations, primarily Communist and Fascist. The 1952 law extended and strengthened screening procedures to prevent the entrance of subversives and security risks.

In his veto message, Truman had condemned the McCarran measure's continued discrimination against immigrants from southern and eastern Europe, characterizing the measure as an affront to NATO allies Italy, Greece, and Turkey. He also criticized its anti-Asian bias and the excessive severity of its security provisions. Over the next decade opposition to ethnic quotas mounted and the national origins system was terminated by the IMMIGRATION ACT OF 1965.

IMMIGRATION POLICY Efforts to guide and control immigration to America often have involved U.S. relations with other countries and influenced the conduct of the nation's foreign affairs. Historians generally divide U.S. immigration policy into four distinct periods: an era of open immigration from 1776 to 1874; an era of increasing federal regulation of immigration from 1875 to 1916; an era of restriction between 1917 and 1964; and an era of liberalization from 1965 to the present.

The United States had a basic policy of free or open immigration throughout its first century. The AMERICAN REVOLUTION contributed to the sense of a unique national identity emerging in the United States. To the young republic's leaders, America and the New World were different from and better than the Old World of Europe. The idea of America as a sanctuary or asylum for the world's oppressed became a central part of the nation's self-image.

Immigrants were needed to settle the frontier and provide laborers for the rapid growth brought by the industrial revolution. Early measures underscored American support for immigration. The Northwest Ordinance (1787) contained land provisions and other measures intended to attract foreigners to the NORTHWEST TERRITORY. The CONSTITUTION, which became effective in 1789, made every elective office but the presidency available to naturalized citizens. Reflecting receptiveness toward immigrants, the NATURALIZATION ACT OF 1790 set the residency requirement for citizenship at two years. Federal land allocations in the 19th century, most notably the Homestead Act (1862), continued to communicate American openness to immigration. The only exceptions to this policy were the ALIEN AND SEDITION ACTS (1798), which imposed stringent controls on aliens during the QUASI-WAR (1798–1800) with France.

The federal government had little direct involvement in the supervision or control of immigration during the first 100 years of the republic. Congress passed a series of maritime laws for ships bringing passengers to American ports, but state governments exercised broad authority over the regulations and administration of immigration. Many states had representatives in Europe to recruit prospective settlers. Organized opposition to the continuing immigration emerged in the wake of the massive Irish and German influx of the 1840s. The nativist KNOW-NOTHING MOVEMENT rose dramatically in the mid-1850s, but quickly receded as the nation's attention turned to the sectional struggle over slavery.

The large number of new immigrants, the need for national immigration procedures, and the relationship of immigration policy to the nation's foreign relations brought greater federal involvement after the Civil War. Regulation by Congress began with the IMMIGRATION ACT OF 1875. Over the next 40 years the federal government imposed progressively tighter rules on the entrance of immigrants. In 1876 the U.S. Supreme Court ruled in HENDERSON V. MAYOR OF NEW YORK that state laws governing immigration were unconstitutional. Congress accepted broad responsibility over immigration in the IMMIGRATION ACT OF 1882. The CHINESE EXCLUSION ACT, passed the same year amid growing opposition on the West Coast to the immigration of Chinese laborers, for the first time blocked the admission of a specific ethnic group.

The great wave of immigrants from southern and eastern Europe beginning in the 1890s sparked increasing debate over stricter limits on new arrivals. Nativist organizations such as the IMMIGRATION RESTRICTION LEAGUE popularized racist theories about the alleged inferiority of the "new" immigrants and pressed for federal legislation to halt their admission. In 1911 the DILLINGHAM COMMISSION submitted its influential report on national immigration policy, calling for restraints on the influx from Europe. Immigration from Asia also remained an issue. Under U.S. pressure, the Japanese government consented in the GENTLEMEN'S AGREEMENT (1907–1908) to prevent the emigration of its laborers to America.

The IMMIGRATION ACT OF 1917 initiated a highly restrictive phase in U.S. immigration policy. The end of the basic American tradition of open borders came amid concerns over the domestic economy and job competition, the continuing transatlantic immigration, and the possible influx of huge numbers of WORLD WAR I refugees from Europe. The 1917 act imposed a literacy test on prospective immigrants, meant to impede less-educated southern and eastern Europeans, and prohibited immigration from a designated ASIATIC BARRED ZONE, which embraced most of Asia. It was followed by the IMMIGRATION ACT OF 1921, which first introduced ethnic quotas on immigration. The IMMIGRATION ACT OF 1924 made the quotas permanent and effectively ended all immigration from Asia. The new limits dramatically reduced immigration from all areas but the north of Europe.

The 1924 act provided the basic framework of U.S. immigration policy over the next four decades. In 1940, on the eve of American entry into WORLD WAR II, Congress voted the ALIEN REGISTRATION ACT as a precaution against foreign espionage. In the war's immediate aftermath, the United States and its allies confronted the problem of millions of refugees in Europe. At the end of 1945, President HARRY S. TRUMAN issued a DIRECTIVE ON DISPLACED PERSONS, authorizing large numbers of refugees to come to America. As COLD WAR tensions mounted in the postwar years, support for refugees fleeing from behind the IRON CURTAIN became an important part of America's anti-Communist foreign policy. Major legislative initiatives included the DISPLACED PERSONS ACT (1948) and the REFUGEE RELIEF ACT (1953).

Measures to prevent the immigration of Communists were included in the 1950 INTERNAL SECURITY ACT. Responding to arguments that discriminatory immigration laws undermined American leadership of the FREE WORLD, Congress enacted a comprehensive update of the nation's immigration code. The IMMIGRATION AND NATIONALITY ACT OF 1952 eliminated all racial barriers to citizenship, but retained the system of ethnic immigration quotas. The movement toward a more open immigration policy continued with the FAIR SHARE REFUGEE ACT (1960) and the MIGRATION AND REFUGEE ASSISTANCE ACT (1962).

Recognition that America's still-restrictive immigration policies hindered the development of good relations with the new postcolonial nations of Africa and Asia helped ensure passage of the IMMIGRATION ACT OF 1965. The 1965 law, which for the first time limited immigration from the Western Hemisphere, removed all ethnic quotas and made family reunification the priority in the allocation of immigrant visas. In following years attention turned to immigration from Latin America. The problem of illegal immigration, primarily from Mexico, figured prominently in the IMMIGRATION REFORM AND CONTROL ACT (1986). This measure granted amnesty to undocumented aliens already in the country. To discourage the further unlawful entry of aliens, the act imposed sanctions on employers hiring illegal workers.

The liberalization of American immigration policy extended to refugee affairs. In the late 1970s, the United States accepted hundreds of thousands of Indochinese BOAT PEOPLE. The REFUGEE ACT OF 1980 provided a permanent legislative apparatus for admitting those fleeing persecution. The same year 130,000 Cuban refugees came to Florida in the MARIEL BOATLIFT. The 1974 JACKSON-VANIK AMENDMENT linked U.S. trade with the USSR to the freedom of Soviet Jews to emigrate. The IMMIGRATION ACT of 1990 increased annual immigration quotas and created a national commission to review U.S. immigration policy.

IMMIGRATION REFORM AND CONTROL ACT (1986) Major reform of U.S. immigration law, representing the first substantive change in U.S. immigration policy since the IMMIGRATION ACT OF 1965. The 1965 act for the first time placed quotas on immigration from Western Hemisphere nations. Throughout the 1970s, illegal immigration from Latin America generally and Mexico in particular increased substantially. By the end of the decade, U.S. census officials estimated there were between three and six million illegal aliens in the country. The SELECT COMMISSION ON IMMIGRATION AND REFUGEE POLICY, created by Congress in early 1981 to study immigration issues, recommended a two-part strategy to deal with illegal immigration. First, the panel supported an amnesty for illegal aliens already in the United States as the only reasonable resolution to the fact of their presence. Second, it advocated penalties on employers hiring undocumented workers as necessary to halt the continuing influx of new illegal aliens. The commission contended that many aliens, without possibility of employment, would have no incentive to enter the country illegally.

Senator Alan K. Simpson (R-WY) and Representative Romano L. Mazzoli (D-KY) introduced legislation in 1981 to revise U.S. immigration law that incorporated the Select Commission's proposals. None of several Simpson-Mazzoli bills submitted over the next five years gained congressional approval. Finally, in 1986, Simpson and Representative Peter W. Rodino, Jr. (D-NJ), sponsored a compromise measure, the Simpson-Rodino Act, that became law on November 6. The Immigration Reform and Control Act of 1986 granted amnesty to illegal aliens in the United States before January 1, 1982; imposed legal sanctions on employers who hired undocumented workers; and tightened procedures for the enforcement of immigration laws. Recognizing the importance of Mexican workers to U.S. agriculture, the act provided for the admission of temporary or seasonal farm laborers. U.S. immigration law was amended further by the IMMIGRATION ACT OF 1990.

IMMIGRATION RESTRICTION LEAGUE Nativist organization active in the first decades of the 20th century. The Immigration Restriction League was formed in 1894 by a group of young Boston patricians who argued open immigration was harming American society. The league remained at the forefront of the restrictionist movement over the next 30 years. Its membership included Senator HENRY CABOT LODGE, SR. (R-MA), who often led the fight in Congress for stricter immigration controls.

Members drew a distinction between "old" and "new" immigrants. Old immigrants were the northern Europeans who founded and built America. In contrast, the league claimed, the growing numbers of new immigrants from southern and eastern Europe were less intelligent and energetic and therefore less deserving or capable of assimilation. Sympathetic academics and intellectuals seized on the emerging fields of anthropology and genetics to construct supporting theories on the racial inferiority of the more recent arrivals.

The league campaigned for a literacy test as a mechanism to exclude unfit and undesirable aliens. Although literacy itself was not an ethnic screen, it generally was understood such a test would limit the immigration of less-educated southern and eastern Europeans. Measures to impose a reading requirement on immigrants received presidential vetoes in 1897, 1913, and 1915. Congress finally enacted a literacy test over President WOODROW WILSON's veto in the IMMIGRATION ACT OF 1917. The league's underlying goal of directly limiting the entrance of new immigrants was realized in the IMMIGRATION ACT OF 1921.

IMPERIALISM Concept in international relations of the forcible extension by a nation of its control over foreign areas and their peoples. The term is often used more broadly to describe any significant extension of a nation's influence and power over other societies through such means as economic exploitation and cultural domination. While America did not pursue an imperialist foreign policy until the time of the SPANISH-AMERICAN WAR (1898), the nation's experience with imperialism dated to the first half of the 19th century. Historians have noted that the continental expansion of the United States represented a form of imperialism in that it entailed the displacement and subjugation of American Indian tribes. The pre–Civil War expansionist doctrine of America's MANIFEST DESTINY became the justifying credo for several early imperialist ventures: the abortive "ALL-OF-MEXICO" MOVEMENT during the MEXICAN WAR (1846–1848), the schemes in the mid-1800s to acquire Spanish colony Cuba, and FILI-

BUSTERING expeditions launched against Latin America. The efforts by Secretary of State WILLIAM H. SEWARD in the immediate post–Civil War years to obtain U.S. possessions in the Caribbean, though unsuccessful, presaged a more imperialist form of national expansion. An attempt in 1870 by President ULYSSES S. GRANT to annex the Dominican Republic was defeated in the Senate, where critics of the initiative noted the break with precedent that the acquisition of already settled foreign territory would represent. Opponents of annexation pointed out the violation of the American commitment to the right of self-government that would occur should the nation chose to rule the Dominican Republic as a colony. The Senate's consideration of Grant's DOMINICAN REPUBLIC ANNEXATION INITIATIVE previewed the later debates on imperialist expansion and revealed a strong anti-imperialist sentiment.

An American imperialism took shape toward the end of the century in the doctrine of expansionism known as NEW MANIFEST DESTINY, which was anchored in a vigorous nationalism, soaring U.S. economic productivity and industrial wealth, and racist theorizing. Many of its adherents embraced the theories of Social Darwinism, which applied British naturalist Charles Darwin's ideas of "natural selection" and "survival of the fittest" to human societies and nations. Social Darwinists contended that various races of people advanced at different rates according to their evolutionary fitness. Social Darwinist thinking underpinned the New Manifest Destiny's assertion of Anglo-Saxon superiority. The United States was said to owe its greatness to its Anglo-Saxon heritage and was presumed to bear an obligation to assume the "white man's burden" of carrying progress to so-called backward areas and civilizing "inferior" peoples.

The connection drawn in the 1890s between expansion and naval power was central to the emerging American imperialism. Influential naval strategist ALFRED THAYER MAHAN and other exponents of an imperialist foreign policy held that America's dynamic economic growth demanded new overseas markets, sources of raw materials, and investment opportunities. The United States, they contended, needed a large merchant marine protected by a great navy to compete commercially with the European powers, which were busy acquiring colonies in Africa, Asia, and among the islands of the Pacific. To support its expanded sea power, the argument continued, America would also need to acquire overseas strategic bases and colonies and construct an isthmian canal in Central America to ease naval and commercial movement between the Atlantic and Pacific oceans. Imperialist ideas were translated into action when a Cuban revolt against Spanish colonial rule embroiled the United States in a brief war with Spain in 1898. Under the TREATY OF PARIS ending the Spanish-American War, the victorious United States gained Spanish possessions Puerto Rico, GUAM, and the Philippine Islands. Cuba was placed under U.S. military occupation pending its transition to independence. In 1902 Cuba effectively became a self-governing U.S. protectorate under terms of the PLATT AMENDMENT (1901), which granted Washington a right of military intervention in the Caribbean island nation. Hawaii, deemed the strategic key to the Pacific, had been annexed by congressional resolution during the war.

The expansionist outcome of the Spanish-American conflict precipitated a national debate over imperialism, with the annexation of the Philippines occasioning the fiercest political battle. Anti-imperialists, whose position was championed by the ANTI-IMPERIALIST LEAGUE, argued that acquisition of the Pacific archipelago marked a break with historic American ISOLATIONISM and contradicted America's commitment to the ideals of self-rule and republican government. Imperialists defended the decision to annex on grounds that the Filipinos, judged unprepared to govern themselves, needed enlightened U.S. rule and that the island chain's proximity to China would facilitate American commercial penetration of what was expected to become a vast market in the future.

America's imperial experience in the Philippines began with the outbreak in 1899 of a revolt against U.S. rule by independence-seeking Filipino insurgents. The bloody PHILIPPINE INSURRECTION, finally crushed by American forces in 1902, ended the enthusiasm in the United States for colonialism. The extension of U.S. influence, rather than territorial aggrandizement, characterized American imperialism after 1900. In the early 20th century, this approach focused on the Caribbean region, where U.S. policy was concerned with safeguarding the strategically key PANAMA CANAL and preventing the expansion of European influence. The United States feared that the chronic fiscal and political instability of the Central American and Caribbean nations would invite European intervention. President THEODORE ROOSEVELT in 1904 proclaimed the ROOSEVELT COROLLARY to the MONROE DOCTRINE (1823), asserting preeminent U.S. influence in the Americas and investing the United States with a right of intercession in the Western Hemisphere to keep order and repel foreign interference. U.S. military interventions and the establishment of American financial protectorates in Cuba, Panama, the Dominican Republic, Haiti, and Nicaragua expanded American hegemony in the Caribbean up through WORLD WAR I. Washington installed U.S. customs collectorships in several Latin American countries, placing their government revenues under American control, and pursued a policy of DOLLAR DIPLOMACY to secure political and economic leverage.

After World War I U.S. imperialism entered a period of retrenchment. Growing anti-imperialism throughout Latin America in the 1920s led the United States to end its Caribbean military occupations. Under the GOOD NEIGHBOR POLICY of the 1930s, the United States dismantled its financial protectorates in Latin America and repudiated its long-standing claim to a right of intervention in the Western Hemisphere. In 1934 Congress passed the TYDINGS-MC-DUFFIE ACT putting the Philippines on course for full independence following a transitional period under a commonwealth status. The unequaled military and economic power with which the United States emerged from WORLD WAR II enabled it to exercise extraordinary influence over international affairs. The COLD WAR prompted America to forge political and military alliances in Europe, Asia, and Latin America and to undertake worldwide defense commitments. The Communist nations, led by the Soviet Union, contended throughout the postwar era that the stationing of U.S. military forces overseas, America's foreign aid program, its economic dominance, and U.S. military interventions constituted imperialism.

IMPRESSMENT British practice of forcibly mustering alleged British deserters serving on American merchant ships into the Royal navy. Often the impressed sailors were not British subjects but Americans. Impressment, viewed by the United States as an affront to its national honor, became a volatile issue in Anglo-American diplomacy between 1790 and 1815 and was a principal cause of troubled relations between the two countries. At war with France almost uninterruptedly for the quarter-century after 1790, Great Britain insisted upon its right as a belligerent to search neutral vessels. Invoking this controversial and disputed right, the British navy regularly stopped and boarded neutral American trade ships at sea and removed sailors deemed to be British. Great Britain defended the practice as a basic national prerogative indispensable to sustaining its superior sea power in the conflict with the French.

British seamen, Royal navy deserters among them, signed on with U.S. merchant ships in increasing numbers at the end of the 19th century, many intending to become American citizens. Britain's strict adherence to the doctrine of inalienable allegiance, meaning that British subjects by birth were British subjects for life, clashed irreconcilably with America's insistence on the right of expatriation, or the right of individuals to change their national allegiance. London refused to recognize naturalized American citizenship as immunity from impressment. Determination of the nationality of suspected seamen was left to the judgment of Royal naval officers, whose indiscriminate methods often resulted i the seizure and forced enlistment of nativ born Americans. An estimated nine of t men impressed from American ships ev tually were found not to be British s jects. When U.S. citizenship could proved, usually at the American gov ment's initiative, the British returne American-born sailors without indemn

By 1796 the United States was is citizenship certificates to its seamen a tection against forced enlistment. Easily lost or sold, the certificates fell into widespread abuse and the British government rejected their validity. Despite protracted U.S. protest over impressmemt, Britain refused to accept any limits on its right to engage in the practice, although it was careful never to insist upon a right to seize natural-born Americans. JAY'S TREATY (1794) and the abortive MONROE-PINKNEY TREATY (1806) failed to resolve the sensitive impressment issue. British abduction of four sailors from the American frigate *Chesapeake* boldly extended the reach of impressment to include U.S. Navy vessels. The CHESAPEAKE AFFAIR (1807) provoked American outrage and helped precipitate U.S. economic retaliation in the form of the EMBARGO ACT (1807). Impressment was a leading cause of the WAR OF 1812. The British largely abandoned the practice after 1815.

INCIDENTS AT SEA AGREEMENT (1972) U.S.-Soviet agreement to avoid incidents at sea involving their armed forces. The Agreement on the Prevention of Incidents On and Over the High Seas was signed May 25, 1972, during the 1972 MOSCOW SUMMIT. It reflected the growing DETENTE between he COLD WAR adversaries. The United ates and Soviet Union agreed to notify 'h other of maneuvers on the high seas posed dangers for navigation, to keep ships and aircraft a safe distance from ther, and to bar their military forces from staging simulated attacks 'he other side's ships and aircraft.

AFFAIRS Relations with Native formed an important aspect of affairs until the late 19th cen-he time of its independence, ates was bordered by Indian 'he steadily advancing Ameri-S. westward territorial ex-1 Indian-white contacts 1800s. The U.S. govern-cessions from the tribes 'ted surrender of Indian formal treaties. The a major cause of war-dian affairs thus in-le ongoing conflicts 's of further fight-lso adamantly op-military contacts

with the Indian nations. In its first half-century, the United States repeatedly protested British and Spanish involvement in Indian resistance to U.S. expansion.

The United States sought allies among the Indian nations in its struggle for independence against Great Britain. The Continental Congress in July 1775 took steps toward creation of a national Indian policy when it assumed control of Indian affairs and commissioned emissaries to negotiate with the tribes for their support in the AMERICAN REVOLUTION. In 1778 the U.S. government completed its first treaty with an Indian nation, a friendship agreement with the Delaware in Ohio. Despite U.S. efforts to forestall Anglo-Indian alliances, the Iroquois in New York and Canada, numbers of other Ohio tribes, and some Indians in the Southeast sided with the British.

The initial aim of U.S. Indian policy after the American Revolution was land acquisition. In victory, America claimed title to all territory west to the Mississippi River. Federal policy assumed that the Indian tribes which joined the British in the war had forfeited their right to possession of lands within the United States. The new nation exacted major INDIAN LAND CESSIONS in the OLD NORTHWEST through treaties dictated at Fort Stanwix in 1784 and Fort McIntosh in 1785 and in North Carolina and Tennessee through the TREATY OF HOPEWELL (1785). In 1789, in the TREATIES OF FORT HARMAR, the federal government returned to the colonial practice of acquiring Indian areas by purchase rather than simply seizing them through right of conquest.

In the 1780s the general principle emerged under the ARTICLES OF CONFEDERATION that the central government should regulate Indian affairs and oversee Indian trade. When states such as New York and Georgia disregarded national authority and continued to conduct their own relations with the Indians, Congress reasserted its primacy over Indian matters in the ORDINANCE FOR THE REGULATION OF INDIAN AFFAIRS (1786) and the Northwest Ordinance (1787). Commerce and treaty-making powers granted by the CONSTITUTION and amplified in a series of laws enacted in 1789 established clear federal control over Indian affairs. Some states continued to defy U.S. authority until the Supreme Court affirmed exclusive federal jurisdiction over the Indians in WORCESTER V. GEORGIA (1832). In a related case decided a year earlier, CHEROKEE NATION V. GEORGIA, the Court ruled that the Indian tribes were not foreign nations, but rather domestic dependent nations under the sovereignty and protection of the United States.

In the 1790s Congress passed the TRADE AND INTERCOURSE ACTS, a series of measures to govern Indian relations, halt abuses of the tribes by traders, and end unlawful white settlement on Indian lands. The federal government in 1795 also set up its own general trade arrangement with the Indian nations when it established the FACTORY SYSTEM, a network of U.S. trading posts intended in part to stop British and Spanish commercial contacts and influence among the tribes. Elimination of the factory system in 1822 briefly left the United States without a central agency to manage Indian relations until creation of the BUREAU OF INDIAN AFFAIRS in 1824.

Mounting Indian resistance in the Old Northwest to the advance of white settlement led to war in the early 1790s between the United States and a confederation of Ohio tribes supported by Great Britain. U.S. forces defeated the Indians at the BATTLE OF FALLEN TIMBERS (1794) in Ohio. In the WAR OF 1812, the United States broke British-allied Indian resistance under Shawnee Chief TECUMSEH in the Indiana Territory, opening the NORTHWEST TERRITORY to greatly expanded American settlement after 1815. The CREEK WAR (1813—1814) also erupted during the hostilities with Great Britain. U.S. victory over the pro-British Creek Nation weakened Indian opposition in the Southeast to white expansion into the Mississippi Valley.

Following the War of 1812, the U.S. government continued to deal with the Indian tribes as separate nations with whom formal treaties were negotiated. The United States worked to replace British trade and influence with the tribes in the Old Northwest. The War Department established American forts along the Great Lakes and northern U.S. border to prevent renewed British agitation of the Indians against U.S. expansionist interests and to halt incursions by British traders into American territory. Victory of federal forces over the Florida Indians in the first of the SEMINOLE WARS (1817–1818) had important ramifica-

tions for U.S.-Spanish diplomacy. The Seminole defeat persuaded Spain to cede Florida to the United States in the ADAMS-ONIS TREATY (1819).

The federal INDIAN REMOVAL POLICY arranged for resettlement after 1835 of southeastern Indians to the INDIAN TERRITORY set aside west of the Mississippi River. The policy established the boundary of a permanent INDIAN COUNTRY and guaranteed U.S. protection of tribal areas against white encroachment. The hoped-for permanent Indian frontier collapsed under pressures brought by U.S. territorial acquisitions in the 1840s. The TEXAS ANNEXATION (1845), resolution of the boundary dispute with Great Britain known as the OREGON QUESTION (1846), and the MEXICAN CESSION (1848) provided vast new areas for settlement and invited large-scale white migration through Indian Country to the Southwest, California, and the Pacific Northwest. The rapid push of whites into these areas led to hostilities with the Indians there. Warfare broke out in Texas, on the central Plains, and in the Oregon and Washington territories in the decade before the Civil War.

By the early 1860s the main outlines of the Indian policy the United States would pursue through the late 19th century had been drawn: secure cessions of Indian lands and locate the tribes on reservations, away from both white settlements and the main overland routes of westward migration. The reservation system was vigorously opposed by the Indians of the Great Plains and the Southwest. Between 1860 and 1890, the United States fought the SIOUX WARS and the APACHE WARS to subjugate the widespread Indian resistance. The costly Sioux conflicts led the U.S. government in the late 1860s to adopt the PEACE POLICY, which sought a negotiated settlement with the Plains Indians as an alternative to the annihilation policy desired by some in the War Department.

The end of Indian warfare and placement of the tribes on reservations by the mid-1880s marked the final transition of Indian relations from a foreign to a domestic policy concern. In 1871 Congress had ended the practice of negotiating treaties with the Indians as though they were independent powers. The General Allotment Act in 1887 provided for the breakup of the Indian tribes. The Indian Reorganization Act restored tribal organizations in 1934.

INDIAN COUNTRY Expression used generally throughout American history to designate territory to which Indian claims had not been ceded to the United States. These areas fell under federal authority and protection and were off limits to settlers and unlicensed traders. As so-called domestic dependent nations, a legal status defined by Chief Justice JOHN MARSHALL in the landmark CHEROKEE NATION V. GEORGIA (1831) case, Indian tribes were guaranteed a continued right to occupy and use lands within Indian Country. While the Indian nations enjoyed internal political independence, the United States asserted territorial sovereignty and barred tribes from ceding property to any person or agent other than the federal government. After 1787, federal acquisition of lands in Indian Country required compensation to the Indian nations and their nominal consent.

The federal INDIAN REMOVAL POLICY established a permanent Indian frontier and defined Indian Country as the western area reserved to the tribes and closed to white settlement. By 1840 a definite Indian Country had been created, extending roughly from the Mississippi River to the U.S. western boundary and reaching from Texas to Canada. The more specific term INDIAN TERRITORY referred to the region set aside for resettlement of the Five Civilized Tribes of the Southeast. The relentless advance of white settlement led to INDIAN LAND CESSIONS that effectively eliminated Indian Country by the end of the 19th century.

INDIAN LAND CESSIONS Territorial transfers from the Indian nations to the United States, wherein the Indians surrendered their limited title to tribal lands through formal treaties with the federal government. After winning its independence from Great Britain, the United States claimed title by so-called right of conquest to all territory from the edge of colonial settlement west to the Mississippi River. A congressional proclamation in September 1783 prohibited any Indian land cessions except those made to the federal government with Congress's authorization. The ORDINANCE FOR THE REGULATION OF INDIAN AFFAIRS (1786) and the Northwest Ordinance (1787) outlined similar constraints and

were intended to thwart individuals, states, and European powers looking to appropriate Indian lands.

By the time the CONSTITUTION was adopted in 1789, federal policy acknowledged that the Indians had a right to the continued occupancy and use of tribal lands. This right could be surrendered only by their consent, as expressed in treaties negotiated between federally appointed U.S. commissioners and Indian leaders, signed by both sides, and ratified by the U.S. Senate. In practice, though, the requirement for Indian consent to land cessions was little more than a formality. Throughout the 19th century, Indian nations on the constantly retreating frontier were forced to relinquish their territories as the pressure of advancing white settlement and the federal Indian removal program overpowered their resistance to loss of their lands.

See also INDIAN COUNTRY, INDIAN TERRITORY.

INDIAN PEACE COMMISSION Special panel appointed by the U.S. Congress in July 1867 to determine the reasons for the outbreak of Indian warfare on the Great Plains in the mid-1860s. Members included the Commissioner of Indian Affairs, senior military officers, and other federal officials. By 1867, organized Indian resistance had closed the Bozeman Trail, shutting off white transit across the northern Plains and impeding U.S. westward expansion. The law creating the commission authorized it to negotiate an end to the costly hostilities with the Plains Indians and to persuade the tribes to settle on reservations.

The commission reported that white mistreatment of the tribes was the major cause of Indian grievances and urged the federal government to pursue a responsible and just PEACE POLICY toward the Indians. The panel concluded the Medicine Lodge Creek Treaty (1867) that brought the CHEYENNE AND ARAPAHO WAR to a close and an agreement at Fort Laramie in 1868 that temporarily halted the SIOUX WARS. The commission was replaced by a permanent Board of Indian Commissioners in 1869.

INDIAN REMOVAL ACT (1830) Widely debated federal legislation that sanctioned the INDIAN REMOVAL POLICY advocated by President ANDREW JACKSON. Enacted May 28,

1830, it cleared the way for negotiation of removal treaties with the southeast Indian tribes. The measure authorized the American president to designate and set aside areas west of the Mississippi River for Indian resettlement. These lands would then be exchanged for Indian territories in the Southeast. Finally, the legislation arranged for the removal of the Southeast tribes to the western districts after 1835. The federal government pledged to absorb the removal costs and to protect the resettled Indians and their western territory from white encroachment. Some 60,000 Indians were transferred beyond the Mississippi River during the 1830s as a consequence of the Indian Removal Act.

INDIAN REMOVAL POLICY Centerpiece of federal Indian policy between 1825 and 1850. Under the policy, the U.S. government transferred Indian tribes located east of the Mississippi River to a designated INDIAN TERRITORY in the West. The long-debated removal program was the federal response to a worsening crisis in INDIAN AFFAIRS in the 1820s. The advance of white settlement had sparked sporadic U.S.-Indian warfare on the frontier since the end of the AMERICAN REVOLUTION. Relations were further strained as land-hungry states and settlers sought to encroach on the remaining Indian areas in the eastern United States.

President ANDREW JACKSON strongly advocated a national removal policy. Congress complied in 1830 in the INDIAN REMOVAL ACT, authorizing the president to set up areas west of the Mississippi and to exchange these districts for Indian-held lands in the East. The law arranged for compensation to the tribes, covered the costs of feeding and transporting the Indians during their removal, and guaranteed their protection following resettlement. Between 1830 and mid-century, the United States negotiated the many separate INDIAN TREATIES that secured the permission and land cessions needed to carry out the removal program.

The Five Civilized Tribes of the Southeast put up strong resistance to the policy. In the late 1830s federal forces battled hostile Creek and Seminole Indians who fought resettlement and the U.S. Army escorted the Cherokees on their forced march in 1838 from Georgia to Oklahoma,

the so-called Trail of Tears. By 1850 the East effectively was cleared of the tribes and the period of Indian removal completed.

INDIAN TERRITORY Region designated for the forced resettlement of Indian tribes in the West. Indian Territory referred generally to the vast unsettled area of the LOUISIANA PURCHASE (1803) considered Indian lands. The term most often was applied to the region, originally comprising most of present-day Oklahoma, Kansas, and Nebraska, set aside in 1834 for Indian resettlement. Key 1830s legislation, notably the INDIAN REMOVAL ACT (1830) and the TRADE AND INTERCOURSE ACT (1834), implemented the federal government's policy of removing the Five Civilized Tribes (Cherokee, Chickasaw, Choctaw, Creek, and Seminole) from the Southeast to the designated western region. The Kansas-Nebraska Act (1854) reduced the Indian Territory to an area covering what is now Oklahoma. Through treaties concluded in the mid-1860s the Five Civilized Tribes ceded the western part of this region to the United States as a home for other tribes affected by resettlement. But under pressure of continued westward expansion, the U.S. government opened this ceded area to white settlement in 1889 and the next year it was organized as the Oklahoma Territory. In 1907 what remained of the Indian Territory was absorbed with the Oklahoma Territory into the new state of Oklahoma.

See also INDIAN COUNTRY, INDIAN LAND CESSIONS, MAP 1.

INDIAN TREATIES Treaties between the United States and American Indian tribes, some 370 of which were formally ratified before Congress terminated treaty-making with the Indians in 1871. From its inception, the U.S. government continued the practice established by Great Britain in the colonial period of negotiating formal diplomatic agreements with the Indian nations. These treaties held the same status and force as treaties with foreign nations. Historically, their principal purpose was to arrange for INDIAN LAND CESSIONS to the United States. Treaties also regulated trade with the tribes, established terms of peace following U.S.-Indian wars, and arranged for the federally sanctioned Indian removal and resettlement in the West starting in the 1830s. Actual negotiations were conducted by special U.S. commissioners acting on the president's behalf. These envoys usually were officials of the BUREAU OF INDIAN AFFAIRS, which was located within the War Department until 1849, when Congress transferred it to the new Department of the Interior.

Development of a national Indian policy after the AMERICAN REVOLUTION initially was hindered as states continued to negotiate independently with tribes within their borders. The CONSTITUTION, adopted in 1789, established federal authority over INDIAN AFFAIRS by granting the president the exclusive power to make treaties with the Senate's advice and consent and by vesting Congress with the power to regulate Indian commerce. The early postwar treaties were based on the premise that Indian territories belonged to the United States and formed part of its national domain. The U.S. sovereignty claim was based on a purported right of conquest. The United States had defeated the British and their Indian allies in the revolution; Great Britain had surrendered its territorial stake in America through the TREATY OF PARIS (1783); the Indian tribes, by supporting the British, had forfeited their land possession rights within U.S. limits. In a shift after 1787, the U.S. government began to reimburse Indian tribes for land cessions. Legislation in 1871 ended the federal practice of negotiating treaties with tribes as though they were independent powers. Importantly, the law did not abrogate existing Indian treaties. Thereafter, the United States made simple agreements with the tribes that required the approval of both chambers of Congress.

INDOCHINA MIGRATION AND REFUGEE ASSISTANCE ACT (1975) Temporary measure passed at the end of the VIETNAM WAR that authorized the admission of Indochinese refugees to the United States. In April 1975, as the Saigon government was collapsing in the face of a North Vietnamese military offensive, the Ford administration established an interagency task force to direct the evacuation of South Vietnamese whose lives would be endangered by the pending Communist takeover. Rescue efforts ended with the fall of Saigon on April 30. Approximately 65,000 former U.S. employees and other "high risk" South Vietnamese were helped to flee while an equal number made their own way to refugee

camps throughout Southeast Asia. There was broad support in Congress for quick action on behalf of the nation's former allies and on May 23 President GERALD R. FORD signed emergency legislation to aid their resettlement. The Indochina Migration and Refugee Assistance Act expanded the legal definition of refugee to include those fleeing Communist Indochina out of fear of persecution and allocated funds for their relocation to the United States. This resettlement, expected to be a one-time initiative, was scheduled to expire in 1977. The steady increase in Indochinese BOAT PEOPLE led to additional interim measures until U.S. refugee provisions were permanently updated in the REFUGEE ACT OF 1980.

INDONESIA REBELLION (1958) Failed attempt by U.S.-supported elements in the Indonesian army to overthrow President Sukarno. Indonesia had been led by Sukarno since its independence from the Netherlands in 1949. In the mid-1950s, the Eisenhower administration grew increasingly disturbed by Sukarno's growing ties with the Indonesian Communist Party and the Communist governments in China and the Soviet Union. In 1957 Sukarno dissolved his nation's parliament and moved to assume dictatorial powers.

With tensions mounting in Indonesia, the United States responded positively to overtures from dissident army officers contemplating rebellion. The CENTRAL INTELLIGENCE AGENCY (CIA) began secret assistance to the rebels. A revolt against Sukarno's rule broke out on Sumatra, Celebes, and other islands in February 1958. Although supported by a clandestine air force of some six B-26 two-engine bombers, the insurgents were unable to overcome military forces loyal to Sukarno. After a CIA pilot, Allen L. Pope, was shot down and captured on May 18, 1958, the Eisenhower administration canceled further U.S. paramilitary aid rather than risk disclosure of the American role in the insurgency. Without U.S. backing the rebels were forced into guerrilla warfare and eventually were crushed. Sukarno remained in power until 1965, when he was replaced by General Suharto during the suppression of an attempted Communist takeover of the government.

INF TREATY See **INTERMEDIATE NUCLEAR FORCES TREATY**.

INHUMANE WEAPONS CONVENTION
(1980)   UNITED NATIONS-sponsored agreement limiting the use of so-called inhumane conventional, or non-nuclear, weapons. The pact, officially titled the Convention on Prohibitions or Restrictions of Use of Certain Conventional Weapons which may be deemed to be Excessively Injurious or have Indiscriminate Effects, was concluded October 10, 1980, by delegates from 72 nations, including the United States, meeting in Geneva, Switzerland. The treaty, which supplements the 1949 GENEVA CONVENTIONS and their 1977 protocols, went into effect in 1983. It has three protocols: Protocol I bans the use of weapons that scatter fragments, such as plastic or glass, which are undetectable by X-ray; Protocol II restricts the use of mines and booby-traps and forbids their employment against civilians; Protocol III prohibits the use of incendiary weapons against a civilian populace. The United States has not ratified and is not a party to the convention.

INMAN, BOBBY RAY (1931–   ) Navy officer and senior intelligence official. Inman graduated from the University of Texas in his native state in 1950. He joined the Navy, was commissioned an ensign in 1952, and advanced rapidly as an intelligence officer. From 1965 to 1967 he was assistant naval attache at the U.S. embassy in Sweden. In 1974 Inman was named director of Naval Intelligence. He became vice-director of the DEFENSE INTELLIGENCE AGENCY in 1976 and then director of the NATIONAL SECURITY AGENCY the following year. In 1981 President RONALD W. REAGAN selected him for promotion to four-star admiral and appointment as deputy director of the CENTRAL INTELLIGENCE AGENCY (CIA) under WILLIAM J. CASEY. Inman oversaw day-to-day agency operations, pressed for improved intelligence on international political and economic trends, and was an early advocate of better safeguards on U.S. TECHNOLOGY TRANSFER. He resigned from the CIA in 1982, reportedly in disagreement over Reagan administration COVERT ACTION and counterintelligence policies, and began a career in private high-technology research. In 1985 he headed a special State Department advisory panel on embassy security. The commission's study, known as the INMAN REPORT, served as the basis for

major 1986 legislation on U.S. overseas diplomatic missions. In 1990 President GEORGE BUSH appointed Inman to the PRESIDENT'S FOREIGN INTELLIGENCE ADVISORY BOARD.

INMAN REPORT (1985) State Department study of U.S. embassy security. Following the terrorist bombings in Lebanon of the U.S. Marine barracks in 1983 and American embassy annex in 1984, Secretary of State GEORGE P. SHULTZ formed a special departmental commission to review U.S. overseas security measures. Chaired by retired Admiral BOBBY R. INMAN, the Advisory Panel on Overseas Security issued its report June 25, 1985. The commission concluded that the continuing rise in international terrorism meant diplomats and other Americans serving abroad would face increasing threat of attack. The panel's report served as the basis for major legislation the next year. On August 27, 1986, President RONALD W. REAGAN signed the omnibus Diplomatic Security and Antiterrorism Act that incorporated key commission recommendations. The measure consolidated existing State Department security offices into a new Bureau of Diplomatic Security, created a Diplomatic Security Service, and funded a major embassy construction program to renovate or replace vulnerable U.S. diplomatic posts. The law also contained an array of initiatives related to terrorism, including financing for government antiterrorism research and victim compensation payments to U.S. hostages held in Iran from 1979 to 1981.

INQUIRY, THE See **FOURTEEN POINTS**.

INSTITUTE OF INTERNATIONAL FINANCE (IIF) Private international organization of bankers that provides its member commercial banks with analysis of the risks involved in lending to developing countries. The institute was established in Washington, D.C., in 1983 by some 37 Western and Japanese banks in response to the THIRD WORLD debt crisis that had rocked the international banking world the preceding year. The crisis had exposed extensive gaps in the information that banks possessed about countries to which they had loaned millions, or even billions, of dollars. In devising the IIF, the predominantly American, West European, and Japanese members looked to avert future debt crises by joining in a collective effort that would make international lending less risky. Since its inception the institute has served mainly as a data-collection service. It seeks to offer member lending institutions a more complete and pertinent profile of economic conditions in nations that are loan candidates. A related IIF objective is to prod borrowing countries to deal with their economic problems in a timely way, rather than delay and face the likely prospect of concerned creditor banks stepping in to impose stringent financial measures. The institute numbers roughly 150 members from some 40 countries. The IIF and its activities are financed through annual members' fees.

INSULAR CASES Series of cases after 1900 in which the U.S. Supreme Court defined the status under American law of outlying U.S. territorial possessions and dependencies. America's acquisition of Hawaii, Puerto Rico, GUAM, and the Philippines in the TREATY OF PARIS (1898) ending the SPANISH-AMERICAN WAR raised the issue of whether the constitutional rights and guarantees enjoyed by U.S. residents extended to the inhabitants of these new territories. The debate turned on a basic question: Did the CONSTITUTION follow the flag?

The first of the Insular Cases, referred to as such because of the islands involved, concerned the continued collection by U.S. port officials of duties on sugar imported from Puerto Rico after its annexation in 1898. Several Puerto Rican sugar companies challenged the tariffs on their exports to the United States. Contending the island was no longer a foreign colony, and noting that Puerto Rico had come under U.S. administration, the sugar owners insisted they were entitled to the full guarantees of American law. By a five-to-four vote on May 27, 1901, the Court in *De Lima* v. *Bidwell* decided that Puerto Rico had ceased to be a foreign country at the end of the Spanish-American War. The sugar tariffs thus had been illegally collected and were ordered lifted. The guiding precedent in the ruling was the court's decision in *Cross* v. *Harrison* (1853), in which it was determined that California had lost its status as a foreign province upon U.S. ratification of its acquisition from Mexico.

In *Downes* v. *Bidwell*, a closely related case decided the same day as *De Lima*, the Court addressed the Constitution's relationship to U.S. overseas possessions and their inhabitants. The specific issue at stake was the constitutionality of the FORAKER ACT (1900), a measure that imposed special import duties on Puerto Rican goods sold in the United States. When the New York port collected the tariff on an orange shipment, the Puerto Rican owners sued, claiming the Foraker law violated the Constitution's mandate that all duties be uniform throughout the United States. The justices by a five-to-four vote upheld the Foraker Act and its fees on Puerto Rican products.

In its majority opinion, the Court asserted that the Constitution did not automatically and instantly apply to the inhabitants of annexed territories; nor did it ipso facto grant them U.S. citizenship. Puerto Rico was no longer a foreign country, but it also was not a part of the United States. The justices held that it was up to Congress to decide where, when, and to what degree to extend the Constitution and its guarantees to American dependencies. In a concurring opinion, Justice Edward D. White for the first time set forth the principle of incorporation, which declared that the full range of constitutional rights applied only to those territories that had been formally incorporated into the United States either by treaty or act of Congress. In the Foraker Act Congress had granted Puerto Rico the status of an unincorporated territory. In dissent, Justice John M. Harlan questioned how Congress could exercise constitutional authority over U.S. acquisitions at the same time it withheld from these territories the complete rights and protections of the Constitution.

White's incorporation doctrine became the basis for rulings in three key subsequent cases. In *Hawaii* v. *Mankichi* (1903), the defendant appealed his manslaughter conviction under Hawaiian law on grounds that he was denied due process during his trial. The Supreme Court rejected the appeal, ruling that since Hawaii was not yet incorporated at the time of the trial, Fifth and Sixth Amendment due process protections had not extended to its residents. A majority of the justices applied the same principle in *Dorr* v. *United States* (1904), deciding against the constitutional appeal of a criminal conviction in the Philippines. In turn, the Court in the 1905 case of *Ras-*

mussen v. *United States* voided six-person jury trials in Alaska, determining that Alaska essentially had been incorporated into the United States and therefore was bound by American legal norms such as the 12-person jury. In a later case, *Balzac* v. *People of Puerto Rico* (1922), the Court ruled that the Constitution's fundamental guarantee against the deprivation of life, liberty, or property without due process of law was applicable to all U.S. possessions regardless of their incorporation status.

INTELLIGENCE COMMUNITY Term used since the 1960s to identify the various agencies and bureaus in the federal executive branch with a role in foreign intelligence. As designated in an executive order signed by President RONALD W. REAGAN in December 1981, the intelligence community encompasses the CENTRAL INTELLIGENCE AGENCY (CIA); the NATIONAL SECURITY AGENCY; the DEFENSE INTELLIGENCE AGENCY; the intelligence components of the armed services; offices involved in satellite reconnaissance; counterespionage elements of the FEDERAL BUREAU OF INVESTIGATION; the Bureau of Intelligence and Research in the DEPARTMENT OF STATE; and intelligence offices in the Department of Energy and the DEPARTMENT OF THE TREASURY. Also often referred to as part of the intelligence community is the DRUG ENFORCEMENT AGENCY, which gathers intelligence on the international narcotics trade. The director of central intelligence, who also serves as head of the CIA, is assisted by an independent intelligence community staff in coordinating and managing the foreign intelligence activities of community members.

INTER-AMERICAN CONFERENCE   See **PAN-AMERICAN CONFERENCE**.

INTER-AMERICAN DEFENSE BOARD See **ORGANIZATION OF AMERICAN STATES** in **APPENDIX E**.

INTER-AMERICAN DEVELOPMENT BANK (IDB) Regional lending institution created to foster economic and social development in capital-poor member countries in Latin America. The agreement chartering the IDB was signed in 1959 by 19 Latin American republics and the United States. The bank, with headquarters in Washington, D.C., formally began operations in October 1960. Membership grew in the last half of the 1970s to include nations outside the Western Hemisphere and now totals 43 countries (27 Western Hemisphere, 16 nonregional) from around the world.

The bank encourages private investment in regional development and provides technical expertise on planning economic growth. When private capital is not available on reasonable terms, the IDB extends financial assistance to spur investment. The agency uses its own regular resources—capital stock and a Fund for Special Operations, both contributed by member countries—together with funds raised on world capital markets through the issuance of securities and sale of bonds, to finance Latin American projects in agriculture, industry, energy production, urban renewal, and health and education. The Fund for Special Operations is used to make loans at lower interest rates with longer repayment periods to less-developed Latin American states. The IDB also administers funds entrusted to it by several donor countries—for example, the Social Progress Trust Fund, a $500 million endowment established by the United States in 1961 under the charter program of the ALLIANCE FOR PROGRESS. All IDB powers are vested in a board of governors, which consists of one representative and one alternate from each member country. A member exercises one vote for each share of the bank's capital stock it holds. The United States, as the largest shareholder, exercises about 34 percent of the total voting power.

INTER-AMERICAN FOUNDATION (IAF) U.S. government corporation created by Congress in 1969 that funds social and economic development in Latin America and the Caribbean. The foundation was established in response to congressional concerns that traditional U.S. development assistance programs were not reaching poor people in the region. The IAF supports local and private organizations involved in self-help projects that directly benefit the poor. The majority of foundation grants are awarded to grass-roots organizations, including agricultural cooperatives, community associations, and small urban enterprises. Other grants go to larger organizations that work with local groups, providing credit, technical assistance, and training. A small amount of funding each year is allocated for scholars researching poverty and local development in the Caribbean and Latin America. Funding of the IAF comes from congressional appropriations and the Social Progress Trust Fund of the INTER-AMERICAN DEVELOPMENT BANK. The corporation was created as an independent federal agency so that its operations would not be subject to short-term swings in U.S. foreign policy. Based in Virginia, the IAF is governed by a nine-member board of directors appointed by the president and confirmed by the Senate. By law six members are from private organizations and three from the government.

INTER-AMERICAN TREATY OF RECIPRO-CAL ASSISTANCE See **RIO TREATY**.

INTERCONTINENTAL BALLISTIC MISSILE (ICBM) Land-based, rocket-propelled missile capable of delivering a nuclear warhead over intercontinental distances, defined under the SALT I (1972) and SALT II (1979) arms control agreements as greater than 5500 kilometers (3300 miles). Developed in the 1950s by the United States and Soviet Union, the missiles enabled each superpower to strike the other's homeland. Most modern ICBMs are equipped with what is called a Multiple Independently Targetable Reentry Vehicle (MIRV), enabling them to carry several separate warheads. ICBMs formed one of the three components of the U.S. strategic nuclear TRIAD and constituted an even more important part of Soviet nuclear forces. The missiles were limited by the SALT I and SALT II accords. Amid domestic debate over the alleged vulnerability of the missiles to surprise attack, the Reagan administration in the 1980s moved to modernize U.S. ICBM forces through deployment of the controversial MX missile. U.S. and Soviet ICBM arsenals were curtailed by the 1991 START Treaty. Following the December 1991 demise of the USSR, Russia and the other erstwhile Soviet republics inheriting the former Soviet nuclear forces agreed to abide by the START limits.

INTERCOURSE ACTS See **TRADE AND INTERCOURSE ACTS**.

INTERGOVERNMENTAL PANEL ON CLIMATE CHANGE See **WORLD METEOROLOGICAL ORGANIZATION**.

INTERMEDIATE NUCLEAR FORCES TREATY (INF Treaty) (1987) U.S.-Soviet arms control agreement eliminating intermediate-range nuclear missiles. In 1977 the Soviet Union began to deploy new SS-20 medium-range missiles capable of striking targets throughout Western Europe. To Western leaders, the missiles, each armed with three highly accurate nuclear warheads, presented a dangerous new political as well as military challenge to the U.S.-European NATO security alliance. Lacking weapons that could match the Soviet missiles, NATO had to rely on the long-range U.S. nuclear arsenal to counteract the SS-20s. NATO planners regarded the SS-20 deployment as part of a Soviet attempt to undermine the political ties between the United States and its allies by playing on European fears that America would not risk its own security to counter a nuclear threat posed only to Europe.

In response to the SS-20 development, NATO foreign ministers on December 12, 1979, unanimously agreed to pursue a two-track policy. Under the so-called Dual-Track Decision, NATO would encourage East-West negotiations to limit intermediate-range nuclear missiles; pending the outcome of such talks, the Western alliance would deploy U.S. medium-range PERSHING II and CRUISE MISSILES in Europe by 1983 to counterbalance the Soviet SS-20s. By NATO's reasoning, deployment of the missiles, both capable of striking the USSR from launch sites in Western Europe, would prevent any decoupling of America's and Western Europe's security and deter Moscow from thinking it could strike Western Europe without inviting U.S. retaliation.

The Soviet invasion of Afghanistan in late December 1979 halted U.S.-Soviet arms control discussions. In 1981 the Reagan administration took office pledging to reverse what it viewed as a decline in U.S. military strength relative to the USSR. President RONALD W. REAGAN strongly supported the scheduled placement of U.S. intermediate-range nuclear missiles in Europe. The controversial missile deployment generated intense opposition from the NUCLEAR FREEZE movement and peace groups in Western Europe. Under mounting domestic and international pressure, the Reagan administration moved to resume arms control negotiations with Moscow. The Kremlin proved receptive, hoping to exploit Western antinuclear sentiment to stop the pending U.S. missile deployment. On November 30, 1981, the United States and Soviet Union opened talks in Geneva on limiting intermediate nuclear forces (INF). In a speech to the National Press Club on November 18, 1981, Reagan had outlined the basic U.S. negotiating position in the INF discussions. In what became known as the Zero Option, the president called for the elimination of all U.S. and Soviet intermediate-range missiles, indicating that if the USSR would scrap its SS-20s, then the United States would not deploy its Pershing II and cruise missiles.

Moscow rejected the Reagan proposal, insisting that any INF agreement must take into account all NUCLEAR WEAPONS in Europe capable of reaching Soviet territory, including the British and French nuclear arsenals. The Western allies rejected the Soviet position as a maneuver to link other kinds of NATO weapons to removal of the SS-20s. In July 1982 chief U.S. negotiator PAUL H. NITZE and his Soviet counterpart Yuli Kvitsinsky held private discussions in Geneva during "informal walks in the woods," in which they moved beyond each side's official negotiating position to develop a proposed formula for INF reductions. Under the so-called walk in the woods agreement, the United States would be authorized 75 cruise missile launchers and the Soviets 75 SS-20 launchers. Washington would forego the deployment of Pershing IIs, while Moscow would abandon its efforts to include limits on British and French systems. The Nitze-Kvitsinsky initiative was rejected by both the U.S. and Soviet governments.

In November 1983 the USSR walked out of the INF talks to protest the arrival of the first U.S. Pershing IIs and cruise missiles in Europe. Negotiations resumed in March 1985 under the aegis of the NUCLEAR AND SPACE TALKS. Mikhail S. Gorbachev's rise to power in the USSR the same month presaged political and social liberalization

within the Communist state and a rapid easing of COLD WAR tensions. Steady improvement in U.S.-Soviet relations brought corresponding progress in arms control deliberations. In January 1986 Moscow offered a plan for the elimination of all U.S. and Soviet INF missiles in Europe over the next five to seven years, with Soviet SS-20s in Asia phased out at a later date. The offer signaled Soviet acceptance that British and French weapons not be included in any INF accord. At the December 1986 REYKJAVIK SUMMIT, Reagan and Gorbachev agreed to remove all INF missiles in Europe and to impose a ceiling of 100 for each side on such missiles deployed elsewhere. The Soviets consented to U.S. demands for stringent on-site verification measures. The agreement fell apart at the end of the two-day gathering, however, when Reagan would not accede to Soviet demands for strict limits on the U.S. STRATEGIC DEFENSE INITIATIVE (SDI).

In February 1987 Gorbachev returned to the Reykjavik formula but dropped his insistence on a link between the INF negotiations and SDI. In light of the dramatic changes taking place in the Soviet Union, the Reagan administration meanwhile had moved away from its earlier opposition to any arms control agreement with Moscow so long as Soviet troops remained in Afghanistan. As prospects for an INF treaty continued to improve, U.S. Secretary of State GEORGE P. SHULTZ and Soviet Foreign Minister Eduard A. Shevardnadze met in Washington in September 1987. After four days of meetings, they announced agreement on the basic framework of a pact that would ban all INF missiles. Reagan and Gorbachev signed the landmark INF Treaty December 8, 1987, on the first day of their WASHINGTON SUMMIT. The agreement required the elimination within three years of all U.S. and Soviet INF missiles, prohibited further manufacture or flight testing of missiles with ranges between 500 and 5,500 kilometers (300 to 3,400 miles), and provided for extensive on-site verification of each side's compliance by teams of inspectors from the other country. Under the pact, which was the first to bar an entire class of weapons, 859 U.S. and 1836 Soviet missiles were to be destroyed. The treaty was ratified by the U.S. Senate on May 27,

1988, and proclaimed in force on June 1 by Reagan and Gorbachev at their Moscow Summit. The destruction of the missiles began in July 1988.

INTERNAL SECURITY ACT (1950) Federal legislation to control subversive activities in the United States. The Alien Registration Act (1940), passed on the eve of World War II, had denied entrance to aliens who advocated the overthrow of the government or belonged to subversive organizations. Immediately after the war, the primary concern became the exclusion of former Nazis. With the onset of East-West Cold War, attention shifted to the question of Communist agents slipping into the country as immigrants. Congressional hearings conducted by the House Un-American Activities Committee and the espionage-related Hiss Case raised public concerns over Communist infiltration of American society and government. Many argued that existing laws were inadequate to meet the threat posed by Communist subversion.

Congress passed comprehensive new internal security legislation in September 1950. President Harry S. Truman vetoed the measure for imposing what he deemed excessively broad and vague constraints on freedoms of speech, press, and assembly. Congress overrode Truman's action and the Internal Security Act became law on September 23, 1950. The statute, known as the McCarran Act after the chairman of the Senate Judiciary Committee, Patrick A. McCarran (D-NV), contained two major parts.

Title I, the Subversive Activities Control Act, required Communist and Communist-front organizations to register with the U.S. attorney general and was based on the presumption that public exposure would undermine their activities. The act created a presidentially appointed five-member Subversive Activities Control Board to determine Communist-affiliated groups. Members of these groups were barred from jobs in defense-related industries or from holding a U.S. passport. The title also blocked the admission of aliens with present or past membership in a Communist or Fascist party or other totalitarian organizations. Title II, the Emergency Detention Act, provided for the internment during national emergencies of people likely to commit espionage or sabotage.

The Communist Control Act of 1954, which denied the Communist Party legal standing, extended the provisions of the Internal Security Act to Communist-infiltrated organizations and was directed primarily at labor unions. In 1961 the Supreme Court upheld the constitutionality of the 1950 act's registration requirements in *Communist Party* v. *Subversive Activities Control Board*. The Court effectively halted enforcement of the Subversive Activities Control Act when it barred the registration of individual members of subversive organizations in *Albertson* v. *Subversive Activities Control Board* (1965) and struck down the ban on defense-industry employment in *United States* v. *Robel* (1967). The Emergency Detention Act was repealed in 1971 while the Subversive Activities Control Board was allowed to lapse in 1973.

INTERNATIONAL ATOMIC ENERGY AGENCY (IAEA) Organization established to foster international cooperation in the development of atomic energy for peaceful purposes. The agency had its origin in the Atoms for Peace proposal made before the United Nations General Assembly by President Dwight D. Eisenhower in December 1953. Eisenhower suggested the formation of a world body devoted to peaceful applications of atomic energy. The statute creating IAEA was approved at an international conference held in New York under U.N. auspices in 1956. The U.N.-affiliated agency formally came into existence in July 1957. The IAEA's main functions are to accelerate and expand atomic energy's contribution to peace and health throughout the world; and to ensure, so far as it is able, that assistance it provides to nations is not used to further any military purpose. Under terms of the Nuclear Non-Proliferation Treaty (1968), the agency bears responsibility for implementing safeguard measures to prevent the diversion by member countries of nuclear materials from peaceful to military purposes.

INTERNATIONAL BANK FOR RECONSTRUCTION AND DEVELOPMENT See **WORLD BANK**.

INTERNATIONAL COMMUNICATION AGENCY See **UNITED STATES INFORMATION AGENCY**.

INTERNATIONAL COOPERATION AD-MINISTRATION See **MUTUAL SECURITY ACT**.

INTERNATIONAL COURT OF JUSTICE See **WORLD COURT**.

INTERNATIONAL COVENANT ON CIVIL AND POLITICAL RIGHTS See **UNIVERSAL DECLARATION OF HUMAN RIGHTS**.

INTERNATIONAL COVENANT ON ECO-NOMIC, SOCIAL, AND CULTURAL RIGHTS See **UNIVERSAL DECLARATION OF HUMAN RIGHTS**.

INTERNATIONAL DEBT CRISIS Major international financial crisis brought on by the inability of THIRD WORLD countries to repay massive loans from the world's commercial banks. In the 1970s so-called middle-income developing nations borrowed billions of dollars from private banks, mostly in the United States, to finance economic development. Oil-producing countries such as Mexico and Venezuela looked to future oil revenues to repay the loans while nations such as Brazil and the Philippines counted on greater earnings through the rapid expansion of their economies. The debt crisis burst on the international scene in August 1982 when Mexico almost defaulted on its $80 billion in foreign obligations. Insolvency was averted only by a complicated restructuring of Mexico's loan payments. It soon became apparent that a combination of dropping oil prices and other commodity prices and high global interest rates had placed in jeopardy more than $500 billion in Third World debt. Of this amount, roughly 60 percent was owed to private lenders by 15 principal borrowers—10 Latin American countries, Morocco, Ivory Coast, Nigeria, Yugoslavia, and the Philippines.

Initially many Western financial experts thought the crisis could be resolved by tighter controls on domestic spending in the debtor nations. Resulting trade surpluses, the experts reasoned, could then be used for loan repayment. The INTERNATIONAL MONETARY FUND (IMF) provided emergency loans to developing nations to enable them to make the payments on their huge debts. The new funds came with strict IMF-mandated austerity programs. The Reagan ad-ministration, philosophically opposed to government intervention in the private sector, supported the IMF-imposed austerity provisions while avoiding direct involvement in the crisis. But the austerity measures, together with a dramatic drop in the flow of new capital, threatened the debtor nations' economies with stagnation and collapse. Widespread defaulting on the massive amounts owed threatened to undermine the entire international financial system.

In an October 1985 address to the annual meeting of the IMF and WORLD BANK, U.S. Secretary of the Treasury JAMES A. BAKER 3RD suggested a new international debt strategy. Arguing that economic expansion rather than belt-tightening held the key to indebted nations being able to generate enough revenue to repay their loans, he outlined a three-pronged plan meant to shift the emphasis from austerity to growth. Baker called for market-oriented reforms in developing nations, most importantly the removal of government controls on economic activities; an increase of $9 billion in IMF and World Bank lending to hard-pressed debtor nations; and the extension of an additional $20 billion in loans from commercial banks over the next three years. Quickly dubbed the Baker Plan, the initiative represented a major departure from the Reagan administration's earlier avoidance of the debt issue. It failed to draw lasting international support and was never fully adopted. Faced with a seemingly insurmountable debt burden, developing nations increasingly maintained that the only solution was an outright reduction in the amount they owed.

At a private conference on international monetary policy in Zurich, Switzerland, in June 1986, Senator Bill Bradley (D-NJ), considered the leading voice in the U.S. Congress on the debt question, proposed an alternative to the Baker Plan. The so-called Bradley Plan accepted the basic premise that debt relief was essential to resolving the financial crisis. Bradley pressed for Third World economic reform but contended that instead of extending new loans, which only compounded the problem, the West should forgive $57 billion in existing obligations. The Bradley proposal added to a growing international debate over the debt crisis. The Reagan administration consistently opposed the idea of debt relief. By 1987 progress on the issue was at a standstill. The major U.S. commercial banks had begun to write off their Third World debt. New loans to debtor nations were limited to the amounts necessary for interest payments on existing debts. In February 1989 economic austerity measures in Venezuela triggered riots in which 300 persons were killed.

Partly in reponse to the violence, U.S. Treasury Secretary Nicholas F. Brady the following month unveiled the new Bush administration's debt strategy. The Brady Plan for the first time gave official U.S. endorsement to the concept of debt reduction. The scheme encouraged voluntary debt relief negotiations between creditor banks and indebted nations. It supported greater involvement by the IMF, World Bank, and Japan in guaranteeing private loans to developing countries and continued the emphasis on market-oriented reforms in debtor nations. Three kinds of debt-reduction transactions were suggested by which banks could exchange their notes for either less valuable bonds, lower interest bonds, or stakes in local businesses. The plan gained favorable reactions from both indebted nations and the international financial community. In July 1989 Mexico completed a historic debt-reduction accord with the IMF and its creditor banks. Similar agreements with other major debtor nations followed, suggesting the Brady approach promised at least a temporary improvement in the debt crisis.

INTERNATIONAL DEVELOPMENT ASSOCIATION See **WORLD BANK**.

INTERNATIONAL DEVELOPMENT COOPERATION AGENCY (IDCA) Federal agency that coordinates most U.S. government foreign aid programs. It also helps plan U.S. policy on international economic issues affecting developing countries. The IDCA was established in 1979 under a foreign aid reorganization plan proposed by President JIMMY CARTER and approved by Congress. The agency, which is independent of the State Department, encompasses the AGENCY FOR INTERNATIONAL DEVELOPMENT, the OVERSEAS PRIVATE INVESTMENT CORPORATION, and the TRADE AND DEVELOPMENT PROGRAM, serving as a coordinating hub for the three independently administered federal organizations. The director of IDCA serves as the principal international development adviser to the president and secretary of state. Responsibility for U.S. participation in multilateral development banks such as the WORLD BANK and the INTER-AMERICAN DEVELOPMENT BANK is shared by the agency director and the secretary of the treasury. The agency also shares responsibility for policy direction of the FOOD FOR PEACE program with the Department of Agriculture. The IDCA guides U.S. participation in UNITED NATIONS and ORGANIZATION OF AMERICAN STATES (OAS) developmental programs, including the U.N. Development Program, the U.N. Children's Fund, the World Food Program, and the OAS Technical Assistance Funds. As head of the principal policy planning agency for U.S. assistance programs, the IDCA director is a member of the National Advisory Committee on International and Monetary Affairs and the Trade Policy Committee. The director also chairs the Development Coordination Committee, a group of representatives from all federal agencies involved with foreign aid programs.

INTERNATIONAL FINANCE CORPORATION See **WORLD BANK**.

INTERNATIONAL GEOPHYSICAL YEAR (IGY) (1957–1958) International scientific enterprise conducted July 1, 1957, to December 31, 1958. The IGY was proposed in 1950 as a successor to the International Polar Year (IPY), the pioneering international cooperative endeavor in meteorology and polar exploration. In the first International Polar Year (1882–1883), scientific expeditions from 11 nations, including the United States, went to the North and South Pole regions. The expeditions provided the first clear picture of polar weather, furnished detailed observations on the atmospheric effect known as the northern lights, or aurora borealis, and yielded valuable discoveries concerning polar magnetic storms. Fifty years later the international scientific community renewed the IPY enterprise. Forty-four nations participated in the second International Polar Year (1932–1933), of which half organized field expeditions. The second IPY generated an interest that continued over the years and culminated in organization of the International Geophysical Year.

The IGY was scheduled to take scientific advantage of a period of maximum solar activity. In 1952 the International Council of Scientific Unions (ICSU) formally adopted the project and broadened its scope to an intensive study of all aspects of the physical environment. The ICSU established an organizing committee and corresponding bodies were formed in each of the 67 nations that finally participated. While many governments took active roles in their own national programs, IGY activities generally were organized through nongovernmental channels by international scientific associations.

The IGY yielded a number of significant scientific discoveries, including detection of the Van Allen radiation belts. Most importantly, it marked the inauguration of the Space Age. In 1955 the United States had disclosed plans to launch several satellites as part of its participation in IGY events. The Soviet Union, which had made a similar announcement in 1956, sent Sputnik, mankind's first satellite, into orbit October 4, 1957. America's first satellite, Explorer 1, lifted off on January 31, 1958. In all, two more Soviet and three more American satellites were launched during the IGY. U.S. government officials later testified they had not considered the nation to be in a contest with the Soviet Union to reach space first. However, intense competition between the U.S. and Soviet space programs quickly escalated into the SPACE RACE. The IGY served as an important example of the positive role scientific exchanges could play in international relations. The only political difficulty occurred when Communist China withdrew after Taiwan joined in 1957.

INTERNATIONAL LABOR ORGANIZATION (ILO) UNITED NATIONS agency concerned with the improvement of working conditions and the promotion of full employment worldwide. The ILO was formed under the TREATY OF VERSAILLES (1919) as an autonomous body affiliated with the LEAGUE OF NATIONS. The United States joined the organization in 1934. At its annual International Labor Conference held in Philadel-

phia in 1944, the ILO adopted the so-called Philadelphia Charter updating and defining the agency's aims and purposes and stating its commitment to worker rights. In 1946 the organization became the first specialized agency associated with the United Nations. National delegations to the ILO are required to include representatives from government, labor, and business. In recent decades the agency's charter has expanded to cover such issues as migrant workers and multinational corporations.

In 1975 the United States threatened to withdraw from the ILO within two years if the organization did not reverse its growing politicization. The Ford administration charged that the agency was being used for political purposes by an anti-Western coalition of the Soviet Union and its Eastern European satellites, Arab states, and THIRD WORLD nations. The administration cited the ILO's anti-Israeli bias and its practice of condemning labor violations in democratic countries while ignoring more serious abuses in totalitarian states. In November 1977 President JIMMY CARTER formally terminated U.S. membership in the ILO. In February 1980 the Carter administration announced that, in view of the organization's avoidance of anti-Israeli actions and more evenhanded adherence to its basic purpose and principles, the United States was rejoining the ILO.

INTERNATIONAL MARITIME ORGANIZATION (IMO) Principal international consultative body responsible for maritime questions. The organization was chartered as the Inter-Governmental Maritime Consultative Organization (IMCO) by a convention signed March 6, 1948, at an international maritime conference held in Geneva, Switzerland, under UNITED NATIONS auspices. Following ratification of the convention by the required 21 countries, including the United States, the IMCO formally came into being on March 17, 1958, as a U.N. specialized agency. It started operations at its London headquarters in January 1959. Under amendments adopted in 1975, the name was changed to the International Maritime Organization on May 22, 1982. The IMO's main functions are to encourage cooperation among its approximately 130 member states on technical matters of all kinds affecting merchant shipping, particularly concerning safety at sea; to prevent and control maritime pollution caused by ships; and to facilitate international maritime traffic. In pursuit of its objectives, the organization periodically convenes international conferences and has adopted a substantial number of conventions relating to marine traffic and protection of the marine environment.

INTERNATIONAL METEOROLOGICAL ORGANIZATION See **WORLD METEOROLOGICAL ORGANIZATION**.

INTERNATIONAL MILITARY TRIBUNAL See **NUREMBURG WAR CRIMES TRIALS**.

INTERNATIONAL MILITARY TRIBUNAL FOR THE FAR EAST See **FAR EAST WAR CRIMES TRIALS**.

INTERNATIONAL MONETARY FUND (IMF) Multinational financial organization responsible for managing the world's money supply. The articles of agreement establishing the IMF, drawn up at the 1944 BRETTON WOODS CONFERENCE, went into effect December 27, 1945, with their ratification by 28 nations, including the United States. Formal operations began at IMF headquarters in Washington, D.C., on March 1, 1947, and the fund became a specialized agency of the UNITED NATIONS on November 15 of the same year. The IMF grew out of the determination of the United States and other industrial powers to replace their economic warfare of the 1930s with a more cooperative international economic system. The economic nationalism that characterized the earlier decade was widely viewed as having contributed to the Great Depression and WORLD WAR II. The fund was formed to promote the orderly and stable exchange of foreign currencies and to aid the expansion of international trade. To accomplish this, the institution maintains a multibillion dollar reserve fund made up of all the currencies of its member states. Member countries can borrow, or draw, from this account to obtain foreign currencies for international financial transactions and to cover foreign balance-of-payments deficits. By the early 1990s, IMF membership had reached some 170 nations. Each country is represented on its Board of Governors, which sets fund policy. The voting power of each member is based on an assigned quota that reflects the size and importance of its economy. This quota also determines the size of a nation's contribution to the IMF's reserve account and its access, or drawing rights, to fund resources. With a quota of roughly 20 percent, the United States exercises a predominant voice in IMF matters.

From 1947 to 1971 the IMF supported the so-called Bretton Woods international monetary system. Devised at the 1944 conference, it provided for fixed currency exchange rates based on a modified gold standard. In recognition of the postwar dominance of the U.S. economy, the value of gold was set at $35 an ounce, making the U.S. dollar the basic international currency. In 1962 the United States and the other leading industrial powers met the need for greater IMF reserves by concluding the General Agreements to Borrow, which pledged its signatories to lend additional monies to the fund as necessary. The same nations thereupon formed the GROUP OF 10 (G-10) to coordinate among themselves on economic policy.

High U.S. inflation rates weakened the dollar and led to the collapse of the Bretton Woods system in 1971. As the real value of the dollar fell, it became increasingly difficult to maintain the price of gold at an artificially low $35 an ounce. When President RICHARD M. NIXON announced on August 15, 1971, that the United States no longer would convert dollars into gold, he effectively severed the dollar, and by extension all other currencies, from a set gold standard. Following Nixon's action, foreign currencies were allowed to "float" against each other, meaning their exchange rates were determined by market forces rather than governmental regulations. Worried that free-floating currencies could precipitate domestic protectionist pressures and cause a breakdown of international economic cooperation, the G-10 nations met in Washington in December 1971 at the Smithsonian Institution. On December 21 delegates concluded the so-called Smithsonian Agreement, establishing a "managed float," whereby the major currencies would not be allowed to fluctuate more than 4.5 percent against each other.

The managed-float system proved incapable of responding to the worldwide inflation of the mid-1970s brought on by the quadrupling of oil prices by the Organization of Petroleum Exporting Countries (OPEC). The huge export earnings of the OPEC countries created serious imbalances in the world economy. Pressures for changes in the international monetary system also were mounting from THIRD WORLD developing countries, which viewed the IMF as largely opposed to their interests. On January 8, 1976, at an IMF meeting in Kingston, Jamaica, agreement was reached on a broad amendment to the fund's charter. Known as the Jamaica Agreement, the amendment went into effect in 1978. It officially severed international exchange rates from any gold standard; authorized member countries to adopt the exchange system of their choosing—fixed, managed, or free-floating—subject to the continued overall control of the IMF; and expanded the organization's role in aiding countries with foreign payments difficulties. In the 1980s the IMF became increasingly involved in the INTERNATIONAL DEBT CRISIS.

The Soviet-dominated Communist bloc long was hostile to the Western-led, market-oriented IMF system. Following the collapse of their Communist regimes, the former Soviet satellites of Eastern Europe joined the fund in the early 1990s. Russia and the other newly sovereign republics of the former Soviet Union became members in 1992.

See also NORTH-SOUTH DIALOGUE.

INTERNATIONAL POLAR YEAR   See **INTERNATIONAL GEOPHYSICAL YEAR**.

INTERNATIONAL REFUGEE ORGANIZATION   See **UNITED NATIONS RELIEF AND REHABILITATION ADMINISTRATION**.

INTERNATIONAL TELECOMMUNICATION UNION (ITU)   Organization whose purpose is to promote international cooperation in the use and improvement of global telecommunications. The United States is among its approximately 165 member states. The origins of the ITU trace back to the International Telegraph Union founded at Paris in 1865 and the International Radio-Telegraph Union established

in Berlin in 1906. In 1932 at Madrid the International Telegraph Convention (1865) and International Radio-Telegraph Convention (1906) were merged into a single International Telecommunication Convention covering radio, telegraph, and telephone. Entering into force January 1, 1934, the Madrid agreement formally established the International Telecommunication Union as the successor to the earlier agencies in the telecommunications field. The union became a specialized agency of the UNITED NATIONS in 1947. The ITU recommends standards and minimum regulations governing international use of telegraph, telephone, and radio services. The union conducts technical studies aimed at improving worldwide means of communication and supports the creation and improvement of telecommunications in developing countries.

See also INTERNATIONAL TELECOMMUNICATIONS SATELLITE ORGANIZATION.

INTERNATIONAL TELECOMMUNICATIONS SATELLITE ORGANIZATION (INTELSAT)   Intergovernmental organization on global satellite telecommunications. The origins of INTELSAT date back to 1964, when an interim International Telecommunications Satellite Consortium was established. All member states of the INTERNATIONAL TELECOMMUNICATION UNION willing to share in the costs of designing, launching into earth orbit, and operating the global communications satellites were permitted to invest. Access to the satellite communications system was open to any nation that agreed to assume the prorated costs of actual use of the facilities. The administration and technical management of the consortium was dominated by the Communications Satellite Corporation (COMSAT), a U.S. agency established by Congress in 1962 and subject to federal control. Other countries party to the system were represented either by their governments or publicly controlled telecommunications organizations. The increasing importance of satellite telecommunications in the 1960s generated international pressure to reorganize the consortium and limit COMSAT's influence over it. Thus the current INTELSAT was created by two international agreements signed at Washington, D.C., on August 20, 1971, and effective February 12,

1973. COMSAT remained the public agency through which U.S. participation in INTEL-SAT is administered. While it lost its role as INTELSAT's operating agency, COMSAT continues to exercise predominant control over the organization's activities. INTEL-SAT's 15-satellite system furnishes about two-thirds of the world's international telecommunications services, including telephone, television, facsimile, data, and telex transmission between more than 700 earth stations in some 170 countries and territories.

INTERNATIONAL TROPICAL TIMBER ORGANIZATION (ITTO) Global organization concerned with the tropical timber industry and the problem of worldwide tropical deforestation. The ITTO was established on April 1, 1985, when the International Tropical Timber Agreement entered into force. This convention had been signed on November 18, 1983, by nations attending a meeting on tropical forestry held in Geneva, Switzerland, under the aegis of the UNITED NATIONS CONFERENCE ON TRADE AND DEVELOPMENT. The United States was one of the original parties to the agreement and became a charter ITTO member. The organization's primary aim is to provide a framework for cooperation and consultation among producing and consuming nations on all relevant aspects of the tropical timber economy. It promotes expansion of international trade in tropical timber. At the same time the organization encourages the development of national policies among members directed at conservation of tropical rain forests and maintenance of ecological balance. The ITTO supports reforestation and sound forest management and promotes the sharing of statistical and market information among its membership. Recognizing the importance of sustainable development to the world tropical timber industry, the United States takes an active part in the ITTO, which has its headquarters in Yokohama, Japan.

INTERNATIONALISM Term for a policy of active involvement in foreign affairs including participation in international organizations and other multinational arrangements. Until WORLD WAR II, the United States followed a largely isolationist foreign policy. America's traditional ISOLATIONISM reflected the nation's desire to avoid entanglement in European political and military developments. This isolationist legacy rested on a strict aversion to foreign alliances. America's dominant position after World War II and its greatly expanded international responsibilities brought a corresponding change in U.S. foreign policy. Under President FRANKLIN D. ROOSEVELT, the United States had moved toward internationalism during the war, assuming a leadership role in the formation of the UNITED NATIONS, INTERNATIONAL MONETARY FUND, WORLD BANK, and other postwar multinational institutions. Continuing the break with America's isolationist past, the Truman administration forged the MARSHALL PLAN (1948), the program of massive U.S. economic aid that helped rebuild war-ravaged Europe. With the onset of the COLD WAR in the late 1940s, Washington spearheaded organization of a series of defensive alliances in Europe and Asia to deter Communist aggression and provide for COLLECTIVE SECURITY. The United States since has pursued an internationalist foreign policy, exercising its dominant military and economic power to shape and influence world events.

INTERVENTION ON THE HIGH SEAS ACT (1974) U.S. environmental protection legislation concerning oil pollution of the high seas. The measure, which became law on February 5, 1974, implemented the International Convention Relating to Intervention on the High Seas in Cases of Oil Pollution Casualties, an agreement concluded under UNITED NATIONS auspices at a parley in Brussels, Belgium, in 1969. The law empowered the U.S. secretary of the treasury, as head of the department housing the Coast Guard, to take necessary steps to prevent or mitigate grave and imminent threats to the U.S. coastline from oil pollution caused by ocean shipping. By its terms the secretary was authorized in emergency situations to detain, disable, or even destroy any vessel that was damaging or posed a severe danger to the American shoreline. In most scenarios the law called for elaborate consultations with other authorities before the treasury secretary took action.

IRAN COUP (1953) U.S.-sponsored over-throw of Iranian Prime Minister Mo-hammed Mossadegh. During WORLD WAR II, British and Soviet forces occupied Iran. Ties to Germany forced the Iranian shah, Reza Pahlavi, to abdicate in favor of his son Mohammed Reza Pahlavi in 1941. At the TEHERAN CONFERENCE (1943), the United States, Great Britain, and Soviet Union agreed the Allies would withdraw from a newly independent Iran after the war. The British departed as pledged by the end of 1945, but the Soviet Union precipitated the IRAN CRISIS by remaining in several northern provinces until forced to leave by Western diplomatic and military pressure in 1946.

In 1951 the Iranian prime minister, General Ali Razmara, was assassinated. Un-der domestic political pressure, the shah named 70-year-old legislator Mohammed Mossadegh as his successor. Mossadegh moved immediately to nationalize the British-controlled Anglo-Iranian Oil Com-pany. The British responded by removing their personnel from the country, effec-tively shutting down oil production and de-priving Iran of its principal source of rev-enue. In the ensuing crisis, Mossadegh was supported by the Tudeh, the Iranian Com-munist Party. The Iranian prime minister broke diplomatic relations with Great Britain in October 1952.

Growing ties between Mossadegh and the Soviet-allied Tudeh heightened fears in Washington of a Communist takeover in Iran. In early 1953 the Eisenhower adminis-tration responded favorably to a British proposal for a joint covert operation to topple Mossadegh. A draft plan, code-named Ajax, prepared by CENTRAL INTELLI-GENCE AGENCY (CIA) agent KERMIT ROOSEVELT, was approved. Roosevelt secretly infiltrated into Iran and met with the increasingly be-leaguered and powerless shah, gaining his participation in the operation. On August 14, 1953, members of the Palace Guard loyal to the shah attempted a coup against Mossadegh, but were repelled by other Iranian military units. The shah fled the country as Communist-led rioting broke out in Teheran. These disturbances had subsided by August 19th when Roosevelt, operating from a clandestine command post, orchestrated pro-shah demonstra-tions. A loyalist column led by General Fa-zollah Zahedi moved on Mossadegh's resi-dence and, after a two-hour battle, drove him into hiding. The deposed Iranian leader surrendered the next day and spent the remainder of his life under house arrest in his native village.

The shah returned from Italy to assume his throne. Zahedi, who became prime minister, restored diplomatic relations with Great Britain and negotiated an agreement more favorable to Iran with Anglo-Iranian. The shah remained a staunch ally of the United States until his downfall in 1979. The success of the Iran Coup encouraged senior U.S. policymakers to undertake simi-lar operations in following years.

IRAN CRISIS (1946) International im-broglio precipitated when the Soviet Union balked at withdrawing its armed forces from northern Iran following WORLD WAR II. After Adolf Hitler's surprise invasion brought the Soviets into the war against Nazi Germany in June 1941, neutral Iran emerged as a vital Allied supply route from the Persian Gulf to the USSR. The pro-Ger-man Iranian ruler, Shah Reza Pahlavi, re-jected an Anglo-Soviet ultimatum to coop-erate with the Allies, whereupon British and Soviet forces jointly invaded and occu-pied Iran in late August 1941 in order to protect the supply route and prevent Ger-man seizure of the Iranian oil fields. The shah was forced to abdicate in mid-Septem-ber in favor of his son Mohammed Reza Pahlavi. In January 1942 Great Britain and the Soviet Union formally agreed to respect Iran's territorial integrity and to withdraw their forces from the country six months af-ter the end of the war. Following U.S. entry into the conflict in December 1941, Ameri-can troops began arriving in Iran to help transport U.S. aid to the USSR. The United States joined in the Anglo-Soviet troop-withdrawal pledge at the TEHERAN CONFER-ENCE in December 1943.

Soviet conduct in Iran in the months just after the war engendered an interna-tional crisis. The USSR, through the Iranian Communist-controlled Tudeh party, pro-moted the separatist revolt that broke out in November 1945 in the northernmost Iranian province of Azerbaijan, thus raising U.S. concerns about possible Soviet territo-rial ambitions and the spread of Soviet influence. While U.S. and British forces proceeded to withdraw, the Soviet troops remained in northern Iran in early 1946, impeding efforts by the Iranian military to suppress the Azerbaijani rebellion. Iran protested to the newly formed UNITED NATIONS Security Council that the USSR was violating its sovereignty by interfering in its internal affairs. At the council's behest, the Soviets and Iranians entered into direct negotiations. Moscow demanded autonomy for Azerbaijan, major Iranian oil concessions, and the right to keep troops in Iran indefinitely. Teheran rejected the demands and with American support renewed its protest before the Security Council. Soviet armed forces remained in Iran past the withdrawal deadline of March 2, as Moscow had announced previously they would. An alarmed Truman administration promptly filed a blunt protest with the USSR, calling for immediate evacuation of the Soviet troops. President HARRY S. TRUMAN feared that Soviet inroads in Iran would imperil the security of Turkey and threaten Western control of the Iranian oil fields.

Facing both firm American opposition and mounting U.N. pressure, the Soviets decided to relent in Iran. As a result of negotiations with the Iranians, the Soviets completed the withdrawal of their troops in May 1946. These negotiations also produced an agreement to form an Iranian-Soviet oil company. The Iranian parliament subsequently rejected the proposed enterprise. The Iran Crisis presaged intense East-West rivalry in the Near and Middle East and contributed toward the development of COLD WAR suspicion and hostility.

IRAN HOSTAGE CRISIS (1979–1981) Ordeal in which 52 Americans were held hostage in Iran for 444 days following seizure of the U.S. embassy in Teheran by militant Iranians. Shah Mohammed Reza Pahlavi's autocratic rule; his repression of political dissent; the gross HUMAN RIGHTS violations of his dreaded secret police (known as SAVAK); and his program for rapid Westernization and modernization of Iran at the expense of Islamic tradition produced a broad-based and growing opposition to his regime in the late 1970s. The opposition comprised members of the Western-educated middle class, various leftist groups, and the fundamentalist Moslem community. A staunch ally of the United States and major purchaser of U.S. military equipment, the shah for decades had been championed in Washington as one whose leadership made Iran an island of stability in the turbulent Middle East. U.S. support of the monarch engendered a strong undercurrent of anti-Americanism in Iran.

Fundamentalist Shiite cleric Ayatollah Ruhollah Khomeini returned to Teheran from exile in Paris on February 1, 1979, to lead a triumphant Islamic revolutionary movement which had forced the shah from power in mid-January. Khomeini's loyalists promptly seized control from an interim government established after the shah fled. The ayatollah assumed supreme authority, appointed a provisional government, formed the ruling Islamic Revolutionary Council, and on April 1, 1979, proclaimed Iran an Islamic republic. Khomeini ordered a nationwide reimposition of Islamic customs and eradication of all forms of Western influence. He also moved quickly to break the extensive bonds the shah had forged with the United States, which was demonized by the revolutionary Islamic leadership for its decades-long support of the deposed Iranian ruler.

The Carter administration's decision to allow the gravely ill shah to enter the United States October 22, 1979, for medical treatment provoked a wave of demonstrations in the Iranian capital by militant students and other anti-American elements. On November 4, a mob stormed the U.S. embassy compound in Teheran, taking 66 American diplomatic personnel hostage. The Iranian militants demanded the extradition of the shah to Iran as the price for the release of the hostages. President JIMMY CARTER flatly rejected the demand. With American public indignation rising, he ordered the deportation of Iranian students who were in the United States illegally, halted imports of Iranian oil, and froze Iranian assets in American banks. Tensions between the countries escalated when, on November 18, Khomeini threatened to try the hostages as spies unless the deposed shah was returned. Several days later the Iranian militants released 13 women and black captives, simultaneously reiterating their demand. Another hostage was released in July 1980 because of illness, leaving 52 Americans captive. As the crisis wore on, the Carter administration labored to increase international diplomatic pressure on Iran. In December the UNITED NATIONS Security Council passed resolutions deploring the holding of the hostages and demanding their release, while the NATO foreign ministers condemned the situation at the U.S. embassy in Teheran as a flagrant violation of international law and human rights. Meanwhile on December 15 the shah flew from New York to Panama at the Panamanian government's invitation following secret diplomatic maneuvering between Washington and Panama City. Notwithstanding this development, Khomeini continued to demand the shah's return.

In February 1980 newly elected Iranian president Abolhassan Bani-Sadr set conditions for the hostages' release: a U.S. admission of guilt for supporting the shah's regime; U.S. acknowledgement of Iran's right to seek the shah's extradition and return of his fortune; and a pledge by the United States not to interfere in Iran's internal affairs. Carter asserted that the United States would not admit guilt for its past policy toward Iran. Hopes of an imminent breakthrough in the crisis were raised, and then dashed, several times in the first few months of the hostage ordeal. A special U.N. investigative commission departed Teheran on March 11, 1980, after a fruitless 17-day stay during which it was unable to win the hostages' release. Domestically Carter faced an erosion of public support for his handling of the hostage situation. Prospects for a settlement of the crisis were dampened by the realization that the Iranian government would not assume direct control of the hostages from the militants. With no end in sight Carter ordered stepped-up U.S. economic and political sanctions throughout April, including severance of diplomatic relations with Teheran and imposition of a near-total trade embargo. These punitive measures failed to coerce the Iranian captors.

Responding to growing American frustration and demands for more decisive action, the president authorized a military rescue mission in April, one that ended in disastrous failure April 25 with the accidental death of 8 members of the U.S. commando team in the Iranian desert. The rescue attempt brought about the resignation of Secretary of State CYRUS R. VANCE, who had opposed the operation from the outset. He was succeeded by EDMUND S. MUSKIE. The crisis remained deadlocked throughout the summer. Following the shah's death in July 1980 in Cairo, where he had been granted permanent asylum in late March, the Iranians shifted from an insistence upon his return to a demand for the repatriation of the deposed monarch's wealth.

The eruption in September of a full-scale war with Iraq prompted Iran to seek a settlement with the United States of the hostage situation. Negotiations for the captives' release began on November 2, 1980, two days before Republican RONALD W. REAGAN overwhelmed Carter in the American presidential election. Voter frustration with the hostage stalemate contributed to Carter's huge margin of defeat. Algeria assumed the role of mediator in the U.S. and Iranian negotiations. Deputy Secretary of State Warren G. Christopher was the chief U.S. representative in the talks. A final agreement on the release of the hostages was concluded in Algiers on January 19, 1981. Under the settlement, known as the Algiers Accords, the United States promised not to interfere in Iran's internal affairs and pledged to return a substantial part of Iran's frozen financial assets in America. The 52 freed American hostages left Teheran aboard two Algerian planes on January 20, just minutes after Reagan's inauguration as president.

Several times since 1981 questions have been raised about the circumstances surrounding the timing of the hostages' release. In 1991 charges resurfaced that senior aides to candidate Reagan met secretly in Paris with Iranian government officials, prior to the November 1980 election, to bargain for a delay in the release of the captives. The Reagan people reportedly sought such a delay to ensure that Carter would not reap the political benefit likely to accrue from a pre-election resolution of the crisis. The allegations, forcefully denied by those implicated, remain unsubstantiated.

IRAN-CONTRA Scandal involving the sale of U.S. arms to Iran and diversion of the proceeds to the Contra rebels battling the Sandinista government in Nicaragua. Separate Reagan administration covert operations to aid the CONTRAS and to open contacts with Teheran would become linked in 1986. In 1981 President RONALD W. REAGAN authorized a program of covert U.S. assistance to anti-Sandinista guerrilla groups. In 1984 Congress passed the third and most restrictive of the BOLAND AMENDMENTS, barring U.S. agencies involved in intelligence activities from providing any aid whatsoever to the Contras. Secretly concluding that the amendment did not apply to the NATIONAL SECURITY COUNCIL (NSC) because the council technically was not an intelligence entity, the Reagan White House turned to the NSC to coordinate continuing covert assistance to the Contras. Between 1984 and 1986 NSC staff member Marine Lieutenant Colonel Oliver L. North directed a secret Contra supply network funded by private and foreign donations.

In 1984 the Reagan administration began a reappraisal of U.S.-Iranian relations, which had been severed during the IRAN HOSTAGE CRISIS (1979–1981). The review reflected U.S. concerns over possible designs by the Soviet Union on Iran. In 1985 National Security Adviser Robert C. McFarlane coordinated U.S. involvement in a secret American-Israeli initiative to sell arms to Iran. Israel aimed to assist Iran in its war with Iraq, long one of the Jewish state's major enemies. The White House wanted to gain influence with moderate elements in Teheran. The Reagan administration also hoped to win the release of American hostages held in Lebanon by radical Iranian-allied Moslem captors as a demonstration of Iranian good faith. Two Israeli shipments of U.S. anti tank and anti aircraft missiles brought the release of one American hostage but otherwise produced no real improvement in U.S.-Iranian relations. McFarlane resigned in December 1985 and was replaced by his deputy, Admiral John M. Poindexter.

In January 1986 Reagan formally approved direct U.S. arms sales to Iran through the CENTRAL INTELLIGENCE AGENCY (CIA) and instructed the CIA not to inform Congress of the COVERT ACTION. The same month North began to implement a secret scheme to divert some of the proceeds from the arms sales to the Contras. Delivery

to Iran of at least four planeloads of U.S. arms between February and October 1986 brought the release of two American hostages. In late May 1986, McFarlane, accompanied by North and several other aides, undertook a secret mission as a special White House envoy to Teheran but was unable to establish contacts with senior Iranian officials. By October 1986, the U.S.-Iranian initiative had become an arms-for-hostages exchange.

In early November 1986 a Beirut magazine published a story on McFarlane's Teheran trip, prompting congressional demands for a full explanation. News of the U.S. arms sales to Iran sparked a firestorm of criticism. Democrats in Congress excoriated the Republican Reagan administration for secretly tradings arms for hostages and violating its own adamant pledge never to make concessions to terrorists. The president attempted to defend the arms sales as part of a gambit for improved U.S.-Iranian relations. The foreign policy crisis worsened on November 25 when Reagan announced the resignation of Poindexter and dismissal of North because of evidence found by Attorney General Edwin Meese 3rd of the diversion of arms sales funds to the Contras. At issue was the possibly illegal circumvention of the congressional ban on aid to the anti-Sandinista forces. Reagan denied any knowledge of the Contra diversion. On November 26 the president appointed the Tower Commission to review the operation of the NSC. The three-member panel was headed by former Senator John G. Tower (R-TX) and included former Secretary of State EDMUND S. MUSKIE and BRENT SCOWCROFT, national security adviser under President GERALD R. FORD.

The growing scandal continued to rock the Reagan administration. In January 1987 both the House and Senate formed special committees to investigate Iran-Contra. Critics charged that Reagan either had lost control of his staff or had authorized possibly illegal activities. In its report of February 26, 1987, the Tower Commission fixed primary blame for the Iran-Contra affair not on systemic flaws in the NSC but on the misconduct of senior Reagan administration aides. It faulted Reagan for lax oversight and management of his staff but uncovered no evidence that he knew of the Contra diversion. Almost from the outset, the panel concluded, the Iran operation had become an arms-for-hostages arrangement.

The congressional Iran-Contra committees, merged into a single panel in March 1987, conducted televised hearings between May and August. North and Poindexter testified under grants of immunity. The hearings revealed the Reagan White House's deliberate attempts to avoid congressional restrictions on U.S. aid to the Contras, including North's secret supply network. North, Poindexter, and others admitted to misleading Congress to conceal from it the Contra resupply effort. North testified to the central role of CIA Director WILLIAM J. CASEY in the Contra operation. Casey, however, had died in May 1987 without appearing before the committee and the full extent of his involvement remained unclear. The congressional panel completed its investigations in November 1987. The bipartisan majority report held Reagan ultimately responsible for the Iran-Contra affair, determining he allowed overzealous subordinates to skirt the law, distort foreign policy-making, and mislead Congress. A minority Republican report concluded the Reagan White House made serious mistakes but maintained it broke no laws. While the committee found no evidence Reagan personally engaged in wrongdoing, the president emerged from the Iran-Contra scandal with his reputation tarnished and effectiveness diminished.

Meanwhile, in December 1986 a federal court, at the request of Attorney General Meese, had appointed Laurence E. Walsh as a special prosecutor to investigate the Iran-Contra affair. On the basis of Walsh's probe, a federal grand jury in March 1988 brought a 23-count indictment against North, Poindexter, and Iran-Contra arms dealers retired Air Force General Richard V. Secord and Albert Hakim. Secord and Hakim each pled guilty to reduced charges under plea bargain arrangements. North was convicted on May 4, 1989, of obstructing a congressional inquiry, shredding documents, and accepting an illegal gift. Poindexter was convicted on April 7, 1990, of five counts of conspiracy, obstruction of Congress, and lying to Congress. The convictions of both men were overturned by appeals courts that cited improper use in their trials of their immunized congressional testimony. McFarlane and Elliot Abrams, former assistant secretary of state for Latin American affairs, pled guilty to charges of withholding information from Congress and were placed on probation.

IRON CURTAIN Metaphor for the barrier dividing Communist Eastern Europe from the West for more than four decades. After WORLD WAR II, the Soviet Union moved to tighten its control over eastern Germany and the countries of Eastern Europe occupied by its armies during the conflict. By early 1946, meetings of the COUNCIL OF FOREIGN MINISTERS of wartime allies—the United States, Great Britain, France, and Soviet Union—had revealed mounting tension between the Western powers and the Communist state over Europe's future. In a famous speech at Westminster College in Fulton, Missouri, on March 5, 1946, former and future British Prime Minister Winston Churchill, with President HARRY S. TRUMAN at his side, alerted the West to the establishment of Soviet Communist hegemony over Eastern Europe. Moscow's aggressive expansionism, Churchill warned, threatened Western security and constituted a menace to the interests of the FREE WORLD. "From Stetin in the Baltic to Trieste in the Adriatic," he said, "an iron curtain has descended across the continent." He urged a resolute Western stand against the Soviets, anchored on an Anglo-American alliance. The term *iron curtain* referred to the hardening postwar division of Europe. In popularizing the expression, Churchill employed a vivid and powerful visual image to describe the Soviet Union's walling off of Eastern Europe. Iron Curtain entered the lexicon of the impending East-West COLD WAR to describe the actual physical barrier constructed by the Communist regimes in Eastern Europe to seal off their nations from the West and prevent their citizens from fleeing. In the 1950s the derivative expression *bamboo curtain* was coined to describe the inaccessibility and isolation of Communist China. The Iron Curtain, including its best-known part, the BERLIN WALL, was torn down in 1989 amid the collapse of communism in Eastern Europe.

IRRECONCILABLES See **RESERVATIONISTS**.

ISOLATIONISM Term referring to a policy of avoiding involvement in international affairs. The United States pursued a basically isolationist foreign policy from the nation's inception until WORLD WAR II. America did not cut itself off completely from the rest of the world or oppose foreign trade or territorial expansion; rather the nation avoided overseas diplomatic and military entanglements or participation in foreign alliances. Shielded from European intervention by geographic separation, the United States concentrated on its own internal development.

GEORGE WASHINGTON gave an early articulation to America's emerging isolationism in a famed message at the end of his presidency. WASHINGTON'S FAREWELL ADDRESS (1796) included the oft-cited admonition to the United States "to steer clear of permanent Alliances." President THOMAS JEFFERSON similarly warned against "entangling alliances" in his first inaugural address in 1801. America's isolationist posture gained formal expression in the MONROE DOCTRINE (1823), which barred further European colonialism in the Western Hemisphere while pledging the United States against interference in Europe. The SPANISH-AMERICAN WAR (1898) marked the arrival of the United States to the status of a world power. With its acquisition of former Spanish colonies in the Caribbean and Pacific, America assumed a greatly expanded international role. But Washington continued to refrain from U.S. participation in alliances or other binding multinational arrangements. The United States proclaimed its neutrality at the outset of WORLD WAR I and did not enter the conflict until April 1917, in response to German submarine attacks on American shipping.

After the war, the Senate, reflecting historic American isolationism, rejected the TREATY OF VERSAILLES (1919) and U.S. membership in the LEAGUE OF NATIONS. With Nazism and fascism casting a threatening shadow over Europe, Congress passed a series of NEUTRALITY ACTS in the late 1930s intended to keep America out of an anticipated conflict there. Following the outbreak of World War II in 1939, the Roosevelt administration declared American neutrality. President FRANKLIN D. ROOSEVELT's subsequent efforts to align the United States behind Great Britain in its struggle against Nazi Germany invited stiff opposition from isolationist groups, most notably the AMERICA FIRST COMMITTEE, which feared that America would be drawn into the war. Roosevelt's movement away from isolationism was supported by the interventionist COMMITTEE TO DEFEND AMERICA BY AIDING THE ALLIES and the FIGHT FOR FREEDOM COMMITTEE.

America's isolationist tradition ended with the Japanese surprise attack on PEARL HARBOR in December 1941 and U.S. entry into World War II. The United States emerged from the war as the world's dominant power with vast global responsibilities. Isolationism gave way to INTERNATIONALISM, as Washington led the drive to form the UNITED NATIONS and other multilateral institutions. With the onset of the COLD WAR in the late 1940s, America committed its military and economic power to the defense of the FREE WORLD and CONTAINMENT of communism. In a fundamental departure from its isolationist past, the United States helped organize NATO and other security alliances as a bulwark against Communist aggression. The outbreak of the KOREAN WAR in 1950 brought a brief resurgence of isolationist arguments, with conservative Republicans advocating a FORTRESS AMERICA strategy wherein the United States would withdraw from Asia and Europe and concentrate on its own security. The Truman administration countered by arguing that U.S. isolationism had contributed to the rise of Nazi Germany and militarist Japan in the 1930s and would encourage Communist aggression in the 1950s. The outcome of the GREAT DEBATE in the U.S. Senate in 1951 over America's defense commitments underscored the broad bipartisan support for the nation's postwar engagement in world affairs.

Internationalism became the mainstay of U.S. foreign policy. Domestic opposition to American intervention in the VIETNAM WAR brought a revival of isolationist themes in the late 1960s and early 1970s. Critics of the war maintained the United States had neither the capability nor the right to serve as the world's policeman. The term neoisolationism was coined to describe advocacy for a policy of U.S. withdrawal from Vietnam in particular and from worldwide commitments in general. Neoisolationism faded with the end of American involvement in Southeast Asia.

ITALIAN ELECTION OPERATION (1948) Secret U.S. operation to influence the 1948 Italian national elections. By the winter of 1947 the Soviet Union had tightened its grip on Eastern Europe and relations between the United States and its former WORLD WAR II ally had deteriorated into COLD WAR confrontation. Senior Truman administration officials were deeply concerned that Soviet-sponsored political subversion also imperiled the security of Western Europe. The immediate worry was the possibility the Italian Communist Party might win parliamentary elections scheduled for April 18, 1948, and thus gain control of the government. Washington foresaw such a result bringing a similar Communist victory in France and eventual Soviet control of the Mediterranean.

In December 1947, in what was the first COVERT ACTION approved by the U.S. government since the end of World War II, the newly formed NATIONAL SECURITY COUNCIL (NSC) sanctioned a secret campaign to ensure the Communists not come to power in Italy. The CENTRAL INTELLIGENCE AGENCY (CIA), established the previous September, was instructed to carry out the election operation. The agency set up a temporary Special Procedures Group in its intelligence branch and subsequently funneled $10 million to the Christian Democrats and other Italian centrist parties. Seeking to negate the clandestine assistance given by the Soviets, the CIA planted news stories and engaged in other propaganda activities designed to discredit the Italian Communists. The success of the operation—the Christian Democrats won a majority of the parliamentary seats—encouraged U.S. policymakers to look to covert action as an effective alternative means to influence international events. In June 1948 the NSC ordered the creation of the OFFICE OF POLICY COORDINATION in the CIA to provide a permanent capability for clandestine operations.

ITATA INCIDENT (1891) Maritime episode that sullied U.S. relations with Chile. Following the outbreak of civil war in Chile in 1891, rebels sent a captured ship, the *Itata*, to San Diego, California, to pick up a weapons shipment from private arms suppliers. Charged with violating U.S. neutrality laws, the crew and its ship were detained in San Diego by federal authorities. After the crew overpowered an American deputy marshal on board and sailed for Chile, President BENJAMIN HARRISON ordered a U.S. cruiser to return the fleeing ship, by force if necessary. When the *Itata* reached Chile, rebel officials surrendered it to the pursuing U.S. Navy party, which escorted the rebel vessel back to San Diego. American courts later released the ship, ruling there had been no violation of the neutrality laws. The incident bred resentment toward the United States among the Chilean rebels who, having been denied guns by the actions of the U.S. government and threatened with American force, were able to assume power with arms obtained from Germany. Lingering anti-American hostility in Chile flared in the BALTIMORE AFFAIR later in 1891.

IVORY TRADE BAN (1989) World ban placed on all trade in elephant ivory. Concern about the plight of the African elephant mounted in 1989 amid estimates that in the preceding decade rampant poaching in east and central Africa had reduced the animal's population from about 1.3 million to roughly 750,000. Throughout the same period the price of ivory had soared, raising the incentive for the well-armed and increasingly violent poachers. Both African and Western governments, urged on by international conservation groups, sought to preserve the dwindling African elephant herds. In May 1989 Kenya and Tanzania, the two African countries where poaching had been most devastating, called for an ivory ban. In June the United States and the European Community announced bans on imports. Under growing international pressure, Japan and Hong Kong, which together accounted for some 75 percent of the world's ivory imports and where large quantities of tusks were used to make jewelry, ornamental carvings, piano keys, and billiard balls, implemented partial curbs.

The CONVENTION ON INTERNATIONAL TRADE IN ENDANGERED SPECIES (CITES), a UNITED NA-

TIONS wildlife preservation agency based in Switzerland, met in Lausanne in October 1989 and voted to proscribe international trade in elephant ivory. More than 90 member countries agreed to abide by the ban. The convention approved a U.S.-proposed resolution to place the African elephant on its most endangered species list. CITES at the same time passed a compromise proposal under which nations able to prove they had flourishing elephant populations could apply later for exemptions from the ivory ban. Five African countries—Zimbabwe, Botswana, Mozambique, Malawi, and Burundi—where elephants were increasing because of effective wildlife management immediately announced that they would form an ivory cartel and not honor the CITES restrictions. They contended that the controlled sale of legal ivory from animals culled from their burgeoning elephant populations was a necessary component of their successful wildlife management program.

The ban formally went into effect in January 1990. Within six months the World Wide Fund for Nature and the African Wildlife Foundation, a pair of conservation watchdog groups that closely monitor the elephant ivory trade, reported that the CITES action had dramatically reduced demand, forced ivory prices down, curbed African poaching, and virtually shut down the major ivory carving factories in Asia.

J

JACKSON AMENDMENT See **STRATEGIC ARMS LIMITATION TALKS I**.

JACKSON, ANDREW (1767–1845) Seventh president of the United States. Jackson was born a few days after his father's death at the Waxhaw settlement in South Carolina. Enlisting in the Continental Army at age 13, he served in the AMERICAN REVOLUTION as a mounted messenger and was taken prisoner by the British. The wartime deaths of his two brothers and mother left Jackson alone. His experience in the revolution filled him with a lifelong enmity toward the British. After the war he read law in North Carolina and, at age 20, was admitted to the bar. Appointed public prosecutor for the western district of North Carolina (now Tennessee), he moved in 1788 to the frontier settlement of Nashville, where, apart from his public duties, he built a prosperous law practice and engaged in land speculation and slave trading.

Jackson's initial political experience came in 1796 as a delegate to the Tennessee constitutional convention. The same year he was elected to Congress as Tennessee's first U.S. representative. Sent to the Senate by the state legislature in 1797, he resigned in 1798 and became a judge on Tennessee's superior court. Jackson left the bench in 1804 and temporarily retreated from politics. Meanwhile, in 1802, he had become a major general in command of the Tennessee militia. He received Aaron Burr in 1805 and for a time was an unwitting accomplice in the latter's ill-fated plot for conquest in the trans-Mississippi Southwest. Jackson disassociated himself from the BURR CONSPIRACY in time to avoid implication in Burr's alleged treason.

A harsh critic of presidents THOMAS JEFFERSON and JAMES MADISON for what he deemed their fainthearted submission to British violations of American neutral shipping rights, Jackson welcomed the outbreak of the WAR OF 1812 with Great Britain. Appointed a major general of Tennesseean volunteers at the war's outset, he commanded the expedition launched against the British-allied Creek Indians after their massacre of white settlers on the frontier in present-day Alabama. Jackson sealed the U.S. victory in the CREEK WAR (1813–1814) when he dealt the Creeks a crushing defeat in the Battle of Horseshoe Bend in March 1814. He was commissioned a major general in the regular U.S. Army in May 1814 and placed in command of the southern frontier. His smashing victory in January 1815 over the invading British at the Battle of New Orleans, which actually was waged after the TREATY OF GHENT had officially ended the war, made him a national hero. His toughness during the war earned him the nickname Old Hickory.

Raids on Georgia settlements by Seminole Indians from sanctuaries in Spanish Florida led President JAMES MONROE in December 1817 to order Jackson to suppress the incursions. Jackson in early 1818 invaded Florida, where he razed Seminole villages, seized Spanish military forts, captured Pensacola, and, in the episode that became known as the AMBRISTER AND ARBUTHNOT AFFAIR, summarily executed British subjects Robert Ambrister and Alexander Arbuthnot for their alleged incitement of the Seminoles. The FLORIDA INVASION, undertaken without express presidential authorization, caused an international furor and brought domestic calls for Jackson's public reprimand or even court-martial. Monroe decided not to discipline the general and several congressional motions to censure Jackson for his conduct during the first of the SEMINOLE WARS failed. Jackson's ulterior annexation objective was realized with Spain's cession of the Floridas to the United States in the ADAMS-ONIS TREATY of 1819. He ended his military career in 1821

when he resigned his commission to accept Monroe's appointment as first territorial governor of Florida. After a six-month tenure presiding over the establishment of American authority in the former Spanish territory, he resigned and returned home to Tennessee. He was elected to the Senate in 1823, where he became chairman of the military affairs committee.

One of four candidates for president in 1824, he finished first in the electoral vote ahead of JOHN QUINCY ADAMS, William H. Crawford, and HENRY CLAY. In the absence of an electoral majority for any of the candidates the election was thrown into the House of Representatives. Clay, House Speaker and a Jackson adversary, gave his support to Adams, who was elected president on the first ballot. After Adams made Clay his secretary of state, Jackson supporters charged that their man had been defeated by a "corrupt bargain." Jackson resigned his Senate seat in 1825 to prepare for a second run at the White House. Nominated for president in 1828 by the nascent Democratic Party, of which he was the founder, he swept to victory over Adams. South Carolinian JOHN C. CALHOUN was elected vice-president.

Jackson's diplomacy produced an agreement with Great Britain that opened the prosperous British West Indies to American commerce. He pursued settlement of long-standing American claims for damages resulting from French assaults on neutral American commercial shipping during the Napoleonic Wars (1803–1815). In a Franco-American treaty concluded in 1831, France agreed to pay the so-called FRENCH SPOLIATION CLAIMS. When the French legislature subsequently refused to appropriate the funds for the indemnity payments, an angry Jackson threatened American reprisal should France fail to abide by terms of the 1831 agreement. Tensions escalated and in late 1835 the two countries broke off diplomatic contacts. Through British mediation, the dispute was resolved in 1836 when France agreed to pay the overdue claims. Jackson made an unsuccessful attempt at purchasing Texas from Mexico. Following the TEXAN REVOLUTION (1836), he recognized the independence of Texas but would not support annexation of the Lone Star Republic for fear of splitting the Democratic Party over the question of slavery.

Immediately after his reelection in 1832 over National Republican candidate Clay, Jackson met head-on the growing tariff controversy that fundamentally framed the issue of states' rights versus federal union. Espousing the doctrine of nullification, which held that a state could refuse to enforce within its territory federal laws it judged to be unconstitutional, South Carolina state legislators in late 1832 moved to nullify the 1828 TARIFF OF ABOMINATIONS and the successor 1832 federal tariff. Jackson responded with a forceful proclamation ordering South Carolina to comply with all federal laws and denouncing nullification as inherently irreconcilable with a system of federal powers. He secured from Congress authorization to use military force to ensure state obedience to federal laws. A final confrontation was averted and the crisis resolved with passage of the COMPROMISE TARIFF in 1833. The tariff controversy forced a break between Jackson and Calhoun, the leading expounder of the nullification doctrine and champion of states' rights. Calhoun resigned in December 1832 amid the Nullification Crisis and was replaced as vice-president by MARTIN VAN BUREN, who emerged as Jackson's heir apparent.

In INDIAN AFFAIRS, Jackson pursued an aggressive policy aimed at removing the Indians, especially the Five Civilized Tribes of the Southeast, from the path of advancing white settlement. He long had faulted the federal government's historical practice of dealing with the Indian tribes as though they were foreign nations. Jackson claimed that the negotiation of INDIAN TREATIES within this framework conferred a measure of independent sovereignty upon the Indian nations that they did not, in his view, actually possess. Rejecting Cherokee assertions of sovereignty in the Southeast, he endorsed Georgia's extension of its laws over all Indian territory within the state. If the Cherokees or other Indians wanted to keep their tribal government and live apart from white society, he declared, they would have to move. He encouraged the various Indian tribes to accept a federal offer of land in the trans-Mississippi West where, he pledged, they would have complete sovereignty. This proposal became the basis for his INDIAN REMOVAL POLICY, which Congress sanctioned through the INDIAN REMOVAL ACT of 1830. The law authorized the president to set aside an INDIAN TERRITORY west of the Mississippi for tribal resettlement; and then swap this area for Indian-held lands in the Southeast. The Jackson administration undertook to negotiate removal treaties with the southeast Indian tribes, several of which put up resistance to the federal policy. In 1835 Jackson involved the U.S. Army in the second Seminole War to subdue the Florida tribe's resistance to the removal program. Under terms of a treaty completed the same year with a minority Cherokee faction, the defiant Cherokee majority eventually was removed by force in 1838 after Jackson left office. Meanwhile, in 1832, U.S. military forces had crushed the Sauk and Fox Indians in Illinois in the BLACK HAWK WAR. Following the inauguration of his handpicked successor Van Buren in March 1937, Jackson retired to his plantation, the Hermitage, near Nashville, where he maintained a keen interest in national politics until his death.

JACKSON-VANIK AMENDMENT (1974) Amendment to the Trade Act of 1974 barring the extension of preferential trade terms to Communist countries that restricted the emigration of their citizens. The measure reflected the concern in the U.S. Congress over the persecution of Jews in the Soviet Union and the difficulties they faced in attempting to leave. In October 1972 U.S. and Soviet negotiators completed a major trade pact, part of the developing DETENTE between the nations, that called for the United States to grant MOST-FAVORED-NATION (MFN) trade status to the Soviet Union.

In the ensuing congressional debate over legislation to implement the trade agreement, Senator Henry M. Jackson (D-WA) introduced an amendment limiting the provision of MFN status or commercial trade credits to only those Communist nations with open emigration policies. Representative Charles A. Vanik (D-OH) submitted a similar measure in the House. The Soviet Union regarded the Jackson-Vanik proposal as an intrusion upon its domestic affairs. At the June 1973 WASHINGTON SUMMIT, Soviet leader Leonid I. Brezhnev met with members of Congress to voice Kremlin objections on the issue.

Throughout the prolonged consideration of the trade bill, both the Nixon and

Ford administrations opposed the Jackson-Vanik measure as congressional interference in the conduct of foreign policy. In October 1974 Jackson and Secretary of State HENRY A. KISSINGER finally reached an agreement on the legislation's terms and the Jackson-Vanik "Freedom of Emigration" Amendment was passed in December. It became law when the Trade Act of 1974 was signed on January 3, 1975. The revised amendment authorized the president to waive its trade-preference restrictions for up to 18 months for countries judged to be moving toward free emigration. The Soviet Union then rejected the trade-emigration linkage established by Congress and repudiated the 1972 trade accord.

Over the next decade, emigration from the Soviet Union fluctuated with the shifting state of superpower relations. By 1979, progress in the SALT II arms control negotiations and a gradual rise in the number of Jews permitted to leave by Moscow led the Carter administration to consider granting MFN trade status to the Soviet Union. The Soviet invasion of Afghanistan in December 1979 ended any prospects for an improvement in trade relations. As U.S.-USSR tensions escalated, Soviet Jewish emigration dropped to an all-time low of some 1000 a year between 1984 and 1986. Political changes under reformist Soviet leader Mikhail S. Gorbachev had led to a steady increase in Soviet Jewish emigration after 1986. At the 1990 WASHINGTON SUMMIT, President GEORGE BUSH and Gorbachev concluded a broad trade agreement that provided MFN status to the USSR. In keeping with Jackson-Vanik, Bush withheld the trade pact from congressional approval pending passage by the Soviet legislature of a law guaranteeing free emigration, which was accomplished in 1991. Following the July 1991 MOSCOW SUMMIT, Bush forwarded the agreement to Congress for enactment. Consideration of Soviet MFN status was derailed by the August 1991 MOSCOW COUP and rendered moot by the disintegration of the USSR in December 1991.

JAMAICA AGREEMENT See **INTERNATIONAL MONETARY FUND**.

JAPANESE AND KOREAN EXCLUSION LEAGUE Organization formed May 7, 1905, in San Francisco during a period of rising anti-Japanese sentiment. The league's primarily union membership advanced arguments against Japanese immigration similar to those used in previous decades to justify the exclusion of Chinese laborers: the Japanese did not fit into American society and their cheap labor undercut the employment of native workers. In 1906 the group helped persuade the San Francisco school board to segregate Japanese and other Asian students. This precipitated a diplomatic crisis with the Japanese government that had to be resolved by the administration of President THEODORE ROOSEVELT the following year in the GENTLEMEN'S AGREEMENT. The organization changed its name to the Asiatic Exclusion League in 1908. Its goals were largely achieved in the IMMIGRATION ACT OF 1924, which effectively barred further Asian immigration. Members continued to advocate exclusionary measures until the late 1940s.

JAPANESE MUTUAL COOPERATION AND SECURITY TREATY See **JAPANESE SECURITY TREATY**.

JAPANESE PEACE TREATY (1951) Peace settlement officially ending WORLD WAR II in the Pacific and restoring Japan's sovereignty. In early 1951 President HARRY S. TRUMAN appointed JOHN FOSTER DULLES to negotiate a Japanese peace treaty. After discussions with American allies and other interested powers, Dulles completed a draft agreement in June, whereupon Truman invited 55 nations, excluding Nationalist and Communist China, to a conference to sign the peace settlement. Fifty-two accepted, including U.S. COLD WAR rival the Soviet Union. The parley opened in San Francisco on September 4, 1951, under the chairmanship of Secretary of State DEAN ACHESON, who thwarted the efforts of the Communist delegates to block the American-sponsored accord. On September 8, 49 nations signed the peace treaty. The USSR and its satellites Poland and Czechoslovakia abstained. The settlement arranged for ending the postwar U.S. military occupation of Japan. Under its terms, Japan acknowledged Korea's independence; renounced all claims to Formosa, the Pescadores, the Kuriles, southern Sakhalin, and the Pacific islands formerly under its mandate; and agreed to a U.S.-administered UNITED NATIONS trusteeship over the Ryukyu and Bonin islands. Other provisions excused the payment of Japanese war reparations and permitted Japan to rearm for self-defense. On the same day the peace settlement was signed, Washington and Tokyo also concluded the JAPANESE SECURITY TREATY allowing U.S. troops to remain in Japan. The U.S. Senate, by 66 to 10, approved the peace treaty on March 20, 1952, and it went into effect April 28.

JAPANESE SECURITY TREATY (1951) Defense pact between the United States and Japan. With the outbreak of the KOREAN WAR in 1950, the Truman administration hastened to extend its policy of CONTAINMENT of communism to Asia. U.S. policymakers viewed Japan as the strategic linchpin in the post–WORLD WAR II security system they undertook to establish in the Pacific. On September 8, 1951, the same day 49 nations concluded the JAPANESE PEACE TREATY, Washington and Tokyo signed a security treaty permitting U.S. armed forces to remain in Japan for an indefinite period to defend it against outside attack. The pact stipulated that the Japanese, through rearmament, would gradually and increasingly assume responsibility for their own defense. In the week before completing the agreement with Japan, the United States had advanced its security arrangement for the Pacific by concluding the PHILIPPINE MUTUAL DEFENSE TREATY and the defensive ANZUS TREATY with Australia and New Zealand.

Japanese disaffection with the pact's infringement on Japan's sovereignty took form over the 1950s in a growing anti-Americanism and finally led Secretary of State JOHN FOSTER DULLES to open negotiations in 1958 on a revision. In January 1960 President DWIGHT D. EISENHOWER and Japanese Premier Nobusuke Kishi signed the Japanese Mutual Cooperation and Security Treaty. The new accord pledged each nation to treat an armed attack against the other as a threat to its own security and to act to meet the common danger. It allowed the United States to base military forces in Japan for 10 years, but also required Washington to consult with Tokyo on their deployment. Japanese leftist opponents of the treaty sought unsuccessfully to block its ratification through violent demonstrations.

JAPANESE-AMERICAN INTERNMENT Incarceration of Japanese-Americans during WORLD WAR II justified on the basis of national security. The war aroused traditional anti-Asian sentiments on the American West Coast. A government report that attributed the success of Japan's surprise attack on PEARL HARBOR in part to Japanese spies in Hawaii fanned existing apprehensions over the loyalty of the Japanese-American community. The extraordinary internment measure grew out of the U.S. government's concern over possible espionage and sabotage.

On February 19, 1942, President FRANKLIN D. ROOSEVELT issued Executive Order 9066. The presidential directive authorized the secretary of war and his designated commanders to identify restricted military areas from which residents could be excluded. Under the order, persons of Japanese ancestry were forcibly relocated from California, Oregon, Washington, and Arizona to internment centers in the U.S. interior. Established by Executive Order 9102 that March, the Wartime Relocation Authority transferred and confined about 120,000 evacuees by November 1942. Many lost their homes, possessions, and businesses.

In December 1944 the Supreme Court in *Korematsu* v. *United States* upheld the constitutionality of the internment for resident aliens, but ruled in *Ex Parte Endo* that loyal citizens could not be held against their will. The same month the federal government announced the relocation centers would be closed by the end of 1945. The Japanese-American Evacuation Claims Act, enacted in 1948 to reimburse those who had lost their property, began a long process of restitution. In 1980 Congress created the Commission on Wartime Relocation and Internment of Civilians to determine whether Japanese-Americans had been wronged under Executive Order 9066. In its 1982 report *Personal Justice Denied*, the commission concluded internment had been a grave injustice and recommended a compensatory payment to its surviving victims. The Japanese-American Internees Reparations Act (1988) offered an official U.S. apology to those incarcerated during the war and authorized a $20,000 payment to each. The first payments were made in 1990.

JAPANESE-AMERICAN TREATY OF 1894
U.S.-Japanese commerce and friendship
pact. The 1858 TREATY OF EDO had established full diplomatic and trade relations
between the United States and Japan, while
similar agreements had opened the isolated
island empire to the major European powers. These pacts had given the United
States and the other Western nations the
privilege of EXTRATERRITORIALITY in Japan as
well as the right to set Japan's tariffs on foreign goods. As Japan modernized under
the Meiji Restoration in the late 19th century, renegotiation of the unequal agreements with the Western powers became a
primary aim of its diplomacy. Japanese successes in the Sino-Japanese War (1894–
1895) persuaded the Western nations of
Japan's emergence as an important power
and brought negotiations to place future
relations on a more equal basis. U.S. Secretary of State WALTER Q. GRESHAM and Japanese envoy Shinichiro Kurino, meeting in
Washington, signed an agreement on November 22, 1894, replacing the 1858 treaty.
Formally titled the Treaty of Commerce
and Navigation of 1894, it rescinded the extraterritoriality provisions of the Edo agreement, restored to Japan control over its tariff rates, provided for greater contacts and
trade between the two nations, and allowed for the free travel and immigration
of their citizens. Similar pacts were concluded by Japan with the European powers. The treaty went into effect in 1899 and
was scheduled to expire after 12 years. It
was succeeded by the TREATY OF WASHINGTON
(1911).

JAY, JOHN (1745–1829) Statesman, diplomat, and first chief justice of the United
States. Descendant of among the wealthiest
and most influential families in colonial
New York, he graduated from King's College (now Columbia University), studied
law, passed the bar in 1768, and began a
successful legal practice in his native New
York City. Thrust into public life by the
AMERICAN REVOLUTION, the patriot Jay was a
New York delegate to the Continental Congress. In December 1778, he was elected its
president, a position he held until his appointment in September 1779 as minister
plenipotentiary to Spain.

Jay's mission to Madrid (1780–1782)
foundered as he was unable to secure
Spanish recognition of U.S. independence,
significant loans, or a military alliance in
the war against the British. He joined BEN-
JAMIN FRANKLIN in Paris in the spring of 1782
as a member of the American commission
to negotiate peace with Great Britain. Suspicious of French diplomatic designs, Jay
orchestrated the commission's decision to
violate its instructions by negotiating with
the British independently of key U.S. ally
France. He influenced fellow commissioners to conclude preliminary articles of
peace in November without the prior consent of the French government. After signing the Anglo-American TREATY OF PARIS
(1783) formally ending the revolution, Jay
declined diplomatic appointments to
Britain and France. Returning to America in
1784, he learned the Continental Congress
had named him secretary of foreign affairs
under the ARTICLES OF CONFEDERATION.

Problems in relations with London and
Madrid preoccupied American diplomacy
during his six-year tenure. The United
States complained persistently about
British incitement of Indian resistance to
U.S. expansion on the northwest frontier.
Jay was unable to win Britain's agreement
to evacuate the military posts it still held in
America's OLD NORTHWEST in violation of the
Treaty of Paris. American noncompliance
with terms of the 1783 agreement concerning treatment of Loyalists and payment of
pre-revolution debts to British creditors effectively prevented Jay and U.S. Minister at
London JOHN ADAMS from gaining British
commercial concessions. Jay negotiated
with Spain's Minister to America Don Diego
de Gardoqui to resolve disputes over the
boundary between the United States and
Spanish Florida, and over Spanish refusal
to acknowledge America's right to navigation of the lower Mississippi River. Bitter
domestic reaction in the South and West
scuttled the proposed JAY-GARDOQUI TREATY
(1786), which would have denied the
United States navigation of Spain's portion
of the Mississippi for 30 years.

Critical of the government under the
Confederation as being too weak, Jay became a strong advocate of the new CONSTI-
TUTION drafted in 1787. He contributed,
with ALEXANDER HAMILTON and JAMES
MADISON, to *The Federalist* papers that
urged the Constitution's adoption by the
states and campaigned successfully for its

ratification by New York. Under the new national government organized in 1789, President GEORGE WASHINGTON appointed Jay as first chief justice of the U.S. Supreme Court. The specter of war with Britain in 1794, arising from continued British occupation of the northwest posts and assaults on neutral American commerce, led Washington to send Jay on a special mission to London to seek a peaceful settlement. The resulting JAY'S TREATY of November 1794, while arranging for British evacuation of the northwest forts, failed to uphold America's neutral rights. Jay's acquiescence in the treaty to the narrow British understanding of FREEDOM OF THE SEAS precipitated a serious crisis in U.S.-French relations. France, at war with Britain, complained bitterly that Jay and the Federalists had abandoned U.S. obligations to the French under the FRANCO-AMERICAN ALLIANCE (1778). Jay and his controversial treaty were vilified by domestic critics, who accused the chief justice of capitulation to British influence. Returning home in 1795, Jay resigned from the Supreme Court to serve as New York's governor (1795–1801), an office to which he had been elected during his London absence. After two terms he returned to private life.

JAY-GARDOQUI TREATY   See **PINCKNEY'S TREATY**.

JAY'S TREATY (1794) Controversial treaty concluded between the United States and Great Britain on November 19, 1794. Negotiated by U.S. Supreme Court Chief Justice JOHN JAY, it addressed the main issues plaguing Anglo-American diplomacy in the decade after the AMERICAN REVOLUTION: violations of the TREATY OF PARIS (1783) that ended the war; commercial conflict; and division over the rights of neutral shipping. Great Britain defied the terms of the Paris agreement by refusing to evacuate its frontier military posts in America's OLD NORTHWEST and by carrying away American slaves during its postwar troop withdrawal from the United States. The British justified maintaining garrisons on U.S. soil and slave confiscations as retaliation for U.S. treaty violations: the United States had failed to protect British Loyalists in America against persecution; and Americans had not yet paid off prewar debts to British creditors.

An unsettled boundary between Maine and Canada was another legacy of the 1783 treaty and a source of growing friction.

To these problems was added the sore point of British restrictions on American trade that had excluded U.S. ships from the British West Indies since 1783. British commercial discrimination prompted Secretary of State THOMAS JEFFERSON at the outset of the 1790s to urge U.S. reciprocal action against British trade with America. Jefferson's threats of reprisal alarmed Great Britain, which in 1791 chose to open full diplomatic relations with its former colony with an eye toward influencing U.S. policy. Talks between first British Minister to America George Hammond and Jefferson resolved nothing. Meanwhile Treasury Secretary ALEXANDER HAMILTON blocked anti-British commerce legislation since the credit and fiscal systems he had devised for the new nation depended heavily on revenues from British trade.

Anglo-American tensions worsened after war broke out between Great Britain and France in February 1793. The British government issued edicts in 1793 and 1794 that targeted French wartime trade with neutrals such as the United States. Enforcement of the orders by British warships led to seizure of American commercial vessels in French Caribbean ports and the IMPRESSMENT of American crews, drawing U.S. outrage. The British also encouraged the establishment of a neutral Indian state in the Old Northwest to act as a buffer against advancing U.S. settlement and thus assure continued British control of the northern posts and the lucrative fur trade in the Great Lakes region. By early 1794, the combination of longstanding peace treaty grievances, lack of an Anglo-American commercial treaty, the Caribbean spoliations, and friction on the northwest frontier had brought a crisis in U.S.-British relations. President GEORGE WASHINGTON, at the urging of Hamilton and other Federalist leaders, sent special envoy Jay on a peace mission to London to negotiate differences and thus avert war.

Under the resulting agreement, known as Jay's Treaty, Great Britain pledged to surrender its northern posts by June 1, 1796, opened the British West Indies to limited American trade, and extended other modest commercial privileges. While the

British agreed to pay for the spoliation of American ships, they did not repudiate the Caribbean raids. In return for the trade concessions, Jay acquiesced on the British interpretation of neutral rights, agreeing that Great Britain could seize enemy property transported on neutral ships provided it paid for the confiscation. Jay in effect consented to British violation of the maritime principle FREE SHIPS MAKE FREE GOODS, an idea earlier endorsed by the United States in both the PLAN OF 1776 and its 1778 commercial treaty with France. The northeast boundary dispute, payment of prewar debts to the British, and the exact sum of British compensation for maritime seizures were referred to joint arbitration commissions. The Anglo-American accord ignored the slave issue, the impressment of American seamen, and British incitement of the Indians.

Jay's Treaty met with bitter opposition in the United States where Democratic-Republican critics assailed the agreement as a sell-out to Great Britain and an abandonment of the American commitment to FREEDOM OF THE SEAS. Angry crowds burned Jay in effigy and threw stones at Hamilton, author of Jay's instructions, when he spoke in support of the accord. The Senate narrowly approved the treaty on June 24, 1795, when Federalist members were able to override Democratic-Republican resistance. Following the exchange of ratifications in October, House of Representative opponents tried to block the pact by attempting to withhold the money needed to enforce its provisions. Their efforts failed as the House approved the appropriation in April 1796. Jay's Treaty brought on a crisis in relations with France, which deplored American capitulation to British rules on neutral trade as a violation of U.S. obligations to the French under the treaties of the FRANCO-AMERICAN ALLIANCE (1778). Despite the protest it engendered, Jay's diplomacy kept the peace and marked the first major step since the American Revolution toward Anglo-American reconciliation.

JCS See **JOINT CHIEFS OF STAFF** in **APPENDIX B**.

JEFFERSON, THOMAS (1743–1826) Revolutionary patriot, diplomat, first secretary of state, vice-president, and third president of the United States. Jefferson graduated from William and Mary College in 1762, studied law, and was admitted to the bar in his native colony of Virginia. From 1769 to 1775, he served in the Virginia House of Burgesses, where he became deeply involved in the politics of the AMERICAN REVOLUTION through membership in a patriot faction fervently opposed to British imperial domination of the American colonies. As a member of the Continental Congress from 1775 to 1776, he drafted the Declaration of Independence, which established the 13 colonies as the United States of America and made the case for the American cause through a vigorous indictment of abuses by King George III. In the landmark document, Jefferson heralded government by popular consent as the foundation of political liberty and asserted fundamental, inalienable human rights.

Determined to push political and social reforms in his own state, he left Congress in September 1776 and the next month returned to the Virginia legislature, where he would serve until his election as governor in 1779. After his two year term, he accepted appointment by the Continental Congress in 1782 as one of the U.S. commissioners authorized to negotiate peace terms with the British. But personal circumstances, notably his wife's death, prevented him from attending the European talks that culminated in the war-ending TREATY OF PARIS (1783). Back in Congress from 1783 to 1784, Jefferson helped draft the Ordinance of 1784, which became the basis for the later organization of the NORTHWEST TERRITORY.

Succeeding BENJAMIN FRANKLIN as minister to France in 1785, and serving in the post until 1789, he negotiated limited trade concessions from the French and concluded an important consular convention in 1788. Jefferson's experience among the French confirmed his view that France was a natural ally of the United States. He came to favor strongly the cultivation of improved Franco-American relations as a counterweight to the British, who Jefferson saw as America's natural rival. Toward the end of his mission he reported on events unfolding in the French Revolution. He left France in October 1789 strongly sympathetic to the cause of French republicanism. Due to his absence in Europe, Jefferson played no direct role in the Constitutional Convention (1787) assembled to strengthen the ARTICLES OF CONFEDERATION. He supported the new CONSTITUTION but objected to the lack of a specific safeguard for individual liberties. His concern was allayed after learning that a bill of rights would be added.

Jefferson in 1790 accepted appointment by President GEORGE WASHINGTON as the first secretary of state. Philosophical differences pitted him against his political nemesis, Treasury Secretary ALEXANDER HAMILTON. The two ranking members in the Washington administration clashed over foreign and domestic policies. The personal division between them evolved into the larger schism in American politics between Jeffersonian Democratic-Republicans and Hamiltonian Federalists. Jefferson, proponent of states' rights and champion of republican government, suspected Hamilton of favoring an American monarchy and resisted the treasury secretary's attempts to concentrate power in the national government at the expense of the states. Jefferson's philosophy of agrarian democracy clashed with Hamiltonian ideas regarding development of American manufacturing and commerce. Hamilton's pro-British outlook and strong antipathy for the French Revolution placed him at loggerheads with the pro-French secretary of state.

The course of U.S. relations with Great Britain and France dominated Jefferson's tenure as secretary of state. He backed the movement in the early 1790s in Congress, led by political ally JAMES MADISON, for commercial discrimination against Britain to pressure it to abandon its military posts in America's OLD NORTHWEST and to make trade concessions. Momentum for anti-British measures mounted in light of British interference with American neutral rights at sea following the outbreak of Anglo-French war in 1793. Jefferson and Madison were thwarted by Hamilton, who, fearing the loss of revenues from British trade, used his influence to block U.S. commercial retaliation. Violent excesses dampened Jefferson's enthusiasm for the French Revolution, though he remained solidly supportive of French republican aspirations. Against counterarguments offered by Hamilton, he persuaded Washington to accept the FRANCO-AMERICAN ALLIANCE (1778) as

still in force and to recognize formally the new revolutionary French government. Having concluded that direct involvement in the Franco-British war would not serve U.S. interests, the secretary of state reluctantly endorsed Washington's NEUTRALITY PROCLAMATION (1793).

French challenges to American neutrality during the GENET AFFAIR (1793) proved embarrassing to Jefferson, who initially had welcomed the arrival of French Minister Edmond C. Genet to the United States. The secretary of state lost patience with the French envoy's meddling in American domestic affairs and helped bring about the minister's dismissal. Concern for navigation of the Mississippi River led Jefferson to prod Spain, which controlled the mouth of the river, to guarantee U.S. access to the waterway through New Orleans. U.S.-Spanish diplomacy bogged down and settlement of the issue awaited negotiation of PINCKNEY'S TREATY (1795) in Washington's second term.

In return for Hamilton's agreement to the eventual location of the nation's capital on the Potomac, Jefferson supported the treasury secretary's plans for funding of the national debt and federal assumption of state debts. Apart from this expedient alliance, Jefferson opposed Hamilton's financial system. Antagonism between the two men hardened through Washington's first term. Resentful of Hamilton's interference in foreign affairs, and convinced that the president had embraced anti-French Federalist sentiments, Jefferson quit the cabinet in December 1793.

He emerged during a three-year retreat to his Virginia home, Monticello, as leader of the opposition Democratic-Republican Party. Jefferson deplored the Washington administration's surrender of American rights to the British in the controversial JAY'S TREATY (1794). He ended his retirement in 1796 to run for president. Finishing second in the voting to Federalist JOHN ADAMS, he became vice-president. Jefferson was critical of the Adams administration's handling of the crisis in U.S.-French relations in the latter 1790s. He suggested initially that the president had exaggerated the XYZ AFFAIR (1797) to turn domestic sympathies against France and thus discredit the traditionally pro-French Democratic-Republicans. The vice-president assailed

Hamiltonian Federalists, who wanted to escalate the undeclared QUASI-WAR (1798–1800) into a full-fledged conflict. The notorious ALIEN AND SEDITION ACTS (1798), Federalist legislation that attempted to suppress free speech and stifle political opposition, drew his condemnation. In the Kentucky Resolutions (1798, 1799), companion measures to Madison's similar Virginia Resolutions (1798), the vice-president denounced the acts as unconstitutional and, in a powerful expression of the principle of states' rights, asserted that a state could nullify federal law.

A tie electoral vote between Jefferson and Aaron Burr threw the historic 1800 election into the House of Representatives, which chose Jefferson president after Hamilton steered Federalist support to his long-standing political adversary, whom the former treasury secretary considered a lesser evil than Burr. In his two terms in office, Jefferson collaborated with Secretary of State Madison on a foreign policy that sought protection for U.S. commercial shipping and neutral rights. Since the end of the American Revolution, the United States had paid money, or so-called tribute, to the North African Barbary states to secure assurances against attacks on American merchant vessels in the Mediterranean Sea by the Barbary pirates. After the Jefferson administration refused Tripoli's demand for increased tribute payments, the piratical state declared war on the United States in 1801. Navy forces sent by Jefferson to the Mediterranean prevailed in the ensuing TRIPOLITAN WAR (1801–1805). The American victory brought an end to further U.S. tribute to Tripoli.

The outstanding achievement of Jefferson's presidency was the LOUISIANA PURCHASE (1803), wherein the United States acquired the vast territory between the Mississippi River and the Rocky Mountains from France for $15 million. The purchase doubled the nation's size and cleared the way for U.S. westward expansion. The Jefferson administration precipitated the WEST FLORIDA CONTROVERSY by staking claim to Spanish West Florida as part of the Louisiana Purchase. Spain dismissed the American claim as illegitimate. Though interested in rounding out the territory of the United States, a hesitant Jefferson decided against a move to try to wrest Florida from Spain by force. To explore the vast trans-Mississippi expanse acquired from Napoleon, the president commissioned the LEWIS AND CLARK EXPEDITION (1804–1806). This historic trek yielded an abundance of geographical and scientific information about the previously uncharted West and spurred the transcontinental expansion of American trade and settlement.

Alerted to the scheming of former Vice-President Burr, who apparently planned either to detach Louisiana from the Union or to invade and conquer Mexico, Jefferson foiled the BURR CONSPIRACY (1804–1807). By refusing to answer Chief Justice JOHN MARSHALL's subpoena ordering him to testify at Burr's treason trial, Jefferson established the precedent of executive privilege. The trial ended in Burr's acquittal. Meanwhile, at Jefferson's recommendation, Congress in March 1807 passed a law banning the importation of slaves to the United States on or after Janury 1, 1808.

Jefferson became preoccupied with the problem of escalating abuses on American merchant shipping by belligerents Great Britain and France during the Napoleonic Wars (1803–1815). Seeking an alternative to either war or U.S. submission, he decided upon a policy of economic coercion to force British and French respect for America's neutral rights. After allowing the NON-IMPORTATION ACT (1806) to go into effect against Britain, the president won congressional passage of the remarkable EMBARGO ACT (1807), which shut off all of America's foreign trade. The embargo caused far greater economic dislocation in the United States than in Britain or France, both of which bore up well under Jefferson's commercial sanctions. The trade ban grew increasingly unpopular since it failed to bring European concessions on neutral rights while crippling the U.S. economy. Bitter congressional opposition to his policy forced Jefferson to approve the total embargo's repeal through the NON-INTERCOURSE ACT, which he signed shortly before leaving office in March 1809.

Jefferson retired to Monticello. Burdensome personal debts led him in the last years of his life to the brink of bankruptcy. At the end of the WAR OF 1812, the lifelong bibliophile sold his 6500-volume book collection to the U.S. government to replace the contents of the Library of Congress, which had been destroyed when the British burned the Capitol in 1814. Jefferson's final great public deed was the founding of the University of Virginia at Charlottesville in 1819. He died on the 50th anniversary of the Declaration of Independence.

JOHNSON ACT See **IMMIGRATION ACT OF 1921**.

JOHNSON, ANDREW (1808–1875) Seventeenth U.S. president. Johnson was born in North Carolina. His father's death in 1811 left the family in poverty. He moved to Tennessee in 1826, settling in Greenville and establishing himself as a tailor. Self-educated and ambitious, he soon plunged into politics as a champion of the workingman and foe of aristocratic privilege. He was elected a Greenville alderman in 1828 and mayor in 1830. Beginning in 1835, the Democrat Johnson served in the state legislature. In 1843 he won a seat in the U.S. House of Representatives, where he spent ten years. He served as Tennessee governor from 1853 until 1857, when he was elected a U.S. Senator. In the Senate, he defended slavery and rejected the theory that the federal government could bar the entrance of slaves into a U.S. territory. In 1860 he was mentioned for the vice-presidential nomination. When the Democratic Party split, he half-heartedly supported John C. Breckenridge, the Southern candidate, while espousing compromise between North and South. Opposed to secession, he was the only Southern senator to support the Union during the Civil War.

In March 1862, President ABRAHAM LINCOLN appointed Johnson military governor of Tennessee. Nominated as Lincoln's running mate in 1864 on the Union ticket, he was elected vice-president. After Lincoln's assassination in April 1865, Johnson became president. His determination to carry out Lincoln's conciliatory plan for reestablishing government in the states that had seceded led him into bitter conflict with the Radical Republicans in Congress, who wanted to impose a harsh program to punish the South for its role in the war. Johnson vetoed initial reconstruction bills passed by the radicals. Strengthened in the congressional elections of 1866, supporters of radical reconstruction pushed through their legislative program over Johnson's objection. They also moved to limit presidential powers by passing, once again over his veto, the Tenure of Office Act (1867), which forbade the president from removing certain public officials from office without the Senate's consent. Johnson defied the law, which he contended was unconstitutional, by dismissing Secretary of War Edwin M. Stanton, a staunch Radical Republican who had been undermining the president's policies. The radicals in the House of Representatives used the episode to impeach Johnson in February 1868 for "high crimes and misdemeanors." He was acquitted by a single vote in May in the impeachment trial before the Senate.

Foreign policy during the turbulent, Reconstruction-dominated Johnson years was conducted almost entirely by Secretary of State WILLIAM H. SEWARD, a Lincoln holdover. An ardent expansionist, Seward completed the ALASKA PURCHASE from Russia in 1867 and annexed the Pacific MIDWAY ISLANDS the same year. His plans for additional territorial acquisitions in the Caribbean were blocked by the administration's Radical Republican foes in Congress. The secretary of state also pursued the ALABAMA CLAIMS against Great Britain for damage inflicted on Union shipping during the Civil War by British-built Confederate ships. Seward negotiated the Anglo-American JOHNSON-CLARENDON CONVENTION (1869), which arranged for arbitration of the claims, but the Senate rejected the agreement. After leaving office in March 1869, Johnson returned to Tennessee. Elected to the U.S. Senate as a Democrat in 1874, he died the following year.

JOHNSON DEBT DEFAULT ACT (1934) Federal legislation barring further loans to nations that had defaulted on debts to the United States. During and immediately after WORLD WAR I Great Britain, France, and the other European Allied countries, unable to sustain the huge costs of the war effort, had borrowed more than $11 billion from America. The worldwide economic crisis of the Great Depression necessitated the HOOVER MORATORIUM, an agreement reached among the United States and the European debtor nations in 1931 to suspend for one year the payment of both U.S.

war debts and German reparations to the European Allies. At the 1932 Lausanne Conference the European nations agreed among themselves to forgive 90 percent of Germany's reparations if the U.S. government in turn canceled their war debts. The Hoover administration declined and, when a joint settlement could not be reached on how to address the debt issue following expiration of the Hoover Moratorium, the European nations, except Finland, defaulted on their loans in December 1932. Unhappy with the lack of progress on resolving the debt question and angered by the European default, Congress passed legislation, sponsored by Senator Hiram W. Johnson (R-CA), prohibiting new loans to governments that failed to repay earlier obligations. President FRANKLIN D. ROOSEVELT signed the measure into law April 13, 1934. The act failed to induce the financially strapped European nations to resume their debt payments and the war debts, which were never repaid, remained a source of U.S.-European tension until WORLD WAR II.

JOHNSON DOCTRINE (1965) Declaration by President LYNDON B. JOHNSON that the United States would not allow the establishment of another Communist government in the Western Hemisphere. His pledge was directed at the Dominican Republic, where a bloody popular revolt had erupted April 24, 1965, against the rightist, Washington-backed government. The Johnson administration initially sent 500 Marines to the island to protect American citizens' lives while insisting U.S. forces would not take sides in the struggle. But on May 2, the president told the nation in a televised address the Dominican revolt had fallen under the control of Communist plotters with links to Fidel Castro's Cuba. Articulating what came to be called the Johnson Doctrine, he said the United States must not, and would not, abide another Castro-style takeover in the Americas.

Johnson's decision under the doctrine to dispatch another 20,000 troops to help thwart the alleged Communist conspiracy tarnished the U.S. image in Latin America. U.S. actions in the DOMINICAN CRISIS were deplored in the region as a violation of the ORGANIZATION OF AMERICAN STATES nonintervention covenant and as resurgent "Yankee

IMPERIALISM." Administration policy lost credibility with American liberals when Johnson was unable to substantiate his claims about the Communist connection in the Dominican Republic uprising.

JOHNSON, LOUIS ARTHUR (1891–1966) Secretary of defense under President HARRY S. TRUMAN. The Virginia native earned a law degree from the University of Virginia and entered practice in Clarksburg, West Virginia. Johnson served in the West Virginia state legislature and saw action as an Army officer in France during WORLD WAR I. After the war he resumed his law practice and became active in veterans' affairs. Appointed assistant secretary of war by President FRANKLIN D. ROOSEVELT in 1937, Johnson pressed for rearmament to build U.S. military preparedness and was a strong advocate of air power. He resigned from government service in July 1940 when new Secretary of War HENRY L. STIMSON decided to bring in his own choice for the assistant's position. Johnson again practiced law between 1940 and 1949, except for several months in 1942 when he headed a U.S. economic advisory mission to India during WORLD WAR II.

In March 1949 Truman named Johnson to succeed JAMES V. FORRESTAL, the nation's first secretary of defense. Stressing his commitment to getting "a dollar's worth of defense for every dollar spent," Johnson set out to reduce defense expenditures. Within a month of taking office, he canceled construction of the Navy's 65,000-ton super aircraft carrier U.S.S. *United States*. Johnson decided the carrier, designed to handle B-29 bombers capable of carrying an atomic bomb, duplicated the strategic bombing mission of the Air Force's new B-36 aircraft.

The cancellation dealt a major blow to Navy plans to participate in strategic air operations, sparking a bitter controversy over the future role of the Navy that became known as the "revolt of the admirals." Secretary of the Navy John L. Sullivan resigned in protest at Johnson's decision. Ranking Navy officials criticized the B-36 and questioned the allocation of defense dollars to the Air Force at the expense of their service. Unidentified Navy sources charged Johnson and Secretary of the Air Force STU-

ART SYMINGTON with corruption in the procurement of the B-36. An investigation by the HOUSE ARMED SERVICES COMMITTEE in the summer of 1949 cleared both officials of any wrongdoing.

Johnson, who supported unification of the armed services, testified in favor of the NATIONAL SECURITY ACT AMENDMENTS OF 1949, which he claimed would result in yearly savings of at least $1 billion. The uproar over further cuts in the Navy budget precipitated by Johnson's economy drive prompted the House Armed Services Committee to hold hearings on defense needs and spending in October 1949. Admiral Louis E. Denfield, the chief of naval operations, testified critically as to Johnson's defense planning and administration. Denfield was fired one week after the end of the hearings by new Secretary of the Navy Francis P. Matthews. The panel's final report condemned the dismissal of the Navy's ranking officer but endorsed Johnson's aims and approved of the secretary's overall performance.

Having weathered the controversy over the Navy, Johnson continued his efforts at trimming defense spending. He helped prepare NSC-68 (1950), a major reassessment of U.S. national security planning, but advised against the report's call for a massive build-up of the nation's military. Johnson altered his opposition to increased defense spending with the outbreak of the KOREAN WAR in June 1950. As American setbacks mounted in the first months of the conflict, he came under increasing attack for the nation's lack of military preparedness. At Truman's request the embattled Johnson resigned in September 1950 and was replaced by GEORGE C. MARSHALL. Johnson returned to private life and his law practice.

JOHNSON, LYNDON BAINES (1908–1973) U.S. representative, senator, vice-president, 36th president. Johnson grew up in the rugged Texas hill country near Austin. After graduating from Southwest Texas State Teachers College in 1930, he taught high school briefly in Houston. From 1931 to 1934 he was an aide in Washington to Representative Richard M. Kleberg (D-TX). In 1935 he returned to Texas to become state director of the National Youth Administration, newly formed as a Great Depression relief program. Campaigning as a New Deal Democrat and ardent supporter of President FRANKLIN D. ROOSEVELT, Johnson won a special election in 1937 to a vacant Texas congressional seat. At the outset of WORLD WAR II he served seven months in the Navy before returning to Washington to resume his legislative duties. Johnson remained in the House of Representatives until 1948, when he was elected to the Senate. He rose quickly in the Senate Democratic hierarchy, becoming majority leader in 1955. His forceful personal style, legislative skill, and ability to construct the compromises necessary to shepherd bills to enactment earned him a reputation as one of the most effective leaders in Senate history. An early advocate of a vigorous American space program, Johnson was an architect of the NATIONAL AERONAUTICS AND SPACE ADMINISTRATION (1958).

In 1960 he made an unsuccessful bid for the Democratic presidential nomination. Selected as his vice-presidential running mate by eventual nominee JOHN F. KENNEDY, Johnson brought geographical balance to the Democratic ticket, helping it to victory in the general election. As vice-president, he chaired executive branch councils on space and the PEACE CORPS and undertook official visits to more than 30 countries. Johnson was sworn in as president on November 22, 1963, shortly after Kennedy's assassination in Dallas.

His presidency early on was marked by domestic accomplishment, including passage of landmark civil rights acts in 1964 and 1965 and inauguration of his Great Society legislative program. Johnson, who took office amid continuing East-West COLD WAR, subscribed to the basic U.S. strategy that since the late 1940s had committed America to the worldwide CONTAINMENT of Communist expansionism. He retained top Kennedy foreign affairs officials Secretary of State DEAN RUSK, Secretary of Defense ROBERT S. MCNAMARA, and National Security Adviser MCGEORGE BUNDY. The new president inherited a worsening situation in Southeast Asia, where U.S.-backed South Vietnam was plagued by political instability following the 1963 DIEM COUP in which South Vietnamese military officers, with tacit U.S. acquiescence, had overthrown the repressive regime of President Ngo Dinh

Diem. Johnson continued Kennedy's policy of providing U.S. military advisers and aid to South Vietnam in its struggle to defeat a two-pronged effort by North Vietnam and an allied insurgency in South Vietnam, known as the Viet Cong, to unify the country under Communist control.

In early August 1964 two U.S. destroyers reported coming under attack by North Vietnamese gunboats while in international waters in the Gulf of Tonkin. Johnson ordered retaliatory air strikes against North Vietnamese coastal bases. He also requested and gained congressional approval of the TONKIN GULF RESOLUTION granting the president broad authority to use force "to prevent further aggression" in Southeast Asia. The Johnson administration subsequently cited the resolution as the legal basis, in the absence of a formal declaration of war, for mounting American military involvement in the VIETNAM WAR.

Johnson swept to a landslide victory over Republican nominee Barry M. Goldwater in the 1964 presidential election. Running a campaign for which he would later be accused of having deceived the American public, Johnson presented himself as a moderate candidate who, unlike the hawkish Goldwater, would not entangle the nation in a wider war in Southeast Asia. Amid burgeoning civil war in the Dominican Republic, Johnson in April 1965 sent some 20,000 U.S. troops to the Caribbean island nation to protect American lives and restore order. His defense of the controversial U.S. intervention in the DOMINICAN CRISIS as necessary to prevent a possible Communist takeover was denounced by Senator J. WILLIAM FULBRIGHT (D-AR) and others as a misleading exaggeration and gave rise to allegations, later exacerbated by Vietnam, of a Johnson "credibility gap." In October he signed into law the IMMIGRATION ACT OF 1965, which broadly updated U.S. immigration laws and eliminated racial barriers to immigration.

Johnson's tenure saw little change in U.S.-Soviet Cold War relations. Under UNITED NATIONS auspices, U.S. and Soviet negotiators reached agreement on the OUTER SPACE TREATY (1967) and the NUCLEAR NON-PROLIFERATION TREATY (1968). Discussions on U.S.-Soviet nuclear arms control negotiations were derailed by the Soviet invasion of Czechoslovakia in 1968. In June

1967 Johnson met Soviet Premier Aleksei N. Kosygin at the impromptu GLASSBORO SUMMIT for two days of talks on the Vietnam War, the recently concluded Arab-Israeli Six-Day War, and other U.S.-Soviet differences. The exchanges produced no breakthroughs. During and after the 1967 Arab-Israeli conflict, Johnson aligned U.S. policy behind clear-cut support of the Jewish state in its bitter confrontation with the surrounding Arab nations.

From 1965 the Vietnam War increasingly consumed Johnson's presidency. Johnson and his senior advisers embraced the DOMINO THEORY, the idea that if South Vietnam was toppled by North Vietnamese aggression, then all of Southeast Asia eventually would fall under Communist domination. In February 1965, in response to Communist guerrilla attacks on U.S. military compounds in South Vietnam, he authorized retaliatory air raids that soon evolved into an almost continuous bombing of the North. In April he sanctioned the use of American ground troops in offensive operations in South Vietnam. Committed to preventing a Communist victory in Vietnam, Johnson over the next three years increased U.S. troop strength in Southeast Asia from 50,000 to more than 500,000. The Johnson administration pursued a strategy of gradual escalation of American involvement in the war, aiming through intensifying U.S. military pressure to force Hanoi to seek a negotiated end to the hostilities.

America's expanding role in the war, and the seeming lack of progress in the protracted and increasingly costly conflict, produced a growing domestic antiwar movement. Opponents charged the war was both unwinnable and unjust. By 1967, Johnson's handling of the conflict was under attack by the liberal wing of his own party in Congress and antiwar demonstrations had effectively deterred the president from making public appearances. Johnson administration assurances that the war was being won were cast in doubt by the suprise Communist TET OFFENSIVE launched in late January 1968. While the enemy attack was repulsed, it brought a reassessment of U.S. policy in the White House. After consultation with a group of senior informal advisers, known as the WISE MEN, Johnson went before a nationwide television audience on March 31, 1968, to announce a deescalation of U.S. military involvement in Vietnam. At the end of his speech, he also revealed he would not seek another term as president. In his remaining months in office he was unable to achieve a breakthrough in U.S.-North Vietnamese peace talks begun in Paris in May 1968. Johnson retired in January 1969 to his Texas ranch. He published his memoirs, *The Vantage Point*, in 1971.

JOHNSON-CLARENDON CONVENTION
See **ALABAMA CLAIMS**.

JOHNSON-REED ACT See **IMMIGRATION ACT OF 1924**.

JOINT CHIEFS OF STAFF See same in **APPENDIX B**.

JONES ACT (1916) See **SCHURMAN COMMISSION**.

JONES ACT (1917) See **FORAKER ACT**.

JORDANIAN CRISIS (1957) Presumed Communist threat to the Arab kingdom of Jordan that the Eisenhower administration met with a show of American military force. In March 1957, following the SUEZ CRISIS (1956), Jordan's King Hussein bowed to domestic and regional Arab nationalist pressures and ended his alliance with Great Britain. In so doing, he forfeited the annual British financial subsidy on which his country had depended. Arab neighbors Egypt, Syria, and Saudi Arabia pledged to assume Jordan's economic burden. An outbreak of unrest, however, apparently fomented by Egypt and Syria, soon imperiled the monarchy. Since both Cairo and Damascus received aid from the Soviet Union, U.S. Secretary of State JOHN FOSTER DULLES linked their involvement in the attempted subversion of Jordan with the Kremlin's drive for greater influence and strategic position in the Middle East.

Acting under the aegis of the recently formulated EISENHOWER DOCTRINE (1957), which declared U.S. determination to defend Mideast countries against Soviet-sponsored Communist aggression, President DWIGHT D. EISENHOWER announced that Jordan's independence was of vital interest to the United States and on April 25, 1957, ordered the 6th Fleet to the eastern Mediterranean. Bolstered by the presence of the U.S. Navy and Eisenhower's firm stance, Hussein promptly put down the opposition and maintained power. Stepping into the breach created by Britain's sudden departure, the United States granted the Jordanian king an immediate $10 million and another $20 million in June 1957. The SYRIAN CRISIS the following September heightened tensions once again in Jordan and prompted further action by the Eisenhower administration in defense of U.S. interests in the region.

JOSEPH, CHIEF (1840–1904) A chief of the Nez Perce Indians and a storied military commander, Joseph led his tribe's fight against the U.S. program to uproot the Nez Perce from their gold-rich lands in Oregon and resettle them on the Lapwai reservation in Idaho. He orchestrated the skillful Indian retreat from the pursuing U.S. Army in the NEZ PERCE WAR (1877). Nez Perce bands under his leadership successfully evaded U.S. military forces during a 1500-mile journey from Oregon to Montana. Exhausted and hungry, Chief Joseph and his followers were overtaken by American troops near the Canadian border in early October 1877. Upon surrender, the Nez Perce chief gave his famous speech that ended: "Hear me my chiefs, I am tired; my heart is sick and sad. From where the sun now stands, I will fight no more forever." In 1878 he and his band were settled on a reservation.
See also MAP 1.

K

KAL FLIGHT 007 (1983) South Korean commercial airliner downed by a Soviet jet fighter on September 1, 1983, over the Sea of Japan. All 269 people aboard Korea Air Line (KAL) Flight 007, enroute from Anchorage, Alaska, to Seoul, were killed, among them Congressman Larry P. McDonald (D-GA) and 60 other Americans. The passenger liner had been shot down after it strayed into Soviet airspace. The incident was deplored in very harsh terms by the U.S. government, which requested a meeting of the UNITED NATIONS Security Council to investigate Soviet conduct. President RONALD W. REAGAN demanded a full explanation by Moscow of "this appalling and wanton deed." Washington released tapes of Soviet radio transmissions intercepted by U S. intelligence revealing the Soviet military deliberately fired on the Korean airliner. On September 13 the Soviet Union, insisting it had not known the plane was a civilian airliner and sticking by its claim that the aircraft had been spying on Soviet military installations on Sakhalin Island, vetoed a Security Council resolution denouncing the downing of Flight 007. A joint U.S. congressional resolution condemning the Soviet action as a "cold-blooded barbarous attack" was passed unanimously September 15 after the White House fended off an attempt by conservative Republicans to include amendments mandating specific punitive U.S. measures against the Soviets. The Reagan administration, determined to avert a serious rupture with the Kremlin, opposed any major retaliatory steps. While the White House sought to limit the practical diplomatic fallout from the airliner downing, the incident set back efforts to ease COLD WAR tensions and improve superpower relations.

KALTENBORN, HANS VON (1878–1965) Radio news commentator familiar to millions of Americans for 30 years. Born in Milwaukee, Wisconsin, Kaltenborn served in the Army during the SPANISH-AMERICAN WAR (1898), although his unit never left the United States. He joined the *Brooklyn Eagle* as a reporter in 1902, leaving three years later to enroll in Harvard University, from which he graduated in 1909. He was rehired by the *Eagle* the following year and remained with the paper until 1930, when he joined the Columbia Broadcasting System (CBS) as a news commentator and correspondent. Throughout the 1930s he reported on events in Europe for CBS. He covered the WORLD ECONOMIC CONFERENCE (1933) and the Spanish Civil War (1936–1939), and interviewed leaders such as Germany's Adolf Hitler, Italy's Benito Mussolini, and Britain's Neville Chamberlain. He won distinction for his up-to-the-minute coverage of the fateful 1938 Munich Conference, where the major European powers provided for Germany's annexation of the Czechoslovakian territory of the Sudentenland. Twenty days of virtual nonstop reporting from the network's New York studio on the Munich crisis made Kaltenborn a household name in America. An internationalist politically, he came under attack from the AMERICA FIRST COMMITTEE in the late 1930s for his endorsement of U.S. involvement in the struggle against German and Japanese aggression. In 1940 he was hired away from CBS by the National Broadcasting Company, where he be-

323

came one of the noted World War II broadcasters. His broadcast career ended in 1955 with his retirement.

KANAGAWA, TREATY OF (1854) Historic agreement negotiated by U.S. Commodore MATTHEW C. PERRY that opened Japan to diplomatic and trade contacts with the United States. It was the first treaty between a western nation and Japan, which had isolated itself from foreign influences for almost two and a half centuries, except for a strictly limited trade with the Dutch. In the 1830s and 1840s American merchants plying the China trade tried unsuccessfully to penetrate the long-secluded empire. Several official U.S. overtures during this period to initiate relations with the Japanese, notably Commodore James Biddle's abortive 1846 mission to the island, failed. Increasing American interest at midcentury in Japan corresponded with the dawning of the United States as a Pacific naval power. Merchant ships sailing between the West Coast and China sought access to Japanese ports to take on fresh water and supplies; the Navy coveted coaling stations in Japan for its steamships; traders wanted to extend their commerce there.

In March 1852 President MILLARD FILLMORE selected Perry to command a naval expedition to Japan to secure an opening. When Perry reached Edo (now Tokyo) Bay on July 8, 1853, with his squadron of four warships, he was under instructions to obtain an agreement that provided for protection of American sailors and property shipwrecked off the Japanese coast, opened Japanese ports for trade, and permitted American vessels trading in Asia to make Japanese ports of call for supplies. While authorized to make a show of military power to demonstrate U.S. determination to open relations, Perry was to use force only in self-defense. He gave Japanese officials a letter from Fillmore addressed to the emperor spelling out American proposals. After announcing he would return early the following year for a formal Japanese response to the president's note, Perry sailed south to China.

He was received cordially on his arrival back at Edo Bay with a seven-ship squadron in February 1854. Perry began treaty talks with Japanese authorities who, influenced by internal politics and increasing external pressures from the West, were inclined to end their isolation. At the town of Kanagawa, on March 31, the two sides signed a simple treaty of friendship that fell well short of initiating full diplomatic and trade relations. It allowed American ships to secure water and other provisions at Hakodate and Shimoda and opened the Japanese ports to limited U.S. commerce. Japan pledged to treat shipwrecked American seamen humanely and agreed to allow stationing of an American consul at Shimoda. The treaty assured the United States MOST-FAVORED-NATION status but said nothing about a coaling station for American steamships. As permitted by the Kanagawa agreement, President FRANKLIN PIERCE made TOWNSEND HARRIS first U.S. consul general at Shimoda. The American envoy concluded the TREATY OF EDO (1858), the first major U.S.-Japanese commercial pact.

KATANGAN CRISIS (1977–1978) Struggle over Shaba (formerly Katanga) Province in the central African nation of Zaire that prompted Western intervention to safeguard the mineral-rich area. In 1963 recently independent Zaire (then the Congo) with UNITED NATIONS assistance had overcome a seccessionist rebellion in its southern province of KATANGA, ending the protracted CONGO CRISIS. Numbers of Katangan rebels fled to neighboring Angola where they formed the Congolese National Liberation Front (known by its French acronym FNLC). In March 1977 between 2000 to 5000 FNLC guerrillas invaded Katanga and seized several major towns. Concern over the threat posed to Katanga's strategically important mining industry, which provided various metals with key military as well as general commercial applications, brought a concerted Western response. The United States announced it was sending emergency medical and other non-lethal supplies to Zaire, while Belgium and France agreed to provide military aid. With American backing, a contingent of 1500 Moroccan troops was flown by French transport planes to Zaire in early April. With the Moroccan reinforcements, the Zairean army by the end of May was able to defeat the invaders and drive them from Katanga.

The Moroccan forces returned to their North African homeland, but the Katangan crisis would reignite the following year. On

May 11, 1978, several thousand FNLC rebels based in Angola again invaded Katanga. Within a week some 2500 French Foreign Legion and Belgian paratroopers, with the approval of Zaire's president Mobutu Sese Seko, were being sent into the country to rescue several thousand Europeans caught in the fighting and to help turn back the invasion. The United States provided 18 transport planes and support personnel to the operation. On May 25 President JIMMY CARTER accused Cuban forces in Angola, there to assist its leftist government remain in power during a civil war, of aiding and training the Katangan guerrillas. Cuban officials denied the charges. By early June the invasion had been crushed in heavy fighting. On June 4, U.S. planes began ferrying in troops from Morocco, Senegal, and other African countries to replace the French and Belgian soldiers. The crisis eased the following month, when Zaire and Angola agreed to prevent further guerrilla activities along their border.

KEARNY See **GREER INCIDENT**.

KELLOGG, FRANK BILLINGS (1856–1937) Lawyer, senator, secretary of state. Born in Potsdam, New York, Kellogg moved with his family to a farm in Minnesota in 1865. He attended public school, read law in a local law office, and was admitted to the bar in 1877. A specialist in corporate law related to Minnesota's rapidly developing iron-mining industry, he gained a reputation over the next 25 years as one of the nation's top jurists. Increasingly active in Republican Party politics, he entered government service under President THEODORE ROOSEVELT as a special counsel responsible for prosecuting antitrust suits. He directed the government's case against Standard Oil Company that resulted in the Supreme Court's landmark decision in 1911 ordering the breakup of the giant trust. Kellogg served as the president of the American Bar Association from 1912 to 1913. In 1916 he was elected as a Republican to the U.S. Senate from Minnesota. During WORLD WAR I he announced his support for the formation of a postwar international organization to preserve the peace. He opposed, however, the proposed LEAGUE OF NATIONS under the TREATY OF VER-

SAILLES (1919), joining the Senate RESERVATIONISTS who first sought unsuccessfully to amend the agreement and then helped block its ratification.

Kellogg was defeated for reelection in 1922. The following year President WARREN G. HARDING named him a U.S. delegate to the fifth PAN-AMERICAN CONFERENCE at Santiago, Chile. On his return he was appointed ambassador to Great Britain. He served in London from January 1924 to February 1925, when he returned to Washington to become secretary of state during CALVIN COOLIDGE's second term. Kellogg confronted difficulties in both Latin America and the Far East. U.S.-Mexican relations, strained by Mexican moves to expropriate American oil and land holdings, began to improve following the 1927 appointment of gifted envoy DWIGHT W. MORROW as ambassador to Mexico City. The same year Kellogg successfully counseled a restrained U.S. reponse to the NANKING INCIDENT, in which Nationalist Chinese forces attacked the foreign community in the city, killing an American and five Europeans. In 1928 Kellogg effectively extended diplomatic recognition to the government that had emerged from China's civil strife under Nationalist leader Chiang Kai-shek. The 1927 GENEVA NAVAL CONFERENCE failed to continue earlier progress among the world's major sea powers on naval disarmament. But the following year Kellogg attained his major diplomatic achievement, formulating with French Foreign Minister Aristide Briand the KELLOGG-BRIAND PACT (1928) renouncing war as an instrument of national policy. The pact gained Kellogg the 1929 Nobel Peace Prize. He left office with the Coolidge administration in 1929 and returned to his Minnesota law practice. From 1930 to 1935 he served as a judge on the PERMANENT COURT OF INTERNATIONAL JUSTICE.

KELLOGG-BRIAND PACT (1928) International agreement to outlaw war. Widespread horror at the carnage of WORLD WAR I led to the emergence of a strong peace movement in the United States in the 1920s. The private American Committee for the Outlawry of War, formed in 1921, waged a campaign to make war illegal by defining any belligerent nation an outlaw state. Noted peace leaders NICHOLAS MURRAY BUTLER, president of Columbia University, and James T. Shotwell, a professor of history there, influenced French Foreign Minister Aristide Briand to consider the idea of abolishing warfare. In an April 1927 speech Briand proposed a Franco-American agreement outlawing war and committing both nations to condemn international aggression. Briand believed such a pact would link the United States and France in a de facto alliance and thereby secure French diplomacy's basic goal of deterring a war with Germany. Secretary of State FRANK B. KELLOGG, observing traditional American opposition to overseas alliances, initially sought to ignore Briand's proposal. U.S. peace groups, however, pressured the Coolidge administration to accept the offer. Kellogg then resolved to counter Briand's attempt at gaining a Franco-American alliance by opening participation in the suggested treaty to other nations.

In December 1927 the secretary of state, who through his involvement in the issue had become an enthusiastic supporter of such a measure, called for a multinational antiwar pact. Although Briand's objective of an alliance with the Americans had been foreclosed, the French foreign minister, who earlier had been awarded the Nobel Peace Prize, felt compelled to respond favorably. By August 1928, 15 nations, including all the major powers except the Soviet Union, had agreed to the Kellogg-Briand initiative. On August 27 delegates from the 15 countries met in Paris to sign a treaty renouncing war as an instrument of national policy and binding its signatories to peaceful settlement of all international disputes. Known both as the Kellogg-Briand Pact and the Pact of Paris, the agreement by 1929 had been accepted by 64 nations, representing most of the world. In ratifying the treaty, the U.S. Senate made explicit its understanding that the pact did not preclude the right of self-defense or implicate the nation in any COLLECTIVE SECURITY arrangement. In 1929 Secretary of State HENRY L. STIMSON sought unsuccessfully to invoke the accord, which lacked an enforcement mechanism and depended entirely on moral suasion, to avert a Sino-Soviet border conflict. In the 1930s Japanese aggression in China and German and Italian belligerency in Europe rendered the pact meaningless.

KENNAN, GEORGE FROST (1904-   ) Diplomat, historian, and influential foreign policy theorist. Kennan was born in Wisconsin, graduated from Princeton in 1925, and entered the FOREIGN SERVICE the following year. He was assigned to minor posts in Germany and the Baltic states before his selection in 1929 for a new program in Russian studies intended to prepare the United States for eventual diplomatic relations with the Soviet Union. Following U.S. diplomatic recognition of the USSR through the 1933 ROOSEVELT-LITVINOV AGREEMENT, Kennan accompanied the first American ambassador to Moscow, WILLIAM C. BULLITT, to the Soviet capital. Posted in the mid-1930s to Vienna and Prague, he was sent to Berlin after the 1939 outbreak of WORLD WAR II in Europe. Following U.S. entry into the conflict in December 1941, he was briefly interned by the Nazis before his repatriation in June 1942. During the war, Kennan served at the U.S. embassy in Portugal and as a member of the American delegation to the EUROPEAN ADVISORY COMMISSION planning for the continent's postwar administration. In 1944 he returned to Moscow, where he was a senior adviser to ambassadors W. AVERELL HARRIMAN and WALTER BEDELL SMITH.

At war's end, with the U.S.-Soviet alliance showing increasing signs of strain, the State Department in February 1946 asked Kennan to prepare an analysis of U.S. policy toward the USSR. His lengthy telegraphed report, dubbed the LONG TELEGRAM, helped convince the Truman administration to adopt a harder line toward the Soviet Union. Kennan was called back to Washington in April 1946 to teach foreign affairs at the National War College. In April 1947 he was selected by Secretary of State GEORGE C. MARSHALL to become the first director of the department's newly formed Policy Planning Staff with responsibility for long-range foreign policy formulation. Kennan outlined his thinking on future U.S.-Soviet relations in a celebrated article, "The Sources of Soviet Conduct," in the July 1947 issue of *Foreign Affairs*. Preferring anonymity, he used the pseudonym "Mr. X," but his identity as the author quickly became known. The article had a profound impact on domestic public debate over the emerging COLD WAR between the Soviet-led Communist bloc and the Western allies. As he had in his earlier telegram, Kennan characterized the Soviet Union as an ideologically expansionist state. He coined the term "containment" to describe a proposed policy of blocking Soviet expansionist tendencies through the application of "counterforce" as necessary. While the West would have to accept the status quo of Soviet hegemony over Eastern Europe, Kennan argued that, once held in check, the Soviet Union eventually would be compelled to liberalize by internal forces.

Kennan's ideas provided the intellectual framework for the Truman administration's CONTAINMENT policy toward the Soviet Union. Kennan envisioned a containment strategy implemented through economic and political means. By 1949 he was in conflict with Secretary of State DEAN ACHESON and other senior Truman administration figures who increasingly were basing containment on military force. Opposed to the creation of the Western security alliance NATO, in 1950 Kennan took a leave of absence at the Institute of Advanced Studies at Princeton. He served briefly as ambassador to the Soviet Union in 1952 before retiring from the Foreign Service the following year when it became apparent he would not be offered a senior position in the new Eisenhower administration. Kennan returned to the Institute of Advanced Studies. He authored several highly regarded works on foreign affairs, including the Pulitzer Prize-winning *Russia Leaves the War* (1956). In 1957 he was a visiting professor at Oxford University. While in England he gave a series of radio lectures in which he laid out a controversial proposal for a policy of DISENGAGEMENT, under which both the United States and Soviet Union would withdraw their military forces from Europe. While never seriously considered by Western policymakers, the proposal brought a vigorous response. Acheson labelled Kennan's approach the "new ISOLATIONISM."

In 1961 President JOHN F. KENNEDY named Kennan ambassador to Yugoslavia. He held the position until 1963, when he resigned in disagreement with what he considered the administration's inflexible Cold War foreign policy. He resumed his aca-

demic career and emerged by mid-decade as a leading critic of American involvement in the VIETNAM WAR. Still active in later years, Kennan enjoyed considerable renown as a key architect of early U.S. postwar foreign policy. His 1947 article is considered one of the most influential documents in American diplomatic history.

KENNEDY BERLIN SPEECH (1963)   Address by President JOHN F. KENNEDY during a visit to West Berlin in which he championed the struggle of the FREE WORLD against the Communist bloc. In an effort to shore up the NATO alliance and win support for an ATLANTIC COMMUNITY based upon the principle of equal partnership, Kennedy undertook a tour of Western Europe from June 23 to July 2, 1963, stopping in Germany, Italy, Great Britain, and Ireland. Everywhere he sought to dispel the doubts raised by the fiercely independent and Eurocentric French President Charles de Gaulle about the willingness of the United States, if necessary, to risk its own nuclear destruction to defend free Europe. Kennedy was greeted enthusiastically by the West Germans, who welcomed his emphatic assurances of continued U.S. military support. On June 26 he spoke in West Berlin to a huge, cheering crowd before the BERLIN WALL, which he called the most vivid demonstration of the failures of the Communist system. His speech extolled West Berlin's 18-year struggle to preserve itself as an island of freedom and democracy behind the IRON CURTAIN. In conclusion, Kennedy remarked "All free men, wherever they may live, are citizens of Berlin, and, therefore, as a free man, I take pride in the words *Ich bin ein Berliner* (I am a Berliner)."

KENNEDY, JOHN FITZGERALD (1917–1963)   U.S. representative, senator, 35th president of the United States. Kennedy was born in Brookline, Massachusetts, to a wealthy family. His father, Joseph P. Kennedy, was active in Democratic Party politics and served President FRANKLIN D. ROOSEVELT as ambassador to Great Britain in the late 1930s. Kennedy graduated from Harvard in 1940. His senior thesis on the British appeasement of Nazi Germany's Adolf Hitler at Munich was published as the book *Why England Slept* (1940), a generally well received work that brought Kennedy early recognition. During WORLD WAR II he served with the Navy in the South Pacific. As the commanding officer of the patrol boat *PT-109*, he was cited for heroism in a celebrated episode following the sinking of his vessel by a Japanese destroyer. Discharged because of a bad back from the Navy in April 1945, he worked briefly as a journalist, covering the SAN FRANCISCO CONFERENCE (1945) and POTSDAM CONFERENCE (1945).

In 1946 Kennedy was elected as a Democrat to the U.S. House of Representatives. He held the seat from Massachusetts for three terms. With the onset of the COLD WAR, he supported the TRUMAN DOCTRINE (1947) and MARSHALL PLAN (1948), the pillars of the Truman administration's emerging strategy for the CONTAINMENT of communism. In 1952 he narrowly defeated incumbent Republican Senator HENRY CABOT LODGE, JR. While convalescing from back surgery, Kennedy wrote *Profiles in Courage* (1956), a study of intrepid politicians in U.S. history who held to their principles in taking unpopular stands. (The work was largely researched and written by aide Theodore C. Sorensen.) The Pulitzer Prize-winning book became a best-seller and brought Kennedy national exposure. He earned additional notice as an unsuccessful candidate for the 1956 Democratic vice-presidential nomination. In the Senate in the late 1950s Kennedy became a critic of the Eisenhower administration's NEW LOOK defense policy and its reliance on nuclear MASSIVE RETALIATION for the DETERRENCE of Communist aggression. He came to espouse a doctrine of FLEXIBLE RESPONSE, whereby the United States would maintain a full range of military forces, enabling it to handle international crises from guerrilla insurgency to all-out war.

Capturing the Democratic presidential nomination in 1960, Kennedy edged out the Republican standardbearer, Vice-President RICHARD M. NIXON, in the general election. During the campaign he blamed the Eisenhower-Nixon administration for an alleged MISSILE GAP between the United States and Soviet Union and for permitting a Communist regime under Fidel Castro to come to power in Cuba. Kennedy's inaugural address on January 20, 1961, underscored his administration's idealistic tone and its Cold War commitment to the defense of the FREE WORLD. He proclaimed American readiness to "pay any price, bear any burden, meet any hardship, support any friend, oppose any foe in order to assure the survival and success of liberty." In its first months the Kennedy administration launched the PEACE CORPS, a program to send American volunteers overseas to aid developing countries, and the ALLIANCE FOR PROGRESS, an initiative to foster economic and social development in Latin America and to improve inter-American relations. The president championed the emerging U.S. manned spaceflight program. In May 1961 he called upon America to prevail in the superpower SPACE RACE, challenging the NATIONAL AERONAUTICS AND SPACE ADMINISTRATION to put a man on the moon by the end of the decade.

The Kennedy White House faced a major foreign policy setback in the Caribbean when, in April 1961, the U.S.-sponsored BAY OF PIGS INVASION by Cuban emigres seeking to overthrow Cuban Communist leader Fidel Castro ended in total failure. A chagrined Kennedy took full responsibility for the fiasco. He secretly ordered OPERATION MONGOOSE, an ultimately unsuccessful clandestine effort to depose Castro. In October 1962 U.S. intelligence overflights discovered Soviet nuclear missile bases under construction in Cuba. Kennedy announced a U.S. naval quarantine of the island to force the Soviet Union to dismantle and withdraw its nuclear arms. After a tense standoff that brought the superpowers to the brink of nuclear confrontation, the CUBAN MISSILE CRISIS was resolved when Soviet Premier Nikita S. Khrushchev, relenting before U.S. pressure, agreed to remove the missiles in return for an American pledge not to invade Cuba. Kennedy's handling of the crisis restored much of the luster he had lost in the Bay of Pigs debacle.

Continued Cold War confrontation marked U.S.-Soviet relations throughout the Kennedy years. Kennedy and Khrushchev met to exchange views and establish personal contacts at the VIENNA SUMMIT in June 1961. The Soviet leader left the parley, which produced no breakthroughs, reportedly believing he could take advantage of the young president. Khrushchev rekindled the BERLIN CRISIS (1958–1962), restating the Kremlin's intention to resolve the divided German city's status on Soviet terms. Kennedy responded by declaring U.S. readiness to defend West Berlin and ordered a buildup of American military forces to communicate U.S. resolve. In August 1961 Communist East Germany began erecting the BERLIN WALL to stem the further flight of its citizens to the West. With the exodus from the Communist bloc halted, Khrushchev decided against testing Western resolve any further, allowing the crisis to ease by the end of the year. In June 1963 Kennedy travelled to Berlin, delivering a famous speech before the wall on the city's symbolic importance to the worldwide struggle for freedom.

Kennedy was a proponent of both arms control and free trade. In September 1961 he signed legislation creating the ARMS CONTROL AND DISARMAMENT AGENCY. The Cuban Missile Crisis, by revealing the need for an emergency superpower communications channel, prompted Washington and Moscow to conclude the first of the "HOT LINE" AGREEMENTS (1963). The United States, Great Britain, and Soviet Union in July 1963 concluded the landmark LIMITED TEST BAN TREATY prohibiting all but underground nuclear explosions. In October 1962 Kennedy secured passage of the TRADE EXPANSION ACT providing for U.S. participation in international trade negotiations under the GENERAL AGREEMENT ON TARIFFS AND TRADE (GATT). The ensuing free-trade talks held from 1964 to 1967 were referred to as the KENNEDY ROUND in his honor.

In Africa the Kennedy administration supported UNITED NATIONS efforts to resolve the CONGO CRISIS (1960–1963). While the U.N. intervention slowly stabilized the former Belgian colony and thwarted Soviet attempts to gain a foothold there, Kennedy confronted a steadily worsening situation in Southeast Asia. In the LAOTIAN CRISIS (1961–1962), Communist and Western-allied factions struggled for control of the former French colony. At the GENEVA CONFERENCE (1961–1962) the United States joined in a multilateral settlement of the crisis involving the formation of a neutral government in Laos. Meanwhile North Vietnam and its allied insurgency in the South, the Viet Cong, were mounting an increasingly effective campaign to unify all of Vietnam under Communist control. Kennedy continued the Eisenhower policy of providing U.S. military aid and advisers to South Vietnam. Following the October 1961 TAYLOR-ROSTOW MISSION, sent to assess conditions in Indochina, the president set in motion a gradual escalation of American involvement in the VIETNAM WAR. Determined to prevent the loss of South Vietnam to communism, he increased the number of U.S. advisers from less than 2000 to more than 16,000 by the end of 1963. In November 1963 the Kennedy administration tacitly approved the DIEM COUP by South Vietnamese military officers that overthrew the repressive regime of President Ngo Dinh Diem. Kennedy's presidency was cut short by his assassination in Dallas on November 22, 1963.

KENNEDY ROUND See **GENERAL AGREEMENT ON TARIFFS AND TRADE.**

KEY WEST AGREEMENT (1948)   Statement defining the roles and missions of the U.S. military services. Enactment of the landmark NATIONAL SECURITY ACT in 1947 had brought the historically independent Army and Navy and the newly created Air Force together into a single defense organization. First Secretary of Defense JAMES V. FORRESTAL faced bitter disagreements among the services as to their respective functions, particularly concerning the conduct of air operations. Seeking to resolve the differences, Forrestal met with the JOINT CHIEFS OF STAFF, the uniformed heads of the armed forces, at Key West, Florida, from March 11 to 14, 1948. Following the discussions, he released a summary paper, "Functions of the Armed Forces and the Joint Chiefs of Staff." The document, soon known as the Key West Agreement, delineated the common and separate functions of the different branches. It granted the Air Force the lead role in strategic air operations involving atomic weapons, while authorizing the Navy to undertake flight operations necessary to a naval campaign. Periodically modified since, the agreement has remained a basic articulation of U.S. military service responsibilities.

KING COTTON DIPLOMACY   Catchphrase for the fundamental diplomacy pursued by the Confederacy during the Civil War, based on the economic strength of its cotton crop. With cotton's rise in the first half of the 19th century as the chief U.S. export, Southern leaders came to regard it as a powerful instrument of leverage in foreign relations, since, by their estimation, the industrializing European countries were so heavily dependent on the American supply of the main fiber for the manufacture of cloth. Senator James H. Hammond (D-SC) expressed the notion in a speech in 1858. Echoing the argument offered in David Christy's work *Cotton Is King* (1855), he asserted that "you dare not make war on cotton. No power on earth dares to make war upon it. Cotton is king."

From the outset of the Civil War Confederate leaders looked to the coercive economic power of cotton, upon which British and French textile industries were critically dependent, as their main diplomatic weapon. Southerners presumed that reliance on their crop would compel the British and French governments to extend recognition and aid to the Confederacy in the interest of preserving their access to the cotton supply. The Confederate leadership welcomed the Union blockade of the Southern coast, surmising the interdiction of cotton exports would hasten European intervention on the South's behalf. The Confederacy, in fact, early in the war resolved to produce a "cotton famine" overseas through a voluntary embargo. State governments and private citizens withheld the crop from market. Southerners refused to plant a new crop and reduced the amount of available cotton by burning large quantities of it. Widespread shortages, Southern leaders calculated, would devastate the British and French economies and thereby force London and Paris to recognize the Confederacy and break the Northern blockade.

Flawed reasoning and miscalculations undermined King Cotton diplomacy, which proved a failure. Bumper crops in the years immediately preceding the war had glutted the marketplace, allowing European mills to stockpile huge surpluses. British and French textile producers, drawing on these stored supplies, did not feel pinched until late 1862, by which time Europe had found ample replacements in cotton from India and Egypt. The Confederate scheme of withholding the crop had only accelerated the European search for substitute sources.

Moreover, neither Great Britain nor France was prepared to risk war with the United States by granting recognition to the Confederacy.

KIRKPATRICK, JEANE DUANE (1926–   ) Educator and diplomat. Jeane Duane Jordan was born in Oklahoma. She received an A.A. degree from Stephens College in Missouri in 1946, a B.A. from Barnard College in 1948, and an M.A. in political science from Columbia University in 1950. She studied at the University of Paris and held research positions at the State Department and George Washington University before marrying fellow political scientist Dr. Evron M. Kirkpatrick in 1955. She became an assistant professor at Trinity College in Washington, D.C., in 1962. In 1967 she joined the faculty at Georgetown University and the following year completed her Ph.D. at Columbia. In 1977 she became a resident scholar at the AMERICAN ENTERPRISE INSTITUTE.

Active in the Democratic Party in the 1970s, she published a controversial article, "Dictatorships and Double Standards," in the November 1979 issue of *Commentary* magazine that brought her to the attention of Republican presidential candidate RONALD W. REAGAN. The article distinguished between rightist authoritarian dictatorships, which Kirkpatrick asserted were less repressive and more open to internal reform, and leftist totalitarian regimes, which she argued ruthlessly suppressed any movement toward democratization or liberalization. She denounced the foreign policy of Democratic President JIMMY CARTER for allegedly undermining pro-American right-wing governments in Nicaragua and Iran and thus paving the way for their replacement by anti-American extremist regimes. Yet at the same time, she maintained, the Carter administration underestimated the threat posed by pro-Soviet totalitarian states and revolutionary movements elsewhere.

Kirkpatrick became an adviser to Reagan during his 1980 presidential campaign. Following his election, he named her the first woman to hold the post of U.S. ambassador to the UNITED NATIONS. Kirkpatrick gained a reputation as an articulate, forceful advocate of American interests and ideals. She enjoyed cabinet rank and took part in the Reagan administration's top-level foreign policy deliberations. Strongly supportive of the administration's staunchly anti-Communist policies, she helped formulate the U.S. policy in Latin America of aiding the CONTRAS and bolstering the government of El Salvador against a leftist insurgency. Informed she was not in line for a more senior position during Reagan's second term, Kirkpatrick resigned in 1985 to resume her teaching career.

KISSINGER COMMISSION Presidential advisory panel on U.S. policy in Central America. President RONALD W. REAGAN established the 12-member National Bipartisan Commission on Central America in July 1983, naming former Secretary of State HENRY A. KISSINGER its chairman. Other members, a mix of Democrats and Republicans, included future Treasury Secretary Nicholas F. Brady, AFL-CIO President Lane Kirkland, and Washington lawyer Robert S. Strauss. Among an additional 11 non-voting "senior counselors" to the panel were JEANE D. KIRKPATRICK, U.S. representative to the UNITED NATIONS, and Representative Jim Wright (D-TX). In forming the panel, Reagan hoped to build a broad national political consensus behind his administration's attempts to counter what it saw as a mounting Communist threat in Central America. White House efforts centered on supporting the El Salvadoran government against leftist guerrillas and pressuring Nicaragua to abandon its pro-Soviet position and democratize.

Following extensive hearings and travels in Central America, the commission on January 11, 1984, issued its report, which generally endorsed the thrust of Reagan's policies. The panel said there was a serious crisis in the region that the United States needed to act boldly to meet. In broad terms, the report embraced the Reagan administration view of why Central America was in turmoil, how that unrest threatened the United States, and what should be done in response. Miserable living conditions for much of the population, the commission observed, made the region "ripe for revolution." But, the report asserted, such conditions had been exploited by hostile outside powers—the Soviet Union and its client Cuba operating through Nicaragua—to expand their political influence and military

presence in Central America. What seriously threatened the United States and the entire Western Hemisphere, the report contended, was not indigenous revolution in Central America but Communist expansionism promoted by the Soviet Union and Cuba. If forced to contend with security threats near its borders, the report reasoned, the United States would either have to assume a permanently increased defense burden or see its capacity to maintain security commitments elsewhere in the world reduced. The panel called such a potential consequence a "strategic coup" for the USSR.

The commission called for more than $8 billion in economic aid to the region through 1989 and urged firm U.S. resistance to the expansion of Soviet and Cuban influence. It endorsed a sharp increase in military aid for El Salvador and recommended continuing the Reagan administration's program of assistance to the CONTRAS fighting to overthrow Nicaragua's Sandinista government. The panel suggested that the insurgency by the anti-Communist Nicaraguan rebels was an incentive working in favor of a regional negotiated settlement. It also called on Reagan to meet with Central American leaders to devise a plan for long-range economic development in the region. While the commission did not recommend committing American military forces into combat in Central America, it did say the United States should consider direct military action against the Nicaraguan government as a "last resort" if the Sandinistas refused to stop sponsoring leftist guerillas movements in neighboring countries. The panel proposed one major departure from Reagan administration policy. It recommended making military aid to El Salvador and Guatemala contingent on demonstrated progress toward democracy, a functional system of equal justice, and an end to HUMAN RIGHTS violations by right wing death squads and government security forces. In a dissent to the recommendation, Kissinger cautioned Congress against suspending military aid to El Salvador if such a cutoff appeared likely to bring a leftist rebel victory.

Embracing most of the Kissinger panel's recommendations, Reagan in February 1984 sent Congress a proposal for an $8.8 billion six-year program of economic and military assistance to Central America. While accepting the commission's proposal that military assistance to the Salvadoran government be linked to improvements in human rights, the president opposed conditions that would leave Congress with the final decision whether El Salvador merited continued aid. Congress enacted only pieces of the sweeping regional aid package. It approved most of the $1 billion-plus in economic and development aid recommended for fiscal year 1985, but rejected the multiyear funding plan, refusing to authorize follow-up aid to Central America for subsequent years.

See also BOLAND AMENDMENTS, CARIBBEAN BASIN INITIATIVE, EL SALVADOR CIVIL WAR, EL SALVADOR WHITE PAPER, IRAN-CONTRA, LINOWITZ REPORT.

KISSINGER, HENRY ALFRED (1923–)
National security adviser, secretary of state. Kissinger, a Jew, was born in Germany. His family fled the Nazi anti-Semitism of Adolf Hitler in 1938 and emigrated to the United States, where they settled in New York City. In 1943 Kissinger was drafted into the U.S. Army and became a naturalized American citizen. He served as an interpreter and intelligence specialist in the European theater during WORLD WAR II. Following Germany's surrender in 1945, he became a district administrator with the military government in the U.S. occupation zone. Discharged in 1946, Kissinger entered Harvard University the same year. Specializing in political science and government, he earned a B.A. in 1950, M.A. in 1952, and Ph.D. in 1954. His doctoral dissertation on 19th century European diplomacy after the defeat of Napoleon was published in 1957 as *A World Restored: Castlereagh, Metternich, and the Problems of Peace*. He remained at Harvard as a member of the faculty and was named a full professor of government in 1962.

In 1954 Kissinger was selected to head a COUNCIL OF FOREIGN RELATIONS study of U.S. nuclear strategy. The results were summarized by Kissinger in *Nuclear Weapons and Foreign Policy* (1957). The book established his reputation as a leading expert on international affairs. In it he criticized the Eisenhower administration's reliance on the threat of MASSIVE RETALIATION with NUCLEAR WEAPONS to deter Communist aggression. He advocated instead a wider range of military options, asserting that defense policy ought to guide the development of weapons technology rather than be determined by it. The work contributed to the formulation of the FLEXIBLE RESPONSE strategy adopted under President JOHN F. KENNEDY. In 1956 Kissinger began a two-year stint as director of the Rockefeller Brothers Fund Special Studies Project. The project's studies helped provide a foundation for New York Governor NELSON A. ROCKEFELLER's unsuccessful 1960 bid for the Republican presidential nomination. Kissinger advised the Eisenhower administration as a consultant on strategic defense issues. He continued his governmental affiliation during the Kennedy and Johnson years, serving as a consultant to the NATIONAL SECURITY COUNCIL (NSC) in 1961 and 1962, the ARMS CONTROL AND DISARMAMENT AGENCY from 1961 to 1968, and the State Department from 1965 to 1969. In 1967 Kissinger attempted unsuccessfully to open a channel through French contacts to Hanoi that might lead to negotiations for ending the VIETNAM WAR.

In November 1968 President-elect RICHARD M. NIXON named Kissinger national security adviser and head of the NSC staff. They both believed that an entrenched foreign affairs bureaucracy stifled innovative policy-making and hampered decisive presidential conduct of international affairs. With Nixon's backing, Kissinger centralized the formulation of U.S. foreign policy within the White House. The NSC became the principal forum for the consideration of foreign policy issues and Kissinger assumed broad responsibility for interdepartmental coordination and the implementation of presidential directives. He practiced a diplomacy known by the German term realpolitik, referring to a foreign policy based on pragmatism rather than an abstract idealism or moralism. He believed world peace and stability depended on a global BALANCE OF POWER and maintained U.S. diplomacy remained credible only when backed by force.

Kissinger viewed relations with COLD WAR rival the Soviet Union as the crux of U.S. foreign policy. He opposed an approach toward Moscow based on a moralistic crusade against communism. Accepting the USSR as a superpower, he sought to engage the Kremlin in the establishment of an international balance of power. Kissinger was a key architect of the Nixon administration's policy of DETENTE with the Soviet Union. His conception of the relationship was based on an idea of "linkage," in which Soviet access to American trade and technology depended on and thus would encourage Soviet cooperation in maintaining international stability. Kissinger played a major role in the negotiation of the SALT I and ABM TREATY arms control agreements and helped lay the groundwork for the landmark 1972 MOSCOW SUMMIT between Nixon and Soviet leader Leonid I. Brezhnev.

He also helped engineer the initiation of ties with Communist China. In 1971 Kissinger made a secret trip to Peking to open top-level U.S.-Chinese contacts and arrange for Nixon's historic 1972 visit to Communist China. Kissinger similarly resorted to secret diplomacy in seeking a negotiated settlement to the Vietnam War. The conflict in Southeast Asia remained the most pressing foreign policy concern throughout Nixon's first term. Nixon and Kissinger realized that a military victory was unattainable but refused to countenance a unilateral withdrawal and abandonment of U.S. ally South Vietnam. Instead, they sought to end the war in a manner that preserved an independent South Vietnam and reaffirmed U.S. readiness to keep its defense commitments. In 1969 the administration devised a new VIETNAMIZATION policy, whereby the South Vietnamese military gradually assumed responsibility from U.S. forces for conducting the war. Kissinger backed the highly controversial CAMBODIAN INCURSION (1970) and LAOTIAN INCURSION (1971), defending the actions as part of the strategy of deescalating the U.S. military role in Indochina. From 1969 he held secret talks in Paris with North Vietnamese negotiator Le Duc Tho. In January 1973 their negotiations culminated in the PARIS PEACE ACCORDS ending U.S. involvement in the Vietnam War. Kissinger and Tho were awarded the 1973 Nobel Peace Prize.

In September 1973 Kissinger succeeded WILLIAM P. ROGERS as secretary of state. He retained his position as national security adviser, becoming the only person ever to hold both posts simultaneously. During the October 1973 YOM KIPPUR WAR, he was instrumental in negotiating the cease-fire halting the Arab-Israeli hostilities. In the war's aftermath he undertook an intensive diplomatic effort to mediate the long-standing Arab-Israeli conflict. His SHUTTLE DIPLOMACY resulted in disengagement agreements separating Arab and Israeli forces in the Sinai and Golan Heights and the restoration of U.S.-Egyptian diplomatic ties, severed since 1967.

When the Watergate scandal brought Nixon's resignation in August 1974, Kissinger remained as secretary of state and national security adviser under President GERALD R. FORD. With Ford's backing Kissinger continued to pursue detente with the Soviet Union. The Ford-Brezhnev VLADIVOSTOK SUMMIT (1974) produced a tentative framework for a SALT II arms control agreement. In 1975 the United States joined in the signing of the HELSINKI ACCORDS intended to cement improved East-West ties. Detente faced mounting domestic criticism, however, from conservatives who charged the USSR was taking advantage of the East-West thaw to forge ahead with a massive military buildup. Liberal detractors contended that Kissinger's realpolitik paid insufficient attention to HUMAN RIGHTS issues within the Communist bloc. In 1974 Congress passed the JACKSON-VANIK AMENDMENT linking U.S. trade concessions to Moscow to the freedom of Soviet Jews to emigrate. Kissinger opposed the measure as a counterproductive intrusion in Soviet internal affairs.

In 1973 he had argued unsuccessfully against congressional legislation barring further U.S. military action in Southeast Asia. In January 1975 North Vietnam launched a full-scale invasion of South Vietnam. Ford and Kissinger were unable to persuade Congress to provide emergency aid to Saigon. South Vietnam fell to the Communist forces in April 1975, marking the final failure of two decades of U.S. policy in Southeast Asia. Washington also was challenged the same year by developments in Africa, where Portugal's withdrawal from its colony Angola precipitated civil war between a newly installed Marxist regime and Western-leaning rebel groups. Kissinger viewed with alarm the appearance of Communist Cuban troops in the ANGOLAN CIVIL WAR. Determined to avoid another Vietnam, Congress passed the CLARK AMENDMENT (1976), halting the administration's program of covert aid for the pro-Western Angolan rebel groups. The measure was approved despite Kissinger's warning about establishment of a possible Communist satellite in Africa. In 1976 Kissinger moved to align U.S. policy more with the aspirations of black Africa, ending American ties with the white minority government in Rhodesia (now Zimbabwe).

In November 1975 Ford revamped his senior foreign policy team. Kissinger continued as secretary of state, but relinquished his post as national security adviser. He left office with the Ford administration in January 1977. Kissinger joined the faculty at Georgetown University and published his memoirs, *The White House Years* (1979) and *Years of Upheaval* (1982). He remained a frequent commentator on world affairs. In 1982 he founded Kissinger Associates, an influential and lucrative international consulting group. In 1983 President RONALD W. REAGAN named him to head the so-called KISSINGER COMMISSION on U.S. policy in Central America.

"KITCHEN DEBATE" (1959) Impromptu debate between U.S. Vice-President RICHARD M. NIXON and Soviet Premier Nikita S. Khrushchev at a U.S. exhibition in Moscow. On July 22, 1959, Nixon left for a 13-day goodwill visit to the USSR. On July 24 he and Khrushchev jointly attended the opening of the American national exhibition in the Soviet capital. The U.S. show was the counterpart of a Soviet exhibition that had recently come to New York. As the two leaders toured the kitchen of the model American home on display, surveying the array of modern appliances and consumer items, they began a spontaneous debate before the assembled press on the virtues of capitalism versus communism. This animated, unscheduled exchange made international headlines. Nixon departed Moscow convinced that the Soviet leader harbored serious misconceptions about the United States and might benefit from a firsthand view of American life. In September, at the invitation of President DWIGHT D. EISENHOWER, Khrushchev visited the United States for the CAMP DAVID SUMMIT and a nationwide tour.

KNOW-NOTHING MOVEMENT Alliance of secret nativist societies that emerged in the 1840s. An influx of German Catholic refugees and Irish immigrants fleeing the potato famine sparked antiforeigner and anti-Catholic sentiments. Nativists feared the loss of jobs, additional tax burdens, and papal influence over American life. Nativist groups expanded rapidly in the early 1850s and a national organization, the American Party, was formed in 1854. The party cloaked itself in secrecy. Newspaper publisher Horace Greeley coined the term "Know-Nothings" to describe its members, who gave the stock reply "I know nothing" to all inquiries about their organization. The Know-Nothings advocated much more severe naturalization laws and exclusion of all but the native born from public office. They carried a number of state governships in the 1855 elections. The slavery issue split apart the American Party the following year and the nativist movement faded as the country's attention turned to the approaching Civil War.

See also AMERICAN PROTECTIVE ASSOCIATION.

KNOX, HENRY (1750–1806) General in the AMERICAN REVOLUTION and President GEORGE WASHINGTON's first secretary of war. At age 12 Knox went to work for a bookseller in his native Boston and in 1771 opened his own shop there. A keen interest in military affairs led to his enlistment in a local militia unit at age 18. Knox joined the American Continental Army in 1775 and took part in nearly all of the revolution's major military engagements, becoming a close adviser and friend of General Washington, who placed him in charge of all American artillery. He earned a commission as brigadier general for his role in the 1776 Battle of Trenton and was promoted to major general following the British surrender at Yorktown in October 1781. In 1782 he took command of the Army post at West Point, New York.

The Continental Congress appointed Knox secretary of war under the ARTICLES OF CONFEDERATION in 1785. Advocate of a strong national government, he backed the new CONSTITUTION and was retained in 1789 as war secretary in Washington's cabinet with responsibility for the Army and Navy. Knox's comprehensive plan in 1790 for a national militia was rejected by Congress. During his tenure, he promoted an adequate Navy and the establishment of a chain of coastal fortifications to protect against superior European seapower. As head of the department responsible for IN-

DIAN AFFAIRS, Knox helped chart an early federal Indian policy that aimed at securing INDIAN LAND CESSIONS through formally negotiated treaties. He left public life in December 1794 and in 1796 settled on his estate in present-day Maine.

KNOX, PHILANDER CHASE (1853–1921) Secretary of state under President WILLIAM HOWARD TAFT. Born in Pennsylvania, Knox graduated from Mount Union College in Ohio in 1872. After reading law in Pittsburgh, he was admitted to the bar in 1875 and the following year became assistant U.S. attorney for the Western Pennsylvania district. He resigned in 1877 to enter private practice. During the next 23 years he was a highly successful corporate lawyer in Pittsburgh. As counsel for the Carnegie Steel Company he played a major part in organizing the U.S. Steel Corporation in 1901. The same year he was appointed U.S. attorney general by President WILLIAM MCKINLEY. Following McKinley's assassination Knox continued in the post under THEODORE ROOSEVELT, earning distinction for his vigorous prosecution of business combines under the Sherman Antitrust Act (1890). In June 1904 the Republican Knox was appointed to fill a vacancy in the U.S. Senate from Pennsylvania and in 1905 was elected to a full term.

He resigned his seat in 1909 to become secretary of state in the incoming Taft administration. During his tenure, Knox undertook a major reorganization of the State Department that included creation of political-geographic divisions for Western European, Near Eastern, and Latin American affairs. His diplomacy helped bring settlement in 1910 of the FISHERIES QUESTION, the long-standing Anglo-American controversy over North Atlantic fisheries, and in 1911 of the BERING SEA DISPUTE, concerning pelagic sealing in the North Pacific. Knox's disapproval thwarted a Japanese syndicate's attempt to purchase the strategically valuable Magdalena Bay in Mexico from American investors. His determination, for reasons of national security, to prevent sale of strategic possessions in the Americas to overseas companies contributed to passage in 1912 of the LODGE COROLLARY, which extended the scope of the MONROE DOCTRINE to non-European powers and foreign corporations.

With Taft, Knox pursued a policy of DOLLAR DIPLOMACY, a program aimed at increasing U.S. diplomatic influence in Latin America and the Far East through the promotion of American commercial expansion. With regard to China, the president and secretary of state sought to check Japanese and Russian influence in Manchuria, boost American investment in the Asian nation, and strengthen the OPEN DOOR policy. At Knox's suggestion, an American banking group was organized to finance railroad concessions in China. The Taft administration's insistent appeal prompted European bankers to allow their American counterparts to participate in the CONSORTIUM LOAN TO CHINA for railroad construction.

Knox believed that unstable public finances, compounded by the burden of heavy indebtedness to European creditors, lay at the root of chronic political unrest in Central America and the Caribbean. In his judgment, such disorder raised the likelihood of European intervention in the Americas and posed a peril to U.S. interests in the region. He encouraged American bankers to take the lead in aiding Haiti, Honduras, and Nicaragua with financial rehabilitation by extending them loans, the repayment of which the U.S. government would guarantee by establishing customs receiverships in the borrowing countries. Knox's scheme for Latin America met with little success. When, in 1911, political unrest threatened the pro-U.S. Nicaraguan regime of Adolfo Diaz, the secretary of state concluded the KNOX-CASTRILLO CONVENTION, which arranged for a private American loan to Diaz's beleaguered government and placed Nicaragua customs collection under U.S. control for the life of the loan. The Knox-Castrillo agreement was rejected by the U.S. Senate, as was a similar one made with Honduras. When a revolt erupted against Diaz in 1912, the Taft administration intervened with military forces to suppress the rebellion and protect American lives and interests in Nicaragua.

Leaving office at the end of Taft's term in 1913, Knox returned to his law practice in Pittsburgh. He was elected again in 1916 to the Senate, where he emerged as a leader of the ultimately successful opposition to ratification of the TREATY OF VERSAILLES (1919) after WORLD WAR I. He drafted the Republican-sponsored ROUND ROBIN resolution rejecting Democratic President WOODROW WILSON's proposed LEAGUE OF NATIONS and later originated a number of the Senate reservations to the league covenant. Knox died in Washington in October 1921 before completing his term.

KNOX-CASTRILLO CONVENTION (1911) Agreement between the United States and Nicaragua to rehabilitate the Central American nation's finances. The treaty, never ratified, was intended to bring about Nicaraguan political stability and represented a prime example of the DOLLAR DIPLOMACY of President WILLIAM HOWARD TAFT and Secretary of State PHILANDER C. KNOX. In October 1909 a revolution broke out against Nicaraguan dictator Jose Santos Zelaya, whose ardent anti-Americanism had made him a nemesis of Washington. During the insurgency, Lee Roy Cannon and Leonard Groce, two Americans who were captured in the private employ of the rebels, were executed by Zelaya's forces at his order. The episode outraged Knox. Denouncing Zelaya's regime both as a "blot on Nicaraguan history" and a menace to Central American peace in a note to the Nicaraguan charge d'affaires in Washington on December 1, 1909, Knox broke off relations with the dictator's government. The Taft administration thereupon lent its moral support to the revolt. Under increasing rebel pressure, Zelaya resigned in mid-December and fled into exile. After continued fighting, the insurgents finally gained control of the country in the summer of 1910.

Events following completion of the U.S.-devised DAWSON AGREEMENTS (1910) culminated in Adolfo Diaz's emergence as Nicaragua's new president in May 1911. Diaz, who enjoyed the backing of American businesses in Nicaragua, promptly appealed for U.S. help to restore his country's troubled public finances to a sound footing. Amid the rebellion to oust Zelaya, Knox had outlined an American plan to take control of Nicaragua's customs revenues as a means of averting future political disorders in the Central American republic. This proposal became the basis for an agreement signed on June 6, 1911, by the secretary of state and the Nicaraguan Minister to the United States Salvador Castrillo. Under the Knox-Castrillo Convention, Nicaragua would seek to stabilize its currency by refinancing its national debt with loans obtained from American bankers. In return, the United States would establish a customs receivership for the life of the loans to guarantee Nicaraguan repayment. This scheme, the Taft administration believed, would eliminate a key incentive to revolt since Nicaraguan customs houses, usually a prized target of insurrectionists, would be under direct U.S. control and protection.

Within a month of signing the convention, Nicaragua defaulted on a debt contracted in 1909 with a British syndicate. An anxious Taft administration, without waiting for formal Senate action on the Knox-Castrillo treaty, persuaded a group of American bankers to assume control of Nicaragua's finances by effectively implementing the provisions of the as-yet unratified convention. The bankers extended a short-term loan to the Nicaraguan government, set up a receivership for customs, and negotiated a repayment arrangement with Nicaragua's European creditors. After the Knox-Castrillo Convention was rejected in May 1912 by the U.S. Senate, American bankers, with the Taft administration's blessing, maintained their virtual protectorate over Nicaraguan finances. When a revolt against the Diaz government erupted in July 1912, Taft intervened, sending 2500 marines into Nicaragua to safeguard U.S. lives and interests and to save Diaz. To discourage future uprisings and ensure regular operation of the nation's finances, a small detachment of marines remained in the Central American country until 1925. Meanwhile in February 1913, as an alternative to the failed Knox-Castrillo Convention, Managua concluded a treaty with Washington that granted the United States naval base concessions and an exclusive right to build and operate a canal through Nicaraguan territory in exchange for $3 million. The U.S. Senate, however, rejected the agreement, which was a precursor to the BRYAN-CHAMORRO TREATY (1914).

See also NICARAGUAN INTERVENTIONS.

KOMER, ROBERT WILLIAM (1922–   ) Intelligence officer and government official. Born in Chicago, Komer graduated from Harvard in 1942 and served in the Army during WORLD WAR II. After earning an

M.B.A. from Harvard in 1947, he joined the CENTRAL INTELLIGENCE AGENCY (CIA). An intelligence analyst, he was assigned to the NATIONAL SECURITY COUNCIL staff from 1961 to 1965. In 1966 he became a special assistant to President LYNDON B. JOHNSON. As American involvement in the VIETNAM WAR escalated, he was given responsibility for redoubling U.S. efforts to defeat the Communist insurgency in South Vietnam. In 1967 Johnson sent Komer to Vietnam with ambassador rank to head a new U.S. PACIFICATION effort. The CIVIL OPERATIONS AND REVOLUTIONARY DEVELOPMENT SUPPORT program, known by its acronym CORDS, brought State Department, military, and CIA counterinsurgency resources together in a single organization. CORDS was credited with significant improvements in the pacification campaign. During his tenure in Saigon, Komer initiated an operation to identify and root out South Vietnamese Communist insurgents, the Viet Cong, that evolved into the controversial PHOENIX PROGRAM. Named U.S. ambassador to Turkey in November 1968, he left office with the Johnson administration in January 1969. Komer worked as a researcher with the RAND CORPORATION until 1977, when he returned to government service as a senior official in the Carter administration Defense Department. In 1981 he joined the faculty of George Washington University.

KOREAGATE Alleged scheme by the South Korean government to buy the influence of members of the U.S. Congress in the early 1970s. The American news media dubbed the lobbying scandal "Koreagate," after the Watergate scandal that culminated in the 1974 resignation of President RICHARD M. NIXON. In October 1976 the *Washington Post* disclosed that the Justice Department was probing sweeping allegations of congressional corruption in connection with influence peddling. The *Post* reported that South Korean agents over a period of several years had dispensed cash and gifts to members of Congress to gain legislative influence and win backing for the Seoul government on Capitol Hill. Other news accounts reported that the lobbying campaign had been devised in the early 1970s by South Korean President Park Chung Hee, businessman Tongsun Park, and Korean Central Intelligence Agency

(KCIA) officials. Park purportedly was worried that the Nixon administration's consideration of a plan to withdraw a third of U.S. troops from the peninsula presaged a weakening of America's commitment to South Korea. Shoring up U.S. congressional support allegedly then became an important objective of his regime.

Amid press reports that as many as 115 members of Congress had taken illegal gifts from South Korean government agents, three congressional commmittees launched investigations in 1977 into the alleged influence-buying activities of Tongsun Park and KCIA operatives. The ethics committees of the House and Senate finished their probes in October 1978 without recommending any harsh disciplinary action against colleagues tied to the scandal. The House ethics panel concluded that the South Korean government had mounted a concerted scheme to solicit influence on Capitol Hill. The committee drew charges of a cover-up when it contended it could not divulge its information without compromising U.S. intelligence sources. The Senate ethics committee, in its final report on the matter, did not call for disciplinary action against any incumbent or former senator. It did refer evidence to the U.S. attorney general of possible illegalities involving several senators and staff aides. The Justice Department never brought charges.

The third committee, the House International Relations Subcommittee on International Organizations, concluded in its November 1978 final report on the scandal that South Korea had run a widespread and frequently illegal campaign in the United States to curry support for President Park Chung Hee's government. But the subcommittee dismissed any connection between recently strengthened U.S. backing for Park and South Korean bribery or influence buying in Washington. The probe ended with the full House membership voting to reprimand (the mildest form of House punishment) three Democratic representatives from California for accepting campaign contributions from Tongsun Park and failing to report them: John J. McFall, Edward R. Roybal, and Charles H. Wilson. Two ex-representatives were indicted for taking money from the South Korean businessman. Former Representative Richard T. Hanna (D-CA) pled guilty and went to prison. Former Representative Otto E. Passman (D-LA) was later acquitted in Federal court. An indictment brought against Tongsun Park was dismissed by the Justice Department in August 1979, thereby ending the government's inquiry into the South Korean influence buying allegations.

KOREAN WAR (1950–1953) Conflict between Communist and UNITED NATIONS forces over control of the Korean peninsula. In 1910 Japan forcibly annexed the neighboring kingdom of Korea, already a Japanese protectorate, into the Japanese Empire. During WORLD WAR II the Allies issued the CAIRO DECLARATION (1943) calling for a free and independent Korea. With Japan's defeat in August 1945, the United States and Soviet Union agreed to divide Korea along the 38TH PARALLEL, roughly the middle of the peninsula, to facilitate the surrender of Japanese forces. Soviet troops occupied north of the line and American troops south of it. The parallel became a de facto makeshift border as the Soviet Union erected fortifications along the line, effectively partitioning the country by the end of 1945.

Moscow installed a Communist regime in its northern sector under Korean Communist Kim Il-Sung. In the South, Washington organized an administration under veteran Korean independence leader Syngman Rhee. With COLD WAR tensions mounting, U.S.-Soviet negotiations on unifying Korea under a single government reached a bitter impasse by 1947. The Truman administration referred the question of Korea to the United Nations. In November 1947 the U.N. General Assembly adopted an American-sponsored resolution providing for a freely elected government for all Korea. After the Soviet Union refused to permit U.N. election commissioners north of the 38th parallel, U.N.-supervised elections were conducted in the south in May 1948. On August 15, 1948, President Rhee proclaimed the Republic of Korea in Seoul, South Korea. On September 9 the Communist Democratic People's Republic of Korea was formed at Pyongyang, North Korea, with Kim as premier.

Both North and South Korea claimed sovereignty over the entire country. The Soviet Union withdrew its occupation forces by the end of 1948 and the United States followed suit by July 1949. American attention increasingly focused not on Asia but on the newly formed NATO Western security alliance and burgeoning U.S. defense commitments in Europe. In a speech to the National Press Club on January 12, 1950, Secretary of State DEAN ACHESON failed to include South Korea within the U.S. defense perimeter in the Far East, an omission that critics later claimed had emboldened the Communist North. Meanwhile serious border clashes between North and South Korea occurred throughout 1949 and into 1950. War erupted on June 25, 1950, when North Korea launched a full-scale surprise invasion of South Korea with at least tacit approval from Soviet Premier Joseph Stalin. Within hours the U.N. Security Council met at the request of the United States to discuss the crisis. The council adopted a resolution ordering an immediate cease-fire and the withdrawal of North Korean forces. Soviet representative Jacob A. Malik was absent, having boycotted the council since the previous January over Communist China's exclusion from the United Nations, and thus did not exercise the Soviet right to veto the measure.

Concluding that Moscow had instigated the North Korean attack, President HARRY S. TRUMAN resolved to take whatever steps necessary to reverse the Soviet-sponsored Communist aggression. The president believed it imperative to demonstrate U.S. resolve to defend the FREE WORLD. An American commitment to safeguarding the security of South Korea was deemed essential to strengthening the will of smaller nations to resist Communist pressure and to upholding the principles of the fledgling United Nations. Recalling the West's failure to stand up to Nazi Germany and Japan in the 1930s, Truman contended that if the invasion of South Korea went unchallenged, it would lead to further Communist aggression and the eventual outbreak of a third world war. On June 27, with the North Korean onslaught rolling over the South Korean defenses, the Security Council approved a U.S.-proposed resolution calling on U.N. members to furnish such assistance "as may be necessary to repel the armed attack and to restore international peace and security in the area." Truman the same day announced he was directing U.S. air and naval units to provide support to the beleaguered South Korean forces. A civil war in neighboring China had ended in 1949 with Communist revolutionaries under Mao Tsetung having driven the Nationalist government of Chiang Kai-shek from power. Chiang's forces fled to the island of Taiwan. Concerned that the fighting in Korea not escalate into a larger conflict, Truman ordered the U.S. 7th Fleet into the Taiwan Strait to prevent any outbreak of hostilities between the rival Communist and Nationalist Chinese regimes.

After capturing Seoul on June 28, North Korean forces continued their drive south to unify the peninsula under Communist rule. On June 30 Truman authorized the commitment of U.S. ground units to the fighting. American forces on occupation duty in Japan deployed to Korea and entered combat on July 5. On July 7 the U.N. Security Council voted to create a unified command for the defense of South Korea. The council asked the United States to designate the overall commander. The following day Truman named General DOUGLAS MACARTHUR, then commander of the U.S. occupation of Japan, to head the U.N. forces. The United States and South Korea furnished the vast bulk of the troops in the U.N. command. Another 15 countries sent small contingents to serve under the U.N. banner. U.S. ground forces in Korea numbered more than 250,000 by June 1951 and reached a peak strength of slightly more than 300,000 in 1953. To support the U.S. war effort, the Truman administration revived the draft, called military reservists to active duty, and increased defense expenditures. While U.S. involvement in Korea initially enjoyed broad domestic support, the president faced criticism from conservative Republicans in Congress who charged he had exceeded his constitutional authority in sending U.S. armed forces into battle without a declaration of war. Truman cited the U.N. resolutions and his authority as commander in chief as justification for his decision to intervene in Korea.

South Korean forces initially were no match for the Soviet-equipped and -trained North Korean units. The first American troops sent into battle also suffered serious reverses. By early August the Communist attack had overrun most of South Korea and driven the U.S.-led U.N. Command back to a final defensive perimeter around the southeastern port city of Pusan. On September 15 MacArthur staged a daring amphibious assault behind enemy lines, landing an invasion force at the port of Inchon on the eastern South Korean coast near Seoul. The U.S. troops quickly moved inland, seizing Seoul and isolating North Korean forces further south. Within days the North Korean army in South Korea disintegrated as its soldiers either surrendered or fled north of the 38th parallel.

With U.N. forces apparently victorious in Korea, the Truman administration made the fateful decision to expand the U.S. objective in the war from the defense of South Korea to the liberation of North Korea and unification of the peninsula under the Rhee government. By early October U.S. units moving northward had crossed the 38th parallel. Soviet representative Malik's return had blocked further U.N. Security Council action on Korea. Instead the General Assembly, where the Soviet Union had no veto power, endorsed the Truman decision, calling on October 7 for establishment of a single democratic government in Korea. U.S. policymakers basically discounted warnings issued by Communist China that it would intervene militarily in North Korea if U.N. forces continued north toward the Yalu River and Chinese border. As U.N. elements advanced on the Yalu, Truman summoned MacArthur to WAKE ISLAND on October 15, 1950, to confer on the course of the conflict. The general mistakenly assured the president there was little chance Communist China would enter the war. In November MacArthur launched an "end-the-war" offensive.

Chinese Communist units, however, had begun to infiltrate into North Korea. On November 25 the Chinese army launched a massive offensive that caught the U.N. command off-guard, inflicting heavy casualties on U.S. units and forcing a full-scale U.N. retreat south. The Chinese intervention dramatically altered the nature of the Korean conflict. MacArthur called it a "new war" and pressed Washington for authority to bomb targets in Chinese Manchuria. Truman, intent on preventing any further escalation of the conflict, withheld the requested authority, underscoring an emerging disagreement with MacArthur over the conduct of the war. Advocating continued adherence to the goal of total military victory in Korea, MacArthur favored an expansion of the war effort, urging Truman in December to approve the blockade and bombardment of Communist China and the use of Nationalist Chinese troops in Korea and against the mainland. The president opted instead for the more limited objective of repulsing the Chinese offensive while confining the war to the Korean peninsula. He and his top advisers saw the Chinese intervention as part of a larger, Soviet-directed worldwide Communist offensive. The administration worried that a protracted ground war in Asia would distract U.S. attention from the defense of Europe, where the massive Soviet army in Eastern Europe was capable of launching a sudden assault on America's West European allies. Truman moved to bolster the U.S. presence in the NATO Western security alliance in Europe. To speed the buildup of U.S. forces in Europe and Asia and the mobilization of the nation's economy to a wartime footing, the president on December 16, 1950, declared a state of national emergency. His actions triggered the GREAT DEBATE in the Senate on U.S. defense policy. In April 1951 the Senate endorsed the deployment of U.S. ground forces to NATO and the underlying commitment of American military power to the CONTAINMENT of Communist aggression.

U.N. forces, after finally halting the Chinese attack along a defensive line below the 38th parallel, resumed the offensive on January 25, 1951. By March U.N. troops had again reached the 38th parallel, whereupon Truman defined America's wartime objective to be the defense of South Korea, signaling U.S. readiness to negotiate a cease-fire. The General Assembly had passed a resolution in February that, in realigning U.N. policy behind a return to the prewar status quo on the peninsula, reflected the growing international sentiment for an end to the hostilities in Korea. Truman's new strategy was opposed by MacArthur, who on March 24 issued a statement that contradicted the president's position by threatening to expand the war to Communist China. After a letter from the general critical of the administration's handling of the conflict was read on the floor of the House of Representatives by Minority Leader Joseph W. Martin, Jr. (R-MA), Truman relieved MacArthur on April 11, 1950,

and replaced him with General MATTHEW B. RIDGWAY.

With the Communists unable to advance and the United Nations committed to a defensive strategy, the two sides settled into a bitter stalemate along a 150-mile front stretching across Korea. Until the war's conclusion in 1953, the front would vary little from its position along the 38th parallel. In June 1951 Communist China indicated its willingness to pursue a negotiated settlement. After Acheson accepted a Soviet proposal in late June for cease-fire discussions, talks between Communist China and North Korea and the U.N. Command got underway at the Korean village of Kaesong near the 38th parallel. They were suspended August 22 amid mutual recriminations but resumed October 25 at the nearby village of Panmunjom. On November 27 agreement was reached on a provisional truce line based on existing military positions. The talks remained deadlocked, however, over the issue of which neutral nations would provide truce inspection teams. In January 1952 the U.N. negotiators proposed the voluntary repatriation of all prisoners of war (POWs) after the completion of an armistice. The Communist side rejected the proposal, claiming the U.N. forces had brainwashed its prisoners. The U.N. Command refused to force unwilling POWs to return to Communist countries. After months of acrimonious debate, the United Nations broke off truce discussions on October 8, 1952.

In November 1952, Republican DWIGHT D. EISENHOWER was elected president. After more than two years of hostilities, and with no end to the conflict in sight, domestic opinion had grown uneasy with the Democratic Truman administration's conduct of the war. Capitalizing on this mood, Eisenhower had declared during the campaign that if elected he would go to Korea, as a former World War II commander, to personally assess the situation. Following his visit to Korea in early December 1952, the president-elect concluded that the war was an unbreakable stalemate and resolved to end it. After taking office in January 1953, Eisenhower secretly informed the Communists that if satisfactory progress toward a peace settlement were not forthcoming, Washington would consider using NUCLEAR WEAPONS and extending the hostilities to the

Chinese mainland. In March 1953 Stalin died and was replaced by a Soviet leadership more inclined to seek a lessening of international tensions. The exact impact of Eisenhower's threat and Stalin's death remain unclear, but on March 28, 1953, the Communist side announced it would accept a U.N. proposal for the exchange of sick and wounded prisoners. Discussions on the exchange led to the resumption of full-scale negotiations on April 26. After the Communist delegates finally accepted the U.N. demand on voluntary POW repatriation, an armistice was signed at Panmunjom on July 27, 1953.

The truce agreement ended hostilities the same day. It established a demilitarized zone (DMZ) across the peninsula separating the two sides and formed a commission of neutral nations Switzerland, Sweden, Czechoslovakia, and Poland to supervise the cease-fire. After three years of fighting, the line between North and South Korea still roughly followed the 38th parallel. The armistice agreement called for an international conference to reach a final settlement of the Korean question. South Korean President Rhee opposed the armistice but reluctantly acquiesced to its implementation after receiving Eisenhower's guarantee of a SOUTH KOREA MUTUAL DEFENSE TREATY binding Washington to Seoul's defense. The 1954 GENEVA CONFERENCE on Korea ended in deadlock and no final resolution of the Korean conflict has been negotiated. The heavily armed border remained the site of recurring North-South clashes. Following the war the United States maintained substantial military forces in South Korea to safeguard that nation's security. The end of the Cold War and demise of the Soviet Union in the early 1990s brought a moderation of North Korea's uncompromising stance. In December 1991 North and South Korea signed a treaty of reconciliation and nonaggression that laid the groundwork for a formal Korean peace settlement.

The United States suffered more than 33,000 killed in action in the Korean War. Chinese and Korean casualties were in the hundreds of thousands. The fighting left a generation-long acrimony between the United States and Communist China. The war marked Communist China's emergence as a world power. The North Korean invasion of South Korea confirmed U.S. fears in the early years of the Cold War of Soviet-sponsored Communist aggression. The Communist attack hastened U.S. involvement in the defense of Western Europe and the strengthening of the NATO security alliance. The Korean War was seen widely as a demonstration of a worldwide U.S. commitment to the defense of freedom. Within a decade, America would again be involved in a war against communism in Asia, this time in Vietnam. The Korean conflict represented an initial attempt by the United Nations at exercising its police power to counter international aggression. Over the next four decades, however, U.N. effectiveness was limited by the veto authority of the major powers.

KOREAN-AMERICAN TREATY OF 1882 Pathbreaking agreement that established relations between the United States and Korea and opened the long-isolated Asian land to the West. A distinct kingdom with its own language and culture, Korea in the mid-19th century was a dependency of its giant Chinese neighbor, sending emissaries and tributes to the emperor in Peking. Known as the Hermit Kingdom, Korea was closed to the outside world except for limited contacts with Japan. As part of its larger goal to expand American trade in the Far East, U.S. diplomacy since the 1850s had aimed at attaining a commercial foothold in Korea. In 1871 the United States sent the LOW-ROGERS EXPEDITION to the remote country in an unsuccessful attempt to open relations. In 1880 Commodore ROBERT W. SHUFELDT undertook a diplomatic and commercial mission aboard the U.S.S. *Ticonderoga* to Japan and China, but likewise failed to achieve an opening with Korea.

Shufeldt returned to China as naval attache in 1881 amid indications Korea was prepared to pursue a commercial treaty with the United States. Concerned by Japanese designs on the strategically located Korean peninsula, China pressed Korea to accept a counterbalancing American presence in the region. Shufeldt negotiated a draft agreement with Chinese official Li Hung Chang that was approved by the Korean government. The American naval officer sailed to Korea, where the treaty was signed on May 22, 1882, in a simple ceremony in a temporary pavilion on the coast. The historic document established diplomatic relations between the two nations, opened three Korean ports to American ships, and provided for the regulation of commerce. The treaty signaled Korea's opening to the West; the next year Great Britain and Germany signed similar measures. In the 1905 TAFT-KATSURA AGREEMENT the United States recognized Japanese hegemony in Korea in return for uncontested American primacy in the Philippines.

KU KLUX KLAN White supremacist vigilante organization formed in 1866 by southerners who resisted the social and political changes brought by the Civil War. The Reconstructionist-era Ku Klux Klan, infamous for its assaults on blacks that included lynchings, had faded by the late 19th century. It was resurrected in Georgia in 1915 as a still secretive fraternal order.

The new Klan was strongly nativist as well as racist, targeting Catholic and Jewish immigrants in addition to blacks. Klansmen portrayed the influx of foreigners from southern and eastern Europe as a corrupting influence on American small-town values.

The Klan's advocacy of an end to open immigration had broad appeal. By the mid-1920s, the organization had approximately three million followers nationwide. Members marched, campaigned politically, and sometimes resorted to such violence as the public flogging of aliens. Klan leaders claimed credit for passage of the IMMIGRATION ACT OF 1924. The enactment of a ban on immigration removed the group's major popular issue and its influence outside the Southeast waned. After WORLD WAR II the Klan's violent resistance to the civil rights movement brought widespread condemnation.

L

LAIRD, MELVIN ROBERT (1922–) Congressman, secretary of defense. Born in Nebraska, Laird was raised in Wisconsin, where his father was a state senator. He graduated from Carleton College in 1942 and served as a Navy officer during WORLD WAR II, seeing action in the Pacific. When his father died in 1946, he waged a successful campaign to fill his vacant seat. He remained a state senator until he won election in 1952 to the U.S. House of Representatives. The conservative Laird was reelected eight times, steadily moving up in

the House Republican leadership and gaining a reputation as a knowledgeable and influential proponent of a strong national defense.

In 1969 President RICHARD M. NIXON named Laird secretary of defense. He took office at the height of the VIETNAM WAR. Committed to achieving "peace with honor" in Indochina, the Nixon administration sought to preserve South Vietnamese independence while gradually disengaging U.S. combat forces. Laird helped develop the administration's VIETNAMIZATION policy, involving the transfer of primary responsibility for the nation's defense to a newly expanded and improved South Vietnamese military and a corresponding steady reduction in U.S. troop levels. Under the program, U.S. troop strength in Vietnam declined from almost 550,000 in 1969 to 70,000 by the spring of 1972. Involved with military planning for the CAMBODIAN INCURSION (1970) and LAOTIAN INCURSION (1971), both intended to speed the Vietnamization process, he also directed the mining of North Vietnamese ports following the 1972 Communist EASTERTIDE OFFENSIVE and the OPERATION LINEBACKER bombing of Hanoi that December after peace negotiations faltered.

With the winding down of the U.S. role in the Vietnam conflict, Laird oversaw broad cuts in the defense budget and a phasing out of the military draft. Under the NIXON DOCTRINE, announced in 1969, the administration emphasized the importance of America's allies bearing a greater share of the collective defense burden. Laird backed the 1972 SALT I and ABM TREATY arms control agreements with the Soviet Union and supported the administration's emerging DETENTE policy with the Communist superpower. Having previously indicated he intended to serve no more than four years, Laird left office at the end of January 1973, two days after the signing of the PARIS PEACE ACCORDS ending U.S. military involvement in Vietnam. He returned briefly to the White House in June 1973 as counselor to the president for domestic affairs. He resigned in February 1974, as the Watergate crisis increasingly gripped the White House, and became a senior executive for *Reader's Digest*.

LANSDALE, EDWARD GEARY (1908–1987) Air Force officer and legendary intelligence agent. Lansdale attended UCLA and worked as an advertising executive before serving as an Army intelligence officer with the OFFICE OF STRATEGIC SERVICES in the Western Pacific during WORLD WAR II. He remained in the Philippines after the war, transferring to the newly formed Air Force in 1947. After a tour back in the United States, he returned to the archipelago in 1950 as part of a CENTRAL INTELLIGENCE AGENCY (CIA) operation to help the recently independent Philippine government over-

come a rebellion by the Communist-dominated Hukbalahap resistance movement. As CIA station chief in Manila from 1951 to 1954, Lansdale developed a theory of counterinsurgency warfare that emphasized social, political, and economic as well as military factors. His image as a slightly larger-than-life forerunner of a new postwar American adviser began during this period. He befriended and worked closely with Ramon Magsaysay, the Philippine defense minister, on civic action projects as part of a successful campaign against the Huk guerrillas. In 1953 he helped organize Magsaysay's landslide election as president.

Following the partition of Vietnam by the 1954 GENEVA CONFERENCE, Lansdale was sent by the Eisenhower administration to assist in the formation of a non-Communist nation in the south. He threw American support behind Ngo Dinh Diem, prime minister in the regime of Emperor Bao Dai that had been installed by the French before they withdrew from their former colony. After a national referendum, Diem became president of a newly proclaimed Republic of Vietnam in 1955. Lansdale helped write the South Vietnamese constitution, established a program for resettlement of refugees from the Communist north, and aided in the development of provincial government administrations. He initially defended Diem against criticism by other American advisers but by 1956 had become disillusioned with the Vietnamese leader's antidemocratic tendencies.

The same year he was recalled to the United States for duty at the Defense Department, where he became involved in coordinating the military's role in clandestine operations. His advocacy of counterinsurgency warfare made him a controversial figure in traditional military circles. In 1961 he was made head of a secret Kennedy administration project, code-named OPERATION MONGOOSE, to remove Cuba's Communist leader Fidel Castro from power. The unsuccessful operation was phased out at the end of 1962. Lansdale retired from the Air Force as a major general the following year. His thinking on the importance of nation-building helped guide early U.S. efforts at defeating the Communist insurgency in Vietnam. He completed his government service as a special assistant to the U.S. ambassador to Vietnam from 1965 to 1968. Lansdale came to embody the debate over U.S. involvement in the VIETNAM WAR. To some he represented the enlightened adviser, to others a well-intentioned but naive and intrusive foreigner who only made things worse. He was the model for characters in two novels on the American presence in Southeast Asia, Graham Greene's *The Quiet American* (1956) and William J. Lederer's and Eugene Burdick's *The Ugly American* (1965).

LANSING, ROBERT (1864–1928)   Secretary of state under President WOODROW WILSON. Lansing was born in Watertown, New York. After graduating from Amherst College in 1886, he read law, was admitted to the bar in 1889, and entered practice with his father's Watertown firm. In 1890 he wed Eleanor Foster, daughter of JOHN W. FOSTER, secretary of state under President BENJAMIN HARRISON. The marriage set him on course for a brilliant career in international law and diplomacy. He represented the United States in many international legal proceedings. His first official appointment was as the U.S. associate counsel before the arbitration commission that met from 1892 to 1893 to adjudicate the BERING SEA DISPUTE over fur-seal hunting. From 1896 to 1897 he was U.S. counsel before the Bering Sea Claims Commission. He represented the United States in 1903 before the tribunal that resolved the ALASKA BOUNDARY DISPUTE and from 1908 to 1910 in the North Atlantic Coast Fisheries Arbitration that disposed of the FISHERIES QUESTION. In addition, Lansing was counsel for the Mexican and Chinese legations in Washington from 1894 to 1895 and 1900 to 1901 respectively. He helped found the American Society of International Law in 1906 and was instrumental in establishing the *American Journal of International Law* in 1907.

A Democrat, Lansing joined the Wilson administration in March 1914 as State Department counselor, in which post he dealt with the complex international legal issues raised by the outbreak of WORLD WAR I the following August. When Secretary of State WILLIAM JENNINGS BRYAN resigned in June 1915 in a dispute over Wilson's diplomatic response to Germany's sinking of the LUSITANIA, Lansing succeeded him. During his tenure he labored in the shadow of Wilson, who determined all important foreign policy matters, and Colonel EDWARD M. HOUSE,

the president's close adviser, who conducted most key diplomatic negotiations for the administration. Lansing supported Wilson's decision to intervene militarily in both Haiti and the Dominican Republic. In 1916 he signed the treaty with Denmark for the DANISH WEST INDIES ACQUISITION. The following year he negotiated with Viscount Ishii of Japan the LANSING-ISHII AGREEMENT, by which the United States recognized Japan's special interests in China and both nations declared their adherence to the OPEN DOOR policy. Seeking to counter German maneuvering for diplomatic favor and influence in Mexico, Lansing persuaded Wilson to extend recognition to the Mexican government of Venustiano Carranza in March 1917. Following the German government's resumption of unrestricted submarine warfare, the president followed Lansing's recommendation and broke diplomatic relations with Germany in February 1917. When a Senate filibuster blocked Wilson's request for authorization to arm American merchant ships, the president, acting on the legal counsel of his secretary of state, proceeded with the arming plan absent specific congressional approval. Wilson, following the advice of Lansing and the rest of his cabinet, asked Congress on April 2, 1917, to declare war on Germany.

After World War I, Lansing was a member of the American delegation that attended the PARIS PEACE CONFERENCE (1919). He and Wilson drifted apart at the conference when his legalistic thinking clashed with the president's idealism. Lansing, favoring compromise on the war-ending settlement, unsuccessfully urged Wilson to relent on the issue of the LEAGUE OF NATIONS in order to win Senate ratification of the TREATY OF VERSAILLES. After Wilson's September 1919 stroke, Lansing on several occasions convened Cabinet meetings on his own authority. When the president learned of this, he demanded Lansing's resignation, which the secretary of state submitted on February 12, 1920. Lansing returned to private law practice in Washington and wrote several books on his experience in government, including *The Peace Negotiations* (1921), a detailed account of his relations with Wilson.

LANSING-ISHII AGREEMENT (1917)   Set of diplomatic notes exchanged between the

United States and Japan regarding the status of China. By the opening years of the 20th century, China had become the site of intense competition among the major European powers, Japan, and the United States for influence and special trade privileges. The ROOT-TAKAHIRA AGREEMENT (1908) had committed the United States and Japan to maintaining the existing status quo in the Pacific, supporting the independence and integrity of China, and upholding the OPEN DOOR principle of equal trade access in the giant Asian nation. Following the August 1914 outbreak of WORLD WAR I in Europe, Japan joined the Allies in the fight against Germany. The Asian power looked to take advantage of the conflict to expand its position in China. Japan attacked and seized German holdings in China's Shantung Province and retained the newly acquired territories under its control. In January 1915 the Japanese government essentially forced on the Chinese government a list of dictates, known as the 21 Demands, that would extend Japanese rights and privileges in China.

America viewed with growing alarm the developments in the Far East. The Wilson administration protested the Japanese action and made clear U.S. refusal to recognize any agreement altering the political or territorial status of China. Japan dropped its more extreme demands, but in May 1915 a reluctant Chinese government was compelled under Japanese pressure to accept a Sino-Japanese treaty acknowledging Japan's position in Shantung. In early 1917 Japan concluded a series of SECRET TREATIES with the Allied powers granting it the rights to the former German concession in Shantung and Germany's Pacific islands north of the equator. The treaties left only the United States opposed to Japan's new acquisitions. After U.S. entry into World War I in April 1917, Washington and Tokyo sought to reconcile their differences on the Far East.

In September 1917 Japan sent Viscount Kikujiro Ishii on a special mission to Washington to secure U.S. recognition of Japan's "paramount interests" in China. The United States, however, remained unreceptive to the idea of Japanese primacy there. After several weeks of discussion, Ishii and Secretary of State ROBERT LANSING reached a general agreement on their nations' mutual interests in China. In an exchange of notes between the two diplomats on November 2, 1917, the United States recognized that "territorial propinquity" allowed Japan to have "special interests" in China and Japan pledged its respect for Chinese sovereignty and the Open Door policy. A secret protocol bound both nations not to take advantage of World War I to acquire special rights in China. The deliberately vague agreement served to preserve U.S.-Japanese relations for the duration of the conflict. At the PARIS PEACE CONFERENCE (1919) Japan pressed successfully to keep its position in Shantung. The Lansing-Ishii correspondence, its key elements effectively incorporated into the 1922 NINE-POWER TREATY on China, was formally canceled in 1923.

LAOS ACCORDS See **GENEVA CONFERENCE (1961–1962)**.

LAOS SECRET WAR U.S.-directed military campaign against Communist forces in Laos during the VIETNAM WAR. The 1954 GENEVA CONFERENCE established Laos, newly independent from French colonial rule, as a neutral nation. The small, constitutional monarchy, strategically located between the two Vietnams, Cambodia, and Thailand, was drawn into the larger East-West struggle over Southeast Asia. In 1957 Prince Souvanna Phouma, the royalist premier, formed a unified government with his half-brother, Prince Souphanouvong, who headed the Laotian Communists, known as the Pathet Lao. The government fell apart the next year amid civil war among Communist, neutralist, and pro-Western factions. In 1959 Communist North Vietnam sent forces into Laotian provinces along its border in support of the Pathet Lao. The North Vietnamese also began construction of a road network through the southern Laotian panhandle, the famous Ho Chi Minh Trail, for infiltrating soldiers and supplies into South Vietnam.

The Eisenhower administration sought to counter Communist gains and advance Western interests in Laos through COVERT ACTION. The CENTRAL INTELLIGENCE AGENCY (CIA) established links with Meo tribal groups in Laos. CIA and U.S. Army Special Forces advisers began to arm and train the mountain tribesmen. A guerrilla force was organized under Meo tribal leader and former Laotian military officer Vang Pao. Secret support also was provided to the royal

Laotian government and army. Pathet Lao battlefield successes in 1961 caused the Kennedy administration to consider direct U.S. military intervention, but a second GENEVA CONFERENCE (1961–1962) temporarily resolved the LAOTIAN CRISIS by reasserting Laotian neutrality and creating a coalition government under Prince Souvanna Phouma.

Agreements reached at the conference called for all foreign forces to be withdrawn from the country. In practice, North Vietnam continued to move men and material down the Ho Chi Minh Trail and to provide support to the Pathet Lao. Over the next decade the United States in turn waged a secret military operation against Communist forces in Laos. The CIA stepped up its assistance to the Meo guerrillas. Huge amounts of supplies were brought in by AIR AMERICA, a covert agency airline. In 1962 Vang Pao commanded roughly 9000 fighters. By 1968 his force, known as the Armee Clandestine or Secret Army, had grown to a peak strength of more than 30,000 tribesmen augmented by some 15,000 Thai mercenaries. With CIA guidance, the Meo conducted attacks along the Ho Chi Minh Trail and engaged the Pathet Lao and North Vietnamese in a prolonged guerrilla war.

With a renewal in hostilities between the royal Laotian government and the Pathet Lao, the United States in December 1964 began a bombing campaign, codenamed Operation Barrel Roll, against Communist forces in northern Laos. In 1965 the U.S. Air Force began Operation Steel Tiger, a bombing assault on the Ho Chi Minh Trail in the Laotian panhandle. By the time the operations ended in 1973, roughly 2 million tons of bombs had been released (equalling the volume of U.S. munitions dropped in WORLD WAR II).

In 1970, press reports, and then congressional hearings, revealed the Laos secret war. Amid mounting domestic opposition to the American involvement in Southeast Asia, the Nixon administration continued U.S. participation in combat operations in Laos. By the early 1970s, Communist offensives were taking their toll on the Meo tribes. In October 1972 the Laotian government began peace talks with the Pathet Lao. A February 1973 peace agreement, concluded in the aftermath of the January PARIS PEACE ACCORDS ending U.S. in-

volvement in the Vietnam War, brought a halt to U.S. operations in Laos. While the secret war had checked the Pathet Lao and disrupted North Vietnamese plans, it failed to halt an eventual Communist victory. The Pathet Lao overthrew a coalition government in 1975, proclaiming a Communist state the same year. More than 50,000 Meo refugees were resettled in the United States.

LAOTIAN CRISIS (1961–1962) Period of heightened East-West tensions over Communist advances in Laos. Following the 1954 GENEVA CONFERENCE that established Laos as an independent constitutional monarchy, rightist, neutralist, and Communist factions struggled for control of the Southeast Asian country. In 1958 a coalition government under neutralist Prince Souvanna Phouma fell and was replaced by a rightist regime. The following year the Laotian Communist liberation movement, the Pathet Lao, under Prince Souphanouvong resumed its insurgency with support from neighboring Communist North Vietnam. The United States provided military assistance to the rightist government. In August 1960, neutralist officers in the Royal Laos Army seized power in a coup and formed a new government headed by Souvanna. By December, rightest forces had retaken the Laotian capital of Vientiane and installed a pro-Western government under Prince Boun Oum.

Full-scale civil war followed as the neutralist and Communist groups joined forces in northern Laos and launched a combined attack against the rightist regime. By March 1961 this offensive was close to gaining control of the country, raising U.S. concerns over a Communist takeover in Laos. Demonstrating American readiness to intervene militarily if necessary to prevent such an outcome, on March 23 President JOHN F. KENNEDY ordered U.S. naval forces to the Gulf of Thailand. At U.S. urging, Great Britain and the Soviet Union, co-chairs of the 1954 Geneva Conference, arranged for a May 3 cease-fire in Laos and the same month convened another international meeting in Geneva on the crisis.

The 1961–1962 GENEVA CONFERENCE met for 15 months. An initial settlement in October 1961 for a neutral Laos under a coalition government fell apart by the end of the year amid renewed fighting. As Pathet Lao successes mounted, Kennedy reaffirmed U.S. opposition to a Communist victory in May 1962, again ordering naval forces to the area and sending 5000 U.S. soldiers to neighboring Thailand. In June the Laotian factions agreed on a coalition government and the crisis ended in July with the signing of measures in Geneva that guaranteed Laotian neutrality and specified the withdrawal of all foreign forces from the country. Hostilities between the various Laotian elements resumed within months. Over the next decade, the United States engaged in the LAOS SECRET WAR to aid the anti-Communist forces and to counter North Vietnamese military operations in the country.

LAOTIAN INCURSION (1971)   U.S.-supported South Vietnamese raid into Laos during the VIETNAM WAR. Since 1959 North Vietnam had constructed an elaborate infiltration route, known as the Ho Chi Minh Trail, to funnel military units and equipment into South Vietnam. Because the trail wound mainly through the neutral nations of Laos and Cambodia, it generally was free from ground attack and became the principal supply route for Communist forces fighting in the South. In 1965 the United States began a concentrated bombing campaign against the trail network in southern Laos. The use of air power slowed but could not halt use of the route. On February 8, 1971, roughly 16,000 South Vietnamese ground troops, with U.S. air support, launched a drive into the southern Laotian panhandle to cut the Ho Chi Minh Trail and attack North Vietnamese supply bases. U.S. ground combat forces had been barred from entering Laos by Congress in the 1970 defense appropriations legislation and did not participate.

After initial success, the operation, code-named Lam Son 719 (after the birthplace of a 15th century Vietnamese hero), met determined North Vietnamese resistance. Suffering heavy losses, the South Vietnamese forces withdrew and ended the operation on March 24. Although the raid fell short of its objectives, President RICHARD M. NIXON, noting the estimates of much heavier Communist casualties, claimed that it demonstrated that VIETNAMIZATION, the U.S. policy of turning over major combat responsibilities to the South Vietnamese army, was working. Nixon also stressed that the disruption of North Vietnam's ability to sustain an offensive would allow the U.S. military withdrawal from Vietnam to continue. The incursion sparked antiwar demonstrations. Congressional opponents of American involvement in the conflict renewed their efforts to bring it to an end. In the fall of 1971 Congress twice approved versions of the MANSFIELD AMENDMENT calling for a halt to U.S. military operations in Southeast Asia.

LEAGUE TO ENFORCE PEACE   Internationalist organization formed during WORLD WAR I that championed the concept of COLLECTIVE SECURITY to prevent aggression and war. Founded in the summer of 1915 in the United States, the league proposed the creation of a world organization which would use the combined economic and military power of member nations to preserve peace and punish aggressors. The league's distinguished membership included American statesmen, lawyers, businessmen, journalists, educators, and religious leaders. Former U.S. President WILLIAM HOWARD TAFT served as its first president. Addressing the league's first national assemblage in Washington, D.C., in May 1916, still 11 months before the United States entered the war, President WOODROW WILSON outlined his nascent ideas for a postwar association of nations to provide collective security. After the war, the organization supported U.S. membership in the LEAGUE OF NATIONS. During the Senate battle over ratification of the war-ending TREATY OF VERSAILLES (1919), however, the group's leadership split over the LODGE RESERVATIONS to American participation in the League of Nations. After the Senate withheld ratification of the treaty in 1920, foreclosing U.S. membership in the league, the organization faded as an effective, active body.

LEAGUE OF NATIONS   International organization formed after WORLD WAR I to preserve peace and promote international cooperation. The cataclysmic war was the impetus for creating a world body to prevent future conflicts. In January 1918 President WOODROW WILSON issued his FOURTEEN POINTS outlining U.S. war aims. The last of these called for an association of nations to maintain peace and deter aggression through a system of COLLECTIVE SECURITY. Wilson headed the commission at the PARIS PEACE CONFERENCE (1919) that drafted the charter for his proposed League of Nations. The resulting Covenant of the League of Nations was adopted on April 28, 1919, and then incorporated into the TREATY OF VERSAILLES ending World War I. The covenant, comprising the first 26 articles of the peace treaty, defined the postwar peacekeeping organization's structure, functions, and powers. It provided for the three principal league organs: an assembly of all member nations, each possessing one vote; the executive council, consisting of permanent seats for the five great powers—the United States, Great Britain, France, Italy, and Japan—and nonpermanent, rotating seats for four other member states, elected by the assembly; and a permanent administrative secretariat.

More than half of the covenant dealt with the maintenance of peace. States joining the league would pledge themselves against aggression and promise to submit for arbitration or judicial settlement all disputes threatening war. Members were to regard an attack on any one of them as an attack on all. The pivotal Article X obligated signatories to guarantee the political independence and territorial integrity of all member nations against outside aggression. In the event of such aggression, the article stipulated the council would advise as to how the league should fulfill its collective security obligation. The mechanism for united action was Article XVI, which provided for military and economic sanctions against nations resorting to war. Other articles called on members to reduce armaments; instructed the council to create a PERMANENT COURT OF INTERNATIONAL JUSTICE; authorized the league to exercise control over the international arms traffic; and established a mandate system over colonies stripped from Germany and Turkey at war's end. The covenant also required all treaties concluded among members to be registered with the secretariat, set forth humanitarian goals relating to improved labor conditions and health standards, and provided for the establishment of the INTERNATIONAL LABOR ORGANIZATION.

Wilson's attempts to secure Senate ratification of the Treaty of Versailles and thereby effect U.S. entry into the league touched off a bitter political struggle. Senate Republican opponents of the proposed organization complained that the system of collective security embodied in the covenant infringed on American sovereignty. They sought reservations to the treaty circumscribing U.S. participation in the league in ways that would preserve U.S. independence of action. Wilson adamantly refused to accept any Senate revisions to the peace treaty. In the end the Senate failed to ratify the Versailles Treaty and the United States never joined the international body.

The league began operations at its headquarters in Geneva, Switzerland, on January 10, 1920, with 42 members. Sixty-three states eventually would join, although the membership at any given time never exceeded 58. The U.S. seat on the executive council was never occupied. When Germany and the Soviet Union were admitted to the organization in 1926 and 1934, respectively, they were granted permanent representation on the council. While eschewing formal membership, the United States maintained a significant informal relationship with the league, sending unofficial representatives to its meetings and at times acting jointly with it, as in the MANCHURIAN CRISIS (1931–1933) or in attempts to promote international disarmament. After the Japanese invasion of Manchuria in 1931 the league criticized Japan's action and recommended that Manchuria be returned to China. Japan responded by withdrawing from the international body. The league took no further steps to enforce its stand. The organization's failure during the 1930s to confront the aggression of Japan, Germany, and Italy or to take decisive steps toward disarmament revealed its ineffectiveness as a peacekeeping body and its incapacity to provide international security.

The discredited league took almost no part in the crises that culminated in the outbreak of WORLD WAR II in Europe in September 1939. It did expel the Soviet Union in 1939 for invading Finland. By early 1940 the organization had ceased to function politically. The league was disbanded on April 18, 1946, whereupon its functions and assets were transferred to the newly created UNITED NATIONS. Some historians have contended that the failure of the United States to join the league crippled the organization from the outset and represented a grave historical miscalculation. By spurning membership and rejecting the Versailles settlement, the argument goes, America forestalled the development of an effective international peacekeeping body that might have prevented the onset of World War II.

LEAHY, WILLIAM DANIEL (1875–1959) Career naval officer, ambassador, and senior military adviser to the president. Leahy graduated from the Naval Academy at Annapolis in 1897. The Iowa native served in the SPANISH-AMERICAN WAR (1898) and commanded the U.S.S. *Dolphin* during the Mexican PUNITIVE EXPEDITION (1916). In 1918 Leahy and then Assistant Secretary of the Navy FRANKLIN D. ROOSEVELT began a lifelong close friendship. President Roosevelt selected Admiral Leahy to be chief of naval operations in 1937. He held the Navy's top uniformed post until his retirement in 1939. The same year Roosevelt named him governor of Puerto Rico.

Appointed ambassador to the Vichy government in France in late 1940, Leahy was recalled to Washington by Roosevelt in May 1942 to serve as the president's military adviser during WORLD WAR II. Roosevelt promoted him to fleet admiral, the Navy's highest rank, and on July 20 formally appointed him to the new position of chief of staff to the commander in chief of the Army and Navy. Leahy presided over meetings of the newly formed JOINT CHIEFS OF STAFF and accompanied the president as his senior military aide at the Allied wartime conferences. Following Roosevelt's death in April 1945, he continued in the same capacity for President HARRY S. TRUMAN. Leahy was among the first to warn of Soviet expansionism in Eastern Europe and pressed for a firm U.S. stance toward the USSR in the immediate postwar period. He served as the president's military assistant until his retirement from government in 1949.

LEBANON CRISIS (1982–1984)   Failed U.S. military and diplomatic efforts intended to bring peace and stability to war-torn Lebanon. Violence between rival Lebanese Christian and Moslem factions continued after the Lebanese Civil War (1975–1976), which had devastated the na-tion's economy and badly weakened its central government. In the late 1970s effective power in Lebanon resided with the dozens of sectarian militias locked in factional strife. Adding to the instability was the presence in Lebanon of the Palestine Liberation Organization (PLO), the principal group representing the Palestinian people and their demand for an independent homeland in Israeli-occupied territories. Following its expulsion from Jordan in 1970, the PLO had migrated into neighboring Lebanon, establishing itself as a virtual state within that state, setting up headquarters in Beirut and military bases throughout the country. The PLO launched cross-border guerrilla raids into northern Israel and orchestrated terrorist attacks against Israeli targets. These led inevitably to reprisals by the Jewish state. Syria, seeking to establish hegemony over Lebanon, was deeply involved in the Lebanese conflict. Syrian forces had occupied Lebanon's Bekaa Valley during the civil war in 1976. Damascus supported various Lebanese factions and sponsored the PLO.

Events in Lebanon compelled the Reagan administration to focus on the violence-plagued country shortly after taking office in January 1981. With Israel and the PLO escalating their cross-border attacks against each other and with Syrian-Israeli tensions dangerously on the rise, President RONALD W. REAGAN sent special diplomatic envoy Philip C. Habib to the Mideast. The administration aspired to the role of mediator in Lebanon and was eager to prevent a Syrian-Israeli clash. Habib brokered a general cease-fire in Lebanon in July 1981. Continuing PLO assaults on northern Israel and Syria's deployment of Soviet-supplied antiaircraft missiles in the Bekaa Valley prompted the Israelis, over U.S. objections, to invade Lebanon in June 1982, with the stated aim of establishing a buffer zone in the south free of Palestinian guerrillas. Israeli forces destroyed the Syrian missiles and advanced to the outskirts of Beirut. Habib arranged several cease-fires, none of which held. After a two-month Israeli siege of Moslem West Beirut, where Palestinian guerrillas were encamped, Habib negotiated a truce agreement providing for the evacuation by sea of PLO forces from Lebanon to Algeria. The evacuation was concluded on September 1 under the supervision of a multinational peacekeeping force comprising U.S., French, and Italian troops. Following the PLO eviction the approximately 800 U.S. marines involved in the operation withdrew from Lebanon.

Violence continued despite the ceasefire. On September 14, Lebanon's president-elect, Maronite Christian Bashir Gemayal, was assassinated. Christian militia took revenge by massacring some 700 Palestinians, mostly civilians, in the Sabra and Shatila refugee camps. The carnage evoked international outrage. Israel came under sharp criticism for the role played by its army, which had allowed the vengeful Christian militia into the Palestinian camps. In late September, Reagan sent some 1200 marines back into Lebanon as part of a multinational peacekeeping force. His move drew criticism from Congress, where some members thought the president was evading the requirements of the WAR POWERS RESOLUTION (1973) by failing to seek congressional approval for the troop commitment. The law prohibits the deployment of U.S. forces to a hostile situation for more than 90 days without express congressional authorization. Reagan administration critics on Capitol Hill voiced concern that the United States, by intervening militarily to shore up the existing Christian-led government, was undermining its ability to assume the role of mediator in Lebanon.

Amid a growing perception in Moslem quarters that U.S. policy was leaning toward the ruling Christian faction and Israel at the expense of the Moslem factions and the Syrians, the American presence in Lebanon came under siege from radical Islamic groups. The U.S. embassy in Beirut was the target of a terrorist bomb in April 1983 that killed 63 people, including 17 Americans. Sniper fire and other hostile acts against the marines escalated. Reagan, despite growing congressional pressure, refused to invoke the war powers measure. Arguing that U.S. forces were needed to help restore Lebanon's sovereignty and territorial integrity, he contended it was impossible to calculate how long the marines would have to remain. In a White House-Capitol Hill compromise, Reagan on October 12, 1983, signed a joint resolution imposing an 18-month limit on the marine deployment. At the same time he declared in writing that he deemed the War Powers Resolution unconstitutional, asserting his authority as commander in chief to deploy American military forces.

On October 23, a terrorist truck bombing of their barracks at the Beirut airport killed 241 American marines. The incident eroded domestic support for an extended U.S. commitment in Lebanon and brought renewed pressure on the Reagan administration to pull out the troops. Some members of Congress argued that the United States must hold its ground, suggesting that an American withdrawal following the bombing would reward and encourage terrorism. Reagan meanwhile portrayed the turmoil in Lebanon as an extension of the East-West conflict. He blamed the Soviet Union for fomenting violence through direct support of its client Syria. The president suggested that U.S. abandonment of Lebanon might lead to expanded Soviet influence in the Middle East. A Defense Department panel, formed in the wake of the barracks bombing to assess the American military mission in Lebanon, concluded in its December 1983 report that the marines had been compromised in their ability to function as neutral peacekeepers because the Lebanese Moslem factions no longer regarded them as evenhanded. The Moslem perception of American partiality, the panel noted, had been shaped by the increasing involvement of U.S. troops in direct combat assistance to the Lebanese army controlled by President Amin Gemayel, a Maronite Christian, who succeeded his assassinated brother. Rival groups saw the Lebanese government's military as a virtual extension of the Maronite Christian faction. With support for administration policy in Lebanon collapsing, Reagan in early February 1984 announced that the marines would be redeployed in stages to ships offshore. On March 30, 1984, he formally ended all U.S. involvement in the multinational peacekeeping force in Lebanon. Following the departure of the marines, Syria emerged as the dominant force in the fractured country.

LEBANON HOSTAGES Scores of Westerners, including 18 Americans, who were abducted and detained in Lebanon by Moslem extremist groups hostile to the United States and the West. The kidnappings of American, British, French, and other Western nationals in the politically fractured and war-torn country spanned from early 1984 until 1988 and were presumed to be the work of Shiite Moslem groups with close ties to Syria and Iran. Most of those abducted were journalists, teachers, academic administrators, or relief-agency employees; almost all were seized in Moslem West Beirut. Their captivity was exploited by the kidnappers to command Western media attention and frustrate the Western nations, particularly the United States, whose staunch support of Israel and predominant influence in the Middle East engendered deep antagonisms in the Arab world. During the 1980s, numbers of the Western hostages were freed by their captors. Others were killed, among them three Americans: Peter Kilburn, librarian of the American University in Beirut, and William Buckley, CENTRAL INTELLIGENCE AGENCY station chief there, both in 1986; and Army Lieutenant Colonel William Higgins, on assignment as head of a UNITED NATIONS truce supervision team, in 1989.

Both presidents RONALD W. REAGAN and GEORGE BUSH publicly stated that they would not countenance any deal with the hostage-takers for the release of the American captives, insisting such a step would amount to a dangerous concession to terrorism. But in 1985 top-level members of the Reagan administration endeavored to arrange a covert exchange with so-called moderates in Iran, involving sales of U.S. weapons to Teheran in expectation that the Iranians would wield their influence among the radical Shiites to secure the release of the U.S. hostages in Lebanon. The ill-fated scheme was exposed as part of the IRAN-CONTRA scandal that rocked the Reagan presidency.

Political developments in the Middle East at the close of the 1980s raised Western hopes that a breakthrough in the hostage ordeal might soon be forthcoming. Following the death of the Islamic fundamentalist ruler Ayatollah Ruhollah Khomeini in July 1989, a more moderate and pragmatic leadership began to emerge in Iran that favored a move toward normalization of relations with the West. The pragmatists in Teheran were said to believe that Iranian cooperation in winning the release of the captives would hasten improved ties with the Western nations, whose investment was badly needed to rebuild the Iran-

ian economy, which had been shattered by the Iran-Iraq War (1980–1988). Syria, confronted at the end of the COLD WAR with the collapse of its main sponsor and arms supplier, the Soviet Union, also grew eager to end its diplomatic estrangement from the West. The presence of the Syrian army in Lebanon made Syria's president, Hafez Assad, the main power broker there. Assad, to court the favor of the Bush administration, joined the U.S.-led coalition against Iraq in the PERSIAN GULF WAR (1991) and agreed to take part in the American-sponsored MIDDLE EAST PEACE CONFERENCE (1991). Damascus, along with Teheran, began to press for the hostages' freedom.

Notwithstanding Bush's disavowal of dealmaking with the radical Shiite captors, the United States pursued behind-the-scenes negotiations to gain the captives' release. The diplomatic maneuvering entered a final phase in August 1991, when the United Nations began intensive negotiations aimed at arranging a swap of the Western hostages for Arab prisoners held by Israel. The U.N. effort, spearheaded by Secretary-General Javier Perez de Cuellar, also involved securing an accounting of Israeli servicemen missing in Lebanon. The U.N.-brokered negotiations by June 1992 had brought the release of all the remaining Western hostages. Those freed included the Briton Terry Waite, the Anglican church hostage negotiator who had himself been taken hostage in Beirut in 1987. For the United States, the eight-year ordeal ended on December 4 with the release of the last and longest-held American hostage, journalist Terry Anderson, who had been in captivity since March 1985. The resolution of the hostage crisis removed the most serious impediment to an improvement in Washington's relationship with Teheran, which had played the decisive role in pressuring the radical Shiite Moslem groups in Lebanon to free the Western captives.

LEBANON INTERVENTION (1958) U.S. military intervention to fortify the Lebanese government against internal strife fomented by the United Arab Republic (UAR). On February 1, 1958, Egypt and Syria, both recipients of military aid from the Soviet Union, joined in forming the UAR, a single state headed by Egyptian President Gamal

Abdel Nasser and dedicated to Arab nationalism and unity. The uneasy political balance in Lebanon between Moslem and ruling Christian factions was upset when a virtual civil war broke out in May 1958. Christian President Camille Chamoun charged the UAR with instigating the violent Moslem opposition to his regime and appealed for UNITED NATIONS intervention to halt the unrest. U.N. observers sent to Lebanon in June were unable to substantiate Chamoun's allegations of massive interference by Nasser in Lebanese internal affairs. Then, on July 14, King Faisal II of Iraq was killed and his pro-Western government overthrown in a UAR-inspired internal coup. Alarmed by the successful Iraqi revolt and its implications for the ongoing turmoil in his own country, Chamoun urgently appealed to President DWIGHT D. EISENHOWER for U.S. help.

Responding immediately, Eisenhower on July 15 ordered 5000 U.S. marines from the 6th Fleet to land in Lebanon. Meanwhile, British troops were flown into neighboring Jordan, which also was under pressure from pro-Nasser elements, at the request of King Hussein, cousin of Iraq's murdered Faisal. Citing U.S. prerogatives under the 1957 EISENHOWER DOCTRINE to explain his action, the president in a message to Congress declared Lebanese independence and territorial integrity as vital to U.S. interests. He said the strife in Lebanon represented "indirect aggression from without." Eisenhower pledged to withdraw U.S. forces as soon as the United Nations was prepared to assume a peacekeeping responsibility in Lebanon. Soviet Premier Nikita S. Khrushchev, warning Washington that the USSR would not stand by idly as events unfolded near its borders in the Middle East, condemned the U.S. intervention and on July 19 called for an immediate summit conference of the heads of government of the Soviet Union, United States, Great Britain, France, and India to deal with the crisis. Eisenhower countered with a proposal that such a five-power meeting be held within the framework of the U.N. Security Council. Khrushchev at first consented. But in early August, after meeting secretly in Peking with Communist Chinese leader Mao Tse-tung, he torpedoed the proposed summit. The U.N. General assembly, summoned into emergency session, approved a compromise Arab-bloc resolution

placing the Lebanon-Jordan problem directly with Secretary-General Dag Hammarskjold. As the political situation in Lebanon eased and began to stabilize, U.S. forces, which had peaked at 15,000 without becoming involved in combat, gradually were reduced and by the end of October 1958 had been entirely withdrawn. British troops simultaneously completed their evacuation from Jordan.

LEMAY, CURTIS EMERSON (1906–1990) U.S. Air Force officer and pioneer in the development of strategic air power. LeMay enrolled in the Reserve Officer's Training Corps (ROTC) at Ohio State University and was commissioned a second lieutenant in the Army in 1928. He completed flight training the following year and was assigned to the Air Corps. During WORLD WAR II the Ohio native commanded bomber units in Europe and the Far East. Promoted to general in 1943, he was a key architect of large-scale bombing tactics. In 1945 he took part in planning the atomic bombing of Japan. After the Air Force was established as a separate service in 1947, LeMay was given command of U.S. Air Force units in Europe. In 1948 he directed the massive BERLIN AIRLIFT that supplied the city after its access on the ground had been cut off by the Soviet Union's blockade.

In October 1948 he was named head of the Strategic Air Command and he held the post until 1957, overseeing the bomber force which then formed the backbone of the U.S. nuclear deterrent. Known as the "Iron Eagle," LeMay in 1961 became Air Force chief of staff. He was an outspoken advocate of using America's air power against North Vietnam to force a settlement of the VIETNAM WAR. In 1965 he suggested informing Hanoi's Communist leadership that the United States was prepared "to bomb them into the Stone Age" if they did not halt their aggression against South Vietnam. LeMay retired the same year. He later contended his controversial Stone Age remark had been taken out of context. In 1968 he was the vice-presidential candidate in Alabama Governor George C. Wallace's unsuccessful third-party presidential campaign.

LEND-LEASE Program of U.S. aid to its allies during WORLD WAR II. While maintaining official American neutrality following the outbreak of war in Europe in 1939, President FRANKLIN D. ROOSEVELT steered U.S. policy toward growing support for Great Britain in its fight against Axis powers Germany and Italy. The Roosevelt administration endorsed the British CASH-AND-CARRY procurement of arms and munitions. In the conflict's first year Great Britain grew increasingly dependent on the purchase of vital war materiel from the United States. In December 1940 British Prime Minister Winston Churchill wrote Roosevelt of his country's need for more armaments and of its dwindling ability to pay cash for war supplies. Churchill pressed the U.S. president to find the means to continue the flow of war materiel to Great Britain. Roosevelt wanted to meet Churchill's request but was mindful of domestic isolationist opposition to any action that might draw America into the war. He conceived of an aid program that would provide assistance to the British much, as he explained at a December 17 news conference, as one would lend a hose to a neighbor fighting a fire. In a national "fireside chat" radio address on December 29, he sought to build support for greater aid to Great Britain, outlining the threat posed to the Western democracies by Fascist aggression. Roosevelt argued that if America did not provide aid to the nations fighting the Axis powers, then it faced the dangerous possibility those nations would be defeated, leaving the United States to face the Fascist alliance alone. The president called for a massive defense production effort that would make the United States "the great arsenal of democracy."

In his annual State of the Union message on January 6, 1941, Roosevelt announced he was sending lawmakers a bill to furnish support to countries resisting Fascist aggression. The measure, which became known as the Lend-Lease Act, was passed by Congress on March 11, 1941. It empowered the president to "sell, transfer title to, exchange, lease, lend, or otherwise dispose of" war materiel to countries whose security was vital to the United States. Repayment was to be "in kind or property, or any other direct or indirect benefit" as determined by the president. The law authorized an initial expenditure of $7 billion in Lend-Lease aid. Presidential aide Harry L. Hopkins directed Lend-Lease activities until October 1941, when the Office of Lend-Lease Administration was es-

tablished under EDWARD R. STETTINIUS, JR. Following U.S. entry into World War II in December 1941, the Lend-Lease program became the principal means for America to funnel material assistance to its wartime allies. At the same time Stettinius became under secretary of state in September 1943, Lend-Lease was placed under the Foreign Economic Administration, headed by Leo T. Crowley. Lend-Lease aid was terminated in August 1945 at war's end. Total assistance provided amounted to slightly more than $50 billion, with $31 billion going to Great Britain and most of the remainder to the Soviet Union, China, and France. In all, aid was sent to 38 countries. Repayment to the United States totaled roughly $10 billion in goods and kind. In 1946 the United States reached an agreement with Great Britain, virtually bankrupt after the war, to settle its Lend-Lease obligations for a final payment of $650 million.

LEWIS AND CLARK EXPEDITION (1804– 1806) Expedition ordered by President THOMAS JEFFERSON to explore the vast trans-Mississippi region acquired from France in the LOUISIANA PURCHASE (1803). Jefferson was eager to learn more about the unknown western country and hoped to discover an overland route to the Pacific Northwest, where the United States, Great Britain, and Russia staked competing claims. He appointed his secretary, Captain Meriwether Lewis, to head the expedition. Lewis selected as an associate his friend Captain William Clark, a younger brother of the frontiersman and Revolutionary War leader George Rogers Clark.

Lewis and Clark set out from St. Louis in the spring of 1804. Proceeding up the Missouri River, they arrived at the present site of Bismarck, North Dakota, and passed the winter there. Following the Columbia River west, the explorers continued beyond the limits of the Louisiana Purchase and reached the Pacific Ocean in present-day Oregon in November 1805. The return trek began in March 1806. After crossing the Rocky Mountains, the party divided into three groups in order to explore separate tributaries of the Missouri before reuniting. The expedition ended back in St. Louis on September 23, 1806.

The Lewis and Clark journey was a landmark episode in western exploration. It had covered thousands of miles of wilderness and added significantly to the store of geographical and scientific knowledge about North America. The expedition served as an impetus to the transcontinental expansion of American trade and settlement.

LIABILITY FOR DAMAGE CAUSED BY SPACE OBJECTS CONVENTION (1972) International treaty spelling out the rules on the liability of countries for damage caused by objects launched into space. Drafted under the auspices of the UNITED NATIONS Committee on Peaceful Uses of Outer Space, the Convention on International Liability for Damage Caused by Space Objects, as the agreement is formally named, was signed March 29, 1972, and entered into force September 1, 1972. With respect to the United States, the treaty went into effect on October 9, 1973. The convention develops in detail the general principle on space liability established by the OUTER SPACE TREATY (1967)—namely, a state that launches or authorizes the launching of an object (a satellite, space vehicle, or space lab) into outer space is responsible for damage caused by the object. Under terms of the convention, a launching nation is absolutely liable for damage caused by its space objects to people or property on the Earth's surface or to airborne aircraft. However, liability for damages sustained in flight by space objects or the people occupying them is borne by the nation found to be at fault. The treaty establishes joint liability in instances where two or more nations have teamed up on a launching. Claims that cannot be settled by diplomatic negotiations are to be submitted to an international claims commission established at the request of either party to a dispute. More than 80 nations have ratified the treaty.

LIBERATION Catchword applied to the U.S. policy advanced for freeing nations under Communist domination. In the aftermath of WORLD WAR II the Soviet Union achieved hegemony over Eastern Europe by installing Moscow-controlled Communist regimes. By the late 1940s the Democratic Truman administration had devised a strategy of CONTAINMENT to block further Soviet expansionism. This strategy came under increasing attack from the Republican Party. In May 1952 JOHN FOSTER DULLES, future sec-

retary of state to Republican President DWIGHT D. EISENHOWER, published a famous article in *Life* magazine. In "A Policy for Boldness" Dulles condemned containment as little more than a strategy for preserving an unacceptable status quo and called for the "liberation" of Eastern Europe. Dulles's ideas were incorporated into the Republican Party's 1952 presidential campaign platform, which characterized containment as an abandonment of Communist satellite nations to "despotism and godless terrorism" and espoused policies for liberating their "captive peoples."

On taking office in 1953, the Eisenhower administration attempted to flesh out a liberation strategy. However, the administration never seriously considered using military force to free Eastern Europe and it quickly became evident that its commitment to "rolling back" postwar Communist gains was largely rhetorical. The administration instead effectively continued the basic U.S. containment policy established by Truman. An early Eisenhower administration proposal for a congressional resolution endorsing the liberation of "captive nations" garnered little support and quietly went without action. The infeasibility of military intervention to free Eastern Europe was dramatically illustrated by American unwillingness to risk a world war in coming to the aid of the Soviet-crushed HUNGARIAN REVOLT (1956).

See also DISENGAGEMENT.

LIBERTY INCIDENT (1967) Attack by Israeli military forces on the American intelligence ship U.S.S. *Liberty*. Following the outbreak of the Arab-Israeli Six-Day War on June 5, 1967, the *Liberty* was in international waters off the Sinai coast in the eastern Mediterranean, apparently monitoring Arab communications. On June 8 the ship came under sudden attack by Israeli jet fighters and torpedo boats. Thirty-four crewmembers were killed and 171 wounded, while the *Liberty* was extensively damaged. The Israeli government apologized for the incident, explaining its military had mistaken the American vessel for the Egyptian transport *El Quseir*, and paid reparations. The United States accepted the official account of its Middle Eastern ally.

LIBYAN BOMBING RAID (1986) Preemptive U.S. air strikes against alleged terrorist installations in Libya. On April 14, 1986, Air Force F-111 bombers from bases in Great Britain and Navy warplanes from aircraft carriers positioned in the southern Mediterranean attacked what the U.S. government characterized as "terrorist-related targets" in Tripoli and Benghazi, Libya. President RONALD W. REAGAN ordered the raid in retaliation for the recent bombing of a West Berlin discotheque in which an American serviceman was killed. He announced his administration had indisputable evidence that Libya had orchestrated the Berlin strike and that Libyan leader Colonel Muammar Qaddafi was plotting further terrorist acts against American installations and tourists. Reagan said the attacks on the North African nation were intended to deter future Libyan-sponsored terrorism and thus had been undertaken in self-defense. He warned of further military action unless Qaddafi ceased his support for anti-American terrorism. An undetermined number of Libyan civilians were killed in the raid, among them, according to Libyan accounts, Qaddafi's adopted daughter. One F-111 was shot down. Condemning the U.S. action, the Soviet Union called off Foreign Minister Eduard A. Shevardnadze's scheduled visit to Washington to confer on details of the upcoming WASHINGTON SUMMIT (1987). In the Libyan bombing's immediate aftermath, terrorist incidents against U.S., British, and Israeli targets occurred in Great Britain, Lebanon, and the Sudan. Western observers generally attributed Qaddafi's less belligerent public posture in the late 1980s to the American bombing raid.

LIMA, DECLARATION OF (1938) Agreement concluded at the Eighth PAN-AMERICAN CONFERENCE in Lima, Peru, that committed the American states to consult with each other in the event of any outside threat to the peace or security of the Western Hemisphere. The United States and the 20 other American republics gathered at the Lima Conference, which met in December 1938, amid the growing threat of war in Europe and Asia. The aggressive actions of Nazi Germany, Fascist Italy, and a militaristic Japan alarmed President FRANKLIN D. ROOSEVELT, who was increasingly concerned about Nazi infiltration in the Western Hemisphere. He sought greater solidarity among the American nations to meet what

he regarded as a serious and common danger. At the instigation of the United States, the Lima gathering focused on the issue of developing improved inter-American cooperation to safeguard hemispheric security. Secretary of State CORDELL HULL, head of the U.S. delegation, urged the Latin American governments to forge a mutual defense pact pledging themselves to resist attack by any non-American country. Argentine resistance, coupled with lingering Latin American suspicion toward the United States, blocked Hull's ambitious proposal.

On December 24 the delegates reached a compromise in the Declaration of Lima, which expanded on the consultative pact adopted at the BUENOS AIRES CONFERENCE in 1936. Also called the Lima Pact, the declaration expressed the determination of the American states to resist all foreign intervention. It provided for consultation among the American foreign ministers in case of an outside threat to the peace or territorial integrity of any of the hemispheric republics. Immediately after the outbreak of WORLD WAR II in Europe in September 1939, the United States called a foreign ministers conference to take steps to preserve peace in the Americas. Held in Panama, the meeting produced the DECLARATION OF PANAMA announcing the neutrality of the Western Hemisphere.

LIMA PACT See **LIMA, DECLARATION OF**.

LIMITED TEST BAN TREATY (1963) Landmark arms control agreement placing strict limits on tests of NUCLEAR WEAPONS. By the mid-1950s growing awareness of the dangers posed by radioactive fallout from nuclear explosions brought mounting international pressure for a halt to nuclear testing. Both the United States and Soviet Union endorsed such a halt, which was viewed widely as an important step toward slowing the East-West arms race and discouraging the spread of nuclear arsenals to other countries. Early negotiations under the auspices of the UNITED NATIONS DISARMAMENT COMMISSION were unable to reconcile Western insistence on a general arms control pact with Soviet advocacy of a separate test ban treaty. From 1958 to 1961, existing nuclear powers the United States, Great Britain, and Soviet Union met almost continuously in the three-way Conference on the Discontinuance of Nuclear Weapons Tests, which was held in Geneva. During most of this period the three nations observed a Soviet-sponsored voluntary NU-CLEAR TESTING MORATORIUM. While the Western powers eventually accepted the Soviet position on a separate treaty, the discussions adjourned in January 1962 with the two sides deadlocked over Western support for, and Soviet opposition to, test ban verification provisions.

Negotiations then shifted to the newly formed EIGHTEEN-NATION COMMITTEE ON DIS-ARMAMENT. France, which had become the fourth nuclear power in 1960, declined to participate in test ban talks and continued to develop its nuclear program. Amid an emerging consensus for confining a test ban agreement to those kinds of explosions verifiable by remote detection systems, the United States, Great Britain, and Soviet Union renewed negotiations in Moscow on July 15, 1963. These talks culminated in the signing in the Soviet capital on August 5 of the Treaty Banning Nuclear Weapon Tests in the Atmosphere, in Outer Space, and Under Water. The accord, known also as the Partial Test Ban Treaty, prohibited all but underground nuclear tests, which were exempt from the ban because they could not be verified by remote sensing or other NA-TIONAL TECHNICAL MEANS. The signatories also agreed not to conduct underground explosions that would spread radioactive debris outside their territorial limits. The treaty, open to all states, was ratified by the U.S. Senate on September 24 and entered into force October 19, 1963. More than 115 nations have become parties. It was followed by the THRESHOLD TEST BAN TREATY (1974) and PEACEFUL NUCLEAR EXPLOSIONS TREATY (1976).

LINCOLN, ABRAHAM (1809–1865) Sixteenth president of the United States. Born in Hardin (now Larue) County, Kentucky, Lincoln was reared on the frontier. He moved with his family to southern Indiana in 1816 and then to Illinois in 1830. By his own estimate, he received altogether about one year of formal schooling. In 1831 he settled in New Salem where he worked as a store clerk. Enlisting for service in the BLACK HAWK WAR (1832), he was made a captain of volunteers but saw no action during his three-month hitch. Returning to New Salem, he became a partner in a gen-

eral store that failed after a brief time. Through appointment he served as a local postmaster from 1833 to 1836, during which time he also worked as a county land surveyor. His introduction to politics came in 1832, when he ran for a seat in the Illinois legislature and lost. In 1834 Lincoln was elected as a Whig to the state legislature, serving there through reelection until 1842. Meanwhile he studied law and was admitted to the bar in 1836. The following year he moved to Springfield where he established a highly successful law practice.

In 1846 he won election as a Whig to the U.S. House of Representatives. Lincoln's single term in Congress was distinguished by his opposition to the MEXICAN WAR (1846–1848). He sided with the Northern Whigs, who accused Democratic President JAMES K. POLK of having provoked the conflict as part of a Southern scheme to wrest territory from Mexico to accommodate the extension of slavery. Lincoln insisted Polk had overstepped his constitutional authority in leading the nation into war and had deceived the American people by pinning the outbreak of the conflict on Mexican provocation. He introduced a series of "spot resolutions" challenging Polk to identify the exact spot where, as the president contended in his 1846 war message, Mexican forces had shed American blood on American soil. Lincoln did not seek reelection. Declining federal appointment as governor of the Oregon Territory, he returned to Springfield and devoted himself to his law practice for the next five years, emerging as one of the best-known trial attorneys in the state.

Passage by Congress of the controversial Kansas-Nebraska Act in 1854 reignited the bitter sectional battle over slavery and abruptly drew Lincoln back into politics. Bitter political disagreement between North and South over the issue of slavery's extension into the territories had brought the nation to the verge of disunion at midcentury. Conflict was averted through the legislative Compromise of 1850, which reaffirmed the provision of the Missouri Compromise (1820) barring slavery's extension to national territories north of the line 36° 30'. In 1854 Senator Stephen A. Douglas (D-IL) introduced a bill to organize the Kansas and Nebraska territories. As enacted, the Kansas-Nebraska measure repealed the Missouri Compromise's slavery restriction and left it to the inhabitants of the territories to decide for themselves by referendum whether to permit slavery, a principle known as popular sovereignty. By opening a vast new area of the country to the introduction of slavery, the Kansas-Nebraska Act provoked a storm of protest from Northern antislavery elements. Lincoln, who ardently objected to the extension of slavery into the territories, was aroused to political action by the new law, which he vehemently denounced. He had always deplored slavery as a moral wrong. His personal conviction was balanced by a sense of pragmatism. He rejected militant abolitionism as a reckless threat to social and political order. He recognized the complexity of the slavery problem, acknowledging the legal protections the peculiar institution enjoyed and the enormous practical difficulties involved in any effort to repeal it. His remedy was to prevent slavery's expansion. Restricting it to the states where it already existed, he reasoned, would gradually and ultimately bring about slavery's extinction.

In 1854 he was elected to the Illinois legislature but promptly resigned to run for the U.S. Senate, only to be defeated. In 1856 he joined the new Republican Party, campaigning actively that year for the first Republican presidential nominee, JOHN C. FREMONT, who lost to Democrat JAMES BUCHANAN. With Senator Douglas up for reelection in 1858, Lincoln was the choice of the Republicans to oppose the author of the Kansas-Nebraska Act. In his speech accepting the nomination on June 17, Lincoln declared "A house divided against itself cannot stand" in reference to the deepening sectional conflict over slavery. Seven famed Lincoln-Douglas debates were held in towns across Illinois. The two candidates agreed on the right of slaveholding in the Southern states and the right to retrieve fugitive slaves. Where they differed fundamentally was on the issue of whether slavery should be permitted to spread to the territories. Moreover, Lincoln scored Douglas for his failure to admit that slavery was morally wrong. Although Douglas won the election, Lincoln had earned national reputation and prominence. In 1860, with the nation edging toward disunion and civil war, Lincoln garnered the Republican nomination because of his relatively moderate position on slavery, beating out front-run-

ner WILLIAM H. SEWARD. The split of the Democratic Party into two factions with separate candidates assured Lincoln's election as president.

His victory touched off the secession crisis. As they had threatened to do in the event Lincoln won the election, states across the Deep South prepared to withdraw from the Union. By the time Lincoln took office on March 4, 1861, seven Southern states had seceded and joined to form the Confederacy under President JEFFERSON DAVIS. In his first inaugural address, Lincoln assured Southerners he had no intention of interfering with slavery where it already existed. At the same time he denied the right of secession under the CONSTITUTION, asserting that the Union was perpetual and indivisible. His order to resupply the federal garrison at Fort Sumter in Charleston Harbor, South Carolina, led Confederate forces under General Pierre G. T. Beauregard to open fire on Sumter on April 12, 1861, forcing its surrender the next day. The episode marked the start of the Civil War.

Lincoln made Seward his secretary of state. He dismissed Seward's fanciful suggestion of war with Europe as a means of uniting the country, a proposal broached by the new secretary in a confidential memo to the president in April 1861. The two worked closely in constructing the Union's CIVIL WAR DIPLOMACY, the overriding goal of which was to prevent foreign recogniton, particularly by Great Britain and France, of the Confederate States as an independent nation. The Lincoln administration sought to isolate the conflict as an internal civil insurrection, denying the South outside help and the legitimizing stamp of foreign diplomatic recognition. For its part, the South aimed to secure such recognition through its own KING COTTON DIPLOMACY, based on the presumed coercive economic strength of the Southern cotton crop. Pressure exerted by the president and secretary of state dissuaded the British from extending recognition to the Confederacy. France, while inclined by economic and imperial self-interest to recognize the South, was unwilling to take this step alone and risk war with the United States.

The issue of slavery had significant bearing on U.S. wartime diplomacy with Britain, which since the early 19th century had led an international antislavery crusade. By issuing the preliminary Emancipation Proclamation on September 22, 1862, Lincoln not only made freedom for the slaves a war aim, but also boosted the Union's moral and political standing in London. The final proclamation on January 1, 1863, and the decisive Union victory at the Battle of Gettysburg in July 1863 foreclosed the possibility of British or French recognition of the South, spelling the failure of King Cotton Diplomacy. Lincoln approved Seward's negotiation with the British government of the AFRICAN SLAVE TRADE TREATY (1862) providing for Anglo-American cooperation in suppressing the illegal international slave traffic.

Early in the war Lincoln had ordered a naval blockade of Southern ports and coastline to cripple Confederate commerce. After taking initial exception with the U.S. position on maritime neutral rights, Britain, the world's foremost naval power, acquiesced in the Lincoln administration's interpretation by accepting the blockade as legally binding. A crisis in Anglo-American diplomacy developed when, in November 1861, a U.S. warship illegally stopped the British mail steamer *Trent*, which was carrying a pair of Confederate diplomatic agents bound for Europe. The Union ship commander removed the Confederate envoys, who were then held in detention. Lincoln was eager to avoid a serious confrontation with the British government over the TRENT AFFAIR. Seward skillfully defused the crisis, averting a possible war with Britain.

The Lincoln administration complained strenuously to London about the construction and arming of naval vessels for the Confederacy by British shipbuilders. Seward's steady pressure eventually led British authorities to take steps to halt the outfitting in British ports of Confederate cruisers, which were exacting a heavy toll on Union maritime shipping. With Lincoln's endorsement, he also pressed the British government to pay the claims of U.S. citizens for the depredations committed by the *Alabama* and other British-built Confederate cruisers against Union seaborne commerce. By allowing these ships to be delivered to the Confederacy, Washington contended, Britain had failed to uphold its obligations as a neutral. The British balked at satisfying the U.S. demand for indemnification. The ALABAMA CLAIMS re-

mained a dispute in Anglo-American relations through the end of Lincoln's presidency. They finally were resolved in 1872 through international arbitration.

France took advantage of civil conflict in the United States to extend its influence in Latin America. The invasion of Mexico by French forces in 1862 presaged French Emperor Napoleon III's 1863 installation of Austrian Archduke Maximilian as emperor of Mexico. Seward protested the French armed occupation and Lincoln refused to recognize Maximilian's puppet government. But the demands of the Civil War would not allow the Lincoln administration to take decisive action against the French. After the war, Seward threatened to use force unless France ended its intervention in Mexico, at which point Napoleon III consented to remove his troops, completing the withdrawal in 1867.

Lincoln was reelected in 1864 over his Democratic opponent, the former Union Army commander General George B. McClellan. On April 14, 1865, five days after Confederate General Robert E. Lee's surrender to Union General ULYSSES S. GRANT at Appomattox marked the end of the Civil War, Lincoln was shot while attending Ford's Theater in Washington, D.C., by the deranged actor John Wilkes Booth, who was an ardent Southern nationalist. The president died the next day and was succeeded by Vice-President ANDREW JOHNSON.

LINCOLN BRIGADE See **ABRAHAM LINCOLN BATTALION**.

LINDBERGH, CHARLES AUGUSTUS (1902–1974) Legendary American aviator who made the first, solo, nonstop transatlantic flight. He was born in Michigan, the son of Charles A. Lindbergh, who served in the U.S. House of Representatives from Minnesota from 1907 to 1917. Reared in Minnesota, the junior Lindbergh learned to fly with the Nebraska Aircraft Corporation and the U.S. Air Service Reserve in Texas and became a pilot with the Army Air Mail Service. Deciding to compete for a $25,000 prize offered for the first successful transatlantic flight, he found supporters to fund the building of a special monoplane. On May 20, 1927, Lindbergh took off from New York in the single-engine *Spirit of St. Louis* and some 33 hours later landed in Paris.

His historic feat caused a worldwide sensation and instantly made him a national hero and international celebrity. As a goodwill ambassador, "Lindy" visited Latin America and the Far East.

In 1929 he married Anne Spencer Morrow, daughter of U.S. Ambassador to Mexico DWIGHT W. MORROW. After completing a U.S. tour for the Guggenheim Foundation, he became a consultant for several air transport companies. The kidnapping and murder of the Lindberghs' child in 1932 was a spectacular case, attracting a crush of publicity. Seeking an escape from the relentless attention of the American press, the Lindberghs secretly moved to Great Britain, where they lived from 1935 to 1938. On a visit to Adolf Hitler's Nazi Germany in 1938, Lindbergh toured German aviation centers at the invitation of Field Marshall Hermann Goering. On a follow-up visit in 1938 he was presented with a special medal of commendation by the German government.

Following the outbreak of WORLD WAR II in Europe in 1939, the outspokenly isolationist Lindbergh returned to the United States to tour the country on behalf of the AMERICA FIRST COMMITTEE, which opposed U.S. intervention in the conflict. Under fire for his vocal ISOLATIONISM and association with Nazi Germany, Lindbergh resigned his commission in the U.S. Army Air Corps Reserve. But after the United States entered the war in 1941, he served as a civilian consultant, testing aircraft and advising on technical and tactical matters. After the war he continued his involvement in aviation and was the author of several books, including his autobiography, *The Spirit of St. Louis* (1953), which captured a Pulitzer Prize.

LINOWITZ REPORT (1983) Report assessing the sources of violent conflict in Central America. Officially titled *The Americas at a Crossroads*, the report was issued April 7, 1983, by the Inter-American Dialogue, a forum of 48 prominent U.S. and Latin American citizens organized by the Smithsonian Institution's Woodrow Wilson International Center for Scholars in Washington, D.C. It was the result of six months of discussions conducted by forum co-chairmen Sol M. Linowitz, former U.S. ambassador to the ORGANIZATION OF AMERICAN STATES, and former President Galo Plaza of Ecuador. The parley examined hostilities ongoing throughout Central America including the EL SALVADOR CIVIL WAR, the conflict in Nicaragua between the Sandinista government and the anti-Communist CONTRAS, and political violence in Guatemala, Honduras, and Panama. Participants addressed the Central American turmoil in the larger context of the geopolitical struggle in the region pitting the United States against the Soviet Union and its client Cuba.

The report advocated the start of a "many-sided dialogue" among the governments of Central America, their political opponents, the United States, the USSR, and Cuba to find ways to end Central American hostilities. It contended that the root causes of unrest in Latin America were indigenous social and economic inequities and an antidemocratic political legacy rather than an East-West struggle over Soviet-sponsored Communist expansionism. The report, in veiled criticism of the Reagan administration's policies in Central America, called on the United States to make a clear commitment to respect national sovereignty in the region and refrain from "covert or overt intervention." It also appealed to the Soviet Union and Cuba to take a pledge against deploying combat forces in Central America. The report urged the superpowers to end their support for all revolutionary and counterrevolutionary movements in the region. It also implored the INTERNATIONAL MONETARY FUND and other international financial institutions to increase their lending in order to spur the flow of private investment into conflict-ridden Central America. The report's U.S. signers included former secretaries of state CYRUS R. VANCE and EDMUND S. MUSKIE and former Secretary of Defense ELLIOT L. RICHARDSON.

See also CARIBBEAN BASIN INITIATIVE, EL SALVADOR WHITE PAPER, KISSINGER COMMISSION.

LIPPMANN, WALTER (1889–1974) Influential political columnist and author. Born in New York City, the brilliant student graduated with honors from Harvard University in 1910. After working briefly for the left-of-center publication *Boston Common*, Lippmann was recruited in the summer of 1910 to *Everybody's* magazine by the famous "muckraker" LINCOLN STEFFENS, who trained his young protege as a cub reporter and writer. He left *Everybody's* in 1912 to accept the position of executive secretary to the new Socialist mayor of Schenectady, New York, the Reverend George R. Lunn. Departing after four months, he completed his first two books, *A Preface to Politics* (1913) and *Drift and Mastery* (1914), in which he rejected the Socialist movement as doctrinaire and sterile. In 1914 he helped form the *New Republic*, a liberal journal of ideas. As associate editor he established a reputation as an authority on foreign affairs. He supported President WOODROW WILSON's determination to avoid U.S. involvement in WORLD WAR I. Lippmann was rumored to have written Wilson's January 1917 "PEACE WITHOUT VICTORY" SPEECH, in which the president described the need for an international organization to ensure lasting world peace. Following America's entry into the war in April 1917, he became an assistant to the secretary of war and member of THE INQUIRY, a special White House panel that helped draft parts of Wilson's FOURTEEN POINTS. At the war's end Lippmann was a member of the U.S. delegation to the PARIS PEACE CONFERENCE.

He joined the editorial staff of the *New York World* in 1921, remaining with the newspaper for a decade and becoming its editor in 1929. Meanwhile he had finished his seminal work *Public Opinion* (1922), a meditation on democracy that asserted the inability of average citizens to understand the complex issues of contemporary national and international politics. Hired by the *New York Herald Tribune* in 1931, he launched his "Today and Tomorrow" column on domestic and world affairs. In 1938 he moved to Washington, D.C., where he continued to write his widely syndicated column, which ran until his retirement in 1967 and twice garnered a Pulitzer Prize for international reporting.

During WORLD WAR II, Lippmann argued against U.S. adoption of a postwar policy of ISOLATIONISM and promoted the idea of an alliance of the ATLANTIC COMMUNITY. In the late 1940s he popularized the term COLD WAR to describe mounting East-West tensions. Lippmann favored coexistence and trade between the United States and Soviet Union, insisting their differences

should be resolved through diplomacy. Commenting in 1961 on deep Soviet-American antagonisms, he remarked "I don't think old men ought to promote wars for young men to fight." On separate occasions in 1958 and 1961 he talked with Soviet leader Nikita S. Khrushchev in Moscow about East-West conflict. Lippmann's early support for President LYNDON B. JOHNSON's handling of the VIETNAM WAR turned to opposition after the 1965 escalation of America's military involvement. Lippmann, who favored a negotiated settlement in Southeast Asia, felt U.S. strategic interests in Vietnam were not sufficient to justify a heavy commitment of American lives and resources. While not advocating an immediate withdrawal, he suggested the United States compromise and settle for limited objectives. In retirement in New York he continued to write columns for *Newsweek*.

LITTLE BELT INCIDENT (1811)   Naval confrontation between the United States and Great Britain. The encounter between U.S. and British warships contributed to the irreversible deterioration in Anglo-American relations that culminated in the WAR OF 1812. The Little Belt Incident occurred in the aftermath of an episode involving British IMPRESSMENT of an American sailor. On May 1, 1811, the British frigate *Guerriere* stopped and boarded the American ship *Spitfire* off New Jersey and seized a native-born U.S. seaman. Captain John Rodgers, commanding the U.S. frigate *President*, received orders to furnish protection to American ships sailing along the coast of the mid-Atlantic states and to search for the culprit *Guerriere*. Rodgers sighted a vessel off Virginia on May 16 that he thought was the *Guerriere* but in actuality was the British sloop-of-war *Little Belt*. Giving chase, the *President* finally overtook the British ship, which failed to make its identity known. The pursuit ended in a lopsided battle. The *President*, emerging largely unscathed, inflicted severe damage on the British sloop, killing nine of its crew and wounding 23.

Britain reacted to news of the incident with outrage. London's protest received little sympathy in America, where anti-British feelings ran strong and where popular sentiment considered the *Little Belt* encounter fitting revenge for the CHESAPEAKE AFFAIR

(1807). In November 1811 the U.S. government offered to settle the matter amicably provided Great Britain agreed to cease its interdiction of neutral U.S. shipping with France, with whom the British were at war. The American proposal proved futile, though, as British Minister at Washington Augustus John Foster reiterated to Secretary of State JAMES MONROE his government's unwillingness to withdraw its wartime trade restrictions.

LITTLE TURTLE (1752–1812) Miami Indian chief who rejected America's territorial claims to the OLD NORTHWEST, he led the violent resistance of the Ohio Indians to the drive of white settlers beyond the Ohio River in the decade after the AMERICAN REVOLUTION. U.S. military operations in the region began in 1790 in response to increasing Indian raids on white settlements. Little Turtle directed the Indian victories over American Generals Josiah Harmar in 1790 and Arthur Saint Clair in 1791. He fought at the BATTLE OF FALLEN TIMBERS (1794), where General "Mad Anthony" Wayne turned the tide and routed the Ohio Indians. In 1795 Little Turtle and his fellow Indian leaders signed the Treaty of Greenville acknowledging their defeat and arranging substantial land cessions to the United States. The Miami chief proclaimed "I am the last to sign the treaty; I will be the last to break it." Thereafter he advocated peace and accommodation, refusing in later years to join TECUMSEH in the Shawnee chief's military opposition to American expansion.

LIVINGSTON, EDWARD (1764–1836) Lawyer, diplomat, and secretary of state under President ANDREW JACKSON. Younger brother of ROBERT R. LIVINGSTON, he graduated from the College of New Jersey (Princeton) in 1781, studied law in his home state of New York, and was admitted to the bar in 1785. Elected to Congress, the Democratic-Republican Livingston served three terms (1795–1801), earning distinction as a critic of such Federalist measures as JAY'S TREATY (1794) with Great Britain and the controversial ALIEN AND SEDITION ACTS (1798). He concurrently held the offices of U.S. attorney for New York and mayor of New York City from 1801 to 1803. When a customs clerk in his federal office misappropriated public funds, Livingston

was forced to sell his own property to make up the deficit. Burdened by heavy personal debts, he moved to New Orleans in 1804, where he resumed law practice and struggled to straighten out his finances.

During the WAR OF 1812 Livingston helped plan the defense of New Orleans and was aide to General Andrew Jackson at the Battle of New Orleans (1815). Elected to the Louisiana legislature in 1820, he won wide acclaim as a legal thinker for his proposed revision of the state legal code. Livingston returned to Congress, where he served in the House (1823–1829) and then the Senate (1829–1831). Appointed secretary of state by President Jackson in 1831, he drafted the landmark Nullification Proclamation (1832), which asserted the federal government's supremacy over state governments and denied South Carolina's right to disregard the TARIFF OF 1832. While getting the French government to acknowledge that U.S. demands for restitution of property losses suffered during the Napoleonic Wars (1803–1815) were valid, Livingston was unable to settle the FRENCH SPOLIATION CLAIMS. He resigned in 1833 to accept appointment as U.S. minister to France, where he continued to work toward a final spoliations resolution. His efforts stalled when the French demanded an apology from Jackson for the American president's threatening posture in the claims issue. Upon returning from France in 1835, Livingston retired from public service to his estate in New York.

LIVINGSTON, ROBERT R. (1746–1813) Statesman, diplomat, and Continental congressman. Brother of EDWARD LIVINGSTON, he was born in New York City, graduated from King's College (now Columbia University) in 1765, and studied law. Admitted to the bar in his native colony, he practiced briefly in partnership with JOHN JAY. In 1773 the British Crown named Livingston to the judicial post of recorder of New York. Dismissed in 1775 for his sympathies with the revolutionary cause in the American colonies, he was elected the same year to the Continental Congress, where he would serve from 1775 to 1781 and 1784 to 1785. Livingston was on the congressional committee that drafted the Declaration of Independence, but lacking instructions from the New York convention, neither voted upon nor signed the document. In high demand as a committee member, he lent his versatile abilities to panels on military affairs, finance, foreign affairs, and legal organization. Livingston served on the SECRET COMMITTEE formed in 1775 to procure war supplies from abroad to sustain the AMERICAN REVOLUTION.

Elected first secretary of the newly created Department of Foreign Affairs, the forerunner of the DEPARTMENT OF STATE, he held the post from 1781 to 1783. In this office Livingston established a bureaucracy and operating procedures that became the practical model for other fledgling executive departments of the national government. As secretary, he approved the instructions sent to Paris by Congress to guide American peace commissioners in negotiations with the British. Livingston supported the resulting TREATY OF PARIS (1783), but chastised the U.S. delegation for having kept aspects of the negotiations secret from America's French allies.

After the war, he devoted his energies to helping govern New York following the British evacuation. Together with ALEXANDER HAMILTON, he led the successful drive for New York's ratification of the federal CONSTITUTION. As chancellor of New York, a judicial position he occupied from 1777 to 1801, Livingston administered the historic first oath of office to President GEORGE WASHINGTON in 1789. Appointed minister to France in 1801 by President THOMAS JEFFERSON, he earned diplomatic distinction by helping U.S. special envoy JAMES MONROE complete the LOUISIANA PURCHASE (1803) from Napoleon Bonaparte. Resigning the French post in 1804, Livingston returned to his New York estate, Clermont. In retirement he helped finance Robert Fulton's pioneering experiments in steam navigation.

LOCKHEED SCANDAL (1976) Major scandal involving bribery of foreign officials by the Lockheed Aircraft Corporation. In February 1976 the Senate Foreign Relations Subcommittee on Multinational Corporations released documents showing that Lockheed, one of the top-ranking U.S. defense contractors, had expended millions of dollars in payoffs in the Netherlands, West Germany, Italy, Turkey, Japan, and elsewhere to win foreign contracts. The

subcommittee had obtained the documents in connection with its ongoing probe, launched in May 1975, of illegal payments abroad by U.S. multinationals. In August 1975, following months of denials, Lockheed finally had acknowledged that since 1970 it had paid more than $22 million to foreign officials and political organizations to promote its overseas business. The firm had refused, however, to comply with Securities and Exchange Commission (SEC) demands for full disclosure of the identities of payoff recipients. In so doing the already financially troubled company had aggravated its problems. Lockheed was saddled with hundreds of millions of dollars in outstanding debts, including a $195 million loan guaranteed by the federal government after the firm almost went bankrupt in 1971. Bankers and federal officials brought pressure on Lockheed to resolve the payoff scandal so financial restructuring of the company could begin.

Following a year of negotiations, Lockheed in April 1976 settled SEC charges that the firm had broken federal statutes by its secret payments to foreign government officials between 1968 and 1975 to secure arms contracts abroad. Under the settlement, Lockheed neither denied nor admitted the charges but vowed not to violate the law in the future. The identities of the payoff recipients remained secret, protected by a court order against disclosure. The U.S. Justice Department between March and May 1976 reached agreements with the governments of the Netherlands, Italy, Greece, Nigeria, and Japan to exchange information on payoffs made by Lockheed to officials in these countries.

LODGE COROLLARY (1912) Senate resolution sponsored by Foreign Relations Committee Chairman HENRY CABOT LODGE, SR. (R-MA) that extended the MONROE DOCTRINE to non-European powers and foreign companies. The corollary, also known as the Magdalena Bay Resolution, came in response to a plan by American investors to sell land on Mexico's Baja California peninsula, including the strategically valuable Magdalena Bay, to a private Japanese syndicate. Opponents of the proposed sale viewed the bay as a potential naval base, warning that its loss could endanger the PANAMA CANAL and threaten American national security. The Lodge resolution, passed on August 2, 1912, by a 51 to 4 vote, declared U.S. determination to bar the sale of such strategic possessions in the Americas to foreign corporations whose governments might use them militarily against the United States. The Japanese canceled the Magdalena transfer. Lodge's measure marked the first time Monroe Doctrine principles were applied to an Asian nation.

LODGE, HENRY CABOT, JR. (1902–1985) Senator, U.S. representative to the UNITED NATIONS, ambassador. Lodge was born in Massachusetts to a distinguished New England family. Grandson of Senator HENRY CABOT LODGE, SR. (R-MA), he graduated from Harvard in 1924 and worked in journalism until his 1932 election to the Massachusetts state legislature. A Republican, he won election to the U.S. Senate in 1936. In the years before WORLD WAR II, Lodge's viewpoint was basically isolationist, although he supported measures to increase U.S. military readiness. Following America's entry in the conflict, he became the first senator since the Civil War to resign his seat in order to go to war, serving as an Army officer in the European theater. In 1946 Lodge was reelected to the Senate, emerging in the postwar years as an internationalist who favored a leading U.S. role in the world. As U.S.-Soviet relations deteriorated into COLD WAR, he joined in the bipartisan foreign policy that committed America to the CONTAINMENT of communism. In 1952 Lodge managed DWIGHT D. EISENHOWER's successful presidential campaign. Neglecting his own Senate reelection bid, he was defeated by Representative JOHN F. KENNEDY (D-MA).

In 1953 President Eisenhower named Lodge ambassador to the United Nations. He remained in the post until 1960, when he became RICHARD M. NIXON's running mate on the unsuccessful Republican presidential ticket. Seeking bipartisan support for his handling of the VIETNAM WAR, President Kennedy in 1963 appointed Lodge ambassador to South Vietnam. He arrived in Saigon in August amid a worsening crisis between the government of President Ngo Dinh Diem and Buddhist protesters. Lodge had an indirect part in the November 1963 DIEM COUP that overthrew the ruling regime, having informed senior South Vietnamese generals that America would tacitly support a change in their nation's leadership. He resigned his position in May 1964, but continued as an informal adviser on Vietnam to President LYNDON B. JOHNSON. Johnson brought Lodge back as ambassador to South Vietnam in July 1965. His second tour in Saigon coincided with a steady escalation in U.S. military involvement in Southeast Asia. Lodge returned home again in April 1967. Following the January 1968 Communist TET OFFENSIVE, he was a member of the informal group of advisers known as the WISE MEN convened by Johnson to assess the future conduct of the Vietnam conflict. In 1969 he was President Nixon's chief negotiator at the PARIS PEACE TALKS with North Vietnam. Lodge finished his long public career as special envoy to the Vatican from 1970 to 1977.

LODGE, HENRY CABOT, SR. (1850–1924) Historian and U.S. senator, grandfather of HENRY CABOT LODGE, JR. Born in Boston into a wealthy and prominent family, Lodge graduated from Harvard in 1871 and obtained a law degree there in 1874. He continued his graduate studies while working from 1873 to 1876 as an assistant editor under eminent historian Henry Adams at the *North American Review*. Granted Harvard's first ever Ph.D. in political science in 1876, he then taught at his alma mater. Among his historical writings were the biographies *Alexander Hamilton* (1882), *Daniel Webster* (1883), and *George Washington* (2 vol., 1889), as well as his *Life and Letters of George Cabot* (1877), a study of his Federalist great-grandfather. Lodge gravitated from academic life to a career in politics as a Republican. He served in the Massachusetts House of Representatives from 1880 to 1883. In 1886 he won election to the U.S. House of Representatives, where he spent six years. He entered the U.S. Senate in 1893 and served there continuously until his death.

His chief interest in the Senate was foreign affairs. A member of the SENATE FOREIGN RELATIONS COMMITTEE from 1896, he exercised a major influence on the development of U.S. foreign policy for a generation. Lodge, as a confirmed protectionist, faithfully supported the Republican policy of high tariffs. He labored concertedly for restrictions on immigration to the United States. A disciple of naval strategist ALFRED THAYER MAHAN, he believed that a powerful modern navy and establishment of bases in the Caribbean and Pacific were indispensable to U.S. security and economic expansion. Lodge embraced the imperialist ambitions of the NEW MANIFEST DESTINY of the 1890s. An ardent nationalist, he vigorously supported the war against Spain in 1898. His influence helped secure ratification of the TREATY OF PARIS (1898) ending the SPANISH-AMERICAN WAR. Under the treaty, the United States acquired from Spain the Philippines, GUAM, and Puerto Rico and assumed control of Cuba.

Lodge was a close friend and adviser to President THEODORE ROOSEVELT, who throughout his tenure placed a high premium on the Massachusetts senator's counsel on foreign affairs. Lodge steered to ratification the second Anglo-American HAY-PAUNCEFOTE TREATY (1901), which granted the United States an exclusive right to build and operate an interoceanic canal in Central America. He served as one of the U.S. representatives on the Alaska Boundary Commission, the joint Anglo-American tribunal that in 1903 arbitrated the ALASKA BOUNDARY DISPUTE. In response to a Japanese syndicate's bid to purchase strategically valuable land in Mexico's Baja California peninsula from American investors, he formulated the LODGE COROLLARY in 1912. The corollary, embodied in a Senate resolution, barred the sale by extending the MONROE DOCTRINE to non-European powers and foreign companies.

Lodge supported U.S. entry into WORLD WAR I in 1917. As majority leader of the Senate and chairman of the Foreign Relations Committee, he led the postwar fight against ratification of the TREATY OF VERSAILLES and the covenant of the LEAGUE OF NATIONS. His opposition to the coupling of the league with the peace treaty embroiled him in a bitter political fight with President WOODROW WILSON, who insisted on the inseparability of the two. Moreover Lodge objected to aspects of the league covenant that he believed infringed on U.S. sovereignty. When the treaty and covenant were submitted in final form for Senate action, he was able to attach the LODGE RESERVATIONS, spelling out various restrictions on U.S. obligations in the league. Ratification

on these terms was unacceptable to Wilson, who adamantly opposed any amendments to the two documents. In the end the treaty and covenant were rejected by the Senate and the United States never joined the League of Nations.

Lodge's account of the controversy was published posthumously as *The Senate and The League of Nations* (1925). He helped secure the Republican presidential nomination for WARREN G. HARDING in 1920 and enjoyed even greater influence in foreign relations following Harding's inauguration in 1921. Lodge steered to ratification the BERLIN TREATY (1921) formally ending the state of war between the United States and Germany. He served as one of the four U.S. delegates to the WASHINGTON NAVAL CONFERENCE (1921–1922) and fought against U.S. membership in the WORLD COURT.

LODGE RESERVATIONS Set of 14 reservations attached to the TREATY OF VERSAILLES (1919) by Senate Republican opponents of the LEAGUE OF NATIONS. The reservations, which circumscribed American participation in the league, were named for Senator HENRY CABOT LODGE, SR. (R-MA), who as chairman of the SENATE FOREIGN RELATIONS COMMITTEE organized Senate Republican opposition to the proposed post–WORLD WAR I international organization for maintaining global peace through COLLECTIVE SECURITY. The league was the brainchild of Democratic President WOODROW WILSON, who at the PARIS PEACE CONFERENCE (1919) had successfully insisted that its covenant be incorporated into the general peace treaty. The RESERVATIONISTS, led by Lodge, complained that the concept of collective security contained in ARTICLE X of the covenant infringed on American sovereignty because it granted an international body ultimate authority to commit U.S. military forces. Defying Wilson, they sought adjustments in the treaty that, with respect to the league, would preserve U.S. independence of action and safeguard Congress's prerogatives in foreign affairs.

The Foreign Relations Committee first reported the Treaty of Versailles to the full Senate in September 1919 with proposals for 45 amendments and 4 reservations. Moderate Republicans who supported Wilson's league joined with Democrats to vote down all of the measures. Lodge and his supporters then formulated a second set of 14 reservations and attached them to the ratification resolution forwarded by the Foreign Relations Committee to the Senate in early November. The Lodge Reservations asserted the Senate's right to advise and consent to league agreements, reaffirmed Congress's authority to appropriate funds for U.S. participation in the league, and declared that the United States should decide unilaterally what matters fell within its national jurisdiction or involved its vital interests. The most significant reservation stated that Congress alone had the right to decide U.S. obligations in each individual instance under Article X of the covenant. Lodge also included a reservation reaffirming the MONROE DOCTRINE as American policy and outside the league's jurisdiction. Opposing Senate revisions to either the treaty or league covenant, Wilson rejected the reservations and urged his supporters to vote against the Lodge ratification resolution. On November 19, 1919, Democrats combined with Republican IRRECONCILABLES to defeat the Treaty of Versailles with Lodge's reservations. Reservationists and irreconcilables then allied to same day to reject the treaty without the reservations. The Senate in February 1920 voted to reconsider the treaty and sent it back to the committee, which promptly reported it with the same Lodge Reservations. Wilson remained unyieldingly opposed to them, insisting that the Senate must not rewrite the treaty. The treaty with the Lodge reservations came to a vote on March 20, when it was defeated a final time.

LOGAN ACT (1799) Federal legislation of January 30, 1799, that barred private American citizens from engaging in unauthorized diplomacy with a foreign government amid a dispute with the United States. Dr. George Logan, a Pennsylvania Quaker and future Democratic-Republican U.S. senator (1801–1807), visited France in 1798 on a personal mission to preserve Franco-American peace in the face of the undeclared QUASI-WAR (1798–1800). In talks with French Foreign Minister Charles Maurice de Talleyrand, Logan indicated Americans by and large were pro-French, suggesting that the administration of Federalist President JOHN ADAMS alone impeded friendly relations between the two countries.

Adams and Secretary of State TIMOTHY PICKERING assailed Logan's freelance diplomatic effort, claiming such contacts sabotaged official administration foreign policy. Congress responded by passing a law promoted by Federalists, the so-called Logan Act. The measure provided a fine and imprisonment for any citizen who, lacking authority, corresponded with a foreign government in an attempt to influence its conduct toward the United States during a period of controversy. The Logan Act, never repealed, remains U.S. law on restricting the diplomatic pursuits of private citizens.

LONDON CLUB See **NUCLEAR SUPPLIERS GROUP**.

LONDON DUMPING CONVENTION (1972) International agreement proscribing ocean dumping of very toxic wastes. Officially called the Convention on the Prevention of Marine Pollution by Dumping, it was negotiated and adopted under the auspices of the Inter-Governmental Maritime Consultative Organization (which became the INTERNATIONAL MARITIME ORGANIZATION) at a conference held in London in October and November 1972. Representatives from some 90 countries, including the United States, attended the gathering, the main aim of which was to prevent indiscriminate disposal at sea of waste chemicals and minerals. The final agreement was concluded on December 29, 1972, and entered into force on August 30, 1975. The United States ratified the measure in September 1973. The London Dumping Convention, as the agreement informally came to be called, barred the disposal of high-level radioactive waste while allowing dumping of low-level waste under strictly limited conditions. A two-year moratorium on low-level radioactive waste disposal was approved in 1983 and extended indefinitely in 1985.

LONDON ECONOMIC CONFERENCE See **WORLD ECONOMIC CONFERENCE**.

LONDON NAVAL CONFERENCES (1930, 1935–1936) International meetings on limiting naval armaments. At the WASHINGTON NAVAL CONFERENCE (1921–1922), the United States, Great Britain, France, Italy, and Japan had concluded the FIVE-POWER TREATY

(1922) restricting the number and size of so-called capital, or large, ships in each country's navy. The world's major sea powers, however, had been unable to agree on limiting lesser vessels such as cruisers, destroyers, and submarines. Following the unsuccessful GENEVA NAVAL CONFERENCE (1927), Great Britain proposed a five-power gathering in London to reach an agreement on smaller warships. The first London Naval Conference was held from January 21 to April 22, 1930. The London Naval Treaty of 1930, signed on the final day of the parley, extended for another five years the Five-Power Treaty's ten-year holiday on the construction of new capital ships and established rules governing submarine warfare. France and Italy, locked in a dispute over the relative strength of their navies, withheld participation from terms of the agreement regarding limits on lesser warships. These provisions fixed the permissible total tonnage for the United States, Great Britain, and Japan respectively at a ratio of 10:10:6 for cruisers and 10:10:7 for other smaller surface ships. The three powers agreed to a single equal tonnage in submarines. Because France and Italy had not subscribed to the limits, an escalator clause allowed each of the three nations to increase its fleet if it felt threatened by the naval construction of Paris or Rome.

The treaty represented the first comprehensive international agreement on naval armaments. By 1934, however, an increasingly militaristic Japan was demanding naval parity with the United States and Great Britain. As called for by the 1930 treaty, the five powers assembled in London on December 9, 1935, to consider revising and renewing the existing accord. When the United States and Great Britain would not accede to Tokyo's demands for parity, Japan withdrew from the meetings on January 15, 1936. Italy, hostile in the face of international condemnation of its conquest of Ethiopia, also proved unreceptive to negotiations. The United States, Great Britain, and France agreed to maintain the principle of naval limitation among themselves and the second London Naval Conference ended on March 25, 1936, with their signing of the London Naval Treaty of 1936. The agreement shifted the emphasis from quantitative to qualitative restrictions on naval armaments, setting limits on the size of warships and the caliber of their guns. The 1930 treaty was allowed to expire as scheduled at the end of 1936. Faced with mounting Japanese and German naval construction, the United States, Great Britain, and France in March 1938 terminated the 1936 treaty. In May 1938 Congress approved the Vinson Naval Act and America embarked on a massive ship-building program in the final years before WORLD WAR II.

LONDON NAVAL TREATIES See **LONDON NAVAL CONFERENCES**.

LONG TELEGRAM (1946) Report submitted by American diplomat GEORGE F. KENNAN, then stationed in Moscow, analyzing U.S.-Soviet relations. The WORLD WAR II alliance between the United States and Soviet Union began to fall apart almost as soon as the conflict had ended. During the war, President FRANKLIN D. ROOSEVELT had pursued a policy of accommodation toward the Soviet Union as part of a larger strategy of defeating the Axis powers. Concerned by increasing U.S.-Soviet confrontation over the shape of postwar Europe, the State Department in February 1946 asked Kennan to draw up an analysis of Soviet behavior and the appropriate U.S. response. The Soviet expert, who had extensive experience in the Communist nation, sent an 8000-word telegram to Washington on February 22. Dubbed the Long Telegram, Kennan's report pressed for fundamental changes in U.S.-Soviet policy. Kennan noted that Soviet ideology regarded socialist-capitalist conflict as inevitable, argued that Soviet foreign policy would remain hostile to the West as long as the USSR remained Communist, and suggested that continued U.S. attempts to accommodate the Soviet leadership were futile. Kennan recommended Washington adopt a firmer stance toward Moscow. The Long Telegram had a powerful impact within the Truman administration, where it provided the intellectual framework for a hardening of U.S. relations with the Soviet Union. The following year President HARRY S. TRUMAN would announce the TRUMAN DOCTRINE of U.S. opposition to Soviet expansionism.

See also CONTAINMENT.

LOUISIANA PURCHASE (1803) U.S. acquisition of the Louisiana territory from France. The purchase, encompassing New

Orleans and the vast area between the Mississippi River, the Rocky Mountains, and Spain's possessions in the Southwest, doubled the nation's size and opened the way for American expansion across the continent. France had ceded Louisiana to Spain at the end of the Seven Years' War in 1763. After a generation in possession, the Spanish found the domain a financial drain and recognized the limits of their power to defend it against advancing American settlement. In the secret October 1800 Treaty of San Ildefonso, Spain returned Louisiana to France in exchange for French leader Napoleon Bonaparte's promise of a kingdom in Italy. The Louisiana acquisition was essential to Napoleon's ambitious plan to plant a new French empire in North America, with France's Caribbean "sugar islands," particularly Santo Domingo, as its commercial base.

Rumors of the San Ildefonso pact alarmed the United States. President THOMAS JEFFERSON and Secretary of State JAMES MADISON mistakenly assumed France had obtained the Floridas as well as the Louisiana province. The Jefferson administration believed such French territorial gains threatened American interests: Napoleon would be situated to dominate the Mississippi Valley and to threaten U.S. settlements east of the river; American continental expansion would be thwarted; and France could cripple American commerce by closing off the Mississippi River. The American president even suggested French control of the critical port city of New Orleans would force the United States into an unwanted military alliance with Great Britain.

Jefferson opted to deal with Napoleon through diplomacy rather than threats. In March 1803 he dispatched special envoy JAMES MONROE to assist U.S. Minister to Paris ROBERT R. LIVINGSTON with negotiations to buy French possessions in North America. Monroe was authorized to offer $10 million for New Orleans and the Floridas. Should France refuse, Monroe and Livingston were directed to seek, at the very least, the establishment of perpetual navigation rights on the Mississippi and a permanent right to deposit merchant goods at New Orleans for transshipment.

By the spring of 1803 Napoleon's scheme for an American empire was unravelling. The French military still had not totally subjugated the black slave rebellion of Toussaint L'Ouverture in Haiti. Facing imminent war with Great Britain and growing U.S. resentment over the Louisiana issue, Napoleon wanted to block an emerging Anglo-American rapprochement and to pull back from his imperial venture in the Americas. When Monroe arrived in Paris on April 13, Napoleon already had informed Livingston of France's willingness to sell all of Louisiana. The American negotiators exceeded their instructions and made the purchase. By a treaty and two conventions dated April 30, 1803, the United States paid $15 million for the territory.

The historic acquisition raised difficult constitutional and legal questions. Jefferson went ahead with the purchase despite his own uncertainty about the extent of the president's power under the CONSTITUTION to buy Louisiana and incorporate it into the United States. Through the 1803 transfer, Napoleon had broken his pledge to the Spanish throne never to sell the domain to a third power. Spain protested to the Jefferson administration to no avail. On December 20, America took possession of Louisiana. Other problems stemmed from the vague boundaries of the purchase. The territory's western limit remained undefined until 1819, when it was clearly drawn to exclude Texas. East of the Mississippi, the United States and Spain made competing claims on West Florida. American annexation of parts of West Florida in 1810 further complicated the dispute. Spain finally relinquished all of present-day Florida to the United States in the ADAMS-ONIS TREATY of 1819.

See also MAP 2.

LOVETT, ROBERT ABERCROMBIE (1895–1986)

Under secretary of state and secretary of defense. A native of Huntsville, Texas, Lovett entered Yale in 1914. He interrupted his studies following U.S. entry into WORLD WAR I, serving as a naval officer and eventually commanding a naval squadron. He graduated from Yale in 1919 and after postgraduate courses in law and business administration at Harvard joined the New York banking firm Brown Brothers Harriman and Company where he quickly rose to become a partner. In December 1940 Lovett was appointed special assistant to Secretary of War HENRY L. STIMSON. In April 1941 he was named assistant secretary of war for air. Primarily responsible for production and procurement, Lovett was credited with the massive expansion of the Army Air Forces during WORLD WAR II. He departed government service at the end of 1945 and resumed his banking career.

Secretary of State GEORGE C. MARSHALL called Lovett back to Washington in July 1947. As under secretary of state, he oversaw the preparation of the MARSHALL PLAN (1948) for European recovery, helped draft the VANDENBERG RESOLUTION (1948) that endorsed U.S. participation in regional defense alliances, and served as the main American representative to discussions laying the groundwork for the formation of NATO (1949). When Marshall resigned in January 1949, Lovett returned to his investment business. U.S. military set-backs early in the KOREAN WAR led President HARRY S. TRUMAN to replace Secretary of Defense LOUIS A. JOHNSON with Marshall in September 1950. Lovett returned to Washington as deputy defense secretary. He succeeded the retiring Marshall in September 1951. As secretary, Lovett continued the major U.S. rearmament program begun in response to both the Korean conflict and wider concerns over the global threat posed by the Soviet Union and international communism. He left the PENTAGON when President DWIGHT D. EISENHOWER took office in January 1953 and again returned to banking. Lovett was a member of two top-level panels on defense issues, the ROCKEFELLER COMMITTEE (1953) and the GAITHER COMMITTEE (1957), during the Eisenhower presidency and served as an informal advisor to President JOHN F. KENNEDY.

LOW-ROGERS EXPEDITION (1871) Unsuccessful U.S. naval expedition to open relations with Korea. America hoped to repeat its historic 1854 opening to Japan with the neighboring, long-isolated Korean "Hermit Kingdom." Acting on information received by the U.S. consul general at Shanghai that the Korean king was ready to make a commercial treaty, the United States in 1871 dispatched Minister to China Frederick F. Low to Korea. Low was accompanied by a U.S. naval squadron under Admiral John Rogers.

The American flotilla arrived off the west coast of Korea on May 30, 1871. The squadron's peaceful intentions were communicated to local officials, but American ships surveying a channel came under fire from Korean coastal forts. When a message from the provincial governor arrived protesting their presence, the American emissaries recognized their mission was doomed to failure. Not wanting to withdraw in seeming retreat, they demanded an apology for the attack by the coastal forts. When this was not forthcoming, a force of 750 men went ashore and destroyed the forts. Three Americans were killed while Korean casualties were estimated at 250. The U.S. squadron returned to China. The entire incident was a serious embarrassment to American diplomacy in Asia. It was learned that the reports given to the U.S. consul general in Shanghai concerning Korean desires for an opening had been fabricated. A decade later the United States succeeded in establishing relations with Korea in the KOREAN-AMERICAN TREATY OF 1882.

LUCE, HENRY ROBINSON (1898–1967) Publisher and editor. Born in Tengchow, China, to a Presbyterian missionary couple, he lived there until age 14. Luce interrupted his undergraduate studies at Yale College to serve with the U.S. Army for a year during WORLD WAR I. Graduating from Yale in 1920, he worked on newspapers in Chicago and Baltimore. In 1923, he and former Yale classmate Briton Hadden co-founded *Time*, the pioneering weekly news magazine that established the two men as journalistic innovators. Following Hadden's death in 1929, Luce charted a successful course for Time Inc. through the Great Depression of the 1930s, launching the business monthly *Fortune* in 1930 and the photojournalism weekly *Life* in 1936. His second wife, whom he married in 1935, was Clare Boothe Luce, the distinguished playwright, journalist, congresswoman, and ambassador to Italy.

As editor-in-chief of his publications, Luce vigorously advanced his views on foreign affairs. With fascism on the march in Europe in the late 1930s, he urged the United States to move beyond its ISOLATIONISM of the post–World War I period and take an active international role. The Republican Luce, who by 1939 regarded Adolf Hitler's Nazi Germany as a grave menace to the United States, advocated early American entry into WORLD WAR II. In a famous February 1941 *Life* magazine essay, he coined the expression AMERICAN CENTURY, arguing that the United States had supplanted Great Britain as the world's most powerful and vigorous nation. Thus, Luce contended, America would bear responsibility at the war's end for exerting global leadership to champion freedom and promote democratic capitalism. These views were anchored in his larger notion of America's moral mission, which stemmed out of his strong Christian beliefs. By 1944 he had come to consider the Soviet Union as the greatest impediment to U.S. postwar geopolitical interests. He grew deeply concerned in the war's late stages about Soviet leader Joseph Stalin's designs on Eastern Europe and the Balkans. After 1945 Luce turned staunchly anti-Communist, becoming a leading COLD WAR apostle. His speeches and magazine pieces in the late 1940s called on U.S. business to invest overseas so as to shore-up non-Communist economies. Advocate of a bold U.S. policy toward the Soviet Union, he criticized as too defensive the Truman administration's strategy of CONTAINMENT.

Luce maintained a lifelong interest in the country of his birth. A loyal supporter of the Nationalist Chinese and their leader, Generalissimo Chiang Kai-shek, he unsuccessfully urged Truman to furnish substantial U.S. military aid to Chiang's forces. After the Chinese Communist victory in 1949, he remained politically committed to the exiled Nationalist Chinese government on Taiwan. Following the successful Soviet launch in October 1957 of Sputnik, the world's first orbiting satellite, Luce's *Life* magazine proclaimed a SPACE RACE between Washington and Moscow and eventually secured exclusive rights to the stories of the seven original American astronauts. Ardent anticommunism remained a Luce trademark. In the early 1960s, his publications advocated a tougher American stance toward Communist Cuba and favored escalating U.S. involvement in the VIETNAM WAR. He retired as editor-in-chief of Time Inc. in 1964.

LUDLOW AMENDMENT (1938) Proposed constitutional amendment. It would have required that any declaration of war by Congress be approved by a majority vote of the American people, except in case of armed attack on the United States, its territories, or the Western Hemisphere. The measure, sponsored by Representative Louis L. Ludlow (D-IN), reflected the strong isolationist sentiment in America in the late 1930s and the corresponding desire to prevent U.S. involvement in the hostilities between China and Japan or the mounting tensions in Europe. Many isolationists believed that a combination of international bankers, munitions makers, and the federal executive branch had drawn the nation into WORLD WAR I and, if left unchecked, could do so again. On January 10, 1938, the House of Representatives voted 209 to 188 against releasing the amendment from committee, effectively killing any chance of its passage. Highlight of the debate leading up to the vote was a letter from President FRANKLIN D. ROOSEVELT, read to the House by Speaker William B. Bankhead (D-AL), arguing the amendment was "impracticable in its application" and "would cripple any president in his conduct of our foreign relations." The close vote on the resolution represented the peak of U.S. ISOLATIONISM in the years before WORLD WAR II.

LUSITANIA (1915)   British transatlantic passenger ship sunk without warning on May 7, 1915, by a German submarine off the Irish coast. Of the 1959 passengers and crew aboard, 1198 died, including 128 Americans. The success of still-experimental German submarines, or U-boats, in sinking British ships in the opening months of WORLD WAR I led German military commanders to urge an escalated submarine warfare campaign as retaliation for the British blockade of German seaborne commerce and to cripple Allied trade in and out of Great Britain. The German government on February 4, 1915, proclaimed the waters around the British Isles a war zone and announced that, after February 18, its submarines would destroy on sight enemy merchant ships within the designated area without regard for the safety of passengers and crew. Germany warned that ships of neutral nations entered the war zone at their own peril. The Germans called their new policy a justified response to Britain's violations of international law on FREEDOM OF THE SEAS, particularly the interdiction of food under its blockade.

Within a week President WOODROW WILSON delivered a stern warning to Germany concerning its war zone decree. He informed Berlin that the United States would regard the destruction of American ships or lives on the high seas by the U-boats as an indefensible breach of neutral rights and would hold Germany "strictly accountable." The German ambassador in Washington, Count Johann Heinrich von Bernstorff, unsuccessfully urged the U.S. State Department to caution Americans against traveling on belligerent ships. Germany's submarines thereafter began exacting a heavy toll on Allied vessels. On March 28, 1915, an American citizen died in the sinking of the British liner *Falaba* in the Irish Sea. On May 1 two Americans died when the U.S. oil tanker *Gulflight* was torpedoed during an encounter between a submarine and a British naval patrol.

Mindful of the resentment created in the United States by these episodes, the German embassy in Washington, on the same day as the *Gulflight* incident, placed an ad in newspapers warning Americans that they took passage on British ships at their own peril. That afternoon the English luxury liner *Lusitania* sailed from New York for Europe carrying small-arms ammunition among its cargo. In a chance encounter near the Irish coast on May 7, the German submarine U-20 torpedoed the passenger liner, which sank in 18 minutes. The catastrophe precipitated widespread outrage in the United States. Wilson on May 13 issued a formal note of protest, demanding Germany stop unrestricted warfare, disavow the *Lusitania* sinking, and pay reparations for the American deaths. In its May 18 reply defending the torpedoing, Germany noted that the vessel had been ferrying contraband munitions and claimed, incorrectly, that it was armed. Judging Berlin's response unsatisfactory, Wilson drafted a second strongly worded protest to the German government. Secre-

tary of State WILLIAM JENNINGS BRYAN objected to the sequel note, which he believed not only was too severe but on principle should be balanced by a formal U.S. protest against British violations of neutral rights. He feared Wilson's tough stand on German submarine policy might lead the United States to war. Refusing to sign the president's message, and failing to persuade Wilson to make a less aggressive reply, Bryan resigned on June 8. The next day the second note, reiterating U.S. demands, was sent over the signature of Bryan's successor, ROBERT LANSING. A final *Lusitania* note on July 21 advised Germany that the U.S. government would regard repetition of an act such as the passenger liner sinking as "deliberately unfriendly."

The German government was unwilling to capitulate publicly on the *Lusitania* matter, but wanted to avoid a critical break with the United States and keep the Americans out of the war. Thus, even as it jousted diplomatically with Washington, Berlin issued secret instructions to submarine commanders not to attack large passenger ships. The new orders failed to prevent the August 1915 U-boat torpedoing of the ARABIC, an incident that heightened the crisis in U.S.-German relations and elicited a German pledge to moderate its submarine warfare policy. In February 1916 the German government apologized for the destruction of the *Lusitania* and agreed to make reparation but adamantly refused to admit that the sinking was illegal. The *Lusitania* dispute remained unsettled when the United States entered World War I in April 1917.

LYTTON COMMISSION See **MANCHURIAN CRISIS**.

M

MacARTHUR, DOUGLAS (1880–1964) Army officer, commander of post–WORLD WAR II occupation forces in Japan, commander of UNITED NATIONS forces in the KOREAN WAR. The son of an Army general, MacArthur was born in Arkansas and raised on frontier posts. He graduated first in his class from West Point in 1903, served in the Philippines and various stateside assignments, and was an aide to President THEODORE ROOSEVELT. He won distinction as a combat leader with the AMERICAN EXPEDITIONARY FORCE during WORLD WAR I and was promoted to general in 1918. From 1919 to 1922 MacArthur was superintendent of West Point. In 1930 he was named Army chief of staff. After completing a five-year tenure in the service's top uniformed post, in 1935 he headed an American military mission to the Philippines to develop a defense program for the U.S. dependency in anticipation of its eventual independence. He retired from the U.S. Army in 1937, but remained in uniform as a field marshal in the Philippine Army. He was recalled to active duty by President FRANKLIN D. ROOSEVELT on the eve of World War II. During the war MacArthur, commander of the Southwest Pacific Theater, fought a brilliant three-year campaign to retake the Philippines from the Japanese. In December 1944 he was promoted to five-star general.

In August 1945 President HARRY S. TRUMAN designated MacArthur Supreme Commander, Allied Powers (SCAP), to accept Japan's surrender and command the occupation of the defeated nation. While overall policy ostensibly was set by the Far Eastern Commission representing the 11 nations that had been at war against Japan, he exercised broad autonomy and authority in implementing and administering the occupation. His six-year tenure as SCAP earned MacArthur international recognition as the architect of modern Japan. He oversaw the elimination of Japanese militarism, guided the drafting of a new Japanese constitution, and instituted political, economic, and social reforms calculated to hasten the development of a democratic, Western-allied nation. Following the outbreak of the Korean War in June 1950, Truman appointed MacArthur commander of the American-led United Nations Command organized to repel the Communist North Korean invasion of South Korea. In September 1950 MacArthur launched a major amphibious assault at Inchon behind enemy lines and U.N. forces quickly drove the North Koreans back across the 38TH PARALLEL. In October the United Nations called for the reunification of Korea and MacArthur sent his armies into North Korea. With victory seemingly in sight, he and Truman conferred on postwar plans at WAKE ISLAND on October 15. In late November 1950, however, Communist China suddenly entered the conflict, its armies forcing the surprised U.N. troops into a general retreat. After months of bitter fighting, the front stabilized roughly along the prewar Korean border.

MacArthur favored pressing the fight until the reunification of Korea and total victory, but Truman decided on the more limited objective of a negotiated settlement. The president, worried over a possible Soviet attack on Western Europe, sought to avoid any further escalation of the fighting between the United States and

Communist China. Tensions between the two men mounted as MacArthur publicly differed with the Truman administration's limited-war strategy. After a letter critical of administration policy from the general to Representative Joseph W. Martin, Jr. (R-MA) was read to Congress, Truman relieved MacArthur of his command on April 11, 1951. He returned to a hero's welcome, including a famed address to a joint session of Congress, but Senate hearings in May and June generally supported Truman's handling of the war and muted the public clamor over MacArthur's dismissal. He retired from public life and became chairman of the Remington Rand corporation.

McCARRAN ACT See INTERNAL SECURITY ACT.

McCARRAN-WALTER ACT See IMMIGRATION AND NATIONALITY ACT OF 1952.

McCARTHY HEARINGS See McCARTHY, JOSEPH RAYMOND.

McCARTHY, JOSEPH RAYMOND (1908–1957)
Controversial U.S. senator whose campaign in the early 1950s against alleged Communist infiltration of the U.S. government brought him notoriety and power. Born in Wisconsin, McCarthy received a law degree from Marquette University in 1935. Entering practice in his native state, he quickly became interested in politics. He ran unsuccessfully in 1936 for county district attorney and three years later was elected as a state circuit court judge. In 1942 he took leave from the bench to join the Marine Corps, serving as an intelligence officer in the Pacific during WORLD WAR II. On his discharge in 1945, he adopted the nickname "Tailgunner Joe" to herald his war record, which he considerably embroidered. In 1946 McCarthy was elected to the U.S. Senate from Wisconsin after having defeated incumbent Robert M. LaFollette, Jr. for the Republican nomination in a suprising upset.

After three undistinguished years in office, he launched his demagogic crusade against alleged Communist subversion in America. In February 1950 he delivered a notorious speech in Wheeling, West Virginia, in which he charged that 205 known Communists were employed in the State Department and claimed to have documentation to prove his allegations. McCarthy's accusations exploited domestic COLD WAR fears of a worldwide Communist threat. Those fears had been engendered by the Soviet Union's subjugation of Eastern Europe and the success in 1949 of a Communist revolution in China. Coming just weeks after the perjury conviction of former State Department official ALGER HISS in the espionage-related HISS CASE, his address created a sensation and catapulted him into the national spotlight. A congressional investigation headed by Senator Millard E. Tydings (D-MD) uncovered no evidence to substantiate McCarthy's initial charges. By attracting widespread publicity, the proceedings enhanced the Wisconsin senator's notoriety and political influence. His blistering attacks against the Democratic Roosevelt and Truman administrations for the purported appeasement of Soviet leader Joseph Stalin at the YALTA CONFERENCE (1945) and loss of China to communism won McCarthy a large following among conservative Republicans. Alleging that Communists had been subverting the nation's foreign policy for some twenty years, he accused numerous government officials of having Communist sympathies or affiliations. His most prominent target was former Secretary of State General GEORGE C. MARSHALL.

Reelected in 1952, McCarthy became chairman of both the Senate Committee on Governmental Operations and its Permanent Subcommittee on Investigations, positions from which he undertook probes aimed at uncovering Communists in government. While these investigations yielded little evidence of subversive conduct, they generated great controversy and attracted enormous publicity. McCarthy came increasingly into conflict with Republican President DWIGHT D. EISENHOWER, who had accepted his support in the 1952 campaign but now wanted to disassociate himself from the senator's demagogic tactics. The crucial turning point in McCarthy's career came when he leveled an accusation of subversion in the U.S. Army. The charge, stemming specifically from the promotion of an Army dentist with alleged Communist sympathies, aroused the indignation of many senior military leaders. To discredit McCarthy, the Army charged that he and his committee's counsel, Roy Cohn, had sought preferential treatment for G. David Schine, a former McCarthy aide recently inducted into military service. The senator countercharged that the Army was using the Schine matter to thwart his investigation. The nationally televised McCarthy hearings, the outgrowth of charges that the Army was lax in rooting out Communist spies, lasted from April to June 1954 and were seen by an audience estimated at 20 million viewers. McCarthy's combative and erratic performance, together with his escalating attacks on the Eisenhower administration, discredited him in the public eye and brought his rapid political demise.

In December 1954 the Senate voted 67 to 22 to condemn McCarthy for his behavior. After a long illness he died in Bethesda, Maryland, in 1957. McCarthy's critics charged him with waging a reckless anti-Communist "witch-hunt" that had created an atmosphere of fear and ruined the careers and lives of many people in and out of government. His defenders praised him for what they contended was a patriotic campaign to expose Communist subversion. The period of anti-Communist fervor that swept the nation in the late 1940s and early 1950s is sometimes referred to as the McCarthy Era. The term McCarthyism refers to the use of innuendo, false charges, and manipulated public hearings to discredit opponents without regard for due process rights.

McCONE, JOHN ALEX (1902–1991) Businessman and government official. McCone received an engineering degree from the University of California at Berkeley in 1922 and joined the Llewellyn Iron Works in Los Angeles. By 1933 the native Californian had risen to the positions of executive vice-president and director. In 1937 he formed his own international engineering and construction firm, Bechtel-McCone. During WORLD WAR II he was involved in aircraft production and directed the building of more than 450 ships.

McCone entered government service in 1947 as a member of President HARRY S. TRUMAN's Air Policy Commission on U.S. air power. In 1948 he served as a special assistant to newly installed first Secretary of Defense JAMES V. FORRESTAL. Appointed under secretary of the air force in June 1950, he

helped double the production of military planes and recommended a major U.S. guided-missile program. Within several years his proposal, which went without action, was recognized as having anticipated the coming missile age. McCone returned to private enterprise in October 1951. In January 1954 he sat on the Wriston Committee on modernizing the diplomatic corps. He joined the Eisenhower administration in 1958, serving as chairman of the Atomic Energy Commission until 1960.

In September 1961, following the failed BAY OF PIGS INVASION of Cuba, President JOHN F. KENNEDY named McCone to replace ALLEN W. DULLES as director of central intelligence and head of the CENTRAL INTELLIGENCE AGENCY (CIA). He gained credit for restoring the agency's morale and reputation after the Bay of Pigs debacle. He placed particular emphasis on intelligence collection and preparation, pressing the development of U.S. SATELLITE RECONNAISSANCE. CIA intelligence reports played a key part in the CUBAN MISSILE CRISIS (1962). McCone's policymaking influence declined following Kennedy's assassination in November 1963 and he resigned from the Johnson administration in April 1965. He resumed his private business interests, becoming a director of ITT. In 1983 he was a member of the SCOWCROFT COMMISSION on U.S. strategic nuclear forces.

McELROY, NEIL HOSLER (1904–1972) Businessman and second secretary of defense in the Eisenhower administration. McElroy earned a bachelors degree in economics from Harvard in 1925. He began a long career with Proctor and Gamble in his native Ohio, advancing to president of the firm in 1948. In 1957 he accepted President DWIGHT D. EISENHOWER's offer to succeed the retiring CHARLES E. WILSON as secretary of defense, with the understanding he would serve only two years. Eisenhower wanted a defense chief who, like Wilson, brought management expertise and experience in industry to the office.

McElroy took office October 9, 1957, just five days after the Soviet launch of Sputnik, the world's first artificial satellite. The rocket that placed Sputnik in orbit also was capable of being used as an INTERCONTINENTAL BALLISTIC MISSILE and throughout his tenure McElroy faced widespread domestic concern over a perceived MISSILE GAP between the United States and the Soviet Union. The new secretary of defense accelerated U.S. missile programs and defended the administration against the claims of congressional Democrats that America had fallen behind in missile technology. He helped formulate the DEFENSE REORGANIZATION ACT OF 1958 and supported Eisenhower's commitment to "security with solvency," holding increases in defense spending to a minimum. McElroy resigned in December 1959 and became chairman of the board of Proctor and Gamble.

McGILLIVRAY, ALEXANDER (1759–1793) Diplomat and head chief of the Creek Nation, McGillivray was the key leader of the southeast Indians' resistance to expanding white settlement in the last quarter of the 18th century. Of Creek, French, and Scottish descent, he served as a British agent in the AMERICAN REVOLUTION and after the war launched a hostile campaign against further westward expansion by whites. In 1784 McGillivray concluded an exclusive trade deal with the Spanish in Florida, acquiring Spanish weapons for Creek armed forays against American settlers in Georgia and Tennessee.

Responding to American overtures, he met with President GEORGE WASHINGTON in 1790 in New York and signed a peace treaty. By its terms, the Creek ceded their territories in Georgia to the federal government and McGillivray was commissioned a brigadier general in the U.S. Army. Two years later the Creek chief repudiated the TREATY OF NEW YORK and renewed his allegiance with Spain. His death from illness thwarted Spanish schemes to unite various southern tribes as an Indian barrier state against the growing American republic.

See also MAP 1.

McGOVERN-HATFIELD AMENDMENT Legislative attempt to end U.S. involvement in the VIETNAM WAR. The April 1970 U.S.-led CAMBODIAN INCURSION fueled domestic antiwar sentiment. On May 2, 1970, Senators George S. McGovern (D-SD) and Mark O. Hatfield (R-OR) announced they were sponsoring an "end-the-war" amendment. The measure to cut off funds for military operations in Southeast Asia on December 31, 1970, was defeated by a 62 to 29 vote

on June 29. A revised version, which would have halted spending and required a U.S. withdrawal from Vietnam by December 31, 1971, was rejected by a 55 to 39 vote on September 1, 1970. Supporters argued that the proposed amendment, attached to a defense procurement bill, would keep pressure on the Nixon administration to fulfill its pledge to extricate America from Southeast Asia. Opponents countered that the measure would undercut the U.S. position at peace negotiations in Paris and would leave the fate of American prisoners of war (POWs) unresolved. The amendment, modified to require the withdrawal of U.S. troops from Vietnam by December 31, 1972, pending the release of American POWs, was voted down a final time by 52 to 44 on June 16, 1971. In 1972 McGovern, running on a strongly antiwar platform, was the unsuccessful Democratic candidate for president.

See also CASE-CHURCH AMENDMENT, COOPER-CHURCH AMENDMENT, MANSFIELD AMENDMENT.

McKINLEY TARIFF (1890) Legislation that continued high U.S. import duties. Since the MORRILL TARIFF of 1861, U.S. trade policy had rested on protectionist duties meant to block foreign imports and thus aid domestic industries. America's rapid internal expansion in the second half of the 19th century enabled the nation to rely primarily on domestic rather than foreign commerce and lessened the need for overseas markets. Named for sponsor Representative WILLIAM McKINLEY (R-OH), the McKinley Tariff maintained U.S. import fees in the 50 percent range. Signed into law October 1, 1890, it also represented the first instance in which reciprocity provisions had been included in a tariff act. Under these provisions, the president could reduce tariff rates on sugar, molasses, coffee, tea, and hide imports from other Western Hemisphere nations. These countries were required to provide the same lower import duties on U.S. goods. The reciprocity measure effectively was negated by the WILSON-GORMAN TARIFF, which removed key item sugar from the lower-duty list. High customs fees were kept under the WILSON-GORMAN TARIFF (1894) and DINGLEY TARIFF (1897).

See also PROTECTIONISM.

McKINLEY, WILLIAM (1843–1901) Twenty-fifth president of the United States. Born in Ohio, McKinley briefly attended Allegheny College. He served in the Union army during the Civil War, attaining the rank of major. After the war he studied law, passed the Ohio bar, and settled in Canton, where he established a successful practice and became active in Republican politics. His first public office, which he held from 1869 to 1871, was Stark County prosecutor. In 1876 he was elected as a Republican to the U.S. House of Representatives. He served in Congress (except for one term after losing a contested election in 1882) until 1891. Proponent of the high protective tariff, he sponsored and helped frame the MCKINLEY TARIFF of 1890. Defeated for reelection in 1890 on the tariff issue, he ran successfully for governor of Ohio in 1891 and was reelected in 1893. He secured the Republican presidential nomination in 1896 and went on to defeat Democrat WILLIAM JENNINGS BRYAN in the general election.

Foreign policy dominated his presidency. A special session of Congress called by McKinley to raise U.S. tariffs continued the Republican legacy of trade PROTECTIONISM when it passed the DINGLEY TARIFF (1897), which established higher customs duties. His administration completed a treaty in June 1897 to annex Hawaii, but Democratic and anti imperialist Republican opposition in the Senate delayed its ratification. The strategic value of the Pacific islands, demonstrated during the SPANISH-AMERICAN WAR (1898), brought a renewed demand for HAWAII ANNEXATION, which was achieved by joint congressional resolution in July 1898. The war, which established the United States as a world power, resulted from mounting Spanish-American conflict over Cuba. In 1895 a rebellion against Spanish colonial rule had broken out on the Caribbean island. Echoing widespread American public sentiment, the president deplored Spain's brutal campaign to suppress the insurrection. Through gradual diplomatic pressure, he tried to persuade Spain to give up its Caribbean colony, but the Spanish government vowed never to grant Cuban independence.

Disclosure on February 9, 1898, in the jingoist American press of the intercepted DE LOME LETTER, in which the Spanish minister to the United States had insulted McKinley, fanned anti-Spanish feeling in America. Following the suspicious destruction of the U.S. battleship *Maine* in Havana harbor on February 15 (for which the Spanish were blamed), the clamor for war grew in the United States. After Spain repeatedly refused U.S. offers to mediate a settlement leading to Cuban independence, McKinley on April 11 asked Congress for authority to use force to restore peace in Cuba. Congress on April 19 approved a resolution that amounted to a virtual declaration of war for the liberation and independence of Cuba. To allay domestic anti imperialist concerns about American war aims, the resolution included the TELLER AMENDMENT disclaiming any U.S. intent to annex Cuba.

The Spanish-American War was brief. By the time a formal armistice ended the fighting, the United States had defeated the Spanish fleet at Manila Bay in the Philippines and had occupied Cuba and Puerto Rico. McKinley sent a five-man commission to Paris to negotiate terms of a final peace. At the war's outset, the president had replaced Secretary of State JOHN SHERMAN with WILLIAM DAY. Day now resigned to head the U.S. negotiating team and was succeeded by JOHN M. HAY. McKinley set aside his earlier reluctance concerning American imperial expansion and endorsed a policy of territorial acquisition. When the American commissioners sought precise instructions on the disposition of the Philippines, he directed them to obtain the archipelago. Under terms of the TREATY OF PARIS (1898) ending the war, the United States acquired Puerto Rico, the Philippine Islands, and GUAM; and Spain relinquished Cuba, which was to remain under U.S. occupation pending the transition to full Cuban independence. McKinley, overcoming anti imperialist and isolationist opposition to American overseas expansion, was able to secure Senate approval of the treaty in February 1899 by one vote more than the required two-thirds majority.

He then turned to the challenge of organizing governments for the new American dependencies. His administration found itself immediately preoccupied with trying to suppress the PHILIPPINE INSURRECTION (1899–1902), the bloody uprising mounted by independence-seeking Filipino rebels under Emilio Aguinaldo. McKinley in

1899 dispatched the SCHURMAN COMMISSION to the Philippines to assess the situation and submit recommendations on setting up civil rule in the islands within a framework of American sovereignty. In early 1900 he sent the TAFT COMMISSION, headed by WILLIAM HOWARD TAFT, to establish civil government in the archipelago and prepare the Filipinos for limited self-rule. In the aftermath of the Spanish-American War, an American military government under General LEONARD WOOD ran Cuba. The task of effecting a shift to Cuban self-government fell to ELIHU ROOT, who was appointed secretary of war in 1899. Determined to safeguard U.S. economic and strategic interests in Cuba, Root, with McKinley, drafted the PLATT AMENDMENT (1901), which gave the United States the right to intervene militarily to preserve stability in the island and prevent possible external challenges to Cuban independence. The FORAKER ACT (1900), meanwhile, provided for the establishment of a temporary civil government in Puerto Rico.

Asserting preeminent American influence in the Caribbean, the McKinley administration in 1900 completed the original HAY-PAUNCEFOTE TREATY with Great Britain. The agreement, replacing the CLAYTON-BULWER TREATY (1850), gave the United States an exclusive right to build and operate an interoceanic canal in Central America, open to all nations. The British rejected the treaty after the U.S. Senate amended it to allow for U.S. fortification of the waterway. A second Hay-Pauncefote Treaty gained approval following McKinley's death in 1901.

In Asia the administration was confronted with the intensifying competition among the major European powers and Japan to carve out spheres of political and economic influence in China. Anxious both to preserve Chinese independence and protect America's trade position in the giant Asian country, Hay won tentative European and Japanese endorsement of the OPEN DOOR policy, under which all foreign powers would have equal commercial access in China and would respect its territorial integrity. In response to the BOXER REBELLION (1900), in which nationalistic Chinese violently sought the expulsion of all foreigners, McKinley sent American troops as part of an international expedition to rescue besieged foreign residents in China. He again defeated Bryan for president in 1900 in an election that was billed by the Democrats as a referendum on IMPERIALISM. On September 6, 1901, during a visit to the Pan-American Exposition in Buffalo, New York, McKinley was shot by anarchist Leon Czolgosz. The president died eight days later and was succeeded by Vice-President THEODORE ROOSEVELT.

McLANE, LOUIS (1786–1857)   Diplomat and secretary of state under President ANDREW JACKSON. Born in Delaware, McLane was a midshipman in the Navy from 1798 to 1801. He attended Newark College (now the University of Delaware), read law, and was admitted to the bar in 1807. His political career began with his election in 1816 as a Democratic-Republican from Delaware to the U.S. House of Representatives, where he spent five successive terms. He served in the U.S. Senate from 1827 until 1829, when he resigned to accept appointment by President Jackson as minister to Great Britain. While in London he negotiated a trade agreement that opened British West Indian ports to U.S. merchant ships. He was recalled by Jackson in 1831 and made secretary of the treasury, a post McLane held until he replaced EDWARD LIVINGSTON as secretary of state in 1833.

The two main diplomatic issues confronting McLane in his new post were the Anglo-American dispute over the boundary between Maine and Canada and the FRENCH SPOLIATION CLAIMS matter. He was unable to make any headway with Great Britain on the boundary dispute, which remained unresolved until Washington and London completed the WEBSTER-ASHBURTON TREATY in 1842. When France refused to fulfill it obligations under an 1831 treaty to pay American claims for shipping losses suffered during the Napoleonic Wars (1803–1815), McLane advised Jackson to order reprisals against French shipping. Others in the cabinet dissuaded the president from taking such drastic action. McLane resigned his office in 1834 and became a bank president in New York City. In 1837 he moved to Maryland, where he was president of the Baltimore and Ohio Railroad Company for ten years. While still in the railroad's employ, he accepted appointment in 1845 by President JAMES K. POLK as minister to Britain. His second London mission was preoccupied with negotiations relating to the OREGON QUESTION. He returned to the United States in 1846 and retired from the railroad the following year.

McMAHON ACT   See **ATOMIC ENERGY ACT**.

McNAMARA, ROBERT STRANGE (1916–) Secretary of defense, president of the WORLD BANK. The California native graduated from the University of California at Berkeley in 1936 and earned an M.B.A. from the Harvard Business School in 1939. The following year he joined the faculty as an accounting instructor. Initially rejected for military service during WORLD WAR II because of poor eyesight, McNamara remained at Harvard to help train Army Air Corps officers. In 1943 he was commissioned an Army captain and sent to England to assist in the planning of U.S. long-range bombing. He subsequently served in the Far East before leaving active duty in 1946 and beginning a management career with the Ford Motor Company. Credited with reorganizing and revitalizing the giant automaker, in 1960 he was named the first president of the firm who was not a member of the Ford family.

The same year President-elect JOHN F. KENNEDY selected McNamara as his secretary of defense. Taking office in January 1961, McNamara wrought major changes in Defense Department organization and management. He asserted greater civilian control over the PENTAGON, centralizing many management functions in the secretary's office. He assigned top-level positions to brilliant young academics and analysts who applied advanced management techniques to the administration of the huge defense bureaucracy. These experts were known derisively as "whiz kids" by senior officers and officials who were uneasy with their lack of experience in military matters. McNamara also sought to minimize interservice rivalries among the armed forces and consolidated overlapping activities by such steps as forming the DEFENSE INTELLIGENCE AGENCY and Defense Supply Agency.

McNamara implemented a basic revision in American warfighting doctrine. The Eisenhower administration's NEW LOOK defense policy, which relied on atomic weapons as the primary component of U.S.

military strength, was replaced by a FLEXIBLE RESPONSE strategy, which emphasized conventional as well as nuclear forces and the ability to react to the full range of possible military threats. McNamara saw the Kennedy administration's handling of the CUBAN MISSILE CRISIS (1962) as an effective demonstration of the new doctrine at work. He also began to shift U.S. nuclear DETERRENCE toward the concept of MUTUAL ASSURED DESTRUCTION and endorsed the partial nuclear LIMITED TEST BAN TREATY (1963). Remaining in office under President LYNDON B. JOHNSON after Kennedy's assassination, he oversaw the deployment of U.S. troops to the Dominican Republic during the 1965 DOMINICAN CRISIS.

McNamara's seven-year tenure was dominated by American involvement in the VIETNAM WAR. He was a principal architect of U.S. policy in Southeast Asia, subscribing to the DOMINO THEORY that Communist aggression in Vietnam imperiled the entire region. He helped formulate the Kennedy administration's decision to increase substantially the number of American military advisers in South Vietnam and later under President Johnson guided the escalating U.S. role in the conflict. He supported the TONKIN GULF RESOLUTION (1964), the 1965 decision to undertake the systematic bombing of North Vietnam, and the deployment the same year of large numbers of U.S. ground combat forces to South Vietnam. Antiwar Senator Wayne Morse (D-OR) dubbed Vietnam "McNamara's War." As domestic antiwar sentiment mounted in the mid-1960s, McNamara came under increasing attack. Critics charged that his extensive reliance on statistical analysis and use of such terms as "body count" to measure battlefield success reflected a detached, computerized approach to the actual horror of war. Exhausted and increasingly troubled by the course of events in Vietnam, McNamara submitted his resignation in November 1967 and left office the following February.

In April 1968 he became president of the World Bank, an international lending agency founded in 1944 to provide funds to member nations for development purposes. Twice reelected its head, he remained at the institution until his retirement in 1981. During his presidency he shifted the bank's emphasis from large scale civil engineering projects to local development programs aimed at providing basic human needs. In retirement McNamara remained active in world affairs, speaking out against the nuclear arms race and apartheid and pressing for progress on East-West relations and global population control.

MACON'S BILL NO. 2 (1810) Legislation adopted by Congress on May 1, 1810, to compel warring powers Great Britain and France to halt their violations of American commercial shipping. The NON-INTERCOURSE ACT (1809) ban on trade relations with the British and French had failed to wrest concessions from the European belligerents. French emperor Napoleon Bonaparte insisted the American law worked to the benefit of his British enemies. In retaliation, he issued the Rambouillet Decree in March 1810 authorizing the seizure of American vessels trading in French ports. Under this decree alone Napoleon confiscated some $10 million in American property. An Anglo-American attempt at a diplomatic settlement of the neutral-rights issue had collapsed when the British disavowed the ERSKINE AGREEMENT (1809). The Non-Intercourse Act, like the repealed EMBARGO ACT (1807), had also caused serious dislocations in the American economy. Congress replaced the unsuccessful measure with Macon's Bill No. 2.

Introduced by Senator Nathaniel Macon from North Carolina, the new law reopened American commerce to the entire world—Britain and France included—but excluded British and French warships from U.S. territorial waters. Under the measure, if either Britain or France pledged to respect American maritime rights prior to March 3, 1811, the president could move to prohibit trade with the other nation. If after a three-month grace period that other nation failed to revoke its restrictions on neutral commerce, the president was authorized to implement the ban.

In Napoleon's view, a uniform relaxation of U.S. trade barriers would favor the British, whose dominant navy would control whatever trade the American law might permit. The French emperor looked to persuade President JAMES MADISON that he intended to rescind his edicts against American shipping. Napoleon directed the French Foreign Minister, the Duc De Cadore, to inform U.S. Minister at Paris JOHN ARMSTRONG that his Berlin and Milan decrees against neutral commerce would be withdrawn after November 1, 1810, on one key condition: the United States prohibit trade with the British unless London revoked its Orders in Council, or executive edicts, that had placed France under blockade. In an ambiguous letter of August 5, 1810, to Armstrong relaying Napoleon's message, Cadore indicated that the French decrees already had been revoked. Madison accepted the French communication on its face. Satisfied that Napoleon had met the terms of Macon's Bill No. 2, the president on November 2, 1810, issued a proclamation announcing that Anglo-American trade would cease on February 2, 1811. Complaining that the United States had been duped by the Cadore Letter, Britain refused to cancel its Orders in Council. Congress formally sanctioned Madison's commercial ban when it approved a second Non-Intercourse Act against Britain on March 2, 1811. The British retaliated with increased raids on American shipping and IMPRESSMENT of American seamen. Anglo-American relations worsened following the rift over Macon's Bill No. 2 and the two countries slid inexorably toward the WAR OF 1812.

MAD See **MUTUAL ASSURED DESTRUCTION**.

MADISON, JAMES (1751–1836) U.S. representative, secretary of state, fourth president of the United States. Born and raised in Virginia, Madison graduated from the College of New Jersey (now Princeton) in 1771. Returning home, he joined the colonial political struggle against Great Britain that erupted in 1775 in the AMERICAN REVOLUTION. After serving as a member of the first Virginia state assembly, he was elected in 1780 to the Continental Congress. He departed the Congress in 1783, following ratification of the TREATY OF PARIS ending the war with Great Britain. From 1784 to 1786 he was a member of the Virginia House of Delegates. Madison soon concluded that the ARTICLES OF CONFEDERATION were inadequate to the task of governing the new nation. He attended the Annapolis Convention in 1786, where he spearheaded the drive that led to the Constitutional Convention at Philadelphia in 1787.

As a delegate to the Philadelphia convention, he earned the sobriquet Father of the CONSTITUTION for his unmatched contributions to the formulation of a new federal government. His Virginia Plan, introduced at the outset, embodied elements of a strong central government and served as the working draft for the document that eventually became the Constitution. Madison's detailed journal, published posthumously, provided the only full account of the convention and stands as the definitive historical record of its proceedings. Following adoption of the Constitution, he played a major role in the struggle to secure its ratification by the states. With ALEXANDER HAMILTON and JOHN JAY, Madison wrote *The Federalist* (1788), a collection of essays interpreting and explaining the Constitution.

Elected in 1789 to the U.S. House of Representatives, where he served four successive terms, he introduced and steered to passage the first 10 amendments to the Constitution, known as the Bill of Rights. Increasingly critical of the financial programs advanced by treasury secretary and Federalist Party head Alexander Hamilton, Madison became a leader, with THOMAS JEFFERSON, of the nascent opposition Democratic-Republican Party. He led the unsuccessful fight in Congress in the early 1790s for commercial sanctions against Great Britain to force it to relinquish its military posts in America's OLD NORTHWEST, as had previously been agreed in the Treaty of Paris, and to end its discriminatory treatment of American trade. A champion of republican government, he was supportive of the aspirations of the French Revolution. Following the outbreak of Anglo-French war in 1793, he strongly opposed the pro-British character of Federalist policy, sympathizing with the French in the conflict. Madison advocated harsh retaliation against British wartime violations of American neutral maritime rights and bitterly opposed the controversial Anglo-American JAY'S TREATY (1794). Retiring from Congress in 1797, he returned to Virginia, where he kept abreast of national developments. He was inspired to vocal political dissent by enactment during the Franco-American QUASI-WAR (1798–1800) of the Federalist-sponsored ALIEN AND SEDITION ACTS (1798), which sought to limit free speech and muzzle Democratic-Republican political opposition. In response he drafted the Virginia Resolutions (1798) declaring the alien and sedition measures unconstitutional. The resolutions, which complemented and closely paralleled Vice-President Jefferson's Kentucky Resolutions (1798, 1799), asserted the right of states to nullify any federal law they judged unconstitutional.

Madison returned to prominent public office following Jefferson's election as president in 1800. Appointed secretary of state in 1801, he served in the post for the length of Jefferson's two terms. He helped guide the negotiations that resulted in the LOUISIANA PURCHASE from France in 1803. With Jefferson, he charted a foreign policy aimed at protecting American commercial shipping and preserving U.S. neutral rights. He backed the president's refusal to make greater tribute payments to the North African Barbary states in order to secure guarantees against attacks on American merchant vessels by Barbary pirates. With its victory in the TRIPOLITAN WAR (1801–1805), the administration ended further U.S. tribute to the piratical state of Tripoli.

With the renewal of war between Great Britain and Napoleonic France in 1803, American merchant shipping became the target of escalating abuses by both of the European belligerents. Madison deplored these maritime depredations and especially denounced the British practice of IMPRESSMENT of American sailors. He had an instrumental hand in devising the policy of economic coercion adopted by the Jefferson administration with the intention of forcing British and French respect for America's neutral rights. The policy hinged on the principle that the United States could preserve its rights by punitive commercial measures rather than by resort to war. The secretary of state vigorously promoted the EMBARGO ACT (1807), the administration-sponsored measure which shut off all of America's foreign trade. The embargo proved a fiasco. It severely damaged the American economy while at the same time failing to wring concessions on neutral rights from either Britain or France, both of which were able to replace the American trade. Fierce congressional opposition finally forced Jefferson to accept repeal of the embargo at the end of his administration in March 1809.

Madison succeeded Jefferson as Democratic-Republican standard-bearer and defeated Federalist candidate CHARLES COTESWORTH PINCKNEY in the 1808 presidential election. With his reelection in 1812 over DeWitt Clinton, he served two full terms. In the wake of the failed trade embargo, Madison hoped to chasten the British and French through enforcement of the NON-INTERCOURSE ACT (1809). Enacted just days before Jefferson left office, the measure allowed U.S. trade with all nations except Great Britain and France but authorized Madison to resume commerce with whichever of the belligerents would pledge to respect America's neutral rights. Nonintercourse proved ineffectual and was repealed through MACON'S BILL NO. 2 (1810), which restored U.S. trade with both the British and French. The new law at the same time stipulated that if either Britain or France should rescind its obnoxious measures against neutral commerce at sea, the United States would reimpose nonintercourse against the other belligerent. On the misleading assurance of French ruler Napoleon Bonaparte that he had revoked his objectionable decrees insofar as they affected American shipping, Madison in November 1810 suspended trade with Britain under terms of Macon's Bill No. 2.

During this time the president promoted the U.S. claim to a part of Spanish West Florida. Rival territorial claims formed the basis of the long-standing WEST FLORIDA CONTROVERSY between Washington and Madrid. In 1810 American settlers at Baton Rouge revolted against Spain, declared West Florida independent, and asked to be annexed to the United States. Madison declared U.S. control over West Florida to the Perdido River and sent troops to occupy the territory. At his urging, Congress in 1811 passed a measure establishing the NO-TRANSFER PRINCIPLE, which expressed American determination to prevent Spanish cession of the Floridas to Great Britain by asserting that colonies in the Western Hemisphere could not be transferred from one European country to another.

With the failure of commercial policy to bring an end to assaults on American shipping, the president in November 1811 advised Congress to begin preparing the nation for possible hostilities with the British. Anglo-American tensions continued to mount. Under pressure from the influential congressional WAR HAWKS, who saw in war an opportunity to seize Canada from Britain and the rest of the Floridas from British ally Spain, Madison on June 1, 1812, asked for a declaration of war, citing impressment, interference with American maritime trade, and British incitement of Indian hostilities in the Old Northwest as principal grievances.

Both unprepared and divided from the outset of the WAR OF 1812, the United States struggled through the conflict's first two years, faring poorly on the battlefield. The president faced growing opposition over the unpopular war, especially from New England Federalists, who derisively dubbed it "Mr. Madison's War." Napoleon's defeat in Europe in 1814 allowed Great Britain to divert reinforcements to North America and focus more intently on the Anglo-American struggle. War weariness and respective domestic political considerations inclined both nations to seek a settlement of hostilities. Madison seized an offer by the British government for direct peace negotiations. Representatives from the two countries met in Ghent, Belgium, where, on December 24, 1814, they concluded the TREATY OF GHENT ending the War of 1812 on the basis of *status quo ante bellum* (restoration of territories held prior to the war). Not a single declared U.S. war aim had been attained; all the main issues over which the conflict had been fought were left unresolved or unaddressed. After leaving office in March 1817, Madison retired from political life to his Virginia estate. He helped Jefferson found the University of Virginia and became its rector in 1826.

MAFIA INCIDENT (1891–1892) Slaying of Italians by a New Orleans mob that caused a diplomatic falling-out between the United States and Italy. Members of Sicily's secret "Mafia Society" were among the large community of Italians who had arrived in New Orleans by 1890. City police chief David C. Hennessy, who had undertaken to crack down on the Sicilian Mafia's local criminal activities, was assassinated in October of that year. A number of Italian suspects were arrested and brought to trial for murder but escaped conviction. Angry New Orleans citizens, insisting on the guilt of the accused, suggested that the Mafia had thwarted justice by improperly interfering in the legal proceedings. On March 14, 1891, a mob of several thousand stormed the city jailhouse, dragged out 11 of the men who had been implicated in the police chief's death, and publicly lynched them. Three of the killed were Italian nationals; the others either were naturalized American citizens or had intended to become American citizens.

An outraged Italian government denounced the lynchings, demanding an indemnity for the families of the victims and punishment of the perpetrators. When the U.S. government was slow to respond to Italian grievances and a Louisiana grand jury handed down no indictments in the killings, Italy withdrew its minister from Washington on March 31. Although the United States then recalled its minister from Rome, diplomatic relations between the nations were not formally severed. In April 1892 Secretary of State JAMES G. BLAINE, at the direction of President BEN-JAMIN HARRISON, expressed regret to Italy for the New Orleans incident and offered a $25,000 indemnity. The Italian government accepted and full diplomatic ties were restored.

MAGDALENA BAY RESOLUTION See **LODGE COROLLARY**.

MAHAN, ALFRED THAYER (1840–1914) Naval officer and historian whose theories on the importance of sea power profoundly influenced U.S. strategic thinking. An 1859 graduate of the U.S. Naval Academy, Mahan gained prominence with the publication of his first book, a naval history of the Civil War, in 1883. The following year he joined the faculty of the recently formed U.S. Navy War College. He subsequently served as president of the school from 1886 to 1889 and again from 1892 to 1894.

Mahan's lectures on naval tactics and history evolved into the two works for which he is most remembered. *The Influence of Sea Power Upon History, 1660–1783* appeared in 1890 amid a national debate on the emergence of America as a world power. Mahan identified naval power as a vital component of a nation's overall strength and prosperity. Without command of the seas, a country would be limited in its ability to favorably influence world affairs. Mahan believed expansion and foreign commerce were essential to a nation on the rise and concluded that a strong navy was necessary to secure and protect access to foreign markets and territorial possessions. His ideas helped to ensure passage of the Naval Act of 1890. This measure, which provided for a series of first-class battleships, marked a key point in the transformation of the U.S. Navy from a coastal defense force to a blue-water fleet capable of exerting U.S. power worldwide. Mahan elaborated his theses two years later in *The Influence of Sea Power Upon the French Revolution and Empire, 1793–1812*.

Beginning in 1890, Mahan authored numerous articles in which he advocated an expanded international role for the United States. He stressed the importance of a powerful navy to the attainment of this objective and called for a transoceanic canal in Panama and bases in Hawaii. He became an informal adviser to THEODORE ROOSEVELT and many of his ideas found expression in the foreign policy of the Roosevelt administration.

Mahan retired as a captain in 1896, but was recalled to active duty to help direct naval operations during the SPANISH-AMERI-CAN WAR (1898). He continued to write prolifically. His works were translated widely and contributed to the growth in his own lifetime of the British, German, and Japanese navies. Considered America's preeminent strategist, his ideas underlie such modern policy initiatives as the use of aircraft carrier task forces to project U.S. power and influence overseas.

MAINE See **SPANISH-AMERICAN WAR**.

MALTA CONFERENCE See **YALTA CONFERENCE**.

MALTA SUMMIT (1989) Shipboard parley December 2 and 3 off the Mediterranean island of Malta between U.S. President GEORGE BUSH and Soviet President Mikhail S. Gorbachev. Meeting against the backdrop of communism's collapse in Eastern

Europe and the dismantling of the Berlin Wall, the two leaders looked to further the thaw in superpower relations and to outline expectations for post–Cold War ties between Washington and Moscow.

Bush spent his first year in office considering how to respond to Gorbachev's far-reaching political and economic reforms and to the dynamic change underway across the Soviet bloc. Critics at home and among America's European allies scored the Bush administration for excessive caution. Citing a softening of Soviet military and foreign policies, they urged the president to capitalize on the opportunity to recast the U.S.-USSR relationship and to end the East-West arms race. The White House, in response, called the end of the Cold War close but not yet at hand and warned against swift steps to relax the West's defenses against Soviet adventurism. But in a series of speeches in May 1989 Bush acknowledged the Soviet military threat to the Western security alliance NATO had declined in the wake of Kremlin policy shifts. At the same time he proposed dramatic mutual cuts on conventional armed forces in Europe.

By the December summit, the Bush administration had concluded American interests were served by U.S. support for Gorbachev's program to liberalize the Soviet political system and revive its troubled economy. The besieged Kremlin leader arrived in Malta shadowed by ethnic unrest and secessionist threats at home and the unravelling of the Soviet empire in Eastern Europe. The U.S. and Soviet leaders gathered for the Mediterranean summit, their first since Bush became president, to discuss East-West affairs and to outline diplomatic goals for the full-scale Washington Summit in June 1990. On arms control, they set several major targets: wrap up a framework START agreement in time for the scheduled June meeting that would cut by half U.S and Soviet strategic nuclear forces; conclude a treaty on reducing NATO and Warsaw Pact conventional forces in Europe by the end of 1990; and strike an interim accord that would cut chemical weapons stockpiles and lead to an eventual international ban on deadly chemical arms.

Bush and Gorbachev made U.S.-Soviet trade a key topic in their talks, agreeing to begin negotiations toward an overall bilateral trade deal. Bush vowed to help the faltering Soviet economy by lifting the curbs on MOST-FAVORED-NATION trade status imposed under the 1974 JACKSON-VANIK AMENDMENT provided the Kremlin liberalized its laws on Soviet Jewish emigration. The American president also pledged U.S. backing for Soviet observer status in the GENERAL AGREEMENT ON TARIFFS AND TRADE (GATT). At the summit's conclusion, the two leaders spoke optimistically of events unfolding in Eastern Europe and of a fresh course in relations between Washington and Moscow. While Gorbachev virtually proclaimed the end of the Cold War, Bush was more cautious when he briefed NATO leaders on his return trip to the United States, pledging a continued U.S. military presence in Europe.

MANCHURIAN CRISIS (1931–1933) International diplomatic crisis over the Japanese seizure of Manchuria. Following its annexation of Korea in 1910, Japan gradually had exerted its dominance over eastern Manchuria, traditionally part of China. On September 18, 1931, Japanese army units guarding a railway in the southeastern Manchurian city of Mukden provoked a clash with Chinese troops. The Mukden Incident served as the pretext for a general Japanese attack on Manchuria. With Japanese forces rapidly occupying the territory, the LEAGUE OF NATIONS Council met in Geneva to seek a resolution to the worsening situation. Although not a league member, the United States participated in the deliberations. In November, Japan, which had justified its action as self-defense and disregarded a council appeal to withdraw its forces, proposed formation of an investigatory commission to visit Manchuria. With China's reluctant assent, the Lytton Commission, headed by Great Britain's Earl of Lytton, was established by the league on December 10, 1931. The panel included a U.S. member, General Frank Ross McCoy.

By early January 1932 Japan was nearing its conquest of all Manchuria. The U.S. government viewed the Japanese aggression as an unacceptable violation of the NINE-POWER TREATY (1922) on China and the KELLOGG-BRIAND PACT (1928) outlawing war. On January 7 Secretary of State HENRY L. STIMSON announced that the United States would not recognize any change in the territorial or political status of China resulting from use of force. The STIMSON DOCTRINE of non-recognition was adopted by the League of Nations Assembly on March 11, but failed to reverse Japan's hold on Manchuria. Meanwhile a Chinese boycott of Japanese goods brought a Japanese attack against the Chinese port of Shanghai. In what became known as the Shanghai Incident, Japanese warplanes on January 28, 1932, bombed the city, causing many civilian deaths. The brutal Japanese assault on and occupation of Shanghai brought international condemnation. Seeking to publicly register American outrage at the incident, Stimson wrote an open letter to Senator William E. Borah (R-ID), chairman of the SENATE FOREIGN RELATIONS COMMITTEE, suggesting that Tokyo's conduct risked the abrogation of the Nine-Power and other treaties.

In May 1932 Japan and China completed an agreement ending the boycott of Japanese goods. Bowing to international pressure, Japan withdrew its forces from Shanghai by the end of the month. By September 1932, Japan had established the nominally independent state of Manchukuo in Manchuria and installed a puppet regime. In October the Lytton Commission submitted its report. The panel's findings criticized Japan's behavior and recommended creation of an autonomous Manchurian government under Chinese sovereignty. The report was approved by the League of Nations Assembly in February 1933, prompting Japan to withdraw from the international organization. The league was unwilling to back its stand with further concrete steps, however, and Japan resumed its aggression against China in 1937. Manchukuo, never recognized by the Western democracies, ceased to exist with Japan's defeat in WORLD WAR II.

MANHATTAN PROJECT U.S.-sponsored program during WORLD WAR II that produced the first atomic, or fission, bomb. Following discovery of the nuclear fission process in late 1938, physicists the world over recognized the potential for harnessing in a weapon of mass destruction the enormous energy released by the splitting of atoms. Concerned that Adolf Hitler's Germany might develop the first atomic bomb, Albert Einstein and other prominent scientists who were refugees from Nazism successfully persuaded President FRANKLIN D. ROOSEVELT in 1939 to increase federal support for nascent American research on a fission weapon. With U.S. entry into World War II in December 1941, British and French scientists were recruited to the American bomb development efforts.

By mid-1942 it was apparent to U.S. planners that special plants capable of producing fissionable materials (uranium and plutonium) would have to be built. Responsibility for construction was assigned to the U.S. Army Corps of Engineers and in August 1942 General Leslie R. Groves was placed in charge of the bomb program. Scientific direction, though, was retained by the National Defense Research Committee and subsequently by the Office of Scientific Research and Development, both under VANNEVAR BUSH. Much of the early U.S. research on a fission weapon was conducted at Columbia University in New York under the management of the Army's Manhattan Engineer District. Thus the bomb development program became known as the Manhattan Project, a code-name that covered all efforts nationwide related to the top-secret atomic weapon enterprise. Work was carried on mainly in three government-supported laboratories—at Columbia, the University of Chicago, and the University of California. Design of the atomic bomb was undertaken at a new weapons laboratory established at Los Alamos, New Mexico, near Santa Fe. Groves named renowned theoretical physicist J. ROBERT OPPENHEIMER director of Los Alamos.

The first atomic test device was exploded at Alamagordo, New Mexico, on July 16, 1945. President HARRY S. TRUMAN was attending the POTSDAM CONFERENCE in Germany, where he was informed of the successful detonation. The Allies had wrapped up their victory in Europe upon Germany's surrender in May. Attention thus was focused on defeating the Japanese in the Pacific. At Truman's order, atomic bombs were exploded over the Japanese cities of Hiroshima on August 6, 1945, and Nagasaki on August 9. The horrific deaths and destruction wrought by the bombs hastened Japan's surrender on August 14.

MANIFEST DESTINY Catchphrase in common use in the mid-19th century to describe the purported inevitability of America's continued westward territorial expansion. The expression was orginated by editor JOHN L. O'SULLIVAN in an article in the July–August 1845 issue of his *United States Magazine and Democratic Review* in which he asserted America's "manifest destiny to overspread the continent allotted by Providence for the free development of our yearly multiplying millions." The article referred specifically to the recent U.S. annexation of Texas, which O'Sullivan, as an ardently expansionist Democrat, endorsed. At the heart of the concept of Manifest Destiny was the notion that Providence had chosen the American people to grow and expand across the North American continent, spreading in their path the blessings of supposedly superior American political institutions and Anglo-Saxon culture.

Once coined, the phrase quickly entered the popular American political lexicon. It was employed by expansionists advocating acquisition of "ALL OREGON" as settlement of the OREGON QUESTION with Great Britain and demanding annexation of Mexican territory after the MEXICAN WAR (1846–1848). The ideology embodied in the term Manifest Destiny was invoked in an expanded form in the 1850s, notably by followers of the nationalist YOUNG AMERICA movement, to rationalize the proposed annexation of Cuba, Central America, and Canada. Although initially and mainly a Democratic Party tenet, Manifest Destiny also had it adherents among Whigs and Republicans. WILLIAM H. SEWARD, secretary of state under Republican presidents ABRAHAM LINCOLN and ANDREW JOHNSON, championed American expansion. He completed the ALASKA PURCHASE from Russia in 1867 and sought during his tenure to annex various Caribbean and Pacific islands.

The spirit of American expansionism was revived in the 1890s by the Republicans in the form of the so-called New Manifest Destiny. This catchphrase connoted the overseas expansion of the United States beyond its continental limits. Embraced by American imperialists, the term came into wide currency in connection with HAWAII ANNEXATION (1898) and the acquisition of Spanish possessions in the Caribbean and Pacific after the SPANISH-AMERICAN WAR (1898).

See also IMPERIALISM.

MANILA PACT See **SOUTHEAST ASIA TREATY ORGANIZATION**.

MANSFIELD AMENDMENT (1971) Congressional measure twice attached to major legislation that called for an end to U.S. military operations in Southeast Asia. The February 1971 U.S.-assisted LAOTIAN INCURSION by South Vietnamese forces provoked debate and criticism in America. Antiwar members of Congress saw the action as a widening of the VIETNAM WAR. On June 22, 1971, the Senate voted 57 to 42 to adopt an amendment to the Selective Service draft extension bill. Introduced by Majority Leader MICHAEL J. MANSFIELD (D-MT), it expressed the "sense of Congress" that all U.S. troops be withdrawn from Indochina within nine months of the bill's passage, subject to the release of American prisoners of war (POW). When the House approved the provision on August 4, it marked the first time Congress formally had urged an end to a war in which the nation was still actively engaged. President RICHARD M. NIXON signed the legislation extending the draft, but made clear he did not consider the attached end-the-war measure binding on U.S. policy. In November 1971 the Congress cleared a modified version of the Mansfield Amendment that stated it was the "policy of the United States," rather than the sense of Congress, that U.S. forces be withdrawn from Indochina within six months after the measure became law, pending the release of the POWs. When signing the defense procurement authorization bill to which the amendment was attached, Nixon reiterated his position that the congressional policy statement was not binding.

See also CASE-CHURCH AMENDMENT, COOPER-CHURCH AMENDMENT, MCGOVERN-HATFIELD AMENDMENT.

MANSFIELD, MICHAEL JOSEPH (1903–) U.S. senator and ambassador. Manfield was born in New York City and grew up in Montana. After service in the Navy during WORLD WAR I and then tours with the Army and Marine Corps, he returned to Montana to work as a miner and then a mining engineer. He earned a bachelor's degree in 1933 and a master's degree in 1937 from the University of Montana, where he became a professor of Far Eastern history. In

1942 Mansfield was elected as a Democrat to the U.S. House of Representatives. In the House he began a lifelong involvement with foreign affairs, undertaking a special mission to assess the political situation in China in 1944 and serving as a delegate to the BOGOTA CONFERENCE in 1948 and the UNITED NATIONS in 1951.

In 1953 Mansfield won election to the U.S. Senate. The following year he was the Senate's Democratic representative to the Manila Conference that established the SOUTHEAST ASIA TREATY ORGANIZATION. Senate majority leader from 1961 to 1977, he emerged in the mid-1960s as a leading critic of the escalating American military involvement in the VIETNAM WAR. In 1971 he sponsored the MANSFIELD AMENDMENT that for the first time expressed the desire of Congress to see America withdraw its troops from Southeast Asia. Mansfield retired from the Senate in 1977. The same year he was named ambassador to Japan by President JIMMY CARTER. During his long tenure in Tokyo he worked to resolve the difficult trade issues threatening to undermine U.S.-Japanese relations. Mansfield retired from his post in 1988.

MARCY, WILLIAM LEARNED (1786–1857) Secretary of state under President FRANKLIN PIERCE. Born in Massachusetts, Marcy graduated from Brown University in 1808. He settled in Troy, New York, practiced law, and after brief service in the WAR OF 1812, became involved in Democratic Party politics. He served successively as state adjutant general in 1821, state comptroller in 1823, and a justice of the state supreme court in 1829. In 1831 he left the bench to accept a seat in the U.S. Senate, where the next year he made a famous speech on behalf of MARTIN VAN BUREN's nomination as minister to Great Britain. Defending Van Buren's practice of political patronage as New York governor and secretary of state under President ANDREW JACKSON, Marcy declared "to the victor belong the spoils of the enemy," a pronouncement that added the expression "spoils system" to the American political lexicon. Marcy resigned from the Senate following his election as New York governor, an office he held from 1833 to 1838. He was secretary of war from 1845 to 1849 under President JAMES K. POLK, earning national recognition for the War Depart-

ment's successful waging of the MEXICAN WAR (1846–1848). Marcy unsuccessfully sought the Democratic nomination for president in 1852. In 1853 he became secretary of state in the Pierce administration.

In his eventful 4-year tenure, Marcy directed the negotiation of 24 treaties, the largest number ratified in the course of an administration up to that time. Significant among them were the agreement completing the GADSDEN PURCHASE (1853) from Mexico; the Anglo-American MARCY-ELGIN TREATY in 1854 concerning U.S. trade with Canada and the FISHERIES QUESTION; an 1855 treaty with the Netherlands opening Dutch colonial ports to American merchant vessels; and the treaty with Denmark in 1857 that freed American ships passing through the Dutch Sound into the Baltic Sea from paying tolls. After the landmark TREATY OF KANAGAWA (1854) opened Japan to the West, Marcy in 1855 appointed TOWNSEND HARRIS as first consul general to the Pacific empire. The Harris mission resulted in the TREATY OF EDO (1858), which laid the groundwork for expanded U.S.-Japanese trade and diplomatic relations.

Amid the explosive domestic sectional politics of slavery in the 1850s, he steered the expansionist Pierce away from a policy bent on the acquisition of Cuba and eventual incorporation of it into the Union as a slave state. When controversial U.S. minister at Madrid PIERRE SOULE tried to exacerbate the diplomatic fallout from the BLACK WARRIOR AFFAIR (1854) in order to give the United States a pretext for annexing Cuba, Marcy curbed his efforts and reached a settlement of the incident with the Spanish government in 1855. Meanwhile, he had repudiated the OSTEND MANIFESTO (1854), the provocative report prepared by Soule and two fellow American diplomats urging the United States to obtain Cuba by purchase or, failing that, by force. Marcy retired with the close of the Pierce administration in March 1857 and died the following July.

MARCY-ELGIN TREATY (1854)   Agreement signed on June 5, 1854, between the United States and Great Britain regarding the FISHERIES QUESTION and U.S. trade with Canada, at the time a British colony. Britain had eliminated preferential treatment for Canadian goods when it adopted a free-trade policy in 1846. Loss of the protected

British market caused great economic hardship in Canada. Canadian merchants then sought outlets for their goods in America but were blocked by high U.S. tariffs. A political group representing Canadian commercial interests saw economic salvation in annexation by the United States. Such a move, the annexationists presumed, would open the vast American market to Canadian products on a tariff-free basis. In 1849 the group called for separation from Britain and union with the United States.

The British government opposed the annexation movement and directed Canadian officials to discourage it. Governor-General of Canada Lord Elgin urged reciprocal free trade with the United States as the best way to quell annexation sentiment. America linked any reciprocity arrangement to British concessions on free navigation of the St. Lawrence River and increased U.S. fishing privileges off the coast of Canada's northeast maritime provinces—privileges that had been granted under the CONVENTION OF 1818 and had been a subject of Anglo-American dispute ever since. The British found these U.S. terms acceptable. When London and Washington were unable, however, to conclude a mutual legislative agreement to lower tariffs on Canadian-American trade, they ended up seeking the same result through a treaty. Off-and-on negotiations spanned five years and were completed in Washington, D.C., by Secretary of State WILLIAM L. MARCY and Lord Elgin from May to June 1854.

As ratified, the Marcy-Elgin agreement extended America's fishing privileges to all the coasts of the maritime provinces, and in return gave British subjects the privileges of fishing along the Atlantic shore as far south as North Carolina at the 36th parallel. Great Britain consented to free navigation of the St. Lawrence River by Americans in equal terms with British subjects, while the United States granted British subjects free navigation of Lake Michigan. The reciprocity provisions permitted the duty-free entry of a large number of agricultural commodities, seafoods, and raw materials (but not manufactured goods) into both the United States and Canada. This reciprocity treaty, the first ever negotiated by the United States, was to remain in force for 10 years, after which time either side could terminate it with a year's notice. It brought

increased U.S.-Canadian trade, helped allay Canada's economic distress, and immediately eased Anglo-American tensions on the fisheries. Anger in the Northern states over supposed British actions to aid the South during the Civil War led the United States to abrogate the agreement in March 1866.

MARIEL BOATLIFT (1980)　　Sealift of Cuban refugees to the United States. On April 1, 1980, a busload of dissident Cubans seeking political asylum crashed into the Peruvian Embassy in Havana. Cuban Communist leader Fidel Castro unexpectedly withdrew the guards around the embassy and within three days another 10,000 Cubans had crowded onto the grounds. Castro agreed to a series of flights to take the refugees out of the country but canceled the program after fewer than 700 had departed. He again reversed himself on April 19, 1980, proclaiming that anyone who so desired could leave Cuba, opening the port at Mariel and encouraging Florida's Cuban exile community to retrieve any relatives still on the island nation.

Within days a "freedom flotilla" of hundreds of small boats launched by the staunchly anti-Castro Cuban-American community had started to transport thousands of Cuban emigres to the United States. The Carter administration decided against trying to limit the unapproved refugee flow and on May 5 President JIMMY CARTER announced that those fleeing Cuba would be welcomed with "an open heart and open arms." The boatlift brought more than 130,000 Cubans to American shores before Castro closed Mariel Bay on September 26. Most were opponents of the Cuban regime or family members of Cubans already in the United States. Roughly 20,000 were criminals and mental patients whom Castro had forced onto the American boats, placing a sudden burden on U.S. health and prison resources and further straining relations between the two countries.

MARPOL CONVENTION (1973)　　International treaty on marine pollution. The agreement, formally titled the Convention for the Prevention of Pollution from Ships, was adopted on November 2, 1973, at an INTERNATIONAL MARITIME ORGANIZATION conference in London attended by delegates from

79 countries. Its provisions strictly regulated discharges of oil and other noxious substances from ocean-going vessels. The convention set forth terms aimed at minimizing the amount of oil which would be released accidently in collisions or strandings of ships. It complemented the LONDON DUMPING CONVENTION (1972), which sought to prevent marine pollution by prohibiting disposal at sea of various harmful, toxic wastes. The MARPOL Convention was modified by a protocol adopted in February 1978 governing oil tanker safety and the prevention of pollution. Both the convention and the protocol entered into force in 1983 and became part of the UNITED NATIONS Law of the Sea on controlling ocean pollution. The United States is party to the MARPOL agreement.

In the course of the 1970s ocean dumping of plastic refuse emerged as a major world environmental problem. Plastic containers, which neither sink nor decompose, were entangling and drowning marine animals, killing other sea life which mistook the items for food, and disrupting valuable fisheries. The United States responded by ratifying the optional Annex V of the MARPOL treaty in November 1978. This annex, which entered into force in 1988, barred dumping of plastics into the ocean and required ships to carry their plastic trash back into port for proper disposal.

See also BASEL CONVENTION.

MARSHALL, GEORGE CATLETT (1880–1959) Army officer, secretary of state, secretary of defense. Born in Pennsylvania, Marshall graduated from the Virginia Military Institute in 1901 and was commissioned a second lieutenant in the Army the following year. His early military career included two tours in the Philippines, assignment as a student and then an instructor at the Army Staff College, and duty with the Massachusetts National Guard. During WORLD WAR I Marshall served with the AMERICAN EXPEDITIONARY FORCE in France, gaining distinction for his planning of the 1918 Meuse-Argonne offensive. From 1919 to 1924 he was aide-de-camp to General JOHN J. PERSHING. Over the next 15 years Marshall saw duty in China and then held a succession of stateside command and staff positions. Promoted to general in 1936, he was

appointed Army chief of staff, the service's top uniformed post, in 1939.

With the outbreak the same year of WORLD WAR II in Europe, Marshall assumed a leading role in the Roosevelt administration's efforts to build America's defenses. Following U.S. entry into the conflict in December 1941, he oversaw the expansion of the Army to a force of more than 8 million. As a member of the wartime U.S. JOINT CHIEFS OF STAFF and the Anglo-American Combined Chiefs of Staff, Marshall was centrally involved in planning and orchestrating the vast worldwide military campaigns that eventually defeated the Axis powers. He accompanied President FRANKLIN D. ROOSEVELT to all the major wartime conferences with British Prime Minister Winston Churchill and Soviet Premier Joseph Stalin. Following the Allied triumph, Churchill called him the "organizer of victory." Promoted to five-star rank during the war, Marshall retired from active duty in November 1945.

The same month President HARRY S. TRUMAN asked that he go to China to attempt to mediate an end to the growing civil war between the Nationalist government under U.S. ally Chiang Kai-shek and insurgent Communist forces under Mao Tse-tung. Named a special presidential envoy with the rank of ambassador, Marshall was instructed to seek formation of a coalition government under the Nationalists, ensure Chinese control over Manchuria as occupying Soviet and defeated Japanese troops withdrew, and formulate an economic aid program for China. By February 1946 Marshall had arranged a tenuous truce between the warring sides. The agreement fell apart, though, while Marshall was back in Washington in March to coordinate U.S. financial assistance. He returned to China, but was unable to prevent a renewal of the fighting. By October 1946 China had plunged into the full-scale civil war that would bring Mao to power in 1949. With Marshall's China mission at an impasse, Truman recalled the retired general to Washington in January 1947 and the same month appointed him secretary of state.

Marshall took office at a time of dramatic upheaval and change. Much of Europe lay devastated from the world war. The wartime U.S.-Soviet alliance had deteriorated into postwar COLD WAR confrontation over Eastern Europe and Germany. The new secretary of state helped formulate the Truman Doctrine, announced by the president in March 1947, that committed the United States to the defense of European nations against Communist takeover. Marshall returned from the 1947 Moscow Conference of the Council of Foreign Ministers convinced both that cooperation with the USSR was futile and that wartorn Western Europe faced economic and political collapse. In a famous commencement address at Harvard University on June 5, 1947, he outlined a program of massive U.S. economic assistance to spur Europe's postwar recovery. The Marshall Plan, a cornerstone of the Truman administration's emerging strategy for the containment of Soviet expansionism, provided billions in aid to the successful reconstruction of Western Europe. In June 1948 Marshall supported the Berlin Airlift as the appropriate response to the Soviet blockade of the German city. The same year he began discussions with America's European allies that culminated in 1949 in the creation of the Western security alliance NATO.

An advocate of unification of the armed services, Marshall backed the 1947 National Security Act forming a single defense establishment. He attended the special inter-American conference that drafted the 1947 Rio Treaty for the mutual defense of the Western Hemisphere. In 1948 he headed the U.S. delegation to the Bogota Conference establishing the Organization of American States. In weakened health, he resigned in January 1949 and became president of the American Red Cross. In July 1950, following the onset of the Korean War, Truman prevailed upon Marshall to accept appointment as secretary of defense. During his 15 months in the post, he helped reverse the early U.S. setbacks in the conflict, endorsed Truman's limited war policy, and approved the president's controversial April 1951 decision to relieve General Douglas MacArthur of his wartime command. Marshall retired from public life in 1951. In the early 1950s he came under attack from demagogic Senator Joseph R. McCarthy (R-WI) for allegedly allowing China to fall to communism. In 1953 Marshall received the Nobel Peace Prize for his European recovery plan.

MARSHALL, JOHN (1755–1835) Secretary of state and Supreme Court chief justice. Born in Virginia, Marshall was privately educated. Following service as an officer in the American Revolution, he studied law, was admitted to the Virginia bar, and began practice in Richmond. He was elected in 1782 to the state legislature, where he served, with brief interruptions, for 15 years. In 1788 he was a delegate to the Virginia convention that ratified the federal Constitution. In the 1790s Marshall emerged as the leader of the Federalists in Virginia. Personal financial problems led him to refuse offers by President George Washington to become attorney general in 1795 and minister to France in 1796.

He accepted appointment in 1797 by President John Adams as a member of a special diplomatic mission sent to Paris to seek a peaceful resolution of the problem of French assaults on American merchant shipping. The mission foundered when, in the notorious episode known as the XYZ Affair (1797), Marshall and his fellow commissioners indignantly rejected French Foreign Minister Charles Maurice de Talleyrand's demand for a bribe. Marshall entered the U.S. House of Representatives from Virginia in 1799. The same year he was named secretary of state, a post he filled for the remainder of the Adams presidency. During his tenure he directed negotiation of the Convention of 1800 which ended the undeclared naval Quasi-War (1798–1800) with France. He also oversaw settlement of a dispute over unpaid American private debts to British lenders dating back to the American Revolution.

In January 1801, shortly before the end of Adams's term, Marshall was named chief justice of the United States, a position he held until his death in 1835. During his 34 years on the bench he established the authority of the Supreme Court and pioneered the development of American constitutional law through written opinions in a series of landmark cases. Two of his opinions stand out as particularly historically significant. In *Marbury* v. *Madison* (1803), he expounded the doctrine of judicial review, which reserved to the federal courts final authority to judge the constitutionality of congressional legislation; in *McCulloch* v. *Maryland* (1819) he set down the theory of implied powers under the Constitution. He presided in 1807 over the famous treason trial of former vice-president Aaron Burr that grew out of the ambiguous BURR CONSPIRACY (1804–1807) and ended in acquittal. Near the end of his tenure Marshall penned the majority opinion in a pair of decisions which clarified the legal standing of American Indians. In CHEROKEE NATION V. GEORGIA (1831), the Court held that Indian tribes were not foreign nations within the meaning of the Constitution. In WORCESTER V. GEORGIA (1832), the Court ruled that the federal government had exclusive jurisdiction over INDIAN AFFAIRS.

MARSHALL PLAN (1948–1952) Program of U.S. economic aid for post–WORLD WAR II Western European recovery devised by Secretary of State GEORGE C. MARSHALL. American foreign aid initiatives in the early postwar years were rooted in the emerging COLD WAR rivalry between the Western alliance and the Soviet bloc. By 1947 the Truman administration had concluded that the USSR sought world domination. Resolving to oppose Soviet expansionism, the administration set forth a policy for the CONTAINMENT of communism. In early 1947 President HARRY S. TRUMAN requested, and Congress approved, $400 million in military and economic assistance to Greece and Turkey to help those countries stave off Communist pressures and thereby thwart presumed Soviet designs on the strategically vital eastern Mediterranean. The president, articulating what soon came to be called the TRUMAN DOCTRINE, declared that the United States would support free people resisting attempted Communist subjugation "by armed minorities or outside pressures."

The watershed Greek-Turkish aid package inaugurated the use of American money to stem the spread of Soviet influence. The second landmark of postwar American foreign aid was the European Recovery Program, or Marshall Plan, which developed out of Truman administration fears that failure to restore and rebuild European nations savaged by the war would invite political collapse and open the way for Soviet domination of Europe through internal subversion. Broached by the American secretary of state in a speech at Har-

vard University on June 5, 1947, the aid plan was aimed at reviving the European economy in order to permit the emergence of social and political conditions under which free institutions could survive. Marshall declared U.S. eagerness to support reconstruction and rehabilitation of Europe both to render the continent less susceptible to Communist subjugation and to increase the volume of international trade. Marshall called on the Europeans to jointly draw up a comprehensive recovery program that the United States would then fund. An offer of U.S. aid even was extended to the USSR and its Eastern European satellites, although the White House had no expectation they would accept.

Soon thereafter the U.S. House of Representatives sent a 19-member Select Committee on Foreign Aid, headed by Representative CHRISTIAN A. HERTER (R-MA), on a fact-finding mission to Europe. The Herter Committee endorsed a Marshall Plan-like initiative for European rehabilitation. On the basis of reports of the Herter panel and other congressional committees, Congress late in 1947 convened a special session to deal with the question of assistance to Europe. Meanwhile, in July 1947, 16 European countries, led by Great Britain and France, had met in Paris, where they established a Committee for European Economic Cooperation, which outlined a four-year master plan for European reconstruction based on massive U.S. financial assistance. The Soviet Union and East bloc countries refused to participate and condemned the Marshall initiative as an imperialist scheme by the Americans to achieve hegemony over all of Europe.

The European committee's report became the basis for the Truman administration's massive $17 billion dollar aid plan. Despite significant opposition to the Marshall initiative from the political right and left in America, the U.S. Congress in April 1948 authorized the European Recovery Program (ERP) and placed it under the control of the Economic Cooperation Administration (ECA), a specialized federal agency established independent of the State Department. Successful American entrepreneur Paul G. Hoffman, appointed head of the ECA, served as the recovery program's principal administrator. The recipient countries reorganized their Committee for European Economic Cooperation as the permanent ORGANIZATION FOR EUROPEAN ECONOMIC COOPERATION to supervise the distribution of ERP aid. The recovery program was enormously successful, actually achieving its objectives ahead of schedule. Between 1948 and 1952 the cumulative gross national product of Western Europe rose some 25 percent. In 1951 the ERP was placed under the MUTUAL SECURITY AGENCY, the federal organization newly created by the MUTUAL SECURITY ACT to administer U.S. foreign aid programs.

MASSIVE RETALIATION Catchphrase that described U.S. strategy in the 1950s for the DETERRENCE of Communist aggression. Following the outbreak of the KOREAN WAR in 1950, the Truman administration had initiated a major U.S. military buildup. President DWIGHT D. EISENHOWER came into office in 1953 committed to reducing defense expenditures and to avoiding future American involvement in costly limited ground wars such as the Korean conflict. The Eisenhower administration adopted the NEW LOOK defense strategy, which emphasized the use of NUCLEAR WEAPONS rather than large conventional Army and Navy forces. In a speech to the COUNCIL ON FOREIGN RELATIONS on January 12, 1954, Secretary of State JOHN FOSTER DULLES explained the new defense policy. Dulles noted that the United States could not afford to defend the entire world or respond to every Communist attack, as in Korea, with traditional military forces. To do so, he contended, would have "grave budgetary, economic, and social consequences." Instead, the United States would rely on the "massive retaliatory power" of its nuclear weapons to deter Communist advances throughout the world. America would retain the initiative to respond to Communist moves "at places and with the means of our choosing." The idea was that Communist nations would be unwilling to undertake or sponsor aggression if, in so doing, they risked provoking a nuclear attack on themselves.

Dulles's speech gave rise to the term "massive retaliation" as shorthand for the Eisenhower administration's nuclear deterrence strategy, although the secretary of state never used the exact phrase in his remarks. The concept of massive retaliation

had come under increasing question by the mid-1950s. Critics pointed out that an excessive reliance on nuclear weapons left the United States without an effective means for dealing with Communist insurgencies and guerrilla warfare. Also, the ability of the United States to threaten its Communist adversaries with nuclear retaliation rested on America sustaining nuclear superiority. As the Soviet Union continued to develop the ability to respond in kind to an American nuclear attack, the United States would be unwilling to risk a possible nuclear war for anything other than vital national interests. In 1961 President JOHN F. KENNEDY replaced the New Look and massive retaliation with a FLEXIBLE RESPONSE strategy.

MATTHEWS, HERBERT LIONEL (1900–1977) Noted American foreign correspondent and author. Born in New York City, he joined the Army tank corps after high school and served overseas in WORLD WAR I as a private. He graduated from Columbia University in 1922 and began a long career in journalism with the *New York Times*. His first foreign assignment was to the Paris bureau in 1931. Matthews's baptism as a war correspondent came when he covered Italy's invasion and conquest of Ethiopia in 1935. He went on to cover the Spanish Civil War from 1936 to 1939. His dispatches from the Republican, or Loyalist, side brought accusations of biased reporting by critics who branded him a devoted Republican sympathizer. He was the first American journalist to disclose the heavy German and Italian military support for the Nationalist forces under General Francisco Franco.

With the outbreak of WORLD WAR II, he went to Italy in early 1940 to head up the *Times* bureau in Rome. Benito Mussolini's government interned Matthews and several other correspondents and prevented them from filing reports after Italy declared war on the United States. A diplomatic exchange returned Matthews to the United States in 1942. Following an 11-month stint in India, he was reassigned by the *Times* in July 1943 to North Africa to cover the Allied invasions of Sicily and Italy. At the war's conclusion he served as London bureau chief before returning to New York in 1949 to write editorials.

He gained national prominence in 1957 for his favorable three-part report in the *Times* on the Cuban revolutionary movement and its leader Fidel Castro, whom Matthews was able to track down in Cuba's Sierra Maestra Mountains and interview at length. Locating the fugitive revolutionary was a journalistic coup. He reported Castro's determination to free Cuba from the dictatorship of General Fulgencio Batista. Castro assured Matthews of his friendship toward the United States and his commitment to free elections and a democratic Cuba. The veteran correspondent was villified after Castro's revolution triumphed and turned the island into a Communist stronghold aligned with America's COLD WAR opponent the Soviet Union. Critics attacked Matthews as a Castro apologist who had misrepresented the true aims and nature of the Cuban revolution. He faced more serious accusations of having promoted Castro's movement and thus aided the eventual Communist victory in Cuba. Matthews responded to the personal attacks in his 1961 book *The Cuban Story*. He conceded that Cuba was not democratic, but suggested that Castro in large part had been driven into the Communist fold by hostile U.S. policies toward his regime. Matthews retired in 1967 after 45 years with the *Times* and moved to Australia, where he died in 1977.

MAYAGUEZ INCIDENT (1975) U.S. military operation to rescue the crew of a captured American freighter. In April 1975 the VIETNAM WAR ended with U.S.-supported governments in South Vietnam and Cambodia falling to Communist forces. On May 12, 1975, Cambodian patrol boats seized the *Mayaguez*, an American merchant ship in transit in the Gulf of Thailand off the Cambodian coast. The vessel was taken to the Cambodian island of Koh Tang and its 39 crewmembers were moved to the mainland. Cambodia's Communist government, with whom the United States did not have diplomatic relations, accused the *Mayaguez* of being on a spy mission. President GERALD R. FORD denounced the capture as an act of piracy and demanded the release of the ship and its crew. When overtures through the UNITED NATIONS and Communist China had no immediate effect, Ford ordered a military response. On May 13 U.S. war-

planes destroyed three Cambodian gunboats. The following day U.S. marines assaulted Koh Tang, where they encountered stiff Cambodian resistance and recaptured the empty *Mayaguez*. At almost the same time the crew was let free from the mainland in a Thai fishing boat and recovered by a U.S. warship. Ford then ordered the operation halted and the marines withdrawn. U.S. casualties were 18 killed in combat and another 23 lost in a related helicopter crash. Critics charged the Ford administration with resorting too quickly to military action, but the operation was approved widely by the American public as a reassertion of U.S. power following the Vietnam debacle.

MEDICINE LODGE CREEK TREATY See **CHEYENNE AND ARAPAHO WAR**.

MELLON, ANDREW WILLIAM (1855–1937) Business magnate, secretary of the treasury, and diplomat. Born in Pittsburgh, he attended Western University of Pennsylvania (now the University of Pittsburgh) before joining the family bank, Thomas Mellon & Sons, in 1874. His father transferred ownership of the bank to him in 1882. Over the next 40 years Mellon built a financial and industrial empire, becoming involved in the development of such industries as steel, coal, petroleum, and aluminum. Among the major companies he founded or helped organize in the second half of the 19th century were the Union Trust Company, the Gulf Oil Corporation, the Aluminum Company of America (Alcoa), and the Pittsburgh Coal Company. In 1902 Thomas Mellon & Sons was incorporated as the Mellon National Bank with Andrew as president.

Appointed secretary of the treasury by President WARREN G. HARDING in 1921, the arch conservative Republican Mellon continued in the post under presidents CALVIN COOLIDGE and HERBERT C. HOOVER. Preaching government thrift, he pushed a domestic program to reduce the swollen national debt from WORLD WAR I and to scale back federal spending to prewar levels. Mellon championed substantial tax cuts for corporations and wealthy individuals to spur business enterprise and promote private investment. His policies came under constant attack from Democrats and progressive Republicans who accused him of favoritism toward big business and the rich. Peace and prosperity through the 1920s helped Mellon steadily to lower the national debt.

On the foreign front he concluded a series of agreements with European governments arranging for repayment of their World War I debts to the United States. However, these settlements from the outset proved inadequate because Mellon and Coolidge rejected any connection between remittance of the debts and the issue of German war reparations to America's European debtors. In the mid-1920s the Europeans were unable to meet their obligations to the United States unless German reparations were collected. Compounding the difficulty was the fact that Mellon refused to ease U.S. tariff barriers to enable the debtor nations to earn enough money through trade to make their debt repayments. Debt settlements became workable only when the United States funneled loans into Germany under the YOUNG PLAN (1929) to fund the reparations payments. Mellon's prestige plummeted in the opening years of the Great Depression. In February 1932 he left the Treasury Department to become U.S. ambassador to Great Britain. His uneventful London stint ended with his resignation in March 1933 after Democratic President FRANKLIN D. ROOSEVELT took office. In 1937 Mellon gave the federal government his extensive art collection together with money to build a National Gallery of Art in Washington, D.C.

MEXICAN CESSION (1848) Vast territory surrendered by Mexico to the United States as a consequence of the MEXICAN WAR (1846–1848). In defeat, the Mexican government was forced to accept the peace terms dictated by the administration of President JAMES K. POLK. The TREATY OF GUADALUPE HIDALGO (1848) ending the U.S.-Mexico conflict outlined the extensive Mexican territorial cession. Mexico relinquished its claim to Texas above the Rio Grande and ceded its California and New Mexico provinces, an area that altogether embraced the present-day states of Arizona, Nevada, California, and Utah, and parts of New Mexico, Colorado, and Wyoming. The transfer amounted to half of Mexico's national territory. The United States paid

$15 million for the California and New Mexico cessions. America had gained approximately 500,000 square miles; including Texas (annexed in 1845) the area amounted to more than one million square miles. A follow-on territorial acquisition was made in the GADSDEN PURCHASE (1853), in which the United States bought the tract of land spanning the southern part of Arizona and New Mexico.

See also TEXAS ANNEXATION, MAP 2.

MEXICAN OIL EXPROPRIATION CONTROVERSY (1938–1942) Diplomatic dispute engended when the Mexican government nationalized the properties of U.S. and British oil companies in 1938. The issue of subsoil mineral rights in Mexico had become a recurring problem in U.S.-Mexican relations after the Mexican Constitution of 1917 limited foreign ownership of lands, mines, and oil fields. Washington and Mexico City reached a compromise, the BUCARELI AGREEMENT (1923), that safeguarded the interests of American property owners in Mexico while affirming the basic Mexican claim of an inalienable national title to subsoil rights. The Bucareli settlement was undermined by Mexican laws passed in 1925 that placed restrictions on alien land ownership and petroleum holdings. By reigniting the subsoil rights dispute, the legislation dealt a serious setback to Mexican-American relations. The goodwill diplomacy of American ambassador to Mexico DWIGHT W. MORROW brought about a new agreement on foreign ownership rights by 1928.

The tenuous understanding ended less than a decade later in a labor dispute. In November 1936 the newly organized Mexican petroleum workers union made demands on the foreign oil companies for wage increases and fringe benefits, threatening an industry-wide strike. When the companies refused to meet the demands, Mexican President Lazaro Cardenas arranged a four-month cooling-off period to avert an industry shutdown and permit further negotiations. The talks stalemated and in May 1937 oil workers struck nationwide. Under Mexican law, the dispute was submitted to a government conciliation and arbitration board, which heard arguments and rebuttals from both the oil companies and the union. The workers returned to their jobs while the panel examined the case. The Mexican conciliation board's ruling, handed down in December 1937, decided in favor of most of the union's demands and was protested by the oil companies. After the petroleum firms rejected terms of a compromise labor settlement offered by his government, Cardenas, under authority of a 1936 Mexican law, expropriated the properties of American and British oil companies on March 18, 1938.

His action touched off a crisis with the United States that played out over four years. The American companies, claiming investments of over $100 million in Mexico, clamored for U.S. government interposition to protect their interests. While troubled by the nationalization of the oil holdings, President FRANKLIN D. ROOSEVELT and Secretary of State CORDELL HULL were determined to maintain America's GOOD NEIGHBOR POLICY and preserve the principle of nonintervention in Latin America. Hull acknowledged Mexico's right of expropriation but insisted on prompt and fair compensation. Cardenas promised to pay but decried the claims of the oil companies for financial restitution as exorbitant. Meanwhile the United States stopped buying Mexican silver at an above-the-world-market price, a move that weakened Mexico's financial stability and was undertaken to pressure Cardenas to give ground on the oil issue.

The controversy remained stalemated until Manuel Avila Camacho succeeded Cardenas in December 1940, whereupon Hull initiated negotiations with the new president. The Roosevelt and Camacho administrations reached a settlement in November 1941. The agreement arranged for the appointment of two experts, one American and one Mexican, to appraise the U.S.-owned oil properties and work out equitable compensation. Announced in April 1942, the expert valuation awarded the American companies almost $24 million, a sum well under what they had sought for their subsoil claims. Under the 1941 agreement Mexico also consented to pay $40 million in settlement of American agrarian claims. For its part the United States promised to help stabilize Mexico's currency by resuming purchases of Mexican silver at a price above the world level, to negotiate a trade pact, and to lend the Mexican government money through the EXPORT-IMPORT BANK for road construction.

MEXICAN WAR (1846–1848) Armed conflict between the United States and Mexico which resulted in vast expansion of the U.S. national domain. U.S. annexation of Texas in 1845 put the neighboring countries on a course for war. Texas had achieved its independence from Mexico by force of arms in the TEXAN REVOLUTION in 1836. The United States became the first nation to establish diplomatic relations with the Lone Star Republic. Newly sovereign Texas's request for U.S. annexation was rejected in 1837 by President MARTIN VAN BUREN, who feared such a step might provoke a confrontation with Mexico, which refused to recognize the independence of its former province.

The proposed annexation of Texas emerged as the dominant issue in the 1844 U.S. presidential campaign, raising as it did the explosive political question of slavery's expansion. The addition of the slave territory of Texas to the Union promised to shift the delicate political equilibrium in Congress between slave states and free states. Advocating immediate annexation of Texas, Democratic candidate JAMES K. POLK swept to victory over Whig standard-bearer HENRY CLAY. As ardent expansionist, Polk championed America's MANIFEST DESTINY to extend its sovereignty over the continent to the Pacific Ocean. Powerful pro-expansion forces prevailed in Congress, which annexed the former Mexican territory of Texas by joint resolution on March 1, 1845, just days before Polk took office.

TEXAS ANNEXATION precipitated a crisis in Mexican-American relations. A resentful Mexico, condemning the move as a virtual act of aggression, promptly broke diplomatic relations with the United States. The long-simmering dispute over the Texan-Mexican boundary formed the immediate flash point for tensions. Texans asserted that their southwest boundary was the Rio Grande. The Mexicans insisted that the Nueces River, some 100 miles east and north of the Rio Grande, marked the true and historical border of Texas. Mexico also adamantly continued to claim all of its former province as part of its national domain. With its formal admission to the United States, Texas had surrendered responsibility for settling its contested borders to the federal government. The state's claim to the Rio Grande was dubious since its southwestern territorial limit, under Mexican sovereignty, had never extended beyond the Nueces. Nonetheless, the Polk administration had accepted the Rio Grande boundary and pledged to uphold it. In July 1845, Polk had ordered several thousand federal troops under General ZACHARY TAYLOR into the disputed region between the Nueces and Rio Grande.

Tensions were exacerbated by the unresolved claims of American citizens against the Mexican government for lives and property lost in Mexico during the periodic revolutions there since the early 1820s. A settlement of these grievances had been reached under a treaty concluded in 1839. But chronic financial troubles had forced Mexico into default on its agreed-on payments. When Polk took office, he pressed the unsettled claims, demanding that the Mexican government make restitution without further delay. The president also had his sights fixed on acquiring Mexico's province of California. At the outset of his administration Polk had made obtaining the coveted territory a major goal of his presidency. Growing American trepidation about suspected British designs on California lent added urgency to Polk's drive to secure it for the United States. He decided on a diplomatic overture aimed both at resolving U.S. differences with Mexico and satisfying his westward expansionist ambitions. In late 1845 he sent envoy JOHN SLIDELL on a special mission to Mexico City with authority to settle boundary and claims questions and negotiate the purchase of California and New Mexico. After the Mexican government twice refused to receive him, a frustrated Slidell departed amid a deepening crisis in U.S.-Mexican diplomacy.

The failure of the SLIDELL MISSION inclined Polk toward the use of force against Mexico. In January 1846 he set the stage for a showdown by ordering General Taylor to advance deeper into the contested region bounded by the Nueces and Rio Grande. With the United States edging inexorably toward confrontation with Mexico, Polk resolved to remove the threat of war with Great Britain over the smoldering OREGON QUESTION involving rival U.S. and British claims to the Oregon Country. Thus he dropped his demand for "ALL OREGON," accepting the compromise boundary of 49° drawn by the Anglo-American OREGON TREATY (1846).

Hostilities broke out in late April 1846 when Mexican forces encountered Taylor's troops in the disputed area in a skirmish that left more than a dozen Americans killed or wounded. On May 11, Polk sent Congress a war message wherein he recited accumulated American grievances against Mexico, scored the Mexican government for having rebuffed Slidell, and charged that Mexico had invaded U.S. territory and "shed American blood on American soil." Complying with the president's request, Congress passed a declaration of war which Polk signed on May 13. Sentiment in Congress toward "Mr. Polk's War," as his critics branded it, was sharply divided along a combination of party and sectional lines. Democrats, particularly Southern expansionists, staunchly supported the administration and its claim that the conflict was just and necessary. Northern Whigs and abolitionists condemned the war as unjust, alleging that Polk had provoked it as part of a Southern conspiracy to wrest from Mexico territory that would then be added to the Union as slave soil. To thwart the suspected scheme of slave interests, they offered in Congress the WILMOT PROVISO to ban slavery forever in any territory acquired from Mexico as a consequence of the war. The controversial amendment repeatedly was introduced during the conflict; each time it was defeated by Southern Democrats who deplored the measure as unnecessary agitation of the slavery question and a threat to states' rights.

American military forces, though outnumbered, readily prevailed over the Mexican army. The U.S. war effort was waged on four main fronts: General Taylor's army struck across the Rio Grande into northern Mexico; a smaller force under General Stephen W. Kearny advanced West to conquer New Mexico; naval forces under Commodore John D. Sloat sought the conquest of California; and an army under General WINFIELD SCOTT fought from Veracruz inland to Mexico City. Taylor scored a series of decisive victories, including his most famous one at the Battle of Buena Vista in February 1847, which made him a national hero and vaulted him to the Whig presidential nomination the following year. General Kearny captured Sante Fe in August 1846, securing New Mexico with almost no loss of life.

In California events were complicated by the so-called BEAR FLAG REVOLT, in which American settlers in the Sacramento Valley rebelled against Mexican rule, proclaiming the area the independent Republic of California, or Bear Flag Republic, in June 1846. Army officer JOHN C. FREMONT, whom the War Department had sent to California in 1845 as head of a well-armed exploring expedition, supported the revolt and assumed its leadership. In July Sloat put forces ashore and declared California part of the United States, whereupon the Bear Flag was supplanted by the Stars and Stripes. He then relinquished his command to Commodore Robert F. Stockton, who teamed with Fremont to complete the conquest of the province by the end of 1846. General Scott landed at Veracruz in March 1847 and after a brief siege captured the port city. His forces then began their inland drive toward the Mexican capital. Scott's victory at the Battle of Chapultepec gave him Mexico City, which he entered on September 14, 1847.

In expectation of an American military victory, Polk in April 1847 had sent State Department chief clerk Nicholas Trist secretly to Mexico to conclude a peace treaty consistent with American territorial demands. After General Scott arranged a cease-fire in August, Trist began negotiations with Mexican representatives. These talks broke down and fighting resumed in early September. Out of concern that Trist was ignoring his instructions, Polk recalled the envoy. But Trist decided to disregard the president's order to return and on his own assumed responsibility for completing a peace agreement. Polk meanwhile faced growing dissent against his administration's territorial goals from opposite political quarters. His disclosure of these aims in full before the end of the year invited strong Whig objections. He was also under pressure from the burgeoning "ALL-OF-MEXICO" MOVEMENT, whose zealous Democratic expansionist adherents were demanding U.S. annexation of the whole of Mexico as slave territory.

Trist entered a new round of negotiations which, after a month, produced a peace settlement. Signed on February 2, 1848, the TREATY OF GUADALUPE HIDALGO established the Rio Grande as the U.S.-Mexican border and gave the United States the Mexican provinces of California and New Mexico, an area embracing present-day California, Nevada, and Utah, most of New Mexico and Arizona, and part of Wyoming and Colorado. In return for the vast MEXICAN CESSION, the United States was to pay $15 million and assume the outstanding claims of its citizens against the Mexican government. Polk, despite Trist's insubordination, decided to accept the treaty after discovering it satisfied his territorial aims. Opposition posed by Democrats who coveted all of Mexico and by Whigs who deplored any territorial acquisition failed to block the Guadalupe Hidalgo agreement in the Senate, where it gained approval on March 10, 1848, by a vote of 38 to 14.

The most important result of the war was the acquisition of more than 500,000 square miles of territory—the largest single addition to the United States after the LOUISIANA PURCHASE (1803). As the wartime debate in Congress had suggested it would, the acquisition precipitated a bitter sectional political battle over whether the new territory should be open to slavery. This struggle, reflecting as it did the profound division between the North and South on the expansion of human bondage beyond the states where it already existed, presaged a deep sectional crisis and, ultimately, the Civil War. The Mexican War left Mexicans humiliated and embittered. With the loss of Texas and cession of California and New Mexico, Mexico had surrendered half its national territory to the Americans. The war provided valuable experience for many American junior officers who would go on to hold command positions on either side in the Civil War. These included ULYSSES S. GRANT, William T. Sherman, George G. Meade, and George B. McClellan with the Union; and Robert E. Lee, Thomas J. "Stonewall" Jackson, Pierre G. T. Beauregard, James Longstreet, and Braxton Bragg with the Confederacy.

MFN See **MOST-FAVORED-NATION**.

MIDDLE EAST PEACE CONFERENCE
(1991–) U.S.- and Soviet-sponsored conference bringing together Israel, its Arab neighbors, and the Palestinians of the Israeli-occupied territories for negotiations aimed at achieving a comprehensive Middle East peace settlement. The parley marked the first time all the major parties to the Arab-Israeli conflict had assembled in one place for peace discussions. The Syrians had boycotted and the Palestinians had been excluded from the only previous attempt at such a forum, the December 1973 GENEVA CONFERENCE ON THE MIDDLE EAST convened after the YOM KIPPUR WAR. The U.S.-mediated CAMP DAVID ACCORDS (1978) had led to the 1979 EGYPTIAN-ISRAELI PEACE TREATY. But ensuing U.S. attempts in the 1980s at building on the Camp David framework, most notably the REAGAN PLAN (1982), made no headway toward resolving the bitter Arab-Israeli conflict.

International developments at the outset of the 1990s, particularly the improvement in U.S.-Soviet relations with the end of the COLD WAR, paved the way for a determined bid by the Bush administration to revive the moribund Mideast peace process. Faced with staggering economic and political crises at home, and eager to secure massive Western economic aid, Soviet President Mikhail S. Gorbachev was ready to cooperate with Washington on the Middle East, where the Soviet Union had historically backed the Arab position and vied with the United States for influence. Moscow's changed Mideast stance confronted Syria with the loss of its long-standing patron and main arms supplier and left the hardline Arab state increasingly isolated. Syrian President Hafez Assad resolved to end his government's diplomatic alienation from the United States, which had condemned Damascus for both its sponsorship of international terrorism and its continuing military intervention in neighboring Lebanon. Courting improved relations with the West, Syria joined the U.S.-led coalition against Iraq in the PERSIAN GULF WAR (1991) and engaged in the behind-the-scenes diplomatic efforts to win the release of the Western LEBANON HOSTAGES.

The lightning-fast victory over Iraq removed the principal threat to Israel's security and strengthened U.S. ties with Saudi Arabia and the Arab gulf states. Exercising its increased leverage in the Middle East following the Persian Gulf War, the Bush administration launched a concerted effort to convene a Mideast peace conference. Secretary of State JAMES A. BAKER 3RD made repeated trips to the region to convince the various parties to participate in direct negotiations. At the summer 1991 MOSCOW SUMMIT, President GEORGE BUSH and Gorbachev made known their intention to jointly sponsor a Mideast gathering. Baker finally won the commitment of all the principals to the Arab-Israeli conflict to attend a peace conference in Madrid under U.S. and Soviet sponsorship. Baker and Soviet Foreign Minister Boris D. Pankin announced the parley on October 18, just hours after Israel and the Soviet Union had renewed diplomatic relations, which Moscow had severed after the 1967 Arab-Israeli Six-Day War.

The opening round of the Middle East Peace Conference was held from October 30 to November 4, 1991, in the Spanish capital. The formal participants were delegates from Israel, Egypt, Jordan, Lebanon, and Syria, as well as representatives of the Palestinians residing in the Israeli-occupied West Bank and Gaza Strip. Bush and Gorbachev attended as sponsors. After delivering their opening addresses October 30, the U.S. and Soviet presidents departed Madrid, leaving Baker and Pankin to chair the gathering. Bush cautioned against expectations of a quick breakthrough and predicted long and difficult negotiations. While pledging America's continued commitment to the peace process, he stressed that a lasting settlement in the region must be reached by the Mideast participants themselves and could not be imposed from without by the United States or any other party. He outlined the approach accepted by all sides as the basis for proceeding at Madrid. It called for direct bilateral negotiations advancing on two tracks: one between Israel and the Arab states, the other between Israel and the Palestinians. These negotiations, Bush noted, would be conducted on the basis of UNITED NATIONS Security Council Resolutions 242 and 338, adopted respectively in 1967 and 1973.

The resolutions called for Israel's withdrawal from Arab territories occupied in the 1967 Six-Day War in return for formal Arab recognition of the Jewish state. The U.N. measures also proclaimed the need to guarantee the territorial integrity and security of all the states in the region and to settle the issue of the Palestinian Arabs, including the more than one million residing in the Israeli-occupied West Bank and Gaza Strip as well as those displaced from historical Palestine by the Arab-Israeli War of 1948.

Bush indicated that shortly after the bilateral talks got underway, multilateral discussions would begin on a series of regional issues, including arms control, water, and economic development. On the difficult question of the Palestinians in the Israeli-occupied territories, he endorsed the general framework outlined in the Camp David Accords: interim Palestinian self-rule for a five-year transition period, during which negotiations would take place to determine the permanent status of the West Bank and Gaza. Bush urged a solution that would give the Palestinian people "meaningful control over their own lives" while at the same time safeguarding Israel's reasonable security needs. Bush took no position on the Palestinian demand for eventual establishment of an independent homeland in the West Bank but suggested territorial compromise was essential for peace.

The USSR's diminished role in the Mideast peace process was underscored by Gorbachev's speech, wherein the Soviet president in effect acknowledged that the United States would be the main diplomatic catalyst as the talks moved forward. The three-day ceremonial first round concluded with the opening addresses of the Israeli and Arab delegations, as each party outlined its demands. Characterized by hostile rhetoric and harsh recriminations, the speeches set an angry and unyielding tone and offered few hints of conciliation or compromise.

In a second phase of the Madrid parley, Israel held separate meetings with Syria, Lebanon, and a joint Jordanian-Palestinian delegation to arrange dates and locations for future direct bilateral negotiations. The parties were unable to agree on where to hold the next round of more substantive bilateral talks, with the Arabs favoring a continuation in Madrid and Israel demanding sessions in the Middle East. The Madrid conference thus adjourned on November 4 with procedural disputes blocking plans for further negotiations. But all sides were publicly committed to continuing the peace process. The Mideast bilateral talks resumed in December 1991 in Washington, D.C.

MIDDLETON, DREW (1913–1990) American journalist who covered WORLD WAR II and postwar European affairs for the *New York Times* and became its long-standing military correspondent. After graduating from Syracuse University in 1935, he worked as a general reporter and sportswriter at several Poughkeepsie, New York, dailies. The New York City native joined the Associated Press in 1937. Sent to its London bureau in April 1939 to report on sports, he turned to covering World War II after Germany invaded Poland later that year. Middleton landed a position with the *New York Times* in London in September 1942. By the end of the war he had accompanied Allied forces in Great Britain, France, North Africa, Sicily, Belgium, and Germany. He covered the CASABLANCA CONFERENCE (1943) on military operations attended by President FRANKLIN D. ROOSEVELT and British Prime Minister Winston Churchill, the Allied invasion of Normandy in June 1944, and the POTSDAM CONFERENCE (1945) on the postwar occupation of Germany by the BIG FOUR.

Middleton became chief *Times* correspondent in Moscow in 1946. Transferred to Germany in 1947, he covered the emerging East-West COLD WAR, the Anglo-American BERLIN AIRLIFT (1948–1949), and the establishment in 1949 of democratic West Germany and Communist East Germany. In 1953 he moved on to London, where he remained for a decade. After assignments to Paris, the UNITED NATIONS in New York, and Brussels, he returned to the United States in 1970 and became the *Times*'s senior military correspondent, a post he held until his official retirement in 1984. He continued to contribute columns on military affairs to the paper until his death in 1990. Middleton authored or co-authored more than a dozen books, including his 1973 memoirs, *Where Has Last July Gone?*

MIDGETMAN See **MISSILE EXPERIMENTAL**.

MIDWAY ISLANDS U.S. unincorporated territory located in the central Pacific Ocean about 1150 miles west by northwest of Honolulu, Hawaii. The Midways comprise the tiny Sand and Eastern islands, which are enclosed by a circular atoll and separated by Brooks Channel. Discovered by American sailors in 1859, Midway formally was annexed by the United States in 1867 and early in the 1900s became a trans-Pacific cable relay station. Established as a U.S. naval and air base in 1941, the islands were the site of the June 1942 Battle of Midway, where U.S. forces repelled an invading Japanese fleet to register America's first decisive victory of WORLD WAR II. Midway remains home to a U.S. Navy station and is under the administrative control of the Navy Department.

See also MAP 7.

MIGRATION AND REFUGEE ASSISTANCE ACT (1962) First comprehensive U.S. refugee legislation, based on a request by President JOHN F. KENNEDY to consolidate and strengthen the nation's various refugee relief efforts. Enacted June 28, 1962, the act continued annual U.S. contributions to the programs of the UNITED NATIONS High Commissioner for Refugees and the Intergovernmental Committee for Migration. The measure increased refugee assistance funding, particularly for the thousands of refugees fleeing to the United States from Fidel Castro's Cuba. It also authorized the president to reallocate foreign aid to meet emergency refugee requirements. The law placed refugee matters under the State Department's Bureau of Security and Consular Affairs and extended the admission guidelines of the FAIR SHARE REFUGEE ACT (1960). Provisions governing refugee admissions subsequently were incorporated into the IMMIGRATION ACT OF 1965. Congress next revised basic American refugee policy in the REFUGEE ACT OF 1980.

MILITARY-INDUSTRIAL COMPLEX Term coined by DWIGHT D. EISENHOWER at the end of his presidency. In a nationally televised Farewell Address on January 17, 1961, Eisenhower described how COLD WAR realities had forced the unprecedented emergence of both a large peacetime military and a permanent arms industry in the United States. The departing president voiced his concern that this new "military-industrial complex" could exercise "unwarranted influence" on American society. He worried about its impact on the nation's politics, economy, and spiritual life. Eisenhower's warning often is invoked by critics who allege fraudulent procurement practices, wasteful spending, and other abuses in the defense establishment. The phrase "military-industrial complex" has come to signify the symbiotic, often mutually beneficial relationship between the DEPARTMENT OF DEFENSE and defense contractors. More recently, critics of defense spending have referred to the "Iron Triangle" of the military, defense industries, and the Congress, noting that domestic politics significantly shapes decisions on how and where defense dollars are to be spent.

MISSILE EXPERIMENTAL (MX) U.S. INTERCONTINENTAL BALLISTIC MISSILE (ICBM). Development of an advanced ICBM began in the early 1970s to replace the Minuteman missiles deployed during the Eisenhower and Kennedy administrations. Dubbed the Missile Experimental, the massive ICBM was designed to carry 10 separate warheads. In 1979 President JIMMY CARTER authorized a full-scale MX program, with the planned production and deployment of 200 missiles. U.S. defense planners had grown concerned, however, over the projected vulnerability of American land-based ICBMs to a first-strike attack by increasingly accurate and lethal Soviet nuclear missiles. To insure the MX's survivability against Soviet attack, the Carter administration proposed a so-called race-track basing system, where the 200 missiles would be shuttled by rail and concealed among 4600 shelters. The Reagan administration scrapped the controversial race-track scheme, opting instead in 1982 for a basing configuration known as Dense Pack, where 100 MXs would be deployed in a single tight missile field in Wyoming. In theory, incoming enemy nuclear warheads striking so close together would destroy each other rather than the U.S. missiles in hardened silos.

When Congress rejected the Dense Pack proposal and withheld MX funding until establishment of an appropriate basing system, President RONALD W. REAGAN appointed the SCOWCROFT COMMISSION to examine U.S. strategic forces. The blue-ribbon panel, reporting in April 1983, acknowledged the MX's vulnerability to attack but characterized the missile as important to U.S. nuclear DETERRENCE and recommended basing 100 of them in existing Minuteman silos. The commission also urged development of a small, single-warhead missile that would be fully mobile and thus invulnerable to Soviet nuclear attack. In May 1983 Congress, endorsing the panel's findings, voted the funds to produce the first 21 MX missiles. Money also was allocated for initial development of the mobile ICBM, dubbed Midgetman. Modernization of the ICBM force, however, remained a contested issue. Liberal arms control advocates opposed MX as an unnecessary, destabilizing weapon system and pressed for cancellation of the costly missile program. Others suggested holding off on MX pending the successful development of Midgetman. In 1985 Reagan and Congress reached an agreement to limit to 50 the number of MXs deployed in existing missile silos. In the late 1980s, Congress approved funding for a mobile MX basing system, involving MX launchers mounted on railroad cars. The 1991 U.S.-Soviet START Treaty barred the deployment of mobile heavy ICBMs, effectively terminating the rail-carried MX program, but left intact the silo-based MXs and the possible deployment of the Midgetman.

MISSILE GAP   Term coined in the late 1950s to describe an alleged disparity between U.S. and Soviet nuclear missile capabilities. The purported gap was at the heart of a controversy over American defense policy. In February 1956 Senators STUART SYMINGTON (D-MO) and Henry M. Jackson (D-WA) warned that the Soviet Union was close to testing its first INTERCONTINENTAL BALLISTIC MISSILE (ICBM) and called for a stepped-up effort if America's own burgeoning missile program was to keep pace. President DWIGHT D. EISENHOWER replied that U.S. missile development was on track and contended that Soviet missile programs posed no immediate danger. The

successful Soviet test firing of an ICBM in August 1957, followed by the Communist nation's dramatic launch that October of Sputnik, the world's first artificial satellite, brought the Eisenhower administration's defense policy under increasing attack. Critics charged that administration complacency and inaction were causing the United States to lag behind its Communist adversary in nuclear missile technology.

Over the next several years senior defense officials in the Republican administration clashed with congressional Democrats who maintained there was a "gap" between U.S. and Soviet missile programs. In 1959 Symington charged the Soviet Union soon could have a three-to-one lead in ICBMs. Eisenhower possessed intelligence on the Soviet Union that supported his claim that no gap existed, but the president was unwilling to release the information and thereby reveal the secret U-2 reconnaissance flights by which it was obtained. In the 1960 presidential election, Democrat JOHN F. KENNEDY made the "missile gap" an important campaign issue. Once in office, the Kennedy administration realized, as Eisenhower had asserted, that there was no real gap. In February 1961 new Secretary of Defense ROBERT S. MCNAMARA quietly acknowledged that the missile gap did not exist and the issue quickly faded.

MISSOURI v. HOLLAND (1920)   U.S. Supreme Court decision addressing the authority of the federal government to enact legislation implementing an international treaty. In 1916 the United States, Canada, and Great Britain concluded a treaty committing each nation to protect certain migratory birds from hunters. Congress in 1918 passed the Migratory Bird Act to implement the agreement. A similar 1913 law regulating migratory bird hunting had been overturned by a federal district court as an unconstitutional infringement on the jurisdiction of state governments. Missouri challenged the constitutionality of the 1918 measure, filing suit against Ray P. Holland, a federal game warden in the state. On April 19, 1920, the Supreme Court by a vote of 7 to 2 ruled the act was constitutional. Writing for the majority, Justice Oliver Wendell Holmes, Jr., noted that a treaty, once ratified, became the supreme law of the land. As early as WARE v. HYLTON

(1796), the Court had found that federal treaties took precedence over state law. Holmes held that a valid treaty could invest Congress with the authority to legislate in areas previously reserved to the states. While consistently upholding a broad federal treaty-making power, the Court in *Reid* v. *Covert* (1957) made clear that such power ultimately was subject to constitutional limits.

MOBY DICK PROGRAM See **GENETRIX PROJECT**.

MODEL TREATY See **PLAN OF 1776**.

MONGOOSE See **OPERATION MONGOOSE**.

MONROE DOCTRINE (1823) Statement of U.S. opposition to European intervention in the Western Hemisphere. Announced by President JAMES MONROE December 2, 1823, in his annual message to Congress, the doctrine expressed what became the basic principle behind U.S. policy in the Americas. Monroe's message evolved out of U.S. concerns over two developments in the early 1820s. Russia's attempt to exclude all but its own ships from the northwest coast of the United States north of 51° latitude clashed with American expansionist aspirations and provoked a diplomatic controversy. During the dispute, Monroe's Secretary of State JOHN QUINCY ADAMS asserted the principle that European governments could establish no new colonies in the Western Hemisphere. A second impetus for the message was the fear that continental European powers planned to reestablish the Spanish colonial empire through reconquest of the newly independent Latin American republics. The British proposed a joint Anglo-American pledge to resist any such intervention, a request the Monroe administration rejected in favor of a unilateral American declaration.

The historic 1823 doctrine set forth three propositions: It restated the noncolonization principle initially laid down by Adams; it declared the United States would view any bid by the European powers to extend their political system to the American continents as threatening to U.S. peace and security; and it pledged the United States not to interfere in Europe's internal affairs

(a vow later abandoned when America emerged as a world power after 1900). Monroe's formulation had little immediate influence, although Russia agreed in the RUSSO-AMERICAN TREATY OF 1824 to withdraw behind a boundary set at 54°40' north latitude. The doctrine, largely ignored in Europe, had no practical bearing until the mid-1840s, when Democrats invoked it against French and British efforts to prevent the annexation of Texas and against Great Britain's Oregon claims. In December 1845 President JAMES K. POLK reaffirmed the Monroe principles in the so-called Polk Corollary, which not only condemned intervention but rejected European arguments about the need to maintain a BALANCE OF POWER in the Western Hemisphere. The corollary expanded the 1823 declaration by barring even voluntary transfers of territory in North America to European powers. Polk cited this restriction in 1848 to discourage possible cession of the Mexican Yucatan peninsula either to Great Britain or Spain.

France challenged the nonintervention dictum during the American Civil War by installing its puppet Archduke Maximilian as the emperor of Mexico in 1864. Under mounting U.S. diplomatic pressure, Napoleon III withdrew the French military presence from Mexico in 1867. The administration of GROVER CLEVELAND invoked the doctrine in 1895 as justification for American intervention to compel Great Britain to arbitrate a dispute with Venezuela over the British Guiana boundary. Secretary of State RICHARD OLNEY, outlining the OLNEY COROLLARY to the Monroe Doctrine, stated U.S. opposition to the increase by any European state of its territory in the Americas. The British acquiesced and the VENEZUELA BOUNDARY DISPUTE was settled peacefully. When joint intervention in Venezuela in December 1902 by Great Britain, Germany, and Italy to collect unpaid debts appeared imminent, President THEODORE ROOSEVELT countered with the threat of U.S. military action on Venezuela's behalf. The Europeans agreed to arbitration, withdrawing their naval forces in February 1903. The VENEZUELA CLAIMS controversy and chronic economic instability among Caribbean and South American nations led the president to proclaim the ROOSEVELT COROLLARY (1904) asserting the U.S. right to intercede in Latin America in order to prevent European intervention. Roosevelt's extension of Monroe's principles was used to justify assorted U.S. military interventions to maintain political stability in Central American countries. The 1912 LODGE COROLLARY for the first time extended the Monroe Doctrine to both foreign syndicates and Asian nations.

Resentment against American involvement in Latin America grew in the decades after WORLD WAR I. Intent on improving relations and dispelling charges of American IMPERIALISM, the Hoover administration revoked the Roosevelt Corollary in 1930 through the CLARK MEMORANDUM. President FRANKLIN D. ROOSEVELT proclaimed the GOOD NEIGHBOR POLICY toward Latin America in 1933. At the Montevideo Conference the same year, the United States joined with other American republics to fashion the CONVENTION ON RIGHTS AND DUTIES OF STATES committing them not to interfere in one another's affairs. During WORLD WAR II, the Western Hemisphere nations other than neutral Argentina united against the Axis powers, eventually adopting the ACT OF CHAPULTEPEC (1945). This mutual-security measure, which declared an attack on one as an attack on all, incorporated the principle of foreign nonintervention as part of a Pan-American defense doctrine. Creation of the ORGANIZATION OF AMERICAN STATES in 1948 provided a permanent Pan-American forum for guaranteeing the Monroe Doctrine. Postwar concerns about Communist inroads in Latin America led the United States to act alone and without prior inter-American approval in the GUATEMALA COUP in 1954, in Fidel Castro's Cuba in the early 1960s, and in the DOMINICAN CRISIS in 1965. U.S. policy in Central America in the 1980s, much criticized in the region, drew on Monroe Doctrine tenets to oppose Soviet-supported Communist movements in Nicaragua and in the EL SALVADOR CIVIL WAR.

See also MANIFEST DESTINY.

MONROE, JAMES (1758–1831) U.S. senator, minister to France and Great Britain, secretary of state, secretary of war, and fifth president of the United States. Born in Virginia, Monroe entered William and Mary College in 1774. Swept up by the patriotic fervor of the AMERICAN REVOLUTION, he left in 1776 to join the Continental Army. He served until 1778, rising from the rank of lieutenant to major. From 1780 to 1783 he

studied law under THOMAS JEFFERSON. His political career began with his election in 1782 to the Virginia assembly. From 1783 to 1786 he was a member of the Confederation Congress. Following his admission to the Virginia bar in 1786, he practiced law at Fredericksburg for four years. A delegate to the Virginia ratifying convention in 1788, he voted against adoption of the U.S. CONSTITUTION because of his sense that it concentrated too much power in the federal government. The same year he was defeated by JAMES MADISON in a race for a seat in the first U.S. Congress. Elected to the U.S. Senate in 1790, he served there four years, aligning himself with the Jeffersonian Democratic-Republicans, who opposed the pro-British Federalist policies of ALEXANDER HAMILTON and sympathized with the republican aspirations of the French Revolution.

Appointed U.S. minister to France by President GEORGE WASHINGTON in 1794, Monroe struggled to square his pro-French orientation with the administration's policy of strict neutrality in the Anglo-French war that had begun in 1793. At his official reception in Paris, Monroe lavished praise on revolutionary France, for which he drew an official reprimand by Secretary of State TIMOTHY PICKERING. Conclusion of the controversial Anglo-American JAY'S TREATY (1794) touched off a crisis in U.S.-French relations. U.S. acquiescence in the agreement to the narrow British interpretation of FREEDOM OF THE SEAS, the French government complained, amounted to an abandonment of American obligations to France under the FRANCO-AMERICAN ALLIANCE (1778). Monroe's failure to defend Jay's Treaty against French objections led Washington to recall him from Paris in 1796.

He was governor of Virginia from 1799 to 1802. In 1803 President Jefferson sent him to Paris as a special envoy to help American Minister ROBERT R. LIVINGSTON negotiate the LOUISIANA PURCHASE from Napoleon Bonaparte. Later the same year Jefferson named Monroe minister to Great Britain. His difficult four-year tenure in London would coincide with a steady deterioration in Anglo-American relations owing to British interference with American neutral maritime rights. In 1804 Monroe undertook a special diplomatic mission to Madrid, where he was unsuccessful in an attempt to purchase the Spanish Floridas.

Returning to his London post in 1805, he sought a settlement of the outstanding differences between the United States and Great Britain. Toward this end, with the assistance of special envoy William Pinkney, he negotiated the MONROE-PINKNEY TREATY (1806). Because the agreement failed to resolve the nettlesome issue of British IMPRESSMENT of American seamen, Jefferson and Secretary of State Madison deemed it unacceptable and never submitted it to the Senate for ratification. In 1808, following his return to the United States, Monroe was an unsuccessful candidate for the Democratic-Republican presidential nomination. Returning to Virginia politics he was elected to the legislature in 1810 and became governor again in January 1811.

He resigned in March to accept President Madison's appointment as secretary of state. Initially of the view that the difficulties between the United States and Great Britain could be resolved peacefully, he soon came to the conclusion that conflict was inevitable. The failure of Anglo-American diplomacy culminated in the WAR OF 1812. In 1814, after the British burned Washington, Monroe took over as secretary of war, replacing JOHN ARMSTRONG, whose resignation had been forced by charges of incompetence and criticism of America's woeful military performance. Monroe held this office while also remaining secretary of state. His energetic efforts in the two cabinet posts enhanced his national reputation as the tide of war turned in U.S. favor. He emerged as the retiring Madison's heir apparent. In 1816 he captured the Democratic-Republican presidential nomination and won an easy victory over Federalist candidate Rufus King.

Monroe's greatest achievements as president were in foreign affairs. His administration was able to dispose of a number of troublesome issues in Anglo-American relations left unresolved by the TREATY OF GHENT (1814) ending the War of 1812. He personally took part in the negotiation with Great Britain of the RUSH-BAGOT AGREEMENT (1817) demilitarizing the Great Lakes. The wide-ranging CONVENTION OF 1818 extended the U.S-Canadian boundary from the Lake of the Woods along the 49th parallel to the Rocky Mountains, dealt with the OREGON QUESTION by leaving the Oregon Country open to joint U.S. and British oc-

cupation for ten years; struck a compromise in the FISHERIES QUESTION by restoring American fishing privileges to certain coastal waters off eastern Canada, and renewed the commercial Convention of 1815 for a decade.

Relations with Spain became a central preoccupation of Monroe's presidency. The independence movement sweeping Latin America augured the end of Spain's New World empire. Monroe strove to capitalize on Spain's deteriorating position in the Western Hemisphere to advance his administration's expansionist aims. He and Secretary of State JOHN QUINCY ADAMS coveted Spanish Florida and sought Spain's formal recognition of U.S. territorial claims under the Louisiana Purchase. The president, while sympathetic to the Latin American revolutions, observed diplomatic caution, withholding U.S. recognition of the independence of Spain's former colonies. He feared that premature recognition could provoke intervention by Spain and its allied European monarchies against the new Latin American republics. Washington initiated negotiations with Madrid in 1817 on territorial questions in North America, highlighted by the issue of the Floridas. Intervening events interrupted the talks. Late in 1817 Monroe ordered General ANDREW JACKSON to suppress hostile cross-border raids on Georgia settlements by Seminole Indians from Spanish Florida. Promptly invading Florida, Jackson crushed the Seminoles, captured Spanish military posts, executed British subjects Robert Ambrister and Alexander Arbuthnot for inciting the Seminoles in the so-called AMBRISTER AND ARBUTHNOT AFFAIR, and stood poised to annex Spanish territory.

The FLORIDA INVASION (1818), mounted without specific presidential authorization, was deplored by both Madrid and London. In Washington, Monroe's entire cabinet, with the exception of Adams, urged that Jackson be reprimanded for his conduct in the Floridas during the first of the SEMINOLE WARS. The president acknowledged that the general had exceeded his instructions and agreed to restore the military posts to Spain but would not discipline Jackson. The general's bold exploit, and Monroe's refusal to repudiate it, convinced the Spanish that the United States posed an imminent annexation threat to Florida and influenced them to negotiate a territorial settlement. The resulting ADAMS-ONIS TREATY (1819) represented a major triumph for the Monroe administration. Under its terms, Spain ceded East and West Florida to the United States. The treaty also fixed the boundary between Spanish and U.S. possessions in North America from the Gulf of Mexico to the Pacific, with Spain relinquishing its claim to Oregon Country and the United States abandoning its claim to Texas. The Adams-Onis agreement, also called the Transcontinental Treaty, established America as a continental nation. Following final approval of the treaty, Monroe discarded his earlier caution and extended diplomatic recognition to the new Latin American states.

He was overwhelmingly reelected in 1820. Suspecting that Spain might attempt to restore its colonial empire in Latin America and concerned by the extension of Russian territorial claims from Alaska down the Pacific northwest coast, the president in his annual message to Congress in 1823 articulated a set of tenets that collectively became known as the MONROE DOCTRINE. Formulated in close collaboration with Adams, the doctrine established U.S. opposition to European intervention in the Western Hemisphere as a fundamental principle of American foreign policy. It asserted that the American continents henceforth would be closed to European colonization and that any foreign effort to acquire further political control in the hemisphere or to violate the independence of existing states would be regarded as a hostile act. Adams settled competing U.S. and Russian territorial claims along America's northwest coast through the RUSSO-AMERICAN TREATY OF 1824, in which Russia accepted 54°40' as Russian Alaska's southern boundary.

Monroe and Adams both wanted to end the African slave trade. Great Britain, which spearheaded the campaign against the traffic in the early 19th century, urged other nations to grant it a right to intercept and search their vessels in the interest of interdicting illegal slave commerce. Sensitive to previous British violations of America's neutral maritime rights, Monroe rejected London's proposal. The United States, instead, acted unilaterally. In 1819 Congress authorized the use of armed vessels to patrol the African coast for slave

traders and the following year passed legislation defining the participation of Americans in the international trade as piracy and thus punishable by death. At the end of his second term in March 1825, Monroe retired to his country estate in Virginia. With his wife's death in 1830, he moved to New York City, where he died in 1831.

MONROE-PINKNEY TREATY (1806) Proposed treaty between the United States and Great Britain to resolve disputes over commerce and neutral rights. Resumption in May 1803 of a decade-long war between Great Britain and France soon posed serious challenges to American neutrality. The British and French imposed restrictions on neutral maritime trade in order to hinder each other's war effort. U.S. commerce and neutral rights faced the greater threat from Great Britain, which enjoyed naval superiority over France. British policy after 1804 aimed at blocking the lucrative American wartime trade with French and Spanish colonies in the West Indies that benefited French ruler Napoleon Bonaparte. Great Britain's highest admiralty court, ruling in 1805 in the case of the seized American trade ship *Essex*, declared that such commerce circumvented the Rule of 1756, a British maritime principle first asserted in the Seven Years' War (1756–1763). The rule, the British court held in its *Essex* decision, prohibited a belligerent nation (in this instance France) from opening trade with a neutral nation (such as the United States) during wartime when that same trade had been forbidden to the neutral (as was the case with the United States) in time of peace. After the *Essex* verdict, British warships in the Caribbean seized increasing numbers of American vessels carrying French or Spanish goods, drawing strong U.S. protest. Anglo-American relations deteriorated in the face of Great Britain's blockade of French-controlled European ports and continuing British IMPRESSMENT, or forced naval recruitment, of American seamen.

Congress retaliated in April 1806 by passing the NON-IMPORTATION ACT, which arranged for a ban on certain British products to the United States effective the following November unless Great Britain settled American grievances. President THOMAS JEFFERSON in May sent Baltimore lawyer

William Pinkney as a special envoy to London to join U.S. Minister to Great Britain JAMES MONROE in negotiating U.S.-British differences. They were instructed to seek an agreement that defined neutral rights, prohibited British impressment of Americans, and secured a British indemnity for seized American vessels. Jefferson suspended enforcement of the Non-Importation Act in November amid the ongoing talks. After Great Britain steadfastly refused to pledge itself against impressment, Monroe and Pinkney strayed from their instructions and on December 31, 1806, concluded an Anglo-American accord.

Under the Monroe-Pinkney Treaty, which made no mention of a British indemnity, the United States surrendered the principle that FREE SHIPS MAKE FREE GOODS while Great Britain moderated its ban on neutral shipping in the West Indies. Displeased with its terms, Jefferson never submitted the treaty to the Senate for ratification. In May 1807 Secretary of State JAMES MADISON directed Monroe and Pinkney to reopen discussion on the basis of the original American demands, but the British rejected further negotiations on those terms. Simmering Anglo-American differences over neutral rights and impressment contributed to the outbreak of the WAR OF 1812.

MONTEVIDEO PLEDGE See **CONVENTION ON RIGHTS AND DUTIES OF STATES**.

MONTREAL PROTOCOL ON SUBSTANCES THAT DEPLETE THE OZONE LAYER See **VIENNA CONVENTION FOR THE PROTECTION OF THE OZONE LAYER**.

MOON TREATY (1979) Multilateral agreement spelling out the status under international space law of the Moon and other celestial bodies. Drafted over a seven-year period by the UNITED NATIONS Committee on the Peaceful Uses of Outer Space, the Agreement Governing the Activites of States on the Moon and Other Celestial Bodies was adopted by the U.N. General Assembly December 5, 1979, and entered into force July 11, 1984. Known informally as the Moon Treaty, it elaborated on and applied principles established in the landmark OUTER SPACE TREATY (1967) to the Moon and other celestial bodies. The agreement states

that all human activities on the Moon and other celestial bodies shall be for peaceful purposes; that the exploration and use of outer space is the province of all mankind and shall be for the benefit of all countries; and that all nations take the necessary steps to avoid disturbing the environmental balance on the Moon and other celestial bodies. Under the treaty, the Moon is demilitarized and nuclear or other weapons of mass destruction cannot be placed in lunar orbit.

Other provisions guarantee freedom of scientific investigation for all nations, reiterate the Outer Space Treaty's ban on claims of national sovereignty over Moon territory, and declare the Moon and its natural resources to be the "common heritage of mankind." Anticipating a point at which technology will open the way to exploitation of the Moon's mineral wealth, the treaty calls for eventual establishment of an international arrangement that would guarantee a fair sharing by all signatories in the benefits derived from lunar resources. To date, the Moon convention has been ratified by a small number of countries with little or no experience in space exploration. The United States and Soviet Union, the world's two leading space powers, did not sign the treaty. Washington and Moscow alike have been concerned that the common-heritage-of-mankind concept would inhibit their ability to independently explore and take unilateral commercial advantage of the Moon.

MOORER, THOMAS HINMAN (1912–   ) U.S. Navy officer, chairman of the JOINT CHIEFS OF STAFF (JCS). An Alabama native, Moorer graduated from the U.S. Naval Academy in 1933. He completed flight training as a naval aviator in 1936. A distinguished combat record in WORLD WAR II was followed by attendance at the Naval War College and, in 1957, promotion to admiral. In 1965 and 1966 Moorer directed U.S. forces deployed to the Caribbean island during the DOMINICAN CRISIS. He was named chief of naval operations in 1967, at a time of extensive Navy involvement in the VIETNAM WAR. In 1970 he became chairman of the JCS, the nation's top military officer. He continued the Nixon administration's policy of VIETNAMIZATION, whereby South Vietnam assumed the burden of fighting in its own defense. In December 1972 he oversaw the heavy U.S. CHRISTMAS BOMBING of Hanoi that hastened North Vietnamese agreement to the 1973 PARIS PEACE ACCORDS. During the 1973 YOM KIPPUR WAR Moorer took part in the U.S. decision to airlift supplies to Israel. He also carried out President RICHARD M. NIXON's order to place U.S. forces on alert, a move that successfully discouraged the Soviet Union from intervening in the conflict. He retired in 1974.

MORATORIUM AGAINST THE VIETNAM WAR See **VIETNAM MORATORIUM**.

MORFONTAINE, TREATY OF See **CONVENTION OF 1800**.

MORGENTHAU, HENRY, JR. (1891–1967) Secretary of the treasury. Morgenthau was born in New York City to a wealthy family. He attended Cornell University for several semesters, worked briefly in his father's real estate business, and then puchased several hundred acres in Dutchess County, New York, much of it an apple orchard, and became a farmer. From 1922 to 1933 he published the *American Agriculturist*, a statewide farm weekly. Morgenthau developed a lifelong friendship and association with his Hudson Valley neighbor, FRANKLIN D. ROOSEVELT. When Roosevelt was elected governor of New York in 1928, he appointed Morgenthau to top state agriculture and conservation positions. In 1933 Morgenthau accompanied President-elect Roosevelt to Washington, where he headed the Farm Credit Administration and helped negotiate the ROOSEVELT-LITVINOV AGREEMENT extending U.S. diplomatic recognition to the Soviet Union. In January 1934 Roosevelt named him secretary of the treasury. Throughout the 1930s Morgenthau was actively involved with Roosevelt's New Deal programs to revitalize the American economy and pull the nation out of the Great Depression. As the worldwide economic crisis brought widespread currency devaluations and a collapse of international trade, he negotiated with Great Britain and France the 1936 Tripartite Stabilization Pact. The agreement represented a precedent-setting multilateral attempt to coordinate on monetary policy. During WORLD WAR II he was centrally involved in financing the massive Allied war effort. In July 1944 he chaired the BRETTON WOODS CONFERENCE that established the INTERNATIONAL MONETARY FUND and the WORLD BANK. The following month he prepared a controversial proposal, known as the MORGENTHAU PLAN, calling for the conversion of postwar Germany into an agrarian state. Following Roosevelt's death in April 1945, Morgenthau found his influence lessened in the new Truman administration. He retired to his New York farm in July 1945.

MORGENTHAU PLAN (1944) Proposal during WORLD WAR II for converting a defeated Germany into an agrarian state. Following the success of the June 1944 D-Day invasion of Nazi-held France, the Allied powers looked forward to impending victory over Germany. By August 1944, U.S. Secretary of the Treasury HENRY MORGENTHAU, JR., reflecting the belief that an industralized Germany would always prove a menace, had drawn up a plan for the postwar dismantling of the German state. The plan called for giving parts of Germany to France, Denmark, Poland, and the Soviet Union. The remainder would be stripped of its heavy industry, effectively reducing it to an agricultural and pastoral country, and divided into two provinces under international control. President FRANKLIN D. ROOSEVELT and British Prime Minister Winston Churchill gave tentative approval to the harsh scheme at the second of their QUEBEC CONFERENCES in September 1944. The German government in its propaganda broadcasts cited leaked details of the plan as proof of an Allied intention to enslave and starve Germany. Roosevelt, heeding the counsel of Secretary of State CORDELL HULL and Secretary of War HENRY L. STIMSON that the plan was vindictive and impracticable, essentially had abandoned the Morgenthau proposal by the February 1945 YALTA CONFERENCE on postwar Europe. With Roosevelt's death in April 1945, HARRY S. TRUMAN became president and aligned U.S. policy behind a reconstructed, industrial Germany as essential to postwar European economic recovery.

MORO WARS (1901–1913) Armed struggle in the Philippine Islands between U.S. forces and the native Moros. Following its defeat in the SPANISH-AMERICAN WAR (1898), Spain ceded the Philippines to the United States, which proclaimed sovereignty over the islands and set up an American military government. Filipino insurgents demanding independence launched the PHILIPPINE INSURRECTION against American annexation in 1899. Before U.S. troops could suppress this four-year rebellion, they faced a second adversary in the Moros, Muslims who inhabited the southern island of Mindanao and lived quite apart from the rest of the mostly Christian Filipino people. An American drive to convert and assimilate the Moros ignited a determined resistance, which began in 1901 as sporadic fighting and escalated into more serious encounters. Some 600 rebellious Moros who had taken refuge on the nearby island of Jolo were slaughtered in 1906 by troops under General LEONARD WOOD. The American military effectively suppressed the Moro uprising by 1906, although intermittent guerrilla fighting continued until 1913.

MORRILL TARIFF (1861) Act that inaugurated a period of high duties on goods imported by the United States. Under pressure from Southern Democrats, who represented the interests of an essentially agricultural economy and thus favored lower tariffs on imported manufactured goods, federal customs fees had declined since the record-high 1828 TARIFF OF ABOMINATIONS. Following the secession of Southern states from the Union in early 1861 and the consequent departure of their representatives from the U.S. Congress, the Republican Party was able to fulfill an 1860 campaign promise to impose higher tariffs to protect domestic industries, located mainly in New England and the mid-Atlantic states, from overseas competition. Enacted March 2, 1861, the Morrill Tariff, named for its sponsor, Representative Justin S. Morrill (R-VT), marked the beginning of a seven-decade commitment to PROTECTIONISM in U.S. trade policy. The act served the more immediate purpose of raising revenues for the North's prosecution of the Civil War. Subsequent revisions increased the average U.S. tariff to almost 50 percent of an import's value by 1869. Tariff acts in 1872 and 1883 and the MCKINLEY TARIFF in 1890 insured high U.S. import duties through the 19th century.

MORROW, DWIGHT WHITNEY (1873–1931) Lawyer and diplomat. Born in Huntington, West Virginia, Morrow graduated from Amherst College in 1895 and from Columbia Law School in 1899. He left

a successful corporate law practice in 1914 to join the banking house of J.P. Morgan where he soon became a partner and remained until 1927. During WORLD WAR I he was a civilian adviser on logistics to General JOHN J. PERSHING. Morrow's wartime contribution to the Allied Maritime Transport Council earned him the Distinguished Service Medal. In 1925 Amherst classmate President CALVIN COOLIDGE named him to chair the Aircraft Board of Inquiry that had been formed to examine aeronautics and its application to national defense. The board's 1926 report led to separate controls for military and private aircraft and the encouragement of commercial aviation.

Appointed U.S. ambassador to Mexico by Coolidge in 1927, he assumed his post amid the seriously strained Mexican-American relations that followed the Mexican Revolution (1910–1920). Through his tact and skillful diplomacy, he earned the trust and friendship of President Plutarco E. Calles and was able to win repeal of the 1925 Mexican law that threatened expropriation of American-held oil rights in Mexico. He also negotiated temporary solutions to the problems of Mexico's confiscation under a land-reform program of American-owned properties and the conflict between the anticlerical Mexican government and the Roman Catholic Church. Morrow enhanced Mexican-American ties by arranging for his son-in-law, aviation hero CHARLES A. LINDBERGH, to make a goodwill flight to Mexico. Following his three-year mission at Mexico City, he served as a member of the U.S. delegation to the first of the LONDON NAVAL CONFERENCES (1930). He was elected as a Republican to the U.S. Senate from New Jersey in 1930 and was considered a possible presidential candidate when he died suddenly of a cerebral hemorrhage in 1931.

MOSCOW CONFERENCE (1942) See **WORLD WAR II CONFERENCES** in **APPENDIX E**.

MOSCOW CONFERENCE (1943) WORLD WAR II meeting of U.S. Secretary of State CORDELL HULL, British Foreign Secretary Anthony Eden, and Soviet Foreign Minister Vyacheslav Molotov. The top foreign affairs officials of the three major Allied powers conferred in Moscow from October 19 to 30, 1943, on wartime strategy and postwar planning. The principal purpose of the gathering was to finalize arrangements for the TEHERAN CONFERENCE of President FRANKLIN D. ROOSEVELT, Prime Minister Winston Churchill, and Soviet Premier Joseph Stalin the following month. The Moscow talks reviewed the preparations for an Anglo-American second front against Nazi Germany in Europe and yielded an agreement to establish a EUROPEAN ADVISORY COMMISSION to formulate postwar Allied policy. Stalin for the first time secretly promised that the Soviet Union would enter the war against Japan once Germany was defeated. Hull, Eden, and Molotov, joined by the Chinese ambassador to Moscow, Foo Ping-sheung, signed a U.S.-sponsored Declaration of Four Nations on General Security. The so-called Moscow Declaration, released November 1, 1943, reaffirmed the Allies' determination to prosecute the war until the unconditional surrender of their Axis enemies and called for the establishment of an international peacekeeping organization at the earliest practical date. The declaration, an important step toward formation of the UNITED NATIONS, was a milestone in America's break with its prewar isolationist tradition.

MOSCOW CONFERENCE (1944)   See **WORLD WAR II CONFERENCES** in **APPENDIX E**.

MOSCOW CONFERENCE (1945)   See **COUNCIL OF FOREIGN MINISTERS**.

MOSCOW CONFERENCE (1947)   See **COUNCIL OF FOREIGN MINISTERS**.

MOSCOW COUP (1991)   Unsuccessful attempt by top Soviet Communist hardliners to oust Soviet President Mikhail S. Gorbachev, whose program of political and economic reforms they opposed. The ill-fated coup raised immediate concerns in Washington and other Western capitals over a possible reversal of improved East-West ties and prompted widespread international opposition. Since the collapse of communism in Eastern Europe at the end of 1989, Gorbachev had struggled to hold in check the restive forces unleashed in the Soviet Union by the process of political liberalization and the nation's worsening economic crisis. Pro-reform liberals unhappy with the pace of change were pressing Gor-

bachev to accelerate the USSR's move toward a market economy and to repudiate the Communist Party and its ideology. The Soviet central government faced mounting challenges to its legitimacy and authority from the Baltic states and other Soviet republics demanding independence from Moscow. The direction of events in the USSR alarmed Communist traditionalists, whose power was threatened and who feared the nation was moving toward disintegration. They urged Gorbachev to deal harshly and decisively with the spreading unrest and suggested that he was losing his grip on events.

The coup attempt began August 19 when a group of senior Soviet Communist officials, all of whom had secured their positions under Gorbachev, had the president detained under house arrest at his dacha in the Crimean peninsula where he had been vacationing. Announcing, dubiously, that Gorbachev was incapacitated with an unspecified illness, the eight conspirators assumed central power by organizing themselves as the so-called State Committee for the State of Emergency. Warning that the country was sliding toward catastrophe, the committee imposed a state of emergency and ordered military units, including hundreds of tanks, positioned throughout Moscow. The overthrow attempt preempted the scheduled August 20 signing in the Soviet capital of Gorbachev's Union Treaty, through which power was to be decentralized from Moscow to the constituent republics. Opposition to the treaty appeared to be a key factor in prompting the hardliners to seize control.

Russian Republic President Boris N. Yeltsin, Gorbachev's chief political rival, led the domestic resistance, galvanizing hundreds of thousands of pro-democracy citizens in Moscow to bravely defy the illegal usurpation of power. Leaders of other Soviet republics joined his stand against the coup and endorsed his call for Gorbachev's restoration as the legitimate leader of the Soviet Union. The developments in the USSR cast a shadow over the course of Soviet relations with the United States and its Western allies. At their MOSCOW SUMMIT meeting just weeks before, Gorbachev and President GEORGE BUSH had signed the historic START Treaty cutting superpower strategic nuclear arsenals, and used the occasion to trumpet the end of the COLD WAR.

Bush joined the other Western leaders in condemning the Soviet coup as illegitimate and regressive. He pledged not to recognize the new Soviet leadership and placed U.S. economic aid to the USSR on hold. In a telephone conversation with Yeltsin on August 20, Bush conveyed his support for the Russian leader's stand against the putsch. The hardliners' action produced apprehension in the West about a possible reversion to Cold War tensions. Questions immediately surfaced in the United States about the coup's implications for the viability of arms control agreements recently concluded with Gorbachev's government, including the START Treaty and CONVENTIONAL FORCES EUROPE TREATY (1990).

The coup collapsed on August 21 amid indications of divided Soviet military loyalties and under the weight of overwhelming opposition both inside and outside the country. Gorbachev, released from house arrest unharmed, declared himself once again in control and arrived back in Moscow safely on August 22. Bush welcomed Gorbachev's return to power and praised Yeltsin for his courageous conduct during the coup as a champion of freedom and democracy. Moving immediately to place U.S.-Soviet relations back on course, Bush lifted the hold on agricultural credit guarantees and other programs imposed at the start of the crisis. Yeltsin emerged as the most popular political figure in the USSR and with his power greatly enhanced. In the turmoil's aftermath, he became virtual co-leader, with Gorbachev, of the Soviet Union. The bungled coup, and the drive for independence it accelerated among the Soviet republics, left the USSR in an unstable and uncertain state, raising concerns in the West over who would control the vast Soviet nuclear arsenal. In September Bush undertook a special NUCLEAR REDUCTION INITIATIVE to facilitate Moscow's control over Soviet nuclear forces. The disintegrating USSR was replaced by the Commonwealth of Independent States in December 1991.

MOSCOW DECLARATION See **MOSCOW CONFERENCE** (1943).

MOSCOW SUMMIT (1972) Historic meeting from May 22 to 29 between President RICHARD M. NIXON and Soviet Communist Party General Secretary Leonid I. Brezhnev in which the two nations endorsed a policy of DETENTE, or relaxation of U.S.-Soviet tensions. The highlight of the summit, the first state visit by an American president to the Soviet Union, was the signing by the post–WORLD WAR II adversaries of the SALT I arms control package. By 1972, after more than a quarter-century of COLD WAR, the superpowers looked to establish a foundation for better two-way relations and to make substantive headway on arms control and disarmament issues. The detailed summit agenda and the seven agreements concluded at the conference largely had been worked out in advance of Nixon's arrival in Moscow on May 22. After five days of wide-ranging talks on U.S.-Soviet relations, Nixon and Brezhnev on May 26 reached final agreement on SALT I, which encompassed two accords: an ABM TREATY to limit the deployment of antiballistic missiles; and an Interim Agreement freezing land- and sea-based offensive missiles at existing levels. Nixon and the Soviet leadership also completed pacts on scientific and technical cooperation, joint space activities, environmental protection, trade, and accidents at sea.

The summit concluded May 29 with the signing of a declaration of principles, in which the two nations pledged to avoid military confrontation and to seek world-wide disarmament. An accompanying joint communique, which summarized summit proceedings and achievements, addressed several outstanding international issues. The U.S. and Soviet leaders acknowledged they were unable to resolve their differences on the VIETNAM WAR. Both sides agreed a European security conference should be held to discuss prospects for MUTUAL AND BALANCED FORCE REDUCTION TALKS in Europe. The communique closed with announcement of Brezhnev's acceptance of Nixon's invitation to visit the United States in 1973.

The Moscow gathering signaled an improvement in relations and a movement toward greater superpower cooperation. Its tangible results surpassed the short-lived and mostly superficial gains of previous top-level U.S.-Soviet parleys. An immediate outgrowth of the summit was finalization in July of an agreement for the sale of $750 million of U.S. grain to the Soviet Union, the largest such transaction to that point between the nations. In October a joint U.S.-Soviet trade commission, established at the Moscow conference, completed a three-year trade pact. The deal outlined a compromise settlement of the Soviet World War II LEND-LEASE debt and a U.S. promise to seek MOST-FAVORED-NATION treatment for Soviet goods. The Kremlin would reject the trade agreement in January 1975 after the U.S. Congress passed the JACKSON-VANIK AMENDMENT (1974), a measure which denied the Soviet Union lower tariff rates until it lifted restrictions on emigration. Nixon and Brezhnev resumed their face-to-face diplomacy in 1973 at the WASHINGTON SUMMIT.

MOSCOW SUMMIT (1974) Third and final summit between President RICHARD M. NIXON and Soviet Communist Party General Secretary Leonid I. Brezhnev. The Moscow parley, held June 27 to July 3, 1974, continued the thaw in Soviet-American relations initiated earlier in the decade and added modestly to the arms control progress made at the prior Moscow and Washington meetings. At the conclusion of their 1973 WASHINGTON SUMMIT, the president and the general secretary agreed to meet again in Moscow the next year to build on the more cooperative U.S.-Soviet relationship. In March 1974, U.S. Secretary of State HENRY A. KISSINGER met with Soviet officials in Moscow to finalize the summer summit agenda. Nixon arrived in Moscow politically weakened by the domestic Watergate scandal and facing questions about his ability to engage in effective negotiations with Brezhnev.

At the outset of talks, the two hailed the development of U.S.-Soviet DETENTE in recent years but acknowledged that many unresolved problems still divided the superpowers. The meetings yielded a number of limited nuclear arms accords, none of which amounted to the long-sought breakthrough toward a permanent agreement on curbing offensive NUCLEAR WEAPONS. Nixon and Brezhnev signed a communique committing their countries to negotiate a new interim pact limiting both the number and destructive capacity of strategic nuclear arms. The existing Interim Agreement, part of SALT I (1972), was scheduled to lapse in 1977. In the separate THRESHOLD TEST BAN TREATY the superpowers agreed not to conduct underground nuclear weapons tests with yields over 150 kilotons.

A 10-year economic accord completed by Nixon and Brezhnev directed Washington and Moscow to facilitate bilateral trade. The pact augmented accords signed in 1972. Soviet and American officials also struck minor agreements on environmental protection, space ventures, cultural exchanges, energy research, and establishing new consulates. On the international front, the leaders discussed the 1973 YOM KIPPUR WAR, urging implementation of UNITED NATIONS Security Council Resolutions 242 and 338, which outlined the framework for a Middle East peace settlement. They called for early completion of the 35-nation CONFERENCE ON SECURITY AND COOPERATION IN EUROPE with results that would allow a final meeting of the heads of state of the participating countries. The summit ended July 3. In the United States, the Watergate scandal had overshadowed the Moscow meetings. Nixon, facing impeachment, resigned the presidency August 9, 1974. His successor, GERALD R. FORD, attended the VLADIVOSTOK SUMMIT in November 1974 to resume Soviet-American negotiations on curtailing the arms race.

MOSCOW SUMMIT (1988) Fourth meeting in 30 months between President RONALD W. REAGAN and Soviet leader Mikhail S. Gorbachev. The Moscow Summit, from May 29 to June 2, continued the East-West dialogue initiated through the previous Reagan-Gorbachev parleys. At the close of their WASHINGTON SUMMIT (1987), the two leaders had announced plans for a Moscow conference in 1988. Bargaining did not produce a breakthrough toward a hoped-for agreement to reduce the U.S. and Soviet strategic nuclear arsenals and in March 1988 the countries acknowledged a START treaty would not be ready for the end-of-May superpower meeting.

Arms control figured as the main item on the Moscow agenda. On June 1 the president and the general secretary exchanged ratification documents for the INTERMEDIATE NUCLEAR FORCES TREATY, the 1987 pact banning medium-range nuclear forces. After making only marginal progress toward a START accord, the two leaders ordered their negotiators in Geneva to resume work on the treaty to cut long-range

NUCLEAR WEAPONS by up to 50 percent. Kremlin objections to the STRATEGIC DEFENSE INITIATIVE (SDI), the U.S. program to develop space-based antimissile defenses, remained the chief impediment to a major deal to reduce strategic nuclear forces. As they had at the 1987 Washington conference, Reagan and Gorbachev sidestepped the question of whether SDI tests in space were permissible under the 1972 ANTIBALLISTIC MISSILE TREATY.

Reagan used his visit to focus attention on HUMAN RIGHTS, particularly the issue of Soviet Jewish emigration, rebuking the USSR for its poor record and meeting with leading Soviet political dissidents and Jewish "refuseniks." An angered Gorbachev chafed at the criticism, claiming Reagan's remarks ignored the recent Kremlin push toward democratization and were based on an outdated understanding of conditions inside the Soviet Union. During the summit, Reagan eased off his staunch anti-Soviet stance and lauded Gorbachev's economic and political reforms. The visiting president also retracted his controversial 1983 comment describing the Soviet Union as an "evil empire."

Discussion of divisive regional issues formed a substantive part of the summit. The two sides negotiated further details of an international agreement reached that April outlining terms for withdrawal of Soviet forces from Afghanistan. On the ANGOLAN CIVIL WAR, the superpowers set an autumn deadline for an international accord to provide for the pullout of Cuban troops from Angola in return for a South African withdrawal from Namibia. Reagan and Gorbachev made no headway on conflicts in Central America and the Middle East.

Gorbachev returned to the United States six months after the Moscow summit to address the UNITED NATIONS General Assembly in New York. In a speech deriding military and ideological struggle in world affairs, the Soviet general secretary revealed Kremlin plans for a dramatic overall troop cut by 1991. The December 7 announcement placed added pressure on President-elect GEORGE BUSH to conclude new arms control deals with Moscow once in office. Gorbachev met briefly with Reagan and Bush at Governor's Island in New York before cutting short his visit to return home in the wake of the devastating earthquake in Soviet Armenia. Bush and Gorbachev would resume the top-level U.S.-Soviet contacts the following year at the MALTA SUMMIT.

MOSCOW SUMMIT (1991) Parley held in Moscow July 30 to 31, 1991, between President GEORGE BUSH and Soviet President Mikhail S. Gorbachev. Preliminary to their meeting in the Soviet capital, the two leaders had conferred in London earlier in July during the annual ECONOMIC SUMMIT of the GROUP OF 7 Western industrial nations. At London, Gorbachev had petitioned for Western economic aid to help resurrect the shattered Soviet economy and reorganize it on free-market principles. The Moscow parley marked the first post–COLD WAR superpower summit. Both Bush and Gorbachev heralded the two-day gathering as the beginning of a new era of cooperation in U.S.-Soviet relations. Highlight of the summit was their signing on July 31 of the historic START Treaty. Under negotiation for almost a decade, the long-awaited arms control agreement mandated cuts in the superpowers' long-range nuclear forces.

The Arab-Israeli conflict was a major topic in the talks between Bush and Gorbachev. In the wake of the U.S.-led coalition's victory in the PERSIAN GULF WAR (1991), the Bush administration had moved to exercise enhanced U.S. leverage in the Mideast to press for a settlement of the bitter Arab-Israeli dispute over the Jewish state's right to exist and Arab demands for a separate Palestinian homeland in Israeli-occupied territories. On the summit's second day, the two leaders announced that their nations were prepared to co-sponsor a Mideast peace conference in October. No date was set for such a gathering nor were invitations formally extended to any of the parties in the region. Bush did disclose that he was sending Secretary of State JAMES A. BAKER 3RD to Israel immediately to discuss the U.S.-Soviet proposal with Prime Minister Yitzhak Shamir. In a related move, Soviet Foreign Minister Aleksandr A. Bessmertnykh on July 31 revealed that his government was prepared to restore full diplomatic relations with Israel provided the Israelis agreed to participate in the proposed conference. The U.S.- and Soviet-sponsored parley came to fruition when the Arabs and Israelis agreed to attend the

MIDDLE EAST PEACE CONFERENCE in October 1991.

In other summit developments, Bush pledged to submit to Congress for its approval a U.S.-Soviet trade pact that would grant the USSR MOST-FAVORED-NATION (MFN) trade status and thereby clear the way for the expansion of the Soviet-American economic relationship. The trade agreement had been concluded at the 1990 WASHINGTON SUMMIT. As required under the JACKSON-VANIK AMENDMENT (1974), which forbade MFN status for any Communist nation that prevented the emigration of its citizens, Bush had withheld the trade pact from Congress until the enactment in 1991 of a Soviet free emigration law. During the Moscow talks Bush urged Gorbachev to find a way to extend freedom to the peoples of the independence-seeking Baltic republics of Latvia, Lithuania, and Estonia and pressed the Soviets to stop sending military aid to Fidel Castro's Communist Cuba. Following the summit, prospects for Senate ratification of the START Treaty were thrown into uncertainty by the MOSCOW COUP in August 1991, in which Soviet hardliners attempted, unsuccessfully, to oust Gorbachev and check the dynamic political and economic changes sweeping the USSR. Meanwhile Bush sent the trade agreement to Congress, where it faced stiff opposition from members who demanded more extensive Soviet economic reforms as the price for normalized trade ties. The failed Moscow Coup brought the collapse of the Soviet Communist Party and the final repudiation of the Communist ideology that had held the USSR together. The State Council, the new Soviet executive body organized in the coup's immediate aftermath, formally recognized the independence of the Baltic states on September 6, 1991. Within a week the Kremlin announced the withdrawal of Soviet military forces from Cuba and an effective halt in unrestricted Soviet economic aid to Castro. In December 1991 a disintegrating Soviet Union was replaced by the Commonwealth of Independent States.

MOSES-LINTHICUM ACT   See **ROGERS ACT**.

MOST-FAVORED-NATION (MFN)   Term used in international agreements to indi-cate the provision of specific rights and privileges. When one country accords another most-favored-nation status, it commits itself to providing that country rights and privileges as favorable as those it extends to any other existing or future treaty partner. MFN is used almost exclusively in connection with trade relations. The United State historically has supported the MFN principle, which serves to mitigate against exclusionary or exploitive trade practices and to promote open trade. The MFN principle was incorporated into the GENERAL AGREEMENT ON TARIFFS AND TRADE that has governed international commerce since 1947. In the JACKSON-VANIK AMENDMENT (1974) the United States linked its provision of MFN trade status to Communist nations to their record on the freedom of their citizens to emigrate. Following Communist China's brutal suppression of the TIANANMEN UPRISING (1989), President GEORGE BUSH resisted domestic pressure to rescind Beijing's MFN status, granted in 1980. The Bush proposal to extend MFN status to the Soviet Union in 1991 was rendered moot by the Communist nation's disintegration the same year.

MULTINATIONAL FORCE AND OB-SERVERS   See **SINAI PEACEKEEPING FORCE**.

MURPHY COMMISSION (1975)   Special blue-ribbon panel that reviewed the organization of the federal government for the handling of foreign affairs. It was established formally as the Commission on the Organization of the Government for the Conduct of Foreign Policy by the Foreign Relations Authorization Act of 1972. The panel began hearings in September 1973. Its 12 members, headed by retired ambassador Robert D. Murphy, were drawn equally from Congress, the executive branch, and the private sector. Other members included Vice-President NELSON A. ROCKEFELLER, Senator MICHAEL J. MANSFIELD (D-MN), and WILLIAM J. CASEY, then president of the EXPORT-IMPORT BANK.

The commission submitted its findings to the president and Congress on June 27, 1975. The report provided a series of recommendations, cornerstone of which was that the DEPARTMENT OF STATE remain the focal point in the U.S. government for the conduct of foreign relations. The panel outlined measures for improving the management of foreign affairs personnel and urged the appointment of more ambassadors with expertise in economics, business, science, and energy. The commission cited the need for greater coordination between the State and Defense departments on political-military issues. It generally endorsed the role of the INTELLIGENCE COMMUNITY in foreign policy and proposed the formation of a joint House-Senate committee on national security to oversee intelligence operations. The commission called for the creation of a single overseas information and cultural affairs agency, stressed the importance of domestic public opinion to foreign policy, and urged greater attention be given to issues of HUMAN RIGHTS. In a written dissent, Mansfield criticized the report's emphasis on the executive branch and its failure to address strengthening the role of the Congress in the formulation of foreign policy.

MURROW, EDWARD ROSCOE (1908–1965) Venerated American broadcast journalist best known for his radio reports from Great Britain during WORLD WAR II. Christened Edgar Roscoe Murrow, the North Carolina native changed his name to Edward while still a speech major at Washington State College, from which he graduated in 1930. He joined the Columbia Broadcasting System (CBS) in 1935 as director of its program for recruiting public figures to speak on the network. Sent to London in 1937 to take charge of the network's European bureau, he was responsible for transmitting cultural programs and special events to America.

His rise to journalistic fame began with Adolf Hitler's annexation of Austria in March 1938. Despite a lack of formal news training, Murrow broadcast vivid eyewitness accounts from Vienna of the Nazi Anschluss. His Austrian reporting immediately established his standing as a gifted and capable foreign correspondent. To help cover the fast-breaking developments leading to World War II, he assembled a European news staff that included correspondents WILLIAM L. SHIRER, Eric Sevareid, Howard K. Smith, and Charles Collingwood. During the war, Murrow broadcast from London, winning distinction for his descriptions of the aerial Battle of Britain (1940–1941) and

the German blitz against the city. His signature opening phrase "This ... is London" became familiar to millions of American listeners.

Back in the United States after the war, he became CBS vice-president in charge of news and public affairs. In 1947 he returned to the air with a nightly radio program of news and commentary. Murrow branched out from radio to the new medium of television. His weekly radio show, the news digest "Hear It Now," produced in collaboration with Fred W. Friendly, became the television program "See It Now" in 1951. Three times Murrow traveled to Korea to report first-hand on the KOREAN WAR. In 1952 he and Friendly produced "Christmas in Korea," the first televised documentary on a U.S. war. The next year they aired a controversial "See It Now" segment widely considered to have contributed to the political demise of demagogic anti-Communist Senator JOSEPH R. MCCARTHY (R-WI). Murrow resigned from CBS in January 1961 to accept appointment by President JOHN F. KENNEDY as director of the UNITED STATES INFORMATION AGENCY. Lung cancer forced his resignation in January 1964.

MUSKIE, EDMUND SIXTUS (1914–   ) Senator, secretary of state. Muskie earned a bachelor's degree at Bates College in 1936 and obtained a law degree at Cornell University in 1939 before opening a law practice in his native Maine. He served as a naval officer during WORLD WAR II. He entered politics following the war as a member of the Maine state legislature. In 1954 he was elected governor. He became the state's first popularly elected Democratic U.S. Senator in 1958. Reelected three more times, he earned a reputation as a pioneering legislator on environmental issues. In the mid-1960s he supported U.S. policy on the VIETNAM WAR. In 1968 Muskie was selected by then Vice-President Hubert H. Humphrey as his running mate on the unsuccessful Democratic presidential ticket. During the Nixon administration Muskie grew increasingly critical of American military involvement in Southeast Asia and pressed for the withdrawal of U.S. forces. In 1972 he failed in a bid to win the Democratic presidential nomination. The following year he had a central role in guiding the

WAR POWERS RESOLUTION through the Senate. Passed over President RICHARD M. NIXON's veto, the legislation was intended to reassert congressional control over the decision to go to war. In April 1980 President JIMMY CARTER named Muskie to replace the resigning CYRUS R. VANCE as secretary of state. His nine-month tenure was dominated by the IRAN HOSTAGE CRISIS and worsening U.S.-Soviet relations following the Communist nation's December 1979 invasion of Afghanistan. He left office with the Carter administration in January 1981 and joined a Washington law firm. In 1986 he served on the TOWER COMMISSION that reported on the IRAN-CONTRA scandal.

MUTUAL ASSURED DESTRUCTION (MAD) Basic principal of U.S.-Soviet nuclear DETERRENCE. The term referred to the ability of the United States and Soviet Union to destroy one another in a nuclear exchange. This capacity for mutual annihilation thus deterred each nation from starting a nuclear conflict. The acronym MAD was often cited with a sense of irony by those who sought to underscore the seeming insanity of a nuclear strategy that relied on a "balance of terror" to prevent nuclear war. In the 1950s America enjoyed overwhelming nuclear superiority over its Communist adversaries. The Eisenhower administration threatened MASSIVE RETALIATION with NUCLEAR WEAPONS to dissuade possible Communist aggression around the world. Continuing improvements in Soviet nuclear capabilities, particularly in INTERCONTINENTAL BALLISTIC MISSILES (ICBMs) undermined the U.S. nuclear advantage. U.S. defense planning became increasingly concerned with the possibility of a Soviet nuclear attack. In recognition of the emerging nuclear parity between the two superpowers, American strategic thinking in the early 1960s shifted to the importance of a strong nuclear force in deterring a Soviet first strike. Secretary of Defense ROBERT S. MCNAMARA spoke of the new U.S. "assured destruction" strategy, which he characterized as the ability of the nation, even after absorbing a surprise attack, to inflict an unacceptable level of damage upon an aggressor. Under this strategy, the United States maintained the capacity to inflict a level of retaliatory destruction sufficient to deter a Soviet nuclear strike.

By the end of the decade the arms race between the United States and Soviet Union had reached a nuclear stalemate. Either side could destroy the other, but neither could defend itself. Strategists on both sides realized that this situation of "mutual assured destruction" actually provided a basis for an effective two-way nuclear deterrence. The MAD doctrine took as its basic premise that the COLD WAR adversaries would achieve security by holding each other nuclear hostage. In 1972 the Nixon administration concluded an arms control agreement with the Soviet Union that locked into place a system of nuclear deterrence based on MAD. The ANTIBALLISTIC MISSILE TREATY barred either side from developing an effective defense against nuclear missiles. As long as neither side could stop the other's attack, then the strategic reality of MAD would work to prevent nuclear war.

In 1983 President RONALD W. REAGAN criticized as fundamentally flawed a strategic defense that would deliberately leave innocent civilians open to attack. He launched the STRATEGIC DEFENSE INITIATIVE (SDI) to develop an effective nuclear missile defense. SDI generated widespread debate over its feasibility and wisdom. The 1991 START Treaty maintained MAD as the cornerstone of U.S.-Soviet nuclear deterrence. With the dissolution of the Soviet Union in December 1991, the Soviet nuclear arsenal came under the control of successor states Russia, Ukraine, Belarus, and Kazakhstan. In 1992 Ukraine, Belarus, and Kazakhstan agreed to eliminate their nuclear weapons by the end of the decade, while the United States and Russia committed to negotiations on further reducing their nuclear forces. Deepening ties between Washington and Moscow pointed to a diminishing need for nuclear deterrence and rendered MAD increasingly obsolete.

MUTUAL AND BALANCED FORCE REDUCTION TALKS See **CONVENTIONAL FORCES EUROPE TREATY**.

MUTUAL DEFENSE ASSISTANCE ACT See **MUTUAL SECURITY ACT**.

MUTUAL SECURITY ACT (1951) Federal law enacted October 10, 1951, that brought a new approach to U.S. foreign aid at a time of heightened COLD WAR tensions. The legislation was first in a decade-long series of annual laws governing authorizations for American foreign assistance programs. Deteriorating East-West relations in the late 1940s prompted a shift in emphasis in America's foreign aid from economic to military. With the 1949 formation of NATO, joining the United States and its allies in Western Europe in a mutual defense pact, President HARRY S. TRUMAN called on Congress to authorize substantial amounts of military aid to America's alliance partners as an investment in his administration's policy of CONTAINMENT of communism. Aside from small-scale military assistance to Nationalist China following WORLD WAR II and to Greece and Turkey starting in 1947 under the TRUMAN DOCTRINE, the entire thrust of U.S. overseas aid in the early postwar years had concerned humanitarian relief and economic recovery. American foreign assistance had encompassed contributions to the UNITED NATIONS RELIEF AND REHABILITATION ADMINISTRATION and the Truman administration's MARSHALL PLAN (1948) for European postwar recovery. Less than six percent of U.S. overseas aid distributed between mid-1945 and mid-1950 went for military purposes.

The president's military aid request underwent acrimonious debate in Congress where members had reservations about a shift toward a costly rearmament effort. Urged by Truman and his top national security advisers, and spurred by the disclosure five days earlier that the USSR had detonated an atomic bomb, ending America's nuclear monopoly, Congress on September 28, 1949, approved the Mutual Defense Assistance Act, authorizing $1.3 billion in U.S. military assistance, of which $1 billion was earmarked for NATO allies. Enactment of the measure launched what was to become a permanent Mutual Defense Assistance program of military aid to nations allied with the United States in resisting Communist expansionism. While precipitated by Cold War stalemate in Europe, the swing in U.S. foreign aid from economic recovery and development to security was accelerated by major developments in Asia—the Communist victory in China in 1949 and the onset of the KOREAN WAR in June 1950. In 1949 the ratio of U.S. economic to military assistance stood at roughly four to one.

By the end of 1950 the ratio was virtually reversed.

In May 1951 Truman submitted all of his administration's foreign aid requests to Congress as a single mutual security program. Under the president's proposal, the Marshall Plan (economic aid), the POINT FOUR program (technical assistance) and the Mutual Defense Assistance program (military aid) were pictured as mutually supporting facets of a single U.S. effort to strengthen FREE WORLD resistance to communism. Congress sanctioned the idea through the Mutual Security Act of 1951, which consolidated all U.S. foreign aid under one annual legislative authorization. The measure created the umbrella Mutual Security Agency (MSA) to administer U.S. foreign aid programs. Only the EXPORT-IMPORT BANK among U.S. aid activities was excluded from the MSA. As part of an executive branch reorganization the MSA was replaced in 1953 by the new Foreign Operations Administration (FOA). The FOA was changed to the International Cooperation Administration (ICA) in 1955 but functionally remained the same agency. Throughout the 1950s the ratio of military to economic aid averaged about two to one. The preponderance of military assistance went to nations along the periphery of the Soviet Union and Communist China—primarily South Korea, Taiwan, South Vietnam, and the NATO allies.

In the years after the death of Soviet ruler Joseph Stalin in 1953, the new Kremlin leadership exhibited increasing interest—through offers of economic credits and technical assistance—in expanding Soviet influence in the underdeveloped world. While the United States had pioneered on this front through its Point Four initiative, American development assistance had been relegated to a minor role during the post-1949 military buildup. The Soviet drive for position in what came to be called the THIRD WORLD sharpened U.S. awareness of the importance of promoting economic development there. Beginning in 1954, rising stocks of surplus farm commodities were channeled into foreign aid through sales and donations to needy countries under the new FOOD FOR PEACE program. With the establishment in 1957 of the Development Loan Fund (DLF) as the lending arm of the ICA, the Eisenhower administration embraced a policy of using long-term, low interest rate loans to spur economic investment and growth in underdeveloped nations.

In the late 1950s, as European decolonization yielded new nations in Asia and Africa that became targets of the East-West contest for political and economic influence, the U.S. foreign aid mix began to shift, with the percentage of military support falling and that of development assistance rising. Acting on the proposal of President JOHN F. KENNEDY, Congress in 1961 replaced the Mutual Security Act with a new annual foreign aid authorization, the FOREIGN ASSISTANCE ACT, which separated military from non-military aid. The legislation transferred the administration of military assistance programs to the Defense Department and placed economic and technical assistance programs under a new AGENCY FOR INTERNATIONAL DEVELOPMENT within the State Department.

MUTUAL SECURITY AGENCY See MUTUAL SECURITY ACT.

MX See MISSILE EXPERIMENTAL.

MY LAI INCIDENT (1968) Massacre of South Vietnamese civilians by U.S. soldiers during the VIETNAM WAR. On March 16, 1968, Army Lieutenant William L. Calley, Jr. led his platoon of approximately 25 men on an operation to secure the hamlet of My Lai. No enemy was encountered, but members of the platoon herded an estimated 150 unarmed civilians into a ditch and gunned them down. In the course of the day additional murders, rapes, and other atrocities were committed. Reports of massive civilian casualties by U.S. helicopter pilots who had flown over the area effectively were covered up by Calley's superiors, who did not investigate or otherwise pursue the evidence of possible war crimes. The incident came to light on March 29, 1969, when Ronald L. Ridenhour, a former combat infantryman, sent copies of a letter to various senior government officials detailing reports he had heard while in Vietnam of the killing at My Lai. The Army convened

a special board of inquiry under General William R. Peers. The investigation gained national and then international attention after journalist Seymour M. Hersh, who won a Pulitzer Prize for his coverage, broke the My Lai story on November 13, 1969.

The Peers inquiry into the concealment of the My Lai massacre resulted in charges of dereliction of duty against 12 officers. Calley's division commander, General Samuel H. Koster, was demoted and the assistant division commander was censored. The brigade commander, Colonel Warren K. Henderson, was acquitted by a court-martial in December 1971. The charges against the other officers eventually were dropped for lack of evidence. Thirteen officers and enlisted men were charged with war crimes in connection with the killings at My Lai. On November 24, 1969, Calley was accused of the premeditated murder of 102 civilians. In March 1971 he was convicted by a court-martial of killing 22 unarmed civilians and sentenced to life imprisonment. His company commander, Captain Ernest L. Medina, the battalion intelligence officer, and three sergeants were found not guilty of murder and other crimes. The charges against the remaining individuals were dismissed.

The entire episode generated intense domestic debate. Many in the antiwar movement saw My Lai as evidence of the illegality and immorality of the U.S. involvement in the Vietnam conflict. Some suggested that the event was representative of atrocities routinely committed by American forces in Southeast Asia. On the other side were supporters of the U.S. war effort who argued that Calley, the only person convicted in the incident, had been singled out as a scapegoat for a breakdown in discipline under difficult guerrilla warfare conditions. Others drew attention to Communist atrocities, such as the murder of more than 3000 civilians at Hue during the 1968 TET OFFENSIVE. Senior military officials condemned the incident, insisting it was an aberration. Calley's conviction was upheld on appeal. His sentence was reduced to 10 years by Secretary of the Army Howard H. Callaway in 1974 and he was released on parole the same year.

N

NAMIBIAN INDEPENDENCE (1990) Attainment of independence by African country Namibia, previously known as South-West Africa, as part of a U.S.-assisted regional political settlement dealing also with Angola. The territory of present day Namibia was a German colony until WORLD WAR I, when it was captured by South Africa. In 1920 South Africa was granted a LEAGUE OF NATIONS mandate to administer the former German possession. After WORLD WAR II the status of South-West Africa became the subject of a protracted dispute between South Africa and the international community. The UNITED NATIONS in 1946 refused Pretoria's request to annex the territory. When, in 1966, the white minority South African government extended its apartheid system of racial segregation and discrimination over the overwhelmingly black South-West Africa, the U.N. Assembly voted to strip South Africa of its mandate. In 1968 the United Nations renamed the territory Namibia. Meanwhile, exiled members of the South-West African People's Organization (SWAPO) had organized a rebel army and in 1966 launched what became a 23-year armed struggle for Namibian independence. In 1978 the U.N Security Council passed Resolution 435, which called for a cease-fire and provided for Namibia's independence following U.N.-sponsored elections. Negotiations were held sporadically over the next 10 years, during which time the South African government proffered several plans for limited internal Namibian self-rule, none of which met with international acceptance.

In the 1980s resolution of the Namibian issue became linked directly to progress toward settlement of the ANGOLAN CIVIL WAR, in which U.S.- and South African-backed rebels of UNITA (National Union for the Total Independence of Angola) were waging an insurgency against the Soviet- and Cuban-supported Angolan Marxist regime. Talks among the United States, Cuba, Angola, and South Africa in 1988 achieved a breakthrough. The discussions, in which the United States mediated between the Angolans and Cubans on one side and the South Africans on the other, brought announcement in August of a scheduled cease-fire in the Namibian war as an opening move toward a peace agreement. Negotiations continued under the chairmanship of U.S. Assistant Secretary of State Chester A. Crocker and yielded a formal agreement in December on a timetable for the withdrawal of Cuban troops from Angola and the independence of Namibia in accordance with U.N. Resolution 435.

The cease-fire in Namibia, the first step in the Namibian independence process, began inauspiciously on April 1, 1989, with a SWAPO incursion from Angola in which hundreds of SWAPO guerrillas were killed or wounded by South African security forces. SWAPO's breach of the cease-fire briefly set back the efforts of the U.N. Transition Group (UNTAG) to oversee the shift to Namibian independence. In national elections for a constituent assembly held in November 1989, under the auspices of UNTAG and a U.N. peacekeeping force, SWAPO won a majority of votes. The constituent assembly drafted a Western-style multiparty constitution with a bill of rights. Namibia became independent on March 21, 1990, with long-standing SWAPO leader Sam Nujoma as its first president.

NANKING INCIDENT (1927) Chinese attack on the foreign community at Nanking. Following the Revolution of 1911, China was wracked by internal strife, as different factions and local warlords struggled for power in the giant Asian nation. By 1927 an alliance of the Nationalist Kuomintang movement headed by Chiang Kai-shek and the Chinese Communist Party was near victory in its struggle to unify China under a single government. On March 29, 1927, soon after Chiang's forces captured Nanking from the regime in Peking, antiforeign riots erupted in the city, killing an American and five Europeans and destroying the U.S. and other consulates. U.S. and British gunboats in the Yangtze River fired on the violent demonstrations as foreigners escaped the area. On April 11 the United States, Great Britain, France, Italy, and Japan presented identical protest notes to the Nationalist foreign minister. U.S. Ambassador to China John Van A. MacMurray counseled more forceful action, but neither President Calvin Coolidge nor Secretary of State Frank B. Kellogg believed the Nanking episode warranted America going to war. Both also recognized that the roughly 13,000 U.S. troops in China, there to protect American lives and property, were insufficient to allow for a more assertive policy. On April 12 Chiang, blaming the Nanking attack on Communist elements, used the incident as a pretext for launching a sudden purge of the Communist Party that left the Nationalists largely in control of China. In 1928 a U.S. settlement with the Nationalist government arranged for Chinese reparation for damages in Nanking and an American apology for the naval bombardment.

NASA See **NATIONAL AERONAUTICS AND SPACE ADMINISTRATION**.

NATIONAL AERONAUTICS AND SPACE ADMINISTRATION (NASA) U.S. government agency responsible for the development of advanced aviation and space technology and for space research and exploration. NASA is concerned with all aspects of manned and unmanned flight both within and beyond the Earth's atmosphere. The Soviet Union's successful October 1957 launch of Sputnik, the first man-made earth-orbiting satellite, dealt a stunning blow to American scientific prestige and inaugurated the start of the Space Race between the Cold War rivals. The Soviet accomplishment spurred President Dwight D. Eisenhower to call for creation of a single civilian agency to conduct space research and exploration for peaceful purposes. NASA was established by the National Aeronautics and Space Act of 1958, which Eisenhower signed into law July 29, 1958. The new agency replaced the National Advisory Committee for Aeronautics (NACA), the federal body created in 1915 to promote advancements in American aeronautics. From the outset NASA comprised a network of centers across the nation with its headquarters in Washington, D.C. The agency currently has 10 major field installations, including the Lyndon B. Johnson Space Center (manned mission control) near Houston, Texas, and the John F. Kennedy Space Center (launch operations) at Cape Canaveral, Florida.

Manned space flight quickly became the focus of NASA's ambitious long-term space exploration program. Project Mercury (1958–1963) and Project Gemini (1962–1966), pioneering agency programs that placed astronauts and equipment in orbit and tested their ability to function in space, laid the groundwork for Project Apollo (1960–1972). This was the bold national effort, formally established as a goal by President John F. Kennedy in 1961, to land Americans on the Moon and return them safely to Earth before the end of the decade. The Apollo 11 mission made history in July 1969 when crew members Neil Armstrong and Edwin (Buzz) Aldrin became the first humans to land on the Moon. After Apollo, public interest in and congressional support for space exploration waned. Despite substantial cuts in its budget, NASA in 1973 was able to launch Skylab, the nation's first manned orbital space laboratory. In an unprecedented instance of international cooperation in space, the United States and Soviet Union in 1975 conducted the joint APOLLO-SOYUZ mission, which involved a two-day linkup of Soviet and American manned spacecraft in earth orbit.

In the late 1970s and early 1980s, NASA developed the reusable space shuttle to make access to space easier and cheaper. The agency came under severe criticism following the explosion of the space shuttle Challenger in January 1986. All seven crewmembers were killed in the accident, the worst in the space program's history. Shuttle flights were halted for two years while NASA worked to improve the shuttle design and overall program safety. International cooperation has become an increasingly important dimension of the U.S. space program. Since its inception in 1958, NASA has undertaken joint projects with more than 100 countries, opening the full range of U.S. civilian space activities to foreign participation. Such cooperation has benefited American aeronautical and space research programs through cost sharing and by stimulating scientific and technical contributions from abroad. Joint ventures in the early 1990s included the Galileo space probe and SPACE STATION FREEDOM.

NATIONAL BIPARTISAN COMMISSION ON CENTRAL AMERICA See **KISSINGER COMMISSION**.

NATIONAL DEFENSE EDUCATION ACT (1958) Federal legislation establishing a $1 billion program for improving the teaching of science, mathematics, and foreign languages at all school levels in the United States. The act was passed at the height of the COLD WAR in response to growing American concern about Soviet leadership in science and space technology, symbolized by the USSR's successful October 1957 launching of Sputnik, the first earth-orbiting satellite. Congress also was spurred by several reports it had received indicating an impending national shortage of scientists. The law was based largely on a special education message delivered to Congress on January 27, 1958, by President DWIGHT D. EISENHOWER requesting a large-scale, federal-state education program stressing science, math, and foreign languages.

Enacted September 2, 1958, the measure: funded a loan program for needy col-

lege students with ability in science, math, engineering, and modern foreign languages; provided matching grants to the states for public schools and loans to private schools for purchase of instructional equipment; established three-year graduate school fellowships, with preference to students planning to teach at the college level; furnished funding to colleges for establishing advanced programs to train public school teachers in instructing modern foreign languages; and authorized grants to the states to help train individuals for employment as skilled technicians in jobs requiring scientific knowledge. Upon signing the law, Eisenhower stressed it would do much to enhance basic national security. The act's programs, periodically amended and extended, eventually were absorbed by the Department of Education, which was established in 1979.

NATIONAL ENDOWMENT FOR DEMOCRACY (NED) Privately run, federally financed organization launched by the Reagan administration to nurture worldwide development of democratic institutions and values. Congress approved the creation of the endowment in 1983. The NED works by providing funds through its different branches to programs and groups around the world. One NED branch, administrated by the AFL-CIO, seeks to promote the development of free labor movements abroad. The Democratic and Republican parties operate divisions that provide advice and support to foreign political parties with the intent of strengthening democratic electoral processes. The U.S. Chamber of Commerce oversees a branch of the NED that sponsors the development of democratic capitalism in nations undertaking the transition from a command to a market economy. A percentage of the NED budget is earmarked for the funding of smaller groups and one-time projects.

In the mid-1980s the NED lent support to the outlawed Polish union Solidarity and helped fund *La Prensa*, the independent newspaper opposed to the Sandinista government in Nicaragua. It aided in the publication of pro-democracy magazines throughout Eastern Europe and funded nascent democratic movements in the Soviet Union. With the collapse of communism in Eastern Europe and demise of the

USSR in the early 1990s, the NED has moved to help construct democratic institutions in the former Communist bloc. In South Africa the endowment has sought to steer black unions clear of Communist influence and advised them on attracting new members. The NED has provided training in building opposition political strength in Turkey, India, and South Korea and has sponsored voter education, registration, and polling in the fledgling democracies of Guatemala, Grenada, and Chile. The NED has absorbed criticism from both ends of the domestic political spectrum. Liberal detractors have voiced objections to its interference in the internal affairs of other nations while conservatives have charged the White House and Congress with chronic underfunding of the endowment at the very moment democracy was "on the march" worldwide.

NATIONAL FOREIGN INTELLIGENCE BOARD (NFIB) Panel comprising the directors of the federal agencies and bureaus involved in foreign intelligence activities. Chaired by the director of central intelligence, who also heads the CENTRAL INTELLIGENCE AGENCY (CIA), the board is concerned primarily with setting intelligence priorities and coordinating the preparation of foreign intelligence estimates among the various members of the INTELLIGENCE COMMUNITY. In 1946 President HARRY S. TRUMAN established an Intelligence Advisory Board to help direct the newly formed CENTRAL INTELLIGENCE GROUP. It included the chiefs of the intelligence offices of the military services and the State Department. With the creation of the CIA the following year, the board was replaced by the Intelligence Advisory Committee. The advisory body evolved into the basic forum for coordinating the activities of the growing number of federal organizations with a role in foreign intelligence. Its membership was expanded to include representatives from the Atomic Energy Commission, the JOINT CHIEFS OF STAFF, and the FEDERAL BUREAU OF INVESTIGATION. In 1958 the committee was merged with the Communications Intelligence Board to form the United States Intelligence Board (USIB). In 1965 the director of the DEFENSE INTELLIGENCE AGENCY joined the board, replacing the representatives of the Army, Navy, and Air Force intelligence services. The director

of the NATIONAL SECURITY AGENCY (NSA), also a Defense Department entity, remained a member of the body. In 1978 the USIB was reconstituted as the National Foreign Intelligence Board. Other members are the representatives of the departments of Justice and the Treasury and the NATIONAL RECONNAISANCE OFFICE.

NATIONAL FOREIGN TRADE COUNCIL (NFTC) Private U.S. business association established in 1914 in Washington, D.C., to promote American foreign commerce. As a representative of U.S. business interests abroad, the council works for federal economic and commercial policies that will encourage growth of the nation's overseas trade and investment. The NFTC seeks the removal of domestic barriers to foreign trade expansion—grain embargoes, restrictions on U.S. business activities in countries that violate HUMAN RIGHTS, limits on TECHNOLOGY TRANSFER, tax provisions—at the same time it lobbies Washington to pressure foreign governments to relax their protectionist policies and open their markets to American goods and services. The council's members comprise a broad cross-section of American business, from manufacturers, oil and mining companies, and agribusinesses to banks and law firms.

NATIONAL INTELLIGENCE AUTHORITY (NIA) First U.S. national intelligence oversight body. The foreign intelligence requirements of WORLD WAR II prompted the formation in 1942 of the OFFICE OF STRATEGIC SERVICES (OSS), the nation's first centralized intelligence agency. Historically the U.S. government had relied on the State Department for information on developments overseas. The Army and Navy also maintained intelligence offices, but these were concerned primarily with military information. OSS director General WILLIAM J. DONOVAN argued for retention of the intelligence service after the war, but President HARRY S. TRUMAN disbanded the OSS in September 1945. An initial administration plan called for a foreign intelligence office in the State Department. It was supplanted by a Navy proposal to establish a central agency for coordination among the various intelligence services of the military and executive departments. The Navy plan became the basis for a presidential directive on foreign intelligence activities signed by Truman on January 22, 1946.

Truman's directive called for the creation of a National Intelligence Authority to oversee the federal government's intelligence activities related to national security. The NIA was composed of the secretaries of state, war, and navy, and a personal representative of the president. Truman appointed military adviser Admiral WILLIAM D. LEAHY as his liaison. To assist the new intelligence coordination body Truman ordered the formation of a CENTRAL INTELLIGENCE GROUP (CIG) consisting of experts drawn from the intelligence services of the State, War, and Navy departments. The intelligence group's primary function was the correlation and evaluation of intelligence information for the NIA. The position of director of central intelligence (DCI) was designated to head the consolidated intelligence staff. The DCI was aided by an Intelligence Advisory Board made up of the chiefs of the principal military and civilian intelligence agencies. Admiral SIDNEY H. SOUERS, who had helped draft the Navy proposal for the new intelligence arrangement, was named the first DCI.

The development of a central intelligence staff was hindered by interdepartmental rivalries and the CIG's effectiveness was limited. Amid concerns about its ability to respond to the mounting foreign intelligence requirements of the COLD WAR, the CIG was replaced by the CENTRAL INTELLIGENCE AGENCY in the NATIONAL SECURITY ACT of 1947. The NIA was absorbed into the NATIONAL SECURITY COUNCIL, also established under the 1947 legislation.

NATIONAL MILITARY ESTABLISHMENT See **NATIONAL SECURITY ACT**.

NATIONAL ORIGINS ACT See **IMMIGRATION ACT OF 1924**.

NATIONAL RECONNAISSANCE OFFICE (NRO) Organization responsible for managing SATELLITE RECONNAISSANCE for the U.S. INTELLIGENCE COMMUNITY. Among the most secret of American intelligence offices, its existence was not officially acknowledged by the U.S. government until 1992, amid a movement for greater openness in U.S. intelligence operations following the end of the COLD WAR. The NRO reportedly was

formed in 1960 following the downing of an American spy plane over the Soviet Union in the U-2 INCIDENT. Its purpose was to coordinate the fledgling U.S. satellite programs and speed their development. A semi-autonomous office in the Defense Department traditionally headed by the under secretary of the air force, the NRO oversees the procurement, scheduling, and operation of intelligence satellites.

See also NATIONAL TECHNICAL MEANS.

NATIONAL SECURITY ACT (1947) Landmark legislation that established the basic modern U.S. national security structure. In its first century and a half, the United States had favored a policy of ISOLATIONISM, avoiding involvement in alliances and disputes outside the Western Hemisphere. The nation traditionally did not maintain a large military in peacetime. WORLD WAR II and its impact on the global political balance brought significant changes in the American approach to international affairs. The United States emerged from the conflict the world's dominant power. The Truman administration and a bipartisan majority in Congress recognized that the United States would have to assume a leading role in preserving peace in the postwar era. The onset of the COLD WAR fortified arguments for maintaining a strong military capability.

World War II had demonstrated the need for greater coordination between the DEPARTMENT OF WAR and DEPARTMENT OF THE NAVY. During the conflict, America's armed forces were directed primarily by an ad hoc wartime JOINT CHIEFS OF STAFF (JCS) composed of the top Army and Navy officers. With the end of hostilities in August 1945, several proposals were advanced to reorganize the nation's defense establishment. In October 1945 the Navy submitted the Eberstadt Report, prepared by Ferdinand Eberstadt, former chairman of the Army-Navy Munitions Board, to the Senate Military Affairs Committee. The report, against unification of the military services, recommended establishment of a cabinet-level national security council to coordinate defense policy and the continuation of the JCS on a permanent basis. In testimony before the committee the same month, General J. Lawton Collins presented the Army position. The Collins plan advocated a single department of armed forces headed by a civilian secretary and retention of the JCS as a strictly advisory body. Both proposals called for the creation of a separate air force.

In December 1945 President HARRY S. TRUMAN submitted a message to Congress endorsing the establishment of a unified defense department. When strong Navy opposition to unification initially blocked reorganization legislation, Truman in May 1946 instructed Secretary of the Navy JAMES V. FORRESTAL and Secretary of War Robert P. Patterson to work together on a unification plan. Following their collaboration, Truman in January 1947 forwarded to Congress a synthesis of the basic Eberstadt and Collins proposals that, after extensive hearings, became the National Security Act of July 26, 1947.

Title I of the act created three new agencies: the NATIONAL SECURITY COUNCIL (NSC), the CENTRAL INTELLIGENCE AGENCY (CIA), and the National Security Resources Board (NSRB). The NSC was designed as a forum to provide the president with advice on foreign, military, and domestic aspects of national security. In addition to the president, its membership included the secretaries of state, army, and navy; the newly designated secretaries of defense and air force; and the chairman of the NSRB. The organization and composition of the NSC staff, directed by a civilian executive secretary, was left to presidential discretion. The CIA replaced the CENTRAL INTELLIGENCE GROUP as the nation's foreign intelligence service. Title I placed the CIA under the NSC and formalized the position of director of central intelligence. The NSRB was responsible for defense mobilization.

Title II redesignated the Department of War as the DEPARTMENT OF THE ARMY, retained the Department of the Navy, and established the DEPARTMENT OF THE AIR FORCE. The three departments, each under a cabinet-level civilian secretary, were grouped together in the National Military Establishment (NME). The NME, headed by a civilian secretary of defense, represented a compromise between Army and Navy views on unification. The new defense organization brought the armed forces into a single coordinated structure but stopped short of their actual merger. The law defined the secretary of defense as the president's primary assistant on national security issues. The JCS gained statutory authority as the principal military advisers to the nation's top civilian leadership.

The National Security Act reflected the postwar consensus that military and foreign policies were inseparable components of the nation's broad national security activities. The NSC and CIA became integral parts of the U.S. national security establishment. The NME was replaced by a unified DEPARTMENT OF DEFENSE in the NATIONAL SECURITY ACT AMENDMENTS OF 1949.

NATIONAL SECURITY ACT AMENDMENTS OF 1949 Legislation that amended the 1947 NATIONAL SECURITY ACT to establish the DEPARTMENT OF DEFENSE. The landmark 1947 law grew out of the recognition that the changing nature of modern warfare and America's post-WORLD WAR II global military commitments required greater coordination among the nation's uniformed services. The act brought the historically separate and independent Army and Navy departments and the newly created Air Force Department into a single NATIONAL MILITARY ESTABLISHMENT (NME) under the general direction of a newly designated secretary of defense. The NME represented an important step toward unification of the armed services, but stopped short of an actual merger and the three military departments remained essentially autonomous.

In 1947 Congress also formed the Hoover Commission to study the organization and operation of the federal government's executive branch. In December 1948 the commission's Task Force on the National Military Establishment, headed by former Chairman of the Army-Navy Munitions Board Ferdinand Eberstadt, submitted its findings of serious waste and inefficiency in the armed services. The commission's final report in February 1949, concerned with eliminating unnecessary duplication and rivalry among the services, recommended strengthening the authority of the secretary of defense and forming the position of chairman of the JOINT CHIEFS OF STAFF (JCS). First Secretary of Defense JAMES V. FORRESTAL also favored greater centralization as the key to unifying the nation's defense establishment. In March 1949 President HARRY S. TRUMAN sent Congress a proposal for a major reorganization of the military.

The National Security Act Amendments of 1949, signed into law by Truman on August 10, adopted the basic elements of his plan. The amendments converted the NME into the cabinet-level Department of Defense. The secretary of defense gained clear control over the departments of the Army, Navy, and Air Force, which were incorporated into the new defense entity. The secretaries of the three military services, who thereafter were to report to the secretary of defense, lost their cabinet rank and membership on the NATIONAL SECURITY COUNCIL (NSC). The 1949 measure also created the position of chairman of the JCS, designated the joint chiefs as the principal military advisers to the president and secretary of defense, and named the vice-president to the NSC. The basic structure of the U.S. defense establishment next was revised by REORGANIZATION PLAN NO. 6 in 1953.

NATIONAL SECURITY AGENCY (NSA)

U.S. intelligence agency responsible for communications intelligence and security. Officially designated as a separate organization in the Defense Department, the highly secretive NSA monitors foreign electronic communications, such as radio messages, and safeguards similar U.S. national security communications from foreign interception. In 1949 Secretary of Defense LOUIS A. JOHNSON moved to consolidate most of the communications intelligence functions of the three military services into a single Armed Forces Security Agency (AFSA) under the JOINT CHIEFS OF STAFF. Difficulties in agency management, evident in the KOREAN WAR, prompted President HARRY S. TRUMAN to issue a presidential directive in 1952 reorganizing the AFSA as the National Security Agency. Its director, who reported to the secretary of defense, coordinated agency activities with the broader INTELLIGENCE COMMUNITY and later represented the NSA on the NATIONAL FOREIGN INTELLIGENCE BOARD.

The new entity rapidly grew into the largest of the nation's intelligence organizations, with facilities and personnel located worldwide. From its inception, the NSA's principal responsibility was to gather information on developments in the Communist world. Its increasingly sophisticated high-technology interception of radio signals, telephone calls, and other electronic communications provided the U.S. government with the bulk of its raw intelligence on the Soviet Union. In the 1980s the agency became involved in efforts to combat the international drug trade, terrorism, and the spread of nuclear and chemical weapons. With the COLD WAR at an end, senior American policymakers in the early 1990s faced a changing world in which U.S. security increasingly rested as much on economic strength as on armed might. It was suggested in government intelligence circles that the NSA begin to turn its electronic surveillance toward the accumulation of economic information useful to the United States in the mounting international economic competition at the close of the 20th century.

NATIONAL SECURITY COUNCIL   See same in **APPENDIX B**.

NATIONAL TECHNICAL MEANS (NTM)

Term referring to intelligence collection systems used to monitor compliance with arms control agreements. Initial U.S.-Soviet disarmament negotiations in the 1950s deadlocked over the USSR's rejection of provisions for on-site verification. By the early 1960s technological advances made it possible for the two superpowers to reach agreement on the use of remote intelligence methods, such as spy satellites and electronic monitoring devices, to verify each other's adherence to arms control measures. Both sides, however, were reluctant publicly to acknowledge or otherwise discuss their top secret reconnaissance programs. The euphemism "national technical means" was coined to avoid direct reference to the remote intelligence systems. The expression first appeared in the 1963 LIMITED TEST BAN TREATY. NTM were designated the official method of verification for the ABM TREATY (1972), SALT I (1972) and SALT II (1979) arms control pacts, and THRESHOLD TEST BAN TREATY (1974). Agreements dependent on NTM verification include clauses committing the signatories not to interfere with each other's satellites or other relevant intelligence means. In the 1980s the Reagan administration revived U.S. emphasis upon on-site verification. The 1987 INTERMEDIATE NUCLEAR FORCES

TREATY marked the first arms control measure with on-site verification provisions.

NATO See **NORTH ATLANTIC TREATY ORGANIZATION** in **APPENDIX C**.

NATURALIZATION ACT OF 1790 Law passed by Congress establishing how aliens could become citizens in the new nation. Enacted March 26, 1790, the measure was meant to standardize the rules for naturalization among the various states and to signal the young republic's openness to immigration. The act set a two-year residency requirement and limited naturalization to "free white persons." The Naturalization Act of 1795 changed the residency requirement to five years. This was expanded to 14 years by the Naturalization Act of 1798, one of the ALIEN AND SEDITION ACTS. The residency period reverted to five years under the Naturalization Act of 1802 and ever since this has remained the basic time requirement.

The racial exclusion did not change until after the Civil War. Congress in 1870 extended the right to naturalization to "aliens of African nativity and to persons of African descent." In 1922 the Supreme Court ruled in OZAWA V. UNITED STATES that Asians and other aliens who were neither white nor African were ineligible for U.S. citizenship. Recognition that discriminatory naturalization practices violated American ideals and undermined the nation's international stature led to the repeal of all racial restrictions on naturalization in the IMMIGRATION AND NATIONALITY ACT OF 1952.

NAVY, DEPARTMENT OF THE See **DEPARTMENT OF THE NAVY** in **APPENDIX B**.

NEOISOLATIONISM See **ISOLATIONISM**.

NEUTRALITY ACTS Series of four acts defining U.S. neutrality amid the mounting international hostilities of the late 1930s and early 1940s. By 1935, the belligerency of Fascist Germany and Italy in Europe, as well as Japanese aggression in Asia, had produced a movement in the U.S. Congress for neutrality legislation to keep America out of foreign wars. Reinforcing traditional American ISOLATIONISM were reports of the Senate NYE COMMITTEE (1934–1936) that suggested U.S. loans to the Allies and other circumventions of American neutrality had drawn the nation into WORLD WAR I. Isolationist and peace groups believed a carefully drawn neutrality law could prevent U.S. entanglement in another overseas conflict. In August 1935 Congress completed work on the first Neutrality Act. The law required a mandatory embargo on "arms, ammunition, or implements of war" to all belligerents in overseas conflicts, restricted U.S. citizens from traveling on belligerent vessels, and established a Munitions Control Board to oversee arms shipments. President FRANKLIN D. ROOSEVELT, who had favored leaving to presidential discretion the authority to embargo arms only to aggressor nations rather than all belligerents, reluctantly signed the Neutrality Act of 1935 into law on August 31. The president nonetheless was given the key power of deciding when foreign hostilities constituted a state of war subject to the legislation's provisions. Planning to return to the question of neutrality in its next session, Congress scheduled the act to expire in six months.

When Italy invaded Ethiopia in October 1935, Roosevelt applied the Neutrality Act, thus prohibiting arms exports to either belligerent. On October 30 the president called for a "moral embargo" on any American trade or commerce with the warring nations. Roosevelt's appeal represented an indirect attempt to curtail Italy's aggression through economic sanctions. The suggested trade embargo bore minor relevance to Ethiopia since the United States had no meaningful economic relations with the African country. Congress considered further neutrality legislation against the backdrop of the Italo-Ethiopian War. The Neutrality Act of 1936, adopted February 29, 1936, revised and extended the 1935 measure until May 1, 1937. A new amendment forbade loans or credits to belligerents. Roosevelt continued to press the "moral embargo" in the Italo-Ethiopian War, but Italy sealed its victory with the capture of Ethiopian capital Addis Ababa in May 1936. The following month, with the war over, the United States lifted its arms embargo but announced it would not recognize the Italian conquest of Ethiopia.

In July 1936 civil war erupted in Spain. Although the 1936 Neutrality Act did not apply to such internal strife, the Roosevelt administration in August declared American neutrality in the conflict and again called for a "moral embargo." On January 8, 1937, Roosevelt signed a congressional resolution formally prohibiting the sale of U.S. armaments to either side in the civil war. Supporters of the Loyalist government in Spain complained to no avail that the measure aided the Nationalist rebels under General Francisco Franco, who were receiving aid from the German and Italian governments. The Roosevelt administration defended the legislation as consistent with U.S. noninterventionist policy. The third Neutrality Act, adopted May 1, 1937, extended the mandatory arms embargo to instances of civil strife found by the president to weaken U.S. security. The 1937 law renewed indefinitely the provisions of the earlier measures and introduced the concept of cash-and-carry. The term referred to the requirement that belligerents purchasing non-military commodities in the United States pay for the items in cash and transport them from America in foreign ships. The Roosevelt administration supported the additional provision, believing it would favor Great Britain and France, with their powerful navies, in the event of war.

When fighting broke out between China and Japan in July 1937, Roosevelt decided against invoking the Neutrality Act of 1937. The president believed official American neutrality in the undeclared Sino-Japanese war would have aided Japan with its larger merchant marine. By 1939, with war looming in Europe, Roosevelt sought revisions in the neutrality law that would allow America more leeway to take steps "short of war" to assist other democratic governments resist Fascist aggression. His administration's efforts were blocked by the isolationist strength in Congress. Following the outbreak of WORLD WAR II in Europe in September 1939, Roosevelt announced American neutrality and imposed an arms embargo, but called a special session of Congress to amend U.S. neutrality legislation. The president argued that permitting Great Britain and France to purchase U.S. arms represented the best chance of keeping America out of war because it would help prevent a German victory that could imperil U.S. security. The Neutrality Act of 1939, enacted November 4, ended mandatory arms embargoes and

empowered the president to sanction cash-and-carry sales of armaments to belligerents. Under the revised law U.S. munitions began to flow to Great Britain and France. With the United States increasingly committed to the support of Great Britain, Congress passed legislation effectively rescinding U.S. neutrality laws that Roosevelt signed on November 17, 1941, just three weeks before the Japanese attack at PEARL HARBOR brought America into the global conflict.

NEUTRALITY PROCLAMATION (1793) Declaration by President GEORGE WASHINGTON of U.S. neutrality in the war between France and Great Britain. France's declaration of war against Great Britain, Spain, and Holland in February 1793 transformed the French Revolutionary Wars (1792–1802) from a continental European conflict into a larger maritime struggle reaching across the Atlantic to the Caribbean Sea and along American shores. When news of the French war declaration reached America in April, Washington and his cabinet convened to confront the question of whether the United States should become involved on either side.

U.S. policy toward revolutionary France had become a divisive issue in American politics in the early 1790s. The French Revolution initially attracted enthusiastic sympathy in America from a public that recalled French support for the United States during the AMERICAN REVOLUTION and that equated the French struggle against monarchy with America's fight for independence from the British. Increasing revolutionary violence by 1793 had begun to erode pro-French sentiment in the United States, drawing the condemnation of Federalists, who were alarmed by the bloody excesses in France known as the Reign of Terror. Despite the guillotine's mounting toll, Democratic-Republicans remained solidly pro-French and continued to endorse the revolution's avowed commitment to liberty, democratic principles, and republican government.

The Washington administration decided that the United States should stay out of the conflict and adopt a policy of strict neutrality. The president was worried that French actions in early 1793 threatened to draw America into the war against the

British. Already French agents in the United States were engaged in possible provocations: commissioning American shipowners and outfitting their vessels as privateers to plunder British wartime shipping; and recruiting U.S. citizens to serve with the French military. Washington, backed by a vote of his cabinet, issued the Neutrality Proclamation on April 22, 1793. Declaring the United States at peace with both the British and French, the neutrality directive called for impartial American conduct toward the warring European powers. It warned that American citizens who took part in hostilities against any of the belligerents would get no protection from the United States and would face prosecution and punishment for actions committed within the jurisdiction of American courts.

At the urging of Secretary of State THOMAS JEFFERSON, the proclamation avoided the word "neutrality"; Jefferson suggested that omission of the word might induce Great Britain to offer more favorable trade terms in order to be certain the United States stayed out of the war. Despite this diplomatic sleight of hand, the British and French recognized the American declaration as an unambiguous statement of neutrality. Democratic-Republican critics, led by JAMES MADISON, denounced the proclamation as a betrayal of America's republican allies in France. They also accused Washington of having overstepped his executive powers. Since the CONSTITUTION gave Congress power to declare war, it was argued, only Congress could declare neutrality.

The proclamation did not resolve the issue of U.S. treaty obligations to the French. Washington anticipated that France might seek to involve the United States by invoking the FRANCO-AMERICAN ALLIANCE (1778), which committed America, if called upon, to defend France's West Indies in time of war. The TREATY OF AMITY AND COMMERCE (1778) permitted French privateers to bring captured property, referred to as "prizes," into American ports and barred France's enemies from outfitting privateers in the United States. Federalist Treasury Secretary ALEXANDER HAMILTON advised Washington that the French treaties were no longer in effect since the government with which they had been completed, the French monarchy, had been overthrown. Democratic-Republican Jefferson contended that the treaties were covenants between nations rather than between particular governments and thus remained in force despite the changes brought by the French Revolution. The president sided with Jefferson and accepted the treaties as still binding.

France, in fact, decided against invoking the alliance. The United States had no navy and could add little militarily to the French maritime war effort. America's greater value to France was as a neutral trade partner able to carry goods between France and the French West Indies under protection of FREEDOM OF THE SEAS. The French Republic did seek an interpretation of the 1778 commerce treaty that would let it freely arm privateers and sell prizes in American ports. Jefferson provided the president the rationale for denying the French. The secretary of state claimed that while the agreement did close American waters to the privateers of French adversaries, it did not thereby automatically grant French privateers the privileges coveted by the French government. Revolutionary France objected to the narrow U.S. treaty interpretation. Franco-American differences over the privateering issue flared during the diplomatic turmoil of the GENET AFFAIR, wherein French Minister to the United States Edmond C. Genet openly challenged Washington's neutrality order. Various executive orders further defining the obligations of American neutrality were brought together in the Neutrality Act of 1794.

NEUTRALITY PROCLAMATIONS (1914) Decrees issued by President WOODROW WILSON proclaiming U.S. neutrality in WORLD WAR I. American isolationist sentiment opposed U.S. involvement in the conflict, which broke out in Europe in early August 1914. From the outset, Wilson embraced a policy of strict U.S. impartiality. Between August 4 and November 6, 1914, as the war expanded in and beyond Europe, Wilson issued a total of 10 proclamations declaring U.S. neutrality toward the various combatants, who were organized in two rival alliances: the Central Powers of Germany, Austria-Hungary, Bulgaria, and Turkey; and the Allied Powers of Great Britain, France, Italy, Russia, and Japan. The proclamations attempted to define activities for which Americans and foreign nationals could be prosecuted under existing U.S. neutrality laws or face expulsion from the United States. The deadly toll exacted by Germany's unrestricted submarine warfare on American shipping overshadowed British infringement of U.S. neutral rights at sea and finally led the United States to enter the war in April 1917.

NEW LOOK Name given to the defense policy adopted by the Eisenhower administration. In the aftermath of WORLD WAR II, American policymakers were preoccupied with the question of how to respond to the threat posed by the Soviet Union to Western European security. By the late 1940s, the United States had undertaken a policy of CONTAINMENT of Soviet expansionism. This policy rested increasingly on the DETERRENCE of possible Soviet aggression through U.S. military strength. Following the outbreak in June 1950 of the KOREAN WAR, viewed in the United States as an extension of a Soviet-sponsored Communist drive for world domination, President HARRY S. TRUMAN initiated a major buildup in both the nation's nuclear arsenal and its traditional, or conventional, non-nuclear forces.

President DWIGHT D. EISENHOWER took office in January 1953 committed to reducing defense expenditures. While Eisenhower supported a powerful military, he insisted that national economic strength was essential to U.S. security and should not be put at risk through excessive defense spending. In July 1953 he ordered a top-level review of the nation's overall military strategy. That October the NATIONAL SECURITY COUNCIL (NSC) adopted the broad outlines of a basic shift in U.S. defense thinking. The council accepted the premise that future wars likely would involve NUCLEAR WEAPONS. Acknowledging the deterrent value and immense destructive power of advanced nuclear arms, the NSC approved a greater emphasis on both strategic and tactical nuclear forces. As later explained by Secretary of State JOHN FOSTER DULLES, America would rely on its capacity for MASSIVE RETALIATION with nuclear weapons to deter Communist aggression around the world. Despite Army and Navy misgivings about pending cuts in their budgets, the Eisenhower administration held to the view that battlefield or tactical nuclear weapons

were a more effective and less expensive alternative to conventional forces.

In remarks at the Press Club in Washington in December 1953, Chairman of the JOINT CHIEFS OF STAFF Admiral Arthur W. Radford referred to the administration's "New Look" defense policy. The term, originally coined to describe a women's fashion trend, quickly stuck. Eisenhower formally presented the New Look in his January 1954 State of the Union address. The policy had several major elements: a general reliance on nuclear weapons; a reduction in conventional ground and naval forces; and an emphasis on economy and long-range defense planning over the "long haul."

The New Look came under increasing scrutiny. National security strategists such as HENRY A. KISSINGER observed that the impending Soviet achievement of nuclear parity with the United States would undermine the general deterrent value of U.S. nuclear weapons. If either superpower could destroy the other, then any threat of nuclear retaliation carried with it the risk of triggering a catastrophic nuclear war. The threat of a nuclear response made sense only to defend vital national interests and to deter the other side from launching a nuclear attack. By 1957, the Eisenhower administration had modified its approach to nuclear deterrence in what became known as the New New Look. Under the revised policy, the United States based its nuclear deterrence on "sufficient" rather than "superior" forces.

Criticism of the New Look mounted during Eisenhower's second term. Former Army Chief of Staff MAXWELL D. TAYLOR and Senators LYNDON B. JOHNSON and JOHN F. KENNEDY among others argued that the policy, with its emphasis on nuclear weapons at the expense of conventional forces, left the United States without the ability to fight in local or limited wars. President Kennedy replaced the New Look with a FLEXIBLE RESPONSE strategy that called for a balanced mix of nuclear and conventional forces to enable a U.S. response to conflicts ranging from guerrilla insurgency to all-out nuclear attack.

NEW MANIFEST DESTINY See **MANIFEST DESTINY**.

NEW YORK TIMES V. UNITED STATES See **PENTAGON PAPERS**.

NEW YORK, TREATY OF (1790) Signed August 7, 1790, by Secretary of War HENRY KNOX and Creek Chief ALEXANDER McGILLIVRAY, this treaty briefly established peaceful relations between the United States and the Creek Indian Nation. Indian hostilities in the southeast, ignited by Georgia's disregard for Creek territorial claims, threatened the U.S. plan for an orderly and peaceful expansion of the southern frontier. Already faced with Indian warfare in the Ohio region, President GEORGE WASHINGTON was determined to avoid a costly confrontation in the southeast. He persuaded McGillivray to come to New York for peace talks.

By terms of the 1790 treaty, the Creeks recognized U.S. sovereignty and McGillivray ceded large tribal territories in Georgia to the federal government. The United States in turn arranged an annuity for the land cession. McGillivray also signed a secret deal that commissioned him as a U.S. brigadier general with a yearly salary. Improved relations lasted until the Creek chief repudiated the New York agreement in 1792 and accepted an appointment as Spain's representative to the tribe.

NEZ PERCE WAR (1877) Also called Chief Joseph's Uprising, the Nez Perce War originated in U.S. efforts in the 1870s to remove the Indian tribe to a small Idaho reservation. In the Stevens Treaty (1855) the Nez Perce had agreed to cede much of their homeland in the region where Idaho, Oregon, and Washington converge in exchange for the promise of a large reservation in Idaho and Oregon. After the discovery of gold in the early 1860s on Nez Perce territory, the U.S. government pressured the tribe to relinquish more lands and to accept a smaller reservation. Some Nez Perce acceded. But bands under Nez Perce CHIEF JOSEPH resisted the American plan and fighting broke out in 1877 when U.S. troops were sent in to dislodge them. Greatly overmatched, Joseph led his followers on an extraordinary 1500-mile retreat from the pursuing U.S. Army toward Canada. The Nez Perce chief was forced to surrender on October 5, 1877, 30 miles short of the Canadian border in Montana. The Nez Perce were sent to a reservation the following year.

See also MAP 1.

NICARAGUA v. UNITED STATES (1986) Case brought before the WORLD COURT by Nicaragua asserting illegal U.S. involvement in efforts to overthrow its government. In the early 1980s the Reagan administration, strongly opposed to the leftist Sandinista regime that had come to power in Managua in 1979, began furnishing military and economic aid to the CONTRAS, antigovernment Nicaraguan rebels based primarily in neighboring Honduras. After U.S. officials acknowledged that CENTRAL INTELLIGENCE AGENCY operatives had assisted in the recent Contra mining of Nicaraguan ports, the Sandinista government on April 9, 1984, asked the World Court to declare U.S. support to the Contra guerrillas a violation of international law and order it halted. The United States accused Nicaragua of attempting to use the U.N. tribunal for propaganda purposes and therefore refused to accept the court's jurisdiction in the matter. On November 26, 1984, the court accepted Nicaragua's suit, maintaining that the 1946 agreement under which the United States had consented to the tribunal's compulsory jurisdiction required six months' notification of termination. The United States refused to participate in the ensuing legal proceedings. President RONALD W. REAGAN on October 7, 1985, announced that America formally was withdrawing its recognition of the World Court's automatic jurisdiction in international political cases. On June 27, 1986, the court ruled that the United States had broken international law and violated Nicaraguan sovereignty by aiding the Contra guerrilla campaign and directed U.S. payment of compensation for damages caused by military action. The U.S. State Department rejected the verdict.

NICARAGUAN INTERVENTIONS U.S. military and political interventions in Nicaragua in the 20th century. In October 1909 a revolt broke out against Nicaraguan dictator Jose Santos Zelaya, whose opposition to U.S. diplomatic interjection in Central America had made him a nemesis of Washington. The Taft administration held Zelaya responsible for fomenting unrest in the region and considered him generally hostile to American business interests in his country. President WILLIAM HOWARD TAFT and Secretary of State PHILANDER C. KNOX denounced the dictator's aggressions against his neighbors and repressive domestic rule as impediments to their attempts at promoting regional peace and stability within the context of the CENTRAL AMERICAN TREATIES OF 1907. Deploring Zelaya's regime as a threat to such a peace, Knox in December 1909 broke off formal relations with the Nicaraguan government. Under mounting rebel pressure, Zelaya in mid-December resigned and went into exile. The insurgents pressed their fight and finally gained control of the country in August 1910.

Zelaya's ouster came as a welcome development for the Taft administration's policy of DOLLAR DIPLOMACY in Latin America. Knox believed Nicaraguan political stability depended on that nation's financial rehabilitation, which he wanted to see effected through loans to Managua from American bankers. Under a scheme he outlined, repayment of the loans would be guaranteed by a U.S.-controlled customs receivership in Nicaragua. Following completion of the U.S.-devised DAWSON AGREEMENTS (1910), Adolfo Diaz emerged as Nicaragua's new president in May 1911. He appealed for American help in stabilizing his country's chronically troubled public finances. Washington and Managua thereupon negotiated the KNOX-CASTRILLO CONVENTION (1911), which provided for American stewardship over Nicaraguan finances. When Nicaragua shortly thereafter defaulted on a debt to British lenders, the Taft administration persuaded American bankers to assume control of the Central American nation's financial matters by effectively implementing terms of the still-unratified convention. Taft and Knox wanted to head off a situation in which European powers might feel compelled to intervene in Nicaragua in violation of the ROOSEVELT COROLLARY (1904) to reclaim their investments. The bankers made a loan to the Nicaraguan government, established a customs receivership, and negotiated a repayment plan with Nicaragua's European creditors. Despite the U.S. Senate's rejection in May 1912 of the Knox-Castrillo treaty, American bankers, with the State Department's endorsement, continued to exercise a virtual protectorate over Nicaragua's finances.

When a revolt broke out against his Conservative government in July 1912, Diaz pleaded for U.S. armed intervention. Taft responded promptly by sending 2500 marines into Nicaragua to suppress the rebellion and bolster Diaz's position. A small detachment of U.S. troops remained in the country on a permanent basis to deter further political unrest. After WOODROW WILSON succeeded Taft in 1913, Diaz approached the new U.S. administration seeking financial relief for his nation's shaky treasury. Ensuing negotiations produced the BRYAN-CHAMORRO TREATY (1914), which granted the United States territorial concessions and exclusive canal rights in Nicaragua in return for $3 million. The U.S. government orchestrated the selection of Conservative successors to Diaz in 1917 and 1921.

Sensitive to growing hostility throughout Latin America toward "Yankee IMPERIALISM," Secretary of State CHARLES EVANS HUGHES grew eager in the early 1920s to end America's military interventions in Nicaragua and elsewhere in the Caribbean region. Following the election and inauguration of Conservative Carlos Solorzano as president, the U.S. marines withdrew from Nicaragua in August 1925. A successful intra-party revolt in October led by Conservative Emiliano Chamorro brought renewed political disorder to the Central American country. After Chamorro became president in January 1926, the opposition Liberals launched an insurrection. Under U.S. pressure, Chamorro resigned in October 1926 and was succeeded by Adolfo Diaz, who returned to power with Washington's backing. The worsening civil war led President CALVIN COOLIDGE to order the marines back to Nicaragua, where they landed in early 1927. Coolidge and Secretary of State FRANK B. KELLOGG then dispatched HENRY L. STIMSON to Nicaragua with instructions to mediate the conflict. After meeting with both Diaz and Liberal leaders, Stimson worked out a political accommodation on May 12, 1927. Concluded at the Nicaraguan village of Tipitapa, the so-called Peace of Tipitapa arranged for Diaz to complete his term, the Liberal rebels to disarm, the United States to supervise a new national election, and the American marines to organize and train an indigenous constabulary. Liberal General Jose M. Moncada won the November 1928 election and became president. Washington chose Anastasio Somoza Garcia to head the constabulary, known as the National Guard.

Meanwhile another Liberal leader, General Augustino Sandino, had rejected the Tipitapa settlement and organized a determined guerrilla resistance in the north to the U.S. marine occupation force. He and his followers were forced to take haven for a time in Mexico after Moncada's election victory. In 1931, Sandino launched another revolt, which the National Guard and U.S. occupation forces effectively suppressed by 1933. That same year the U.S. marines were withdrawn from Nicaragua following the inauguration of Liberal Juan Sacasa as Moncada's successor. In 1934 Somoza's National Guard assassinated Sandino in Managua during negotiations between the rebels and the government. After seizing leadership of the Liberal party and engineering Sacasa's overthrow, Somoza assumed the presidency in 1937, establishing a military dictatorship.

See also CONTRAS.

NINE-POWER TREATY (1922) Agreement reached at the WASHINGTON NAVAL CONFERENCE (1921–1922) guaranteeing the sovereignty, independence, and territorial integrity of China. By the early 20th century the major European powers had extracted various commercial and related territorial concessions from the weak Chinese Manchu dynasty. Japan took advantage of WORLD WAR I to attack and seize German holdings in China's Shantung Province. Though sanctioned by its wartime allies Great Britain, France, and Russia, Japan's action drew opposition from the United States. After America entered the war in April 1917, Washington and Tokyo concluded the LANSING-ISHII AGREEMENT, which recognized Japan's "special interests" in China while reaffirming mutual U.S.-Japanese respect for the independence and integrity of China and the OPEN DOOR principle of equal trade access for outside powers in the giant Asian nation. The PARIS PEACE CONFERENCE (1919) allowed Japan to keep the former German concession, or sphere of influence, in Shantung, but required that Japanese troops be withdrawn from the province.

When the world's major naval powers—the United States, Great Britain, France, Italy, and Japan—convened in Washington in 1921 to discuss naval disarmament, the question of China's status remained a pressing issue. Great Britain, France, and Japan were concerned to preserve their existing spheres of influence,

while the United States was committed to maintaining the Open Door policy. Because Far Eastern questions were included in the conference agenda, the Netherlands, Belgium, Portugal, and China also attended. On February 6, 1922, all nine participants reached agreement on a pact regarding China. The Nine-Power Treaty recognized China's sovereignty and independence; upheld the Open Door principle; and bound its signatories not to seek special rights or privileges for their citizens in China.

While guaranteeing Chinese integrity and the Open Door, the agreement left intact the various spheres of influence in China. Because the pact incorporated the key provisions of the Lansing-Ishii Agreement, the United States and Japan formally canceled the earlier understanding the following year. The United States protested the Japanese seizure of Manchuria in 1931 as a violation of the treaty. Japan's 1937 invasion of China drew similar condemnation at the BRUSSELS CONFERENCE (1937). The contest over China and the deteriorating situation in the Far East culminated in WORLD WAR II.

NITZE, PAUL HENRY (1907–   ) Senior State and Defense department official, arms control negotiator. Nitze was born in Amherst, Massachusetts. He graduated from Harvard in 1928 and the following year joined the Wall Street investment banking firm Dillon, Read and Company. During WORLD WAR II he held a succession of top government economic posts in Washington. Following the war he remained in government service, accepting the position in 1946 of deputy director of the office of international trade policy in the State Department. He helped formulate the MARSHALL PLAN (1948) for postwar European economic recovery. From 1950 to 1953 he was director of the department's policy planning staff, where he chaired an interdepartmental committee charged with reviewing U.S. foreign and defense policy. The study group's influential report, NSC-68 (1950), provided the framework for the Truman administration's subsequent defense buildup in support of its strategy of CONTAINMENT of Communist aggression.

Nitze left office with the Truman administration in January 1953. He remained active in foreign affairs, serving as president of the private Foreign Service Education Foundation and as an adviser to the 1957 GAITHER COMMITTEE on U.S. strategic forces. In 1961 President JOHN F. KENNEDY appointed Nitze assistant secretary of defense for international security affairs. He became Navy secretary in 1963 and deputy secretary of defense in 1967, remaining in the post until President LYNDON B. JOHNSON left office in January 1969.

The same year President RICHARD M. NIXON named him a member of the U.S. delegation to strategic arms control discussions with the Soviet Union. Nitze assisted in the successful negotiation of the 1972 SALT I arms control agreements before returning to private life in 1974. In 1976 he helped found the COMMITTEE ON THE PRESENT DANGER, a private bipartisan advocacy group concerned with allegedly declining U.S. defenses in the face of a mounting Soviet military buildup. He became a leading critic of the 1979 SALT II arms control accord, which he contended left U.S. strategic nuclear forces at a dangerous disadvantage, and was an adviser to Republican candidate RONALD W. REAGAN during the 1980 presidential campaign. In 1981 President Reagan brought Nitze out of retirement to head the American negotiating team at U.S.-Soviet arms control talks in Geneva, Switzerland. In 1982 he was involved in the abortive WALK IN THE WOODS agreement to limit intermediate-range nuclear missiles. Nitze stepped down from his full-time position in 1984 but continued as a special adviser on arms control until 1989.

NIXON DOCTRINE (1969) Statement of U.S. policy meant to guide American military involvement in armed conflicts in the THIRD WORLD. President RICHARD M. NIXON introduced the Nixon Doctrine, also known as the Guam Doctrine, at a news conference held July 25, 1969, during a stopover on Guam at the outset of an eight-nation tour of Asia and Europe. The doctrine outlined the parameters of U.S. support for non-Communist governments under Communist attack. Unless another major power intervened, America would not commit combat forces to the hostilities. The United States would furnish military and economic aid to friendly states as necessary to defeat Soviet-sponsored insurgencies, but the country under attack had to do its own

fighting. If a nation was unable or unwilling to defend itself, Nixon contended, then direct U.S. intervention would make little difference.

Nixon's pronouncement was viewed widely as a recognition that the United States needed to curtail and reconfigure its global defense commitments. America's difficult Vietnam experience formed the context for the Nixon dictum. Domestic opposition to the protracted U.S. involvement in the VIETNAM WAR had mounted in the late 1960s. In his first months in office, Nixon had initiated a policy of VIETNAMIZATION, which called for a gradual U.S. troop withdrawal as South Vietnamese forces assumed more and more of the combat burden. Although formulated as a general rule for U.S. involvement worldwide, the Nixon Doctrine was interpreted to apply primarily to Asia. It maintained the U.S. nuclear umbrella in the Pacific and provided for continued U.S. military and economic contributions toward Southeast Asian and Japanese defense. Nixon informed America's Asian allies they would have to assume primary responsibility for defending themselves in a land war. He said the shift in America's defense policy would await the end of the Vietnam War and would not compromise U.S. treaty obligations.

Nixon believed that after Vietnam the United States would be unwilling to commit its troops against guerrilla forces. He insisted his policy did not represent a disengagement from the Third World, but instead outlined a realistic basis for continued American involvement in efforts to halt Communist aggression. In the 1980s, U.S. assistance to the Salvadoran government during the EL SALVADOR CIVIL WAR was cited as an example of the Nixon Doctrine at work.

NIXON, RICHARD MILHOUS (1913–   ) U.S. representative, senator, vice-president, 37th president of the United States. A native of California, Nixon graduated from Whittier College in 1934 and Duke Law School in 1937. He passed the California bar and entered private practice in his hometown of Whittier. During WORLD WAR II he served as a naval officer in the Pacific. Nixon was elected to the House of Representatives as a Republican from California in 1946 and reelected in 1948. He supported the TRUMAN DOCTRINE (1947) committing the United States to the CONTAINMENT of Soviet expansionism and served on the HERTER COMMITTEE that helped formulate the MARSHALL PLAN (1948), the program of massive U.S. economic aid for the postwar reconstruction of Europe. As a member of the HOUSE UN-AMERICAN ACTIVITIES COMMITTEE, he rose to national prominence for his role in the HISS CASE involving charges of Communist espionage against former State Department official ALGER HISS. Nixon's determined investigation of Hiss, who was convicted in 1950 of perjury, cemented his reputation as a leading anti-Communist but also earned him the lasting enmity of liberals and others who believed Hiss the victim of a witch-hunt.

In 1950 he won election to the U.S. Senate. He backed the Truman administration's decision to intervene in the KOREAN WAR but criticized its conduct of the Asian conflict as too restrained and scored President HARRY S. TRUMAN when he dismissed U.S. wartime commander General DOUGLAS MACARTHUR in 1951. The following year Republican presidential nominee DWIGHT D. EISENHOWER selected Nixon as his running mate. The ticket swept to victory in the general election and won a second term in 1956. As vice-president, Nixon traveled extensively, visiting some 54 countries and developing his reputation as a student of foreign affairs. In 1958 he received high marks for his handling of the CARACAS EPISODE, in which he came under attack by anti-American demonstrators while on a goodwill trip to Venezuela. During a visit to the Soviet Union in 1959, he exchanged views with Soviet leader Nikita S. Khrushchev in their celebrated "KITCHEN DEBATE" on the relative merits of their nations' political systems. In 1960 Nixon gained the Republican presidential nomination before losing to Democrat JOHN F. KENNEDY in a close race. In 1962 he was defeated in a bid for the governorship of California. Nixon returned to private law practice but remained active in Republican politics. In 1968 he again captured the Republican nomination and was elected president over Democratic standard-bearer Hubert H. Humphrey.

Nixon entered the White House in January 1969 eager to reshape U.S. foreign policy. He appointed as national security adviser Harvard professor HENRY A. KISSINGER, who shared his views on the need to streamline an entrenched foreign affairs bureaucracy to allow for innovative and decisive policy-making. With Nixon's backing, Kissinger centralized the formulation of U.S. foreign policy within the White House. Both men believed effective diplomacy rested on the exercise of power rather than abstract ideals. Nixon fashioned a foreign policy based on a pragmatic approach to world affairs.

The most pressing problem facing the new president was the VIETNAM WAR. Nixon had campaigned in 1968 on a platform of ending America's involvement in the increasingly unpopular conflict in a way that attained "peace with honor." He recognized that the United States could not gain a military victory in Vietnam but opposed a unilateral U.S. withdrawal that abandoned Saigon or undermined confidence in America's worldwide defense commitments. The new administration adopted a policy of VIETNAMIZATION, whereby South Vietnamese forces would be trained and equipped to assume reponsibility for the ground fighting as the American military gradually withdrew from Indochina. From a strength of 540,000 in 1969, U.S. troop levels in Southeast Asia were cut to 25,000 by the end of 1972. Vietnamization became part of a new U.S. strategy for the containment of Communist aggression in the THIRD WORLD, announced by Nixon in July 1969. Under the NIXON DOCTRINE, America would furnish military and economic aid to friendly nations facing leftist insurgencies, but the country under attack was expected to do its own fighting.

Nixon continued U.S. participation in the PARIS PEACE TALKS with Communist North Vietnam that had begun under predecessor LYNDON B. JOHNSON. With negotiations at a stalemate, he authorized Kissinger to begin secret discussions in August 1969 with North Vietnamese representatives in Paris. In 1970 U.S. and South Vietnamese forces struck at Communist sanctuaries along the border in neutral Cambodia. Domestic critics accused the Nixon administration of a further widening of the war. The president defended the CAMBODIAN INCURSION as necessary to protect U.S. troops and ensure the success of Vietnamization. He similarly approved the controversial LAOTIAN INCURSION in 1971.

Throughout his first term Nixon staved off efforts by a growing antiwar movement in Congress to enact legislation terminating American involvement in Vietnam. In March 1972, with U.S. ground forces largely having exited, North Vietnam launched a massive assault against the South. In response to the EASTERTIDE OFFENSIVE, Nixon resumed U.S. bombing of the North and directed the mining of its key ports. In October 1972 Kissinger announced a tentative peace settlement. When final peace talks stalled, Nixon ordered the CHRISTMAS BOMBING to force Hanoi back to the negotiating table. In January 1973 Kissinger and North Vietnamese envoy Le Duc Tho concluded the PARIS PEACE ACCORDS providing for a cease-fire and ending the long U.S. military intervention in Vietnam. Nixon and Congress subsequently clashed over a continued American role in Southeast Asia. The CASE-CHURCH AMENDMENT (1973) barred future U.S. military operations in Indochina. The WAR POWERS RESOLUTION, passed over Nixon's veto in November 1973, restricted the president's ability to commit U.S. forces to hostilities without congressional authorization.

Long identified with hardline anti-Communist policies, Nixon stunned many observers with his dramatic reorientation of U.S. COLD WAR foreign policy toward a more pragmatic accommodation with the Communist bloc. He concluded that the Soviet Union's emergence as a nuclear superpower necessitated East-West negotiation rather than confrontation. Guided by realism rather than moralism, he sought to engage the Kremlin in a BALANCE OF POWER arrangement that would enhance international peace and stability by recognizing each side's vital security concerns. Nixon also believed it unwise and unrealistic for the United States to continue refusing to recognize the existence of Communist China. On taking office he discreetly signaled America's readiness to end its two-decade-long isolation of the Communist nation. When Peking responded favorably, Nixon dispatched Kissinger on a secret mission to Communist China in 1971 to open top-level contacts. The president stunned the world when he announced in July 1971 that he would visit mainland China the fol-

lowing year. Nixon met with Chinese leaders Mao Tse-tung and Chou En-lai at the historic 1972 PEKING SUMMIT. The SHANGHAI COMMUNIQUE issued at the end of the parley guided the subsequent normalization of U.S.-Chinese relations.

Nixon pursued a policy of DETENTE with the Soviet Union. In 1969 the two sides began bilateral strategic arms control negotiations. In 1970 the two superpowers spearheaded conclusion of the multilateral SEABED ARMS CONTROL TREATY banning NUCLEAR WEAPONS from the ocean floor. In 1972 Nixon journeyed to the USSR for the landmark MOSCOW SUMMIT. At the gathering he and Soviet leader Leonid I. Brezhnev signed the SALT I arms control agreement and a series of trade, cultural, and scientific measures. The meeting underscored a remarkable improvement in U.S.-Soviet relations and marked a period of enhanced East-West ties lasting through the decade. Nixon and Brezhnev conferred again at the 1973 WASHINGTON SUMMIT and 1974 MOSCOW SUMMIT.

The Nixon White House in 1971 was confronted with a worsening American economy. High U.S. inflation made it increasingly difficult to maintain the dollar at a set gold value. In August 1971 Nixon announced the United States would no longer keep the dollar on a gold standard. His action ended the fixed currency exchange rate system that had served as the basis of the international monetary structure since the 1944 BRETTON WOODS CONFERENCE. In December 1971 the leading members of the INTERNATIONAL MONETARY FUND met in Washington and concluded the SMITHSONIAN AGREEMENT establishing a revised international monetary policy.

Nixon won reelection by a landslide over Democrat George S. McGovern in 1972. His presidency was soon rocked, however, by the growing Watergate scandal, involving a White House cover-up of an illegal break-in at the Democratic National Headquarters and related unlawful political activities. The Middle East commanded Washington's attention in October 1973 when a surprise Egyptian and Syrian attack on Israel initiated the YOM KIPPUR WAR. Nixon ordered a massive U.S. airlift of emergency military supplies and equipment to Israel. When Moscow threatened to intervene in the conflict to prevent

Egypt's defeat, the president placed U.S. forces on worldwide alert to deter any Soviet action. Following the war, Kissinger launched an intensive round of SHUTTLE DIPLOMACY in an effort to mediate the long-standing Arab-Israeli conflict. Washington's central role in the negotiation of a January 1974 Egyptian-Israeli troop disengagement agreement helped bring an end to the ARAB OIL EMBARGO (1973–1974).

Meanwhile Nixon was increasingly consumed by the widening Watergate controversy that had come to preoccupy the country. Numbers of administration officials, including the president's two senior White House aides and his former attorney general, would be indicted by a Watergate special prosecutor and ultimately convicted for their part in the scandal. In testimony before the Senate select committee on Watergate, White House Counsel John Dean in June 1973 directly implicated Nixon by accusing him of involvement in the cover-up. Following a full inquiry into Nixon's conduct, the House Judiciary Committee voted in July 1974 to recommend impeachment of the president on charges that included obstruction of justice and abuse of power. Rather than face an impeachment trial, Nixon resigned on August 9, 1974, becoming the only president ever to relinquish the office. In his parting address he admitted only errors of judgment. He was succeeded by Vice-President GERALD R. FORD, who the following month granted Nixon a pardon for any crimes he might have committed while president. Nixon retired to California and later moved to New Jersey. He traveled extensively abroad and, after a period of seclusion, gradually reemerged as a respected foreign policy thinker and informal adviser. He published *RN: The Memoirs of Richard Nixon* (1978) and a half-dozen books on foreign affairs. Following the disintegration of the USSR in December 1991, he forcefully advocated greater U.S. assistance to the fledgling democratic governments in Russia and other newly sovereign former Soviet republics.

NON-IMPORTATION ACT (1806) Legislation passed by Congress on April 18, 1806, to force Great Britain to respect America's neutral rights. U.S. merchant shipping suffered abuses by European belligerents following the outbreak of renewed Anglo-French warfare in 1803. Governments in London and Paris aimed to limit one another's war-making ability by restricting the neutral maritime trade then dominated by the United States. Britain, with naval power vastly superior to France's, posed the greater threat to American commerce and neutral rights. After 1804 the British pursued a policy targeted at cutting off U.S. neutral trade with France. Britain seized American vessels, confiscated cargoes, partially blockaded American harbors, and, in a particularly galling affront to U.S. national honor, continued to abduct American seamen through IMPRESSMENT.

British conduct drew angry U.S. protests and pressured President THOMAS JEFFERSON to respond. Secretary of State JAMES MADISON in January 1806 issued a report condemning London's infringement on neutral commerce and its impressment of American sailors. Congress followed by passing a series of resolutions, the first two of which assailed British maritime raids as "unprovoked aggression" and a "direct encroachment upon America's national independence." The third resolution was the retaliatory Non-Importation Act, which authorized a ban on certain British imports to the United States, including hemp, flax, tin, brass, and some woolens, effective November 15, 1806, unless Britain settled American grievances. At Jefferson's urging, Congress suspended enforcement of the law pending conclusion of negotiations on the abortive MONROE-PINKNEY TREATY (1806). These discussions failed to resolve Anglo-American differences on neutral rights. Following several more delays and suspensions the Non-Importation Act finally took effect on December 14, 1807, a week prior to Jefferson's more extensive EMBARGO ACT. Non-importation remained nominally in force through the period leading to the WAR OF 1812. The weak measure proved ineffectual and brought no concessions in British policy.

NON-INTERCOURSE ACT (1809) Legislation signed on March 1, 1809, by President THOMAS JEFFERSON repealing the unpopular EMBARGO ACT (1807). The overriding intent behind Jefferson's total ban on American foreign trade had been to compel warring powers Great Britain and France to respect America's neutral rights. When the embargo caused widespread economic distress in the United States while failing to coerce any concessions from either London or Paris, popular domestic opposition to Jefferson's policy soared. With support for the embargo collapsing in Congress, sentiment for replacing the Embargo Act with a milder measure prevailed. The Non-Intercourse Act, enacted three days before Jefferson left office, reopened trade with all nations except France and Great Britain. The measure barred American ships from trading with either of the European belligerents and closed American ports to British and French vessels and goods.

The new law authorized the president to resume trade with whichever of the two warring countries first stopped violating America's neutral rights. Thus the Non-Intercourse Act offered to reward British or French cooperation even as it kept up pressure on them. After British Minister to the United States David M. Erskine gave assurances that his government soon would revoke its measures against neutral American shipping, President JAMES MADISON in April 1809 proclaimed the renewal of legal trade with Great Britain. British Foreign Secretary George Canning disavowed the so-called ERSKINE AGREEMENT and recalled the minister to London, prompting Madison to revive the Non-Intercourse Act against Great Britain in August 1809. America's economy suffered most under the non-intercourse legislation, which proved too weak to force British or French concessions. Congress replaced the law in May 1810 with MACON'S BILL NO. 2.

NON-INTERCOURSE ACT (1811)   See **MACON'S BILL NO. 2**.

NON-PROLIFERATION TREATY See **NUCLEAR NON-PROLIFERATION TREATY**.

NO-TRANSFER PRINCIPLE (1811) Maxim of U.S. diplomacy aimed at reducing European influence in the Americas. The principle barred the transfer of existing colonies in the American continents from one European nation to another. The United States in the 1790s viewed with growing unease the possibility that a weak Spain's colonial possessions in the Caribbean and North America might come under the control of a powerful Great Britain or France. President

THOMAS JEFFERSON, alarmed by the prospect of a new French empire on the continent, strongly opposed Napoleon's acquisition of the Louisiana territory from Spain in 1802. The next year the United States preempted French ambitions by purchasing the vast Louisiana expanse from Napoleon.

President JAMES MADISON sanctioned the no-transfer policy in 1811 when it appeared Great Britain was poised to obtain Florida. On January 15 he signed a joint resolution declaring that the United States would consider Spanish cession of Florida to another European state a threat to American security interests. Madison also asserted that under certain circumstances the United States might use force to prevent such a transaction. The Spanish government eventually sold Florida to the United States in the ADAMS-ONIS TREATY (1819). The no-transfer principle became a basic tenet of American foreign policy and emerged in the course of the 19th century as an essential part of the MONROE DOCTRINE.

NOOTKA SOUND CONTROVERSY (1790) Anglo-Spanish territorial dispute in North America that threatened to involve the United States. The conflict arose out of competing claims by Great Britain and Spain to Nootka Sound, located on the west coast of Vancouver Island in present-day British Columbia, Canada. British traders, arriving in 1789 to establish a post on the sound, had their ships seized and were driven out by Spanish authorities who had recently arrived in the Pacific Northwest. Spain and Great Britain braced for war, each petitioning its allies for pledges of support.

President GEORGE WASHINGTON invited his cabinet's advice on setting up U.S. policy in the event of war. Washington presumed the British would seek to move troops from Canada across the neutral United States to strike at the Spanish possessions of the Floridas, New Orleans, and the Louisiana province. Such a development seemed certain to carry the conflict to American soil. Treasury Secretary ALEXANDER HAMILTON, who wanted improved Anglo-American relations and prized British trade as a vital revenue source for the young American republic, endorsed giving Great Britain permission to send its forces through U.S. territory. Secretary of State

THOMAS JEFFERSON was wary of British territorial designs on America's frontier and opposed the scheme to allow their forces to traverse the United States.

When revolution-torn France turned down a Spanish request for help, Spain opted for a diplomatic settlement rather than fight the British alone. In the Nootka Sound Convention of October 28, 1790, the Spanish agreed to pay an indemnity for British property and acknowledged British rights to trade and settle along the northwest coast of North America. The settlement spared Washington from having to make a decision on American involvement in the controversy. The Nootka Sound Convention later surfaced during the OREGON QUESTION, a predominant issue in Anglo-American diplomacy from 1818 to 1846. The British contended they had inherited all Spanish claims to the Oregon Country in the 1790 accord. The United States, meanwhile, insisted it had acquired Spanish claims to the region in the ADAMS-ONIS TREATY (1819).

NORTH ATLANTIC FISHERIES CONVENTION See **FISHERIES QUESTION**.

NORTH ATLANTIC TREATY See **NORTH ATLANTIC TREATY ORGANIZATION** in **APPENDIX C**.

NORTH ATLANTIC COOPERATION COUNCIL See **NORTH ATLANTIC TREATY ORGANIZATION** in **APPENDIX C**.

NORTH ATLANTIC TREATY ORGANIZATION See same in **APPENDIX C**.

NORTH PACIFIC SEALING CONVENTION See **BERING SEA DISPUTE**.

NORTH-SOUTH DIALOGUE   Discussion on international economic issues between wealthier industrialized countries generally located in the Northern Hemisphere and poorer THIRD WORLD countries found mainly in the Southern Hemisphere. In 1974, French President Valery Giscard d'Estang, responding to the recent massive rise in world oil prices, suggested a three-way conference of developed, oil-producing, and developing nations to address energy costs and international inflation. At the developing nations' urging, the proposed

meeting's agenda was expanded to include international development questions and the structure of the world economy. The first Conference on International Economic Cooperation (CIEC) was held in Paris from December 16 to 19, 1975. Commonly referred to as the North-South Dialogue, the gathering was attended by representatives from 26 nations: 7 industrialized nations, including the United States, which together with a delegation from the European Economic Community formed the so-called Group of 8; and 7 oil-producing and 12 developing nations, collectively known as the Group of 19. The conference established four expert commissions to draw up proposals on energy, raw materials, development, and finance.

The second and final CIEC session met in Paris from May 30 to June 2, 1977. Agreement was reached on providing increased aid to developing countries and on establishing a Common Fund under the UNITED NATIONS CONFERENCE ON TRADE AND DEVELOPMENT (UNCTAD) to stabilize international commodity prices. Many Third World countries depended on commodities as their primary source of export earnings. Developing nations called for establishment of a New International Economic Order (NIEO), a broad restructuring of the world's financial institutions and reallocation of its resources meant to narrow the gap between rich and poor countries. The industrialized nations rejected NIEO as little more than a plan for the redistribution of wealth from North to South and not a true development program.

At the suggestion of WORLD BANK President ROBERT S. MCNAMARA, an Independent Commission on International Development Issues under former West German Chancellor Willy Brandt was created in November 1977 to continue research on North-South questions. The Brandt Commission's call in 1980 for an international meeting to revive the North-South Dialogue led to the 1982 CANCUN SUMMIT on economic cooperation and development. The Cancun parley failed to resolve North-South differences over the structure of the world's economy. President RONALD W. REAGAN enunciated U.S. opposition to government-run economic plans, such as the NIEO, and argued for private sector, market-oriented economic activity as the key to Third World growth.

With the advent of the INTERNATIONAL DEBT CRISIS in 1982, the focus of North-South discussions in such forums as UNCTAD and the INTERNATIONAL MONETARY FUND turned to measures for reducing the massive Third World indebtedness while maintaining the flow of desperately needed investment capital to developing nations.

NORTHWEST ORDINANCES See **NORTHWEST TERRITORY**.

NORTHWEST TERRITORY Area north and west of the Ohio River extending to the Mississippi River, it absorbed surging U.S. westward expansion in the late 18th and early 19th centuries. The territory, encompassing the OLD NORTHWEST, was part of Great Britain's huge land cession to the United States in the TREATY OF PARIS (1783) ending the AMERICAN REVOLUTION. Congress arranged for the settlement and political development of the national domain in a series of Northwest Ordinances in the 1780s. The ordinances established a framework for the absorption of additional territories as the United States advanced across the continent.

The Ordinance of 1784 provided for the division of the newly acquired west into districts, each eligible for statehood upon achieving a population of 20,000. It planned for the establishment of temporary governments, under Congress's oversight, until statehood might be attained. The 1784 act was blocked by the refusal of several southern states to surrender their western territorial claims and it never took effect. The Ordinance of 1785 set guidelines for the survey and subdivision of western lands into townships with clear-cut boundaries and titles to ownership. The historic Ordinance of 1787 established the Northwest Territory and outlined provisions for its government: initially, Congress would exercise authority through its own appointees; future division of the territory would be limited to between three and five states; once any division attained a population of 60,000, it would join the Union as a state; and slavery would be forbidden in the territory. The act's guarantees of religious freedom and public education were meant in part to encourage immigration from abroad.

The approximately 45,000 Indians across the Northwest Territory offered stiff resistance to white expansion between 1783 and the WAR OF 1812. Treaties at Fort Stanwix (1784) and Fort McIntosh (1785) secured significant land cessions from the Indians. To help avert conflict on the frontier, Congress mandated just treatment of the Indians in the 1787 ordinance. But white pressure on Indian territories sparked warfare in the early 1790s. General "Mad Anthony" Wayne's victory at the BATTLE OF FALLEN TIMBERS in 1794 yielded the TREATY OF GREENVILLE (1795), which opened up the Ohio region to advancing settlement. The presence of British forts in the Northwest Territory, in violation of the 1783 Treaty of Paris, remained a challenge to U.S. sovereign claims until Great Britain agreed to withdraw the posts in JAY'S TREATY in 1794. The United States broke effective Indian resistance in the Old Northwest at the BATTLE OF TIPPECANOE (1811), thwarting British hopes for an Indian buffer state between Canada and America's western boundary. The Northwest Territory gained local self-rule in 1799, eventually becoming the states of Ohio (1803), Indiana (1816), Illinois (1818), Michigan (1837), and Wisconsin (1848).

See also MAP 3.

NSA See **NATIONAL SECURITY AGENCY**.

NSC See **NATIONAL SECURITY COUNCIL** in **APPENDIX B**.

NSC-68 (1950) Report prepared for the National Security Council (NSC) on U.S. defense policy. In the immediate aftermath of WORLD WAR II, the United States moved rapidly to demobilize its huge wartime military. The Soviet Union's postwar seizure of much of Eastern Europe brought increasing American involvement in efforts to halt the further spread of Soviet communism. U.S. membership in NATO, the Western military alliance formed in April 1949, cemented American commitment to the defense of Western Europe and the CONTAINMENT of Soviet expansionism. U.S. policy rested on the concept of DETERRENCE, or using the threat of certain and costly military conflict to discourage Soviet aggression. The United States relied on the fact it was the only power with NUCLEAR WEAPONS. The nuclear monopoly enabled the nation to keep its armed forces and defense budgets at traditionally low peacetime levels.

The situation changed in August 1949 when the Soviet Union exploded its first atomic bomb. Concern over the effectiveness of America's defense strategy was heightened when the Communist revolution led by Mao Tse-tung came to power in China the same year. In January 1950 President HARRY S. TRUMAN directed the NSC to undertake a major reassessment of U.S. national security policy. A joint State and Defense department study group was formed, headed by PAUL H. NITZE, director of the State Department's Policy Planning Staff. The interdepartmental committee submitted its findings in April 1950. The report, NSC-68, identified the Soviet Union as the principal risk to the West's security and recommended an immediate, massive build up in American military strength. The committee's analysis rested on several key assumptions: the Soviet Union was an expansionist power; the Soviet leadership would refuse to negotiate outstanding issues; and the USSR would have the nuclear capability to destroy the United States by 1954. The report concluded that America would have to assume primary responsibility for the defense of the non-Communist world and warned of the danger of local wars.

Truman accepted the committee's evaluation of the strategic situation but was reluctant to initiate major increases in defense spending. The outbreak of the KOREAN WAR in June 1950 was viewed as confirmation of the basic thrust of NSC-68 and the document provided an initial framework for large-scale U.S. rearmament. The emphasis in NSC-68 on a broad military buildup was replaced by the more economy-minded NEW LOOK defense policy adopted under President DWIGHT D. EISENHOWER. But the report's assessment of the threat posed by the Soviet Union remained a basic tenet of U.S. strategic thinking until the end of the COLD WAR in the late 1980s.

NUCLEAR ACCIDENTS AGREEMENT (1971) U.S.-Soviet accord to prevent the accidental outbreak of nuclear war. An outgrowth of SALT I arms control negotiations, the Agreement on Measures to Reduce the Risk of Outbreak of Nuclear War was signed in Washington on September 30, 1971. The agreement bound the United States and the Soviet Union to notify each other immediately in the event of any accidental, unauthorized, or other incident involving a nuclear weapon that raised the risk of nuclear war; take the necessary steps to render any such weapon harmless; and inform each other of planned test missile launches extending beyond national territory in the direction of the other party.

NUCLEAR FREEZE Catchphrase expressing the goal of a grassroots movement to freeze NUCLEAR WEAPONS as a first step toward nuclear disarmament. In 1980 U.S. peace groups joined in a campaign for an international freeze on the development, testing, production, and deployment of nuclear weapons. They argued such a freeze would halt the East-West nuclear arms race and provide an impetus to meaningful arms control negotiations on the eventual elimination of nuclear armaments. The nuclear freeze movement grew rapidly in the early 1980s, drawing support from political and advocacy organizations, religious groups, environmental activists, educators, scientists, and politicians. Many criticized the Reagan administration's defense buildup and the absence of U.S.-Soviet arms control talks. President RONALD W. REAGAN strongly opposed the idea of a nuclear freeze, arguing it would lock into place a dangerous Soviet superiority in certain kinds of strategic nuclear arms. By 1982, 11 state legislatures and more than 600 town meetings and city councils had passed resolutions endorsing a nuclear freeze. The political pressure generated by the campaign was credited with helping persuade Reagan to pursue START arms control discussions with the Soviet Union. The movement reached the peak of its influence when the U.S. House of Representatives on March 8, 1983, approved a resolution calling for the United States and the Soviet Union to undertake a mutual and verifiable freeze. A similar proposal was rejected in the Senate. Attention faded after the mid-1980s as rapidly improving U.S.-Soviet relations resulted in the INF TREATY (1987) cutting nuclear arsenals in Europe.

NUCLEAR MATERIAL CONVENTION (1980) Multilateral agreement on the safeguarding of nuclear materials. The pact reflected international concern, amid the growing worldwide use of nuclear energy, that a non-nuclear-armed country or a terrorist group could acquire enough nuclear fuel to build a nuclear weapon. First proposed by the United States in 1974 and endorsed by the 1975 review conference of the NUCLEAR NON-PROLIFERATION TREATY, the Convention on the Physical Protection of Nuclear Material was drafted in Vienna from 1977 to 1979 under the auspices of the INTERNATIONAL ATOMIC ENERGY AGENCY and opened for signature on March 3, 1980. With its ratification by 21 nations, including the United States, it entered into force February 8, 1987. The convention made the unlawful taking or use of nuclear materials an international offense subject to extradition and punishment among the pact's signatories. It established specific levels of protection to be accorded different categories of nuclear fuel, required that appropriate steps be taken to safeguard nuclear supplies within national terrritories and during international transport, and called for international cooperation to recover missing nuclear materials.

NUCLEAR NON-PROLIFERATION ACT (1978) Federal legislation to tighten controls on U.S. exports of nuclear materials. India's surprise 1974 detonation of a nuclear device, the emergence of ambitious regional powers seeking to acquire nuclear arsenals, and the growing worldwide use of nuclear fuels that might be diverted from peaceful to military purposes raised U.S. concerns over the global spread of NUCLEAR WEAPONS. At the urging of the Carter administration, Congress gave near unanimous approval to strict new restrictions on U.S. nuclear fuel exports. President JIMMY CARTER signed the non-proliferation measure into law on March 10, 1978. The act further restricted the transfer of plutonium and enriched uranium, which could be used in nuclear weapons. It effectively prohibited the export of processing facilities capable of producing either fuel and mandated prior U.S. approval of any retransfer to a third party of U.S.-supplied nuclear materials. Importing countries were required to accept international safeguards before they could receive U.S. nuclear supplies. Under the law the United States reaffirmed its commitment to remaining a reliable source of nuclear fuel to nations adhering to non-

proliferation policies. The legislation's call for the negotiation of additional international controls on nuclear supplies was realized in part with the NUCLEAR MATERIAL CONVENTION (1980).

NUCLEAR NON-PROLIFERATION TREATY (1968) International arms control agreement to prevent the spread of NUCLEAR WEAPONS. Negotiated under auspices of the EIGHTEEN-NATION COMMITTEE ON DISARMAMENT, the treaty adopted by the UNITED NATIONS General Assembly on June 12, 1968, was signed by 59 nations in Washington, London, and Moscow on July 1, 1968, and entered into force on March 5, 1970. More than 120 nations are party to the agreement, including all the declared nuclear powers. The treaty commits nuclear states not to transfer nuclear weapons or the means for their manufacture to non-nuclear states and bars non-nuclear states from accepting or acquiring nuclear weapons. It empowered the INTERNATIONAL ATOMIC ENERGY AGENCY to establish guidelines for the international transfer of nuclear fuels and required non-nuclear states to conclude inspection agreements with the agency so as to prevent the diversion of nuclear materials from peaceful to military purposes. As provided for under the treaty, review conferences have been held every five years in Geneva beginning in 1975. India's surprise detonation of a nuclear device in 1974 revealed the need for additional safeguards against nuclear proliferation, resulting in the formulation of the multilateral NUCLEAR MATERIAL CONVENTION (1980).

NUCLEAR REDUCTION INITIATIVE (1991) Plan advanced by President GEORGE BUSH to unilaterally cut some 24,000 weapons from the U.S. nuclear arsenal. He announced the planned reduction in a nationally televised address from the White House on September 27, 1991. Most of the weapons encompassed by his initiative were outside the scope of the two major U.S.-Soviet nuclear arms control agreements concluded in the prior four years, the INTERMEDIATE NUCLEAR FORCES TREATY (1987) and START Treaty (1991). The initiative's main elements included removal from Europe and Asia of U.S. tactical missiles (also known as battlefield or theater weapons) and nuclear-tipped artillery shells, all to be destroyed; removal from

Navy surface ships and attack submarines of nuclear-armed CRUISE MISSILES; abandonment of the effort to develop a rail-based mode for the 10-warhead U.S. MX missile; and an end to the 24-hour alert status of U.S. strategic bomber aircraft. The day after Bush's address the PENTAGON ordered an immediate stand-down of the 40 strategic bombers on round-the-clock ground alert in the United States, leaving the nation with no long-range bombers in a state of nuclear-attack readiness for the first time since 1957.

Bush's move marked a break from previous U.S. practice of making arms cuts only as part of reciprocal agreements negotiated with the Soviet Union. While emphasizing that his initiative was not contingent on Soviet reciprocation, he did call upon the USSR to respond in kind. Explaining the geopolitical impetus for his plan, Bush observed that a Soviet invasion of Western Europe could no longer be deemed a realistic threat in view of communism's demise in Eastern Europe, the end of the COLD WAR, and the collapse just weeks before of the attempted MOSCOW COUP. In the abortive coup, Communist hardliners had tried to oust Soviet President Mikhail S. Gorbachev and arrest the process of political and economic liberalization sweeping the USSR. Serious questions had been raised by the United States and its Western allies as to who controlled the Soviet nuclear arsenal during the coup. The failure of the putsch, heralded in the West as a victory for democratic forces in the Soviet Union, hastened the disintegration of Soviet central authority, as any number of Soviet republics moved to establish their independence from Moscow.

Bush's decision to cut U.S. tactical NUCLEAR WEAPONS reportedly stemmed out of post-coup concern about the security of similar Soviet arms, given that several Soviet republics were challenging the Kremlin's control over the nuclear forces on their soil. Bush was said to have figured that a unilateral destruction of U.S. tactical nuclear arms would encourage prompt Soviet reciprocation. The president's initiative drew strong bipartisan support in Congress and was welcomed in the capitals of Western Europe. Gorbachev responded on October 5 with a corresponding Soviet plan that surpassed in scope and numbers the Bush arms control initiative. The Soviet

leader took his country's strategic bombers off alert; directed the destruction of tactical nuclear missiles, artillery shells, and mines; and, in a step that eased apprehensions in the West, moved to further centralize control over Soviet nuclear arms. Bush and the other Western leaders hailed Gorbachev's measures. Following the December 1991 dissolution of the Soviet Union, Washington coordinated closely with Russia and other newly sovereign Soviet republics on the disposition and control of the former Soviet nuclear arsenal.

NUCLEAR AND SPACE TALKS See UMBRELLA TALKS.

NUCLEAR SUPPLIERS GROUP Affiliation of the principal suppliers of nuclear fuels and technologies. Following India's surprise 1974 explosion of an atomic device, the seven leading nuclear exporters, including the United States and the Soviet Union, met in London the following year to tighten international nuclear safeguards and prevent the further spread of materials and facilities capable of producing NUCLEAR WEAPONS. Of particular concern was the burgeoning international transfer of nuclear fuel and equipment for use in nuclear energy. The group, which has expanded to some 15 members, convenes annually in London. Also known as the London Club, it has served as a forum for the development of a common nuclear export policy. In 1977 members adopted a stringent set of rules and guidelines governing the transfer of nuclear items.

See also NUCLEAR MATERIAL CONVENTION.

NUCLEAR TESTING MORATORIUM (1958–1961) Voluntary moratorium on nuclear testing observed by the United States, Great Britain, and the Soviet Union. In the mid-1950s the world's three existing nuclear powers, amid mounting international concern over the dangers posed by radioactive nuclear fallout, began protracted, off-and-on negotiations over a nuclear test ban. On March 31, 1958, the Soviet Union announced an indefinite suspension of its nuclear testing, while retaining the right to resume if other nations did not follow suit. The United States continued with a previously scheduled test series through the end of October. In early November 1958 the USSR exploded several nuclear devices. On

November 7 President DWIGHT D. EISEN-HOWER stated that, while the Soviet tests relieved America of any obligation to reciprocate, the United States would abide by the informal moratorium. Over the next three years the United States, Great Britain, and the Soviet Union adhered to the voluntary suspension. France, which became the fourth nuclear power with a test explosion in 1960, did not join in the moratorium. Amid heightened COLD WAR tensions, the Soviet government on August 30, 1961, declared it was ending the suspension. Soviet testing began again the following day and was followed two weeks later by renewed U.S. tests. In 1963 the LIMITED TEST BAN TREATY brought a formal halt to all but underground nuclear testing.

NUCLEAR TRIAD See **TRIAD**.

NUCLEAR WEAPONS Explosive devices deriving their fearsome destructive power from the splitting (fission) or joining (fusion) of atomic nuclei. Development of the atomic (fission) bomb by the United States in 1945, in the final stages of WORLD WAR II, was followed by U.S. creation of the hydrogen (fusion) bomb in 1952. The more powerful hydrogen device has become the common nuclear warhead. Nuclear weapons, referring to both warheads and their means of delivery, generally are grouped into three categories according to range: tactical or battlefield nuclear weapons with a range of several hundred miles or less; intermediate or theater nuclear weapons capable of reaching targets up to several thousand miles away within a given military theater of operations, such as Europe; and strategic nuclear weapons, designed by the United States and Soviet Union to travel intercontinental distances and strike each other's homeland. Since the 1950s the United States has maintained a strategic nuclear TRIAD of long-range manned bombers, INTERCONTINENTAL BALLISTIC MISSILES, and SUBMARINE-LAUNCHED BALLISTIC MISSILES. Nuclear weapons have defined and dominated postwar arms control negotiations.

See also INTERMEDIATE NUCLEAR FORCES TREATY, SALT I, SALT II, START.

NUREMBURG WAR CRIMES TRIALS Post–WORLD WAR II trials of German Nazis accused of committing war crimes during the conflict. On August 8, 1945, representa-tives from the United States, Great Britain, France, and the Soviet Union meeting in London established an International Military Tribunal and adopted legal guidelines for the prosecution and punishment of the major German war criminals, defined as those who had made, influenced, or advanced the Third Reich's criminal government policies. Twenty-two Nazi civil and military leaders were charged variously with "conventional war crimes," such as the mistreatment of prisoners; "crimes against peace," involving the waging of aggressive war; and "crimes against humanity," entailing the extermination of six million Jews in the Holocaust and other atrocities. Their trial before an international tribunal of justices appointed by the victorious Allied powers was held at Nuremburg, Germany, between November 20, 1945, and October 1, 1946. U.S. Attorney General Francis Biddle served as the American representative on the tribunal and Supreme Court Associate Justice Robert A. Jackson acted as the principal U.S. prosecutor. Three defendants were acquitted. Of the 19 found guilty, 12, including Hermann Goering, were sentenced to death, and the others received long prison sentences. The trials marked the first time in which individuals acting as members of a government were held responsible for war crimes. Following the proceedings, Army General Telford Taylor replaced Jackson as chief U.S. prosecutor. In a series of trials before an American tribunal in the U.S. occupation zone in Germany, Taylor prosecuted lesser German war criminals including military officers, government officials, and members of Nazi organizations. Similar proceedings against German and other Axis war criminals were held in courts across Europe.

See also FAR EAST WAR CRIMES TRIALS.

NYE COMMITTEE (1934–1936) U.S. Senate panel that investigated the munitions industry as a cause of war. By the early 1930s, a broad movement of peace organizations, proponents of disarmament, and critics of big business and finance, led by the WOMEN'S INTERNATIONAL LEAGUE FOR PEACE AND FREEDOM, had generated considerable pressure for a congressional investigation of arms manufacturers and their war-making influence. Advocates of an inquiry believed that munitions makers and powerful financiers, in their quest for profits, encouraged international arms races and the wars that resulted. They hoped that if it could be demonstrated that the arms industry and international bankers, working through the federal executive branch, had drawn the United States into WORLD WAR I, then legislation could be enacted to keep the nation out of future conflicts.

In April 1934 the Senate approved the formation of the Special Committee Investigating the Munitions Industry to look into the arms makers' connection to America's entry into the world war in 1917. The committee was headed by isolationist Senator Gerald P. Nye (R-ND). Other members of the panel, soon known as the Nye Committee, were W. Warren Barbour (R-NJ), Homer T. Bone (D-WA), Bennett Champ Clark (D-MO), and ARTHUR H. VANDENBERG (R-MI). The committee held hearings from

September 1934 to February 1936, gaining national attention with the appearance of such well-known figures as the four du Pont brothers from the chemical firm bearing their name and the renowned Wall Street financier J.P. Morgan. In all, the panel questioned nearly 250 witnesses and prepared several voluminous reports. Though able to document large wartime profits for the munitions industry, the committee could not establish a direct link between arms manufacturers and the American decision to go to war. In its majority report, the panel favored government ownership of the armaments industry. The committee's well-published investigation helped bring passage of the first of the NEUTRALITY ACTS in 1935 and contributed to the prevailing American ISOLATIONISM of the period.

O

OAS See **ORGANIZATION OF AMERICAN STATES** in **APPENDIX C.**

ODER-NEISSE LINE De facto boundary drawn between Poland and Germany at the close of WORLD WAR II. Named for the Oder and Neisse rivers, which run from the Baltic Sea to the border of Czechoslovakia, the boundary line came to symbolize the postwar political division of Europe and the West's inability to prevent the establishment of Soviet hegemony behind the IRON CURTAIN.

At the YALTA CONFERENCE in February 1945, the United States and Great Britain accepted the so-called Curzon Line as the

new Soviet-Polish border by consenting to changes in Poland's eastern frontier that let the USSR keep a slice of territory formerly under Polish control. Soviet leader Joseph Stalin suggested the Poles receive part of eastern Germany as compensation for their loss. While President FRANKLIN D. ROOSEVELT and British Prime Minister Winston Churchill indicated interest, they withheld definite approval of the proposal pending resolution of Poland's postwar political status.

The POTSDAM CONFERENCE, convened by the BIG THREE in July 1945 to consider postwar Allied treatment of a defeated Germany, yielded a compromise whereby the

United States and Great Britain agreed to the Oder-Neisse Line as the temporary Polish-German border pending a conclusive peace settlement and final boundary determination. Under the Potsdam agreement, Poland retained control of German territory east of the Oder-Neisse, a development that resulted in the eventual forced expulsion westward of several million resident ethnic Germans.

The onset of the COLD WAR resulted in the partition of Germany in 1949 into democratic West Germany and Communist East Germany. The division of Europe and mounting East-West conflict blocked prospects for a negotiated adjustment of the Oder-Neisse Line, making Polish postwar annexation of German lands a fait accompli. Formal recognition of the Oder-Neisse boundary by the Western allies and the Soviet bloc was made for the first time in the landmark HELSINKI ACCORDS (1975), in which both sides confirmed the postwar European political geography. Under the FINAL SETTLEMENT WITH RESPECT TO GERMANY TREATY that cleared the way to German reunification in October 1990, Germany vowed to respect the Oder-Neisse Line and pledged never to try to reclaim the lands lost to Poland.

OFFICE OF THE COORDINATOR OF INFORMATION See **OFFICE OF STRATEGIC SERVICES**.

OFFICE OF FACTS AND FIGURES See **OFFICE OF WAR INFORMATION**.

OFFICE OF POLICY COORDINATION (OPC) Agency responsible for U.S. COVERT ACTION in the opening years of the COLD WAR. In December 1947 the recently formed CENTRAL INTELLIGENCE AGENCY (CIA) was directed by the NATIONAL SECURITY COUNCIL (NSC) to help secretly prevent a Communist victory in upcoming Italian national elections. The success of the ad hoc ITALIAN ELECTION OPERATION in April 1948 caused U.S. policymakers to conclude that covert action represented an effective alternative between diplomacy and war for halting Soviet expansionism. On June 18, 1948, the NSC issued a directive authorizing a permanent U.S. covert action capability. The Office of Policy Coordination was established September 1 under the direction of veteran intelligence officer FRANK G. WISNER. Its purpose was to conduct covert political, economic, and paramilitary operations to undermine the Soviet Union's hold over Eastern Europe and weaken the international Communist movement.

Although its budget and staff were drawn from the CIA, the covert action office functioned as a separate entity. Policy guidance and instructions came from a special joint State and Defense department panel. Primary supervisory responsibility rested with State Department official GEORGE F. KENNAN. By the time WALTER BEDELL SMITH took charge of the CIA in October 1950, OPC had grown to a staff of several hundred with a budget of nearly $5 million. Among its covert projects was the secret establishment and funding of RADIO FREE EUROPE. Smith ended the organization's semi-autonomous status, bringing it under his direct control. In January 1951 OPC was placed under the new CIA post of deputy director of plans and in August 1952 it was merged into the plans division, the agency department responsible for clandestine operations.

OFFICE OF SCIENCE AND TECHNOLOGY POLICY See same in **APPENDIX B**.

OFFICE OF STRATEGIC SERVICES (OSS) U.S. intelligence service during WORLD WAR II. Prior to the war, the U.S. government traditionally had relied on the State Department for information on foreign developments. The intelligence branches of the War and Navy departments concerned themselves with information of military value. In 1940 President FRANKLIN D. ROOSEVELT sent Wall Street lawyer and WORLD WAR I Army hero WILLIAM J. DONOVAN to Europe to assess the fighting between Great Britain and Nazi Germany. British intelligence operations impressed Donovan. Believing America should prepare for its probable involvement in World War II, he suggested to Roosevelt in 1941 the formation of a centralized U.S. intelligence service patterned on the British model.

Roosevelt took a major step toward implementing Donovan's proposal by issuing a directive on July 11 of that year establishing the position of coordinator of information. Donovan was appointed to the new post, gaining authority to spend secret funds and assemble a staff to coordinate the federal government's foreign intelligence activities. While Roosevelt's directive stopped short of approving a separate intelligence agency, Donovan quickly developed the Office of the Coordinator of Information (soon referred to as COI) into his proposed intelligence service. The COI had four major functional divisions: Secret Intelligence; Research and Analysis; FOREIGN INFORMATION SERVICE; and Special Operations, responsible for unconventional warfare.

America's entry into World War II exposed the need for a special organization to carry out intelligence activities traditionally not undertaken by the military. On June 13, 1942, Roosevelt signed Executive Order 9182, which redesignated Donovan's intelligence operation as the Office of Strategic Services. The new organization, made formally responsible for intelligence, espionage, unorthodox warfare, and other clandestine activities, was placed under the recently formed JOINT CHIEFS OF STAFF. The Foreign Information Service was made a separate entity as the OFFICE OF WAR INFORMATION.

The OSS played a major role in the U.S. war effort. Numbering more than 30,000 people at its peak, the service gathered and prepared vital information, ran subversion and propaganda programs, and conducted guerrilla operations behind enemy lines. Its research and analysis branch pioneered the use of geographic area studies. Numerous future high-ranking intelligence officials, including CIA directors ALLEN W. DULLES and WILLIAM J. CASEY, began their intelligence careers in the OSS.

In November 1944, Donovan submitted a memorandum to Roosevelt recommending the creation of a permanent peacetime intelligence agency. His desire to see the OSS retained after the war was thwarted, however, when President HARRY S. TRUMAN disbanded the organization by executive order on September 20, 1945. Often referred to as America's first centralized intelligence service, the OSS left an enduring mark. It helped establish intelligence as a distinct profession; laid the groundwork for the use of COVERT ACTION as an acceptable alternative between diplomacy and military action in postwar U.S. international relations; and served as prece-

dent for the CENTRAL INTELLIGENCE AGENCY formed in 1947.

OFFICE OF WAR INFORMATION (OWI) U.S. WORLD WAR II propaganda agency. Distinguished American literary figures Archibald MacLeish and Robert E. Sherwood, among the interventionists who favored U.S. entry into the war even before the December 1941 Japanese attack on PEARL HARBOR, set up the prewar U.S. government information organs that were the antecedents of the OWI. Both men were committed to the triumph of democratic ideals over Fascist aggression and each urged that preservation of human freedom be embraced as a fundamental purpose of the world war. MacLeish, an accomplished poet who was still serving as Librarian of Congress, in 1941 became head of a new Office of Facts and Figures (OFF), which was responsible for providing Americans with information on the war and explaining their vested interest in its outcome. The Pulitzer Prize-winning playwright Sherwood, a speechwriter for President FRANKLIN D. ROOSEVELT, the same year organized and directed the Foreign Information Service, whose principal mission was to trumpet democracy's virtues to audiences abroad.

Neither agency functioned very effectively in the months after the conflict engulfed America. Responding to demands within his administration for a better coordinated and more focused U.S. propaganda effort, Roosevelt signed an executive order on June 13, 1942, that created the Office of War Information by consolidating the OFF, the Foreign Information Service, and several other related federal information agencies. Elmer Davis, the popular CBS radio newscaster, was named OWI director. The new organization, comprising domestic and overseas branches, presented the global conflict as a struggle between forces of good and evil. Roosevelt's FOUR FREEDOMS and the principles contained in the Allied ATLANTIC CHARTER formed the ideological foundation for the OWI's assault on fascism. Under Davis, the agency tried to popularize the idea of U.S. leadership in a hoped-for postwar democratic world order. The OWI championed the concept of a UNITED NATIONS.

The domestic branch, headed by MacLeish until 1943, undertook to educate

Americans on major wartime issues and on the ominous menace posed by the Axis powers of Germany, Italy, and Japan. The domestic propagandists sought to shore up public morale through films, radio programming, posters, and publications that depicted a homogeneous United States unified in support of the war effort. American middle class values were celebrated and Roosevelt's New Deal accomplishments were prominently featured. The president was highlighted as leader of a free and democratic people. Hollywood was an active domestic branch ally. The film industry produced government propaganda shorts and permitted hundreds of feature length motion pictures to be altered by the OWI to fit American policy. These home front activities attracted criticism from several political quarters. Republicans protested that the OWI was being used to muster support for Roosevelt's re-election to a fourth term. Southern Democrats objected to what they termed the agency's sympathies for greater racial equality and the progress of black Americans. Congress reined in the increasingly controversial domestic branch in 1943 by slashing its budget.

The OWI's overseas branch, under Sherwood, directed its propaganda toward audiences in war-torn Europe and Asia through its *Victory* magazine and VOICE OF AMERICA broadcasts. The branch was the mouthpiece for official U.S. policy. Its idealized portrayal of Americans and their way of life was intended to counter distorted Axis propaganda depictions. Sherwood and his staff concentrated on the basic message that the United States and Allies would prevail in the war and that their victory would benefit the whole world. In conjunction with the Allied military command in Europe, the OWI set up a psychological warfare branch that employed leaflet programs and loudspeaker broadcasts to erode enemy troop morale. The OWI, planned at its inception as a temporary agency, was disbanded at the war's end in August 1945.

See also UNITED STATES INFORMATION AGENCY.

OGDENSBURG CONFERENCE (1940) Meeting between President FRANKLIN D. ROOSEVELT and Canadian Prime Minister W. L. Mackenzie King to discuss common defense issues. The two leaders conferred in Roosevelt's railway car near Ogdensburg, New York, on August 18, 1940. The meeting occurred against the backdrop of the Battle of Britain, as Germany's air assault on Great Britain and the spread of WORLD WAR II across Europe raised concerns over the dangers posed to Western Hemisphere security. Canada already was a belligerent in the war against Germany. Roosevelt and King agreed to establish a Joint Board on Defense to coordinate the defense of the northern half of the Western Hemisphere. The Joint Board provided for close U.S.-Canadian cooperation throughout World War II.

See also DECLARATION OF PANAMA.

OLD NORTHWEST Region between the Ohio and Mississippi rivers and the Great Lakes embracing the present-day states of Ohio, Indiana, Illinois, Michigan, and Wisconsin. Great Britain relinquished the area to the United States in the TREATY OF PARIS (1783) following the AMERICAN REVOLUTION. After the states had ceded their various claims to the Old Northwest to the central government, it became a public domain and was organized under the Northwest Ordinance (1787) as the NORTHWEST TERRITORY. The Old Northwest and the Northwest Territory covered the same geography and often are used interchangeably in historical accounts.

See also MAP 3.

OLIVE BRANCH PETITION See **AMERICAN REVOLUTION**.

OLNEY COROLLARY See **VENEZUELA BOUNDARY DISPUTE**.

OLNEY, RICHARD (1835–1917) Attorney general and secretary of state in the second term of President GROVER CLEVELAND. A graduate of Brown University in 1856 and Harvard Law School in 1858, the Massachusetts native was admitted to the bar in 1859 and entered corporate law practice. Olney served in the Massachusetts legislature in 1874 as a Democrat. Named attorney general by Cleveland in 1893, he held the post until 1895, when he was selected to replace WALTER Q. GRESHAM, who had died, as secretary of state.

Commissioned in his new office on June 8, he inherited the VENEZUELA BOUND-

ARY DISPUTE. With the firm support of Cleveland he pressured Great Britain to arbitrate the contested boundary between Venezuela and British Guiana. The secretary contended that the British, by refusing to submit the entire disputed territory at issue to arbitration, were effectively extending their colonization in the Americas in violation of the MONROE DOCTRINE. In a threatening note to London, Olney warned that the United States had a right to intervene in the controversy under what became known as the OLNEY COROLLARY to the Monroe dictum. The collorary asserted virtual U.S. hegemony over the Western Hemisphere. His firm stand succeeded in securing international arbitration and settlement of the dispute.

During his tenure, Olney was confronted by difficulties connected to the outbreak in 1895 of the Cuban insurrection against Spain. He was concerned to prevent FILIBUSTERING expeditions mounted by Cuban rebels from U.S. soil with the help of private American funding. The secretary of state resisted domestic pressure to recognize the belligerent status of the Cuban insurgents, whom he felt lacked the organization necessary to form a responsible government. He strove without much effect to persuade Spain to implement a program of humane reforms in Cuba. After leaving the State Department at the end of Cleveland's term in March 1897, Olney returned to his law practice and never again held political office. He declined an offer extended by President WOODROW WILSON to be ambassador to Great Britain.

OLYMPIC BOYCOTT (1980) U.S.-led boycott of the 1980 Moscow Summer Olympic Games in protest of the Soviet Union's invasion of Afghanistan in late December 1979. The Soviet move surprised the U.S. government, which scrambled in the first days of 1980 to devise a coherent response. The invasion prompted the Carter administration to cancel efforts at furthering DETENTE with the USSR. On January 2 President JIMMY CARTER recalled the U.S. ambassador from Moscow for consultations. The next day the president asked the Senate to defer its ratification vote on the U.S.-Soviet SALT II arms control agreement in light of events in Afghanistan. The Senate complied and SALT II was shelved in-

definitely. In a televised speech to the nation January 4, Carter outlined a set of retaliatory measures meant to exact a concrete price from the USSR for its actions. He announced an immediate embargo on sales of American grain and high-technology items to the Soviets. He also warned that the United States would consider withdrawing from the 1980 Summer Olympics, scheduled to be held in Moscow, if Soviet aggression continued. Secretary of State CYRUS R. VANCE reiterated the warning January 14 when he urged the Kremlin to withdraw its troops from Afghanistan within a month or face a possible American boycott of the Summer Olympics.

On January 20 Carter declared unequivocally that America would not attend the summer games unless Soviet forces were pulled out of Afghanistan by February 20. He simultaneously called on the rest of the world to join in the boycott. On February 12 the International Olympic Committee (IOC), rejecting a U.S. request that the games be either moved, postponed, or canceled absent a prompt Soviet exodus from Afghanistan, announced that the Olympics would take place in Moscow as scheduled. The Carter administration, expressing regret at the IOC decision, indicated it would spearhead an international boycott. The February 20 deadline passed without any Soviet retreat. Meanwhile Carter's boycott plan came under increasing criticism at home and abroad. Detractors objected to the politicization of an event that was supposed to symbolize friendly competition among nations and represent an oasis from political conflict. Unswayed, Carter on March 21 informed a group representing America's Olympic athletes that his decision not to send a U.S. contingent to Moscow was irreversible.

The games were staged as planned in Moscow from July 19 to August 3. Eighty-one countries took part; 55 stayed away expressly because of the Afghanistan invasion. The U.S.-orchestrated boycott was a major embarrassment to the Kremlin, which had invested heavily in the Olympics, the first ever held in a Communist country, and had staked Soviet prestige on a smooth-running, successful event. In retaliation, the USSR and other East bloc nations boycotted the 1984 Summer Olympics held in Los Angeles.

OMNIBUS TRADE ACT (1988) Comprehensive federal trade legislation. In 1985 Congress began work on a successor trade bill to the TRADE ACT OF 1974 and the TRADE AGREEMENTS ACT OF 1979, which together governed U.S. international commerce. Broad bipartisan support for new trade legislation in the mid-1980s reflected mounting congressional discontent over hundred-billion dollar U.S. trade deficits and their connection to alleged unfair foreign trade practices. Many legislators favored mandatory U.S. retaliation against unfair overseas competition. Action on the proposed measure stalled, however, as Congress turned its attention in 1986 to tax reform and in 1987 to the federal budget deficit crisis. By early in the presidential election year of 1988, congressional attention had refocused on politically sensitive trade issues. The final draft of the pending trade bill included a controversial provision, sponsored by Representative Richard A. Gephardt (D-MO), that would have imposed limits on imports from nations that ran trade surpluses with the United States while refusing to modify unfair trade policies. The Gephardt Amendment drew charges of PROTECTIONISM from America's top trading partners, the European Economic Community and Japan, who argued that unfair trade policies could only be addressed through negotiations under the multilateral GENERAL AGREEMENT ON TARIFFS AND TRADE (GATT).

Under pressure from the Reagan White House, which opposed the measure as contrary to America's commitment to free trade and the expansion of international markets, Congress dropped the Gephardt Amendment from the final version of the trade bill passed in April 1988. In an election year showdown with the Democratic congressional leadership, Republican President RONALD W. REAGAN vetoed the legislation because of his objections to a section requiring advance notice to workers of plant closings. Unable to override the veto, Congress approved an almost identical trade bill without the plant-closing provision. Signed into law by Reagan on August 23, 1988, the massive trade package extended until 1993 the president's authority to negotiate trade agreements with other nations, thus allowing continued U.S. participation in the ongoing URUGUAY ROUND of GATT trade talks; provided for special relief to import-damaged domestic industries; and tightened controls on the export of technology vital to U.S. national security. Responding to the TOSHIBA AFFAIR (1987), the law imposed sanctions on the Japanese Toshiba Corporation and the Norwegian Kongsberg firm as punishment for their illegal sale of machinery useful in submarine design to the Soviet Union. Section 301 of the act, relating to overseas trade barriers, required the executive branch to identify unfair foreign trade practices, take steps to eliminate them through negotiation, and then resort to retaliatory measures if necessary. Under the so-called Super 301 provisions, President GEORGE BUSH in 1989 cited Japan for unfair trade policies, leading to special U.S.-Japanese STRUCTURAL IMPEDIMENT INITIATIVE trade discussions.

OPEN DOOR U.S. policy regarding China in the first half of the 20th century, entailing support for equal foreign trade access in the Asian nation and maintenance of Chinese independence and territorial integrity. With the opening of China to outside commerce during the 19th century, the major trading nations subscribed to the principle, commonly referred to as the Open Door, of equal commercial opportunity in the giant country. The United States gained Open Door trading privileges in China under the TREATY OF WANGHIA (1844), although its volume of trade remained relatively minor. China's defeat in the Sino-Japanese War (1894–1895) revealed the growing military and political weakness of the Manchu Dynasty. In the last years of the century the major European powers and Japan scrambled to carve China into spheres of influence, forming virtual trade monopolies in their zones and securing other valuable commercial concessions from the Manchu government.

This partitioning threatened China with dismemberment and thus jeopardized America's emerging Pacific commercial and strategic interests. Victory in the SPANISH-AMERICAN WAR (1898) had left the United States in possession of the Philippines and with a greatly expanded stake in the Far East. American business interests saw in China's huge population a potentially vast market for future trade. The McKinley administration's decision to retain the Philippines after the war had been influenced in part by the expectation that the archipelago would facilitate U.S. commerce in China. Supporters of a vigorous U.S. foreign policy in Asia argued that the plunder of China by the major powers would diminish the value of the Philippines to Washington.

In 1898 President WILLIAM MCKINLEY, evincing traditional U.S. opposition to participation in foreign alliances, rejected a British overture for an Anglo-American guarantee of the Open Door in China. Great Britain, as the world's principal trading nation, stood to profit from preservation of Open Door principles. On the recommendation of Far Eastern affairs adviser William W. Rockhill, Secretary of State JOHN M. HAY decided to incorporate the British proposal into an American diplomatic initiative to win international backing for the Open Door. With McKinley's approval, Hay in September 1899 sent notes to Great Britain, Germany, and Russia seeking formal assurances they would respect the principle of the Open Door. He did not propose an end to already established spheres of influence but rather requested that the powers allow equal trade opportunities for all nations within their zones. In November Hay circulated the memorandum to France, Italy, and Japan.

The replies to the first Open Door note were generally ambiguous and evasive. Hay nonetheless decided to construe the responses as acceptance and thereby, by his thinking, commit the great powers to support for the Open Door. On March 20, 1900, he announced that he had received "final and definitive" international approval to an American call for adherence to the Open Door in China. In June 1900 a violent antiforeign uprising, fomented by a secret Chinese society known as the Boxers, erupted against the spreading Western presence and influence in China. The United States participated in the international armed expedition sent to rescue the besieged foreign legations and suppress the BOXER REBELLION. Hay worried that foreign powers would use the Boxer revolt as a pretext for expanding their spheres of influence in China. In July 1900, in the midst of the Boxer crisis, the secretary sent a circular letter to the major powers informing them of the U.S. commitment to restoring peace and security to China and pre-

serving Chinese territorial and administrative integrity. The second Open Door note, which did not ask for a reply, also reaffirmed U.S. support for "the principle of equal and impartial trade with all parts of the Chinese Empire."

Hay's two notes established the basic Open Door policy pursued by the United States over the next half-century. The Russo-Japanese War (1904–1905) brought initial international recognition of the Open Door after the belligerents sought American mediation. President THEODORE ROOSEVELT secured both Russian and Japanese endorsement of the Open Door before agreeing to arbitrate an end to the war at the PORTSMOUTH CONFERENCE (1905). In the ROOT-TAKAHIRA AGREEMENT (1908) the United States and Japan pledged to respect each other's Pacific possessions and uphold the Open Door. In practice, however, Japan and the other major powers continued to maneuver for advantage in China. Following the outbreak of WORLD WAR I, Japan attacked and seized German holdings in China and, in 1915, presented Peking with a list of 21 Demands that, if acceded to, would have amounted to a virtual Chinese surrender of sovereignty to Tokyo. U.S. pressure helped persuade Japan to withdraw the more extreme demands. Under the LANSING-ISHII AGREEMENT (1917) Tokyo reaffirmed its commitment to the Open Door, while Washington acknowledged Japan's unique relationship with China based on their geographical proximity. At the WASHINGTON NAVAL CONFERENCE (1921–1922), the twin Open Door principles of Chinese territorial integrity and equal trade access were formally adopted in the NINE-POWER TREATY (1922). Over the next two decades, relations between Tokyo and Washington steadily worsened in the face of mounting Japanese aggression against China. In 1931 Japan launched a major military offensive against the Chinese province of Manchuria. The Hoover administration issued the STIMSON DOCTRINE (1932) stating U.S. refusal to recognize the Japanese conquest of Manchuria and establishment of the puppet state of Manchukuo. Japan's invasion of China in 1937 elicited further U.S. protests against the violation of the Open Door. Growing tensions in the Pacific between Japan and the United States culminated in WORLD WAR II.

OPEN SKIES Concept of mutual East-West aerial surveillance, first proposed by President Dwight D. Eisenhower in 1955 and eventually incorporated into an international agreement in 1992. By the early 1950s Cold War adversaries the United States and Soviet Union both possessed growing nuclear arsenals. Initial efforts toward East-West arms control had foundered over Soviet rejection of U.S. demands for strict verification provisions for any disarmament agreement. In 1955 Eisenhower fastened on the idea of joint aerial inspection as a way of breaking the East-West disarmament deadlock. Sanctioned intelligence overflights of each other's territory, he reasoned, would provide an unobtrusive means for arms control verification and would lessen international tensions by reducing the fear of surprise nuclear attack. At Eisenhower's direction, a team of U.S. experts under presidential aides Nelson A. Rockefeller and Harold E. Stassen worked out the details of an aerial inspection plan at Quantico, Virginia, in May and June 1955. The president presented the proposal to the four-nation Geneva Summit on July 21, 1955. Under the plan, soon dubbed Open Skies, East and West would exchange detailed information on their military installations, facilities, and bases. Each participating nation would then permit the stationing of reconnaissance aircraft and crews from the other side at selected airfields in its territory. These aircraft would be authorized to fly designated surveillance missions determined by mutual agreement. U.S. allies Great Britain and France endorsed the Open Skies idea. The Soviet Union, however, rejected the proposal outright as nothing more than a brazen Western espionage scheme. Aspects of Eisenhower's Open Skies concept were later realized in the SATELLITE RECONNAISSANCE tacitly accepted by both superpowers in the 1960s.

Against a backdrop of rapidly improving East-West relations, President George Bush in May 1989 revived the Open Skies idea as a means of building trust between NATO and the Communist Warsaw Pact. Representatives of the 16 NATO and 7 Warsaw Pact countries met at the so-called Open Skies Conference in Ottawa, Canada, from February 12 to 28, 1990, and negotiated the basic outline of a mutual aerial inspection regime. Talks on a final agreement continued over the next two years amid the collapse of communism in Eastern Europe and dissolution of the Warsaw Pact, end of the East-West Cold War, and disintegration of the USSR. The United States, its NATO allies, former Warsaw Pact members Poland, Czechoslovakia, Hungary, Romania, and Bulgaria, and newly independent Soviet republics Russia, Belarus, Ukraine, and Georgia signed the Open Skies Treaty in Helsinki, Finland, on March 24, 1992. The pact provides for extensive aerial reconnaissance of each signatory's territory. The reciprocal overflights, by aircraft with cameras and other special viewing equipment, are designed to build international confidence and security by making each nation's military open to outside inspection.

OPEN SKIES TREATY See **OPEN SKIES**.

OPERATION CHAOS See **ANGLETON, JAMES JESUS**.

OPERATION DESERT SHIELD See **PERSIAN GULF WAR**.

OPERATION DESERT STORM See **PERSIAN GULF WAR**.

OPERATION JUST CAUSE See **PANAMA INVASION**.

OPERATION LINEBACKER (1972) Code name for two distinct U.S. air operations over North Vietnam during the Vietnam War. In response to the Communist Eastertide Offensive that began March 30, 1972, President Richard M. Nixon ordered Operation Linebacker I, an extensive aerial bombing campaign against North Vietnamese ports, supply facilities, airfields, and other military targets. Amid indications peace talks in Paris were near to reaching a settlement of the conflict, the United States in October 1972 scaled back its bombing, limiting it to the part of North Vietnam below the 20th parallel. By mid-December 1972 the Paris negotiations, however, had broken down in stalemate. On December 18 Nixon authorized Operation Linebacker II, a massive air campaign against the Hanoi area meant to persuade the North Vietnamese to conclude a peace agreement. Over the next two weeks U.S. B-52 strategic bombers pounded the North Vietnamese capital in the heaviest bombardment of the war. The American anti-war movement strongly condemned the so-called Christmas Bombing. Operation Linebacker II was halted on December 30, when it was announced the United States and North Vietnam would resume negotiations. Defenders of the controversial bombing maintain that it hastened the PARIS PEACE ACCORDS ending U.S.-North Vietnamese hostilities signed one month later. Detractors argue the air operation was unnecessary and that North Vietnam already was prepared to accept the peace agreement.

OPERATION MONGOOSE U.S. secret operation in the early 1960s to overthrow the Castro regime in Cuba. Fidel Castro had come to power in January 1959 at the head of a revolution that drove Cuban dictator Fulgencio Batista into exile. As Castro moved to impose a Communist system on the island nation, senior U.S. officials began to consider ways to remove him from power. Apparently as early as 1960, the CENTRAL INTELLIGENCE AGENCY (CIA) was involved in efforts to assassinate the Cuban leader. In April 1961 the U.S.-backed BAY OF PIGS INVASION by Cuban exile forces ended in embarrassing failure. The following November the Kennedy administration authorized a broad COVERT ACTION plan intended to topple the Castro government. The operation, code-named Mongoose, was closely supervised by Attorney General Robert F. Kennedy, while its execution was entrusted to veteran intelligence operative EDWARD G. LANSDALE. Through propaganda, sabotage, and paramilitary activities, Mongoose aimed to bring about an open revolt against Castro by the end of 1962. A large covert organization was established, support was provided to Cuban exile political groups in the United States, and exile forces were trained and sent on commando raids in Cuba. The operation was proving largely ineffective when it was overwhelmed by the CUBAN MISSILE CRISIS in October 1962. Following resolution of the crisis, Mongoose was officially terminated. However, CIA attempts to assassinate Castro, part of the Mongoose operation, continued until 1965.

OPERATION PAPER (1951–1954) U.S. covert operation in support of Nationalist Chinese guerrillas. Following the defeat of Chiang Kai-shek's army by the Communists under Mao Tse-tung in 1949, General Li Mi fled with some four thousand Nationalist troops into neighboring Burma. In February 1951 the CENTRAL INTELLIGENCE AGENCY began to equip Li Mi's army for guerrilla warfare in adjacent Chinese provinces. The U.S. government hoped the operation, code-named Paper, would force China to divert military units from the KOREAN WAR as well as disrupt and harass Communist rule in the south of China. Li Mi's forces moved into China's Yunan province in May, but were turned back with heavy casualties. Similar forays two months later and in the summer of 1952 likewise were repulsed. The presence of the ragged Li Mi army increasingly strained relations between Washington and the Burmese government. U.S. Ambassador to Thailand WILLIAM J. DONOVAN oversaw its secret evacuation to Taiwan by 1954.

OPERATION POISED HAMMER See **PERSIAN GULF WAR**.

OPERATION PROVIDE COMFORT See **PERSIAN GULF WAR**.

OPERATION TROPIC (1951–1953) U.S.-directed guerrilla operations against China. In November 1950 Communist Chinese military units entered the KOREAN WAR on the side of North Korea against the U.S.-led UNITED NATIONS forces. In 1951 the CENTRAL INTELLIGENCE AGENCY (CIA) undertook a secret guerrilla warfare campaign as a way of striking directly at China without overt American involvement. Operation Tropic involved the recruitment and training by the CIA of anti-Communist Chinese agents in Hong Kong for infiltration into China. Neither the agents nor the so-called "third force" guerrilla elements they were to organize and lead on the mainland were affiliated with the Nationalist Chinese government on Taiwan. The first agents were sent into China in the spring of 1952. In November, CIA agents John T. Downey and Richard G. Fecteau were shot down in an agency DC-3 airplane and captured while trying to recover a Chinese agent from the mainland. Both were sentenced by Communist China to long prison terms for espionage. Fecteau was released in 1971 and Downey two years later. Operation Tropic was terminated in 1953.

OPERATION URGENT FURY See **GRENADA INVASION**.

OPPENHEIMER, J. ROBERT (1904–1967) Nuclear physicist who directed development of the first atomic bomb during WORLD WAR II. J. (an initial not standing for any name) Robert Oppenheimer was born in New York City. After graduating from Harvard University in 1925, he studied at Cambridge University in England and at Georg August Universitat in Gottingen, Germany, where he earned his Ph.D. in 1927. In 1929 he joined the faculties of both the California Institute of Technology (Caltech) and the University of California at Berkeley. During the 1930s Oppenheimer became a political and social activist. Reacting to the Great Depression, Nazism's rise, and the Spanish Civil War, he championed liberal causes and made acquaintances with many Communists and others on the political left.

In 1941 he was enlisted by the federal government as a research consultant on development of an atomic, or fission, bomb. In 1942 Army General Leslie R. Groves, in charge of the newly formed MANHATTAN PROJECT, as the bomb program was codenamed, made Oppenheimer director of the atomic bomb laboratory established at Los Alamos, New Mexico. On academic leave for the two years it took to construct the weapon, he earned the appellation the "father of the atomic bomb" for his management of the extraordinary task. The project culminated in the first atomic bomb test at Alamagordo, New Mexico, in July 1945 and the atomic bombing of the Japanese cities Hiroshima and Nagasaki the next month. He returned to Caltech and Berkeley in 1946 and the following year accepted the directorship of the Institute for Advanced Study in Princeton, New Jersey, a post he held until his death in 1967.

As a consultant to the State Department he helped author the ACHESON-LILIENTHAL REPORT (1946), which outlined a plan for international control of atomic energy that became official U.S. policy on the issue. From 1947 to 1952, he was chairman of the key General Advisory Committee of the civilian Atomic Energy Commission (AEC). After the Soviet Union exploded its first atomic bomb in 1949, the committee was asked to consider whether the United States should undertake to build a hydrogen, or fusion, weapon. Asserting that the manufacture of a fusion bomb was at that time technically infeasible, and urging a delay in the development of mass-destruction weapons, the panel unanimously recommended that U.S. thermonuclear research be confined to the theoretical level. In 1950 President HARRY S. TRUMAN overrode Oppenheimer's committee and ordered work accelerated on a fusion devise. Physicist EDWARD TELLER oversaw development of the hydrogen bomb by 1952.

In the climate of suspicion created by Wisconsin Republican Senator JOSEPH R. MCCARTHY's demagogic campaign against alleged Communist subversion in the early 1950s, Oppenheimer faced charges that his positions on U.S. NUCLEAR WEAPONS policy had been influenced by underlying Soviet sympathies. Detractors pointed to the Princeton physicist's prior left-wing associations. In December 1953 the AEC notified Oppenheimer that his security clearance had been suspended. A special inquiry was conducted in April and May 1954. While explicitly stating that Oppenheimer's loyalty was not in doubt, the hearing board concluded on June 28 that, in view of his past Communist contacts, his conduct during deliberations on the hydrogen bomb, and his purportedly sometimes "less than candid" testimony before the investigative panel, he represented a potential security risk. The commission rescinded Oppenheimer's access to secret information, effectively ending his government service. The decision was condemned as an injustice by many distinguished figures in American science and education who portrayed Oppenheimer as a victim of McCarthyism. In December 1963, in what was seen widely as a gesture of redress, President LYNDON B. JOHNSON presented the celebrated nuclear physicist with the AEC's prestigious Enrico Fermi Award for outstanding contributions to the field of atomic energy.

ORANGE WAR PLAN U.S. contingency war plan for possible armed conflict with Japan. The plan, first formulated by the Navy Department in 1906, identified the Western Pacific as vital to U.S. interests. While color-coded war plans were developed for other possible contingencies, U.S. strategists thought Japan posed the greatest potential threat and the Orange War Plan represented basic U.S. naval strategy. Following WORLD WAR I, Japan again was seen as the most likely American enemy in a future conflict. In 1921 a revised Orange War Plan became the basis for Army and Navy strategic planning. The plan, with its "Japan First" emphasis, was replaced in 1939 by the RAINBOW WAR PLANS, which shifted U.S. strategy to a "Europe First" focus.

ORDINANCE FOR THE REGULATION OF INDIAN AFFAIRS (1786) Law providing for the Confederation Congress's management of INDIAN AFFAIRS under the ARTICLES OF CONFEDERATION. Its enactment was spurred by the defiance of federal authority on Indian matters by several states and mistreatment of Indian tribes by settlers and land speculators. Escalating Indian hostility, fueled by white encroachment on their lands and the often unscrupulous practices of traders, threatened U.S. hopes after the AMERICAN REVOLUTION for a peaceful and orderly westward expansion. Seeking to avoid the great expense of continuous Indian war, Congress acted to restrain the offending states and frontiersmen. The ordinance, enacted August 7, 1786, created Indian districts north and south of the Ohio River, each under a superintendent. These officials were authorized to grant trade licenses to whites and to take necessary steps to protect Indian rights and property. The 1786 measure was undermined by inadequate enforcement and open flouting of its provisions. The worsening situation on the frontier led to implementation of the federal TRADE AND INTERCOURSE ACTS in the 1790s.

OREGON QUESTION Issue from 1818 to 1846 of conflicting U.S. and British claims to the Oregon Country, which embraced the territory north of the 42nd parallel, south of 54°40', and between the Rocky Mountains and the Pacific Ocean. Both the United States and Great Britain staked competing claims to the region by virtue of discovery, exploration, and settlement. The early 19th-century British proposal to divide the disputed territory on the basis of possession rewarded Great Britain's larger presence in Oregon and was rejected by the American government. In the Anglo-American CONVENTION OF 1818, which extended the U.S.-Canadian boundary along the 49th parallel west to the Rockies, the two countries agreed to joint occupation of

the Oregon Country for 10 years. Spain surrendered its long-standing claims north of the 42nd parallel to the United States in the ADAMS-ONIS TREATY (1819); and Russia abandoned its claims below 54°40' through treaties with the United States in 1824 and Great Britain in 1825. Thus by 1827 Washington and London were the only remaining rivals for Oregon, and that year they completed an agreement to extend joint occupation indefinitely. Either country could break the arrangement by giving one year's notice of its intention to do so.

The United States opposed British insistence through the 1830s on a division of the Oregon Country at the Columbia River. America sought a harbor on the West Coast for strategic and commercial reasons. When the WILKES EXPEDITION confirmed that the Strait of Juan de Fuca, located between Vancouver Island and the Olympic peninsula in present-day Washington State, was safe and well-suited to shipping, the United States made a northern boundary of the 49th parallel the core demand of its Oregon diplomacy. A line at 49° north latitude would ensure U.S. access to the harbors of the valued strait.

Public interest in the Pacific Northwest soared with the influx of American pioneers in the early 1840s. The Oregon settlers invited U.S. annexation and westerners across the frontier held "Oregon Conventions," demanding American occupation of the territory to 54°40'. President JOHN TYLER in his annual message to Congress in December 1843 asserted a U.S. right to the entire region between 42° and 54°40'. Expansionist Democrats popularized the political slogan "ALL OREGON" in the 1844 campaign and Democratic nominee JAMES K. POLK was elected president on a platform that endorsed exclusive American claims to Oregon.

In his inaugural address in 1845, Polk challenged British claims by declaring U.S. title to the whole of Oregon "clear and unquestionable." But later that year he offered Great Britain a compromise boundary of the 49th parallel, with Vancouver Island south of 49° also under British control. When British Minister in Washington Richard Pakenham rejected the proposal, Polk withdrew the offer and reasserted the U.S. claim to all of Oregon. Meanwhile western Democrats and other expansionists had found further justification for their Oregon ambitions in the emerging idea at mid-19th century of America's MANIFEST DESTINY. After 1845 they adopted the phrase "54°40' OR FIGHT", a slogan which expressed a willingness to risk war with Great Britain in order to gain the whole of the Oregon territory.

Facing imminent war with Mexico, the Polk administration began to seek an Oregon compromise. In April 1846, Congress passed a resolution authorizing the president to terminate the 1827 joint occupation agreement. Polk in May gave Great Britain the required one year's notice, at the same time expressing hope for a friendly resolution of the Oregon issue. The British government, inclined toward settlement in order to preserve important trade relations, responded by renewing negotiations. The Anglo-American OREGON TREATY of June 1846 settled the territorial dispute by extending the 49th parallel boundary from the Rocky Mountains west to the middle of the channel between the mainland and Vancouver Island, leaving the entire island in British hands.

See also MAP 2.

OREGON TREATY (1846) Signed June 15, 1846, by Secretary of State JAMES BUCHANAN and Great Britain's Minister to the United States Richard Pakenham, it settled the OREGON QUESTION by resolving conflicting American and British claims to ownership of the Oregon Country. Under the CONVENTION OF 1818, renewed in 1827, the United States and Great Britain had agreed to joint occupation of the territory running west from the Rocky Mountains between the 42nd parallel and 54°40'.

To hasten settlement of the long-standing Anglo-American contest for Oregon, President JAMES K. POLK in May 1846 gave Great Britain one year's notice that America intended to terminate the joint occupation agreement. British Foreign Secretary Lord Aberdeen responded by drafting a compromise treaty, which Polk received in early June and quickly accepted without changes on the Senate's advice. Formal Senate consent to the Oregon Treaty, or Buchanan-Pakenham Treaty, came on June 18 by a 41 to 14 vote. The agreement divided the Oregon Country by extending the U.S.-Canadian boundary of the 49th parallel west to

mid-channel between the mainland and Vancouver Island, then south through the Strait of Juan de Fuca to the Pacific Ocean. Vancouver Island went to Great Britain. The British also secured navigation rights to the Columbia River, most of which now lay within American territory. Both countries were guaranteed free navigation of the Juan de Fuca Strait. Unhappy American expansionists and British nationalists alike characterized the treaty as a surrender and charged their governments with capitulation.

See also MAP 2.

ORGANIZATION OF AMERICAN STATES See same in **APPENDIX B**.

ORGANIZATION FOR ECONOMIC CO-OPERATION AND DEVELOPMENT (OECD) International organization whose membership comprises 24 market-economy nations from Europe, North America, and the Far East. Established in Paris in 1961, the OECD replaced the Organization for European Economic Cooperation (OEEC), which had been created in 1948 to implement the U.S. MARSHALL PLAN for post–WORLD WAR II European recovery. By 1960 the OEEC, of which the United States and Canada were only associate members, had fulfilled its objectives. The increased economic interdependence of the ATLANTIC COMMUNITY, however, suggested the need for a permanent cooperative economic agency in which Western nations would participate on an equal footing. Thus the OEEC was transformed into the OECD. Eighteen European countries, Canada, and the United States were charter members. Since 1961 Japan, Finland, Australia, and New Zealand have joined the organization. The organization's principal aims are to promote economic growth among members through intergovernmental coordination on monetary and fiscal policy; spur economic expansion in member and nonmember countries; expand world trade; and oversee members' foreign aid contributions to less developed countries. In recent years it has been involved in efforts to combat unstable currencies, huge international trade imbalances, THIRD WORLD indebtedness, and high levels of unemployment in industrialized countries.

**ORGANIZATION FOR EUROPEAN ECO-
NOMIC COOPERATION** See **ORGANIZA-
TION FOR ECONOMIC COOPERATION
AND DEVELOPMENT**.

OSCEOLA (c. 1804–1838) Seminole Indian leader, he headed resistance to the
U.S. program in the 1830s to remove the
tribe from Florida to the INDIAN TERRITORY.
Under terms of the Treaty of Payne's Landing (1832) and the Treaty of Fort Gibson
(1833), the Seminoles were to be resettled
after 1835 on land beyond the Mississippi
River. Osceola repudiated these agreements and directed the tribe's tenacious
fight against the United States in the second of the SEMINOLE WARS (1835–1842). En
route to peace talks in 1837 under a flag of
truce, he was arrested and imprisoned by
U.S. forces and died under suspect circumstances. Absent Osceola's leadership, Seminole opposition finally folded in 1842.

See also MAP 1.

OSS See **OFFICE OF STRATEGIC SER-
VICES**.

OSTEND MANIFESTO (1854) Controversial memorandum prepared by three American diplomats that recommended the
United States seize Cuba should Spain
refuse to sell its island colony. In the mid-
1800s Southern Democratic expansionists
wanted the United States to annex Cuba
and bring it into the Union as a slave state.
Pro-expansion Democratic President
FRANKLIN PIERCE, a champion of America's
MANIFEST DESTINY, took office in 1853 committed to obtaining Cuba. His administration, concerned about rumored British territorial designs on Cuba and a Spanish plan
to emancipate Cuban slaves, regarded acquisition of the trade-rich island as vital to
U.S. security and protection of American
economic interests.

The evolving domestic sectional politics of slavery in the 1850s constrained
Pierce's Cuban policy. After signing the
controversial Kansas-Nebraska Act (1854)
on admitting newly organized U.S. territories as slave or free states, a measure that
decidedly favored Southern pro-slavery interests and aroused bitter "Free Soil" opposition in the North, he dared not risk further Northern political ire by support of a
pro-slavery drive to take the island. Pierce

withdrew his backing for private FILIBUSTER-
ING expeditions to grab Cuba as slave territory for the United States. He warned, as
well, that the U.S. government would vigorously prosecute anyone violating American
neutrality laws by interfering with the Spanish colony.

His administration turned to diplomatic efforts to obtain Cuba. In April 1853
Secretary of State WILLIAM L. MARCY authorized U.S. Minister to Spain PIERRE SOULE, a
fervent Southern expansionist who advocated Cuba's outright annexation, to offer
the Spanish government up to $130 million
for the island. If Spain turned this down,
Soule was to direct his attention to what
the secretary of state termed "the next most
desireable object, which is to detach the island from the Spanish dominion." When
the administration's initial attempts at purchase failed, Marcy instructed Soule to confer with U.S. Minister to Great Britain JAMES
BUCHANAN and U.S. Minister to France John
Y. Mason about ways to advance U.S. efforts
at acquiring Cuba. Meeting in Ostend, Belgium, in October 1854, the three ministers
drafted a report, later dubbed the Ostend
Manifesto, and sent it as a confidential dispatch to the State Department. The communique, after restating arguments about
Cuba's value to the United States, suggested Washington offer Madrid no more
than $120 million for the island. If the
Spanish government rejected these terms,
the ministers urged the United States to
take Cuba by military force. Soule was principally responsible for the aggressive views
expressed in the report. News of the "manifesto" soon became public, intensifying
Spanish resentment over U.S. annexationist
designs and causing a domestic political
furor. The Northern antislavery press and
newly formed Republican Party denounced
the diplomats' dispatch as proof of a South-
ern-inspired Democratic Party scheme for
slavery's extension. Marcy repudiated the
Ostend report and forced Soule's resignation. Politically damaged at home and
abroad, the Pierce administration abandoned all plans to obtain Cuba.

O'SULLIVAN, JOHN LOUIS (1813–1895)
Journalist and diplomat. Son of an American merchantman, he was born on a ship
in the harbor of Gibraltar. After attending
schools in France and Great Britain, he

earned undergraduate and advanced degrees in 1831 and 1834 from Columbia College in New York. Admitted to the bar, he practiced law in New York City from 1835 until 1837, when he founded and became editor of the *United States Magazine and Democratic Review*. O'Sullivan distinguished himself as a leading proponent of nationalism and expansionism in the 1840s. His publication glorified the "genius" of American democracy. In an 1845 editorial, he orginated the expression MANIFEST DESTINY, which became the catchphrase in the mid-19th century for advocates of U.S. territorial growth across the continent.

Twice in the early 1850s he was indicted for violating U.S. neutrality laws through his sponsorship of FILIBUSTERING expeditions to Cuba. He escaped conviction and in 1854 was named U.S. minister to Portugal, a post he held until 1858. During the American Civil War, he lived in Europe, penning pamphlets in which he voiced sympathy for the Southern cause and urged the British government to extend diplomatic recognition to the Confederacy. O'Sullivan lived in obscurity in New York from 1879 until his death.

OUTER SPACE TREATY (1967) First major treaty on outer space, the Treaty on Principles Governing the Activities of States in the Exploration and Use of Outer Space, Including the Moon and Other Celestial Bodies, or Outer Space Treaty, remains the most comprehensive and important international agreement on space law. The advent of the Space Age in the late 1950s added an entirely new arena to the problems of international relations. In 1963 the United States and the Soviet Union concluded the LIMITED TEST BAN TREATY, prohibiting nuclear testing in outer space. Both nations separately pledged not to station nuclear or other weapons of mass destruction in space. Recognizing the need for a set of general principles to guide the growing exploration and use of space, the world's two space powers referred the issue to the UNITED NATIONS in May 1966. Multilateral negotiations were conducted successfully under the auspices of the United Nations Committee on the Peaceful Uses of Outer Space and the Outer Space Treaty was approved by the General Assembly in December of the same year. The

United States, Soviet Union, and 58 other nations signed the treaty on January 27, 1967. Some 98 nations are now signatories to the agreement.

The treaty established space as a common heritage and outlawed claims of national sovereignty. It extended international law to outer space and guaranteed all nations free access to all celestial bodies and areas. A key provision formalized the prohibition on weapons of mass destruction in space and expanded it to include military bases and activities on celestial bodies. Reflecting the desires of both the United States and the Soviet Union, the agreement did not preclude the use of satellites for intelligence purposes. Other articles provided for the safe return of astronauts who accidently landed in other nations, identified the launching state as liable for damages its space activities might cause, and outlined procedures to limit experiments potentially harmful to the earth's environment.

See also MOON TREATY.

OVERSEAS PRIVATE INVESTMENT CORPORATION (OPIC) U.S. government corporation chartered in 1979 to encourage American private investment in developing countries. OPIC, an independent agency within the INTERNATIONAL DEVELOPMENT COOPERATION AGENCY, promotes investment projects intended to help social and economic development. The corporation seeks to make investing in developing nations attractive to U.S. business by two principal means: insuring private U.S. investors against the political risks of expropriation, inconvertibility of local currencies to U.S. dollars, and damage from war or revolution; and guaranteeing payment to U.S. lenders of the principal and interest on loans (up to $50 million) made to eligible private investors. OPIC also offers loans and loan guarantees to small- and medium-sized American businesses to help finance development projects. The corporation is governed by a board of directors comprising appointees from both the federal government and the private sector.

OZAWA v. UNITED STATES (1922) U.S. Supreme Court decision that held Asian aliens were ineligible for U.S. citizenship. In a case involving a Japanese man who had resided in the United States 20 years and wished to become an American citizen, the Court found that the Naturalization Act of 1790 and its subsequent revisions applied only to those who were white or of African descent. Ozawa, the Court reasoned, did not meet the racial qualifications for citizenship set by U.S. law. The unanimous ruling, delivered November 13, 1922, provoked substantial protest in Japan. The Immigration Act of 1924 further strained relations by making indirect use of the *Ozawa* decision. The legislation prohibited the entry of aliens ineligible for citizenship, thereby effectively excluding the Japanese and other Asians. All racial barriers to citizenship were removed by the Immigration and Nationality Act of 1952.

P

PACIFIC CHARTER See **SOUTHEAST ASIA TREATY ORGANIZATION**.

PACIFIC DOCTRINE See **FORD DOCTRINE**.

PACIFICATION Term used during the Vietnam War to describe the basic U.S. and South Vietnamese strategy for defeating the Communist Viet Cong insurgency. Pacification referred to gaining the allegience of the South Vietnamese populace away from the Viet Cong. It involved a combination of military, political, social, and economic actions designed to root out the covert Communist infrastructure in the countryside and install in its place government institutions under South Vietnamese control. This included identifying and destroying Viet Cong cadres, providing defense against guerrilla attack, and initiating civic action and economic development projects. It was thought that key to undermining the appeal of communism was improving the lives of the South Vietnamese peasantry. Architects of this approach spoke of "winning the hearts and minds of the people." The effectiveness of allied pacification efforts improved substantially when U.S. counterinsurgency resources were consolidated in the Civil Operations and Revolutionary Development Support program in 1967.

PACKARD COMMISSION (1986) Blue-ribbon panel named by President Ronald W. Reagan to study the U.S. military establishment. Formation of the 11-member Commission on Defense Management followed several years of highly publicized disclosures of fraud and waste in Pentagon spending and came amid a growing congressional debate over the command structure in the Defense Department. The commission quickly became known by the name of its chairman, David Packard, a former deputy secretary of defense and head of Hewlett-Packard, a major defense contractor. Other members included ranking Reagan administration national security figures Frank C. Carlucci 3rd and William P. Clark, Jr.; retired Air Force General Brent Scowcroft; and Carla A. Hills, later U.S.

trade representative. The panel submitted its report in February 1986. Its findings found fault with U.S. national security planning, military organization, and defense procurement. Commission recommendations for strengthening the position of the chairman of the JOINT CHIEFS OF STAFF, creating the post of vice-chairman, and improving weapons acquisition procedures were incorporated the same year into the GOLDWATER-NICHOLS DEFENSE REORGANIZATION ACT.

PACT OF PARIS See **KELLOGG-BRIAND PACT**.

PALMER RAIDS (1919–1920) The apprehension and arrest of alleged political and labor agitators by federal agents under the direction of U.S. Attorney General A. Mitchell Palmer. The raids took place during the so-called "Red Scare" of 1919 to 1920, red being the color associated with radical political movements connected to the Russian Revolution (1917) and widely thought to threaten American society. Many worried that Bolsheviks, Communists, and others deemed subversive were entering the country as part of the massive immigration from Europe. The membership of Socialist organizations then forming in the United States mostly was foreign-born and immigrants commonly were identified with radical ideologies.

Public concerns were heightened in early 1919 by widespread labor unrest and a nationwide series of bombings and attempted bombings. Palmer and his assistant J. Edgar Hoover linked the bombings to an alleged radical conspiracy. Under pressure from Congress and the press to take action, the Wilson administration decided on the apprehension and deportation of radical aliens. Agents from the Justice Department began mass arrests across the country, seizing thousands of purported radicals. Those who were aliens were processed for deportation under the ANARCHIST ACT (1918). In December 1919 the U.S. transport *Buford*, nicknamed "The Soviet Ark," sailed for Russia with 249 deportees. The raids, which peaked on January 2, 1920, when more than 2700 people were taken into custody in 33 cities, ended that May amid mounting protests over the violation of civil liberties and as fears over the immediate danger of foreign subver-

sion subsided. Continuing concerns over the admission of radical elements from eastern Europe contributed to the restrictive provisions of the IMMIGRATION ACT OF 1921.

PAN AM FLIGHT 103 (1988) Pan Am jetliner flying from London to New York City that crashed into the village of Lockerbie, Scotland, on December 21, 1988, after a terrorist bomb on board exploded. All 259 people aboard the airliner, mostly Americans, and 11 Lockerbie inhabitants on the ground were killed. A week passed before British investigators could confirm conclusively that the crash had been caused by the detonation of a powerful plastic explosive of a type favored by terrorist groups. The incident, occurring at the height of the winter holiday season, raised fears in Europe and the United States about the susceptibility of air travel to international terrorist attack.

On December 22 the Federal Aviation Administration (FAA) excited a controversy with its revelation that the U.S. embassy in Finland had received a warning on December 5 from an anonymous phone caller that a Pan Am plane flying from Frankfurt, West Germany, to the United States would be the target of a bombing attempt within two weeks. The U.S. government had decided against publicly divulging the phone message. The FAA's post-crash disclosure of the warning, together with the fact that an earlier leg of Flight 103 had originated in Frankfurt on a different Pan Am plane, prompted widespread complaints that the public had not been informed of the possible risk.

President GEORGE BUSH in August 1989 formed the seven-member Presidential Commission on Aviation Security and Terrorism, chaired by former U.S. Labor Secretary Ann McLaughlin, to examine the Lockerbie bombing. Its final report, submitted May 15, 1990, faulted Pan Am and the FAA for security lapses and charged that the overall security system of U.S. civil aviation was seriously flawed. The panel outlined an array of new steps to improve aviation security and urged preemptive and retaliatory U.S. military strikes against terrorist targets. In addition to the report, the commission gave Bush a confidential memorandum with classified suggestions for combating terrorism. The White House endorsed the panel's broad findings without committing to any of the specific recommendations. In October 1990 Congress passed legislation deriving from the commission's recommendations to tighten security procedures at major airports. The measure called for the establishment of federal guidelines on public notification of terrorist threats against airlines and greater emphasis on the development of technology to detect explosives in luggage and cargo.

Extensive probes uncovered evidence that led U.S., British, and French investigators to suspect that Libya had masterminded the bombing, presumably in retaliation for the LIBYAN BOMBING RAID, the 1986 U.S. air strike from which Libyan leader Muammer Qaddafi narrowly escaped with his life. With Libya's emergence as the prime suspect, the U.S. government backed away from its initial supposition that either Iranian radicals or a Syrian-backed Palestinian group had been responsible. In November 1991 U.S. and British authorities issued indictments against two Libyan intelligence officers believed to have engineered the downing of Flight 103 and demanded their extradition. In a related move French officials issued arrest warrants for four other Libyan agents linked to the September 1989 bombing of a French UTA passenger jet over Niger in which 171 people were killed.

The Libyan government detained the two Pan Am and four UTA suspects but refused to turn them over, noting that Libya had no extradition treaty with the United States, Great Britain, or France. Qaddafi's proposal that the Libyan agents be tried domestically or before the WORLD COURT was rejected as unsatisfactory by the U.S. State Department. By year's end the United States and its European allies had begun to consider economic sanctions or even military reprisal against Libya to force Qaddafi's government to surrender the suspects. Efforts to compel Libyan compliance soon moved to the UNITED NATIONS, where the United States, Great Britain, and France sought to enlist international support for pressure on Tripoli. On March 31, 1992, the U.N. Security Council passed a resolution authorizing imposition of limited sanctions against Libya if it did not turn over the bombing suspects by April 15. The mea-

sure, the toughest action ever undertaken by the international body to combat state-sponsored terrorism, also demanded that Libya renounce all forms of terrorist activity and all aid to terrorist groups.

Meanwhile, on March 26, the World Court had begun hearings on Libyan allegations that the U.S. and British efforts to force Libya to turn over the bombing suspects violated international law. The Libyans contended that U.S. and British threats of punitive economic and military action were illegal because Libya bore no obligation to extradite the accused agents. On the eve of the U.N. deadline, the World Court denied Libya's bid to block the sanctions. Rejecting a last-minute Libyan appeal, the Security Council allowed a ban on commerical air traffic in and out of Libya—the main feature of the U.N. punitive embargo—to take effect as scheduled on April 15. The United Nations was authorized to implement an oil embargo if the limited sanctions failed to compel Libyan cooperation.

PANAMA CANAL See **CANAL ZONE**.

PANAMA CANAL COMMISSION   See **PANAMA CANAL TREATIES**.

PANAMA CANAL TREATIES (1977) Two treaties providing for U.S. transfer of the PANAMA CANAL to Panama in the year 2000. Under the HAY-BUNAU-VARILLA TREATY (1903), newly independent Panama granted America perpetual control over a 10-mile wide CANAL ZONE, within which the U.S. government gained the right to build and operate an interoceanic waterway. In return, Panama would receive an annual fee from the canal revenues. To defend the Panama Canal, which was completed in 1914, the United States stationed military forces in the zone.

U.S.-Panamanian relations grew increasingly strained over the question of sovereignty in the Canal Zone. The United States insisted it exercised complete authority within the zone, while Panama maintained the 1903 treaty gave Washington only limited jurisdiction. Mounting Panamanian discontent with the U.S. presence in the Canal Zone culminated in the January 1964 PANAMA RIOTS, large-scale anti-American disturbances that left 4 U.S. soldiers and 21 Panamanians dead. In December 1964 President LYNDON B. JOHNSON announced U.S. readiness to negotiate a new treaty governing the canal. U.S.-Panamanian talks over the next decade made little headway, however. In 1974 Secretary of State HENRY A. KISSINGER and Panamanian Foreign Minister Juan A. Tack signed an agreement on the principles to serve as the basis for a final settlement, including the return of the Canal Zone to Panama. In 1977 U.S. negotiators ELLSWORTH BUNKER and Sol M. Linowitz finally reached agreement with their Panamanian counterparts on a pair of canal treaties. President JIMMY CARTER and Panamanian leader General Omar Torrijos Herrera signed the landmark measures on September 7, 1977, in Washington.

The Panama Canal Treaty, which superseded the Hay-Bunau-Varilla Treaty, stated that the United States would maintain possession of the waterway until December 31, 1999, when Panama would assume total control of the Canal Zone. In the interim Panama would gradually assume a greater role in the operation, maintenance, and defense of the canal. The treaty established the Panama Canal Commission to manage the waterway until the year 2000. The joint U.S.-Panamanian agency would be headed by an American until 1990, when a Panamanian would assume the position. The United States would continue to collect canal revenues during the transition period, providing an increasing percentage of the income to Panama. The Panama Canal Neutrality Treaty, officially the Treaty Concerning the Permanent Neutrality and Operation of the Panama Canal, obligated Panama to keep the canal permanently neutral and open to all nations. The United States and Panama jointly pledged to guarantee the canal's neutrality. Moreover, the treaty promised American warships and auxiliary vessels would receive priority handling.

Panama ratified the treaties by a national plebiscite in October 1977. Powerful opposition was mounted in the United States, however, by conservatives who contended that yielding America's position in Panama was a major strategic error. The Carter administration argued the treaties marked a new U.S. relationship with Latin America based on mutual respect and co-

operation. After protracted debate, the Senate ratified the Neutrality Treaty on March 16, 1978, by a vote of 68 to 32, one more than the two-thirds needed. Reflecting members' apprehensions over America's ability to ensure the security of the waterway under the treaty, the Senate attached a reservation that authorized use of military force in Panama to reopen the canal or restore its operation. Sponsored by Senator Dennis DeConcini (D-AZ), the reservation was decried in Panama as an infringement on Panamanian sovereignty. The Senate approved the Panama Canal Treaty on April 18, 1978, again by a 68 to 32 vote. To assuage Panamanian objections to the DeConcini Reservation, the Senate included in the resolution of ratification the statement that any action the United States might take to assure the security of the Panama Canal should not be interpreted as a right of intervention in the affairs of Panama.

See also PANAMA INVASION.

PANAMA CONGRESS (1826) Pioneering inter-American conference. In 1824 South American liberator Simon Bolivar invited the newly independent Latin American republics to meet to consider establishing a confederation that would provide mutual security against attack by previous colonial ruler Spain or other continental European powers. The proposed gathering in Panama was planned also as a forum for promoting Pan-American trade and affirming a shared commitment to democracy. Bolivar's original invitation was extended by Mexico and Colombia in 1825 to include the United States. An enthusiastically receptive President JOHN QUINCY ADAMS and Secretary of State HENRY CLAY accepted, believing U.S. preeminence in the Western Hemisphere, as articulated in the MONROE DOCTRINE (1823), demanded American representation at the Congress.

Notifying the Senate in late December 1825 of the scheduled parley, the president nominated two delegates to the Panama meeting and emphasized that U.S. participation would be merely consultative. Senators were displeased that Adams had accepted the invitation without first formally canvassing their body. Several members argued that since the Panama Congress would have governmental status, American attendence would mark a break from the nation's traditions of nonentanglement and neutrality. In January 1826, after considerable debate, the Senate backed the Adams administration by approving the mission. Continuing political opposition, however, held up House approval of the necessary appropriations for the American delegation until late March. As events transpired, the congressional delay precluded U.S. participation in the inter-American conference, which met from mid-June to mid-July 1826. Of the two American delegates dispatched, Richard C. Anderson died en route and John Sergeant had only reached Mexico City when the Panama Congress adjourned.

PANAMA, DECLARATION OF (1939) Proclamation of Pan-American neutrality adopted at the first Meeting of American Foreign Ministers in Panama. After WORLD WAR II broke out in Europe on September 1, 1939, U.S. President FRANKLIN D. ROOSEVELT initiated the inter-American consultative process sanctioned under the DECLARATION OF LIMA (1938) by calling a conference of foreign ministers to chart a policy for preserving peace and neutrality in the Western Hemisphere. Secretary of State CORDELL HULL and the foreign ministers of the other 20 American republics opened their 8-day meeting in Panama on September 21. There was broad consensus among the attending nations for keeping out of the European conflict. On October 3 the conference issued the Declaration of Panama, decreeing a safety zone roughly 300 miles wide around the Western Hemisphere. All belligerent powers were barred from taking naval action within the designated neutral area. The zone did not encompass Canada, which was a belligerent in the world war. This scheme for insulating the Americas from the conflict was Roosevelt's brainchild. The security zone, which exceeded the normal coastal limits recognized under international law, was unprecedented in international relations. The belligerents insisted the zone had no validity under international law and never accepted it.

PANAMA INVASION (1989) U.S. armed invasion of Panama to oust ruling Panamanian military strongman General Manuel Antonio Noriega. U.S.-Panamanian rela-

tions disintegrated during President RONALD W. REAGAN's second term as the willful and autocratic Noriega, whose previous clandestine work for the CENTRAL INTELLIGENCE AGENCY had linked him to the Reagan administration's anti-Communist policy in Central America, became an increasing irritant and embarrassment to Washington. Escalating U.S. criticism of the general included allegations of his involvement in illegal drug trafficking to the United States. In 1988 the U.S. government imposed economic sanctions against Panama as part of an effort to drive Noriega from power. The general drew U.S. condemnation when, in May 1989, he overturned the presidential election victory of main opposition candidate Guillermo Endara. President GEORGE BUSH thereupon stepped up U.S. economic sanctions and called for Noriega's resignation. With the inauguration in September 1989 of Noriega's frontmen as the nominal president and vice-president of Panama, the U.S. government broke off diplomatic relations. In early October a military coup attempt against the general was thwarted. The Bush administration faced sharp domestic criticism for failing to intervene with U.S. forces stationed in Panama to aid the anti-Noriega uprising. A spate of encounters between American military personnel and their dependents and Panamanian troops heightened tensions, leading Noriega to declare that a virtual state of war existed between the two countries.

Early on December 20 U.S. forces mounted the largest American military operation since the VIETNAM WAR when five task forces invaded Panama from air and sea. Codenamed Operation Just Cause, the invasion, involving some 24,000 troops, half of which already were stationed in Panama, had three declared purposes: to protect the lives of American citizens in Panama; to safeguard the PANAMA CANAL, which was scheduled, by terms of the PANAMA CANAL TREATIES, to come under Panama's preponderant control on January 1, 1990; and to capture General Noriega and bring him to justice. Following the invasion, Endara proclaimed himself president of Panama and received immediate U.S. recognition of his government. U.S. forces met determined resistance before establishing effective control in the country. Twenty-three American troops were killed and more than 200 wounded in the fighting. Panamanian casualties numbered in the hundreds. Noriega eluded capture and on December 23 took refuge in the Vatican embassy in Panama City. On January 3, 1990, the deposed military leader left the papal diplomatic mission and surrendered to U.S. occupation forces. He was immediately flown to the United States to face trial on drug charges.

In mid-February, with the return of order to the streets, the White House announced the withdrawal of the last intervention forces from Panama. The invasion was very popular with the American public. In Latin America, opponents of the U.S. action rebutted Bush administration claims that the operation was justified within the terms of international law. Critics have charged the Bush administration and Congress with failing to deliver on their promise to Endara of large-scale U.S. aid to help rebuild Panama and boost its ailing economy. In April 1992 Noriega was convicted by a Miami jury on eight counts of drug trafficking.

PANAMA RIOTS (1964) Violent clashes in Panama over the issue of sovereignty in the Panama CANAL ZONE. Under the HAY-BUNAU-VARILLA TREATY (1903), the United States gained perpetual control over the Canal Zone, the 10-mile-wide strip through which the interoceanic waterway was built. From the outset, disagreement arose over the question of sovereignty in the zone, with Panama insisting on an interpretation of limited U.S. jurisdiction and the United States claiming full powers. While the two countries twice adjusted provisions of the 1903 treaty, in 1936 and 1955, they failed to settle the sovereignty dispute. To assuage growing Panamanian discontent, evidenced by riots in Panama City and a march on the Canal Zone in November 1959, President DWIGHT D. EISENHOWER in September 1960 ordered that Panama's flag henceforth be flown side-by-side with the American flag at a designated site in the zone. An order in December 1963 by the American governor barred the flying of any flags in front of Canal Zone schools. An attempt by U.S. students to raise an American flag over the American high school triggered large-scale Panamanian riots on January 9 and 10, 1964, in which 4 U.S. soldiers

and 21 Panamanians were killed. Panama broke relations with the United States and demanded a new canal treaty. Attempts to reach a basis for renegotiating the Canal Zone's status were unsuccessful. After President LYNDON B. JOHNSON agreed to review all issues in U.S.-Panamanian treaty relations, the two nations resumed normal diplomatic ties on April 3, 1964.

See also PANAMA CANAL TREATIES.

PANAMA TOLLS CONTROVERSY (1912–1914) Anglo-American dispute over toll payments for use of the PANAMA CANAL. With construction of the canal nearing completion, Congress in August 1912 passed a law exempting American vessels engaged in the domestic coastwide trade (e.g., from New York to California) from payment of tolls. The British government protested the exemption, insisting it violated the Anglo-American HAY-PAUNCEFOTE TREATY of 1901, which held that the canal should be free and open to the ships of all nations on "terms of entire equality." Contending the U.S. action would lead to higher tolls for foreign ships, London asked for either repeal of the exemption legislation or arbitration of the dispute. In the 1912 presidential campaign, both major parties endorsed the right of the United States under existing treaties to discriminate in favor of its ships. In America, supporters of exemption maintained that the equality provisions referred merely to uniformity of rates. Opponents, on the other hand, argued that the United States was honor-bound not to discriminate. Troubled by charges of bad faith leveled against the U.S. government, and eager to win British support for other policies, President WOODROW WILSON went before a joint session of Congress on March 5, 1914, to ask for repeal of the tolls exemption. After considerable debate, the House of Representatives and Senate complied. A bill repealing the exemption was cleared June 11 for the president's signature.

PAN-AMERICAN CONFERENCE Regular meeting of the American republics; formally called the International Conference of American States. PAN-AMERICANISM and the Pan-American movement were inaugurated in Washington, D.C., at the First International Conference of American States

(1889–1890), otherwise known as the First Pan-American Conference. Delegates from the United States and 17 Latin American countries took the initial steps at the Washington Conference toward formulating inter-American political and economic cooperation by creating the International Union of American States and the COMMERCIAL BUREAU OF AMERICAN REPUBLICS, the latter of which was the forerunner of the PAN-AMERICAN UNION. Eight more Pan-American Conferences were held in major Latin American cities over the first half of the 20th century, at about five-year intervals. These meetings functioned as the main forum for consideration of issues in inter-American relations. At the Ninth Pan-American parley, held in Bogota, Colombia, in 1948, the ORGANIZATION OF AMERICAN STATES (OAS) was established as the hub of the post–WORLD WAR II inter-American system. The Pan-American Conference continued as a regular institutional feature under the OAS but henceforward became known as the Inter-American Conference. Under a revision of the OAS charter in 1967, the annual meetings of the organization's general assembly replaced the quinquennial Pan-American gatherings.

See also INTER-AMERICAN CONFERENCES in APPENDIX E.

PAN-AMERICAN UNION Agency of Western Hemisphere nations that has functioned as an integral component of the inter-American system. The First PAN-AMERICAN CONFERENCE, held in Washington from 1889 to 1890 under U.S. sponsorship, founded the Commercial Bureau of American Republics to collect and distribute commercial information and promote trade among member countries. In 1910 at the Fourth Pan-American Conference in Buenos Aires, the bureau was reorganized and renamed the Pan-American Union. The union, with headquarters in Washington, became the administrative agency of the quinquennial Pan-American conferences and bore responsibility for facilitating various political, economic, and cultural contacts among the American states. In 1948 the Pan-American Union became the permanent secretariat of the newly created ORGANIZATION OF AMERICAN STATES (OAS). Under the direction of the OAS permanent council, the union fosters economic, legal, social, and cultural relations among organization members and

also prepares the programs and regulations of OAS conferences.

PAN-AMERICANISM Diplomatic concept of unity and cooperation among the republics of the Western Hemisphere in the interests of peace, mutual security, and common commercial advantage. The Pan-American movement was inaugurated at the First PAN-AMERICAN CONFERENCE, convened in Washington in 1889 at the behest of Secretary of State JAMES G. BLAINE, who sought an alliance of American states based on a shared commitment to stable republican government and aversion to European IMPERIALISM in the Western Hemisphere. The Washington Conference established the COMMERCIAL BUREAU OF AMERICAN REPUBLICS, predecessor to the PAN-AMERICAN UNION, to promote inter-American trade. The idea of Pan-Americanism foreshadowed the GOOD NEIGHBOR POLICY toward Latin America that took shape in the 1930s. The Pan-American Union and the various agreements and agencies produced by general and special Pan-American conferences coalesced into a broad inter-American system, the hub of which became the ORGANIZATION OF AMERICAN STATES created in 1948.

PANAY INCIDENT (1937) Japanese attack on the U.S. gunboat *Panay*. During the MANCHURIAN CRISIS (1931–1933) an increasingly militaristic and aggressive Japan had seized Manchuria, traditionally under Chinese control, and formed the puppet state of Manchukuo. In July 1937 hostilities broke out between Japanese and Chinese forces in northern China. By September Japan had launched a full-scale assault on the Chinese coast. In November 1937 the *Panay* sailed up the Yangtze River to Nanking to evacuate the American embassy to the new Nationalist Chinese capital at Hankow. On December 12, 1937, Japanese warplanes attacked and sank the *Panay* while it was moored in the river above Nanking, killing 2 Americans and wounding 30 others. The Roosevelt administration, neither ready nor willing to go to war in Asia over the incident, responded cautiously. Tokyo claimed its pilots had mistaken the ship for a Chinese vessel, apologized for the raid, and promised to pay indemnities. Having learned the U.S. vessel was clearly marked, Secretary of State

Cordell Hull did not believe the Japanese account. Nevertheless he accepted Tokyo's apology and indemnity offer on December 24, 1937, ending the episode.

See also Brussels Conference.

PARIS AGREEMENTS (1954) Multilateral agreements providing for West German sovereignty and integration into NATO. Following its defeat in World War II, Nazi Germany was divided in 1945 into four occupation zones by victorious allies the United States, Great Britain, France, and the Soviet Union. By 1947 cooperation among the wartime allies had given way to mounting East-West Cold War confrontation over the future status of Germany and Eastern Europe. The Soviet Union installed a Communist regime in its zone in Eastern Germany while the Western powers at the Six-Nation Conference on Germany (1948) moved to unify their zones under a democratic federal government. The formal partition of Germany into two separate states was realized in 1949 with the establishment of the Federal Republic of Germany in the Western zone and the German Democratic Republic in the Soviet zone. The same year the Western allies formed the NATO security alliance to protect Western Europe against Communist aggression. Communist North Korea's surprise invasion of South Korea in June 1950 initiating the Korean War raised Western concerns over a possible Soviet attack in Europe as part of a worldwide Communist offensive. In order to offset an overwhelming Soviet advantage in ground forces on the European continent, the United States pressed for the formation and integration of West German military units into the NATO command. Fellow alliance member France, influenced by the still-powerful memory of its occupation by German armies during World War II, opposed immediate West German rearmament.

After protracted discussion, the NATO allies, meeting in Bonn in 1952, agreed on the creation of West German armed forces within the context of their inclusion in a West European military command. On May 27, 1952, France, Belgium, the Netherlands, Luxembourg, Italy, and West Germany signed a pact forming a European Defense Community (EDC) with a joint European army. The EDC command would be separate from but report directly to NATO. While West Germany did not become a part of NATO, its security was guaranteed under a NATO protocol signed by alliance members the same day. The United States, Great Britain, France, and West Germany also completed four related agreements, known as the Bonn Conventions, providing for broad West German sovereignty, the end of the Allied military occupation in West Germany, and the stationing and support of NATO forces there. The U.S. Senate ratified the NATO protocol and conventions on July 1, 1952.

The French parliament balked at approving the EDC, delaying both West German rearmament and the implementation of the Bonn agreements and thereby straining U.S.-French relations. In August 1954 the French National Assembly rejected ratification of the EDC. Faced with the collapse of the Bonn arrangements, the NATO allies and West Germany sought a new formula for West German rearmament at the nine-power London Conference from September 28 to October 3, 1954. Negotiations continued at the Paris Conference from October 20 to 23, 1954, culminating in an interlocking set of accords. Signed on the last day of the conference, the Paris Agreements established a Western European Union (WEU) as the European component of NATO, with West Germany as a member; revised the Bonn Conventions to provide for full West Germany sovereignty; and authorized West Germany to join NATO. The WEU did not constitute a separate joint European military force and West German units were to be integrated directly into the NATO command. The Senate ratified U.S. approval of West German membership on March 29, 1955. West Germany gained full sovereignty on May 5, 1955, and entered NATO the next day.

See also Final Settlement with Respect to Germany Treaty.

PARIS CLUB See **GROUP OF 10**.

PARIS, DECLARATION OF See **FREEDOM OF THE SEAS**.

PARIS PEACE ACCORDS (1973) Agreement ending U.S. involvement in the Vietnam War. In 1965 the Johnson administration began a major escalation of the

American military presence in Southeast Asia to prevent a Communist North Vietnamese victory over U.S. ally South Vietnam. The same year the United States launched a systematic bombing campaign against North Vietnam. Washington offered to end the bombing provided Hanoi halted its aggression against the South and agreed to negotiate an end to the hostilities. North Vietnam, however, continued its military operations in the South, rejected various U.S. overtures for negotiations, and insisted instead that America withdraw from Southeast Asia. With U.S. forces locked in a costly and seemingly interminable ground war in Vietnam, and with domestic opposition to the conflict mounting, President LYNDON B. JOHNSON in September 1967 unveiled the so-called SAN ANTONIO FORMULA, promising to suspend the bombing of North Vietnam if it would enter peace negotiations. But Hanoi dismissed the U.S. offer.

By 1968 more than 500,000 U.S. troops were in Vietnam. Washington remained confident it could prevail militarily. The surprise Communist TET OFFENSIVE in late January 1968 further eroded support for the war at home and prompted the Johnson administration to reexamine its Vietnam policy. Having decided to deescalate American involvement in the conflict, Johnson on March 31, 1968, announced a partial bombing halt of the North as a peace initiative. His overture led to the start of U.S.-North Vietnamese negotiations in Paris on May 13, 1968. Veteran diplomat W. AVERELL HARRIMAN headed the American delegation to the Paris Peace Talks. Johnson's declaration on October 31 of a complete halt to the bombing of North Vietnam was the key development leading to expanded negotiations involving, in addition, both South Vietnam and the National Liberation Front (NLF), the Communist insurgency in South Vietnam known popularly as the Viet Cong.

These talks opened in Paris on January 25, 1969, five days after RICHARD M. NIXON had assumed the presidency. Nixon appointee HENRY CABOT LODGE, JR. had replaced Harriman as chief U.S. representative. Lodge himself was later succeeded by diplomats DAVID K. E. BRUCE and William J. Porter. North Vietnam demanded total withdrawal of U.S. forces from Vietnam, the removal of Nguyen Van Thieu as president of South Vietnam, and the NLF's inclusion in a new South Vietnamese government. The United States insisted on the mutual withdrawal of U.S. and North Vietnamese forces from South Vietnam and supported the Thieu government. Washington vetoed any participation of the NLF (renamed the Provisional Revolutionary Government of South Vietnam in 1969) in South Vietnamese politics. In an effort to break the deadlock, U.S. National Security Adviser HENRY A. KISSINGER and chief North Vietnamese negotiator Le Duc Tho held a series of secret meetings in Paris beginning in August 1969. Their diplomacy yielded no breakthrough and on March 24, 1972, Nixon called for an indefinite suspension of the Paris talks until North Vietnam was prepared to enter "serious discussions."

Meanwhile the Nixon administration had altered the U.S. conduct of the war, adopting a policy of VIETNAMIZATION, whereby primary responsibility for the ground fighting was transferred to the South Vietnamese military. By March 1972 U.S. troop strength in Southeast Asia had been reduced to roughly 70,000. On March 30 North Vietnam launched its EASTERTIDE OFFENSIVE against the South. Both the public Paris talks and private Kissinger-Tho contacts resumed in mid-July 1972, after Hanoi's military offensive had stalled. At a White House press conference on October 26 Kissinger revealed that discussions with Tho had produced a tentative agreement on a nine-point peace settlement. Kissinger's comment that "peace is at hand" later was scored by Democrats as a misleading assessment issued to influence the presidential election the following week. When negotiations to finalize an agreement reached an impasse on December 13, 1972, Nixon ordered a resumption of U.S. bombing of the North to force a peace settlement. The so-called CHRISTMAS BOMBING continued until December 30, when the White House announced Kissinger and Tho would meet in Paris in January.

The Kissinger-Tho talks culminated in the signing of a peace agreement among the United States, North Vietnam, South Vietnam, and Viet Cong on January 27, 1973. The Paris Peace Accords, officially the Agreement on Ending the War and Restoring Peace in Vietnam, implemented an internationally supervised cease-fire through-out Vietnam effective the same day. It speci-fied that all U.S. military forces would be withdrawn from South Vietnam within 60 days, allowed the North Vietnamese forces already in South Vietnam to remain there but barred their reinforcement, permitted U.S. military and economic aid to South Vietnam, and provided for the release of all prisoners of war (POWs) within 60 days. The parties stated their commitment to the reunification of Vietnam through peaceful means and reaffirmed the 17TH PARALLEL as the provisional dividing line between North and South. Hanoi tacitly accepted the con-tinued existence of the South Vietnamese government. Washington acquiesced to Viet Cong participation in a national recon-ciliation council to be established within 90 days. It was to oversee national elections meant to fulfill the right of the South Viet-namese people to self-determination. The United States indicated its readiness for im-proved relations with North Vietnam fol-lowing the war's end. The accords called for the withdrawal of all foreign troops from Laos and Cambodia and international respect for Laotian and Cambodian sover-eignty and neutrality. An International Commission of Control and Supervision (ICCS), composed of representatives from Canada, Poland, Hungary, and Indonesia, was created to supervise implementation of the agreement. Finally, an international peace conference on Indochina was to be held within 30 days. Invited to participate, besides the four signatories, were Great Britain, France, the Soviet Union, Commu-nist China, the four countries on the ICCS, and the UNITED NATIONS secretary-general.

Kissinger disputed critics who claimed the accords could have been concluded the previous October, thus avoiding the inten-sive bombing of North Vietnam that fol-lowed. He contended that Hanoi had sought to alter substantially the agreed-upon terms. Nixon refuted charges that a peace settlement could have been achieved four years earlier, noting that only at the end had North Vietnam dropped its insis-tence on the removal of the South Viet-namese government. The final American troops were withdrawn from Vietnam on March 29, 1973. The same day Hanoi re-leased what it claimed were its remaining 67 U.S. POWs. The accords extricated America from the war but did not end the fighting in Vietnam. Kissinger and Tho met in Paris in May and June for ultimately fruitless discussions on numerous Com-munist violations of the cease-fire. Due to the continuing hostilities, the international peace conference was never held and the national reconciliation council never estab-lished. Kissinger and Tho were awarded the Nobel Peace Prize in 1973. Tho de-clined to accept the award because Vietnam was not unified.

PARIS PEACE CONFERENCE (1919) Meeting of victorious Allied Powers that concluded the TREATY OF VERSAILLES (1919) with Germany ending WORLD WAR I. Facing imminent defeat, Germany in October 1918 appealed directly to President WOODROW WILSON for an end to hostilities on the basis of the peace terms outlined in his FOURTEEN POINTS (1918). The points, which provided a framework for a liberal peace settlement, called for open diplomacy, free trade, worldwide arms reductions, the right of na-tional self-determination, and impartial ad-justment of territorial claims. The final point proposed creation of a postwar LEAGUE OF NATIONS to maintain world peace and deter aggression through COLLECTIVE SE-CURITY. Wilson won Allied consent in the so-called pre-armistice agreement that the principles forming his peace program should serve as the basis for a permanent peace, with two exceptions. The Allies in-sisted that FREEDOM OF THE SEAS be left sub-ject to discussion and demanded that Ger-many pay reparations for damage done to Allied civilian populations. On November 11, 1918, Germany and the Allies signed the armistice agreement ending the fight-ing. Through ensuing consultations, Allied governments completed plans to meet in Paris to draw up a final peace treaty.

Believing his own presence a key to se-curing a just peace, the Democrat Wilson resolved to attend the peace conference. His decision, announced November 18, provoked strong criticism from leading Re-publicans who contended that the presi-dent's leadership and foreign policies had been repudiated in the just-completed con-gressional elections, in which Republicans captured majorities in both the House and Senate. The criticism intensified when Wil-son revealed that in addition to himself, the five-member U.S. peace commission would consist of presidential adviser Colonel ED-WARD M. HOUSE; Secretary of State ROBERT LANSING; General Tasker Bliss, who was a member of the Allied Supreme War Council in Paris; and veteran diplomat Henry White, the only Republican delegate. No senator or prominent Republican was included. Wilson also brought along THE IN-QUIRY, a group of technical experts, for information and advice. But he himself dominated the peace commission, making all of its key decisions.

The 32-nation peace conference convened in the French capital on January 18, 1919. The hundreds of delegates in attendance met periodically in plenary session, but the responsibility for all major decisions was vested in a supreme executive COUNCIL OF TEN, consisting of two representatives from each of the five major powers: the United States, Great Britain, France, Italy, and Japan. The Council of Ten was in time replaced by the even more powerful COUNCIL OF FOUR, consisting of Wilson, British Prime Minister David Lloyd George, French Premier Georges Clemenceau, and Italian Premier Vittorio Orlando. Wilson dominated the first phase of the conference with his efforts to gain priority consideration for his proposed association of nations, which he believed the cornerstone of any lasting peace settlement. At his insistence, the conference voted on January 25 to include the league as an integral part of the general peace treaty. Wilson assumed the chairmanship of the commission established to draw up the charter or covenant of the League of Nations.

It became necessary in framing the covenant to reach a decision on the status of Germany's colonies. While concurring with the Allied leaders that its prewar possessions not be restored to Germany, Wilson at the same time felt strongly that they not be parceled out as spoils of war. Initially he favored making the colonies the common possession of the league with its smaller member nations acting as trustees. The American president encountered opposition from Japan and members of the British Dominions, which wanted to annex the territories outright. Japan sought Germany's Pacific islands north of the equator, Australia desired German New Guinea and the German Pacific islands south of the

equator, and the Union of South Africa hoped to take possession of German South-West Africa. Delegates reached a consensus that all German colonies would be transferred to the jurisdiction of the league, which would then assign an administrative mandate over each to a member state. Under the compromise formula, Japan, the British Dominions, and other states were virtually guaranteed to obtain mandates over the territories they coveted. The commission subsequently produced a draft charter based largely on a plan initially put forward by Wilson. Under the covenant, all states were to be admitted as members of the League of Nations, which would hear all disputes arising between two or more member states. For Wilson the most important element of the charter was ARTICLE X, which embodied the idea of collective security. It obligated members to regard an attack on any one of them as an attack on all and to cooperate to preserve peace against external aggression. On February 14, 1919, President Wilson presented the completed draft Covenant of the League of Nations to a plenary session of the conference.

He then departed Paris for a short visit to the United States, where he encountered nascent Republican opposition to the league and its incorporation into the treaty. At a White House meeting on February 26 with members of the House and Senate committees on foreign relations, the president was grilled by his Republican critics, who suggested that the covenant infringed on U.S. sovereignty and might involve the United States in future wars fomented by the European powers. On March 4, 1919, with Wilson preparing to return to France, Senator HENRY CABOT LODGE, SR. (R-MA), chairman of the SENATE FOREIGN RELATIONS COMMITTEE, introduced the ROUND ROBIN, a resolution declaring the league covenant unacceptable in its proposed form. It was signed by 39 Republican senators or senators-elect, more than the one-third plus one of the Senate necessary to prevent ratification of any peace treaty. A defiant Wilson responded by forecasting that the covenant would be tied to so many parts of the final peace treaty that the two could not be separated without destroying the whole structure of a permanent settlement. By the time he arrived back in Paris on March 14, the president acknowledged the need to modify the original covenant to overcome Senate opposition. Promptly reconvening the League of Nations Commission, Wilson won approval of amendments that exempted domestic matters such as immigration and tariffs from the league's jurisdiction, allowed the United States to refuse a mandate over conquered colonies, permitted members to withdraw from the league upon two years' notice, and explicitly recognized the MONROE DOCTRINE.

In return for accepting these amendments, various delegations sought Wilson's support for further revisions in the covenant or pressed him for concessions on other aspects of the peace treaty. The Japanese wanted language formally recognizing the principle of racial equality inserted in the league covenant. Swayed by strong opposition among the British Dominions to the addition of such a statement, Wilson, as chairman of the League of Nations Commission, denied the Japanese appeal. To placate Japan and secure its support for his coveted league, however, he withdrew his opposition to Japanese acquisition of German rights, such as railroad and mining concessions, in China's Shantung Province, which Japanese forces had occupied during the war. Wilson did exact a pledge that Shantung eventually would be restored to China, with Japan retaining only economic concessions in the province.

The French demanded clear guarantees for their security against Germany, which had invaded France twice in the preceding half-century. France wanted the land west of the Rhine River detached from Germany and converted into a buffer state or permanent Allied occupation zone. Wilson adamantly opposed the proposal, contending it would violate the principle of self-determination by placing the five million Germans living in the Rhineland under French rule. A prolonged dispute followed, during which Clemenceau accused Wilson of being pro-German, and the American president threatened to walk out of the conference. The French finally accepted an arrangement whereby the Rhineland would be permanently demilitarized and occupied by Allied troops for 15 years. Wilson and Lloyd George, who backed the American president on the Rhineland question, agreed to a pair of virtually identical treaties obligating the United States and

Great Britain to defend France against an unprovoked German attack. The U.S. Senate never ratified the Franco-American version of the so-called Treaty of Guarantee.

The second major French demand concerned the issue of reparations. The British and French delegations insisted that Germany pay the full cost of the war to the Allied peoples. The United States itself sought no reparations. Acquiescing in the Anglo-French position, Wilson endorsed the idea that the war's cost should include such items as pensions to disabled Allied veterans and payments to the widows and children of those killed. This expansion of the definition of civilian damages agreed on in the armistice promised to double Germany's reparations. Wilson favored assessing Germany a fixed dollar sum and incorporating that figure in the peace treaty. Clemenceau and Lloyd George opposed establishment of a definite amount. The Council of Four ultimately agreed that the peace treaty itself would neither fix the amount of reparations nor set a time limit on payments; rather, a Reparations Commission would subsequently assess the sums that Germany was to pay.

With respect to Central Europe and the problems of national unity and defensible frontiers it presented, the U.S. and British delegations appealed for boundaries that would follow discernible lines of nationality. Wilson ended up compromising on the principle of self-determination when he supported the territorial settlement for that region worked out by conference. The new state of Czechoslovakia, which was formed through the dismemberment of the Austrian-Hungarian empire at the end of World War I, absorbed the Sudetenland, home to more than three million Germans. Poland, proclaimed an independent republic in 1918 in the wake of the Central Powers' defeat, obtained the German province of Posen (Poznan) and also the Polish Corridor, a strip separating East Prussia from the rest of Germany that gave the Poles access to the Baltic. Danzig (Gdansk), largely German in population, was made a free city under League of Nations jurisdiction.

Premier Orlando insisted that the BIG FOUR resolve certain issues of vital concern to Italy. He sought a pledge that the territorial provisions of the Treaty of London (1915), one of the so-called SECRET TREATIES, would be honored. The London Treaty promised Italy the South Tyrol up to the Brenner Pass, an area within which lived about 200,000 Austrian Germans, as well as territory at the head of and along the eastern shore of the Adriatic. At the conference Italy expanded its demand to include the port city of Fiume. Wilson accepted the Italian claim to the Brenner line before realizing that this new boundary violated his principle of self-determination. He objected strenuously, however, to Italy's bid for Fiume, which had a large Italian population but which was encircled by Yugoslav territory and, moreover, was the primary Adriatic port for the new state of Yugoslavia. With Orlando and his foreign minister, Sidney Sonnino, continuing to press their demand for Fiume, Wilson on April 23, 1919, appealed directly to the Italian people to repudiate their leaders and endorse what he termed a fair and just peace. An infuriated Orlando and Sonnino walked out of the conference and left Paris. The final details of the German treaty thus were worked out by Wilson, Clemenceau, and Lloyd George. With the Fiume question still unresolved, the Italians returned to the conference on May 6. Italy later negotiated an interim solution with Yugoslavia and ultimately, in 1924, gained control of Fiume.

The completed Treaty of Versailles was presented to the Germans on May 7, 1919. The final text embodied the league covenant, stripped Germany of its colonies, incorporated the reparations and territorial provisions worked out by the Big Four, forced Germany to admit its war guilt, and substantially disarmed it. After reviewing the treaty, Germany complained that its terms were exceedingly harsh and failed to constitute the just peace promised by the Allies in the armistice agreement. Under the threat of renewed Allied military action, the German government finally signed the treaty in Versailles's Hall of Mirrors on June 28, marking the end of the peace conference.

PARIS PEACE CONFERENCE (1946) International gathering of Allied nations after WORLD WAR II to finalize peace treaties for minor Axis powers Italy, Hungary, Bulgaria, Romania, and Finland. At the POTSDAM CONFERENCE (1945), the United States, Great Britain, and the Soviet Union formed a

COUNCIL OF FOREIGN MINISTERS to prepare draft peace settlements with the defeated Axis countries. At the December 1945 MOSCOW CONFERENCE, the BIG THREE agreed that the treaties for the lesser Axis countries, once drawn up by the council, would be submitted to an international peace conference for final approval. The council, comprising the foreign ministers of the Big Three and France, met in Paris from April 25 to May 16 and again from June 15 to July 12, 1946. The preliminary Paris Conference produced draft settlements for the former Axis satellites and laid the groundwork for the Paris Peace Conference, which convened in the French Capital on July 29, 1946, with the 21 nations that had fought against the European Axis powers in attendance. Held at a time of nascent COLD WAR tensions, the gathering was marked by increasingly acrimonious East-West debate over the future of Eastern Europe. The delegates were unable to resolve such questions as the disputed Italian-Yugoslav border and navigation of the Danube River. The conference adjourned October 15, 1946, without having completed the peace settlements. The treaties with the minor Axis powers finally were concluded at a meeting of the four-power Council of Foreign Ministers in New York from November 4 to December 12, 1946. The measures were signed in Paris on February 10, 1947, and came into force on September 16 of the same year.

PARIS PEACE TALKS See **PARIS PEACE ACCORDS**.

PARIS SUMMIT (1960)   Aborted May 1960 meeting of President DWIGHT D. EISENHOWER, British Prime Minister Harold MacMillan, French President Charles de Gaulle, and Soviet Premier Nikita S. Khrushchev. The parley was canceled on its first day as a result of the diplomatic fallout from the U-2 INCIDENT. Plans for a spring 1960 gathering of the four powers to address the East-West impasse on the status of Berlin were finalized in late December 1959. Preparations for the summit were disrupted at the last moment by a major international episode that proved a great embarrassment to the United States. On May 1, 1960, a U.S. U-2 spy plane was downed over the Soviet Union and its pilot, Gary Francis Powers, captured. The initial CENTRAL INTELLIGENCE AGENCY cover story of a lost weather research plane unravelled before evidence of U.S. espionage activities revealed by Khrushchev on May 7. The premier, expressing outrage over the violation of Soviet sovereignty, offered Eisenhower the opportunity to disavow the overflight. But on May 11, about to depart for Paris, the American president acknowledged he had authorized the spy mission and others like it and defended such surveillance as necessary to protect against a surprise Soviet attack. He also pledged to renew his 1955 OPEN SKIES proposal at the summit.

The Paris conference convened May 16 under a diplomatic cloud. In the opening session Khrushchev denounced the U-2 mission. He demanded Eisenhower apologize, punish those responsible for the overflight, and vow to halt further U.S. aerial surveillance of the USSR. Eisenhower announced the U-2 flights had been suspended and would not be resumed, but rejected the other Soviet demands as unacceptable to the United States. Khrushchev then withdrew an earlier invitation to the American president to visit his country in June. Deadlocked at the outset, the summit collapsed after its initial session and the leaders departed. The spy plane revelation and the abandoned Paris gathering ended immediate prospects for relaxation of COLD WAR tensions.

PARIS, TREATY OF (1783) Treaty signed on September 3, 1783, between the United States and Great Britain that formally ended the AMERICAN REVOLUTION and consummated American independence. Under the settlement, also known as the Peace of Paris and the Definitive Treaty of Peace, the United States gained title to a continental territory extending from the Atlantic to the Mississippi River and from Canada to Spanish Florida. The boundaries inherited by the new nation accommodated westward expansion after 1783 and were a key to early U.S. growth.

By 1780 Great Britain was formally at war with the United States, U.S. ally France, French ally Spain, and the unallied Netherlands, and found itself diplomatically isolated from most of the rest of Europe. British hopes for victory in America evaporated at the decisive Battle of Yorktown with the surrender of General Charles

Cornwallis's army in October 1781. Yorktown and British military setbacks to the French in the West Indies raised dissatisfaction in Great Britain with the already unpopular conflict. On February 27, 1782, Parliament approved a measure that demanded an end to the war and renounced further imperial efforts to hold the former American colonies. A bill adopted March 5 authorized the Crown to make peace. Prime Minister Lord North resigned under pressure on March 20 and was succeeded by the Marquis of Rockingham, whose new ministry moved swiftly to pursue a diplomatic settlement with the Americans. British envoy Richard Oswald was dispatched to Paris on April 12, 1782 to open negotiations with an American peace commission.

The Continental Congress in June 1781 had appointed a five-member commission—JOHN ADAMS, BENJAMIN FRANKLIN, JOHN JAY, Henry Laurens, and THOMAS JEFFERSON—to replace a single negotiator, John Adams, who was selected two years earlier when peace plans were initially contemplated. Congress at the same time had modified the peace terms it first drafted in 1779. Those included American independence, total British military evacuation from American territory, free navigation of the Mississippi River for both countries, and certain minimum boundaries in North America. Under the amended peace instructions, only independence remained an essential American demand; the handling of all other issues was left to the discretion of the commission. Influenced by the diplomatic supplications of French Foreign Minister Charles Gravier Comte de Vergennes, Congress also had ordered the commissioners to consult closely with America's ally France on all negotiations and to take no action without the "knowledge and concurrence" of the French foreign ministry.

Oswald opened informal talks with Franklin, who was the only commission member in Paris in the spring of 1782. Franklin and Vergennes made clear to the British envoy that the FRANCO-AMERICAN ALLIANCE (1778) precluded either the United States or France from completing a separate peace with Great Britain. In outlining American aims, Franklin distinguished between "necessary" terms, including independence, evacuation of troops from the United States, a generous territorial boundary, and fishing rights for Americans in Newfoundland waters; and "desirable" terms, such as a war indemnity for property damage, a commerce treaty, and British cession of Canada to the United States. The British government accepted the so-called "necessary" terms as grounds for discussions. Jay, arriving in Paris in June 1782 from a fruitless two-year diplomatic mission to Madrid, delayed the start of formal negotiations by insisting that Oswald's instructions first be changed to empower the British diplomat to deal officially with the United States of America rather than with the "Colonies."

Wary of the aims of French diplomacy, Jay doubted France's commitment to helping secure a treaty favorable to U.S. interests. He suspected Vergennes was prepared to defer, or even sacrifice, American independence to achieve French diplomatic goals. Evidence that France supported Spanish claims to the territory in America between the Appalachian Mountains and the Mississippi River fueled Jay's concerns, as did news of a secret trip in early September by Vergennes's secretary, Joseph Rayneval to London, which Jay took as proof of a French plan to divide the trans-Appalachian West between Spain and Great Britain. Believing protection of American interests demanded that Vergennes be excluded from negotiations, Jay decided to disregard Congress's instructions about French involvement. Without consulting Franklin, he communicated to Prime Minister Lord Shelbourne, who had come to power following Rockingham's death in July, his willingness to discuss terms with Oswald independently of France provided London would agree to imminent negotiations. A consenting British ministry on September 19 authorized Oswald to "treat with commissioners of the United States"—an instruction that satisifed Jay and was tantamount to recognition of American sovereignty. In early October, Jay and Oswald opened official talks and soon were joined by Franklin, who voiced mild objections to Jay's brash diplomacy but agreed with the initiative. Adams entered the discussions at month's end after arriving in Paris from the Netherlands, where he had concluded a commerce treaty and gained Dutch diplomatic recognition of the United States. Laurens reached Paris from London in November in the waning days of negotiations.

Jefferson, prevented by personal reasons from going to France, had no role in the peace talks.

On November 30, 1782, the four American commissioners and Oswald signed a preliminary peace treaty that was not to take effect until France also reached settlement with the British. The terms were a triumph for U.S. diplomacy. Great Britain recognized American independence and pledged to withdraw its military forces from U.S. territory "with all convenient speed." The United States gained the right to fish in waters off Newfoundland and Nova Scotia, and the privilege to dry and cure fish on Labrador and the Magdalen Islands. Generous British territorial cessions left the United States with a domain stretching from the Atlantic seaboard to the Mississippi River and from Canada to Spanish Florida at the 31st parallel. The preliminary settlement also satisfied two key British demands. First, the United States validated all private prewar debts owed to British creditors by American citizens; second, the American negotiators obligated the national government to press the state legislatures to restore fully the rights and property of Loyalists, or those American colonists who had not broken allegiance with Britain.

After learning of the terms of the preliminary treaty, Vergennes reproved the American commissioners for proceeding without French consultation. A personal letter from Franklin reaffirming America's commitment to the French alliance mollified Vergennes. Desiring a quick end to the war, the French foreign minister accepted the Anglo-American pact without serious objections. When France and Spain signed preliminary peace terms with Great Britain on January 20, 1783, the U.S. preliminary articles went into effect. The initial Anglo-American, Anglo-French, and Anglo-Spanish settlements served as armistice agreements that formally ended hostilities. The Continental Congress ratified the provisional treaty April 15 following a debate in which the commission's deliberate exclusion of the French from negotiations came under sharp criticism.

A final, formal peace was delayed while the Dutch and British negotiated a preliminary accord, which they finally concluded on September 2, 1783. The next morning the United States and Britain signed the definitive Treaty of Paris ending the Revolutionary War. That afternoon the French and Spanish signed separate, similar definitive treaties with the British. Terms of the final Anglo-American Peace of Paris were the same as those of the preliminary agreement.

Diplomatic problems fostered by ambiguities in the treaty were an important legacy of the historic Paris agreement. Mutual charges of noncompliance with the terms concerning British military withdrawal from America, the treatment of Loyalists, and payment of prewar debts beset Anglo-American relations for a decade after the war. These differences were addressed and largely resolved through the controversial JAY'S TREATY in 1794. U.S.-Spanish disputes over Spanish Florida's northern boundary and over navigation rights to the Mississippi River simmered until the two countries reached a settlement in PINCKNEY'S TREATY (1795). The Paris treaty's vague or faulty geographical descriptions invited competing U.S.-British territorial claims. Location of the Canadian-American boundary west of the Lake of the Woods in present-day Minnesota remained in dispute until the CONVENTION OF 1818. Disagreement over the boundary between Maine and Canada finally was cleared up through the WEBSTER-ASHBURTON TREATY (1842). The Peace of Paris failed to address the territorial rights or political status of the North American tribes that had allied with the British in the war, leaving to early U.S. diplomacy the issue of relations with the Indian nations.

See also MAP 2.

PARIS, TREATY OF (1898) Treaty of December 10, 1898, that ended the SPANISH-AMERICAN WAR and secured U.S. territorial acquisitions in the Caribbean and Pacific. After Spain sued for peace in late July 1898, President WILLIAM MCKINLEY demanded that Madrid relinquish Cuba and cede Puerto Rico and one of the Mariana Islands to the United States. He also insisted on U.S. occupation of Manila Bay pending a final determination on the status of the Philippines. Spain protested the severity of the initial terms but was forced to accept them, signing a preliminary peace protocol on August 12. The protocol, which ended the fighting, arranged for peace talks in Paris to conclude a final treaty that would resolve the Philippines question and the issue of the Cuban foreign debt of $400 million.

Formal negotiations began in the French capital October 1. The five-member American commission, led by former Secretary of State WILLIAM R. DAY, included Senators George Gray (D-DE), William P. Frye (R-ME), and Cushman K. Davis (R-MN), and *New York Tribune* owner WHITELAW REID. Their Spanish counterparts accepted the U.S. demand for Cuban independence and agreed to assume Cuba's past debts. On October 26 McKinley clarified U.S. designs regarding the Philippines by instructing his negotiators to demand Spanish cession of the archipelago. The president sided with expansionists who, advocating America's NEW MANIFEST DESTINY, coveted the islands for their strategic value as a naval outpost and for their commercial importance as a link to Asian trade. The Treaty of Paris was completed in December. Under its terms, a weakened Spain surrendered sovereignty over Cuba, ceded Puerto Rico and GUAM to the United States as a war indemnity, and reluctantly relinquished the Philippines in return for $20 million. The U.S. Senate ratified the treaty on February 6, 1899, by a vote of 57 to 27, or one more than the required two-thirds majority. Approval followed a bitter congressional debate in which anti-imperialist foes of U.S. expansionism in the Pacific offered stiff resistance to the pact.

See also IMPERIALISM, MAP 6, MAP 7.

PARIS UNION See **WORLD INTELLECTUAL PROPERTY ORGANIZATION**.

PARTIAL TEST BAN TREATY See **LIMITED TEST BAN TREATY**.

PASSENGER CASES (1849) U.S. Supreme Court ruling in two related cases striking down state laws that imposed a head tax on foreign passengers arriving by ship. In CITY OF NEW YORK V. MILN (1836), the Court had allowed the states wide latitude in controlling immigration. Massachusetts and New York had resorted to head taxes as a means of funding their immigration expenses. In a decision released February 7, 1849, a five to four majority found that these taxes infringed on the federal power to regulate foreign commerce. The involvement of state governments in the administration of immigration basically was brought to a halt by the Supreme Court in HENDERSON V. MAYOR OF NEW YORK (1876).

PAX AMERICANA Catchphrase conveying America's dominant global position since WORLD WAR II, particularly in the immediate postwar years. The expression (Latin for American Peace) derived from the similar Pax Britannica, describing leading world power Great Britain's maintenance of international peace and stability from the end of the Napoleonic Wars (1803–1815) to the onset of WORLD WAR I. Pax Britannica in turn was coined from Pax Romana, referring to an extended period of peace prevailing in the ancient world under Roman rule. The United States emerged from World War II unequaled in terms of military and economic power. Washington's ability to shape world events and serve as a global policeman meant it could, in effect, impose a Pax Americana on much of the world. Successive postwar American presidents exercised overwhelming U.S. military and economic strength to influence world affairs. The United States was unable to prevent the Soviet Union's postwar subjugation of Eastern Europe or the success of Mao Tse-tung's Communist revolution in China. With the onset of the COLD WAR, American power was committed to the CONTAINMENT of Communist expansionism.

By the mid-1960s fellow superpower and Communist adversary the Soviet Union, economically resurgent Europe and Japan, and the THIRD WORLD were all challenging American supremacy. The postwar Pax Americana generally is considered to have ended with America's disastrous involvement in the VIETNAM WAR. The collapse of communism and breakdown of the Soviet Union in the early 1990s left the United States as the only superpower, leading to suggestions of a possible return to a Pax Americana. Notwithstanding America's unquestioned military superiority, many experts argued that the nation's weakened economic position had diminished the U.S. capacity to dominate world affairs.

PAYNE-ALDRICH TARIFF (1909) Legislation that lowered U.S. import duties and began a brief period of moderated PROTECTIONISM in U.S. trade policy. The DINGLEY TARIFF (1897) had set customs fees at record-high levels. Wisconsin Senator Robert M. LaFollette and other progressive Republicans attacked protective tariffs as benefitting big business and other special interests and pressed for lower rates. Representative Sereno E. Payne (R-NY) introduced a tariff reform bill in 1909. Before its final passage, the measure was refashioned in the Senate by Nelson W. Aldrich (R-RI). Signed into law April 9, 1909, the act reduced import duties, but left rates at a still-protectionist average level of 40 percent. Further easing of customs charges occurred with the UNDERWOOD TARIFF (1913).

PAYNE'S LANDING, TREATY OF   See **OSCEOLA**.

PEACE CORPS Independent agency of the U.S. government that trains and sends American volunteers abroad to help the peoples of developing countries meet their needs for skilled manpower. During the 1960 presidential campaign the Democratic candidate, Massachusetts Senator JOHN F. KENNEDY, promoted the idea of a volunteer corps of skilled technicians devoted to improving the living conditions in THIRD WORLD countries. After becoming president, Kennedy established the Peace Corps by executive order on March 1, 1961, and appointed brother-in-law Sargent Shriver as its first director. The agency, an elaboration on the Truman administration's POINT FOUR program of technical assistance to underdeveloped areas, was made permanent on September 22, 1961, with the passage by Congress of the Peace Corps Act. In 1971 the Peace Corps was placed under ACTION, an umbrella federal agency set up by President RICHARD M. NIXON to coordinate U.S. volunteer programs, both domestic and overseas. Congress returned the corps to independent status in 1981.

Its stated purpose, beyond the functional objective of furnishing technical know-how to less-developed nations, is to foster better mutual understanding among Americans and the people they aid. From the agency's inception, adult Americans of all ages have been eligible to volunteer. The program's original orientation, however, was on youth. Kennedy envisioned the corps as a vehicle for mobilizing the idealism of young Americans in a service that would promote a positive image of America in the Third World, which had become a major new front in the COLD WAR ideological competition between Moscow and Washington. Participants, the president explained in 1961, would live under the same "hardship conditions" as the citizens of the countries to which they were sent.

Volunteers undergo 9 to 14 weeks of preliminary training in the language of their host country and its economy, geography, history, and customs, as well as in the technical skills needed for their specific overseas assignments. Recruits generally serve for two years. Since 1961 Peace Corps personnel have worked on projects in agriculture, food production, health, natural resource conservation, community development, and elementary education. The corps currently has about 7000 volunteers posted in some 60 countries throughout Latin America, Africa, Eastern Europe, the Near East, Asia, and the Pacific.

PEACE DIVIDEND Catchphrase coined to identify money in the U.S. budget that, with the end of the COLD WAR, could be shifted from defense outlays to other purposes. With the political and economic liberalization of the Soviet Union under Mikhail S. Gorbachev, the steady improvement in U.S.-Soviet relations, and the collapse of communism in Eastern Europe in 1989, American civilian and military leaders generally concurred that the United States no longer needed to maintain large military forces to defend Western Europe. By early 1990, public discussion of the federal budget centered on the possibility of freeing substantial sums from defense spending and applying these savings, dubbed the "peace dividend," to domestic programs. The focus on defense budget cuts was interrupted in late 1990 by the PERSIAN GULF WAR. Following the conflict, attention returned to the issue of reductions in U.S. armed forces. Talk of a peace dividend faded, however, as it became apparent that the need to continue to maintain a sizable military, the inherent difficulties and delays in cutting defense programs, and domestic political pressures against military spending reductions in local areas meant any savings realized would fall well short of the previously anticipated windfall.

See also MILITARY-INDUSTRIAL COMPLEX.

PEACE OF PARIS See **PARIS, TREATY OF** (1783).

PEACE POLICY U.S. approach to INDIAN AFFAIRS framed in the decade after the Civil War. The federal government developed the Peace Policy to relieve the problem of continuing warfare with the Plains Indians from Montana to Texas. It prevailed after Congress determined that the alternative, attempting to subdue the Indians by military force, would be excessively costly and time-consuming. The policy drew on the recommendations of the INDIAN PEACE COMMISSION established by Congress in July 1867. The new approach called for a negotiated end to the Plains Indian wars, an American commitment to honor its treaty obligations, and substantial U.S. financial support for the transition of the Indians to a settled agricultural life. The basic goal of confining the Indians to reservations guided U.S. policy until the late 1880s, at which point all the tribes had been subjugated.

PEACE OF TIPITAPA See **NICARAGUAN INTERVENTIONS**.

"PEACE WITHOUT VICTORY" SPEECH (1917) Address to the U.S. Senate on January 22, 1917, in which President WOODROW WILSON outlined his proposal for a desirable peace settlement of WORLD WAR I. At the war's outset in August 1914 he had proclaimed American neutrality. Thereafter the Wilson administration's goal had been to keep the United States from getting drawn into the conflict. Frustrated by his abortive diplomatic efforts in 1915 and 1916 to end the military struggle between the Allies and Central Powers, Wilson went before the Senate in January 1917 to explain to Americans and the world his ideas on what kind of peace should result. This must be, he insisted, a "peace without victory." He argued that a conqueror's imposed peace would humiliate the loser and would not endure. "Only a peace between equals can last," Wilson contended. The president maintained that a durable peace would be based upon national self-determination, the equality of all nations, FREEDOM OF THE SEAS, and an overall reduction of armaments worldwide. Raising the concept of COLLECTIVE SECURITY, he asserted the need for an organization of nations at war's end to guarantee a peaceful world.

His speech drew immediate objection in the Senate from Republican members unalterably opposed to collective security. Senator William E. Borah (R-ID) on January 25 proposed a resolution stating the United States must abide by its historic commitment to avoiding entanglement in European politics. Senator HENRY CABOT LODGE, SR. (R-MA) followed by suggesting that U.S. participation in any postwar association of nations organized to safeguard world security would involve an unacceptable surrender of American sovereignty. Developments soon preempted both Wilson's appeal for "peace without victory" and Borah's resolution. Germany's announcement on January 31, 1917 that after February 1 it would resume unrestricted submarine warfare began a chain of events that ended with America's entry into World War I in April 1917 on the Allied side.

PEACEFUL NUCLEAR EXPLOSIONS TREATY (1976) U.S.-Soviet agreement governing underground nuclear explosions for peaceful purposes. The 1963 LIMITED TEST BAN TREATY prohibited all nuclear tests other than those conducted underground. The 1974 THRESHOLD TEST BAN TREATY placed a maximum size on underground test explosions of 150 kilotons (150,000 tons of TNT). Because no essential difference existed between a nuclear device used as a weapon and one employed for peaceful purposes, such as large-scale excavation, the United States and the Soviet Union undertook to draft a parallel agreement to the threshold treaty placing similar restrictions on peaceful nuclear explosions. The Treaty on Underground Nuclear Explosions for Peaceful Purposes was signed May 28, 1976, by President GERALD R. FORD in Washington and Soviet General Secretary Leonid I. Brezhnev in Moscow. The pact limited individual peaceful nuclear explosions to 150 kilotons. Group explosions similarly were held to 150 kilotons unless their component blasts could be separately identified and measured. Both sides agreed to abide by the provisions pending the treaty's formal ratification. U.S. Senate approval was delayed, however, first by the Carter administration, which as an alternative sought to negotiate a COMPREHENSIVE TEST BAN TREATY,

and then by the Reagan administration, which argued the agreement's verification procedures were inadequate. At their 1990 WASHINGTON SUMMIT, President GEORGE BUSH and Soviet President Mikhail S. Gorbachev on June 1 agreed on a detailed protocol to the treaty strengthening its verification provisions. The amended pact, together with the companion threshold treaty, was ratified by the Senate on September 25, 1990.

PEARL HARBOR (1941) U.S. naval base on the Hawaiian island of Oahu, site of a Japanese surprise attack that brought the United States into WORLD WAR II. U.S.-Japanese relations deteriorated steadily in the late 1930s and early 1940s over Japanese aggression in the Far East. While neither country was yet a belligerent in the world war, Japan allied itself with Axis powers Germany and Italy and the United States sided with Great Britain. In early November 1941, the Japanese government decided that unless ongoing U.S-Japanese discussions promptly yielded American endorsement of Japanese hegemony in the Western Pacific, it would resort to war. On November 25 a naval task force secretly left Japan with plans to attack the U.S. fleet at Pearl Harbor. On November 27, with Japanese military preparations and intercepted communications both indicating possible hostilities, Washington issued a war warning to U.S. Pacific commanders. U.S. officials surmised any attack would come in the Southwest Pacific. Meanwhile U.S.-Japanese negotiations had reached an impasse. On the morning of December 7, 1941, Japanese warplanes struck without warning at Pearl Harbor. Nineteen U.S. ships were sunk or disabled, about 175 planes destroyed, and roughly 3000 soldiers and sailors killed or wounded. Japanese losses were very light. The attack failed to cripple the U.S. Pacific fleet, however, since its critical aircraft carriers were at sea that morning.

On December 8 America formally declared war on Japan. In his famous address before a joint session of Congress, President FRANKLIN D. ROOSEVELT called December 7 a "date which will live in infamy." The sneak attack at Pearl Harbor sparked widespread outrage and anger in the United States, unifying the country behind the war effort. On December 11 Japan's Axis allies

Germany and Italy declared war on the United States. The U.S. Congress responded with declarations of war against the two nations the same day. In January 1942 a presidential commission headed by Supreme Court Justice Owen J. Roberts criticized the local Army and Navy commanders at Hawaii for failing to implement adequate defensive measures. Persistent questions about the failure of U.S. prewar military preparations led Congress in September 1945 to appoint a Joint Committee on the Investigation of the Pearl Harbor Attack. In its report submitted in July 1946, the committee absolved the Roosevelt administration of direct responsibility for the military disaster. Continuing allegations that Roosevelt in late 1941 concealed warnings about the impending Japanese attack so as to allow America to be drawn into the war have never been substantiated.

PEARL HARBOR TREATY See **HAWAIIAN RECIPROCITY TREATY**.

PEKING SUMMIT (1972) Historic meeting February 21 to 28, 1972, between President RICHARD M. NIXON and Chinese leaders Chairman Mao Tse-tung and Premier Chou En-lai that marked a shift toward normalized Sino-American relations after more than 20 years of antagonism and diplomatic stalemate. Nixon's visit, first by an American president to Communist China, was a dramatic symbol of the beginning of a thaw between Washington and Peking.

Since 1949, when Mao's Communist forces completed the takeover of the mainland and established the People's Republic of China, the United States had recognized the nationalist Republic of China with its capital in Taiwan. Affirming U.S. support of the nationalists, the Eisenhower administration completed the UNITED STATES-TAIWAN MUTUAL DEFENSE PACT in 1954. The deadlock in Sino-American relations after 1955 hardened in the 1960s with America's escalating involvement in the VIETNAM WAR. The Nixon administration in its first term took discreet steps toward reconciliation and a more pragmatic relationship between Washington and Peking. In 1971 the U.S. government lifted a ban on American travel to China, eased a 21-year trade embargo with the mainland, and engaged in PING-PONG DIPLOMACY. Nixon believed U.S.-Chinese rapprochement would serve U.S. strategic in-

terests and perceived that the increasingly hostile Sino-Soviet split in the late 1960s had opened the Chinese leadership to a relaxation of tensions with the United States.

Nixon in mid-July 1971 stunned the world with the surprise announcement he would attend a Peking Summit with Chinese leaders in early 1972 to seek the normalization of relations between the two countries and to confer on issues of mutual concern, such as Vietnam, Soviet designs on Asia, Sino-American cultural exchanges, and bilateral trade. Arrangements for the parley had been set during national security adviser HENRY A. KISSINGER's secret talks in Peking July 9 to 11 with Chou En-lai. At a follow-up Kissinger visit in October, the two sides finalized the agenda and itinerary for the Nixon trip. Addressing himself to the problem posed by U.S. support for Nationalist China in pre-summit remarks, the president stressed the new Sino-American relationship would not result in Washington's abandonment of Taiwan.

Nixon arrived in Peking February 21. Following a week of private talks, public banquets, and sight-seeing, Nixon and Chou issued the joint SHANGHAI COMMUNIQUE spelling out agreement on the need for increased contacts between their nations. The communique included U.S. acceptance of Peking's claim that Taiwan was part of China and outlined a U.S. pledge ultimately to withdraw its military advisers from the island. Generally favorable domestic reaction to the summit was partly offset by strong conservative Republican criticism, which charged Nixon with deserting the Nationalist Chinese government. Taiwan denounced the Shanghai Communique. Nixon sent senior diplomats on a tour of Asian countries to explain the Peking talks and assure America's allies in the region of U.S. determination to uphold its strategic and commercial interests in East Asia.

Progress toward normal relations continued after 1972 through increased trade and cultural contacts. In May 1973 the two countries established nondiplomatic liaison offices in Peking and Washington. President GERALD R. FORD's trip to the 1975 PEKING SUMMIT reconfirmed the U.S. commitment to closer contacts with mainland China.

PEKING SUMMIT (1975) Four days of talks on key issues in U.S.-Chinese diplomacy between President GERALD R. FORD and the leadership of the People's Republic of China, including Chairman Mao Tse-tung and Deputy Premier Deng Xiaoping. Premier Chou En-lai, a major presence at the historic PEKING SUMMIT in 1972, was ill and did not take part in the parley. Ford's Peking visit from December 1 to 4 continued the U.S. push for normalization of relations begun by the Nixon administration in the early 1970s. The U.S.-Soviet relationship was a major topic on the summit agenda. The Chinese criticized the American policy of DETENTE with the USSR and pressed the president to adopt a harder stance against the Soviets, whom Deng called the greatest threat to global peace. The two sides remained deadlocked on Korea, as Ford rejected the Chinese proposal for withdrawal of U.S. troops from South Korea and direct talks between the United States and North Korea.

Discussion ended without substantive new agreement on Sino-American contacts. This contrasted sharply with the 1972 Peking gathering, which yielded the landmark SHANGHAI COMMUNIQUE establishing guidelines for improvement of U.S.-China relations. The 1975 parley also resulted in no new initiatives on the Taiwan issue. In closing toasts on December 4, Ford and Deng reaffirmed the Shanghai accord, which acknowledged Chinese claims to Taiwan. On a stopover in Honolulu on the return from the People's Republic, the president delivered a speech in which he declared the so-called FORD DOCTRINE. The new doctrine asserted that world stability and U.S. security depended on American commitments in Asia. The next face-to-face meeting of U.S. and Chinese leaders was at the WASHINGTON SUMMIT in 1979.

PEKING SUMMIT (1984)   See **BEIJING SUMMIT**.

PENTAGON   Name of the massive five-sided Defense Department headquarters building outside Washington, D.C. The structure was completed in 1943 during WORLD WAR II. Since the establishment of the Defense Department in 1949, the term has become a synonym for the department itself and for the American military establishment.

PENTAGON PAPERS   Defense Department study of U.S. policy during the VIETNAM WAR.

In June 1967 Secretary of Defense ROBERT S. MCNAMARA directed the preparation of a comprehensive internal review of U.S. military involvement in Southeast Asia. Completed in January 1969, the 47-volume *History of the United States Decision-Making Process on Vietnam Policy* chronicled the deepening American role in Vietnam from 1945 to 1968. Dubbed the Pentagon Papers after the Defense Department's headquarters building outside Washington, D.C., the top-secret study included both extensive analysis and numerous classified government documents.

In March 1971 Daniel Ellsberg, who had worked on the Pentagon Papers as a researcher at the RAND CORPORATION, furnished a copy to Neil Sheehan, a reporter for the *New York Times*. A one-time hawkish supporter of the war who had come to oppose U.S. involvement in Vietnam, Ellsberg believed disclosure of the papers would spur the growing antiwar movement. On June 13, 1971, the *Times* began printing excerpts from the still highly classified government study. Seeking both to protect secret intelligence sources revealed in the documents and to prevent the further erosion of public support for the war, the Nixon administration went to court to halt publication. On June 30, 1971, the U.S. Supreme Court ruled 6 to 3 in *The New York Times* v. *United States* that the newspaper had a First Amendment right to publish the material. The *Times* and other newspapers subsequently ran extensive extracts and the *Times* published a condensed book version. An offical 12-volume Government Printing Office edition also was released in 1971. The Pentagon Papers provided the American public a detailed, inside account of government decision making. The U.S. link to the DIEM COUP (1963) and the Johnson administration's manipulation of the TONKIN GULF INCIDENT (1964) were among the revelations cited by antiwar critics as evidence of a credibility gap in U.S. policy in Southeast Asia. Meanwhile defenders of the war suggested that the papers showed the consistency of basic U.S. policy over four presidential administrations to aid South Vietnam.

The Pentagon Papers and other unauthorized disclosures of classified information to the press prompted President RICHARD M. NIXON to form a special White House unit known as the "Plumbers" to halt the leaks. Illegal acts by the "Plumbers" culminated in the Watergate scandal, which forced Nixon's resignation in 1974. Ellsberg was arrested in June 1971 and charged with theft of government property and violations of the ESPIONAGE ACT. His case ended in a mistrial in May 1973 when it was learned that the White House in 1971 had ordered an improper break-in and search of the Los Angeles office of Ellsberg's psychiatrist and the tapping of Ellsberg's phone conversations.

PER CENTUM LIMIT ACT See **IMMIGRATION ACT OF 1921**.

PERDICARIS AFFAIR (1904) Diplomatic incident in the independent North African sultanate of Morocco that President THEODORE ROOSEVELT exploited to enhance his reputation for strength in foreign affairs. In May 1904 Ion Perdicaris, a Greek native holding American naturalization papers, was abducted and held for ransom by a Moroccan chieftan named Raisuli. The United States rushed a warship to Moroccan waters and demanded that Morocco's sultan help win Perdicaris's freedom. Even though arrangements for the captive's release were concluded promptly and with Roosevelt's knowledge, the president advised Secretary of State JOHN M. HAY to deliver a further message of protest through the American consul general in Tangier. Hay's famous June 22 telegram, sent just as Perdicaris was being freed, ended with the dramatic exclamation that the United States would see "Perdicaris alive or Raisuli dead." Hay's ultimatum to Tangier stirred delegates at the Republican National Convention then meeting in Chicago. The delegates, about to nominate Roosevelt for a second term, cheered the forceful Morocco dispatch as an example of the president's BIG STICK diplomacy at work.

PERMANENT COURT OF ARBITRATION See **WORLD COURT**.

PERMANENT COURT OF INTERNATIONAL JUSTICE See **WORLD COURT**.

PERRY, MATTHEW CALBRAITH (1794–1858) Naval officer best remembered for his path-breaking expedition to Japan in the early 1850s. Born in Newport, Rhode Island, he entered the U.S. Navy in 1809 and saw his first action in the Anglo-American LITTLE BELT INCIDENT (1811). A younger brother of Naval Commodore Oliver Hazard Perry, he served during the WAR OF 1812 aboard the *President* and the *United States*. Afterward he filled a variety of assignments with the Navy. Perry helped convoy freed American slaves to the haven of Liberia in West Africa, pursued pirates in the West Indies in 1822, cruised the Mediterranean in the mid-1820s, and in 1830 made a voyage to Russia, where he declined an offer of a commission in the Russian navy.

Serving ashore for the most part from 1833 to 1841, Perry devised the enlisted naval training system finally adopted by Congress in 1837 and organized the first American naval engineering corps. A founder of the U.S. Naval Lyceum for officer education, he later helped plan the curriculum at the U.S. Naval Academy established at Annapolis in 1845. An early proponent of steam warships, he is sometimes called the father of the steam navy. He commanded the American squadron sent to Africa in 1843 to help the British navy suppress the slave trade under terms of the WEBSTER-ASHBURTON TREATY (1842). During the MEXICAN WAR (1846–1848) Commodore Perry led U.S. naval forces operating on Mexico's east coast. His squadron supported General WINFIELD SCOTT's landing at Veracruz and seige of the city.

In 1852 Perry embarked on the course that brought him fame when he accepted command of a pioneering American expedition to Japan, a country closed to the West for more than two centuries. Directed by President MILLARD FILLMORE to secure a treaty opening Japan to commercial and diplomatic ties with the United States, he sailed from Norfolk, Virginia, with four warships. He was instructed initially to try persuasion in quest of U.S. aims. Failing that, he was expected to impress on the Japanese, through a show of force, America's determination to initiate relations. Perry's armada arrived in the Bay of Edo (later Tokyo) in July 1853 and the American commander delivered a letter from Fillmore to the Japanese emperor outlining American proposals. Perry informed imperial officials he would return early the following year for a definitive reply, then withdrew with his ships to China. He sailed into Edo Bay a second time in February 1854 with seven ships. Japanese authorities, yielding to American insistence, decided to end their isolation and on March 31, 1854, signed the TREATY OF KANAGAWA. This historic agreement, Perry's crowning accomplishment, opened the Pacific island empire to U.S. trade and laid a foundation for diplomatic contacts. After returning to the United States, he was honored before Congress. In retirement in New York, Perry completed a three-volume narrative of his expedition.

PERSHING, JOHN JOSEPH (1860–1948) Army general, commander of U.S. forces sent to Europe in WORLD WAR I. Pershing graduated from West Point in 1886. After serving with the cavalry in the final actions against the Apache Indians in Arizona and the Sioux in the Dakotas, he became a military instructor at the University of Nebraska, where he also earned a law degree, and returned to West Point as a tactical officer. Cadets gave the demanding Pershing the nickname "Black Jack" for his prior service with black cavalry units. The name stuck, coming to signify his harsh toughness. During the SPANISH-AMERICAN WAR (1898) he won distinction for his combat performance in the invasion of Cuba. He returned to Washington and was assigned to head the newly formed Bureau of Insular Affairs in the War Department. He helped develop early U.S. policies for the administration of the territories won from Spain in the war.

Pershing reported to the Philippines in 1901 as the PHILIPPINE INSURRECTION against U.S. rule was drawing to an end. He participated in the initial efforts to subdue the fiercely independent Moro tribespeople on Mindanao Island. In 1905 he was named U.S. military attache to Japan, where he became an official observer of the Russo-Japanese War (1904–1905). His dispatches on the conflict impressed President THEODORE ROOSEVELT, who selected him for promotion to general over more senior officers in 1906. Pershing returned to the Philippines where, as commander of the Mindanao department, he helped conclude the MORO WARS (1901–1913).

While stationed in Texas in 1915, he learned that his wife and three of his four young children had been killed in a fire in San Francisco. Following Francisco (Pancho) Villa's surprise raid on Columbus, New Mexico, in March 1916, Pershing commanded the PUNITIVE EXPEDITION that pur-

sued the Mexican guerrilla leader across Mexico until February 1917. Villa eluded capture by Pershing but his band was dispersed and his ability to stage attacks across the border into U.S. territory curtailed. In May 1917 Pershing was selected to head U.S. forces in Europe in World War I. He arrived in France in June in advance of the AMERICAN EXPEDITIONARY FORCE (AEF). While resolutely insisting American forces remain in a separate command rather than serve as replacements for British and French units, he built the AEF into a 2-million-man army. The AEF was sent into battle in the spring of 1918, playing a critical role in halting the final German offensive in France. That September it was part of the Allied offensive that ended the war. Pershing's generalship in organizing, training, and leading the AEF won wide renown.

In 1919 he became the first general since GEORGE WASHINGTON to be promoted to five-star rank. Named Army chief of staff in 1921, he retired in 1924. The following year he headed a special commission on an unsuccessful mission to South America to settle a boundary dispute between Chile and Peru. In retirement he served as chairman of the American Battle Monuments Commission and penned *My Experiences in the World War* (1931), which garnered a Pulitzer Prize for history.

PERSHING II U.S. intermediate-range nuclear missile. The weapon system, named for General JOHN J. PERSHING, became an important and highly visible factor in U.S.-Soviet relations. Under its 1979 DUAL-TRACK DECISION, the NATO Western security alliance resolved to deploy newly developed Pershing II missiles in Western Europe if similar Soviet missiles were not withdrawn from Eastern Europe. The Soviet response was unfavorable and the first Pershing II's appeared in Western Europe in 1983. Deployment of the missiles, with a range of about 1100 miles and thus capable of reaching targets in the USSR, prompted a Soviet walk-out from superpower arms control discussions in Geneva. Following the resumption of negotiations, the Pershing II's were eliminated, along with their Soviet counterparts, under the INTERMEDIATE NUCLEAR FORCES TREATY (1987).

PERSIAN GULF INTERVENTION (1987–1988) Commitment of U.S. forces to the

Persian Gulf during the Iran-Iraq War (1980–1988) to protect neutral shipping. The intervention came in response to the increasingly frequent attacks on international commercial shipping in the area as a result of the long-standing conflict. Kuwait, virtually allied with Iraq, in late 1986 had approached both the United States and Soviet Union seeking military protection from Iranian assault on its fleet of oil tankers. Moscow responded by leasing Kuwait three tankers that would carry Kuwaiti oil under the Soviet flag and by sending several warships to the gulf to escort the Soviet transport vessels. The Soviet naval presence alarmed the United States, which feared an increase in the Kremlin's political influence in the area. Eager both to discourage an enlarged Soviet role and to prevent an Iranian military victory in the strategic gulf region, the Reagan administration early in 1987 proposed a scheme to reregister Kuwait's tankers as U.S.-owned ships eligible for protection by U.S. forces. The White House began briefing key congressional committees on the reflagging initiative in March 1987. But the plan drew little notice in Congress until the STARK INCIDENT on May 17, in which an American frigate on patrol in the region was struck by two deadly missiles fired from an Iraqi jet. Three days later the Reagan administration announced formally that Kuwaiti tankers would fly the American flag and be escorted in the gulf by Navy warships.

In the ensuing weeks the proposal became the focus of intense bipartisan congressional opposition. Many members argued that the reflagging policy presented substantial risks of a direct military confrontation between the United States and Iran. President RONALD W. REAGAN acknowledged the possibility of conflict but insisted that a failure to proceed posed a greater threat to American interests. He fended off House and Senate attempts to delay his Persian Gulf initiative and the reflagging operation began in July 1987. Democratic lawmakers took exception to Reagan's assertion of far-reaching presidential authority to commit U.S. armed forces without prior congressional consultation or approval. They suggested that the deployment of the protective naval escorts skirted the WAR POWERS RESOLUTION, the 1973 law intended to guarantee an integral role for

Congress in decisions to send American forces into harm's way. Apprehensions on Capitol Hill were heightened when from the outset the U.S.-led convoys encountered such gulf hazards as Iranian mines and missile attacks. The PENTAGON responded by sending minesweeping helicopters to the area and striking at Iranian oil platforms used as bases for laying mines and staging assaults on neutral commerce. Abandoning their initial refusal to take part in the operation, Great Britain, France, Italy, the Netherlands, and Belgium soon contributed ocean-going minesweeping and other forces to the U.S. initiative. The European actions, together with pledges of financial support by Japan and several Arab oil states, quieted intense criticism in the United States over the nonparticipation of American allies.

In October 1987 the Senate adopted a resolution expressing general concern over the reflagging of Kuwaiti tankers. But it deferred a vote on whether to invoke the War Powers Resolution and thereby trigger the legislation's 90-day deadline for the withdrawal of U.S. forces unless Congress authorized them to remain. The convoy operations settled into a relatively uneventful routine that was interrupted abruptly in April 1988 when a Navy ship struck a mine and was disabled. The White House met with senior congressional leaders to plot retaliatory action. Ensuing U.S. strikes on Iranian targets enjoyed broad bipartisan support in Congress. The VINCENNES INCIDENT on July 3 exacerbated U.S.-Iranian tensions. But the conclusion in late August 1988 of a formal truce in the Iran-Iraq War represented a major breakthrough in the Persian Gulf and prompted the Defense Department to begin reducing the size of the U.S. force there.

See also PERSIAN GULF WAR.

PERSIAN GULF WAR (1991) Conflict in which a U.S.-led multilateral coalition forced Iraq to end its occupation of Kuwait. Long-standing Iraqi expansionist designs on Kuwait fueled mounting tensions in 1990 between the neighboring Arab countries. On August 2, 1990, Iraqi forces invaded and seized Kuwait. President GEORGE BUSH joined in the immediate international condemnation of the Iraqi aggression. The UNITED NATIONS Security Council unanimously called for Iraq's unconditional withdrawal from Kuwait. Defying the United Nations, Iraqi President Saddam Hussein declared that Iraq had annexed Kuwait. The Bush administration grew alarmed over a possible further Iraqi military thrust to seize the oil fields of U.S.-ally Saudi Arabia. Bush made clear the United States would not accept Saddam gaining control over much of the world's oil reserves. On August 7 he dispatched U.S. forces to the defense of Saudi Arabia. Dubbed Operation Desert Shield, the deployment quickly became the largest American overseas military commitment since the VIETNAM WAR. By mid-October U.S. forces in the Persian Gulf numbered some 200,000.

Iraq's invasion of Kuwait represented the first post–COLD WAR international crisis. Washington and Moscow, historically rivals in the Middle East, coordinated closely on their response to the Iraqi aggression. Bush and Soviet leader Mikhail S. Gorbachev met at the HELSINKI SUMMIT in September 1991 to discuss the Persian Gulf situation. The United States spearheaded formation of a broad international political and military coalition committed to reversing Iraq's annexation of Kuwait. U.S.-Soviet cooperation yielded a series of U.N. Security Council resolutions denouncing Iraqi actions in Kuwait and imposing economic sanctions on Baghdad. The defense of Saudi Arabia and use of sanctions to compel Iraq to pull back from Kuwait enjoyed wide support in the U.S. Congress. But Bush's announcement on November 8 that the administration was roughly doubling the size of the U.S. combat forces in the Gulf in preparation for possible offensive operations against Iraq raised fears among Democratic lawmakers that the nation was sliding toward war. Bush justified deepening American involvement in the Gulf by citing the strategic importance of the region and its oil resources and the need to provide for the security of U.S. allies. Confronting Iraq's aggression, he asserted, was a test of the post–Cold War world's ability to keep the peace. The president coined the phrase "new world order" to describe his idea of a "new partnership of nations . . . based on consultation, cooperation, and collective action." He established Iraqi withdrawal from Kuwait as the objective of U.S. policy. While vilifying Saddam as a present-day

Adolf Hitler, Bush stopped short of making the Iraqi leader's ouster an explict American goal.

On November 29, 1990, the Security Council passed Resolution 678 authorizing the U.S.-led coalition to use armed force to remove Iraq from Kuwait if it had not withdrawn by January 15, 1991. By the end of 1990 the 28-nation coalition had assembled a powerful force of more than a half-million troops in the Saudi Arabian desert, including units from Great Britain, France, Egypt, Syria, and the Arab Gulf states. The Soviet Union committed no forces to the operation. U.S. Army General H. Norman Schwarzkopf was placed in overall command of the coalition forces, the bulk of which were from the United States. As the U.N. deadline approached, U.S. Secretary of State JAMES A. BAKER 3RD met with Iraqi Foreign Minister Tariq Aziz in Geneva on January 9, 1991, in a final unsuccessful attempt to get Baghdad to leave Kuwait and avert hostilities.

Bush meanwhile was forced to contend with a sizable domestic opposition to the nation becoming involved in a war with Iraq. "No blood for oil" became the popular chant of antiwar protesters, who suggested that the U.S. government bore considerable responsibility for Iraq's expansionist aggression because Washington had tolerated Saddam's repressive regime throughout the 1980s when doing so served U.S. strategic interests. While maintaining he had the constitutional authority to commit U.S. troops to a U.N. peacekeeping mission, Bush was eager to avoid a confrontation with Congress over its war-making powers. On January 8 the president formally asked Congress to approve the participation of U.S. forces in impending U.N. military action in the Persian Gulf. On January 12 the House by 250 to 183 and Senate by 52 to 47 approved a resolution authorizing the president to use military force if Iraq had not complied with all U.N. resolutions by January 15. The close vote in the Senate reflected the desire of many legislators to postpone military action in order to give economic sanctions more time to work.

Iraq steadfastly refused to withdraw from Kuwait. The Persian Gulf War began on January 16, 1991, when Bush ordered an aerial bombing campaign launched against Iraq. With the start of hostilities, Operation Desert Shield was redesignated Operation Desert Storm. Coalition aircraft and missiles struck at Iraq around the clock, encountering little effective resistance and inflicting devastating damage. Iraq attempted to split the allied coalition by launching Scud missile attacks against Israel. Heeding diplomatic appeals from Washington, the Jewish state refused to be drawn into the conflict, recognizing that its participation might drive Arab members from the coalition. After weeks of sustained bombing, Iraq on February 15 signaled a readiness to negotiate its departure from Kuwait. The United States rejected the Iraqi initiative, claiming it contained unacceptable conditions and demands. For the first time, Bush also called on the Iraqi people to overthrow Saddam. The Soviet Union then interceded in an effort to mediate an end to the conflict. Aziz flew to Moscow and several Soviet-Iraqi peace plans were drafted, each of which Bush rejected as incompatible with the U.N. demand for unconditional Iraqi withdrawal. When Baghdad ignored a final ultimatum, the president gave the go-ahead on February 23, 1991, for a massive ground offensive to liberate Kuwait. In a lightning-fast 100-hour ground war, the coalition forces recaptured Kuwait and routed the occupying Iraqi army. The frontline Iraqi soldiers offered almost no resistance and tens of thousands surrendered to coalition units. On February 27 Bush declared Kuwait free and announced a cease-fire.

On March 3 Iraq accepted a U.N. resolution which formally rescinded its annexation of Kuwait. Meanwhile revolts against Saddam's predominantly Sunni Moslem regime broke out in largely Shiite Moslem southern Iraq and among Kurds seeking an independent homeland in northern Iraq. Notwithstanding the fact that Bush had urged Saddam's ouster, the White House on March 26 emphasized that the United States would not interfere in Iraq's internal affairs and thus would not aid the rebels. On April 6 Iraq acceded to U.N. conditions for a permanent cease-fire, bringing the Persian Gulf War to an end. The terms provided for a U.N. observer force along the Iraq-Kuwait border and required the destruction of all Iraqi biological, chemical, and NUCLEAR WEAPONS. The United States and four other permanent members of the Security Council agreed to contribute soldiers to the 1400-member peacekeeping force.

Iraqi forces loyal to Saddam had crushed the Kurdish and Shiite rebellions by early April. More than a million Kurdish refugees fled toward Turkey and Iran to escape the Iraqi army. Responding in part to criticism that it had encouraged the Kurds to revolt and then abandoned them to slaughter by Saddam's superior forces, the Bush administration on April 6 warned the Iraqi government not to take any military action against Kurdish refugees above the 36th parallel in northern Iraq. Hundreds of thousands of refugees huddled in mountain camps along the Turkish-Iraq border, with as many as a thousand dying each day of disease and exposure. The U.S. Air Force began dropping food and other supplies to the refugees. As the magnitude of the problem became apparent, the United States in mid-April initiated Operation Provide Comfort, a massive relief campaign involving some 8000 U.S. military personnel deployed to Turkey to provide food, shelter, and clothing to some 700,000 Kurds. On April 16 the White House announced that U.S., British, and French troops would establish a "safe zone" in northern Iraq to encourage Kurdish refugees stranded along the Turkish border to return to their homes. The allied task force crossed into northern Iraq and took control of several hundred square miles of territory. With the United States and its allies providing security against Iraqi attack, the Kurds began to return home. Under international pressure, Iraq consented in May to the stationing of some 500 U.N. guards in the Kurdish safe zone. With the rebel Kurdish leadership and Saddam's government engaged in discussion on greater Kurdish autonomy within Iraq, the last coalition forces withdrew from the safe zone by July 15, 1991. To deter future Iraqi attack against the Kurds, the United States and its European allies joined in Operation Poised Hammer, the deployment of a small multinational military force along the Turkish-Iraq border. Throughout 1991 U.N. experts dismantled the Iraqi war machine. Confronted with evidence of a secret Iraqi nuclear weapons project, the U.N. Security Council on October 11, 1991, banned all Iraqi atomic programs.

PHILIPPINE CRISIS (1986) Popular political uprising that drove Philippine President Ferdinand E. Marcos into exile. His dictatorial rule and reputed personal corruption presented a quandary in the early 1980s for the Reagan administration, which professed support for HUMAN RIGHTS and democracy overseas but was loath publicly to criticize friendly governments when they failed to meet American standards. Although a long-standing and loyal U.S. ally, Marcos resisted diplomatic appeals from Washington for meaningful political and economic reforms, thus fueling a growing Communist insurgency in the Philippines that troubled American policymakers. The brazen assassination in August 1983 of non-Communist Filipino opposition leader Benigno S. Aquino, Jr. on his return from self-imposed exile in the United States galvanized domestic political dissent. Marcos met the growing challenges to his regime with repressive countermeasures.

He surprised his detractors in late 1985 when he agreed to hold "snap" presidential elections early the next year. The non-Communist opposition united behind Corazon Aquino, widow of the murdered leader, as its candidate. Marcos claimed victory in the February 7, 1986, election. But most official observers, including a U.S. delegation led by Senator Richard G. Lugar (R-IN), chairman of the SENATE FOREIGN RELATIONS COMMITTEE, had witnessed widespread ballot fraud and concluded that Marcos had rigged the outcome. With protests mounting in the Philippines and on Capitol Hill, U.S. President RONALD W. REAGAN called for an honest tally of the vote. Declaring the election fraudulent, senior Philippine military leaders defected on February 22 and pledged their loyalty to Aquino. Large crowds flocked to the support of the growing military rebellion. By February 24 some one million Filipinos supporting Marcos's ouster had massed around rebel headquarters in Manila. The dissension in the armed forces and mobilization of "people power" left Marcos isolated both at home and abroad. Reagan publicly and privately urged the dictator to step down. Under

mounting pressure to quit, the beleaguered Marcos finally capitulated. On February 25, shortly after his inauguration to a new term as president, he fled the Philippines for exile in Hawaii. The United States and other nations promptly recognized Aquino as president and she announced a new cabinet February 26.

PHILIPPINE INSURRECTION (1899–1902) Conflict between U.S. military forces and independence-seeking Filipino rebels over American annexation of the archipelago following the SPANISH-AMERICAN WAR (1898). In 1896, Philippine nationalists had turned to armed revolt to free their islands from Spanish colonial rule. The rebellion ended when the two sides agreed to a truce in December 1897. Under its terms, the rebel leadership, headed by Emilio Aguinaldo, went into exile in Hong Kong in return for Spanish promises of governmental reforms in the archipelago. These pledges went unfulfilled. Following the outbreak of the Spanish-American War, Aguinaldo returned to the islands and organized a Filipino army that fought alongside U.S. forces against the Spanish. Aguinaldo proclaimed the Philippines independent on June 12, 1898, and after the Spanish defeat in August the nationalist Filipino leadership established the Philippine Republic.

By late 1898, the administration of WILLIAM MCKINLEY had decided the United States would retain control of the islands, deemed increasingly vital to American strategic and commercial interests. In the TREATY OF PARIS (1898) ending the Spanish-American War, Spain ceded the Philippine Islands to the United States for $20 million. Aguinaldo and his followers, having anticipated U.S. support for Philippine independence, rejected American annexation. The Philippine Insurrection against U.S. rule began on February 4, 1899, when widespread fighting broke out between Filipino and U.S. troops near Manila. A brutal four-year struggle ensued. Overmatched by U.S. forces, the Filipinos resorted to guerrilla tactics and the American military had its first experience with the difficulties of counterinsurgency warfare. The capture of Aguinaldo in March 1901 broke the rebellion, although fighting continued for another year before U.S. forces gained full control of the islands. On July 4, 1902, President THEODORE ROOSEVELT issued a proclamation ending the Philippine Insurrection and granting amnesty to the rebels.

PHILIPPINE INTERVENTION (1989) U.S. military action undertaken to help defeat a bid by rebel Philippine army troops to oust the government of President Corazon Aquino. The coup attempt was the sixth and most serious against Aquino since she came to power in February 1986 following the PHILIPPINE CRISIS. It apparently was prompted by widespread sentiment within the armed forces that Aquino's administration was both corrupt and incompetent and had failed to deal effectively with the Communist insurgency in the archipelago. The uprising began December 1 with rebel soldiers attacking military positions around Manila and planes bombing several targets in the capital including the presidential palace. That same day, responding to an appeal from Aquino, President GEORGE BUSH authorized American jet fighters from Clark Air Base in the Philippines to provide air support. The fighters, seeking to keep rebel aircraft from taking off, also buzzed rebel positions. Coup organizers were apprised that American planes would fire on any aircraft attempting to strike at loyalist troops. The coup collapsed on December 7 when most of the rebel soldiers surrendered under an agreement reached between the Aquino government and the leaders of the uprising. The U.S. intervention came under severe criticism in the Philippines, where some opposition leaders unsuccessfully urged Aquino's impeachment for having requested U.S. military support. She retained control of the government but was substantially weakened by the coup attempt.

PHILIPPINE MUTUAL DEFENSE TREATY (1951) Mutual defense pact between the United States and the Republic of the Philippines. After WORLD WAR II, President HARRY S. TRUMAN pledged U.S. aid toward the economic recovery of the war-devastated Philippines and vowed to proceed with existing plans for Philippine independence. In April 1946 the U.S. Congress passed a pair of laws defining economic relations between the United States and a sovereign Philippines. The Philippine Rehabilitation Act authorized $620 million for the repair of war damages and restoration of public services and property. The Philippine Trade Act established the framework for future commercial relations. Following enactment of these measures, and completion of a treaty governing general U.S.-Philippine relations, the islands became fully independent on July 4, 1946, in fulfillment of the terms of the TYDINGS-McDUFFIE ACT of 1934.

The United States continued to provide for the defense of the new republic. Under the Philippine Military Assistance Act passed by Congress in June 1946, America had assumed responsibility for training the Philippine armed forces. In March 1947 Washington concluded a military assistance treaty with Manila that gave the United States long-term leases on 23 army and navy bases in the archipelago. Following the Communist victory in China in 1949 and the outbreak of the KOREAN WAR in 1950, the Truman administration resolved to extend its policy of CONTAINMENT to Asia through the establishment of a Pacific security structure. U.S. foreign policy emphasized the vital strategic importance of the Philippines. On August 30, 1951, the U.S. and Philippine governments signed the Philippine Mutual Defense Treaty. Ratified by both nations the following year, it committed the United States to come to the defense of the islands in the event of an outside attack. The treaty represented one link in the chain of Pacific mutual security arrangements forged by America in 1951. On September 1, the United States concluded the defensive ANZUS TREATY with Australia and New Zealand and on September 8 signed the bilateral JAPANESE SECURITY TREATY.

PHOENIX PROGRAM See **CIVIL OPERATIONS REVOLUTIONARY DEVELOPMENT SUPPORT**.

PICKERING, TIMOTHY (1745–1829) Soldier, secretary of state, and member of Congress. Born in Salem, Massachusetts, Pickering graduated from Harvard College in 1763, studied law, and was admitted to the bar in his native colony in 1768. An early supporter of the movement for American independence, he contributed his talents as a pamphleteer in the years before the AMERICAN REVOLUTION. A colonel in the Massachusetts militia, Pickering participated in the initial fighting against the British in April 1775 and went on to serve as adjutant general (1777) and quartermaster general (1780–1785) of the Continental Army. In 1787 he moved to the Wyoming Valley area of Pennsylvania, where he earned a reputation as a skilled Indian negotiator through his dealings with the Senecas.

Becoming active in Federalist politics, he was appointed U.S. postmaster general in 1791. President GEORGE WASHINGTON named Pickering secretary of war in 1795. During his brief tenure, he promoted construction of the frigates that would form the foundation of U.S. naval power in the WAR OF 1812. In August 1795 he became secretary of state, replacing EDMUND RANDOLPH, who was pressured to resign following disclosure of suspicious contacts with French Minister to the United States Joseph Fauchet that suggested Randolph had come under French influence. A staunch Federalist and admiring disciple of ALEXANDER HAMILTON, Pickering ardently opposed the French Revolution and deplored pro-French sympathies of the Democratic-Republicans.

As secretary of state, he clashed with President JOHN ADAMS over American policy toward France. Pickering favored a deepening of the division that had developed in Franco-American relations in the mid-1790s. After the XYZ AFFAIR (1797), he advocated full-fledged war with France and suggested a possible United States alliance with Great Britain. When Adams refused to declare war and looked for a negotiated way out of the maritime QUASI-WAR (1798–1800), Pickering corresponded with the president's adversaries within Federalist ranks in order to weaken Adams politically and undercut his policies. As a consequence, Adams dismissed him in May 1800. After moving back to his native Massachusetts, Pickering was elected to the U.S. Senate, where he served from 1803 to 1811, distinguishing himself as a vigorous critic of Democratic-Republican presidents THOMAS JEFFERSON and JAMES MADISON. He concluded his public career with two terms in the U.S. House of Representatives (1813–1817), where he voiced adamant opposition to the WAR OF 1812. Pickering retired to his Massachusetts farm.

PIERCE, FRANKLIN (1804–1869)   Fourteenth president of the United States. Pierce was born in New Hampshire, son of Benjamin Pierce, who had fought in the AMERICAN REVOLUTION and was twice New Hampshire governor. Franklin graduated from Bowdoin College in 1824, studied law, and was admitted to the bar in 1827. Entering politics as a Jacksonian Democrat, he was elected in 1829 to the New Hampshire legislature. He served in the U.S. House of Representatives from 1833 until 1837, when he entered the Senate. Pierce resigned his seat in 1842 to return to Concord, where he practiced law with great success and became the leader of the Democratic Party in the state. Declining an appointment by President JAMES K. POLK to become U.S. attorney general, he volunteered for duty in the MEXICAN WAR (1846–1848). Enlisting as a private, he rose to the rank of brigadier general, serving under General WINFIELD SCOTT.

When Pierce returned to New Hampshire at war's end, he found the nation in the throes of a worsening sectional political crisis over the issue of slavery and its extension into the territories. Since his days in the Senate, Pierce had rebuked the abolitionist movement in the North as a threat to the Union, opposed federal attempts to curb slavery in the territories, and respected Southern states' rights. He vigorously supported the Compromise of 1850, the legislative plan devised to end the agitation over slavery by balancing respective political interests of the North and South. In 1852 Pierce captured the Democratic presidential nomination as a compromise candidate on the 49th ballot over JAMES BUCHANAN, Stephen A. Douglas, and LEWIS CASS. Running in the general election on a platform that embraced the Compromise of 1850 as the final settlement of the slavery question, he defeated Whig nominee Winfield Scott.

On entering office in March 1853, Pierce promised to pursue a vigorous foreign policy aimed at territorial acquisition. His successful candidacy had benefited from the loyal support of YOUNG AMERICA, the movement within the Democratic Party that advocated an aggressive U.S. expansionism, and he embraced the idea of America's MANIFEST DESTINY to extend its sovereignty over the whole continent.

Pierce's goal of acquiring land from Mexico for a proposed southern transcontinental railroad was realized through the GADSDEN PURCHASE in 1853. The purchase, covering territory in present-day southern Arizona and New Mexico, completed the modern outline of the 48 contiguous states. Relations with Great Britain during Pierce's tenure were mixed. Secretary of State WILLIAM L. MARCY negotiated the Anglo-American MARCY-ELGIN TREATY (1854), covering U.S. trade reciprocity with Canada, then a British dominion, and the status of American fishing privileges in Canadian waters. Pierce protested the continued British colonial presence in Central America as a violation of the CLAYTON-BULWER TREATY (1850). He dismissed the British minister in Washington for recruitment during the Crimean War of troops in America in alleged violation of U.S. neutrality laws, drawing a strong objection from the British government. During Pierce's term, Commodore MATTHEW C. PERRY completed his historic mission to Japan, the fruit of which was the landmark TREATY OF KANAGAWA (1854) inaugurating U.S.-Japanese trade and diplomatic relations.

His administration's expansionist foreign policy goals were curtailed by the domestic political crisis precipitated by the Kansas-Nebraska Act (1854). The controversial measure repealed the Missouri Compromise (the federal legislation that had barred slavery's extension to territory north of 36°30', organized the new territories of Kansas and Nebraska, and permitted the settlers in the territories to decide for themselves whether to permit slavery). Pierce endorsed the act in hopes of securing support in Congress for other policies. The law reopened with renewed intensity the bitter sectional debate over the slavery question and brought a wild rush of pro-slavery and antislavery adherents into Kansas to vie for control. Armed conflict broke out between the slave-state and free-state advocates. In the face of worsening civil strife in "Bleeding Kansas," Pierce sent federal troops in an effort to maintain order.

Free soil opposition in the North forced the president to abandon his goal of acquiring Cuba as slave territory. In 1853, after the Spanish government spurned his administration's offer to buy the island, Pierce had instructed his European ministers PIERRE SOULE in Spain, John Y. Mason in Paris, and James Buchanan in London to confer on ways to detach Cuba from Spain. The three American diplomats produced the OSTEND MANIFESTO (1854), a controversial memorandum recommending forceable annexation of the island should Spain continue to refuse to sell. When the report raised a domestic storm about the extension of slavery, Pierce and Marcy repudiated it. Pierce also ended his support for private FILIBUSTERING expeditions in the Caribbean and Central America. Under pressure from antislavery forces in Congress, he revoked his administration's diplomatic recognition of the government of WILLIAM WALKER, the pro-slavery American filibuster who had led a successful rebellion in Nicaragua and emerged in 1856 as its self-appointed president. Regarded as badly weakened politically by the Kansas-Nebraska Act, Pierce was denied renomination in 1856 by the Democrats, who instead turned to James Buchanan. He left the White House in March 1857 and, after traveling in Europe, settled permanently in New Hampshire, resuming his law practice.

PIKE COMMITTEE Special U.S. House of Representatives investigation of the INTELLIGENCE COMMUNITY. Following the publication of allegations of illegal U.S. intelligence activities in the *New York Times* in December 1974, President GERALD R. FORD named the ROCKEFELLER COMMISSION to determine whether the CENTRAL INTELLIGENCE AGENCY (CIA) had violated its charter. Not content to entrust the investigation to a presidential panel, the Senate the same month formed the CHURCH COMMITTEE to probe U.S. intelligence agencies. On February 19, 1975, the House similarly voted to create a select committee to examine suspected unlawful or improper intelligence operations. An initial Select Committee on Intelligence was prevented from getting underway by a controversy surrounding its chairman, Representative Lucien N. Nedzi (D-MI), who stepped down when other Democrats on the panel requested his resignation following the disclosure he earlier had received a secret CIA briefing on past agency misconduct.

A new panel was established on July 17 with Representative Otis G. Pike (D-NY) as chairman. The 13-member Pike Committee included Representatives Les Aspin (D-WI),

Ronald V. Dellums (D-CA), Robert McClory (R-IL), and Robert W. Kasten, Jr. (R-WI). The committee conducted public hearings and prepared a detailed study of U.S. intelligence organization, management, and prior abuses and illegalities. Its work was aided by the CIA's own record of agency transgressions, known as the FAMILY JEWELS, furnished by CIA director WILLIAM E. COLBY. On January 19, 1976, the full House, over Pike's objections, voted against public release of the panel's final report because of the highly sensitive information it contained. In early February the New York weekly *Village Voice* published substantial excerpts from the classified document. CBS news correspondent Daniel Schorr acknowledged that he had provided the *Voice* with the material. Schorr was called before a House ethics committee investigating the circumstances surrounding the report's publication, but refused to answer how he had obtained a copy. The committee deplored Schorr's conduct, but took no further action.

The Pike Committee submitted 20 proposals to the House on reforming U.S. intelligence activities. Key recommendations included: having the director of central intelligence concentrate on overall management of the intelligence community and no longer also head the CIA, separating the NATIONAL SECURITY AGENCY from the Defense Department, and abolishing the DEFENSE INTELLIGENCE AGENCY. While the reorganization ideas were not adopted, committee emphasis on continuing congressional oversight resulted in the formation on July 14, 1977, of the House Permanent Select Committee on Intelligence.

PINCKNEY, CHARLES COTESWORTH (1746–1825) American soldier and diplomat; brother of Thomas, who negotiated PINCKNEY'S TREATY (1795) with Spain. Born in Charleston, South Carolina, Charles Cotesworth Pinckney was educated in Great Britain and France. Returning to America in 1769, he was admitted to the South Carolina bar and began a successful law practice. He served in the colony's provincial assembly before the AMERICAN REVOLUTION. In the war, he rose quickly to colonel in the South Carolina militia, went north to join General GEORGE WASHINGTON as an aide, and in 1778 returned to command a South Carolina regiment.

Commissioned a brigadier general before his discharge from the army in November 1783, Pinckney resumed his law practice in Charleston and stayed active in state politics.

He was a delegate to the federal Constitutional Convention in 1787 and the following year played a key role in securing South Carolina's ratification of the CONSTITUTION. In 1791 he declined President Washington's offer to command a federal army dispatched to quell an uprising of Ohio Indian tribes on the northwest frontier. He turned down Washington's subsequent offers to become secretary of war in 1794 and secretary of state in 1795. Pinckney accepted the president's appointment in July 1796 to replace JAMES MONROE as minister to France. He arrived at Paris in December amid worsening U.S.-French diplomatic tensions over the Anglo-American JAY'S TREATY (1794), which France condemned as a violation of the FRANCO-AMERICAN ALLIANCE (1778) and evidence of U.S. partiality toward French adversary Great Britain. After the French government refused to recognize him, an indignant Pinckney left France for Amsterdam in 1797. Later that year President JOHN ADAMS named Pinckney, Elbridge Gerry, and JOHN MARSHALL to a special mission to France aimed at resolving the deepening crisis in relations. The mission collapsed following the XYZ AFFAIR, in which agents of French Foreign Minister Charles Maurice de Talleyrand demanded a bribe from the American commissioners as the price for starting formal negotiations. The Americans refused and Pinckney returned home.

In July 1798, with the undeclared U.S.-French QUASI-WAR (1798–1800) threatening to become a full-fledged conflict, he accepted command of U.S. military forces in the American south. He left the post in June 1800 after the crisis had eased and the two nations had moved toward a diplomatic settlement. Pinckney was the Federalist Party's unsuccessful candidate for vice-president in 1800. Nominated for president in 1804 and 1808, he lost to THOMAS JEFFERSON and JAMES MADISON respectively. In the meantime Pinckney had resumed his South Carolina law practice.

PINCKNEY'S TREATY (1795) Treaty concluded October 27, 1795, by U.S. Minister to Great Britain Thomas Pinckney which settled a number of disputes between the United States and Spain that had simmered since the end of the ANNERICAN REVOLUTION. Following the war, Spain would not recognize a U.S. right to navigate through the Spanish-owned lower Mississippi River and port of New Orleans. The United States contended the economic life of its western settlements depended on free navigation of the Mississippi and access in and out of the Gulf of Mexico. By closing the waterway, the U.S. government protested, Spain unfairly abridged legitimate U.S. sovereign rights upstream.

Friction over the new nation's southwestern boundary stemmed from Spanish objections to the TREATY OF PARIS (1783) between the United States and Great Britain. The agreement fixed the boundary between the United States and Spanish West Florida at the 31st parallel. Through the Anglo-Spanish Definitive Treaty of Peace of 1783, the British ceded the Floridas to Spain. The Spanish government declared itself not bound by the terms of the Anglo-American treaty, ignored the 31st parallel limit, and claimed territory as far north as the Tennessee and Ohio rivers. In the decade after the American Revolution, Spain held military posts in Alabama, Mississippi, and Tennessee and supported Indian resistance to American settlement in the region. Through its encouragement of the Creek and Seminole tribes, Spain hoped to develop an Indian barrier against further U.S. expansion to the south and west.

The two nations sought a settlement of their differences through negotiations between U.S. Secretary for Foreign Affairs JOHN JAY and Spanish Minister to the United States Don Diego de Gardoqui. The draft Jay-Gardoqui Treaty (1786) required the United States to drop its claims to lands east of the Mississippi and south of the Yazoo rivers in present-day Louisiana and Mississippi; and to refrain from using Spain's portion of the Mississippi River for 30 years. In return, Spain would grant the United States trade concessions. Violent protest in the south and threat of rebellion in the west over the proposed pact's terms forced Jay to cancel his talks with Gardoqui before the treaty could be concluded.

The navigation and boundary issues remained unresolved until 1795 when special envoy Thomas Pinckney arrived in Spain in response to a conciliatory invitation by Madrid to renew negotiations. Expecting war with Great Britain and concerned that JAY'S TREATY (1794) signaled an emerging Anglo-American alliance, Spain looked to end its conflict with the United States and deter a possible American attack on thinly defended Spanish possessions in North America. The resulting Treaty of San Lorenzo, known as Pinckney's Treaty, represented a major U.S. diplomatic victory. By its terms, the United States gained unrestricted navigation of the Mississippi River and secured the right to deposit merchant goods at New Orleans for transshipment. Spain agreed to accept the 31° latitude as the West Florida boundary and pledged not to provoke Indian attacks on frontier American settlements. Both countries endorsed the principle FREE SHIPS MAKE FREE GOODS and arranged a plan for settlement of claims. The U.S. Senate approved the treaty unanimously in March 1796. Territorial dispute between the United States and Spain continued with the WEST FLORIDA CONTROVERSY.

See also ADAMS-ONIS TREATY.

PING-PONG DIPLOMACY Expression referring to the role table tennis played in the historic 1971 opening between the United States and Communist China. America had refused to recognize the Communist state installed on the Chinese mainland in 1949 and for more than two decades there was almost no contact between the COLD WAR adversaries. President RICHARD M. NIXON took office in 1969 interested in exploring a possible improvement in U.S.-Communist Chinese relations as part of his administration's overall foreign policy. After several discreet signals sent through third-party countries had alerted Peking of U.S. readiness for contacts, Nixon authorized the State Department on March 15, 1971, to lift the ban on Americans traveling to Communist China. Peking responded to the overture the following month when, at the world table tennis championships in Japan, the Chinese team invited the American team to come play it in China. With State Department approval, the U.S. team arrived in Peking on April 10, becoming the first Americans officially to visit the mainland since 1949. The group played several exhibition matches and met with Premier Chou En-lai before departing one week later.

Chou told them they had "opened a new page in the relations of the Chinese and American people." Nixon moved quickly to build on what was dubbed the ping-pong diplomacy, declaring on April 14 a relaxation of a 20-year U.S. trade embargo on China. After a secret trip to China by National Security Adviser HENRY A. KISSINGER in early July, Nixon announced to a surprised world on July 15 that he would visit the Communist nation in 1972 to confer with Chinese leaders on the normalization of relations and other issues.

See also PEKING SUMMIT *(1972).*

PITTMAN-BLOOM RESOLUTION See HAVANA, ACT OF.

PLAN OF 1776 Model set of articles for treaties to be entered into by the newly independent United States. At the same time it adopted the Declaration of Independence, the Second Continental Congress appointed a special committee to fashion principles for a standard amity and commerce treaty to be negotiated with European foreign powers, particularly France. Committee members JOHN ADAMS, BENJAMIN FRANKLIN, John Dickinson, and Robert Morris submitted the Plan of 1776, also known as the Model Treaty or "Plan of Treaties," on July 18 and Congress approved it with slight modifications on September 17. The plan defined concepts of maritime neutral rights and FREEDOM OF THE SEAS championed by the United States in the late 1700s.

The main elements of the Model Treaty were drawn from 18th-century European practices favored in the treaties of the small-navy powers: the doctrine of FREE SHIPS MAKE FREE GOODS; the freedom of neutrals to trade in noncontraband goods in the ports of a belligerent; and restricted contraband items carefully defined to exclude food stuffs and naval stores. These principles were incorporated into the Franco-American TREATY OF AMITY AND COMMERCE in 1778 and, with the notable exception of the Anglo-American JAY'S TREATY (1794), served as the basis for U.S. agreements to 1800.

PLATT AMENDMENT (1901) U.S.-devised amendment to the Cuban constitution which served as the basis for Cuban-American relations from 1901 to 1934. Its victory in the SPANISH-AMERICAN WAR (1898) left the United States in control of Cuba. American expansionists wanted to forsake the TELLER AMENDMENT, the congressional measure passed on the eve of the war disclaiming any U.S. intent to exercise sovereignty or control over Cuba once peace was restored, and annex the island. President WILLIAM MCKINLEY resisted the imperialist demands and stuck with plans for an independent Cuba, but one with strong ties to America. General LEONARD WOOD, American military governor of Cuba, implemented reforms for public works, education, sanitation, and local government that were intended in part to bind the island to the United States. Despite the tangible benefits Wood's rule brought, most Cubans resented the U.S. occupation. Increasing Cuban demands for freedom and sovereignty, coupled with anti imperialist pressure at home, prompted Wood to convene Cuban leaders in November 1900 to prepare a constitution. Wood particularly instructed them to make provision for special relations between the United States and Cuba. The resulting Cuban proposal was unsatisfactory to the McKinley administration, which proceeded to draw up its own plan. Although most of it was drafted by Secretary of War ELIHU ROOT, it became known as the Platt Amendment after Senator Orville H. Platt (R-CT), chairman of the Senate committee on Cuban relations. The measure became law as a rider attached to the Army appropriations bill of March 2, 1901.

Under terms of the amendment, Cuba could not make any treaty with a foreign power that would impair its independence; cede any of its territory to a foreign power; or incur public debt beyond its ability to repay lest it invite foreign intervention. Other provisions deferred to the future a decision on ownership of the Isle of Pines off Cuba's southwest coast; required Cuba to ratify all acts of the American military government; obligated Cuba to sell or lease coaling or naval stations on the island to the U.S. government; and, most important, granted the United States the right to intervene militarily in Cuba to maintain order and preserve independence. When the Cuban leadership responsible for drafting a constitution initially rejected the Platt measure, characterizing it as an affront to Cuban sovereignty, the United States vowed to continue its military occupation until the Cubans accepted the amendment. Under U.S. pressure, the members of the Cuban constituent assembly in June 1901 adopted it as an appendix to their new constitution. After U.S. troops were withdrawn from the island in May, 1902, the Platt Amendment was incorporated into a permanent Cuban-American treaty concluded in 1903.

The one-sided agreement made the island a quasi-protectorate of the United States. Under the measure America promptly acquired lease of a naval base at Guantanamo Bay on Cuba's southeast coast. The Platt Amendment was invoked by Washington to justify armed U.S. interventions in Cuba from 1906 to 1909 and in 1917 and was used numerous other times to exercise influence over the island's policies and affairs. In 1925 the United States relinquished all claims to the Isle of Pines and Cuba assumed sovereignty over the island. American interference under the amendment bred deep resentment in Cuba and strengthened demands for its repeal in the 1920s. As part of its Good Neighbor Policy toward Latin America, the administration of President Franklin D. Roosevelt signed a treaty with Cuba in 1934 abrogating the measure and thus removing the limitations on Cuban sovereignty. The United States retained its lease at Guanatanamo Bay, which remains home to a major U.S. Navy base.

See also Cuban Interventions.

PLAZA ACCORD (1985) Agreement reached by the Group of 5 (G-5) finance ministers on September 22, 1985, at the end of two days of meetings at the Plaza Hotel in New York City. In the early 1980s, high U.S. interest rates, resulting in large measure from the massive borrowing necessary to finance growing U.S. federal budget deficits, caused the dollar to climb in value against other currencies. The stronger dollar made imports into the United States less expensive, while it increased the price of American exports overseas. The Reagan administration, philosophically committed to free-market economic activity, initially opposed government intervention to regulate international currency exchange rates. By 1985, however, massive U.S. foreign trade deficits had threatened international economic stability and given rise to mounting PROTECTIONISM in

the U.S. Congress. Reflecting a shift in U.S. policy, Secretary of the Treasury James A. Baker 3rd successfully pressed for coordinated G-5 action to redress the trade imbalances. Under the so-called Plaza Accord, the major industrial nations agreed to work together to drive down the value of the U.S. dollar and thus increase the competitiveness of American goods; to resist domestic protectionist pressures; and to open their markets to greater international trade. The United States pledged to reduce its excessive budget deficits, which were identified as the principal cause of the dislocations in the world economy. The subsequent devaluation of the dollar brought minor improvement in the U.S. trade deficit, but was largely offset by continuing huge federal budget shortfalls.

POINT FOUR Program of U.S. technical assistance to underdeveloped countries. In his inaugural address of January 20, 1949, President Harry S. Truman identified the four major elements of his administration's foreign policy. The first three points were support for the United Nations, continuing implementation of the Marshall Plan, and participation in the emerging North Atlantic Treaty Organization. The fourth point was a proposal for American technical aid to poor nations worldwide to foster their economic development. Truman appealed for a "bold new program" to make U.S. scientific and industrial know-how available for the improvement and growth of underdeveloped areas. His proposal was promptly dubbed "Point Four" by the American press.

By 1949 geopolitical competition between the United States and Soviet Union for influence among the countries of Latin America, the Middle East, Africa, and Asia loomed as an important new front in the Cold War. The Truman administration was concerned that poverty and economic stagnation in these nations would breed political unrest and might turn them toward communism and the Soviet fold. Point Four, as proposed, rested on the premise that U.S. technical assistance would contribute to economic development, which would in turn promote political stability. By helping free peoples around the world become more productive and prosperous, Truman suggested, the United States would contribute to democracy and world peace.

Point Four also was framed as a sound investment that would serve U.S. strategic and economic interests by ensuring the continued flow of vital raw materials from underdeveloped nations and by promoting the development of potentially vast new markets for U.S. exports.

In June 1949 the president asked Congress to enact his Point Four initiative with a modest initial funding level. Qualms about the uncertain duration and cost of the program made Congress hesitant to adopt it. After strong lobbying by Truman, Point Four passed in May 1950 as the Act for International Development. The president signed the legislation on June 5. The act established the Technical Cooperation Administration (TCA) within the State Department to administer the program. By the end of 1951 the United States had concluded Point Four agreements with more than 30 nations. The TCA conducted advisory missions in the areas of health, education, public administration, agriculture, mining, and industrial development. Point Four technicians, so-called shirt-sleeve diplomats, took their skills to such countries as Peru, Egypt, Iran, and India.

From its inception, however, the program had a limited impact as international conditions pushed it to the margin of American foreign policy. Deepening Cold War tensions in Europe, the Communist victory in China, and the onset of the Korean War brought a shift in U.S. overseas aid from economic to military assistance. After 1950 military aid constituted the largest share of U.S. foreign assistance programs. In 1953 the TCA was merged into the Mutual Security Agency. Point Four functions eventually were inherited by the Agency for International Development following its creation in 1961.

POLIGNAC MEMORANDUM (1823) Diplomatic note dated October 9, 1823, from the French ambassador to Great Britain, the Prince de Polignac, to British Foreign Secretary George Canning. The memorandum eased British and U.S. trepidations over French ambitions in the Western Hemisphere. After French forces invaded Spain in April 1823 and restored the authority of King Ferdinand VII, it appeared that France might be plotting a military intervention in South America either to reimpose Spanish authority over the newly

independent Spanish American states or to extend French dominion over them. Canning, anxious to forestall expansion of Franco-Spanish power in the New World and concerned to preserve British trade with the rich markets of Latin America, insisted that France clarify its intentions toward the former Spanish colonies. He cautioned Polignac against any aggressive French designs on South America.

In August, the foreign secretary invited the United States to deliver a warning in tandem with Britain to France and other continental European powers to stay out of Latin America. Secretary of State John Quincy Adams, believing America should proceed independently in order to assert its preeminence in the hemisphere, persuaded President James Monroe to decline the British proposal and, instead, issue a unilateral statement. Meanwhile Polignac answered Canning. The October memorandum disclaimed any French intentions to conquer or annex Spain's former colonies in the Americas. Canning, equipped with these French assurances, abandoned his efforts to obtain a joint Anglo-American declaration. In December 1823 the president enunciated his Monroe Doctrine forbidding further European colonization in the Western Hemisphere.

POLK COROLLARY See **MONROE DOCTRINE**.

POLK, JAMES KNOX (1795–1849) Eleventh president of the United States. Born in North Carolina, he moved with his family to central Tennessee in 1806. After graduating from the University of North Carolina in 1818, he read law in Nashville, was admitted to the bar in 1820, and started practice in Columbia, Tennessee. He served his political apprenticeship as a member of the state legislature from 1823 to 1825, during which time he became a friend of fellow Tennessean Andrew Jackson. Entering the U.S. House of Representatives in 1825 as a staunch Jacksonian Democrat, he held his seat 14 years, serving as speaker from 1835 to 1839. After Jackson became president in 1829, Polk was a leader of administration supporters in the House.

Elected Democratic governor of Tennessee in 1839, he was defeated for reelection in 1841 and again two years later. In

1844 he bested favorite MARTIN VAN BUREN for the Democratic presidential nomination on the ninth ballot, becoming the first successful dark horse candidate in U.S. history. The proposed U.S. annexation of Texas was the major issue in the 1844 campaign, presaging as it did the addition of slave territory to the Union and, consequently, a shift in the political balance in Congress between slave and free states. Running on a platform that advocated immediate annexation of Texas, he defeated Whig candidate HENRY CLAY.

An ardent expansionist, Polk came to office a champion of America's MANIFEST DESTINY to extend its sovereignty over the whole continent. His vigorous policy of territorial acquisition ultimately extended the nation's boundaries to the shores of the Pacific. On the long-standing OREGON QUESTION, involving competing Anglo-American claims to the territory west of the Rockies and between 42° and 54°40', he initially would settle for nothing less than the whole of Oregon Country, a stand aggressively endorsed by Democratic expansionists in the slogan "54°40' OR FIGHT." Faced with a deepening crisis in U.S.-Mexican relations over Texas, Polk did not want to risk war with Britain. The Oregon controversy was resolved when his secretary of state, JAMES BUCHANAN, successfully negotiated the OREGON TREATY (1846), which established a compromise boundary along the 49th parallel. Suspicions about British designs in the mid-1840s on Central America and Mexico's Yucatan Peninsula led the president to declare the POLK COROLLARY to the MONROE DOCTRINE. The corollary expanded the scope of the U.S. pledge to block further European territorial acquisitions in the Western Hemisphere.

Just days before Polk's inauguration in March 1845, Congress had annexed the former Mexican province of Texas by joint resolution. TEXAS ANNEXATION embittered Mexico, which broke diplomatic relations with the United States. The ensuing dispute over the Texas-Mexico boundary put the neighboring countries on course for a confrontation. The United States claimed the Rio Grande as its southwest border. Mexico fixed the border at the Nueces River north of the Rio Grande. In a bid to settle the issue peaceably while at the same time satisfying his westward expansionist ambitions,

the president in November 1845 dispatched JOHN SLIDELL on a special diplomatic mission to Mexico City to negotiate the boundary question and offer to purchase New Mexico and California. When the Mexican government frustrated the SLIDELL MISSION (1845–1846) by refusing to receive the American envoy, Polk readied for a showdown, sending federal troops under General ZACHARY TAYLOR into the disputed region between the Rio Grande and Nueces. Mexican troops engaged Taylor's forces in a skirmish in late April 1846, leading Polk to charge that Mexico had shed American blood on American soil. At his urging, Congress declared war on May 13, 1846.

While Democrats enthusiastically supported the MEXICAN WAR (1846–1848), Northern Whigs and abolitionists voiced vehement opposition. They denounced the conflict as unjust, alleging it had been provoked by Polk as part of a Southern plot to spread slavery into lands wrested from Mexico. The outnumbered U.S. armies used superior skill to win the war. In victory, Polk disclaimed the bold demands of the "ALL-OF-MEXICO" MOVEMENT, whose Democratic extremist adherents wanted to annex Mexico in its entirety. His own more limited, but still extensive, territorial demands were met in the TREATY OF GUADALUPE HIDALGO (1848) ending the war. Under its terms, Mexico accepted the Rio Grande as the Texas boundary and ceded its California and New Mexico provinces, an area embracing all or part of present-day California, New Mexico, Arizona, Nevada, Utah, Colorado, and Wyoming. The United States paid $15 million for the MEXICAN CESSION. The vast acquisition, the largest single addition to the nation since the LOUISIANA PURCHASE (1803), touched off the fierce sectional political struggle at the end of the 1840s over whether to permit slavery's extension into the newly won territory.

A long-standing free-trade advocate, Polk achieved a reduction in U.S. import duties when he signed into law the WALKER TARIFF in 1846. He did not seek reelection. Leaving office in March 1849 near collapse from physical exhaustion, he died three months later in Tennessee.

POLLARD SPY CASE Israeli espionage in the United States that strained relations between the two countries. On November 21, 1985, Jonathan J. Pollard, a civilian intelligence analyst with the U.S. Navy, was seized outside the Israeli embassy in Washington and charged with selling classified information to its government. His wife, Anne Henderson Pollard, was arrested as an accomplice the following day. Further investigation revealed that the American couple had been part of an Israeli intelligence operation and had furnished hundreds of secret documents to Israeli agents. The Pollards pleaded guilty to espionage charges in June 1986. Jonathan Pollard was sentenced to life in prison, while Anne Pollard received a five-year term. Four Israelis were named as unindicted conspirators in the case, including senior intelligence officer Rafael Eitan and Aviem Sella, a colonel in the Israel Air Force. Responding to U.S. protests, Israeli officials characterized the affair as an unauthorized, renegade intelligence operation. Under U.S. pressure, Eitan and Sella were removed from their government positions, but otherwise the matter was allowed to fade. Anne Pollard, suffering from a rare stomach disorder, was released from prison in January 1990.

PORTSMOUTH CONFERENCE   See **PORTSMOUTH TREATY**.

PORTSMOUTH TREATY (1905)   Settlement mediated by President THEODORE ROOSEVELT that ended the Russo-Japanese War (1904–1905), a conflict waged for control of Korea and Manchuria. Concluded on September 5, 1905, at the Portsmouth Conference, the treaty restored peace, upheld the principles of the OPEN DOOR, and preserved the balance of power in the Far East.

Roosevelt, at Japan's invitation, had brought the belligerents together in August 1905 at Portsmouth, New Hampshire, for peace talks. He had conditioned his participation on prior Japanese endorsement of America's Open Door policy in China. Japan, as de facto military victor, forced the Russians to agree to withdraw from Korea and to surrender their interests in southern Manchuria, including Port Arthur. The talks stalled when Japan demanded all of the island of Sakhalin and a large monetary indemnity. Russia threatened to abandon the conference and renew fighting. Roosevelt, troubled by the implications of decisive

Japanese gains in East Asia, prevailed on Japan to drop the indemnity demand and struck a compromise that restored half of Sakhalin to Russia.

Roosevelt's diplomacy won him the Nobel Peace Prize in 1906 and raised his international prestige. But many in Japan, expecting an indemnity, felt the settlement had denied them just compensation for their nation's victory. Lingering resentment strained U.S.-Japanese relations. The treaty was a landmark in the history of the contemporary Far East. For the first time an Asian nation had defeated a major European power. Japan had established itself as a rising world force. The terms of the agreement confirmed the island nation as the dominant presence in Manchuria and Korea. Japan's development as a major Pacific power would be of great significance to the United States in the decades to follow.

See also TAFT-KATSURA AGREEMENT.

POTSDAM CONFERENCE (1945)   Third and final WORLD WAR II meeting of the leaders of the three major Allied powers, held from July 17 to August 2, 1945. The BIG THREE heads of government had last conferred at the YALTA CONFERENCE in February 1945. In May Nazi Germany surrendered, ending the war in Europe. As agreed at Yalta, the United States, Great Britain, and the Soviet Union, joined by newly liberated France, then established occupation zones in the defeated Axis power. U.S. President HARRY S. TRUMAN, British Prime Minister Winston Churchill, and Soviet Premier Joseph Stalin convened at Potsdam, Germany, near Berlin to discuss the occupation and future status of Germany, the resolution of European political and territorial issues, and the prosecution of the war against Japan. The delegations included U.S. Secretary of State JAMES F. BYRNES, British Foreign Secretary Anthony Eden, and Soviet Foreign Minister Vyacheslav Molotov. Following his party's defeat in a British general election, Churchill was replaced at the conference on July 28 by new British Prime Minister Clement Attlee, whose choice for foreign secretary, Ernest Bevin, succeeded Eden.

The United States, Great Britain, and the Republic of China issued the Potsdam Declaration on July 26, reiterating their demand for Japan's unconditional surrender. Nationalist Chinese leader Chiang Kai-shek, who did not attend the Potsdam gathering, approved the document by wire from China. The Soviet Union was not yet at war with Japan and was not a party to the declaration. Stalin secretly reaffirmed the Soviet pledge made at Yalta to enter the war against Japan within three months of Germany's defeat. On August 2, Truman, Attlee, and Stalin signed a final agreement summarizing the results of the conference. The three leaders adopted a set of political and economic principles to govern the initial postwar administration of Germany. These included the complete disarmament and demilitarization of the country, the uniform treatment of the German populace throughout the four occupation zones, the destruction of Nazism and creation of democratic self-rule, and treatment of occupied Germany as a "single economic unit." The conference sanctioned the payment of German war reparations through Allied removal of industrial property and equipment from the defeated Axis nation. The German navy and merchant marine were divided among the Big Three and Allied intentions to try war criminals were reconfirmed. The decision was reached to forceably resettle in Germany ethnic Germans, numbering more than 6 million, living in Poland, Czechoslovakia, and Hungary.

The conferees agreed to establish a COUNCIL OF FOREIGN MINISTERS to prepare draft peace treaties with minor Axis powers Italy, Hungary, Finland, Romania, and Bulgaria. The council, which as conceived was to include France and China, was further charged with drawing up a peace settlement for Germany once an adequate German government had been established. It was also to oversee the withdrawal of Allied troops from Iran. As determined at Yalta, the Soviet Union gained possession of a sizable part of Poland. German East Prussia was divided between Poland and the USSR. As compensation for its loss of territory to Moscow, Poland was given administrative control of German areas east of the ODER-NEISSE LINE, pending their formal transfer in a future peace treaty. The Big Three called for UNITED NATIONS membership for the former lesser Axis powers, following the conclusion of peace treaties, and for all "peace-loving states."

Truman was troubled by signs the Soviets were failing to abide by the DECLARATION ON LIBERATED EUROPE, the statement formulated at Yalta calling for self-determination and democratic institutions in areas freed from Nazi rule. The Soviets were tightening their grip on the countries in Eastern Europe occupied by the Red Army. Truman and Attlee extended diplomatic recognition to the Soviet-installed government in Poland after winning assurances that representatives of the democratic Polish government-in-exile in London would be included. The Western allies declined to recognize Soviet-sponsored regimes in Romania and Bulgaria. The United States and Great Britain rebuffed Soviet attempts to gain a base on the Dardenelles Straits or one of Italy's former colonies in Northern Africa.

On August 6, four days after the conference, the United States dropped the first atomic bomb on the Japanese city of Hiroshima. On August 8 the USSR declared war on Japan. The following day America dropped a second atomic bomb on Nagasaki, causing Japan on August 10 to accept the Potsdam Declaration terms of surrender. With the final defeat of the Axis menace, the wartime U.S.-Soviet alliance quickly began to unravel. The Council of Foreign Ministers meeting in London in September 1945 underscored fundamental East-West differences over Germany and Eastern Europe and presaged postwar hostility and confrontation between the Western alliance and Soviet bloc. By 1947 U.S.-Soviet relations had hardened into COLD WAR. U.S. and Soviet heads of government did not meet again until the GENEVA SUMMIT in 1955.

POWELL, COLIN LUTHER (1937–   )
Army officer and national security adviser. Powell was born in New York City, where he attended City College and enrolled in the Reserve Officers' Training Corps (ROTC). He graduated in 1958 and was commissioned an officer in the U.S. Army. He served in South Vietnam from 1962 to 1963 and again in 1968 to 1969 at the height of the VIETNAM WAR. In 1971 he completed a master's degree at George Washington University and the following year was selected as a White House Fellow, a coveted position in which promising offi-

cers were groomed for larger responsibilities. During his year-long internship he worked as an assistant to FRANK C. CARLUCCI 3RD, the deputy director of the Office of Management and Budget. Over the next decade Powell held a variety of command and staff positions and earned promotion to general.

In July 1983 he was named senior military assistant to Secretary of Defense CASPAR W. WEINBERGER. During his three-year tenure he was involved in planning the GRENADA INVASION (1983) and the LIBYAN BOMBING RAID (1986). In June 1986 Powell took command of the Army's 5th Corps in West Germany. He was called back to Washington in January 1987 to become the deputy to Carlucci, who had replaced Admiral John M. Poindexter as national security adviser amidst the burgeoning IRAN-CONTRA scandal. The ensuing investigations determined that Powell, who had a peripheral role while at the PENTAGON in the sale of arms to Iran, had acted properly and he was one of the few participants to emerge with his reputation intact. He was charged with implementing the TOWER COMMISSION's (1987) recommendations for reorganization of the NATIONAL SECURITY COUNCIL staff.

In November 1987 Carlucci succeeded Weinberger as secretary of defense and Powell was elevated to national security adviser. He held the position through the end of the Reagan administration, taking a lead role in the coordination of U.S.-Soviet arms control issues. President GEORGE BUSH in August 1989 nominated him for chairman of the JOINT CHIEFS OF STAFF. Powell became the first black American to hold the nation's highest military position. He presided over the successful prosecution by U.S. armed forces of the PANAMA INVASION (1989) and the PERSIAN GULF WAR (1991).

PRESIDENTIAL COMMISSION ON AVIATION SECURITY AND TERRORISM See **PAN AM FLIGHT 103**.

PRESIDENTIAL DIRECTIVE 59 (PD–59) (1980) Statement of U.S. strategy for using NUCLEAR WEAPONS in the event of war. Since the 1960s U.S. DETERRENCE of a possible nuclear attack by the Soviet Union had rested on the concept of MUTUAL ASSURED DESTRUCTION (MAD). The MAD doctrine held that neither superpower could launch a nuclear strike without absorbing a devastating counterstrike by its rival. Each nation, in effect, held the other hostage, thus rendering nuclear war an untenable military option. In the mid-1970s U.S. defense planners, worried that Soviet strategic doctrine increasingly contemplated the possibility of limited nuclear war, began to develop a more flexible U.S. nuclear policy. President JIMMY CARTER on July 25, 1980, issued Presidential Directive 59 setting forth a revised U.S. nuclear war-fighting strategy. While withholding details of the top secret plan, the administration underscored that the United States was not retreating from its long-standing position that nuclear war was unthinkable. Defense Secretary HAROLD BROWN explained that PD–59 would ensure continued U.S. deterrence of any possible nuclear conflict by enabling America to respond selectively to any level or type of Soviet nuclear attack. The directive authorized a wider range of U.S. limited nuclear war-fighting options, instructed defense planners to prepare to fight a protracted nuclear war lasting up to 60 days, and ordered improvements in the survivability of U.S. command and control facilities. Critics charged PD–59 had made nuclear war more plausible and thus more likely, while supporters characterized it a necessary precaution that enhanced U.S. security and deterrence.

PRESIDENT'S FOREIGN INTELLIGENCE ADVISORY BOARD (PFIAB) Panel of private citizens that advises the president on intelligence matters. On the recommendation of the second Hoover Commission on the organization of the government, President DWIGHT D. EISENHOWER established the advisory body in 1956 to review periodically the activities of the U.S. INTELLIGENCE COMMUNITY. Known as the President's Board of Consultants on Foreign Intelligence Activities, the eight-member panel was chaired by Dr. James R. Killian, Jr., president of the Massachusetts Institute of Technology.

The board lapsed at the end of the Eisenhower administration but was revived by President JOHN F. KENNEDY following the disastrous BAY OF PIGS INVASION (1961). Renamed the President's Foreign Intelligence Advisory Board, it was chaired by General James H. Doolittle. Other distinguished figures who have headed the panel include CLARK M. CLIFFORD during the Johnson administration, General MAXWELL D. TAYLOR in the Nixon years, and economist Leo Cherne during the Ford presidency. President JIMMY CARTER disbanded the board in 1977. It was reestablished by President RONALD W. REAGAN in 1981 and placed under the direction of former Ambassador to Great Britain Anne Armstrong. Believing the 14-member body too unwieldy, President GEORGE BUSH scaled it back to a 6-member panel in July 1990. Former Senator John G. Tower (R-TX) was selected to head the new group, composed largely of veteran intelligence officials and scientists. The PFIAB is credited with spurring development of the U-2 and SR-71 spy planes and promoting the use of SATELLITE RECONNAISSANCE. It proposed the influential 1976 TEAM A/TEAM B study of the threat posed by the Soviet Union.

PRESIDENT'S INTELLIGENCE OVERSIGHT BOARD (PIOB) Panel in the office of the White House that monitors U.S. intelligence activities. The board was established by President GERALD R. FORD in 1976 in the wake of revelations of past improprieties committed by the CENTRAL INTELLIGENCE AGENCY and other intelligence services. Its membership consists of three distinguished private citizens who are appointed by the president and serve without compensation. The board reviews the activities of the INTELLIGENCE COMMUNITY and reports to the president any findings of possibly illegal or improper behavior.

PREVENTION OF NUCLEAR WAR AGREEMENT (1973) U.S.-Soviet declaration of a joint commitment to prevent nuclear war. The agreement, in essence a statement of principles, was signed by President RICHARD M. NIXON and General Secretary Leonid I. Brezhnev on June 22, 1973, during the 1973 WASHINGTON SUMMIT. The United States and Soviet Union pledged to conduct their foreign relations so as to preclude the development of situations that might lead to nuclear conflict. They also agreed to refrain from the threat or use of force in circumstances endangering international peace and security and to hold urgent consultations whenever any international development appeared to carry the risk of nuclear war. While the document reflected growing

U.S.-Soviet DETENTE, the two superpowers were careful to include an article affirming their inherent right of self-defense and their continued adherence to existing security arrangements and treaties.

PROJECT SOCRATES U.S. Defense Department program that monitors the advanced technologies of America's major economic competitors. Project Socrates was created within the DEFENSE INTELLIGENCE AGENCY in 1988 to collect data on the world's most advanced technologies. The information it gathers is intended to help planners in the private sector gauge the status of American high technology compared with the foreign competition. The program brings together both government and corporate experts to assess how the United States is faring across a range of key technological areas. It has concentrated on tracking developments in microelectronics, exotic structural materials, superconductors, high-performance computers, and high-definition television.

Since its inception the program has come under discussion as part of a larger debate over what role, if any, the federal government should play in support of critical high technology industries. Proponents of a national industrial policy contend that the government should continue initiatives like Project Socrates that are geared toward restoring America as a major force in the consumer electronics industry and at defending the U.S. position within the semiconductor and computer industries. Detractors argue against any government coordinated effort at promoting particular technologies. They contend that strategic planning on research and development should be left to the private sector and ought to be guided by free-market forces.

PROTECTIONISM Term used to describe the use by a government of tariffs and other trade measures to restrict imports and thus protect domestic industries from foreign competition. Protectionism historically has been employed to shelter newly formed, or so-called infant, industries and to prevent the loss of jobs in industries unable to compete with overseas competitors. Since the early 19th century, classical economic theory has maintained that protectionism ultimately stifles domestic economic development while free trade, by contrast, encourages productivity and growth.

Historians divide U.S. trade policy into four periods. During the first era, from 1789 until the WAR OF 1812, the newly formed federal government sought to expand American maritime commerce and access to British and French markets. The nation's first import duty, the TARIFF OF 1789, was designed principally to raise revenues for the federal government. The second period, from the TARIFF OF 1816 until the Civil War, saw the initial rise of protectionist duties, intended largely to bolster nascent textile and other industries in the North. Bitter sectional rivalry developed over higher tariffs, which were favored by Northern manufacturing interests, but opposed in the South, where the agricultural economy depended on low-cost imported finished goods. The sectional differences resulted in a compromise policy of mild protectionism. The outbreak of the Civil War and secession of the South from the Union left the Northern-dominated Congress free to impose steeper import duties. The 1861 MORRILL TARIFF inaugurated a third period of high protectionism that lasted until the SMOOT-HAWLEY TARIFF (1930) was enacted at the beginning of the Great Depression. Except for a brief period following the passage of the 1913 UNDERWOOD TARIFF, the federal government maintained very high tariffs on an extensive range of imported items.

The worldwide financial collapse of the early 1930s brought passage of the TRADE AGREEMENTS ACT (1934), ushering in a fourth shift in U.S. trade policy that continues to the present. The act allowed the president to negotiate reciprocal tariff reductions with other nations, thus stimulating international trade and, by extension, the American economy. The legislation signaled the end of traditional American protectionism and a growing commitment to free trade. Acting on the belief that economic nationalism in the 1930s had worsened the Great Depression and helped cause WORLD WAR II, the United States joined with other nations in 1947 to form the GENERAL AGREEMENT ON TARIFFS AND TRADE (GATT) to promote and regulate international commerce. In subsequent years seven separate GATT "rounds," or multilateral trade negotiations, have reduced tariffs and other barriers to worldwide trade. Postwar U.S. presidential administrations have maintained a consistent commitment to free trade policies. In the mid-1980s, however, huge trade imbalances between America and Japan raised protectionist sentiments in the U.S. Congress. At issue were alleged Japanese use of such unfair trading practices as dumping goods at below market prices and providing government subsidies to aid exports. In 1990 the two nations completed special STRUCTURAL IMPEDIMENTS INITIATIVE talks meant to improve trade relations. The UNITED STATES-CANADA FREE TRADE AGREEMENT, concluded in 1988, and ongoing negotiations with Mexico for a similar pact reflect the basic U.S. goal of broad North American trade liberalization.

PUBLIC LAW 480   See **FOOD FOR PEACE**.

PUEBLO INCIDENT (1968)   Seizure of U.S. intelligence ship by North Korea. On January 5, 1968, the U.S.S. *Pueblo*, a small freighter converted by the Navy for use as an electronic surveillance vessel, left Japan on an intelligence mission to be conducted in international waters off the eastern coast of North Korea. The *Pueblo* was part of an operation in the northern Pacific, code-named Clickbeetle, to intercept the electronic communications of U.S. Communist adversaries China, North Korea, and the Soviet Union. On January 23, the *Pueblo* was fired on by North Korean torpedo boats, submarine chasers, and jet fighters. Commander Lloyd M. Bucher was forced to surrender the lightly armed ship and its crew of 83. Four of the crew members were wounded, one fatally. The North Koreans captured secret documents and electronics equipment which the crew had been unable to destroy.

The United States condemned the attack, insisting it had occurred in international waters, and demanded the release of the crew. North Korea defended its action, claiming the *Pueblo* had violated its territorial limits. The crew was freed in December 1968 after the United States publicly admitted, in a statement it later disavowed, that the *Pueblo* had intruded into North Korean waters. Bucher and other crewmembers revealed they had been tortured during their 11 months in captivity and forced to sign confessions written by their Communist jailers.

See also EC-121 INCIDENT.

PUNITIVE EXPEDITION (1916–1917) U.S. military intervention in Mexico to stop bandit raids into the United States by Mexican revolutionary Francisco "Pancho" Villa. Villa gained the upper hand in the struggle for power among competing factions in the Mexican Revolution (1910–1920) in 1914 when he drove Constitutionalist leader Venustiano Carranza from Mexico City and won the political support of President WOODROW WILSON. Carranza regained the capital in February 1915, forcing Villa and his forces to flee northward. In the following months, Carranza strengthened his position and established control over much of Mexico. In October 1915 the United States abandoned Villa and recognized Carranza's regime as Mexico's de facto government. Villa continued guerrilla warfare in the north against Carranza. Resentful of the Wilson administration's recognition of the Constitutionalist leader, he retaliated by attacking Americans. In January 1916, Villa stopped a train at Santa Ysabel in northern Mexico, removed 17 American mining engineers, and shot and killed them. He also staged cross-border assaults on Texas and New Mexico. In a raid on Columbus, New Mexico, on March 9, 1916, his men killed some 15 Americans and burned the town. Mounting domestic demands for military intervention to stop the loss of American life compelled Wilson to take action.

After securing Carranza's reluctant consent, the American president ordered General JOHN J. PERSHING to lead a punitive expedition into Mexico in pursuit of Villa. The expedition began March 15. Pershing's force of 10,000 penetrated more than 300 miles into Mexico on the trail of the elusive Villa. This size and strength of Pershing's expedition surprised and alarmed Carranza, who came under great political pressure at home to effect a withdrawal of the American soldiers from Mexican soil. As weeks wore on Mexican popular sentiment became increasingly hostile to the Pershing campaign. Carranza demanded that the U.S. force be pulled out under threat of war and ordered his troops to block Pershing if he moved in any direction except north toward the border.

In June 1916 Wilson mobilized the National Guard and stationed it along the Texan-Mexican border in anticipation of a conflict. Neither side, however, wanted war. Since the United States did not face a critical threat to its security from the situation in northern Mexico, and since U.S. entry into WORLD WAR I against Germany appeared imminent, Wilson in January 1917 ordered the withdrawal of the U.S. expeditionary force. By the first week of February, the last of Pershing's troops left Mexico having failed to capture Villa, whose raids continued until 1920. Meanwhile, a new Mexican Constitution was proclaimed on February 5. 1917. Carranza was elected President a month later, and the United States extended immediate recognition to the new Government.

Q

QUADRIPARTITE AGREEMENT ON BERLIN (1971) Milestone East-West accord on the German city. Following WORLD WAR II, Allied powers the United States, Great Britain, France, and the Soviet Union divided Germany into four occupation zones. The German capital of Berlin, located in the Soviet zone, likewise was separated into four sectors. Negotiations toward a final peace settlement with the defeated Axis power gave way to increasingly acrimonious debate over Moscow's imposition of Communist regimes in the areas of Eastern Europe occupied by its armies during the war. Amid mounting COLD WAR confrontation over Germany, the Soviet Union in 1948 blockaded the Western sectors in Berlin. The United States and Great Britain responded with the BERLIN AIRLIFT, resupplying West Berlin by air until the blockade was lifted in 1949. The same year the postwar partition of Germany was formalized when the three Western allies formed the democratic state of West Germany in their zones and the USSR established Communist East Germany in its zone. The next two decades saw continuing East-West confrontation in Central Europe, with no progress made on the question of Germany and each side refusing to recognize the German state created by the other.

In 1969 new West German Chancellor Willy Brandt pursued a policy of improved relations with the Soviet Union and Communist Eastern Europe, including East Germany. His diplomatic initiative, known as *Ostpolitik*, resulted in the signing in 1970 of treaties with the Soviet Union and Poland and the first top-level contacts between the two German states. Brandt's overtures contributed to a nascent U.S.-Soviet DETENTE and overall lessening of East-West tensions. In March 1970 the United States, Great Britain, France, and Soviet Union began negotiations on a Berlin settlement. On September 3, 1971, representatives of the four powers concluded an agreement governing the future status of the divided city. The measure, known as the Quadripartite Agreement, bound its signatories to forego the use or threat of force in Berlin. The accord recognized the economic, judicial, and cultural ties between West Germany and West Berlin but affirmed that West Berlin was not a formal part of the West German state. Moscow pledged to allow unimpeded Western access to Berlin, improve communications between the city's halves, and permit greater numbers of visitors to East Berlin.

In December 1971 East and West Germany completed a set of accords supplementing the Quadripartite Agreement's provisions on access to Berlin and visits to East Berlin. On June 3, 1972, the foreign ministers of the United States, Great Britain, France, and Soviet Union signed a comprehensive agreement on Berlin that incorporated the four-way accord and German pacts negotiated the previous year. The 1972 measure effectively recognized the existence of separate East and West German states. In November the four powers agreed on UNITED NATIONS membership for both Germanies. The United States and East Germany established diplomatic relations in 1974.

See also FINAL SETTLEMENT WITH RESPECT TO GERMANY TREATY.

QUARANTINE SPEECH (1937) Address by President FRANKLIN D. ROOSEVELT on the worsening international situation delivered at a public rally in Chicago on October 5, 1937. Following clashes between Japanese and Chinese forces in July 1937, Japan launched an undeclared war against its Asian neighbor. Invading Japanese army units moved against the Nationalist Chinese capital at Nanking. The Roosevelt administration, reflecting the strong American ISOLATIONISM of the period, limited the U.S. response to the Japanese aggression to verbal condemnation. The other major Western powers similarly avoided direct involvement in the Sino-Japanese hostilities. Roosevelt worried that American inaction only encouraged Japanese militarism, as well as the growing bellicosity of Fascist Germany and Italy in Europe. In his Chicago speech, the president sought to alert the American people to the dangers posed by mounting international lawlessness and to the need for a greater U.S. role in world affairs. Employing a medical metaphor, Roosevelt called for "peace-loving nations" to "quarantine" aggressor countries spreading the "epidemic of world lawlessness." The address, dubbed the Quarantine Speech, drew immediate criticism from isolationists, peace groups, and others concerned the president was leading the nation into war. Sensing the domestic opposition to greater American overseas involvement, the Roosevelt administration refrained from advocating more forceful measures, such as economic sanctions, against the Japanese aggression. The United States adopted a restrained position at the November 1937 BRUSSELS CONFERENCE on the Sino-Japanese war. The international meeting concluded without taking any concrete action and the Japanese conquest of China continued until WORLD WAR II.

QUASI-WAR (1798–1800) Undeclared naval war between the United States and France stemming from French interference with neutral American commerce. U.S.-French relations deteriorated in the mid-1790s over American policy toward the war between Great Britain and France, the predominant conflict in the French Revolutionary Wars (1792–1802) then embroiling Europe. France insisted that strict American impartiality, outlined by President GEORGE WASHINGTON in the NEUTRALITY PROCLAMATION (1793), effectively favored Great Britain, whose naval superiority made it less reliant upon the trans-Atlantic transport of goods by American trade vessels. The French deplored the Anglo-American JAY'S TREATY (1794) as a diplomatic betrayal that violated the treaties of the FRANCO-AMERICAN ALLIANCE (1778). By the terms of Jay's Treaty, the United States had bowed to British wartime restrictions on FREEDOM OF THE SEAS that greatly reduced the flow of American merchant ships between the French West Indies and France. Accusing the Federalist Washington administration of pro-British leanings, the French government in November 1796 suspended diplomatic relations with the United States and decreed that French naval vessels and privateers could raid America's neutral shipping with Great Britain. After Federalist JOHN ADAMS outdistanced pro-French Democratic-Republican THOMAS JEFFERSON in the December election to succeed Washington, France stepped up its capture of American vessels and confiscation of their neutral cargoes. Continuing French maritime depredations along America's Atlantic coast and in the Caribbean pushed the nations toward a serious conflict.

Adams's bid after taking office in March 1797 for a diplomatic solution foundered when French Foreign Minister Charles Maurice de Talleyrand refused to negotiate formally with visiting American peace commissioners unless they paid a bribe and satisfied other French demands. News of the French government's attempt at extortion, known as the XYZ AFFAIR, reached the United States in the spring of 1798, outraging Adams and inspiring ardent anti-French feelings. So-called extreme Federalists, including Secretary of State TIMOTHY PICKERING, clamored for an immediate war declaration against France. But the president was reluctant to commit America's inadequate military forces to conflict. With the protection of American commerce from French attack as the top priority, Adams emphasized a substantial naval buildup. From March through July 1798 Congress took steps in preparation for a possible war. It created the separate DEPARTMENT OF THE NAVY; appropriated sufficient funds to complete three frigates requisitioned in March 1797; authorized construction or purchase of more than 20 additional warships; permitted American merchant ships to arm themselves against French raids; and for the first time empowered American Navy ships and privateers to prey on armed French vessels. Congress also approved raising a 10,000-man army and enlisting an additional 50,000 men in a provisional force that might be activated in the event of a war declaration or French invasion. George Washington consented to come out of retirement if need arose to command the new army, which was to be organized by ALEXANDER HAMILTON, named as second in command. Moreover, the United States unilaterally suspended its 1778 treaties of alliance and commerce with France.

By November 1798 U.S. warships and armed privateers were engaged in an undeclared quasi-war, or "partial war," with French ships in U.S. coastal waters and the Caribbean. American forces fought under strict constraints: Navy ships and privateers alike were barred from attacking unarmed French vessels and could not capture private property. Adams fended off efforts by the extreme Federalists to escalate the limited maritime war into a full-scale conflict and to push the United States toward an alliance with Great Britain. Pro-war Federalists figured to exploit a larger Franco-American showdown to damage the rival Democratic-Republican Party, with its record of pro-French sentiment. Federalist majorities in Congress passed the ALIEN AND SEDITION ACTS (1798), controversial internal-security legislation aimed at suppressing enemy aliens and muzzling political dissent in the Democratic-Republican press.

The surge of anti-French sentiment in America and a string of U.S. naval successes in the West Indies concerned the French, who especially feared the prospect of an Anglo-American alliance. Talleyrand in late 1798 began to send signals to Adams through U.S. Minister to the Netherlands William Vans Murray of a French desire for negotiations. Adams responded to Talleyrand's overture by sending a U.S. peace commission to Paris over strong Federalist opposition in both his cabinet and the Senate. The American envoys negotiated the CONVENTION OF 1800, which ended the Quasi-War and restored normal Franco-American diplomatic relations.

QUEBEC CONFERENCES See **WORLD WAR II CONFERENCES** in **APPENDIX E**.

QUEMOY-MATSU CRISES (1954–1955, 1958) Armed clashes over the Nationalist Chinese-held Quemoy and Matsu islands in the Taiwan Strait off the coast of Communist China. After a protracted civil war, the Chinese Communists under Mao Tse-tung drove the Nationalist Chinese government headed by Chiang Kai-shek from power in 1949. Chiang fled with his remaining forces to the island of Taiwan (then still referred to in the West by its Portuguese name, Formosa) some 135 miles off China's southeastern coast. The Nationalists also retained control of a string of small islands just off China's coast in the Taiwan Strait. As Mao established the Communist People's Republic of China on the mainland, Chiang made Taiwan the temporary seat of the Nationalist Republic of China, which he claimed remained the legitimate government of all China.

Amid mounting COLD WAR tensions, the Truman administration refused to recognize the Chinese Communist government, maintaining it was a puppet regime of the Soviet Union. The administration had avoided U.S. involvement in the internal Chinese conflict. Following the outbreak of the KOREAN WAR in June 1950, Washington anxiously anticipated a larger Communist offensive in the Far East. President HARRY S. TRUMAN ordered the U.S. 7th Fleet to defend Taiwan, declaring that a Communist occupation of the island would pose a grave threat to FREE WORLD interests in the West Pacific. Eager to preclude any escalation of the hostilities in Asia, Truman also instructed the fleet to prevent Nationalist Chinese attacks against the mainland. In November 1950 Communist China entered the Korean conflict against the U.S.-led UNITED NATIONS forces. The bitter fighting fueled U.S.-Communist Chinese enmity. In an effort to pressure Peking to accept an armistice in Korea, newly elected President DWIGHT D. EISENHOWER in February 1953 announced he was directing the 7th Fleet no longer to block Nationalist attacks against the Communist Chinese mainland.

Tensions between the rival Chinese states intensified over the next 18 months. When Communist Chinese Premier Chou En-lai in August 1954 called for the liberation of Taiwan, Eisenhower responded that "any invasion of Formosa would have to run over the 7th Fleet." The next month the Communist threat shifted to the Nationalist-held Quemoy, Matsu, and Tachen island groups. On September 3, 1954, the Communists began shelling the offshore islands. The Nationalists retaliated with air and sea raids along the mainland coast. To deter a Communist Chinese assault on Taiwan, the Eisenhower administration in December 1954 concluded the TAIWAN MUTUAL DEFENSE TREATY with the Nationalist government. The pact effectively extended a guarantee of U.S. protection to Taiwan.

As the Communist Chinese shelling increased, Eisenhower in a special message to Congress on January 24, 1955, asked for explicit authority to use U.S. military forces to protect Taiwan, the adjoining Pescadore islands, and "related positions and territories." The request was deliberately vague concerning the offshore islands, since Eisenhower at one and the same time wanted to communicate U.S. resolve to Peking and avoid committing America to a possible war over militarily unimportant islands. Congress passed the Formosa Resolution on January 28 authorizing the president to employ U.S. armed forces as he deemed necessary to defend Taiwan. In February 1955 the 7th Fleet helped the Nationalist Chinese evacuate the Tachen islands, which were not considered vital to Taiwan's security. Chinese clashes over the Quemoy and Matsu islands continued unabated and the Eisenhower administration braced for a Communist assault. Concerted diplomatic intercession by Great Britain and India, both of which recognized Communist China, helped resolve the crisis. Indian efforts at mediation in particular led Chou on April 22, while at the Bandung Conference of non-aligned nations, to call for U.S.-Communist Chinese negotiations on relaxing tensions in the Taiwan area. The United States responded favorably and the Communist shelling of the offshore is-

lands gradually abated. U.S.-Communist Chinese contacts began at the ambassadorial level in Geneva in August 1955. The talks proved inconclusive and were suspended by the United States in December 1957.

In August 1958 Communist China resumed its shelling of the Quemoy and Matsu islands, whereupon the Eisenhower administration moved beyond its 1954 stance and declared its readiness to defend the island groups. Eisenhower reinforced the 7th Fleet and authorized it to escort Nationalist supply ships to the islands. As part of an internationally supported effort to resolve the second Quemoy-Matsu Crisis, the United States and Communist China on September 15, 1958, resumed ambassadorial talks in Warsaw, Poland. In October U.S. Secretary of State JOHN FOSTER DULLES went to Taiwan to impress on Chiang the need for a lessening in Nationalist-Communist confrontation. In a communique released October 23, Chiang announced a reduction in the Nationalist military presence on the offshore islands and an end to Nationalist attempts to return to the mainland by force. Peking responded by curtailing the shelling of the islands, effectively bringing the crisis to a halt.

During the 1960 presidential campaign, Democratic candidate JOHN F. KENNEDY and Republican nominee RICHARD M. NIXON debated U.S. defense of the Quemoy and Matsu island groups. Kennedy argued against an unequivocal commitment that risked pulling the United States into a world war over the nonessential islands, while Nixon contended their loss could not be allowed because it would lead to further Communist aggression against Taiwan. In the face of a Communist military buildup along the Taiwan Strait in 1962, the Kennedy administration warned Peking against any attack against the offshore islands. What is sometimes referred to as the third, and last, Quemoy-Matsu Crisis ended without major incident.

See also SHANGHAI COMMUNIQUE.

QUOTA ACT See **IMMIGRATION ACT OF 1921.**

R

RADIO FREE EUROPE (RFE) U.S.-funded anti-Communist network that since the early 1950s has broadcast news, commentary, and entertainment to the peoples of Eastern Europe. Radio Free Europe transmitted native-language programs from its headquarters in Munich, Germany, to Poland, Czechoslovakia, Hungary, Romania, and Bulgaria. Supplementing its efforts was a companion anti-Communist network located in Munich called Radio Liberty (RL), which broadcast to the USSR in Russian and the languages of other Soviet ethnic groups.

The OFFICE OF POLICY COORDINATION, the element within the CENTRAL INTELLIGENCE AGENCY (CIA) responsible for COVERT ACTION in the first years of the COLD WAR, enlisted post–WORLD WAR II East European refugees from communism to aid the West's propaganda campaign against the Soviet Union's satellites in Eastern Europe. In 1950 East bloc emigres launched RFE in West Germany with financing secretly provided by the CIA. The network set out to encourage aspirations for democracy and liberty behind the IRON CURTAIN. RFE beamed accurate news items and Western popular music to countries whose totalitarian governments allowed only doctored accounts of domestic and foreign affairs, and barred contemporary West European and American cultural offerings.

In 1951 Soviet refugees used clandestine CIA funds to found Radio Liberation. The station changed its name to Radio Liberty in 1959. RFE and RL, removed from any overt links to the U.S. government, were able to denounce Soviet and East European Communist regimes without directly implicating Washington, which could plausibly deny any responsibility for the efforts of the twin networks. The stations drew a broad listenership by satisfying a demand for uncensored news otherwise not available within the Soviet orbit. From their inception the networks attracted aggressive countermeasures by East bloc Communist officials, who electronically jammed RFE and RL signals and even resorted to sabotage in unsuccessfully attempting to disrupt the stations' operations. CIA sponsorship of the radio networks, widely rumored throughout the 1960s, was publicly disclosed in 1971 by Senator Clifford P. Case (R-NJ), who proposed legislation to fund them openly and thereby bring them under direct congressional oversight. RFE and RL were removed from CIA control in 1973 when Congress created the Board for International Broadcasting to assume budgetary and policy authority over the stations. The board, comprising the directors of RFE and RL and a number of presidential appointees, takes its direction from the State Department and reports yearly to the president and Congress.

With the collapse of communism in Eastern Europe by 1990, Radio Free Europe faced an uncertain future. Senior officials responsible for U.S. worldwide broadcasting operations and interested members of Congress joined an emerging debate at the outset of the 1990s on whether democratization in the East bloc and the newfound openness of its societies might have rendered RFE obsolete. The station rejected suggestions it had outlived its usefulness. To persuade Congress of its continuing value in the post–Cold War era, RFE stressed the role it could fill in helping former Soviet bloc countries to nurture democracy and its institutions.

See also VOICE OF AMERICA, UNITED STATES INFORMATION AGENCY.

RADIO LIBERTY See **RADIO FREE EUROPE**.

RADIO MARTI U.S.-financed radio station that broadcasts news, public affairs, and entertainment programming in Spanish to Cuba. Named for Jose Marti, a 19th century hero of the island's independence struggles against Spain, Radio Marti is an instrument of the U.S. government's public information campaign against the Communist regime of Cuban leader Fidel Castro. In 1983, Congress established the station to provide the people of Cuba with news and commentary unavailable to them through state-controlled, censored journalism. Located in Miami and staffed largely by members of the Cuban-American community in South Florida, Radio Marti is under the jurisdiction of the VOICE OF AMERICA (VOA). Cuban officials consistently have condemned the station's efforts as part of a larger U.S. propaganda scheme to destabilize Castro's government. The U.S. government in March 1990 launched the Miami-based Television Marti on a trial basis. Like its radio counterpart, the TV station beams programming directly to Cuba. VOA supervises Television Marti's production. The Cuban government has denounced the U.S.-funded project as illegal on the grounds the station violates international telecommunications agreements by using Cuban broadcast frequencies. Castro's regime has electronically jammed Television Marti telecasts and threatened to disrupt American domestic programming in retaliation.

See also RADIO FREE EUROPE, UNITED STATES INFORMATION AGENCY.

RAINBOW WAR PLANS U.S. contingency war plans in the years before WORLD WAR II. By late 1937, the rise of Fascist powers Germany and Italy had caused the Roosevelt administration to consider revising the ORANGE WAR PLAN which since WORLD WAR I had focused U.S. defense preparations on a potential conflict with Japan. In May 1939 the administration adopted a set of five contingency plans, known collectively as the Rainbow War Plans, that shifted U.S. strategic thinking toward the possibility of war in Europe. The plans envisioned the United States fighting a defensive war against Japan until, either alone or with Great Britain and France as allies, America had defeated the Axis alliance in Europe. In September 1939 war broke out between Great Britain and France on one side and Germany and Italy on the other. From January to March 1941, high-ranking American, British, and Canadian military staff officers met in secret in Washington to formulate joint strategy in the event the United States entered the conflict. The resulting ABC-1 war plan (its code-name formed by taking the first letter of the three countries involved) called for a primary Allied war effort against Germany. In April 1941 similar planning, which included Dutch military officers, produced the ABCD-1 war plan for the Pacific, outlining Allied defensive responsibilities in the theater. After PEARL HARBOR brought America into World War II in December 1941, the United States and Great Britain consulted at the WASHINGTON CONFERENCE (1941–1942), where they formally adopted a "Germany First" strategy and integrated their military operations through establishment of an Anglo-American Combined Chiefs of Staff.

RAND CORPORATION Independent public policy research organization. Founded in 1948 in Santa Monica, California, the corporation studies current issues involving U.S. national security and international relations. Major areas emphasized in its scholarship are geopolitics, international economic policy, strategic and tactical military forces, defense policy, and terrorism. The cooperative RAND/UCLA Center for Soviet Studies has specialized in Soviet-American and Soviet-East European relations, Soviet foreign policy, and East-West military and arms control issues. RAND (for *Re*search *AN*d *D*evelopment) provides policy analysis to both businesses and government policymakers. Its flagship publication, *RAND Research Review*, appears three times a year.

RANDOLPH, EDMUND JENNINGS (1753–1813) Attorney general and secretary of state under President GEORGE WASHINGTON.

The Virginia native attended William and Mary College, read law, and was admitted to the bar in 1774. With the start of the AMERICAN REVOLUTION, the staunch patriot Randolph served as an aide-de-camp to General Washington in New England in 1775. Returning to Virginia, he was the youngest member of the state constitutional convention in 1776. He served as Virginia attorney general from 1776 to 1786 and concurrently was a member of the Continental Congress from 1779 to 1782. Elected Virginia governor in 1786, he held the post for two years. Joining the movement for a revision of the ARTICLES OF CONFEDERATION, he represented his state as a delegate to the Annapolis Convention in 1786 and the federal Constitutional Convention in Philadelphia in 1787. Randolph also was a member of the Virginia Convention in 1788 that ratified the new CONSTITUTION.

Appointed first U.S. attorney general by President Washington, he served in the post from 1789 to 1794, striving through his tenure to remain impartial in the pervasive political contest between Secretary of State THOMAS JEFFERSON and Treasury Secretary ALEXANDER HAMILTON. When Randolph succeeded the retiring Jefferson at the State Department in January 1794, American foreign affairs were dominated by Anglo-French war and its impact on U.S. relations with the two belligerents. He forced the recall of Edmond C. Genet as French minister to the United States in the wake of the notorious GENET AFFAIR, but then granted the controversial French diplomat asylum to spare him from arrest by the revolutionary French government. Randolph recalled U.S. Minister at Paris Gouverneur Morris, whose pro-British sympathies had antagonized the French, and replaced him with the pro-French JAMES MONROE. Randolph unsuccessfully objected to the appointment of U.S. Supreme Court Chief Justice JOHN JAY as special envoy to London to negotiate outstanding difficulties in Anglo-American relations. Though personally friendly with the chief justice, the secretary of state believed that as a matter of propriety Jay should resign his judicial office before taking the diplomatic post. Putting aside his opposition, Randolph worked with Hamilton in drafting the instructions for Jay's mission, endorsed the resultant JAY'S TREATY (1794),

and sought to assure Paris that this Anglo-American agreement did not violate existing Franco-American treaty obligations. He initiated negotiations with Spain that culminated, shortly after he left office, in PINCKNEY'S TREATY (1795). The accord opened the Mississippi River to free navigation by Americans and established the U.S. boundary with Spanish Florida.

Allegations of illicit contacts with the French minister to the United States Joseph Fauchet led to Randolph's resignation as secretary of state in August 1785. Following his ignominious departure, he published a long self-defense titled *A Vindication of Mr. Randolph's Resignation* (1795). He withdrew to Richmond, Virginia, and resumed the practice of law. In 1807 he defended former Vice-President Aaron Burr at his treason trial stemming from the BURR CONSPIRACY.

RAPIDAN CONFERENCE (1929) Meeting between British Prime Minister Ramsay MacDonald and U.S. President HERBERT C. HOOVER. MacDonald made an official visit to the United States from October 4 to October 10, 1929, to improve Anglo-American ties and confer with Hoover on naval disarmament. Relations between the two nations had been strained by their inability to agree on naval arms limitations at the GENEVA NAVAL CONFERENCE (1927). The two leaders met on October 6 in the rustic quiet of Hoover's fishing camp on the Rapidan River in Virginia. Their discussions centered on naval disarmament, but also addressed the maritime rights of neutrals in wartime, British naval bases in the Western Hemisphere, and the strengthening of the KELLOGG-BRIAND PACT (1928) outlawing war. While no issues were resolved, the so-called Rapidan Conference paved the way for the first of the LONDON NAVAL CONFERENCES. On October 7 MacDonald, with Hoover's backing, issued invitations to France, Italy, and Japan, which were promptly accepted, for a five-power conference on naval armaments in London the following year. MacDonald's trip generated considerable goodwill and presaged increasing coordination between America and Great Britain on naval and other defense matters.

REAGAN DOCTRINE (1985) U.S. pledge to support indigenous anti-Communist insurgencies battling Soviet-backed Marxist regimes in the THIRD WORLD. The doctrine emerged as a leading foreign policy prerogative under President RONALD W. REAGAN, who outlined its premises most forcefully in 1985 in his State of the Union message and in an October address to the UNITED NATIONS General Assembly. The policy evolved out of the Reagan administration's determination to stem Soviet expansionist influence in Africa, Asia, and Latin America. He advocated U.S. aid to anti-Communist guerrilla "proxies" as a cheaper, more politically tenable option for achieving national security aims than the direct commitment of American armed forces. Reagan related the doctrine to a purported "democratic revolution" underway worldwide in the 1980s. He claimed the United States bore a special obligation to defend liberty and democracy and thus to support so-called freedom fighters opposing Soviet-sponsored totalitarianism.

The Reagan dictum served as the rationale for U.S. economic and military assistance to the anti-Sandinista CONTRAS in Nicaragua; to the Mujahedeen resistance in Soviet-occupied Afghanistan; to rebel factions arrayed against Vietnam's client government in Cambodia; and, following the repeal of the CLARK AMENDMENT in 1985, to the UNITA guerrilla forces seeking the overthrow of the Soviet- and Cuban-supported regime in Angola. Critics contended the doctrine ignored possible diplomatic solutions and amounted to American funding of low-cost mercenaries whose devotion to democratic principles frequently was dubious. The electoral defeat of the Sandinista government, Soviet withdrawal from the AFGHANISTAN WAR, and favorable political settlements in the ANGOLAN CIVIL WAR and CAMBODIAN CIVIL WAR were attributed by Reagan and Bush administration policymakers to the success of the Reagan policy.

REAGAN PLAN (1982) Middle East initiative proposed by U.S. President RONALD W. REAGAN as the basis for negotiating a settlement of the Arab-Israeli conflict. In June 1982 Israeli military forces invaded Lebanon in a drive to smash the Palestine Liberation Organization (PLO), a quasi-governmental association of groups representing the Palestinian people and their aspirations for Palestinian nationhood. The

sworn enemy of the Jewish state, the PLO had its headquarters in the Lebanese capital of Beirut and guerrilla bases throughout the country. Israel defended the invasion as necessary to secure its northern border against PLO-directed guerrilla raids and terrorist strikes. In August, the Reagan administration responded to the LEBANON CRISIS by sending U.S. troops to help with the evacuation of the PLO guerrillas from Israeli-besieged West Beirut. The expulsion of the PLO from the divided Lebanese city was carried out under an arrangement negotiated by Reagan's special envoy to the Mideast, Philip C. Habib. On September 1, the day the PLO evacuation was completed, Reagan sought to reinvigorate the Arab-Israeli peace process by floating a major initiative in a televised speech in which he set forth U.S. views on resolving the Palestinian issue.

The United States, he announced, would endorse self-government for Palestinians in the Israeli-occupied West Bank and Gaza Strip provided it was accomplished in association with Jordan. Reagan emphasized America would not support either an independent Palestinian state or Israeli sovereignty in the occupied territories. He urged the Israelis to freeze further Jewish settlement in the West Bank, which Israel had seized in the 1967 Arab-Israeli Six-Day War, as a step to encourage Arab participation in the peace process outlined by the CAMP DAVID ACCORDS (1978). Reagan reiterated U.S. support for the Camp David plan to grant self-rule to the Palestinians in the West Bank and Gaza for five years while Israel, Egypt, Jordan, and the United States negotiated the final disposition of the territories. The president broke with earlier U.S. policy by stating in advance that the United States regarded Palestinian self-government in the occupied territories in association with Jordan as offering the best prospect for a just and durable peace in the region. The U.S. position, Reagan explained, was based on a belief that negotiations toward resolving the Arab-Israeli conflict ought to involve an exchange of land for peace as set out in UNITED NATIONS Security Council Resolution 242, adopted in 1967. The resolution's call for Israeli withdrawal from territories occupied in the Six-Day War, he observed, applied clearly to the West Bank and Gaza. He added that the final status of Jerusalem should be decided through negotiations, at the same time emphasizing that the United States believed the city should remain undivided.

Reagan strongly reaffirmed the U.S. commitment to Israel and implored its Arab enemies to recognize the Jewish state's right to exist. The Israeli government promptly rejected the Reagan plan as inconsistent with the Camp David Accords and a threat to Israeli security. The Reagan administration, moreover, proved unable to persuade Jordan's King Hussein to begin peace talks with Israel as an opening step toward broader negotiations within the Camp David framework. The PLO rejected the Reagan proposal, demanding instead the formation of an independent Palestinian state. In the ensuing years the administration made various unsuccessful attempts to revive the Mideast peace process. In August 1988 King Hussein announced that Jordan was severing its legal and administrative links to the West Bank and relinquishing its claims to the territory to the PLO.

REAGAN, RONALD WILSON (1911–   )
Governor, 40th president of the United States. Reagan graduated from Eureka College in his native Illinois in 1932 and became a radio sportscaster in Iowa. In 1937 he moved to Hollywood and began a 25-year career as a movie actor, appearing in some 50 films. During WORLD WAR II he served in an Army picture unit that made military training films. Reagan first became active in politics as president of the Screen Actors Guild from 1947 to 1952. A leader in efforts to purge Communists from the film industry, he testified before the HOUSE UN-AMERICAN ACTIVITIES COMMITTEE during its investigation of Communist influence in Hollywood. From 1954 to 1962 Reagan served as host of General Electric's weekly television theater series and toured the country as a corporate spokesman. During this period he completed his transformation from New Deal Democrat to staunch conservative Republican.

Reagan was elected Republican governor of California in 1966 and reelected in 1970. During his two terms he emerged as the nation's most prominent conservative political figure. In 1968 he mounted a brief, unsuccessful bid for the Republican

presidential nomination. In 1975 he was a member of the ROCKEFELLER COMMISSION that investigated the INTELLIGENCE COMMUNITY. Reagan challenged President GERALD R. FORD for the 1976 Republican presidential nomination. During the campaign he criticized the Ford administration's policy of DÉTENTE with the Soviet Union. Ford weathered Reagan's challenge before losing to Democratic candidate JIMMY CARTER in the general election. During the Carter presidency Reagan was an outspoken critic of the PANAMA CANAL TREATIES (1977) and the administration's defense budgets, which he termed inadequate in the face of growing Soviet military capabilities. Reagan easily captured the 1980 Republican presidential nomination and went on to defeat Carter, whose candidacy was seriously weakened by the continuing IRAN HOSTAGE CRISIS (1979–1981).

Reagan took office in January 1981 determined to reverse the weakness and vacillation he believed had characterized American foreign policy since the nation's troubled experience in the VIETNAM WAR. The new administration reasserted U.S. readiness to defend American interests worldwide. The Soviet invasion of Afghanistan in 1979 had reinforced Reagan's view that Communist aggression sponsored and directed by Moscow posed the greatest threat to U.S. and Western security. The administration began a major defense buildup to counter what it contended was a dangerous Soviet lead in both nuclear and conventional military forces. Reagan restored funding for the B-1 bomber, which Carter had canceled, continued deployment of the MX missile, and pressed the development of ANTISATELLITE WEAPONS. In 1983 he launched the controversial STRATEGIC DEFENSE INITIATIVE (SDI), a program to develop a space-based defensive shield against nuclear missile attack. The president fully recovered from a gunshot wound suffered during an assassination attempt in March 1981 by deranged assailant John Hinkley.

Relations with the Soviet Union remained strained throughout Reagan's first term. The return to East-West COLD WAR confrontation that followed the Soviet intervention in the AFGHANISTAN WAR intensified in the early 1980s. Reagan adopted a hardline stance toward Moscow, terming the USSR an "evil empire." In September 1983 he condemned the Soviet downing of the civilian KAL FLIGHT 007. Reagan opposed the U.S.-Soviet SALT II arms control measure concluded under Carter in 1979, maintaining it locked in place a Soviet advantage in INTERCONTINENTAL BALLISTIC MISSILES. He proposed, instead, negotiations for a START agreement that would actually reduce rather than just limit superpower nuclear arsenals. To counterbalance recently installed Soviet missiles, the administration in November 1983 began deploying PERSHING II and CRUISE MISSILES to NATO forces in Europe, overcoming concerted opposition by both domestic and European NUCLEAR FREEZE advocates. The Kremlin the same month suspended all U.S.-Soviet arms talks.

Central America also commanded Reagan's early attention. The president viewed with alarm the leftist Sandinista regime that had emerged in Nicaragua following the 1979 overthrow of strongman and longtime U.S. ally General Anastasio Somoza. In April 1981 Reagan cut U.S. aid to the Sandinista government, charging that Managua was secretly providing arms and training to Marxist FMLN guerrillas in the EL SALVADOR CIVIL WAR. Accusing the Soviet Union and Communist Cuba of fomenting and aiding leftist insurgencies in Central America, the administration greatly increased U.S. military and economic assistance to El Salvador. In December 1981 Reagan authorized a program of covert U.S. aid to the CONTRAS, anti-Sandinista Nicaraguan rebel groups then forming in the region. U.S. support for the Contras, opposed by many liberals in Congress, remained a matter of bitter debate throughout the Reagan presidency. Responding to criticism that U.S. policy ignored the social and economic causes of unrest in Central America, the White House in 1982 unveiled the CARIBBEAN BASIN INITIATIVE to promote regional development. In 1983 Reagan ordered the GRENADA INVASION to reverse a Cuban-supported leftist military coup and evacuate several hundred Americans on the Caribbean island. In 1984 the presidentially appointed KISSINGER COMMISSION on Central America identified Soviet- and Cuban-sponsored Communist expansionism as the chief menace to the region. The panel endorsed Reagan's hardline anti-Communist policies, while also stressing the impor-

tance of addressing pressing regional social and economic problems.

Reagan sought unsuccessfully to find a solution to the long-standing Arab-Israeli conflict in the Middle East. Following the Israeli invasion of Lebanon in 1982, he committed U.S. marines to an international peacekeeping force in the war-torn country. The so-called REAGAN PLAN, his proposal the same year for a Middle East peace settlement based on Palestinian self-rule in the West Bank in association with Jordan, drew little support from either Israel or the Arabs. In October 1983 a suicidal bombing by a Moslem fundamentalist terrorist killed 241 marines at their barracks in Beirut. Reagan withdrew the marines in February 1984, ending U.S. intervention in the LEBANON CRISIS. The same year radical Islamic factions in Beirut began to abduct Americans and other Westerners, hoping to use the LEBANON HOSTAGES to coerce changes in U.S. Mideast policy.

The Reagan administration from the start proclaimed a tough antiterrorism stance that included a refusal either to negotiate with or make concessions to terrorists. Reagan singled out Libya and Iran as terrorist states. In April 1981 and again in January 1989 U.S. Navy jets clashed with and shot down Libyan fighters in separate GULF OF SIDRA INCIDENTS. In 1985 the administration was confronted with both the Moslem extremist hijacking of TWA FLIGHT 847 and the ACHILLE LAURO AFFAIR, in which Palestinian terrorists seized an Egyptian cruise ship and murdered an American passenger. In response to alleged Libyan involvement in a West Berlin terrorist bombing that killed an American and wounded 60 others, Reagan in April 1986 ordered the LIBYAN BOMBING RAID. The disclosure in November 1986 that the White House had secretly sold arms to Iran in return for the release of American hostages in Lebanon undercut the president's antiterrorism policy. Revealed at the same time was the fact that NATIONAL SECURITY COUNCIL staff members between 1984 and 1986 had operated a secret supply network to circumvent congressional restrictions on aid to the Contras. Proceeds from the Iran arms sales were diverted to Contra aid. The IRAN-CONTRA affair tarnished Reagan's reputation and credibility and damaged his administration's effectiveness. Reagan had defended the Iranian arms sales as part of a U.S. diplomatic overture to supposedly moderate elements in Teheran. In 1987, as the Iran-Iraq War (1980–1988) intensified, he ordered the U.S. Navy to escort neutral shipping in the PERSIAN GULF INTERVENTION.

Reagan throughout his presidency was an apostle of democracy and free market economics. He promulgated the REAGAN DOCTRINE stating U.S. readiness to support anti-Communist insurgencies worldwide. Under the doctrine U.S. military aid was funneled to the Contras, pro-Western UNITA rebels in the ANGOLAN CIVIL WAR, and Mujahedeen guerrillas in Afghanistan. In 1986 the administration assisted the emergence of democratic governments in Haiti and the Philippines by facilitating the peaceful removal from power of authoritarian rulers Jean-Claude Duvalier and Ferdinand E. Marcos. Domestic critics charged that Reagan's policy of CONSTRUCTIVE ENGAGEMENT with the white minority government of South Africa acquiesced in that country's system of racial separatism, known as apartheid. Congress rejected the policy in 1986 when it voted economic sanctions against Pretoria over Reagan's veto. At the 1981 CANCUN SUMMIT on North-South economic issues, Reagan advanced market-based economies as the key to THIRD WORLD development. Similarly, he favored free-market solutions to the mounting INTERNATIONAL DEBT CRISIS involving developing nations. In 1988 he concluded the UNITED STATES-CANADA FREE TRADE AGREEMENT.

Reagan continued the steady improvement in U.S.-Communist Chinese relations begun under President RICHARD M. NIXON. He met with the Communist Chinese leadership at the BEIJING SUMMIT in 1984, the same year he won a landslide reelection. His second term witnessed a stunning improvement in U.S-Soviet relations. Washington and Moscow agreed to resume arms control negotiations in January 1985. In March Mikhail S. Gorbachev became leader of the USSR, inaugurating a program of sweeping political liberalization within the Communist nation and pursuing improved ties with the West. Reagan and Gorbachev conferred at the GENEVA SUMMIT (1985) and REYKJAVIK SUMMIT (1986). At the 1987 WASHINGTON SUMMIT they signed the landmark INTERMEDIATE NUCLEAR FORCES TREATY eliminating an entire class of NUCLEAR WEAPONS and

cutting superpower nuclear arsenals in Europe. In April 1988 Washington and Moscow joined in an agreement concluded under UNITED NATIONS auspices providing for Soviet military withdrawal from Afghanistan. Reagan's May 1988 visit to the Soviet Union for the MOSCOW SUMMIT capped the remarkable change in the U.S.-Soviet relationship occurring during his tenure. He retired to California on leaving office in January 1989 and published his memoirs, *An American Life* (1990).

RECIPROCAL TRADE AGREEMENTS ACT See **TRADE AGREEMENTS ACT**.

RED CLOUD'S WAR See **SIOUX WARS**.

RED EAGLE   See **WEATHERFORD, WILLIAM**.

RED SCARE See **PALMER RAIDS**.

REED, JOHN (1887–1920) American journalist and revolutionary. He was born in Oregon to a wealthy and socially prominent family. After graduating from Harvard College in 1910, he became deeply interested in social problems through the work of "muckraking" American journalists LINCOLN STEFFENS and Ida M. Tarbell. In 1913 Reed joined the staff of the radical journal *The Masses*. The first of his numerous arrests for political agitation came in 1914 for speaking in support of striking silkweavers in Paterson, New Jersey. Sent the same year by *Metropolitan Magazine* to report on the Mexican Revolution, he established a national reputation as a war correspondent through his four-month-long coverage of Pancho Villa's rebel army. He reported on WORLD WAR I from Europe for the same magazine until illness forced his return to American in 1916.

Reed and his wife, journalist Louise Bryant, arrived in St. Petersburg, Russia, in autumn 1917 in time to observe the October Revolution, in which the Bolsheviks took power. His famous eyewitness account of the event, *Ten Days That Shook the World* (1919), offered an impassioned and enthusiastic description of the Bolshevik victory. Returning to America, he plunged into Socialist Party politics. When the party expelled Reed and other radicals in 1919, he helped organize the Communist Labor Party, becoming its leader and editor of its paper *The Voice of Labor* Indicted for sedition, he evaded the U.S. government and fled to Russia. He died in Moscow in October 1920 after a brief bout with typhus and was buried in the Kremlin.

REFUGEE ACT OF 1980 Comprehensive revision of U.S. refugee policy. The legislation, signed by President JIMMY CARTER on March 17, 1980, was the first thorough overhaul of U.S. refugee law since the MIGRATION AND REFUGEE ASSISTANCE ACT. That 1962 act had been supplemented in 1975 by the INDOCHINA MIGRATION AND REFUGEE ASSISTANCE ACT, providing aid to refugees from nations formerly allied with the United States in the VIETNAM WAR. The sudden influx of hundreds of thousands of Indochinese BOAT PEOPLE in the late 1970s overwhelmed U.S. refugee programs, requiring additional interim assistance measures and pointing out the need for new permanent refugee provisions. The Refugee Act of 1980 raised to 50,000 the number of refugees regularly allowed into the United States each year. The president was authorized to increase the annual total in consultation with Congress, and to admit refugees on an emergency basis. The definition of refugee formally was expanded to include anyone who had a well-founded fear of racial, ethnic, religious, or political persecution. By extending refugee status to people worldwide, the act superseded the provisions of the 1962 law restricting refugee assistance to those from Communist countries or the Middle East. An office of U.S. Coordinator for Refugee Affairs was created to oversee refugee issues.

REFUGEE RELIEF ACT (1953) Special legislation to admit refugees to the United States. The problem of refugees in Europe following WORLD WAR II had led to passage of the DISPLACED PERSONS ACT in 1948. When the nation's first major refugee law expired at the end of 1951, President HARRY S. TRUMAN appealed for legislation that would allow refugees to continue to come to America. The Truman administration asserted foreign policy interests would be served by

aiding those who escaped from Communist regimes in Eastern Europe. In June 1952 Congress overrode Truman's veto of the IMMIGRATION AND NATIONALITY ACT OF 1952. This measure, a major overhaul of American immigration law, retained ethnic immigration quotas favoring northern and western Europeans and offered no special protection for refugees. The same year Truman appointed a seven-member Presidential Commission on Immigration and Naturalization headed by former Solicitor General Philip B. Perlman. In its report, *Whom We Shall Welcome*, submitted in January 1953, the panel concluded refugee admissions were crucial to the West's struggle against the spread of communism in Europe.

Shortly after assuming office, President DWIGHT D. EISENHOWER sent Congress a message requesting "emergency" refugee legislation. The new administration successfully persuaded lawmakers the refugee situation in Europe required immediate action. The Refugee Relief Act, signed into law August 7, 1953, authorized 209,000 special immigrant visas through the end of 1956. Half of the visas were allocated for "escapees" and refugees from Eastern Europe. In a major departure from basic immigration policy, the new arrivals were to be admitted outside existing quota limits. Congress enacted similar specific measures in the late 1950s to accept Hungarian refugees fleeing the failed HUNGARIAN REVOLT (1956) and Dutch-Indonesians displaced by Indonesian independence. Refugee policy was addressed next in the FAIR SHARE REFUGEE ACT in 1960.

REGISTRATION OF SPACE OBJECTS TREATY (1974) International agreement drafted under UNITED NATIONS auspices that established a mandatory system of registering objects launched into outer space. Formally named the Convention on Registration of Objects Launched into Outer Space, the treaty was opened for signature on January 14, 1975, and went into effect September 15, 1976, following ratification by five nations, one of which was the United States. More than 40 countries, including all the space powers, and the European Space Agency currently are parties to the convention. The agreement, which implemented terms of the OUTER SPACE TREATY (1969) relating to registration of space objects, obligates each launching country to keep a national record showing details (such as date and location of launch, orbital parameters, general functions) of all satellites and other space objects it puts into earth orbit or beyond. Launching nations also are required to furnish the U.N. secretary-general with the same detailed information, which is then recorded in a central register accessible to other U.N. members.

REID, WHITELAW (1837–1912) Journalist and diplomat. Reid was born near Xenia, Ohio. After graduating from Miami University in his native state in 1856, he edited the weekly *Xenian News*. Hired by the *Cincinnati Gazette* as a reporter in 1861, he covered the Civil War as a field correspondent. He was at the battles of Shiloh (1861) and Gettysburg (1863) and was among the first newspapermen to reach the abandoned Confederate capital of Richmond, Virginia, after it fell to the Union in 1865. Following abortive attempts at running cotton plantations in Louisiana and Alabama he returned to journalism, joining the *New York Tribune* in 1868 as a top editorial assistant to owner and editor Horace Greeley. With Greeley's death in 1872, Reid took over editorship of America's most profitable newspaper.

A staunch Republican and political ally of Secretary of State JAMES G. BLAINE, he was appointed U.S. minister to France in 1889. Returning to the United States after three uneventful years in Paris, he was the unsuccessful Republican vice-presidential candidate in 1892. By the mid-1890s he had become an ardent expansionist who advocated U.S. acquisition of Cuba and HAWAII ANNEXATION. He and the *Tribune* stood behind the McKinley administration's decision to wage the SPANISH-AMERICAN WAR (1898) and from the conflict's outset favored U.S. territorial gains in the Caribbean and Pacific. President WILLIAM MCKINLEY named Reid a member of the five-man American peace delegation that negotiated the TREATY OF PARIS (1898) ending the war. When differences surfaced among the American representatives in Paris about the treaty's territorial provisions, his arguments helped persuade McKinley to demand U.S. retention of the entire Philippines.

Political and social ties with Secretary of State JOHN M. HAY and President THEODORE ROOSEVELT landed Reid appointment in 1905 as U.S. minister to Great Britain. Before departing, he relinquished active editorship of the *Tribune*. His diplomatic mission was distinguished by his involvement in negotiating the January 1909 agreement with the British to submit the long-standing North Atlantic FISHERIES QUESTION to international arbitration. After a brief illness, Reid died at his post in London in 1912.

REISCHAUER,   EDWIN   OLDFATHER (1910–1990)   U.S. ambassador to Japan; scholar of East Asian affairs and a leading authority on Japan. Born in Tokyo, the son of American missionaries, he graduated from Oberlin College in Ohio in 1931 and earned a master's degree in history from Harvard University the next year. After studying in France, Japan, and China, he taught at Harvard, where he received his Ph.D. in Far Eastern languages in 1939. With U.S. entry into WORLD WAR II in 1941, he served as a research analyst on the Far East for the State Department and as a senior Army intelligence officer. Following the war he returned to Harvard to resume teaching and research.

In 1961 he was named ambassador to Japan by President JOHN F. KENNEDY, who reportedly decided on the appointment after reading a 1960 article by Reischauer in the journal FOREIGN AFFAIRS. In the piece, the Harvard professor described a "broken dialogue" between the United States and Japan in the wake of discord over the postwar JAPANESE SECURITY TREATY (1951). In his five-year tenure at Tokyo, he helped bring about a marked improvement in U.S.-Japanese relations. His fluency in the language and deep understanding of Japanese culture and society endeared him to his host country. Reischauer urged the Japanese government to assert greater political and economic leadership in East Asia and encouraged an improvement in relations between Japan and South Korea. Upon his return to the United States in 1966 he rejoined the faculty at Harvard, where he began to speak out against U.S. involvement in the VIETNAM WAR. Reischauer retained a close affiliation with the university until his death. An author or coauthor of some dozen books, his works included *Japan, Past and Present* (1946); *The Japanese* (1977); and the classic volumes *East Asia: The Great Tradition* (1960), written with Harvard colleague JOHN K. FAIRBANK, and *East Asia: The Modern Transformation* (1965), done in collaboration with Fairbank and Albert Craig.

REORGANIZATION PLAN NO. 6 (1953) Broad restructuring of the DEPARTMENT OF DEFENSE (DOD). The NATIONAL SECURITY ACT AMENDMENTS OF 1949 had created a centralized Defense Department that brought the nation's land, naval, and air forces together in a single organization. The KOREAN WAR spotlighted the problem of continuing interservice rivalries and revealed organizational shortcomings in the U.S. defense establishment. President DWIGHT D. EISENHOWER in February 1953 directed the formation of a special panel, known as the ROCKEFELLER COMMITTEE, to propose improvements in DOD's organization. The committee, under chairman NELSON A. ROCKEFELLER, completed its report in April 1953.

On April 30, 1953, President Eisenhower sent Congress his plan for overhauling the Defense Department. The sixth blueprint for revamping of the executive branch submitted that year, it was designated Reorganization Plan No. 6. The proposal incorporated the key recommendations of the Rockefeller Committee. Under reorganization legislation then in place, it was scheduled to go into effect by executive order unless formally rejected by Congress in 60 days. In an accompanying message, Eisenhower identified three basic goals in the reorganization of the defense establishment: "clear and unchallenged civilian responsibility"; "maximum effectiveness at minimum cost"; and "the best possible military plans." When Congress declined to cancel the proposed restructuring, Reorganization Plan No. 6 took effect June 30, 1953. The measure shifted the nation's top military officers, the JOINT CHIEFS OF STAFF (JCS), from direct command of the armed forces to an advisory and planning role. It drew a clear civilian line of authority over DOD, running from the president, to the secretary of defense, to the secretaries of the military services. The plan in-

creased the responsibilities of the JCS chairman and, reflecting the emphasis on cost effectiveness of the Eisenhower administration's NEW LOOK defense strategy, consolidated several major DOD logistics offices. Advances in military science and technology brought further restructuring of the defense establishment in the DEFENSE REORGANIZATION ACT OF 1958.

RESERVATIONISTS Group of Republican Senators led by SENATE FOREIGN RELATIONS COMMITTEE Chairman HENRY CABOT LODGE, SR. (R-MA), who in the debate over ratification of the TREATY OF VERSAILLES (1919) ending WORLD WAR I would not accept U.S. participation in the LEAGUE OF NATIONS without reservations protecting American sovereignty. Through the insistence of Democratic President WOODROW WILSON, the PARIS PEACE CONFERENCE incorporated the proposed league, a postwar international organization to deter aggression through COLLECTIVE SECURITY, into the Versailles peace settlement concluded in late June 1919. During the conference strong Republican opposition to the league and its integration into the peace treaty had begun to take shape in the Senate. The Republican ROUND ROBIN, introduced by Lodge in March 1919, had declared the league covenant unacceptable as initially devised and opposed further consideration of it until after the final peace settlement. The resolution kicked off the bitter political fight between Senate Republicans and Wilson over the league.

When the Treaty of Versailles was referred to the Senate Foreign Relations Committee in July 1919 for its consideration, Lodge and other influential Republicans mobilized opposition to Wilson's League of Nations. Lodge led the so-called reservationists, a group of more than 30 Republican senators that included WARREN G. HARDING of Ohio, Charles C. Curtis of Kansas, and FRANK B. KELLOGG of Minnesota, who wanted to attach reservations to the treaty that would redress their main objection to Wilson's coveted postwar body. They contended that the idea of collective security embodied in ARTICLE X of the league covenant sacrificed U.S. sovereignty by vesting the power to commit U.S. military forces to an international body. The covenant, the reservationists complained, would limit America's independence of action during an international conflict because league members would collectively determine who was the aggressor and how and whether to respond. Another Republican group, small but powerful, advocated outright rejection of the league in any form. Known as the irreconcilables, their ranks numbered some 15, including prominent Senators Hiram W. Johnson of California, William E. Borah of Idaho, Robert M. La Follette of Wisconsin, and PHILANDER C. KNOX of Pennsylvania. Proponents of historic American ISOLATIONISM, they adamantly opposed U.S. participation in a system of collective security. The irreconcilables, generally disillusioned with the peace treaty, believed America was strong and self-sufficient and should hew to its traditional policy of avoiding foreign entanglements.

The reservationists, with the support of the irreconcilables, adopted a strategy of delay, tying up the treaty in the Foreign Relations Committee for two months in expectation that public opinion toward the league would grow increasingly negative as the political debate dragged on. In September 1919 Lodge's committee reported the treaty to the Senate with recommendations for extensive amendments and reservations. Moderate Republicans who basically backed Wilson on the league joined with Democrats to vote down all the measures. Following this rejection, Lodge then reported a ratification resolution accompanied by 14 reservations, the so-called LODGE RESERVATIONS, circumscribing American obligations under the league covenant. Ratification on these terms was unacceptable to Wilson, who contended that the Lodge Reservations would lead to the treaty's nullification. The president thus urged defeat of the Lodge resolution. On November 19, 1919, a combination of loyal Democrats and Republican irreconcilables rejected the treaty with reservations. When the treaty without reservations was put to a vote the same day, reservationists and irreconcilables then joined to prevent its passage.

REUBEN JAMES See **GREER INCIDENT**.

REYKJAVIK SUMMIT (1986)   So-called pre-summit October 11 to 12 between President RONALD W. REAGAN and Soviet Communist Party General Secretary Mikhail S. Gorbachev that developed into a major round of superpower arms control negotiations. At the conclusion of their GENEVA SUMMIT in 1985, the two leaders tentatively agreed to meet in the United States the following year. Fixing a date for the next conference proved difficult as the modest goodwill generated at Geneva in 1985 faded through the first half of 1986. Stalemated U.S.-Soviet arms control talks adjourned in March with no immediate prospect for progress. Moscow delayed negotiations on a superpower summit after the U.S. bombing raid on Libya in April. Soviet-American relations deteriorated further when the Kremlin rebuked the Reagan administration for arming anti-Communist rebels in Afghanistan and Angola and when the United States announced it would no longer abide by the 1979 SALT II agreement.

Summit prospects dimmed in early September after the Soviets arrested and detained American journalist Nicholas Daniloff as a spy. The Daniloff incident, seen as Kremlin retaliation for the U.S. arrest a week prior of Soviet UNITED NATIONS employee Gennadi F. Zakharov on espionage charges, dominated Soviet-American relations for weeks. Reagan vowed there would be no summit as long as Daniloff remained captive. The two governments reached an agreement on September 30 to exchange their detained citizens. The same day Reagan and Gorbachev revealed they would attend an October preliminary summit meeting, or pre-summit, in Iceland to establish a framework and agenda for an anticipated summit in the United States. Gorbachev refused to hold a formal conference with Reagan unless it resulted in concrete agreements. The general secretary had proposed the Reykjavik parley as a vital interim step toward a major accord on NUCLEAR WEAPONS.

In two days of talks the Soviet and U.S. leaders achieved no breakthrough on the main issue of arms control. But the detailed discussions at Reykjavik transformed the pre-summit into a true summit. Reagan and Gorbachev nearly concluded a historic agreement to make sweeping reductions in their respective offensive nuclear arsenals. Both sides accepted the principle that there should be dramatic two-way cuts in the numbers of strategic and intermediate-range nuclear forces. The discussions broke down over long-standing differences concerning limits on the STRATEGIC DEFENSE INITIATIVE (SDI), the U.S. program for developing space-based antimissile defenses. Gorbachev demanded a 10-year ban on field tests of SDI. Reagan, who offered to delay SDI deployment for a decade, would not agree to restrict the program to laboratory research, even in return for major cuts in Soviet weapons levels. The general secretary's insistence on SDI limits led Reagan to suggest the elimination of all ballistic missiles over a 10-year period. The president later backed off this idea when NATO allies complained a ballistic-missile ban would remove the protective U.S. nuclear umbrella and leave Europe vulnerable to superior Soviet conventional forces.

The Iceland parley ended in deadlock, each side accusing the other of intransigence on SDI. Domestic critics scored Reagan for his adamant position on the issue and accused him of having missed a landmark opportunity in Reykjavik to strike a major arms control agreement. The summit marked a temporary setback in the East-West arms control dialogue and clouded the prospects for progress on other key Soviet-American issues. A negotiating breakthrough on medium-range nuclear weapons led to completion of the INTERMEDIATE NUCLEAR FORCES TREATY at the WASHINGTON SUMMIT in 1987.

RICHARDSON, ELLIOT LEE (1920–)
Lawyer, diplomat, senior government official who held various cabinet posts. Born into a prominent Boston family, Richardson graduated from Harvard in 1941. After distinguished service as an Army officer during WORLD WAR II, he earned a degree from Harvard Law School in 1947 and clerked for U.S. Supreme Court Justice Felix Frankfurter before entering private practice. In 1957 President DWIGHT D. EISENHOWER appointed him assistant secretary for legislation in the Department of Health, Education, and Welfare (HEW), where he helped draft the NATIONAL DEFENSE EDUCATION ACT (1958). From 1959 to 1961 he was U.S. attorney for Massachusetts. Returning to private practice, he was elected his state's lieutenant governor as a Republican in 1964 and attorney general two years later.

In 1969 Richardson joined the Nixon administration as under secretary of state.

He took an active part in preparations for the SALT I arms control talks that began in Helsinki in November 1969 and supported administration efforts to extricate the United States from direct involvement in the VIETNAM WAR. In June 1970 President RICHARD M. NIXON named Richardson secretary of HEW. He remained at the department until January 1973, when he became secretary of defense. Three months later he was selected by Nixon to replace Richard G. Kleindienst as attorney general. Kleindienst had resigned because of his close ties with several White House aides implicated in the worsening Watergate scandal. In October 1973 Richardson gained wide renown when he refused Nixon's order to fire Watergate special prosecutor Archibald Cox and resigned instead in what became known as the Saturday Night Massacre. Richardson returned to government service in December 1974 as ambassador to Great Britain under President GERALD R. FORD. He became secretary of commerce in November 1975 and held the post until the end of the Ford administration, when he returned to private law practice. From 1977 to 1980 he served as U.S. representative to the UNITED NATIONS CONFERENCE ON THE LAW OF THE SEA. In February 1990 he headed the U.N. observer team that monitored the elections in Nicaragua in which the Sandinista government was unseated.

RIDGWAY, MATTHEW BUNKER (1895–) Army officer, commander of allied forces in the KOREAN WAR, supreme commander of NATO. Born at Fort Monroe, Virginia, where his father, an Army officer, was stationed, Ridgway graduated from West Point in 1917. He spent WORLD WAR I with an infantry regiment on the Mexican border, returned to West Point as an instructor, and served overseas tours in China, Nicaragua, the CANAL ZONE, and the Philippines. Assigned to the War Department's General Staff at the time of U.S. entry in WORLD WAR II, he was promoted to general in 1942 and took command of the 82nd Airborne Division. He parachuted with the division into Normandy on D-Day in 1944. In 1946 he was appointed U.S. Army representative to the newly formed Military Staff Committee of the UNITED NATIONS, where he helped prepare a report on U.N. Security Council use of military force. The same year he also was named senior U.S. delegate to the INTER-AMERICAN DEFENSE BOARD responsible for co-ordinating Western Hemisphere security.

In December 1950 Ridgway became commander of U.S. forces in the Korean War, replacing General Walton H. Walker, who had been killed in a vehicle accident. A Chinese Communist offensive had just dealt the American 8th Army a serious defeat. Ridgway moved quickly to reverse the situation, recapturing the South Korean capital of Seoul by March 1951. The following month he succeeded General DOUGLAS MACARTHUR, who had been relieved by President Harry S. Truman, as head of the overall U.N. command in Korea. In July 1951 he oversaw the start of the armistice talks that finally ended the war two years later. In 1952 Ridgway became the commander of NATO forces in Europe. He returned to Washington in 1953 to become Army chief of staff. During his tenure he voiced increasing disagreement with the Eisenhower administration's NEW LOOK defense strategy that emphasized NUCLEAR WEAPONS over traditional Army and Navy conventional forces. He retired in 1955 and became a business executive.

RIO DE JANEIRO CONFERENCE (1942) Third Meeting of American Foreign Ministers convened to consider cooperative action against the Axis powers following the Japanese attack on PEARL HARBOR and U.S. entry into WORLD WAR II. At the instigation of the United States, the foreign ministers met in Rio de Janeiro, Brazil, from January 15 to 28, 1942, to consult on measures for preserving the unity and territorial integrity of the Western Hemisphere. The U.S. delegation, headed by Under Secretary of State SUMNER WELLES, sought the consent of the other 20 American republics to a resolution pledging themselves to break off relations with the Axis powers. Nine Latin American countries already had declared war on the Axis, and three others had severed relations. As anticipated, Chile and Argentina refused to accept the U.S.-sponsored measure mandating diplomatic rupture. To preserve inter-American unity, the conference agreed to a compromise. On January 28, the delegates unanimously approved a resolution that merely recommended a break in relations with the Axis powers. The conference also created an INTER-AMERICAN DE-FENSE BOARD to consult on measures for strengthening hemispheric security, recommended an economic boycott against the Axis nations, and endorsed the ATLANTIC CHARTER.

By the time the Rio de Janeiro meeting adjourned, all the attending countries, with the exception of Chile and Argentina, had severed relations with the Axis. Chile did so in January 1943. Argentina, ruled by a pro-Fascist government sympathetic to Nazi Germany, followed a policy of neutrality for much of the war and was an impediment to Allied solidarity in the Americas. Fellow Latin American nations and the United States condemned its failure to repudiate the Axis. Buenos Aires finally yielded to U.S. pressure and broke relations with Germany and Japan in January 1944.

See also ACT OF CHAPULTEPEC.

RIO TREATY (1947) A pact for COLLECTIVE SECURITY drafted at the Inter-American Conference for the Maintenance of Peace and Security, held near Rio de Janeiro from August 15 to September 2, 1947. In fulfillment of the ACT OF CHAPULTEPEC (1945), representatives of the nations of the PAN-AMERICAN UNION met after WORLD WAR II in Brazil to establish a permanent mutual-defense system for the Western Hemisphere. Delegates from the United States and the Latin American republics signed the Inter-American Treaty of Reciprocal Assistance on September 2, 1947. Generally known as the Rio Treaty, it stated that an attack against one American state would be considered an attack against all. The pact provided for an Organ of Consultation to meet in the event of a threat to regional peace to consider collective measures that might be taken. By a two-thirds vote of signatories, this body could decide on joint action to meet aggression. No country, however, would be required to commit armed forces without its consent. The treaty also defined the territorial limits of the mutual-defense system by creating a hemispheric security zone. The Rio agreement was the first comprehensive inter-American collective-security pact and the first regional defense arrangement under the UNITED NATIONS CHARTER. President HARRY S. TRUMAN testified to the significance of the developments at Rio by flying there to address the conference before it adjourned. Congress overwhelmingly approved the treaty in December 1947. The Pan-American Bogota Conference in 1948 established the ORGANIZATION OF AMERICAN STATES, an umbrella regional organization that absorbed the Rio mutual-security machinery.

ROCKEFELLER COMMISSION (1975) Special panel that investigated the CENTRAL INTELLIGENCE AGENCY (CIA). In December 1974 the *New York Times* published reports of a "massive illegal domestic intelligence operation" conducted by the CIA against the anti-VIETNAM WAR movement and other sources of domestic political dissent. Responding to calls for an official inquiry, President GERALD R. FORD announced in early January 1975 he was naming Vice-President NELSON A. ROCKEFELLER to head an eight-member commission charged with determining whether the CIA had engaged in illegal or improper activities. Other members were former Secretary of the Treasury C. Douglas Dillon; retired General Lyman L. Lemnitzer; former California governor RONALD W. REAGAN; John T. Connor, chairman of Allied Chemical Corporation; attorney Erwin N. Griswold; labor leader Lane Kirkland; and educator Edgar F. Shannon, Jr. Ford's hope of forestalling a congressional investigation ended when Congress formed the CHURCH COMMITTEE in the Senate and the PIKE COMMITTEE in the House to examine possible CIA transgressions.

The commission began hearings on January 13 and completed its probe on May 12. Its investigation was aided by an internal CIA document, known as the FAMILY JEWELS, that detailed agency improprieties since the late 1940s. In its 300-page report, issued on June 10, the panel found that the CIA had engaged in unlawful or improper activities including the opening of private mail, extensive domestic surveillance of groups and individuals targeted as politically suspect, and the testing of mind-altering drugs on unknowing subjects. Ford withheld the section of the report concerning agency involvement in assassination plots against foreign leaders, terming it too sensitive for release. Commission recommendations included tighter controls on CIA operations and better oversight to prevent future abuses. In February 1976 Ford issued Executive Order 11905 that governed authorized intelligence activities and established the PRESIDENT'S INTELLIGENCE OVERSIGHT BOARD.

ROCKEFELLER COMMITTEE (1953) Committee appointed early in the Eisenhower administration by Secretary of Defense CHARLES E. WILSON to recommend changes in the DEPARTMENT OF DEFENSE. During the 1952 presidential campaign, victorious Republican candidate DWIGHT D. EISENHOWER criticized PENTAGON waste, inefficiency, and haphazard planning and promised to create a top-level panel to study ways to improve the nation's defense establishment. The Committee on Department of Defense Organization was formed February 19, 1953, with NELSON A. ROCKEFELLER as its chairman. Other members were former Secretary of Defense ROBERT A. LOVETT; chairman of the JOINT CHIEFS OF STAFF (JCS) General Omar N. Bradley; scientist and government advisor Dr. VANNEVAR BUSH; the director of the Office of Defense Mobilization, Dr. Arthur S. Flemming; David Sarnoff, chairman of the board of RCA; and the president's brother, Milton S. Eisenhower, then president of Pennsylvania State University. The committee submitted its report April 11, 1953. Key proposals—clear civilian control of the Defense Department, assignment of the JCS to strictly planning and advisory roles, and consolidation of many support functions and offices—were incorporated by President Eisenhower into REORGANIZATION PLAN NO. 6, a major restructuring of the defense establishment that went into effect June 30, 1953.

ROCKEFELLER, NELSON ALDRICH (1908–1979) Government official, governor, vice-president. The grandson of industrialist John D. Rockefeller, Nelson was born in Maine to one of the nation's wealthiest families. He graduated from Dartmouth in 1930 and worked in various family enterprises. In 1935 he became a director of Creole Petroleum Corporation, which had large holdings in Venezuela, and developed a lifelong interest in Latin American affairs. He was named by President FRANKLIN D. ROOSEVELT in 1940 to head the newly created Office of the Coordinator of Inter-American Affairs. As coordinator, Rockefeller was responsible for administering economic assistance and cultural exchange programs. In 1944 he became assistant secretary of state for Latin American affairs, in which post he directed U.S. participation in the Mexico City Conference (1945) that yielded the ACT OF CHAPULTEPEC on hemispheric security. He left government service in August 1945, but continued his involvement in Latin American affairs, founding several private organizations to stimulate economic growth and improve living conditions in the region.

In 1950 President HARRY S. TRUMAN appointed Rockefeller chairman of an advisory board for the POINT FOUR program. He resigned from his position with the federal foreign assistance program in 1951 to concentrate on the private sector's role in international economic development. In 1953 Rockefeller was selected by President DWIGHT D. EISENHOWER to head a special panel on defense reorganization. The ROCKEFELLER COMMITTEE's report served as the basis for a major restructuring of the defense establishment. Rockefeller was under secretary of the Department of Health, Education, and Welfare and a special assistant on foreign policy before leaving the administration in 1955 to pursue a political career. Elected governor of New York in 1958, he won reelection in 1962, 1966, and 1970, becoming a national figure in the process. In 1960, 1964, and 1968 he was an unsuccessful candidate for the Republican Party presidential nomination.

Rockefeller announced his resignation as governor in December 1973 to devote his attention to two national study groups, his own Commission on Critical Choices for America and the congressionally established Commission on Water Quality. When GERALD R. FORD succeeded to the presidency following the resignation of RICHARD M. NIXON in August 1974, he nominmated Rockefeller for the vice-presidency. Confirmed by the Congress, Rockefeller was sworn in as the 41st vice-president in December. In January 1975 Ford assigned him responsibility for undertaking a special investigation of the U.S. INTELLIGENCE COMMUNITY following allegations of widespread improprieties. The ROCKEFELLER COMMISSION's report, released in June, concluded that while illegalities and other abuses had occurred, the vast majority of U.S. intelligence activities had been conducted correctly. Under pressure from the conservative wing

of the Republican Party, Rockefeller withdrew from consideration as Ford's running mate in the 1976 presidential election. He retired to private life the next year and died suddenly in 1979.

ROGERS ACT (1924) Legislation that combined the U.S. diplomatic service, responsible for political functions, and the consular service, responsible for commercial and business relations, to create the modern FOREIGN SERVICE. In the aftermath of WORLD WAR I the diplomatic and consular services inherited new and expanded responsibilities that underscored the need for reform of the foreign relations machinery. In particular, the lack of any provision for shifting personnel between the diplomatic and consular branches handicapped efforts at ensuring proper and competent staffing of the State Department and overseas posts. The more prestigious diplomatic service remained the almost exclusive club of the wealthy and politically well-connected. Many diplomatic postings carried substantial social and entertainment obligations. With the limited diplomatic salaries, only individuals with large private incomes could afford to fill the posts. Although slightly higher, the salaries of the less prestigious consular service were not enough to lure highly capable individuals from private enterprise.

Representative John J. Rogers (R-MA), who had witnessed the problems besetting the diplomatic and consular services during a visit to Europe in 1919, championed reform. Over several years he worked with the State Department to fashion legislation that would establish a single career foreign service free from political influence. Signed into law May 24, 1924, the Rogers Act amalgamated the diplomatic and consular services into the unified Foreign Service of the United States. Permanent officers below the rank of minister were designated as Foreign Service officers (FSOs) and made subject to diplomatic or consular assignments interchangeably. The act arranged for appointment by open, competitive examination with promotion based strictly on merit, established new salary and retirement scales, and authorized entertainment allowances, thus placing the service on a secure professional basis for the first time. The act substantially improved service quality and morale. But administrative flaws remained which became manifest in a promotion rate for ex-diplomats that was twice as fast as that for ex-consuls. The SENATE FOREIGN RELATIONS COMMITTEE strongly criticized this discrepancy in a 1928 report. A series of proposals to redress personnel and other inequities culminated in the Moses-Linthicum Act of 1931. Sponsored by Senator George H. Moses (R-NH) and Representative J. Charles Linthicum (D-MD), the law assured an impartial promotion process and provided for increases in both salaries and allowances.

ROGERS, BERNARD WILLIAM (1921–   )

Army officer, commander of NATO forces in Europe. A Kansas native, Rogers graduated from West Point in 1943. After assignments stateside and as an aide to General Mark Clark in Austria, he attended Oxford University on a Rhodes scholarship. He saw action during the KOREAN WAR as an infantry battalion commander. Following VIETNAM WAR service and promotion to general, he was assigned command of the 5th Infantry Division in Colorado in 1969. He addressed racial, drug, and training issues then troubling the military and instituted reforms that improved morale and discipline, gaining a reputation as an innovative leader. In 1976 Rogers became Army chief of staff. He devoted his three-year tenure to refurbishing and rebuilding the service following its demoralization in the Vietnam conflict.

In June 1979 he succeeded General ALEXANDER M. HAIG, JR. as NATO supreme allied commander. Concerned by the Warsaw Pact's mounting military strength, Rogers pressed for the continuing modernization of NATO defenses, strongly supporting the December 1979 DUAL-TRACK DECISION to deploy U.S. intermediate range PERSHING II and CRUISE MISSILES. The following year he won praise for his diplomatic skill in gaining renewed Greek membership in the alliance. Greece had withdrawn from NATO's military command in 1974 in protest over the Turkish invasion of Cyprus. Rogers oversaw the early-1980s Reagan administration defense buildup in Europe. The final years of his tenure were marked by improving U.S.-Soviet relations and a gradual lessening of East-West tensions. His command ended with his retirement in 1987.

ROGERS PLAN (1969)

Proposal advanced by U.S. Secretary of State WILLIAM P. ROGERS for achieving a comprehensive Arab-Israeli peace settlement. Rogers presented his plan on December 9, 1969, at the height of the so-called War of Attrition (1968–1970) between Egyptian and Israeli forces along the Suez Canal. Egypt's President Gamal Abdel Nasser had initiated the hostilities in a bid to gradually wear down the Jewish state following its overwhelming victory over neighboring Arab nations in the June 1967 Six-Day War. In that conflict Israel had captured the Sinai Peninsula and Gaza Strip from Egypt, the West Bank (including East Jerusalem) from Jordan, and the Golan Heights from Syria. Rogers and President RICHARD M. NIXON were concerned that the heavy and escalating assistance provided by U.S. COLD WAR adversary the Soviet Union to the Egyptians and Syrians would bring a shift in the Mideast military balance against Israel. The Nixon administration, committed to preserving Israeli security and containing Soviet influence, moved on the diplomatic front in an effort to secure a breakthrough in the Arab-Israeli conflict. The Rogers Plan called for Israeli withdrawal from Arab lands occupied in the June 1967 war in return for a binding peace with the Arab states that assured Israel's territorial integrity and security. The secretary of state, opposing Israel's absorption of East Jerusalem, proposed that Jerusalem remain united under an administration that would acknowledge the interests of the holy city's three religious communities (Christian, Jewish, Moslem). Under his initiative, Israeli shipping would be guaranteed freedom of navigation through regional waterways, including the Suez Canal. The parties to the Arab-Israeli conflict would work out the specific details of security arrangements, including demilitarization of the Sinai Peninsula and safeguarding the access of all Mideast states to the Gulf of Aqaba.

The Rogers proposal was promptly rejected as unacceptable by Israel and Egypt, each contending that its interests were not adequately protected under the American plan. The regional BALANCE OF POWER was significantly altered in early 1970 when more than 20,000 Soviet troops were stationed in Egypt. Nasser hoped to counter Israel's total air superiority through the introduction of Soviet-manned surface-to-air missiles (SAMs) and Soviet-flown MiG fighter jets. The expanded Soviet military presence marked a dangerous intensification of the Arab-Israeli conflict, presaging a possible superpower Mideast clash. In response, the Nixon administration bolstered Israel's defenses by replacing Israeli aircraft lost in the War of Attrition. In early August 1970 Rogers succeeded in securing an Egyptian-Israeli cease-fire along the canal. Hostilities had no sooner stopped than Egypt deployed SAMs along the Suez in violation of the truce. The Egyptian action forestalled any prospect for further progress within the Rogers Plan framework.

See also GENEVA CONFERENCE ON THE MIDDLE EAST, YOM KIPPUR WAR.

ROGERS, WILLIAM PIERCE (1913–) U.S. attorney general, secretary of state. A New York native, Rogers graduated from Colgate in 1934 and earned a law degree from Cornell in 1937. From 1938 to 1942 he was an assistant attorney on the staff of Thomas E. Dewey, New York district attorney and future Republican presidential candidate. During WORLD WAR II he served as a Navy officer in the Pacific theater. Following the war he went to Washington as a counsel for several Senate committees and then entered private practice in 1950. He was active in DWIGHT D. EISENHOWER'S successful 1952 presidential campaign and was appointed deputy attorney general in the new administration. He held the number two position in the Justice Department until 1957, when Eisenhower named him attorney general. He left office with the Eisenhower administration in January 1961 and returned to his private law practice.

Rogers gained some exposure to foreign affairs through his handling of international law cases and in 1965 was a U.S. delegate to the 20th session of the UNITED NATIONS's General Assembly. In light of his limited foreign policy experience, his selection as secretary of state in 1968 by president-elect RICHARD M. NIXON came as a surprise. Nixon defended Rogers as a superb negotiator, while many observers suggested the appointment revealed the new president's intention to keep his own hand on foreign relations. During his four-and-one-

half-year tenure, Rogers maintained a low profile as Nixon and his national security adviser, HENRY A. KISSINGER, dominated the formulation and direction of American foreign policy. Rogers supported the administration's prosecution of the VIETNAM WAR, but had little direct role in the negotiation of the 1973 PARIS PEACE ACCORDS ending U.S. involvement in the conflict. Similarly, he was on the periphery of Nixon's opening to mainland Communist China, the SALT I and ANTIBALLISTIC MISSILE TREATY agreements with the Soviet Union, and the summits with both Communist nations.

His most prominent initiative was his 1969 ROGERS PLAN for peace in the Middle East. The plan called for Israel to withdraw from territories occupied during the 1967 Arab-Israeli Six-Day War in return for Arab commitment to a permanent peace settlement. The proposal was rejected by both Israel and the Arab states, but in 1970 Rogers succeeded in securing a cease-fire that lasted until the 1973 YOM KIPPUR WAR. Rogers also defused a 1969 crisis with Peru over that country's expropriation of oilfields belonging to the American-owned International Petroleum Company. Finding a loophole in the HICKENLOOPER AMENDMENT (1962), which mandated a cut-off of U.S. aid in such circumstances, he avoided applying its sanctions while fashioning a diplomatic solution to the dispute, thus averting possible damage to America's relations with Latin America. Rogers resigned in September 1973 and resumed his law career, effectively retiring from politics. In 1986 he chaired the presidential commission that investigated the space shuttle Challenger disaster.

ROGUE RIVER WAR (1855–1856) Conflict in the Oregon Territory between the Rogue River Indians and white settlers organized as volunteer militia. The war marked the climax of friction between settlers and Indians over surging white immigration into Oregon following resolution of the OREGON QUESTION in 1846. The Rogue tribes opposed the territorial governor's plan to acquire Indian lands, remove the resisting Indians, and make way for expansion of settlements and mining operations.

Initially, U.S. Army forces interposed between the warring tribes and volunteer militia to prevent assaults on peaceful Indians and settlers. Brutalities inflicted by both sides in the winter of 1855–1856 drew the American military further into the conflict. In a series of actions in the spring of 1856, notably at Big Meadows in late May, U.S. troops and militia broke the Indian resistance. Forced to surrender, the Rogue River tribes abandoned their homeland and were removed to reservations on the Pacific Coast.

See also MAP 1.

ROOSEVELT COROLLARY (1904) Statement of principle, precipitated by the VENEZUELA CLAIMS controversy (1902–1903), that extended the MONROE DOCTRINE (1823) to encompass the right of the United States to intercede in Latin America in order to prevent intervention by a European nation. President THEODORE ROOSEVELT announced the corollary on December 6, 1904, in his annual message to Congress. He proclaimed the intention of the United States to exercise exclusive international police power in the Western Hemisphere.

At the turn of the century, financially troubled Latin American nations increasingly were unable to repay their European creditors. The European countries threatened intervention to force settlement of the debts. Roosevelt viewed the European ultimatums as a challenge to America's sovereign influence in its own backyard. Possible foreign encroachment loomed as a threat to both U.S. security interests and economic prerogatives, especially in the area of the proposed PANAMA CANAL.

Roosevelt first invoked the corollary early in 1905 when the Dominican Republic, in default to European lenders and fearful of military invasion, appealed to the United States for protection. Against the protests of domestic non-interventionists, Roosevelt concluded an agreement with the Dominican Republic in February 1905 that effectively placed the Caribbean nation under American control. For several years the United States collected the Dominican Republic's customs, paid its debts, and assured its security and territorial integrity.

The Dominican Republic experience set an important American foreign policy precedent. Within a decade the United States found itself, through the Roosevelt Corollary, deeply involved in the domestic affairs of other Caribbean and Central American states. In 1930 Republican President HERBERT C. HOOVER, who favored a non-interventionist foreign policy, endorsed the CLARK MEMORANDUM, a State Department report repudiating the Roosevelt Corollary.

ROOSEVELT, FRANKLIN DELANO (1882–1945) Governor, 32nd president of the United States. Roosevelt was born at the family estate on the Hudson River at Hyde Park, New York, a fifth cousin of President THEODORE ROOSEVELT. He graduated from Harvard in 1904 and entered Columbia Law School. He left before graduation on passing the bar in 1907 and joined a prominent New York City law firm. In 1910 Roosevelt was elected to the New York State legislature as a Democrat from Hyde Park's district. He won reelection in 1912 before accepting appointment by President WOODROW WILSON as assistant secretary of the Navy in 1913. Serving in the post throughout WORLD WAR I, he oversaw the Navy's wartime expansion. In 1914 he lost a bid for the Democratic nomination for a U.S. Senate seat from New York. He resigned his Navy position to campaign as the vice-presidential candidate on the unsuccessful 1920 Democratic presidential ticket.

Roosevelt returned to private law practice. Stricken with polio in 1921, his legs were left permanently paralyzed. After a prolonged convalescence, he resumed his political career. He was elected Governor of New York in 1928 and was returned to the state house two years later. In 1932 he garnered the Democratic presidential nomination and swept to victory over incumbent Republican HERBERT C. HOOVER. Roosevelt was reelected in 1936 and won unprecedented third and fourth terms in 1940 and 1944. His 12 years in the White House constitute the longest tenure of any president.

He assumed the presidency in March 1933 at the height of the worst economic crisis in the nation's history. In his first term, Roosevelt launched the New Deal, a program of sweeping federal economic and social legislation devised to help America surmount the Great Depression. His administration promoted foreign trade as part of its scheme for economic resurrection. Free trade advocate Secretary of State

CORDELL HULL attended the WORLD ECONOMIC CONFERENCE, which convened in London in June 1933 to address the worldwide economic depression. The gathering adjourned without meaningful action in July after Roosevelt opposed international currency stabilization on grounds it would reduce his flexibility in domestic economic policy. Motivated in part by hopes for increased trade with the Soviet Union, the president in November 1933 concluded the ROOSEVELT-LITVINOV AGREEMENT extending U.S. diplomatic recognition to the Communist government in Moscow. Through Hull's efforts, the administration in June 1934 gained passage of the TRADE AGREEMENTS ACT authorizing the president to negotiate tariff reductions with other nations. The same month the WORLD DISARMAMENT CONFERENCE (1932-1934) ended in failure, a casualty of resurgent European rivalries. The abortive parley strengthened U.S. aversion to involvement in European power politics.

Hoover had moved to improve U.S. relations in Latin America, where U.S. military and economic intervention from the turn of the century had engendered deep resentment and hostility. Expanding on his predecessor's efforts, Roosevelt in 1933 inaugurated the GOOD NEIGHBOR POLICY. The same year at the Seventh PAN-AMERICAN CONFERENCE at Montevideo, Uruguay, Hull signed the CONVENTION ON RIGHTS AND DUTIES OF STATES to the principle of nonintervention in the Western Hemisphere. In 1934 Roosevelt abrogated the PLATT AMENDMENT, which had given Washington a right to intercede in Cuba, and withdrew the last U.S. marines from Haiti, ending U.S. military intervention in Latin America. The president in 1936 proposed a special Pan-American conference on strengthening regional ties and safeguarding hemispheric security. In December, he attended the resultant BUENOS AIRES CONFERENCE, where delegates adopted a convention providing for Pan-American consultation in the event of an outside threat to peace in the Western Hemisphere. Eager to improve relations with Mexico, the Roosevelt administration in 1941 negotiated the final resolution of the long-standing MEXICAN OIL EXPROPRIATION CONTROVERSY.

Developments in Asia also commanded Roosevelt's attention. In March 1934 the president signed the TYDINGS-MCDUFFIE ACT granting the Philippines their full independence in 1946 following a 10-year transitional period as a U.S. commonwealth. An increasingly militaristic Japan sought to revise the FIVE-POWER TREATY (1922) and 1930 London Naval Treaty limiting the navies of the major sea powers. When the United States and Great Britain would not accede to the Japanese demand for naval parity, Tokyo withdrew from the second of the LONDON NAVAL CONFERENCES in January 1936. In July 1937 Japan began a full-scale invasion of China. Washington denounced the Japanese aggression as a violation of the NINE-POWER TREATY (1922). In October Roosevelt delivered his QUARANTINE SPEECH, in which he called for the isolation of nations breaking international law. At the November 1937 BRUSSELS CONFERENCE on the Sino-Japanese conflict, however, the United States and fellow Western democracies limited themselves to a verbal condemnation of Japan's actions. In December 1937 Roosevelt, unwilling and unprepared to commit America to a possible war in Asia, accepted Tokyo's explanation and restitution for the PANAY INCIDENT, in which Japanese warplanes sank a U.S. gunboat in Chinese waters.

While economic crisis continued to grip the nation, events in Europe increasingly dominated Roosevelt's second term. The president viewed with alarm the growing belligerency of Nazi Germany under Adolf Hitler and Fascist Italy under Benito Mussolini. The strength of traditional American ISOLATIONISM led Congress in 1935 to pass the first of the NEUTRALITY ACTS, intended to keep America out of a possible foreign war. Roosevelt declared U.S. neutrality in the Italo-Ethiopian War (1935–1936), but refused to recognize Italy's conquest of the African country. He likewise proclaimed U.S. neutrality in the Spanish Civil War (1936–1939). He decided against invoking U.S. neutrality following the onset of Sino-Japanese hostilities in 1937, maintaining that to do so would aid Japan with its larger merchant marine. In 1938 Nazi Germany annexed Austria and, with British and French acquiescence, absorbed the Western part of Czechoslovakia. Concerned about the growing threat of war in Europe and possible Nazi infiltration of the Western Hemisphere, the Roosevelt administration secured adoption in December 1938 of the DECLARATION OF LIMA further committing the American states to consult on their mutual defense.

Roosevelt declared official U.S. neutrality following the outbreak of WORLD WAR II in Europe in September 1939. In October Washington was the driving force behind the DECLARATION OF PANAMA proclaiming Pan-American neutrality and establishing a 300-mile safety zone around the Western Hemisphere. Certain that Nazi Germany posed a grave menace to the U.S. and world security, Roosevelt gradually steered American policy toward support for Great Britain in its struggle against Hitler. When France fell to German invasion in June 1940, the White House stepped up its efforts to strengthen U.S. defenses and military preparedness. The same month, in an attempt to fashion a bipartisan defense policy, Roosevelt brought Republicans HENRY L. STIMPSON and Frank Knox into his cabinet as secretary of war and secretary of navy. In July 1940 a special Pan-American consultive meeting approved the U.S.-proposed ACT OF HAVANA barring German acquisition of existing European colonies in the Western Hemisphere. Determined to provide Great Britain with desperately needed warships, Roosevelt in September announced the BASES-FOR-DESTROYERS AGREEMENT whereby old U.S. destroyers would be exchanged for British military bases. In December, he called on American economic might to serve as a great ARSENAL OF DEMOCRACY and the following month enunciated the nation's commitment to the worldwide attainment of the FOUR FREEDOMS. Under the March 1941 LEND-LEASE Act, authorizing U.S. assistance to countries deemed vital to America's security, the president funneled extensive aid to Great Britain. The deepening Anglo-American ties were underscored at the August 1941 ATLANTIC CONFERENCE, where Roosevelt and British Prime Minister Winston Churchill drafted the ATLANTIC CHARTER outlining their common postwar aims. Meanwhile U.S.-Japanese tensions had mounted over Tokyo's continued military onslaught on China. Roosevelt gradually restricted U.S. exports to Japan in an effort to restrain its expansionist behavior, but negotiations between the two Pacific powers had reached an impasse by November 1941. On December 7, 1941, Japan launched a surprise attack against the U.S.

fleet at PEARL HARBOR, bringing America into World War II. Roosevelt orchestrated the massive U.S. wartime mobilization. Together with Churchill he formulated a "Germany First" strategy, whereby the Allies would concentrate on defeating the Nazi power and then turn their full attention to Japan. Trepidation about possible Japanese espionage and subversion led Roosevelt to order a program of JAPANESE AMERICAN INTERNMENT, which later was criticized as a massive abridgement of civil liberties. The president also approved the top-secret MANHATTAN PROJECT that developed the first atomic bomb.

Roosevelt met with the other major Allied leaders at a series of wartime conferences to map strategy and plan for the postwar world. At the January 1943 CASABLANCA CONFERENCE with Churchill he declared the Allied goal to be the unconditional surrender of the Axis powers. Roosevelt, Churchill, and Soviet Premier Joseph Stalin met at the TEHERAN CONFERENCE in November 1943 to finalize plans for the Anglo-American invasion of France and discuss the postwar shape of Europe and the formation of postwar international security. Roosevelt championed the establishment of the UNITED NATIONS as the cornerstone of postwar international security. The Roosevelt administration also guided the creation of the INTERNATIONAL MONETARY FUND and WORLD BANK, the pillars of the postwar international financial and economic system. Roosevelt, Churchill, and Stalin conferred again in February 1945 at the YALTA CONFERENCE where the president gained Stalin's agreement to the basic UNITED NATIONS CHARTER and a firm Soviet pledge to enter the war against Japan, but acquiesced to postwar Soviet hegemony in Eastern Europe.

Roosevelt died in office on April 12, 1945, on the eve of Allied victory in World War II. He was succeeded by Vice-President HARRY S. TRUMAN. His widow, Eleanor Roosevelt, accepted Truman's appointment later in the year to serve as a member of the U.S. delegation to the United Nations. She took special interest in the plight of war refugees and, as chairwoman of the Human Rights Commission of the Economic and Social Council, played an instrumental role in gaining passage of the UNIVERSAL DECLARATION OF HUMAN RIGHTS (1948).

ROOSEVELT, KERMIT (1916–   ) Intelligence officer. Roosevelt was born in Buenos Aires, Argentina. The grandson of President THEODORE ROOSEVELT, he graduated from Harvard in 1938. He taught history at his alma mater and the California Institute of Technology until 1941. During WORLD WAR II he served in the OFFICE OF STRATEGIC SERVICES (OSS). After the war he wrote the official history of the OSS and then joined the newly formed CENTRAL INTELLIGENCE AGENCY (CIA). In 1953 he orchestrated the IRAN COUP that overthrew Iranian Prime Minister Mohammed Mossadegh. Roosevelt left the CIA in 1957 for a career in business.

ROOSEVELT, THEODORE (1858–1919) Twenty-sixth president of the United States. Roosevelt was born into a wealthy family in New York City. After graduating from Harvard University in 1880, he read law briefly and then turned to historical writing, authoring the *Naval History of the War of 1812* (1882) and the four-volume *Winning of the West* (1889–1896). He was elected in 1881 as a Republican to the New York legislature, where he served for three sessions. Grief-stricken by the deaths of his mother and wife on the same day in 1884, he retreated for two years to his cattle ranch in Dakota Territory (present-day North Dakota). Returning to New York City, he ran unsuccessfully for mayor in 1886, whereupon he resumed his writing. His political career was revived when President BENJAMIN HARRISON appointed him to the U.S. Civil Service Commission in 1889. Roosevelt remained on the commission until 1895, when he was named president of the board of police commissioners of New York City. Appointed assistant secretary of the Navy in 1897 by President WILLIAM MCKINLEY, he helped prepare U.S. naval forces for the expected conflict with Spain. When the SPANISH-AMERICAN WAR (1898) broke out, Roosevelt resigned his post and, with his friend LEONARD WOOD, organized the 1st U.S. Volunteer Cavalry. In action in Cuba, Colonel Roosevelt led his "Rough Riders" on the famed charge up San Juan Hill. Just back from the war, Roosevelt received the Republican nomination for governor of New York and won the election in 1898. In 1900 he was elected vice-president as McKinley's running mate on the Republi-

can ticket. Following McKinley's assassination, Roosevelt became president on September 14, 1901, and went on to gain reelection in 1904.

In foreign affairs Roosevelt articulated broadened American international responsibilities as a consequence of recent U.S. acquisitions in the Caribbean and the Pacific. His vigorous foreign policy, extending the NEW MANIFEST DESTINY of the 1890s, accelerated America's rise to the status of a world power in the decade after 1900. He perceived the growing interdependence of the world at the turn of the century and necessity for a greater involvement of the United States in global affairs. In Latin America, Roosevelt renewed U.S. commitment to the MONROE DOCTRINE (1823) and enlarged its scope. He served notice on Europe of America's claim to preeminent power and influence in the Western Hemisphere. Roosevelt defined protection of the Caribbean as fundamental to U.S. national security. When Great Britain, Germany, and Italy moved militarily against Venezuela in 1902 to force settlement of debts owed them, he interceded and persuaded the Europeans to settle their claims through arbitration. The VENEZUELA CLAIMS incident and the chronic problem of Latin American default on foreign loans led Roosevelt to formulate the ROOSEVELT COROLLARY (1904) to the Monroe Doctrine. The corollary proclaimed the U.S. right to intercede in a Latin American nation in order to prevent intervention by a European state. He first exercised the corollary in the Dominican Republic in 1905 when the United States, under an EXECUTIVE AGREEMENT, took control of the insolvent island nation and collected its customs, made payments on its debts to European creditors, and assured its territorial integrity. Roosevelt's willingness to use force to ensure U.S. hegemony in the Western Hemisphere was an expression of his BIG STICK diplomacy.

Roosevelt's major achievement in Latin American policy, accomplished in concert with Secretary of State JOHN M. HAY, was acquisition of the Panama CANAL ZONE in 1903, which opened the way for America's construction of an interoceanic canal. The HAY-PAUNCEFOTE TREATY (1901) with the British granted the United States an exclusive right to build and fortify an isthmian waterway. The HAY-BUNAU-VARILLA TREATY

(1903), concluded with newly independent Panama, provided the United States a Canal Zone "in perpetuity," thus reversing the setback to American policy aims suffered when Colombia rejected the HAY-HERRAN TREATY (1902).

In the Far East, Roosevelt continued the policy of the OPEN DOOR, which strove to keep China territorially intact, commercially accessible, and politically sovereign. European and Japanese expansion in East Asia jeopardized America's blossoming interests there. Roosevelt sought to prevent shifts in the BALANCE OF POWER that might result in restriction of American strategic and commercial access in the Pacific. The Russo-Japanese War (1904–1905), waged over Manchuria and Korea, posed a clear threat to the Asian status quo. At Japan's urging, Roosevelt mediated a settlement of the conflict. The PORTSMOUTH TREATY of 1905, while recognizing Japan's military triumph, limited Japanese territorial gains and maintained a measure of balance in the Far East. Roosevelt received the Nobel Peace Prize in 1906 for his diplomatic efforts.

Roosevelt's East Asian policy called for improved relations with Japan. The TAFT-KATSURA AGREEMENT (1905), secretly negotiated between Secretary of War WILLIAM HOWARD TAFT and Foreign Minister Count Taro Katsura, informally committed the two nations to acceptance of one another's position in the Pacific. America acknowledged Japan's dominion over Korea. In turn, Japan recognized American hegemony in the Philippines. Ties with Japan nearly unraveled in 1907 over discrimination against Japanese immigrants in California. Roosevelt defused the crisis through the GENTLEMEN'S AGREEMENT (1907–1908). At the height of the controversy, Roosevelt had dispatched a GREAT WHITE FLEET of 16 battleships on a worldwide cruise to remind Japan of America's burgeoning sea power. Subsequently, the ROOT-TAKAHIRA AGREEMENT (1908) addressed U.S. and Japanese concerns in Asia. By its terms, both countries agreed neither to seek total control of the Pacific nor to violate the territorial integrity of China.

At the invitation of Germany, Roosevelt intervened in 1905 in the dispute among the major European powers over the status of Morocco. He arranged the ALGECIRAS CONFERENCE (1906), where his personal envoy, Henry White, helped construct a compromise settlement on the North African sultanate which ended the threat of European war. Roosevelt was pivotal in the development of the modern American Navy. A devotee of ALFRED THAYER MAHAN, the naval philosopher of the new IMPERIALISM, he related sea power to national policy and strategy. Roosevelt expanded the size of the fleet and made important improvements in firepower, tactics, and equipment. New strategic considerations led him to concentrate the main naval forces in separate Atlantic and Pacific fleets.

Leaving office upon the inauguration of his hand-picked successor, William Howard Taft, in March 1909, Roosevelt went on an African safari and tour of Europe. He returned to the United States a year later and soon reentered politics, becoming a leader of the progressive Republican movement that sought to block the conservative Taft's renomination in 1912. After failing to wrest the nomination from Taft, Roosevelt bolted the Republican ranks to run as candidate of the newly formed Progressive, or Bull Moose, Party. While campaigning in Milwaukee, he was shot in the chest by a deranged assailant but was not badly wounded and quickly recovered. By splitting the Republican vote with Taft, he ensured the election of Democrat WOODROW WILSON. With the outbreak of WORLD WAR I in Europe in 1914, he advocated American military preparedness and support of the Allies and criticized Wilson's neutrality policy. He decided not to seek the Republican presidential nomination in 1916 and instead supported CHARLES EVANS HUGHES. Upon U.S. entry into the war in 1917, Roosevelt offered to organize and lead a group of volunteers but Wilson rejected his request. After the armistice in 1918, he spoke out vehemently against Wilson's proposal for a LEAGUE OF NATIONS. He died at his home in Oyster Bay, New York, in 1919.

ROOSEVELT-LITVINOV AGREEMENT (1933) Exchange of notes establishing diplomatic relations between the United States and Soviet Union. Following Bolshevik victory in the 1917 Russian Revolution, U.S. presidents from WOODROW WILSON to HERBERT C. HOOVER refused to recognize the Soviet Communist regime, citing its repudiation of former Russian debts, confiscation of private property, and advocacy of world-wide Communist revolution. In 1933 the Roosevelt administration conceived of official U.S.-Soviet ties as opening the way to joint cooperation on restraining Japanese aggression in the Far East. The administration also hoped to develop U.S.-Soviet trade and thus boost the depressed American economy. The Soviet government, concerned over the rise of German fascism and looking to expand its international contacts, was receptive to U.S. overtures. At President FRANKLIN D. ROOSEVELT's invitation, Soviet Foreign Minister Maxim Litvinov came to Washington for discussions in November 1933. On November 16 Roosevelt and Litvinov signed a series of notes normalizing U.S.-Soviet relations. The Soviet Union pledged to settle previous financial claims on debts, to refrain from supporting subversive activities in the United States, and to protect the religious freedom of Americans in the USSR. The new U.S.-Soviet ties did not result in either a meaningful increase in trade or a cooperative policy of opposition to Japanese militarism. Roosevelt came under criticism when Joseph Stalin's Soviet regime subsequently failed to live up to the terms of the 1933 agreement.

ROOT ARBITRATION TREATIES (1908–1909)   Series of 25 bilateral arbitration agreements entered into by the United States. In 1908 and 1909 Secretary of State ELIHU ROOT negotiated the treaties with all of the leading nations of the world except Germany. In general, the Root pacts bound the parties to refer disputes which could not be resolved through diplomacy to the PERMANENT COURT OF ARBITRATION established in 1899 by the first of the HAGUE PEACE CONFERENCES. The agreements excluded from arbitration all questions relating either to the vital interests, independence, or honor of the signatory nations or to the interests of third parties (other countries). Jealous of any infringement of its treaty power, the U.S. Senate ratified the Root agreements after adding a reservation requiring its approval for the arbitration of every individual case under each treaty. Senate insistence on a similar reservation in 1905 had blocked ratification of a set of arbitration treaties negotiated by then Secretary of State JOHN M. HAY. Root, grasping the Senate's adamant stance on the issue, per-

suaded President THEODORE ROOSEVELT to accept the reservation.

See also BRYAN *"COOLING OFF" TREATIES.*

ROOT, ELIHU (1845–1937)   Leading political figure whose long and varied career in foreign affairs included service as secretary of war and secretary of state. Born in Clinton, New York, Root graduated from Hamilton College in 1864. He received his law degree from New York University in 1867, was admitted to the bar the same year, and began an extremely successful practice in New York City, specializing in corporate law. From 1883 to 1885 he was U.S. attorney for the southern district of New York. A Republican, he acted as legal advisor to THEODORE ROOSEVELT during much of the latter's political career in New York.

Appointed secretary of war by President WILLIAM MCKINLEY in 1899, Root continued in the post under Roosevelt, who succeeded the assassinated McKinley in 1901. During his War Department tenure, he was responsible for overseeing the administration of the former Spanish colonies of Cuba, Puerto Rico, and the Philippines, which had come under U.S. control following the SPANISH-AMERICAN WAR (1898). He selected General LEONARD WOOD as American military governor of Cuba and formulated the controversial PLATT AMENDMENT (1901) to the Cuban constitution, which served as the basis for U.S.-Cuban relations until 1934. He oversaw the U.S. military campaign that suppressed the PHILIPPINE INSURRECTION (1899–1902) and helped draft the federal Philippine Government Act of 1902, which established the Pacific archipelago as an unorganized U.S. territory under America's colonial administration. He supervised, as well, the establishment of temporary civil government in Puerto Rico as provided for by the FORAKER ACT. He also undertook a fundamental reorganization of the Army, creating both a general staff and the Army War College. In 1903 Root served as a member of the joint arbitration tribunal that decided the ALASKA BOUNDARY DISPUTE with Canada in favor of the United States.

He resigned in 1904 to resume his law practice but returned to Roosevelt's administration in 1905 as secretary of state, a post he held until 1909. Establishment of friendly relations with Latin America became a primary aim of Root's diplomacy. He made a goodwill tour of South America in 1906, attending the Third PAN-AMERICAN CONFERENCE at Rio de Janeiro. The outbreak of war in Central America led Root to convene a conference in Washington to seek peace and political stability in the chronically unstable area. This parley produced the CENTRAL AMERICAN TREATIES OF 1907, a series of eight agreements designed to restore peace and settle future disputes among the five Central American republics. In keeping with the Roosevelt administration's goal of maintaining good relations with Japan, he negotiated the GENTLEMEN'S AGREEMENT (1907–1908), which resolved a worsening dispute over the status of Japanese immigration to the United States, and the ROOT-TAKAHIRA AGREEMENT (1908), which obligated the United States and Japan to respect each other's territorial positions in the Pacific and to uphold the OPEN DOOR policy in China. During his tenure he also reorganized the U.S. consular service and negotiated the ROOT ARBITRATION TREATIES, a series of 25 bilateral agreements entered into by the United States that arranged for submission of deadlocked diplomatic disputes to the PERMANENT COURT OF ARBITRATION.

Elected U.S. Senator from New York in 1909, Root held his seat until 1915. While in the Senate he remained active in foreign affairs. In 1910 he served as chief U.S. counsel in the North Atlantic Fisheries Arbitration at The Hague, Netherlands, which settled the FISHERIES QUESTION between America and Canada. The same year he was appointed a member of the Permanent Court of Arbitration. From 1910 to 1925 he was president of the private CARNEGIE ENDOWMENT FOR INTERNATIONAL PEACE. He was awarded the Nobel Peace Prize in 1912 for contributions to the world peace movement and international arbitration. Following U.S. entry into WORLD WAR I in April 1917, President WOODROW WILSON sent Root to Russia as head of a special diplomatic mission to exhort that country, in the throes of the Russian Revolution, to stay in the war against Germany. The mission failed when the Bolsheviks took power and moved to withdraw Russia from the conflict. A leading Republican advocate of U.S. participation in the proposed LEAGUE OF NATIONS, Root urged acceptance of the league covenant with reservations. He was a member of the international commission of jurists which met at The Hague in 1920 to devise the first WORLD COURT. The following year President WARREN G. HARDING named him one of the U.S. delegates to the WASHINGTON NAVAL CONFERENCE (1921–1922). After serving in 1929 on the commission that met in Geneva to revise the original World Court statute, he withdrew from public life.

ROOT-TAKAHIRA AGREEMENT (1908) EXECUTIVE AGREEMENT between the United States and Japan concerning the BALANCE OF POWER in the Far East. A crisis developed in Japanese-American relations in the aftermath of the PORTSMOUTH CONFERENCE (1905), the parley convened by President THEODORE ROOSEVELT to negotiatie a settlement of the Russo-Japanese War (1904–1905). Dissatisfaction among the Japanese with the resulting PORTSMOUTH TREATY (1905), which they felt did not sufficiently reward their military victory over Russia, engendered strong anti-American feelings. Developments within the United States added to antagonism between the two powers. Racial discrimination against Japanese in California and a campaign to legally exclude Japanese immigrants produced a bitter anti-Americanism in Japan. The GENTLEMEN'S AGREEMENT (1907–1908) helped lift some of the tension by striking a compromise on the immigration issue. But anti-Japanese agitation on the Pacific Coast continued and the two countries appeared headed for confrontation. Roosevelt was eager to defuse the crisis. To impress Japan with a demonstration of American naval power, he ordered the GREAT WHITE FLEET on a worldwide cruise. While the fleet was at sea, Roosevelt's Secretary of State, ELIHU ROOT, moved on the diplomatic front to head off a possible Japanese-American showdown in the Far East.

In Washington, D.C., on November 30, 1908, Root concluded an accord with Japan's ambassador to the United States, Baron Kogoro Takahira, that expanded on the earlier TAFT-KATSURA AGREEMENT (1905). It stipulated that the United States and Japan would respect one another's territorial possessions in the Pacific; maintain the existing status quo in the region; uphold the OPEN DOOR policy in China; and support by peaceful means the independence and territorial integrity of China. The Root-Takahira Agreement embodied Roosevelt's balance-of-power concept for East Asia. Its "existing status quo" clause signaled U.S. recognition of Japan's paramount influence and position in Korea and southern Manchuria. The agreement, which helped ease the strain in U.S.-Japanese relations, marked an American concession to the realities of Japan's strong position in the Far East.

ROSENBERG CASE Espionage case involving the transfer of U.S. atomic bomb secrets to the Soviet Union. Electrical engineer Julius Rosenberg and his wife, Ethel, were native New Yorkers who by 1940 had become active in the Communist Party. In 1950 they were arrested and charged with heading a Soviet espionage ring that included Ethel's brother David Greenglass, Harry Gold, Morton Sobell, and German-born British physicist Klaus Fuchs. The Rosenbergs were accused of transmitting information in 1944 and 1945 to the Soviet Union on the U.S. atomic bomb program.

The 1951 trial of the Rosenbergs was conducted at a time of intense domestic concern over the perceived threats posed by Soviet subversion and international communism. In the preceding year former State Department official ALGER HISS had been found guilty of lying over his involvement in Soviet espionage, Senator JOSEPH R. MCCARTHY (R-WI) had launched his allegations of Communist infiltration of the federal government, and the Communist invasion of South Korea had started the KOREAN WAR. The Rosenbergs were convicted March 29, 1951, and sentenced to death. The other members of the espionage network received extended prison sentences.

The Rosenberg case attracted worldwide attention. An international campaign against their death sentence included many who thought their penalty was too harsh and others who believed they were the victims of an anti-Communist witch-hunt. Their conviction was upheld on appeal. President DWIGHT D. EISENHOWER linked any grant of clemency to the Rosenbergs admitting their guilt. They declined, continuing to maintain their innocence, and were executed June 19, 1953. While found guilty of wartime espionage, the Rosenbergs remain the only Americans ever put to death

in peacetime for spying. The following year Congress further strengthened the nation's espionage laws in the ESPIONAGE AND SABOTAGE ACT. The Rosenbergs' sons, Robert and Michael Meeropol, have been at the forefront of the continuing debate over the case, steadfastly insisting on their parents' innocence. In 1990 a transcript of remarks by Nikita S. Khrushchev was published in which the former Soviet leader praised the Rosenbergs for what he called their assistance to his nation.

ROSTOW, EUGENE VICTOR (1913–   ) Lawyer, educator, government official. Rostow was born in New York City. He graduated from Yale in 1933 and, after studying economics in England, returned to his alma mater to earn a law degree in 1937. He joined the law school faculty the following year. During WORLD WAR II he served as an adviser to the State Department. Resuming his teaching career, he became dean of the Yale Law School in 1955. In 1966 he was named under secretary of state for political affairs. His brother, WALT W. ROSTOW, also served in the Johnson administration as national security adviser. Both Rostows strongly supported U.S. involvement in the VIETNAM WAR, believing it essential to halt Communist aggression in Southeast Asia. Rostow returned to a law professorship at Yale in 1969. In the late 1970s he was a member of the COMMITTEE ON THE PRESENT DANGER, a private panel formed to draw attention to the growing military threat posed by the Soviet Union. In 1981 he was named director of the ARMS CONTROL AND DISARMAMENT AGENCY in the new Reagan administration. Rostow was dismissed from his post in 1983, allegedly for pressing for greater flexibility in the administration's hardline negotiating stance toward Moscow, and returned to Yale.

ROSTOW THESIS   See **ROSTOW, WALT WHITMAN**.

ROSTOW, WALT WHITMAN (1916–   ) Educator, State Department official, and national security adviser. Rostow was born in New York City. He graduated from Yale in 1936, was a Rhodes Scholar at Oxford in England, and returned to his alma mater to earn a Ph.D. in 1940. During WORLD WAR II he served as an Army major with the OFFICE

OF STRATEGIC SERVICES, the nation's wartime intelligence service. After a brief stint with the State Department and additional studies in England, he became a professor of economic history at the Massachusetts Institute of Technology, where he was associated with the Center for International Studies. In 1957 he joined Senator JOHN F. KENNEDY's (D-MA) Massachusetts-based brain trust, the "Cambridge group," and was credited with originating the slogan "the New Frontier" for Kennedy's 1960 presidential campaign.

Kennedy brought Rostow to the White House with him in January 1961 as the deputy to National Security Adviser MC-GEORGE BUNDY. Rostow took part throughout 1961 in the formulation of U.S. policy toward the mounting Communist insurgencies in Southeast Asia. In October he accompanied General MAXWELL D. TAYLOR on a special fact-finding trip to South Vietnam. The report of the TAYLOR-ROSTOW MISSION advocated an increased U.S. role in the VIETNAM WAR. In November 1961 Rostow moved to the State Department as counselor and chairman of the Policy Planning Council. In 1964 he was appointed to the additional post of U.S. representative to the Inter-American Committee on the ALLIANCE FOR PROGRESS. This special panel of the ORGANIZATION OF AMERICAN STATES was formed to improve Latin American participation in directing the alliance. While at the State Department, Rostow developed what came to be called the "Rostow Thesis." His influential theory on Vietnam-type situations held that an externally supported insurgency, such as the Communist Viet Cong guerrillas in South Vietnam, could be defeated only by military action against the external source of support, in this instance North Vietnam. Rostow's thinking underlay the gradual escalation in the use of U.S. military force in the mid-1960s to pressure the North Vietnamese to abandon their support of the Viet Cong insurgents.

In March 1966 President LYNDON B. JOHNSON named Rostow to succeed Bundy as national security adviser. In September his brother, EUGENE V. ROSTOW, was appointed under secretary of state for political affairs. Walt Rostow became one of the president's closest aides, accompanying him to the June 1967 GLASSBORO SUMMIT with Soviet Premier Aleksei N. Kosygin. He supported a policy of continued U.S. bombing of North Vietnam, arguing that the raids were key to halting Communist infiltration of the South and would compel the North Vietnamese to enter peace negotiations. Rostow left government service at the end of the Johnson administration in 1969. He accepted a teaching position at the University of Texas and authored books on history, economics, and international affairs.

ROUND ROBIN (1919) Senate resolution rejecting the LEAGUE OF NATIONS as initially proposed at the PARIS PEACE CONFERENCE (1919), where negotiations were in progress on a settlement to end WORLD WAR I. President WOODROW WILSON led the U.S. delegation to Paris. From the start of the conference in January 1919, the overriding issue for Wilson was the creation of his proposed league, an organization of nations to deter aggression and preserve peace through a system of COLLECTIVE SECURITY. At his adamant insistence, the conference voted on January 25 to make the League of Nations an integral part of the general peace treaty. Wilson himself was made chairman of the commission formed to draw up the Covenant of the League of Nations, outlining the projected organization's functions and powers. On February 14, 1919, he read the completed draft of the league covenant to the full conference. The Democratic president then returned to the United States briefly for the purpose of signing legislation and explaining the covenant to the American people. In Congress, strong Republican opposition to the league and its incorporation into the peace treaty already was taking shape. Wilson invited members of the House and Senate committees on foreign relations to dine with him and discuss the proposed postwar organization. At the White House dinner, held on February 26, he was interrogated at length by his Republican foes, none of whom was persuaded to support the president's coveted league.

On March 4, 1919, just before Wilson was to return to France, Foreign Relations Committee Chairman HENRY CABOT LODGE, SR. (R-MA) read in the Senate a resolution, known as the Round Robin, declaring the league covenant unacceptable in its existing form and opposing further consideration of the league until after the peace settlement. Drafted by PHILANDER C. KNOX (R-PA), the Round Robin was signed by 39 Republican senators or senators-elect, more than the one-third plus one of the Senate necessary to block ratification of any treaty completed at Paris. The Republican membership thus served notice that it would in all likelihood turn down any peace accord embodying the league covenant. That night, an angry Wilson responded defiantly in an address in New York, predicting that the covenant would be tied to so many elements of the final peace treaty that the two could not be separated. The president then departed for Paris. The Round Robin was the opening salvo in the bitter fight that ensued between Wilson and the Senate Republicans over the league and over his insistence upon the inseparability of the covenant and the TREATY OF VERSAILLES (1919).

RUMSFELD, DONALD HAROLD (1932–) Congressman, secretary of defense. Rumsfeld graduated from Princeton in 1954 and spent the next three years as a Navy pilot and flight instructor. The Illinois native then worked in Washington as a congressional aide before joining a Chicago investment banking firm in 1960. In 1962 he won election as a Republican to the U.S. House of Representatives. He served in Congress until 1969 when he entered the Nixon administration as a member of the White House staff. In 1973 he was appointed U.S. ambassador to NATO. Following President RICHARD M. NIXON's resignation in August 1974, Rumsfeld headed President GERALD R. FORD's transition team and then became White House chief of staff. In a shake-up of his senior advisers, Ford in November 1975 named Rumsfeld to replace JAMES R. SCHLESINGER as secretary of defense. During his 14-month tenure, Rumsfeld stressed the importance of balancing Secretary of State HENRY A. KISSINGER's policies of DETENTE with a continuing emphasis on DETERRENCE and a strong military. Leaving office with the Ford administration in January 1977, he taught briefly at Northwestern University before embarking on a career as a top corporate executive. In November 1983 he agreed to succeed Robert C. McFarlane as the Reagan administration's special Middle East envoy.

With Arab-Israeli negotiations at a standstill, Rumsfeld resigned in May 1984 and was not replaced. He resumed his business activities.

RUSH, RICHARD (1780–1859) Political figure who held diverse diplomatic and senior government posts. A Philadelphia native and son of prominent physician Benjamin Rush, he graduated from the College of New Jersey (now Princeton) in 1798. Admitted to the Pennsylvania bar in 1800, he practiced law until 1811, when he entered politics through appointment as Pennsylvania attorney general. President JAMES MADISON brought the Democratic-Republican Rush into his administration in 1812 as comptroller of the U.S. Treasury. Named U.S. attorney general in 1814, he held the office for three years. As acting secretary of state from March to September 1817, he negotiated the Anglo-American RUSH-BAGOT AGREEMENT (1817) establishing limits for naval armaments on the Great Lakes.

Appointed U.S. minister to Great Britain by President JAMES MONROE in October 1817, he enjoyed a successful eight-year tenure in London, during which he helped bring substantial progress on a variety of unresolved diplomatic difficulties remaining from the WAR OF 1812. He negotiated the CONVENTION OF 1818, which arranged for joint occupation of the Oregon Country and guided Anglo-American understanding on the OREGON QUESTION for almost 30 years. The 1818 settlement also secured important British concessions on the North Atlantic FISHERIES QUESTION. He adroitly handled discussions with the British government that limited the diplomatic fallout from the AMBRISTER AND ARBUTHNOT AFFAIR (1818), the execution of British subjects by U.S. General ANDREW JACKSON during the FLORIDA INVASION. Rush also figured importantly in U.S.-British consultations concerning the two nations' shared suspicion of a continental European plan to intervene in Latin America to restore the Spanish colonial empire. These negotiations preceded U.S. enunciation of the MONROE DOCTRINE in 1823.

Returning to the United States, he served as secretary of the treasury under President JOHN QUINCY ADAMS from 1825 to 1829. He went down to defeat in 1828 as vice-presidential candidate on the ticket with Adams. Retiring to private life, Rush periodically returned to public service. In 1835 President Andrew Jackson named him to the commission that settled the so-called Toledo War, a boundary controversy between Ohio and Michigan. He spent from 1836 to 1838 in Britain, where as U.S. legal representative he secured wealthy Englishman James Smithson's bequest to the United States, which later was used to establish the Smithsonian Institution in Washington. In 1847 he accepted appointment by President JAMES K. POLK as U.S. minister to France, a post he held for two years. After the February 1848 revolution forced out the French monarchy, Rush recognized the new French republic without awaiting instructions from Washington, a bold stroke that strengthened the new government's position and subsequently was applauded by the United States.

RUSH-BAGOT AGREEMENT (1817) Anglo-American diplomatic agreement to demilitarize the Great Lakes. Acting Secretary of State RICHARD RUSH and British Minister to the United States Charles Bagot sealed the disarmament understanding through an exchange of notes on April 28 and 29, 1817. The TREATY OF GHENT (1814), ending the WAR OF 1812, left unaddressed the issue of restricting naval armaments on the Great Lakes, which had been the scene of major Anglo-American maritime battles. U.S. and British determination to prevent one another from gaining naval superiority on the lakes threatened to touch off a postwar seaborne military buildup there. Eager to avoid a costly naval race, Secretary of State JAMES MONROE had U.S. Minister at London JOHN QUINCY ADAMS propose mutual disarmament to the British government in January 1817. After British Foreign Secretary Lord Castlereagh embraced the suggestion, Monroe and Bagot began negotiations that produced a preliminary arms limitation agreement. London's final consent did not reach Washington until after Monroe had become president, and thus Rush concluded the formal U.S.-British understanding with Bagot.

By its terms, the two nations limited their naval forces on the Great Lakes to a very few light vessels necessary for police functions and enforcements of customs laws. The deal did not extend to forts or armaments along the U.S-Canadian land frontier surrounding the lakes. To dispel British suspicions that the United States might not regard the agreement as binding, the Senate on April 16, 1818, unanimously approved the pact and thereby gave it the status of a treaty. The Rush-Bagot Agreement, still in force today, marked the first instance in the history of international relations of reciprocal naval disarmament.

RUSK, DAVID DEAN (1909–   ) Secretary of state. Born in Cherokee County, Georgia, Rusk graduated from Davidson College in North Carolina in 1931. A Rhodes Scholar, he studied at Oxford University in England, where he earned a B.S. degree in 1933 and an M.A. degree in 1934. He became a professor of government and international relations at Mills College, Oakland, California, and in 1938 was made dean of the faculty. During WORLD WAR II Rusk attained the rank of Army colonel and served on the staff of General JOSEPH STILWELL in the China-Burma-India theater. In 1946 he joined the State Department as assistant chief of the division of international security affairs. The same year he became a special assistant to Secretary of War Robert P. Patterson. In 1947 he returned to the State Department as director of the office of special political affairs, which subsequently became the office of UNITED NATIONS affairs. In 1949 he was appointed deputy under secretary of state. The following year he was elevated to the post of assistant secretary of state for Far Eastern Affairs, where he helped formulate Truman administration policy during the KOREAN WAR. He was an adviser to JOHN FOSTER DULLES in the negotiation of the 1951 JAPANESE PEACE TREATY.

Rusk left the State Department in March 1952 to become president of the Rockefeller Foundation. During his tenure at the philanthropic organization, he oversaw the expansion of foundation aid to agriculture, education, and health projects in developing nations in Latin America, Africa, and Asia. In December 1960 President-elect JOHN F. KENNEDY named Rusk his secretary of state. The selection of Rusk rather than a more prominent figure was said to signal Kennedy's intention to exercise close personal control over his administration's foreign policy. Rusk entered office at a time of continuing East-West COLD WAR confrontation. He took no active part in the deliberations leading to the failed

U.S.-sponsored BAY OF PIGS INVASION in April 1961 to remove Cuban leader Fidel Castro from power. The following year Rusk counseled a hard-line stance toward the Soviet Union during the CUBAN MISSILE CRISIS. He supported Kennedy's clear commitment to the defense of West Berlin during the final stages of the Berlin Crisis (1958–1962) and helped maintain U.S. policy behind U.N. peacekeeping efforts in the CONGO CRISIS (1960–1963).

Rusk's attention increasingly was drawn to events in Southeast Asia. He assisted in the resolution of the LAOTIAN CRISIS (1961–1962), whereby Laos was declared neutral, and endorsed the commitment of U.S. military force to halt the North Vietnamese effort to seize South Vietnam and unify Vietnam under Communist control. Rusk saw the VIETNAM WAR as stemming ultimately from an attempt by the Communist Chinese government, espousing a radical ideology of world revolution, to extend its influence over Indochina. He concurred in the U.S. policy of CONTAINMENT of communism in Southeast Asia and argued that the American presence in Vietnam was essential to demonstrate the resolve of the FREE WORLD to oppose Communist aggression. His belief in the need for a military victory led him to endorse the escalation of U.S. involvement in the Vietnam conflict.

Rusk continued as secretary of state under LYNDON B. JOHNSON. His influence on policy-making increased, as he developed a closer working relationship with Johnson than he had enjoyed with Kennedy. He became the new president's key foreign policy adviser. He recommended in favor of the U.S. military intervention in the Dominican Republic during the DOMINICAN CRISIS (1965–1966) and guided the unsuccessful U.S. diplomatic efforts to avert the 1967 Arab-Israeli Six-Day War. In the war's aftermath, he helped chart U.S. involvement in the passage of U.N. Resolution 242 calling for Israel's withdrawal from territories it occupied during the conflict in return for Arab recognition of the Jewish state's right to exist.

The Vietnam War increasingly dominated Johnson's presidency. Following the TONKIN GULF INCIDENT in August 1964, Rusk backed Johnson's decision to order retaliatory air strikes against North Vietnam and to obtain congressional approval of the TONKIN GULF RESOLUTION authorizing U.S. military action in Southeast Asia. Rusk emerged as the leading defender of the administration's policies in Southeast Asia. Appearing before the SENATE FOREIGN RELATIONS COMMITTEE in 1966, he justified the escalating U.S. military role in the conflict, disputing Senator J. WILLIAM FULBRIGHT'S (D-AR) claim that America had no vital strategic interests at stake in Indochina. As domestic criticism of the war mounted, Rusk remained steadfast in support of the administration's position. In 1968 he opposed Johnson's decision, following the TET OFFENSIVE, to deescalate U.S. involvement in Vietnam and played little part in the PARIS PEACE TALKS begun with North Vietnam the same year. Rusk left office with the Johnson administration in January 1969 and became a professor of international law at the University of Georgia.

RUSSO-AMERICAN TREATY OF 1824
Treaty signed April 17, 1824, that resolved conflicting U.S. and Russian claims to territory along America's northwest coast. In the late 18th century, Russian traders began to establish settlements in Russian America, or present-day Alaska. The Russian government in 1789 chartered the Russian-American Company, granting it exclusive trade rights and sovereignty in the coastal region as far south as the 55th parallel. In 1812 the company advanced south into Spanish California and set up the Fort Ross trading post just north of San Francisco. Czar Alexander I issued an imperial edict in September 1821 on the Russian syndicate's behalf. It extended the company's exclusive claim down the Pacific Coast to 51° north latitude and barred all foreign ships from coming within 100 miles of Russian America north of the 51st parallel. The royal declaration pushed the Alaska southern boundary into the Oregon Country, an area claimed jointly by the United States and Great Britain, provoking American and British protests.

Secretary of State JOHN QUINCY ADAMS informed the Russian minister to Washington that the United States would contest Russia's right to any territorial establishments in North America and considered the American continents forever closed to further European colonization. Adams's noncolonization dictum became one of the fundamental principles of the 1823 MONROE

DOCTRINE. The Adams warning led to a series of negotiations that yielded a Russo-American settlement at St. Petersburg, Russia, in April 1824. In the treaty, Russia abandoned its claim to Fort Ross and accepted 54°40' as the southern boundary of its territory in North America. Both countries agreed to a reciprocal right of trade along the entire northwest coast for 10 years. The British concluded a similar treaty with Russia the next year. Russia ceded Alaska to the United States in 1867.

See also ALASKA PURCHASE.

RUSSO-AMERICAN TREATY OF 1867 See **ALASKA PURCHASE.**

S

SACKVILLE-WEST INCIDENT (1888) Episode during the 1888 U.S. presidential election campaign that briefly sullied Anglo-American relations. In September 1888 British Minister to Washington Sir Lionel Sackville-West received a letter, signed Charles F. Murchison, saying the writer was an English-born naturalized American who wanted the diplomat's private and confidential advice on how to vote in the approaching election. The "Murchison letter" actually had been written by a Republican fruit grower from California named George A. Osgoodby. The unsuspecting Sackville-West fell for the hoax. He replied that the incumbent, Democratic President GROVER CLEVELAND, would be friendlier to Great Britain than Republican nominee BENJAMIN HARRISON. The Republicans published Sackville-West's letter shortly before the election, hoping its contents would damage Cleveland with Irish voters. The correspondence brought a sharp public outcry against foreign interference in America's domestic politics. Republicans suggested the letter showed Cleveland to be a tool of Britain. For his part the president demanded Sackville-West's replacement. When the British foreign secretary refused to recall the embattled diplomat, Cleveland dismissed Sackville-West to dispell any idea that he and the Democratic Party were unduly inclined toward Britain. Harrison won the election.

SALISBURY, HARRISON EVANS (1908–) American journalist and author noteworthy as an expert on Russian history and Soviet affairs. Upon graduating from the University of Minnesota in 1930, he went to work as a reporter for the United Press (UP), serving in a succession of domestic assignments. The Minnesota native was dispatched to UP's London bureau in 1942. He spent eight months in the Soviet Union in 1944 reporting on conditions there late in WORLD WAR II. Back in the United States after the war, he completed his first book, *Russia on the Way* (1946), based on his Soviet observations.

In January 1949 he joined the *New York Times* as its Moscow correspondent. Salisbury labored under the strict censorship imposed by the totalitarian Communist regime of Joseph Stalin. He returned to the United States in 1954, at which point the *Times* published his descriptions of the Soviet Union under Stalin in an acclaimed series called "Russia Re-viewed." The series garnered Salisbury the 1955 Pulitzer Prize for international reporting and led the Kremlin to bar him from the Soviet Union for five years. He returned at the outset of the 1960s and traveled extensively throughout the country, gathering impressions that became the basis for two books, *To Moscow—and Beyond: A Reporter's Narrative* (1960) and *A New Russia?* (1962).

As American involvement in the VIETNAM WAR escalated in the mid-1960s, Salisbury became skeptical of President LYNDON B. JOHNSON's predictions of an imminent U.S. victory. He went to North Vietnam in December 1966 to report on the effects of American bombing. His dispatches from Hanoi described substantial civilian casualties and property damage, contradicting Johnson administration claims that U.S. warplanes were only attacking strategic military targets. He suggested that the U.S. bombing was strengthening rather than weakening the resolve of the North Vietnamese to fight the war. Salisbury's war coverage stoked the increasingly divisive domestic debate over America's role in the conflict. Critics impugned his patriotism and called into question the accuracy of his reporting.

In 1970 he was named first editor of the *Times* Op-Ed, or "opposite editorial," page of opinion and commentary. As an editorial board member, he endorsed the paper's 1971 decision to publish the PENTAGON PAPERS, the classified U.S. government report on American involvement in Vietnam. Made associate editor in 1972, he officially retired from the *Times* at the end of 1973. Salisbury has authored several dozen books, including the best-sellers *The 900 Days: The Siege of Leningrad* (1969), about the Nazi bombardment and blockade of Leningrad during World War II, and *Black Night, White Snow: Russia's Revolutions 1905–1917*(1978); and his memoirs, *Journey for Our Times* (1983).

SALT I See **STRATEGIC ARMS LIMITATION TALKS I**.

SALT II See **STRATEGIC ARMS LIMITATION TALKS II**.

SAMOA See **CONVENTION OF 1899**.

SAN ANTONIO FORMULA (1967) Proposal made by President LYNDON B. JOHNSON in a September 29, 1967, speech in San Antonio, Texas, to halt the U.S. bombing of North Vietnam during the VIETNAM WAR. In what became known as the "San Antonio Formula," Johnson said America would cease its aerial and naval bombardment of the Communist North if that country would promptly begin "productive discussions" on ending hostilities and agree not to take military advantage of the stop in bombing. The speech made public the offer the Johnson administration privately had extended to Hanoi through diplomatic and other channels the previous month. Johnson had decided to undertake the initiative amid indications the North Vietnamese were prepared to negotiate. The formula marked an important shift in U.S. requirements for ending the bombing of North Vietnam. Since the start of the U.S. air campaign in 1965, America had conditioned any halt in its bombing on North Vietnam first ending its infiltration of South Vietnam. The North Vietnamese government in October rejected Johnson's overture.

SAN FRANCISCO CONFERENCE (1945) Major international gathering held before the end of WORLD WAR II from April 25 to June 26, 1945, at which the UNITED NATIONS CHARTER was drafted. At the conclusion of the YALTA CONFERENCE (1945), the BIG THREE announced that an international gathering would convene in San Francisco in late April 1945 to finalize the preliminary proposals drafted at the DUMBARTON OAKS CONFERENCE (1944) for a permanent postwar organization to replace the LEAGUE OF NATIONS. On April 25, delegates of 50 nations assembled as scheduled in San Francisco for the parley that was known officially as the United Nations Conference on International Organization. The United States, Great Britain, Soviet Union, and China acted as the sponsoring powers and were joined by 46 other states, comprising those that either had signed the UNITED NATIONS DECLARATION (1942) or had declared war on the Axis powers by March 1, 1945. The 50 participating states, together with Poland, became the 51 original members of the UNITED NATIONS.

Working with the Dumbarton Oaks proposals and the Yalta agreement, the delegates hammered out the 111-article charter. The major point of contention at San Francisco concerned use of the veto in the Security Council, one of six principal U.N. organs and the one vested with primary responsibility for exercising the organization's COLLECTIVE SECURITY mandate. The deadlock on this issue was broken when the Soviet Union finally abandoned its demand that the veto power of the five permanent members extend not only to Security Council action but also to topics of debate. Instead, the BIG FIVE adopted the so-called Yalta formula, which stated that the veto could not be used to prevent discussion of any dispute brought to the council's attention. The conference also approved a statute creating the INTERNATIONAL COURT OF JUSTICE as one of the United Nation's principal organs. The delegates unanimously approved the U.N. charter on June 25 and signed it the following day. The charter, the basic constitution for the United Nations, came into force on October 24, 1945 (since designated United Nations Day), after a majority of the original signers, including the Big Five, had ratified it. The first session of the U.N. General Assembly convened in London in January 1946.

See also UNITED NATIONS PARTICIPATION ACT.

SAN JUAN ISLANDS CONTROVERSY Dispute between the United States and Great Britain over a group of islands midway in the Strait of Juan de Fuca, the channel separating Canada's Vancouver Island from present-day Washington State. The vague boundary through the channel drawn by the OREGON TREATY (1846) had precipitated an Anglo-American argument over rightful ownership of the San Juan Islands. Washington and London negotiated a temporary settlement of their territorial rivalry in 1860 by arranging for joint occupation of the islands. Terms of the TREATY OF WASHINGTON (1871) turned the San Juan controversy over to the German Emperor Wilhelm I for arbitration. In October 1872 he decided on a boundary line that gave the disputed islands to the United States.

SAN LORENZO, TREATY OF See **PINCKNEY'S TREATY**.

SANE/FREEZE American peace organization active in arms control issues. SANE, a shorthand name derived from its formal title, the Committee for a Sane Nuclear Policy, was formed in 1957 by citizens concerned over the above-ground testing of NUCLEAR WEAPONS in the American Southwest. The tests caused the spread of deadly radioactive particles in the atmosphere. The group is credited with helping to build support for the LIMITED TEST BAN TREATY (1963). In the 1960s SANE was an early and outspoken opponent of U.S. involvement in the VIETNAM WAR. The organization emerged as a leading advocate of nuclear arms reductions and was at the forefront of the NUCLEAR FREEZE movement in the early 1980s. SANE merged with the Nuclear Weapons Freeze Campaign in 1987 to form SANE/FREEZE, with the Reverend WILLIAM SLOANE COFFIN, JR. as its first president. The group, the largest peace organization in the United States with upwards of 150,000 members, is involved in education, information, and lobbying activities.

SATELLITE RECONNAISSANCE Use of satellites for intelligence purposes. In the opening years of the COLD WAR, the U.S. government had only a very limited knowledge of military developments in the Soviet bloc. At the 1955 GENEVA SUMMIT, President DWIGHT D. EISENHOWER suggested an OPEN SKIES arrangement between the United States and Soviet Union, whereby each superpower would allow the other to conduct intelligence flights over its territory. Eisenhower's proposal, presented as a means of easing tensions raised by each side's uncertainty and apprehension over the other's military activities, was rejected by the USSR as a pretense for espionage. In 1956 the United States, alarmed by the Soviet development of ballistic nuclear missiles, began top-secret overflights of the Soviet Union with the newly fielded U-2 reconnaissance aircraft. The flights were stopped after one of the spy planes was downed over the USSR in the May 1960 U-2 INCIDENT. The United States maintained and actually enhanced its ability to monitor Soviet developments, however, as the same year it deployed the first reconnaissance satellite into orbit.

The Soviet Union soon followed suit, while negotiations under UNITED NATIONS auspices established the basic principle that satellites were above territorial limits and thus had a right of unrestricted transit through space. In ensuing decades both superpowers came to rely on increasingly sophisticated satellites for various intelligence purposes, including early warning of missile attack and verification of compliance with arms control agreements. Both tacitly accepted observation by the other's satellites as essential to international stability, in effect implementing Eisenhower's Open Skies concept. When cited as the means of verification in arms control pacts, the secrecy-shrouded systems traditionally have been identified by the euphemism NATIONAL TECHNICAL MEANS. The highly classified U.S. program is directed by the NATIONAL RECONNAISSANCE OFFICE.

SCHLESINGER, JAMES RODNEY (1929–   ) Director of the CENTRAL INTELLIGENCE AGENCY (CIA), secretary of defense, first secretary of energy. Schlesinger was educated at Harvard where he earned bachelor's (1950), master's (1952), and doctoral (1956) degrees in economics. He was on the faculty at the University of Virginia from 1955 until 1963, when he joined the RAND CORPORATION as a senior staff member. He became the think tank's director of strategic studies in 1967. Schlesinger entered the Nixon administration in 1969 as assistant director of the Bureau of the Budget, helping guide the agency's 1970 reorganization into the Office of Management and Budget. In 1971 he was appointed chairman of the Atomic Energy Commission.

Schlesinger became head of the CIA in February 1973. During his brief tenure, he shifted emphasis from clandestine operations to the collection and analysis of strategic intelligence. Following press disclosure of CIA agent involvement in illegal domestic intelligence activities, he launched an internal investigation into past agency improprieties. The resulting report, known as the FAMILY JEWELS, later aided congressional probes into U.S. INTELLIGENCE COMMUNITY misconduct. In May 1973, President RICHARD M. NIXON named Schlesinger to replace ELLIOT L. RICHARDSON as secretary of defense. Richardson in turn had become attorney general in a cabinet shake-up related to the worsening domestic Watergate scandal.

Schlesinger took office at the very end of direct U.S. military involvement in the VIETNAM WAR. He worked to revitalize the armed forces, largely demoralized by the difficult Vietnam experience, and maintained that, DETENTE notwithstanding, the Soviet Union continued to pose a dangerous military threat. He moved to modernize U.S. nuclear warfare doctrine and capabilities, then linked to the concept of MUTUAL ASSURED DESTRUCTION. While continuing to adhere to the basic strategic precept that a nuclear war was unwinnable and therefore should never be initiated, the Nixon administration in 1974 unveiled a more flexible nuclear strategy that targeted Soviet military facilities as well as cities, thus allowing America to respond to a limited Soviet nuclear attack with less than-all-out retaliation. Noting the two superpowers had roughly equivalent nuclear arsenals, Schlesinger stressed that NATO no longer could rely primarily on nuclear arms for DETERRENCE and pressed for improvements in the western security alliance's conventional forces.

In October 1973 Schlesinger directed the massive U.S. airlift of military supplies to Israel during the YOM KIPPUR WAR and, at Nixon's order, placed the American military on worldwide alert to prevent Soviet intervention in the conflict. He remained at the Defense Department following Nixon's August 1974 resignation. In April 1975 the Ford administration was powerless to halt the North Vietnamese invasion that finally subdued South Vietnam and reunified the country under Communist control. Schlesinger and other senior administration figures argued unsuccessfully for congressional approval of a resumption of U.S. aid to Saigon. In May 1975 the U.S. military reacted quickly to the seizure by Communist Cambodian forces of an unarmed American freighter in the MAYAGUEZ INCIDENT, freeing the ship and its crew.

President GERALD R. FORD dismissed Schlesinger in November 1975 as part of a reshuffling of the cabinet. His departure was attributed largely to differences with the White House on the defense budget. In 1977 President JIMMY CARTER designated Schlesinger the first head of the newly created Department of Energy. He served in the post until 1979, when he returned to private life as a consultant. In 1983 he was a member of the SCOWCROFT COMMISSION on strategic nuclear forces.

SCHURMAN COMMISSION (1899)   Special U.S. commission on the future status of the Philippine Islands. Under the TREATY OF PARIS (1898) ending the SPANISH-AMERICAN WAR (1898), a defeated Spain ceded the Philippines to the United States for $20 million. The McKinley administration's annexation of the islands ignited a fierce debate between American imperialists, who vigorously supported U.S. expansion into the Pacific, and anti-imperialists, who deplored the acquisition as a retreat from historic U.S. ISOLATIONISM and inimical to American principles of freedom and self-government. The Paris treaty won narrow Senate ratification on February 6, 1899, just two days after independence-seeking forces under Filipino rebel leader Emilio Aguinaldo had launched the armed PHILIPPINE INSURRECTION against U.S. rule. The depth of domestic American opposition to annexation was revealed on February 14, when the U.S. Senate barely defeated a resolution to grant independence to the islands. Meanwhile, on January 20, 1899, President WILLIAM McKINLEY had appointed Cornell University president Jacob G. Schurman to head a Philippine Commission charged with assessing the situation in the islands and preparing a report for setting up a civil government. On its return the following August from a Pacific tour, the Schurman Commission recommended ultimate independence for the islands, but urged continuation of U.S. rule for an indefinite period until the Filipinos could be prepared for self-government.

On April 1, 1900, McKinley appointed a second Philippine Commission, headed by Federal Circuit Judge WILLIAM HOWARD TAFT. Instructed to establish a territorial government in the archipelago, in accord with the Schurman panel's recommendations, the Taft Commission assumed legislative powers the following September and, with the end of American military rule, took over as civil authority in July 1901. Taft became the first civil governor of the Philippines. Under the close guidance of Secretary of War ELIHU ROOT, the commission forged a government for the islands and made preparations for a phased transition to limited Filipino self-rule. The federal Philippine Government Act of 1902, also called the Organic Act, established the islands as an unorganized U.S. territory. The law guaranteed increased self-government by arranging for the formation of a popular assembly once local rebellion was put down and peace restored. In 1907 an elective assembly was introduced. It served as the lower house of the Philippine bicameral legislature, with the Taft Commission becoming the upper house. The head of the commission, given the new title of governor-general of the Philippines, acted as the chief executive.

By 1913 a broad American consensus had emerged in favor of Philippine independence. The Jones Act of August 29, 1916, named after its sponsor, Representative William A. Jones (D-VA), affirmed the U.S. intention to grant the archipelago independence as soon as a stable government could be achieved. The legislation, known also as the Organic Act of the Philippine Islands, gave all Filipino males the vote, established an elective Senate to replace the Philippine Commission, and vested supreme executive authority in the American governor-general, who was to be appointed by the U.S. president. The islands achieved complete independence in 1946 under terms outlined in the TYDINGS-McDUFFIE ACT of 1934.

SCOTT ACT (1888) Measure adopted by Congress in the aftermath of unsuccessful negotiations with the Chinese government over immigration issues. In March 1888, Chinese and American negotiators reached preliminary agreement on a treaty to authorize much tighter restrictions on Chinese immigration to the United States. When the Chinese government balked at the proposed accord, Representative William L. Scott (D-PA) sponsored a bill to implement one of the draft treaty's provisions.

The Scott Act, which became law on October 1, 1888, denied reentry to Chinese laborers who departed the United States to visit their native land. The legislation also applied to an estimated 20,000 Chinese out of the country at the time it was passed. In the 1894 GRESHAM-YANG TREATY the United States agreed to allow departing Chinese workers to return. China for its part accepted the strict U.S. limitations on Chinese immigration then in effect. See also CHINESE EXCLUSION ACT.

SCOTT, WINFIELD (1786–1866) Army general, diplomatic envoy, and presidential candidate. A native Virginian, Scott briefly attended William and Mary College and then studied law before enlisting in the Army in 1807. He was commissioned a captain the following year. During the WAR OF 1812 he distinguished himself at the battles of Chippewa and Lundy's Cave along the U.S.-Canadian border and was promoted to general. He served in the BLACK HAWK WAR (1832) and led American forces in the initial stages of the second of the SEMINOLE WARS (1835–1842). In 1838 he was dispatched as a special envoy on a successful mission to calm U.S.-Canadian border tensions following the CAROLINE AFFAIR. The same year he was given responsibility for removal of the Cherokee Indians from Georgia to the newly created INDIAN TERRITORY west of the Mississippi. Recalled before the relocation had been completed, he was sent to Maine, where he mediated a peaceful resolution of the so-called AROOSTOOK WAR (1838–1839) over the U.S.-Canadian boundary.

In 1841 Scott was named commanding general of the U.S. Army. He was referred to as "Old Fuss and Feathers" because of his insistence on strict discipline and formality. During the MEXICAN WAR (1846–1848) he commanded the amphibious operation that seized Veracruz and led U.S. forces on the victorious campaign across Mexico to Mexico City. In 1852 he was the unsuccessful Whig Party candidate for president. He demonstrated considerable diplomatic skill when he journeyed to Oregon in 1859 to defuse the Anglo-American controversy over competing U.S. and British claims to San Juan Island in the Puget Sound. Although a southerner by birth, he remained loyal to the Union in the Civil War and oversaw its initial military preparations before retiring in November 1861.

SCOWCROFT, BRENT (1925–) National security adviser in both the Ford and Bush administrations. A native of Utah, Scowcroft graduated from West Point in 1947 and was commissioned a second lieutenant in the Air Force. After an aviation mishap cut short his career as a military pilot, he received an M.A. in international relations from Columbia University in 1953. Over the next two decades he held various teaching assignments at West Point and the Air Force Academy, was a military attaché at the U.S. embassy in Yugoslavia, and served in senior national security affairs positions at the Defense Department. He also earned his Ph.D. in international relations from Columbia in 1967. In 1971 Scowcroft was named military aide to President RICHARD M. NIXON. Promoted to general the following year, he accompanied Nixon on his historic 1972 trips to Communist China and the Soviet Union. In January 1973 Scowcroft became the deputy to HENRY A. KISSINGER, the president's national security adviser and head of the NATIONAL SECURITY COUNCIL (NSC) staff. When Kissinger relinquished the NSC post in 1975 to turn his full energies to his duties as secretary of state, Scowcroft left active military duty to become national security adviser under President GERALD R. FORD. While Kissinger's powerful presence commanded the public spotlight, Scowcroft quietly remained in the background, coordinating the executive branch's foreign affairs machinery.

Scowcroft left office at the close of the Ford administration in January 1977. He served informally during the Carter years as a member of the president's general advisory committee on arms control. In 1982 he became vice-chairman of Kissinger Associates, an international consulting firm headed by the former secretary of state. The following year President RONALD W. REAGAN asked Scowcroft to head a special government panel charged with evaluating U.S. strategic nuclear forces. The influential report of the SCOWCROFT COMMISSION, issued in April 1983, helped resolve the controversial MX missile basing issue while providing a blueprint for U.S. nuclear modernization and arms control negotiations. Reagan again called on Scowcroft in 1986 to serve as one of three members of the TOWER COMMISSION formed to investigate the NSC and the IRAN-CONTRA scandal. In January 1989 President GEORGE BUSH brought him back for a second tour as national security adviser. Scowcroft helped orchestrate the arms-control negotiations leading to the CONVENTIONAL FORCES EUROPE TREATY (1990) and START Treaty (1991) and was one of the small group of top aides advising Bush on the conduct of the PERSIAN GULF WAR (1991).

SCOWCROFT COMMISSION (1983) Presidential blue-ribbon panel on U.S. strategic nuclear forces. Since the mid-1970s American defense planners had been concerned about the possible vulnerability of U.S. land-based INTERCONTINENTAL BALLISTIC MISSILE (ICBM) forces to a preemptive strike by increasingly accurate and lethal Soviet nuclear missiles. Both the Carter and Reagan administrations had struggled to find a survivable basing mode for the latest U.S. ICBM, the massive 10-warhead MX missile scheduled for deployment in the early 1980s. In December 1982 Congress rejected the Reagan administration's Dense Pack proposal, under which 100 MXs would be deployed in a theoretically invulnerable compact formation, and withheld production funding for the missile until an acceptable basing scheme was developed. On January 3, 1983, President RONALD W. REAGAN appointed a special bipartisan panel to assess the MX program and U.S. ICBM forces within a broad review of American strategic NUCLEAR WEAPONS. The Presidential Commission on Strategic Forces was headed by Brent Scowcroft, a retired Air Force general and former and future national security adviser. Among those on the distinguished 11-member panel were former Secretary of State ALEXANDER M. HAIG, JR. and RICHARD M. HELMS, former director of the CENTRAL INTELLIGENCE AGENCY. Reagan also named seven senior counselors to the commission, including former Secretary of State HENRY A. KISSINGER and former secretaries of defense HAROLD BROWN, MELVIN R. LAIRD, DONALD H. RUMSFELD, and JAMES R. SCHLESINGER. The Scowcroft Commission submitted its report on April 11, 1983. While confirming the increasing vulnerability of U.S. land-based missiles, the panel stressed that the TRIAD of American strategic forces continued to guarantee U.S. nuclear DETERRENCE. The commission described the MX as essential to countering the Soviet Union's advantage in ICBM capabilities, urging the deployment of 100 of the missiles in existing Minuteman III ICBM silos. To ensure the future survivability of U.S. ICBM forces, it recommended the development of a mobile, single-warhead missile, dubbed the MIDGETMAN. The report also proposed shifting the focus of U.S.-Soviet arms control discussions to limits on the number of nuclear warheads rather than on the number of delivery vehicles, such as missiles and bombers. Reagan endorsed the commission's findings on April 19 and directed its arms control proposals be incorporated into U.S. START negotiating posi-

tions. Congress approved the initial funding for MX deployment in May 1983.

SDI See **STRATEGIC DEFENSE INITIATIVE**.

SEABED ARMS CONTROL TREATY (1971) International agreement to prevent the placement of NUCLEAR WEAPONS on the ocean floor. Negotiated under the auspices of the CONFERENCE OF THE COMMITTEE ON DISARMAMENT in Geneva, the Treaty on the Prohibition of the Emplacement of Nuclear Weapons and Other Weapons of Mass Destruction on the Seabed and the Ocean Floor and in the Subsoil Thereof, was approved by the UNITED NATIONS General Assembly on December 7, 1970. It was signed in Washington, London, and Moscow on February 11, 1971, and entered into force on May 18, 1972. The parties to the treaty, numbering more than 90 nations, are prohibited from emplacing any nuclear or other weapons of mass destruction beyond the 12-mile territorial limit from their shores. The ban extends, as well, to any related launch, testing, or storage facilities. The treaty does not apply to nuclear-armed submarines.

SEATO See **SOUTHEAST ASIA TREATY ORGANIZATION**.

SECRET COMMITTEE Committee formed September 18, 1775, by the Continental Congress to procure war supplies for the AMERICAN REVOLUTION. Members included its two eventual chairmen, Thomas Willing and Robert Morris, BENJAMIN FRANKLIN, and ROBERT R. LIVINGSTON. The committee's name referred to its anticipated undercover purchase of materials from nations unwilling to risk hostilities with Great Britain by open support of the American rebellion. Charged initially with obtaining munitions, the panel by January 1776 was also responsible for importing medical supplies, blankets, and other basic provisions and soon exercised broad control over foreign trade.

In April 1776 the Congress authorized the committee to outfit and dispatch vessels for privateering. The same month, together with the COMMITTEE OF SECRET CORRESPONDENCE, the panel sent SILAS DEANE to France to seek French military aid. Clandestine French assistance to the Americans in the war's first years was channeled through the dummy trade firm HORTALEZ AND COM-PANY. The Secret Committee was renamed the Committee of Commerce in July 1777. By bringing France into the conflict, the 1778 FRANCO-AMERICAN ALLIANCE removed the need to conceal trade relations between Paris and the insurgent colonies. The Commerce Committee's functions were assumed by a superintendent of finance in 1781. Roberts Morris, called the "financier of the Revolution," held the post until 1784, when he resigned due to ill health and was replaced by a board of three commissioners. Responsibility for the regulation of commerce fell to the departments of State and Treasury in the federal government that took shape after 1789. A separate DEPARTMENT OF COMMERCE was established in 1903.

SECRET TREATIES (1915–1917) Controversial pacts made by the Allies during WORLD WAR I for apportioning the anticipated territorial spoils of war. Between 1915 and 1917, Great Britain, France, Italy, Romania, Serbia, Montenegro, Russia, and Japan entered into a series of secret agreements spelling out how various territories and colonies of the major Central Powers (Germany, Austria-Hungary, and Turkey) would be divided up in the event of an Allied victory. When the United States entered the war in April 1917, Allied leaders feared that President WOODROW WILSON, who in his war message had declared that the United States was fighting to make the world "safe for democracy" and sought no conquests, would ask them to surrender their territorial objectives as the price for full American participation.

The Wilson administration was informed of the pacts in broad outline shortly after the U.S. declaration of war against Germany. At the end of April British Foreign Secretary Arthur J. Balfour discussed the secret treaties in Washington with Wilson and his close foreign policy adviser Colonel EDWARD M. HOUSE. The president indicated he did not consider the United States bound by any secret Allied arrangements. He concurred with House that to take up the issue of the pacts would invite disputes among the Allies and divert attention from the war effort at what was a critical juncture. Balfour later sent copies of the treaties to Wilson, who neither offered criticism nor made any U.S. demands.

Following the November 1917 Russian Revolution, the Bolsheviks, having seized power, immediately called for a World War I armistice on the basis of no annexations and no indemnities. They soon discovered the secret treaties between czarist Russia and the Allies in the official Russian archives. Bolshevik leaders published the texts of the agreements, condemning them as evidence of ulterior Allied imperialistic designs. Exposure of the treaties prompted widespread disillusionment in Allied countries. Wilson became convinced of the urgent need for a statement of Allied war aims that would dispel the Bolshevik charge of IMPERIALISM and capture the imagination of the world. Acting independently, he formulated the idealistic FOURTEEN POINTS (1918) outlining a liberal peace program. Embodying such principles as open diplomacy, national self-determination, and impartial adjustment of colonial claims, the Fourteen Points constituted a rejection of the secret treaties.

SEDITION ACT (1918) Amendment to the ESPIONAGE ACT of 1917 that made seditious statements about American participation in WORLD WAR I a serious crime. The measure became law May 16, 1918, amid concerns that domestic dissension and political agitation threatened to undermine the nation's war effort. The act prohibited false statements that could be deemed to interfere with the war's conduct. It barred use of "disloyal, profane, scurrilous, or abusive language" about the U.S. government, CONSTITUTION, flag, or armed forces; and forbade anyone from urging a cutback in war production or from advocating or teaching subversive activities. The Supreme Court in *Abrams* v. *United States* (1919) upheld the wartime limits on free speech. More than 1500 people were arrested under the act's provisions including Socialist Party leader Eugene V. Debs, who received a prison sentence of 10 years for antiwar agitation. Debs was pardoned by President WARREN G. HARDING in 1921.

See also ALIEN REGISTRATION ACT.

SELECT COMMISSION ON IMMIGRATION AND REFUGEE POLICY Panel created by Congress October 5, 1978, to study and make recommendations concerning U.S. immigration policy and laws. Its formation stemmed from concerns about the ability of existing immigration law to respond to the continuing upsurge in illegal immigration from Latin America and the growing refugee problem posed by Indochinese BOAT PEOPLE. The Select Commission was chaired by the Reverend Theodore M. Hesburgh, then president of the University of Notre Dame. The 16-member body included presidential appointees from the private sector and local government, cabinet officials, and members of Congress. The commission submitted its findings March 1, 1981. Key proposals included a modest increase in annual immigration quotas and a one-time amnesty for illegal aliens coupled with legal sanctions against employers who hired undocumented workers. The report served as the basis for the IMMIGRATION REFORM AND CONTROL ACT of 1986.

SEMINOLE WARS Trio of wars waged between the United States and the Seminole Indians in Florida between 1817 and 1858. U.S. troop forays into Spanish-held Florida to pursue runaway slaves harbored by the Seminoles were met by retaliatory Indian ambushes. These border skirmishes escalated into the First Seminole War (1817–1818). An American military expedition under General ANDREW JACKSON, after capturing Spanish forts at St. Marks and Pensacola, quickly penetrated INDIAN COUNTRY and broke the Seminole resistance by April 1818. The war's outcome persuaded Spain to sell Florida to the United States. In 1819, the countries completed the ADAMS-ONIS TREATY, which transferred all of Spain's territory east of the Mississippi River to the United States for $5 million.

The federal decision to remove the Seminole Indians from their homelands to territory west of the Mississippi sparked the Second Seminole War (1835–1842). Fighting erupted in 1835 when Seminole Chief OSCEOLA refused to recognize the treaties of Payne's Landing (1832) and Fort Gibson (1833) with the U.S. government arranging for the tribe's resettlement. Retreating into the Everglades, the Seminoles resisted the U.S. Army for seven years. The conflict, among the costliest and most deadly Indian wars ever fought by U.S. troops, dragged on after Osceola's 1837 imprisonment and death in 1838. The U.S. military campaign finally defeated the Seminoles in 1842.

Most of the tribe was forced to emigrate westward. The Indians who refused to leave were hunted down and removed by the United States in the Third Seminole War (1855–1858). A small number still held on in the Everglades and did not make peace with the federal government until 1934.

See also MAP 1.

SENATE ARMED SERVICES COMMITTEE See same in **APPENDIX D.**

SENATE FOREIGN RELATIONS COMMITTEE See same in **APPENDIX D.**

SERVICE, JOHN STEWART (1909–   ) FOREIGN SERVICE officer and China expert who became embroiled in a protracted controversy over whether he posed a security risk as a government official. Service was born in China, the son of American missionaries. After graduation from Oberlin College in 1931, he entered the Foreign Service and was posted to the U.S. consulate in Kunming. Remaining in China until 1945, he observed firsthand the civil war between the Nationalist government of Chiang Kai-shek and revolutionary Communist forces led by Mao Tse-tung. Service correctly predicted an eventual Communist victory over the corrupt Nationalist regime. During WORLD WAR II he argued unsuccessfully for the extension of American aid to Mao. With Chiang already receiving U.S. assistance, Service suggested that support for Mao would both abet the fight against Japan and enable the United States to develop contacts with China's likely future leadership.

Following his return to Washington, Service was arrested in June 1945 and charged with passing confidential documents to Philip J. Jaffe, editor of *Amerasia*, a political journal sympathetic to the Chinese Communists. Service defended his contacts with Jaffe as the routine provision by a government official of background information to a journalist preparing an article. The charges were dropped for lack of evidence. As concerns over Communist infiltration of the U.S. government mounted in the late 1940s, Service underwent a series of security checks by the State Department. In each instance he received a favorable evaluation. In the spring of 1950

Senator JOSEPH R. MCCARTHY (R-WI) cited Service and the AMERASIA CASE in his allegations of Communist espionage in the State Department. Another department hearing again cleared Service, but an audit of the proceedings by the Loyalty Review Board of the Civil Service found "reasonable doubt" as to his loyalty. On the board's recommendation, he was dismissed from the Foreign Service by Secretary of State DEAN ACHESON in December 1951. In 1957 the U.S. Supreme Court ruled in *Service* v. *Dulles* that Acheson's decision was in error. A lower court then ordered Service reinstated with full back pay. He retired in 1962 and became a resident China scholar at the University of California at Berkeley.

17TH PARALLEL Boundary line between North and South Vietnam. The 1954 GENEVA CONFERENCE temporarily divided Vietnam into two zones. The northern half subsequently became the Communist Democratic Republic of Vietnam (North Vietnam) while the U.S.-supported Republic of Vietnam (South Vietnam) was established in the south. The actual demarcation line roughly followed the 17th parallel—thus the boundary became identified commonly with the geographic latitude. A five-mile-wide demilitarized zone, or DMZ, was centered on the demarcation line. The United States sought to halt North Vietnamese infiltration across the border during the VIETNAM WAR and the entire area was the scene of frequent combat. In 1975 the boundary was eliminated when Vietnam was unified under the Communist North.

SEWARD, WILLIAM HENRY (1801–1872) Secretary of state under Presidents ABRAHAM LINCOLN and ANDREW JOHNSON. Seward was born in Orange County, New York. After graduating from Union College in 1820, he read law, was admitted to the bar in 1822, and went into practice in Auburn, New York, the following year. He gradually became involved in state politics and in the late 1820s was drawn into the Anti-Masonic movement. As a protege of Anti-Masonic leader Thurlow Weed, he was elected in 1830 to the New York state senate, where he served four years. Rebounding from a failed gubernatorial bid in 1834, Seward was elected governor of New York in 1838 as a Whig and reelected in 1840. He de-

clined renomination in 1841 and returned to his law practice.

His advanced antislavery stand attracted the support of the growing Free Soil movement in the North and helped secure his election in 1848 to the U.S. Senate from New York. In the great Senate debate on the Compromise of 1850, HENRY CLAY's legislative plan to end the sectional struggle over the issue of slavery and its extension into the territories, Seward opposed accommodation of the South. In a speech on March 11, 1850, he made his famous remark about the existence of a "higher law than the CONSTITUTION" that demanded slavery's exclusion from new states joining the Union. Following his reelection in 1854 Seward joined the newly formed Republican Party, emerging as one of its national leaders. From his Senate seat he continued to attack slavery on moral grounds and came to embody the growing antislavery sentiment of the North in the years just preceding the outbreak of the Civil War. In a renowned speech at Rochester, New York, in October 1858, he declared that the national divisiveness over slavery was an "irrepressible conflict." Seward was defeated for the Republican presidential nomination in 1860 by Abraham Lincoln. In March 1861 he joined Lincoln's cabinet as secretary of state, believing he would be the dominant figure in the administration.

Outlining his views to the president in a confidential April 1861 memo, he proposed war with Europe as a means of unifying the country, but Lincoln disregarded the suggestion. Seward weathered this inauspicious start and went on to conduct the administration's CIVIL WAR DIPLOMACY with great skill. He successfully dissuaded the European powers from extending diplomatic recognition to the Confederacy. His steady pressure gradually moved the British government to take action against outfitting of Confederate cruisers in British ports. Seward adroitly defused the crisis in Anglo-American relations brought on by the TRENT AFFAIR (1861), in which a U.S. warship illegally intercepted and seized a British vessel carrying two Confederate emissaries enroute to Europe. He also pressed London to settle the claims of U.S. citizens for damages caused to Union commercial shipping by the *Alabama* and other British-built Confederate ships. The

ALABAMA CLAIMS remained a major source of contention in Anglo-American diplomacy until their resolution through international arbitration in 1872. Seward invoked historic American prerogatives under the MONROE DOCTRINE to protest the French armed intervention in Mexico in 1862. The demands of the Civil War, however, constrained the Lincoln administration from moving decisively against France. With the improvement in the North's military situation in 1864, the secretary of state asserted U.S. opposition to the French presence in Mexico with greater resolve. At the end of the war, Seward backed with threat of force the U.S. demand that France end its Mexican venture, whereupon the French agreed to withdraw their troops.

At the same time Lincoln was fatally shot by John Wilkes Booth in April 1865, Seward was attacked and wounded by a Booth co-conspirator. On his recovery he continued in the Johnson administration, where he pursued an expansionist postwar foreign policy. In 1867 he concluded the ALASKA PURCHASE from Russia. His critics pilloried the acquisition as needless and wasteful, dubbing it "Seward's Folly." The same year he oversaw the annexation of the MIDWAY ISLANDS in the Pacific. He advocated similar U.S. acquisition of Hawaii. His efforts to incorporate the Dominican Republic into the United States were thwarted by a lack of political support in Congress, while a treaty negotiated for the acquisition of the Danish West Indies failed to win Senate ratification. Seward loyally supported Johnson against the Radical Republicans, who bitterly opposed the president and his reconciliatory policy toward the South under Reconstruction. At the end of Johnson's term in March 1869, Seward retired from public life. After a trip around the world he returned to his home in New York.

SHANGHAI COMMUNIQUE (1972) Joint U.S.-Chinese statement released at the end of President RICHARD M. NIXON's historic 1972 visit to the People's Republic of China. Following the Communist Chinese victory over the Nationalist Chinese in 1949, the United States had refused to recognize the mainland Communist state, supporting instead the Nationalist regime that fled to Taiwan as the legitimate government of China. The February 1972 PEKING SUMMIT between Nixon and Communist Chinese leaders Chairman Mao Tse-tung and Premier Chou En-lai marked the end of two decades of U.S. diplomatic isolation of Communist China and signaled a dramatic shift in U.S. policy.

On February 27, 1972, at the end of the week-long summit, Nixon and Chou journeyed to Shanghai, where they issued a joint communique summarizing their deliberations. The statement comprised five sections: (1) a general account of the Nixon trip; (2) separate statements by each nation of its positions on Asian issues; (3) an agreement on basic principles governing international relations; (4) separate statements by each nation on the status of Taiwan; (5) a review of joint discussions on future cooperation in such areas as science, culture, sports, and journalism. In the second section, the United States reiterated its support of South Vietnam in the VIETNAM WAR and its commitment to defend South Korea. China reaffirmed its backing for North Vietnam and for North Korean proposals for the "peaceful unification" of Korea. The key fourth section reflected a careful resolution by Nixon and Chou of U.S.-Chinese differences over Taiwan. China reasserted its claim to the island and declared U.S. support for the Nationalist regime the basic obstacle to the normalization of relations between Peking and Washington. While seeking improved ties with the mainland, Nixon was not prepared to abandon the Nationalist Chinese and the American statement straddled the Taiwan question. The United States acknowledged that "all Chinese on either side of the Taiwan Strait maintain there is but one China and that Taiwan is part of China" and stated its ultimate objective to withdraw American military forces from Taiwan as tensions in the area diminished. The U.S. position drew strong condemnation from Taiwan and its conservative Republican allies in the United States. The Shanghai Communique served as the basis for U.S.-Chinese relations until U.S. recognition of the Communist government and establishment of full diplomatic ties in 1979.

SHANGHAI INCIDENT   See **MANCHURIAN CRISIS**.

SHERMAN, JOHN (1823–1900) Congressman, senator, and first secretary of state under President WILLIAM McKINLEY. Born in

Ohio, younger brother of Civil War general William T. Sherman, he never attended college. He read law and was admitted to the bar in 1844 in his native state, where he practiced for the next decade. Sherman's long congressional career began with his election in 1854 to the House of Representatives from Ohio as a Republican. He was chairman of the first Republican convention in Ohio in 1855 and helped organize the national Republican Party. He left the House with his election in 1861 to the U.S. Senate, where he served until 1877, becoming chairman of the Senate Finance Committee and an authority on federal financial affairs. Appointed secretary of the treasury by President RUTHERFORD B. HAYES in 1877, Sherman supported the Republican protective tariff policy.

He unsuccessfully sought the party's presidential nomination in 1880, 1884, and 1888. Again elected to the Senate in 1881, he held his seat for the next 16 years. He sponsored and helped draft the Sherman Antitrust Act of 1890 and the Sherman Silver Purchase Act of the same year. In 1897 President McKinley named the 73-year-old Sherman as secretary of state. His anti-expansionist views were at odds with the McKinley cabinet's increasing inclination toward war with Spain. In failing health, Sherman resigned his post at the outset of the SPANISH-AMERICAN WAR in April 1898 and was replaced by his assistant secretary, WILLIAM R. DAY. He lived in retirement in Washington, D.C., until his death.

SHIRER, WILLIAM LAWRENCE (1904–   ) Correspondent, radio commentator, and author. After graduating Phi Beta Kappa from Coe College in Iowa in 1925, the Chicago native set out for Europe, where he landed a job as a reporter with the Paris edition of the *Chicago Tribune*. In 1927 he became roving European correspondent for the newspaper, winning notice for his coverage of famed American aviator CHARLES A. LINDBERGH's historic trans-Atlantic landing at Paris (1927), LEAGUE OF NATIONS sessions in Geneva, and the 1928 winter and summer Olympics. Touring India in 1930 and 1931, he reported on Mahatma Gandhi's emerging civil disobedience movement against British colonialism.

Shirer joined the *Universal News Service* in 1935 as its chief correspondent in Berlin, where he covered the rise of Adolf Hitler's Nazi Germany. His dispatches increasingly alerted the West to Hitler's expansionist ambitions. Hired by the Columbia Broadcasting System (CBS) in 1937, he reported from Vienna and Prague on the tide of European developments that presaged the start of WORLD WAR II in September 1939. Shirer broadcast news of the German annexation of Austria in 1938 and the British appeasement of Hitler at Munich the same year. He covered the early course of the war from Germany as a foreign correspondent attached to the westward-invading German army. Confronted with tightening German censorship, he left Berlin in December 1940 and returned to the United States. He completed his first book, *Berlin Diary: The Journal of a Foreign Correspondent, 1939–1941* (1941), an eyewitness account of Germany under Hitler, that became an international bestseller.

Shirer remained with CBS until 1947 as a network news commentator. From 1942 to 1948 he also wrote a syndicated column for the *New York Herald Tribune*. At the end of World War II he returned to Germany to cover the NUREMBURG WAR CRIMES TRIALS. During Senator JOSEPH R. MCCARTHY's (R-WI) demagogic investigations into alleged Communist subversion in the early 1950s, he was blacklisted from journalism for his liberal views and outspoken support of individuals in the American media and entertainment world accused of Communist affiliations. He subsequently worked as a freelance writer, contributing articles to various magazines and authoring numerous books, including *The Rise and Fall of the Third Reich* (1960), his monumental history of Nazi Germany.

SHUFELDT, ROBERT WILSON (1822–1895) U.S. Navy officer and diplomat. A native of New York, Shufeldt entered the Navy as a midshipman in 1839. He resigned his commission in 1853 to serve as a captain in commercial shipping. At the start of the Civil War in 1861, he was appointed consul general to Cuba. In 1863 he rejoined the Navy, participating in several operations off the Confederate coast. He remained in the service after the war, becoming a strong advocate of the Navy's role in the extension of American commerce. In 1878 Shufeldt embarked on a two-year diplomatic and commercial mission aboard the U.S.S. *Ticonderoga*. Sailing to the Far East, he sought unsuccessfully to establish U.S. relations with Korea. He returned to Asia in 1881 as U.S. naval attaché to China. With Chinese assistance he was able to complete the historic KOREAN-AMERICAN TREATY OF 1882 that opened Korea to the West. Shufeldt retired as a rear admiral in 1884.

SHULTZ, GEORGE PRATT (1920–) Secretary of the treasury, secretary of state. A native of New York City, Shultz graduated from Princeton University in 1942 and was a Marine Corps officer in the Pacific during WORLD WAR II. He earned a doctorate in economics from the Massachusetts Institute of Technology in 1949 and began a teaching career at the school. In 1957 he became a professor at the University of Chicago and in 1962 was named dean of the graduate business school. Shultz served as an economic adviser to the Eisenhower, Kennedy, and Johnson administrations. In 1969 President RICHARD M. NIXON brought him into government full-time as secretary of labor. The following year he became director of the newly created Office of Management and Budget and in 1972 was appointed secretary of the treasury. As a top economic policymaker Shultz was involved in the administration's 1971 move to take the U.S. dollar off the gold standard and in the initial stages of the TOKYO ROUND of trade negotiations under the GENERAL AGREEMENT ON TARIFFS AND TRADE. He resigned his post in March 1974 and became president of Bechtel, an international construction firm.

In June 1982 President RONALD W. REAGAN named Shultz to succeed ALEXANDER M. HAIG, JR. as secretary of state. He took office at a time of increased U.S. involvement in the Middle East. Shultz helped design the abortive REAGAN PLAN for Arab-Israeli peace and supported the commitment of American troops as part of a multinational peacekeeping force in Beirut during the LEBANON CRISIS (1982–1984). In the wake of the October 1983 suicide bombing of the U.S. Marine barracks in Beirut, he became a forceful advocate of direct retaliatory action against terrorists and their state sponsors and endorsed the 1986 LIBYAN BOMBING RAID.

Shultz's tenure spanned a dramatic evolution in U.S.-Soviet relations from the

heightened COLD WAR tensions of the early 1980s to the rapidly improving ties between Reagan and Soviet leader Mikhail S. Gorbachev later in the decade. He met with Soviet Foreign Minister Andrei A. Gromyko at the 1985 UMBRELLA TALKS that brought a resumption of stalled superpower arms control discussions. Shultz accompanied Reagan to his first meeting with Gorbachev at the 1985 GENEVA SUMMIT and was the president's principal adviser throughout the succession of Reagan-Gorbachev summits that marked deepening U.S.-Soviet ties. He had a central role in the negotiation of the INTERMEDIATE NUCLEAR FORCES TREATY (1987) cutting U.S. and Soviet nuclear arsenals in Europe.

He was an architect of the REAGAN DOCTRINE of providing U.S. aid to anti-Communist insurgencies in Latin America, Africa, and Asia. In 1987 Shultz appeared before the congressional committee investigating the burgeoning IRAN-CONTRA scandal involving the covert sale of arms to Iran and diversion of the proceeds to the CONTRAS, the U.S.-backed rebels battling the leftist Sandinista government in Nicaragua. He testified that he had opposed the idea of providing arms to Iran in return for the release of American hostages in Lebanon and had been kept in the dark regarding the secret operation. In 1988 he helped conclude the UNITED NATIONS-mediated agreement providing for the withdrawal of Soviet military forces from the AFGHANISTAN WAR. Shultz left office with the Reagan administration in January 1989 and joined the faculty at Stanford University.

SHUTTLE DIPLOMACY (1974–1975) Term coined to describe the diplomatic effort undertaken by U.S. Secretary of State HENRY A. KISSINGER following the YOM KIPPUR WAR (1973) to secure troop disengagement agreements between Israel and its Arab foes Egypt and Syria. The expression derived from Kissinger's shuttling back and forth by plane between Jerusalem and various Arab capitals. The Yom Kippur War began in early October 1973 when Egypt and Syria mounted a surprise attack against the Jewish state to avenge their humiliating defeat in the 1967 Six-Day War. In that conflict, Israel had smashed three neighboring Arab armies and captured Arab territories, including the Sinai Peninsula and Gaza

Strip from Egypt, the West Bank (including East Jerusalem) from Jordan, and the Golan Heights from Syria. The Egyptian and Syrian forces, seeking to retake Israeli-occupied lands, both received abundant weapons and supplies from the Soviet Union, which was eager to expand its influence in the strategically vital Middle East. Soviet sponsorship of the Arab armies placed the October war in the larger East-West context of the COLD WAR. The United States responded by launching a major airlift of armaments and equipment to Israel, which since its creation as an independent state in 1948 had enjoyed solid U.S. support.

After absorbing the initial Arab assault, Israeli forces counterattacked, driving into Syria and crossing the Suez Canal to encircle an Egyptian army. With Israel winning the war decisively on both fronts, the UNITED NATIONS Security Council on October 25 approved a cease-fire resolution. Accepting the U.N. action, the Israelis and Egyptians stopped fighting. The Syrians refused to observe the cease-fire unless and until the Israelis withdrew from the territories occupied since 1967. The October 25 resolution established a U.N. peacekeeping force to police the Egyptian-Israeli truce. This U.N. Emergency Force (UNEF), comprising troops from several smaller member nations, took up positions between the Israeli and Egyptian armies in the Sinai and along the Suez. In talks with the Soviet leadership in Moscow, Kissinger had worked out the Security Council cease-fire resolution, implementation of which was assured only after President RICHARD M. NIXON placed U.S. armed forces worldwide on increased alert to deter unilateral Soviet military action in the Middle East to relieve the surrounded Egyptian army.

With the cease-fire in effect, Kissinger travelled to the USSR, Israel, and throughout the Arab world in an attempt to initiate a Mideast peace process, in accordance with Security Council Resolution 338. Adopted on October 22, 1973, the resolution called for an immediate start of negotiations among the parties to the Arab-Israeli conflict aimed at achieving a permanent peace in the Middle East. The secretary sought Egyptian-Israeli and Syrian-Israeli accords on the disengagement of armed forces as stepping stones toward a compre-

hensive and durable regional peace settlement. On November 11, 1973, Egypt and Israel signed the so-called six-part agreement devised to strengthen the cease-fire. Under the accord, which had been drawn up by Kissinger and Egyptian President Anwar Sadat during talks in Cairo on November 7, both sides agreed to open discussions immediately on the U.N.-supervised disengagement of their armies along the Suez and in the Sinai. Kissinger and Sadat also negotiated a restoration of full U.S.-Egyptian diplomatic relations, broken in 1967 at the time of the Six-Day War. The ensuing Egyptian-Israeli talks on the disposition of military forces on either side of the cease-fire line reached an impasse and were broken off at the end of November.

In fulfillment of an agreement reached at the December 1973 GENEVA CONFERENCE ON THE MIDDLE EAST, the first ever Arab-Israeli peace parley, Israel and Egypt resumed their negotiations with Kissinger serving as intermediary. He flew back and forth repeatedly between Aswan (where Sadat was spending part of the winter) and Jerusalem for separate meetings with Egyptian and Israeli officials. His efforts led to the signing on January 18, 1974, of an Egyptian-Israeli disengagement agreement. The accord provided for the withdrawal of all Israeli forces from west of the Suez Canal and established a narrow Egyptian zone in the Sinai. It created a slim U.N. buffer zone between the Egyptian and Israeli armies patrolled by UNEF troops. Both countries consented to U.S. aerial surveillance over the disengagement area to ensure compliance. The process of troop separation and withdrawal was completed, as scheduled, within 40 days.

There was continued fighting in the Golan Heights area in the first part of 1974 as Kissinger moved to mediate between the Israelis and Syrians. Israel balked at entering into talks until Syria both provided a list of Israeli prisoners of war (POWs) and allowed the International Red Cross (IRC) to visit them. The Syrians initially would meet neither Israeli demand. During a stopover in Damascus at the end of February, Kissinger secured from Syrian President Hafez Assad a list of Israeli POWs and assurances the IRC would be free to visit the captives beginning March 1. Assad's actions satisfied Israeli conditions for entering discussions with Syria and U.S.-brokered negotiations promptly got underway. Kissinger engaged in shuttle diplomacy through April and May, jetting between Damascus and Jerusalem numerous times. His labors culminated on May 31, 1974, when Israel and Syria signed a troop disengagement agreement that effected a cease-fire between their forces and left the Israelis in control of virtually all of the Golan Heights. The accord provided for Israeli withdrawal from Syrian territory occupied during the Yom Kippur War and restoration to Syria of a small strip of the Golan Heights. It set up a U.N. buffer zone, policed by a newly created peacekeeping force called the U.N. Disengagement Observer Force (UNDOF). Israel and Syria agreed to return all POWs within 24 hours and to complete the pullback of armed forces within 20 days.

Through Kissinger's continued shuttle diplomacy, a second disengagement accord, the so-called Interim Agreement, was formally concluded between Israel and Egypt on September 1, 1975. The pact, which elaborated on the January 1974 agreement, was intended to reduce the likelihood of renewed Egyptian-Israeli hostilities. It required an Israeli withdrawal in the Sinai to the eastern end of the key Gidi and Mitla Passes. The Israeli-vacated territory was included in an expanded U.N. buffer zone. Israel still retained control of almost 90 percent of the Sinai Peninsula. Under the agreement, the Israelis consented to return to the Egyptians the Abu Rudeis oil fields along the Gulf of Suez. The Egyptians promised not to blockade the Gulf of Aqaba and agreed to allow nonmilitary Israeli cargo to pass through the Suez Canal, opening the waterway to the Jewish state for the first time since 1956. Both sides pledged not to resort to use of force for three years and declared their determination to reach a final peace settlement through negotiations.

The Interim Agreement also set forth a plan for U.S. supervision of an early-warning surveillance system in the Sinai. The proposal called for deployment of two electronic early-warning observation stations operated separately by Egypt and Israel; and three other stations in the Gidi and Mitla passes manned by up to 200 American civilians. The U.S. observers were to monitor Egyptian and Israeli military activity in the vicinity of the U.N. buffer zone and to report to the UNEF any detected movement of Egyptian or Israeli armed forces into the Gidi and Mitla passes. The American personnel also were delegated responsibility for verifying that the Israeli and Egyptian stations were being used only for surveillance. Congress initially raised strong objections to the proposal to involve Americans directly in the volatile Middle East, but in the end authorized President GERALD R. FORD to send U.S. civilian volunteers for the early-warning surveillance mission.

Accompanying the Interim Agreement was a memorandum of understanding between the United States and Israel. It contained specific U.S. pledges of aid to the Jewish state including arms shipments, economic support, and assistance in meeting Israel's oil requirements. The memorandum also affirmed unequivocal U.S. political commitment to Israel in the event of direct Soviet military involvement in the Middle East. The United States, moreover, pledged neither to recognize nor negotiate with the Palestine Liberation Organization (PLO) so long as it refused to recognize Israel's right to exist.

See also CAMP DAVID ACCORDS.

SIBERIAN INTERVENTION (1918–1920) Allied military intervention in Russia during and after WORLD WAR I. After seizing power in November 1917 during the Russian Revolution, Nikolai Lenin's Bolshevik regime withdrew Russia from the world war, concluding the separate Brest-Litovsk Treaty with Germany in March 1918, and moved to consolidate its hold amid the civil war sweeping the giant nation. In August 1918 a small British-French-American military expedition occupied the northern Russian cities of Murmansk and Archangel to keep Allied war materials from falling into German hands. The same month some 8000 American troops joined a largely Japanese Allied force at Vladivostok in Russian Siberia. President WOODROW WILSON sent the U.S. soldiers to prevent Japanese inroads in Siberia as well as to aid in the rescue of approximately 100,000 Czech prisoners of war escaped from Russia. The Allies harbored hopes of a White Russian victory over the Bolsheviks in the Russian civil war that would bring Russia back into the fight against Germany. Wilson, however, opposed any Allied intervention in Russian internal affairs and the U.S. forces in Siberia limited their operations to guarding the Trans-Siberian Railway and evacuating the Czechs. After the end of the world war in November 1918, Wilson resisted British and French pressures for large-scale intervention against the Bolsheviks and the U.S. troops under General William S. Graves carefully avoided supporting the White Russian government in Siberia under Admiral Alexander Kolchak. American forces were withdrawn from northern Russia in August 1919 and, following the final rescue of the Czechs, from Siberia in April 1920. Japan followed in 1922 as the Bolshevik armies exerted increasing control over Siberia.

SIMPSON-RODINO ACT See **IMMIGRATION REFORM AND CONTROL ACT**.

SINAI PEACEKEEPING FORCE Multinational peacekeeping contingent stationed since 1982 in the Sinai Peninsula. Israel captured the Sinai from Egypt in the June 1967 Six-Day War. The EGYPTIAN-ISRAELI PEACE TREATY, concluded March 26, 1979, in fulfillment of the U.S.-mediated CAMP DAVID ACCORDS (1978), provided for Israel to return the peninsula to Egypt in stages over a three-year period. The peace pact called for the UNITED NATIONS Emergency Force (UNEF) to observe the phased Israeli pullout. The peacekeeping unit had been formed after the YOM KIPPUR WAR (1973) to enforce the Egyptian-Israeli cease-fire and patrol a U.N. buffer zone in the Sinai. A new plan for overseeing the Israeli withdrawal had to be devised after the Soviet Union in July 1979 vetoed an extension of UNEF's mandate. Moscow's action reflected the strong opposition among Soviet-allied states in the Arab world to the Camp David peace process. A Security Council proposal for UNEF's replacement by the U.N. Truce Supervisory Organization (UNTSO) was rejected by Israel, which maintained the small unarmed group was inadequate for the task.

With UNEF almost withdrawn and negotiations within the United Nations at an impasse, the United States, Egypt, and Is-

rael on September 19 reached a separate agreement on monitoring the Sinai transfer. Under the accord, an observer team of 200 U.S. civilian technicians already in the Sinai was given responsibility for overseeing the Israeli withdrawal and the disposition of Egyptian and Israeli forces during the transition. The U.S. field mission had been operating an early-warning surveillance system between Egyptian and Israeli lines in the Sinai since 1975 under terms of the so-called Interim Agreement, a second Egyptian-Israeli troop disengagement accord reached through the SHUTTLE DIPLOMACY of U.S. Secretary of State HENRY A. KISSINGER. The U.S. observer team, which had been scheduled for disbandment in early 1980, had its term extended and functions expanded in view of its new mission.

The Security Council remained deadlocked over a U.N. role in the Sinai. The United States consequently in 1981 organized a multinational peacekeeping force to patrol the peninsula and the Egyptian-Israeli border once Israel had completed its withdrawal in April 1982. U.S. allies Canada, Great Britain, France, the Netherlands, Italy, Australia, and New Zealand agreed to participate in the peacekeeping operation. In December 1981 the U.S. Congress authorized the president to contribute up to 1200 American troops to the 3000-strong Sinai force. The first contingent of U.S. soldiers arrived in the Sinai in March 1982. The peacekeeping force, officially the Multinational Force and Observers, assumed its mission as scheduled in April, replacing the U.S. civilian observer group that had overseen the Israeli withdrawal.

SIOUX WARS Series of conflicts spanning almost 40 years between U.S. forces and the Sioux tribes along the Great Plains. America's vast territorial expansion in the 1840s was followed by the large-scale westward movement of settlers and prospectors across Indian lands to California and Oregon. The Sioux opposed the white migration over the Plains and fought the U.S. efforts after 1850 to obtain their territories and isolate them on reservations.

War followed the Sioux ambush of a small American military force in the 1854 Grattan Massacre in Wyoming. A U.S. retaliatory expedition in 1855 led to a peace settlement and a period of relative calm. Fighting erupted again in 1862 in Minnesota and North Dakota. Sioux opposition to the influx of white settlers in the area was crushed by 1864. Sioux assaults on American emigrant traffic on the Bozeman Trail in Wyoming and Montana escalated after 1865 and ignited Red Cloud's War, named for the Ogala Sioux Chief. In 1867 Congress established the INDIAN PEACE COMMISSION to negotiate an end to the costly conflict. Peace came the next year when Red Cloud signed the Treaty of Fort Laramie, in which the Sioux agreed to move to designated reservations by 1876 and the United States pledged to abandon its Bozeman Trail forts.

The Fort Laramie agreement also guaranteed that the United States would respect the sacred position the Black Hills in South Dakota held for the Sioux Indians. When gold prospectors rushed into the area after 1874, the Sioux raided the trespassers and finally refused to move to the reservations by 1876, sparking the Black Hills War. Troops under General George A. Custer were annihilated at the Battle of Little Big Horn in June 1876 by Sioux and Cheyenne forces under chiefs Sitting Bull and Crazy Horse. Sioux resistance folded in 1877 under the pressure of the military campaign by U.S. reinforcements. When the U.S. military intervened to suppress a violent religious fervor that was sweeping the reservations, inspired by the prediction of a coming Indian saviour, the Sioux rebelled in a final uprising. Indian surrender in this 1890 Messiah War followed the U.S. Army massacre of several hundred Sioux at the Battle of Wounded Knee.

See also MAP 1.

SIX-NATION CONFERENCE ON GERMANY (1948) Meeting of Western nations in London on the future status of Germany. In 1945, following its defeat in WORLD WAR II, Germany was divided into U.S., British, French, and Soviet occupation zones. The four occupying powers established an ALLIED CONTROL COUNCIL to coordinate the administration of their areas. At the POTSDAM CONFERENCE (1945), the Allies formed a four-power COUNCIL OF FOREIGN MINISTERS to negotiate the final postwar shape of Germany. The council's ensuing deliberations soon revealed fundamental East-West differences over the disposition of Germany and Eastern Europe. East-West talks on Germany reached an impasse by the end of 1947 amid mounting COLD WAR confrontation over the Soviet Union's imposition of Communist regimes in Eastern European countries. Western proposals for a democratic German state were unacceptable to the Soviet Union, while the West rejected Soviet hegemony over Eastern Europe.

The United States, Great Britain, and France met in London from February 23 to March 5 and again from April 20 to June 2, 1948, to discuss plans for merging their occupation zones into a single German political entity. The inclusion at the conference of representatives from Belgium, the Netherlands, and Luxembourg signaled the emergence of a Western political alliance. Delegates of the six nations reached agreement on uniting the French zone with the previously joined U.S. and British zones (known as BIZONIA) and on forming a federal German government to administer the newly merged Western zone. The six-nation conference also laid plans for the European Coal and Steel Community. The Soviet Union vehemently denounced the conference as a violation of four-power control over Germany and withdrew from the Allied Control Council. The Federal Republic of Germany, or West Germany, was established in the Western zone in May 1949 with its capital at Bonn. The following October the Soviets formed the Communist German Democratic Republic, or East Germany, in the Eastern zone. In May 1952 delegates from the United States, Great Britain, France, and West Germany, meeting in the West German capital, signed the BONN CONVENTIONS providing for broad West German sovereignty. West Germany gained full sovereignty under the 1954 PARIS AGREEMENTS.

See also FINAL SETTLEMENT WITH RESPECT TO GERMANY TREATY.

SLBM See **SUBMARINE-LAUNCHED BALLISTIC MISSILE.**

SLIDELL, JOHN (1793–1871) Politician, diplomat, and Confederate envoy. Born in New York City, he graduated from Columbia College in 1810. After a failed trade venture he moved in 1819 to New Orleans, where he became a lawyer and served from 1829 to 1833 as federal district attorney. He mounted several unsuccessful races for Congress before winning a seat in the U.S. House of Representatives in 1843 as a Democrat from Louisiana. In 1845 President JAMES K. POLK sent him as a personal emissary to Mexico with instructions to resolve the Texas boundary dispute and purchase New Mexico and California. A hostile Mexican government rebuffed Slidell, officially refusing to receive him. Failure of the SLIDELL MISSION hastened the outbreak of the MEXICAN WAR in 1846.

He served from 1853 to 1861 in the U.S. Senate, where he supported an annexationist U.S. policy toward Cuba and favored giving the president limited power to suspend American neutrality laws in order to promote FILIBUSTERING expeditions in Latin America. Early in the Civil War, Slidell was selected to represent the Confederacy as its agent in France. Captured enroute to Europe and imprisoned by the Union in the celebrated TRENT AFFAIR (1861), he eventually was released and made it to Paris, where he failed to secure French emperor Napoleon III's diplomatic recognition of the South. Slidell remained in Europe following the war. He died in Great Britain in 1871.

SLIDELL MISSION (1845–1846) Abortive diplomatic mission of Louisiana political figure JOHN SLIDELL to resolve the Texas-Mexico boundary controversy and acquire Mexican territory. Following the TEXAN REVOLUTION, the Republic of Texas claimed the Rio Grande as its southern and western boundary with Mexico. The United States annexed Texas and incorporated it in the Union in 1845, accepting the border claim of its newest addition. Mexico, embittered by the loss of Texas, refused to recognize any boundary with the new American state. Mexican rejection of U.S. territorial claims to the Rio Grande placed the neighboring countries on a course for hostile confrontation. President JAMES K. POLK in July 1845 sent several thousand federal troops into southern Texas to occupy the contested region. He then considered a diplomatic overture to resolve the Texas-Mexico boundary question and, at the same time, to satisfy his expansionist designs on other Mexican territory.

Polk in November 1845 dispatched Slidell, a New Orleans lawyer and Democratic member of the U.S. House of Representatives, on a special mission to Mexico City with full diplomatic powers to settle the boundary dispute and negotiate U.S. purchase of New Mexico and California. Slidell was also instructed to seek resolution of the outstanding claims of American citizens against the Mexican government for property losses incurred during Mexico's struggle for independence from Spain. Polk suggested that Mexico could satisfy the claims by ceding California and New Mexico to the United States. Before sending Slidell, Polk had received formal assurances from Mexico that it was prepared to resume diplomatic relations suspended after the TEXAS ANNEXATION and that it would receive an American envoy for talks on U.S.-Mexican differences. News of Slidell's mission aroused fierce opposition within Mexico to the scheduled negotiations. Under great internal political pressure not to deal with America, the government of President Jose J. Herrara rebuffed Slidell when he arrived in December, refusing any official contacts with Polk's envoy. After Herrara fell from power in the last days of December, Slidell was instructed by Polk to approach the successor Mexican government. He did and again was rejected. A frustrated Slidell finally withdrew from Mexico in March 1846. His failed diplomatic trek presaged the start of the MEXICAN WAR.

SMITH ACT See **ALIEN REGISTRATION ACT**.

SMITH, ROBERT (1757–1842) Secretary of the Navy, secretary of state. Born in Pennsylvania, Smith graduated from the College of New Jersey (now Princeton) in 1781. He served briefly during the AMERICAN REVOLUTION as a private with the Continental Army. After studying law, he was admitted to the Maryland bar and built a large admiralty practice in Baltimore. From 1793 to 1800 he was a member of the Maryland state legislature. A loyal Democratic-Republican, he was named secretary of the navy by President THOMAS JEFFERSON in 1801. At the beginning of Jefferson's second term in 1805, Smith was nominated and confirmed as attorney general. But when Jefferson's replacement choice to head the Navy Department fell through, Smith continued to act concurrently as Navy secretary. After several months, he gave up the attorney-generalship and continued as Navy chief until 1809.

In his tenure he oversaw U.S. warships sent to the Mediterranean to fight the TRIPOLITAN WAR (1801–1805), maintaining the vigorous naval blockade of Tripoli that ended the conflict over assaults by Barbary pirates on American commercial shipping. Though opposed to Jefferson's embargo against the British and French during the Napoleonic Wars (1803–1815), Smith sought dutifully to enforce it. He was Jefferson's intermediary in fruitless diplomatic discussions with the British Foreign Office over British IMPRESSMENT of American seamen.

With the inauguration of JAMES MADISON as president in March 1809, Smith became secretary of state. He clashed with Madison over the policy to be pursued to protect U.S. interests threatened by the Anglo-French war. Smith generally opposed the president's plans for commercial restrictions against the European belligerents. The secretary of state's major diplomatic undertaking was negotiation of the ERSKINE AGREEMENT (1809), the rejection of which by the British government dealt a further blow to Anglo-American relations. He became embroiled in an acrimonious political battle with Treasury Secretary ALBERT GALLATIN, who had been a vocal critic of Smith's performance as Navy secretary. When Gallatin tendered his resignation in March 1811, Madison refused to accept it. The president then summoned Smith, criticized him for inefficiency and causing discord within the administration, and requested his resignation. Smith left the cabinet in April and returned to private life in Baltimore, where he died in 1842.

SMITH, WALTER BEDELL (1895–1961) Army and intelligence officer, ambassador, and state department official. After service in the National Guard in his native Indiana, Smith received an Army commission in 1917 and saw action in WORLD WAR I. He continued on a military career, eventually rising to the rank of lieutenant general and serving as chief of staff during WORLD WAR II to General DWIGHT D. EISENHOWER. In this position he largely was responsible for planning and coordinating the North Africa, Sicily, and Normandy invasions. In 1946 President HARRY S. TRUMAN appointed him ambassador to the Soviet Union. American envoy to the Kremlin at the outset of the COLD WAR, he was involved in U.S.-Soviet confrontation over the IRAN CRISIS (1946) and BERLIN AIRLIFT (1948–1949) and took part in the 1947 MOSCOW CONFERENCE.

Smith returned to the United States as commander of the 1st Army in 1949. His memoir *My Three Years in Moscow* (1950) included his assessment of the threat posed by the Soviet Union and the need to maintain a strong national defense. In 1950 Truman chose the tough-minded, forceful administrator to head the recently formed CENTRAL INTELLIGENCE AGENCY (CIA). Smith presided over the rapid growth in the agency during the KOREAN WAR. He undertook a major reorganization, bringing the quasi-independent OFFICE OF POLICY COORDINATION that was responsible for covert operations under CIA control, while establishing administration, intelligence, and plans divisions that set the agency's basic structure for the next 20 years. In February 1953 President Eisenhower named Smith under secretary of state. He led the U.S. delegation to the GENEVA CONFERENCE (1954) on Indochina before retiring from government service in October 1954.

SMITH-MUNDT ACT See **UNITED STATES INFORMATION AGENCY**.

SMITHSONIAN AGREEMENT See **INTERNATIONAL MONETARY FUND**.

SMOOT-HAWLEY TARIFF (1930) Federal act that imposed record duties on items imported into the United States. Named for co-sponsors Senator Reed Smoot (R-UT) and Congressman Willis C. Hawley (R-OR), the legislation was signed by President HERBERT C. HOOVER on June 17, 1930. Reflecting American protectionist sentiment in the period following WORLD WAR I, the act raised the already steep tariffs of the FORDNEY-MCCUMBER TARIFF (1922) to the highest levels in U.S. history. By 1932 U.S. duties on imported goods averaged nearly 60 percent. Other nations retaliated with similar measures. The resulting decrease in international trade aggravated the worldwide economic depression of the 1930s. The Smoot-Hawley Act was the last time U.S. tariffs were set by the Congress. In an effort to revitalize the economy, the administration of President FRANKLIN D. ROOSEVELT, led by free trade advocate Secretary of State CORDELL HULL, proposed that Congress delegate to the president some of its constitutional power to regulate foreign commerce. This was accomplished by the TRADE AGREEMENTS ACT of 1934, which authorized the president to negotiate tariff-reducing trade agreements with other nations.

See also GENERAL AGREEMENT ON TARIFFS AND TRADE, PROTECTIONISM.

SNOW, EDGAR PARKS (1905–1972) American journalist and author who was an authority on Communist China. Originally from Kansas City, Missouri, he attended the University of Missouri before going East to the Columbia School of Journalism, from which he graduated in 1927. By 1928 the freelancing Snow had made his way to China, where he remained for 12 years, working as a newspaper correspondent and magazine writer for sundry American and British publications. He achieved renown when, in 1936, he became the first Westerner to search out and report on the little-known Chinese Communists in their remote headquarters in Yenan province. Snow interviewed revolutionary leaders Mao Tse-tung and Chou En-lai. He reported that the insurgents enjoyed great popular support in the Chinese countryside, were highly disciplined and politically devoted, and represented a strong nationalist and anti-Japanese force. The American journalist predicted an eventual Communist Chinese triumph over Chiang Kai-shek's ineffectual Nationalist government. Snow's firsthand observations of Communist programs and actions became the basis of his classic book *Red Star Over China* (1937).

From the time of the final Communist victory in 1949 until the first steps were taken toward normalization of U.S.-Chinese relations in the early 1970s, Snow was among a handful of Americans who enjoyed intermittent access to mainland China. His books *The Other Side of the River: Red China Today* (1962) and *The Long Revolution* (1972) were based on impressions gathered during return visits to

the country in 1960, 1965, and 1970. Long sympathetic toward the Chinese Revolution, Snow remained friendly with Mao and Chou and thus was able to gain exclusive interviews with the two leaders. Critics accused Snow of being an apologist or even propagandist for the Chinese Communist regime. He denied the allegations, insisting he was not a Communist but an honest observer of events on the mainland. He died in 1972 in Switzerland, where he had resided since 1959.

SON TAY RAID (1970) Secret attempt to rescue U.S. prisoners of war (POWs) during the VIETNAM WAR. After months of special training, a volunteer Army commando force under Colonel Arthur D. (Bull) Simons on November 21, 1970, flew roughly 400 miles in Air Force helicopters to assault the Son Tay prison compound 20 miles northwest of Hanoi. The daring nighttime foray into North Vietnam found the prison camp recently abandoned. The American POWs held there had been relocated. After a brief fire-fight with North Vietnamese soldiers in the area, the raiders returned to their base in Thailand without any losses. The unsuccessful raid, reported by Secretary of Defense MELVIN R. LAIRD on November 24, underscored the importance attached to the recovery by America of its POWs.

SONNENFELDT DOCTRINE (1975) Name coined in the American media for comments made by U.S. State Department Counselor Helmut Sonnenfeldt in December 1975 in London regarding the political outlook for Eastern Europe. Sonnenfeldt asserted that the USSR-Eastern Europe relationship was unnatural and unstable because it rested overwhelmingly upon sheer Soviet military power. He observed that any drive by the Eastern European states for autonomy from Moscow could lead to World War III. The State Department official contended it was in the long-term interests of the United States to wield its influence in the Soviet bloc to avoid an explosive confrontation there. He called for a U.S. policy of responding to Eastern Europe's aspiration for greater independence within the context of Soviet geopolitical influence and armed might. Sonnenfeldt warned overzealous U.S. encouragement of East European liberalization might trigger developments leading to a Soviet crackdown and a setback for the course of autonomy in the region. Conservative voices in American politics and the press criticized the so-called Sonnenfeldt Doctrine, which carried no official weight, as a formula for abandoning Eastern Europe and accepting Soviet domination behind the IRON CURTAIN.

SOUERS, SIDNEY WILLIAM (1892–1973) Naval and intelligence officer who held senior national security positions in the Truman administration. Souers graduated from Miami University in his native Ohio in 1914 and launched a successful business career. He received a commission as a lieutenant commander in the U.S. Naval Reserve in 1929. Volunteering for active duty in July 1940, he served in various intelligence positions during WORLD WAR II. He was promoted to admiral in 1943 and became deputy chief of naval intelligence in 1945.

Souers took part in the planning for a permanent postwar national intelligence agency. In January 1946 he accepted appointment as the first director of central intelligence (DCI) and head of the newly formed CENTRAL INTELLIGENCE GROUP with the understanding he would shortly return to civilian life. Replaced as DCI by General HOYT S. VANDENBERG in June 1946, he was called back to Washington by President HARRY S. TRUMAN in May 1947 to establish an intelligence office for the Atomic Energy Commission. In September 1947 Souers became the first executive secretary of the new NATIONAL SECURITY COUNCIL (NSC). In 1949 he began the tradition of the secretary, later redesignated the national security advisor, conducting the daily briefing for the president on national security developments. He took part in the major review of U.S. foreign and defense policy that culminated in NSC-68 (1950), an NSC report that identified the Soviet Union as the overriding threat to the nation's security. Souers again returned to private life in January 1950.

SOULE, PIERRE (1801–1870) Controversial diplomat and political leader. Born and educated in France, the young lawyer and republican activist was forced into exile in 1825 for political agitation against the Bourbon monarchy. Emigrating the same year to the United States, he settled in New Orleans, where he prospered as a lawyer, orator, and financier and became active in Democratic Party politics. He won election to the Louisiana state senate in 1846 and the U.S. Senate in 1848. In Washington, Soule succeeded South Carolina's JOHN C. CALHOUN as standard-bearer of the states' rights Southern Democrats and earned distinction as an ardent pro-slavery Southern expansionist. He also became a leader of YOUNG AMERICA, the nationalist movement which emerged after the MEXICAN WAR (1846–1848). Its adherents both embraced the idea of America's MANIFEST DESTINY and advocated monarchy's replacement in Europe by republican government.

Soule left the Senate in April 1853 to accept appointment by President FRANKLIN PIERCE as U.S. minister to Spain. The Louisianan's outspoken support for U.S. annexation of the Spanish colony of Cuba meshed with the Pierce administration's prime foreign policy objective of acquiring the island. Soule's turmoil-filled tenure in Madrid was marked by his sponsorship of European republican revolutionaries and by diplomatic missteps committed in his zealous quest for Cuba. During the BLACK WARRIOR AFFAIR (1854), he exceeded instructions from Secretary of State WILLIAM L. MARCY by delivering American demands to the Spanish government as an aggressive ultimatum. He thereby sought unsuccessfully to fan the diplomatic dispute into a more serious conflict that would offer the United States a pretext for seizing Cuba.

At Marcy's direction, Soule met with JAMES BUCHANAN and John Y. Mason, U.S. ministers to Great Britain and France, in Ostend, Belgium, in October 1854 to confer on ways to advance Pierce administration efforts at obtaining Cuba. Under Soule's leadership, the three American diplomats drafted the OSTEND MANIFESTO (1854), which urged U.S. annexation of the island by force should Spain balk at selling its colony. Public disclosure of their recommendation provoked a domestic political uproar. After Marcy repudiated the Ostend Manifesto and Pierce abandoned plans for Cuba's acquisition, Soule resigned as minister to Spain in December 1854. Returning to New Orleans and private law practice, in 1857 he successfully defended WILLIAM WALKER, the adventurer notorious for FILIBUSTERING expeditions to Nicaragua, against a charge of violating U.S. neutrality laws. During the Civil War, Soule served as a

Confederate official and, though never in the field, as a brigadier general.

SOUTH KOREA MUTUAL DEFENSE TREATY (1953) Bilateral agreement committing the United States to the defense of South Korea. During the KOREAN WAR (1950–1953), U.S. military forces constituted the major part of the UNITED NATIONS command fighting to repel the Communist North Korean invasion of South Korea. While the United States supported the unification of Korea under a single non-Communist government, the entry of Communist China into the war in November 1950 on the side of North Korea had forced the Truman administration to accept the more limited objective of restoring South Korea's border at the 38TH PARALLEL. After almost two years of difficult negotiations, an armistice agreement on July 27, 1953, brought an end to the hostilties, fixing the demarcation line between the two Koreas roughly where it had been at the outset of the conflict. The South Korean government, bitterly opposed to any agreement that left Korea divided or allowed Chinese troops to remain in the North, reluctantly agreed to the armistice when guaranteed a U.S. mutual defense pact and long-term U.S. economic and military aid. The U.S.-South Korean defense treaty, signed in Seoul on August 8, 1953, by South Korean President Syngman Rhee and U.S. Secretary of State JOHN FOSTER DULLES bound the two nations to respond jointly to external armed attack and allowed the continued presence of U.S. military forces in South Korea. The pact, closely paralleling the PHILIPPINE MUTUAL DEFENSE TREATY (1951) and ANZUS TREATY (1951), was viewed by the United States as part of an interconnected set of agreements providing for a comprehensive regional security system in the western Pacific. The treaty was ratified by the Senate on January 26, 1954, and has served since as the basic framework for the continued U.S. military commitment to the defense of South Korea.

SOUTHEAST ASIA COLLECTIVE DEFENSE TREATY See **SOUTHEAST ASIA TREATY ORGANIZATION**.

SOUTHEAST ASIA TREATY ORGANIZATION (SEATO) COLLECTIVE SECURITY arrangement formed at the 1954 Manila Conference by the United States and seven other nations. Concerned over Communist China and its support of Communist insurgencies in Indochina, the Eisenhower administration since early in 1954 had sought to establish a regional security alliance as a mechanism for achieving the CONTAINMENT of communism in Asia. Action on an alliance had been deferred, however, by Great Britain and France, both of which preferred to await the results of the impending international GENEVA CONFERENCE on Indochina. The Geneva parley, which ended in July 1954, granted Cambodia, Laos, and Vietnam their independence; and arranged a temporary division of Vietnam that left the Communist Viet Minh in control of the northern half. Intent on preventing further Communist advances in the region, representatives of the three Western powers, Pakistan, Thailand, the Philippines, Australia, and New Zealand met in Manila and on September 8, 1954, concluded the Southeast Asia Collective Defense Treaty.

Also known as the Manila Pact, the agreement pledged joint action in the event of an attack on any member nation. The treaty provided for collective defense against either external aggression or foreign-sponsored subversion. In an attached statement, the United States made clear that its military involvement in the alliance applied only to countering Communist aggression. In the case of other hostilities, America committed only to consultations with its allies. A protocol to the agreement extended its protections to Cambodia, Laos, and South Vietnam, each of which had been barred at the Geneva Conference from entering military alliances. Reflecting their uncertain relationship to mainland China, British colony Hong Kong and Nationalist Chinese Taiwan were not included under the pact's security arrangements. India, Burma, and Indonesia elected not to participate. At the suggestion of Philippine President Ramon Magsaysay, the eight treaty members also signed a Pacific Charter, a statement of their common commitment to the independence, self-government, and economic development of Asian nations.

The treaty called for a council to consult on military matters. This became the Southeast Asia Treaty Organization (SEATO), headquartered in Bangkok, Thailand. Unlike NATO, its Atlantic counterpart, SEATO had no joint forces and was essentially a coordinating body. While the alliance did not become militarily involved in the VIETNAM WAR, the United States cited its SEATO commitments in the TONKIN GULF RESOLUTION (1964) authorizing use of American armed force to defend South Vietnam from Communist aggression. By the late 1960s SEATO's effectiveness had been undercut by increasing foreign policy differences among its members. Pakistan formally withdrew in 1973. Viewed as no longer necessary following the Vietnam War and the lessening of tensions that accompanied the resumption of U.S.-Chinese relations, the organization was dissolved in 1977.

SPACE RACE U.S.-Soviet competition in space. The Space Race was inaugurated with the Soviet Union's launch of Sputnik, mankind's first earth-orbiting satellite, in 1957. The Soviet feat, heralded by Moscow as proof of the Communist system's superior capacity for technological achievement, stunned the United States and transformed space into a new front in the East-West COLD WAR. Space technology had clear military applications, namely the use of rockets for INTERCONTINENTAL BALLISTIC MISSILES, and thus the race for supremacy in space involved national security as well as prestige. Congress responded to Sputnik, and the domestic political fallout it produced, by creating the NATIONAL AERONAUTICS AND SPACE ADMINISTRATION and launching a concerted civilian space program. The Space Race reached its peak in the 1960s with the superpower competition, captured by the United States in 1969 with its successful Apollo 11 lunar mission, to land a man on the moon. The U.S.-Soviet DETENTE of the early 1970s resulted in the joint APOLLO-SOYUZ (1975) manned space venture. U.S.-Soviet space coordination, derailed by the strained superpower relations of the early 1980s, resumed with the 1987 signing of an agreement for cooperation in the exploration and use of outer space.

SPACE STATION FREEDOM Proposed Earth-orbiting space station under development by the NATIONAL AERONAUTICS AND SPACE ADMINISTRATION (NASA). The multi-billion dollar space platform, named Freedom, is the projected centerpiece of America's program for manned exploration of the solar system. Planning for the station began in 1984 after President RONALD W. REAGAN called on NASA to build the nation's first permanently manned space outpost "within the decade." The station was envisioned as an orbiting laboratory for scientific research and experimentation and as a base from which astronauts would venture to the Moon, Mars, or other planets within the solar system. Construction will require a series of space shuttle flights to carry Freedom's component pieces into orbit. Assembly is scheduled for completion by 1999 at the earliest. As planned the station would orbit about 250 miles above the earth and is supposed to last 30 years. It is one of the largest international cooperative scientific efforts ever mounted. Japan, Canada, and the European Space Agency (ESA) are major foreign partners brought into the project by the United States through agreements negotiated by NASA and the State Department. The foreign participants, who are providing personnel and equipment and sharing the cost, have made Space Station Freedom a major focus of their space planning into the 21st century.

Through the end of the 1980s the program's schedule repeatedly was delayed by increases in Freedom's anticipated cost and complexity. The project was dealt a setback in March 1990 when federal experts announced they had found a major flaw in the space station design. NASA investigators had concluded that the space platform's vast array of parts would begin to fail well before assembly was completed, forcing an elaborate and costly program of repairs and preventive maintenance. Exposure of the flawed design brought a congressional directive to NASA in October 1990 to make Freedom simpler, cheaper, and safer. In March 1991 the agency unveiled a revised space station design. NASA contended the new plan, by reducing the crew size from eight to four, scaling back the number of shuttle flights needed for assembly, and minimizing maintenance, would cut the station's overall cost from earlier estimates of $38 billion to $30 billion through 1999. Recurring problems with the space station's planning have eroded its once-solid political support in Congress, where in June 1991 the House Appropriations Committee voted to cut virtually all funding for the project. The funding survived intact after President GEORGE BUSH lobbied lawmakers, telling them that shelving Space Station Freedom would have dire economic and diplomatic consequences. His message was echoed by an alarmed Japan, Canada, and the ESA, whose top officials warned that U.S. abandonment of the project would jeopardize future international scientific ventures.

SPANISH-AMERICAN WAR (1898) Brief war with Spain from which the victorious United States emerged as a world power with far-flung colonial possessions. The armed conflict grew out of U.S. determination to end Spain's colonial hold on Cuba. American popular opinion had sympathized with Cuban rebels during their unsuccessful decade-long struggle for independence from Spanish rule, known as the Ten Years' War (1868–1878). But President ULYSSES S. GRANT had resisted domestic political pressure to intervene on the insurrectionists' behalf, not wanting to embroil the United States in a major diplomatic crisis with Spain.

Economic hardship caused by a depression in Cuba's sugar market, added to latent discontent with Spanish colonial authority, sparked a new and bloody insurrection in February 1895. The renewal of the Cuban fight for independence rekindled American sympathy for the rebels. Cuban refugees established revolutionary committees, or juntas, in America that raised money, procured munitions, organized FILIBUSTERING expeditions, and spread anti-Spanish propaganda. In Cuba the rebels waged war on property, plundering and destroying Spanish loyalist holdings and burning sugar plantations, many of them American-owned, in a drive to render the island virtually worthless to Spain. Madrid charged Washington with failure to uphold its policy of neutrality since the money and arms sustaining the insurrection came mainly from the United States. The U.S. government labored to enforce its neutrality laws, ordering Navy patrols of the American coastline to interdict smugglers and gunrunners bound for Cuba.

When its initial more restrained approach failed to suppress the insurrection, the Spanish government sent ruthless General Valeriano Weyler to Cuba to crush the rebels. To counter the guerrilla insurgency and control the rural populace, Weyler implemented a harsh policy of herding Cubans into concentration camps, where many died from malnutrition and disease owing to primitive sanitation and woefully inadequate food, shelter, and medical care. The Spanish army waged its own assault on property, destroying villages and farms. News of the human misery in the concentration camps evoked outrage among Americans. The sensationalist American "yellow press" championed the rebels' cause. Joseph Pulitzer's *New York World* and WILLIAM RANDOLPH HEARST's, *New York Journal*, locked in a circulation war, published sensational accounts of Spanish atrocities against the insurgents while ignoring the brutal excesses of the rebels. Both papers editorialized for U.S. intervention on humanitarian grounds to stop the war in Cuba and ensure Spain's expulsion from the island. Keying on the squalid concentration camps, Hearst's *Journal* pinned the sobriquet "Butcher" on Spanish General Weyler.

The influential yellow press fomented American anti-Spanish sentiment and encouraged the growing demand for U.S. intervention. Despite the rising clamor, President GROVER CLEVELAND was committed to keeping the United States out of the Cuban struggle and thus refused to formally recognize the belligerency of the rebels. His administration offered to mediate between Spain and its rebellious colony, but the Spanish government spurned the overture, resenting U.S. intrusion and suspecting U.S. imperial designs on the island. The Cuban question was interjected into the 1896 national election, with the Republican platform calling for the U.S. government to use its influence to restore peace in Cuba and secure the island's independence. Republican proponents of NEW MANIFEST DESTINY wanted to drive Spain from the Western Hemisphere and establish a U.S. territorial stronghold in the Caribbean. However, the victorious Republican presidential candidate, WILLIAM MCKINLEY, opposed the jingoist sentiment in his party and disclaimed imperialist designs on Cuba.

Prospects for a peaceful settlement of the Cuban rebellion seemed to brighten when, in the fall of 1897, a more liberal Spanish government came to power and inaugurated reforms in Cuba. It promptly replaced General Weyler and promised eventual home rule for the Cubans. The concessions were dismissed as insufficient by the insurgents, who demanded complete independence. But Spain's efforts at conciliation were welcomed by President McKinley, who in his annual message to Congress in December 1897 urged that Spain be given a reasonable opportunity to reach a satisfactory solution in Cuba.

A succession of incidents in early 1898 brought a rapid deterioration in Spanish-American relations. On February 9, Hearst's *New York Journal* published a pilfered private letter written by Enrique Dupuy de Lome, Spanish minister in Washington, in which he disparaged McKinley. The Spanish diplomat's immediate resignation did little to dampen the anti-Spanish feeling unleashed in the United States by the sensational DE LOME LETTER. Less than a week later, on February 15, a mysterious explosion blew up the U.S. battleship *Maine* in Havana Harbor, killing 260 men. The interventionist yellow press suggested that Spain was behind the disaster and sensationalized the incident to stir up popular sentiment in the United States for war. On March 17, while the nation awaited the findings of a special naval court of inquiry's probe into the *Maine* explosion, Senator Redfield Proctor (R-UT) gave a speech in the U.S. Senate that refocused attention on the plight of the native Cuban population. Proctor, recently returned from a tour of Cuba, described the death and misery he had witnessed in the concentration camps. His graphic account boosted domestic sentiment for U.S. intervention to help the Cubans secure their freedom from Spanish misrule. The naval court of inquiry issued its report on March 28, 1898, determining that the *Maine* had been destroyed by a mine or torpedo. The finding was interpreted by an outraged American public as confirmation of Spanish culpability. The investigation actually uncovered no evidence as to the specific identity of a responsible party.

McKinley had resisted the increasing domestic clamor for intervention, but the drift toward U.S.-Spanish confrontation was gaining momentum. Before the end of March, his administration delivered an ultimatum to Madrid demanding an immediate armistice in Cuba, an end to the concentration camp policy, and U.S. mediation of the rebellion. In a subsequent message the president made clear that the United States considered Cuban independence the only acceptable outcome. Spain, neither militarily or financially equipped to fight the United States, wanted to avoid war but was constrained from meeting all the U.S. demands by Spanish domestic opinion, which would not tolerate total capitulation on Cuba. Thus the Spanish government spurned the proposed U.S. mediation and placed conditions on granting an armistice. Following the Spanish rejection of U.S. demands, McKinley came under mounting domestic political pressure to involve the nation in a war with Spain to liberate Cuba and avenge the *Maine*. He yielded to the forces for war, heeding also the admonition of Republicans who suggested he risked splitting the party if he failed to act.

On April 11, 1898, two days after the Spanish government had made a further concession by ordering an armistice in Cuba, McKinley sent a message to Congress requesting authority to use American military power to restore peace in Cuba. Intervention, he contended, was warranted by humanitarian concern for the native Cuban populace, by the need to protect American lives and property on the island, by the insurrection's devastating toll on U.S. commerce in Cuba, and by the purported "constant menace" to peace posed by the Cuban turmoil. Congress responded on April 19 by passing a series of four resolutions which McKinley signed the following day. The first three recognized Cuban independence, demanded that Spain immediately relinquish its sovereignty over Cuba and withdraw from the island, and empowered the president to employ U.S. armed forces to compel Spanish compliance. The fourth, the TELLER AMENDMENT, was enacted to ease anti-imperialist trepidations about U.S. war aims. It disclaimed any U.S. intent to annex Cuba. Spain promptly severed diplomatic relations and on April 24 declared war on the United States. The next day Congress responded with a declaration of war, retroactive to April 21, when McKinley had proclaimed a blockade of the Cuban coast.

Spain was unprepared for war with a formidable naval power such as the United

States, which had more battleships and overall boasted a more modern and better trained navy. Since geography made sea power the decisive factor in the conflict, Spain from the outset was on a course for certain defeat. The war's first action occurred not in Cuba but in the Pacific, in Spain's Philippine Islands. Commmodore George Dewey, in command of the U.S. Asiatic squadron, sailed from Hong Kong on April 27 for the Philippines. His ships entered Manila Bay, where on May 1 they destroyed the Spanish fleet lying at anchor. Lacking the troops necessary to take Manila, Dewey awaited Army reinforcements, which arrived in strength by the end of July. American forces, encountering token Spanish resistance, captured Manila on August 13. To support U.S. operations in the Philippines, the Navy had occupied GUAM in the Spanish Marianas in June and Congress by joint resolution had annexed Hawaii on July 7.

Meanwhile in the Caribbean, a small Spanish fleet eluded American patrols and on May 19 entered the harbor of Santiago on Cuba's southern coast, where it promptly was blockaded by U.S. naval forces. American troops under General William R. Shafter landed in Cuba in late June and pressed toward the city of Santiago. This force comprised both regular Army units and special volunteer regiments, the most celebrated of which went by the name the "Rough Riders" and was led by Colonels LEONARD WOOD and THEODORE ROOSEVELT. Following hard-fought victories at the battles of El Caney and San Juan Hill on July 1, the American army was poised on the outskirts of Santiago. Two days later the Spanish fleet made a futile dash from the harbor to elude the U.S. blockade. American naval forces within hours totally decimated the Spanish flotilla. In the battle, the Spanish suffered 323 killed and 151 wounded, compared to just one American fatality. The overwhelming U.S. victory virtually ended the war. On July 17, under threat of U.S. bombardment, Santiago and its garrison formally surrendered. On July 25 American troops landed in Puerto Rico and within a few days occupied the Spanish island. With its armies in the Philippines and Cuba isolated by the destruction of its fleets at Manila Bay and Santiago, Madrid sued for peace.

Hostilities formally ended with the signing on August 12 of an armistice protocol. Its terms, dictated by the McKinley administration, required Spain to relinquish Cuba, cede Puerto Rico and one of the Mariana Islands to the United States, and consent to U.S. occupation of the city and harbor of Manila until the final disposition of the Philippines was settled in a definitive peace treaty. During the ensuing peace negotiations in Paris, influential Republican proponents of American imperial expansion waged a campaign demanding the United States keep the Philippines. They emphasized the strategic and commercial value of the islands as a prime site for a naval base in the West Pacific and gateway to the potentially lucrative China trade and warned that Germany or Japan was likely to seize them if the United States did not. Imperialists further contended that the Filipinos were unfit for self-government and thus would require America's civilizing tutelage. Persuaded by the imperialist arguments, McKinley abandoned his earlier disinclination to expansion and in late October instructed the American negotiators to demand the cession of the entire archipelago.

The peace talks yielded the TREATY OF PARIS, signed on December 10, 1898. Spain surrendered its sovereignty over Cuba, ceded Puerto Rico and Guam to America, and parted with the Philippines in return for U.S. payment of $20 million. In the United States the treaty encountered stiff opposition from anti-imperialists, who argued that extension of U.S. sovereignty over the Philippines contradicted American democratic principles, and who moreover suggested that the "inferior" Filipinos were inassimilable into American society. After extended debate, the Senate narrowly approved the treaty on February 6, 1899. Two days before, independence-seeking Filipino nationalists under rebel leader Emilio Aguinaldo had launched an armed revolt against the U.S. occupation. U.S. forces finally crushed the bloody PHILIPPINE INSURRECTION in 1902. Meanwhile Cuba was placed under temporary American military administration. Reminded of the Teller Amendment pledge against U.S. colonial designs on Cuba, the McKinley administration explained that the step was necessary to prepare the island for independence.

The "splendid little war," as Secretary of State JOHN M. HAY dubbed it, marked a turning point for America. With its victory, the United States established itself as strategically dominant in the Caribbean and a major power in the Far East. The course of the war contributed to the growth and modernization of the Navy and paved the way for construction of the PANAMA CANAL. The acquisition of overseas possessions signaled the emergence of an American IMPERIALISM and presaged a deepening U.S. involvement in world affairs.

SPECIAL INTELLIGENCE SERVICE See **FEDERAL BUREAU OF INVESTIGATION**.

SPOONER ACT See **HAY-BUNAU-VARILLA TREATY**.

STANDING CONSULTATIVE COMMISSION (SCC) (1972) Joint U.S.-Soviet body set up to help administer bilateral arms control agreements. The ABM TREATY and SALT I Interim Agreement, both signed March 26, 1972, provided for the prompt formation of a Standing Consultative Commission to promote implementation of the two measures and to advance their overall objectives. The commission was established by a U.S.-Soviet memorandum of understanding dated December 21, 1972. Each side is represented by a commissioner and deputy commissioner, supported by a staff of advisers and administrative personnel. The SCC, which meets at least twice a year in Geneva, serves as a forum for resolving questions on compliance; reviewing instances of possible unintended interference with NATIONAL TECHNICAL MEANS of verification; and considering proposals for improving the existing accords or for further arms control measures. The 1972 memorandum assigned the commission similar responsibility for the NUCLEAR ACCIDENTS AGREEMENT (1971), while Article XVII of the SALT II Treaty (1979) did the same for that arms control pact.

"STANDSTILL" AGREEMENT See **HOOVER MORATORIUM**.

STAR WARS See **STRATEGIC DEFENSE INITIATIVE**.

STARK INCIDENT (1987) Deadly attack on a U.S. Navy ship by an Iraqi warplane. Thirty-seven U.S. sailors were killed when the American frigate *Stark*, part of a small U.S. naval force stationed in the region, was struck on May 17, 1987, while cruising in the northern Persian Gulf by two Exocet missiles fired from an Iraqi Mirage F-1 jet. The incident added another vessel to the more than 200 noncombatant ships that had come under Iraqi or Iranian attack during the long Iran-Iraq War (1980–1988). Baghdad apologized for what it insisted was an accidental assault in a war zone. The Reagan administration accepted the Iraqi government's explanation, but moved quickly after the *Stark* episode to implement a controversial new policy of committing the American Navy to a potential combat role in the gulf region. Under the PERSIAN GULF INTERVENTION, additional U.S. warships were deployed to the region and assumed responsibility for the escort and protection of neutral shipping.

START See **STRATEGIC ARMS REDUCTION TALKS**.

STATE, DEPARTMENT OF See **DEPARTMENT OF STATE** in **APPENDIX B**.

STEEL SEIZURE CASE (1952) U.S. Supreme Court decision regarding the extent of the president's power to take action in support of U.S. foreign policy. After negotiations with the steel companies failed to produce a new collective bargaining agreement, the United Steelworkers of America in December 1951 gave notice of their intention to strike at year's end. President HARRY S. TRUMAN referred the labor dispute to federal mediation. When the government's intervention proved unsuccessful, the steel unions called a nationwide strike for April 9, 1952. Identifying the production of steel as critical to the nation's effort in the KOREAN WAR, Truman on April 8 issued an executive order directing Secretary of Commerce Charles Sawyer to seize the steel mills and keep them running. The president based his directive on his broad powers as commander in chief during a war emergency. The steel industry on April 29 obtained on injunction in federal district court blocking the seizure. The Truman administration appealed and the Supreme Court, because of the gravity of the situation, immediately heard the case. The unions remained at work during the legal proceedings. On June 2, 1952, the Court ruled by 6 to 3 in *Youngstown Sheet and Tube Co.* v. *Sawyer* that Truman's seizure order was unconstitutional. Writing for the majority, Justice Hugo Black held that in taking possession of private property without explicit statutory authority, the president had infringed on the constitutional prerogatives of the legislative branch. While affirming the president's extensive powers as commander in chief, the Court underscored their ultimate submission to constitutional restraint. Control of the steel mills reverted to the industry and the workers went out on strike until July 24, 1952, when a settlement finally was reached.

STEFFENS, JOSEPH LINCOLN (1866–1936) American journalist and author. After graduating from the University of California in 1889, the San Francisco native studied and travelled in Europe. On his return to the United States in 1892, he worked as a newspaper reporter and editor in New York City. Joining the staff of *McClure's Magazine*, he began to write articles exposing corruption in American politics and economic life that established him as the first and best-known of the "muckrakers," American journalists of the early 20th century who attacked dishonesty and greed in government and business and who crusaded for progressive social reforms. His "muckraking" pieces appeared in book form as *The Shame of the Cities* (1904) and *The Struggle for Self-Government* (1906). Steffens suggested that government corruption stemmed inevitably from America's ruthlessly competitive economic system.

With fellow muckrakers Ida M. Tarbell and Ray Stannard Baker, he took over the *American Magazine* in 1906, but left the next year to devote himself to freelance writing. Mentor to journalists WALTER LIPPMANN and JOHN REED, he grew interested in comparing the merits of reform and revolution as means for redressing social wrongs. Twice between 1914 and 1916 he made excursions to observe firsthand the progress of the Mexican Revolution. In 1919, as part of American emissary WILLIAM C. BULLITT's mission, he journeyed to Russia to assess the state of its unfolding revolution. He met and interviewed Bolshevik leader Nikolai Lenin. Much impressed by Communist achievements, he returned to America and remarked "I have seen the future and it works." Steffens lectured extensively throughout the United States on his Mexican and Russian observations. His *Autobiography* (1931) became an American bestseller. With the onset of the Great Depression of the 1930s, Steffens became an increasing admirer of the Soviet Union, extolling its brand of communism as the only effective solution to the social ills wrought by capitalism. In the last decade of his life he wrote columns for several California journals.

STETTINIUS, EDWARD REILLY, JR. (1900–1949) Industrialist, secretary of state, ambassador to the UNITED NATIONS. Stettinius was born in Chicago, Illinois, the son of a wealthy partner of the J.P. Morgan banking firm. He left the University of Virginia in 1924 before graduating to begin a business career with General Motors. In 1934 he accepted a senior executive position with United States Steel and became chairman of the corporation in 1938. The following year President FRANKLIN D. ROOSEVELT selected him to head a special War Resources Board established to study U.S. wartime industrial mobilization. In 1940 Stettinius entered the Roosevelt administration as a member of the newly formed National Defense Commission. Following U.S. entry into WORLD WAR II, he held high-ranking defense production posts and served as administrator of the LEND-LEASE program of U.S. aid to its wartime allies. In 1943 he was appointed under secretary of state. In 1944 he headed the American delegation to the DUMBARTON OAKS CONFERENCE that laid the groundwork for formation of the United Nations.

Stettinius succeeded an ailing CORDELL HULL as secretary of state in December 1944. In February 1945 he accompanied Roosevelt to the YALTA CONFERENCE and the following month attended the Mexico City Conference that drafted the ACT OF CHAPULTEPEC. When HARRY S. TRUMAN became president following Roosevelt's death in April 1945, he was concerned that Stettinius, who had never held elective office, was next in line to be president due to the vacancy in the vice-presidency. Truman retained Stettinius as secretary of state until the June 1945 close of the SAN FRANCISCO CONFERENCE inaugurating the United Nations, where Stettinius had chaired the U.S.

delegation, and then replaced him with the more politically experienced JAMES F. BYRNES. Stettinius in turn was named the first U.S. representative to the United Nations. He resigned in June 1946 and served as rector of the University of Virginia until his death from a heart ailment in 1949.

STEVENSON, ADLAI EWING, 2ND (1900–1965)   Statesman and diplomat. Stevenson was born in Los Angeles, California. Named after his grandfather, who was vice-president during GROVER CLEVELAND's second term, he grew up in Illinois, attended the private Choate School in Connecticut, and graduated from Princeton in 1922. After two years at Harvard Law School, he returned to Illinois, where he worked on a family newspaper and completed his law degree at Northwestern University in 1927. Except for service in Washington from 1933 to 1935 as a special counsel with several New Deal administrations, Stevenson practiced as a member of a Chicago law firm until 1941. A student of world affairs, he was active in the final years before U.S. entry into WORLD WAR II in the COMMITTEE TO DEFEND AMERICA BY AIDING THE ALLIES, which opposed traditional American ISOLATIONISM and favored assistance to Great Britain in its fight against Nazi Germany. During the war Stevenson was a special assistant to Navy Secretary Frank Knox. Transferred to the State Department in 1945, he participated in planning for the UNITED NATIONS. He attended the SAN FRANCISCO CONFERENCE (1945) where the international organization was formally inaugurated, and was a member of the U.S. delegation to the opening sessions of the U.N. General Assembly in 1946 and 1947.

In 1948 Stevenson was elected Democratic governor of Illinois. His four-year term won him national recognition as an innovative and articulate political figure. He was the Democratic presidential candidate in 1952 and 1956, both times losing to Republican DWIGHT D. EISENHOWER. During the 1950s Stevenson practiced international law, traveled widely, and authored several books, including an account of his 1958 trip to the Soviet Union, *Friends and Enemies: What I Learned in Russia* (1959). He was an early advocate of nuclear disarmament and of greater U.S. economic aid to the developing world. In 1960 he lost the Democratic presidential nomination to JOHN F. KENNEDY, whereupon he became a foreign policy adviser to the Kennedy campaign. In December 1960 President-elect Kennedy named Stevenson ambassador to the United Nations with cabinet rank. In this post he pressed for U.N. resolution of the CONGO CRISIS (1960–1963) and supported Secretary General Dag Hammarskjold against Soviet criticism. Initially unaware of American involvement in the BAY OF PIGS INVASION (1961), he endured the embarrassment of publicly denying any U.S. role. In 1962 he captured international attention for his dramatic confrontation with the Soviet U.N. ambassador during the CUBAN MISSILE CRISIS. Stevenson remained at his U.N. post under President LYNDON B. JOHNSON, defending U.S. policy in the VIETNAM WAR and DOMINICAN CRISIS (1965). He died suddenly of a heart attack in London in July 1965.

STILWELL, JOSEPH WARREN (1883–1946)   Army officer, U.S. commander in China during WORLD WAR II. Stilwell was born in Florida and grew up in Yonkers, New York. He graduated from West Point in 1904. After duty in the Philippines, where he saw combat in the MORO WARS (1901–1913), he returned to West Point as an instructor. He served in the AMERICAN EXPEDITIONARY FORCE in France during WORLD WAR I. A gifted linguist, Stilwell in 1920 was appointed under a new program as the Army's first language officer in China. He spent a three-year tour traveling throughout China, learning the language, and gaining unusual insight into the East Asian country. He was back in China from 1926 to 1929 and again from 1935 to 1939, when he was U.S. military attaché. In the early 1930s he served under future Army Chief of Staff GEORGE C. MARSHALL at Fort Benning, Georgia. Brilliant and demanding, Stilwell earned the nickname "Vinegar Joe" for his acid tongue.

In 1939 he was promoted to general. In 1941 he took command of the 3rd Corps, headquartered in California, gaining a reputation as the Army's best large-unit leader. The first months of World War II brought serious Allied military reverses in the Pacific. President FRANKLIN D. ROOSEVELT and Marshall enlisted Stilwell to check Japanese advances on the Asian mainland.

In February 1942 he was named commanding general of U.S. forces in the China-Burma-India theater and chief of staff to Nationalist Chinese leader Generalissimo Chiang Kai-shek. The United States was unable to commit ground forces to the theater. Stilwell's primary mission was to assist Chiang in building an effective Chinese army. By 1944 Chinese forces trained and led by Stilwell had defeated the Japanese in northern Burma.

Stilwell found himself in increasing disagreement with Chiang. The American general was concerned with China's role in the struggle against Japan. Chiang's first priority, however, was preserving sufficient forces to be able to defeat his Communist Chinese adversaries once the war with Japan was concluded. Chiang also opposed reforms of the Chinese army urged by Stilwell that threatened to undermine his control. Following a renewed Japanese offensive in China in 1944, Roosevelt recommended that Stilwell be appointed overall commander of Allied forces there. Chiang refused and instead demanded Stilwell's recall. Unwilling to sever relations with a critical wartime ally, Roosevelt was forced to accede and Stilwell was withdrawn in October 1944. The differences between Chiang and Stilwell underscored the limits of American influence in China. Chiang's inflexible policies, while not fatal in the fight against Japan, helped insure the eventual Chinese Communist rise to power in 1949. Stilwell commanded the U.S. 10th Army on Okinawa from June 1945 until the end of the war in August. He died in 1946 following an operation for stomach cancer.

STIMSON DOCTRINE (1932) Doctrine of nonrecognition adopted by the Hoover administration to protest Japan's seizure of Manchuria. The United States deplored Japanese expansionist aggression in China during the MANCHURIAN CRISIS (1931–1933) as a violation of the NINE-POWER TREATY and the KELLOGG-BRIAND PACT of 1928, the latter of which renounced war as a means of achieving national aims. Antiinterventionist President HERBERT C. HOOVER, determined to keep the United States out of the Far East crisis, opposed a direct U.S. response on Manchuria, favoring instead a negotiated settlement between Japan and China. Secretary of State HENRY L. STIMSON in No-

vember 1931 told the LEAGUE OF NATIONS, to which the United States did not belong, that America would neither join nor oppose a proposed economic embargo of the Japanese. As the league debated possible responses, Japan continued its invasion and by the end of the year its military effectively controlled Manchuria.

With the situation worsening, Hoover and Stimson resorted to the nonrecognition doctrine, a principle previously invoked by Secretary of State WILLIAM JENNINGS BRYAN in May 1915 to protest Japan's 21 Demands, a diplomatic ploy to strengthen the Japanese position in China. On January 7, 1932, Stimson sent diplomatic notes to both China and Japan stating that the United States would not accept any Manchurian arrangement that impaired American treaty rights; and would not recognize territorial gains or other privileges brought about by the use of armed force. The declaration of American intentions, known either as the Stimson Doctrine or the Hoover-Stimson Doctrine, carried no threat of armed intervention or other forceful measures and basically amounted to a moral sanction against aggression. Undeterred, Japan proclaimed the nominally independent state of Manchukuo on February 18. Stimson announced America's refusal to recognize Tokyo's puppet government in Manchuria. U.S. diplomacy received a modest boost in March when the League of Nations adopted an anti-Japanese resolution that incorporated the nonrecognition principle. The Stimson Doctrine failed to check Japanese expansionism in China through the end of the 1930s. The inability of the United States and European powers to act together against Japanese aggression demonstrated the weakness of the Kellogg-Briand Pact.

STIMSON, HENRY LEWIS (1867–1950) Secretary of war, governor general of the Philippines, secretary of state. Born in New York City, Stimson graduated from Yale in 1888. He earned a master's degree at Harvard in 1889 and attended Harvard Law School briefly before passing the bar in 1891, whereupon he joined ELIHU ROOT's New York law firm. Stimson entered government service in 1906 when President THEODORE ROOSEVELT appointed him U.S. district attorney for southern New York. In

1910 he was defeated as the Republican candidate for governor of the state. On Root's recommendation, President WILLIAM HOWARD TAFT made him secretary of war in 1911. In his two years in the post, Stimson worked to modernize the Army's organization, tactics, and training. He departed office with the Taft administration in 1913. During WORLD WAR I Stimson served as an artillery officer with the AMERICAN EXPEDITIONARY FORCE in France. After the war he returned to his law firm. In 1927 President CALVIN COOLIDGE named him a special envoy to Nicaragua to mediate the civil war there. Stimson succeeded in negotiating the PEACE OF TIPITAPA temporarily halting the fighting. The same year he became governor general of the Philippines. Stimson was recalled from the U.S. territory in 1929 to become secretary of state under incoming president HERBERT C. HOOVER.

The Hoover presidency coincided with the onset of the worldwide Great Depression and much of the administration's attention was devoted to economic issues. Stimson supported the HOOVER MORATORIUM (1931) temporarily suspending the payment of debts to the United States by financially strapped European countries. He headed U.S. delegations to the first of the LONDON NAVAL CONFERENCES in 1930 that concluded an agreement on naval disarmament and to the opening sessions of the ultimately ineffective WORLD DISARMAMENT CONFERENCE (1932–1934). In 1931 Japan invaded Manchuria, precipitating the international MANCHURIAN CRISIS (1931–1933) over the disputed Chinese territory. As Japan moved to install the puppet state of Manchukuo, the secretary of state in January 1932 issued the STIMSON DOCTRINE, declaring that the United States would not recognize any government or international agreement brought about by aggression. U.S. pressure helped bring widespread condemnation of Japan, but the Asian power retained its hold over Manchuria until the end of WORLD WAR II.

Stimson left his position at the end of the Hoover administration in 1933 and resumed his law practice. Following the outbreak of WORLD WAR II in Europe in 1939, he emerged as an outspoken critic of American isolationism and a leading member of the COMMITTEE TO DEFEND AMERICA BY AIDING THE ALLIES. In June 1940 Democratic President FRANKLIN D. ROOSEVELT, seeking to fashion a bipartisan foreign policy in support of greater aid to Great Britain in its fight against Germany, brought the Republican Stimson into his cabinet as secretary of war. With U.S. entry into the world conflict in 1941, Stimson oversaw the massive buildup of U.S. ground and air forces and helped devise U.S. wartime strategy. Having witnessed the final victory over the Axis Powers, he retired from public life on his 78th birthday in September 1945.

STOCKHOLM CONFERENCE See **UNITED NATIONS ENVIRONMENT PROGRAM**.

STOCKHOLM DECLARATION (1986) East-West agreement to adopt additional steps, known as confidence-building measures (CBMs), to reduce the risk of military confrontation in Europe. The 1975 HELSINKI ACCORDS concluded by the CONFERENCE ON SECURITY AND COOPERATION IN EUROPE (CSCE) first provided for CBMs between the massive forces of the Western security alliance, NATO, and its Communist counterpart, the Warsaw Pact, arrayed against each other in central Europe. Early CBMs included prior notification of military maneuvers involving more than 25,000 troops and the exchange of observers for military exercises. In 1983, the CSCE decided to convene a conference in Stockholm to negotiate additional CBMs between NATO and the Warsaw Pact. The Conference on Confidence and Security-Building Measures in Europe was conducted in phases from 1984 to 1986. Agreement was reached on a new set of CBMs, which were outlined in a final document released September 19, 1986, at the end of the 12th and concluding session. These measures included prior notification of military maneuvers involving more than 13,000 troops; one year's advance warning of exercises involving more than 40,000 troops and two years' warning for more than 75,000 troops; exchange of observers for exercises above 17,000 troops; and the requirement for each nation to allow up to three short-notice air and ground inspections of its announced maneuvers by members of the other military alliance. The Stockholm Declaration entered into effect on January 1, 1987. The agreement subsequently was rendered moot by the collapse of communism in Eastern Europe in 1989, the disbandment of the Warsaw Pact, and the completion of the CONVENTIONAL FORCES EUROPE TREATY (1990) providing for broad disarmament on the continent.

STRATEGIC ARMS LIMITATION TALKS I

(SALT I) (1969–1972)   U.S.-Soviet arms control negotiations leading to the ABM TREATY and Interim Agreement. The two superpowers first explored possible strategic arms discussions at the EIGHTEEN-NATION COMMITTEE ON DISARMAMENT in the 1960s. President LYNDON B. JOHNSON, at the signing of the NUCLEAR NON-PROLIFERATION TREATY on July 1, 1968, announced U.S.-Soviet agreement on strategic arms talks, but preparations were indefinitely postponed following the Soviet Union's August 1968 invasion of Czechoslovakia. In 1969 both the U.S. and Soviet governments signaled their readiness for arms control negotiations. Formal Strategic Arms Limitation Talks on strategic NUCLEAR WEAPONS and antiballistic missile (ABM) defenses began in Helsinki in November 1969. The director of the ARMS CONTROL AND DISARMAMENT AGENCY, Gerard C. Smith, headed the U.S. delegation throughout the three-year negotiations.

The SALT I sessions (as they were later designated to distinguish them from the successor SALT II negotiations), held alternately in Helsinki and Vienna, culminated in the two landmark arms control agreements, which were signed by President RICHARD M. NIXON and General Secretary Leonid I. Brezhnev on May 26, 1972, at the MOSCOW SUMMIT. The ABM Treaty placed strict restraints on the development and deployment of ABM systems. The Interim Agreement on Certain Measures with Respect to the Limitation of Strategic Offensive Arms, set to last five years, was designed to hold each side's strategic nuclear arsenal at agreed-upon levels pending negotiation of a comprehensive SALT accord. The first arms control accord to limit nuclear weapons, the Interim Agreement froze each side's number of INTERCONTINENTAL BALLISTIC MISSILES at existing levels. It established ceilings on the number of SUBMARINE-LAUNCHED BALLISTIC MISSILES at 710 for the United States and 910 for the Soviet Union. The agreement did not address strategic nuclear bombers. While negoti-

ated as an EXECUTIVE AGREEMENT rather than a treaty, Nixon submitted the measure to Congress for ratification. Approved September 30, 1972, it entered into force, together with the ABM Treaty, on October 3, 1972. An amendment to the resolution of endorsement, known as the Jackson Amendment after its sponsor Henry M. Jackson (D-WA), expressed the Congress's understanding and insistence that U.S.-Soviet long-term strategic arrangements be based on the principle of equality. SALT II negotiations began in November 1972 and concluded with the signing of the SALT II Treaty in June 1979.

STRATEGIC ARMS LIMITATION TALKS II

(SALT II) (1972–1979)   U.S.-Soviet arms control discussions culminating in the SALT II Treaty. As provided for in the SALT I Interim Agreement, SALT II negotiations on a comprehensive pact limiting strategic offensive NUCLEAR WEAPONS began in Geneva in November 1972. A major milestone was reached at the VLADIVOSTOK SUMMIT when President GERALD R. FORD and General Secretary Leonid I. Brezhnev on November 24, 1974, concluded an agreement establishing the basic framework for a SALT II pact. The Vladivostok Accord limited each side to a total of 2400 strategic nuclear delivery systems—INTERCONTINENTAL BALLISTIC MISSILES (ICBMs), SUBMARINE-LAUNCHED BALLISTIC MISSILES (SLBMs), and heavy bombers; banned the construction of new ICBM launchers; and restricted the deployment of new types of strategic offensive arms. A final SALT II agreement was delayed by differences over how to address CRUISE MISSILES and a new Soviet aircraft, the Backfire bomber, and by the transition from the Ford to the Carter administration.

After various high-level meetings in Washington and Moscow and nearly continuous negotiating sessions in Geneva, the Treaty on the Limitation of Strategic Offensive Arms was signed by President JIMMY CARTER and Brezhnev on June 18, 1979, during their VIENNA SUMMIT. The pact, effective until the end of 1985, provided for an initial ceiling of 2400 on the number of strategic nuclear delivery vehicles allowed each side, to be lowered to 2250 by the end of 1981; detailed limits on the number of launchers for missiles capable of carrying more than one warhead; a ban on various additional ICBM launchers; restrictions on the flight-testing or deployment of new types of ICBMs; and advance notification of certain ICBM test launches. Verification of compliance was left to each side's NATIONAL TECHNICAL MEANS. An accompanying protocol barred for three years the deployment of mobile ICBM launchers and of cruise missiles with a range in excess of 600 kilometers (360 miles). A Joint Statement of Principles called for further SALT III negotiations on strategic arms. Carter forwarded the SALT II agreement to the U.S. Senate for its ratification in late June 1979. Following the Soviet Union's December 1979 invasion of Afghanistan, he withdrew the treaty from consideration on January 3, 1980 and it was never ratified.

Despite the hardening of relations between the superpowers in the early 1980s, both sides pledged to observe the unratified SALT II limits. The further SALT III discussions called for under the pact never took place. Instead, new START negotiations began in 1982. In May 1986 President RONALD W. REAGAN announced the United States would no longer abide by the SALT II terms. Reagan defended the step as a necessary response to repeated Soviet violations of the treaty. Rapidly improving U.S.-Soviet ties in the late 1980s brought a new impetus to strategic arms negotiations, culminating in the 1991 START agreement.

STRATEGIC ARMS REDUCTION TALKS (START) (1982–1991)   U.S.-Soviet arms control negotiations on strategic NUCLEAR WEAPONS culminating in the 1991 START Treaty. The SALT II arms control agreement, concluded in 1979, had called for further SALT III discussions on strategic offensive weapons systems. In protest over the Soviet Union's December 1979 invasion of Afghanistan, the Carter administration withdrew the SALT II pact from Senate consideration, effectively suspending the SALT process. President RONALD W. REAGAN took office in 1981 determined to reverse what he believed was a growing Soviet nuclear superiority. As a candidate he had campaigned against the SALT II treaty, claiming it locked into place a dangerous Soviet advantage in INTERCONTINENTAL BALLISTIC MISSILES (ICBMs). When the Reagan administration embarked on a major U.S. defense buildup, it was criticized at home and abroad for

paying insufficient attention to nuclear arms control. Reagan replied that the rearmament program was necessary as insurance against an inferior U.S. negotiating position. The NUCLEAR FREEZE movement and other proponents of disarmament discounted such reasoning, observing that both superpowers already had massive nuclear arsenals capable of annihilating one another. Under mounting domestic political pressure to balance his strategic nuclear forces buildup with corresponding arms control initiatives, Reagan in May 1982 proposed new U.S.-Soviet negotiations to actually reduce rather than merely limit, as with SALT I and SALT II, the total number of nuclear missiles on each side. When Soviet leader Leonid I. Brezhnev responded favorably, new arms control discussions, dubbed START rather than SALT III, began June 29, 1982, in Geneva.

The Soviets broke off the negotiations on December 8, 1983, in protest against U.S. deployment in Western Europe of PERSHING II and CRUISE MISSILES capable of reaching the USSR. Following the 1985 UMBRELLA TALKS between U.S. Secretary of State GEORGE P. SHULTZ and Soviet Foreign Minister Andrei A. Gromyko, START discussions resumed in March 1985. At the REYKJAVIK SUMMIT (1986), Reagan and Soviet General Secretary Mikhail S. Gorbachev agreed on a basic framework for major reductions in the U.S. and Soviet strategic arsenals, but the two sides remained deadlocked over Soviet insistence that any START agreement be linked to strict restrictions on the STRATEGIC DEFENSE INITIATIVE (SDI), the U.S. program for nuclear-missile defense. The Soviets dropped their SDI demand in 1989, but reiterated their readiness to withdraw from a START pact if the United States, in moving to deploy SDI, terminated the 1972 ABM TREATY.

Meeting in London in conjunction with the July 1991 ECONOMIC SUMMIT of the GROUP OF 7 Western industrialized powers, President GEORGE BUSH and Gorbachev announced completion of a START agreement capping more than six years of negotiations. The same month the two leaders signed the Strategic Arms Reduction Treaty in ceremonies on July 31 at their MOSCOW SUMMIT. The historic pact represented the first agreement to impose actual cuts in each side's nuclear stocks, providing for reductions of roughly 30 percent from existing levels. To reach the treaty's overall ceiling for each country of 6000 nuclear warheads carried by no more than 1600 long-range missiles and bombers, the United States would have to retire more than 600 intercontinental ballistic missiles and SUBMARINE-LAUNCHED BALLISTIC MISSILES while the Soviet Union would have to slash its heavy ICBM force by 50 percent. The pact set tight guidelines on the development of new strategic delivery systems. Each side had one weapon system it refused to include under START limits but that the other side insisted be restricted. In separate binding declarations, the United States and Soviet Union accepted limits on their deployment, respectively, of long-range cruise missiles and Backfire jet bombers. The treaty was scheduled to run for 15 years, open to extension for successive five-year periods.

U.S. Senate ratification of the agreement was placed on hold in the wake of the dramatic political upheaval in the Soviet Union following the failed August 1991 MOSCOW COUP. The disintegration of the USSR in December 1991 raised the fundamental questions of whether and how the newly independent states emerging from the former Communist nation would observe the terms of the START pact. Washington began negotiations with the four erstwhile Soviet republics—Russia, Ukraine, Belarus, and Kazakhstan—exercising control over the former Soviet arsenal. On May 23, 1992, the United States concluded an agreement with the four former Soviet republics committing them to abide by the START Treaty. Ukraine, Belarus, and Kazakhstan pledged to sign the NUCLEAR NON-PROLIFERATION TREATY (1968) and to become nuclear-free by the end of the decade. Each promised to eliminate all long-range nuclear weapons within seven years. All three had already transferred their short-range nuclear arms to Russia for dismantling. The United States and Russia committed to further negotiations on reducing their strategic nuclear forces below START levels. The May 1992 agreement cleared the way for U.S. Senate approval of the START accord.

STRATEGIC DEFENSE INITIATIVE (SDI)
U.S. defense program to develop a space-based shield against nuclear missile attack. In 1972 the United States and the Soviet Union signed the ABM TREATY placing strict limits on each side's deployment of antiballistic missiles (ABM). The ban on missile defenses effectively marked an acceptance of the strategic doctrine of MUTUAL ASSURED DESTRUCTION (MAD) as the basis for nuclear DETERRENCE between the two superpowers. Under the MAD doctrine, neither side could risk a nuclear attack against the other for fear of certain devastating retaliation. In 1983 President RONALD W. REAGAN proposed a major defense program, known as the Strategic Defense Initiative, as a means of moving beyond the nuclear balance-of-terror underpinning MAD to a more secure method of deterrence. In a nationwide televised speech on March 23, 1983, announcing SDI, Reagan asked, "What if free people could live secure in the knowledge that their security did not rest upon the threat of instant U.S. retaliation to deter a Soviet attack, that we could intercept and destroy strategic ballistic missiles before they reached our own soil or that of our allies?"

Reagan presented a vision of a space-based defensive system made up of exotic new technologies, such as directed-energy weapons, that would be able to shoot down incoming ballistic missiles throughout their flight trajectory. Because of the emphasis on futuristic technologies, the program soon acquired the label Star Wars. The SDI proposal brought considerable opposition. Critics charged variously that SDI was technologically infeasible and that its expensive space weapons could be easily and cheaply countered by the USSR. A coalition of arms control experts, disarmament groups, and members of Congress suggested that SDI threatened U.S.-Soviet nuclear stability. Many argued it would violate the ABM Treaty. The Soviet Union condemned SDI as dangerous and destabilizing and insisted that any START agreement to cut strategic nuclear weapons be linked to strict limits on ABM systems. In response the Reagan administration argued that SDI was fully feasible within the realm of emerging technologies and that the Soviets already were engaged in similar research. The administration interpreted the 1972 ABM pact as permitting the development of new ABM systems based on advanced technologies and contended SDI would promote international stability by rendering ballistic missiles obsolete.

The Reagan administration in the 1980s was able to secure congressional funding for SDI, but the project remained highly controversial. In 1987 Congress mandated that the program conform to a strict interpretation of the ABM Treaty. By 1989, the emphasis had begun to shift toward a more limited system. The same year the USSR dropped its demand that SDI and START be linked, but stressed that the deployment of any new American ABM system would jeopardize U.S.-Soviet arms control. By the early 1990s, rapidly improving U.S.-Soviet relations and corresponding arms control breakthroughs suggested to many a fading need for an expensive ABM system. Iraq's use of Scud missiles during the PERSIAN GULF WAR (1991), however, and the success of the U.S. Patriot missile in shooting them down, provided new momentum for a scaled-back SDI program. In his January 1991 State of the Union address, President GEORGE BUSH announced he was refocusing SDI on a more limited ground- and space-based ABM system capable of protecting U.S. territory, forces, and allies against missile attack by a regional power such as Iraq or by a renegade military command in the Soviet Union.

STRUCTURAL IMPEDIMENTS INITIA-TIVE (SII) U.S.-Japanese trade talks. In May 1989 President GEORGE BUSH, acting under the so-called Super 301 provision of the 1988 OMNIBUS TRADE ACT, identified Japan as an unfair trading partner in the area of satellites, supercomputers, and forest products. Bush's move set in motion a process whereby the unfair trading practices, if left uncorrected, would draw eventual U.S. retaliatory measures. After a series of sharp exchanges between the major trading partners and close allies, the United States and Japan agreed to hold formal talks on the various "structural impediments" to trade between them. The wideranging negotiations opened September 4, 1989, in Tokyo. Known as the Structural Impediments Initiative, the discussions aimed at identifying changes that might be effected in both nations' economies to resolve trade differences and narrow the substantial annual U.S. trade deficit with Japan. The negotiations concluded June 28, 1990,

with the signing of a final agreement meant to eliminate major structural barriers to trade. In general, the pact sought to make the American economy more productive and to promote greater consumption in the Japanese economy. Japan promised to allocate several trillion dollars over the next 10 years on domestic public works projects and to facilitate U.S. access to Japanese markets. The United States pledged to reduce its budget deficit and to spend more on research and development.

STUDIES AND OBSERVATION GROUP (SOG) Unconventional warfare unit during the VIETNAM WAR. Part of the U.S. military command in South Vietnam, the group was formed in 1964 to conduct secret operations against Communist forces in the neighboring countries of Cambodia, Laos, and North Vietnam, where American forces were not openly involved in ground combat. Missions assigned to the joint Army-Navy-Air Force SOG included commando raids and the interdiction of enemy supply lines along the Ho Chi Minh Trail. South Vietnamese forces also took part. At peak strength the unit comprised 2000 U.S. and 8000 South Vietnamese personnel. The group was dissolved prior to the 1973 U.S. withdrawal from Southeast Asia.

SUBMARINE-LAUNCHED BALLISTIC MISSILE (SLBM) Ballistic missile carried in and launched by a submarine. SLBMs, which form one of the three legs of the U.S. strategic nuclear forces TRIAD, are believed to be invulnerable to surprise attack and thus considered essential to American nuclear DETERRENCE. In the early 1980s the United States began to replace its Poseidon SLBMs with highly advanced Trident I and Trident II missiles, each with a range of more than 4000 miles. SLBMs are limited by the SALT I (1972), SALT II (1979), and START (1991) arms control agreements.

SUBVERSIVE ACTIVITIES CONTROL ACT See **INTERNAL SECURITY ACT**.

SUEZ CRISIS (1956) International crisis precipitated when Egypt seized the Suez Canal. The showdown emerged from several interrelated developments after WORLD WAR II: the growth of Arab nationalism and hostility to the Western-supported state of

Israel; the Communist bloc's push to expand its influence in the Middle East; and the waning influence of once-dominant colonial powers Great Britain and France in the region. Egyptian President Gamal Abdel Nasser, who had directed the coup that deposed King Farouk in 1952, set out to make his country, previously a British colony, the dominant force in the Middle East. His regime, seeking economic and military aid from both East and West, adopted a nonaligned foreign policy that appealed to the rising tide of Egyptian nationalism. Nasser was determined to build the Aswan High Dam on the Nile River, a $1.3 billion project to increase Egypt's arable land by one-third and to supply electrical power. Since Egypt lacked the resources to finance this vast undertaking, he turned to foreign assistance.

The Eisenhower administration had looked expectantly toward Nasser as an independent figure whose strong leadership might emerge as a stabilizing force in the Middle East. In December 1955 the United States offered Egypt a loan of $56 million for construction of the dam. Britain followed with a $14 million offer and the WORLD BANK signaled its willingness to lend another $200 million. Nasser, meanwhile, had arranged a number of arms purchases from the Communist bloc and increased Egypt's trade with the Soviet Union. Troubled by the Egyptian leader's deepening ties with the USSR and by his increasingly anti-Western posture, U.S. Secretary of State JOHN FOSTER DULLES in July 1956 abruptly canceled the Aswan loan offer. Britain did likewise and the World Bank funding, contingent on the others, was withdrawn.

On July 26, 1956, a chagrined Nasser retaliated by nationalizing the Universal Suez Canal Company, the international corporation that long had operated the Suez Canal and whose major stockholders were British and French. While promising to compensate the stockholders, he declared that henceforth Egyptians would operate and control the 103-mile-long waterway linking the Mediterranean and the Red Sea. He also said he would use canal revenues to finance the Aswan dam. Britain and France, heavily dependent on oil supplies transported through the canal, condemned the seizure, characterizing as intolerable

the prospect that an international waterway so vital to their economies should fall under the control of someone whom they distrusted and who was fostering links to the Communist world. London and Paris reacted to Nasser's deed by freezing Egyptian assets within their reach and began talks on a joint military operation to seize the Suez. Emphatically opposed to armed intervention by its allies, the United States sought a diplomatic solution. There followed three months of intensive international negotiations initiated by Dulles. These efforts ended in stalemate when neither side would budge on the question of control over the canal. Nasser insisted it remain with Egypt, while British Prime Minister Anthony Eden and French Premier Guy Mollet demanded a form of international authority.

During this period Great Britain, France, and Israel secretly laid plans for joint military action against Egypt if negotiations failed. The crisis came to a head on October 29 when Israel, which faced continuous fighting on its borders with Egypt, Jordan, and Syria, and which feared an upsurge in hostile Arab raids into its territory from Egypt, invaded the Gaza Strip and Sinai Peninsula. The next day, without informing the United States in advance, Britain and France, using the Israeli action as a pretext for moving to protect the Suez, issued an ultimatum threatening intervention unless all armed forces were kept 10 miles from the canal. Americans, in the midst of the final days of a presidential campaign, were stunned by Israel's attack on Egypt. Suspecting Israeli collusion with the British and French, the United States rushed a resolution before the UNITED NATIONS Security Council on October 30 calling for an immediate cease-fire and withdrawal of Israel's troops from Egypt. Britain and France vetoed it and a similar resolution proposed by the USSR. When Nasser rejected the joint Anglo-French ultimatum, British and French aircraft began bombing Egyptian military targets on October 31. The two nations continued these air strikes for four days and then landed troops at Port Said and along the canal. Israeli forces, meanwhile, routed the Egyptians and overran the Sinai Peninsula.

President DWIGHT D. EISENHOWER on October 31 condemned the Anglo-French-Israeli assault, calling it irreconcilable with the principles of the United Nations. The Eisenhower administration sought an end to the crisis through the veto-free U.N. General Assembly, which on November 2 approved a U.S.-sponsored proposal for an immediate cease-fire and exit of all foreign troops from Egypt. London and Paris spurned this appeal. The Soviet Union then threatened to use force against the British, French, and Israelis. On November 5, Soviet Premier Nikolai A. Bulganin suggested joint military intervention with the United States to end the so-called aggression against Egypt. Eisenhower rejected the proposal as "unthinkable," characterizing it as an attempt by the Kremlin to distract world attention from Moscow's brutal suppression of the HUNGARIAN REVOLT (1956). November 5th also saw the General Assembly vote to create a U.N. Emergency Force (UNEF) to supervise a cease-fire. Yielding to U.S. pressure Britain, France, and Israel accepted a halt to hostilities effective midnight November 6 and consented to pull their forces out of Egypt. UNEF arrived to oversee the troop withdrawals and ultimately remained until 1967, acting as a buffer between Israel and Egypt. By Christmas 1956 the British and French had removed the last of their forces. Israel's troops were withdrawn by March 1957 and in June of the same year Egypt approved terms for use of the canal by all nations.

The Suez invasion proved a fiasco for Great Britain and France, exposing their fall from the ranks of great powers. America's anticolonial stand in the crisis earned it new respect in the Arab world. Its relations with the British and French, though, plummeted to their lowest point since before World War II. Despite his army's poor showing against the Israelis, Nasser emerged a hero of Arab nationalism. By its staunch support of Egypt and condemnation of Western colonialism, the Soviet Union won new prestige in the Middle East. The Anglo-French retreat after Suez left a power vacuum in the region that Moscow, with its enhanced stature, looked to fill. Soviet inroads during and after the crisis threatened Western security and economic interests, prompting the president's declaration in January 1957 of the EISENHOWER DOCTRINE, which announced the United States would defend Middle East nations against Communist aggression.

SULLIVAN PRINCIPLES (1977) Recommended code for fair employment practices by American companies with operations in South Africa. Formulated in March 1977 by Reverend Leon Sullivan, a Baptist minister from Philadelphia and the first black member of the General Motors board of directors, the principles constituted voluntary guidelines meant to promote an end to discrimination against South Africa's blacks under that nation's system of institutionalized racial segregation and inequality, known as apartheid. The principles included nonsegregation in the workplace, equal pay for equal work, equal and fair employment practices for all employees, special training for prospective black supervisors and administrators, accelerated black promotions, and improvement in the living conditions of employees. Sullivan subsequently added two principles: one supporting the formation of black labor unions; another advocating change in South Africa's migrant worker laws.

He called on U.S. firms doing business in South Africa to adopt his guidelines. By 1985 more than 150 American companies working in South Africa had voluntarily subscribed to the Sullivan principles. In September of that year, under intensifying domestic anti-apartheid political pressure, President RONALD W. REAGAN signed an executive order that imposed limited U.S. economic sanctions on South Africa and endorsed the Sullivan code. The order urged American businesses to adhere to the principles without making compliance a legal requirement. In 1987 Sullivan concluded that after a decade, South Africa had made no significant progress toward redressing its racial injustices and urged all U.S. corporations to pull out of the country.

See also CONSTRUCTIVE ENGAGEMENT.

SUSSEX (1916) French passenger steamer torpedoed without warning by a German U-boat on March 24, 1916, in the English Channel. Several Americans who had taken passage on the ship were injured in the sinking, which marked a continuation of Germany's controversial WORLD WAR I submarine warfare campaign and caused a serious crisis in U.S.-German relations. The United States regarded the *Sussex* incident as a violation of the so-called ARABIC Pledge, the promise rendered by the German government after the August 1915 sinking of the British liner *Arabic* to cease surprise submarine attacks on unarmed Allied passenger vessels. Secretary of State ROBERT LANSING recommended a drastic U.S. response, unsuccessfully urging President WOODROW WILSON to break off relations with Germany without further delay. Wilson on April 18, 1916, delivered a virtual ultimatum to Berlin, threatening to sever diplomatic ties unless Germany immediately halted its U-boat attacks on merchant and passenger ships. Following a bruising internal debate, the German government bowed to U.S. pressure and on May 4 promised that its submarines would not torpedo such vessels without sufficient warning and without attempting to save lives.

This *Sussex* Pledge, as it came to be known, also contained the proviso that the United States must compel Great Britain to lift its food blockade on Germany in accordance with the "rules of international law." Wilson accepted the German pledge but not the added condition. The *Sussex* promise averted war between the United States and Germany in the short term. America entered World War I in April 1917 following Germany's resumption of unrestricted submarine warfare.

SYMINGTON AIR POWER HEARINGS (1956) U.S. Senate investigation into the relative strength of American and Soviet air power. In early May 1955 the Defense Department announced the appearance of high-performance jet fighters and bombers at the Soviet Union's annual May Day celebration in Moscow. Senator STUART SYMINGTON (D-MO) took the floor on May 17th to warn that America "may have lost control of the air." Charging the Eisenhower administration with having underestimated Soviet capabilities, the former secretary of the air force and outspoken advocate of U.S. air power called for an inquiry into U.S. defense planning. As the Congressional debate over the adequacy of U.S. air forces mounted, the SENATE ARMED SERVICES COMMITTEE acted on Symington's proposal. On February 25, 1956, the panel appointed a special five-member subcommittee, headed by Symington, to investigate U.S. and Soviet air power. The subcommittee conducted extensive hearings from April until July. The testimony of ranking Air Force officers tended to support Symington's contention that more funding was needed if

America was not to fall behind in air power, while Secretary of Defense CHARLES E. WILSON made the case for U.S. existing air strength and the economy-minded Eisenhower defense budgets. The hearings prompted Congress to vote an additional $800 million that year for B-52 bombers. The subcommittee's majority report, released in January 1957, concluded: the USSR had the lead in combat aircraft and would soon close the "quality gap"; the United States was becoming vulnerable to a surprise air attack; and the Eisenhower administration had placed balancing the budget ahead of national security. The findings contributed to the intensifying debate over defense issues between the Republican administration and congressional Democrats in the late 1950s.

See also MISSILE GAP.

SYMINGTON, WILLIAM STUART (1901–1988) Secretary of the air force and U.S. senator from Missouri. Symington was born in Amherst, Massachusetts. After service in the Army during WORLD WAR I, he graduated from Yale in 1923 and began a business career with Symington Company, a family-owned railroad equipment plant in New York. In 1935 he moved to St. Louis to take over the Emerson Electrical Manufacturing Company. Emerson's impressive production performance during WORLD WAR II brought Symington to the attention of Senator HARRY S. TRUMAN (D-MO). After Truman became president in 1945, he named Symington chairman of the Surplus Property Board, a government body responsible for disposing of excess war items. In 1946 Truman appointed him assistant secretary of war for air. Following passage of the 1947 NATIONAL SECURITY ACT, Symington became first secretary of the newly formed DEPARTMENT OF THE AIR FORCE.

He resigned the post in April 1950 in disagreement over defense spending reductions, but remained with the Truman administration to direct U.S. mobilization efforts for the KOREAN WAR. In 1952 he won election to the Senate. The Missouri Democrat was among the early opponents of Senator JOSEPH R. MCCARTHY (R-WI) and his investigations into alleged Communist subversion in the U.S. government. By the mid-1950s, Symington had emerged as a leading spokesman for U.S. air power. In 1956 he chaired a congressional inquiry into the comparative strength of U.S. and Soviet air forces. The SYMINGTON AIR POWER HEARINGS concluded America faced a dangerous "bomber gap." In the late 1950s Symington spearheaded congressional Democrat charges that the Republican Eisenhower White House had allowed a MISSILE GAP to develop between the United States and Soviet Union.

In September 1960 Symington became head of a special Democratic Party committee on defense organization. The Symington Committee reported to President-elect JOHN F. KENNEDY that December. Its recommendations for sweeping changes in Defense Department structure were politically infeasible, but many of its proposals for streamlining operations and improving budget procedures later were adopted. An early supporter of U.S. involvement in Southeast Asia, Symington became an ardent critic of the VIETNAM WAR. By 1967 he believed the war was not vital to U.S. security interests and was harming the nation's economy. In the early 1970s he spoke out against its extension to Cambodia and Laos. Symington retired from the Senate in 1976.

SYRIAN CRISIS (1957) International showdown over suspected Communist-inspired plots by Syria against its pro-Western neighbors. Following the JORDANIAN CRISIS (1957), attention in the Middle East quickly shifted to Syria, where the presence of an active and growing Communist Party concerned the Eisenhower administration. Under a recently concluded agreement, the Syrians were receiving military and economic aid from America's COLD WAR rival the Soviet Union. Tensions between Washington and Damascus increased during the summer of 1957, leading the Eisenhower administration to surmise that a Communist takeover was imminent in the Arab country. In mid-August Syria accused three officials of the American embassy of plotting to overthrow its government and forced them to leave the country. The

United States retaliated by expelling the Syrian ambassador in Washington.

The Eisenhower administration became convinced that the Syrian regime, with the Kremlin's assistance and encouragement, planned aggression against several neighboring states. Acting within the framework of the EISENHOWER DOCTRINE on the Middle East, President DWIGHT D. EISENHOWER on September 5, 1957, announced plans to airlift arms to Jordan and assured Turkey, Iraq, and Lebanon that the United States would help defend them against Communist attack or subversion. In addition, U.S. air forces were sent to a base in Turkey and the 6th Fleet was ordered to the eastern Mediterranean. Bolstered by the American president's pledge, the Turks, Iraqis, Jordanians, and Lebanese amassed military forces around Syria's borders. The Syrian foreign minister accused the United States of seeking to dominate his country and complained before the UNITED NATIONS that the foreign troop buildup around Syria imperiled peace. While the Arab nations disclaimed any intention of invading Syria, the Turks continued to increase their forces on the Syrian frontier. Soviet leader Nikita S. Khrushchev on October 8 charged the United States with fomenting conflict by inciting a Turkish attack on Syria. He warned Turkey that the USSR would use force to safeguard its interests in the Middle East. Secretary of State JOHN FOSTER DULLES responded by announcing that the United States, as a member of NATO, would go to Turkey's defense in the event it was attacked. Efforts in the United Nations to mediate the tense standoff were unsuccessful. Neither superpower, however, favored further escalation of the confrontation and the Syrian crisis eased by the end of the month. Turkey reduced its forces along the Syrian border. While no Communist takeover occurred in Damascus, the Soviet Union had augmented considerably its influence there.

See also LEBANON INTERVENTION.

T

TAFT COMMISSION See **SCHURMAN COMMISSION**.

TAFT, WILLIAM HOWARD (1857–1930) Twenty-seventh president of the United States, and the nation's tenth chief justice. Born in Cincinnati, Ohio, he graduated from Yale in 1878 and Cincinnati Law School in 1880, whereupon he was admitted to the bar. A Republican, he was appointed to his first public office, Hamilton County assistant prosecutor, in 1881. He was briefly tax collector for Cincinnati in 1882 and then practiced law from 1883 until 1887, when he was selected to fill a vacancy on the Ohio Supreme Court. The next year he was elected to a term of his own. He left the state bench in 1890 to accept appointment by President BENJAMIN HARRISON as U.S. solicitor general. Two years later he became a federal circuit court judge.

In 1900 President WILLIAM MCKINLEY named him to head the second Philippine Commission. The five-man panel, generally dubbed the TAFT COMMISSION, was directed to end American military rule by establishing civil government in the Philippine Islands, which had become a U.S. possession after the SPANISH-AMERICAN WAR (1898). In 1901 Taft became the first civil governor of the Philippines. During his three-year governorship, he championed public education and economic improvements, oversaw the restoration of peace following the PHILIPPINE INSURRECTION (1899–1902), and took steps toward establishing limited self-government for the archipelago. In 1904 he joined the Roosevelt administration as secretary of war and quickly became a close friend and adviser of President THEODORE ROOSEVELT. In the cabinet post, Taft was in direct charge of construction of the PANAMA CANAL. On a visit to Tokyo in 1905 as the president's emissary, he negotiated the TAFT-KATSURA AGREEMENT regarding respective U.S. and Japanese interests in the Far East. When a rebellion destabilized Cuba in 1906, Roosevelt ordered American military intervention under the PLATT AMENDMENT (1901), whereupon Taft formally declared U.S. occupation and oversaw the establishment of a provisional American government on the island.

Nominated for president in 1908 as Roosevelt's hand-picked successor, he defeated Democratic candidate WILLIAM JENNINGS BRYAN. Upon taking office, Taft turned to the issue of tariff revision. After signing the PAYNE-ALDRICH TARIFF (1909), he defended the legislation during a nationwide speaking tour against criticism that it was a token measure which only marginally lowered U.S. duties. He negotiated the CANADIAN RECIPROCITY AGREEMENT in 1911, only to see the pact rejected by the Canadians following his impolitic comments about free trade paving the way to eventual U.S. annexation of Canada. Together with Secretary of State PHILANDER KNOX, he implemented a policy of DOLLAR DIPLOMACY, a program devised to increase U.S. diplomatic influence in the Far East and Latin America through government-promoted American commercial expansion.

Taft won renomination in 1912 after beating back a challenge by Roosevelt at the Republican national convention. Roosevelt then left the party to run as the new Bull Moose Party candidate. Democrat

WOODROW WILSON won the three-way election, with Taft finishing a distant third. Upon leaving office in March 1913, Taft retired to Yale University as Kent professor of law. In 1921 he was named chief justice of the Supreme Court by President WARREN G. HARDING. Illness forced Taft's resignation from the court in February 1930 and he died a month later.

TAFT-KATSURA AGREEMENT (1905) Understanding reached between the United States and Japan regarding their respective interests in the Far East. The Russo-Japanese War (1904–1905), waged for control over Manchuria and Korea, jeopardized the OPEN DOOR policy. In February 1904 the United States appealed unsuccessfully for a mutual pledge by the belligerents to respect China's neutrality and independence. As Japanese military successes mounted, President THEODORE ROOSEVELT came to the conclusion that the Open Door and U.S. interests in the Far East would not be served by a total Russian defeat that would leave Japan dominant in East Asia. Tokyo's victories over Moscow engendered fears in the Roosevelt administration about the safety of the Philippines, which the United States had acquired following the SPANISH-AMERICAN WAR (1898) and which represented the key to American trade and naval power in the Pacific. Roosevelt's diplomatic efforts to end the conflict received a boost when, in April 1905, the Japanese government informed the United States that it would preserve the Open Door in Manchuria and restore the province to China. A month later Japan, its basic war aims attained by a major victory over the Russian fleet, formally asked Roosevelt to take the initiative in acting as mediator of the conflict.

He won quick Russian consent to his role as go-between in peace negotiations. Roosevelt then invited both powers to open joint peace talks at Portsmouth, New Hampshire, under his personal mediation. Prior to the PORTSMOUTH CONFERENCE, which convened in August, Secretary of War WILLIAM HOWARD TAFT, while on a trip to the Philippines, visited Tokyo as Roosevelt's emissary to consult with Japanese Prime Minister Count Taro Katsura on the Far East. On July 29, 1905, they concluded the secret Taft-Katsura Agreement, or what is sometimes called the Taft-Katsura Agreed

Memorandum. Under its terms, the United States accepted Japanese dominion over Korea. For its part Japan recognized American hegemony in the Philippines, disavowing any aggressive designs on the archipelago. On July 31 Roosevelt approved the memorandum, which was simply an executive agreement and therefore did not require Senate ratification. The Taft-Katsura Agreement was supplemented in 1908 by the ROOT-TAKAHIRA AGREEMENT.

See also PORTSMOUTH TREATY.

TAIWAN MUTUAL DEFENSE TREATY (1954) Bilateral security pact between the United States and Nationalist China. With its overthrow in 1949 by the Chinese Communist revolution headed by Mao Tse-tung, the National Chinese government under Chiang Kai-shek fled to the island of Taiwan, where it reestablished the Republic of China. The United States refused to recognize the mainland Communist People's Republic of China and instead maintained ties with the Taiwan regime, supporting its claim as the sole legitimate government of all China. The Nationalist Chinese harbored hopes of returning to the mainland, while Mao's new Communist government sought to eliminate the last opposition to its rule and bring all China under its control. Communist Chinese shelling of the Nationalist-controlled islands of Quemoy and Matsu in September 1954 triggered the first of the QUEMOY-MATSU CRISES, raising fears in both Taipei and Washington of a Communist assault on Taiwan.

On December 2, 1954, U.S. Secretary of State JOHN FOSTER DULLES and Nationalist Foreign Minister George K. C. Yeh, meeting in Washington, signed a mutual defense treaty committing the United States to the defense of Taiwan. The pact, ratified by the Senate on February 9, 1955, called for common action in the event of external armed attack against either nation in the Western Pacific and authorized the United States to station military forces in and around Taiwan as jointly agreed necessary for its defense. Under the treaty, the U.S. 7th Fleet, patrolling the Taiwan Strait, guaranteed Nationalist Chinese security for more than three decades.

On December 15, 1978, President JIMMY CARTER announced the extension of U.S. diplomatic recognition to Communist

China effective January 1, 1979. As part of this step, the United States severed its official ties with Nationalist China. Carter also indicated America would give Taiwan the required one-year notice for termination of the mutual defense treaty effective December 31, 1979. Senator Barry M. Goldwater (R-AZ) and 14 other legislators filed suit in U.S. District Court to block Carter's cancellation of the 1954 agreement, arguing the president lacked the authority under the CONSTITUTION to end a treaty without congressional approval. On December 13, 1979, the Supreme Court declined to hear arguments in *Goldwater* v. *Carter*, dismissing the suit and upholding an appellate court ruling that had backed the president's right to terminate the defense pact. Meanwhile, on April 10, 1979, Carter had signed the Taiwan Relations Act redefining U.S. ties with Nationalist China. The act created a private, non-profit corporation, the American Institute, to conduct future U.S. relations with Taiwan. Generally, U.S. financial, legal, cultural, and other contacts were no longer under an intergovernmental aegis but otherwise remained unchanged. The 1979 legislation also communicated continued U.S. commitment to the security of Taiwan and the resolution of its status through peaceful means.

TAIWAN RELATIONS ACT See **TAIWAN MUTUAL DEFENSE TREATY**.

TAMPICO INCIDENT See **VERACRUZ INCIDENT**.

TARIFF OF ABOMINATIONS (1828) Federal act that levied very high tariffs on imported goods. With the TARIFF OF 1816 and then the Tariff of 1824, Congress had imposed progressively steeper import duties to protect U.S. manufacturing from overseas competition. The growth of American PROTECTIONISM generated bitter sectional debate, pitting the agricultural South, which opposed higher tariffs, against the increasingly industrial North, which favored them. In 1828 conflicting political interests in Congress resulted in passage of tariff legislation that imposed very high rates and extended them to many items not previously subject to custom charges. Signed into law by President JOHN QUINCY ADAMS on May 19, 1828, the measure's higher import taxes on

finished goods angered Southern interests while its new duties on raw materials brought opposition in the North. The widely unpopular tariff was denounced by political figures as an "abomination," thus earning its popular title. The South Carolina legislature in December 1828 declared the tariff act unconstitutional, sparking the Nullification Controversy over a state's right to nullify a federal law it found objectionable. The constitutional crisis ultimately was resolved by passage of the COMPROMISE TARIFF (1833), which revised the most controversial features of the 1828 tariff.

TARIFF OF 1789 First U.S. tariff. The ARTICLES OF CONFEDERATION, under which the United States was governed from 1781 to 1789, did not grant the federal government the authority to impose tariffs. This restriction left the government without the means either to raise revenues or to manage trade with other nations. The new national government formed under the CONSTITUTION in 1789 was given exclusive power to regulate foreign commerce and levy tariffs. In its initial session, the U.S. Congress passed a tariff bill, introduced by Virginia Representative JAMES MADISON, intended primarily to provide monies for the operation of the government. Enacted July 4, 1789, it placed duties of 5 percent to 11 percent on items imported into the new nation. The tariff measure also represented the first limited use of import duties for protectionist purposes. Customs were imposed on some 30 commodities to discourage their importation and encourage their domestic production. To spur development of the American merchant fleet, a 10 percent reduction in duties was included for articles carried on U.S. shipping. U.S. tariffs were adjusted periodically until 1812, when they were roughly doubled to help finance the WAR OF 1812. Following the war, import duties were realigned broadly in the TARIFF OF 1816.

See also PROTECTIONISM.

TARIFF OF 1816 Legislation that revised U.S. import duties following the WAR OF 1812 with Great Britain. During the conflict, U.S. tariffs had been doubled to roughly 20 percent of an imported item's value. The 1816 tariff act, which marked the rise of PROTECTIONISM in U.S. trade policy, retained the higher duties so as to assist the development of domestic industries. A minimum tax on cotton cloth effectively excluded it from importation and protected fledgling U.S. textile mills from overseas competition. The measure, adopted April 27, 1816, represented an uneasy balance between Southern agriculture and New England shipping interests, which opposed higher tariffs, and Northern manufacturing, which favored them. Import duties were increased further in the Tariff of 1824 and again in the 1828 TARIFF OF ABOMINATIONS.

TAYLOR, MAXWELL DAVENPORT (1901–1987) Army officer, chairman of the JOINT CHIEFS OF STAFF (JCS), ambassador. A native of Missouri, Taylor graduated from West Point in 1922. After service with engineer and artillery units, he returned to his alma mater as an instructor of foreign languages. From 1935 to 1939 he was attached to the U.S. embassy in Tokyo to study Japanese and learn about the Japanese military. In 1937 he was assigned briefly as assistant U.S. military attaché in China. During WORLD WAR II Taylor was promoted to general and commanded the 101st Airborne Division in extensive combat in Europe. Following the war he was named superintendent of West Point. In 1949 he returned to Europe as American military governor in Berlin. After a tour with the Army staff in Washington, he became commander of U.S. forces in the KOREAN WAR in 1953.

Taylor was appointed Army chief of staff in 1955. During his four-year tenure as the service's top officer, he found himself increasingly in disagreement with the Eisenhower administration's NEW LOOK defense strategy. He worried that the strategy's extensive reliance on atomic weapons left America without conventional, or non-nuclear, forces sufficient to handle lesser threats to the nation's security that might not warrant an atomic response. He argued that, in the face of the Soviet Union's expanding atomic arsenal, the United States would no longer enjoy clear nuclear superiority and consequently needed to develop its conventional capabilities. Taylor retired in 1959. The same year he published *The Uncertain Trumpet*. The influential book outlined his thinking on national security, calling for a FLEXIBLE RESPONSE strategy that would provide America a mix of forces capable of meeting military challenges from nuclear war to Communist insurgency. Taylor's ideas were incorporated by Senator JOHN F. KENNEDY (D-MA) into his 1960 presidential campaign and subsequently formed the foundation of the Kennedy administration's defense policy.

In January 1961 Taylor became president of the Lincoln Center for the Performing Arts in New York City. That April President Kennedy called him to Washington to head an investigation into the failed BAY OF PIGS INVASION of Communist Cuba. In July, Taylor joined the White House staff in the newly formed position of military representative of the president, becoming one of Kennedy's key advisers. In October 1961 he led a small group of senior officials on a special fact-finding trip to South Vietnam to assess the Communist threat there. The recommendations of the TAYLOR-ROSTOW MISSION, largely adopted by the Kennedy administration, brought a deepening American military involvement in the VIETNAM WAR.

Taylor returned to active military duty as chairman of the JCS in October 1962. He held the nation's highest uniformed post until July 1964, when he again retired and was named U.S. ambassador to South Vietnam by President LYNDON B. JOHNSON. As both JCS chairman and then ambassador, he pressed for a vigorous counterinsurgency campaign in Vietnam. In 1965 Taylor was succeeded in Saigon by HENRY CABOT LODGE, JR. Taylor continued as a special consultant to Johnson throughout his presidency. In 1968 he opposed the majority recommendation of the WISE MEN, an informal group of senior advisers to the Johnson administration, for U.S. disengagement from Vietnam. Taylor retired to private life in 1969, but was a member and chairman of the PRESIDENT'S FOREIGN INTELLIGENCE ADVISORY BOARD during the Nixon administration.

TAYLOR, ZACHARY (1784–1850) Twelfth president of the United States. Born in Virginia and raised in Kentucky, Taylor received little formal schooling. His acceptance in 1808 of a commission as an infantry first lieutenant marked the start of 40 years service in the U.S. Army. Promoted to captain in 1810, he won distinction in

September 1812 for his successful defense of Ft. Harrison, Indiana Territory, against Indian attack. During the WAR OF 1812, he served under General WILLIAM HENRY HARRISON in defense of the OLD NORTHWEST. Taylor was promoted to colonel in 1832 and that year took part in the BLACK HAWK WAR. He acquired the nickname "Old Rough and Ready" fighting Florida's Seminole Indians from 1837 to 1840 in the second of the SEMINOLE WARS. Following his victory at the Battle of Okeechobee in December 1837 he was made brigadier general.

U.S. annexation of Texas in 1845 led to Taylor's most important military assignment, commanding the Army detachment in Texas that early in 1846 was sent into the region between the Nueces River and Rio Grande, then claimed by both the United States and Mexico. Hostilities between his forces and Mexican troops touched off the MEXICAN WAR (1846–1848). Promoted to major general and put in command of the Army of the Rio Grande, he disregarded orders to remain on the defensive and advanced southward into Mexico, finally defeating Mexican forces under General Santa Anna at the key battle of Buena Vista in February 1847. The victory made him a national hero and the Whig Party nominated him as its presidential candidate in 1848. Taylor won the election over Democratic nominee LEWIS CASS and Free Soil candidate MARTIN VAN BUREN.

When he was inaugurated in March 1849, the nation was absorbed with the issue of whether to allow slavery's extension into the vast area ceded by Mexico to the United States after the war in the TREATY OF GUADALUPE HIDALGO (1848). Although himself a slaveholder, Taylor opposed extension of the "peculiar institution" and gave indications he would not veto the WILMOT PROVISO, which would prohibit slavery in the MEXICAN CESSION, should Congress pass it. While he assured the South that slavery faced no threat wherever it already existed, Taylor made clear that he would not hesitate to use force to quell Southern rebellion over the slavery question. He was steadfastly committed to the Union and denied the right of secession. Falling suddenly ill, he died July 9, 1850, before Congress had finished work on the Compromise of 1850, the legislative package devised to alleviate the sectional crisis over

slavery. Opposing concessions to the South, Taylor had stood against the compromise proposal. He was succeeded by Vice-President MILLARD FILLMORE. The one notable diplomatic achievement of Taylor's presidency was the Anglo-American CLAYTON-BULWER TREATY (1850) providing for joint protection and control of any future interoceanic canal across Central America.

TAYLOR-ROSTOW MISSION (1961) Special top-level team dispatched to South Vietnam in October 1961 by President JOHN F. KENNEDY to assess the Communist threat there and make recommendations concerning U.S. policy. Following the 1954 GENEVA CONFERENCE that divided Vietnam in two, the United States began providing limited military and economic assistance to the anti-Communist nation formed in the south. Confronted with an intensification of the Communist Viet Cong insurgency in his country, President Ngo Dinh Diem in June 1961 asked for substantial additional U.S. aid to equip and train South Vietnamese military forces. As the Kennedy administration considered this request, Diem followed with the suggestion of a bilateral U.S.-Vietnamese defense treaty.

In early October 1961 Kennedy decided to send his personal military adviser, General MAXWELL D. TAYLOR, on a fact-finding trip to South Vietnam. Taylor headed a small group of senior national security officials that included the mission's deputy, WALT W. ROSTOW, and veteran counterinsurgency expert EDWARD G. LANSDALE. The report of the Taylor-Rostow visit was submitted November 3, 1961. Characterizing the situation in South Vietnam as dire but not hopeless, it concluded that prompt and energetic U.S. action was necessary to turn the tide. A vigorous response was also described as essential to demonstrate U.S. resolve in halting Communist aggression in Southeast Asia. Key recommendations included additional economic and technical assistance; increased numbers of U.S. military advisers and support troops; and an 8000-soldier task force that primarily would provide flood relief, but would be available, if necessary, for combat operations. On November 22, 1961, Kennedy approved a "First Phase of Vietnam Program" that incorporated all the proposals except the combat unit. Kennedy's decision marked an important milestone in the deepening American involvement in the VIETNAM WAR. From a total of approximately 1350 personnel at the time of the Taylor-Rostow mission, U.S. military strength in South Vietnam grew to more than 16,000 by the end of 1963.

TEAM A/TEAM B (1976) Intelligence analysis of the military threat posed by the Soviet Union. By 1975 debate was mounting in the INTELLIGENCE COMMUNITY over CENTRAL INTELLIGENCE AGENCY (CIA) estimates of Soviet capabilities and intentions. Concerned that these CIA studies tended to underestimate Soviet strength, the PRESIDENT'S FOREIGN INTELLIGENCE ADVISORY BOARD in August 1975 proposed to President GERALD R. FORD that a "competitive analysis" of the Soviet threat be conducted. Ford concurred and the following year the NATIONAL SECURITY COUNCIL set up an intelligence exercise in which two separate teams were involved in preparing the annual national intelligence estimate (NIE) on the USSR. Team A was the group of CIA analysts normally responsible for drafting the NIE. Team B was made up of outside experts enlisted for the competitive study. The independent panel was chaired by Dr. Richard E. Pipes, professor of Russian history at Harvard University. Other members included veteran security official PAUL H. NITZE and General Daniel O. Graham from the DEFENSE INTELLIGENCE AGENCY.

Both teams were provided access to the same intelligence information. Their findings, however, differed markedly. Team B argued that no evidence existed to support the CIA conclusion that Soviet missiles were less accurate than their American counterparts. If, in fact, Soviet missiles were more accurate than the CIA estimated, then U.S. forces could be vulnerable to a Soviet surprise attack. In its overall assessment, Team B found that, contrary to Team A predictions, Soviet strategic programs revealed an intention to develop a "war-winning capability."

Team B input was incorporated into the final 1976 NIE on the USSR. The substance of the team's thinking was leaked to the press in January 1977, prompting debate in the Congress and elsewhere over the actual Soviet menace. Convinced the threat was real, Nitze helped found the COMMITTEE ON THE PRESENT DANGER, a private group committed to raising support for improved U.S. defenses. Incoming President JIMMY CARTER ordered his own review of Soviet capabilities. While the Carter administration took an increasingly dim view of Soviet behavior, the more hawkish perspective articulated by Team B came to the fore with the inauguration of President RONALD W. REAGAN in 1981, helping to provide the impetus for the new administration's massive defense buildup.

TECHNICAL COOPERATION ADMINISTRATION See **POINT FOUR**.

TECHNOLOGY TRANSFER Transfer of technological knowledge from one nation to another. This exchange, whether authorized or unauthorized, occurs in three basic ways: open information sources such as professional journals and conferences, the sale or licensing of items such as patents and blueprints, and industrial espionage. Beginning in the 1950s the Western industrialized nations took steps to prevent the transfer of militarily useful technologies to the Soviet Union and the Communist bloc. The Western security alliance NATO formed the Coordinating Committee for Multilateral Export Controls (COCOM) to oversee East-West trade and restrict the sale of sensitive items. The United States imposed additional safeguards on the transfer of strategic U.S. technologies. The TOSHIBA AFFAIR (1987) involving the illegal sale to the Soviet Union of machinery useful in submarine design brought U.S. sanctions against the offending Japanese and Norwegian firms. The collapse of communism in Eastern Europe in the late 1980s brought a relaxation of COCOM constraints. Technology transfer also has been an issue in the NORTH-SOUTH DIALOGUE, with THIRD WORLD nations demanding greater access to Western technology. Various UNITED NATIONS forums, including the UNITED NATIONS CONFERENCE ON TRADE AND DEVELOPMENT, have sought unsuccessfully to devise a code for technology transfer that reconciles Western emphasis on private ownership and enterprise with Third World calls for the sharing of technological resources.

TECUMSEH (1768–1813) Shawnee warrior chief who waged a lifelong battle to stop U.S. westward expansion in the OLD

NORTHWEST. After 1805, Tecumseh sought a wide-ranging confederation of midwestern Indian tribes to resist further white encroachment on Indian lands. Traveling extensively, he implored neighboring tribes to lay aside rivalries and unite to protect territory that Tecumseh believed all Indians held in common. When his supporters were turned back in October 1811 by General WILLIAM HENRY HARRISON at the BATTLE OF TIPPECANOE, the Shawnee chief's plans for Indian union effectively died and Indian resistance faltered. Tecumseh next joined the British and fought against the United States in the WAR OF 1812. As a brigadier general he commanded 2000 warriors in a series of major engagements in the Old Northwest. Tecumseh was killed in the Battle of the Thames in Canada in August 1813. The U.S. victory at Thames broke the Indian opposition to settlement between the Ohio and Mississippi rivers and ended the slain Shawnee leader's dream of one Indian nation united against the advancing whites.

See also MAP 1.

TEHERAN CONFERENCE (1943)   First WORLD WAR II conference among U.S. President FRANKLIN D. ROOSEVELT, British Prime Minister Winston Churchill, and Soviet Premier Joseph Stalin. The leaders of the three major Allied powers met in Teheran from November 28 to December 1, 1943, to discuss both their common military strategy against Nazi Germany and plans for the postwar world. It marked the first meeting between Roosevelt and Stalin. Roosevelt in particular had urged the gathering in hopes of establishing an informal working relationship with his Soviet counterpart. En route to the conference, which was held in the Iranian capital largely because Stalin refused to venture any further from the Soviet Union, Roosevelt and Churchill conferred in Cairo from November 22 to 26. They were joined at the First Cairo Conference by Nationalist Chinese leader Generalissimo Chiang Kai-shek. In a joint communique, known as the Cairo Declaration, the three leaders reaffirmed their resolve to wage war relentlessly against Japan; declared all Chinese territories seized by Japan, including Manchuria and Formosa (Taiwan), should be returned to China; and stated their determination that Korea, then under Japanese annexation, become independent and free.

Since the Soviet Union was not at war with Japan, Stalin wanted to avoid any appearance of Soviet involvement in an anti-Japanese alliance. The Soviet premier thus barred Chiang from attending the Teheran parley. Stalin did, however, secretly pledge at Teheran that the USSR would enter the war against Japan once Germany had been defeated. The decision was made at the conference to launch Operation Overlord, the Anglo-American invasion of German-occupied France, in late spring 1944. Stalin had long sought the creation of a second front in Europe to relieve German military pressure on the Soviet Union. The BIG THREE considered, but reached no decision upon, the postwar shape of Germany; determined the eastern Polish boundary, with Roosevelt and Churchill acquiescing to Soviet acquisition of part of eastern Poland; laid preliminary plans for a UNITED NATIONS peacekeeping organization, championed by Roosevelt; and agreed to support Marshall Josip Tito's partisan forces in Yugoslavia. In a joint declaration, released following the conference, the three leaders affirmed their commitment to the independence and sovereignty of Iran, then under Allied wartime occupation and control.

Roosevelt, Churchill, and Stalin next met at the YALTA CONFERENCE (1945). On their way back from Teheran, Roosevelt and Churchill again conferred in the Egyptian capital. The Second Cairo Conference, from December 4 to 6, 1943, largely concerned Anglo-American military planning for the 1944 invasion of France. Roosevelt named General DWIGHT D. EISENHOWER to command the operation. Roosevelt and Churchill also held conversations with Turkish President Ismet Inonu, whose country was then officially neutral in the world war. The three heads of government reiterated their nations' close ties.

TELLER AMENDMENT (1898)   Disclaimer added to the congressional resolution authorizing war with Spain. In his message to Congress on April 11, 1898, President WILLIAM MCKINLEY asked for authority to intervene militarily to establish peace in Cuba, which was fighting for its independence from Spanish colonial rule. On April 19, Congress passed a joint resolution that recognized Cuban independence, demanded Spanish withdrawal from the island, and empowered the president to use force. An additional clause proposed by Senator Henry M. Teller (R-CO) was affixed, without dissent, to the war measure. The Teller Amendment stated that the United States had no intention of annexing or exercising sovereignty over Cuba. Control of the island, the amendment asserted, would be left to the Cubans once peace and order were restored. McKinley signed the joint resolution on April 20. Under the TREATY OF PARIS (1898) ending the SPANISH-AMERICAN WAR (1898), the United States assumed temporary authority over Cuba, pending a determination on how to effect the transition to full Cuban sovereignty. An American military government was established on the island and remained there until the formation of a nominally independent Cuba in 1903. America retreated from its Teller Amendment pledge when it engineered the attachment to the Cuban constitution of the PLATT AMENDMENT (1901), which granted the United States a right to intervene in Cuba.

TELLER, EDWARD (1908–) Hungarian-born American nuclear physicist known as the "father of the hydrogen bomb." Educated in Hungary and Germany, Teller received his Ph.D. in 1930 from the University of Leipzig. Leaving Germany to escape persecution as a Jew by the Nazis, he studied in 1934 under pioneering Danish nuclear physicist Niels Bohr at the University of Copenhagen. The following year he moved to the United States, taking a post as professor of physics at George Washington University. As WORLD WAR II broke out in Europe, Teller joined with Albert Einstein and other distinguished scientists in urging the United States to take the lead in nuclear weapons research. He became an American citizen in 1941, the same year he was recruited to work on the MANHATTAN PROJECT to develop the first atomic, or fission, bomb. In 1943 he joined the prestigious scientific staff under J. ROBERT OPPENHEIMER at the newly formed Los Alamos laboratories in New Mexico, where atomic bombs were to be produced and tested.

In the course of the project, Teller grew interested in the untapped potential of nuclear fusion to yield a greatly more powerful hydrogen bomb. To his displeasure, research at Los Alamos in the fusion process effectively was shelved as attention focused on the construction of an atomic weapon. He continued to advocate development of a fusion "superbomb" even after the dropping of atomic bombs on the Japanese cities of Hiroshima and Nagasaki in August 1945 brought World War II to an end. Disagreement with Oppenheimer, who opposed fusion-bomb research, prompted Teller to leave Los Alamos in 1946 for a professorship at the University of Chicago. He returned to the New Mexico laboratories in 1949, the same year the Soviet Union exploded its first atomic device. When, in early 1950, President HARRY S. TRUMAN called for accelerated development of a fusion weapon, Teller was named director of the U.S. hydrogen bomb program. In 1952 he became director of the University of California's Lawrence Radiation Laboratory, newly established in Livermore, California, where further work on the hydrogen bomb led to its successful detonation in 1952 at Eniwetok on the Pacific Marshall Islands.

In 1953 Teller also became a professor of physics at Berkeley. From 1956 to 1958 he served on the General Advisory Committee of the Atomic Energy Commission (AEC). Throughout the COLD WAR he tirelessly advocated a vigorous U.S. defense policy to counter what he regarded as a Soviet Communist drive for world domination. In the early 1960s he opposed limitations on NUCLEAR WEAPONS tests, which he contended were indispensable to the development of less-expensive and lighter weapons with reduced radioactive fallout. In 1963 he urged the U.S. Senate to reject the LIMITED TEST BAN TREATY. He retired from Berkeley and his activities at Livermore in 1975. The same year he became a senior research fellow at the HOOVER INSTITUTION ON WAR, REVOLUTION, AND PEACE at Stanford University. In the early 1980s he became an outspoken proponent of basing U.S. nuclear DETERRENCE on sophisticated defensive weapons rather than on the concept of MUTUAL ASSURED DESTRUCTION. He enthusiastically endorsed President RONALD W. REAGAN's call in 1983 for U.S. development of the STRATEGIC DEFENSE INITIATIVE, a space-based defensive shield to protect against ballistic missiles.

TEN-NATION COMMITTEE ON DISAR-MAMENT See **CONFERENCE ON DISAR-MAMENT**.

TET OFFENSIVE (1968) Pivotal North Vietnamese military campaign during the VIETNAM WAR. In 1965 President LYNDON B. JOHNSON began a steady escalation of U.S. involvement in Southeast Asia, building U.S. troop levels to more than 500,000 by 1968 and committing American forces to direct combat in defense of South Vietnam against Communist North Vietnamese and Viet Cong aggression. By late 1967 the U.S. commander in Vietnam, General WILLIAM C. WESTMORELAND, and other senior American officials were presenting an optimistic picture of the war's progress. At the end of January 1968, U.S. and South Vietnamese units began observance of the customary annual truce in commemoration of the traditional Vietnamese lunar new year holiday of Tet. Communist forces broke the ceasefire on January 30, 1968, launching a surprise offensive that by the next day brought major cities and military bases throughout South Vietnam under attack. In Saigon, Communist assault teams struck the U.S. embassy and the Presidential Palace. Communist troops overran the historic city of Hue and hit 39 other provincial capitals. Recovering from the sudden attack, U.S. forces in fierce fighting turned back the offensive. Hue was not retaken until February 24. While American casualties were heavy, the Communists suffered devastating battlefield reverses, with estimated losses of more than 45,000 soldiers. The Communist Viet Cong guerrillas, having come into the open, were effectively eliminated as a fighting force.

The Tet offensive, although a major defeat for North Vietnam, marked a turning point for U.S. involvement in the Vietnam War. The well-executed, country-wide Communist attack undermined previous rosy reports on the situation in Vietnam and convinced many in Washington the conflict was unwinnable. Antiwar protests mounted. Noted journalist WALTER CRONKITE reflected the growing unease among many Americans when, on his nightly newscast, he questioned U.S. aims in the war and the feasibility of achieving them. A request by Westmoreland for 200,000 additional soldiers prompted a Johnson administration

reappraisal of its Vietnam policy. In March 1968 Johnson accepted the recommendation of a panel of informal senior advisers, known as the WISE MEN, for American disengagement from the conflict. The president limited to 30,000 the number of American reinforcements to be sent to Vietnam and, on March 31, 1968, announced in a television address a halt of U.S. bombing of North Vietnam above the 20th parallel. The actions marked the end of an expanding U.S. role in the war. Johnson, who had only narrowly defeated antiwar Senator EUGENE J. MCCARTHY (D-MN) in the New Hampshire presidential primary on March 12, also revealed in the speech his decision not to seek reelection.

TEXAN REVOLUTION (1836) War that brought Texas its independence from Mexico; also called the Texan War of Independence. Spain opened Texas, part of the Spanish colony of Mexico, to colonization in January 1821, when it granted American Moses Austin a charter to settle 200 families in the territory. Following Austin's death in June, his son, Stephen F. Austin, persuaded the newly independent Mexican government to renew the settlement charter and in the autumn of 1821 the first American colonists began arriving in Texas. After Mexico passed a law in 1824 inviting expanded colonization, more and more settlers poured into Texas, attracted by generous grants of land.

By 1835 about 20,000 American colonists, with some 4000 slaves, had settled in the Mexican territory. The Mexican government then resolved to stop the American immigration and establish more centralized control over Texas. Mexican attempts in the early 1830s to limit colonization by restricting slavery in Texas and barring further settlement by U.S. citizens had encountered strong opposition and proved ineffective. The Mexican government's efforts at mid-decade to reassert its authority in Texas stiffened the settlers' resistance. Texans began to organize militarily and, at conventions in the fall of 1835, resolved to separate from Mexico. Fighting in Texas between the settlers and Mexican forces broke out in October 1835. About 6000 troops under Mexican military dictator General Antonio Lopez de Santa Anna marched into the territory to crush the rebellion. On March 2, 1836, insurgent leaders, meeting at Washington, Texas, issued a declaration of independence and drafted a constitution. On March 4 they established a provisional government and named SAM HOUSTON to command the Texas army. Meanwhile, on February 23 Santa Anna had begun his SIEGE OF THE ALAMO, the fortified Mexican mission at San Antonio captured and held by a small rebel force. For 12 days the vastly outnumbered Texans at the Alamo held off the Mexican army before being overwhelmed and slaughtered. Soon afterward Santa Anna's forces massacred some 300 surrendering Texan troops at Goliad.

Moving east the Mexican army encountered the forces under Sam Houston on April 21, 1836, at the Battle of San Jacinto. Houston's troops won a commanding victory in what was the war's decisive engagement. Santa Anna, taken prisoner, signed a treaty May 14 pledging his country's recognition of Texas's independence. While the Mexican Congress subsequently repudiated the agreement, Texan independence was an unchallenged fact after San Jacinto. In October 1836 a permanent government was established and Houston became the first president of the independent Republic of Texas. The U.S. government extended diplomatic recognition to the Lone Star Republic in March 1837. Following its annexation by the United States in 1845, Texas became the 28th state.

See also TEXAS ANNEXATION.

TEXAS ANNEXATION (1845) Acquisition of Texas by the United States. Early U.S. relations with Mexico were dominated by the dispute over the Texas region. The United States had abandoned its vague claims to the territory in the Spanish-American ADAMS-ONIS TREATY (1819). But U.S. designs on Texas were revived after Mexico gained its independence from Spain in 1821. The Mexican government spurned attempts in the 1820s by Presidents JOHN QUINCY ADAMS and ANDREW JACKSON to purchase the province. Mexico's offer of inexpensive land grants lured some 20,000 largely slave-holding American settlers to Texas by the mid-1830s. Measures pushed by the Mexican government in the early 1830s to banish slavery in the territory, to restrict Protestant worship there, to impose bur-

densome customs duties, and to limit settlers' legal rights caused widespread resentment. In 1835, after Mexican dictator Antonio Lopez de Santa Anna had suspended the constitution and sent troops above the Rio Grande to put down growing unrest, Texas revolted. On March 2, 1836, Texas declared its independence and established itself as the Republic of Texas, or Lone Star Republic.

In the ensuing war, Texans under SAM HOUSTON routed Mexican forces and captured Santa Anna at the decisive Battle of San Jacinto in April 1836. In return for his life the imprisoned leader recognized an independent Texas with its boundary at the Rio Grande. But Mexico soon repudiated Santa Anna's pledge. Congress recognized Texas independence on March 3, 1837, and the United States became the first nation to strike diplomatic relations with the Lone Star Republic. President MARTIN VAN BUREN in August that same year rejected a request by Texas for U.S. annexation. He feared such an action could provoke war with Mexico and likely would force a split in the Democratic Party between pro-slavery and antislavery elements.

The annexation issue resurfaced in Washington in 1842 after Texas completed treaties of commerce and friendship with Great Britain and France. The United States, concerned generally by increasing Lone Star contacts with foreign nations, was particularly wary of British designs on Texas. Negotiations reopened by President JOHN TYLER yielded an annexation treaty in April 1844, which the U.S. Senate promptly rejected over the slavery issue. Texas annexation became the major issue in the 1844 presidential campaign and emerged as the rallying cry for advocates of the MANIFEST DESTINY of American continental expansion. Democrat JAMES K. POLK was elected on a platform promoting annexation of Texas and the Oregon Country. The House and Senate annexed Texas by joint resolution, which outgoing President Tyler signed March 1, 1845.

Texas in July approved the U.S. annexation. On December 29, it was admitted to the Union as the 28th state. Annexation brought a crisis in Mexican-American relations. Mexico, calling the action equal to a war declaration, broke diplomatic ties with the United States in late March 1845. The dispute over Texas was a precursor to the MEXICAN WAR (1846–1848).

See also MAP 2.

THE INQUIRY See **FOURTEEN POINTS**.

THIRD WORLD Term used to refer to nations with low per capita incomes and developing economies. The Third World initially was distinguished from the First World (the United States and other industrialized countries) and the Second World (the Soviet Union and other Communist countries). The term Fourth World emerged in the 1970s to indentify very poor countries with extremely low per capita incomes and little economic growth. The expression Third World (*tiers monde*) originated in France after WORLD WAR II to describe nations that were neutral or otherwise outside the mounting East-West COLD WAR. The idea of the Third World as a distinct entity separate from either the U.S.-led West or Soviet-led Communist bloc grew out of the 1955 Bandung Conference of African and Asian leaders. The gathering provided an early impetus to the nonaligned movement formally inaugurated at the first Conference of Nonaligned Countries held in Belgrade, Yugoslavia, in 1961. During the Eisenhower years, Secretary of State JOHN FOSTER DULLES adamantly opposed the basic premise that any state could be neutral in the struggle of the FREE WORLD against communism. By the 1960s, America had come to view the Third World, expanding rapidly with the gaining of independence by numerous former European colonies, as the next Cold War battleground, where Western democracy would prove superior to Soviet communism in the development of new nations. In the 1970s the nonaligned movement emerged as an important international political force, capitalizing on its large numbers to dominate the voting in the UNITED NATIONS General Assembly.

As development issues moved to the forefront of the international agenda, the Third World was characterized increasingly in economic terms. In 1964, 77 developing nations formed the Group of 77 (G-77) to serve as a caucus on economic matters and advance their joint interests in such forums as the UNITED NATIONS CONFERENCE ON TRADE AND DEVELOPMENT. While the group's membership has grown to more than 120 nations, it has kept the designation G-77. The United States participted in the NORTH-SOUTH DIALOGUE of the mid-1970s between the mainly Northern Hemisphere industrialized nations and the developing nations located mostly in the Southern Hemisphere. America led Western opposition that blocked adoption of the developing nations' suggested redistribution of the world's wealth under a proposed New International Economic Order, favoring instead free market solutions to spark Third World growth. In recent years the term Third World has been de-emphasized in favor of "developing countries" or "less developed countries."

38th PARALLEL Latitude dividing South Korea from North Korea since 1945. At the end of WORLD WAR II, the Allies adopted the 38th parallel as a temporary boundary to mark separate zones in Korea where the Japanese would surrender to U.S. and Soviet occupation forces. Plans to reunite the country foundered as America and the Soviet Union sought to influence the political future of the peninsula. In 1948 a Communist government took root in the north while in the south a democratic pro-Western government emerged. North Korea's invasion of the south on June 25, 1950, initiated the KOREAN WAR.

The conflict became a critical test of America's post-World War II policy of CONTAINMENT. President HARRY S. TRUMAN committed American troops to aid South Korea as part of the UNITED NATIONS military response. Communist China entered the war in November 1950 in support of North Korea. Peace talks began in July 1951 at Kaesong and dragged on for two years while the fighting continued. Negotiators finally concluded an armistice at Panmunjom on July 27, 1953. After three years of bitter struggle, the border between the two Koreas had shifted little from its prewar location around the 38th parallel. Since the Korean War, sporadic talks between the nations on reunification have ended in deadlock.

THOMSON-URRUTIA TREATY (1921) Settlement by which the United States paid Colombia $25 million recompense for U.S. involvement in the Panamanian revolution of 1903. The Colombian senate's rejection of the HAY-HERRAN TREATY (1903), which called for U.S. construction of an isthmian canal across Colombia's province of Panama, frustrated U.S. plans for a Central American waterway. President THEODORE ROOSEVELT, determined to locate the canal in Panama, threw unspoken U.S. support behind the successful November 1903 Panamanian revolt against Colombia and quickly extended diplomatic recognition to the newly independent Central American state. Over bitter Colombian objections, the United States and Panama completed the HAY-BUNAU-VARILLA TREATY (1903) clearing the way for an American-built and -controlled interoceanic waterway.

Roosevelt's exercise of BIG STICK diplomacy in securing the Panama Canal rights incurred Colombian resentment and fanned sentiment across Latin America against U.S. IMPERIALISM. After a decade of strained relations, President WOODROW WILSON made an overture to mollify the South American country and win general Latin American confidence. U.S. Minister to Colombia Thaddeus A. Thomson and Colombian Foreign Minister Jose Urrutia negotiated a treaty in April 1914 in which the United States expressed regret for its role in the 1903 Panamanian uprising and offered to pay an indemnity of $25 million. Former President Roosevelt deplored the proposed agreement as "blackmail." Republican senators, notably HENRY CABOT LODGE, SR. of Massachusetts, spearheaded strong congressional objections to the treaty and the Senate blocked its ratification.

Congress, after a seven-year interval, revived the Thomson-Urrutia agreement. On April 20, 1921, the Senate approved a modification of the original treaty. Under the Senate's amended version, the United States consented to pay $25 million to Colombia as compensation for events in Panama but refused to offer a formal apology. Colombia accepted the U.S. revisions and ratified the settlement in 1922, thereby recognizing Panama's independence. A provision in the final agreement granted the United States oil concessions in Colombia that previously had been denied to American firms by the Colombian government.

303 COMMITTEE See **COVERT ACTION**.

THRESHOLD TEST BAN TREATY (1974) U.S.-Soviet agreement to limit the size of underground nuclear tests. The 1963 LIMITED TEST BAN TREATY barred nuclear test explosions except those conducted underground. In the favorable climate of U.S.-Soviet DETENTE, President RICHARD M. NIXON and General Secretary Leonid I. Brezhnev concluded the Treaty on the Limitation of Underground Nuclear Weapons Tests on July 3, 1974, at the 1974 MOSCOW SUMMIT. The arms control pact established an underground testing "threshold," prohibiting nuclear blasts with an explosive force greater than 150 kilotons (150,000 tons of TNT). The United States and Soviet Union agreed to limit the number of underground tests to a minimum and to pursue negotiations toward a comprehensive testing ban. Forwarded to the U.S. Senate in 1976, the treaty's ratification was variously delayed. The same year both sides pledged to abide by the 150-kiloton limit pending the pact's final approval. The Carter administration effectively shelved the agreement while seeking a COMPREHENSIVE TEST BAN TREATY. The Reagan administration maintained that the treaty's verification procedures were inadequate and pressed for further negotiations. On June 1, 1990, President GEORGE BUSH and Soviet President Mikhail S. Gorbachev, meeting at the WASHINGTON SUMMIT (1990), signed a lengthy protocol to the treaty tightening its verification procedures. The Senate ratified the amended pact, as well as the companion PEACEFUL NUCLEAR EXPLOSIONS TREATY (1976), on September 25, 1990.

TIANANMEN UPRISING (1989) Student-led pro-democracy movement that was brutally crushed by the Communist Chinese government. The Chinese army's slaughter on the night of June 3, 1989, of hundreds—possibly thousands—of protestors and civilian bystanders in Beijing's Tiananmen Square was undertaken to end peaceful, antigovernment demonstrations that had begun in mid-April. The student-led uprising had captured world attention and raised premature hopes in the West that the Communist regime might be pressed into permitting serious political reforms. When hardliners prevailed and tightened their hold on the government, however, China appeared to be descending into a new period of repression. The bloody military crackdown drew swift and widespread international condemnation. In the wake of the Beijing massacre, U.S. President GEORGE BUSH imposed sanctions against the Chinese government, including suspension of arms sales and a ban on visits between U.S. and Chinese military leaders. But the president, who had served as the U.S. representative to Communist China from 1974 to 1975, emphasized that he did not want to break the relationship with China that America had nurtured since 1972, insisting that a rupture between Washington and Beijing would neither serve U.S. interests nor promote democracy and respect for HUMAN RIGHTS in the Asian nation.

Congress felt Bush's actions did not go far enough in protesting the Tiananmen suppression. Both chambers moved in 1989 to approve tougher economic and political sanctions against the Chinese. After extended debate, a congressional package of sanctions, moderated to win the White House's approval, was enacted in early 1990. Meanwhile, in 1989 the Bush administration had taken steps toward ending Beijing's diplomatic isolation. BRENT SCOWCROFT, the president's national security adviser, led a top-level U.S. delegation on a secret trip to China to begin mending U.S.-Chinese relations. Disclosure of the visit rekindled congressional criticism of the administration, which was faulted for being too conciliatory and morally detached. In 1990, Bush renewed China's MOST-FAVORED-NATION trade status under a storm of criticism and thwarted efforts on Capitol Hill aimed at forcing him to adopt a harder line toward China. Under pressure from lawmakers, Bush issued an executive order April 11, 1990, allowing Chinese students who had been in the United States since the 1989 crackdown to remain until at least January 1, 1994.

TIBET OPERATION U.S. support to anti-Chinese forces in Tibet in the 1950s and 1960s. In 1951, two years after seizing power in Peking, Communist Chinese troops invaded neighboring Tibet, incorporating the ancient mountain country into China as an autonomous region. By 1953, the CENTRAL INTELLIGENCE AGENCY (CIA) had begun to train and equip refugee Khamba tribesmen and other Tibetans for guerrilla

operations against the Chinese. U.S. policymakers hoped ultimately to undermine the Chinese occupation of Tibet. A Chinese move in 1959 to replace the traditional Tibetan leader, the Dalai Lama, was met with widespread rebellion. After fierce fighting the Tibetan uprising was crushed and the Dalai Lama fled with CIA assistance to India. The Chinese Communists systematically suppressed Tibetan Buddhism and in 1964 imposed a secular government. CIA support for the Tibetan guerrilla resistance subsequently was phased out amid the realization its goals were unattainable.

TIENTSIN, TREATIES OF (1858) Treaties forced on China by the United States, Great Britain, France, and Russia. Hostility toward foreign commercial and political encroachment after 1850 led the Chinese imperial government to evade some of its obligations under agreements completed with the major western countries in the early 1840s, including the Sino-American TREATY OF WANGHIA (1844). In 1856 the British and French went to war against China to force its compliance with the earlier treaties and to coerce further Chinese concessions. The Europeans attained a swift victory in the naval conflict. Although the United States had declined Britain's invitation to join the Anglo-French military alliance against China and remained neutral, it sent diplomats, as did Russia, to take part with French and British representatives in negotiating new pacts with the defeated Chinese.

The four foreign powers signed separate commercial agreements with China in 1858 at the city of Tientsin on the Pei-ho River. In order, treaties were concluded by Russia on June 13; the United States on June 18; Great Britain on June 26; and France on June 27. Through the MOST-FAVORED-NATION clauses contained in their agreements, nonbelligerents America and Russia received the same privileges as Britain and France. The treaties opened 11 additional Chinese ports to unrestricted foreign commerce, legalized the opium trade, and established a five-percent fixed tariff on imports into China. Among other provisions, foreigners were granted freedom to travel in China's interior; visiting European and American citizens were exempted from Chinese law by EXTRATERRITORI-

ALITY provisions; foreign diplomats gained the right to reside in Peking, the imperial capital; and Christian missionaries were permitted to worship, teach, and convert Chinese free of government interference. The unequal terms, virtually dictated at Tientsin, stoked Chinese antiforeignism and cleared the way for western commercial domination and cultural penetration of the empire to the end of the 19th century. The U.S.-Chinese Treaty of Tientsin was amended in 1868 by the BURLINGAME TREATY.

TIPPECANOE, BATTLE OF (1811) Key engagement in frontier hostilities between the United States and an Indian confederation under Shawnee Chief TECUMSEH. By 1811, mounting Indian opposition to the steady advance of American settlers in the Indiana Territory had brought a U.S. military response. General WILLIAM HENRY HARRISON set out north from Vincennes in September 1811 with one thousand troops to stamp out the British-backed Indian resistance and to forestall Tecumseh's plans for a powerful Indian union to fight the whites. On November 7, 1811, Tecumseh's brother, known as The Prophet, staged a surprise attack on Harrison's camp along the Tippecanoe Creek. The U.S. general repelled the assault, dispersing the Indians. The next day he destroyed the abandoned nearby Indian capital at Prophetstown. While not militarily decisive, the outcome at Tippecanoe effectively halted Tecumseh's efforts to unite midwestern tribes to block U.S. territorial expansion.

British support of Tecumseh's confederation movement further strained Anglo-American relations on the eve of the WAR OF 1812. After Tippecanoe, embittered northern Indians under Tecumseh aligned with Great Britain and fought against the United States in the 1812 conflict. The British and Indian defeat at the Battle of the Thames in October 1813, also the scene of Tecumseh's death, signaled the end of Indian resistance between the Ohio and Mississippi rivers, opening the entire Midwest to American settlement after the war.

See also MAP 1.

TLATELOLCO, TREATY OF (1967) Multilateral agreement to ban NUCLEAR WEAPONS from Latin America. Following the 1962 CUBAN MISSILE CRISIS, various Latin American nations, including Mexico and Brazil, proposed a formal pact barring nuclear weapons from the region. Negotiations begun in 1965 culminated in the Treaty for the Prohibition of Nuclear Weapons in Latin America, signed at Tlatelolco, a section of Mexico City, on February 14, 1967. The first agreement to bar nuclear weapons from an inhabited part of the Earth, it prohibited the nations of the Western Hemisphere south of the 35° North latitude, excluding the United States, from developing, acquiring, testing, or storing any nuclear device either on their own behalf or for any other party. While the treaty, which requires the ratification of all Latin American and Caribbean states to take effect, officially remains in abeyance pending the participation of Cuba and Guyana, it has been regarded in operation for its adherents since April 22, 1968. Two protocols to the agreement apply to outside states. The United States is a party to both Protocol I, which calls for nations with possessions in Latin America to abide by the treaty's provisions, and Protocol II, which requests that nuclear powers pledge not to use or threaten to use nuclear weapons in the region.

TOKYO ROUND See **GENERAL AGREEMENT ON TARIFFS AND TRADE**.

TONKIN GULF INCIDENT (1964) U.S.-North Vietnamese naval encounter that served as justification for the TONKIN GULF RESOLUTION and direct American involvement in the VIETNAM WAR. In July 1964, amid a worsening situation in South Vietnam, the Johnson administration announced it was raising from 16,000 to 21,000 the total number of U.S. military advisers committed to helping the Southeast Asian nation resist Communist North Vietnamese aggression. On August 2 the U.S. destroyer *Maddox* was on patrol in international waters in the Gulf of Tonkin off North Vietnam's coast when it came under attack from North Vietnamese torpedo boats. The attack was repulsed and several gunboats were damaged or destroyed. Two nights later the *Maddox,* joined by the U.S. destroyer *Turner Joy,* reported another assault by North Vietnamese torpedo boats in the Tonkin Gulf. The American ships escaped harm while two Communist gunboats were sunk. President LYNDON B. JOHNSON ordered an immediate retaliatory airstrike against North Vietnam that destroyed another 25 gunboats at their bases. On August 5 Johnson sent to Congress a draft resolution that would authorize him as president and commander in chief to use armed force as necessary to repel attacks against the U.S. military and to defend America's Southeast Asian allies from aggression. The Tonkin Gulf Resolution was passed by Congress on August 7 and signed into law on August 10.

The measure served as the legal basis for the Johnson administration's subsequent escalation of the U.S. military role in Vietnam. As opposition to the war mounted, intense debate erupted over the meaning of the resolution and attention turned to the incident behind its enactment. In 1968 the SENATE FOREIGN RELATIONS COMMITTEE under chairman J. WILLIAM FULBRIGHT (D-AR) conducted hearings into the 1964 incident. Senior administration defense officials refuted Fulbright's suggestion that the second attack on August 4 might not have occurred. Fulbright's charge that the administration might have provoked the naval engagement to allow it to escalate the war also was denied. Experts continue to debate whether the second encounter was actually a mistaken sonar reading. Publication of the PENTAGON PAPERS in 1971 revealed that in February 1964 the United States and South Vietnam had undertaken a joint program of clandestine operations, referred to as Plan 34A, against North Vietnam. In late July and early August 1964 South Vietnamese patrol boats staged secret commando raids on the North Vietnamese coast in the Tonkin Gulf. Some Vietnam observers surmise that the North Vietnamese may have attacked the U.S. destroyers in the gulf believing they were part of the 34A operations.

TONKIN GULF RESOLUTION (1964) Act of Congress that served as the constitutional justification for the escalation of U.S. military involvement in the VIETNAM WAR. In early August 1964 two American destroyers reported they had been attacked by North Vietnamese torpedo boats in international waters off the coast of North Vietnam in what became known as the TONKIN GULF INCIDENT. President LYNDON B. JOHNSON ordered retaliatory air strikes and sent before Congress a draft resolution authorizing the president, as commander in chief, to "take all necessary measures to repel an armed attack against the forces of the United States and to prevent further aggression." Congress passed the proposed Southeast Asia Resolution on August 7. The House approved by a unanimous voice vote of 416 to 0, while the Senate voted 88 to 2, with Senators Ernest H. Gruening (D-AK) and Wayne Morse (D-OR) the only dissenters. Johnson signed the measure into law on August 10. Commonly referred to as the Tonkin Gulf Resolution, it stated that the United States was prepared, at the determination of the president, to use armed force if necessary to defend the freedom of any state protected under the SOUTHEAST ASIA TREATY ORGANIZATION (SEATO).

The Johnson administration cited the resolution as the legal basis for its growing commitment in the mid-1960s of American combat forces to the conflict in Southeast Asia. South Vietnam was not a formal participant in SEATO, but had been included in the organization's collective security guarantees. As opposition to U.S. involvement in the Vietnam War mounted, use of the resolution came under increasing scrutiny. Senator J. WILLIAM FULBRIGHT (D-AR) led a growing number of legislators who argued that the resolution did not constitute a declaration of war and therefore could not be construed as congressional authority for waging a war in Indochina. Amid widespread dissatisfaction over the course of the Vietnam conflict, Congress repealed the measure in June 1970. Its termination, however, was largely symbolic and did not halt U.S. involvement in the war. President RICHARD M. NIXON, who did not oppose repeal, instead cited his constitutional powers as commander in chief to continue American combat operations in Vietnam until the PARIS PEACE ACCORDS in January 1973. Debate over the respective war powers of the executive and legislative branches led to passage by Congress in November 1973 of the WAR POWERS RESOLUTION, which limited the ability of the president to engage U.S. armed forces in hostilities without congressional approval.

See also CASE-CHURCH AMENDMENT, COOPER-CHURCH AMENDMENT.

TORQUAY ROUND See **GENERAL AGREEMENT ON TARIFFS AND TRADE**.

TORTURE TREATY (1984) Multilateral agreement making torture a criminally punishable offense under international law. The Convention Against Torture and Other Cruel, Inhuman, or Degrading Treatment or Punishment was approved unanimously by the UNITED NATIONS General Assembly on December 10, 1984. The treaty, which defined torture as "any act by which severe pain or suffering, whether physical or mental, is intentionally inflicted on a person," created a Committee Against Torture under U.N. auspices to investigate alleged violations. Member nations were bound to prevent torture in any territory under their jurisdiction and to prosecute or extradite for prosecution those accused of the crime. The United States signed the measure April 18, 1988, but its ratification was delayed in the U.S. Senate by conservatives concerned that provisions of the pact might supersede the U.S. CONSTITUTION. After attaching several reservations restricting the treaty from any infringement on U.S. sovereignty or law, the Senate approved a resolution of ratification on October 27, 1990.

TOSHIBA AFFAIR (1987) Episode involving the illegal sale by Japanese and Norwegian companies of militarily useful technology to the Soviet Union. In May 1987 the Japanese government revealed that the Toshiba Machine Company of Japan had transferred restricted technology to the Soviet Union in contravention of international agreements and Japanese law. Toshiba Machine, an independent subsidiary of the giant Japanese Toshiba Corporation, admitted selling highly sophisticated metal-milling machinery to the Soviets in 1983 and 1984. The USSR had acquired the computers and software needed to run the machines from Kongsberg Trade, a subsidiary of the state-owned Norwegian weapons firm Kongsberg Vaapenfabrikk. U.S. defense experts claimed the technology had enabled the Soviets to produce finely honed propeller blades for their submarines. The blades made the vessels much quieter and thus far more difficult for the United States to track. The transactions had violated regulations established by the 16-nation COORDINATING COMMITTEE ON EXPORT CONTROLS (COCOM). The U.S. Defense Department estimated that the sales could end up forcing the replacement of as much as $5 billion in American defense equipment rendered obsolete by the Soviet leap in submarine technology.

Disclosure of the matter served to escalate the already sharp trade tensions between the United States and Japan and drew an angry protest from the U.S. Congress. The House and Senate initiated efforts during the remainder of 1987 to punish Toshiba and Kongsberg. Sanctions against the firms were incorporated in a catch-all appropriations bill signed into law December 22. The measure barred the Defense Department from importing goods or services from Toshiba, Kongsberg, or any of their subsidiaries unless the defense secretary decided, on a case-by-case basis, that such action would adversely impact U.S. national security. Tougher penalities were included in the OMNIBUS TRADE ACT (1988), terms of which prohibited the parent Toshiba and Kongsberg firms from selling goods or services to the U.S. government for three years. The legislation also imposed a three-year ban on imports from Toshiba Machine and Kongsberg Trade, and on U.S. government contracting or procurement from these subsidiaries. Exceptions were made for essential defense-related goods and for commercial spare and component parts that U.S. industries could not acquire elsewhere.

See also TECHNOLOGY TRANSFER.

TOWER COMMISSION See **IRAN-CONTRA**.

TRADE ACT OF 1974 Federal legislation granting the president broad authority to negotiate trade agreements with foreign nations. Under the TRADE EXPANSION ACT (1962), the United States had participated in the KENNEDY ROUND (1964–1967) of trade negotiations among the member states of the GENERAL AGREEMENT ON TARIFFS AND TRADE (GATT) held in Geneva, Switzerland. The presidential power to enter into trade agreements conferred by the 1962 act expired in 1967. Attempts to renew this authority were blocked by an increasingly protectionist Congress in 1967 and 1970. In 1971 the United States ran its first trade deficit, with the nation's imports exceeding its exports, since 1888. The deteriorating U.S. trade position stemmed partly from the erection of various import barriers by the European Economic Community, or Common Market, and Japan.

In April 1973 President RICHARD M. NIXON asked Congress for wide new negotiating powers to enable U.S. representatives to join in GATT trade talks scheduled to begin in Tokyo later the same year. Nixon opposed the rising PROTECTIONISM in Congress, arguing that the key to reversing U.S. trade deficits was increased international commerce through the removal of trade barriers. As part of its comprehensive trade proposal, the administration also called for the relaxation of certain restrictions on trade with the Soviet Union. Nixon sought to extend MOST-FAVORED-NATION tariff concessions and EXPORT-IMPORT BANK credits to the Communist nation as part of a 1972 U.S.-Soviet trade agreement. The president described the trade pact as a cornerstone of the developing U.S.-Soviet DETENTE. Passage of the proposed trade bill was delayed by the 1973 YOM KIPPUR WAR and by congressional efforts, opposed by the White House, to link trade concessions to the USSR to the lessening of Soviet restrictions on Jewish emigration. In 1974 the Watergate scandal dominated the national agenda before forcing Nixon's resignation from office in August. Meanwhile the TOKYO ROUND of trade negotiations, intended primarily to reduce non-tariff trade barriers, had started as scheduled in September 1973 with the United States in attendance. The Ford administration, responding to concerns among other GATT members about the lack of U.S. negotiating authority, pressed for final action on the long-stymied trade legislation before the end of 1974. In October 1974 Secretary of State HENRY A. KISSINGER reached a compromise agreement with congressional leaders providing for attachment to the trade bill of the JACKSON-VANIK AMENDMENT linking trade concessions to Soviet Jewish emigration.

Approved by Congress in December 1974, the trade legislation was signed into law by President GERALD R. FORD on January 3, 1975. The act gave the president authority, good for five years, to conclude trade agreements with other nations to reduce tariffs by as much as 60 percent and to eliminate non-tariff trade barriers. The

Tokyo Round trade negotiations were completed in 1979 and the results implemented by the United States in the TRADE AGREEMENTS ACT OF 1979. The USSR rejected the Jackson-Vanik Amendment, effectively terminating the 1972 U.S.-Soviet trade agreement.

TRADE AGREEMENTS ACT (1934)   Federal legislation authorizing the president to negotiate tariff-reduction agreements with other nations. The U.S. CONSTITUTION granted the power to set import duties to Congress, which exercised this prerogative in a series of tariff acts from 1789 to 1930. Since the mid-1800s, America had pursued a policy of trade PROTECTIONISM, relying on high tariffs to discourage imports and thus stimulate domestic industries. This policy culminated in the 1930 SMOOT-HAWLEY TARIFF, which imposed record steep tariff rates and inspired retaliatory construction of trade barriers by other nations. The resulting drop in international commerce exacerbated the deepening worldwide Great Depression of the 1930s. President FRANKLIN D. ROOSEVELT took office in 1933 committed to reversing the decline in international trade as part of his broad New Deal program to revitalize the American economy. The administration, guided by free-trade advocate Secretary of State CORDELL HULL, drafted a comprehensive trade bill delegating to the president much of the Congress's constitutional power to regulate foreign commerce. While opposed by traditional protectionists among the Republican congressional delegation, the legislation received broad support from New Deal Democrats and was signed into law June 12, 1934.

The measure represented a break with America's protectionist past. It empowered the president to conclude reciprocal agreements with other governments to reduce tariffs by as much as 50 percent and remove other trade barriers. The act, originally in effect for three years, was extended periodically until its replacement by the TRADE EXPANSION ACT in 1962. The legislation had the desired effect of increasing U.S. foreign trade. In 1947 President HARRY S. TRUMAN relied on the Trade Agreements Act to authorize U.S. participation in negotiations establishing the GENERAL AGREEMENT ON TARIFFS AND TRADE, a set of principles and rules governing international commerce.

TRADE AGREEMENTS ACT OF 1979 Federal legislation that made changes in U.S. law to permit implementation of the agreements reached at the TOKYO ROUND of multilateral trade negotiations. The international trade talks, conducted under the auspices of the GENERAL AGREEMENT ON TARIFFS AND TRADE (GATT), had begun in the Japanese capital in September 1973 and culminated in a package of agreements signed by the major trading nations in Geneva, Switzerland, on April 12, 1979. The agreements, intended to liberalize world commerce, included a phased reduction in tariffs among GATT member nations by an average 33 percent, a series of measures to eliminate non-tariff barriers to trade, and reforms in GATT rules and procedures. Several of the agreements required that the United States amend its existing trade laws. In the TRADE ACT OF 1974, which authorized U.S. participation in the Tokyo Round, Congress had established a special "fast-track" procedure, whereby it would consider any resulting trade bill under rules prohibiting amendments to the measure. In June 1979 the Carter administration submitted trade legislation to Congress to bring U.S. trade laws into conformity with the GATT agreements. The bill met with quick congressional approval and was signed into law by President JIMMY CARTER on July 26, 1979. The act revised U.S. countervailing duties (designed to protect domestic industries against foreign government-subsidized imported goods) and anti-dumping laws (which barred imports at below-home-market prices); restricted discrimination against foreign suppliers in bidding for government contracts; and extended for eight years the president's authority to negotiate trade agreements with other nations. The measure was succeeded in 1988 by the OMNIBUS TRADE ACT.

TRADE AND DEVELOPMENT PROGRAM U.S. federal agency whose purpose is to promote economic development in, and U.S. exports to, THIRD WORLD countries. The program was established in 1980 as a component organization of the INTERNATIONAL DEVELOPMENT COOPERATION AGENCY (IDCA). Under the OMNIBUS TRADE ACT of 1988, it was made an independent agency within the IDCA. The program funds feasibility studies by U.S. firms of development projects that will be financed by the WORLD BANK or other international lending institutions. Within the federal bureaucracy it has principal responsibility for coordinating government-to-government technical assistance under U.S. foreign economic development programs. The agency also helps U.S. companies become involved in development projects that have the potential to create new outlets for U.S. exports.

TRADE EXPANSION ACT (1962) Legislation reauthorizing U.S. participation in international tariff-reduction negotiations. In 1947 the United States joined in the formation of the GENERAL AGREEMENT ON TARIFFS AND TRADE (GATT), a set of principles and rules governing international commerce. Subsequent tariff-cutting conferences of GATT-subscribing nations, referred to as "rounds," brought substantial reductions in import duties among member countries. Greater U.S. involvement in international trade was thwarted in the 1950s, however, by several developments. Congressional Republicans, reflecting their party's traditionally protectionist orientation, succeeded in attaching to the periodic extensions of the TRADE AGREEMENTS ACT (1934) measures limiting the president's authority to conclude tariff-reducing agreements. The creation in 1957 of the European Common Market resulted in the erection by its members of a tariff on the goods of non-member nations such as the United States.

President JOHN F. KENNEDY, a free-trade advocate, wanted to expand overseas markets through the removal of international trade barriers. In a special message to Congress on January 25, 1962, he asked for a new trade law giving the president enlarged, unencumbered authority to negotiate reciprocal tariff concessions with the Common Market. Placing trade issues in a broad international context, Kennedy appealed for the development of expanded commercial ties among ATLANTIC COMMUNITY members as a preferable alternative to a separate European trading block. He noted the mutual benefits to be realized from the free exchange of goods and stressed the importance of common economic growth to the development of the FREE WORLD. Concerned about the worsening U.S. foreign balance of payments (the sum total of the nation's economic transactions with other countries) and the emergence of an increasingly protectionist European Common Market, Congress approved the Trade Expansion Act of 1962.

As signed into law by Kennedy on October 11, 1962, the act extended the president's authority to conduct trade negotiations for five years; empowered the president to reach agreements reducing tariffs by up to 50 percent of their 1962 levels and eliminating duties in entire categories of goods traded mainly between the United States and the Common Market; and established the office of the UNITED STATES TRADE REPRESENTATIVE. The KENNEDY ROUND, trade talks held in Geneva from 1964 to 1967 among the United States, the Common Market countries, and other GATT members, resulted in an average 35-percent lowering of import duties.

See also PROTECTIONISM, TRADE ACT OF 1974.

TRADE AND INTERCOURSE ACTS Series of laws passed by Congress starting in the 1790s designed to further the federal government's aims of peace and order in its relations with the Indians. The measures helped implement INDIAN TREATIES and enforce their terms against the actions of unscrupulous whites on the frontier. The legislation formed the foundation of federal Indian policy in the 19th century. The Act of July 2, 1790, provided for the regulation of Indian trade through the licensing of white traders. It invalidated any acquisition of Indian lands by individuals unless authorized by public treaty with the United States and set punishments for crimes committed by whites against Indians in INDIAN COUNTRY. The Act of March 1, 1793, banned white settlement on Indian lands and authorized the president to remove unlawful settlers. The measure enacted May 19, 1796, defined Indian Country in detail and required passports for whites traveling there.

The permanent Trade and Intercourse Act of March 30, 1802, replaced the temporary measures of the 1790s and remained the basic law regulating Indian-white relations for more than a generation. Trade abuses and encroachment on Indian lands continued through the 1820s, leading Congress to pass the Trade and Intercourse Act of June 30, 1834. This legislation, which helped clear the way for the federal INDIAN

REMOVAL POLICY of the 1830s, set aside a permanent Indian Country in the West and guaranteed it against white settlement. It strengthened the licensing system for the Indian trade and, for the first time, authorized use of U.S. military force to prevent or end fighting among the Indian tribes.

TRADING WITH THE ENEMY ACT (1917) Federal legislation regulating U.S. foreign trade during wartime or national emergency. Following U.S. entry into WORLD WAR I in April 1917, President WOODROW WILSON sought and Congress passed a series of emergency measures granting the executive branch broad powers in directing the American war effort. The Trading with the Enemy Act, signed into law October 6, 1917, was designed to support the Allied blockade of Germany and prevent any U.S. commerce that would aid the enemy Central Powers. The act authorized the president to employ a wide range of economic measures during wartime or a presidentially declared national emergency. These included an embargo on trade with another nation and the regulation of U.S. companies with overseas business connections. Reflecting concerns over German espionage and subversion in the United States, the legislation also empowered the president to control and censor mail, cable, and radio communications between the United States and foreign countries. The postmaster general was given sweeping censorship powers over the American foreign-language press.

During WORLD WAR II Congress extended the president's power under the act to expropriate, freeze, or otherwise control foreign property and accounts in the United States. Following the onset of the KOREAN WAR, President HARRY S. TRUMAN in 1950 declared a state of emergency and imposed trade embargoes on Communist China and North Korea. After the fighting ended in 1953, the embargoes were kept in place as a component of the U.S. COLD WAR struggle against the Communist bloc. The act served as the basis for bans placed on trade with Communist Cuba in 1963 and with North Vietnam in 1964 early in the VIETNAM WAR. President RICHARD M. NIXON reopened trade with Communist China in 1971 as part of his diplomatic initiative ending a two-decade break in U.S.-Chinese relations. Congress in 1977 amended the act to confine to wartime most of the president's authority to impose economic controls. The revised law left intact the peacetime embargoes already in place on Communist nations.

TRADING HOUSE ACT See **FACTORY SYSTEM**.

TRANSCONTINENTAL TREATY See **ADAMS-ONIS TREATY**.

TREASURY, DEPARTMENT OF THE See **DEPARTMENT OF THE TREASURY** in **APPENDIX B**.

TREATY OF ... See **..., TREATY OF**.

TRENT AFFAIR (1861) Maritime incident during the American Civil War that involved the United States in a diplomatic crisis with Great Britain over FREEDOM OF THE SEAS. At the war's outset London proclaimed its neutrality, thereby acknowledging, against Union objections, the Confederacy's belligerent status. The North's primary wartime diplomatic objective was to prevent Europe's two leading powers, Britain and France, from recognizing the South as an independent nation. From the beginning of the conflict the Confederate government sent diplomatic agents to Europe to work for recognition and to purchase ships and supplies. European statesmen received the South's commissioners, but only unofficially.

In August 1861 the Confederacy appointed James M. Mason an agent to Britain and JOHN SLIDELL an agent to France. Setting out from Charleston, South Carolina, the two envoys successfully evaded the Union blockade of the Confederate coast and reached Havana, Cuba, where on November 7, 1861, they took passage on the British mail steamer *Trent,* bound for Britain. The next day Captain Charles Wilkes aboard the Union warship *San Jacinto,* acting without specific instructions from Washington, stopped the *Trent,* searched it, and arrested and removed Mason and Slidell. The *Trent* was allowed to resume its voyage, but the commissioners were taken to Boston and imprisoned. The North celebrated news of the agents' capture. Wilkes was hailed as a hero in the House of Representatives and President

ABRAHAM LINCOLN's cabinet commended the Navy captain's conduct. An outraged Britain, by contrast, greeted word of the *Trent* Affair with indignation. Wilkes's action was deplored as a violation of neutral rights and an insult to the British flag. The British government, after ordering the Royal Navy to make war preparations, demanded an apology and release of Slidell and Mason. If the demands were not swiftly met, the British minister in Washington, Richard B. Pemmel, was under instructions to break off diplomatic relations and return to London.

Lincoln and Secretary of State WILLIAM H. SEWARD meanwhile had recognized America's shaky legal position in the *Trent* episode. While Wilkes had been within his rights under international law to stop and search the neutral British vessel at sea on suspicion of neutrality violations, he had failed, as the doctrine of freedom of the seas required, to bring the ship into port for adjudication by an official prize court before arbitrarily seizing the Confederate agents as contraband. Meeting on Christmas Day 1861 to consider the British ultimatum, Lincoln's cabinet agreed unanimously that the United States must release Mason and Slidell rather than risk probable war with the British. In a communication dated December 26, Seward acknowledged Wilkes's error and informed British Foreign Secretary Lord John Russell that the commissioners would be freed immediately. Russell's acceptance of Seward's reply as satisfactory resolved the Anglo-American crisis.

See also CIVIL WAR DIPLOMACY.

TRIAD Term used to describe the three components of U.S. strategic nuclear forces: manned bombers, land-based INTERCONTINENTAL BALLISTIC MISSILES (ICBMs), and SUBMARINE-LAUNCHED BALLISTIC MISSILES (SLBMs). Maintenance of the triad followed the development in the mid-1950s of ballistic missile technology. In ensuing decades the trio of NUCLEAR WEAPONS systems formed the foundation of U.S. military strategy for the DETERRENCE of nuclear attack by the Soviet Union. The basic premise of the triad was that at least one of its three legs would survive any Soviet surprise attack. The USSR therefore could not risk a nuclear first strike against the United States for fear of a devastating U.S. counterattack. Periodic modernization of the triad remained at the forefront of U.S. national security. Debate over the vulnerability of U.S. strategic forces and deployment of the MX missile led to the appointment of the SCOWCROFT COMMISSION (1983), which endorsed continued reliance on the triad concept.

See also NUCLEAR REDUCTION INITIATIVE, START.

TRILATERAL COMMISSION Private international organization of approximately 300 prominent labor leaders, businesspersons, scholars, and political figures from the world's three major industrialized regions—North America, Western Europe, and Japan. Founded in New York City in 1973, it grew directly out of a 1972 gathering of distinguished Americans, Canadians, Japanese, and West Europeans convened by Chase Manhattan Bank head David Rockefeller to devise a plan for bringing, in his words, "the best brains in the world to bear on the problems of the future." It took its name from the term trilateralism, a concept of "natural" partnership among the United States, Western Europe, and Japan. The commission's avowed purpose is to encourage closer political and economic cooperation among the three regions by analyzing major issues of common concern and developing practical proposals to deal with them. A closely linked goal has been to foster greater economic and political ties with the THIRD WORLD. The group has published reports on such subjects as monetary policy, trade, East-West relations, energy, international security, and arms control.

Conservative critics long have suggested that the commission is involved in a conspiracy to gain control of the U.S. government and establish a new international order—an allegation rejected repeatedly by the group. Many current or former senior U.S. statesmen are, or have been, members of the organization, including presidents JIMMY CARTER and GEORGE BUSH, Carter's national security adviser ZBIGNIEW BRZEZINSKI, secretaries of defense HAROLD BROWN and CASPAR W. WEINBERGER, and Secretary of State CYRUS R. VANCE.

TRIPARTITE DECLARATION (1950) A pledge by the United States, Great Britain, and France to uphold the status quo in Palestine. In November 1947 the UNITED NATIONS General Assembly recommended a three-way partition of Palestine into an Arab state, a Jewish state, and the city of Jerusalem, which would be placed under an international trusteeship. The proposal won Jewish acceptance but met with fierce opposition from the member nations of the Arab League (an organization formed in 1945 which vowed to resist the Zionist goal of realizing a Jewish state in Palestine). A U.S.-supported plan to establish a temporary U.N. trusteeship over Palestine fell through and Arab-Jewish fighting spread throughout the disputed territory. On May 14, 1948, as it had announced it would the previous December, Great Britain formally ended its LEAGUE OF NATIONS mandate over Palestine. Jewish residents in Palestine immediately proclaimed the independent state of Israel. Within minutes, President HARRY S. TRUMAN granted Israel de facto diplomatic recognition. Troops from Arab League states then moved into Palestine and a full-fledged war ensued. The Israelis routed the Arab armies and much of the Arab population in Palestine fled to refugee camps in neighboring Arab lands.

The United States kept out of the war but held to its support for an independent Israel. In January 1949 Truman extended the Israelis de jure, or full legal, recognition. Following several failed mediation attempts, the United Nations worked out an armistice in Palestine between Israel and the Arab states in July 1949. American RALPH J. BUNCHE headed the U.N. negotiations and played a central role in brokering the Arab-Israeli truce. A shaky and partial peace followed, marked by constant raids and reprisals across the armistice lines. The defeated Arabs harbored bitter resentment against Israel and against the United States for its support of Zionism. Refusing to recognize Israel's existence, the Arab states imposed an economic blockade against the Jewish state and threatened to destroy it in a second war. When U.S. efforts to achieve a true Middle East peace foundered, the United States and its Western allies interceded with a view toward guaranteeing the armistice settlement. In the Tripartite Declaration, issued in May 1950, the American, British, and French governments announced that if either the Arabs or Israelis moved to violate the armistice lines in Palestine, they would take immediate military action "both within and outside the United Nations" to prevent such transgressions.

TRIPOLITAN WAR (1801–1805) Naval conflict between the United States and the North African state of Tripoli. In the late 18th century the pirates of the Barbary states of Morocco, Algiers, Tunis, and Tripoli regularly preyed on merchant traffic in the Mediterranean Sea, plundering ships and capturing crews of nations that refused to pay tribute money in return for a guarantee of immunity from attack or interference. After the AMERICAN REVOLUTION, the commercial shipping of the United States became the target of Barbary assaults. A newly independent America no longer had the maritime protection it had enjoyed as a British colony. The United States, following the European custom, made tribute payments to secure safe passage for its trade vessels along the Barbary Coast of North Africa. American diplomacy also yielded a series of BARBARY TREATIES after 1785, including one with Tripoli in 1796. In each of these "peace and friendship" agreements, the United States in effect purchased assurances against Barbary attacks on American commerce in the Mediterranean.

In 1800 the pasha of Tripoli increased America's protection payments. When the Tripolitan ruler's sudden demand for more money was rejected, he declared war on the United States in May 1801. Naval forces dispatched to the Mediterranean by President THOMAS JEFFERSON began to make headway against the Tripolitan corsairs after Commodore Edward Preble took command in 1803. With losses mounting, and squeezed by a vigorous American blockade, the pasha agreed to negotiate a settlement of the conflict. On June 4, 1805, the United States and Tripoli concluded a peace treaty that brought an end to U.S. tribute payments. To win the release of the crew of its captured frigate *Philadelphia,* the United States agreed to pay a $60,000 ransom. Over the next decade, unprotected American shipping fell victim to pirate attacks even as the United States continued to pay tribute to the other Barbary states. America's Barbary troubles ended after the U.S. victory in the ALGERINE WAR (1815).

TRUMAN DOCTRINE (1947) Statement of American determination to assist countries in repelling Soviet expansion or internal Communist subversion. Announced by President HARRY S. TRUMAN before a joint session of Congress on March 12, 1947, the doctrine marked U.S. acknowledgement of the dawning COLD WAR with the Soviet Union. The president's message confronted crises in Turkey and Greece in the years immediately after WORLD WAR II that Truman claimed imperiled American and world security. Pressure exerted by the Soviet Union on Turkey since 1945 to relinquish the Dardanelles, the Turkish-held passageway between the Black Sea and the Mediterranean, had prompted the United States in August 1946 to dispatch a naval task force to the region in support of the Turks. Truman feared that either Turkey or Greece, the latter torn by civil war, could follow the Eastern European countries as the next "casualty" of Soviet aggression. By the end of 1946, with the Athens government under siege from Soviet-supported Greek Communist factions, Greece had emerged as the most pressing U.S. concern. When Great Britain announced in February 1947 that economic woes would force London to end its military and financial commitments in Greece and Turkey, Truman moved to fill the breach in the eastern Mediterranean.

Appearing before the full Congress in March, he called for $400 million in U.S. economic and military aid to bolster the Greek and Turkish regimes. Truman made the request part of a broader ideological declaration and call-to-action. He said that in the postwar world a struggle was underway between "two alternative ways of life," one free and the other totalitarian. Global peace and the national security, he asserted, depended on American willingness "to help free peoples maintain their free institutions and national integrity" against Communist-led aggression and totalitarianism. The president's remarks were directed mainly at a Europe economically shattered by World War II and thus vulnerable to local Communist movements abetted by Moscow.

Congress approved the aid package to Greece and Turkey in May. The peacetime commitment of economic and military support broke with U.S. foreign policy tradition and marked a shift away from the American ISOLATIONISM of the pre-World War II period. Critics scored the Truman program on grounds it provided aid to undemocratic governments and bypassed the

UNITED NATIONS. The Truman Doctrine appeal for U.S. resolve to oppose the spread of communism signaled the start of the CONTAINMENT policy. Greek and Turkish aid foreshadowed massive U.S. contributions toward European recovery in the MARSHALL PLAN announced in June 1947.

TRUMAN, HARRY S. (1884–1972) Senator, vice-president, 33rd president of the United States. Born and raised in Missouri, Truman graduated from high school in Independence in 1901. After working several years as a clerk, he helped run the family farm near Grandview for more than a decade. A member of the Missouri National Guard, he served during WORLD WAR I as commander of an artillery battery in France and was discharged with the rank of major in 1919. Back in Missouri, he became active in Democratic politics and was elected a district judge, an administrative post tantamount to a county executive, in 1922. He was defeated for reelection in 1924. From 1923 to 1925 he studied at the Kansas City Law School. In 1926 he won election as presiding judge of Jackson County. He held the post until 1934, when he captured a seat in the U.S. Senate. Truman was a strong supporter throughout the 1930s of President FRANKLIN D. ROOSEVELT and the New Deal. Following U.S. entry into WORLD WAR II, he gained national attention as chairman of the Senate's Special Committee to Investigate the National Defense Program. The Truman Committee was credited with preventing mismanagement and corruption in war production totaling billions of dollars. Chosen as Roosevelt's running mate in 1944, Truman was elected vice-president. He succeeded to the presidency upon Roosevelt's death on April 12, 1945.

Truman's first months as president were marked by dramatic international developments. He presided over the ending of World War II and occupied a central role in the final Allied planning for the postwar world. On May 8 Nazi Germany surrendered, terminating hostilities in Europe. Truman strongly supported the work of the SAN FRANCISCO CONFERENCE, which in June completed the UNITED NATIONS CHARTER providing for the formation of an international peacekeeping organization. In July he attended the POTSDAM CONFERENCE with British Prime Minister Winston Churchill (who was replaced by new Prime Minister Clement Attlee during the parley) and Soviet Premier Joseph Stalin. The last wartime meeting of the BIG THREE Allied powers finalized plans for the occupation of Germany, laid the groundwork for the negotiation of peace treaties with the defeated Axis powers, and reviewed preparations for Soviet entry into the war against Japan. At Truman's order, atomic bombs were dropped on Japanese cities Hiroshima and Nagasaki in early August 1945, leading to Japan's capitulation the same month. He defended the decision to use the atomic bomb as necessary to force Tokyo's surrender and thus avert hundreds of thousands of projected Allied casualties in an invasion of Japan.

The United States emerged from the war as the dominant world power. Truman continued the shift begun under Roosevelt away from historic American ISOLATIONISM and toward a foreign policy of INTERNATIONALISM. The Truman administration committed the United States to leadership in the establishment of the pillars of the postwar international economic structure: the INTERNATIONAL MONETARY FUND, WORLD BANK, and GENERAL AGREEMENT ON TARIFFS AND TRADE. Truman initially followed Roosevelt's accommodating approach toward the Soviet Union. But relations between the wartime allies quickly deteriorated over fundamental U.S.-Soviet differences regarding the postwar shape of Central Europe. Negotiations over the reunification of the Western and Soviet occupation zones in Germany soon reached a bitter impasse. With tensions mounting over Moscow's subjugation of Eastern Europe, Truman adopted a tougher stance toward the Communist power. The Kremlin's delay in withdrawing Soviet forces from their wartime occupation of northern Iran precipitated the IRAN CRISIS (1946). In an early East-West confrontation, the USSR removed its troops under strong U.S. pressure.

By 1947 U.S.-Soviet relations had deteriorated into COLD WAR. Alarmed by the Kremlin's tightening grip on Eastern Europe and the possibility of Communist inroads in Turkey, Greece, and Western Europe, the Truman administration committed U.S. policy to the CONTAINMENT of Soviet expansionism. In March 1947 the president announced the TRUMAN DOCTRINE, stating it was "the policy of the United States to support free peoples who are resisting attempted subjugation by armed minorities or by outside pressures." The containment policy at first relied largely on political and economic measures. In June Secretary of State GEORGE C. MARSHALL unveiled a U.S. proposal to help rebuild the war-ravaged countries of Europe. The MARSHALL PLAN funneled some $12 billion in reconstruction aid to European recovery. In 1948 Moscow imposed a blockade on the Western-administered sector of Berlin. The Truman administration responded by mounting the BERLIN AIRLIFT, in which U.S. and British planes resupplied West Berlin until the blockade was lifted the following year. The city became a symbol of Western resolve to resist Communist aggression. In 1949 Washington spearheaded formation of the NATO military alliance to provide for the defense of U.S.-allied Western Europe.

The Truman administration had departed from America's prewar tradition of avoiding overseas alliances when it signed the RIO TREATY, the inter-American mutual defense pact. The following year the United States joined in the establishment of the ORGANIZATION OF AMERICAN STATES. Responding to criticism that U.S. aid favored Europe at the expense of Latin America, Truman in 1949 launched the POINT FOUR program to channel U.S. assistance to less-developed areas. In the Middle East he aligned U.S. policy firmly behind support of Israel, extending diplomatic recognition to the Jewish state minutes after its proclamation of independence on May 14, 1948.

The Truman administration oversaw a major restructuring of America's national security institutions. Both the experiences of World War II and the demands of America's postwar global defense responsibilities led to passage of the NATIONAL SECURITY ACT in 1947. The landmark legislation unified the armed forces in a single defense establishment and created the CENTRAL INTELLIGENCE AGENCY and NATIONAL SECURITY COUNCIL. The NATIONAL SECURITY ACT AMENDMENTS OF 1949 formed the DEPARTMENT OF DEFENSE. After the Soviet explosion of an atomic bomb in August 1949 ended the U.S. nuclear monopoly, Truman directed the development of a more powerful hydrogen weapon. The first hydrogen bomb was detonated in 1952. In 1950 the Truman ad-

ministration drew up NSC-68, a secret study of U.S. national security that identified the Soviet-led Communist bloc as an immediate and dangerous threat and urged a massive U.S. defense buildup. The report served as the basis for U.S. rearmament following the outbreak of the KOREAN WAR in June 1950.

Truman waged a spirited reelection campaign in 1948 to overcome a huge deficit in the polls and defeat Republican candidate New York Governor Thomas E. Dewey. His second term was largely dominated by developments in Asia. In 1949 Communist forces under Mao Tse-tung won their long struggle for control of China, driving the Nationalist regime of Chiang Kai-shek to the island of Taiwan. Truman, who had avoided direct U.S. involvement in the Chinese civil war, came under domestic attack from conservatives who charged he had lost China to communism. In June 1950 Communist North Korea launched a surprise invasion of U.S.-allied South Korea. The United States gained U.N. backing for the use of military action to repel the North Korean aggression. Truman, perceiving the Korean War as a test of U.S. readiness to resist Communist aggression, committed U.S. combat units to the defense of South Korea. Concerned that the North Korean assault was part of a larger Soviet-directed Communist offensive, he sped U.S. aid to France in its fight against the Communist Viet Minh in French Indochina and approved the deployment of U.S. ground forces to NATO in Europe.

A U.S.-led U.N. Command under General DOUGLAS MACARTHUR by November 1950 had expelled the North Koreans from the South and was driving north in a campaign to unify the country under non-Communist control. The same month, however, Communist China entered the conflict on the side of North Korea. Communist Chinese armies initially inflicted serious reverses on the U.N. forces. By April 1951 the U.N. Command had halted the Chinese onslaught and established a defensive line roughly along the 38TH PARALLEL, the prewar boundary. Deciding against a further expansion of the U.S. war effort, Truman sought negotiations with the Communists to end the hostilities. When MacArthur publicly criticized the president's strategy and advocated continued pursuit of a military victory, Truman relieved the general for insubordination. Armistice negotiations began in July 1951 but remained deadlocked throughout Truman's presidency.

Truman's second term coincided with the emergence of demagogic Senator JOSEPH R. MCCARTHY (R-WI). The postwar Soviet use of subversion in Eastern Europe raised domestic fears over possible Communist infiltration of America. In 1947 Truman implemented a loyalty-security program for employees of the federal government. The administration itself came under attack in 1950 when McCarthy launched his sensational campaign against alleged Communist subversion, charging U.S. foreign policy had been compromised by Communist agents and sympathizers in the State Department. Truman and his top aides refuted the allegations. While himself staunchly anti-Communist, the president criticized the anti-Communist excesses of the early 1950s. He vetoed both the INTERNAL SECURITY ACT (1950) and IMMIGRATION AND NATIONALITY ACT OF 1952, contending they violated civil liberties. Congress, however, overrode both vetoes. Truman decided against seeking a third term and retired to Independence in 1953. He published his memoirs, *Years of Decision* (1955) and *Years of Trial and Hope* (1956), and became an elder statesman.

TRUST TERRITORY OF THE PACIFIC IS-LANDS UNITED NATIONS trusteeship administered by the United States since 1947. Its more than 2000 small islands are scattered over 3 million square miles of the western Pacific Ocean north of the equator between the international date line and the Philippines. Total land area is only 700 square miles (about half the size of Rhode Island) and less than 100 of the islands are inhabited. The region, known also as Micronesia, embraces three main island groups: the Carolines, the Marianas, and the Marshalls. GUAM, in the Marianas chain, has separate status as a U.S. commonwealth.

In the late 19th century, Spain gained sovereignty over the Carolines and the Marianas while Germany took control of the Marshalls. Following the SPANISH-AMERICAN WAR (1898), Spain ceded Guam to the United States and sold its remaining Micronesian possessions to Germany. Japanese forces occupied the German Marianas,

Carolines, and Marshalls early in WORLD WAR I. Japan administered the islands during the interwar period under a LEAGUE OF NATIONS mandate granted in 1920. Fighting in the Western Pacific in WORLD WAR II pointed up the vital strategic importance of the archipelagos. As American forces began in 1944 to drive Japan from the area, interim military governments run by the U.S. Navy were established in the islands. After the war the United States placed the islands under the newly created U.N. trusteeship system because of their strategic military value. Under an agreement approved by the U.N. Security Council in 1947, Micronesia became the Trust Territory of the Pacific Islands with the United States as administering authority.

The U.S. government assumed responsibility for promoting the economic, social, and educational progress of the territory's inhabitants and their development toward self-rule. Provisions of the U.N. arrangement safeguarded U.S. security interests. The trusteeship permitted America to establish military bases in the islands and authorized the United States to close for "security reasons"—and thereby exempt from U.N. oversight—any part of the territory. American use of the Marshalls for atomic-weapons testing had started in July 1946 at Bikini Atoll and was continued under American administration of the islands. The Pacific Proving Grounds, established at Eniwetok Atoll in 1947 and expanded in 1953 to incorporate Bikini, were closed to U.N. inspection. NUCLEAR WEAPONS trials through the 1950s forced the displacement of hundreds of Marshallese and caused serious health problems among others. President JOHN F. KENNEDY in 1962 directed that atmospheric nuclear testing be discontinued in the Trust Territory.

In 1951 President HARRY S. TRUMAN transferred responsibility for civil administration of the islands from the Navy Department to the Interior Department. Executive authority over local government was vested in a high commissioner, appointed by the president and under the interior secretary's supervision. In 1965, a bicameral, popularly elected Congress of Micronesia was formed, with limited legislative powers. Creation of the lawmaking body marked the first significant step toward separate political status for the trusteeship. Formal negotiations between the United States and the Micronesian Congress on the issue of self-determination began in 1969 but stalled in the early 1970s. By 1979 the territory had divided into four self-governing entities: The Northern Marianas in 1976 voted to become a commonwealth of the United States and two years later adopted a constitution allowing them to elect their own governor and legislature; the Republic of the Marshall Islands, the Federated States of Micronesia (comprising the eastern Carolines), and the Republic of Belau each in turn approved constitutions establishing a large measure of local autonomy. In 1980 the Marshalls, the Federated States of Micronesia, and Belau concluded so-called compacts of free association with the United States. Under free-association status, the Micronesian entities were to become independent constitutional states with full internal self-government. The United States, meanwhile, would retain responsibility for defending the islands and would continue to provide federal economic assistance.

The compacts were approved by plebiscites in the three regions during 1983. The U.S. Congress approved the instruments in 1985 and 1986. In June 1986 the U.N. Trusteeship Council determined the United States had fulfilled its obligations and endorsed termination of the trusteeship. Washington declared the compacts with the Marshalls and the Federated States to be effective from October 21 and November 3, 1986, respectively. A declaration on the Belau Compact was delayed by disputes over an amendment to the Belau Constitution banning U.S. nuclear forces in the islands. Belau consequently has continued as the one remaining part of the Trust Territory, with its final status unresolved.

See also MAP 7.

TURNER, STANSFIELD (1923–) Naval officer and head of the CENTRAL INTELLIGENCE AGENCY (CIA). Turner graduated from the U.S. Naval Academy in 1946, where he was a classmate of future president JIMMY CARTER. A Rhodes scholar, the Illinois native studied at Oxford University before embarking on a distinguished naval career that included promotion to admiral, service as president of the Naval War College, and command of NATO forces in southern Eu-

rope. Turner was nominated for director of the CIA by President Carter after the first choice for the post, Theodore C. Sorensen, met stiff congressional opposition over his prior draft status as a conscientious objector. Turner took the helm in March 1977 at a time when the CIA was continuing to recover from congressional investigations of the mid-1970s into agency misdeeds. He emphasized intelligence collection and preparation over covert operations and essentially cleaned house in the agency's clandestine services branch. In October 1977 he released some two hundred officers, including many with long service, in what quickly became known as the Halloween Massacre. Turner retired from the Navy in 1978. With the inauguration of President RONALD W. REAGAN in 1981, he was succeeded at the CIA by WILLIAM J. CASEY. He has since served on the boards of several corporations.

TWA FLIGHT 847 (1985) Trans World Airlines (TWA) jet carrying 153 passengers and crew, 104 of them Americans, that was hijacked by two Lebanese Shiite Moslem gunmen on June 14, 1985, while enroute from Athens to Rome. The hijackers, associated with an Iranian-backed Islamic fundamentalist group linked to prior terrorist strikes against U.S. targets in Lebanon, forced the Boeing 727 to fly to Beirut, where they freed the women and children on board and made known their demands. Key among them was the release of 766 Lebanese Shiite prisoners held by Israel in exchange for the freedom of the remaining TWA Flight 847 captives. The airliner then was flown to Algiers. Following a five-hour stop in Algeria, during which the gunmen freed more passengers and threatened to kill the rest unless their demands were promptly satisfied, the jet was forced back to Beirut, where an American passenger, U.S. Navy enlisted man Robert D. Stethem, was shot dead and dumped from the plane.

The airliner returned to Algiers on June 15. Thereupon Algerian government officials negotiated the release of more than half of the hostages. Meanwhile, President RONALD W. REAGAN announced the United States would make no concessions to the hijackers and reiterated his administration's policy of never negotiating with terrorists. On June 16 the plane suddenly left Algiers and returned to Beirut for the third and final time amid indications the gunmen feared a U.S. military attempt to rescue the hostages. In the war-torn Lebanese capital the less extreme Shiite Amal militia, led by Nabih Berri, quickly stepped in and adopted the cause of the hijackers, on whose behalf Berri declared he would negotiate. At his order, the remaining TWA passengers were removed from the plane by Amal militiamen and hidden in Beirut to preclude a possible U.S. rescue attempt.

As the Beirut crisis wore on and prospects for a quick resolution faded, the situation evoked comparisons to the IRAN HOSTAGE CRISIS (1979–1981) that had consumed President JIMMY CARTER and politically derailed his administration. To raise the pressure on the United States and Israel to meet Shiite demands, Berri and the hijackers staged a succession of "media events." On June 20, a day after Western journalists were allowed to interview the TWA crew, five passengers were put before a chaotic Beirut press conference to say that they and the other captives were alive and well treated and to urge the United States not to try a military rescue mission.

Anxious to achieve a breakthrough in the crisis, Berri on June 26 released an ill American hostage and proposed moving the remaining 39 to a western embassy in Beirut or to Syria, where they would stay until Israel freed the more than 700 Shiite Lebanese prisoners. Back-channel diplomatic negotiations with Syrian President Hafez Assad brought a settlement of the crisis on June 30. The hostages were taken from Beirut to Damascus and then flown to an American military base in West Germany enroute to the United States. The Reagan administration had made no public concession to the hijackers but had given private assurances to Syria, the dominant military and political power inside Lebanon, that once the Americans were released, Israel would promptly begin to free the Lebanese Shiite prisoners. Equipped with this informal U.S. guarantee, Assad had interceded to secure the freedom of the captives. On July 1, the Israeli government announced it would release 300 of the Lebanese detainees within days. Israeli officials stressed the move was not part of a deal with the hijackers, Syria, or the United States, con-

tending that all along Israel had planned to free the Lebanese Shiites.

TWO-PLUS-FOUR   See **FINAL SETTLEMENT WITH RESPECT TO GERMANY TREATY**.

TYDINGS-McDUFFIE ACT (1934) U.S. law under which the Philippine Islands gained their independence in 1946 following a transition period as a commonwealth. In the JONES ACT of 1916, the United States had promised the Filipinos independence as soon as they should achieve a stable government. Several U.S domestic political groups joined forces in the early 1930s to exert pressure for giving the Philippines their freedom. American agricultural producers and labor organizations, seeking the exclusion of the archipelago's agricultural exports and strict curbs on Filipino immigration, agitated for granting the Philippines independence, as did anti-imperialists and isolationists. Congress responded by passing the Hawes-Cutting Act in January 1933 over the veto of President HERBERT C. HOOVER. The legislation provided for complete Philippine independence following a 10-year transitional commonwealth period, during which the United States would maintain sovereignty over the islands. Hoover had opposed the measure out of the belief that the Philippines were not yet ready for freedom and probably would not be able to defend themselves against Japanese aggression. Dissatisfied with several features of the independence law, particularly a high U.S. tariff, immigration curbs to the United States, and provisions for permanent U.S. military bases in the islands, the Philippine legislature rejected it in October 1933.

As a substitute, Congress passed the Tydings-McDuffie Act, which President FRANKLIN D. ROOSEVELT signed on March 24, 1934. The new legislation offered the Filipinos only marginally better terms. Aside from arranging for the removal of U.S. Army bases and for a negotiated settlement of the future status of U.S. naval bases, it substantially duplicated the Hawes-Cutting measure. The Philippine legislature unanimously accepted the Tydings-McDuffie law. As called for under the independence act, the Filipinos framed and ratified a constitution in 1935. In November of that year the

Philippine Commonwealth was inaugurated with newly elected Manuel Quezon as president. The brutal Japanese invasion and occupation of the Philippines during WORLD WAR II interrupted the commonwealth period, which was scheduled to end in 1946. Following the liberation of the war-ravaged islands in 1945, President HARRY S. TRUMAN declared U.S. intent to aid in Philippine economic recovery and to proceed with plans to grant the archipelago full independence, which was effected on July 4, 1946, when the Republic of the Philippines formally came into existence.

See also MAP 7.

TYLER, JOHN (1790–1862) Tenth president of the United States. Born in Virginia, Tyler graduated from William and Mary College in 1807. He read law and was admitted to the Virginia bar in 1809. Entering politics as a Jeffersonian Democratic-Republican, he was elected to the Virginia House of Delegates in 1811. During the WAR OF 1812 he served briefly in a local militia unit. He left the state legislature in 1816 after capturing a seat in the U.S. House of Representatives where he served until 1821. Tyler stood for states' rights and supported strict limits on the federal government's powers. While opposed to the international slave trade, he believed that the national government lacked the constitutional authority to restrict slavery in any U.S. territory. In 1820 he voted against adoption of the Missouri Compromise that barred slavery in new territories above the 36° 30' latitude.

Tyler became governor of Virginia in 1825 and two years later was elected to the U.S. Senate, where he achieved national prominence. Sharing the general aversion of Southern agricultural interests to high protective duties, Tyler voted against the steep TARIFF OF ABOMINATIONS (1828). His rejection of the theory of nullification (that a state could refuse to enforce within its boundaries federal laws it deemed unconstitutional) put him in opposition to South Carolina's move to declare the 1828 and 1832 federal tariffs null and void. But Tyler considered President ANDREW JACKSON's strong proclamation against South Carolina's stand objectionable and was the only senator to vote against the 1833 Force Act, passed by Congress during the Nullification Crisis, authorizing the use of force to compel states to uphold federal laws.

Tyler endorsed Jackson's opposition to rechartering the Bank of the United States. However, when the president removed the federal government's deposits from its vaults, Tyler protested bitterly and supported resolutions in the Senate condemning Jackson's action. Unwilling to follow the Virginia legislature's order to vote for a Senate motion expunging these resolutions, Tyler resigned his seat in 1836 and left the Democratic Party. He joined the ranks of a Southern states' rights faction that, for reasons of political expediency, cooperated with the emerging, anti-Jacksonian Whig Party but did not embrace Whig nationalist doctrines. Defeated in a bid for the Senate in 1839, Tyler was nominated as the vice-presidential candidate the following year on the Whig ticket with standard-bearer WILLIAM HENRY HARRISON. They won the election running on the famous campaign slogan "Tippecanoe and Tyler, too." When Harrison died in April 1841, within a month of taking office, Tyler acceded to the presidency.

His states' rights views conflicted with the nationalist ideas of Kentucky Senator HENRY CLAY, the Whig leader in Congress. After Tyler twice vetoed bills to recharter the Bank of the United States and blocked other key parts of Clay's legislative program, the Kentuckian declared the president disloyal to Whig principles and persuaded the entire cabinet, except Secretary of State DANIEL WEBSTER, to resign in protest in September 1841. The mass defection left Tyler a president without a party. Though politically weakened by this internecine battle, Tyler attained a number of foreign affairs successes. In 1842 the long-standing Anglo-American dispute over the Northeast boundary between the United States and Canada was resolved through the WEBSTER-ASHBURTON TREATY. Following his successful negotiation of the agreement, Webster resigned his post and was replaced by ABEL P. UPSHUR. In 1844 the Tyler administration concluded with China the TREATY OF WANGHIA, opening the Asian nation's ports to American commerce.

Tyler made a central goal of his presidency the annexation of Texas, which had remained an independent republic since winning its freedom from Mexico in the

TEXAN REVOLUTION (1836). Secretary of State Upshur nearly had finished an annexation treaty with Texas when he was killed by an accidental explosion aboard a Navy ship in February 1844. His successor, JOHN C. CALHOUN, concluded the negotiations on the annexation agreement. Bitter sectional division over the extension of slavery into newly acquired U.S. territories brought the so-called UPSHUR-CALHOUN TREATY's defeat in the Senate. TEXAS ANNEXATION was achieved in March 1845 by a joint resolution of Congress, which Tyler signed just days before leaving office. He retired to Virginia, where he practiced law and tended to his estate. When the slavery dispute brought the country to the brink of civil war, he helped organize a convention of border states in Washington in February 1861 to seek a compromise to save the Union. After serving as chairman of that fruitless gathering, and when all other efforts at compromise failed, Tyler supported secession in the Virginia Convention. He served in the provisional Congress of the Confederacy and was elected to the Confederate House of Representatives but died in 1862 before he could take his seat.

U

UMBRELLA TALKS (1985) Unofficial name given to discussions between U.S. Secretary of State GEORGE P. SHULTZ and Soviet Foreign Minister Andrei A. Gromyko on resuming stalled arms control negotiations. The Soviet Union had walked out of U.S.-Soviet talks on both intermediate-range and strategic NUCLEAR WEAPONS in late 1983 in protest against deployment of U.S. PERSHING II and CRUISE MISSILES in Western Europe. With both sides evincing interest in a return to the bargaining table, President RONALD W. REAGAN and Gromyko conferred in Washington in September 1984. Shultz and Gromyko then met in Geneva on January 7 to 8, 1985, for what were dubbed the "umbrella" talks because they covered the full range of possible U.S.-Soviet arms control negotiations. Afterward it was announced that the two superpowers would begin new arms control discussions, known as the Nuclear and Space Talks (NST), comprising three separate, but interrelated, sets of negotiations on strategic forces, intermediate nuclear forces in Europe, and space weapons. The NST sessions, which opened in Geneva on March 12, 1985, culminated in the INTERMEDIATE NUCLEAR FORCES TREATY (1987) and START Treaty (1991).

UNCLOS See **UNITED NATIONS CONFERENCE ON THE LAW OF THE SEA**.

UNCTAD See **UNITED NATIONS CONFERENCE ON TRADE AND DEVELOPMENT**.

UNDERWOOD TARIFF (1913) Major tariff legislation that revised U.S. trade policy. The 1909 PAYNE-ALDRICH TARIFF had lowered U.S. import duties from 50 percent to a still protectionist level of 40 percent. The 1912

Democratic presidential candidate WOODROW WILSON opposed PROTECTIONISM as the tool of trusts and other financial interests. Wilson favored free trade and the development of overseas markets for American goods. Following his March 1913 inauguration, he called a special session of Congress to consider new tariff legislation. Breaking with established tradition, he became the first president since JOHN ADAMS in 1800 to appear in person before Congress, doing so on April 8 to deliver a message advocating tariff revision. A reform bill introduced by Representative Oscar W. Underwood (D-AL) was signed into law by Wilson on October 3, 1913. Passage of the tariff act was aided by adoption the same year of the 16th Amendment to the U.S. CONSTITUTION authorizing a federal income tax. The new source of revenue meant that tariffs, apart from their protectionist role, no longer need serve as the primary means of financing the government. The Underwood measure reduced import fees below 30 percent, their lowest levels since before the Civil War. While still moderately protectionist, the lesser rates reflected a brief American movement toward greater international commerce in the years before WORLD WAR I. Following the war, demand to protect domestic industries from renewed foreign competition brought enactment of the 1921 EMERGENCY TARIFF.

UNESCO See **UNITED NATIONS EDUCATIONAL, SCIENTIFIC, AND CULTURAL ORGANIZATION**.

UNION OF CONCERNED SCIENTISTS (UCS) National association of scientists and other citizens concerned about the impact of certain advanced technologies on modern society and international relations. Founded by scientists and students at the Massachusetts Institute of Technology (MIT) in 1969, UCS has evolved into an influential advocacy organization. Its two primary interests are U.S. energy policy and the prevention of nuclear war. The organization runs educational programs, engages in public interest litigation and lobbying, and conducts research and analysis of technical issues. UCS has actively participated in the debate over nuclear arms control. The group has supported the idea of a NUCLEAR FREEZE, opposing development of the MX missile and ANTISATELLITE WEAPONS, and

called for an American policy of no first use of NUCLEAR WEAPONS. In the 1980s the organization emerged as a leading critic of the STRATEGIC DEFENSE INITIATIVE. UCS argued that efforts to develop a space-based shield against nuclear missile attack risked destabilizing superpower nuclear DETERRENCE and contended the project ultimately was technologically infeasible.

UNITED NATIONS See same in **APPENDIX C**.

UNITED NATIONS CHARTER (1945) Basic constitution for the UNITED NATIONS organization. Drafted at the SAN FRANCISCO CONFERENCE, the charter was signed on June 26, 1945, the gathering's closing day, by the 50 attending nations. The document, consisting of a preamble and 111 articles, proclaimed the new permanent international organization's purposes and principles and provided for establishment of its six principal organs: (1) a General Assembly, in which all member nations would be represented and have one vote; (2) an 11-member Security Council, vested with primary responsibility for maintaining world peace and security, on which the BIG FIVE Powers (United States, Great Britain, France, Soviet Union, and China) would hold permanent seats and each wield a veto over all substantive matters; (3) an 18-member Economic and Social Council, operating under the General Assembly, to coordinate U.N. economic and social programs; 4) an INTERNATIONAL COURT OF JUSTICE for adjudicating international legal disputes; (5) a Trusteeship Council to supervise the administration of trust territories; and (6) a Secretariat, headed by the secretary-general, to handle the organization's routine administrative work. The charter entered into force on October 24, 1945, with ratification by the five permanent members of the Security Council and a majority of the other original signatories. The charter was revised by amendments incorporated in 1965 which increased the memberships of the Security Council to 15 and the Economic and Social Council to 27 and by an amendment in 1973 which further enlarged the Economic and Social Council to 54.

UNITED NATIONS CONFERENCE ON INTERNATIONAL ORGANIZATION See **SAN FRANCISCO CONFERENCE**.

UNITED NATIONS CONFERENCE ON THE LAW OF THE SEA (UNCLOS) Periodic UNITED NATIONS-sponsored conferences on international maritime questions. UNCLOS I, held in Geneva in 1958, adopted four conventions and a protocol on the settlement of disputes. Together these formed the basis of international sea law regarding territorial waters, the continental shelf, fishing and conservation, and the high seas. Conferees were unable to reach agreement on the width of the territorial waters at either UNCLOS I or UNCLOS II, conducted in Rome in 1960. UNCLOS III opened in 1973 and concluded nine years later after more than a dozen negotiating sessions in New York and Geneva with adoption of the Convention on the Law of the Sea. The treaty was signed by 117 nations on December 10, 1982, at a final UNCLOS III session at Montego Bay, Jamaica. It set a 12-mile boundary for territorial waters, created an exclusive economic zone for coastal states extending out 200 miles from their shorelines, granted coastal states limited rights over the adjacent continental shelf, and defined the area beyond the continental shelf as the "common heritage of mankind." Embracing the idea advanced by THIRD WORLD nations that all countries should benefit from the commercial exploitation of the seabed, the convention called for creation of an International Seabed Authority (ISA) to control and direct sea mining and other seabed enterprises. The United States, endorsing private free-market development of the seabed, refused to sign the agreement because of the ISA provisions. By 1991, the convention had been ratified by 45 of the 60 countries necessary for it to go into effect.

UNITED NATIONS CONFERENCE ON TRADE AND DEVELOPMENT (UNCTAD) Special body of the UNITED NATIONS General Assembly formed to promote international trade and development and serve as a forum for the discussion and resolution of the multilateral issues involved. UNCTAD began as a special U.N. trade conference attended by 122 nations, including the United States, in Geneva from March to June 1964. The meeting was convened in response to mounting demands from THIRD WORLD developing countries for redress of alleged inequities in the international economic system. UNCTAD became a permanent General Assembly organ in December 1964. All U.N. states are members. Formal sessions of the full conference are held every four years. UNCTAD has become the major venue for the NORTH-SOUTH DIALOGUE on economic matters between developed and developing nations. Since the mid-1970s the Group of 77, the principal caucus representing developing nations in international economic parleys, has pressed for establishment of a New International Economic Order (NIEO). The major industrial powers, led by the United States, have opposed the NIEO proposal, arguing the answer to Third World development is not to transfer wealth from the developed to the developing world but to generate new wealth through adoption of free-market economic solutions. With the emergence of the INTERNATIONAL DEBT CRISIS in the 1980s, UNCTAD also became a forum for developing nations' debt-reduction proposals.

UNITED NATIONS DECLARATION (1942) Pledge of cooperation and common purpose among Allied nations to defeat the Axis powers. After Japan's attack on PEARL HARBOR on December 7, 1941, brought the United States into WORLD WAR II, British Prime Minister Winston Churchill hurried to Washington, D.C., to confer with President FRANKLIN D. ROOSEVELT on joint strategy and to draft the basis for an international alliance against the Axis. On January 1, 1942, representatives of 26 countries, including the United States, Great Britain, Soviet Union, and China, signed the Declaration by United Nations at Washington. In the document, the signatory governments affirmed the purposes and principles embodied in the ATLANTIC CHARTER (1941), expressly endorsed the need to promote international respect for HUMAN RIGHTS, pledged the employment of their full military and economic resources against the Axis nations, and promised not to conclude a separate armistice or peace. The declaration marked the first official use of the term UNITED NATIONS, which had been suggested by President Roosevelt. Twenty-one more nations eventually signed the document as they joined the war against the Axis.

UNITED NATIONS DISARMAMENT COMMISSION Principal UNITED NATIONS deliberative body on arms control issues. Established by the General Assembly in 1952, its original membership included the 11 nations then on the Security Council and Canada. In 1954 a Disarmament Subcommittee—comprising the three nuclear powers, the United States, Great Britain, and Soviet Union, and two other major military powers, Canada and France—was formed to undertake arms control negotiations. The subcommittee met without success until its termination in 1957. The same year the commission was enlarged to 25 members. In 1958 its membership was extended to include all U.N. states. The commission functioned intermittently until 1965 when it became inactive. In 1978 it was revived by the first U.N. Special Session on Disarmament. The commission, again composed of all U.N. members, serves as the organization's main forum for disarmament discussions and works closely with the CONFERENCE ON DISARMAMENT, the international body for arms control negotiations.

UNITED NATIONS EDUCATIONAL, SCIENTIFIC, AND CULTURAL ORGANIZATION (UNESCO) Specialized agency of the UNITED NATIONS. The genesis of UNESCO was the concern of the European allies after WORLD WAR II to restore the educational and cultural systems of territories that had been occupied by Nazi Germany. The organization was established in November 1945 at a U.N.-sponsored conference in London, England, and formally came into being a year later following ratification of its constitution by 20 nations, including the United States. UNESCO's stated purpose is to contribute to world peace and security by promoting cooperation among nations in education, science, culture, and communications. The organization encourages international exchanges of knowledge and ideas through conferences and other contacts among educators, scientists, artists, and writers around the world. UNESCO assists member governments with national projects aimed at combating illiteracy, training teachers, upgrading scientific and technical education, and developing the scope and quality of print and broadcast journalism. It also sponsors research in such areas as racial conflict, disarmament, and HUMAN RIGHTS. UNESCO's governing body is a General Conference of all members. National commissions link UNESCO with the educational, scientific, and cultural life in each country. The organization numbers some 160 members. Critical of what it character-

ized as the politicization of UNESCO policies and mismanagement of organization activities, the United States withdrew in protest in 1985. Washington had adamantly opposed a campaign within UNESCO to establish a so-called New World Information and Communication Order, which called for an international code of conduct for journalists. America objected to the proposal as a threat to the free flow of information. Acting against the recommendations of a domestic panel, which reported that UNESCO was bringing its policies more in line with the views of the Western industrial nations, the United States announced in 1990 that it would not rejoin the organization.

UNITED NATIONS ENVIRONMENT PROGRAM (UNEP) Organization within the UNITED NATIONS that coordinates environmental activities. UNEP was formally established in December 1972 in fulfillment of a proposal approved at the U.N. Conference on the Human Environment held in Stockholm, Sweden, from June 5 to 16, 1972. Representatives from some 112 nations, including the United States, had attended the parley, which was convened in response to growing world concern over man-made destruction of the environment. The conference represented a landmark in the emergence of the environment as an important international issue. Other major results of the meeting included establishment of a global Earthwatch program to monitor trends in air and water pollution, land use, and human health as it related to the environment; implementation of a worldwide environmental information service to help countries exchange knowledge; creation of a $100 million U.N. environmental fund for pollution control, with a 40 percent U.S. contribution; and a U.S. sponsored recommendation for a 10-year ban on commercial whaling (the proposed moratorium failed to materialize). The conference concluded with adoption by the delegates of the Declaration on the Human Environment, a document outlining principles to guide future international efforts against pollution.

UNITED NATIONS MONETARY AND FINANCIAL CONFERENCE See **BRETTON WOODS CONFERENCE**.

UNITED NATIONS OFFICE OF HIGH COMMISSIONER FOR REFUGEES See UNITED NATIONS RELIEF AND REHABILITATION ADMINISTRATION.

UNITED NATIONS PARTICIPATION ACT (1945) Law under which the United States was authorized to take part in the UNITED NATIONS. As the first step toward American participation in the post–WORLD WAR II organization for maintaining world peace and security, President HARRY S. TRUMAN in early July 1945 submitted the just completed UNITED NATIONS CHARTER to the Senate to be considered as a treaty. The SENATE FOREIGN RELATIONS COMMITTEE voted 20 to 1 to approve it without amendments or reservations. On July 28, 1945, following six days of formal debate, the full Senate approved the charter by 89 to 2, a margin that reflected the overwhelming public sentiment in favor of the new international system of COLLECTIVE SECURITY. Congress next went to work on a measure to implement U.S. membership in the United Nations. Debate focused on Article 43 of the U.N. Charter pledging member states to make troops available to the Security Council, at its summons and in accordance with special agreements concluded between the member and the United Nations, for the purpose of collective security. Opponents voiced fears that such agreements would deprive Congress of its constitutional authority to declare war. To allay these concerns, Truman assured lawmakers that any agreement completed under Article 43 would be sent to Congress for its legislative consent. Attempts in the Senate to amend the bill to require congressional approval of the commitment of U.S. forces in every case in which the Security Council proposed to take action were rejected. As signed into law December 20, 1945, the participation act provided for Senate confirmation of the U.S. representative to the Security Council as well as delegates to the General Assembly and other U.N. agencies; granted the president authority both to impose economic sanctions voted by the Council and to deploy military forces under agreements approved by Congress; and authorized U.S. payment of the nation's share of U.N. expenses.

UNITED NATIONS RELIEF AND REHABILITATION ADMINISTRATION (UNRRA) Agency established on November 9, 1943, in Washington, D.C., by 44 nations allied in the struggle against the Axis powers in WORLD WAR II. Its purpose was to provide food, clothing, shelter, medical aid, and other assistance to war-devastated countries liberated from Axis control. This charter was later expanded to include caring for the growing number of refugees, or displaced persons, created by the war. Member nations furnished the funding for UNRRA, with more than half the eventual $4 billion total contributed by the United States. The agency's first director general was former New York Governor Herbert H. Lehman. UNRRA was most active in Europe in 1945 and 1946, where it helped care for millions of displaced persons. On December 15, 1946, the newly formed UNITED NATIONS approved the constitution of the International Refugee Organization (IRO), which assumed the functions of the UNRRA on July 1, 1947. The IRO was replaced by the United Nations Office of High Commissioner for Refugees (UNHCR), which was created on December 3, 1949, and commenced operations January 1, 1951. UNHCR remains the U.N. agency responsible for refugee issues.

UNITED STATES v. BELMONT (1937) Case in which the U.S. Supreme Court ruled that EXECUTIVE AGREEMENTS, international compacts entered into by the president but not submitted to the Senate for ratification, enjoy the force of law. In 1918 the Soviet government nationalized the Petrograd Metal Works and appropriated its holdings, including an account deposited with August Belmont, a private banker in New York City. The monies, however, were not recovered and Belmont died in 1924. In 1933 President FRANKLIN D. ROOSEVELT concluded the ROOSEVELT-LITVINOV AGREEMENT extending American diplomatic recognition to the Soviet government. Under the agreement, the Soviet Union transferred to the U.S. government its claim to any amounts allegedly owed the USSR by American nationals to include the Belmont account. When federal authorities moved to take possession of the assets, the executors of Belmont's will resisted handing over the funds on grounds it constituted confiscation under New York State law. On May 3, 1937, a unanimous Supreme Court decided against the executors, finding that Roosevelt's executive agreement with the Soviet government was a valid international pact. In WARE V. HYLTON (1796) the Court had established that treaties took precedence over conflicting state laws. In the *Belmont* opinion, Justice George Sutherland emphasized the president's primary role in foreign relations and extended a similar constitutional status to executive agreements.

UNITED STATES v. CURTIS-WRIGHT EXPORT CORPORATION (1936) Major U.S. Supreme Court decision regarding federal authority over foreign affairs. In 1932 armed conflict had broken out between Bolivia and Paraguay over the disputed Chaco border region. Both sides in the undeclared war depended on outside arms shipments. In May 1934 the U.S. Congress approved a joint resolution authorizing President FRANKLIN D. ROOSEVELT to embargo American arms sales to the belligerents. Roosevelt subsequently imposed the embargo and its various penalties of fines or imprisonment for violators. Convicted of selling aircraft machine guns to Bolivia in violation of the embargo, the Curtis-Wright Export Corporation challenged Roosevelt's action as an unconstitutional extension of federal power. By a 7 to 1 vote on December 21, 1936, the Supreme Court upheld the embargo resolution. In the majority opinion, Justice George Sutherland asserted the federal government had sweeping powers over foreign affairs that derived ultimately not from the CONSTITUTION but from the basic fact of the nation's sovereignty. These powers, he argued, were an inherent prerogative of nationality and as such did not require expression in the Constitution. Congress thus had broad latitude to delegate foreign affairs responsibilities to the president. Sutherland went on to characterize the president as the "sole organ of the federal government in the field of international relations" with exclusive authority to represent the nation abroad and negotiate treaties. In the STEEL SEIZURE CASE (1952), the Court made clear that regardless of its source this executive authority was subject to constitutional limits. *Reid v. Covert* (1957) affirmed the same principle for federal foreign powers in general.

UNITED STATES GLOBAL CHANGE RESEARCH PROGRAM (US/GCRP) Ongoing U.S. scientific research effort launched in 1989 to assess global climate change. The program developed out of growing international trepidation about the greenhouse effect, the warming of the Earth's atmosphere caused by concentrations of carbon dioxide and other so-called greenhouse gases emitted into the air. These gases form a blanketing layer that traps the sun's heat, causing a rise in average global temperatures. Environmentalists the world over fear that such warming of the planet could have dire long-term consequences. The greenhouse effect is a complex issue, however, and uncertainties exist about the offsetting impact of cloud cover and various ocean and atmospheric dynamics. Recognition of the need for international cooperation to deal with global climate change prompted the establishment in 1988 of the INTERGOVERNMENTAL PANEL ON CLIMATE CHANGE (IPCC) under the joint auspices of the WORLD METEOROLOGICAL ORGANIZATION (WMO) and the UNITED NATIONS ENVIRONMENT PROGRAM. The IPCC promptly called upon nations to undertake coordinated research to resolve the unanswered scientific questions relating to global climate change and to yield more reliable predictions upon which sound policy responses to climate change could be based. Washington took the world lead in developing a research program when it organized the US/GCRP in 1989. Other countries followed suit and have worked with the United States to coordinate research efforts through international forums such as the WMO's World Climate Research Program. The goal of the US/GCRP, the largest research undertaking of its kind in the world, is to establish the scientific basis for national and international environmental policy making as it relates to man-made and natural changes in the Earth's climate. The research program was an integral component of the comprehensive U.S. Climate Change Strategy announced by President GEORGE BUSH in 1990. The strategy was built around a series of actions intended, among other aims, to curb greenhouse gas emissions.

UNITED STATES INFORMATION AGENCY (USIA) Federal agency responsible for the U.S. government's overseas information, educational exchange, and cultural programs. America emerged from WORLD WAR II with a vastly enlarged international role. The OFFICE OF WAR INFORMATION, the wartime agency that pioneered U.S. dissemination of information abroad, was disbanded in August 1945. In the early postwar years the State Department oversaw expanding U.S. propaganda and foreign educational and cultural affairs. The mounting East-West COLD WAR brought congressional action to strengthen the U.S. government's ability to win the "war of words" with the Communist bloc. The Smith-Mundt Act, signed into law January 27, 1948, formally established within the State Department the nation's first peacetime overseas information program. On August 1, 1953, Congress created the independent United States Information Agency to carry out the federal government's international information activities. The agency, which since its inception has been known overseas as the United States Information Service, did not take control of the educational and cultural programs from the State Department until 1978, when USIA, as part of a larger bureaucratic restructuring, was renamed the International Communication Agency. In 1983 the name was changed back to USIA.

The agency's basic functions since 1953 have been to improve understanding abroad of American society and to help advance U.S. foreign policy aims by influencing public attitudes in other nations. USIA employs diverse communications means, including radio, television, direct satellite transmission, motion pictures, seminars, exhibits, libraries, publications, and English-language instruction, to develop public support abroad for U.S. goals and to counter distorted or skewed presentations of U.S. policies by America's adversaries. The agency's international radio service, the VOICE OF AMERICA, beams programming around the clock in more than 40 languages to listeners worldwide. Its international press service supplies news stories and photos to thousands of overseas publications, and produces magazines, newspapers, pamphlets, leaflets, and cartoons for foreign distribution. Television and film services furnish agency-produced programs, movies, and documentaries about the United States to foreign networks. The agency sponsors cultural and academic exchanges, including the prestigious FULBRIGHT SCHOLARSHIPS. USIA is responsible, as

well, for advising the president, secretary of state, and NATIONAL SECURITY COUNCIL on the impact of worldwide public opinion on American policies. In a related capacity, it provides members of the official U.S. foreign affairs community with daily summaries of foreign media coverage of U.S. actions. The agency, with headquarters in Washington, has some 200 posts located at U.S. diplomatic missions in more than 120 countries.

UNITED STATES INSTITUTE OF PEACE Independent, federal corporation established to develop and spread knowledge about the peaceful resolution of international conflict. Created by Congress in 1984, the institute is governed by a bipartisan board of directors, whose 15 members are appointed by the president subject to Senate confirmation. Board members include the director of the ARMS CONTROL AND DISARMAMENT AGENCY, the assistant secretary of state for HUMAN RIGHTS and humanitarian affairs, and the assistant secretary of defense for national security policy. The institute runs a program of grants to nonprofit organizations, public and private institutions, and individuals researching peace, war, and international conflict management. It also administers an internal research and studies program and a fellowship program for scholars. Among other activities are education and public information and a research library program. Institute publications include a biennial report and a newsletter, *The United States Institute of Peace Journal.* Congress appropriates all funding for the institute and its activities.

UNITED STATES INTERNATIONAL TRADE COMMISSION Independent agency of the U.S. government that serves the president and Congress as a fact-finding advisory body on tariffs and foreign trade. Established originally by Congress in 1916 as the United States Tariff Commission, the agency was renamed the International Trade Commission under the TRADE ACT OF 1974. The commission comprises six members, appointed by the president and confirmed by the Senate, who serve nine-year terms. No more than three members may be from the same political party. In its fact-finding capacity the agency has broad authority to study and investigate all aspects of U.S. foreign trade, the competitiveness of American products, and foreign and domestic customs laws. While it does not make policy, the commission's technical advice is incorporated into federal policy decisions on international trade. Agency investigations assess the impact of rising imports on U.S. industry and examine whether importers are infringing on U.S. patents, copyrights, or trademarks. The commission also probes whether foreign companies are involved in the practice of "dumping" goods—selling them in the United States at prices lower than they would charge in their home market. If so, and if a U.S. industry is being harmed by unfairly priced imports, the Commerce Department is empowered to place a duty on the items equal to the price discrepancy.

UNITED STATES TARIFF COMMISSION See **UNITED STATES INTERNATIONAL TRADE COMMISSION**.

UNITED STATES TRADE REPRESENTATIVE See same in **APPENDIX B**.

UNITED STATES-CANADA FREE TRADE AGREEMENT (1988) Sweeping trade pact concluded between the United States and Canada in 1988. In 1984 President RONALD W. REAGAN and Canadian Prime Minister Brian Mulroney had agreed to pursue an agreement that would liberalize Canadian-American commerce. Each country was the other's largest trading partner. Since taking office in 1981, Reagan had envisioned the creation of a free-trade zone encompassing the United States, Canada, and possibly Mexico. The U.S.-Canada agreement, negotiated in 1987, was signed on January 2, 1988, by the two leaders. The accord was scheduled to take effect on January 1, 1989, provided the legislatures of both countries had formally approved it and enacted the laws necessary for its implementation.

Under the pact, the neighbors pledged to phase out virtually all remaining tariffs between them over a 10-year period. The agreement eliminated some barriers to cross-border investment and trade in services, such as banking and insurance, and barred new restrictions in these areas. In addition, it guaranteed U.S. access to Canadian oil, gas, and uranium and outlined

new procedures for settling U.S.-Canadian trade disputes in a systematic and timely manner. The accord did not address government subsidies, which were more widely used in Canada than in the United States, calling instead for follow-up negotiations on the thorny issue.

In the United States the agreement met with modest opposition from industries fearful of Canadian competition, especially in lumbering and fishing. At the end of July, Reagan formally submitted the pact to Congress, where it was given special expedited status reserved for trade bills. Under the "fast-track" procedures, the House of Representatives and Senate had 90 days from the date of formal submission to either accept or reject the pact and could neither amend it nor block it by a filibuster. After limited debate, Congress approved the agreement and passed legislation bringing American laws into conformity with it. Reagan signed the measure on September 28, 1988, hailing it as a hallmark of free trade.

Meanwhile in Canada the pact ran into stiff dissent and touched off a year-long political struggle. Its foes argued that the elimination of remaining duties would deal a damaging blow to the Canadian economy, since Canada traditionally had relied on higher tariff barriers to protect its industries from bigger U.S. competitors. When opposition parties in the Canadian Parliament blocked ratification, Mulroney called for a national election—10 months before it was scheduled—that amounted to a referendum on the trade issue. His Conservative Party's commanding victory in the November 21 election assured acceptance of the free-trade agreement. A special session of Parliament met in late December and approved the accord, which went into force as scheduled on January 1, 1989. It was the second U.S. bilateral free-trade agreement. The first, with Israel, began in 1985.

UNIVERSAL DECLARATION OF HUMAN RIGHTS (1948) Landmark UNITED NATIONS proclamation on HUMAN RIGHTS. The Universal Declaration was adopted by the U.N. General Assembly on December 10, 1948, as a "common standard of achievement for all peoples and all nations." The document consisted of a preamble and 30 articles setting down basic human rights and freedoms to which, it asserted, all men and women everywhere were entitled without discrimination. Two international covenants subsequently were drafted by the U.N. Commission on Human Rights between 1948 and 1954. The International Covenant on Civil and Political Rights and the International Covenant on Economic, Social, and Cultural Rights, both of which were unanimously adopted by the General Assembly in December 1966, put into binding legal form, and in some instances elaborated on, the rights set forth in the Universal Declaration. One key right put forward in both covenants, and not contained in the declaration, is the right of peoples to self-determination. The two covenants entered into force in 1976. The one on civil and political rights became effective simultaneously with its Optional Protocol, which provides for consideration by a U.N. Human Rights Committee of complaints from individuals who purport to be victims of violations of any rights contained in the covenant. As of 1991, more than 100 states had acceded to the two covenants. The United States has not ratified either measure.

UNIVERSAL POSTAL UNION (UPU) UNITED NATIONS specialized agency responsible for organizing and improving world postal services and promoting international postal collaboration. UPU member countries are united in a single postal territory for the exchange of mail. The union sets uniform international rates for sending mail overseas and guarantees freedom of postal transit. All members must agree to common rules governing regular letter mail, while a series of special agreements, binding only on UPU members which accede to them, cover such areas as insured letters, parcels, money orders, and periodicals. The union traces its origins to an international conference held in Paris, France, in 1863 to address the growing need for a set of established principles to govern international postal exchange. The United States participated in the first International Postal Congress at Bern, Switzerland, in 1874. This Bern Conference yielded a treaty establishing a General Postal Union (GPU). At the second International Postal Congress, held in Paris in 1878, the GPU was renamed the Universal Postal Union. By an agreement concluded in 1947, the UPU became part of the United Nations. The union has the largest membership of any of the U.N. specialized agencies. Virtually all U.N. members and various dependent territories participate.

UPSHUR, ABEL PARKER (1791–1844) Secretary of state under President JOHN TYLER. A Virginia native, Upshur attended both the College of New Jersey (now Princeton) and Yale but did not graduate. He read law, was admitted to the bar in 1810, and began practice in Richmond. He served in the Virginia legislature from 1812 to 1813 and again from 1825 to 1827. Upshur was a justice of the Virginia supreme court from 1826 to 1841. Throughout this period, he was a strong proponent of the extreme states' rights, pro-slavery stance. In September 1841 President Tyler named him secretary of the navy. In 1843 Upshur succeeded DANIEL WEBSTER as secretary of state. In office, he ardently advocated the annexation of Texas, which he wanted added to the Union as slave territory as a means to secure the South's economic and political interests. He initiated negotiations with the Lone Star Republic for a treaty of annexation. Before he could conclude the agreement, Upshur was killed in an accidental explosion aboard the warship *Princeton* on the Potomac River on February 28, 1844. His successor, JOHN C. CALHOUN, on April 12 signed the completed annexation measure that largely had been Upshur's work. Bitter sectional division over the issue of slavery's extension into newly acquired U.S. territories led to the defeat of the Upshur-Calhoun Treaty in the Senate in June 1844. TEXAS ANNEXATION was accomplished by a joint resolution of Congress in 1845.

UPSHUR-CALHOUN TREATY   See **UPSHUR, ABEL PARKER**.

URUGUAY ROUND   See **GENERAL AGREEMENT ON TARIFFS AND TRADE**.

"USES OF MILITARY POWER" (1984) Speech delivered at the National Press Club on November 28, 1984, by Defense Secretary CASPAR W. WEINBERGER outlining six major tests to be applied when weighing a decision whether to send U.S. troops into combat abroad. The speech was prompted by growing concern among congressional Democrats that the Reagan administration would commit American troops to the

EL SALVADOR CIVIL WAR or to the anti-Sandinista Contra insurgency in Nicaragua.

Weinberger asserted, first, that the United States should send forces into battle only where it was in the nation's vital interest to fight. Second, he emphasized that once committed, American troops should enter combat with the unequivocal intention of winning; if the nation lacked the will to commit the forces required to prevail, the secretary argued, then it should not commit them at all. Third, he insisted that in advance of any combat deployment the country should have clearly defined military and political objectives, and should be prepared to send the forces necessary to accomplish them. Fourth, he stressed that, in the event of a combat commitment, the United States must be ready to adjust the size and disposition of its forces in response to shifts in American objectives. Invoking the lesson of America's experience in the VIETNAM WAR to frame his fifth test, Weinberger contended that there must be a reasonable assurance that any military action would enjoy the support of the American public and Congress. Finally, he declared that commitment of U.S. forces to combat must be a last resort undertaken only when political and diplomatic means had failed or had no prospect of succeeding.

He argued that the six criteria he had outlined, if applied carefully, would keep the United States from being drawn into an "endless morass" where it was not required by national interest to use force of arms. His tests were endorsed by senior military officers and defense officials who since the end of the Vietnam conflict had advocated that before the nation embark again on military intervention, it set well-defined goals and then allocate the forces necessary to accomplish them.

See also VIETNAM SYNDROME.

USIA See **UNITED STATES INFORMATION AGENCY**.

U-2 INCIDENT (1960) Downing of an American spy plane over the Soviet Union. In 1956 the CENTRAL INTELLIGENCE AGENCY (CIA) initiated a secret series of high-altitude reconnaissance flights by the newly developed U-2 single-pilot jet to provide information on the Soviet military. On May 1, 1960, a U-2 flown by Francis Gary Powers on an aerial photography mission was shot down near Sverdlovsk by a Soviet missile. Soviet Premier Nikita S. Khrushchev publicly disclosed the aircraft's downing on May 5 and accused the United States of violating Soviet airspace for espionage purposes. In Washington the State Department denied the Soviet charges and NASA handed out a CIA cover story of a lost weather research plane. This fabrication fell apart on May 7 when Khrushchev displayed photos of Soviet airfields recovered from the wreckage of the U-2 and revealed that Powers, captured after parachuting safely to earth, had confessed to being on a CIA mission.

Caught in an obvious and embarrassing lie, President DWIGHT D. EISENHOWER decided to reveal the truth about the U-2 program. At a May 11 news conference he acknowledged extensive U.S. aerial surveillance of the Soviet Union, accepted responsibility for the overflights, defended U.S. intelligence activities as a necessary precaution against surprise attack, and renewed his 1955 OPEN SKIES proposal. The U-2 episode brought to a halt the gradual improvement in East-West relations dating back to the CAMP DAVID SUMMIT between Eisenhower and Khrushchev the previous fall. A scheduled PARIS SUMMIT of the leaders of the United States, Great Britain, France, and Soviet Union went ahead as planned on May 16, 1960. The conference collapsed after one session when Eisenhower, who had given assurances that the intelligence flights had been discontinued, rejected Khrushchev's demands that the United States apologize for its past actions and punish those responsible. The U-2 flights, though terminated, were soon replaced on both sides by more effective SATELLITE RECONNAISSANCE. Powers was released in February 1962 in exchange for Soviet spy Rudolph Abel. In 1977 he was killed in the crash of a traffic helicopter he was piloting in California.

V

VAN BUREN, MARTIN (1782–1862) Secretary of state, vice-president, eighth president of the United States. Born in New York, Van Buren became a legal clerk at age 14, read law, and was admitted to the bar in 1803. He developed a successful practice in his home village of Kinderhook near Albany and entered local Democratic-Republican politics. Elected to the state senate in 1812, he held his seat until 1820 and served concurrently as state attorney general from 1816 to 1819. During his eight years in Albany he helped forge and headed the Albany Regency, the powerful Democratic-Republican Party machine that came to dominate New York State politics through the practice of patronage. Elected to the U.S. Senate in 1821, he became a supporter and political confidant of ANDREW JACKSON, whose successful presidential campaign in 1828 he helped manage. Following his election to the governorship of New York the same year, Van Buren resigned from the Senate. His two-month tenure as governor ended with his resignation in March 1829 to accept appointment as Jackson's secretary of state.

He quickly became the most influential and trusted of Jackson's close advisers, a group known as the "kitchen cabinet." At the State Department he introduced the political spoils system which the Albany Regency had operated with such success in New York. Van Buren in 1830 negotiated an Anglo-American treaty that settled an old commercial dispute by reopening the British West Indies to U.S. trade. The same year he concluded a commercial treaty with Turkey providing for free access to the Black Sea for American merchant ships. He secured the French government's agreement to pay the FRENCH SPOLIATION CLAIMS in compensation for damages inflicted upon American maritime commerce during the Napoleonic Wars (1803–1815), but failed in an attempt to purchase Texas from Mexico.

With Jackson's reluctant acceptance, Van Buren resigned his post in April 1831 to enable the president to reorganize his cabinet and thereby remove the supporters of Vice-President JOHN C. CALHOUN, who had split with Jackson over the federal tariff. He promptly was nominated as U.S. minister to Great Britain, but the Senate rejected his appointment for partisan political reasons, with Vice-President Calhoun casting the deciding vote. He was elected vice-president in 1832 as Jackson's running mate. Van Buren garnered the Democratic presidential nomination in 1836 as Jackson's hand-picked successor, and defeated a trio of Whig candidates in the general election.

He took office in 1837 amid deepening sectional division over slavery exacerbated by an upsurge in abolitionist sentiment in the North. Van Buren favored a compromise on the volatile issue, which he foresaw as a threat to both the Democratic Party and national unity. While assuring the South he would protect slaveholding in the states where it existed, he opposed the extension of the "peculiar institution." Accordingly he rejected a plan to annex Texas, which had achieved independence from Mexico in 1836, and admit it to the Union as a slave state. Van Buren opposed annexation, as well, out of concern it might provoke war with Mexico. Seeking peace with America's southern neighbor, he adopted a policy of conciliation aimed at alleviating tensions over Texas and the separate matter of outstanding American property claims against Mexico.

Relations with Great Britain during his term were threatened by two diplomatic crises involving Canada, at the time a British colony. Eager to avoid a major Anglo-American rift, Van Buren successfully defused the 1837 CAROLINE AFFAIR, during which Canadian militia ventured into U.S. waters to destroy an American steamship that had been supplying Canadian rebels against British rule. He also was able to resolve peacefully the bloodless 1839 AROOSTOOK WAR over the disputed Maine-New Brunswick boundary. Van Buren forged ahead with implementation of Jackson's INDIAN REMOVAL POLICY, the U.S. program to relocate the southeast Indian tribes to areas west of the Mississippi River. In 1838 he sent federal forces under General WINFIELD SCOTT to supervise the forced removal of Cherokee Indians who refused to leave their Georgia homeland voluntarily. Thousands of Cherokees died of disease and exposure during the arduous six-month trek on the "Trail of Tears." The Van Buren administration vigorously continued to wage the second of the SEMINOLE WARS (1835–1842) against Seminole Indians resisting removal from Florida.

Renominated in 1840, Van Buren was defeated decisively by Whig presidential candidate WILLIAM HENRY HARRISON. In retirement he continued to harbor national political ambitions. His opposition to the immediate annexation of Texas cost him the Democratic nomination in 1844, which went to pro-annexation, expansionist candidate JAMES K. POLK. The sectional quarrel over the extension of slavery intensified when the United States acquired vast new territories following the MEXICAN WAR (1846–1848). Van Buren became active among the "Barnburners," a breakaway faction of New York Democrats opposed to slavery's expansion. In 1848 he was the unsuccessful presidential candidate of the Free Soil Party, which the "Barnburners" had helped forge and which embraced the nonextension-of-slavery principle of the WILMOT PROVISO. Concerned that the slavery issue threatened to split the Union, Van Buren parted with the Free Soilers when he supported the Compromise of 1850, the legislative package sponsored by Kentucky's Whig Senator HENRY CLAY to avert a sectional crisis. After several years spent traveling in Europe, he retired in 1855 to his New York estate.

VANCE, CYRUS ROBERTS (1917–   ) Secretary of the Army, secretary of state. Born in West Virginia, Vance graduated from Yale University in 1939. After earning a law degree from his alma mater in 1942, he served as a naval officer during WORLD WAR II. In 1947 he joined a Wall Street law firm. From 1957 to 1960 he was a special counsel to the SENATE ARMED SERVICES COMMITTEE. In 1958, as a counsel to the Senate Special Committee on Space and Astronautics, he helped formulate the legislation establishing the NATIONAL AERONAUTICS AND SPACE ADMINISTRATION. In 1961 Vance entered full-time government service with the Kennedy administration as general counsel for the DEPARTMENT OF DEFENSE. He became secretary of the army in 1962. In 1964 President Lyndon B. Johnson appointed him deputy secretary of defense. A key architect of Johnson administration policy in the VIETNAM WAR, he strongly supported the growing American involvement in the conflict. Johnson sent him to the CANAL ZONE in 1964 to aid in the resolution of the PANAMA RIOTS. The following year he was a member of a special U.S. fact-finding mission to the Dominican Republic during the DOMINICAN CRISIS.

Vance stepped down from his post in June 1967, citing financial and health considerations, including a painful spinal condition. He returned to his New York law firm, but continued to serve Johnson as a special diplomatic troubleshooter. In November 1967 he successfully mediated a Greek-Turkish dispute over Cyprus and in February 1968 went to South Korea to reaffirm U.S. defense commitments there in the wake of the PUEBLO INCIDENT. From May 1968 to January 1969 he was deputy chief American delegate at the newly launched PARIS PEACE TALKS on ending the Vietnam War. By 1968 Vance's views on Vietnam had begun to change. He advocated a general cease-fire and supported Johnson's March 1968 decision to deescalate the U.S. role in the conflict. In subsequent years he came to characterize the U.S. intervention in Vietnam as a mistake.

Vance remained in private practice during the Nixon and Ford administrations. In 1976 he became a foreign policy adviser to

Democratic presidential candidate JIMMY CARTER and took office as secretary of state with the Carter administration in January 1977. Vance moved promptly to integrate Carter's emphasis on HUMAN RIGHTS into U.S. foreign policy, announcing in February 1977 that American foreign aid would be tied to the human rights records of recipient countries. Amid conservative criticism that the Carter administration's uncompromising stance on human rights ignored vital national security concerns, he made clear that State Department decisions on foreign aid would fully take into account U.S. strategic interests. Vance endorsed the repeal in 1977 of the BYRD AMENDMENT and the reimposition of full economic sanctions on the white minority government of Rhodesia (now Zimbabwe) in keeping with the administration's open support for black majority rule in Africa. In 1978 he helped secure Senate ratification of the controversial PANAMA CANAL TREATIES and assisted in the negotiation of the CAMP DAVID ACCORDS bringing peace between Egypt and Israel.

Vance strongly supported a continued policy of DETENTE with the Soviet Union and played a central role in the finalization of the 1979 SALT II arms control agreement limiting U.S. and Soviet nuclear arsenals. He also favored the normalization of relations with Communist China and aided in the negotiations leading to Carter's recognition of the Beijing government in January 1979. Vance's final six months in office were dominated by events in Southwest Asia. The storming of the U.S. embassy in Teheran in November 1979 brought about the protracted IRAN HOSTAGE CRISIS and was followed a month later by the Soviet invasion of Afghanistan. In January 1980 he helped formulate the CARTER DOCTRINE committing the United States to the defense of the Persian Gulf.

Vance resigned in April 1980 over his opposition to the administration's failed military mission to rescue the American hostages in Iran. He resumed his law practice and published his memoirs, *Hard Choices*, in 1983. In October 1991 he was appointed UNITED NATIONS special envoy to the Yugoslav civil war. Vance brokered a tenuous cease-fire between newly independent Croatia and Serbia-dominated Yugoslavia and was centrally involved in the deployment of a U.N. peacekeeping force to the region. In March 1992 he assumed the additional responsibility of U.N. mediator in the conflict between former Soviet republics Armenia and Azerbaijan.

VANDENBERG,   ARTHUR   HENDRICK (1884–1951) U.S. senator, chairman of the SENATE FOREIGN RELATIONS COMMITTEE. Vandenberg was born in Michigan. Forced to withdraw from the University of Michigan in 1901 for financial reasons, he began a career in journalism, quickly rising to editor and publisher of the Grand Rapids *Herald* newspaper. He became active in Michigan Republican politics and in 1928 was appointed to fill a vacant U.S. Senate seat. He won election in his own right that fall and was reelected to three more terms. In the 1930s Vandenberg was an isolationist, supporting the NEUTRALITY ACTS and opposing U.S. involvement in the political upheavals enveloping Europe and the Far East. His views began to shift following American entry into WORLD WAR II, coming to hold U.S. participation in a postwar international organization as essential to world security. In January 1945 he delivered a celebrated speech on the Senate floor formally renouncing his ISOLATIONISM in favor of INTERNATIONALISM and signaling bipartisan support for the Democratic Roosevelt administration's foreign policy.

President FRANKLIN D. ROOSEVELT appointed him a delegate to the April 1945 SAN FRANCISCO CONFERENCE on the UNITED NATIONS. Vandenberg was responsible for the insertion of provisions authorizing regional COLLECTIVE SECURITY arrangements in Article 51 of the UNITED NATIONS CHARTER. In 1947 he became chairman of the Senate's foreign relations panel. He supported the TRUMAN DOCTRINE and helped secure passage in the Congress of the MARSHALL PLAN for economic aid to war-torn Europe. In August 1947 he accompanied Secretary of State GEORGE C. MARSHALL to the Inter-American Conference in Brazil that concluded the RIO TREATY on Western Hemisphere defense. In early 1948 Vandenberg worked with Under Secretary of State ROBERT A. LOVETT on a draft resolution that would express the support of the Senate for U.S. participation in a regional security alliance in Europe. The measure, known as the VANDENBERG RESOLUTION, was approved by a 64 to 4 vote in June 1948, paving the way for U.S. membership in NATO the following year. Vandenberg died in office in 1951.

VANDENBERG, HOYT SANFORD (1899–1954) Military and intelligence officer. Vandenberg graduated from West Point in 1923 and entered the Army Air Corps. He was promoted to general during WORLD WAR II and after combat command became chief of Army intelligence in January 1946. In June 1946 President HARRY S. TRUMAN appointed him director of central intelligence (DCI). As DCI, Vandenberg served as a member of the NATIONAL INTELLIGENCE AUTHORITY, at the time the nation's senior intelligence oversight body, and headed the CENTRAL INTELLIGENCE GROUP (CIG), the precursor to the CENTRAL INTELLIGENCE AGENCY established by Truman in a January 1946 presidential directive.

The nephew of influential Senator ARTHUR H. VANDENBERG (R-MI), Vandenberg proved an aggressive and assertive director who expanded CIG's scope and authority. During his brief tenure the new agency acquired its own budget, began to conduct intelligence research and analysis, gained an espionage capability, and assumed responsibility from the FEDERAL BUREAU OF INVESTIGATION for intelligence operations in Latin America. Vandenberg left the intelligence post in May 1947 to return to duty with the newly formed Air Force as vicechief and then chief of staff. He directed U.S. participation in the massive BERLIN AIRLIFT (1948–1949) during the Soviet blockade of the divided German city and oversaw the commitment of U.S. air power in the KOREAN WAR until his retirement in June 1953. He died of cancer the following year.

VANDENBERG RESOLUTION (1948) Senate declaration endorsing U.S. participation in regional security alliances. WORLD WAR II had ended the nation's traditionally isolationist foreign policy and brought U.S. membership in the UNITED NATIONS. As the Soviet Union consolidated its postwar hold on Eastern Europe and East-West relations deteriorated into COLD WAR, the Truman administration began to consider U.S. involvement in a West European COLLECTIVE SECURITY arrangement designed to halt further Communist expansion. The United States had signed the RIO TREATY for the collective defense of the Western Hemisphere in 1947. The administration worried, however, that historic American reluctance to enter a European military alliance might undercut backing for such a step in Con-

gress. The bipartisan nature of American foreign policy in the early Cold War years prevailed when, in the spring of 1948, Michigan Senator ARTHUR H. VANDENBERG, chairman of the SENATE FOREIGN RELATIONS COMMITTEE and a leading Republican, drafted a resolution affirming Senate support for the contemplated European defense pact. He was aided on the measure by ROBERT A. LOVETT, under secretary of state in the Democratic administration. The Vandenberg Resolution was approved by the Senate on June 11, 1948, by a 64 to 4 vote. The policy declaration, which called for "regional and other collective" security arrangements, marked an important milestone in America's assumption of worldwide defense responsibilities and paved the way for U.S. participation in the formation of NATO the following year.

VENEZUELA BOUNDARY DISPUTE Longstanding dispute between Great Britain and Venezuela over the western border of British Guiana (now Guyana) that drew American intervention. The boundary had remained unfixed ever since Great Britain annexed British Guiana in 1814. A survey done in 1840 by British geographer Sir Robert Schomburgk drew a boundary favorable to his country and the British government soon adopted this so-called Schomburgk line as its definitive claim. Venezuela refused to accept the Schomburgk survey and made a massive counterclaim to lands in the neighboring British colony.

In the mid-1880s, following the discovery of gold in the contested territory, Great Britain enlarged its claims to include an area west of the Schomburgk line. Venezuela severed diplomatic relations with the British in 1887 and invited the United States to arbitrate the boundary rift. American offers through the early 1890s to help forge a settlement were rejected by Great Britain, which insisted areas east of the Schomburgk boundary were closed to arbitration. As American sentiment mounted against the inflexible British position, President GROVER CLEVELAND in 1894 pledged to renew U.S. attempts at breaking the deadlock. A joint congressional resolution on February 20, 1895, which urged British-Venezuelan arbitration, signaled the start of intensified American involvement in the boundary controversy.

Secretary of State RICHARD OLNEY in July 1895 sent Great Britain an aggressive note demanding it submit the issue to U.S. arbitration. He declared that British pressure on lands claimed by Venezuela violated the MONROE DOCTRINE (1823). The secretary of state's assertion, later dubbed the Olney Corollary, broadened the scope of Monroe's principles by making it U.S. policy to oppose the increase by European powers of their territorial holdings in the Americas. According to Olney, the Monroe Doctrine granted the United States a virtual protectorate over the American continents. He relied on the doctrine to justify U.S. intervention in the Venezuela controversy.

In a reply that arrived December 7, Great Britain denied the Monroe Doctrine's validity under international law and again rejected arbitration. Cleveland then gained permission from Congress to appoint an independent commission to decide the Venezuela boundary and to enforce the panel's recommendations. Cleveland's determination to force a settlement brought a shift in British policy. Preoccupied by worsening relations with Germany and by its troubles with the Boers in South Africa, Great Britain wanted to maintain peaceful ties with the United States and thus consented to negotiate the boundary problem with Olney.

Great Britain finally agreed to submit the dispute to an arbitration tribunal with the understanding that areas under British or Venezuelan settlement for at least 50 years would be exempted. Great Britain and Venezuela signed an arbitration treaty in February 1897 approving the 50-year formula. In October 1899 the tribunal made a unanimous ruling that gave Great Britain some 90 percent of the contested territory, awarded Venezuela control over the mouth of the Orinoco River, and placed the boundary roughly along the Schomburgk line. The Cleveland-Olney diplomacy during the controversy won effective British recognition of the predominant U.S. position in the Western Hemisphere. Settlement of the dispute marked the beginning of a new Anglo-American rapprochement at the close of the 19th century.

VENEZUELA CLAIMS (1902–1903) Controversy over the principle of European intervention in the Western Hemisphere for the collection of debts. The crisis arose when Venezuelan dictator Cipriano Castro failed to pay his country's debts to several European nations. In December 1902 Great Britain, Germany, and Italy sent combined naval forces to the Caribbean in an attempt to force settlement of their claims. This armada sank part of the Venezuelan navy, sealed off major Venezuelan ports, and bombarded the coastline.

Castro appealed to the United States for assistance. At first President THEODORE ROOSEVELT declined. But mounting American concern over suspected German territorial designs on Venezuela prompted Roosevelt to act. Secretary of State JOHN M. HAY, wielding the threat of U.S. military involvement on Venezuela's behalf, persuaded the intervening nations to consent to arbitration of the dispute. The Europeans submitted their claims to the Hague PERMANENT COURT OF ARBITRATION, which finally settled the matter. Germany's willingness to reduce its cash demands hastened the negotiations. On February 14, 1903, the three powers lifted their naval blockade and withdrew.

The Venezuela Claims incident had important consequences. The spectre of European intervention had alarmed all of Latin America. Argentine Foreign Minister Dr. Luis M. Drago implored the United States to endorse the so-called Drago Doctrine, which denounced the use of armed force by a European power to collect public debts from an American state. In 1904 Roosevelt, mindful of the lessons of the Venezuela Claims incident, announced the ROOSEVELT COROLLARY to the MONROE DOCTRINE. The corollary spelled out America's right of intercession in the Western Hemisphere in order to prevent European intervention.

VERACRUZ INCIDENT (1914) U.S. military occupation of Veracruz, Mexico, amid the Mexican Revolution (1910–1920). In 1911 a revolution led by democratic reformer Francisco I. Madero overthrew Mexican dictator Porfirio Diaz and established a liberal government, which received U.S. diplomatic recognition. Reactionary General Victoriano Huerta seized power in February 1913 after staging a successful coup d'etat against Madero, who was assassinated. The major European powers recognized Huerta's regime, but President WILLIAM HOWARD TAFT declined to do the same despite pressure for such action by American business interests with investments in Mexico. When WOODROW WILSON became president in March 1913, he rebuked Huerta by declaring a policy whereby the United States would not recognize governments that had come to power by force against the will of the people.

Huerta, surrounded by revolutionary upheaval, did not control all of the country. General Venustiano Carranza led an opposition revolt in northern Mexico. He and his followers, calling themselves Constitutionalists, vowed to depose Huerta and reestablish constitutional government. Wilson, concluding that Huerta must be forced from power, sought to mediate Mexico's civil war in a way that would ensure his ouster. In August 1913 Wilson proposed an immediate armistice to be followed by a free election in which Huerta would not be a candidate. At the same time he called on the European powers to pressure the Mexican ruler to accept American mediation. When Huerta refused Wilson's scheme, vowing armed resistance against any U.S. attempt to interfere in Mexico, the American president adopted a policy of nonintervention. He also imposed a strict arms embargo to all sides in Mexico's civil conflict.

In October 1913, Huerta dissolved Mexico's congress and imposed a military dictatorship. Wilson in November informed governments with diplomatic missions in Mexico that he was committed to driving Huerta from rule. He asked these countries to withdraw or withhold recognition from Huerta's regime. In the ensuing months Wilson sought to further isolate the Mexican dictator diplomatically while encouraging the Constitutionalist fight against him. Early in 1914 he selectively lifted the arms embargo against Carranza's forces and stationed U.S. naval units in the Gulf of Mexico to interdict shipments of arms and munitions from Europe to the Huerta government.

Increasingly, however, force seemed to offer the only immediate prospect for toppling the resilient dictatorship. An episode at Tampico became Wilson's pretext for military action. On April 9, 1914, an unarmed party from the warship U.S.S. *Dolphin*, among the vessels stationed in Mexican waters, went ashore at the Mexican port city, without permission, to buy supplies.

By mistake the sailors entered a restricted area and were arrested by Huerta's Federalist troops. When local Federalist commander General Morelos Zarazoga learned of the arrest, he immediately released the Americans and relayed a personal apology to Admiral Henry T. Mayo, commander of the American squadron off Tampico. Mayo spurned Zarazoga's gesture and, on his own initiative, demanded a formal apology by the Mexican government and a 21-gun salute to the American flag. Wilson supported Mayo's ultimatum, thereby converting a minor episode into an issue of national honor. Huerta rebuffed the American demands despite warnings that his refusal might bring U.S. military reprisal.

Congress on April 22, 1914, granted Wilson's request for authority to use force against Huerta's regime to uphold U.S. rights and avenge the purported insult of the Tampico incident. Meanwhile U.S. forces had landed on Mexican soil the day before. Informed that the German merchant steamer *Ypiranga* was approaching Veracruz with a cargo of munitions for Huerta, Wilson had ordered the Navy to seize the Mexican port city's customs house to prevent delivery of the shipment. On April 21 American warships shelled Veracruz while some 1000 marines went ashore, where they met determined resistance by Mexican garrison troops. By midday April 22, the Americans had overcome the Mexican forces and taken control of the entire city. The dead and wounded, mostly Mexicans, totalled more than 400. The American occupation of Veracruz, to Wilson's dismay, united Mexican popular sentiment behind Huerta and elicited condemnation throughout Latin America of Yankee IMPERIALISM. Carranza himself denounced the U.S. intervention as foreign aggression. When U.S. Army General Frederick Funston was sent to Veracruz with an expeditionary force to contend with rising anti-American violence, a major U.S.-Mexican conflict appeared probable.

The United States did not want war. When Argentina, Brazil, and Chile, the so-called ABC Powers, offered to mediate the dispute, Wilson accepted, as did Huerta. Delegates from the United States, Mexico, and the ABC Powers met in a conference at the neutral site of Niagara Falls, Ontario, from May 20 to June 30, 1914. The South

American mediators proposed U.S. withdrawal from Veracruz contingent upon Huerta's abdication and establishment of a provisional Mexican government chosen by the country's contending revolutionary factions. The ABC Mediation failed because Carranza refused to negotiate peace with Huerta and rejected its plan for a provisional government. On July 15, however, Huerta, his regime besieged by rival revolutionary forces, resigned and went into exile. A month later the Constitutionalists entered Mexico City and Carranza assumed the presidency. He then was driven from power by Mexican revolutionary leader Francisco "Pancho" Villa, who took over the government. The Wilson administration swung its support to Villa. On November 23, 1914, the U.S. occupation forces withdrew from Veracruz. Carranza fought back and regained power in Mexico City in February 1915. Thereupon Wilson adopted an official policy of neutrality. The United States formally recognized Carranza's regime as the de facto Mexican government in October 1915.

See also BUCARELI AGREEMENT, PUNITIVE EXPEDITION.

VERSAILLES, TREATY OF (1919) Comprehensive peace treaty imposed by the victorious Allied Powers on Germany at the end of WORLD WAR I. The armistice with Germany of November 11, 1918, recognized the FOURTEEN POINTS, U.S. President WOODROW WILSON's blueprint for a liberal peace, as the basis for a final peace settlement. The treaty was negotiated among the Allied delegations attending the PARIS PEACE CONFERENCE (1919). The parley was dominated by the COUNCIL OF FOUR, comprising Wilson, British Prime Minister David Lloyd George, French Prime Minister Georges Clemenceau, and Italian Prime Minister Vittorio Orlando, who made all the major decisions on the peace terms. Wilson labored to preserve intact the Fourteen Points but was compelled to compromise, bowing to various demands by Allied statesmen in order to gain their support for his coveted LEAGUE OF NATIONS, the proposed postwar international organization to maintain peace and deter aggression through COLLECTIVE SECURITY. The completed draft treaty, comprising 400 articles, was presented to a German delegation on May 7, 1919, for its

review. The German government protested that the settlement violated many of the Fourteen Points, imposed crushing economic burdens, and generally was vengeful rather than just. The BIG FOUR dismissed most of these objections and implemented only minor changes in response to the German complaints. Under threat of renewed Allied military action, Germany reluctantly signed the treaty on June 28, 1919, in the Hall of Mirrors at Versailles Palace, outside Paris.

The Covenant of the League of Nations, defining the body's structure, powers, and functions, constituted the first part of the treaty. The covenant established a mandate system to administer former German colonies under league supervision. These colonies were stripped from Germany by other sections of the peace settlement. Mandates over the former German overseas possessions were awarded to the Allied powers which had occupied them during the war. Terms defining German frontiers in Europe forced Germany to cede Alsace-Lorraine to France; three small areas to Belgium; and Posan and West Prussia, including the so-called Polish Corridor (a strip of land giving an otherwise landlocked Poland access to the Baltic Sea), to Poland. Danzig, largely German in population, was made a free city under League of Nations jurisdiction.

Germany accepted permanent demilitarization of the Rhineland, which was to be occupied by the Allies for 15 years. France was given ownership of the Saar coal mines as compensation for the wanton destruction of French mines by invading German armies. Germany's Saar Valley was for 15 years to be administered by France under League of Nations supervision and occupied by Allied forces. At the end of this period, the region's inhabitants would decide their destiny by a plebiscite. Japan obtained Germany's leasehold in China's Shantung Province, which Japanese forces had occupied during the war. (Japan promised to restore Shantung to Chinese sovereignty in the near future, a pledge the Japanese delivered on in 1922 at the WASHINGTON NAVAL CONFERENCE.)

Germany was required to pay much larger reparations than those contemplated in the armistice agreement, which implied that the Germans would be liable only for civilian damages and not the entire cost of the war to the Allied Powers. The United States itself had not sought and did not expect to receive indemnities. The mechanism establishing German legal liability for reparations was the controversial Article 231, the so-called War Guilt Clause, which forced Germany and its allies to accept responsibility for all the losses and damage incurred by the Allied peoples and governments as a consequence of the war. A Reparations Commission was given responsibility for determining the total sum Germany was to pay. In the meantime, Germany was to relinquish $5 billion in property to the Allies. Other treaty terms dictated drastic German disarmament, bound Germany to respect Austria's independence, and directed the Allies to indict Wilhelm II, the former German Kaiser, for alleged crimes against international morality and the sanctity of treaties. (No trial ever materialized because the Netherlands, where the deposed German emperor went into exile after the war, refused to extradite him.) The Treaty of Versailles entered into force January 10, 1920, following ratification by Germany and four of the great Allied powers: Great Britain, France, Italy, and Japan. The Allies subsequently concluded separate peace treaties with other Central Powers—Austria, Hungary, Bulgaria, and Turkey.

The treaty met with wide-ranging criticism in the United States. Many Americans condemned it as too lenient. Liberals, on the other hand, regarded it as too harsh and vengeful. They attacked Wilson for retreating from his idealistic principles, particularly that of self-determination, and settling for a compromise peace that bowed to power politics and indulged the territorial aims of the victorious Allied Powers. Wilson had been compelled to compromise on the Fourteen Points in order to save his coveted League of Nations, which he fully expected would reconsider the decisions reached at Paris and iron out the treaty's more serious flaws and injustices. The president calculated, moreover, that the United States through its participation in the league would exert a moderating influence on the implementation of the final peace. The debate over ratification of the Treaty of Versailles became one of the greatest political battles in American history, pitting Wilson against Senate Republi-

cans. When the president submitted the treaty to the SENATE FOREIGN RELATIONS COMMITTEE on July 10, 1919, for its consideration, committee chairman HENRY CABOT LODGE, SR. (R-MA), Wilson's political arch-enemy, mobilized Republican opposition to the League of Nations. Lodge and other influential Senate Republicans earlier had issued the ROUND ROBIN (1919) declaring the league covenant unacceptable as initially framed and urging that it be considered apart from and after the final peace settlement. Wilson, insisting on the indivisibility of the league and treaty, had stood his ground and fought successfully at Paris for the incorporation of the covenant into the Versailles accord.

Lodge and his fellow RESERVATIONISTS would not abide U.S. participation in the international body without reservations safeguarding American independence of action. They contended that the idea of collective security embodied in the covenant infringed on U.S. sovereignty. Another Republican group, the ardently isolationist IRRECONCILABLES, advocated rejection of the league in any form. The reservationists, with the cooperation of the irreconcilables, bottled up the treaty in the Foreign Relations Committee for two months, surmising correctly that public opposition to the league would grow as the political fight in Washington wore on. Amid indications that public support for his cherished league was eroding, Wilson decided to take his case directly to the people. On September 4, 1919, he embarked on a 9500-mile rail tour of the Midwest and West, during which he delivered more than 35 speeches in 29 cities. Leading irreconcilable Senators William E. Borah of Idaho and Hiram W. Johnson of California trailed after the president in many cities to speak against the league and treaty. Wilson's trek ended abruptly when he collapsed at Pueblo, Colorado, on September 25 and was rushed back to Washington, where on October 2 he suffered an incapacitating stroke. Meanwhile, on September 10 Lodge's committee had reported the treaty to the full Senate with recommendations for 45 amendments and reservations. A combination of Democrats and moderate Republicans voted down all of the proposed revisions. Lodge and his cohorts then drafted a set of 14 reservations circumscribing U.S. obligations under the league covenant and attached them to a ratification resolution submitted by the Foreign Relations Committee to the Senate in early November. Uncompromisingly opposed to any Senate modifications of the treaty or covenant, the infirm Wilson rejected the LODGE RESERVATIONS and appealed to his supporters to defeat the Lodge ratification resolution. On November 19, 1919, Wilson Democrats combined with Republican irreconcilables to vote down the Treaty of Versailles with reservations. An attempt the same day to ratify the treaty without reservations was turned back by an alliance of reservationists and irreconcilables.

In February 1920 the Senate elected to reconsider the treaty, referring it back to the committee. Without delay the panel reported it with the Lodge Reservations intact. Wilson would not budge from his position, despite the appeals of supporters and close advisers who urged him to accept the relatively modest Senate reservations rather than see the entire treaty fail ratification. He reiterated his opposition to any Senate revision of the final peace settlement. The treaty with reservations was rejected a final time by the Senate on March 19, 1920. The state of war between Germany and the United States was formally ended in 1921 by the TREATY OF BERLIN. The Senate's rejection of the Versailles Treaty preempted Wilson's intention that the United States should exert a moderating influence on the Reparations Commission. The total reparations bill was set in 1921 at $33 billion, more than double what U.S. experts had figured at the Paris Peace Conference and well beyond Germany's capacity to pay. German delinquency in payment necessitated formulation of the DAWES PLAN (1924) and YOUNG PLAN (1929) rescheduling and reducing reparations obligations. An embittered Germany chafed under the imposed peace settlement. Following the collapse of its currency in the early 1920s, Germany began to press for revision of the treaty. British economist John Maynard Keynes criticized the debilitating economic impact of the final peace on Germany in his celebrated work *The Economic Consequences of the Peace* (1919), in which he argued that the harshness of the treaty would sow the seeds of a future war in Europe. Keynes's views contributed significantly to growing sentiment in the 1920s in the United States and Great Britain that the Versailles terms were too severe and should be moderated. Nazi leader Adolf Hitler stridently denounced the treaty to powerful effect during his political ascendancy. In the 1930s he dismantled the peace settlement, repudiating its reparations and disarmament provisions. Many historians contend that the harshness of the treaty contributed fundamentally to Hitler's rise to power and WORLD WAR II.

VIENNA CONVENTION FOR THE PROTECTION OF THE OZONE LAYER (1985) International environmental agreement for safeguarding the ozone layer, the belt of gas about 15 miles above the Earth's atmosphere that shields the planet from the sun's harmful ultraviolet rays. The convention was signed March 22, 1985, at a UNITED NATIONS conference in Vienna, Austria, and entered into force February 27, 1987, following ratification by 20 nations including the United States. By its terms, signatories agreed to pursue measures to protect human health and the natural environment against the adverse effects of ozone shield depletion. The measure emphasized research and monitoring and mandated a 20-percent cut in production of man-made chlorofluorocarbons (CFCs)—ozone-destroying chemicals used in spray cans, refrigerators, and air conditioners—by the early 1990s.

A supplemental agreement was concluded in September 1987 at a meeting in Montreal and followed detection of an ozone hole above Antarctica caused by CFCs. The United States and some 30 other nations signed the Montreal Protocol on Substances that Deplete the Ozone Layer, which called for a 50-percent reduction in production and consumption of CFCs by the end of the century. At a conference on ozone preservation held in London in March 1989, the United States, Canada, Australia, and the 12-nation European Community announced dramatic unilateral cuts in CFC use. Another conference in May of the same year in Helsinki, Finland, the first official gathering of the parties to the 1987 Montreal Protocol, yielded a nonbinding declaration of intent to halt completely the production and use of CFCs by the year 2000.

VIENNA SUMMIT (1961) Meeting between President JOHN F. KENNEDY and Soviet Premier Nikita S. Khrushchev in Vienna in early June 1961, in which the two leaders established personal contacts and exchanged views on the key issues and trouble spots in U.S.-Soviet relations. Shortly after Kennedy's inauguration in January 1961, Khrushchev released two downed American airmen as a goodwill gesture and communicated that he would welcome the chance to meet with the new president. Kennedy concurred and after conferring with British, French, and West German leaders, scheduled talks for June 3 to 4 in Vienna with his Soviet counterpart. As President DWIGHT D. EISENHOWER had done prior to his 1959 CAMP DAVID SUMMIT conference with Khrushchev, Kennedy assured the European allies that Vienna would not be a formal parley and that he would not negotiate unilaterally with the Soviet premier.

For two days the U.S. and Soviet leaders held frank discussions on the major COLD WAR issues. On disarmament, Khrushchev rejected updated U.S. proposals for a comprehensive ban on NUCLEAR WEAPONS testing. The talks largely focused on Germany and the BERLIN CRISIS. Berlin's status had remained a pressing source of conflict ever since the Soviet premier in November 1958 demanded the imminent end of post-WORLD WAR II U.S., British, and French occupation of the city. At Vienna, Khrushchev threatened to sign a separate peace treaty with East Germany cutting off Western access rights to Berlin by the end of the year. Kennedy insisted the United States and its allies would keep their postwar commitments in Germany. The meeting ended with no shift in the positions staked out by the Cold War competitors on Berlin. Afterward, Kennedy outlined what he described as the Soviet intent to drive the United States, Great Britain, and France from their one outpost behind the IRON CURTAIN and he rallied allied support to withstand Soviet pressure on Berlin. The long hiatus in top-level U.S.-Soviet diplomacy that followed the Vienna talks ended in 1967 with the GLASSBORO SUMMIT of President LYNDON B. JOHNSON and Soviet Premier Aleksei N. Kosygin.

VIENNA SUMMIT (1979) Gathering from June 15 to 18 at which U.S. President JIMMY CARTER and Soviet General Secretary Leonid I. Brezhnev signed the SALT II agreement concluding seven years of strategic arms limitation talks. The Vienna parley was the first face-to-face meeting of the two leaders and the first top-level U.S.-Soviet conference since the VLADIVOSTOK SUMMIT in 1974. Relations between the countries had declined steadily following the August 1974 resignation of President RICHARD M. NIXON. The Soviet-American DETENTE of the early 1970s eroded in the face of several key developments through the end of the decade: the large-scale Russian military buildup; increasing Soviet involvement in regional conflicts in Africa and Central America; and Washington's criticism of Moscow's HUMAN RIGHTS record. Brezhnev and Carter convened in Austria to discuss these issues and the status of East-West arms control efforts.

The major achievement of the summit was the signing of the SALT II Treaty limiting strategic offensive arms. The treaty, negotiated as the replacement for the SALT I (1972) Interim Agreement, was a compromise between the basic framework worked out in the VLADIVOSTOK ACCORD (1974) and subsequent U.S. proposals for more comprehensive weapons limits. The discussions between the two leaders produced no breakthrough on any of the major points of Soviet-American conflict. Privately Carter and Brezhnev agreed in the future to hold regular U.S.-Soviet summits rather than wait for special occasions.

The Vienna talks and the completion of a major arms pact briefly interrupted the growing tension between Washington and Moscow. The Soviet invasion of Afghanistan in December 1979 precluded Senate ratification of the SALT II accord and caused the most serious rift in relations between the superpowers since the end of the VIETNAM WAR. The heads of government of the two nations would not meet again until the GENEVA SUMMIT in 1985.

VIETNAM MORATORIUM (1969) Nationwide protest against U.S. participation in the VIETNAM WAR. Escalating U.S. military involvement in Southeast Asia in the mid-1960s precipitated a growing domestic antiwar movement. In 1967, large demonstrations were staged in New York, San Francisco, and Washington. The 1968 Democratic National Convention in Chicago was the scene of violent clashes between police and antiwar protesters. In 1969 Sam Brown, a 26-year-old antiwar activist who had worked in Senator EUGENE J. MC-CARTHY's (D-MN) 1968 presidential campaign, helped found and became coordinator for the Vietnam Moratorium Committee, an umbrella organization of antiwar groups. The committee's call for a nationwide non-violent "moratorium" against the war to be held on October 15, 1969, drew the endorsement of politicians, academics, and religious leaders. On the designated day an estimated million Americans attended demonstrations, conducted peace vigils and teach-ins, or otherwise protested the war. The Moratorium, as it became known, marked the first coordinated, nationwide antiwar event and underscored mounting opposition to the conflict. The Nixon administration's policy of gradually winding down the U.S. military role in Vietnam brought a decline in antiwar demonstrations, although large protests flared after both the CAMBODIAN INCURSION (1970) and LAOTIAN INCURSION (1971). Antiwar activity continued until the U.S. military withdrawal from the conflict in 1973.

VIETNAM SYNDROME Expression used to describe the impact of America's prolonged, traumatic experience in the VIETNAM WAR on the national psyche. Since the 1973 withdrawal of American forces from South Vietnam, the term generally has referred to a widespread preoccupation with avoiding involvement in another protracted military conflict. Liberal political figures who came of age in the 1960s have tended to view all subsequent U.S. military interventions as potential Vietnam-like quagmires. Conservatives have used the phrase to refer to a purported dangerous paralysis of American will. The Reagan administration took office in 1981 committed to reasserting U.S. readiness to defend its interests overseas. But as Secretary of Defense CASPAR W. WEINBERGER underscored in his "USES OF MILITARY POWER" speech in 1984, U.S. willingness to use military force remained subject to national concerns about the possible repetition of another Vietnam. The successful U.S. military operations in the GRENADA INVASION (1983) and PANAMA INVASION (1989) were viewed as too brief and

small to be taken as evidence America had put the Vietnam conflict behind it. In 1991 President GEORGE BUSH contended that U.S. victory in the PERSIAN GULF WAR had ended the Vietnam Syndrome.

VIETNAM WAR (1959–1975)   Protracted armed struggle in which North Vietnam, aided by a Communist insurgency in the South, ultimately defeated U.S.-allied South Vietnam and unified all Vietnam under Communist control. The United States at the peak of its involvement committed more than a half-million military personnel to the defense of South Vietnam in what was the longest and most divisive foreign war in American history. The conflict also engulfed neighboring Laos and Cambodia.

In the 19th century, France had colonized Vietnam, Laos, and Cambodia and joined them in an Indochinese Union. During WORLD WAR II French Indochina fell under the control of the Japanese military. In 1941 Vietnamese Communist leader Ho Chi Minh united various nationalist groups in the Viet Minh movement for Vietnamese independence. In 1945 the U.S. OFFICE OF STRATEGIC SERVICES funneled aid to Ho's forces fighting a guerrilla campaign against the Japanese. Following Japan's surrender to the Allies, Ho proclaimed the establishment of an independent Democratic Republic of Vietnam in September 1945. But the British and Chinese forces which accepted the Japanese army's capitulation in Vietnam also permitted the return of French military units and reimposition of French colonial rule. Negotiations between the French government and Ho over the future status of Vietnam proved unsuccessful and the French Indochinese War between France and the Viet Minh erupted in 1946.

During World War II President FRANKLIN D. ROOSEVELT had stated U.S. opposition to a postwar restoration of French colonialism in Indochina. The Truman administration, however, acquiesced to renewed French rule. President HARRY S. TRUMAN avoided challenging Paris on Indochina lest he undermine the French government or strengthen the already powerful French Communist Party. Truman moreover sought French support for Washington's hardening stance against the Soviet Union. At the same time, the White House was unwilling to link America with European colonialism; thus the United States initially adopted a neutral position in the French-Viet Minh conflict. The onset of the East-West COLD WAR, however, brought a deepening U.S. involvement in Vietnam. The emergence of a Communist Chinese government in 1949 raised concerns in Washington over the Communist threat in Asia.

The Viet Minh meanwhile waged a successful guerrilla war against the French. In January 1950 the Soviet Union and Communist China recognized Ho's government. In February 1950 France established Vietnam as an autonomous state within the French Union. Thereupon the United States extended diplomatic recognition to the State of Vietnam and its government headed by former Emperor Bao Dai. Noting Ho's ties with Moscow and Peking, Washington came to view the Viet Minh as part of a Soviet-directed worldwide Communist offensive. In May the Truman administration approved a program of U.S. military and economic aid to France to help it defeat the Viet Minh. The outbreak in June 1950 of the KOREAN WAR heightened American worries over Communist expansionism in Asia and brought greatly expanded U.S. assistance to the French in Indochina.

Despite substantial U.S. aid, France by early 1954 was nearing defeat in Vietnam. In April 1954 the French government requested direct American action to save the French garrison under seige by the Viet Minh at Dien Bien Phu. President DWIGHT D. EISENHOWER conditioned U.S. military intervention on joint British participation and strong congressional support for the policy. When neither was forthcoming, he decided against unilateral U.S. action. On May 7, 1954, Dien Bien Phu fell, signalling the collapse of the French military position in Indochina. The international GENEVA CONFERENCE (1954) on Korea and Indochina negotiated an end to the French Indochinese War. France granted Vietnam its full independence. The GENEVA ACCORDS, concluded in July 1954, temporarily divided Vietnam at the 17TH PARALLEL between the Democratic Republic of Vietnam, or North Vietnam, and the State of Vietnam, or South Vietnam, pending national elections in 1956 to unify the country.

The United States declined to sign the accords, not wanting to endorse the emergence of a Communist state in the North. With the formation of the SOUTHEAST ASIA TREATY ORGANIZATION (SEATO) in September 1954, Washington formally extended the U.S. policy of CONTAINMENT of communism to Indochina. The following month the Eisenhower administration initiated U.S. economic and military aid to the South Vietnamese government formed under the anti-Communist nationalist leader Ngo Dinh Diem. The aid marked the start of a growing U.S. commitment to the defense of South Vietnam, which Diem formally proclaimed the Republic of Vietnam in 1955. Between 1954 and 1956 the United States replaced France as South Vietnam's key ally and benefactor. Eisenhower deployed several hundred U.S. military advisers to train the South Vietnamese armed forces. The White House backed Diem's refusal to hold the Geneva-mandated national elections, concurring in the South Vietnamese president's assertion that the Communists would not permit a fair vote.

By 1957 the temporary partition of Vietnam had hardened into a permanent division between Communist North Vietnam and non-Communist South Vietnam. Ho and the fervently nationalist Communist leadership in Hanoi remained committed to the goal of uniting Vietnam. In January 1959 North Vietnam launched a Communist insurgency in the South aimed at toppling the government in Saigon and replacing it with a regime that would agree to national reunification under Ho. In 1960 Hanoi announced the formation in the South of the National Liberation Front (NLF), a Communist-led coalition of anti-Diem insurgent groups. The NLF became widely known as the Viet Cong (for Vietnamese Communist). Taking office in January 1961, the Kennedy administration grew alarmed over the Communist guerrilla movement's growing success in the South Vietnamese countryside, especially in view of Soviet Premier Nikita S. Khrushchev's public declaration that Moscow would support "wars of national liberation." President JOHN F. KENNEDY foresaw the THIRD WORLD becoming the next locus of ideological struggle between the FREE WORLD and the Communist bloc; he believed Vietnam represented a critical test of a U.S.-allied government's ability to withstand a Communist insurgency. The administration's new FLEXIBLE RESPONSE defense strategy included an emphasis on counterinsurgency operations. Kennedy reaffirmed Eisenhower's commitment to the defense of South Vietnam. Following the TAYLOR-ROSTOW MISSION report in November 1961 on the worsening situation in Southeast Asia, he authorized the dispatch of additional military advisers and the first U.S. combat support units to Vietnam.

The conflict in Indochina spread to Laos, where pro-Western and Communist factions struggled for control. A second GENEVA CONFERENCE (1961–1962) reached an agreement ending the LAOTIAN CRISIS (1960–1962) and providing for Laotian neutrality. The fighting in Laos soon resumed between U.S.- and North Vietnamese-allied groups and continued until 1975. By 1963 U.S. military strength in Vietnam had risen to more than 16,000. Believing efforts to defeat the Viet Cong were being undermined by Diem's increasingly repressive regime, the Kennedy administration tacitly backed the military coup that overthrew the South Vietnamese leader in November 1963. The DIEM COUP was followed by a prolonged period of political instability in South Vietnam, lasting until a strong government emerged under President Nguyen Van Thieu in 1967. Meanwhile President LYNDON B. JOHNSON continued the deepening U.S. involvement in Southeast Asia.

The nature of the Vietnam War changed in 1964 when North Vietnamese regular army units began to infiltrate into South Vietnam. North Vietnam received a steady flow of military supplies and armaments from the Soviet Union and Communist China. Following the August 1964 TONKIN GULF INCIDENT, in which two U.S. destroyers reportedly came under attack by North Vietnamese gunboats, Johnson prevailed on Congress to pass the TONKIN GULF RESOLUTION authorizing the president to take whatever measures necessary to repel further aggression and defend America's SEATO allies. The Johnson administration thereafter cited the resolution as the mandate for the steadily expanding U.S. role in the fighting in Vietnam. In February 1965 Johnson ordered air strikes against North Vietnam in retaliation for Communist raids on U.S. military installations in South Vietnam. In March he authorized a sustained bombing campaign meant both to interdict infiltration from the North and force Hanoi to negotiate a cease-fire. The same month the first U.S. ground combat troops were

deployed to South Vietnam to help the outnumbered and largely ineffectual South Vietnamese military engage the North Vietnamese. Major U.S. and North Vietnamese units first clashed in October 1965. The conflict escalated rapidly, with U.S. military strength in Vietnam climbing in 1965 from roughly 25,000 to more than 180,000. The Johnson administration enlisted the support of America's Pacific allies in the growing war. The U.S. forces eventually were joined by contingents from South Korea, the Philippines, Australia, New Zealand, and Thailand.

Between 1965 and 1968 U.S. combat units assumed the major burden of the fighting in South Vietnam, with the South Vietnamese army concentrating on PACIFICATION. Despite periodic assurances by Johnson that victory was in sight, the American military presence in Vietnam continued to expand, prompting critics to charge the administration with a "credibility gap." The conflict's seeming interminability and mounting U.S. casualties fueled a growing domestic antiwar movement that eventually brought Johnson's political downfall. The proliferation of antiwar demonstrations across the country after 1967 revealed a deep national division over Vietnam. Opponents of American involvement in the war, representing a cross-section of opinion, included pacifists, religious groups, college students, mainstream political figures, and radical activists. Critics on the left contended that the United States had intervened unjustly in what was said to be an indigenous civil war with deep historical roots. Other detractors argued that the nation was mired in a costly and ultimately unwinnable conflict in which its own interests were not vitally at stake. Johnson defended his administration's Vietnam policy against the criticism. The president subscribed to the DOMINO THEORY, which held that if one country in the region fell to communism the others would be toppled in succession. U.S. involvement in Southeast Asia, he maintained, was essential to checking Communist aggression and demonstrating America's readiness to fulfill its security commitments.

Under intensifying domestic pressure, Johnson vigorously pursued a peace settlement with Hanoi. The two sides, though, were unable to agree on a basic framework for negotiations. The Johnson administration's confidence was dealt a serious blow in late January 1968 by the Communist TET OFFENSIVE. Although ultimately repelled, the surprise countrywide attack inflicted serious losses on U.S. and South Vietnamese forces and underscored a continuing Communist capacity and resolve to fight. U.S. Commander WILLIAM C. WESTMORELAND asked for substantial reinforcements. The Tet offensive heightened domestic unease about the course of the war and led to a White House reappraisal of Vietnam policy. After consultation with a group of senior informal advisers known as the WISE MEN, Johnson concluded that America could not prevail militarily in Vietnam and thus decided upon a deescalation of the U.S. role there. In a nationwide television address on March 31, 1968, the president announced a partial halt in the bombing of the North and signaled Washington's renewed interest in peace negotiations. Hanoi responded favorably and the PARIS PEACE TALKS began in May 1968.

President RICHARD M. NIXON took office in January 1969 committed to achieving "peace with honor" in Vietnam, a position he had campaigned on in the 1968 election. He sought to disengage the United States from the war in a way that both preserved South Vietnam's independence and retained America's international standing and credibility. The Nixon administration adopted a policy of VIETNAMIZATION, whereby the South Vietnamese army would be trained and equipped to gradually assume responsibility for the ground fighting, thus permitting U.S. forces to be withdrawn from Vietnam. With the Paris Peace Talks stalled, National Security Adviser HENRY A. KISSINGER began secret negotiations with North Vietnamese representatives in Paris in August 1969. In 1970 Nixon authorized U.S. and South Vietnamese attacks against Communist sanctuaries along the border in neutral Cambodia. The president defended the CAMBODIAN INCURSION as necessary to speed Vietnamization and safeguard U.S. forces. The operation aroused intense domestic criticism for, it was contended, widening the war. The United States began providing military assistance to the pro-Western government in Phnom Penh in its fight against the Communist Khmer Rouge insurgency. In 1971 Nixon sanctioned the LAOTIAN INCURSION, a U.S.-supported South Vietnamese assault on the Ho Chi Minh Trail, the Communist supply line running through Laos. Antiwar members of Congress attempted unsuccessfully in the early 1970s to pass the McGOVERN-HATFIELD AMENDMENT and similar measures devised to terminate U.S. involvement in Vietnam.

By the spring of 1972 U.S. forces in South Vietnam had been reduced from a peak of 540,000 in 1969 to approximately 70,000. In March 1972 North Vietnam launched the EASTERTIDE OFFENSIVE, a major invasion of the South. Nixon directed a resumption of U.S. bombing of the North and the mining of its key harbors. With U.S. air support the South Vietnamese army succeeded in halting the Communist offensive. In October 1972 Kissinger announced a breakthrough in U.S.-North Vietnamese negotiations. When talks to iron out the final details reached an impasse, Nixon in December ordered OPERATION LINEBACKER, a massive bombing campaign intended to force Hanoi's agreement to peace terms. In January 1973 Kissinger and North Vietnamese negotiator Le Duc Tho concluded the PARIS PEACE ACCORDS arranging for a cease-fire and ending U.S. involvement in the Vietnam War. Remaining U.S. forces were withdrawn from Vietnam by March 29, 1973. Nixon and Congress thereafter clashed over continued U.S. bombing raids in support of the Lon Nol government in Cambodia. Starting in June 1973, Congress passed a series of measures, most notably the CASE-CHURCH AMENDMENT, barring further U.S. military action in Southeast Asia. In November 1973 Congress overrode Nixon's veto to enact the watershed WAR POWERS RESOLUTION limiting the president's authority to commit U.S. forces to hostilities without express congressional approval.

The 1973 cease-fire never took hold as fighting between North and South Vietnam flared over the next two years. In January 1975 Hanoi unleashed an all-out invasion of the South. President GERALD R. FORD was unable to convince a wary Congress to increase U.S. aid to Saigon or otherwise respond to the North Vietnamese violation of the Paris Peace Accords. In April 1975 Ford ordered an emergency helicopter evacuation of U.S. embassy personnel and other Americans in South Vietnam. Saigon fell to

Communist forces on April 30, 1975. Cambodia came under Communist control the same month and a Communist government was installed in Laos in August.

The United States suffered 55,000 killed and 300,000 wounded in the war. Vietnamese casualties on both sides ran to the hundreds of thousands. The reunification of Vietnam in 1975 under Communist control represented the final failure of three decades of U.S. policy in Southeast Asia. The lessons to be drawn from America's bitter Vietnam experience remained a matter of debate. Liberals cited Vietnam in warning against U.S. military intervention in Third World insurgencies. Conservatives pointed to the brutal Communist regimes imposed in Indochina as proof of the need for a U.S. worldwide commitment to the containment of communism. The uncertainty and deep reluctance to commit American military forces that characterized U.S. foreign policy in the war's aftermath became known as the VIETNAM SYNDROME. In the late 1970s the United States became involved in efforts to aid the tens of thousands of refugees, or BOAT PEOPLE, fleeing Communist rule in Vietnam. Washington steadfastly refused to recognize the Vietnamese government. Progress on resolving the status of U.S. military personnel still missing in Southeast Asia, the end of the Cold War, and settlement of the CAMBODIAN CIVIL WAR raised prospects for the normalization of U.S.-Vietnamese relations in the early 1990s.

VIETNAMIZATION U.S. policy for transferring to South Vietnam responsibility for its own defense. As the Johnson administration steadily escalated U.S. military involvement in Southeast Asia in the mid-1960s, American forces effectively took over the fighting of the VIETNAM WAR. On taking office in 1969, the Nixon administration thoroughly reviewed U.S. strategy in Vietnam, concluding that America should end its direct military participation in the conflict and instead help South Vietnam to assume the lead role in defending itself against Communist aggression. The term "Vietnamization" was coined by Secretary of Defense MELVIN R. LAIRD to describe the process.

Meeting with South Vietnamese President Nguyen Van Thieu on Midway Island,

President RICHARD M. NIXON announced the new policy on June 8, 1969. It involved the gradual withdrawal of U.S. forces from South Vietnam and the training and equipping of the South Vietnamese military to take their place. To disrupt North Vietnam's ability to launch attacks during this transition, American and South Vietnamese forces conducted the controversial CAMBODIAN INCURSION (1970) and LAOTIAN INCURSION (1971). U.S. troop strength dropped from roughly 540,000 in 1969 to about 25,000 by 1972. While Vietnamization achieved the goal of extricating America from Vietnam, its overall success remains a matter of debate. The South Vietnamese army, with U.S. air power, defeated the major 1972 North Vietnamese EASTERTIDE OFFENSIVE. In 1975 South Vietnam, without U.S. support, collapsed before the final North Vietnamese assault.

VINCENNES INCIDENT (1988) Accidental downing of an Iranian commercial airliner over the southern Persian Gulf by a U.S. Navy vessel. In 1987, amid the Iran-Iraq War (1980–1988), President RONALD W. REAGAN committed American naval forces to the Gulf to protect Kuwaiti oil tankers sailing under the American flag from Iranian attack. In the PERSIAN GULF INTERVENTION, U.S. warships kept sea lanes open and protected neutral shipping. From the outset, U.S.-led convoys in the Gulf encountered Iranian mines, missile attacks, and speedboat raids. American forces met these hazards with minesweeping operations and retaliatory strikes against Iranian oil platforms and naval vessels. When the U.S. frigate *Samuel Rogers* was disabled by a mine in April 1988 during an escort operation, the Defense Department promptly launched what it described as a "measured response" against Iranian targets. Teheran complained to the UNITED NATIONS and threatened retaliation, while Reagan warned that the Iranians would continue to absorb losses if they imperiled American interests in the Gulf.

On July 3, 1988, the U.S. cruiser *Vincennes* shot down an Iranian passenger liner over the Strait of Hormuz after mistaking it for an attacking F-14 fighter jet. All 290 people aboard the airliner were killed. While President Reagan expressed regret at the loss of innocent life, and pledged compensation for the families of the victims, the U.S. government defended the decision of *Vincennes* Captain Will C. Rogers 3rd to open fire and indicated there would be no change in the overall U.S. policy of defending neutral shipping in the Gulf as a result of the mishap. The United States explained that the *Vincennes* had been engaged in a skirmish with several Iranian gunboats when its radar detected the Iranian Airbus approaching head on, outside any commercial air corridor. When the aircraft did not respond to radio warnings on both military and civilian frequencies, it was assumed to be hostile and was destroyed with a surface-to-air missile attack.

The Iranian government, incredulous that the U.S. cruiser's state-of-the-art Aegis radar system had been unable to distinguish between a wide-bodied jetliner and an F-14 less than a quarter its size, accused the United States of a premeditated massacre and vowed revenge. In the days after the incident, key details of the initial U.S. account that fixed the primary blame on Iran—the exact altitude, flight path, and electronic signals of the Iranian plane—were called into question, placing the Reagan administration on the defensive. On August 19, 1988, the Defense Department released the results of the official Navy investigation of the downing. The report determined that human errors caused by combat stress and lack of experience had led the U.S. crew to misidentify the airliner as an attacking Iranian F-14 fighter. Experts suggested the downing in December 1989 of PAN AM FLIGHT 103 was possibly the work of terrorists carrying out Iran's promised revenge. In 1991 U.S. and British authorities charged two Libyan intelligence agents with the Pan Am bombing.

VIRGINIUS AFFAIR (1873) Violent episode that threatened to precipitate a war between the United States and Spain. In the early 1870s Cuban insurgents seeking the overthrow of Spanish colonial rule on their island were engaged in a rebellion against Spain known as the Ten Years' War (1868–1878). From the war's outset, exiled rebels had launched FILIBUSTERING expeditions from U.S. soil with the support and funding of American sympathizers. In October 1873 the *Virginius,* a steamer flying the American flag that was ferrying rebel arms

to Cuba, was captured in waters near Jamaica by a Spanish warship and brought into the harbor at Santiago, Cuba. Following swift court-martial trials, Spanish authorities executed 53 crew members and passengers, some of them U.S. citizens, as pirates.

The seizure of the *Virginius* and the summary executions, violations of international law, excited indignation among Americans and drew quick U.S. condemnation. President ULYSSES S. GRANT ordered the Navy mobilized for possible hostilities. In a virtual ultimatum delivered to Madrid, Secretary of State HAMILTON FISH threatened to break diplomatic relations unless the Spanish government released the *Virginius* and its survivors, paid an indemnity for the killings, and saluted the American flag. When Fish subsequently learned that the *Virginius* belonged to Cuban revolutionaries, had been fraudulently registered under the American banner, and was carrying filibusters in violation of American neutrality law, he softened the Grant administration's position and negotiated a compromise with Spanish Minister at Washington Jose Polo de Bernabe in November 1873. The United States dropped the flag salute demand. Spain in return released the *Virginius* and the surviving prisoners, acknowledged the capture had been illegal, and agreed to pay an $80,000 indemnity to the families of the executed Americans.

VLADIVOSTOK ACCORD See **STRATEGIC ARMS LIMITATION TALKS II**.

VLADIVOSTOK SUMMIT (1974) Talks held by President GERALD R. FORD and General Secretary Leonid I. Brezhnev November 23 to 24 at the port city of Vladivostok in the eastern Soviet Union. The superpower leaders used their meetings to get acquainted and to reaffirm the bilateral commitment to DETENTE established by Brezhnev and President RICHARD M. NIXON between 1972 and 1974. Ford had become president in August 1974 following Nixon's resignation in the face of the Watergate scandal.

High mark of the summit was the signing by the two leaders of the VLADIVOSTOK ACCORD establishing the principle of equivalency in strategic, or long-range, nuclear forces. The accord amounted to a tentative agreement to limit the numbers of all

U.S. and Soviet strategic offensive NUCLEAR WEAPONS and delivery systems through 1985. U.S. Secretary of State HENRY A. KISSINGER called the arms agreement a breakthrough development that imposed a ceiling on the arms race for a decade. Ford and Brezhnev announced negotiations on a final accord would take place at the SALT II talks scheduled to resume in Geneva in January 1975. In the summit's final communique, the two nations stressed their determination to sustain and build upon the Soviet-American cooperation of recent years. The Vladivostok parley was the last bilateral U.S.-Soviet conference until President JIMMY CARTER and Brezhnev met at the June 1979 VIENNA SUMMIT to sign the SALT II agreement.

VOA See **VOICE OF AMERICA**.

VOICE OF AMERICA (VOA) Global radio service of the UNITED STATES INFORMATION AGENCY (USIA). The Roosevelt administration launched Voice of America in February 1942 to counter propaganda of the Axis powers and explain U.S. goals in WORLD WAR II to listeners throughout war-torn Europe and Asia. At its wartime peak VOA broadcast in 40 languages. The SMITH-MUNDT ACT (1948) made VOA a permanent agency under the DEPARTMENT OF STATE. In its postwar incarnation the broadcast service, through its news, editorials, and entertainment programming, strove to win support abroad for American foreign policies and to strengthen foreign understanding of American society by offering a clear picture of life in the United States. With the advent of the COLD WAR, VOA joined the U.S. anti-Communist propaganda effort against the Soviet Union and its East European satellites that was spearheaded by RADIO FREE EUROPE and RADIO LIBERTY.

In 1953 VOA became a separate entity under USIA, the newly established federal agency given responsibility for the U.S. government's overseas information programs. VOA currently transmits 24 hours a day, beaming news, features, commentary, and cultural programs in more than 40 languages to a vast worldwide audience. The flagship U.S. broadcast service, it has jurisdiction over RADIO MARTI and Television Marti, the companion Miami-based anti-Communist stations that broadcast directly to Cuba. VOA throughout its history has enjoyed great independence. It lost a significant measure of autonomy in December 1990 when USIA assumed control of the service's budget, personnel management, and public affairs. The USIA move was an early step in the Bush administration's plan to consolidate all of the government's international broadcasting operations under one authority.

W

WAKE ISLAND U.S. possession in the north Pacific Ocean, situated some 2100 miles west of Honolulu, Hawaii. Wake Island, comprising a coral atoll and the islets of Wake, Wilkes, and Peale, covers a total land area of about three square miles. Discovered in 1796 by British Captain William Wake, it was charted in 1841 by U.S. Navy Lieutenant Charles Wilkes during the exploratory WILKES EXPEDITION. (The third islet was named after Titian Ramsay Peale, the expedition's naturalist.) The United States in 1899 formally annexed Wake, which for years hence served as a cable relay station on the trans-Pacific telegraph. It was established in 1934 as a U.S. naval reservation, becoming a key civilian aviation station the following year when Pan American Airways opened a seaplane base there.

With WORLD WAR II erupting in the Pacific, Japanese forces captured Wake from the U.S. Navy garrison on December 23, 1941. Japan surrendered it to the United States in September 1945. Following the war, and particularly before the advent of long-range jets, the U.S. unincorporated territory emerged as an important refueling stop for commercial and military flights between Hawaii, GUAM, and Japan. President HARRY S. TRUMAN traveled to Wake Island in October 1950 to confer with General DOUGLAS MACARTHUR in the course of the KOREAN WAR. Under the jurisdiction of the DEPARTMENT OF THE AIR FORCE since 1972, it remains the site of an Air Force base.

See also MAP 7.

WALK IN THE WOODS See **INTERMEDIATE NUCLEAR FORCES TREATY**.

WALKER COMMISSION See **HAY-BUNAU-VARILLA TREATY**.

WALKER SPY RING Soviet espionage ring in the U.S. Navy. On May 20, 1985, retired Navy warrant officer John A. Walker, Jr. was arrested in Baltimore, Maryland, on charges of passing classified documents to the Soviet Union. Walker, who had been a Soviet agent for more than 17 years, headed a family spy ring based in Norfolk, Virginia. His son Michael L. Walker, a Navy seaman, was detained aboard the U.S.S. *Nimitz* on May 22, while his brother, retired naval officer Arthur J. Walker, was seized in Norfolk on May 29. A fourth member of the espionage cell, family friend Jerry A. Whitworth, also a former Navy man, was arrested on June 3 in California. Under a plea bargain arrangement, John and Michael Walker pleaded guilty on October 28, 1985, and were sentenced to life and 25 years respectively. Following his conviction on espionage charges, Arthur Walker received a life term on November 12. Whitworth was found guilty on August 28, 1986, and given a 365-year sentence. The Walker spy ring furnished the Soviet Union with information on U.S. communications and codes and the movement of American fleets. Senior government officials characterized it the most damaging espionage conspiracy in decades and among the gravest security breaches in the history of the Navy.

WALKER TARIFF (1846) Federal legislation that lowered U.S. tariffs. Following their gradual reduction under the 1833 COMPROMISE TARIFF, import duties were raised again under the Tariff of 1842. In 1846 President JAMES K. POLK demonstrated the Democratic Party's growing commitment to free trade by seeking to reverse the protectionist trend of the 1842 measure. Similar developments overseas aided the movement for a more open commercial policy. The vote on the 1846 act came after Great Britain repealed its Corn Laws, which had blocked the importation of foreign grains. The Walker Tariff, named for Secretary of the Treasury Robert J. Walker, was enacted July 30, 1846. It reduced import duties, dropped the imposition of a minimum tariff on selected commodities, and added items to the so-called free list of imports not subject to customs. Import duties were lowered again under the Tariff of 1857 before being raised dramatically by the MORRILL TARIFF (1861).

See also PROTECTIONISM.

WALKER, WILLIAM (1824–1860) American adventurer remembered for his FILIBUSTERING exploits in Central America. He graduated from the University of Nashville in his hometown in 1838 and five years later received a medical degree from the University of Pennsylvania. Following postgraduate medical study in Europe, he went to New Orleans, where he took up the study of law and was admitted to the Louisiana bar. He practiced briefly before becoming editor of a New Orleans newspaper in the late 1840s. In 1850 Walker moved to California where, imbued with the spirit of MANIFEST DESTINY and animated by great personal ambition, he turned to filibustering. In October 1853 he commanded an armed colonizing expedition against the Mexican province of Lower California, which Walker proclaimed an independent republic with himself as president. He was forced to retreat northward into the United States and surrender to the American military after U.S. authorities blocked his flow of supplies from San Francisco. Brought to trial for violating American neutrality laws, he was acquitted in May 1854 by a sympathetic jury.

Soon after, Walker jumped at the opportunity presented by a revolution in Nicaragua. At the invitation of a revolutionary Nicaraguan faction in need of outside help, he led an armed band of some 60 men from the United States to the Central American country in 1855 and joined in the fighting. Aided and subsidized by the Accessory Transit Company, an American transportation firm operating in Nicaragua, he seized control of the country and, after the United States formally recognized his regime in May 1856, declared himself Nicaragua's president. Southern expansionists welcomed Walker's move as a prelude to Nicaragua's annexation by the United States and eventual incorporation into the Union as a slave state. Walker encouraged such thinking when he repealed an earlier Nicaraguan decree abolishing slavery and proposed a revival of the African slave trade, steps calculated, in his words, "to bind the Southern states to Nicaragua as if she were one of themselves." But antislavery forces in the North forced President FRANKLIN PIERCE to revoke American recognition of Walker's government.

Walker harbored grandiose visions of a military empire comprising the small Central American states. He planned an interoceanic canal that would attract the world's commercial shipping traffic and contemplated use of slave labor to develop Central America's agricultural economy. His schemes were cut short when he became locked in a struggle with American commercial baron Cornelius Vanderbilt for control of the Accessory Transit Company. A coalition of neighboring Central American republics supported by Vanderbilt drove Walker from power in May 1857. He returned to the United States and later that year launched another expedition against Nicaragua, of which he still claimed to be the lawful president. Arrested upon arrival by the U.S. Navy, he was sent back to America. Walker's last Central American foray ended in September 1860 with his capture in Honduras by the British navy, which turned him over to Honduran authorities. Condemned by a court-martial, he was executed by firing squad on September 12.

WALTERS, VERNON ANTHONY (1917–   ) Military officer, intelligence official, ambassador. Born in New York City, Walters spent his youth in Europe and was educated in France and England. He demonstrated an exceptional aptitude for languages, becoming fluent in French, Italian, Spanish, Portuguese, and German. He enlisted in the Army in 1941 and was commissioned a second lieutenant the following year. During WORLD WAR II his language abilities landed him assignments in intelligence and as an interpreter. He remained in the Army after the war, holding various military attaché posts and serving on occasion as the translator for senior American officials. In 1958 he was with RICHARD M. NIXON when the vice-president's car came under attack during the CARACAS EPISODE. Named the senior military attaché at the American embassy in Paris in 1967, Walters assisted HENRY A. KISSINGER in secret negotiations in France with the North Vietnamese for ending the VIETNAM WAR.

In 1972 President Nixon appointed him deputy director of the CENTRAL INTELLIGENCE AGENCY (CIA). Walters later earned praise during the various Watergate investigations for resisting White House pressure to involve the CIA in the cover-up of the domestic political scandal. He left the agency and retired as an Army general in 1976. He worked as a consultant and wrote his memoirs, *Silent Missions* (1978). In 1981 President RONALD W. REAGAN named Walters an ambassador-at-large. Over the next four years he visited more than 100 countries as the president's special envoy, in particular rallying support for the administration's anti-Communist policies in Latin America and Africa. In 1985 Walters became U.S. ambassador to the UNITED NATIONS, where he pressed U.S. opposition to the Soviet military invasion of Afghanistan, lobbied for the cause of HUMAN RIGHTS in Cuba, and promoted efforts to curtail international terrorism. Named ambassador to West Germany by President GEORGE BUSH in 1989, Walters took his new post in time to witness the fall of the BERLIN WALL and the collapse of communism in Eastern Europe. He retired in 1991.

WANGHIA, TREATY OF (1844) First treaty between the United States and China. America was content to trade with the east Asian country on an informal basis until the First Opium War (1839–1842) between Great Britain, whose merchants dominated the lucrative opium trade in China and thus wanted it preserved, and the imperial Chinese government which sought to ban the trafficking. The victorious British compelled Chinese acceptance of the Treaty of Nanking (1842). Its terms forced China to

cede Hong Kong to the British, pay a war indemnity, open five ports to unrestricted British commerce, and recognize the principle of unhampered trade opportunity for foreign merchants. American traders in China worried that their British counterparts had secured advantages. Despite Chinese assurances that the U.S. would enjoy the same trading privileges, the United States moved diplomatically to protect American commercial interests.

President JOHN TYLER appointed Massachusetts Congressman CALEB CUSHING as first U.S. commissioner to the Chinese empire in 1843. Cushing was instructed to win the same commercial concessions by treaty, and without resort to force, that the British had wrested through war. He succeeded in this when, after five months of negotiation, he persuaded Chinese officials to sign a commercial agreement on July 3, 1844, at Wanghia, a village near the seaport of Macao. The treaty authorized the United States to station consuls and trade freely in the Chinese ports of Canton, Amoy, Ningpo, Foochow, and Shanghai. By its terms, America was granted the right of EXTRATERRITORIALITY, or legal jurisdiction over its citizens living in China, and MOST-FAVORED-NATION status. The United States, unlike the British in the Nanking agreement, acquired no Chinese territory. Approved unanimously by the U.S. Senate, the treaty established U.S.-Chinese economic contacts on a diplomatic foundation. Its emphasis on a principle of equal trade access among foreign powers operating in China presaged the OPEN DOOR policy articulated by the United States at the end of the 19th century. The agreement regulated Sino-American relations until the TREATIES OF TIENTSIN were concluded in 1858.

WAR BRIDES ACT (1945) Federal immigration measure signed December 28, 1945, that authorized the admission of alien spouses and children of members of the U.S. armed forces who had served honorably during WORLD WAR II. The law exempted the close relatives from having to wait for one of the scarce immigration quotas then available. The GI Fiancees Act the following year extended the same status to the men and women engaged to U.S. veterans. In 1947 Congress amended the War Brides Act to permit the entrance of Asian spouses who otherwise were barred by the racial exclusions then mandated under U.S. immigration law.

WAR, DEPARTMENT OF See **DEPART-MENT OF WAR** in **APPENDIX B**.

WAR OF 1812 (1812–1814) War between the United States and Great Britain. The conflict was precipitated by British interference with America's neutral maritime commerce and alleged British incitement of Indians on the American frontier. Since the end of the AMERICAN REVOLUTION, Washington and London had clashed on the issue of FREEDOM OF THE SEAS. The United States favored an expansive interpretation of neutral maritime rights in wartime anchored on the principle FREE SHIPS MAKE FREE GOODS. From the outset of the French Revolutionary Wars (1792–1802), the United States endured violations of its neutral rights at sea by both Great Britain and France, the two main European belligerents. The American merchant marine nonetheless profited handsomely from the expanded opportunities for neutral shipping produced by the protracted conflict. Renewed Anglo-French warfare with the start of the Napoleonic Wars (1803–1815) subjected American seaborne commerce to escalating and more serious abuses. The British and French sought to hinder each other's ability to fight by curbing the neutral maritime trade then dominated by the United States. U.S. commerce faced the greater threat from Great Britain, which enjoyed naval superiority over France.

British policy after 1804 resolved to stop the prosperous American wartime trade with the French West Indies that so benefited French ruler Napoleon Bonaparte. Britain's highest admiralty court, ruling in the 1805 case of the seized American trade ship *Essex*, insisted such commerce circumvented the Rule of 1756, a unilaterally proclaimed British maritime principle. The rule held that a belligerent nation could not open trade with a neutral nation in wartime when the same trade had been denied the neutral nation in peacetime. American ships, the British thus contended, were barred from carrying goods from the French Caribbean to France since this traffic had been closed to the United States before the Anglo-French war. After the *Essex*

verdict Great Britain seized American ships, partially blockaded American ports, confiscated France-bound cargoes, and continued its IMPRESSMENT of sailors from American ships.

British conduct invited strong U.S. protests and brought a marked deterioration in relations between the two nations. Congress struck back with the NON-IMPORTATION ACT (1806) authorizing a ban on assorted British products to the United States. Efforts at a negotiated settlement of Anglo-American differences on neutral rights produced the abortive MONROE-PINKNEY TREATY (1806), terms of which President THOMAS JEFFERSON found so unsatisfactory that he never submitted it to the Senate. America's neutral trade meanwhile fell prey to intensifying Anglo-French economic warfare. Britain precipitated the commercial fight in May 1806 when it imposed a blockade on all European ports under French control. Napoleon retaliated in November with the Berlin Decree, which initiated the so-called Continental system for strangling British commerce with the rest of Europe. Britain countered with a series of Orders in Council, or edicts, tightening its blockade on the French. Napoleon then responded with tougher decrees against British trade. American neutral commerce with Europe became the main casualty of the escalating Anglo-French battle of blockades.

Anglo-American tensions reached new heights in 1807 when the British ship *Leopard* attacked the U.S. vessel *Chesapeake* and impressed four seamen, three of them American citizens. The CHESAPEAKE AFFAIR outraged the American public and brought demands for redress. Unwilling to resort to war, Jefferson pursued a policy of economic pressure intended to win British—and French—respect for U.S. neutral rights. At his request, Congress in December 1807 passed the EMBARGO ACT virtually cutting off America's foreign trade by closing U.S. ports to all commerce except domestic coastal trade. His administration anticipated, incorrectly, that reliance on U.S. commerce would compel the British and French to recognize U.S. rights as the price for having the embargo lifted. The trade ban was a flop, injuring the United States far more than the European belligerents and failing to wring any concession from either London or Paris. Soaring domestic opposition to the embargo, especially among the economically hard-hit commercial classes of the northeast, forced its repeal after 14 months. It was immediately replaced by the milder NON-INTERCOURSE ACT (1809), which reopened trade with all nations except Great Britain and France and empowered Jefferson's successor, JAMES MADISON, to resume commerce with either or both of the belligerents once they agreed to stop violating America's neutral maritime rights.

After restoring legal trade with the British in April 1809 as a consequence of the ERSKINE AGREEMENT, an embarrassed and angry Madison several months later was forced to reverse himself and reimpose non-intercourse when the British government disavowed the Erskine understanding. This clumsy diplomatic episode widened the chasm between Washington and London. The Non-Intercourse Act also caused serious damage to the American economy without bringing European concessions. Congress replaced the measure in May 1810 with MACON'S BILL NO. 2, which reopened U.S. trade with Great Britain and France. The law stated that if one of the belligerents took steps to end its interference with legal American trade, and the other failed to do likewise within a given period of time, the president would be authorized to reimpose a trade ban on the recalcitrant party. Napoleon used this proviso to manipulate Madison. By pretending that the French decrees affecting American shipping had been revoked, the French ruler inveigled the president into reimposing non-intercourse against Great Britain in November 1810. The British contended that Madison had been duped by the French and thus refused to revoke their Orders in Council. Ensuing Anglo-American negotiations were fruitless.

With the United States and Great Britain at an impasse on impressment and the rights of neutral commerce, Madison called Congress into session a month early, in November 1811, and suggested it prepare the nation for possible hostilities. The Congress was dominated by the WAR HAWKS, a group of young, nationalistic representatives, chiefly from the South and West, who demanded action to avenge the wrongs inflicted on the nation by Great Britain.

These legislators harbored distinct sectional grievances against the British. On the frontier in the OLD NORTHWEST an Indian confederation organized and led by the enterprising Shawnee chief TECUMSEH was mounting hostile resistance to further white westward expansion. British agents in Canada were sympathetic to the Indians, who were known to receive British arms and ammunition. As a matter of policy, Great Britain continued to endorse the creation of a neutral Indian buffer state in the NORTHWEST TERRITORY as a barrier against advancing U.S. settlement. Westerners suspected that the British were actively inciting Indian attacks on American settlers.

In November 1811, as Congress met, an army under General WILLIAM HENRY HARRISON sustained heavy losses as it drove off a surprise Indian attack at the BATTLE OF TIPPECANOE in the Indiana Territory. The West blamed Great Britain for the bloodshed and demanded the expulsion of the British from Canada as the solution to the frontier Indian problem. The Western call for the conquest of British colony Canada, ostensibly an act of self-defense, was mirrored by Southern demands for the seizure of Spanish East and West Florida. The Floridas were coveted because of their strategic position and navigable rivers draining into the Gulf of Mexico. The United States had asserted a questionable claim to a section of West Florida as part of the LOUISIANA PURCHASE (1803). In 1810, ignoring Spanish protests, U.S. forces had occupied a portion of the territory, thereby exacerbating the long-standing WEST FLORIDA CONTROVERSY. That Spain was then allied with Great Britain, Southerners suggested, offered grounds for conquering the rest of the Floridas in the event of war.

In his message to Congress on June 1, 1812, requesting a declaration of war against Great Britain, Madison cited impressment, interference with neutral commerce, and intrigues with the western Indians as major grievances. The House of Representatives approved the declaration on June 4 by a vote of 79 to 49. The Senate, delayed by pro-British Federalist sentiment among the New England and neighboring maritime states, finally voted for war on June 17 by a 19 to 3 margin. Madison signed the war declaration on June 18. Two days earlier Great Britain had announced its intention to revoke its edicts against U.S. shipping. But news of this concession did not reach America until several weeks after hostilities had begun. The United States entered the war ill-prepared. Congress had spent months debating without making adequate military preparations. When the conflict began, America had a regular army of fewer than 10,000 men, a navy of 16 warships, and no national bank—a situation that seriously hampered the government's ability to borrow to finance the war effort.

In the war's first year, the United States suffered a series of major military setbacks. A three-pronged U.S. attack on Canada was a total failure. During this ill-conceived campaign, General William Hull surrendered his army and the garrison at Detroit to the British. The suprisingly successful showing of the U.S. Navy in the first year offered some consolation and bolstered flagging American confidence. In 1813 General William Henry Harrison recovered control of the Detroit area when he decisively defeated the British in October at the Battle of the Thames. His success had been made possible by the September naval triumph of Commodore Oliver Hazard Perry over the British squadron on Lake Erie. Tecumseh's death in the Thames engagement spelled the end of effective Indian resistance in the Old Northwest. The war in the south centered on action against British-allied Indians on the frontier. The Creeks, with British encouragement, launched assaults in early 1813 on American settlers in the Mississippi and Alabama territories. General ANDREW JACKSON led the retaliatory U.S. campaign to subdue the Indians. He dealt the Creeks a crushing defeat at the Battle of Horseshoe Bend in March 1814. U.S. victory in the CREEK WAR weakened Indian resistance in the southeast to advancing white settlement.

A new situation took shape in 1814 with Napoleon's defeat in Europe, which enabled Great Britain to send veteran reinforcements to North America. Several major British efforts during the summer to invade the United States from Canada were turned back by American forces. Meanwhile a British army landed in Chesapeake Bay in August, routed the American militia defending Washington, and then marched into the capital, where they burned the White House and other public buildings before

withdrawing. The American force at Fort McHenry repulsed a subsequent attack on Baltimore. It was during the British bombardment of the fort that Francis Scott Key wrote the *Star Spangled Banner*. The U.S. Navy continued to prove its mettle with victories in a series of notable single-ship actions. These successes, however, could not overcome the overwhelming superiority of the British fleet, which tightened its crippling blockade of the American coast. The impact on both private business and government revenues was devastating. By the war's late stages, most of the ships in the American Navy were either captured or bottled up in U.S. ports and American maritime trade had been effectively driven from the high seas.

Russia's offer to mediate the conflict led indirectly to the convening of American and British commissioners in Ghent, Belgium, in August 1814 for peace talks. The British pressed for boundary readjustments and for a permanent Indian barrier state on the northwest frontier. The Americans, while rejecting the British demands, were themselves in no position to seek territorial gains and soon found it diplomatically necessary to abandon U.S. insistence on concessions regarding maritime rights and impressment. The British commissioners at length dropped their demands and accepted the American proposal for a peace on the basis of *status quo ante bellum* (restoration of territories held prior to war). The TREATY OF GHENT, returning territory occupied by either side, was signed December 24, 1824, officially ending the war. News of the peace treaty was slow to reach British and American commanders on the southern frontier. Thus at New Orleans on January 8, 1815, two weeks after the Ghent settlement had been concluded, General Andrew Jackson inflicted an overwhelming defeat on an invading British force. Jackson's smashing victory at the Battle of New Orleans made him a national hero and ended the war on a glorious note for most Americans.

Federalist New England, a stronghold of pro-British sentiment, had offered the greatest domestic opposition to the conflict, which it derisively dubbed "Mr. Madison's War." This opposition culminated in the Hartford Convention, which brought together Federalist delegates from the New

England states to discuss grievances against Democratic-Republican policies. Conducted in secrecy in the Connecticut city from December 1814 to January 1815, the convention outlined supposed constitutional infractions alleged to have been committed by the Madison administration in its conduct of the war. The gathering, resisting the call of extremist delegates to consider secession from the Union, went only so far as to propose certain amendments to the Federal CONSTITUTION intended to protect sectional interests. The end of the war abruptly halted the work of the convention and discredited the whole movement it represented.

Measured by the terms of the peace treaty, which granted the United States none of its original war aims, the War of 1812 amounted to a failure. But it was not entirely so. Although the Ghent settlement ignored the issue of maritime rights, the British in practice stopped impressments with the end of the war. The power of the Indians on the northwest frontier had been broken, clearing the way for the advance of American settlement after 1815. Jackson's victory over the Creeks weakened southern Indian resistance to American expansion and set into motion events leading to Spain's cession of the Floridas to the United States through the ADAMS-ONIS TREATY (1819). A widespread feeling among Americans that the young nation had successfully defended its rights and independence engendered a strong new sense of national unity.

WAR HAWKS Group of U.S. legislators who emerged in the 12th Congress (1811–1813) as staunch advocates of war with Great Britain. Through the exercise of their political influence, they contributed significantly to the eventual U.S. decision to confront the British in the WAR OF 1812. When Congress convened in 1811, an anti-British mood predominated in America, fueled by British violations of U.S. neutral rights. The 12th Congress came under the leadership of a body of new Democratic-Republican members, whom Representative John Randolph collectively dubbed the "war hawks" for their bellicosity. Among them were HENRY CLAY and Richard M. Johnson of Kentucky; JOHN C. CALHOUN and Langdon Cheves of South Carolina; Felix Grundy of Tennessee; and Peter B. Porter

of New York. Mostly young and primarily from the lower south and west, the war hawks were ardent nationalists and fervent expansionists who viewed British maritime restrictions and IMPRESSMENT of American sailors as galling assaults upon national rights and honor. Members of this political fraternity in Congress also raised regional grievances against the British. Southerners and westerners complained London's edicts against the U.S. maritime trade had cut off overseas markets for their agricultural products. War hawks from the OLD NORTHWEST denounced suspected British encouragement of Indian resistance to American territorial expansion and advocated the conquest of Canada. Meanwhile pro-expansion southern war hawks favored a U.S. move to annex the Floridas from Britain's ally Spain. Although a minority in Congress, the war hawks wielded substantial clout, especially in the House, where they controlled the key Navy and foreign relations committees and where Clay was elected speaker. Thus the war hawks were well positioned to thwart diplomacy and press their demand for war with the British.

WAR POWERS RESOLUTION (1973) Federal legislation governing the commitment of U.S. combat forces abroad. Under the U.S. CONSTITUTION, the war-making authority is divided between the legislative and executive branches. Congress is vested with the power to declare war, while the president is designated the commander in chief of the armed forces. Congress has voted a declaration of war five times: WAR OF 1812, MEXICAN WAR (1846–1848), SPANISH-AMERICAN WAR (1898), WORLD WAR I, and WORLD WAR II. During the 19th century, it became accepted practice for presidents on their own authority to employ U.S. military forces for limited actions such as suppressing piracy and the slave trade and protecting American lives and property abroad. In the early 20th century, presidents exercised this discretion in undertaking a series of U.S. military interventions in the Caribbean and Central America.

Since World War II, presidents have assumed broad authority to involve the military in hostilities overseas. U.S. forces fought in the KOREAN WAR and VIETNAM WAR without congressional declarations of war. The Johnson administration cited the TONKIN GULF RESOLUTION (1964) as the legal basis for U.S. military involvement in Southeast Asia. The protracted conflict led growing numbers of legislators to assert that the White House had overstepped the intent of the resolution to wage an undeclared war in Vietnam. Pressure mounted on Capitol Hill for legislation to reassert Congress's constitutional role in committing the nation to war.

After several years of debate, lawmakers in October 1973 passed the War Powers Resolution. The measure stated that the president's constitutional power as commander in chief to commit U.S. armed forces to hostilities could be exercised only in connection with a declaration of war, specific statutory authorization, or in a national emergency involving an enemy attack. The law contained three provisions meant to curtail the president's ability independently to send U.S. armed forces into combat. The resolution directed the president to consult "in every possible instance" with Congress before committing U.S. forces to imminent or actual hostilities. It required the president to submit a written report to Congress within 48 hours of introducing U.S. forces into a hostile or potentially hostile situation and stipulated that the troop commitment had to be ended within 60 days of the written report unless Congress specifically authorized its continuation. The deadline could be extended by 30 days to allow for the safe disengagement of U.S. forces from combat. The law also provided Congress a so-called legislative veto over any commitment of U.S. forces to hostilities undertaken without specific congressional approval. Thus lawmakers gave themselves power to order a withdrawal of American troops at any time through passage of a concurrent resolution.

President RICHARD M. NIXON vetoed the war powers bill on October 24, 1973, contending the measure represented an unconstitutional infringement on executive branch powers. He further asserted that the bill would dangerously weaken the nation's ability to respond decisively and effectively in an international crisis. Nixon's political influence had been seriously weakened, however, by the unfolding Watergate scandal and Congress was able to override his veto on November 7, enacting the resolution into law. The controversial war powers measure has been the subject of ardent debate. Liberal critics have assailed it for per-

mitting the president to fight a war without restraint for up to 60 days. Conservatives have charged that it hamstrings the president's ability to conduct foreign policy.

In practice, presidents have avoided complying fully with the act's terms while questioning its constitutionality. In the first real test of the resolution, President GERALD R. FORD did not consult with Congress before ordering military action against Communist Cambodian forces in the MAYAGUEZ INCIDENT (1975). Neither did President JIMMY CARTER confer with lawmakers before the abortive April 1980 U.S. rescue mission during the IRAN HOSTAGE CRISIS. Both presidents reported to Congress, but the military operations were concluded well before other provisions of the war powers act took effect. While President RONALD W. REAGAN informed Congress of his deployment of U.S. marines to Lebanon in 1982 as part of a multinational peacekeeping force, he avoided acknowledging the validity of the War Powers Resolution. As the marines' involvement in hostilities during the LEBANON CRISIS (1982–1984) expanded, Reagan resisted congressional efforts to invoke the 60-day limit under the war powers act, but agreed to a compromise congressional resolution restricting the deployment to 18 months.

In 1983 the U.S. Supreme Court ruled in *Immigration and Naturalization Service* v. *Chadha* that legislative vetoes over presidential policy are unconstitutional. Legal scholars have construed this decision as effectively striking down at least the concurrent resolution provision of the war powers legislation. Presidents Reagan and GEORGE BUSH reported to Congress on the GRENADA INVASION (1983) and PANAMA INVASION (1989) respectively, but in each case hostilities were concluded before the war powers act deadlines became an issue. During the PERSIAN GULF INTERVENTION (1987–1988) the Reagan administration persuaded Congress that U.S. protection of neutral shipping in the gulf did not merit invoking the War Powers Resolution. In the PERSIAN GULF WAR (1991) Congress voted a joint resolution expressly authorizing U.S. involvement.

WARE v. HYLTON (1796) U.S. Supreme Court ruling that federal treaties took precedence over state law. As part of its confiscation of British property during the AMER-

ICAN REVOLUTION, Virginia had passed a statute stipulating that private debts owed by its residents to British creditors be paid instead to the state. The 1783 Anglo-American TREATY OF PARIS ending the conflict authorized the citizens of either nation to bring suit in the other to collect past debts. In a 4 to 0 decision delivered March 7, 1796, the Supreme Court ruled that the treaty provision nullified the Virginia law. In the unanimous opinion, Justice Samuel Chase observed that under the CONSTITUTION treaties were the supreme law of the land. Subsequent Court decisions consistently have upheld the primacy of the federal treaty-making power over state sovereignty.

See also MISSOURI V. HOLLAND.

WARNKE, PAUL CULLITON (1920–   ) Director of the ARMS CONTROL AND DISARMAMENT AGENCY (ACDA). Born in Massachusetts, Warnke graduated from Yale University in 1941. After serving in the Coast Guard during WORLD WAR II, he earned a law degree from Columbia University in 1948 and joined a Washington law firm. In 1966 President LYNDON B. JOHNSON named him the Defense Department's general legal counsel. The following year he became an assistant secretary for international security affairs, the department's third-ranking position. Increasingly disenchanted with American involvement in the VIETNAM WAR, Warnke argued for U.S. disengagement from the conflict. He left office with the Johnson administration in January 1969 and opened an influential Washington law practice with former Secretary of Defense CLARK CLIFFORD. Warnke became an outspoken critic of U.S. policy in Southeast Asia. A strong advocate of arms control negotiations with the Soviet Union, he opposed the development of new U.S. strategic weapons which might destabilize the superpower nuclear balance. In February 1977 President JIMMY CARTER selected Warnke to head the ACDA and serve as chief U.S. negotiator at strategic arms talks with the Soviet Union. The nomination sparked bipartisan opposition from conservative senators who characterized Warnke as weak on defense. After extensive debate, he won Senate confirmation the following month. His tenure was marked by efforts to conclude a final SALT II arms control accord. With negotiations on an agreement almost completed, Warnke resigned in October 1979, citing personal reasons, and returned to his law practice.

WASHBURNE, ELIHU BENJAMIN (1816–1887) Congressman, briefly secretary of state during the Grant administration, and diplomat. Born in Maine, he was a printer's apprentice before attending Harvard Law School in 1839. Washburne was admitted to the Massachusetts bar in 1840 and later the same year moved to Galena, Illinois, where he practiced law, invested successfully in western lands, and turned his energies to politics. Elected to the U.S. House of Representatives from Illinois in 1852 as a Whig, he served there 16 years and became a Republican upon the founding of that party in 1854.

During the Civil War, he was a political adviser to his personal friend President ABRAHAM LINCOLN and sponsored the rise of fellow Galena townsman ULYSSES S. GRANT to the rank of general and command of the Union Army. Washburne was a staunch supporter of Grant's successful run for president in 1868. Named secretary of state in 1869, he held the post from March 5 to March 16, a period of just 12 days. This courtesy appointment was a prelude to his selection by Grant on March 17 as U.S. minister to France and was intended to give him prestige in the French capital.

Washburne's mission to France lasted eight years. He witnessed the downfall in 1870 of Emperor Napoleon III amid political unrest in the wake of French reverses in the Franco-Prussian War (1870–1871). He won distinction as the only official representative of a foreign government to stay in Paris during the German siege and the days of the Commune, a bloody revolt by French radicals, in 1871. In addition to successfully maintaining U.S. neutrality during the Franco-Prussian conflict, Washburne looked out for the safety and interests of German residents of France. On his return to the United States in 1877, he settled in Chicago and devoted himself to literary and historical pursuits. Washburne's last political venture was his unsuccessful bid for the Republican presidential nomination in 1880.

WASHINGTON CONFERENCE (1941-1942) See **WORLD WAR II CONFERENCES** in **APPENDIX E.**

WASHINGTON CONFERENCE (1942) See **WORLD WAR II CONFERENCES** in **APPENDIX E**.

WASHINGTON CONFERENCE (1943) See **WORLD WAR II CONFERENCES** in **APPENDIX E**.

WASHINGTON, GEORGE (1732–1799) Commander in chief during the AMERICAN REVOLUTION and first president of the United States. By 1748 the home-educated Virginia native had embarked on his early career as a land surveyor. He was commissioned a major in the Virginia militia in 1752, the same year he inherited the family estate, Mount Vernon. Sent by Governor Robert Dinwiddie in 1753 to demand French withdrawal from land in the Ohio Valley claimed by Great Britain, Washington served in the ensuing French and Indian War (1754–1763). He achieved regimental command and the rank of colonel but failed to gain a regular commission in the Royal army. Following his election to the Virginia House of Burgesses in 1758, he resigned from the Virginia militia and returned to civilian life.

A member of the House until 1774, he emerged as a leader of Virginia resistance to the British government's policy of colonial taxation and tightening imperial administration. He was a delegate to the Continental Congress in 1774 and 1775, serving on various committees charged with military preparations for the impending rebellion. On June 15, 1775, Congress made Washington a general and unanimously elected him commander in chief of the newly formed Continental Army. Refusing all pay for his services, he assumed command on July 3. After forcing a British evacuation of Boston in March 1776, he was unable to defend New York City and had to withdraw with his army into New Jersey. Morale-boosting successes at Trenton in December 1776 and Princeton in January 1777 were followed by defeats in Pennsylvania at Brandywine and Germantown that fall and the loss of Philadelphia. These military setbacks tarnished Washington's standing in the Continental Congress. Richard Henry Lee and Benjamin Rush among other delegates schemed to replace him with General Horatio Gates, who had defeated the British at the Battle of Saratoga in October 1777. Washington's congressional supporters thwarted the so-called Conway Cabal, leaving the general securely in command. Meanwhile Washington and his troops endured a winter of hardship and near starvation at Valley Forge, Pennsylvania (1777–1778). The Continental Army emerged from its rough winter camp well-drilled and revitalized by word of the FRANCO-AMERICAN ALLIANCE (1778). With French support, Washington pressed the fight against the British, finally forcing the surrender of General Charles Cornwallis at Yorktown, Virginia, in October 1781, which effectively ended the war. Resigning his military commission, Washington bade farewell to his officers at Fraunces Tavern in New York on December 4, 1783, and returned to Mount Vernon.

Convinced that problems plaguing the new American nation in the 1780s stemmed from the weakness of decentralized government under the ARTICLES OF CONFEDERATION, Washington advocated a strengthened central government. He was a Virginia delegate to the Constitutional Convention (1787), serving as its president and distinguishing himself by his support for a strong federal government. Afterward he promoted ratification of the new CONSTITUTION by the Virginia legislature.

Unanimously elected the first president, Washington was inaugurated in New York City on April 30, 1789, and held office for two terms (1789–1797). With Congress he undertook to establish the three initial executive departments of the new federal government, the DEPARTMENT OF STATE, DEPARTMENT OF WAR, and DEPARTMENT OF THE TREASURY, each of which bore responsibilities for the conduct of U.S. foreign relations. Washington endorsed the landmark fiscal policies designed by Secretary of the Treasury ALEXANDER HAMILTON to restore public credit, repay the national debt, and foster nascent domestic industries. The TARIFF OF 1789 and Tonnage Act (1789) protected fledgling American manufactures from European competition and raised valuable operating revenues for the young republic.

Washington forged his foreign policy under the pressure of the war that erupted in 1792 between Great Britain and France. Determined to keep the United States from becoming embroiled in the conflict, he issued his NEUTRALITY PROCLAMATION (1793) declaring strict American neutrality. Domestic critics of the proclamation charged

Washington with reneging on U.S. obligations to France under the Franco-American Alliance. French Minister to the United States Edmond C. Genet flouted the president's neutrality policy during the notorious GENET AFFAIR (1793), prompting Washington to demand the French diplomat's recall. While France would decide not to invoke its alliance with the United States, the president concurred with Secretary of State THOMAS JEFFERSON that the two treaties of the alliance were still binding despite the overthrow of the French monarchy with which they had been completed. By supporting Jefferson's assertion that treaties were a compact between nations rather than between specific governments, Washington established an enduring principle of American diplomacy.

When a combination of British interference with U.S. neutral shipping and mutual violations of the TREATY OF PARIS (1783) ending the American Revolution brought a crisis in Anglo-American relations, Washington sent JOHN JAY to London to negotiate differences and avert war. JAY'S TREATY (1794), under which the United States accepted the narrow British interpretation of FREEDOM OF THE SEAS, was denounced by the Democratic-Republican opposition as a surrender to Britain and abandonment of the French-American alliance. Washington withstood ardent protest at home and in Paris and upheld the controversial accord. British agreement in Jay's Treaty to abandon the posts they had held in America's OLD NORTHWEST since the revolution removed a chief obstacle to further U.S. westward expansion and marked an important diplomatic victory for Washington. The president settled several long-standing difficulties with Spain through PINCKNEY'S TREATY (1795), which fixed the disputed boundary between the United States and Spanish Florida at the 31st parallel and granted U.S. ships free access to the length of the Mississippi River and to the port of New Orleans.

Washington and Secretary of War HENRY KNOX favored peaceful federal relations with the American Indian tribes. The administration aimed to purchase tribal lands through formal INDIAN TREATIES to accommodate continued westward expansion of the United States. Washington wanted to avoid war while achieving an orderly advance of the American frontier. His personal meeting with Chief ALEXANDER MCGILLIVRAY in 1790 preceded the signing of the TREATY OF NEW YORK, which established peaceful ties between the United States and the Creek Nation and arranged for Creek territorial cessions in Georgia to the federal government.

In the early 1790s Washington moved militarily in the Old Northwest against Ohio Indians who, with encouragement from the British in Canada, staged hostile resistance to white settlement beyond the Ohio River. U.S. forces dispatched under General Arthur Saint Claire to subdue the Indians were routed in November 1791. Washington turned to General "Mad Anthony" Wayne, whose expedition overwhelmed Indian tribes confederated under Miami Chief LITTLE TURTLE at the decisive BATTLE OF FALLEN TIMBERS in 1794. In the TREATY OF GREENVILLE (1795), the defeated Indians ceded most of present-day Ohio, clearing the way for further U.S. expansion into the NORTHWEST TERRITORY. Meanwhile, under the Washington administration's stewardship, Congress passed a series of TRADE AND INTERCOURSE ACTS through the mid-1790s to furnish a framework for administrating INDIAN LAND CESSIONS and regulating trade with the Indians.

WASHINGTON'S FAREWELL ADDRESS (1796) revealed the president's precedent-setting decision not to seek a third term. His celebrated valedictory to the nation urged America to avoid permanent alliances abroad and to stay politically detached from Europe. This "great rule of conduct" concerning foreign policy endured into the 20th century as the basic statement of U.S. ISOLATIONISM. When war loomed with France in 1798, Washington interrupted his retirement at Mount Vernon to accept command of a provisional army organized to fight in the anticipated conflict. Full-scale hostilities were avoided when President JOHN ADAMS settled the undeclared QUASI-WAR (1798–1800) through diplomacy. Thus Washington never personally assumed command of the American forces. In 1976 Congress posthumously promoted him to six-star General of the Armies to ensure that he would outrank all other American generals.

WASHINGTON NAVAL CONFERENCE (1921–1922) International meeting on naval armaments and the Far East. The United States, Great Britain, and Japan emerged from WORLD WAR I as the leading sea powers. Eager to avoid a costly and potentially destabilizing naval armaments race, the three nations agreed, together with major sea powers France and Italy, to hold an international conference on naval limitation. Because each nation's position in the western Pacific was connected to its naval power, Far Eastern affairs were included on the meeting's agenda. The United States sought the termination of the Anglo-Japanese military alliance, a relationship that American leaders worried could threaten U.S. interests in Asia. Japan, on the other hand, regarded continued naval primacy in its home waters in the western Pacific as essential to its security.

The gathering, officially titled the Conference on the Limitation of Armament, was held in Washington, D.C., from November 12, 1921, to February 6, 1922. Also in attendance for the discussions on the Far East were Belgium, the Netherlands, Portugal, and China. Germany, recently defeated in the world war, and Russia, whose new Bolshevik government was not yet recognized by the other participants, were not invited. The U.S. delegation was headed by Secretary of State CHARLES EVANS HUGHES and included former Secretary of State ELIHU ROOT and Senators HENRY CABOT LODGE, SR. (R-MA), and Oscar W. Underwood (D-AL).

The conference yielded three major agreements: the FOUR-POWER TREATY that committed the United States, Great Britain, France, and Japan to respect each other's Pacific island possessions, effectively abrogating the Anglo-Japanese alliance; the FIVE-POWER TREATY that set limits on the navies and Pacific fortifications of the major sea powers; and the NINE-POWER TREATY, signed by all the conferees, that guaranteed the sovereignty and territorial integrity of China. Several minor agreements also were reached, including a treaty between the United States and Japan ending the YAP ISLAND CONTROVERSY concerning cable relay station rights on the Pacific island.

See also GENEVA NAVAL CONFERENCE, LONDON NAVAL CONFERENCES.

WASHINGTON NAVAL TREATY See **FIVE-POWER TREATY**.

WASHINGTON SUMMIT (1973)   Week-long meetings between President RICHARD M. NIXON and Soviet General Secretary Leonid I. Brezhnev which yielded a series of agreements expanding the Soviet-American DETENTE of the early 1970s. The Washington parley, second of three U.S.-Soviet summits during the Nixon administration, was characterized by optimism and continued the trend begun in Moscow the year before toward improved superpower relations. Brezhnev's visit from June 16 to 25, 1973, repaid Nixon's trip to the MOSCOW SUMMIT in 1972, at which the two leaders signed the SALT I agreement limiting offensive NUCLEAR WEAPONS and the ABM TREATY. At the outset of the Washington talks, the president and the general secretary vowed to build on the successes of their 1972 meeting and to seek long-term world peace. The centerpiece of the summit was the signing by Nixon and Brezhnev on June 21 of a declaration on offensive nuclear arms. Under this agreement, both sides pledged to accelerate ongoing SALT II talks in Geneva. The declaration called for completion by the end of 1974 of a permanent accord limiting offensive strategic weapons to replace the Interim Agreement fashioned under SALT I. The two leaders also signed a pact on the peaceful uses of atomic energy. In the course of the conference, U.S. and Soviet officials finalized a series of less significant agreements on oceanography, transportation, cultural exchanges, agriculture, and income taxes.

Trade emerged as a key summit issue when Brezhnev met with House and Senate members in an attempt to win MOST-FAVORED-NATION tariff treatment for Soviet goods. The general secretary lobbied congressional leaders to drop their insistence on unrestricted Soviet Jewish emigration as a precondition to the granting of trade concessions to the USSR. But in 1974 Congress would pass the JACKSON-VANIK AMENDMENT, mandating that most-favored-nation trade privileges be withheld from countries not permitting the free emigration of their citizens. The Kremlin's restrictive policy on Jewish emigration remained a perennial source of conflict with successive U.S. administrations. The 1973 Washington gathering ended with Nixon accepting Brezhnev's invitation to a MOSCOW SUMMIT in 1974.

WASHINGTON SUMMIT (1979)   Talks between President JIMMY CARTER and Chinese Deputy Premier Deng Xiaoping held amid the first official visit to the United States by a top Chinese Communist leader. Deng's January 28 to February 6 stay followed the establishment of diplomatic relations between the United States and the People's Republic of China on January 1. The summit aimed at solidifying the new contacts between the United States and mainland China and continuing the improvement of the Sino-American relationship.

In the course of their meetings, Carter and Deng signed a series of agreements on cultural and scientific exchanges. These included an accord to establish consulates in several major cities in each country; a science and technology pact; a space accord enabling the Chinese to pay NASA to launch civilian communications satellites; and an arrangement intended to increase cultural and educational contacts. Beyond these formal agreements, Peking consented in principle to permit American news organizations to set up bureaus in China. On international issues, the United States insisted on softening the indirect criticism of Soviet expansionism expressed in the February 1 joint press communique summarizing the Carter-Deng talks. During the summit the Chinese leader had described the USSR as a menace to world peace and stressed the Sino-American duty to cooperate to oppose Soviet hegemony. U.S. Secretary of State CYRUS R. VANCE afterward assured the Soviet ambassador to the United States that Deng's remarks did not signal an alignment of Washington and Peking against Moscow. The deputy premier also caused the host Carter administration diplomatic problems by suggesting the Chinese might use force against Vietnam in response to its invasion of Cambodia and to Chinese-Vietnamese border tensions. Deng's comments foreshadowed China's incursion into Vietnam on February 17, which ended as a decisive military setback for the mainland.

In the summit's aftermath, the United States and Communist China continued to expand their contacts. In July the countries concluded a pact granting the Chinese MOST-FAVORED-NATION trade status. Diplomatic relations were strengthened when Vice-President Walter F. Mondale visited Peking in late August for talks with China's top leadership. These discussions yielded a broadened cultural exchange agreement. U.S. and Chinese leaders next met in 1984 when President RONALD W. REAGAN and Pre-

mier Zhao Ziyang convened for the WASHINGTON SUMMIT.

WASHINGTON SUMMIT (1984) Talks between Premier Zhao Ziyang and U.S. officials during the Chinese leader's friendship tour of the United States from January 9 to 16, 1984. Zhao's U.S. stay was the first by a top-level Chinese Communist official since Deng Xiaoping attended the WASHINGTON SUMMIT in January 1979 following the establishment of formal diplomatic ties between the two countries. Improvement of Sino-American relations and expansion of two-way trade predominated Zhao's discussions with President RONALD W. REAGAN, Secretary of State GEORGE P. SHULTZ, and congressional leaders.

Reagan and Zhao signed a new accord on industrial cooperation and renewed a pact on science and technology exchanges. Negotiations also made headway on a U.S.-Chinese nuclear power agreement. Addressing prospects for trade with his Communist nation, Zhao assured American business leaders the People's Republic of China had moved irreversibly in opening up to the West. He stressed China's great need for U.S. capital and advanced technology to achieve its modernization program. Reagan reciprocated Zhao's visit when he attended the BEIJING SUMMIT in April 1984, centerpiece of a self-described "journey of peace" to mainland China.

WASHINGTON SUMMIT (1987) Meeting in Washington, D.C., from December 8 to 10, 1987, at which President RONALD W. REAGAN and Soviet General Secretary Mikhail S. Gorbachev signed the landmark INTERMEDIATE NUCLEAR FORCES TREATY (INF Treaty) abolishing medium-range nuclear forces. When the October 1986 REYKJAVIK SUMMIT did not achieve a breakthrough in U.S.-Soviet arms control negotiations, prospects for a follow-up superpower summit were left in doubt. The Iceland talks had foundered on the issue of the STRATEGIC DEFENSE INITIATIVE (SDI), the U.S. program to develop a space-based shield for nationwide protection against ballistic missiles. The Reagan administration rejected the Kremlin's demand for SDI limits and the two sides departed Reykjavik accusing each other of intransigence on space arms.

The summit outlook remained uncertain through much of 1987. The COLD WAR adversaries clashed in April over reciprocal allegations of embassy buggings. The controversy, which followed the discovery of extensive electronic listening devices in the new American embassy in Moscow, overshadowed a spring mission by U.S. Secretary of State GEORGE P. SHULTZ to Moscow to speed progress on a bilateral arms deal covering medium-range missiles. In October, following months of discussions, the superpowers announced Reagan and Gorbachev would meet in Washington in December to conclude a long-awaited treaty scrapping intermediate-range nuclear forces. Scheduling of the summit had been delayed by a Soviet demand, rejected by the Reagan administration, that there be a draft agreement on strategic and space weapons treaties for consideration at the December parley.

Arms control was the focus of the third Reagan-Gorbachev meeting. Centerpiece of the summit was the December 8 signing of the INF Treaty eliminating all U.S. and Soviet shorter- and medium-range nuclear missiles. The two leaders also made modest headway on several disputes hindering negotiations to cut strategic nuclear forces. Reagan and Gorbachev reaffirmed weapons ceilings agreed on at Reykjavik for a START deal and directed negotiators to work out a verification and compliance system for an accord on long-range nuclear force reductions. The superpowers avoided a confrontation on SDI, the main obstacle to a strategic arms agreement, by deferring the question of whether further program testing and development was consistent with the 1972 ANTIBALLISTIC MISSILE TREATY (ABM Treaty). The Soviets maintained that the ABM pact barred SDI tests in space; the Reagan administration interpreted the treaty less restrictively, contending it permitted space trials.

The president and the general secretary failed to resolve any major regional or HUMAN RIGHTS issues. While restating Soviet willingness to pull its 115,000 troops out of Afghanistan within a year, Gorbachev refused to set a specific timetable for withdrawal. Reagan pledged continued U.S. aid to anti-Soviet Afghan rebels until the Kremlin began its exodus. Gorbachev also withheld Soviet support for a U.S.-endorsed UNITED NATIONS arms embargo against Iran for refusing to negotiate a cease-fire in its war with Iraq. Reagan was unable to obtain Gorbachev's assurance of pending further liberalization of Soviet policies on human rights and the emigration of Soviet Jews. On bilateral affairs, the Washington talks yielded agreements on joint air service between the countries, oceanographic research, and monitoring of underground nuclear tests.

In a final communique, Reagan and Gorbachev announced plans for a MOSCOW SUMMIT in 1988. The Washington parley marked a turn in superpower dealings from harsh Cold War rhetoric and mutual suspicion toward frank discussion and practical negotiation. The warm reception given the visiting Soviet leader by the public and media alike demonstrated growing American responsiveness to the thaw in U.S.-Soviet relations since Gorbachev came to power in 1985 and initiated dramatic political and economic reforms.

WASHINGTON SUMMIT (1990) Second meeting between President GEORGE BUSH and Soviet President Mikhail S. Gorbachev, held May 31 to June 3, 1990, in the U.S. capital. The two leaders completed significant arms control and trade accords during four days of talks on the swift transformation in U.S.-Soviet relations since Bush took office in January 1989. They welcomed the thaw between the superpowers that had accelerated with the preceding year's dramatic developments: sweeping political change in the Soviet Union and Eastern Europe, the fall of the BERLIN WALL, and the easing of East-West military tensions.

Covering an agenda outlined at their December 1989 MALTA SUMMIT, Bush and Gorbachev discussed the post-COLD WAR military and political order in Europe, airing their differences on the issue of German reunification. Gorbachev restated Soviet opposition to the idea, favored by the United States, of a single Germany with membership in NATO. Bush in turn objected to the Kremlin leader's proposal to eventually replace NATO and its Soviet-block counterpart, the Warsaw Pact, with a pan-European council under the 35-nation CONFERENCE ON SECURITY AND COOPERATION IN EUROPE (CSCE).

Moving to aid the badly faltering Soviet economy, the presidents concluded a pact to normalize U.S.-USSR trade and grant the Soviet Union MOST-FAVORED NATION (MFN) trade status. Bush backed off a pre-summit threat to delay signing of the accord because of the Kremlin's economic embargo on Lithuania, the Baltic republic that had declared its independence from Moscow. But Bush reportedly informed Gorbachev he would neither forward the pact to Congress for approval nor waive the JACKSON-VANIK AMENDMENT (1974) limits on MFN eligibility until the Kremlin lifted restrictions on Soviet Jewish emigration to Israel.

The summit yielded a series of arms control accords. A framework START agreement on cutting U.S. and Soviet strategic nuclear forces nailed down the major terms to be contained in a final strategic-arms reduction pact. Numbers of unresolved details and technical issues prevented completion at the Washington meeting of a formal treaty on long-range NUCLEAR WEAPONS. A chemical-weapons agreement directed the superpowers immediately to halt production of chemical arms and eventually to destroy their stockpiles, following the completion of an international accord banning chemical weapons. In a joint statement, the two sides called for stepped-up negotiations in Vienna toward a treaty cutting conventional forces in Europe.

At the end of the parley, both leaders acknowledged remaining differences on arms issues and Europe's future but stressed that the summit had underscored greater cooperation in U.S.-Soviet relations. From Washington, Gorbachev embarked on a brief cross-country tour. In a meeting with 145 American business leaders in Minnesota, he outlined Soviet economic reforms and urged more U.S. investment in the USSR. Gorbachev then flew to California, where he visited former President RONALD W. REAGAN and conferred with South Korea President Roh Tae Woo about normalizing relations between Moscow and Seoul. Bush and Gorbachev next met on short notice at the HELSINKI SUMMIT in September 1990 in response to Iraq's invasion of Kuwait.

WASHINGTON, TREATY OF (1871) Agreement concluded between the United States and Great Britain that provided for the settlement of outstanding differences in Anglo-American relations. The major item concerned the unresolved ALABAMA CLAIMS, the U.S. financial grievances against Great Britain for damages inflicted on Union shipping during the Civil War by British-built Confederate warships. London had resisted Washington's repeated demands for redress and rejected as groundless U.S. appeals for collateral damages. The issue of the Civil War claims remained at an impasse until January 1871, when U.S. Secretary of State HAMILTON FISH made arrangements with visiting British emissary Sir John Rose for submitting all Anglo-American disputes to a joint high commission empowered to negotiate a settlement. Apart from the Alabama Claims, the principal matters at issue were the FISHERIES QUESTION, the long-standing dispute over American fishing rights in Canadian waters; the SAN JUAN ISLANDS CONTROVERSY, concerning the contested northwestern water boundary between the Canadian province of British Columbia and the United States; and other British and American claims, particularly those stemming from U.S. seizure of British property during the Civil War. The 10-member commission, comprising five representatives from each nation, convened for the first time in Washington in late February 1871. Following numerous formal meetings in the U.S. capital, the commissioners signed an agreement on May 8, 1871.

The treaty arranged for creation of a five-member international tribunal that would meet in Geneva, Switzerland, to arbitrate the Alabama Claims. In the pact's preamble, the British government expressed regret for the escape of the *Alabama* and other Confederate raiders from British ports and for the depredations committed by the vessels. At U.S. insistence, the British agreed to three rules of international law that were to guide the arbitrators. The first asserted that a neutral nation had to use "due diligence" to prevent the departure from its ports of armed ships intending to wage war on another nation; the second said it was a neutral's duty to stop any belligerent from using its ports as bases for naval operations or for arming or supplying; the third contended that neutral governments were under an obligation to exercise "due diligence" over all people in its jurisdiction to prevent violations of its neutrality laws. On the fisheries question, the treaty guaranteed American inshore fishing privileges in Canada and opened U.S. waters in the Atlantic north of 39° to Canadian fishermen. Since the United

States secured the more lucrative fishing rights, the Washington settlement arranged for an international arbitration commission to rule on how much Canada should receive in additional compensation. The agreement submitted the San Juan Island dispute to the German emperor for arbitration. Finally, it called for a joint commission to settle those British and American claims distinct from the Alabama grievances.

The U.S. Senate ratified the treaty on May 24, 1871, by a vote of 50 to 12. The arbitration tribunal met as scheduled in Geneva and announced its decision in September 1872. Finding the British government responsible for the damages wrought by the *Alabama* and other cruisers, the arbitrators awarded the United States a $15.5 million indemnity. In the case of the San Juan Islands dispute, the German emperor in October 1872 gave the islands to the United States. The general claims commission in September 1873 dismissed all American claims while awarding the British some $1.9 million for their property losses during the Civil War. The fisheries commission, after meeting in Halifax, Nova Scotia, decided in November 1877 to award Canada $5.5 million to compensate for the fishing privileges earlier conceded to the United States.

WASHINGTON, TREATY OF (1911)

U.S.-Japanese commerce and friendship pact. The JAPANESE-AMERICAN TREATY OF 1894 had established broad commercial relations between the two nations. With the 1894 agreement due to expire, Secretary of State PHILANDER C. KNOX and Japanese Ambassador to the United States Yasuya Uchida concluded a successor pact at Washington on February 21, 1911. Known formally as the Treaty of Commerce and Navigation of 1911, it provided for full and equal commercial relations and guaranteed the right of each nation's citizens to travel and reside in the other country. U.S.-Japanese relations deteriorated in the 1930s over Japanese aggression against China. When Japan's assault on its Asian neighbor in 1937 developed into a full-scale invasion, the Roosevelt administration began to consider a U.S. trade embargo to compel Japanese withdrawal. U.S. policymakers were concerned, however, that such action might violate the 1911 treaty. On July 26, 1939, Washington

gave Tokyo the required six-months notice of U.S. termination of the commerce pact, effective January 26, 1940. America imposed an increasingly restrictive embargo on Japan in the period leading up to the December 1941 Japanese surprise attack at PEARL HARBOR and U.S. entry into WORLD WAR II.

WASHINGTON'S FAREWELL ADDRESS

(1796)   Parting message of President GEORGE WASHINGTON to the nation. Published September 19, 1796, in the Philadelphia *Daily American Advertiser,* it contained among the most enduringly influential statements on foreign policy in American history. As Washington's second term in office drew to a close, his administration remained preoccupied with the domestic political debate over what direction U.S. diplomacy should take toward the French Revolutionary Wars (1792–1802). Washington's NEUTRALITY PROCLAMATION of 1793, issued shortly after France had declared war on Great Britain, Spain, and Holland, had stated America's impartiality toward all belligerents and was formulated primarily to keep the United States from becoming embroiled in the conflict on behalf of either the British or the French.

The opposing sentiments of America's emerging political parties jeopardized U.S. ability to chart a neutral course in the mid-1790s. Pro-British Federalists and pro-French Democratic-Republicans each sought to steer diplomatic developments to the advantage of the side where their respective political sympathies lay. Against this backdrop, and amid the 1796 presidential campaign, Washington tendered his Farewell Address. Drafted with the help of the president's longtime aide, former Treasury Secretary ALEXANDER HAMILTON, the historic valedictory to the nation was never delivered orally, appearing only in the newspapers of the day.

The message, much of which dwelled on domestic affairs, opened with Washington's revelation that he would not be a candidate for a third term. He warned of the threat posed by sectionalism in American politics, calling a strong union the foundation of American liberty and the nation's best insurance against vulnerability to unwanted foreign entanglements. Washington deplored the dangers of factional party policies, which he contended promoted geographic divisions and invited foreign influence and intrigues; and, in a salvo aimed at Federalist and Democratic-Republican conduct, asserted that U.S. interests were best served by avoiding either passionate attachment or intense opposition to other nations.

The address outlined the president's "great rule of conduct" regarding foreign policy: the United States, in extending its trade relations, should forge as little political connection as possible with foreign nations. Washington in particular urged U.S. political detachment from Europe, arguing that American and European interests were remote and frequently incompatible. While emphasizing that the United States must uphold faithfully its existing obligations abroad, he advised the nation in the future to avoid permanent alliances with any foreign countries. But Washington conceded that "extraordinary emergencies" might warrant the establishment of temporary alliances. The Farewell Address thus presented what became the fundamental expression of American ISOLATIONISM until well into the 20th century.

WEATHERFORD, WILLIAM (1780–1824) The half-blood Weatherford, also known as Red Eagle, was a Creek Indian chief best remembered for his leadership in the CREEK WAR (1813–1814) against the United States. A disciple of Shawnee Chief TECUMSEH, the apostle of Indian unity to oppose U.S. westward expansion, Weatherford spearheaded Creek resistance to advancing white settlement across the southeast. In the Creek War he directed the Indians' assault in August 1813 on Fort Mims, Alabama, in which more than 500 white soldiers and civilians were killed. Weatherford next led Creek forces in the decisive Battle of Horseshoe Bend on the Tallapoosa River. There, on March 27, 1814, the Creeks were routed by General ANDREW JACKSON. The defeated Indians were forced to cede half of their lands in Alabama through the TREATY OF FORT JACKSON (1814). Weatherford, who had surrendered to Jackson, was pardoned and became an advocate of peaceful Indian-white relations.

See also MAP 1.

WEBB-POMERENE ACT (1918) Federal law enacted on April 10, 1918, that ex-empted America's foreign commerce from antitrust restrictions. Sponsored in Congress by Representative Edwin Y. Webb (D-NC) and Senator Atlee Pomerene (D-OH), the legislation authorized U.S. industries to organize themselves as combinations for export trade without becoming subject to the Sherman Antitrust Act, the landmark U.S. law passed in 1890 against economic monopoly. The Webb-Pomerene measure specified that export combinations would enjoy the exemption provided they neither restricted trade within the United States nor hurt domestic competitors. The act was intended primarily to help American corporations compete more effectively in international markets against British and German cartels. Endorsed by President WOODROW WILSON and business leaders, it illustrated the push by American manufacturers for expanded exports and presaged the economic nationalism that characterized U.S. foreign relations in the 1920s and 1930s.

Congress passed a corollary law in December 1919 to accommodate American banks that wanted to spread the risks of making loans to European countries for post-WORLD WAR I reconstruction by forming banking consortiums. The Edge Act, sponsored by Senator Walter E. Edge (R-NJ), permitted such combining of financial assets by exempting U.S. banks from antitrust rules whenever they joined together for the purpose of foreign financial transactions.

WEBSTER, DANIEL (1782–1852) Lawyer, prominent senator, and twice secretary of state. Born in New Hampshire, Webster graduated from Dartmouth College in 1801, read law in Boston, and was admitted to the bar there in 1805. In 1807 he moved to Portsmouth, New Hampshire, where he established a highly successful practice and engaged in politics as a Federalist. He became spokesman for New England merchant and shipping interests that objected to the embargo and other restrictions on Anglo- and Franco-American trade imposed by Democratic-Republican presidents THOMAS JEFFERSON and JAMES MADISON. His famous Rockingham Memorial (1812), a forceful statement of opposition to the WAR OF 1812, helped him win election as a Federalist from New Hampshire in 1812 to the U.S. House of Representatives, where he served two terms. As a member of the foreign relations committee, he continued his vigorous criticism of the conflict with the British and opposed the high protective duties of the TARIFF OF 1816 as harmful to New England commerce.

Upon leaving Congress in 1817, Webster settled in Boston and devoted himself to his law practice. He appeared before the U.S. Supreme Court in numerous landmark cases, including *McCulloch* v. *Maryland* (1819) and *Dartmouth College* v. *Woodward* (1819), gaining a reputation as one of the foremost constitutional lawyers of his time. Elected to the House of Representatives from Massachusetts, he took his seat in 1823 and joined the antiprotectionist opposition to the Tariff of 1824. In 1827 the state legislature chose Webster to fill a vacancy in the U.S. Senate, where he served through successive reelection until 1841. With the rise of industry in New England, he reversed his long-standing antiprotectionist position. He supported and helped win passage of the controversial TARIFF OF ABOMINATIONS (1828) and thereafter advocated PROTECTIONISM as a national policy. A champion of nationalism, Webster engaged states' rights proponent Senator Robert Y. Hayne of South Carolina in a renowned debate in January 1830 over nullification. This was the doctrine advanced by Hayne's South Carolina colleague JOHN C. CALHOUN asserting the right of a state to judge federal laws unconstitutional and thus refuse to enforce them within its sovereign boundaries. Insisting that nullification would result inevitably in violence and civil war, Webster upheld the powers of the federal government and concluded with the famous words "Liberty and Union, now and forever, one and inseparable." Siding with President ANDREW JACKSON, he favored use of force by the federal government against South Carolina when it moved in 1832 and 1833 to nullify the tariff laws. Webster voted against the COMPROMISE TARIFF of 1833 that defused the nullification crisis.

Along with perennial Senate rival HENRY CLAY of Kentucky, he was a leader of the loose anti-Jackson political coalition that developed into the new Whig Party. In 1836 Webster was an unsuccessful contender for the Whig presidential nomination. He campaigned for WILLIAM HENRY HARRISON in the 1840 presidential race and was rewarded with appointment as secretary of state. When, after Harrison's death, states' rights southerner JOHN TYLER became president and promptly vetoed measures sponsored by Clay for rechartering the Bank of the United States, the entire cabinet save Webster resigned in protest. He continued in office in order to complete negotiation with Great Britain over the Maine-New Brunswick boundary dispute. These efforts culminated in the WEBSTER-ASHBURTON TREATY (1842), which resolved the border issue and also established an Anglo-American understanding on trying to stop the African slave trade. Webster also laid the groundwork for the opening of U.S. trade and diplomatic relations with China by preparing CALEB CUSHING's mission to the Far East. Under pressure from fellow Whigs to resign, he left the cabinet in May 1843 and resumed his law practice.

Reelected to the U.S. Senate from Massachusetts in 1845, he opposed TEXAS ANNEXATION. As he had feared, the acquisition of Texas both moved the nation closer to a sectional political showdown over the issue of slavery's extension to newly acquired territories and led to conflict with Mexico. An ardent critic of the MEXICAN WAR (1846–1848), he assailed Democratic President JAMES K. POLK's expansionist designs on America's southern neighbor. In the postwar dispute over whether to permit slavery in the territories gained by the United States through the MEXICAN CESSION, he favored a solution that would prevent sectional confrontation. Webster considered slavery a "great moral and political evil," but felt also that the "peculiar institution" was, within the southern states, a matter with which the federal government should not interfere. He grew alarmed over the deepening sectional crisis that in the late 1840s appeared likely to bring southern secession. Deploring political radicals in both the North and South, Webster voted for the Compromise of 1850, the package of measures sponsored in the Senate by Henry Clay to avert disunion by balancing competing northern and southern interests on the slavery issue. On March 7, 1850, he delivered his famous speech in defense of Clay's legislative compromise. Appealing for national unity, Webster said he spoke "not as a Massachusetts man, not as a northern man, but as an American." Slavery was an evil, he observed, but not as great an evil as disunion. He warned the South there could be no peaceful secession and reproved northern antislavery forces for their uncompromising severity.

When MILLARD FILLMORE succeeded to the presidency in 1850, Webster again became secretary of state. The most noteworthy act of his two-year tenure was the drafting in 1850 of the Hulsemann Letter, a forceful State Department note to the Austrian charge d'affaires in Washington, Chevalier J. G. Hulsemann, upholding the right of the U.S. government to express sympathy for the participants in the liberal Hungarian revolt (1848–1849) against Austria. He bid unsuccessfully for the Whig presidential nomination in 1852. In failing health, Webster died later the same year while still secretary of state.

WEBSTER-ASHBURTON TREATY (1842) Completed in Washington on August 9, 1842, by Secretary of State DANIEL WEBSTER and British special envoy Lord Ashburton (Alexander Baring), it settled the northeast boundary dispute. Both the United States and Great Britain claimed a roughly 12,000-square-mile tract of land between Maine and the Canadian province of New Brunswick. For some 60 years, the two countries had been unable to resolve diplomatically the location of the northeast boundary, defined ambiguously in the TREATY OF PARIS (1783) at the end of the AMERICAN REVOLUTION. Dutch arbitration, arranged through the Anglo-American CONVENTION OF 1827, failed when the United States in 1831 rejected the King of Netherlands's decision. The festering border disagreement brought Maine and New Brunswick to the verge of armed conflict in 1839 before the bloodless AROOSTOOK WAR ended in a truce.

The Maine-New Brunswick boundary, together with the diplomatic fallout from Anglo-American confrontation in the CAROLINE AFFAIR (1837–1842) and the CREOLE AFFAIR (1841–1842), prompted Washington and London to initiate negotiations toward settlement of several outstanding problems in U.S.-British relations. Talks begun in June 1842 between Webster and Ashburton culminated in their August treaty. Its terms fixed the northeast boundary along the present-day line. The United States re-

ceived about 7000 square miles of the disputed territory and secured navigation rights on the St. John River through New Brunswick. Great Britain gained some 5000 square miles and thus retained its prized military route between Quebec and the maritime provinces. The U.S. government arranged to pay Maine and Massachusetts $150,000 each to surrender their claims to the contested border area.

The accord also cleared up several other Anglo-American boundary disputes. The British conceded a stretch of territory at the head of the Connecticut River in New Hampshire; accepted a line between Lake Superior and Lake of the Woods that awarded America lands in Minnesota; and agreed to a boundary line along northern New York and Vermont just above the 45th parallel that allowed the United States to retain Fort Montgomery on Lake Champlain, called "Fort Blunder" because it was built mistakenly on Canadian soil. Responding to the problem throughout the 1830s of anti-British Canadian rebels taking refuge across the border in American territory, the treaty provided for the extradition of fugitive criminals between the United States and Canada. In addition, it obligated the United States to keep a naval presence in African waters to work cooperatively with British forces in suppressing the slave trade along the African coast. Through an exchange of notes, Webster and Ashburton unofficially disposed of the Creole and Caroline affairs.

An authentic copy of the original 1782 map defining the northeast boundary surfaced one year after the exchange of final ratifications in October 1842. This map confirmed the long-standing American claim to the disputed territory, and showed that the United States had surrendered land to which it held valid title. The Webster-Ashburton Treaty, sharply criticized by expansionists in America as a capitulation to British demands, resolved long-simmering problems in Anglo-American diplomacy and helped restore the relationship to friendlier terms at the approach of the mid-19th century.

WEINBERGER, CASPAR WILLARD (1917–) Secretary of defense under President RONALD W. REAGAN. Weinberger graduated from Harvard in 1938 and stayed on to earn a law degree there in 1941. He served as an Army officer in the Pacific theater during WORLD WAR II and then joined a law firm in his native San Francisco. In 1952 he was elected as a Republican to the California State Assembly. After an unsuccessful bid for state attorney general in 1958, he remained active in politics, becoming California Republican Party chairman in 1962. In 1968 Governor Reagan appointed him state director of finance. In 1969 President RICHARD M. NIXON brought Weinberger to Washington as chairman of the Federal Trade Commission. The following year he moved to the Office of Management and Budget (OMB). As deputy director (1970–1972) and director (1972–1973) at OMB he earned the nickname "Cap the Knife" for his ability to cut federal programs and spending. In 1973 he was made secretary of health, education, and welfare. He remained at the department under President GERALD R. FORD before returning to private life in 1975 as a senior executive with Bechtel, the international construction firm based in California.

Named President Reagan's first secretary of defense in 1981, Weinberger oversaw the new administration's massive military buildup in the early 1980s. Congress initially approved large increases in the defense budgets submitted by Weinberger for funding improvements in both strategic and conventional forces. The administration restored the B-1 strategic bomber, canceled during the Carter presidency in 1977, initiated plans for a 600-ship Navy, and pressed for deployment of the MX missile. In 1983 Weinberger lent ardent support to Reagan's newly announced STRATEGIC DEFENSE INITIATIVE (SDI), a proposed space-based defensive shield against nuclear missiles. SDI and the testing of ANTISATELLITE WEAPONS became recurring points of disagreement between the defense secretary, who believed both systems were necesary to counter threats posed by the Soviet Union, and liberal members of Congress who believed they undermined arms control negotiations.

Weinberger was part of the senior Reagan team that sought to end the nation's post–VIETNAM WAR reluctance to use military power as an instrument of foreign policy and reassert America's readiness to defend its interests worldwide. In 1981 U.S. war planes shot down two Libyan jet fighters in the first of the GULF OF SIDRA INCIDENTS. The following year U.S. marines were dispatched to Beirut as part of an international peacekeeping force during the LEBANON CRISIS (1982–1984). In October 1983 U.S. military forces staged the GRENADA INVASION to remove a newly installed leftist government on the Caribbean island with links to Communist Cuba. Weinberger in November 1984 quieted concerns in Congress over the possible commitment of U.S. troops to conflicts in Central America when he delivered a major policy address entitled the "USES OF MILITARY POWER," outlining six stringent requirements that should be met before U.S. forces were deployed into combat.

By the mid-1980s Weinberger's unwillingness to curb increases in the Defense Department's funding requests brought growing criticism from members of Congress confronted by enormous budget deficits. Improving East-West relations also brought pressure for reduced defense spending. Weinberger's later tenure was marked by further U.S. military action. In line with the Reagan administration's anti-terrorist policy, U.S. warplanes in 1986 conducted the LIBYAN BOMBING RAID in retaliation for an alleged terrorist incident. In 1987 the administration embarked on the PERSIAN GULF INTERVENTION, committing U.S. warships to protect neutral shipping imperiled by the Iran-Iraq War (1980–1988). Weinberger resigned in November 1987 to spend more time with his ill wife. He supported the INTERMEDIATE NUCLEAR FORCES TREATY concluded by Reagan and Gorbachev at the WASHINGTON SUMMIT that December. In 1988 he became publisher of *Forbes* magazine. Indicted in June 1992 by the IRAN-CONTRA special prosecutor on charges of having lied to Congress regarding the scandal, he was pardoned by President GEORGE BUSH that December.

WELLES, BENJAMIN SUMNER (1892–1961) Career U.S. diplomat who figured most prominently in Latin American affairs, Welles was born in New York City and graduated from Harvard University in 1914. Entering the State Department the following year, he held minor diplomatic posts in Tokyo and Buenos Aires. In June 1920 he was named assistant chief of the department's Division of Latin American Affairs and in September became chief. In 1922 he was assigned by Secretary of State CHARLES

EVANS HUGHES to draw up plans for the withdrawal of U.S. troops and military government from the Dominican Republic. Welles's mission culminated in the establishment of an independent Dominican government in July 1924 and an end to the American military occupation. The same year he mediated a political settlement of the civil war in Honduras that had prompted U.S. military intervention to protect American lives and property in the Central American country.

Welles left the government in 1925 and spent the next two years writing *Naboth's Vineyard: The Dominican Republic 1844–1924* (1928), which included an appeal for a more cooperative U.S. policy in Latin America. In 1933 President FRANKLIN D. ROOSEVELT named him an assistant secretary of state and he became an architect and leading proponent of the administration's GOOD NEIGHBOR POLICY toward Latin America. Before he could assume his new post, Welles was sent in April 1933 as U.S. ambassador to Cuba. Amid worsening disorder and violence on the island, he was instructed to negotiate a truce between President Gerardo Machado and his political opponents. Machado was ousted in a military coup and replaced by interim President Dr. Carlos Manuel de Cespedes y Quesada, whom the American ambassador deemed friendly to U.S. interests and thus endorsed. When, in September 1933, Cespedes was overthrown by a coalition of Cuban noncommissioned officers and left-wing students, Welles persuaded Roosevelt to withhold recognition from the new government on grounds it was too radical and lacked popular backing. Roosevelt and Secretary of State CORDELL HULL rejected Welles's recommendation that the United States intervene militarily in Cuba under authority of the PLATT AMENDMENT (1901) to restore Cespedes to power.

After Colonel Fulgencio Batista emerged as Cuban strongman and de facto leader, Welles left the island in December 1933 and took up his post as assistant secretary for hemispheric policy. He negotiated the treaty with Cuba in May 1934 that abrogated the Platt Amendment, thereby restoring full sovereignty and independence to the Caribbean nation. He assisted Secretary of State Hull at the BUENOS AIRES CONFERENCE (1936), the special inter-American peace parley convened at Roosevelt's urging. At Buenos Aires, Welles helped win support for a declaration establishing the principle of inter-American consultation in the event of a threat to hemispheric peace. He was appointed under secretary of state in 1937. Following the outbreak of WORLD WAR II in Europe in September 1939, Welles represented the United States at a special meeting of the American republics in Panama, at which the DECLARATION OF PANAMA establishing inter-American neutrality was concluded.

In early 1940 Roosevelt sent him on a much publicized but ultimately fruitless fact-finding mission to the belligerent European nations to explore the possibility of an early end to the war. Welles accompanied Roosevelt at the shipboard ATLANTIC CONFERENCE with British Prime Minister Winston Churchill off the Newfoundland coast in August 1941 and helped draft the ATLANTIC CHARTER. After America entered the war, Welles attended the special Rio Conference (1942), where the American foreign ministers created the INTER-AMERICAN DEFENSE BOARD. Acrimonious disagreements with Hull over both policy and access to the president finally forced Welles's resignation in September 1943. The secretary of state seized on a reported homosexual encounter involving Welles as the immediate reason for demanding the diplomat's exit from the administration. In retirement Welles devoted himself to writing about foreign affairs in such books as *The Time for Decision* (1944) and *Seven Decisions that Shaped History* (1950).

See also CUBAN INTERVENTIONS, DOMINICAN INTERVENTIONS, HONDURAN INTERVENTIONS.

WEST FLORIDA CONTROVERSY Dispute between the United States and Spain from 1783 to 1819 over the disposition of West Florida. Great Britain ceded the Floridas to Spain in 1783. Under the British, West Florida had covered the area that stretched between the Mississippi and Apalachicola Rivers and extended north from the Gulf of Mexico to a line above the 32nd parallel. Spain claimed these same boundaries when it took possession. But the Anglo-American TREATY OF PARIS (1783) ending the AMERICAN REVOLUTION fixed the U.S. southern border at the 31st parallel. The boundary disagreement strained Spanish-American relations for more than a decade.

Confronted with an increasingly powerful United States and facing war in Europe, Spain agreed in PINCKNEY'S TREATY in 1795 to accept the 31st parallel as West Florida's northern limit.

At the outset of the 19th century, the United States desired control of the strategically valuable and rich West Florida coast with its network of rivers emptying into the Gulf of Mexico. After 1803, the U.S. government claimed West Florida between the Mississippi and Perdido Rivers as part of the LOUISIANA PURCHASE. Spain refuted the American interpretation of the Louisiana boundary and dismissed the U.S. claim as an illegitimate bid for rightful Spanish territory. By the Mobile Act of 1804, Congress authorized President THOMAS JEFFERSON to take control of the disputed zone, but he refrained before strong Spanish protests. Subsequent negotiations between Washington and Madrid brought no settlement of the controversy through the end of the Jefferson presidency.

In 1810, American settlers in the Baton Rouge district rebelled against Spain, declared West Florida independent, and requested U.S. annexation. Asserting American ownership of West Florida to the Perdido, President JAMES MADISON declared U.S. control over the territory on October 27, 1810, and American troops took possession in December as far as the Pearl River. Faced with European criticism of the American occupation, the Madison administration defended its action as a move to preempt British seizure of the region. At Madison's urging, Congress passed important two-fold legislation in January 1811. A secret resolution, by declaring American determination to block Spanish cession of the Floridas to another foreign power, established the NO-TRANSFER PRINCIPLE that colonies in the Western Hemisphere could not be exchanged from one European country to another. A separate act authorized Madison to take West Florida east of the Perdido and all of East Florida if necessary to prevent foreign annexation. The United States seized the area between the Pearl and Perdido rivers in 1813 and occupied the rest of West Florida during the FLORIDA INVASION (1818). Spain finally ceded the Floridas to the United States in 1819 in the ADAMS-ONIS TREATY.

See also MAP 4.

WESTERN HEMISPHERE ACT (1976) Federal law signed by President GERALD R. FORD on October 20, 1976, that aligned U.S. immigration practices for the Western Hemisphere with those in effect for the Eastern Hemisphere. The IMMIGRATION ACT OF 1965 had set an annual ceiling of 170,000 on Eastern Hemisphere immigration. It made 20,000 the maximum quota for any one country in a given year and introduced a visa preference system that favored, in order, family reunification and special job skills. While the 1965 act for the first time imposed an overall quota of 120,000 on Western Hemisphere immigration, it did not apply the per-country limit or preference system to the region. Lack of priority treatment for family members subjected many relatives of U.S. residents to prolonged waiting periods for visas. The 1976 law extended both individual country quotas and the preference system to the Western Hemisphere, thereby standardizing U.S. immigration procedures. The legislation's per-country quota limits had the effect of halving authorized Mexican immigration to the United States. The act did not address illegal immigration, but a steep increase in undocumented aliens from Latin America dating from the early 1970s became a major impetus for the IMMIGRATION REFORM AND CONTROL ACT OF 1986.

WESTMORELAND, WILLIAM CHILDS (1914–) Army officer and commander of U.S. forces in the VIETNAM WAR. Westmoreland graduated from West Point in 1936. During WORLD WAR II, the South Carolina native commanded an artillery battalion in combat in North Africa and Europe. He was an instructor at the Army War College, again held field command in the KOREAN WAR, and was promoted to general in 1952. After tours of duty with the Army staff in Washington and as a division commander, he served from 1960 to 1963 as superintendent at West Point. The following year he was named to head the U.S. Military Assistance Command in South Vietnam.

Westmoreland took command of the approximately 20,000 U.S. military personnel in the Southeast Asian nation in June 1964. At the time American forces were serving in advisory and support roles meant to assist South Vietnam defend itself from Communist North Vietnamese aggression. Within two months the U.S. mission had begun to change. Following reports of North Vietnamese attacks on U.S. Navy destroyers in international waters off North Vietnam's coast, the Congress in early August 1964 passed the TONKIN GULF RESOLUTION authorizing a direct U.S. combat role in the Vietnam conflict. Westmoreland oversaw a steady escalation in American military involvement. The first combat units arrived in 1965, with U.S. troop strength eventually reaching a peak of more than 540,000 in 1969.

Throughout his four-year tenure, Westmoreland struggled to find a combination of tactics that would defeat both regular North Vietnamese units infiltrating into the South and the Communist Viet Cong guerrilla insurgency in the countryside. While the South Vietnamese army concentrated on local security, U.S. forces undertook "search and destroy" operations, attempting to pin down and engage an elusive enemy. When battlefield successes did not seem to translate into any long-term gain and American casualties mounted, Westmoreland became an increasingly controversial figure. His reports of progress in the war were contradicted by the TET OFFENSIVE, the surprise Communist assault in January 1968 that caught U.S. forces off guard. Although the offensive eventually was defeated with heavy Communist losses, it convinced many in Washington that the Vietnam conflict was unwinnable.

Westmoreland became a target of growing domestic antiwar sentiment and was widely blamed for U.S. military difficulties in Southeast Asia. In July 1968 he was named Army chief of staff and was replaced in Saigon by General CREIGHTON W. ABRAMS, JR. Westmoreland retired from the Army's top uniformed post in 1972. Although Communist forces did not finally prevail until 1975, he remained closely identified with America's defeat in Indochina. In retirement he criticized the Johnson administration's handling of the war, arguing that its restraints on U.S. military action prevented the defeat of North Vietnam. In January 1982 CBS broadcast a TV documentary, "The Uncounted Enemy: A Vietnam Deception," which suggested that Westmoreland, while in command in Saigon, had presented manipulated and misleadingly low enemy troop strength figures to support falsely optimistic reports on the war. Westmoreland sued CBS for libel. After an 18-week trial, the two sides reached an out-of-court settlement in February 1985 in which no money changed hands. In a statement agreed to by both sides, CBS stood by its broadcast while stating that it never meant to impugn Westmoreland's patriotism or loyalty.

WHALING MORATORIUM (1985)   Proposed international suspension of commercial whaling undertaken to stop the decimation of the mammal. The United States was among the 15 nations that signed the International Convention for the Regulation of Whaling in December 1946. Terms of the agreement, which remains the basis for international cooperation in this area, provided for total protection of certain whale species; made specific ocean areas whale sanctuaries; prescribed open and closed seasons for whaling; set the maximum number of whales which may be taken in a season; and banned the capture of baby whales and female whales accompanied by their calves. The convention also established the International Whaling Commission (IWC) to provide for proper conservation of whale stocks and to develop regulations for the control of the whaling industry.

Disturbed by evidence of dwindling whale populations, the IWC voted in 1982 to implement a five-year moratorium on commercial whaling, starting in October 1985. Several IWC member countries, notably Iceland, Norway, the Soviet Union, South Korea, and Japan objected to the moratorium for economic reasons and challenged conservationist claims about the impact of commercial whaling on the size of the stocks. These nations initially either ignored the moratorium or exploited loopholes in the IWC rules allowing whales to be captured for scientific research. In 1987 the IWC approved a U.S.-sponsored nonbinding resolution urging governments not to issue licenses for "scientific" whaling. Nations failing to abide by the measure have faced a threat of U.S. economic sanctions and have risked exclusion from fishing in U.S. waters. Under growing international pressure, Norway and the Soviet Union decided to end commercial whaling in 1987 and Japan followed suit the following year. Nonetheless Japan, along with Iceland and South Korea, has declared its intention to continue scientific whaling.

WHEELER, EARLE GILMORE (1908–1975)
U.S. Army officer who served as chairman
of the JOINT CHIEFS OF STAFF (JCS). A native
of Washington, D.C., Wheeler graduated
from West Point in 1932. While holding a
variety of command and staff positions, he
rose to prominence in the Army chiefly on
his skills as an administrator. Promoted to
general in 1952, he was appointed director
of the JCS staff in 1960. A protege of General MAXWELL D. TAYLOR, Wheeler became
Army chief of staff in 1962. His testimony in
support of the LIMITED TEST BAN TREATY the
following year contributed to its eventual
Senate approval. In 1964 he succeeded
Taylor as chairman of the JCS. Wheeler's
tenure as the nation's top military officer
spanned the height of America's involvement in the VIETNAM WAR. He strongly supported the expanding U.S. role in the conflict in the mid-1960s, believing it possible
to defeat Communist aggression on the battlefield and guarantee South Vietnamese independence. In 1969 he began implementation of the Nixon administration's
VIETNAMIZATION strategy, whereby South
Vietnamese forces assumed an increasing
share of the fighting. Wheeler retired in
1970.

WHITE, HARRY DEXTER (1892–1948)
U.S. treasury official who was accused of involvement in Soviet espionage. White grew
up in Boston, where he worked in his family's hardware business. Following service
overseas in the Army during WORLD WAR I,
he earned bachelor's and master's degrees
in economics from Stanford. He completed
his doctorate at Harvard and became a professor of economics at Lawrence College in
Wisconsin. In 1934 he began a distinguished career at the Treasury Department
as a special economic analyst. Within four
years he had become director of the newly
formed Division of Monetary Research.

In 1941 Secretary of the Treasury
HENRY MORGENTHAU, JR. assigned White responsibility for foreign economic policy.
During WORLD WAR II he worked closely
with his British counterpart, the renowned
economist John Maynard Keynes, in planning for the postwar international financial
order. He was a key participant at the BRET-
TON WOODS CONFERENCE (1944), which approved creation of the INTERNATIONAL MONE-
TARY FUND (IMF) and the WORLD BANK. White
also helped draft the MORGENTHAU PLAN

(1944) for Allied policy toward postwar
Germany. The plan, which President HARRY
S. TRUMAN rejected in 1945, called for transforming Germany from an industrial to an
agricultural nation. White was appointed
assistant secretary of the treasury in January
1945. Truman named him the first American executive director of the IMF in May
1946. He resigned from government the
following year and went into financial consulting.

In July 1948 former Communist spy
Elizabeth Bentley testified before the HOUSE
UN-AMERICAN ACTIVITIES COMMITTEE that White
had belonged to the same wartime Soviet
espionage network as she. In early August
another self-confessed former Soviet agent,
WHITTAKER CHAMBERS, accused White of
membership in an underground Communist cell in the 1930s. White vehemently denied the charges in a dramatic appearance
before the committee on August 13. He
died of a heart attack three days later. In
November Chambers produced a memorandum by White as part of a cache of secret government documents allegedly
handed over to him in the 1930s. The revelation drew modest notice, though, as attention gravitated to the controversy surrounding ALGER HISS and other accused
spies. The White case resurfaced briefly in
1953 when U.S. Attorney General Herbert
Brownell, Jr. and former President Truman
took part in a bitter public exchange over
whether White was known to be a security
risk when he was selected for the IMF post
in 1946.

WHITE, THEODORE HAROLD (1915–
1986) Journalist and author. Born in
Boston, White studied Chinese history and
oriental languages at Harvard University,
earning his undergraduate degree in 1938.
Recipient of a fellowship that enabled him
to travel widely, he began a journalism career in China, filing free-lance dispatches to
the *Boston Globe* and *Manchester Guard-
ian*. Recruited to *Time* magazine in 1939 by
JOHN HERSEY, the war correspondent and
novelist, White covered East Asia until
1945, reporting on the course of WORLD
WAR II and becoming chief of *Time*'s China
bureau. His increasing disenchantment
with Chiang Kai-shek's Nationalist Chinese
government placed him at sharp odds politically with *Time* publisher HENRY R. LUCE,
a fervent friend and supporter of Chiang.

This disagreement prompted White's resignation from *Time* in 1946.

Returning to the United States he wrote *Thunder Out of China* (1946), a highly critical examination of Chiang and his ruling Kuomintang Party, in collaboration with colleague Annalee Jacoby. After a brief stint as senior editor at the *New Republic,* he edited *The Stilwell Papers* (1948), the World War II writings of U.S. General JOSEPH W. STILWELL. In 1948 he moved to Paris, where he reported for the Overseas News Agency and penned the best-selling *Fire in the Ashes* (1953), an analysis of Europe's postwar recovery. He returned to the United States in 1953 and began covering the American political scene, first for the *Reporter* and then for *Colliers.* In 1956 he turned to writing novels. With income from his fiction he embarked on an ambitious 20-year project to chronicle in detail American presidential campaigns. *The Making of the President 1960* (1961), the hugely successful first entry in White's landmark series, garnered the 1962 Pulitzer Prize for nonfiction. Subsequent volumes followed the 1964, 1968, and 1972 presidential races. His 1978 memoir *In Search of History* recounted his career as both journalist and historian.

WHO See **WORLD HEALTH ORGANIZATION.**

WILKES EXPEDITION (1838–1842) Congressionally-sponsored scientific expedition that explored extensively in the Pacific. Authorized officially as the U.S. Exploring Expedition in 1836, the maritime journey was conceived as an opportunity to demonstrate to the world, and Europe in particular, America's ability to contribute significantly to science and discovery. U.S. naval officer Charles Wilkes accepted command of the excursion and set sail with a fleet of six ships from Virginia in August 1838. The four-year expedition charted and surveyed more than 200 South Pacific islands, the Antarctic coastal areas known today as Wilkes Land, the Hawaiian island chain, and the west coast of North America. It returned to New York in the summer of 1842 with enormous collections amassed by civilian scientists among the crew in such areas of natural history as mineralogy, geology, and biology. Wilkes's exploration of the coastal region along the Pacific northwest directly contributed to American insistence on a settlement of the OREGON QUESTION with Great Britain that would secure U.S. access to the harbors of the Juan de Fuca Strait.

WILLIAMS, WILLIAM APPLEMAN (1921–1990) Historian best known as a gadfly of American foreign policy. The Iowa native was a 1944 graduate of the U.S. Naval Academy. After serving as a Navy line officer in the Pacific during WORLD WAR II, he completed master's (1948) and doctoral (1950) degrees in history at the University of Wisconsin and went on to teach at half a dozen colleges. Williams was a professor at Wisconsin from 1960 to 1968 and at Oregon State University from 1968 until his retirement in 1986. A so-called revisionist historian, he authored a dozen books, wherein he portrayed the United States as an imperialist power bent on forcing its economic and political will around the world. Williams, generally acknowledged as the founder of the New Left school of American history, especially criticized America's role in the COLD WAR and the VIETNAM WAR. His works include *The Shaping of American Diplomacy 1750–1955* (1956), *The Tragedy of American Diplomacy* (1959), and *America Confronts a Revolutionary World: 1776–1976.*

WILMOT PROVISO (1846) Amendment offered in the U.S. Congress to ban slavery in territory acquired from Mexico as a result of the MEXICAN WAR (1846–1848). Soon after the war began, Democratic President JAMES K. POLK requested $2 million from Congress with which to negotiate peace. It was well known that the expansionist Polk administration sought territorial gains as a basic war aim and planned to use the money to obtain land from Mexico. When a bill to appropriate the $2 million was submitted in the House of Representatives on August 8, 1846, Pennsylvania Democrat David Wilmot introduced an amendment prohibiting slavery in any territory that might be acquired from Mexico. The language of the Wilmot Proviso was derived from the Ordinance of 1787 forbidding slavery in the NORTHWEST TERRITORY. The proviso won the support of abolitionist legislators, Northern Whigs who condemned the war as the centerpiece of a Southern Democratic drive to add slave soil to the Union in order to tip the sectional political balance in Congress, and unhappy Northern Democrats who felt the Polk administration had betrayed them by accepting the compromise Oregon boundary in settlement of the Anglo-American OREGON QUESTION. Southern Democrats opposed Wilmot's amendment as a threat to states' rights and unnecessary agitation of the slavery question.

The Wilmot Proviso was adopted in the House but the Senate adjourned without taking any action. In the next Congress in 1847, a $3 million appropriation bill with the attached proviso was passed by the House and presented to the Senate, where it was defeated by Southern Democratic opposition. The Senate passed its own appropriation measure minus the slavery-restriction amendment. After bitter debate, the House concurred in the Senate bill and the $3 million was appropriated to Polk without Wilmot's conditions. While never approved in Congress, the proviso forced to the fore the profound sectional division over the question of slavery in the territories. The fundamental principle of the Wilmot Proviso continued to frame the national debate on slavery and became a fundamental plank in the platforms of the Free Soil and Republican parties.

WILSON, CHARLES ERWIN (1890–1961) Businessman and secretary of defense in the Eisenhower administration. Wilson was born in Minerva, Ohio. He graduated from the Carnegie Institute of Technology in 1909 and began work at the Westinghouse Electric Company, where he directed the engineering of automobile electrical equipment. In 1919 he joined General Motors, eventually rising to become president of the automotive giant in 1941. During WORLD WAR II he oversaw General Motor's massive production of armaments for the war effort.

In late 1952 President-elect DWIGHT D. EISENHOWER selected Wilson to be his first secretary of defense. During confirmation hearings before the SENATE ARMED SERVICES COMMITTEE, Wilson came under question for his large stockholdings in General Motors. Asked if he could make decisions contrary to the interests of his former company, Wil-

son replied that "For years I thought what was good for the country was good for General Motors and vice versa." His remark later often was misquoted as "What's good for General Motors is good for the country." Wilson agreed to sell his stock and was confirmed in January 1953.

Eisenhower, former five-star general and supreme allied commander of NATO, took the lead in formulating his administration's defense policy. Wilson was expected to concentrate on management of the DEPARTMENT OF DEFENSE. In February 1953 he appointed the ROCKEFELLER COMMITTEE to evaluate the Defense Department as part of the president's pledge to reorganize and improve the defense establishment. The committee's recommendations were incorporated into REORGANIZATION PLAN NO. 6 (1953) which granted the secretary of defense greater responsibility for supervising the nation's armed forces. Wilson also supported Eisenhower's NEW LOOK defense policy, which sought to contain defense spending and limit U.S. involvement in local conflicts such as the KOREAN WAR by emphasizing strategic and tactical NUCLEAR WEAPONS rather than more costly conventional forces. Wilson indicated his desire to resign at the start of Eisenhower's second term. He left office in October 1957, resuming business activities that included membership on the board of directors of General Motors.

WILSON PLAN See **FORT MISSIONS**.

WILSON, THOMAS WOODROW (1856–1924) Twenty-eighth president of the United States. Wilson was born in Virginia, son of a Presbyterian minister. After graduating from Princeton University in 1879, he studied law at the University of Virginia, was admitted to the Georgia bar, and entered practice in Atlanta in 1882. He abandoned law in 1883 to enter Johns Hopkins University graduate school, where he studied government and history in preparation for an academic career. In 1885 he finished his first book, the esteemed *Congressional Government*, which was his doctoral dissertation. After teaching history at Bryn Mawr College from 1885 to 1888 and then at Wesleyan University for two years, he became professor of jurisprudence and political economy at Princeton in 1890. In 1902 he was appointed president of Princeton. He resigned the post in 1910 to accept the Democratic nomination for governor of New Jersey. Aligning himself with progressive forces, he was elected in a landslide and quickly wrested control of the party in New Jersey from the state Democratic political machine. During his two-year term Wilson steered to enactment a far-reaching liberal reform program.

His success in the statehouse thrust him into contention in 1912 for the Democratic presidential nomination. The backing of Democratic leader WILLIAM JENNINGS BRYAN and the party's more progressive elements helped Wilson garner the nomination. Benefiting from the split in the Republican ranks, he won the general election over incumbent Republican President WILLIAM HOWARD TAFT and Progressive Party candidate THEODORE ROOSEVELT. Bryan was rewarded with appointment as secretary of state. Wilson, however, dominated the conduct of his administration's foreign policy. A proponent of free trade, he called Congress into a special session early in his first term to consider dramatic tariff reform legislation. The resulting UNDERWOOD TARIFF (1913) effected a move away from traditional American PROTECTIONISM by reducing U.S. import duties to their lowest levels since before the Civil War. He endorsed the negotiation by his secretary of state of the BRYAN "COOLING OFF" TREATIES (1913–1914), a series of some 30 bilateral agreements designed to prevent the outbreak of war during periods of worsening international tensions. These pacts were swept aside by the cataclysm of WORLD WAR I.

Latin America frequently commanded Wilson's attention during his two terms. His administration in 1914 negotiated the original U.S.-Colombian THOMSON-URRUTIA TREATY, in which the United States apologized for its complicity in the 1903 Panamanian revolution and offered to pay Colombia an indemnity of $25 million. Republican opposition in the Senate, however, blocked ratification of the accord. The president disposed of the PANAMA TOLLS CONTROVERSY (1912–1914) with Great Britain by successfully pressuring Congress to repeal a 1912 law exempting certain American vessels from payment of tolls for use of the PANAMA CANAL. The British government had contended that the exemption constituted a violation of the HAY-

PAUNCEFOTE TREATY of 1901, which called for equal access to the waterway on equal terms for all nations. Notwithstanding his denunciation of DOLLAR DIPLOMACY, Wilson pursued an interventionist policy in Latin America aimed at achieving political stability and protecting U.S. economic and security interests in the Western Hemisphere. In response to violent political upheavals, he ordered American military interventions in Haiti in 1915 and the Dominican Republic in 1916, exacerbating resentment throughout the Caribbean region over U.S. IMPERIALISM.

The turbulent Mexican Revolution (1910–1920) formed the backdrop to U.S.-Mexican relations during Wilson's presidency. In early 1913 Mexican General Victoriano Huerta took power after deposing and arranging the assassination of liberal President Francisco Madero. His moral sensibilities offended by the coup d'etat, Wilson refused to recognize the Huerta government. After the Mexican strongman rejected a U.S. offer to mediate the Mexican civil war and then imposed a military dictatorship in October 1913, Wilson became committed to forcing Huerta's ouster. The Wilson administration worked to isolate Huerta diplomatically and supported his rivals, the Constitutionalists. U.S.-Mexican relations deteriorated further in the wake of the TAMPICO INCIDENT (1914), in which Mexican troops arrested and detained U.S. sailors in the Mexican city. Wilson used the episode as the pretext for dispatching marines in April 1914 to occupy the Mexican port city of Veracruz. The American occupation raised a serious threat of war between the neighboring nations. The crisis produced by the VERACRUZ INCIDENT was defused in the course of the ABC MEDIATION. Unable to consolidate control over Mexico, Huerta resigned in July 1914 and went into exile.

The Constitutionalists occupied Mexico City the following month, with Venustiano Carranza assuming the presidency. His regime was recognized by the United States as Mexico's de facto government in 1915. Rival Mexican revolutionary Francisco "Pancho" Villa, upset by American acceptance of Carranza, retaliated by staging deadly cross-border raids into U.S. territory. Wilson responded by dispatching the PUNITIVE EXPEDITION (1916–1917) under General JOHN J. PERSHING in pursuit of Villa and his raiders. Pershing drove hundreds of miles into northern Mexico but was unable to capture the elusive Villa. The American military intervention alarmed Carranza, who demanded that the U.S. troops pull out under threat of war. Rather than risk a confrontation, Wilson ordered the expedition withdrawn in January 1917. Carranza was elected president under a new Mexican constitution in March 1917, whereupon the Wilson administration immediately extended recognition to his government.

Following the outbreak of World War I in August 1914, Wilson strove to keep America out of the conflict, proclaiming official U.S. neutrality and appealing to Americans to remain impartial in thought as well as action. Infringement of American neutral maritime rights by the European belligerents led Wilson to protest strenuously the British blockade policy and Germany's submarine warfare. The torpedoing of the British passenger liner LUSITANIA by a German submarine in May 1915 resulted in the loss of 1200 lives, including more than 120 Americans. Wilson demanded a German disavowal of the sinking and reparations for the American deaths. His strong protests to the German government prompted the resignation of Secretary Bryan, who feared the president's tough stand on German submarine policy would draw the United States into the war. Wilson replaced Bryan with ROBERT LANSING. The torpedoing of the British liner ARABIC in August 1915 heightened U.S.-German tensions. Wilson's protests led the German government to pledge that its U-boats would no longer attack unarmed passenger ships without warning. A German submarine's sinking of the French passenger steamer SUSSEX in March 1916 violated the so-called Arabic Pledge causing a serious crisis in U.S.-German relations. Wilson condemned the attack and threatened to sever diplomatic ties unless Germany immediately halted its policy of unrestricted submarine warfare. In response to U.S. pressure, the German government in May 1916 promised that its submarines would not torpedo unarmed merchant and passenger ships without sufficient warning. This Sussex Pledge in the short term averted war. Meanwhile Wilson sent his closest adviser, Colonel EDWARD M. HOUSE, to Europe in 1915 and 1916 to explore the possibility of an American-mediated peace. House's missions proved unsuccessful.

Running on the campaign slogan "He kept us out of war," Wilson was reelected in 1916. Frustrated by his inability to mediate an end to the fighting between the Allied and Central powers, Wilson in January 1917 delivered an address before the Senate in which he called on the belligerents to accept "peace without victory" and outlined his proposal for a desirable settlement of the conflict. His appeal was ignored by Germany, which on January 31 announced a resumption of unrestricted submarine warfare. Wilson promptly broke off diplomatic relations. The continuing German U-boat scourge and publication of the ZIMMERMANN TELEGRAM, a secret German message seeking an alliance with Mexico, led him to a decision for war. He went before Congress on April 2, 1917, to ask for a declaration of war against Germany. Wilson's message deplored the German submarine campaign against neutral maritime commerce as a war against mankind. "The world must be made safe for democracy," the president declared in calling for American participation in the Allied fight against the Central Powers. Congress adopted the war resolution on April 6.

Under Wilson's leadership, the nation undertook an unprecedented military and industrial mobilization to mount the American war effort. The president assumed a central role in the formulation of Allied war aims. As early as January 1917, in his "PEACE WITHOUT VICTORY" SPEECH, he had appealed for an association of nations to prevent future wars through COLLECTIVE SECURITY. On January 8, 1918, he set forth FOURTEEN POINTS as the basis for a lasting peace. Wilson's idealistic program voiced the aspirations of liberals worldwide for a just peace based on self-determination, without annexations or indemnities. The 14th point called for establishment of a LEAGUE OF NATIONS to guarantee the political independence and territorial integrity of all members. Germany in October 1918 appealed for peace on the basis of the Fourteen Points. Wilson then won Allied acceptance of his program in the so-called pre-armistice agreement. The ensuing armistice, signed November 11, 1918, provided that the final peace settlement with Germany would be founded on Wilson's principles.

Believing his presence indispensable to attaining the goal of a liberal peace and a viable postwar international system of collective security, Wilson personally headed the U.S. delegation to the PARIS PEACE CONFERENCE (1919). He, British Prime Minister David Lloyd George, French Prime Minister Georges Clemenceau, and Italian Prime Minister Vittorio Orlando together formed the COUNCIL OF FOUR, which dominated the proceedings and made all major decisions on the drafting of the peace treaty. At Paris, Wilsonian idealism clashed with self-interested European power politics. The president was forced to compromise numerous of the Fourteen Points in order to secure approval for his coveted League of Nations. The league covenant was incorporated into the TREATY OF VERSAILLES (1919) with Germany formally ending World War I. By the time Wilson returned from France to the United States in July 1919, Senator HENRY CABOT LODGE, SR. (R-MA) had organized and mobilized Senate Republican opposition to the peace settlement and league. Lodge led the fight to attach reservations to the treaty designed to guarantee American independence of action by imposing constraints on American participation in the league. Wilson adamantly opposed any Senate revision to the Versailles Treaty.

In September 1919 the president embarked on a grueling speaking tour of the American West, the goal of which was to generate public support for ratification of the Versailles accord without amendments or reservations. After a speech at Pueblo, Colorado, on September 25 he physically collapsed. Returning to Washington, he suffered a stroke on October 2 from which he never fully recovered. The convalescent Wilson unyieldingly refused to accept ratification of the Versailles Treaty with the LODGE RESERVATIONS. As a consequence the Senate twice failed to approve the peace settlement and the United States never joined the League of Nations. Wilson was awarded the Nobel Peace Prize in 1919 for his efforts to achieve world peace and establish the league. He retired from office in March 1921 and spent the last years of his life in Washington in virtual seclusion. He formed a law partnership with BAINBRIDGE COLBY, who had served as his last secretary of state, but was unable to work on account of his shattered health.

WILSON-GORMAN TARIFF (1894) Legislation that moderately reduced import duties while leaving U.S. trade PROTECTIONISM in place. President GROVER CLEVELAND, representing the tariff-reform mainstream of the Democratic Party, favored lower U.S. customs fees, particularly on raw materials used by American industry. Since the Civil War the United States had followed a protectionist trade policy, relying on high tariffs to shield domestic markets from foreign competition. As recently as 1890 Congress had enacted the MCKINLEY TARIFF, which maintained steep duties on imported items. Cleveland argued that high fees on imported raw materials, apart from protecting domestic producers, raised the cost of manufactured goods for American consumers. Representative William L. Wilson (D-WV) sponsored a bill in the House of Representatives that provided for numerous duty-free materials. The measure was amended extensively in the Senate, however, by protectionist Senators led by Arthur P. Gorman (D-MD). The resulting act, passed August 28, 1894, limited duty-free treatment of raw materials to copper, lumber, and wool. Although dissatisfied with its final shape, Cleveland allowed the legislation to become law because it generally reduced import fees from roughly 50 percent to 40 percent. Duties were raised to new highs three years later by the DINGLEY TARIFF (1897).

WISE MEN Informal group of senior advisers during the Johnson years. President LYNDON B. JOHNSON turned to the former high-ranking government officials, popularly known as the "Wise Men," for counsel on the VIETNAM WAR. In March 1968, following the TET OFFENSIVE, the Johnson administration undertook a full reevaluation of U.S. policy in Southeast Asia. A special committee under new Secretary of Defense CLARK M. CLIFFORD concluded that there was no prospect of a readily attainable military solution to North Vietnamese Communist aggression against South Vietnam. The panel recommended a halt to the steadily escalating American military involvement in the conflict. Johnson decided to consult with his private advisory group. In late March the outside advisers were assembled in Washington and briefed on the situation in Vietnam. Present were former Secretary of State DEAN ACHESON; former Under Secretary of State GEORGE W. BALL; Arthur Dean, a New York lawyer who had helped negotiate the KOREAN WAR settlement; veteran diplomats Robert D. Murphy and HENRY CABOT LODGE, JR.; former Secretary of the Treasury C. Douglas Dillon; CYRUS R. VANCE, former deputy defense secretary; former national security adviser MCGEORGE BUNDY; and retired generals Omar Bradley, MATTHEW B. RIDGWAY, and MAXWELL D. TAYLOR. After considering the uncertain military prospects and the erosion of public support at home, a majority of the advisers favored U.S. disengagement from the war. Up to this point, the group had strongly supported U.S. actions in Vietnam. Johnson was influenced greatly by the change in position. On March 31, 1968, he went on nationwide television to announce a halt to U.S. bombing above the 20th parallel in North Vietnam and to propose new negotiations to end the war. From this point it was clear that the U.S. goal in Vietnam no longer was to win the war but to find a way to withdraw.

WISNER, FRANK GARDINER (1909–1965) Intellegence officer. Wisner earned his undergraduate (1931) and law degrees (1934) from the University of Virginia. The native Mississippian became a member of a Wall Street law firm and in 1941 joined the U.S. Naval Reserve. During WORLD WAR II he served in the OFFICE OF STRATEGIC SERVICES, the nation's wartime intelligence service. In 1946 he returned to his law practice. The following year he accepted the position of deputy assistant secretary of state for occupied areas, with responsibility for the Soviet-dominated nations of Eastern Europe.

In September 1948 Wisner reentered the intelligence service as the head of the newly-formed OFFICE OF POLICY COORDINATION (OPC) at the CENTERAL INTELLIGENCE AGENCY (CIA). The OPC was created to enable U.S. policymakers to undertake covert operations in the mounting COLD WAR struggle with the Soviet Union. Under Wisner the agency rapidly expanded, founding RADIO FREE EUROPE (1950) and participating in the unsuccessful ALBANIA OPERATION (1950–1952) to unseat the Communist government there. In 1952 OPC was merged into CIA's Plans Directorate and Wisner became chief of the new COVERT ACTION organization. The plans division was behind the successful IRAN COUP (1953) and GUATEMALA COUP (1954), both of which installed pro-Western leaders.

Wisner was deeply depressed by the failure of the West to intervene in the HUNGARIAN REVOLT (1956) on behalf of the anti-Soviet uprising. He returned to his old post after hospitalization, but suffered a nervous breakdown following the failed covert attempt to overthrow President Sukarno in the INDONESIA REBELLION (1958). Wisner was transferred to the CIA station in London in 1959. He resigned in 1961 and four years later committed suicide at his Maryland farm.

WOMEN'S INTERNATIONAL LEAGUE FOR PEACE AND FREEDOM (WILPF) International organization active in peace and social justice issues. The WILPF evolved out of the International Congress of Women convened at The Hague, Netherlands, in 1915 to seek an end to WORLD WAR I. The gathering, presided over by noted American peace activist and social reformer JANE ADDAMS, was attended by more than 1100 women from 12 nations. It formed the International Women's Committee for a Durable Peace. Delegates were sent to the heads of various belligerent and neutral nations in an unsuccessful effort to urge peace negotiations to halt the fighting. At a second congress in Zurich, Switzerland, in 1919, women from 16 nations voted to make the committee a permanent organization and the present title was adopted. Addams served as president of the WILPF until her death in 1935. In the 1920s the league mounted a massive petition drive in favor of the WORLD DISARMAMENT CONFERENCE (1932–1934). The group supported the establishment of the UNITED NATIONS and other international organizations devoted to keeping world peace. Since the 1970s the WILPF has been involved in the NUCLEAR FREEZE movement and HUMAN RIGHTS issues. Headquartered in Geneva, Switzerland, the organization has twenty-two chapters worldwide including one in the United States.

WOOD, LEONARD (1860–1927) Army officer and military governor. Wood attended Harvard Medical School and received his M.D. in 1884. He joined the Army Medical Corps and reported to Arizona, participating in the Indian campaign that forced Apache chief Geronimo's surrender in 1886. Wood was awarded the Congressional Medal of Honor for his service as both a surgeon and cavalry commander. In 1895 he was transferred to Washington, where he became the physician to President WILLIAM MCKINLEY and formed a close friendship with THEODORE ROOSEVELT, then assistant secretary of the navy. Following the outbreak in April 1898 of the SPANISH-AMERICAN WAR, Wood and Roosevelt organized the 1st U.S. Volunteer Cavalry, known as the "Rough Riders," with Wood in command and Roosevelt his deputy. The Rough Riders took part in the invasion of Cuba, winning fame at the Battle of San Juan Hill, and Wood was promoted to general. Following the surrender of Santiago in July 1898, he was made military governor of the city. In October he assumed responsibility for eastern Cuba and in December 1899 was named military governor of the entire island.

Wood brought dramatic changes to the former Spanish colony. He established a public education system, made significant advances in sanitation, undertook the construction of highways and railroads, and laid the foundation for democratic government. With the end of the American occupation in 1902, he transferred the administration of the island to Cuban officials. Years later, after his death, the Cuban government voted his widow a pension in recognition of his accomplishments.

In 1903 Wood was sent to the Philippines as military governor of Moro Province, where the Moro tribespeople on Midanao and neighboring islands were waging resistance to American rule in the so-called MORO WARS (1901–1913). While improving conditions in the province, Wood ruthlessly crushed the main Moro rebellion, drawing criticism for the heavy Filipino death toll. In 1906 he became commander of Army troops in the Philippines. He returned to the United States in 1908. From 1910 to 1914 he served as Army chief of staff. President WOODROW WILSON chose General JOHN J. PERSHING to lead U.S. forces in WORLD WAR I, bypassing the more senior Wood. Named governor general of the Philippines in 1921, Wood died following an operation for a brain tumor in 1927.

WORCESTER v. GEORGIA (1832) Second of the two landmark Cherokee Nation cases in which the U.S. Supreme Court ruled that the federal government had exclusive jurisdiction over INDIAN AFFAIRS. Samuel Worcester, a missionary who worked among the Cherokees, had been sentenced to prison for violating a Georgia statute that required whites living in Indian territory to pay a state license fee. Worcester petitioned the Supreme Court to reverse his conviction on the grounds the Cherokees were an autonomous nation and their areas were not subject to Georgia laws. The Court agreed, voiding the statute and ordering Worcester released. In CHEROKEE NATION V. GEORGIA (1831), the Court had defined the status of the Indian tribes as domestic dependent nations under the protection of the United States. The *Worcester* decision, spelled out in Chief Justice JOHN MARSHALL's majority opinion, established that under this special arrangement the individual states had no authority to pass laws affecting the Indian nations.

WORLD BANK International organization that provides loans to its member nations. Officially titled the International Bank for Reconstruction and Development (IBRD), it was chartered, together with its sister institution, the INTERNATIONAL MONETARY FUND, during WORLD WAR II at the BRETTON WOODS CONFERENCE (1944) to prevent a postwar repetition of the international financial chaos of the 1930s. The World Bank, as it soon became known, was devised to aid in the reconstruction of war-torn nations and to promote international economic development. The agreement forming the IBRD went into effect December 27, 1945, following ratification by the required 28 countries, including the United States. The bank commenced operations at its Washington, D.C. headquarters on June 25, 1946, and became a specialized agency of the UNITED NATIONS on November 15, 1947.

When the new organization's resources proved insufficient to meet the capital needs of postwar Europe, the United States assumed primary responsibility under the massive MARSHALL PLAN for aiding the continent's recovery. By 1949 the World Bank had focused on fostering economic growth by funding major projects in less-developed parts of the world. As required by the bank's charter, loans went only to member governments or to private firms where repayment was guaranteed by a member state. In 1956 the International Finance Corporation (IFC) was established as an affiliate of the World Bank to lend to private enterprises without the requirement for government guarantees, thus spurring private economic development. A second affiliate, the International Development Association (IDA), was formed in 1960 to provide so-called soft loans—zero interest, a small service charge, and a long repayment period (normally 50 years)—to very low income developing countries which otherwise could not obtain investment capital. The majority of the IDA loans have gone to improving physical infrastructure and for rural development. In the 1970s World Bank President ROBERT S. MCNAMARA shifted the institution's emphasis away from such large-scale engineering projects as dams and bridges and toward smaller grassroots initiatives, such as schools and clinics. Since the early 1980s, the IBRD has been at the forefront of efforts to resolve the INTERNATIONAL DEBT CRISIS.

By the early 1990s, the World Bank had some 170 member countries. Each is represented on its Board of Governors, which sets policy. Voting is by a weighted system that reflects a nation's capital contributions to the bank's reserve. With slightly more than 16 percent of the voting power, almost double that of Japan with the next highest amount, the United States has a dominant role in IBRD affairs. Routine operations are delegated to the bank's 22 executive directors, who in turn elect a president, by tradition an American, for a five-year renewable term. Roughly 90 percent of its funds for making loans are obtained from private sources in world capital markets, with the other 10 percent coming from contributions by wealthier nations. As affiliates, the IDA and IFC share the same institutional structure, management, and staff with the IBRD. The organizations together have become known as the World Bank Group. A third affiliate, the Multilateral Investment Guarantee Agency (MIGA), was charted in 1985 to protect borrowers against noncommercial risks such as war and government expropriation.

The Soviet-led Communist bloc historically opposed the World Bank. Communist China became a member in 1980. The collapse of communism in Eastern Europe in the late 1980s opened the way to membership for the region's former Soviet satellites. Following the 1991 disintegration of the USSR, Russia and the other newly independent erstwhile Soviet republics joined the bank in 1992.

See also NORTH-SOUTH DIALOGUE.

WORLD BANK GROUP   See **WORLD BANK**.

WORLD COURT   Principal judicial organ of the UNITED NATIONS. Formally the International Court of Justice (ICJ), it provides a forum for resolving international legal disputes. Delegates to the first of the HAGUE PEACE CONFERENCES (1899) initially broached the idea of an international court. The conference, with the support of the U.S. delegation, established the Permanent Court of Arbitration, a tribunal that nations might call upon to arbitrate their differences. Although used only rarely, the court still exists and assists principally in the nomination of justices for the ICJ. In 1921 the LEAGUE OF NATIONS formed the Permanent Court of International Justice (PCIJ), the first international forum organized as a court of law. The PCIJ, soon referred to commonly as the World Court, met at The Hague, Netherlands. The United States was never a member of the league or the court. Under the UNITED NATIONS CHARTER, the PCIJ was succeeded by the ICJ in 1946.

The new tribunal, also known as the World Court, has continued to reside at the Hague Peace Palace. Composed of 15 judges of different nationalities, elected to staggered 9-year terms, the court considers cases involving disputes between nations. Its jurisdiction encompasses the interpretation of international agreements, breaches of international obligations, and questions of international law. It has no separate enforcement power, relying on the U.N. Security Council to implement its judgments as necessary. Members of the United Nations enjoy automatic access to the court; other countries may apply to become party to its jurisdiction. Under the 1946 CONNALLY AMENDMENT, America accepted the court's rulings as binding in all matters except those pertaining to U.S. domestic jurisdiction. In an action related to U.S. refusal to participate in the case of NICARAGUA V. UNITED STATES (1984), the Reagan administration in 1985 rescinded U.S. acceptance of the court's compulsory jurisdiction.

WORLD DISARMAMENT CONFERENCE (1932–1934) Major international gathering on disarmament. The victorious Allied powers emerged from WORLD WAR I determined to prevent a reoccurrence of the conflict's terrible carnage. The 1919 TREATY OF VERSAILLES ending the war created the LEAGUE OF NATIONS to keep world peace. The new organization's covenant called for general disarmament. In 1921 the league established a civilian-military Temporary Mixed Commission for the Reduction of Armaments. With international pressure for a worldwide disarmament meeting mounting, the advisory Temporary Commission was succeeded in 1925 by the Preparatory Commission for the Disarmament Conference. The preparatory panel was charged with drawing up draft disarmament plans. Though not a member of the league, the United States starting in 1924 sent representatives to its disarmament commissions.

The international peace movement that developed in the 1920s endorsed the Preparatory Commission's work. The WOMEN'S INTERNATIONAL LEAGUE FOR PEACE AND FREEDOM undertook a massive petition drive in support of a disarmament conference. The commission, however, was unable to agree on a draft disarmament treaty to guide negotiations at an international gathering. French delegates argued that multilateral security arrangements should precede disarmament; American and British representatives, on the other hand, sought disarmament first with security discussions to follow. In December 1930 the commission finally decided to leave key issues unresolved and called for the disarmament gathering to be held in 1932.

The Conference for the Reduction and Limitation of Armaments, better known as the World Disarmament Conference, convened at Geneva, Switzerland, on February 2, 1932. Attending the parley, which was also referred to as the Geneva Disarmament Conference, were representatives from 59 nations, making it the largest international gathering up to that time. The U.S. delegation included diplomats Norman H. Davis and Hugh S. Gibson and Dr. Mary E. Wooley, president of Mount Holyoke College. The conference, which opened

against a backdrop of Japanese aggression in Manchuria, became deadlocked over French calls for security agreements prior to disarmament and demands by Germany, which had been disarmed under the Versailles Treaty, for arms equality with other nations. To break the stalemate, President HERBERT C. HOOVER in late June sent the conference a proposal to reduce all armaments by one-third. The initiative failed to gather support and in July the talks were recessed until the following February.

During the interim a Bureau of the General Disarmament Conference was formed to continue discussions. Germany asserted it would not attend the 1933 sessions if it were treated like a defeated power, while France adamantly opposed German rearmament without additional security guarantees. After extensive negotiations, the United States, Great Britain, France, Germany, and Italy issued a Five-Power Declaration on December 11, 1932, that reaffirmed their commitment to every country's "equality of rights in a system which would provide security for all nations" and the conference reconvened as scheduled in February 1933. A general disarmament agreement, however, proved increasingly elusive. Adolf Hitler had come to power in Berlin in January 1933 and Germany's position asserting its right to rearm hardened throughout the 1933 sessions, which ended in June. On October 14, 1933, Germany withdrew from both the disarmament conference and the League of Nations. The conference met again in May and June 1934 before ending in failure. The inability of France and Germany to put aside their differences strengthened America's historic aversion to involvement in European affairs.

WORLD ECONOMIC CONFERENCE (1933) International meeting in London to address the worsening worldwide economic depression. Planning for the conference began in 1932, when President HERBERT C. HOOVER and European leaders concurred on the need for top-level discussions on a range of economic questions. Of pressing concern was the pending expiration in December 1932 of the HOOVER MORATORIUM on the payment of both European WORLD WAR I debts to the United States and German war reparations. Following Hoover's defeat in the 1932 presidential election, the scheduled gathering was postponed until after the inauguration of President-elect FRANKLIN D. ROOSEVELT in March 1933. Roosevelt entered office focused on implementing his New Deal program for domestic economic recovery. In his inaugural address he stated that international trade relations, while vital, were "secondary to the establishment of a sound national economy."

Roosevelt named Secretary of State CORDELL HULL to head the U.S. delegation to the world economic parley slated to begin in London on June 12. Hull's instructions limited him to the negotiation of bilateral tariff reductions. Roosevelt, having taken the United States off the gold standard, nixed any American involvement in international currency stabilization and steadfastly opposed any readjustment of Allied war debts owed the United States. During the gathering, known also as the London Economic Conference, France and the other "gold bloc" nations of continental Europe pressed for establishment of a world gold standard, while Great Britain urged stabilization among the dollar, franc, and sterling-based pound. Roosevelt, placing domestic considerations first, was adamant on retaining the ability to devalue the dollar as necessary to stimulate the American economy. In a message relayed to the conference on July 3, he stated his clear opposition to currency stabilization, forestalling further European monetary initiatives and effectively ending the gathering. The conference formally adjourned on July 27 having achieved no progress on international economic cooperation.

WORLD HEALTH ORGANIZATION (WHO) Global health agency. The World Health Organization was established on July 22, 1946, at an international health conference convened in New York by the UNITED NATIONS Economic and Social Council. WHO officially came into being on April 7, 1948, when its constitution entered into force. The United States became a member on June 21, 1948, by joint resolution of Congress. The declared objective of WHO, which is a U.N. specialized agency, is to help all peoples of the world to attain the highest possible level of physical and mental health. WHO assists governments to expand health services; prevent and eradicate

diseases; promote maternal and child health, family planning, mental health, environmental health, and health education; and improve standards of nutrition, sanitation, and housing. The organization serves as a global clearinghouse for health information and statistics. It has authority to establish international quality-control standards for food, drugs, and vaccines. WHO, often in conjunction with the United Nations Children's Fund, has sponsored ambitious programs aimed at immunizing children worldwide against disease. In recent years, one of the most publicized aspects of WHO activity has been its coordination of international efforts to cope with the worldwide AIDS epidemic. In 1987 the organization launched a global public information campaign to halt transmission of the Human Immunodeficiency Virus (HIV) that causes AIDS.

WORLD INTELLECTUAL PROPERTY ORGANIZATION (WIPO) Organization responsible for promoting the protection of intellectual property throughout the world. Intellectual property, referring to the product of intellectual activity in industry, science, and the creative arts, comprises two main branches: industrial property (technological patents, scientific discoveries, industrial designs, trademarks, commercial names), and copyright and neighboring rights (literary, musical, and artistic works; artistic performances; films, records, and broadcasts). The convention establishing WIPO was signed by 51 countries, including the United States, in Stockholm, Sweden, in 1967 and entered into force in April 1970. The organization effectively succeeded the United International Bureau for the Protection of Intellectual Property, or BIRPI (the French acronym), which had been set up in 1893 to administer the two main international intellectual property treaties: the Paris Convention for the Protection of Industrial Property of 1883 (last revised in 1967), and the Bern Convention for the Protection of Literary and Artistic Works of 1886 (last revised in 1971). BIRPI oversaw the Paris Union and the Bern Union, the respective executive secretariats created by the two basic intellectual property covenants. In December 1974 WIPO became a specialized agency of the UNITED NATIONS.

The organization's overall objective is to build international cooperation by promoting respect for intellectual property rights worldwide. WIPO works closely with the Paris and Bern unions to provide registration services for all forms of intellectual property, monitor compliance with existing treaties, encourage the dissemination of artistic works across national boundaries, and facilitate TECHNOLOGY TRANSFER from the industrialized world to developing countries. Membership is open to any nation that belongs to either the Paris or Bern Union, or that participates in the organizations of the U.N. system.

WORLD METEOROLOGICAL ORGANIZATION (WMO) Flagship international organization on meteorology. The WMO's predecessor, the pioneering International Meteorological Organization (IMO), was established in 1878. Delegates to an IMO conference in Washington, D.C., in 1947, drafted the World Meteorological Convention creating the WMO. The agreement entered into force March 23, 1950, and the WMO was formally established in April 1951 at the first session of its main political organ, the World Meteorological Congress, in Paris. The United States was an original signer of the WMO convention and a charter member of the organization. The WMO became a UNITED NATIONS specialized agency under an agreement concluded in December 1951.

With headquarters in Geneva, Switzerland, the organization serves several major purposes. It facilitates worldwide cooperation in the establishment of networks of stations for making meteorological observations; promotes rapid exchange among members of weather information; and supports the standardization of meteorological observations to ensure uniform publication of statistics. The organization also seeks to improve and expand applications of meteorology to aviation, fishing, and agriculture. Activities of the WMO include the World Weather Watch Program, the World Climate Program, and a Global Observing System (including land stations, aircraft, ships, and satellites). More recently the organization has become involved in global environmental issues. Since the Chernobyl nuclear power plant accident in the Soviet Union in 1986, it has collaborated with the INTERNA-

TIONAL ATOMIC ENERGY AGENCY on research relating to the dissemination of hazardous materials in the atmosphere. In 1988 the organization jointly established the Intergovernmental Panel on Climate Change (IPCC) with the UNITED NATIONS ENVIRONMENT PROGRAM. The IPCC was created to review and assess available scientific information on climate warming, to gauge the environmental and socio-economic impact of such change, and to formulate possible international responses.

WORLD REFUGEE YEAR LAW See **FAIR SHARE REFUGEE ACT**.

WORLD WAR I (1914–1918) Global conflict waged between the Allied and Central powers. Among its many and complex causes were the rise of nationalism in Europe, the hardening of the European alliance system, BALANCE OF POWER politics, colonial rivalries of the great powers, growing Anglo-German naval and economic rivalry, the instability of the Balkans, and the gradual collapse of the Turkish Ottoman Empire. The assassination of Austrian Archduke Franz Ferdinand by a Serbian nationalist in July 1914 triggered a chain of events that brought about the outbreak of war in Europe in early August. The fighting quickly expanded to many different fronts and eventually involved virtually all of the world's major powers. The struggle was waged between two rival alliances: the Central Powers of Germany, Austria-Hungary, Bulgaria, and Turkey; and the Allied Powers of Great Britain, France, Italy, Russia, and Japan (later joined by the United States).

From the outset opinion in the United States was overwhelmingly opposed to U.S. involvement in the hostilities. Most Americans were isolationist, not believing their interests vitally at stake in the European conflict. President WOODROW WILSON immediately adopted a policy of strict U.S. neutrality. He promptly issued formal NEUTRALITY PROCLAMATIONS and also offered to mediate the conflict, but was turned down by the belligerents. On August 19 he issued an appeal to Americans to be impartial. Such impartiality in reality proved difficult. Americans in the main sympathized with Great Britain, France, and other Allied Powers because of bonds of ancestry, culture, language, and historical friendship. German- and Irish-Americans, on the other hand, tended to be pro-German, or at least anti-British. U.S. relations with Berlin had been strained since the 1880s by rivalry in SAMOA and by suspected German territorial ambitions in the Caribbean. By the time World War I began there was widespread mistrust in America of German militarism and IMPERIALISM. Germany's brutal invasion of Belgium at the conflict's outset, in violation of a treaty obligation to respect the latter's neutrality, confirmed American suspicions and increased popular antipathy in the United States toward the Central Powers. Both Wilson and Secretary of State WILLIAM JENNINGS BRYAN resolved at the war's start to be exactingly evenhanded, cognizant that any action the United States might take would likely benefit one side or the other. Except for Bryan, Wilson's cabinet had definite pro-Allied leanings. The president believed that the United States must aspire to the role of peacemaker. U.S. partiality in the conflict, he realized, would foreclose any chance for American mediation. While determined to chart a neutral course, Wilson would find his sympathies becoming more pro-Allied as the fighting continued.

Anticipating an infringement of the U.S. export trade, Bryan in the war's first months proposed that the belligerents endorse the rules of naval wartime contained in the Declaration of London, which had been drafted in 1909 and signed by the leading powers but never ratified. The measure, embodying an expansive interpretation of neutral maritime rights, generally favored neutrals and so-called small navy powers. The Central Powers agreed to abide by the declaration provided the Allies also would. Determined to exploit their unrivaled sea power to deprive Germany of vital goods and raw materials borne on American ships, the British resisted all such overtures which might offset their naval superiority. London attached so many conditions to its acceptance of Bryan's request as to in effect reject it. In its drive to strangle all trade with the Central Powers, the British government unilaterally modified prevailing maritime law, virtually eliminating the distinction between contraband and free goods and expanding a belligerent's right to stop and search neutral ships.

London in March 1915 ordered a blockade of all German ports, subjecting to seizure and confiscation all merchant vessels venturing in or out of Germany. By mid-1915, British maritime policy had cut off almost all American trade with the Central Powers and the European neutral states. Washington protested repeatedly the British interference with American seaborne commerce, but Great Britain defended its actions as legally and morally justified. Ultimately the Wilson administration was unwilling to threaten use of force against London and thus ended up acquiescing in the British interpretation of maritime neutral rights.

At the same time the Allies stifled American trade with the Central Powers, they fortified their own economic ties with the United States. The depressed American economy received a boost from Allied purchases of supplies and munitions. Under international law, the munitions trade was legal for neutrals. When, early in the war, France sought a loan from an American bank to pay for American goods, the Wilson administration stymied the transaction by announcing that private loans to belligerents were inconsistent with the nation's strict neutrality. This policy, disadvantageous to the Allies, was substantially modified by the State Department in mid-October 1914. By month's end American bankers began extending commercial credits to Allied governments. With dwindling gold balances, the British and French needed more credits and outright loans to sustain their purchases. In September 1915 Wilson agreed to allow the Allies to float large loans in the United States, accepting the State Department's argument that without such financing the Allies would be unable to continue buying American goods, to the detriment of U.S. business.

In early 1915 Germany retaliated against the tightening British blockade with a submarine campaign aimed at crippling Allied and neutral maritime trade in and out of Great Britain. The Germans complained that American neutrality in practice worked to the disadvantage of the Central Powers and thus was unfair. Only the Allies benefited from U.S. neutral trade, Berlin observed, because the British controlled the seas. Germany contended, moreover, that U.S. impartiality was undermined by the fact that the Allied war effort depended so heavily on private American loans. On February 4, 1915, the German government proclaimed the waters around the British Isles a war zone and announced that starting February 18 its submarines, or U-boats, would destroy enemy merchant ships within the designated area without regard for the safety of passengers and crew. Ships of neutral nations, Germany warned, entered the war zone at their own peril. Wilson on February 10 issued a strong protest, warning Germany that the United States would regard the destruction of American ships or lives on the high seas by U-boats as an indefensible breach of neutral rights and would hold Berlin "strictly accountable." Launched as scheduled, the German U-boat campaign exacted a heavy toll on Allied vessels.

On May 7, 1915, a German submarine sank without warning the British passenger liner LUSITANIA in the North Atlantic, causing the deaths of almost 1200 passengers and crew, including 128 Americans. The catastrophe precipitated widespread public outrage and revulsion in the United States, where it was condemned as an unprecedented violation of neutral rights. Wilson issued forceful notes of protest demanding that Germany quit its unrestricted submarine warfare, disavow the *Lusitania* sinking, and pay indemnities for the American deaths. Bryan, worried that Wilson's tough stand on German submarine policy would draw America into the war, resigned in protest in June 1915 and was replaced by State Department Counselor ROBERT LANSING. Unwilling to publicly concede to Washington on the *Lusitania* episode, yet loath to risk a major diplomatic split that could bring the United States into the war, the German government secretly ordered a halt to U-boat attacks on large passenger ships. The instructions did not prevent the torpedoing in August 1915 of the British liner ARABIC, in which two Americans were killed. The incident elicited further American denunciations of German policy and led the German government to pledge that its U-boats would cease surprise attacks on unarmed Allied passenger vessels.

Germany subsequently declared that after March 1, 1916, its U-boats would sink armed Allied merchant ships without warning. This announcement raised fears among some congressional Democrats that Wilson's insistence on upholding the right of Americans to take passage on Allied ships without restriction would invariably result in further loss of American lives and thus draw the United States into the war. They introduced the GORE-McLEMORE RESOLUTIONS (1916) aimed at limiting Americans from traveling on armed merchant vessels. Wilson refused to countenance any U.S. retreat on the issue of neutral rights and bristled at the challenge to his control of foreign policy from within party ranks. He successfully pressured congressional leaders to shelve the resolutions in early March 1916. The torpedoing in late March 1916 of the French passenger ship SUSSEX, in which several Americans were injured, touched off a serious crisis in U.S.-German diplomacy. Washington regarded the attack as a deliberate violation of the so-called Arabic Pledge. On April 18 Wilson threatened to break relations unless Germany immediately abandoned its policy of unrestricted submarine warfare. Eventually yielding to U.S. pressure, the German government on May 7 promised that its submarines would not sink merchant ships without warning and without providing for the safety of passengers and crews. This Sussex Pledge in the short run averted an armed confrontation.

Developments in the first year of the war had persuaded Wilson that the only sure way to keep the United States out of the conflict was to bring it to an end through diplomacy. Toward this goal he dispatched his close diplomatic adviser Colonel EDWARD M. HOUSE to London, Paris, and Berlin in early 1915 to offer American mediation. Nothing came of House's months-long negotiations with the major belligerents. Wilson sent his trusted aide on a second European peace mission in January 1916 to confer with British, French, and German leaders. House's talks with British Foreign Secretary Sir Edward Grey yielded the HOUSE-GREY MEMORANDUM, an Anglo-American proposal for gaining a negotiated peace. The House-Grey scheme went nowhere, however, since the Allied and Central powers both remained confident in 1916 that they could break the military stalemate and go on to victory. The memorandum did reveal the Wilson administration's increasing partiality toward the

Allies. The war figured prominently in the 1916 presidential campaign. Voters, both parties realized, overwhelmingly wanted peace. Running on the slogan "He kept us out of war," Wilson was reelected, narrowly defeating Republican CHARLES EVANS HUGHES.

Following his election victory, he attempted unsuccessfully to convene a peace conference among the belligerents. With his diplomatic efforts at an impasse, Wilson delivered an address before the Senate in January 1917 in which he explained to Americans and the world his concept of a peace settlement. His "PEACE WITHOUT VICTORY" SPEECH, suffused with Wilsonian idealism, envisioned a durable peace based on worldwide arms reductions, national self-determination, FREEDOM OF THE SEAS, and a postwar organization of nations to deter aggression. The president's peacemaking hopes were dealt a critical blow when the German government notified Washington of its decision to resume unrestricted submarine warfare on February 1 against all ships, whether neutral or belligerent, in a broad war zone around Great Britain and the other Allied countries. Unable to break the stalemate in the land war, Germany's military leaders had concluded that their only chance was to seek a swift victory by waging an all-out submarine campaign against Allied maritime commerce. While surmising that unrestricted U-boat attacks would probably drive the United States into the war on the Allied side, the German high command calculated that the submarine offensive would cripple Britain and force it to sue for peace before U.S. military power could become effective. Wilson deplored the submarine warfare decision as a violation of the Sussex Pledge and on February 3 announced the severing of diplomatic relations with Germany.

When the menace of the German unrestricted warfare campaign succeeded in driving fearful American shippers from the seas in increasing numbers, the Wilson administration came under mounting pressure to furnish government protection. The president initially resisted pleas that he seek congressional authority to arm American merchant vessels. He changed his thinking after learning of the ZIMMERMANN TELEGRAM, a secret diplomatic message from Berlin to Mexico City. Intercepted by

British intelligence and turned over to the State Department on February 24, the Zimmermann cable revealed a German scheme to strike an alliance with Mexico in the event that unrestricted submarine warfare resulted in war between Germany and the United States. Appearing before Congress on February 26, Wilson asked for authority to place defensive arms on American merchant ships destined for the German-designated war zone. A group of senators, led by Robert M. La Follette (R-WI) viewed Wilson's proposed armed neutrality as a dangerous step toward war and prevented passage of the measure by a filibuster that lasted until the end of the congressional session on March 4. Wilson ordered the arming anyway on March 9 under authority of an old antipiracy law and within days authorized American merchant vessels to take action against the submarines.

From the end of February through the first three weeks in March, Germany waged a relentless underseas attack against all ships passing through the war zone. In mid-March submarines torpedoed three American merchant ships with heavy loss of life. The deadly submarine campaign convinced Wilson that armed neutrality was not sufficient to protect American lives and commerce. Germany's flagrant offenses, he concluded, left no alternative but war. The destruction of American property and lives galvanized public opinion across the country into a mounting demand for war. On April 2 the president went before a special joint session of Congress to ask for a declaration of war. He condemned the German submarine policy as "warfare against mankind" and exclaimed that the United States was joining the fight to secure a just peace, declaring "The world must be made safe for democracy." On April 6 Congress passed a formal war declaration. The United States declared war against Austria-Hungary in December 1917.

The strong pull of America's isolationist tradition kept the United States from formally joining the Allies. Instead it became a so-called associated power in what henceforth was officially termed the "Allied and Associated Powers." This distinction, made at U.S. insistence, was merely technical, since the United States participated as a full member of the Allied coalition. That fact notwithstanding, the Wilson administration wanted to advertise that America had entered the war for its own principled reasons and not for either territorial conquest or to engage in power politics.

U.S. entry into the war provided the Allies with a vital infusion of manpower, munitions, and new loans as well as a boost to morale, which had plummeted in the face of the conflict's terrible carnage and seeming interminability. Wilson named General JOHN J. PERSHING to organize and command U.S. overseas forces, which were designated the AMERICAN EXPEDITIONARY FORCE (AEF). The destruction of Allied shipping by German U-boats reached its peak as the United States joined the war. The U.S. Navy contributed destroyers to the Allied antisubmarine campaign, convoyed merchant ships and troop transports across the Atlantic, helped tighten the blockade on Germany, and aided the British fleet in closing off the North Sea to German U-boats. During the war, U.S. armed forces swelled to some 5 million personnel with roughly 2 million serving overseas. U.S. land and naval forces figured decisively in the eventual Allied victory.

In war-weary Europe, political pressure mounted throughout 1917 for a negotiated peace. The November 1917 Russian Revolution had far-reaching consequences for the Allied cause and the war's future course. The Bolsheviks, having seized power in Russia, appealed to all belligerents for a peace based on no territorial conquests or indemnities. The revolutionary leadership then published the SECRET TREATIES (1915–1917), a series of pacts made between czarist Russia and the other Allies (excluding the United States) that arranged for the apportioning of territorial spoils in the event of an Allied victory. The Bolsheviks denounced the treaties as evidence of Allied imperialistic designs and in early December entered into negotiations with the Central Powers for an armistice. The Allied governments, after refusing an invitation to join these negotiations and spurning a Soviet request to declare their war objectives, were unable to settle on a joint statement of aims. Meanwhile, revelation of the secret treaties had disillusioned liberal opinion in Allied countries. Convinced of the pressing need for a formulation of war aims that would rebut the Bolshevik allegations of imperialism, captivate world opinion, and

perhaps draw Russia back into the Allied fold, Wilson decided to act on his own. In Janury 1918 he set forth the idealistic FOURTEEN POINTS as the proposed basis for a just and enduring peace. Wilson's liberal program embraced open diplomacy, a right of national self-determination, and freedom of the seas and prescribed territorial adjustments in Europe and the Near East. His 14th point urged creation of a LEAGUE OF NATIONS to preserve the postwar peace through COLLECTIVE SECURITY.

In March 1918 Russia and Germany concluded a separate peace, the Treaty of Brest-Litovsk. Russia's withdrawal from the war allowed the Germans to redeploy a half-million troops to the Western front, where they achieved numerical superiority in preparation for their series of great offensives that spring and summer. Bolstered by U.S. forces, the Allied armies weathered the German onslaught and launched a major summer counteroffensive, forcing Germany into retreat. Meanwhile in August 1918 Wilson committed American troops to the SIBERIAN INTERVENTION (1918–1920), a joint Allied military expedition mounted in Russia to prevent Allied war materials from ending up in German possession. With defeat rapidly closing in, the Germans in October 1918 appealed to Wilson for an end to hostilities on the basis of his Fourteen Points. The American president informed Berlin that he would not deal with the existing German government because it did not, he suggested, represent the German people. Wilson then sent Colonel House as his representative to inter-Allied meetings in Paris at which a reply to Germany's peace appeal was drafted. House won Allied consent in the so-called pre-armistice agreement to Wilson's liberal program as the blueprint for a final peace, subject to reservations on freedom of the seas and the issue of German war reparations. Germany's Kaiser Wilhelm II abdicated on November 9, whereupon the Germans proclaimed a republican government. On November 11, in France's forest of Compiegne, Germany and the Allies signed the armistice ending the fighting and setting the groundwork for a peace conference.

Wilson led the U.S. delegation to the extraordinary PARIS PEACE CONFERENCE in 1919, where the victorious Allied and Associated Powers concluded the TREATY OF VER-

SAILLES (1919) with Germany marking the formal end of World War I. Wilson's coveted League of Nations was incorporated as an integral part of the final peace settlement. The U.S. Senate failed to ratify the Versailles Treaty and thus America never joined the league. Following the Paris parley, the Allies signed separate peace treaties with the other Central Powers. The United States and Germany concluded the TREATY OF BERLIN in August 1921, ending the state of war between them. The same month the United States also signed separate peace settlements with Austria and Hungary.

WORLD WAR II (1939–1945) Global conflict precipitated by Axis powers Germany, Italy, and Japan that ended in their defeat by Allied nations the United States, Great Britain, France, Soviet Union, and China. The origins of the war lay in the aftermath of WORLD WAR I. The harsh terms imposed by the TREATY OF VERSAILLES on a defeated Germany engendered bitterness and resentment and ultimately would aid the rise to power of Nazi leader Adolf Hitler. The Versailles Treaty created the LEAGUE OF NATIONS to provide for COLLECTIVE SECURITY and keep the peace. The United States never ratified the treaty and did not join the league. The international organization proved ineffectual. A member of the victorious Allies that had drafted the Versailles settlement at the PARIS PEACE CONFERENCE (1919), Japan harbored grievances, believing its interests had not received ample consideration from the United States and European powers.

In 1931 Japan exhibited an increasing militarism as it moved to expand its influence in the Far East. Japanese forces seized Manchuria from China and transformed it into the puppet state of Manchukuo under Tokyo's control. The United States reaffirmed its commitment to the OPEN DOOR policy guaranteeing China's sovereignty and territorial integrity. The Hoover administration formulated the STIMSON DOCTRINE (1932), declaring U.S. refusal to recognize any change in China's status resulting from force. The League of Nations also attempted to respond to Japan's aggression, undertaking an investigation of the MANCHURIAN CRISIS (1931–1933). A league vote in 1933 calling for the return of Manchuria to Chinese sovereignty prompted Japan to withdraw from the international body. League members were unable to agree on further action, underscoring the organization's inability to maintain international peace and stability. Within four years, Germany and Italy had also quit the league and by the eve of World War II it effectively had ceased to function.

Hitler became dictator of Germany in 1933 and began to rearm the country in violation of the Versailles Treaty. In 1935 Italian Fascist leader Benito Mussolini launched an invasion of Ethiopia. Italy completed its conquest of the African country in 1936. The same year Hitler, emboldened by British and French failures to challenge German rearmament, remilitarized the Rhineland in direct contravention of the Versailles terms. President FRANKLIN D. ROOSEVELT viewed with alarm the growing belligerency of Germany and Italy. Americans, however, strongly opposed U.S. involvement in the developments in Europe. Reflecting the strength of traditional American ISOLATIONISM in the 1930s, Congress in 1935 passed the first of the NEUTRALITY ACTS, a series of measures designed to keep the United States out of a possible foreign war. Roosevelt proclaimed U.S. neutrality in the Italo-Ethiopian War (1935–1936), but withheld U.S. recognition of Mussolini's colonial regime in Ethiopia. The president again declared American neutrality in the Spanish Civil War (1936–1939).

In July 1937 Japan resumed its expansionist aggression in Asia, unleashing a full-scale invasion of China. Washington denounced the Japanese action as a violation of the NINE-POWER TREATY (1922) on the Far East. In his October 1937 QUARANTINE SPEECH, Roosevelt issued a call for the international isolation of lawbreaking nations. At the BRUSSELS CONFERENCE (1937) on the Sino-Japanese conflict, however, the United States and fellow Western powers limited themselves to a verbal condemnation of Tokyo and the Japanese assault on China continued unabated. In December 1937 Japanese warplanes sank a U.S. gunboat in Chinese waters. The Roosevelt administration, unwilling and unprepared to commit America to possible hostilities in Asia, was compelled to accept Japan's explanation and offer of restitution for the PANAY INCIDENT. Tensions also were mounting in Europe. In March 1938 Germany annexed

Austria. At the Munich Conference in September 1938, Great Britain and France followed a policy of appeasement toward Nazi Germany. They acquiesced in Berlin's absorption of the Sudetenland, the German-populated western part of Czechoslovakia, in the belief Hitler's territorial ambitions would thus be satisfied. The United States, concerned about the growing threat of war and possible Nazi infiltration of the Western Hemisphere, spearheaded adoption in December 1938 of the DECLARATION OF LIMA providing for consultation among the American states on their mutual defense.

In March 1939 Hitler forced Czechoslovakia to accept German occupation. The same month Great Britain and France, finally convinced of the need to confront Hitler, pledged to aid Poland in the event of German attack. After signing the Molotov-Ribbentrop non-aggression pact with the Soviet Union in August 1939, Germany invaded Poland in September, triggering World War II. Roosevelt proclaimed official American neutrality. In October 1939 the American states adopted the U.S.-proposed DECLARATION OF PANAMA, affirming Pan-American neutrality and creating a 300-mile safety zone around the Western Hemisphere. Roosevelt believed Nazi Germany posed a grave danger to U.S. and world security. He gradually steered American policy toward support of the Allies in the fight against Hitler. The fall of France in June 1940 further alerted Washington to the growing menace of the German war machine. The Roosevelt administration accelerated efforts to strengthen U.S. defenses and military preparedness. The same month the president laid the groundwork for a bipartisan defense policy, bringing Republicans HENRY L. STIMSON and Frank Knox into his cabinet to head the War and Navy departments. At an inter-American parley in July 1940, delegates approved the U.S.-sponsored ACT OF HAVANA, which barred Germany from gaining control over the Western Hemisphere colonies of conquered European powers.

Roosevelt was determined to provide a beleaguered Great Britain with all possible aid short of war. His efforts were opposed by the isolationist AMERICA FIRST COMMITTEE, which feared the United States would be drawn into the war, and supported by the interventionist COMMITTEE TO DEFEND AMERICA BY AIDING THE ALLIES and the FIGHT FOR FREEDOM COMMITTEE. In September 1940 the White House announced the DESTROYERS-FOR-BASES AGREEMENT, under which aged American naval destroyers were exchanged for British bases in the Western Hemisphere. The same month Germany, Italy, and Japan signed the Tripartite Pact forming the Axis alliance. Roosevelt continued to align the United States with the Allied cause, declaring in December 1940 that American industrial might would serve as a great ARSENAL OF DEMOCRACY.

In March 1941 Congress passed the LEND-LEASE Act authorizing the president to furnish military and economic aid to any country deemed vital to U.S. security. Under the lend-lease program America funneled vast amounts of assistance to Great Britain and, following the June 1941 German invasion of the Soviet Union, to the USSR. The Roosevelt administration announced the stationing of U.S. defensive forces on Greenland in April 1941 and on Iceland in July 1941. The deepening Anglo-American ties were reinforced the following month at the ATLANTIC CONFERENCE, where Roosevelt and British Prime Minister Winston Churchill drafted the ATLANTIC CHARTER articulating their common postwar aims. At the gathering Roosevelt agreed to increase the U.S. Navy's role in the protection of British convoys in the North Atlantic. Following an armed clash between an American destroyer and German submarine in the September 1941 GREER INCIDENT, the president authorized U.S. warships in the North Atlantic to engage Axis vessels on sight in what became known as the "Undeclared War."

U.S.-Japanese relations meanwhile worsened over Tokyo's continued aggression in China. In January 1940 the Roosevelt administration terminated the 1911 TREATY OF WASHINGTON governing U.S.-Japanese commerce. Roosevelt subsequently restricted American exports to Japan in an attempt to restrain its expansionist behavior. Following the movement of Japanese troops into French Indochina in September 1940, he placed an embargo on the sale of U.S. steel and scrap iron to Japan. When Tokyo expanded its presence in Indochina in July 1941, Roosevelt froze Japanese assets in the United States. In October 1941 he suspended U.S. oil shipments to Japan.

U.S.-Japanese negotiations over their growing differences reached an impasse in November 1941. On December 7, 1941, Japan launched a surprise attack against the U.S. Pacific fleet at PEARL HARBOR. The following day, after hearing Roosevelt describe December 7 as "a date which will live in infamy," Congress voted a declaration of war against Japan. Within days Germany and Italy would declare war on the United States and Congress would reciprocate, thus completing the war's expansion into a global conflict.

Roosevelt and Churchill met later in the month at the WASHINGTON CONFERENCE, where they solidified planning for joint Anglo-American military operations and gave final approval to a "Germany First" strategy. The Allies would concentrate on destroying the Nazi power and then turn their full energies to the defeat of Japan. The UNITED NATIONS DECLARATION, signed in January 1942 by the United States, Great Britain, the Soviet Union, China and 22 other countries, formalized the Allied coalition opposed to the Axis powers. Some 50 nations ultimately would join the Allied side while several East European countries enlisted in the Axis alliance. The United States undertook a massive war mobilization. More than 16 million Americans eventually served in uniform. World War II was waged across Europe, North Africa, and Asia and on all the major oceans. After initial Axis successes, the tide turned in the Allied favor in 1942. German advances in the Soviet Union and North Africa were stopped at the battles of Stalingrad and El Alamein and the U.S. Navy destroyed the striking power of the Japanese fleet at the Pacific Battle of Midway. As a prelude to entering the fighting in Europe, U.S. forces landed in North Africa in Operation Torch in November 1942.

The leaders of the major Allied powers held a series of wartime conferences to map out strategy and plan for the postwar world. At the January 1943 CASABLANCA CONFERENCE, Roosevelt and Churchill proclaimed Allied policy to be the unconditional surrender of the Axis powers. An Anglo-American invasion of Italy in September 1943 led to the surrender of the Fascist Italian government the same month. In the Pacific, U.S. forces fought a bloody island-hopping campaign toward Japan. Roose-velt, Churchill, and Soviet Premier Joseph Stalin first met at the November 1943 TEHERAN CONFERENCE. The BIG THREE finalized planning for an Anglo-American invasion of France in 1944 and agreed on the formation of a postwar UNITED NATIONS peacekeeping organization. Representatives from the various Allied nations gathered in 1944 to lay the groundwork for a postwar international economic and political order. The BRETTON WOODS CONFERENCE established the INTERNATIONAL MONETARY FUND and WORLD BANK, while the DUMBARTON OAKS CONFERENCE framed the UNITED NATIONS CHARTER. In June 1944 Anglo-American forces under General DWIGHT D. EISENHOWER successfully launched the D-Day invasion of France.

Roosevelt, Churchill, and Stalin conferred a final time in February 1945 at the YALTA CONFERENCE. Roosevelt gained Stalin's renewed pledge that the Soviet Union would enter the war against Japan once Germany was defeated, a key goal of U.S. planners who forecast a costly struggle to invade and finally subdue the Japanese home islands. The president acquiesced to Moscow's hegemony in Eastern Europe. Roosevelt died in April 1945 and was succeeded by Vice-President HARRY S. TRUMAN. At the SAN FRANCISCO CONFERENCE the same month, delegates completed planning for the United Nations. Crushed between U.S. and British armies in the West and Soviet armies in the East, Germany surrendered on May 7, 1945. The U.S., British, and Soviet leaders gathered at the POTSDAM CONFERENCE in July 1945 to address postwar Europe and review preparations for Soviet entry into the war against Japan. On the eve of the parley the top-secret U.S. MANHATTAN PROJECT successfully detonated the first atomic bomb. Truman ordered atomic bombs dropped on two Japanese cities: Hiroshima on August 6 and Nagasaki on August 9. Japan sued for peace on August 10 and formally capitulated on September 2, 1945, ending World War II.

The war left much of Europe and Asia in ruins. America suffered almost 300,000 killed in action. Military and civilian casualties on all sides ran to the tens of millions. The Potsdam Conference established the COUNCIL OF FOREIGN MINISTERS to prepare peace treaties with the defeated Axis nations. The PARIS PEACE CONFERENCE (1946) and New York Conference (1946) concluded peace settlements for minor Axis powers Italy, Hungary, Bulgaria, Romania, and Finland. The United States emerged from the conflict as the world's dominant power. The Truman administration completed the fundamental shift in U.S. foreign policy from isolationism to INTERNATIONALISM, committing America to a leading role in international affairs. A generation of American leaders resolved not to repeat the mistakes of the 1930s and allow international aggression to go unchecked. The lessons of World War II were cited by U.S. presidents committing American forces to the postwar defense of Western Europe and to halting Communist aggression in the KOREAN WAR and VIETNAM WAR.

The U.S.-Soviet wartime alliance was quickly shattered by fundamental disagreements over the future status of Germany and Eastern Europe. The onset of the East-West COLD WAR blocked negotiation of a German peace treaty and left Germany divided between Western-allied democratic and Soviet-dominated Communist states. The JAPANESE PEACE TREATY was concluded in 1951 and the AUSTRIAN STATE TREATY, which reestablished Austria as an independent nation, in 1955. The collapse of communism in Eastern Europe led to the FINAL SETTLEMENT WITH RESPECT TO GERMANY TREATY (1990) reuniting Germany and bringing to a close the remaining unresolved issue of World War II.

WRIGHT-REAGAN PLAN See **CONTRAS**.

WRISTON REPORT See **FOREIGN SERVICE**.

X

X See **KENNAN, GEORGE FROST**.

XYZ AFFAIR (1797) Diplomatic incident between the United States and France that triggered the QUASI-WAR (1798–1800). JOHN ADAMS succeeded GEORGE WASHINGTON as president in 1797 amid deteriorating Franco-American relations attributable to a series of developments in Washington's second term. Washington's NEUTRALITY PROCLAMATION (1793), which was intended to keep the United States from direct involvement in the French Revolutionary Wars (1792–1802) in general and the conflict between France and Great Britain in particular, had drawn French objection because strict American impartiality essentially favored superior British sea power. France angrily deplored the controversial Anglo-American JAY'S TREATY (1794), which the French insisted violated the FRANCO-AMERICAN ALLIANCE (1778) and undermined the TREATY OF AMITY AND COMMERCE (1778). WASHINGTON'S FAREWELL ADDRESS (1796), recommending American detachment from European politics and avoidance of permanent alliances, together with the recall of U.S. Minister at Paris JAMES MONROE, a Democratic-Republican and ardent French supporter, fed growing French suspicion that the Federalist Washington administration favored a pro-British policy.

The revolutionary French government refused to receive Monroe's replacement, Federalist CHARLES COTESWORTH PINCKNEY, when he arrived in December 1796. After the Federalist Adams defeated pro-French Democratic-Republican presidential candidate THOMAS JEFFERSON the same month, French naval vessels and privateers began confiscatory raids on American trade ships bound to or from British ports, especially in the West Indies. On March 2, 1797, France decreed it no longer recognized the principle of FREE SHIPS MAKE FREE GOODS and henceforth would permit its ships to capture any U.S. vessels trading with Great Britain. Increasing French seizures of American cargoes pushed the two countries toward conflict.

Adams in May 1797 called a special session of Congress to deal with the French crisis. He requested limited military preparations in case war broke out and, over the protest of so-called extreme Federalists, asked for approval of a special diplomatic mission to France to seek a peaceful solution and improved relations. Congress authorized a series of modest defense measures, including construction of naval frigates, strengthening of coastal fortifications, and placing state militias on alert, and approved the mission. Adams on May 31 appointed a commission to France comprising Pinckney, JOHN MARSHALL, and Elbridge Gerry. The American envoys were instructed to seek compensation for losses suffered by American commerce and to win French consent to freeing the United States from its obligation under the 1778 alliance to defend the French West Indies. In return the commission was authorized to offer France concessions on trade and neutral rights similar to those secured by the British in Jay's Treaty.

The commissioners arrived at Paris on October 4, 1797, but French Foreign Minister Charles Maurice de Talleyrand refused to receive them officially. On October 18 three agents of the foreign minister approached the American envoys to demand a bribe of $250,000 and a sizeable loan to France as the price for beginning formal negotiations. The Americans rejected the solicitation. A prolonged impasse followed as Talleyrand persisted in his demand for money, prompting an indignant Pinckney to respond "No! No! Not a sixpence!" (His words inspired the popular American slogan "Millions for defense, but not one cent for tribute.") In March 1798 a frustrated Pinckney and Marshall broke off their abortive diplomatic effort and departed Paris. Gerry remained behind in hopes his presence might help avert a war. Meanwhile, the commissioners' correspondence had arrived at the capital in Philadelphia, informing an angered Adams of the French bid at diplomatic extortion.

The president appeared before Congress March 19 to reveal how the French had rebuffed the U.S. peace commission. Assailing the insult to America's national honor, he sought permission for measures to strengthen U.S. military forces. Skeptical Democratic-Republicans, suspecting Adams was exaggerating the episode as a pretext for declaring war, demanded to see the commissioners' diplomatic correspondence. On April 3 the president submitted the dispatches to Congress after substituting the letters X, Y, and Z for the names of Talleyrand's agents. Publication of the dispatches by order of the Senate sparked a widespread public uproar, deeply damaging French support in America. Extreme Federalists, led by Secretary of State TIMOTHY PICKERING, pressed for an immediate war declaration against France. But Adams advocated a peaceful course while the nation fortified its limited defenses. The widening schism in U.S.-French relations that followed the XYZ Affair prompted Congress to abrogate the 1778 treaties with France, suspend trade, sanction U.S. seizure of armed French vessels, and expand the American military. As 1798 wore on, the United States found itself embroiled in the undeclared Quasi-War with France. This maritime conflict over neutral rights finally was settled through the CONVENTION OF 1800.

Y

YAKIMA WAR (1855–1858) Indian resistance to the rapid advance of settlers and miners in the Washington Territory after 1846 led to warfare between the United States and an alliance of the Yakima and several neighboring tribes. The Indian confederation opposed federal plans to relocate the tribes and open territory along the Columbia and Yakima rivers to white settlement. Hostilities broke out when the Yakimas repudiated an 1855 treaty made at Camp Stevens that ceded their lands to the United States and arranged for their placement on a reservation. Indian forces fought off U.S. troops for three years. Finally, the tribes suffered a pivotal defeat at the Battle of Four Lakes near Spokane, Washington, in September 1858. Their power broken, the Indians were removed to reservations.

See also MAP 1.

YALTA CONFERENCE (1945) Second WORLD WAR II conference of U.S. President FRANKLIN D. ROOSEVELT, British Prime Minister Winston Churchill, and Soviet Premier Joseph Stalin. The leaders of the three major Allied powers first met in late 1943 at the TEHERAN CONFERENCE, where they reviewed their joint military strategy for the defeat of Nazi Germany and began planning for the postwar world. At Teheran, Stalin pledged to join the war against Japan once Germany surrendered. Germany's imminent collapse and the need to finalize plans for the postwar administration of Europe led Roosevelt and Churchill in late 1944 to press for another BIG THREE meeting. Roosevelt also was eager to secure Soviet entry in the Pacific war and to hasten the planning for the establishment of a UNITED NATIONS international peacekeeping organization. In view of Stalin's refusal to venture far from the Soviet Union, agreement was reached to hold the proposed conference at the Soviet resort city of Yalta on the Black Sea.

En route to Yalta, Roosevelt, Churchill and their advisers rendezvoused at Malta in the Mediterranean for preliminary discussions. The Malta Conference, from January 30 to February 2, 1945, largely involved Anglo-American military staff coordination. The Yalta Conference took place from February 4 to 11, 1945. The American delegation included Secretary of State EDWARD R. STETTINIUS, JR., Army Chief of Staff GEORGE C. MARSHALL, presidential aide Harry L. Hopkins, and State Department officials CHARLES E. BOHLEN and ALGER HISS. After difficult negotiations that revealed fundamental differences on postwar Europe within the wartime alliance, the three leaders signed an EXECUTIVE AGREEMENT on the final day encapsulating and announcing the decisions reached.

The Yalta agreement reaffirmed the Allied commitment to Germany's unconditional surrender, provided for Germany's division into four postwar occupation zones among the Big Three and France, and established an ALLIED CONTROL COUNCIL for the joint administration of the defeated Axis power. It endorsed the payment of war reparations by Germany and the punishment of German war criminals. The conference reconfirmed the Soviet acquisition of part of eastern Poland agreed to at Teheran. In return, Poland was to receive as yet unspecified territories from Germany. The United States and Great Britain were committed to the formation of a democratic government in a postwar Poland freed from Nazi occupation. Confronted at Yalta with the fact that Poland was already under the Soviet Red Army's control, Roosevelt and Churchill consented to a Soviet-dominated provisional governing committee as the basis for a postwar Polish government. Roosevelt was prepared to defer final resolution of the issue of Poland's future status to ensure Soviet entry into the war against Japan. The Western allies won Soviet acceptance of an American-sponsored Declaration on Liberated Europe binding the conferees to respect the principles of democracy and self-determination in the areas liberated from Nazi rule.

The three delegations also addressed key issues left unresolved from the 1944 DUMBARTON OAKS CONFERENCE on the formation of the United Nations. The Anglo-American position that the veto power of permanent members of the Security Council apply to substantive and not merely procedural matters prevailed. The Western leaders for their part acquiesced to Stalin's demand that the Soviet republics of the Ukraine and Byelorussia be admitted separately to the General Assembly, thus giving the USSR three votes in the body. The Yalta agreement called for an international conference to meet at San Francisco to prepare the UNITED NATIONS CHARTER. The SAN FRANCISCO CONFERENCE convened as proposed in April 1945. At Roosevelt's request, the Yalta decisions on the U.N. veto and USSR General Assembly membership were not made public, presumably so he could first soften any adverse reaction their disclosure might bring in the United States. Also concealed for security reasons was a Soviet pledge to enter the war against Japan within three months of Germany's surrender. In return, the Western leaders secretly agreed the Soviet Union would regain the southern half of Sakhalin Island, which it had lost in the Russo-Japanese War (1904–1905); retain control over Outer Mongolia; receive concessions in China; and obtain the Kurile Islands from Japan.

The Yalta parley was followed in July 1945 by the POTSDAM CONFERENCE, the final Big Three wartime meeting. Details of the arrangements reached at Yalta regarding the United Nations had leaked by the end

of February 1945, raising persistent questions in the United States, despite Roosevelt administration denials, as to what other secret agreements might have been concluded at the conference. The Yalta decisions on Poland and Germany, and the failure to address in greater detail the fate of areas occupied by the Red Army, came under mounting U.S. domestic criticism as Moscow moved after World War II to impose Communist regimes throughout Eastern Europe. Roosevelt's defenders argued that the imperative necessity of bringing the USSR into the war against Japan had limited the president's ability to constrain Stalin with respect to Eastern Europe. When postwar East-West relations deteriorated into COLD WAR, Yalta was singled out by critics as the infamous occasion at which Eastern Europe had been abandoned by the West to the new tyranny of communism. In the early 1950s demagogic Senator JOSEPH R. MCCARTHY (R-WI) cited the conference as evidence of alleged Communist subversion of American foreign policy from within the State Department. Throughout the Cold War Yalta remained, particularly for conservatives, a symbol of U.S. appeasement of the Soviet Union.

YAP ISLAND CONTROVERSY (1919–1922) Diplomatic dispute between the United States and Japan concerning control of the North Pacific island. At the PARIS PEACE CONFERENCE after WORLD WAR I, Japan received a LEAGUE OF NATIONS mandate over German islands in the North Pacific, including the Marshall, Mariana, and Caroline groups. Among the Carolines was tiny Yap Island, a key cable center important to the United States as a communications link to GUAM, the Philippines, and China. During the peace talks, President WOODROW WILSON had objected to Yap's inclusion under the Japanese mandate, insisting it should be placed under international control as a cable station. After the Paris Conference the American government strenuously protested the disposition of Yap. When in 1920 the European allies backed Japan's right to the island, the United States disclaimed the entire Japanese North Pacific mandate. America had not ratified the TREATY OF VERSAILLES and contended it was not bound to accept the League of Nations award to Japan.

The controversy was resolved through a U.S.-Japanese treaty concluded on February 11, 1922, following the WASHINGTON NAVAL CONFERENCE. Under the pact, the United States received cable, radio, and residential rights on Yap on an equal basis with the Japanese. In return, America formally recognized all terms of Japan's mandate, including Japanese sovereignty over Yap Island.

YOM KIPPUR WAR (1973) Major armed conflict in the Middle East between Israel and Arab states. Since Israel's creation as a nation in 1948, Arabs had proclaimed their unyielding determination to destroy the Jewish state and restore an Arab Palestine. The war erupted when Egypt and Syria, seeking to regain territories captured by Israeli forces in the 1967 Arab-Israeli Six-Day War, launched simultaneous surprise attacks against Israel on October 6, 1973, the Jewish holy day of Yom Kippur. Syrian troops struck from the North through the Golan Heights while Egyptian forces attacked from the West across the Suez Canal. The Arab armies, each of which was receiving huge amounts of arms and supplies from the Soviet Union, dealt the Israelis heavy losses in the war's first week. To counter Soviet support for the Egyptians and Syrians, the Nixon administration mounted a massive airlift of weapons and equipment to Israel. The U.S. intervention helped the Israelis reverse the military tide. Counterattacking, the Israeli army drove deep into Syria and encircled the Egyptian forces by crossing the Suez into Egypt.

With the reeling Arabs and their Soviet patron eager for an end to hostilities, U.S. Secretary of State HENRY A. KISSINGER went to Moscow to confer with Soviet Communist Party leader Leonid I. Brezhnev on the Middle East war. They drafted a cease-fire proposal which was acceptable to both sides and which the UNITED NATIONS Security Council adopted on October 22. Fighting continued, though, as the cease-fire fell through. The Soviets, concerned that the Israelis were poised to decimate the surrounded Egyptian army, endorsed Egyptian President Anwar Sadat's plea for joint Soviet-American military intervention in his country to restore peace. Steadfastly opposed to direct Soviet involvement in the Middle East, the Nixon administration re-

jected the proposal. The Kremlin then threatened to intervene unilaterally to save Sadat's troops. Anticipating imminent Soviet action, President RICHARD M. NIXON on October 24 warned the USSR to keep out of the region. U.S. policy would not tolerate Soviet military inroads near the strategically vital Suez Canal. To dissuade Moscow from moving militarily, Nixon ordered all U.S. forces worldwide placed on heightened alert. Crisis was averted when the Soviets backed down and the two superpowers supported a Security Council resolution that was adopted on October 25. The measure effected an Egyptian-Israeli cease-fire and established a U.N. peacekeeping force made up of contingents from smaller nations to enforce the truce.

Although the Israeli-Egyptian fighting stopped, clashes between the Syrians and Israelis continued into 1974. Kissinger assumed the role of mediator in peace negotiations between Israel and neighboring Arab nations. Through several rounds of SHUTTLE DIPLOMACY, he helped broker the agreement signed in January 1974 by Israel and Egypt to separate their forces along the Suez and in the Sinai. Turning to the ongoing Israeli-Syrian hostilities, Kissinger shuttled back and forth between Damascus and Jerusalem in search of a peace settlement. The culmination of his efforts was the cease-fire agreement signed by the Syrians and Israelis on May 31, 1974. By terms of the accord, a U.N. buffer zone was created between the two countries and both sides agreed to disengage their armies in the disputed Golan Heights.

See also ARAB OIL EMBARGO.

YOUNG AMERICA Name given to a faction within the Democratic Party after the MEXICAN WAR (1846–1848). The movement, active until the mid-1850s, was identified with an aggressive nationalism. It advocated a vigorous, "spread eagle" expansionist foreign policy, championing the idea of America's MANIFEST DESTINY. Imbued with republican ideas, Young America's followers sympathized deeply with the unsuccessful liberal revolutions against conservative monarchical rule that swept Europe in 1848. Adherents urged expressions of U.S. support for the liberal revolutionary movements and went so far as to propose American intervention on behalf of forces in Europe struggling to replace despotism with republican governments.

Young America reached its apogee in the election year of 1852, when it formulated a platform espousing U.S. expansionism in Latin America, aid to the world's liberal political movements, and free trade. It supported winning presidential candidate FRANKLIN PIERCE, who on taking office in March 1853 promised to pursue a vigorous expansionist policy. The movement wholeheartedly endorsed the Pierce administration's ultimately abortive efforts to acquire Cuba and promoted American FILIBUSTERING expeditions south of the border. Young America faded in the latter 1850s as the sectional political conflict between North and South intensified and the nation moved closer to civil war.

YOUNG, ANDREW JACKSON, JR. (1932–   ) Civil rights leader, congressman, ambassador to the UNITED NATIONS. Young was born and raised in New Orleans. He graduated from Howard University in 1951, completed divinity studies at Hartford Theological Seminary in 1955 and was ordained in the United Church of Christ. He served as a pastor in Georgia and Alabama and as a social worker with the National Council of Churches in New York City. Active in the civil rights movement, he joined the Southern Christian Leadership Conference in 1961 and became a top aide to Dr. Martin Luther King, Jr. In 1972 Young won election to the U.S. House of Representatives as a Democrat from an Atlanta district, becoming the first black to represent Georgia in Congress since the 1870s. Twice reelected, he had an important part in JIMMY CARTER's successful 1976 presidential campaign.

President-elect Carter named him the first black U.S. representative to the United Nations. Young's tenure was marked by controversy over his outspoken condemnation of racism in international affairs and his support for black nationalist movements in Africa, notably the African National Congress in South Africa. He resigned his post in August 1979 amid the uproar generated by disclosure of unauthorized contacts he had with representatives of the Palestine Liberation Organization. The meetings drew domestic political criticism from American Jewish groups and strained U.S. relations

with Israel. Young was elected mayor of Atlanta in 1981 and held the position until 1989. In 1990 he unsuccessfully sought the governorship of Georgia.

YOUNG PLAN (1929) Agreement meant to finalize German WORLD WAR I reparations. By 1923 Germany, its postwar economy in shambles, had defaulted on its massive reparations payments to Great Britain, France, and its other Allied wartime foes. The 1924 DAWES PLAN established a temporary financial arrangement under which Germany successfully met a reduced payments schedule. As provided for under the interim Dawes scheme, the Allies formed a committee of financial experts in 1929 to draft recommendations for a final German reparations settlement. The group, similar to the earlier panel that had drawn up the Dawes Plan, included representatives from Great Britain, Belgium, France, Italy, Japan, and Germany. Although America had declined any reparations and was not involved formally in the issue, the U.S. government, as it had in 1924, supported the participation of private American citizens on the committee. U.S. corporate executive and lawyer Owen D. Young became chairman of the gathering. While it officially opposed any connection between reparations and Allied war debts owed to the United States, Washington recognized that the ability and inclination of European nations to repay their U.S. obligations was linked to the successful resolution of German reparations.

The committee met in Paris from February 9 to June 7, 1929. Its report was approved by international conferences, attended by the United States as an observer, at The Hague, Netherlands, in August 1929 and January 1930. The Young Plan went into effect May 17, 1930. It reduced the total reparations Germany owed from the original $33 billion sum to slightly more than $8 billion; provided for payment to be spread out over 58 1/2 years; and created the Bank of International Settlements to handle the financial transactions. In 1931, the worldwide Great Depression would induce President HERBERT C. HOOVER to devise the so-called HOOVER MORATORIUM on repayment of both Allied war debts and German reparations. The European Allies effectively canceled the reparations at the 1932 Lausanne Conference.

Z

Z Pseudonym used by the author of a widely discussed article in the winter 1989–1990 issue of *Daedalus,* scholarly journal of the American Academy of Arts and Sciences, that addressed the U.S. response to the demise of Communist systems worldwide. The piece, "The Soviets' Terminal Crisis," contended that the momentous political and economic changes underway in the USSR and Eastern Europe marked the beginning of communism's irrevocable collapse, not only in the Soviet bloc, but from the "Baltic to the China Sea and from Berlin to Beijing." The article was pessimistic about the efforts of Soviet President Mikhail S. Gorbachev to transform Soviet society. His policies of economic restructuring and political openness, perestroika and glasnost, were criticized by Z as half-way measures calculated to maintain the supremacy of the Soviet Communist Party and preserve the Soviet Union rather than to effect a transition to democracy and free-market institutions. Communism, Z insisted, was inherently incapable of self-reform and consequently was in the process of disintegration. Since Gorbachev's policies were destined to failure, the article argued, any aid the United States might provide to help him would be futile and even counterproductive; such assistance would, in Z's judgement, only delay the historic makeover of the Soviet Union and "prolong the agony" of the restive Soviet peoples.

The appearance of the pseudonymous article aroused great curiosity in academia, the media, and the foreign policy establishment about the author's identity and set off a flurry of speculation. The piece evoked memories of an earlier contribution to the debate over U.S. policy toward the Soviet Union—the famous 1947 article in FOREIGN AFFAIRS by GEORGE F. KENNAN, who at the time identified himself only as "X," on the CONTAINMENT of communism. In an August 1990 column on the Op-Ed page of the *New York Times,* Martin E. Malia, a professor of Russian history at the University of California at Berkeley, revealed himself as the *Daedalus* article's author. He explained the pseudonym as a precaution taken to protect his Soviet friends from reprisal in the event of a possible reactionary crackdown by the Soviet government, and suggested that developments in the USSR in 1990 had vindicated his analysis.

ZERO OPTION See **INTERMEDIATE NUCLEAR FORCES TREATY**.

ZIMMERMANN TELEGRAM (1917) Infamous coded note from Germany to Mexico that helped precipitate American entry into WORLD WAR I. On January 9, 1917, the German high command decided on a resumption of unrestricted submarine warfare as its best and only means for breaking the European military stalemate and defeating the Allies, even at the risk of drawing the United States into the war. On January 31, German Ambassador to Washington Count Johann Heinrich von Bernstorff notified Secretary of State ROBERT LANSING that, effective February 1, his nation's U-boats would renew their attacks against all Allied and neutral shipping without warning. President WOODROW WILSON, condemning the German government's decision as a violation of the pledge it had made against unrestricted submarine warfare following the sinking of the French passenger steamer SUSSEX (1916), broke off diplomatic relations with Berlin on February 3.

Meanwhile on January 17 German Foreign Secretary Arthur Zimmermann had sent a telegram to the German minister in Mexico Heinrich von Eckhardt. Should the United States join the war against Germany, the note said, von Eckhardt was to propose a military alliance with Mexico and to ask Mexican president Venustiano Carranza to urge Japan to desert the Allies and switch sides in the conflict. If the Central Powers were victorious, Zimmermann wrote, Mexico's reward for aiding Germany would be recovery of Arizona, Texas, and New Mexico, the historic Mexican territory ceded to the United States after the MEXICAN WAR (1846–1848).

The telegram was intercepted and decoded by British intelligence and passed on to the U.S. government on February 24. Its contents persuaded Wilson of German treachery and prompted him to ask a joint session of Congress on February 26 for permission to arm American merchant ships. Made public on March 1, the Zimmermann cable aroused strong anti-German sentiment throughout the country and figured as a major factor in the U.S. decision on April 6, 1917, to declare war against Germany.

ZUMWALT, ELMO RUSSEL, JR. (1920–)
U.S. Navy officer, chief of naval operations (CNO). Zumwalt graduated from Annapolis in 1942 and saw action in the Pacific during WORLD WAR II. The California native held a variety of sea and shore assignments before appointment in 1963 as executive assistant to Secretary of the Navy PAUL H. NITZE. He was promoted to admiral in 1965 and took command of U.S. naval forces in the VIETNAM WAR in 1968. He became the youngest

CNO in history when President RICHARD M. NIXON named him to the position in 1970. During his controversial four-year tenure as the Navy's top uniformed officer, Zumwalt undertook a series of reforms meant to bring the service more into line with changing American lifestyles. He issued a series of directives, known as "Z-Grams," that liberalized regulations regarding conduct, discipline, and personal appearance and pressed the recruitment of women and minorities.

Zumwalt strongly advocated advanced new weapons systems such as the Trident SEA-LAUNCHED BALLISTIC MISSILE to counter a perceived mounting Soviet military threat. Shortly before his retirement in 1974 he questioned the ability of the Navy to control the seas in the event of war with the USSR. In retirement Zumwalt criticized the Ford administration's national security policies, arguing that they failed to address the Soviet military buildup, and engaged in public debate with Secretary of State HENRY A. KISSINGER over possible Soviet violations of the 1972 SALT I arms control agreement. Zumwalt claimed the administration was withholding information on Soviet non-compliance, which Kissinger denied. Kissinger also disavowed remarks attributed to him by Zumwalt that America was on the decline and the Soviet Union on the rise.

In 1976 he was the unsuccessful Democratic candidate for the U.S. Senate in Virginia, losing to independent incumbent Harry F. Byrd, Jr. In the 1980s Zumwalt, who had ordered the use of Agent Orange in Vietnam, became active in efforts to help U.S. service people suffering from exposure to the defoliant. His son Elmo R. Zumwalt III, who had been exposed to Agent Orange while a naval officer in Vietnam, died at age 42 of cancer in 1988.

$=$ *Appendix A* $=$

Timeline

*T*his timetable portrays the major developments in U.S foreign affairs from 1776 to the present. Items are included under six broad categories: International Affairs; Presidential Administration; Diplomacy and Foreign Relations; National Security; Economy, Trade, and Development; and Science, Technology, and Environment. Dictionary entries are indicated by SMALL CAPS.

International
Affairs

———————————————————————— Continental Congress ————————————————————————

Presidential
Administration

Declaration of
Independence
●
4 JUL

Diplomacy and
Foreign Relations

DELAWARE INDIAN TREATY
●
17 SEP

PLAN OF 1776
●
17 SEP

TREATY OF AMITY AND COMMERCE
●
6 FEB

———————————————————————— AMERICAN REVOLUTION ————————————————————————

National
Security

Economy, Trade,
and Development

Science, Technology,
and Environment

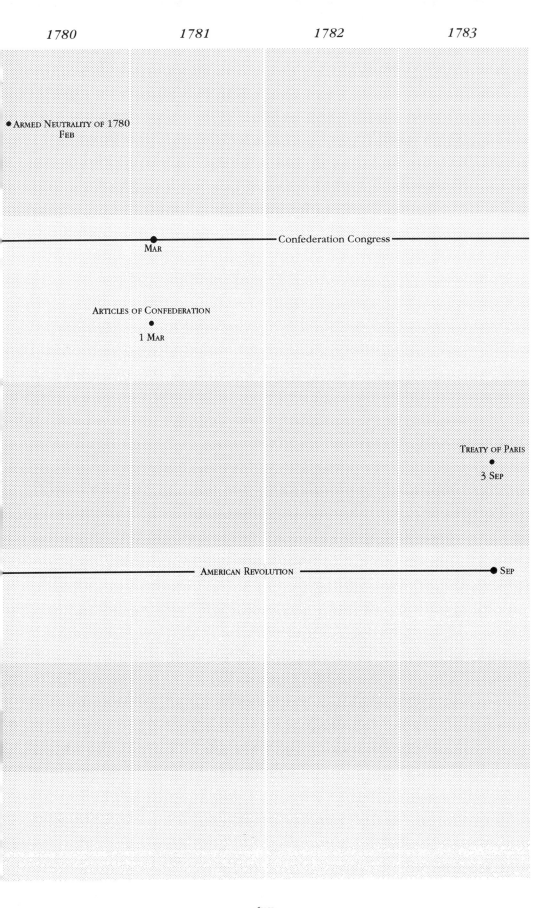

1780 1781 1782 1783

● Armed Neutrality of 1780
      Feb

MAR ————————————— Confederation Congress ——————————————

Articles of Confederation
            ●
      1 Mar

Treaty of Paris
       ●
     3 Sep

———————————— American Revolution ———————————————— ● Sep

International Affairs

————————————— Confederation Congress —————————————

Presidential Administration

ORDINANCE FOR
THE REGULATION OF
INDIAN AFFAIRS
●
7 AUG

CONSTITUTION
●
17 SEP

Diplomacy and Foreign Relations

TREATY OF FORT STANWIX
●
22 OCT

TREATY OF
HOPEWELL
●
28 NOV

JAY-GARDOQUI
TREATY
●
AUG

National Security

Economy, Trade, and Development

Science, Technology, and Environment

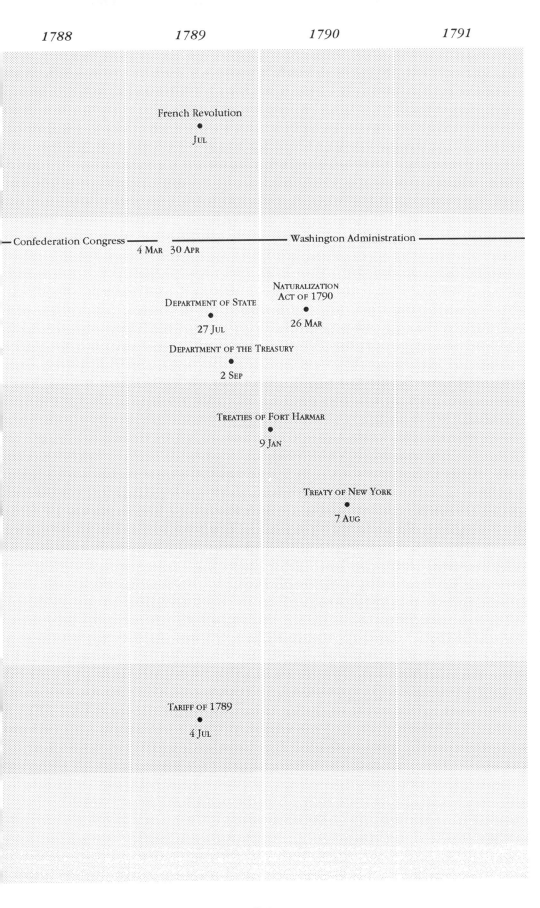

1788 1789 1790 1791

French Revolution
•
Jul

Confederation Congress ————   ———————— Washington Administration ————
4 Mar 30 Apr

Naturalization
Act of 1790
Department of State •
• 26 Mar
27 Jul

Department of the Treasury
•
2 Sep

Treaties of Fort Harmar
•
9 Jan

Treaty of New York
•
7 Aug

Tariff of 1789
•
4 Jul

	1792	1793	1794	1795

International Affairs

APR ——————————————— French Revolutionary Wars ———————————————

Presidential Administration

——————————————— Washington Administration ———————————————

NEUTRALITY PROCLAMATION
•
22 APR

Diplomacy and Foreign Relations

JAY'S TREATY
•
19 NOV

TREATY OF GRENVILLE
•
3 AUG

APR ——— GENET AFFAIR ——— JUN

PINCKNEY'S TREAT
•
27 OCT

National Security

BATTLE OF FALLEN TIMBES
•
20 AUG

Economy, Trade, and Development

Science, Technology, and Environment

Invention Cotton Gin
•
APR

1796	1797	1798	1799

———— French Revolutionary Wars ————

— Washington Administration ———●——————— Adams Administration ————
                                4 MAR

WARE V. HYLTON
      ●
   7 MAR

   WASHINGTON'S FAREWELL ADDRESS
                  ●
              19 SEP

                                                        LOGAN ACT
                    OCT—— XYZ AFFAIR ——APR   ●
                                                          30 JUN

                    MAR ———————— QUASI-WAR ————

                    ALIEN AND SEDITION ACTS
                       JUN —— JUL

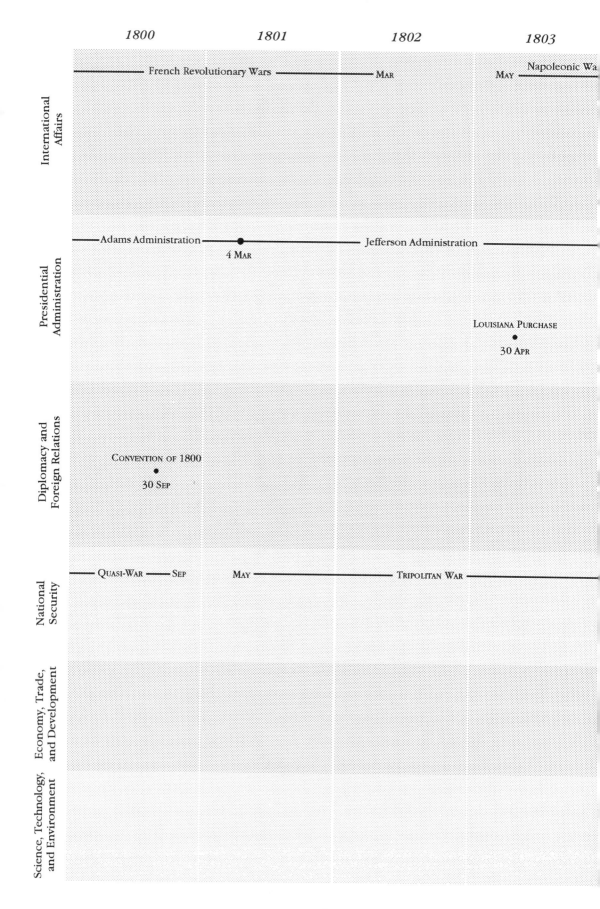

International Affairs

—— French Revolutionary Wars —————— MAR   MAY —— Napoleonic Wa

Presidential Administration

—— Adams Administration ——●—————— Jefferson Administration ——————
4 MAR

LOUISIANA PURCHASE
●
30 APR

Diplomacy and Foreign Relations

CONVENTION OF 1800
●
30 SEP

National Security

—— QUASI-WAR —— SEP   MAY ———————— TRIPOLITAN WAR ——————

Economy, Trade, and Development

Science, Technology, and Environment

——————— Napoleonic Wars ———————

——————— Jefferson Administration ———————

MAY ——————— LEWIS AND CLARK EXPEDITION ——————— SEP

MONROE-PINKNEY TREATY
●
31 DEC

——— TRIPOLITAN WAR ——————— JUN

CHESAPEAKE AFFAIR
●
22 JUN

NON-IMPORTATION ACT
●
18 APR

EMBARGO ACT
●
22 DEC

First Commercially
Successful Steamboat
●
AUG

683

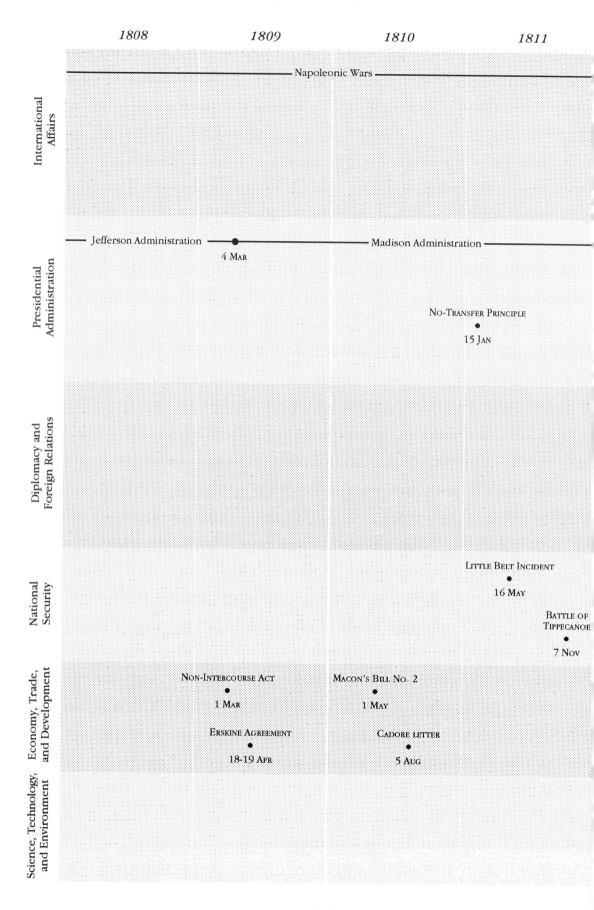

1808   1809   1810   1811

Napoleonic Wars

International Affairs

Jefferson Administration ————●———— Madison Administration
                              4 Mar

Presidential Administration

No-Transfer Principle
●
15 Jan

Diplomacy and Foreign Relations

Little Belt Incident
●
16 May

National Security

Battle of Tippecanoe
●
7 Nov

Non-Intercourse Act   Macon's Bill No. 2
●   ●
1 Mar   1 May

Erskine Agreement   Cadore letter
●   ●
18-19 Apr   5 Aug

Economy, Trade, and Development

Science, Technology, and Environment

Napoleonic Wars —————————————— Jun

Sep — Congress of Vienna — Jun

Madison Administration ——————————————

Treaty of Ghent
•
24 Dec

Jun —————————— War of 1812 ——————————— Dec

Algerine War
Mar ——— Jun

Feb ——— Creek War ——— Mar

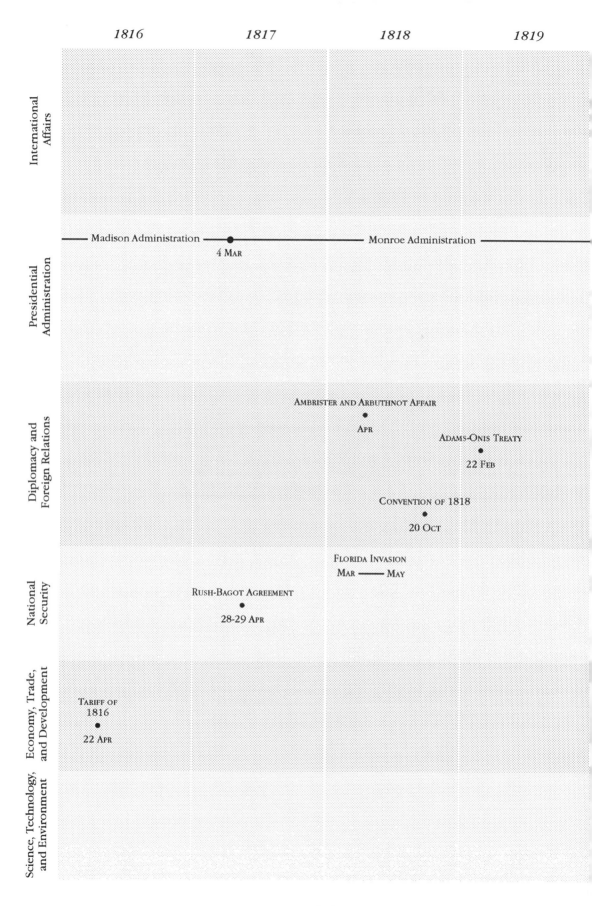

1816   1817   1818   1819

International Affairs

Presidential Administration

—— Madison Administration —— ● 4 MAR —— Monroe Administration ——

Diplomacy and Foreign Relations

AMBRISTER AND ARBUTHNOT AFFAIR
●
APR

ADAMS-ONIS TREATY
●
22 FEB

CONVENTION OF 1818
●
20 OCT

National Security

FLORIDA INVASION
MAR —— MAY

RUSH-BAGOT AGREEMENT
●
28-29 APR

Economy, Trade, and Development

TARIFF OF 1816
●
22 APR

Science, Technology, and Environment

Mexican Independence
from Spain
●
24 Aug

Polignac
Memorandum
●
9 Oct

— Monroe Administration —

Monroe
Doctrine
●
2 Dec

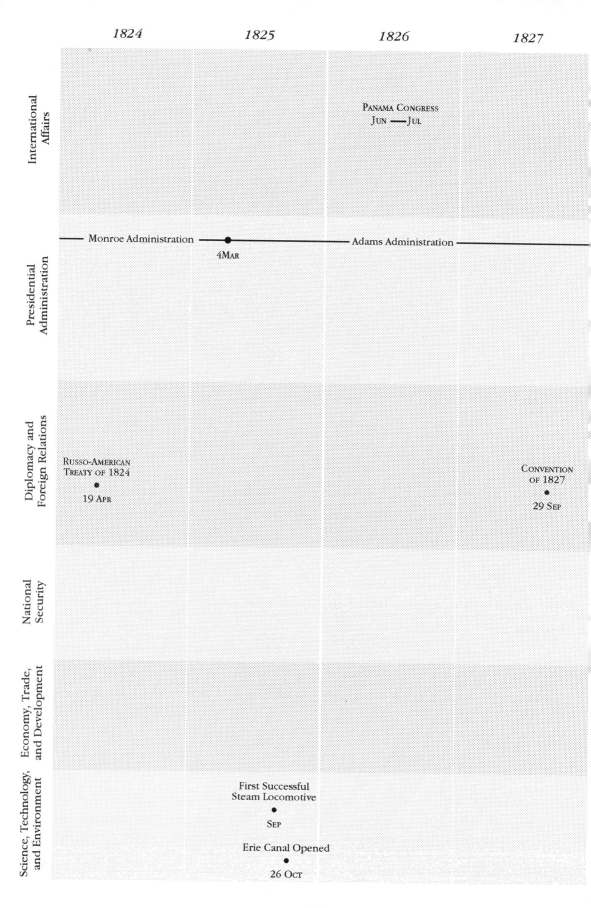

	1824	1825	1826	1827

International Affairs

PANAMA CONGRESS
JUN ——— JUL

Presidential Administration

——— Monroe Administration ——————●———————— Adams Administration ———————
4 MAR

Diplomacy and Foreign Relations

RUSSO-AMERICAN
TREATY OF 1824
●
19 APR

CONVENTION
OF 1827
●
29 SEP

National Security

Economy, Trade, and Development

Science, Technology, and Environment

First Successful
Steam Locomotive
●
SEP

Erie Canal Opened
●
26 OCT

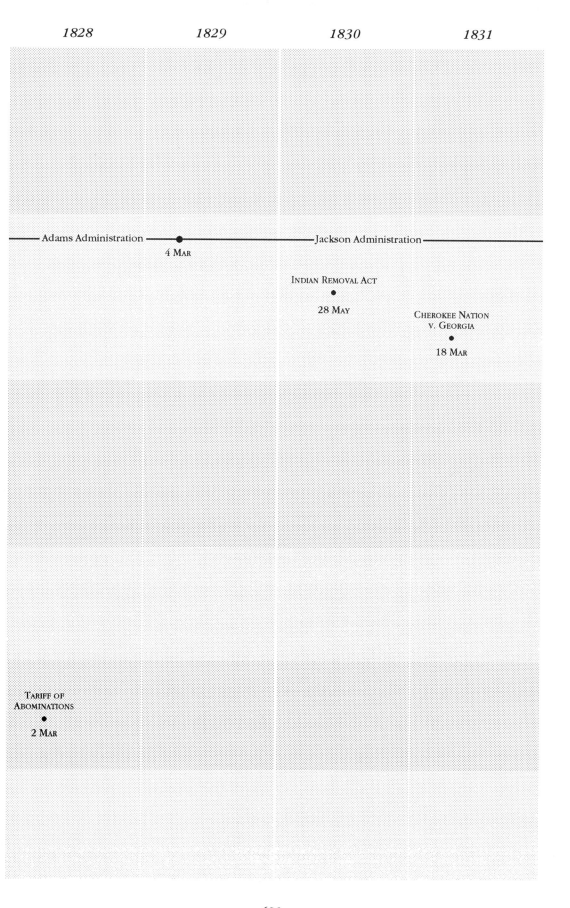

1828   1829   1830   1831

—— Adams Administration ———●——————Jackson Administration————
                          4 Mar

                                    Indian Removal Act
                                           ●
                                        28 May

                                                    Cherokee Nation
                                                    v. Georgia
                                                        ●
                                                    18 Mar

Tariff of
Abominations
    ●
  2 Mar

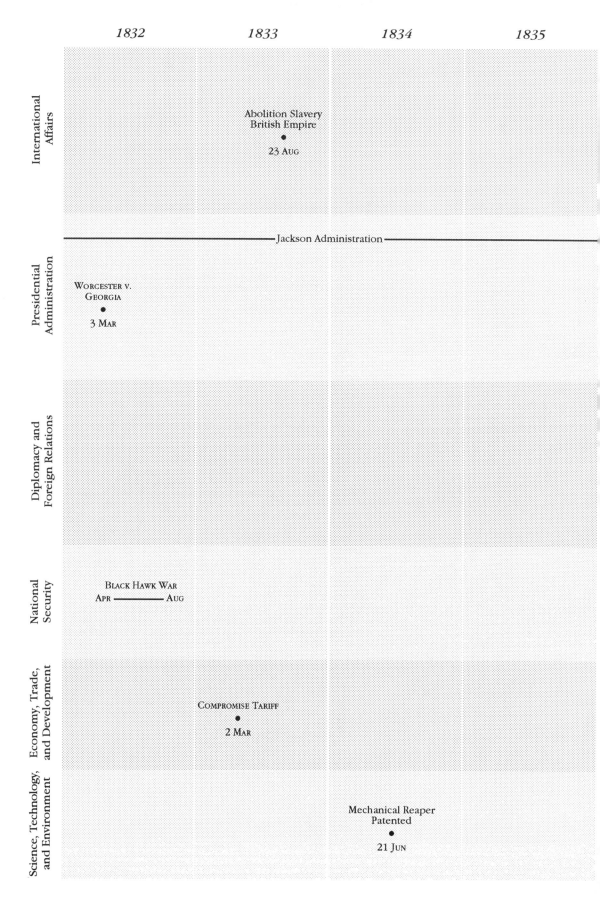

	1832	1833	1834	1835

International Affairs

Abolition Slavery
British Empire
●
23 AUG

―――――Jackson Administration―――――

Presidential Administration

WORCESTER V.
GEORGIA
●
3 MAR

Diplomacy and Foreign Relations

National Security

BLACK HAWK WAR
APR ――――― AUG

Economy, Trade, and Development

COMPROMISE TARIFF
●
2 MAR

Science, Technology, and Environment

Mechanical Reaper
Patented
●
21 JUN

TEXAN REVOLUTION
FEB ———— MAY

First Opium War
NOV ————

SIEGE OF ALAMO
———— 6 MAR
26 FEB

———— Jackson Administration ———●——— Van Buren Administration ————
4 MAR

CITY OF NEW YORK V. MILN
●
FEB

CAROLINE AFFAIR
●
29 DEC

AMISTAD AFFAIR
●
JAN

AROOSTOOK WAR
FEB ———— MAR

AUG ———— WILKES EXPEDITION ————

Colt Revolver
Patented
●
25 FEB

Development Photography
●
JAN

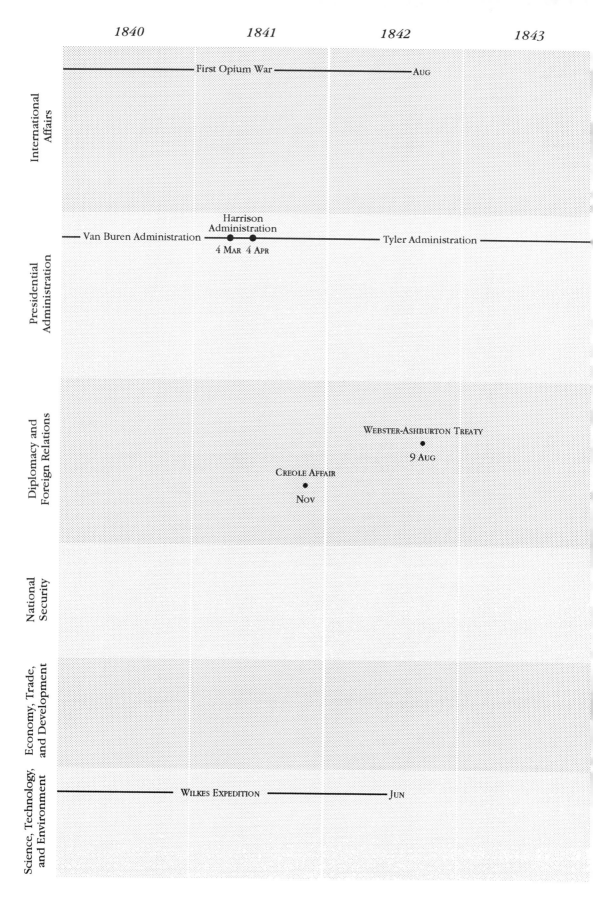

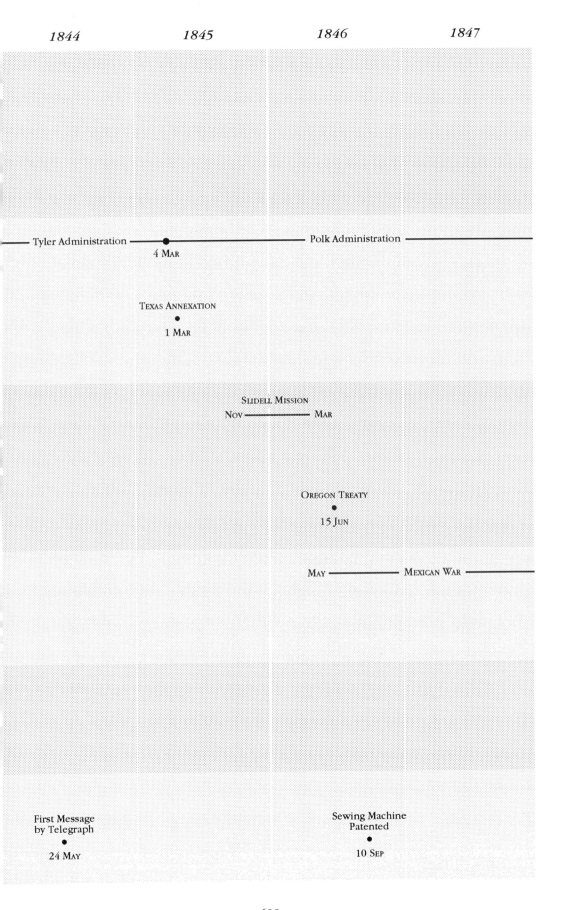

1844   1845   1846   1847

Tyler Administration ——————— ● ————————— Polk Administration ———————
                               4 Mar

Texas Annexation
                ●
             1 Mar

Slidell Mission
Nov ——————— Mar

Oregon Treaty
                ●
             15 Jun

May ——————— Mexican War ———————

First Message   Sewing Machine
by Telegraph   Patented
     ●   ●
 24 May   10 Sep

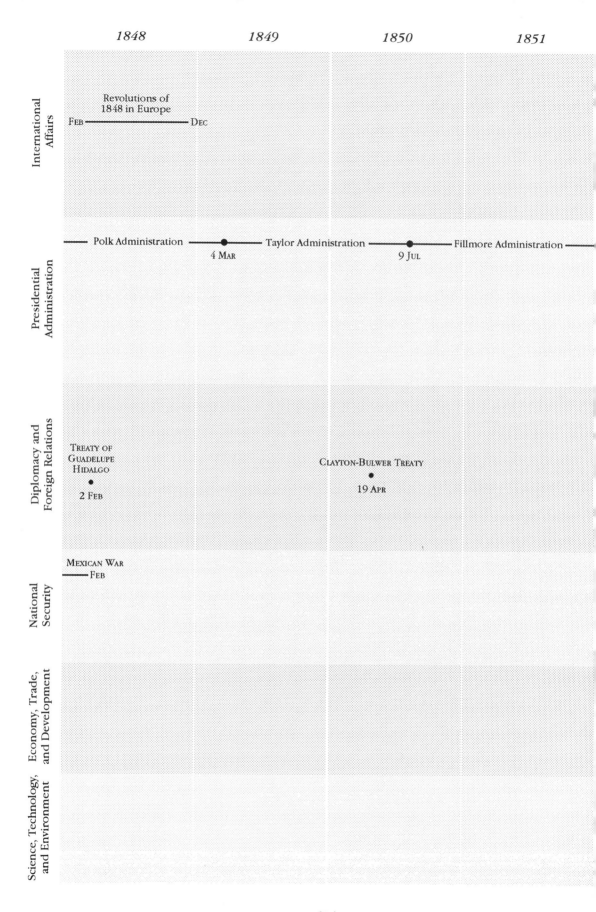

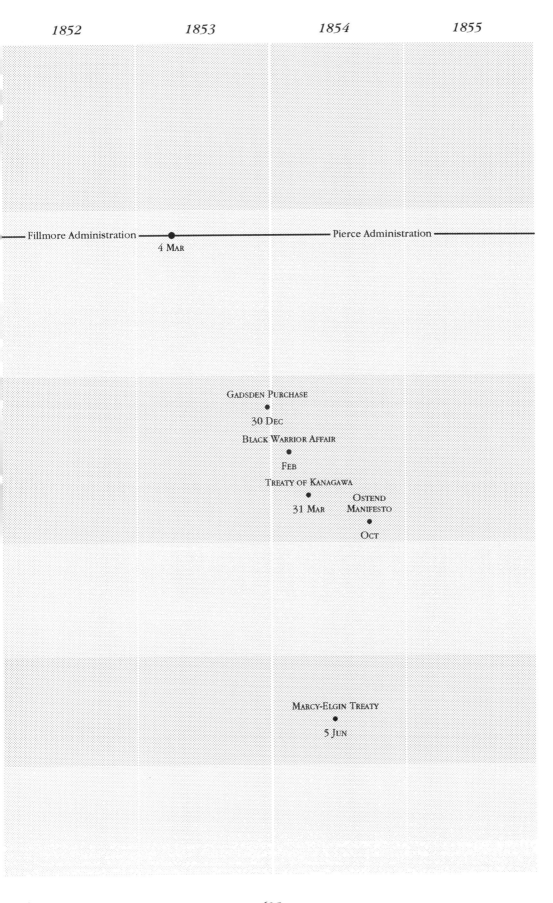

1852   1853   1854   1855

Fillmore Administration ——●—— Pierce Administration ——
4 MAR

GADSDEN PURCHASE
●
30 DEC

BLACK WARRIOR AFFAIR
●
FEB

TREATY OF KANAGAWA
●
31 MAR

OSTEND
MANIFESTO
●
OCT

MARCY-ELGIN TREATY
●
5 JUN

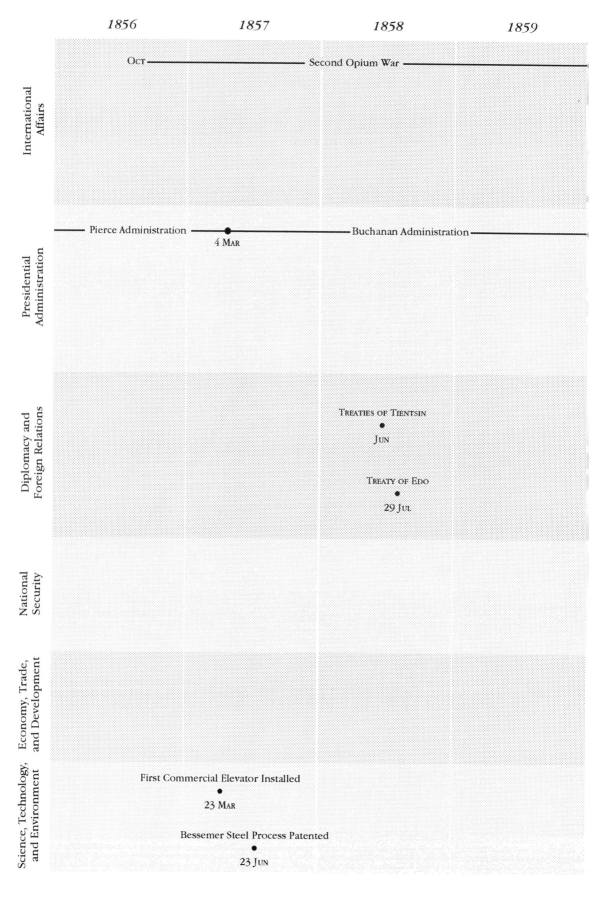

Second Opium War
———————————— Oct   Dec ———————— French Intervention in Mexico ————

—— Buchanan Administration ———●————————— Lincoln Administration ————
4 Mar

TRENT AFFAIR
●
8 Nov

AFRICAN SLAVE TRADE TREATY
●
7 Apr

Apr ————————————— Civil War ————

MORRILL TARIFF
●
2 Mar

Monitor and Merrimack,
First Ironclad Warships
●
9 Mar   First
Machine Gun
●
Nov

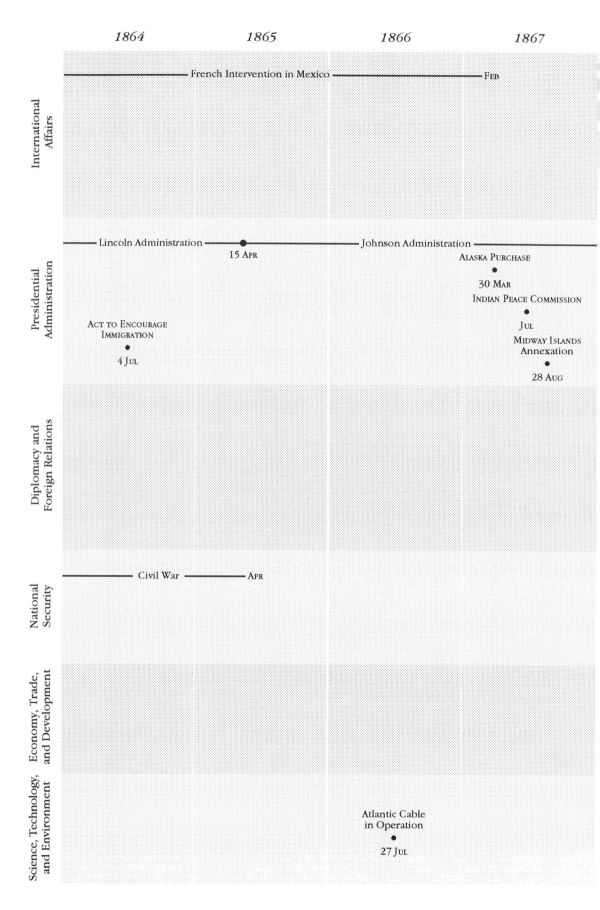

1864 1865 1866 1867

International Affairs

French Intervention in Mexico — Feb

Presidential Administration

Lincoln Administration — 15 Apr — Johnson Administration

Alaska Purchase
30 Mar

Indian Peace Commission
Jul

Act to Encourage Immigration
4 Jul

Midway Islands Annexation
28 Aug

Diplomacy and Foreign Relations

National Security

Civil War — Apr

Economy, Trade, and Development

Science, Technology, and Environment

Atlantic Cable in Operation
27 Jul

Jul — Franco-Prussian War — May

● Meiji Restoration
Jan

Oct———————————————— Ten Years' War ——————————————

———— Johnson Administration ————●———————— Grant Administration ————————
4 Mar

Low-Rogers Expedition
●
May

Burlingame Treaty
●
28 Jul

Treaty of Washington
●
8 May

Transcontinental
Railway Completed
●
10 May

Suez Canal
Opened
●
17 Nov

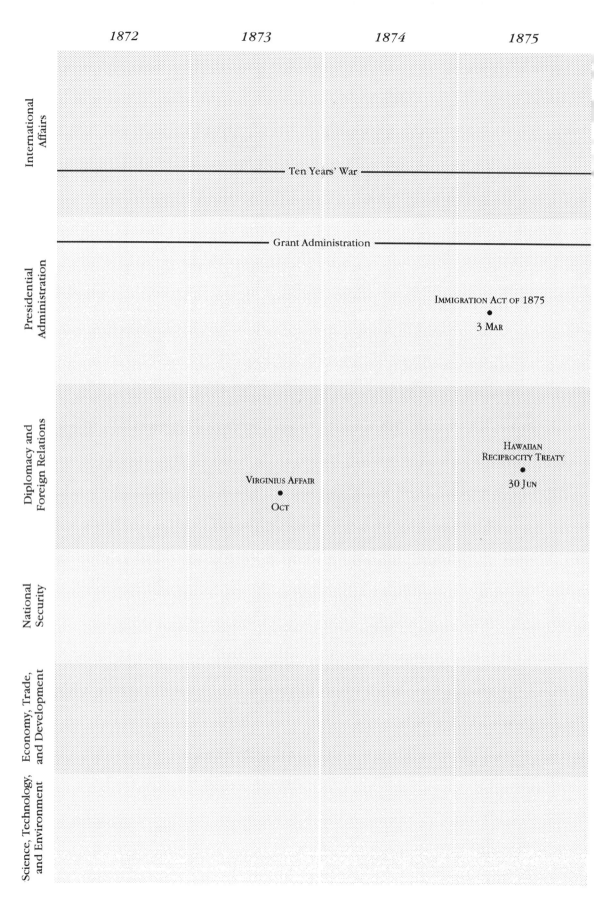

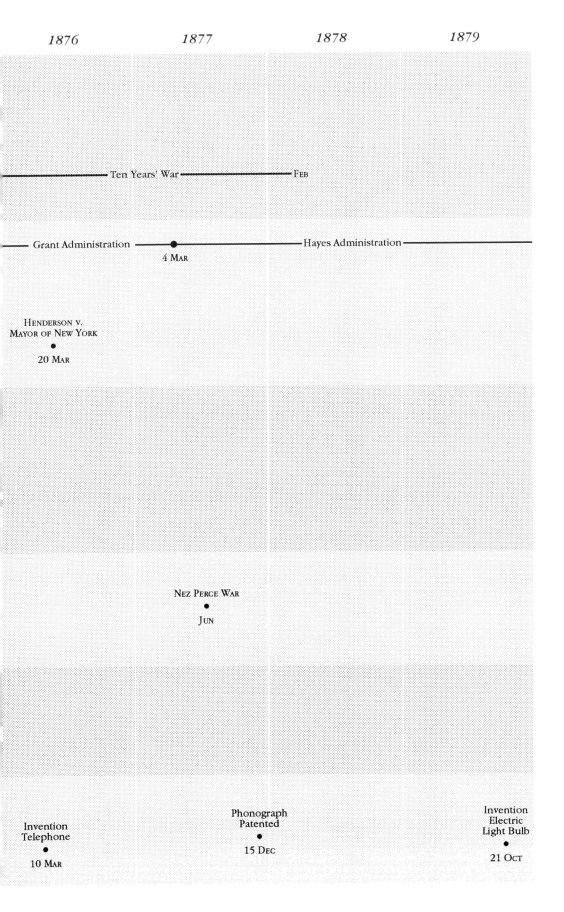

Ten Years' War ———————————— Feb

Grant Administration ———●——— Hayes Administration —————
4 Mar

Henderson v.
Mayor of New York
●
20 Mar

Nez Perce War
●
Jun

Phonograph
Patented
●
15 Dec

Invention
Telephone
●
10 Mar

Invention
Electric
Light Bulb
●
21 Oct

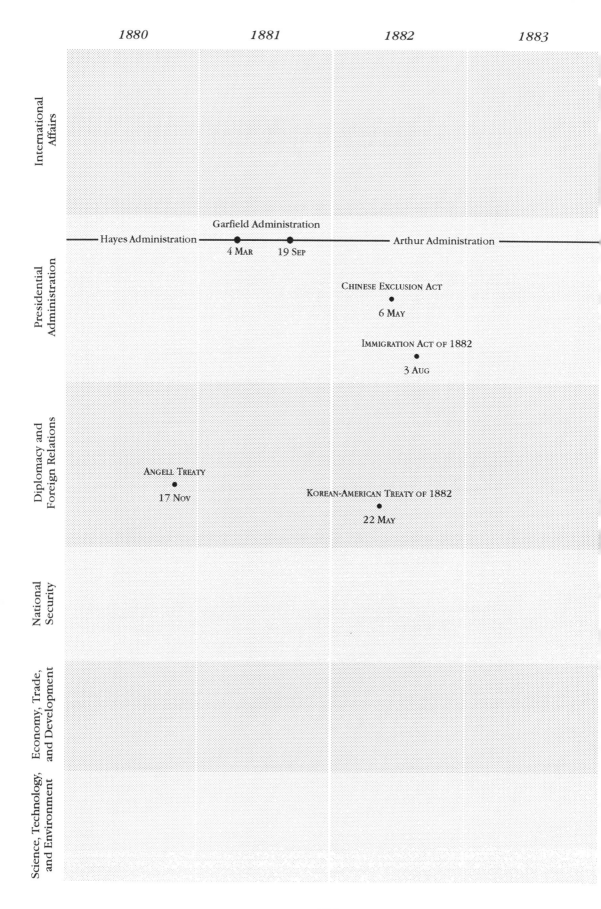

	1880	1881	1882	1883

International Affairs

Garfield Administration

Hayes Administration ● ● Arthur Administration
4 MAR 19 SEP

Presidential Administration

CHINESE EXCLUSION ACT
●
6 MAY

IMMIGRATION ACT OF 1882
●
3 AUG

Diplomacy and Foreign Relations

ANGELL TREATY
●
17 NOV

KOREAN-AMERICAN TREATY OF 1882
●
22 MAY

National Security

Economy, Trade, and Development

Science, Technology, and Environment

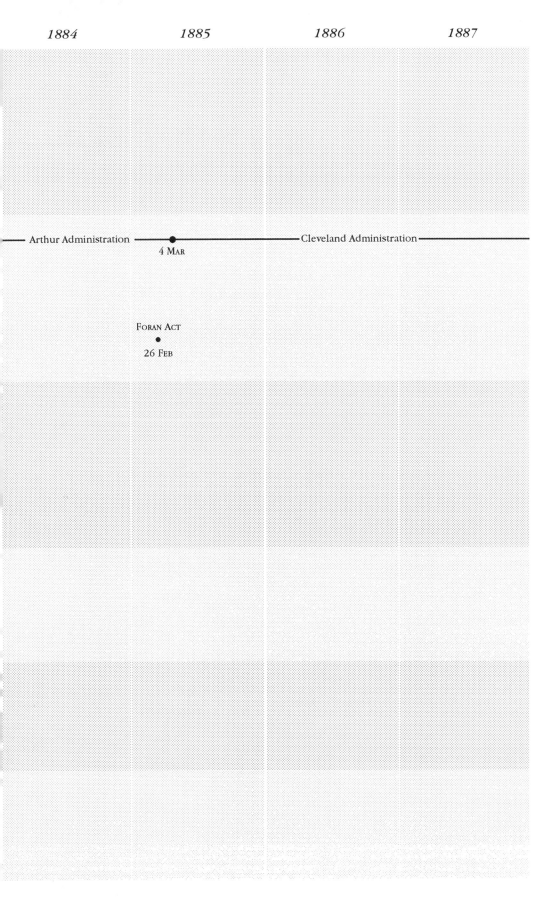

1884   1885   1886   1887

Arthur Administration 4 Mar Cleveland Administration

Foran Act
26 Feb

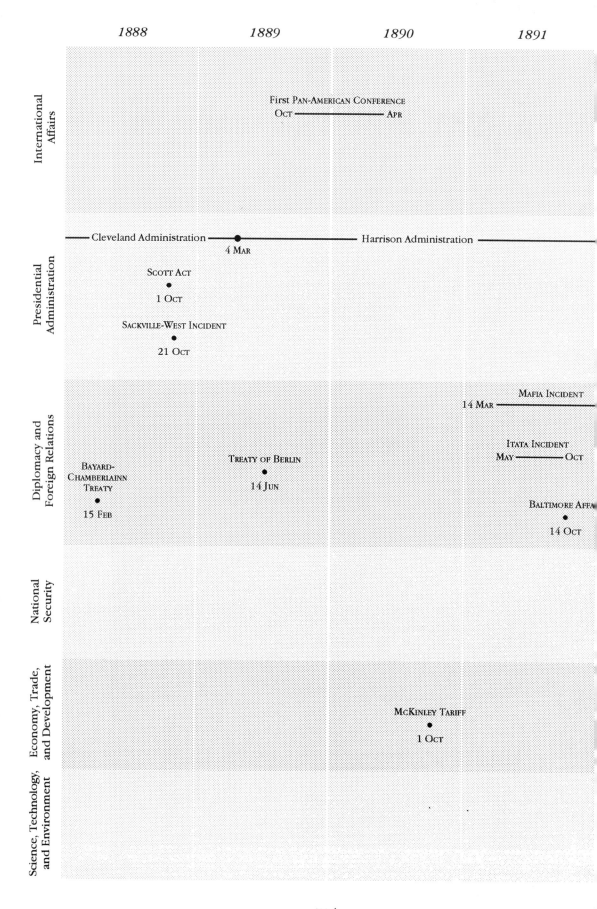

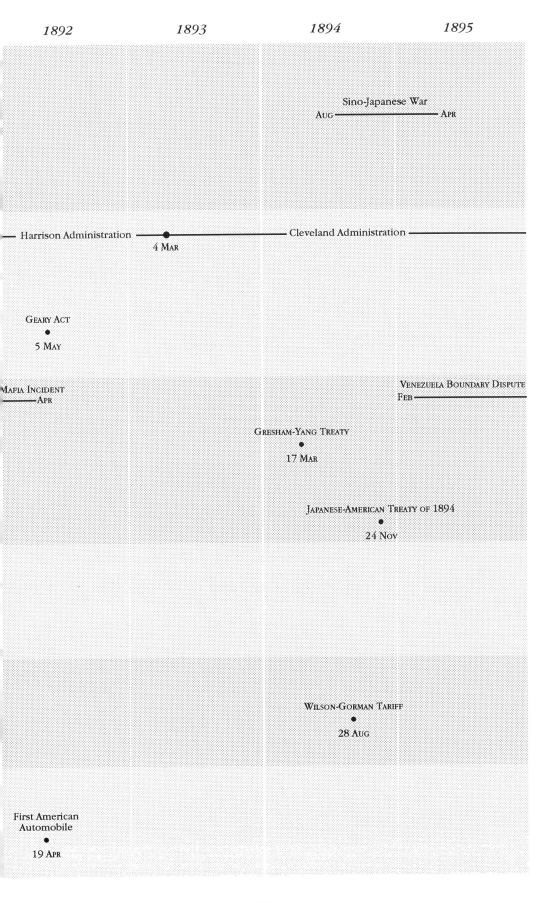

1892   1893   1894   1895

Sino-Japanese War
Aug——————————————Apr

Harrison Administration ———●——————— Cleveland Administration ———
4 Mar

Geary Act
●
5 May

Mafia Incident
——Apr

Venezuela Boundary Dispute
Feb——————————

Gresham-Yang Treaty
●
17 Mar

Japanese-American Treaty of 1894
●
24 Nov

Wilson-Gorman Tariff
●
28 Aug

First American
Automobile
●
19 Apr

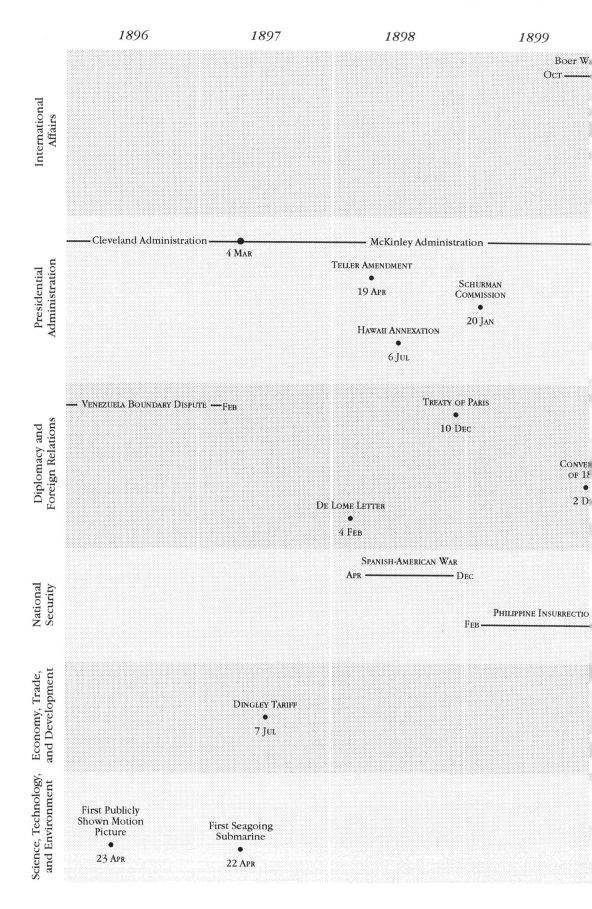

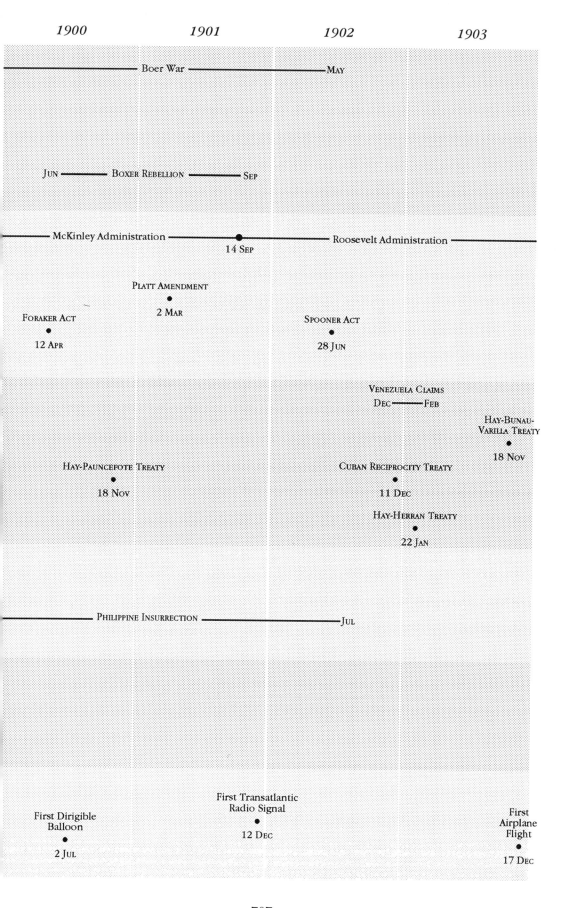

1900 1901 1902 1903

Boer War — MAY

JUN — BOXER REBELLION — SEP

McKinley Administration — 14 SEP — Roosevelt Administration

PLATT AMENDMENT
2 MAR

FORAKER ACT
12 APR

SPOONER ACT
28 JUN

VENEZUELA CLAIMS
DEC — FEB

HAY-BUNAU-
VARILLA TREATY
18 NOV

HAY-PAUNCEFOTE TREATY
18 NOV

CUBAN RECIPROCITY TREATY
11 DEC

HAY-HERRAN TREATY
22 JAN

PHILIPPINE INSURRECTION — JUL

First Transatlantic
Radio Signal
12 DEC

First Dirigible
Balloon
2 JUL

First
Airplane
Flight
17 DEC

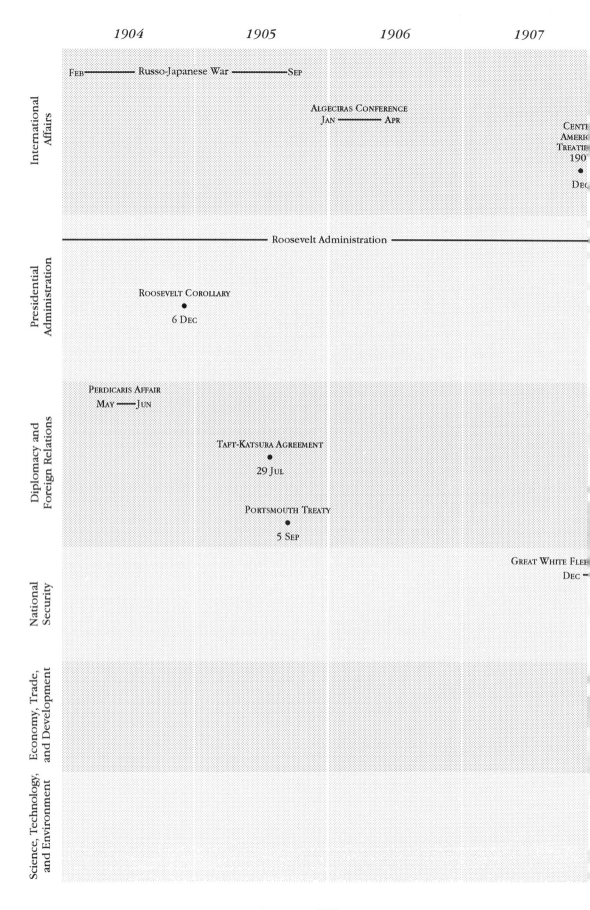

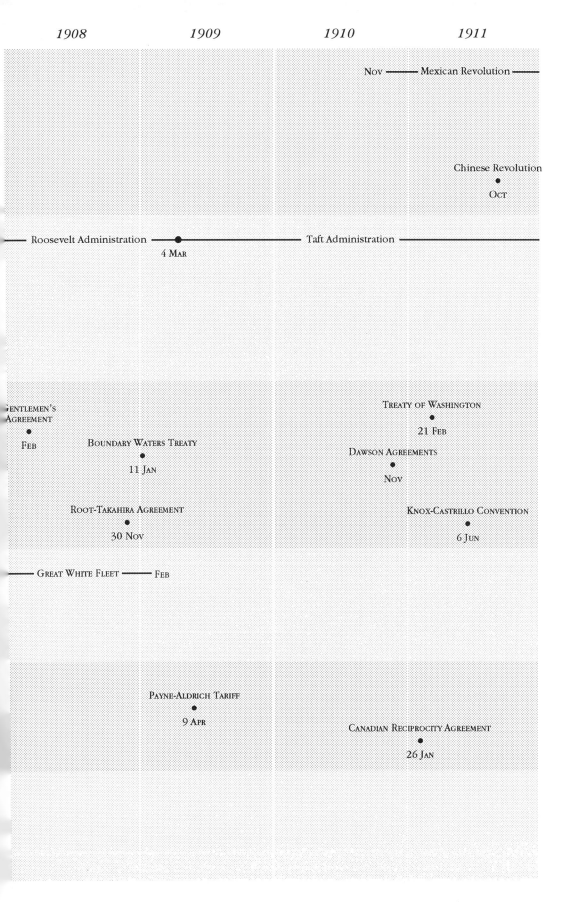

1908   1909   1910   1911

Nov ——— Mexican Revolution ———

Chinese Revolution
●
Oct

— Roosevelt Administration ——●—— Taft Administration ———
4 Mar

Gentlemen's
Agreement
●
Feb

Treaty of Washington
●
21 Feb

Boundary Waters Treaty
●
11 Jan

Dawson Agreements
●
Nov

Root-Takahira Agreement
●
30 Nov

Knox-Castrillo Convention
●
6 Jun

— Great White Fleet ——— Feb

Payne-Aldrich Tariff
●
9 Apr

Canadian Reciprocity Agreement
●
26 Jan

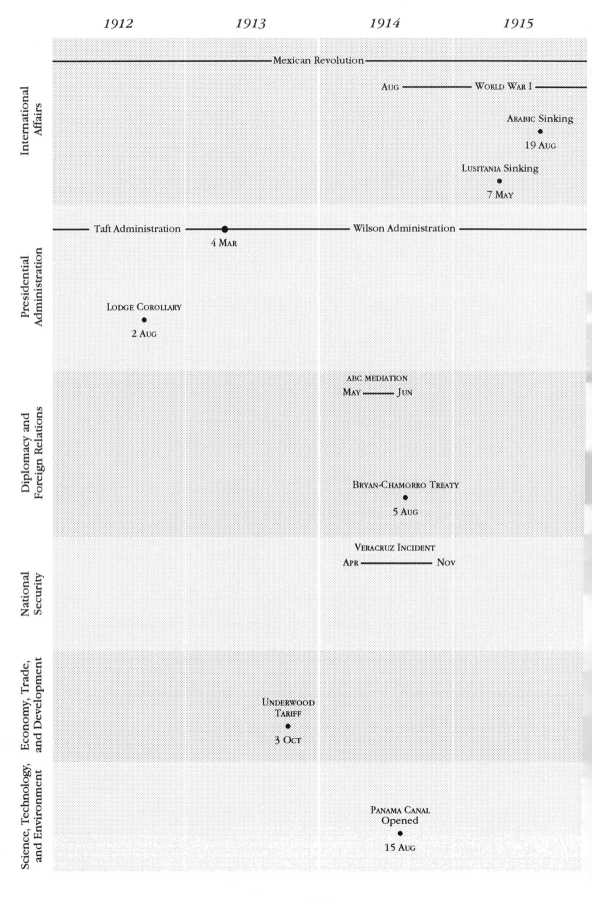

———————————— Mexican Revolution ————————————

———————— World War I ———————— Nov

Zimmerman Telegram

17 Jan

Paris Peace Conference
Jan ————— Jun

Sussex Sinking

24 Mar

Russian Revolution

Nov

Treaty of Versailles

28 Jun

———————— Wilson Administration ————————

Danish West Indies Acquisition

4 Aug

"Peace Without
Victory" Speech

22 Jan

Fourteen Points

8 Jan

Immigration Act
of 1917

5 Feb

House-Grey
Memorandum

22 Feb

Lansing-Ishii Agreement

2 Nov

Lodge
Reservations

Sep

Gore-McLemore
Resolutions

Feb

Round Robin

4 Mar

Sedition Act

16 May

Siberian Intervention
Aug ————

Mar —— Punitive Expedition —— Feb

American Entry World War I

6 Apr

Espionage Act

15 Jun

Anarchist Act

16 Oct

Webb-Pomerene Act

10 Apr

American Relief
Administration

2 Mar

Trading with the Enemy Act

6 Oct

Introduction Tank in Battle

15 Sep

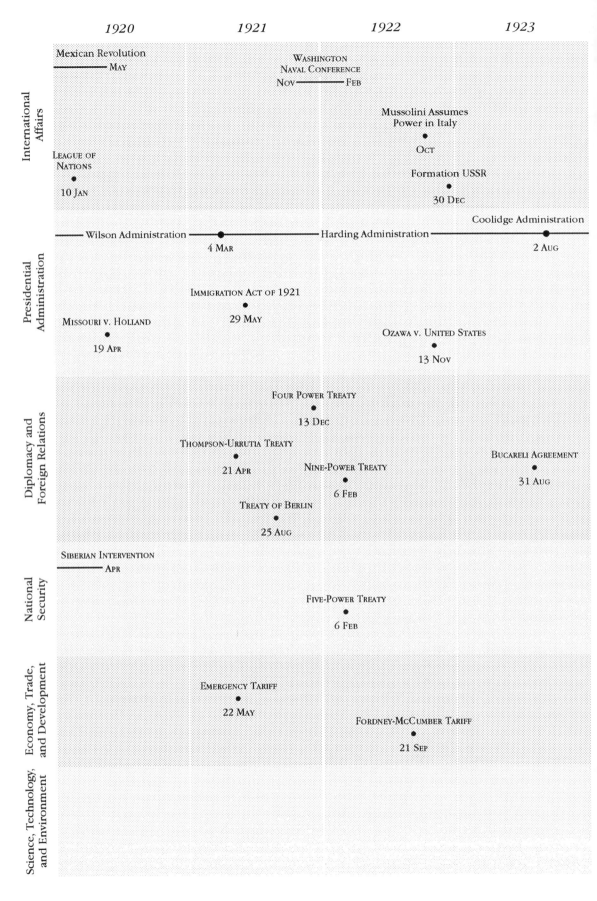

International Affairs

Mexican Revolution
—————— MAY

WASHINGTON
NAVAL CONFERENCE
NOV ——————— FEB

Mussolini Assumes
Power in Italy
●
OCT

LEAGUE OF
NATIONS
●
10 JAN

Formation USSR
●
30 DEC

Presidential Administration

Coolidge Administration
●
——— Wilson Administration ———●——————— Harding Administration ———————●
4 MAR   Harding Administration   2 AUG

IMMIGRATION ACT OF 1921
●
29 MAY

MISSOURI v. HOLLAND
●
19 APR

OZAWA v. UNITED STATES
●
13 NOV

Diplomacy and Foreign Relations

FOUR POWER TREATY
●
13 DEC

THOMPSON-URRUTIA TREATY
●
21 APR

NINE-POWER TREATY
●
6 FEB

BUCARELI AGREEMENT
●
31 AUG

TREATY OF BERLIN
●
25 AUG

National Security

SIBERIAN INTERVENTION
—————— APR

FIVE-POWER TREATY
●
6 FEB

Economy, Trade, and Development

EMERGENCY TARIFF
●
22 MAY

FORDNEY-MCCUMBER TARIFF
●
21 SEP

Science, Technology, and Environment

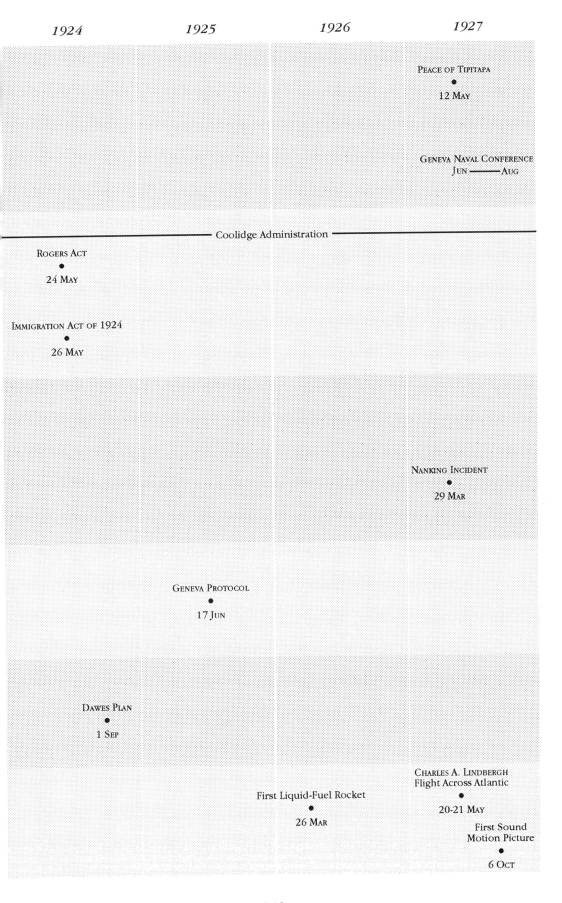

1924   1925   1926   1927

PEACE OF TIPITAPA
●
12 MAY

GENEVA NAVAL CONFERENCE
JUN ———— AUG

———————— Coolidge Administration ————————

ROGERS ACT
●
24 MAY

IMMIGRATION ACT OF 1924
●
26 MAY

NANKING INCIDENT
●
29 MAR

GENEVA PROTOCOL
●
17 JUN

DAWES PLAN
●
1 SEP

CHARLES A. LINDBERGH
Flight Across Atlantic
●
20-21 MAY

First Liquid-Fuel Rocket
●
26 MAR

First Sound
Motion Picture
●
6 OCT

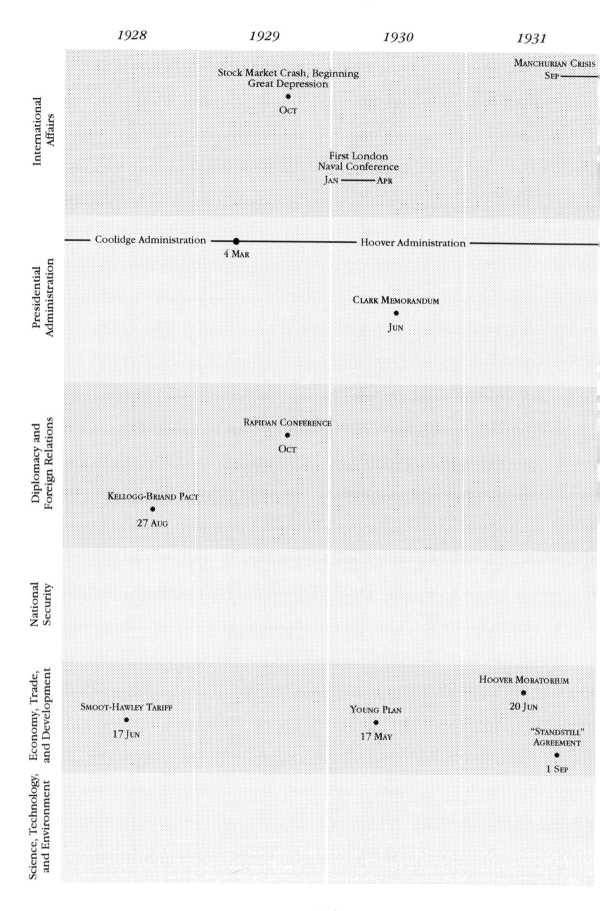

1928 1929 1930 1931

International Affairs

Stock Market Crash, Beginning Great Depression
Ocт

Manchurian Crisis
Sep

First London Naval Conference
Jan ——— Apr

Presidential Administration

Coolidge Administration ——●—— Hoover Administration
4 Mar

Clark Memorandum
Jun

Diplomacy and Foreign Relations

Rapidan Conference
Ocт

Kellogg-Briand Pact
27 Aug

National Security

Economy, Trade, and Development

Hoover Moratorium
20 Jun

Smoot-Hawley Tariff
17 Jun

Young Plan
17 May

"Standstill" Agreement
1 Sep

Science, Technology, and Environment

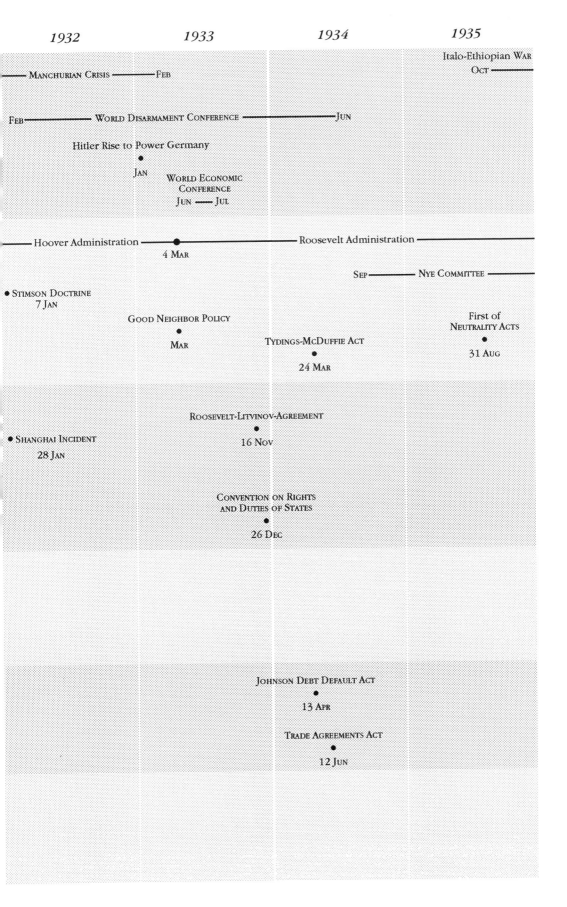

1932   1933   1934   1935

Italo-Ethiopian War
Oct

— Manchurian Crisis ——— Feb

Feb ———— World Disarmament Conference ———— Jun

Hitler Rise to Power Germany
●
Jan

World Economic
Conference
Jun —— Jul

— Hoover Administration ——●—— Roosevelt Administration ——
4 Mar

Sep ——— Nye Committee ——

● Stimson Doctrine
7 Jan

Good Neighbor Policy
●
Mar

First of
Neutrality Acts
●
31 Aug

Tydings-McDuffie Act
●
24 Mar

Roosevelt-Litvinov-Agreement
●
16 Nov

● Shanghai Incident
28 Jan

Convention on Rights
and Duties of States
●
26 Dec

Johnson Debt Default Act
●
13 Apr

Trade Agreements Act
●
12 Jun

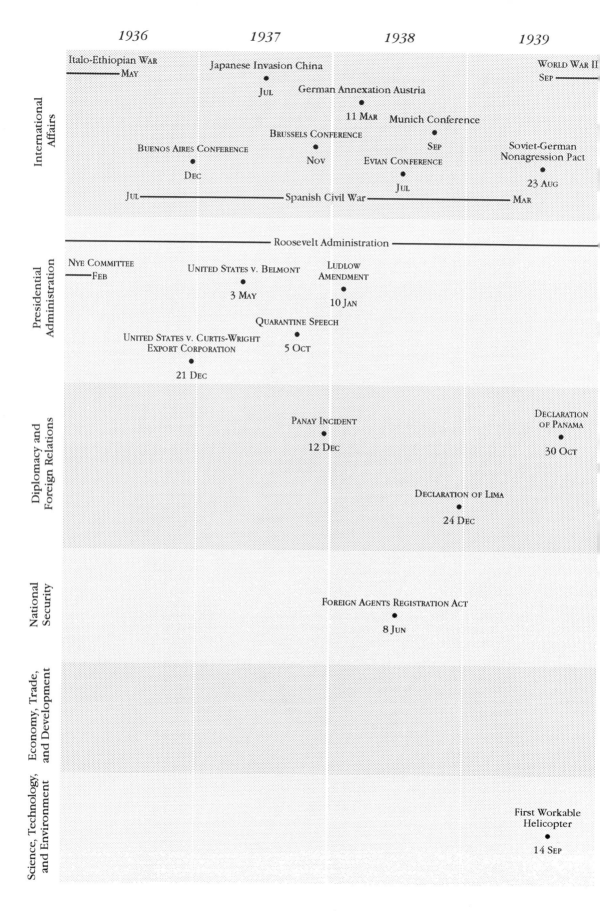

1936   1937   1938   1939

International Affairs

Italo-Ethiopian War
— May

Japanese Invasion China
Jul

German Annexation Austria
11 Mar

World War II
Sep —

Munich Conference
Sep

Brussels Conference
Nov

Buenos Aires Conference
Dec

Evian Conference
Jul

Soviet-German Nonagression Pact
23 Aug

Jul — Spanish Civil War — Mar

— Roosevelt Administration —

Presidential Administration

Nye Committee
— Feb

United States v. Belmont
3 May

Ludlow Amendment
10 Jan

Quarantine Speech
5 Oct

United States v. Curtis-Wright Export Corporation
21 Dec

Diplomacy and Foreign Relations

Panay Incident
12 Dec

Declaration of Panama
30 Oct

Declaration of Lima
24 Dec

National Security

Foreign Agents Registration Act
8 Jun

Economy, Trade, and Development

Science, Technology, and Environment

First Workable Helicopter
14 Sep

——————— WORLD WAR II ———————

MOSCOW CONFERENCE
•
OCT

UNITED NATIONS DECLARATION
•
1 JAN

TEHERAN CONFERENCE
NOV DEC

RIO DE JANEIRO CONFERENCE
•
JAN

——————— Roosevelt Administration ———————

LEND-LEASE
•
11 MAR

CONNALLY RESOLUTION
•
5 NOV

DESTROYERS-FOR-BASES AGREEMENT
•
3 SEP

OGDENSBURG CONFERENCE
•
18 AUG

ATLANTIC CHARTER
•
14 AUG

ACT OF HAVANA
•
30 JUL

GREER INCIDENT
•
11 SEP

ALIEN REGISTRATION ACT
•
28 JUN

PEARL HARBOR
•
7 DEC

MANHATTAN PROJECT
•
AUG

First Nuclear Reactor
•
2 DEC

First Jet Airplane
•
MAY

First Guided Missile
•
24 DEC

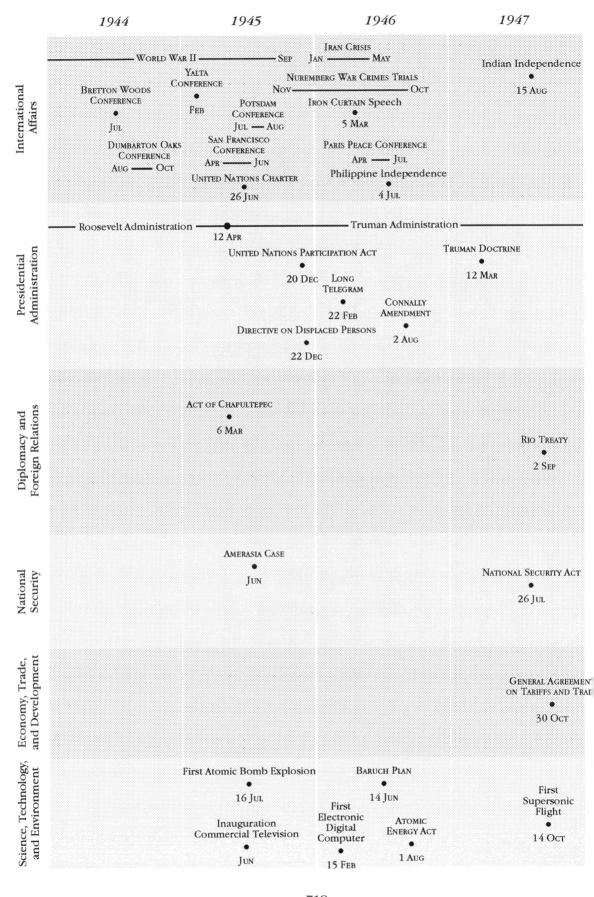

	1944	1945	1946	1947

International Affairs

WORLD WAR II ——————— SEP

IRAN CRISIS
JAN ————— MAY

Indian Independence
15 AUG

YALTA CONFERENCE
FEB

NUREMBERG WAR CRIMES TRIALS
NOV ————————— OCT

BRETTON WOODS CONFERENCE
JUL

POTSDAM CONFERENCE
JUL —— AUG

IRON CURTAIN Speech
5 MAR

DUMBARTON OAKS CONFERENCE
AUG ——— OCT

SAN FRANCISCO CONFERENCE
APR ——— JUN

PARIS PEACE CONFERENCE
APR —— JUL

UNITED NATIONS CHARTER
26 JUN

Philippine Independence
4 JUL

Presidential Administration

Roosevelt Administration ——————●————— Truman Administration ——————
12 APR

UNITED NATIONS PARTICIPATION ACT
20 DEC

TRUMAN DOCTRINE
12 MAR

LONG TELEGRAM
22 FEB

CONNALLY AMENDMENT
2 AUG

DIRECTIVE ON DISPLACED PERSONS
22 DEC

Diplomacy and Foreign Relations

ACT OF CHAPULTEPEC
6 MAR

RIO TREATY
2 SEP

National Security

AMERASIA CASE
JUN

NATIONAL SECURITY ACT
26 JUL

Economy, Trade, and Development

GENERAL AGREEMENT ON TARIFFS AND TRADE
30 OCT

Science, Technology, and Environment

First Atomic Bomb Explosion
16 JUL

BARUCH PLAN
14 JUN

First Supersonic Flight
14 OCT

Inauguration Commercial Television
JUN

First Electronic Digital Computer
15 FEB

ATOMIC ENERGY ACT
1 AUG

718

JUN ———— BERLIN AIRLIFT ————MAY   JUN ———————— KOREAN WAR —————

Israeli Statehood
Proclaimed
●
14 MAY   UNIVERSAL   People's Republic
         DECLARATION OF   of China Proclaimed
         HUMAN RIGHTS   ●

SIX–NATION   ●   1 OCT
CONFERENCE ON   10 DEC
GERMANY
FEB ————————JUN

——————————————— Truman Administration ———————————————

                CHINA WHITE PAPER
                   ●
DISPLACED PERSONS ACT   6 AUG
●
25 JUN

GENOCIDE TREATY
●
9 DEC   TRIPARTITE DECLARATION
                   ●
                MAY   JAPANESE PEACE
                                      TREATY
GENEVA CONVENTIONS   ●
●
12 AUG   8 SEP

KEY WEST AGREEMENT   NATO Formed   GREAT DEBATE   ANZUS
●   NSC–68   JAN ———— APR   TREATY
MAR   ●   ●   ●
VANDENBERG RESOLUTION   4 APR   APR   1 SEP
●   PHILIPPINE MUTUAL DEFENSE TREATY ●
11 JUN   NATIONAL SECURITY ACT   30 AUG
      AMENDMENTS OF 1949   JAPANESE SECURITY TREATY ●
HISS CASE   ●   INTERNAL SECURITY ACT ●   8 SEP
●   10 AUG   23 SEP   MUTUAL SECURITY ACT ●
AUG   1 OCT

POINT FOUR
●
MARSHALL PLAN   20 JAN
●
APR

Development
Transistor
●
JUL

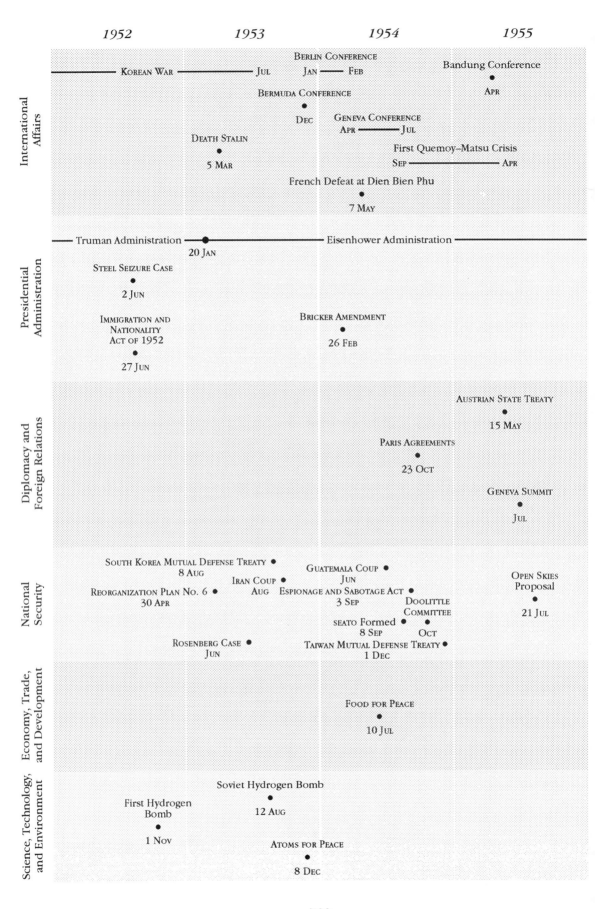

	1952	1953	1954	1955

International Affairs

BERLIN CONFERENCE

KOREAN WAR ——— JUL JAN —— FEB

Bandung Conference

APR

BERMUDA CONFERENCE

DEC GENEVA CONFERENCE

APR ——— JUL

DEATH STALIN

First Quemoy–Matsu Crisis

SEP ——————— APR

5 MAR

French Defeat at Dien Bien Phu

7 MAY

Presidential Administration

Truman Administration ——— Eisenhower Administration ———

20 JAN

STEEL SEIZURE CASE

2 JUN

IMMIGRATION AND
NATIONALITY
ACT OF 1952

BRICKER AMENDMENT

26 FEB

27 JUN

Diplomacy and Foreign Relations

AUSTRIAN STATE TREATY

15 MAY

PARIS AGREEMENTS

23 OCT

GENEVA SUMMIT

JUL

National Security

SOUTH KOREA MUTUAL DEFENSE TREATY ●
8 AUG

GUATEMALA COUP ●
JUN

OPEN SKIES
Proposal

IRAN COUP ●
AUG ESPIONAGE AND SABOTAGE ACT ●

REORGANIZATION PLAN NO. 6 ●
30 APR

3 SEP DOOLITTLE
COMMITTEE

21 JUL

SEATO Formed ●
8 SEP OCT

ROSENBERG CASE ●
JUN

TAIWAN MUTUAL DEFENSE TREATY ●
1 DEC

Economy, Trade, and Development

FOOD FOR PEACE

10 JUL

Science, Technology, and Environment

Soviet Hydrogen Bomb

First Hydrogen
Bomb

12 AUG

1 NOV

ATOMS FOR PEACE

8 DEC

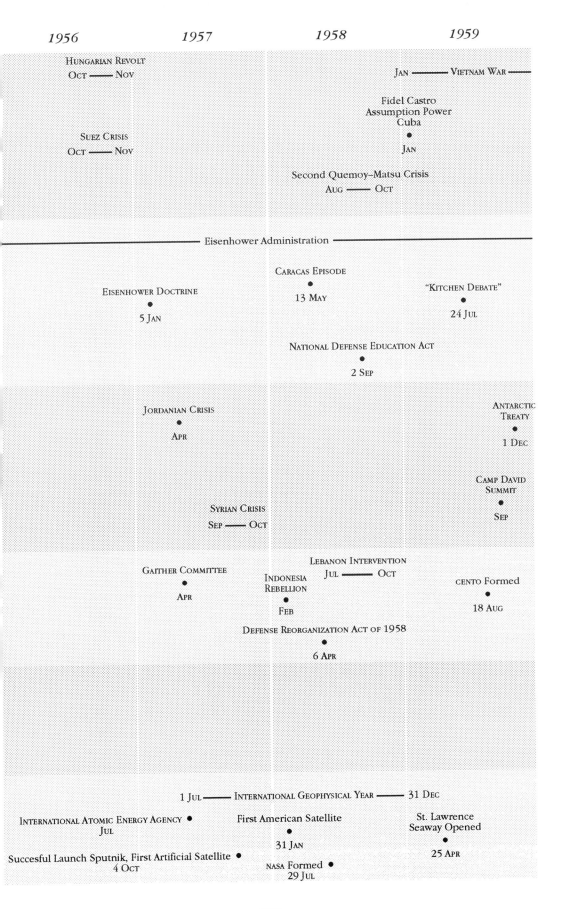

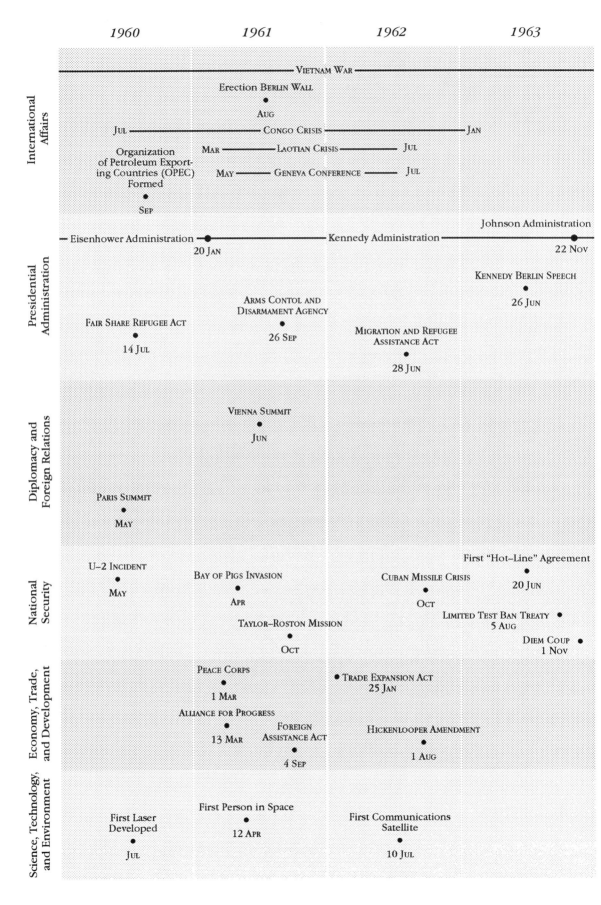

	1960	1961	1962	1963

International Affairs

Vietnam War

Erection Berlin Wall
Aug

Jul ——— Congo Crisis ——— Jan

Mar ——— Laotian Crisis ——— Jul

Organization of Petroleum Exporting Countries (OPEC) Formed
Sep

May ——— Geneva Conference ——— Jul

Presidential Administration

Johnson Administration

— Eisenhower Administration ——— Kennedy Administration ———
20 Jan   22 Nov

Kennedy Berlin Speech
26 Jun

Arms Contol and Disarmament Agency
26 Sep

Fair Share Refugee Act
14 Jul

Migration and Refugee Assistance Act
28 Jun

Diplomacy and Foreign Relations

Vienna Summit
Jun

Paris Summit
May

National Security

U–2 Incident
May

Bay of Pigs Invasion
Apr

First "Hot–Line" Agreement
20 Jun

Cuban Missile Crisis
Oct

Taylor–Roston Mission
Oct

Limited Test Ban Treaty
5 Aug

Diem Coup
1 Nov

Economy, Trade, and Development

Peace Corps
1 Mar

Trade Expansion Act
25 Jan

Alliance for Progress
13 Mar

Foreign Assistance Act
4 Sep

Hickenlooper Amendment
1 Aug

Science, Technology, and Environment

First Laser Developed
Jul

First Person in Space
12 Apr

First Communications Satellite
10 Jul

1964	1965	1966	1967

──────────────── Vietnam War ────────────────

Arab–Israeli
Six–Day War
•
Jun

──────────────── Johnson Administration ────────────────

Johnson Doctrine
•
2 May

San Antonio
Formula
•
29 Sep

Tonkin Gulf Resolution
•
7 Aug

Immigration Act of 1965
•
3 Oct

Panama
Riots
•
Jan

Glassboro Summit
•
Jun

Treaty of
Tlatelolco
•
14 Feb

Apr ──────── Dominican Crisis ──────── Sep

Tonkin Gulf Incident
•
Aug

Liberty Incident
•
8 Jun

Outer Space Treaty
•
27 Jan

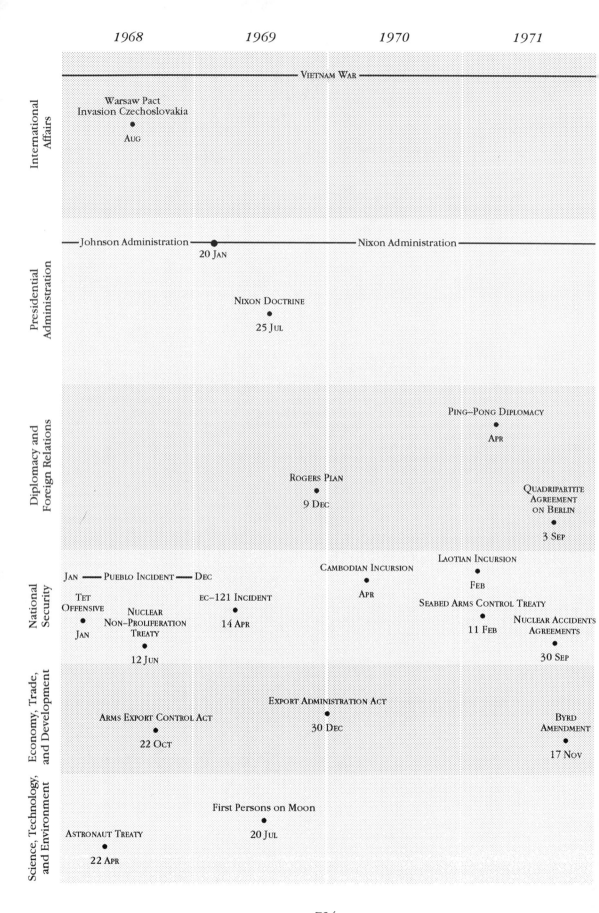

	1968	1969	1970	1971

International Affairs

VIETNAM WAR

Warsaw Pact
Invasion Czechoslovakia
AUG

Presidential Administration

Johnson Administration ——●—— Nixon Administration
20 JAN

NIXON DOCTRINE
25 JUL

Diplomacy and Foreign Relations

PING–PONG DIPLOMACY
APR

ROGERS PLAN
9 DEC

QUADRIPARTITE
AGREEMENT
ON BERLIN
3 SEP

National Security

LAOTIAN INCURSION
FEB

CAMBODIAN INCURSION
APR

JAN —— PUEBLO INCIDENT —— DEC

TET
OFFENSIVE
JAN

EC–121 INCIDENT
14 APR

SEABED ARMS CONTROL TREATY
11 FEB

NUCLEAR
NON–PROLIFERATION
TREATY
12 JUN

NUCLEAR ACCIDENTS
AGREEMENTS
30 SEP

Economy, Trade, and Development

EXPORT ADMINISTRATION ACT
30 DEC

ARMS EXPORT CONTROL ACT
22 OCT

BYRD
AMENDMENT
17 NOV

Science, Technology, and Environment

First Persons on Moon
20 JUL

ASTRONAUT TREATY
22 APR

724

VIETNAM WAR ——————————————— APR

Opening CSCE ●
JUN

YOM KIPPUR WAR
●
OCT

ARAB OIL EMBARGO
OCT —————— MAR

GENEVA CONFERENCE ON THE MIDDLE EAST ●
DEC

———— Nixon Administration ———————— ● ———— Ford Administration ————
9 AUG

CASE ACT
●
22 AUG

INDOCHINA MIGRATION AND
REFUGEE ASSISTANCE ACT
●
23 MAY

FORD
DOCTRINE

WAR POWERS RESOLUTION
●
7 NOV

●
7 DEC

PEKING
SUMMIT
●
FEB

PARIS PEACE ACCORDS
●
27 JAN

JAN ——————— SHUTTLE DIPLOMACY ——————— SEP

MOSCOW SUMMIT
●
JUN–JUL

HELSINKI
ACCORDS

SHANGHAI
COMMUNIQUE
●
27 FEB

●
1 AUG

WASHINGTON SUMMIT
●
JUN

VLADIVOSTOK SUMMIT
●
NOV

PEKING
SUMMIT
●
DEC

MOSCOW
SUMMIT
●
MAY

● EASTERTIDE OFFENSIVE
20 MAR

PREVENTION OF NUCLEAR
WAR AGREEMENT
●
22 JUN

THRESHOLD TEST
BAN TREATY
●
3 JUL

MAYAGUEZ INCIDENT
●
12 MAY

● BIOLOGICAL WEAPONS
CONVENTION
12 APR

CHILE
COUP
●
11 SEP

HUGHES–RYAN AMMENDMENT
●
30 DEC

● SALT I
26 MAY

JACKSON–VANIK AMENDMENT ●
20 DEC

TRADE ACT OF 1974
●
3 JAN

HARKIN
AMMENDMENT
●
9 DEC

CITES ●
3 MAR

INTERVENTION ON
THE HIGH SEAS ACT
●
5 FEB

REGISTRATION OF
SPACE OBJECTS TREATY
●
14 JAN

LIABILITY FOR DAMAGE
CAUSED BY SPACE OBJECTS
CONVENTION
●
29 MAR

U.S. Skylab Launched ●
14 MAY

APOLLO–SOYUZ
●
15 JUL

MARPOL CONVENTION ●
2 NOV

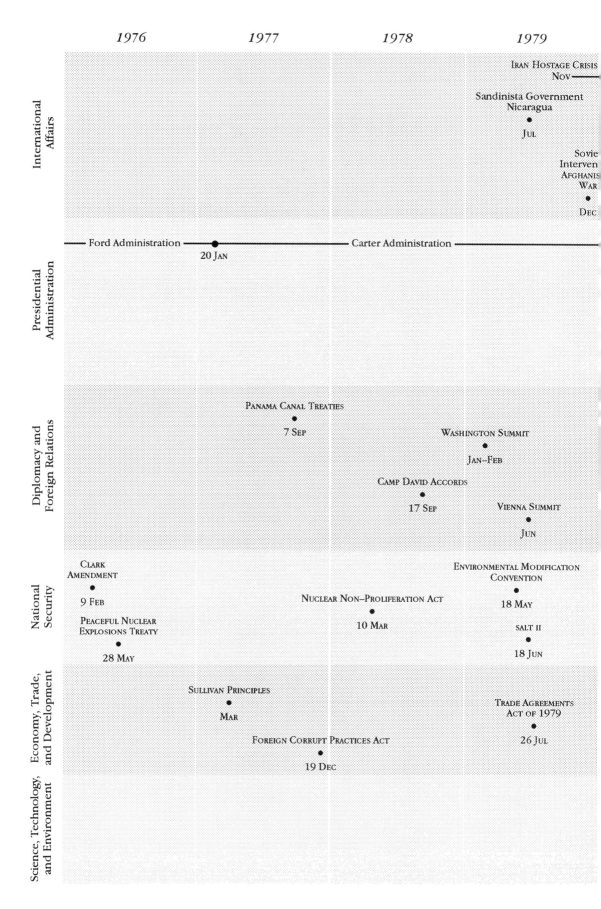

1976   1977   1978   1979

International Affairs

IRAN HOSTAGE CRISIS
NOV ——

Sandinista Government
Nicaragua
•
JUL

Sovie
Interven
AFGHANIS
WAR
•
DEC

Presidential Administration

—— Ford Administration ——●—— Carter Administration ——
20 JAN

Diplomacy and Foreign Relations

PANAMA CANAL TREATIES
•
7 SEP

WASHINGTON SUMMIT
•
JAN–FEB

CAMP DAVID ACCORDS
•
17 SEP

VIENNA SUMMIT
•
JUN

National Security

CLARK
AMENDMENT
•
9 FEB

PEACEFUL NUCLEAR
EXPLOSIONS TREATY
•
28 MAY

NUCLEAR NON–PROLIFERATION ACT
•
10 MAR

ENVIRONMENTAL MODIFICATION
CONVENTION
18 MAY

SALT II
•
18 JUN

Economy, Trade, and Development

SULLIVAN PRINCIPLES
•
MAR

FOREIGN CORRUPT PRACTICES ACT
•
19 DEC

TRADE AGREEMENTS
ACT OF 1979
•
26 JUL

Science, Technology, and Environment

Iran Hostage Crisis ———— Jan   Jun ———— Lebanon Crisis ————

Martial Law Poland
•
Dec

Olympic Boycott
Jul —— Aug

KAL FLIGHT 007
•
1 Sep

Falklands War
Apr ——— Jun

— Carter Administration ————•———————— Reagan Administration ————
20 Jan

Linowitz Report
•
7 Apr

Carter
Doctrine
•
23 Jan

El Salvador White Paper
•
23 Feb

Reagan Plan
•
1 Sep

Refugee Act of 1980
•
17 Mar

Nuclear Material
Convention
•
3 Mar

U.S. Support contras
•
Dec

Grenada Invasion
Oct ——— Dec

SDI
•
23 Mar

Inhumane Weapons Convention
•
10 Oct

Scowcroft Commission Report
•
11 Apr

Caribbean Basin Initiative
•
24 Feb

Cancun Summit
•
Oct

Export Trading Company Act
•
8 Oct

Maiden Launch
U.S. Space Shuttle
•
12 Apr

	1984	1985	1986	1987

International Affairs

LEBANON CRISIS
—MAR

PHILIPPINE CRISIS
●
FEB

GORBACHEV ASSUMPTION
POWER USSR
●
MAR

TWA FLIGHT 847
●
14 JUN

— Reagan Administration —

Presidential Administration

HOSTAGE TAKING ACT
●
12 OCT

IMMIGRATION REFORM
AND CONTROL ACT
●
6 NOV

INMAN REPORT
●
25 JUN

IRAN–CONTRA
●
NOV

Diplomacy and Foreign Relations

● WASHINGTON SUMMIT
JAN

● KISSINGER COMMISSION REPORT
11 JAN

WASHINGTON SUMMIT
●
DEC

GENEVA SUMMIT
●
NOV

BEIJING SUMMIT
●
APR–MAY

TORTURE TREATY
●
10 DEC

REYKJAVIK SUMMIT
●
OCT

National Security

ACHILLE–LAURO AFFAIR ●
7 OCT

STARK INCIDENT
●
17 MAY

LIBYAN BOMBING RAID ●
14 APR

STOCKHOLM DECLARATION ●
19 SEP

PERSIAN GULF INTERVENTION
●
MAY

INF TREAT
●
8 DEC

GOLDWATER–NICHOLS DEFENSIVE REORGANIZATION ACT ●
1 OCT

Economy, Trade, and Development

AFRICAN FAMINE
RELIEF AND RECOVERY
ACT
●
2 APR

PLAZA ACCORD
●
22 SEP

Science, Technology, and Environment

VIENNA CONVENTION FOR THE
PROTECTION OF THE OZONE LAYER
●
22 MAR

DRIFTNET IMPACT MONITORING, ●
ASSESSMENT, AND CONTROL ACT
29 DEC

WHALING MORATORIUM
●
OCT

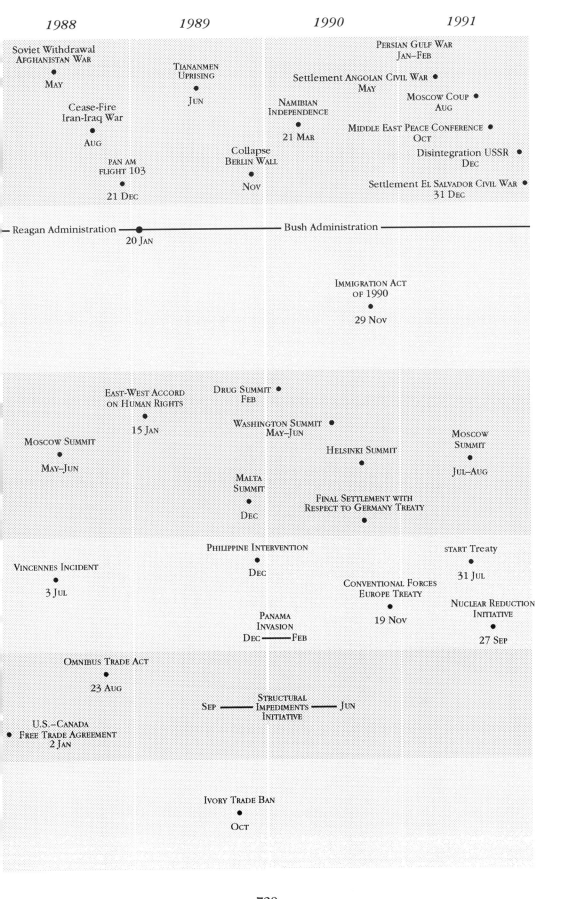

1988 **1989** **1990** **1991**

PERSIAN GULF WAR
JAN–FEB

Soviet Withdrawal
AFGHANISTAN WAR

MAY

Settlement ANGOLAN CIVIL WAR
MAY

TIANANMEN
UPRISING

JUN

MOSCOW COUP
AUG

Cease-Fire
Iran-Iraq War

AUG

NAMIBIAN
INDEPENDENCE

MIDDLE EAST PEACE CONFERENCE
OCT

21 MAR

DISINTEGRATION USSR
DEC

PAN AM
FLIGHT 103

Collapse
BERLIN WALL

21 DEC

NOV

Settlement EL SALVADOR CIVIL WAR
31 DEC

— Reagan Administration —————————————— Bush Administration ——————
20 JAN

IMMIGRATION ACT
OF 1990

29 NOV

EAST-WEST ACCORD
ON HUMAN RIGHTS

DRUG SUMMIT
FEB

15 JAN

WASHINGTON SUMMIT
MAY–JUN

MOSCOW SUMMIT
MAY–JUN

MOSCOW
SUMMIT

HELSINKI SUMMIT

JUL–AUG

MALTA
SUMMIT

FINAL SETTLEMENT WITH
RESPECT TO GERMANY TREATY

DEC

PHILIPPINE INTERVENTION

START Treaty

DEC

31 JUL

VINCENNES INCIDENT

CONVENTIONAL FORCES
EUROPE TREATY

3 JUL

NUCLEAR REDUCTION
INITIATIVE

PANAMA
INVASION

19 NOV

DEC —————— FEB

27 SEP

OMNIBUS TRADE ACT

23 AUG

STRUCTURAL
SEP ——————— IMPEDIMENTS ——————— JUN
INITIATIVE

U.S.–CANADA
FREE TRADE AGREEMENT
2 JAN

IVORY TRADE BAN

OCT

Appendix B

Executive Branch

This appendix contains brief summaries of the key foreign policy departments, offices, and agencies within the executive branch of the U.S. government. Included are comprehensive listings of the individuals who have held the senior position in each organization. Items and persons in SMALL CAPS are separate dictionary entries.

ARMS CONTROL AND DISARMAMENT AGENCY (ACDA) With the onset of the East-West COLD WAR after WORLD WAR II, arms control and disarmament seldom occupied the agenda of senior American policymakers. The Eisenhower administration created the Office of the Special Assistant to the President for Disarmament in 1955, authorizing first director Harold E. Stassen to undertake a complete review of U.S. disarmament policy. But the JOINT CHIEFS OF STAFF and the State Department looked skeptically on bold arms initiatives and

thus curbed the disarmament office's influence.

In the late 1950s Senator Hubert H. Humphrey (D-MN), chairman of the subcommittee on disarmament of the SENATE FOREIGN RELATIONS COMMITTEE, and others in Congress drew attention to the relative lack of focus within the government foreign policy establishment on arms control and disarmament. By the early 1960s, interest in forming an agency devoted to this policy area had gained wide support. On September 26, 1961, President JOHN F. KENNEDY

ACDA DIRECTOR	DATES	ADMINISTRATION
William C. Foster	1961–1969	Kennedy L. B. Johnson
Gerard C. Smith	1969–1973	Nixon
Fred C. Ikle	1973–1977	Nixon Ford
PAUL C. WARNKE	1977–1978	Carter
George C. Seignious	1978–1980	Carter
Ralph W. Earle 2nd	1980–1981	Carter
EUGENE V. ROSTOW	1981–1983	Reagan
Kenneth L. Adelman	1983–1987	Reagan
William F. Burns	1988–1989	Reagan
Ronald F. Lehman 2nd	1989–	Bush

signed the Arms Control and Disarmament Act, establishing the Arms Control and Disarmament Agency within the executive branch. From its inception, the ACDA has functioned as the federal government's principal administrative office on arms control issues. The agency has figured in the formulation of the major bilateral and multilateral arms control accords involving the United States since the early 1960s, including the NUCLEAR NON-PROLIFERATION TREATY (1968), SALT I (1972) and SALT II (1979), INTERMEDIATE NUCLEAR FORCES TREATY (1987), and START Treaty (1991).

The ACDA makes recommendations to the president, the secretary of state, and Congress on arms control policy and its projected impact on America's foreign affairs, national security, and economy. The agency gathers and assesses relevant scientific, political, legal, military, and other information on which arms policy is based. Subject to guidance from the president and secretary of state, the ACDA has the authority under its charter to prepare and manage U.S. participation in international arms control discussions. In practice, the agency has been incorporated into the State Department's overall direction of international negotiations.

The ACDA director, who is appointed by the president with the Senate's approval, serves under the direction of the secretary of state but enjoys access to the president when necessary and may deal directly with other executive agencies on matters outside the State Department's expertise. The director attends all meetings of the NATIONAL SECURITY COUNCIL on weapons procurement, arms sales, and the defense budget; coordinates ACDA's contacts with Congress; and functions as the agency's liaison to key House and Senate committees. The legislation forming the ACDA authorized the president to appoint a General Advisory Committee (GAC), a special 15-member consultative panel that advises the president, secretary of state, and ACDA director on issues of arms control and world peace. The GAC has never had any direct influence on policy-making.

CENTRAL INTELLIGENCE AGENCY (CIA) The Central Intelligence Agency is the principal federal organization responsible for gathering and analyzing foreign intelligence relevant to U.S. national security. It reports to the president through the NATIONAL SECURITY COUNCIL (NSC). A director and deputy director, only one of whom may be from the military, head the agency. Both are appointed by the president and confirmed by the Senate. The CIA director, who bears the title of director of central intelligence (DCI), serves as the president's main intelligence adviser. In addition to running the CIA, the DCI oversees the U.S. INTELLIGENCE COMMUNITY, a sizable and diverse body that includes the federal government's various civilian and military intelligence services and the intelligence elements of several cabinet departments. In this capacity, the DCI directs the NATIONAL FOREIGN INTELLIGENCE BOARD, a panel comprising the chiefs of the other intelligence units. Designated a statutory adviser to the NSC, the central intelligence head usually attends its meetings.

The origins of the CIA date to the establishment during WORLD WAR II of the OFFICE OF STRATEGIC SERVICES (OSS), the United States' first government-wide, independent intelligence organization. This forerunner of the CIA initially was set up as the OFFICE OF THE COORDINATOR OF INFORMATION (COI) in July 1941. President FRANKLIN D. ROOSEVELT reorganized and renamed it the OSS on June 13, 1942, placing it under the direction of the JOINT CHIEFS OF STAFF. Following the Allied victory, President HARRY S. TRUMAN dismantled the OSS in September 1945. His decision went against the advice of senior officials such as General WILLIAM J. DONOVAN, director of both COI and OSS, who recommended the creation of a permanent and unified peacetime intelligence service patterned on the wartime organization.

America's greatly expanded postwar world role, however, generated broad new demands for foreign intelligence. Truman formed the CENTRAL INTELLIGENCE GROUP by executive order in January 1946. This temporary agency, headed by a director of central intelligence, served under the supervision of the NATIONAL INTELLIGENCE AUTHORITY, which consisted of the secretaries of war, state, and navy and the president's military chief of staff. In July 1947 Congress passed the landmark NATIONAL SECURITY ACT, establishing the CIA as an independent executive agency under the newly formed NSC. Under the legislation, the DCI post was given a legal basis. The agency's major functions,

DIRECTOR OF CENTRAL INTELLIGENCE	DATES	ADMINISTRATION
SIDNEY W. SOUERS	1946	Truman
HOYT S. VANDENBERG	1946–1947	Truman
ROSCOE H. HILLENKOETTER	1947–1950	Truman
WALTER BEDELL SMITH	1950–1953	Truman Eisenhower
ALLEN W. DULLES	1953–1961	Eisenhower Kennedy
JOHN A. MCCONE	1961–1965	Kennedy L. B. Johnson
William F. Raborn, Jr.	1965–1966	L. B. Johnson
RICHARD M. HELMS	1966–1973	L. B. Johnson Nixon
JAMES R. SCHLESINGER	1973	Nixon
WILLIAM E. COLBY	1973–1976	Nixon
GEORGE BUSH	1976–1977	Ford
STANSFIELD TURNER	1977–1981	Carter
WILLIAM J. CASEY	1981–1987	Reagan
William H. Webster	1987–1991	Reagan Bush
Robert M. Gates	1991–	Bush

laid out in the law, were to serve as the federal government's clearinghouse for foreign intelligence and to advise the president and the NSC on foreign intelligence issues and developments. The CIA was not at first granted intelligence-gathering responsibilites, acquiring this role only through later directives and reorganizations.

As U.S.-Soviet COLD WAR tensions mounted, the CIA gained authority to conduct covert activities including political, psychological, and economic warfare and paramilitary operations. The principal target of CIA clandestine operations was international communism promoted and subsidized by the Soviet Union. The clandestine branch's mission was to support anti-Communist political elements and governments the world over. The Intelligence Community justified secret measures as a necessary counterforce to similar Soviet intelligence methods. A 1954 report of the DOOLITTLE COMMITTEE, the panel commissioned by President DWIGHT D. EISENHOWER to study U.S. intelligence activities, concluded that the CIA must build a COVERT ACTION service

"more ruthless and effective" than the intelligence agencies of America's adversaries. Throughout the 1950s, the covert operations branch would take an active role in funding and directing campaigns aimed at controlling political events in Iran, Guatemala, and Indonesia. A number of failed missions staged in the early 1960s, notably the U-2 INCIDENT (1960) over the Soviet Union and the BAY OF PIGS INVASION (1961) of Cuba, tarnished the agency's image and raised questions about CIA competence and overall command and control of covert activities.

Starting in the mid-1970s, Congress spearheaded important reforms. Revelations during the probe of the domestic Watergate political scandal exposed longstanding CIA involvement in unsavory and illegal activities. These actions, known to intelligence insiders as the FAMILY JEWELS, included assassination plots against foreign leaders, spying on Americans in the United States, interception and opening of mail, and testing of mind-altering drugs on human subjects. Federal lawmakers, acting to strengthen legislative oversight of intelligence matters, passed the HUGHES-RYAN AMENDMENT in 1974, requiring the president to notify appropriate House and Senate committees prior to CIA participation in overseas covert missions. In another important step the same year, Congress created special investigating committees in each of its chambers to look into alleged abuses by the Intelligence Community. The Senate and House panels, under respective chairmen FRANK CHURCH (D-ID) and Otis G. Pike (D-NY), yielded the most detailed accounts ever of secret CIA operations. The twin committees made extensive recommendations for reforming oversight of the intelligence system. Meanwhile the ROCKEFELLER COMMISSION, appointed by President GERALD R. FORD to examine CIA domestic intelligence excesses, released its final report in June 1975, calling for explicit limitations on the domestic role of the CIA and a stronger supervision of the agency by Congress and the PRESIDENT'S FOREIGN INTELLIGENCE ADVISORY BOARD.

In May 1976 the Senate established a permanent select committee on intelligence to oversee the CIA and the larger Intelligence Community. The House followed suit in July 1977. These new panels effectively supplanted the Armed Services subcommittees of the Senate and House that were responsible for monitoring intelligence matters. In the 1980s the CIA devoted increasing intelligence resources to combating international terrorism and drug trafficking and to monitoring worldwide economic developments. The end of the Cold War and disintegration of the Soviet Union in the early 1990s prompted an ongoing reexamination of the U.S. Intelligence Community.

DEPARTMENT OF THE AIR FORCE The origin of the Air Force dates to 1907 when the U.S. Army, then under the DEPARTMENT OF WAR, formed an Aeronautical Division within the Signal Corps. The Navy began a similar program for naval aviation. Air power proved an important new facet of

SECRETARY OF THE AIR FORCE	DATES	ADMINISTRATION
W. STUART SYMINGTON	1947-1950	Truman
Thomas K. Finletter	1950-1953	Truman
Harold E. Talbott	1953-1955	Eisenhower
Donald A. Quarles	1955-1957	Eisenhower
James H. Douglas	1957-1959	Eisenhower
Dudley C. Sharp	1959-1961	Eisenhower
Eugene M. Zuckert	1961-1965	Kennedy L. B. Johnson
HAROLD BROWN	1965-1969	L. B. Johnson
Robert C. Seamans, Jr.	1969-1973	Nixon
John L. McLucas	1973-1976	Nixon Ford
Thomas C. Reed	1976-1977	Ford Carter
John C. Stetson	1977-1979	Carter
Hans Mark	1979-1981	Carter
Verne Orr	1981-1985	Reagan
Russell A. Rourke	1985-1986	Reagan
Edward C. Aldridge, Jr.	1986-1988	Reagan
Donald B. Rice	1989-	Bush

warfare during WORLD WAR I. Following U.S. entry into the conflict in 1918, the War Department established a separate Air Service to direct the Army's burgeoning aviation forces. The Air Service became the Air Corps in 1926 and the Army Air Forces (AAF) in 1941. Military aviation came of age in WORLD WAR II. During the conflict, ROBERT A. LOVETT, assistant secretary of war for air, oversaw the expansion of the AAF into an essentially autonomous force of more than 2 million personnel and 80,000 aircraft.

The experiences of World War II as well as the demands of America's postwar global security requirements underscored the need for both an integrated national military establishment and a distinct air service. The landmark 1947 NATIONAL SECURITY ACT transferred the AAF to a newly created Department of the Air Force. The War Department was redesignated the Department of the Army. The civilian secretary of the Air Force briefly enjoyed cabinet rank and membership on the NATIONAL SECURITY COUNCIL (NSC). The NATIONAL SECURITY ACT AMENDMENTS OF 1949 made the Air Force, together with the Army and Navy, subordinate military departments within the newly formed DEPARTMENT OF DEFENSE. The Air Force secretary has since reported to the secretary of defense, who became the sole defense representative in the cabinet and NSC. Since the 1950s the Air Force has been responsible for the bomber and missile legs of the U.S. nuclear TRIAD, cornerstone of U.S. nuclear DETERRENCE throughout the COLD WAR. The department has also been centrally involved in the development of U.S. SATELLITE RECONNAISSANCE.

DEPARTMENT OF COMMERCE The rapidly expanding American economy in the late 19th century brought calls for a federal department to promote U.S. foreign trade. Congress established the cabinet-level Department of Commerce and Labor

in 1903 to represent the interests of both business and labor in the national government. The department proved unwieldy and in 1913 it was divided into the Department of Commerce and the Department of Labor. The first commerce secretary, William C. Redfield, inaugurated the department's formal study of foreign markets and created a corps of overseas commercial attachés. Under HERBERT C. HOOVER, secretary during the Harding and Coolidge administrations, the department was built into a key component of the executive branch with broad responsibility for international economics. The department prepared a wide range of economic information and statistics and maintained some 50 offices around the world to facilitate U.S. trade. With the dramatic decline in international commerce in the 1930s as a result of the Great Depression, the Roosevelt administration reduced the department's activities. In 1939 President FRANKLIN D. ROOSEVELT consolidated all U.S. overseas attachés within the DEPARTMENT OF STATE. Since WORLD WAR II the Commerce Department has concentrated on U.S. economic growth and international trade. The DEPARTMENT OF THE TREASURY is responsible for U.S. international monetary and fiscal policy while the UNITED STATES TRADE REPRESENTATIVE handles international trade negotiations. Within the Commerce Department, the International Trade Administration helps formulate U.S. trade policy, facilitates overseas commerce, and monitors unfair foreign trade practices. The Bureau of Export Administration controls the export of items and technologies vital to U.S. security.

DEPARTMENT OF DEFENSE (DOD) The Department of Defense is in charge of U.S. armed forces. Largest of the cabinet departments in both funding and personnel, DOD is headed by the secretary of defense. The civilian secretary also serves as a member of

SECRETARY OF COMMERCE AND LABOR	DATES	ADMINISTRATION
George B. Cortelyou	1903–1904	T. Roosevelt
Victor H. Metcalf	1904–1906	T. Roosevelt
Oscar S. Straus	1906–1909	T. Roosevelt
Charles Nagel	1909–1913	Taft Wilson

SECRETARY OF COMMERCE	DATES	ADMINISTRATION
William C. Redfield	1913–1919	Wilson
Joshua W. Alexander	1919–1921	Wilson
HERBERT C. HOOVER	1921–1928	Harding Coolidge
William F. Whiting	1928–1929	Coolidge
Robert P. Lamont	1929–1932	Hoover
Roy D. Chapin	1932–1933	Hoover
Daniel C. Roper	1933–1938	F. D. Roosevelt
Harry L. Hopkins	1938–1940	F. D. Roosevelt
Jesse H. Jones	1940–1945	F. D. Roosevelt
Henry A. Wallace	1945–1946	F. D. Roosevelt Truman
W. AVERELL HARRIMAN	1946–1948	Truman
Charles Sawyer	1948–1953	Truman
Sinclair Weeks	1953–1958	Eisenhower
Lewis L. Strauss	1958–1959	Eisenhower
Frederick H. Mueller	1959–1961	Eisenhower
Luther H. Hodges	1961–1965	Kennedy L. B. Johnson
John T. Connor	1965–1967	L. B. Johnson
Alexander B. Trowbridge	1967–1968	L. B. Johnson
C. R. Smith	1968–1969	L. B. Johnson
Maurice H. Stans	1969–1972	Nixon
Peter G. Peterson	1972–1973	Nixon
Frederick B. Dent	1973–1975	Nixon Ford
Rogers C. B. Morton	1975–1976	Ford
Thomas S. Kleppe	1976–1977	Ford
Juanita M. Kreps	1977–1980	Carter
Philip M. Klutznick	1980–1981	Carter
Malcolm Baldrige	1981–1987	Reagan
C. William Verity	1987–1989	Reagan
Robert A. Mosbacher	1989–1992	Bush
Barbara H. Franklin	1992–	Bush

the NATIONAL SECURITY COUNCIL (NSC). The major elements of the Defense Department include the Office of the Secretary; the JOINT CHIEFS OF STAFF (JCS); and the departments of Army, Navy, and Air Force. The JCS, comprising the senior military officers of the Army, Navy, Air Force, and Marine Corps, acts as the defense secretary's immediate military staff. Its members serve as the link between the PENTAGON's top civilian admin-

SECRETARY OF DEFENSE	DATES	ADMINISTRATION
JAMES V. FORRESTAL	1947–1949	Truman
LOUIS A. JOHNSON	1949–1950	Truman
GEORGE C. MARSHALL	1950–1951	Truman
ROBERT A. LOVETT	1951–1953	Truman
CHARLES E. WILSON	1953–1957	Eisenhower
NEIL H. MCELROY	1957–1959	Eisenhower
THOMAS S. GATES, JR.	1959–1961	Eisenhower
ROBERT S. MCNAMARA	1961–1968	Kennedy L. B. Johnson
CLARK M. CLIFFORD	1968–1969	L. B. Johnson
MELVIN R. LAIRD	1969–1973	Nixon
ELLIOT L. RICHARDSON	1973	Nixon
JAMES R. SCHLESINGER	1973–1975	Nixon Ford
DONALD H. RUMSFELD	1975–1977	Ford
HAROLD BROWN	1977–1981	Carter
CASPAR W. WEINBERGER	1981–1987	Reagan
FRANK C. CARLUCCI 3RD	1987–1989	Reagan
RICHARD B. CHENEY	1989–	Bush

istrators and the armed forces. The chairman of the JCS is the chief military adviser to the secretary of defense, the NSC, and the president. The three military departments function under the general direction of the defense secretary. Each is organized separately under its own civilian secretary.

The Department of Defense emerged in response to new political and military realities at mid-century. Until 1941, the departments of War and Navy functioned separately and independently. America's experience in WORLD WAR II showed the need for greater coordination among U.S. armed forces. The advent of NUCLEAR WEAPONS and the growing U.S. role in international affairs following the war underlined the need for a centralized defense establishment. President HARRY S. TRUMAN in December 1945 proposed the creation of a Department of National Defense with three coordinated branches for land, naval, and air forces. The Navy in particular resisted unification, but after extended debate Congress passed the NATIONAL SECURITY ACT in July 1947. The law created the NATIONAL MILITARY ESTABLISHMENT (NME), headed by a secretary of defense, and legalized the wartime JCS. The Air Force was made a separate and co-equal service and the War Department became the Department of the Army. The Marines remained part of the Navy. The three service departments were grouped under the NME, but each continued under the control of its own cabinet-level service secretary. The NATIONAL SECURITY ACT AMENDMENTS OF 1949 replaced the NME with a cabinet-level Department of Defense. The Army, Navy, and Air Force were converted from executive to military departments, still administered by their civilian service secretaries, but under the strengthened authority, direction, and control of the secretary of defense. The service secretaries lost their cabinet rank and membership on the NSC. The 1949 amendments also established the posts of the JCS chairman and deputy secretary of defense.

Interservice rivalries hindered the new defense department. The ROCKEFELLER COM-

MITTEE, formed by President DWIGHT D. EISENHOWER to analyze DOD's problems, recommended significant organizational and procedural changes in April 1953. The panel's proposals were adopted that June in REORGANIZATION PLAN No. 6, which provided for a half-dozen new assistant secretaries of defense and fortified the powers of the defense secretary and the JCS organization. Escalating defense spending, technical advances in weapons systems, and concern about Soviet primacy in space following the October 1957 launch of the first unmanned satellite Sputnik prompted calls for further changes in the U.S. defense program. Congress passed the DEFENSE REORGANIZATION ACT OF 1958, which gave the defense secretary broadened authority to curb waste and duplication of effort by the three military services.

The 1958 measure was the last major revision of the military establishment until the mid-1980s. Responding to Army, Air Force, and Navy parochialism that hindered cooperation among the services and undermined the JCS, Congress implemented the GOLDWATER-NICHOLS DEFENSE REORGANIZATION ACT in 1986. The legislation created the position of vice-chairman of the JCS, gave the military staff increased bureaucratic clout, and strengthened the authority of its chairman over the other JCS members.

DEPARTMENT OF THE NAVY The Continental Congress founded the Continental Navy on October 13, 1775, to contend

SECRETARY OF THE NAVY	DATES	ADMINISTRATION
Benjamin Stoddert	1798–1801	J. Adams
ROBERT SMITH	1801–1809	Jefferson Madison
Paul Hamilton	1809–1812	Madison
William Jones	1813–1814	Madison
Benjamin W. Crowninshield	1815–1818	Madison Monroe
Smith Thompson	1819–1823	Monroe
Samuel L. Southard	1823–1829	Monroe J. Q. Adams
John Branch	1829–1831	Jackson
Levi Woodbury	1831–1834	Jackson
Mahlon Dickerson	1834–1838	Jackson Van Buren
James K. Paulding	1838–1841	Van Buren
George E. Badger	1841	W. H. Harrison Tyler
ABEL P. UPSHUR	1841–1843	Tyler
David Henshaw	1843–1844	Tyler
Thomas W. Gilmer	1844	Tyler
John Y. Mason	1844–1845	Tyler
George Bancroft	1845–1846	Polk
John Y. Mason	1846–1849	Polk Taylor
William B. Preston	1849–1850	Taylor Fillmore

SECRETARY OF THE NAVY	DATES	ADMINISTRATION
William A. Graham	1850–1852	Fillmore
John P. Kennedy	1852–1853	Fillmore Pierce
James C. Dobbin	1853–1857	Pierce Buchanan
Isaac Toucey	1857–1861	Buchanan Lincoln
Gideon Welles	1861–1869	Lincoln A. Johnson
Adolph E. Borie	1869	Grant
George M. Robeson	1869–1877	Grant Hayes
Richard W. Thompson	1877–1881	Hayes
Nathan Goff, Jr.	1881	Hayes
William H. Hunt	1881–1882	Arthur
William E. Chandler	1882–1885	Arthur Cleveland
William C. Whitney	1885–1889	Cleveland B. Harrison
Benjamin F. Tracy	1889–1893	B. Harrison Cleveland
Hilary A. Herbert	1893–1897	Cleveland McKinley
John D. Long	1897–1902	McKinley T. Roosevelt
William H. Moody	1902–1904	T. Roosevelt
Paul Morton	1904–1905	T. Roosevelt
Charles J. Bonaparte	1905–1906	T. Roosevelt
Victor H. Metcalf	1906–1908	T. Roosevelt
George von L. Meyer	1909–1913	Taft Wilson
JOSEPHUS DANIELS	1913–1921	Wilson Harding
Edwin Denby	1921–1924	Harding Coolidge
Curtis D. Wilbur	1924–1929	Coolidge Hoover
Charles F. Adams	1929–1933	Hoover
Claude A. Swanson	1933–1939	F. D. Roosevelt
Charles Edison	1939–1940	F. D. Roosevelt
Frank Knox	1940–1944	F. D. Roosevelt

SECRETARY OF THE NAVY	DATES	ADMINISTRATION
JAMES V. FORRESTAL	1944–1947	F. D. Roosevelt Truman
John L. Sullivan	1947–1949	Truman
Francis P. Matthews	1949–1951	Truman
Dan A. Kimball	1951–1953	Truman
Robert B. Anderson	1953–1954	Eisenhower
Charles S. Thomas	1954–1957	Eisenhower
THOMAS S. GATES, JR.	1957–1959	Eisenhower
William B. Franke	1959–1961	Eisenhower
John B. Connally	1961	Kennedy
Fred H. Korth	1962–1963	Kennedy
PAUL H. NITZE	1963–1967	L. B. Johnson
Paul R. Ignatius	1967–1969	L. B. Johnson
John H. Chafee	1969–1972	Nixon
John Warner	1972–1974	Nixon
J. Wm. Middendorf 2nd	1974–1977	Nixon Ford
W. Graham Claytor, Jr.	1977–1979	Carter
Edward Hidalgo	1979–1981	Carter
John Lehman	1981–1987	Reagan
James H. Webb, Jr.	1987–1988	Reagan
William L. Ball 3rd	1988–1989	Reagan Bush
H. Lawrence Garrett 3rd	1989–	Bush

with British naval power during the AMERICAN REVOLUTION. With the formation of the federal government under the CONSTITUTION in 1789, America's ships and sailors came under the control of the DEPARTMENT OF WAR. The Department of the Navy was established following assaults throughout the 1790s on American merchant ships by Great Britain, France, and the Barbary pirates of North Africa. French attacks on American shipping culminated in an undeclared maritime QUASI-WAR (1798–1800) between the United States and France. The U.S. Congress, recognizing the need for an independent executive department to administer naval forces, formed the Navy Department on April 30, 1798. Benjamin Stoddert became the first secretary of the navy, a civilian post with cabinet standing.

The WAR OF 1812 with Great Britain revealed the need for greater involvement of naval officers in the direction of the department. A remedy arrived in 1815, when federal lawmakers formed a three-man Board of Naval Commissioners to assist the secretary with fleet operations and policy. The board was replaced in 1842 by a network of technical bureaus, each led by a Navy officer directly responsible to the civilian secretary. At intervals between 1815 and the Civil War, the Navy dispatched its forces to the Mediterranean, Caribbean, South Atlantic, Pacific, Far East, and off the African Coast. These missions were undertaken mainly to protect broadening overseas commerce. A series of special operations, notably the exploratory WILKES EXPEDITION (1838–1842) and the voyages in the early 1850s of MATTHEW C. PERRY to Japan, promoted the expansion of scientific knowledge and worldwide American trade.

A continuing lack of institutional authority of career officers over strategy and general fleet operations hindered the department to the end of the 19th century. In the 1890s the United States began to develop a first-class naval force as part of the nation's assumption of a major world role. The Naval Act of 1890 began a long-term capital shipbuilding program. Legislative reform led to the creation in 1900 of a General Board of the Navy to support the secretary. This advisory group of high-ranking officers assisted in drafting war plans and offered counsel on general policy. But its members held no executive powers. Operational authority remained firmly with the secretary. Establishment in 1915 of a chief of naval operations (CNO) contributed to improved overall coordination within the department. Congress gave the CNO authority equal to his responsibilities as the secretary's main adviser and as the officer in overall charge of fleet operations.

WORLD WAR II brought only marginal changes in department organization. The U.S. Navy emerged from the war as the most powerful maritime force in the world. The authority of the Navy command for the most part was relinquished to the unified defense establishment forged by the NATIONAL SECURITY ACT of 1947. Under this legislation and its 1949 amendments, the Department of the Navy was placed under the newly formed DEPARTMENT OF DEFENSE and the navy secretary lost both cabinet rank and membership on the NATIONAL SECURITY COUNCIL. The Marine Corps, established in November 1775 as naval infantry for service at sea, has remained an integral part of the Navy since.

DEPARTMENT OF STATE The Department of State is the senior department in the executive branch. It is headed by the secretary of state, long considered the most prestigious position in the cabinet. As America's ranking diplomat, the secretary acts as principal adviser to the president on the formulation and execution of U.S. foreign policy and is responsible for the over-

all direction and supervision of American foreign relations. The State Department represents the United States in international forums and is responsible for the negotiation of treaties and agreements with foreign nations. The secretary, a member of the NATIONAL SECURITY COUNCIL, often conducts major diplomatic negotiations personally. The department also is in charge of the FOREIGN SERVICE and its network of embassies and consulates.

The Continental Congress's COMMITTEE OF SECRET CORRESPONDENCE managed U.S. foreign relations until the establishment, under the ARTICLES OF CONFEDERATION, of a permanent executive department of foreign affairs and secretary for foreign affairs in 1781. The cabinet-level Department of Foreign Affairs was created on July 27, 1789, by the first Congress in its initial session under the new CONSTITUTION. In September 1789, Congress changed the name to the Department of State and renamed the secretary for foreign affairs the secretary of state. Until the creation of the Department of Interior in 1849, the secretary handled some domestic affairs, including responsibility for the Patent Office and the census.

The State Department began to expand considerably as the United States assumed a more active role in world affairs following the SPANISH-AMERICAN WAR (1898). The ROGERS ACT in 1924 contributed to the development of a professional diplomatic corps by combining the diplomatic and consular services in the single Foreign Service. WORLD WAR II thrust the United States into a position of world leadership, which brought a tremendous growth in department activities and the creation after 1945 of the modern State Department. Reflecting America's superpower status, postwar secretaries of state have occupied a prominent place in international diplomacy. Secretary DEAN ACHESON, acting on the recommendations of the Hoover Commission (1947–1949) on executive branch reorganization, established the department's current structure of both regional, or geographic, and functional bureaus. A series of influential studies of American diplomacy and state department organization, most notably the WRISTON REPORT (1954), HERTER REPORT (1962), and MURPHY COMMISSION (1975), brought additional improvements in the

SECRETARY OF STATE	DATES	ADMINISTRATION
JOHN JAY	1784–1790	Confederation Congress Washington
THOMAS JEFFERSON	1790–1793	Washington
EDMUND RANDOLPH	1794–1795	Washington
TIMOTHY PICKERING	1795–1800	Washington J. Adams
JOHN MARSHALL	1800–1801	J. Adams
JAMES MADISON	1801–1809	Jefferson
ROBERT SMITH	1809–1811	Madison
JAMES MONROE	1811–1817	Madison
JOHN QUINCY ADAMS	1817–1825	Monroe
HENRY CLAY	1825–1829	J. Q. Adams
MARTIN VAN BUREN	1829–1831	Jackson
EDWARD LIVINGSTON	1831–1833	Jackson
LOUIS MCLANE	1833–1834	Jackson
JOHN FORSYTH	1834–1841	Jackson Van Buren
DANIEL WEBSTER	1841–1843	W. H. Harrison Tyler
ABEL P. UPSHUR	1843–1844	Tyler
JOHN C. CALHOUN	1844–1845	Tyler
JAMES BUCHANAN	1845–1849	Polk
JOHN M. CLAYTON	1849–1850	Taylor Fillmore
DANIEL WEBSTER	1850–1852	Fillmore
EDWARD EVERETT	1852–1853	Fillmore
WILLIAM L. MARCY	1853–1857	Pierce
LEWIS CASS	1857–1860	Buchanan
JEREMIAH S. BLACK	1860–1861	Buchanan
WILLIAM H. SEWARD	1861–1869	Lincoln A. Johnson
ELIHU B. WASHBURNE	1869	Grant
HAMILTON FISH	1869–1877	Grant
WILLIAM M. EVARTS	1877–1881	Hayes
JAMES G. BLAINE	1881	Garfield Arthur
FREDERICK T. FRELINGHUYSEN	1881–1885	Arthur
THOMAS F. BAYARD	1885–1889	Cleveland
JAMES G. BLAINE	1889–1892	B. Harrison

SECRETARY OF STATE	DATES	ADMINISTRATION
JOHN W. FOSTER	1892–1893	B. Harrison
WALTER Q. GRESHAM	1893–1895	Cleveland
RICHARD OLNEY	1895–1897	Cleveland
JOHN SHERMAN	1897–1898	McKinley
WILLIAM R. DAY	1898	McKinley
JOHN M. HAY	1898–1905	McKinley T. Roosevelt
ELIHU ROOT	1905–1909	T. Roosevelt
ROBERT BACON	1909	T. Roosevelt
PHILANDER C. KNOX	1909–1913	Taft
WILLIAM JENNINGS BRYAN	1913–1915	Wilson
ROBERT LANSING	1915–1920	Wilson
BAINBRIDGE COLBY	1920–1921	Wilson
CHARLES EVANS HUGHES	1921–1925	Harding Coolidge
FRANK B. KELLOGG	1925–1929	Coolidge
HENRY L. STIMSON	1929–1933	Hoover
CORDELL HULL	1933–1944	F. D. Roosevelt
EDWARD R. STETTINIUS, JR.	1944–1945	F. D. Roosevelt Truman
JAMES F. BYRNES	1945–1947	Truman
GEORGE C. MARSHALL	1947–1949	Truman
DEAN ACHESON	1949–1953	Truman
JOHN FOSTER DULLES	1953–1959	Eisenhower
CHRISTIAN A. HERTER	1959–1961	Eisenhower
DEAN RUSK	1961–1969	Kennedy L. B. Johnson
WILLIAM P. ROGERS	1969–1973	Nixon
HENRY A. KISSINGER	1973–1977	Nixon Ford
CYRUS R. VANCE	1977–1980	Carter
EDMUND S. MUSKIE	1980–1981	Carter
ALEXANDER M. HAIG, JR.	1981–1982	Reagan
GEORGE P. SHULTZ	1982–1989	Reagan
JAMES A. BAKER 3RD	1989–	Bush

formal procedures used in department policy-making and in the management of the professional foreign service corps.

DEPARTMENT OF THE TREASURY The cabinet-rank secretary of the treasury heads the United States's premier financial

SECRETARY OF THE TREASURY	DATES	ADMINISTRATION
ALEXANDER HAMILTON	1789–1795	Washington
Oliver Wolcott	1795–1800	Washington J. Adams
Samuel Dexter	1801	J. Adams Jefferson
ALBERT GALLATIN	1801–1814	Jefferson Madison
George W. Campbell	1814	Madison
Alexander J. Dallas	1814–1816	Madison
William H. Crawford	1816–1825	Madison Monroe
RICHARD RUSH	1825–1829	J. Q. Adams
Samuel D. Ingham	1829–1831	Jackson
LOUIS MCLANE	1831–1833	Jackson
William J. Duane	1833	Jackson
Roger B. Taney	1833–1834	Jackson
Levi Woodbury	1834–1841	Jackson Van Buren
Thomas Ewing	1841	W. H. Harrison Tyler
Walter Forward	1841–1843	Tyler
John C. Spencer	1843–1844	Tyler
George M. Bibb	1844–1845	Tyler Polk
Robert J. Walker	1845–1849	Polk
William M. Meredith	1849–1850	Taylor Fillmore
Thomas Corwin	1850–1853	Fillmore
James Guthrie	1853–1857	Pierce
Howell Cobb	1857–1860	Buchanan
Philip F. Thomas	1860–1861	Buchanan
John A. Dix	1861	Buchanan
Salmon P. Chase	1861–1864	Lincoln
William P. Fessenden	1864–1865	Lincoln
Hugh McCulloch	1865–1869	Lincoln A. Johnson
George S. Boutwell	1869–1873	Grant
William A. Richardson	1873–1874	Grant
Benjamin H. Bristow	1874–1876	Grant
Lot M. Morrill	1876–1877	Grant Hayes

SECRETARY OF THE TREASURY	DATES	ADMINISTRATION
JOHN SHERMAN	1877–1881	Hayes
William Windom	1881	Garfield Arthur
Charles J. Folger	1881–1884	Arthur
WALTER Q. GRESHAM	1884	Arthur
Hugh McCulloch	1884–1885	Cleveland
Daniel Manning	1885–1887	Cleveland
Charles S. Fairchild	1887–1889	Cleveland
William Windom	1889–1891	B. Harrison
Charles Foster	1891–1893	B. Harrison Cleveland
John G. Carlisle	1893–1897	Cleveland McKinley
Lyman J. Gage	1897–1902	McKinley T. Roosevelt
L. M. Shaw	1902–1907	T. Roosevelt
George B. Cortelyou	1907–1909	T. Roosevelt
Franklin MacVeagh	1909–1913	Taft
W. G. McAdoo	1913–1918	Wilson
Carter Glass	1918–1920	Wilson
David F. Houston	1920–1921	Wilson
ANDREW W. MELLON	1921–1932	Harding Coolidge Hoover
Ogden L. Mills	1932–1933	Hoover
William H. Woodin	1933	F. D. Roosevelt
HENRY MORGANTHAU, JR.	1934–1945	F. D. Roosevelt Truman
Fred M. Vinson	1945–1946	Truman
John W. Snyder	1946–1953	Truman
George M. Humphrey	1953–1957	Eisenhower
Robert B. Anderson	1957–1961	Eisenhower
C. Douglas Dillon	1961–1965	Kennedy L. B. Johnson
Henry H. Fowler	1965–1968	L. B. Johnson
Joseph W. Barr	1968–1969	L. B. Johnson
David M. Kennedy	1969–1971	Nixon
John B. Connally	1971–1972	Nixon
GEORGE P. SHULTZ	1972–1974	Nixon
William E. Simon	1974–1977	Nixon Ford

SECRETARY OF THE TREASURY	DATES	ADMINISTRATION
W. Michael Blumenthal	1977–1979	Carter
G. William Miller	1979–1981	Carter
Donald T. Regan	1981–1985	Reagan
JAMES A. BAKER 3RD	1985–1988	Reagan
Nicholas F. Brady	1988–	Reagan Bush

agency, the Department of the Treasury, which manages the federal government's money resources. Under this broad charter, the department functions as the nation's accountant, revenue collector, money producer, and leading economic policy formulator. The treasury secretary, the president's top adviser on fiscal issues, works closely with the White House and Congress on shaping the nation's increasingly interconnected domestic and international financial, economic, and tax policies. The independent Federal Reserve System, created by the 1913 Federal Reserve Act, has primary responsibility for monetary policy and the nation's banking industry.

Though formally established on September 2, 1789, by the first Congress under the U.S. CONSTITUTION, the Treasury Department originated in the early stages of the AMERICAN REVOLUTION. In February 1776, the Continental Congress appointed a standing committee to manage the rebellious colonies' finances, particularly the debt incurred to fund the war for independence from Great Britain. A single superintendent of finance directed the Treasury Office between 1781 and 1784. A board of three commissioners then handled the fiscal affairs of the confederated states until the ratification of the Constitution in 1788. Following creation of the permanent Treasury Department in the executive branch, ALEXANDER HAMILTON became the first treasury secretary.

The Treasury Department developed a major role in American foreign relations in the 20th century, as global commerce flourished and issues of international trade, economic development, and currency exchange emerged as first-rank foreign policy concerns with consequences for national security. Treasury Secretary HENRY MORGEN-

THAU, JR., in a demonstration of his department's growing clout, chaired the BRETTON WOODS CONFERENCE in July 1944. This meeting of the Allied nations yielded the post–WORLD WAR II international monetary system and established the INTERNATIONAL MONETARY FUND (IMF) and WORLD BANK. In the late 1940s, the Treasury Department helped structure and implement the massive U.S. economic aid efforts, most notably the MARSHALL PLAN, that largely rebuilt wartorn Europe and Japan.

Against the backdrop of an increasingly competitive global economy, the treasury secretary acts as the principal architect of U.S. international fiscal policies. Each year the Treasury Department works with the State Department, the Office of Management and Budget, and Congress to coordinate the substantial U.S. foreign economic aid programs. On the trade front, the department enforces the tariff laws and collects duties on imported goods. The involvement of international economic developments in America's security interests frequently places the treasury secretary at meetings of the NATIONAL SECURITY COUNCIL. As the nation's ranking financial officer, the secretary represents the United States at meetings of the finance ministers of the GROUP OF 7, the leading Western industrial democracies. The secretary serves as U.S. governor of the International Monetary Fund, the World Bank, the INTER-AMERICAN DEVELOPMENT BANK, the AFRICAN DEVELOPMENT BANK, and the ASIAN DEVELOPMENT BANK.

DEPARTMENT OF WAR The Department of War, forerunner of the Department of the Army, was created by the first U.S. Congress in August 1789 to direct the armed forces of the young republic. America's experience with a national military extended back to

SECRETARY OF WAR	DATES	ADMINISTRATION
HENRY KNOX	1789–1794	Washington
TIMOTHY PICKERING	1795	Washington
James McHenry	1796–1800	Washington
Samuel Dexter	1800–1801	J. Adams
Henry Dearborn	1801–1809	Jefferson
William Eustis	1809–1813	Madison
JOHN ARMSTRONG	1813–1814	Madison
JAMES MONROE	1814–1815	Madison
William H. Crawford	1815–1816	Madison
JOHN C. CALHOUN	1817–1825	Monroe
JAMES BARBOUR	1825–1828	J. Q. Adams
Peter B. Porter	1828–1829	J. Q. Adams
John H. Eaton	1829–1831	Jackson
LEWIS CASS	1831–1836	Jackson
Joel R. Poinsett	1837–1841	Van Buren
John Bell	1841	W. H. Harrison Tyler
John C. Spencer	1841–1843	Tyler
James M. Porter	1843–1844	Tyler
William Wilkins	1844–1845	Tyler
WILLIAM L. MARCY	1845–1849	Polk
George W. Crawford	1849–1850	Taylor Fillmore
Charles M. Conrad	1850–1853	Fillmore
JEFFERSON DAVIS	1853–1857	Pierce
John B. Floyd	1857–1860	Buchanan
Joseph Holt	1861	Buchanan
Simon Cameron	1861–1862	Lincoln
Edwin M. Stanton	1862–1868	Lincoln A. Johnson
John M. Schofield	1868–1869	A. Johnson
John A. Rawlins	1869	Grant
William W. Belknap	1869–1876	Grant
Alphonso Taft	1876	Grant
James D. Cameron	1876–1877	Grant
George W. McCrary	1877–1879	Hayes
Alexander Ramsey	1879–1881	Hayes
Robert T. Lincoln	1881–1885	Garfield Arthur

SECRETARY OF WAR	DATES	ADMINISTRATION
William C. Endicott	1885–1889	Cleveland
Redfield Proctor	1889–1891	B. Harrison
Stephen B. Elkins	1891–1893	B. Harrison
Daniel S. Lamont	1893–1897	Cleveland
Russell A. Alger	1897–1899	McKinley
ELIHU ROOT	1899–1904	McKinley T. Roosevelt
WILLIAM HOWARD TAFT	1904–1908	T. Roosevelt
Luke E. Wright	1908–1909	T. Roosevelt
Jacob M. Dickinson	1909–1911	Taft
HENRY L. STIMSON	1911–1913	Taft
Lindley M. Garrison	1913–1916	Wilson
Newton D. Baker	1916–1921	Wilson
John W. Weeks	1921–1925	Harding Coolidge
Dwight F. Davis	1925–1929	Coolidge
James W. Good	1929	Hoover
Patrick J. Hurley	1929–1933	Hoover
George H. Dern	1933–1936	F. D. Roosevelt
Harry H. Woodring	1936–1940	F. D. Roosevelt
HENRY L. STIMSON	1940–1945	F. D. Roosevelt
Robert P. Patterson	1945–1947	Truman
Kenneth C. Royall	1947	Truman

June 1775, when the Continental Congress established the Continental Army to fight the British in the AMERICAN REVOLUTION. A year later the Congress founded a Board of War and Ordnance, composed of five sitting legislators, to oversee the U.S. war effort. In 1781, American lawmakers abolished this board and created a War Office under the direction of a single secretary at war. When Congress formed the War Department in 1789 it changed the title of the department head from secretary at war to secretary of war. The Department of War exercised administrative control over both land and sea forces until the DEPARTMENT OF THE NAVY was created in 1798. INDIAN AFFAIRS also initially fell under the War Department's jurisdiction but in 1849 was shifted to the newly created Department of the Interior.

In the first half of the 1800s, the secretary presided over the steady growth of the War Department bureaucracy and staff and the emergence of a professionally competent officer corps. The U.S. Military Academy was founded at West Point in 1803. Secretaries JOHN C. CALHOUN and JEFFERSON DAVIS brought major advances in department administration. At the close of the 19th century, the U.S. Army increasingly aspired to the professional standards of the major European armies. Thus the War Department upgraded officer education and sought organizational changes. Secretary of War ELIHU ROOT in 1903 pushed through key reforms that reinvigorated the National Guard (system of state militias), chartered the Army War College, and established the office of Army chief of staff to provide a mil-

SECRETARY OF THE ARMY	DATES	ADMINISTRATION
Kenneth C. Royall	1947–1949	Truman
Gordon Gray	1949–1950	Truman
Frank Pace, Jr.	1950–1953	Truman
Robert T. Stevens	1953–1955	Eisenhower
Wilber M. Brucker	1955–1961	Eisenhower
Elvis J. Stahr, Jr.	1961–1962	Kennedy
Cyrus R. Vance	1962–1964	Kennedy L. B. Johnson
Stephen Ailes	1964–1965	L. B. Johnson
Stanley R. Resor	1965–1971	L. B. Johnson Nixon
Robert F. Froehlke	1971–1973	Nixon
Howard H. Callaway	1973–1975	Nixon Ford
Martin R. Hoffmann	1975–1977	Ford
Clifford L. Alexander, Jr.	1977–1981	Carter
John O. Marsh, Jr.	1981–1989	Reagan
Michael P. W. Stone	1989–	Bush

itary link between the War Department and the field commands.

Following WORLD WAR I, in which 2 million troops served in the AMERICAN EXPEDITIONARY FORCE in France, the War Department entered a period of lean budgets and retrenchment. With the onset of the Great Depression in the late 1920s, funding of the Army declined and troop strength plummeted. Army and air forces began to grow in reponse to the outbreak of WORLD WAR II in Europe in 1939 and expanded rapidly after the United States entered the conflict in December 1941. Beyond training and equipping the large American Army and helping conduct the Allied war effort, the War Department oversaw the top-secret MANHATTAN PROJECT that produced the first atomic bomb. By the end of the war, the U.S. Army was the world's most powerful and the War Department had become the largest federal bureaucracy.

The NATIONAL SECURITY ACT of 1947 and its 1949 amendments wrought major changes in the organization of the War Department. The Air Force was detached from the Army and established as a separate and equal military department. The War Department became the Department of the Army, which was in turn made subordinate to the newly created DEPARTMENT OF DEFENSE. The secretary of war was redesignated secretary of the army. All three service secretaries — Army, Navy, and Air Force—lost their cabinet status. Kenneth C. Royall, incumbent secretary of war at the time of the military overhaul, managed the transition to become the first secretary of the army.

JOINT CHIEFS OF STAFF (JCS) The Joint Chiefs of Staff functions within the DEPARTMENT OF DEFENSE (DOD) as the top-level advisory council to the president and secretary of defense on America's armed forces. The military staff agency includes the four senior officers of the armed services — the Army and Air Force chiefs of staff, the chief of naval operations, and the commandant of the Marine Corps — and a chairman (CJCS) and vice-chairman, both appointed by the president from among the service branches and confirmed by the Senate. Members bring the perspectives of their parent services to a collective consideration

JCS CHAIRMAN	DATES	ADMINISTRATION
Adm. WILLIAM D. LEAHY, USN (Chief of Staff to the Commander in Chief of the Army and Navy)	1942–1949	F. D. Roosevelt Truman
Gen. Omar N. Bradley, USA	1949–1953	Truman Eisenhower
Adm. Arthur W. Radford, USN	1953–1957	Eisenhower
Gen. Nathan F. Twining, USAF	1957–1960	Eisenhower
Gen. Lyman L. Lemnitzer, USA	1960–1962	Eisenhower Kennedy
Gen. MAXWELL D. TAYLOR, USA	1962–1964	Kennedy L. B. Johnson
Gen. Earle G. Wheeler, USA	1964–1970	L. B. Johnson Nixon
Adm. Thomas H. Moorer, USN	1970–1974	Nixon
Gen. George S. Brown, USAF	1974–1978	Nixon Ford Carter
Gen. David C. Jones, USAF	1978–1982	Carter Reagan
Gen. John W. Vessey, Jr., USA	1982–1985	Reagan
Adm. William J. Crowe, Jr., USN	1985–1989	Reagan Bush
Gen. COLIN L. POWELL, USA	1989–	Bush

of U.S. defense needs and capabilities. The staff is responsible for integrating these views into recommendations and advice that take account of America's overall security requirements.

The CJCS presides over meetings of the Joint Chiefs, setting the agenda and working to resolve disagreements among members. Since 1986, the chairman, rather than the entire JCS, has acted as the principal military adviser to the president and the NATIONAL SECURITY COUNCIL (NSC). Other members, however, may individually submit their views to senior civilian policymakers when such views conflict with those of the CJCS. Traditionally, the chairman represents the JCS before the key congressional committees involved with military issues. The CJCS's responsibilities include aiding the president and defense secretary with strategic direction and planning for the military; evaluating the preparedness of the armed forces; and representing the United States on the UNITED NATIONS Military Staff Committee. The vice-chairman functions as a key aide to the chairman, performing tasks assigned by the CJCS with the defense secretary's approval.

The JCS was an offspring of America's involvement in WORLD WAR II. President FRANKLIN D. ROOSEVELT in early 1942 empaneled the senior officers of the Army, Navy, and Army Air Forces to advise him collectively on wartime strategy and operations and ensure coordination among U.S. land, sea, and air forces. In July 1942, the president's personal military adviser, Admiral WILLIAM D. LEAHY, was added to the JCS to preside over its meetings and to act as a direct liaison to the White House. Emergence of the United States as a postwar world power and the demands of global warfare accelerated the governmental drive for an integrated national security system. Legislation creating a unified NATIONAL MILITARY ESTABLISHMENT (NME) under a secretary of defense also formally authorized the JCS. The law, the NATIONAL SECURITY ACT of 1947, kept the staff's wartime composition and designated its members the chief military advisers to the president and defense secretary, with responsibilities for the strategic planning and direction of U.S. forces. A multiservice Joint Staff was attached to the JCS to support the senior military advisory agency.

The NATIONAL SECURITY ACT AMENDMENTS OF 1949, which reorganized the NME as the Department of Defense and strengthened the defense secretary's authority over the military services, also established the chairman's position. After June 1952, the Marine Corps commandant was included in the JCS and treated as the equal of the other service chiefs whenever the staff took matters directly concerning the Marines under consideration. Though the commandant soon became, for all intents and purposes, a de facto member, Congress did not pass a measure making the Marine leader a full partner in the JCS until October 1978.

In the immediate postwar years, the JCS had continued to exercise direct authority over the uniformed services. REORGANIZATION PLAN NO. 6, implemented in 1953 to improve overall military planning and enhance civilian control of America's defenses, removed the JCS from the chain of command and restricted it to an advisory role. In order to improve interservice coordination, the DEFENSE REORGANIZATION ACT OF 1958 assigned the JCS responsibility for the strategic planning and direction of the military's major multiservice commands. A major overhaul of the Joint Chiefs system occurred under the GOLDWATER-NICHOLS DEFENSE REORGANIZATION ACT of 1986. The landmark bill gave the CJCS greater control over the Joint Staff and increased the chairman's authority at the expense of the four service chiefs. The 1986 measure also created the vice-chairman post.

NATIONAL SECURITY COUNCIL (NSC) Created under the NATIONAL SECURITY ACT of 1947, the National Security Council is the topmost advisory body on national security affairs in the executive branch. Members advise the president on the integration of U.S. domestic, foreign, and military activities as they relate to America's security objectives and commitments. The NSC staff

has been a key agent in the coordination of national security policy, but its powers are strictly advisory and it has no independent policy-making authority.

By law, members of the council include the president, vice-president, secretary of state, and secretary of defense. The director of central intelligence (DCI) and the chairman of the JOINT CHIEFS OF STAFF (JCS) serve as formal advisers, while the assistant to the president for national security affairs (better known as the national security adviser), the treasury secretary, and the White House chief of staff all regularly take part in NSC meetings. On occasion other government officials may attend at the request of the president.

The NSC staff is headed by the national security adviser. This group of several dozen people, recruited from the civilian government, the military, and academia, carries out the administrative tasks of the council. The national security adviser, who is appointed by the president and does not require congressional confirmation, traditionally figures as one of the leading officials in the foreign policy structure of the executive branch. Often the adviser is a close confidant of the president on national security issues, with direct access and significant influence.

The NSC emerged out of America's experience in WORLD WAR II. President FRANKLIN D. ROOSEVELT largely had administered the U.S. war effort through a combination of personal advisers and ad hoc agencies. By 1945, leaders in Congress, the armed services, and the executive branch saw the need for a formal, accountable, high-level body to formulate national security policy. On July 26, 1947, President HARRY S. TRUMAN signed the landmark National Security Act, overhauling the nation's defense and intelligence establishments and providing for the NSC.

The council's organization and role have evolved over time according to the concepts of each president. The Eisenhower White House was first to institutionalize the NSC and make it integral to the executive foreign policy apparatus. In 1953 President DWIGHT D. EISENHOWER replaced the council's executive secretary position with the newly formed post of national security adviser. He was also responsible for establishing a significant NSC adjunct, the

NATIONAL SECURITY ADVISER	DATES	ADMINISTRATION
SIDNEY W. SOUERS	1947–1950	Truman
James S. Lay, Jr.	1950–1953	Truman
Robert Cutler	1953–1955	Eisenhower
Dillon Anderson	1955–1956	Eisenhower
William A. Jackson	1956	Eisenhower
Robert Cutler	1957–1958	Eisenhower
Gordon Gray	1958–1961	Eisenhower
MCGEORGE BUNDY	1961–1966	Kennedy L. B. Johnson
WALT W. ROSTOW	1966–1969	L. B. Johnson
HENRY A. KISSINGER	1969–1975	Nixon Ford
BRENT SCOWCROFT	1975–1977	Ford
ZBIGNIEW BRZEZINSKI	1977–1981	Carter
Richard V. Allen	1981	Reagan
William P. Clark, Jr.	1981–1983	Reagan
Robert C. McFarlane	1983–1985	Reagan
John M. Poindexter	1985–1986	Reagan
FRANK C. CARLUCCI	1986–1987	Reagan
COLIN L. POWELL	1987–1989	Reagan
BRENT SCOWCROFT	1989–	Bush

Board of Consultants on Foreign Intelligence Activities — later renamed the PRESIDENT'S FOREIGN INTELLIGENCE ADVISORY BOARD. Presidents JOHN F. KENNEDY and LYNDON B. JOHNSON made comparatively little use of the NSC. President RICHARD M. NIXON revitalized the council. His national security adviser, HENRY A. KISSINGER, was particularly influential in shaping and directing national security policy. Kissinger owns the distinction of having been the only adviser to serve simultaneously as secretary of state. President JIMMY CARTER gave the national security adviser cabinet rank. His successor, RONALD W. REAGAN, downgraded the position, rescinding the cabinet status.

In 1986 the NSC found itself at the center of the IRAN-CONTRA scandal. Council staff members had conducted covert operations involving secret arms sales to Iran and the diversion of part of the proceeds to the U.S.-backed Contra guerrillas in Nicaragua. The NSC, as part of the president's executive office, traditionally has remained beyond congressional scrutiny. Congressional committees criticized the Reagan administration's use of the NSC to avoid legislative oversight of its intelligence activities and to circumvent legal bans on aiding the CONTRAS. The TOWER COMMISSION, appointed by Reagan to investigate the affair, concluded in its 1987 report that Iran-Contra represented a failure of senior executive-branch officials to fulfill their responsibilities rather than a problem with the NSC structure itself.

OFFICE OF SCIENCE AND TECHNOLOGY POLICY (OSTP) WORLD WAR II and the increasingly diverse and complex demands of modern warfare focused interest in the White House on science and technology. VANNEVAR BUSH, head of the wartime Office of Scientific Research and Development, first fulfilled the role of a presidential science assistant, informally advising

SCIENCE ADVISER	DATES	ADMINISTRATION
James R. Killian, Jr.	1957–1961	Eisenhower
Jerome B. Wiesner	1961–1964	Kennedy L. B. Johnson
Donald F. Hornig	1964–1969	L. B. Johnson
Lee A. Dubridge	1969–1970	Nixon
Edward E. David, Jr.	1970–1973	Nixon
H. Guyford Stever	1976–1977	Ford
Frank Press	1977–1981	Carter
George A. Keyworth 2nd	1981–1985	Reagan
William R. Graham, Jr.	1986–1989	Reagan
D. Allan Bromley	1989–	Bush

FRANKLIN D. ROOSEVELT on science and technology matters. Various proposals were advanced in the early postwar years to institutionalize scientific advice to the federal government. In 1950 President HARRY S. TRUMAN signed legislation establishing the National Science Foundation. Believing that scientific expertise on defense issues was needed on the White House staff, Truman created the Science Advisory Committee the following year, placing it within the presidential Office of Defense Mobilization.

America received a jolt in 1957 when the Soviet Union launched Sputnik, the first artificial satellite. Responding to concerns about U.S. scientific prowess in the wake of the Soviet feat, President DWIGHT D. EISENHOWER the same year formed the President's Scientific Advisory Committee (PSAC). The PSAC was a panel of distinguished private scientists and engineers who met periodically to advise the White House on technical issues pertaining to defense, space, and civilian enterprise. Eisenhower also created the position of special assistant to the president for science and technology and appointed James R. Killian, Jr., president of the Massachusetts Institute of Technology, to the post. The science adviser served as chairman of PSAC. In 1962 President JOHN F. KENNEDY formed the Office of Science and Technology (OST) within the executive office of the president. The president's science adviser was also director of OST, which had its own staff and budget. In 1973 President RICHARD M. NIXON, unhappy with PSAC criticism of administration policies,

abolished the committee, OST, and the position of science adviser.

President GERALD R. FORD in 1975 introduced legislation to reestablish a science advisory position within the White House. The 1976 National Science and Technology Policy, Organization, and Priorities Act created a permanent Office of Science and Technology. Its director, the president's science adviser, is subject to Senate confirmation. OSTP advises the president on science and technology with respect to national security, foreign relations, the economy, energy, the environment, and health. The director acts as an adviser to the NATIONAL SECURITY COUNCIL and serves as a member of the National Space Council, an executive branch panel responsible for U.S. space policy.

UNITED STATES TRADE REPRESENTATIVE (USTR) Acknowledging the need for an administrative agency within the White House devoted to increasingly complex U.S. trade activities, Congress created the Office of the Special Trade Representative for Trade Negotiations in 1962 under the TRADE EXPANSION ACT. This measure authorized the special trade representative to direct all trade negotiations and to administer the nation's trade-agreements program. The new agency marked an important gain for antiprotectionist forces in Congress and pleased advocates of a liberal trade policy in the foreign policy establishment. With the TRADE ACT OF 1974, Congress established the office as a cabinet-level agency

U.S. TRADE REPRESENTATIVE	DATES	ADMINISTRATION
CHRISTIAN A. HERTER	1962–1966	Kennedy L. B. Johnson
William M. Roth	1967–1969	L. B. Johnson Nixon
Carl J. Gilbert	1969–1971	Nixon
William D. Eberle	1971–1975	Nixon Ford
Frederick B. Dent	1975–1977	Ford Carter
Robert S. Strauss	1977–1979	Carter
Reubin O. Askew	1979–1980	Carter
William E. Brock 3rd	1981–1985	Reagan
Clayton Yeutter	1985–1989	Reagan
Carla A. Hills	1989–	Bush

within the executive office of the president and granted it further powers for coordinating U.S. trade policy. In 1980 lawmakers renamed the agency the Office of the U.S. Trade Representative. President JIMMY CARTER's executive order of January 4, 1980, made the trade office responsible for setting and implementing overall trade policy.

The agency is led by the U.S. trade representative, a cabinet-level official with the rank of ambassador, who is directly responsible to the president and Congress. The president relies on the USTR for policy guidance on the expansion of U.S. exports, unfair trade practices, bilateral trade and commodity issues, and direct investment matters. The trade representative reports to the Congress in appearances before the Senate Finance Committee and the House Ways and Means Committee. As America's principal trade negotiator, the USTR serves as the chief U.S. representative at major international conferences and negotiations, including all activities of the GENERAL AGREEMENT ON TARIFFS AND TRADE (GATT); trade-related discussions and meetings in the ORGANIZATION FOR ECONOMIC COOPERATION AND DEVELOPMENT (OECD); and trade- and commodity-linked activities of the UNITED NATIONS CONFERENCE ON TRADE AND DEVELOPMENT. The USTR, by virtue of the office, is a member of the board of directors of the OVERSEAS PRIVATE INVESTMENT CORPORATION (OPIC) and the EXPORT-IMPORT BANK. A trio of deputy U.S. trade representatives assists the incumbent USTR. All three hold the rank of ambassador: two are located in Washington, D.C., and one in Geneva, Switzerland. A chief textile negotiator, also with ambassador's rank, is primarily responsible for negotiating textile agreements with foreign governments.

Appendix C

Diplomatic Corps

This appendix reviews the course of U.S. relations with the nations that have figured most prominently in American foreign affairs: China, France, Germany, Great Britain, Japan, Mexico, Russia (Soviet Union), and Spain. Also covered are the three key international organizations of which the United States is a member: the North Atlantic Treaty Organization, Organization of American States, and United Nations. Following each overview is a historical listing of the U.S. representatives to that nation or organization. The use of SMALL CAPS throughout indicates that item or person is the subject of a separate dictionary entry.

America's earliest envoys were the secret agents appointed by the Continental Congress during the AMERICAN REVOLUTION to buy war supplies and seek European support in the conflict with Great Britain. Because the young republic associated ambassadors with monarchy, no American diplomatic representatives of this highest grade were appointed for more than 100 years. The United States sent ministers instead. By the close of the 19th century, America had emerged as a major international power with widening foreign policy horizons. In 1893 the United States commissioned its first full-fledged ambassadors to Great Britain, France, Germany, and Italy.

CHINA The prosperous East Asia trade in the decades after 1790 marked the earliest American contacts with China. CALEB CUSHING, first U.S. envoy to China, concluded the TREATY OF WANGHIA in July 1844, which granted America generous commercial concessions and most favorable diplomatic status. Alexander Everett replaced Cushing in 1845 and served as the first permanent American emissary to China. The BURLINGAME TREATY (1868) spelled out broadened agreements on commerce, travel, consular affairs, and immigration. But a swelling tide of Chinese immigrant labor into America in the 1870s provoked strong, even violent, anti-Chinese sentiments in the United States. Passage of the CHINESE EXCLUSION ACT (1882) and other restrictive immigration measures raised diplomatic tensions between the countries in the late 1800s.

At the turn of the century, America's OPEN DOOR policy safeguarded the expanding U.S. commercial stake in China and called on the United States, the major European powers, and Japan to respect and preserve China's political and territorial integrity. In 1900, the American military joined with European and Japanese forces to quell the bloody, antiforeigner BOXER REBELLION of Chinese ultranationalists. The Nationalist Revolution of 1911 overthrew the Chinese monarchy and resulted in the establishment in 1912 of the short-lived Chinese republic under revolutionary figure Sun Yat-sen. Political factionalism brought the period of the warlords after 1916, when rival provincial military groups contended for control of China and sought the support of various Western powers. Under the NINE-POWER TREATY, concluded in 1922 at the WASHINGTON NAVAL CONFERENCE,

MINISTER TO CHINA	DATES	ADMINISTRATION
CALEB CUSHING	1844	Tyler
Alexander H. Everett	1846–1847	Polk
John W. Davis	1848–1850	Polk
		Taylor
Humphrey Marshall	1853–1854	Pierce
Robert M. McLane	1854	Pierce
Peter Parker	1856–1857	Pierce
		Buchanan
William B. Reed	1858	Buchanan
John E. Ward	1859–1860	Buchanan
Anson Burlingame	1862–1867	Lincoln
		A. Johnson
J. Ross Browne	1868–1869	A. Johnson
Frederick F. Low	1870–1873	Grant
Benjamin P. Avery	1874–1875	Grant
George F. Seward	1876–1880	Grant
		Hayes
James B. Angell	1880–1881	Hayes
		Garfield
John Russell Young	1882–1885	Arthur
Charles Denby	1885–1898	Cleveland
		B. Harrison
		Cleveland
		McKinley
Edwin H. Conger	1898–1905	McKinley
		T. Roosevelt
William W. Rockhill	1905–1909	T. Roosevelt
		Taft
William James Calhoun	1910–1913	Taft
Paul S. Reinsch	1913–1919	Wilson
Charles R. Crane	1920–1921	Wilson
Jacob Gould Schurman	1921–1925	Harding
		Coolidge
John Van A. MacMurray	1925–1929	Coolidge
		Hoover

the United States and the other major Pacific powers pledged to respect the sovereignty and independence of China. The pact also committed its signatories to uphold free-trade principles and to help a fragmented and war-torn China achieve a stable government.

In the Chinese Civil War that erupted again after WORLD WAR II, the United States backed Chiang Kai-shek's Nationalist regime with sporadic military and economic aid in its fight against the Chinese Communists led by Mao Tse-tung. The late 1945 diplomatic mission of General GEORGE C. MAR-

AMBASSADOR TO CHINA	DATES	ADMINISTRATION
Nelson T. Johnson	1930–1941	Hoover F. D. Roosevelt
Clarence E. Gauss	1941–1944	F. D. Roosevelt
Patrick J. Hurley	1945	F. D. Roosevelt Truman
J. Leighton Stuart	1945	Truman
Karl L. Rankin	1953–1957	Eisenhower
Everett F. Drumright	1958–1962	Eisenhower Kennedy
Alan G. Kirk	1962–1963	Kennedy
Jerauld Wright	1963–1965	Kennedy L. B. Johnson
Walter P. McConaughy	1966–1974	L. B. Johnson Nixon
Leonard Unger	1974–1979	Nixon Ford Carter
Leonard F. Woodcock	1979–1981	Carter
Arthur W. Hummel, Jr.	1981–1985	Reagan
Winston Lord	1985–1989	Reagan Bush
James R. Lilley	1989–	Bush

SHALL to China to mediate a settlement between Chiang and Mao failed. Chiang fled mainland China in 1949 with his Kuomintang forces and set up a Nationalist government-in-exile on the island of Taiwan, proclaiming it the Republic of China. In October 1949 the victorious Communists established the mainland People's Republic of China. The Communist triumph, a blow to America's COLD WAR strategy of CONTAINMENT, aroused alarm in the United States and provoked charges and countercharges in Congress and the foreign policy establishment about "who lost China." President HARRY S. TRUMAN broke with an American tradition of acknowledging de facto governments and refused to recognize Red China. The official U.S. diplomatic presence withdrew in early 1950 and prospects for normalized relations were scuttled when American and Chinese Communist forces fought on opposing sides in the KOREAN WAR.

The diplomatic chasm between the United States and mainland China was nar-

CHIEF OF U.S. LIAISON OFFICE IN PEKING	DATES	ADMINISTRATION
DAVID K. E. BRUCE	1973–1974	Nixon
GEORGE BUSH	1974–1975	Ford
THOMAS S. GATES, JR.	1976–1977	Ford Carter
Leonard F. Woodcock	1977–1979	Carter

rowed by the visit of President RICHARD M. NIXON in February 1972 for the PEKING SUMMIT. The two nations, through the SHANGHAI COMMUNIQUE, pledged to work toward the normalization of relations. In 1973 they opened nondiplomatic liaison offices in each other's capital as a step toward regular two-way contacts. Finally in December 1978, President JIMMY CARTER and Chinese leader Deng Xiaoping announced an agreement to initiate full diplomatic relations. On January 1, 1979, the United States shifted diplomatic recognition from Taiwan to mainland China, acknowledging Beijing's claim of one China with Taiwan as part of that single China. America's "one China" affirmation came with the understanding that the United States would continue to have trade, cultural, and other unofficial contacts with the Taiwanese. Rapidly expanding ties followed diplomatic recognition, aided by China's move toward economic reform and greater receptiveness to Western capital investment and technology and by a joint interest in opposing Soviet influence in Asia. The Chinese Communist regime's brutal suppression of the pro-democracy TIANANMEN UPRISING in the summer of l989 and hostile defiance of Western criticism of the crackdown strained U.S.-Chinese relations and threatened to undermine the diplomatic advances of the preceding decade.

FRANCE The United States has maintained formal diplomatic relations with France since the TREATY OF AMITY AND COMMERCE (1778) first secured that nation's recogni-tion of American independence. French military forces provided critical support to the colonies in the AMERICAN REVOLUTION. Diplomatic ties unraveled during the XYZ AFFAIR (1797), when the two countries clashed over French assaults on American commercial shipping. The United States posted no minister to Paris for the length of the undeclared maritime QUASI-WAR (1798 – 1800). Full contacts finally were restored through the CONVENTION OF 1800. Friction over the enduring French presence on the American continent at the onset of the 19th century eased after the Jefferson administration completed the LOUISIANA PURCHASE from Napoleon Bonaparte in 1803.

French imposition of hand-picked dictator Maximilian in Mexico in the mid-1860s defied the MONROE DOCTRINE ban on European expansion in the Western Hemisphere and thus strained Franco-American relations. The two countries avoided conflict when Napoleon III withdrew French troops from Mexico in 1867. French neutrality in the SPANISH-AMERICAN WAR (1898) benefited the victorious United States and contributed to the rapprochement between Washington and Paris in the decade after 1898. Relations were strengthened in this period by American mediation at the ALGECIRAS CONFERENCE (1906) of the dispute between France and Germany over Morocco.

The two countries fought as allies in WORLD WAR I. In 1942, following its entrance into WORLD WAR II, America withdrew its ambassador from Nazi-occupied France. From 1942 to 1944, the United States remained in contact with the puppet

MINISTER TO FRANCE	DATES	ADMINISTRATION
BENJAMIN FRANKLIN	1778–1785	Continental Congress Confederation Congress
THOMAS JEFFERSON	1785–1789	Confederation Congress Washington
William Short	1790–1792	Washington
Gouverneur Morris	1792–1794	Washington
JAMES MONROE	1794–1796	Washington
ROBERT R. LIVINGSTON	1801–1804	Jefferson
JOHN ARMSTRONG	1804–1810	Jefferson Madison
Joel Barlow	1811–1812	Madison

MINISTER TO FRANCE	DATES	ADMINISTRATION
William H. Crawford	1813–1815	Madison
ALBERT GALLATIN	1816–1823	Madison Monroe
James Brown	1823–1829	Monroe J. Q. Adams
William C. Rives	1829–1832	Jackson
Levett Harris	1833	Jackson
EDWARD LIVINGSTON	1833–1835	Jackson
LEWIS CASS	1836–1842	Jackson Van Buren W. H. Harrison Tyler
William R. King	1844–1846	Tyler Polk
RICHARD RUSH	1847–1849	Polk
William C. Rives	1849–1853	Taylor Fillmore
John Y. Mason	1854–1859	Pierce Buchanan
Charles J. Faulkner	1860–1861	Buchanan
William L. Dayton	1861–1864	Lincoln
John Bigelow	1865–1866	A. Johnson
John A. Dix	1866–1869	A. Johnson
ELIHU B. WASHBURNE	1869–1877	Grant
Edward F. Noyes	1877–1881	Hayes
Levi P. Morton	1881–1885	Garfield Arthur
Robert M. McLane	1885–1889	Cleveland
WHITELAW REID	1889–1892	B. Harrison
T. Jefferson Coolidge	1892–1893	B. Harrison

Vichy government through lower-ranking officials. In October 1944 the United States recognized General Charles de Gaulle's Committee of National Liberation as the provisional government of France. Normal Franco-American diplomatic relations resumed in 1945 with the establishment of the French Fourth Republic (1945–1958). U.S. aid channeled through the MARSHALL PLAN was vital to the rebuilding of France during the early postwar period. France joined NATO in 1949 and stood with the Western alliance against Soviet expansionism in the 1950s. The more independent French foreign policy pursued by President de Gaulle after 1958 challenged U.S. leadership of the Atlantic alliance and resulted in France's withdrawal of its forces from NATO's integrated military structure in 1966. Beginning in the 1970s U.S.-French ties were strengthened by the annual ECONOMIC SUMMITS of the GROUP OF 7 Western industrialized nations. France participated in the U.S.-led UNITED NATIONS coalition that defeated Iraq in the PERSIAN GULF WAR (1991).

AMBASSADOR TO FRANCE	DATES	ADMINISTRATION
James B. Eustis	1893–1897	Cleveland
Horace Porter	1897–1905	McKinley T. Roosevelt
Robert S. McCormick	1905–1907	T. Roosevelt
Henry White	1907–1909	T. Roosevelt
ROBERT BACON	1909–1912	Taft Wilson
Myron T. Herrick	1912–1914	Taft Wilson
William G. Sharp	1914–1919	Wilson
Hugh Campbell Wallace	1919–1921	Wilson
Myron T. Herrick	1921–1929	Harding Coolidge
Walter E. Edge	1929–1933	Hoover
Jesse Isidor Straus	1933–1936	F. D. Roosevelt
WILLIAM C. BULLITT	1936–1940	F. D. Roosevelt
WILLIAM D. LEAHY	1941–1942	F. D. Roosevelt
Jefferson Caffery	1944–1949	F. D. Roosevelt Truman
DAVID K. E. BRUCE	1949–1952	Truman
James C. Dunn	1952–1953	Truman
C. Douglas Dillon	1953–1957	Eisenhower
Amory Houghton	1957–1961	Eisenhower
James M. Gavin	1961–1962	Eisenhower
CHARLES E. BOHLEN	1962–1968	Kennedy L. B. Johnson
R. Sargent Shriver, Jr.	1968–1970	L. B. Johnson Nixon
Arthur K. Watson	1970–1972	Nixon
John N. Irwin 2nd	1973–1974	Nixon
Kenneth Rush	1974–1977	Ford
Arthur A. Hartman	1977–1981	Carter
Evan G. Galbraith	1981–1985	Reagan
Joe M. Rodgers	1985–1989	Reagan Bush
Walter J. P. Curley	1989–	Bush

GERMANY U.S. diplomatic recognition of Prussia, in effect since June 1797, was transferred in May 1871 to the newly united German Empire under Chancellor Otto von Bismarck. President WOODROW WILSON severed diplomatic ties with Germany in February 1917 in response to its unrestricted submarine warfare against

MINISTER TO GERMANY	DATES	ADMINISTRATION
JOHN QUINCY ADAMS	1797–1801	J. Adams
Henry Wheaton	1835–1846	Jackson Van Buren W. H. Harrison Tyler Polk
Andrew J. Donelson	1846–1849	Polk Taylor
Edward A. Hannegan	1849–1850	Taylor
Daniel D. Barnard	1850–1853	Fillmore Pierce
Peter D. Vroom	1853–1857	Pierce Buchanan
Joseph A. Wright	1857–1861	Buchanan Lincoln
Norman B. Judd	1861–1865	Lincoln A. Johnson
Joseph A. Wright	1865–1867	A. Johnson
George Bancroft	1867–1874	A. Johnson Grant
J. C. Bancroft Davis	1874–1877	Grant Hayes
Bayard Taylor	1878	Hayes
Andrew D. White	1879–1881	Hayes Garfield
A. A. Sargent	1882–1884	Arthur
John A. Kasson	1884–1885	Arthur Cleveland
George H. Pendleton	1885–1889	Cleveland
William Walter Phelps	1889–1893	B. Harrison Cleveland

neutral shipping in WORLD WAR I. In April America joined the Allied fight against the Central Powers. The United States restored relations with the postwar Weimar Republic in November 1921. America's entrance into WORLD WAR II following the Japanese attack on PEARL HARBOR led Adolf Hitler's Nazi Germany, allied with Japan, to declare war on the United States on December 11, 1941, rupturing diplomatic contacts for the length of the conflict.

Following Germany's unconditional surrender in May 1945, the victorious Allies gave much of eastern Germany to Poland and divided the remainder of the country into occupation zones. The United States, Great Britain, France, and the Soviet Union each administered affairs within its own area and dealt with matters affecting all of Germany through the collective ALLIED CONTROL COUNCIL (ACC). Berlin, located in the Soviet zone, was jointly run by the four powers, each occupying a sector of the city. Cooperation between the Western allies and USSR on the issue of Germany's future soon foundered over fundamental ideological and political differences. With Cold War tensions mounting in the late 1940s, the division between the U.S., French, and British zones in the West and Soviet zone in the East hardened into a permanent boundary. In 1948 the Soviets withdrew from the ACC and blockaded Berlin, isolat-ing the city from all ground transportation links to the West. The Berlin Airlift, the U.S. and British effort to supply West Berlin with food and fuel, finally broke the 10-month Soviet blockade in May 1949.

In September 1949 the Western powers established the democratic Federal Re-

AMBASSADOR TO GERMANY	DATES	ADMINISTRATION
Theodore Runyon	1893–1896	Cleveland
Edwin F. Uhl	1896–1897	Cleveland McKinley
Andrew D. White	1897–1902	McKinley T. Roosevelt
Charlemagne Tower	1902–1908	T. Roosevelt
David Jayne Hill	1908–1911	T. Roosevelt Taft
John G. A. Leishman	1911–1913	Taft Wilson
James W. Gerard	1913–1917	Wilson
Ellis L. Dresel	1921–1922	Harding
Alanson B. Houghton	1922–1925	Harding Coolidge
Jacob Gould Schurman	1925–1930	Coolidge Hoover
Frederic M. Sackett	1930–1933	Hoover
William E. Dodd	1933–1937	F. D. Roosevelt
Hugh R. Wilson	1938	F. D. Roosevelt
James B. Conant	1955–1957	Eisenhower
David K. E. Bruce	1957–1959	Eisenhower
Walter C. Dowling	1959–1963	Eisenhower Kennedy
George C. McGhee	1963–1968	Kennedy L. B. Johnson
Henry Cabot Lodge, Jr.	1968–1969	L. B. Johnson
Kenneth Rush	1969–1972	Nixon
Martin J. Hillenbrand	1972–1976	Nixon Ford
Walter J. Stoessel, Jr.	1976–1981	Ford Carter
Arthur F. Burns	1981–1985	Reagan
Richard R. Burt	1985–1989	Reagan
Vernon A. Walters	1989–1991	Bush
Robert M. Kimmitt	1991–	Bush

AMBASSADOR TO GERMAN DEMOCRATIC REPUBLIC	DATES	ADMINISTRATION
JOHN SHERMAN COOPER	1974–1976	Ford
David B. Bolen	1977–1980	Carter
Herbert S. Okun	1980–1983	Carter Reagan
Rozanne L. Ridgway	1983–1985	Reagan
Francis J. Meehan	1985–1988	Reagan
Richard C. Barkley	1988–1990	Reagan Bush

public of Germany, or West Germany. A month later, under Soviet direction, the eastern zone organized itself as the Communist German Democratic Republic, or East Germany, thus finalizing the split of historic Germany in the postwar era. In May 1955, after West Germany gained full sovereignty and joined the Western security alliance NATO, the United States posted its first ambassador to West German capital Bonn.

Between 1949 and 1970 West Germany refused to recognize the German Democratic Republic. West Germany, proclaiming itself the single legitimate government of all of Germany, would not establish ties with nations that maintained diplomatic links with East Germany. The exodus of East Germans to the West in the early 1950s prompted the Soviet-backed Communist regime to undertake construction of barbed-wire fencing along the East-West boundary. Recurring conflict over the divided German city's status led to Soviet instigation in 1958 of the BERLIN CRISIS and the eventual raising of the BERLIN WALL in 1961. West German Chancellor Willy Brandt in 1969 inaugurated a policy of rapprochement with East Germany that resulted in the first meeting of German leaders in 1970. In 1972 the two Germanys concluded a treaty acknowledging one another's sovereignty and postwar borders. In September 1974 the United States established diplomatic relations with East Germany.

Strong political and economic ties, a thriving trade partnership, NATO membership, and mutual security concerns closely bound the United States and West Germany in the postwar period. The large and long-standing American military presence in West Germany underscored the U.S. commitment to the defense of the Federal Republic of Germany and Western Europe against a Communist Warsaw Pact strike. The fall of the Berlin Wall in November 1989 under the pressure of collapsing governments in East Germany and Eastern Europe set in motion German reunification and presaged the end of the Cold War. In February 1990 the two Germanys and the four World War II Allies outlined plans for negotiating German unity. The FINAL SETTLEMENT WITH RESPECT TO GERMANY TREATY providing for German reunification was signed in September 1990. International concerns over historic German nationalism were assuaged by a unified Germany's membership in NATO. Final agreements struck by West and East Germany established Berlin as the post-merger capital and confirmed Germany's commitment to democratic and free-market institutions. Official reunification took place October 3, 1990. With economic might assuming greater importance in the post–Cold War world, Germany's powerful economy assured it a leading role in European affairs and greater stature in relations with the United States.

GREAT BRITAIN The United States won its independence from Great Britain in the AMERICAN REVOLUTION. Following the British military surrender at Yorktown in October 1781, negotiators reached peace terms in the TREATY OF PARIS, concluded on September 3, 1783. Under the treaty, Great Britain

MINISTER TO GREAT BRITAIN	DATES	ADMINISTRATION
JOHN ADAMS	1785–1788	Confederation Congress
Thomas Pinckney	1792–1796	Washington
Rufus King	1796–1803	Washington J. Adams Jefferson
JAMES MONROE	1803–1807	Jefferson
William Pinkney	1808–1811	Jefferson Madison
Jonathan Russell	1811–1812	Madison
JOHN QUINCY ADAMS	1815–1817	Madison
RICHARD RUSH	1818–1825	Monroe
Rufus King	1825–1826	J. Q. Adams
ALBERT GALLATIN	1826–1827	J. Q. Adams
JAMES BARBOUR	1828–1829	J. Q. Adams Jackson
LOUIS MCLANE	1829–1831	Jackson
MARTIN VAN BUREN	1831–1832	Jackson
Aaron Vail	1832–1836	Jackson
Andrew Stevenson	1836–1841	Jackson Van Buren W. H. Harrison Tyler
EDWARD EVERETT	1841–1845	Tyler
LOUIS MCLANE	1845–1846	Polk
George Bancroft	1846–1849	Polk Taylor
Abbott Lawrence	1849–1852	Taylor Fillmore
Joseph R. Ingersoll	1852–1853	Fillmore Pierce
JAMES BUCHANAN	1853–1856	Pierce
George M. Dallas	1856–1861	Pierce Buchanan
CHARLES FRANCIS ADAMS	1861–1868	Lincoln A. Johnson
Reverdy Johnson	1868–1869	A. Johnson
J. Lothrop Motley	1869–1870	Grant
Robert C. Schenck	1871–1876	Grant
Edwards Pierrepont	1876–1877	Grant Hayes
John Welsh	1877–1879	Hayes
James Russell Lowell	1880–1885	Hayes Garfield Arthur

MINISTER TO GREAT BRITAIN	DATES	ADMINISTRATION
Edward J. Phelps	1885–1889	Cleveland B. Harrison
Robert T. Lincoln	1889–1893	B. Harrison

AMBASSADOR TO GREAT BRITAIN	DATES	ADMINISTRATION
THOMAS F. BAYARD	1893–1897	Cleveland
JOHN M. HAY	1897–1898	McKinley
Joseph Choate	1899–1905	McKinley T. Roosevelt
WHITELAW REID	1905–1912	T. Roosevelt Taft
Walter Hines Page	1913–1918	Wilson
John W. Davis	1918–1921	Wilson
George Harvey	1921–1923	Harding Coolidge
FRANK B. KELLOGG	1924–1925	Coolidge
Alanson B. Houghton	1925–1929	Coolidge
CHARLES G. DAWES	1929–1931	Hoover
ANDREW W. MELLON	1932–1933	Hoover
Robert Worth Bingham	1933–1937	F. D. Roosevelt
Joseph P. Kennedy	1938–1940	F. D. Roosevelt
John G. Winant	1941–1946	F. D. Roosevelt
W. AVERELL HARRIMAN	1946	Truman
Lewis W. Douglas	1947–1950	Truman
Walter S. Gifford	1950–1953	Truman
Winthrop W. Aldrich	1953–1957	Eisenhower
John Hay Whitney	1957–1961	Eisenhower
DAVID K. E. BRUCE	1961–1969	Kennedy L. B. Johnson
Walter H. Annenberg	1969–1974	Nixon Ford
ELLIOT L. RICHARDSON	1975–1976	Ford
Anne L. Armstrong	1976–1977	Ford
Kingman Brewster, Jr.	1977–1981	Carter
John J. Louis, Jr.	1981–1983	Reagan
Charles H. Price 2nd	1983–1989	Reagan
Henry E. Catto, Jr.	1989–1991	Bush
Raymond G. H. Seitz	1991–	Bush

recognized U.S. independence; consented to American territorial boundaries to the west and north of the Mississippi River and the Canadian border; and granted the United States fishing privileges in the North Atlantic around Newfoundland. The United States initiated diplomatic ties when it named JOHN ADAMS the first American minister to Great Britain in February 1785. Shunned by the British government, Adams left London in February 1788 after an unproductive stay. Anglo-American relations were temporarily discontinued, resuming in January 1792 when Congress commissioned THOMAS PINCKNEY as Adams's successor.

British harassment of neutral U.S. commercial shipping and IMPRESSMENT of American seamen in Great Britain's navy provoked the June outbreak of the WAR OF 1812. Within weeks the United States suspended relations with Great Britain. By the terms of the TREATY OF GHENT, which formally ended the stalemated conflict in December 1814, Great Britain reaffirmed its recognition of U.S. independence. The United States reestablished diplomatic ties to Great Britain with the appointment of JOHN QUINCY ADAMS as envoy to London in February 1815. The two nations removed a source of diplomatic friction when they settled long-standing disputes over the U.S.-Canada border through the WEBSTER-ASHBURTON TREATY of 1842 and the OREGON TREATY of 1846.

In 1861 Great Britain declared itself neutral in the American Civil War, recognizing the Confederacy's belligerent status but refusing to acknowledge its independence. The TRENT AFFAIR and the manufacture of Confederate warships in English shipyards nearly led to diplomatic rupture and war between London and Washington. To the end of the 19th century, the U.S.-British relationship endured the ALASKA BOUNDARY DISPUTE, the VENEZUELA CLAIMS episode, competition for construction rights to a transoceanic canal in Central America, and jockeying for hegemony in Latin America and the Caribbean. Settlement of these issues led to a period of improved relations, the so-called Anglo-American entente, in the decade after 1900.

Allies in WORLD WAR I and WORLD WAR II, the United States and Great Britain since 1945 have maintained a staunch political and diplomatic partnership as anchors of the Western alliance and members of NATO.

The two countries consult closely on foreign policy issues and global problems and generally share major foreign and security policy objectives. Important economic ties bind the Anglo-American relationship. Great Britain remains the United States' largest trading partner in the European Community (EC), while only Canada receives more in U.S. foreign direct investment. In turn, Great Britain is the largest source of foreign direct investment in the United States.

JAPAN U.S. Commodore MATTHEW C. PERRY's historic missions to Japan culminated in the TREATY OF KANAGAWA in March 1854 opening the self-isolated Pacific nation to American trade and contacts. TOWNSEND HARRIS, who would become America's first resident minister to Japan in January 1859, concluded a path-breaking commercial treaty in 1858 that also arranged for reciprocal diplomatic recognition. Japan modernized rapidly after the Meiji Restoration in 1868 and by the turn of the century U.S.-Japanese diplomacy was concerned with the evolving strategic and commercial interests of the two countries in the western Pacific. President THEODORE ROOSEVELT in 1905 mediated talks between Russia and Japan that resulted in the PORTSMOUTH TREATY, which ended the Russo-Japanese War (1904–1905) and preserved the BALANCE OF POWER in the Far East. The TAFT-KATSURA AGREEMENT (1905) and ROOT-TAKAHIRA AGREEMENT (1908) committed the United States and Japan to respect one another's territorial possessions and spheres of influence in East Asia, to preserve the Pacific status quo, and to uphold China's territorial integrity. Japanese expansionist aims in China from the turn of the 20th century were a recurring source of friction with the United States. Backing the principle of Chinese sovereignty, the Wilson administration opposed the 21 Demands issued in January 1915, a Japanese ploy to strengthen its position in China. Tensions were defused temporarily by the LANSING-ISHII AGREEMENT (1917), wherein the United States acknowledged Japan's special interests in China and both Washington and Tokyo endorsed Chinese territorial sovereignty.

Japan's invasion of Manchuria in 1931 was deplored by the United States through the STIMSON DOCTRINE of nonrecognition.

MINISTER TO JAPAN	DATES	ADMINISTRATION
TOWNSEND HARRIS	1859–1862	Buchanan Lincoln
Robert H. Pruyn	1862–1865	Lincoln
Robert B. Van Valkenburgh	1867–1869	A. Johnson Grant
Charles E. De Long	1869–1873	Grant
John A. Bingham	1873–1885	Grant Hayes Garfield Arthur
Richard B. Hubbard	1885–1889	Cleveland
John F. Swift	1889–1891	B. Harrison
Frank L. Coombs	1892–1893	B. Harrison
Edwin Dun	1893–1897	Cleveland
Alfred E. Buck	1897–1902	McKinley T. Roosevelt
Lloyd C. Griscom	1903–1905	T. Roosevelt

Japanese aggression in China violated the NINE-POWER TREATY (1922) and the OPEN DOOR principles and foreshadowed Toyko's push for military conquest of all of Asia. Declarations of war followed Japan's surprise bombing of PEARL HARBOR on December 7, 1941. U.S. and Japanese forces fought one another throughout the Pacific theater in WORLD WAR II. Japan formally surrendered on September 2, 1945, after the American atomic bombing in August of Hiroshima and Nagasaki. In the war's aftermath, U.S. occupation forces under General DOUGLAS MACARTHUR oversaw the rebuilding of Japan and the transformation of its society. The JAPANESE PEACE TREATY and the JAPANESE SECURITY TREATY were completed in September 1951, clearing the way in 1952 for restoration of full sovereignty to a largely demilitarized Japan.

A stable relationship with Japan continues to be a key foundation of American policy in Asia. Japan's economic might and expanding international role underline the importance for the United States of close contacts between Washington and Tokyo.

AMBASSADOR TO JAPAN	DATES	ADMINISTRATION
Luke E. Wright	1906–1907	T. Roosevelt
Thomas J. O'Brien	1907–1911	T. Roosevelt Taft
Charles Page Bryan	1911–1912	Taft
Larz Anderson	1913	Taft
George W. Guthrie	1913–1917	Wilson
Roland S. Morris	1917–1920	Wilson
Charles Beecher Warren	1921–1922	Harding
Cyrus E. Woods	1923–1924	Harding Coolidge

AMBASSADOR TO JAPAN	DATES	ADMINISTRATION
Edgar A. Bancroft	1924–1925	Coolidge
Charles MacVeagh	1925–1928	Coolidge
William R. Castle, Jr.	1930	Hoover
W. Cameron Forbes	1930–1932	Hoover
JOSEPH C. GREW	1932–1941	Hoover F. D. Roosevelt
Robert D. Murphy	1952–1953	Truman Eisenhower
John M. Allison	1953–1957	Eisenhower
Douglas MacArthur 2nd	1957–1961	Eisenhower
EDWIN O. REISCHAUER	1961–1966	Kennedy L. B. Johnson
U. Alexis Johnson	1966–1969	L. B. Johnson
Armi H. Meyer	1969–1972	Nixon
Robert S. Ingersoll	1972–1973	Nixon
James D. Hodgson	1974–1977	Nixon Ford
MICHAEL J. MANSFIELD	1977–1988	Carter Reagan
Michael Armacost	1989–	Bush

The nations, with increasingly interdependent economies, are major trade partners. Swelling U.S. trade deficits with Japan and American anxieties over Japanese economic and technological prowess raised tensions between the trans-Pacific allies through the 1980s and into the 1990s. Domestic protectionist pressures and the quest for greater access to Japanese markets have provoked U.S. government efforts to get Japan to lift its restrictions on U.S. goods. Japan has responded with pointed criticism of America's soaring federal deficit, short-sighted economic planning, low savings rate, and lack of productivity. To forestall further deterioration in the relationship, the two sides in 1989 undertook the high-level STRUCTURAL IMPEDIMENTS INITIATIVE to settle major differences on trade issues.

MEXICO The United States forged diplomatic ties with recently independent Mexico in March 1825, posting Joel R. Poinsett as the first American envoy to Mexico City. Texas dominated the stormy U.S.-Mexican relationship in its first quarter century, with both nations staking claim to the territory. American presidents JOHN QUINCY ADAMS and ANDREW JACKSON failed in bids to purchase it from the Mexican government in the 1820s and early 1830s. By 1835, 30,000 Americans had arrived in Texas, lured by Mexico's offer of land grants. The settlers mounted the armed TEXAN REVOLUTION against Mexico and on March 2, 1836, proclaimed the independent Lone Star Republic under first President SAM HOUSTON. After suffering crushing defeats at the Alamo and Goliad in February and March 1836, the Texans turned the military tide at San Jacinto in late April, routing the Mexican forces. Captured Mexican leader Santa Anna, in return for his own life, pledged recognition of Lone Star independence. While Mexico renounced Santa Anna's promise as illegitimate, it did not pursue its claim on Texas.

Following the U.S. annexation of Texas by joint resolution of Congress on March 1, 1845, the Mexicans protested strenuously

MINISTER TO MEXICO	DATES	ADMINISTRATION
Joel R. Poinsett	1825–1830	J. Q. Adams Jackson
Anthony Butler	1830–1835	Jackson
Powhatan Ellis	1839–1842	Van Buren W. H. Harrison Tyler
Waddy Thompson	1842–1844	Tyler
Wilson Shannon	1844–1845	Tyler Polk
Nathan Clifford	1848–1849	Polk Taylor
Robert P. Letcher	1850–1852	Taylor Fillmore
Alfred Conkling	1852–1853	Fillmore Pierce
JAMES GADSDEN	1853–1856	Pierce
JOHN FORSYTH	1856–1858	Pierce Buchanan
Robert M. McLane	1859–1860	Buchanan
John B. Weller	1861	Buchanan
Thomas Corwin	1861–1864	Lincoln
Marcus Otterbourg	1867	A. Johnson
William S. Rosencrans	1868–1869	A. Johnson Grant
Thomas H. Nelson	1869–1873	Grant
JOHN W. FOSTER	1873–1880	Grant Hayes
Philip H. Morgan	1880–1885	Hayes Garfield Arthur Cleveland
Henry R. Jackson	1885–1886	Cleveland
Thomas C. Manning	1886–1887	Cleveland
Edward S. Bragg	1888–1889	Cleveland
Thomas Ryan	1889–1893	B. Harrison
Issac P. Gray	1893–1894	Cleveland
Matt W. Ransom	1895–1897	Cleveland

and within weeks broke diplomatic links with the United States. A long-simmering dispute over the location of the Texan border fanned U.S.-Mexican tensions. American special envoy JAMES SLIDELL, dispatched by pro-expansionist President JAMES K. POLK in November 1845 to negotiate a resolution of the border rift, twice was shunned by a suspicious Mexican government and hostilities broke out in April 1846. The TREATY OF

AMBASSADOR TO MEXICO	DATES	ADMINISTRATION
Powell Clayton	1897–1905	McKinley T. Roosevelt
Edwin H. Conger	1905	T. Roosevelt
David E. Thompson	1906–1909	T. Roosevelt Taft
Henry Lane Wilson	1910–1913	Taft
Henry P. Fletcher	1917–1919	Wilson
Charles Beecher Warren	1924	Coolidge
James R. Sheffield	1924–1927	Coolidge
DWIGHT W. MORROW	1927–1930	Coolidge Hoover
J. Reuben Clark, Jr.	1930–1933	Hoover
JOSEPHUS DANIELS	1933–1941	F. D. Roosevelt
George S. Messersmith	1942–1946	F. D. Roosevelt Truman
Walter Thurston	1946–1950	Truman
William O'Dwyer	1950–1952	Truman
Francis White	1953–1957	Eisenhower
Robert C. Hill	1957–1960	Eisenhower
Thomas C. Mann	1961–1963	Kennedy
Fulton Freeman	1964–1969	L. B. Johnson
Robert H. McBride	1969–1974	Nixon
Joseph J. Jova	1974–1977	Nixon Ford
Patrick J. Lucey	1977–1979	Carter
Julian Nava	1980–1981	Carter Reagan
John A. Gavin	1981–1986	Reagan
Charles J. Pilliod, Jr.	1986–1989	Reagan Bush
John N. Negroponte	1989–	Bush

GUADALUPE HIDALGO, concluded in February 1848, marked the end of the MEXICAN WAR. By its terms, a defeated Mexico recognized the U.S. annexation of Texas, accepted the Rio Grande as the Texan-Mexican border, and ceded the New Mexico and California territories to the United States in return for $15 million. Quick adoption of the treaty by the U.S. Senate forestalled the extremist "ALL-OF-MEXICO" MOVEMENT, whose advocates campaigned for America's annexation of the whole of its southern neighbor in the name of MANIFEST DESTINY. Full diplomatic contacts were restored in July 1848. Mexico made a final territorial concession to the United States in the GADSDEN PURCHASE (1853).

France moved during the American Civil War to enlarge its influence in Latin America. Secretary of State WILLIAM H. SEWARD protested the French intervention in Mexico in 1862 as imperial meddling in the

Western Hemisphere. President ABRAHAM LINCOLN refused to recognize the puppet regime of Austrian Archduke Maximilian, whom French Emperor Napoleon III enthroned as emperor of Mexico in 1864. The burdens of the Civil War kept the Lincoln administration from taking decisive action against France. Under growing U.S. pressure, Napoleon III ended the French intervention in 1867.

The turbulent and violent Mexican Revolution (1910–1920), which included among its casualties American nationals and their property, interrupted normal U.S.-Mexican relations. The TAMPICO INCIDENT (1914), involving the arrest and detention of U.S. sailors in the Mexican city, strained already frayed U.S.-Mexican relations. The episode prompted President WOODROW WILSON to order U.S. marines ashore in April 1914 to occupy the Mexican port of Veracruz. The U.S. occupation pushed the neighboring countries to the brink of war. The crisis fueled by the VERACRUZ INCIDENT was defused in the course of the ABC MEDIATION. After a series of deadly cross-border raids into U.S. territory by Francisco "Pancho" Villa, Wilson dispatched General JOHN J. PERSHING in 1916 on his PUNITIVE EXPEDITION to track down the elusive Mexican revolutionary. Wilson withdrew the fruitless expedition in early 1917 rather than risk a confrontation with the government of Venustiano Carranza, which had grown alarmed by the large American military presence.

Recurring threats by the Mexican government after 1917 to expropriate the vast property holdings of American oil companies generated alarm and anger in the United States. The 1923 BUCARELI AGREEMENT, which reestablished normal U.S.-Mexican diplomatic ties, resolved the issue of subsoil rights ownership. When the Mexican government revived the petroleum dispute in the mid-1920s, U.S. Ambassador DWIGHT W. MORROW used skillful diplomacy to achieve a temporary settlement of the subsoil rights conflict. In 1938 crisis flared again when Mexican President Lazaro Cardenas, espousing economic independence for his country, nationalized petroleum and expropriated U.S. oil properties. The nations reached a compromise resolution of the MEXICAN OIL EXPROPRIATION CONTROVERSY in 1941, in which Mexico agreed to reimburse American companies for their oil holdings.

Despite their historical differences, Mexico and the United States have had close and mostly friendly relations since WORLD WAR II. The neighbors are bound by substantial trade ties and work together on such sensitive issues as narcotics traffic into the United States, immigration, and border environmental matters. Mexico's large foreign debt of the late 1970s and 1980s, a source of friction with the United States, led Mexican governments to seek relief from American banks and the INTERNATIONAL MONETARY FUND. Throughout the 1980s Mexico disagreed with American policy in Central America, criticizing U.S. support of the anti-Sandinista Nicaraguan CONTRAS and the El Salvadoran military and condemning America's PANAMA INVASION in late December 1989 to oust dictator Manuel Antonio Noriega. In the early 1990s Washington and Mexico City pursued negotiations on a free-trade agreement.

NORTH ATLANTIC TREATY ORGANIZATION (NATO) This regional alliance, encompassing 13 West European nations together with the United States, Canada, and Turkey, provides for the security of its members in the North Atlantic area. Since 1949 NATO has served as the cornerstone of the West's collective defense system. The alliance was formed to discourage, and if necessary repel, a Soviet military assault on West Europe by the combined conventional forces of its members and by extending the U.S. nuclear deterrent to the West European states. NATO's charter enjoins member nations to regard an attack on one as an attack on all. The organization also is a forum for regular consultation on political, economic, and other nonmilitary issues. Member nations have approached the alliance as a channel through which to resolve differences in their individual foreign and defense policies.

NATO, with headquarters in Brussels, is organized into three major components. The North Atlantic Council, a political body vested with supreme authority, seats the permanent civilian representatives, or NATO ambassadors, of the member nations. The council sets and implements basic alliance policies. The NATO Secretariat is directed by the secretary-general, who

AMBASSADOR TO NATO	DATES	ADMINISTRATION
William H. Draper, Jr.	1952–1953	Truman Eisenhower
John C. Hughes	1953–1955	Eisenhower
George W. Perkins	1955–1957	Eisenhower
W. Randolph Burgess	1957–1961	Eisenhower Kennedy
Thomas K. Finletter	1961–1965	Kennedy L. B. Johnson
Harlan Cleveland	1965–1969	L. B. Johnson Nixon
Robert Ellsworth	1969–1971	Nixon
David M. Kennedy	1972–1973	Nixon
DONALD H. RUMSFELD	1973–1974	Nixon Ford
DAVID K. E. BRUCE	1974–1976	Ford
Robert Strausz–Hupe	1976–1977	Ford Carter
W. Tapley Bennett, Jr.	1977–1983	Carter Reagan
David M. Abshire	1983–1987	Reagan
Alton G. Keel, Jr.	1987–1989	Reagan Bush
William H. Taft 4th	1989–	Bush

also serves as chairman of the NATO council. Finally, there is the integrated military structure, which comprises three strategic-area commands: Atlantic Command, European Command, and English Channel Command. A fourth element, the Canada-U.S. Regional Planning Group, develops plans for North American security. France is not part of the integrated military arrangement. While remaining militarily independent, the French nonetheless cooperate with NATO forces. All other members are full military partners.

Concern over their security amid the Soviet imposition after WORLD WAR II of Communist regimes in Eastern Europe led the West European nations of Great Britain, France, Belgium, Luxembourg, and the Netherlands in March 1948 to conclude the Brussels Treaty for collective self-defense. A Canadian initiative, broached a month later, proposed that the Brussels Treaty Or-

ganization be replaced by an Atlantic defense system incorporating the North American countries. On April 4, 1949, the United States, Canada, Iceland, Norway, Portugal, Italy and the five Brussels Pact members signed the North Atlantic Treaty creating the Atlantic security organization. Greece and Turkey joined in 1952 followed by West Germany in 1955. France pulled out of the integrated military structure in 1966, prompting the organization the following year to transfer NATO headquarters from Paris to Brussels. Greek military forces withdrew from NATO in August 1974 after Turkey's invasion of Cyprus but rejoined in 1980. Spain was admitted to the alliance in 1982.

The collapse of communism in Eastern Europe in 1989, end of the East-West COLD WAR, and disintegration of the Soviet Union prompted a review of NATO's purpose and future. Upon reunification in October

1990, Germany maintained its membership in the organization, in part to reassure neighbors apprehensive over historic German expansionism. At an annual NATO summit in November 1991, the 16 member states endorsed a new alliance strategy that emphasized the organization's increasingly political and diplomatic focus and reaffirmed the alliance's importance as a mechanism for preserving close U.S.-European ties. The continued presence of American conventional and nuclear forces was viewed as essential to European security. At the conference NATO leaders also approved the creation of a new institution, the North Atlantic Cooperation Council, as a forum for security contacts with the former Eastern bloc. The council was slated to include all NATO members plus Bulgaria, Romania, Hungary, Czechoslovakia, Poland, the Baltic states — Lithuania, Estonia, and Latvia—and the Soviet Union.

ORGANIZATION OF AMERICAN STATES (OAS) The Ninth Pan-American Conference, held in Bogota, Colombia, in 1948, established the Organization of American States as a regional organization under the United Nations Charter to promote political, economic, and cultural cooperation among the member states. The OAS, with headquarters in Washington, D.C., became the hub of the post–World War II inter-American system. The hemispheric mutual-defense arrangement forged by the Rio Treaty of 1947 was made the fulcrum of the new organization's system for regional collective security. The OAS charter also outlined procedures for the peaceful settlement of disputes between organization members and prohibited military action by one state against another except in immediate self-defense. The OAS from its inception was resolutely anti-Communist. The delegates at Bogota took a strong stand against communism in the Western Hemisphere, declaring it incompatible with inter-American political principles. In 1962 the organization expelled the Cuban Communist government of Fidel Castro.

The OAS comprises several key constituent bodies. The General Assembly meets annually to set basic organization policies. The Permanent Council, which seats a representative with ambassador's rank from each country, functions as the executive coordinating agency of the organization. The Meeting of Consultation of

AMBASSADOR TO OAS	DATES	ADMINISTRATION
Paul C. Daniels	1948–1951	Truman
John C. Drier	1951–1960	Truman Eisenhower
deLesseps S. Morrison	1961–1963	Kennedy
Ellsworth Bunker	1964–1966	L. B. Johnson
Sol M. Linowitz	1966–1969	L. B. Johnson Nixon
Joseph J. Jova	1969–1974	Nixon
William S. Mailliard	1974–1977	Nixon Ford Carter
Gale W. McGee	1977–1981	Carter Reagan
J. William Middendorf 2nd	1981–1985	Reagan
Richard T. McCormack	1985–1989	Reagan Bush
Luigi R. Einaudi	1989–	Bush

Ministers of Foreign Affairs (known generally as the Meeting of American Foreign Ministers) convenes to consider urgent problems bearing on regional peace or security. Collective action cannot be taken without two-thirds approval of the foreign ministers. The PAN-AMERICAN UNION is the permanent secretariat. The Inter-American Defense Board, established at the 1942 RIO DE JANEIRO CONFERENCE, remains independent of the OAS. Part of the inter-American system, the board provides for military coordination among American nations on the defense of the hemisphere against external aggression.

The chief U.S. envoy to the OAS, who bears the title of permanent representative and carries the rank of ambassador, is appointed by the president. Historically the United States has exercised a dominant role in the organization, particularly in security affairs and economic development, where the Latin American states have relied heavily on U.S. funding. OAS membership includes the United States and 32 Caribbean and Latin American nations. Twenty-five other countries from the Americas, Europe, Africa, and Asia are permanent observers to the organization.

See also INTER-AMERICAN CONFERENCES in APPENDIX E.

RUSSIA / SOVIET UNION The earliest American envoy to Russia was Francis Dana, who resided in the Russian capital of St. Petersburg between 1781 and 1783 but was never officially received at court. The United States initiated formal diplomatic relations in 1809 when it posted JOHN QUINCY ADAMS as the first U.S. minister to Russia. Expanding Russian territorial and trade claims in Alaska and the Pacific Northwest in the early 19th century conflicted with U.S. interests and helped prompt formulation of the MONROE DOCTRINE (1823), which declared U.S. determination to oppose European expansion in the Americas. The RUSSO-AMERICAN TREATY OF 1824, the first formal agreement between the countries, settled the dispute by limiting Russian influence to areas north of 54°40'. The ALASKA PURCHASE by the United States in 1867 ended the Russian presence in the region.

The mediation of President THEODORE ROOSEVELT at the 1905 PORTSMOUTH CONFERENCE yielded the PORTSMOUTH TREATY ending the Russo-Japanese War (1904–1905) over competing interests in Korea and Manchuria. The United States suspended diplomatic relations following the tumultuous Russian Revolution of November 1917. After the Bolsheviks withdrew Russia from WORLD WAR I by completing a separate peace with Germany in March 1918, the United States committed some 8000 troops to the Allied SIBERIAN INTERVENTION (1918–1920). America withheld recognition of the new Union of Soviet Socialist Republics (USSR) until President FRANKLIN D. ROOSEVELT concluded the ROOSEVELT-LITVINOV AGREEMENT with Soviet Foreign Minister Maxim Litvinov in November 1933, whereupon WILLIAM C. BULLITT was appointed first U.S. ambassador to the Soviet Union. The United States and USSR were allied against Nazi Germany in WORLD WAR II. In the immediate postwar years, a struggle over boundaries and the political order in Europe drove a wedge between the United States and West European powers on one side and the Soviet Union on the other. The division of Germany and the Soviet drive to subjugate Eastern Europe brought a dramatic deterioration in East-West relations in the late 1940s, marking the opening phase of the long COLD WAR. America responded to Soviet expansionism with a strategy of Communist CONTAINMENT. The East-West breach spawned the rival NATO and Warsaw Pact security alliances, with the United States as the cornerstone of the Western alliance and the USSR as the anchor of the Communist bloc.

Ideological conflict and military competition divided the two major nuclear superpowers for more than 40 years. They narrowly averted a nuclear confrontation in 1962 in the CUBAN MISSILE CRISIS and clashed over escalating U.S. involvement after 1965 in the VIETNAM WAR. Cold War hostilities eased amid the U.S.-Soviet DETENTE of the 1970s. The historic 1972 MOSCOW SUMMIT between President RICHARD M. NIXON and Soviet leader Leonid I. Brezhnev marked both a major step toward rapprochement and the emergence of top-level summitry as a staple of Soviet-American diplomacy. The thaw in relations brought increased cultural contacts and two-way trade and led to completion of the SALT I and SALT II arms control accords. However, indirect confrontation in numerous

MINISTER TO RUSSIA	DATES	ADMINISTRATION
JOHN QUINCY ADAMS	1809–1814	Madison
William Pinkney	1817–1818	Madison Monroe
George W. Campbell	1819–1820	Monroe
Henry Middleton	1821–1830	Monroe J. Q. Adams Jackson
JAMES BUCHANAN	1832–1833	Jackson
William Wilkins	1834–1835	Jackson
John Randolph Clay	1836–1837	Jackson Van Buren
George M. Dallas	1837–1839	Van Buren
Churchill C. Cambreleng	1840–1841	Van Buren W. H. Harrison Tyler
Charles S. Todd	1841–1846	Tyler Polk
Ralph I. Ingersoll	1847–1848	Polk
Arthur P. Bagby	1849	Polk Taylor
Neill S. Brown	1850–1853	Fillmore Pierce
Thomas H. Seymour	1854–1858	Pierce Buchanan
Francis W. Pickens	1858–1860	Buchanan
John Appleton	1860–1861	Buchanan Lincoln
Cassius M. Clay	1861–1862	Lincoln
Simon Cameron	1862	Lincoln
Cassius M. Clay	1863–1869	Lincoln A. Johnson Grant
Andrew G. Curtin	1869–1872	Grant
James L. Orr	1873	Grant
Marshall Jewell	1873–1874	Grant
George H. Boker	1875–1878	Grant Hayes
Edwin W. Stoughton	1878–1879	Hayes
JOHN W. FOSTER	1880–1881	Hayes Garfield
William H. Hunt	1882–1884	Arthur

MINISTER TO RUSSIA	DATES	ADMINISTRATION
Alphonso Taft	1884–1885	Arthur Cleveland
George V. N. Lothrop	1885–1888	Cleveland
Lambert Tree	1889	Cleveland
Charles Emory Smith	1890–1892	B. Harrison
Andrew D. White	1892–1894	B. Harrison Cleveland
Clifton R. Breckinridge	1894–1897	Cleveland McKinley

regional conflicts in Asia, Africa, Latin America, and the Middle East; the continuing arms race; and U.S. condemnation of the Kremlin HUMAN RIGHTS record demonstrated the limits of Soviet-American cooperation. The Soviet invasion of Afghanistan in 1979 and subsequent U.S. support for anti-Communist Mujahedeen rebels in the AFGHANISTAN WAR damaged superpower relations and derailed arms control efforts through the early 1980s.

After Mikhail S. Gorbachev became leader of the USSR in 1985, U.S.-Soviet relations steadily began to improve, hastening a decline in East-West tensions through the late 1980s. He won U.S. confidence with his emphasis on opening up the Soviet system and restructuring the Soviet command economy, a pair of processes known as glasnost and perestroika. At the WASHINGTON SUMMIT in 1987, he and President RONALD W. REAGAN completed the historic INF TREATY abolishing an entire class of NUCLEAR WEAPONS. Gorbachev's program of political and economic reform touched off dynamic movements for political freedom across the Soviet bloc. The forces thus unleashed brought the demise of communism in Eastern Europe and the reunification of Germany. The collapse of the BERLIN WALL and the Soviet retreat from an adventurist foreign policy accelerated the thaw in superpower relations and enhanced the prospects for major conventional and strategic arms reductions. President GEORGE BUSH and Gorbachev met at the MALTA SUMMIT in December 1989 to consult on the course of post–Cold War ties between their countries. Completion in 1990 of the FINAL SETTLEMENT WITH RESPECT TO GERMANY TREATY and the CONVENTIONAL FORCES EUROPE TREATY

ended the protracted East-West struggle over Europe. Moscow's political cooperation with Washington in the PERSIAN GULF WAR (1991) demonstrated the transformation in the U.S.-Soviet relationship. At the MOSCOW SUMMIT in July 1991, Bush and Gorbachev took another major step toward disarmament by signing the historic START Treaty cutting superpower nuclear arsenals.

Meanwhile, a beleaguered Gorbachev, struggling to resurrect the shattered Soviet economy, faced growing domestic challenges to his policies and leadership. The weakening of Communist central authority accelerated independence movements across the USSR, with the Baltics and other republics moving to break free from Moscow. Russian Republic President Boris N. Yeltsin's courageous leadership in defense of democracy helped foil the August 1991 MOSCOW COUP, in which Communist hardliners in the Kremlin attempted to oust Gorbachev and seize power. Bush had backed the Russian leader's stand against the putsch and refused to recognize the cabal that had confined Gorbachev at his Crimean dacha. Yeltsin emerged from the crisis not only a hero but the most powerful political figure in the unraveling Soviet Union. The abortive coup, illustrative of profound instability and uncertainty in the USSR, raised serious concerns in Washington as to who controlled the massive Soviet nuclear arsenal. Addressing these worries, Bush issued his NUCLEAR REDUCTION INITIATIVE in September 1991 and sought assurances from the Soviet authorities about the security of atomic weapons. In the coup's aftermath Gorbachev tried in vain to stave off the disintegration of the USSR. Strug-

AMBASSADOR TO RUSSIA	DATES	ADMINISTRATION
Ethan A. Hitchcock	1897–1899	McKinley
Charlemagne Tower	1899–1902	McKinley T. Roosevelt
Robert S. McCormick	1903–1905	T. Roosevelt
George L. Meyer	1905–1907	T. Roosevelt
John W. Riddle	1907–1909	T. Roosevelt Taft
William W. Rockhill	1910–1911	Taft
Curtis Guild	1911–1913	Taft
George T. Marye	1914–1916	Wilson
David R. Francis	1916–1917	Wilson

AMBASSADOR TO USSR	DATES	ADMINISTRATION
WILLIAM C. BULLITT	1933–1936	F. D. Roosevelt
Joseph E. Davies	1937–1938	F. D. Roosevelt
Laurence A. Steinhardt	1939–1941	F. D. Roosevelt
William H. Standley	1942–1943	F. D. Roosevelt
W. AVERELL HARRIMAN	1943–1946	F. D. Roosevelt Truman
WALTER BEDELL SMITH	1946–1948	Truman
Alan G. Kirk	1949–1951	Truman
GEORGE F. KENNAN	1952	Truman
CHARLES E. BOHLEN	1953–1957	Eisenhower
Llewellyn E. Thompson	1957–1962	Eisenhower Kennedy
Foy D. Kohler	1962–1966	Kennedy L. B. Johnson
Llewellyn E. Thompson	1967–1969	L. B. Johnson
Jacob D. Beam	1969–1973	Nixon
Walter J. Stoessel, Jr.	1974–1976	Nixon Ford
Malcolm E. Toon	1977–1979	Carter
Thomas J. Watson, Jr.	1979–1981	Carter
Arthur A. Hartman	1981–1987	Reagan
Jack F. Matlock, Jr.	1987–1991	Reagan Bush
Robert S. Strauss	1991–	Bush

gling to keep pace with the extraordinary course of events within the Soviet Union, the Bush administration began to reorient U.S. policy in anticipation of Gorbachev's imminent political demise. The USSR collapsed in December 1991 when the leaders of the three Slavic republics — Russia, Ukraine, and Byelorussia—signed an agreement forming a new Commonwealth of Independent States. By the end of the year Gorbachev had resigned his now defunct office and 11 former Soviet republics had joined the commonwealth as sovereign members. The United States recognized Russia as the successor state to the Soviet Union.

SPAIN During the AMERICAN REVOLUTION, Spain withheld recognition of U.S. independence out of concern for the impact of America's revolutionary example on Spanish colonies in the New World. Madrid established diplomatic relations with Washington in 1783. The new American republic found itself bordered on the south and west by Spanish territories the Floridas and Louisiana. PINCKNEY'S TREATY (1795) disposed of a number of disputes that had beset Spanish-American relations since the end of the American Revolution. By its terms, Spain granted U.S. citizens free navigation of the Mississippi River, accepted the 31st parallel as the boundary between the United States and West Florida, and vowed not to incite Indian attacks on American frontier settlements. The WEST FLORIDA CONTROVERSY was joined in full when the U.S. government claimed West Florida between the Mississippi and Perdido rivers as part of the LOUISIANA PURCHASE (1803). Spain dismissed the U.S. claim as illegitimate. In

1810 President JAMES MADISON directed American troops to occupy the region as far as the Pearl River. The United States captured the area between the Pearl and Perdido in 1813 and occupied the rest of West Florida during the FLORIDA INVASION (1818). Spain ceded the Floridas to the United States in the ADAMS-ONIS TREATY (1819). This landmark agreement also defined the boundary between Spanish and U.S. possessions in North America from the Gulf of Mexico to the Pacific Ocean, with Spain accepting 42 degrees as the northern extent of its territory and the United States surrendering its claim to Texas.

President JAMES MONROE withheld U.S. recognition of the independence of Spain's rebellious Latin American colonies until after the Adams-Onis Treaty was ratified. When an alliance of European monarchies appeared to be plotting an invasion of Latin America to restore Spain's colonies, the president proclaimed the MONROE DOCTRINE (1823), asserting opposition to European intervention in the Western Hemisphere as a basic tenet of U.S. foreign policy. American acquisition of Cuba from Spain became a goal in the mid-19th century of Southern expansionists who wanted to add the island to the Union as slave territory. Various schemes to purchase or annex the Spanish colony fell through. The OSTEND MANIFESTO (1854), in which three American diplomats urged the United States to take Cuba by force if Spain refused to sell it, sullied U.S.-Spanish rela-

MINISTER TO SPAIN	DATES	ADMINISTRATION
William Short	1794–1795	Washington
David Humphreys	1797–1801	J. Adams
		Jefferson
Charles Pinckney	1802–1804	Jefferson
George W. Erving	1816–1819	Madison
		Monroe
JOHN FORSYTH	1819–1823	Monroe
Hugh Nelson	1823–1825	Monroe
		J. Q. Adams
Alexander H. Everett	1825–1829	J. Q. Adams
		Jackson
Cornelius P. Van Ness	1829–1836	Jackson
John H. Eaton	1837–1840	Jackson
		Van Buren

MINISTER TO SPAIN	DATES	ADMINISTRATION
Aaron Vail	1840–1842	Van Buren W. H. Harrison Tyler
Washington Irving	1842–1846	Tyler Polk
Romulus M. Saunders	1846–1849	Polk Taylor
Daniel M. Barringer	1849–1853	Taylor Fillmore Pierce
PIERRE SOULE	1853–1855	Pierce
Augustus C. Dodge	1855–1859	Pierce
William Preston	1859–1961	Buchanan
Carl Schurz	1861	Lincoln
Gustavus Koerner	1862–1864	Lincoln
John P. Hale	1865–1869	A. Johnson Grant
Daniel E. Sickles	1869–1874	Grant
CALEB CUSHING	1874–1877	Grant
James Russell Lowell	1877–1880	Hayes
Lucius Fairchild	1880–1881	Hayes
Hannibal Hamlin	1881–1882	Garfield Arthur
JOHN W. FOSTER	1883–1885	Arthur Cleveland
Jabez L. M. Curry	1885–1888	Cleveland
Perry Belmont	1889	Cleveland
Thomas W. Palmer	1889–1890	B. Harrison
E. Burd Grubb	1890–1892	B. Harrison
A. Loudon Snowden	1892–1893	B. Harrison Cleveland
Hannis Taylor	1893–1897	Cleveland McKinley
Stewart L. Woodford	1897–1898	McKinley
Bellamy Storer	1899–1902	McKinley T. Roosevelt
Arthur S. Hardy	1903–1905	T. Roosevelt
William M. Collier	1905–1909	T. Roosevelt Taft
Henry Clay Ide	1909–1913	Taft Wilson

AMBASSADOR TO SPAIN	DATES	ADMINISTRATION
Joseph E. Willard	1913–1921	Wilson Harding
Cyrus E. Woods	1921–1923	Harding
Alexander P. Moore	1923–1925	Harding Coolidge
Ogden H. Hammond	1926–1929	Coolidge
Irwin B. Laughlin	1929–1933	Hoover
Claude G. Bowers	1933–1939	F. D. Roosevelt
Alexander W. Weddell	1939–1942	F. D. Roosevelt
Carlton J. H. Hayes	1942–1945	F. D. Roosevelt
Norman Armour	1945	F. D. Roosevelt
Stanton Griffis	1951–1952	Truman
Lincoln MacVeagh	1952–1953	Truman Eisenhower
James C. Dunn	1953–1955	Eisenhower
John Lodge	1955–1961	Eisenhower Kennedy
Anthony J. D. Biddle, Jr.	1961	Kennedy
Robert F. Woodward	1962–1965	Kennedy L. B. Johnson
Angier B. Duke	1965–1968	L. B. Johnson
Robert F. Wagner	1968–1969	L. B. Johnson
Robert C. Hill	1969–1972	Nixon
Horacio Rivero	1972–1974	Nixon Ford
Wells Stabler	1975–1978	Ford Carter
Terence A. Todman	1978–1983	Carter Reagan
Thomas O. Enders	1983–1986	Reagan
Reginald Bartholomew	1986–1989	Reagan Bush
Joseph Zappala	1989–	Bush

tions. Under domestic political fire, President FRANKLIN B. PIERCE was forced to repudiate the controversial memorandum.

The American public sympathized with Cuban insurgents who fought unsuccessfully for their independence from Spanish rule in the Ten Years' War (1868 – 1878). President ULYSSES S. GRANT, however, refused to grant belligerent status to the rebels for fear of involving the nation in a major diplomatic crisis with Spain. Spanish attempts to crush the Cuban revolt that erupted in 1895 met with strong American protest. Madrid and Washington went to war over U.S. insistence that Spain grant Cuba independence and evacuate the island. By terms of the Treaty of Paris (1898) ending the Spanish-American War (1898), a defeated Spain ceded Puerto Rico, Guam, and the Philippine Islands to the United States and relinquished Cuba, which was placed under the administration of an American military government until 1902.

Following the outbreak of the Spanish Civil War in 1936, the United States pursued a policy of nonintervention. Congress in 1937 extended the second of the Neutrality Acts to the Spanish conflict, thus depriving the recognized Republican government of the ability to purchase arms and ammunition in America. The Nationalists won the civil war in 1939, whereupon Washington recognized the Fascist government of Francisco Franco. During World War II, Franco's regime sympathized with the Axis powers but was persuaded by the Allies to remain neutral. At the war's end, the United States led efforts to isolate Spain diplomatically and deny it admission to the United Nations and to encourage the rise of democratic rule in Madrid.

The advent of the Cold War and outbreak of the Korean War expanded Western security concerns, prompting Washington to shift its position toward Madrid. In November 1950 the United States resumed full diplomatic relations with Spain. In 1953 the two nations concluded an agreement, renewed in 1963, permitting U.S. construction of several air and naval bases in Spain. In 1955 Spain was admitted to the United Nations. Franco died in 1975 and was replaced by his designated successor, Prince Juan Carlos de Borbon, who became head of state as King Juan Carlos I. Franco's death hastened a process of political liberalization that had taken root in the last years of his life. The first Spanish democratic elections in 40 years took place in 1977. Spain joined the Western security alliance NATO in 1982. The U.S. military presence became a controversial issue in Spanish politics in the 1980s. In January 1988 the United States agreed, at Spain's request, to withdraw 72 jet fighters based near Madrid. Later that year the two nations concluded a new eight-year pact governing U.S. bases in Spain.

UNITED NATIONS (U.N.) Formed during World War II by the Allied powers, the United Nations replaced the moribund League of Nations, the international organization created at the end of World War I to ensure global peace through collective security. At the Moscow Conference in October 1943, the United States, Great Britain, Soviet Union, and China concluded the Moscow Declaration, in which they agreed on the need for a permanent organization to deal with international problems threatening world peace. The concept took shape in further talks at the Dumbarton Oaks Conference (1944) and the Yalta Conference (1945). At the San Francisco Conference in 1945, the Allies framed the United Nations Charter, which was signed that June by 50 countries and ratified in October. A U.S. delegation attended when the United Nations convened for its first regular session in London in January 1946. In December of the same year, the organization established its permanent seat in New York City.

The U.N. charter outlines the major structures within the organization, notably the General Assembly, the Security Council, and the Secretariat. All member nations are represented in the General Assembly, which considers political, administrative, and budget issues. The Security Council deals with international security matters and is responsible for maintaining global peace. It consists of five permanent members — the United States, Great Britain, France, Russia, and the People's Republic of China—and another 10 members elected biennially by the General Assembly. Following the USSR's disintegration at the end of 1991, Russia assumed the Soviet Union's seat on the Security Council. Each country on the council has one representative and exercises one vote. Since all key decisions require unanimous approval of the five permanent members, each exercises complete veto power. The Secretariat, under the direction of the U.N. secretary-general, primarily handles administrative matters.

The permanent U.S. Mission to the United Nations, established under the United Nations Participation Act (1945), is headed by the U.S. representative to the United Nations, a presidential appointee who generally is referred to as America's U.N. ambassador. The U.S. delegation is responsibile for articulating American policy on issues that come before the world body

AMBASSADOR TO U.N.	DATES	ADMINISTRATION
Edward R. Stettinius, Jr.	1945–1946	Truman
Warren R. Austin	1947–1953	Truman
Henry Cabot Lodge, Jr.	1953–1960	Eisenhower
James J. Wadsworth	1960–1961	Eisenhower
Adlai E. Stevenson	1961–1965	Kennedy L. B. Johnson
Arthur J. Goldberg	1965–1968	L. B. Johnson
George W. Ball	1968	L. B. Johnson
James Russell Wiggins	1968–1969	L. B. Johnson
Charles W. Yost	1969–1971	Nixon
George Bush	1971–1973	Nixon
John A. Scali	1973–1975	Nixon Ford
Daniel P. Moynihan	1975–1976	Ford
William W. Scranton	1976–1977	Ford
Andrew J. Young	1977–1979	Carter
Donald F. McHenry	1979–1981	Carter
Jeane J. Kirkpatrick	1981–1985	Reagan
Vernon A. Walters	1985–1989	Reagan Bush
Thomas R. Pickering	1989–1992	Bush
Edward J. Perkins	1992–	Bush

and keeping the president and State Department apprised of major developments at U.N. headquarters.

See also UNITED NATIONS CONFERENCES in APPENDIX E.

Appendix D

Congressional Committees

The CONSTITUTION *secures Congress a multifaceted involvement in foreign affairs. Through the power of the purse lawmakers authorize and appropriate funding for foreign aid, defense, and intelligence activities. The Congress as a whole has sole authority to declare war, while the Senate must ratify all treaties and confirm all presidential nominations to top foreign policy positions. Congress exercises its foreign affairs influence mainly through a handful of key House and Senate committees. This appendix profiles the major panels on national security and foreign policy: House Armed Services; House Foreign Affairs; Senate Armed Services; and Senate Foreign Relations. Names of committee chairmen and their dates of service appear at the end of each profile. The use of* SMALL CAPS *indicates a separate entry in the dictionary.*

HOUSE ARMED SERVICES COMMITTEE Among the most influential committees in the House of Representatives, the Armed Services Committee deals with national defense and military affairs. The panel, with substantial budget and defense-policy oversight responsibilities, reviews the legislation, programs, and government activities related to U.S. national security. House rules assign the committee jurisdiction over the DEPARTMENT OF DEFENSE and the armed forces. The Secretary of Defense, chairman of the JOINT CHIEFS OF STAFF, and military service secretaries all regularly appear before Armed Services to testify on America's defense needs and preparedness and to present the administration's military budget proposals. The committee also acts as overseer for the House on arms control and disarmament and military applications of atomic energy. The panel's jurisdiction over intelligence was curtailed sharply with the creation in 1977 of the House Permanent Select Committee on Intelligence.

Every year the Armed Services Committee, in conjunction with its Senate counter-part, prepares the two authorization bills that set the ceilings for Defense Department spending on weapons, manpower, and military facilities. Armed Services does not exercise total control over defense outlays, since the House Budget and Appropriations panels are included in the funding process. It does, however, largely determine how and where the money will be spent.

The House Armed Services Committee was established on January 2, 1947, under the Legislative Reorganization Act of 1946. Federal lawmakers formed the new panel by merging the committees on Military Affairs and Naval Affairs, which together had covered national defense matters since 1822. A strong pro-defense coalition of southern Democrats and conservative Republicans controlled Armed Services in its first quarter century, under the leadership of a string of powerful southern Democratic chairmen. Some changes in the panel's composition began in the early to mid-1970s, at the end of the VIETNAM WAR, with the arrival of a faction of more liberal Democrats who alleged wasteful and excessive

HASC CHAIRMAN	DATES	ADMINISTRATION
Walter G. Andrews	1947–1949	Truman
Carl Vinson	1949–1953	Truman
Dewey Short	1953–1955	Eisenhower
Carl Vinson	1955–1965	Eisenhower Kennedy L. B. Johnson
L. Mendel Rivers	1965–1971	L. B. Johnson Nixon
F. Edward Hebert	1971–1975	Nixon Ford
Melvin Price	1975–1985	Ford Carter Reagan
Les Aspin	1985–	Reagan Bush

military spending and criticized the committee majority's routine support of the defense establishment.

The 1980s were a dynamic period for Armed Services. Under Chairman Melvin Price (D-IL), the committee oversaw the Reagan administration's first-term defense buildup, when United States military spending soared to cover expensive new weapons systems, hardware, and personnel costs. By mid-decade, growing federal budget deficits pressured the White House and Congress to reduce defense outlays and led Armed Services to explore manpower cuts, military base closings, and weapons systems delays and cancellations. Les Aspin (D-WI) assumed the chairmanship as reform-minded committee members joined in the call for changes in a PENTAGON procurement system beset by waste, mismanagement, and fraud. The elimination of the Soviet military threat with the end of the COLD WAR presaged major cuts in defense spending in the early 1990s. The Armed Services Committee joined the emerging national policy debate over reducing and restructuring the U.S. armed forces for the post–Cold War world.

HOUSE FOREIGN AFFAIRS COMMITTEE

The House Foreign Affairs Committee has foremost responsibility for foreign relations within the House of Representatives. Federal legislation, programs, initiatives, and actions on foreign policy fall within the committee's purview. It functions as the House expert overseer on American foreign affairs. The panel's jurisdiction, similar to that of the SENATE FOREIGN RELATIONS COMMITTEE, covers U.S. diplomatic relations, international conferences, wars, international economic policy, overseas trade, export controls, and international organizations. Unlike Senate Foreign Relations, which generally is the far more influential panel, House Foreign Affairs does not have a constitutional role in the approval of treaties or presidential appointments, but it does exercise the power of the purse. In collaboration with its Senate counterpart, House Foreign Affairs determines the funding of foreign aid programs and other outlays tied to U.S. foreign relations.

By precedent, the panel keeps watch over the State Department and other executive branch agencies involved in the conduct of foreign affairs. House rules authorize the Foreign Affairs Committee to monitor the president's handling of foreign policy to ensure it adheres to the law and takes account of congressional concerns. Members stay abreast of foreign affairs developments through frequent meetings with the government's top civil and military

HFAC CHAIRMAN	DATES	ADMINISTRATION
Jonathan Russell	1822–1823	Monroe
John Forsyth	1823–1827	Monroe J. Q. Adams
EDWARD EVERETT	1827–1829	J. Q. Adams
William S. Archer	1829–1834	Jackson
James M. Wayne	1835	Jackson
EDWARD EVERETT	1835	Jackson
Churchill C. Cambreleng	1835	Jackson
John Y. Mason	1835–1837	Jackson
Benjamin C. Howard	1837–1839	Jackson Van Buren
Francis W. Pickens	1839–1841	Van Buren
CALEB CUSHING	1841	W. H. Harrison Tyler
JOHN QUINCY ADAMS	1842–1843	Tyler
Samuel W. Inge	1843–1847	Tyler Polk
Truman Smith	1847–1849	Polk
John A. McClernand	1849–1851	Taylor Fillmore
Thomas H. Bayly	1851–1855	Fillmore Pierce
Alexander C. M. Pennington	1855–1857	Pierce
Thomas L. Clingman	1857–1858	Buchanan
George W. Hopkins	1858–1859	Buchanan
Thomas Corwin	1859–1861	Buchanan
John J. Crittenden	1861–1863	Lincoln
Henry Winter Davis	1863–1865	Lincoln
Nathaniel P. Banks	1865–1873	Lincoln A. Johnson Grant
Leonard Myers	1873	Grant
Godlove S. Orth	1873–1875	Grant
Thomas Swann	1875–1879	Grant Hayes
Samuel S. Cox	1879–1881	Hayes
Charles G. Williams	1881–1883	Garfield Arthur
Andrew G. Curtin	1883–1885	Arthur

HFAC CHAIRMAN	DATES	ADMINISTRATION
Perry Belmont	1885–1888	Cleveland
James B. McCreary	1888–1889	Cleveland
Robert R. Hitt	1889–1891	B. Harrison
James H. Blount	1891–1893	B. Harrison
James B. McCreary	1893–1895	Cleveland
Robert R. Hitt	1895–1907	McKinley T. Roosevelt
Robert G. Cousins	1907–1909	T. Roosevelt
James B. Perkins	1909–1910	Taft
David J. Foster	1910–1911	Taft
William Sulzer	1911–1912	Taft
Charles B. Smith	1912–1913	Taft
Henry D. Flood	1913–1919	Taft Wilson
Stephen G. Porter	1919–1931	Wilson Harding Coolidge Hoover
J. Charles Linthicum	1931–1932	Hoover
Samuel D. McReynolds	1932–1939	Hoover F. D. Roosevelt
Sol Bloom	1939–1947	F. D. Roosevelt Truman
Charles A. Eaton	1947–1949	Truman
Sol Bloom	1949	Truman
John Kee	1949–1951	Truman
James P. Richards	1951–1953	Truman
Robert B. Chiperfield	1953–1955	Eisenhower
James P. Richards	1955–1957	Eisenhower
Thomas S. Gordon	1957–1959	Eisenhower
Thomas E. Morgan	1959–1977	Eisenhower Kennedy L. B. Johnson Nixon Ford
Clement J. Zablocki	1977–1983	Carter Reagan
Dante B. Fascell	1983–	Reagan Bush

officials, hearings on American programs and policies, fact-finding missions abroad, and involvement as official U.S. delegates to a range of international conferences and events.

The House of Representatives initially dealt with foreign affairs through a series of ad hoc panels. In 1807 members established the special Foreign Relations Committee, or so-called Aggression Committee, in response to assaults on American commercial shipping by Great Britain and France during the Napoleonic Wars (1803–1815). In 1822 the Aggression panel was made a standing committee and renamed the Committee on Foreign Affairs. In the 1970s Foreign Affairs briefly changed its title, redesignating itself the Committee on International Relations in 1975, and then reverting to the Committee on Foreign Affairs in 1979. Once deemed a minor committee, the importance of House Foreign Affairs rose gradually with the expansion of the U.S. role in world affairs in the 20th century and especially after WORLD WAR II.

SENATE ARMED SERVICES COMMITTEE

In the U.S. Senate, responsibility for review of national defense and the military resides first and foremost with the Armed Services Committee. Its oversight includes the DEPARTMENT OF DEFENSE and the armed forces,

nuclear energy when it poses issues of national security, and arms control. Space-based military operations, defense research and development, and the maintenance and operation of the PANAMA CANAL also fall within the panel's purview. The Armed Services Committee and its majority party chairman review proposed legislation, presidential actions, and all related issues and developments linked to defense.

The Senate relies on Armed Services regularly to examine overall U.S. defense policy. Since 1987, the committee has held major hearings on national security strategy at the beginning of each Congress. The defense secretary, the chairman of the JOINT CHIEFS OF STAFF, and other top officials often come before the panel to present the president's proposed military budgets and to report on the administration's programs and policies. In addition, foreign policy and defense experts in and out of government are frequently invited to testify before the committee.

Senate Armed Services' power and influence stem primarily from its yearly preparation with the HOUSE ARMED SERVICES COMMITTEE of funding legislation for the Defense Department and military construction. The two authorization bills, which set caps on spending for weapons, manpower, and military facilities, earmark in detail how and where PENTAGON dollars are to be

SASC CHAIRMAN	DATES	ADMINISTRATION
Chan Gurney	1947–1949	Truman
Millard E. Tydings	1949–1951	Truman
Richard B. Russell	1951–1953	Truman
Leverett Saltonstall	1953–1955	Eisenhower
Richard B. Russell	1955–1969	Eisenhower Kennedy L. B. Johnson
John C. Stennis	1969–1981	Nixon Ford Carter
John G. Tower	1981–1985	Reagan
Barry M. Goldwater	1985–1987	Reagan
Sam Nunn	1987–	Reagan Bush

allocated. The committee has special responsibility for assisting the Senate screen presidential nominations to the top executive branch defense posts, such as the secretary of defense and the chairman of the Joint Chiefs of Staff. After its confirmation hearings, the panel recommends either approval or rejection to the full chamber. In a related function, Armed Services advises the Senate on proposed arms control agreements with other nations.

Three separate committees on Military Affairs, Naval Affairs, and the Militia, established in December 1816, were the Senate's first standing panels on defense and the armed forces. The military affairs and militia committees were merged in 1858 to form, appropriately, the Military Affairs and Militia Committee. In 1872, this panel dropped militia from its name. Military Affairs and Naval Affairs existed until 1947 when, under the Legislative Reorganization Act of 1946, they were combined into a new permanent committee, today's Armed Services Committee.

From the start Senate Armed Services has enjoyed a legacy of powerful chairmen, who have directed the Senate's defense positions from this leadership perch. First of these was Georgia Democrat Richard B. Russell, who in his 16 years at the helm dominated defense issues in the Senate. John G. Tower (R-TX), who became chairman in 1981 after the Republicans gained a majority, was an influential force in shepherding the Reagan administration's massive defense buildup through the Senate in the early 1980s. Later Tower helped forestall major defense cuts when, in the mid-1980s, federal budget deficits threated Pentagon funding. Sam Nunn (D-GA), chairman since 1987, parlayed his expertise on both strategic and technical issues into a commanding position as the Senate's major voice on national defense through the close of the 1980s. The end of the COLD WAR and collapse of the Soviet Union eliminated the Soviet military threat, compelling the U.S. defense establishment to reexamine its strategic assumptions, worldwide commitments, size, and role at the start of the 1990s. Armed Services assumed leadership in the Senate in the emerging national debate over how to reduce and retool American military forces in view of impending major cuts in defense spending.

SENATE FOREIGN RELATIONS COMMITTEE The Senate's involvement in foreign affairs ranges beyond its constitutional power of approval over treaties and related nominations. The Foreign Relations Committee is the major channel through which the Senate exercises its influence on international affairs and American foreign policy. Its jurisdiction embraces foreign economic and military aid, wars and military interventions, arms control, international scientific and environmental matters, international terrorism, and international organizations for development assistance, such as the WORLD BANK. The panel is responsible for regularly reviewing and studying U.S. national security, international economic involvement, and foreign policy. In this context, the committee also advises the president on the conduct of U.S. foreign relations. Panel members of the same party as the president generally advance the administration's programs before both the committee and the full Senate.

Members are kept abreast of issues and activities through testimony of the nation's top foreign policy officials at committee hearings. Also important are overseas fact-finding missions, participation as American delegates to foreign conferences, and private meetings with visiting heads of state. Key legislative duties include the drafting of all foreign economic and military aid bills and preparing the yearly authorization measure for funding of the many agencies and programs under the committee's jurisdiction.

The Foreign Relations Committee has a special responsibility to help the Senate carry out its constitutionally assigned approval authority over treaties. A treaty sent by the president to the Senate for advice and consent is referred to the Foreign Relations panel for review. Members then report it back to the full Senate with their recommendation for either approval or rejection. The panel exercises much the same role on nominations, holding confirmation hearings on presidential appointees to the top executive branch foreign policy posts.

In its first decades the Senate had no system of permanent committees. Between 1789 and the early 1800s, some 200 ad hoc panels dealt with specific foreign affairs issues as they arose. On December 10, 1816, senators created the Committee on Foreign

SFRC CHAIRMAN	DATES	ADMINISTRATION
James Barbour	1816–1818	Madison
Nathaniel Macon	1818–1819	Monroe
James Brown	1819–1820	Monroe
James Barbour	1820–1821	Monroe
Rufus King	1821–1822	Monroe
James Barbour	1822–1825	Monroe
Nathaniel Macon	1825–1826	Adams
Nathan Sanford	1826–1827	J. Q. Adams
Nathaniel Macon	1827–1828	J. Q. Adams
Littleton W. Tazewell	1828–1832	J. Q. Adams Jackson
John Forsyth	1832–1833	Jackson
William Wilkins	1833–1834	Jackson
Henry Clay	1834–1836	Jackson
James Buchanan	1836–1841	Jackson Van Buren
William C. Rives	1841–1842	W. H. Harrison Tyler
William S. Archer	1842–1845	Tyler
William Allen	1845–1846	Polk
Ambrose H. Sevier	1846–1848	Polk
Edward A. Hannegan	1848–1849	Polk
William R. King	1849–1850	Taylor
Henry S. Foote	1850–1851	Fillmore
James M. Mason	1851–1861	Fillmore Pierce Buchanan
Charles Sumner	1861–1871	Lincoln A. Johnson Grant
Simon Cameron	1871–1877	Grant
Hannibal Hamlin	1877–1879	Hayes
William W. Eaton	1879–1881	Hayes
William Windon	1881–1883	Arthur
John F. Miller	1883–1887	Arthur Cleveland
John Sherman	1887–1893	Cleveland B. Harrison
John T. Morgan	1893–1895	Cleveland
John Sherman	1895–1897	Cleveland
Cushman K. Davis	1897–1901	McKinley

SFRC CHAIRMAN	DATES	ADMINISTRATION
Shelby M. Cullom	1901–1913	T. Roosevelt Taft
Augustus O. Bacon	1913–1914	Wilson
William J. Stone	1914–1919	Wilson
HENRY CABOT LODGE, SR.	1919–1924	Wilson Harding Coolidge
William E. Borah	1925–1933	Coolidge Hoover
Key Pittman	1933–1940	F. D. Roosevelt
Walter F. George	1940–1941	F. D. Roosevelt
Tom Connally	1941–1947	F. D. Roosevelt Truman
ARTHUR H. VANDENBERG	1947–1949	Truman
Tom Connally	1949–1953	Truman
Alexander Wiley	1953–1955	Eisenhower
Walter F. George	1955–1957	Eisenhower
Theodore F. Green	1957–1959	Eisenhower
J. WILLIAM FULBRIGHT	1959–1975	Eisenhower Kennedy L. B. Johnson Nixon Ford
John Sparkman	1975–1979	Ford Carter
FRANK CHURCH	1979–1981	Carter
Charles H. Percy	1981–1985	Reagan
Richard G. Lugar	1985–1987	Reagan
Claiborne Pell	1987–	Reagan Bush

Relations as one of the original 11 select committees. On December 13, Virginia Senator JAMES BARBOUR became the panel's first chairman. The prestigious committee historically has drawn prominent leaders of the Senate and nation. Six presidents, nine vice-presidents, and nineteen secretaries of state have served as members.

In the late 19th century, the Foreign Relations Committee wielded considerable influence over foreign policy through its treaty power, rejecting an unprecedented 10 agreements between 1860 and 1897. When WOODROW WILSON submitted the TREATY OF VERSAILLES (1919) for ratification, Chairman HENRY CABOT LODGE, SR. (R-MA) sought changes to the agreement ending WORLD WAR I that were unacceptable to the president. After a bitter battle between Lodge and Wilson, the Senate rejected the treaty in 1919 and again in 1920, thus blocking America from joining the LEAGUE OF NATIONS. Between World War I and WORLD WAR II, the committee reflected the national mood of ISOLATIONISM. Lodge's successor, William E. Borah (R-ID), fought throughout the 1920s against U.S. involvement in internationalist ventures. In the

1930s, Chairman Key Pittman (D-NV) sponsored neutrality legislation meant to keep the United States out of European conflicts. The views of committee internationalists began to prevail by 1940, a key factor contributing to the decision by the United States to modify its neutrality and enact LEND-LEASE, the program to materially aid the Allied powers at the start of World War II.

America's own war experience and fears of postwar Soviet-sponsored Communist expansion changed some of the panel's leading isolationists, such as Senator ARTHUR H. VANDENBERG (R-MI), into internationalists. Vandenberg became Foreign Relations chairman in 1947 and helped secure bipartisan support for the MARSHALL PLAN, NATO, and other major cornerstones of the U.S. postwar foreign policy of CONTAINMENT. Growing concern by the mid-1960s over the escalating U.S. role in the VIETNAM WAR led the Foreign Relations Committee to seek a greater Senate role in the shaping and conduct of American foreign policy. Chairman J. WILLIAM FULBRIGHT (D-AK), a high-profile critic of American involvement in Vietnam, held nationally televised hearings on the war. In 1973 the Foreign Relations Committee endorsed the WAR POWERS RESOLUTION. The controversial measure, which Congress passed over a presidential veto, required the president to recall within 60 days any U.S. forces committed to hostilities unless Congress authorized their continued deployment. Richard G. Lugar (R-IN) demonstrated the continuing influence of the panel's chairman when he successfully pressed the Reagan administration to support the ouster of Philippine dictator Ferdinand E. Marcos in the PHILIPPINE CRISIS in 1986.

Appendix E

Conferences and Summits

This appendix provides charts of the major international conferences and summits at which the United States was a participant. The use of SMALL CAPS *indicates a separate dictionary entry.*

1. EARLY CONFERENCES

Conference	Date	Location	Participants	Significance
BERN CONFERENCE	1874	Switzerland	International	Establishment General Postal Union, renamed UNIVERSAL POSTAL UNION in 1878
Berlin Conference	1885	Berlin	United States European Powers	Agreement on freedom of trade in the Congo area, abolition slave traffic central Africa
Washington Conference	1887	Washington, DC	United States Great Britain Germany	Discussion disposition of SAMOA
Berlin Conference	1889	Berlin	United States Great Britain Germany	TREATY OF BERLIN on Samoa
First Hague Peace Conference	1899	The Hague	International	HAGUE CONVENTIONS governing warfare, establishment PERMANENT COURT OF ARBITRATION
PORTSMOUTH CONFERENCE	1905	Portsmouth, NH	United States Russia Japan	PORTSMOUTH TREATY ending Russo-Japanese War (1904–1905)
ALGECIRAS CONFERENCE	1906	Spain	United States European Powers	U.S.-assisted mediation of Franco-German dispute over Morocco
Second Hague Peace Conference		The Hague	International	Update, expansion HAGUE CONVENTIONS
Washington Conference	1907	Washington, DC	United States Central American Nations	CENTRAL AMERICAN TREATIES OF 1907
ABC Conference	1914	Niagara Falls, Ontario	United States Argentina Brazil Chile	ABC MEDIATION OF VERACRUZ INCIDENT
International Congress of Women	1915	The Hague	International	Formation predecessor to WOMEN'S INTERNATIONAL LEAGUE FOR PEACE AND FREEDOM

2. PAN-AMERICAN CONFERENCES

Conference	Date	Location	Significance
First	1889-1890	Washington, DC	Established COMMERCIAL BUREAU OF AMERICAN REPUBLICS
Second	1901-1902	Mexico City	Resolution favoring the voluntary arbitration of disputes
Third	1906	Rio de Janeiro	Discussion on opposing the use of force to collect international debts
Fourth	1910	Buenos Aires	Commercial Bureau reorganized as PAN-AMERICAN UNION
Fifth	1923	Santiago	Gondra Treaty (ratified by the United States in 1924) for the prevention of conflict between American states
Sixth	1928	Havana	Discussion of a ban on intervention in other member states
Seventh	1933	Montevideo	CONVENTION ON RIGHTS AND DUTIES OF STATES
Eighth	1938	Lima	DECLARATION OF LIMA providing for consultative meetings among foreign ministers on security issues
Ninth	1948	Bogota	Charter of the ORGANIZATION OF AMERICAN STATES
Tenth	1954	Caracas	Condemnation of international communism as incompatible with inter-American ideals; Declaration of Caracas, adopted March 28, 1954, reaffirming inter-American democratic principles

3. MEETINGS OF CONSULTATION OF MINISTERS OF FOREIGN AFFAIRS

Meeting	Date	Location	Significance
First	1939	Panama	DECLARATION OF PANAMA
Second	1940	Havana	ACT OF HAVANA
Third	1942	Rio de Janeiro	Consultation on cooperative action in WORLD WAR II, establishment INTER-AMERICAN DEFENSE BOARD

Subsequent meetings conducted within the OAS framework, including, notably:

Meeting	Date	Location	Significance
Fourth	1951	Washington, DC	Coordination on the threat to the Western Hemisphere posed by international communism
Eighth	1962	Punta del Este, Uruguay	Resolution excluding Communist Cuba from the inter-American System

4. OTHER INTER-AMERICAN CONFERENCES

Conference	Date	Location	Significance
Pan-American Commemorative Congress	1926	Panama	Commemoration 1826 PANAMA CONGRESS
Conference for the Maintenance of Peace	1936	Buenos Aires	CONVENTION FOR THE MAINTENANCE, PRESERVATION, AND REESTABLISHMENT OF PEACE
Chapultepec Conference	1945	Mexico City	ACT OF CHAPULTEPEC
Conference for the Maintenance of Peace and Continental Security	1947	Rio de Janeiro	RIO TREATY

5. INTERWAR CONFERENCES

Conference	Date	Location	Participants	Significance
PARIS PEACE CONFERENCE	1919	Paris	WORLD WAR I Allied and Associated Powers	TREATY OF VERSAILLES
WASHINGTON NAVAL CONFERENCE	1921–1922	Washington, DC	United States European Powers Japan	FOUR-POWER TREATY, FIVE-POWER TREATY, NINE-POWER TREATY
Geneva Conference	1925	Geneva	International	GENEVA PROTOCOL
RAPIDAN CONFERENCE	1929	Virginia	President HERBERT C. HOOVER British Prime Minister Ramsay MacDonald	Discussion naval disarmament
First London Naval Conference	1930	London	United States Great Britain France Italy Japan	London Naval Treaty of 1930
WORLD DISARMAMENT CONFERENCE	1932–1934	Geneva	International	Unsuccessful general disarmament negotiations
WORLD ECONOMIC CONFERENCE	1933	London	International	Discussion world economic crisis
Second London Naval Conference	1935–1936	London	United States Great Britain France Italy Japan	London Naval Treaty of 1936
BRUSSELS CONFERENCE	1937	Brussels	International	Discussion Japanese invasion China
EVIAN CONFERENCE	1938	France	International	Discussion issue of Jewish and other refugees from fascism
OGDENSBURG CONFERENCE	1940	Ogdensburg, NY	President FRANKLIN D. ROOSEVELT Canadian Prime Minister W. L. MacKenzie King	Coordination joint defense issues

6. WORLD WAR II CONFERENCES

Conference	Code Name	Date	Nations	Participants	Significance
ATLANTIC CONFERENCE		1941	United States / Great Britain	President FRANKLIN D. ROOSEVELT / Prime Minister Winston Churchill	ATLANTIC CHARTER
Washington Conference	Arcadia	1941–1942	United States / Great Britain	Roosevelt / Churchill	"Europe First" strategy confirmed; UNITED NATIONS DECLARATION
Washington Conference		1942	United States / Great Britain	Roosevelt / Churchill	Discussion Anglo-American second front in Europe; agreement on 1942 invasion North Africa (Operation Torch)
Moscow Conference		1942	United States / Great Britain / Soviet Union	Special Envoy W. AVERELL HARRIMAN / Churchill / Soviet Premier Joseph Stalin	Review Allied war planning
Casablanca Conference	Symbol	1943	United States / Great Britain	Roosevelt / Churchill	Agreement on 1943 Anglo-American invasion of Sicily and Italy, 1944 invasion France; Roosevelt calls for unconditional surrender of Axis Powers
Washington Conference	Trident	1943	United States / Great Britain	Roosevelt / Churchill	1944 date set for Anglo-American cross-channel invasion of France (Operation Overlord) opening second front in Europe
Quebec Conference	Quadrant	1943	United States / Great Britain	Roosevelt / Churchill	Anglo-American military planning; agreement to step up operations in the Far East
MOSCOW CONFERENCE		1943	United States / Great Britain / Soviet Union	Secretary of State CORDELL HULL / Foreign Secretary Anthony Eden / Foreign Minister Vyacheslav Molotov	Formation EUROPEAN ADVISORY COMMISSION; preparation TEHERAN CONFERENCE; MOSCOW DECLARATION, signed also by China, calling for international peacekeeping organization
Cairo Conference	Sextant	1943	United States / Great Britain / China	Roosevelt / Churchill / Generalissimo Chiang Kai-shek	Discussion China-Burma-India Theater; CAIRO DECLARATION calling for the return of all Chinese territories seized by Japan and for Korean independence

6. WORLD WAR II CONFERENCES (Cont.)

Conference	Code Name	Date	Nations	Participants	Significance
TEHERAN CONFERENCE	Eureka	1943	United States Great Britain Soviet Union	Roosevelt Churchill Stalin	Discussion Allied military strategy; planning for postwar Europe; Soviet pledge to enter war against Japan following Germany's defeat
Cairo Conference		1943	United States Great Britain Turkey	Roosevelt Churchill President Ismet Inonu	Discussion Turkish neutrality; reaffirmation close mutual ties
Quebec Conference	Octagon	1944	United States Great Britain	Roosevelt Churchill	Review strategy final defeat Germany, prosecution war against Japan; discussion postwar treatment Germany, tentative approval MORGANTHAU PLAN
Moscow Conference		1944	United States Great Britain Soviet Union	Ambassador Harriman Churchill Stalin	Discussion postwar status Eastern Europe
MALTA CONFERENCE		1945	United States Great Britain	Roosevelt Churchill	Anglo-American military staff coordination; preparation YALTA CONFERENCE
YALTA CONFERENCE	Argonaut	1945	United States Great Britain Soviet Union	Roosevelt Churchill Stalin	Final planning for defeat Germany; renewal Soviet pledge to enter war against Japan; discussion postwar status Eastern Europe; preparation DECLARATION ON LIBERATED EUROPE; designation Allied occupation zones Germany; creation ALLIED CONTROL COUNCIL; resolution remaining issues on formation UNITED NATIONS, agreement to convene SAN FRANCISCO CONFERENCE
POTSDAM CONFERENCE	Terminal	1945	United States Great Britain Soviet Union	President HARRY S. TRUMAN Churchill, Prime Minister Clement Attlee Stalin	POTSDAM DECLARATION reaffirming Allied unconditional surrender terms for Japan; discussions on postwar Europe, agreement on postwar German and Polish boundaries, German reparations, trial Nazi war criminals; formation COUNCIL OF FOREIGN MINISTERS

7. COUNCIL OF FOREIGN MINISTERS CONFERENCES

Conference	Date	Nations	Participants	Significance
London	1945	United States Great Britain France Soviet Union China	Secretary of State James F. Byrnes Foreign Secretary Ernest Bevin Foreign Minister Georges Bidault Foreign Minister Vyacheslav Molotov Foreign Minister Dr. Wang Shih Chieh	Stalemated over Soviet efforts to limit French and Chinese participation in council deliberations
Moscow	1945	United States Great Britain France	Byrnes Bevin Molotov	Compromise agreement among Big Three to exclude China from the formulation of European peace treaties
Paris	1946	United States Great Britain France Soviet Union	Byrnes Bevin Bidault Molotov	Peace treaties for minor Axis Powers drafted in preparation for Paris Peace Conference (1946)
New York	1946	United States Great Britain France Soviet Union	Byrnes Bevin Bidault Molotov	Peace Treaties for minor Axis Powers Italy, Hungary, Bulgaria, Romania, Finland completed; commission of deputies established to prepare peace settlements for Germany and Austria
Moscow	1947	United States Great Britain France Soviet Union	Secretary of State George C. Marshall Bevin Bidault Molotov	Mounting East-West Cold War tensions over Germany and Eastern Europe; formation Austrian Treaty Commission
London	1947	United States Great Britain France Soviet Union	Marshall Bevin Bidault Molotov	Increasingly acrimonious debate on Eastern Europe culminating in council's indefinite adjournment
Paris	1949	United States Great Britain France Soviet Union	Secretary of State Dean Acheson Bevin Foreign Minister Robert Schuman Foreign Minister Andrei Y. Vyshinsky	Resolution Berlin Airlift; agreement on basic outline of Austrian Peace Treaty; the council, which never reconvened, ended in impasse on Germany

8. UNITED NATIONS CONFERENCES

Conference	Date	Location	Significance
United Nations Conference on Food and Agriculture	1943	Hot Springs, VA	Established FOOD AND AGRICULTURE ORGANIZATION OF THE UNITED NATIONS
Washington Conference	1943	Washington, DC	Established UNITED NATIONS RELIEF AND REHABILITATION ADMINISTRATION
BRETTON WOODS CONFERENCE	1944	Bretton Woods, NH	Established INTERNATIONAL MONETARY FUND, WORLD BANK
DUMBARTON OAKS CONFERENCE	1944	Washington, DC	Draft UNITED NATIONS CHARTER
International Civil Aviation Conference	1944	Chicago	Drafted Convention for International Civil Aviation Organization
SAN FRANCISCO CONFERENCE	1945	San Francisco	Formation UNITED NATIONS
United Nations Educational and Cultural Conference	1945	London	Drafted constitution for UNITED NATIONS EDUCATIONAL, SCIENTIFIC, AND CULTURAL ORGANIZATION (UNESCO)
International Health Conference	1946	New York	Drafted Constitution for WORLD HEALTH ORGANIZATION
United Nations Conference on Trade and Employment	1947	Geneva	Formation GENERAL AGREEMENT ON TARIFFS AND TRADE (GATT)
United Nations Conference on Trade and Employment	1947-1948	Havana	Drafted Charter for INTERNATIONAL TRADE ORGANIZATION
United Nations Maritime Conference	1948	Geneva	Established INTERNATIONAL MARITIME ORGANIZATION
International Atomic Energy Conference	1956	New York	Formation INTERNATIONAL ATOMIC ENERGY AGENCY
UNITED NATIONS CONFERENCE ON THE LAW OF THE SEA	1958	Geneva	First UNCLOS session, subsequent conferences in 1960 and 1973 leading to U.N. Convention on the Law of the Sea (1982)
UNITED NATIONS CONFERENCE ON TRADE AND DEVELOPMENT	1964	Geneva	First UNCTAD session, subsequently established as General Assembly Special Body convening quadrennially
STOCKHOLM CONFERENCE	1972	Stockholm	Established UNITED NATIONS ENVIRONMENT PROGRAM

9. POSTWAR CONFERENCES

Conference	Date	Location	Participants	Significance
PARIS PEACE CONFERENCE	1946	Paris	WORLD WAR II Allies	Peace treaties with minor Axis Powers
SIX-NATION CONFERENCE ON GERMANY	1948	London	United States, Great Britain, France, Belgium, Netherlands, Luxembourg	Agreement on formation of West German state
BERMUDA CONFERENCE	1953	Bermuda	President DWIGHT D. EISENHOWER, British Prime Minister Winston Churchill, French Premier Joseph Laniel	Discussions NATO, ATOMS FOR PEACE, BERLIN CONFERENCE
BERLIN CONFERENCE	1954	Berlin	United States, Great Britain, France, Soviet Union	Agreement on holding the 1954 GENEVA CONFERENCE
GENEVA CONFERENCE	1954	Geneva	International	GENEVA ACCORDS on Indochina
Manila Conference	1954	Manila	International	Formation SEATO
Paris Conference	1954	Paris	United States, Western European Allies	PARIS AGREEMENTS on West German sovereignty, membership NATO
GENEVA CONFERENCE	1961-1962	Geneva	International	LAOS ACCORDS
Manila Conference	1966	Manila	United States, Asian Allies	Review conduct VIETNAM WAR
GENEVA CONFERENCE ON THE MIDDLE EAST	1973	Geneva	International	First Arab-Israeli Peace Conference, convened in aftermath of YOM KIPPUR WAR
Helsinki Conference	1975	Helsinki	International	CSCE summit meeting to sign HELSINKI ACCORDS
CONFERENCE ON INTERNATIONAL ECONOMIC COOPERATION	1975, 1977	Paris	International	NORTH-SOUTH DIALOGUE on international economic issues
CANCUN SUMMIT	1981	Mexico	International	Discussion North-South economic issues
DRUG SUMMIT	1990	Columbia	United States, Columbia, Peru, Bolivia	Declaration pledging cooperation in the fight against illegal narcotics trafficking
MIDDLE EAST PEACE CONFERENCE	1991	Multiple sites	International	Arab-Israeli peace negotiations

10. GENERAL AGREEMENT ON TARIFFS AND TRADE (GATT) ROUNDS

Round	Date	Location	Significance
Geneva	1947	Switzerland	Formation GATT; reductions in tariffs on some 45,000 items
Annecy	1949	France	35 percent reduction in tariffs on some 5000 items
Torquay	1950-1951	England	25 percent reduction in tariffs on some 10,000 items
Geneva	1955-1956	Switzerland	Tariff reductions on approximately 15 percent of all dutiable items
Dillon	1960-1962	Switzerland	20 percent reduction in industrial tariffs
Kennedy	1964-1967	Switzerland	35 percent overall reduction in tariffs; negotiations for first time on broad categories of products rather than single items
Tokyo	1973-1979	Japan; Switzerland	Broad elimination non-traffic barriers to trade; comprehensive update GATT rules and procedures
Uruguay	1986-	Uruguay; Switzerland	Negotiations on unfair trade practices

11. ECONOMIC SUMMITS

Summit	Date	Host	Participants	Significance
Rambouillet	1975	France	Group of 5 (G5) and Italy	First economic summit major non-Communist industrial powers
Puerto Rico	1976	United States	Group of 7 (G7)	Discussion North-South Dialogue
London	1977	Great Britain	G7	Agreement henceforth to include the president of the European Community in relevant discussions
Bonn	1978	West Germany	G7	Statement of joint commitment to combatting international terrorism
Tokyo	1979	Japan	G7	Discussions on energy policy and common strategy to reduce oil consumption
Venice	1980	Italy	G7	Condemnation of December 1979 Soviet intervention in the Afghanistan War and taking of diplomatic hostages in the Iran Hostage Crisis
Ottawa	1981	Canada	G7	Joint commitment to economic revitalization, increased aid to Third World
Versailles	1982	France	G7	Discussions on the continuing Western recession, Falklands War, and Israeli-Lebanonese border conflict
Williamsburg	1983	United States	G7	Renewed commitment to market-based economic growth
London	1984	Great Britain	G7	Expression of concern over continuing Iran-Iraq War (1980-1988)
Bonn	1985	West Germany	G7	Discussion international monetary system
Tokyo	1986	Japan	G7	Statement on international terrorism
Venice	1987	Italy	G7	Endorsement freedom of navigation in the Persian Gulf, denunciation of apartheid in South Africa
Toronto	1988	Canada	G7	Communique supporting expansion of East-West trade, INF Treaty
Paris	1989	France	G7	Support for financial aid to Poland and Hungary; condemnation of brutal Communist Chinese suppression of Tiananmen Uprising; discussion debt-for-nature swaps
Houston	1990	United States	G7	Discussion Uruguay Round trade talks, global warming, German reunification; establishment joint task force to study possible aid to the Soviet Union
London	1991	Great Britain	G7	Collective commitment to completion of the Uruguay Round Trade Talks; special meeting with Soviet President Mikhail S. Gorbachev, endorsement Soviet associate membership in the International Monetary Fund and World Bank

12. U.S.-SOVIET SUMMITS

Summit	Date	Nations	Participants	Significance
GENEVA SUMMIT	1955	United States Great Britain France Soviet Union	President DWIGHT D. EISENHOWER Prime Minister Anthony Eden Premier Edgar Faure Premier Nikolai A. Bulganin	Discussion German reunification, European security, disarmament, U.S. OPEN SKIES proposal
CAMP DAVID SUMMIT	1959	United States Soviet Union	President Eisenhower Premier Nikita S. Khrushchev	Moderation BERLIN CRISIS
PARIS SUMMIT	1960	United States Great Britain France Soviet Union	President Eisenhower Prime Minister Harold MacMillan President Charles de Gaulle Premier Khrushchev	Terminated over U-2 INCIDENT
VIENNA SUMMIT	1961	United States Soviet Union	President JOHN F. KENNEDY Premier Khrushchev	Discussion Berlin Crisis
GLASSBORO SUMMIT	1967	United States Soviet Union	President LYNDON B. JOHNSON Premier Aleksei N. Kosygin	Discussion Middle East, VIETNAM WAR, East-West relations
MOSCOW SUMMIT	1972	United States Soviet Union	President RICHARD M. NIXON General Secretary Leonid I. Brezhnev	DETENTE, SALT I arms control agreement, U.S.-Soviet trade pact
WASHINGTON SUMMIT	1973	United States Soviet Union	President Nixon General Secretary Brezhnev	PREVENTION OF NUCLEAR WAR AGREEMENT
MOSCOW SUMMIT	1974	United States Soviet Union	President Nixon General Secretary Brezhnev	THRESHOLD TEST BAN TREATY
VLADIVOSTOK SUMMIT	1974	United States Soviet Union	President GERALD R. FORD General Secretary Brezhnev	VLADIVOSTOK ACCORD

12. U.S.-SOVIET SUMMITS (*Cont.*)

Summit	Date	Nations	Participants	Significance
VIENNA SUMMIT	1979	United States Soviet Union	President JIMMY CARTER General Secretary Brezhnev	SALT II arms control agreement
GENEVA SUMMIT	1985	United States Soviet Union	President RONALD W. REAGAN General Secretary Mikhail S. Gorbachev	Resumption top-level U.S.-Soviet contacts
REYKJAVIK SUMMIT	1986	United States Soviet Union	President Reagan General Secretary Gorbachev	Discussion arms control
WASHINGTON SUMMIT	1987	United States Soviet Union	President Reagan General Secretary Gorbachev	INF TREATY
MOSCOW SUMMIT	1988	United States Soviet Union	President Reagan General Secretary Gorbachev	Discussion arms control, HUMAN RIGHTS, regional issues
MALTA SUMMIT	1989	United States Soviet Union	President GEORGE BUSH President Gorbachev	Discussion collapse of communism in Eastern Europe, ending COLD WAR
WASHINGTON SUMMIT	1990	United States Soviet Union	President Bush President Gorbachev	Post-COLD WAR East-West relations, U.S.-Soviet trade pact
HELSINKI SUMMIT	1990	United States Soviet Union	President Bush President Gorbachev	Coordinated response to Iraqi invasion of Kuwait
MOSCOW SUMMIT	1991	United States Soviet Union	President Bush President Gorbachev	START Treaty

13. U.S.-CHINESE SUMMITS

Summit	Date	Participants	Significance
PEKING SUMMIT	1972	President RICHARD M. NIXON Chairman Mao Tse-tung Premier Chou En-lai	Initiation U.S.-Communist Chinese ties; SHANGHAI COMMUNIQUE
PEKING SUMMIT	1975	President GERALD R. FORD Chairman Mao Deputy Premier Deng Xiaoping	Normalization relations
WASHINGTON SUMMIT	1979	President JIMMY CARTER Deputy Premier Deng	Establishment diplomatic relations
WASHINGTON SUMMIT	1984	President RONALD W. REAGAN Premier Zhao Ziyang	Discussions on trade, strengthening Sino-American ties
BEIJING SUMMIT	1984	President Reagan "Supreme Leader" Deng Premier Zhao	Widening Sino-American relations

Appendix F

Glossary

Foreign affairs in general, and diplomacy in particular, have their own unique lexicons. This glossary concisely defines the most commonly encountered foreign affairs terms. Items in italics are explained separately in the glossary, while those in SMALL CAPS *receive dictionary entries.*

ACCORD International *agreement* between two or more states. Originally, an accord addressed subjects of lesser importance than those covered in treaties. Now the term is used virtually interchangeably, in general parlance, with *treaty*.

AGREEMENT In international relations, the general term for a binding *accord* of any kind. An agreement may be *bilateral or multilateral*.

ALLIANCE *Agreement* between countries to support each other diplomatically and militarily in defense of common interests and against attack.

AMBASSADOR *Chief of mission* of the highest diplomatic rank. An ambassador is accredited by a head of state as that nation's official representative to a foreign government or international organization. Historically, resident ambassadors were called "ordinary" and ambassadors on special missions were "extraordinary." This distinction later was dropped. "Plenipotentiary" simply means possessed of full powers to do an ambassador's normal job.

ARMISTICE Cessation of hostilities by mutual agreement of the belligerents. An armistice may temporarily halt the fighting to permit direct peace negotiations between belligerents or to allow for *mediation* by a third party. Other terms for armistice are *cease-fire* and *truce*.

ATTACHE Technical specialist attached to an *embassy* or *legation*. Attaches, who serve with diplomatic rank, specialize in political, economic, military, agricultural, cultural, or other fields.

BILATERAL Indicates participation of two nations or parties, as in bilateral *treaty* or bilateral *negotiation*.

BLOCKADE Naval action undertaken to stop supplies from reaching an enemy. A nation imposes a blockade by deploying its navy to interdict the maritime traffic in and out of an enemy's ports. Blockades are regulated by international law, which requires that they be maintained by forces sufficient to make them effective; otherwise, neutral ships are not legally bound to respect them. The term has also been used to describe the denial of transit or access on land, most notably with the Soviet Union's 1948 ground blockade of Berlin necessitating the BERLIN AIRLIFT.

BOYCOTT Refusal to buy products from or do business with a country or group of countries. Undertaken as a protest measure, a boycott may be either government-inspired or privately organized.

CARTEL An agreement among independent countries to restrict commercial competition through monopolistic regulation of prices, production, and the marketplace.

CEASE-FIRE Cessation of hostilities by mutual agreement of the belligerents. Another term for *armistice*.

CHARGE D'AFFAIRES Diplomatic officer who, for the period of time until an *ambassador* or *minister* has been appointed, serves as *chief of mission*. A charge d'affaires ad interim is the senior official who takes charge temporarily in the absence of the regular chief of mission.

CHARTER Document outlining the structure, powers, and functions of an international organization, for example the UNITED NATIONS CHARTER. Also, a document stating international goals or policies, such as the ATLANTIC CHARTER.

CHIEF OF MISSION Ranking officer in a permanent diplomatic mission, for example the *ambassador* in an *embassy* or the *minister* in a *legation*.

COMITY Courtesies extended by one nation to another. Acts of comity between states are said to reflect respect for one another's laws and institutions.

COMMONWEALTH A voluntary federation or association of independent states united by common interests, values, or heritage.

COMMUNIQUE Statement issued following an important international meeting or *conference* that summarizes what was discussed at the gathering and outlines any achievements.

CONDOMINIUM Joint administration of a dependent territory by two or more foreign powers. In a condominium, jurisdiction over the subject territory is divided among the foreign sovereigns.

CONFERENCE Meeting between the representatives of two or more states or among the members of an international organization. A conference generally convenes to address specific matters and extends over at least several sessions.

Conference diplomacy refers to the conduct of *negotiation*s through such meetings rather than through normal diplomatic channels. In diplomacy, a congress is the same as a conference.

CONSORTIUM An international partnership or association of financial institutions. Banks of different nations organize themselves in a consortium usually for the purpose of a joint venture that requires large commitments of capital.

CONSUL Public official sent abroad by a nation to promote its commercial interests in another country and to assist its nationals living or traveling there. Consuls principally seek to open markets in the host country for their own nation's exports. Their responsibilities include administrative functions relating to commercial shipping, granting visas, and aiding nationals accused of crimes in the host country.

CONSULATE Office of a *consul*. Consulates are normally established in the major cities of a foreign country. Administratively, they are under the *embassy*, which is located in the capital city.

CONSULATE GENERAL A larger and more important *consulate*, presided over by a consul general, who outranks a *consul*.

CONVENTION *Agreement* between two or more states, usually specific in nature, relating to matters such as international postage, copyright law, and law of the sea. A convention, in general diplomatic parlance, is the same as a *treaty*.

DECLARATION In diplomacy, a joint statement by two or more states that can have the same binding effect as a *treaty*. Declarations may be issued in their own right or appended to a treaty as a clarification or interpretation.

DOCTRINE Term used throughout American history to denote a significant presidential foreign policy statement or initiative, as in the MONROE DOCTRINE or REAGAN DOCTRINE.

EMBARGO Official edict forbidding trade with a country or countries. An embargo may be either partial, where it applies only to select products, or a total ban on trade. It is an economic weapon used by nations to achieve their political or strategic objectives.

EMBASSY Official residence of an *ambassador*. Often inaccurately used to denote the office where the ambassador and ambassador's staff work, which is properly called the chancery. Historically, when diplomatic missions were smaller, the residence and offices were usually housed in the same building. Nowadays confusion is avoided through use of the terms "embassy residence" and "embassy office."

EMISSARY General term for a diplomatic agent sent as an official messenger by a government or head of state.

ENTENTE A close understanding in relations between two or more nations. It suggests diplomatic cooperation and compatibility of national objectives. Entente generally denotes an informal relationship although it may be formalized in a *treaty* or other binding agreement.

ENVOY General term for a senior diplomat sent by one government or international organization as its representative to another government or organization.

EXTRADITION Return by one nation to another of a person accused of a crime. Extradition is initiated through a formal request from one country to another and is governed by specific terms set forth in extradition treaties between the states.

GOOD OFFICES A procedure for peaceful settlement of an international dispute whereby a third state, or an international body, seeks to bring the disputants together. An offer by a third party of its good offices involves diplomatic efforts aimed at "breaking the ice" between disputing nations and getting them into direct discussions. The third party serves as a go-between only, neither involving itself in substantive negotiations nor suggesting a solution. A nation's offer of its good offices is frequently a prelude to its *mediation* of the dispute.

LEASEHOLD An area leased by a foreign state under an arrangement with the territorial sovereign. In each case, a specific *agreement* stipulates the extent of authority to be exercised over the area by the lessee.

LEGATION Technically the official residence of a diplomatic *minister*. In general parlance, legation also refers to the offices where the minister and staff work.

MEDIATION Procedure for peaceful settlement of a conflict between nations in which a third party acts as an intermediary. A mediator tries to help the disputants reach a solution by making substantive suggestions and promoting compromise on both sides.

MINISTER A chief of diplomatic mission who heads a *legation* rather than an *embassy*. The full official title is *envoy* extraordinary and minister plenipotentiary. A minister ranks below an ambassador and above a minister resident. With legations now a rarity, the title is used generally to denote the second-ranking officer at a larger embassy.

MISSION A nation's permanent diplomatic establishment in another country, either an *embassy* or *legation*. The official in charge of the mission is the *chief of mission*. Nations also maintain missions to various international organizations, for example, the U.S. mission to the UNITED NATIONS.

MULTILATERAL Indicates participation of more than two nations or parties, as in a multilateral treaty.

NEGOTIATION Diplomatic technique for peacefully resolving differences between nations and for advancing national interests. The aims of negotiation are achieved by compromises reached through direct personal contact. The process implies a willingness on both sides to make concessions.

NEUTRALITY Legal standing of a nation that does not join in a war between other states. Under international law, the status of neutrality confers on a nation both rights and obligations with respect to the belligerents.

NONALIGNED Term denoting those nations which adopted a stance or pursued a policy of independence and nonalignment with respect to the East-West Cold War struggle. Nonaligned states refused to side with either the United States or Soviet Union.

NUNCIO *Ambassador* of the Vatican at a foreign capital; often called a papal nuncio. A Vatican representative of the rank of *minister* is an internuncio.

PACT An *agreement* or *treaty* between two or more nations. Pact is also used to refer to a military *alliance*.

PLEBISCITE Vote to determine the will of the entire population of an area on a major public issue. Plebiscites often have been used in international relations in connection with territorial cessions and boundary adjustments.

PROTECTORATE Relationship in which one nation has established control over another, weaker country and is providing it with protection. The stronger state exercises various degrees of authority in the subordinated state without actually annexing it. The protectorate country usually takes charge of foreign affairs, defense, and public finances.

PROTOCOL Expression used in two contexts. First, it denotes a formal international agreement, similar to a *treaty*, but generally less important. Second, it refers to the ceremonial side of international diplomacy, including matters of etiquette, courtesy, and precedence.

RAPPROCHEMENT Establishment of improved or cordial relations between nations after a period of diplomatic tension or estrangement.

RATIFICATION Act by which a state formally confirms and approves terms of a *treaty*. Each signatory carries out ratification in accordance with its constitutional system. A treaty ordinarily enters into force when the signatories exchange documents of ratification.

RECOGNITION Process whereby a nation establishes diplomatic relations with a new foreign state or a new political regime in an existing state. In the United States the recognition power is vested in the president, who under the Constitution has sole authority to send and receive ambassadors.

REPARATIONS Financial indemnities imposed by the winners upon the losers following a war. Reparations, which may take the form of either property transfers or cash payments, are supposed to represent compensation to the victors for the cost of damages and property loss they incurred in the conflict. They also are levied as a means of reducing a defeated nation's further war-making capacity.

SANCTIONS Collective international punitive actions against a law-breaking state involving diplomatic, economic, or military measures.

SOVEREIGNTY Concept of a nation's political independence and supreme authority within its own borders, free from external interference.

SPHERE OF INFLUENCE Territorial area in which one power, with the general acquiescence of others, exercises a dominant influence.

SUMMIT Meeting between two or more heads of state. Summit diplomacy refers to direct face-to-face *negotiations* between the heads of state at such a gathering.

TARIFF Tax levied on imports to help protect a nation's industry, business, labor, and agriculture from foreign competition or to raise revenue.

TREATY Formal mutually binding *agreement* between countries that establishes or defines their mutual obligations and rights. A treaty may be *bilateral* or *multilateral* and of specific or indefinite duration.

TRUCE Suspension of hostilities by mutual agreement of the belligerents. Another term for *armistice*.

WHITE PAPER Statement of official government policy or position with background documentation.

Appendix G

Guide to Further Sources

There is a range of general sources that will be useful to anyone doing research in American foreign affairs. The exhaustive *Guide to U.S. Foreign Relations* (Santa Barbara, CA: ABC-CLIO, 1983), edited by Richard Dean Burns, is a superb annotated bibliography covering the vast literature on the field through 1982. For a condensed historical overview of U.S. foreign relations see *Encyclopedia of American History* 6th ed. (New York: Harper & Row, 1982) edited by Richard B. Morris. Works by two eminent American historians are staple narrative overviews: Thomas A. Bailey's *A Diplomatic History of the American People* 10th ed. (Englewood Cliffs, NJ: Prentice-Hall, 1980) and Alexander DeConde's *A History of American Foreign Policy* 3rd ed. (New York: Charles Scribner's, 1978). Lester Brune's two-volume *Chronological History of U.S. Foreign Relations* (New York: Garland, 1985) covers developments in detail year by year from 1776 to 1981.

The three-volume *Encyclopedia of American Foreign Policy* (New York: Charles Scribner's, 1978), edited by Alexander DeConde, is a compendium of topical essays on major concepts, themes, ideas, and policies by diplomatic historians and other specialists. *The Reader's Companion to American History* (New York: Houghton Mifflin, 1991), edited by Eric Foner and John A. Garraty, provides a wide range of entries pertaining to U.S. foreign affairs. *The International Relations Dictionary* 4th ed. (Santa Barbara, CA: ABC-CLIO, 1988), edited by Jack C. Plano and Roy Olton, contains conceptual entries on diplomacy, international economics, war, arms control, international law, American foreign policy, international organizations, and other related

areas. John E. Findling's *Dictionary of American Diplomatic History* 2nd ed. (Westport, CT: Greenwood Press, 1989) comprises short entries on incidents, policies, ideas, treaties, etc.; it also includes brief biographical sketches of American diplomats.

The classic work on U.S. secretaries of state is the 10-volume *The American Secretaries of State and Their Diplomacy* (New York: Alfred Knopf, 1928). Edited by Samuel Flagg Bemis, the series spans from 1789 to 1925. It is continued as the multivolume *American Secretaries of State and Their Diplomacy* (New York: Cooper Square, 1963–), edited by Bemis and Robert H. Ferrell. See also *An Uncertain Tradition: American Secretaries of State in the Twentieth Century* (New York: McGraw-Hill, 1961), a series of profiles (through John Foster Dulles) edited by Norman A. Graebner; and *Makers of American Diplomacy from Ben Franklin to Henry Kissinger* (New York: Charles Scribner's, 1974), biographical essays edited by Frank J. Merli and Theodore A. Wilson.

The U.S. government offers several valuable sources. *Foreign Relations of the United States* is the official documentary record of American foreign policy and diplomacy. Over 350 volumes have been published since the State Department began the series in 1861. The most recent volumes cover the last years of the Eisenhower administration. The monthly *Department of State Bulletin* has chronicled U.S. foreign policy and involvement in world affairs since 1938. *American Foreign Policy: Current Documents*, issued in annual volumes, presents the major foreign policy messages, addresses, statements, speeches, reports, press conferences, and briefings by officials in the White House, State Department, and other foreign affairs agencies. For the texts of U.S. treaties see the 13-volume *Treaties and Other International Agreements of the United States, 1776–1949,* compiled by Charles I. Bevans, and *United States Treaties and Other International Agreements,* which has been the official place of publication since 1950. The handiest source on multilateral agreements is N.J. Rengger's *Treaties and Alliances of the World* 5th ed. (Harlow, Essex, United Kingdom: Longman Group UK Limited, 1990). See the annual *Political Handbook of the World* (Binghamton, NY: CSA Publications, current year), edited by Arthur S. Banks, for key political information about every country and for a description of major intergovernmental organizations.

Several reference works offer a solid journalistic account of contemporary American foreign affairs. The weekly *Facts on File World News Digest with Index,* accumulated annually as the *Facts on File Yearbook,* covers developments throughout the world. *Congress and the Nation* (Washington, DC: Congressional Quarterly, 1964–) is an excellent multivolume series that provides a detailed overview of the federal government's activities since the end of World War II. Each volume contains sections on foreign affairs and national defense. The work is especially useful on legislative histories and the development of U.S. policies. The *Congressional Quarterly Almanac* (Washington, DC: Congressional Quarterly, 1959–) is a complementary source. Published annually, it summarizes the interplay between Congress and the executive branch in formulating U.S. foreign policy. *Congressional Quarterly's Guide to the U.S. Supreme Court* (Washington, DC: Congressional Quarterly, 1989) is a good starting point for research on the legal aspects of U.S. foreign relations. Following are selective lists of works on foreign affairs organized by major topical areas.

DIPLOMACY

Historical

General

Bailey, Thomas A. *A Diplomatic History of the American People.* 10th ed. Englewood Cliffs, NJ: Prentice-Hall, 1980.

Bemis, Samuel Flagg. *A Diplomatic History of the United States.* 4th ed. New York: Holt, 1955.

Cole, Wayne S. *An Interpretive History of American Foreign Relations.* 2nd ed. Homewood, IL: Dorsey, 1974.

Davids, Jules. *America and the World of Our Time: United States Diplomacy in the Twentieth Century.* 3rd ed. New York: Random House, 1970.

DeConde, Alexander. *A History of American Foreign Policy.* 3rd ed. New York: Charles Scribner's, 1978.

Ferrell, Robert H. *American Diplomacy: A History.* 3rd ed. New York: Norton, 1975.

———. *American Diplomacy: The Twentieth Century.* New York: Norton, 1988.

Jones, Howard. *The Course of American Diplomacy from the Revolution to the Present.* New York: Franklin Watts, 1985.

LaFeber, Walter. *The American Age: United States Foreign Policy at Home and Abroad Since 1750.* New York: Norton, 1989.

Leopold, Richard W. *The Growth of American Foreign Policy: A History.* New York: Alfred Knopf, 1962.

Paterson, Thomas G., ed. *Major Problems in American Foreign Policy—Documents and Essays.* 2 vols. 3rd ed. Lexington, MA: D.C. Heath, 1989.

Pratt, Julius W.; De Santis, Vincent P.; and Siracusa, Joseph M. *A History of United States Foreign Policy.* 4th ed. Englewood Cliffs, NJ: Prentice-Hall, 1980.

Rappaport, Armin. *A History of American Diplomacy.* New York: Macmillan, 1975.

Smith, Daniel M. *The American Diplomatic Experience.* Boston: Houghton Mifflin, 1972.

Wells, Samuel F., Jr.; Ferrell, Robert H.; and Trask, David F. *The Ordeal of World Power: American Diplomacy Since 1900.* Boston: Little, Brown, 1975.

Williams, William A., ed. *From Colony to Empire: Essays in the History of American Foreign Relations.* New York: Wiley & Sons, 1972.

———. *The Tragedy of American Diplomacy.* New York: Dell, 1972.

American Revolution

Bemis, Samuel Flagg. *The Diplomacy of the American Revolution.* 3rd ed. Bloomington: Indiana University Press, 1957.

Kaplan, Lawrence S. *Colonies into Nation: American Diplomacy, 1763–1801.* New York: Macmillan, 1972.

Middlekauff, Robert. *The Glorious Cause: The American Revolution, 1763–1789*. New York: Oxford University Press, 1982.

Morris, Richard B. *The Peacemakers: The Great Powers and American Independence*. New York: Harper & Row, 1965.

Stinchcombe, William C. *The American Revolution and the French Alliance*. Syracuse, NY: Syracuse University Press, 1969.

Confederation and Federalist Periods

DeConde, Alexander. *Entangling Alliance: Politics and Diplomacy Under George Washington*. Durham, NC: Duke University Press, 1958.

———. *The Quasi-War: The Politics and Diplomacy of the Undeclared War with France*. New York: Charles Scribner's, 1966.

McDonald, Forrest. *The Presidency of George Washington*. Lawrence: University Press of Kansas, 1974.

Marks, Frederick W., 3rd. *Independence on Trial: Foreign Affairs and the Making of the Constitution*. Baton Rouge: Louisiana State University Press, 1973.

Miller, John C. *The Federalist Era, 1789–1801*. New York: Harper & Row, 1960.

Smith, Page. *John Adams*. 2 vols. New York: Doubleday, 1962.

Varg, Paul A. *Foreign Policies of the Founding Fathers*. East Lansing: Michigan State University Press, 1963.

1800 to Civil War

Ammon, Harry. *James Monroe: The Quest for National Identity*. New York: McGraw-Hill, 1971.

Bemis, Samuel Flagg. *John Quincy Adams and the Foundations of American Foreign Policy*. New York: Alfred Knopf, 1949.

———. *John Quincy Adams and the Union*. New York: Alfred Knopf, 1956.

Billington, Ray A. *The Far Western Frontier, 1830–1860*. New York: Harper & Row, 1956.

Brant, Irving. *James Madison*. 6 vols. Indianapolis, IN: Bobbs-Merrill, 1941–1961.

Burt, Alfred L. *The United States, Great Britain, and British North America from the Revolution to the Establishment of Peace after the War of 1812*. New Haven, CT: Yale University Press, 1940.

Connor, Seymour V., and Faulk, Odie B. *North America Divided: The Mexican War, 1846–1848*. New York: Oxford University Press, 1971.

Dangerfield, George. *The Era of Good Feelings*. New York: Harcourt Brace Jovanovich, 1952.

Egan, Clifford L. *Neither Peace nor War: Franco-American Relations 1803–1812*. Baton Rouge: Louisiana State University Press, 1983.

Graebner, Norman A. *Empire on the Pacific: A Study in American Continental Expansion*. New York: Ronald Press, 1955.

Kaplan, Lawrence. *Entangling Alliances with None: American Foreign Policy in the Age of Jefferson*. Kent, OH: Kent State University Press, 1987.

McCoy, Charles A. *Polk and the Presidency*. Austin: University of Texas Press, 1960.

Malone, Dumas. *Jefferson the President: First Term, 1801–1805*. Boston: Little, Brown, 1970.

———. *Jefferson the President: Second Term, 1805–1809*. Boston: Little, Brown, 1974.

May, Ernest R. *The Making of the Monroe Doctrine*. Cambridge, MA: Harvard University Press, 1975.

Merk, Frederick. *Manifest Destiny and Mission in American History: A Reinterpretation*. New York: Alfred Knopf, 1963.

———. *The Monroe Doctrine and American Expansion 1843–1849*. New York: Alfred Knopf, 1966.

Perkins, Bradford. *Castlereagh and Adams: England and the United States, 1812–1823*. Berkley: University of California Press, 1964.

———. *Prologue to War: England and the United States, 1805–1812*. Berkeley: University of California Press, 1961.

Pletcher, David M. *The Diplomacy of Annexation: Texas, Oregon, and the Mexican War*. Columbia: University of Missouri Press, 1973.

Potter, David. *The Impending Crisis, 1848–1861*. New York: Harper & Row, 1976.

Remini, Robert V. *Andrew Jackson and the Course of American Freedom, 1822–1832*. New York: Harper & Row, 1981.

———. *Andrew Jackson and the Course of American Democracy, 1833–1845*. New York: Harper & Row, 1984.

Schroeder, John H. *Mr. Polk's War: American Opposition and Dissent, 1846–1848*. Madison: University of Wisconsin Press, 1973.

Sellers, Charles G. *James K. Polk: Continentalist, 1843–1846*. Princeton, NJ: Princeton University Press, 1966.

Stagg, J.C.A. *Mr. Madison's War: Politics, Diplomacy, and Warfare in the Early American Republic 1783–1830*. Princeton, NJ: Princeton University Press, 1983.

Van Deusen, Glyndon G. *The Jacksonian Era, 1828–1848*. New York: Harper & Row, 1959.

Varg, Paul A. *United States Foreign Relations, 1820–1860*. East Lansing: Michigan State University Press, 1979.

Civil War Diplomacy

Case, Lynn M., and Spencer, Warren F. *The United States and France: Civil War Diplomacy*. Philadelphia: University of Pennsylvania Press, 1970.

Crook, David P. *The North, the South, and the Powers 1861–1865*. New York: Wiley, 1974.

Duberman, Martin B. *Charles Francis Adams 1807–1886*. Boston: Houghton Mifflin, 1961.

Ferris, Norman B. *Desperate Diplomacy: William Seward's Foreign Policy, 1861*. Knoxville, TN: University of Tennessee Press, 1976.

Jenkins, Brian. *Britain and the War for the Union*. 2 vols. Montreal: McGill-Queen's University Press, 1974–1980.

MacPherson, James M. *Battle Cry of Freedom: The Civil War Era*. New York: Oxford University Press, 1988.

Owsley, Frank L. *King Cotton Diplomacy: Foreign Relations of the Confederate States of America*. 2nd ed. Chicago: University of Chicago Press, 1959.

Van Deusen, Glyndon G. *William Henry Seward*. New York: Oxford University Press, 1967.

1865 Through Spanish-American War

Beisner, Robert L. *From the Old Diplomacy to the New, 1865–1900*. New York: Crowell, 1975.

———. *Twelve Against Empire: The Anti-Imperialists, 1898–1900*. New York: McGraw-Hill, 1968.

Campbell, Charles S., Jr. *The Transformation of American Foreign Relations, 1865–1900*. New York: Harper & Row, 1976.

Dobson, John M. *America's Ascent: The United States Becomes a Great Power, 1880–1914*. De Kalb: Northern Illinois University Press, 1978.

Dulles, Foster Rhea. *The Imperial Years*. New York: Crowell, 1956.

———. *Prelude to World Power: American Diplomatic History, 1860–1900*. New York: Macmillan, 1965.

Foner, Philip S. *The Spanish-Cuban-American War and the Birth of American Imperialism, 1895–1902*. 2 vols. New York: Monthly Review Press, 1972.

Healy, David. *U.S. Expansionism: The Imperialist Urge in the 1890s*. Madison: University of Wisconsin Press, 1970.

LaFeber, Walter. *The New Empire: An Interpretation of American Expansion 1860–1898*. Ithaca, NY: Cornell University Press, 1963.

Langer, William L. *The Diplomacy of Imperialism, 1890–1902*. 2d ed. New York: Alfred Knopf, 1968.

May, Ernest R. *Imperial Democracy: The Emergence of America as a Great Power*. New York: Harcourt Brace Jovanovich, 1961.

Morgan, H. Wayne. *America's Road to Empire: The War with Spain and Overseas Expansion*. New York: Wiley, 1965.

———. *William McKinley and His America*. Syracuse, NY: Syracuse University Press, 1963.

Paolino, Ernest N. *The Foundations of the American Empire: William Henry Seward and U.S. Foreign Policy*. Ithaca, NY: Cornell University Press, 1973.

Pletcher, David M. *The Awkward Years: American Foreign Relations under Garfield and Arthur*. Columbia: University of Missouri Press, 1962.

Pratt, Julius W. *America's Colonial Experiment*. New York: Prentice-Hall, 1950.

———. *Expansionists of 1898: The Acquisition of Hawaii and the Spanish Islands*. Baltimore: Johns Hopkins Press, 1936.

1900 Through World War II

Adler, Selig. *The Uncertain Giant, 1921–1941: American Foreign Policy Between the Wars*. New York: Macmillan, 1965.

Bailey, Thomas A. *Woodrow Wilson and the Lost Peace*. New York: Macmillan, 1944.

Beale, Howard K. *Theodore Roosevelt and the Rise of America to World Power*. Baltimore: Johns Hopkins Press, 1956.

Bendiner, Elmer. *A Time for Angels: The Tragicomic History of the League of Nations*. New York: Alfred Knopf, 1975.

Birdsall, Paul. *Versailles Twenty Years After*. New York: Reynal & Hitchcock, 1941.

Buehnig, Edward H., ed. *Wilson's Foreign Policy in Perspective*. Bloomington: Indiana University Press, 1957.

Dallek, Robert. *Franklin D. Roosevelt and American Foreign Policy, 1932–1945*. New York: Oxford University Press, 1979.

Divine, Robert A. *Roosevelt and World War II*. Baltimore: Johns Hopkins Press, 1969.

Dulles, Foster Rhea. *America's Rise to World Power, 1898–1954*. New York: Harper & Row, 1954.

Duroselle, Jean-Baptiste. *From Wilson to Roosevelt: Foreign Policy of the United States 1913–1945*. Cambridge, MA: Harvard University Press, 1963.

Ellis, L. Ethan. *Republican Foreign Policy, 1921–1933*. New Brunswick, NJ: Rutgers University Press, 1968.

Feis, Herbert. *Churchill, Roosevelt, Stalin: The War They Waged and the Peace They Sought*. Princeton, NJ: Princeton University Press, 1957.

Ferrell, Robert H. *American Diplomacy in the Great Depression: Hoover-Stimson Foreign Policy 1929–1933*. New Haven, CT: Yale University Press, 1957.

———. *Woodrow Wilson and World War I, 1917–1921*. Harper & Row, 1985.

Gregory, Ross. *The Origins of American Intervention in the First World War*. New York: Norton, 1971.

Howe, Quincy. *Ashes of Victory: World War II and its Aftermath*. New York: Simon and Schuster, 1972.

Kennan, George F. *American Diplomacy, 1900–1950*. Chicago: University of Chicago Press, 1951.

Link, Arthur S. *Woodrow Wilson: Revolution, War, and Peace*. Arlington Heights, IL: AHM, 1979.

Marks, Frederick W., 3rd. *Velvet on Iron: The Diplomacy of Theodore Roosevelt*. Lincoln: University of Nebraska Press, 1980.

May, Ernest R. *World War and American Isolationism, 1914–1917*. Cambridge, MA: Harvard University Press, 1959.

Mayer, Arno J. *Politics and Diplomacy at Peacemaking: Containment and Counterrevolution at Versailles 1918–1919*. New York: Alfred Knopf, 1967.

Nevins, Allan. *The New Deal in World Affairs, 1933–1945*. New Haven, CT: Yale University Press, 1950.

Offner, Arnold A. *The Origins of the Second World War: American Foreign Policy and World Politics, 1914–1941*. New York: Praeger, 1975.

Scholes, Walter V., and Scholes, Marie V. *The Foreign Policies of the Taft Administration*. Columbia: University of Missouri Press, 1970.

Seymour, Charles. *American Diplomacy During the World War*. Baltimore: Johns Hopkins Press, 1934. Reprint 1964.

Smith, Daniel M. *Great Departure: United States and World War I, 1914–1920*. New York: Wiley, 1965.

Smith, Gaddis. *American Diplomacy During the Second World War, 1941–1945*. New York: Wiley, 1965.

Taylor, F. Jay. *The United States and the Spanish Civil War, 1936–1939*. New York: Bookman, 1956.

Traina, Richard P. *American Diplomacy and the Spanish Civil War*. Bloomington: Indiana University Press, 1968.

Walworth, Arthur. *America's Moment: 1918, American Diplomacy at the End of World War I*. New York: Norton, 1977.

———. *Wilson and His Peacemakers: American Diplomacy at the Paris Peace Conference*. New York: Norton, 1986.

1945 To Present

Ambrose, Stephen E. *Eisenhower. Vol. 2, The President*. New York: Simon and Schuster, 1984.

———. *Rise to Globalism: American Foreign Policy Since 1938*. 5th ed. New York: Penguin Books, 1988.

Beschloss, Michael. *The Crisis Years: Kennedy and Khrushchev, 1960–1963*. New York: HarperCollins, 1991.

Divine, Robert A. *Eisenhower and the Cold War*. New York: Oxford University Press, 1981.

Donovan, Robert J. *Conflict and Crisis: The Presidency of Harry S. Truman 1945–1948*. New York: Norton, 1978.

Gaddis, John Lewis. *The Long Peace*. New York: Oxford University Press, 1987.

———. *Strategies of Containment*. New York: Oxford University Press, 1982.

———. *The United States and the End of the Cold War: Implications, Reconsiderations, Provocations*. New York: Oxford University Press, 1992.

———. *The United States and the Origins of the Cold War, 1941–1947*. New York: Columbia University Press, 1972.

Graebner, Norman A. *Cold War Diplomacy: American Foreign Policy, 1945–1975*. 2nd ed. New York: Van Nostrand, 1977.

————, ed. *The National Security: Its Theory and Practice, 1945–1960*. New York: Oxford University Press, 1986.

Hammond, Paul Y. *Cold War and Detente: The American Foreign Policy Process Since 1945*. 2d ed. New York: Harcourt Brace Jovanovich, 1975.

Horowitz, David. *Free World Colossus: A Critique of American Foreign Policy in the Cold War*. Rev. ed. New York: Hill & Wang, 1965.

Hyland, William G. *The Cold War Is Over*. New York: Random House, 1990.

Kolko, Joyce, and Kolko, Gabriel. *The Limits of Power: The World and United States Foreign Policy, 1945–1954*. New York: Harper & Row, 1972.

LaFeber, Walter. *America, Russia, and the Cold War, 1945–1975*. 4th ed. New York: Wiley, 1987.

————, ed. *The Origins of the Cold War*. New York: Wiley, 1971.

Nathan, James A., and Oliver, James K. *United States Foreign Policy and World Order*. 2nd edition. Boston: Little, Brown, 1981.

Osgood, Robert E., et al. *America and the World: From the Truman Doctrine to Vietnam*. Baltimore: Johns Hopkins Press, 1970.

Paterson, Thomas G., ed. *Containment and the Cold War: American Foreign Policy Since 1945*. Reading, MA: Addison-Wesley, 1973.

Spanier, John W. *American Foreign Policy Since World World*. 7th ed. New York: Praeger, 1977.

Ulam, Adam B. *Expansion and Coexistence*. 2nd ed. New York: Holt, Rinehart & Winston, 1974.

Walton, Richard J. *Cold War and Counterrevolution: The Foreign Policy of John F. Kennedy*. New York: Viking, 1972.

Geographical

Africa

Chester, Edward W. *Clash of Titans: Africa and U.S. Foreign Policy*. Maryknoll, NY: Orbis, 1974.

Clendenen, Clarence C.; Collins, Robert; and Duignan, Peter. *Americans in Africa, 1865–1900*. Stanford, CA: Hoover Institution, 1966.

————, and Duignan, Peter. *Americans in Black Africa up to 1865*. Stanford, CA: Hoover Institution, 1964.

Coker, Christopher. *The U.S. and South Africa, 1968–1985*. Durham, NC: Duke University Press, 1986.

Duignan, Peter, and Gann, Lewis H. *The United States and Africa: A History*. New York: Cambridge University Press, 1984.

Gallagher, Charles F. *The United States and North Africa: Morocco, Algeria and Tunisia*. Cambridge, MA: Harvard University Press, 1963.

Howe, Russell W. *Along the African Shore: An Historic Review of Two Centuries of U.S.-African Relations*. New York: Barnes & Noble, 1975.

Noer, Thomas J. *Britain, Boer and Yankee: The United States and South Africa 1870–1914*. Kent, OH: Kent State University Press, 1978.

Asia

Bonner, Raymond. *Waltzing with a Dictator: The Marcoses and the Making of American Policy*. New York: Times Books, 1987.

Borg, Dorothy. *The United States and the Far Eastern Crisis of 1933–1938*. Cambridge, MA: Harvard University Press, 1964.

Brown, W. Norman. *The United States and India, Pakistan and Bangladesh*. Cambridge, MA: Harvard University Press, 1972.

Dulles, Foster Rhea. *American Policy Toward Communist China, 1949–1969*. New York: Crowell, 1972.

————. *Yankees and Samurai: America's Role in the Emergence of Modern Japan 1791–1900*. New York: Harper & Row, 1965.

Etzold, Thomas H., ed. *Aspects of Sino-American Relations Since 1784*. New York: New Viewpoints, 1978.

Fairbank, John K. *The United States and China*. 4th ed. Cambridge, MA: Harvard University Press, 1983.

Foster, John W. *American Diplomacy in the Orient*. Boston: Houghton Mifflin, 1903.

Friend, Theodore W. *Between Two Empires: The Ordeal of the Philippines, 1929–1946*. New Haven, CT: Yale University Press, 1965.

Israel, Jerry. *Progressivism and the Open Door: America and China, 1905–1921*. Pittsburgh: University of Pittsburgh Press, 1971.

May, Ernest R., and Thomas, James C., Jr., eds. *American-East Asian Relations: A Survey*. Cambridge, MA: Harvard University Press, 1972.

Neu, Charles E. *The Troubled Encounter: the United States and Japan*. New York: Wiley, 1975.

Reischauer, Edwin O. *The United States and Japan*. 3rd ed. Cambridge, MA: Harvard University Press, 1965.

Tuchman, Barbara W. *Stilwell and the American Experience in China, 1911–1945*. New York: Macmillan, 1970.

Canada

Callahan, James M. *American Foreign Policy in Canadian Relations*. New York: Macmillan, 1937.

Craig, Gerald M. *The United States and Canada*. Cambridge, MA: Harvard University Press, 1968.

Doran, Charles F., and Siegler, John H., eds. *Canada and the United States*. New York: American Assembly, 1985.

————. *Forgotten Partnership*. Baltimore: Johns Hopkins Press, 1985.

Europe

Adams, Henry M. *Prussian-American Relations, 1775–1871*. Cleveland: Press of Western Reserve University, 1960.

Allen, Harry C. *Conflict and Concord: The Anglo-American Relationship Since 1783*. New York: St. Martin's Press, 1959.

————. *Great Britain and the United States: A History of Anglo-American Relations (1783–1952)*. New York: St. Martin's Press, 1955.

Blumenthal, Henry. *France and the United States: Their Diplomatic Relations, 1789–1914*. Chapel Hill: University of North Carolina Press, 1970.

Campbell, Charles S., Jr. *From Revolution to Rapprochement: The United States and Great Britain, 1783–1900*. New York: Wiley, 1974.

Cortada, James W. *Two Nations Over Time: Spain and the United States, 1776–1977*. Westport, CT: Greenwood Press, 1978.

DeConde, Alexander. *This Affair of Louisiana*. New York: Charles Scribner's, 1976.

Duroselle, Jean-Baptiste. *France and the United States: From the Beginnings to the Present*. Chicago: University of Chicago Press, 1978.

Gatzke, Hans W. *Germany and the United States: A "Special Relationship"?* Cambridge, MA: Harvard University Press, 1980.

Jones, Howard T. *To the Webster-Ashburton Treaty: A Study in Anglo-American Relations, 1783–1843*. Chapel Hill: University of North Carolina Press, 1977.

Morgan, Roger. *The United States and West Germany 1945–1973*. London: Oxford University Press, 1974.

Zahniser, Marvin R. *Uncertain Friendship: American-French Relations through the Cold War*. New York: Wiley, 1975.

Latin America

Bemis, Samuel Flagg. *The Latin American Policy of the United States: An Historical Interpretation*. New York: Harcourt Brace Jovanovich, 1943.

Callcott, Wilfrid H. *The Western Hemisphere: Its Influence on United States Policies to the End of World War II*. Austin: University of Texas Press, 1968.

Foner, Philip S. *A History of Cuba and its Relations with the United States*. 2 vols. New York: International Publishers, 1962–1963.

Gellman, Irwin F. *Good Neighbor Diplomacy: United States Policies in Latin America, 1933–1945*. Baltimore: Johns Hopkins Press, 1979.

Inman, Samuel Guy. *Inter-American Conferences, 1826–1954: History and Problems*. Washington, DC: University Press, 1965.

Kryzanek, Michael J. 2nd ed. *U.S.-Latin American Relations*. Westport, CT: Greenwood Press, 1985.

LaFeber, Walter. *Inevitable Revolutions: The United States in Central America*. New York: Norton, 1984.

————. *The Panama Canal: The Crisis in Historical Perspective*. Updated ed. New York: Oxford University Press, 1989.

Langley, Lester D. *Struggle for the American Mediterranean: United States-European Rivalry in the Gulf-Caribbean, 1776–1904*. Athens: University of Georgia Press, 1976.

————. *The United States and the Caribbean, 1900–1970*. Athens: University of Georgia Press, 1980.

May, Ernest R. *The Making of the Monroe Doctrine*. Cambridge, MA: Harvard University Press, 1975.

Munro, Dana G. *Intervention and Dollar Diplomacy in the Caribbean, 1900–1921.* Princeton, NJ: Princeton University Press, 1964.

———. *The United States and the Caribbean Republics, 1921–1933.* Princeton, NJ: Princeton University Press, 1974.

Pastor, Robert A. *Condemned to Repetition: The United States and Nicaragua.* Princeton, NJ: Princeton University Press, 1987.

Perkins, Dexter. *A History of the Monroe Doctrine.* Rev. ed. Boston: Houghton Mifflin, 1963.

———. *The United States and the Caribbean.* 2nd ed. Cambridge, MA: Harvard University Press, 1966.

Schmitt, Karl M. *Mexico and the United States, 1821–1973: Conflict and Coexistence.* New York: Wiley, 1974.

Stuart, Graham H., and Tigner, James L. *Latin America and the United States.* 6th ed. Englewood Cliffs, NJ: Prentice-Hall, 1975.

Whitaker, Arthur P. *The United States and the Independence of Latin America, 1800–1830.* Baltimore: Johns Hopkins Press, 1941.

Middle East

Bryson, Thomas A. *American Diplomatic Relations with the Middle East, 1784–1975: A Survey.* Metuchen, NJ: Scarecrow Press, 1977.

De Novo, John A. *American Interests and Policies in the Middle East, 1900–1939.* Minneapolis: University of Minnesota Press, 1963.

Field, James A., Jr. *America and the Mediterranean World, 1776–1882.* Princeton, NJ: Princeton University Press, 1969.

Friedman, Thomas. *From Beirut to Jerusalem.* New York: Farrar, Straus, & Giroux, 1989.

Kupchan, Charles A. *The Persian Gulf and the West.* New York: Unwin Hyman, 1987.

Reich, Bernard, *Quest for Peace: United States-Israel Relations and the Arab-Israeli Conflict.* New Brunswick, NJ: Transaction, 1977.

Rubenberg, Cheryl. *Israel and the American National Interest.* Champaign, IL: University of Illinois Press, 1986.

Stockey, Robert W. *America and the Arab States: An Uneasy Encounter.* New York: Wiley, 1975.

Yergin, Daniel. *The Prize: The Epic Quest for Oil, Money and Power.* New York: Simon and Schuster, 1991.

Russia/Soviet Union

Bailey, Thomas A. *America Faces Russia: Russian-American Relations from Early Times to Our Day.* Ithaca, NY: Cornell University Press, 1950.

Dulles, Foster Rhea. *The Road to Teheran: The Story of Russia and America, 1781–1943.* Princeton University Press, 1944.

Garthoff, Raymond L. *Detente and Confrontation.* Washington, DC: Brookings, 1985.

Gaddis, John Lewis. *Russia, the Soviet Union and the United States: An Interpretive History.* New York: Wiley, 1978.

Hyland, William G. *Mortal Rivals: Superpower Relations from Nixon to Reagan.* New York: Random House, 1987.

Unterberger, Betty M. *America's Siberian Expedition, 1918–1920.* New York: Greenwood, 1969.

Williams, William Appleman. *American-Russian Relations, 1781–1947.* New York: Rinehart, 1952.

Document Collections

Bevans, Charles I., comp. *Treaties and Other International Agreements of the United States of America, 1776–1949.* 12 vols. Washington, DC: GPO, 1968–.

Challener, Richard D., ed. *From Isolation to Containment, 1921–1951: Three Decades of American Foreign Policy from Harding to Truman.* Columbia: University of South Carolina Press, 1971.

Documents on American Foreign Relations. New York: Simon and Schuster, 1939–. (Continued as the series *American Foreign Relations, A Documentary Record.* New York: New York University Press, 1971–.)

Documents on International Affairs. 31 vols. New York: Oxford University Press, 1929–1973.

Ferrell, Robert H., ed. *America as a World Power, 1872–1945.* Columbia: University of South Carolina Press, 1971.

Historic Documents of 19–. Washington, DC: Congressional Quarterly, 1972–.

Schlesinger, Arthur M., Jr., ed. *The Dynamics of World Power: A Documentary History of United States Foreign Policy, 1945–*

1973. 5 vols. New York: Chelsea House, 1973.

United States Treaties and Other International Agreements. Washington, DC: GPO, 1950–.

United States in World Affairs, 1931–. New York: Simon and Schuster, 1932–.

U.S. Department of State. *A Decade of American Foreign Policy Basic Documents, 1941–1949.* Rev. ed. Washington, DC: GPO, 1985.

U.S. Department of State. *American Foreign Policy, 1950–1955: Basic Documents.* 2 vols. Pub. no. 6446. Washington, DC: GPO, 1957.

U.S. Department of State. *American Foreign Policy: Current Documents, 1956–1967.* 12 vols. Washington, DC: GPO, 1959–1969.

U.S. Department of State. *Department of State Bulletin.* Washington, DC: GPO, 1939–.

U.S. Department of State. *Foreign Relations of the United States.* Washington, DC: GPO, 1861–.

U.S. President. *Public Papers of the President of the United States.* Washington, DC: GPO, 1960–.

UNITED NATIONS

Bloomfield, Lincoln P. *The United Nations and U.S. Foreign Policy: A New Look at the National Interest.* 3rd ed. London: University of London Press, 1969.

Divine, Robert A. *Second Chance: The Triumph of Internationalism in America during World War II.* New York: Atheneum, 1967.

Everyone's United Nations. 10th ed. New York: United Nations, 1986.

Finger, Seymour M. *American Ambassadors at the U.N.* New York: Holmes & Meier, 1987.

Gati, Toby T., ed. *The United States, the United Nations, and the Management of Global Change.* New York: New York University Press, 1983,

Luard, Evan. *A History of the United Nations.* 2 vols. New York: St. Martin's Press, 1982–1989.

Osmanczyk, Edmund Jan. *Encyclopedia of the United Nations and International Agreements.* 2nd ed. New York: Taylor and Francis, 1990.

Schiavone, Giuseppe. *International Organizations: A Dictionary and Directory.* 2nd ed. Chicago: St. James Press, 1983.

U.S. Department of State. *United States Contributions to International Organizations Annual Report.* Washington, DC: GPO, 1952–.

Yearbook of the United Nations 19–. New York: United Nations, 1947–.

NATIONAL SECURITY

General

Buckley, Thomas H., and Strong, Edwin, B., Jr. *American Foreign and National Security Policies, 1914–1945.* Knoxville: University of Tennessee Press, 1987.

Destler, I. M.; Gelb, Leslie H.; and Lake, Anthony. *Our Own Worst Enemy.* New York: Simon and Schuster, 1984.

Falk, Stanley. *The Presidency and the Management of National Security.* New York: Free Press, 1988.

Freedman, Lawrence. *The Evolution of Nuclear Strategy.* 2nd ed. New York: St. Martin's Press, 1989.

George, Alexander L., and Smoke, Richard. *Deterrence in American Foreign Policy: Theory and Practice.* New York, Columbia University Press, 1974.

Graebner, Norman A., ed. *The National Security.* New York: Oxford University Press, 1986.

Prados, John. *Keepers of the Keys: A History of the National Security Council from Truman to Bush.* New York: William Morrow, 1991.

Spanier, John. *Games Nations Play.* Washington, DC: Congressional Quarterly, 1990.

Arms Control and Disarmament

Bechhoefer, Bernard G. *Postwar Negotiations for Arms Control.* Washington, DC: Brookings Institution, 1961.

Blacker, Coit D. *Reluctant Warriors: The United States, the Soviet Union, and Arms Control.* New York: W.H. Freeman, 1987.

Dupuy, Trevor N., and Hammesman, Gay M. *A Documentary History of Arms Control and Disarmament.* New York: Bowker, 1973.

Elliot, Jeffrey M., and Reginald, Robert. *The Arms Control, Disarmament, and Military Security Dictionary.* Santa Barbara, CA: ABC-CLIO, 1989.

Goldblat, Jozef. *Arms Control Agreements: A Handbook.* New York: Praeger, 1983.

Mayers, Teena. *Understanding Nuclear Weapons and Arms Control*. Arlington, VA: Education in World Issues, 1984.

Menos, Dennis. *Arms Control Fact Book*. Jefferson, NC: McFarland, 1985.

Miller, Steven E., and Van Evera, Stephen, eds. *The Star Wars Controversy*. Princeton, NJ: Princeton University Press, 1986.

Quester, George H. *Nuclear Diplomacy: The First Twenty-five Years*. New York: Dunellen, 1970.

Roberts, Chalmers M. *The Nuclear Years: The Arms Race and Arms Control, 1945–1970*. New York: Praeger, 1970.

Talbott, Strobe. *Deadly Gambits*. New York: Alfred Knopf, 1984.

———. *The Inside Story of SALT II*. New York: Harper & Row, 1979.

U.S. Arms Control and Disarmament Agency. *Arms Control and Disarmament Agreements: Texts and Histories of Negotiations*. Washington, DC: GPO, 1982.

U.S. Arms Control and Disarmament Agency. *Documents on Disarmament*. Washington, DC: GPO, 1960–.

Military Affairs

Blaufarb, Douglas S. *The Counterinsurgency Era: U.S. Doctrine and Performance, 1950 to the Present*. New York: Free Press, 1977.

Dupuy, R. Ernest, and Dupuy, Trevor N. *The Encyclopedia of Military History*. 2nd rev. ed. New York: Harper & Row, 1986.

Hagan, Kenneth J., ed. *In Peace and War: Interpretations of American Naval History, 1775–1984*. Westport, CT: Greenwood Press, 1984.

Matloff, Maurice, ed. *American Military History*. Washington, DC: GPO, 1969.

Millet, Allan R. and Maslowski, Peter. *For the Common Defense: A Military History of the United States*. New York: Free Press, 1984.

O'Connor, Raymond G., ed. *American Defense Policy in Perspective: From Colonial Times to the Present*. New York: Wiley, 1965.

Perret, Geoffrey. *A Country Made by War: From the Revolution to Vietnam—The Story of America's Rise to Power*. New York: Random House, 1989.

Vagts, Alfred. *Defense and Diplomacy: The Soldier and the Conduct of Foreign Relations*. New York: Columbia University Press, 1956.

Wars

Bauer, K. Jack. *The Mexican War, 1846–1848*. New York: Macmillan, 1974.

Blair, Clay. *The Forgotten War: America in Korea 1950–1953*. New York: Times Books, 1987.

Calvocoressi, Peter, and Wint, Guy. *Total War: The Story of World War II*. New York: Pantheon, 1972.

Catton, Bruce. *The Centennial History of the Civil War*. 3 vols. New York: Doubleday, 1961–1965.

Coffman, Edward M. *The War to End All Wars: The American Military Experience in World War I*. New York: Oxford University Press, 1968.

De Weerd, Harvey A. *President Wilson Fights His War: World War I and the American Intervention*. New York: Macmillan, 1968.

Higginbotham, Don. *The War of American Independence: Military Attitudes, Policies, and Practices, 1763–1789*. New York, Macmillan, 1972.

Horseman, Reginald. *The Causes of the War of 1812*. Philadelphia: University of Pennsylvania Press, 1962.

———. *The War of 1812*. New York: Alfred Knopf, 1964.

Kahin, George McT. *Intervention: How America Became Involved in Vietnam*. New York: Alfred Knopf, 1986.

Karnow, Stanley. *Vietnam: A History*. New York: Viking, 1983.

Liddell Hart, Basil. *History of the Second World War*. New York: Putnam's, 1970.

Olson, James S., ed. *Dictionary of the Vietnam War*. Westport, CT: Greenwood Press, 1988.

Palmer, Bruce, Jr. *The 25-Year War: America's Military Role in Vietnam*. Lexington: University Press of Kentucky, 1984.

Pentagon Papers. Gravel edition. Boston: Beacon Press, 1971.

Summers, Harry G., Jr. *Korean War Almanac*. New York: Facts on File, 1990.

———. *Vietnam War Almanac*. New York: Facts on File, 1985.

Toland, John. *In Mortal Combat: Korea, 1950–1953*. New York: William Morrow, 1991.

INTELLIGENCE

Ambrose, Stephen E. *Ike's Spies: Eisenhower and the Espionage Establishment*. Garden City, NY: Doubleday, 1981.

Bamford, James. *The Puzzle Palace.* Boston: Houghton Mifflin, 1982.

Becket, Henry S. A. *The Dictionary of Espionage.* Briarcliff Manor, NY: Stein and Day, 1986.

Cline, Ray S. *The CIA Under Reagan, Bush, and Casey.* Washington, DC: Acropolis, 1981.

———. *Secrets, Spies, and Scholars: Blueprint of the Essential CIA.* Washington, DC: Acropolis, 1976.

Corson, William R. *The Armies of Ignorance: The Rise of the American Intelligence Empire.* New York: Dial Press, 1977.

De Silva, Peter. *The CIA and the Uses of Intelligence.* New York: Times Books, 1978.

Jeffreys-Jones, Rhodri. *American Espionage: From Secret Service to CIA.* New York: Free Press, 1977.

Kirkpatrick, Lyman B., Jr. *The U.S. Intelligence Community: Foreign Policy and Domestic Activities.* New York: Hill and Wang, 1973.

Leary, William M. *The Central Intelligence Agency—History and Documents.* Huntsville: University of Alabama Press, 1984.

Miller, Nathan. *Spying for America: The Hidden History of U.S. Intelligence.* New York: Dell, 1989.

O'Toole, G.J.A. *The Encyclopedia of American Intelligence and Espionage from the Revolutionary War to the Present.* New York: Facts on File, 1988.

Powers, Thomas. *The Man Who Kept the Secrets: Richard Helms and the CIA.* New York: Alfred Knopf, 1979.

Prados, John. *Presidents' Secret Wars: CIA and Pentagon Covert Operations Since World War II.* New York: William Morrow, 1986.

———. *The Soviet Estimate: U.S. Intelligence Analysis and Soviet Strategic Forces.* Princeton, NJ: Princeton University Press, 1986.

Ranelagh, John. *The Agency: The Rise and Fall of the CIA.* New York: Simon and Schuster, 1986.

Richelson, Jeffrey T. *America's Secret Eyes in Space: The U.S. Keyhole Spy Satellite Program.* New York: Harper & Row, 1990.

———. *The U.S. Intelligence Community.* Cambridge, MA: Ballinger, 1985.

Smith, R. Harris. *OSS: The Secret History of America's First Central Intelligence Agency.* Berkeley, CA: University of California Press, 1972.

Treverton, Gregory F. *Covert Action.* New York: Basic Books, 1989.

Watson, Bruce W.; Watson, Susan M.; and Hopple, Gerald W., eds. *United States Intelligence: An Encyclopedia.* New York: Garland, 1990.

ECONOMY, TRADE, AND DEVELOPMENT

Bauer, Robert A. *The Interaction of Economics and Foreign Policy.* Charlottesville: University of Virginia Press, 1975.

Becker, William H., and Wells, Samuel F., Jr., eds. *Economics and American Diplomacy: An Assessment.* New York: Columbia University Press, 1981.

Cohen, Benjamin J., ed. *American Foreign Economic Policy: Essays and Comments.* New York: Harper & Row, 1968.

Cohen, Stephen D. *The Making of United States International Economic Policy: Principles, Problems, and Proposals for Reform.* New York: Praeger, 1977.

Destler, I.M. *Making Foreign Economic Policy.* Washington, DC: Brookings Institution, 1980.

de Vries, Margaret G. *The IMF in a Changing World, 1945–1985.* Ann Arbor, MI: Books on Demand, 1986.

Friesen, Connie M. *The Political Economy of East-West Trade.* New York: Praeger, 1976.

Gardner, Richard N. *Sterling-Dollar Diplomacy: The Origins and Prospects of Our International Economic Order.* Rev. ed. New York: McGraw-Hill, 1969.

Hogan, Michael J. *The Marshall Plan: America, Britain, and the Reconstruction of Europe, 1947–1952.* New York: Cambridge University Press, 1987.

Kindleberger, Charles P. "U.S. Foreign Economic Policy, 1776–1976." *Foreign Affairs* 55:2 (1977), 395–417.

Mason, Edward S. *Foreign Aid and Foreign Policy.* New York: Harper & Row, 1964.

Miller, William J. *Encyclopedia of International Commerce.* Centreville, MD: Cornell Maritime Press, 1985.

Painter, David S. *Oil and the American Century.* Baltimore: Johns Hopkins Press, 1986.

Pastor, Robert A. *Congress and the Politics of Foreign Economic Policy, 1929–1976.* Berkeley: University of California Press, 1980.

Peterson, Peter G. *The United States in the Changing World Economy*. 2 vols. in 1. Washington, DC: GPO, 1971.

Porter, Glenn, ed. *Encyclopedia of American Economic History*. 3 vols. New York: Charles Scribner's, 1980.

Randall, Stephen J. *U.S. Foreign Oil Policy, 1919–1984*. Toronto: University of Toronto Press, 1985.

Stanley, Robert G. *Food for Peace: Hope and Reality of U.S. Food Aid*. New York: Gordon and Breach, 1973.

Taussig, Frank W. *The Tariff History of the United States*. New York: Putnam's, 1931.

Wilhelm, John, and Feinstein, Gerry. *U.S. Foreign Assistance: Investment or Folly*. Westport, CT: Greenwood Press, 1984.

Wilson, Theodore A. *The Marshall Plan, 1947–1951*. Headline Series, no. 236. New York: Foreign Policy Association, 1977.

Woodruff, William. *America's Impact on the World: A Study of the Role of the United States in the World Economy, 1750–1970*. New York: Wiley, 1975.

SCIENCE, TECHNOLOGY, AND ENVIRONMENT

Averch, Harvey A. *A Strategic Analysis of Science and Technology Policy*. Baltimore, MD: Johns Hopkins Press, 1985.

Barfield, Claude E. *Science Policy from Ford to Reagan: Change and Continuity*. Washington, DC: American Enterprise Institute, 1982.

Barke, Richard. *Science, Technology, and Public Policy*. Washington, DC: Congressional Quarterly, 1986.

Brown, Lester R., et al. *State of the World*. New York: Norton, 1984–.

Bush, Vannevar. *Modern Arms and Free Men*. New York: Simon and Schuster, 1949.

Hiskes, Anne L., and Hiskes, Richard P. *Science, Technology, and Policy Decisions*. Boulder, CO: Westview Press, 1986.

Killian, James R., Jr. *Sputnik, Scientists, and Eisenhower*. Cambridge, MA: MIT Press, 1977.

Kuehn, Thomas J., and Porter, Alan C., eds. *Science, Technology, and National Policy*. Ithaca, NY: Cornell University Press, 1981.

Logsdon, John M. *The Decision to Go to the Moon: Project Apollo and the National Interest*. Cambridge, MA: MIT Press, 1970.

McDougall, Walter A. *The Heavens and the Earth: A Political History of the Space Age*. New York: Basic Books, 1985.

Penik, James L., et al., eds. *The Politics of American Science, 1939 to the Present*. Rev ed. Cambridge, MA: MIT Press, 1972.

Rhodes, Richard. *The Making of the Atomic Bomb*. New York: Simon amd Schuster, 1986.

Skolnikof, Eugene B. *Science, Technology, and American Foreign Policy*. Cambridge, MA: MIT Press, 1967.

Smith, Bruce L. R. *American Science Policy Since World War II*. Washington, DC: Brookings Institution, 1990.

Stares, Paul B. *The Militarization of Space: U.S. Policy, 1945–1984*. Ithaca, NY: Cornell University Press, 1985.

INDIAN AFFAIRS

Debo, Angie. *A History of the Indians of the United States*. Norman: University of Oklahoma Press, 1970.

Deloria, Vine, Jr., and Lytle, C. M. *American Indians, American Justice*. New York: Random House, 1983.

Dillon, Richard. *North American Indian Wars*. New York: Gallery Books, 1983.

Horseman, Reginald. *Expansion and American Indian Policy, 1783–1812*. East Lansing: Michigan State University Press, 1967.

Kappler, Charles J., ed. *Indian Affairs: Law and Treaties*. 5 vols. Washington, DC: GPO, 1904–1941.

Kelly, Lawrence C. *Federal Indian Policy*. New York: Chelsea House, 1990.

Priest, Loring B. *Uncle Sam's Stepchildren: The Reformation of United States Indian Policy, 1865–1887*. New Brunswick, NJ: Rutgers University Press, 1942.

Prucha, Francis Paul. *American Indian Policy in Crisis: Christian Reformers and the Indian, 1865–1900*. Norman: University of Oklahoma Press, 1976.

———. *American Indian Policy in the Formative Years: The Indian Trade and Intercourse Acts, 1790–1834*. Cambridge, MA: Harvard University Press, 1962.

Royce, Charles. *Indian Land Cession in the United States*. New York: Arno Press, 1971.

Satz, Ronald N. *American Indian Policy in the Jacksonian Era*. Lincoln: University of Nebraska, 1975.

Sturtevant, William C., ed. *Handbook of North American Indians. Vol. 4, History of Indian-White Relations.* Washington, DC: Smithsonian Institution, 1988.

Tyler, S. Lyman. *A History of Indian Policy.* Washington, DC: Department of the Interior, Bureau of Indian Affairs, 1973.

Van Every, Dale. *Disinherited: The Lost Birthright of the American Indian.* New York: William Morrow, 1966.

Washburn, Wilcomb E., ed. *The American Indian and the United States: A Documentary History.* 4 vols. New York: Random House, 1973.

————. *The Indian in America.* New York: Harper & Row, 1975.

————. *Red Man's Land/White Man's Law: A Study of the Past and Present Status of the American Indian.* New York: Charles Scribner's, 1971.

IMMIGRATION

Bernard, William S. "Immigration: History of U.S. Policy." In *Harvard Encyclopedia of American Ethnic Groups.* Cambridge, MA: Belknap Press, 1980.

Cafferty, Pastora San Juan, et al. *The Dilemma of American Immigration: Beyond the Golden Door.* New Brunswick, NJ: Transaction Books, 1983.

Congressional Research Service. *Immigration Law and Policy, 1952–1979.* Washington, DC: GPO, 1979.

Divine, Robert A. *American Immigration Policy, 1924–1951.* New Haven, CT: Yale University Press, 1957.

Greene, Victor. "Immigration Policy." In *Encyclopedia of American Political History.* New York: Charles Scribner's, 1984.

Handlin, Oscar. *The Uprooted.* Boston: Little, Brown, 1973.

Higham, John. *Strangers In the Land.* New Brunswick, NJ: Rutgers University Press, 1988.

Hull, Elizabeth. *Without Justice for All: The Constitutional Rights of Aliens.* Westport, CT: Greenwood Press, 1985.

Hutchinson, E. P. *Legislative History of American Immigration Policy 1798–1965.* Philadelphia: University of Pennsylvania Press, 1981.

Kraut, Alan N. *The Huddled Masses: The Immigrant in American Society, 1889–1921.* Arlington Heights, IL: Haran Davidson, 1982.

Loescher, Gilburt D., and Scanlon, John A. *Calculated Kindness: Refugees and America's Half-open Door, 1945 to the Present.* New York: Free Press, 1986.

Zucker, Norman L., and Zucker, Naomi Flink. *The Guarded Gate: The Reality of American Refugee Policy.* New York: Harcourt Brace Jovanovich, 1987.

MEMOIRS

Acheson, Dean. *Present at the Creation: My Years in the State Department.* New York: Norton, 1969.

Alsop, Joseph W., with Platt, Adam. *I've Seen the Best of It.* New York: Norton, 1992.

Ball, George W. *The Past Has Another Pattern.* New York: Norton, 1982.

Baruch, Bernard M. *Baurch.* 2 vols. New York: Holt, Rinehart & Winston, 1957–1960.

Bohlen, Charles E. *Witness to History: 1929–1969.* New York: Norton, 1973.

Bowles, Chester. *Promises to Keep: My Years in Public Life, 1941–1969.* New York: Harper & Row, 1971.

Brzezinski, Zbigniew K. *Power and Principle.* New York: Farrar, Straus, & Giroux, 1983.

Butler, Nicholas Murray. *Across the Busy Years: Recollections and Reflections.* 2 vols. New York: Charles Scribner's, 1939–1940.

Byrnes, James F. *All in One Lifetime.* New York: Harper & Row, 1958.

Carter, Jimmy. *Keeping Faith.* New York, Bantam, 1982.

Clifford, Clark M. *Counsel to the President.* New York: Random House, 1991.

Colby, William E., and Forbath, Peter. *Honorable Men: My Life in the CIA.* New York: Simon and Schuster, 1978.

Daniels, Josephus. *Shirt-Sleeve Diplomat.* Chapel Hill: University of North Carolina Press, 1947.

Eisenhower, Dwight D. *The White House Years.* 2 vols. Garden City, NY: Doubleday, 1963–1965.

Ford, Gerald R. *A Time to Heal.* New York: Harper & Row, 1979.

Forrestal, James. *The Forrestal Diaries.* Ed. by Walter Millis. New York: Viking, 1951.

Grew, Joseph C. *Turbulent Era: A Diplomatic Record of Forty Years, 1904–1945.* 2 vols. London: Hammond, 1953.

Haig, Alexander M., Jr. *Caveat*. New York: Macmillan, 1984.

Harriman, W. Averell, and Abel, Elie. *Special Envoy to Churchill and Stalin, 1941–1946*. New York: Random House, 1975.

Hay, John M. *The Life and Letters of John Hay*. 2 vols. Ed. by Roscoe R. Thayer. Boston: Houghton Mifflin, 1915.

Hoover, Herbert C. *Memoirs*. 3 vols. New York: Macmillan, 1951–1952.

Hull, Cordell. *Memoirs*. 2 vols. New York: Macmillan, 1948.

Johnson, Lyndon B. *The Vantage Point*. New York: Holt, Rhinehart, & Winston, 1971.

Kennan, George F. *Memoirs, 1925–1963*. 2 vols. Boston: Little, Brown, 1967, 1972.

Kissinger, Henry A. *White House Years*. Boston: Little, Brown, 1979.

———. *Years of Upheaval*. Boston: Little, Brown, 1979.

Landsdale, Edward G. *In the Midst of Wars*. New York: Harper & Row, 1972.

Lansing, Robert. *War Memoirs of Robert Lansing, Secretary of State*. Indianapolis: Bobbs Merrill, 1935.

Leahy, William D. *I Was There*. New York: Whittlesay House, 1950.

Lodge, Henry Cabot, Jr. *The Storm Has Many Eyes: A Personal Narrative*. New York: Norton, 1973.

MacArthur, Douglas. *Reminiscences*. New York: McGraw-Hill, 1964.

Nitze, Paul H. *From Hiroshima to Glasnost: At the Center of Decision*. New York: Weidenfeld & Nicolson, 1989.

Nixon, Richard M. *RN: The Memoirs of Richard Nixon*. New York: Grosset & Dunlap, 1978.

———. *Six Crises*. Garden City, NY: Doubleday, 1962.

Reagan, Ronald. *An American Life*. New York, Simon and Schuster, 1990.

Ridgway, Matthew B., with Martin, Harold H. *Soldier: The Memoirs of Matthew B. Ridgway*. New York: Harper & Row, 1956.

Rostow, W. W. *The Diffusion of Power: An Essay in Recent History*. New York: Macmillan, 1972.

Seymour, Charles. *The Intimate Papers of Colonel House Arranged as a Narrative*. 4 vols. Boston: Houghton Mifflin, 1926–1928.

Smith, Walter Bedell. *My Three Years in Moscow*. Philadelphia: Lippincott, 1950.

Stimson, Henry L., and Bundy, McGeorge. *On Active Service in Peace and War*. New York: Harper & Row, 1949.

Taylor, Maxwell D. *Swords and Ploughshares*. New York: Norton, 1972.

Truman, Harry S. *Memoirs*. 2 vols. Garden City, NY: Doubleday, 1955–1956.

Vance, Cyrus R. *Hard Choices*. New York: Simon and Schuster, 1983.

Walters, Vernon A. *Silent Missions*. Garden City, NY: Doubleday, 1978.

Welles, Sumner. *The Time for Decision*. New York: Harper & Row, 1944.

Westmoreland, William C. *A Soldier Reports*. Garden City, NY: Doubleday, 1976.

Appendix H

Maps

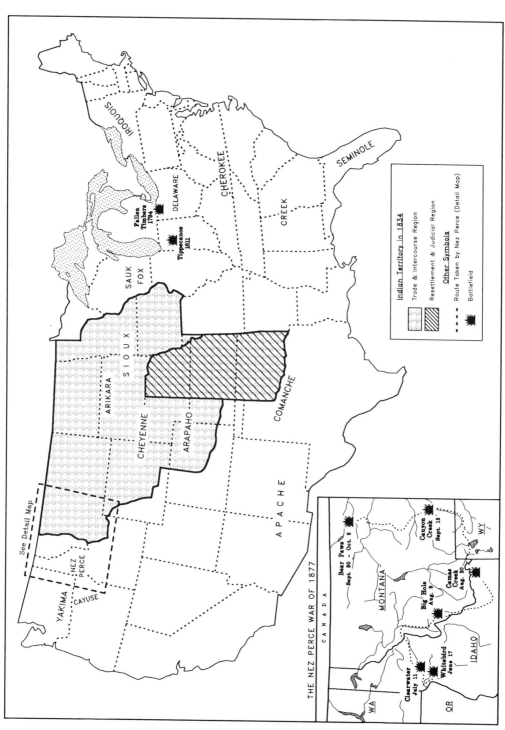

Map 1   Indian Affairs

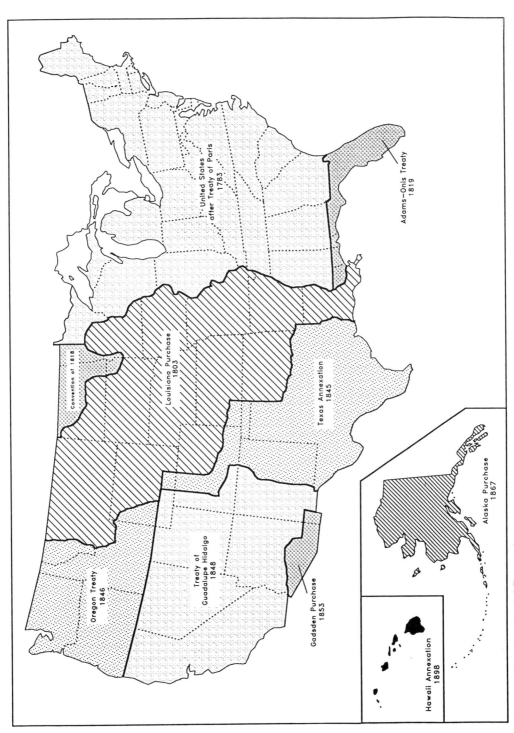

Map 2   U.S. Territorial Expansion

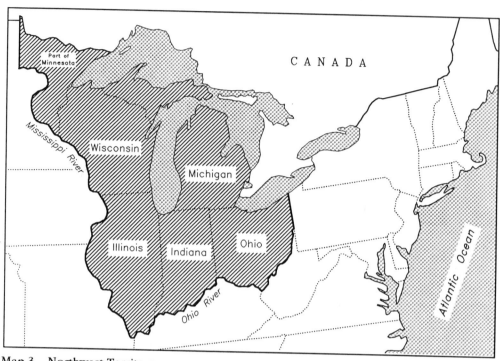

Map 3   Northwest Territory

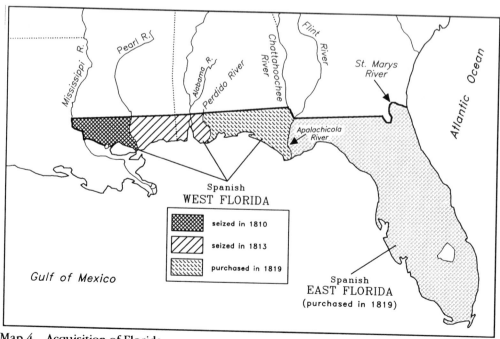

Spanish
WEST FLORIDA

▓	seized in 1810
⧄	seized in 1813
▒	purchased in 1819

Gulf of Mexico

Spanish
EAST FLORIDA
(purchased in 1819)

Map 4   Acquisition of Florida

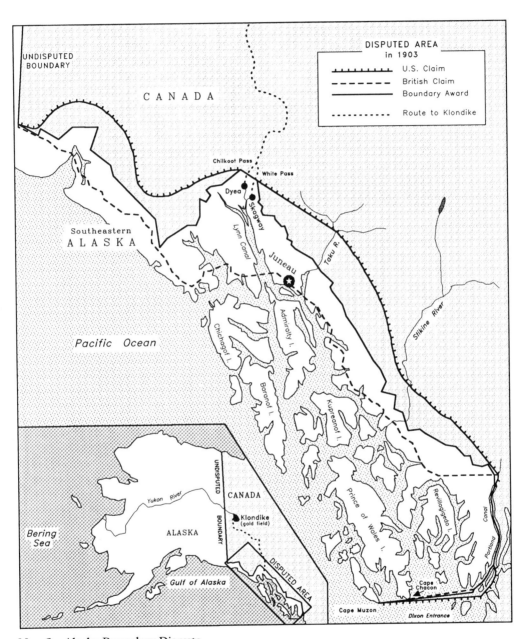

Map 5 Alaska Boundary Dispute

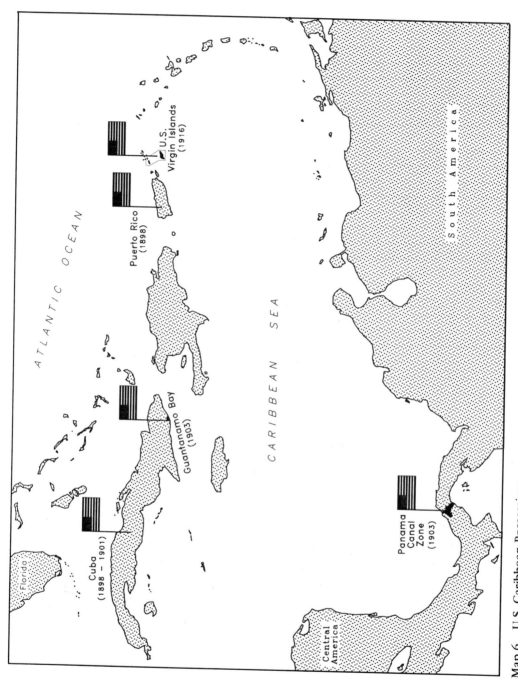

Map 6   U.S. Caribbean Possessions

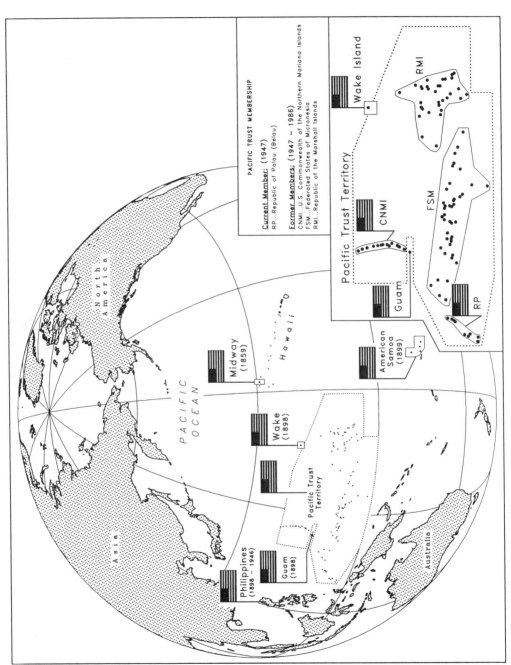

PACIFIC TRUST MEMBERSHIP

Current Member: (1947)
RP...Republic of Palau (Belau)

Former Members: (1947 – 1986)
CNMI...U.S. Commonwealth of the Northern Mariana Islands
FSM...Federated States of Micronesia
RMI...Republic of the Marshall Islands

Wake Island

Pacific Trust Territory

RMI

CNMI

FSM

Guam

RP

American Samoa
(1899)

Midway
(1859)

Wake
(1898)

Pacific Trust Territory

Philippines
(1898 – 1946)

Guam
(1898)

North America

Asia

PACIFIC OCEAN

Hawaii

Australia

Map 7   U.S. Pacific Possessions

The Winner

David Baldacci is the internationally acclaimed author of more than 20 bestselling novels. With his books published in at least 45 different languages, and with over 90 million copies in print, he is one of the world's favourite storytellers. His family foundation, the Wish You Well Foundation, a non-profit organization, works to eliminate illiteracy across America. Still a resident of his native Virginia, he invites you to visit him at www.DavidBaldacci.com, and his foundation at www.WishYouWellFoundation.org, and to look into its programme to spread books across America at www.FeedingBodyandMind.com.

DAVID BALDACCI

The Winner

PAN BOOKS

First published 1997 by Warner Books, USA

First published in Great Britain 1998 by Simon & Schuster UK Ltd

This edition published 2011 by Pan Books
an imprint of Pan Macmillan, a division of Macmillan Publishers Limited
Pan Macmillan, 20 New Wharf Road, London N1 9RR
Basingstoke and Oxford
Associated companies throughout the world
www.panmacmillan.com

ISBN 978-0-330-54516-7

1 3 5 7 9 8 6 4 2

A CIP catalogue record for this book is available from
the British Library.

Printed in the UK by CPI Group (UK), Croydon, CR0 4YY

To Collin,
my buddy, my boy, my son

The Winner

ONE

Jackson studied the shopping mall's long corridor, noting haggard mothers piloting loaded strollers and the senior citizens group walking the mall both for exercise and conversation. Dressed in a gray pinstriped suit, the stocky Jackson stared intently at the north entrance to the shopping mall. That would no doubt be the one she would use since the bus stop was right in front. She had, Jackson knew, no other form of transportation. Her live-in boyfriend's truck was in the impoundment lot, the fourth time in as many months. It must be getting a little tedious for her, he thought. The bus stop was on the main road. She would have to walk about a mile to get there, but she often did that. What other choice did she have? The baby would be with her. She would never leave it with the boyfriend, Jackson was certain of that.

While his name always remained Jackson for all of his business endeavors, next month his appearance would change dramatically from the hefty middle-aged man he was currently. Facial features of course would again be altered; weight would probably be lost; height added or taken away, along with hair. Male or female? Aged or youthful? Often, the persona would be taken from people whom he knew, either wholly or bits of thread from different ones, sewn together until the delicate quilt of fabrication was complete. In school, biology had been a favorite subject. Specimens belonging to that rarest of all classes, the hermaphrodite, had never ceased to fascinate him. He smiled as he dwelled for a moment on this greatest of all physical duplicities.

Jackson had received a first-rate education from a prestigious Eastern school. Combining his love of acting with his natural acumen for science and chemistry, he had achieved a rare double major in drama and chemical engineering. Mornings would find him hunched over pages of complex equations or malodorous concoctions in the university's chemistry lab, while the evenings would have him energetically embroiled in the production of a Tennessee Williams or Arthur Miller classic.

Those accomplishments were serving him very well. Indeed, if his classmates could only see him now.

In keeping with today's character – a middle-aged male, overweight and out of shape from leading a sedentary lifestyle – a bead of perspiration suddenly sprouted on Jackson's forehead. His lips curled into a smile. This physical reaction pleased him immensely, aided as it was by the insulation of the padding he was wearing to provide bulky proportions and to conceal his own wiry frame. But it was something more than that too: He took pride in the fact that he became the person totally, as though different chemical reactions took place within him depending on who and what he was pretending to be.

He didn't normally inhabit shopping malls; his personal tastes were far more sophisticated. However, his clientele were most comfortable in these types of surroundings, and comfort was an important consideration in his line of work. His meetings tended to make people quite excited, sometimes in negative ways. Several interviews had become extremely animated, compelling him to think on his

2

feet. These reminiscences brought another smile to Jackson's lips. You couldn't argue with success, though. He was batting a thousand. However, it only took one to spoil his perfect record. His smile quickly faded. Killing someone was never a pleasant experience. Rarely was it justified, but when it was, one simply had to do it and move on. For several reasons he hoped the meeting today would not precipitate such an outcome.

He carefully dabbed his forehead with his pocket handkerchief and adjusted his shirt cuffs. He smoothed down a barely visible tangle in the synthetic fibers of his neatly groomed wig. His real hair was compressed under a latex skullcap.

He pulled open the door to the space he had rented in the mall and went inside. The area was clean and orderly – in fact too much so, he thought suddenly as he slowly surveyed the interior. It lacked the look of a true working space.

The receptionist seated behind the cheap metal desk in the foyer looked up at him. In accordance with his earlier instructions, she didn't attempt to speak. She had no idea who he was or why she was here. As soon as Jackson's appointment showed up, the receptionist had been instructed to leave. Very soon she would be on a bus out of town, her purse a little fatter for her minimal troubles. Jackson never looked at her; she was a simple prop in his latest stage production.

The phone beside her sat silent, the typewriter next to that, unused. Yes, absolutely, too well organized, Jackson decided with a frown. He eyed the stack of paper on the receptionist's desk. With a sudden motion he spread some of the papers around the desk's surface. He then cocked the phone around just so and put a piece of paper in the typewriter, winding it through with several quick spins of the platen knob.

Jackson looked around at his handiwork and sighed. You couldn't think of everything all at once.

Jackson walked past the small reception area, quickly hitting the end of the shallow space, and then turned right. He opened the door to the tiny interior office, slipped across the room, and sat down behind the scuffed wooden desk. A small TV sat in one corner of the room, its blank screen staring back at him. He pulled a cigarette from his pocket, lit it, and leaned far back in the chair, trying his best to relax despite the constant flow of adrenaline. He stroked his thin, dark mustache. It too was made of synthetic fiber ventilated on a lace foundation and attached to his skin with spirit gum. His nose had been changed considerably as well: a putty base highlighted and shadowed, to make his nose's actual delicate and straight appearance bulky and slightly crooked. The small mole resting next to the altered bridge of his nose was also fake: a concoction of gelatin and alfalfa seeds mixed in hot water. His straight teeth were covered with acrylic caps to give them an uneven and unhealthy appearance. All of these illusions would be remembered by even the most casual observer. Thus when they were removed, he, in essence, disappeared. What more could someone wholeheartedly engaged in illegal activities want?

Soon, if things went according to plan, it would all begin again. Each time was a little different, but that was the exciting part: the not knowing. He checked his watch again. Yes, very soon. He expected to have an extremely productive meeting with her; more to the point, a mutually beneficial meeting.

He only had one question to ask LuAnn Tyler, one simple question that carried the potential for very complex repercussions. Based upon his experience, he was reasonably certain of her answer, but one just never knew. He dearly hoped, for her sake, that she would give the right one. For there was only one "right" answer. If she said no? Well, the baby would never have the opportunity to know its mother, because the baby would be an orphan. He smacked the desktop with the palm of his hand. She would say yes. All the others had. Jackson shook his head vigorously as he thought it through. He would make her see, convince her of the inescapable logic of joining with him. How it would change everything for her. More than she could ever imagine. More than she could ever hope for. How could she say no? It was an offer that simply no one could refuse.

If she came. Jackson rubbed his cheek with the back of his hand, took a long, slow drag on the cigarette, and stared absently at a nail pop in the wall. But, truth be known, how could she not come?

TWO

The brisk wind sailed straight down the narrow dirt road between the compression of thick woods on either side. Suddenly the road curved north and then just as abruptly dipped to the east. Over a slight rise the view yielded still more trees, some dying, bent into what seemed painful shapes by wind, disease, and weather; but the majority were ramrod straight, with thickening girths and soaring, leafy branches. On the left side of the road, the more diligent eye could discern a half circle of open space consisting of mud interspersed with patches of new spring grass. Also nestled with nature into this clearing were rusted engine blocks, piles of trash, a small mountain of bone-dry beer cans, discarded furniture, and a litany of other debris that served as visual art objects when covered with snow, and as home to snakes and other creatures when the mercury made its way north. Smack in the middle of that semicircular island rested a short, squat mobile trailer atop a crumbling cinder block foundation. Seemingly its only touch with the rest of the world were the electrical and telephone lines that ran down from the thick, leaning poles along the road and collided with one side of the trailer. The trailer was a decided eyesore in the middle of nowhere. Its occupants would have agreed with that description: The middle of nowhere was aptly applied to themselves as well.

Inside the trailer, LuAnn Tyler looked at herself in

the small mirror perched atop the leaning chest of drawers. She held her face at an unusual angle, not only because the battered piece of furniture listed to one side with a broken leg, but also because the mirror was shattered. Meandering lines grew outward on the surface of the glass like the slender branches of a sapling such that if LuAnn had looked head-on into the mirror she would have seen not one but three faces in the reflection.

LuAnn didn't smile as she studied herself; she could never really remember smiling at her appearance. Her looks were her only asset – that had been beaten into her head ever since she could remember – although she could have used some dental work. Growing up on unfluoridated well water and never stepping foot inside a dentist's office had contributed to that situation.

No smarts, of course, her father had said over and over. No smarts, or no opportunity to use them? She had never broached the subject with Benny Tyler, dead now these past five years. Her mother, Joy, who had passed away almost three years ago, had never been happier than after her husband died. That should have completely dispelled Benny Tyler's opinions of her mental ability, but little girls believed what their daddy told them, mostly unconditionally.

She looked over to the wall where the clock hung. It was the only thing she had of her mother's; a family heirloom of sorts, as it had been given to Joy Tyler by her own mother on the day she married Benny. It had no intrinsic value; you could buy one in any pawnshop for ten bucks. Yet LuAnn treasured it. As a little girl LuAnn had listened to the slow, methodical ticks of that clock far into the night. Knowing that in the middle of all the darkness it would always be there, it would always soothe her into sleep and greet her in the morning. Throughout her growing up it had been one of her few anchoring points. It had a connection, too, in that it went back to her grandmother, a woman LuAnn had adored. Having that clock around was like having her grandmother around forever. As the years had gone by, its inner workings had worn down considerably so that it produced unique sounds. It had carried LuAnn through more bad times than good, and right before Joy died she had told LuAnn to take it, to take good care of it. And now LuAnn would keep it for her daughter.

She pulled her thick auburn hair straight back, tried a bun, and then dexterously knotted a French braid. Not satisfied with either of these looks, she finally piled her thick tresses on top and secured them with a legion of bobby pins, frequently cocking her head to test the effect. At five feet ten inches tall, she also had to stoop to see herself in the mirror.

Every few seconds she looked over at the small bundle on the chair next to her. She smiled as she took in the droopy eyes, the curved mouth, the chipmunk cheeks, and doughy fists. Eight months and growing up fast. Her daughter had already started to crawl with the funny, back-and-forth gyrations of infancy. Walking would soon replace that. LuAnn stopped smiling as she looked around. It would not take Lisa long to navigate the boundaries of this place. The interior, despite LuAnn's diligent efforts to keep it clean, resembled the exterior largely due to the temperamental outbursts of the man sprawled on the bed. Duane Harvey had twitched once or twice since staggering into the house at four A.M., throwing off his clothes, and climbing into bed, but otherwise he had remained motionless. She recalled fondly that on one night early in their relationship, Duane had not come home drunk: Lisa had been the

8

result. Tears glimmered for the briefest time in LuAnn's hazel eyes. She hadn't much time or sympathy for tears, particularly her own. At twenty years of age she had already cried enough of them to last her until the end of her days, she figured.

She turned back to the mirror. While one of her hands played with Lisa's tiny fist, LuAnn used the other to pull out all the bobby pins. She swept her hair back and then let her bangs fall naturally forward over her high forehead. It was a style she had worn in school, at least through the seventh grade, when she had joined many of her friends in the rural county in dropping out and seeking work and the paycheck that came with it. They had all thought, wrongly as it turned out, that a regular paycheck beat the hell out of an education any day of the week. For LuAnn, there hadn't been much choice. Half her wages went to help her chronically unemployed parents. The other half went to pay for things her parents couldn't afford to give her, such as food and clothes.

She eyed Duane carefully as she undid her tattered robe, revealing her naked body. Seeing no sign of life from him, she swiftly pulled on her underwear. As she grew up, her blossoming figure had been a true eye-opener for the local boys, making them press for manhood even before the natural order of things would allow them official entry.

LuAnn Tyler, the movie-star-slash-supermodel-to-be. Many of the residents of Rikersville County, Georgia, had thoroughly considered the issue of LuAnn and bestowed upon her that title, weighted down as it was with the highest of expectations. She was not long for their way of life, it was plain to see, proclaimed the wrinkled, thick local women holding court on their broad, decaying porches, and no one

9

disagreed with them. The natural beauty she possessed would hold out for nothing less than the glossiest of all brass rings. She was the vicarious hope for the locals. New York or maybe Los Angeles would beckon to *their* LuAnn, it was only a matter of time. Only she was still here, still in the very same county where she had lived all her life. She was a disappointment of sorts without ever – despite being barely out of her teens – having had the opportunity to realize any of her goals. She knew the townsfolk would have been surprised to realize that her ambitions did not include lying naked in bed next to Hollywood's hunk of the month or treading the models' catwalk wearing the latest creations of the haute couture crowd. Although, as she slipped into her bra, it occurred to her that, right about now, sliding into the latest fashions in exchange for ten thousand dollars a day was not such a bad deal.

Her face. And her body. Her father had often commented on that attribute too. Voluptuous, full-figured, he had described it, as though it were an entity distinct from her. Weak mind, dazzling body. Thankfully, he had never gone beyond those verbalizations. Late at night she sometimes wondered if he had ever wanted to but simply lacked the courage or the opportunity. Sometimes the way he would look at her. On rare occasions, she would venture into the deepest parts of her subconscious and sense, like the sudden, scary prick of a needle, the disjointed pieces of memory that made her wonder if the opportunity maybe had presented itself. At that point she would always shudder and tell herself that thinking such evil of the dead was not a good thing.

She studied the contents of the small closet. Really, she owned only one dress that would be appropriate for her appointment. The short-sleeve, navy blue with white trim around the collar and hemline. She remembered the day she bought it. A whole paycheck blown. *Sixty-five entire dollars*. That was two years ago and she had never repeated that insane extravagance, in fact it was the last dress she had bought. The garment was a little frayed now, but she had done a nice touch-up job with needle and thread. A strand of small, fake pearls, a birthday gift from a former admirer, encircled her long neck. She had stayed up late methodically coloring in the nicks on her only pair of high heels. They were dark brown and didn't match the dress but they would have to do. Flip-flops or sneakers, her only other two choices, were not going to cut it today, although she would wear the sneakers on the mile-long trek to the bus stop. Today could be the start of something new, or at least different. Who knew? It could lead to somewhere, anywhere. It could carry her and Lisa away to something other than the Duanes of the world.

LuAnn took a deep breath, opened up the zippered interior pocket of her purse, and carefully unfolded the piece of paper. She had written down the address and other information from the phone call from someone who had identified herself as a Mr. Jackson, a call she had almost not answered after pulling the midnight to seven shift as a waitress at the Number One Truck Stop.

When the phone call came LuAnn's eyes had been welded shut as she sat on the kitchen floor breast-feeding Lisa. The little girl's teeth were coming in and LuAnn's nipples felt like they were on fire, but the baby formula was too damn expensive and they were out of milk. At first, LuAnn had no desire to answer the phone. Her job at the popular truck stop right off the interstate kept her running nonstop, with Lisa meanwhile tucked safely under the counter in her baby seat. Luckily, the little girl could

11

hold a bottle and the diner's manager liked LuAnn enough that the arrangement hadn't jeopardized her position. They didn't get many calls. Mostly Duane's buddy looking for him to go drinking or strip a few cars that had broken down on the highway. Their Bud and Babe money they called it, and often right to her face. No, it was not Duane's boys calling this early. Seven A.M. would find them three hours into the deep sleep of another drinking binge.

After the third ring, for some reason, her hand had reached out and plucked up the phone. The man's voice was crisp and professional. He had sounded as though he were reading from a script and her sleep-clouded mind had pretty much reasoned that he was trying to sell her something. That was a joke! No charge cards, no checking account, just the little bit of cash hung in a plastic bag inside the hamper she used for Lisa's dirty diapers. It was the only place Duane would never search. Go ahead, mister, you just try to sell me something. Credit card number? Well let me just make one up right now. Visa? MasterCard? AmEx? Platinum. I've got 'em all, at least in my dreams. But the man had asked for her by name. And then he had mentioned the work. He wasn't selling her anything. He, essentially, was offering her employment. *How did you get my phone number?* she had asked him. The information was readily available, he had replied, so authoritatively that she instantly believed him. But she already had a job, she had told him. He asked what her salary was. She refused to answer at first and then, opening her eyes while Lisa suckled contentedly, she told him. She wasn't sure why. Later, she would think that it was a premonition of things to come.

Because that's when he had mentioned the pay.

One hundred dollars per weekday for a guaranteed two weeks. She had quickly done the arithmetic in her head. A total of one thousand dollars with the very real possibility of more work to come at those same rates. And they weren't full days. The man had said four hours tops, per day. That wouldn't affect her job at the truck stop at all. That came to twenty-five dollars per hour. No one she knew had ever earned such money. Why, at a full year that was twenty-five thousand dollars! And really, she would only be working half-time. So the rate was more like fifty thousand dollars per year! Doctors, lawyers, and movie stars earned such gigantic sums, not a high school dropout mother residing in the hopeless grip of poverty with someone called Duane. As if responding to her unspoken thoughts, Duane stirred for an instant, looking at her through brick-red eyes.

"Where the hell you going?" Duane's voice was thick with the drawl of the area. It seemed that she had heard those same words, that same tone, all her life from a variety of men. In response she picked up an empty beer can off the chest of drawers.

"How 'bout another beer, bay-bee?" She smiled coyly and arched her eyebrows wickedly. Her thick lips dangled each syllable seductively. It had the desired effect. Duane groaned at the sight of his malt and aluminum God and slumped back into the grip of his coming hangover. Despite his frequent drinking binges, he never could hold his liquor. In another minute he was asleep once more. The baby-doll smile instantly faded and LuAnn looked at the note again. The work, the man had said, involved trying new products, listening to some ads, getting her opinion on things. Sort of like a survey. Demographic analysis, he had termed it, whatever the hell that was. They did it all the time. It was connected to advertising rates, and television commercials, things like that. A hundred dollars a day for just giving her opinion, something she did for free just about every minute of her life.

Too good to be true, really. She had thought that a number of times since his phone call. She was not nearly as dumb as her father had thought. In fact, housed behind her comely face was an intellect far more powerful than the late Benny Tyler could have imagined, and it was coupled with a shrewdness that had allowed her to live by her wits for years now. However, only rarely did anyone go beyond her looks. She often dreamed of an existence where her boobs and butt weren't the first, last, and only thing anyone ever noticed about her, ever commented on.

She looked over at Lisa. The little girl was awake now, her eyes darting around the bedroom until they came to rest with much glee upon her mother's face. LuAnn's eyes crinkled back at her little girl. After all, could it be worse than her and Lisa's present reality? She normally held a job for a couple of months or, if she was really lucky, half a year, and then a layoff came with the promise of a rehire when times got better, which they never seemed to do. Without a high school diploma she was immediately categorized as stupid. By virtue of living with Duane, she had long ago decided she deserved that label. But he was Lisa's father even if he had no intention of marrying LuAnn, not that she had pushed him on that. She was not overeager to take Duane's last name or the man-child that came with it. However, having grown up in something less than the embrace of a happy, caring household, LuAnn was firmly convinced that the family unit was vitally important to a child's well-being. She had read all the magazines and watched numerous talk shows on the subject. In Rikersville, LuAnn was one step ahead of the welfare rolls most of the time; there were about twenty people for every lousy job. Lisa could and would do far better than her mother

– LuAnn had dedicated her life to making that a reality. But with a thousand dollars, perhaps LuAnn would do all right for herself. A bus ticket to somewhere else. Some money to live off until she could find a job; the little nest egg she had so desperately wanted over the years but had never been able to accumulate.

Rikersville was dying. The trailer was Duane's unofficial sepulcher. He would never have it any better and probably would have it much worse before the ground swallowed him up. It could be her crypt too, LuAnn realized, only it wouldn't be. Not after today. Not after she kept her appointment. She folded up the piece of paper and put it back in her purse. Sliding a small box out of one of the drawers, she found enough change for bus fare. She finished with her hair, buttoned her dress, swooped up Lisa, and quietly left the trailer, and Duane, behind.

THREE

There was a sharp knock on the door. The man quickly stood up from behind the desk, adjusted his tie, and opened a file folder lying in front of him. In the ashtray next to him were the remains of three cigarettes.

"Come in," he said, his voice firm and clear.

The door opened and LuAnn stepped into the room and looked around. Her left hand clutched the handle of the baby carrier where Lisa lay, her eyes looking around the room with obvious curiosity. Over LuAnn's right shoulder hung a large bag. The man observed the vein plunging down LuAnn's long, sinewy biceps until it connected with a maze of others in her muscular forearm. The woman was obvious strong, physically. What about her character? Was it as strong?

"Are you Mr. Jackson?" LuAnn asked. She looked directly at him as she spoke, waiting for his eyes to take the inevitable inventory of her face, bosom, hips, and so on. It didn't matter from what walk of life they came, in that regard men were all the same. She was thus very surprised when his gaze did not leave her face. He held out his hand and she shook it firmly.

"I am. Please sit down, Ms. Tyler. Thank you for coming. Your daughter is quite beautiful. Would you care to put her down over here?" He pointed to a corner of the room.

"She just woke up. The walk and the bus ride

16

makes her go to sleep every time. I'll just keep her beside me, if that's okay." As if in agreement, Lisa began to jabber and point.

He nodded his assent and then sat back down and took a moment to peruse the file.

LuAnn put Lisa and the large bag down next to her, pulled out a set of plastic keys, and handed them to her daughter to play with. LuAnn straightened back up and studied Jackson with considerable interest. He was dressed expensively. A line of perspiration was strung across his forehead like a miniature set of pearls and he appeared a little nervous. She ordinarily would put that down to her looks. Most of the men she encountered either acted like fools in attempts to impress her or shut down within themselves like wounded animals. Something told her that neither was the case with this man.

"I didn't see a sign over your office. People might not know you're even here." She looked at him curiously.

Jackson smiled tightly at her. "In our business we don't cater to foot traffic. It doesn't matter to us if people in the mall know we're here or not. All of our business is conducted via appointments, phone calls, that sort of thing."

"I must be the only appointment right now then. Y'all's waiting room is empty."

Jackson's cheek twitched as he formed a steeple with his hands. "We stagger our appointments so as not to keep people waiting. I'm the only member of the firm at this location."

"So you got other places of business?"

He nodded absently. "Would you mind filling out this information sheet for me? Take your time." He slid a piece of paper and pen over to her. LuAnn quickly filled out the form, making short, tight

17

motions with the pen. Jackson watched as she did so. He reviewed her information after she finished. He already knew everything on it.

LuAnn looked around the place. She had always been observant. Being the object of many males' desires, she typically studied the configuration of every place she was in, if only to determine the fastest exit.

When he looked up he noted her scrutinizing the office surroundings. "Something wrong?" he asked.

"It's kinda funny."

"I'm afraid I don't understand."

"You've got a funny office, is all."

"How do you mean?"

"Well, there's no clock anywhere, no trash can, no calendar, and no phone. Now, I ain't worked in any places where people wear neckties on the job, but even Red over at the truck stop keeps a calendar, and he's on the phone more than he's not. And the lady out front, she don't got a clue as to what's going on. Hell, with those three-inch nails, using that type-writer would be mighty hard anyway." LuAnn caught the stunned look on his face and quickly bit her lip. Her mouth had gotten her in trouble before, and this was one job interview she couldn't afford to blow. "I don't mean nothing by it," she said quickly. "Just talking. Guess I'm a little nervous, is all."

Jackson's lips moved for an instant and then he smiled grimly. "You're very observant."

"Got two eyes like everybody else." LuAnn smiled prettily, falling back on the old reliable.

Jackson ignored her look and rustled his papers. "You recall the terms of employment I gave to you over the phone?"

She snapped back to business. "One hundred dollars per day for two weeks, with maybe some more weeks at that same pay. I work until seven in

18

the morning right now. If it's all right I'd like to come and do this job in the early afternoon. Around about two? And is it okay if I bring my little girl? She takes her big nap around then, she won't be no trouble at all. Cross my heart." With an automatic motion LuAnn reached down and picked up the toy keys from the floor where the little girl had flung them and handed them back to Lisa. Lisa thanked her mother with a loud grunt.

Jackson stood up and put his hands in his pockets. "That's fine. It's all fine. You're an only child and your parents are dead, correct?"

LuAnn jerked at the abrupt change in subject. She hesitated and then nodded, her eyes narrowing.

"And for the better part of two years you have lived with one Duane Harvey, an unskilled laborer of sorts, currently unemployed, in a trailer in the western part of Rikersville." He looked at her as he recounted this information. He was not waiting for affirmation now. LuAnn sensed this and merely stared back at him. "Duane Harvey is the father of your daughter, Lisa, age eight months. You quit school in the seventh grade and have held numerous low-paying jobs since that time; all of them I think would be accurately summed up as dead-ends. You are uncommonly bright and possess admirable survival skills. Nothing is more important to you than your daughter's well-being. You are desperate to change the circumstances of your life and you are just as desperate to leave Mr. Harvey far behind. Right now you are wondering how to accomplish any of this when you lack the financial means to do so and likely always will. You feel trapped and well you should. You are most assuredly trapped, Ms. Tyler." He stared across the desk at her.

LuAnn's face was flushed as she stood up. "What the hell's going on here? What right do you have—"

He impatiently broke in. "You came here because I offered you more money than you've *ever* earned before. Isn't that right?"

"How come you know all those things "bout me?" she demanded.

He crossed his arms and studied her intently before answering. "It's in my best interests to know everything I can about someone with whom I'm about to do business."

"What does knowing about me have to do with my opinions and surveys and such?"

"Very simple, Ms. Tyler. To know how to evaluate your opinion on things I need to know intimate details about the opinion maker. Who you are, what you want, what you know. And don't know. The things you like, dislike, your prejudices, your strengths, and weaknesses. We all have them, in varying degrees. In sum, if I don't know all about you, I haven't done my job." He came around the corner of the desk and perched on the edge. "I'm sorry if I offended you. I can be rather blunt; however, I didn't want to waste your time."

Finally the anger in LuAnn's eyes passed away. "Well, I guess if you put it that way—"

"I do, Ms. Tyler. May I call you LuAnn?"

"That's my name," she said brusquely. She sat back down. "Well, I don't want to waste your time either, so what about the hours? Is the afternoon okay?"

Jackson abruptly returned to his seat and looked down at the desk, rubbing his hands slowly over its cracked surface. When he looked back up at her, his countenance was even more serious than it had been seconds before.

"Have you ever dreamed of being rich, LuAnn? I mean rich beyond all your wildest fantasies. So wealthy in fact that you and your daughter could literally do anything in the world you wanted to do, when you wanted to do it? Have you ever had that dream?"

LuAnn started to laugh until she caught the look in his eyes. There was no humor, no diffidence, no sympathy in their depths, merely an intense desire to hear her answer.

"Hell, yes. Who hasn't had that dream?"

"Well, those who are already filthy rich rarely do, I can tell you that. However, you're right, most other people, at some point in their lives, have that fantasy. Yet virtually no one ever makes that fantasy a reality. The reason is simple: They can't."

LuAnn smiled disarmingly. "But a hundred bucks a day ain't bad either."

Jackson stroked his chin for several seconds, coughed to clear his throat, and then asked a question. "LuAnn, do you ever play the lottery?"

She was surprised by the inquiry but readily replied. "Now and then. Everybody around here does. It can get expensive, though. Duane plays every week, sometimes half his paycheck – that is when he pulls a paycheck, which ain't usually the case. He's all-fired certain he's going to win. Plays the same numbers every time. Says he saw them in a dream. I say he's just dumber than dirt. Why?"

"Have you ever played the national Lotto?"

"You mean the one for the whole country?"

Jackson nodded, his eyes fixed on her. "Yes," he said slowly, "that's exactly the one I mean."

"Once in a while. But the odds are so big I got a better chance of going for a stroll on the moon than I do of winning that thing."

"You're absolutely right. In fact, the odds this month are approximately one in thirty million."

"That's what I mean. I'd rather go for the dollar scratch-offs. At least then you got a chance to make

21

a quick twenty bucks. No sense throwing good money after bad. I always say, particularly when you don't get none to speak of."

Jackson licked his lips and leaned his elbows on the desk as he looked at her. "What would you say if I told you I could drastically better your chances of winning the lottery?" He kept his eyes trained resolutely on her.

"Excuse me?" Jackson said nothing. LuAnn looked around the room as if expecting to see a surveillance camera somewhere. "What's this got to do with the job? I didn't come here to play no games, mister."

"In fact," Jackson continued, ignoring her queries, "what if I could lower your odds to one in one? Would you do it?"

LuAnn exploded. "Is this some kind of big joke? If I didn't know better I'd think maybe Duane was behind this. You better tell me what the hell's going on before I really get mad."

"This is no joke, LuAnn."

LuAnn rose out of the chair. "You durn sure got something else on the burner and I don't want no parts of it. No parts! Hundred bucks a day or not," she said with deep disgust, mingled with deeper disappointment as her plans for the thousand-dollar pay-day rapidly faded away. She picked up Lisa and her bag and turned to leave.

The quiet tones of Jackson's voice rippled across her back. "I am guaranteeing that you will win the lottery, LuAnn. I am guaranteeing that you will win, *at minimum*, fifty million dollars."

She stopped. Despite her brain's telling her to run as fast as she could out of the place, she found herself slowly turning to face him.

Jackson had not moved. He still sat behind the desk, his hands clasped in front of him. "No more

Duanes, no more graveyard shifts at the truck diner, no more worrying about having food and clean clothes for your daughter. Anything you want, you can have. Anywhere you want to go, you can go. Anyone you want to become, you can." His tone remained quiet and steady.

"You mind telling me how can you do that?" *Had he said fifty million dollars? Lord Almighty!* She placed one hand against the door to steady herself.

"I need an answer to my question."

"What question?"

Jackson spread his hands. "Do you want to be rich?"

"Are you a crazy man or what? I'm strong as all get out so if you try anything I'll kick your little butt all the way down the street and leave you with half the brains you started the day with."

"Do I take that as a no?" he said.

LuAnn tossed her hair to one side and switched Lisa's carrier from her right to her left hand. The little girl was looking back and forth at them, as though absorbed in the heated conversation. "Look, there is no way in hell that you can guarantee me something like that. So I'm just gonna walk on out of here and call the nut house to come get you."

In response, Jackson looked at his watch and walked over to the TV and turned it on.

"In one minute the national daily drawing will be held. It's *only* a one million dollar payoff; however, it will serve to illustrate a point nonetheless. Understand, I do not profit from this, it's used only for demonstration purposes, to quell your quite understandable skepticism."

LuAnn turned to look at the screen. She watched as the lottery drawing began and the ball machines fired up.

Jackson glanced over at her. "The winning

23

numbers will be eight, four, seven, eleven, nine, and six, in that order." He pulled a pen and paper from his pocket and wrote the numbers down. He handed the paper to LuAnn.

She almost laughed and a loud snort did escape her mouth. It stopped just as quickly when the first number announced was eight. In rapid succession the four, seven, eleven, nine, and six balls were kicked out and announced as the winning combination. Her face pale, LuAnn stared down at the paper and then at the winning numbers on the screen.

Jackson turned off the TV. "I trust that your doubts about my abilities are now satisfied. Perhaps we can get back to my offer."

LuAnn leaned back against the wall. Her skin seemed to be humming against her bones, as though a million bees had plunged into her body. She looked at the TV. She saw no special wires or contraptions that could have aided him in predicting the outcome. No VCR. It was just plugged into the wall. She swallowed hard and looked back at him.

"How the hell did you do that?" The words came out in a hushed, fearful tone.

"You have no possible need to know that information. Just answer my question, please." His voice rose slightly.

She took a deep breath, tried to calm her twitching nerves. "You're asking me if I want to do something wrong. Then I'm telling you flat-out that I won't. I ain't got much, but I'm no criminal."

"Who says it's anything wrong?"

"Excuse me, but are you saying that guaranteeing to win the lottery ain't wrong? Sure as hell sounds like a fix to me. You think just because I work crap jobs I'm stupid?"

"I actually have a high opinion of your intelligence. That's why you're here. However, someone

24

has to win that money, LuAnn. Why not you?"

"Because it's wrong, that's why."

"And who exactly are you hurting? Besides, it's not wrong, technically, if no one ever finds out."

"I'd know."

Jackson sighed. "That's very noble. However, do you really want to spend the rest of your life with Duane?"

"He has his good points."

"Really? Would you care to enumerate them?"

"Why don't you go straight on to hell! I think my next stop's gonna be at the police station. I got a friend who's a cop. I betcha he'll be real interested to hear about all this." LuAnn turned and gripped the doorknob.

This was the moment Jackson had been waiting for. His voice continued to rise. "So Lisa grows up in a filthy trailer in the woods. Your little girl will be extra-ordinarily beautiful if she takes after her mother. She reaches a certain age, the young men start to get interested, she drops out of school, a baby perhaps comes along, the cycle starts anew. Like your mother?" He paused. "Like you?" Jackson added very quietly.

LuAnn turned slowly around, her eyes wide and glimmering.

Jackson eyed her sympathetically. "It's inevitable, LuAnn. I'm speaking the truth, you know I am. What future do you and Lisa have with him? And if not him, another Duane and then another and another. You'll live in poverty and you'll die in poverty and your little girl will do the same. There's no changing that. It's not fair of course, but that doesn't make it any less certain. Oh, people who have never been in your situation would say that you should just pack up and go. Take your daughter and just leave. Only they never tell you how you're supposed to do that. Where will the money for bus fare and motel rooms and food come from? Who'll watch your child, first while you look for work, and then when you find it, if you ever do?" Jackson shook his head in sympathy and slid the back of one hand under his chin as he eyed her. "Of course, you can go to the police if you want. But by the time you get back, there will be no one here. And do you think they'll really believe you?" An expression of condescension played across his features. "And then what will you have accomplished? You'll have missed the opportunity of a lifetime. Your only shot at getting out. Gone." He shook his head sadly at her, as if to say, "Please don't be that stupid."

LuAnn tightened her grip on the baby carrier. An agitated Lisa was starting to struggle to get out and her mother automatically started rocking the little girl back and forth. "You talking about dreams, Mr. Jackson, I got me my own dreams. Big ones. Damn big ones." Her voice was trembling though. LuAnn Tyler had a very tough exterior built up over long, hard years of scrapping for an existence and never getting anywhere; however, Jackson's words had hurt LuAnn, or rather the truth in those words.

"I know you do. I said you were bright and you've done nothing at this meeting but reinforce that opinion. You deserve far better than what you have now. However, rarely do people get what they deserve in life. I'm offering you a way to achieve your big dreams." He abruptly snapped his fingers for effect. "Like that."

She suddenly looked wary. "How do I know you're not the police trying to set me up? I ain't going to no prison over money."

"Because it would be a clear case of entrapment, that's why. It would never hold up in court. And why in the world would the police target *you* for such an elaborate scheme?"

LuAnn leaned up against the door. Under her

dress she felt her heart beating erratically between her breasts.

Jackson stood up. "I know you don't know me, but I take my business very, very seriously. I never do anything without a very good reason. I would not be here wasting your time with some joke, and I most certainly never waste my time." Jackson's voice carried an unmistakable ring of authority and his eyes bored into LuAnn with an intensity that was impossible to ignore.

"Why me? Out of all the people in the whole friggin' world, why'd you come knocking on my door?" She was almost pleading.

"Fair question; however, it's not one I'm prepared to answer, nor is it particularly pertinent."

"How can you know I'm going to win?"

He looked at the TV. "Unless you think I was incredibly lucky with that drawing, then you shouldn't doubt the outcome."

"Huh! Right now, I doubt everything I'm hearing. So what if I play along and I still don't win?"

"Then what have you lost?"

"The two bucks it costs to play, that's what! It might not sound like much money to you, but that's bus fare for almost a whole week!"

Jackson pulled four singles from his pocket and handed them to her. "Then consider that risk eliminated and a hundred percent return on top of it."

She rubbed the money between her fingers. "I wanta know what's in it for you. I'm a little too old to believe in good fairies and wishes on a star." LuAnn's eyes were clear and focused now.

"Again, a good question, but one that only becomes applicable if and when you agree to participate. You're right, however: I'm not doing this out of the goodness of my heart." A tiny smile escaped his lips. "It's a business transaction. And in all good business

27

transactions, both sides benefit. However, I think you'll be pleased at how generous the terms will be."

LuAnn slid the money into her bag. "If you need my answer right this very minute, it's going to be a big, fat no."

"I realize that my proposition has certain complexities. Therefore, I will give you some time to think about it." He wrote a toll-free phone number down on a piece of paper and held it out to her. "But not too much time. The monthly lottery drawing takes place in four days. I have to have your answer by ten A.M. the day after tomorrow. This number will reach me anywhere."

She looked at the paper in his hand. "And if I still say no in two days, which I probably will?"

Jackson shrugged. "Then someone else will win the lottery, LuAnn. Someone else will be at least fifty million dollars richer and they certainly won't waste any time feeling guilty about it, I can assure you." He smiled pleasantly. "Believe me when I tell you that a lot of people would gladly take your place. *Gladly*." He put the paper in her hand and closed her fist around it. "Remember, one minute past ten A.M. and the offer to you is gone. Forever." Jackson of course did not mention the fact that if LuAnn said no, he would have her immediately killed. His tone was almost harsh, but then he quickly smiled again and opened the door for her, glancing at Lisa as he did so. The little girl stopped thrashing and stared wide-eyed at him. "She looks just like you. I hope she got your brains as well." As she passed through the doorway, he added, "Thank you for coming, LuAnn. And have a nice day."

"What makes me think your name ain't Jackson?" she said, giving him a piercing stare.

"I sincerely hope to hear from you soon, LuAnn. I like to see good things happen to deserving people. Don't you?" He shut the door softly behind her.

FOUR

On the bus ride home, LuAnn clutched both Lisa and the piece of paper bearing the phone number with equal tenacity. She had the very uncomfortable feeling that everyone on the bus was acutely aware of what had just happened to her and was judging her harshly as a result. An old woman wearing a battered coat and droopy, torn knee-high stockings gripped her plastic shopping bags and glared at LuAnn. Whether she was really privy to LuAnn's interview or simply resented her youths, looks, and beautiful baby girl, LuAnn couldn't be sure.

She sat back in her seat and let her mind race ahead to examine her life if she said yes or no to the proposal. While declining the offer seemed to carry with it certain consequences, all of them emblazoned with Duane-like features, acceptance seemed to bear its own problems. If she actually won the lottery and came into incalculable wealth, the man had said she could have anything she wanted. Anything! Go anywhere. Do anything. God! The thought of such unbridled freedom only a phone call and four days away made her want to run screaming with joy through the bus's narrow aisle. She had put aside the notion that it was all a hoax or some bizarre scheme. Jackson had asked for no money, not that she had any to give. He had also given no indication that he desired any sexual favors from her, although the full terms had not, as yet, been disclosed. However,

Jackson did not strike her as being interested in her sexually. He had not tried to touch her, had not commented on her features, at least not directly, and seemed, in every way, professional and sincere. He could be a nut, but if he was he certainly had done an admirable job of feigning sanity in front of her. Plus, it had cost money to rent the space, hire the receptionist, and so forth. If Jackson was certifiable, he definitely had his normal moments. She shook her head. And he had called every number correctly on the daily drawing, before the damn machines had even kicked them out. She couldn't deny that. So if he was telling the truth, then the only catch was that his business proposal resonated with illegality, with fraud, with more bad things than she cared to think about. That was a big catch. And what if she went along and then was caught somehow, the whole truth coming out? She could go to prison, maybe for the rest of her life. What would happen to Lisa? She suddenly felt miserable. Like most people, she had dreamt often of the pot of gold. It was a vision that had carried her through many a hopeless time when self-pity threatened to overtake her. In her dreams, though, the pot of gold had not been attached to a ball and chain. "Damn," she said under her breath. A clear choice between heaven and hell? And what were Jackson's conditions? She was sure the man would exact a very high price in exchange for transforming her from penniless to a princess.

So if she accepted and actually won, what would she do? The potential of such freedom was easy to see, taste, hear, feel. The actual implementation of it was something altogether different. Travel the world? She had never been outside Rikersville, which was best known for its annual fair and reeking slaughterhouses. She could count the times on one hand that she had ridden in an elevator. She had never owned a house or a car; in fact, she had never really owned anything. No bank account had ever borne her name. She could read, write, and speak the king's English passably, but she clearly wasn't Social Register material. Jackson said she could have anything. But could she really? Could you really pluck a toad from the mud in some backwater and deposit it in a castle in France and really believe it could actually work? But she didn't need to do it all, change her life so dramatically, become something and someone that she decidedly wasn't. She shuddered.

That was the thing, though. She flipped her long hair out of her face, leaned against Lisa, and played her fingers over her daughter's forehead where the golden hairs drifted across. LuAnn took a deep breath, filling her lungs with the sweet spring air from the open bus window. The thing was, she wanted desperately to be someone else, anyone other than who she was. Most of her life she had felt, believed, and hoped that one day she would do something about it. With each passing year, however, that hope grew more and more hollow, more and more like a dream that one day would break completely free from her and drift away until finally, when she was the shrunken, wrinkled owner of a quickly fading, unremarkable life, she would no longer remember she had ever possessed such a dream. Every day her bleak future became more and more graphic, like a TV with antenna finally attached.

Now things had abruptly changed. She stared down at the phone number as the bus rolled down the bumpy street, carrying her and Lisa back to the dirt road that would lead to the dirtier trailer, where Duane Harvey lurked, awaiting their return in what she was certain would be a foul temper. He would want beer money. But she brightened as she recalled she had two extra singles riding in her pocket. Mr. Jackson had already provided her with some benefit. Having Duane out of the way so she could think things through would be a start. Tonight was dollar pitcher night at the Squat and Gobble, his favorite hangout. With two bucks, Duane would happily drink himself into oblivion. She looked out the window at the world awakening from winter. Spring was here. A new beginning. Perhaps for her as well? To occur at or before ten A.M., two days from now. She and Lisa locked eyes for a long moment and then mother and daughter exchanged tender smiles. She laid her head gently down on Lisa's chest not knowing whether to laugh or cry and yet wanting very much to do both.

FIVE

The busted screen door creaked open and LuAnn passed through carrying Lisa. The trailer was dark, cool, and quiet. Duane might still be asleep. However, as she navigated through the narrow passageway, she kept her eyes and ears on high alert for movement or sound. She wasn't anything close to being afraid of Duane unless he got the drop on her. In a fair fight, she could more than hold her own. She had kicked the crap out of him on more than one occasion when he had been particularly drunk. He normally didn't try anything too outrageous when he was sober, which he would be now, or as close to it as he usually got. It was a strange relationship to have with someone who could be categorized as her significant other. However, she could name ten other women she knew who had similar arrangements, based more on pure economics, limited options, and in essence, inertia, than on anything approaching tender emotions. She had had other offers; but rarely was the grass greener elsewhere, she knew that firsthand. She picked up her pace as she heard the snores coming from the bedroom and leaned her head in the small room. She sucked in her breath as she eyed the twin figures lying under the sheets. Duane's head was visible on the right. The other person was completely covered by the sheet; however, the twin humps in the chest region suggested it was not one of Duane's male drinking buddies sleeping it off.

LuAnn quietly stepped down the hallway and placed an anxious-looking Lisa and her carrier down in the bathroom, then closed the door. LuAnn didn't want her little girl to be disturbed by what was about to happen. When she again opened the bedroom door, Duane was still snoring loudly; however, the body beside him had moved, and the dark red hair was clearly visible now. It only took a second for LuAnn to clamp a hand around the thick mane, and then she pulled with all her immense strength and the unfortunate owner of those long locks was hauled out of the bed to crash buck-naked against the far wall.

"Shit!" the woman bellowed as she landed on her butt and was immediately pulled across the rough, ragged carpet by a grim-looking LuAnn. "Dammit, LuAnn, let go."

LuAnn looked back at her for a split second. "Shirley, you slut around here again, and I swear to God I'll break your neck."

"Duane! Help me for chrissakes! She's crazy!" Shirley wailed, pulling and clawing at her hair in a futile effort to make LuAnn let go. Shirley was short and about twenty pounds overweight. Her chubby legs and full, wobbly breasts slapped back and forth against each other as the two women made their way to the bedroom door.

Duane stirred as LuAnn passed by. "What's going on here?" he said sleepily.

"Shut up," LuAnn snapped back.

As his eyes focused on the situation, Duane reached across to the nightstand and pulled out a pack of Marlboros from the drawer. He grinned at Shirley as he lit up.

"Going home so soon, Shirl?" He wiped his droopy hair out of his face as he sucked contentedly on his cigarette.

Facing to the rear as she was, Shirley glared at him, her fat cheeks a deep burgundy. "You're a piece of crap."

Duane blew her an imaginary kiss. "I love you too, Shirl. Thanks for the visit. Made my morning." He belly-laughed and slapped his thigh as he propped himself up on the pillow. Then LuAnn and Shirley disappeared through the doorway.

After depositing Shirley next to a rusted-out Ford engine block in the front yard, LuAnn turned back to the trailer.

Shirley stood up and shrieked, "You pulled half my hair out, you bitch." LuAnn kept walking, not looking back. "I want my clothes. Give me my damned clothes, LuAnn."

LuAnn turned around. "You didn't need 'em while you were here, so I can't see no reason why you'd need 'em now."

"I can't go home like this."

"Then don't go home." LuAnn went up the cinder block steps to the trailer and slammed the door behind her.

Duane met her in the hallway, dressed in his boxers, an unlit Marlboro dangling from his mouth. "Does a man good to have two alleycats fighting over him. Got my blood going, LuAnn. How 'bout you stepping up to the plate? Come on, baby, give me a kiss." He grinned at her and tried to slide an arm around her long neck. His next breath was a tortured one as her right fist smashed into his mouth, loosening a couple of his teeth. As painful as that blow was, it did not come close on the hurt scale to the knee that planted itself violently between his legs. Duane dropped heavily to the floor.

LuAnn hovered over him. "If you pull that crap again, Duane Harvey, so help me God, I'll rip it right off and flush it down the toilet."

"Crazy-ass woman," he half-sputtered, half-whimpered, clutching at his groin; blood seeped through his lips.

She reached down and clamped an iron grip across his cheeks. "No, *you're* crazy if you think for one second I'm gonna put up with that shit."

"We ain't married."

"That's right, but we live together. We got a kid together. And this place is as much mine as it is yours."

"Shirl don't mean nothing to me. What do you care?" He stared up at her, small tears gathering in the corners of his eyes as he continued to clutch his privates.

"Because that little fat piece of bacon is gonna waddle on down to the IGA and the beauty parlor and the damned Squat and Gobble and tell everybody that will listen all about it and I'm gonna look like the biggest piece of trash in the world."

"You shouldn't have left me this morning." He struggled up off the floor. "See, this here's all your fault. She came by to see you about something. What was I supposed to do?"

"I don't know, Duane, how about giving her a cup of coffee instead of your dick?"

"I don't feel so good, babe. I really don't." He leaned up against the wall.

She roughly pushed past him on her way to check on Lisa. "Best news I've heard all day."

A minute later she marched past him again and entered the bedroom, where she proceeded to rip the sheets off the bed.

Duane sulkily watched her from the doorway. "Go ahead and throw 'em away. I don't give a crap, you bought 'em."

She didn't look at him as she answered. "I'm taking 'em over to Wanda's to wash. If you're gonna sleep around with sluts, it ain't gonna cost me nothing."

As she lifted the mattress, a flash of green caught her eye. She shoved the mattress off the bed frame and then looked over at Duane. "What the hell is this?" she demanded.

Duane looked at her coldly. He sauntered into the room, scooped up the piles of cash, and stuffed them in a paper bag that had been sitting on the table beside the bed. He continued to eye her as he closed the bag. "Let's just say I won the lottery," he said arrogantly.

She perceptibly stiffened at his words as though she'd been slapped flush in the face. For a moment she felt as though she would topple right over in a dead faint. Had Duane actually been behind all of this? Were he and Jackson in this together? She could not have envisioned a more unlikely pair. It couldn't possibly be. She quickly recovered and crossed her arms. "Bull. Where'd you get it, Duane?"

"Let's just say it's a real good reason to be nice to me and to keep your mouth shut."

Angrily pushing him from the room, she locked the door. She changed into jeans, sneakers, and a sweatshirt and then quickly packed an overnight bag. When she unlocked and threw open the door, Duane hadn't budged; the bag was still clutched in his hand. She moved quickly past him, opened the door to the bathroom, and scooped up a wriggling Lisa in one arm; the dirty linen and overnight bag in her other hand, she headed for the front door.

"Where you going, LuAnn?"

"None of your damned business."

"How long you gonna be pissed about this? I didn't get mad at you for kicking me in the balls, did I? I done already forgot about it, in fact."

She whirled around for a second. "Duane, you

have got to be the dumbest person on the face of this earth."

"Is that right? Well who do you think you are? Princess Di? Why, if it weren't for me, you and Lisa wouldn't even have a damned place to stay. I took you in or you wouldn't have nothing." He lit up another cigarette but warily kept out of range of her fist. He scrunched the match out on the tattered carpet. "So maybe instead of bitching all the time, you oughta try being nice to me." He held up the paper bag stuffed with cash. "There's plenty more where this came from, too, little girl. I ain't gonna be living in this craphole much longer. You best think about it. You best think real good about that. I ain't taking crap from you or anybody else anymore. You hear me?"

She opened the front door. "Duane, I'll start being nice to you right now. You know how? I'm gonna leave before I kill you!" Lisa started to cry at her mother's angry tones as though she thought they were directed at her. LuAnn kissed the little girl and cooed in her ear to calm her down.

Duane watched LuAnn march across the muddy yard, admiring her soft behind in the tight jeans. For a moment he looked around for Shirley, but she had evidently already made a run for it, naked and all.

"I love you, babe," he yelled after LuAnn, grinning.

"Go to hell, Duane."

SIX

The mall was far busier than it had been during her visit the day before. LuAnn was grateful for the crowds as she made a wide berth around the office she had visited earlier, though she did glance in its direction as she passed by. Through the glass panes on either side of the door it seemed dark inside. She supposed if she tried the door, it would be locked. She didn't imagine that Jackson would have hung around long after she had left, and she assumed she had been his sole "client."

She had called in sick to work and spent a sleepless night at a friend's house alternating between staring at a full moon and Lisa's tiny mouth as it randomly produced smiles, grimaces, and every expression in between while the little girl slept heavily. She had finally decided not to make a decision on Jackson's proposal until she had some more information. One conclusion had come fairly rapidly: She would not go to the police. She could prove nothing, and who would believe her? There was no upside potential to such a move and at least fifty million reasons against it. For all her sense of right and wrong, she could not get past that one inescapable temptation: Incredible, sudden wealth was perhaps staring her in the face. She felt guilty that the decision wasn't more black and white. However, her latest episode with Duane had only reinforced to her that Lisa could not be allowed to grow up in such an environment. Something had to give.

The mall office was at the end of a corridor on the south side of the building. LuAnn swung open the door and went in.

"LuAnn?"

LuAnn stared at the source of this exclamation. Behind the counter, the young man was dressed neatly in a short-sleeve shirt, necktie, and black slacks. In his excitement, he repeatedly clicked a pen in his right hand. LuAnn stared at him, but no recognition was forthcoming.

The young man almost vaulted over the counter. "I didn't expect you to remember me. Johnny Jarvis. I go by John now." He extended a hand in a professional manner and then, grinning, he gave her a solid hug and spent a full minute cooing over Lisa. LuAnn pulled out a small blanket from her bag, set her daughter down on it, and gave her a stuffed animal.

"I can't believe it's you, Johnny. I haven't seen you since, what, the sixth grade?"

"You were in the seventh, I was in the ninth."

"You look good. Real good. How long you been working here?"

Jarvis grinned proudly. "After high school I went on to the community college and got my A.S. That stands for associate degree in science. Been at the mall for two years now. Started out as a data inputter but now I've moved up to sort of the assistant manager of mall operations."

"Congratulations. That's wonderful, Johnny – I mean John."

"Oh hell, you can call me Johnny. I can't believe you just walked on in that door. When I saw you, I thought I was gonna fall over and die. I never thought I'd see you again. I supposed you'd just gone on to New York City or something."

"Nope, still here," she said quickly.

"I'm kinda surprised I've never seen you around the mall before then."

"I don't get up here much. It's a pretty long way from where I live now."

"Have a seat and tell me what you been up to. I didn't know you had a baby. Didn't even know you were married."

"I'm not married."

"Oh." Jarvis's face reddened slightly. "Uh, you want some coffee or something? I just put on a fresh pot."

"I'm kind of in a hurry, Johnny."

"Oh, well, what can I do for you?" He suddenly looked surprised. "You aren't looking for a job, are you?"

She looked pointedly at him. "What if I was? Something wrong with that?"

"No, I mean, course not. I just meant, you know, I never expected you to hang around here, working in no mall, that's all." He smiled.

"A job's a job, ain't it? *You* work here. And while we're talking about it, exactly what am I supposed to be doing with my life?"

Jarvis's smile quickly faded and he rubbed his hands nervously down the legs of his pants. "I didn't mean nothing by it, LuAnn. I just always thought of you living in some castle somewhere wearing fancy clothes and driving fancy cars. I'm sorry."

LuAnn's anger faded as she thought back to Jackson's proposition. Castles might be within her reach now. "It's okay, Johnny, it's been a long week, you know what I mean? I'm not looking for a job. What I'm looking for is a little information about one of your renters here."

Jarvis glanced over his shoulder at the rear office area where the sounds of phones and clattering keyboards could be heard mixed with short bursts of

41

conversation, and then he turned back to her. "Information?"

"Yeah. I came by here yesterday morning. Had an appointment."

"With who?"

"That's what I want you to tell me. It was that business on the right as you come in the mall next to the bus stop. It ain't got no sign or anything, but it's next to the ice cream place."

Jarvis looked puzzled for a second. "I thought that space was still vacant. We got a lot of that. This mall isn't exactly in the middle of a booming area."

"Well, it wasn't vacant yesterday."

Jarvis walked over to the computer on the counter and started punching buttons. "What was the appointment for?"

LuAnn's reply was immediate. "Oh, it was a sales job, you know. Pushing products door-to-door."

"Yeah, we've had some people like that come in on a temporary basis. More like an interview room than anything else. If we have the space, which we usually do, we rent it out, sometimes just for the day. Especially if it's already been built out, you know, ready-made office space."

He pulled up a screen and studied it. As voices continued to filter in from the back office he went over and shut the door. He looked a little apprehensively at LuAnn. "So what'd you want to know?"

She noted his concerned look and glanced in the direction of the door he had just shut. "You're not going to get in trouble over this, are you, Johnny?"

He waved his hand dismissively. "Hell, no. Remember, I'm the assistant manager here," he said importantly.

"Well, just tell me whatever you can. Who the people are. What the business is. An address somewhere. Stuff like that."

Jarvis looked confused. "Well, didn't they tell you that during the interview?"

"Some of it," she said slowly. "But I just want to make sure it's all legit, you know. Before I accept or not. I got to buy some nicer clothes and maybe get me a car. I don't want to do that if it's not on the up-and-up."

Jarvis snorted. "Well, you're smart to do that. I mean just because we rent space to these people, it don't mean they're shooting straight with you." He added anxiously, "They didn't ask for money from you, did they?"

"No, as a matter of fact, the money they were talking about me getting was pretty unbelievable."

"Probably too good to be true then."

"That's what I'm afraid of." She watched his fingers sail across the computer keyboard. "Where'd you learn to do that stuff?" she said with admiration.

"What, this? That's when I was at the community college. They got programs over there that teach you just about anything. Computers are cool."

"I wouldn't mind going back to school one day."

"You were always real smart in school, LuAnn. I bet you'd pick it up like nobody's business."

She gave him a pretty look. "Maybe one day. Now what'cha got for me?"

Jarvis studied the screen again. "Company's name is Associates, Inc. At least that's what they put on the rental agreement. They leased for a week, starting yesterday in fact. Paid in cash. Didn't give any other address. When they pay in cash we don't really care."

"They ain't nobody there now."

Jarvis nodded absently as he tabbed down the screen. "Guy named Jackson signed the lease agreement," he said.

"About my height with black hair, sort of fat?"

"That's right. I remember him now. He seemed very professional. Anything out of the way happen during your interview?"

"Depends on what you call out of the way. But he was real professional to me, too. Anything else you can tell me?"

Jarvis studied the screen again, hoping to find a few more kernels of information with which to entice LuAnn. Finally, strong disappointment etched across his features, he looked at her and sighed. "Not really, I guess."

LuAnn hoisted up Lisa and then eyed a stack of steno pads and a cup of pens on the counter. "Could I have one of those pads and a pen, Johnny? I could pay you something for them."

"You kidding? Good golly, take all you want."

"One of each is all I need. Thanks." She put the pad and pen in her handbag.

"No problem at all, we got tons of that stuff."

"Well, I appreciate what you told me. I really do. And it was real nice seeing you, Johnny."

"Hell, you made my whole year walking in the door like that." He took a peek at his watch. "I take my lunch break in about ten minutes. They got a nice Chinese place down at the food court. You have time? My treat. We could talk some more, catch up."

"Maybe another time. Like I said, I'm kind of in a hurry."

LuAnn observed Jarvis's disappointment and felt a little guilty. She put Lisa down and gave him a big hug. She smiled as she listened to him breathe deeply into her freshly washed hair. As he pressed his hands against the small of her back, and the warmth and softness of her chest spread over his, Jarvis's spirits were instantly rekindled. "You've done real well for yourself, Johnny," LuAnn said as she stepped back. "Always knew you'd do just fine."

Things might have been different, she thought, if she had come across Johnny a while back.

Jarvis was now treading across fine white clouds. "You did? I'm kind of surprised you even thought about me at all."

"There you go, I'm just full of surprises. Take care of yourself, maybe I'll see you around." She picked up Lisa, who was rubbing the stuffed animal against her mother's cheek and jabbering happily, and headed for the door.

"Hey, LuAnn?"

She turned back around.

"You gonna take that job?"

She considered the question for a moment. "I don't know yet. But I expect you'll probably hear about it if I do."

LuAnn's next stop was the public library, a place she had frequented when in school, but it had been years since she had last been there. The librarian was very pleasant and complimented LuAnn on her daughter. Lisa snuggled against her mother while she looked around at all the books.

"Da. Da, ooh."

"She likes books," said LuAnn. "I read to her every day."

"She's got your eyes," the woman said looking back and forth between mother and child. LuAnn's hand gently slid against Lisa's cheek.

The woman's smile faded when she saw no ring on LuAnn's finger. LuAnn noted the look. "Best thing I've ever done. I ain't got much, but this little girl's never gonna be hurting for love."

The woman smiled weakly and nodded. "My daughter is a single mother. I do what I can to help out but it's very hard. There's never enough money to go around."

45

"Tell me about it." LuAnn dug a bottle and a container of water out of her diaper bag, mixed some formula she had gotten from a friend together, and helped Lisa get a grip on it. "If I ever get to the end of a week with more money than I started with, I'm not going to know what to do with myself."

The woman shook her head wistfully. "I know they say that money is the root of all evil, but I often think how nice it would be not to have to worry about the bills. I can't imagine the feeling. Can you?"

"I can imagine it. I imagine it must feel pretty durn good."

The woman laughed. "Now, how can I help you?"

"You keep copies of different newspapers here on that film stuff, don't you?"

The woman nodded. "On microfilm. It's in that room." She pointed to a doorway at the far end of the library.

LuAnn hesitated.

"Do you know how to use the microfilm machine? If not, I can show you. It's not very difficult."

"That'd be real nice. Thank you."

They entered the room, which was vacant and dark. The woman turned on the overhead light, seated LuAnn at one of the terminals, and picked out a microfilm spool from one of the files. It only took a minute to insert the spool, and information appeared on the lit screen. The woman worked the controls and lines of text flashed across the screen. LuAnn watched her carefully as she removed the spool and turned the machine off. "Now, you try it," the woman said.

LuAnn expertly inserted the spool and manipulated the controls as the film advanced.

"That's very good. You learn quickly. Most people don't get the hang of it right away."

"I've always been good with my hands."

46

"The catalogue files are clearly marked. We carry the local paper, of course, and some of the national ones. The publication dates are printed on the outside of the file drawers."

"Thank you very much."

As soon as the woman left, LuAnn carried Lisa, who was still slurping on the bottle, and started exploring the rows of file cabinets. She set Lisa down and watched in amusement as the little girl rolled to a cabinet, put down the bottle, and tried to pull herself up. LuAnn located a major newspaper in one of the cabinets and proceeded to check the boxes housing the spools until she found the dates corresponding to the last six months. She took a minute to change and burp Lisa and then inserted the first spool into the microfilm machine. With Lisa perched on her lap and pointing excitedly and jabbering on about the sights on the screen, LuAnn's eyes scanned the front page. It didn't take long to locate the story and the accompanying two-inch headline. "Lottery Winner Nets Forty-five Million Dollars." LuAnn quickly read the story. Outside, the sound of a sudden rainstorm assailed her ears. Spring brought a lot of rain to the area, usually in the form of thunderstorms. As if in response to her thoughts, thunder boomed and the entire building seemed to shake. LuAnn glanced anxiously over at Lisa, but the little girl was oblivious to the sounds. LuAnn pulled a blanket from her bag, set it down on the floor with some toys, and put Lisa down. LuAnn turned back to the headline. She pulled the steno pad and pen out of her handbag and started scribbling notes. She flipped to the next month. The U.S. Lotto drawing was held on the fifteenth of each month. The dates she was looking at were for the sixteenth through the twentieth. Two hours later she had completed her review of the past six winners.

She unwound the last spool and replaced it in the file drawer. She sat back and looked at her notes. Her head was pounding and she wanted a cup of coffee. The rain was still coming down hard. Carrying Lisa, she went back into the library, pulled some children's books down, and showed Lisa the pictures in them and read to the little girl. Within twenty minutes, Lisa had fallen asleep and LuAnn put her in the baby carrier and set it on the table next to her. The room was quiet and warm. As LuAnn felt herself starting to doze she put one arm protectively across Lisa and gripped the little girl's leg in a gentle squeeze. The next thing she knew she was startled awake when a hand touched her shoulder. She looked up into the eyes of the librarian.

"I'm sorry to wake you, but we're closing up."

LuAnn looked around bewildered for a moment. "Good Lord, what time is it?"

"A little after six, dear."

LuAnn quickly packed up. "I'm sorry for falling asleep in here like that."

"Didn't bother me a bit. I'm just sorry I had to wake you, you looked so peaceful there with your daughter and all."

"Thanks again for all your help." LuAnn cocked her head as she listened to the rain pounding on the roof.

The woman looked at her. "I wish I could offer you a ride somewhere, but I take the bus."

"That's okay. The bus and me know each other real good."

LuAnn draped her coat over Lisa and left. She sprinted to the bus stop and waited until the bus pulled up a half hour later with a squeal of brakes and a deep sigh of its air-powered door. She was ten cents short on the fare, but the driver, a heavyset black man whom she knew by sight, waved her on after dropping in the rest from his own pocket.

"We all of us need help every now and again," he said. She thanked him with a smile. Twenty minutes later, LuAnn walked into the Number One Truck Stop several hours before her shift.

"Hey, girl, what you doing here so soon?" asked Beth, LuAnn's fiftyish and very matronly coworker, as she wiped a wet cloth across the Formica counter.

A three-hundred-pound truck driver appraised LuAnn over the rim of his coffee cup and, even soaked as she was from her jaunt in the rain, he came away dutifully impressed. As always. "She come early so she wouldn't miss big old Frankie here," he said with a grin that threatened to swallow up his whole wide face. "She knew I got on the earlier shift and couldn't bear the thought of not seeing me no more."

"You're right, Frankie, it'd just break her heart if LuAnn didn't see your big old hairy mug on a regular basis," Beth rejoined, while prying between her teeth with a swizzle stick.

"Hi, Frankie, how you?" LuAnn said.

"Just fine, now," Frankie replied, the smile still cemented on his features.

"Beth, can you watch Lisa for a minute while I change into my uniform?" LuAnn asked as she wiped her face and arms down with a towel. She checked Lisa and was relieved to find her dry and hungry. "I'm going to make her up a bottle in just a minute and mix up some of that oatmeal. Then she should be ready to go down for the night even though she had a pretty big nap not too long ago."

"You bet I can take that beautiful little child into my arms. Come here, darling." Beth hoisted up Lisa and settled her against her chest, where Lisa proceeded to make all manner of noises and pull at the pen stuck behind Beth's ear. "Really, now,

LuAnn, you ain't got to be here for hours. What's up?"

"I got soaked and my uniform's the only clean thing I got. Besides, I felt bad about missing last night. Hey, is there anything left over from lunch? I sorta can't remember eating yet today."

Beth gave LuAnn a disapproving look and planted one hand on a very full hip. "If you took half as good care of yourself as you do this baby. My Lord, child, it is almost eight o'clock."

"Don't nag, Beth. I just forgot, that's all."

Beth grunted. "Right, Duane drank your money away again, didn't he?"

"You oughta drop that little sumbitch, LuAnn," Frankie grumbled. "But let me kick his ass first for you. You deserve better than that crap."

Beth raised an eyebrow that clearly signaled her agreement with Frankie.

LuAnn scowled at them. "Thank you both for your vote on *my* life, now if you'll excuse me?"

Later that evening, LuAnn sat at the far corner booth finishing a plate of food Beth had rounded up for her. She finally pushed the dinner away and sipped a cup of fresh coffee. The rain had started again and the clattering sound against the diner's tin roof was comforting. She pulled a thin sweater tighter around her shoulders and checked the clock behind the counter. She still had two hours before she went on duty. Normally, when she got to the diner early she'd try to catch a little overtime, but the manager wasn't letting her do that anymore. Hurt the bottom line, he had told LuAnn. Well, you don't want to know about my bottom line, she had told him right back, but to no avail. But that was okay, he let her bring Lisa in. Without that, there'd be no way she could work at all. And he paid her in cash. She knew he was avoiding payroll taxes that way, but she made little enough money as it was without the government taking any. She had never filed a tax return; she had lived her entire life well below the poverty line and rightly figured she didn't owe any taxes.

Lisa was in her carrier across from her. LuAnn tucked the blanket more snugly around her sleeping daughter. LuAnn had fed Lisa parts of her meal; her daughter was taking to solid food real well, but she hadn't made it through the mushed carrots before falling asleep again. LuAnn worried that her daughter wasn't getting the right kind of sleep. And she wondered, Was putting her baby under the counter of a noisy, smoky truck stop every night going to mess up Lisa's head years from now? Lower her self-esteem and do other damage LuAnn had read about in the magazines or seen on TV. That nightmarish thought had cost LuAnn more sleep than she could remember. And that wasn't all. When Lisa turned to solid food for good would there always be enough? Not having a car, always scrounging change for the bus, walking, or running through the rain. What if Lisa caught something? What if LuAnn did? What if she were laid up for a while? Who would take care of Lisa? She had no insurance. She took Lisa to the free county clinic for her shots and checkups, but LuAnn hadn't been to a doctor in over ten years. She was young, strong, and healthy, but that could change quickly. You never knew. She almost laughed when she thought of Duane trying to navigate the endless details of Lisa's daily requirements. The boy would run screaming into the woods after a few minutes. But it really wasn't a laughing matter.

While she looked at the tiny mouth opening and closing, LuAnn's heart suddenly felt as heavy as the semis parked in the diner's parking lot. Her daughter depended on her for everything and the truth was LuAnn had nothing. One step from the edge every day of her life and getting closer all the time. A fall was inevitable; it was only a matter of time. She thought back to Jackson's words. A cycle. Her mother. Then LuAnn. Duane resembled Benny Tyler in more ways than she cared to think about. Next up was Lisa, her darling little girl for whom she would kill, or be killed, whatever it took to protect her. America was full of opportunity, everybody said. You just had to unlock it. Only they forgot to give out keys for LuAnn's kind. Or maybe they didn't forget at all. Maybe it was intentional. At least that's how she usually saw things when she was more than a little depressed, like now.

She shook her head clear and squeezed her hands together. That kind of thinking wasn't going to help her now. LuAnn pulled her handbag over and slid out the steno pad. What she had found at the library had greatly intrigued her.

Six lottery winners. She had started with the ones last fall and continued up to the present. She had written down their names and backgrounds. The articles had carried a photo of each winner; their smiles had seemed to stretch across the width of the page. In reverse order of winning they were: Judy Davis, age twenty-seven, a welfare mother with three young children; Herman Rudy, age fifty-eight, a former truck driver on disability with massive medical bills from an injury on the job; Wanda Tripp, sixty-six, widowed and subsisting on Social Security's "safety net" of four hundred dollars a month; Randy Stith, thirty-one, a recent widower with a young child, who had recently been laid off from his assembly line job; Bobbie Jo Reynolds, thirty-three, a waitress in New York who after winning the article said had given up her dream of starring on Broadway to take up painting in the south of France. Finally, there was Raymond Powell, forty-four, a recent bankrupt who had moved into a homeless shelter.

LuAnn slumped back in her seat. *And LuAnn, twenty years old, single mother, dirt poor, uneducated, no prospects, no future.* She would fit in perfectly with this desperate group.

She had only gone back six months. How many more of them were there? It made for great stories, she had to admit. People in dire straits hit the jackpot. Old people with newfound wealth. Young children with a suddenly bright future. All their dreams coming true. Jackson's face appeared in her thoughts. *Someone has to win. Why not you, LuAnn?* His calm, cool tones beckoned to her. In fact, those two sentences reverberated over and over in her head. She felt herself beginning to slide over the top of an imaginary dam. What was awaiting her in the deep waters below, she was not sure. The unknown both scared her and drew her, fiercely. She looked at Lisa. She could not shake the image of her little girl growing into a woman in a trailer with no way to escape while the young wolves circled.

"What'cha doing, sweetie?"

LuAnn jerked around and stared into Beth's face. The older woman expertly juggled plates full of food in both hands.

"Nothing much, just counting up all my fortune," LuAnn said.

Beth grinned and looked at the steno pad, which LuAnn quickly closed. "Well, don't forget the little people when you hit the big time, Miss LuAnn Tyler." Beth cackled and then carried the food orders to the waiting customers.

LuAnn smiled uneasily. "I won't, Beth. I swear," she said quietly.

SEVEN

It was eight o'clock in the morning on *the day*. LuAnn stepped off the bus with Lisa. This was not her usual stop, but it was close enough to the trailer that she could walk it in half an hour or so, which was nothing to her. The rain had passed and left the sky a brilliant blue and the earth a lush green. Small clusters of birds sang the praises of the changing season and the exit of another tedious winter. Everywhere LuAnn turned as she tramped along under the newly risen sun there was fresh growth. She liked this time of the day. It was calm, soothing, and she tended to feel hopeful about things.

LuAnn looked ahead to the gently rolling fields and her manner grew both somber and expectant. She walked slowly through the arched gateway and past the patinated sign proclaiming her entrance into the Heavenly Meadows Cemetery. Her long, slender feet carried her automatically to Section 14, Lot 21, Plot 6; it occupied a space on a small knoll in the shadow of a mature dogwood that would soon begin showing its unique wares. She laid Lisa's carrier down on the stone bench near her mother's grave and lifted out the little girl. Kneeling in the dewy grass, she brushed some twigs and dirt off the bronze marker. Her mother, Joy, had not lived all that long: thirty-seven years. It had seemed both brief and an eternity for Joy Tyler, that LuAnn knew. The years with Benny had not been pleasant, and had, LuAnn firmly believed now, hastened her mother's exit from the living.

"Remember? This is where your grandma is, Lisa. We haven't been for a while because the weather was so bad. But now that it's spring it's time to visit again." LuAnn held up her daughter and pointed with her finger at the recessed ground. "Right there. She's sleeping right now, but whenever we come by, she sort of wakes up. She can't really talk back to us but if you close your eyes tight as a baby bird's, and listen real, real hard, you can kinda hear her. She's letting you know what she thinks about things."

After saying this, LuAnn rose up and sat on the bench with Lisa on her lap, bundled against the chill of the early morning. Lisa was still sleepy; it usually took her a while to wake up, but once she did, the little girl wouldn't stop moving or talking for several hours. The cemetery was deserted except for a workman LuAnn could see far in the distance, cutting grass on a riding mower. The sounds of the mower's engine didn't reach her and there were few cars on the roadway. The silence was peaceful and she closed her eyes tight as a baby bird's and listened as hard as she could.

At the diner she had made up her mind to call Jackson right after she got off work. He had said anytime and she figured he would answer the phone on the first ring regardless of the time. Saying yes had seemed like the easiest thing in the world to do. And the smartest. It was her turn. After twenty years filled with grief, disappointment, and depths of despair that seemed to have endless elasticity, the gods had smiled upon her. Out of the masses of billions, LuAnn Tyler's name had turned the hat trick on the slot machine. It would never happen again, of that she was dead certain. She was also sure that the other people she had read about in the paper had made a similar phone call. She hadn't read anything about them getting in trouble. That sort of news would have been all over, certainly in as poor an area as she lived in, where everyone played the lottery in a frantic effort to throw off the bitter hopelessness of being a have-not. Somewhere between leaving the diner and stepping on the bus, however, she had felt something very deep inside of here prompting her to not pick up the phone but, instead, to seek counsel other than her own. She came here often, to talk, to lay flowers she had picked, or to spruce up her mother's final resting place. In the past, she had often thought she actually did communicate with her mother. She had never heard voices; it was more levels of feelings, of senses. Euphoria or deep sadness sometimes overtook her here, and she had finally put it down to her mother reaching out to her, letting her opinion on things having to do with LuAnn seep into her child's body, into her mind. Doctors would probably call her crazy, she knew, but that didn't take away from what she felt.

Right now she hoped for something to speak to her, to let her know what to do. Her mother had raised her right. LuAnn had never told a lie until she had started living with Duane. Then the fabrications seemed to just happen; they seemed to be an inextricable part of simply surviving. But she had never stolen anything in her life, never really done anything wrong that she knew of. She had kept her dignity and self-respect through a lot over the years and it felt good. It helped her get up and face the toil of another day when that day contained little in the way of hope that the next day and the next would be any different, any better.

But today, nothing was happening. The noisy lawn mower was drawing closer and the traffic on the road had picked up. She opened her eyes and sighed. Things were not right. Her mother apparently was not going to be available today of all days. She stood up and was preparing to leave when a feeling came over her. It was like nothing she had ever experienced before. Her eyes were automatically drawn to another section of the cemetery, to another plot that lay about five hundred yards away. Something was pulling her there, and she had no doubt what it was. Eyes wide, and her legs moving of their own accord, LuAnn made her way down the narrow, winding asphalt walkway. Something made her clutch Lisa tightly to her bosom, as though if she didn't the little girl would be snatched away by the unseen force compelling LuAnn to its epicenter. As she drew nearer to the spot, the sky seemed to turn a terrible dark. The sounds of the mowing were gone, the cars had stopped coming down the road. The only sound was the wind whistling over the flat grass and around the weathered testaments to the dead. Her hair blowing straight back, LuAnn finally stopped and looked down. The bronze marker was similar in style to her mother's, and the last name on it was identical: Benjamin Herbert Tyler. She had not been to this spot since her father had died. She had tightly clutched her mother's hand at his funeral, neither woman feeling the least bit saddened and yet having to display appropriate emotions for the many friends and family of the departed. In the strange way the world sometimes worked, Benny Tyler had been immensely popular with just about everyone except his own family because he had been generous and cordial with everyone except his own family. Seeing his formal name etched in the metal made her suck in her breath. It was as though the letters were stenciled over an office door and she would soon be ushered in to see the man himself. She started to draw back from the sunken earth, to retreat from the sharp jabs that seemed to sink in deeper with each step she had taken toward his remains. Then the intense feeling she had not realized beside her mother's grave suddenly overtook her. Of all places. She could almost see wisps of gauzy membrane swirling above the grave like a spiderweb picked up by the wind. She turned and ran. Even with Lisa, she hit an all-out sprint three steps into a run that would have made many an Olympian bristle with envy. Without missing a step and gripping Lisa to her chest, LuAnn snatched up Lisa's baby carrier and flew past the gates of the cemetery. She had not closed her eyes tight like a baby bird. She had not even been listening particularly hard. And yet the immortal speech of Benny Tyler had risen from depths so far down she could not contemplate them, and had made its way ferociously into the tender ear canals of his only child.

Take the money, little girl. Daddy says take it and damn everyone and everything else. Listen to me. Use what little brain you've got. When the body goes, you got nothing. Nothing! When did I ever lie to you, baby doll? Take it, dammit, take it, you dumb bitch! Daddy loves you. Do it for Big Daddy. You know you want to.

The man on the mower paused to watch her race away under a sky of pristine blue that begged to be photographed. The traffic on the road had picked up considerably. All the sounds of life, which had disappeared so inexplicably for LuAnn during those few moments, had once again reappeared.

The man looked over at the grave from which LuAnn had fled. Some people just got spooked in a graveyard, he figured, even in broad daylight. He went back to his mowing.

LuAnn was already out of sight.

The wind chased the pair down the long dirt road. Sweat drenched LuAnn's face as the sun bore down

58

on her from gaps in the foliage; her long legs ate up the ground with a stride that was both machine-like in its precision and wonderfully animalistic in its grace. Growing up she had been able to outrun just about everybody in the county, including most of the varsity football team. God-given world-class speed, her seventh-grade gym teacher had told her. What exactly she was supposed to do with that gift no one ever told her. For a thirteen-year-old girl with a woman's figure it had just meant if she couldn't beat up the boy who was trying to feel her up, at least she could probably outrun him.

Now her chest was burning. For a minute she wondered if she would keel over from a heart attack, as her father had. Perhaps there was some physical flaw buried deep within all the descendants of the man, just waiting for the opportunity to cleave another Tyler from the ranks. She slowed down. Lisa was bawling now and LuAnn finally stopped running and hugged her baby hard, whispering soothing words into the little girl's small pink ear while she made slow, wide circles in the dense shadows of the forest until the cries finally stopped.

LuAnn walked the rest of the way home. The words of Benny Tyler had made up her mind. She would pack what she could from the trailer and send somebody back for the rest. She would stay with Beth for a while. Beth had offered before. She had an old ramshackle house, but it had a lot of rooms and after the death of her husband her only companions were a pair of cats that Beth swore were crazier than she was. LuAnn would take Lisa into the classroom with her if need be, but she was going to get her GED and then maybe take some classes at the community college. If Johnny Jarvis could do it then she could, too. And Mr. Jackson could find somebody else to "gladly" take her place. All these answers to her life's dilemmas had come roaring in upon her so fast she could barely keep her head from exploding off her shoulders with relief. Her mother had spoken to her, in a roundabout manner perhaps, but the magic had been worked. "Never forget about the dearly departed, Lisa," she whispered to the little girl. "You just never know."

LuAnn slowed as she neared the trailer. Duane had been rolling in money the day before. She wondered how much he had left. He was quick to buy rounds at the Squat and Gobble when he had a few bucks in his pocket. Lord only knew what he had done with the wad he had under the bed. She didn't want to know where he had gotten it. She figured it was only an additional reason to get the hell out.

As she rounded the bend, a flock of blackbirds scattered from the trees overhead and scared her. She looked up at them angrily for a moment and then kept walking. As the trailer came into her line of sight, she abruptly stopped. There was a car parked out front. A convertible, big and wide, shiny black with white side-walls, and on the hood a huge chrome ornament that from a distance looked vaguely like a woman engaged in some indecent sexual act. Duane drove a battered Ford pickup truck which had been in the impoundment lot the last LuAnn had seen it. None of Duane's cronies drove anything like this crazy machine. What in the world was going on? Had Duane gone flat-out loco and bought this boat? She stole up to the vehicle and examined it, keeping one eye on the trailer. The seats were covered in a white leather with inlays of deep burgundy. The inside of the car was spotless, the dashboard clock polished enough to hurt your eye when the sunlight hit it just so. There was nothing in the front or rear seats to identify the owner. The keys hung in the ignition, a tiny Bud can attached to the ring. A phone rested in a device built specifically to hold it and attached to the hump between the front seat and the dashboard. Maybe this thing did belong to Duane. But she figured it would've taken all the cash under his mattress and then some to buy this rig.

She moved quickly up the steps and listened for sounds from within before venturing farther. When she didn't hear anything, she decided finally to brave it. She had kicked his butt the last time, she could do it again.

"Duane?" She slammed the door loudly. "Duane, what the hell did you do? Is that thing out there yours?" There was still no answer. LuAnn put an agitated Lisa down in her baby carrier and moved through the trailer. "Duane, are you here? Come on, answer me, will you, please. I don't have time to play around."

She went into the bedroom, but he wasn't there. Her eyes were riveted by her clock on the wall. It took her an instant to stuff it in her bag. She wasn't going to leave it with Duane. She exited the bedroom and moved down the hallway, passing Lisa as she did so. She stopped to calm the little girl down and placed her bag next to the baby carrier.

She finally saw Duane, lying on the raggedy couch. The TV was on, but no sound came from the battered box. A grease-stained bucket of chicken wings was on the coffee table next to what LuAnn assumed was an empty can of beer. A mess of fries and an overturned bottle of ketchup were next to the bucket of wings. Whether this was breakfast or the remnants of dinner from last night, she didn't know.

"Hey, Duane, didn't you hear me?"

She saw him turn his head, very, very slowly, toward her. She scowled. Still drunk. "Duane, ain't you never going to grow up?" She started forward. "We got to talk. And you ain't going to like it, but that's too bad becau—" She got no further as the big hand clamped over her mouth, cutting off her scream. A thick arm encircled her waist, pinning her arms to her sides. As her panicked eyes swept the room, she noted for the first time that the front of Duane's shirt was a mass of splotchy crimson. As she watched in horror, he fell off the couch with a small groan and then didn't move again.

The hand shot up to her throat and pushed her chin up so hard she thought her neck was going to snap under the pressure. She sucked in a huge breath as she saw the other hand holding the blade that descended toward her neck.

"Sorry, lady, wrong time, wrong place." LuAnn didn't recognize the voice. The breath was a mixture of cheap beer and spicy chicken wings. The foul odor pressed against her cheek as fiercely as the hand against her mouth. He had made a mistake, though. With one hand bracing her chin and the other holding the knife, he had left her arms free. Perhaps he thought she would be paralyzed with fear. She was far from it. Her foot crunched backward against his knee at the same moment her bony elbow sunk deep into his flabby gut, hitting right at the diaphragm.

The force of her blow caused his hand to jerk suddenly and the knife slashed her chin. She tasted blood. The man dropped to the floor, spitting and coughing. The hunting knife clattered to the bare carpet next to him. LuAnn hurtled toward the front door, but her attacker managed to snag a leg as she passed by and she tumbled to the floor a few feet from him. Despite being doubled over, he clamped thick fingers around her ankle and dragged her back toward him. Finally, she got a good look at him as she turned over on her back, kicking at him with all her might: sunburned skin, thick, caterpillar eyebrows, sweaty, matted black hair, and full, cracked lips that were at the moment grimacing in pain. She couldn't see his eyes, which were half-closed as his body shrugged off her blows. LuAnn took in those features in an instant. What was even more evident was that he was twice her size. In the grip that tightened around her leg, she knew she had no chance against him, strength-wise. However, she wasn't about to leave Lisa to face him alone; not without a lot more fight than she had already given him.

Instead of resisting further, she threw herself toward him, screaming as loudly as she could. The scream and her sudden leap startled him. Off-balance, he let go of her leg. Now she could see his eyes; they were deep brown, the color of old pennies. In another second they were shut tightly again as she planted her index fingers in both of them. Howling again, the man fell backward against the wall but then he ricocheted off like a bounced ball and slammed blindly into her. They both pitched over the couch. LuAnn's flailing hand seized an object on the way down. She couldn't see exactly what it was, but it was solid and hard and that's all she cared about as she swung with all her might and smashed it against his head right before she hit the floor, barely missing Duane's limp body, and then she slammed headfirst into the wall.

The telephone had shattered into pieces upon impact with the man's thick skull. Seemingly unconscious, her attacker lay facedown on the floor. The dark hair was now a mass of red as the blood poured from the head wound. LuAnn lay on the floor for a moment and then sat up. Her arm tingled where she had hit the coffee table, and then it went numb on her. Her buttocks ached where she had slammed into the floor. Her head pounded where it had struck the wall. "Damn," she said as she struggled to regain her equilibrium. She had to get out of here, she told herself. Grab Lisa and keep running until her legs or lungs gave out. Her vision blurred for an instant and her eyes rolled up into her head. "Oh, Lord," she moaned as she felt it coming. Her lips parted and she sank back down to the floor, unconscious.

EIGHT

LuAnn had no idea how long she had been out. The blood that had poured out of the wound on her chin hadn't yet hardened against her skin so it couldn't have been all that long. Her shirt was ripped and bloody; one breast hung loose from her bra. She slowly sat up and rearranged herself with her good arm. She wiped her chin and touched the cut; it was jagged and painful. She slowly lifted herself up. She could not seem to catch her breath as lingering terror and physical trauma battered her from within and without.

The two men lay side by side; the big man was clearly still breathing, the expansions and contractions of his huge gut were easy to see. LuAnn wasn't sure about Duane. She dropped to her knees and felt for his pulse, but if it was there, she couldn't find it. His face looked gray, but it was hard to tell in the darkness. She jumped up and flipped on a light, but the illumination was still poor. She knelt down beside him again and touched his chest gingerly. Then she lifted his shirt. She quickly pulled it back down, nauseated at the sight of all the blood there. "Oh, Lord, Duane, what have you gone and done? Duane, can you hear me? Duane!" In the dim light she was able to see that no more blood was flowing from his wounds: a sign that his heart was probably no longer beating. She felt his arm; it was still warm to the touch, but she felt his fingers and they were already beginning to curl and grow cold. She eyed the remnants of the phone. There was no way to call the ambulance now, although it didn't look like Duane was going to need one. She should probably go fetch the police, though. Find out who the other man was, why he had cut up Duane and tried to kill her.

When LuAnn rose to leave, she noticed the small pile of bags that had been hidden behind the greasy bucket of chicken. They had fallen off the table in the scuffle. LuAnn stooped down and picked one up. It was clear plastic. Inside was a small amount of white powder. Drugs.

Then she heard the whimpering. Oh God, where was Lisa? But there was another sound. LuAnn sucked in her breath as she jerked around and looked down. The big man's hand was moving, he was starting to rise. He was coming for her! Oh sweet Lord, he was coming for her! She dropped the bag and raced to the hallway. Using her good arm to snatch up Lisa, who started screaming when she saw her mother, LuAnn bolted through the front door, slamming it back against the side of the trailer. She ran past the convertible, stopped, and turned back. The massive wall of flesh she had clocked with the phone didn't explode through the door. At least not yet. Her eyes shifted slightly to the car; the dangling keys glimmered temptingly in the sunlight. She hesitated for only an instant, then she and Lisa were in the car. LuAnn gunned the motor and fishtailed out of the muck and on to the road. She took a minute to get her nerves under control before she turned on to the main highway into town.

Now Duane's sudden wealth made a lot of sense. Selling drugs was obviously far more lucrative than stripping cars for a living. Only Duane had apparently gotten greedy and kept a little too much of the drugs or green for himself. The stupid idiot! She had to call the police. Even if Duane was alive, which she doubted, she was probably only saving him for a long spell in jail. But if he was still alive, she couldn't just leave him to die. The other fellow she didn't give a damn about. She only wished she had hit him harder. As she sped up, she looked over at Lisa. The little girl sat wide-eyed in her baby carrier, the terror still clearly observable in her quivering lips and cheeks. Lisa settled her injured arm over her daughter, biting back the pain this simple movement caused her. Her neck felt as though a car had run over it. Then her eyes alighted on the cellular phone. She pulled off the road and snatched it up.

After quickly figuring out how to work it, she started to dial 911. Then she slowly put down the phone. She looked down at her fingers. They were shaking so hard she couldn't make a fist. They were also covered with blood, and probably not just her own. It was suddenly dawning on her that she could easily be implicated in all of this. Despite his starting to move, the guy could have slumped back down, dead, for all she knew. She would have killed him in self-defense, she knew that, but would anyone else? A drug dealer. She was driving his car.

This thought made her look around suddenly to see if anyone was watching. Some cars were heading towards her. The top! She had to close the ragtop. She jumped into the backseat and gripped the stiff fabric. She pulled upward, and then the big white convertible top descended down upon them like a clam closing up. She hit the ragtop's clamps, jumped back into the driver's seat, and tore down the road.

Would the police believe that she knew nothing about Duane's selling drugs? Somehow Duane had kept the truth from her, but who would accept that as the truth? She didn't believe it herself. This reality swept over her like a fire raging through a paper house; there seemed to be no escape. But maybe there was. She almost shrieked as she thought of it. For an instant her mother's face appeared in her thoughts. It was with immense difficulty that she pushed it away. "I'm sorry, Momma. I ain't got no choices left." She had to do it: the call to Jackson.

That's when her gaze came to rest on the dashboard. For several seconds she could not even manage a breath. It was like every ounce of blood had evaporated from her body as her eyes stayed locked on the shiny clock.

It was five minutes *past* ten.

Gone. Forever, Jackson had said, and she didn't doubt for an instant he had meant it. She pulled off the road and slumped over the steering wheel in her misery. What would happen to Lisa while she was in prison? Stupid, stupid Duane. Screwed her in life, and now in death.

She slowly raised her head up and looked across the street, wiping her eyes so she could make out the image: a bank branch, squat, solid, all-brick. If she had owned a gun, she would have seriously contemplated robbing it. Even that was not an option, though; it was Sunday and the bank was closed. As her eyes drifted over the front of the bank her heart started to beat rapidly again. The change in her state of mind was so sudden as to feel almost drug-induced.

The bank clock showed four minutes *before* ten.

Bankers were supposed to be steady, reliable folk. She hoped to God their clocks were reliable as well. She snatched up the phone, at the same time digging frantically in her pocket for the slip of paper with the number on it. Her coordination seemed to have totally deserted her. She could barely force her fingers to punch in the numbers. It seemed to take forever for the line to begin ringing. Fortunately for her nerves, it rang only once before being answered.

"I was beginning to wonder about you, LuAnn," Jackson said. She could envision him checking his watch, probably marveling at how close she had cut it.

She forced herself to breathe normally. "I guess the time just got away from me. I had a lot going on."

"Your cavalier attitude is refreshing, although, quite frankly, it's a bit amazing to me."

"So what now?"

"Aren't you forgetting something?"

LuAnn looked puzzled. "What?" Her brain was near serious burnout. A series of pains shot throughout her body. *If all this turned out to be a joke . . .*

"I made you an offer, LuAnn. In order to have a legally enforceable arrangement, I need an acceptance from you. A formality, perhaps, but one on which I have to insist."

"I accept."

"Wonderful. I can tell you with complete assurance that you will never regret that decision."

LuAnn looked nervously around. Two people walking on the other side of the highway were staring at the car. She put the vehicle in gear and headed down the road. "So now what?" she again asked Jackson.

"Where are you?"

Her tone was wary. "Why?" Then she added quickly, "I'm at home."

"Fine. You are to go to the nearest outlet selling lottery tickets. You will purchase one."

"What numbers do I play?"

"That doesn't matter. As you know, you have two options. Either accept a ticket with numbers automatically dispensed by the machine or pick whatever numbers you want. They're all fed into the same central computer system with up-to-the-second results and no duplicate combinations are allowed; that ensures only one winner. If you opt for a personalized combination and your first choice has already been taken, simply pick another combination."

"But I don't understand. I thought you were gonna tell me what numbers to play. The winning numbers."

"There is no need for you to understand anything, LuAnn." Jackson's voice had risen a notch higher. "You are simply to do what you're told. Once you have the combination, call me back and tell me what the numbers are. I'll take care of the rest."

"So when do I get the money?"

"There will be a press conference—"

"Press conference!" LuAnn almost flipped the car over. She fought to keep it under control with her good arm as she cradled the phone under her chin.

Now Jackson sounded truly exasperated. "Haven't you ever watched one of these things? The winner attends a press conference, usually in New York. It's televised across the country, the world. You'll have your photo taken holding a ceremonial check and then reporters will ask questions about your background, your child, your dreams, what you'll do with the money. Quite nauseating, but the Lottery Commission insists. It's terrific PR for them. That's why ticket sales have been doubling every year for the last five years. Everybody loves a deserving winner, if for no other reason than most people believe themselves to be quite deserving."

"Do I have to do it?"

"Excuse me?"

"I don't want to be on TV."

"Well, I'm afraid you don't have a choice. Keep in mind that you're going to be at least fifty million dollars richer, LuAnn. For that kind of money, they expect you to be able to handle *one* press conference. And, frankly, they are right."

"So I have to go?"

"Absolutely."

"Do I have to use my real name?"

"Why wouldn't you want to?"

"I've got my reasons, Mr. Jackson. Would I?"

"Yes! There is a certain statute, LuAnn, not that I would expect you to be aware of it, popularly termed the 'right to know' law. To put it simply, it says that the public is entitled to know the identities, the *real* identities, of all lottery winners."

LuAnn let out a deep breath filled with disappointment. "Okay, so when do I get the money?"

Now Jackson discernibly paused. The hair on the back of LuAnn's neck started to bristle. "Listen, don't try pulling no crap on me here. What about the damn money?"

"There's no cause to get testy, LuAnn. I was merely pondering how to explain it to you in the simplest terms possible. The money will be transferred into an account of your designation."

"But I don't have any account. I've never had enough money to open a damn account."

"Calm down, LuAnn, I'll take care of all of that. You don't have to worry about it. The only thing you have to do is win." Jackson's voice tried to sound upbeat. "Go to New York with Lisa, hold that big check, smile, wave, say nice, humble things, and then spend the rest of your life on the beach."

"How do I get to New York?"

"Good question; however, one for which I have already prepared. There's no airport near where you live, but there is a bus station. You'll take a bus to the train station in Atlanta. That's on Amtrak's Crescent line. The Gainsville station is closer to you, but they don't sell tickets there. It's a long ride, about

71

eighteen hours or so with numerous stops; however, a good part of it will be while you're sleeping. It will take you to New York and you won't have to change trains. I'd put you on a plane to New York, but that's a little more complicated. You have to show identification, and, frankly, I don't want you in New York that quickly. I'll make all the arrangements. A reserved ticket will be waiting for you at each station. You can leave for New York right after the lottery drawing takes place."

The prone figures of Duane and the man who had tried his best to kill her flashed across LuAnn's mind. "I'm not sure I want to hang around here that long."

Jackson was startled. "Why not?"

"That's my business," she said sharply, then her tone softened. "It's just that if I'm gonna win this thing, I don't want to be around here when people find out, is all. It'll be like a pack of wolves on a calf, if you know what I mean."

"That won't happen. You won't be publicly identified as the winner until the press conference occurs in New York. When you arrive in the city, someone will be waiting for you and will take you to the lottery headquarters. Your winning ticket will be confirmed and then the press conference will occur the next day. It used to take weeks to verify the winning ticket. With the technology they have today, it takes hours."

"How about if I drive to Atlanta and take the train up today?"

"You have a car? My goodness, what will Duane say?" There was considerable mirth in Jackson's tone.

"Let me worry about that," LuAnn snapped.

"You know, LuAnn, you might want to act a little more grateful, unless, of course, someone makes you

72

rich beyond your wildest dreams on a routine basis."

LuAnn swallowed hard. She was going to be rich all right. By cheating. "I am," she said slowly. "It's just now that I made up my mind, everything's going to change. My whole life. And Lisa's, too. It's a little mind-boggling."

"Well, I understand that. But keep in mind that this particular change is definitely of the positive variety. It's not like you're going to prison or anything."

LuAnn fought back the catch in her throat and clenched her bottom lip between her teeth. "Can't I please take the train up today? Please?"

"Hold on for one minute." He clicked off. LuAnn looked up ahead. A police cruiser sat on the side of the road, a radar gun perched on the door. LuAnn automatically checked her speedometer and, although she was under the speed limit, slowed down slightly. She didn't breathe again until she was several hundred yards down the road. Jackson clicked back on, his abrupt tones startling her.

"The Crescent pulls into Atlanta at seven-fifteen this evening and arrives in New York at one-thirty tomorrow afternoon. Atlanta is only a couple hours' drive from where you are." He paused for an instant. "You're going to need money for the ticket, though, and I'm assuming you'll need additional funds, perhaps for some travel-related incidentals."

LuAnn unconsciously nodded at the phone. "Yes." She suddenly felt very dirty, like a whore pleading for some extra cash after an hour's work.

"There's a Western Union office near the train station. I'll wire you five thousand dollars there." LuAnn gulped at the amount. "Remember my initial job offer? We'll just call it your salary for a job well done. You just have to show proper identification—"

"I don't have any."

"Just a driver's license or passport. That's all they need."

LuAnn almost laughed. "Passport? You don't need a passport to go from Piggly-Wiggly to the Wal-Mart, do you? And I don't have a driver's license either."

"But you're planning to drive a car to Atlanta." Jackson's astonished tone was even more amusing to her. Here the man was, orchestrating a multi-million-dollar scam, and he could not comprehend that LuAnn would operate an automobile without a license.

"You'd be surprised how many people ain't got a license for anything and they still do it."

"Well, you can't get the money without proper identification."

"Are you anywhere nearby?"

"LuAnn, I only came to glorious Rikersville to conduct my meeting with you. Once it was done, I didn't hang around." He paused again and LuAnn could hear the displeasure in his voice when he spoke next. "Well, we have a problem then."

"Well, how much would the train ticket be?"

"About fifteen hundred."

Remembering Duane's money hoard, a sudden thought struck LuAnn. She again pulled off the road, put down the phone, and quickly searched the car's interior. The brown leather bag she pulled from underneath the front seat didn't disappoint her. There was enough cash in there probably to buy the train.

"A woman I work with, her husband left her some money when he passed on. I can ask her for the money. A loan. I know she'll give it to me," she told Jackson. "I won't need no ID for cash, will I?" she added.

"Money is king, LuAnn. I'm sure Amtrak will accommodate you. Just don't use your real name, of course. Use something simple, but not too phony sounding. Now go buy the lottery ticket and then call me back immediately. Do you know how to get to Atlanta?"

"It's a big place, or so I've heard. I'll find it."

"Wear something to hide your face. The last thing we need is for you to be recognized."

"I understand, Mr. Jackson."

"You're almost there, LuAnn. Congratulations."

"I don't feel much like celebrating."

"Not to worry, you have the rest of your life to do that."

LuAnn put down the phone and looked around. The car windows were tinted so she didn't think anyone had actually seen her, but that could change. She had to ditch the car as fast as possible. The only question was where. She didn't want to be seen getting out of the car. It would be pretty hard to miss a tall, blood-caked woman hauling a baby out of a car with tinted windows and a chrome figure doing nasty things on the vehicle's hood. An idea finally hit her. A little dangerous perhaps, but right now she didn't have much alternative. She did a U-turn and headed in the opposite direction. Within twenty minutes she was pulling slowly down the dirt road, and straining to see ahead as she drew nearer to her destination. The trailer finally came into view. She saw no other vehicle, no movement. As she pulled in front of the trailer cold dread poured over her as she once again felt the man's hands around her throat, as she watched the blade swooping toward her. "You see that man coming out that house," LuAnn said out loud to herself, "you're gonna run right over his butt, let his lips kiss the oil pan on this thing."

She rolled down the passenger window so she

could check for sounds coming from within but heard nothing. She pulled a diaper wipe out of Lisa's bag and methodically rubbed down all of the car's surfaces that she had touched. She had watched a few episodes of *America's Most Wanted*. If it hadn't been too dangerous she would have gone back inside the trailer and wiped down the telephone. But she had lived there for almost two years. Her fingerprints would be all over the place, anyway. She climbed out of the car, stuffing as much cash from the bag as she could under the liner of Lisa's baby seat. She pulled her torn shirt together as best she could. She noiselessly closed the car door and, holding Lisa with her good arm, she quickly made her way back down the dirt road.

From within the trailer, the pair of dark eyes watched LuAnn's hasty departure, taking in every detail. When she suddenly glanced around the man stepped back into the shadow of the trailer's interior. LuAnn didn't know him, but he wasn't taking any chances at being observed. His dark leather jacket was zipped halfway up the front, the butt of a 9-mm visible sticking out of the inside pocket. He stepped quickly over the two men lying on the floor, careful to avoid the pools of blood. He had happened along at an opportune time. He was left with the spoils of a battle he had not even had to fight. What could be better? He scooped the drug packets off both the coffee table and the floor and deposited them in a plastic bag that the man pulled from his jacket. After thinking about it for a moment, he put half the stash back where he had found it. No sense being greedy, and if the organization these boys worked for got wind that no drugs had been discovered by the police in the trailer they might start looking for who took it. If only part of the stash was missing they'd probably assume the cops had sticky fingers.

He eyed the fight scene and then noted the torn

fabric on the floor; recognition spread across his features. It was from the woman's shirt. He put it in his pocket. She owed him now. He looked at the remnants of the phone, the position of each man's body, the knife and the dents in the wall. She must have walked right into the middle of this, he deduced. Fat man got the little man, and LuAnn somehow got the fat man. His admiration for her increased as he noted the man's bulk.

As if he sensed this observation, the fat man started to stir again slowly. Not waiting for the fat man to recover further, the other man stooped down, used a cloth to snatch up the knife, and then plunged it repeatedly into the man's side. The dying man grew momentarily stiff, his fingers digging into the threadbare carpet, hanging on to the last seconds of his life, desperately unwilling to let go. After a few moments, though, his entire body shook for an instant and then slowly relaxed, his fingers uncurled and splayed out, his palms flush against the floor. His face was turned to the side; one lifeless, blood-filled eye stared up at his killer.

Next, he roughly flipped over Duane, squinting in the dim light as he tried to determine if the chest was moving up or down. Just to be safe he used several carefully aimed thrusts to make certain Duane Harvey joined the fat man in the hereafter. He tossed the knife down.

In another few seconds, he was through the front door and around the back of the trailer where he plunged into the woods. His car was parked off a little-used dirt trail that snaked through the heavy woods. It was windy and rough, but it would deliver him on to the main road in plenty of time to take up his real task: following LuAnn Tyler. When he climbed into his car, his car phone was ringing. He picked it up.

"Your duties are at an end," Jackson said. "The hunt has officially been called off. The balance of your payment will be sent to you via the usual channels. I thank you for your work and I'll keep you in mind for future employment."

Anthony Romanello gripped the phone hard. He debated whether to tell Jackson about the two bodies in the trailer and then decided not to. He might have stumbled on to something really interesting.

"I saw the little lady tearing out of here on foot. But she doesn't look like she has the resources to go very far," Romanello said.

Jackson chuckled. "I think money will be the least of her worries." Then the line went dead.

Romanello clicked off his phone and pondered the matter for a moment. Technically, he had been called off. His work was at an end and he could just return home and wait for the rest of his money. But there was something screwy going on here. Everything about the job was somehow off. Sending him down here to the sticks to kill some hick chick. And then being told not to. And there was Jackson's passing reference to money. Dollars were something that always held Romanello's interest. He made up his mind and put the car in gear. He was going to follow LuAnn Tyler.

NINE

LuAnn stopped at a gas station rest room and cleaned up as best as she could. She cleaned the wound on her jaw, pulled a Band-Aid out of Lisa's diaper bag, and covered the cut with it. While Lisa slurped contentedly on a bottle, LuAnn bought her lottery ticket and some ointment and gauze at the local 7-Eleven. As part of the ten numbers she picked, she used her own and Lisa's birthdays.

"People been coming in here like damn cattle," said the clerk, who was a friend of hers named Bobby.

"What happened there?" he asked, pointing to the large Band-Aid on her face.

"Fell and cut myself," she said quickly. "So what's the jackpot up to?" LuAnn asked.

"A cool sixty-five mil and counting." Bobby's eyes gleamed with anticipation. "I got a dozen tickets myself. I'm feeling good about this one, LuAnn. Hey, you know that movie where the cop gives the waitress half his lottery winnings? LuAnn, tell you what, darling, I win this thing, I'll give half to you, cross my heart."

"I appreciate that, Bobby, but what exactly do I have to do for the money?"

"Why, marry me, o' course." Bobby grinned as he handed her the ticket she had purchased. "So what do you say, how about half of yours if you win? We'll still get hitched."

"I think I'll just play this one all by myself.

Besides, I thought you were engaged to Mary Anne Simmons."

"I was, but that was last week." Bobby looked her up and down in obvious admiration. "Duane is dumb as dirt."

LuAnn jammed the ticket far down into her jeans. "You been seeing much of him lately?"

Bobby shook his head. "Nah, he's been keeping to himself lately. I heard he's been spending a lot of time over Gwinnett County way. Got some business over there or something."

"What kind of business?"

Bobby shrugged. "Don't know. Don't want to know. Got better things to do with my time than worry about the likes of him."

"Duane come into some money that you know of?"

"Come to think of it, he was flashing some cash around the other night. I thought maybe he won the lottery. If he did, I think I'll just go kill myself right now. Damn, she looks just like you." Bobby gave Lisa's cheek a gentle rub. "You change your mind about splitting the pot or marrying me, you just let me know, sweet cheeks. I get off at seven."

"I'll see you around, Bobby."

At a nearby pay phone, LuAnn dialed the number again and once again Jackson picked it up on the first ring. She gave him the ten digits from her ticket and she could hear him rustling paper on the other end of the line as he wrote them down.

"Read them to me once more, slowly," he said. "As you can understand, we can't have any mistakes now."

She read them again and he read them back to her.

"Good," he said. "Very good. Well, now the hard part is over. Get on the train, do your little press conference, and sail away into the sunset."

"I'm going to the train station right now."

"Someone will meet you at Penn Station and take you to your hotel."

"I thought I was going to New York."

"That's the name of the train station in New York, LuAnn," Jackson said impatiently. "The person meeting you will have a description of you and Lisa." He paused. "I'm assuming you're bringing her."

"She don't go, I don't go."

"That's not what I meant, LuAnn, of course you can bring her. However, I trust you did not include Duane in the travel plans."

LuAnn swallowed hard as she thought back to the bloodstains on Duane's shirt, how he had fallen off the couch and never moved again. "Duane won't be coming," she said.

"Excellent," Jackson said. "Enjoy your trip."

The bus dropped off LuAnn and Lisa at the train station in Atlanta. After her phone call with Jackson, she had stopped at the Wal-Mart and purchased some essentials for herself and Lisa, which were in a bag slung over her shoulder; her own torn shirt had been replaced with a new one. A cowboy hat and a pair of sunglasses hid her face. She had thoroughly cleaned and dressed the knife wound in the rest room. It felt a lot better. She went to the ticket counter to purchase her train ticket to New York. And that's when LuAnn made a big mistake.

"Name, please," the agent said.

LuAnn was fiddling with a fussing Lisa and thus answered automatically, "LuAnn Tyler." She caught her breath as soon as she said it. She looked at the clerk, who was busily typing the information into her computer. LuAnn couldn't change it now. That would obviously make the woman suspicious. She swallowed hard and hoped to God the slip would not come back to haunt her. The woman recommended the Deluxe sleeping car accommodations since LuAnn was traveling with a baby. "There's one available and it has a private shower and all," the woman said. LuAnn quickly agreed. While the ticket was being processed, the sales agent raised an eyebrow when LuAnn pulled some bills from under Lisa's baby seat to pay for the ticket, stuffing the rest in her pocket.

LuAnn observed the woman's look, thought quickly, and smiled at her. "My rainy day money. Figured I might as well use it while the weather's nice. Go up to New York and see the sights."

"Well, enjoy yourself," the woman said, "but be careful. You shouldn't be carrying a lot of cash up there. My husband and I made that mistake when we went years ago. We weren't five minutes out of the train station when we got robbed. Had to call my mother to send us some money so we could come home."

"Thanks, I'll be real careful."

The woman looked behind LuAnn. "Where's your luggage?"

"Oh, I like to travel light. Besides, we got family up there. Thanks again." LuAnn turned and walked toward the departure area.

The woman stared after her and then turned back and was startled by the person who had seemingly appeared from nowhere and was now standing in front of her window. The man in the dark leather jacket put his hands on the counter. "One-way ticket to New York City, please," Anthony Romanello said politely and then stole a sideways glance in LuAnn's direction. He had watched through the plate glass of the 7-Eleven as LuAnn had purchased her lottery ticket. Next, he had observed her make the phone call from the pay phone, although he had not risked getting close enough to overhear the conversation. The fact that she was now on her way to New York had piqued his curiosity to the maximum. He had many reasons for wanting to leave the area as quickly as possible, anyway. Even though his assignment was over, finding out what LuAnn Tyler was up to and why she was going to New York was just an added inducement. It was all the more convenient because he happened to live there. It could be she was simply running from the bodies in the trailer. Or it could be more. Much more. He took the train ticket and headed toward the platform.

LuAnn stood well back from the tracks when the train came noisily into the station a bit behind schedule. With the aid of a conductor she found her compartment. The Deluxe Viewliner sleeping compartment had a lower bunk, an upper bunk, an armchair, sink, toilet, and private shower. Because of the lateness of the hour, and with LuAnn's permission, the attendant changed the compartment to its sleeping configuration. After he was finished, LuAnn closed the door to the room, sat down in the armchair, pulled out a bottle, and started feeding Lisa as the train slid smoothly out of the station half an hour later. The train gathered speed and soon LuAnn was watching the countryside sail by through the two large picture windows. She finished feeding Lisa and cradled the little girl against her chest to burp her. That accomplished, LuAnn turned Lisa around and started playing with her, doing patty cake and singing songs, which the delighted little girl joined in on in her own unique fashion. They passed an hour or so playing together until Lisa finally grew tired and LuAnn put her in the baby carrier.

LuAnn sat back and tried to relax. She had never

been on a train before, and the gliding sensation and rhythmic click of the wheels was making her drowsy as well. It was hard to remember the last time she had slept, and she started to drift off. LuAnn awoke with a start several hours later. It must be nearly midnight, she thought. She suddenly recalled that she hadn't eaten all day. It hadn't seemed important with everything that had happened. She popped her head out the compartment door, spied an attendant, and asked if there was food on the train. The man looked a little surprised and glanced at his watch. "They made the last call for dinner several hours ago, ma'am. The dining car is closed now."

"Oh," LuAnn said. It wouldn't be the first time she had gone hungry. At least Lisa had eaten.

However, when the man caught sight of Lisa and then looked at how tired LuAnn seemed, he smiled kindly and told her to wait just a bit. Twenty minutes later he came back with a tray loaded with food and even set it out for her, using the lower bunk as an impromptu table. LuAnn tipped him generously from her stash of funds. After he left, she devoured her meal. She wiped off her hands and reached carefully into her pocket and pulled out the lottery ticket. She looked over at Lisa; the little girl's hands were gently swaying in her slumber, a smile played across the small features. Must be a nice dream, LuAnn thought, smiling at the precious sight.

LuAnn's features grew softer and she leaned down and spoke quietly into Lisa's tiny ear. "Momma's gonna be able to take care of you now, baby, like I should've been doing all along. The man says we can go anywhere, do anything." She stroked Lisa's chin and nuzzled her cheek with the back of her hand. "Where you wanta go, baby doll? You name it, we'll go. How's that sound? That sound good?"

LuAnn locked the door and laid Lisa down on the bed, checking to make sure the straps on the baby seat were tight. LuAnn lay back on the bed and curled her body protectively around her daughter. While the train made its way to New York City, she stared out the window into the darkness, wondering mightily about what was going to come next.

TEN

The train had been delayed at several points along the route and it was nearly three-thirty in the afternoon when LuAnn and Lisa emerged into the frenzy of Penn Station. LuAnn had never seen this many people in one place in all her life. She looked around, dazed, as people and luggage flew past her like sprays of buckshot. She tightened her grip on Lisa's carrier as the train ticket agent's warning came back to her. Her arm was still throbbing painfully, but she figured she could still deck just about anybody who tried something. She looked down at Lisa. With so many interesting things going on around her, the little girl seemed ready to explode out of her seat. LuAnn moved slowly forward, not knowing how to get out of the place. She saw a sign for Madison Square Garden and vaguely recalled that several years ago she had watched a boxing match on TV that had been telecast from there. Jackson said someone would be here, but LuAnn couldn't imagine how the person would find her in the middle of all this chaos.

She jerked slightly as the man brushed against her. LuAnn looked up into dark brown eyes with a silvery mustache resting below the broad, flattened nose. For an instant LuAnn wondered if he was the man she had seen fighting at the Garden; however, she quickly realized that he was much too old, at least in his early fifties. He had the breadth of shoulders, flattened, crusty ears, and battered face, though, that marked the man as an ex-boxer.

"Miss Tyler?" His voice was low but clear. "Mr. Jackson sent me to pick you up."

LuAnn nodded and put out her hand. "Call me LuAnn. What's your name?"

The man started for an instant. "That's not really important. Please follow me, I have a car waiting." He started to walk away.

"I really like to know people's names," LuAnn said, without budging.

He came back to her, looking slightly irritated, although somewhere in his features she thought she discerned the beginnings of a smile. "Okay, you can call me Charlie. How's that?"

"That's fine, Charlie. I guess you work for Mr. Jackson. Do you use your real names with each other?"

He didn't answer as he led her toward the exit. "You want me to carry the little girl? That thing looks heavy."

"I've got it okay." She winced as another stab of pain shot through her injured arm.

"You sure?" he asked. He eyed her bandaged jaw. "You look like you've been in a fight."

She nodded. "I'm okay."

The pair exited the train station, moved past the line of people waiting in the cab stand, and Charlie opened the door of a stretch limo for LuAnn. She gawked for a minute at the luxurious vehicle before climbing in.

Charlie sat across from her. LuAnn couldn't help staring at the vehicle's interior.

"We'll be at the hotel in about twenty minutes. You want something to eat or drink in the meantime? Train food sucks," said Charlie.

"I've had a lot worse, although I am kinda hungry. But I don't want you to have to make a special stop."

He looked at her curiously. "We don't have to stop." He reached into the refrigerator and pulled out soda, beer, and some sandwiches and snack foods. He unlocked a section of the limo's interior paneling and a table materialized. As LuAnn watched in astonishment, Charlie laid the food and drink out and completed the repast with a plate, silverware, and napkin, his big hands working quickly and methodically.

"I knew you were bringing the baby, so I had the limo stocked with milk, bottles, and stuff like that. At the hotel they'll have everything you need."

LuAnn made up a bottle for Lisa, cradled her against one arm, and fed her with one hand while she devoured a sandwich with the other.

Charlie watched the tender way she handled her daughter. "She's cute, what's her name?"

"Lisa, Lisa Marie. You know, after Elvis's daughter."

"You look a little young to be a fan of the King."

"I wasn't – I mean, I don't really listen to that kind of music. But my momma did. She was a big fan. I did it for her."

"She appreciated it, I guess."

"I don't know, I hope she does. She died before Lisa was born."

"Oh, sorry." Charlie fell silent for a moment. "Well, what kind of music do you like?"

"Classical. I really don't know nothing about that kinda music. I just like the way it sounds. The way it makes me feel, sorta clean and graceful, like swimming in a lake somewhere up in the mountains, where you can see all the way to the bottom."

Charlie grinned. "I never thought about it that way. Jazz is my thing. I actually play a little horn myself. Outside of New Orleans, New York has some of the best jazz clubs around. Play until the sun comes up, too. A couple of them not too far from the hotel."

"Which hotel are we going to?" she asked.

"Waldorf-Astoria. The Towers. You ever been to New York City?" Charlie took a swig of club soda and sat back against the seat, unbuttoning the front of his suit coat.

LuAnn shook her head and swallowed a bite of sandwich. "I ain't never really been anywhere."

Charlie chuckled softly. "Well then, the Big Apple is a helluva place to start."

"What's the hotel like?"

"It's real nice. First-rate, especially the Towers. Now it's not the Plaza, but then what is? Maybe you'll be staying at the Plaza one day, who knows." He laughed and wiped his mouth with a napkin. She noticed that his fingers were abnormally large and thick, the knuckles massive and knobby.

LuAnn looked at him nervously as she finished her sandwich and took a sip of Coke. "Do you know why I'm here?"

Charlie settled a keen gaze upon her. "Let's just say I know enough not to ask too many questions. Let's leave it at that." He smiled curtly.

"Have you ever met Mr. Jackson?"

Charlie's features grew grim. "Let's just leave it alone, okay?"

"Okay, just curious, is all."

"Well, you know what curiosity did to that old cat." The dark eyes glittered briefly at LuAnn as the words rolled off his tongue. "Just stay cool, do what you're told, and you and your kid have no problems, ever again. Sound good to you?"

"Sounds good to me," LuAnn said meekly, cradling Lisa closer to her hip.

Right before they climbed out of the limo, Charlie pulled out a black leather trench coat and matching wide-brimmed hat and asked LuAnn to put them on. "For obvious reasons, we don't want you to be observed right now. You can ditch the cowboy hat."

LuAnn put on the coat and hat, cinching the belt up tight.

"I'll check you in. Your suite is under the name of Linda Freeman, an American business executive with a London-based firm traveling with her daughter on a combination of business and pleasure."

"A business executive? I hope nobody asks me no questions."

"Don't worry, nobody will."

"So that's who I'm supposed to be? Linda Freeman?"

"At least until the big event. Then you can go back to being LuAnn Tyler."

Do I have to? LuAnn wondered to herself.

The suite Charlie escorted her to after he checked her in was on the thirty-second floor and was mammoth in size. It had a large sitting room and a separate bedroom. LuAnn looked around in wonderment at the elegant furnishings, and almost fell over when she saw the opulent bathroom.

"You get to wear these robes?" She fingered the soft cotton.

"You can have it if you want. For seventy-five bucks or so a pop that is," Charlie replied.

She walked over to the window and partially drew back the curtains. A goodly slice of the New York City skyline confronted her. The sky was overcast and it was already growing dark. "I ain't never seen so many buildings in all my life. How in the world do people tell 'em apart? They all look the same to me." She looked back at him.

Charlie shook his head. "You know, you're real funny. If I didn't know better, I'd think you were the biggest hick in the world."

LuAnn looked down. "I am the biggest hick in the world. At least the biggest one you'll probably ever see."

He caught her look. "Hey, I didn't mean anything by it. You grow up here, you get an attitude about things, you know what I mean?" He paused for a minute while he watched LuAnn go over and stroke Lisa's face. "Look, here's the refreshment bar," he finally said. He showed her how it worked. Next, he opened the thick closet door. "Over here is the safe." He indicated the heavy metal door inserted into the wall. He punched in a code and the cylinders whirled into place. "It's a real good idea to keep your valuables in there."

"I don't think I have anything worth putting in there."

"How about that lottery ticket?"

LuAnn gulped, dug into her pocket, and produced the lottery ticket. "So you know that much, huh?"

Charlie didn't answer her. He took the ticket, barely glancing at it, before thrusting it in the safe. "Pick a combo – nothing obvious like birthdays or stuff like that. But choose something you'll remember off the top of your head. You don't want to be writing the numbers down anywhere. Got that?" He opened the safe again.

LuAnn nodded, and input her own code and waited until the safe was in the lock mode before shutting the closet door.

Charlie headed to the door. "I'll be back tomorrow morning about nine. In the meantime, you get hungry or anything, just order up room service. Don't let the waiter get a good look at your face, though. Put your hair up in a bun or wear the shower cap, like you're about to jump in the tub. Open the door, sign the bill as Linda Freeman, and then go into the bedroom. Leave some tip money on the table. Here." Charlie took a wad of bills from his pocket and handed them to her. "Generally, keep a low profile. Don't go walking around the hotel or stuff like that."

"Don't worry, I know I don't sound like no executive person." LuAnn pulled her hair out of her eyes and tried to sound flippant, although her low self-esteem was as plain as the hurt tones in Charlie's response.

"That's not it, LuAnn. I didn't mean . . ." He finally shrugged. "Look, I barely finished high school. I never went to college and I did okay for myself. So neither one of us could pass as a Harvard grad, so who the hell cares?" He touched her lightly on the shoulder. "Get a good night's sleep. When I come back tomorrow, we can go out and see some of the sights and you can talk your head off, how about that?"

She brightened. "Going out would be nice."

"It's supposed to be chilly tomorrow, so dress warmly."

LuAnn suddenly looked down at her wrinkled shirt and jeans. "Uh, these are all the clothes I have. I, uh, left home kind of quick." She looked embarrassed.

Charlie said kindly, "That's all right: No luggage, no problem." He sized her up quickly. "What, you're about five ten, right? Size eight?"

LuAnn nodded and blushed slightly. "Maybe a little bigger on top than that."

Charlie's eyes hovered over her chest area for a moment. "Right," he said. "I'll bring some clothes with me tomorrow. I'll get some things for Lisa, too. I'll need a little extra time though. I'll be here around noon."

"I can take Lisa with us, right?"

"Absolutely, the kid comes with us."

"Thanks, Charlie. I really appreciate it. I wouldn't have the nerve to go out on my own. But I'm kind of itching to, if you know what I mean. I never seen a place this big in my whole life. I betcha there's probably more people in this one hotel than in my whole hometown."

Charlie laughed. "Yeah, I guess being from here, I kind of take it for granted. But I see what you mean. I see it exactly."

After he left, LuAnn gently lifted Lisa out of her carrier and laid her in the middle of the king-size bed, stroking her hair as she did so. She quickly undressed her, gave her a bath in the oversize tub, and dressed Lisa in her pajamas. After laying the little girl back down on the bed, covering her with a blanket, and propping big pillows on either side of her so she wouldn't roll off, LuAnn debated whether to venture into the bathroom and perhaps give the tub a try as well to work the pains out of her body. That's when the phone rang. She hesitated for an instant, feeling guilty and trapped at the same time. She picked it up. "Hello?"

"Miss Freeman?"

"Sorry, you've—" LuAnn mentally kicked herself. "Yes, this is Miss Freeman," she said quickly, trying to sound as professional as possible.

"A little faster next time, LuAnn," Jackson said. "People rarely forget their own names. How are things? Are you being taken care of?"

"Sure am. Charlie's wonderful."

"Charlie? Yes, of course. You have the lottery ticket?"

"It's in the safe."

"Good idea. Do you have pen and paper?"

LuAnn looked around the room and then pulled a sheet of paper and a pen from the drawer of the antique-looking desk against the window.

Jackson continued: "Jot down what you can. Charlie will have all the details as well. You'll be happy to know that everything is in place. At six P.M. the day after tomorrow, the winning ticket will be announced nationwide. You can watch it on TV from your hotel room; all the major networks will be carrying it. I'm afraid there won't be much drama in the proceedings for you, however." LuAnn could almost envision the tight little smile on his lips as he said this. "Then the entire country will eagerly wait for the winner to come forward. You won't do it immediately. We have to give you time, in theory of course, to calm down, start thinking clearly, perhaps get some advice from financial people, lawyers, et cetera, and then you make your joyous way up to New York. Winners aren't required to come to New York, of course. The press conference can be held anywhere, even in the winner's hometown. However, many past winners have voluntarily made the trek and the Lottery Commission likes it that way. It's far easier to hold a national press conference from here. Thus, all your activities will take a day or two. Officially, you have thirty days to claim the money, so there's no problem there. By the way, in case you haven't figured it out, that's why I wanted you to wait before coming. It would not look good if people were aware you arrived in New York *before* the winning number was announced. You'll have to remain incognito until we're ready to present you as the winner." He sounded upset that his plans had been altered.

LuAnn scribbled down notes as fast as she could. "I'm sorry, but I really couldn't wait, Mr. Jackson," LuAnn said hurriedly. "I told you what it would be like back home. It's such a small place and everything. People would know I'd got the winning ticket, they just would."

"All right, fine, there's no sense wasting time discussing it now," he said brusquely. "The point is we have to keep you under cover until a day or so after the lottery drawing. You took the bus to Atlanta, correct?"

"Yes."

"And you took suitable precautions to disguise your appearance?"

"Big hat and glasses. I didn't see anybody I knew."

"And you of course didn't use your real name when buying your ticket?"

"Of course not," LuAnn lied.

"Good. I think your tracks have been effectively erased."

"I hope so."

"It won't matter, LuAnn. It really won't. In a few days, you'll be much farther away than New York."

"Where exactly will I be?"

"As I said before, you tell me. Europe? Asia? South America? Just name it and I'll make all the arrangements."

LuAnn thought for a moment. "Do I have to decide now?"

"Of course not. But if you want to leave immediately after the press conference, the sooner you let me know the better. I've been known to work miracles with travel arrangements, but I'm not a magician, particularly since you don't have a passport or any other identification documents." He sounded incredulous as he said this. "Those will have to be prepared as well."

"Can you get them made up? Even like a Social Security card?"

"You don't have a Social Security number? That's impossible."

"It ain't if your parents never filled out the paperwork for one," she fired back.

"I thought the hospital wouldn't let a baby leave without that paperwork having been completed."

LuAnn almost laughed. "I wasn't born in no hospital, Mr. Jackson. They say the first sight I saw was the dirty laundry stacked in my momma's bedroom because that's right where my grandma delivered me."

"Yes, I suppose I can get you a Social Security number," he said huffily.

"Then could you have them put another name on the passport, I mean with my picture on it, but with a different name? And on all the other paperwork too?"

Jackson said slowly, "Why would you want that, LuAnn?"

"Well, because of Duane. I know he looks stupid and all, but when he finds out I won all this money, he's gonna do everything he can to find me. I thought it'd be best if I disappeared. Start over again. Fresh, so to speak. New name and everything."

Jackson laughed out loud. "You honestly think Duane Harvey will be able to track you down? I seriously doubt if he could find his way out of Rikersville County if he had a police escort."

"Please, Mr. Jackson, if you could do it that way, I'd really appreciate it. Of course, if it's too hard for you, I'll understand." LuAnn held her breath desperately, hoping that Jackson's ego would take the bait.

"It's not," Jackson snapped. "It's quite simple, in fact, when you have the right connections, as I do. Well, I suppose you haven't thought of the name you want to use, have you?"

She surprised him by rattling one off immediately, as well as the place where the fictitious person was from.

"It seems you've been thinking about doing this for a while. Perhaps with or without the lottery money. True?"

"You got secrets, Mr. Jackson. Why not me, too?"

She heard him sigh. "Very well, LuAnn, your request is certainly unprecedented, but I'll take care of it. I still need to know where you want to go."

"I understand. I'll think real hard about it and let you know real soon."

"Why am I suddenly worried that I will regret having selected you for this little adventure?" There was a hint of something in his tone that caused LuAnn to shudder. "I'll be in touch after the lottery drawing, to let you know the rest of the details. That's all for now. Enjoy your visit to New York. If you need anything just tell . . ."

"Charlie."

"Charlie, right." Jackson hung up.

LuAnn went immediately to the wet bar and uncapped a bottle of beer. Lisa started to make a noise and LuAnn let her down on the floor. LuAnn watched with a big smile on her face as Lisa moved around the room. Just in the last few days, her little girl had started to really get the hang of crawling and now she was exploring the large dimensions of the suite with considerable energy. Finally, LuAnn got down on the floor and joined her. Mother and daughter made the circuit of the hotel room for about an hour until Lisa grew tired and LuAnn put her down for the night.

LuAnn went into the bathroom and started running water in the tub while she checked the cut on her jaw in the mirror. It was healing okay, but it would probably leave a scar. That didn't bother her; it could have been a lot worse. She got another beer from the refrigerator and walked back into the bathroom. She slid into the hot water and took a sip of the cold beer. She figured she would need plenty of both alcohol and steamy, soothing water to get through the next couple of days.

Promptly at twelve o'clock, Charlie arrived with several bags from Bloomingdale's and Baby Gap. During the next hour, LuAnn tried on several outfits that made her tingle all over.

"You certainly do those clothes justice. More than justice," Charlie said admiringly.

"Thank you. Thanks for all this stuff. You got the size just right."

"Hell, you got the height and figure of a model. They make these clothes for people like you. You ever think about doing that for a living? Modeling, that is?"

LuAnn shrugged as she put on a cream-colored jacket over a long, pleated black skirt. "Sometimes, when I was younger."

"Younger? My God, you can't be far out of your teens."

"I'm twenty, but you feel older after having a baby."

"I guess that's true."

"No, I ain't cut out for modeling."

"Why not?"

She looked at him and said simply, "I don't like getting my picture taken, and I don't like looking at myself."

Charlie just shook his head. "You are definitely one strange young woman. Most girls your age, with your looks, you couldn't drag them away from the mirror. Narcissus personified. Oh, but you need to wear those big sunglasses and keep the hat on; Jackson said to keep you under wraps. We probably shouldn't be going out, but in a city of seven million I don't think we're going to have a problem." He held up a cigarette. "You mind?"

She smiled. "Are you kidding? I work in a truck diner. They don't even let you in unless you got your smokes and plan to use 'em. Most nights the place looks like it's on fire."

"Well, no more truck diners for you."

"I guess not." She pinned a wide-brimmed, floppy hat to her hair. "How do I look?" She posed for him.

"Better than anything in *Cosmo*, that's for sure."

"You ain't seen nothing yet. You just wait till I dress my little girl," she said proudly. "Now that *is* something I dream about. A lot!"

An hour later, LuAnn put Lisa, who was decked out in the latest Baby Gap fashions, in her baby carrier and hefted it. She turned to Charlie. "You ready?"

"Not just yet." He opened the door to the suite and then looked back at her. "Why don't you close your eyes. We might as well do the whole production." LuAnn looked strangely at him. "Go on, just do it," he said, grinning.

She obeyed. A few seconds later he said, "Okay, open them up." When she did, she was staring at a brand new and very expensive baby carriage. "Oh, Charlie."

"You keep lugging that thing around much longer," he said, pointing at the baby carrier, "your hands are going to scrape the ground."

LuAnn gave him a big hug, loaded Lisa in, and they were off.

ELEVEN

Shirley Watson was madder than hell. In seeking appropriate revenge for her humiliation at the hands of LuAnn Tyler, Shirley had taxed her ingenuity, to the extent she had any, to the maximum. She parked her pickup in an out-of-the-way spot about a quarter of a mile from the trailer and got out, a metal canister held tightly in her right hand. She looked at her watch as she made her way toward the trailer, where she was pretty certain LuAnn would be deeply sleeping after working at the diner all night. Where Duane was she didn't really care. If he was there, then she might get a piece of him too for not defending her against the Amazon-like LuAnn.

With each step, the short, squat Shirley grew even angrier. She had gone to school with LuAnn, and had also dropped out before graduating. Also like LuAnn, she had lived in Rikersville all her life. Unlike LuAnn, however, she had no desire to leave it. Which made what LuAnn had done to her even more awful. People had seen her sneaking home, completely naked. She had never been more humiliated. She had gotten more crap than she knew how to deal with. She was going to have to live with that the rest of her life. Stories would be told again and again until she would be the laughingstock of her hometown. The abuse would continue until she was dead and buried; maybe even then it wouldn't stop. LuAnn Tyler was going to pay for that. So she was screwing around with Duane, so what? Everybody knew Duane had no intention of marrying LuAnn. And everyone else knew that LuAnn would probably kill herself before she would ever walk down the aisle with that man. LuAnn stayed because she had nowhere else to go, or lacked the courage to make a change, Shirley knew that – at least she believed she did – for a fact. Everyone thought LuAnn was so beautiful, so capable. Shirley fumed and grew even more flushed in the face despite the cool breeze flickering across the road. Well, she was going to love to hear what people had to say about LuAnn's looks after she got done with her.

When she drew close to the trailer, Shirley bent low and made her way from tree to tree. The big convertible was still parked in front of the trailer. Shirley could see the tire marks in the hardened mud where something had spun out. She passed the car, taking a moment to peer inside before continuing her stealthy approach. What if somebody else was there? She suddenly smiled to herself. Maybe LuAnn was getting some on the side while Duane was away. Then she could pay LuAnn back even steven. She smiled even more broadly as she envisioned a naked LuAnn running screaming from the trailer. Suddenly, everything became very quiet, very still. As if on cue, even the breeze stopped. Shirley's smile disappeared and she looked around nervously. She gripped the canister even more firmly and reached in her jacket pocket and pulled out the hunting knife. If she missed with the battery acid she was carrying in the canister, then she most assuredly wouldn't miss with the knife. She had been cleaning game and fish most of her life and could wield a blade with the best of them. LuAnn's face would get the benefit of that expertise, at least in the areas the acid missed.

"Damn," she said as she moved up to the front steps and the smell hit her right in the face. She looked around again. She hadn't experienced such an odor even when working a brief stint at the local landfill. She slipped the knife back in her pocket, unscrewed the top to the canister, and then took a moment to cover her nose with a handkerchief. She had come too far to turn back now, smell or not. She silently moved into the trailer, and made her way down to the bedroom. Edging open the door, she looked in. Empty. She closed the door softly and turned to head down the other way. Maybe LuAnn and her beau were asleep on the couch there. The hallway was dark and she felt her way along the wall. As she drew closer, Shirley steeled herself to strike. She lurched forward and, instead, stumbled over something and fell to the floor, coming face-to-face with the decaying source of the stench. Her scream could be heard almost to the main road.

"You sure didn't buy much, LuAnn." Charlie surveyed the few bags on the chaise longue in her hotel room.

LuAnn came out of the bathroom where she had changed into a pair of jeans and a white sweater, her hair done up in a French braid. "I just like looking. That was fun enough. Besides, I flat out can't believe the prices up here. Good God!"

"But I would've paid for it," Charlie protested. "I told you that a hundred times."

"I don't want you spending money on me, Charlie."

Charlie sat down in a chair and stared at her. "LuAnn, it's not *my* money. I told you that, too. I'm on an expense account. Whatever you wanted, you could have."

"Is that what Mr. Jackson said?"

"Something like that. Let's just call it an advance on your future winnings." He grinned.

LuAnn sat down on the bed and played with her hands, a deep frown on her face. Lisa was still in her baby carriage playing with some toys Charlie had bought her. Her happy sounds filled the room.

"Here." Charlie handed LuAnn a package of photos from their day in New York. "For the memory book."

LuAnn looked at the photos and her eyes crinkled. "I never thought I'd see a horse and buggy in this city. It was lots of fun riding around that big old park. Smack dab in the middle of all them buildings, too."

"Come on, you'd never heard of Central Park?"

"Sure I had. *Heard*, leastways. Only I just thought it was all made up." LuAnn handed him a double photo of herself that she picked out of the pack.

"Whoops, thanks for reminding me," said Charlie.

"That's for my passport?"

He nodded as he slipped the photo into his jacket pocket.

"Don't Lisa need one?"

He shook his head. "She's not old enough. She can travel under yours."

"Oh."

"So I understand you want to change your name."

LuAnn put the photos away and started fiddling with the packages. "I thought it'd be a good idea. A fresh start."

"That's what Jackson said you said. I guess if that's what you want."

LuAnn suddenly plopped down on the chaise longue and put her head in her hands.

Charlie looked keenly at her. "Come on, LuAnn, changing your name isn't that traumatic. What's bothering you?"

103

She finally looked up. "Are you sure I'm gonna win the lottery tomorrow?"

He spoke carefully. "Let's just wait until tomorrow, LuAnn, but I don't think you'll be disappointed."

"All that money, but I don't feel good about it, Charlie, not one bit."

He lit a cigarette and puffed on it as he continued to watch her. "I'm gonna order up some room service. Three courses, a bottle of wine. Some hot coffee, the works. You'll feel better after you've eaten." He opened up the hotel services book and began to peruse the menu.

"Have you done this before? I mean, looked after people that . . . Mr. Jackson has met with?"

Charlie looked up from the menu. "I've worked with him for a while, yeah. I've never met him in person. We communicate solely over the phone. He's a smart guy. A little anal for my tastes, a bit paranoid, but real sharp. He pays me well, real well. And baby-sitting people in fancy hotels and ordering room service isn't such a bad life." He added with a big smile, "I've never looked after anybody I had this much fun with, though."

She knelt down beside the baby carriage and pulled out a giftwrapped package from the storage bin underneath. She handed it to him.

Charlie's mouth gaped in surprise. "What's this?"

"I got you a present. Actually, it's from me and Lisa. I was looking for something for you and she started pointing and squealing at it."

"When did you do this?"

"Remember, while you were over looking at the men's clothing."

"LuAnn, you didn't have to—"

"I know that," she said quickly. "That's why it's called a gift, you're not supposed to have to."

Charlie gripped the box tightly in his hands, his eyes riveted on her. "Well, go ahead and open it for gosh sakes," she said.

While Charlie carefully pulled off the wrapping paper, LuAnn heard Lisa stir. She went over and picked up the little girl. They both watched Charlie as he took off the box top.

"Damn!" He gently lifted out the dark green fedora. It had an inch-wide leather band on the outside and a ribbon of cream-colored silk lining the inside.

"I saw you trying it on at the store. I thought you looked real nice in it, real sharp. But then you put it back. I could tell you didn't want to."

"LuAnn, this thing cost a lot of money."

She waved him off. "I had some saved up. I hope you like it."

"I love it, thank you." He gave her a hug and then took one of Lisa's dimpled fists in his. He gave it a gentle, formal shake. "And thank you, little lady. Excellent taste."

"Well, try it on again. Make sure you still like it."

He slid it over his head and checked himself out in the mirror.

"Slick, Charlie, real slick."

He smiled. "Not bad, not bad." He fussed with it a little until he caught the proper angle. Then he took it off and sat back down. "I've never gotten a gift from the people I've looked after. I'm usually only with them for a couple of days anyway, then Jackson takes over."

LuAnn quickly picked up on the opening. "So how'd you come to be doing this kind of work?"

"I take it you'd like to hear my life story?"

"Sure. I've been bending your ear enough."

Charlie settled back in the chair and assumed a comfortable look. He pointed to his face. "Bet you didn't guess I used to ply my skills in the boxing ring." He grinned. "Mostly, I was a sparring partner – a punching bag for up-and-comers. I was smart enough to get out while I still had my brains, at least some of them. After that, I took up semipro football. Let me tell you, that isn't easier on the body, but at least you get to wear helmets and pads. I'd always been athletic, though, and to tell you the truth I liked making my living that way."

"You look like you're in real good shape?"

Charlie slapped his hard stomach. "Not bad for being almost fifty-four. Anyway, after football, I coached a little, got married, floated around here and there, never finding anything that fit, you know?"

LuAnn said, "I know that feeling real good."

"Then my career path took a big turn." He paused to crush out his cigarette and immediately lit another.

LuAnn took the opportunity to put Lisa back in the baby carriage. "What'd you do?"

"I spent some time as a guest of the U.S. government." LuAnn looked at him curiously, not getting his meaning. "I was in a federal prison, LuAnn."

She looked astonished. "You don't look the type, Charlie."

He laughed. "I don't know about that. Besides, there are lots of different types doing time, LuAnn, let me tell you."

"So what'd you do?"

"Income tax evasion. Or fraud I guess they'd call it, at least the prosecutor did. And he was right. I guess I just got tired of paying it. Never seemed like there was enough to live on, let alone giving a chunk to the government." He brushed his hair back. "That little mistake cost me three years and my marriage."

"I'm sorry, Charlie."

He shrugged. "Probably the best thing that ever happened to me, really. I was in a minimum security facility with a bunch of other white collar criminal types so I didn't have to worry every minute about somebody cutting my head off. I took a bunch of classes, started thinking about what I wanted to do with my life. Really only one bad thing happened to me on the inside." He held up the cigarette. "Never smoked until I got to prison. There, just about everybody did. When I got out I finally quit. For a long time. Took it back up about six months ago. What the hell. Anyway, when I got out, I went to work for my lawyer, sort of as an in-house investigator. He knew I was an honest, reliable sort, despite my little conviction. And I knew a lot of people up and down the socioeconomic scale, if you know what I mean. A lot of contacts. Plus I learned a lot while I was in the slammer. Talk about your education. I had professors in every subject from insurance scams to auto chop shops. That experience helped out a lot when I jumped to the law firm. It was a good gig, I enjoyed the work."

"So how'd you hook up with Mr. Jackson?"

Now Charlie didn't look so comfortable. "Let's just say he happened to call one day. I had gotten myself in a little bit of trouble. Nothing real serious, but I was still on parole and it could've cost me some serious time inside. He offered to help me out and I accepted that offer."

"Kind of like I did," said LuAnn, an edge to her voice. "His offers can be kind of hard to refuse."

He glanced at her, his eyes suddenly weary. "Yeah," he said curtly.

She sat down on the edge of the bed and blurted out, "I've never cheated on anything in my whole life, Charlie."

Charlie dragged on his cigarette and then put it

out. "I guess it all depends on how you look at it."

"What do you mean by that?"

"Well, if you think about it, people who are otherwise good, honest, and hardworking cheat every day of their lives. Some in big ways, most in small ones. People fudge on their taxes, or just don't pay 'em, like me. Or they don't give money back when somebody figures up a bill wrong. Little white lies, folks tell almost automatically on a daily basis, sometimes just to get through the day with their sanity. Then there's the big cheat: Men and women have affairs all the time. That one I know a lot about. I think my ex-wife majored in adultery."

"I got a little taste of that, too," LuAnn said quietly.

Charlie stared at her. "One dumb SOB is all I can say. Anyway, it all adds up over a lifetime."

"But not to no fifty million dollars' worth."

"Maybe not in dollar terms, no. But I might take one big cheat in a lifetime over a thousand little ones that eat away at you eventually, make you not like yourself too much."

LuAnn hugged herself and shivered.

He studied her for a moment and then looked once more at the room service menu. "I'm gonna order dinner. Fish okay with you?"

LuAnn nodded absently and stared down at her shoes while Charlie conveyed their dinner order over the phone.

That done, he flipped another cigarette out of the pack and lit up. "Hell, I don't know one single person who would turn down the offer you got. As far as I'm concerned you'd be stupid to." He paused and fiddled with his lighter. "And from the little I've seen of you, maybe you can redeem yourself, at least in your eyes. Not that you'd need much redeeming."

She stared up at him. "How can I do that?"

108

"Use some of the money to help other people," he said simply. "Maybe treat it like a public trust, or something like that. I'm not saying don't enjoy the money. I think you deserve that." He added, "I saw some background info on you. You haven't exactly had the easiest life."

LuAnn shrugged. "I got by."

Charlie sat down beside her. "That's exactly right, LuAnn, you're a survivor. You'll survive this, too." He looked at her intently. "You mind me asking a personal question now that I've spilled my guts to you?"

"Depends on the question."

"Fair enough." He nodded. "Well, like I said, I looked at some of your background stuff. I was just wondering how you ever hooked up with a guy like Duane Harvey. He has 'loser' stamped all over him."

LuAnn thought of Duane's slender body lying facedown on the dirty carpet, the small groan he had made before plummeting over, as though he were calling to her, pleading for help. But she hadn't answered that call. "Duane's not so bad. He had a bunch of bad breaks." She stood up and paced. "I was going through a real bad time. My momma had just died. I met Duane while I was thinking of what to do with my life. You either grow up in that county and die there or you get out just as fast as you can. Ain't nobody ever moved *into* Rikersville County, least not that I ever heard of." She took a deep breath and continued. "Duane had just moved into this trailer he had found. He had a job then. He treated me nice, we talked some about getting married. He was just different."

"You wanted to be one of the ones who was born and died there?"

She looked at him, shocked. "Hell, no. We were going to get out. I wanted to and that's what Duane

109

wanted, at least that's what he said." She stopped pacing and looked over at Charlie. "Then we had Lisa," she said simply. "That kinda changed things for Duane. I don't think having a kid was part of his plan. But we did and it's the best thing that ever happened to me. But after that, I knew things weren't going to work out between us. I knew I had to leave. I was just trying to figure out how when Mr. Jackson called."

LuAnn looked out the window at the twinkling lights etched against the darkness. "Jackson said there were some conditions with all this. With the money. I know he's not doing this because he loves me." She looked over her shoulder at Charlie.

Charlie grunted. "No, you're absolutely right about that."

"You got any idea what the conditions are?"

Charlie was shaking his head before she finished asking the question. "I do know that you'll have more money than you'll know what to do with."

"And I can use that money any way I want, right?"

"That's right. It's yours, free and clear. You can clean out Saks Fifth Avenue and Tiffany. Or build a hospital in Harlem. It's up to you."

LuAnn looked back out the window and her eyes began to shine as the thoughts plowing through her head seemed to dwarf the skyline staring back at her. Right that very instant, everything seemed to click! Even the massive number of buildings in New York City seemed far too small to hold the things she wanted to do with her life. With all that money.

TWELVE

"We should've just stayed at the hotel and watched it from there." Charlie looked around nervously. "Jackson would kill me if he knew we were here. I have strict orders never to take any of the 'clients' here." "Here" was the headquarters of the United States National Lottery Commission located in a brand new state-of-the-art, needle-thin skyscraper on Park Avenue. The huge auditorium was filled with people. Network news correspondents were scattered throughout, microphones clamped in their fists, as were representatives from magazines, newspapers, and cable TV.

Near the front of the stage, LuAnn cradled Lisa against her chest. She wore the glasses Charlie had bought for her and a baseball cap turned backward under which her long hair was balled up. Her memorable figure was hidden under the full-length trench coat.

"It's okay, Charlie, nobody's gonna remember me under all this stuff."

He shook his head. "I still don't like it."

"I had to come see. It just wouldn't be the same sitting in the hotel room watching on TV."

"Jackson's gonna probably call the hotel right after the drawing," he grumbled.

"I'll just tell him I fell asleep and didn't hear the phone."

"Right!" He lowered his voice. "You're gonna win at least fifty million bucks and you fall asleep?"

"Well, if I already *know* I'm gonna win, what's so exciting about it?" she shot back.

Charlie had no ready answer for that so he clamped his mouth shut and again took up a careful scrutiny of the room and its occupants.

LuAnn looked at the stage where the lottery pinball machine was set up on a table. It was about six feet long and comprised ten large tubes, each one rising above an attached bin of Ping-Pong balls. Each ball had a number painted on it. After the machine was activated, the air would circulate the balls until one made its way through the tiny hatch, popped up into the tube, and was caught and held by a special device inside the tube. Once a ball was thus captured, a bin of balls below that tube would immediately shut down and the next bin would automatically activate. Down the line it would go, the suspense building, until all ten winning numbers were finally revealed.

People were nervously looking at their lottery tickets; many held at least a dozen in their hands. One young man had an open laptop computer in front of him. The screen was filled with hundreds of lottery combinations he had purchased as he reviewed his electronic inventory. LuAnn had no need to look at her ticket; she had memorized the numbers: 0810080521, which represented her and Lisa's birthdays, and the age LuAnn would be on her next birthday. She didn't feel any more guilt as she observed the hopeful looks on the faces surrounding her. She would be able to handle their imminent disappointment. She had made up her mind, set her plan, and that decision had bolstered her spirits incredibly and it was the reason she was standing in the middle of this sea of tense people instead of hiding under the bed back at the Waldorf.

She stirred out of her musings as a man walked on

to the stage. The crowd instantly hushed. LuAnn had half-expected to see Jackson striding across the stage, but the man was younger and far better looking. LuAnn wondered for a moment if he was in on it. She and Charlie exchanged tight smiles. A blond woman in a short skirt, black nylons, and spike heels joined the man and stood next to the sophisticated-looking machine, hands clasped behind her back.

The man's announcement was brief and clear as the TV cameras focused on his handsome features. He welcomed everyone to the drawing and then he paused, stared dramatically out at the crowd, and delivered the real news of the evening: The official jackpot, based upon ticket sales up to the very last minute, was a record-setting one hundred million dollars! A collective gasp went up from the crowd at the mention of the gigantic sum. Even LuAnn's mouth dropped open. Charlie looked over at her, shook his head slightly, and a small grin escaped his lips. He playfully elbowed her, leaned close, and whispered into her ear. "Hell, you can clean out Saks and Tiffany *and* still build that hospital, just with the friggin' interest."

It was indeed the largest jackpot ever and someone, one incredibly fortunate person, was about to win it, the lottery man declared with a beaming smile and a ton of showmanship. The crowd cheered wildly. The man gestured dramatically to the woman, who hit the power switch on the side of the machine. LuAnn watched as the balls in the first bin started bouncing around. When the balls started attacking the narrow pathway into the tubes, LuAnn felt her heart race and her breathing constrict. Despite the presence of Charlie beside her, the calm, authoritative manner of Mr. Jackson, his correct predicting of the daily lottery, and all the other things she had been through in the last several days, she suddenly felt that her being here was totally crazy. How could Jackson or anyone else control what those gyrating balls would do? It occurred to her that what she was witnessing resembled sperm dive-bombing an egg, something she had seen once on a TV program. What were the chances of correctly picking the one that would break through and impregnate? Her spirits plummeted as she confronted a very distinct set of options: travel back home and somehow explain the deaths of two men in a drug-filled trailer she happened to call home; or seek the hospitality of the nearest homeless shelter here in the city and contemplate what to do with the wrecked state of her life.

She clutched Lisa even more tightly and one of her hands drifted over and clasped Charlie's thick fingers. A ball squirted through the opening and was caught in the first tube. It was the number zero. It was shown on a large screen suspended over the stage. As soon as this occurred, the second bin of balls started popping. In a few seconds, it too had produced a winner: the number eight. In quick succession, six more of the balls popped through into their respective tubes and were caught. The tally now stood as follows: 0-8-1-0-0-8-0-5. LuAnn mouthed the familiar numbers silently. Sweat appeared on her forehead and she felt her legs begin to give way. "Oh my God," she whispered to herself, "it's really gonna happen." Jackson had done it; somehow, some way, the uppity anal little man had done it. She heard many moans and groans next to her as lottery tickets were torn up and thrown to the floor as the numbers stared back at the crowd from the stage. LuAnn watched, completely mesmerized, as the ninth bin of balls started bouncing. The entire process now seemed to be occurring in the slowest of slow motion. Finally, the number two ball kicked out and held in tube number nine. There were no hopeful faces left in the crowd. Except for one.

The last bin fired up and the number one ball quickly fought its way right against the hatch of the last tube and appeared to be ready to shoot through to victory at any moment. LuAnn's grip on Charlie's fingers began to loosen. Then, like a pricked balloon hemorrhaging air, the number one ball suddenly slid back down to the bottom and was replaced near the hatch by a suddenly energetic and determined number four ball. With sharp, jerky motions, it grew closer and closer to the open pathway leading into the number ten and final tube, although it appeared to be repeatedly repelled from the opening. The blood slowly drained from LuAnn's face and for a moment she thought she would end up on the floor. "Oh, shit," she said out loud, although not even Charlie could hear her over the crowd noise. LuAnn squeezed Charlie's fingers so tightly he almost yelled out in pain.

Charlie's own heart was racing as if in sympathy for LuAnn. He had never known Jackson to fail, but, well, you never knew. *What the hell, it couldn't hurt*, he thought. He moved his free hand up and quietly felt under his shirt for the thick, silver crucifix he had worn for as long as he could remember. He rubbed it for good luck.

Ever so slowly, even as LuAnn's heart threatened to cease beating, the two balls, as though carefully choreographed, again swapped places with each other in the swirling spray of hot air, even ricocheting off one another at one point. After this momentary collision, the number one ball, mercifully for LuAnn, finally shot through the opening and was caught in the tenth and final tube.

It was all LuAnn could do not to scream out loud from pure relief, rather than from the excitement of having just become one hundred million dollars

115

richer. She and Charlie looked at each other, their eyes wide, both bodies shaking, faces drenched with perspiration, as though they had just finished making love. Charlie inclined his head toward her, his eyebrows arched as if to say "You won, didn't you?"

LuAnn nodded slightly, her head swaying slowly as if to the tunes of a favorite song. Lisa kicked and squirmed as though she sensed her mother's exhilaration.

"Damn," Charlie said, "I thought I was going to pee in my pants waiting for that last number to drop." He led LuAnn out of the room and in a couple of minutes they were walking slowly down the street in the direction of the hotel. It was a beautiful, brisk night; the cloudless sky housed a stretch of stars that seemingly had no end. It matched LuAnn's mood precisely. Charlie rubbed at his hand. "God, I thought you were going to snap my fingers off. What was that all about?"

"You don't wanta know," said LuAnn firmly. She smiled at him, sucked in huge amounts of the sweet, chilly air, and gave Lisa a tender kiss on the cheek. She suddenly elbowed Charlie in the side, a mischievous grin on her face. "Last one to the hotel pays for dinner." She took off like a blue streak, the trench coat billowing out like a parachute in her wake. Even as she left him in the dust, Charlie could hear her shrieks of joy flowing back to him. He grinned and then bolted after her.

Neither one would have been so happy had they seen the man who had followed them to the lottery drawing and was watching from across the street. Romanello had figured that tailing LuAnn might result in some interesting developments. But even he had to admit that his expectations had so far been exceeded.

THIRTEEN

"**Y**ou're certain that's where you want to go, LuAnn?"

LuAnn spoke earnestly into the phone. "Yes sir, Mr. Jackson. I've always wanted to go to Sweden. My momma's people came from there, a long time ago. She always wanted to go there, but never had the chance. So I'd sort of be doing it for her. Is that much trouble?"

"Everything is trouble, LuAnn. It's just a matter of degrees."

"But you can get it done, can't you? I mean I'd like to go to other places, but I'd really like to start in Sweden."

Jackson said testily, "If I can arrange for someone like *you* to win one hundred million dollars, then I can certainly take care of travel plans."

"I appreciate it. I really do." LuAnn looked over at Charlie, who was holding Lisa and playing with her.

She smiled at him. "You look real good doing that."

"What's that?" Jackson asked.

"I'm sorry, I was talking to Charlie."

"Put him on, we need to arrange for your visit to the lottery office so they can confirm the winning ticket. The sooner that's accomplished, the sooner we can get on with the press conference and then you can be on your way."

"The conditions you talked about—" LuAnn began.

Jackson interrupted, "I'm not ready to discuss that right now. Put Charlie on, I'm in a hurry."

LuAnn swapped the phone for Lisa. She watched closely as Charlie spoke in low tones into the phone, his back to her. She saw him nod several times and then he hung up.

"Everything okay?" Her tone was anxious as she held a rambunctious Lisa.

He looked around the room for a moment before his eyes finally met hers. "Sure, everything's A-okay. You have to go over to see the lottery people this afternoon. Enough time has passed."

"Will you go with me?"

"I'll go over in the cab with you, but I won't go in the building. I'll hang around outside until you come out."

"What all do I have to do?"

"Just present the winning ticket. They'll validate it and issue you an official receipt. There'll be witnesses there and all. You'll be confirmed every which way from Sunday. They go over the ticket with a high-tech laser to verify it's authentic. They got special fiber threads in the tickets, some of them right under the row of numbers. Kind of like U.S. currency, to prevent counterfeiting. It's impossible to duplicate, especially in a short time frame. They'll call the outlet where you bought the ticket to confirm that lottery number was indeed purchased at that site. They'll ask for background info on you. Where you're from, kids, parents, that sort of thing. It takes a few hours. You don't have to wait. They'll get in touch when the process is complete. Then they'll release a statement to the press that the winner has come forward, but they won't release your name until the press conference. You know, keep the suspense building. That stuff really sells tickets for the next drawing. You don't have to hang around for that either. The actual press conference will be the next day."

"Do we come back here?"

"Actually, 'Linda Freeman' is checking out today. We'll go to another hotel where you can check in as LuAnn Tyler, one of the richest people in the country. Fresh in town and ready to take on the world."

"You ever been to one of these press conferences before?"

He nodded. "A few. They can be a little crazy. Especially when the winners bring family with them. Money can do strange things to people. But it doesn't last too long. You get asked a bunch of questions and then off you go." He paused and then added, "That's nice what you're doing, going to Sweden for your mom like that."

LuAnn looked down as she played with Lisa's feet. "I hope so. It's sure gonna be different."

"Well, sounds like you can use a little different."

"I don't know how long I'll stay."

"Stay as long as you want. Hell, you can stay forever if you want to."

"I'm not sure I can do that. I don't think I'd fit in."

He gripped her shoulders and looked her in the face. "Listen, LuAnn, give yourself some credit. Okay, so you don't have a bunch of fancy degrees, but you're sharp, you take great care of your kid, and you got a good heart. In my book, that puts you ahead of about ninety-nine percent of the population."

"I don't know how good I'd be doing right now if you weren't here helping me out."

He shrugged. "Hey, like I said, it's part of the job." He let go of her shoulders and fished a cigarette out of his pack. "Why don't we have some quick lunch and then you go claim your prize? What do you say, you ready to be filthy rich, lady?"

119

LuAnn took a deep breath before answering. "I'm ready."

LuAnn emerged from the Lottery Commission building, walked down the street, and turned a corner, where she met Charlie at a prearranged spot. He had kept Lisa for her while she had gone in.

"She's been watching everything going by. She's a real alert kid," he said.

"Won't be long before I'm running every which way after her."

"She was doing her best to get down and crawl off, swear to God." Charlie smiled and put a very exuberant Lisa back in her carriage. "So how'd it go?"

"They were real friendly. Treated me real special. 'You want coffee, Ms. Tyler?' 'You want a phone to make calls?' One woman asked me if I wanted to hire her as my personal assistant." She laughed.

"You better get used to that. You have the receipt?"

"Yep, in my purse."

"What time's the press conference?"

"Tomorrow at six o'clock, they said." She eyed him. "What's wrong?"

As they walked, Charlie had glanced surreptitiously over his shoulder a couple of times. He looked over at her. "I don't know. When I was in prison and then doing the PI stuff I developed this kind of built-in radar that tells me when somebody's paying a little too close attention to me. My alarm's going off right now."

LuAnn started to look around, but he cut her off. "Don't do that. Just keep walking. We're fine. I checked you in at another hotel. It's another block down. Let's get you and Lisa in okay and then I'll snoop around a little. It's probably nothing."

LuAnn looked at the worry creases around his eyes and concluded his words did not match his feelings. She gripped the baby carriage tighter as they continued down the street.

Twenty yards behind and on the other side of the street, Anthony Romanello debated whether or not he had been spotted. The streets were filled with people at this hour, but something in the sudden rigidity of the people he was tracking had set off his own warning bell. He hunkered in his jacket and dropped back another ten yards, still keeping them well in sight. He kept a constant lookout for the closest taxi in case they decided to snare one. He had the advantage though, in that it would take some time to load the baby carriage and baby in. He would have plenty of opportunity to hail a cab in that time. But they continued on foot until they reached their destination. Romanello waited outside the hotel for a moment, looked up and down the street, and then went in.

"When did you get these?" LuAnn stared at the new set of luggage stacked in a corner of the hotel suite.

Charlie grinned. "You can't go on your big trip without the proper baggage. And this stuff is super-durable. Not that expensive crap that falls apart if you look at it wrong. One bag is already packed with things you'll need for the trip over. Things for Lisa and what-not. I had a lady friend of mine do it. We'll have to do some more shopping today to fill up the other bags, though."

"My God, I can't believe this, Charlie." She gave him a hug and a peck on the cheek.

He looked down in embarrassment, his face flushed. "It wasn't such a big deal. Here." He

121

handed her passport to her. She solemnly looked at the name inside, as though the fact of her reincarnation were just sinking in, which it was. She closed the small blue book. It represented a gateway to another world, a world she would soon, with a little luck, be embracing.

"Fill that sucker up, LuAnn, see the whole damned planet. You and Lisa." He turned to leave. "I'm going to check on some things. I'll be back shortly."

She fingered the passport and looked up at him, her cheeks slightly red. "Why don't you come with us, Charlie?"

He turned slowly back around and stared at her. "What?"

LuAnn looked down at her hands and spoke hurriedly. "I was thinking I got all this money now. And you been real nice to me and Lisa. And I never been anywhere before and all. And, well, I'd like you to come with us – that is, if you want to. I'll understand if you don't."

"That's a very generous offer, LuAnn," he said softly. "But you don't really know me. And that's a big commitment to make to someone you don't really know."

"I know all I need to," she said stubbornly. "I know you're a good person. I know you been taking care of us. And Lisa took to you like nobody's business. That counts for a durn lot in my book."

Charlie smiled in the little girl's direction and then looked back at LuAnn. "Why don't we both think on it, LuAnn. Then we'll talk, okay?"

She shrugged and slid several strands of hair out of her face. "I ain't proposing marriage to you, Charlie, if that's what you think."

"Good thing, since I'm almost old enough to be your grandfather." He smiled at her.

"But I really like having you with me. I ain't had that many friends, least that I can count on. I know I can count on you. You're my friend, ain't you?"

There was a catch in his throat when Charlie answered. "Yes." He coughed and assumed a more businesslike tone. "I hear what you're saying, LuAnn. We'll talk about it when I get back. Promise."

When the door closed behind him, LuAnn got Lisa ready for her nap. While the little girl drifted off to sleep, LuAnn restlessly walked the parameters of the hotel suite. She looked out the window in time to see Charlie exit the building and head down the street. She followed him with her eyes until he was out of sight. She had not seen anyone who appeared to be tracking him, but there were so many people around, she couldn't be sure. She sighed and then frowned. She was out of her element here. She just wanted to see him back safe and sound. She began to think about the press conference, but as she envisioned a bunch of strangers asking her all sorts of questions, her nerves began to jangle too much and she quit thinking about it.

The knock at the door startled her. She stared at the door, unsure what to do.

"Room service," the voice said. LuAnn went to the door and squinted through the peephole. The young man standing there was indeed dressed in a bellman's uniform.

"I didn't order anything," she said, trying hard to keep her voice from quaking.

"It's a note and package for you, ma'am."

LuAnn jerked back. "Who from?"

"I don't know, ma'am. A man in the lobby asked me to give it to you."

Charlie? LuAnn thought. "Did he ask for me by name?"

"No, he pointed you out when you were walking

123

to the elevator, and just said give it to you. Do you want it, ma'am?" he said patiently. "If not, I'll just put it in your box behind the registration desk."

LuAnn opened the door slightly. "No, I'll take it." She stuck out her arm and the bellman put the package in it. She immediately closed the door. The young man stood there for a moment, upset that his errand and patience had not resulted in a tip. However, the man had already rewarded him handsomely for it, so it had worked out okay.

LuAnn tore open the envelope and unfolded the letter. The message was brief and written on hotel stationery.

Dear LuAnn, how's Duane feeling lately? And the other guy, what'd you hit him with anyway? Dead as a doornail. Sure hope the police don't find out you were there. Hope you enjoy the story, a little hometown news. Let's chat. In one hour. Take a cab to the Empire State Building. It's truly a landmark worth seeing. Leave the big guy and the kid at home. XXXOOOs

LuAnn ripped off the brown packing paper and the newspaper fell out. She picked it up and looked at it: It was the *Atlanta Journal and Constitution*. It had a page marked with a yellow piece of paper. She opened to that page and sat down on the sofa.

In her agitation at seeing the headline, she jumped up. Her eyes fed voraciously on the words, occasionally darting to the accompanying photo. If possible, the trailer looked even dingier captured in grainy black and white; in fact it looked like it had actually collapsed and was merely awaiting the dump truck to cart it and its occupants away for burial. The convertible was also in the photo, its long hood and obscene ornament pointed straight at the trailer like some hunting dog telling its master: There's the kill.

Two men dead, the story said. Drugs involved. As LuAnn read the name Duane Harvey, a teardrop splattered on to the page and blurred some of the text. She sat down and did her best to compose herself. The other man had not yet been identified. LuAnn read quickly, and then she stopped searching when she found her name. The police were looking for her right now; the paper didn't say she had been charged with any crime, although her disappearance had probably only increased the police's suspicions. She flinched when she read that Shirley Watson had discovered the bodies. A canister of battery acid had been found on the floor of the trailer. LuAnn's eyes narrowed. *Battery acid*. Shirley had come back to avenge herself and had brought that acid to do the job, that was clear. She doubted, though, if the police would care about a crime that had not occurred when they had their hands full with at least two that had.

While she sat staring in shock at the paper, another knock on the door almost made LuAnn jump out of her chair.

"LuAnn?"

She took a deep breath. "Charlie?"

"Who else?"

"Just a minute." LuAnn jumped up, hastily ripped the news article out of the paper and stuffed it in her pocket. She slid the letter and the rest of the newspaper under the couch.

She unlocked the door and he entered the room and shrugged off his coat. "Stupid idea, like I'm going to be able to spot somebody out on those streets." He slid a cigarette from its pack and lit up, thoughtfully staring out the window. "Still can't shake the feeling that somebody was tailing us, though."

"It could've just been somebody looking to rob us, Charlie. You got a lot of that up here, don't you?"

He shook his head. "Crooks have gotten more daring lately, but if that was the case, they would've hit us and run. Grabbed your purse and disappeared. It's not like they were going to pull a gun and stick us up in the middle of a million people. I had the sense whoever it was was tracking us for a while." He turned to stare at her. "Nothing unusual happened to you on the way up, did it?"

LuAnn shook her head, staring back at him with wide eyes, afraid to speak.

"Nobody followed you up to New York that you know of, did they?"

"I didn't see anybody, Charlie. I swear I didn't." LuAnn started to shake. "I'm scared."

He put a big arm around her. "Hey, it's okay. Probably just paranoid Charlie going off on nothing. But sometimes it pays to be paranoid. Look, how about we go do some more shopping? It'll make you feel better."

LuAnn nervously fingered the newspaper article in her pocket. Her heart seemed to be climbing up her throat, seeking a larger space in which to explode. However, when she looked up at him, her face was calm, bewitching. "You know what I really want to do?"

"What's that? Name it and it's done."

"I want to get my hair done. And maybe my nails. They both look kinda crappy. And with the press conference going on across the whole country and all, I'd like to look good."

"Damn, why didn't I think of that? Well, let's just look up the fanciest beauty parlor in the phone book—"

"There's one in the lobby," LuAnn said hurriedly. "I saw it coming in. They do hair and nails and feet,

126

and facials, stuff like that. It looked real nice. Real nice."

"Even better then."

"Could you watch Lisa for me?"

"We can come down and hang out with you."

"Charlie, I swear. Don't you know nothing?"

"What? What'd I say?"

"Men don't come down to the beauty parlor and watch the goings-on. That's for us females to keep secret. If you knew how much trouble it takes to get us all pretty, it wouldn't be nearly as special. But you got a job to do."

"What's that?"

"You can 'ooh' and 'ahh' when I get back and tell me how beautiful I look."

Charlie grinned. "I think I can handle that one."

"I don't know how long I'll be. I might not be able to get in right away. There's a bottle ready in the refrigerator for Lisa for when she gets hungry. She's gonna want to play for a while and then you can put her down for a nap."

"Take your time, I've got nothing else on the agenda. A beer and cable TV" – he went over and lifted Lisa out of the baby carriage – "and the company of this little lady, and I'm a happy man."

LuAnn picked up her coat.

Charlie said, "What do you need that for?"

"I need to buy some personal things. There's a drug store across the street."

"You can just get them in the gift shop in the lobby."

"If they're anything like the prices at the last hotel, I'll go across the street and save myself some money, thank you very much."

"LuAnn, you're one of the richest women in the world, you could buy the whole damned hotel if you wanted."

"Charlie, I've been scraping pennies all my life. I

127

can't change overnight." She opened the door and glanced back at him, trying her best to hide the rising anxiety she was experiencing. "I'll be back as soon as I can."

Charlie moved over to the door. "I don't like it. If you go out, I'm supposed to go with you."

"Charlie, I'm a grown woman. I can take care of myself. Besides, Lisa's going to have to take a nap soon and we can't leave her here by herself, can we?"

"Well, no, but—"

LuAnn slid an arm across his shoulder. "You look after Lisa and I'll be back as soon as I can." She gave Lisa a kiss on the cheek and Charlie a gentle squeeze on the arm.

After she left, Charlie grabbed a beer from the wet bar and settled into his chair with Lisa on his lap and the TV remote in hand. He suddenly paused and looked over at the doorway, a frown appearing on his features as he did so. Then he turned back and did his best to interest Lisa in channel surfing.

FOURTEEN

When LuAnn stepped from the cab she looked up at the towering presence of the Empire State Building. She didn't have long to dwell upon the architecture, though, as she felt the arm slide around hers.

"This way, we can talk." The voice was smooth, comforting, and it made every hair on her neck stiffen.

She pulled her arm free and looked at him. Very tall and broad shouldered, his face was clean-shaven, the hair thick and dark, matching the eyebrows. The eyes were big and luminous.

"What do you want?" Now that she could actually see the man behind the note, LuAnn's fear quickly receded.

Romanello looked around. "You know, even in New York, we're bound to attract attention if we conduct this conversation out in the open. There's a deli across the street. I suggest we continue our chat there."

"Why should I?"

He crossed his arms and smiled at her. "You read my note and the news article, obviously, or you wouldn't be here."

"I read it," LuAnn said, keeping her voice level.

"Then I think it's clear we have some things to discuss."

"What the hell do you have to do with it? Were you involved in that drug dealing?"

The smile faded from the man's lips and he stepped back for a moment. "Look—"

"I didn't kill nobody," she said fiercely.

Romanello looked around nervously. "Do you want everybody here to know our business?"

LuAnn looked around at the passersby and then stalked toward the deli with Romanello right behind.

Inside they found an isolated booth far in the back. Romanello ordered coffee and then looked at LuAnn. "Anything interest you on the menu?" he asked pleasantly.

"Nothing." She glared back at him.

After the waitress departed, he looked at her. "Since I can understand your not wanting to prolong this discussion, let's get to the heart of it."

"What's your name?"

He looked startled. "Why?"

"Just make up one, that's what everybody else seems to be doing."

"What are you talking—" He stopped and considered for a moment. "All right, call me Rainbow."

"Rainbow, huh, that's a different one. You don't look like no rainbow I've ever seen."

"See, that's where you're wrong." His eyes gleamed for an instant. "Rainbows have pots of gold at the end."

"So?" LuAnn's tone was calm, but her look was wary.

"So, you're my pot of gold, LuAnn. At the end of my rainbow." He spread apart his hands. She started to get up.

"Sit down!" The words shot out of his mouth. LuAnn stopped in midrise, staring at the man. "Sit down unless you want to spend the rest of your life in prison instead of paradise." The calm returned to his manner and he politely gestured for her to resume her seat. She did so, slowly, her eyes squarely on his.

"I ain't never been real good at games, Mr. Rainbow, so why don't you say whatever the hell it is you want to say and let's be done with it."

Romanello waited for a moment as the waitress returned with his coffee. "You sure you don't want some? It's quite chilly outside."

The chill in LuAnn's eyes compelled him to move on. He waited until the waitress had set the coffee and cream down and asked if they wanted anything else. After she left, he leaned across the table, his eyes bare inches from LuAnn's. "I was at your trailer, LuAnn. I saw the bodies."

She flinched for an instant. "What were you doing there?"

He sat back. "Just happened by."

"You're full of crap and you know it."

"Maybe. The point is, I saw you drive up to the trailer in that car, the same one in the newspaper photo. I saw you pull a wad of cash out of your kid's baby seat at the train station. I saw you make a number of phone calls."

"So what? I'm not allowed to make phone calls?"

"The trailer had two dead bodies and a shitload of drugs in it, LuAnn. That was *your* trailer."

LuAnn's eyes narrowed. *Was Rainbow a policeman sent to get her to confess?* She fidgeted in her seat. "I don't know what you're talking about. I never seen no bodies. You musta seen somebody else get out of that car. And who says I can't keep my money wherever the hell I want to keep it." She dug her hand into her pocket and pulled out the newspaper article. "Here, why don't you take this back and go try scaring somebody else."

Romanello picked up the piece of paper, glanced at it, and put it in his pocket. When his hand

131

returned to view, LuAnn could barely keep from trembling as she saw the torn piece of bloody shirt.

"Recognize this, LuAnn?"

She struggled to maintain her composure. "Looks like a shirt with some stains on it. So what?"

He smiled at her. "You know, I didn't expect you to remain this calm about it. You're a dumb chick from Hooterville. I pictured you dropping to your knees pleading for mercy."

"Sorry I ain't what you imagined. And if you call me a dumb anything again, I'll knock you flat on your ass."

His face suddenly became hard and he slid down the zipper of his jacket until the butt of his 9-mm was revealed. "The last thing you want to do, LuAnn, is make me upset," he said quietly. "When I get upset, I can be very unpleasant. In fact I can be downright violent."

LuAnn barely glanced at the weapon. "What do you want from me?"

He zipped the jacket back up. "Like I said, you're my pot of gold."

"I ain't got any money," she said quietly.

He almost laughed. "Why are you in New York, LuAnn? I bet you've never been out of that god-forsaken county before. Why of all places did you take off for the Big Apple?" He cocked his head at her, waiting for an answer.

LuAnn rubbed her hands nervously across the uneven surface of the table. She didn't look at him when she finally spoke. "Okay, maybe I knew what happened in that trailer. But I didn't do nothing wrong. I had to get out, though, because I knew it might look real bad for me. New York seemed as good as anyplace." She looked up to test his reaction to her explanation. The mirth was still there.

"What are you going to do with all the money, LuAnn?"

She nearly crossed her eyes. "What are you talking about? What money? In the baby seat?"

"I would hope you weren't going to try and stuff one hundred million dollars in a baby seat." He eyed her chest. "Or, despite its obvious capacity, your bra." She just stared at him, her mouth open a notch. "Let's see," he continued, "what's the going price for blackmail these days? Ten percent? Twenty percent? Fifty percent? I mean, even at half, you're still talking millions in your bank account. That'll keep you and the kid in jeans and sneakers for life, right?" He took a sip of his coffee and sat back, idly fingering the edges of his napkin while he watched her.

LuAnn clamped a fist around the fork in front of her. For a moment she thought about attacking him, but that impulse subsided.

"You're crazy, mister, you really are."

"The press conference is tomorrow, LuAnn."

"What press conference?"

"You know, that's where you're going to hold that big old check and smile and wave to the disappointed masses."

"I've gotta go."

His right hand shot across and gripped her arm. "I don't think you can spend that money from a prison cell."

"I said I gotta go." She jerked her hand free and stood up.

"Don't be a fool, LuAnn. I saw you buy the lottery ticket. I was at the lottery drawing. I saw the big smile on your face, the way you ran down the street whooping and hollering. And I was inside the lottery building when you went to get your winning ticket validated. So don't try to bullshit with me. You walk out of here and the first thing I'm going to do is place a call to that Podunk county and that Podunk sheriff and tell them everything I saw. And then I'm going to send them this piece of shirt. You can't believe the high-tech stuff they've got in the lab these days. They'll start piecing it together. And when I tell them you just won the lottery and maybe they should grab you before you disappear, then you can just kiss your new life good-bye. Although I guess you can afford to put your kid up somewhere nice while you rot in jail."

"I didn't do nothing wrong."

"No, what you did was stupid, LuAnn. You ran. And when you run, the cops always figure you're guilty. It's how cops think. They'll believe you were in it up to your pretty little ass. Right now, they haven't gotten around to you. But they will. It's up to you to decide whether they start focusing on you ten minutes from now, or ten days from now. If it's ten minutes, you're dead. If it's ten days, I figure your plan is to disappear forever. Because that's what I intend to do. You only pay me once, that I'll guarantee. I couldn't spend all that money even if I tried and neither could you. We all win that way. The other way, you lose, slamdunk. So what's it gonna be?"

She stood frozen for a moment halfway out of her chair. Slowly, inch by inch, she sat back down.

"Very smart of you, LuAnn."

"I can't pay you half."

His face darkened. "Don't be greedy, lady."

"It's got nothing to do with that. I can pay you, I just don't know how much, but it'll be a lot. Enough for you to do whatever the hell you want to."

"I don't understand—" he began.

LuAnn interrupted, borrowing phraseology from Jackson. "You don't have to understand nothing. But if I do this I want you to answer one question for

134

me and I want the truth or you can just go and call the cops, I don't care."

He eyed her cautiously. "What's the question?"

LuAnn leaned across the table, her voice low but intense. "What were you doing in that trailer? You just didn't happen on by, I know that sure as I'm sitting here."

"Look, what does it matter why I was there?" He threw his arm up in a casual motion.

LuAnn reached out as quickly as a striking rattler and grabbed his wrist. He winced as she squeezed it with a strength he had not anticipated. Big and strong as he was, it would've taken all his might to break that grip. "I said I wanted an answer, and it better be the right one."

"I earn my living" – he smiled and corrected himself – "I *used* to earn my living by taking care of little problems for people."

LuAnn continued to grip the waist. "What problems? Did this have to do with the drugs Duane was dealing?"

Romanello was already shaking his head. "I didn't know anything about the drugs. Duane was already dead. Maybe he was holding out on his supplier or maybe skimming off the top and the other guy cut him up. Who knows? Who cares?"

"What happened to the other guy?"

"You were the one who hit him, weren't you? Like I said in the note, dead as a doornail." LuAnn didn't answer. He paused and took a breath. "You can let go of my wrist any time now."

"You haven't answered my question. And unless you answer it, you can just go call the sheriff, because you ain't getting one red cent from me."

Romanello hesitated, but then his greed won out over his better judgment. "I went there to kill you," he said simply.

135

She slowly let go of his wrist after giving it one more intense ratchet. He took a minute to rub the circulation back in.

"Why?" LuAnn demanded fiercely.

"I don't ask questions. I just do what I'm paid to do."

"Who told you to kill me?"

He shrugged. "I don't know." She reached for his wrist again, but this time he was ready for her and jerked it out of danger. "I'm telling you I don't know. My clients don't just drop by and have coffee and chat about who they want me to take out. I got a call, I got half the money up front. Half when the job was done. All through the mail."

"I'm still alive."

"That's right. But only because I got called off."

"By who?"

"By whoever hired me."

"When did you get the call?"

"I was in your trailer. I saw you get out of the car and take off. I went to my car and got the call then. Around ten-fifteen."

LuAnn sat back as the truth dawned on her: Jackson. So that's how he took care of those who refused to go along.

When she didn't say anything, Romanello leaned forward. "So now that I've answered all your questions, why don't we discuss the arrangements for our little deal?"

LuAnn stared at him for a full minute before speaking. "If I find out you're lying to me, you won't like it one bit."

"You know, somebody who kills for a living usually strikes a little more fear into people than what you're showing," he said, his dark eyes flickering at her. He partially unzipped his jacket again so that the butt of the 9-mm was once more

136

visible. "Don't push it!" His tone was menacing.

LuAnn glanced at the pistol with contempt before settling her eyes back on his. "I growed up surrounded by crazy people, *Mr. Rainbow*. Rednecks getting drunk and pointing twelve-gauge shotguns in people's faces and then pulling the trigger just for fun, or cutting somebody up so bad their momma wouldn't have knowed them and then betting on how long they'd take to bleed to death. Then there was the black boy who ended up in a lake with his throat slashed and his private parts gone, 'cause somebody thought he was too uppity hanging around a white girl. I'm pretty sure my daddy had something to do with that, not that the police down there gave a damn. So your little gun and your big man bullshit don't mean crap to me. Let's just get this over with and then you can get the hell out of my life."

The danger in the depths of Romanello's eyes rapidly dissipated. "All right," he said quietly, zipping his jacket back up.

FIFTEEN

A half hour later Romanello and LuAnn exited the deli. LuAnn climbed into a cab and headed back to her hotel where, to follow through on her cover story to Charlie, she would spend the next several hours at the beauty salon. Romanello walked down the street in the opposite direction, silently whispering to himself. Today had been a very good day. The arrangements he had made with LuAnn weren't a hundred percent foolproof, but his gut told him she would honor the deal she had made. If the first installment of the money wasn't in his account by close of business two days from now, then he would be on the phone to the police in Rikersville. She would pay, Romanello was sure of that. Why bring all that grief on yourself?

Since he was in a festive mood, he decided to stop and buy a bottle of Chianti on the way to his apartment. His thoughts were already focused on the mansion he would buy in some faraway land to replace it. He had earned good money over the years exterminating human beings, but he had to be careful in how he spent it or where he kept it. The last thing he wanted was the IRS knocking on his door asking to see his W-2s. Now that problem was behind him. Instant, massive wealth allowed one to soar beyond the reach of the Revenue boys, and everyone else. Yes, it had been a great day, Romanello concluded.

Not finding a cab handy, he opted for the subway. It was very crowded and he could barely find standing room in one of the train cars. He rode the subway for a number of stops before pushing through the masses and once again hitting the street. He turned the key in his door, closed and locked it, and walked into the kitchen to drop off the bottle. He was about to take off his jacket and pour himself a glass of Chianti when someone knocked at the door. He squinted through the peephole. The brown uniform of the UPS man filled his line if vision.

"What's up?" he asked through the door.

"Got a delivery for an Anthony Romanello, this address." The UPS man was busily scanning the package, an eight-by-eleven-inch container that bulged out at the center.

Romanello opened the door.

"You Anthony Romanello?"

He nodded.

"Just sign right here, please." He handed Romanello a pen attached to what looked to be an electronic clipboard.

"You're not trying to serve me with legal papers, are you?" Romanello grinned as he signed for the package.

"They couldn't pay me enough to do that," the UPS man replied. "My brother-in-law used to be a process server up in Detroit. After he was shot the second time, he went to work driving a bakery truck. Here you go. Have a good one."

Romanello closed the door and felt the contents of the package through the thin cardboard. A smile broke across his lips. The second installment of his LuAnn Tyler hit. He had been told of the possibility of being called off. But his employer had assured him that the rest of the money would be forthcoming regardless. The smile froze on his face as it suddenly

139

struck him that the payment should have been mailed to his post office box. Nobody was supposed to know where he lived. Or his real name.

He whirled around at the sound behind him.

Jackson emerged from the shadows of the living room. Dressed as immaculately as when he had interviewed LuAnn, Jackson leaned against the doorway to the kitchen and looked Romanello up and down behind a pair of dark glasses. Jackson's hair was streaked with gray and a neatly trimmed beard covered his chin. His cheeks were large and puffy, the ears red and flattened-looking, both the result of carefully designed latex molds.

"Who the hell are you and how did you get in here?"

In response, Jackson pointed one gloved hand at the package. "Open it."

"What?" Romanello growled back.

"Count the money and make certain it's all there. Don't worry, you won't hurt my feelings by doing so."

"Look—"

Jackson slipped off the glasses and his eyes bored into Romanello. "Open it." The voice was barely above a whisper and spoken in an entirely non-threatening manner that made Romanello wonder why he was shivering inside. After all, he had murdered six people in premeditated fashion over the span of the last three years. Nobody intimidated him.

He quickly ripped open the package and the contents spilled out. Romanello watched as the cut-up newspaper drifted to the floor.

"Is this supposed to be funny? If it is, I'm not laughing." He glowered at Jackson.

Jackson shook his head sadly. "As soon as I hung up with you I knew my little slip over the phone

140

would prove to be serious. I made mention of LuAnn Tyler and money, and money, as you well know, makes people do strange things."

"What exactly are you talking about?"

"Mr. Romanello, you were hired to perform a job for me. Once that task was called off, your participation in my affairs was at an end. Or let me rephrase that: Your participation in my affairs was *supposed* to be at an end."

"They were at an end. I didn't kill the lady and all I get from you is cut-up newspaper. I'm the one who should be pissed."

Jackson ticked the points off with his fingers. "You followed the woman back to New York. You, in fact, have been following her all over the city. You sent her a note. You met with her, and while I wasn't privy to the conversation itself, from the looks of things the subject matter wasn't pleasant."

"How the hell do you know all that?"

"There isn't much I don't know, Mr. Romanello. There really isn't." Jackson put the glasses back on.

"Well, you can't prove anything."

Jackson laughed, a laugh that sent every hair on Romanello's neck skyward and made him reach for his gun, a gun that was no longer there.

Jackson looked at the man's amazed face and shook his head sadly. "Subways are so crowded this time of night. Pickpockets, I understand, can stalk honest people with impunity. There's no telling what else you might find missing."

"Well, like I said, you can't prove it. And it's not like you can just go to the cops. You hired me to kill someone. That doesn't do a whole lot for your credibility."

"I have no interest in going to the authorities. You disobeyed my instructions and in doing so jeopardized my plans. I came here to inform you that I was

141

aware of this, to plainly show you that the rest of your money has been forfeited because of your improper actions, and that I have decided upon the appropriate punishment. A punishment that I fully intend to mete out now."

Romanello drew himself up to his full six feet three inch height, towering over Jackson, and laughed heartily. "Well, if you came here to punish me, I hope you brought somebody else with you to do the punishing."

"I prefer to handle these matters myself."

"Well, then this is going to be your last job." In a flash, Romanello's hand went down to his ankle and he was erect again in a second, the jagged-edge blade in his right hand. He started forward and then stopped as he eyed the device in Jackson's hand.

"The touted advantages of strength and superior size are so often overrated, wouldn't you agree?" said Jackson. The twin darts shot out from the taser gun and hit Romanello dead center in the chest. Jackson continued to squeeze the trigger, sending 120,000 volts of electricity along the thin metal cords that were attached to the darts. Romanello went down as though poleaxed, and he lay there staring up as Jackson stood over him.

"I've held the trigger down for a full minute now, which will incapacitate you for at least fifteen minutes, more than ample for my purposes."

Romanello watched helplessly as Jackson knelt down beside him and gingerly pulled the two darts free and packed the apparatus back in his pocket. He carefully opened Romanello's shirt. "Quite hairy, Mr. Romanello. A medical examiner will never pick up on the extremely small holes in your chest." The next item Jackson withdrew from his coat would have left Romanello numb if he hadn't already been. With his tongue feeling as big as a knobby tree root,

Romanello thought he had suffered a stroke. His limbs were useless to him: there was no physical sensation at all. He could still see clearly, however, and suddenly wished he had been blinded as well. He watched in horror as Jackson methodically checked the hypodermic needle he held in his hand.

"It's mostly an innocuous saline solution, you know," Jackson said as though he were addressing a science class. "I say mostly, because what's lurking in here can be quite deadly under certain conditions." He smiled down at Romanello and paused for a moment as he considered the import of his own words and then continued. "This solution contains prostaglandin, a substance produced naturally in the body. Normal levels are measured in micrograms. I'm about to give you a dose several thousand times that, measured in milligrams in fact. When this dose hits your heart it will cause the coronary arteries to severely constrict, triggering what doctors would technically term a myocardial infarction or coronary occlusion, also known as a heart attack of the most devastating kind. To tell you the truth, I've never combined the effects of electrification caused by the stun gun with this method of inflicting death. It might be interesting to observe the process." Jackson was betraying no more emotion than if he were about to dissect a frog in biology class. "Since prostaglandin occurs naturally in the body, as I mentioned, it's also naturally metabolized by the body, meaning there will be no suspiciously high traces left for a medical examiner to detect. I'm currently working on a poison to which I will attach an enzyme, encapsulated by a special coating. The protective cover is quickly broken down by the components in the bloodstream; however, the poison will have ample time to do its work before that occurs. Once the protective coating is gone the enzymes will instantly react with the poison compound and break it down, in effect destroying it. They use a similar process to clean up oil slicks. It's absolutely untraceable. I was planning to use it on you tonight; however, the process is not yet perfected and I hate to rush things of that nature. Chemistry, after all, requires patience and precision. Hence, the fallback to the old reliable: prostaglandin."

Jackson held the needle very close to Romanello's neck, seeking the perfect entry site. "They will find you here, a young, strapping man felled in his prime by natural causes. Another statistic in the ongoing health debate."

Romanello's eyes almost exploded out of his head as he struggled with every ounce of will to break the grip of inertia the stun gun had caused. The veins stood out on his neck with the effort he was exerting and Jackson quietly thanked him for providing such a convenient place, right before the needle plunged into the jugular vein and its contents poured into his body. Jackson smiled and gently patted Romanello on the head as his pupils shot back and forth like a metronome.

From his bag, Jackson extracted a razor blade. "Now, a sharp-eyed medical examiner might pick up on the hypodermic's entry site, so we will have to address that." Using the razor, Jackson nicked Romanello's skin at the precise place the needle had gone in. A drop of blood floated to the surface of the skin. Jackson replaced the razor in the bag and pulled out a Band-Aid. He pressed it across the fresh cut and sat back to study his handiwork, smiling as he did so.

"I'm sorry that it's come to this, as your services might have been useful to me in the future." Jackson picked up one of Romanello's limp hands and made the sign of the cross over the stricken man's chest. "I know that you were raised Roman Catholic, Mr. Romanello," he said earnestly, "although you obviously have strayed from the teachings of the Church, but I'm afraid a priest to administer last rites is out of the question. I hardly think it matters where you're going anyway, do you? Purgatory is such a silly notion after all." He picked up Romanello's knife and placed it back in the sheath strapped to his ankle.

Jackson was about to stand up when he noted the edge of the newspaper sticking out from the inside of Romanello's jacket pocket. He nimbly plucked it out. As he read the article detailing the story of the two murders, drugs, LuAnn's disappearance, and the police's search for her, his features became grim. That explained a lot. Romanello was blackmailing her. Or attempting to. Had he discovered this piece of information a day earlier, Jackson's solution would have been simple. He would've executed LuAnn Tyler on the spot. Now he could not do that and he hated that he had lost partial control of the situation. She had already been confirmed as the winning ticket holder. She was scheduled to appear to the world in less than twenty-four hours as the lottery's newest winner. Yes, now her requests made more sense. He folded up the piece of paper and put it in his pocket. Like it or not, he was wedded to LuAnn Tyler, warts and all. It was a challenge, and, if nothing else, he loved a challenge. However, he would take control back. He would tell her exactly what she had to do, and if she didn't follow his instructions precisely, then he would kill her after she won the lottery.

Jackson gathered up the shredded newspaper and remnants of the UPS package. The dark suit he was wearing came off with a tug on certain discreet parts of the garment, and together with the now revealed body moldings that had given Jackson his girth, all of these items were packed in a pizza carrier bag that Jackson pulled from a corner of the living room. Underneath, a much slimmer Jackson was wearing the blue and white shirt proclaiming him to be a Domino's Pizza delivery person. From one of his pockets, he pulled out a piece of thread and, edging it carefully under the putty on his nose, lifted the piece cleanly off and stuck it in the pizza box. The mole, beard, and ear pieces he similarly discarded. He swabbed his face down with alcohol from a bottle pulled from his pocket, removing the shadows and highlights that had aged his face. His hands worked quickly and methodically from years of long practice. Last, he combed a gel through his hair that effectively removed the sprayed-on streaks of gray. He checked his altered appearance in a small mirror hanging on the wall. Then this chameleon landscape was swiftly altered by a small bristly mustache applied with spirit gum, and a hair extender hung in a long ponytail out from under the Yankee baseball cap he was now putting on. Dark glasses covered his eyes; dress shoes were replaced with tennis shoes. He once again checked his appearance: completely different. He had to smile. It was quite a talent. When Jackson quietly left the building a few seconds later, Romanello's features were relaxed, peaceful. They would forever remain so.

SIXTEEN

"Everything will be all right, LuAnn." Roger Davis, the young, handsome man who had announced the lottery drawing, said these words as he patted her on the hand. "I know you have to be nervous but I'll be right there with you. We'll make it as painless as possible for you, I give you my word," he said gallantly.

They were in a plush room inside the lottery building, just down the corridor from the large auditorium where a mass of press and regular folk awaited the latest lottery winner's arrival. LuAnn wore a pale blue knee-length dress with matching shoes, her hair and makeup impeccable thanks to the in-house staff at the Lottery Commission. The cut on her jaw had healed enough that she had opted for makeup instead of the bandage.

"You look beautiful, LuAnn," said Davis. "I can't remember a winner looking so ravishing, I mean that." He sat down right next to her, his leg touching hers.

LuAnn flashed him a quick smile, slid a couple of inches away and turned her attention to Lisa. "I don't want Lisa to have to go out there. All them lights and people would just scare her to death."

"That's fine. She can stay in here. We'll have someone watching her of course, every minute. Security is very tight here as you can imagine." He paused while he once again took in LuAnn's shapely form. "We'll announce that you have a daughter,

147

though. That's why your story is so great. Young mother and daughter, all this wealth. You must be so happy." He patted her on the knee and then let his hand linger for a moment before pulling it away. She wondered again whether he was in on all of it. Whether he knew she had won an enormous fortune by cheating. He looked the type, she concluded. The kind who would do anything for money. She imagined he would be very well paid for helping to pull off something this big.

"How long until we go out there?" she asked.

"About ten minutes." He smiled at her again and then said as casually as possible, "Uh, you weren't exactly clear on your marital status. Will your husband—"

"I'm not married," LuAnn said quickly.

"Oh, well, will the father of the child be attending?" He added quickly, "We just have to know for scheduling purposes."

LuAnn looked dead at him. "No, he won't."

Davis smiled confidently and inched closer. "I see. Hmmm." He made a steeple with his hands and rested them against his lips for a moment and then he laid one arm casually across the back of her seat. "Well, I don't know what your plans are, but if you need anyone to show you around town I am absolutely here for you, LuAnn, twenty-four hours a day. I know after living all your life in a small town, that the big city" – Davis lifted his other arm dramatically toward the ceiling – "must be very overwhelming. But I know it like the back of my hand. The best restaurants, theaters, shopping. We could have a great time." He edged still closer, his eyes hugging the contours of her body as his fingers drifted toward her shoulder.

"Oh, I'm sorry, Mr. Davis, I think maybe you got the wrong idea. Lisa's father ain't coming for the

148

press conference, but he's coming up after. He had to get leave first."

"Leave?"

"He's in the Navy. He's with the SEALs." She shook her head and stared off as if digging up some shocking memories. "Let me tell you, it downright scares me some of the stuff he's told me about. But if there's anybody that can take care of himself it's Frank. Why, he beat six guys unconscious in a bar one time 'cause they were coming on to me. He probably would've killed them if the police hadn't pulled him off, and it took five of them to do it, big, strong cops, too."

Davis's mouth dropped open and he scooted away from LuAnn. "Good Lord!"

"Oh, but don't say nothing about that at the press conference, Mr. Davis. What Frank does is all top-secret-like and he'd get real pissed at you if you said anything. Real pissed!" She stared intently at him, watching the waves of fear pour over his pretty-boy features.

Davis stood up abruptly. "No, of course not, not one word. I swear." Davis licked his lips and put a shaky hand through his heavily moussed hair. "I'd better go check on things, LuAnn." He managed a weak smile and gave her a shaky thumbs-up.

She returned the gesture. "Thanks so much for understanding, Mr. Davis." After he had gone, LuAnn turned back to Lisa. "You ain't never gonna have to do that, baby doll. And pretty soon, your momma ain't gonna have to do it no more either." She cradled Lisa against her chest and stared across at the clock on the wall, watching the time tick down.

Charlie glanced around the crowded auditorium while he methodically pushed his way toward the

149

front of the stage. He stopped at a spot where he could see clearly and waited. He would've liked to be up on the stage with LuAnn, giving her what he knew would be much needed moral support. However, that was out of the question. He had to remain in the background; raising suspicion was not part of his job description. He would see LuAnn after the press conference was completed. He also would have to tell her his decision about whether he would accompany her or not. The problem was he hadn't made up his mind yet. He stuffed his hand in his pocket for a cigarette and then remembered smoking wasn't permitted in the building. He really was craving the soothing influences of the tobacco and for a brief instant he contemplated sneaking outside for a quick one, but there wasn't enough time.

He sighed and his broad shoulders collapsed. He had spent the better part of his life roaming from point to point with nothing in the way of a comprehensive plan, nothing resembling long-term goals. He loved kids and would never have any of his own. He was paid well, but while money went a long way toward improving his physical sur-roundings it didn't really contribute to his genuine overall happiness. At his age, he figured this was as good as it was going to get. The avenues he had taken as a young man had pretty much dictated what the remaining years of his life would be like. Until now. LuAnn Tyler had offered him a way out of that. He held no delusions that she was interested in him sexually, and in the cold face of reality, away from her unpretentious and yet incredibly seductive presence, Charlie had concluded that he did not want that either. What he wanted was her sincere friendship, her goodness – two elements that had been appallingly lacking in his life. And that brought

150

him back to the choice. Should he go or not? If he went, he had little doubt that he would enjoy the hell out of LuAnn and Lisa, with an added plus of being a father figure for the little girl. For a few years anyway. But he had sat up most of the night thinking about what would happen after those first few years.

It was inevitable that beautiful LuAnn, with her new wealth, and the refinement that would come from those riches, would be the target of dozens of the world's most eligible men. She was very young, had one child, and would want more. She would marry one of these men. That man would assume the responsibility of fathering Lisa, and properly so. He would be the man in LuAnn's life. And where would that leave Charlie? He edged forward, squeezing between two CNN cameramen as he thought about this again. At some point, Charlie figured, he would be compelled to leave them. It would be too awkward. It wasn't like he was family or anything. And when that time came it would be painful, more painful than allowing his body to be used for a punching bag during his youth. After spending only a few days with them, he felt a bond with LuAnn and Lisa that he had not managed to form in over ten years of marriage with his ex-wife. What would it be like after three or four years together? Could he calmly walk away from Lisa and her mother without suffering an irreparably broken heart, a screwed-up psyche? He shook his head. What a tough guy he had turned out to be. He barely knew these simple people from the South and he was now engulfed in a life-churning decision the consequences of which he was extrapolating out years into the future.

A part of him said simply go for the ride and enjoy the hell out of yourself. You could be dead from a heart attack next year, what the hell did it matter? The other part of him, though, he was afraid, was winning the day. He knew that he could be LuAnn's friend for the rest of his life, but he didn't know if he could do it close-up, every day, with the knowledge that it might end abruptly. "Shit," he muttered. It came down to pure envy, he decided. If he were only twenty – he shrugged – okay, thirty years younger. Envy of the guy who would eventually win her. Win her love, a love that he was sure would last forever, at least on her side. And heaven help the poor man who betrayed her. She was a hellcat, that was easy to see. A firecracker with a heart of gold, but that was a big part of the attraction: Polar opposites like that in the same fragile shell of skin and bones and raw nerve endings was a rare find.

Charlie abruptly stopped his musings and looked up at the stage. The entire crowd seemed to tense all at once, like a biceps flexing and forming a ridge of muscle. Then the cameras started clicking away as LuAnn, tall, queenly, and calm, walked gracefully into their field of vision and stood before them all. Charlie shook his head in silent wonderment. "Damn," he said under his breath. She had just made his decision that much harder.

Sheriff Roy Waymer nearly spit his mouthful of beer clear across the room as he watched LuAnn Tyler waving back at him from the TV. "Jesus, Joseph, Mary!" He looked over at his wife, Doris, whose eyes were boring into the twenty-seven-inch screen.

"You been looking for her all over the county and there she is right there in New York City," Doris exclaimed. "The gall of that girl. And she just won all that money." Doris said this bitterly as she wrung her hands together; twenty-four torn-up lottery tickets resided in the trash can in her back yard.

Waymer wrestled his considerable girth out of his

La-Z-Boy and headed toward the telephone. "I phoned up to the train stations around here and at the airport in Atlanta, but I hadn't heard nothing back yet. I didn't take her to be heading up to no New York, though. I didn't put no APB out on LuAnn because I didn't think she'd be able to get out of the county, much less the state. I mean, the girl ain't even got a car. And she had the baby and all. I thought for sure she'd just hightailed it over to some friend's house."

"Well, it sure looks like she slipped right out on you." Doris pointed at LuAnn on the TV. "Right or wrong there ain't many people that look like that, that's for sure."

"Well, Mother," he said to his wife, "we don't exactly have the manpower of the FBI down here. With Freddie out with his back I only got two uniformed officers on duty. And the state police are up to their eyeballs in work; they couldn't spare nobody." He picked up the phone.

Doris looked at him anxiously. "You think LuAnn killed Duane and that other boy?"

Waymer held the phone up to his ear and shrugged. "LuAnn could kick the crap out of most men I know. She sure as hell could Duane. But that other guy was a hoss, almost three hundred pounds." He started punching in numbers on the phone. "But she coulda snuck up behind him and smashed that phone over his head. She'd been in a fight. More than one person saw her with a bandage on her chin that day."

"Drugs was behind it, that's for sure," Doris said. "That poor little baby in that trailer with all them drugs."

Waymer was nodding his head. "I know that."

"I bet'cha LuAnn was the brains behind it all. She's sharp, all right, we all know that. And she was always too good for us. She tried to hide it, but we could all see through that. She didn't belong here, she wanted to get out, but she didn't have no way. Drug money, that was her way, you mark my words, Roy."

"I hear you, Mother. Except she don't need drug money no more." He nodded toward the TV.

"You best hurry up then, before she gets away."

"I'll contact the police up in New York to go pick her up."

"Think they'll do that?"

"Mother, she's a possible suspect in a double murder investigation," he said importantly. "Even if she ain't done nothing wrong, she's probably gonna be what they call a material witness."

"Yeah, but you think those Yankee police up in New York gonna care about that? Huh!"

"Police is police, Doris, North or South. The law's the law."

Unconvinced of the virtues of her Northern compatriots, Doris snorted and then suddenly looked hopeful. "Well, if she's convicted wouldn't she have to give back the money she won?" Doris looked back at the TV, at LuAnn's smiling face, wondering whether to go out to the trash and try to reconstruct all those lottery tickets. "She sure as heck wouldn't need all that money in prison, would she?"

Sheriff Waymer didn't answer. He was now trying to get through to the NYPD.

LuAnn held the big check, waved, and smiled at the crowds and answered a barrage of questions thrown at her from all sides of the vast room. Her picture was transported across the United States and then across the world.

Had she definitive plans for the money? If so, what were they?

"You'll know," LuAnn answered. "You'll see, but you'll just have to wait."

There were a series of predictably stupid questions such as "Do you feel lucky?"

"Incredibly," she responded. "More than you'll ever know."

"Will you spend it all in one place?"

"Not likely unless it's a really, really big place."

"Will you help your family?"

"I'll help all the people I care about."

Three times her hand was sought in matrimony. She answered each suitor differently and with polite humor but the bottom line was always "No." Charlie silently fumed at these exchanges; and then, checking his watch, he made his way out of the room.

After more questions, more photos, and more laughter and smiles, the press conference was finally over and LuAnn was escorted off the stage. She returned to the holding room, quickly changed into slacks and a blouse, erased all the makeup from her face, piled her long hair under a cowboy hat, and picked up Lisa. She checked her watch. Barely twenty minutes had passed since she had been introduced to the world as the new lottery winner. She expected that the local sheriff would be contacting the New York police by now. Everyone from LuAnn's hometown watched the lottery drawing religiously including Sheriff Roy Waymer. The timing would be very tight.

Davis leaned his head in the door. "Uh, Ms. Tyler, there's a car waiting for you at the rear entrance to the building. I'll have someone escort you down if you're ready."

"Ready as I'll ever be." When he turned to leave, LuAnn called after him. "If anybody shows up asking for me, I'll be at my hotel."

Davis looked at her coldly. "Are you expecting anyone?"

"Lisa's father, Frank."

Davis's face tightened. "And you're staying at?"

"The Plaza."

"Of course."

"But please don't tell anybody else where I am. I haven't seen Frank in a while. He's been on maneuvers for almost three months. So we don't want to be disturbed." She arched her eyebrows wickedly and smiled. "You know what I mean?"

Davis managed a very insincere smile and made a mock bow. "You can trust me implicitly, Ms. Tyler. Your chariot awaits."

Inwardly, LuAnn smiled. Now she was certain that when the police came for her, they would be directed as fast as possible to the Plaza Hotel. That would gain her the precious moments she would need to escape this town, and this country. Her new life was about to begin.

SEVENTEEN

The rear exit was very private and thus very quiet. A black stretch limo confronted LuAnn as she left the building. The chauffeur tipped his hat to her and held open the door. She got in and settled Lisa in the seat next to her.

"Good work, LuAnn. Your performance was flawless," Jackson said.

LuAnn nearly screamed out as she jerked around and stared into the dark recesses of the limo's far corner. All the interior lights in the rear of the limo were off except for a solitary one directly over her head that suddenly came on, illuminating her. She felt as though she were back on the stage at the lottery building. She could barely make out his shape as he hunkered back into his seat.

His voice drifted out to her. "Really very poised and dignified, a touch of humor when it was called for, the reporters eat that up, you know. And of course the looks to top it all off. *Tres* marriage proposals during one press conference is certainly a record as far as I'm aware."

LuAnn composed herself and settled back into her seat as the limo proceeded down the street. "Thank you."

"Quite frankly I was concerned that you would make a complete fool of yourself. Nothing against you of course. As I said before, you are an intelligent young woman; however, anyone, no matter their sophistication, thrust into a strange situation, is more apt to fail than not, wouldn't you agree?"

"I've had a lot of practice."

"Excuse me?" Jackson leaned forward slightly but still remained hidden from her view. "Practice with what?"

LuAnn stared toward the darkened corner, her vision blocked by the shining light. "Strange situations."

"You know, LuAnn, you really do amaze me sometimes, you really do. In some limited instances your perspicacity rivals my own and I don't say that lightly." He stared at her for several more seconds and then opened a briefcase lying on the seat next to him and pulled out several pieces of paper. As he sat back against the soft leather, a smile played across his features and a sigh of contentment escaped his lips.

"And now, LuAnn, it's time to discuss the conditions."

LuAnn fumbled with her blouse before crossing her legs. "We need to talk about something first."

Jackson cocked his head. "Really? And what might that be?"

LuAnn let out a deep breath. She had stayed awake all night deciding how best to tell him about the man calling himself Rainbow. She had first wondered whether Jackson needed to know at all. Then she decided that since it was about the money, then he would probably find out at some point. Better it be from her.

"A man came and talked to me yesterday."

"A man, you say. What about?"

"He wanted money from me."

Jackson laughed. "LuAnn, my dear, everybody will want money from you."

"No, it's not like that. He wanted half of my winnings."

"Excuse me? That's absurd."

"No it ain't. He . . . he had some information about me, things that had happened to me, that he said he would tell, if I didn't pay him."

"My goodness, what sorts of things?"

LuAnn paused and looked out the window. "Can I have something to drink?"

"Help yourself." A gloved finger came out of the darkness and pointed to the door built into one side of the limo. LuAnn did not look in his direction as she opened the refrigerator door and pulled out a Coke.

She took a long drink, wiped her lips, and continued. "Something happened to me right before I called to tell you I was going to take your offer."

"Would that possibly be the two dead bodies in your trailer? The drugs there? The fact that the police are looking for you? Or perhaps something else you tried to hide from me?" She didn't answer at first, nervously cradling the soda in her lap, the astonishment clear on her face.

"I didn't have nothing to do with those drugs. And that man was trying to kill me. I was just protecting myself."

"I should have realized when you wanted to leave town so quickly, change your name, all that, that there was something up." He shook his head sadly. "My poor, poor LuAnn. I guess I would've left town quickly too, confronted with those circumstances. And who would have thought it of our little Duane. Drugs! How terrible. But I tell you what, out of the goodness of my heart, I won't hold it against you. What's past is past. However" – here Jackson's tone became starkly forceful – "don't ever try to hide anything from me again, LuAnn. Please don't do that to yourself."

"But this man—"

Jackson spoke impatiently. "That's taken care of. You certainly won't be giving any money to him."

She stared into the darkness, amazement spreading across her face. "But how could you have done that?"

"People are always saying that about me: How could I have done that?" Jackson looked amused and said in a slightly hushed voice, "I can do anything, LuAnn, don't you know that by now? Anything. Does that frighten you? If it doesn't, it should. It even frightens me sometimes."

"The man said he was sent to kill me."

"Indeed."

"But then he got called off."

"How terribly peculiar."

"Timewise, I figure he got called off right after I called you and said I'd do it."

"Life is chock full of coincidences, isn't it?" Jackson's tone had become mocking.

Now LuAnn's features took on their own glint of ferocity. "I get bit, I bite back, real hard. Just so we understand each other, Mr. Jackson."

"I think we understand each other perfectly, LuAnn." In the darkness, she heard papers rustling. "However, this certainly complicates matters. When you wanted your name changed, I thought we could still do everything aboveboard."

"What do you mean?"

"Taxes, LuAnn. We do have the issue of taxes."

"But I thought all that money was mine to keep. The government couldn't touch it. That's what all the ads say."

"That's not exactly true. In fact the advertising is very misleading. Funny how the government can do that. The principal is not tax-free, it's *tax-deferred*. But only for the first year."

"What the hell does that mean?"

160

"It means that for the first year the winner pays no federal or state taxes, but the amount of that tax is simply deferred until the next year. The underlying tax is still owed, it's just the timing that's affected. No penalties or interest will accrue of course, so long as payment is made on a timely basis during the next tax year. The law states that the tax must be paid over ten years in equal installments. On one hundred million dollars, for example, you will owe roughly fifty million dollars in state and federal income tax, or one half the total amount. You're obviously in the highest tax bracket now. Divided by ten years the tax payment comes to five million dollars per year. In addition to that, generally speaking, any money you earn from the principal amount is taxable without any type of tax-deferred status.

"And I must tell you, LuAnn, I have plans for that principal, rather grand plans. You will make a great deal more money in the coming years; however, it will almost all be taxable income, dividends, capital gains, interest from taxable bonds, that sort of thing. That ordinarily would not present a problem, since law-abiding citizens who are not on the run from the police under an assumed name can file their tax returns, pay their fair share of tax, and live quite nicely. You can no longer do that. If my people filed your tax return under the name LuAnn Tyler with your current address and other personal inform-ation, don't you think the police might come knocking on your door?"

"Well, can't I pay tax under my new name?"

"Ah, potentially a brilliant solution; however, the IRS tends to get quite curious when the very first tax return filed by someone barely out of her teens has so many zeros on it. They might wonder what you were doing before and why all of a sudden you're richer than a Rockefeller. Again, the result would probably be the police, or even more likely the FBI, knocking on your door. No, that won't really do."

"So what do we do?"

When Jackson next spoke, the tone that reached LuAnn's ears made her tighten her grip on Lisa.

"You will do exactly as I tell you, LuAnn. You are ticketed on a flight that will take you out of the country. You will never return to the United States. This little mess in Georgia has bestowed upon you a life on the move. Forever, I'm afraid."

"But—"

"There's no *but* to it, LuAnn, that is the way it will be. Do you understand?"

LuAnn sat back against the leather seat and said stubbornly, "I got enough money now to where I can handle myself okay. And I don't like people telling me what to do."

"Is that right?" Jackson's hand closed around the pistol he had lifted from his briefcase. In the darkness he could have swung it up in an instant: mother and child obliterated. "Well, then why don't you take your chances on getting out of the country by yourself. Would you like to do that?"

"I can take care of myself."

"That's not the point. You made a deal with me, LuAnn. A deal I expect you to honor. Unless you're a fool you will work with me and not against me. You will see that in the long run your and my interests are the same. Otherwise, I can stop the limo right here, toss you and the child out, and I'll phone the police to come and pick you up. It's your choice. Decide. Now!"

Confronted with that option, LuAnn looked desperately around the interior of the limo. Her eyes finally settled on Lisa. Her daughter looked up at her with big, soft eyes; there was complete faith there.

162

LuAnn let out a deep breath. What choice did she really have?

"All right."

Jackson again rustled the papers he held. "Now, we have just enough time to go over these documents. There are a number of them for you to sign, but let me discuss the principal terms first. I will try to be as simple in my explanation as possible.

"You have just won one hundred million dollars and change. As we speak, that money has been placed in a special escrow account set up by the Lottery Commission under your name. By the way, I have obtained a Social Security number for you, under your *new* name. It makes life so much easier when you have one of those. Once you execute these papers my people will be able to transfer the funds out of that account and into one over which I will have complete and total control."

"But how do *I* get to the money?" LuAnn protested.

"Patience, LuAnn, all will be explained. The money will be invested as I see fit and for my own account. However, from those investment funds you will be guaranteed a minimum return of twenty-five percent per annum, which comes to approximately twenty-five million dollars per year. Those funds will be available to you all during the course of the year. I have accountants and financial advisors who will handle all of that for you, don't worry." He held up a cautionary finger. "Understand that that is income from principal. The one hundred million is never touched. I will control that principal amount for a period of ten years and invest it however I choose. It will take several months or more to fully implement my plans for the money, so the ten-year period will commence approximately in the late fall of this year. I will provide you with the exact date later. Ten years from that date, you will receive the full one hundred million dollars back. Any of the yearly income you've earned over the ten years is of course yours to keep. We will invest that for you as well, free of charge. I'm sure you're ignorant of this, but at that rate, your money, compounded, less even an exorbitant personal allowance, will double approximately every three years, particularly when you don't pay any taxes. Under practically any reasonable projection, you will be worth hundreds of millions of dollars at the end of the ten-year period, risk-free." Jackson's eyes sparkled as he rattled off the figures. "It's positively intoxicating, isn't it, LuAnn? It just beats the hell out of a hundred dollars a day, doesn't it? You've come a long way in less than a week, you truly have." He laughed heartily. "To start you off, I will advance you the sum of five million dollars, interest-free. That should be sufficient to keep you until the investment earnings come rolling in."

LuAnn swallowed hard at the mention of the gigantic sums. "I don't know nothing about investing, but how can you guarantee me so much money each year?"

Jackson looked disappointed. "The same way I could *guarantee* that you would win the lottery. If I can perform that magic, I think I can handle Wall Street."

"What if something should happen to me?"

"The contract you will be signing binds your heirs and assigns." He nodded at Lisa. "Your daughter. However, that income would go to her and at the end of the ten-year period so would the principal amount. There's also a power of attorney form. I took the liberty of already having filled in the notary panel. I'm a man of many talents." He chuckled lightly. From out of the darkness, Jackson extended the packet of documents and a pen to her. "They're clearly marked where your signature is required. I trust that you are satisfied with the terms. I told you from the start that they would be generous, didn't I?"

LuAnn hesitated for an instant.

"Is there a problem, LuAnn?" Jackson asked sharply.

She shook her head, quickly signed the documents, and handed them back. Jackson took the documents and slid open a compartment in the console of the limo.

LuAnn heard Jackson make some tapping sounds and a loud screech ensued and then stopped.

Jackson said, "Faxes are wonderful things especially when time is of the essence. Within ten minutes the funds will be wired into my account." He picked the papers up as they slid out of the machine and placed them back into his briefcase.

"Your bags are in the trunk. I have your plane tickets and hotel reservations with me. I have planned your itinerary out for the first twelve months. It will be a great deal of travel; however, I think the scenery will be pleasant enough. I have honored your request to travel to Sweden, the land of your maternal ancestors. Think of it all as an extremely long vacation. I may have you end up in Monaco. They have no personal income tax. However, out of an abundance of caution I'm putting together and thoroughly documenting an intricate cover story for you. In sum, you left the States as a very young girl. You met and married a wealthy foreign national. The money will be kept only in foreign banks and offshore accounts. U.S. banks have stringent reporting requirements to the IRS. None of your money will ever, ever be kept in the United States. However, keep in mind that you will be traveling under a United States passport as a

United States citizen. Some accounts of your wealth may well trickle back here. We have to be prepared for that. However, if the money is all your husband's, who is not an American citizen, who does not reside at any time in this country, who earns no income directly in America, or from investments or business endeavors connected to this country, then, generally speaking, the IRS cannot touch you. I won't bore you with the complex tax rules having to do with U.S. source income such as interest on bonds issued by U.S. concerns, dividends paid by U.S. corporations, other transactions and sales of property having some tangible connection to the United States that could trip up the unwary. My people will take care of all that. Believe me when I say it won't be a problem."

LuAnn reached out for the tickets.

"Not quite yet, LuAnn, we have some steps to take. The police," he said pointedly.

"I took care of that."

"Oh, did you now?" His tone was one of amusement. "Well, I would be very surprised if New York's Finest weren't stationing themselves at every airport, bus, and train station right this very minute. Since you're a felon fleeing across state lines, they've probably called the FBI in as well. They're sharp. It's not like they'll be waiting patiently at your hotel for you to show up." He looked out the window of the limo. "We have some preparations to take care of. It'll give the police additional time to set up their net; however, it's a trade-off we have to make."

As Jackson was talking, LuAnn felt the limo slow down and then stop. Then she heard a long, slow clanking sound, as though a door were being raised. When it stopped, the limo pulled through and then stopped again.

The limo phone rang and Jackson quickly

answered it. He listened for a few moments and then hung up. "Confirmation that the hundred million dollars has been received; though it's after regular banking hours, I'd had special arrangements in place. Omniscience is such a rewarding gift."

He patted the seat. "Now I need you to sit next to me. First, close your eyes and then give me your hand so I can guide you," Jackson said, reaching for it out of the darkness.

"Why do I have to close my eyes?"

"Indulge me, LuAnn. I can't resist a little drama in life, particularly since it's so rare. I can assure you that what I'm about to do will be absolutely essential to your safely evading the police and starting your new life."

LuAnn started to question him again but then thought better of it. She took his hand and closed her eyes.

He settled her down beside him. She could feel a light shine down on her features. She jerked as she felt the scissors cut into her hair. Jackson's breath was right next to her ear. "I would advise you not to do that again. It's hard enough to do this in such a small space with limited time and equipment. I wouldn't want to do you serious damage." Jackson continued cutting until her hair stopped just above her ears. He periodically stuffed the cut hair into a large trash bag. A wet substance was continually run through the remaining strands and then it quickly hardened almost like concrete. Jackson used a styling brush to manipulate the remaining strands into place.

Jackson next clamped a portable mirror surrounded by non-heating light bulbs to the edge of the limo's console. Ordinarily, with the nose job he was going to perform, he would employ two mirrors to test profile constantly; however, he didn't have that luxury sitting in a limo in a Manhattan underground parking garage. He opened up his kit, a ten-tray case filled with makeup supplies and a myriad of tools with which to apply them and then set to work. She felt his nimble fingers flying over her face. He blocked out her eyebrows with Kryolan's eyebrow plastic, covered them with a sealer, dressed the area with a creme stick, and then powdered it. Then he created totally new ones using a small brush. He thoroughly cleansed the lower part of her face with rubbing alcohol. He applied spirit gum to her nose, and let it dry. While it did so, he applied K-Y lubricating jelly to his fingers so the putty he was going to use wouldn't stick to them. He let the putty heat up in his hand, and then commenced applying the malleable substance to her nose, methodically kneading and pressing until a satisfactory shape was created. "Your nose is long and straight, LuAnn, classic, really. However, a little putty, a little shadowing and highlighting and, *voilà*, we have a thick, crooked piece of cartilage that isn't nearly as becoming. However, it's only temporary. Everyone, after all, is only temporary." He chuckled lightly at this philosophical statement as he went through the process of stippling the putty with a black stipple sponge, powdering the surface, stippling in a foundation color, and adding rouge to the nares to give a natural appearance. Using subtle shadowing and highlights, he made LuAnn's eyes seem closer together, and made her chin and jawline seem less prominent with the aid of powders and creams. Rouge was placed skillfully on the cheekbones to lessen their impact on her overall appearance.

She felt him gently examining the wound on her jaw. "Nasty cut. Souvenir from your trailer experience?" When LuAnn didn't answer, he said, "You know this will require some stitching. Even with that, it's deep enough that it probably will scar. Don't worry, after I'm done, it will be invisible. But eventually, you may want to consider plastic surgery." He chuckled again and added, "In my professional opinion."

Next, Jackson carefully painted her lips. "A little thinner, I'm afraid, than the classical model, LuAnn. You may want to consider collagen at some point."

It was all LuAnn could do not to jump up and run screaming from him. She had no idea what she was going to look like; it was as though he were some mad scientist bringing her back from the dead.

"I'm stippling in freckles now, along the forehead, around the nose and cheeks. If I had time, I'd do your hands as well, but I don't. No one would notice anyway, most people are so unobservant." He spread open the collar of her shirt and applied foundation and stippling around her neck. Then he buttoned her shirt up, repacked his equipment, and guided her back to her seat.

"There's a small mirror in the compartment next to you," Jackson informed her.

LuAnn slowly pulled out the mirror and held it up in front of her face. She gasped. Looking back at her was a redheaded woman with short, spiky hair, a very light, almost albino complexion, and an abundance of freckles. Her eyes were smaller and closer together, her chin and jawline less prominent, the cheeks flat and oval. Her lips were a deep red and made her mouth look huge. Her nose was much broader and bore a distinctive curve to the right. Her dark eyebrows were now tinted a much lighter color. She was completely unrecognizable to herself.

Jackson tossed something on her lap. She looked down. It was a passport. She opened it. The photo staring back at her was the same woman whom she had looked at in the mirror.

169

"Wonderful work, wouldn't you say?" Jackson said.

As LuAnn looked up, Jackson hit a switch and a light illuminated him. Or her, rather, as LuAnn received a second jolt. Sitting across from her was her double, or the double of the woman she had just become. The same short red hair, facial complexion, crooked nose, everything – it was as though she had suddenly discovered a twin. The only difference was she was wearing jeans and her twin was wearing a dress.

LuAnn was too amazed to speak.

Jackson quietly clapped his hands together. "I've impersonated women before, but I believe this is the first time I've impersonated an impersonation. That photo of me, by the way. Taken this morning. I think I hit it rather well, although I don't think I did your bust justice. Well, even 'twins' needn't be identical in every respect." He smiled at her shocked look. "No need to applaud, however I do think that considering the working conditions, it does deserve some degree of acclaim."

The limo started moving again. They exited the garage and a little more than half an hour later, they arrived at JFK.

Before the driver opened the door, Jackson looked sharply at LuAnn. "Don't put on your hat or your glasses, as that suggests attempting to hide one's features and you could conceivably mess up the makeup. Remember, rule number one: When trying to hide, make yourself as obvious as possible, put yourself right out in the open. Seeing adult twins together is fairly rare, however, but while people – the police included – will notice us, perhaps even gawk, there will be no levels of suspicion. In addition, the police will be looking for one woman. When they see two together, and twins at that, even with a child, they'll discount us entirely, even as they stare at us. It's just human nature. They have a lot of ground to cover and not much time."

Jackson reached across for Lisa. LuAnn automatically blocked his hand, looking at him suspiciously.

"LuAnn, I am trying my best to get you and this little girl safely out of the country. We will shortly be walking through a squadron of police and FBI agents who will be doing their best to apprehend you. Believe me, I have no interest in keeping your daughter, but I do need her for a very specific reason."

Finally, LuAnn let go. They climbed out of the limo. In high heels Jackson was a little taller than LuAnn. She noted that he had a long, lean build that, she had to admit, looked good in the stylish clothing. He put a black coat on over his dark dress.

"Come on," he said to LuAnn. She stiffened at the new tone of his voice. Now he also *sounded* exactly like her.

"Where's Charlie?" LuAnn asked as they entered the terminal a few minutes later, a chubby skycap with the bags in tow.

"Why?" Jackson said quietly. He expertly maneuvered in the high heels.

LuAnn shrugged. "Just wondering. He'd been taking me around before. I thought I'd see him today."

"I'm afraid Charlie's duties with you are at an end."

"Oh."

"Don't worry, LuAnn, you're in much better hands." They entered the terminal and Jackson glanced up ahead. "Please act natural; we're twin sisters, if anyone asks, which they won't. However, I

171

have identification to support that cover just in case they do. Let me do the talking."

LuAnn looked up ahead and swallowed quickly as she eyed the quartet of police officers carefully scrutinizing each of the patrons at the crowded airport.

They passed by the officers, who did indeed stare at them. One even took a moment to check out Jackson's long legs as the coat he was wearing flapped open. Jackson seemed pleased at the attention. Then, just as Jackson had predicted, the police quickly lost interest in them and focused on other persons coming into the terminal.

Jackson and LuAnn stopped near the international flight check-in for British Airways. "I'll check in at the ticket counter for you while you wait over near that snack bar." Jackson pointed across the broad aisle of the terminal.

"Why can't I check in myself?"

"How many times have you flown overseas?"

"I ain't never flown."

"Precisely. I can get through the process a lot faster than you. If you messed up something, said something you weren't supposed to, then we might attract some attention that we don't really need right now. Airline personnel aren't the most security conscious people I've ever run across but they're not idiots either and you'd be surprised what they pick up on."

"All right. I don't want to mess nothing up."

"Good, now give me your passport, the one I just gave you." LuAnn did so and watched as Jackson, the skycap behind him, swung Lisa's baby carrier in one hand as he sauntered over to the ticket counter. Jackson had even picked up that mannerism of hers. LuAnn shook her head in awe and moved over to the spot designated by Jackson.

Jackson was in the very short first-class line and it

moved very quickly. He rejoined LuAnn in a few minutes. "So far, so good. Now, I wouldn't recommend changing your appearance for several months. You can wash the red dye out of course, although, frankly, I think the color works well on you." His eyes twinkled. "Once things die down, and your hair grows out, you can use the passport I originally made up for you." He handed a second U.S. passport to her, which she quickly put in her bag.

From the corner of his eye, Jackson watched as two men and a woman all dressed in suits moved down the aisle, their eyes sweeping the area. Jackson cleared his throat and LuAnn glanced in their direction and then away again. LuAnn had spied, in one of their hands, a piece of paper. On it was a picture of her, no doubt taken at the press conference. She froze until she felt Jackson's hand inside hers. He gave it a reassuring squeeze. "Those are FBI agents. But just remember that you don't look anything like that photo now. It's as if you're invisible." His confident tones assuaged her fears. Jackson moved forward. "Your flight leaves in twenty minutes. Follow me." They went through security and down to the departure gate and sat down in the waiting area.

"Here." Jackson handed her the passport, along with a small packet. "There's cash, credit cards, and an international driver's license in there, all in your new name. And your new appearance with respect to the driver's license." He took a moment to toy with her hair in a completely clinical fashion. He scrutinized her altered features and came away duly impressed with himself again. Jackson took a moment to grip her by the hand and even patted her shoulder. "Good luck. If you find yourself in difficulty at any time, here is a phone number that will reach me anywhere in the world day or night. I will tell you, though, that unless there is a problem you and I will never meet or speak to each other again." He handed her the card with the number on it.

"Isn't there something you want to say to me, LuAnn?" Jackson was smiling pleasantly.

She looked at him curiously and shook her head. "Like what?"

"Perhaps, thank you?" he said, no longer smiling.

"Thank you," she said very slowly. It was difficult pulling her gaze away from him.

"You're welcome," he said very slowly back, his eyes riveted to hers.

Finally, LuAnn nervously looked down at the card. She hoped she would never have to use it. If she never looked upon Jackson's face again, it would be all right with her. The way she felt around the man was too close to the feeling she had experienced at the cemetery when her father's grave had threatened to swallow her up. When she looked up again, Jackson had disappeared into the crowd.

She sighed. She was already tired of running and now she was about to start a lifetime of just that.

LuAnn took out her passport and looked at its blank pages. That would soon change. Then she turned back to the first page and stared at the strange photo and the stranger name underneath it. A name that would not be so unusual after a while: Catherine Savage from Charlottesville, Virginia. Her mother had been born in Charlottesville before moving as a young girl into the deep South. Her mother had spoken to LuAnn often of the good times she had as a child in the beautiful, rolling countryside of Virginia. Moving to Georgia and marrying Benny Tyler had abruptly ended those good times. LuAnn thought it appropriate that her new identity should call that city her hometown as well. Her new name had been well thought out too. A savage she was and a savage she would remain despite an enormous fortune at her command. She

174

looked at the photo again and her skin tingled as she remembered that it was Jackson staring back at her. She quickly closed the passport and put it away.

She touched her new face gingerly and then looked away after she eyed another policeman making his way toward her. She couldn't tell if he was one of the ones who might have seen Jackson check in for her. If so, what if he watched her get on the plane instead of Jackson? Her mouth went dry and she silently wished that Jackson hadn't left. Her flight was called. As the policeman approached, LuAnn willed herself to stand. As she picked up Lisa her packet of documents tumbled to the floor. Her heart trembling, she bent down to retrieve them with one hand, at the same time awkwardly balancing Lisa in her car seat with her other. She suddenly found herself staring at a pair of black shoes. The cop bent down and looked her over. In one hand he held a photo of her. LuAnn froze for an instant as his dark eyes bored into hers.

A kindly smile emerged on his face. "Let me help you, ma'am. I've got kids of my own. Traveling with them is never easy."

He scooped up the papers, replaced them in the packet, and handed it to her. LuAnn thanked him and he tipped his cap to her before moving off.

LuAnn was sure that if someone had cut her at that instant no blood would have come out. It was all frozen inside her.

Since first-class passengers could board at their leisure, LuAnn took some time to look around; however, her hopes were fading. It was clear that Charlie wasn't coming. She walked down the jet-walk and the flight attendant greeted her warmly while LuAnn marveled at the interior size of the Boeing 747.

"Right this way, Ms. Savage. Beautiful little girl." LuAnn was led up a spiral staircase and escorted to her seat. With Lisa in the seat next to her, LuAnn accepted a glass of wine from the cabin attendant. She again looked around the lavish space in awe and noted the built-in TV and phone at each seat. She had never been on a plane before. This was quite a princely way to experience it for the first time.

The darkness was rapidly gathering as she looked out the window. For now Lisa was content to look around the cabin and LuAnn used the time to think while she sipped on her wine. She took a series of deep breaths and then studied the other passengers as they entered the first-class compartment. Some were elderly and expensively dressed. Others were in business suits. One young man wore jeans and a sweatshirt. LuAnn thought she recognized him as a member of a big-time rock band. She settled back in her seat and then jumped a bit as the plane pushed back from its moorings. The flight attendants went through their pre-flight safety drill and within ten minutes the giant plane was lumbering down the runway. LuAnn held on to the sides of her seat and gritted her teeth as the plane rocked and swayed while it gathered speed. She didn't dare look outside the window. Oh Lord, what had she done? One of her arms flew protectively over Lisa, who appeared far calmer than her mother. Then with a graceful motion, the plane lifted into the air and the lurching and swaying stopped. LuAnn felt as though she were floating into the sky on an enormous bubble. A princess on a magic carpet; the image swept into her mind and stayed there. Her grip relaxed, her lips parted. She looked out the window and down at the twinkling lights of the city, the country she was leaving behind. Forever, according to Jackson. She gave a symbolic wave out the window and then leaned back against the seat.

Twenty minutes later she had put on her headphones and was gently swaying her head to some classical music. She jerked upright when the hand fell upon her shoulder and Charlie's voice filtered down to her. He wore the hat she had bought him. His smile was big and genuine, but there was a nervousness evident in his body language, the twitching of his eyes. LuAnn took off the headphones.

"Good gosh," he whispered. "If I hadn't recognized Lisa I would've passed right by you. What the hell happened?"

"A long story." She gripped his wrist tightly and let out a barely audible sigh. "Does this mean you're finally gonna tell me your real name, Charlie?"

A light rain had started to fall on the city shortly after the 747 had lifted off. Walking slowly down the street in midtown Manhattan with the aid of a cane, the man in the black trench coat and waterproof hat seemed not to notice the inclement weather. Jackson's appearance had changed drastically since his last encounter with LuAnn. He had aged at least forty years. Heavy pouches hung under his eyes, a fringe of brittle white hair circled the back of his bald head, which was mottled all over with age spots. The nose was long and saggy, the chin and neck equally so. His gait, slow and measured, matched the feebleness of his character. He often aged himself at night, as though when darkness came he felt compelled to shrink down, to draw nearer to old age, to death. He looked up into the cloudy sky. The plane would be over Nova Scotia about now as it traveled along its convex path to Europe.

And she had not gone alone; Charlie had gone off with her. Jackson had stayed behind after dropping off LuAnn and watched Charlie board the aircraft, not knowing his employer was only a few feet away. That arrangement might work out all right after all, Jackson

177

thought. He had doubts about LuAnn, serious doubts. She had withheld information from him, usually an unpardonable sin. He had managed to avoid a serious problem by eliminating Romanello, and he had to concede that the difficulty had been partially his in the making. He had, after all, hired Romanello to kill his chosen one if she had failed to accept his offer. However, he had never before had a winner on the run from the police. He would do what he always did when confronted with a possible disaster: He would sit back and observe. If things continued to run smoothly he would do nothing. At the slightest sign of trouble, however, he would take immediate and forceful action. So having capable Charlie along with her might prove to be a good thing. LuAnn was different from the others, that was certain.

Jackson pulled his collar up and slowly ambled down a side street. New York City in the darkness and rain held no terror for him. He was heavily armed and expertly skilled in innumerable ways of killing anything that breathed. Anyone targeting the "old man" as easy pickings would painfully realize the mistake. Jackson had no desire to kill. It was sometimes necessary, but he took no pleasure in it. Only the attainment of money, power, or ideally both, would suffice as justification in his mind. He had far better things to do with his time.

Jackson turned his face once again to the sky. The light rain fell on the latex folds of his "face." He licked at them; they were cool to the touch, felt good against his real skin. Godspeed to you both, he said under his breath and then smiled.

And God help you if you ever betray me.

He continued down the street, thinking intently and whistling while he did so. It was now time to plan for next month's winner.

PART TWO

Ten Years Later

EIGHTEEN

The small private jet landed at the airstrip at Charlottesville-Albemarle Airport and taxied to a halt. It was nearly ten o'clock at night and the airport had pretty much shut down for the day. The Gulfstream V was the day's last incoming flight in fact. The limousine was waiting on the tarmac. Three people quickly exited the plane and climbed into the limo, which immediately drove off and a few minutes later was heading south on Route 29.

Inside the limo, the woman took off her glasses and laid her arm across the young girl's shoulder. Then LuAnn Tyler slumped back against the seat and took a deep breath. Home. Finally, they were back in the United States. All the years of planning had finally been executed. She had thought about little else for some time now. She glanced over at the man who sat in the rear-facing seat. His eyes stared straight ahead, his thick fingers drummed a somber rhythm across the car's window. Charlie looked concerned, and he was concerned, but he still managed a smile, a reassuring grin. If nothing else he had always been reassuring for her over the last ten years.

He put his hands in his lap and cocked his head at her. "You scared?" he asked.

LuAnn nodded and then looked down at ten-year-old Lisa, who had immediately slumped over her mother's lap and fallen into an exhausted sleep. The trip had been a long and tedious one.

"How about you?" she asked back.

He shrugged his thick shoulders. "We prepared as well as we could, we understand the risks. Now we just live with it." He smiled again, this time more broadly. "We'll be okay."

She smiled back at him, her eyes deep and heavy. They had been through a lot over the last decade. If she never climbed aboard another airplane, never passed through another Customs post, never again wondered what country she was in, what language she should be trying to muddle through, it would be perfectly fine with her. The longest trip she wanted to take for the rest of her life was strolling down to the mailbox to pick up her mail, or driving down to the mall to go shopping. God, if it could only be that easy. She winced slightly and rubbed in a distracted fashion at her temples.

Charlie quickly picked up on this. Over the years he had acquired a heightened sensitivity to the subtle tracks of her emotions. He scrutinized Lisa for a long moment to make sure she was indeed sleeping. Satisfied, he undid his seat belt, sat down next to LuAnn, and spoke in soft tones.

"He doesn't know we've come back. Jackson doesn't know."

She whispered back to him. "We don't know that, Charlie. We can't be sure. My God, I don't know what's scaring me the most: the police or him. No, that's a lie. I know, it's him. I'd take the police over him any day. He told me never to come back here. Never. Now I am back. We all are."

Charlie laid his hand on top of hers and spoke as calmly as he could. "If he knew, do you think he'd have let us get this far? We took about as circuitous a route as anybody could take. Five plane changes, a train trip, four countries, we zigzagged halfway across the world to get here. He doesn't know. And

182

you know what, even if he does he's not going to care. It's been ten years. The deal's expired. Why should he care now?"

"Why should he do any of the things he's done? You tell me. He does them because he wants to."

Charlie sighed, undid his jacket button, and lay back against the seat.

LuAnn turned to him and gently rubbed his shoulder. "We're back. You're right, we made the decision and now we're going to live with it. It's not like I'm going to announce to the whole world that I'm around again. We're going to live a nice, quiet life."

"In considerable luxury. You saw the photos of the house."

LuAnn nodded. "It looks beautiful."

"An old estate. About ten thousand square feet. Been on the market for a long time, but with an asking price of six million bucks, can't say I'm surprised. Let me tell you, we got a deal at three point five mil. But then I drive a hard bargain. Although, of course, we dumped another million into renovation. About fourteen months' worth, but we had the time, right?"

"And secluded?"

"Very. Almost three hundred acres, plus or minus as they say. About a hundred of those acres are open, 'gently rolling land.' That description was in the brochure. Growing up in New York, I never saw so much green grass. Beautiful Piedmont, Virginia, or so the realtor kept telling me on all those trips I took over here to scout for homes. And it was the prettiest home I saw. True it took a lot of work to get it in shape, but I got some good people, architects and what-not representing our interests. It's got a truckload of outbuildings, caretaker's house, three-stall horse barn, a couple of cottages, all vacant by

183

the way; I don't see us taking in renters. Anyway, all those big estates have that stuff. It's got a pool. Lisa will love that. Plenty of room for a tennis court. The works. But then there's dense forest all around. Look at it as a hardwood moat. And I've already started shopping around for a firm to construct a security fence and gate around the property line fronting the road. Probably should have already gotten that done."

"Like you didn't have enough to do. You do too much as it is."

"I don't mind. I kind of like it."

"And my name's not on the ownership papers?"

"Catherine Savage appears nowhere. We used a straw man for the contract and closing. Deed was transferred in the name of the corporation I had set up. That's untraceable back to you."

"I wish I could have changed my name again, just in case he's on the lookout for it."

"That would've been nice except the cover story he built for you, the same one we used to appease the IRS, has you as Catherine Savage. It's complicated enough without adding another layer to it. Geez, the death certificate we had made up for your 'late' husband was hell to get."

"I know." She sighed heavily.

He glanced over at her. "Charlottesville, Virginia, home to lot of rich and famous, I hear. Is that why you picked it? Private, you can live like a hermit, and nobody'll care?"

"That was one of two reasons."

"And the other?"

"My mother was born here," LuAnn said, her voice dropping a notch as she delicately traced the hem of her skirt. "She was happy here, at least she told me she was. And she wasn't rich either." She fell silent, her eyes staring off. She jolted back and looked at Charlie, her face reddening slightly. "Maybe some of that happiness will rub off on us, what do you think?"

"I think so long as I'm with you and this little one," he said, gently stroking Lisa's cheek, "I'm a happy man."

"She's all enrolled in the private school?"

Charlie nodded. "St. Anne's-Belfield. Pretty exclusive, low student-to-teacher ratio. But, hell, Lisa's educational qualifications are outstanding. She speaks multiple languages, been all over the world. Already done things most adults will never do their whole life."

"I don't know, maybe I should have hired a private tutor."

"Come on, LuAnn, she's been doing that ever since she could walk. She needs to be around other kids. It'll be good for her. It'll be good for you too. You know what they say about time away."

She suddenly smiled at him slyly. "Are you feeling claustrophobic with us, Charlie?"

"You bet I am. I'm gonna start staying out late. Might even take up some hobbies like golf or something." He grinned at LuAnn to show her he was only joking.

"It's been a good ten years, hasn't it?" Her voice was touched with anxiety.

"Wouldn't trade 'em for anything," he said.

Let's hope the next ten are just as good, LuAnn said to herself. She laid her head against his shoulder. When she had stared out at the New York skyline all those years ago, she had been brimming with excitement, with the potential of all the good she could do with the money. She had promised herself that she would and she had fulfilled that promise. Personally, however, those wonderful dreams had not been met. The last ten years had only been good to her if you defined good as constantly on the move, fearful of discovery, having pangs of guilt every time she bought something because of how she had come by the money. She had always heard that the incredibly rich were never really happy, for a variety of reasons. Growing up in poverty LuAnn had never believed that, she simply took it to be a ruse of the wealthy. Now, she knew it to be true, at least in her own case.

As the limo drove on, she closed her eyes and tried to rest. She would need it. Her "second" new life was about to commence.

NINETEEN

Thomas Donovan sat staring at his computer screen in the frenetic news room of the *Washington Tribune*. Journalistic awards from a number of distinguished organizations dotted the walls and shelves of his cluttered cubicle, including a Pulitzer he had won before he was thirty. Donovan was now in his early fifties but still possessed the drive and fervor of his youth. Like most investigative journalists, he could dish out a strong dose of cynicism about the workings of the real world, if only because he had seen the worst of it. What he was working on now was a story the substance of which disgusted him.

He was glancing at some of his notes when a shadow fell across his desk.

"Mr. Donovan?"

Donovan looked up into the face of a young kid from the mail room.

"Yeah?"

"This just came in for you. I think it's some research you had requested."

Donovan thanked him and took the packet. He dug into it with obvious zeal.

The lottery story he was working on had so much potential. He had already done a great deal of research. The national lottery took in billions of dollars each year in profits and the amount was growing at more than twenty percent a year. The government paid out about half its revenue in prize

187

money, about ten percent to vendors and other operating costs, and kept forty percent as profit, a margin most companies would kill for. Surveys and scholars had argued for years about whether the lottery amounted to a regressive tax with the poor the chief loser. The government maintained that, demographically, the poor didn't spend a disproportionate share of their income on the game. Such arguments didn't sit well with Donovan. He knew for a fact that millions of the people who played the game were borderline poverty-level, squandering Social Security money, food stamps, and anything else they could get their hands on to purchase the chance at the easy life, even though the odds were so astronomically high as to be farcical. And the government advertisements were highly misleading when it came to detailing precisely what those odds were. But that wasn't all. Donovan had turned up an astonishing seventy-five percent bankruptcy rate per year for the winners. Nine out of every twelve winners each year subsequently had declared bankruptcy. His angle had to do with financial management companies and other scheming, sophisticated types getting hold of these poor people and basically ripping them off. Charities calling up and hounding them relentlessly. Purveyors of every type of sybaritic gratification selling them just about anything they didn't need, calling their wares "must-have" status items for the nouveaux riches and charging a thousand percent markup for their trouble. It didn't stop there. The sudden wealth had destroyed families and life-time friendships as greed supplanted all rational emotions.

And the government was just as much to blame, Donovan felt, for these financial crashes. About twelve years ago they had bestowed the initial prize in one lump sum and given it tax-deferred status for one year to attract more and more players. The advertisements had played up this fact dramatically, touting the winnings as "tax-free" in the large print and counting on the "fine print" to inform the public that the amounts were actually tax-deferred and only for one year. Previously, the winnings had been paid out over time and taxes taken out automatically. Now the winners were on their own as far as structuring the payment of taxes went. Some, Donovan had learned, thought they owed no tax at all and went out and spent the money freely. All the earnings on that principal were subject to numerous taxes as well, and hefty ones. The Feds just hung the winners out there with a pat on the back and a big check. And when the winners weren't astute enough to set up sophisticated accounting and financial systems, the tax boys would come after them and take every last dime they had, under the guise of penalties and interest and what-not, and leave them poorer than when they started out.

It was a game designed for the ultimate destruction of the winner and it was done under the veil of the government's doing good for its people. It was the devil's game and our own government was doing it to us, Donovan was firmly convinced. And the government did it for one reason and one reason only: money. Just like everybody else. He had watched other papers give the problem lip service. And whenever a real attack or exposé was formed in the news media, government lottery officials quickly squelched it with oceans of statistics showing how much good the lottery monies were doing. The public thought the money was earmarked for education, highway maintenance, and the like, but a large part of it went into the general purpose funds and ended up in some very interesting places, far away from buying school books and filling potholes.

Lottery officials received fat paychecks and fatter bonuses. Politicians who supported the lottery saw large funds flow to their states. All of it stunk and Donovan felt it was high time the truth came out. His pen would defend the less fortunate, just as it had over his entire career. If he did nothing else, Donovan would at least shame the government into reconsidering the morals of this gargantuan revenue source. It might not change anything, but he was going to give it his best.

He refocused on the packet of documents. He had tested his theory on the bankruptcy rate going back five years. The documents he was holding took those results back another seven years. As he paged through year after year of lottery winners, the results were almost identical, the ratio staying at virtually nine out of twelve a year declaring personal bankruptcy. Absolutely astonishing. He happily thumbed through the pages. His instincts had been dead-on. It was no fluke.

Then he abruptly stopped and stared at one page, his smile disappearing. The page represented the list of twelve consecutive lottery winners from exactly ten years ago. It couldn't be possible. There must be some mistake. Donovan picked up the phone and made a call to the research service he had engaged to do the study. No, there was no mistake, he was told. Bankruptcy filings were matters of public record.

Donovan slowly hung up the phone and stared again at the page. Herman Rudy, Bobbie Jo Reynolds, LuAnn Tyler, the list went on and on, twelve winners in a row. Not one of them had declared personal bankruptcy. Not one. Every twelve-month period for the lottery except this one had resulted in nine bankruptcies.

Most reporters of Thomas Donovan's caliber lived or died by two intangibles: perseverance and instincts. Donovan's instinct was that the story he might be on to right now would make his other angle seem about as exciting as an article on pruning.

He had some sources to check and he wanted to do them in more privacy than the crowded newsroom allowed. He threw the file in his battered briefcase and quickly left the office. In non-rush hour traffic he reached his small apartment in Virginia in twenty minutes. Twice divorced with no children, Donovan led a life focused solely on his work. He had a relationship slowly percolating with Alicia Crane, a well-known Washington socialite from a wealthy family, which had once been politically well connected. He had never been fully comfortable moving in these circles; however, Alicia was supportive and devoted to him, and truth be known, flitting around the edges of her luxurious existence wasn't so bad.

He settled into his home office and picked up the phone. There was a definite way to obtain information on people, particularly rich people, no matter how guarded their lives. He dialed the number of a longtime source at the Internal Revenue Service. Donovan gave that person the names of the twelve consecutive lottery winners who had not declared bankruptcy. Two hours later he got a call back. As he listened, Donovan checked off the names on his lists. He asked a few more questions, thanked his friend, hung up, and looked down at his list. All the names were crossed off except for one. Eleven of the lottery winners had duly filed their tax returns each year, his source had reported. That was as far as his source would go, however. He would tell Donovan no specifics except to add that the income reported on all of the eleven tax returns was enormous. While the question still intrigued Donovan as to how all of them had avoided bankruptcy and apparently done very well over the last ten years, another more puzzling question had emerged.

He stared down at the name of the sole lottery winner that wasn't crossed off. According to his source, this person had not filed any tax returns, at least under her own name. In fact this person had outright disappeared. Donovan had a vague recollection of the reason why. Two murders, her boyfriend in rural Georgia and another man. Drugs had been involved. The story had not interested him all that much ten years ago. He would not have recalled it at all except that the woman had disappeared just after winning a hundred million dollars and the money had disappeared with her. Now his curiosity was much greater as he eyed that particular name on his list: "LuAnn Tyler." She must have switched identities on her run from the murder charge. With her lottery winnings she could easily have invented a new life for herself.

Donovan smiled for an instant as it suddenly occurred to him that he might have a way of discovering LuAnn Tyler's new identity. And maybe a lot more. At least he could try.

The next day Donovan telephoned the sheriff in Rikersville, Georgia, LuAnn's hometown. Roy Waymer had died five years ago. Ironically, the current sheriff was Billy Harvey, Duane's uncle. Harvey was very talkative with Donovan when the subject of LuAnn came up.

"She got Duane killed," he said angrily. "She got him involved in those drugs sure as I'm talking to you. The Harvey family ain't got much, but we got our pride."

"Have you heard from her in any way over the last ten years?" Donovan asked.

Billy Harvey paused for a lengthy moment. "Well, she sent down some money."

"Money?"

"To Duane's folks. They didn't ask for it, I can tell you that."

"Did they keep it?"

"Well, they're on in years and poorer'n dirt. You don't just turn your back on that kind of money."

"How much are we talking about?"

"Two hundred thousand dollars. If that doesn't show LuAnn's guilty conscience, I don't know what would."

Donovan whistled under his breath. "Did you try to trace the money?"

"I wasn't sheriff then, but Roy Waymer did. He even had some local FBI boys over to help, but they never turned up a durn thing. She's helped some other people round here too, but we could never get a handle on her whereabouts from them either. Like she was a damned ghost or something."

"Anything else?"

"Yeah, you ever talk to her, you tell her that the Harvey family ain't forgot, not even after all these years. That murder warrant is still outstanding. We get her back to Georgia, she'll be spending some nice quality time with us. I'm talking twenty to life. No statute of limitations on murder. Am I right?"

"I'll let her know, Sheriff, thanks. Oh, I'm wondering if you could send me a copy of the file on the case. The autopsy reports, investigative notes, forensics, the works?"

"You really think you can find her after all this time?"

"I've been doing this kind of stuff for thirty years and I'm pretty good at it. I'm sure going to try."

"Well, then I'll send it up to you, Mr. Donovan."

Donovan gave Harvey the *Trib*'s FedEx number

and address, hung up, and wrote down some notes. Tyler had a new name, that was for certain. In order even to begin to track her down, he had to find out what that name was.

He spent the next week exploring every crevice of LuAnn's life. He got copies of her parents' death notices from the *Rikersville Gazette*. Obituaries were full of interesting items: birthplaces, relatives, and other items that could conceivably lead him to some valuable information. Her mother had been born in Charlottesville, Virginia. Donovan talked to the relatives listed in the obituary, at least the few who were alive, but received few useful facts. LuAnn had never tried to contact them.

Next, Donovan dug up as many facts as he could on LuAnn's last day in the country. Donovan had conversations with personnel from the NYPD and the FBI field office in New York. Sheriff Waymer had seen her on TV and immediately notified the police in New York that LuAnn was wanted in Georgia in connection with a double murder and drug trafficking. They, in turn, had put a blanket over the bus and train stations, and the airports. In a city of seven million, that was the best they could do; they couldn't exactly put up roadblocks. However, there hadn't been one sign of the woman. That had greatly puzzled the FBI. According to the agent Donovan talked to who was somewhat familiar with the file, the Bureau wanted to know how a twenty-year-old woman with a seventh-grade education from rural Georgia, carrying a baby no less, had waltzed right through their net. An elaborate disguise and cover documents were out of the question, or so they thought. The police had thrown out their net barely a half hour after she had appeared on national television. No one was that fast. And all the money had disappeared as well. At the time, some at the FBI had wondered whether she had had help. But that lead had never been followed up as other crises of more national importance had swallowed up the Bureau's time and manpower. They had officially concluded that LuAnn Tyler had not left the country, but had simply driven out of New York or taken the subway to a suburb and then lost herself somewhere in the country or perhaps Canada. The NYPD had reported its failure to Sheriff Waymer and that had been the end of it. Until now. Now, Donovan was greatly intrigued. His gut told him that LuAnn Tyler had left the country. Somehow she had gotten past the law. If she had gotten on a plane, then he had something to work with.

He could narrow the list down in any event. He had a certain day to work with, even a block of hours on that day. Donovan would begin with the premise that LuAnn Tyler had fled the country. He would focus on international flights departing from JFK during that time frame, ten years ago. If the records at JFK turned up nothing, he would focus on LaGuardia and then Newark International Airport. At least it was a start. There were far fewer international flights than domestic. If he had to start checking domestic flights, he concluded he would have to try another angle. There were simply too many. As he was about to start this process a package arrived from Sheriff Harvey.

Donovan munched on a sandwich at his cubicle while he looked through the files. The autopsy photos were understandably gruesome; however, they didn't faze the veteran reporter. He had seen far worse in his career. After an hour of reading he laid the file aside and made some notes. From the looks of it, he believed LuAnn Tyler to be innocent of the charges for which Harvey wanted to arrest her. He had done some independent digging of his own into

195

Rikersville, Georgia. By virtually all accounts, Duane Harvey was a lazy good-for-nothing with no greater ambition than to spend his life drinking beer, chasing women, and adding nothing whatsoever of value to mankind. LuAnn Tyler, on the other hand, had been described to him by several persons who had known her as hardworking, honest, and a loving, caring mother to her little girl. Orphaned as a teenager, she seemed to have done as well as she could under the circumstances. Donovan had seen photos of her, had even managed to dig up a video-tape of the press conference announcing her as the lottery winner ten years ago. She was a looker all right, but there was something behind that beauty. She hadn't scraped by all those years on her physical assets alone.

Donovan finished his sandwich and took a sip of his coffee. Duane Harvey had been cut up badly. The other man, Otis Burns, had also died from knife wounds to his upper torso. There had been serious but nonfatal head trauma also present, and the clear signs of a struggle. LuAnn's fingerprints had been found on the broken phone receiver and also all over the trailer. No surprise since she happened to live there. There had been one witness account of seeing her in Otis Burns's car that morning. Despite Sheriff Harvey's protests to the contrary, Donovan's research led him to believe that Duane was the drug dealer in the family and had been caught skimming. Burns was probably his supplier. The man had a lengthy rap sheet in neighboring Gwinnett County, all drug related. Burns had probably come to settle the score. Whether LuAnn Tyler knew of Duane's drug dealing was anybody's guess. She had worked at the truck stop up until the time she had bought her lottery ticket and disappeared only to resurface, however briefly, in New York City. So if she had known of Duane's sideline, she hadn't reaped any discernible benefits from it. Whether she had been in the trailer that morning and had had anything to do with either man's death was also unclear. Donovan really didn't care one way or another. He had no reason to sympathize with Duane Harvey or Otis Burns. At this point he didn't know what he felt about LuAnn Tyler. He did know that he wanted to find her. He wanted that very much.

TWENTY

Jackson sat in a chair in the darkened living room of a luxurious apartment in a prewar building overlooking Central Park. His eyes were closed, his hands neatly folded in his lap. Approaching forty years of age he was still lean and wiry in build. His actual facial features were androgynous, although the years had etched fine lines around his eyes and mouth. His short hair was cut stylishly, his clothing was quietly expensive. His eyes, however, were clearly his most distinctive feature, which he had to disguise very carefully when he was working. He rose and moved slowly through the amply proportioned apartment. The furnishings were eclectic: English, French, and Spanish antiques mixed liberally with Oriental art and sculpture.

He entered an area of his apartment reminiscent of a Broadway star's dressing room. It was his makeup room and workshop. Special recessed lighting covered the ceiling. Multiple mirrors with their own special nonheating bulbs ringed the room. Two padded reclining leather chairs sat in front of two of the largest mirrors. The chairs had casters which allowed them to be rolled about the room. Innumerable photos were neatly pinned to cork bulletin boards on the walls. Jackson was an avid photographer, and many of his subjects were the basis for most of the identities he had created over the years. Both full wigs and hairpieces, neatly separated into toupees and falls, lined one wall, each hanging on special cotton-covered wire. Customized wall cabinets housed dozens of latex caps and other body pieces along with acrylic teeth, caps, and molds, and other synthetic materials and putties. One massive storage unit contained absorbent cotton, acetone, spirit gum, powders, body makeup; large, medium, and small brushes with bristles of varying rigidity; cake makeup, modeling clay, collodion to make scars and pock marks; crepe hair to make beards, mustaches, and even eyebrows; Derma wax to alter the face, creme makeup, gelatin, makeup palettes; netting, toupee tape, sponges, ventilating needles to knot hair into net or gauze for beards and wigs; and hundreds of other devices, materials, and substances designed solely to reshape one's appearance. There were three racks of clothing of all descriptions and several full-length mirrors to test the effect of any disguise. In a specially built case with multiple drawers were over fifty complete sets of identification documents that would allow Jackson to travel the world as a man or a woman.

Jackson smiled as he noted various articles in the room. This was where he was most comfortable. Creating his numerous roles was the one constant pleasure in his life. Acting out the part, however, ran a close second as his favorite endeavor. He sat down at the table and ran his hand along its top. He stared into a mirror. Unlike anyone else looking into a mirror, Jackson didn't see his reflection staring back at him. Instead, he saw a blank countenance, one to be manipulated, carved, painted, covered, and massaged into someone else. Although he was perfectly content with his intellect and personality, why be limited to one physical identity one's whole life, he thought, when there was so much more out there to experience? Go anywhere, do anything. He had told that to all twelve of his lottery winners. His baby ducklings all in a row. And they had all bought it, completely and absolutely, for he had been dead right.

Over the last ten years he had earned hundreds of millions of dollars for each of his winners, and billions of dollars for himself. Ironically, Jackson had grown up in very affluent circumstances. "Old money" his family had been. His parents were long dead. The old man had been, in Jackson's eyes, a typical example of those members of the upper class whose money and position had been inherited rather than earned. Jackson's father had been both arrogant and insecure. A politician and insider in Washington for many years, the old man had taken his family connections as far as he could until his decided lack of merit and marketable skills had done him in and the escalator had stopped moving upward. And then he had spent the family money in a futile attempt to regain that upward momentum. And then the money was gone. Jackson, the eldest, had often taken the brunt of the old man's wrath over the years. Upon turning eighteen, Jackson discovered that the large trust fund his grandfather had set up for him had been raided illegally so many times by his father that there wasn't anything left. The continuing rage and physical abuse the old man had wielded after Jackson had confronted him with this discovery had left a profound impression on the son.

The physical bruises eventually had healed. The psychological damage was still with Jackson and his own inner rage seemed to grow exponentially with each year, as though he were trying to outdo his elder in that regard.

It might seem trite to others, Jackson understood that. Lost your fortune? So what? Who gives a damn? But Jackson gave a damn. Year after year he had counted on that money to free him from his father's tyrannical persecution. When that long-held hope was abruptly torn away, the absolute shock had carved a definite change in him. What was rightfully his had been stolen from him, and by the one man who shouldn't have done it, by a man who should have loved his son and wanted the best for him, respected him, wanted to protect him. Instead Jackson had gotten an empty bank account and the hate-filled blows of a madman. And Jackson had taken it. Up to a point. But then he hadn't taken it anymore.

Jackson's father had died unexpectedly. Parents killed their small children every day, never with good reason. By comparison, children killed their parents only rarely, usually with excellent purpose. Jackson smiled lightly as he thought of this. An early chemical experiment, administered through his father's beloved scotch, the rupturing of a brain aneurysm the result. As with any occupation, one had to start somewhere.

When those of average or below-average intelligence committed crimes such as murder, they usually did so clumsily, with no long-range planning or preparation. The result was typically swift arrest and conviction. Among the highly intelligent, serious crimes evolved from careful planning, long-term approaches, many sessions of mental gymnastics. As a result, arrests were rare, convictions even rarer. Jackson was definitely in the latter category.

The eldest son had been compelled to go out and earn the family fortune back. A college merit scholarship to a prestigious university and graduation at the top of his class had been followed by his careful nurturing of old family contacts, for those embers could not be allowed to die out if Jackson's long-range plan was to succeed. Over the years he had devoted himself to mastering a variety of skills, both corporeal and cerebral, that would allow him to pursue his dream of wealth and the power that came with it. His body was as fit and strong as his mind, the one in precise balance with the other. However, ever mindful of not following in his father's footsteps, Jackson had set a far more ambitious goal for himself: He would do all of it while remaining completely invisible from scrutiny. Despite his love of acting, he did not crave the spotlight as his politician father had. He was perfectly content with his audience of one.

And so he had built his invisible empire albeit in a profoundly illegal manner. The results were the same regardless of where the dollars had originated. Go anywhere, do anything. It didn't only apply to his ducklings.

He smiled at this thought as he continued to move through the apartment.

Jackson had a younger brother and sister. His brother had inherited their father's bad habits and consequently expected the world to offer up its best for nothing of comparable value in return. Jackson had given him enough money to live a comfortable but hardly luxurious existence. If he ran through that money there would be no more. For him, that well was dry. His sister was another matter. Jackson cared deeply for her, although she had adored the old man with the blind faith a daughter often shows to her father. Jackson had set her up in grand style but never visited her. The demands on his time were too immense. One night might find him in Hong Kong, the next in London. Moreover, visits with his sister would necessitate conversation and he had no desire to lie to her about what he had done and continued to do for a living. She would never be a part of that world of his. She could live out her days in idle luxury and complete ignorance looking for someone to replace the father she believed had been so kind, so noble.

Still, Jackson had done right by his family. He had no shame, no guilt there. He was not his father. He had allowed himself one constant reminder of the old man, the name he used in all his dealings: Jackson. His father's name was Jack. And no matter what he did, he would always be Jack's son.

As he continued to drift around his apartment he stopped at a window and looked out at a spectacular evening in New York. The apartment he was living in was the very same one he had grown up in, although he had completely gutted it after purchasing it; the ostensible reason had been to modernize and make it suitable for his particular needs. The more subtle motivation had been to obliterate, to the extent he could, the past. That compulsion did not only apply to his physical surroundings. Every time he put on a disguise, he was, in effect, layering over his real self, hiding the person his father had never felt deserved his respect or love. None of the pain would ever be fully wiped away, though, so long as Jackson lived, as long as he could remember. The truth was, every corner of the apartment held the capability of flinging painful memories at him at any moment. But that wasn't so bad, he had long since concluded. Pain was a wonderful motivational tool.

Jackson entered and exited his penthouse by private elevator. No one was ever allowed in his apartment under any circumstances. All mail and other deliveries were left at the front desk; but there was very little of that. Most of his business was conducted by means of phone, computer modem, and fax. He did his own cleaning, but with his traveling schedule and spartan habits, these were not overly time-consuming chores, and were certainly a small price to pay for absolute privacy.

Jackson had created a disguise for his real identity and used it whenever he left his apartment. It was a worst-case scenario plan, in the event the police ever came calling at his door. Horace Parker, the elderly doorman who greeted Jackson each time he left his apartment, was the same one who had tipped his cap to the shy, bookish boy clutching his mother's hand all those years ago. Jackson's family had left New York when he was a teenager, because his father had fallen on bad times, so the aged Parker had accepted Jackson's altered appearance as simply maturation. Now with the "fake" image firmly in people's minds, Jackson was confident that no one could ever identify him.

For Jackson, hearing his given name from Horace Parker was comforting and troubling at the same time. Juggling so many identities was not easy, and Jackson occasionally found himself not responding when he heard his real name uttered. It was actually nice being himself at times, however, since it was an escape of sorts where he could relax, and explore the never-ending intricacies of the city. But no matter which identity he assumed, he always took care of business. Nothing came before that. Opportunities were everywhere and he had exploited them all.

With such limitless capital, he had made the world his playpen for the last decade, and the effects of his manipulations could be felt in financial markets and political paradigms all across the globe. His funds had propelled enterprises as diverse as his identities, from guerrilla activities in Third World countries to the cornering of precious metal markets in the industrialized world. When one could mold world events in that way, one could profit enormously in the financial markets. Why gamble on futures markets, when one could manipulate the underlying product itself, and thereby know precisely which way the winds would be blowing? It was predictable and logical; risk was controlled. These sorts of climates he loved.

He had exhibited a distinctly benevolent side as well, and large sums of money had been funneled to deserving causes across the globe. But even with those situations he demanded and received ultimate control however invisible it was, figuring that he could exercise far better judgment than anyone else. With so much money at stake, who would deny him? He would never appear on any power list or hold any political office; no financial magazine would ever interview him. He floated from one passion to another with the utmost ease. He could not envision a more perfect existence, although he had to admit that even his global meanderings were becoming a little tedious lately. Redundancy was beginning to usurp originality in his numerous lines of business and he had begun searching around for a new pursuit that would satisfy an ever-growing appetite for the unusual, for the extremely risky, if only to test and retest his skills of control, of domination, and ultimately, of survival.

He entered a smaller room which was filled floor to ceiling with computer equipment. This represented the nerve center of his operation. The flat screens told him in real time how his many worldwide interests were doing. Everything from stock exchanges to futures markets to late-breaking news stories was captured, catalogued, and eventually analyzed here by him.

He craved information, absorbed it like a three-year-old learning a foreign language. He only needed to hear it once and he never forgot it. His eyes scanned each of the screens, and from long habit he was able to separate the important from the mundane, the interesting from the obvious in a matter of minutes. Investments of his colored in soft blue on the screens meant he was doing very well; those mired in harsh red meant he was doing less well. He sighed in satisfaction as a sea of blue blinked back at him.

He went into another, larger room that housed his collection of mementos from past projects. He pulled out a scrapbook and opened it. Inside were photographs of and background information on his twelve precious pieces of gold – the dozen individuals upon whom he had bestowed great wealth and new lives; and who, in turn, had allowed him to recoup his family's fortune. He flipped idly through the pages, occasionally smiling as various pleasant memories flickered through his mind.

He had handpicked his winners carefully, culling them from welfare rolls and bankruptcy filings; logging hundreds of hours tramping through poor, desolate areas of the country, both urban and rural, searching for desperate people who would do anything to change their fortunes – normal law-abiding citizens who would commit what was technically a financial crime of immense proportion without blinking an eye. It was wonderful what the human mind could rationalize given the appropriate inducement.

The lottery had been remarkably easy to fix. It was often that way. People just assumed institutions like that were absolutely above corruption or reproach. They must have forgotten that government lotteries had been banned on a wholesale basis in the last century because of widespread corruption. History did tend to repeat itself, if in a more sophisticated and focused manner. If Jackson had learned one thing over the years it was that nothing, absolutely nothing, was above corruption so long as human beings were involved, because, in truth, most people were not above the lure of the dollar or other material enticements, particularly when they worked around vast sums of money all day. They tended to believe that part of it was rightfully theirs anyway.

And an army of people wasn't required to carry out his plans. Indeed, to Jackson, the notion of a "widespread conspiracy" was an oxymoron anyway.

He had a large group of associates working for him around the globe. However, none of them knew who he really was, where he lived, how he had come by his fortune. None of them were privy to the grand plans he had laid, the worldwide machinations he had orchestrated. They simply performed their small slice of the pie and were very well compensated for doing so. When he wanted something, a bit of information not readily available to him, he would contact one of them and within the hour he would have it. It was the perfect setting for contemplation, planning, and then action – swift, precise, and final.

He completely trusted no one. And with his ability to create flawlessly more than fifty separate identities, why should he? With state-of-the-art computer and communications technology at his fingertips, he could actually be in several different places at the same time. As different people. His smile broadened. Could the world be any more his personal stage?

As he perused one page of the scrapbook his smile faded and was replaced with something more understated; it was a mixture of discernible interest and an emotion that Jackson almost never experienced: uncertainty. And something else. He would never have characterized it as fear; that particular demon never bothered him. Rather he could adequately describe it as a feeling of destiny, of the unmistakable conviction that two trains were on a collision course and no matter what one or the other did, their ominous meeting would take place in a very memorable manner.

Jackson stared at the truly remarkable countenance of LuAnn Tyler. Of the twelve lottery winners, she had been by far the most memorable. There was danger in that woman, danger and a definite volatility that drew Jackson like the most powerful magnet in the world. He had spent several weeks in Rikersville, Georgia, a locale he had picked for one simple reason: its irreversible cycle of poverty, of hopelessness. There were many such places in America, so well documented by the government under such categories as "lowest per capita income levels," "below standard health and education resources," "negative economic growth." Stark fiscal terms that did little or nothing to enlighten anyone as to the people behind the statistics; to shed light on a large segment of the population's free fall into misery. Ever the capitalist, Jackson surprisingly did not mind the added element of his actually doing some good here. He never picked rich people to win, although he had no doubt most of them would have been far easier to persuade than the poor he solicited.

He had discovered LuAnn Tyler as she rode the bus to work. Jackson had sat across from her, in disguise, of course, blending into the background in his torn jeans, stained shirt, and Georgia Bulldogs cap, a scruffy beard covering the lower part of his face, his piercing eyes hidden behind thick glasses. Her appearance had struck him immediately. She seemed out of place down here; everyone else looked so unhealthy, so hopeless, as though the youngest among them were already counting the days until burial. He had watched her play with her daughter; listened to her greet the people around her, and watched their dismal spirits noticeably lifted by her thoughtful comments. He had proceeded to investigate every element of LuAnn's life, from her impoverished background to her life in a trailer home with Duane Harvey. He had visited that trailer several times while LuAnn and her "boyfriend" had not been there. He had seen the small touches LuAnn had employed to keep the place neat and clean despite Duane Harvey's slovenly lifestyle. Everything having to do with Lisa was kept separate and immaculate by LuAnn. Jackson had seen that clearly. Her daughter was her life.

Disguised as a truck driver, he had spent many a night in the roadside diner where LuAnn worked. He had watched her carefully, seen the terms of her life grow more and more desperate, observed her stare woefully into her infant daughter's eyes, dreaming of a better life. And then, after all this observation, he had chosen her as one of the fortunate few. A decade ago.

And then he had not seen or spoken to her in ten years; however, a rare week went by that he did not at least think of her. At first he had kept quite a watchful eye on her movements, but as the years went by and she continued to move from country to country in accordance with his wishes, his diligence had lessened considerably. Now, she was pretty much off his radar screen entirely. The last he had heard she was in New Zealand. Next year could find her in Monaco, Scandinavia, China, he well knew. She would float from one locale to the next until she died. She would never return to the United States, of that he was certain.

Jackson had been born to great wealth, to every material advantage, and then it had all been taken away. He had had to earn it back through his skill, his sweat, his nerve. LuAnn Tyler had been born to nothing, had worked like a dog for pennies, no way out, and look at her now. He had given LuAnn Tyler the world, allowing her to become who she had always wanted to be: someone other than LuAnn Tyler. Jackson smiled. With his complete love of deception, how could he not appreciate that irony? He had spent most of his adult life pretending to be other people. LuAnn had spent the last ten years of hers living another life, filling in the dimensions of another identity. He stared into the lively hazel eyes, studied the high cheekbones, the long hair; he traced with his index finger the slender yet strong neck and began to wonder once more about those trains, and the truly wonderful collision they might one day create. His eyes began to shine with the thought.

TWENTY-ONE

Donovan entered his apartment and sat down at the dining room table, spreading the pages he had taken out of his briefcase in front of him. His manner was one of subdued excitement. It had taken several weeks, dozens of phone calls, and a massive amount of leg work to accumulate the information he was now sifting through.

Initially, the task seemed more than daunting; indeed it had seemed destined for failure through sheer numbers. During the year LuAnn Tyler had disappeared, there had been over seventy thousand scheduled international passenger-aircraft movements at JFK. On the day she presumably fled there had been two hundred flights, or ten per hour, because there had been no flights between one and six A.M. Donovan had whittled down the parameters of his search at JFK to include women between the ages of twenty and thirty traveling on an international flight on the date of the press conference ten years ago, between the hours of seven P.M. and one A.M.. The press conference had lasted until six-thirty and Donovan doubted she could have made a seven o'clock flight, but the flight could have been delayed, and he wasn't taking any chances. That meant checking sixty flights and about fifteen thousand passengers. Donovan had learned during his investigation that most airlines kept active records of passengers going back five years. After that the information was archived. His task promised to be easier because most airline records had been computerized in the mid-seventies. However, Donovan had met a stone wall in seeking passenger records from ten years ago. The FBI could get such records, he had been told, but usually only through a subpoena.

Through a contact at the Bureau who owed him a favor, Donovan had been able to pursue his request. Without going into particulars and naming names with his FBI contact, Donovan had been able to convey the precise parameters of his search, including the fact that the person he was seeking had probably been traveling under a newly issued passport and traveling with a baby. That had narrowed things down considerably. Only three people satisfied those very narrow criteria and he was now looking at a list of them together with their last known addresses.

Next, Donovan pulled out his address book. The number he was calling was a firm called Best Data, a well-known national credit check agency. Over the years the company had amassed a large database of names, addresses, and, most important, Social Security numbers. They serviced numerous firms requiring that information, including collection agencies and banks checking up on the credit of potential borrowers. Donovan gave the three names and last known addresses of the people on his list to the person at Best Data, and then provided his credit card number to pay for Best Data's fee. Within five minutes he was given the Social Security numbers for all three people, their last known addresses, and five "nearbys," or neighbors' addresses. He checked those against the records from the airlines. Two of the women had moved, which wasn't surprising given their ages ten years ago; in the interim they had probably moved on to careers and marriages.

One woman, however, had not changed her address. Catherine Savage was still listed as living in Virginia. Donovan called directory assistance in Virginia, but no number came up for that name and address. Undeterred, he next called the Virginia Department of Motor Vehicles, or DMV, and gave the woman's name, last known address, and Social Security number, which in Virginia was also the driver's license number. The person at DMV would only tell Donovan that the woman had a current, valid Virginia driver's license but would not reveal when it had been issued or the woman's current address. Unfortunate, but Donovan had chased lots of leads into brick walls in the past. At least he knew she was now living in Virginia or at least had a driver's license in the commonwealth. The question now was Where in the commonwealth might she be? He had ways of finding that out, but decided in the meantime to dig up some more information on the woman's history.

He returned to the office where he had an on-line account through the newspaper and accessed the Social Security Administration's PEBES, or Personal Earnings and Benefit Estimate Statement database on the World Wide Web. Donovan was from the old school when it came to research methods, but even he occasionally lumbered out to do some Net surfing. All one needed to find out information on a person was their Social Security number, mother's maiden name, and the birthplace of the person. Donovan had all of these facts in hand. LuAnn Tyler had been born in Georgia, that he knew for certain. However, the first three digits of the Social Security number he had been given identified Catherine Savage as having been born in Virginia. If LuAnn Tyler and Catherine Savage were one and the same, then Tyler had obtained a phony SSN. It wasn't all that difficult to do, but he doubted whether the woman would've had the connections to do it. The PEBES listed a person's earnings going back to the early fifties, their contributions to the Social Security fund, and their expected benefits upon retirement based upon those contributions. That was normally what was shown. However, Donovan was looking at a blank screen. Catherine Savage had no history of wage earnings of any kind. LuAnn Tyler had worked, Donovan knew that. Her last job had been at a truck diner. If she had received a paycheck, her employers should have withheld payroll taxes, including amounts for Social Security. Either they hadn't or LuAnn Tyler didn't have a Social Security number to begin with. Or both. He called up Best Data again and went through the same process. The answer this time, however, was different. As far as the Social Security Administration was concerned, LuAnn Tyler didn't exist. She simply did not have a Social Security number. There was no more to be learned here. It was time for Donovan to take some more serious steps.

That evening Donovan returned home, opened a file, and took out IRS form 2848. The form was entitled "Power of Attorney and Declaration of Representative." A relatively simple form as Internal Revenue documents went, but one that carried extraordinary power. With it Donovan could obtain all sorts of confidential tax documents on the person he was investigating. True, he would have to stretch the truth a little in filling out the form, and a little falsification of signature was involved, but his motives were pure, and, thus, his conscience was clear. Besides, Donovan knew that the IRS received tens of millions of requests a year from taxpayers for information about their tax returns. The fact that somebody would take the time to match signatures

214

was beyond the realm of probability. Donovan smiled. The odds of it would be greater even than the odds of winning the lottery. He filled out the form, listing the woman's name and last known address, put in her Social Security number, listed himself as the woman's representative for tax purposes, and requested the woman's federal income tax returns for the last three years, and mailed it off.

It took two months and numerous prodding phone calls, but the wait was worth it. Donovan had devoured the contents of the package from the IRS when it finally came. Catherine Savage was an awfully wealthy woman and her tax return from the prior year, at a full forty pages in length, reflected that wealth and the financial complexities that level of income bore. He had requested her last three years' worth of returns, but the IRS had only sent one for the simple reason that she had only filed one return. The mystery behind that had been cleared up quickly, because Donovan, as Catherine Savage's tax representative, had been able to contact the IRS and ask virtually every question that he wanted about the taxpayer. Donovan had learned that Catherine Savage's tax situation had sparked a great deal of initial interest with the IRS. A U.S. citizen with such an extraordinary level of income filling a tax return for the first time at age thirty was enough to jump-start even the most drone-like of Revenue agents into action. There were over a million Americans living abroad who simply never filed returns, costing the government billions in unpaid taxes, and consequently this was an area that always received the IRS's attention. However, the initial interest had been quickly dissipated as every question the agency had asked had been answered and every question had been supported by substantial documentation, Donovan had been told.

Donovan looked at his notes from the conversation with the IRS agent. Catherine Savage had been born in the United States, in Charlottesville, Virginia, in fact, and then left the country as a young girl when her father's business had taken him overseas. As a young woman living in France, she had met and married a wealthy German businessman who was a resident of Monaco at the time. The man had died a little over two years ago and his fortune had duly passed to his young widow. Now, as a U.S. citizen with control of her own money, all of which was passive, unearned income, she had begun paying her income taxes to her homeland. The documents in the file were numerous and legitimate, the IRS agent had assured Donovan. Everything was aboveboard. As far as the IRS was concerned, Catherine Savage was a responsible citizen who was lawfully paying her taxes although residing outside the United States.

Donovan leaned back in his chair and studied the ceiling, his hands clasped behind his head. The agent had also provided Donovan with another piece of interesting news. The IRS had very recently received a change of address form for Catherine Savage. She was now in the United States. In fact, she had returned, at least according to her records, to the town of her birth: Charlottesville, Virginia. The same town where LuAnn Tyler's mother had been born. That was far too much of a coincidence for Donovan.

And with all that information in hand, Donovan was fairly certain of one thing: LuAnn Tyler had finally come home. And now that he was so intimately familiar with virtually every facet of her life, Donovan felt it was time that they actually meet. How and where was what he started to think about.

TWENTY-TWO

Sitting in his pickup truck parked on the side of a sharp bend in the road, Matt Riggs surveyed the area through a pair of lightweight field binoculars. The tree-filled, steeply graded land was, to his experienced eye, impenetrable. The half mile of winding asphalt private road running to his right formed a T-intersection with the road he was on; beyond that, he knew, sat a grand country estate with beautiful vistas of the nearby mountains. However, the estate, surrounded by thick woods, couldn't be seen from anywhere except overhead. Which made him wonder again why the owner would want to pay for an expensive perimeter security fence in the first place. The estate already had the very best of nature's own handiwork for protection.

Riggs shrugged and bent down to slip on a pair of Overland boots, then pulled on his coat. The chilly wind buffeted him as he stepped from his truck. He sucked the fresh air in and put a hand through his unkempt dark brown hair, working a couple of kinks out of his muscular frame before donning a pair of leather gloves. It would take him about an hour to walk the front location of the fence. The plans called for the fence to be seven feet high, made of solid steel painted glossy black, with each post set in two feet of concrete. The fence would have electronic sensors spaced randomly across its frame, and would be topped by dangerously sharp spike finials. The front gates, set on six-foot-high, four-foot-square concrete monuments with a brick veneer, would be of similar style and construction. The job also called for a video camera, intercom system, and a locking mechanism on the huge gates that would ensure that nothing less than the head-on impact of an Abrams tank could ever open it without the permission of the owner. From what he could tell, Riggs didn't expect such permission to be granted very often.

Bordered by Nelson County on the southwest, Greene County to the north, and Fluvanna and Louisa counties on the east, Albemarle County, Virginia, was home to many wealthy people, some famous and some not. However, they all had one thing in common: They all craved privacy and were more than willing to pay for it. Thus, Riggs was not entirely surprised at the precautions being undertaken here. All the negotiations had been handled through a duly authorized intermediary. He reasoned that someone who could afford a fence such as this, and the cost was well into the hundreds of thousands of dollars, probably had better things to do with his time than sit down and chat with a lowly general contractor.

Binoculars dangling around his neck, he dutifully trudged down the road until he found a narrow pathway into the woods. The two most difficult parts of the job were clear to him: getting the heavy equipment up here and having his men work in such cramped surroundings. Mixing concrete, punching postholes, laying out the frames, clearing land, and angling sections of a very heavy fence, all of that took space, ample space that they would not have here. He was very glad to have added a healthy premium to the job, plus a provision for a cost overrun for exactly those reasons. The owner, apparently, had not set a limit as to the price, because the representative had promptly agreed to the huge dollar amount Riggs had worked up. Not that he was complaining. This single job would guarantee his best year ever in business. And although he had only been on his own for three years, his operation had been growing steadily ever since the first day. He got to work.

The BMW pulled slowly out from the garage and headed down the drive. The road going down was lined on either side with four-board oak fencing painted a pristine white. Most of the cleared land was surrounded by the same style of fencing, the white lines making a stunning contrast to the green landscape. It was not quite seven in the morning and the stillness of the day remained unbroken. These early morning drives had become a soothing ritual for LuAnn. She glanced back at the house in her rearview mirror. Constructed of beautiful Pennsylvania stone and weathered brick with a row of new white columns bracketing a deep front porch, a slate roof, aged-looking copper gutters, and numerous French doors, the house was elegantly refined despite its imposing size.

As the car passed down the drive and out of sight of the house, LuAnn turned her eyes back to the road and suddenly took her foot off the gas and hit the brake. The man was waving at her, his arms crisscrossing themselves as he flagged her down. She inched forward and then stopped the car. He came up to the driver's side window and motioned for her to open it. Out of the corner of her eye she saw the black Honda parked on a grass strip bordering the road.

She eyed him with deep suspicion but hit the button and the window descended slightly. She kept one foot on the accelerator ready to mash it down if the situation called for it. His appearance was innocent enough: middle-aged and slight of build, with a beard laced around the edges with gray.

"Can I help you?" she asked, her eyes attempting to duck his gaze at the same time she tried her best to note any sudden movements on his part.

"I think I'm lost. Is this the old Brillstein Estate?" He pointed up the road toward where the house was.

LuAnn shook her head. "We just recently moved in, but that wasn't the name of the owners before us. It's called Wicken's Hunt."

"Huh, I could've sworn this was the right place."

"Who were you looking for?"

The man leaned forward so that his face filled her window. "Maybe you know her. The name is LuAnn Tyler, from Georgia."

LuAnn sucked in a mouthful of air so quickly she almost gagged. There was no hiding the astonishment on her face.

Thomas Donovan, his face full of satisfaction, leaned even closer, his lips right at her eye level. "LuAnn, I'd like to talk to you. It's important and—"

She hit the accelerator and Donovan had to jump back to avoid having his feet crushed by the car tires.

"Hey!" he screamed after her. The car was almost out of sight. Donovan, his face ashen, ran to his car, started it up, and roared off down the road. "Christ!" he said to himself.

Donovan had tried directory assistance in Charlottesville, but they had no listing for Catherine Savage. He would have been shocked if they had. Someone on the run all these years didn't ordinarily give out her phone number. He had decided, after much thought, that the direct approach would be, if not the best, at least the most productive. He had watched the house for the last week, noted her pattern of early morning drives, and chosen today to make contact. Despite being almost run over, he had the satisfaction of knowing that he had been right. Throwing the question at her out of the blue like that, he knew, was the only sure way to get the truth. And now he had it. Catherine Savage was LuAnn Tyler. Her looks had changed considerably from the video and photos he had seen from ten years ago. The changes were subtle, no one single alteration really dramatic, yet the cumulative effect had been marked. Except for the look on her face and her abrupt departure, Donovan wouldn't have known it was her.

He now focused on the road ahead. He had just glimpsed the gray BMW. It was still far ahead, but on the curvy mountain road his smaller and more agile Honda was gaining. He didn't like playing the daredevil role; he had disdained it in his younger days when covering dangerous events halfway around the world, and he disliked it even more now. However, he had to make her understand what he was trying to do. He had to make her listen. And he had to get his story. He hadn't worked twenty-hour days the last several months tracking her down simply to watch her disappear again.

Matt Riggs stopped for a moment and again studied the terrain. The air was so clean and pure up here, the sky so blue, the peace and quiet so ethereal, he again marveled at why he had waited so long to chuck the big city, and come to calmer, if less exciting, parts. After years of being in the very center of millions of tense, increasingly aggressive people, he now found being able to feel like you were all alone in the world, for even a few minutes, was more soothing than he could have imagined. He was about to pull the property survey out of his jacket to study in more detail the dimensions of the property line when all thoughts of work amid the peaceful countryside abruptly disappeared from his mind.

He jerked his head around and whipped the binoculars up to his eyes to focus on what had suddenly destroyed the morning's calm. He quickly located the origin of the explosion of sound. Through the trees he spied two cars hurtling down from the road where the country estate was situated, their respective engines at full throttle. The car in front was a big BMW sedan. The car behind it was a smaller vehicle. What the smaller car lacked in muscle power to the big Bimmer, it more than made up for in agility around the winding road. At the speeds the two were doing, Riggs thought it most likely they would both end up either wrapped around a tree or upside down in one of the steep ditches that bordered either side of the road.

The next two visuals he made through his binoculars made him turn and run as fast as he could back to his truck.

The look of raw fear on the woman's face in the Bimmer, the way she looked behind to check her pursuer's progress, and the grim countenance of the man apparently chasing her were all he needed to kick-start every instinct he had ever gained from his former life.

He gunned the engine, unsure exactly what his plan of action would be, not that he had much time to come up with one. He pulled on to the road, strapping his seat belt across him as he did so. He normally carried a shotgun in the truck to ward off snakes, but he had forgotten it this morning. He had some shovels and a crowbar in the truck bed, although he hoped it wasn't going to come to that.

As he flew down the road, the two cars appeared in front of him on the main road. The Bimmer took the turn almost on two wheels before stabilizing, the other car right behind it. However, now on the straightaway, the three hundred plus horses of the BMW could be fully used, and the woman quickly opened a two-hundred-yard gap between herself and her pursuer, a gap that grew with every second. That wouldn't last, Riggs knew, because a curve that would qualify for deadman's status was fast approaching. He hoped to God the woman knew it; if she didn't he would be watching the BMW turn into a fireball as it sailed off the road and crashed into an army of unyielding hardwoods. With that prospect nearly upon them, his plan finally came together. He punched the gas, the truck flew forward, and he gained on what he now saw was a black Honda. The man apparently had all of his attention focused on the BMW, because when Riggs passed him on the left, the man didn't even look over. However, he took abrupt and angry notice when Riggs cut in front of him and immediately slowed down to twenty miles an hour. Up ahead, Riggs saw the woman glance back in her rearview mirror, her eyes riveted on Riggs and his fortuitous appearance on the scene as the truck and Honda fought a pitched battle for supremacy of the road. Riggs tried to motion to her to slow down, to make her understand what he was trying to do. Whether she got the message or not, he couldn't tell. Like the coils of a sidewinder, the truck and the Honda swayed back and forth across the narrow roadway, coming dangerously close to the sheer drop on the right side. Once, the truck's wheel partially skidded in the gravel shoulder and Riggs braced himself for the plunge over, before he barely managed to regain control. The driver of the Honda tried mightily to pass, leaning on his horn the whole time. But in his past career Riggs had done his share of dangerous, high-speed driving and he expertly matched the other man maneuver for maneuver. A minute later they rounded the almost V-shaped curve, a wall of sheer jutting rock on his left and an almost vertical drop to the right. Riggs anxiously looked down that steep slope for any sight of the Bimmer's wreckage. He breathed a sigh of relief as he saw none. He looked up the once again straight road. He saw the glint of a bumper far up ahead and then the big sedan was completely out of sight. Admiration was his first thought. The woman hadn't slowed down much, if any, coming around that curve. Even at twenty miles an hour Riggs hadn't felt all that safe. Damn

Riggs reached across to his glove box and pulled out his portable phone. He was just about to punch in 911 when the Honda now took the very aggressive tack of ramming his truck from behind. The phone flew out of his hand and smashed into several pieces against the dashboard. Riggs cursed, shook off the impact, clenched the wheel hard, shifted into low gear, and slowed down even more as the Honda repeatedly smashed into him. What he was hoping would happen eventually did, as the Honda's front bumper and the truck's heavy-duty rear one locked together. He could hear the gears grinding in the Honda as the driver tried to extricate his vehicle without success. Riggs peered into the rearview mirror and he saw the man's hand slide over to his glove compartment. Riggs wasn't going to wait around to see whether a weapon emerged from it or not. He jerked the truck to a stop, slammed the gear in reverse, and the two vehicles roared backward down the road. He watched with satisfaction as the man in the Honda jerked back upright and gripped the steering wheel in a panic. Riggs slowed as he came to the curve, cleared it and then shot forward again. As he came to a straightaway, he cut the wheel sharply to the left and slammed the Honda into the rocky side of the road. The force of that collision uncoupled the two vehicles. The driver appeared unhurt. Riggs slammed the truck into drive and quickly disappeared down the road in pursuit of the BMW. He continually looked back for several minutes but there was no sign of the Honda. Either it had been disabled upon impact, or the driver had decided not to pursue his reckless actions further.

The adrenaline continued to course through Riggs's body for several minutes until it finally dissipated. Five years removed from the dangers of his former profession, Riggs was aware that this morning's five-minute episode had reminded him vividly of how many close calls he had survived. He had neither expected nor ever wanted to rekindle that anxious feeling in the sleepy morning mists of central Virginia.

His damaged bumper clanking loudly, Riggs finally slowed down, as further pursuit of the BMW was hopeless. There were innumerable roads off the main track and the woman could have taken any one of them and be long gone by now. Riggs pulled off the road and stopped, plucked a pen from his shirt pocket and wrote the license plate numbers of the Honda and BMW down on the pad of paper he kept affixed to his dashboard. He ripped the paper off the pad and tucked it in his pocket. He had a pretty good idea who was in the Bimmer. Someone who lived in the big house. The same big house he had been hired to surround with a state-of-the-art security fence. Now the owner's request started to make a whole lot more sense to Riggs. And the question he was most interested in now was why? He drove off, deep in thought, the morning's peacefulness irretrievably shattered by the look of sheer terror on a woman's face.

TWENTY-THREE

The BMW had indeed pulled off on a side road several miles away from where Riggs and the Honda had tangled. The driver's side door was open, the motor running. Arms clutched tightly around her sides, LuAnn walked in tight, frenetic circles in the middle of the road, shooting frosty breaths skyward in her agitation. Anger, confusion, and frustration raced across her features. All traces of fear were gone, however. The present emotions were actually far more damaging to her. Fear almost always passed; these other mental battering rams did not retreat so easily. She had learned this over the years, and had even managed to cope with it as best as she could.

Now thirty years old, LuAnn Tyler still carried the impulsive energy and sleek animal movements of her youth. The years had grafted on to her a more complete, mature beauty. However, the basic elements of that beauty had been discernibly altered. Her body was leaner, the waist even tighter. The effect was to make her appear even taller than she already was. Her hair had grown out and now was far more blond than auburn, and cut in a sophisticated manner that highlighted her more defined facial features, including the minor nose job done for disguise rather than aesthetics. Her teeth were now perfect, having benefitted from years of expensive dentistry. There was, however, one imperfection.

She had not followed Jackson's advice regarding

the knife wound to her jaw. She had had it stitched, but let the scar remain. It wasn't all that noticeable, but every time she looked in the mirror, it was a stark reminder of where she had come from, how she had gotten here. It was her most visible tie to the past, and not a pleasant one. That was the reason she would not cover it over with surgery. She wanted to be reminded of the unpleasantness, of the pain.

People she had grown up with would probably have recognized her; however, she never planned to see anyone like that here. She had resigned herself to wearing a big hat and sunglasses whenever she ventured out into public, which wasn't very often. A lifetime of hiding from the world: that had come with her deal.

She went and sat back down on the front seat of the BMW, rubbing her hands back and forth across the padded steering wheel. She continually looked back down the road for any sign of her pursuer; however, the only sounds were her car's engine and her own uneven breathing. Huddled in her leather jacket, she hitched up her jeans, swung her long legs inside the car, and closed the door and locked it.

She took off and for a few moments as she drove her thoughts centered on the man in the truck. He had obviously helped her. Was he just a good Samaritan who had happened along at the right time? Or was he something else, something more complex than that? She had lived with this paranoia for so long now that it was like an exterior coating of paint. All observations had to pass through its screening first, all conclusions were based in some way upon how she perceived the motivation of anyone colliding unexpectedly with her universe. It all came down to one grim fact: fear of discovery. She took one long, deep breath and wondered for the hundredth time if she had made a grievous mistake by returning to the United States.

Riggs drove his battered truck up the private road. He had kept a close eye out for the Honda on his return down the road, but the car and driver had not reappeared. Going up to the house, he figured, was the quickest way to find a telephone, and perhaps also seek an explanation of sorts for this morning's events. Not that he deserved one, but his intervention had helped the woman and he felt that was worth something. In any event, he couldn't exactly let it rest now. He was surprised that no one stopped him on the drive up. There was no private security, apparently. He had met with the owner's representative in town; this was his first visit to the estate, which had been christened Wicken's Hunt long ago. The home was one of the most beautiful in the area. It had been constructed in the early 1920s with craftsmanship that was simply nonexistent today. The Wall Street magnate who had had it built as a summer retreat had jumped off a New York skyscraper during the stock market crash of '29. The home had passed through several hands, and had been on the market six years before being sold to the current owner. The place had required substantial renovation. Riggs had talked to some of the subcontractors employed to do that work. They had spoken with awe of the craftsmanship and beauty of the place.

Whatever moving trucks had hauled the owner's possessions up the mountain road had apparently done so in the middle of the night, because Riggs could find no one who had seen them. No one had seen the owner, either. He had checked at the courthouse land records. The home was owned by a corporation that Riggs had never heard of. The usual channels of gossip had not yielded an answer to the mystery, although St. Anne's-Belfield School had admitted a ten-year-old girl named Lisa Savage who had given Wicken Hunt as her home address. Riggs had heard that a tall young woman would occasionally drop off and pick up the child; although she had always worn sunglasses and a large hat. Most often picking up the little girl would be an elderly man who had been described to Riggs as built like a linebacker. A strange household. Riggs had several friends who worked at the school but none of them would talk about the young woman. If they knew her name, they wouldn't say what it was.

When Riggs rounded a curve, the mansion suddenly appeared directly in front of him. His truck resembled a plain, squat tug bearing down on the *QEII*. The mansion stood three stories tall, with a double doorway spanning at least twenty feet.

He parked his truck in the wraparound drive that encircled a magnificent stone fountain that, on this cold morning, was not operating. The landscaping was as lush and as carefully planned as the house; and where annuals and even late-blooming perennials had died out, evergreens and other hardy foliage of all descriptions filled in the spaces.

He slid out of his seat, making sure he had the piece of paper with the license plate numbers still in his pocket. As he walked up to the front door, he wondered if a place like this would condescend to have a doorbell; or would a butler automatically open the door at his approach? Actually, neither happened, but as he cleared the top step, a voice did speak to him from a brand new-looking intercom built into the side of the wall next to the door.

"Can I help you?" It was a man's voice, big, solid, and, Riggs thought, slightly threatening.

"Matthew Riggs. My company was hired to build the privacy fence on the property's perimeter."

229

"Okay."

The door didn't budge, and the tone of the voice made clear that unless Riggs had more information to impart, this status was not going to change. He looked around, suddenly conscious that he was being observed. Sure enough, above his head, recessed within the back of one of the columns, was a video camera. That looked new as well. He waved.

"Can I help you?" the voice said again.

"I'd like to use a telephone."

"I'm sorry, that's not possible."

"Well, I'd say it should be possible since I just crashed my truck into a car that was chasing a big charcoal gray BMW that I'm pretty sure came from this house. I just wanted to make sure that the woman driving the car was okay. She looked pretty scared the last time I saw her."

The next sound Riggs heard was the front door being unbolted and thrown open. The elderly man facing him matched the six foot one Riggs in height, but was far broader across the shoulders and chest. However, Riggs noted that the man moved with a slight limp as though the legs and, perhaps, the knees in particular were beginning to go. The possessor of a very strong, athletic body himself, Riggs decided he would not want to have to take this guy on. Despite his advancing age and obvious infirmities, the man looked strong enough to break Riggs's back with ease. This was obviously the guy seen at the school picking up Lisa Savage. The doting linebacker.

"What the hell are you talking about?"

Riggs pointed toward the road. "About ten minutes ago, I was out doing a preliminary survey of the property line in advance of ordering up men and equipment when this BMW come bolting down the road, a woman driving, blond from what I could see, and scared to death. Another car, a black Honda Accord, probably a 1992 or '93 model, right on her butt. A guy was driving that one and he looked determined as hell."

"The woman, is she all right?" The elderly man edged forward perceptibly. Riggs backed up a notch, unwilling to let the guy get too close until he had a better understanding of the situation. For all he knew, this guy could be in cahoots with the man in the Honda. Riggs's internal radar was all over the place on this one.

"As far as I know. I got in between them and took the Honda out, banged the crap out of my truck in the process." Riggs briefly rubbed his neck as the recollection of his collision brought several distinct painful twinges to that location. He would have to soak in the tub tonight.

"We'll take care of the truck. Where's the woman?"

"I didn't come up here to complain about the truck, mister—"

"Charlie, call me Charlie." The man extended his hand, which Riggs shook. He had not under-estimated the strength the old guy possessed. As he took his hand back Riggs observed the indentations in his fingers caused by the other man's vise-like grip. Whether he was merely anxious about the safety of the woman, or he mangled visitors' fingers on a routine basis, Riggs didn't know.

"I go by Matt. Like I said, she got away, and as far as I know, she's fine. But I still wanted to call it in."

"Call it in?"

"The police. The guy in the Honda was breaking at least several laws that I know of, including a couple of felonies. Too bad I didn't get to read him his rights."

"You sound like a cop."

231

Had Charlie's face darkened, or was that his imagination, Riggs wondered.

"Something like that. A long while back. I got the license plate number of both cars." He looked at Charlie, studying the battered and grizzled face, trying to get beyond the solid stare he was getting in return. "I'm assuming the BMW belongs to this house, and the woman."

Charlie hesitated for a moment and then nodded. "She's the owner."

"And the Honda?"

"Never seen it before."

Riggs turned and looked back down the road. "The guy could've been waiting partially down the entry road. There's nothing stopping him from doing that." Riggs turned and looked back at Charlie.

"That's why we contracted with you to build the fence and gate." A glint of anger rose in Charlie's eyes.

"Now I can see why that might be a good idea, but I only got the signed contract yesterday. I work fast, but not that fast."

Charlie relaxed at the obvious logic of Riggs's words and looked down for a moment.

"What about using that phone, Charlie?" Riggs took a step forward. "Look, I know a kidnap attempt when I see one." He looked up at the facade of the house. "It's not hard to see why either, is it?"

Charlie took a deep breath, his loyalties sharply divided. He was sick with worry about LuAnn – *Catherine*, he corrected himself mentally; despite the passage of ten years, he had never been comfortable with her new name. He was finding it close to impossible to allow the police to be called in.

"I take it you're her friend or family—"

"Both actually," Charlie said with renewed vigor as he stared over Riggs's shoulder, a smile breaking across his face.

The reason for that change in attitude reached Riggs's ears a second later. He turned and watched the BMW pull up behind his truck.

LuAnn got out of the car, glanced at the truck for a moment, until her eyes riveted on the damaged bumper; then she strode up the steps, passing over Riggs to focus on Charlie.

"This guy said you ran into some trouble," said Charlie, pointing at Riggs.

"Matt Riggs." Riggs extended his hand. In her boots, the woman wasn't much shorter than he. The impression of exceptional beauty he had gotten through his binoculars was considerably magnified up close. The hair was long and full, with golden highlights that seem to catch every streak of the sun's rays as it slowly rose over them. The face and complexion were flawless to the point of seeming impossible to achieve naturally, yet the woman was young so the cut of the plastic surgeon's knife could not have beckoned to her yet. Riggs reasoned the beauty must be all her own. Then he spotted the scar that ran along her jawline. That surprised him, it seemed so out of place with the rest of her. The scar also intrigued Riggs because, to his experienced eye, the wound seemed to have been made by a knife with a serrated edge. Most women, he figured, especially those who had the kind of money she obviously did, would have paid any amount to cover up that blemish.

The pair of calm, hazel eyes that stared into Riggs made him conclude that this woman was different. The person he was looking at was one of those rare creations: a very lovely woman who cared little about her looks. As his eyes continued to sweep over her, he noted the lean, elegant, body; but from the smallish hips and waist there grew a breadth of

233

shoulders that suggested exceptional physical strength. When her hand closed around his, he almost gasped. The grip was almost indistinguishable from Charlie's.

"I hope you're okay," said Riggs. "I got the plate number of the Honda. I was going to call it in to the cops, but my cell phone got broken when the guy hit me. The car's probably stolen anyway. I got a good look at the guy. This is a pretty isolated place. We should be able to nail him, if we act fast enough."

LuAnn looked at him, confusion on her face. "What are you talking about?"

Riggs blinked and stepped back. "The car that was chasing you."

LuAnn looked over at Charlie. Riggs watched closely but he saw no discernible signals passing between them. Then LuAnn pointed over at Riggs's truck. "I saw that truck and another car driving erratically, but I didn't stop to ask any questions. It was none of my business."

Riggs gaped for a moment before he responded. "The reason I was doing the two-step with the Honda was because he was trying his best to run you off the road. In fact, I almost took your place as the wreck of the week."

"Again, I'm sorry, but I don't know what you're talking about. Don't you think I would know if someone were trying to run me off the road?"

"So you're saying that you always drive eighty miles an hour around curvy, mountainous roads just for the fun of it?" Riggs asked heatedly.

"I don't think my driving methods are any of your concern," she snapped back. "However, since you happen to be on my property, I think it is my concern to know why you're here."

Charlie piped in. "He's the guy who's building the security fence."

LuAnn eyed Riggs steadily. "Then I would strongly suggest you concentrate on that task rather than come up here with some outrageous account of my being chased."

Riggs's face flushed and he started to say something, but then decided against it. "Have a good day, ma'am." He turned and headed back to his truck.

LuAnn didn't look back. She passed by Charlie without a glance and walked quickly into the house. Charlie stared after Riggs for a moment before shutting the door.

As Riggs climbed back in his truck another car pulled up the drive. An older woman was driving. The back seat of the car was stacked with groceries. The woman was Sally Beecham, LuAnn's live-in housekeeper, just back from early-morning grocery shopping. She glanced over at Riggs in a cursory fashion. Though his features were laced with anger, he curtly nodded at her and she returned the gesture. As was her custom, she pulled around to the side-load garage and hit the garage door opener clipped to the car's visor. The door in from the garage led directly to the kitchen, and Beecham was an efficient person who detested wasted effort.

As Riggs pulled off he glanced back up at the massive house. With so many windows staring back at him he didn't catch the one framing LuAnn Tyler, arms folded across her chest, looking resolutely at him, a mixture of worry and guilt on her face.

TWENTY-FOUR

The Honda slowed down, turned off the back road, then made its way over a rustic wooden bridge spanning a small creek, and then disappeared into the thickness of the surrounding forest. The antenna clipped some of the overhanging branches, sending a shower of dewdrops on to the windshield. Up ahead, under an umbrella of oak trees, a small, ramshackle cottage was visible. The Honda pulled into the tiny backyard and then into a small shed located behind the cottage. The man closed the doors of the shed and walked up to the house.

Donovan rubbed his lower back and then worked his neck around some in an attempt to overcome the aftereffects of his early morning escapade. He was still visibly shaking. Donovan stamped into the house, threw off his coat, and proceeded to make coffee in the small kitchen. Nervously smoking a cigarette while the coffee percolated, he looked outside the window with a slight feeling of apprehension, although he was fairly certain no one had followed him. He rubbed his brow. The cottage was isolated and the landlord didn't know his real name or the reason he had decided to take up temporary residence here.

The guy in the truck, who the hell had he been? Friend of the woman or some guy who had happened by? Since he had been seen, Donovan would have to shave off his beard and do something with his hair. He would also have to rent another car. The Honda was damaged and the guy in the truck could've gotten the license plate number. But the Honda was a rental, and Donovan had not used his real name in leasing it. He wasn't worried about the woman doing anything about it, but the guy might put a crimp in his plans. He wouldn't risk driving the Honda back into town to exchange it for another rental. He didn't want to be spotted driving it, and he didn't want to have to explain the damage to the bumper right now. Tonight, he'd walk to the main road and catch a bus into town, where he would pick up another rental car.

He poured a cup of coffee and walked into the dining room that had been set up as an office. A computer terminal, printer, and fax and phone were set up on one table. File boxes were stacked neatly in one corner. On two walls hung several large bulletin boards. They were filled with newspaper clippings.

The car chase had been stupid, Donovan muttered to himself. It was a miracle both of them weren't dead in some ravine right now. Tyler's reaction had absolutely astonished him. Although, thinking about it now, it probably shouldn't have. She was scared, and she had ample reason to be. Donovan's next problem was apparent. What if she disappeared again? Finding her the first time had been part hard work and part luck. There was no guarantee he would be as fortunate the next time. However, there was nothing he could do about that now. He could only wait and watch.

He had established a contact at the regional airport who would advise Donovan if any person matching LuAnn Tyler's description or traveling under the name Catherine Savage was headed out of the area via plane. Unless she had another identity already set up, it would be difficult for Tyler to travel any time soon except under the name Catherine Savage, and that would leave him a trail. If she left the area by means other than airplane, well, he could watch the house, but he couldn't do it twenty-four hours a day. He briefly contemplated calling in reinforcements from the *Trib*, but there were many factors that cautioned him against doing that. He had worked alone for almost thirty years, and bringing in a partner now was not very appealing, even if the newspaper would consent to do it. No, he would do what he could to dog her movements, and he would work very hard to set up another face-to-face. He was convinced that he could make the woman trust him, work with him. He didn't believe that she had killed anybody. But he was fairly certain that she and perhaps some of the other winners were hiding something about the lottery. He wanted that story, wherever it led him.

A fire blazed in the hearth of the spacious two-story library, which had floor-to-ceiling maple bookcases on three walls and inviting, overstuffed furniture arranged in intimate conversation patterns. LuAnn sat on a leather sofa, her legs drawn up under her, bare feet protruding, an embroidered cotton shawl covering her shoulders. A cup of tea and a plate of uneaten breakfast sat on the table next to her. Sally Beecham, dressed in a gray uniform with a sparkling white apron, was just leaving, carrying the serving tray. Charlie closed the arched double doors behind her and sat down next to LuAnn.

"Listen, are you gonna tell me what really happened or not?" When LuAnn didn't answer, Charlie gripped one of her hands. "Your hands are like ice. Drink the tea." He rose and stoked the fire until the flames made his face redden. He looked at her expectantly. "I can't help you if you don't tell me what's wrong, LuAnn."

Over the last ten years a lasting bond had been built between the two that had seen them through many crises, both minor and major, in their travels. From the time Charlie had touched her shoulder as the 747 climbed into the skies, until they had arrived back in America, they had been inseparable. Even though his given name was Robert, he had taken "Charlie" as his accepted name. It wasn't too far from the truth, as his middle name was Charles. What was in a name anyway? However, he referred to her as LuAnn only in private, as now. He was her closest friend and confidant, really her only one, since there were things she could not even tell her daughter.

As he sat back down, Charlie winced in pain. He was acutely aware that he was slowing down, a process that was exacerbated by the rough treatment of his body in his youth. The difference in years between the two was now more pronounced than ever, as nature took its toll on him. Even with all that, he would do anything for her, would face any danger, confront any enemy she had with every ounce of strength and ingenuity he had left.

It was the look in Charlie's eyes as LuAnn read these very thoughts that made her finally start talking.

"I had just left the house. He was standing in the middle of the driveway waving for me to stop."

"And you did?" Charlie's tone was incredulous.

"I didn't get out of the car. I couldn't exactly run over the man. If he tried anything, or pulled a gun, you can bet I would've done just that."

Charlie hitched one leg up over the other, an action that was accompanied by another painful wince. "Go on. Eat while you're talking, and drink your tea! Your face is white as a sheet."

LuAnn did as he said, managing to get some bites of egg and toast down and a few sips of the hot tea. Putting the cup back down, she wiped her mouth with a napkin. "He motioned for me to roll the window down. I cracked it a bit and asked him what he wanted."

"Wait a minute, what'd he look like?"

"Medium height, full beard, a little gray at the edges. Wire-rimmed glasses. Olive complexion, maybe a hundred sixty pounds. Probably late forties or early fifties." Over the last ten years, memorizing minute details of people's appearances had become second nature to LuAnn.

Charlie mentally filed away her description of the man. "Go on."

"He said he was looking for the Brillstein Estate." She hesitated and took another sip of tea. "I told him that this wasn't the place."

Charlie leaned forward. "What'd he say then?"

Now LuAnn was perceptibly shaking. "He said he was looking for somebody."

"Who? Who?" Charlie asked again as LuAnn's blank stare dropped to the floor.

She finally looked up at him. "LuAnn Tyler from Georgia."

Charlie sat back. After a decade, they had pretty much put the fear of exposure on the back burner, though it was still there and always would be. Now that flame had just been rekindled.

"Did he say anything else?"

LuAnn rubbed the napkin across her dry lips and then sat back up. "He said something about wanting to talk to me. Then . . . I . . . I just went blank, slammed the accelerator, and almost ran over him." She let all the air drain out of her after speaking. She looked over at Charlie.

"And he chased you?"

She nodded. "I've got strong nerves, Charlie, you know that, but they have their limits. When you're going out for a relaxing early morning drive and you get hit with something like that instead?" She cocked her head at him. "God, I was just starting to feel comfortable here. Jackson hasn't shown up, Lisa loves school, this place is so beautiful." She fell silent.

"What about the other guy, Riggs? Is his story true?"

Suddenly agitated, LuAnn stood up and paced the room. She stopped and ran her hand fondly along a row of finely bound novels resting on the shelves. Over the years, she had read just about every book in the room. Ten years of intensive education with some of the finest private tutors had produced an articulate, polished, cosmopolitan woman far removed from the one who had run from that trailer, from those bodies. Now those bloody images would not budge from her mind.

"Yes. He just jumped right into the middle of it. I probably would've lost the guy, anyway." She added quietly, "But he did help me. And I would've liked to have thanked him. But I couldn't exactly do that, could I?" She threw up her hands in frustration and sat back down.

Charlie rubbed his chin as he pondered the situation.

"You know, legally, the lottery scam amounts to a bunch of felonies, but the statute of limitations has expired on all of them. The guy can't really hurt you there."

"What about the murder charge? There's no statute of limitations on that. I did kill the man, Charlie. I did it in self-defense, but who the hell would believe me now?"

"True, but the police haven't pursued the case in years."

"Okay, do you want me to go turn myself in?"

"I'm not saying that. I just think you might be blowing this out of proportion."

LuAnn trembled. Going to jail over the money or the killing was not her biggest concern. She put her hands together and looked over at Charlie.

"My daddy probably never said one word to me that was true. He did his best to make me feel like the most worthless piece of trash in the world and any time I built up some confidence he'd come along and tear it down. The only thing I was good for according to him was making babies and looking pretty for my man."

"I know you had it rough, LuAnn–"

"I swore to myself that I would never, ever do that to any child of mine. I swore that to God on a stack of Bibles, said it on my mother's grave, and whispered it to Lisa while I was carrying her and every night for six months after she was born." LuAnn swallowed hard and stood up. "And you know what? Everything I've told her, everything she knows about herself, you, me, every damned molecule of her existence is a lie. It's all made up, Charlie. Okay, maybe the statute of limitations is expired, maybe I won't go to jail because the police don't care that I killed a drug dealer. But if this man has found out my past and he brings it all out into the open, then Lisa will know. She'll know that her mother told her more lies than my daddy probably ever thought of in his entire life. I'll be a hundred times worse than Benny Tyler, and I'll lose my little girl as certain as the sun comes up. I'll lose Lisa." After this outburst, LuAnn shuddered and closed her eyes.

"I'm sorry, LuAnn, I hadn't thought about it like that." Charlie looked down at his hands.

LuAnn's eyes opened and they held a distinctly fatalistic look. "And if that happens, if she finds out, then it's over for me. Jail will seem like a day in the park, because if I lose my little girl, then I won't have any reason to be anymore. Despite all this." She swept her arms around the room. "No reason at all."

LuAnn sat back down and rubbed at her forehead.

Charlie finally broke the silence. "Riggs got the license plate number. On both cars." He fiddled with his shirt and added, "Riggs is an ex-cop, LuAnn."

Her head in her hands, LuAnn looked at him. "Oh God! And I didn't think it could get any worse."

"Don't worry, he runs your plate, he gets nothing except Catherine Savage with this address, legit Social Security number, the works. Your identity has no holes in it. Not after all this time."

"I think we have a very big hole, Charlie. The guy in the Honda?"

Charlie conceded the point with a quick nod of his head. "Right, right, but I'm talking about Riggs. Your end with him is okay."

"But if he tracks the other guy down, maybe talks to him?"

"Then maybe we got a big problem." Charlie finished the thought for her.

"You think Riggs might do that?"

"I don't know. I do know that he didn't buy your story about not knowing you were being chased. Under the circumstances, I don't blame you for not acknowledging it, but an ex-cop? Hell, he's got to be suspicious. I don't think we can count on him letting it lie."

LuAnn rubbed the hair out of her eyes. "So what do we do?"

Charlie gently took one of her hands. "*You* do nothing. You let old Charlie see what he can find us. We've been in tight places before. Right?"

She slowly nodded and then licked her lips nervously. "But this might be the tightest one of them all."

Matt Riggs walked quickly up the steps of the old Victorian with a wraparound porch that he had meticulously restored over the last year. He had had a few years of carpentry and woodworking experience before coming to Charlottesville. They had been pursuits he had taken up to alleviate the stress that had come with what he used to do for a living. He wasn't thinking about the graceful lines of his home right now, however.

He went inside and down the hall to his office, for his home also housed his business. He shut the door, grabbed the phone, and placed a call to an old friend in Washington, D.C. The Honda had D.C. tags. Riggs was pretty sure what running the license plate would reveal: either a rental or stolen. The BMW would be another matter. At least he would find out the woman's name, since it had suddenly occurred to him on the drive home that neither the man calling himself Charlie nor the woman had ever mentioned it. He was assuming the last name would be Savage and that the woman in the BMW was either Lisa Savage's mother or perhaps, from her youthful looks, an older sister.

A half hour later he had his answers. The Honda was indeed a rental out of the nation's capital. Tom Jones was the name of the lessee and he had rented the vehicle two weeks ago. Tom Jones! That was real clever, Riggs thought. The address he had for the man would be as phoney as the name, he was certain. A total deadend; he had expected nothing less.

Then he stared down at the woman's name he had written on a piece of paper. Catherine Savage. Born in Charlottesville, Virginia. Age: thirty. Social Security number had checked out, current address was correct: Wicken's Hunt. Unmarried. Excellent credit, no priors. No red flags at all in her background. He had a good slice of her past right there in his hand in less than half an hour. Computers were wonderful. And yet . . .

He looked at her age again. Thirty years old. He thought back to the house and substantial grounds, three hundred acres of prime Virginia real estate. He knew the asking price for Wicken's Hunt had been six million dollars. If she had struck a wonderful deal, Ms. Savage could conceivably have gotten it for between four and five million, but from what he heard the renovation work had easily run to seven figures. Where the hell does a woman that young get that kind of money? She wasn't a movie star or rock star; the name Catherine Savage meant nothing to him, and he wasn't that far out of the loop on popular culture.

Or was it Charlie who had the bucks? They weren't husband and wife, that was clear. He had said he was family, but something was off there too. He leaned back in his chair, slid open a drawer of his desk, and popped a couple of aspirin, as his neck threatened to stiffen up again. It could be she had inherited serious family money or been the extraordinarily rich widow of some old duffer. Recalling her face, he could easily see that. A lot of men would shower her with everything they had.

So what now? He looked out the window of his office at the beauty of the surrounding trees with their vibrant fall colors. Things were going well for him: An unhappy past behind him; a thriving business in a place he loved. A low-key lifestyle that he figured would add lots of quality years to his life. And now this. He held the piece of paper with her name on it up to eye level. Despite having no material incentive to care at all about her, Riggs's curiosity was at a high pitch.

"Who the hell are you, Catherine Savage?"

TWENTY-FIVE

"You about ready, honey?" LuAnn peeked in the door and cast her gaze fondly on the back of the young girl who was finishing dressing.

Lisa looked around at her mother. "Almost."

With a face and athletic build that mirrored LuAnn's, Lisa Savage was the one immovable landmark in her mother's life.

LuAnn stepped into the room, closed the door, and settled on the bed. "Miss Sally says you didn't eat much breakfast, are you feeling all right?"

"I have a test today. I guess I'm just a little nervous." One result of having lived all over the world was that her speech carried myriad traces of the different cultures, dialects, and accents. The mesh was a pleasing one, although several months in Virginia had already started to graft upon Lisa the beginnings of a mild Southern inflection.

LuAnn smiled. "I would've thought that by now, after so many straight A's, you wouldn't get so nervous." She touched her daughter's shoulder. During the time spent traveling, LuAnn had thrown every ounce of energy and a great deal of money into reshaping herself to be who she had always wanted to be, which was as far from Southern white trash named LuAnn Tyler as she could get. Well-educated, able to speak two foreign languages, she noted with pride that Lisa could speak four, as much at home in China as in London. She had covered several lifetimes in the last ten years. With this morning's developments, maybe that was a good thing. Had she run out of time?

Lisa finished dressing and sat down with her back to her mother. LuAnn picked up a brush and started doing her daughter's hair, a daily ritual between the two that allowed them to talk and catch up with each other.

"I can't help it, I still do get nervous. It's not always easy."

"Most things worthwhile in life aren't easy. But, you work hard and that's the important thing. You do your best, that's all I'll ever ask, regardless of what your grades are." She combed Lisa's hair into a thick ponytail and then clipped on a bow. "Just don't bring home any B's." They both laughed.

As they walked downstairs together, Lisa looked over at her mother. "I saw you talking to a man outside this morning. You and Uncle Charlie."

LuAnn tried to hide her apprehensiveness. "You were up? It was pretty early."

"Like I said, I was nervous about the test."

"Right."

"Who was he?"

"He's putting up the security fence and gate around the property. He had some questions about the plans."

"Why do we need a security fence?"

LuAnn took her hand. "We've talked about this before, Lisa. We're, well, we're very well-off financially. You know that. There are some bad people in the world. They might try to do things, to get money from us."

"Like robbing us?"

"Yes, or maybe something else."

"Like what?"

LuAnn stopped and sat down on the steps,

beckoning Lisa to join her. "Remember how I'm always telling you to be careful, watch out for people?" Lisa nodded. "Well, that's because some bad people might try to take you away from me."

Lisa looked frightened. "I'm not telling you that to scare you, baby, but in a way I guess I do want you to be concerned, to be aware of what's going on. If you use your head and keep your eyes open, everything will be fine. Me and Uncle Charlie won't let anything happen to you. Mommy promises. Okay?"

Lisa nodded and they went down the stairs hand in hand.

Charlie met them in the hallway. "My, don't we look extra pretty this morning."

"I've got a test."

"You think I don't know that? I was up last night until ten-thirty with you going over the stuff. You're gonna ace it, sure as anything. Go get your coat, I'll be out front in the car."

"Isn't Mommy taking me today?"

Charlie glanced over at LuAnn. "I'm gonna give your mom a break this morning. Besides, it'll give us one more time to go over the test stuff, right?"

Lisa beamed. "Right."

After Lisa had gone, Charlie turned a very serious face to LuAnn. "I'm gonna check some things out in town after I drop Lisa off."

"You think you can find this guy?"

Charlie shrugged as he buttoned up his overcoat. "Maybe, maybe not. It's not a big town, but it's got lots of hiding places. One reason *we* picked it, right?"

LuAnn nodded. "What about Riggs?"

"I'll save him for later. I go knock on his door now, he might get more suspicious than he already is. I'll call from the car if I find out anything."

LuAnn watched the two climb into Charlie's Range Rover and drive off. Deep in thought, she pulled on a heavy coat, walked through the house and out the back. She passed the Olympic-size pool with surrounding flagstone patio and three-foot-high brick wall. At this time of year, the pool was drained and protected by a metal cover. The tennis court would probably go in next year. LuAnn cared little for either activity. Her underprivileged childhood had yielded no opportunities to idly hit a yellow ball around or lounge in chlorinated water. But Lisa was an avid swimmer and tennis player, and upon arriving at Wicken's Hunt, she had pressed eagerly for a tennis court. Actually, it was nice to know she was going to be around in one spot long enough actually to plan something like the construction of a tennis court down the road.

The one activity LuAnn had picked up in her travels was what she was heading to do right now. The horse barn was about five hundred yards behind the main house and surrounded on three sides by a thick grove of trees. Her long strides took her there quickly. She employed several people full-time to care for the grounds and horse barn, but they were not yet at work. She pulled the gear from the tack room and expertly saddled her horse, Joy, named for her mother. She snagged a wide-brimmed Stetson hat and leather gloves off the wall, and swung herself up on to her ride. She had had Joy for several years now; the horse had traveled with them to several countries, not an easy task, but one that was quite manageable when your pocketbook was bottomless. LuAnn and company had arrived in the United States via plane. Joy had made the crossing by boat.

One reason she and Charlie had decided upon the property was its myriad of riding trails, some probably dating from Thomas Jefferson's days.

She started off at a good pace and soon left the

house behind. Twin clouds of breath escorted the pair as they made their way down a gradual decline and then around a curve, the trees hugging either side of the trail. The morning's briskness helped to clear LuAnn's head, let her think about things.

She had not recognized the man, not that she had expected to. Counterintuitively, she had always expected discovery to come from unknown quarters. He had known her real name. Whether that was a recent discovery on his part or he had found out long ago, she had no way of knowing.

Many times she had thought about going back to Georgia and telling the truth, just making a clean breast of it and attempting to put all of it behind her. But these thoughts had never managed to work themselves into cohesive actions and the reasons were clear. Although she had killed the man in self-defense, the words of the person calling himself Mr. Rainbow had continually come back to her. She had run. Thus, the police would assume the worst. On top of that, she was vastly rich, and who would have any sympathy or compassion for her now? Especially people from her hometown. The Shirley Watsons of the world were not so rare. Added to that was the fact that she had done something that was absolutely wrong. The horse she was riding, the clothes she was wearing, the home she was living in, the education and worldliness she had obtained over the years for herself and Lisa, all had been bought and paid for with what amounted to stolen dollars. In stark fiscal terms, she was one of the biggest crooks in history. If need be, she could endure prosecution for all that, but then Lisa's face sprung up in her thoughts. Almost simultaneously, the imagined words of Benny Tyler that day at the graveyard came filtering back to her.

Do it for Big Daddy. When did I ever lie to you,

baby doll? Daddy loves you.

She pulled Joy to a halt and sunk her head in her hands as a painful vision entered her head.

Lisa, sweetheart, your whole life is a lie. You were born in a trailer in the woods because I couldn't afford to have you anywhere else. Your father was a no-account loser who got murdered over drugs. I used to stick you under the counter at the Number One Truck Stop in Rikersville, Georgia, while I waited tables. I've killed a man and run from the police over it. Mommy stole all this money, more money than you could dream of. Everything you and I have came from that stolen money.

When did Mommy ever lie to you, baby doll? Mommy loves you.

LuAnn slowly dismounted and collapsed on a large stone that jutted at an angle from the ground. Only after several minutes did she slowly come around, her head swaying in long, slow movements, as though she were drunk.

She finally rose and took a handful of pebbles from the ground. She idly skipped the stones across the smooth surface of a small pond, sending each one farther and farther with quick, graceful flicks of her wrist. She could never go back now. There was nothing to go back to. She had given herself a new life, but it had come with a terrifyingly high cost. Her past was total fabrication, thus her future was uncertain. Her day-to-day existence vacillated between fear of total collapse of the flimsy veneer shrouding her true identity and immense guilt for what she had done. But if she lived for anything, it was to ensure that Lisa's life would not be harmed in any way by her mother's past – or future – actions. Whatever else happened, her little girl would not suffer because of her.

LuAnn remounted Joy, cantering along until she slowed the mare down to a walk as they passed through some overhanging tree branches. She guided Joy to the edge of the trail and watched the swift, powerful thrust of the swollen creek that cut a jagged path across her property. There had been recent heavy rains, and early snow in the mountains had turned the usually docile water into a dangerous torrent. She backed Joy away from the edge and continued on.

Ten years ago, just after she, Charlie, and Lisa had landed in London, they had immediately boarded a plane for Sweden. Jackson had given them detailed marching orders for the first twelve months and they had not dared to deviate from them. The next six months had been a whirlwind zigzag through western Europe and then several years in Holland and then back to Scandinavia where a tall, light-haired woman would not seem so out of place. They had also spent time in Monaco and surrounding countries. The last two years had them in New Zealand, where they had all enjoyed the quiet, civilized, and even somewhat old-fashioned lifestyle. While Lisa knew multiple languages, English had been her primary one; LuAnn had been firm on that. LuAnn was an American despite spending so much time away.

It had indeed been fortunate that Charlie was a seasoned traveler. It had been largely through his efforts that potential disaster had been avoided at several different times. They had not heard from Jackson, but both assumed that he knew Charlie was with her. Thank God he was. If he hadn't gotten on that plane, LuAnn didn't know what she would've done. As it stood now, she couldn't function without him. And he wasn't getting any younger. She shook at the thought of life without the man. To be robbed of the one person in her life who shared her secret, who loved her and Lisa. There was nothing Charlie wouldn't do for them, and when his life ended and that void erupted . . . She drew in a deep breath.

Their new identities had been cemented over the years as LuAnn had taken great pains to establish the history Jackson had concocted for her and her daughter. The toughest part by far had been Lisa. Lisa believed her father to have been an extremely wealthy European financier who had died when Lisa was very young and who had left behind no family other than them. Charlie's role, while never fully explained, was clearly one of family and the "uncle" label had seemed a natural one. There were no photographs of Mr. Savage. LuAnn had explained to Lisa that her father was very reclusive and a touch eccentric and had allowed none to be taken. LuAnn and Charlie had long debated whether actually to create a man, photos and all, but had decided that it would be too dangerous. A wall with holes punched through it would eventually fall. Thus, Lisa believed her mother to be the very young widow of an extremely wealthy man, whose wealth, in turn, had made her mother one of the wealthiest women in the world. And one of the most generous.

LuAnn had sent Beth, her former coworker, enough money to start her own chain of restaurants. Johnny Jarvis from the mall had received enough to pay for several advanced degrees at the country's most prestigious universities. Duane's parents had received enough money to keep them secure in their retirement. LuAnn had even sent money to Shirley Watson, a guilty reaction to having lashed the woman with a negative reputation in the only place where Shirley would ever have the ambition or courage to live. Finally, LuAnn's mother's gravesite was now marked with a far more elaborate monument. The police, she was sure, had done all they could to track her down through this largesse, but

253

without success. Jackson had hidden the money well and there had been absolutely no trace for the authorities to follow.

In addition, half her yearly income had been donated anonymously to a number of charities and other good works that she and Charlie had identified over the years. They were ever on the lookout for more deserving homes for the lottery money. LuAnn was determined to do as much good as she could with the money to atone, at least in part, for the manner in which she had acquired it. Even with all that, the money came in far faster than they could dispose of it. Jackson's investments had paid off more handsomely than even he had envisioned and the anticipated twenty-five million dollars in earnings each year had actually exceeded forty million per annum. All money unspent by LuAnn had also been reinvested by Jackson and the surplus had kept compounding until the assets LuAnn now held in her own name were almost half a billion dollars. She shook her head at the thought of the staggering sum. And the original lottery prize money, one hundred million dollars, was to be returned to her very shortly, the ten-year period having expired, as her contract with Jackson had stated. That mattered little to LuAnn. Jackson could keep it; it wasn't as though she needed it. But he would return it. The man, she had to admit, had been utterly faithful to his promise.

Over all these years, every quarter the detailed financial statements had arrived, no matter where they happened to be in the world. But since only the papers and never the man showed up, LuAnn's anxiety finally had passed. The letter accompanying all the financial packets was from an investment company with a Swiss address. She had no idea of Jackson's ties to this firm, nor did she care to explore that area further. She had seen enough of him to be respectful of his volatility; and more disturbingly, of the extreme consequences which he was capable of causing. She also remembered how he had been prepared to kill her if she had rejected his offer. There was something not quite natural about him. The powers he seemed to possess could hardly be of this world.

She stopped at a large oak. From one of its branches a long knotted rope dangled. LuAnn gripped the rope and lifted herself off the saddle, while Joy, already quite familiar with this ritual, waited patiently. Her arms moving like wonderfully calibrated pistons, LuAnn swiftly climbed to the other end of the rope, which was tied around a thick branch almost thirty feet off the ground, and then made her way back down. She repeated the process twice more. She had a fully equipped gymnasium in her home where she worked out diligently. It wasn't vanity; she had little interest in how it made her look. She was naturally strong, and that physical strength had carried her through many a crisis. It was one of the few constant things in her life and she was loath to let it disappear.

Growing up in Georgia, she had climbed many trees, run through miles of countryside, and jumped many ravines. She had just been having fun; the concept of exercise hadn't come into the equation. And so, in addition to pumping the iron, she had built a more natural exercise course across her extensive grounds. She pulled herself up the rope one more time, the muscle cords in her arms and back tight as rebar.

Breathing hard, she settled lightly back into the saddle and made her way back to the horse barn, her heart lightened and her spirits raised by the invigorating ride through the countryside and the strenuous rope climb.

In the large storage building next to the horse barn, one of the groundspeople, a beefy man in his early thirties, had just started splitting logs with a sledgehammer and wedge. LuAnn glanced at him through the open doorway as she rode by. She quickly unsaddled Joy and returned the horse to its stall. She walked over to the doorway of the outbuilding. The man briefly nodded to her and then continued his work. He knew she lived in the mansion. Other than that, he knew nothing about her. She watched the man for a minute and then took off her coat, lifted a second sledgehammer off the wall, squeezed a spare wedge between her fingers, testing its weight, set a log up on the block, tapped the wedge into its rough surface, stepped back, and swung cleanly. The wedge bit deep, but didn't cleave the log in two. She hit it again, dead center, and then again. The log broke clean. The man glanced at her in surprise, then shrugged and kept splitting. They both pounded away, barely ten feet from each other. The man could split a log with one swing of the hammer, while it continued to take LuAnn two and sometimes three blows. He smiled over at her, the sweat showing on his brow. She kept pounding away, though, her arms and shoulders working in precise unity, and within five minutes she was cracking a log with one blow, and before he knew it she was doing it faster than he.

The man picked up his pace, the sweat falling faster across his brow, his grin gone as his breaths became more painful. After twenty minutes, he was taking two and three strikes to crack a log as his big arms and shoulders started to tire rapidly, his chest heaving and his legs rubbery. He watched in growing amazement as LuAnn continued, her pace steady, the strength of her blows against the wood totally undiminished. In fact, she seemed to be hitting the wedge harder and harder. The sound of metal on metal rang out louder and louder. Finally, the man dropped the sledgehammer and leaned back against the wall, his gut heaving, his arms dead, his shirt drenched in perspiration despite the chilly weather. LuAnn finished her pile of logs and, barely missing a stroke, finished off his stack as well. Her work complete, she wiped her forehead and replaced the sledgehammer on the wall hook before glancing over at the puffing man as she shook out her arms.

"You're very strong," she said, looking at the substantial pile of wood he had split as she put her coat back on.

He looked at her in surprise and then started laughing. "I was thinking that too before you came along. Now I've half a mind to go work in the kitchen."

She smiled and patted him on the shoulder. She had chopped wood virtually every day of her life from the time she had started school until she was sixteen. She hadn't done it for exercise, like now; back then she had done it to keep warm. "Don't feel bad, I've had a lot of practice."

As she walked back up to the house she took a moment to admire the rear facade of the mansion. The purchase and renovation of this house had been, by far, her greatest extravagance. And she had done it for two reasons. First, because she was tired of traveling and wanted to settle down, although she would've been happy in something far less magnificent than what she was staring at. Second, and most important, she had done it for the same reason she had done most things over the years: for Lisa. To give her a real home with a sense of permanence where she could grow up, marry, and have children of her own. Home the last ten years had been hotels, rented villas, and chalets, not that LuAnn was complaining about existing in such luxury, but none of them were home. The tiny trailer in the middle of the woods all those years ago had had far deeper roots for her than the most extravagant residence in Europe. Now they had this. LuAnn smiled at the sight: big, beautiful, and safe. At the thought of the last word, LuAnn suddenly huddled in her coat as a wind broke through the stand of trees.

Safe? When they had gone to bed last night they had been safe and secure, or as much as one could be living the kind of existence they all did. The face of the man in the Honda sprang up before her and she closed her eyes tightly until it finally went away. In its place came another image. The man's face stared at her with many emotions passing across it. Matthew Riggs had risked his life for her and the best she could do was accuse him of lying. And with that response she had only served to make him more suspicious. She pondered a moment, and then sprinted toward the house.

Charlie's office was straight out of a men's club in London, with a magnificent wet bar of polished walnut occupying one corner. The custom-built mahogany desk had neatly sorted piles of correspondence, bills, and other household matters. LuAnn quickly flipped through his card file until she found the one she wanted and plucked it out. She then took out a key Charlie kept high up on a shelf and used it to open a drawer in his desk. She took out the .38 revolver, loaded it, and carried it upstairs with her. The weight of the compact weapon restored some of her confidence. She showered, changed into a black skirt and sweater, threw on a full-length coat, and went down to the garage. As she drove down the private road, one hand tight around the pistol in her coat pocket, LuAnn anxiously looked around, for the Honda could be lurking. She breathed a sigh of relief when she hit the main road and was still all alone. She glanced at the address and phone number on the business card and wondered whether she should call first. Her hand hesitated over the car phone and then she decided just to chance it. If he wasn't there, then maybe it was best. She didn't know whether what she was planning would help or hurt matters. Ever one to choose action over passivity, she couldn't change her ways now. Besides, it was her problem, not anyone else's. She would have to deal with it eventually.

Eventually, she would have to deal with it all.

TWENTY-SIX

Jackson had just arrived back from a cross-country trip and was in his makeup room divesting himself of his most recent disguise when the phone rang. It was not his residential phone. It was his business line, an untraceable communications linkage, and it almost never rang. Jackson called out on the line often during the business day to convey precise instructions to his associates across the globe. Almost no one ever called him, however; and that was the way he wanted it. He had a myriad of other ways to ascertain whether his instructions were being carried out. He snatched up the phone.

"Yes?"

"I think we might have a problem here, or it may be nothing," the voice said.

"I'm listening." Jackson sat down and used a long piece of string to lift the putty off his nose. Then he removed the latex pieces adhering to his face by tugging gently on their edges.

"As you know, two days ago we wired income from the last quarter to Catherine Savage's account in the Caymans. To Banque Internacional. Just like always."

"So? Is she complaining about the rate of return?" Jackson said sarcastically. He tugged firmly on the back edges of his snow white wig and then pulled up and then forward. He next removed the latex skullcap and his own hair sprang free.

"No, but I got a call from the wire department at

Banque and they wanted to confirm something."

"What was that?" Jackson cleansed his face while he was listening, his eyes scanning the mirror as layer after layer of concealment was removed.

"That they had wired all the monies from Savage's accounts to Citibank in New York."

New York! As he absorbed this stunning news, Jackson opened his mouth wide and removed the acrylic caps. Instantly, dark, misshapen teeth became white and straight. His dark eyes glittered menacingly and he stopped removing his disguise. "First, why would they call you if it was her account?"

"They shouldn't have. I mean they never have before. I think the guy at the wire desk down there is new. He must have seen my name and phone number on some of the paperwork and figured I was a principal on the receiving account instead of being on the other end of the transaction, the sending account."

"What did you tell him? I hope you didn't excite any suspicion."

"No, not at all," the voice said nervously. "I simply thanked him and said that was correct. I hope I did the right thing, but of course I wanted to report it to you right away. It seemed unusual."

"Thank you."

"Anything you want me to do on follow-up?"

"I'll handle it." Jackson hung up the phone. He sat back and fiddled absently with the wig. None of LuAnn's money was ever, ever supposed to end up in the United States. Money in the United States was traceable. Banks filed 1099s with the IRS, and other documents detailing income and account balances. Social Security numbers were communicated and kept as part of the official record; filings with the IRS on behalf of the taxpayer were required. None of that was ever supposed to happen in LuAnn's case.

LuAnn Tyler was a fugitive. Fugitives did not return to their homeland and start paying their taxes, even under assumed names.

He picked up his phone and dialed a number.

"Yes, sir?" the voice asked.

Jackson said, "The taxpayer's name is Catherine Savage." Jackson provided her Social Security number and other pertinent information. "You will find out immediately whether she has filed a U.S. tax return or any other type of documents with the IRS. Use all the sources at your disposal, but I need this information within the hour."

He hung up again. For the next forty-five minutes, he walked around his apartment, wearing the portable phone and headset, a requirement when you liked to pace and your apartment was as large as Jackson's was.

Then the phone rang again.

The voice was crisp. "Catherine Savage filed an income tax return last year. I couldn't get full particulars in such a short time frame; however, according to my source, the income reported was substantial. She also recently filed a change of address form with the IRS."

"Give it to me." Jackson wrote the Charlottesville, Virginia, address down on a piece of paper and put it in his pocket.

"One more thing," the voice said. "My source pulled up a very recent filing in connection with Savage's tax account."

"By her?"

"No. It was a Form 2848. It gives a third party a power of attorney to represent the taxpayer with respect to just about anything having to do with their tax matters."

"Who was the requesting party?"

"A fellow named Thomas Jones. According to the

file, he's already received information on her account, including her change of address and last year's income tax return. I was able to get a facsimile of the 2848 form he filed. I can send it to you right now."

"Do so."

Jackson hung up and a minute later had the fax in his hands. He looked at Catherine Savage's signature on the form. He pulled out the originals of the documents LuAnn had signed ten years earlier in connection with their agreement for the lottery winnings. The signatures weren't even close, not that the IRS, cumbersome institution that it was, would ever have taken the time to compare signatures. A forgery. Whoever the man was, he had filed this document without the woman's knowledge. Jackson studied the address and phone number that Tom Jones had given for himself. The address was a P.O. box. Jackson was certain that would also be another dead end. The man was privy to Catherine Savage's tax situation and her new address and his background was a complete sham.

That startling fact was not what annoyed Jackson the most, troubling as it was. He sat down in a chair and studied the wall as his mind moved in ever expanding circles of thought. LuAnn had come back to the United States, despite his explicit instructions to the contrary. She had disobeyed him. That was bad enough. The problem was compounded by the fact that someone else was now interested in her. For what reason? Where was this person now? Probably the same place Jackson was just about to head to: Charlottesville, Virginia.

The lights of the two trains were becoming clearer. The possibility of that collision with LuAnn Tyler crept closer and closer to reality. Jackson went back to his makeup room. It was time for another creation.

TWENTY-SEVEN

After dropping Lisa off at St. Anne's, taking care to walk her directly into the classroom, as was his and LuAnn's practice, Charlie had wheeled the Range Rover out of the parking lot and headed into town. Over the last few months while LuAnn had remained reclusive inside their mountainside fortress, Charlie had been the point man, meeting with prominent townsfolk, making the rounds of businesses and charities and university officials. He and LuAnn had decided that they could not keep secret her wealth and presence in this small, albeit cosmopolitan town and any attempt to do so would invite more suspicion rather than less. Thus, Charlie's task was to lay the groundwork with the town's leaders for the eventual emergence of LuAnn into their society. However, it would only be a very limited emergence. Everyone could understand the need for privacy of the extremely wealthy. And there were many organizations very eager to receive donations from LuAnn, so that maximum cooperation and understanding would likely be forthcoming. That pipeline had already been opened, as LuAnn had donated over a hundred thousand dollars to several local causes. As he headed down the road Charlie shook his head wearily. All these plans, strategies, and what-not. Being phenomenally wealthy was a big pain in the ass. Sometimes he yearned for the old days. A few bucks in his pocket, a beer nearby, and a pack of smokes when he wanted it; a fight on the tube. He smiled wryly. LuAnn had finally gotten him to stop smoking about eight years ago and he knew that had prolonged his life considerably. But he was allowed an occasional cigar. She wasn't about to mother him to death.

Charlie's earlier forays into Charlottesville society had produced one contact in an extremely useful position, a contact that he now intended to pump for information that would allow him and LuAnn to check out her pursuer and, if possible, forestall any real problem. If the man wanted money, that was one thing. Money was not an issue. LuAnn's pocketbook was more than sufficient to satisfy even the most outrageous blackmailer. But what if the issue wasn't simply money? The problem was, Charlie was unsure exactly what the man knew or didn't know. He had mentioned LuAnn's real name. Did he also know about Duane Harvey's murder and LuAnn's relationship to the dead man? The warrant that had been issued for LuAnn's arrest ten years ago? And how had he tracked LuAnn down after all these years? The next issue was even more critical: Did the man know about the lottery fix? LuAnn had told Charlie all about the man calling himself Rainbow. Rainbow might have figured it out. He had followed her, watched her buy a lottery ticket, leave immediately for New York, and win a fortune. Had the man known it was rigged? And had he told anyone? LuAnn had not been sure.

And what had happened to Rainbow? Charlie licked his lips nervously. He had never really known Jackson, never even seen him. But while he had worked for him, he had talked to the man often. The tones of Jackson's voice had been unremarkable: even, calm, direct, supremely confident. Charlie had known people just like that. These men weren't the

265

blusterers, the ones who always said a hell of a lot more than they ever had the courage or ability to back up in reality. They were the ones who looked you dead in the eye, said precisely what they intended to do with little fanfare or hyperbole, and then simply did it. These types would efficiently disembowel you and not lose any sleep over it. Jackson, Charlie had long ago decided, was one of those. Despite his own toughness and strength, Charlie shivered slightly. Wherever Rainbow was, it wasn't among the living, that was for damn sure. Charlie drove on, lost in thought.

TWENTY-EIGHT

uAnn pulled her car into the driveway and
stopped in front of the house. She didn't see
the pickup truck anywhere. He probably was
off at another job. She was about to leave, but the
simple beauty of Matt Riggs's home made her stop,
get out of the BMW, and go up the plank steps. The
graceful lines of the old structure, the obvious care
and skill which had gone into rehabbing it, made her
eager to explore the place, even if its owner was
absent.

She moved around the broad porch, running her
hand along its intricate wooden scrollwork. She
opened the screen door and knocked at the front
door, but there was no answer. She hesitated and
then tried the doorknob. It turned easily in her hand.
People had not locked their doors where she had
grown up either. As security conscious as she was
now, it was good to know there were still places like
that left in the world. She hesitated again. Entering
the man's home without his knowledge might only
compound matters. However, if he never found out?
She might be able to obtain some useful information
about him, something she could use to help extricate
herself from this potential disaster.

She pushed open the front door and then closed it
softly behind her. The living room had random-
width oak flooring splotched and mottled with age.
The furnishings were simple but carefully arranged
and each was of excellent quality. LuAnn wondered

whether Matt Riggs bought the pieces in broken condition and then worked on them. She moved through the rooms, stopping to admire the man's handiwork here and there. The slight smell of varnish hovered over various pieces of furniture. The place was neat and clean. There were no pictures of family: no wife, no kids. She didn't know why but this struck her as odd. She reached his office and peered inside. Quietly moving over to his desk, she stopped for a moment as she thought she heard a sound come from somewhere within the house. Her heart started to race and she briefly contemplated fleeing. The sound wasn't repeated, however, and she calmed down and seated herself behind the desk. The first thing that caught her eye was the paper on which Riggs had jotted down the notes. Her name and other information about her. Then she glanced at the information on the Honda. She looked at her watch. Riggs was clearly not a man who believed in idleness. And he was able to get information from sources that were obviously more than a little sophisticated. That was troubling. LuAnn jerked her head up as she looked out the broad window into the backyard. There was a barn-like structure there. The door was open slightly. LuAnn had thought she had noted movement there. As she got up to go outside, her hand dipped into her jacket pocket and closed around the .38.

When she exited the house she started to head back to her car. Then her curiosity got the better of her and she crept over to the barn door and peered inside. An overhead light illuminated the area well. It was set up as a workshop and storage facility. In front of two entire walls were sturdy work benches and tables and more tools than LuAnn had ever before seen in one place. The two other walls had shelving where wood supplies and other materials were stacked in precise configurations. As LuAnn moved inside she eyed the staircase at the rear of the structure. In former times she was certain it would have led to a hayloft. Riggs, however, had no animals in need of hay, at least that she could see. She wondered what it housed now.

She took the steps slowly. When she reached the top, she stared in amazement. The place was set up as a small study and observation area. Two bookcases, a beat-up leather chair and ottoman, and an ancient potbellied stove stared back at her. In one corner, an old-fashioned telescope was set up to look out a huge window in the rear of the barn. As LuAnn climbed up and looked through the window, her heart started to pound. Riggs's truck was parked behind the barn.

As she turned to run down the stairs, she found herself staring down the barrel of a twelve-gauge shotgun.

When Riggs saw who it was he slowly lowered the weapon. "What the hell are you doing here?" She tried to move past him, but Riggs grabbed her arm. She just as quickly pulled it free.

"You scared me to death," she said.

"Sorry. Now what the hell are you doing here?"

"Is this how you usually welcome company into your home?"

"Company usually comes in through the front door, and only after I've opened it." He looked around. "This sure as hell isn't my front door, and I don't remember inviting you in."

LuAnn moved away from him as she looked around the space and then returned her gaze to his angry features.

"This is a nice place to come and think. How would you like to build me something like this at my house?"

Riggs leaned up against the wall. He still held the shotgun in the down position but he could swing it up into a firing position in the matter of a second. "I would think you'd want to see my work on the fence before you hired me for something else, Ms. Savage."

She feigned surprise at the sound of her name but apparently not enough to satisfy Riggs.

"So, did you find anything else of interest in my office besides my homework on you?"

She looked at him with even more respect. "I'm a little paranoid about my privacy."

"So I noticed. Is that why you carry a pistol?"

LuAnn looked down at her pocket. A sliver of the .38 was visible.

"You have good eyes."

"A thirty-eight doesn't have such great stopping power. If you're serious about your privacy, and your security, you might want to step up to a nine millimeter. A semiautomatic over a revolver is a no-brainer." The hand holding the shotgun twitched for an instant. "I tell you what, you take the revolver out, muzzle first, and I'll stop fussing with my shotgun here."

"I'm not going to shoot you."

"That's absolutely right, you're not," he said evenly. "Please do as I say, Ms. Savage. And do it very slowly."

LuAnn took the pistol out, holding it by the barrel.

"Now unload it and put the bullets in one pocket and the pistol in the other. And I can count to six so don't try to be cute."

LuAnn did as she was told, looking at him angrily. "I'm not used to being treated like a criminal."

"You break into my house carrying a weapon, that's exactly how I'm going to treat you. Count yourself lucky that I didn't shoot first and ask questions later. Buckshot can be very irritating to the skin."

"I didn't break in. The door was open."

"Don't try that one in a court of law," he fired back.

When Riggs had confirmed that she had emptied the revolver, he broke open the shotgun and laid it down on the bookcase. He crossed his arms and studied her.

Slightly unnerved, LuAnn went back to her original train of thought. "My circle of friends is very small. When somebody intrudes on that circle I tend to get curious."

"That's funny. You call it intrusion, but what I did this morning ordinarily would be called coming to the rescue."

LuAnn brushed a strand of hair out of her face and looked away for a moment. "Look, Mr. Riggs—"

"My friends call me Matt. We're not friends, but I'll allow you the privilege," he said coolly.

"I'd rather call you Matthew. I don't want to break any of your rules."

Riggs looked startled for a moment before settling back down. "Whatever."

"Charlie said you were a cop."

"I never said so."

She looked at him, surprise now clear on her features. "Well, were you?"

"What I was really isn't any of your business. And you still haven't told me what you're doing here."

She rubbed her hand across the old leather chair. She didn't answer right away and Riggs was content to let the silence endure until she broke it. "What happened this morning is a little more complicated than it appeared. It's something that I'm taking care of." She paused and looked up at him, her eyes searching his. "I appreciate what you did. You helped me and you didn't have to. I came here to thank you."

Riggs relaxed a little bit. "Okay, although I didn't expect any thanks. You needed some help and I was around to give it. One human being to another. The world would be a hell of a lot better place if we all lived by that rule."

"I also came to ask a favor."

Riggs inclined his head toward her, waiting.

"The situation this morning, I would appreciate it if you'd just forget about it. Like I said, Charlie and I are taking care of it. If you got involved, it might make things more difficult for me."

Riggs took this in for a few moments.

"Do you know the guy?"

"I really don't want to get into it."

Riggs rubbed his chin. "You know, the guy banged me up. So I already feel like I'm involved."

LuAnn moved closer to him. "I know you don't know me, but it would mean a lot if you would just drop it. It really would." Her eyes seemed to widen with each word spoken.

Riggs felt himself drawing closer to her although he hadn't physically budged an inch. Her gaze seemed to be pasted on to his face, all the sunlight streaming through the window seemed to be blocked out as though an eclipse were occurring.

"I'll tell you what: Unless the guy gives me any more trouble, I'll forget it ever happened."

LuAnn's tensed shoulders slumped in relief. "Thank you."

She moved past him toward the stair. The scent of her perfume drifted through his nostrils. His skin started to tingle. It had been a long time since that had happened.

"Your home is beautiful," she said.

"It certainly doesn't compare to yours."

"Did you do it all yourself?"

"Most of it. I'm pretty handy."

272

"Why don't you come by tomorrow and we can talk about you doing some more work for me."

"Ms. Savage—"

"Call me Catherine."

"Catherine, you don't have to buy my silence."

"Around noon? I can have some lunch ready."

Riggs gave her a searching look and then shrugged. "I can make that."

As she started down the stairs, he called after her. "That guy in the Honda. Don't assume he's going to give up."

She glanced back at the shotgun for one significant moment before settling her gaze on him.

"I never assume anything anymore, Matthew."

"Well, it's a good cause, John, and she likes to help good causes." Charlie leaned back in his chair and sipped the hot coffee. He was sitting at a window table in the dining room of the Boar's Head Inn, off Ivy Road a little west of the University of Virginia. Two plates held the remnants of breakfast. The man across from him beamed.

"Well, I can't tell you how much it means to the community. Having her here – both of you – is just wonderful." Wearing a costly double-breasted suit, with a colorful handkerchief dangling from the outer pocket and matching his polka-dot tie, the wavy-haired John Pemberton was one of the area's most successful and well-connected real estate agents. He also sat on the boards of numerous charities and local committees. The man knew virtually everything that happened in the area, which was precisely the reason Charlie had asked him to breakfast. Further, the commission on the sale of LuAnn's home had landed six figures in Pemberton's pocket and he was, thus, an eternal friend.

Now he looked down at his lap and a sheepish grin appeared on his handsome features when he looked back up at Charlie. "We are hoping to actually *meet* Ms. Savage at some point."

"Absolutely, John, absolutely. She's looking forward to meeting you too. It'll just take some time. She's a very private person, you understand."

"Of course, of course, this place is full of people like that. Movie stars, writers, people with more money than they know what to do with."

An involuntary smile played across Pemberton's lips. Charlie assumed the man was daydreaming about future dollars of commission when these wealthy folk moved in or out of the area.

"You'll just have to live with my company for a little while longer." A grin creased Charlie's features.

"And very enjoyable company it is too," Pemberton replied automatically.

Charlie put down his coffee cup and pushed his breakfast plate away. If he still smoked cigarettes he would've stopped to light one up. "We have Matt Riggs doing some work for us."

"Putting in the security fence. Yes, I know. Undoubtedly his biggest job to date."

Upon noting Charlie's surprised look, Pemberton smiled in an embarrassed fashion. "Despite its cosmopolitan appearance, Charlottesville really is a small town. There is very little that happens that isn't known by most people soon thereafter."

At those words, Charlie's spirits plummeted. *Had Riggs already told someone? Had they made a mistake coming here? Should they have planted themselves amid the seven million residents of New York City instead?*

With an effort, he shook off these numbing thoughts and plunged ahead. "Right. Well, the guy had some terrific references."

"He does very good work, dependable and

professional. He hasn't been here all that long by the standards of most locals, about five years, but I've never heard a bad word said about him."

"Where'd he come from?"

"Washington. D.C., not the state of." Pemberton fingered his teacup.

"So he was a builder up there then?"

Pemberton shook his head. "No, he got his general contractor's license after he got here."

"Still, he could've apprenticed up there."

"I think he had some natural talent for the trade. He's a first-rate carpenter, but he apprenticed with Ralph Steed, one of our best local builders for two years. Ralph passed away about that time and that's when Riggs went out on his own. He's done very well. He's a hard worker. And landing that fence job doesn't hurt any."

"True. Still, the guy just shows up in town one day and plunges into something new. That takes some balls. I mean I've met him, and it wasn't like he would've been fresh out of college when he came here."

"No, he wasn't." Pemberton looked around the small dining area. When he spoke next it was with a lowered voice. "You're not the first person who has been curious about Riggs's origins."

Charlie leaned forward, adding to the conspiratorial image of the pair. "Is that right? What do we have here, a little local intrigue?" Charlie tried to make his tone appear light and unconcerned.

"Of course rumors come and go, and you know the questionable veracity of most of them. Still, I have heard from various sources that Riggs held some important position in Washington." Pemberton paused for effect. "In the intelligence community."

Behind the stone mask Charlie fought the urge to abruptly give back his breakfast. Although LuAnn

275

had had the good luck to be one of the recipients of Jackson's control of the lottery, she might have just matched that luck with a dose of incredibly bad fortune. "In intelligence, you say? Like a spy?"

Pemberton threw up his hands. "Who knows. Secrets are a way of life with people like that. Torture them and they won't say a thing. Probably bite on their cyanide pill or whatever and go peacefully into the night." Pemberton obviously enjoyed a touch of the dramatic mixed in with elements of danger and intrigue, particularly at a safe distance.

Charlie rubbed at his left knee. "I had heard he was a cop."

"Who told you that?"

"I don't recall. Just heard it in passing."

"Well, if he was a policeman that's something that can be checked. If he was a spy, there'd be no record of it, would there?"

"So he never talked to anyone here about his past?"

"Only in vague terms. That's probably why you heard he was a policeman. People hear bits and pieces, they start to fill in the holes themselves."

"Well, son of a gun." Charlie sat back, trying hard to appear calm.

"Still, he's an exceptional builder. He'll do good work for you." Pemberton laughed. "Just so long as he doesn't start snooping around. You know if he was a spy, those habits probably die hard. I've led a pretty squeaky clean life, but everybody has skeletons in their closet, don't you think?"

Charlie cleared his throat before answering. "Some more than others."

Charlie leaned forward again, his hands clasped in front of him on the table; he was quite eager to change the subject and had the vehicle to do so.

276

"John," Charlie's voice dipped low, "John, I've got a small favor to ask of you."

Pemberton's smile broadened. "Just ask it, Charlie. And consider it done."

"A man came by the house the other day asking for a donation to a charitable foundation he said he headed."

Pemberton looked startled. "What was his name?"

"He wasn't local," Charlie said quickly. "He gave me a name but I'm not sure it was his real one. It all seemed suspicious, you understand what I'm saying."

"Absolutely."

"Someone in Ms. Savage's position has to be careful. There are a lot of scams out there."

"Don't I know it. How upsetting."

"Right. Well, anyway, the guy said he was staying in the area for a while. Asked for a follow-up meeting with Ms. Savage."

"I hope you're not going to agree to that."

"I haven't yet. The guy left a phone number, but it's not a local one. I called it. It was an answering service."

"What was the name of the foundation?"

"I don't remember exactly, but it had something to do with medical research of some kind."

"That's so easy to concoct," Pemberton said knowingly. "Of course I have no personal experience with frauds like that," he added huffily, "but I understand that there is a proliferation of them."

"That was exactly my read. Well, to make a long story short, since the guy said he was going to be around awhile, I thought it probable that he was renting someplace hereabouts, instead of sacking out at a hotel. That gets to be expensive after a while, especially if you're living scam to scam."

"And you want to know if I can find out where he might be staying?"

"Exactly. I wouldn't ask it if it weren't real important. With things like this I'm never too careful. I want to know who I'm dealing with in case he shows up again."

"Of course, of course." Pemberton let out a shallow breath and sipped at his tea. "I'll certainly look into it for you. My sympathies lie with you and Ms. Savage."

"And we will be very grateful for any assistance you can give us. I've mentioned several of the other charities you head up to Ms. Savage and she spoke very positively about all of them and your work with them."

Pemberton was glowing now. "Why don't you give me a description of the man? I have the morning free and I can start my own little investigation. If he's within fifty miles of here, with my connections, I'm certain I can find him."

Charlie described the man, laid some cash on the table for the meal, and stood up. "We really appreciate it, John."

TWENTY-NINE

Thomas Donovan scanned the city streets for a parking spot. Georgetown was not known for its abundance of places to leave one's vehicle. He was driving a new rental car, a late model Chrysler. He turned right from M Street on to Wisconsin Avenue, and finally managed to snag a spot on a side street not too far from where he was heading. A light rain began to fall as he walked down the street. The quiet area he soon found himself in harbored an elite neighborhood of towering brick and clapboard residences which were home to high-ranking businessmen and political types. He eyed some of the homes as he walked along. In the lights visible through intricately designed windows Donovan could make out well-dressed owners settling down in front of warm fires, coddling drinks and exchanging light kisses as they went through their rituals of relaxation after another day of perhaps changing the world, or merely adding to their already hefty investment portfolios.

So much wealth and power rested in this area that an energy seemed to wash up from the brick sidewalks and hurtle Donovan along at a furious clip. Money and power had never been overriding ambitions of his. Despite that, his occupation often placed him in close proximity to those who held the attainment of one or both of these prizes above all else. It was a wonderful position from which to play the altruistic cynic and Donovan often played that role to the fullest for the simple reason that he genuinely believed in what he did for a living. The irony of this was not lost on him. For without the rich and powerful and their evil ways, at whom would he throw his sharp-edged stones?

Donovan finally stopped at one formidable residence: a one-hundred-year-old three-story brick townhouse sitting behind a waist-high brick wall topped by black wrought-iron fencing of a style found throughout the area. He inserted a key into the gate's lock and went up the sidewalk. Another key allowed him entry through the massive wooden front door and he shook off his coat.

The housekeeper appeared immediately and took the wet coat from him. She wore a traditional maid's uniform and spoke with a practiced degree of deference.

"I'll tell the missus you're here, Mr. Donovan."

He nodded quickly and moved past her into the drawing room where he took a moment to warm himself before the blazing fire and then looked around with contentment. His upbringing had been decidedly blue collar but he did not attempt to hide his pleasure at occasionally dabbling in luxury. It was an incongruity in his nature that had bothered him greatly in his youth, but much less so now. Some things did become better as one aged, he mused, including layers of personal guilt that one ended up shedding like peeling an onion.

By the time he had mixed himself a drink from the stock housed behind a cabinet in one corner of the drawing room, the woman had appeared.

She moved quickly to him and gave him a deep kiss. He took her hand and caressed it lightly.

"I missed you," she said.

He led her over to the large sofa against one wall. Their knees touched as they sat close together.

Alicia Crane was petite, in her mid-thirties, with long hair that was looking more ash than blond with each passing day. Her dress was costly and the jewelry clinging to her wrists and ears easily matched the richness of the garment; however, the image was one of quiet wealth and sophistication. Her features were delicate, the nose so small as to be barely noticeable between the deep luster of the dark brown eyes. While she was not a traditional beauty, her obvious wealth and refinement had inspired a certain look that was pleasant enough. On her best days she would be described as very well put together.

Her cheek trembled slightly as he stroked it.

"I missed you too, Alicia. A lot."

"I don't like it when you have to be away." Her voice was cultured and dignified, its cadence slow and exact. It was a voice seemingly too formal for a relatively young woman.

"Well, it's part of the job." He smiled at her. "But you're making that job a lot more difficult to do." He *was* attracted to Alicia Crane. While not the brightest star in the universe, she was a good person, without the pretenses and airs that her level of wealth usually stamped on its possessors.

With a start, she stared. "Why in the world did you shave off your beard?"

Donovan rubbed his hand across the smooth skin. "Change of pace," he said quickly. "You know men go through their own form of menopause. I think it took about ten years off the mug. What do you think?"

"I think you're just as handsome without it as you were with it. In fact, you remind me a little of Father. When he was a younger man, of course."

"Thanks for lying to an *old* man." He smiled. "But being compared to him, well that's high praise."

"I can have Maggie put on some supper. You must be starved." She gripped his hand with both of hers.

"Thank you, Alicia. And maybe a hot bath after that."

"Of course, the rain is so chilling at this time of year." She hesitated for a moment. "Will you have to leave again soon? I was thinking we could go down to the islands. It's so beautiful this time of year."

"That sounds wonderful, but I'm afraid it'll have to keep. I have to leave tomorrow."

Her disappointment shone through on her face before her gaze dropped. "Oh, I see."

He tucked one hand under her chin and stared into her eyes. "Alicia, I had a breakthrough today. A breakthrough that I wasn't sure would happen. It was a risk on my part, but sometimes you have to take risks if you want the payoff." He remembered from that morning, the haunted look in LuAnn Tyler's eyes. "All that sniffing around, never sure if anything's going to turn up. But that's all part of the game."

"That's wonderful, Thomas, I'm so happy for you. But I hope you didn't place yourself in personal danger. I don't know what I would do if anything happened to you."

He sat back as he contemplated his daredevil morning. "I can take care of myself. But I don't take unnecessary risks. I leave that for the kiddies coming up." His voice was calming.

He glanced over at her; the look on her face was that of a child listening to her favorite hero recount a past adventure. Donovan finished his drink. A hero. He liked the feeling. Who wouldn't? Who didn't need that kind of unadulterated admiration every now and then? He smiled deeply and gripped Alicia's small hand in his.

"I promise you something. After I break this story,

we're going to take a long vacation. Just you and me. Someplace warm, with plenty to drink, and I can dust off my talents as a sailor. I haven't done that in a long time and I can't think of anyone I'd rather do it with. How's that sound?"

She laid her head against his shoulder and squeezed his hand tightly. "Wonderful."

THIRTY

"You invited him for lunch?" Charlie stared at LuAnn with a mixture of anger and frustration on his grizzled face. "Would you mind telling me why you did that? And would you mind telling me why the hell you went there in the first place?"

They were in Charlie's office. LuAnn stood next to the bulky desk while Charlie sat in front of it. He had unwrapped a thick cigar and was about to light it when LuAnn had delivered the news of her excursion that morning.

Defiance was all over LuAnn's features as she scowled back at him. "I couldn't just sit around and do nothing."

"I told you I was going to handle it. What, you don't trust my judgment anymore?"

"Of course I do, Charlie, it's not that." LuAnn dropped her defiant stance, perched on the edge of his chair and ran her fingers through his thinning hair. "I figured if I could get to Riggs before he had a chance to do anything, apologize and then get him to drop it, we'd be free and clear."

Charlie shook his head, wincing as a small pain worked at his left temple. He took a deep breath and put an arm around her waist. "LuAnn, I had a very informative conversation with John Pemberton this morning."

"Who?"

"Real estate agent. Guy who sold us the house.

That's not important. What is relevant is the fact that Pemberton knows everybody and everything that goes on in this town. He's trying to track down the guy in the Honda for us right now."

LuAnn jerked back. "You didn't tell him—"

"I concocted a cover story and fed it to him. He slurped it up like it was the sweetest ice cream in the world. We both have gotten real good with making up stuff over the years, haven't we?"

"Sometime too good," LuAnn said gloomily. "It's getting harder and harder to remember what's true and what's not."

"I also talked to Pemberton about Riggs. Trying to get some of the guy's history out, to try and get a feel for the guy."

"He's not a cop. I asked him and he said he wasn't. You said he was."

"I know, a screw-up on my part, but Riggs led me to believe he was."

"So what the heck was he? And why all the secrecy?"

"A funny question coming from you." LuAnn jabbed an elbow playfully into Charlie's side. Her smile disappeared with Charlie's next words. "Pemberton thinks Riggs was a government spy."

"A spy? Like the CIA?"

"Who the hell knows. It's not like the guy's gonna advertise what outfit he was with. Nobody really knows for sure. His background is kind of a blur as far as Pemberton can tell."

LuAnn shuddered, remembering the info Riggs had gathered on her so quickly. Now it perhaps made sense. But she was still unconvinced. "And now he builds fences in rural Virginia. I didn't think they ever let spies retire."

"You've been watching too many mob movies. Even spies change jobs or retire, especially with the

Cold War ending. And there are a lot of specialities in intelligence gathering. Not all of them involve trench coats, pistols up the sleeve, and assassination plots working against foreign dictators. He could've been just some schlep working in an office looking at aerial photos of Moscow."

LuAnn recalled her meeting with Riggs at his home. The way he had handled the shotgun, his observation skills and his knowledge of firearms. And finally his confident and cool demeanor. She shook her head firmly. "He doesn't strike me as the office type."

Charlie sighed deeply. "Me either. So how did it go?"

LuAnn stood back up and leaned against the doorjamb, her fingers hooked through the belt loops on the jeans she had changed into. "He had already dug up some info on me and the Honda. The cover stuff came up on me, so we're okay there."

"Anything on the Honda?"

LuAnn shook her head. "Rental up in D.C. Name looked phony. Probably a dead-end."

"Riggs moves fast. How'd you find that out?"

"I did a little snooping around his office. When he caught me he was holding a shotgun."

"Good gosh, LuAnn, if the guy was a spy you're lucky he didn't blow your head off."

"It didn't seem so risky while I was doing it. It turned out all right anyway."

"You and your risk-taking. Like going to the drawing that night in New York. I should really start putting my foot down around here. What else?"

"I admitted to him that the car chase was something we were concerned about and that we were handling it."

"And he accepted that? No questions?" Charlie's tone was skeptical.

"I was telling the truth, Charlie," she said heatedly. "I get kind of tingling all over when the rare occasion happens along that I can do that."

"Okay, okay. I didn't mean to put a stick in your spokes. God, we sound like an old married couple here."

LuAnn smiled. "We *are* an old married couple. We just have a few more secrets to share than most."

Charlie flashed her a quick grin and took a moment to light his cigar. "So you really think Riggs is okay? He won't keep nosing around?"

"I think he's very curious, and he should be. But he told me he wasn't going to pursue it and I believe him. I'm not exactly sure why, but I do. There doesn't appear to be much B.S. in the man."

"And him coming over for lunch tomorrow? I take it you want to get to know him a little better."

LuAnn studied Charlie's face for a moment. Was there a touch of jealousy there? She shrugged her shoulders. "Well, it's a way to keep an eye on him, and maybe learn a little more about him. Maybe he's got some secrets, too. It certainly sounds like it, anyway."

Charlie puffed on his cigar. "So if things are cool with Riggs then we got only the guy in the Honda to worry about."

"Isn't that enough?"

"It's better than two headaches at one time. If Pemberton can trace him maybe we have clear sailing."

LuAnn looked nervously at him. "If he finds him, what are you going to do?"

"I've been thinking about that. I think I've decided to play straight with the man, call his hand and see what the hell he wants. If it's money, maybe we see what we can work out."

"And if it's not just money he wants?" She had

287

difficulty getting the next part out. "What if he knows about the lottery?"

Charlie took the cigar from his mouth and stared at her.

"I can't see how he could. But in the billion to one chance he does, there are a lot of other places in the world we can live, LuAnn. We could be gone tomorrow if need be."

"On the run again," she said, her tone bone-tired.

"Consider the alternative. It's not pleasant."

She reached out and plucked the cigar from between his fingers. Clenching it between her teeth, she drew the smoke in and then let it slowly out. She handed it back to him.

"When is Pemberton supposed to get back to you?"

"No set time. Could be tonight, could be next week."

"Let me know when you hear from him."

"You'll be the first to know, milady."

She turned to leave.

"Oh, am I invited to this lunch tomorrow?" he asked.

She glanced back. "I was kind of counting on it, Charlie." She smiled prettily and left. He stood up and watched her glide gracefully down the hallway. Then he closed the door to his study and sat down at his desk puffing thoughtfully on his stogie.

Riggs had put on a pair of chino pants, and the collar of his button-down shirt peeked out from under his patterned sweater. He had driven over in a Jeep Cherokee he had borrowed while his pickup truck was in the shop having its bumper repaired. The Jeep seemed more fitting to the affluent surroundings than his battered truck anyway. He smoothed down his freshly washed hair before climbing out of the Cherokee and walking up the steps of the mansion. These days he didn't usually dress up, except for the occasional social event he attended in town. He had finally decided a jacket and dress slacks was too pretentious. It was only lunch after all. And who knew? The lady of the house might ask him to do some on-site work.

The door was answered by the maid who escorted Riggs to the library. Riggs wondered if he had been watched as he had pulled up in the circle. Maybe there were video cameras trained on that area as well, with Catherine Savage and her sidekick Charlie sitting in some observation room crammed floor to ceiling with TV monitors.

He looked around the spacious area and noted with due respect the numerous volumes lining the walls. He wondered if they were for show only. He had been in places where that was the case. Somehow he didn't think that was true here. His attention fell upon the photos lining the fireplace mantel. There were ones there of Charlie and a little girl who strongly resembled Catherine Savage, but none of Catherine Savage. That seemed odd, but the woman was odd, so there was some semblance of consistency there.

He turned when the double doors to the library opened. His first real encounter with the woman, in his reconfigured hayloft, had not prepared him for his second.

The golden hair tumbled down the stylishly flared shoulders of a black one-piece dress that ended at her bare calves and didn't miss any contour of her long, curvy body along the way. It struck him that on her the garment would have seemed equally appropriate at a state fair or a White House dinner. She wore matching black low heel shoes. The image of a sleek, muscular panther gliding toward him held fast in his mind. After giving it some thought, Riggs had decided that the woman's beauty was undeniable, but wasn't perfect. After all, whose was? And another remarkable detail now emerged: While there were fine lines beginning to carve themselves around her eyes, Riggs noticed the almost complete absence of lines around her mouth, as though she had never smiled.

Curiously, the small scar on her jaw considerably heightened her attraction, he felt. Perhaps by silently forging a layer of danger, of adventure into her past?

"I'm glad you could make it," she said, moving briskly forward and extending a hand, which Riggs shook. He was again amazed at the strength he felt in that grip; her long fingers seemed to swallow his big, callused hand. "I know contractors have numerous emergencies during the day. Your time is never your own."

Riggs eyed the walls and ceilings of the library. "I heard about some of the renovations you had done here. I don't care how good the G.C. is, something this complex, things get out of whack every now and then."

"Charlie handled all of that. But I think things went fairly smoothly. I'm certainly pleased with the end product."

"I could see that."

"Lunch will be ready in a few minutes. Sally is setting it up in the rear verandah. The dining room seats about fifty and I thought it might be a little overwhelming for three. Would you like something to drink beforehand?"

"I'm okay." He pointed at the photos. "Is that your daughter? Or younger sister?"

She blushed and then followed his gesture, but settled herself on the couch before answering. "My daughter, Lisa. She's ten years old. I can't believe that, the years go by so quickly."

Riggs looked her over in an unassuming manner. "You must have had her very young then."

"Younger than I probably should have, but I wouldn't give her back for anything in the world. Do you have children?"

Riggs shook his head quickly and looked down at his hands. "Never been that lucky."

LuAnn had noted the absence of a wedding ring, although some men never wore them. She assumed a man who worked with his hands all day might not wear it simply for safety reasons.

"Your wife—"

"I'm divorced," he interjected. "Almost four years now." He put his hands in his pockets and again ran his eyes around the room. He could sense her following the path of his observations. "You?" he asked, settling his eyes back upon her.

"Widowed."

"I'm sorry."

She shrugged. "It was a long time ago," she said simply. There was a ring in her voice that told Riggs the years had not managed to diminish the impact of the loss.

"Ms. Savage—"

"Please, call me Catherine." She smiled impishly. "All my close friends do."

He smiled back and sat down next to her. "So where's Charlie?"

"He's out running some errands. He'll be joining us for lunch though."

"So he's your uncle?"

LuAnn nodded. "His wife passed on years ago. Both my parents are dead. We're really all the family left."

"I take it your late husband did very well for himself. Or maybe you did. I don't want to sound

291

politically incorrect." Riggs grinned suddenly. "Either that, or one of you won the lottery."

LuAnn's hand tightened perceptibly on the edge of the couch. "My husband was a brilliant business-man who obviously left me very well-off." She managed to say this with a casual air.

"He sure did," Riggs agreed.

"And you? Have you lived here all your life?"

"Gee, after my visit here yesterday I thought you would have checked out my background thor-oughly."

"I'm afraid I don't have quite the level of sources you obviously do. I didn't think builders had such an information network." Her eyes remained fixed on his.

"I moved here about five years ago. Apprenticed with a local builder who taught me the trade. He died about three years ago and that's when I set up my own shop."

"Five years. So your wife lived here with you for a year."

Riggs shook his head. "The divorce was *final* four years ago, but we had been separated for about fourteen months. She's still up in D.C. Probably always will be."

"Is she in politics?"

"Attorney. Big partner, at a big firm. She has some politically connected clients. She's very successful."

"She must be good then. That's still very much a man's world. Like a lot of other ones."

Riggs shrugged. "She's smart, a great business-getter. I think that's why we broke up. The marriage thing got in the way."

"I see."

"Not what you'd call an original story, but it's the only one I have. I moved down here and never looked back."

"I take it you like what you do."

"It can be a hassle sometimes, just like any job. But I like putting things together. It's therapeutic. And peaceful. I've been lucky, got some good word of mouth and the business has been steady. As you probably know, there's a lot of money in this area. Even before you came."

"So I understand. I'm glad your career change has worked out."

He sat back while he digested her words, his lips pursed, his hands balled up into fists, but not in a threatening way.

He chuckled. "Let me guess, you heard that I was either a CIA operative or an international assassin who abruptly decided to chuck all that and take up hammering and sawing in more placid sur-roundings."

"Actually, I hadn't heard the assassin angle."

They exchanged brief smiles.

"You know if you just told people the truth, they'd stop speculating." She couldn't believe she had just made that statement, but there it was. She looked at him with what she hoped was an air of complete innocence.

"You're assuming that I care if people speculate about me. I don't."

"That's beneath you, I take it."

"If I've learned anything in life, it's that you don't worry about what other people think or say. You worry about yourself and that's good enough. Otherwise you're setting yourself up to be a basket case. People can be cruel. Especially people who supposedly cared about you. Believe me, I speak from experience."

"I take it the divorce wasn't exactly amicable?"

He didn't look at her when he spoke. "I'm not taking anything away from you, but sometimes

293

losing a spouse isn't as traumatic or painful as going through a divorce. They each have their own degrees of hurt, I guess."

He looked down at his hands. There was a definite ring of sincerity in his words and LuAnn felt instant guilt that she in fact had not been widowed, at least not by the falsehood of losing a wealthy husband. It was as though he were baring his wounds in return for LuAnn baring hers. As usual, it was all lies on her part. Could she even speak the truth anymore? In fact how could she? Speaking the truth would destroy her, all the lies would immediately fall to earth like those old buildings demolished by explosives that caused them to implode.

"I can understand that," she said.

Riggs didn't appear inclined to continue.

LuAnn finally looked at her watch. "Lunch should be just about ready. I thought after we eat you could look at a site at the rear grounds where I'm thinking of having you build a small studio." She stood up and Riggs did too. He appeared immeasurably relieved that this particular conversation was over.

"That sounds good, Catherine. In my business, work is always welcome."

As they walked to the rear of the house, Charlie joined them. The two men shook hands. "Glad to see you again, Matt. I hope you're hungry. Sally usually puts out a good spread."

Lunch was devoted to enjoying the food and drink and discussing innocuous subjects of local interest. However, there was an energy between Charlie and Catherine Savage that was unmistakable to Riggs. A strong bond, he concluded. Unbreakable, in fact. They were family, after all.

"So what're we looking at timewise on the fence, Matt?" Charlie asked. He and Riggs were on the rear terrace overlooking the grounds. Lunch was over and LuAnn had gone to pick up Lisa. School had ended early because of a scheduled teacher workshop. She had asked Riggs to remain until she returned so they could talk about the studio construction. Riggs wondered if her going to get Lisa had been a deliberate maneuver to leave Charlie behind to pump him for information. Whatever the reason, he remained on guard.

Before Riggs had a chance to answer him about the fence, Charlie extended a cigar. "You smoke these things?"

Riggs took it. "After a meal like that, and a gorgeous day like this, even if I didn't, I'd be tempted." He snipped off the end with a cutter Charlie handed him and they took a moment to get their respective smokes going.

"I figure a week to dig all the postholes. Two weeks clearing land, and assembling and installing the fencing. That includes pouring the cement for the posts. Another week to install the gate and security systems. One month total. That's about what I estimated in the contract."

Charlie looked him over. "I know, but sometimes what you put on paper doesn't work exactly that way in reality."

"That pretty much sums up the construction business," Riggs agreed. He puffed on his cigar. "But we'll get in before the frost, and the lay of the land isn't as bad as I originally thought." He paused and eyed Charlie. "After yesterday, I wish I could have that sucker in today. I'm sure you do too."

It was an open invitation for discussion and Charlie didn't disappoint Riggs. "Have a seat, Matt." Charlie indicated a pair of white wrought-iron chairs next to the balustrade. Charlie sat down gingerly. "God these suckers are uncomfortable as hell, and for what they cost you'd think they were made out of gold. I'm thinking the interior designer we used must've gotten some kind of kickback on them." He smoked his cigar while he looked over the landscape. "Damn, it's beautiful here."

Riggs followed his gaze. "It's one reason I came here. A big reason."

"What were the other reasons?" Charlie grinned at him. "I'm just kidding. That's *your* business." The emphasis on the word was not lost on Riggs. Charlie wriggled in the seat until he managed to find a semicomfortable position. "Catherine told me about your little discussion yesterday."

"I assumed she would. She shouldn't go sneaking around people's houses, though. That's not always a healthy thing to do."

"That's exactly what I told her. I know it might be hard to see, but she's rather headstrong."

The two men exchanged knowing chuckles.

"I do appreciate your agreeing not to pursue it," Charlie said.

"I told her so long as the guy didn't bother me, I wouldn't bother him."

"Fair enough. I'm sure you can see that with all of Catherine's wealth, she's a target for a variety of scams, hustles, or downright threats. We have Lisa to worry about too. We keep a real close eye on her."

"You sound like you speak from experience."

"I do. This isn't the first time. And it won't be the last. But you can't let it get to you. I mean Catherine could buy a deserted island somewhere and make it impossible for anyone to reach her, but what kind of life would that be? For her or Lisa?"

"And you. It's not like you're tapping on the grave, Charlie. You look like you could suit up for the Redskins on Sunday."

Charlie beamed at the compliment. "I actually

296

played some semipro ball way back when. And I take care of myself. And Catherine nags me about my diet. I think she lets me smoke these things out of pity." He held up the cigar. "Although lately I'm feeling old beyond my years. But yeah, I don't want to live on a deserted island."

"So any luck finding the guy in the Honda?" Riggs asked.

"I'm working on it. Got some inquiries going."

"Don't take offense at this, but if you find him, what do you plan on doing about it?"

Charlie looked over at him. "What would you do?"

"Depends on his intentions."

"Exactly. So until I find him and determine what his intentions are, I don't know what I'm going to do." There was a slight trace of hostility in Charlie's tone that Riggs chose to ignore. He looked back over the countryside.

"Catherine says she wants to put up an outdoor studio. Do you know where?"

Charlie shook his head. "I really haven't discussed it with her. I think it was a recent impulse on her part."

Riggs again looked over at him. Had that been a conscious slip on his part? It was as though Charlie were telling him pointblank that the potential new piece of business was the payoff for Riggs keeping his mouth shut. Or was there another reason?

"What would she be using it for, the studio?"

Charlie glanced at him. "Does it matter?"

"Actually it does. If it's an art studio, I'd make sure there was sufficient lighting, maybe put in some skylights, and a ventilation system to carry the paint fumes out. If she just wants to use it to get away, read or sleep, I'd configure it differently."

Charlie nodded thoughtfully. "I see. Well, I don't

know what she plans to use it for. But she doesn't paint, that I know."

The men fell silent until that silence was interrupted by the sounds of LuAnn and Lisa approaching. The door to the terrace opened and the pair came out.

In person, Lisa Savage resembled her mother even more than in the photo. They both walked the same way, easy glides, no wasted energy.

"This is Mr. Riggs, Lisa."

Riggs had not been around many children in his life, but he did what came naturally. He put out his hand. "Call me Matt, Lisa. Pleased to meet you."

She smiled and squeezed his hand in return. "Pleased to meet you, Matt."

"That's quite a grip." He glanced up at LuAnn and then Charlie. "That particular attribute must run in the family. If I keep coming over here I might have to start wearing a steel glove."

Lisa smiled.

"Matthew is going to build a studio for me, Lisa. Out there somewhere." She pointed toward the rear grounds.

Lisa looked up at the house in undisguised wonderment. "Isn't our house big enough?"

All the adults burst into laughter at that one and finally Lisa joined in too.

"What's the studio for?" Lisa asked.

"Well, maybe it'll be kind of a surprise. In fact, I might let you use it too, sometimes."

Lisa grinned broadly at the news.

"But only if you keep your grades up," said Charlie. "By the way, how'd your test go?" Charlie's tone was gruff, but it clearly was all a facade. It was obvious to Riggs that the old guy loved Lisa as much as he did her mother, if not more.

Lisa's mouth dropped into a pout. "I didn't get an A."

298

"That's okay, sweetie," Charlie said kindly. "Probably my fault. I'm not all that good with math."

Lisa suddenly broke into a big smile. "I got an A plus."

Charlie playfully cuffed her head. "You got your mother's sense of humor, that's for sure."

LuAnn said, "Miss Sally has some lunch ready for you. I know you didn't get a chance to eat at school. Run along and I'll see you after I finish up with Matthew."

LuAnn and Riggs walked through the rear grounds. Charlie had begged off. He had some things to do, he had said.

After Riggs had walked the property he pointed to a clearing that was level, had an unobstructed view of the distant mountains, but still had shade trees on two sides. "That looks like a nice spot. Actually, with this much land, you probably have a number of potential locations. By the way, if I knew what you were going to use the place for I could make a more informed choice for the site." He looked around. "And you have a number of outbuildings already. Another option would be to convert one of those into a studio."

"I'm sorry, I thought I was clear on that. I want it done from scratch. None of the other buildings would really do. I want it set up like yours. Two stories. The first floor could be set up as a workshop for some of my hobbies, that is, when I get around to having some hobbies. Lisa is into drawing and she's getting pretty good. Maybe I could take up sculpting. That seems like a very relaxing pastime. On the second level I want a woodstove, a telescope, comfortable furniture, built-in bookcases, maybe a small kitchen, bay windows."

Riggs nodded and looked around. "I saw the pool area. Are you planning on a poolhouse and maybe tennis courts?"

"Next spring. Why?"

"I was just thinking that we might want to tie those and the studio into an overall plan. You know, use the same materials or some combo thereof with the poolhouse and the studio."

LuAnn shook her head. "No, I want it separate. We'll put in a large gazebo for outdoor entertaining and all that. It'll be mostly Lisa using the pool and tennis courts. I want those facilities closer to the main house. The pool is already close. The studio I want farther away. Sort of hidden."

"That's fine. You certainly have the land." He checked out the slope of the property. "So do you swim or play tennis?"

"I can swim like a fish, but I've never played tennis and I really don't have any desire to start."

"I thought all rich people played tennis. That and golf."

"Maybe if you're born with money. I haven't always been wealthy."

"Georgia."

LuAnn looked sharply at him. "What?"

"I've been trying to place your accent. Lisa's is all over the place. Yours is very faint, but it's still there. I'd guess you spent a lot of years in Europe, but you know what they say, you can take the girl out of Georgia but you can't take Georgia out of the girl."

LuAnn hesitated for a moment before replying. "I've never been to Georgia."

"I'm surprised. I'm usually pretty good at gauging that."

"Nobody's perfect." She flicked her hair out of her eyes. "So what do you think?" She looked at the clearing.

Riggs stared at her curiously for a moment before answering. "We'll have to draw up plans. They'll help you get it exactly the way you want, although it

300

sounds like you have a pretty good idea already. Depending on the size and complexity, it could take anywhere from two to six months."

"When could you start?"

"Not any time this year, Catherine."

"You're that busy?"

"It's got nothing to do with that. No sane builder would start on a project like that now. We need architectural plans and we also need to get building permits. The ground will be freezing soon and I don't like to pour footers after that. And we wouldn't be able to get it framed and under roof before winter set in. Weather can get real nasty up here. This is definitely a next spring project."

"Oh." LuAnn sounded deeply disappointed. She stared off at the site as though she were seeing her hideaway fully completed.

Trying to make her feel better Riggs said, "Spring will be here before you know it, Catherine. And the winter will allow us to work up a really good set of plans. I know a first-rate architect. I can set up a meeting."

LuAnn was hardly listening. Would they even be here next spring? Riggs's news about the construction schedule had dissipated much of her enthusiasm for the project.

"I'll see. Thanks."

As they walked back to the house Riggs touched her shoulder. "I take it you're not into delayed gratification. If I could put it up for you right now, I would. Some sleazy builders might take on the job and charge you a healthy premium and then proceed to turn out a piece of crap that'll fall down in a year or two. But I take pride in my work and I want to deliver a quality job for you."

She smiled at him. "Charlie said you had excellent references. I guess I can see why."

301

They were passing by the horse barn. LuAnn pointed at it and said, "I guess that counts as a hobby. You ride?"

"I'm no expert, but I won't fall off either."

"We should go for a ride sometime. There are some beautiful trails around here."

"I know," was Riggs's surprising reply. "I used to walk them before this property was sold. You made an excellent choice in real estate, by the way."

"Charlie found it."

"He's a good person to have around."

"He makes my life a lot easier. I don't know what I'd do without him."

"Nice to have somebody like that in your life."

She cast a furtive glance at him as they continued back to the house.

THIRTY-ONE

Charlie met them at the rear entrance. There was a suppressed excitement in his manner, and the darting glances he gave LuAnn told her the reason: Pemberton had found where the man in the Honda was staying.

While not showing it, Riggs picked up on the subtle undercurrents.

"Thanks for the lunch," he said. "I'm sure you've got things to do and I've got some appointments to take care of this afternoon." He looked over at LuAnn. "Catherine, let me know about the studio."

"I will. Call me about going for a ride."

"I'll do that."

After he left, Charlie and LuAnn went into Charlie's study and closed the door.

"Where is the guy?" she asked.

"He's our neighbor."

"What?"

"A little rental cottage. Pretty isolated. It's not more than four miles from here up Highway Twenty-two. I looked at some land up near there when we were thinking of building. Used to be a big estate up there but now there's just the caretaker's cottage. Remember, we took a drive up there a while back?"

"I remember exactly. You could walk or ride it through the back trails. I've done it. The guy could have been spying on us for a while."

"I know. That's what worries me. Pemberton gave

303

me exact directions to the place." Charlie laid the paper with the directions down on his desk while he pulled on his coat.

LuAnn took the opportunity to scan surreptitiously the directions and commit them to memory.

Charlie unlocked a drawer of his desk. LuAnn's eyes widened as she watched him pull out the .38. He proceeded to load it.

"What are you going to do?" she said fiercely.

He didn't look at her as he checked the safety and put the gun in his pocket. "Like we planned, I'm going to go check it out."

"I'm going with you."

He looked at her angrily. "The hell you are."

"Charlie, I am."

"What if there's trouble?"

"You're saying that to me?"

"You know what I mean. Let me check it out first, see what the guy's up to. I'm not going to do anything dangerous."

"So why the gun?"

"I said *I'm* not going to do anything dangerous. I don't know about him."

"I don't like it, Charlie."

"You think I do? I'm telling you, it's the only way. Something happens, the last thing I want is you in the middle of it."

"I've never expected you to fight my battles for me."

He touched her cheek gently. "You're not exactly twisting my arm here. I want you and Lisa to be safe and sound. In case you hadn't noticed, I've kind of made that my life's work. By choice." He smiled.

She watched him open the door and start to head out. "Charlie, please be careful."

He looked back, noting the worry in her features.

"LuAnn, you know I'm always careful."

As soon as he left, LuAnn went to her room, changed into jeans and a warm shirt, and pulled on sturdy boots.

In case you hadn't noticed, Charlie, my life's work is to make sure you and Lisa are safe and sound.

She grabbed a leather jacket from her closet and raced out of the house in the direction of the horse barn. She saddled Joy and then galloped off toward the maze of trails behind the mansion.

As soon as Charlie hit the main road, Riggs started to follow from a safe distance in the Cherokee. Riggs had thought it a fifty-fifty possibility that something was going to happen as soon as he left. A friend of Riggs had mentioned seeing Pemberton and Charlie having breakfast the day before. That was smart on Charlie's part, and indeed, was probably the path Riggs would have taken to track down the man in the Honda. That and Charlie's excited manner had been enough to convince Riggs that something was up. If he had been wrong, he wouldn't have wasted much time. He kept the Range Rover just in sight as it turned north on to Highway 22. It wasn't easy being invisible on the rural road, but Riggs was confident he could manage it. On the seat next to him was his shotgun. This time he would be prepared.

Charlie glanced to the right and left as he pulled the Range Rover underneath the cover of trees and then stopped. He could see the cottage up ahead. He might have wondered who would have built the place in the middle of nowhere, but Pemberton had informed him that the house had been a caretaker's cottage for a vast estate that was no longer in existence. Ironic that the tiny structure had outlived the main house. He gripped the pistol in his pocket

305

and got out. Threading his way through the thick trees behind the cottage, he made his first stop the shed. Rubbing away the dirt and grime on the window he was able barely to make out the black Honda inside. For this, he and LuAnn owed Pemberton a nice little donation to a charity of his choice.

Charlie waited about another ten minutes, his gaze glued to the small cottage, looking for any movement, any shadows falling across the windows. The place appeared unoccupied but the car in the shed belied that appearance. Charlie moved forward cautiously.

He glanced around but did not notice Riggs crouched behind a stand of thick holly bushes to the left of the house.

Riggs lowered his binoculars and surveyed the area. Like Charlie, he had detected no movement or sound coming from the cottage but that didn't mean anything. The guy could be in there just waiting for Charlie to put in an appearance. Shoot first and ask questions later. Riggs gripped his shotgun and waited.

The front door was locked. Charlie could have smashed a glass pane next to the door and unlocked the door from the inside, or simply kicked the door until it tore loose from the doorjamb – it didn't look all that sturdy. However, if the house was indeed occupied, knocking down the door might prompt a deadly response. And, if it wasn't occupied, he didn't want to leave any evidence that he had been to the cottage. Charlie knocked on the door, his pistol half out of his pocket. He waited and knocked again. There was no answer. He slid the gun back in his pocket and looked at the lock, a common pin tumbler, to his expert eye. He pulled out two items from his inner coat pocket: a straight pick and a tension tool. Fortunately, arthritis had not yet set into his fingers or he would not have had the dexterity needed to pick the lock. He first slid the pick into the keyhole and then eased the tension tool underneath the pick. Using the pick, Charlie raised the tumbler pins to their open position, and the constant pressure from the tension tool kept the tumbler pins open. Charlie manipulated the pick, sensing the subtle vibrations of the pins until he was rewarded with a click. He turned the doorknob and the door swung open. He replaced his tools in his coat. His State Pen degree had once again worked its magic. All the while he listened intently. He was well aware that a trap could be awaiting him. His hand closed around the .38. If the guy gave Charlie the opportunity to use it he would. The ramifications of such an act were too numerous to analyze; however, at least a few of them would be better than outright exposure.

The cottage's interior was of a simple configuration. The hallway ran from front to back, splitting the space into roughly equivalent halves. The kitchen was in the back on the left; the small dining room fronted that. On his right was an equally modest living room. Tacked on to the rear of that was a combination mud room/laundry room. Plain wooden stairs on the right made their way to the bedrooms on the second floor. Charlie observed little of this, because his attention was riveted on the dining room. He stared in amazement at the computer, printer, fax, and stacks of file boxes. He moved closer as his eyes swept to the bulletin board with all the news clippings and photos affixed to it.

He mouthed the headlines. LuAnn's face was prominent among the various photos. The whole story was there: the murders, LuAnn winning the lottery, her disappearance. Well, that had confirmed his suspicions. Now it remained to discover who the man was and, more important, what he wanted from them.

He made his way around the room, carefully lifting papers here and there, studying the clippings, examining the file boxes. His eyes diligently searched for anything that would identify the man; however, there was nothing. Whoever was pursuing them knew what he was doing.

Charlie moved to the desk and carefully slid open a drawer. The papers in there yielded nothing new. He tried the other drawers with similar results. For a moment he thought about turning on the computer but his skills with that technology were about nil. He was about to begin a search of the rest of the house when a solitary box in the far corner caught his eye. He might as well hit that too, he figured.

Lifting off the top, Charlie's eyes immediately started to twitch uncontrollably. The word "shit" passed almost silently from between his lips and his legs made a serious threat of giving out on him.

A single piece of paper stared back at him. The names were listed neatly on it. LuAnn's name was there. Most of the remaining names represented people Charlie was also familiar with: Herman Rudy, Wanda Tripp, Randy Stith, Bobbie Jo Reynolds among others. All past lottery winners. Most of them Charlie had personally escorted, like LuAnn. All of them, he knew, had won their fortunes with Jackson's help.

Charlie steadied himself by placing a shaking hand on top of the windowsill. He had been prepared to find evidence of the man knowing all about the murders and LuAnn's involvement. He had not been at all prepared to learn that the lottery scam had been uncovered. The hairs on his forearms felt like they had suddenly been electrified.

How? How could the guy have found out? Who the hell was he? He quickly put the boxtop back, turned, and headed out the door. He made sure it was locked before shutting it. He swiftly retraced his steps to the Range Rover, climbed in, and drove off.

Donovan headed down Route 29. He had been on the road the better part of two hours on his return trip from Washington and he was anxious to get back on the hunt. He sped up as he neared his final destination. On the drive down, he had thought of the next steps he would employ against LuAnn Tyler. Steps designed to make her cave in and do so quickly. If one approach failed, he would find another. The saving grace in all of this – a look of deep satisfaction came to his features as he thought of it – was that he had LuAnn Tyler over a barrel. The oft-quoted phrase was quite true: A chain was only as strong as its weakest link. And LuAnn, you are that rusty link, he said to himself. And you're not going to get away. He checked his watch. He would be at the cottage shortly. On the seat next to him was a small-caliber pistol. He didn't like guns, but he wasn't stupid either.

THIRTY-TWO

As Riggs watched Charlie drive off he caught only a glimpse of the man's face. However, it was enough to tell him that something was up. And that what was up was all bad. After the Range Rover disappeared from his line of sight, Riggs turned around and stared at the cottage. Should he make an attempt as well to search the place? It might answer a lot of questions. He had almost decided to flip a coin when another development caused him to crouch down behind the holly tree again and return to his role of observer.

LuAnn had tethered Joy to a tree in the woods about a hundred yards from the clearing in which the cottage stood. She emerged from outside the tree line with the same graceful movements Riggs had observed in her before. She squatted down on her haunches and waited, surveying the area with quick, darting movements of her head. Despite the impenetrable bulk of the holly tree, Riggs almost felt naked before her intense gaze.

LuAnn studied the road at the same time Riggs studied her. Was she aware that Charlie had already come and gone? Probably not. However, her features gave away nothing.

LuAnn silently watched the cottage for a time before moving over to the shed. Glancing through the same window Charlie had, she looked over the Honda. Then she lifted some dirt and grime from the windowsill and covered over the small opening

Charlie had made in the filth. Riggs watched this procedure with growing respect. Even he might not have thought to do that. Charlie certainly hadn't.

LuAnn turned her attention to the house. Both hands were in the pockets of her coat. She knew Charlie had been here but had already left. The smeared window had told her that. She also deduced he hadn't stayed very long because she had ridden Joy hard on the way over, and her route had been far more direct than the one Charlie had had to drive, although he had had a head start. His short stay meant he had found either nothing, or something highly incriminating. Her instincts told her that it was almost undoubtedly the latter. Should she leave and return home and let him fill her in? While that would have been the most prudent thing to do, LuAnn quickly made her way to the front porch and her hand closed around the doorknob. It didn't budge despite the immense pressure she was exerting. She had no special tools to jimmy it as Charlie had; thus she moved on, looking for another way in and finding it at the rear of the cottage. The window finally opened under her persistent tuggings and she quickly climbed inside.

She silently descended from the windowsill to the floor and immediately crouched down. From her line of sight she could make out the kitchen. She had very acute hearing, and if someone had been in the small house she was certain she would have heard his breathing no matter how shallow. She edged forward until she reached what should have been the dining room but had been set up as an office. LuAnn's eyes widened as she saw the news clippings on the bulletin board. As LuAnn's gaze swept around the room, she sensed there was something more at work here than a blackmail scheme.

* * *

311

"Oh, hell." Riggs ducked down after saying the words and watched in dismay as the Chrysler passed by him on the way to the cottage. The man was hunched over the steering wheel, but Riggs had no trouble recognizing him despite the beard's having been shaved off. Thinking quickly, Riggs gripped his shotgun and hurried to his Cherokee.

LuAnn flew to the back of the cottage as soon as she heard the car drive up. She raised her head a few inches above the windowsill; her heart sank. "Dammit!" She watched Donovan pull around to the rear of the cottage and climb out of the Chrysler. Her eyes were riveted on the pistol he held in his right hand. He headed straight for the rear door. LuAnn backed away, her eyes darting every which way, looking desperately for an exit. The problem was there wasn't any, at least none that would be unobserved. The front door was locked and if she attempted to open it, he would hear her. There was no time to wriggle through a window. The cottage was so small that he couldn't possibly fail to see her if she remained on the first floor.

Donovan inserted the key in the door lock. If he had glanced through the paned door window, he would have spotted LuAnn immediately. The door began to open.

LuAnn edged back into the dining room and was about to head upstairs and try for an escape from the second floor when she heard it.

The car horn was loud and shrill and the sound pattern kept repeating itself, like a car alarm that had been activated. She crept back to the window and watched as Donovan jerked to a halt, slammed the door closed, and then ran around to the front of the cottage.

LuAnn lost no time. She launched herself through

the same window she had used to enter, did a roll, and came up running. She made it to the shed and crouched down. The horn was still beeping. She ran to the far side of the shed, peered around the edge, and watched as Donovan advanced down the road, away from her, toward the sound, his pistol making wide sweeps as he did so.

The hand that suddenly gripped LuAnn's shoulder almost made her scream.

"Where's your horse?" Riggs's voice was even and calm.

She looked at him, the whiplash of fear receding as quickly as it had appeared. "About a hundred yards that way." She jerked her head in the direction of the thick woods. "Is that your car alarm?"

Riggs nodded and gripped his car keys tightly. One eye on Donovan and the other on their avenue of escape, Riggs rose to his feet and pulled LuAnn up with him. "Ready, go." Bursting out from their cover they raced across the open ground. Keeping his eyes on Donovan's back, Riggs unfortunately caught his foot on a root and he went down, his finger gripping the key ring, accidentally pressing the alarm's shut-off button. Donovan whipped around and stared at them. LuAnn had Riggs up again in a moment and they raced off into the woods. Donovan lurched toward them, his pistol making broad sweeps. "Hey," he screamed. "Dammit, hold it right there." Donovan waved the gun around, but he wasn't going to shoot; he wasn't a killer.

LuAnn ran like the wind and Riggs found it impossible to keep up with her. He had slightly twisted his ankle, he told himself, but truth be known, even at full speed he probably could not have caught her. They reached Joy, who stood patiently awaiting her owner's arrival. LuAnn quickly released the tether and jumped into the saddle without even bothering to use the stirrup. She flicked out a hand and hauled Riggs up behind her. The next moment they were racing up the trail astride the fleet mare. Riggs looked back for an instant, but Donovan was nowhere in sight. They had moved so fast he wasn't surprised. Riggs gripped LuAnn's waist with both hands and hung on for dear life as she whipped Joy at a breakneck pace through the swerving trails.

They had returned Joy to the horse barn and were walking back to the main house before Riggs broke the silence. "I take it that's how you handle those kind of situations. Break into the place. See what you can find. I don't know why I should be surprised. That's what you did with me." He looked at LuAnn with angry eyes.

She matched the look. "I didn't break into your place. And I don't remember asking you to follow me."

"I followed Charlie, not you," he corrected her. "But it's a damn good thing I was there, wasn't it? Two times in two days. At this rate you'll wear out your nine lives in a week." She kept walking, her arms crossed in front of her, her eyes staring resolutely ahead. Riggs stopped.

She stopped too and looked down for an instant. When she looked up there was a far softer countenance confronting him. "Thank you. Again. But the more distance you put between the three of us and yourself, the better off you'll be, I guarantee it. Forget the fence. I don't think we'll be staying on here. Don't worry, I'll pay you for it anyway." She stared at him for a moment longer, trying to push away feelings that had been strangers to her for so long that they now simply frightened her. "Have a good life, Matthew." She turned and headed for the house.

314

"Catherine?" She kept walking. "Catherine," he said again.

She finally stopped.

"Would you please tell me what's going on? I might be able to help you."

"I don't think so."

"You never know."

"Believe me, I know."

She started toward the house again.

Riggs stood there staring after her. "Hey, in case you forgot, I don't have a car to get home in."

When she turned around, the key ring was already sailing through the air. Riggs caught it in the palm of his hand.

"Take my car. It's parked out front. Keep it as long as you like. I've got another one."

On that she spun back around and disappeared into the house.

Riggs slowly pocketed the keys, shaking his head in absolute frustration.

THIRTY-THREE

"Where the hell have you been?" Charlie came out of his study and leaned up against the doorjamb. His face was still pale, a detail LuAnn picked up on immediately.

"Same place you were," she said.

"What? LuAnn, I told you—"

"You weren't alone. Riggs followed you. In fact he managed to save me again. If he happens to do it once more, I might have to consider marrying the man."

Charlie went a shade paler. "Did he go inside the house?"

"No, but I did."

"How much did you see?" Charlie asked nervously.

LuAnn swept past him and into the office. "I don't want Lisa to hear."

Charlie closed the door behind them. He went straight over to the liquor stand and poured himself a drink. LuAnn watched his movements in silence for a moment before speaking.

"Apparently, you saw more than I did."

He turned to her and downed the drink in one motion. "The news clippings on the lottery? The murders?"

LuAnn nodded. "I saw them. After my first encounter with the man, I wasn't very surprised to see that."

"I wasn't either."

"Apparently there was more, though." She looked

at him pointedly at the same time she sat down on the sofa, folding her hands in her lap and collecting her nerves as best she could.

There was a haunted look in Charlie's features, as though he had awoken from a nightmare and attempted to laugh it off, only to find out he wasn't dreaming. "I saw some names. A list of them in fact. Yours was on there." He paused and put the glass down. His hands were shaking. LuAnn braced herself. "Herman Rudy. Wanda Tripp. Randy Stith. They were on there too. I escorted them all in New York."

LuAnn slowly rested her head in her hands.

Charlie sat down beside her, put one beefy hand on her back, and slowly rubbed it.

She sat back and slumped against him; a painful weariness laced her words. "We have to go, Charlie. We have to pack up and go. Tonight."

He considered the request before running a hand across his forehead. "I've been thinking about that. We can run, like we've done before. But there's a difference now."

LuAnn's response was immediate. "He knows about the lottery fix *and* he knows LuAnn Tyler and Catherine Savage are one and the same. Our cover isn't going to work anymore."

Charlie nodded glumly. "We've never been confronted with both of those before. It makes disappearing a little trickier."

She suddenly stood up and started her ritualistic pacing, moving in fluid circles around the room. "What does he want, Charlie?"

"I've been thinking about that too." He went over to the liquor stand with his empty glass, hesitated, and decided against a second round. "You saw the guy's setup. What did it look like to you?" he asked.

LuAnn stopped pacing and leaned up against the

317

fireplace mantel. In her mind, she went through every detail of the place.

"His car was a rental, under an assumed name. So he doesn't want us to be able to trace his real identity. I didn't recognize the man, but there must be another reason he's going incognito."

"Right." Charlie studied her. Over the years, he had learned that LuAnn missed almost nothing and her instincts were first-rate.

"He tried to spook me, which he did. I take that as a warning, a message that he's a player and he wants us to be aware of that for the next time he calls."

"Go on," he encouraged.

"The place, the little I saw of it, was set up like an office. Very neat, very orderly. Computer, fax, printer, files. It was like he had made all of this some special research project."

"Well, he would've had to do a ton of research to figure out the lottery scam. Jackson is no dummy."

"How do you think he did it, Charlie?"

He rubbed his chin and sat down in front of his desk. "Well, we don't know for absolute certain that he has figured it all out. I just saw the list. That's all."

"With the names of all those lottery winners? Come on. How long did Jackson run the scam anyway?"

Charlie shook his head. "I don't know. I mean, I was there for nine of them, including you. Started in August. You were Miss April, my last gig."

LuAnn shook her head stubbornly. "He knows, Charlie; we have to assume that to be true. However he did it, he did it."

"Okay. So it seems pretty clear the guy wants money."

She shook her head. "We don't know that. I mean, why would he set up shop here and bring all that stuff with him? He didn't need to do that. He could just send me a letter from parts unknown with the same info, and a demand for money to be wire-transferred to his bank account."

Charlie sat back, his face carrying extreme confusion. He had not looked at the matter in that light. "That's true."

"And I don't think the guy's hurting for money. He was wearing really nice clothes. Two leased cars, the rent on that cottage isn't cheap, I'm thinking, and all that equipment he had. He's not digging his dinner out of garbage cans."

"Right, but unless he's already a. millionaire, going after you would significantly enrich his bank account," said Charlie.

"But he hasn't done that. He hasn't asked for anything. I wish I knew why." She was lost deep in thought for a moment and then looked up. "How long did Pemberton say the cottage had been rented?"

"About a month."

"That makes it even more unlikely he was going to blackmail us. Why wait? Why come right out and warn me that he knows everything? How does he know I won't just disappear in the middle of the night? If I do that, he's not going to be filling up his bank account with my funds."

Charlie sighed deeply. "So what do we do now?"

"Wait," was finally the answer from LuAnn's lips. "But make arrangements for us to leave the country on a moment's notice. By private jet. And since he knows about Catherine Savage, we're going to need another set of identification papers. Can you get them?"

"I'll have to look up some old contacts, but I can do it. It'll take a few days."

LuAnn stood up.

"What about Riggs?" Charlie asked. "The man's not going to let it go now."

"There's nothing we can do about that. He doesn't trust us and I don't blame him."

319

"Well, I doubt if he'll do anything that'll end up hurting you."

She looked sharply at him. "How do you know that?"

"Look, LuAnn, it doesn't take a rocket scientist to see Riggs has a thing for you." A hint of resentment tinged his response. His tone softened, however, with his next words. "Seems like a nice guy. Under different circumstances, who knows. You shouldn't spend your life alone, LuAnn."

A flush swept over her face. "I'm not alone. I've got Lisa and I've got you. I don't need anybody else. I can't handle anybody else." She looked away. How could she invite anyone into her life? It was impossible. Half truths competing with complete falsehoods. She was no longer a real person. She was a thirty-year-old shell, period. Everything else had been bartered away. Jackson had taken the rest of it. He and his offer. If she hadn't made that call way back when. If she hadn't panicked? She wouldn't have spent ten years turning herself into the woman she always wanted to be. She wouldn't be living in a million-dollar mansion. But as ironic as it sounded, she would probably have far more of a life than she had now. Whether it was to be spent in another wrecked mobile trailer or slinging fried foods at the truck stop, LuAnn Tyler, the pauper, would probably have been happier than Catherine Savage, the princess, ever dreamt of being. But if she hadn't accepted the offer, Jackson would have had her killed. There was no way out. She turned back to Charlie and spread her arms wide.

"That's the trade-off, Charlie. For this. For all this. You, me, and Lisa."

"The Three Musketeers." Charlie attempted a smile.

"Let's pray for a happy ending." LuAnn opened the door and disappeared down the hallway in search of her daughter.

THIRTY-FOUR

"Thank you for meeting with me on such short notice, Mr. Pemberton."

"John, please call me John, Mr. Conklin." Pemberton shook the other man's hand and they sat down at the small conference table in Pemberton's real estate office.

"I go by Harry," the other man said.

"Now you mentioned over the phone that you were interested in a house, but you really didn't say what area or price range."

Without seeming to do so, Pemberton looked Harry Conklin over. Probably in his sixties, expensive clothing, air of assurance, undoubtedly liked the good things in life. Pemberton swiftly calculated his potential commission.

"I got your name on good reference. I understand that you specialize in the upper-end market around here," Conklin said.

"That's correct. Born and raised here. Know everybody and every property worth knowing about. So would that be a price range you're interested in? The upper end?"

Conklin assumed a comfortable look. "Let me tell you a little about myself. I make my living on Wall Street and it's a damn good living if I do say so myself. But it's also a young man's game and I'm not a young man anymore. I've made my fortune and it's substantial. I've got a penthouse in Manhattan, a place in Rio, a home on Fisher Island in Florida, and a country estate outside London. But I'm looking to get out of New York and radically simplify my life. And this place is about as beautiful as they come."

"Absolutely right," Pemberton chimed in.

"Now, I do a lot of entertaining, so it would have to be a substantial place. But I want privacy as well. Something old, and elegant, but restored. I like old things, but not old plumbing, you understand me?"

"Perfectly."

"Now, I'm assuming that there are probably a number of properties around here that fit the bill."

"There are. Most assuredly," Pemberton said excitedly.

"But see, I've got one in mind. One I heard about from my father, in fact. He was in the stock market too. Back in the twenties. Made a bundle and was fortunate to get out before the crash. He used to come here and stay with a good friend of his who was in the market too. My father, God rest his soul, loved it there, and I thought it would be appropriate for his son to buy it and live in it."

"What a truly inspiring idea. Certainly makes my job easier. Do you know the name of the place?" Pemberton's smile was broadening.

"Wicken's Hunt."

Pemberton's smile quickly faded.

"Oh." He licked his lips, made a clicking sound with his tongue against his teeth. "Wicken's Hunt," he repeated, looking depressed.

"What's the matter? Did it burn down or something?"

"No, no. It's a beautiful place, wonderfully restored." Pemberton sighed deeply. "Unfortunately it's no longer on the market."

"You sure?" Conklin sounded skeptical.

"I'm certain. I was the selling agent."

"Damn, how long ago?"

"About two years, although the people have only been in it for several months. There was a lot of renovation work to do."

Conklin looked at him slyly, eyebrows cocked. "Think they might want to sell?"

Pemberton's mind raced through the possibilities. Flipping a property like that within the relatively short span of two years? What a wonderful impact on his wallet.

"Anything's possible. I've actually gotten to know them – well, one of them anyway – fairly well. Just had breakfast with him, in fact."

"So it's a couple then, old like me, I guess. Wicken's Hunt isn't exactly a starter home from what my father told me."

"Actually, they're not a couple. And he's older, but the property doesn't belong to him. It belongs to her."

Conklin leaned forward. "To her?"

Pemberton looked around for a moment, got up and fully shut the door to his conference room, and then sat back down.

"You understand that I'm telling you this in confidence."

"Absolutely. I didn't survive all those years on Wall Street without understanding confidences."

"While the land records show a corporation as the title holder, the real owner of Wicken's Hunt is a young woman. Catherine Savage. Obviously incredibly wealthy. Quite frankly, I'm not certain what the source of that wealth is, nor is it my business to ask. She lived abroad for years. Has a little girl about ten. Charlie Thomas – the older man – he and I have had some nice little discussions. They've been very generous with several local charities. She doesn't come out in public very much, but that's understandable."

323

"Sure is. If I moved here, you might not see me for weeks on end."

"Exactly. They seem to be real good people, though. They seem very happy here. Very happy."

Conklin sat back and it was his turn to sigh. "Well, I guess they won't be looking to move any time soon. Damn shame too." He eyed Pemberton intently. "Real damn shame, since I make it my practice to pay a finder's fee on top of any real estate commission you might collect from the seller."

Pemberton perked up noticeably. "Is that right?"

"Now, there aren't any ethical considerations that would prevent you from accepting such an inducement, are there?"

"None that I can think of," Pemberton said quickly. "So, how much would that inducement come to?"

"Twenty percent of the purchase price." Harry Conklin drummed his fingers on the tabletop and watched Pemberton's face turn different colors.

If Pemberton hadn't been sitting down, he would've toppled to the floor. "That's very generous," he finally managed to say.

"If I want something done, I find the best way to accomplish my goal is to provide decent incentives to those in a position to help me achieve that goal. But from the looks of things here, I don't think it's likely. Maybe I'll try North Carolina, I hear good things about it." Conklin started to get up.

"Wait a minute. Please wait just a minute."

Conklin hesitated and then slowly resumed his seat.

"Actually, your timing may be perfect."

"Why's that?"

Pemberton leaned even closer to him. "There have been recent developments, very recent developments, that might give us an opening to approach them about selling."

"If they just moved in, seem happy here, what kind of developments are we talking about? The place isn't haunted, is it?"

"No, nothing like that. As I said, I had a breakfast meeting with Charlie. He was concerned about a person who had come to visit them. Asking for money."

"So? That happens to me all the time. You think that'll make them pack up and leave?"

"Well, I wouldn't have thought so at first either, but the more I thought about it, the more unusual it sounded. I mean, you're right, the rich get approached all the time, so why should this man upset them so? But he obviously did."

"How do you know that?"

Pemberton smiled. "In many ways, in fact, in more ways than people around here care to admit, Charlottesville is a small town. Now I know for a fact that very recently Matt Riggs was up surveying Ms. Savage's property line when he became engaged in a reckless chase with another car that almost got him killed."

Conklin shook his head in confusion. "Who's Matt Riggs?"

"A local contractor hired by Ms. Savage to install a security fence around her property."

"So he was chasing another car? How does that tie in with Catherine Savage?"

"A friend of mine was heading to work that morning. He lives up in that same area and works in town. He was about to turn on to the main road heading into town when a charcoal gray BMW flew by. He said it must've been doing eighty. If he had pulled out a second sooner that BMW would've torn his car in half. He was so shaken, he couldn't budge for a full minute. Good thing too, because while he's sitting there trying to keep his breakfast down, Matt

Riggs's pickup comes barreling by and another car is locked on his bumper. They were obviously going at it."

"Do you know who was in the BMW?"

"Now, I've never met her but I know people who have seen her. Catherine Savage is a tall, blond woman. Real good-looking. My friend only got a glimpse of the driver, but he said she was blond and pretty. And I saw a charcoal gray BMW parked up at Wicken's Hunt when I went up to do a preclosing walk-through with Charlie."

"So you think somebody was chasing her?"

"And I think Matt Riggs must've run smack into it. I know that his truck's in the shop with a busted bumper. I also know that Sally Beecham – she's the maid up at Wicken's – saw Riggs walking off in a huff from the house later that same morning."

Conklin stroked his chin. "Very interesting. Guess there's no way to find out who was chasing her?"

"Yes there is. I mean I did. At least his location. You see, it gets even more interesting. As I said, Charlie invited me to breakfast. That's when he told me about this man who had come by the house wanting money. Charlie wanted my help in finding out if the man was staying in the area. Of course, I agreed to do what I could. At that point I didn't know about the car chase. I found that out later."

"You said you were able to find the man? But how could you? Lots of places to hide around here, I would think." Conklin asked this in a nonchalant manner.

Pemberton smiled triumphantly. "Not much escapes my notice, Harry. Like I said, I was born and raised here. Charlie gave me a description of the man and the car. I used my contacts and in less than twenty-four hours I had located him."

"Probably holed up pretty far away, I'll bet."

Pemberton shook his head. "Not at all. He was right under their noses. A small cottage. It's barely ten minutes from Wicken's Hunt by car. But very isolated."

"Help me out here. I don't have my bearings here yet. Is it near Monticello?"

"Well, in the general vicinity, but the area I'm talking about is north of that, north of Interstate Sixty-four, in fact. The cottage isn't too far from the Airslie Estate, off Highway Twenty-two, the Keswick Hunt area it's called. The man had leased the cottage about a month ago."

"Good gosh, did you get a name?"

"Tom Jones." Pemberton smiled knowingly. "Obviously false."

"Well, I guess they appreciated your help. So what happened?"

"I don't know. My business keeps me hopping. I really haven't talked to them about it any more."

"Well, this Riggs fellow, I bet he's sure sorry he got involved."

"Well, he can take care of himself."

"Maybe so, but getting banged around in a car in a high-speed chase? Most general contractors don't do that."

"Well, Riggs wasn't always a G.C."

"Really?" Conklin said, his features inscrutable. "You really do have the Peyton Place here. So what's his story?"

Pemberton shrugged his shoulders. "Your guess is as good as mine. He never talks about his past. He just appeared one day about five years ago, started learning the building trade and he's been here ever since. Pretty mysterious. Charlie thought he was a policeman. Frankly, I think he was with the government in some secret capacity and they put him out to pasture. Call it my gut."

"That's real interesting. Old guy then."

"No. Mid- to late thirties. Tall, strong, and very capable. Excellent reputation."

"Good for him."

"Now about our arrangement. If this man really is dogging them, I can talk to Charlie, see what he has to say. Maybe they will agree to move. It's certainly worth asking."

"I tell you what, you let me think about it for a few days."

"I can get the process started anyway."

Conklin put up one hand. "No, I don't want you doing that. When I'm ready to move, we'll move fast, don't you worry about that."

"I just thought—"

Conklin abruptly got up. "You'll hear from me very soon, John. I appreciate the insight, I really do."

"And if they won't move, there are at least a dozen other estates I can show you. They would serve your purposes equally well, I'm sure."

"This fellow in the cottage intrigues me. You wouldn't happen to have an exact address and directions, would you?"

Pemberton was startled by the question. "You certainly don't want to talk to him, do you? He might be dangerous."

"I can take care of myself. And I've learned in my business that you never know where you might find an ally." Conklin looked at him keenly until understanding spread across Pemberton's face. He wrote the information down on a piece of paper and handed it to the other man.

Conklin took an envelope out of his pocket and handed it to Pemberton, motioning for him to open it.

"Oh my God." Pemberton sat there gaping at the wad of cash that spilled out. "What's this for? I haven't done anything yet."

Conklin eyed Pemberton steadily. "You've given me information, John. Information is always worth a great deal to me. I'll be in touch." The men shook hands and Conklin took his leave.

Back at the country inn where he was staying, Harry Conklin walked into the bathroom, closed the door, and turned on the water. Fifteen minutes later the door opened and Jackson emerged, the remnants of Harry Conklin bundled in a plastic bag which Jackson deposited in a side pouch of his luggage. His conversation with Pemberton had been very enlightening. His encounter with the man had not been by chance. Upon arriving in Charlottesville, Jackson had made discreet inquiries around town that had quickly identified Pemberton as the selling agent for Wicken's Hunt. He sat on the bed and opened a large, detailed map of the Charlottesville area, noting and committing to memory the places he and Pemberton had discussed and the written directions to the cottage. Before talking to Pemberton he had educated himself on some of the history of Wicken's Hunt, which had been nicely detailed in a book on local area estates and their original owners at the county library. It had given him enough background information to form his cover story and draw out Pemberton on the subject.

Jackson closed his eyes, deep in thought. Right now he was planning how best to begin his campaign against LuAnn Tyler and the man who was pursuing her.

THIRTY-FIVE

Riggs had given it a day before he had attempted to retrieve his Jeep. Just in case the guy was still around, he went armed and he went at night. The Cherokee looked undamaged. Riggs made a quick check of it before heading toward the cottage. The Chrysler was nowhere to be seen. He shone his flashlight in the window of the shed. The Honda was still there. Riggs went up to the front door and wondered for the hundredth time if he should just leave this business alone. Dangerous things seemed to happen around Catherine Savage. He had had his fill of such events and he had come to Charlottesville in search of other things. Still, he could not stop his hand from carefully turning the doorknob. The door swung open.

The flashlight in one hand, his pistol in the other, Riggs moved forward slowly. He was reasonably certain that the place was empty, but assumptions like that could earn you an unwanted trip to the morgue with a tag around your big toe. He could see most of the first floor from where he was standing. He shone his flashlight slowly around the room. There was a light switch on the wall, but he wasn't about to use it. In what had been the dining room, he discerned dust patterns on the floor that showed certain objects had been removed. He ran his fingers over these areas and then moved on. He moved into the kitchen where he lifted the phone. There was no

330

dial tone. He moved back into the dining room.

As Riggs's eyes swept the room, they passed right over the figure dressed all in black standing just inside the half-opened closet door next to the stairs.

Jackson closed his eyes the second before the light moved across his hiding place so that his pupils would not reflect off it. When the arc of illumination had passed, Jackson reopened his eyes and gripped the handle of the knife tightly. He had heard Riggs before he had ever set foot on the porch. It was not the man who had leased the cottage. He was long gone; Jackson had already searched the place thoroughly. This man had come to reconnoiter the place as well. Riggs, it must be, Jackson concluded. In fact, Jackson found Riggs almost as interesting as the man he had come to kill tonight. Ten years ago Jackson had predicted that LuAnn would be a problem, and now that prediction was coming true. He had done some preliminary checking on Riggs's background after his discussion with Pemberton. The fact that there was little to find out had intrigued him greatly.

When Riggs passed within a few feet of him, Jackson contemplated killing him. It would take just a flick of the razor-sharp blade against his throat. But as quickly as the homicidal impulse flared through his system, it passed. Killing Riggs would further no purpose, at least not at present. Jackson's hand gripping the knife relaxed. Riggs would live another day. If there was a next time, Jackson decided, the outcome might be far different. He didn't like people meddling in his business. If nothing else, he would now check into Riggs's background with far greater intensity.

Riggs left the cottage and headed toward his Cherokee. He glanced back at the cottage. A sensation had just come over him, as though he had just survived a close call. He shrugged it off. He had once lived by his instincts; however, he assumed they had rusted somewhat since his occupation had changed. It was an empty house and nothing more.

Watching from the window, Jackson picked up on Riggs's slight hesitation, and with it his curiosity grew even more. Riggs would possibly make an interesting project, but he would have to wait. Jackson had something more pressing to take care of. From the floor of the closet Jackson picked up what looked like a doctor's bag. He moved to the dining room, crouched down, and unpacked the contents of a first-rate fingerprint kit. Jackson then moved over to the light switch and hit it from various angles with a handheld laser carried in his jacket pocket. Several latent prints sprang to life under the beam. Jackson dusted the area with a fiberglass brush dipped in black powder and gently brushed around the area of the light switch, outlining the latent prints. The kitchen counter, telephone, and doorknobs were subjected to the same process. The telephone, especially, evidenced very clear fingerprints. Jackson smiled. Riggs's real identity would not be a mystery much longer. Using pressure-wound tape, he then lifted the prints from each of the areas and transferred them to separate index cards. Humming quietly to himself, Jackson marked the cards with special identification hieroglyphics and placed them in separate plastic-lined containers. He then carefully removed all evidence of the fingerprint powder from each of the surfaces. He loved the methodology of it all. Precise steps that reached a precise conclusion. It took him only a few minutes to repack his kit and then he left the cottage. He took a side trail to his waiting car and drove off. It was not often that one captured two birds with one stone. Tonight's work was beginning to look like precisely that.

THIRTY-SIX

"I like Mr. Riggs, Mom."

"Well, you don't really know him, do you?"

LuAnn sat on the edge of her daughter's bed and fingered the bed covers absentmindedly.

"I have good instincts about these things."

Mother and daughter exchanged smiles. "Really? Well, maybe you can share some of your insights with me."

"Seriously, is he going to come back soon?"

LuAnn took a deep breath. "Lisa, we may have to go away soon."

Lisa's hopeful smile faded away at this abrupt change of subjects. "Go away? Where?"

"I'm not sure just yet. And it's not for certain. Uncle Charlie and I haven't finished talking about it yet."

"Were you going to include me in those discussions?"

The unfamiliar tone in her daughter's voice startled LuAnn. "What are you talking about?"

"How many times have we moved in the last six years? Eight? And that's just as far back as I can remember. God knows how many times we did when I was really little. It's not fair." Lisa's face colored and her voice shook.

LuAnn swept an arm around her shoulders. "Sweetie, I didn't say it was for certain. I just said maybe."

"That's not the point. Okay, so it's maybe now. Or maybe next month. But then one day it'll be 'we're moving' and there's nothing I can do about it."

LuAnn put her face in Lisa's long hair. "I know it's hard on you, baby."

"I'm not a baby, Mom, not anymore. And I'd really like to know what we're running from."

LuAnn stiffened and raised her head back up, her eyes searching out Lisa's.

"We're not running from anything. What would we possibly be running from?"

"I was hoping you would tell me. I like it here, I don't want to leave, and unless you can give me a really good explanation why we have to, I'm not going."

"Lisa, you're ten years old and even though you're a very intelligent and mature ten-year-old, you're still only a child. So where I go, you go."

Lisa turned her face away. "Do I have a big trust fund?"

"Yes, why?"

"Because when I turn eighteen I'm going to have my own home and I'm going to stay there until I die. And I don't want you to ever visit me."

LuAnn's cheeks reddened. "Lisa!"

"I mean it. And then maybe I'll have friends and can do the things I want to do."

"Lisa Marie Savage, you've been all over the world. You've done things most people will never get a chance to do their entire lives."

"Well, you know what?"

"What?" LuAnn shot back.

"Right now, I'd trade with them in a heartbeat."

Lisa lay down in the bed and put the covers up almost over her head. "And right now, I'd like to be alone."

LuAnn started to say something and then thought

better of it. Biting her lip hard, she raced down the hallway to her room, where she collapsed on the bed.

It was unraveling. She could feel it, like a big ball of twine someone had tossed down a long set of stairs. She rose, went into the bathroom, and started the shower. She pulled off her clothes and stepped under the steaming water. Leaning up against the wall she closed her eyes and tried to tell herself that it would be okay, that in the morning Lisa would be all right, that her love for her mother remained undiminished. This was not the first serious argument mother and daughter had had over the years. Lisa did not just share her mother's physical attributes; LuAnn's independence and stubborn streak had been replicated in her daughter. After a few minutes LuAnn finally calmed down and let the soothing water envelop her.

When she opened her eyes another image invaded her thoughts. Matthew Riggs must believe her to be insane by now. Insane and dishonest as hell. Quite a combination if you were trying to make an impression. But she wasn't. If anything, she felt sorry for him, having risked his life twice and gotten kicked in the gut both times for his trouble. He was a very attractive man, but she wasn't looking for a relationship. How could she? How could she even contemplate partnering with someone? She'd be afraid to speak for fear of letting a secret scurry free. With all that, the image of Matt Riggs remained fixed in her head. A very handsome man. Strong, honest, courageous. And there was secrecy in his background too. And hurt. She suddenly cursed out loud that her life wasn't normal. That she couldn't attempt even a friendship with him.

She moved her hands fiercely along her limbs as she soaped up and released her frustrations at the same time. The harsh movements against her skin rekindled a disturbing revelation. The last man she had slept with was Duane Harvey over ten years ago. As her fingers moved over her breasts, Riggs's face appeared again in her thoughts. She shook her head angrily, closed her eyes again, and laid her face against the wall of the shower. The costly imported tile was wet and warm. She remained in that position despite danger signs flashing in her mind. So wet. So warm. So safe. Almost unconsciously her hands dipped to her waist and then over her buttocks and all the while Matthew Riggs resided in her thoughts. She kept her eyes scrunched tight. The fingers of her right hand slithered around to her navel. Her breaths became heavier. Under the sounds of the water, a low moan passed over her lips. A large tear made its way down her face before it was washed away. Ten years. Ten damned years. The fingers of her two hands were touching now, intermeshed in a way, like the gears of a clock. Slow, methodical, reliable. Back and forth . . . She jerked straight up so quickly she almost smashed her skull against the showerhead.

"Good Lord, LuAnn!" She exclaimed this to herself. She cut off the water and stepped out of the shower. She sat down on the lid of the toilet and hung her head between her knees; the lightheadedness was already passing. Her wet hair sprawled across her long, bare legs. The floor became sopping wet as the water poured off her body. She glanced over at the shower, a guilty look on her face. The muscles in her back bunched together, the veins in her arms swelled large. It wasn't easy. It just wasn't easy at all.

She rose on unsteady legs, toweled off, and went into the bedroom.

Among the costly furnishings of her bedroom was

a very familiar object. The clock her mother had given her ticked away, and as LuAnn listened, her nerves began to reassemble themselves. Thank God she had stuffed it in her bag right before almost being killed in that trailer so many years ago. Even now she would lie awake at night listening to its clunkiness. It skipped every third beat and at around five o'clock in the afternoon it would make a noise like someone had lightly smacked a cymbal. The gears and wires, the guts of the contraption, were tired; but it was like listening to an old friend strum on a weathered guitar, the notes not what they should be, ideally, but holding comfort for her, some peace.

She pulled on a pair of panties and then went back into the bathroom to dry her hair. Looking in the mirror she saw a woman on the brink of something: disaster probably. Should she start seeing a shrink? Didn't you have to be truthful in therapy in order to make any progress? She mouthed this question to her reflection in the mirror. No, psychotherapy wasn't going to be an option. As usual, she would just go it alone.

She traced the scar on her face, letting her finger feel each contour of the ridged, damaged skin, in essence reliving the painful events of her past. *Never forget*, she told herself. *It's all a sham. All a lie.*

She finished drying her hair, and was about to go back into the bedroom and collapse on to the bed when Lisa's words came back to her. She just couldn't let that resentment and anger fester all night. She had to talk to her daughter again. Or at least try to.

She went back into the bedroom to put on her robe before heading for Lisa's room.

"Hello, LuAnn."

So stunned was LuAnn that she had to reach out

337

and grip the doorjamb or she would've sagged to the floor. As LuAnn stared at him, she found that the muscles in her face had ceased to function. She couldn't even form a response, as though she had just suffered a stroke.

"It's been a long time." Jackson stepped away from the window and sat down on the edge of the bed.

His casual movements finally broke LuAnn free from her inertia. "How the hell did you get in here?"

"Not relevant." The words and tone were instantly familiar to her. All those years ago came rushing back with such speed that the effect was nearly incapacitating.

"What do you want?" She forced the words to come out.

"Ah, very relevant. However, we have much to discuss, and I would suggest you do so in the comfort of some clothing." He stared pointedly at her body.

LuAnn found it extremely difficult to take her eyes off him. Being half naked in front of the man was far less disturbing than having to turn her back on him. Finally, she threw open her closet door, pulled out a knee-length robe, and quickly put it on. She cinched the robe tightly around her waist and turned back around. Jackson wasn't even looking at her. His eyes roamed the spectacular parameters of her boudoir; his gazed rested on the clock on the wall briefly and then moved on. Apparently, the brief view of her body – a sight many men would have paid hard cash for – had inspired in him nothing more than extreme diffidence.

"You've done well for yourself. If I remember correctly, your previous decorating tastes were limited to dirty linoleum and Goodwill castoffs."

"I don't appreciate this intrusion."

He swiveled his head around and his eyes flashed into hers. "And I don't appreciate having to take time away from a very busy schedule to rescue you yet again, LuAnn. By the way, do you prefer LuAnn or Catherine?"

"I'll let you choose," she said sharply. "And I don't need to be rescued by anyone, certainly not by you."

He rose from the bed and scrutinized her altered appearance closely. "Very good. Not quite as good as I could have done, but I won't nit-pick," he finally said. "Still, the look is very chic, very sophisticated. Congratulations."

LuAnn responded by remarking, "The last time I saw you, you were wearing a dress. Other than that, you haven't changed much."

Jackson still had on the dark clothing he had worn at the cottage. His features were the same as for their first meeting, although he had not covered his lean frame with padding. He thrust his head forward; the smile seemed to engulf his entire face. "Didn't you know?" he said. "Aside from my other remarkable abilities, I also never age." His smile receded as quickly as it had appeared. "Now, let's talk." He once again perched on the edge of the bed and motioned for LuAnn to sit at a small antique writing desk situated against one wall. She did so.

"What about?"

"I understand you had a visitor. A man who chased you in a car?"

"How the hell do you know that?" LuAnn said angrily.

"You just won't accept the fact that you can't conceal information from me. Like the fact that you have reentered the United States against my most explicit instructions."

"The ten years are up."

"Funny, I don't remember setting an expiration date on those instructions."

"You can't expect me to run for the rest of my life."

"On the contrary, that is exactly what I expect. That is exactly what I *demand*."

"You cannot run my life."

Jackson looked around the room again and then stood up. "First things first. Tell me about the man."

"I can handle this situation by myself."

"Is that right? From what I can tell, you've committed one blunder after another."

"I want you to leave right now. I want you to get the hell out of my house."

Jackson calmly shook his head. "The years have done nothing to ameliorate your temper. An unlimited supply of money can't purchase good breeding or tact, can it?"

"Go to hell."

In response Jackson reached one hand inside his jacket.

In an instant LuAnn had snatched up a letter opener from her writing desk. She cocked her arm back in preparation to hurl it. "I can kill you with this from twenty feet. Money *can* buy a lot of things."

Jackson shook his head sadly. "Ten years ago I found you, a young girl with a good head on her shoulders in very difficult circumstances. But you were still white trash, LuAnn. And, I'm afraid to say, some things just don't change." His hand slowly came out of his jacket. In it he held a slip of paper. "You can put your little toy away. You won't need it." He looked at her with a calmness that managed, under the circumstances, to paralyze her. "At least not tonight." He unfolded the paper. "Now, I understand that two men have recently entered your life: Matthew Riggs is one; the other is as yet unidentified."

LuAnn slowly dropped her arm, but she still clutched the letter opener in her hand.

Jackson looked up from the paper. "I have a vested interest in ensuring that your secret never be found out. I have a number of ongoing business activities, and above all I value anonymity. You're one in a line of dominoes. And when they start to fall, they tend to keep falling until they reach the end. I am that end. Do you understand?"

LuAnn sat back down in the chair and crossed her legs. "Yes," she answered curtly.

"You have unnecessarily complicated my life by coming back to the United States. The man who is following you discovered your identity, in part, through your tax records. That is why I never wanted you to come back."

"I probably shouldn't have," LuAnn conceded. "But you try moving just about every six months, a new country, a new language. And try doing it with a little girl."

"I appreciate your difficulties; however, I assumed that being one of the richest women on earth would more than make up the difference."

"Like you said, money can't buy everything."

"You never met the man before? In your extensive travels? You're absolutely certain?"

"I would've remembered. I've remembered everything the last ten years." She said this softly.

Jackson studied her closely. "I believe you. Do you have any reason to think that he knows about the lottery?"

LuAnn hesitated a second. "No."

"You're lying. Tell me the truth immediately or I'll kill everyone in this house starting with you." This abrupt threat, delivered calmly and precisely, made her suck in her breath.

She swallowed with difficulty. "He had a list. A

list with twelve names on it. Mine, Herman Rudy, Bobbie Jo Reynolds, and some others."

Jackson assimilated this information rapidly and then looked down at the paper. "And the man Riggs?"

"What about him?"

"There's some confusion as to his background."

"Everyone has secrets."

Jackson smiled. "Touché. Under other circumstances that would not bother me. However, in this instance it does."

"I'm not following you."

"Riggs has a mysterious past and he just happens to be around when you need assistance. I take it he did help you."

LuAnn looked at him quizzically. "Yes, but he's been here for five years, long before I got here."

"That's not the point. I'm not suggesting the man is a plant. I am suggesting that he could well be something entirely different than what he claims. Now he coincidentally collides with your world. That's what worries me."

"I don't think it was anything other than a coincidence. He was hired to do a job for me. It was perfectly natural that he would be nearby when the other man started chasing me."

Jackson shook his head. "I don't like it. I saw him tonight." LuAnn stiffened perceptibly. "At the cottage. I was this close to him." He spread his hands about two feet apart. "I contemplated killing him on the spot. It would have been extremely easy."

LuAnn's face turned white and she licked dry lips. "There's no reason to do that."

"You have no way of knowing that. I'm going to check him out and if I find anything in his background to suggest trouble for me, then I will eliminate him. It's that simple."

"Let me get that information for you."

"What?" Jackson looked startled.

"Riggs likes me. He's already helped me, probably saved my life. It would be natural for me to show my gratitude. Get to know him better."

"No, I don't like it."

"Riggs is a nobody. A local builder. Why trouble yourself with him? Like you said, you're busy."

Jackson studied her intensely for a moment. "All right, LuAnn, you do that. However, any information you obtain better be reported to me in a timely fashion or, with respect to Mr. Riggs, I will take matters into my own very capable hands. Clear?"

LuAnn let out a deep breath. "Clear."

"The other man, of course, I must find. It shouldn't be too terribly difficult."

"Don't do that."

"Excuse me?"

"You don't have to do that. Find him."

"I am very much certain that I do."

The memory of Mr. Rainbow came flooding back to her. She did not want another death on her conscience. She wasn't worth it. "If he shows up again, we're just going to leave the country."

Jackson refolded the paper and replaced it in his pocket. He made a precise steeple with his hands. "You obviously do not fully understand the situation. Were you the only one he was on to, then perhaps your simplistic solution might resolve the matter, at least temporarily. However, the man has a list with the names of eleven other people with whom I worked. I would submit that a resolution involving all of them fleeing the country almost simultaneously would be essentially unworkable."

LuAnn drew in a sharp breath. "I could pay the man. How much money can he want? That would take care of it."

343

Jackson smiled tightly. "Blackmailers are a bad lot. They never seem to go away." He added sharply, "Unless they receive extreme persuasion to do so."

"Mr. Jackson, please don't do it," she said again.

"Don't do what, LuAnn? Ensure your survival?" He glanced around. "And with it all of this?" He rested his gaze back upon her. "How is Lisa, by the way? As beautiful as her mother?"

LuAnn felt her throat constrict. "She's fine."

"Excellent. Let's keep it that way, shall we?"

"Can't you just let it go? Let me handle it."

"LuAnn, many years ago we were confronted with a situation regarding another would-be blackmailer. I took care of that incident and I will take care of this one. In matters like this I almost never opt for delegation. Count your blessings that I'm allowing Riggs to live. For now."

"But that man can't prove anything. How can he? And even if he could, they'll never be able to trace anything to you. Maybe I'll go to jail, but you won't. Hell, I don't even know who you really are."

Jackson stood up, his lips pursed. He took a moment to rub his left hand delicately along the edge of the bedspread.

"Beautiful needlework here," Jackson commented. "Indian isn't it?"

Distracted for an instant by his query, LuAnn was suddenly staring down the barrel of a 9-mm, a suppressor attached to its muzzle.

"One potential solution could involve my killing all twelve of you. That would certainly qualify as a startling dead-end for our inquisitive friend. Remember that the ten-year period is up. The lottery's principal amount has already been returned to a Swiss account that I have set up in your name. I would strongly advise against transferring that money into the United States." He pulled another slip of paper from his pocket and put it down on her bed. "Here are the authorization codes and other account information that will enable you to access it. The funds are untraceable. There you have it. As agreed." Jackson's fingers curled around the trigger of his weapon. "However, now I really don't have any incentive to keep you around, do I?" He advanced toward her. LuAnn's fingers tightened around the letter opener.

"Put it down, LuAnn. Granted, you're remarkably athletic, but you're not faster than a bullet. Put it down. *Now!*"

She dropped the letter opener and backed up against the wall.

Jackson stopped a few inches from her. While he lined up the pistol with her left cheekbone, he ran a gloved hand along her right cheek. There was no sexual content to the motion. Even through the glove, LuAnn could sense the purely clinical chill of his touch.

"You should have thrown it the first time, LuAnn. You really should have." His eyes were mocking.

"I'm not going to kill someone in cold blood," said LuAnn.

"I know. You see, that is your greatest short-coming, because that's precisely when you should strike."

He removed his hand and looked at her.

"Ten years ago I felt you were the weak link in the chain. During the intervening years, I thought perhaps I was wrong. Everything was going so smoothly. But now I find my initial intuition was correct. Even if I were in no personal danger of discovery, were I to let this man blackmail you or perhaps even expose the manipulations of the lottery, then that would be a failure on my part. I do not fail. Ever. And I do not let other people have any control whatsoever over plans of mine, for that, in itself, would be a form of failure. Besides, I couldn't bear to let such a grand performance be ruined.

"Just think about the wonderful life I've given you, LuAnn. Remember what I told you all those years ago: 'Go anywhere, do anything.' I gave that to you. The impossible. All yours. Look at you now. Flawless beauty." His hand went to the front of her robe. With slow movements he undid the strap and the robe fell open, fully exposing her quivering breasts and flat belly. He slid the robe over her shoulders and it fell to the floor.

"The most prudent action on my part, of course, would be to kill you. Right here and right now. In fact, what the hell." He pointed the gun directly at her head and pulled on the trigger. LuAnn jerked back, her eyes slamming shut.

When she reopened them, Jackson was studying her reaction. She was shaking terribly; her heart was thumping around inside her, she couldn't catch her breath.

Jackson shook his head. "Your nerves don't seem to be as strong, LuAnn, as when we were last together. And nerves, or a lack thereof, really are the whole ball of wax." He looked at the pistol for a moment, slipped off the safety, and continued speaking calmly. "As I was saying, the most prudent thing, when one is confronted with a weak link, is to snip it out." He paused and then continued, "I'm not going to do that with you, at least not yet. Not even after you've disobeyed me, jeopardized everything. Would you like to know why?"

LuAnn remained planted against the wall, afraid to move, her eyes fixed on his.

He took her silence for assent. "Because I feel you have a greater destiny to fulfill. A dramatic statement, but I'm a dramatic person; I think I'll allow

346

myself that. It's really as simple as that. And in very large measure, you are a creation of mine. Would you be living in this house, speaking and thinking as an educated person, traveling the world on a whim, without me? Of course not. In killing you, I would, in effect, be killing part of myself. That, as I'm sure you can appreciate, I am loath to do. Nevertheless, please keep in mind that a wild animal, when trapped, will ultimately sacrifice a limb in order to escape and survive. Don't think for one moment that I am not capable of that sacrifice. If you do, you're a fool. I sincerely hope that we are able to extricate you from this little problem." He shook his head sympathetically, much as he had ten years earlier during their very first meeting. "I really do, LuAnn. However, if we can't, we can't. Problems come up in business all the time, and I'm counting on you to do your part, to do all you can to ensure that we successfully navigate this one." Jackson's tone once again became businesslike as he ticked off items with his fingers. "You will not leave the country. You obviously went to a great deal of trouble to get back in, so stay and enjoy it for a while. You will immediately report to me any further contact with our mysterious stranger. The number I gave you ten years ago will still reach me. I will be in touch on a regular basis. Whatever additional instructions I give you, you will follow precisely. Understood?"

She quickly nodded.

"I'm quite serious, LuAnn. If you disobey me again, I will kill you. And it will be slow and unbelievably painful." He studied her reaction to these words for a moment. "Now go into the bathroom and compose yourself."

She started to turn away.

"Oh, LuAnn?"

She looked back.

347

"Keep in mind that if we do fail to contain this problem and I have to eliminate that weak link, there will be no reason that I can see to stop there." He glanced ominously in the direction of the doorway leading to the hallway, where barely twenty feet away Lisa lay sleeping. He turned back to her. "I like to give my business associates as much incentive as possible to achieve success. I find that they're much more likely not to disappoint."

LuAnn ran into the bathroom, locking the door after her. She gripped the cold marble of the vanity, every limb shaking uncontrollably, as though she had left her skeleton back there with him. Wrapping a thick, full-length towel around her, she sank down to the floor. Her natural courage was tempered with a strong dose of common sense and she understood quite clearly the serious personal jeopardy she was in. But that was far from her greatest fear. The fact that Jackson might set his murderous sights on Lisa made her nearly delirious with terror.

Curiously enough it was with this thought that LuAnn's features grew deadly still in their own right. Her eyes stared across at the doorway, on the other side of which stood a person to whom she was probably more similar than dissimilar. They both had secrets; they both were incredibly rich from ill-gotten gains. They both had mental and physical abilities above and beyond the norm. And perhaps most telling, they both had killed someone. Her act had been spontaneous, survival the only motive. Jackson's had been premeditated, but survival of sorts had also been his motivation. Perhaps not as wide a chasm as it looked on the surface. The results, after all, had been the deaths of two human beings.

She slowly rose from the floor. If Jackson ever came after Lisa, then either he would die or LuAnn would; there would be no other possibilities. She let the towel fall to the floor. She unlocked the door. There seemed to exist an ethereal connection between Jackson and LuAnn Tyler that defied a logical explanation. It was as though, even after all this time apart, that their synapses had become fused together at a certain, almost psychic level. For she was absolutely certain what she would find when she returned to the bedroom. She threw open the door.

Nothing. Jackson was gone.

LuAnn pulled on some clothes and hurried down the hallway to check on Lisa. The little girl's steady breathing told her mother that she was asleep. For a while, LuAnn simply hovered over Lisa, afraid to leave her. She didn't want to wake her. She wouldn't be able to hide the terror she was feeling from her daughter. Finally, LuAnn made certain the windows were locked and left the room.

Next she made her way to Charlie's bedroom and gently roused him from sleep.

"I just had a visitor."

"What? Who?"

"We should've known he'd find out," she said wearily.

When the meaning behind her words worked through his grogginess, Charlie sat straight up in bed, almost knocking over the lamp on the nightstand. "Good God, he was here? Jackson was here?"

"When I finished my shower I found him waiting for me in my bedroom. I don't think I've ever been that scared in my life."

"Oh, God, LuAnn, baby." Charlie hugged her tightly for several moments. "How the hell – how the hell did he find us?"

"I don't know, but he knows everything. The man who chased me. About Riggs. I, I told him about the list of lottery winners. I tried to lie, but he knew I was. He threatened everyone in the house if I didn't tell him the truth."

"What's he going to do?"

"He's going to find the guy and then he's going to kill him."

Charlie leaned up against the headboard and LuAnn sat down next to him. Charlie put a big hand across his face and shook his head. He looked over at her. "What else did he say?"

"That we weren't to do anything. Be careful around Riggs and to let him know if the other guy showed up again."

"Riggs? Why'd he mention him?"

She looked over at him. "Jackson seemed very suspicious of him. Like maybe he has an ulterior motive for being involved."

"Son of a bitch," Charlie moaned and abruptly rolled out of bed. He stood up and started getting dressed.

"What are you doing?"

"I don't know, but I feel like I've got to do something. Warn Riggs. If Jackson's after him—"

She reached up and gripped his arm. "If you tell Riggs about Jackson, then all you're doing is guaranteeing his death. Somehow, some way, Jackson will find out. He always does. I've got Riggs safe, at least for now."

"How'd you do that?"

"Jackson and I worked out a little arrangement. At least I think he bought it. Who can tell with him?"

Charlie stopped pulling on his pants and looked over at her.

LuAnn continued, "For now anyway, Jackson's going to focus on the other man. He'll find him, and it's not like we can warn him, because we don't even know who he is."

Charlie sat back down on the bed. "So what do we do?"

LuAnn took his hand in hers. "I want you to take Lisa away. I want both of you to go away."

"There's no way I'm leaving you alone with that guy in the neighborhood. No way in hell."

"Yes you will, Charlie, because you know I'm right. By myself, I'm okay. But if he were to get hold of Lisa . . ." She didn't need to finish the thought.

"Why don't you go with her and let me stay here and handle it?"

LuAnn shook her head. "That won't work. If I leave Jackson will come looking. Looking hard. So long as I'm around, he's not going to stray too far. In the meantime, you two can get away."

"I don't like it. I don't want to abandon you, LuAnn. Not now."

She put her arms around his burly shoulders. "My God, you're not abandoning me. You're going to be taking care of the most precious thing I have—" She broke off here, as Jackson's face planted itself squarely in her thoughts.

Finally Charlie took her hand. "Okay. When do you want us to leave?"

"Right now. I'll go get Lisa ready while you pack. Jackson just left, so I doubt if he's going to be watching the place. He probably figures I'm too frozen with fear to do anything. Actually, he wouldn't be too far from the truth."

"Where do we go?"

"You pick the place. I don't want to know. That way nobody can get the information out of me. Call when you get there and then we'll make arrangements to safely communicate after that."

Charlie shrugged. "I never thought it would come to this."

She kissed him lightly on the forehead. "We'll be

okay. We just need to be really careful."

"And what about you? What are you going to do?"

LuAnn took a deep breath. "Whatever it takes to make sure we all survive this."

"And Riggs?"

She looked squarely at him. "Especially Riggs."

"I hate this, Mom. I hate it." Lisa stomped around the room in her pajamas as LuAnn hurriedly packed her daughter's bags.

"I'm sorry, Lisa, but you're just going to have to trust me on this."

"Trust, ha, that's a funny one coming from you." Lisa glared at her from across the room.

"I don't need that kind of talk right now, young lady."

"And I don't need this." Lisa sat down on the bed and stubbornly crossed her arms.

"Uncle Charlie is ready, you need to get a move on."

"But we're having a party at school tomorrow. Can't it at least wait until after that?"

LuAnn slammed the suitcase shut. "No, Lisa, I'm afraid it really can't."

"When is this going to stop? When are you going to stop dragging me all over the place?"

LuAnn ran a shaky hand through her hair and sat down next to her daughter, putting an arm around Lisa's quaking form. She sensed the pain coursing through the small body. Could the truth hurt her daughter any worse than this? LuAnn clenched her fist and pushed it against her right eye as she tried to stop her nerves from pouring right out of her body.

She turned to her daughter. "Lisa?" The little girl refused to look at her mother.

"Lisa, please look at me."

Finally, Lisa looked at her mother, her small face a blend of anger and disappointment, a combination that was crushing to LuAnn.

LuAnn spoke slowly. The words she was uttering would have been unthinkable an hour ago. But then Jackson had shown up and his appearance had changed a lot of things. "I promise that one day, very soon, I will tell you everything you want to know. In fact, more than you will ever want to know about me, about you, about everything. All right?"

"But why—"

LuAnn put her hand gently across her daughter's mouth, silencing her. "But I'm telling you right now that when I do it will shock you, it will hurt you and you might never understand or appreciate why I did what I did. You may hate me for it, you may be sorry I'm your mother" – she paused, biting hard into her lip – "but however you feel, I want you to know that I did what I thought was best at the time. I did what I thought was best for you. I was very young and I really didn't have anyone to help me make my decision."

She cupped Lisa's chin with her hand and tilted her daughter's face up to hers. Lisa's eyes were now filled with tears. "I know I'm hurting you now. I don't want you to go away, but I will die before I'd let anything happen to you. So would Uncle Charlie."

"Mom, you're scaring me."

LuAnn gripped Lisa with both hands. "I love you, Lisa. More than I've ever loved anything in my whole life."

"I don't want anything to happen to you." Lisa touched her mother's face. "Mom, will you be okay?"

LuAnn managed a reassuring smile. "A cat always lands on its feet, sweetie. Mommy'll be just fine."

THIRTY-SEVEN

The next morning LuAnn rose early after a mostly sleepless night. Saying good-bye to her daughter had been the most wrenching thing she had ever done; however, she knew that task would seem easy compared to the day she would tell Lisa the truth about her life, about her mother's life. LuAnn hoped she would have the opportunity to do that. And yet a huge wave of relief had swept over her when she had watched the lights of the Range Rover disappear down the road the night before.

Now her biggest concern was devising a way to reapproach Riggs without making him even more suspicious. But she didn't have much time. If she didn't report back to Jackson with some information soon, then he would turn his attention fully on Riggs. She was not going to let that happen.

She was thinking this through as she drew back her bedroom curtains and peered out on to the rear lawn. Her bedroom was on the third floor and provided an inspiring view of the surrounding countryside. A balcony opened off the bedroom through a pair of French doors. LuAnn wondered if that was how Jackson had gained access to the room last night. Normally she activated the burglar alarm right before she went to bed. She might start doing it earlier, although she had little hope that any security system would pose much of a challenge for the man. He seemed to be able to walk right up and then through walls.

She brewed a pot of coffee in the small kitchenette next to her dressing room. Then she put on a silk robe and, holding a cup of steaming coffee in one hand, she stepped out on to the balcony. A table and two chairs were set up there; however, she chose to perch on the marble railing and look out over her property. The sun was on its way up and the rays of pink and gold formed a backdrop to a sea of equally colorful foliage. The view was almost enough to raise her sagging spirits. What she saw next almost caused her to fall off the balcony.

Matthew Riggs was kneeling in the grass near the spot where she had wanted her studio to be built. From her vantage point LuAnn watched in amazement as Riggs unrolled a thick set of blueprints and eyed the lay of the land. LuAnn clambered up on top of the railing and, one hand clinging to the brick wall of the house for support, she stood on tip-toe for a better look. Now she could make out stakes planted in the ground at various points. While she watched, Riggs unraveled some twine and, tying one end to a stake, he started laying out what looked to be the footprint of a building.

She tried calling to him, but her voice couldn't carry far enough.

LuAnn jumped down from the railing, raced through her bedroom, not even pausing to put on shoes. She took the stairs two at a time and unlocked the back door. Sprinting across the dewy grass in her bare feet, the silk robe clung to her form, showing a good deal of her long legs in the process.

Breathing hard, she reached the spot where Riggs had been and looked around. Her breaths were visible in the early morning chill and she pulled the sheer robe tight around her.

Where the hell had he gone? She hadn't imagined it. The stakes were there, the string affixed to them.

She stared at them as if they would eventually reveal the secret of the man's whereabouts.

"Morning."

LuAnn whirled around and stared at him as he emerged from the stand of trees, a large rock in his hand. He set it down ceremoniously in the middle of the staked-out area.

"Your stone chimney," he proclaimed, grinning.

"What are you doing?" LuAnn asked in an amazed tone.

"You always run around outside in that? You're going to catch pneumonia." He stared at her and then discreetly looked away as the emerging sun's rays cleared the tops of the trees and made the thin robe virtually transparent; she wasn't wearing anything underneath. "Not to mention what it's doing to me," he muttered to himself.

"I don't usually see someone on my property at the crack of dawn putting stakes into the ground."

"Just following orders."

"What?"

"You wanted a studio, I'm building you a studio."

"You said there wasn't enough time before winter set in. And you needed plans and permits."

"Well, you admired mine so much, I had the brilliant idea of using those diagrams for this one. That'll save a lot of time. And I've got contacts at the inspector's office so we can expedite the approval process." He paused and looked at her as she stood there shivering. "Now don't rush to thank me," he said.

She crossed her arms. "It's not that, I—" She shuddered again as a brisk wind sailed down the tree line. Riggs took off his heavy coat and draped it around her shoulders.

"You know you really shouldn't be outside in your bare feet."

"You don't have to do this, Matthew. I think I've

intruded on your time and patience enough."

He shrugged and looked down at the ground, tapping one of the stakes lightly with his foot. "I don't really mind, Catherine." He coughed in an embarrassed fashion and looked up at the tree line. "There are a lot worse things than hanging out with a woman like you." He shot her a quick glance and then looked away.

LuAnn blushed, biting nervously at her bottom lip while Riggs shoved his hands in his pockets and stared off at nothing. The pair unconsciously emulated two teens nervously feeling each other out for that vital first date.

She looked over at the staked-out area. "So, it'll be just like yours?"

Riggs nodded. "I had the time since you fired me on the fence job."

"I told you I'd pay you and I meant it."

"I'm sure you meant it, but I have a policy of not accepting payment for a job I didn't do. I'm kind of funny that way. Don't worry, I'll charge you plenty for this one."

Riggs once again looked at the surrounding country. "It doesn't get much prettier than this, I can tell you that. Once I build this thing, you probably won't want to leave it."

"That sounds very nice, but hardly realistic."

He glanced over at her. "I guess you travel a lot. A person in your position."

"It's not that. But I do travel a lot." She added wearily, "Too much."

Riggs looked around again. "It's good to see the world. But it's nice to come home too."

"You sound like you speak from experience." She looked at him curiously.

He grinned sheepishly. "Me? I haven't really been anywhere."

"But you still like to come home. For some peace?" she said quietly, her big eyes locked on his.

His grin disappeared and he looked at her with renewed respect. "Yes," he finally said.

"How about some breakfast?"

"I already ate, but thanks."

"Coffee?" She was balancing on one bare foot and then the other as the cold ate at her skin.

Riggs watched her movements and then said, "I'll take you up on that one." Riggs tugged off his work gloves and stuffed them in his pants pocket. He turned around and bent down. "Climb on."

"Excuse me?"

"Climb on." He patted his back. "I know I'm not as bulky as your horse but just pretend."

LuAnn didn't budge. "I don't think so."

Riggs turned and looked at her. "Will you come on? I'm not kidding about the pneumonia. Besides, I do this with billionaires all the time, I'm telling you."

LuAnn laughed, pulled his coat on all the way, and hoisted herself up piggyback style, wrapping her arms around his neck. He locked his arms around her bare thighs. "Are you sure you're up to it? It's a pretty long way and I'm not exactly petite."

"I think I can manage, just don't shoot me if I collapse." They started off.

Halfway there she jabbed him playfully in the sides with her knees.

"What the hell was that for?"

"I'm pretending, just like you said. So giddy-up."

"Don't push it," he groused back and then smiled.

In the woods near the horse barn, Jackson re-packed his sound wand and made his way through the woods to his car parked on a side road. He had watched in some amusement as Riggs carried LuAnn back to the house. He had also noted the rough footprint for the structure Riggs was apparently building for her. Considering how she was dressed, Jackson thought it likely that LuAnn and the handsome Riggs would probably be enjoying an intimate moment very shortly. That was good, since it would give her an opportunity to pump him for information. Using the sound wand, he had also recorded Riggs's voice, an asset that might prove valuable later. He reached his car and drove off.

Riggs sipped on a cup of coffee in the kitchen while LuAnn munched on a piece of buttered toast. She rose and fixed herself another cup of coffee and freshened his.

Riggs couldn't help but stare when her back was turned. She hadn't changed her clothes and the clingy robe was making him think about things he probably shouldn't be. He finally looked away, his face hot.

"If I get another horse, I think I'll name it after you," LuAnn said.

"Thanks bunches." He looked around. "Everybody else still sleeping?"

She put the coffeepot back down and took a moment to sponge up a bit of spillage on the counter. "Sally has the day off. Charlie and Lisa went on a little vacation."

"Without you?"

She sat back down, her eyes roaming the room before she looked back at him and spoke casually. "I had some things to take care of. I might have to leave for Europe soon. If I do, I'll meet up with them and then we'll all go together. Italy is beautiful this time of year. Have you ever been?"

"The only Rome I've been to is in New York."

"In your past life?" She looked at him over the top of her coffee cup.

"There we go with that past life thing again. It's really not all that exciting."

"So why not tell me about it then?"

"So what's the quid pro quo?"

"Ah, I assume you learned that phrase from your attorney ex-wife."

"Assumptions are dangerous things. I like facts a lot better."

"So do I. So shower me with them."

"Why are you so interested in what I did before I came to Charlottesville?"

Because I'm doing my best to keep you alive, and it sickens me every time I think how close you came to being dead because of me. LuAnn struggled to keep her tone at an even level despite that painful reality. "I'm just a naturally curious person."

"Well, so am I. And I have a hunch your secrets are a lot more interesting than mine."

She tried her best to look surprised. "I don't have any secrets."

He put down his coffee cup. "I can't believe you can actually say that with a straight face."

"I have a lot of money. Some people would like to take it away from me any way they can. That doesn't exactly qualify for shocker status."

"So, you've concluded the guy in the Honda was a potential kidnapper."

"Maybe."

"Funny kidnapper."

"What do you mean?"

"I've been thinking a lot about it. The guy looked like a college professor. He rented a place in the area and furnished it. When he attempted to 'kidnap' you he wasn't even wearing a mask. And when I showed up on the scene, instead of hightailing it off, he tried to drive right through me even though he had no chance of catching you. And in my experience most

360

kidnappers don't work solo. Logistically, it's difficult to go it alone."

"In your experience?"

"See, I'm showering you with secrets."

"Maybe he was trying to frighten me before he actually made the kidnap attempt."

"Don't think so. Why put you on your guard? Kidnappers kind of like the element of surprise."

"If he's not a kidnapper, what then?"

"I was hoping you could tell me. Charlie went into the cottage and so did you. What did you find?"

"Nothing."

"That's bullshit and you know it."

LuAnn stood up and glared at him. "I don't appreciate being called a liar."

"Then stop lying."

Her lips trembled and she abruptly turned away from him.

"Catherine, I'm trying to help you here. Okay, in my past life I did deal with the criminal class quite a bit. I've got some insights and some skills that might prove useful if you'd just tell me the truth."

He rose and put a hand on her shoulder. He turned her around to face him. "I know you're scared. And I also know you've got stronger nerves and more spirit than just about anybody I've ever run across, so I'm assuming whatever you're facing is pretty bad. And I want to help you. I *will* help you, if you'll just let me." He cupped her chin with his hand. "I'm playing straight with you, Catherine. I really am."

She winced slightly as he said her name again. Her *fake* name. She finally reached up and lightly caressed his fingers with her own. "I know you are, Matthew, I know." She looked up at him and her lips parted slightly. Their eyes did not budge from each other as their fingers exchanged touches that were

361

suddenly electrifying both their bodies. The spontaneity of the sensation absolutely immobilized them. But not for long.

Riggs swallowed hard, dropped his hands to her bottom, and abruptly pulled LuAnn against him. The warmth and softness of her breasts burned invisible holes through his thick flannel shirt. Their mouths erupted against each other as he yanked the robe free and it fell to the floor. LuAnn moaned and closed her eyes, her head swaying drunkenly from side to side as Riggs attacked her neck. She pulled at his hair and then wrapped her arms around his head as he hoisted her up in the air, his face buried in her chest. She wrapped her legs around his torso.

Following her frantic, whispered directions, Riggs lunged blindly along the hallway to the small first-floor guest bedroom. Riggs pushed open the door. LuAnn jerked away from him and sprawled flat on her back on the bed, the muscles in her long legs tensing in anticipation. She reached up and pulled at him.

"Dammit, Matthew, hurry!" At his subconscious level Riggs noticed the abrupt return of the Georgia drawl but he was far too intoxicated with the passion of the moment to do anything about it.

Riggs's heavy work boots hit the hardwood floor with a loud thump and his pants followed immediately. She jerked his shirt off, popping several buttons in the process, then slid his boxers down. They didn't bother with the bed covers although Riggs did manage to back-kick the door closed before he plunged on top of her.

THIRTY-EIGHT

Jackson sat at the table and studied the laptop's small screen. His suite was large and airy and furnished with eighteenth-century reproductions. The aged hardwood floors were partially covered with area rugs stitched with early American colonial themes. A large wooden carving of a duck in flight hung on one wall. A set of framed prints, each depicting a Virginia native who had gone on to become president of his country long ago, was on another wall. The inn was located in close proximity to his area of focus, was quiet, and allowed Jackson the greatest freedom of unobserved movement. The night before, he had checked out as Harry Conklin and checked back in under another name. He liked to do that. He became uncomfortable staying in one character too long. Besides, he had met with Pemberton in the Conklin role and he didn't want to run into the man again. Now a baseball cap covered his head. Heavy latex eye pouches bracketed the fake nose. The hair was blondish-gray and tied in a ponytail that sprouted out the back of the cap. His neck was long and wrinkled and his build was stocky. He looked like an aging hippie. His luggage was stacked neatly in one corner. He had a practice of not unpacking when he traveled; his line of work sometimes necessitated rapid exits.

Two hours earlier he had scanned one set of fingerprints lifted from the cottage into his hard drive and transmitted them via modem to one of his information contacts. He had already called this person and told him what was coming. This particular contact had access to a database that housed oceans of the most interesting facts, the sole reason that Jackson had enlisted his services many years ago. It wasn't certain that the man who was pursuing LuAnn would have his fingerprints on file anywhere, but Jackson had nothing to lose by checking. If the man did, Jackson's task of tracking him down would become far easier.

Jackson smiled as his computer screen started filling up with data. A digitized photo of the man had even accompanied the personal details.

Thomas J. Donovan. The photo was three years old, but Jackson reckoned that at this time of life, Donovan wouldn't have changed all that much. He studied the nondescript features of the man carefully and then checked the contents of his portable makeup kit and various hairpieces he had brought with him. Yes, if it came down to it, he could impersonate the man. Donovan's name was actually familiar to Jackson. Donovan was an award-winning journalist at the *Washington Tribune*. In fact, about a year ago he had done an in-depth piece on Jackson's father's career as a United States senator.

Jackson had read the story and quickly condemned it as a fluff piece that came nowhere near to addressing the personal side of his father and his monstrous behavior. The history books would smile upon the man; his son knew better.

Jackson's hunch had proven correct. He had figured the man trailing LuAnn wasn't your typical blackmailer. It had taken a lot to track her down and an investigative journalist or perhaps ex-law enforcement person would have the skills, knowledge, and more important, the informational resources to have successfully done so.

Jackson sat back and mused for a moment. Actually, a true blackmailer would have posed less of a difficulty for him. Donovan was undoubtedly on to a story, an enormous story, and he would not stop until he achieved his goal. Or until someone stopped him. It was an interesting challenge. Simply killing the man wouldn't do any good, however. That might make people suspicious. Also, Donovan might have told others of his investigations, although most journalists of Donovan's capabilities, Jackson was aware, kept their cards close to the vest until they broke the story, for a variety of reasons not the least of which was the fear of being scooped.

He had to determine how much Donovan knew and whether he had told anyone else. He picked up the phone, got the number for the *Trib*, and dialed it. He asked for Thomas Donovan. He was told that Donovan had taken a leave of absence. He slowly hung up the phone. He wouldn't have talked to the man if he had come on the phone. He did want to hear his voice, though, in case that knowledge should become useful later. Jackson was also an accomplished mimic and impersonating someone's voice was a wonderful way to manipulate others.

According to Pemberton, Donovan had been in the Charlottesville area for at least a month. Jackson focused briefly on one obvious question: Of all the lottery winners why had the man targeted LuAnn? Jackson almost immediately answered his own query. Because she was the only one running from a murder charge. The only one who had disappeared for ten years and then resurfaced. But how could Donovan possibly have picked up her trail? The cover had been deep and it had been buried even deeper with the passage of ten years, even though LuAnn had committed a tremendous blunder by coming back to the States.

He had a sudden thought. Donovan apparently knew the names of all or some of the lottery winners for the year Jackson had fixed the game. What if he attempted to contact some of the others? If he didn't get what he wanted from LuAnn, and Jackson felt reasonably sure he wouldn't, the next logical step would be to seek out the others. Jackson took out his electronic Rolodex and started making phone calls. After half an hour he had finished contacting the other eleven. Compared to LuAnn, they were sheep to be led around. What he told them to do, they did. He was their savior, the man who had led them to the Promised Land of wealth and leisure. Now, if Donovan bit, the trap would spring.

Jackson began to pace the room. He paused and opened his briefcase. He pulled out the photos. They had been taken on his first day in Charlottesville, even before meeting with Pemberton. The quality of the photos was good considering he had been using a long-range lens and the early morning light had not been the best. The faces stared back at him. Sally Beecham looked tired and bothered. In her forties, tall and slender, she was LuAnn's live-in housekeeper. Her suite was on the first floor on the north side of the mansion. He studied the next two photos. The two young Hispanic women constituted the cleaning staff. They came at nine and left at six. Finally came the photos of the groundspeople. Jackson studied each of their faces. When taking the photographs, he had watched the people intently; how they moved, how they gestured. His handheld sound wand had picked up their voices perfectly. He had listened to their voices over and over as he had just listened to Riggs's. Yes, it was coming together nicely. Like pieces in a strategic battle plan, he was positioning his soldiers to optimal advantage. Possibly, none of the information he had painstakingly gathered about Catherine Savage's daily world would ever come into play. But, on the chance that it might, he would be more than ready. He put the photos away and closed the briefcase.

From a hidden compartment in his suitcase he drew out a short-handled throwing knife. Hand-crafted in China, the blade was so sharp it couldn't even be touched by a bare hand without drawing blood; it was thrown by means of the perfectly balanced teak handle. Jackson strolled around the room, as his mind was sidetracked for a moment. LuAnn was uncommonly fast, lithe, agile, words that would equally be applied to himself. Yes, she had certainly upgraded herself. What else had she learned? What other skills had she acquired? He wondered whether she had experienced the same premonition he had: that their paths would cross again one day like two trains colliding. And had she done her utmost to prepare for that eventuality? Twenty feet. Using the letter opener, she could have killed him from that distance. Fast as he was, the blade would have been imbedded in his heart before he had a chance to react.

On this last thought Jackson wheeled around and let the knife fly. It sailed across the room, splitting the duck's head completely in half upon impact and burrowing several inches into the wall. Jackson eyed the distance between himself and his target: At least *thirty* feet, he estimated. He smiled. LuAnn would have been far wiser to have killed him. She had, no doubt, been constrained by her conscience. That was her greatest weakness and Jackson's greatest advantage, for he had no such parallel compunction.

Ultimately, if it came down to it, he knew that would be the difference.

THIRTY-NINE

LuAnn watched Riggs, who lay dozing next to her. She let out a small breath and stretched her neck. She had felt like a virgin while they made love. An incredibly energetic display of sex, she was surprised the bed hadn't caved in; they'd probably be sore tomorrow. A grin spread over her face. She stroked his shoulder and huddled next to him, putting one of her bare legs across both of his. With this movement he finally stirred and looked over at her.

A boyish smile cracked his face.

"What?" she asked, her eyes impish.

"I'm just trying to remember how many times I said 'oh, baby.'"

She rubbed her hand across his chest, letting the nails bite in just enough to make him playfully grab her hand. LuAnn said, "I think it was more often than I screamed 'yes, yes,' but that was only because I couldn't catch my breath."

He sat up and put a hand through her hair. "You make me feel young and old all at the same time."

They kissed again and Riggs lay back while LuAnn nestled on his chest. She noticed a scar on his side.

"Let me guess, old war wound?"

He looked up surprised and then followed her gaze to the scar. "Oh, yeah, real exciting, appendicitis."

"Really? I didn't think people came with two appendixes."

"What?"

She pointed to another scar on his other side.

"Hey, can we just enjoy the moment here and stop with the observations and questions?" His tone was playful, but she noted the serious intent just below the surface.

"Well, you know, if you come over every day to work on the studio, we might make this a regular thing, sort of like breakfast." LuAnn smiled and then almost immediately caught herself. *What was the chance of that happening?* The impact of this thought was crushing.

She quickly moved away from him and started to get up.

Riggs could hardly miss this dramatic transformation.

"Was it something I didn't say?"

She turned to find him looking at her. As if suddenly self-conscious about her nakedness, she pulled the bedspread off the bed and draped it around her. "I've got a lot to do today."

Riggs sat up and grabbed at the bedspread. "Well, excuse the hell out of me. I didn't mean to get in the way of your schedule. I guess I had the six A.M. to seven A.M. slot. Who's up next? The Kiwanis Club?"

She jerked the bedspread free. "Hey, I don't deserve that."

Riggs rubbed his neck and started to pull on his clothes. "Okay. It's just that I'm having trouble switching gears as fast as you. Going nonstop from the most intensive passion I can ever remember to discussing the day's workload sort of rubbed me the wrong way. I'm sorry as hell if I offended you."

LuAnn looked down and then moved over and sat next to him. "That's how it was for me too, Matthew," she said quietly. "I'm embarrassed to tell you how long it's been." She paused and then said almost to herself, "Years."

369

He looked at her incredulously. "You've gotta be kidding." She didn't answer and he was reluctant to break the silence. The ringing phone did.

Hesitating for a moment, LuAnn picked it up. She hoped to God it was Charlie and not Jackson. "Hello?"

It turned out to be neither. "We're going to talk, Ms. Tyler, and we're going to do it today," Thomas Donovan said.

"Who is this?" LuAnn demanded.

Riggs quickly looked over at her.

"We had a brief meeting the other day when you were out driving. The next time I saw you was when you were sneaking out of my place with your boyfriend."

"How did you get this number? It's unlisted."

Donovan silently laughed. "Ms. Tyler, no information is safe, if you know where to look. I'm assuming by now that you realize I know where to look."

"What do you want?"

"Like I said, I want to talk."

"I don't have anything to say to you."

Riggs went over to the phone and held the receiver with her. At first LuAnn tried to push him off but Riggs held firm.

"Sure you do. And I have a lot to say to you. I can understand your reaction the other day. Maybe I should have approached you differently, but that's past. I know beyond a doubt that you're sitting on a story of immense importance, and I want to know what it is."

"I have nothing to say to you."

Donovan considered this for a moment. He ordinarily didn't like to take this tack, but right now he couldn't think of an alternative strategy. He made up his mind. "I'll give you this as an inducement. If

370

you talk to me, I'll give you forty-eight hours to leave the country before I go public. If you don't talk to me then I go public with everything I have as soon as I get off the phone." He struggled internally for a moment and then added quietly, "Murder doesn't have a statute of limitations, LuAnn."

Riggs stared over at LuAnn, wide-eyed. She looked away from him.

"Where?" she asked.

Riggs was shaking his head fiercely but LuAnn ignored him.

"Let's make it a very public place," Donovan said. "Michie's Tavern. I'm sure you know where that is. One o'clock. And don't bring anyone with you. I'm way too old for guns and speeding cars. I catch a whiff of your boyfriend or anyone else, the deal is off and I call the sheriff in Georgia. Do you understand?"

LuAnn ripped the phone free from Riggs and slammed it down.

Riggs faced her. "Would you like to fill me in on what's going on? Who are you supposed to have murdered? Someone in Georgia?"

LuAnn stood up and pushed past him, her face crimson from the abrupt revealing of this secret. Riggs grabbed her arm and pulled her back roughly. "Dammit, you're going to tell me what's going on."

She snapped around and, quick as a ferret, connected her right fist flush with his chin, causing his head to snap back and hit hard against the wall.

When he came to Riggs was lying on the bed. LuAnn sat next to him holding a cold compress to his bruised chin and then pressed it against the growing knot on his head.

"Damn!" he said as the cold went through his system.

"I'm sorry, Matthew. I didn't mean to do that. I just—"

371

He rubbed his head in disbelief. "I can't believe you knocked me out. I'm not a chauvinist, but I can't believe a woman just flattened my butt with one punch."

She managed a feeble smile. "I had a lot of practice growing up, and I'm pretty strong." She added kindly, "But I think your head hitting the wall had a lot to do with it."

Riggs rubbed his jaw and sat up. "Next time we're having an argument and you're thinking about popping me, just let me know and I'll surrender on the spot. Deal?"

She touched his face gently and kissed him on the forehead. "I'm not going to hit you anymore."

Riggs looked over at the phone. "Are you going to meet him?"

"I don't have a choice – that I can see."

"I'm going with you."

LuAnn shook her head. "You heard him."

Riggs sighed. "I don't believe you murdered anyone."

LuAnn took a deep breath and decided to tell him. "I didn't murder him. It was self-defense. The man I was living with ten years ago was involved in drugs. I guess he was skimming off the top and I walked right into the middle of it."

"So you killed your boyfriend?"

"No, the man who killed my boyfriend."

"And the police—"

"I didn't stay around long enough to find out what they were going to do."

Riggs looked around the room. "The drugs. Is that where all this came from?"

LuAnn almost laughed. "No, he was a small-timer. Drug money didn't have anything to do with this."

Riggs wanted desperately to ask what did, but

refrained from doing so. He sensed that she had divulged enough of her past life for now. Instead he watched in silent frustration as LuAnn slowly got up and started to leave the room, the bedspread dragging behind her, the well-defined muscles in her bare back tensing with each stride.

"LuAnn? That's your real name?"

She turned to look at him and nodded faintly. "LuAnn Tyler. You were right about Georgia. Ten years ago I was a lot different. A lot."

"I believe it, although I bet you've always had that right cross." He attempted a smile, but neither of them was buying it.

She watched Riggs as he dug into his pants pocket. He tossed something to her. She caught the keys in the palm of her hand. "Thanks for letting me use your BMW; you might need the horsepower in case he starts chasing you again."

She frowned, looked down, and then walked out of the room.

FORTY

Wearing a long black leather coat and a matching hat, her eyes hidden behind a pair of Ray-Bans, LuAnn stood outside the "Ordinary," an aged wooden building that was part of Michie's Tavern, a historic structure originally built in the late 1700s and later moved to its current location down the road from Monticello in the late 1920s. It was lunchtime and the place was starting to fill up with tourists either lining their stomachs with the fried chicken buffet offered there after touring Jefferson's home and its neighbor Ash Lawn, or fueling up before setting out on the tour. Inside, a fire blazed in the hearth and LuAnn, who had arrived early to check things out, had soaked in the warmth from the flames before deciding to wait for him outside. She looked up when the man walked toward her. Even without his beard she recognized him.

"Let's go," Donovan said.

LuAnn looked at him. "Go where?"

"You follow me in your car. I'll be checking my rearview mirror. If I see anyone who remotely looks like they're following us, then I pick up my cell phone and you go to prison."

"I'm not following you anywhere."

He leaned into her face and said quietly, "I think you might want to reconsider."

"I don't know who you are or what you want. You said you wanted to meet. Well, I'm here."

Donovan looked around at the line of people making their way into the tavern. "I had in mind a little more privacy than this."

"You picked the place."

"That I did." Donovan jammed his hands in his pocket and stared at her in obvious discomfort.

LuAnn broke the silence. "I'll tell you what, we'll go for a drive in my car." She stared at him ominously and spoke in low tones. "But don't try anything because if you do, I *will* hurt you."

Donovan snorted for a moment and then just as quickly stopped as he stared into her eyes. An involuntary shiver swept over him. He followed her long strides to her car.

LuAnn got on Interstate 64 and put the big sedan on cruise control.

Donovan turned to her. "You know, you threatened me back there with bodily injury. Maybe you did kill that guy in the trailer."

"I didn't *murder* anyone. I didn't do anything wrong in that trailer."

Donovan studied her features and then looked away. When he spoke next, his tone was softer, calmer. "I didn't spend the last several months tracking you down, LuAnn, in order to destroy your life."

She glanced over at him. "Then what did you track me down for?"

"Tell me what did happen in that trailer."

LuAnn shook her head in frustration and remained silent.

"I've dug through a lot of dirt over the years, and I can read between the lines with the best of them. I don't believe you murdered anyone," Donovan said. "Come on, I'm not a cop. You can check me for a wire if you want. I've read all the newspaper accounts. I'd like to hear your version."

LuAnn let out a deep sigh and looked over at him. "Duane was dealing drugs. I didn't know anything about it. I just wanted to get out of that life. I went to the trailer to tell him so. Duane was cut up very badly. A man grabbed me, tried to cut my throat. We fought. I hit him with the telephone and he died."

Donovan looked puzzled. "You just hit him with the telephone?"

"Really hard. I guess I cracked his skull."

Donovan rubbed his chin thoughtfully. "The man didn't die from that. He was stabbed to death."

The BMW almost ran off the road before LuAnn regained control. LuAnn stared over at him, her eyes wide. "What?" she gasped.

"I've seen the autopsy reports. He did have a wound to the head, but it wasn't fatal. He died from multiple stab wounds to his chest. No doubt about it."

It didn't take LuAnn long to realize the truth. *Rainbow*. Rainbow had killed him. And then lied to her. She shook her head. Why should that be such a big surprise, she thought. "All these years, I believed that I had killed him."

"That's a horrible thing to carry around inside. I'm glad I could clear your conscience on it."

"The police can't still be interested in all this. It's been ten years," LuAnn said.

"That's where you've run into some incredibly bad luck. Duane Harvey's uncle is the sheriff in Rikersville now."

"Billy Harvey is sheriff?" LuAnn said in astonishment. "He's one of the biggest crooks down there. He had an auto chop shop. He ran gambling in the back rooms of the bars; he was into everything you could earn a buck from illegally. Duane kept trying to get in on it, but Billy knew Duane was too stupid and unreliable. That's probably why he ended up

376

selling drugs over in Gwinnett."

"I don't doubt it. But the fact is he's sheriff. Probably figured the best way to avoid trouble with the police was to become the police."

"So you talked to him?"

Donovan nodded. "According to him, the whole family has never gotten over poor Duane and his hasty exit from the living. He said the drug dealing sort of besmirched the whole family. And the money you sent? Instead of salving over those wounds, they took it as pouring salt on them, like you were trying to buy them off somehow. I mean they spent it and all, but they still didn't like it, at least according to the illustrious Billy Harvey. Bottom line is, he told me that the investigation is still active and he's not going to rest until LuAnn Tyler is brought in for trial. From what I can tell his theory is that you're the one who was involved in the drug dealing because you wanted to escape Duane and the boring life. Duane died trying to protect you and then you murdered the other guy, who allegedly was your partner."

"That's a bunch of lies."

Donovan shrugged. "You know it is, I know it is. But the people deciding that will be a jury of your peers down in Rikersville, Georgia." He took a moment to appraise her expensive clothing. "Or a jury of whom your peers *used* to be. I wouldn't recommend that you wear that outfit to the trial. It might rub people the wrong way. Duane being flower food and all these last ten years while you were living the high life and doing a pretty good impersonation of Jackie O, it just wouldn't sit well with the good folks down there."

"Tell me something I don't know." She paused for a moment. "So is that your deal? If I don't talk, you're going to throw me to Billy Harvey?"

Donovan patted the dashboard. "It may surprise

you to know that I don't give a damn about all that stuff. If you hit that man, you did it in self-defense. That I believe."

LuAnn lifted her sunglasses and stared across at him. "Then what do you care about?"

He leaned toward her. "The lottery." His eyebrows arched.

LuAnn spoke evenly. "What about it?"

"You won it ten years ago. One hundred million dollars."

"So?"

"So, how'd you do it?"

"I bought a ticket that turned out to be the winning number, how else do you do it?"

"I don't mean that. Let me fill you in on something. Without getting too technical, I went back through years' worth of lottery winners. There's a constant rate of bankruptcy declared by all those winners. Nine out of twelve every year. Bang, bang, you can set your clock by it. Then I run across twelve consecutive winners who somehow managed to avoid the big 'B' and you were smack in the middle of that unique group. Now how is that possible?"

She glanced over at him. "How should I know? I've got good money managers. Maybe they do too."

"You haven't paid taxes on your income nine out of the last ten years; I guess that helps."

"How do you know that?"

"Again, all sorts of information is available. You just have to know where to look. I know where to look."

"You'd have to talk to my financial people about that. I was in other parts of the world during that time, maybe the income wasn't taxable in the U.S."

"I doubt that. I've written enough financial stories to know that there's almost nothing Uncle Sam won't tax, if he can find it, that is."

"So call up the IRS and report me."

"That's not the story I'm looking for."

"Story?"

"That's right. I forgot to fill you in on the reason I came to visit you. My name's Thomas Donovan. You probably haven't heard of me, but I'm a journalist for the *Washington Trib* going on thirty years now and a damned good one even if I am blowing my own horn. A while back I decided to do a story on the national lottery. Personally, I think the whole thing is a travesty. Our own government doing that to the poorest among us. Dangling carrots like that, all the catchy ads, enticing people to cash in their Social Security checks to play something with odds at millions to one. Excuse the soapbox, but I only write about things I feel passionate about. Anyway, my original angle was the rich sucking it back out of the poor after they hit the jackpot. You know, investment shysters, people peddling one scheme after another, and the government just letting them go right ahead and do it, and then when the winners' finances are so screwed up, they haven't paid enough tax or what-not, the IRS comes in and takes every last dime, leaving them poorer than before they won. A good story, and one I feel needs to be told. Well, while I'm researching the story, I find out this interesting coincidence about all the lottery winners from your year: They didn't lose a dime of their money. In fact, using their tax returns as a gauge, they're all richer now. A lot richer. So I track you down and here I am. What I want is simple: the truth."

"And if I don't tell you, I end up in a Georgia prison, is that it? That's what you implied over the phone."

Donovan stared across at her angrily. "I won two Pulitzers before I was thirty-five. I've covered Vietnam, Korea, China, Bosnia, South Africa. Gotten my ass shot up twice. I've spent my life chasing every hot spot in the world. I'm as legit as they come. I'm not going to blackmail you, because I don't operate that way. I told you that over the phone just to get you to meet with me. If Sheriff Billy catches up to you it's not going to be with my help. Personally, I hope he never does."

"Thank you."

"But if you don't tell me the truth, I'll find it out someplace else. And then I'm going to write that story. And if you don't tell me your side of things, I can't guarantee how flatteringly I can portray you. I report the facts, guilt will fall where it may. If you're willing to talk to me, I can guarantee only one thing: that your side of the story will be heard. But if you've broken the law somehow, there's nothing I can do about that. I'm not a cop, and I'm not a judge." He paused and looked at her. "So what's it going to be?"

She didn't speak for several minutes, her eyes staring down the road. He could see the conflict going on inside her.

Finally she looked over at him. "I want to tell you the truth. God, I want to tell somebody the truth." She took a deep breath that almost turned into a shudder. "But I can't."

"Why not?"

"You're already in a great deal of danger. If I were to talk to you, that danger would turn to an absolute certainty that you're going to die."

"Come on, LuAnn, I've been in dangerous spots before. It comes with the territory. What is it, and who's behind it?"

"I want you to leave the country."

"Excuse me?"

"I'll pay. You pick a place, I'll make all the arrangements. I'll set up an account for you."

"Is that your way of dealing with problems? Send them off to Europe? Sorry, but I've got a life right here."

"That's just it. If you stay you're not going to have a life."

"You're really going to have to do better than that. If you'd work with me, we could really accomplish something here. Just talk to me. Trust me. I didn't come down here to shake you down. But I also didn't come down here to be thrown a bunch of bullshit."

"I'm telling you the truth. You are in serious danger!"

Donovan wasn't listening now. He rubbed his chin as he thought out loud. "Similar backgrounds. All poor, desperate. It made for great stories, really picked up the numbers of players." He looked at her, clutched her arm. "Come on, LuAnn, you had help leaving the country ten years ago. You've gotten a whole lot richer. I can smell the story here, if you'd just give me the right angle. This could rank right up there with the Lindbergh baby and who shot JFK. I've got to know the truth. Is the government behind this, whatever this is? They're making billions off this thing every month, sucking it out of the rest of us. Taxation without representation." Donovan rubbed eager hands together. "Are we talking all the way to the White House? Please tell me we are."

"I'm not telling you anything. And I'm doing it to keep you as safe as I can."

"If you work with me, we both win."

"I don't consider being murdered winning. Do you?"

"Last chance."

"Will you please believe me?"

"Believe what? You haven't told me anything," he bellowed.

"If I tell you what I know, it's like I'm putting a pistol against your head and pulling the trigger myself."

Donovan sighed. "Then why don't you take me

back to my car. I don't know, LuAnn, I guess I expected more from you. You grew up dirt-poor, raised a kid by yourself, and then got this incredible break. I thought you might give a crap."

LuAnn put the car in gear and they started off again. She glanced once or twice at him and then started speaking in a very low voice, as though she were afraid of being overheard. "Mr. Donovan, the person who is looking for you right this very minute is not someone you want to mess around with. He told me he's going to kill you because you might know too much. And he will. Unless you leave right now, he'll find you for sure and when he does it won't be pretty. This person can do anything. Anything."

Donovan snorted and then his face froze. He slowly turned and looked at her as the answer finally hit him. "Including making a poor woman from Georgia rich?"

Donovan saw LuAnn jerk slightly as he said the words. His eyes widened. "Jesus, that's it, isn't it? You said this man can do anything. He made you the lottery winner, didn't he? A woman barely out of her teens running from the police after believing she committed a murder—"

"Mr. Donovan, please."

"She stops to buy a lottery ticket and then just happens to travel to New York where the lottery drawing is being held. And what do you know, she wins a hundred million bucks." Donovan slapped the dashboard with the palm of his hand. "Good God, the national lottery was fixed."

"Mr. Donovan, you have got to let it drop."

Donovan's face flushed crimson. "No way, LuAnn. No way am I letting this drop. Like I said, you couldn't have eluded the NYPD and the FBI all by yourself. You had help, a lot of help. This elaborate cover story you had in Europe. Your 'perfect' money managers.

This guy set all of it up. All of it, didn't he? Didn't he?"
LuAnn didn't answer. "God, I can't believe I didn't see
it all before. Sitting here talking to you, it just all fell
into place. I've been drifting in circles for months and
now—" He turned sideways in his seat. "You're not
the only one either, are you? The other eleven non-
bankrupts? Maybe more. Am I right?"

LuAnn was shaking her head hard. "Please stop."

"He didn't do it for free. He must've gotten some
of your winnings. But, Christ, how did he fix it?
Why? What's he doing with all that money? It can't
be just one guy." Donovan fired questions left and
right. "Who, what, when, why, how?" He gripped
her shoulder. "Okay, I'll accept your statement that
whoever is behind this is one very dangerous
individual. But don't discount the power of the
press, LuAnn. It's toppled crooks bigger than this
guy. We can do it, if we work together." When
LuAnn didn't respond, Donovan let go of her
shoulder. "All I'm asking is that you think about it,
LuAnn. But we don't have a lot of time."

When they returned to his car Donovan got out
and then poked his head back in the door. "This
number will reach me." He handed across a card.
LuAnn didn't take it.

"I don't want to know how to reach you. You'll be
safer that way." LuAnn suddenly reached across
and grabbed his hand. Donovan winced from the
pressure of her fingers.

"Will you please take this?" She reached in her
purse and took out an envelope. "There's ten
thousand dollars in here. Pack your bags, go to an
airport, get on a plane, and get the hell out of here.
Call me when you get to wherever you're going and
I'll send enough money to keep you in hotels and
restaurants for as long as you want."

"I don't want money, LuAnn. I want the truth."

LuAnn pushed back the urge to scream. "Dammit I'm trying my best to save your life."

He dropped the card on to her front seat. "You warned me and I appreciate that. But if you won't help me, I'll get it from somewhere else. One way or another, this story is being told." He looked at her ominously. "If this person is half as dangerous as you say he is, you might want to think about getting the hell out of here. My butt may be in the crosshairs now, but it's only my butt. You've got a kid." He paused again and right before he turned to leave he said, "I hope we both make it through this, LuAnn. I mean that."

He walked across the parking lot to his car, got in, and drove off. LuAnn watched him go. She took a deep breath, trying to calm her shaken nerves. Jackson was going to kill the man unless she did something. But what could she do? For one thing, she wasn't going to tell Jackson about her meeting with Donovan. She looked around the parking lot for any sign of him. But what was the use? He could be anyone. Her heart took another jolt. He could've tapped her phone lines. If so he would know about Donovan's phone call, that they had planned to meet. If he knew that, it was highly likely that he had followed her. Then Jackson would already be tracking Donovan. She looked down the road. Donovan's car was already out of sight. She slammed her fists into the steering wheel.

Although LuAnn didn't know it, Jackson had not tapped her phone line. However, as she drove off, she also had no inkling that directly beneath her seat a small transmitter had been affixed to the floorboard. Her entire conversation with Donovan had just been heard by someone else.

FORTY-ONE

Riggs turned off the receiving unit and the sounds of LuAnn's BMW coming through his earphones vanished. He slowly took off the headphones, sat back in his desk chair, and let out a long breath. He had anticipated obtaining some information about LuAnn Tyler and her discussions with the man he now knew to be Thomas Donovan, a newspaper reporter. The name was familiar to Riggs; he had seen the guy's byline in past years. However, Riggs hadn't anticipated stumbling across something that had all the earmarks of a major conspiracy.

"Damn." Riggs stood up and looked out the window of his home office. The trees were stunning, the sky a pale blue that was both dazzling and soothing. To the right a squirrel scampered up a tree, a chestnut secured between its jaws. Farther back, through the thickness of the trees, Riggs could make out a slender procession of deer headed by a six-point buck as they made their way cautiously toward the small spring-fed pond situated on Riggs's property. So peaceful, so serene, all that he had hoped for. He looked back at the receiving device he had used to listen in on LuAnn and Donovan's conversation. "LuAnn Tyler," Riggs said out loud. Not Catherine Savage, not even close, she had said. New identity, new life, far, far away. That was something Riggs could certainly relate to. He eyed the phone, hesitated, then picked it up. The number he was calling had been given to him five years ago, for emergencies, just as, unknown to Riggs, Jackson had provided one to LuAnn ten years ago. Just for emergencies. Well, Riggs decided as he punched in the numbers, he supposed this qualified as such.

An automated voice came on the line. Riggs left a series of numbers and then his name. He spoke slowly in order to let the computer verify the authenticity of his voice patterns. He put down the phone. One minute later it rang. He picked it up.

"That was fast," Riggs said, sitting back down.

"That number gets our attention. What's the situation? You in trouble?"

"Not directly. But I've come across something I need to check up on."

"Person, place, or thing?"

"Person."

"I'm ready, who is it?"

Riggs took a silent breath and hoped to God he was doing the right thing. He would at least hedge his bets until he understood matters a little better. "I need to find out about someone named LuAnn Tyler."

LuAnn's car phone buzzed as she was driving back home.

"Hello?"

The voice on the other end of the line made her breathe easier.

"Don't tell me where you are, Charlie, we can't be sure this line is safe." She checked where she was on the road. "Give me twenty minutes and then call me at the prearranged spot." She hung up. When they had come to the area, they had identified a pay phone at a McDonald's that would receive incoming calls. That was their safe phone.

Twenty minutes later she was standing at the pay phone, snatching it up on the first ring.

"How's Lisa?"

Charlie's tone was low. "Fine, we're both okay. She's still bumming, but who can blame the kid."

"I know. Did she talk to you at all?"

"A little. Although, I think we're both the enemy as far as she's concerned right now. That little girl's playing it close to the vest. Chip off the old block, right?"

"Where is she?"

"Crashed on the bed. We drove all night, and she didn't sleep much, just stared out the car window."

"Where are you?"

"Right now we're at a motel on the outskirts of Gettysburg, Pennsylvania, just across the Maryland state line. We had to stop, I was falling asleep at the wheel."

"You didn't use a credit card, did you? Jackson can trace that."

"You think I'm a novice at being on the run? All cash."

"Any sign that you've been followed?"

"I've varied my route, gone the interstate, back roads, lots of stops in very public places. I've checked every car that even looks remotely familiar. No one's on to us. How's it on your end? You hook up with Riggs?"

LuAnn blushed at the question. "You could say that." She paused and cleared her throat. "I met up with Donovan."

"Who?"

"The guy from the cottage. His name is Donovan. He's a reporter."

"Aw, crap!"

"He knows about the twelve lottery winners."

"How?"

"It gets complicated, but basically because none of us declared bankruptcy. In fact we all became a lot richer through shrewd investment advice. I guess that's pretty unusual with lottery winners."

"Damn, I guess Jackson isn't infallible."

"That's a comforting thought. I've got to go. Give me the number there." Charlie did so.

"I brought the portable cell phone too, LuAnn. You've got the number, right?"

"Memorized."

"I don't like it that you're all alone in this. I really don't."

"I'm holding my own. I've just got to think things through a little. When Jackson shows up again, I want to be ready."

"I'm not sure that's possible. The guy's not human."

LuAnn hung up the phone and walked back to her car. As unobtrusively as she could, she scanned the parking lot for anyone looking remotely suspicious. But that was the problem: Jackson never looked suspicious.

Charlie hung up the phone, checked on Lisa, and then went to the window of the ground-floor motel room. The building was constructed in the shape of a horseshoe so that Charlie was looking out not only at the parking lot but also at the motel units on the other side of the parking lot. He had a habit of checking the parking lots every thirty minutes to see who had pulled in after them. He had selected fairly isolated places that would make it easier to flush out someone who was following them. Despite his sharp scrutiny he could not have seen the pair of binoculars focused on him from the dark recesses of the motel room directly across from his. This person's car was not in the parking lot because he was not a paying guest of the motel. He had broken into the room when Charlie and Lisa had gone out to eat. The man put down the binoculars and jotted some words down in a notebook before taking up his sentry once again.

FORTY-TWO

The BMW pulled into the front drive. LuAnn sat in the car and stared up at the house. She had not gone home. After driving around for a while, she had decided to come here. The Jeep was there, so he must be as well. She got out of the sedan and walked up the wide steps of the Victorian.

Riggs heard her coming. He was just finishing up his phone call, the paper in front of him covered with notes, more information than he had ever wanted to know. His gut was cramping up just thinking about it all.

He opened the door to her knock and she passed through the doorway without looking at him.

"How'd it go?" he asked.

LuAnn drifted around the room before settling down on the couch and looking up at him with a shrug. "Not all that well, really." Her voice was listless. Riggs rubbed his eyes and sat down in the chair opposite her.

"Tell me about it."

"Why? Why in the hell would I want to get you involved in all this?"

He paused and briefly considered what he was about to say. He could walk away from this. She was obviously giving him the opportunity to do so. He could just say you're right and escort her to the door and out of his life. As he looked at her, so tired, so alone, he spoke quietly and intensely.

"I want to help you."

"That's nice, but I really wouldn't know where to begin."

"How about ten years ago, Georgia, and you're running from the cops for a murder you didn't commit."

She stared at him, biting her lip. She wanted desperately to trust the man; it was an almost physiologically compelling need. And yet, as she stared down the hallway to where his study was, where she had previously seen the information he had obtained on her so easily, so quickly, the doubts came flooding back to her. Jackson was suspicious of the man. Who was he? Where had he come from? What had he done in his past life?

When she looked back over at him, he was watching her closely. He read the uncertainty, the suspicions there.

"LuAnn, I know you really don't know me. Yet. But you *can* trust me."

"I want to, Matthew. I really do. It's just—" She stood up and started her ritualistic pacing. "It's just that I've made a habit the last ten years of never trusting anyone. Anyone other than Charlie."

"Well, Charlie's not here, and from the looks of things, you're not going to be able to handle this alone."

She stiffened at the words. "You'd be surprised at what I can handle."

"I don't doubt that. Not at all," he said in a sincere, if disarming, manner.

"And getting you involved means, ultimately, placing you in danger. That's not something I want on my conscience."

"You'd be surprised at how accustomed I am to dangerous things. And people."

She stared at him, a glimmer of a smile on her lips. Her deep hazel eyes were intoxicating to him, calling up the fresh memory of their lovemaking.

"I still don't want you to get hurt."

"Then why are you here? In spite of how terrific this morning was, I doubt if you're here for a nooner. You've got other things on your mind, I can tell."

She sat back down and clasped her hands together. After thinking the matter over a minute she started speaking earnestly. "The man's name was Thomas Donovan. He's a reporter of some kind. He started investigating me."

"Why? Why you? The murder?"

LuAnn hesitated before answering. "That was part of it."

"What was the other part?"

LuAnn didn't answer now; she looked at the floor. Imparting personal information to anyone other than Charlie went against every instinct she possessed.

Riggs decided to take a shot. "Did it have to do with the lottery?"

She slowly looked up, the astonishment starkly on her face.

"I knew your real name; something clicked. You won a hundred million dollars ten years ago, a lot of stories about you back then. Then you disappeared."

She studied him warily, alarm bells ringing. His face, though, was one of complete sincerity, and finally that look subdued her suspicions, at least temporarily.

"Yes, I won that money."

"So what did Donovan want? Your story on the killing?"

"Partly."

"What was the other part?" he asked persistently.

Now the alarm bells started ringing again, and this time Riggs's honest features did not silence them. LuAnn rose. "I've got to be going."

"Come on, LuAnn. Talk to me."

"I think I've said more than I should have."

Riggs knew far more than she had already told him, but he had wanted to hear it from her. His source for the information on LuAnn had naturally desired to know why he wanted it. He had lied, or gotten close to it. He wasn't going to give LuAnn Tyler away, at least not yet. He had no reason to trust her, and many reasons not to. But he did trust her. He did believe in her.

As her hand closed over the doorknob he called to her.

"LuAnn, if you change your mind, I'll be here."

She didn't look at him, fearful of what might happen if she did. She wanted to tell him everything. She wanted his help, she wanted to make love to him again. After all these years of fabrication, of lies, deceit, and constant fear of exposure, she just wanted to be held; to be loved for herself, not for the enormous wealth she possessed.

Riggs watched the BMW pull out of his driveway. When it had disappeared from view he turned and went back to his study. Because of his inquiries into LuAnn Tyler, Riggs knew the Feds would undoubtedly get around to dispatching some agents to Charlottesville to talk to him or at least get the local FBI office involved. But because of his special status, they would have to jump through some bureaucratic hoops before that could be accomplished. He had some time, but not much. And once the Bureau boys showed up, it was over for LuAnn Tyler. All of her diligent work over the last ten years to remain hidden Riggs could blow up in the next few days. A very strong emotion told Riggs he could not allow that to happen, despite what he knew about the woman. In the course of his past career, deception had become a way of a life. So also had reading people, telling the good ones from the bad, to the extent you could. LuAnn was a good person, Riggs had long ago concluded. Even if she didn't want his help, she was going to get it. But she was obviously involved with some very dangerous people. And now, Riggs thought to himself, so was he.

FORTY-THREE

When LuAnn arrived home it was late; the household staff had gone, and Sally Beecham would not return until tomorrow. She went in the house through the garage, punched in the alarm code, and threw her coat and purse down on the kitchen island. She went upstairs to shower and change. She had a lot of things to think through right now.

In the shrubs bordering the edge of the expensive lawn by the garage side of the house, Jackson knelt in the mulch and smiled to himself. He lowered the small piece of equipment he was holding in his hand. On its digital face were the six numbers constituting LuAnn's pass code for the home's alarm system. The scanner had picked up the electrical impulses thrown off when LuAnn inputted her pass code and then it had unscrambled them. With the pass code Jackson could come and go freely.

When he got back to his rental car, his cell phone buzzed. He spoke for a few minutes and then hung up. Charlie and Lisa were at a motel outside of Gettysburg. They would probably be on the move again soon. LuAnn had tried to get them away from him, or rather Lisa away from him. Charlie could take care of himself, Jackson well knew. If it came to it, Lisa was the Achilles' heel of her mother.

LuAnn had watched out the window as the figure

made its way down the tree line toward the main road. The steps had been animal-like in their stealth and precision, much as hers would have been. She didn't know what had drawn her to the window at that precise instant. She felt no fear or even apprehension as she watched Jackson move down the hillside. She had expected him to be there. For what specific reason or for how long Jackson had been watching the house, she wasn't sure; but it was completely logical that he should be. She was now his main focus, she knew. And to be the main focus of the man was akin to treading on the very edge of the grave. She drew the curtains shut and sat on her bed. The enormous house felt cold and threatening, as though she were all alone in a mausoleum of immense proportion, just waiting for something unspeakably horrible to happen to her.

Was Lisa truly safe, beyond the reach of the man? The answer to that question was so obvious that it hit her like a hard slap in the face.

I can do anything, LuAnn.

The mocking words came back to her after all these years and sent a shiver through her. Riggs was right, she couldn't get through this alone. He had offered help, and this time she needed it. Whether she was making the right decision or not, she didn't care. Right now, she just needed to do something. She jumped up, grabbed her car keys, unlocked a box in her closet, and placed the loaded nickel-plated .44 Magnum in her purse. She ran down the stairs and into the garage. A minute later the BMW was flying down the road.

Riggs was in the room over his barn when he heard the car drive up and park next to the garage. He watched out the window as LuAnn came into view. She started toward the house but then, as if sensing his presence, she turned to stare at him.

Their eyes stayed locked for a long time as each silently probed the other. A minute later she was sitting across from him, warming her hands from the heat of the stove.

This time Riggs felt no compunction to mince words.

"The lottery was fixed, wasn't it? You knew you were going to win, didn't you?"

LuAnn jolted upright for an instant, but then let out an almost simultaneous breath of relief.

"Yes." With that one word she felt as though the last ten years of her life had suddenly evaporated. It was a cleansing feeling. "How'd you figure it out?"

"I had some help."

LuAnn tensed and slowly rose. Had she just made the biggest mistake of her life?

Riggs sensed her sudden change and put up a hand. As calmly as he could, he said, "Nobody else knows right now. I pulled some pieces of information from different sources and then took a wild stab." He hesitated and then added, "I also bugged your car. I heard your entire conversation with Donovan."

"Who the hell are you?" LuAnn hissed, her hand feeling for her purse catch and the gun inside even as she stared at him.

Riggs just sat there and stared back at her. "I'm someone very much like you," was his surprising reply. Those words stopped her cold. Riggs stood and put his hands in his pockets, leaned up against the bookcase, and eyed the gently swaying trees through the window. "My past is a secret, my present is all made up." He looked over at her. "A lie. But for a good reason." He raised his eyebrows. "Like you."

LuAnn trembled for an instant. Her legs felt weak and she abruptly sat down on the floor. Riggs swiftly knelt beside her, taking her hand in his. "We don't have a lot of time so I'm not going to sugarcoat things. I made some inquiries about you. I did it discreetly, but it's going to have ripple effects none-theless." He looked at her intently. "Are you ready to hear this?"

LuAnn swallowed hard and nodded; the fear passed from her eyes and was replaced with an inexplicable calmness.

"The FBI has been interested in you ever since you fled the country. The case has been dormant for a while, but that's not going to last. They know some-thing is up with you, and maybe with how you won the money, but they don't know what, and they haven't been able to prove anything."

"If you bugged the car, you know how Donovan got on to it."

Riggs nodded and helped her up. They both sat on the couch. "Bankruptcy. Pretty clever. I know the Feds haven't latched on to that angle yet. Do you know how it was rigged?"

LuAnn shook her head.

"Is it a group, an organization behind it? Donovan thought it was the government. Please don't tell me it is. That gets way too complicated."

"It's not." LuAnn was speaking clearly now, although traces of fear, the effect of the sudden expo-sure of long-held secrets, flitted over her features. "It's one person, as far as I know."

Riggs sat back with an amazed look. "One person. That isn't possible."

"He had some people working for him, at least two that I know of, but I'm pretty sure he was the boss." That was an understatement. LuAnn could not imagine Jackson taking orders from anyone.

"Was Charlie one of those people?"

LuAnn started again. "What makes you say that?"

397

Riggs shrugged. "The uncle story was a little lame. And you two seemed to be sharing a secret. There wasn't any mention in all my research about you of any uncle, so I assumed he came into the picture after the lottery scam."

"I'm not going to answer that." The last thing she was going to do was incriminate Charlie.

"Fair enough. What about this person behind it? What can you tell me about him?"

"He calls himself Jackson." LuAnn stopped suddenly, astonished that she was telling anyone this. As the name passed over her lips, she closed her eyes and imagined for an instant what Jackson would do to her, to all of them, if he had any idea what she was revealing. She instinctively looked over her shoulder.

Riggs gripped her arm. "LuAnn, you're not alone anymore. He can't hurt you now."

She almost laughed out loud. "Matthew, if we're the luckiest people in the world, he'll kill us quick instead of making us suffer."

Riggs felt her arm shaking. As strong and resourceful as he knew her to be, she was clearly afraid.

"If it makes you feel any better," he said, "I've dealt with some pretty bad people in my time, and I'm still here. Everyone has weaknesses."

"Sure, right." LuAnn's voice was hushed, her words lifeless.

Riggs's tone was harsh. "Well, if you want to roll over for him and play dead, go ahead. I don't see how that's going to help Lisa, though. If this guy's as scary as you say, you think he's going to let her walk?"

"I haven't told her about any of this."

"Jackson's not going to assume that. He's going to assume that she knows everything, and that she's going to have to be eliminated if things turn against him."

"I know," she finally said. She rubbed her face and glanced wearily at him. "I don't understand. Why do you want to help me? You don't even know me. And I just told you I did something illegal."

"Like I said, I checked you out. I know your background. Jackson took advantage of you. Hell, if it had been me in your same position, I would've jumped at the chance to be rich too."

"That's just it, I didn't. I had decided not to go along, but then I walked into Duane's drug deal, and the next thing I know two men are dead and I'm running as fast as I can with a baby in my arms. I . . . I didn't think I had any choice left. I just wanted to get away."

"I can understand that, LuAnn. I really can."

"I've been running ever since, scared of my shadow, afraid somebody would find everything out. It's been ten years, but it's felt like a hundred." She shook her head and gripped her hands together.

"So I take it Jackson's in the area."

"He was in my garden about forty-five minutes ago."

"What?"

"I'm not sure what he was up to, but I'm assuming he's laying the groundwork for whatever plan he's about to implement."

"What sort of plan?"

"He's going to kill Donovan for starters."

"So I heard you tell Donovan."

"And then Jackson will probably come after us." LuAnn put her face in her hands.

"Well, you won't be seeing him again."

"You're wrong there, Matthew. I have to meet with him. And very soon."

He looked at her in absolute shock. "Are you crazy?"

"Jackson suddenly appeared in my bedroom last night. We had quite a lengthy discussion. I told him I was going to get to know you better. I don't think he had sex in mind, it just worked out that way."

"LuAnn, you don't—"

"He was going to kill you. In the cottage last night. I guess you went back for your truck. He said he was two feet from you. You're lucky to be alive. Very lucky."

Riggs sat back. His instincts had been right. That was a little heartening, despite the close call he had unwittingly experienced.

"He was going to check you out. He was concerned about your background, it was fuzzy. He was going to look into your background, and if he found anything worrisome, he was going to kill you."

"But?"

"But I told him I'd check you out instead."

"You took a risk there."

"Not as many as you've taken for me. I owed you. And I didn't want anything to happen to you. Not because of me."

Riggs spread his hands wide. "So why? Why the lottery fix? Did you give him some of your winnings?"

"All of it." Riggs looked blankly at her. LuAnn said, "He had control of the money for ten years; that period just ended. He invested the money and paid me some of the income from those investments."

"He had a hundred million to invest. How much did you earn each year?"

"Around forty million on the initial principal. He also invested any amounts I didn't spend. I earned tens of millions more on that each year."

Riggs gaped at her. "That's a forty percent return on your lottery money alone."

"I know. And Jackson made a lot more than that, I'm certain. He wasn't in this out of the goodness of

400

his heart. It was a business transaction, plain and simple."

"So if you made forty percent, he probably made at least that and maybe more. That's a minimum of eighty percent return on your money. He could only have done that through illegal channels."

"I don't know about that."

"And at the end of ten years?"

"I got the hundred million back."

Riggs rubbed at his brow. "And if there were twelve of you at, say, an average of seventy million dollars each, this guy had almost one billion dollars to invest."

"He's got a lot more than that now, I'm sure." She looked at him, saw the worry lines. "What, what are you thinking?"

He looked at her steadily. "Another thing that's had the FBI's dander up." She looked puzzled. Riggs started to explain. "I know for a fact that for years now the FBI, Interpol, and a few other foreign law enforcement agencies have been aware of something: Tremendous amounts of money have been funneled into lots of activities across the globe, some legit, others not. At first the Feds thought it was drug cartel money, either from South America or Asia, partly to launder it. That didn't turn out to be the case. They picked up threads here and there, but the leads always fizzled. Someone with that much money can cover himself really well. Maybe that someone is Jackson." Riggs fell silent.

"You're sure the Feds don't know about the lottery?"

Riggs looked uneasy. "I can tell you, if they do, they didn't learn it from me. But they do know of my inquiries about you. There was no getting around that."

"And if they've figured it out for themselves?

Then we have Jackson *and* the federal government coming for us. Right?"

Riggs looked away for a moment and then stared her directly in the eye. "Right."

"And to tell you the truth, I'm not sure which one frightens me more."

They looked at each other, similar thoughts running through their minds. Two people against all of this.

"I need to go now," LuAnn said.

"Go where?"

"I'm pretty certain that Jackson's been following my movements closely. He'll know we've seen each other several times. He may know I've met with Donovan. If I don't report back to him right away" – here she took a painful swallow – "well, it won't be pretty."

Riggs gripped her shoulders tightly. "LuAnn, this guy is a psycho, but he must be brilliant as well. That makes him even more dangerous. You walk in there, the guy gets the least bit suspicious . . ."

She gently rubbed his arms with her hands. "Well, I just have to make sure he doesn't get suspicious."

"How in the hell are you going to do that? He already must be. I say we bring in the troops, set the guy up and take him."

"And me, what about me?"

Riggs stared at her. "I'm sure you could probably work a deal with the authorities," he said lamely.

"And the folks down in Georgia? You heard Donovan, they want to lynch me."

"The Feds could talk to them, they . . ." Riggs broke off as he realized absolutely none of what he was saying could be guaranteed.

"And maybe I work a deal with all of them. I give back the money. It might surprise you, but I really don't care about that. And then maybe I get a sympathetic judge, or judges, and they give me a break. Cumulatively what could I be looking at? Twenty years?"

"Maybe not that much."

"How much then?"

"I can't tell you that. I don't know."

"I'd make a real sympathetic defendant, wouldn't I? I can see the headlines now: Drug dealer-turned-murderess-turned-dream-stealer-turned-fugitive LuAnn Tyler living like a queen while people blow their Social Security checks on the lottery. Maybe they'd give me a prize instead of throwing away the key. What do you think?"

Riggs didn't answer and he couldn't manage to look at her either.

"And let's say we set Jackson up? What if we miss and he gets away? Or what if we nail him? Do you think with all his money, all his power, he might beat the rap? Or maybe he just might pay someone to carry out his revenge for him. Given that, what do you think my life is worth? And my daughter's life?"

Riggs did answer this time. "Nothing. Okay, I hear where you're coming from. But listen, why can't you report back to the guy over the phone? You don't need to see him in person."

LuAnn considered this for a minute. "I'll try," was all she could promise.

LuAnn stood up to her full height and gazed down at him. She looked twenty again, strong, rangy, confident. "Despite having zillions of dollars and traveling all over the world, I'm not the FBI. I'm still just a dumb girl from Georgia, but you might be a little surprised at what I can do when I set my mind to it." Lisa's face was conjured up in her thoughts. "And I've got a lot to lose. Too much." Her eyes seemed to look right through his, seeing something far, far down the road. When she spoke, her voice carried the full measure of her deep Southern roots. "So I'm not going to lose."

FORTY-FOUR

George Masters stared down at the file intently. He was sitting in his office at the Hoover Building in Washington. Masters had been with the FBI for over twenty-five years. Ten of those years had been spent in the FBI's New York office. And now Masters was staring down at a name that he had become intimately familiar with ten years ago: LuAnn Tyler. Masters had been part of the federal investigation of Tyler's flight from the United States, and although the investigation had been officially closed years ago due to basic inertia, Masters had never lost interest mainly because none of it made sense. Things that didn't make sense bothered the veteran FBI agent greatly. Even after transferring to Washington, he had kept the case in the back of his mind. Now there were recent events that had ignited that spark of interest into a full flame. Matthew Riggs had made inquiries about LuAnn Tyler. Riggs, Masters knew, was in Charlottesville, Virginia. Masters knew Riggs, or who Riggs used to be, very well. If someone like Riggs was interested in Tyler, so was Masters.

After failing to prevent LuAnn Tyler's escape from New York, Masters and his team had spent considerable time trying to reconstruct the last several days leading up to her disappearance. He had figured that she would have either driven up from Georgia to New York or taken the train. She didn't have a driver's license or a car. The big convertible she had been spotted in had been found in front of the trailer, so she hadn't used that vehicle. Masters had then focused on the trains. At the station in Atlanta, Masters had hit the jackpot. LuAnn Tyler had taken the Amtrak Crescent to New York City on the day the authorities believed the murders were committed. But that wasn't all she had done. LuAnn had made a phone call from Otis Burns's car phone. Burns was the other dead man in the trailer. The FBI had traced the phone call. The number was an eight hundred number, but it had already been disconnected. Investigations into who had leased the phone number had run into a complete dead-end. That had gotten Masters's curiosity up even more.

Now that he was once again focused on LuAnn Tyler, Masters had instructed his men to go over NYPD records looking for any unusual events occurring around the time of LuAnn's disappearance. One item his men had just discovered had interested Masters greatly. A man named Anthony Romanello had been found dead in his New York apartment the night before the press conference announcing LuAnn as the lottery winner. The discovery of a dead body in New York City was hardly news; however, the police had been suspicious of Romanello's death because he had a long arrest record and was suspected of hiring himself out as an assassin. The police had probed into the details of what he had done on his last day among the living. Romanello and a woman had been seen at a restaurant shortly before Romanello had died; they had been observed having a serious argument. Barely two hours later, Romanello was dead. The official cause of death had been ruled cardiac arrest; however, the autopsy had revealed no sign of heart trouble in the youthful and strongly built man. None of these details had gotten Masters excited. What had gotten his adrenaline going was the description of the woman: It matched LuAnn Tyler precisely.

Masters shifted uncomfortably in his chair and lit up a cigarette. And then came the kicker: Found on Romanello's person was a receipt for a train ticket. Romanello had been in Georgia and returned to New York on the very same train with LuAnn, although they had been seated in separate compartments. Was there a connection? Drawing on information that had been long buried in his mind, the veteran FBI agent was beginning to piece things together from a clearer perspective. Maybe being away from the case all these years had been a good thing.

He had finished poring over the files he had accumulated on LuAnn Tyler, including records from the lottery. The winning ticket had been purchased at a 7-Eleven in Rikersville, Georgia, on the day of the trailer murders, presumably by LuAnn Tyler. Pretty nervy for her to stop and buy a ticket after a double homicide, Masters thought. The winning ticket had been announced on the following Wednesday at the drawing in New York. The woman fitting LuAnn's description had been seen with Romanello on Friday evening. And the press conference announcing LuAnn as the winner had been held on Saturday. But the thing was, according to Amtrak records and the ticket found on Romanello, both Tyler and Romanello had taken the Crescent train on the *previous* Sunday getting them into New York on Monday. If so, that meant LuAnn had left for New York City *before* she had known she had even won the lottery. Was she just running from a possible murder charge and coincidentally chose New York in which to hide, and then just happened to win a hundred million bucks? If so, she must be the luckiest person in the world. George Masters did not believe that anyone could be that lucky. He ticked off the points on his hand. Murders. Telephone call. Purchase of lottery ticket. Train to New York before winning ticket announced. LuAnn Tyler wins the lottery. Romanello and Tyler argue. Romanello dies. LuAnn Tyler, a twenty-year-old with a seventh-grade education and a baby, walks right through a massive police net and successfully disappears. She could not, Masters decided, have done that alone. All of this had been planned well in advance. And that meant one thing. Masters suddenly gripped the arms of his chair tightly as the conclusion hit him.

LuAnn Tyler knew that she was going to win the lottery.

The implications of that last thought sent a deep shudder through the grim-faced agent. He couldn't believe he hadn't seen that possibility ten years ago, but he had to admit it had never even occurred to him. He was looking for a potential murderer and nothing else. He drew solace from the fact that ten years ago he didn't have the Romanello angle to chew on.

Masters obviously wasn't old enough to remember all the lottery corruption from the last century, but he certainly remembered the game show scandals in the 1950s. Those would seem laughable by comparison to what the country might be now facing.

Ten years ago someone may have corrupted the United States Lottery. At least once, possibly more. The ramifications were truly terrifying to think about. The federal government depended on the revenue from that lottery to fund a myriad of programs, programs that were now so entrenched politically that it would be impossible to repeal them. But if the source of those funds was contaminated? If the American People ever discovered that fact?

Masters's mouth went dry with the thought. He swallowed some water from a carafe on his desk and downed a couple of aspirin to combat the beginnings of what would still become a torturous headache. He composed himself and picked up his phone. "Get me the director," he instructed. While he waited for the call to go through, Masters sat back in his chair. He knew this eventually would have to go up to the White House. But he'd let the director talk to the attorney general and the A.G. could talk to the president. If his conclusions were right, so much shit would hit the fan that everyone would eventually be covered in it.

FORTY-FIVE

J ackson was again in his suite and was again staring at his laptop. LuAnn had met with Riggs several times now. Jackson would give her another few hours to call. He was disappointed in her nonetheless. He had not tapped LuAnn's phone line, an oversight that he had decided was not worth remedying at this point. She had caught him a little off-guard by sending Lisa away so quickly. The associate he had retained to track LuAnn's movements had been compelled to follow Charlie and Lisa, thereby depriving Jackson of a valuable pair of eyes. Thus, he did not know that LuAnn and Donovan had already met.

He had contemplated sending for more people so that all bases would be covered, but too many strangers lurking around town would probably raise suspicion. He wanted to avoid that if possible. Particularly because there was a wild card out there he was unsure of: Matt Riggs. He had transmitted Riggs's fingerprints to the same information source and was awaiting a reply.

Jackson's mouth sagged as the information spread over the screen. The name that appeared as the owner of the fingerprints was not Matthew Riggs. For a moment Jackson wondered if he could have lifted someone else's prints in the cottage by mistake. But that was impossible; he had seen the exact area the man calling himself Matt Riggs had touched. There could have been no mistake there. He quickly decided to check the other source of a

409

possible mistake. He dialed the number and spoke at length to the person on the other end.

"This one was tricky," the voice said. "We went through normal channels initially to avoid any suspicions. We believe the request was kicked to senior level and we received back a 'no-fingerprint-found' reply."

"But a person was identified," Jackson said.

"Right, but only after we went back through other channels." Jackson knew that meant hacking into a database. "That's when we pulled up the inform-ation we transmitted to you."

"But it's a different name than the one he's using now and it lists him as being deceased."

"Right, but the thing is, when a criminal dies, the standard procedure is to fingerprint the corpse and transmit the prints to the FBI for verification. When that's completed, the pointer – the linkage used to retrieve the print from the database – is deleted. The result is that there are, technically, no prints of deceased criminals on the database."

"So how do you explain what you just sent me? Why would they want to have this person listed as deceased but under another name?"

"Well, that tells me that the name listed on the database is his real one and the one he's using now is phony. The fact that he's listed as dead tells me that the Feds want people to believe he's dead, including anyone who might try to get access to their database to check. I've seen the Feds do that before."

"Why?"

The answer the man gave him caused Jackson to slowly hang up the phone. Now it all made sense. He stared at the screen.

Daniel Buckman: Deceased.

It was less than three minutes after LuAnn left that

Riggs received a telephone call. The message was terse, but still managed to chill Riggs to the bone.

"Someone just made an unauthorized access of your fingerprint file through the Automated Fingerprint Identification System. And it was somebody who knew what he was doing because we didn't realize it happened until after the fact. Exercise extreme care, we're checking it out right now."

Riggs slammed down the phone and grabbed his receiving unit. He took a moment to unlock a drawer of his desk. He pulled out two pistols, two ammo clips, and an ankle holster. The larger pistol he put in his pocket and the smaller one he inserted in the holster he belted around his ankle. Then he ran for his Jeep. He hoped to God LuAnn hadn't found and removed the transmitter from her car.

FORTY-SIX

From the car phone LuAnn called the number Jackson had given her. He buzzed her back less than a minute later.

"I'm on the move too," he said. "We need to talk."

"I'm reporting back to you, like you said."

"I'm sure you are. I trust you have a good deal to tell me."

"I don't think we have a serious problem on our hands."

"Oh, really, I'm so very glad to hear it."

LuAnn responded testily. "Do you want to hear it or not?"

"Yes, but in person."

"Why?"

"Why not?" he fired back. "And I have some information that might be of interest to you."

"About what?"

"No, about whom. Matt Riggs. Like his real name, his real background, and why you should take every caution in dealing with him."

"You can tell me all that over the phone."

"LuAnn, perhaps you didn't hear me. I said you're going to meet me in person."

"Why should I?"

"I'll give you a wonderful reason. If you don't I'll find Riggs and kill him in the next half hour. I'll cut off his head and mail it to you. If you call to warn him, then I'll go to your home and kill everyone there from the maids to the gardeners and then I'll

412

burn it to the ground. Then I'll go to your precious daughter's exclusive school and slaughter everyone there. You can keep calling, trying to warn the whole town, and I'll just start killing people at random. Is that a good enough reason, LuAnn, or do you want to hear more?"

LuAnn, pale and trembling at this verbal onslaught, had to force her next breath out. She knew that he meant every insane word. "Where and when?"

"Just like old times. Speaking of old times, why don't you ask Charlie to join us. This applies to him as well."

LuAnn held the phone away from her, staring at it as though she wanted to melt it down along with the man on the other end. "He's not around right now."

"My, my. And I thought he never left your side, the faithful sidekick."

Something in his tone touched a chord in LuAnn's memory. She couldn't think of what it was. "We're not exactly joined at the hip. He's got a life to live."

For now, Jackson thought. *For now, just like you. I'm having my doubts, though, I really am.*

"Let's meet at the cottage where our inquisitive friend was nesting. Thirty minutes, can you manage it?"

"I'll be at the cottage in thirty minutes."

Jackson hung up the car phone and with an automatic motion felt for the knife hidden in his jacket.

Ten miles away LuAnn almost mirrored that movement, slipping off the safety on her .44.

Dusk was gathering as LuAnn drove down the tree-lined, leaf-strewn dirt road. The area was very dark. It had rained heavily the night before and a spray of water kicked up on her windshield as she

drove through a deep puddle; she was momentarily
startled. The cottage was up ahead. She slowed
down and swept the terrain with her eyes. She saw
no car, no person. She knew that meant nothing.
Jackson seemed to appear and disappear whenever
he damn well pleased with less rippling than a
pebble flung across the ocean. She pulled the BMW
to a stop in front of the ramshackle structure and
climbed out. She knelt down for a moment and eyed
the dirt. There were no other tire tracks and the mud
would have shown any very clearly.

LuAnn studied the exterior of the cottage. He was
already there, she was certain. It was as though the
man carried a scent that was detectable only to her.
It smelled like the grave, moldy and dank. She took
one last breath and started toward the door.

Upon entering the cottage, LuAnn surveyed the
small area.

"You're early." Jackson stepped from the shadows.
His face was the same one from each of their face-to-
face encounters. He liked to be consistent. He wore a
leather jacket and jeans. A black ski cap covered the
top of his head. Dark hiking boots were on his feet.
"But at least you came alone," he added.

"I hope the same can be said of you." LuAnn
shifted slightly so that her back was against a wall
rather than the door.

Jackson interpreted her movements and smiled
slightly. He folded his arms and leaned against the
wall, his lips pursed. "You can start delivering your
report," he ordered.

LuAnn kept her hands in her jacket, one fist closed
around her pistol; she managed to point the muzzle
at Jackson through the pocket.

Her movements were slight but Jackson cocked
his head and smiled. "Now I distinctly remember
you saying you wouldn't kill in cold blood."

414

"There are exceptions to everything."

"Fascinating, but we don't have time for games. The report?"

LuAnn started speaking in short bursts. "I met with Donovan. He's the man who was following me, Thomas Donovan." LuAnn assumed that Jackson had already run down Donovan's identity. She had decided on the drive over that the best approach was to tell Jackson mostly the truth and to only lie at critical junctures. Half truths were a wonderful way to inspire credibility, and right now she needed all she could muster. "He's a reporter with the *Washington Tribune*."

Jackson squatted on his haunches, his hands pressed together in front of him. His eyes remained keenly on her. "Go on."

"He was doing a story on the lottery. Twelve of the winners from ten years ago." She nodded toward Jackson. "You know the ones; they've all flourished financially."

"So?"

"So, Donovan wanted to know how, since so many of the other winners have gone belly-up. A very consistent percentage, he said. So your twelve sort of stuck out."

Jackson hid his chagrin well. He didn't like having loose ends, and this one had been glaring. LuAnn studied him closely. She read the smallest of self-doubts in his features. That was enormously comforting to her, but this was not the time to dwell on it.

"What did you tell him?"

"I told him I had been referred to an excellent investment firm by someone from the lottery. I gave him the name of the investment firm you used. I'm assuming they're legitimate."

"Very," Jackson replied. "At least on the surface. And the others?"

"I told Donovan I didn't know about them, but that they could have been referred to the same firm for all I knew."

"And he bought that?"

"Let's just say that he was disappointed. He wanted to write a story about the wealthy screwing the poor – you know, they win the lottery and then parasitic investment firms churn their accounts, earn their pieces of the pie, and leave the winner with nothing but attorney fees for filing bankruptcy. I told him that I certainly didn't support that conclusion. I had done just fine."

"And he knew about your situation in Georgia?"

"That's what drew him to me initially, I would imagine." LuAnn drew in a small breath of relief as she saw Jackson nod slightly at this remark. He apparently had arrived at the same conclusion. "He thought I would confess to some big conspiracy, I guess."

Jackson's eyes glittered darkly. "Did he mention any other theories, like the lottery being fixed?"

To hesitate now would be disastrous, LuAnn knew, so she plunged ahead. "No. Although he thought he had a big story. I told him to talk directly to the investment firm, that I had nothing to hide. That seemed to take the wind out of his sails. I told him if he wanted to contact the Georgia police he could go ahead. Maybe it was time to get things out in the open."

"You weren't being serious."

"I wanted him to believe I was. I figured if I made a big deal out of resisting or wanting to hide anything, he'd get even more suspicious. As it was, everything sort of fizzled for him."

"How did you leave it?"

"He thanked me for meeting with him, even apologized for troubling me. He said he might

416

contact me later, but kind of doubted it." Once again LuAnn saw Jackson incline his head slightly. This was working out better than she could have expected. "He got out of my car and into his. That's the last I saw of him."

Jackson was silent for several moments and then he slowly rose, silently clapping his hands together. "I love a good performance and I think you handled the situation very well, LuAnn."

"I had a good teacher."

"What?"

"Ten years ago. The airport, where you impersonated an impersonation. You told me the best way to hide is to stick out, because it runs counterintuitive to human nature. I used the same principle. Be overly open, cooperative, and honest, and even suspicious people tend to rethink things."

"I am honored that you remembered all that."

A little ego-stroking went a long way with most men, LuAnn knew, and Jackson, exceptional though he was in many ways, was no exception in that regard. In an understatement of mammoth proportions, LuAnn said, "You're a little hard to forget. So you don't have to do anything with Donovan, he's harmless. Now tell me about Riggs."

A smile formed on the man's lips. "I witnessed your impromptu meeting with Riggs on the rear grounds this morning. It was rather picturesque. From your state of undress, I imagine he had quite a pleasant morning."

LuAnn hid her anger at this barb. Right now she needed information. She replied, "All the more reason why I should know all about him."

"Well, let's start with his real name: Daniel Buckman."

"Buckman? Why would he have a different name?"

417

"Funny question coming from you. Why do people change their names, LuAnn?"

Perspiration sprouted on her forehead. "Because they have something to hide."

"Precisely."

"Was he a spy?"

Jackson laughed. "Not quite. Actually, he's not anything."

"What do you mean by that?"

"I mean that dead men, technically, can't be anything other than dead, correct?"

"Dead?" LuAnn's entire body froze. *Had Jackson killed Matthew? It couldn't be.* She fought with all her might not to plunge to the floor. Luckily, Jackson continued.

"I obtained his fingerprints, had them run through a database and the computer told me that he's dead."

"The computer's wrong."

"The computer only relays what it's been told. Someone wanted it to appear that Riggs was dead in case anyone came looking."

"Came looking? Like who?"

"His enemies." When LuAnn didn't respond, Jackson said, "Have you ever heard of the Witness Protection and Relocation Program?"

"No. Should I?"

"You've lived abroad for so long, I suppose not. It's run by the federal government, more particularly by the United States Marshal's Service. It's to protect persons testifying against dangerous criminals or organizations. They get new identities, new lives. Officially, Riggs is dead. Shows up in a small town, starts a new life under a new identity. Maybe his features have been altered somewhat. I don't know for certain, but it's an educated guess on my part that Riggs is a member of that select group."

418

"Riggs – Buckman – was a witness? To what?"

Jackson shrugged. "Who knows? Who cares? What I'm telling you is that Riggs is a criminal. Or was a criminal. Probably drugs or something like that. Maybe Mafia informant. Witness Protection isn't used for purse snatchers."

LuAnn settled back against the wall to keep herself from falling. *Riggs was a criminal.*

"I hope you haven't confided anything to him. There's no telling what his agenda might be."

"I haven't," LuAnn managed to say.

"So what can you tell me about the man?"

"Not as much as you just told me. He doesn't know any more than he did before. He's not pushing the issue. He thinks Donovan was a potential kidnapper. From what you just said, I'm sure he doesn't want to draw any attention to himself."

"True, that's very good for us. And I'm sure your little rendezvous this morning didn't hurt at all."

"That's really none of your business," she retorted hotly. With their exchange of information at an end, she wasn't going to let that remark pass.

"Ah, your first mistake this session. You just can't make it through without committing some blunder, can you?" He pointed a slender finger at her. "Everything about you is my business. I made you. And in a real sense I feel responsible for your well-being. I don't take that responsibility lightly."

LuAnn blurted out, "Look, the ten years is up. You've made your money. I've made mine. I say we call it a day, forever. In thirty-six hours I'll be on the other side of the world. You go your way, I'll go mine, because I'm more than real tired of this."

"You disobeyed me."

"Right, well I spent ten damn years in twenty different countries, constantly looking over my shoulder, obeying *your* instructions. And I guess

419

now I'll spend the rest of my life doing the same thing. So let me get to it." The two engaged in a stare-down of prolonged duration.

"You'll leave right away?"

"Just give me time to pack my bags. We'll be gone by tomorrow morning."

Jackson rubbed his chin as he considered this proposal. "Tell me something, LuAnn, tell me why I shouldn't kill you right now."

She had been prepared for that question. "Because Donovan might find it a little peculiar that right after he talks to me I end up a corpse. He's not suspicious now. I think I can guarantee you that would get his radar going. You really want that kind of trouble?"

Jackson pursed his lips for a moment and then motioned to the door. "Go pack."

LuAnn looked at him and motioned to the door. "You first."

"Let's leave together, LuAnn. That way, we'll each have a reasonable chance at reciprocating in kind in the event one of us tries something violent."

They went to the door together, their gazes glued to each other.

Right when Jackson put his hand on the door-knob, the door burst open, almost knocking him down.

Riggs stood there, his gun leveled on Jackson. Before he could fire, Jackson pulled LuAnn in front of him, his hand edging downward.

"Matthew, don't," LuAnn cried out.

Riggs shot her a glance. "LuAnn—"

LuAnn sensed rather than saw Jackson cock his arm. He was using an underhand throwing method to hurl the knife, but it wouldn't be any less deadly that way.

Her hand shot out, partially colliding with Jackson's forearm. The next instant Riggs was grunting in pain, the knife sticking out of his arm. He dropped to the floor, clutching at the blade's handle. LuAnn pulled her gun out of her pocket and whipped around, trying to draw a bead on Jackson. At the very same time, Jackson pulled her backward against him.

Their combined momentum sent Jackson and LuAnn crashing through the glass window. LuAnn landed on top of him as they hit the porch, hard. LuAnn's pistol squirted free from her hand and slid across the porch. Each felt the subtle but undeniable strength of the other as they wrestled amid the thick, slippery shards of glass, trying to gain some footage. He clutched at her neck, she kicked at his groin, one of her elbows levered against his chin. Locked tightly together, they both rose slowly, each seeking an advantage. She noted the blood pouring from the grisly wound on Jackson's hand; he must have cut it going through the window. His grip couldn't be a hundred percent, she thought. With a sudden burst of strength that seemed to astonish even Jackson, LuAnn tore free from him, seized him by his belt and shirt front, and threw him face first against the side of the cottage where he slumped down, momentarily stunned from the impact. Without wasting an instant or any unnecessary motion, LuAnn propelled herself forward, straddled his back, gripped his chin with both hands, and pulled it backward, trying her best to crack his spine. Jackson screamed in pain as she pulled harder and harder. Another inch and he was a dead man. Her hands, however, suddenly slipped and she fell backward, landing in the glass. She exploded up and then froze as she looked down. In her hands was Jackson's face.

Jackson staggered up. For one terrible instant their eyes locked on each other. And for the first time, LuAnn was staring at Jackson's real face.

Jackson looked down at her hands. He touched his face, felt his own skin, his own hair, his breath coming in great gasps. Now she could identify him. Now she had to die.

The same thought occurred to LuAnn. She dove for the gun at the same time Jackson pounced on her; they slid together along the porch, both straining for the gun.

"Get off her, you bastard!" Riggs screamed. LuAnn turned to see the man, deathly pale, standing at the window, his shirt entirely red, the gun in his shaky hands. With an enviable bit of speed Jackson leapt over the porch railing. Riggs fired an instant too late, the bullets striking the porch instead of flesh.

"Shit!" Riggs groaned and dropped to his knees, disappearing from LuAnn's line of sight.

"Matthew!" LuAnn sprung to the window. Meanwhile, Jackson had disappeared into the woods.

LuAnn raced through the door, pulling off her jacket as she did so. She was next to Riggs in an instant. "Wait, don't pull it out, Matthew." Using her teeth, she tore her jacket sleeve apart and into strips. Next, she ripped open his shirtsleeve and exposed the wound. At first she tried to staunch the bleeding with the cloths, but she couldn't. She searched under Riggs's armpit and applied pressure with her finger at a certain spot. The flow of blood finally stopped. As gently as she could LuAnn pulled the knife free while Riggs's fingers dug into her arm, his teeth almost biting through his lip. She tossed the blade down.

"Matthew, hold your finger right here, don't push too hard, you need to allow a little blood to flow through." She guided his finger to the pressure point under his arm that she had been pressing against.

"I've got a first-aid kit in my car. I'll dress it as best

as I can. Then we need to get you to a doctor."

LuAnn retrieved her gun from the porch and they hustled out to the BMW, where LuAnn cleaned and dressed the wound using the first-aid kit from her glove compartment. As she cut the last piece of tape off with her teeth and wound it around the gauze, Riggs looked at her. "Where did you learn to do this stuff?"

LuAnn grunted. "Hell, the first time I ever saw a doctor was when Lisa was born. And even then it was only for about twenty minutes. You live in the boonies with no money, you have to learn how to do this just to survive."

When they got to an urgent care center off Route 29, LuAnn started to get out of the car to help Riggs in. He stopped her.

"Look, I think it'll be better if I go in alone. I've been to this place before, they know me. General contractors get hurt a lot. I'll tell 'em I slipped and stuck a hunting knife in my arm."

"You're sure?"

"Yeah, I think I made a big enough mess for you already."

He struggled out of the car.

"I'll be here when you get out, I promise," she said.

He smiled weakly, and holding his injured arm, he went inside.

LuAnn pulled the BMW around and backed into the parking space so she could see anyone coming in. She locked the doors and then swore under her breath. Riggs had come to her rescue, for that she could hardly fault him. But right before that she had Jackson convinced that everything was okay. Another minute and they would've been home free. God, the timing. She slumped against the seat. It was possible that she could explain Riggs's sudden and armed presence away. Riggs had been concerned for her safety, followed her, thinking maybe that the man she was meeting was Donovan. But Riggs had done something else, something that she couldn't explain away. She let out a loud groan as she watched the traffic pass by on Route 29.

In front of Jackson, Riggs had called her LuAnn. That one word had destroyed everything. There was no way he would've missed that. Now, Jackson knew she had lied to him about what Riggs knew. She had no doubt what the punishment for that would be. Her spirits had been so high barely thirty minutes ago. Now all bets were off.

She glanced down at the seat and saw the white piece of paper there. She picked up Donovan's card and looked at the phone number. She thought for a moment and then picked up the phone. She silently cursed when she only got the answering machine. She left a lengthy message telling Donovan what had happened. She implored him once again to go underground, that she would pay for everything. He was a good man looking for the truth. She didn't want him to die. She didn't want anyone else to die because of her. She hoped to God he would live to get the message.

Jackson pressed the cloth against his palm. He had indeed badly cut his hand going through the glass. Damn the woman. Riggs would've been dead if she hadn't hit Jackson's arm a millisecond before he released the knife.

He gingerly touched his real skin. A small lump had appeared thanks to one of her blows. He had finally felt her raw strength and he had to admit, it exceeded his own. Who would have thought it? The big muscle-bound types never possessed genuine God-given strength like that; the kind you couldn't manufacture in a health spa. It was a combination of both inner and outer phenomena, working in precise, albeit spontaneous, bursts when called upon. One couldn't measure it or quantify it, because it came and went upon demand by its owner and varied in its intensity depending on the situation, rising to the occasion and mustering just enough reserve so that failure was never a possibility. Either you had that type of power or you didn't. LuAnn Tyler clearly did. He would not forget that. He would not seek to conquer her that way, but, as always, he would adapt around it. And the stakes were as high as they were ever likely to climb, for one specific reason.

The irony was he had believed her. He had been prepared to let her walk away. LuAnn had confided in Riggs, that was clear. Riggs knew her real name. There were few actions that angered Jackson more than prevarication by his own people. Disloyalty could not and would not be tolerated. If she had lied about Riggs, it was more than probable that she had lied about Donovan. Jackson had to assume that the *Trib* reporter was closing in on the truth. Thus, he had to be stopped as well.

As these thoughts were going around in Jackson's mind, his portable phone rang. He picked it up. He listened, asked a few questions, conveyed some clear instructions, and when he hung up, a deep look of satisfaction graced his true features. The timing couldn't have been better: His trap had just been sprung.

FORTY-SEVEN

The Bell Ranger helicopter landed in a grassy field where three black sedans bearing government license plates were waiting. George Masters alighted from the chopper, another agent, Lou Berman, right at his elbow. They climbed in one of the cars and started off. Riggs had seriously underestimated the quickness of the response time from Washington.

Twenty minutes later the procession made its way down the gravel road and stopped in front of Riggs's home. Car doors swung open and serious-looking men, weapons out and ready, swarmed the front and back of the house and barn.

Masters strode up to the front door. When his knocks were not answered, he motioned to one of the men. The burly agent planted one foot directly against the lock and the door flew open, crashing against the interior wall. After they searched the house thoroughly, they finally converged in Riggs's office.

Masters sat down at the desk and quickly rustled through the papers, his eyes alighting on one set of notes. Masters leaned back in the chair and intently studied Riggs's scribbles on LuAnn Tyler and someone named Catherine Savage. He looked up at Berman. "Tyler disappears and Catherine Savage reappears. That's the cover."

"We can check the airports, see if Catherine Savage flew out ten years ago," Berman said.

Masters shook his head. "We don't need to do that. They're one and the same. Tyler is here. Find out Savage's address pronto. Call up some of the high-end real estate agents around here. I don't think her highness will be living in another trailer."

Berman nodded, pulled out a portable phone, and went to confer with the local FBI agents who had accompanied them here.

Masters ran his eyes around Riggs's office. He was wondering how Riggs fit into all this. He had it nice here, new life, new career, peaceful, lot of good years left to live. But now? Masters had been at the White House meeting with the president, the attorney general, and the director of the FBI. As Masters had outlined his theory, he had watched each of their faces go sickly pale. A scandal of horrific proportions. The government lottery, fixed. The American people would believe that their own government had done it to them. How could they not? The president had publicly announced his support for the lottery, even appeared in a TV commercial touting it. So long as the billions flowed in, and a few lucky people were elevated to millionaire status, who cared?

The concept of the lottery had received attacks claiming that what it spent on furthering the public welfare was largely negated by what it cost in others: breakup of families, gambling addiction, making poor people even poorer, causing people to eschew hard work and industriousness for the unrealistic dream of winning the lottery. One critic had said it was much like inner city kids striving for the NBA instead of an MBA. However, the lottery had remained bulletproof from those attacks.

If it came out, however, that the game was fixed, then the bullets would rapidly shatter that bubble. There would be a tremendous blood-letting and everyone from the president on down was going to take a major hit. As Masters had sat in the Oval Office he saw that clearly in all their features: the FBI director, the nation's top lawman; the attorney general, the nation's top lawyer; the president, the number one of all. The responsibility would fall there and it would fall heavily. So Masters had been given explicit instructions: Bring in LuAnn Tyler, at any cost and by any means possible. And he intended to do just that.

"How's it feel?"

Riggs climbed slowly into the car. His right arm was in a sling. "Well, they gave me enough pain-killers to where I'm not sure I can feel anything."

LuAnn put the car in gear and they sped out on to the highway.

"Where are we going?" he asked.

"McDonald's. I'm starving and I can't remember the last time I had a Big Mac and fries. Sound good?"

"Sounds good."

She pulled into the drive-through of a McDonald's, ordering some burgers, fries, and two coffees.

They ate as they drove. Riggs put down his coffee, wiped his mouth, and nervously fingered the dashboard with his good arm. "So tell me, how badly did I screw things up for you?"

"Matthew, I'm not blaming you."

"I know," he said sheepishly. He slapped the seat. "I thought you were walking into a trap."

She stared over at him. "And why's that?"

Riggs looked out the window for a long moment before answering. "Right after you left I got a call."

"Is that right? Who from, and what did it have to do with me?"

He sighed deeply. "Well, for starters, my name's not Matthew Riggs. I mean it's been my name for the last five years, but it's not my real name."

"Well, at least we're even on that score."

He said with a forced grin, "Daniel Buckman." He held out his hand. "My friends call me Dan."

LuAnn didn't take it. "You're Matthew to me. Do your friends also know that technically you're dead and that you're in the Witness Protection Program?"

Riggs slowly withdrew his hand.

She flipped him an impatient look. "I told you that Jackson can do anything. I wish you'd start believing me."

"I was betting he was the one who tapped into my file. That's why I followed you. If he knew about me, I didn't know how he'd react. I thought he might kill you."

"That's always a possibility with the man."

"I got a good look at him."

LuAnn was exasperated. "That wasn't his real face. Dammit, it's never his real face." She thought of the rubbery flesh she had held. She had seen his real face. *His real face.* She knew what that meant. Jackson would now do everything in his power to kill her.

She slid her hands nervously over the steering wheel. "Jackson said you were a criminal. So what'd you do?"

"Are you telling me you believe everything that guy says to you? Just in case you didn't notice, he's a psycho. I haven't seen eyes like that since they executed Ted Bundy."

"Are you saying you're not in Witness Protection?"

"No. But the program isn't just for the bad guys."

She looked at him, puzzled. "What does that mean?"

"Do you think criminals can pick up the phone and get the sort of info I got on you?"

"I don't know, why can't they?"

"Pull over."

429

"What?"

"Just pull the damn car over!"

LuAnn turned into a parking lot and stopped the car.

Riggs leaned over and pulled out the listening device from under LuAnn's seat. "I told you I had bugged your car." He held up the sophisticated device. "Let me tell you, they almost never give out equipment like this to felons."

LuAnn looked at him, her eyes wide.

Riggs took a deep breath. "Up until five years ago, I was a special agent with the FBI. I'd like to think a *very* special agent. I worked undercover infiltrating gangs operating both in Mexico and along the Texas border. These guys were into everything from extortion to drugs to murder for hire; you name it, they were doing it. I lived and breathed with that scum for a year. When we busted the case open, I was the lead witness for the prosecution. We knocked out the entire operation, sent a bunch of them to prison for life. But the big bosses in Colombia didn't take all that kindly to my depriving them of about four hundred million a year in disposable income from the drug operation component. I knew how badly they'd want me. So I did the brave, honorable thing. I asked to disappear."

"And?"

"And the Bureau turned me down. They said I was too valuable in the field. Too experienced. They did have the courtesy to set me up in another town, in another gig. A desk job for a while."

"So there was no wife. That was all made up."

Riggs rubbed his injured arm again. "No, I was married. After I relocated. Her name was Julie."

LuAnn said very quietly, "Was?"

Riggs shook his head slowly and took a weary sip

430

on his coffee. The steam from the liquid fogged the window and he traced his real initials in it, forming the D and the B for Dan Buckman with great care as though doing it for the very first time. "Ambush on the Pacific Coast Highway. Car went over the cliff with about a hundred bullet holes in it. Julie was killed by the gunfire. I took two slugs; somehow neither of them hit any vitals. I was thrown clear of the car, landed on a ledge. Those were the scars you saw."

"Oh, God. I'm so sorry, Matthew."

"Guys like me, we probably shouldn't get married. It wasn't something I was looking for. It just happened. You know, you meet, you fall in love, you want to get married. You expect everything to sort of click after that. Things that you know might come up to ruin it, you sort of will them away. If I had resisted that impulse, Julie would still be alive and teaching first grade." He looked down at his hands as he spoke. "Anyway, that was when the brilliant higher-ups at the Bureau decided I just might want to retire and change my identity. Officially, I died in the ambush. Julie's six feet under in Pasadena and I'm a general contractor in safe, pastoral Charlottesville." He finished his coffee. "Or at least it used to be safe."

LuAnn slid her hand across the front seat and took his in a firm grip.

He squeezed back and said, "It's tough wiping out so many years of your life. Trying not to think about it, forgetting people and places, things that were so important to you for so long. Always afraid you're going to slip up." He stared at her. "It's damn tough," he said wearily.

She raised her hand up and stroked his face. "I never realized how much we had in common," she said.

431

"Well, here's another one." He paused for a second as their eyes locked. "I hadn't been with a woman since Julie."

They kissed tenderly and slowly.

"I want you to know," Riggs said, "that that wasn't the reason this morning happened. I've had other opportunities over the years. I just never felt like doing anything about them." He added quietly, "Until you."

She traced his jaw line with her index finger and then her finger curled up to his lips. "I've had other chances too," she said. They kissed again and then their bodies instinctively embraced and held tightly like two pieces from a mold, joined at last. They sat and rocked together for several minutes.

When they finally pulled away, Riggs checked the parking lot, refocusing on the present situation.

"Let's get to your house, pack some clothes, and whatever else you need. Then we'll go to my house and I'll do the same. I left the notes I made from my phone calls about you on my desk. I don't want to leave a trail for anyone."

"There's a motel off twenty-nine about four miles north of here."

"That's a start."

"So, what do you think Jackson's going to do now?"

"He knows I lied about you. He has to assume I lied about Donovan. Since I have every reason not to reveal the truth and Donovan is trying his best to do that, Jackson will go after him first and me second. I called Donovan and left a message warning him."

"Boy, that's real encouraging, being number two on Master Psycho's hit list," Riggs said, tapping his hand against the gun in his pocket.

A few minutes later they pulled up the private drive to Wicken's Hunt. The house was dark. LuAnn parked in front and she and Riggs got out. LuAnn

432

punched in the home's security code and they went inside.

Riggs sat alertly on the bed while LuAnn stuffed some things in a small travel bag.

"You're sure Lisa and Charlie are okay?"

"As sure as I can be. They're far away from here. And him. That can only be a good thing."

Riggs went over to the window that overlooked the front drive. What he saw coming up the drive-way made his knees buckle for an instant. Then he snatched LuAnn by the hand and they were racing down the stairs and out the rear entrance.

The black sedans stopped in front of the house and the men quickly scrambled out. George Masters laid a hand on the BMW's hood and immediately scanned the area. "It's warm. She's here somewhere. Find her." The men fanned out and surrounded the house.

LuAnn and Riggs were racing past the horse barn and were headed into the deep woods when LuAnn pulled up.

Riggs stopped too, clutching at his arm, sucking in air. They were both trembling.

"What are you doing?" he gasped.

She motioned toward the horse barn. "You can't run with that arm. And we can't just go floundering around in the woods."

They entered the horse barn. Joy immediately started to make some noise and LuAnn quickly darted over and soothed the animal. While LuAnn readied their mount, Riggs pulled a pair of binoculars off the wall and went outside. Setting up in some thick bushes that hid the horse barn from the house, Riggs focused the binoculars. He automatically jerked back as he saw, under the flood lights that fully illuminated the entire rear law, the man moving across the back of the house, rifle in hand and the letters "FBI" emblazoned across his jacket. The next sight made Riggs mutter under his breath. It was five years since he had seen the man. George Masters hadn't changed much. The next instant the men disappeared from view as they entered the house.

Riggs hustled back to the horse barn where LuAnn was checking the cinches on the saddle. She patted Joy's neck, whispering calming words to the horse as she slid on the bridle.

"You ready?" she asked Riggs.

"Better be. As soon as they find the house empty, they're going to check the grounds. They know we're around somewhere – the car's engine would've still been warm."

LuAnn planted a wooden crate next to Joy, swung up, and reached out a hand for Riggs. "Step on that crate and hold on tight to me."

Riggs managed to struggle up in this fashion, clutching his arm as he did so. He planted his good arm around LuAnn's waist.

"I'll go as slow as I can, but it's going to jostle you a lot regardless. Horseback riding does that."

"Don't worry about me. I'll take a little pain to having to try and explain everything to the FBI."

As they started off on the trail LuAnn said, "So that's who it was? Your old friends?" Riggs nodded.

"At least one old friend in fact. Used to be a friend anyway. George Masters. He's the one at the Bureau who said I was too valuable in the field, who wouldn't let me enter Witness Protection until my wife was dead."

"Matthew, it's not worth it. There's no reason you should be running from them, you haven't done anything wrong."

"Look, LuAnn, it's not like I owe those guys anything."

"But if I'm caught and you're with me?"

"Well, we just won't get caught." He grinned.

"What's so funny?"

"I was just thinking how bored I'd been the last few years. I guess I'm not really happy unless I'm doing something where I have a reasonable shot at getting my head blown off. I might as well own up to it."

"Well, you picked the right person to hang with then." She looked up ahead. "The motel's probably out of the question."

"Yep, they'll cover every place like that. Besides, riding up on a horse might make the motel manager suspicious."

"I've got another car back at the house, fat lot of good that'll do us."

"Wait a minute. We do have a car."

"Where?"

"We've got to get to the cottage, pronto."

When they arrived at the cottage, Riggs said, "Keep a sharp eye out in case you know who decided to come back." He opened up the doors to the rear shed and went inside. In the darkness, LuAnn couldn't see what he was doing. Then she heard a motor turn over and then die. Then it kicked over again and this time it kept running. A moment later, Donovan's black Honda, torn-up front bumper and all, appeared in the doorway. Riggs pulled it to a stop outside the shed doors and climbed out.

"What do you want to do with the horse?"

LuAnn looked around. "I could send her back up the trail. She'd probably go back to the horse barn on her own, but in the dark like this, she might miss the trail or wander off and fall in a hole or maybe the creek."

"How about we put her in the shed and then you can call somebody to come get her?" he offered.

"Good idea." She swung down and led Joy inside the shed.

She looked around and noted the watering trough, tack wall, and two small bales of hay stored in the back of the shed.

"It's perfect. The tenant before Donovan must have kept a horse and used this as a stable."

Lifting off the saddle and slipping off the horse's bridle, LuAnn tethered Joy to a hook on the wall with a piece of rope she found. LuAnn scrounged up a bucket and, using water from the outside tap, she filled up the watering trough, and laid out the hay in front of Joy. The horse immediately dipped her head to the trough and then started to munch the hay. LuAnn shut the doors and climbed in the driver's seat of the Honda while Riggs eased in the other side.

There was no key in the ignition. LuAnn glanced under the steering column and saw a bundle of exposed wires hanging down. "They teach hot wiring at the FBI?"

"You learn a lot of things going through life."

She put the car in gear. "Tell me about it."

They were silent and still for a moment and then Riggs stirred. "We may only have one shot at getting out of this relatively intact."

"And what's that?"

"The FBI can be accommodating to people who cooperate."

"But, Matthew—"

He broke in, "But they can be absolutely forgiving to people who give them what they really want."

"Are you suggesting what I think you are?"

"All we need to do is deliver Jackson to them."

"That's good to hear. For a minute there I thought it might be something difficult."

They drove off in the Honda.

FORTY-EIGHT

It was ten o'clock in the morning. Donovan stared through a pair of binoculars at the large Southern colonial home set amid mature trees. He was in McLean, Virginia, one of the most affluent locales in the United States. Million-dollar properties were the norm here and that was typically only on one acre of land or less. The home he was staring at rested on five secluded acres. You have to have substantial wealth for a place like this. As he looked at the columned portico, Donovan knew without a doubt that the current owner had more than enough.

As he watched, a brand new Mercedes drove down the street from the opposite direction and approached the massive gates to the property. As the Mercedes nosed toward the entrance, the gates parted and the car entered the private drive. Through the binoculars, Donovan eyed the woman driving. In her forties now, she still matched her lottery photo from ten years ago pretty well. Lots of money could slow down the aging process, Donovan figured.

He checked his watch. He had gotten here early just to scope things out. He had checked his answering machine and had listened to LuAnn Tyler's warning. He wasn't going to run yet, but he had taken her advice quite seriously. He would've been a fool to think there weren't some serious forces behind all this. He took out the gun from his pocket and checked to make sure it was fully loaded. He scanned the area intently once more. He waited a few more minutes to give her time to get settled, then tossed his cigarette out the window, rolled it

437

up, and drove toward the house.

He pulled up to the gates and spoke into an intercom. The voice answering him sounded nervous, agitated. The gates opened and a minute later he was standing inside the foyer that rose a full three stories above his head.

"Ms. Reynolds?"

Bobbie Jo Reynolds was trying her best not to meet his eye. She didn't speak, but simply nodded. She was dressed in a way Donovan would describe as very put together. You wouldn't have suspected that barely ten years ago she had been a starving actress wannabe hustling tables. She had been back in the country for almost five years now after a lengthy sojourn in France. During his investigation into the lottery winners, Donovan had checked her out thoroughly. She was now a very respected member of the Washington social community. He suddenly wondered if Alicia Crane and she knew each other.

After failing to get anywhere with LuAnn, Donovan had contacted the eleven other lottery winners. They had been far easier to track down than LuAnn; none of them were fugitives from the law. Yet.

Reynolds was the only one who had agreed to speak with him. Five of the winners had hung up on him. Herman Rudy had threatened bodily harm and used language Donovan hadn't heard since his Navy days. The others hadn't called back after he had left messages.

Reynolds escorted him into what Donovan figured was the living room – large, airy, and filled, presumably under an interior designer's tasteful eye, with contemporary furnishings, sprinkled here and there with costly antiques.

Reynolds sat down in a wingback chair and motioned Donovan to the settee across from her. "Would you like some tea or coffee?" She still didn't look at him, her hands nervously clasping and unclasping.

"I'm fine." He hunched forward, took out his notebook, and slipped a tape recorder from his pocket. "You mind if I record this conversation?"

"Why is that necessary?" Reynolds was suddenly showing a little backbone now, he thought. Donovan quickly decided to squelch that tendency before it gained any further strength.

"Ms. Reynolds, I assumed when you called me back that you were prepared to talk about things. I'm a reporter. I don't want to put words in your mouth, I want to get the facts exactly straight, can you understand that?"

"Yes," she said nervously, "I suppose I can. That's why I called you back. I don't want my name besmirched. I want you to know that I've been a very respectable member of this community for years. I've given generously to numerous charities, I sit on several local boards—"

"Ms. Reynolds," Donovan interrupted, "do you mind if I call you Bobbie Jo?"

There was a perceptible wince on Reynolds's face. "I go by Roberta," she said primly.

Reynolds reminded Donovan so much of Alicia he was tempted to ask if they knew each other. He decided to pass on that impulse.

"All right, Roberta, I know you've done a ton of good for the community. A real pillar. But I'm not interested in the present. I want to talk about the past, specifically ten years ago."

"You mentioned that on the phone. The lottery." She swept a shaky hand through her hair.

"That's right. The source of all this." He looked around at the opulence.

"I won the lottery ten years ago, that's hardly news now, Mr. Donovan."

"Call me Tom."

"I would prefer not."

"Fine. Roberta, do you know someone named LuAnn Tyler?"

Reynolds thought a moment and then shook her head. "It doesn't seem familiar. Should I know her?"

"Probably not. She won the lottery too, in fact two months after you did."

"Good for her."

"She was a lot like you. Poor, not a lot to look forward to. No way out, really."

She laughed nervously. "You make it sound like I was destitute. I was hardly that."

"But you weren't exactly rolling in dough, were you? I mean that's why you played the lottery, right?"

"I suppose. It's not like I expected to win."

"Didn't you, Roberta?"

She looked startled. "What are you talking about?"

"Who manages your investments?"

"That's none of your business."

"Well, my guess is it's the same person who manages the money of eleven other lottery winners, including LuAnn Tyler."

"So?"

"Come on, Roberta, talk to me. Something's up. You know all about it and I want to find out all about it. In fact, you knew you were going to win the lottery."

"You're crazy." Her voice was trembling badly.

"Am I? I don't think so. I've interviewed lots of liars, Roberta, some very accomplished. You're not one of them."

Reynolds stood up. "I don't have to listen to this."

Donovan persisted. "The story's going to come out, Roberta. I'm close to breaking through on a variety of fronts. It's only a matter of time. The question is: Do you want to cooperate and maybe get out of this whole thing relatively unscathed or do you want to go down with everybody?"

"I . . . I . . ."

Donovan continued in a steady voice. "I'm not looking to wipe out your life, Roberta. But if you participated in a conspiracy to fix the lottery, in whatever manner, you're going to take some lumps. But I'll offer you the same deal I offered Tyler. Tell me all you know, I go and write my story and you do whatever you want to do until the story hits. Like disappear. Consider the alternative. It's not nearly as pretty."

Reynolds sat back down and looked around her home for a moment. She took a deep breath. "What do you want to know?"

Donovan turned on the recorder. "Was the lottery fixed?" She nodded. "I need an audible response, Roberta." He nodded toward the recorder.

"Yes."

"How?" Donovan was almost shaking as he waited for the answer.

"Would you mind pouring me a glass of water from that carafe over there?"

Donovan jumped up, poured the water, and set the glass down in front of her. He sat back down.

"How?" he repeated.

"It had to do with chemicals."

Donovan cocked his head. "Chemicals?"

Reynolds pulled a handkerchief from her pocket and wiped at a sudden cluster of tears in her eyes.

As Donovan watched her, he figured she was near the breaking point. Ironic that the one to call him back would be the nervous Nellie type.

"I'm no scientist, Roberta, give it to me as simply as you can."

441

Reynolds gripped the handkerchief tightly. "All but one ball, the one with the winning number, was sprayed with some chemical. And the passageway through which the ball traveled was sprayed with something. I can't explain it exactly, but it made certain that only the ball that wasn't sprayed with anything went through. It was the same for all the other ball bins."

"Damn!" Donovan stared at her in amazement. "Okay, Roberta, I got a million questions. Do the other winners know about this? How it was done? And by whom?" He thought back to LuAnn Tyler. She knew, that was for damned sure.

"No. None of the winners knew how it was done. Only the people who did it knew." She pointed to his tape recorder. "Your recorder's stopped." She added bitterly, "I'm sure you don't want to miss one word of this."

Donovan picked up the recorder and studied it as he reflected on her words. "But that's not exactly right, because you knew how the lottery was fixed, Roberta, you just told me. Come on, give me the whole truth."

The crunching blow to his upper torso sent Donovan over the top of the settee. He landed hard on the oak floor, his breath painfully gone. He could feel shattered ribs floating inside him.

Reynolds hovered over him. "No, the truth is only the *person* who came up with the whole scheme knew how it was done." The feminine hair and face came off and Jackson stared down at the injured man.

Donovan tried desperately to get up. "Christ."

Jackson's foot slammed into his chest, knocking him back against the wall. Jackson stood erect. "Kick-boxing is a particularly deadly art form. You can literally kill someone without using your

442

hands."

Donovan's hand slipped down to his pocket, fumbling for his gun. His limbs would barely respond, his broken ribs were prodding internal organs they weren't meant to touch. He couldn't seem to catch his breath.

"Really, you're obviously not feeling well. Let me help you." Jackson knelt down and, using the handkerchief, pulled the gun out of Donovan's pocket. "This actually is perfect. Thank you."

He kicked Donovan viciously in the head and the reporter's eyes finally closed. Jackson pulled plastic locking binds from his pocket and within a minute had Donovan secured.

He pulled off the rest of the disguise, packed it carefully in his bag pulled from under the couch, and went up the stairs two at a time. He raced down the hallway and opened the bedroom door at the far end.

Bobbie Jo Reynolds lay spread-eagled on the bed, her arms and legs tied to the bedposts, tape over her mouth. She looked wildly up at Jackson, her body twitching in uncontrollable fear.

Jackson sat down next to her. "I want to thank you for following my directions so precisely. You gave the staff the day off and made the appointment with Mr. Donovan just as I requested." He patted her hand. "I knew that I could count on you, the most faithful of my little flock." He looked at her with soft, comforting eyes until her trembling subsided. He unloosened her straps and gently removed the tape.

He stood up. "I have to attend to Mr. Donovan downstairs. We'll be gone very soon and won't trouble you anymore. You will stay here until we're gone, do you understand?"

She nodded in a jerky motion, rubbing her wrists. Jackson stood up, pointed Donovan's gun at her, and squeezed the trigger until the firing pin had no bullets left to ignite.

He watched for a moment as blood spread over the sheets. Jackson shook his head sadly. He did not enjoy killing lambs. But that was how the world worked. Lambs were made for sacrifice. They never put up a fight.

He went back downstairs, pulled out his makeup kit and mirror, and spent the next thirty minutes hovering over Donovan.

When the reporter finally came to his head was splitting; he could feel the internal bleeding but at least he was still alive.

His heart almost stopped when he found himself staring up at . . . Thomas Donovan. The person even had his coat and hat on. Donovan refocused his eyes. His initial impression had been one of staring at his twin. Now he could see subtle differences, things that weren't exactly right. However, the impersonation was still remarkable.

Jackson knelt down. "You look surprised, but I assure you, I'm very adept at this. Powders, creams, latex, hairpieces, spirit gum, putty. It really is amazing what one can do, even if it is all an illusion of sorts. Besides, in your case it wasn't all that difficult. I don't mean this in a negative way, but you have quite an ordinary face. I didn't have to do anything special and I've been studying your features for several days now. You did surprise me by shaving off your beard, though. However, instead of beard we have beard stubble courtesy of crepe hair and adhesive."

He grabbed Donovan under his armpits and lifted him up to the couch and sat down across from him. The groggy journalist listed to one side. Jackson gently propped him up with a pillow.

"It certainly wouldn't pass the closest of scrutiny;

however, the result isn't bad for a half hour's work."

"I need to get to a doctor." Donovan managed to get the words out through blood-caked lips.

"I'm afraid that's not going to happen. But I will take a couple of minutes to explain some things to you. For what it's worth, I believe that I owe you that. You were quite ingenious in figuring out the bankruptcy angle. That, I admit, had never occurred to me. My main concern was to ensure that none of my winners would want for money. Any shortage of funds might give them motivation to tell all. Fat and happy people rarely double-cross their benefactor. You found the hole in that plan."

Donovan coughed and, with a sudden motion, managed to sit up straight. "How'd you pick up my trail?"

"I knew LuAnn would tell you basically nothing. What would you do next? Ferret out another source. I phoned all my other winners and alerted them that you might call. Ten of them I instructed to blow you off. I told Bobbie Jo – excuse me, Roberta – to meet with you."

"Why her?"

"Simple enough. Geographically, she was the closest one to me. As it is, I had to drive through the night to get here and set everything up. That was me in the Mercedes, by the way. I had a description of you. I thought that was you in the car watching the house."

"Where's Bobbie Jo?"

"Not relevant." Jackson smiled both in his eagerness to explain and in his triumph and total control over the veteran reporter. "Now, to continue. The substance applied to nine of the ten balls was a clear light acrylic. If you care for precise details, it was a diluted solution of polydimethyl siloxane that I made a few modifications to, a turbocharged version if you will. It builds up a powerful static charge and also increases the size of the ball by approximately one thousandth of an inch without, however, a measurable change in weight or appearance or even smell. They do weigh the balls, you know, to ensure that all are of equal weight. In each bin the ball with the winning number on it had no chemicals applied to it. Each passageway through which the winning ball must travel was given a small trace of the modified polydimethyl siloxane solution as well. Under those precisely controlled conditions, the nine balls with the static charge could not enter a passageway coated with the same substance; indeed, they repelled each other, much like a force field. Thus they could not be part of the winning combination. Only the uncoated ball would be able to do so."

The awe was clear on Donovan's face, but then his features clouded. "Wait a minute: If the nine balls were coated with the same charge, why wouldn't they be repelling each other in the bin? Wouldn't that make people suspicious?"

"Wonderful question. I thrive on the details. I further modified the chemical so that it would be instantly activated by the heat given off by the air flow into the machines to make the balls gyrate. Until then, the balls would remain motionless."

Jackson paused, his eyes shining. "Inferior minds seek convoluted scenarios; it takes a brilliant one to achieve simplicity. And I'm sure your background research revealed that all of my winners were poor, desperate, searching for a little hope, a little help. And I gave it to them. To all of you. The lottery loved it. The government looked like saints helping the impoverished like that. You people in the media got to write your teary-eyed stories. Everybody won. Including me." Donovan half expected the man to take a bow.

"And you did this all by your lonesome?" Donovan sneered.

Jackson's retort was sharp. "I didn't need anyone else, other than my winners. Human beings are infinitely fallible, completely unreliable. Science is not. Science is absolute. Under strict principles, if you do A and B, then C will occur. That rarely happens if you inject the inefficiencies of humanity into the process."

"How'd you get the access?" Donovan was starting to slur his words as his injuries took their toll.

Jackson's smile broadened. "I was able to gain employment as a technician at the company that provided and maintained the ball machines. I was drastically overqualified for the position, which was one reason I got it. No one really cared about the geeky little techie, it was like I wasn't even there. But I had complete and unrestricted access to the machines. I even bought one of the ball machines so that I could experiment in private as to the right combinations of chemicals. So there I am, mister technician, spraying the balls with what everyone thought was a cleansing solution to get rid of dust and other grime that might have gotten into the bins. And all I had to do was hold the winning ball in my hand while I did so. The solution dries almost immediately. I surreptitiously drop the winning ball back into the bin and I'm all set."

Jackson laughed. "People really should respect the technicians of the world more, Mr. Donovan. They control everything because they control the machines that control the flow of information. In fact, I use many of them in my work. I didn't need to buy off the leaders. They're useless because they're incompetent showpieces. Give me the worker bees

447

any day."

Jackson stood up and put on a pair of thick gloves. "I think that covers everything," he said. "No, after I finish with you, I'm going to visit LuAnn."

Damn me for a fool for not listening to you, LuAnn, Donovan thought to himself.

Through the glove Jackson rubbed his injured hand where the glass had cut him. He had many paybacks planned for LuAnn.

"Piece of advice, A-hole," Donovan sputtered, "tangle with that woman and she'll cut your balls off."

"Thank you for your point of view." Jackson gripped Donovan tightly by the shoulders.

"Why're you keeping me alive, you son of a bitch?" Donovan tried to pull back from him, but was far too weak.

"Actually, I'm not." Jackson suddenly placed both hands around the sides of Donovan's head and gave it an abrupt twist. The sound of bone cracking was slight but unmistakable. Jackson lifted the dead man up and over his shoulder. Carrying him down to the garage, Jackson opened the front door of the Mercedes and pressed Donovan's fingers against the steering wheel, dash, cock, and several other surfaces that would leave good prints. Finally, Jackson clinched the dead man's hand around the gun he had used to kill Bobbie Jo Reynolds. Wrapping the body in a blanket, Jackson loaded it in the trunk of the Mercedes. He raced back into the house, retrieved his bag and Donovan's recorder, then returned to the garage and climbed behind the wheel of the Mercedes. In a few minutes the car had left the very quiet neighborhood behind. Jackson stopped by the side of the road, rolled down the window, and hurled the gun into the woods before pulling off again. Jackson would wait until nightfall and then a certain local incinerator he had found on an earlier reconnaissance would prove to be Thomas Donovan's final resting place.

As he drove on, Jackson thought briefly of how he would deal with LuAnn Tyler and her new ally, Riggs. Her disloyalty was now firmly established and there would be no more reprieves. He would focus his undivided attention on that matter shortly. But first he had something else to take care of.

Jackson entered Donovan's apartment, closed the door, and took a moment to survey the premises. He was still wearing the dead man's face. Thus, even if he had been spotted, it was of no concern to him. Donovan's body had been incinerated, but Jackson had a limited amount of time to complete his search of the late reporter's apartment. A journalist kept records, and those records were what Jackson had come for. Very soon the housekeeper would discover Bobbie Jo Reynolds's body and would call the police. Their search would very quickly, largely through Jackson's efforts, lead to Thomas Donovan.

He searched the apartment rapidly but methodically and soon found what he was looking for. He stacked the record boxes in the middle of the small foyer. They were the same ones Donovan had kept in the cottage in Charlottesville, filled with the results of his investigation into the lottery. Next he logged on to Donovan's computer and did a search of the hard drive. Thankfully, Donovan had not bothered to employ any passwords. The hard drive was clear. He probably kept everything on disk for portability. He looked at the back of the computer and then behind the desk. No phone modem. Just to be sure, Jackson again checked the icon screen. No computer services like America Online were present. Thus there was no e-mail to search. How old-fashioned of Donovan, he thought. Next he checked a stack of floppies in the desk drawer and piled them all in one of the boxes. He would look at them later.

He was preparing to leave when he noted the phone answering machine in the living room. The red light was blinking. He went over to the phone and hit the playback button. The first three messages were innocuous. The voice on the fourth message made Jackson jerk around and bend his head low to catch every single word.

Alicia Crane sounded nervous and scared. Where were you, Thomas, she implored. You haven't called. What you were working on was too dangerous. Please, please call me, the message said.

Jackson rewound the tape and listened to Alicia's voice again. He hit another button on the machine. Finally, he picked up the boxes and left the apartment.

FORTY-NINE

LuAnn looked at the Lincoln Memorial as she drove the Honda over the Memorial Bridge. The water of the Potomac River was dark and choppy. Flecks of white foam appeared but then quickly dissipated. It was the morning rush hour and the traffic over the bridge was heavy. They had spent one night in a motel near Fredericksburg while they decided what to do. Then they had driven to the outskirts of Washington, D.C., and spent the night at a motel near Arlington. Riggs had made some phone calls and visited a couple of retail establishments preparing for the events that would take place the next day. Then they had sat in the motel room eating while Riggs had gone over the plan, the details of which LuAnn quickly memorized. With that completed they had turned out the lights. One slept while the other kept watch. That was the plan at least. However, neither one got much rest. Finally, they both sat up, one curled around the other. Under any other circumstances they would have probably made love. As it was they spent the night looking out the window on to the dark street, listening for any sound that might herald another wave of danger.

"I can't believe I'm doing this," LuAnn said as they drove along.

"Hey, you said you trusted me."

"I do. I do trust you."

"LuAnn, I know what I'm doing. There are two

things I know: how to build things, and how the Bureau works. This is the way to do it. The only way that makes sense. You run, they'll eventually find you."

"I got away before," she said confidently.

"You had some help and a better head start. You'd never get out of the country now. So if you can't run, you do the reverse, you go right at them, take the offensive."

LuAnn focused on the traffic at the same time she was thinking intently about what they were about to do. What she was about to do. The only man she had ever absolutely trusted was Charlie. And that complete trust had not come quickly, it had been built and then cemented over a ten-year period. She had only known Riggs for a very short time. And yet he had earned her trust, even in a matter of days. His actions reached her far more deeply than any words he could try to tempt her with.

"Aren't you nervous?" she asked. "I mean you don't really know what you're going to be walking into."

He grinned at her. "That's the really great part, isn't it?"

"You're a crazy man, Matthew Riggs, you really are. All I want in my life is a little predictability, a semblance of tranquillity, of normalcy even, and you're salivating over walking along the edge of the cliff."

"It's all in how you look at it." He looked out the window. "Here we are." He pointed to an open spot on the curb and she pulled over and parked. Riggs got out and then poked his head back in. "You remember the plan?"

LuAnn nodded. "Going over everything last night helped. I can find it with no trouble."

"Good, see you soon."

As Riggs walked down the street to the pay phone,

452

LuAnn looked up at the large, ugly building. The J. EDGAR HOOVER BUILDING was stenciled on its facade. Home of the Federal Bureau of Investigation. These people were looking for her everywhere and here she was parked ten feet from their damned headquarters. She shivered and put on her sunglasses. Putting the car in gear, she tried to keep her nerves in check. She hoped to hell the man really knew what he was doing.

Riggs made the phone call. The man on the other end was understandably excited. Within a few minutes Riggs was inside the Hoover Building and being escorted by an armed guard to his destination.

The conference room he was deposited in was large but sparsely furnished. He passed by the chairs gathered around the small table, and remained standing waiting for them to arrive. He took a deep breath and almost cracked a smile. He had come home, in a manner of speaking. He scanned the room for any hidden cameras, and saw nothing obvious, which meant the room was probably under both audio and video surveillance.

He swung around when the door opened and two men dressed in white shirts and similar ties entered.

George Masters extended his hand. He was large, nearly bald, but his figure was trim. Lou Berman sported a severe crew cut and a grim demeanor.

"It's been a long time, Dan."

Riggs shook his hand. "It's Matt now. Dan's dead, remember, George?"

George Masters cleared his throat, looked nervously around, and motioned Riggs to sit down at the nicked-up table. After they were all seated, George Masters inclined his head toward the other man. "Lou Berman, he's heading up the investigation we discussed over the phone." Berman nodded curtly at Riggs.

Masters looked at Berman. "Dan" – Masters

paused, correcting himself – "Matt was one of the best damned undercover agents we ever had."

"Sacrificed a lot in the name of justice, didn't I, George?" Riggs eyed him evenly.

"Gave it up, too dangerous." He looked over at Berman. "George here will tell you I stayed in the ball game one inning too many. Right, George? Sort of against my will, though."

"That was all a long time ago."

"Funny, it still seems like yesterday to me."

"Goes with the territory, Matt."

"That's easy to say when you haven't watched your wife get her brains blown out because of what her husband did for a living. How's your wife by the way, George? Three kids too, right? Having kids and a wife must be nice."

"All right, Matt. I get your point. I'm sorry."

Riggs swallowed hard. He was feeling far more emotion than he had expected, but it did feel like yesterday and he had waited half a decade to say this. "It would've meant a lot more if you had said it five years ago, George."

Riggs's stare was so intense that Masters finally had to look away.

"Let's get down to it," Riggs finally said, breaking out of the past.

Masters put his elbows up on the table and glanced over at him. "FYI, I was in Charlottesville two nights ago."

"Beautiful little college town."

"Visited a couple of places. Thought I might see you."

"I'm a working man. Gotta keep busy."

Masters eyed the sling. "Accident?"

"The construction business can be very hazardous. I'm here to strike a deal, George. A mutually satisfactory deal."

454

"Do you know where LuAnn Tyler is?" Berman leaned forward, his eyes darting all over Riggs's face.

Riggs cocked his head at the other man. "I've got her down in the car, Lou, you want to go check? Here." Riggs reached in his pocket, pulled out a set of keys, and dangled them in front of the FBI agent. They were the keys to his house, but Riggs figured Berman wouldn't take him up on the offer.

"I'm not here to play games," Berman snarled.

Riggs put the keys away and leaned forward. "Neither am I. Like I said, I'm here to make a deal. You want to hear it?"

"Why should we deal? How do we know you're not working with Tyler?"

"What do you care if I am?"

Berman's face turned red. "She's a criminal."

"I worked with criminals most of my career, Lou. And who says she's a criminal?"

"The state of Georgia."

"Have you really looked at the case? I mean really looked at it. My sources say it's bullshit."

"Your sources?" Berman almost laughed.

Masters intervened. "I've looked at it, Matt. It probably *is* bullshit." He glowered over at Berman. "And even if it isn't, it's Georgia's problem, not ours."

"Right, and your interests should lie elsewhere."

Berman refused to give it up. "She's also a tax evader. She won a hundred million bucks and then disappeared for ten years and hasn't paid Uncle Sam a dime."

"I thought you were an FBI agent, not an accountant," Riggs shot back.

"Let's settle down, guys," Masters said.

Riggs leaned forward. "I thought you'd be a lot more interested in the person behind LuAnn Tyler,

455

the person behind a lot of people. The invisible guy with billions of dollars running around the planet playing games, causing havoc, making your lives miserable. Now, do you want to get to him, or do you want to talk to LuAnn Tyler about her itemized deductions?"

"What are you suggesting?"

Riggs sat back. "Just like old times, George. We reel in the big fish and let the little one go."

"I don't like it," Berman grumbled.

Riggs's eyes played over the man's features. "Based upon my experience at the Bureau, catching the big fish gets you promoted and, more important, gets you pay raises; delivering the small fry doesn't."

"Don't lecture me on the FBI, Riggs, I've been around the block a few times."

"Good, Lou, then I shouldn't have to waste time on this crap. We deliver you the man and LuAnn Tyler walks. And I mean from everything – federal, taxes, and the state of Georgia."

"We can't guarantee that, Matt. The boys at the IRS go their own way."

"Well, maybe she pays some money."

"Maybe she pays a lot of money."

"But no jail. Unless we agree on that, it's a no go. You have to make the murder charge go away."

"How about we arrest you right now and hold you until you tell us where she is?" Berman was inching forward, crowding Riggs.

"Then how about you never break the biggest case of your career. Because LuAnn Tyler will disappear again and you'll be stuck at point A again. And on what charge would you be holding me by the way?"

"Accessory," Berman fired back.

"Accessory to what?"

Berman thought for a moment. "Aiding and abetting a fugitive."

"What proof do you have of that? What actual proof do you have that I even know where she is, or have ever even met her?"

"You've been investigating her. We saw the notes in your house."

"Oh, so you came by my house on your visit to Charlottesville? You should've called ahead. I would've fixed up something nice for dinner."

"And we found lots of interesting stuff," Berman snapped.

"Good for you. Can I see the search warrant you used to enter my premises without permission?"

Berman started to say something and then clamped his mouth shut.

A thin smile broke across Riggs's face. "Great. No search warrant. All inadmissible. And since when is it a crime to make a phone call and get some *public* information on someone? Considering that I got that information from the Feds."

"Your WPP handler, not us," Berman said threateningly.

"I guess I treat all you guys as one big, happy family."

Masters started speaking slowly. "Supposing we do go along, you haven't given us the connection between Tyler and this other person."

Riggs had been expecting this question and was surprised it hadn't come up before. "He had to get the money from somewhere."

Masters considered this statement for a moment, and then his eyes flickered. "Listen, Matt, this is a little bigger than you probably know." He looked over at Berman briefly before continuing. "We know – or rather we think – the lottery was . . ." Masters paused, searching for the right words. "We believe

457

the lottery may have been compromised. Was it?"

Riggs sat back in his chair and tapped his fingers on the table. "Maybe."

Masters again chose his words carefully. "Let me make this real clear to you. The president, the A.G., the director of the FBI, they've all been apprised of this possibility. I can tell you that their collective reaction was one of absolute shock."

"Bully for them."

Masters ignored Riggs's sarcastic tone. "If the lottery was fixed, then this situation has to be handled very delicately."

Riggs chuckled. "Translation: If it ever gets out to the public, half the guys in Washington, including the president, the A.G., the director, and you two guys, will probably be looking through the want ads. So what you're suggesting is a major cover-up."

"Hey, this all probably happened ten years ago. It didn't occur on our watch," Berman said.

"Gee, Lou, that'll go over real big with John Q. Public. All of your butts are on the line here and you know it."

Masters banged his fist down on the table. "Do you realize what would happen if it becomes public that the lottery was fixed?" Masters said hotly. "Can you imagine the lawsuits, the investigations, the scandals, the blow it would give the old U.S. of A. right in the gut? It would almost be like the country defaulting on its debt. It cannot be allowed to happen. It *will not* be allowed to happen."

"So what's your suggestion, George?"

Masters rapidly calmed down and ticked off the points with his fingers. "You bring in Tyler. We question her, we get her cooperation. With that information in hand we bring in the people—"

"*Person*, George," Riggs interrupted. "There's just one of him, but let me tell you, he's a very special one."

"Okay, so with Tyler's help we nail him."

"And what happens to LuAnn Tyler?"

Masters spread his hand helplessly. "Come on, Matt, she's got a state murder warrant out. She hasn't paid taxes for almost a decade. I have to assume she was in on the lottery scam. That all adds up to a few lifetimes in prison, but I'll settle for just one, maybe half of one if she's real cooperative, but I can't guarantee it."

Riggs stood up. "Well, guys, it was nice talking to you."

Berman was up in an instant and he slid over to the door, blocking Riggs's exit.

"Lou, I've still got one good arm, and the fist attached to it is just itching like hell to plant one right across your face." Riggs started to advance menacingly toward the door.

"Wait a minute, just hold it. Both of you sit down," Masters bellowed.

Riggs and Berman engaged in a suitably lengthy stare-down and then slowly returned to their seats.

Riggs stared over at Masters. "If you think the woman's going to waltz in here so she can risk her life in order to bring this guy down and then be rewarded by spending the rest of her life in prison, then you've hung around the Bureau too long, George. Your brains are gone."

Riggs pointed a finger at him. "Let me fill you in on something. It's the game of life and it's called 'who's got the leverage.' You call up the state of Georgia and tell them that LuAnn Tyler is no longer wanted for murder there, or for anything else. If she's got a friggin' parking ticket outstanding, then it's wiped out. You understand me? Squeaky clean. Then you call up the IRS and you tell them that she'll pay what she owes, but they can forget jail time. As far as being involved in any lottery scam, if the statute of limitations hasn't already expired, then that goes away too. The tiniest infraction that could possibly put her in jail for even a second gets blotted out. Gone. She's a free person."

"Are you nuts?" Berman said.

"Or?" Masters said quietly, his eyes fixed on Riggs.

"Or, we go public with everything, George. What does she have to lose? If she's going to go to prison for life, then she's going to have to have some hobbies to fill up her days. I'm thinking appearances on *Sixty Minutes*, *Dateline*, *Prime Time Live*, maybe even *Oprah*. A book deal would probably be in the cards too. She can just talk her little heart out about the lottery being fixed, how the president and the A.G. and the FBI director wanted to cover it all up to save their jobs and how they were stupid enough to let a master criminal who's been wreaking world-wide havoc for years walk away so they could put a young woman who grew up dirt-poor in prison for doing something all of us would've done in an instant!"

Riggs sat back and looked at both men. "That, gentlemen, is what I mean by leverage."

While Masters considered this, Berman snorted. "One guy? I don't believe that. We're looking at a big organization. No way could one person do all the stuff I've been seeing on my radar screen. We haven't been able to prove anything, but we know there are multiple players."

Riggs thought back to the cottage, right before the knife sliced into his arm. He had stared right into the most deadly pair of eyes he had ever seen. Over the years working undercover in some very dangerous situations, he had been scared before; he was only human after all. But he had never before felt the nervous terror those eyes had aroused in him. If he had had a crucifix handy, he would have pulled it out to ward the guy off.

He looked at Berman. "You know, Lou, you'd be surprised. This guy is a master of disguise. He can probably play enough roles to fill a Broadway musical. And by going it alone, he never has to worry about anyone turning snitch on him or trying to cut him out."

Masters started speaking in low tones as he tried a different tack. "Remember, Matt, not so long ago, you were one of us. You might want to think about that. You've obviously gained Tyler's confidence. You bring her in, well, let's just say your government would be very grateful. No more sawing and hammering to make a living."

"Let me think about that for a second, George." Riggs closed his eyes, reopened them almost instantaneously, and said, "Go to hell."

He and Masters locked eyes. "What do you say, George? Is it a deal? Or do I go and phone Oprah?"

Slowly, almost imperceptibly, Masters nodded.

"I'd really love to hear you *say* it, George."

Berman started to cut in, but Masters stared him into silence.

"Yes, it's a deal," Masters said, "no jail."

"Georgia too?"

"Georgia too."

"You sure you can do that? I know your authority is limited there." Riggs's tone was taunting.

"Mine is, but I don't think the president of the United States has that same problem. My instructions are to avoid public exposure at all costs. I guarantee that either he or the A.G. will make that phone call."

"Good, now get the director and the attorney general in here, because I want to hear the same things from them. By the way, is the president busy today?"

461

"There's no way in hell the president is meeting with you."

"Then get the director and the A.G. in here, George. Right now."

"You don't trust my word?"

"Let's just say your track record hasn't inspired my confidence all that much. And I take comfort in numbers." He nodded at the phone. "Make the call."

Masters and Riggs stared across at each other for at least a minute. Then Masters slowly picked up the phone and spoke into it at length. It took some schedule-juggling, but within thirty minutes the director of the FBI and the attorney general of the United States were sitting across from Riggs. Riggs presented the same deal to them he had presented to Masters, and he extracted the same promises.

Riggs rose. "Thank you for your cooperation."

Berman got up too. "All right, if we're working together now, bring Tyler in, we can wire her, get a team together, and go get this 'one man crime wave.'"

"Uh-uh, Lou. The deal was *I'd* bring him in, not the FBI."

Berman looked ready to explode. "Listen you—"

"Shut up, Lou!" The FBI director's eyes bored into him and then he turned to look at Riggs. "You really think you can pull this off?"

Riggs smiled. "Have I ever let you guys down before?" He glanced over at Masters.

Masters didn't return the smile, but just continued to study Riggs's face. "If you don't, all bets are off. For Tyler." He paused and then added ominously, "And you. Your cover's blown. And I'm not sure how much incentive we'd have to reestablish it. And your enemies are still plenty active."

Riggs walked across the room to the door, but then turned back. "Well, George, I never really

462

expected anything less from you guys. Oh, and don't try to have me followed. That'll just piss me off and waste a lot of time. Okay?"

Masters nodded quickly. "Sure, don't sweat it."

The big-voiced attorney general asked a final question. "Was the lottery fixed, Mr. Riggs?"

Riggs looked back at her. "You bet it was. And you want to know the kicker? It looks like the United States Lottery was used to finance the plans of one of the most dangerous psychopaths I've personally ever seen. I truly hope this never makes it on to the six o'clock news." His eyes swept the room taking in the steadily rising panic in each of their faces. "Have a good day." Riggs closed the door behind him.

The rest of the group looked around at each other. "Holy shit," was all the director could say, his head swaying from side to side.

Masters picked up the phone and spoke into it. "He's leaving the building now. He'll know he's being followed. Make it a short leash, but give him some room. He's an expert at this stuff, so he'll take you for a waltz around the city and then try to lose you. Be alert! When he hooks up with Tyler, communicate with me immediately. Keep them under surveillance, but don't approach them." He looked over at the A.G., who nodded her assent. Masters hung up the phone and took a deep breath.

"Do you believe Riggs's story that it's only one man behind all this?" the director asked, looking nervously at Masters.

"It sounds incredible, but I hope to God it's true," said Masters. "I'd rather be dealing with one guy than some worldwide crime syndicate." The A.G. and director both nodded in agreement.

Berman looked around with questioning eyes. "So what's the plan here?"

The director cleared his throat heavily and said,

"We can't ever let this come out, you all know that. No matter what happens. No matter who gets hurt. Even if Riggs is successful and we are able to apprehend this person and any others involved in the scheme, then we still face a major problem."

The A.G. folded her arms across her chest and picked up this line of thought. "Even if we can build a case against him on all the other activities this person will know he has 'leverage,' to use Riggs's terms. And he'll use the same threat Riggs used. Deal with him or he goes public. I can just see his defense lawyer salivating over that one." She involuntarily shuddered.

"So what you're saying is this thing can never go to trial," Berman said. "What then?"

The A.G. ignored the question and instead asked Masters, "You think Riggs is playing straight with us?"

Masters shrugged. "He was one of the best at undercover operations. To do that you have to lie on a regular basis and appear not to be. Truth takes a backseat. Sometimes reality becomes blurred. And old habits die hard."

"Meaning we can't completely trust him," the A.G. said.

Masters looked thoughtful for a moment. "No more than he can trust us."

"Well," the director said, "there's the strong possibility that we won't bring this guy in alive." He looked around the room. "Right?"

They all nodded. Masters ventured, "If he's half as dangerous as Riggs says he is, I'd shoot first and ask no questions later. Then maybe our problem goes away."

"And what about Riggs and Tyler?" the A.G. asked.

Berman answered, "Well, if we're going to go that

route, you never know who might get caught in the crossfire. I mean none of us wants that to happen, of course," he quickly added, "but like Riggs's wife, you know, innocent people sometimes die."

"Tyler is hardly innocent!" the director said angrily.

"That's right," Masters said. "And if Riggs is tying his allegiances to her instead of us, well then he has to accept the consequences. Whatever they may be."

All of them looked at each other uneasily. Under normal circumstances, none of them would have been remotely contemplating any of this. They had dedicated their lives to apprehending criminals and then seeing them receive a fair trial before a court of law for their offenses. Their now silently praying that justice wouldn't happen this time, that instead several human beings would die before a judge or jury ever heard their case, was not sitting well with any of them. However, in this present case, they were all confronted with something much larger than merely hunting down a criminal. Here the truth was far more dangerous.

"Whatever the consequences may be," the director quietly repeated.

FIFTY

Walking down the street, Riggs looked at his watch. The clock housing was actually a sophisticated recording device; the tiny perforations in the leather strap were the speaker component. The day before, he had spent some time in a well-known "spy shop" four blocks from the FBI building. The technology had certainly gotten better over the years. At least his deal with the government was recorded somewhere other than in his memory. With operations like this, he shouldn't put too much faith in anyone, no matter which side he was on.

Riggs knew that the government could never allow the truth to come out. In this case capturing the criminal alive was just as bad as not capturing him, maybe worse. And anyone who knew the truth was in serious jeopardy, and not just from Jackson. Riggs knew that the FBI would never intentionally gun down an innocent person. But he knew the FBI hardly regarded LuAnn as innocent. And since Riggs had thrown his support her way, he was automatically lumped with her as the enemy. If it got dicey toward the end, which Riggs knew it would, and if LuAnn were anywhere near Jackson, well, the FBI might not be real careful about who they were firing at. Riggs didn't expect Jackson to go down quietly. He would take out as many agents as he could. Riggs had seen that in his eyes at the cottage. The man had no respect for human life. To him a person was merely a factor to be manipulated and eliminated if circumstances called for it. As an undercover agent, Riggs had dealt with people like that for years. People almost as dangerous as Jackson. Given those elements, the FBI would err on the side of killing the man rather than taking him alive; they wouldn't risk the life of an agent in order to ensure that the man would stand trial. Riggs was well aware that the government had no incentive to bring Jackson to trial and every incentive not to. So Riggs's job was to flush out Jackson and then the Feds could do what they wanted. If that was pumping the man full of lead, Riggs would be glad to help them do so. But he was going to keep LuAnn as far away from the man as humanly possible. She was not going to be caught in the crossfire. He had been through that once. History was not going to repeat itself.

Riggs didn't bother to look behind him. He knew he was already under surveillance. Despite Masters's assurances to the contrary, he would have immediately ordered a tail. Riggs would've done the same thing in his position. Now he had to beat the trail before meeting up with LuAnn. He smiled. Just like old times.

While Riggs had been dealing with the FBI, LuAnn had driven to another pay phone and dialed a certain phone number. It rang several times and LuAnn thought she would probably get the standard automated message. Then a voice answered. She could barely recognize it, the connection was so bad.

"Charlie?"

"LuAnn?"

"Where are you?"

"On the road. I can barely hear you. Hold on, I'm passing some power lines."

In a moment, the connection was much clearer.

"That's better," LuAnn said.

"Hang on, there's someone who wants to talk to you."

"Mom?"

"Hello, baby."

"Are you okay?"

"I'm fine, sweetie, I told you Mommy would be fine."

"Uncle Charlie said you and Mr. Riggs saw each other."

"That's right. He's helping me. With things."

"I'm glad you're not alone. I miss you."

"I miss you too, Lisa, I can't tell you how much."

"Can we come home soon?"

Home? Where was home now? "I think so, baby. Mommy's working really hard on that right now."

"I love you."

"Oh, sweetie, I love you too."

"Here's Uncle Charlie."

"Lisa?"

"Yes?"

"I mean to keep my promise to you. I'm going to tell you everything. The truth. Okay?"

The voice was small, a little scared. "All right, Mom."

When Charlie came back on the phone, LuAnn told him to just listen. She filled him in on the latest events including Riggs's plan and his real background.

Charlie could barely contain himself. "I'm pulling over at a rest stop in two minutes. Call me back."

When LuAnn did so, Charlie's tone was heated. "Are you crazy?"

"Where's Lisa?"

"In the rest room."

"Is it safe?"

468

"I'm right outside the door and the place is packed with families. Now answer my question."

"No, I don't think I'm crazy."

"You let Riggs, an ex-FBI agent, walk into the Hoover Building and cut a deal for you. How in hell do you know he's not selling you down the river right now?"

"I trust him."

"Trust him?" Charlie's face turned crimson. "You barely know him. LuAnn, this is a big mistake, darling. A damned big one."

"I don't think so. Riggs is playing straight. I know he is. I've learned some things about him in the last few days."

"Like he's an experienced undercover agent who's an expert at lying."

LuAnn blinked for a second as these words sunk in. A small seed of doubt suddenly grew, invading her confidence in Matthew Riggs.

"LuAnn, are you there?"

She gripped the phone hard. "Yes. Well, if he did sell me down the river, it won't be long before I find out."

"You've got to get out of there. You said you've got the car. Get the hell out of there."

"Charlie, he saved my life. Jackson almost killed him while he was trying to help me."

Charlie was silent for a moment. He was having an internal conflict and was highly uncomfortable with it. From everything LuAnn had just told him, Riggs probably was going to bat for her. Charlie thought he knew why: The man was in love with her. Was LuAnn in love with him? Why shouldn't she be? And where did that leave him? The fact was, Charlie wanted Riggs to be lying. He wanted the man out of their lives. That thought was skewing his whole mental process. But Charlie did love LuAnn.

And he loved Lisa too. He had always put his own interests behind theirs. And with that thought his inner conflict disappeared. "LuAnn, I'll go with your instincts. Riggs is probably okay, now that I think about it. Just keep your eyes open, will you?"

"I will, Charlie. Where are you?"

"We headed through West Virginia, then into Kentucky, skirted the edge of Tennessee, and now we're floating back toward Virginia."

"I've gotta go now. I'll call later today and fill you in."

"I hope the rest of today isn't as exciting as the last two were."

"You and me both. Thanks, Charlie."

"For what? I haven't done anything."

"Now who's lying?"

"Take care of yourself."

LuAnn hung up the phone. She would be meeting Riggs soon if everything went according to plan. As she walked back to the car, Charlie's initial reaction came back to her. Could she trust Riggs? She slid into the front seat of the Honda. She had left it running because she had no keys and didn't share Riggs's skills at hot-wiring automobiles. She was about to put the car in gear when her hand stopped. This was no time for doubts, and yet she was suddenly overwhelmed with them. Her hand refused to move.

FIFTY-ONE

Riggs walked slowly down Ninth Street, looking casually around, as if he had all the time in the world. A gust of freezing air hit him. He stopped, gingerly slipped off the sling, and put his injured arm in the sleeve of his overcoat, buttoning it all the way up. As the bitter wind continued to blow down the street, Riggs pulled up the collar of his overcoat, took a knit cap emblazoned with the Washington Redskins logo from his pocket, and pulled it tightly over his head so that only the lower part of his reddening face was visible. He entered a corner convenience store.

The two teams of agents that were following him, one on foot, the other in a gray Ford, swiftly moved into position. One team covered the front of the store, the other the rear. They knew Riggs was an experienced undercover agent and they weren't taking any chances.

Riggs appeared carrying a newspaper under his arm, walked down the street, and hailed a taxi. The agents quickly climbed into the sedan, and it followed the taxi.

Moments after the sedan disappeared, the real Matt Riggs, wearing a dark felt cap, emerged from the store and walked quickly in the opposite direction. The key had been the brightly colored knit cap. His pursuers would have focused on the burgundy and gold colors like a ship's beacon to pinpoint their man and would not notice the subtle

471

differences in the overcoats, pants, and shoes. He had called in a favor last night from an old friend who had thought Riggs long dead. The FBI was now tailing that old friend to his job at a law firm near the White House. The man lived near the FBI building, so his being in the vicinity would not be difficult to explain. And a lot of Washingtonians wore Redskins knit caps this time of year. Finally, the FBI couldn't possibly know of the long ago connection between the two men. The agents would question him briefly, realize their mistake, report back to Masters and the director, and get their heads handed to them for their morning troubles.

Riggs climbed in a cab and gave an address. The car sped off. He ran a hand through his hair. He was glad to get that one under his belt. He and LuAnn were a long way from being home free, but it felt good to know he still had it, at least in small doses. As the cab stopped at a red light, Riggs opened the newspaper he had purchased at the store.

Staring back at him from the front page were two photos. One person he knew, the other was a stranger to him. He quickly read the story and then looked at the pictures again. With a press badge dangling around his neck and a small notepad and pen peeking out from his shirt pocket, a sleepy-eyed Thomas Donovan looked like he had just climbed off a plane from covering some major news event on the other side of the world.

The woman in the photo next to him could not have struck a greater contrast to the reporter's disheveled image. The dress was elegant, the hair and makeup obviously professionally done and thus impeccable, the background almost surreal in its abundant luxury: a charity event where the rich and famous caucused to raise money for the less fortunate. Roberta Reynolds had been a longtime participant in such events and the story said her brutal murder had robbed the Washington area's charitable community of a great benefactor. Only one line of the story recounted the source of Reynolds's wealth: a sixty-five-million-dollar lottery win ten years earlier. She was apparently worth far more than that now. Or, at least, now her estate was.

She had been murdered – allegedly, the story reported, by one Thomas Donovan. he had been seen around the woman's home. A message from Donovan requesting an interview was on the dead woman's answering machine. Donovan's prints had been found on a carafe of water and a glass in Reynolds's home, which indicated the two had indeed met. And, finally, the pistol apparently used to slaughter Roberta Reynolds had been found in a wooded area about a mile from her home, along with her Mercedes, with Donovan's prints all over both of them. The murdered woman had been discovered lying on her bed. Evidence indicated she had been bound and held for some period of time, so that the crime was obviously premeditated, the paper said. There was an APB out on Donovan and the police were confident they would soon apprehend him.

Riggs finished reading the story and slowly folded up the newspaper. He knew the police were completely wrong. Donovan hadn't killed Reynolds. And it was highly likely that Donovan was dead as well. Riggs took a deep breath and thought about how he would break the news to LuAnn.

FIFTY-TWO

The burly man looked around at the other pricey homes in the Georgetown neighborhood. Fiftyish with pale skin and a neatly trimmed mustache, the man hitched up his pants, tucked his shirt in, and rang the bell to the front door.

Alicia Crane opened the door, looking anxious and tired.

"Yes?"

"Alicia Crane?"

"Yes."

The man flashed his identification. "Hank Rollins, homicide detective, Fairfax County, Virginia."

Alicia stared at the man's photo and the badge affixed to it. "I'm not sure—"

"Are you an acquaintance of Thomas Donovan?"

Alicia closed her eyes and bit her lip on the inside. When she reopened her eyes she said, "Yes."

Rollins rubbed his hands together. "Ma'am, I've got some questions to ask you. We can either do it down at the station or you can ask me in before I freeze to death, it's your call."

Alicia immediately opened the door. "Of course, I'm sorry." She led him down the hallway to the living room. After settling him down on the sofa she asked him if he wanted coffee.

"That'd be great, yes, ma'am."

As soon as she left the room, Rollins lurched to his feet and looked around the room. One item commanded his immediate attention. The photo of Donovan, his arm around Alicia Crane. It looked to be of recent vintage. They both looked extremely happy.

Rollins was holding the photo in his hands when Alicia walked back in carrying a tray with two cups of coffee and some creamer and two blue packets of Equal.

She lowered the tray to the coffee table. "I couldn't find the sugar. The housekeeper ran an errand. She'll be back in about an hour and I don't usually—" Her eyes caught the photo.

"May I have that?" she asked. She set down the tray and held out her hand.

Rollins quickly passed the photo over and returned to his seat. "I'll get to the point, Ms. Crane. You've read the newspaper, I assume?"

"You mean that pack of lies." Her eyes flashed for an instant.

"Well, I'll agree that it's all largely speculation at this time; however, there's a lot of things pointing toward Thomas Donovan having killed Roberta Reynolds."

"His fingerprints and his gun?"

"It's an active homicide investigation, Ms. Crane, so I can't really go into it with you, but, yes, things like that."

"Thomas wouldn't hurt anyone."

Rollins shifted his bulk around, picked up a cup of coffee, and stirred some cream into it. He tasted the result and then poured the contents of an Equal pack into the cup before he resumed speaking. "But he did go visit Roberta Reynolds."

Alicia crossed her arms and glared at him. "Did he?"

"He never mentioned it to you, that he was going to meet with her?"

"He told me nothing."

Rollins pondered this for a moment. "Ma'am, we got your name off Donovan's answering machine at his apartment. You sounded upset, said what he was working on was dangerous." Alicia didn't take the bait. "Also his place had been ransacked, all his records, files, everything gone."

Alicia started to shake, finally steadying herself by grasping the arm of the chair she was sitting in.

"Ms. Crane, you might want to have some of that coffee. You don't look too good."

"I'm all right." However, she did raise the cup and take several nervous sips.

"Well, if, as you say, someone went through Thomas's apartment, then there must be someone else involved. You should focus your efforts on apprehending that person."

"I'm not arguing with you on that point, but I have to have something to go on. I guess I don't have to tell you that Ms. Reynolds was a very prominent member of the community and we're getting a lot of heat to find her killer, pronto. Now I've already talked to someone at the *Trib*. He told me Donovan was working on a story having to do with lottery winners. And Roberta Reynolds was one of those winners. Now, I'm not a reporter, but when you're talking that kind of money, maybe somebody would have a motive for murder."

Alicia smiled for an instant.

"Something you want to tell me?"

Alicia returned to her prim manner and shook her head.

"Ms. Crane, I've been working homicide since my youngest was born and now he's got his own kids. Don't take this the wrong way, but you're holding out on me and I'd like to know why. Murder isn't something you want to screw around with." He looked at the elegant room. "Murderers and those

476

who *assist* murderers don't end up in places nearly as nice as this one."

Alicia's eyes bulged at him. "What are you implying?"

"I'm not implying a damn thing. I came here looking for facts. I listened to your voice on Donovan's answering machine. That voice told me two things: First, you were scared for him; second, you knew exactly why you were scared for him."

Alicia kneaded and kneaded her lap with her fisted hands. She closed and opened her eyes several times. Rollins waited patiently while she went through her decision-making process.

When she started speaking it was in quick bursts. Rollins whipped out his notebook and scribbled.

"Thomas had initially started investigating the lottery because he was convinced that several top money management firms were taking the winners' money and either losing it or charging such huge commissions, churning, he called it, that the winners were left with nothing. He also hated the government for, in essence, leaving these poor people exposed to all of that. And then so many of them not understanding how to handle their taxes, and then the IRS coming in and taking everything back. And more. Leaving them with nothing."

"How did he arrive at that conclusion?"

"Bankruptcies," she said simply. "All these people were winning all this money and then they were declaring bankruptcy."

Rollins scratched his head. "Well, I've read about that from time to time. I always chalked it up to the winners' not being money savvy. You know, spend everything they get, forget to pay taxes, that kind of stuff, like you said. Pretty soon, you can work your way right through all those winnings. Hell, I'd probably do the same thing, just go nuts."

"Well, Thomas didn't think that was all there was to it. But then he discovered something else." She took another sip of coffee, her face coloring prettily as she recalled Thomas Donovan's cleverness.

"Which was?" Rollins prodded.

"Which was the fact that twelve lottery winners in a row didn't declare bankruptcy."

"So?"

"So Thomas's research went back many years. In all that time the ratio of winners to bankrupt was completely consistent. Then, right in the middle of this consistency were twelve who didn't. Not only didn't they declare bankruptcy but they grew far wealthier."

Rollins rubbed his chin, unconvinced. "I'm still not seeing a story here."

"Thomas wasn't clear in his mind about that yet. But he was getting closer. He called me regularly from the road to let me know how things were going, what he had found out. That's why I was so worried when I hadn't heard from him."

Rollins looked at his notebook. "Right. You mentioned danger in your phone message."

"Thomas tracked down one of the twelve lottery winners." Alicia paused and struggled to remember the name. "LuAnn somebody. Tyler, that's right, LuAnn Tyler. He said she was charged with murdering somebody right before she won the lottery and then she disappeared. He tracked her down, partly through her tax records. He went to visit her."

"Now, where was this?" Rollins was again scribbling in his notebook.

"Charlottesville. Lovely country, some of the most beautiful estates. Have you ever been?"

"On my salary, I'm not really into estate shopping. What next?"

"He confronted the woman."

"And?"

"And she cracked. Or almost did. Thomas said you can always tell by the eyes."

"Uh-huh." Rollins rolled his own eyes. "So what was Donovan's angle?"

"Excuse me?"

"His angle. What story was he going to write that you thought put him in danger?"

"Oh, well, the woman was a murderer. She had killed once, she could kill again."

Rollins smiled lightly. "I see."

"I don't think you're taking this seriously."

"I take my work very seriously. I just don't see the connection. Are you suggesting that this LuAnn person killed Roberta Reynolds? Why would she do that? We don't even know if they knew each other. Are you suggesting that she may have threatened Donovan?"

"I'm not suggesting that LuAnn Tyler threatened or murdered anyone. I mean I have no proof of that."

"Then what?" Rollins was struggling to maintain his patience.

Alicia looked away. "I . . . I don't know. I mean I'm not sure."

Rollins stood up, closing his notebook. "Well, if I need any more information I'll be in touch."

Alicia just sat there, her face pale, her eyes shut. Rollins was almost at the door when she spoke. "The lottery was fixed."

Rollins slowly turned and walked back into the living room. "Fixed?"

"He called two days ago and told me that. Thomas made me promise not to breathe a word to anyone." She clutched at the hem of her skirt in anxiety. "That LuAnn Tyler person practically admitted that the lottery was fixed. Thomas sounded, well, he sounded a little frightened. And now, I'm just so worried about him. He was supposed to call again, but never did."

Rollins parked his bulk on the sofa once more. "What else did he tell you?"

"That he had contacted the other eleven winners, but that only one had called him back." Her lips trembled. "Roberta Reynolds."

"So Donovan did meet with her." His tone was accusatory.

Alicia rubbed a tear from her eye. She didn't speak but merely shook her head. Finally she said, "He had been working on this story for a long time, but he only recently confided in me. He was scared. I could tell in his voice." She cleared her throat. "He had at least arranged to meet with Roberta Reynolds. The meeting was to take place yesterday morning. I haven't heard from him since that time, and he'd promised to call me right after it was over. Oh, God, I know something terrible has happened."

"Did he tell you who fixed the lottery?"

"No, but LuAnn Tyler told him to watch out for somebody. A man. That this person would kill him, that he was on Thomas's trail and would find him. That he was very dangerous. I'm sure this person had something to do with that woman's death."

Rollins sat back and stared sadly at her and took a big gulp of the hot coffee.

Alicia didn't look up. "I told Thomas to go to the police with what he knew."

Rollins sat forward. "Did he?"

She shook her head fiercely. "Dammit no!" A huge breath escaped her lungs. "I pleaded with him to. If someone had fixed the lottery, all that money. I mean people would kill for that. You're a policeman, aren't I right about that?"

"I know people who'd cut your heart out for a couple of singles," was Rollins's chilling reply. He looked down at his empty coffee cup. "Got any more?"

Alicia started. "What? Oh, yes, I just made a fresh pot."

Rollins took out his notepad again. "Okay, when you get back, we'll have to go over every detail and then I'm calling in some reinforcements. I'm not afraid to admit that this one is looking like it's way over my head. You up for a trip to police head-quarters?"

Alicia nodded without much enthusiasm and left the room. She came back a couple of minutes later balancing the wooden tray, her eyes focused on the filled coffee cups, trying not to spill them. When she looked up her eyes widened in utter disbelief and she dropped the entire tray on the floor.

"Peter?"

The remnants of Detective Rollins – wig, mustache, facial mask, and malleable rubber pad-ding – were neatly positioned on the wingback chair. Jackson, or Peter Crane, Alicia Crane's elder brother, was looking back at her, his features infinitely troubled as his right cheek rested on his right palm.

Donovan's observation that Bobbie Jo Reynolds had looked a lot like Alicia Crane was right on the mark. However, it had been Peter Crane's alias, Jackson, disguised as Bobbie Jo Reynolds, who looked a lot like Alicia Crane. The family resem-blance was remarkable.

"Hello, Alicia."

She stared at the discarded disguise. "What are you doing? What is all this?"

"I think you should sit down. Would you like me to clean up that mess?"

"Don't touch it." She put one hand against the doorjamb to steady herself.

"I didn't mean to upset you so," said Jackson with

sudden sincere remorse. "I . . . I guess when faced with confrontation, I'm just more comfortable not being myself." He smiled weakly.

"I don't appreciate this at all. I almost had a heart attack."

He rose quickly, encircled her waist with one of his arms, and guided her over to the sofa. He patted her hand kindly. "I'm sorry, Alicia, I really am."

Alicia again stared over at the remains of the beefy homicide detective. "What is this all about, Peter? Why were you asking me all those questions?"

"Well, I needed to know how much you knew about everything. I needed to know what Donovan had told you."

She jerked her hand from under his. "Thomas? How do you know about Thomas? I haven't seen or spoken to you in three years."

"Has it been that long?" he said evasively. "You don't need anything, do you? You just had to ask."

"Your checks come like clockwork," she said, a bit bitterly. "I don't need any more money. It would have been nice to have seen you once in a while. I know you're very busy, but we are family."

"I know." He looked down for a moment. "I always said I would take care of you. And I always will. Family is family."

"Speaking of, I spoke with Roger the other day."

"And how is our decadent, undeserving younger brother?"

"He needed money, like always."

"I hope you didn't send him any. I gave him enough to last a lifetime, even invested it for him. All he had to do was stay within a reasonable budget."

"There's nothing reasonable about Roger, you know that." She looked at him a little nervously. "I sent him some money." Jackson started to say something, but she hurried on. "I know what you

482

said all those years ago, but I just couldn't let him be thrown out on the street."

"Why not? It might be the best thing that ever happened to him. He shouldn't live in New York. It's too expensive."

"He wouldn't survive. He's not strong, not like Father."

Jackson held his tongue at the mention of their father. The years had not cleared up his sister's blindness in that regard. "Forget it, I'm not going to waste my time discussing Roger."

"I want you to tell me what's going on, Peter."

"When did you meet Donovan?"

"Why?"

"Please just answer the question."

"Almost a year ago. He did a lengthy piece on Father and his distinguished career in the senate. It was a wonderful, compelling testimonial."

Jackson shook his head in disbelief. She would have viewed it that way: the exact opposite of the truth.

"So I called Thomas up to thank him. We had lunch and then dinner and, well, it's been wonderful. Extraordinarily wonderful. Thomas is a noble man with a noble purpose in life."

"Like Father?" Jackson's mouth curled into a smirk.

"Very much like him," she said indignantly.

"It's truly a small world." He shook his head at the irony.

"Why do you say that?"

Jackson stood up and spread his arms to show the entire sweep of the room. "Alicia, where exactly do you think all of this came from?"

"Why, from the family money, of course."

"The family money? That was gone. All of it. Has been for years."

"What are you talking about? I know that Father

483

ran into some financial difficulties along the way, but he recovered. He always did."

Jackson looked at her with contempt. "He recovered shit, Alicia. He didn't earn a dime of it. It was all made long before he was around. All he did was blow it. My inheritance, your inheritance. He pissed it away on himself and his lousy dreams of greatness. He was a fake and a loser."

She jumped up and slapped his face. "How dare you! Everything you have is because of him."

Jackson slowly rubbed his skin where she had hit him. His real skin was pale, smooth as though he had lived his life in a temple like a Buddhist monk, which in one sense he had.

"Ten years ago, *I* fixed the national lottery," he said quietly, his dark eyes glittery as he stared at her small, stunned face. "All that money, everything you have came from that money. From me. Not dear old Dad."

"What do you mean? How could you—"

Jackson pushed her down on the sofa as he interrupted.

"I collected almost one billion dollars from twelve lottery winners, the very same ones Donovan was investigating. I took their winnings and I invested the money. You remember Grandfather's network of Wall Street elite? He actually *earned* his money. I maintained those contacts over the years for a very specific purpose. With the fortune I amassed from the lottery winners, which Wall Street assumed came from the 'family money,' I was one of their preferred customers. I negotiated the best deals, was given first choice of all the initial public offerings, the sure-fire winners. That's a well-kept secret of the rich, Alicia. They get first dibs on everything: A stock that I get at ten dollars a share right before it hits the market goes to seventy dollars a share in the twenty-four hours after it hits the market. I sell it to the ordinary folks, collect my six hundred percent return, and move on to the next windfall. It was like printing money; it's all in who you know and what you bring to the table. When you bring a billion dollars, believe me, everybody sits up and takes notice. The rich get richer and the poor never will."

Alicia's lips had begun trembling halfway through her brother's explanation, as his speech and mannerisms grew more and more intense, more and more feverish. "Where is Thomas?" Her question was barely audible.

Jackson looked away and licked his dry lips. "He was no good for you, Alicia. No good at all. An opportunist. And I'm sure he loved all of this. All that you had. All that I had given you."

"*Was? Was* no good?" Alicia stood up, her hands clamped so tightly together the skin looked boiled.

"Where is he? What have you done to him?"

Jackson stared at her, searching her features for something. It suddenly occurred to him that he was looking for some redeeming quality. From afar he had long held idyllic visions of his only sister, putting her perhaps on a pedestal. Face-to-face with her he found that image was unsustainable. The tone of his response was casual, his words far from casual, as he finally made up his mind.

"I killed him, Alicia."

She stood there frozen for an instant and then started toppling to the floor. He grabbed her and laid her on the couch, this time not so gently. "Now don't be this way. There will be other men. I can assure you of that. You can walk the earth searching for Father. Donovan wasn't him, but I'm sure you'll keep trying." He didn't try to hide the sarcasm.

She wasn't listening to him, however. The tears stained her cheeks.

485

He continued despite her tears, pacing in front of her, the professor in front of his class of one. "You'll have to leave the country, Alicia. I erased your phone message to Donovan, so the police won't have that to go on. However, since your relationship has endured for a year, it must be well known to others. The police will come calling at some point. I'll make all the arrangements. As I recall, you've always loved New Zealand. Or perhaps Austria. We had several lovely times there as children."

"Stop it! Stop it, you animal."

He turned to find her on her feet.

"Alicia—"

"I'm not going anywhere."

"Let me be quite clear. You know too much. The police will ask questions. You have no experience in these matters. They will get the truth from you quite easily."

"You're right about that. I intend to call them right now and tell them everything."

She started for the phone, but he blocked her way. "Alicia, be reasonable."

She hit him with her fists as violently as she could. They did no physical damage to him; however, the blows conjured up the memory of another violent confrontation with another family member. His father, back then, had been physically stronger than he, was able to dominate him in ways that Jackson had never let himself be dominated since.

"I loved him, damn you! I loved Thomas," Alicia shrieked in his face.

Jackson focused a pair of watery eyes upon her. "I loved someone too," he said. "Someone who should have loved me back, respected me, but who didn't." Despite the years of pain, of guilt and embarrassment, Jack's son still held long-buried feelings for the old man. Feelings that he had never dwelt upon or vocalized until now. The resurgence of this emotional maelstrom had a violent impact on him.

He grabbed her by the shoulders and threw her roughly on the sofa.

"Peter—"

"Shut up, Alicia." He sat down next to her. "You're leaving the country. You are not going to call the police. Do you understand?"

"You're crazy, you're insane. Oh, God, I don't believe this is happening."

"Actually, right now, I'm absolutely certain I'm the most rational member in the family." He stared into her eyes and repeated the words very slowly. "You're not talking to anyone, Alicia, do you understand?"

She looked at his eyes and suddenly shivered to the depths of her soul. For the first time during this confrontation, terror had suddenly replaced her anger. It had been a long time since she had seen her brother. The boy she had happily romped with, and whose maturity and intelligence she had been fascinated by, was now unrecognizable to her. The man across from her was not her brother. This manifestation was something else altogether.

She hastily changed course and spoke as calmly as she could. "Yes, Peter, I understand. I . . . I'll pack tonight."

Jackson's face took on a level of despair that it had not carried for many years. He had read her thoughts, her fears; they were so plainly written on the thin parchment of her soft features. His fingers clutched the large throw pillow on the sofa between them.

"Where would you like to go, Alicia?"

"Anywhere, Peter, anywhere you say. New Zealand, you mentioned New Zealand. That would be fine."

"It is a beautiful country. Or Austria, as I said, we had good times there, didn't we?" He tightened his grip on the pillow. "Didn't we?" he asked again.

"Yes we did." Her eyes dipped to follow his movements and she tried to swallow but her throat was too dry. "Perhaps I could travel there first and then on to New Zealand."

"And not a word to the police? You promise?" He lifted up the pillow.

Her chin trembled uncontrollably as she watched the pillow come toward her. "Peter. Please. Please don't."

His words were stated very precisely. "My name is Jackson, Alicia. Peter Crane doesn't live here anymore."

With a sudden pounce, he pushed her flat against the couch, the pillow completely covering her face. She fought hard, kicking, scratching, gyrating her body, but she was so small, so weak; he barely felt her fighting for her life. He had spent so many years making his body hard as rock; she had spent that time waiting for a precise replica of her father to stride gallantly into her life, her muscles and her mind growing soft in the process.

Soon, it was over. As he watched, the violent movements diminished quickly and then stopped altogether. Her pale right arm slid down to her side and then dangled off the couch. He removed the pillow and forced himself to look down at her. She at least deserved that. The mouth was partially open, the eyes wide and staring. He quickly closed them and sat there with her, patting her hand gently. He did not try to hold back his own tears. That would've done no good. He struggled to remember the last time he had cried but couldn't. How healthy was it when you couldn't even recall?

He placed her arms across her chest but then

decided to have them clasped at her waist instead. He carefully lifted her legs up on the sofa and put the pillow he had used to kill her under her head, arranging her pretty hair so that it swept out evenly over the pillow. He thought she was very lovely in death despite the utter stillness. There was a peace there, a serenity that was at least heartening to him, as though what he had just done wasn't all that terrible.

He hesitated for a moment and then went ahead: He checked her pulse and laid her hand back down. If she'd still been alive, then he would've left the room, fled the country, and left it at that. He wouldn't have touched her like that again. She was family after all. But she was dead. He rose and looked down at her one last time.

It needn't have ended this way. Now all the family he had left was the useless Roger. He should go kill his brother right now. It should have been him lying there, not his cherished Alicia. However, Roger wasn't worth the effort. He froze for an instant as an idea occurred to him. Perhaps his brother could play a supporting role in this production. He would call Roger and make him an offer. An offer he knew his younger brother would be unable to resist as it would be all cash; the most potent drug in existence.

He gathered up the elements of his disguise, and methodically reapplied them, all the time making little darting glances at his dead sister. He had coated his hands with a lacquer-like substance, so he wasn't concerned about leaving fingerprints. He left by the back door. They would find her soon enough. Alicia had said her housekeeper had gone out to run an errand. It was a better than even chance that the police would think Thomas Donovan had continued his homicidal rampage by murdering his lady friend, Alicia Morgan Crane. Her obituary would be extensive, her family had been very important; there would be much to write about. And at some point, Jackson would have to come back, as himself once more, to bury her. Roger could hardly be trusted to do that. *I am sorry, Alicia. It shouldn't have come to this.* This unexpected turn of events had come closer than anything he could remember to completely immobilizing him. Above all else he cherished complete control and it suddenly had been stripped from him. He looked down at his hands, the instruments of his sister's death. His sister. Even now his legs felt rubbery, his body not in sync with his mind.

As he walked down the street, still reeling from what he had just done, Jackson's mental energies finally were able to focus on the one person he clearly saw as responsible for all of it.

LuAnn Tyler would experience the brunt of everything he was now feeling. The pain that slashed so viciously through him would be multiplied a hundredfold upon her until she would beg him to just finish her, make her stop breathing because every breath would be a hell, would be beyond what any person could endure. Even her.

And the grand part of it all was that he would not have to go looking for her. She would come to him. She would run to him with all the speed and strength her extraordinary physical specimen of a body could inspire. For he would have something that LuAnn would go anywhere, do anything for. He would hold something that LuAnn Tyler would die for. *And so you will LuAnn Tyler slash Catherine Savage.* As he disappeared down the street he swore this, over the mental image of a still-warm body whose dear face strongly resembled his own.

FIFTY-THREE

For the tenth time Riggs looked around the Mall and then checked his watch. In cutting his deal with the FBI, he had just shimmied out on to the most fragile limb in the world and LuAnn was three hours late. If she never showed up, where did that leave him? Jackson was still out there, and Riggs doubted if the knife would miss its mark a second time. If he didn't produce Jackson, fulfill his deal with his former employer, and have his cover reestablished, the cartel members who had sworn to kill him five years ago would soon learn that he was alive and they would surely try again. He couldn't return to his house. His business was probably already going to hell, and to top it off, he had five bucks in his pocket and no car. If he could have screwed up his life to any greater degree he was at a loss as to how.

He slumped on a bench and stared up at the Washington Monument while the cold wind whipped up and down the flat, open space that stretched from the Lincoln Memorial to the United States Capitol. The sky was overcast; it would be raining again soon. You could smell it in the air. Just wonderful. *And you're right between a rock and a hard place, Mr. Riggs*, he said to himself. His emotional barometer had dropped to its lowest point since finding out his wife had perished in the gang attack five years ago. Had it really been less than one week ago that he had been leading a relatively normal life?

Building things for wealthy people, reading books by his woodstove, attending a few night classes at the university, thinking seriously about taking a real vacation for a change?

He blew on his cold fingers and stuffed them in his pockets. His injured shoulder ached. He was just about to leave when the hand touched his neck.

"I'm sorry."

As he turned his head, his spirits soared with such swiftness that he felt dizzy. But he couldn't help smiling. He needed desperately to smile.

"Sorry for what?"

He watched as LuAnn settled in beside him, slipping her arm through his. She didn't answer right away. After staring off for a minute and then taking a heavy breath, she turned to him, stroked his hand with hers.

"I had some misgivings."

"About me?"

"I shouldn't have. After all you've done, I shouldn't have any doubts left."

He looked at her kindly. "Sure you should. Everybody has doubts. After the last ten years, you should have more than most." He patted her hand, looked into her eyes, noted their moist edges, and then said, "But you're here now. You came. So it must be okay, right? I passed the test?"

She simply nodded her head, unable to speak.

"I vote for finding a warm place where I can fill you in on developments and we can discuss our plan of attack. Sound good?"

"I'm all yours." Her grip tightened on his hand as though she would never let go. And right now, that was just fine with him.

They ditched the Honda, which was acting up, and rented a sedan. Riggs was getting tired of hot-wiring the car anyway.

492

They drove to the outskirts of western Fairfax County and stopped for lunch at a nearly empty restaurant. On the drive out Riggs filled her in on the meeting at the Hoover Building. They walked past the bar area and sat at a table in the corner. LuAnn absently watched the bartender tinker with the TV to better the reception of a daytime soap he was watching. He slouched against the bar and pried between his teeth with a swizzle stick as he watched the small screen. It would be wonderful, she thought, to be that relaxed, that laid back.

They ordered food and then Riggs pulled out the newspaper. He didn't say a word until LuAnn had read the entire story.

"Good Lord."

"Donovan should have listened to you."

"You think Jackson killed him?"

Riggs nodded grimly. "Probably set him up. Had Reynolds call him, say she was gonna spill her guts. Jackson is there and pops them both with the result that Donovan gets blamed for it all."

LuAnn let her head rest in her hands.

Riggs gently touched her head. "Hey, LuAnn, you tried to warn the guy. There was nothing else you could do."

"I could have said no to Jackson ten years ago. Then none of this would've happened."

"Yeah, but I bet if you had, he would've done you right then and there."

LuAnn wiped her eyes with her sleeve. "So now I've got this great deal with the FBI you negotiated for me, and in order to finalize it all we need to do is drop a net over Lucifer." She sipped on her coffee. "Would you care to tell me how we're going to do that?"

Riggs put away the paper. "I've been giving it a lot of thought as you might have guessed. The problem is we can't be too simplistic or too complicated. Either way, he'll smell a trap."

"I don't think he'll take another meeting with me."

"No, I wasn't going to suggest that. He wouldn't show, but he'd send somebody to kill you. That's way too dangerous."

"Didn't you know, I like danger, Matthew. If I wasn't constantly smothered in the stuff, I wouldn't know what to do with myself. Okay, no meeting, what else?"

"Like I said before, if we can find out who he really is, track him down, then we might be in business." Riggs paused as their food came. After the waitress left he picked up his sandwich and started talking in between bites. "You don't remember anything about the guy? I mean anything that could start us in the right direction to finding out who he really is?"

"He was always disguised."

"The financial documents he sent you?"

"They were from a firm in Switzerland. I've got some back at the house, which I guess I can't get to. Even with our deal?" She raised an eyebrow.

"I wouldn't advise that, LuAnn. The Feds run across you now, they might forget all about our little deal."

"I've got some other documents at my bank in New York."

"Still too risky."

"I could write the firm in Switzerland, but I don't think they're going to know anything. And if they do, I don't think they're going to talk. I mean, that's why people bank in Switzerland, right?"

"Okay, okay. Anything else? There's gotta be something you remember about the guy. The way he dressed, smelled, talked, walked. Any particular interests? How about Charlie? Would he have any ideas?"

LuAnn hesitated. "We could ask him," she said, wiping her hands on her napkin, "but I wouldn't bet on it. Charlie told me he'd never even met Jackson face-to-face. It was always over the phone."

Riggs slumped back and touched his injured arm. "I just don't see any way to get to him, Matthew."

"There is a way, LuAnn. In fact I had already concluded it was the only way. I was just going through the motions with all those questions."

"How?"

"You have a phone number where you can reach him?"

"Yes. So?"

"We set up a meeting."

"But you just said—"

"The meeting will be with me, not you."

LuAnn half stood up in her anger. "No way, Matthew, there is no way in hell I'm going to let you near that guy. Look what he did to you." She pointed at his arm. "The next time will be worse. A lot worse."

"It would've been a lot worse if you hadn't messed up his aim." He smiled tenderly at her. "Look, I'll call him. I tell him that you're leaving the country and all these problems behind. You know Donovan is dead, so Jackson doesn't have that issue anymore. Everybody's home free." LuAnn was vigorously shaking her head as she sat back down.

"Then I'll tell him," Riggs continued, "that I'm not such a happy camper. I've got it all figured out: I'm a little tired of construction work, and I want my payoff."

"No, Matthew, no!"

"Jackson figures I'm a criminal anyway. Trying to extort him wouldn't seem out of line at all. I'll tell him I bugged your bedroom, that I've got a recording of a conversation he had with you, that night at your house, where you both talked a lot about things."

"Are you nuts?"

"I want money. Lots of it. Then he gets the tape."

"He will kill you."

Now Riggs's face darkened. "He'll do that anyway. I don't like sitting around waiting for the other shoe to drop. I'd rather go on the offensive. Make him sweat for a change. And I may not be the killing machine he is, but I'm no slouch either. I'm a veteran FBI agent. I've killed before, in the line of duty, and if you think I'd hesitate one second before blowing his brains out, then you really don't know me."

Riggs looked down for a moment, trying to make himself calm down. His plan was risky, but what plan wouldn't be? When he looked back up at LuAnn, he was about to say something else but the look on her face froze the words in his mouth.

"LuAnn?"

"Oh, no!" Her voice was filled with panic.

"What is it? What's the matter?" Riggs grabbed her shoulder, which was quivering. She didn't answer him. She was looking at something over his shoulder. He whirled around, expecting to see Jackson coming for them, foot-long knives in either hand. He scanned the nearly empty restaurant and then his eyes settled on the TV where a special news report was being broadcast.

A woman's face spread across the screen. Two hours ago, Alicia Crane, prominent Washingtonian, had been found dead in her home by her house-keeper. The evidence collected so far suggested that she had been murdered. Riggs's eyes widened as he listened to the broadcaster mention that Thomas Donovan, prime suspect in the Roberta Reynolds murder, apparently had been dating Alicia Crane.

LuAnn could not pull her eyes away from that face. She had seen those features, those eyes staring at her from the front porch of the cottage. Jackson's eyes bored into her.

His real face.

She had shuddered when she had actually seen it, or realized what she was seeing. She had hoped to never lay eyes on those features again. Now she was staring at them. They were planted on the TV.

When Riggs looked back at her, she raised a shaky finger toward the screen. "That's Jackson," she said, her voice breaking. "Dressed up like a woman."

Riggs looked back at the screen. That couldn't be Jackson, he thought. He turned back to LuAnn. "How do you know? You said he was always in disguise."

LuAnn could barely take her eyes away from the face on the screen. "At the cottage, when he and I went through the window. We fought and his face, plastic, rubber, whatever, came off. I saw his real face. That face." She pointed to the screen.

Riggs's first thought was the correct one. *Family?* God, could it be? The connection to Donovan couldn't be a coincidence, could it? He raced to the phone.

"Sorry I lost your boys, George. Hope that didn't cost you any brownie points with the top brass."

"Where the hell are you?" Masters demanded.

"Just listen." Riggs recounted the news story he had just heard.

"You think he's related to Alicia Crane?" Masters asked, the excitement echoing in his voice, his anger at Riggs completely gone, for now.

"Could be. Ages are about right. Older or younger brother maybe, I don't know."

"Thank God for strong genes."

497

"What's your game plan?"

"We check her family. Shouldn't be too hard to do. Her father was a U.S. senator for years. Very prominent lineage. If she has brothers, cousins, whatever, we hit 'em fast. Bring them in for questioning. Hell, it can't hurt."

"I don't think he's going to be waiting for you to knock on the front door."

"They never do, do they?"

"If he is around, be careful, George."

"Yeah. If you're right about all this—"

Riggs finished for him: "The guy just killed his own sister. I'd hate to see what he'd do to a non-family member."

Riggs hung up. For the very first time he actually felt hopeful. He was under no delusions that Jackson would be around for the FBI to take into custody. He would be flushed out, cut off from his home base. He'd be pissed, full of revenge. Well, let him be. He'd have to cut Riggs's heart out before he'd get to LuAnn. And they wouldn't be sitting targets. Now was the time to keep on the move.

Ten minutes later they were in the car heading for points unknown.

FIFTY-FOUR

Jackson boarded the Delta shuttle for New York. He needed additional supplies and he was going to pick up Roger. He couldn't count on him to travel by himself and get to where he was supposed to be. Then they would head back south. During the short flight Jackson checked in with the man following Charlie and Lisa. They had made a rest stop. Charlie had talked on the phone. No doubt checking in with LuAnn. They had gone on and were now close to reentering Virginia on the southern side. It was all working out very well. An hour later, Jackson was in a cab threading its way through Manhattan toward his apartment.

Horace Parker looked around with intense curiosity. A doorman for over fifty years at a building where average apartments covered four thousand square feet and went for five million, and the penthouse that covered triple that space and went for twenty mil, he had never seen anything like this before. He watched as the small army of men in FBI windbreakers swept through the lobby and into the private elevator that went only to the penthouse. They looked deadly serious and had the weaponry to prove it.

He went back outside and looked up and down the street. A cab pulled up and out stepped Jackson. Parker immediately went over to him. The doorman had known him for most of his life. Years ago he had

499

skipped pennies in the lobby's massive fountain with Jackson and his younger brother, Roger. To earn extra money he had baby-sat them and taken them to Central Park on the weekends; he had bought them their first beers when they were barely into puberty. Finally, he had watched them grow up and then leave the nest. The Cranes, he had heard, had fallen on hard times, and they had left New York. Peter Crane, though, had come back and bought the Penthouse. Apparently, he had done awfully well for himself.

"Good evening, Horace," Jackson said cordially.

"Evening, Mr. Crane," Parker said and tipped his cap.

Jackson started past him.

"Mr. Crane, sir?"

Jackson turned to him. "What is it? I'm in a bit of a hurry, Horace."

Parker looked upward. "There's some men come to the building, Mr. Crane. They went right up to your apartment. A bunch of them. FBI. Guns and everything, never seen nothing like it. They're up there right now. I think they're waiting for you to get home, sir."

Jackson's reply was calm and immediate. "Thank you for the information, Horace. Simply a misunderstanding."

Jackson put out his hand, which Parker took. Jackson immediately turned and walked away from the apartment building. When Parker opened his hand, there was a wad of hundred-dollar bills there. He looked around discreetly before stuffing the cash in his pocket and taking up his position by the door once more.

From the shadows of an alley across the street, Jackson turned and looked up at his apartment building. His eyes kept going up and up until they

500

came to rest upon the windows of the penthouse. His penthouse. He could see the silhouettes move slowly across the windows, and his lips started to tremble at this outrageous invasion of his home. The possibility that they could have traced him to his personal residence had not occurred to him. How in the hell? He couldn't worry about it now, though. He went down the cross street and made a phone call. Twenty minutes later a limousine picked him up. He called his brother and told him to leave his apartment immediately – not even bothering to pack a bag – and meet Jackson in front of the St. James Theater. Jackson wasn't sure how the police had found out his identity, but he couldn't be sure they wouldn't wind up at Roger Crane's apartment at any minute. Then he made a quick stop to gather together some necessary supplies from another smaller apartment he kept under a phony name. Under the ownership of one of his myriad corporate shells he maintained a private jet and full-time crew at La Guardia. He called ahead so that the pilot on duty would be able to file his flight plan as quickly as possible. Jackson did not intend to spend time twiddling his thumbs in the waiting area. The limo would take them right to the plane. That accomplished, he collected his brother from in front of the theater.

Roger was two years younger and slimly built but wiry like his older brother. He also shared the same shock of dark hair and delicate facial features. He was certainly curious about his brother's abrupt return to his life. "I couldn't believe you called like that out of the blue. What's up, Peter?"

"Shut up, I need to think." He suddenly turned to his younger brother. "Have you seen the news?"

He shook his head. "I don't usually watch TV. Why?"

He obviously didn't know of Alicia's death. That was good. Jackson didn't answer his brother; he settled back in the seat, his mind racing through a seemingly infinite number of scenarios.

In a half hour they were at La Guardia Airport. Soon they had left the Manhattan skyline behind on their way south.

The FBI did converge on Roger Crane's small apartment building, but a little too late. Yet they were far more intrigued by what they had discovered at Peter Crane's penthouse.

Masters and Berman, walking around the massive penthouse, came across Jackson's makeup and archives rooms and his computerized control center.

"Holy shit," Berman said, his hands in his pockets as he stared at the masks, makeup bins, and racks of clothing.

Masters held the scrapbook gingerly in his gloved hands. FBI technicians roamed everywhere collecting evidence.

"Looks like Riggs was right. One guy. Maybe we *can* survive all this," Masters said.

"So what's our next move?"

Masters answered immediately. "We focus on Peter Crane. Put a blanket on the airports and train and bus stations. I want road blocks posted on all the major arteries leading out of town. You're to instruct all the men that he's extremely dangerous and a master of disguise. Send out photos of the guy everywhere, fat lot of good that'll do us. We've cut off his home base, but he's obviously got enormous financial resources. If we do manage to track him down, I want no unnecessary chances. Tell the men that if there's the slightest threat, to shoot him down."

"How about Riggs and Tyler?" Berman asked.

"So long as they don't get in the way, they'll be okay. If they get mixed up with Crane along the way, well, there's no guarantee. I'm not going to jeopardize my men to make sure they don't get hurt. As far as I'm concerned LuAnn Tyler belongs in jail. But that's why we've got some ammo with her. We can send her to jail or threaten to. I think she'll keep her mouth shut. Why don't you go oversee the rest of the evidence collection."

While Berman did so, Masters sat down and read the background information on LuAnn that accompanied her photo.

He was finishing up when Berman returned.

"You think Crane's going to go after Tyler now?" Berman asked.

Masters didn't answer. Instead he looked down at the picture of LuAnn Tyler staring back at him from the photo album. He now understood why she had been picked as a lottery winner. Why they had all been picked. He now had a much clearer idea of who LuAnn Tyler was and why she had done what she had. She had been destitute, stuck in a cycle of poverty, with an infant daughter. No hope. All of the chosen winners had shared this common denominator: no hope. They were ripe for this man's scheme. Masters's features betrayed the emotions he was feeling. Right at that very moment, and for a number of reasons, George Masters was starting to feel immense guilt.

It was nearing midnight when Riggs and LuAnn stopped at a motel. After checking in, Riggs phoned George Masters. The FBI agent had just returned from New York and he detailed to Riggs what had happened since they had last spoken. After receiving this briefing Riggs hung up the phone and looked over at a very anxious LuAnn.

503

"What happened? What did they say?"

Riggs shook his head. "As expected. Jackson wasn't there, but they found enough evidence to keep him in prison for the rest of his life and then some. Including a scrapbook on all the lottery winners."

"So he *was* related to Alicia Crane."

Riggs nodded grimly. "Her older brother, Peter. Peter Crane is Jackson. Or at least everything points that way."

LuAnn was wide-eyed. "Then he murdered his own sister."

"Looks that way."

"Because she knew too much? Because of Donovan?"

"Right. Jackson couldn't take a chance on that. Maybe he shows up disguised or maybe as his true self. He gets what he wants out of her, maybe he tells her he killed Donovan. Who knows. She apparently was dating the guy. She might have gone nuts, threatened to go to the police. At some point he murdered her, I feel sure of that."

LuAnn shuddered. "Where do you think he is?"

Riggs shrugged. "The Feds got to his house, but from the looks of the place the man has money to burn, a million different places he could go, a dozen faces and identities he could go there under. It's not going to be easy to catch him."

"To finish our deal?" LuAnn's tone was slightly sarcastic.

"We handed the Feds his friggin' identity. They're at his 'world' headquarters right now. When I said we'd deliver him, I didn't necessarily mean in a box with a ribbon on it, laid on the doorstep of the Hoover Building. As far as I'm concerned we've lived up to our end of the bargain."

LuAnn let out a deep breath. "So does that mean

504

everything's square? With the FBI? And Georgia?"

"We'll have some details to work out, but yeah, I think so. Unknown to them, I recorded the entire meeting at the Hoover Building. I've got Masters, the director of the FBI, and the attorney general of the United States herself, acting upon the authority of the president of the United States no less, all on tape agreeing to the deal I proposed. They've got to play straight with us now. But I've gotta be straight with you too. The IRS is going to put a big dent in your bank account. In fact after so many years of compounded penalties and interest, I'm not sure how much money you're going to have left, if any."

"I don't care about that. I want to pay my taxes, even if it takes everything I've got. The truth is, I stole the money to begin with. I just want to know if I have to keep looking over my shoulder for the rest of my life."

"You're not going to prison, if that's what you mean." He touched her cheek with his hand. "You don't look too happy."

She blushed and smiled at him. "I am." Her smile quickly faded though.

"I know what you're thinking."

She blurted out, "Until they catch Jackson, my life's not worth spit. Or yours. Or Charlie's." Her lips trembled. "Or Lisa's." She suddenly jumped up and grabbed the phone.

"What are you doing?" Riggs asked.

"I need to see my daughter. I need to know that she's safe."

"Wait a minute, what are you going to tell them?"

"That we can meet up somewhere. I want her near me. Nothing's going to happen to her without it happening to me first."

"LuAnn, look—"

"This subject isn't open for discussion." Her tone was ferocious.

"All right, all right, I hear you. But where are we going to meet them?"

LuAnn passed a hand over her forehead. "I don't know. Does it matter?"

Riggs said, "Where are they now?"

"The last I heard, they were heading back into southern Virginia."

He rubbed his chin. "What's Charlie driving?"

"The Range Rover."

"Terrific. It'll hold all of us. We'll meet them wherever they are right now. We'll leave the rental and head out. Go somewhere and wait for the FBI to do its thing. So call them and I'll run up to that all-night burger place we saw on the way in and get us some food."

"Good enough."

When Riggs got back with two bags of food, LuAnn was no longer on the phone.

"You reach them?"

"They're at a motel on the outskirts of Danville, Virginia. But I need to call them back and let them know when we're going to be there." She looked around. "Where the hell are we?"

"We're in Edgewood, Maryland, north of Baltimore. Danville is a little over a hundred miles south of Charlottesville, which means we're about five or six hours from Danville."

"Okay, if we start right now—"

"LuAnn, it's after midnight. They're probably in bed, right?"

"So?"

"So, we can catch some sleep, which we both really need, get up early, and meet them tomorrow around noon."

"I don't want to wait. I want Lisa safe with me."

"LuAnn, driving when you're exhausted isn't real safe. Even if we start right now, we won't make it

506

until five or six in the morning. Nothing's going to happen between now and then. Come on, I think we've had enough excitement for one day. And if Lisa knows you're coming tonight, she won't get a wink of sleep."

"I don't care. I'd rather she be sleepy and safe."

Riggs shook his head slowly. "LuAnn, there's another reason we might not want to hook up with them right now, and it has to do with keeping Lisa safe."

"What are you talking about?"

Riggs put his hands in his pockets and leaned up against the wall. "Jackson is somewhere out there, that we know. Now, the last time we saw him he was running off into the woods. He could have easily come back and followed us."

"But what about Donovan and Bobbie Jo Reynolds and Alicia Crane? He killed them."

"We believe he killed them, or had someone kill them. Or he could've killed all of them personally and hired someone to follow us. That man has a deep pocketbook; there isn't much he can't buy."

LuAnn reflected briefly on Anthony Romanello. Jackson had hired him to kill her. "So Jackson could know about your meeting with the FBI? He could know where we are right now?"

"And if we go running off to see Lisa, then we lead him right to her as well."

LuAnn slumped down on the bed. "We can't do that, Matthew," she said wearily.

He rubbed her shoulders. "I know."

"But I want to see my little girl. Can't I do that?"

Riggs thought for a few minutes and then sat on the bed beside her and held her hands with his. "Okay, we'll stay here for the night. It would be a lot easier for someone to follow us at night and remain unseen. Tomorrow, we'll get an early start and head

507

down to Danville. I'll keep an eagle eye out for anyone remotely suspicious. As an undercover agent, I got pretty good at that. We'll take secondary roads, make frequent stops, and occasionally take the interstate. It'll be impossible for anyone to trail us. We'll meet Charlie and Lisa at the motel and then we'll have Charlie take her directly to the local FBI office in Charlottesville. We'll follow in our car but we won't go in. I don't want them getting hold of you just yet. But since we struck a deal with the Feds, we might as well avail ourselves of some of their protection resources. How's that sound?"

She smiled. "So I'll see Lisa tomorrow?"

He cupped her chin in his hand. "Tomorrow."

LuAnn called Charlie back, setting the meeting time at one o'clock the following day at the motel in Danville. With Charlie, Riggs, and herself around her little girl, Jackson could just come on and try something, because she liked their odds of survival under those circumstances.

They slid into bed and Riggs wrapped his good arm around her slim waist and snuggled against her. His 9-mm was under his pillow, a chair wedged tightly under the door lock. He had unscrewed a light bulb, broken it, and sprinkled the remains in front of the door. Although he didn't expect anything to happen, he wanted as much advance warning as he could get if it did.

As he lay next to her he was both confident and uneasy. She apparently sensed this and turned to face him, her hand gently stroking his face.

"Got something on your mind?"

"Anticipation, I guess. When I was with the FBI I had to work hard to keep my patience. I seem to have a natural aversion to delayed gratification."

"That all?" Riggs slowly nodded. "You sure you're not sorry you got involved in all this?"

He pulled her closer to him. "Why in the world would I be?"

"Well, let me list some things for you. You've been stabbed, and came within an inch of dying. A madman is probably going to try his best to kill us. You stuck your neck out with the FBI for me and your cover is blown, with the result that the people who tried to kill you before may try again. You're running around the country with me trying to stay one step ahead of everybody and your business is going to hell and it doesn't look like I'll have two dimes to rub together to even begin to repay you for everything you've done. That cover it?"

Riggs stroked her hair and figured he might as well say it now. Who knew how things were going to go. He might not get another chance.

"You left out the part about me falling in love with you."

Her breath caught as her eyes drifted over him, taking in every subtle quiver, trying to give them all simultaneous meaning. All the while his words echoed in her head. She tried to say something but couldn't.

He filled in the silence. "I know it's probably the world's worst timing, but I just wanted you to know."

"Oh, Matthew," she finally managed to say. Her voice was trembling, everything about her was.

"I'm sure you've heard those words before. Lots of times, from guys probably a lot better suited—"

She covered his mouth with her hand but she didn't say anything for a long minute. He gently kissed her fingers.

Her voice was husky as though she were reaching down deep in order to utter the words. "Other men have said them. But this is the first time I've really been listening."

509

She stroked his hair and then her lips searched out and found his in the darkness and sunk in, slowly and deeply. They blindly undressed each other, their fingers probing and gently caressing. LuAnn began to softly cry as the unlikely twins of nervous fear and intense happiness fought for dominance. Finally, she just stopped thinking and gave herself over to what she had been looking for for so many years, across so many countries; from precious dreams that rudely dissolved into nightmares, which viciously framed realities that never came close to inspiring in her any more than an extreme ambivalence about her life. She clutched Matthew Riggs hard, as if realizing that this might be her last chance. Their bodies gripped each other for a long time before relaxing. They fell into an exhausted sleep safely in each other's arms.

FIFTY-FIVE

Charlie rubbed the sleep from his eyes and stared over at the phone. It had been a couple of hours since LuAnn had filled him in on all the recent developments and he still couldn't get to sleep. So Jackson was really Peter Crane. That information personally did him no good, but Charlie figured it would help immeasurably the authorities' efforts to track the man down. On the downside, if Jackson knew his identity had been discovered, Charlie figured he would be one pissed-off person. And Charlie wouldn't want anyone he cared for to be in the vicinity of the gentleman if that was the case.

He pulled himself up from the couch. His knees were aching more than usual. All the driving was getting to him. He was very much looking forward to seeing LuAnn. And Riggs too, he supposed. Sounded like the guy had really come through for LuAnn. If he could pull all this off, well, it would be a miracle.

He went into the adjoining room and checked on Lisa. She was still sleeping soundly. He looked at her delicate features, seeing so much of her mother in them. She was going to be tall too. The last ten years had gone by so fast. Where would they all be next week? Where would he be? Maybe with Riggs in the equation, his run was coming to an end. He had no doubt that LuAnn would take care of him financially, but it would never be the same. But what the hell, the whirlwind that represented the last ten years with her and Lisa had been far more than he deserved anyway.

The ringing phone startled him. He checked his watch. Almost two A.M. He snatched up the receiver.

"Charlie?"

Charlie didn't recognize the voice at first. "Who's this?"

"Matt Riggs."

"Riggs? Where's LuAnn? Is she okay?"

"She's more than okay. They caught him. They caught Jackson." His tone was one of unbridled joy.

"Christ Almighty. Hallelujah! Where?"

"In Charlottesville. The FBI had put a team of agents together at the airport and he and his brother walked right into it. I guess he was coming to pay LuAnn back."

"His brother?"

"Roger. The FBI doesn't know if he's involved in all this, but I don't think they care. They've got Peter Crane. They want LuAnn to come to Washington in the morning to give a deposition."

"Tomorrow? What about meeting us down here?"

"That's why I called. I want you and Lisa to get packed up right now and meet us in Washington. At the Hoover Building. Ninth Street and Pennsylvania Avenue. They'll be expecting you. I set it all up. If you leave now, you can meet us for breakfast. I personally want to celebrate."

"And the FBI? The murder charge?"

"All taken care of, Charlie. LuAnn's home free."

"That's great, Riggs. That's the most wonderful news I've heard in I can't remember how long. Where's LuAnn?"

"She's on the other phone talking to the FBI. Tell Lisa that her mother loves her and can't wait to see her."

"You got it." He hung up and immediately started to pack. He would've loved to have seen Jackson's face when the FBI busted him. The prick. He figured he'd pack the car before waking Lisa. Might as well let her sleep as long as possible. When she heard the news about her mother Charlie was sure further sleep would not be possible for the little girl. It looked like Riggs had come through after all.

His heart lighter than it had been in years, Charlie, a bag under each arm, opened the front door.

He immediately froze. The man was standing in the doorway, his face covered by a black ski mask, a pistol in his hand. With a scream of rage, Charlie threw the bag at him, knocking the gun free. Next, Charlie grabbed the man by the mask and hurled him into the room, where he slammed against a wall and went down. Before the man could get up, Charlie was on top of him, hammering him with lefts and rights, his old boxing skills coming back as though he had never left the ring.

The piston-like battering took its toll as the man slumped down, groaning from the furious beating, and lay still. Charlie turned his head as he felt the second presence in the room.

"Hello, Charlie." Jackson closed the door behind him.

As soon as he recognized the voice, Charlie leapt for him, surprising Jackson with his quickness. The twin darts from the stun gun hit Charlie in the chest, but not before his massive fist collided with Jackson's chin, knocking him back against the door. However, Jackson continued to squeeze the trigger, sending the massive electrical current into Charlie's body.

Charlie was on his knees using all of his strength to try to rise, to kick the shit out of the man, to beat him into oblivion where he could hurt no one else.

He tried to propel himself forward, every mental impulse in his brain craving nothing less than the man's complete destruction. But his body refused to follow his orders. As he slowly sank to the floor, he stared at a terrified Lisa standing in the doorway leading into the bedroom.

He tried to say something, tried to scream to her to run, to run like hell, but all that came out was something that would hardly qualify as a whisper.

He watched in horror as Jackson staggered up, flew over to Lisa, and pressed something against her mouth. The girl struggled valiantly but it was no use. As her nostrils sucked in the chloroform she was soon on the floor next to Charlie.

Jackson wiped the blood from his face and roughly pulled his associate up. "Take her to the car and don't let anyone see you."

The man nodded dully, his entire body one large hurt from Charlie's fists.

Charlie watched helplessly as the man carried the unconscious Lisa out. Then his eyes slid over to Jackson, who knelt down next to him, rubbing his chin gingerly.

Then, speaking in a voice that exactly impersonated Riggs, he said, "They caught Jackson. They caught him. I feel like celebrating." Then Jackson laughed out loud.

Charlie didn't say anything. He just lay there, watching, waiting.

In his own voice, Jackson said, "I knew my phone call would make you drop your guard just enough. Opening the door without checking first, no gun ready. How lax. You were really very diligent about not being followed, though. I knew you would be. That's why on the very first night I was in Charlottesville, I entered the garage at Wicken's Hunt and placed a transmitter inside the wheel well

514

of each vehicle there, including your Range Rover. This particular transmitter was originally designed for military use and employs satellite-tracking technology. I could have followed you around the globe. It was very expensive, but obviously was well worth it.

"I knew after I met with LuAnn that she would send Lisa off with you and I needed to know exactly where you were just in case I needed little Lisa for the final showdown. I love strategic thinking, don't you? It's so rare when someone does it correctly. As it turns out, I do need her. That's why I'm here."

Charlie winced slightly when Jackson pulled the knife from his coat and he flinched again when Jackson pulled up the sleeve of Charlie's shirt.

"I really love this device," Jackson said, looking at the stun gun. "It's one of the few instruments I'm aware of that allows one to have full control over another without seriously injuring them and still leaving them fully conscious."

Jackson packed the stun gun away in his coat. He left the darts in Charlie. He wasn't worried about leaving any evidence behind this time.

"You sided with the wrong person." As Jackson said this he ripped open the shirtsleeve up to Charlie's shoulder to give himself a clear space in which to work. "You were loyal to LuAnn and look where it got you." Jackson shook his head sadly, but the smile on his face betrayed his true feelings of glee.

As slowly as he could, Charlie tried to flex his legs. He grimaced a little, but he could feel something down there. It hurt, but at least he could feel it. What Jackson didn't know was that one of the darts had hit Charlie's thick Crucifix, imbedding completely in it. The other dart had partially hit the medallion before entering his chest, with the result that the voltage that had rocked his body was far less than Jackson had counted on it to be.

"Now, the stun charge will last approximately fifteen minutes," Jackson lectured him. "Unfortunately, the cut I'm about to inflict upon you will only take about ten minutes to cause you to bleed to death. However, you won't feel anything, physically. Mentally, well, it might be rather unnerving watching yourself bleed to death and being absolutely powerless to do anything about it. I could kill you quick, but this way seems far more gratifying to me personally."

As he spoke, Jackson made a precise and deep gash in Charlie's upper arm. Charlie bit the inside of his jaw as he felt the sharp blade slice through his skin. As Charlie's blood started to pour out in a steady flow, Jackson rose.

"Good-bye, Charlie, I'll tell LuAnn you said hello. Right before I kill her." Jackson snapped this last sentence out, his face a twisted mass of hatred. Then he smiled and closed the door.

Inch by agonizing inch, Charlie managed to roll over on to his back. Then, after an equally hard struggle, he brought his massive hands up, up until they closed around the darts. He was already dizzy from the blood loss. The sweat pouring off his brow, he pulled with all his strength and, little by little, the darts came loose and he tossed them aside. That didn't lessen the numbness of his body, but it felt good nonetheless. With what little control he had over his limbs, he slid over to the wall backward and inched his torso up to a sitting position by levering himself against this solid surface. His legs were on fire, the equivalent of a million burning needles stuck in them, and his body was covered in blood, but he managed to thrust himself upward as though he were squatting weights and his legs held, his knees locked in place. Ironically, the stun gun's impact had made his knees feel better than they had in years. Keeping himself pressed against the wall for support, he made it to the closet, which he managed to throw open. He pushed himself into the closet and gripped a wooden suit hanger with his teeth. All his limbs were on fire now, which was exhilarating because the slow return of his motor functions was becoming evident all over his body. He managed to grip the suit hanger in one hand and rip off the slender stem that normally kept trousers neatly in place. Dropping the rest of the hanger, he pushed off from the wall, propelling himself to the bed. Using his teeth and one of his hands, he shredded the bed sheet into strips. He worked more quickly now as his limbs returned to a semblance of normalcy. He was starting to feel nauseated; the blood loss was taking its toll. He was running out of time. As quickly as he could he wound a long strip directly above the cut and then used the thin piece of wood to torque down on it. The rude tourniquet worked its life-saving magic and the flow of blood finally halted. Charlie knocked the phone receiver off and punched in 911. After giving his location he sat back on the bed, sweat pouring off him, his entire body crimson from his own blood. He was still uncertain whether he was going to live or not, and yet all he could think about was the fact that Jackson had Lisa. He knew exactly what Jackson was going to do with her. The girl was bait. Bait to lure the mother. And when LuAnn went for that bait, Charlie knew exactly what would happen: Jackson would slaughter them both.

This terrifying thought was his last before he lost consciousness.

As the van moved down the highway, Jackson looked over at the unconscious Lisa, finally shining a penlight on her features so he could see them more clearly. "The spitting image of her mother," he said to himself. "She has her fighting spirit too," he added.

Jackson reached over and touched the young girl's face. "You were just an infant when I last saw you." He paused for a moment and looked out into the darkness before returning his gaze to her. "I'm very sorry it had to come to this."

He rubbed her cheek lightly, before slowly withdrawing his hand. Roberta, Donovan, his sister, Alicia, and now the little girl. How many more people was he going to have to kill? After this was all over, he told himself, he would go to the most remote location he possibly could find and do nothing for the next five years. When he had cleansed his mind of the events of this past week, he would go on with his life. But first he had to take care of LuAnn. That was one death he was not going to lose much sleep over.

"I'm coming, LuAnn," he said to the darkness.

LuAnn sat bolt upright in bed feeling as if every nerve were on fire. Her breath came in big chunks, her heart pounding out of control.

"Sweetie, what is it?" Riggs sat up and wrapped an arm around her quivering shoulders.

"Oh, God, Matthew."

"What? What is it?"

"Something's happened to Lisa."

"What? LuAnn, you were dreaming. You had a bad dream, that's all."

"He's got her. He's got my baby. Oh, God, he was touching her. I saw it."

Riggs pulled her around to face him. Her eyes were careening all over the room. "LuAnn, there's nothing wrong with Lisa. You had a nightmare.

Perfectly natural under the circumstances." He tried to sound as calm as possible, although being wakened out of a dead sleep by this hysterical outburst had certainly unnerved him.

She pushed him off, jumped up, and started tossing things off the table next to the bed.

"Where's the phone?"

"What?"

"Where's the damned phone?" she screamed. As soon as she said it, she uncovered the phone.

"Who are you calling?"

She didn't answer. Her fingers flew across the face of the receiver as she punched in the cell phone number. She was almost vibrating off the ground as she waited for an answer. "They're not answering."

"So? Charlie probably turned off the phone. Do you know what time it is?"

"He wouldn't turn off the phone. He *never* turns off the damned phone." She redialed, with the same result.

"Well, if that's the case, maybe the battery's dead. If he didn't plug it in when he got to the motel."

LuAnn was shaking her head. "Something's happened. Something's wrong."

Riggs got up and went over to her. "LuAnn, listen to me." He shook her to the extent his wound would allow him. "Will you listen for a minute?"

She finally calmed down a bit and managed to look at him.

"Lisa is fine. Charlie is fine. You had a nightmare and that's all." He put his arm around her, squeezed her tightly to him. "We're going to see them tomorrow. And everything is going to be fine, okay? If we go tonight and we are being followed, we'll never know it. Don't let a nightmare make you do something that could end up *really* putting Lisa in danger."

She stared at him, terror still in her eyes.

He continued to murmur in her ear and his soothing tones finally reached her. She let him draw her back over to the bed and they climbed in. As he settled back to sleep, however, LuAnn stared at the ceiling, silently praying that it really had only been a nightmare. Something deep within her kept telling her it wasn't. In the darkness she could see what looked to be a hand reaching out for her. Whether in a friendly gesture or not she couldn't tell, because it never fully formed and then it was gone. She put an arm around the sleeping Riggs, holding him protectively. She would have given anything to be doing the same for her daughter.

FIFTY-SIX

The two FBI agents sipped hot coffee and enjoyed the late morning calm and beauty of the area. The winds were whipping up, however, as a storm system approached with the promise of even higher winds and a lot of rain, that night and into the next day. Stationed at the road leading up to LuAnn's home, the veteran agents had seen little activity, but they kept alert despite the tedium.

At eleven o'clock a car approached their checkpoint and stopped. The window came down on the driver's side.

Sally Beecham, LuAnn's housekeeper, looked expectantly at one of the agents and he quickly waved her through. She had gone out two hours before to run some errands. When she had passed the checkpoint earlier she had been very nervous. The FBI hadn't explained much to her, but they had made it clear that she wasn't in trouble. They wanted her to go about her normal duties, keep everything the same. They had given her a number to call in case she noticed anything suspicious.

As she passed through the checkpoint this time, she looked more comfortable, perhaps even a touch self-important with all of this official attention.

One of the agents commented to the other, "I don't think Tyler's going to be coming back to eat any of that food." His colleague smirked knowingly.

The next vehicle that came down the road and

stopped at the checkpoint drew some special attention. The older man driving the van explained that he was the groundskeeper. The younger man in the passenger seat was his assistant. They produced ID, which the agents checked thoroughly, then made some phone calls to verify. The agents opened the back of the van and it was indeed filled with tools, boxes, and old rolled-up tarps. Just to make sure, one of the agents followed the van up the road.

Sally Beecham's car was parked in front; a shrill beep emanated from the house. The front door was open and the agent could see her just inside the door deactivating the alarm system, he presumed. He was proven correct when the beep stopped. The agent watched the men get out of the van, pull some tools from the back of the vehicle, stack them in a wheelbarrow, and head around to the back of the house. Then the agent got in his car and drove back to the checkpoint.

LuAnn and Riggs were standing in the parking lot of the motel outside Danville, Virginia. Riggs had talked to the motel manager. The police had been summoned the night before. The man in Room 112 had been attacked and badly injured. Because of the severity of the wound, a medevac helicopter had been called to airlift out the man. The name the man had given was not Charlie's; however, that meant nothing. And the manager was not aware of a young girl being with the man.

"You're sure they were in room one twelve?"

LuAnn whirled around. "Of course I'm sure."

She closed her eyes, stopped pacing, and rocked on her heels. She knew! She knew what had happened. The thought of Jackson touching Lisa, hurting her, all because of what LuAnn had done or hadn't done. It was numbing, absolutely and totally incapacitating.

"Look, how was I supposed to know you have some kind of psychic connection with this guy?" Riggs replied.

"Not him dammit. Her! My daughter."

This statement stopped Riggs dead in his tracks. He looked down and then watched her resume her pacing.

"We need some information, Matthew. Right now."

Riggs agreed, but he didn't want to go to the police. That would entail wasting a lot of time in explanations and the end result might very well be the local cops taking LuAnn into custody.

Finally, Riggs said, "Come on."

They went into the motel office and Riggs walked over to a pay phone. Riggs phoned Masters. The FBI still had no leads on Jackson and Roger Crane still had not surfaced, Riggs was told.

Riggs briefly explained the situation at the motel the night before to Masters.

"Hold on," Masters said.

While Riggs did so he looked over at LuAnn staring at him. She was silently waiting for the worst news she could possibly receive, of that he was certain. He tried to smile reassuringly at her, but then stopped. The last thing he could be right now was reassuring, particularly since he had nothing to base it upon. Why set her up even further for the long fall.

When Masters came back on, his tone was low and nervous. Riggs turned away from LuAnn while he listened.

Masters said, "I just checked with the local police in Danville. Your information is correct, a man was stabbed at that motel on the outskirts of town. The ID found on him gave his name as Robert Charles Thomas."

523

Charlie? Riggs licked his lips, gripped the phone. "His ID? He couldn't tell the police?"

"He was unconscious. Lost a lot of blood. Damn miracle he's even alive, they tell me. The wound was professionally administered, designed to slow-bleed the person. They found darts from a stun gun in the room. Guess that was how he was incapacitated. As of early this morning, they weren't sure if he was going to make it."

"What's he look like?" Riggs heard some paper rustling over the line. He was almost certain it was Charlie, but he needed to be absolutely sure.

Masters started speaking again. "Over six feet, in his sixties, strongly built, must be strong as an ox to have survived to this point."

Riggs breathed deeply. No doubt now. It was Charlie. "Where is he now?"

"The medevac took him to the UVA trauma center in Charlottesville."

Riggs felt the presence next to him. He turned to find Lisa staring at him; the look in her eyes was scary.

"George, was there any mention of a ten-year-old girl being with him?"

"I asked. The report said that the man came to for a few seconds and started shouting a name."

"Lisa?"

Riggs heard Masters clear his throat. "Yes." Riggs remained silent. "It was her daughter, wasn't it? This guy's got her, doesn't he?" Masters asked.

"Looks like it," Riggs managed to get out.

"Where are you?"

"Look, George, I don't think I'm ready to give you that information yet."

Masters started speaking more forcefully. "He's got the little girl. You two could be next, Matt. Think about it. We can protect you both. You have got to come in."

"I don't know."

"Look, you can go back to her house. I've got the entrance under twenty-four-hour guard. If she agrees to go there, I'll fill the place up with agents."

"Hold on, George." Riggs held the phone against his chest and looked at LuAnn. His eyes told her all she needed to know.

"Charlie?"

"Unconscious. They don't know if he's going to make it. The good news is that a medevac helicopter flew him to the trauma center at UVA hospital."

"He's in Charlottesville?" she asked.

Riggs nodded. "It's only a short hop from Danville by air, and the trauma unit there is top-notch. He'll get the best care."

She continued to stare at him, waiting. And he knew exactly what for.

"Jackson probably has Lisa." He moved on quickly. "LuAnn, the FBI wants us to come in. So they can protect us. We can go to Wicken's Hunt if you want. Agents are already guarding the entrance. They think—"

She snatched the phone out of his hand.

She screamed into it. "I don't want protection. I don't need your damned protection. He's got my daughter. And the only thing I'm going to do is find her. I'm going to get her back. You hear me?"

"Ms. Tyler, I'm assuming this is LuAnn Tyler—" Masters started to say.

"You just stay out of the way. He'll kill her sure as hell if he even *thinks* you're around."

Masters tried to remain calm even as he said the awful words. "Ms. Tyler, you can't be sure he hasn't already done something to her."

Her reply was surprising, both for its content and its intensity. "I know he hasn't hurt her. Not yet."

"The man's a psycho. You can't be sure—"

"The hell I can't. I know exactly what he wants. And it's not Lisa. You just stay out of the way, FBI man. If my daughter dies because you got in the way, there won't be any place on this earth that I won't find you."

Sitting at his desk in the heavily guarded Hoover Building, with twenty-five years of high-level criminal detection work behind him, during which he'd confronted more than his share of evil, now surrounded by a thousand superbly trained, hardened FBI special agents, George Masters actually shivered as he listened to those words.

The next sound he heard was the phone slamming down.

Riggs raced after LuAnn as she stormed to the car.

"LuAnn, will you wait a damned minute?" She whirled around, waiting for him to speak. "Look, what George said makes a lot of sense."

LuAnn threw up her hands and started to get in the car.

"LuAnn, you go in to the FBI. Let them protect you from this guy. Let me stay on the outside. Let me track him down."

"Lisa is my daughter. I'm the reason she's in this danger and I'm the one who's going to get her out. Just me. Nobody else. Charlie's almost dead. You were almost killed. Three other people have been slaughtered. I'm not involving anybody else in my screwed up, miserable, sonofabitchin' excuse for a life." She screamed the words at him; when she stopped, both their chests were heaving.

"LuAnn, I'm not letting you go after him alone. If you don't want to go to the FBI, fine. I won't go either. But you're not, repeat not, going after him alone. That way you both die."

"Matthew, did you hear me? Just get out of this.

Go to your buddies at the FBI and let them get you a new life somewhere the hell away from all of this. The hell away from me. Do you want to die? Because if you hang around me, you're going to, sure as I'm looking at you." The polished facade had fallen away, shed like a snake's skin in autumn. She was one long, raw muscle standing alone.

"He'll come after me, regardless, LuAnn," Riggs said quietly. "He'll find me and he'll kill me whether I go to the FBI or not." She didn't respond so he continued. "And to tell you the truth, I'm too old, too tired of running and hiding to start it up again. I'd rather go down the cobra's hole and meet him head-on. I'll take my chances with you next to me. I'd rather have you than every agent at the Bureau, than every cop in the country. We're probably only going to have one shot at this, and I'll take that shot with you." He paused for a moment as she stared at him, her eyes wild, her long hair billowing in the wind, her strong hands balling up into fists and then uncurling. Then he said, "If you'll take that shot with me."

The wind was really picking up now. They each stood barely two feet apart from the other. The gap would either swell or diminish with LuAnn's answer. Despite the chill, cold sweat clung to each of their faces. She finally broke the silence.

"Get in."

The room was completely dark. Outside the rain was pouring down and had been for most of the day. Sitting in the very center of the space, her body bound tightly to a chair, Lisa was trying, without much success, to use her nose to inch up the mask that covered her eyes. The intense darkness – being totally and completely blind – was unnerving to her. She had the impression that perilous things were lurking very near her. In that regard she was completely right.

"Are you hungry?" The voice was right at her elbow and her heart nearly stopped.

"Who is it? Who are you?" Her voice quavered.

"I'm an old friend of your mother's." Jackson knelt beside her. "These bindings aren't too tight, are they?"

"Where's Uncle Charlie? What did you do to him?" Lisa's courage suddenly resurfaced.

Jackson quietly chuckled. "Uncle, is it?" He stood back up. "That's good, very good."

"Where is he?"

"Not relevant," Jackson snapped. "If you're hungry, tell me so."

"I'm not."

"Something to drink then?"

Lisa hesitated. "Maybe some water."

She heard some tinkling of glass in the background and then she felt a coldness against her lips and jerked back.

"It's only water. I'm not going to poison you." Jackson said this in such a commanding fashion that Lisa quickly opened her mouth and drank deeply. Jackson patiently held the cup until she was finished.

"If you need anything else, to use the bathroom for instance, then just say so. I'll be right here."

"Where are we?" When Jackson didn't answer, she asked, "Why are you doing this?"

Standing there in the darkness, Jackson considered the question carefully before answering. "Your mother and I have some unfinished business. It has to do with things that occurred a long time ago, although there have been repercussions of a very recent vintage that are motivating me."

"I bet my mom didn't do anything to you."

"On the contrary, while she owes her entire life to me, she has done everything in her power to hurt me."

"I don't believe that," Lisa said hotly.

"I don't expect you to," Jackson said. "You're loyal to your mother, as you should be. Family ties are very important." He crossed his arms and thought for a moment on the status of his own family, of Alicia's sweet, peaceful face. *Sweet and peaceful in death.* With an effort he shrugged the vision off.

"My mom will come and get me."

"I certainly expect her to."

Lisa blinked rapidly as his meaning suddenly dawned upon her. "You're going to hurt her, aren't you? You're going to try and hurt my mom when she comes to get me." Her voice had risen.

"Call if you need anything. I don't intend to make you suffer unduly."

"Don't hurt my mom, please." The tears materialized behind the mask.

Jackson did his best to ignore the pleas. Finally, the crying turned to bawling and then dissolved into exhausted whimpering. He had first seen Lisa as an eight-month-old infant. She had certainly grown up into a lovely child. Had LuAnn not accepted his offer, the orphaned Lisa would probably be in a foster home somewhere. He looked over at her, suffering terribly inside, her head slumped on to her chest in her private agony. A lot for a ten-year-old to handle. Maybe she would have been better off in that foster home, without ever really having known her mother. The woman Jackson was going to now eliminate from her life. He had no desire to cause pain to the daughter, but such was life. It wasn't fair. He had told LuAnn that the very first day they had met: Life was not fair. If you wanted something you had to take it. Before someone else took from you.

Neatly dissected down to its essence, life was one long series of lily pad hoppings. The quick and the resourceful were able to adapt and survive; all others were simply crushed as a more nimble creature landed on the lily pad they had occupied for too long.

He stood completely motionless as though conserving all his energies for what lay ahead. He stared off into the darkness. Very soon it would all begin. And very soon it would all end.

FIFTY-SEVEN

The medical facility at the University of Virginia was a teaching component of the medical school as well as a highly regarded public hospital with a level-one trauma center. LuAnn raced down the corridor. Riggs was parking the car and then would follow her in. She reflected briefly on the fact that she had never before been in a hospital. She quickly concluded that she didn't care for either the smell or atmosphere. A lot of that was probably due to the reason she was here: to see Charlie.

He was in a private room. A member of the Charlottesville police force stood guard outside his door. LuAnn shot right past him and started to enter the room,.

"Whoa, there, ma'am. No visitors," said the police officer, a solidly built man in his early thirties, holding out a beefy arm for emphasis.

LuAnn had whirled around ready for a fight when Riggs hustled up.

"Hey, Billy."

The officer turned around. "Hey, Matt, how you doing?"

"Not so good. Won't be playing basketball at the Y with you for a while."

Billy looked at his sling. "How'd you do that?"

"Long story. The guy in there is her uncle." He nodded at LuAnn.

Billy looked embarrassed. "I'm sorry, ma'am, I

didn't know. They told me no visitors, but I know they didn't mean family. You go on in."

"Thanks, Billy," Riggs said.

LuAnn pushed open the door and went in. Riggs was right behind her.

LuAnn stared across at Charlie lying in the bed. As if he sensed her presence, he looked over and a smile spread across his face. He looked pale but his eyes were quick and active.

"Damn, now that's a real pleasant sight," he said.

LuAnn was next to him in an instant, taking his big hand in hers. "Thank God, you're okay."

Charlie was about to say something when the door opened and a middle-aged man in a white coat popped his head in. "Just making rounds, folks." He opened the door all the way and came in. He carried a clipboard.

"Dr. Reese," he said, introducing himself.

"Matt Riggs. This is Charlie's niece, Catherine." Riggs pointed at LuAnn, who shook the doctor's hand.

Dr. Reese checked Charlie's vital signs while he spoke. "Well, it's very lucky Charlie was so good with a tourniquet. Stopped the blood loss before things got really nasty."

"So he's going to be okay?" LuAnn asked anxiously.

Reese peered at her over his glasses. "Oh, yes. He's in no danger. We replaced the blood he lost, the wound is all stitched up. All he needs is some rest, get his strength back." Reese noted his findings on Charlie's record log.

Charlie half-sat up. "I feel fine. When can I check out?"

"I think we'll give you a couple of more days to get back on your feet."

Charlie was clearly not pleased with that answer.

"I'll be back in the morning," Reese said. "Don't stay too long, folks, let him get some rest."

As soon as Reese was gone, Charlie sat all the way up. "Any word on Lisa?"

LuAnn closed her eyes and looked down. Thick tears slid out from under her eyelids. Charlie looked over at Riggs for the first time.

"We think he has her, Charlie," said Riggs

"I *know* he has her. I told the cops everything I knew as soon as I came to."

"I'm sure they're working on it," Riggs said lamely.

Charlie banged his fist against the metal sides of the bed. "Dammit, they're not going to catch him. He's long gone. We've got to do something. He hasn't tried to contact you?"

"I'm going to contact him," LuAnn said, opening her eyes. "But I had to come see you first. They said – they said you might not make it." Her voice shook and her hand gripped his tighter.

"It'd take a lot more than one cut to send yours truly into oblivion." He paused, struggling with what he was about to say. "I'm sorry, LuAnn. That bastard's got her and it's my fault. He called in the middle of the night, impersonated Riggs's voice. Said that the FBI had Jackson. That I was to come up to Washington and rendezvous with you at the FBI building. I dropped my guard. I walked right into his trap." Charlie shook his head. "God, I should've suspected something, but he sounded just like Riggs."

LuAnn leaned over and hugged him. "Damn you, Charlie, you almost got yourself killed for her. And for me."

Charlie wrapped his big arms around her while Riggs watched in respectful silence as the two shook and swayed together.

"Lisa will be okay, Charlie." She sounded a lot more confident than she actually felt. However, it would do Lisa no good if LuAnn allowed herself to become hysterical and thus useless.

"LuAnn, you know that guy. He could do anything to her."

"He wants me, Charlie. His whole world is falling apart. The Feds are on to him, he killed Donovan and Bobbie Jo Reynolds and probably his own sister as well. And I know he thinks I'm the cause of all of it."

"That's nuts."

"It's not nuts if he believes it."

"Well, you can't just walk in there and give yourself to him."

Riggs piped in, "My sentiments exactly. You can't just call the guy up and say 'Don't worry, I'll be right over so you can kill me.'"

LuAnn didn't answer him.

"He's right, LuAnn," Charlie said. He started to get up.

"What the hell are you doing?" she said sharply.

"Getting dressed."

"Excuse me, didn't you hear the doctor?"

"I'm old, my hearing's going. And so am I. Going, that is."

"Charlie—"

"Look," he said angrily as he stumbled trying to get his pants on. LuAnn gripped his good arm, while Riggs steadied him on the other side. "I'm not going to lie here in this bed while that son of a bitch has Lisa. If you don't understand that, I really don't care."

LuAnn nodded in understanding and helped him get his pants on. "You're a big old ornery bear, you know that?"

"I've got one good arm, and just let me get it around that guy's neck."

Riggs held up his own injured arm. "Well, between us we have two good arms. I owe the guy too."

LuAnn put her hands on her hips and looked around. "There's a cop outside."

"I can take care of him," Riggs said.

LuAnn picked up the rest of Charlie's belongings, including the portable cell phone, and put them in a plastic hospital bag.

When Charlie was finished dressing, Riggs stepped out the door and spoke to Billy.

"Billy, you mind going down to the cafeteria and getting a couple of coffees and maybe some stuff to munch on? I'd go but I can't carry anything with this bum arm." He jerked his head toward the room. "And she's pretty hysterical right now. I don't want to leave her."

"I'm really not supposed to leave my post, Matt."

"I'll hang out here, Billy, it'll be okay." Riggs held up some money. "Here, get yourself something too. Last time we played hoops I remember you eating a whole pizza by yourself afterward." He eyed Billy's healthy dimensions. "I don't want you to wilt away to nothing."

Billy took the money and laughed. "You sure know the way to a fella's heart."

As soon as Billy got into the elevator and the doors closed, Charlie, LuAnn, and Riggs left the room and made their way out by the back stairs. With LuAnn and Riggs supporting Charlie, they quickly walked through the pouring rain to the car. With the thick clouds, it was already dark and the visibility was getting worse every minute.

Shortly, the three of them were in the car heading down Route 29. Charlie used the opportunity to tell them everything that had happened at the motel, including the fact that Jackson had had another man

535

with him. After he finished, Charlie leaned forward from the back seat. "So what's the plan?" He winced as the car bounced over a pothole and jostled his arm.

LuAnn pulled into a gas station. She pulled out a slip of paper from her pocket. "I'm going to call him."

"And then what?" Riggs asked.

"I'll let him tell me," she replied.

"You know what the hell he's going to say," Charlie rejoined. "He's going to set up a meeting, just you and him. And if you go, he's going to kill you."

"And if I don't go, he's going to kill Lisa."

"He'll kill her anyway," Riggs said hotly.

LuAnn looked over at him. "Not if I get him first." She thought back to her last encounter with Jackson, at the cottage. She was stronger than he was. Not by much, but she had the clear advantage there. However, he knew that too. She had seen that in his eyes. That meant he would not go toe-to-toe with her again, at least not physically. She would have to remember that. If he could adapt, so could she.

"LuAnn, I have a lot of confidence in you," Riggs said, "but this guy is something else again."

"He's right, LuAnn," Charlie added.

"Thanks for the vote of confidence, guys." She didn't wait for them to answer. She pulled the portable phone out of the bag and punched in the number. Before it started ringing, she looked at both of them. "But remember, I've got *two* good arms."

Riggs slid his hand down into his coat until it touched the reassuring metal of his pistol. His aim would have to be a lot better this time around. He hoped not to have the painful distraction of a knife sticking out of his arm.

He and Charlie watched as LuAnn spoke into the

receiver, leaving the number of the cell phone. She hung up and waited, still not looking at them. Barely three minutes had passed before the phone rang.

Before LuAnn could say anything, Jackson said, "Please know that I have a device attached to my phone that will indicate whether this call is being traced, just in case you happen to be sitting at police headquarters. It will tell me in about five seconds if that is occurring. If you are, I will immediately hang up and slit your daughter's throat."

"I'm not at the police and I'm not tracing your call."

He didn't say anything for five seconds. She could envision him eyeing his device, perhaps hoping she was lying to him. "I applaud you for avoiding the obvious," he finally said quite pleasantly.

"When and where?" LuAnn said.

"No greeting? No small talk? Where are your manners? Has the expensively constructed princess deteriorated that suddenly? Like a flower without water? Without sunshine?"

"I want to talk to Lisa. Right now."

"Sorry about Uncle Charlie," Jackson said. He was sitting on the floor almost in total darkness. He held the phone close to his mouth, speaking slowly and in as casual a tone as he could muster. He wanted her panic level to rise steadily, he wanted her to feel his absolute control of the situation. When the time came he wanted her to come obediently forward to receive her punishment. He wanted her to come meekly to confront her executioner.

She wasn't about to tell Jackson that Charlie was sitting right behind her wanting nothing more than to wring the life out of him. "I want to talk to Lisa!"

"How can you be sure I haven't killed her already?"

"What?" she gasped.

"You can talk to her, but how will you know it's not me mimicking her voice? 'Mommy, Mommy,' I could say. 'Come help me.' I could say all those things. So if you want to talk to her, you can, but it will prove nothing."

"You son of a bitch!"

"Would you still like to talk to her?"

"Yes," LuAnn said pleadingly.

"Manners now. Yes, what?"

She hesitated for an instant, taking a deep breath, trying to keep her wits and her nerves together. "Yes, please," she said.

"Just a minute. Now where have I put that child?"

Riggs was doing his best to listen in. Exasperated, LuAnn finally opened the door and got out of the car.

She strained to hear any sound in the background.

"Mom, Mom, is that you?"

"Honey, baby, it's Mom. Oh, God, sweetie, I'm so sorry."

"Oh, excuse me, LuAnn, that's still me," Jackson said. "Oh, Mom, Mommy, are you there?" he said again, mimicking Lisa's voice precisely.

LuAnn was too stunned to say anything.

The next voice she heard was Jackson's real one. His tone almost bit into her ear it was said with such forcefulness. "I'll let you talk to her, really talk to her. You can have your mother–daughter emotional exchange. But when you're done I will tell you exactly what you will do. If you deviate in any way from my instructions . . ."

He didn't finish. He didn't have to. They both sat there on the phone, not saying anything, simply listening to each other's breathing, two trains careening out of control, about to slam into each other across the wireless void. LuAnn tried with all her might to hold back the thick gush of air that was

538

ramming against her throat. She knew what he was doing. What he was doing to her mind. But she was equally aware that she could do nothing about it. At least not right now.

"Do you understand?"

"Yes." As soon as she said the word, she heard it. She heard the sound in the background that made her both smile and grimace simultaneously. She looked at her watch. Five o'clock. The smile increased at the same time her eyes took on a gleam. A gleam of hope.

The next minute she was talking to Lisa, quickly asking her questions that only her little girl would know the answer to. They both desperately wanted to reach through the darkness that separated them.

And then Jackson came back on the line and gave her the instructions, the where and the when. None of it surprised her as she focused again on the sounds occurring in the background on his end. He ended the call by saying, with daunting finality, "See you soon."

She clicked off the phone and got back in the car. She spoke with a calmness that astonished the two men, particularly under the circumstances.

"I'm to call him tomorrow ten A.M. He'll give me the meeting place then. He'll let Lisa go if I come alone. If he even thinks anyone else is around, he'll kill her."

"So it's you for Lisa," Riggs said.

She looked at both of them. "That's the way it's going to be."

"LuAnn—"

"That's the way it's going to be," she said more forcefully.

"How do you know he'll let her go? You can't trust him," Charlie implored.

"On this I can. He just wants me."

"There's got to be another way," Riggs exclaimed.

"There's only one way, Matthew, and you know it." She looked at him sadly before putting the car in gear and driving off.

She had one more card to play. But Charlie and Riggs weren't going to be invited to the game. They had already sacrificed too much for her. Jackson had nearly killed both men, and she wasn't about to give the man another try on either. If Jackson were given an extra shot, she knew what the outcome would be. It was now up to her. It was up to her to save her daughter, and that, she felt, was the way it should be. She had been self-reliant for most of her life, and truth be known, that was the way she liked it. That knowledge was reassuring. And she knew something else.

She knew where Jackson and Lisa were.

FIFTY-EIGHT

The rain had finally slackened off but the spring showers were far from over. LuAnn had tacked up a blanket over the shattered window of the cottage. Riggs had turned the heat fully on and it was comfortable enough. The remnants of a meal rested on the kitchen sink. Riggs eyed the stains on the dining room floor. His blood. Charlie and Riggs had pulled mattresses down from the upstairs bedroom and laid them out on the floor. They had decided the cottage was the best place to spent the night. Charlie and Riggs had argued with LuAnn for hours trying to change her mind. Finally, she said she would call the FBI in the morning before she called Jackson. It was possible the FBI could trace the call. That had appeased the men enough that they agreed to let LuAnn keep the first watch. Riggs would relieve her in two hours.

Exhausted, both men soon began snoring deeply. LuAnn stood with her back to the window and silently observed them. She looked at her watch; it was after midnight. She made sure her gun was loaded, then she knelt next to Charlie and gave him a light kiss on the cheek. He barely moved.

She moved over to Riggs and watched the even rise and fall of his chest. Brushing the hair out of his eyes, she watched him a while longer. She knew the odds were not good that she would ever see either man again. She kissed him gently on the lips and then rose. For one long moment she leaned back against the wall, taking deep breaths as everything she was confronted with threatened to simply overwhelm her.

Then she was on the move again, climbing through the window to avoid the squeaky front door. She put up her hood against the fine rain falling. Ignoring the car and the unavoidable noise it would make, she went to the shed and opened the door. Joy was still there. LuAnn had forgotten to call anyone to come get the horse; however, the shed was dry and warm and there was still water and hay left. She quickly saddled the animal and swung on to Joy's back. Easing her out of the shed, they made it to the woods with scarcely any noise.

When she reached the edge of her property, she dismounted and led Joy back to the horse barn. She hesitated for a moment and then she took the binoculars off the wall, edged through the thick brush, and set up surveillance in a narrow break in the tree line, exactly where Riggs had earlier. She scanned the rear of the house. She jerked back as a car's headlights glinted off the binoculars. The car pulled around to the garage side, but the garage doors didn't budge. As LuAnn watched, a man got out of the car and walked around the rear of the house as if on patrol. Under the rear floods, LuAnn could see the FBI insignia emblazoned on his windbreaker. Then the man got back in the car and it pulled off.

LuAnn broke from the trees and raced across the open ground. She made it to the side of the house in time to see the car head back down the private drive toward the main road, the one where she had fled from Donovan, the encounter that had started this whole nightmare. The FBI was guarding the entrance to her home. She suddenly remembered that Riggs had mentioned that to her during his

542

conversation with Masters. She would have dearly loved to have enlisted the agents' very able assistance, but they no doubt would have arrested her on the spot. Yet fear of arrest wasn't the chief factor. She simply refused to involve anyone else in her problems. No one else was going to be stabbed or killed because of her. Jackson wanted her and only her. She knew he expected her to walk meekly to him, to receive her punishment in exchange for her daughter's release. Well, in this case, he was going to get more than he wanted. A lot more. She and Lisa were going to survive this. He wasn't.

As she started to head back to the rear of the house, she noticed something else. Sally Beecham's car out front. That puzzled her. She shrugged and went around to the rear door.

The sound she had heard in the background during Jackson's call to her was what had brought her here. The absolutely unique sounds of the old clock, the family heirloom, passed down to her from her mother, the very same one LuAnn had diligently refused ever to part with. It had proved to be the most valuable possession she had because she had heard it in the background during her phone conversation with Jackson.

Jackson had been in her house, had called from her house. And LuAnn was absolutely convinced that Lisa was there now. Jackson was here too, she knew. LuAnn had to admire the man's nerve, to come here, with the FBI waiting just down the road. In a very few minutes, she would come face-to-face with her worst nightmare.

She pressed herself flat against the brick wall and peered in the side door, squinting hard through the pane of glass to see if the alarm light that was visible from this point was red or green. She breathed a quiet sigh of relief when she saw the friendly green.

She knew the code to disarm it of course, but disarming it would produce one shrill beep that might jeopardize everything.

LuAnn inserted her key in the lock and slowly opened the door. She paused for a minute; the gun she held made quick, darting movements all around. She heard nothing. It was well past midnight now so that wasn't so surprising. Something was bothering her, however.

Being back in her own house should have brought some comfort to her, but it didn't. If anything it was close to unnerving. Letting her guard down now, letting herself be lulled by the familiarity of the surroundings, could easily result in her and Lisa's not being around to see the sun come up.

She continued down the hallway and then froze. She heard voices clearly. Several people; she recognized none of them. She slowly let out her breath as the music from a commercial came on. Someone was watching TV. A glint of light came from a doorway at the end of the hallway. LuAnn quietly moved forward, stopping right before her shadow would pass across the small opening between door and wall. She listened for a few seconds more. Then she edged open the door with her left hand as she pointed her gun through the opening with her right. The door swung silently inward and LuAnn leaned in. The room was dark, the only light coming from the TV. What she saw next made her freeze once again. The dark hair, cut short around the neck and built high up in the form of a modified beehive, was directly in front of her. Sally Beecham was in her bedroom watching TV. Or was she? She was sitting so still that LuAnn couldn't tell if she was alive or not.

For an instant: the image of LuAnn threading her way through that trailer ten years ago, spotting

Duane on the couch. Going toward him, walking right up to him. And seeing him turn, turn so slowly toward her, the blood all over his chest, his face as gray as a Navy ship. And watching him fall off that couch, dying. And then the hand clamping over her mouth from behind. From behind!

She whirled but there was no one there; however, her abrupt movements had made some noise. When she looked back Sally Beecham was staring at her with horror in her eyes. When she recognized LuAnn she seemed to catch her breath. A hand fluttered up to her chest, which was heaving.

She started to say something, but LuAnn put a finger up to her lips and whispered, "Shh."

"There's someone here," LuAnn said. Sally looked confused. "Have you seen anyone here?" Sally shook her head and pointed to herself, the worry lines sprouting all over her ghastly pale face.

And that's when it hit LuAnn, and her own face went pale.

Sally Beecham never parked in front of the house. She always parked in the garage which led directly into the kitchen. LuAnn's hand tightened on the gun. She looked at the face again. It was hard to tell in the dark light, but she wasn't taking any chances. "I'll tell you what, Sally. I want you to get in the kitchen pantry and I'm going to lock you in. Just to be safe."

LuAnn watched as the eyes darted over her face. Then one of the hands started to move behind the woman's back.

LuAnn thrust the gun forward. "And we're going to do it right now or I'll shoot you right here. And pull out the gun, butt-first."

When the pistol emerged, LuAnn motioned to the floor. The gun clunked when it hit the hardwood.

When the person moved in front of LuAnn,

LuAnn quickly reached out and jerked the wig off, revealing the man. He had short, dark hair. He jerked around for an instant, but LuAnn shoved the gun in his ear.

"Move, Mr. Jackson! Or should I say, Mr. Crane?" She had no false hopes as to the fate of Sally Beecham, but with everything else confronting her, LuAnn did not have the opportunity to dwell on it. She hoped she would have the chance to grieve for the woman.

When they reached the kitchen, LuAnn shoved him inside the pantry and locked the door from the outside. The door was an original from the house, solid oak, three inches thick with a deadbolt. It would hold him. At least for a while. She didn't need long.

She raced to the end of the hallway and flew up the carpeted stairs. LuAnn made her way from door to door. She was fairly certain that Lisa was in her mother's bedroom but she couldn't take any chances. Her eyes had adjusted well to the darkness and she quickly surveyed room after room. All empty. She went on. There was only one more bedroom left: hers. LuAnn willed her hearing to the highest possible acuity. All she wanted to hear was Lisa sighing, mumbling, breathing, anything to let her mother know she was okay. She couldn't call out, that was too dangerous. She recalled that Jackson now had someone with him. Where was that person?

She reached the door, slid her hand around the doorknob, took a deep breath, and turned it.

A long bolt of lightning cut across the sky, followed by a deafening clap of thunder. At the same instant, the blanket was blown off the window and rain started coming in. The combination of these events finally woke Riggs. He sat up, disoriented for a moment, and then looked around. He saw the open window, the wind and rain coming through. He glanced over at Charlie, who was still sleeping. Then it hit him.

He staggered up. "LuAnn? LuAnn?" His cries roused Charlie.

"What the hell?" he said.

In a minute they had searched the small cottage.

"She's not here," he screamed to Charlie.

They both raced outside. The car was still there. Riggs looked around bewildered.

"LuAnn," Charlie screamed over the sounds of the storm.

Riggs looked over at the shed. The doors were open. It hit him. He raced over and looked in the empty shed. He looked down at the mud in front of the shed. Even in the darkness, he could make out the hoof prints. He followed the tracks to the edge of the woods. Charlie ran up beside him.

"Joy was in the shed," he told Charlie. "It looks like she's gone back to the house."

"Why would she do that?"

Riggs thought hard for a minute. "Were you surprised she agreed to finally calling the FBI tomorrow?"

"Yes," Charlie said, "but I was too damn tired and too relieved to think much about it."

"Why would she go to the house?" Riggs repeated Charlie's question. "The FBI is guarding the place. What would be there that she'd take that sort of risk?"

Charlie went pale and he staggered slightly.

"What is it, Charlie?"

"LuAnn once told me something Jackson had told her. A rule he lived by."

"What was it?" Riggs demanded.

"If you want to hide something, put it out in plain sight because no one would see it."

Now it was Riggs's turn to go pale as the truth hit him. "Lisa's at the house."

"And so is Jackson."

They raced to the car.

As the sedan flew down the road Riggs picked up the portable phone. He dialed the police and then the local FBI. He was shocked to hear Masters's voice come on the line.

"He's here, George. Crane's at Wicken's Hunt. Bring everything you got." Riggs heard the phone drop to the desk and footsteps running off. Then he clicked off the phone and floored the car.

As the door swung open, LuAnn darted into the room. Smack in the center was a chair and in that chair was Lisa, slumped over, exhausted. The next sound LuAnn heard was the labored ticking of that clock, that wonderful, beautiful clock. She closed the door behind her and ran to her daughter, hugged her. Her face dissolved into a big smile when her daughter's eyes met her mother's.

And then a loop of thick cord was around LuAnn's neck, was pulled tight, and LuAnn's breath was suddenly gone; her gun fell to the floor.

Lisa screamed and screamed in agonizing silence, the tape still tightly across her mouth. She kicked at her chair, trying to topple it over, trying to reach her mother, help her in some way before this man killed her.

Jackson was fully behind LuAnn now. He had watched from the darkness next to the dresser as LuAnn had sailed toward Lisa, oblivious to his presence in the room. Then he had struck. The cord had a piece of wood attached to it and Jackson was winding it tighter and tighter. LuAnn's face was

548

turning blue, her senses were slipping away as the cord dug deeply into the skin of her neck. She tried to punch him but it was too awkward, her fists flailed helplessly, sapping away what remaining strength she had. She kicked at him, but he was too quick and dodged those blows as well. She dug at the rope with her strong fingers but it was so imbedded in her skin that there was no space left to get a grip.

He whispered into her ear. "Tick-tock, LuAnn. Tick-tock of the little clock. Like a magnet, it led you right to me. I held the phone right next to it so you couldn't help but hear it. I told you I find out everything about someone I do business with. I visited your trailer in good old Rikersville. I listened to the rather unique sounds of that timepiece several times. And then seeing it on the wall of the bedroom the night I visited you. Your little, cheap family heirloom." He laughed. "I would have loved to have seen your face when you thought you had outsmarted me. Was it a happy face, LuAnn? Was it?"

Jackson's smile deepened as he felt her giving way, her vaunted strength almost gone. "Now don't forget your daughter. There she is." He hit a light switch and swung her around violently so that she could see Lisa reaching for her. "She'll watch you die, LuAnn. And then it will be her turn. You cost me a family member. Someone I loved. How does it feel to be responsible for her death?" He yanked on the cord harder and harder. "Die, LuAnn. Just give in to it. Close your eyes and just stop breathing. Just do it. It's so easy. Just do it. Do it for me. You know you want to," he hissed.

LuAnn's eyes were close to erupting out of their sockets now, her lungs almost dead. She felt like she was deep under water; she would give anything to take one breath, just one long drink of air. As LuAnn listened to those taunting words she was swept back to a graveyard, to a plot of dirt, to a small brass marker in the ground many years ago. Exactly where she was heading. *Do it for Big Daddy, LuAnn. It's so easy. Come and see Big Daddy. You know you want to.*

From the corner of her blood-filled right eye she could barely see Lisa silently screaming for her mother, reaching for her across a chasm that was barely seconds from becoming eternal. At that very moment and from a place so deep that LuAnn never even knew she possessed it, there came a rush of strength so unbelievably powerful that it almost knocked her over. With a shriek, LuAnn jerked upright and then bent forward, lifting an astonished Jackson completely off the floor in the process. She clamped her arms around his legs so that she was carrying him piggyback style. Then she exploded backward, her legs pumping like a long jumper about to erupt into flight until she slammed Jackson violently into the heavy dresser against the wall. The sharp wooden edge caught him dead on the spine.

He screamed in pain but hung on to the cord. LuAnn reached up and dug her fingernails right into the recent wound on his hand – the one from the fight at the cottage – tearing the cut wide open. Jackson screamed again and this time he let go of the cord. Feeling the rope go lax, LuAnn whipped her torso forward and Jackson went flying over her shoulders and crashing into a mirror hanging on the wall.

LuAnn staggered drunkenly around in the middle of the room sucking in huge amounts of air. She reached up to her throat and pulled off the cord. Then her eyes settled dead center on the man.

Jackson grabbed at his injured back and struggled

to stand up. It was too little too late, as with a guttural scream LuAnn pounced. She flattened him to the floor and pinned him there. Her legs clamped against his, immobilizing them. Her hands encircled his throat and now *his* face started to turn blue. The grip he felt against his throat was ten times as strong as the one he had battled on the cottage porch. He looked into her blood-filled eyes, red with burst capillaries from her near strangling, and he knew there was no way he could ever break her choke hold. His hands groped the floor as she continued to squeeze the life out of him. A series of visions proceeded across his mind, but there was no rush of strength to accompany it. His body started to go limp. His eyes rolled in their sockets, his neck constricted to the breaking point under the ever increasing pressure. His fingers finally closed around a bit of glass from the shattered mirror and held. He swung it upward, catching her in the arm and cutting through her clothing and into her skin. She didn't release her grip. He cut her again and then again but to no avail. She was beyond pain; she would simply not let go.

Finally, with the last bit of strength he had left, his fingers felt under her arm and he pressed as hard as he could. Suddenly, LuAnn's arms went dead as Jackson found the pressure point and her grip was abruptly broken. In an instant he had pushed her off and sprinted across the room, gasping for breath.

LuAnn watched in horror as he grabbed Lisa's chair and dragged it across the room to the window. She got to her feet, flying toward them. She knew exactly what he was going to do, but damn if she was going to let him do it. He was lifting the chair and Lisa with it, and LuAnn dove for it, her hand closing around her daughter's leg as the chair smashed against the window that overlooked the brick patio almost thirty feet below. LuAnn and Lisa crashed to the floor amid the shattered glass.

Jackson tried to snatch up her gun but LuAnn was one step ahead of him. LuAnn's leg flew up and caught Jackson, who had strayed a little too close, directly in the crotch. He bent down, groaning. She jumped up and landed a powerful right hand squarely against Jackson's chin. He went down to the floor.

In the distance they all heard the police sirens coming. Jackson swore under his breath, picked himself up, and, clutching his privates, raced through the doorway and then slammed and locked the door.

LuAnn let him go. Screaming and crying in relief, she gently pulled off the tape and undid the ropes holding Lisa. Mother and daughter held each other tightly. LuAnn clutched at Lisa's body, she pushed her face in Lisa's hair, her nose drank in every wonderful smell of her little girl. Then LuAnn stood and picked up her gun and fired two shots out the window.

Riggs and Charlie and the FBI agents were engaged in an animated discussion at the entrance to the private road when they heard the shots. Riggs threw the car into gear and roared up the road. The FBI agents ran to their car.

Jackson bolted down the hallway, suddenly stopped, and looked in Sally Beecham's bedroom. Empty. He spied the gun on the floor and snatched it up. Then he heard the pounding. He raced to the kitchen and unlocked and threw open the pantry door. Roger Crane, squinting and quivering, stumbled out.

"Thank God, Peter. She had a gun. She put me in here. I . . . I did exactly as you told me."

552

"Thank you, Roger." He lifted up the pistol. "Tell Alicia I said hello." Then he fired point blank into his brother's face. The next instant he was out the door and racing across the lawn for the woods.

As they jumped out of their car Riggs saw Jackson first and sprinted after him. Charlie, despite his weakened state, was right behind. When the lawmen pulled up seconds later, they ran to the house.

LuAnn met them on the stairs. "Where are Matthew and Charlie?"

The men looked at each other. "I saw somebody running into the woods," one of them answered.

They all ran out on to the front lawn. That's when they heard it, the drone of the helicopter as the blades cut through the rain and wind. It landed on the front lawn. They all saw the FBI insignia on the side. The group raced over; LuAnn and Lisa reached it first.

Several police cars pulled up next to the fountain and a small army of officers poured out.

George Masters climbed out of the helicopter followed by a team of FBI agents. He looked at her. "LuAnn Tyler?" She nodded. Masters looked at Lisa. "Your daughter?"

"Yes," LuAnn said.

"Thank God." He let out a deep sigh of relief and held out his hand. "George Masters, FBI. I came into town to interview Charlie Thomas. When I got to the hospital he was gone."

"We've got to go after Jackson, I mean Peter Crane. He went into the woods," LuAnn said. "Matthew and Charlie went after him. But I want Lisa safe. I can't leave her without knowing she'll be completely safe."

Masters looked between mother and daughter, spitting images of each other. Then he looked at the helicopter.

"We'll transport her to the FBI office here in Charlottesville in this helicopter. I'll put her smack in the center of a room with a half dozen heavily armed FBI agents. That good enough?" He smiled weakly.

A grateful look crossed her face. "Yes. Thanks for understanding."

"I've got children too, LuAnn."

While Masters gave instructions to the pilot, LuAnn gave Lisa one more hug and kiss and then turned and raced for the woods, a swarm of FBI agents and police officers right behind her. As fleet of foot as she was, and knowing the terrain as well as she did, she soon left them far behind.

Riggs could hear the feet flying in front of him. Charlie had dropped back a bit, but Riggs could hear his heavy breathing not far behind. The woods were wreathed in almost complete darkness and the rain continued to pour down. Riggs blinked his eyes rapidly to gain some degree of night vision. He pulled his gun, slipped the safety off with a quick punch of his finger. Then he halted abruptly as the sounds ahead of him stopped. He crouched and swept the area with his eyes, his gun making wide arcs. He heard the sound behind him an instant too late as the foot slammed into his back, sending him lunging forward and then down. He hit the wet ground hard, his face sliding painfully across the grass and dirt, and he ended up slamming against a tree, his gun smacking hard against the trunk. The impact caused his wounded arm to start bleeding again. When he flipped over on his back, he saw the man flying at him, the foot poised to deliver another crunching blow. Then Charlie blindsided Jackson and the two men went sprawling.

An incensed Charlie pounded Jackson with his fists and then cocked his arm back to deliver a

554

knock-out punch. Quick as an eel, Jackson made a direct hit on Charlie's wound, a blow that made him scream and double over. Then, with the same motion employed in striking a cymbal, Jackson smashed both palms against Charlie's ears, forcing a sudden, painful rush of air into his ear canals and rupturing an eardrum. Nauseated and dizzy from the combined blows, Charlie fell off Jackson and lay on the ground groaning.

"I should've slit your throat at the motel," Jackson spat down at him. Jackson was about to deliver a crushing kick to Charlie's head when he heard Riggs scream at him.

"Get the hell away from him before I blow your damn head off."

When Jackson looked over, Riggs's gun was pointed directly at him. Jackson stepped away from Charlie.

"Finally, we meet. Riggs the criminal. How about discussing a financial arrangement that will make you very rich?" Jackson said. His voice was hoarse and weak from his near strangling by LuAnn. He clutched at his torn hand; his face was bleeding from Charlie's blows.

"I'm not a criminal, asshole. I was an FBI agent who testified against a cartel. That's why I was in Witness Protection."

Jackson circled closer to Riggs. "Ex-FBI? Well, then at least I'm certain you won't shoot me down in cold blood." He pointed a warning finger at Riggs. "Understand though, if I go down, so does LuAnn. I'll tell your former employers that she was in on everything, even helped me plan it. I'll paint a picture so dark that she'll be grateful for a life sentence. My attorneys will see to that. But don't worry, I understand you can have yearly conjugal visits in some prisons now."

"You're going to rot in jail."

"I hardly think that. I can only imagine what sort of deal I can cut with the Feds. I would think they'd do anything to avoid public disclosure of all this. When this is all over, I'm sure I'll be seeing you again. In fact, I look forward to it."

Jackson's mocking tones burned through every fiber of Riggs's body. What was even more maddening was the fact that everything Jackson had predicted could very well happen. But it wouldn't, Riggs swore to himself. "That's where you're wrong," Riggs said.

"About what?"

"About killing you in cold blood." Riggs pulled the trigger. The sound that *didn't* occur seemed to drive all the blood from Riggs's body. The gun didn't fire; the impact with the tree had jammed it. He pulled the trigger again with the same sickening result.

Jackson instantly drew his own gun and pointed it at Riggs.

Riggs dropped the useless pistol and backed up as Jackson advanced. He finally stopped retreating when his foot felt nothing but air. He looked behind him: a sheer drop. Down below, the fast-moving water. He looked back at Jackson, who smiled and then fired.

The bullet hit right in front of Riggs's feet and he stepped back a half inch, teetering on the edge.

"Let's see how well you swim with no arms." The next shot hit Riggs's good arm. He grunted in pain and doubled over, clutching it, trying to maintain his balance. Then he looked up at the sneering face of Jackson.

"Take the bullet or the jump, it's your choice. But do it quick, I don't have much time."

Riggs had only an instant. As he crouched over,

the arm that had just been hit slid up the length of his sling – a very natural movement under the circumstances. Jackson had underestimated his resourcefulness. Jackson wasn't the only one who had lived by his wits, who had gotten himself out of tight spots by acting nimbly. What Riggs was about to do had saved his life while working undercover during a drug deal that had gone sour. It would not save his life this time. But it would save several others, including one that he cared more about than his own: LuAnn's.

He locked eyes with Jackson. His anger was so intense that it blocked out the pain in both arms. His hand closed around the butt of the compact gun taped inside his sling, the one he had originally had in his ankle holster. Its muzzle was pointed right at Jackson. Wounded arm and all, his aim was as sharp as ever. And Jackson was only a few feet away. But Riggs had to make the first shot count.

"Riggs!" Charlie screamed.

Jackson didn't take his eyes off Riggs. "You're next, *Uncle Charlie*."

Matt Riggs would never forget the look on Jackson's face as the first shot Riggs fired erupted through the sling and hit the man flush in the face, tearing first through the powder, putty, and spirit gum, and then slamming a microsecond later into real flesh and bone. The gun fell from an astonished Jackson's hand.

Riggs kept pulling the trigger, sending bullet after bullet slamming into Jackson. Head, torso, leg, arm – there wasn't a piece of him Riggs missed until the firing pin banged empty twelve shots later. And all the time Jackson's countenance held a look of supreme disbelief as blood mixed with fake hair and skin; creams and powders mutated into a dull crimson. The total effect was eerie, as though the

557

man were dissolving. Then Jackson dropped to his knees, blood pouring from a dozen wounds, and then he fell face forward to the ground and did not move again. His last performance.

That's when Riggs went fully over the edge. The multiple kicks from the pistol were enough to completely unsettle his balance, and his feet were unable to counter the slippery red clay. But as he went over, a look of grim satisfaction came over his face even as he stared down at the abyss he was plummeting toward. Two useless arms, both bleeding him to death, deep, fast, icy water, nothing to grab. It was over.

He heard Charlie scream his name one more time, and then he heard nothing else. He felt no pain now, only peace. He hit the water awkwardly and went under.

Charlie scrambled over and was just about to plunge in when a body hurtled by him and went over the edge.

LuAnn broke the surface of the water cleanly and almost instantly reappeared. She scanned the surface of the rapidly moving water that was already pulling her downstream.

From the bank, Charlie stumbled along through the thick trees and heavy underbrush, trying to keep up. The shouts of the FBI agents and police officers were getting louder, but it didn't look as though their help would arrive in time.

"Matthew!" LuAnn screamed. Nothing. She dove under, methodically pushing off from bank to bank searching for him. Twenty seconds later she re-surfaced, sucking in air.

"LuAnn!" Charlie yelled at her.

She ignored his cries. As the cold rain pelted her, she sucked in another lungful of air and went under again. Charlie stopped, his eyes darting everywhere, trying to pinpoint where she would come up. He wasn't about to lose both of them.

When LuAnn broke the surface again she wasn't alone. She gripped Riggs tightly around the chest as the current swept them along. He gagged and spit up water as his lungs struggled to function again. She tried to swim cross-current but was making little progress. She was freezing. In another minute hypothermia could well incapacitate her. Riggs was sheer dead weight, and she felt his strength fading. She scissored her legs around his upper torso, angling just enough that his face was above the water's surface. She kept putting pressure on his stomach, making his diaphragm kick up and down, helping him clear his lungs.

She looked desperately behind her, searching for some way out. Her eyes fell upon a fallen tree, and, more important, the thick branch that was suspended partially out over the water. It would be close. She readied herself, gauging the distance and height. She tensed her legs around Riggs and then made her lunge. Her hands closed around the branch and held. She raised herself up. She and Riggs were now partially out of the water. She tried to pull herself up more, but couldn't; Riggs was too heavy. She looked down and saw him staring at her, his breath coming in short gasps. Then she watched horrified as he started to unwrap her legs from around him.

"Matthew, don't! Please!"

Through blue lips that moved in a painfully slow manner he said, "We're not going to both die, LuAnn." He pushed her legs again and she was now fighting him and the current and the weary ache in her limbs as the numbing cold settled deeply within her. Her lips were trembling with both rage and helplessness. She looked down at him again as he

559

tried desperately to free himself, to rid her of the burden. She could simply let go, fall with him, but what about Lisa? She had seconds to make a choice, but then she didn't have to. For the first time in her life, her strength failed, and her grip was broken. She started to plummet downward.

The thick arm that clamped around her body ended her fall and the next thing she felt was herself and Riggs being lifted completely out of the water.

She cocked her head back and her eyes fell upon his face.

Straddling the tree trunk, Charlie, bad arm and all, grunted and grimaced and finally pulled them safely to a narrow dirt bank where they all three collapsed, the water inches from them. LuAnn's legs were still locked in a death grip around Riggs She lay back, her head on Charlie's chest, which was heaving mightily from his efforts. LuAnn slid her right hand down to Riggs, who took it, laying it against his cheek. Her left hand went up and gripped Charlie's shoulder. He covered her hand with his. None of them said a word.

FIFTY-NINE

"Well, it's all done," Riggs said, gingerly hanging up the phone. They were in his home office, LuAnn, Charlie, and Lisa. A gentle snow was falling outside. Christmas was rapidly closing in.

"So what's the bottom line?" LuAnn asked.

LuAnn and Charlie were healed. Riggs was out of his sling, and the cast he had had to wear to mend the bone Jackson's bullet had broken had recently been removed as well. He still moved slowly, though.

"Not great. The IRS finished its calculations of the back taxes you owed, penalties and interest all compounded for the last eight or so years."

"And?"

"And it came to all the cash you had, all the investments you had, and all the property you had, including Wicken's Hunt." He managed a grin, trying to ease the impact of the depressing news. "You were actually short sixty-five cents so I threw it in for you, no charge."

Charlie snorted. "What a Christmas present. And the other lottery winners get to keep all their money. That's not fair."

"They paid their taxes, Charlie," Riggs replied.

"She's paid taxes."

"Only since coming back to this country and only under the name Catherine Savage."

"Well, she couldn't before. Not without probably going to prison for a crime she didn't commit."

561

"Well, gee, that's a real winning argument."

"Yeah, but they all won by cheating too," Charlie retorted.

"Well, the government isn't about to announce that to the world. They make billions off the lottery. Telling the truth might just mess that up, don't you think?"

"How about all the millions she gave to charity, doesn't that count for something?" Charlie said angrily.

"The IRS applauded LuAnn's generosity but said they really couldn't help on that because she had never filed a return. I'm telling you it's not a bad deal. She could have gone to prison for a long time over this. Except for that fact, she probably could have kept some of the money. But that was a very real threat over her head. Sheriff Harvey didn't go away very easily."

"I can't believe this crap. After all she's been through. She broke up Crane's worldwide criminal syndicate, the FBI looks like heroes, they confiscated all his property, billions of bucks into the Treasury, and she winds up with nothing. Not even a pat on the back. It's not fair!"

LuAnn put a hand on a seething Charlie's shoulder. "It's okay, Charlie. I didn't deserve any of that money. And I wanted to pay what I owed. I just want to be LuAnn Tyler again. I told Matthew that. But I didn't murder anyone. All the charges against me are gone, right?" She looked at Riggs for confirmation.

"That's right. Federal, state, everything. Free as a bird."

"Yeah, and poor as a church mouse," Charlie added angrily.

"Is that it, Matthew? They can't come back on me later? The IRS, I mean? For more money?"

"All the papers are signed. They dropped everything. It's over. They confiscated all your accounts, they foreclosed on the house. Anyway, even if they came after you, which they can't, you don't have any more money."

Lisa looked at him. "Maybe we can move in here, Mom." She added quickly, "I mean for a little while." She looked between LuAnn and Riggs nervously. LuAnn smiled at Lisa. Telling her daughter the entire truth had been the hardest thing she had ever had to do. But the second she had finished, she had never felt greater relief. Lisa had taken the news admirably. Now at least their relationship could take on a semblance of normalcy.

Riggs looked at LuAnn, a little nervous himself. "I was thinking along those lines myself." He swallowed hard. "Can you excuse us for a minute?" he asked Charlie and Lisa.

He took LuAnn by the arm and they left the room. Charlie and Lisa watched them go and then exchanged smiles.

Riggs sat LuAnn down by the fireplace and stood in front of her. "I'd love for all of you to move in here. There's plenty of room. But—" He looked down.

"But what?" she asked.

"I was thinking about a more permanent arrangement."

"I see."

"I mean, I earn a good living and, well, now that you don't have all that money." She cocked her head at him as he blew out a deep breath. "I just never wanted you to think I was after you because of your wealth. It would've driven me crazy. It was like this big roadblock I couldn't get around. I don't want you to think that I'm happy you're not rich anymore.

563

If there had been some way for you to keep the money, that would've been great. But, now that you don't have it, I just want you to know . . ." Here he stumbled again, unable to continue, suddenly terrified at the deep waters he had ventured into.

"I love you, Matthew," LuAnn said simply.

Riggs's features fully relaxed. He didn't look terrified anymore. In fact, he couldn't remember ever being this happy before. "I love you too, LuAnn Tyler."

"Have you ever been to Switzerland?" she asked.

He looked surprised. "No. Why?"

"I always thought about honeymooning there. It's so romantic, so beautiful. Especially at Christmas time."

Riggs looked troubled. "Well, sweetie, I work hard, but small-town, one-man-shop general contractors don't make enough money to do those sorts of things. I'm sorry." He licked his lips nervously. "I'll understand if you can't accept that, after all these years of being so rich."

In response, LuAnn opened her purse and took out a slip of paper. On it was an account number at a bank in Switzerland. The account had been opened with one hundred million dollars: Jackson's return of her principal. It was all there, just waiting. It cranked out six million a year in interest alone. She would retain her lottery prize after all. And she wasn't feeling any guilt about it this time around. Right now in fact, it seemed like she had earned it. She had spent the last ten years trying to be someone she wasn't. It had been a life of great wealth and great misery. Now she was going to spend the rest of her life being who she really was and enjoying it. She had a beautiful, healthy daughter and *two* men who loved her. No more running, no more hiding for LuAnn Tyler. She was truly blessed.

She smiled at him, stroked his face.

"You know what, Matthew?"

"What?"

Right before she kissed him she said, "I think we'll be just fine."

ACKNOWLEDGMENTS

To Michelle, for keeping everything going while I'm off in my dream world.

To Jennifer Steinberg, for superb research, as always.

To Catherine Broome, M.D., for taking the time from a very busy schedule to talk poisons with me over lunch.

To Steve Jennings, for his always sharp editorial eye.

To Carl Patton, my favourite accountant, and Tom DePont of NationsBank, for much needed help on complex tax issues.

To Larry Kirshbaum, Maureen Egen, and the rest of the Warner crew, for being so supportive and just plain, good people.

To Aaron Priest, for being my sage, my mentor, and, most important, my friend.

To Frances Jalet-Miller, for once again making the story immeasurably better.

To the rest of my family and friends, for their continued love and support.

www.panmacmillan.com